Encyclopedia of Business Information Sources

ISSN 0071-0210

Encyclopedia of Business Information Sources

A Bibliographic Guide to Nearly 25,000 Citations Covering Over 1,100 subjects of Interest to Business Personnel

Includes: Abstracts and Indexes, Almanacs and Yearbooks, Bibliographies, Biographical Sources, CD-ROM Databases, Directories, E-Books, Encyclopedias and Dictionaries, Financial Ratios, Handbooks and Manuals, Internet Databases, Online Databases, Periodicals and Newsletters, Price Sources, Research Centers and Institutes, Statistics Sources, Trade and Professional Societies, and Other Sources of Information on Each Topic

32nd EDITION
Volume 1

Virgil L. Burton III

GALE
CENGAGE Learning

Farmington Hills, Mich • San Francisco • New York • Waterville, Maine
Meriden, Conn • Mason, Ohio • Chicago

Encyclopedia of Business Information Sources 32nd Edition, Volume 1

Project Editor: Virgil L. Burton III

Composition and Electronic Prepress: Gary Leach

Manufacturing: Rita Wimberley

WCN: 01-100-101

Gale
27500 Drake Rd.
Farmington Hills, MI, 48331-3535

ISBN-13: 978-1-57302-543-0 (2V SET)
ISBN-13: 978-1-57302-544-7 (V1)
ISBN-13: 978-1-57302-545-4 (V2)

ISSN 0071-0210

Printed in the United States of America
1 2 3 4 5 19 18 17 16 15

Contents

Volume 1

Introduction

As the information needs of business managers and information professionals continue to increase, timely and convenient access becomes more valuable. The *Encyclopedia of Business Information Sources (EBIS)* is designed to assist these individuals in locating material relevant to today's rapidly-changing business environment.

EBIS now includes nearly 25,000 citations, dealing with more than 1,100 business, financial, and industrial topics. The subjects cover a variety of business-related concerns. These include, for example:

- Business functions—Accounting; Administration; Personnel Management
- Computer-related subjects—Computer Graphics; Computer Software Industry; Local Area Networks
- Foreign trade—International Marketing; Latin American Markets; North American Free Trade Agreement (NAFTA)
- Information industry topics—Electronic Publishing; Internet; Multimedia

Easy to Use

A convenient and accessible grouping of information sources is provided for each business topic. Within these topics, there is the additional convenience of type-of-material categories: directories, periodicals, handbooks, and so forth. An extensive *Outline of Contents* (see p. xiii) makes the exact heading for any subject easy to locate. Many cross-references provide additional assistance in finding needed information.

EBIS thus serves two kinds of information needs: for a quick survey of publications and organizations relating to a particular topic, and for reference to a specific source that will provide a single fact or statistic.

"Sources Cited" Section

For users with a specific title, organization, or service in mind, an alphabetic list of sources follows the main text. This *Sources Cited* section repeats all entries from the main text, sorting them alphabetically by publication title or organization name. The *Sources Cited* section also includes complete contact information.

Extensive Updating

Thousands of changes and additions were required to update this edition of *EBIS*. Information was verified through reliable sources and independent research of the editorial staff. Current editions of *Gale's Encyclopedia of Associations and Research Centers Directory* were used to update nonprint sources in the categories of "Trade Associations and Professional Societies" and "Research Centers and Institutes."

Standard business or economic compilations, such as the annual *Economic Report of the President* and *Risk Management Association's Annual Statement Studies,* have been carefully examined and entered under topics for which these publications contain significant data. Many out-of-print and discontinued items have been deleted from this edition of *EBIS*, although a few titles considered to be unique or of particular interest have been retained. Should it be desirable to consult these works, they may be available at local libraries.

New material for this edition has been collected in various ways. These include examining publishers' catalogs or brochures, reviewing material in business libraries, scanning lists of recommended titles, and discussing publications with business librarians. Publishers' Internet Web pages have also been useful.

Available in Electronic Formats

The Directory is also available as part of the Gale Directory Library. For more information, call 1-800-877-GALE

Suggestions Are Welcome

If you have suggestions, concerns, or comments about the *Encyclopedia of Business Information Sources*, please contact:

Encyclopedia of Business Information Sources

Gale, Cengage Learning

27500 Drake Road

Farmington Hills, MI 48331-3535

Phone: 248-699-4253

Toll-free: 800-877-GALE

Fax: 248-699-8070

Primary Listings

In the main section of the *Encyclopedia of Business Information Sources (EBIS)*, entries are arranged alphabetically by **▮1▮** topic, and further subdivided by **▮2▮** type of source and **▮3▮** publication title or organization name. For example:

▮1▮ CORPORATE FINANCE

▮2▮ DIRECTORIES

▮3▮ *America's Corporate Finance Directory.* National Register Publishing Co., Reed Elsevier Inc. Annual. $730.00. A directory of financial information, covering 5,000 major U. S. corporations.

▮3▮ *Corporate Finance Sourcebook.* National Register Publishing Co., Reed Elsevier Inc. Annual. $650.00. Lists more than 3,700 organizations providing corporate capital.

▮2▮ ONLINE DATABASES

▮3▮ *ABI/INFORM.* Proquest Co. Provides online indexing to business-related material occurring in more than 1,000 periodicals from 1971 to the present. Inquire as to online cost and availability.

▮2▮ RESEARCH CENTERS AND INSTITUTES

▮3▮ Bendheim Center for Finance. Princeton University, Dept. of Economics, Princeton, NJ 08544. Phone: (609)258-4023. Fax: (609)258-6419.

Locate Topics in the Outline of Contents Section

The *Encyclopedia of Business Information Sources* covers more than 1,100 topics. The efficient way to locate a particular topic is to scan the *Outline of Contents* section, which follows this *User's Guide*. The *Outline of Contents* lists topics alphabetically.

Users can determine at a glance the specific form of the subject term that has been employed. Numerous cross-references provide assistance where necessary. For instance, if the term being sought is Cellular Telephones, the *Outline of Contents* provides a cross-reference directing users to the heading "Mobile Telephone Industry," where information on cell phones may be found.

19 Kinds of Sources

Material under each topic is grouped according to the type of source or form in which the information is provided. A user can look under the topic of interest (Corporate Finance, for example) to find key information sources arranged as follows:

- Abstracts and Indexes
- Almanacs and Yearbooks
- Bibliographies
- Biographical Sources
- CD-ROM Databases
- Directories
- E-Books
- Encyclopedias and Dictionaries
- Financial Ratios
- General Works
- Handbooks and Manuals
- Internet Databases
- Online Databases
- Other Sources
- Periodicals and Newsletters
- Price Sources
- Research Centers and Institutes
- Statistics Sources
- Trade/Professional Associations

Content of the Entries

The content of the entries is described here and illustrated in the sample that appears on the previous page.

Entries for publications and online databases list the title of the work, the name of the author (where applicable), the name of the publisher or provider, frequency or year of publication, and price. Brief descriptive notes are often added to clarify listings. Entries included in the "Internet Databases" category provide the name of the Web site, the name of the provider or host, telephone/fax numbers, E-mail address, the URL address, and information on content and cost (most are free).

Entries for trade associations and research centers provide the organization name, address, telephone/fax numbers, and Internet information where available. Many of these entries include a brief description of the organization.

Sources Cited Section

Arrangement—In the Sources Cited section, all entries from the primary listings in *EBIS* are arranged alphabetically by publication title, database title, or organization name.

Contact Information—The Sources Cited section provides contact information—including URL addresses and e-mail in most instances—for print publishers and for publishers or providers of online databases.

Many of the online databases referenced in EBIS are available through the widely used service providers listed below.

ONLINE DATABASE VENDORS

DIALOG
Dialog/Thomson Corp.
11000 Regency Parkway, Suite 10
Cary, NC 27518
(800)334-2564 or (919)462-8600
Fax: (919)468-9890
http://www.dialog.com

DIALOG DataStar
Dialog/Thomson Corp.
11000 Regency Parkway, Suite 10
Cary, NC 27518
(800)334-2564 or (919)462-8600
Fax: (919)468-9890
http://www.dialog.com/products/datastar

InfoTrac OneFile
Gale, Cengage Learning
27500 Drake Road
Farmington Hills, MI 48331-3535
(800)877-4253 or (248) 699-4253
Fax: (800) 414-5043 or (248)699-8096
gale.cengage.com

LEXIS-NEXIS
Reed-Elsevier Inc.
P. O. Box 933
Dayton, OH 45401-0933
(800)227-4908 or (937)865-6800
Fax: (937)865-6909
http://www.lexisnexis.com

OCLC FirstSearch
OCLC Online Computer Library Center, Inc.
6565 Kilgour Place
Dublin, OH 43017-3395
(800)848-5878 or (614)764-6000
Fax: (614)764-6096
http://www.oclc.org/firstsearch

Ovid Technologies, Inc.
333 Seventh Ave., 20th Floor
New York, NY10001
(800)950-2035 or (646)674-6300
Fax: (646)674-6301
http://www.ovid.com

Questel-Orbit, Inc.
1725 Duke Street, Suite 625
Alexandria, VA22314
(800)456-7248 or (703)519-1820
Fax: (703)519-1821
http://www.questel.orbit.com

WESTLAW
West Group
610 Opperman Drive
Saint Paul, MN 55123
(800)328-4880 or (651)687-7000
Fax: (651)687-7849
http://www.westlaw.com

Outline of Contents

A

ABBREVIATIONS

ENCYCLOPEDIAS AND DICTIONARIES

Acronyms, Initialisms, & Abbreviations Dictionary. Cengage Learning Inc. • Annual. $1474.00. Provides more than 780,000 definitions in all subject areas. eBook also available.

INTERNET DATABASES

Acronym Finder: The Web's Most Comprehensive Database of Acronyms, Abbreviations, and Initialisms. Mountain Data Systems. Phone: (970)586-5556; Email: acronyms@mtnds.com • URL: http://www.acronymfinder.com • Web site provides more than 750,000 definitions. Searching offers a choice of "exact acronym," "acronym begins with," "acronym (wildcard)", or "reverse lookup (keywords)." Fees: Free.

ABRASIVES INDUSTRY

ABSTRACTS AND INDEXES

Alloys Index. CSA. • Monthly. $775 print and online.

Chemical Abstracts. American Chemical Society Chemical Abstracts Service. • Available via CAS' electronic products including SciFinder and STN.

Metals Abstracts. CSA. • Monthly. $3,575.00 per year. Includes print and online editions.

FINANCIAL RATIOS

Annual Statement Studies. Risk Management Association. • Annual. Compiled from over 280,000 financial statements.

Annual Statement Studies: Industry Default Probabilities and Cash Flow Measures. Risk Management Association. • Annual. $405 Nonmembers. Serves as a companion volume to the original *Annual Statement Studies*. Gives probability of default estimates on a percentage scale for more than 450 industries. Includes changes in position year-by-year for eight financial statement line items and provides percentage measures of cash flow.

OTHER SOURCES

Abrasive Engineering Society Conference Proceedings. Abrasive Engineering Society. • Irregular. Price on application.

PERIODICALS AND NEWSLETTERS

Grinding and Abrasive Magazine. Abrasive Magazine, Inc. • Eight times a year. $27.00 per year. Formerly *Abrasive Magazine*.

Grits and Grinds. Saint-Gobain Abrasives Inc. • Quarterly. Free.

Visons. Unified Abrasives Manufacturers' Association - Grain Committee. • Irregular. Newsletter. Price on application.

PRICE SOURCES

Chemical & Engineering News. American Chemical Society. • Weekly Annual. $265 Nonmembers print, North America. Magazine on chemical and engineering news.

STATISTICS SOURCES

United States Census of Mineral Industries. Bureau of the Census, U.S. Department of Commerce. U. S. Government Printing Office. • Quinquennial.

TRADE/PROFESSIONAL ASSOCIATIONS

United Abrasives Manufacturers Association. 30200 Detroit Rd., Cleveland, OH 44145-1967. Phone: (440)899-0010; Fax: (440)892-1404; Email: contact@uama.org • URL: http://www.uama.org • Formerly *Coated Abrasives Manufacturers Institute*.

ABSENTEEISM

ABSTRACTS AND INDEXES

Business Periodicals Index Retrospective. EBSCO Publishing Inc. • 11/year. Quarterly and annual cumulations.

ONLINE DATABASES

Wilson Business Abstracts Online. H.W. Wilson Co. • Indexes and abstracts 600 major business periodicals, plus the *Wall Street Journal* and the business section of the *New York Times*. Indexing is from 1982, abstracting from 1990, with the two newspapers included from 1993. Updated weekly. Inquire as to online cost and availability. (*Business Periodicals Index* without abstracts is also available online.).

PERIODICALS AND NEWSLETTERS

HR Magazine (Human Resources): Strategies and Solutions for Human Resource Professionals. Society for Human Resource Management. • Monthly. $70. Formerly *Personnel Administrator*.

TRADE/PROFESSIONAL ASSOCIATIONS

American Management Association. 1601 Broadway, New York, NY 10019-7420. Phone: 877-566-9441 or (212)586-8100 or (518)891-5510; Fax: (212)903-8168 or (518)891-0368; Email: customerservice@amanet.org • URL: http://www.amanet.org • Provides educational forums worldwide where members and their colleagues learn superior, practical business skills and explore best practices of world-class organizations through interaction with each other and expert faculty practitioners. Maintains a publishing program providing tools individuals use to extend learning beyond the classroom in a process of life-long professional growth and development through education.

ACADEMIC DEGREES

See also COLLEGES AND UNIVERSITIES

ABSTRACTS AND INDEXES

Current Index to Journals in Education (CIJE). Oryx Press. • Monthly. $245.00 per year. Semiannual cumulations, $475.00.

Education Index. H.W. Wilson Co. • 10 times a year. Quarterly and annual cumulations. Price varies.

DIRECTORIES

A Guide to College Programs in Hospitality, Tourism, & Culinary Arts. International Council on Hotel, Restaurant, and Institutional Education. • Biennial. Covers: About 500 secondary and technical institutes, colleges, and universities; international coverage. Entries include: School name, address, areas of study, degrees offered, name and title of contact, program description, financial aid information, tuition and fees, admission and graduation requirements.

The Guide to Graduate Environmental Programs. Island Press-Center For Resource Economics. • $19.99 Individuals. Covers: Graduate study facilities and 160 programs in the environmental sciences in the U.S. Entries include: Facility name, address, phone, program name, profile, Number of students and faculty in the program, requirements for master's and doctoral degrees, faculty/advisee ratio, e-mail contact and Web site address, special program features, auxiliary services.

ONLINE DATABASES

Education Index Online. H.W. Wilson Co. • Indexes a wide variety of periodicals related to schools, colleges, and education, 1984 to date. Monthly updates. Inquire as to online cost and availability.

PERIODICALS AND NEWSLETTERS

Resources in Education. Educational Resources Information Center. U. S. Government Printing Office. • Monthly. Reports on educational research.

STATISTICS SOURCES

Occupational Projections and Training Data. U. S. Government Printing Office. • Biennial. $31.50. Issued by Bureau of Labor Statistics, U. S. Department of Labor. Contains projections of employment change and job openings over the next 15 years for about 500 specific occupations. Also includes the number of associate, bachelor's, master's, doctoral, and professional degrees awarded in a recent year for about 900 specific fields of study.

ACADEMIC DISSERTATIONS

See DISSERTATIONS

ACCIDENT INSURANCE

See also AUTOMOBILE INSURANCE; CASUALTY INSURANCE

ALMANACS AND YEARBOOKS

Insurance Almanac: Who, What, When and Where in Insurance. Criterion Publishing Co. • Annual. $195. Lists insurance agencies and brokerage firms; U.S. and Canadian insurance companies, adjusters, appraisers, auditors, investigators, insurance officials and insurance organizations.

BIBLIOGRAPHIES

Insurance and Employee Benefits Literature. Special Libraries Association. • Bimonthly. $15.00 per year. Lists a wide variety of literature in all branches of the insurance industry. Includes annotations.

FINANCIAL RATIOS

Best's Key Rating Guide. A.M. Best Company Inc. • Annual. $200 Individuals regular service. Financial information and ratings on thousands of major property/casualty insurers.

ONLINE DATABASES

I.I.I. Data Base Search. Insurance Information Institute. • Provides online citations and abstracts of insurance-related literature in magazines, newspapers, trade journals, and books. Emphasis is on property and casualty insurance issues, including highway safety, product safety, and environmental liability. Inquire as to online cost and availability.

OTHER SOURCES

Life, Health, and Accident Insurance Law Reports. Wolters Kluwer Law & Business CCH. • $835.00 per year. Looseleaf service. Monthly updates.

STATISTICS SOURCES

Injury Facts. National Safety Council. • Annual. $109.85 Nonmembers.

TRADE/PROFESSIONAL ASSOCIATIONS

American Insurance Association. 2101 L St. NW, Ste. 400, Washington, DC 20037. Phone: (202)828-7100; Fax: (202)293-1219 • URL: http://www.aiadc.org/aiapub • Represents companies providing property and casualty insurance and suretyship. Monitors and reports on economic, political, and social trends; serves as a clearinghouse for ideas, advice, and technical information. Represents members' interests before state and federal legislative and regulatory bodies; coordinates members' litigation.

Council of Insurance Agents and Brokers. 701 Pennsylvania Ave. NW, Ste. 750, Washington, DC 20004-2608. Phone: (202)783-4400; Fax: (202)783-4410; Email: ciab@ciab.com • URL: http://www.ciab.com • Represents the interests of the leading commercial property and casualty insurance agencies and brokerage firms in the U.S. and around the world.

ACCIDENTS

See also ACCIDENT INSURANCE; SAFETY; TRAFFIC ACCIDENTS AND TRAFFIC SAFETY

ABSTRACTS AND INDEXES

Health and Safety Science Abstracts. Institute of Safety and Systems Management. Cambridge Information Group. • Monthly. Provides coverage of world literature on general safety, environmental and ecological safety, industrial hygiene and occupational safety, transportation safety, aviation and aerospace safety, and medical safety. Formerly *Safety Science Abstracts Journal.*

CD-ROM DATABASES

OSH-ROM: Occupational Safety and Health Information on CD-ROM. SilverPlatter Information Inc. • Price and frequency on application. Produced in Geneva by the International Occupational Safety and Health Information Centre, International Labour Organization (www.ilo.org). Provides about two million citations and abstracts to the worldwide literature of industrial safety, industrial hygiene, hazardous materials, and accident prevention. Material is included from journals, technical reports, books, government publications, and other sources. Time span varies.

INTERNET DATABASES

National Center for Health Statistics: Monitoring the Nation's Health. National Center for Health Statistics, Centers for Disease Control and Prevention. Phone: (301)458-4000; Email: nchsquery@cdc.gov • URL: http://www.cdc.gov/nchswww • Web site provides detailed data on diseases, vital statistics, and health care in the U. S. Includes a search facility and links to many other health-related Web sites. "Fastats A to Z" offers quick data on hundreds of topics from Accidents to Work-Loss Days, with links to Comprehensive Data and related sources. Frequent updates. Fees: Free.

ONLINE DATABASES

Embase. Elsevier. • Worldwide medical literature, 1974 to present. Weekly updates. Inquire as to online cost and availability.

PERIODICALS AND NEWSLETTERS

Accident Analysis and Prevention. Elsevier. • Monthly. $461 Individuals print. Provides wide coverage of the general areas relating to accidental injury and damage, including the pre-injury and immediate post-injury phases.

Accident Prevention. Flight Safety Foundation. • Monthly. Description: Carries items of particular value to professional pilots: general air safety material and reports of dangerous situations, incidents, near misses by professional pilots, ground crew, or other persons involved.

EHS Today. Penton Media Inc. • Monthly. $55.00 per year. Industrial safety and security management.

Human Factors and Aviation Medicine. Flight Safety Foundation. • Bimonthly. $120 Members. Contains information important to the training and performance of all aviation professionals.

Journal of System Safety. System Safety Society. • Bimonthly. $100 for nonmembers (in U.S. Canada and International). Contains technical information, industry reports, expert opinions, book reviews and conference previews. Formerly *Hazard Prevention.*

Safety and Health. National Safety Council. • Monthly. Qualified professionals may receive free for one year.

STATISTICS SOURCES

Injury Facts. National Safety Council. • Annual. $109.85 Nonmembers.

Occupational Injuries and Illnesses by Industry. Bureau of Labor Statistics, U.S. Department of Labor. U. S. Government Printing Office. • Annual.

Report on the American Workforce. U. S. Government Printing Office. • Annual. Issued by the U. S. Department of Labor (www.dol.gov). Appendix contains tabular statistics, including employment, unemployment, price indexes, consumer expenditures, employee benefits (retirement, insurance, vacation, etc.), wages, productivity, hours of work, and occupational injuries. Annual figures are shown for up to 50 years.

Vital Statistics of the United States. Public Health Service, U.S. Dept. of Health and Human Services. Bernan Press. • Biennial. $110.

TRADE/PROFESSIONAL ASSOCIATIONS

Personal Injury Lawyers Marketing and Management Association. 607 Briarwood Dr., Ste. 4, Myrtle Beach, SC 29572. Phone: 800-497-1890 or (843)361-1700; Fax: (866)859-8126; Email: info@pilmma.org • URL: http://www.pilmma.org • Represents personal injury lawyers and disability attorneys. Provides members with the necessary tools, information and education to help grow and manage a successful contingency-based injury and disability law practice. Seeks to fulfill the marketing and management needs of members by granting access to sources of credible information and educational events.

ACCOUNTABILITY, SOCIAL

See SOCIAL RESPONSIBILITY

ACCOUNTANTS

See CERTIFIED PUBLIC ACCOUNTANTS

ACCOUNTING

See also AUDITING; CERTIFIED PUBLIC ACCOUNTANTS; COMPUTERS IN ACCOUNTING; COST ACCOUNTING; GOVERNMENT ACCOUNTING; WOMEN ACCOUNTANTS

ABSTRACTS AND INDEXES

Accounting and Tax Index. ProQuest L.L.C. • Quarterly. Indexes accounting, auditing, and taxation literature appearing in journals, books, pamphlets, conference proceedings, and newsletters.

Accounting Articles. Wolters Kluwer Law & Business CCH. • Monthly. $624. Covers accounting news.

Business Periodicals Index Retrospective. EBSCO Publishing Inc. • 11/year. Quarterly and annual cumulations.

ALMANACS AND YEARBOOKS

Yearbook. Association of Government Accountants. • Annual.

CD-ROM DATABASES

Business Abstracts with Full Text. EBSCO Publishing Inc. • Includes full text articles from more than 460 business publications from 1982 to present. Indexing for nearly 880 publications.

DIRECTORIES

Academy of Accounting Historians--Membership Directory. Academy of Accounting Historians. • Annual. Covers: over 900 member individuals and organizations concerned with accounting and business history. Entries include: Member name, address, phone, and fax.

Accounting and Bookkeeping General Services Directory. InfoGroup Inc. • Annual. Number of listings: 27,213. Entries include: Name, address, phone, size of advertisement, name of owner or manager, number of employees, year first in "Yellow Pages." Compiled from telephone company "Yellow Pages," nationwide.

Accounting and Bookkeeping Systems (Wholesale) Directory. InfoGroup Inc. • Annual. Number of listings: 547. Entries include: Name, address, phone, size of advertisement, name of owner or manager, number of employees, year first in "Yellow Pages." Compiled from telephone company "Yellow Pages," nationwide.

American Society of Women Accountants--Membership Directory. Accounting and Financial Women's Alliance. • Annual. Covers: Approximately 5,000 members in accounting and accounting-related fields. Entries include: Name, address, phone, fax, e-mail.

The Association of Chartered Certified

Accountants--Directory of Business Advisers. Association of Chartered Certified Accountants. • Annual. $20. Covers practicing accounting firms and individual accountants acting as non-executive directors.

Directory of Chartered Accountants in Business. Institute of Chartered Accountants in Australia. • Annual. $35. Covers business members in Australia and overseas.

Emerson's Directory of Leading U.S. Accounting Firms. Emerson Co. • Biennial. $195.00. Provides information on 500 major CPA firms.

National Society of Public Accountants - Yearbook. National Society of Accountants. • Annual. Free to members, government agencies and libraries; not available to others.

ENCYCLOPEDIAS AND DICTIONARIES

Encyclopedia of American Business. Cengage Learning Inc. • 2013. eBook. 2 volumes. 800 essays. A guide to the nuts and bolts of business jargon. Difficult ideas are explained in straightforward language to help non-specialists, students, and general readers understand the complex and sometimes confusing concepts and terms that are used in business. Five general areas of business are covered: accounting, banking, finance, marketing, and management.

Encyclopedia of Business and Finance. Cengage Learning Inc. • 2014. $485. 3rd edition. Two volumes. Published by Macmillan Reference USA. Contains articles on accounting, business administration, banking, finance, management information systems, and marketing.

FINANCIAL RATIOS

Income and Fees of Accountants in Public Practice. National Society of Accountants. • Contains info on fees charged for tax and accounting services by geography. Members, $49.00; non-members, $125.00.

GENERAL WORKS

Accounting and Business Research. Routledge. • 6/year. $137 Individuals print. Publication for the banking, finance, and accounting industries.

Business I. ITHAKA JSTOR, the Journal Storage Project. • Contains more than 2 million pages from 47 titles in the fields of economics and finance, accounting, labor relations, marketing, management, operations research, and risk assessment.

Small Business Controller. Thomson RIA. • Quarterly. $76 Individuals. Source for technical information in accounting and financial management. For financial managers in growing and emerging businesses.

HANDBOOKS AND MANUALS

Accountant's Business Manual. American Institute of Certified Public Accountants. • $198.75. Looseleaf. Two volumes. Semiannual updates. Covers a wide variety of topics relating to financial and accounting management, including types of ownership, business planning, financing, cash management, valuation, retirement plans, estate planning, workers' compensation, unemployment insurance, social security, and employee benefits management.

Applying GAAP and GAAS. Matthew Bender and Company Inc. • $898 Print. In-depth explanations of generally accepted accounting principles (GAAP) and generally accepted auditing standards (GAAS).

GAAP Guide. Aspen Publishers, Inc. • Annual. $364. Also available in eBook format. Provides information on understanding GAAP literature in clear language.

Miller European Accounting Guide. Aspen Publishers, Inc. • Annual. $159.00. Presents analysis of accounting standards in 25 European and Eastern European countries.

Not-for-Profit Entities - Best Practices in Presentation and Disclosure. American Institute of Certified Public Accountants. • $86.25 Nonmembers Print/Online. Provides preparers and auditors with the tools they need to work through the process of creating and verifying the format and accuracy of their company or clients' financial statements.

Practitioner's Guide to GAAS. John Wiley & Sons Inc. • Annual. $105 paperback. Covers GAAS: Generally Accepted Auditing Standards, promulgated by the American Institute of Certified Public Accountants. (Includes CD-ROM.).

SEC Accounting Rules. Wolters Kluwer Law & Business CCH. • $448.00. Looseleaf service.

INTERNET DATABASES

Rutgers Accounting Web. Rutgers University Accounting Research Center. Phone: (973)353-5172; Fax: (973)353-1283 • URL: http://www.rutgers.edu/accounting • RAW Web site provides extensive links to sources of national and international accounting information, such as the Big Six accounting firms, the Financial Accounting Standards Board (FASB), SEC filings (EDGAR), journals, publishers, software, the International Accounting Network, and "Internet's largest list of accounting firms in USA." Searching is offered. Fees: Free.

ONLINE DATABASES

Accounting and Tax Database. ProQuest L.L.C. • Provides indexing and abstracting of the literature of accounting, taxation, and financial management, 1971 to date. Updating is weekly. Especially covers accounting, auditing, banking, bankruptcy, employee compensation and benefits, cash management, financial planning, and credit. Inquire as to online cost and availability.

Wilson Business Abstracts Online. H.W. Wilson Co. • Indexes and abstracts 600 major business periodicals, plus the *Wall Street Journal* and the business section of the *New York Times.* Indexing is from 1982, abstracting from 1990, with the two newspapers included from 1993. Updated weekly. Inquire as to online cost and availability. (*Business Periodicals Index* without abstracts is also available online.).

OTHER SOURCES

Accounting Research Studies. American Institute of Certified Public Accountants. • Irregular.

Finance and Accounting for Nonfinancial Managers. American Management Association Extension Institute. • $19.95. Looseleaf. Self-study course. Emphasis is on practical explanations, examples, and problem solving. Quizzes and a case study are included.

Financial Accounting Series. Financial Accounting Standards Board. • Monthly. Price on application.

Forensic Accounting and Financial Fraud. American Management Association Extension Institute. • Looseleaf. $159.00. Self-study course. Emphasis is on practical explanations, examples, and problem solving. Quizzes and a case study are included.

Management Advisory Services Guideline Series. American Institute of Certified Public Accountants. • Irregular. Price varies.

PERIODICALS AND NEWSLETTERS

Abacus: A Journal of Accounting, Finance and Business Studies. John Wiley & Sons Inc. Wiley-Blackwell. • Quarterly. $597 Institutions Australia & New Zealand, print and online. Journal covering academic and professional aspects of accounting, finance and business.

Accounting and Financial Planning for Law Firms. ALM Media Properties LLC. • Monthly. $499 /year. Covers budgeting, liability issues, billing systems, benefits management, and other topics relating to law firm administration. (A Law Journal Newsletter, formerly published by Leader Publications).

The Accounting Review. American Accounting Association. • Bimonthly. $450 Individuals print. Accounting education, research, financial reporting, and book reviews.

Accounting Today: The Business Newspaper for the Tax & Accounting Community. SourceMedia Inc. • Biweekly. $99.00 per year. Covers news affecting tax and accounting professionals.

Journal of Accountancy. American Institute of Certified Public Accountants. • Monthly. $75 Individuals. Accounting journal.

Journal of Accounting Research. Institute of Professional Accounting. Blackwell Publishing Inc. • Five times a year. Institutions, $425.00 per year. Includes online edition. Annual *Supplement* available. Accepts for review unpublished research in the fields of empirical and experimental accounting.

Journal of Government Financial Management. Association of Government Accountants. • Quarterly. $95 Individuals. *Government Accountants Journal.*

Main Street Practitioner. National Society of Accountants. • Bimonthly. For accounting and tax practitioners.

NSPA Washington Reporter. National Society of Accountants. • Monthly. Membership.

The Practical Accountant: Providing the Competitive Edge. SourceMedia Inc. • Monthly. $65.00 per year. Covers tax planning, financial planning, practice management, client relationships, and related topics.

Public Accounting Report: Competitive Intelligence for Accounting Firms. Strafford Publications Inc. • Presents news and trends affecting the accounting profession.

Schmalenbach Business Review. Verlagsgruppe Handelsblatt GmbH. • Quarterly. $135 Institutions.

RESEARCH CENTERS AND INSTITUTES

Accounting Research Program. UCLA Anderson School of Management, 110 Westwood Plz., Los Angeles, CA 90095-1481. Phone: (310)206-8711; Fax: (310)825-3165 • URL: http://www.anderson.ucla.edu.

Columbia University - Columbia Business School - Center for Excellence in Accounting and Security Analysis. 608 Uris Hall, 3022 Broadway, New York, NY 10027. Phone: (212)854-3832; Fax: (212)316-9219; Email: ceasa@gsb.columbia.edu • URL: http://www8.gsb.columbia.edu/ceasa • Financial reporting that reflects economic reality and investment advice that communicates sound valuations.

Connecticut Society of Certified Public Accountants Education and Research Foundation. 845 Brook St., Bldg. 2, Rocky Hill, CT 06067-3405. Phone: 800-232-2232 or (860)258-4800; Fax: (860)258-4859; Email: artr@cs-cpa.org • URL: http://www.cs-cpa.org • Accounting.

Monash University - Centre for Research in Accounting and Finance. Wellington Rd., Bldg. 11E, Clayton, VIC 3168, Australia. Phone: 61 3 99052389; Fax: 61 3 99055475; Email: kim.langfield-smith@buseco.monash.edu.au • URL: http://www.buseco.monash.edu.au/aaf/research/ • Accounting and finance.

Rutgers University - Rutgers Accounting Research Center. Rutgers Business School, Rm. 919, 1 Washington Park, Newark, NJ 07102-3122. Phone: (973)353-5172; Fax: (973)353-1283; Email: miklosv@andromeda.rutgers.edu • URL: http://raw.rutgers.edu • Accounting theory and practice, especially digital accounting, continuous reporting and continuous audit.

Stockholm School of Economics - Department of Accounting - Center for Accounting and Managerial Finance. PO Box 6501, SE-113 83 Stockholm, Sweden. Phone: 46 8 7369000; Fax: 46 8 318186; Email: info@hhs.se • URL: http://www.economicresearch.se/amf • Accounting theory, management accounting, financial accounting, and financial markets.

Universitat Pompeu Fabra - Research Center in Financial Economics and Accounting. Ramon Trias Fargas, 25-27, E-08005 Barcelona, Spain. Phone: 34 93 5421619; Fax: 34 93 5421746; Email: xavier.freixas@upf.edu • URL: http://www.crefc.upf.edu • Financial economics, accounting, and business.

University of Illinois at Urbana-Champaign - Center for International Education and Research in Accounting. 320 Wohlers Hall, 1206 S 6th St., Champaign, IL 61820. Phone: (217)333-4545; Fax: (217)244-6565; Email: ciera@uiuc.edu • URL: http://www.cba.uiuc.edu.

University of Newcastle upon Tyne - Cultures, Imperialism and Accounting Practice Research Group. Ridley Bldg., Business School, Newcastle upon Tyne NE1 7RU, United Kingdom. Phone: 44 191 2227586; Email: s.s.k.davie@newcastle.ac.uk • URL: http://www.ncl.ac.uk/niassh/ciap/index.htm • History of accounting across cultures and its relation to economics, politics, and society.

TRADE/PROFESSIONAL ASSOCIATIONS

Accounting and Auditing Organization for Islamic Financial Institutions. Yateem Center, Blk. 304, Al Muthana Rd., Manama, Bahrain. Phone: 973 17 244 496; Fax: 973 17 250 194 • URL: http://www.aaoifi.com • Represents central banks, Islamic financial institutions, and other participants from the international Islamic banking and finance industry. Aims to uphold the accounting and auditing standards of Islamic financial institutions. Provides its members the necessary resources needed to improve and maintain the quality of service of Islamic financial institutions.

American Institute of Certified Public Accountants. 1211 Avenue of the Americas, New York, NY 10036-8775. Phone: 888-777-7077 or (212)596-6200; Fax: (212)596-6213; Email: service@aicpa.org • URL: http://www.aicpa.org • Professional society of accountants certified by the states and territories. Responsibilities include establishing auditing and reporting standards; influencing the development of financial accounting standards underlying the presentation of U.S. corporate financial statements; preparing and grading the national Uniform CPA Examination for the state licensing bodies. Conducts research and continuing education programs and oversight of practice. Maintains over 100 committees including Accounting Standards, Accounting and Review Services, AICPA Effective Legislation Political Action, Auditing Standards, Taxation, Consulting Services, Professional Ethics, Quality Review, Women and Family Issues, and Information Technology.

American Society of Cost Segregation Professionals. 1101 Pennsylvania Ave. NW, 6th Fl., Washington, DC 20004. Phone: (203)671-7372; Fax: (203)745-0724; Email: info@ascsp.org • URL: http://www.ascsp.org • Seeks to address the growing need for credentials, educational programs, technical standards and a code of ethics for the cost segregation industry. Establishes a measurable standard by which cost segregation consultants will be evaluated. Develops benchmark technical standards for reporting that are aligned with the IRS Audit Techniques Guide for Cost Segregation.

Association for Accounting Administration. 136 S Keowee St., Dayton, OH 45402. Phone: (937)222-0030; Fax: (937)222-5794; Email: aaainfo@cpaadmin.org • URL: http://www.cpaadmin.org • Members are accounting and office systems executives.

Association of Government Accountants. 2208 Mt. Vernon Ave., Alexandria, VA 22301-1314. Phone: 800-AGA-7211 or (703)684-6931; Fax: (703)548-9367; Email: agamembers@agacgfm.org • URL: http://www.agacgfm.org • Members are employed by federal, state, county, and city government agencies. Includes accountants, auditors, budget officers, and other government finance administrators and officials.

Financial Managers Society. 1 N La Salle St., Ste. 3100, Chicago, IL 60602-4003. Phone: 800-275-4367 or (312)578-1300; Fax: (312)578-1308; Email: info@fmsinc.org • URL: http://www.fmsinc.org • Works for the needs of finance and accounting professionals from banks, thrifts and credit unions. Offers career-enhancing education, specialized publications, national leadership opportunities and worldwide connections with other industry professionals.

National Association of Certified Public Bookkeepers. 140 N Union Ave., Ste. 240, Farmington, UT 84025-2954. Phone: 866-444-9989; Fax: (801)451-4688; Email: info@nacpb.org • URL: http://www.nacpb.org • Aims to protect the public interest by ensuring that only qualified individuals provide public bookkeeping services. Fosters the professional development of public bookkeepers. Offers certification programs in bookkeeping.

National Society of Accountants. 1010 N Fairfax St., Alexandria, VA 22314. Phone: 800-966-6679 or (703)549-6400; Fax: (703)549-2984; Email: members@nsacct.org • URL: http://www.nsacct.org • Formerly *National Society of Public Accountants.*

ACCOUNTING, BANK

See BANK ACCOUNTING

ACCOUNTING, COMPUTERS IN

See COMPUTERS IN ACCOUNTING

ACCOUNTING, COST

See COST ACCOUNTING

ACCOUNTING, GOVERNMENT

See GOVERNMENT ACCOUNTING

ACCOUNTING RESEARCH

ABSTRACTS AND INDEXES

Business Periodicals Index Retrospective. EBSCO Publishing Inc. • 11/year. Quarterly and annual cumulations.

ALMANACS AND YEARBOOKS

Research in Accounting Regulation. Reed Elsevier Inc. • Irregular. Dates vary. Price varies. 15 volumes.

DIRECTORIES

The Association of Chartered Certified Accountants--Directory of Business Advisers. Association of Chartered Certified Accountants. • Annual. $20. Covers practicing accounting firms and individual accountants acting as non-executive directors.

INTERNET DATABASES

Rutgers Accounting Web. Rutgers University Accounting Research Center. Phone: (973)353-5172; Fax: (973)353-1283 • URL: http://www.rutgers.edu/accounting • RAW Web site provides extensive links to sources of national and international accounting information, such as the Big Six accounting firms, the Financial Accounting Standards Board (FASB), SEC filings (EDGAR), journals, publishers, software, the International Accounting Network, and "Internet's largest list of accounting firms in USA." Searching is offered. Fees: Free.

ONLINE DATABASES

Wilson Business Abstracts Online. H.W. Wilson Co. • Indexes and abstracts 600 major business periodicals, plus the *Wall Street Journal* and the business section of the *New York Times*. Indexing is from 1982, abstracting from 1990, with the two newspapers included from 1993. Updated weekly. Inquire as to online cost and availability. (*Business Periodicals Index* without abstracts is also available online.).

PERIODICALS AND NEWSLETTERS

CPA Technology and Internet Tax Advisor. Wolters Kluwer Law and Business. • Monthly. $261.00 per year. Newsletter. Describes hardware and software products and makes recommendations. Formerly *CPA Technology and Internet Advisor.*

Journal of Accounting Research. Institute of Professional Accounting. Blackwell Publishing Inc. • Five times a year. Institutions, $425.00 per year. Includes online edition. Annual *Supplement* available. Accepts for review unpublished research in the fields of empirical and experimental accounting.

RESEARCH CENTERS AND INSTITUTES

Accounting Research Program. UCLA Anderson School of Management, 110 Westwood Plz., Los Angeles, CA 90095-1481. Phone: (310)206-8711; Fax: (310)825-3165 • URL: http://www.anderson.ucla.edu.

Rutgers University - Rutgers Accounting Research Center. Rutgers Business School, Rm. 919, 1 Washington Park, Newark, NJ 07102-3122. Phone: (973)353-5172; Fax: (973)353-1283; Email: miklosv@andromeda.rutgers.edu • URL: http://raw.rutgers.edu • Accounting theory and practice, especially digital accounting, continuous reporting and continuous audit.

University of Illinois at Urbana-Champaign - Bureau of Economic and Business Research. 430 Wohlers Hall, Office of Research, College of Business, 1206 S 6th St., Champaign, IL 61820. Phone: (217)333-2330; Fax: (217)333-7410; Email: lhuff@uiuc.edu • URL: http://business.illinois.edu/research • Economics and business, including studies in business expectations, health economics, forecasting and planning, innovation, entrepreneurship, consumer behavior, poverty problems, small business operations and problems, investment and growth, productivity, research methodology, organizational behavior, and international business and banking.

University of Iowa - McGladrey Institute of Accounting Education and Research. 108 John Pappajohn Business Bldg., Henry B. Tippie College of Business, Iowa City, IA 52242-1994. Phone: 800-553-4692 or (319)335-0958 or (319)335-0862; Fax: (319)335-1956; Email: mark-penno@uiowa.edu • URL: http://tippie.uiowa.edu/accounting/mcgladrey/index.cfm • Accounting, auditing, and financial reporting by public and private organizations.

TRADE/PROFESSIONAL ASSOCIATIONS

American Woman's Society of Certified Public Accountants. 136 S Keowee St., Dayton, OH 45402. Phone: 800-297-2721 or (937)222-1872; Fax: (937)222-5794; Email: info@awscpa.org • URL: http://www.awscpa.org • Citizens who hold Certified Public Accountant certificates as well as those who have passed the CPA examination but do not have certificates. Works to improve the status of professional women and to make the business community aware of the professional capabilities of the woman CPA. Conducts semiannual statistical survey of members; offers specialized education and research programs.

ACID RAIN

See also ENVIRONMENT

ABSTRACTS AND INDEXES

Environment Abstracts. University Publications of America. • Monthly. Price varies. Provides multidisciplinary coverage of the world's environmental literature. Incorporates *Acid Rain Abstracts*.

Environment Abstracts Annual: A Guide to the Key Environmental Literature of the Year. University Publications of America. • Annual. $495.00. A yearly cumulation of *Environment Abstracts*.

Pollution Abstracts. Cambridge Information Group. • Monthly. $1,390.00 per year. Includes print and online editions; with index, $1,515.00 per year.

CD-ROM DATABASES

Environment Abstracts on CD-ROM. University Publications of America. • Quarterly. $1,295.00 per year. Contains the following CD-ROM databases: *Environment Abstracts*, *Energy Abstracts*, and *Acid Rain Abstracts*. Length of coverage varies.

ACOUSTICAL ENGINEERING

See NOISE CONTROL

ACQUISITIONS AND MERGERS

See MERGERS AND ACQUISITIONS

ACTUARIAL SCIENCE

ALMANACS AND YEARBOOKS

American Yearbook and Leadership Manual. American Academy of Actuaries. • Annual. $15.00.

Casualty Actuarial Society Yearbook and Proceedings. Casualty Actuarial Society. • Annual. $40. Approximately 2,500 actuaries working in insurance other than life insurance.

Society of Actuaries Yearbook. Society of Actuaries. • Annual. The yearbook houses information from each department within the SOA. Background information, bylaws, statements and other governing documents, recipients of awards and past officer listings are all easily accessible.

PERIODICALS AND NEWSLETTERS

The Actuary. Society of Actuaries. • Bimonthly. Description: Features information about actuaries practicing in life and health insurance, pensions, and investments in the U.S. and Canada. Recurring features include letters to the editor, news of research and education, a calendar of events, reports of meetings, notices of publications available, and puzzles.

Contingencies: The Magazine of the Actuarial Profession. American Academy of Actuaries. • Bimonthly. $24 Nonmembers. Provides non-technical articles on the actuarial aspects of insurance, employee benefits, and pensions.

STATISTICS SOURCES

Vital Statistics of the United States: Life Tables. U. S. Government Printing Office. • Annual. $64. Produced by the National Center for Health Statistics, Public Health Service, U. S. Department of Health and Human Services. Provides detailed data on expectation of life by age, race, and sex. Historical data is shown annually from the year 1900. (Vital Statistics, volume 2.).

TRADE/PROFESSIONAL ASSOCIATIONS

Casualty Actuarial Society. 4350 N Fairfax Dr., Ste. 250, Arlington, VA 22203. Phone: (703)276-3100; Fax: (703)276-3108; Email: office@casact.org • URL: http://www.casact.org • Professional society of property/casualty actuaries. Seeks to advance the body of knowledge of actuarial science applied to property, casualty and similar risk exposures, to maintain qualification standards, promote high standards of conduct and competence, and increase awareness of actuarial science. Examinations required for membership.

Conference of Consulting Actuaries. 3880 Salem Lake Dr., Ste. H, Long Grove, IL 60047-5292. Phone: (847)719-6500; Email: conference@ccactuaries.org • URL: http://www.ccactuaries.org • Formerly Conference of Actuaries of Public Practice.

ADDITIVES AND FLAVORINGS

ABSTRACTS AND INDEXES

Applied Science and Technology Index. EBSCO Publishing Inc. • 11/year. Indexes a wide variety of English language technical, industrial, and engineering periodicals.

Current Contents: Engineering, Computing and Technology. Thomson Reuters Intellectual Property and Science. • Weekly. $730 per year. Reproductions of contents pages of technical journals. Includes *Author Index*, *Address Directory*, *Current Book Contents*, and *Title Word Index*. Formerly *Current Contents: Engineering, Technology and Applied Sciences*.

Food Science and Technology Abstracts. Ovid Technologies Inc. • Monthly. $1,780.00 per year. Provides worldwide coverage of the literature of food technology and food production.

Foods Adlibra: Key to the World's Food Literature. General Mills, Inc. Foods Adlibra Publications. • Semimonthly. $240.00 per year. Provides journal citations and abstracts to the literature of food technology and packaging.

ALMANACS AND YEARBOOKS

Feed Additive Compendium. Miller Publishing Co. • Annual. $260 U.S. and Canada. Covers the use of drugs as additives to livestock and poultry feed.

DIRECTORIES

Directory of African Importers of Food Additives and Aromatics. EXIM Infotek Private Ltd. • $150 Individuals. Covers: 40 African importers of aromatic chemicals, bakery and pastry ingredients, food additives, food colors, food colouring, fragrances, flavors, and yeast. Entries include: Company name, postal address, telephone, fax, e-mail, website, contact person, designation, and product details.

Directory of Asian Importers of Food Additives and Aromatics. EXIM Infotek Private Ltd. • $750 Individuals. Covers: 410 Asian importers of agar, agar-agar, aromatic chemicals, chemical for food, essence, flavor and fragrance chemicals, flavoring materials, flavoring essence, food additives, food colors, food flavors, food ingredients, food raw materials, fragrances, fruit powder, natural coloring matters, oleoresin, raw material for flavors, raw materials for food colors, tapioca starch, vanillin (pollar BR), whey powder, xylitol, and yeasts. Entries include: Company name, postal address, telephone, fax, e-mail, website, contact person, designation, and product details.

Directory of Australia and New Zealand Importers of Food Additives and Aromatic Chemicals. EXIM Infotek Private Ltd. • $150 Individuals. Covers: 30 Australian and New Zealand importers of bakery raw materials, baking improvers, carbohydrates derivatives, citrates, essence, flavor and fragrance chemicals, flavors, flower essences, food additives, food colors, food chemicals, food colors, food ingredients, fragrances, industrial food flavors, and industrial food ingredients. Entries include: Company name, postal address, telephone, fax, e-mail, website, contact person, designation, and product details.

Directory of Chinese Manufacturers & Exporters of Food Additives & Aromatic Chemicals. EXIM Infotek Private Ltd. • $5 Individuals. Covers: 40 Chinese manufacturers and exporters of essence, flavors, food additives, food flavor, food ingredients, and yeast. Entries include: Company name, postal address, city, country, phone, fax, e-mail and websites, contact person, designation, and product details.

Directory of Chinese Manufacturers & Exporters of Spices, Seasonings & Flavorings. EXIM Infotek Private Ltd. • $5 Individuals. Covers: 30 Chinese manufacturers and exporters of chili, dried chili, dried ginger, garlic powder, pepper, salt, seasonings, spices. Entries include: Company name, postal address, city, country, phone, fax, e-mail and websites, contact person, designation, and product details.

Directory of Indian Importers of Food Additives and Aromatics. EXIM Infotek Private Ltd. • $5 Individuals. Covers: 40 Indian importers of aroma chemicals, flavors, food additives, food colors, fragrances, and vanillin (pollar Br). Entries include: Company name, postal address, telephone, fax, e-mail, website, contact person, designation, and product details.

Directory of Japanese Importers of Food Additives and Aromatic Chemicals. EXIM Infotek Private Ltd. • $350 Individuals. Covers: 145 Japanese importers of agar-agar, aromatic chemicals, essence, food additives, food colors, food flavors, food ingredients, fragrances, natural coloring matters, raw materials for food colors, and yeasts. Entries include: Company name, postal address, telephone, fax, e-mail, website, contact person, designation, and product details.

Directory of Japanese Manufacturers & Exporters of Food Additives & Aromatic Chemicals. EXIM Infotek Private Ltd. • $5 Individuals. Covers: 30 Japanese manufacturers and exporters of aromatic chemicals, dairy farming products, food additives, food flavoring. Entries include: Company name, postal address, city, country, phone, fax, e-mail and websites, contact person, designation, and product details.

Directory of Middle East Importers of Food Additives and Aromatics. EXIM Infotek Private Ltd. • $250 Individuals. Covers: 90 Middle East importers of additives, aromatic chemicals, artificial sweeteners, food additives, food colors, food chemicals, margarine, and yeast. Entries include: Company name, postal address, telephone, fax, e-mail, website, contact person, designation, and product details.

Directory of Middle East Importers of Photographic Equipment and Supplies. EXIM Infotek Private Ltd. • $350 Individuals. Covers: 130 Middle East importers of cameras, lens and accessories, photographic chemicals, motion picture and theater equipment, cinematographic equipment and accessories, film, microfilm and blueprint equipment, motion picture film, photo processing and developing equipment, photographic apparatus and accessories, and photographic equipment. Entries include: Company name, postal address, telephone, fax, e-mail, website, contact person, designation, and product details.

Directory of North American Importers of Food Additives and Aromatics. EXIM Infotek Private Ltd. • $250 Individuals. Covers: 80 North American importers of aromatic chemicals, aromatics, baking ingredients, citric acid, flavor ingredients, flavoring extracts, food additives, food colors, food ingredients, food preparations, fragrances, preservatives, and starches. Entries include: Company name, postal address, telephone, fax, e-mail, website, contact person, designation, and product details.

Directory of Taiwanese Manufacturers & Exporters of Food Additives & Aromatic Chemicals. EXIM Infotek Private Ltd. • $5 Individuals. Covers: 40 Taiwanese manufacturers and exporters of aromo compounds, chemicals for food and beverages, colorants for food and beverages, and natural additives for the food and beverages. Entries include: Company name, postal address, city, country, phone, fax, e-mail and websites, contact person, designation, and product details.

Food Processing Guide and Directory. Putman Media Inc. • Annual. $90. Lists over 5,390 food ingredient and equipment manufacturers.

Major Food and Drink Companies of the World. Cengage Learning Inc. • 12th edition. eBook. Published by Graham & Whiteside. Contains profiles and trade names for more than 9,200 important food and beverage companies in various countries. In addition to foods, includes both alcoholic and nonalcoholic drink products.

ONLINE DATABASES

Applied Science and Technology Index Online. H.W. Wilson Co. • Provides online indexing of 500 major scientific, technical, industrial, and engineering periodicals. Time period is 1983 to date. Monthly updates. Inquire as to online cost and availability.

Food Science and Technology Abstracts (online). IFIS North American Desk. • Produced by International Food Information Service. Provides about 500,000 online citations, with abstracts, to the international literature of food science, technology, commodities, engineering, and processing. Approximately 2,000 periodicals are covered. Time period is 1969 to date, with monthly updates. Inquire as to online cost and availability.

PERIODICALS AND NEWSLETTERS

Flavour and Fragrance Journal. John Wiley and Sons, Inc., Journals Div. • Bimonthly. Individuals, $890.00 per year; institutions, $1,185.00 per year.

Food Additives and Contaminants: Analysis, Surveillance, Evaluation, Control. Taylor & Francis Ltd. • Monthly. Institutions $2,038.00 per year.

Food Distribution Magazine. Phoenix Media Network Inc. • Monthly. $49.00 per year. Edited for marketers and buyers of domestic and imported, specialty or gourmet food products, including ethnic foods, seasonings, and bakery items.

Food Processing. Putman Media Inc. • Monthly. $89 others. Edited for executive and operating personnel in the food processing industry.

The Monell Connection: From the Monell Chemical Senses Center, a Nonprofit Scientific Institute Devoted to Research on Taste and Smell. Monell Chemical Senses Center. • Three times a year. Free. Newsletter. Includes brief summaries of selected papers describing ongoing work of Monell scientists.

Perfumer and Flavorist. Allured Business Media. • Monthly. $135.00 per year. Provides information on the art and technology of flavors and fragrances, including essential oils, aroma chemicals, and spices.

RESEARCH CENTERS AND INSTITUTES

Institute of Food Science. Cornell University, 114 Stocking Hall, Ithaca, NY 14853-7201. Phone: (607)255-7900; Fax: (607)254-4868; Email: ddm2@cornell.edu • URL: http://www.nysaes.cornell.edu/cifs • Research areas include the chemistry and processing of food commodities, food processing engineering, food packaging, and nutrition.

University of Wisconsin—Madison - College of Agricultural and Life Sciences - Food Research Institute. Microbial Sciences Bldg., 1550 Linden Dr., Madison, WI 53706. Phone: (608)263-7777; Fax: (608)263-1114; Email: czuprync@svm.vetmed.wisc.edu • URL: http://fri.wisc.edu • Food microbiology and toxicology, with emphasis on practical problems of food producers and distributors, including studies on foodborne diseases; food safety, preservation, processing, handling, spoilage, quality, and allergens; mycotoxins; heat induced mutagens in food; and anti-carcinogens in food.

TRADE/PROFESSIONAL ASSOCIATIONS

Chemical Sources Association. 3301 Rte. 66, Ste. 205, Bldg. C, Neptune, NJ 07753. Phone: (732)922-3008; Fax: (732)922-3590 • URL: http://www.chemicalsources.org • Representatives of flavor and fragrance manufacturers. Purpose is to find suppliers and manufacturers for rare or hard-to-obtain chemicals and essential oils used in the flavor and fragrance industry. Compiles statistics.

National Association of Flavors and Food-Ingredient Systems. 3301 Rte. 66, Bldg. C, Ste. 205, Neptune, NJ 07753. Phone: (732)922-3218; Fax: (732)922-3590; Email: info@naffs.org • URL: http://www.naffs.org • Manufacturers of fruit and syrup toppings, flavors and stabilizers for the food industry. Formerly National Association of Fruits, Flavors and Syrups.

ADHESIVES

ABSTRACTS AND INDEXES

Applied Science and Technology Index. EBSCO Publishing Inc. • 11/year. Indexes a wide variety of English language technical, industrial, and engineering periodicals.

Chemical Abstracts. American Chemical Society Chemical Abstracts Service. • Available via CAS' electronic products including SciFinder and STN.

CPI Digest: Key to World Literature Serving the Coatings, Plastics, Fibers, Adhesives, and Related Industries. CPI Information Services. • Monthly. $397.00 per year. Abstracts of business and technical articles for polymer-based, chemical process industries. Includes a monthly list of relevant U. S. patents. International coverage.

NTIS Alerts: Materials Sciences. U.S. Department of Commerce National Technical Information Service. • Biweekly. $130 per year. Covers ceramics, glass, coatings, composite materials, alloys, plastics, wood, paper, adhesives, fibers, lubricants, and related subjects.

DIRECTORIES

Adhesives Age Buyers Guide. Chemical Week Associates. • Annual. Lists manufacturers and suppliers of raw materials, chemicals, equipment, and machinery for the adhesives industry.

Assembly Buyers Guide. Reed Elsevier Group plc Reed Business Information. • Annual. $68.00. Lists manufacturers and suppliers of equipment relating to assembly automation, fasteners, adhesives, robotics, and power tools.

Directory of American Manufacturers & Exporters of Adhesive, Glues & Sealants. EXIM Infotek Private Ltd. • $30 Individuals. Covers: 390 American manufacturers and exporters of adhesive applicators, adhesive chemicals, adhesive fastening systems, adhesive paper rolls, adhesive products, adhesives, adhesives for duct insulation, adhesives for leather and rubber, adhesives-bonding, adhesives-bushing, adhesives-canvas, adhesives-ceramic, adhesives-concrete, adhesives-cyanocrylates, adhesives-electrical, adhesives-electrically conductive, adhesives-epoxy, adhesives-gasket, adhesives-gasoline resistant, adhesives-glass block, adhesives-graphite, adhesives-grinding and polishing wheel, adhesives-heat seal, adhesives-hot melt, adhesives-latex, adhesives-leather, adhesives-linoleum, adhesives-metal, adhesives-oil resistant, adhesives-paper, adhesives-patching and repair, adhesives-plastic, adhesives-pressure sensitive products, adhesives-raw materials, adhesives-resin, adhesives-structural laminating, adhesives-textile bonding, adhesives-therosetting and thermoplastic, adhesives-ultra violet curing, adhesives-urethane, adhesives-vinyl, adhesives-water resistant, adhesives-waterproofing, adhesives-wood and plywood, aerosol, animal glue, carpet and ceramic flooring, carton sealing adhesives, cyanoacrylates, cyanocrylate adhesives, epoxy, epoxy adhesives, epoxy solvent, eva and polyamide based adhesives for product assembly, floor covering installation adhesives, flooring adhesives, fluid applied roofing, glue, glue-bookbinders, glue-casein, heat seal adhesives, high temp adhesives, hot melt adhesives, industry adhesives, packaging adhesive, polishing wheel and belt inorganic adhesives, polyurethane adhesives, potting compounds, precision torque strength sealing, sealants, structural adhesives, stuffing box sealant, threadlocking and retaining anaerobic, tire sealants, white glue, wire self adhesive backed clips, and woodworking adhesive. Entries include: Company name, postal address, city, country, telephone, fax, e-mail and websites, contact person, designation, and product details.

Directory of Chinese Manufacturers & Exporters of Adhesive, Glues, Sealants. EXIM Infotek Private Ltd. • $10 Individuals. Covers: 50 Chinese manufacturers and exporters of adhesive products, adhesives, bone glue, epoxy resins, glue, glue products, hot melt adhesives, polyurethane adhesive, and sealing materials. Entries include: Company name, postal address, city, country, phone, fax, e-mail and websites, contact person, designation, and product details.

Directory of Japanese Manufacturers & Exporters of Adhesive, Glues & Sealants. EXIM Infotek Private Ltd. • $5 Individuals. Covers: 20 Japanese manufacturers & exporters of adhesives, epoxy resins, glue, plastic adhesives. Entries include: Company name, postal address, city, country, phone, fax, e-mail & websites, contact person, designation, products detail.

Directory of South Korean Manufacturers & Exporters of Adhesive, Glues & Sealants. EXIM Infotek Private Ltd. • $5 Individuals. Covers: 30 South Korean manufacturers and exporters of processed rubber-solution and adhesives, synthetic adhesives. Entries include: Company name, postal address, city, country, phone, fax, e-mail and websites, contact person, designation, and product details.

Directory of Taiwanese Manufacturers & Exporters of Adhesive, Glues & Sealants. EXIM Infotek Private Ltd. • $20 Individuals. Covers: 190 Taiwanese manufacturers and exporters of adhesives-instant settings, adhesive packing materials, glue, processed rubber-solution and adhesives, and synthetic adhesives. Entries include: Company name, postal address, city, country, phone, fax, e-mail and websites, contact person, designation, and product details.

Glues Directory--Wholesalers. InfoGroup Inc. • Annual. Number of listings: 916. Entries include: Name, address, phone, size of advertisement, name of owner or manager, number of employees, year first in "Yellow Pages." Compiled from telephone company "Yellow Pages," nationwide.

FINANCIAL RATIOS

Annual Statement Studies. Risk Management Association. • Annual. Compiled from over 280,000 financial statements.

Annual Statement Studies: Industry Default Probabilities and Cash Flow Measures. Risk Management Association. • Annual. $405 Nonmembers. Serves as a companion volume to the original *Annual Statement Studies*. Gives probability of default estimates on a percentage scale for more than 450 industries. Includes changes in position year-by-

For publishers' addresses, refer to SOURCES CITED section at the back of the book.

year for eight financial statement line items and provides percentage measures of cash flow.

ONLINE DATABASES

CA Search. American Chemical Society Chemical Abstracts Service. • Guide to chemical literature, 1967 to present. Inquire as to online cost and availability.

World Surface Coatings Abstracts (Online). Paint Research Association of Great Britain. • Indexing and abstracting of the literature of paint and surface coatings, 1976 to present. Monthly updates. Inquire as to online cost and availability.

PERIODICALS AND NEWSLETTERS

Adhesives Age. Chemical Week Associates. • Monthly. $60 Individuals.

The Composites and Adhesives Newsletter. T/C Press. • Quarterly. $190.00. Presents news of the composite materials and adhesives industries, with particular coverage of new products and applications.

International Journal of Adhesion and Adhesives. Elsevier. • $1,858.40 Institutions. Six times a year. Published in England.

Journal of Adhesion. Taylor & Francis Ltd. • Monthly. $3,193 Individuals. Monthly. Three volumes. Individuals, $1,575.00 per year; institutions, $3,056.00 per year; corporations, $6,760.00 per year.

U.S. Glass, Metal, and Glazing. AutoGlass Repair and Replacement Key Communications Inc. • Monthly. $35.00 per year. Edited for glass fabricators, glaziers, distributors, and retailers. Special feature issues are devoted to architectural glass, mirror glass, windows, storefronts, hardware, machinery, sealants, and adhesives. Regular topics include automobile glass and fenestration (window design and placement).

STATISTICS SOURCES

U.S. Industry and Trade Outlook. U.S. Department of Commerce National Technical Information Service. • Annual. Produced by the International Trade Administration, U.S. Department of Commerce, in a "public-private" partnership with DRI/ McGraw-Hill and Standard & Poor's. Provides basic data, outlook for the current year, and "Long-Term Prospects" (five-year projections) for a wide variety of products and services. Includes high technology industries. Formerly *U.S. Industrial Outlook.*

ADMINISTRATION

See also BUSINESS; EXECUTIVES; INDUSTRIAL MANAGEMENT; PUBLIC ADMINISTRATION

ABSTRACTS AND INDEXES

Business Periodicals Index Retrospective. EBSCO Publishing Inc. • 11/year. Quarterly and annual cumulations.

CD-ROM DATABASES

Business Abstracts with Full Text. EBSCO Publishing Inc. • Includes full text articles from more than 460 business publications from 1982 to present. Indexing for nearly 880 publications.

DIRECTORIES

Management Professionals Association--Directory of MPA Members. Management Professionals Association. • Annual. Covers: 26,000 members worldwide. Entries include: Company name, member name and title, address, phone, biographical information.

Reference Book of Corporate Managements. • Annual. Libraries, $650.00 per year; others, $795.00 per year. Lease basis. Management executives at over 12,000 leading United States companies.

INTERNET DATABASES

EBSCO Information Services. EBSCO Publishing Inc. 10 Estes St., Ipswich, MA 01938-2106. Phone: 800-653-2726 or (978)356-6500; Fax: (978)356-6565; Email: information@ebscohost.com • URL: http://www.ebscohost.com • Fee-based Web site providing Internet access to a wide variety of databases, including business-related material. Full text is available for many periodical titles, with daily updates. Fees: Apply.

InSite 2. Intelligence Data/Thomson Financial. Phone: 800-654-0393 or (617)856-1890; Fax: (617)737-3182; Email: intelligence.data@tfn.com • URL: http://www.insite2.gale.com/ • Fee-based Web site consolidates information in a "Base Pack" consisting of Business InSite, Market InSite, and Company InSite. Optional databases are Consumer InSite, Health and Wellness InSite, Newsletter InSite, and Computer InSite. Includes fulltext content from more than 2,500 trade publications, journals, newsletters, newspapers, analyst reports, and other sources. Continuous updating. Formerly produced by The Gale Group.

ProQuest. ProQuest L.L.C. 789 E Eisenhower Pkwy., Ann Arbor, MI 48106-1346. Phone: 800-521-0600 or (734)761-4700; Fax: (734)662-4554; Email: info@proquest.com • URL: http://www.proquest.com • Fee-based Web site providing Internet access to more than 3,000 periodicals, newspapers, and other publications. Many items are available full-text, with daily updates. Includes extensive corporate and financial information. Fees: Apply.

ONLINE DATABASES

Wilson Business Abstracts Online. H.W. Wilson Co. • Indexes and abstracts 600 major business periodicals, plus the *Wall Street Journal* and the business section of the *New York Times.* Indexing is from 1982, abstracting from 1990, with the two newspapers included from 1993. Updated weekly. Inquire as to online cost and availability. (*Business Periodicals Index* without abstracts is also available online.).

OTHER SOURCES

How to Manage Conflict in the Organization. American Management Association Extension Institute. • Looseleaf. $139.00. Self-study course. Emphasis is on practical explanations, examples, and problem solving. Quizzes and a case study are included.

PERIODICALS AND NEWSLETTERS

Academy of Management Journal. Academy of Management. • Bimonthly. $180 /year for individuals and academic libraries (print only). Presents research papers on management-related topics.

Academy of Management Perspectives. Academy of Management. • Quarterly. $130 /year for individuals in U.S. (print only). Contains articles relating to the practical application of management principles and theory.

Administrative Science Quarterly. Cornell University, Johnson Graduate School of Management. • Quarterly. $299 Institutions combined (print & e-access).

California Management Review. University of California at Berkeley. • Quarterly. $122 Individuals print and online.

Church Executive: The First Source of Information for Business Administrators of America's Largest Churches. Power Trade Media L.L.C. • Monthly. $39 Individuals. Magazine for church leaders.

Forbes. Forbes Inc. • Biweekly. $29.99 Individuals. Magazine reporting on industry, business and finance management.

Fortune Magazine. Time Inc., Business Information Group. • Biweekly. $19.99 all access. Edited for top executives and upper-level managers.

Harvard Management Update. Harvard Business School Publishing. • Description: Provides information on current management techniques and trends.

SAM Advanced Management Journal. Society for Advancement of Management. Society for Advancement of Management. • Quarterly. $64 Individuals one year. Provides information on leading business topics for practicing managers.

RESEARCH CENTERS AND INSTITUTES

Board of Research. Babson College, 204 Babson, Babson Park, MA 02457-0310. Phone: (781)235-1200; Fax: (718)239-6416; Email: chern@babson.edu • URL: http://www.babson.edu/bor • Research areas include management, entrepreneurial characteristics, and multi-product inventory analysis.

Financial Executives Research Foundation. Financial Executives International, 1250 Headquarters Plz., West Tower, 7th Fl., Morristown, NJ 07960. Phone: (973)765-1000; Fax: (973)765-1018; Email: mhollein@financialexecutives.org • URL: http://www.financialexecutives.org • Publishes research in business management, with emphasis on corporate financial management issues. Maintains inquiry services.

TRADE/PROFESSIONAL ASSOCIATIONS

Alpha Kappa Psi. 7801 E 88th St., Indianapolis, IN 46256-1233. Phone: (317)872-1553; Fax: (317)872-1567; Email: mail@akpsi.org • URL: http://www.akpsi.org • Professional fraternity - business administration. Conducts educational and charitable programs. Focuses on leadership development.

American Management Association. 1601 Broadway, New York, NY 10019-7420. Phone: 877-566-9441 or (212)586-8100 or (518)891-5510; Fax: (212)903-8168 or (518)891-0368; Email: customerservice@amanet.org • URL: http://www.amanet.org • Provides educational forums worldwide where members and their colleagues learn superior, practical business skills and explore best practices of world-class organizations through interaction with each other and expert faculty practitioners. Maintains a publishing program providing tools individuals use to extend learning beyond the classroom in a process of life-long professional growth and development through education.

Association of Latino Administrators and Superintendents. PO Box 65204, Washington, DC 20035. Phone: (202)466-0808; Email: contact@alasedu.org • URL: http://www.alasedu.net • Represents the interests of Latino superintendents and administrators. Provides professional development programs to strengthen the skills of superintendents, principals and other administrators. Advocates for policies to ensure the quality of the public education system.

Canadian Institute of Certified Administrative Managers. 15 Collier St., Lower Level, Toronto, ON, Canada M4T 2T5. Phone: (705)725-8926; Fax: (705)725-8196; Email: office@cim.ca • URL: http://www.cicam.org • Certified administrative managers. Promotes excellence in the practice of administrative management. Facilitates communication and cooperation among members; makes available continuing professional development courses.

Delta Mu Delta Honor Society. 9217 Broadway Ave., Brookfield, IL 60513-1251. Phone: 866-789-7067 or (708)485-8494; Fax: (708)221-6183; Email: dmd@dmd-ntl.org • URL: http://deltamudelta.org • Serves as honor society for business administration.

European Women's Management Development Austria. Schmiedinger strasse 67, 5020 Salzburg, Austria. Email: austria@ewmd.org • URL: http://www.ewmd.org/chapter/104 • Aims to improve the quality of management with respect to people, children, age and the cultural diversity of Europe. Provides a forum for collecting and exchanging information about trends management development in Europe and worldwide. Promotes women in management. Facilitates communication among individuals involved in the development of new role models for better work-life-balance.

European Women's Management Development Switzerland. Stockerstrasse 56, 8002 Zurich, Switzerland. Email: switzerland@ewmd.org • URL: http://www.ewmd.org • Aims to improve the quality of management with respect to people, children, age and the cultural diversity of Europe. Provides a forum for collecting and exchanging information about trends management development in Europe and worldwide. Promotes women in management. Facilitates communication among individuals involved in the development of new role models for better work-life-balance.

EWMD ITALY: European Women's Management Development. c/o EWMD Brescia, via Papa Giovanni XXIII 74, Rezzato, I-25086 Brescia, Italy. Phone: 39 30 2793124; Email: italy@ewmd.org • URL: http://www.ewmd.org/chapter/106 • Aims to improve the quality of management with respect to people, children, age and the cultural diversity of Europe. Promotes the best practices for work-life-balance management. Provides a forum for collecting and exchanging information about trends management development in Europe and worldwide. Promotes women in management. Facilitates communication among individuals involved in the development of new role models for better work-life-balance.

Graduate Management Admission Council. 11921 Freedom Dr., Ste. 300, Reston, VA 20190. Phone: 866-505-6559 or (703)668-9600; Fax: (703)668-9601; Email: customercare@gmac.com • URL: http://www.gmac.com • Graduate schools of management and business administration. Works to establish criteria for use in admission to graduate management programs. Provides professional development for academic administrators and seminars for admissions officers. Maintains Graduate Management Admission Search Service, a program that provides institutions with the names of qualified students with desirable characteristics. Employs Educational Testing Service to develop and administer the Graduate Management Admission Test. Conducts research on student selection issues and political and social issues related to graduate management education.

Institute of Administrative Management. Halesfield 7, Coppice House, Telford TF7 4NA, United Kingdom. Phone: 44 20 70912600 or 44 20 70912606; Fax: 44 20 70917340; Email: info@instam.org • URL: http://www.instam.org • Seeks to promote and develop, for the public benefit, the science of administrative management in all branches; encourage the attainment of professional academic qualifications. Provides the latest techniques and developments in the field of administrative management via conferences, seminars, meetings and publications.

Phi Gamma Nu. 6745 Cheryl Ann Dr., Seven Hills, OH 44131-3720. Phone: (216)524-0019; Email: pgnexecutivedirector@gmail.com • URL: http://www.phigammanu.com • Professional fraternity - business administration and economics.

Sigma Iota Epsilon. c/o Dr. G. James Francis, President, Colorado State University, 213 Rockwell Hall, Fort Collins, CO 80523. Phone: (970)491-6265 or (970)491-7200; Fax: (970)491-3522; Email: jim.francis@business.colostate.edu • URL: http://www.sienational.com • Honorary and professional fraternity for students in all management concentrations (business, construction management, etc.) Provides competitions, educational and charitable programs, and speakers' bureau on a local level. Student division of the Academy of Management.

Society for Advancement of Management. 6300 Ocean Dr., OCNR 330, Unit 5807, Corpus Christi, TX 78412. Phone: 888-827-6077 or (361)825-3045; Fax: (361)825-5609; Email: moustafa.abdelsamad@tamucc.edu • URL: http://www.samnational.org • Represents management executives in industry commerce, government, and education. Fields of interest include management education, policy and strategy, MIS, international management, administration, budgeting, collective bargaining, distribution, incentives, materials handling, quality control, and training.

ADMINISTRATIVE DECISION MAKING

See DECISION-MAKING

ADMINISTRATIVE LAW AND REGULATION

See also BUSINESS LAW; CORPORATION LAW AND REGULATION; LABOR LAW AND REGULATION; LAWS; LAWYERS

ABSTRACTS AND INDEXES

Current Law Index. Cengage Learning Inc. • $1,332 Individuals. Monthly. $1269.00 per year. Produced in cooperation with the American Association of Law Libraries. Indexes more than 900 law journals, legal newspapers, and specialty publications from the U.S., Canada, U.K., Ireland, Australia, and New Zealand.

Index to Legal Periodicals and Books. H.W. Wilson Co. • Monthly. $490.00 per year. Quarterly and annual cumulations.

BIBLIOGRAPHIES

Current Publications in Legal and Related Fields. American Association of Law Libraries. Fred B. Rothman and Co. • Looseleaf service. Annual cumulation.

CD-ROM DATABASES

Authority on Administrative Law. Matthew Bender and Company Inc. • Periodic updates. Price on request. Full text CD-ROM provides detailed information on Federal administrative procedural law. Contains a large number of judicial, regulatory, and statutory references.

Index to Legal Periodicals and Books. EBSCO Publishing Inc. • Contains indexing of more than 1,400 English language legal periodicals from 1981 to date and 2,500 books.

INTERNET DATABASES

Lexis.com Research System. Lexis-Nexis Group. Phone: 800-227-4908 or (937)865-6800; Fax: (937)865-6909; Email: webmaster@prod.lexis-nexis.com • URL: http://www.nexis.com • Fee-based Web site offers extensive searching of a wide variety of legal sources. Additional features include Daily Opinion Service, lexis.com Bookstore, Career Center, CLE Center, Law Schools, and Practice Pages ("Pages specific to areas of specialty").

OTHER SOURCES

Administrative Law. Matthew Bender and Company Inc. • Three times a year. $1,416.00. Six looseleaf volumes. Covers investigations, adjudications, hearings, licenses, judicial review, and so forth.

PERIODICALS AND NEWSLETTERS

Administrative Law Review. American Bar Association. • Quarterly. $10 Single issue. Scholarly legal journal on developments in the field of administrative law.

Federal Register. Office of the Federal Register. U. S. Government Printing Office. • Daily except Saturday and Sunday. $764.00 per year. Publishes regulations and legal notices issued by federal agencies, including executive orders and presidential proclamations. Issued by the National Archives and Records Administration (www.nara.gov).

ADULT EDUCATION

See also CORRESPONDENCE SCHOOLS AND COURSES; GRADUATE WORK IN UNIVERSITIES; TRAINING OF EMPLOYEES; VOCATIONAL EDUCATION

ABSTRACTS AND INDEXES

Current Index to Journals in Education (CIJE). Oryx Press. • Monthly. $245.00 per year. Semiannual cumulations, $475.00.

Education Index. H.W. Wilson Co. • 10 times a year. Quarterly and annual cumulations. Price varies.

CD-ROM DATABASES

ERIC SilverPlatter. U.S. Department of Education Institute of Education Sciences Education Resources Information Center. • Opinion papers, evaluations, speeches.

ONLINE DATABASES

Education Index Online. H.W. Wilson Co. • Indexes a wide variety of periodicals related to schools, colleges, and education, 1984 to date. Monthly updates. Inquire as to online cost and availability.

ERIC. U.S. Department of Education Institute of Education Sciences Educational Resources Information Center. • Funded by the U.S. Department of Education, Institute of Education Sciences (formerly Office of Educational Research and Improvement). Provides access to more than one million online records covering education-related journal and report literature, 1966 to date. Updating is monthly. Inquire as to online cost and availability.

PERIODICALS AND NEWSLETTERS

AAACE Adult Learning. American Association for Adult and Continuing Education. • Quarterly. $216 Institutions print and online.

Adult and Continuing Education Today. Learning Resources Network. • Biweekly. $95 Individuals.

Adult Education Quarterly: A Journal of Research and Theory. American Association for Adult and Continuing Education. Pine Forge Press. • Quarterly. $445 Institutions combined (print & e-access). Scholarly journal committed to advancing the understanding and practice of adult and continuing education.

Journal of Library and Information Services in Distance Learning. The Haworth Press Inc. • Quarterly. $150.00 per year to libraries; $48.00 per year to individuals.

Resources in Education. Educational Resources Information Center. U. S. Government Printing Office. • Monthly. Reports on educational research.

RESEARCH CENTERS AND INSTITUTES

FHI 360 - National Institute for Work and Learning. 1825 Connecticut Ave. NW, Washington, DC 20009. Phone: (202)884-8184; Fax: (202)884-8422; Email: icharner@fhi360.org • URL: http://www.niwl.org • Research areas include adult education, training, unemployment insurance, and career development.

TRADE/PROFESSIONAL ASSOCIATIONS

Association for Continuing Higher Education. OCCE Admin Bldg., Rm. 233, 1700 Asp Ave., Norman, OK 73072-6407. Phone: 800-807-2243 or (405)329-0249; Fax: (405)325-4888; Email: admin@acheinc.org • URL: http://www.acheinc.org • Institutional members are accredited colleges or universities that offer credit and non-credit continuing education; individual members are persons currently or formerly on the faculty or staff of a university continuing education division and those interested in supporting the association's work. Promotes high standards for professional excellence, stimulates faculty leadership in constructive support of continuing higher education programs, and cooperates with other groups and organizations in the achievement of these goals.

ADVERTISING

See also ADVERTISING AGENCIES; ADVERTISING MEDIA; ADVERTISING SPECIALTIES; DIRECT MAIL ADVERTISING; INDUSTRIAL ADVERTISING; MARKETING; OUTDOOR ADVERTISING; PUBLIC RELATIONS AND PUBLICITY; RADIO AND TELEVISION ADVERTISING

ABSTRACTS AND INDEXES

Business Periodicals Index Retrospective. EBSCO Publishing Inc. • 11/year. Quarterly and annual cumulations.

Communication Abstracts: An International Information Service. Pine Forge Press. • Bimonthly. Institutions, $1,150.00 per year. Provides broad coverage of the literature of communications, including broadcasting and advertising.

What's New in Advertising and Marketing. Special Libraries Association - Advertising and Marketing Div. • Quarterly. Non-profit organizations, $20.00 per year; corporations, $30.00 per year. Lists and briefly describes a wide variety of free or inexpensive material relating to advertising, marketing, and media.

ALMANACS AND YEARBOOKS

Advances in Library Administration and Organization. Delmus E. Williams and Janine Golden, editors. Emerald Group Publishing Ltd. • Annual. Price varies per volume. 31 volumes.

CD-ROM DATABASES

Advertiser and Agency Red Books Plus. National Register Publishing Co. • Quarterly. $1,295.00 per year. The CD-ROM version of *Standard Directory of Advertisers, Standard Directory of Advertising Agencies*, and *Standard Directory of International Advertisers and Agencies*.

Business Abstracts with Full Text. EBSCO Publishing Inc. • Includes full text articles from more than 460 business publications from 1982 to present. Indexing for nearly 880 publications.

OECD Statistical Compendium. Organization for Economic Cooperation and Development. • Semiannual. $1,905.00 per year for 1 to 10 users. CD-ROM contains more than 730,000 monthly, quarterly, and annual time series for OECD countries, 1960 to date. Includes fully searchable data on agriculture, food, economic indicators, national accounts, employment, energy, finance, industry, technology, and foreign trade. Results can be displayed in various forms.

DIRECTORIES

Addressing & Letter Service Directory. InfoGroup Inc. • Annual. Number of listings: 8,077. Entries include: Name, address, phone, size of advertisement, name of owner or manager, number of employees, year first in "Yellow Pages." Compiled from telephone company "Yellow Pages," nationwide.

Advertiser & Agency Red Books Plus. LexisNexis. • Quarterly. $2,195 Individuals. CD-ROM. Covers 15,750 of the world's top advertisers, their products and what media they use, as well as 13,900 U.S. and international ad agencies and nearly 100,000 key executives worldwide in management, creative, and media positions. Entries include: For advertisers--Company name, job function/title, product/brand name, advertising expenditures by media. For personnel--Name and title.

Advertiser's Yearbook. Oekonomisk Literatur Norge A/S. • Annual. $780. Covers: Advertising agencies in Norway. Entries include: Company name, address, phone, fax, management/ad/text, list of customers, special services, number of employees, share capital, sales.

Advertising Age--Agencies Ranked by Gross Income Issue. Crain Communications Inc. • Annual. $25 Individuals PDF. Covers: More than 600 advertising agencies. Publication includes: Ranked lists of about 650 U.S advertising agencies, 1,600 foreign agencies, the world's Top 50 advertising organizations, top media services companies in the U.S. and worldwide, top U.S. healthcare agencies, and multicultural agencies, which reported billings and gross income, or whose billings and gross incomes were ascertained through research. Entries include: For agencies with gross income over three million dollars: agency name, rank for two years, billing, gross income, and number of employees.

Advertising & Press Annual in Africa. International Publications Service. • Annual. Covers: African newspapers, magazines, radio and television stations, annuals, poster and transportation advertising and exhibits and shows; leading advertisers and professionals in the field in Africa; associations involved in a variety of fields of advertising and publicity in Africa.

Advertising Companies Contact Lists. Sheila Greco Associates L.L.C. • $65. Consists of 3 individually-priced lists covering advertising companies in the U.S. Each list features details for one company and includes global headquarter name, address, phone, fax, U.S. headquarter phone number, URL, company description, ticker symbol, revenues reported, industry type, key executive names and titles. All lists downloadable via PDF format.

Advertising Consultants Directory. InfoGroup Inc. • Annual. Number of listings: 51,839. Entries include: Name, address, phone, size of advertisement, name of owner or manager, number of employees, year first in "Yellow Pages." Compiled from telephone company "Yellow Pages," nationwide.

Advertising--Displays Directory. InfoGroup Inc. • Annual. Number of listings: 4,029. Entries include: Name, address, phone, size of advertisement, name of owner or manager, number of employees, year first in "Yellow Pages." Compiled from telephone company "Yellow Pages," nationwide.

Advertising (Promotional) Directory. InfoGroup Inc. • Annual. Number of listings: 6,226. Entries include: Name, address, phone, size of advertisement, name of owner or manager, number of employees, year first in "Yellow Pages." Compiled from telephone company "Yellow Pages," nationwide.

Advertising (Signs) Directory. InfoGroup Inc. • Annual. Number of listings: 28,945. Entries include: Name, address, phone, size of advertisement, name of owner or manager, number of employees, year first in "Yellow Pages." Compiled from telephone company "Yellow Pages," nationwide.

American Business Directory for the USSR. Amtorg Trading Corp. • Publication consists of paid advertisements and business reply cards from U.S. companies wishing to do business with the U.S.S.R.

Answering Bureaus Directory. InfoGroup Inc. • Annual. Number of listings: 5,102. Entries include: Name, address, phone, size of advertisement, name of owner or manager, number of employees, year first in "Yellow Pages." Compiled from telephone company "Yellow Pages," nationwide.

Catalogue of Manufacturers and Exporters. Durban Regional Chamber of Business. • Publication includes: Company listings of manufacturing members that do business with Africa in the following categories: basic metal, chemicals, clothing, food and beverages, furniture, hair care products, hardware, household, and investment, among others. Entries include: Company name, address, phone, fax. Principal content of publication is advertisements.

Directory of French Importers of Advertising and Display Articles and Supplies. EXIM Infotek Private Ltd. • $150 Individuals. Covers: 35 French importers of advertising articles, displays, flags, banners, and signs. Entries include: Company name, postal address, telephone, fax, e-mail, website, contact person, designation, and product details.

International Advertising Association Membership Directory. International Advertising Association. • Annual. Membership. Available only online. Over 3,600 advertisers, advertising agencies, media, and other firms involved in advertising.

Internet Resources and Services for International Marketing and Advertising: A Global Guide. Greenwood Electronic Media. • $75 Individuals hardcover. Covers: Over 2,000 Web sites with information pertaining to marketing and advertising in more than 150 countries.

Outdoor Advertising Directory. InfoGroup Inc. • Annual. Number of listings: 2,647. Entries include: Name, address, phone, size of advertisement, name of owner or manager, number of employees, year first in "Yellow Pages." Compiled from telephone company "Yellow Pages," nationwide.

Real Estate Advertisers Directory. InfoGroup Inc. • Annual. Number of listings: 7,204. Entries include: Name, address, phone, size of advertisement, name of owner or manager, number of employees, year first in "Yellow Pages." Compiled from telephone company "Yellow Pages," nationwide.

Standard Directory of Advertisers: The Advertiser Red Book. LexisNexis. • Annual. $1,399 Individuals classified 2010. Covers over 14,000 U.S. and Canadian companies that place over $200,000 worth of national and/or regional advertising.

E-BOOKS

Ads to Icons. Cengage Learning Inc. • 2011. eBook. 2nd edition. Published by Kogan Page. Examines current and future trends in advertising. Through 50 international case studies of new and iconic advertising campaigns, author Paul Springer identifies why these campaigns were successful and analyzes their contribution to the continued development of advertising.

INTERNET DATABASES

Business 2.0 Web Guide to the Best Business Links. Business 2.0 Media Inc. Phone: (415)293-4800; Email: support@business2.com • URL: http://www.business2.com/webguide • Web site presents an extensive, searchable directory of links to "the best, most informative, and authoritative web pages." Twenty main categories cover business, finance, career, company information, people, and technology topics, with thousands of subtopics, all linking to Web sites recommended by experienced business researchers. Fees: Free.

ONLINE DATABASES

Business Media Advertising Source®. Kantar Media SRDS. • Contains in-depth information on advertising opportunities in healthcare trade media throughout the world.

Wilson Business Abstracts Online. H.W. Wilson Co. • Indexes and abstracts 600 major business periodicals, plus the *Wall Street Journal* and the business section of the *New York Times*. Indexing is from 1982, abstracting from 1990, with the two newspapers included from 1993. Updated weekly. Inquire as to online cost and availability. (*Business Periodicals Index* without abstracts is also available online.).

PERIODICALS AND NEWSLETTERS

Advertising Age: The International Newspaper of Marketing. Crain Communications Inc. • Weekly.

$178.50 Individuals. Includes supplement *Creativity*.

Advertising Age's Euromarketing. Crain Communications Inc. • Weekly. $295 Individuals. Newsletter on European advertising and marketing.

ADWEEK. Nielsen Business Media Inc. • Weekly. $149 Individuals. Covers local, national, and international advertising news and trends. Includes critiques of advertising campaigns.

IAA National & World News. International Advertising Association. • Description: Supplies information on Association policies and activities. Includes reviews of publications and reports from the 62 chapters worldwide.

International Journal of Advertising: The Quarterly Review of Marketing Communications. Advertising Association. NTC Publications Ltd. • Quarterly. $490 standard subscription. Advertising journal.

An Introduction to the Advertising Business. Japan Advertising Agencies Association. • Biennial. Contains advertising information for employees newly recruited to member companies.

Journal of Advertising. M.E. Sharpe Inc. • Quarterly. $90 per year. An academic journal devoted to advertising theory and research.

Journal of Advertising Research. Advertising Research Foundation. • Quarterly. $365 Individuals standard subscription. Journal of advertising, marketing, and media research.

The Licensing Letter (TLL). EPM Communications Inc. • Description: Concerned with all aspects of licensed merchandising, "the business of associating someone's name, likeness or creation with someone else&'s product or service, for a consideration." Recurring features include statistics, research, events, mechanics, available properties, and identification of licensors, licensing agents, and licensees.

Med Ad News. Engel Publishing Partners. • Monthly. $225.00 per year. Covers the field of pharmaceutical advertising and marketing.

Media Industry Newsletter. Access Intelligence L.L.C. • Description: Covers the media industry, including advertising, marketing, publishing, radio, and television. Recurring features include weekly box scores of advertising pages in major magazines, salaries of top executives, earnings reports, and news of people in the industry.

Promotional Products Business. Promotional Products Association International. • Monthly. $58 /year for members. Magazine covering news, trends, new products and business issues affecting the promotional products industry. Official magazine of the Promotional Products Assoc. International.

STATISTICS SOURCES

Advertising Age: National Expenditures in Newspapers. Crain Communications Inc. • Annual.

U.S. Industry and Trade Outlook. U.S. Department of Commerce National Technical Information Service. • Annual. Produced by the International Trade Administration, U.S. Department of Commerce, in a "public-private" partnership with DRI/ McGraw-Hill and Standard & Poor's. Provides basic data, outlook for the current year, and "Long-Term Prospects" (five-year projections) for a wide variety of products and services. Includes high technology industries. Formerly *U.S. Industrial Outlook*.

TRADE/PROFESSIONAL ASSOCIATIONS

Association of National Advertisers. 708 3rd Ave., 33rd Fl., New York, NY 10017. Phone: (212)697-5950; Fax: (212)687-7310 • URL: http://www.ana.net • Serves the needs of members by providing marketing and advertising industry leadership in traditional and e-marketing, legislative leadership, information resources, professional development and industry-wide networking. Maintains offices in New York City and Washington, DC.

Digital Screenmedia Association. 13100 Eastpoint Park Blvd., Louisville, KY 40223. Phone: (502)489-3915 or (502)241-7545; Fax: (502)241-2795 • URL: http://www.digitalscreenmedia.org • Promotes the interests and serves the needs of companies engaged in the self-service and kiosk industry. Encourages its members to exercise effective and ethical business practices. Fosters the growth and health of the self-service and kiosk industry.

Direct Marketing Association. 1120 Ave. of the Americas, New York, NY 10036-6700. Phone: (212)768-7277; Fax: (212)302-6714; Email: info@the-dma.org • URL: http://www.thedma.org • A division of the Direct Marketing Association. Members include publishers and circulation directors.

National Advertising Review Board. 112 Madison Ave., 3rd ft., New York, NY 10016. Phone: (212)705-0115; Fax: (212)705-0136 • URL: http://www.asrcreviews.org/asrc-contact-us • Individuals from industry and the public. Sponsored by the National Advertising Review Council for the purpose of sustaining high standards of truth and accuracy in national advertising. Aims to maintain a self-regulatory mechanism that responds constructively to public complaints about national advertising and which significantly improves advertising performance and credibility.

ADVERTISING AGENCIES

See also ADVERTISING

CD-ROM DATABASES

Advertiser and Agency Red Books Plus. National Register Publishing Co. • Quarterly. $1,295.00 per year. The CD-ROM version of *Standard Directory of Advertisers*, *Standard Directory of Advertising Agencies*, and *Standard Directory of International Advertisers and Agencies*.

DIRECTORIES

Triangle Business Journal's Book of Lists. Greater Raleigh Chamber of Commerce. • $45 Members. Provides 25 listings for 75 different business sectors in Raleigh and Durham area including advertising agencies, architects, banks, real estate agencies, hotels, accountants, and golf courses.

FINANCIAL RATIOS

Annual Statement Studies. Risk Management Association. • Annual. Compiled from over 280,000 financial statements.

Annual Statement Studies: Industry Default Probabilities and Cash Flow Measures. Risk Management Association. • Annual. $405 Nonmembers. Serves as a companion volume to the original *Annual Statement Studies*. Gives probability of default estimates on a percentage scale for more than 450 industries. Includes changes in position year-by-year for eight financial statement line items and provides percentage measures of cash flow.

HANDBOOKS AND MANUALS

Advertising Agency. Entrepreneur Press. • Looseleaf. $69.00. A practical guide to starting a small advertising agency. Covers profit potential, start-up costs, market size evaluation, pricing, accounting, advertising, promotion, etc. (Start-Up Business Guide No. E1223.).

PERIODICALS AND NEWSLETTERS

American Advertising. American Advertising Federation. • Quarterly. Membership.

ADVERTISING ART

See COMMERCIAL ART

ADVERTISING, COOPERATIVE

See COOPERATIVE ADVERTISING

ADVERTISING COPY

ABSTRACTS AND INDEXES

Business Periodicals Index Retrospective. EBSCO Publishing Inc. • 11/year. Quarterly and annual cumulations.

DIRECTORIES

The ADWEEK Directory: The Directory of U.S. Advertising Agencies, Public Relations Firms and Media Buying Services. ADWEEK Magazines. • Annual. $499 Individuals 1 Directory. Covers: Over 23,000 personal listings and it has information on more than 5,900 full-service advertising agencies, public relations firms, media buying services, direct marketing and related organizations. Database includes: List of over 30,000 major accounts managed by agencies. Entries include: Agency name, address, phone, fax/e-mail, URL; names and titles of key personnel; major accounts; Ultimate parent company; headquarters location; major subsidiaries and other operating units; year founded; number of employees; fee income; billings; percentage of billings by medium. Individual listings for each agency branch.

ONLINE DATABASES

Wilson Business Abstracts Online. H.W. Wilson Co. • Indexes and abstracts 600 major business periodicals, plus the *Wall Street Journal* and the business section of the *New York Times*. Indexing is from 1982, abstracting from 1990, with the two newspapers included from 1993. Updated weekly. Inquire as to online cost and availability. (*Business Periodicals Index* without abstracts is also available online.).

PERIODICALS AND NEWSLETTERS

Print: America's Graphic Design Magazine. Krause Publications Inc. • Bimonthly. $57.00 per year. Emphasizes creative trends.

ADVERTISING, INDUSTRIAL

See INDUSTRIAL ADVERTISING

ADVERTISING LAW AND REGULATION

See also BUSINESS LAW

ABSTRACTS AND INDEXES

Business Periodicals Index Retrospective. EBSCO Publishing Inc. • 11/year. Quarterly and annual cumulations.

Current Law Index. Cengage Learning Inc. • $1,332 Individuals. Monthly. $1269.00 per year. Produced in cooperation with the American Association of Law Libraries. Indexes more than 900 law journals, legal newspapers, and specialty publications from the U.S., Canada, U.K., Ireland, Australia, and New Zealand.

Index to Legal Periodicals and Books. H.W. Wilson Co. • Monthly. $490.00 per year. Quarterly and annual cumulations.

ALMANACS AND YEARBOOKS

Advertising Law Guide. Wolters Kluwer Law & Business CCH. • Monthly. $2,115. Contains full-text reporting of state and federal laws as well as federal regulations.

DIRECTORIES

Lawyer's Register International by Specialties and Fields of Law Including a Directory of Corporate Counsel. Lawyer's Register Publishing Co. • Annual. $359 Individuals. Referral source for law firms.

For publishers' addresses, refer to SOURCES CITED section at the back of the book.

INTERNET DATABASES

Lexis.com Research System. Lexis-Nexis Group. Phone: 800-227-4908 or (937)865-6800; Fax: (937)865-6909; Email: webmaster@prod.lexis-nexis.com • URL: http://www.nexis.com • Fee-based Web site offers extensive searching of a wide variety of legal sources. Additional features include Daily Opinion Service, lexis.com Bookstore, Career Center, CLE Center, Law Schools, and Practice Pages ("Pages specific to areas of specialty").

OTHER SOURCES

Advertising Compliance Service Newsletter. John Lichtenberger. • Bimonthly. $495.00 per year.

Lindey on Entertainment, Publishing and the Arts. Alexander Lindey, editor. Thomson West. • $1,582.86 Full Set. Provides basic forms, applicable law, and guidance.

PERIODICALS AND NEWSLETTERS

Media and the Law. SIMBA Information Inc. • Semimonthly. $327.00 per year. Newsletter.

RESEARCH CENTERS AND INSTITUTES

Center for Study of Responsive Law. PO Box 19367, Washington, DC 20036. Phone: (202)387-8030; Fax: (202)234-5176 • URL: http://csrl.org • A consumer-oriented research group.

TRADE/PROFESSIONAL ASSOCIATIONS

National Advertising Review Board. 112 Madison Ave., 3rd ft., New York, NY 10016. Phone: (212)705-0115; Fax: (212)705-0136 • URL: http://www.asrcreviews.org/asrc-contact-us • Individuals from industry and the public. Sponsored by the National Advertising Review Council for the purpose of sustaining high standards of truth and accuracy in national advertising. Aims to maintain a self-regulatory mechanism that responds constructively to public complaints about national advertising and which significantly improves advertising performance and credibility.

National Consumer Law Center. 7 Winthrop Sq., Boston, MA 02110-1245. Phone: (617)542-8010; Fax: (617)542-8028; Email: consumerlaw@nclc.org • URL: http://www.nclc.org • Serves as a specialized resource in consumer and energy law funded by federal, state, and foundation grants and donations. Lawyers provide research, technical consulting, and in-depth assistance to legal services, private lawyers, and state agencies throughout the nation. Defines recurring patterns in the problems of low-income consumers and develops a series of alternative solutions utilizing litigation, legislation, lawyer training, and development of new service delivery systems. Seeks consultants for an interdisciplinary approach to problems. Conducts analyses of weatherization and energy assistance programs for low-income homeowners, renters, and state and federal agencies.

ADVERTISING MEDIA

See also ADVERTISING; MASS MEDIA; RADIO AND TELEVISION ADVERTISING

DIRECTORIES

Hispanic Media & Market Source. Kantar Media SRDS. • Quarterly. $445 per year. Provides detailed information on the following Hispanic advertising media in the U.S.: TV, radio, newspapers, magazines, direct mail, outdoor, and special events.

International Media Guide: Business-Professional: Asia/Pacific, Middle East, Africa. Kantar Media SRDS. • $553 Individuals online; 1 year. Provides information on 3,800 trade publications "from Africa to the Pacific Rim," including advertising rates and circulation data.

International Media Guide Business-Professional Publications: Europe. Kantar Media SRDS. • $553 Individuals online; 1 year. Describes 8,800 trade journals from Eastern and Western Europe, with advertising rates and circulation data.

International Media Guide: Business/Professional Publications: The Americas. Kantar Media SRDS. • $553 Individuals online; 1 year. Describes over 4,400 trade publications from North, South, and Central America, with advertising rates and circulation data.

International Media Guide: Newspapers Worldwide. Kantar Media SRDS. • $553 Individuals online; 1 year. Covers over 3,400 papers in every major city in the world.

SRDS Interactive Advertising Source. Kantar Media SRDS. • Quarterly. $569.00 per year. Provides descriptive profiles, rates, audience, personnel, etc., for producers of various forms of interactive or multimedia advertising: online/Internet, CD-ROM, interactive TV, interactive cable, interactive telephone, interactive kiosk, and others.

VNU Business Media. ADWEEK Media. • Annual. $100.00. Presents cost, circulation, and audience statistics for various mass media segments, including television, radio, magazines, newspapers, telephone yellow pages, and cinema.

ONLINE DATABASES

Arbitron Radio County Coverage. Arbitron Inc. • Ratings of radio and TV stations plus audience measurement data, updated frequently. Inquire as to online cost and availability.

PERIODICALS AND NEWSLETTERS

Advertising Age: The International Newspaper of Marketing. Crain Communications Inc. • Weekly. $178.50 Individuals. Includes supplement *Creativity*.

B to B: The Magazine for Marketing and E-Commerce Strategists. Crain Communications Inc. • Monthly. $59.00 per year. Formerly *Advertising Age's Business Marketing*.

Broadcasting and Cable. NewBay Media, LLC. • 51 times a year. $179.00 per year; includes print and online editions. Formerly *Broadcasting*.

Interactive Marketing and P R News: News and Practical Advice on Using Interactive Advertising and Marketing to Sell Your Products. Access Intelligence L.L.C. • Biweekly. $495.00 per year. Newsletter. Provides information and guidance on merchandising via CD-ROM ("multimedia catalogs"), the Internet, and interactive TV. Topics include "cybermoney," addresses for e-mail marketing, "virtual malls," and other interactive subjects. Formerly *Interactive Marketing News*.

Internet Business Report: Software, Tools and Platforms. Jupitermedia Corp. • Semimonthly. $695.00 per year; with electronic software, $795.00 per year. Newsletter. Covers Internet advertising, fee collection, and attempts in general to make the Internet/World Wide Web profitable. Includes news of how businesses are using the Internet for sales promotion and public relations.

Medical Marketing and Media. Haymarket Media, Inc. • Monthly. $148 U.S. 1-year subscription. Contains articles on marketing, direct marketing, advertising media, and sales personnel for the healthcare and pharmaceutical industries.

SHOOT: The Leading Newsweekly for Commercial Production and Postproduction. Nielsen Business Media Inc. • Weekly. $125 /year. Covers animation, music, sound design, computer graphics, visual effects, cinematography, and other aspects of television and motion picture production, with emphasis on TV commercials.

TRADE/PROFESSIONAL ASSOCIATIONS

Advertising Media Credit Executives Association. 24600 Detroit Rd., Ste. 100, Bay Village, OH 44140-0036. Email: amcea@tx.rr.com • URL: http://www.amcea.org • Credit executives for advertising media such as newspapers, magazines, radio, and television. Provides information for exchange of ideas on credit management methods and procedures; encourages study in advanced educational courses in fundamentals, such as business law, finance, banking, accounting, and economics.

Association of Free Community Papers. 7445 Morgan Rd., Ste. 203, Liverpool, NY 13090. Phone: 877-203-2327; Fax: (781)459-7770 • URL: http://www.afcp.org • Represents publishers of nearly 3,000 free circulation papers and shopping/advertising guides. Offers national classified advertising placement service and national marketing for industry recognition. Conducts charitable programs. Sponsors competitions and compiles industry statistics.

MPA - The Association of Magazine Media. 757 3rd Ave., 11th Fl., New York, NY 10017. Phone: (212)872-3700 or (212)872-3745; Email: mpa@magazine.org • URL: http://www.magazine.org • Members are publishers of consumer and other periodicals. Affiliated with American Society of Magazine Editors; Media Credit Association; Publishers Information Bureau. Formerly Magazine Publishers Association.

Radio Advertising Bureau. 1320 Greenway Dr., Ste. 500, Irving, TX 75038-2587. Phone: 800-232-3131 or (972)753-6786 or (516)753-6782; Fax: (972)753-6727 or (212)753-6727; Email: efarber@rab.com • URL: http://www.rab.com • Includes radio stations, radio networks, station sales representatives, and allied industry services, such as producers, research firms, schools, and consultants. Calls on advertisers and agencies to promote the sale of radio time as an advertising medium. Sponsors program to increase professionalism of radio salespeople, awarding Certified Radio Marketing Consultant designation to those who pass examination. Sponsors regional marketing conferences. Conducts extensive research program into all phases of radio sales. Issues reports on use of radio by national, regional, and local advertisers. Speaks before conventions and groups to explain benefits of radio advertising. Sponsors Radio Creative Fund. Compiles statistics.

ADVERTISING, POINT-OF-SALE

See POINT-OF-PURCHASE ADVERTISING

ADVERTISING RESEARCH

See also MARKET RESEARCH; MEDIA RESEARCH

ABSTRACTS AND INDEXES

Business Periodicals Index Retrospective. EBSCO Publishing Inc. • 11/year. Quarterly and annual cumulations.

PERIODICALS AND NEWSLETTERS

Journal of Advertising. M.E. Sharpe Inc. • Quarterly. $90 per year. An academic journal devoted to advertising theory and research.

Journal of Advertising Research. Advertising Research Foundation. • Quarterly. $365 Individuals standard subscription. Journal of advertising, marketing, and media research.

Journal of Website Promotion: Innovations in Internet Business Research, Theory, and Practice. The Haworth Press Inc. • Semiannual. $250.00 per year to libraries; $45.00 per year to individuals. Presents a scholarly view of such items as spam, banner ads, pop-ups, click rates, and the use of search engines for advertising.

Mediaweek: The News Magazine of the Media. Nielsen Business Media Inc. • Published for advertising media buyers and managers.

ADVERTISING SPECIALTIES

See also ADVERTISING

DIRECTORIES

PROMO Annual SourceBook: The Only Guide to the $70 Billion Promotion Industry. Primedia Business Magazines and Media. • Annual. $49.95. Lists service and supply companies for the promotion industry. Includes annual salary survey and award winning campaigns.

FINANCIAL RATIOS

Annual Statement Studies. Risk Management Association. • Annual. Compiled from over 280,000 financial statements.

Annual Statement Studies: Industry Default Probabilities and Cash Flow Measures. Risk Management Association. • Annual. $405 Nonmembers. Serves as a companion volume to the original *Annual Statement Studies.* Gives probability of default estimates on a percentage scale for more than 450 industries. Includes changes in position year-by-year for eight financial statement line items and provides percentage measures of cash flow.

HANDBOOKS AND MANUALS

Specialty Advertising. Entrepreneur Press. • Looseleaf. $59.50. A practical guide to starting a business dealing in advertising specialties. Covers profit potential, market size evaluation, start-up costs, pricing, accounting, advertising, promotion, etc. (Start-Up Business Guide No. E1292.).

PERIODICALS AND NEWSLETTERS

Incentive: Managing and Marketing Through Motivation. Nielsen Business Media Inc. • Monthly. $59.00 per year.

Retail Ad World. Visual Reference Publications Inc. • Monthly. $299.00 per year. Weekly report on outstanding advertising by department stores, specialty stores and shopping centers with reprints of current advertising. Formerly *Retail Ad Week.*

TRADE/PROFESSIONAL ASSOCIATIONS

Promotional Products Association International. 3125 Skyway Cir. N, Irving, TX 75038-3526. Phone: 888-426-7724 or (972)252-0404; Fax: (972)258-3004 or (972)258-3003; Email: membership@ppai.org • URL: http://www.ppai.org • Suppliers and distributors of promotional products including incentives, imprinted ad specialties, premiums, and executive gifts. Promotes industry contacts in 60 countries. Holds executive development and sales training seminars. Conducts research and compiles statistics. Administers industry advertising and public relations program. Maintains speakers' bureau. Conducts trade shows, regional training, publishes educational resources.

ADVISORY SERVICES

See INVESTMENT ADVISORY SERVICES

AEROSOL INDUSTRY

See PRESSURE PACKAGING

AEROSPACE INDUSTRY

See also AIRPLANE INDUSTRY; AVIATION INDUSTRY; DEFENSE INDUSTRIES; ROCKET INDUSTRY

ABSTRACTS AND INDEXES

Air University Library Index to Military Periodicals. U.S. Air Force. • Quarterly. Annual cumulation.

Applied Science and Technology Index. EBSCO Publishing Inc. • 11/year. Indexes a wide variety of English language technical, industrial, and engineering periodicals.

Engineering Index Monthly: Abstracting and Indexing Services Covering Sources ofthe World's Engineering Literature. Engineering Information Inc. • Monthly. Institutions, $5,279.00 per year. Provides indexing and abstracting of the world's engineering and technical literature.

International Aerospace Abstracts. American Institute of Aeronautics and Astronautics, Inc. CSA. • 11 times a year. $2,260.00 per year. Includes print and online editions.

ALMANACS AND YEARBOOKS

Progress in Aerospace Sciences: An International Journal. Elsevier. • $2,631 Individuals Print. Aerospace journal. Text in English, French and German.

CD-ROM DATABASES

OECD Statistical Compendium. Organization for Economic Cooperation and Development. • Semiannual. $1,905.00 per year for 1 to 10 users. CD-ROM contains more than 730,000 monthly, quarterly, and annual time series for OECD countries, 1960 to date. Includes fully searchable data on agriculture, food, economic indicators, national accounts, employment, energy, finance, industry, technology, and foreign trade. Results can be displayed in various forms.

DIRECTORIES

Aerospace Consultants Directory. InfoGroup Inc. • Annual. Number of listings: 10,653. Entries include: Name, address, phone, size of advertisement, name of owner or manager, number of employees, year first in "Yellow Pages." Compiled from telephone company "Yellow Pages," nationwide.

GENERAL WORKS

Space Sciences: Macmillan Science Library. Cengage Learning Inc. • $690 Individuals. 2012. $629. 00. Four volumes. Includes business and economic aspects of aerospace technology. (Macmillan Reference USA imprint, Macmillan Science Library). eBook also available.

INTERNET DATABASES

Business 2.0 Web Guide to the Best Business Links. Business 2.0 Media Inc. Phone: (415)293-4800; Email: support@business2.com • URL: http://www.business2.com/webguide • Web site presents an extensive, searchable directory of links to "the best, most informative, and authoritative web pages." Twenty main categories cover business, finance, career, company information, people, and technology topics, with thousands of subtopics, all linking to Web sites recommended by experienced business researchers. Fees: Free.

Fedstats. Federal Interagency Council on Statistical Policy. Phone: (202)395-7254 • URL: http://www.fedstats.gov • Web site features an efficient search facility for full-text statistics produced by more than 100 federal agencies, including the Census Bureau, the Bureau of Economic Analysis, and the Bureau of Labor Statistics. Boolean searches can be made within one agency or for all agencies combined. Links are offered to international statistical bureaus, including the UN, IMF, OECD, UNESCO, Eurostat, and 20 individual countries. Fees: Free.

FreeLunch.com. Economy.com, Inc. Phone: (610)696-8700; Fax: (610)696-1678 • URL: http://www.freelunch.com • Web site provides free access to more than 200 million economic and financial data series, covering industry, demographics, labor markets, prices, retail sales, government spending, trade, interest rates, housing starts, the stock market, etc. Data is available in either chart or table form. Searching is offered. Free, but registration required. Economy.com, Inc. also offers fee-based economic analysis at *The Dismal Scientist* site (www.dismal.com).

Manufacturing Profiles. U. S. Bureau of the Census. Phone: (301)763-4636 or (301)763-4100; Fax: (301)763-4794; Email: webmaster@census.gov • URL: http://www.census.gov/prod/www/abs/mfg-prof.html • The Census Bureau makes available free on PDF (Portable Document Format) an annual consolidation of the entire Current Industrial Report series, presenting "all the data compiled." Contains statistics on production, shipments, inventories, consumption, exports, imports, and orders for a wide variety of manufactured products.

ONLINE DATABASES

Aerospace America Magazine. American Institute of Aeronautics and Astronautics. • Monthly. $200 Institutions non member, domestic. Covers aeronautics and space technology with special attention to aerospace defense, design, and electronics.

Aerospace Database. American Institute of Aeronautics and Astronautics. • Contains abstracts of literature covering all aspects of the aerospace and aircraft industry 1983 to date. Monthly updates. Inquire as to online cost and availability.

PERIODICALS AND NEWSLETTERS

Advanced Composites Monthly. Composite Market Reports Inc. • Description: Covers advanced composite materials processes and markets in the aerospace industry worldwide. "Prepared for engineering, program, and manufacturing management at primes and their subcontractors where aerospace components made of high-performance composite materials are designed, fabricated, or assembled." Discusses subcontract opportunities of interest to U.S., Canadian, and overseas aerospace companies. Recurring features include a calendar of events, reports of meetings, interviews, news of research, and application case histories.

Aerospace America Magazine. American Institute of Aeronautics and Astronautics. • Monthly. $200 Institutions non member, domestic. Covers aeronautics and space technology with special attention to aerospace defense, design, and electronics.

Aerospace Daily. McGraw Hill Financial Inc. • Description: Reports on developments in the aerospace industry in the U.S. and overseas. Covers related political decisions. **Remarks:** Available in print, e-mail, and URL format.

Air Force Journal of Logistics. U. S. Government Printing Office. • Quarterly. $15.00 per year. Issued by the Air Force Logistics Management Center, Air Force Department, Defense Department. Presents research and information of interest to professional Air Force logisticians.

Defense Daily Network: The Business Source for Aerospace and Defense. Access Intelligence L.L.C. • Daily. Covers the global defense industry.

Flying Safety. U.S. Air Force. U. S. Government Printing Office. • Monthly. $50.00 per year. Published in the interest of safer flying. Articles cover many fields of flight, aircraft engineering, training and safety measures in the air and on the ground.

Satellite News: The Monthly Newsletter Covering Management, Marketing Technology and Regulation. Access Intelligence L.L.C. • 50 times a year. $1,097.00 per year. Newsletter. Covers business applications in space, including remote sensing and satellites. Incorporates (Space Business News).

RESEARCH CENTERS AND INSTITUTES

California Institute of Technology. Caltech 17-6, 1200 E Califoria Blvd., Pasadena, CA 91125. Phone:

For publishers' addresses, refer to SOURCES CITED section at the back of the book.

800-514-2665 or (626)395-6811 or (818)395-6811: Fax: (818)393-4218 or (626)395-5768: Email: feefback@jpl.nasa.gov • URL: http://www.caltech.edu.

Joint Institute for Advancement of Flight Sciences. 725 23rd St. NW. 227 Hunting Ave., Washington. DC 20052. Phone: (202)994-6080: Fax: (202)994-3394: Email: jiafs@seas.gwu.edu • Conducts research in aeronautics, astronautics, and acoustics (flight-produced noise).

Massachusetts Institute of Technology - Kavli Institute for Astrophysics and Space Research. 77 Massachusetts Ave., 37-241. Cambridge, MA 02139. Phone: (617)253-7501; Fax: (617)253-3111: Email: jhewitt@mit.edu • URL: http://space.mit.edu • Space sciences, including theoretical astrophysics. Experimental studies include X-ray astronomy, gravitational waves, interplanetary plasmas, optical and infrared astronomy, very-long-baseline interferometry, synthetic aperture radar, human/machine system interaction, response of human systems to zero-gravity environment, and space environmental studies.

Ohio Aerospace Institute. 22800 Cedar Point Rd., Cleveland, OH 44142. Phone: (440)962-3000: Fax: (216)962-3120 or (440)962-3120: Email: info@oai.org • URL: http://www.oai.org • Aerospace-related research, education, and technology transfers. Formerly Ohio Aerospace Institute.

Space Institute - University of Tennessee. B.H. Goethert Pky:, MS01. Tullahoma, TN 37388-9700. Phone: (931)393-7213: Fax: (931)393-7211: Email: tmccay@utsi.edu • URL: http://www.utsi.edu.

STATISTICS SOURCES

Aerospace Facts and Figures. Aerospace Industries Association of America. • Annual. $35 Individuals. Includes financial data for the aerospace industries.

Standard & Poor's Industry Surveys. Standard & Poor's Financial Services L.L.C. • Semiannual. $1,800.00. Two looseleaf volumes. Includes monthly *Supplements*. Provides detailed, individual surveys of 52 major industry groups. Each survey is revised on a semiannual basis. Also includes "Monthly Investment Review" (industry group investment analysis) and monthly "Trends & Projections" (economic analysis).

Survey of Current Business. U. S. Government Printing Office. • Published by Bureau of Economic Analysis, U. S. Department of Commerce. Presents a wide variety of business and economic data.

TRADE/PROFESSIONAL ASSOCIATIONS

ASM International. 9639 Kinsman Rd., Materials Park, OH 44073-0002. Phone: 800-336-5152 or (440)338-5151: Email: memberservicecenter@asminternational.org • URL: http://www.asminternational.org • Metallurgists, materials engineers, executives in materials producing and consuming industries; teachers and students. Disseminates technical information about the manufacture, use, and treatment of engineered materials. Offers in-plant, home study, and intensive courses through Materials Engineering Institute.

European Organisation for the Exploitation of Meteorological Satellites. Eumetsat-Allee 1, D-64295 Darmstadt, Germany. Phone: 49 6151 8077: Fax: 49 6151 807555; Email: press@eumetsat.int • URL: http://www.eumetsat.int • Seeks to establish and maintain the long-term continuity of European systems of operational meteorological satellites. Contributes to a global meteorological satellite observing system coordinated with other space-faring nations, for operational meteorology and the monitoring of climate change. Sponsors students attending the International Space University.

AFFIRMATIVE ACTION PROGRAMS

See also EQUAL EMPLOYMENT OPPORTUNITY

OTHER SOURCES

Affirmative Action Compliance Manual for Federal Contractors. Bloomberg BNA. • Monthly. Resource guide for employers and attorneys so that they can more easily monitor and measure affirmative action requirements, implement policies, and quickly access other compliance information.

BNA Fair Employment Practices. Bloomberg BNA. • Biweekly. $938.00 per year. Looseleaf service.

Practical Guide to Equal Employment Opportunity. ALM Media Properties LLC. • $570 two volumes. Serves as a legal manual for EEO compliance. "Volume one analyzes discrimination on the basis of race, religion, sex, age, and physical handicaps including AIDS." Provides information relating to an employer's liability in cases of sexual harassment of employees, including same-sex harassment. Covers affirmative action and reverse discrimination issues. Volume two contains model affirmative action plans, a sample EEO compliance manual, checklists, and other documents. (Law Journal Press).

PERIODICALS AND NEWSLETTERS

Affirmative Action Register: The E E O Recruitment Publication. INSIGHT Into Diversity. • Monthly. $15 Individuals. "The *Affirmative Action Register* is the only nationwide publication that provides for systematic distribution to mandated minorities, females, handicapped, veterans, and Native Americans." Each issue consists of recruitment advertisements placed by equal opportunity employers (institutions and companies).

Civil Rights: State Capitals. Wakeman/Walworth Inc. • 50 times a year. $245.00 per year: print and online editions. $350.00 per year. Newsletter. Includes coverage of state affirmative action programs. Formerly *From the State Capitals: Civil Rights*.

MBI: The National Report on Minority, Women-Owned and Disadvantaged Business. Community Development Services, Inc. CD Publications. • Semimonthly. $379.00 per year. Newsletter. Provides news of affirmative action, government contracts, minority business employment, and education/training for minorities in business. Formerly *Minorities in Business*.

School Law News. Wolters Kluwer Law and Business. • Biweekly.

TRADE/PROFESSIONAL ASSOCIATIONS

National Association for Equal Opportunity in Higher Education. 209 3rd St. SE, Washington, DC 20003. Phone: (202)552-3300; Fax: (202)552-3330 • URL: http://www.nafeo.org/community/index.php • Provides a unified framework representing historically and predominantly black universities and colleges and similarly situated institutions in their attempt to continue as viable forces in American society. Seeks to build a case for securing increased support from federal agencies, philanthropic foundations, and other sources, and to increase black leadership of educational organizations and membership on federal boards and commissions relating to education. Offers placement service. Maintains biographical data on member colleges/universities and presidents/chancellors. Compiles statistics on black graduates.

AFFLUENT MARKET

ABSTRACTS AND INDEXES

Business Periodicals Index Retrospective. EBSCO Publishing Inc. • 11/year. Quarterly and annual cumulations.

ONLINE DATABASES

Wilson Business Abstracts Online. H.W. Wilson Co. • Indexes and abstracts 600 major business periodicals, plus the *Wall Street Journal* and the business section of the *New York Times*. Indexing is from 1982, abstracting from 1990, with the two newspapers included from 1993. Updated weekly. Inquire as to online cost and availability. (*Business Periodicals Index* without abstracts is also available online.).

PERIODICALS AND NEWSLETTERS

City & Country Club Life: The Social Magazine for South Florida. Club Publications, Inc. • Five times a year. Controlled circulation.

Fortune Magazine. Time Inc., Business Information Group. • Biweekly. $19.99 all access. Edited for top executives and upper-level managers.

Money. • 13 times a year. $19.95 per year. Covers all aspects of family finance; investments, careers, shopping, taxes, insurance, consumerism, etc.

Palm Beach Illustrated: The Best of Boca Raton to Vero Beach. Palm Beach Media Group. • 11 times a year. $39.95 per year. Includes *Palm Beach Social Observer*. Formerly *Illustrated*.

Private Asset Management. Institutional Investor Inc. Journals Group. • Biweekly. $2,335.00 per year. Newsletter. Includes print and online editions. Edited for managers investing the private assets of wealthy ("high-net-worth") individuals. Includes marketing, taxation, regulation, and fee topics.

Profit Investor Portfolio: The International Magazine of Money and Style. Profit Publications, Inc. • Bimonthly. $29.95 per year. A glossy consumer magazine featuring specific investment recommendations and articles on upscale travel and shopping.

Robb Report. CurtCo Robb Media. • Monthly. $65 U.S. /year subscription (Online). Consumer magazine featuring advertisements for expensive items-antique automobiles, boats, airplanes, large houses, etc.

Robb Report Home Entertaining & Design. CurtCo Robb Media. • Monthly. $65. Covers "high end" home theaters, audio, video, wireless home networks, and custom installations.

Robb Report Motorcycling. CurtCo Robb Media. • Semiannual. Price on application. Contains reviews of the "newest high-quality motorcycles.".

Robb Report Worth: Wealth in Perspective. CurtCo Robb Media. • Monthly. $54.95 per year. Glossy magazine featuring articles for the affluent on personal financial management, investments, estate planning, trusts, private bankers, taxes, travel, yachts, and lifestyle. Formerly *Worth: Financial Intelligence*.

Town and Country. The Hearst Corp. • Monthly. $24.00 per year.

Travel and Leisure. American Express Publishing Corp. • Monthly. $39.00 per year. In three regional editions and one demographic edition.

Vanity Fair. Conde Nast Publications. • Monthly. $18.00 per year.

AFTER-DINNER SPEAKING

See PUBLIC SPEAKING

AGE AND EMPLOYMENT

See EMPLOYMENT OF OLDER WORKERS

AGING

See RETIREMENT

AGREEMENTS

See CONTRACTS

AGRIBUSINESS

ABSTRACTS AND INDEXES

World Agricultural Economics and Rural Sociology Abstracts (WAERSA). CABI. • Monthly. Print and online available. Published in England by CABI Publishing. Provides worldwide coverage of the literature.

ALMANACS AND YEARBOOKS

Research in Domestic and International Agribusiness Management. Elsevier. • Dates vary. $73.25. 12 volumes.

CD-ROM DATABASES

OECD Statistical Compendium. Organization for Economic Cooperation and Development. • Semiannual. $1,905.00 per year for 1 to 10 users. CD-ROM contains more than 730,000 monthly, quarterly, and annual time series for OECD countries, 1960 to date. Includes fully searchable data on agriculture, food, economic indicators, national accounts, employment, energy, finance, industry, technology, and foreign trade. Results can be displayed in various forms.

DIRECTORIES

Directory of American Agribusiness. Agricultural Resources & Communications Inc. • $64.95. Covers: Over 7,200 leading companies in agricultural chemicals, implements, seed, grain, feed, food processing, animal health and services, including public relations and consulting in 27 different types of agribusinesses in the U.S. Entries include: Company name, address, phone, fax, type of business, key company contacts.

Kompass Agribusiness, Food, and Beverage. APN News & Media Group Ltd. APN Business Information Group. • Annual. $85. Covers: Agricultural food and beverage companies and their products and services.

E-BOOKS

Encyclopedia of American Industries. Cengage Learning Inc. • 2011. $807.00. 6th edition. Three volumes. Volume one is Manufacturing Industries and volume two is Service and Non-Manufacturing Industries. Provides the history, development, and recent status of approximately 1,000 industries. Includes statistical graphs, with industry and general indexes. Also available as eBook.

FINANCIAL RATIOS

Agri-Business Update. Kings County Farm Bureau. • Monthly. Covers agricultural business information.

GENERAL WORKS

Agribusiness Connections. Agribusiness Association of Australia. • Peer-reviewed journal dealing with resource management and economic issues in the food and fibre sectors.

INTERNET DATABASES

Business 2.0 Web Guide to the Best Business Links. Business 2.0 Media Inc. Phone: (415)293-4800; Email: support@business2.com • URL: http://www.business2.com/webguide • Web site presents an extensive, searchable directory of links to "the best, most informative, and authoritative web pages." Twenty main categories cover business, finance, career, company information, people, and technology topics, with thousands of subtopics, all linking to Web sites recommended by experienced business researchers. Fees: Free.

Fedstats. Federal Interagency Council on Statistical Policy. Phone: (202)395-7254 • URL: http://www.fedstats.gov • Web site features an efficient search facility for full-text statistics produced by more than 100 federal agencies, including the Census Bureau, the Bureau of Economic Analysis, and the Bureau of Labor Statistics. Boolean searches can be made within one agency or for all agencies combined. Links are offered to international statistical bureaus, including the UN, IMF, OECD, UNESCO, Eurostat, and 20 individual countries. Fees: Free.

FreeLunch.com. Economy.com, Inc. Phone: (610)696-8700; Fax: (610)696-1678 • URL: http://www.freelunch.com • Web site provides free access to more than 200 million economic and financial data series, covering industry, demographics, labor markets, prices, retail sales, government spending, trade, interest rates, housing starts, the stock market, etc. Data is available in either chart or table form. Searching is offered. Free, but registration required. Economy.com, Inc. also offers fee-based economic analysis at *The Dismal Scientist* site (www.dismal.com).

PERIODICALS AND NEWSLETTERS

Ag Executive. Ag Executive Inc. • Description: Focuses on financial, personnel, and risk management issues for commercial agriculture. Covers business analysis and practical management ideas for improving profitability. Includes such topics as accounting, farm business organization, financing, economic forecasting, resource/risk control, and taxes.

Ag Lender. Doane Agricultural Services Co. • Monthly. $139 Individuals.

AgExporter. U. S. Government Printing Office. • Monthly. $44 Individuals. Issued by the Foreign Agricultural Service, U. S. Department of Agriculture. Edited for U. S. exporters of farm products. Provides practical information on exporting, including overseas trade opportunities.

Agri Marketing: The Magazine for Professionals Selling to the Farm Market. Doane Agricultural Services Co. • Monthly. $30 Individuals.

Agribusiness Fieldman. Agricultural Publishing Co. • Monthly. $19.95 per year.

Agribusiness Worldwide. Keller International Publishing L.L.C. • Bimonthly. $30 Individuals. Trade magazine for those involved in agriculture and livestock development in Asia, Africa, Latin America, and the Middle East. Subjects covered include agricultural production, financing, marketing, and handling.

Amber Waves. Economic Research Service Hazard Analysis and Critical Control Points. • Quarterly. Replaces *Agricultural Outlook; Food Review*; and *Rural America.* Provides research and analysis from the U.S. Department of Agriculture's Economic Research Service. Includes economic data on agriculture, food, trade, and environmental factors.

The Delmarva Farmer: The Agribusiness Newspaper of the Mid-Atlantic Region. American Farm Publications Inc. • Biweekly. $31 Individuals /year. Newspaper (tabloid) featuring news of interest to agricultural concerns in Maryland, Delaware, Virginia, New Jersey, and Pennsylvania.

Farm & Country: The Farm Business Resource. Agricultural Publishing Company Ltd. • $26 Individuals. Agricultural business magazine.

Farm Industry News. Primedia Business Magazines and Media. • Monthly. $25.00 per year. Includes new products for farm use.

The Kiplinger Agriculture Letter. Kiplinger Washington Editors Inc. • Description: Publishes information on actions and proposals by the administration, U.S. Department of Agriculture, and Congress affecting all aspects of agriculture. Includes analysis and forecasts on a broad range of issues affecting the farm/food industry, government production and price support programs, commodity production and consumption data, food marketing and processing, consumer trends, taxes, farm credit, and financial matters.

Outlook for United States Agricultural Trade. U. S. Government Printing Office. • Quarterly. $15.00 per year. Issued by the Economic Research Service, U. S. Department of Agriculture. (Situation and Outlook Reports.).

The Washington Agricultural Record. Washington Agricultural Record. • Description: Focuses on Washington farm issues and developments, reporting international congressional and United States Department of Agriculture (U.S.D.A.) news and international agricultural developments.

STATISTICS SOURCES

Standard & Poor's Industry Surveys. Standard & Poor's Financial Services L.L.C. • Semiannual. $1,800.00. Two looseleaf volumes. Includes monthly *Supplements.* Provides detailed, individual surveys of 52 major industry groups. Each survey is revised on a semiannual basis. Also includes "Monthly Investment Review" (industry group investment analysis) and monthly "Trends & Projections" (economic analysis).

Survey of Current Business. U. S. Government Printing Office. • Published by Bureau of Economic Analysis, U. S. Department of Commerce. Presents a wide variety of business and economic data.

TRADE/PROFESSIONAL ASSOCIATIONS

Agribusiness Association of Australia. 1 Torrdale Rd., Farrell Flat, SA 5416, Australia. Fax: 61 8 81278052; Email: agri@agribusiness.asn.au • URL: http://www.agribusiness.asn.au • Works to raise knowledge on issues affecting the development of an efficient and competitive agri-food value chain.

Agribusiness Council. PO Box 5565, Washington, DC 20016-1165. Phone: (202)296-4563; Email: info@agribusinesscouncil.org • URL: http://agribusinesscouncil.org • Business organizations, universities and foundations, and individuals interested in stimulating and encouraging agribusiness in cooperation with the public sector, both domestic and international. Seeks to aid in relieving the problems of world food supply. Supports coordinated agribusiness in the developing nations by identifying opportunities for investment of U.S. private-sector technology management and financial resources. Advises agribusiness leaders about selected developing countries with good investment climates; brings potential investment opportunities to the attention of U.S. agribusiness firms; coordinates informal network of state agribusiness councils and grassroots organization; encourages companies to make investment feasibility studies in agribusiness; provides liaison and information exchange between agribusiness firms, governments, international organizations, universities, foundations, and other groups with the objective of identifying areas of cooperation and mutual interest; encourages projects geared to the conversion of subsistence farming to intensive, higher income agriculture in order to bring the world's rural populations, wherever feasible, into the market economy.

American Society of Agricultural Consultants. N78 W 14573 Appleton Ave., Ste. 287, Menomonee Falls, WI 53051. Phone: (262)253-6902; Fax: (262)253-6903; Email: cmerry@agconsultants.org • URL: http://www.agconsultants.org • Members are independent, full-time consultants in many specialty areas serving agribusiness interests throughout the world. Strives to maintain high standards of ethics and competence in the consulting field. Provides referral service to agribusiness interests seeking consultants having specific knowledge, experience, and expertise. Maintains liaison with governmental agencies utilizing consultants and with legislative and administrative acts affecting consultants.

Association for the Development of International

Exchange of Food and Agricultural Productions and Techniques. 41 rue de Bourgogne, F-75007 Paris, France. Phone: 33 1 44180888; Fax: 33 1 44180889; Email: adepta@adepta.com • URL: http://www.adepta.com • Individuals involved in agribusiness. Promotes partnerships and networks among skilled agribusiness professionals.

Bahamas Agricultural and Industrial Corporation. Levy Bldg., E Bay St., Nassau, Bahamas. Phone: (242)322-3740; Fax: (242)322-2123; Email: baic@bahamas.net.bs • URL: http://www.bahamas.gov.bs • Assists in the development of commerce and industry in the Bahamas and works to expand the economic opportunities available to Bahamians. Sponsors seminars; disseminates information.

Canadian Western Agribition. Canada Centre Bldg., 2nd Fl., Evraz Pl., Regina, SK, Canada S4P 3J8. Phone: (306)565-0565; Fax: (306)757-9963; Email: info@agribition.com • URL: http://www.agribition.com • Agribusinesses. Aims create and maintain an effective, hospitable and entertaining atmosphere to market Canadian agriculture products and expertise to the world. Promotes the expansion, development and interest in agriculture and encourages the breeding and improvement of livestock. Promotes interest in agriculture and stock raising, and particularly to organize, sponsor and host an annual agriculture show. Encourages competition within and among various breeds of livestock, and among producers of other agricultural products. Focuses attention on the outstanding qualities of various agricultural products and breeds of livestock and promote the sale of agricultural products and livestock. Seeks to promote the export of agricultural products, foster improved urban-rural relations within the agricultural industry, and provide a forum in which to channel educational information to the agricultural industry and to the public generally.

Central Association of Agricultural Valuers. Market Chambers, 35 Market Pl., Gloucestershire, Coleford GL16 8AA, United Kingdom. Phone: 44 1594 832979; Fax: 44 1594 810701; Email: enquire@caav.org.uk • URL: http://www.caav.org.uk • Members are land agents, agricultural valuers and auctioneers which awards the qualification FAAV on examination. Publishes technical guidance and briefings. Engages with government and others in professional matters.

Communicating for America. 112 E Lincoln Ave., Fergus Falls, MN 56537. Phone: 800-432-3276 or (218)739-3241; Fax: (218)739-3832; Email: memberbenefits@cainc.org • URL: http://www.communicatingforamerica.org • Promotes the general health, well being and advancement of people in agriculture and agribusiness. Participates in federal and state issues that affect the quality of life in rural America and provides members with a variety of money-saving benefit programs. Conducts grants program, research on rural issues, and international exchange programs with an agricultural focus.

CUMELA Nederland. Postbus 1156, NL-3860 BD Nijkerk, Netherlands. Phone: 31 33 2474900; Fax: 31 33 2474901; Email: info@cumela.nl • URL: http://www.cumela.nl • Agricultural and rural contractors. Seeks to advance the interests of agribusinesses. Represents members' commercial and regulatory interests at the national level.

National Agri-Marketing Association. 11020 King St., Ste. 205, Overland Park, KS 66210. Phone: (913)491-6500 or (815)422-0321; Fax: (913)491-6502; Email: agrimktg@nama.org • URL: http://www.nama.org • Persons engaged in agricultural marketing for manufacturers, advertising agencies and the media. Promotes the highest standards of agricultural marketing; provides for the exchange of ideas; encourages the study and better understanding of agricultural advertising, selling and marketing; works to broaden understanding of the economic importance of agriculture; encourages careers in agricultural marketing. Provides agri-marketing short courses.

National Association of Agricultural Contractors. The Old Cart Shed, Easton Lodge Farm, Old Oundle Rd., Wansford, Peterborough PE8 6NP, United Kingdom. Phone: 44 1780 784631; Fax: 44 1780 784933; Email: members@naac.co.uk • URL: http://www.naac.co.uk • Represents agricultural and amenity contractors in United Kingdom and their commercial and regulatory interests at the national level.

National Association of Farm Business Analysis Specialists. PO Box 467, Camp Point, IL 62320. Phone: (217)593-7233; Fax: (217)593-7239 • URL: http://www.nafbas.org • Aims to advance comparative farm business analysis techniques. Provides opportunities for farm business analysis specialists to exchange ideas and methods. Encourages and promotes the professional competence of members.

National Council of Agricultural Employers. 8233 Old Courthouse Rd., Ste. 200, Vienna, VA 22182. Phone: (703)790-9039; Email: info@ncaeonline.org • URL: http://www.ncaeonline.org • Growers of agricultural commodities who employ hand labor for field crops; processors and handlers, farm and commodity organizations, and others whose business is related to labor-intensive farming in the U.S. Aims to improve the position and image of U.S. agriculture as an employer of labor and to facilitate and encourage the establishment and maintenance of an adequate force of agricultural employees. Serves as clearinghouse for exchange of information on labor supply, length of employment, and other conditions of work. Does not engage in recruitment, housing, supplying, or employment of agricultural workers, and does not represent its members or others in negotiating with labor unions or other organizations, or in agreeing to any contract relating to hours, wages, or working conditions. Keeps member abreast of national legislation affecting agricultural labor.

Processors' and Growers' Research Organisation. The Research Station, Great North Rd., Thornhaugh, Peterborough PE8 6HJ, United Kingdom. Phone: 44 1780 782585; Fax: 44 1780 783993; Email: info@pgro.org • URL: http://www.pgro.org • Farmers, food processors, merchant seedsmen, agrochemical companies, higher education institutes and research stations. Provides research, evaluation and advice on the growing, harvesting and usage of different types of peas and beans. This includes the evaluation of new varieties, crop protection products and growing and harvesting techniques. Provides technical services including seed and soil testing and instrument calibration.

Royal Agricultural Society of New Zealand. PO Box 54, Woodend 7461, New Zealand. Phone: 64 3 3131004; Fax: 64 3 3131003 • URL: http://www.ras.org.nz • Promotes and rewards excellence in agribusiness in New Zealand.

Samuel Roberts Noble Foundation. 2510 Sam Noble Pkwy., Ardmore, OK 73401. Phone: (580)223-5810 or (580)224-6230; Fax: (580)224-6265; Email: jacalaway@noble.org • URL: http://www.noble.org • Strives to promote agriculture, the ranching industry, and plant biology. Hosts the "Junior Beef Excellence Program."

Southern U.S. Trade Association. 701 Poydras St., Ste. 3725, New Orleans, LA 70139. Phone: (504)568-5986; Fax: (504)568-6010; Email: susta@susta.org • URL: http://www.susta.org • The Southern U.S. Trade Association (SUSTA) promotes the export of high-value food and agricultural products internationally. SUSTA works closely on an individual basis with its export company members to develop and expand their share of agricultural export markets through partnering with the Department of Agriculture to provide southern U.S. companies discounted booth space at international trade exhibitions, and inbound and outbound trade missions. SUSTA facilitates the MAP Branded Program that reimburses up to 50% of certain international marketing and promotion expenses, including eligible tradeshows, in-store displays, and required label changes.

UNIMA. 10, Cours Aristide Briand, BP 402, F-08107 Charleville-Mezieres, France. Phone: 33 324 328563; Fax: 33 324 327692; Email: sgi@unima.org • URL: http://www.unima.org/en/home • Agricultural contractors, farm workers, farmers, farm equipment manufacturers, and other providers of support and services to agricultural industries. Seeks to advance the interests of agribusinesses. Represents members' commercial and regulatory interests at the national level.

United Agribusiness League. 54 Corporate Park, Irvine, CA 92606-5105. Phone: 800-223-4590 or (949)975-1424; Fax: (949)975-1573 or (949)975-1671; Email: marketing@aul.org • URL: http://www.ual.org • Agricultural industries and businesses. Promotes the development and common interest of the agricultural industry. Works to coordinate members' activities to advance agribusiness in general; provides services and benefits to enable members to realize greater productive efficiency. Serves as a clearinghouse on international agribusiness. Provides employee health care plans and other insurance to agribusinesses.

AGRICULTURAL CHEMICALS

See also CHEMICAL INDUSTRIES; FERTILIZER INDUSTRY; POTASH INDUSTRY

ABSTRACTS AND INDEXES

Biological and Agricultural Index. H.W. Wilson Co. • 11 times a year. Annual and quarterly cumulations. Price varies.

DIRECTORIES

The Agrochemical Companies Fact File. Hemming Information Services. • $695. Covers: 300 agrochemical manufacturers; formulators; biopesticide manufacturers, and agrochemical trading companies worldwide. Entries include: Details on key executives, financial data, operating locations, main markets, products, subsidiaries, joint ventures, and portfolios.

Directory of American Manufacturers & Exporters of Agro Chemicals. EXIM Infotek Private Ltd. • $10 Individuals. Covers: 50 American manufacturers and exporters of agricultural chemicals, agricultural deodorants for swine and manure, biochemicals, fungicides, insecticides, pesticides, and phosphatic chemicals. Entries include: Company name, postal address, city, country, phone, fax, e-mail and websites, contact person, designation, and product details.

Directory of Chinese Manufacturers & Exporters of Agro Chemicals, Fertilizers, Pesticides, Insecticides. EXIM Infotek Private Ltd. • $20 Individuals. Covers: 210 Chinese manufacturers and exporters of agricultural chemical products, agricultural chemicals, agrochemicals, biochemical products, biological pesticides, bio-pesticides, chemical fertilizers, farm chemicals, fertilizers, herbicides, insecticide, nitrogen fertilizer, pesticide intermediates, pesticides, and phosphate fertilizers. Entries include: Company name, postal address, city, country, phone, fax, e-mail and websites, contact person, designation, and product details.

Directory of South Korean Manufacturers & Exporters of Agro Chemicals. EXIM Infotek Private Ltd. • $5 Individuals. Covers: 20 South Korean manufacturers and exporters of fertilizers, fungicides/insecticides/bactericides, and herbicides/

plant growth control substances. Entries include: Company name, postal address, city, country, phone, fax, e-mail and websites, contact person, designation, and product details.

Directory of Taiwanese Manufacturers & Exporters of Agro Chemicals. EXIM Infotek Private Ltd. • $10 Individuals. Covers: 50 Taiwanese manufacturers and exporters of agrochemicals, fertilizers, fungicides/insecticides/bactericides destroyers, and herbicides/plant growth control substances. Entries include: Company name, postal address, city, country, phone, fax, e-mail and websites, contact person, designation, and product details.

Major Chemical and Petrochemical Companies of the World. Cengage Learning Inc. • Annual. $1,460 Individuals. 2008. 12th edition. eBook. Published by Graham & Whiteside. Contains profiles of more than 8,500 important chemical and petrochemical companies in various countries. Subject areas include general chemicals, specialty chemicals, agricultural chemicals, petrochemicals, industrial gases, and fertilizers.

FINANCIAL RATIOS

Industry Norms and Key Business Ratios. Dun & Bradstreet Inc. • Annual. Five volumes. Covers over 800 kinds of businesses, arranged by Standard Industrial Classification number. More detailed editions covering longer periods of time are also available.

ONLINE DATABASES

Agricola. U.S. National Agricultural Library World List of Agricultural Serials. • Covers worldwide agricultural literature. Over 3.3 million citations, 1970 to present, with monthly updates. Inquire as to online cost and availability.

CA Search. American Chemical Society Chemical Abstracts Service. • Guide to chemical literature, 1967 to present. Inquire as to online cost and availability.

Derwent Crop Protection File. Derwent Information Ltd. • Provides citations to the international journal literature of agricultural chemicals and pesticides from 1968 to date, with updating eight times per year. Formerly *PESTDOC*. Inquire as to online cost and availability.

PERIODICALS AND NEWSLETTERS

Croplife. Meister Media. • Monthly. $36.00 per year. Formerly *Farm Chemicals*.

Dealer Progress: How Smart Agribusiness is Growing. The Fertilizer Institute. • Bimonthly. Free to qualified personnel; others, $40.00 per year. Published in association with the Fertilizer Institute. Includes information on fertilizers and agricultural chemicals, including farm pesticides. Formerly *Progress*.

Soil Science: An Interdisciplinary Approach to Soils Research. Lippincott Williams & Wilkins. • Monthly. Monthly. Individuals, $182.00 per year; institutions, $336.00 per year.

RESEARCH CENTERS AND INSTITUTES

Ohio State University - Laboratory for Pest Control Application Technology. Ohio Agricultural Research & Development Ctr., 1680 Madison Ave., Wooster, OH 44691. Phone: (330)263-3931; Fax: (330)263-3686; Email: downer.2@osu.edu • URL: http://www.oardc.ohio-state.edu/lpcat • Conducts pest control research in cooperation with the U. S. Department of Agriculture.

Tennessee Agricultural Experiment Station - University of Tennessee, Knoxville. 103 Morgan Hall, Knoxville, TN 37996-4506. Phone: (865)974-4520; Fax: (865)974-6451; Email: AgResearch@tennessee.edu • URL: http://taes.tennessee.edu.

University of Massachusetts at Amherst - West Experiment Station - Soil and Plant Tissue Testing Laboratory. 682 N Pleasant St., Amherst, MA 01003. Phone: (413)545-2311; Fax: (413)545-1931; Email: veneman@psis.umass.edu • URL: http://soiltest.umass.edu • Soil and plant tissue.

STATISTICS SOURCES

U.S. Industry and Trade Outlook. U.S. Department of Commerce National Technical Information Service. • Annual. Produced by the International Trade Administration, U.S. Department of Commerce, in a "public-private" partnership with DRI/McGraw-Hill and Standard & Poor's. Provides basic data, outlook for the current year, and "Long-Term Prospects" (five-year projections) for a wide variety of products and services. Includes high technology industries. Formerly *U.S. Industrial Outlook*.

TRADE/PROFESSIONAL ASSOCIATIONS

AOAC International. 481 N Frederick Ave., Ste. 500, Gaithersburg, MD 20877-2417. Phone: 800-379-2622 or (301)924-7077; Fax: (301)924-7089; Email: aoac@aoac.org • URL: http://www.aoac.org • Government, academic, and industry analytical scientists who develop, test, and collaboratively study methods for analyzing fertilizers, foods, feeds, pesticides, drugs, cosmetics, and other products related to agriculture and public health. Offers short courses for analytical laboratory personnel in chemical and microbiological quality assurance, lab waste management, statistics, giving expert testimony, and technical writing.

CropLife America. 1156 15th St. NW, Washington, DC 20005. Phone: (202)296-1585; Fax: (202)463-0474 • URL: http://www.croplifeamerica.org • Fosters the interests of the general public and member companies by promoting innovative and environmentally sound manufacture, distribution and use of crop protection and production technologies for safe, high quality, affordable, abundant food, fiber and other crops.

AGRICULTURAL CREDIT

See also AGRICULTURAL ECONOMICS; CREDIT

ABSTRACTS AND INDEXES

Biological and Agricultural Index. H.W. Wilson Co. • 11 times a year. Annual and quarterly cumulations. Price varies.

ALMANACS AND YEARBOOKS

The Debt Finance Landscape for U.S. Farming and Farm Businesses. U.S. Department of Agriculture Economic Research Service. • Annual.

INTERNET DATABASES

USDA. U.S. National Institute of Standards and Technology. 100 Bureau Dr., Gaithersburg, MD 20899-1070. Phone: 800-877-8339 or (301)975-6478 or (202)720-2791; Fax: (301)975-8295; Email: inquiries@nist.gov • URL: http://www.nist.gov • The USDA home page has six sections: News and Information; What's New; About USDA; Agencies; Opportunities; Search and Help. Keyword searching is offered from the USDA home page and from various individual agency home pages. Agencies are the Economic Research Service, Agricultural Marketing Service, National Agricultural Statistics Service, National Agricultural Library, and about 12 others. Updating varies. Fees: Free.

ONLINE DATABASES

Agricola. U.S. National Agricultural Library World List of Agricultural Serials. • Covers worldwide agricultural literature. Over 3.3 million citations, 1970 to present, with monthly updates. Inquire as to online cost and availability.

PERIODICALS AND NEWSLETTERS

Ag Lender. Doane Agricultural Services Co. • Monthly. $139 Individuals.

Banker News. American Bankers Association. • Biweekly. $48 Members.

STATISTICS SOURCES

Agricultural Statistics. U.S. Department of Agriculture National Agricultural Statistics Service. • Annual. $46 Individuals. Provides a wide variety of statistical data relating to agricultural production, supplies, consumption, prices/price-supports, foreign trade, costs, and returns, as well as farm labor, loans, income, and population. In many cases, historical data is shown annually for 10 years. In addition to farm data, includes detailed fishery statistics.

AGRICULTURAL ECONOMICS

ABSTRACTS AND INDEXES

NTIS Alerts: Agriculture & Food. U.S. Department of Commerce National Technical Information Service. • Biweekly. $130 per year. Covers agricultural economics, horticulture, fisheries, veterinary medicine, food technology, and related subjects.

World Agricultural Economics and Rural Sociology Abstracts (WAERSA). CABI. • Monthly. Print and online available. Published in England by CABI Publishing. Provides worldwide coverage of the literature.

ALMANACS AND YEARBOOKS

Agricultural Policy Monitoring and Evaluation. Organization for Economic Cooperation and Development. Organisation for Economic Co-operation and Development Publications and Information Center. • Annual. Provides estimates of support to agriculture as well as chapters on agricultural policy developments.

CD-ROM DATABASES

AGRICOLA on SilverPlatter. Ovid Technologies Inc. • Updated monthly. Price varies. Produced by the National Agricultural Library. Provides over 4 million citations to the literature of agriculture, agricultural economics, animal sciences, entomology, fertilizer, food, forestry, nutrition, pesticides, plant science, water resources, and other topics.

EconLit. Ovid Technologies Inc. • Updated monthly. Lists journal articles, book reviews, disserations of economic literature. Over 1,400 journals covered.

DIRECTORIES

Agronomists Directory. InfoGroup Inc. • Annual. Number of listings: 1,029. Entries include: Name, address, phone, size of advertisement, name of owner or manager, number of employees, year first in "Yellow Pages." Compiled from telephone company "Yellow Pages," nationwide.

ENCYCLOPEDIAS AND DICTIONARIES

Encyclopedia of Food and Culture. Cengage Learning Inc. • 2003. $657.00. Three volumes. Contains 600 articles covering various aspects of food and its place in society, from agronomy to zucchini. Includes illustrations and a detailed index. eBook also available, updated in 2004.

INTERNET DATABASES

USDA. U.S. National Institute of Standards and Technology. 100 Bureau Dr., Gaithersburg, MD 20899-1070. Phone: 800-877-8339 or (301)975-6478 or (202)720-2791; Fax: (301)975-8295; Email: inquiries@nist.gov • URL: http://www.nist.gov • The USDA home page has six sections: News and Information; What's New; About USDA; Agencies; Opportunities; Search and Help. Keyword searching is offered from the USDA home page and from various individual agency home pages. Agencies are the Economic Research Service, Agricultural Marketing Service, National Agricultural Statistics Service,

National Agricultural Library, and about 12 others. Updating varies. Fees: Free.

ONLINE DATABASES

CAB Abstracts. CABI. • Contains 46 specialized abstract collections covering over 10,000 journals and monographs in the areas of agriculture, horticulture, forest products, farm products, nutrition, dairy science, poultry, grains, animal health, entomology, etc. Time period is 1972 to date, with monthly updates. Inquire as to online cost and availability. *CAB Abstracts on CD-ROM* also available, with annual updating.

OTHER SOURCES

Agricultural Law. Matthew Bender and Company Inc. • Semiannual. $2,501.00. 15 looseleaf volumes. Covers all aspects of state and federal law relating to farms, ranches and other agricultural interests. Includes five volumes dealing with agricultural estate, tax and business planning.

PERIODICALS AND NEWSLETTERS

Amber Waves. Economic Research Service Hazard Analysis and Critical Control Points. • Quarterly. Replaces *Agricultural Outlook; Food Review*; and *Rural America*. Provides research and analysis from the U.S. Department of Agriculture's Economic Research Service. Includes economic data on agriculture, food, trade, and environmental factors.

RESEARCH CENTERS AND INSTITUTES

Poland Ministry of Agriculture and Food Economy - Institute of Agricultural and Food Economics. ul. Świetokrzyska 20, 00-002 Warsaw, Poland. Phone: 48 22 5054444; Fax: 48 22 8271960; Email: andrzej.kowalski@ierigz.waw.pl • URL: http://www.ierigz.waw.pl • Agricultural and food policy, forecasting of agriculture and food economy development, farm and food industry economics, regional analyses, ownership transformations, analysis and prognosis of agricultural and food markets, and social transformation in agricultural and rural populations.

STATISTICS SOURCES

Agricultural Statistics. U.S. Department of Agriculture National Agricultural Statistics Service. • Annual. $46 Individuals. Provides a wide variety of statistical data relating to agricultural production, supplies, consumption, prices/price-supports, foreign trade, costs, and returns, as well as farm labor, loans, income, and population. In many cases, historical data is shown annually for 10 years. In addition to farm data, includes detailed fishery statistics.

Agriculture Fact Book. U. S. Government Printing Office. • Annual. $26 Individuals. Issued by the Office of Communications, U. S. Department of Agriculture. Includes data on U. S. agriculture, farmers, food, nutrition, and rural America. Programs of the Department of Agriculture in six areas are described: rural economic development, foreign trade, nutrition, the environment, inspection, and education.

TRADE/PROFESSIONAL ASSOCIATIONS

Agricultural Economics Association of South Africa. Private Bag x935, Pretoria 0001, South Africa. Phone: 27 12 3411115 • URL: http://www.aeasa.org.za • Represents the interests of agricultural economists. Promotes training, research and interest in agricultural economics. Fosters the applications of scientific principles of agricultural economics in solving agricultural and rural problems of Southern Africa.

Agricultural Economics Society. Holtwood, Red Lion St., Cropredy, Banbury OX17 1PD, United Kingdom. Phone: 44 1295 750182 • URL: http://www.aes.ac.uk • Agricultural economists in the UK, students of agricultural economics, and interested individuals. Promotes the study and teaching of all disciplines relevant to agricultural economics. Areas of interest include agricultural industry; food and related industries; rural communities. Conducts studies in fields of economics, statistics, marketing, business management, politics, history, and sociology.

French Society of Agricultural Economics. 19 Av. du Maine, F-75732 Paris, France. Phone: 33 1 45498840; Fax: 33 1 45498841; Email: sfer.asso@orange.fr • URL: http://www.sfer.asso.fr • Educators, social scientists, civil servants, and other interested persons. Promotes research and instruction in the economic, political, and social applications of agriculture and rural space. Acts as a forum for the exchange of ideas and information. Conducts colloquia.

Indian Society of Agricultural Economics. C-104, 1st Fl., Sadguru Complex -1, Gen. A. K. Vaidya Marg, Goregaon E, Mumbai 400 063, Maharashtra, India. Phone: 91 22 28493723; Fax: 91 22 28493724; Email: isae@bom7.vsnl.net.in • URL: http://www.isaeindia.org • Agricultural economists in India. Seeks to further the study of the social and economic problems of agriculture and rural areas and promotes technical competence for teaching and research in agricultural economics and related fields.

AGRICULTURAL EXTENSION WORK

ONLINE DATABASES

Agricola. U.S. National Agricultural Library World List of Agricultural Serials. • Covers worldwide agricultural literature. Over 3.3 million citations, 1970 to present, with monthly updates. Inquire as to online cost and availability.

AGRICULTURAL FOREIGN TRADE

See FOREIGN AGRICULTURE

AGRICULTURAL MACHINERY

ABSTRACTS AND INDEXES

Agricultural Engineering Abstracts. CABI Publishing North America. • Bimonthly. Published in England by CABI Publishing.

DIRECTORIES

Directory of American Manufacturers & Exporters of Tractors, Parts & Accessories. EXIM Infotek Private Ltd. • $5 Individuals. Covers: 25 American manufacturers and exporters of agricultural tractors and spare parts, farm tractors, tractor parts, and tractors. Entries include: Company name, postal address, city, country, phone, fax, e-mail and websites, contact person, designation, and product details.

Directory of Japanese Manufacturers & Exporters of Tractors, Parts & Accessories. EXIM Infotek Private Ltd. • $5 Individuals. Covers: 30 Japanese manufacturers and exporters of used agricultural tractor, used farm tractors, used tractors. Entries include: Company name, postal address, city, country, phone, fax, e-mail and websites, contact person, designation, and product details.

The International Directory of Importers - Agricultural Machinery & Implements Importers. Interdata. • $220 Individuals print. Covers: 2,300 international firms importing agricultural equipment. Entries include: Company name and address, contact person, email, number of employees, year established, phone and telefaxes, business activity, bank references, as well as a listing of agricultural machinery & implements currently being imported.

Milking Machines--Wholesalers Directory. InfoGroup Inc. • Annual. Number of listings: 956. Entries include: Name, address, phone, size of advertisement, name of owner or manager, number of employees, year first in "Yellow Pages." Compiled from telephone company "Yellow Pages," nationwide.

NAEDA Buyer's Guide. North American Equipment Dealers Association. • Annual. $35 print only. List of manufacturers and suppliers of agricultural, outdoor power equipment and construction equipment.

FINANCIAL RATIOS

Annual Statement Studies. Risk Management Association. • Annual. Compiled from over 280,000 financial statements.

Annual Statement Studies: Industry Default Probabilities and Cash Flow Measures. Risk Management Association. • Annual. $405 Nonmembers. Serves as a companion volume to the original *Annual Statement Studies*. Gives probability of default estimates on a percentage scale for more than 450 industries. Includes changes in position year-by-year for eight financial statement line items and provides percentage measures of cash flow.

Industry Norms and Key Business Ratios. Dun & Bradstreet Inc. • Annual. Five volumes. Covers over 800 kinds of businesses, arranged by Standard Industrial Classification number. More detailed editions covering longer periods of time are also available.

HANDBOOKS AND MANUALS

Regional Official Guides: Tractors and Farm Equipment. Iron Solutions, LLC. • Quarterly. Quarterly. Membership.

INTERNET DATABASES

Manufacturing Profiles. U. S. Bureau of the Census. Phone: (301)763-4636 or (301)763-4100; Fax: (301)763-4794; Email: webmaster@census.gov • URL: http://www.census.gov/prod/www/abs/mfg-prof.html • The Census Bureau makes available free on PDF (Portable Document Format) an annual consolidation of the entire Current Industrial Report series, presenting "all the data compiled." Contains statistics on production, shipments, inventories, consumption, exports, imports, and orders for a wide variety of manufactured products.

ONLINE DATABASES

Agricola. U.S. National Agricultural Library World List of Agricultural Serials. • Covers worldwide agricultural literature. Over 3.3 million citations, 1970 to present, with monthly updates. Inquire as to online cost and availability.

Thomas Register Online. Thomas Publishing Company L.L.C. • Provides concise information on approximately 194,000 U. S. companies, mainly manufacturers, with over 50,000 product classifications. Indexes over 115,000 trade names. Information is updated semiannually. Inquire as to online cost and availability.

PERIODICALS AND NEWSLETTERS

Farm Equipment. Cygnus Business Media Inc. • Seven times a year. $48.00 per year. Includes annual *Product* issue.

Implement and Tractor: The Business Magazine of the Farm and Industrial Equipment Industry. Agra USA. • Bimonthly. $35.00 per year. Includes annuals *Product File* and *Red Book*.

NAEDA Equipment Dealer. North American Equipment Dealers Association. • Monthly. $45 Individuals ground delivery. Covers power equipment for farm, outdoor, and industrial use. Formerly *Farm and Power Equipment Dealer*.

PRICE SOURCES

PPI Detailed Report. Periodical covering business. Bureau of Labor Statistics, U.S. Department of

Labor. U. S. Government Printing Office. • Monthly. $55 Individuals.

RESEARCH CENTERS AND INSTITUTES

Biological and Agricultural Engineering. Texas A & M University, 2117 TAMU, 201 Scoates Hall, College Station, TX 77843-2117. Phone: (979)845-3931; Email: info@baen.tamu.edu • URL: http://baen.tamu.edu.

Tennessee Agricultural Experiment Station - University of Tennessee, Knoxville. 103 Morgan Hall, Knoxville, TN 37996-4506. Phone: (865)974-4520; Fax: (865)974-6451; Email: AgResearch@tennessee.edu • URL: http://taes.tennessee.edu.

U.S. Department of Agriculture Agricultural Research Service - National Soil Dynamics Laboratory. c/o Henry Allen Torbert, Scientist, 411 S Donahue Dr., Auburn, AL 36832-5806. Phone: (334)844-3979 • URL: http://www.ars.usda.gov/main/site_main.htm?modecode=64-20-05-00.

STATISTICS SOURCES

United States Census of Manufactures. U.S. Department of Commerce U.S. Census Bureau. • Quinquennial. Results presented in reports, tape, CD-ROM, and Diskette files.

U.S. Industry and Trade Outlook. U.S. Department of Commerce National Technical Information Service. • Annual. Produced by the International Trade Administration, U.S. Department of Commerce, in a "public-private" partnership with DRI/McGraw-Hill and Standard & Poor's. Provides basic data, outlook for the current year, and "Long-Term Prospects" (five-year projections) for a wide variety of products and services. Includes high technology industries. Formerly *U.S. Industrial Outlook*.

TRADE/PROFESSIONAL ASSOCIATIONS

North American Equipment Dealers Association. 1195 Smizer Mill Rd., Fenton, MO 63026-3480. Phone: (636)349-5000; Fax: (636)349-5443; Email: naeda@naeda.com • URL: http://www.naeda.com • Retailers of farm equipment, implements, light industrial equipment, outdoor power equipment and related supplies. Conducts programs on management training and governmental and trade relations.

AGRICULTURAL MARKET

See FARM MARKETS

AGRICULTURAL PRODUCTS

See FARM PRODUCE

AGRICULTURAL STATISTICS

See also BUSINESS STATISTICS

CD-ROM DATABASES

OECD Statistical Compendium. Organization for Economic Cooperation and Development. • Semiannual. $1,905.00 per year for 1 to 10 users. CD-ROM contains more than 730,000 monthly, quarterly, and annual time series for OECD countries, 1960 to date. Includes fully searchable data on agriculture, food, economic indicators, national accounts, employment, energy, finance, industry, technology, and foreign trade. Results can be displayed in various forms.

INTERNET DATABASES

USDA. U.S. National Institute of Standards and Technology. 100 Bureau Dr., Gaithersburg, MD 20899-1070. Phone: 800-877-8339 or (301)975-6478 or (202)720-2791; Fax: (301)975-8295; Email: inquiries@nist.gov • URL: http://www.nist.gov • The USDA home page has six sections: News and Information; What's New; About USDA; Agencies; Opportunities; Search and Help. Keyword searching is offered from the USDA home page and from various individual agency home pages. Agencies are the Economic Research Service, Agricultural Marketing Service, National Agricultural Statistics Service, National Agricultural Library, and about 12 others. Updating varies. Fees: Free.

STATISTICS SOURCES

Agricultural Statistics. U.S. Department of Agriculture National Agricultural Statistics Service. • Annual. $46 Individuals. Provides a wide variety of statistical data relating to agricultural production, supplies, consumption, prices/price-supports, foreign trade, costs, and returns, as well as farm labor, loans, income, and population. In many cases, historical data is shown annually for 10 years. In addition to farm data, includes detailed fishery statistics.

Agriculture Fact Book. U. S. Government Printing Office. • Annual. $26 Individuals. Issued by the Office of Communications, U. S. Department of Agriculture. Includes data on U. S. agriculture, farmers, food, nutrition, and rural America. Programs of the Department of Agriculture in six areas are described: rural economic development, foreign trade, nutrition, the environment, inspection, and education.

United States Census of Agriculture. U.S. Department of Agriculture National Agricultural Statistics Service. • Quinquennial. Provides uniform, comprehensive farming and ranching operations data for every U.S. state and county, including production expenses, market value of products, and operator characteristics.

AGRICULTURAL SURPLUSES

See FARM PRODUCE

AGRICULTURE

See also COOPERATIVES; FOREIGN AGRICULTURE

ABSTRACTS AND INDEXES

Agrindex: International Information System for the Agricultural Sciences and Technology. Food and Agriculture Organization of the United Nations. Bernan Press. • Monthly. $500.00 per year. Text in English, French, and Spanish.

Biological and Agricultural Index. H.W. Wilson Co. • 11 times a year. Annual and quarterly cumulations. Price varies.

ALMANACS AND YEARBOOKS

Advances in Agronomy. American Society for Agronomy, Inc. Elsevier. • Annual. $193. A leading reference and a first-rate source for the latest research in agronomy.

The State of Food and Agriculture. Bernan Associates. • Annual. $75. Published by the Food and Agriculture Organization of the United Nations (FAO). A yearly review of world and regional agricultural and food activities. Includes tables and graphs. Text in English.

Yearbook of Agriculture. U.S. Department of Agriculture. U. S. Government Printing Office. • Annual.

CD-ROM DATABASES

AGRICOLA on SilverPlatter. Ovid Technologies Inc. • Updated monthly. Price varies. Produced by the National Agricultural Library. Provides over 4 million citations to the literature of agriculture, agricultural economics, animal sciences, entomology, fertilizer, food, forestry, nutrition, pesticides, plant science, water resources, and other topics.

Biological & Agricultural Index Plus. EBSCO Publishing Inc. • Full text of literature in biology and agriculture. Also includes podcasts, indexing and abstracts.

DIRECTORIES

Agricultural and Mineral Commodities Year Book. Routledge Reference. • $420 Individuals Hardback. Publication includes: List of international commodity organizations. Entries include: Name, address, phone, fax, e-mail, URL, publications, name of the chairperson, and description. Principal content of publication is a gathering of information about 40 commodities traded internationally, including barley, phosphates, soybeans, wool, zinc, lead, and natural gas.

Agricultural Producers Directory. InfoGroup Inc. • Annual. Number of listings: 22,572. Entries include: Name, address, phone, size of advertisement, name of owner or manager, number of employees, year first in "Yellow Pages." Compiled from telephone company "Yellow Pages," nationwide.

Delaware Agricultural Trade Directory. Delaware Department of Agriculture. • Irregular. Covers: about 300 producers, processors, and distributors of agricultural products in Delaware; includes exporters. Entries include: Company name, address, phone, type of product or service, quantity, variety, other information.

Directory of California Agricultural Exporters. • Biennial. $50. Covers: Approximately 1,600 California companies in the growing, processing, and trading of food and fiber products in the worldwide market. Entries include: Company name, address, phone, fax, E-mail/web address, name and title of contact, number of employees, year established, products grown, processed, or traded, names and titles of key personnel, type of company.

Directory of Chinese Manufacturers & Exporters of Agro Commodities. EXIM Infotek Private Ltd. • $10 Individuals. Covers: 80 Chinese manufacturers and exporters of agricultural products, beans, broad beans, buckwheat, farm products, grains, maize, rice, soy beans, sugar, and wheats. Entries include: Company name, postal address, city, country, phone, fax, e-mail and websites, contact person, designation, and product details.

Directory of Chinese Manufacturers & Exporters of Flowers, Plants & Trees, Seeds & Bulbs. EXIM Infotek Private Ltd. • $5 Individuals. Covers: 35 Chinese manufacturers and exporters of artificial flowers, artificial plants, asparagus, flower plants, flowers-cut, flowers-dried, flowers-manmade, flowers-various, lotus roots, ornamental plants, plants, plants-natural, potpourri, roses. Entries include: Company name, postal address, city, country, phone, fax, e-mail and websites, contact person, designation, and product details.

Economic Guide--Tunisia. Information Economique Africaine. • Biennial. $50. Covers: Industrial, commercial and agricultural entities in Tunisia. Entries include: Company name, address, phone.

Israel Agro and Biotechnology Industry Export-Import Directory. International Business Publications, USA. • Annual. $99.95 Individuals hardcover, e-book, CD-ROM. Covers: Information on strategic economic, investment, export-import, and business opportunities. Contains important export-import, government, and business contacts. Ultimate directory for conducting export-import operations in the country.

GENERAL WORKS

Journal of Agribusiness in Developing and Emerging Economies. Emerald Group Publishing Ltd. • Peer-reviewed journal publishing information on agriculture and food chains and their implications for economic and societal development and public policy in Asia, Africa, Latin America and Eastern Europe.

INTERNET DATABASES

FedWorld: A Program of the United States Department of Commerce. National Technical Information Service. Phone: 800-553-NTIS or (703)605-6000; Fax: (703)605-6900; Email: webmaster@fedworld.gov • URL: http://www.fedworld.gov • Web site offers "a comprehensive central access point for searching, locating, ordering, and acquiring government and business information." Emphasis is on searching the Web pages, databases, and government reports of a wide variety of federal agencies. Fees: Free.

FirstGov: Your First Click to the U. S. Government. General Services Administration. Phone: 800-333-4636 or (202)501-0705; Email: public.affairs@gsa.gov • URL: http://www.gsa.gov • Free Web site provides extensive links to federal agencies covering a wide variety of topics, such as agriculture, business, consumer safety, education, the environment, government jobs, grants, health, social security, statistics sources, taxes, technology, travel, and world affairs. Also provides links to federal forms, including IRS tax forms. Searching is offered, both keyword and advanced.

USDA. U.S. National Institute of Standards and Technology. 100 Bureau Dr., Gaithersburg, MD 20899-1070. Phone: 800-877-8339 or (301)975-6478 or (202)720-2791; Fax: (301)975-8295; Email: inquiries@nist.gov • URL: http://www.nist.gov • The USDA home page has six sections: News and Information; What's New; About USDA; Agencies; Opportunities; Search and Help. Keyword searching is offered from the USDA home page and from various individual agency home pages. Agencies are the Economic Research Service, Agricultural Marketing Service, National Agricultural Statistics Service, National Agricultural Library, and about 12 others. Updating varies. Fees: Free.

WilsonWeb Periodicals Databases. H.W. Wilson Co. 950 University Ave., Bronx, NY 10452-4224. Phone: 800-367-6770 or (718)588-8400 or (718)558-8400; Fax: (718)590-1617 or (800)590-1617; Email: custserv@hwwilson.com • URL: http://www.hwwilson.com • Web sites provide fee-based access to *Wilson Business Full Text, Applied Science & Technology Full Text, Biological & Agricultural Index, Library Literature & Information Science Full Text,* and *Readers' Guide Full Text, Mega Edition.* Daily updates.

ONLINE DATABASES

Agricola. U.S. National Agricultural Library World List of Agricultural Serials. • Covers worldwide agricultural literature. Over 3.3 million citations, 1970 to present, with monthly updates. Inquire as to online cost and availability.

CAB Abstracts. CABI. • Contains 46 specialized abstract collections covering over 10,000 journals and monographs in the areas of agriculture, horticulture, forest products, farm products, nutrition, dairy science, poultry, grains, animal health, entomology, etc. Time period is 1972 to date, with monthly updates. Inquire as to online cost and availability. *CAB Abstracts on CD-ROM* also available, with annual updating.

OTHER SOURCES

Agricultural Law. Matthew Bender and Company Inc. • Semiannual. $2,501.00. 15 looseleaf volumes. Covers all aspects of state and federal law relating to farms, ranches and other agricultural interests. Includes five volumes dealing with agricultural estate, tax and business planning.

PERIODICALS AND NEWSLETTERS

Agricultural Research. U. S. Government Printing Office. • Monthly. $50 Individuals. Issued by the Agricultural Research Service of the U. S. Department of Agriculture. Presents results of research projects related to a wide variety of farm crops and products.

Agronomy Journal: An International Journal. American Society of Agronomy. • Bimonthly. $216 Nonmembers.

Amber Waves. Economic Research Service Hazard Analysis and Critical Control Points. • Quarterly. Replaces *Agricultural Outlook; Food Review;* and *Rural America.* Provides research and analysis from the U.S. Department of Agriculture's Economic Research Service. Includes economic data on agriculture, food, trade, and environmental factors.

CSANews. American Society of Agronomy. • Monthly. Description: Publishes information on agronomy, crop science, soil science, and related topics. Provides news of the societies and members; reports of annual meetings; listings of publications; announcements of awards, retirements, and deaths; job listings; and a calendar of events.

Journal of Agricultural and Food Information. The Haworth Press Inc. • Quarterly. Institutions, $95.00 per year. A journal for librarians and others concerned with the acquisition of information on food and agriculture.

The Kiplinger Agriculture Letter. Kiplinger Washington Editors Inc. • Description: Publishes information on actions and proposals by the administration, U.S. Department of Agriculture, and Congress affecting all aspects of agriculture. Includes analysis and forecasts on a broad range of issues affecting the farm/food industry, government production and price support programs, commodity production and consumption data, food marketing and processing, consumer trends, taxes, farm credit, and financial matters.

National Farmers Union News. National Farmers Union. • Description: Provides news, legislation, and tax information in relation to the farming industry.

The Washington Agricultural Record. Washington Agricultural Record. • Description: Focuses on Washington farm issues and developments, reporting international congressional and United States Department of Agriculture (U.S.D.A.) news and international agricultural developments.

RESEARCH CENTERS AND INSTITUTES

Cornell University - Agricultural Experiment Station. 240 Roberts Hall, Ithaca, NY 14853-5905. Phone: (607)255-2552; Fax: (607)255-9499; Email: cuaes@cornell.edu • URL: http://www.cuaes.cornell.edu/cuaes.

Economic Research Service - Canada Division. 1800 M St. NW, Washington, DC 20036. Phone: 800-999-6779 or (202)694-5227; Email: jwainio@ers.usda.gov • URL: http://www.ers.usda.gov/Briefing/canada/ • Canadian agricultural supply, consumption, and trade, including Canadian policies related to agriculture.

Tennessee Agricultural Experiment Station - University of Tennessee, Knoxville. 103 Morgan Hall, Knoxville, TN 37996-4506. Phone: (865)974-4520; Fax: (865)974-6451; Email: AgResearch@tennessee.edu • URL: http://taes.tennessee.edu.

University of California - California Agricultural Experiment Station. 1111 Franklin St., Rm. 6402, Oakland, CA 94607-5200. Phone: (510)987-0036 or (510)987-0060; Fax: (510)465-2659 or (510)451-2317; Email: steve.nation@ucop.edu • URL: http://ucanr.org/AES.shtml • Plant and animal biology, agricultural engineering and economics, soils, and water, including basic and applied studies directed toward solving problems of agriculture involved in production, storage, and transportation of over 300 commodities produced in California. Studies problems relating to forestry, human welfare and nutrition, pest management, mosquito control, and outdoor recreation. Operates on a statewide basis, with main units on Berkeley, Davis, and Riverside campuses of the University and ten research and extension centers throughout the state.

University of Wisconsin - Madison - College of Agricultural and Life Sciences - Wisconsin Agricultural Experiment Station. 212 Agricultural Hall, 1450 Linden Dr., Madison, WI 53706. Phone: (608)261-1432; Fax: (608)265-9534; Email: waes@cals.wisc.edu • URL: http://www.cals.wisc.edu/waes.

STATISTICS SOURCES

Agricultural Statistics. U.S. Department of Agriculture National Agricultural Statistics Service. • Annual. $46 Individuals. Provides a wide variety of statistical data relating to agricultural production, supplies, consumption, prices/price-supports, foreign trade, costs, and returns, as well as farm labor, loans, income, and population. In many cases, historical data is shown annually for 10 years. In addition to farm data, includes detailed fishery statistics.

Agriculture Fact Book. U. S. Government Printing Office. • Annual. $26 Individuals. Issued by the Office of Communications, U. S. Department of Agriculture. Includes data on U. S. agriculture, farmers, food, nutrition, and rural America. Programs of the Department of Agriculture in six areas are described: rural economic development, foreign trade, nutrition, the environment, inspection, and education.

Statistical Yearbook. United Nations Publications. • Annual. $125.00. Contains statistics for about 200 countries on a wide variety of economic, industrial, and demographic topics. Compiled by United Nations Statistical Office.

United States Census of Agriculture. U.S. Department of Agriculture National Agricultural Statistics Service. • Quinquennial. Provides uniform, comprehensive farming and ranching operations data for every U.S. state and county, including production expenses, market value of products, and operator characteristics.

TRADE/PROFESSIONAL ASSOCIATIONS

Agricultural Development Initiatives. PO Box 50006, Nashville, TN 37205. Phone: (615)599-2015; Email: adi@onepost.net • URL: http://www.agri-develop.org • Aims to serve rural households by teaching them sustainable agriculture. Encourages enterprise development among local entrepreneurs toward the end goal of financial freedom. Facilitates the transfer of appropriate technology to local agricultural enterprises.

American Farm Bureau Federation. 600 Maryland Ave. SW, Ste. 1000W, Washington, DC 20024-2555. Phone: (202)406-3600 or (202)406-3614; Fax: (202)406-3602 or (202)406-3604; Email: fbnews@fb.org • URL: http://www.fb.org • Federation of 50 state farm bureaus and Puerto Rico, with membership on a family basis. Analyzes problems of members and formulates action to achieve educational improvement, economic opportunity, and social advancement. Maintains speakers' bureau; sponsors specialized education program.

American Society of Agronomy. 5585 Guilford Rd., Madison, WI 53711-5801. Phone: (608)273-8080 or (608)273-8085; Fax: (608)273-2021; Email: headquarters@sciencesocieties.org • URL: http://www.agronomy.org • Professional society of agronomists, plant breeders, physiologists, soil scientists, chemists, educators, technicians, and others concerned with crop production and soil management, and conditions affecting them. Sponsors fellowship program and student essay and speech contests. Provides placement service.

Australian Institute of Agricultural Science and Technology. PO Box 576, Sydney, NSW 1585, Australia. Phone: 61 2 94318657; Fax: 61 2 94318677; Email: admin@aginstitute.com.au • URL: http://www.aginstitute.com.au • Provides expert services to its clients and the community, together with ways that these are enhanced through professional development, networking, and representation of the interests of agricultural industries.

British Crop Protection Council. c/o Chris Todd, Manager, 7 Omni Business Centre, Omega Park, Alton GU34 2QD, United Kingdom. Phone: 44 1420 593 200 or 44 1420 593200; Fax: 44 1420 593 209 or 44 1420 593209; Email: md@bcpc.org • URL: http://www.bcpc.org • Promotes the knowledge and understanding of crop protection/production through conferences, publications, teaching resources for schools, training manuals, identifying R&D needs for policy makers.

Canadian Agri-Marketing Association - Manitoba. 3336 Portage Ave., Ste. 509, Winnipeg, MB, Canada R3K 2H9. Phone: (204)782-6618 or (204)837-2853; Email: camamb@mymts.net • URL: http://www.cama.org/manitoba/ManitobaHome.aspx • Represents and supports individuals involved in agricultural marketing.

Canadian Agri-Marketing Association - Ontario. c/o Mary Thornly, Executive Director, 22 Guyers Dr., RR 3, Port Elgin, ON, Canada N0H 2C7. Phone: (519)389-6552; Email: camaont@bmts.com • URL: http://www.cama.org/Ontario/OntarioHome.aspx • Represents and supports individuals involved in agricultural marketing.

Communicating for America. 112 E Lincoln Ave., Fergus Falls, MN 56537. Phone: 800-432-3276 or (218)739-3241; Fax: (218)739-3832; Email: memberbenefits@cainc.org • URL: http://www.communicatingforamerica.org • Promotes the general health, well being and advancement of people in agriculture and agribusiness. Participates in federal and state issues that affect the quality of life in rural America and provides members with a variety of money-saving benefit programs. Conducts grants program, research on rural issues, and international exchange programs with an agricultural focus.

Coordinating Committee of Agriculture, Commercial, Industrial and Financial Associations. Route 6, 9-21, Zone 4, Level 9, 01004 Guatemala City, Guatemala. Phone: 502 2201-0000; Email: unice@cacif.org.gt • URL: http://www.cacif.org.gt.

CropLife Australia. AMP Bldg., Level 2, 1 Hobart Pl., Locked Bag 916, Canberra, ACT 2601, Australia. Phone: 61 2 62306399; Fax: 61 2 62306355 • URL: http://www.croplifeaustralia.org.au • Works for a fair, science-based regulatory system, encourages research and development.

CUMELA Nederland. Postbus 1156, NL-3860 BD Nijkerk, Netherlands. Phone: 31 33 2474900; Fax: 31 33 2474901; Email: info@cumela.nl • URL: http://www.cumela.nl • Agricultural and rural contractors. Seeks to advance the interests of agribusinesses. Represents members' commercial and regulatory interests at the national level.

Demeter Biodynamic Trade Association. PO Box 264, Talmage, CA 95481-0264. Email: info@demeterbta.com • URL: http://www.demeterbta.com • Represents Demeter Certified Biodynamic farms, vineyards, wineries, dairies, food processors, traders and distributors. Aims to further interest and education in Demeter Certified Biodynamic farming. Strives to promote Demeter Certified Biodynamic products in the marketplace. Supports and advocates for the protection of the Demeter certification marks.

Farm Financial Standards Council. c/o Carroll Merry, N78 W14573 Appleton Ave., No. 287, Menomonee Falls, WI 53051. Phone: (262)253-6902; Fax: (262)253-6903 • URL: http://www.ffsc.org • Aims to create and promote uniformity and integrity in financial reporting and analysis for agricultural producers. Strives to be recognized as the definitive resource of financial guidelines to benefit agricultural producers.

International Farm Management Association. c/o Tony King, Honorary Secretary, 38 West End, Cambridge CB22 4LX, United Kingdom. Phone: 44 1223 832527; Email: honsecretary@ifmaonline.org • URL: http://www.ifmaonline.org • Farmers, extension workers, academics, resource use planners, and managers in 68 countries concerned with the planning, production, and marketing in agriculture. Furthers the knowledge and understanding of farm business management and fosters the exchange of ideas and information about farm management theory and practice worldwide.

National Alliance of Independent Crop Consultants. 349 E Nolley Dr., Collierville, TN 38017. Phone: (901)861-0511; Fax: (901)861-0512; Email: jonesnaicc@aol.com • URL: http://www.naicc.org • Independent crop consultants and contract researchers united to promote agriculture and professionalism in the field. Seeks to: assist in the formation of state and national policies relating to agricultural production and of crop management philosophies; support agricultural crop producers by the most ecologically sound, environmentally safe, and economical means. Encourages members to expand their knowledge concerning crop management practices and techniques; participates in research in this area. Provides assistance in the formation of state and regional consultant organizations; offers referral system for members. Compiles statistics; sponsors educational programs.

National Association of Agricultural Contractors. The Old Cart Shed, Easton Lodge Farm, Old Oundle Rd., Wansford, Peterborough PE8 6NP, United Kingdom. Phone: 44 1780 784631; Fax: 44 1780 784933; Email: members@naac.co.uk • URL: http://www.naac.co.uk • Represents agricultural and amenity contractors in United Kingdom and their commercial and regulatory interests at the national level.

National Association of State Departments of Agriculture. 1156 15th St. NW, Ste. 1020, Washington, DC 20005. Phone: (202)296-9680; Fax: (202)296-9686; Email: nasda@nasda.org • URL: http://www.nasda.org • Directors of state and territorial departments of agriculture. Coordinates policies, procedures, laws, and activities between the states and federal agencies and Congress. Conducts research.

National Grange. 1616 H St. NW, Washington, DC 20006. Phone: 888-447-2643 or (202)628-3507; Fax: (202)347-1091; Email: info@nationalgrange.org • URL: http://www.nationalgrange.org • Rural family service organization with a special interest in agriculture. Promotes mission and goals through legislative, social, educational, community service, youth and member services programs. Sponsors needlework and stuffed toy contests.

Organization for Competitive Markets. PO Box 6486, Lincoln, NE 68506. Phone: (402)817-4443 • URL: http://www.competitivemarkets.com • Works for increased competition and protection for the agricultural marketplace. Works against "abuse of corporate power and consolidation of the agricultural market."

Processors' and Growers' Research Organisation. The Research Station, Great North Rd., Thornhaugh, Peterborough PE8 6HJ, United Kingdom. Phone: 44 1780 782585; Fax: 44 1780 783993; Email: info@pgro.org • URL: http://www.pgro.org • Farmers, food processors, merchant seedsmen, agrochemical companies, higher education institutes and research stations. Provides research, evaluation and advice on the growing, harvesting and usage of different types of peas and beans. This includes the evaluation of new varieties, crop protection products and growing and harvesting techniques. Provides technical services including seed and soil testing and instrument calibration.

Samuel Roberts Noble Foundation. 2510 Sam Noble Pkwy., Ardmore, OK 73401. Phone: (580)223-5810 or (580)224-6230; Fax: (580)224-6265; Email: jacalaway@noble.org • URL: http://www.noble.org • Strives to promote agriculture, the ranching industry, and plant biology. Hosts the "Junior Beef Excellence Program."

Spanish Confederation of Business Organisations. Calle Diego de Leon, 50, E-28006 Madrid, Spain. Phone: 34 91 5663400; Fax: 34 91 5622562; Email: ceoe@ceoe.es • URL: http://www.ceoe.es • Represents the Spanish business community in all sectors, including agriculture, industry and services.

UNIMA. 10, Cours Aristide Briand, BP 402, F-08107 Charleville-Mezieres, France. Phone: 33 324 328563; Fax: 33 324 327692; Email: sgi@unima.org • URL: http://www.unima.org/en/home • Agricultural contractors, farm workers, farmers, farm equipment manufacturers, and other providers of support and services to agricultural industries. Seeks to advance the interests of agribusinesses. Represents members' commercial and regulatory interests at the national level.

Women Organizing for Change in Agriculture and Natural Resource Management. 1775 K St. NW, Ste. 410, Washington, DC 20006. Phone: (202)331-9099; Fax: (202)331-9366 • URL: http://www.wocan.org • Builds leadership among women and men in agriculture and natural resource management towards gender equality. Seeks to empower women as leaders and agents in adapting to, mitigating and reducing the adverse effects of climate change. Creates global awareness campaigns on the impact of climate change in women. Conducts and publishes gender-specific climate change research.

AGRONOMY

See AGRICULTURE

AIDS POLICY

ABSTRACTS AND INDEXES

Business Periodicals Index Retrospective. EBSCO Publishing Inc. • 11/year. Quarterly and annual cumulations.

Current Law Index. Cengage Learning Inc. • $1,332 Individuals. Monthly. $1269.00 per year. Produced in cooperation with the American Association of Law Libraries. Indexes more than 900 law journals, legal newspapers, and specialty publications from the U.S., Canada, U.K., Ireland, Australia, and New Zealand.

Readers' Guide to Periodical Literature. EBSCO Publishing Inc. • Provides indexing for over 400 periodicals dating back to 1983.

Social Sciences Citation Index. Thomson Reuters Corp. • Weekly. Product is accessed via *Web of Science*.

Social Sciences Index Retrospective: 1907-1983. EBSCO Publishing Inc. • Indexing for 1,000,000 articles. Coverage includes international index and social sciences and humanities index.

BIBLIOGRAPHIES

AIDS Literature and Law Review. University Publishing Group Inc. • Monthly. $225.00 per year. Contains abstracts of journal and newspaper articles. Formerly *AIDS Literature and News Review*.

CD-ROM DATABASES

AGRICOLA on SilverPlatter. Ovid Technologies Inc. • Updated monthly. Price varies. Produced by the National Agricultural Library. Provides over 4 million citations to the literature of agriculture, agricultural economics, animal sciences, entomology, fertilizer, food, forestry, nutrition, pesticides, plant science, water resources, and other topics.

Readers' Guide to Periodical Literature. EBSCO Publishing Inc. • Provides indexing for over 400

For publishers' addresses, refer to SOURCES CITED section at the back of the book.

periodicals dating back to 1983.

Social Sciences Abstracts. EBSCO Publishing Inc. • Provides indexing from 1983 and abstracting from 1994 of more than 750 periodicals covering economics, area studies, community health, public administration, public welfare, urban studies, and many other topics related to the social sciences.

Social Sciences Citation Index. Thomson Reuters Corp. • Weekly. Product is accessed via *Web of Science*.

HANDBOOKS AND MANUALS

AIDS Reference Guide: A Sourcebook for Planners and Decision Makers. Frances Fernald, editor. • $448.00 Looseleaf Service. Two volumes. Includes twelve updates and twelve newsletters. Covers a wide range of AIDS topics, including "Employment Policies and Issues," "Legal Issues," "Financing Issues," "Impact on Healthcare Providers," "Global Issues," and "Legislative, Regulatory, and Governance Issues."

INTERNET DATABASES

Lexis.com Research System. Lexis-Nexis Group. Phone: 800-227-4908 or (937)865-6800; Fax: (937)865-6909; Email: webmaster@prod.lexis-nexis.com • URL: http://www.nexis.com • Fee-based Web site offers extensive searching of a wide variety of legal sources. Additional features include Daily Opinion Service, lexis.com Bookstore, Career Center, CLE Center, Law Schools, and Practice Pages ("Pages specific to areas of specialty").

ONLINE DATABASES

Wilson Business Abstracts Online. H.W. Wilson Co. • Indexes and abstracts 600 major business periodicals, plus the *Wall Street Journal* and the business section of the *New York Times*. Indexing is from 1982, abstracting from 1990, with the two newspapers included from 1993. Updated weekly. Inquire as to online cost and availability. (*Business Periodicals Index* without abstracts is also available online.).

Wilson Social Sciences Abstracts Online. H.W. Wilson Co. • Provides online abstracting and indexing of more than 500 periodicals covering area studies, community health, public administration, public welfare, urban studies, and many other social science topics. Time period is 1994 to date for abstracts and 1983 to date for indexing, with updates weekly. Inquire as to online cost and availability.

OTHER SOURCES

AIDS Litigation Reporter (Acquired Immune Deficiency Syndrome): The National Journal of Record of AIDS-Related Litigation. Andrews Publications. • Semimonthly. $951.00 per year. Newsletter. Provides reports on a wide variety of legal cases in which AIDS is a factor.

PERIODICALS AND NEWSLETTERS

AIDS and Public Policy Journal. University Publishing Group Inc. • Quarterly. Individuals, $59.00 per year; institutions, $115.00 per year.

AIDS Policy and Law: The Biweekly Newsletter on Legislation, Regulation, and Litigation Concerning AIDS. LRP Publications Library. • 11/year. Newsletter for personnel managers, lawyers, and others.

RESEARCH CENTERS AND INSTITUTES

Center for Women Policy Studies. 1776 Massachusetts Ave. NW, Ste. 450, Washington, DC 20036. Phone: (202)872-1770; Fax: (202)296-8962; Email: cwps@centerwomenpolicy.org • URL: http://www.centerwomenpolicy.org • Conducts research on the policy issues that affect the legal, economic, educational, and social status of women, including sexual harassment in the workplace, and women and AIDS.

TRADE/PROFESSIONAL ASSOCIATIONS

American Foundation for AIDS Research. 120 Wall St., 13th Fl., New York, NY 10005-3908. Phone: (212)806-1600; Fax: (212)806-1601 • URL: http://www.amfar.org • Purpose is to raise funds to support AIDS research.

AIR BASES

See AIR FORCE

AIR CARGO

See AIR FREIGHT

AIR CONDITIONING INDUSTRY

See also HEATING AND VENTILATION; REFRIGERATION INDUSTRY

ABSTRACTS AND INDEXES

Applied Science and Technology Index. EBSCO Publishing Inc. • 11/year. Indexes a wide variety of English language technical, industrial, and engineering periodicals.

NTIS Alerts: Energy. U.S. Department of Commerce National Technical Information Service. • Biweekly. $130 per year. Covers electric power, batteries, fuels, geothermal energy, heating/cooling systems, nuclear technology, solar energy, energy policy, and related subjects.

DIRECTORIES

Air Conditioning & Heating & Refrigeration Equipment Directory. InfoGroup Inc. • Annual. Number of listings: 689. Entries include: Name, address, phone, size of advertisement, name of owner or manager, number of employees, year first in "Yellow Pages." Compiled from telephone company "Yellow Pages," nationwide.

Air Conditioning Contractors of America--Membership Directory. Air Conditioning Contractors of America. • Annual. Covers: Member air conditioning and heating contractors, manufacturers, vocational technical schools. Entries include: Company name, address, phone, fax, names and titles of key personnel, description of fields, and types of work performed.

E-BOOKS

Macmillan Encyclopedia of Energy. Cengage Learning Inc. • 2003. eBook. Published by Macmillan Reference USA. Covers the business, technology, and history of a wide variety of energy sources. Inquire as to price and availability.

FINANCIAL RATIOS

American Supply Association Operating Performance Report. American Supply Association. • Annual. $399 Members. Report provides details on operating performance.

Annual Statement Studies. Risk Management Association. • Annual. Compiled from over 280,000 financial statements.

Annual Statement Studies: Industry Default Probabilities and Cash Flow Measures. Risk Management Association. • Annual. $405 Nonmembers. Serves as a companion volume to the original *Annual Statement Studies*. Gives probability of default estimates on a percentage scale for more than 450 industries. Includes changes in position year-by-year for eight financial statement line items and provides percentage measures of cash flow.

Industry Norms and Key Business Ratios. Dun & Bradstreet Inc. • Annual. Five volumes. Covers over 800 kinds of businesses, arranged by Standard Industrial Classification number. More detailed editions covering longer periods of time are also available.

INTERNET DATABASES

Manufacturing Profiles. U. S. Bureau of the Census. Phone: (301)763-4636 or (301)763-4100; Fax: (301)763-4794; Email: webmaster@census.gov • URL: http://www.census.gov/prod/www/abs/mfg-prof.html • The Census Bureau makes available free on PDF (Portable Document Format) an annual consolidation of the entire Current Industrial Report series, presenting "all the data compiled." Contains statistics on production, shipments, inventories, consumption, exports, imports, and orders for a wide variety of manufactured products.

OTHER SOURCES

ASHRAE Transactions. American Society of Heating, Refrigerating and Air-Conditioning Engineers. • Semiannual. Members, $169.00 per year; non-members, $211.00 per year.

Major Energy Companies of the World. Cengage Learning Inc. • Annual. $1,460 Individuals. 2008. 12th edition. eBook. Published by Graham & Whiteside. Contains detailed information on more than 4,850 important energy companies in various countries. Industries include electricity generation, coal, natural gas, nuclear energy, petroleum, fuel distribution, and equipment for energy production.

PERIODICALS AND NEWSLETTERS

Air Conditioning, Heating, and Refrigeration News: The HVACR Contractor's Weekly Newsmagazine. BNP Media. • Weekly. $87.00 per year. Includes *Supplement*.

Dealerscope: Product and Strategy for Consumer Technology Retailing. North American Publishing Co. • Monthly. $79 /year. Formerly *Dealerscope Consumer Electronices Marketplace*. Provides product information and valuable strategy for consumer technology retailers.

Heating/Piping/Air Conditioning Engineering: The Magazine of Mechanical Systems Engineering. Penton Media Inc. • Monthly. Covers design, specification, installation, operation, and maintenance for systems in industrial, commercial, and institutional buildings. Formerly (Heating, Piping and Air Conditioning).

Shop Talk. International Mobile Air Conditioning Association. • Monthly. $20 /year for domestic. Description: Carries news briefs on happenings in the motor vehicle air conditioning and installed accessories industry. Publishes technical as well as management-oriented articles and listings of manuals, technical services, and training opportunities available. Recurring features include reports of meetings, company and personnel news, reports on the Association's activities and professional interest groups, and monthly supplements on specific topics.

RESEARCH CENTERS AND INSTITUTES

Purdue University - Ray W. Herrick Laboratories. School of Mechanical Engineering, 140 S Martin Jischke Dr., West Lafayette, IN 47907-2031. Phone: (765)494-2132; Fax: (765)494-0787; Email: rhlab@ecn.purdue.edu • URL: http://engineering.purdue.edu/Herrick/index.html • Mechanical engineering, including studies on heating, air conditioning, and refrigeration equipment and systems, engineering acoustics, noise and vibration control (including vehicle and engine noise), sound quality, positive displacement compressor technology, mechanical reliability, precision measurements, mechanics of materials, tribology, noise control materials, electro-hydraulic and engine controls, emissions, and automatic control.

STATISTICS SOURCES

Refrigeration, Air Conditioning, and Warm Air Heating Equipment. U. S. Bureau of the Census. • Annual. Provides data on quantity and value of shipments by manufacturers. Formerly *Air Conditioning and Refrigeration Equipment*. (Current Industrial Reports, MA-333M.).

U.S. Industry and Trade Outlook. U.S. Department of Commerce National Technical Information Service. • Annual. Produced by the International Trade Administration, U.S. Department of Commerce, in a "public-private" partnership with DRI/McGraw-Hill and Standard & Poor's. Provides basic data, outlook for the current year, and "Long-Term Prospects" (five-year projections) for a wide variety of products and services. Includes high technology industries. Formerly *U.S. Industrial Outlook.*

TRADE/PROFESSIONAL ASSOCIATIONS

American Society of Heating, Refrigerating and Air-Conditioning Engineers. 1791 Tullie Cir. NE, Atlanta, GA 30329. Phone: 800-527-4723 or (404)636-8400; Fax: (404)321-5478; Email: ashrae@ashrae.org • URL: http://www.ashrae.org • Represents Technical society of heating, ventilating, refrigeration, and air-conditioning engineers. Sponsors numerous research programs in cooperation with universities, research laboratories, and government agencies on subjects such as human and animal environmental studies, effects of air-conditioning, quality of inside air, heat transfer, flow, and cooling processes. Conducts professional development seminars. Writes method of test standards and other standards addressing energy conservation in buildings, indoor air quality, and refrigerants. Publishes extensive literature and electronic products.

AIR FORCE

ABSTRACTS AND INDEXES

Air University Library Index to Military Periodicals. U.S. Air Force. • Quarterly. Annual cumulation.

PERIODICALS AND NEWSLETTERS

Air Force Magazine. Air Force Association. • Monthly. Magazine for personnel of United States Air Force, government agencies, and aerospace industry.

Air Force Times. Gannett Government Media Corp. • Weekly (Mon.). $55 Individuals print and online. Independent newspaper serving Air Force personnel worldwide.

Airman: Official Magazine of the U.S. Air Force. U. S. Government Printing Office. • Monthly. $41.00 per year.

STATISTICS SOURCES

Annual Report of the Secretary of Defense. U.S. Department of Defense - Office of the Secretary. • Annual.

AIR FREIGHT

See also FREIGHT TRANSPORT

ABSTRACTS AND INDEXES

Business Periodicals Index Retrospective. EBSCO Publishing Inc. • 11/year. Quarterly and annual cumulations.

DIRECTORIES

Air Freight Directory. Air Cargo Inc. • Bimonthly. $34.50 single copy. Publication includes: Directory of more than 500 motor carriers contracting with Air Cargo, Inc. for delivery and pick up of freight. Air Cargo is a ground service specialist organization jointly owned by 18 major air carriers. Entries include: Airport city and code, firm name, address, phone, and services offered. Principal content of publication is chart of service points and rates.

National Customs Brokers and Forwarders Association of America Membership Directory. National Customs Brokers and Forwarders Association of America. • Annual. $55.00. Lists about 600 customs brokers, international air cargo agents, and freight forwarders in the U.S.

ONLINE DATABASES

TRIS: Transportation Research Information Service. The National Academies National Research Council. • Contains abstracts and citations to a wide range of transportation literature, 1968 to present, with monthly updates. Includes references to the literature of air transportation, highways, ships and shipping, railroads, trucking, and urban mass transportation. Formerly *TRIS-ON-LINE.* Inquire as to online cost and availability.

OTHER SOURCES

Aviation Law Reports. Wolters Kluwer Law & Business CCH. • Semimonthly. Four looseleaf volumes covering aviation law.

PERIODICALS AND NEWSLETTERS

Air Cargo News. Air Cargo News, Inc. • Monthly. $39.95 per year.

Air Cargo World: International Trends and Analysis. • Monthly. $58.00 per year. Provides news and information concerning air freight carriers, freight forwarding, and cargo operations at airports.

Air Transport World. Intertec Publishing. • Monthly. $89 Individuals print and online. Includes supplement *World Airline Reports.*

Cargo Facts: The Airfreight and Express Industry Newsletter of Record. Air Cargo Management Group. • Monthly. $445 per year. Provides analysis of developments in the air freight and express industry.

RESEARCH CENTERS AND INSTITUTES

Northwestern University - Transportation Center. 600 Foster St., Evanston, IL 60208-4055. Phone: (847)491-7287; Fax: (847)491-3090; Email: masmah@northwestern.edu • URL: http://transportation.northwestern.edu • Transportation, including information technology, air, rail, motor carrier, ocean and inland shipping, pipeline, telecommunications, and public transit. Focuses on the movement of materials, people, energy, and information. Emphasizes development of advanced models in logistics (vehicle routing, scheduling, inventory management, facility location), analyses of safety in the motor carrier and airline industries, evaluation of the impact of delivery restrictions in congested areas, use of advanced information technologies as competitive weapons in transportation management, studies of the impact of regulatory reform on industry economy, models of intercity travel behavior and suburban congestion, transportation planning.

STATISTICS SOURCES

Air Transport. Airlines for America. • Annual. $20. Airline industry information.

TRADE/PROFESSIONAL ASSOCIATIONS

Regional Airline Association. 2025 M St. NW, Ste. 800, Washington, DC 20036-3309. Phone: (202)367-1170; Fax: (202)367-2170; Email: raa@raa.org • URL: http://www.raa.org • Regional air carriers engaged in the transportation of passengers, cargo, or mail on a scheduled basis; persons, companies and organizations engaged in pursuits related to commercial aviation; colleges and universities, state and local governments and state aviation associations. Responds to community, consumer and public needs for air transportation and aviation facilities and to help establish a healthy business, regulatory and legislative climate that enables members to profit through service to the nation and the flying public. Supports programs for improving safety and reliability of air transportation and air commerce; provides a forum for exchange of ideas and information.

AIR PILOTS

BIBLIOGRAPHIES

Aviation. U. S. Government Printing Office. • Annual. Free. Lists government publications. (GPO Subject Bibliography Number 18).

DIRECTORIES

Airport/Facility Directory. U.S. National Ocean Service. • Covers: Non-military airports in the continental United States; separate volumes cover the southeast, northeast, northwest, east central, north central, southwest, and south central states (including Puerto Rico and the Virgin Islands). Entries include: Airport name, location, weather service phone number, control center frequencies, and information concerning navigational and other aids and systems.

Jet and PropJet Business Aircraft Directory. Avcom International Inc. • Annual. $26.95. Owners of business jet and turboprop aircraft. Worldwide coverage. Formerly *Propjet.*

List of Certificated Pilot Schools. Federal Aviation Administration. U. S. Government Printing Office. • Lists FAA-approved ground and flight schools and the pilot training courses each school offers.

PERIODICALS AND NEWSLETTERS

Air Line Pilot; The Magazine of Professional Flight Deck Crews. Air Line Pilots Association Engineering and Air Safety Resource Center. • 10 times a year. $30.00 per year.

FAA Aviation News. Federal Aviation Administration. U. S. Government Printing Office. • Bimonthly. $28.00. per year. Designed to help airmen become safer pilots. Includes updates on major rule changes and proposals.

Flight International. Reed Business Information Ltd. • Weekly. $140.00 per year. Technical aerospace coverage.

Flying. Bonnier Corp. • Monthly. $14 Individuals print. General aviation magazine. Includes three *Special Issues.* Price on application.

Plane and Pilot. Werner Publishing Corp. • 11/year. $14.97 per year.

Professional Pilot Magazine. Queensmith Communications Corp. • Monthly. $50 Individuals. Edited for career pilots in all areas of aviation: airline, corporate, charter, and military. Includes flying technique, avionics, navigation, accident analysis, career planning, corporate profiles, and business aviation news.

TRADE/PROFESSIONAL ASSOCIATIONS

Lawyer-Pilots Bar Association. PO Box 1510, Edgewater, MD 21037. Phone: (410)571-1750; Fax: (410)571-1780; Email: lpba@comcast.net • URL: http://www.lpba.org • Lawyers who are licensed pilots and engaged in the practice of aviation law or interested in aviation. Is concerned with law, safety, and general aviation.

National Association of Flight Instructors. 3101 E Milham Ave., Portage, MI 49002. Phone: 866-806-6156; Email: nafi@nafinet.org • URL: http://www.nafinet.org • Flight instructors certified by the Federal Aviation Administration. Works to raise the professional standards of the flight instructor through education and organization. Serves as a central point for dissemination of knowledge, methodology, and new information relative to flight instruction. Supports improved legislation concerning pilot training, certification, and aviation regulations. Works with all segments of the industry for improvement of flight education, efficiency, and safety. Compiles statistics.

Ninety Nines, International Organization of Women Pilots. 4300 Amelia Earhart Dr., Ste. A, Oklahoma City, OK 73159. Phone: 800-994-1929 or (405)685-7969; Fax: (405)685-7985; Email: 99s@ninety-nines.org • URL: http://www.ninety-nines.org • Licensed women pilots. Formerly Ninety-Nines International Women Pilots.

For publishers' addresses, refer to SOURCES CITED section at the back of the book.

AIR POLLUTION

See also ENVIRONMENT

ABSTRACTS AND INDEXES

Environment Abstracts. University Publications of America. • Monthly. Price varies. Provides multidisciplinary coverage of the world's environmental literature. Incorporates *Acid Rain Abstracts*.

Environment Abstracts Annual: A Guide to the Key Environmental Literature of the Year. University Publications of America. • Annual. $495.00. A yearly cumulation of *Environment Abstracts*.

Excerpta Medica: Environmental Health and Pollution Control. Elsevier. • 16 times a year. Institutions, $3,246.00 per year. Section 46 of *Excerpta Medica*. Covers air, water, and land pollution and noise control.

NTIS Alerts: Environmental Pollution & Control. U.S. Department of Commerce National Technical Information Service. • Biweekly. $130 per year. Covers the following categories of environmental pollution: air, water, solid wastes, radiation, pesticides, and noise.

Pollution Abstracts. Cambridge Information Group. • Monthly. $1,390.00 per year. Includes print and online editions; with index, $1,515.00 per year.

CD-ROM DATABASES

Environment Abstracts on CD-ROM. University Publications of America. • Quarterly. $1,295.00 per year. Contains the following CD-ROM databases: *Environment Abstracts, Energy Abstracts*, and *Acid Rain Abstracts*. Length of coverage varies.

ENCYCLOPEDIAS AND DICTIONARIES

Environmental Encyclopedia. Cengage Learning Inc. • $327 Individuals. 2011. $298.00. 4th edition. Provides over 1,300 articles on all aspects of the environment. Written in non-technical style. eBook also available. Inquire for pricing.

Pollution A to Z. Cengage Learning Inc. • 2003.Two volumes. Provides encyclopedic coverage of many aspects of environmental pollution, including air, water, noise, and soil. Inquire as to price and availability.

INTERNET DATABASES

Manufacturing Profiles. U. S. Bureau of the Census. Phone: (301)763-4636 or (301)763-4100; Fax: (301)763-4794; Email: webmaster@census.gov • URL: http://www.census.gov/prod/www/abs/mfg-prof.html • The Census Bureau makes available free on PDF (Portable Document Format) an annual consolidation of the entire Current Industrial Report series, presenting "all the data compiled." Contains statistics on production, shipments, inventories, consumption, exports, imports, and orders for a wide variety of manufactured products.

PERIODICALS AND NEWSLETTERS

Air and Waste Management Association Journal. • Monthly. Individuals, $150.00 per year; institutions, $329.00 per year: nonprofit institutions, $229.00 per year. Includes annual *Directory of Governmental Air Pollution Agencies*.

Air Pollution Control. Bloomberg BNA. • Biweekly. $798.00 per year. Newsletter.

Environmental Business Journal: Strategic Information for a Changing Industry. Environmental Business International Inc. • Monthly. $250 Single issue. Includes both industrial and financial information relating to individual companies and to the environmental industry in general. Covers air pollution, wat es, U. S. Department of Health and Human Services. Provides conference, workshop, and symposium proceedings, as well as extensive reviews of environmental prospects.

Environmental Regulation: State Capitals. Wakeman/Walworth Inc. • 50 times a year. $245.00 per year; print and online editions, $350.00 per year. Newsletter. Formerly *From the State Capitals: Environmental Regulation*.

RESEARCH CENTERS AND INSTITUTES

Center for Energy and Environmental Studies - Carnegie Mellon University Department of Engineering and Public Policy. Baker Hall 128-A, Pittsburgh, PA 15213. Phone: (412)268-5897; Fax: (412)268-1089; Email: rubin@cmu.edu.

University of California, Riverside - Air Pollution Research Center. 205 Fawcett Laboratory, Riverside, CA 92521. Phone: (951)827-4191 or (909)787-5124; Fax: (951)827-5004 or (909)787-5004; Email: roger.atkinson@ucr.edu • URL: http://www.aprc.ucr.edu • Atmospheric chemistry and the effects of pollutants on plant systems and modeling of photochemical smog formation to yield information relevant to the development of rational and cost-effective air pollution control strategies. Research program includes studies of chemical and physical transformations of pollutants in the atmosphere, chemical composition and related mutagenicity of gaseous and particulate organic pollutants, spectroscopic identification and measurement of atmospheric constituents, effects of pollutants on agricultural crops, definition of tolerance levels for specified plant species and description of symptom expression of plants, modeling atmospheric transformations of pollutants, and translation of research results into models suitable for direct application to control strategies by state and federal agencies and public officials.

University of Rhode Island - Air Pollution Research Laboratory. 121 Wales Hall, Kingston, RI 02881. Phone: (401)874-2535; Fax: (401)874-2355 • URL: http://ww2.uri.edu.

STATISTICS SOURCES

Air Quality Data. U.S. Environmental Protection Agency. • Annual.

Standard & Poor's Industry Surveys. Standard & Poor's Financial Services L.L.C. • Semiannual. $1,800.00. Two looseleaf volumes. Includes monthly *Supplements*. Provides detailed, individual surveys of 52 major industry groups. Each survey is revised on a semiannual basis. Also includes "Monthly Investment Review" (industry group investment analysis) and monthly "Trends & Projections" (economic analysis).

U.S. Industry and Trade Outlook. U.S. Department of Commerce National Technical Information Service. • Annual. Produced by the International Trade Administration, U.S. Department of Commerce, in a "public-private" partnership with DRI/McGraw-Hill and Standard & Poor's. Provides basic data, outlook for the current year, and "Long-Term Prospects" (five-year projections) for a wide variety of products and services. Includes high technology industries. Formerly *U.S. Industrial Outlook*.

TRADE/PROFESSIONAL ASSOCIATIONS

National Association of Clean Air Agencies. 444 N Capitol St. NW, Ste. 307, Washington, DC 20001. Phone: (202)624-7864; Fax: (202)624-7863; Email: 4cleanair@4cleanair.org • URL: http://www.cleanairworld.org • State, local and territorial air pollution program administrators and members of their staffs. Provides an opportunity for state and local officials who are responsible for implementing air pollution control programs established under the Clean Air Act to share air quality-related experiences and to discuss problems. Encourages communication and cooperation among federal, state, and local regulatory agencies.

AIR TRAFFIC

See AIR TRAVEL

AIR TRAVEL

See also AIRLINE INDUSTRY

ABSTRACTS AND INDEXES

Business Periodicals Index Retrospective. EBSCO Publishing Inc. • 11/year. Quarterly and annual cumulations.

BIBLIOGRAPHIES

Travel and Tourism. U. S. Government Printing Office. • Annual. Free. Issued by the Superintendent of Documents. A list of government publications on the travel industry and tourism. Formerly *Mass Transit, Travel and Tourism*. (Subject Bibliography No. 302.).

DIRECTORIES

ASU.com. Airline Services Unlimited. • Quarterly. $44.95 book plus 1 bonus issue and 16 months. Covers: Over 25,000 listings for airlines, lodgings, tours, car rental companies, and cruise lines, which allow travel discounts to airline employees worldwide. Entries include: Name, address, and phone of facility or service; description; regular price and type and amount of discount; credit cards accepted; validity dates; booking procedures; whether parents and retired airline employees are eligible.

HANDBOOKS AND MANUALS

Health Information for International Travel. U.S. Dept. of Health and Human Services - Centers for Disease Control and Prefabricated. • Annual. $38. Produced by the Centers for Disease Control and Prevention (CDC). Primarily edited for "healthcare providers who administer pre- and post-travel counseling and care." Also serves as a reference for airlines, cruise lines, and the travel industry in general. Covers such items as injuries during travel, motion sickness, disabilities, vaccines, insect repellents, and travel with children. Sometimes known as "The Yellow Book.".

ONLINE DATABASES

United States International Air Travel Statistics. U. S. Department of Transportation, Center for Transportation Information. • Provides detailed statistics on air passenger travel between the U. S. and foreign countries for both scheduled and charter flights. Time period is 1975 to date, with monthly updates. Inquire as to online cost and availability.

OTHER SOURCES

Travel Law. ALM Media Properties LLC. • $555. Emphasis is on the legal rights of travelers, including a consideration of class action suits. Includes such matters as tour operator liability, hotel responsibilities, overbooking by airlines, and frequent-flyer issues. (Law Journal Press).

PERIODICALS AND NEWSLETTERS

Frequent Flyer: For Business People Who Must Travel. Official Airline Guides. • Monthly. $89.00 per year to individuals. Also known as *OAG Frequent Flyer*. Edited for business travelers. Contains news of frequent flyer programs, airport developments, airline services, and business travel trends. Available only with *OAG Flight Guide*.

Front Row Advisor: Business and First Class Air Travel and the Alluring World of Free Upgrades. Diversified Specialties Inc. • Bimonthly. $145.00 per year. Newsletter. Contains information on opportunities provided by airlines to upgrade coach seats to business class, including frequent flyer upgrades.

Inside Flyer. • Monthly. $36.00 per year. Newsletter. Provides information relating to frequent flyer awards and air travel.

Jax Fax Travel Marketing Magazine: The Official Leisure Travel Booking Magazine. Jet Airtransport Exchange Inc. • Monthly. $15.00 per year. Trade magazine for travel agents.

Newsline: Research News from the U. S. Travel Data Center. U.S. National Research Council. • Monthly. $55.00 per year. Newsletter. Covers trends in the U. S. travel industry.

Summary of Health Information for International Travel. U.S. Department of Health and Human Services. • Biweekly. Formerly *Weekly Summary of Health Information for International Travel.*

Travel Smart: Pay Less, Enjoy More. Dunan Communications, Inc. • Monthly. $39.00 per year. Newsletter. Provides information and recommendations for travelers. Emphasis is on travel value and opportunities for bargains. Incorporates *Joy of Travel.*

RESEARCH CENTERS AND INSTITUTES

U.S. Travel Association. 1100 New York Ave. NW, Ste. 450, Washington, DC 20005-3934. Phone: (202)408-8422; Fax: (202)408-1255; Email: feedback@ustravel.org • URL: http://www.ustravel.org • Conducts economic, statistical, and market research relating to the U. S. travel industry. Affiliated with the Travel Industry Association of America.

STATISTICS SOURCES

Air Carrier Traffic Statistics Monthly. U.S. Department of Transportation. • Monthly. Provides passenger traffic data for large airlines.

Air Transport. Airlines for America. • Annual. $20. Airline industry information.

Outlook for Travel and Tourism. U.S. Travel Association. • Annual. Members, $100.00; nonmembers, $175.00. Contains forecasts of the performance of the U. S. travel industry, including air travel, business travel, recreation (attractions), and accomodations.

Summary of International Travel to the United States. International Trade Administration, Tourism Industries. U.S. Department of Commerce. • Monthly. Quarterly and annual versions available. Provides statistics on air travel to the U.S. from 90 countries. Formerly *Summary and Analysis of International Travel to the United States.*

TRADE/PROFESSIONAL ASSOCIATIONS

Air Transport Association of Canada. 255 Albert St., Ste. 700, Ottawa, ON, Canada K1P 6A9. Phone: (613)233-7727; Fax: (613)230-8648; Email: atac@atac.ca • URL: http://www.atac.ca/web/en • Air transport companies. Promotes a business climate beneficial to members. Represents' members interests before government agencies. Conducts research and educational programs; compiles industry statistics.

National Air Carrier Association. 1000 Wilson Blvd., Ste. 1700, Arlington, VA 22209. Phone: (703)358-8060; Fax: (703)358-8070 • URL: http://www.naca.cc • Represents U.S. certificated airlines specializing in low-cost scheduled and air charter operations. Assists members in the promotion of air transportation and serves as a liaison between members and U.S. government bodies that regulate air transportation.

AIRCRAFT INDUSTRY

See AIRPLANE INDUSTRY

AIRLINE INDUSTRY

See also AIR TRAVEL

ABSTRACTS AND INDEXES

Business Periodicals Index Retrospective. EBSCO Publishing Inc. • 11/year. Quarterly and annual cumulations.

NTIS Alerts: Transportation. U.S. Department of Commerce National Technical Information Service. • Biweekly. $130 per year. Covers air, marine, highway, inland waterway, pipeline, and railroad transportation.

BIBLIOGRAPHIES

Federal Aviation Regulations. U. S. Government Printing Office. • Annual. Free. Lists government publications. GPO Subject Bibliography Number 12.

CD-ROM DATABASES

OECD Statistical Compendium. Organization for Economic Cooperation and Development. • Semiannual. $1,905.00 per year for 1 to 10 users. CD-ROM contains more than 730,000 monthly, quarterly, and annual time series for OECD countries, 1960 to date. Includes fully searchable data on agriculture, food, economic indicators, national accounts, employment, energy, finance, industry, technology, and foreign trade. Results can be displayed in various forms.

DIRECTORIES

Airline Handbook. Aerotravel Research. • Annual. Covers: 2,000 commercial airlines (scheduled and chartered) serving over 200 nations and territories worldwide. Entries include: Airline name, address of main office, phone, telex, financial keys, number of employees, routes and destinations, aircraft fleets, passenger traffic totals, company history.

ASU.com. Airline Services Unlimited. • Quarterly. $44.95 book plus 1 bonus issue and 16 months. Covers: Over 25,000 listings for airlines, lodgings, tours, car rental companies, and cruise lines, which allow travel discounts to airline employees worldwide. Entries include: Name, address, and phone of facility or service; description; regular price and type and amount of discount; credit cards accepted; validity dates; booking procedures; whether parents and retired airline employees are eligible.

National Air Transportation Association Official Membership Directory. National Air Transportation Association. • Annual. List more than 1,000 regular, associate, and affliate members; regular members include airport service organizations, air taxi operators, and commuter airlines.

Plunkett's Airline, Hotel, and Travel Industry Almanac. Plunkett Research Ltd. • Annual. $349.99. Contains profiles of 300 leading companies, including airlines, hotels, travel agencies, theme parks, cruise lines, casinos, and car rental companies.

FINANCIAL RATIOS

Annual Statement Studies. Risk Management Association. • Annual. Compiled from over 280,000 financial statements.

Annual Statement Studies: Industry Default Probabilities and Cash Flow Measures. Risk Management Association. • Annual. $405 Nonmembers. Serves as a companion volume to the original *Annual Statement Studies.* Gives probability of default estimates on a percentage scale for more than 450 industries. Includes changes in position year-by-year for eight financial statement line items and provides percentage measures of cash flow.

Industry Norms and Key Business Ratios. Dun & Bradstreet Inc. • Annual. Five volumes. Covers over 800 kinds of businesses, arranged by Standard Industrial Classification number. More detailed editions covering longer periods of time are also available.

INTERNET DATABASES

Business 2.0 Web Guide to the Best Business Links. Business 2.0 Media Inc. Phone: (415)293-4800; Email: support@business2.com • URL: http://www.business2.com/webguide • Web site presents an extensive, searchable directory of links to "the best, most informative, and authoritative web pages." Twenty main categories cover business, finance, career, company information, people, and technology topics, with thousands of subtopics, all linking to Web sites recommended by experienced business researchers. Fees: Free.

Fedstats. Federal Interagency Council on Statistical Policy. Phone: (202)395-7254 • URL: http://www.fedstats.gov • Web site features an efficient search facility for full-text statistics produced by more than 100 federal agencies, including the Census Bureau, the Bureau of Economic Analysis, and the Bureau of Labor Statistics. Boolean searches can be made within one agency or for all agencies combined. Links are offered to international statistical bureaus, including the UN, IMF, OECD, UNESCO, Eurostat, and 20 individual countries. Fees: Free.

FreeLunch.com. Economy.com, Inc. Phone: (610)696-8700; Fax: (610)696-1678 • URL: http://www.freelunch.com • Web site provides free access to more than 200 million economic and financial data series, covering industry, demographics, labor markets, prices, retail sales, government spending, trade, interest rates, housing starts, the stock market, etc. Data is available in either chart or table form. Searching is offered. Free, but registration required. Economy.com, Inc. also offers fee-based economic analysis at *The Dismal Scientist* site (www.dismal.com).

ONLINE DATABASES

TRIS: Transportation Research Information Service. The National Academies National Research Council. • Contains abstracts and citations to a wide range of transportation literature, 1968 to present, with monthly updates. Includes references to the literature of air transportation, highways, ships and shipping, railroads, trucking, and urban mass transportation. Formerly *TRIS-ON-LINE.* Inquire as to online cost and availability.

OTHER SOURCES

Aviation Law Reports. Wolters Kluwer Law & Business CCH. • Semimonthly. Four looseleaf volumes covering aviation law.

PERIODICALS AND NEWSLETTERS

Air Transport World. Intertec Publishing. • Monthly. $89 Individuals print and online. Includes supplement *World Airline Reports.*

Airline Business: The Voice of Airline Managements. Reed Aerospace. • Monthly. $130.00 per year. Published in England by Reed Business Information. Covers management and financial topics for international airline executives.

Frequent Flyer: For Business People Who Must Travel. Official Airline Guides. • Monthly. $89.00 per year to individuals. Also known as *OAG Frequent Flyer.* Edited for business travelers. Contains news of frequent flyer programs, airport developments, airline services, and business travel trends. Available only with *OAG Flight Guide.*

Professional Pilot Magazine. Queensmith Communications Corp. • Monthly. $50 Individuals. Edited for career pilots in all areas of aviation: airline, corporate, charter, and military. Includes flying technique, avionics, navigation, accident analysis, career planning, corporate profiles, and business aviation news.

Regional Airline World. Shephard Press Ltd. • 10 times a year. $130.00 per year. Covers the business, financial, and technical aspects of regional, short-haul, and commuter airline operations.

RESEARCH CENTERS AND INSTITUTES

Massachusetts Institute of Technology - Center for Transportation and Logistics. 77 Massachusetts Ave., E40-276, Cambridge, MA 02139. Phone: (617)253-5320; Fax: (617)253-4560; Email: sheffi@mit.edu • URL: http://ctl.mit.edu • Transportation and logistics, with emphasis on problem-oriented, interdisciplinary, and multi-

For publishers' addresses, refer to SOURCES CITED section at the back of the book.

model studies, including studies on innovative urban transportation systems, transport technology innovations, railroad systems operations, trucking, energy policies, regional transportation planning and programming, highway location and design, flight transportation, ocean shipping, transportation systems analysis, logistics, supply chain management, logistics organizations, shipper/carrier relationships and logistics information technology.

Northwestern University - Transportation Center. 600 Foster St., Evanston, IL 60208-4055. Phone: (847)491-7287; Fax: (847)491-3090; Email: masmah@northwestern.edu • URL: http://transportation.northwestern.edu • Transportation, including information technology, air, rail, motor carrier, ocean and inland shipping, pipeline, telecommunications, and public transit. Focuses on the movement of materials, people, energy, and information. Emphasizes development of advanced models in logistics (vehicle routing, scheduling, inventory management, facility location), analyses of safety in the motor carrier and airline industries, evaluation of the impact of delivery restrictions in congested areas, use of advanced information technologies as competitive weapons in transportation management, studies of the impact of regulatory reform on industry economy, models of intercity travel behavior and suburban congestion, transportation planning.

STATISTICS SOURCES

Air Carrier Industry Scheduled Service Traffic Statistics. U.S. Department of Transportation. • Quarterly. Includes data for commuter airlines.

Air Carrier Traffic Statistics Monthly. U.S. Department of Transportation. • Monthly. Provides passenger traffic data for large airlines.

Air Transport. Airlines for America. • Annual. $20. Airline industry information.

Airport Activity Statistics of Certificated Route Air Carriers. U. S. Department of Transportation. U. S. Government Printing Office. • Annual. $58 Individuals.

Standard & Poor's Industry Surveys. Standard & Poor's Financial Services L.L.C. • Semiannual. $1,800.00. Two looseleaf volumes. Includes monthly *Supplements*. Provides detailed, individual surveys of 52 major industry groups. Each survey is revised on a semiannual basis. Also includes "Monthly Investment Review" (industry group investment analysis) and monthly "Trends & Projections" (economic analysis).

Standard & Poor's Statistical Service. Current Statistics. Standard & Poor's Financial Services L.L.C. • Monthly. $688.00 per year. Includes 10 *Basic Statistics* sections, *Current Statistics Supplements* and *Annual Security Price Index Record*.

Survey of Current Business. U. S. Government Printing Office. • Published by Bureau of Economic Analysis, U. S. Department of Commerce. Presents a wide variety of business and economic data.

TRADE/PROFESSIONAL ASSOCIATIONS

Air Transport Association of Canada. 255 Albert St., Ste. 700, Ottawa, ON, Canada K1P 6A9. Phone: (613)233-7727; Fax: (613)230-8648; Email: atac@atac.ca • URL: http://www.atac.ca/web/en • Air transport companies. Promotes a business climate beneficial to members. Represents' members interests before government agencies. Conducts research and educational programs; compiles industry statistics.

Airport Minority Advisory Council. 2001 Jefferson Davis Hwy., Ste. 500, Arlington, VA 22202. Phone: (703)414-2622; Fax: (703)414-2686; Email: amac.info@amac-org.com • URL: http://www.amac-org.com • Advocates for equal opportunity for minorities and women in airport contracting and employment.

National Air Carrier Association. 1000 Wilson Blvd., Ste. 1700, Arlington, VA 22209. Phone: (703)358-8060; Fax: (703)358-8070 • URL: http://www.naca.cc • Represents U.S. certificated airlines specializing in low-cost scheduled and air charter operations. Assists members in the promotion of air transportation and serves as a liaison between members and U.S. government bodies that regulate air transportation.

National Air Transportation Association. 4226 King St., Alexandria, VA 22302. Phone: 800-808-6282 or (703)845-9000; Fax: (703)845-8176 • URL: http://www.nata.aero • Represents the interests of aviation businesses nationwide. Provides vital aviation services to the airlines, the military, and business/corporate/individual aircraft owners and operators; services includes fueling, maintenance, and flight instruction.

Regional Airline Association. 2025 M St. NW, Ste. 800, Washington, DC 20036-3309. Phone: (202)367-1170; Fax: (202)367-2170; Email: raa@raa.org • URL: http://www.raa.org • Regional air carriers engaged in the transportation of passengers, cargo, or mail on a scheduled basis; persons, companies and organizations engaged in pursuits related to commercial aviation; colleges and universities, state and local governments and state aviation associations. Responds to community, consumer and public needs for air transportation and aviation facilities and to help establish a healthy business, regulatory and legislative climate that enables members to profit through service to the nation and the flying public. Supports programs for improving safety and reliability of air transportation and air commerce; provides a forum for exchange of ideas and information.

AIRPLANE ELECTRONICS

See AVIONICS

AIRPLANE INDUSTRY

See also AEROSPACE INDUSTRY; AVIATION INDUSTRY

ABSTRACTS AND INDEXES

Applied Science and Technology Index. EBSCO Publishing Inc. • 11/year. Indexes a wide variety of English language technical, industrial, and engineering periodicals.

Business Periodicals Index Retrospective. EBSCO Publishing Inc. • 11/year. Quarterly and annual cumulations.

Science Citation Index. Thomson Reuters Intellectual Property and Science. • Weekly. Includes *Source Index*, *Citation Index*, *Permuterm Subject Index*, and *Corporate Index*. Provides researchers, administrators, faculty, and students with quick, powerful access to the bibliographic and citation information they need to find research data, analyze trends, journals and researchers, and share their findings.

CD-ROM DATABASES

OECD Statistical Compendium. Organization for Economic Cooperation and Development. • Semiannual. $1,905.00 per year for 1 to 10 users. CD-ROM contains more than 730,000 monthly, quarterly, and annual time series for OECD countries, 1960 to date. Includes fully searchable data on agriculture, food, economic indicators, national accounts, employment, energy, finance, industry, technology, and foreign trade. Results can be displayed in various forms.

Science Citation Index. Thomson Reuters Intellectual Property and Science. • Weekly. Includes *Source Index*, *Citation Index*, *Permuterm Subject Index*, and *Corporate Index*. Provides researchers, administrators, faculty, and students with quick, powerful access to the bibliographic and citation information they need to find research data, analyze trends, journals and researchers, and share their findings.

DIRECTORIES

ABD--Aviation Buyer's Directory. Air Service Directory Inc. • Quarterly. Covers: aircraft, parts, and equipment manufacturers and dealers, and service firms in the aviation industry. Entries include: Company name, address, phone.

Aircraft Parts & Auxiliary Equipment NEC Directory. InfoGroup Inc. • Annual. Number of listings: 1,412. Entries include: Name, address, phone, size of advertisement, name of owner or manager, number of employees, year first in "Yellow Pages." Compiled from telephone company "Yellow Pages," nationwide.

The International Directory of Importers--Aircraft and Aviation Equipment and Accessories Importers. Interdata. • $200 Individuals print. Covers: 500 international firms importing aircraft and aviation equipment and accessories. Entries include: Company name and address, contact person, email, number of employees, year established, phone and telefaxes, business activity, bank references, as well as listing of aircraft equipment currently being imported.

FINANCIAL RATIOS

Annual Statement Studies. Risk Management Association. • Annual. Compiled from over 280,000 financial statements.

Annual Statement Studies: Industry Default Probabilities and Cash Flow Measures. Risk Management Association. • Annual. $405 Nonmembers. Serves as a companion volume to the original *Annual Statement Studies*. Gives probability of default estimates on a percentage scale for more than 450 industries. Includes changes in position year-by-year for eight financial statement line items and provides percentage measures of cash flow.

Industry Norms and Key Business Ratios. Dun & Bradstreet Inc. • Annual. Five volumes. Covers over 800 kinds of businesses, arranged by Standard Industrial Classification number. More detailed editions covering longer periods of time are also available.

INTERNET DATABASES

Business 2.0 Web Guide to the Best Business Links. Business 2.0 Media Inc. Phone: (415)293-4800; Email: support@business2.com • URL: http://www.business2.com/webguide • Web site presents an extensive, searchable directory of links to "the best, most informative, and authoritative web pages." Twenty main categories cover business, finance, career, company information, people, and technology topics, with thousands of subtopics, all linking to Web sites recommended by experienced business researchers. Fees: Free.

Fedstats. Federal Interagency Council on Statistical Policy. Phone: (202)395-7254 • URL: http://www.fedstats.gov • Web site features an efficient search facility for full-text statistics produced by more than 100 federal agencies, including the Census Bureau, the Bureau of Economic Analysis, and the Bureau of Labor Statistics. Boolean searches can be made within one agency or for all agencies combined. Links are offered to international statistical bureaus, including the UN, IMF, OECD, UNESCO, Eurostat, and 20 individual countries. Fees: Free.

FreeLunch.com. Economy.com, Inc. Phone: (610)696-8700; Fax: (610)696-1678 • URL: http://www.freelunch.com • Web site provides free access to more than 200 million economic and financial data series, covering industry, demographics, labor markets, prices, retail sales, government spending, trade, interest rates, housing starts, the stock market, etc. Data is available in either chart or table form. Searching is offered. Free, but registration required. Economy.com, Inc. also offers fee-based economic analysis at *The Dismal Scientist* site (www.dismal.com).

Manufacturing Profiles. U. S. Bureau of the Census. Phone: (301)763-4636 or (301)763-4100; Fax: (301)763-4794; Email: webmaster@census.gov • URL: http://www.census.gov/prod/www/abs/mfg-prof.html • The Census Bureau makes available free on PDF (Portable Document Format) an annual consolidation of the entire Current Industrial Report series, presenting "all the data compiled." Contains statistics on production, shipments, inventories, consumption, exports, imports, and orders for a wide variety of manufactured products.

ONLINE DATABASES

Aerospace America Magazine. American Institute of Aeronautics and Astronautics. • Monthly. $200 Institutions non member, domestic. Covers aeronautics and space technology with special attention to aerospace defense, design, and electronics.

Aerospace Database. American Institute of Aeronautics and Astronautics. • Contains abstracts of literature covering all aspects of the aerospace and aircraft industry 1983 to date. Monthly updates. Inquire as to online cost and availability.

OTHER SOURCES

Aviation Law Reports. Wolters Kluwer Law & Business CCH. • Semimonthly. Four looseleaf volumes covering aviation law.

Jane's All the World's Aircraft. Jane's Information Group, Inc. • Annual. $630.00; CD-ROM edition, $1,455.00; online edition, $1,566.00; microfiche edition, $3,075.00. Lists civil and military aircraft, helicopters, airships, and aero engines.

PERIODICALS AND NEWSLETTERS

A/C Flyer: Best Read Resale Magazine Worldwide. McGraw Hill Financial Inc. • Monthly. Individuals $49.00 per year; students, $28.00 per year. Lists used airplanes for sale by dealers, brokers, and private owners. Provides news and trends relating to the aircraft resale industry. Special issues include "Product & Service Buyer's Guide" and "Dealer/Broker Directory.".

Aerospace America Magazine. American Institute of Aeronautics and Astronautics. • Monthly. $200 Institutions non member, domestic. Covers aeronautics and space technology with special attention to aerospace defense, design, and electronics.

Aerospace Engineering Magazine. Society of Automotive Engineers. • Monthly. $66.00 per year. Provides technical information that can be used in the design of new and improved aerospace systems.

AIAA Journal. American Institute of Aeronautics and Astronautics. • Monthly. $80 Members /year for members in the U.S.; print and online. Technical journal providing original archival research papers on new theoretical developments and/or experimental results in the fields of aeronautics and astronautics. For research-oriented readers.

Air Market News. General Publications Inc. • Bimonthly. Free to qualified personnel. Subject matter is news of aircraft products and services.

Flight International. Reed Business Information Ltd. • Weekly. $140.00 per year. Technical aerospace coverage.

Flying. Bonnier Corp. • Monthly. $14 Individuals print. General aviation magazine. Includes three *Special Issues*. Price on application.

Trade-a-Plane. • 36 issues per year. $36.00 per year. Subject matter is aircraft for sale or trade.

RESEARCH CENTERS AND INSTITUTES

Ohio Aerospace Institute. 22800 Cedar Point Rd., Cleveland, OH 44142. Phone: (440)962-3000; Fax: (216)962-3120 or (440)962-3120; Email: info@oai.org • URL: http://www.oai.org • Aerospace-related research, education, and technology transfers. Formerly Ohio Aerospace Institute.

University of Texas at Austin - Center for Aeromechanics Research. WRW 201B, Mail Code C060, Department of Aerospace Engineering and Engineering Mechanics, Cockrell School of Engineering, Austin, TX 78712-1085. Phone: (512)471-3110 or (512)471-5962; Fax: (512)471-3788; Email: varghese@mail.utexas.edu • URL: http://research.ae.utexas.edu/car • Aeroelasticity and structural dynamics; control of flexible structures; flight structures; supersonic and hypersonic shock-induced separated flows; turbulence; combustion; transient chemically reacting flow models for the study of glow discharges and semiconductor process plasmas; plasma thrusters; micro-plasma discharges; rarefied and non-equilibrium flows; low density planetary atmospheres; optical diagnostics and laser-based sensor development.

STATISTICS SOURCES

Aerospace Facts and Figures. Aerospace Industries Association of America. • Annual. $35 Individuals. Includes financial data for the aerospace industries.

Standard & Poor's Statistical Service. Current Statistics. Standard & Poor's Financial Services L.L.C. • Monthly. $688.00 per year. Includes 10 *Basic Statistics* sections, *Current Statistics Supplements* and *Annual Security Price Index Record*.

Survey of Current Business. U. S. Government Printing Office. • Published by Bureau of Economic Analysis, U. S. Department of Commerce. Presents a wide variety of business and economic data.

TRADE/PROFESSIONAL ASSOCIATIONS

American Institute of Aeronautics and Astronautics. 1801 Alexander Bell Dr., Ste. 500, Reston, VA 20191-4344. Phone: 800-639-2422 or (703)264-7500; Fax: (703)264-7551; Email: custserv@aiaa.org • URL: http://www.aiaa.org • Represents scientists and engineers in the field of aeronautics and astronautics. Facilitates interchange of technological information through publications and technical meetings in order to foster overall technical progress in the field and increase the professional competence of members. Operates Public Policy program to provide federal decision-makers with the technical information and policy guidance needed to make effective policy on aerospace issues. Public Policy program activities include congressional testimony, position papers, section public policy activities, and workshops. Offers placement assistance; compiles statistics; offers educational programs. Provides abstracting services through its AIAA Access.

National Business Aviation Association. 1200 G St. NW, Ste. 1100, Washington, DC 20005-3830. Phone: (202)783-9000; Fax: (202)331-8364; Email: info@nbaa.org • URL: http://www.nbaa.org • Companies owning and operating aircraft for business use, suppliers, and maintenance and air fleet service companies. Compiles statistics; provides literature for researchers and students.

AIRPLANES, BUSINESS

See BUSINESS AVIATION

AIRPORTS

ABSTRACTS AND INDEXES

Business Periodicals Index Retrospective. EBSCO Publishing Inc. • 11/year. Quarterly and annual cumulations.

DIRECTORIES

Airport/Facility Directory. U.S. National Ocean Service. • Covers: Non-military airports in the continental United States; separate volumes cover the southeast, northeast, northwest, east central, north central, southwest, and south central states (including Puerto Rico and the Virgin Islands). Entries include: Airport name, location, weather service phone number, control center frequencies, and information concerning navigational and other aids and systems.

Jane's Air Traffic Control. IHS Global Ltd. IHS Jane's: Defense & Security Intelligence & Analysis. • Annual. $495.00. International coverage of equipment and supplies for both civil and military airports. Formerly *Jane's Airport and ATC Equipment*.

FINANCIAL RATIOS

Annual Statement Studies. Risk Management Association. • Annual. Compiled from over 280,000 financial statements.

Annual Statement Studies: Industry Default Probabilities and Cash Flow Measures. Risk Management Association. • Annual. $405 Nonmembers. Serves as a companion volume to the original *Annual Statement Studies*. Gives probability of default estimates on a percentage scale for more than 450 industries. Includes changes in position year-by-year for eight financial statement line items and provides percentage measures of cash flow.

PERIODICALS AND NEWSLETTERS

Airport Business. Cygnus Business Media Inc. • 10 times a year. $55.00 per year.

Airports: The Weekly for Airport Users, Managers, and Suppliers. Aviation Week Business Intelligence Services. • Weekly. $649.00 per year. Newsletter. Covers news of worldwide airport development, financing, operations, marketing, bidding, improvements, and personnel.

Homeland Security and Defense: Weekly Intelligence for the Global Homeland Security and Defense Community. Aviation Week Business Intelligence Services. • Weekly. $595.00 per year. Newsletter. Emphasis is on airline and airport programs (federal, state, and local). Also covers counterterrorism, protection of military units, Department of Homeland Security activities, industrial security, communications equipment, and other topics related to homeland security.

Jane's Airport Review: The Global Airport Business Magazine. Jane's Information Group, Inc. • 10 times a year. $190.00 per year. CD-Rom edition, $775.00 per year. Edited for airport managers. Covers all aspects of airport operations.

STATISTICS SOURCES

Airport Activity Statistics of Certificated Route Air Carriers. U. S. Department of Transportation. U. S. Government Printing Office. • Annual. $58 Individuals.

TRADE/PROFESSIONAL ASSOCIATIONS

National Air Transportation Association. 4226 King St., Alexandria, VA 22302. Phone: 800-808-6282 or (703)845-9000; Fax: (703)845-8176 • URL: http://www.nata.aero • Represents the interests of aviation businesses nationwide. Provides vital aviation services to the airlines, the military, and business/corporate/individual aircraft owners and operators; services includes fueling, maintenance, and flight instruction.

ALARMS

See ELECTRONIC SECURITY SYSTEMS

ALCOHOL AS FUEL

See FUEL

ALCOHOLIC BEVERAGES

See DISTILLING INDUSTRY

ALCOHOLISM

See also DRUG ABUSE AND TRAFFIC

ABSTRACTS AND INDEXES

Excerpta Medica: Drug Dependence, Alcohol Abuse, and Alcoholism. Elsevier. • Bimonthly. Section 40 of *Excerpta Medica.*

Psychological Abstracts. American Psychological Association. • Monthly. Members, $815.00 per year; individuals and institutions, $1,207.00 per year. Covers the international literature of psychology and the behavioral sciences. Includes journals, technical reports, dissertations, and other sources.

BIBLIOGRAPHIES

International Bibliography of Studies on Alcohol. Sarah S. Jordy, compiler. Rutgers Center of Alcohol Studies Publications. • $200.00. Three volumes. Volume one, *References*, 1901-1950; volume two, *Indexes*, 1901-1980; volume three, *References* and *Indexes*, 1951-1960.

DIRECTORIES

National Directory of Drug and Alcohol Abuse Treatment Programs. Substance Abuse and Mental Health Services Administration Data, Outcomes and Quality. • Annual. Lists federal, state, local, and privately funded agencies administering or providing drug abuse and alcoholism treatment services. Formerly *National Directory of Drug Abuse and Alcoholism Treatment and Prevention Programs.*

ENCYCLOPEDIAS AND DICTIONARIES

Encyclopedia of Drugs, Alcohol, and Addictive Behavior. Cengage Learning Inc. • $820 Individuals. 2009. 3rd Edition. eBook. Published by Macmillan Reference USA. Covers the social, economic, political, and medical aspects of addiction. Inquire for price and availability.

GENERAL WORKS

Drugs, Alcohol & Tobacco: Learning About Addictive Behavior. Edited by Rosalyn Carson-Dewitt, M.D. Cengage Learning Inc. • $512. Three volumes. Contains 200 articles on various aspects of addiction. Includes color illustrations, a glossary, and comprehensive indexing. Macmillan Reference USA imprint. eBook also available. Inquire for pricing.

ONLINE DATABASES

Embase. Elsevier. • Worldwide medical literature, 1974 to present. Weekly updates. Inquire as to online cost and availability.

PERIODICALS AND NEWSLETTERS

Addiction Research Foundation Journal: Addiction News for Professionals. Addiction Research Foundation of Ontario, Subscription-Marketing Dept. • Six times a year. $19.00 per year. News and opinions from the drug and alcohol field around th world. Formerly *Alcoholism and Drug Addiction Research Foundation Journal.*

Alcohol Research and Health. U. S. Government Printing Office. • Quarterly. $33.00 per year. Issued by the National Institute on Alcohol Abuse and Alcoholism. Presents alcohol-related research findings and descriptions of alcoholism prevention and treatment programs.

Alcoholism: Clinical and Experimental Research. Research Society on Alcoholism. Lippincott Williams & Wilkins. • Monthly. Individuals, $331.00 per year; institutions, $639.00 per year.

Alcoholism Treatment Quarterly: The Practitioner's Quarterly for Individual, Group, and Family Therapy. The Haworth Press Inc. • Quarterly. $535.00 per year. Edited for professionals working with alcoholics and their families. Formerly *Alcoholism Counseling and Treatment.*

Counselor: The Magazine for Addiction Professionals. Health Communications, Inc. • Bimonthly. $9.95 Individuals /year, online only. Covers both clinical and societal aspects of substance abuse.

Drug and Alcohol Abuse Education. Editorial Resources Inc. • Monthly. $84.00 per year. Newsletter covering education, prevention, and treatment relating to abuse of drugs and alcohol.

A Journal of Ethnicity in Substance Abuse. The Haworth Press Inc. • Quarterly. $380.00 per year. Includes print and online editions. Edited for researchers and practitioners. Covers various areas of susbstance abuse, including alcoholism. Formerly *Drugs and Society.*

Journal of Workplace Behavior Health. The Haworth Press Inc. • Quarterly. $160 Individuals print + online. An academic and practical journal focusing on employee alcoholism and mental health problems. Formerly *Labor-Management Alcoholism Journal.*

Workplace Substance Abuse Advisor. LRP Publications Library. • Description: Reviews federal, state, and local laws and regulations concerning alcohol and drug use, testing, and policies. Discusses significant court decisions. Contains information on the drug enforcement budgets at all levels of government. Examines employee assistance plans and other educational programs designed to help substance abusers.

RESEARCH CENTERS AND INSTITUTES

Addiction Research Unit. University at Buffalo, Dept. of Psychology, Buffalo, NY 14260-4110. Phone: (716)887-2566; Fax: (716)887-2252; Email: connors@ria.org • URL: http://wings.buffalo.edu/aru.

TRADE/PROFESSIONAL ASSOCIATIONS

International Plant Nutrition Institute. 3500 Parkway Ln., Ste. 550, Norcross, GA 30092-2844. Phone: (770)447-0335; Fax: (770)448-0439; Email: info@ipni.net • URL: http://www.ipni.net • Formerly Potash and Phosphate Institute.

National Council on Alcoholism and Drug Dependence. 217 Broadway, Ste. 712, New York, NY 10007. Phone: 800-622-2255 or (212)269-7797; Fax: (212)269-7510; Email: national@ncadd.org • URL: http://www.ncadd.org • Works for the prevention and treatment of alcoholism and other drug dependence through programs of public education, information and public policy advocacy.

ALKALI INDUSTRY

See also POTASH INDUSTRY

ONLINE DATABASES

CA Search. American Chemical Society Chemical Abstracts Service. • Guide to chemical literature, 1967 to present. Inquire as to online cost and availability.

ALLOYS

See METAL INDUSTRY

ALUMINUM FOIL

See ALUMINUM INDUSTRY

ALUMINUM INDUSTRY

ABSTRACTS AND INDEXES

Aluminum Industry Abstracts: A Monthly Review of the World's Technical Literature on Aluminum. Aluminum Association. • Monthly. $975.00 per year. Includes print and online editions. Formerly *World Aluminum Abstracts.*

ALMANACS AND YEARBOOKS

CRB Commodity Yearbook. Commodity Research Bureau. CRB. • Annual. $179 plus $10.00 shipping cost. The single most comprehensive source of commodity and futures market information available.

CD-ROM DATABASES

METADEX Materials Collection: Metals-Polymers-Ceramics. Cambridge Scientific Abstracts L.P. • Quarterly. Provides CD-ROM citations to the worldwide literature of materials science and metallurgy. Corresponds to *Metals Abstracts, Alloys Index, Steels Alert, Nonferrous Alert, Polymers/Ceramics/Composites Alert,* and *Engineered Materials Abstracts.* (Formerly produced by ASM International.).

DIRECTORIES

Aluminum Extrusion Press Directory. Aluminum Association. • Irregular. $70 Members. Covers: Locations of 496 aluminum presses at 217 plants in 148 US companies; details on extruders, locations, press sizes, anodizing, painting and billet casting facilities. Entries include: Names of extruders and plant addresses.

Dun's Industrial Guide: The Metalworking Directory. Dun & Bradstreet Inc. • Annual. Libraries, $485; commercial institutions, $795.00. Lease basis. Three volumes. Lists about 65,000 U. S. manufacturing plants using metal and suppliers of metalworking equipment and materials. Includes names and titles of key personnel. Products, purchases, and processes are indicated.

INTERNET DATABASES

Manufacturing Profiles. U. S. Bureau of the Census. Phone: (301)763-4636 or (301)763-4100; Fax: (301)763-4794; Email: webmaster@census.gov • URL: http://www.census.gov/prod/www/abs/mfg-prof.html • The Census Bureau makes available free on PDF (Portable Document Format) an annual consolidation of the entire Current Industrial Report series, presenting "all the data compiled." Contains statistics on production, shipments, inventories, consumption, exports, imports, and orders for a wide variety of manufactured products.

PERIODICALS AND NEWSLETTERS

Metal Center News. Sackett Business Media Inc. • Monthly. $109 U.S. 1-year subscription (12 MCN magazine plus 1 annual directory). The trade magazine of the metals distribution industry: the service centers that warehouse, process and distribute carbon and stainless steels, aluminum and copper and brass.

33 Metalproducing: For Primary Producers of Steel, Aluminum, and Copper-Base Alloys. Penton Media Inc. • Monthly. $65.00 per year. Covers metal production technology and methods and industry news. Includes a bimonthly *Nonferrous Supplement.*

PRICE SOURCES

Chemical & Engineering News. American Chemical Society. • Weekly Annual. $265 Nonmembers print, North America. Magazine on chemical and engineering news.

Platt's Metals Week. Platts Global Energy. • Weekly. $770 Individuals.

STATISTICS SOURCES

Aluminum Standards and Data. Aluminum Association. • Biennial. $75 Members.

Aluminum Statistical Review. Aluminum Association. • Annual. $95 Members.

Standard & Poor's Industry Surveys. Standard & Poor's Financial Services L.L.C. • Semiannual. $1,800.00. Two looseleaf volumes. Includes monthly *Supplements.* Provides detailed, individual surveys of 52 major industry groups. Each survey is revised on a semiannual basis. Also includes "Monthly Investment Review" (industry group investment analysis) and monthly "Trends & Projections" (economic analysis).

United States Census of Mineral Industries. Bureau of the Census, U.S. Department of Commerce. U. S. Government Printing Office. • Quinquennial.

U.S. Industry and Trade Outlook. U.S. Department of Commerce National Technical Information Service. • Annual. Produced by the International Trade Administration, U.S. Department of Commerce, in a "public-private" partnership with DRI/McGraw-Hill and Standard & Poor's. Provides basic data, outlook for the current year, and "Long-Term Prospects" (five-year projections) for a wide variety of products and services. Includes high technology industries. Formerly *U.S. Industrial Outlook.*

TRADE/PROFESSIONAL ASSOCIATIONS

European Aluminum Foil Association. Am Bonneshof 5, 40474 Dusseldorf, Germany. Phone: 49 211 4796150; Fax: 49 211 4796408; Email: enquiries@alufoil.org • URL: http://www.alufoil.org • Represents the European aluminum foil industry.

AMERICAN STOCK EXCHANGE

See STOCK EXCHANGES

AMUSEMENT INDUSTRY

See also CONCESSIONS; FAIRS; MOTION PICTURE INDUSTRY; RADIO BROADCASTING INDUSTRY; RECREATION INDUSTRY; SHOW BUSINESS; TELEVISION BROADCASTING INDUSTRY

DIRECTORIES

Entertainment Sourcebook: An Insider's Guide on Where to Find Everything. Applause Theatre & Cinema Books. • Annual. $45.00. Compiled by the Association of Theatrical Artists and Craftspeople (www.entertainmentsourcebook.com/ATAC.htm). Lists more than 5,000 sources of theatrical and entertainment supplies and services, such as props, costumes, publicity agencies, scenic shops, amusement park equipment, audio/video products, balloons, wigs, make-up, magic supplies, etc.

The Grey House Performing Arts Directory. Grey House Publishing. • Annual. $250 Individuals Softcover. Covers: More than 8,500 dance companies, instrumental music programs, opera companies, choral groups, theatre companies, performing arts series, and performing arts facilities. Database includes: Information resources section covering hundreds of performing arts associations, publications, and Web sites. Entries include: Mailing address, telephone and fax numbers, e-mail addresses, Web sites, mission statement, key management contacts, and facility information such as capacity, season, and attendance.

International Association of Amusement Parks and Attractions International Directory and Buyers' Guide. International Association of Amusement Parks and Attractions. • Annual. Over 1,800 member amusement parks, attractions and industry suppliers.

Magicians Directory. InfoGroup Inc. • Annual. Number of listings: 1,133. Entries include: Name, address, phone, size of advertisement, name of owner or manager, number of employees, year first in "Yellow Pages." Compiled from telephone company "Yellow Pages," nationwide.

Plunkett's Airline, Hotel, and Travel Industry Almanac. Plunkett Research Ltd. • Annual. $349.99. Contains profiles of 300 leading companies, including airlines, hotels, travel agencies, theme parks, cruise lines, casinos, and car rental companies.

Roller Rinks Directory. InfoGroup Inc. • Annual. Number of listings: 2,944. Entries include: Name, address, phone, size of advertisement, name of owner or manager, number of employees, year first in "Yellow Pages." Compiled from telephone company "Yellow Pages," nationwide.

FINANCIAL RATIOS

Annual Statement Studies. Risk Management Association. • Annual. Compiled from over 280,000 financial statements.

Annual Statement Studies: Industry Default Probabilities and Cash Flow Measures. Risk Management Association. • Annual. $405 Nonmembers. Serves as a companion volume to the original *Annual Statement Studies.* Gives probability of default estimates on a percentage scale for more than 450 industries. Includes changes in position year-by-year for eight financial statement line items and provides percentage measures of cash flow.

OTHER SOURCES

Lindey on Entertainment, Publishing and the Arts. Alexander Lindey, editor. Thomson West. • $1,582.86 Full Set. Provides basic forms, applicable law, and guidance.

Westlaw Journal Entertainment Industry. Thomson Reuters Westlaw. • Monthly. *Sports and Entertainment Litigation Reporter.* Provides concise, unbiased coverage of litigation involving such issues as breach of contract, First Amendment, invasion of privacy, unfair competition, misappropriation of funds, and copyright and trademark issues.

PERIODICALS AND NEWSLETTERS

Funworld. International Association of Amusement Parks and Attractions. • Monthly 11/year. $70 Members. Analysis and statistics of the international amusement park industry. Text in English; sections in French, German, Japanese and Spanish.

IEG's Sponsorship Report: The International Newsletter of Event Sponsorship and Lifestyle Marketing. IEG LLC. • $499 multi-user subscription. Newsletter reporting on corporate sponsorship of special events: sports, music, festivals, and the arts. Edited for event producers, directors, and marketing personnel.

TRADE/PROFESSIONAL ASSOCIATIONS

Amusement Industry Manufacturers and Suppliers International. 3026 S Orange, Santa Ana, CA 92707. Phone: (714)425-5747; Fax: (714)276-9666; Email: info@aimsintl.org • URL: http://www.aimsintl.org • Represents manufacturers and suppliers of amusement riding devices and equipment used by amusement parks, carnivals, and traveling amusement companies. Exchanges information on safety, maintenance, state laws, transportation, and credit. Works to develop safety programs and codes at the federal and state levels; carries out public relations activities; and cooperates with the ASTM to develop voluntary standards for amusement rides and devices.

Association of Theatrical Artists and Craftspeople. 48 Fairway St., Bloomfield, NJ 07003-5515. Phone: (212)234-9001 • URL: http://www.atacbiz.com • Members are artists and craftspeople working in theatre, film, TV, and advertising. Areas of expertise include props, costumes, millinery, puppetry, display, and special effects.

International Amusement and Leisure Defense Association. PO Box 4563, Louisville, KY 40204. Phone: (502)473-0956; Fax: (502)473-7352; Email: info@ialda.org • URL: http://www.ialda.org • Promotes and protects the interests of the amusement and leisure industries. Encourages members to exchange information, share experiences and develop litigation strategies regarding the amusement and leisure industry. Serves as a clearinghouse for speakers and authors on industry-specific topics.

Outdoor Amusement Business Association. 1035 S Semoran Blvd., Ste. 1045A, Winter Park, FL 32792. Phone: 800-517-OABA or (407)681-9444; Fax: (407)681-9445; Email: oaba@oaba.org • URL: http://www.oaba.org • Represents executives and employees of carnivals and fairs; ride owners; independent food and games concessionaires; manufacturers and suppliers of equipment. Promotes and lobbies on behalf of the interests of the outdoor amusement industry; provides a center for dissemination of information.

AMUSEMENT PARKS

See AMUSEMENT INDUSTRY

ANIMAL INDUSTRY

See LIVESTOCK INDUSTRY

ANIMATION, COMPUTER

See COMPUTER ANIMATION

ANNIVERSARIES AND HOLIDAYS

See CHRONOLOGY; SPECIAL EVENT PLANNING

ANNUAL REPORTS OF CORPORATIONS

See CORPORATION REPORTS

ANNUAL WAGE PLANS

See WAGES AND SALARIES

ANNUITIES

ALMANACS AND YEARBOOKS

Investment Company Yearbook. Thomson Financial Inc. • Annual. $310.00. Provides an "entire history of recent events in the mutual funds industry," with emphasis on changes during the past year. About 100 pages are devoted to general information and advice for fund investors. Includes 600 full-page profiles of popular mutual funds, with brief descriptions of 10,000 others, plus 7,000 variable annuities and 500 closed-end funds. Contains a glossary of technical terms, a Web site index, and an overall book index. Also known as *Wiesenberger Investment Companies Yearbook.*

INTERNET DATABASES

ACGA: Partners in Philanthropy. American Council on Gift Annuities. Phone: (317)269-6271; Fax: (317)269-6276; Email: acga@acga-web.org • URL: http://www.acga-web.org • Web site provides detailed information on gift annuities, including suggested charitable gift annuity rates for use by charities and their donors. Rates for immediate and deferred annuities are presented in the form of tables for ages 20 to 90 (and over), for both "Single Life" and "Two Lives - Joint and Survivor." Other items covered include the philosophy of gift annuities, state regulations, "What's New," and a search site. Fees: Free.

Free Insurance Advice. InsWeb, Inc. 2868 Prospect Park Dr., Ste. 650, Rancho Cordova, CA 95670.

For publishers' addresses, refer to SOURCES CITED section at the back of the book.

Phone: (916)853-3300; Fax: (916)853-3300; Email: customercare@insweb.com • URL: http://www.insweb.com • Web site offers a wide variety of advice and information on automobile, life, health, and "other" insurance. Includes glossaries of insurance terms, Standard & Poor's ratings of individual insurance companies, and "Financial Needs Estimators." Searching is available. Fees: Free.

PERIODICALS AND NEWSLETTERS

Annuity Market News. SourceMedia Inc. • Monthly. $625.00 per year. Newsletter. Edited for investment and insurance professionals. Covers the marketing, management, and servicing of variable and fixed annuity products.

Broker World. Insurance Publications Inc. • Bimonthly. $6.00 per year. Edited for independent insurance agents and brokers. Special feature issue topics include annuities, disability insurance, estate planning, and life insurance.

Financial Planning: The Magazine for Financial Service Professionals. SourceMedia Inc. • Monthly. $79.00 per year. Edited for independent financial planners and insurance agents. Covers retirement planning, estate planning, tax planning, and insurance, including long-term healthcare considerations. Special features include a Retirement Planning Issue, Mutual Fund Performance Survey, and Variable Life and Annuity Survey.

Guide to Life, Health, and Annuity Insurers: A Quarterly Compilation of Insurance Company Ratings and Analysis. Weiss Research Inc. • Quarterly. $499. Emphasis is on rating of financial safety and relative risk. Includes annual summary.

National Underwriter. • Weekly. Two editions: *Life* or *Health*. $86.00 per year, each edition.

On Wall Street. SourceMedia Inc. • Monthly. $96.00 per year. Edited for securities dealers. Includes articles on financial planning, retirement planning, variable annuities, and money management, with special coverage of 401(k) plans and IRAs.

TRADE/PROFESSIONAL ASSOCIATIONS

Association for Advanced Life Underwriting. 11921 Freedom Dr., Ste. 1100, Reston, VA 20190. Phone: 888-275-0092 or (703)641-9400; Fax: (703)641-9885 • URL: http://www.aalu.org • Represents advanced life underwriters who specialize in the more complex fields of estate analysis, business insurance, pension planning, employee benefit plans, and other subjects related to the sale and service of large volumes of life insurance. Serves as conference of the National Association of Life Underwriters.

ANNUITY TABLES

See INTEREST

ANSWERING SERVICE

See TELEPHONE ANSWERING SERVICE

ANTHRACITE COAL

See COAL INDUSTRY

ANTIMONY INDUSTRY

See METAL INDUSTRY

ANTIQUES AS AN INVESTMENT

See also ART AS AN INVESTMENT

DIRECTORIES

Antique Shop Guide--Central Edition. Mayhill Publications Midcountry Media. • Annual. $6.25 Individuals. Covers: Antique shops in Illinois, Indiana, Iowa, Kentucky, Michigan, Minnesota, Missouri, Ohio, Tennessee, Wisconsin, western Pennsylvania, and West Virginia. Entries include: For antique shops--Shop name, address, map reference, specialty, whether reproductions are stocked, hours and seasons open, phone. Listings for other categories have similar detail.

Cards--Baseball Directory. InfoGroup Inc. • Annual. Number of listings: 4,538. Entries include: Name, address, phone, size of advertisement, name of owner or manager, number of employees, year first in "Yellow Pages." Compiled from telephone company "Yellow Pages," nationwide.

Glassware (Collectible) Directory. InfoGroup Inc. • Annual. Number of listings: 12,366. Entries include: Name, address, phone, size of advertisement, name of owner or manager, number of employees, year first in "Yellow Pages." Compiled from telephone company "Yellow Pages," nationwide.

National Antique & Art Dealers Association of America--Membership Directory. National Antique and Art Dealers Association of America. • Continuous. Provides a list of members and their areas of specialization in the decorative arts.

Warman's Antiques & Collectibles Price Guide. Krause Publications Inc. • Annual. $20 Individuals Paperback. Covers: Over 50,000 antiques and collectibles, plus listings for collector's clubs. Database includes: 1,500 color photos. Entries include: Description, price.

PRICE SOURCES

Kovels' on Antiques and Collectibles: The Newsletter for Dealers, Collectors, and Investors. Antiques Inc. • Monthly. $27 Individuals.

Miller's Antiques Shops, Fairs and Auctions. Antique Collector's Club. • Annual. $35 Individuals.

Warman's Antiques and Collectibles Price Guide. Krause Publications Inc. • Annual. $20 Individuals. Manufacturer profiles, key events, current status, collector's clubs, museums, resources available for Americana and collectibles.

TRADE/PROFESSIONAL ASSOCIATIONS

Appraisers Association of America. 212 W 35th St., 11th Fl. S, New York, NY 10001. Phone: (212)889-5404; Fax: (212)889-5503; Email: referrals@appraisersassociation.org • URL: http://www.appraisersassociation.org • Professional society of appraisers of personal property such as: Americana; antiques; armor; art objects; bibelot; books; bronzes; china and porcelain; clocks and watches; coins; crystal and glass; curios; diamonds and jewelry; enamels; etchings; fine art; firearms; furniture; furs; graphic art; guns; household furnishings; ivories; leather goods; lighting fixtures; linens and lace; miniatures; music; musical instruments; oriental art; paintings; pewter; pianos; primitive art; prints; rugs; sculpture; Sheffield plate; silver and silverware; stamps; steins and tankards; taxes; and woodcarvings.

Art and Antique Dealers League of America. Lennox Hill Sta., New York, NY 10021. Phone: (212)879-7558; Fax: (212)772-7197; Email: secretary@artantiquedealersleague.com • URL: http://www.artantiquedealersleague.com • Members are retailers and wholesalers of antiques and art objects.

The Questers. 210 S Quince St., Philadelphia, PA 19107-5534. Phone: (215)923-5183; Email: questers210@questers1944.org • URL: http://www.questers1944.org • Promotes the study and appreciation of antiques and objects of art and their historical backgrounds; aids in the restoration and preservation of historical places. Has donated several antique pieces to the White House and has contributed financially to historic houses, villages, and foundations. Sponsors annual scholarship at Columbia University for graduate studies in the field of architectural restoration.

ANTITRUST ACTIONS

ABSTRACTS AND INDEXES

Current Law Index. Cengage Learning Inc. • $1,332 Individuals. Monthly. $1269.00 per year. Produced in cooperation with the American Association of Law Libraries. Indexes more than 900 law journals, legal newspapers, and specialty publications from the U.S., Canada, U.K., Ireland, Australia, and New Zealand.

HANDBOOKS AND MANUALS

Antitrust Division Manual. U. S. Government Printing Office. • Looseleaf. $60.00. Includes basic manual, with supplementary material for an indeterminate period. Serves as a guide to the operating policies and procedures of the Antitrust Division of the U. S. Department of Justice (www.usdoj.gov). Covers suggested methods of conducting investigations and litigation.

Antitrust-Intellectual Property Handbook. Alan J. Weinschel. Glasser LegalWorks. • Looseleaf. $175.00. Periodic supplementation. Covers patent licensing, patent antitrust issues, innovation markets, intervention by government agencies, standard-setting activities, royalty arrangements, and related intellectual property/antitrust topics. Provides explanations, legal guidance, and historical background.

Antitrust Law Handbook. Thomson West. • $699.30. Designed for practitioners and students.

Antitrust Laws and Trade Regulation: Desk Edition. Matthew Bender and Company Inc. • $1,999 Print (2 Volumes). Includes the history and organization of the antitrust laws.

INTERNET DATABASES

Lexis.com Research System. Lexis-Nexis Group. Phone: 800-227-4908 or (937)865-6800; Fax: (937)865-6909; Email: webmaster@prod.lexis-nexis.com • URL: http://www.nexis.com • Fee-based Web site offers extensive searching of a wide variety of legal sources. Additional features include Daily Opinion Service, lexis.com Bookstore, Career Center, CLE Center, Law Schools, and Practice Pages ("Pages specific to areas of specialty").

OTHER SOURCES

Antitrust and Trade Regulation Report. Bloomberg BNA. • Weekly. $1,479.00 per year. Looseleaf service.

Antitrust Basics. ALM Media Properties LLC. • $535 /year. Discusses "business practices consistently upheld, as well as those consistently condemned." Covers a wide variety of antitrust legal topics. (Law Journal Press).

Antitrust Counseling and Litigation Techniques. Matthew Bender and Company Inc. • Annual. Guide to corporate antitrust counseling and successful antitrust litigation.

Antitrust Laws and Trade Regulation. Matthew Bender and Company Inc. • $1,990.00. 11 looseleaf volumes. Periodic supplementation. Covers provisions and applications of the Sherman, Clayton, Robinson-Patman, and Federal Trade Commission Acts. Also covers state antitrust laws.

Antitrust Litigation Reporter: The National Journal of Record on Antitrust Litigation. Andrews Publications. • Monthly. $775.00 per year. Newsletter. Provides reports on federal and state antitrust statutes.

Callmann on Unfair Competition, Trademarks and Monopolies. Louis Altman and Rudolf Callmann. Thomson West. • Semiannual. $2,973. Covers various aspects of anti-competitive behavior.

Intellectual Property and Antitrust Law. William C. Holmes. Thomson West. • Semiannual. $1,347 full set. Includes patent, trademark, and copyright practices.

White Collar Crime: Business and Regulatory Offenses. ALM Media Properties LLC. • $740 print + online + ebook. Covers such legal matters as criminal tax cases, securities fraud, computer crime, mail fraud, bank embezzlement, criminal antitrust activities, extortion, perjury, the criminal liability of corporations, and RICO (Racketeer Influenced and Corrupt Organization Act). (Law Journal Press).

APARTMENT HOUSES

See also BUILDING INDUSTRY; CONDOMINIUMS; REAL ESTATE BUSINESS

CD-ROM DATABASES

Sourcebooks America CD-ROM. CACI Marketing Systems. • Annual. $1,250.00. Provides the CD-ROM version of *The Sourcebook of ZIP Code Demographics: Census Edition* and *The Sourcebook of County Demographics: Census Edition*.

OTHER SOURCES

Apartment Building Income-Expense Analysis. Institute of Real Estate Management. • Annual.

PERIODICALS AND NEWSLETTERS

Affordable Housing Finance. Alexander & Edwards Publishing. • 10/year. $119 Individuals. Provides advice and information on obtaining financing for lower-cost housing. Covers both government and private sources.

Building Business & Apartment Management. Home Builders Association of Southeastern Michigan. • Monthly. $48 Individuals. Construction and apartment industry magazine.

Buildings: The Source for Facilities Decision-Makers. Stamats Communications Inc. • Monthly. $70.00 per year. Serves professional building ownership/management organizations.

Housing the Elderly Report. Community Development Services, Inc. CD Publications. • Monthly. $249.00 per year. Newsletter. Edited for retirement communities, apartment projects, and nursing homes. Covers news relative to business and property management issues.

Managing Housing Letter. Community Development Services, Inc. CD Publications. • Description: Provides news and advice for owners and managers of rental housing--public, private, and subsidized--including news from Washington and practical management tips. Recurring features include news of research.

Metropolitan Home: Style for Our Generation. Hachette Filipacchi Media U.S., Inc. • Bimonthly. $17.94 per year.

Multi-Housing News. Nielsen Business Media Inc. • Individuals and firms primarily engaged in the development, construction, planning and management of multi-housing.

PRICE SOURCES

National Real Estate Index. CB Richard Ellis Group Inc. • Price and frequency on application. Provides reports on commercial real estate prices, rents, capitalization rates, and trends in more than 65 metropolitan areas. Time span is 12 years. Includes urban office buildings, suburban offices, warehouses, retail properties, and apartments.

STATISTICS SOURCES

American Housing Survey for the United States in (year). U. S. Government Printing Office. • Biennial. $51.00. Issued by the U. S. Census Bureau (www.census.gov). Covers both owner-occupied and renter-occupied housing. Includes data on such factors as condition of building, type of mortgage, utility costs, and housing occupied by minorities. (Current Housing Reports, H150.).

Characteristics of Apartments Completed (year). U.S. Department of Commerce U.S. Census Bureau. • Annual. Covers privately financed, nonsubsidized apartments in buildings with five units or more.

U.S. Housing Markets. DoveTale Publishers. • Monthly. $345.00 per year. Includes eight interim reports. Provides data on residential building permits, apartment building completions, rental vacancy rates, sales of existing homes, average home prices, housing affordability, etc. All major U. S. cities and areas are covered.

Value of Construction Put in Place. U.S. Bureau of the Census. U. S. Government Printing Office. • Monthly.

TRADE/PROFESSIONAL ASSOCIATIONS

Community Associations Institute. 6402 Arlington Blvd., Ste. 500, Falls Church, VA 22042. Phone: 888-224-4321 or (703)970-9220; Fax: (703)970-9558; Email: cai-info@caionline.org • URL: http://www.caionline.org • Condominium and homeowner associations, cooperatives, and association-governed planned communities of all sizes and architectural types; community or property managers and management firms; individual homeowners; community association managers and management firms; public officials; and lawyers, accountants, engineers, reserve specialists, builder/developers and other providers of professional services and products for CAs. Seeks to educate and represent America's 250,000 residential condominium, cooperative and homeowner associations and related professionals and service providers. Aims to foster vibrant, responsive, competent community associations that promote harmony, community and responsible leadership.

APPARATUS, SCIENTIFIC

See SCIENTIFIC APPARATUS AND INSTRUMENT INDUSTRIES

APPAREL, CHILDREN'S

See CHILDREN'S APPAREL INDUSTRY

APPAREL INDUSTRY

See CLOTHING INDUSTRY

APPAREL, MEN'S

See MEN'S CLOTHING INDUSTRY

APPAREL, WOMEN'S

See WOMEN'S APPAREL

APPLE INDUSTRY

See also FRUIT INDUSTRY

ALMANACS AND YEARBOOKS

CRB Commodity Yearbook. Commodity Research Bureau. CRB. • Annual. $179 plus $10.00 shipping cost. The single most comprehensive source of commodity and futures market information available.

DIRECTORIES

Major Food and Drink Companies of the World. Cengage Learning Inc. • 12th edition. eBook. Published by Graham & Whiteside. Contains profiles and trade names for more than 9,200 important food and beverage companies in various countries. In addition to foods, includes both alcoholic and nonalcoholic drink products.

FINANCIAL RATIOS

Industry Norms and Key Business Ratios. Dun & Bradstreet Inc. • Annual. Five volumes. Covers over 800 kinds of businesses, arranged by Standard Industrial Classification number. More detailed editions covering longer periods of time are also available.

INTERNET DATABASES

USDA. U.S. National Institute of Standards and Technology. 100 Bureau Dr., Gaithersburg, MD 20899-1070. Phone: 800-877-8339 or (301)975-6478 or (202)720-2791; Fax: (301)975-8295; Email: inquiries@nist.gov • URL: http://www.nist.gov • The USDA home page has six sections: News and Information; What's New; About USDA; Agencies; Opportunities; Search and Help. Keyword searching is offered from the USDA home page and from various individual agency home pages. Agencies are the Economic Research Service, Agricultural Marketing Service, National Agricultural Statistics Service, National Agricultural Library, and about 12 others. Updating varies. Fees: Free.

ONLINE DATABASES

Agricola. U.S. National Agricultural Library World List of Agricultural Serials. • Covers worldwide agricultural literature. Over 3.3 million citations, 1970 to present, with monthly updates. Inquire as to online cost and availability.

CAB Abstracts. CABI. • Contains 46 specialized abstract collections covering over 10,000 journals and monographs in the areas of agriculture, horticulture, forest products, farm products, nutrition, dairy science, poultry, grains, animal health, entomology, etc. Time period is 1972 to date, with monthly updates. Inquire as to online cost and availability. *CAB Abstracts on CD-ROM* also available, with annual updating.

Food Science and Technology Abstracts (online). IFIS North American Desk. • Produced by International Food Information Service. Provides about 500,000 online citations, with abstracts, to the international literature of food science, technology, commodities, engineering, and processing. Approximately 2,000 periodicals are covered. Time period is 1969 to date, with monthly updates. Inquire as to online cost and availability.

PERIODICALS AND NEWSLETTERS

American Fruit Grower. Meister Media. • Monthly. $27.47 per year.

Good Fruit Grower. Fruit Commission. • $35 Individuals.

PRICE SOURCES

PPI Detailed Report. Periodical covering business. Bureau of Labor Statistics, U.S. Department of Labor. U. S. Government Printing Office. • Monthly. $55 Individuals.

STATISTICS SOURCES

Agricultural Statistics. U.S. Department of Agriculture National Agricultural Statistics Service. • Annual. $46 Individuals. Provides a wide variety of statistical data relating to agricultural production, supplies, consumption, prices/price-supports, foreign trade, costs, and returns, as well as farm labor, loans, income, and population. In many cases, historical data is shown annually for 10 years. In addition to farm data, includes detailed fishery statistics.

For publishers' addresses, refer to SOURCES CITED section at the back of the book.

United States Census of Agriculture. U.S. Department of Agriculture National Agricultural Statistics Service. • Quinquennial. Provides uniform, comprehensive farming and ranching operations data for every U.S. state and county, including production expenses, market value of products, and operator characteristics.

TRADE/PROFESSIONAL ASSOCIATIONS

Apple Products Research and Education Council. 1100 Johnson Ferry Rd., Ste. 300, Atlanta, GA 30342. Phone: (404)252-3663; Email: jpa@kellencompany.com • URL: http://www.appleproducts.org • Represents processors of apple products and suppliers to the industry. Conducts program to improve business conditions in the apple products industry and to enable the industry to serve the interests of consumers. Conducts research programs on the health benefits of apple products.

APPLIANCES

See ELECTRIC APPLIANCE INDUSTRY

APPLICATIONS FOR POSITIONS

See JOB RESUMES

APPRAISAL (ALL PROPERTY)

See VALUATION

APPRAISAL OF REAL ESTATE

See REAL PROPERTY VALUATION

AQUACULTURE

ABSTRACTS AND INDEXES

Aquatic Sciences and Fisheries Abstracts: Aquatic Pollution and Environmental Quality. Food and Agriculture Organization of the United Nations. CSA. • Bimonthly. Part three. Includes print and online editions.

ONLINE DATABASES

ASFA Aquaculture Abstracts (Online). Cambridge Scientific Abstracts L.P. • Indexing and abstracting of the literature of marine life, 1984 to present. Inquire as to online cost and availability.

PERIODICALS AND NEWSLETTERS

Journal of Aquatic Food Product Technology: An International Journal Devoted to Foods from Marine and Inland Waters of the World. The Haworth Press Inc. • Quarterly. $375.00 per year.

North American Journal of Aquaculture. American Fisheries Society. • Quarterly. $419 Institutions print & online. Covers research and new developments relating to aquaculture.

RESEARCH CENTERS AND INSTITUTES

Auburn University - Alabama Agricultural Experiment Station - Department of Fisheries and Allied Aquacultures. 203 Swingle Hall, Auburn, AL 36849. Phone: (334)844-4786; Fax: (334)844-9208; Email: fish@auburn.edu • URL: http://www.ag.auburn.edu/fish • Aquaculture in fresh, brackish, and marine water; fisheries management in large and small impoundments, and rivers; aquatic plants management; nutrition and feeds; parasites and disease; limnology; water quality and management for aquaculture; international development for fisheries and aquaculture; aquatic ecology and environmental assessment; environmental education.

Texas A&M University - College of Agriculture and Life Sciences - Department of Wildlife and Fisheries Sciences - Aquacultural Research and Teaching Facility. 210 Nagle Hall, College Station, TX 77843. Phone: (979)272-3422 or (979)845-7471; Fax: (979)845-3786 or (979)845-7103; Email: d-gatlin@tamu.edu • URL: http://wfsc.tamu.edu/facilities/aquacultural-research-and-teaching-facility • Warm water aquaculture, including basic and applied studies in nutrition, bioenergetics, environmental physiology, and developmental biology. Species of interest include channel catfish, crawfish, tilapia, red drum, hybrid striped bass, and largemouth bass.

TRADE/PROFESSIONAL ASSOCIATIONS

American Fisheries Society. 5410 Grosvenor Ln., Bethesda, MD 20814. Phone: (301)897-8616; Fax: (301)897-8096; Email: main@fisheries.org • URL: http://fisheries.org • International scientific organization of fisheries and aquatic science professionals, including fish culturists, fish biologists, water quality scientists, fish health professionals, fish technologists, educators, limnologists, and oceanographers. Promotes the development of all branches of fishery science and practice, and the conservation, development, and wise utilization of fisheries, both recreational and commercial. Strengthens professional standards by certifying fisheries scientists, stressing professional ethics, and providing forums for the exchange of scientific and management information. Represents members through written and verbal testimony before legislative and administrative bodies concerning aquatic environmental issues. Maintains over 30 committees.

Aquatic Research Interactive. 1100 W Columbus Dr., East Chicago, IL 46312. Phone: (219)391-4138; Fax: (219)391-4168; Email: fishmail@arii.org.

ARBITRATION

DIRECTORIES

Martindale-Hubbell International Dispute Resolution Directory: A Unique Guide to International ADR Professionals and Procedures. LexisNexis Martindale-Hubbell. • Annual. $250 Individuals. Covers: Service providers in over 90 countries of international arbitration and dispute resolution at both international levels and within the individual's national jurisdiction: Professionals and their credentials. Database covers: Judges, attorneys, law firms, and other neutral experts that specialize in alternative dispute resolution. Database includes: Information on the processes of dispute resolution and the rules which govern it. Entries include: Contact information.

OTHER SOURCES

Labor Arbitration Awards. Wolters Kluwer Law & Business CCH. • Weekly. $1,239.00 per year. Looseleaf service.

PERIODICALS AND NEWSLETTERS

Dispute Resolution Journal. American Arbitration Association. • Quarterly. $55 /year for nonmembers. Professional journal covering topics on dispute resolution. Formerly *Arbitration Journal.*

Labor Relations Bulletin. Aspen Publishers Inc. • Description: Provides information and insight to management and labor officials to help them avoid or resolve conflicts. Recurring features include reports on current developments in labor law and relations, discipline and grievance cases based on actual arbitration, a question and answer column on labor and employment relations, and a column titled Reflections of an Arbitrator, offering the insight and experience of prominent national arbitrators.

Securities Arbitration Commentator. Richard P. Ryder. • Monthly. $695.00 per year. Newsletter. Edited for attorneys and other professionals concerned with securities arbitration.

Summary of Labor Arbitration Awards. American Arbitration Association. • Monthly. Periodical covering private sector arbitration decisions and collective bargaining issues.

RESEARCH CENTERS AND INSTITUTES

Massey University - Dispute Resolution Centre. College of Business, Private Bag 11222, Palmerston North, New Zealand. Phone: 64 6 3505799; Fax: 64 6 3505809; Email: dispute@massey.ac.nz • URL: http://www.massey.ac.nz/massey/learning/colleges/college-business/international-students/specialisation/dispute-resolution.cfm • Negotiation, mediation, and arbitration.

TRADE/PROFESSIONAL ASSOCIATIONS

National Academy of Arbitrators. NAA Operations Ctr., Ste. 412, 1 N Main St., Cortland, NY 13045. Phone: 888-317-1729 or (607)756-8363; Email: naa@naarb.org • URL: http://www.naarb.org • Labor-management arbitrators. Works to improve general understanding of the nature and use of arbitration as a means of settling labor disputes. Conducts research and educational programs.

ARCHITECTURE

See also BUILDING INDUSTRY

ABSTRACTS AND INDEXES

Art Index. EBSCO Publishing Inc. • Quarterly. Annual cumulations. Price varies. Subject and author index to periodicals in art, architecture, industrial design, city planning, photography, and various related topics.

Avery Index to Architectural Periodicals. Columbia University, Avery Architectural Library. • Annual. $995.

NTIS Alerts: Building Industry Technology. U.S. Department of Commerce National Technical Information Service. • Biweekly. $130 per year. Covers architecture, construction management, building materials, maintenance, furnishings, and related subjects.

FINANCIAL RATIOS

Annual Statement Studies. Risk Management Association. • Annual. Compiled from over 280,000 financial statements.

Annual Statement Studies: Industry Default Probabilities and Cash Flow Measures. Risk Management Association. • Annual. $405 Nonmembers. Serves as a companion volume to the original *Annual Statement Studies.* Gives probability of default estimates on a percentage scale for more than 450 industries. Includes changes in position year-by-year for eight financial statement line items and provides percentage measures of cash flow.

ONLINE DATABASES

Art Index Online. H.W. Wilson Co. • Indexes a wide variety of art-related periodicals, 1984 to date. Monthly updates. Inquire as to online cost and availability.

Avery Architectural Periodicals Index. Columbia University Avery Architectural and Fine Arts Library. • Indexes a wide range of periodicals related to architecture and design. Subjects include building design, building materials, interior design, housing, land use, and city planning. Time span: 1977 to date. *bul* URL: www-rlg.stanford.edu/cit-ave.html.

OTHER SOURCES

Forms and Agreements for Architects, Engineers and Contractors. Albert Dib. Thomson West. • $2,687.25 full set. Three times a year. Five looseleaf volume. Covers evaluation of construction documents and alternative clauses. Includes pleadings for litigation and resolving of claims. (Real Property Law Series).

PERIODICALS AND NEWSLETTERS

Design Cost Data. DC & D Technologies Inc. • Bimonthly. $149 U.S. /year plus online access to archive. Provides a preliminary cost estimating system for architects, contractors, builders, and developers, utilizing historical data. Includes case studies of actual costs. Formerly *Design Cost and Data*.

HQ: Good Design is Good Business. McGraw-Hill Inc. • Quarterly. Design magazine for C-level executives, building owners and developers, and design and construction professionals.

Journal of Architectural Education. Association of Collegiate Schools of Architecture. The MIT Press. • Quarterly. Free to members; non-members, $50. 00. Articles on architectural education, theory and practice.

PRICE SOURCES

Building Construction Cost Data. RSMeans. • Annual. $194.95 Individuals. Lists over 20,000 entries for estimating.

RESEARCH CENTERS AND INSTITUTES

University of California at Berkeley - Center for Environmental Design Research. 390 Wurster Hall, MC 1839, Berkeley, CA 94720-1839. Phone: (510)642-2896; Fax: (510)643-5571; Email: cedr@ced.berkley.edu • URL: http://ced.berkeley.edu/research/center-for-environmental-design-research.

TRADE/PROFESSIONAL ASSOCIATIONS

American Institute of Architects. 1735 New York Ave. NW, Washington, DC 20006-5209. Phone: 800-AIA-3837 or (202)626-7300; Fax: (202)626-7547; Email: infocentral@aia.org • URL: http://www.aia.org • Represents architects, licensed architects, graduate architects, not yet licensed and retired architects. Fosters professionalism and accountability among members through continuing education and training. Promotes design excellence by influencing change in the industry. Sponsors educational programs with schools of architecture, graduate students, and elementary and secondary schools. Advises on professional competitions. Supplies construction documents. Established the American Architectural Foundation. Sponsors Octagon Museum; operates bookstore; stages exhibitions; compiles statistics. Provides monthly news service on design and construction. Conducts professional development programs, research programs, charitable activities, and children's services.

Business Architects Association. 727 S Dearborn St., Ste. 710, Chicago, IL 60605-3826. Email: info@businessarchitects.org • URL: http://www.businessarchitectsassociation.org • Aims to promote and advance the business architecture profession through education, research, and application of methodologies. Provides educational and networking opportunities for the continuing education of members. Offers professional training and certification programs.

National Architectural Accrediting Board. 1101 Connecticut Ave. NW, Ste. 410, Washington, DC 20036. Phone: (202)783-2007; Fax: (202)783-2822; Email: info@naab.org • URL: http://www.naab.org • Formed by the American Institute of Architects, Association of Collegiate Schools of Architecture, and National Council of Architectural Registration Boards to stimulate the improvement of architectural education. Conducts continuing program of accreditation of programs of architecture. Compiles statistics; maintains library of 100 volumes of descriptions and self-evaluations of architecture schools.

Public Art Fund. 1 E 53rd St., New York, NY 10022. Phone: (212)223-7800; Fax: (212)223-7801; Email: info@publicartfund.org • URL: http://www.publicartfund.org • Works with artists, architects, city planners, and community groups to explore and develop programs that bring art of both a temporary and permanent nature directly into the public environment. Provides public information and consultation on public art to governmental agencies, private businesses, and community groups, both in New York City and across the country.

ARCHIVES MANAGEMENT

See RECORDS MANAGEMENT

AREA DEVELOPMENT

See INDUSTRIAL DEVELOPMENT

ARMAMENT AND DEFENSE

See DEFENSE INDUSTRIES

ARMAMENTS MARKET

See MILITARY MARKET

ARMY

DIRECTORIES

Carroll's Federal & Federal Regional Directory. Caroll Publishing. • Semiannual. $500 Individuals. Lists more than 23,000 U. S. government officials throughout the country, including military installations.

Carroll's Federal Regional Directory. Caroll Publishing. • Annual. $500 Individuals. Covers: Over 32,000 officials in federal congressional, judicial, and executive branch departments and agencies outside the District of Columbia. Database includes: Regional maps showing states covered in each federal region and Federal Information Centers. Entries include: Organization or agency name; names, addresses, and phone numbers of key personnel.

Federal Regional Yellow Book: Who's Who in the Federal Government's Departments, Agencies, Military Installations, and Service Academies Outside of Washington, DC. Leadership Directories Inc. • Semiannual. $465 Individuals annual. Lists over 35,000 federal officials and support staff at 8,000 regional offices.

OTHER SOURCES

Army AL&T: Professional Publication of the AL&T Community. U. S. Government Printing Office. • Quarterly. $21 U.S.. Produced by the U.S. Army Materiel Command (www.amc.army.mil). Reports on Army research, development, and acquisition. Formerly *Army RD&A*.

STATISTICS SOURCES

Annual Report of the Secretary of Defense. U.S. Department of Defense - Office of the Secretary. • Annual.

Quarterly Labour Force Statistics. Organization for Economic Cooperation and Development. Organisation for Economic Co-operation and Development Publications and Information Center. • Quarterly. $90.00 per year. Provides current data for OECD member countries on population, employment, unemployment, civilian labor force, armed forces, and other labor factors.

TRADE/PROFESSIONAL ASSOCIATIONS

American Armed Forces Mutual Aid Association. 102 Sheridan Ave., Fort Myer, VA 22211-1110. Phone: 800-522-5221 or (703)707-4600; Fax: (888)210-4882; Email: info@aafmaa.com • URL: http://www.aafmaa.com • A mutual aid organization providing aid to families of deceased career Army and Air Force officers and noncommissioned officers.

Army Aviation Association of America. 593 Main St., Monroe, CT 06468-2830. Phone: (203)268-2450; Email: aaaa@quad-a.org • URL: http://www.quad-a.org • Commissioned officers, warrant officers, and enlisted personnel serving in U.S. Army aviation assignments in the active U.S. Army, Army National Guard, and Army Reserve; Department of Army civilian personnel and industry representatives affiliated with army aviation. Fosters fellowship among military and civilian persons connected with army aviation, past or present; seeks to advance status, overall esprit, and general knowledge of professionals engaged in army aviation. Activities include locator and placement services, technical assistance, and biographical archives. Sponsors speakers' bureau; maintains hall of fame.

Army Emergency Relief. 200 Stovall St., Rm. 5S33, Alexandria, VA 22332-4005. Phone: 866-878-6378 or (703)428-0000; Fax: (703)325-7183; Email: aer@aerhq.org • URL: http://www.aerhq.org/dnn563 • A private organization whose primary purpose is to relieve distress of members of the Army (active and retired) and their dependents, and to provide assistance to needy spouses and orphans of deceased Army members; a secondary purpose is to make available educational assistance (scholarships) to unmarried dependent children of soldiers (active, retired, or deceased) who need such assistance to pursue undergraduate studies.

Association of the United States Army. 2425 Wilson Blvd., Arlington, VA 22201. Phone: 800-336-4570 or (703)841-4300 • URL: http://www.ausa.org/Pages/default.aspx • Professional society of: active, retired, and reserve military personnel; West Point and Army ROTC cadets; civilians interested in national defense. Seeks to advance the security of the United States and consolidate the efforts of all who support the United States Army as an indispensable instrument of national security. Conducts industrial symposia for manufacturers of Army weapons and equipment, and those in the Department of the Army who plan, develop, test, and use weapons and equipment. Symposia subjects have included guided missiles, army aviation, electronics and communication, telemedicine, vehicles, and armor. Sponsors monthly PBS TV series, America's Army.

ART AS AN INVESTMENT

See also ANTIQUES AS AN INVESTMENT

ABSTRACTS AND INDEXES

Art Index. EBSCO Publishing Inc. • Quarterly. Annual cumulations. Price varies. Subject and author index to periodicals in art, architecture, industrial design, city planning, photography, and various related topics.

BIOGRAPHICAL SOURCES

Who's Who in American Art. Marquis Who's Who L.L.C. • Biennial. $297. Lists over 14,000 people active in visual arts.

Who's Who in Art. Cengage Learning Inc. • Biennial. $190 Individuals cloth bound. Contains about 3,000 brief biographies of artists, designers, curators, critics, and other art-related individuals. International coverage, with British emphasis. Published by Hilmarton Manor Press.

DIRECTORIES

Art Now Gallery Guides. Louise Blouin Media Inc. • Monthly. $35 Individuals. Covers: in 'Art Now

For publishers' addresses, refer to SOURCES CITED section at the back of the book.

Gallery Guide--International Edition' current exhibitions in over 1,800 museums and galleries. Separate regional editions cover metropolitan New York, Boston and New England, the Philadelphia area, the southeast, Chicago and the midwest, the southwest, California and the northwest, Latin America, and Europe. Listings are paid. Entries include: Gallery or museum name, address, phone, days and hours of operation, artist's name or name of the exhibit, medium, and dates of showing.

National Antique & Art Dealers Association of America--Membership Directory. National Antique and Art Dealers Association of America. • Continuous. Provides a list of members and their areas of specialization in the decorative arts.

ONLINE DATABASES

Art Index Online. H.W. Wilson Co. • Indexes a wide variety of art-related periodicals, 1984 to date. Monthly updates. Inquire as to online cost and availability.

PRICE SOURCES

Leonard's Annual Price Index of Art Auctions. Auction Index Inc. • Annual. $245.00. List major auction houses.

TRADE/PROFESSIONAL ASSOCIATIONS

Art and Antique Dealers League of America. Lennox Hill Sta., New York, NY 10021. Phone: (212)879-7558; Fax: (212)772-7197; Email: secretary@artantiquedealersleague.com • URL: http://www.artantiquedealersleague.com • Members are retailers and wholesalers of antiques and art objects.

Art Dealers Association of America. 205 Lexington Ave., Ste. 901, New York, NY 10016. Phone: (212)488-5550; Fax: (646)688-6809 • URL: http://www.artdealers.org • Art dealers united to promote the highest standards of connoisseurship, scholarship, and ethical practice within the profession and to increase public awareness of the role and responsibilities of reputable art dealers. Works with museums and scholars on activities and problems of mutual concern; cooperates with domestic and international government agencies on art matters and offers assistance and expertise to these agencies; advises on legislation and other governmental activity regarding the fine arts; seeks to identify and remove fake works of art from the marketplace. Appraises, for tax purposes only, works of art donated to nonprofit institutions.

National Association of Women Artists. 80 5th Ave., Ste. 1405, New York, NY 10011. Phone: (212)675-1616; Email: office@thenawa.org • URL: http://www.thenawa.org • Formerly Women's Art Club of the City of New York.

ART BUSINESS

See also ARTS MANAGEMENT

ABSTRACTS AND INDEXES

Art Index. EBSCO Publishing Inc. • Quarterly. Annual cumulations. Price varies. Subject and author index to periodicals in art, architecture, industrial design, city planning, photography, and various related topics.

BIBLIOGRAPHIES

Subject Bibliography: Art and Artists. U. S. Government Printing Office. • Annual. Free. Lists books, pamphlets, periodicals, and other government publications on art-related topics. (Subject Bibliography No. SB-107.).

BIOGRAPHICAL SOURCES

Who's Who in American Art. Marquis Who's Who L.L.C. • Biennial. $297. Lists over 14,000 people active in visual arts.

Who's Who in Art. Cengage Learning Inc. • Biennial. $190 Individuals cloth bound. Contains about 3,000 brief biographies of artists, designers, curators, critics, and other art-related individuals. International coverage, with British emphasis. Published by Hilmarton Manor Press.

CD-ROM DATABASES

Art Index. EBSCO Publishing Inc. • Indexing for over 600 periodicals and 13,000 art dissertations.

DIRECTORIES

Art Marketing Sourcebook: Where to Sell Fine Art. ArtNetwork. • Biennial. $23.95 plus 4 shipping. Covers: over 2,000 representatives, consultants, galleries, architects, interior designers, museums, and specialty markets. Entries include: Company name, address, phone, description of services, style represented, mediums, years in business, types of companies dealt with, geographical limitations, number of clients, requirements for viewing slides.

Art Now Gallery Guides. Louise Blouin Media Inc. • Monthly. $35 Individuals. Covers: in 'Art Now Gallery Guide--International Edition' current exhibitions in over 1,800 museums and galleries. Separate regional editions cover metropolitan New York, Boston and New England, the Philadelphia area, the southeast, Chicago and the midwest, the southwest, California and the northwest, Latin America, and Europe. Listings are paid. Entries include: Gallery or museum name, address, phone, days and hours of operation, artist's name or name of the exhibit, medium, and dates of showing.

Money to Work II--Funding for Visual Artists. Art Resources International. • Irregular. $8.95 plus $3.25 shipping. Covers: about 225 organizations offering grants for painters, sculptors, photographers, printmakers, and other visual and craft artists. Entries include: Organization name, description of grant, application and selection procedures.

Warner Business Association--Business Directory. Warner Business Association. • List of businesses, artists, and artisans in Warner, New Hampshire.

GENERAL WORKS

Art Business News. Advanstar Communications Inc. • Monthly. $55 Canada and Mexico. Trade magazine covering art business news.

Art Business Today. Fine Art Trade Guild. • 5/year. £29 Individuals. Trade magazine covering the art business in the UK.

Source Directory of Indian, Eskimo, and Aleut Owned-and-Operated Arts and Crafts Businesses. U.S. Indian Arts and Crafts Board. • Irregular. Covers over 250 Native American-owned businesses specializing in arts and crafts products.

ONLINE DATABASES

Art Index Online. H.W. Wilson Co. • Indexes a wide variety of art-related periodicals, 1984 to date. Monthly updates. Inquire as to online cost and availability.

PERIODICALS AND NEWSLETTERS

Picture Framing Magazine. Hobby Publications, Inc. • Monthly. $20 per year. Published for retailers, wholesalers, and manufacturers of picture frames.

RESEARCH CENTERS AND INSTITUTES

International Foundation for Art Research. 500 5th Ave., Ste. 935, New York, NY 10110. Phone: (212)391-6234; Fax: (212)391-8794 • URL: http://www.ifar.org • Research fields are art theft and the authenticity of art objects. Maintains an information archive on stolen art and operates an authentication service.

STATISTICS SOURCES

United States Census of Service Industries. U.S. Department of Commerce U.S. Census Bureau. • Quinquennial. Various reports available.

TRADE/PROFESSIONAL ASSOCIATIONS

Americans for the Arts. 1000 Vermont Ave. NW, 6th Fl., Washington, DC 20005. Phone: (202)371-2830; Fax: (202)371-0424; Email: info@artsusa.org • URL: http://www.americansforthearts.org • Members are arts organizations and interested individuals. Conducts research and provides information and clearinghouse services relating to the visual arts.

Art and Antique Dealers League of America. Lennox Hill Sta., New York, NY 10021. Phone: (212)879-7558; Fax: (212)772-7197; Email: secretary@artantiquedealersleague.com • URL: http://www.artantiquedealersleague.com • Members are retailers and wholesalers of antiques and art objects.

Art and Creative Materials Institute. 99 Derby St., Ste. 200, Hingham, MA 02043-4216. Phone: (781)556-1044; Fax: (781)207-5550; Email: debbieg@acminet.org • URL: http://www.acminet.org • Members are manufacturers of school and professional art and craft materials.

Art Dealers Association of America. 205 Lexington Ave., Ste. 901, New York, NY 10016. Phone: (212)488-5550; Fax: (646)688-6809 • URL: http://www.artdealers.org • Art dealers united to promote the highest standards of connoisseurship, scholarship, and ethical practice within the profession and to increase public awareness of the role and responsibilities of reputable art dealers. Works with museums and scholars on activities and problems of mutual concern; cooperates with domestic and international government agencies on art matters and offers assistance and expertise to these agencies; advises on legislation and other governmental activity regarding the fine arts; seeks to identify and remove fake works of art from the marketplace. Appraises, for tax purposes only, works of art donated to nonprofit institutions.

National Antique and Art Dealers Association of America. 220 E 57th St., New York, NY 10022. Phone: (212)826-9707; Fax: (212)832-9493; Email: inquiries@naadaa.org • URL: http://www.naadaa.org • Art and antique dealers who handle antiques and works of art of the highest quality. Safeguards the interests of those who buy, sell, and collect antiques and works of art. Sponsors periodic exhibitions; maintains speakers' bureau.

Professional Organization of Women in the Arts. 365 Bridge St., Ste. 7F, Brooklyn, NY 11201. Email: powarts@gmail.com • URL: http://www.powarts.org • Promotes the advancement of women in the visual arts industry. Aims to educate, empower and promote leadership among women employed in the visual arts. Serves as a medium for the communication and exchange of ideas between women in the visual arts industry.

ART, COMMERCIAL

See COMMERCIAL ART

ART DEALERS

See ART BUSINESS

ART IN INDUSTRY

See also ARCHITECTURE; COMMERCIAL ART; DESIGN IN INDUSTRY; GRAPHIC ARTS INDUSTRY

ABSTRACTS AND INDEXES

Art Index. EBSCO Publishing Inc. • Quarterly. Annual cumulations. Price varies. Subject and author index to periodicals in art, architecture, industrial design, city planning, photography, and various related topics.

CD-ROM DATABASES

Art Index. EBSCO Publishing Inc. • Indexing for over 600 periodicals and 13,000 art dissertations.

DIRECTORIES

ASA Artisan. American Society of Artists. • Quarterly. Publication includes: Lists of shows and competitions accepting fine art, art and craft work and other information for and about members. Entries include: Show or competition name, location, sponsor, name and address of contact, dates, requirements, supple exhibit info, etc. Principal content of publication is information for and about ASA members.

International Directory of Corporate Art Collections. International Art Alliance. • $115. Contains information on about 1,300 corporate art collections maintained or sponsored in the U. S., Canada, Europe, and Japan.

ONLINE DATABASES

Art Index Online. H.W. Wilson Co. • Indexes a wide variety of art-related periodicals, 1984 to date. Monthly updates. Inquire as to online cost and availability.

OTHER SOURCES

Arts Management. Alvin H. Reiss. • Five times a year. $22.00 per year. National news service for those who finance, manage and communicate the arts.

TRADE/PROFESSIONAL ASSOCIATIONS

American Institute of Graphic Arts. 164 5th Ave., New York, NY 10010-5901. Phone: (212)807-1990; Fax: (212)807-1799 • URL: http://www.aiga.org • Graphic designers, art directors, illustrators and packaging designers. Sponsors exhibits and projects in the public interest. Sponsors traveling exhibitions. Operates gallery. Maintains library of design books and periodicals; offers slide archives.

Arts SA. GPO Box 2308, Adelaide, SA 5001, Australia. Phone: 61 8 84635444; Fax: 61 8 84635420; Email: artssa@sa.gov.au • URL: http://arts.sa.gov.au • Works to develop, facilitate and administer the Government's vision and strategy for the arts and cultural sector.

Craft Retailers Association for Tomorrow. PO Box 293, Islamorada, FL 33036. Phone: (305)664-3650; Fax: (305)664-0199; Email: info@craftonline.org • URL: http://www.craftonline.org • Represents a network of galleries, shops and artists. Supports and encourages creativity and artistic excellence in American craftspeople. Promotes awareness of American crafts through communication programs, education, networking and marketing.

Public Art Fund. 1 E 53rd St., New York, NY 10022. Phone: (212)223-7800; Fax: (212)223-7801; Email: info@publicartfund.org • URL: http://www.publicartfund.org • Works with artists, architects, city planners, and community groups to explore and develop programs that bring art of both a temporary and permanent nature directly into the public environment. Provides public information and consultation on public art to governmental agencies, private businesses, and community groups, both in New York City and across the country.

ARTIFICIAL INTELLIGENCE

See also MICROCOMPUTERS AND MINICOMPUTERS; ROBOTS

ABSTRACTS AND INDEXES

Applied Science and Technology Index. EBSCO Publishing Inc. • 11/year. Indexes a wide variety of English language technical, industrial, and engineering periodicals.

Business Periodicals Index Retrospective. EBSCO Publishing Inc. • 11/year. Quarterly and annual cumulations.

Computer and Information Systems Abstracts Journal: An Abstract Journal Pertaining to the Theory, Design, Fabrication and Application of Computer and Information Systems. CSA. • Monthly. $1,750 per year.

Computer Science Index. EBSCO Publishing Inc. • Quarterly. $245 per year. Contains brief abstracts of book and periodical literature covering all phases of computing, including approximately 70 specific application areas.

Current Contents: Engineering, Computing and Technology. Thomson Reuters Intellectual Property and Science. • Weekly. $730 per year. Reproductions of contents pages of technical journals. Includes *Author Index*, *Address Directory*, *Current Book Contents*, and *Title Word Index*. Formerly *Current Contents: Engineering, Technology and Applied Sciences.*

Inspec Direct. Institution of Engineering and Technology. • Monthly. $2,400 per year. Section C of *Science Abstracts*.

Key Abstracts: Artificial Intelligence. The Insititution of Engineering and Technology. • Monthly. $250.00 per year. Provides international coverage of journal and proceedings literature, including material on expert systems and knowledge engineering. Published in England by the Institution of Electrical Engineers (IEE).

NTIS Alerts: Biomedical Technology & Human Factor Engineering. U.S. Department of Commerce National Technical Information Service. • Biweekly. $130 per year. Covers biotechnology, ergonomics, bionics, artificial intelligence, prosthetics, and related subjects.

Science Citation Index. Thomson Reuters Intellectual Property and Science. • Weekly. Includes *Source Index*, *Citation Index*, *Permuterm Subject Index*, and *Corporate Index*. Provides researchers, administrators, faculty, and students with quick, powerful access to the bibliographic and citation information they need to find research data, analyze trends, journals and researchers, and share their findings.

CD-ROM DATABASES

Science Citation Index. Thomson Reuters Intellectual Property and Science. • Weekly. Includes *Source Index*, *Citation Index*, *Permuterm Subject Index*, and *Corporate Index*. Provides researchers, administrators, faculty, and students with quick, powerful access to the bibliographic and citation information they need to find research data, analyze trends, journals and researchers, and share their findings.

DIRECTORIES

The AI Week Directory. R.R. Bowker L.L.C. • Irregular. $99. Covers: The US and international artificial intelligence community and related businesses. Entries include: Company name, size, and financial status; names of key personnel; products and services.

The Annual Directory of the Information Industry Association. Software and Information Industry Association. • Annual. Members, $75.00; non-members, $125.00.

ONLINE DATABASES

Applied Science and Technology Index Online. H.W. Wilson Co. • Provides online indexing of 500 major scientific, technical, industrial, and engineering periodicals. Time period is 1983 to date. Monthly updates. Inquire as to online cost and availability.

Wilson Business Abstracts Online. H.W. Wilson Co. • Indexes and abstracts 600 major business periodicals, plus the *Wall Street Journal* and the business section of the *New York Times*. Indexing is from 1982, abstracting from 1990, with the two newspapers included from 1993. Updated weekly. Inquire as to online cost and availability. (*Business Periodicals Index* without abstracts is also available online.).

PERIODICALS AND NEWSLETTERS

AI Magazine. American Association for Artificial Intelligence. Association for the Advancement of Artificial Intelligence. • Quarterly. Information on artificial intelligence research and innovative applications of the science.

Computer Languages, Systems and Structures. Elsevier. • Quarterly. Contains papers on all aspects of the design, implementation and use of programming languages, from theory to practice.

Computers in Human Behavior. Elsevier. • Bimonthly. Qualified personnel, $242.00 per year; institutions, $1,100.00 per year.

EDP Weekly: The Leading Weekly Computer News Summary. Computer Age and EDP News Services. • Weekly. $495.00 per year. Newsletter. Summarizes news from all areas of the computer and microcomputer industries.

Intelligent Systems Report. Lionheart Publishing Inc. • Monthly. $299.00 per year. Newsletter. Formed by merger of *Neural Network News* and *AI Week*.

International Journal of Intelligent Systems. John Wiley and Sons, Inc., Journals Div. • Monthly. $1,925.00 per year; with online edition, $2,022.00 per year.

Release 1.0 Esther Dysons Monthly Report. EDventure Holdings Inc. • Description: Reports on technology, communications, and the Internet. Reviews and analyzes the technology business. Recurring features include a calendar of events.

Report. Robinson and Associates. • Monthly. $295.00 per year. Newsletter. Articles cover the artificial intelligence field. Formerly Artificial Intelligence Report.

Telematics and Informatics: An International Journal on Telecommunications and Internet Technology. Elsevier. • Four times a year. Institutions, $938.00 per year.

RESEARCH CENTERS AND INSTITUTES

Carnegie Mellon Research Institute-The Robotics Institute. 5000 Forbes Ave., Pittsburgh, PA 15213. Phone: (412)268-3818; Fax: (412)268-6436; Email: robotics@ri.cmu.edu • URL: http://www.ri.cmu.edu • Multidisciplinary research activities include expert systems applications, minicomputer and microcomputer systems design, genetic engineering, and transportation systems analysis.

Carnegie Mellon University - College of Fine Arts - Studio for Creative Inquiry. 5000 Forbes Ave., Rm. 111, Pittsburgh, PA 15213-3890. Phone: (412)268-3451; Fax: (412)268-2829; Email: mmbm@andrew.cmu.edu • URL: http://studioforcreativeinquiry.org • Research areas include artificial intelligence, virtual reality, hypermedia, multimedia, and telecommunications, in relation to the arts.

Center for Artificial Intelligence. University of Pennsylvania, Computer and Information Science Dept., Moore School of Electrical Engineering, 200 S 33rd St., Philadelphia, PA 19104-6389. Phone: (215)898-3191; Fax: (215)898-0587 • URL: http://www.upenn.edu.

Digital Image Analysis Laboratory. University of Arizona, Dept. of Electrical and Computer Engineering, 1230 E Speedway Blvd., Tucson, AZ 85721. Phone: (520)621-4554; Fax: (520)621-8076; Email: dial@ece.arizona.edu • URL: http://www.ece.arizona.edu • Research fields include image processing, computer vision, and artificial intelligence.

Imaging and Computer Vision Center. Drexel University, 3141 Chestnut St., Philadelphia, PA 19104. Phone: (215)895-2215; Fax: (215)895-4983; Email: icvc-support@cbis.ece.drexel.edu • URL: http://www.biomed.drexel.edu • Fields of research include computer vision, robot vision, and expert systems.

Massachusetts Institute of Technology - Computer Science and Artificial Intelligence Laboratory. The Stata Ctr., Bldg. 32, 32 Vassar St., Cambridge, MA 02139. Phone: (617)253-5851; Fax: (617)258-8682; Email: rus@csail.mit.edu • URL: http://www.csail.mit.edu • Research is in four areas: Intelligent Systems; Parallel Systems; Systems, Languages, and Networks; and Theory. Emphasis is on the application of online computing.

McGill Centre for Intelligent Machines. McGill University, McConnell Engineering Bldg., Rm. 410, 3480 University St., Montreal, QC, Canada H3A 2A7. Phone: (514)398-6319; Fax: (514)398-7348; Email: cim@cim.mcgill.ca • URL: http://www.cim.mcgill.ca.

Purdue University - Robot Vision Laboratory. Electrical Engineering Bldg., School of Electrical and Computer Engineering, 465 Northwestern Ave., West Lafayette, IN 47907-2035. Phone: (765)494-4600 or (765)494-3456; Fax: (765)494-6440; Email: kak@purdue.edu • URL: http://engineering.purdue.edu/RVL • Advanced automation with robotics and artificial intelligence, including studies in sensory feedback for intelligent robot manipulation and fundamental research in computer vision.

Techsolve Inc. 6705 Steger Dr., Cincinnati, OH 45237. Phone: 800-345-4482 or (513)948-2000; Fax: (513)948-2109 or (800)345-4482; Email: perkins@techsolve.org • URL: http://www.techsolve.org • Fields of research include quality improvement, computer-aided design, artificial intelligence, and employee training.

University of Florida - Center for Intelligent Machines and Robotics. Department of Mechanical Engineering, Gainesville, FL 32611. Phone: (352)392-9461; Fax: (352)392-1071; Email: ccrane@ufl.edu • URL: http://cimar.mae.ufl.edu/CIMAR/index.html • Robotics and artificial intelligence, including studies in industrial robotics, nuclear reactor maintenance, interactive animated display of man-controlled and autonomous robots, light machinery, hazardous area manipulation, and human augmentation.

University of Michigan - Collaboratory for Research on Electronic Work. School of Information N, Rm. 2226, 1075 Beal Ave., Ann Arbor, MI 48109-2112. Phone: (734)764-6131; Fax: (734)647-8045; Email: finholt@umich.edu • URL: http://www.crew.umich.edu/about.html • Concerned with the design and use of computer-based tools for thinking and planning in the professional office.

University of Texas at Austin - Artificial Intelligence Laboratory. Department of Computer Science, 2317 Speedway, 2.302, Austin, TX 78712. Phone: (512)471-9565; Fax: (512)471-8885; Email: porter@cs.utexas.edu • URL: http://www.cs.utexas.edu/ai-lab • Artificial intelligence, physics problem solving, automatic programming, natural language understanding, neural networks, automatic theorem proving, machine learning, logical foundations of artificial intelligence, qualitative reasoning, and robotics.

STATISTICS SOURCES

U.S. Industry and Trade Outlook. U.S. Department of Commerce National Technical Information Service. • Annual. Produced by the International Trade Administration, U.S. Department of Commerce, in a "public-private" partnership with DRI/McGraw-Hill and Standard & Poor's. Provides basic data, outlook for the current year, and "Long-Term Prospects" (five-year projections) for a wide variety of products and services. Includes high technology industries. Formerly *U.S. Industrial Outlook.*

TRADE/PROFESSIONAL ASSOCIATIONS

Cognitive Science Society. 10200 W 44th Ave., Ste. 304, Wheat Ridge, CO 80033-2840. Phone: (303)327-7547; Fax: (720)881-6101; Email: info@cognitivesciencesociety.org • URL: http://cognitivesciencesociety.org • Represents published PhD's; students and PhD's not actively publishing in the fields of psychology, artificial intelligence, and cognitive science. Promotes the dissemination of research in cognitive science and allied sciences. (Cognitive science is a branch of artificial intelligence that seeks to simulate human reasoning and associative powers on a computer, using specialized software).

ARTIFICIAL LIMBS

See PROSTHETICS INDUSTRY

ARTS MANAGEMENT

See also ART BUSINESS; FOUNDATIONS; FUND-RAISING; GRANTS-IN-AID

ABSTRACTS AND INDEXES

Art Index. EBSCO Publishing Inc. • Quarterly. Annual cumulations. Price varies. Subject and author index to periodicals in art, architecture, industrial design, city planning, photography, and various related topics.

DIRECTORIES

Guide to Arts Administration Training and Research. Americans for the Arts. • Triennial. $12.95. Lists 33 institutions.

GENERAL WORKS

Business in the Arts Award Brochures. Business Committee for the Arts. • $4 plus shipping and handling. Presents highlights of theatre-support programs developed by businesses receiving the national Business in the Arts Awards.

ONLINE DATABASES

Art Index Online. H.W. Wilson Co. • Indexes a wide variety of art-related periodicals, 1984 to date. Monthly updates. Inquire as to online cost and availability.

OTHER SOURCES

Arts Management. Alvin H. Reiss. • Five times a year. $22.00 per year. National news service for those who finance, manage and communicate the arts.

Lindey on Entertainment, Publishing and the Arts. Alexander Lindey, editor. Thomson West. • $1,582.86 Full Set. Provides basic forms, applicable law, and guidance.

PERIODICALS AND NEWSLETTERS

Journal of Arts Management, Law, and Society. Helen Dwight Reid Educational Foundation. • Quarterly. $108 Individuals print only. Addresses current and ongoing issues in arts policy, management, low and governance from a range of philosophical and national perspectives encompassing diverse disciplinary viewpoints. Formerly *Journal of Arts Management and Law.*

Variety: The International Entertainment Weekly. Reed Elsevier Group plc Reed Business Information. • Weekly. $199 Individuals print + online. Contains national and international news of show business, with emphasis on motion pictures and television. Includes *Market* and *Special Focus* issues.

Washington International Arts Letter. Allied Business Consultants Inc. • Description: Publishes information about cultural developments; personalities in the arts; and the workings and actions of the National Endowments of the Arts and Humanities, Congress, and federal offices as they affect this field. Recurring features include announcements of jobs, scholarships, grants, and other forms of assistance available in the arts and humanities; bibliographies; publications reviews; and listings of names and addresses of businesses and organizations that contribute to the arts.

RESEARCH CENTERS AND INSTITUTES

Florida State University - Department of Art Education - Center for Arts Administration Program. 1033 William Johnston Bldg., Tallahassee, FL 32306. Phone: (850)644-5473 or (850)644-2158; Fax: (850)644-5067 • URL: http://arted.fsu.edu/Programs/Arts-Administration-Change-your-World • Serves as an administrative and resource base for the development of research, service, and education in arts administration. Provides psychological, social, business, governance, and art related information to private and public arts agencies. Administers research capabilities at the University in arts, business, and public administration.

TRADE/PROFESSIONAL ASSOCIATIONS

Americans for the Arts. 1000 Vermont Ave. NW, 6th Fl., Washington, DC 20005. Phone: (202)371-2830; Fax: (202)371-0424; Email: info@artsusa.org • URL: http://www.americansforthearts.org • Members are arts organizations and interested individuals. Conducts research and provides information and clearinghouse services relating to the visual arts.

Association of Performing Arts Presenters. 1211 Connecticut Ave. NW, Ste. 200, Washington, DC 20036-2716. Phone: 888-820-2787 or (202)833-2787; Fax: (202)833-1543; Email: info@artspresenters.org • URL: http://www.apap365.org/Pages/APAP365.aspx • Arts organizations involved in presentation of the professional performing arts; artists and artist management companies. Explores the roles, responsibilities, and opportunities for presenters, artists' managers, and artists, in order "to enable and celebrate the rich and diverse presenting field in its service to the public." Administers Lila Wallace/Reader's Digest Arts Partners regranting program.

ASBESTOS INDUSTRY

ABSTRACTS AND INDEXES

Environment Abstracts. University Publications of America. • Monthly. Price varies. Provides multidisciplinary coverage of the world's environmental literature. Incorporates *Acid Rain Abstracts.*

Environment Abstracts Annual: A Guide to the Key Environmental Literature of the Year. University Publications of America. • Annual. $495.00. A yearly cumulation of *Environment Abstracts.*

Pollution Abstracts. Cambridge Information Group. • Monthly. $1,390.00 per year. Includes print and online editions; with index, $1,515.00 per year.

CD-ROM DATABASES

Environment Abstracts on CD-ROM. University Publications of America. • Quarterly. $1,295.00 per year. Contains the following CD-ROM databases: *Environment Abstracts, Energy Abstracts,* and *Acid Rain Abstracts.* Length of coverage varies.

ONLINE DATABASES

CA Search. American Chemical Society Chemical Abstracts Service. • Guide to chemical literature, 1967 to present. Inquire as to online cost and availability.

Toxline. National Library of Medicine. • Weekly. Abstracting service covering human and animal toxicity studies, 1965 to present (older studies available in *Toxback* file). Weekly updates. Inquire as to online cost and availability.

OTHER SOURCES

Asbestos Litigation Reporter: The National Journal of Record of Asbestos Litigation. Andrews Publications. • Semimonthly. $995.00 per year. Provides reports on legal cases involving asbestos as a health hazard.

PRICE SOURCES

Chemical & Engineering News. American Chemical Society. • Weekly Annual. $265 Nonmembers print, North America. Magazine on chemical and engineering news.

ASIAN MARKETS

ABSTRACTS AND INDEXES

F & S Index: International. Cengage Learning Inc. • $2,659 Individuals. Monthly. $2,532.00 per year, including quarterly and annual cumulations. Provides annotated citations to marketing, business, financial, and industrial literature. Coverage of international business activity includes trade journals, financial magazines, business newspapers, and special reports. Areas included are Asia, Latin America, Africa, the Middle East, Oceania, and Canada.

PAIS International. ProQuest L.L.C. • Monthly. $850.00 per year; cumulations three times a year. Provides topical citations to the worldwide literature of public affairs, economics, demographics, sociology, and trade. Text in English; indexed materials in English, French, German, Italian, Portuguese and Spanish.

ALMANACS AND YEARBOOKS

People's Republic of China Year Book. Current Publications Ltd. • Annual. $98.00. Serves as the official yearbook of the People's Republic of China. Covers developments in various aspects of life in China, including the economy, industry, transportation, telecommunications, agriculture, technology, demographics, the legal system, health, and foreign relations. Includes many statistical tables and photographs. Text in Chinese.

CD-ROM DATABASES

Asia Pacific Kompass on Disc. Kompass USA, Inc. • Annual. CD-ROM provides information on more than 200,000 companies in Australia, China, Hong Kong, India, Korea, Malaysia, New Zealand, Philippines, Singapore, Thailand, and Taiwan. Classification system covers approximately 50,000 products and services.

Kompass CD-ROM Editions. Kompass USA, Inc. • Semiannual or annual. Prices vary. CD-ROM versions of Kompass international trade directories are available for each of 36 major countries and nine world regions. Searching is provided for 50,000 product/service items and for many company details.

PAIS International. ProQuest L.L.C. • Monthly. $1,995.00 per year. Contains over 650,000 citations to the literature of contemporary social, political, and economic issues.

DIRECTORIES

Asia Pacific Autos Directory. Business Monitor International Ltd. • $975 Individuals CD. Covers: 1,612 top autos executives on 519 leading automotive companies from China, Hong Kong, India, Indonesia, Malaysia, Pakistan, Philippines, Singapore, Taiwan, Thailand, and Vietnam. Entries include: Parent company head offices; full company name and address; telephone, fax, email, and website address; senior contact personnel; full description of company activity; company profile; nationality; and ownership status and parentage.

Asia Pacific Food and Drink Directory. Business Monitor International Ltd. • $895 Individuals CD. Covers: 2,022 top food and drink executives on 688 leading food and drink companies from Asia Pacific. Entries include: Company name and address; phone, fax, email and website address; senior contact personnel; full description of company activity; local company profile; nationality; and ownership status and parentage.

Asia Pacific Oil and Gas Directory. Business Monitor International Ltd. • $895 Individuals. Covers: 1,329 top oil and gas executives on 445 leading oil and gas companies from Asia Pacific. Entries include: Company name and address; phone, fax, email and website address; senior contact personnel; full description of company activity; local company profile; nationality; and ownership status and parentage.

Asia Pacific Pharmaceuticals and Healthcare Directory. Business Monitor International Ltd. • $895 Individuals. Covers: 3,353 top pharmaceutical executives at 1,120 leading pharmaceutical companies from China, Hong Kong, India, Indonesia, Malaysia, the Philippines, Singapore, South Korea, Taiwan, Thailand and Vietnam. Entries include: Company name and address; phone, fax, email and website address; senior contact personnel; full description of company activity; local company profile; nationality; and ownership status and parentage.

Asia Pacific Telecommunications Directory. Business Monitor International Ltd. • $895 Individuals. Covers: 2,438 top telecommunications executives at 893 leading telecommunications companies from Asia Pacific. Entries include: company name and address; phone, fax, email and website address; senior contact personnel; full description of company activity; local company profile; nationality; and ownership status and parentage.

Asian Business League of San Francisco--Membership Directory. Asian Business League of San Francisco. • Includes contact information of Asian-American members.

Asia's 7,500 Largest Companies. GAP Books. • Annual. $180. Covers: top 7,500 companies of Hong Kong, Indonesia, Japan, Korea, Malaysia, the Philippines, Singapore, Taiwan, Thailand, and China. Entries include: Company name, address, line of business, International SIC numbers, financial data including assets, turnover, and capital.

Blue Book of the East--Asia, Africa, Middle East and Far East Directory. Indian Export Trade Journal. • Biennial. $750. Covers: Trade and industry in Asia, Africa, the Middle East and Far East.

Directory for Setting Up Enterprises in Japan. • Covers: Approximately 700 companies in Japan that offer market research, direct investment planning, and incorporation and other professional services. Entries include: Name, address, phone, fax, profile, services offered, and contact persons/divisions.

Directory of Asian Importers of Fodder and Animal Foodstuffs. EXIM Infotek Private Ltd. • $450 Individuals. Covers: 210 Asian importers of alfalfa, alfalfa hay cubes, animal and foodstuff aditives, animal feeds, feed additives, animal food, cottonseed meal, feeder calves, fodder, cereals, and livestock breeding supplies, livestock products, and whey. Entries include: Company name, postal address, telephone, fax, e-mail, website, contact person, designation, and product details.

Directory of Asian Importers of Photographic Equipment and Supplies. EXIM Infotek Private Ltd. • $500 Individuals. Covers: 170 Asian importers of cameras, lens and accessories, photographic chemicals, motion picture and theater equipment, colored film, black and white film, digital camera, plate and photographic papers, graphic films, microfilm and blueprint equipment, motion picture films, photo film, photo finishing equipment, photo finishing paper and chemicals, photographic equipment, photographic goods, photographic materials, photographic paper, and tripod. Entries include: Company name, postal address, telephone, fax, e-mail, website, contact person, designation, and product details.

Directory of Asian Importers of Wax & Wax Products. EXIM Infotek Private Ltd. • Covers: 90 Asian importers of micro waxes, normal paraffin, paraffin waxes, polishes and creams, and slack waxes. Entries include: Company name, postal address, telephone, fax, e-mail, website, contact person, designation, and product details.

Doing Business in Today's Hong Kong. American Chamber of Commerce in Hong Kong. • Publication includes: In an appendix lists of business organizations in Hong Kong, including quality and standards organizations, government agencies, chambers of commerce, and industry-specific associations. Entries include: Organization name, address, phone, fax, telex. Principal content of publication is information on investment, business, sales and manufacturing trade, real estate, and the electronics industry in Hong Kong.

Hong Kong Classified Business Telephone Directory. Hong Kong Telephone Company Ltd. • Covers: Company listings for Hong Kong businesses.

Hoover's Handbook of World Business. Dun & Bradstreet Inc. Hoover's Inc. • Annual. $225 Individuals Hardcover. Covers: Hundreds of companies headquartered outside the U.S., including many with substantial activity in the U.S.; global enterprises, businesses that dominate their respective industries, and representative companies from all major industries. Entries include: Company name, overview, history, exchange and stock symbols, fiscal year-end date, names and titles of key personnel, name of auditors, number of employees, headquarters address, phone, fax, description of where the company does business, specific products/services/brand names produced, key competitors, 10 years of key financial data.

International Media Guide: Business-Professional: Asia/Pacific, Middle East, Africa. Kantar Media SRDS. • $553 Individuals online; 1 year. Provides information on 3,800 trade publications "from Africa to the Pacific Rim," including advertising rates and circulation data.

Japan Company Handbook. Toyo Keizai Inc. • Quarterly. $148 per issue; airmail postpaid. Covers: In two sections: over 3,700 Japanese corporations listed on the 'First Section' of Tokyo, Osaka, and Nagoya stock exchanges, listed in one volume; about 900 firms, smaller in capital but 'considered promising' and listed on the 'Second Section,' are given in a separate volume titled 'Japan Company Handbook--Second Section'; 800 over-the counter companies; and nearly 80 local market companies. Entries include: Company name, address, phone, fax, telex, description, outlook, year established, fiscal year, overseas offices, president, references, capital, other financial data, stock exchanges on which listed, underwriters, number of employees, names of major stockholders and percentage of Japanese and foreign ownership, principal products, and export ratio.

Orient Trade Directory. Selective Books International. • $19.95 Individuals. Covers: Suppliers of over 4,000 products in Japan, Korea, Malaysia, China, India, Thailand, Indonesia and Singapore. Entries include: Photos, names, addresses, phones and fax.

GENERAL WORKS

Economic and Social Survey of Asia and the Pacific. United Nations Publications. • Annual. $85 print. Emphasis is on trends in economic policy and economic development strategies.

INTERNET DATABASES

Trade Show Center. Global Sources/Trade Media Holdings Ltd. Phone: (656)574-2800; Email: service@globalsources.com • URL: http://www.globalsources.com/TRADESHW/TRDSHFRM.HTM • Free Web site provides current, detailed information on more than 1,000 major trade shows worldwide, including events in the U. S., but with an emphasis on "Asia and Greater China." Searching is offered by product, supplier, country, and month of year. Includes links to "Trade Information.".

OTHER SOURCES

Japanese Company Factfinder: Teikoku Databank. Teikoku Databank America, Inc. • Monthly. $60 Individuals per connect hour + US$ 5.60/record. CD-ROM provides detailed financial and descriptive information on more than 186,000 Japanese companies doing business overseas.

PERIODICALS AND NEWSLETTERS

Business Week China. Ministry of Foreign Economic Relations and Trade, Institute of International Trade. McGraw Hill Financial Inc. • Bimonthly. Price on application. Edited for business and government officials in the People's Republic of China. Selected Chinese translation of *Business Week.*

Business Week International: The World's Only International Newsweekly of Business. McGraw Hill Financial Inc. • Weekly. $95.00 per year.

China Business Review. United States-China Business Council. • Bimonthly. $99 per year. Covers trends and issues affecting U. S. investment and trade with China and Hong Kong.

Emerging Markets Quarterly. Institutional Investor Inc. Journals Group. • Quarterly. Price on application. Newsletter on financial markets in developing areas, such as Africa, Latin America, Southeast Asia, and Eastern Europe. Topics include institutional investment opportunities and regulatory matters. Formerly *Emerging Markets Weekly.*

Far Eastern Economic Review. Dow Jones International Marketing Service. • Weekly. $205.00 per year (air mail). Published in Hong Kong by Review Publishing Co., a Dow Jones subsidiary (GPO Box 160, Hong Kong). Covers Asian business, economics, politics, and international relations. Includes reports on individual countries and companies, business trends, and stock price quotations.

Hong Kong Week. Dow Jones & Co., Inc. • Weekly. $260.00 per year (air mail). A guide to investing in Hong Kong and China. Provides stock prices, market analysis, and commentary. Edited and published in Hong Kong by the *Asian Wall Street Journal.*

Institutional Investor International Edition: The Magazine for International Finance and Investment. Institutional Investor Inc. Journals Group. • Monthly. $475.00 per year. Covers the international aspects of professional investing and finance. Emphasis is on Europe, the Far East, and Latin America.

International Economic Scoreboard. The Conference Board. • Description: Provides current data on the business outlook in 11 major industrial countries: Australia, Canada, France, West Germany, Italy, Japan, Korea, New Zealand, Taiwan, the United Kingdom, and the U.S. **Remarks:** A source for additional information on this indicator system and its uses is available at the Center for International Business Cycle Research, Columbia University Business School.

The Japan Times. • Weekly. $120.00 per year. Provides news and commentary on Japan's economy, trade policies, and Japanese life in general. Regular features include "Business Briefs," "Market Reports," "Lifestyle," and "Issue Analysis." Supplement available *The Japan Times Weekly.* Text in English.

Journal of Asia-Pacific Business. The Haworth Press Inc. • Quarterly. $225.00 per year. Includes print and online editions. An academic and practical journal concerned with marketing, finance, and other aspects of doing business in Asia.

Journal of Asian Business. Southeast Asia Business Program. University of Michigan. • 3/year. An international academic journal covering business in all parts of Asia.

Market: Asia Pacific. Edimax. • Description: Concerned with demographics, lifestyles, and business opportunities in the Asia Pacific region. Profiles a particular city or country in each issue, providing consumer market trends, surveys results, and articles on direct marketing and marketing management.

The Nikkei Weekly: Japan's Leading Business Newspaper. Nikkei America, Inc. • Weekly. $129 Individuals. A newspaper in English "dedicated to all aspects of Japanese business and its influence on people, markets and political trends around the world." Includes English versions of articles appearing in leading Japanese business newspapers, such as *Nihon Keizai Shimbun, Nikkei Marketing Journal* and *Nikkei Financial Daily.*

RESEARCH CENTERS AND INSTITUTES

Brookings Institution - Center for Northeast Asian Policy Studies. 1775 Massachusetts Ave. NW, Washington, DC 20036. Phone: (202)797-6055; Fax: (202)797-2485; Email: communications@brookings.edu • URL: http://www.brookings.edu/cnaps.aspx • Security and architecture of Northeast Asia; U.S.-China strategic relations; the dynamics of relations across the Taiwan Strait; integrating China into the world economy and the international political system; Japan's structural rigidities; and U.S. foreign policy on the Korean peninsula.

California State Polytechnic University, Pomona - Industrial Research Institute for Pacific Nations. School of Business Administration, 3801 W Temple Ave., Pomona, CA 91768. Phone: (909)869-2350 or (909)869-2399; Fax: (909)869-6799; Email: hkjin@csupomona.edu • URL: http://www.csupomona.edu • Conducts research on the Pacific nations marketplace.

Columbia University - Columbia Business School - Center on Japanese Economy and Business. Uris Hall, Rm. 2M9, 3022 Broadway, New York, NY 10027. Phone: (212)854-3976; Fax: (212)678-6958; Email: dew35@columbia.edu • URL: http://www8.gsb.columbia.edu/cjeb • Research areas include Pacific Basin trade policy.

Republic of Korea Ministry of Health and Welfare - Korea Institute for Health and Social Affairs. Jinhungro 235, Bulgwang-dong, Eunpyeonggu, Seoul 122-705, South Korea. Phone: 82 2 3808000; Fax: 82 2 3522181; Email: master@kihasa.re.kr • URL: http://www.kihasa.re.kr/html/jsp/english/main.jsp • National health, social welfare, and population. Also provides information and guidelines for the formulation of government policy in these fields. Health Policy, Social Insurance, Social Welfare, Population and Family, and Survey and Statistics. Also provides information and guidelines for the formulation of government policy in these fields.

STATISTICS SOURCES

Statistical Indicators for Asia and the Pacific. United Nations Publications. • Quarterly. Quarterly. $80.00 per year. Provides data on economic and demographic trends in the region. Text in English.

Statistical Yearbook for Asia and the Pacific. United Nations Publications. • Annual. $90.00. Includes 56 countries of the region. Contains data on national accounts, trade, industry, banking, wages, consumption, population, and other economic and demographic subjects. Text in English and French.

TRADE/PROFESSIONAL ASSOCIATIONS

American Indonesian Chamber of Commerce. 317 Madison Ave., Ste. 1619, New York, NY 10017. Phone: (212)687-4505; Fax: (212)867-5844; Email: wayne@aiccusa.org • URL: http://www.aiccusa.org • Holds briefings on new trade policies in Indonesia and offers orientation workshops to company personnel traveling in Indonesia.

American-Kuwaiti Alliance. 2550 M St. NW, Washington, DC 20037. Phone: (202)429-4999; Email: info@americankuwaitialliance.org • URL: http://ww.american-kuwaitialliance.com • Aims to expand and deepen the political, commercial and cultural ties between the U.S. and Kuwait. Fosters the existing U.S.-Kuwaiti relations by facilitating expanded political relationships and policies. Promotes increased trade and commerce, and creates opportunities for American and Kuwaiti citizens to exchange cultural experiences.

Asia Pacific Network for Global Change Research. East Bldg., 4th Fl., 1-5-2 Wakinohama Kaigan Dori, Chuo-ku, Kobe, Hyogo 651 0073, Japan. Phone: 81 78 2308017; Fax: 81 78 2308018; Email: info@apn-gcr.org • URL: http://www.apn-gcr.org • Promotes, encourages and supports research activities on long-term global changes in climate, ocean and terrestrial systems, and on related physical, chemical, biological and socio-economic processes. Fosters global environmental change research in the Asia-Pacific region; increases developing country participation in research; strengthens interactions between the science community and policy makers. Cooperates closely with various scientific programmers and other networks.

Asian Clearing Union. 47, 7th Negarestan Alley, Pasdaran Ave., Tehran, Iran. Phone: 98 21 2842076 or 98 21 2854509; Fax: 98 21 2847677; Email: acusecret@cbi.ir • URL: http://www.asianclearingunion.org • Central banks, monetary authorities, and treasuries of Asian countries. Works to economize on the use of exchange reserves; promotes shifting of national banking services to domestic banks; seeks to enhance economic, financial, and commercial cooperation among Asian nations. Provides short-term credit facilities.

Asian Financial Society. 32 Broadway, Ste. 1701, New York, NY 10004-1610. Phone: (646)580-5066; Email: event@afstoday.org • URL: http://afstoday.org • Fosters business relationships and opportunities for growth for professionals in the Asian financial community.

Fiji Commerce and Employers Federation. PO Box 575, Suva, Fiji. Phone: 679 679 3313188; Fax: 679 679 3302183; Email: employer@fcef.com.fj • URL: http://www.fcef.com.fj • Employers. Seeks to create and maintain a domestic political and social climate conducive to business. Represents members' interests before government agencies, labor and industrial organizations, and the public; gathers and disseminates information.

Korea Employers Federation. KEF Bldg., 276-1 Daehung-dong Mapo-ku, Seoul 121-726, South Korea. Phone: 82 2 32707310 or 82 2 32707324; Fax: 82 2 32707431 • URL: http://eng.kef.or.kr • Represents bus owners and operators. Seeks to establish and maintain a domestic political, labor, and social climate conducive to business. Represents members' interests; conducts lobbying activities; gathers and disseminates economic information.

Malaysian Employers' Federation. PO Box 11026, 50732 Kuala Lumpur, Malaysia. Phone: 60 3 79557778; Fax: 60 3 79556808; Email: mef-hq@mef.org.my • URL: http://www.mef.org.my/public/default.aspx • Employers (3470) and employers' associations (10). Seeks to ensure a domestic political, business, and labor climate conducive to economic growth. Works to safeguard the rights and interests of Malaysian employers. Represents members in negotiations with labor organizations, at the Industrial Court, Labour Court, and conciliation proceedings; provides consultancy and advisory services to members; gathers and disseminates information; conducts lobbying activities. Sponsors human resources and industrial relations training programs; conducts surveys on salaries and compensation packages.

United States-China Chamber of Commerce. 55 W Monroe St., Ste. 630, Chicago, IL 60603. Phone:

(312)368-9911; Fax: (312)368-9922; Email: info@usccc.org • URL: http://www.usccc.org • Members are individuals interested in improving trade between the U. S. and the People's Republic of China.

ASPHALT INDUSTRY

BIBLIOGRAPHIES

Catalog of Asphalt Institute Publications. Asphalt Institute. • Annual. Free.

DIRECTORIES

Asphalt Emulsion Manufacturers Association--Membership Directory. Asphalt Emulsion Manufacturers Association. • Biennial. Covers: About 100 member manufacturers and their plants and suppliers to the industry; international coverage. Entries include: Company name, address, phone, names and titles of representatives. Plant listings include address and phone.

Asphalt Paving Technologists. Association of Asphalt Paving Technologists. • Annual. $50 Members. Covers: About 850 member engineers and chemists engaged in paving or related fields, such as paving materials and construction equipment; international coverage. Entries include: Name, affiliation, address, phone.

Asphalt Recycling & Reclaiming Association--Membership Directory. Asphalt Recycling and Reclaiming Association. • Annual. Covers: About 200 contractors, manufacturers, consulting engineers, and public works officials involved in asphalt reclaiming and recycling. Entries include: Name of company, address, phone; key personnel; type of organization or company; product line, or contact person.

PERIODICALS AND NEWSLETTERS

Asphalt Pavement. National Asphalt Pavement Association. • Bimonthly. Free.

Oil Daily: Daily Newspaper of the Petroleum Industry. Energy Intelligence Group. • Daily. Email, $1,595.00 per year; fax, $2,395.00 per year, online, $1,495.00 per year. Newspaper for the petroleum industry.

PRICE SOURCES

PPI Detailed Report. Periodical covering business. Bureau of Labor Statistics, U.S. Department of Labor. U. S. Government Printing Office. • Monthly. $55 Individuals.

RESEARCH CENTERS AND INSTITUTES

Texas Transportation Institute, Systems Planning - Texas A & M University. 3135 TAMU, College Station, TX 77843-3135. Phone: (979)845-6002 or (979)845-9356; Fax: (979)945-6008; Email: k-turnbull@tamu.edu • URL: http://www.tti.tamu.edu.

TRADE/PROFESSIONAL ASSOCIATIONS

Asphalt Emulsion Manufacturers Association. No. 3 Church Cir., Annapolis, MD 21401. Phone: (410)267-0023; Fax: (410)267-7546 • URL: http://www.aema.org • Seeks to foster advancement and improvement of the asphalt emulsion industry.

Asphalt Institute. 2696 Research Park Dr., Lexington, KY 40511-8480. Phone: (859)288-4960; Fax: (859)288-4999; Email: info@asphaltinstitute.org • URL: http://www.asphaltinstitute.org • Composed of petroleum asphalt/bitumen producers, manufacturers and affiliated businesses. Promotes the use, benefits, and quality performance of petroleum asphalt through environmental marketing, research, engineering, and technical development, and through the resolution of issues affecting the industry.

Association of Asphalt Paving Technologists. 6776 Lake Dr., Ste. 215, Lino Lakes, MN 55014-1191. Phone: (651)293-9188; Fax: (651)293-9193; Email: aaptinfo@gmail.com • URL: http://www.asphalttechnology.org • Represents engineers and chemists engaged in asphalt paving or related fields such as materials and construction equipment.

National Asphalt Pavement Association. 5100 Forbes Blvd., Lanham, MD 20706. Phone: 888-468-6499 or (301)731-4748; Fax: (301)731-4621; Email: napa@hotmix.org • URL: http://www.hotmix.org • Manufacturers and producers of scientifically proportioned Hot Mix Asphalt for use in all paving, including highways, airfields, and environmental usages. Membership includes hot mix producers, paving contractors, equipment manufacturers, engineering consultants, and others. Supports research and publishes information on: producing, stockpiling, and feeding of the aggregate to the manufacturing facility; drying; methods of screening, storing, and proportioning in the manufacturing facility; production of the hot mix asphalt; transporting mix to paver; lay down procedure and rolling; general workmanship; and related construction practices and materials. Commits to product quality, environmental control, safety and health, and energy conservation. Conducts training programs on a variety of technical and managerial topics for industry personnel. Maintains speakers' bureau and Hot Mix Asphalt Hall of Fame.

ASSOCIATIONS

See also CLUBS; WOMEN'S CLUBS

BIOGRAPHICAL SOURCES

Who's Who in Association Management. ASAE: The Center for Association Leadership. • Annual. $160. Lists paid executives who are members of the association and suppliers of products and services to the association.

DIRECTORIES

Asian Directory of Trade & Business Associations. Asia Pacific Infoserv. • $245 Individuals book only. Covers: Trade associations and service sectors in every Asia Pacific country. Entries include: Association name, address, telephone number, fax number, e-mail, year of establishment, President and General Secretary, number of members, memberships of international associations, and field of activity.

Association for University Business and Economic Research--Membership Directory. Association for University Business and Economic Research. • Annual. $10. Covers: member institutions in the United States and abroad with centers, bureaus, departments, etc., concerned with business and economic research. Entries include: Name of bureau, center, etc., sponsoring institution name, address, phone, names and titles of director and staff, publications and frequency.

Building & Loan Associations Directory. InfoGroup Inc. • Annual. Number of listings: 11,966. Entries include: Name, address, phone, size of advertisement, name of owner or manager, number of employees, year first in "Yellow Pages." Compiled from telephone company "Yellow Pages," nationwide.

Directory of Trade and Professional Associations in the European Union - The Blue Book. Euroconfidentiel S. A. • Annual. $160.00. Includes more than 9,000 EU-related associations.

Encyclopedia of Associations: International Organizations. Cengage Learning Inc. • Annual. $1,144 Individuals. 2010. eBook. Covers multinational and national membership organizations worldwide. Contact for pricing.

Encyclopedia of Associations: National Organizations of the U.S. Cengage Learning Inc. • Annual. $778 Individuals. Provides detailed information on nonprofit American membership organizations of national scope. eBook also available.

Encyclopedia of Associations: Regional, State and Local Organizations. Cengage Learning Inc. • 2013. $278. 5 volumes. Covers more than 100,000 U.S. nonprofit membership organizations with interstate, state, intrastate, city or local scope and interest, including trade and professional associations, social welfare and public affairs organizations and religious, sports, and hobby groups with voluntary members.eBook also available.

Isle of Man: General Information Factfile. Commercial Development Div. The Treasury Isle of Man Government. • Annual. Covers: financial institutions, insurance companies, real estate agencies, legal and accounting firms, shipowners, manufacturer, and other service trades on the Isle of Man; government service agencies. Database includes: Summaries of economic activity and opportunity; government policies regarding trade and industry; information on education and social issues. Entries include: Company or agency name, address, phone; shipowners and stockbrokers also include telex and fax numbers; financial institutions and real estate agencies include names of contact or other key personnel; banks and insurance companies include branch office and subsidiary names, addresses, and phone numbers.

Management Professionals Association--Directory of MPA Members. Management Professionals Association. • Annual. Covers: 26,000 members worldwide. Entries include: Company name, member name and title, address, phone, biographical information.

National Association for Drama Therapy--Membership List. North American Drama Therapy Association. • Annual. Covers: About 400 registered drama therapists and NADT members. Entries include: Name, address, membership category.

National Trade and Professional Associations Directory. Columbia Books and Information Services. • Annual. $299. Provides key facts on approximately 7,800 trade associations, labor and professional organizations.

Washington: A Comprehensive Directory of the Key Institutions and Leaders in th e National Capitol Area. Columbia Books Inc. • Annual. $149.00. Provides information on about 5,000 Washington, DC key businesses, government offices, non-profit organizations, and cultural institutions, with the names of about 25,000 principal executives. Includes Washington media, law offices, foundations, labor unions, international organizations, clubs, etc.

Washington Information Directory. CQ Press. • Annual. $175 Individuals print cloth, standing order. Covers: 10,000 governmental agencies, congressional committees, and non-governmental associations considered competent sources of specialized information. Entries include: Name of agency, committee, or association; address, phone, fax, and Internet; annotation concerning function or activities of the office; and name of contact.

World Directory of Trade and Business Association. Euromonitor Publications Ltd. • $750 Individuals. Covers: publication and membership details of each association. Entries include: full contact details of trade and business associations world wide.

HANDBOOKS AND MANUALS

Professional Corporations and Associations. Berrien C. Eaton. Matthew Bender and Company Inc. • Semiannual. $3,211 ebook. Detailed information on forming, operating and changing a professional corporation or association.

ONLINE DATABASES

Industry Insider. Thomson Financial. • Contains full-text online industry research reports from more than 200 leading trade associations, covering 50 specific industries. Reports include extensive

For publishers' addresses, refer to SOURCES CITED section at the back of the book.

statistics and market research data. Inquire as to online cost and availability.

OTHER SOURCES

Company of Military Historians. • Represents professional society of military historians, museologists, artists, writers, journalists, military personnel, teachers, researchers, and other individuals interested in the history of American military units, organization, tactics, uniforms, arms, and equipment. Maintains museum.

Orders and Medals Society of America. • Persons, including 300 members outside the U.S., interested in collecting and studying insignias of the orders of knighthood and merit, the decorations of valor and honor, the medals of distinction and service, and allied material and historical data.

PERIODICALS AND NEWSLETTERS

Nonprofit Issues. Donald W. Kramer. • Description: Presents legal information for nonprofit executives and their professional advisors.

RESEARCH CENTERS AND INSTITUTES

University of Bristol - Centre for Market and Public Organisation. 2 Priory Rd., Bristol BS8 1TX, United Kingdom. Phone: 44 117 3310799; Fax: 44 117 3310705; Email: simon.burgess@bristol.ac.uk • URL: http://www.bristol.ac.uk/cmpo • Reform of activities on the boundaries of the state, regulation, privatization, and incentives in the public sector.

TRADE/PROFESSIONAL ASSOCIATIONS

Advertising Media Credit Executives Association. 24600 Detroit Rd., Ste. 100, Bay Village, OH 44140-0036. Email: amcea@tx.rr.com • URL: http://www.amcea.org • Credit executives for advertising media such as newspapers, magazines, radio, and television. Provides information for exchange of ideas on credit management methods and procedures; encourages study in advanced educational courses in fundamentals, such as business law, finance, banking, accounting, and economics.

Afghan Peace and Democracy Act. 220 St. 9, District 4, Taimani, Kabul, Afghanistan. Email: info@afghanact.org • URL: http://www.alternatives.ca/en/about-us • Enhances the role of civil society organizations. Helps the NGOs in advocating peace and democracy in Afghanistan. Provides direct support and collaboration to Afghan NGOs and civil societies.

Afghanistan Microfinance Association. House No 547 St. 3, Taimani Project, District 4, Kabul, Afghanistan. Phone: 93 799 308876; Email: info@ama.org.af • URL: http://www.ama.org.af • Promotes the microfinance sector of Afghanistan. Seeks to enhance the security measures between microfinance institutions (MFIs) and increase government support in terms of securing microfinance operations. Develops and delivers a number of training modules in local languages to ensure the best use of the training programs by employees of the microfinance sector.

African Private Equity and Venture Capital Association. The Banking Hall, Cropthorne Ct., 26 Maide Vale, London, United Kingdom. Phone: 44 20 3632 0408; Email: avca@avca-africa.org • URL: http://www.avcanet.com • Advances, develops and stimulates private equity and venture capital in Africa. Promotes high ethical standards of business conduct and professional competence in the private equity and venture capital industries.

Agribusiness Association of Australia. 1 Torrdale Rd., Farrell Flat, SA 5416, Australia. Fax: 61 8 81278052; Email: agri@agribusiness.asn.au • URL: http://www.agribusiness.asn.au • Works to raise knowledge on issues affecting the development of an efficient and competitive agri-food value chain.

Agricultural Economics Association of South Africa. Private Bag x935, Pretoria 0001, South Africa. Phone: 27 12 3411115 • URL: http://www.aeasa.org.za • Represents the interests of agricultural economists. Promotes training, research and interest in agricultural economics. Fosters the applications of scientific principles of agricultural economics in solving agricultural and rural problems of Southern Africa.

American Accounts Payable Association. 660 N Main Ave., Ste. 200, San Antonio, TX 78205-1217. Phone: (210)630-4373; Fax: (210)630-4410; Email: membership@americanap.org • URL: http://www.americanap.org • Seeks to uphold the standards of practice in the accounts payable profession. Fosters the professional development of members. Offers comprehensive educational programs for accounts payable professionals.

American Association of Individual Investors. 625 N Michigan Ave., Chicago, IL 60611. Phone: 800-428-2244 or (312)280-0170; Fax: (312)280-9883 or (312)280-1625; Email: members@aaii.com • URL: http://www.aaii.com • Individuals who make their own investment decisions. Assists individuals in becoming effective managers of their own assets through educational programs and research. Provides programs to help individuals develop an investment philosophy and decision-making process based on their objectives, capabilities and attitudes. Offers home-study curriculum on investment topics and a videotape course on investing fundamentals and mutual funds.

American Association of Inside Sales Professionals. 14530 Florissant Path, Apple Valley, MN 55124. Phone: 800-604-7085; Email: info@aa-isp.org • URL: http://www.aa-isp.org • Serves as an authoritative resource to leaders and individual sales representatives. Aims to perfect the skills of inside sale professionals. Conducts leadership and career development trainings, member forums and networking, conferences, education and accreditation programs that will help advance the inside sales profession.

American Association of Professional Technical Analysts. 10621 Big Canoe, 5516 Red Fox Dr., Big Canoe, GA 30143. Phone: 800-222-7636; Email: membership@aapta.com • URL: http://www.aapta.com • Aims to promote the use of technical analysis. Provides a forum for members to share ideas, information, research and analytical techniques. Encourages the highest professional ethics and competence among technical analysts.

American Fair Credit Council. 100 W Cypress Creek Rd., Ste. 700, Fort Lauderdale, FL 33309. Phone: 888-657-8272; Fax: (954)343-6960; Email: info@americanfaircreditcouncil.org • URL: http://www.americanfaircreditcouncil.org • Promotes good practice in the debt settlement industry. Protects the interests of consumer debtors. Advances the application of consumer protection, principals in marketing, sales, and fulfillment of debt settlement services.

American Home Business Association. 53 W 9000 S, Sandy, UT 84070. Phone: 866-396-7773 or (801)273-2350; Fax: (866)396-7773 or (801)273-2399; Email: info@homebusinessworks.com • URL: http://www.homebusinessworks.com • Offers benefits and services dedicated to supporting the needs of home business, small business and entrepreneurs. Benefits include health-auto-home insurance, legal, low long distance and 800 numbers, business line of credit, merchant accounts, tax programs, office supply and travel discounts and more. Seeks to provide members access to the best traditional benefits and timely information that is critical to conduct a successful home, small or Internet business.

American Legal Finance Association. 228 Park Ave. S, No. 23315, New York, NY 10003. Phone: (212)837-2911 • URL: http://www.americanlegalfin.com • Develops an awareness of the legal funding industry. Works to establish legal and regulatory frameworks to meet the needs and concerns of all parties interested in legal funding. Establishes and maintains ethical standards and fair business practices within the legal funding industry.

American Management Association. 1601 Broadway, New York, NY 10019-7420. Phone: 877-566-9441 or (212)586-8100 or (518)891-5510; Fax: (212)903-8168 or (518)891-0368; Email: customerservice@amanet.org • URL: http://www.amanet.org • Provides educational forums worldwide where members and their colleagues learn superior, practical business skills and explore best practices of world-class organizations through interaction with each other and expert faculty practitioners. Maintains a publishing program providing tools individuals use to extend learning beyond the classroom in a process of life-long professional growth and development through education.

ASAE: The Center for Association Leadership. 1575 I St. NW, Washington, DC 20005-1103. Phone: 888-950-ASAE or (202)371-0940; Fax: (202)371-8315; Email: mbrshpsec@asaenet.org • URL: http://www.asaecenter.org • Professional society of paid executives of international, national, state, and local trade, professional, and philanthropic associations. Seeks to educate association executives on effective management, including: the proper objectives, functions, and activities of associations; the basic principles of association management; the legal aspects of association activity; policies relating to association management; efficient methods, procedures, and techniques of association management; the responsibilities and professional standards of association executives. Maintains information resource center. Conducts resume, guidance, and consultation services; compiles statistics in the form of reports, surveys, and studies; carries out research and education.

Asia Pacific Loan Market Association. Jardine House, 32nd Fl., One Connaught Pl., Central, Hong Kong, Hong Kong, China. Phone: 852 28263500 • URL: http://www.aplma.com • Promotes growth and liquidity in the primary and secondary loan markets. Facilitates the standardization of primary and secondary loan documentation. Develops standard trading, settlement and valuation procedures. Organizes educational and social functions for syndicated loan professionals. Acts as a liaison between major loan market players and regional regulators.

Associacao Brasileira de Private Equity and Venture Capital. Avenida Rio Branco, 123, Rm. 1505, 20040-005 Rio de Janeiro, RJ, Brazil. Phone: 55 21 39702432 • URL: http://www.abvcap.com.br • Promotes and develops the private equity and venture capital industry in Brazil. Represents the interests of the Brazilian private equity and venture capital community.

Association des Femmes Chefs d'Entreprises du Cote d'Ivoire. BP 8232, Abidjan 08, Côte d'Ivoire. Phone: 225 3 327571; Email: fcem_ci@yahoo.fr • URL: http://www.fcem.org/en/pays-membres.html • Promotes women's entrepreneurial initiatives. Reinforces national associations of women business entrepreneurial potentials. Lobbies before the public and private institutions, policy makers and governments on issues that impede women's entrepreneurial potentials. Facilitates the development of business, partnership and trade. Fosters professional growth and business skills perfection. Encourages women to create enterprises.

Association des Femmes Chefs d'Entreprises du Maroc. Residence El Amri, Rue du 6 octubre, Quartie Racine, Casablanca, Morocco. Phone: 212 22 397593; Fax: 212 22 397736; Email: afem@afem.ma • URL: http://afem.ma • Promotes women's entrepreneurial initiatives. Reinforces national associations of women business entrepreneurial potentials. Lobbies before the public and private institutions, policy makers and governments on issues that impede women's entrepreneurial potentials. Facilitates the development of business, partnership and trade. Fosters professional growth and business skills perfection. Encourages women to create enterprises.

Association des Femmes d'Affaires et Chefs d'Entreprises du Benin. BP 1226, Cotonou, Benin. Phone: 229 331617; Fax: 229 332627; Email: hotelgl@leland.bj • URL: http://fcem.org/en/pays-membres/195-pays-membres/fiche-pays-details/afrique-membres/1523-republique-de-benin-afrique-membres.html • Promotes women's entrepreneurial initiatives. Reinforces national associations of women business entrepreneurial potentials. Lobbies before the public and private institutions, policy makers and governments on issues that impede women's entrepreneurial potentials. Facilitates the development of business, partnership and trade. Fosters professional growth and business skills perfection. Encourages women to create enterprises.

Association des Femmes d'Affaires et Chefs d'Entreprises du Gabon. B.P. 6023, Libreville, Gabon. Phone: 241 6 264216; Fax: 241 723883; Email: refegcham@yahoo.fr • URL: http://www.fcem.org/en/pays-membres.html • Promotes women's entrepreneurial initiatives. Reinforces national associations of women business entrepreneurial potentials. Lobbies before the public and private institutions, policy makers and governments on issues that impede women's entrepreneurial potentials. Facilitates the development of business, partnership and trade. Fosters professional growth and business skills perfection. Encourages women to create enterprises.

Association des Femmes Entrepreneurs Chefs d'Entreprises. Ave. Le Marinel N 9-11, Commune de la Gombe, Kinshasa, Republic of the Congo. Phone: 243 998911092; Fax: 243 3225667; Email: bismura2@yahoo.fr • URL: http://www.fcem.org/en/pays-membres.html • Promotes women's entrepreneurial initiatives. Reinforces national associations of women business entrepreneurial potentials. Lobbies before the public and private institutions, policy makers and governments on issues that impede women's entrepreneurial potentials. Facilitates the development of business, partnership and trade. Fosters professional growth and business skills perfection. Encourages women to create enterprises.

Association for Better Insulation. 3906 Auburn Hills Dr., Greensboro, NC 27407. Phone: (603)768-3984; Fax: (270)721-0022; Email: service@betterinsulation.com • Informs homeowners about better insulation choices to help them make educated decisions. Promotes a green and more sustainable growth in the insulation industry. Acts as a proponent of green building products, environment responsibility and long term savings of energy and resources in the building industry.

Association for Corporate Growth - Toronto Chapter. 720 Spadina Ave., Ste. 202, Toronto, ON, Canada M5S 2T9. Phone: (416)868-1881; Fax: (416)391-3633; Email: acgtoronto@acg.org • URL: http://www.acg.org/toronto • Professionals with a leadership role in strategic corporate growth. Seeks to facilitate the professional advancement of members, and the practice of corporate growth management. Fosters communication and cooperation among members; conducts continuing professional education programs.

Association for Financial Markets in Europe. St. Michael's House, 1 George Yard, London EC3V 9DH, United Kingdom. Phone: 44 207 7439300; Fax: 44 207 7439301 • URL: http://www.afme.eu • Principal trade association in the UK for firms active in the investment banking and securities industry. Represents the interests of its members on all aspects of their business and promotes their views to the authorities in the UK, the European Union, and elsewhere.

Association for Financial Professionals. 4520 E West Hwy., Ste. 750, Bethesda, MD 20814. Phone: (301)907-2862; Fax: (301)907-2864 • URL: http://www.afponline.org • Seeks to establish a national forum for the exchange of concepts and techniques related to improving the management of treasury and the careers of professionals through research, education, publications and recognition of the treasury management profession through a certification program. Conducts educational programs. Operates career center.

Association for Project Management. Ibis House, Regent Park, Summerleys Rd., Princes Risborough HP27 9LE, United Kingdom. Email: info@apm.org.uk • URL: http://www.apm.org.uk • Strives to develop and promote the professional disciplines of project and programme management for the public benefit.

Association for Project Management Hong Kong. c/o Agee Leung, 35/F Central Plaza, 18 Harbour Rd., Wan Chai, Hong Kong, China. Phone: 852 51810371; Email: agee.leung@apm.org.uk • URL: http://www.apm.org.uk/group/apm-hong-kong-branch • Aims to establish project management as the recognized profession essential for managing beneficial change in every type of business. Provides career development to project and management professionals.

Association for the Development of International Exchange of Food and Agricultural Productions and Techniques. 41 rue de Bourgogne, F-75007 Paris, France. Phone: 33 1 44180888; Fax: 33 1 44180889; Email: adepta@adepta.com • URL: http://www.adepta.com • Individuals involved in agribusiness. Promotes partnerships and networks among skilled agribusiness professionals.

Association Mauricienne des Femmes Chefs d'Entreprise. Regency Sq., 1st Fl., 4 Conal and McIrvine St., Beau Bassin, Mauritius. Email: cheelichop@intnet.mu • URL: http://fcem.org/en/pays-membres/195-pays-membres/fiche-pays-details/afrique-membres/1517-ile-maurice-afrique-membres.html • Promotes women's entrepreneurial initiatives. Reinforces national associations of women business entrepreneurial potentials. Lobbies before the public and private institutions, policy makers and governments on issues that impede women's entrepreneurial potentials. Facilitates the development of business, partnership and trade. Fosters professional growth and business skills perfection. Encourages women to create enterprises.

Association of African American Financial Advisors. PO Box 4853, Capitol Heights, MD 20791. Phone: (240)396-2530; Fax: (888)392-5702; Email: info@aaafainc.cm • URL: http://aaafainc.com • Seeks to develop and foster professional relationships among African American professionals working in the financial advisory industry. Provides assistance and nurturing for those families that seek to improve their opportunities for participating and prospering financially in an economically progressive society. Strives to create support networks for minority financial professionals. Provides a forum for further education, training and visibility of its members.

Association of Appraiser Regulatory Officials. c/o Larry Disney, President, 135 W Irvin St., Ste. 301, Richmond, KY 40475. Phone: (605)773-4608; Fax: (605)773-5369 • URL: http://www.aaro.net • Represents real estate appraiser licensing agencies in the United States and its territories. Seeks to improve the administration and enforcement of real estate appraisal laws. Provides education, research, communication and cooperation among appraiser regulatory officials.

Association of Business Executives. 5th Fl., CI Tower, St. George Sq., New Maiden, Surrey, London KT3 4TE, United Kingdom. Phone: 44 20 83292930; Fax: 44 20 83292945; Email: info@abeuk.com • URL: http://www.abeuk.com • Student membership sitting examinations.

Association of Business Process Management Professionals. 1000 Westgate Dr., Ste. 252, Saint Paul, MN 55114. Phone: (651)288-3420; Fax: (651)290-2266; Email: president@abpmp.org • URL: http://www.abpmp.org • Fosters the advancement of business process management concepts and its practices. Seeks to develop a common body of knowledge in business process management. Provides educational and networking activities for the continuing education of its members and their professional colleagues.

Association of Business Women in Iceland. Kringlunni 7, IS-103 Reykjavik, Iceland. Email: fka@fka.is • URL: http://www.fka.is • Promotes women's entrepreneurial initiatives. Reinforces national associations of women business entrepreneurial potentials. Lobbies before the public and private institutions, policy makers and governments on issues that impede women's entrepreneurial potentials. Facilitates the development of business, partnership and trade. Fosters professional growth and business skills perfection. Encourages women to create enterprises.

Association of Business Women of Serbia. Volgina 15, 11060 Belgrade, Serbia. Phone: 38 11 2776801; Fax: 38 11 2776801; Email: upz.office@pupin.rs • URL: http://www.poslovnezene.org.rs/en • Promotes women's genuine business interests. Establishes links with similar associations in Europe and worldwide. Trains women in starting and running a business.

Association of Certified Adizes Practitioners International. 1212 Mark Ave., Carpinteria, CA 93013. Phone: (805)565-2901; Fax: (805)565-0741; Email: paula@adizes.com • URL: http://www.adizes.com • Professional management consultants who are certified to practice the Adizes Method of management. (The Adizes method, devised by Dr. Ichak Adizes, is a comprehensive approach to creating and managing healthy change within a company.) Promotes organizational transformation (consulting) as a profession. Facilitates discussion of ideas and exchange of information among members. Conducts research and educational programs.

Association of Certified Treasury Managers. 52, Nagarjuna Hills, Hyderabad 500 082, Telangana, India. Phone: 91 40 23435368 or 91 40 23435374; Fax: 91 40 23352521; Email: info@actmindia.org • URL: http://www.qfinance.com/information-sources/association-of-certified-treasury-managers-india • Develops and regulates the growth of the treasury management profession. Organizes seminars, workshops, and training programs in treasury management, foreign exchange management, risk management, and allied areas. Provides placement assistance to members and students.

Association of Chinese Finance Professionals. 240 Hazelwood Ave., San Francisco, CA 94127. Email: acfp_us@yahoo.com • URL: http://www.acfp.net • Promotes cooperation between U.S. and China in the fields of commercial and investment banking, asset management, insurance, corporate finance, financial planning and financial software. Provides a forum for finance professionals to exchange ideas and discuss experiences.

Association of Corporate Treasurers. 51 Moorgate, London EC2R 6BH, United Kingdom. Phone: 44 20 7847 2540; Fax: 44 20 7374 8744; Email: enquiries@treasurers.co.uk • URL: http://www.treasurers.org • Professional body supporting those working in treasury, risk and corporate finance in the international marketplace. Promotes the study and best practice of finance and treasury management: offers education and examination, conferences, publications and training for financial professionals.

Association of Corporate Treasurers of Southern Africa. PO Box 5853, Cresta 2118, South Africa. Phone: 27 11 4821512; Fax: 27 11 4821996 • URL: http://www.actsa.org.za • Provides a forum for the promotion of the common interests of corporate treasurers in Southern Africa. Provides learning and networking opportunities for its members.

Association of Corporate Treasurers Singapore. Block 51, Telok Blangah Dr., No. 06-142, Singapore 100051, Singapore. • URL: http://www.act.org.sg • Provides a platform for the exchange of ideas and information relating to treasury. Enhances treasury management skills through training and education. Facilitates a platform for dialogue between the industry and the government. Promotes the growth of the treasury profession to help Singapore develop into a financial hub in the region.

Association of Divorce Financial Planners. 514 Fourth St., East Northport, NY 11731-2342. Phone: 888-838-7773; Email: adfp@divorceandfinance.org • URL: http://www.divorceandfinance.org • Aims to create awareness of the benefits of divorce financial planning. Provides members with continuing education. Promotes communication, networking and peer review.

Association of European Businesses. Krasnoproletarskaya ul 16, Bldg. 3, entrance 8, 4th Fl., 127473 Moscow, Russia. Phone: 7 495 2342764; Fax: 7 495 2342807; Email: info@aebrus.ru • URL: http://www.aebrus.ru • Represents and promotes the interests of European companies conducting business in the Russian Federation.

Association of Ghana Industries. Trade Fair Centre, 2nd Fl., Addison House, Accra, Ghana. Phone: 233 21 779023 or 233 21 779024; Fax: 233 21 773143 or 233 21 763383; Email: agi@agighana.org • URL: http://www.agighana.org • Voluntary business association, providing policy advocacy and advisory services, market development/market clinic, industrial sub-contracting, management training, business plan preparation, export market promotion, information gathering, analysis and dissemination, media planning and events management, and networking.

Association of Governmental Risk Pools. 9 Cornell Rd., Latham, NY 12110. Phone: (518)389-2782; Email: info@agrip.org • URL: http://www.agrip.org • Works to promote risk pooling as a practical extension of a public entity's obligation to be a good steward of public funds. Aims to act as an advocate for the advancement of intergovernmental pooling as the most appropriate risk financing mechanism for most public entities. Seeks to provide meaningful and significant educational and professional support for the governing bodies and employees of intergovernmental risk pools.

Association of Independent Asset Managers in Liechtenstein. PO Box 134, FL-9496 Balzers, Liechtenstein. Phone: 423 3882350; Fax: 423 3882359; Email: info@vuvl.li • URL: http://www.vuvl.li/CFDOCS/cmsout/admin/content.cfm?GroupID=141 • Aims to protect and promote the reputation of independent asset managers in Liechtenstein and abroad. Seeks to establish professional guidelines within the framework of the Asset Management Accounting. Facilitates exchange of information within the business community.

Association of Internal Management Consultants. 824 Caribbean Ct., Marco Island, FL 34145. Phone: (239)642-0580; Fax: (239)642-1119 • URL: http://www.aimc.org • Consists of internal management consultants. Seeks to develop and encourage the professional practice of internal management-consulting; establish high standards of professional performance; serve as a forum for the exchange of information and the sharing of professional methods and techniques; cooperate with commercial, educational, and governmental bodies on matters of common interest. Conducts educational seminars.

Association of Latino Administrators and Superintendents. PO Box 65204, Washington, DC 20035. Phone: (202)466-0808; Email: contact@alasedu.org • URL: http://www.alasedu.net • Represents the interests of Latino superintendents and administrators. Provides professional development programs to strengthen the skills of superintendents, principals and other administrators. Advocates for policies to ensure the quality of the public education system.

Association of MBAs. 25 Hosier Ln., London EC1A 9LQ, United Kingdom. Phone: 44 20 72462686 or 44 20 72462691; Fax: 44 20 72462687; Email: info@mbaworld.com • URL: http://www.mbaworld.com • Consists of students and graduates of Association of MBAs-approved MBA programmes, business schools, companies and organizations who share the objectives of the Association and who wish to contribute towards them. Seeks to enhance quality in management and provide a unique network of contracts for members. Provides a range of services including a membership book, networking/educational events, career opportunities, accreditation of MBA programmes, salary research, administration of a preferential rate MBA loan scheme for students of accredited programmes and an MBA information service.

Association of Microfinance Organizations of Tajikistan. 14 Firuz St., 734003 Dushanbe, Tajikistan. Phone: 992 44 6005794; Fax: 992 44 6005793; Email: office@amfot.tj • URL: http://www.amfot.tj • Facilitates the development of the microfinance sector in Tajikistan. Serves as a forum for interrelation and network of microfinance organizations in Tajikistan. Provides professional services for training and consultations and assists in the introduction of national standards of microfinance activity.

Association of Moroccan Professionals in America. PO Box 77254, San Francisco, CA 94107. Fax: (801)996-6334; Email: jaridati@amp-usa.org • URL: http://www.amp-usa.org • Promotes networking opportunities among Moroccan professionals. Advances the social and professional development of Moroccan professionals. Encourages bilateral commercial exchanges between the U.S. and Morocco. Provides community service and education initiatives in Morocco.

Association of Productivity Specialists. 521 5th Ave., Ste. 1700, New York, NY 10175. Email: inquire@apsworld.org • URL: http://www.apsworld.org • Firms and individuals engaged in the Productivity Specialist segment of the management consultant profession. Seeks to promote greater public knowledge of the productivity specialist profession (productivity specialists develop management systems to achieve business objectives in numerous areas, including production levels, quality performance, inventory costs, operating costs and manufacturing lead times); to improve professional capabilities of member firms by promoting educational and research and development programs; to cooperate with federal, state, and local government agencies on matters of interest to members; to help member firms improve, develop and review skills of their professional employees. Has established standards of ethics and competence for productivity specialists.

Association of Proposal Management Professionals. PO Box 77272, Washington, DC 20013-8272. Phone: (202)450-2549; Email: rick.harris@apmp.org • URL: http://www.apmp.org • Proposal managers, proposal planners, proposal writers, consultants, desktop publishers and marketing managers. Encourages unity and cooperation among industry professionals. Seeks to broaden member knowledge and skills through developmental, educational and social activities. Maintains speakers' bureau. Provides current information and developments in the field.

Association of Residential Cleaning Services International. c/o Ernie Hartong, 7870 Olentangy River Rd., Ste. 301, Columbus, OH 43235. Phone: (614)547-0887; Fax: (614)505-7136; Email: chris@arcsi.org • URL: http://www.arcsi.org • Represents residential cleaning service owners and professionals. Advances and improves the residential cleaning industry. Shares knowledge and information to ensure the growth and development of cleaning service businesses.

Association of Slovenia Entrepreneurs. PO Box 40-95, 1000 Ljubljana, Slovenia. Phone: 386 1 5443678; Fax: 386 1 5443680; Email: marta.turk1@guest.arnes.si • URL: http://fcem.org • Promotes women's entrepreneurial initiatives. Lobbies before the public and private institutions, policy makers and governments on issues that impede women's entrepreneurial potentials. Facilitates the development of business, partnership and trade. Fosters professional growth and business skills perfection. Encourages women to create enterprises.

Association of Small and Medium Enterprises. 167 Jalan Bukit Merah, Tower 4, No.03-13, Singapore 150167, Singapore. Phone: 65 65130388; Fax: 65 65130399; Email: enquiries@edc-asme.sg • URL: http://www.asme.org.sg • Seeks to bring together entrepreneurs of various industries and service sectors for information exchange; promotes relationship between various national interest bodies; provides continuous business education and training; fosters entrepreneurship networking both locally and internationally; works toward the institutionalization of ASME as a business association network body.

Association Senegalaise des Femmes Chefs d'Entreprise. B.P. 30081, Dakar, Senegal. Phone: 221 338241010; Fax: 221 8257246; Email: hadjadiordiop2000@yahoo.fr • URL: http://www.fcem.org/en/pays-membres.html • Promotes women's entrepreneurial initiatives. Lobbies before the public and private institutions, policy makers and governments on issues that impede women's entrepreneurial potentials. Facilitates the development of business, partnership and trade. Fosters professional growth and business skills perfection. Encourages women to create enterprises.

Association to Advance Collegiate Schools of Business. 77 S Harbour Island Blvd., Ste. 750, Tampa, FL 33602. Phone: (813)769-6500; Fax: (813)769-6559; Email: events@aacsb.edu • URL: http://www.aacsb.edu • Represents educational institutions, businesses, and other entities devoted to the advancement of management education. Works to advance quality management education worldwide through accreditation.

Association Women and Business in Russia. 8, Zaozernaya str., 196084 Saint Petersburg, Russia. Phone: 7 812 3162733; Fax: 7 812 7101191; Email: info@demetra.su • URL: http://www.fcem.org/en/pays-membres.html • Advances and supports businesswomen's interests in public, political and business circles of Russia. Helps develop women's business in Russia. Raises well-being and establishes a civilized, socially-responsible business in Russia.

Australian Venture Capital Association Limited. Level 10, Kyle House, 27-31 Macquarie Pl., Sydney, NSW 2000, Australia. Phone: 61 2 82437000 or 61 2 82382600; Email: members@avcal.com.au • URL: http://www.avcal.com.au • Promotes the venture capital and private equity industry in Australia. Provides networking events for members, industry tools (non-disclosure agreement, valuation guidelines, Standard Industry Trust Deed and

Standard VCLP), information for entrepreneurs seeking capital and employment database.

Battery Recycling Association of North America. 12505 N Main St., Ste. 212, Rancho Cucamonga, CA 91739. • URL: http://www.brana-online.org • Represents companies that handle, recycle, transport and manage portable power batteries. Seeks to establish guidance and training on the proper methods and regulations governing the safe handling of batteries. Fosters dialogue with battery handlers, recyclers, manufacturers and the regulatory community.

Bermuda Business Development Agency. Maxwell Roberts Bldg., 6th Fl., 1 Church St., Hamilton HM 11, Bermuda. Phone: (441)292-0632; Fax: (441)292-1797; Email: info@bermudabda.com • URL: http://bermudabda.com • Professionals and businesses. Promotes and supports high business standards among professionals in international business.

BEST Employers Association. 2505 McCabe Way, Irvine, CA 92614. Phone: 866-706-2225; Email: bestassoc@bestlife.com • URL: http://www.beassoc.org • Provides small independent businesses with managerial, economic, financial and sales information helpful for business improvement. Organizes and sponsors healthcare alliances for small employers. (The acronym BEST stands for Beneficial Employees Security Trust).

British Association of Women Entrepreneurs. 112 John Player Bldg., Stirling FK7 7RP, United Kingdom. Phone: 44 18 2725 5170; Email: deb@bawe-uk.org • URL: http://www.bawe-uk.org • Encourages the personal development of member entrepreneurs. Provides opportunities for members to expand their business through informal and formal networking. Represents and promotes British entrepreneurship worldwide.

British Cheque Cashers Association. Portal Business Ctr., Dallam Ct., Dallam Ln., Warrington WA2 7LT, United Kingdom. Phone: 44 1925 426090; Email: info@bcca.co.uk • URL: http://www.bcca.co.uk • Provides representation of its members' interests to government whether in London or Brussels - and its regulatory bodies. Also seeks to enhance understanding of the industry and to promote the interests of check cashers generally by helping to shape a climate of opinion which enables members to conduct their business profitably.

British Sociological Association. Bailey Ste., Palatine House, Belmont Business Park, Durham DH1 1TW, United Kingdom. Phone: 44 191 383 0839; Fax: 44 191 383 0782; Email: enquiries@britsoc.org.uk • URL: http://www.britsoc.co.uk • Individuals interested or employed in the fields of psychology, sociology, and other social sciences. Promotes the study of sociology and works to create a favorable climate for sociological research. Acts as a communication and information network.

British Venture Capital Association. 5th Fl. E, Chancery House, 53-64 Chancery Ln., London WC2A 1QS, United Kingdom. Phone: 44 20 74920400; Fax: 44 20 74201801; Email: bvca@bvca.co.uk • URL: http://www.bvca.co.uk • Venture capital, private equity, and professional firms connected with the venture capital industry. Represents virtually every major source of venture capital in the UK. Provides information about members to entrepreneurs and investors; represents members' views in discussions with Government and other bodies; provides a forum for the exchange of views among members; develops and maintains the highest standards of professional practice and provides training for members' employees.

Business Architects Association. 727 S Dearborn St., Ste. 710, Chicago, IL 60605-3826. Email: info@businessarchitects.org • URL: http://www.businessarchitectsassociation.org • Aims to promote and advance the business architecture profession through education, research, and application of methodologies. Provides educational and networking opportunities for the continuing education of members. Offers professional training and certification programs.

Business Industry Promotion Association of Pakistan. 455 Shadman 1, Lahore, Pakistan. Phone: 92 42 7581288; Fax: 92 42 7581288; Email: bipap@brain.net.pk • Seeks to integrate the activities of professionals in the fields of trade, industry, manufacturing, exporting, engineering, investment, finance and general services. Facilitates cooperation and networking among business professionals.

Businesswomen's Association. Oakhurst Bldg., W Wing, 2nd Fl., Rm. 2004, 11/13 St. Andrews Rd., Johannesburg 2193, South Africa. Phone: 27 11 484 4945; Email: admin@bwasa.co.za • URL: http://www.bwasa.co.za • Represents businesswomen in South Africa. Creates opportunities to advance the interests of women in business. Provides local and national forums where members can exchange ideas and be informed about current issues.

BVI Association of Compliance Officers. Road Town, Tortola, British Virgin Islands. • URL: http://www.bviaco.com • Promotes the role and importance of compliance in the British Virgin Islands. Encourages education, training and standards of practice within the BVI financial industry. Provides a forum for the exchange of ideas among members.

Canadian Agri-Marketing Association - Manitoba. 3336 Portage Ave., Ste. 509, Winnipeg, MB, Canada R3K 2H9. Phone: (204)782-6618 or (204)837-2853; Email: camamb@mymts.net • URL: http://www.cama.org/manitoba/ManitobaHome.aspx • Represents and supports individuals involved in agricultural marketing.

Canadian Agri-Marketing Association - Ontario. c/o Mary Thornly, Executive Director, 22 Guyers Dr., RR 3, Port Elgin, ON, Canada N0H 2C7. Phone: (519)389-6552; Email: camaont@bmts.com • URL: http://www.cama.org/Ontario/OntarioHome.aspx • Represents and supports individuals involved in agricultural marketing.

Canadian Payroll Association. 250 Bloor St. E, Ste. 1600, Toronto, ON, Canada M4W 1E6. Phone: 800-387-4693 or (416)487-3380; Fax: (416)487-3384; Email: Membership@payroll.ca • URL: http://www.payroll.ca • Represents the payroll community in Canada; offers education programs, advocacy efforts, products and services to help members enhance and adapt payroll operations, meet new legislative requirements, address changing workplace needs and take advantage of emerging technologies.

Cayman Finance. Fidelity Financial Ctre., 2nd Fl., 1 Gecko Link, West Bay Rd., Grand Cayman, Cayman Islands. Phone: (345)623-6725; Email: enquiries@caymanfinance.ky • URL: http://caymanfinances.com • Represents Cayman's financial services industry. Promotes the integrity and quality of financial services in the Cayman Islands. Offers the media and the financial services industry with information on issues that affect Cayman's financial services.

Cayman Islands Directors Association. George Town, Grand Cayman, Cayman Islands. Phone: (345)945-0012; Fax: (345)947-7328 • URL: http://www.cida2008.com • Represents individuals who hold office as directors of one or more Cayman Islands registered companies. Promotes and safeguards the interests of directors of Cayman Islands registered companies. Maintains code of conduct and best practice among members to ensure corporate governance.

Central Association of Agricultural Valuers. Market Chambers, 35 Market Pl., Gloucestershire, Coleford GL16 8AA, United Kingdom. Phone: 44 1594 832979; Fax: 44 1594 810701; Email: enquire@caav.org.uk • URL: http://www.caav.org.uk • Members are land agents, agricultural valuers and auctioneers which awards the qualification FAAV on examination. Publishes technical guidance and briefings. Engages with government and others in professional matters.

China Association of Microfinance. RDI of CASS, Rm. 1343, 5 Jianguomennei St., Beijing 100732, Hebei, China. Phone: 86 10 8519 6476 or 86 10 8519 5660; Fax: 86 10 8519 6476; Email: cam.net@163.com • URL: http://www.chinamfi.net • Represents and supports the microfinance industry. Promotes governmental support and strengthens international cooperation on microfinance. Raises funds for microfinance development and provides financial services to populations living with poverty and low income. Enhances the management capacity of microfinance institutions.

China Venture Capital and Private Equity Association. Office Tower E1, 21/F, Rm. 2109, 1 E Chang An Ave., Beijing 100738, Hebei, China. Phone: 86 10 85183584; Fax: 86 10 85150835 • URL: http://www.cvca.com.cn • Promotes the interests and the development of venture capital and private equity industry in the Greater China Region. Fosters understanding of the importance of venture capital and private equity to the vitality of the Greater China economy and global economies.

Chinese Finance Association. Church Street Station, New York, NY 10008. • URL: http://www.tcfaglobal.org • Promotes Chinese finance, business, economy, financial institutions and financial markets.

Chinese Women's Business Association. 11F, 157-1, Section 1, Xin-Shen South Rd., Taipei, Taiwan. Phone: 886 937 515276; Fax: 886 2 23821655; Email: taimay@ms16.hinet.net • URL: http://www.fcem.org/en/pays-membres.html • Promotes women's entrepreneurial initiatives. Lobbies before the public and private institutions, policy makers and governments on issues that impede women's entrepreneurial potentials. Facilitates the development of business, partnership and trade. Fosters professional growth and business skills perfection. Encourages women to create enterprises.

ChristianTrade Association International. PO Box 62187, Colorado Springs, CO 80962-2187. Phone: (719)432-8428; Email: info@christiantrade.com • URL: http://www.ctaintl.org • Forms, develops and recognizes national organizations committed to the growth of the Christian trade. Encourages the industry to grow based on fairness, equally accessible markets, and a biblical model. Facilitates networking and sharing of ideas publishes directory. Designs and develops training programs leading to professional excellence for participants in the Christian trade.

Collision Industry Electronic Commerce Association. 3149 Dundee Rd., No. 181, Northbrook, IL 60062-2402. Phone: (847)498-6945; Fax: (847)897-2094 • URL: http://cieca.com • Aims to facilitate electronic commerce within the collision industry. Works to provide a forum and methods to develop and maintain objective and uniform electronic commerce standards and guidelines. Encourages and supports open competition and free choice for the mutual benefit of all parties.

Community College Business Officers. 3 Boar's Head Ln., Ste. B, Charlottesville, VA 22903-4604. Phone: (434)293-2825; Fax: (434)245-8453; Email: info@ccbo.org • URL: http://www.ccbo.org • Represents business officers. Works to support business officers.

Community Development Bankers Association. 1444 Eye St., Ste. 201, Washington, DC 20005. Phone: (202)689-8935; Email: info@cdbanks.org • URL: http://www.cdbanks.org • Represents the interests of the community development bank sector.

Educates policy makers on how to deliver credit and financial services to low and moderate income communities.

Community Managers International Association. PO Box 848, Dana Point, CA 92629-0848. Phone: (949)940-9263; Email: cmiamanager@gmail.com • URL: http://www.cmiamanager.org • Aims to promote the community management profession. Provides an environment for the exchange of ideas among members. Collaborates with other national and state organizations. Sponsors seminars and workshops.

Construction Management Association of America. 7926 Jones Branch Dr., Ste. 800, McLean, VA 22102. Phone: (703)356-2622; Fax: (703)356-6388; Email: info@cmaanet.org • URL: http://cmaanet.org • Promotes the growth and development of construction management as a professional service; encourages high professional standards. Conducts conferences and forums on construction management topics. Sponsors a professional certification program.

Consultants Association for the Natural Products Industry. PO Box 4014, Clovis, CA 93613-4014. Phone: (559)325-7192; Email: info@cani-consultants.org • URL: http://www.cani-consultants.org • Works to enhance the growth and integrity of the natural products industry. Offers professional services to help manufacturers, distributors, retailers, and non-profit organizations thrive in the nutraceutical marketplace. Promotes education and ethical standards for the improvement of manufacturing, distribution, marketing and advertising to help the industry develop safe and beneficial products for the public.

Consumer Data Industry Association. 1090 Vermont Ave. NW, Ste. 200, Washington, DC 20005-4905. Phone: (202)371-0910; Fax: (202)371-0134; Email: cdia@cdiaonline.org • URL: http://www.cdiaonline.org • Serves as international association of credit reporting and collection service offices. Maintains hall of fame and biographical archives; conducts specialized educational programs. Offers computerized services and compiles statistics.

Corporate Responsibility Association. 123 S Broad St., Ste. 1930, Philadelphia, PA 19109. Phone: (215)606-9520; Fax: (267)800-2701 • URL: http://www.croassociation.org • Seeks to advance the corporate responsibility officers (CRO) community and its role within corporations. Strengthens the community of practice across all corporate responsibility disciplines. Establishes professional development and certification programs for corporate responsibility officers.

Corporate Social Responsibility Association. 155 E Boardwalk Dr., No. 544, Fort Collins, CO 80525. Phone: (303)944-4225; Fax: (303)496-0437; Email: jhall@csrassn.com • URL: http://csrassn.com • Promotes information gathering, networking and implementation of corporate social responsibility. Works to integrate ethical, social and environmental concerns in business. Supports best management practices in consolidating corporate social responsibility.

Craft Retailers Association for Tomorrow. PO Box 293, Islamorada, FL 33036. Phone: (305)664-3650; Fax: (305)664-0199; Email: info@craftonline.org • URL: http://www.craftonline.org • Represents a network of galleries, shops and artists. Supports and encourages creativity and artistic excellence in American craftspeople. Promotes awareness of American crafts through communication programs, education, networking and marketing.

CUMELA Nederland. Postbus 1156, NL-3860 BD Nijkerk, Netherlands. Phone: 31 33 2474900; Fax: 31 33 2474901; Email: info@cumela.nl • URL: http://www.cumela.nl • Agricultural and rural contractors. Seeks to advance the interests of agribusinesses. Represents members' commercial and regulatory interests at the national level.

Decorative Plumbing and Hardware Association. 7508 Wisconsin Ave., 4th Fl., Bethesda, MD 20814-3561. Phone: (301)657-3642; Fax: (301)907-9326; Email: info@dpha.net • URL: http://www.dpha.net • Advances the business and professional development of independent dealers, manufacturers, representatives and others involved in the decorative plumbing and hardware industry. Offers educational programs to train staff, create career paths and provide recognition.

Deep Draft Lubricant Association. c/o Shawn Konrad, Director, Belle Chasse Marine Transportation, 5813 Citrus Blvd., Harahan, LA 70123-5810. Phone: (504)837-3125; Email: information@ddla.org • URL: http://www.ddla.org • Promotes the interests of persons and firms engaged in the delivery of petroleum lubricants to deep draft vessels in the waters of the United States. Strives to create awareness of the individual operators, their suppliers and the industry of operational efficiencies and environmental regulations. Works to develop and improve performance standards and business methods.

Delhi Management Association. India Habitat Ctre., Core 6A, 1st Fl., Lodi Rd., New Delhi 110 003, Delhi, India. Phone: 91 11 24649552; Fax: 91 11 24649553; Email: dmadelhi@sify.com • URL: http://www.dmadelhi.org • Unites to participate in an exciting venture of institution-building, evolving a unique equation of synergy within the India Habitat Centre complex. Shares common concern for habitat.

Demeter Biodynamic Trade Association. PO Box 264, Talmage, CA 95481-0264. Email: info@demeterbta.com • URL: http://www.demeterbta.com • Represents Demeter Certified Biodynamic farms, vineyards, wineries, dairies, food processors, traders and distributors. Aims to further interest and education in Demeter Certified Biodynamic farming. Strives to promote Demeter Certified Biodynamic products in the marketplace. Supports and advocates for the protection of the Demeter certification marks.

Digital Screenmedia Association. 13100 Eastpoint Park Blvd., Louisville, KY 40223. Phone: (502)489-3915 or (502)241-7545; Fax: (502)241-2795 • URL: http://www.digitalscreenmedia.org • Promotes the interests and serves the needs of companies engaged in the self-service and kiosk industry. Encourages its members to exercise effective and ethical business practices. Fosters the growth and health of the self-service and kiosk industry.

Dutch Association of Corporate Treasurers. PO Box 279, 1400 AG Bussum, Netherlands. Phone: 31 35 6954101; Fax: 31 35 6945045 • URL: http://www.dact.nl • Represents the Dutch treasury community. Promotes the development of treasury in The Netherlands.

Dutch Corporate Finance Association. Koopvaardijweg 2, 4906 CV Oosterhout, Netherlands. Email: secretariaat@dcfa.nl • URL: http://www.dcfa.nl • Represents the interests of financial professionals. Facilitates sharing of knowledge and information among members. Creates a platform for managers within the financial sector.

Eastern Finance Association. PO Box 244023, Montgomery, AL 36124-4023. Phone: (850)644-4220; Fax: (850)644-4225; Email: membershipservices@blackwellpublishers.co.uk • URL: http://etnpconferences.net/efa • College and university professors and financial officers; libraries. Provides a meeting place for persons interested in any aspect of finance, including financial management, investments, and banking. Sponsors research competitions.

Economics, Business and Enterprise Association. Adur Business Ctre., Little High St., Shoreham-by-Sea BN43 5EG, United Kingdom. Phone: 44 1273 467542; Email: office@ebea.org.uk • URL: http://www.ebea.org.uk/home • Teachers of economics, business studies and related subjects in schools and colleges. Represents teachers of economics, business studies and related subjects in schools and colleges throughout the UK and provides its members with the professional support they need in the classroom. Aims to encourage and promote the teaching and study of economics and related subjects within a broadly based curriculum.

Estonian Business Association. Sadama 5/7, EE-10111 Tallinn, Estonia. Email: esea@esea.ee • URL: http://www.esea.ee • Fosters active business community in the country. Develops cooperation with foreign business associations. Keeps its members updated through local and international seminars and workshops. Meets with state authorities to advance the organization's interests.

Ethics and Compliance Officer Association. 411 Waverley Oaks Rd., Ste. 324, Waltham, MA 02452-8420. Phone: (781)647-9333; Fax: (781)647-9399; Email: membership@theecoa.org • URL: http://www.theecoa.org • Managers of ethics, compliance, and business conduct programs. Offers educational business ethics and compliance programs; conducts national research; and provides free job-listing service.

European Association for Personnel Management. c/o Chartered Institute of Personnel and Development, 151 The Broadway, Wimbledon, London SW19 1JQ, United Kingdom. Phone: 44 20 86126200; Fax: 44 20 86126201 • URL: http://www.eapm.org • Represents national personnel management associations. Seeks to maintain professional standards of personnel management and act as representative for personnel management associations in Europe. Disseminates information.

European Federation of Financial Analysts Societies. c/o Claudia Stinnes, Secretary, Mainzer Landstrasse 47a, DE-60329 Frankfurt, Germany. Phone: 49 69 264848300; Fax: 49 69 264848335; Email: info@effas.com • URL: http://effas.net • Associations and individuals active in the area of financial analysis. Objectives are to provide investors with accurate and comprehensive data on financial matters and to develop a general methodology of financial analysis based on approaches utilized in different European countries.

European Federation of Management Consultancies Associations. Kunstlaan Ave. des Arts 3-5, B-1210 Brussels, Belgium. Phone: 32 2 2500650 or 32 2 2500651; Email: feaco@feaco.org • URL: http://www.feaco.org • European associations of national management consultancy associations. Purposes are to: promote and develop the profession of management consultancy; foster high standards of professional practice and ethics; mediate the exchange of information and experience among member associations and companies and individuals within member associations; establish relations with other organizations interested in management practice. Upholds professional Guidelines for Business Ethics; studies, promotes, and protects the professional interests of members. Maintains liaison with other management consultancy organizations.

European Financial Management and Marketing Association. 8, rue Bayen, F-75017 Paris, France. Phone: 33 1 47425272; Fax: 33 1 47425676; Email: info@efma.com • URL: http://www.efma.com • European financial organizations in 17 countries. Goals are to: establish communication among individuals working with European financial organizations and supporting the concept of marketing; encourage innovation in the field; foster initiation of financial marketing research projects; represent the interests of European financial marketing. Sponsors seminars and professional training sessions. Maintains documentation center.

Compiles data on credit card systems.

European International Business Academy. c/o EIASM, Hotel Metropole, 2nd Fl., Pl. de Brouckere Plein, 31, B-1000 Brussels, Belgium. Phone: 32 2 2266660; Fax: 32 2 5121929 • URL: http://www.eiba-online.org • Individuals and associations involved in international business. Encourages exchange of ideas; fosters communication among members; serves as an information clearinghouse for those interested in education and research of international business.

European Operations Management Association. c/o EIASM, Pl. de Brouckere Plein 31, B-1000 Brussels, Belgium. Phone: 32 2 2266660; Fax: 32 2 5121929; Email: euroma@eiasm.be • URL: http://www.euroma-online.org • Advances operations management in both manufacturing and service through research, education and practice.

Executives Association of Great Britain. The Limes, High Rd., Orsett, London RM16 3ER, United Kingdom. Phone: 44 1375 893414 • URL: http://www.eagb.co.uk • Executives of businesses in the United Kingdom. Provides a forum for the exchange of information between members.

Facility Management Association of Australia. 313 La Trobe St., Level 6, Melbourne, VIC 3000, Australia. Phone: 61 3 86416666; Fax: 61 3 86416600; Email: info@fma.com.au • URL: http://www.fma.com.au/cms • Promotes the facility management profession in Australia.

Federation of European Risk Management Associations. Ave. de Tervuren, 237 B-12, B-1150 Brussels, Belgium. Phone: 32 2 7619432; Fax: 32 2 7718720; Email: info@ferma.eu • URL: http://www.ferma.eu • Exists to widen and raise the culture of Risk Management throughout Europe to its members and to the risk management and insurance community.

Financial Markets Association. 333 2nd St. NE, No. 104, Washington, DC 20002. Phone: (202)544-6327; Email: dp-fma@starpower.net • URL: http://www.fmaweb.org • Accountants, brokers, retail and investment bankers. Dedicated to meeting the needs of the financial industry for capital markets, fiduciary services, data processing, banking, asset/liability management, broker/dealer activities and investment advisory services. Offers educational seminars.

Financial Markets Association of Pakistan. Treasury Management Group, National Bank of Pakistan, NBP Head Office, 1st Flr.,, I.I. Chundrigar Rd., Karachi 74000, Pakistan. Phone: 92 21 143738; Fax: 92 21 1439440 • URL: http://www.fma.com.pk • Represents the interest of financial markets. Aims to promote educational, professional, ethical and social interests of the financial markets and the banking industry. Provides training and development support and conducts survey studies and research of the various fields of financial markets.

Financial Planning Association. 7535 E Hampden Ave., Ste. 600, Denver, CO 80231. Phone: 800-322-4237 or (303)759-4900; Fax: (303)759-0749; Email: webfeedback@fpanet.org • URL: http://www.plannersearch.org/Pages/home.aspx • Works to support the financial planning process in order to help people achieve their goals and dreams. Believes that everyone needs objective advice to make smart financial decisions and that when seeking the advice of a financial planner, the planner should be a CFP professional.

Financial Publishers Association. 15430 Endeavor Dr., Jupiter, FL 33478-6402. Phone: (561)515-8555; Fax: (561)282-4509; Email: support@financialpublishers.org • URL: http://www.financialpublishers.org • Aims to enhance the financial publishing industry's reputation for excellence. Shares knowledge of business best practices to help members. Provides financial information to guide investors.

Financial Women's Association of New York. 355 Lexington Ave., 15th Fl., New York, NY 10017. Phone: (212)297-2133; Fax: (212)370-9047 or (212)982-3008; Email: fwaoffice@fwa.org • URL: http://www.nywici.org/links/link_fwa.html • Persons of professional status in the field of finance in the New York metropolitan area. Works to promote and maintain high professional standards in the financial and business communities; provide an opportunity for members to enhance one another's professional contacts; achieve recognition of the contribution of women to the financial and business communities; encourage other women to seek professional positions within the financial and business communities. Activities include educational trips to foreign countries; college internship program including foreign student exchange; high school mentorship program; Washington and international briefings; placement service for members. Maintains speakers' bureau.

French Bruneian Business Association. Kompleks Jalan Sultan, Rm. 301-306, 3rd Fl., Jalan Sultan, Bandar Seri Begawan BS8811, Brunei. Phone: 673 2240924 or 673 2220960; Fax: 673 2243373 • URL: http://www.fbbabrunei.com • Brings together people actively involved in trade and commerce between France and Brunei Darussalam. Provides a mutual forum for French and Bruneian business partners. Disseminates economic information to members on matters of interest. Develops business opportunities between Brunei Darussalam and France.

Geosynthetics Materials Association. c/o Industrial Fabrics Association International, 1801 County Rd. B W, Roseville, MN 55113-4061. Phone: 800-225-4324 or (651)222-2508; Fax: (651)631-9334; Email: generalinfo@ifai.com • URL: http://www.ifai.com/groups/gma • Represents members of the geosynthetics industry including manufacturers, testing firms and service companies. Aims to promote the acceptance and use of geosynthetic materials in a variety of applications. Provides resources and offers networking opportunities among members.

German Private Equity and Venture Capital Association. Residenz Deutschen Theater, Reinhardtstrasse 27c, D-10117 Berlin, Germany. Phone: 49 30 3069820; Fax: 49 30 30698220; Email: bvk@bvkap.de • URL: http://www.bvkap.de • Represents the venture capital and private equity companies in Germany. Aims to create a favorable environment for the industry through publications and cooperation with other institutions.

Gibraltar Association of Compliance Officers. PO Box 1493, Gibraltar, Gibraltar. Phone: 350 200 74518; Email: info@gaco.gi • URL: http://www.gaco.gi • Represents and protects the interests of compliance officers. Seeks to promote the exchange of views and the professional development of officers engaged in the performance of a compliance function within the Gibraltar Finance Centre.

Gift and Home Trade Association. 2550 Sandy Plains Rd. Ste. 225, Marietta, GA 30066. Phone: 877-600-4872; Email: info@giftandhome.org • URL: http://www.giftandhome.org • Aims to ensure the viability of the gift and home industry. Promotes business practices and professional development. Establishes standards and ethical guidelines.

Gift Sales Manager Association. 14710 Quaker Bottom Rd., Sparks, MD 21152. Phone: (410)472-3593; Email: ldcolson@comcast.net • URL: http://www.giftsalesmanagers.org • Represents the interests of sales managers in the gift and home decor industry. Works to improve company operations and increase sales. Serves as a forum to exchange information and ideas among members.

Government Investment Officers Association. 10655 Park Run Dr., Ste. 120, Las Vegas, NV 89144. Phone: (702)255-3224; Fax: (702)575-6670; Email: mday@gioa.us • URL: http://www.gioa.us • Provides education and training to government investment officers to assist them in their responsibilities. Promotes educational and professional development among investment officers in state and local governments. Seeks to instill higher levels of investment management skills, ethics and efficiency. Interacts with the public investment community and other public investment officers so that members will have the opportunity to gain the skills, knowledge and contacts that will greatly aid them in discharging their duties.

Graduate Management Association of Australia. PO Box 6328, Melbourne, VIC 8008, Australia. Phone: 61 3 95363109; Fax: 61 3 95253656; Email: service@gmaa.com.au • URL: http://www.gmaa.asn.au • Promotes the standing graduate schools and postgraduate management. Enhances the value of graduate management qualifications. Contributes to the development of Australia and its managerial resources. Provides a forum for the interaction of members and students from various management schools. Pursues the regular exchange of ideas and knowledge between members and leaders in industry and management education.

Healthcare Financial Management Association. 3 Westbrook Corporate Ctr., Ste. 600, Westchester, IL 60154. Phone: 800-252-4362 or (708)531-9600; Fax: (708)531-0032; Email: memberservices@hfma.org • URL: http://www.hfma.org • Financial management professionals employed by hospitals and long-term care facilities, public accounting and consulting firms, insurance companies, medical groups, managed care organizations, government agencies, and other organizations. Conducts conferences, including annual conference in late June and audio teleconferences. Publishes books on healthcare financial issues. A Fellowship in Healthcare Financial Management (FHFMA) as well as the Certified Healthcare Professional (CHFP) in Finance and Accounting, Financial Management of Physician Practices, Managed Care, and Patient Financial Services are offered.

Hong Kong Venture Capital and Private Equity Association. Rm. 2001, Wilson House, 19 - 27 Wyndham St., Central, Hong Kong, Hong Kong, China. Phone: 852 21677518; Fax: 852 21677530 ; Email: hkvca@hkvca.com.hk • URL: http://web.hkvca.com.hk/en • Promotes and protects the interests of the venture capital industry in Hong Kong. Educates enterprises about venture capital/private equity as a partner in creating value in the business. Seeks to improve the investment environment in Hong Kong and in the People's Republic of China.

Hong Kong Women Professionals and Entrepreneurs Association. Kingswell Commercial Tower, 171-173 Lockhart Rd., Rm. B, 18 Fl., Hong Kong, Hong Kong, China. Phone: 852 28822555; Fax: 852 28824673; Email: info@hkwpea.org • URL: http://www.hkwpea.org • Works to create practical and innovative learning and business opportunities for members and for others. Promotes high professional standards. Reaches out and establishes relationships with counterparts in Mainland China and abroad.

Hungarian Venture Capital and Private Equity Association. 11 Pauler St., H-1013 Budapest, Hungary. Phone: 36 1 4750924; Email: hvca@hvca.hu • URL: http://www.hvca.hu • Promotes the interests and the development of the venture capital and private equity industry in Hungary. Creates a set of professional and ethical standards for member companies. Provides a regular forum for the exchange of ideas among members.

Indian Venture Capital Association. C-7, Pashchimi Marg, Vasant Vihar, New Delhi 110 057, Delhi, India. Phone: 91 11 46160389; Email: aakriti@indiavca.org • URL: http://www.indiavca.org • Facilitates the growth of venture capital and private

For publishers' addresses, refer to SOURCES CITED section at the back of the book.

equity activities in India. Encourages and assists in the creation of more venture capital and private equity funds in India. Works to increase the skills of India's entrepreneurs.

Industrial Auctioneers Association. 3213 Ayr Ln., Dresher, PA 19025. Phone: 800-805-8359 or (215)366-5450; Fax: (215)657-1964; Email: info@industrialauctioneers.org • URL: http://www.industrialauctioneers.org • Represents industrial machinery and equipment auctioneers. Promotes the use of auction sales in idle industrial equipment. Maintains ethical and professional standards among member auctioneers.

Industrialists' Association of Panama. Apartado 0819-05411, Panama City, Panama. Phone: 507 230-0169; Email: sip@cableonda.net • URL: http://www.industriales.org.

Information Technology Services Marketing Association. 91 Hartwell Ave., Lexington, MA 02421-3137. Phone: (781)862-8500; Fax: (781)674-1366; Email: info@itsma.com • URL: http://www.itsma.com • Supports marketing executives who market and sell technology-related services and solutions. Provides research, consulting and training to the world's leading technology, communications, and professional services providers. Facilitates peer sharing and networking opportunities among members.

Interim Management Association. Dorset House, 1st Fl., 27-45 Stamford St., London SE1 9NT, United Kingdom. • URL: http://www.interimmanagement.uk.com • Recruitment consultancies specializing in interim managers for industry and commerce at senior level.

International Air Filtration Certifiers Association. c/o Michael Alleman, 129 S Gallatin, Liberty, MO 64068. Phone: 888-679-1904; Fax: (816)792-8105 • URL: http://www.iafca.com • Promotes professionalism in the biological safety cabinet industry. Establishes and maintains certification program for biological safety cabinet certifiers. Provides information and guidance to legislative and regulatory agencies with regard to laws and standards affecting the industry.

International Amusement and Leisure Defense Association. PO Box 4563, Louisville, KY 40204. Phone: (502)473-0956; Fax: (502)473-7352; Email: info@ialda.org • URL: http://www.ialda.org • Promotes and protects the interests of the amusement and leisure industries. Encourages members to exchange information, share experiences and develop litigation strategies regarding the amusement and leisure industry. Serves as a clearinghouse for speakers and authors on industry-specific topics.

International Association for Chinese Management Research. Kogod School of Business, 4400 Massachusetts Ave. NW, Washington, DC 20016. Phone: (316)978-6788; Fax: (316)978-3349; Email: iacmrus@gmail.com • URL: http://www.iacmr.org • Promotes scholarly studies of organization and management of firms in the Chinese context. Fosters the development of management research capabilities in and on China. Facilitates international collaboration between management researchers from around the globe.

International Association of CFOs and Corporate Treasurers China. c/o Mr. Francis Ho, CLP Holdings, Group Treasury Dept., 147 Argyle St., Mongkok, Kowloon, Hong Kong, China. • URL: http://www.iacctchina.com • Promotes the development of professional corporate treasury practice in China. Fosters exchange and sharing among a network of corporate treasurers and CFOs in both mainland Chinese. Supports financial reforms in China by developing a platform for dialogue between members and financial regulators.

International Association of Directional Drilling. 525 Sam Houston Pkwy. E, Ste. 525, Houston, TX 77060. Phone: (281)931-8811 or (281)288-6484; Email: dallen@iadd-intl.org • URL: http://www.iadd-intl.org • Represents the interests of the directional drilling industry. Encourages members to share ideas and develop safety and performance standards. Fosters collaboration among operators, directional drilling vendors and suppliers.

International Association of Financial Executives Institutes. 1003 Pasong Tamo Tower, 10th Fl., 2210 Don Chino Roces Ave., Makati City 1231, Philippines. Phone: 63 2 7280315 • URL: http://www.iafei.org • Seeks to build and improve mutual understanding internationally among financial executives through the exchange of financial information, experience, and ideas. Provides a basis for international cooperation among financial executives towards making financial systems and regulations more uniform, compatible, and harmonious worldwide. Promotes ethical considerations in the practice of financial management throughout the world.

International Association of Registered Financial Consultants. Financial Planning Bldg., 2507 N Verity Pkwy., Middletown, OH 45042-0506. Phone: 800-532-9060; Fax: (513)424-5752; Email: info@iarfc.org • URL: http://www.iarfc.org • Financial professionals gathered to foster public confidence in the financial planning profession. Helps financial consultants exchange planning techniques. Offers educational programs and professional certifications.

International Association of Women in Family Enterprises. 1906 Vista Del Lago Dr., No. L-119, Valley Springs, CA 95252. Phone: (209)772-9200 or (209)772-2810; Fax: (209)772-2810; Email: info@iawife.com • URL: http://www.iawife.com • Aims to support women who are building and growing family businesses. Offers opportunities to help members become successful in family enterprises. Provides support, education and networking among members.

International Bridal Manufacturers Association. 118 W 20th St., 3rd Fl., New York, NY 10011-3627. Email: info@ibma.us • URL: http://ibma.us • Represents wedding apparel and accessory manufacturers. Promotes economic opportunities and fosters better relationships between manufacturers and retailers of bridal apparel. Coordinates and sets non-conflicting dates for bridal industry markets.

International Factoring Association. 6627 Bay Laurel Pl., Ste. C, Avila Beach, CA 93424-0039. Phone: 800-563-1895; Fax: (805)773-0021; Email: info@factoring.org • URL: http://www.factoring.org • Represents the interests of the factoring industry. Assists the factoring community by providing information, training, purchasing power and resources. Provides opportunities for members to discuss issues and concerns in the industry.

International Farm Management Association. c/o Tony King, Honorary Secretary, 38 West End, Cambridge CB22 4LX, United Kingdom. Phone: 44 1223 832527; Email: honsecretary@ifmaonline.org • URL: http://www.ifmaonline.org • Farmers, extension workers, academics, resource use planners, and managers in 68 countries concerned with the planning, production, and marketing in agriculture. Furthers the knowledge and understanding of farm business management and fosters the exchange of ideas and information about farm management theory and practice worldwide.

International Janitorial Cleaning Services Association. 2011 Oak St., Wyandotte, MI 48192. Phone: (734)252-6189; Email: info@ijcsa.com • URL: http://www.ijcsanetwork.com • Represents the interests of the janitorial industry. Promotes professionalism and ethics in the janitorial and cleaning services field. Provides training and education for cleaning professionals.

International Ombudsman Association. 111 Deer Lake Rd., Ste. 100, Deerfield, IL 60015. Phone: (847)509-7991; Fax: (847)480-9282; Email: info@ombudsassociation.org • URL: http://www.ombudsassociation.org/home.aspx • Individuals actively engaged in the practice of organizational ombudsmanry, as designated neutrals. Works to enhance the quality and value of the ombudsman function by: establishing and communicating appropriate standards of excellence for the profession; developing and disseminating ethical guidelines for organizational ombudspeople; training new and experienced ombuds practitioners in complaint handling skills and principles of effective practice; communicating the latest developments of the profession; and fostering appropriate forums to share common interests and strengthen skills.

International Photovoltaic Equipment Association. PO Box 771507, Orlando, FL 32877. Phone: (407)856-9100; Email: ekus@ipvea.com • URL: http://www.ipvea.org • Represents manufacturers and suppliers of photovoltaic (PV) fabrication equipment and related raw materials used in PV ingot, wafer, cell and panel manufacturing. Fosters the development of the photovoltaic equipment manufacturing industry. Provides members with a forum for information, discussion and exchange of ideas to develop business opportunities and strategic partnerships.

International Project Management Association. PO Box 7905, 1008 AC Amsterdam, Netherlands. Phone: 31 33 2473430; Fax: 31 33 2460470; Email: info@ipma.ch • URL: http://www.ipma.ch • National project management associations in 43 countries. Liaises the international exchange of project management information and promotes the advancement of project management methods, systems, and practical application techniques. Encourages the development of and cooperates with national organizations with common interests; provides for individual participation in countries without national societies.

IQNet Association - International Certification Network. Bollwerk 31, CH-3000 Bern, Switzerland. Phone: 41 31 3102440; Fax: 41 31 3102449; Email: headoffice@iqnet.ch • URL: http://www.iqnet-certification.com • National management systems certification bodies. Seeks to advance the practice of corporate and organizational management and business excellence. Evaluates management systems and bestows certification upon qualified organizations; serves as a clearinghouse on management systems.

Ireland China Association. 28 Merrion Sq., Dublin 2, Dublin, Ireland. Phone: 353 1 6424178; Fax: 353 1 6612315; Email: info@irelandchina.org • URL: http://www.irelandchina.org • Aims to bring together Irish and Chinese businesspeople for the purpose of exploring business opportunities and making contracts. Promotes greater economic ties and increases trade and commerce between Ireland and China. Furthers the cultural links and greater knowledge of both countries.

Ireland Japan Association. 28 Merrion Sq., Dublin 2, Dublin, Ireland. Phone: 353 1 6424178; Email: info@ija.ie • URL: http://www.ija.ie • Aims to enhance and develop relations between Ireland and Japan. Promotes economic and business ties and increases trade and commerce between Ireland and Japan. Fosters mutual understanding between the peoples of both countries. Creates a forum for Irish and Japanese people to interact in both business and social environments.

Israel Advanced Technologies Industries. PO Box 12591, 46733 Herzliya, Israel. Phone: 972 73 7136313; Fax: 972 73 7136314; Email: orit@iati.co.il • URL: http://www.iati.co.il • Promotes the development of the venture capital industry in Israel. Supports and enhances the growth of Israeli high-technology industries. Secures special conditions and privileges for members from service organizations in Israel and abroad.

I.T. Financial Management Association. PO Box 30188, Santa Barbara, CA 93130. Phone: (805)687-7390; Fax: (805)687-7382; Email: info@itfma.com • URL: http://www.itfma.com • Individuals and corporations interested in the financial management of information technology (IT) organizations. Works for the education and improvement of members and the industry. Offers certification in IT financial management. Conducts peer studies, in-house seminars, and chargeback system reviews. Operates educational programs.

Japan Association of Corporate Executives. 1-4-6, Marunouchi, Chiyoda-ku, Tokyo 100-0005, Japan. Phone: 81 3 32111271 or 81 3 32840220; Fax: 81 3 32132946 or 81 3 32123774; Email: kdcontact1207@doyukai.or.jp • URL: http://www.doyukai.or.jp • Businesspersons in Japan. Formulates social, economic, policy proposals through research and discussion among members.

Japan Business Incubation Association. Shiba-Koen, Minato-ku 3-5-8 Kikai, Tokyo 105 0011, Japan. Phone: 81 50 36021751; Email: reception@jbia.jp • URL: http://jbia.jp • Promotes new business creation in local communities and encourages the exchange of information among major international organizations. Conducts studies and makes proposals on new business creation and implements training programs for incubation managers. Provides consulting support, implementation, and policy proposals related to business incubation.

Japan Securities Dealers' Association. 1-5-8, Kayaba-cho Nihonbashi, Chuo, Tokyo 103-0025, Japan. Phone: 81 3 3667-8537; Email: international@wan.jsda.or.jp • URL: http://www.jsda.or.jp/en • Represents securities companies and registered financial institutions. Aims to protect investors by ensuring fair and smooth trading in securities and other transactions by members of the association. Promotes the implementation of policy measures for the revitalization of the Japanese securities markets in order to contribute to the growth and development of the Japanese economy.

Korean Standards Association. Korean Technology Ctr., 701-7, Yeoksam-Dong, Gangnam-Gu, Seoul 135-513, South Korea. Phone: 82 2 60094513; Fax: 82 2 69194006; Email: ksaicd@ksa.or.kr • URL: http://www.ksa.or.kr/eng • Provides industrial research and survey, education and training on quality and standardization; serves as the national KS certification body; promotes globalization of local enterprises.

Korean Women Entrepreneurs Association. 7F, 733-24, Yeoksam-dong, Gangnam-Gu, Seoul, South Korea. Phone: 82 2 3690922; Fax: 82 2 3690950; Email: ceo@wbiz.or.kr • URL: http://www.womanbiz.or.kr • Represents Korean businesswomen and provides full-support for the growth and development of their businesses. Helps entrepreneurs gain confidence and improve their competitiveness through counseling and training. Implements government-commissioned projects.

Latin American Venture Capital Association. 589 8th Ave., 18th Fl., New York, NY 10018. Phone: (646)315-6735; Fax: (646)349-1047; Email: info@lavca.org • URL: http://www.lavca.org • Promotes the growth of the private equity and venture capital industry in Latin America and the Caribbean. Advocates on behalf of the industry by disseminating information to the media, promoting the region to investors and supporting efforts to improve the regulatory framework. Conducts research on industry trends, performance and policy environment. Develops model documents, industry guides and standards.

Latvian Venture Capital and Private Equity Association. Skolas St. 25-1, LV-1010 Riga, Latvia. Phone: 371 6 29477979 or 371 6 29265627; Email: info@lvca.lv • URL: http://www.lvca.lv • Promotes the development of the venture capital sector in Latvia. Informs businessmen and the society about venture capital financing possibilities. Promotes the exchange of information among members.

LCD TV Association. 16055 SW Walker Rd., Ste. 264, Beaverton, OR 97006-4942. Phone: (215)206-6506; Email: membership@lcdtvassociation.org • URL: http://www.lcdtvassociation.org • Aims to help the LCD TV supply chain and retail channel as well as the end customer. Creates and promotes new features and functions for the industry. Provides methods to improve members' products and services.

Malaysia South-South Association. Bangunan AmBank Group, 17th Fl., Jaalan Raja Chulan, 50200 Kuala Lumpur, Malaysia. Phone: 60 3 20783788; Fax: 60 3 20728411; Email: mail@massa.net.my • URL: http://www.massa.net.my • Promotes and enhances knowledge and understanding of economic, trade and investment policies and conditions of South-South countries. Acts as an informal liaison body between the private sector and the government in the promotion of trade and investment. Provides a forum for the dissemination of ideas and for the discussion of trade, economy and culture. Enhances trade and investment relations and fosters friendship and cooperation in South-South countries.

Malaysian Venture Capital and Private Equity Association. 54-3, Jalan 27/70A, Desa Sri Hartamas, 50480 Kuala Lumpur, Malaysia. Phone: 60 3 23006550; Fax: 60 3 62062484; Email: info@mvca.org.my • URL: http://www.mvca.org.my • Promotes, develops and maintains the venture capital industry in Malaysia as a source of equity financing for the start-up or development of small and medium-sized enterprises. Encourages the promotion, research, and analysis of venture capital in Malaysia and other countries. Serves as a forum for the exchange of views among members. Represents the members to all governmental institutions or public authorities.

Malta Association of Women in Business. TaL-Imriekeb, Ramla Rd., Naxxar NXR 08, Malta. Phone: 356 21 422009 or 356 21 334394; Email: info@mawb.eu • URL: http://www.mawb.eu • Encourages reciprocal support, exchange of ideas, sharing of experiences and business and economic opportunities among its members both nationally and internationally. Organizes seminars, workshops, social and informative evenings. Promotes an environment for women to grow and develop in their businesses and professions. Promotes the interests of its members in the pursuit of innovative and effective changes in business, economic, social and public policy.

Management Consultancies Association. 36-38 Cornhill, 5th Fl., London EC3V 3NG, United Kingdom. Phone: 44 20 76457950; Fax: 44 20 76457951; Email: info@mca.org.uk • URL: http://www.mca.org.uk • Enhances the consultancy management profession. Furthers the collective objectives and interests of its members. Acts as a focal point for individuals wishing to seek advice on management consultancy. Serves as a forum for members to discuss matters of current interest and future policy.

Media Financial Management Association. 550 W Frontage Rd., Ste. 3600, Northfield, IL 60093. Phone: (847)716-7000; Fax: (847)716-7004; Email: info@mediafinance.org • URL: http://www.mediafinance.org • Members are accountants and other financial personnel in the radio and television broadcasting industries. Formerly Broadcast Financial Management Association.

Moscow International Business Association. Office 505, Ilyinka d.5/2, 109012 Moscow, Russia. Phone: 7 495 6200130; Fax: 7 495 6200552; Email: miba@mibas.ru • URL: http://www.mibas.ru • Strives to create an environment for Russian and foreign businessmen operating in Moscow. Boosts the Russian economy by helping businessmen engaged in productive endeavors.

Mountains and Plains Independent Booksellers Association. 3278 Big Spruce Way, Park City, UT 84098. Phone: (435)649-6079; Fax: (435)649-6105; Email: info@mountainsplains.org • URL: http://www.mountainsplains.org • Supports independent bookstores; promotes literacy and defends freedom of speech and of the press.

National Aboriginal Capital Corporation Association. 75 Albert St., Ste. 908, Ottawa, ON, Canada K1P 5E7. Phone: (613)688-0894; Fax: (613)688-0895 • URL: http://www.nacca.net • Assists Aboriginal Financial Institutions (AFIs) in promoting the growth and development of Aboriginal businesses. Provides products and services to AFIs and Aboriginal-focused organizations including institutional capacity-building, training, access to capital, advocacy, partnerships, and member services with quality and accountability.

National Aboriginal Lands Managers Association. 1024 Mississauga St., Curve Lake, ON, Canada K0L 1R0. Phone: 877-234-9813 or (705)657-7660; Fax: (705)657-7177; Email: info@nalma.ca • URL: http://www.nalma.ca • Advances the professional development and technical expertise in the field of land management. Provides a working environment to all First Nations Lands Managers. Creates opportunities for networking between land managers on land related issues. Creates a system that will assist First Nations interests in various land management functions.

National Alliance of Craftsmen Associations. 816 Camaron St., Ste. 212, San Antonio, TX 78212. Phone: (210)271-9100; Fax: (210)212-9250 • Works to create and promote community empowerment, sustainability and growth through the development of employment, economic and educational opportunities in blighted communities. Concentrates on the barriers that perpetuate the underutilized, underemployed, unemployed, unskilled and underskilled community. Aims to build a stronger and healthier country one community at a time.

National Association for Business Teacher Education. 1914 Association Dr., Reston, VA 20191-1596. Phone: (703)860-8300; Fax: (703)620-4483; Email: nbea@nbea.org • URL: http://www.nabte.org • An institutional division of National Business Education Association. Represents colleges and universities with programs for the education of business teachers. Works to improve and advance business teacher education. Operates Business Education Research Foundation.

National Association for Moisture Management. 76 D St., Hull, MA 02045. Phone: (781)925-0354; Fax: (781)925-0650 • URL: http://na4mm.com • Educates and protects the consumer from problems associated with moisture. Works with state, federal and local officials to develop standards and practices in the moisture management industry. Offers continuing education programs for moisture management professionals.

National Association of Agricultural Contractors. The Old Cart Shed, Easton Lodge Farm, Old Oundle Rd., Wansford, Peterborough PE8 6NP, United Kingdom. Phone: 44 1780 784631; Fax: 44 1780 784933; Email: members@naac.co.uk • URL: http://www.naac.co.uk • Represents agricultural and amenity contractors in United Kingdom and their commercial and regulatory interests at the national level.

National Association of Blessed Billionaires. Presbyterian Church of Mt. Vernon, 199 N Columbus Ave., Mount Vernon, NY 10553. Phone: (914)633-4417 or (347)933-3000; Email: nabb10m@aol.com • URL: http://blessedbillionaires.org • Aims to build self-esteem and good moral character among young people. Helps young men and women gain the skills they need to become successful and responsible adults. Provides a vehicle for inner-city youth to learn about and participate in the competitive market through leadership and entrepreneurial training. Conducts training on all aspects of business and money management.

National Association of Certified Public Bookkeepers. 140 N Union Ave., Ste. 240, Farmington, UT 84025-2954. Phone: 866-444-9989; Fax: (801)451-4688; Email: info@nacpb.org • URL: http://www.nacpb.org • Aims to protect the public interest by ensuring that only qualified individuals provide public bookkeeping services. Fosters the professional development of public bookkeepers. Offers certification programs in bookkeeping.

National Association of Commercial Finance Brokers. Hamilton House, 1 Temple Ave., London EC4Y 0HA, United Kingdom. Phone: 44 20 74892056; Email: admin@nacfb.org.uk • URL: http://www.nacfb.org • Seeks to protect consumer from fraud and malpractice in the commercial finance industry. Raises professional standards of commercial finance brokers. Provides training, education and information.

National Association of Farm Business Analysis Specialists. PO Box 467, Camp Point, IL 62320. Phone: (217)593-7233; Fax: (217)593-7239 • URL: http://www.nafbas.org • Aims to advance comparative farm business analysis techniques. Provides opportunities for farm business analysis specialists to exchange ideas and methods. Encourages and promotes the professional competence of members.

National Association of Financial and Estate Planning. 515 E 4500 S, No. G-200, Salt Lake City, UT 84107. Phone: 800-454-2649; Fax: (877)890-0929 or (801)266-9900; Email: info@accuplan.net • URL: http://www.nafep.com • Represents financial and estate planners.

National Association of Financial Services. Tauentzienstrasse 12, D-10787 Berlin, Germany. Phone: 49 30 23003504 or 49 30 20454403; Fax: 49 30 23003562 or 49 30 20634759; Email: fifaeg@t-online.de • URL: http://www.fifa.de • Promotes the financial industry in Germany. Seeks to develop the field of financial services. Provides information on the financial industry.

National Association of Independent Real Estate Brokers. 7102 Mardyke Ln., Indianapolis, IN 46226. Phone: (317)547-4679; Email: director@nationalrealestatebrokers.org • URL: http://nationalrealestatebrokers.org • Aims to educate independent real estate brokers and real estate agents. Promotes the value of independent real estate brokers and real estate agents nationwide through national promotional campaigns. Works to introduce the general public to independent real estate brokers and real estate agents, their real estate companies and the benefits they offer.

National Association of Minority Automobile Dealers. 9745 Lottsford Rd., Ste. 150, Largo, MD 20774. Phone: (301)306-1614; Fax: (301)306-1493 • URL: http://www.namad.org • Automobile dealers. Acts as liaison between membership, the federal government, the community, and industry representatives; seeks to better the business conditions of its members on an ongoing basis. Serves as a confidential spokesperson for dealers. Offers business analysis, financial counseling, and short- and long-term management planning. Conducts research programs; compiles statistics.

National Association of Minority Government Contractors. PO Box 44609, Washington, DC 20026. Email: info@namgc.org • URL: http://www.namgc.org • Focuses on enhancing diversification in the workplace. Provides opportunities for the federal, state and local government sector to find key resources in order to engage in contracting opportunities. Provides members with networking, information and services which will connect them with federal, state and local government contracting opportunities.

National Association of Mortgage Processors. 1250 Connecticut Ave. NW, Ste. 200, Washington, DC 20036. Phone: 800-977-1197 or (202)261-6505; Fax: (202)318-0655; Email: contact@mortgageprocessor.org • URL: http://www.mortgageprocessor.org • Represents mortgage processors. Assists contract loan processors as well as in-house mortgage loan processors in all aspects of their businesses. Offers services such as training classes, blog cafe, community discussion, certification programs and download library.

National Association of Pharmaceutical Sales Representatives. 2020 Pennsylvania Ave. NW, Ste. 5050, Washington, DC 20006-1811. Phone: 800-284-1060; Email: contact@napsronline.org • URL: http://www.napsronline.org • Represents sales representatives, sales managers and sales trainers who work in the pharmaceutical industry. Provides Continuing Medical Education to members as well as candidates who wish to start a pharmaceutical sales career. Aims to educate, train, create standards and provide current information for professional pharmaceutical sales representatives as well as for individuals who want to gain entry into the industry.

National Association of Professional Asian American Women. 304 Oak Knoll Terr., Rockville, MD 20850. Phone: (301)785-8585; Email: napaw@comcast.net • URL: http://www.napaw.org • Represents the professional interests of Asian-American women. Promotes continued personal and professional development; works to enhance career opportunities. Encourages greater visibility of Asian-American women in public decision-making. Conducts educational programs.

National Association of Real Estate Consultants. 404 4th Ave., Lewiston, ID 83501. Phone: (208)746-7963; Fax: (208)746-4760 • URL: http://www.narec.com • Works to assist real estate professionals in reframing their focus as real estate consultants to better meet the needs of today's savvy consumer. Helps promote alternative or fee-for-service real estate business models.

National Association of Settlement Purchasers. c/o Susan Barnes, Association Administrator, 720 Collier Dr., Dixon, CA 95620. Phone: (707)888-2647; Email: susan@barnescompany.com • URL: http://www.nasp-usa.com • Finance companies that purchase structured settlements from individuals for a lump sum (structured settlements are received by individuals as redress for personal injury or other liability). Seeks to insure ethical practice in the trading of structured settlements; promotes advancement of the structured settlement purchasing industry. Serves as a clearinghouse on the purchase of structured settlements; lobbies for reform of regulations governing the trade in structured settlements.

National Association of Small Business Contractors. 700 12th St. NW, Ste. 700, Washington, DC 20005. Phone: 888-861-9290 • URL: http://www.nasbc.org • Serves and advances the interests of small business contractors. Seeks to establish opportunities for small business owners to meet with state and federal agencies, prime contractors, potential teaming partners and procurement experts. Strives to create a strong and respected voice for advocacy in support of small business' interests.

National Association of State and Local Equity Funds. 1970 Broadway, Ste. 250, Oakland, CA 94612. Phone: (510)444-1101; Fax: (510)444-1191; Email: info@naslef.org • URL: http://www.naslef.org • Promotes efficient management of state and local equity funds. Represents individuals, public and private corporations and professional associations with an interest in the tax credit program or an active involvement with a state or local equity fund. Fosters greater understanding of the Low Income Housing Tax Credit (LIHTC).

National Association of Supervisor of Business Education. c/o Melissa Scott, Treasurer, 9890 S Maryland Pkwy., Ste. 221, Las Vegas, NV 89183. Phone: (702)486-6625 or (303)982-6654; Fax: (702)668-4321 • URL: http://www.nasbe.us • Acts as a representative voice for local supervisors of business and office education programs in public and private schools. Supports programs and activities in cooperation with the American Vocational Association and other business education organizations.

National Association of Women MBAs. Rice University, PO Box 2932, Houston, TX 77251-2932. Email: philana.kiely@mbawomen.org • URL: http://www.mbawomen.org • Provides networking opportunities for its members. Increases communication among graduate business schools regarding their initiatives to educate and support women in business.

National Black MBA Association. 1 E Wacker Ste. 3500, Chicago, IL 60601. Phone: (312)236-2622; Fax: (312)236-0390; Email: info@nbmbaa.org • URL: http://www.nbmbaa.org • Creates educational opportunities to form professional and economic growth of African-Americans. Develops partnerships to its members and provides educational programs to increase the awareness on business field.

National Business Education Association. 1914 Association Dr., Reston, VA 20191-1596. Phone: (703)860-8300; Fax: (703)620-4483; Email: nbea@nbea.org • URL: http://www.nbea.org • Teachers of business subjects in secondary and postsecondary schools and colleges; administrators and research workers in business education; businesspersons interested in business education; teachers in educational institutions training business teachers; high school and college students preparing for careers in business.

National Business Incubation Association. 340 W State St., Unit 25, Athens, OH 45701-1565. Phone: (740)593-4331; Fax: (740)593-1996; Email: info@nbia.org • URL: http://www.nbia.org • Incubator developers and managers; corporate joint venture partners, venture capital investors; economic development professionals. (Incubators are business assistance programs providing business consulting services and financing assistance to start-up and fledgling companies.) Helps newly formed businesses to succeed. Educates businesses and investors on incubator benefits; offers specialized training in incubator formation and management. Conducts research and referral services; compiles statistics; maintains speakers' bureau; publishes information relevant to business incubation and growing companies.

National Business Officers Association. 1400 L St. NW, Ste. 850, Washington, DC 20005. Phone: (202)407-7140 or (202)407-7141; Fax: (202)354-4944; Email: jeff.shields@nboa.net • URL: http://www.nboa.net • Independent school business officers. Helps members streamline business and strategic operations.

National Chemical Credit Association. 1100 Main St., Buffalo, NY 14209-2356. Phone: (716)887-9547; Fax: (716)878-0479 • URL: http://www.ncca1.org/document_1.html • Represents chemical companies. Aims to facilitate the exchange of commercial credit information among leaders of the chemical industry, as well as provide continual professional education to its members. Sponsors monthly educational programs at divisional meetings.

National Council of Asian American Business Associations. 475 N Whisman Rd., Ste. 200, Mountain View, CA 94043. Phone: (650)303-6164; Fax: (650)350-1545; Email: info@national-caaba.

org • URL: http://www.national-caaba.org • Serve as the voice of Asian Pacific American business owners in the United States. Works to effect positive change in the areas of economic development, public contracting and private procurement, and public and fiscal policies that impact Asian Pacific American businesses and communities at large. Seeks to create opportunities in the social, political, and economic sectors for the Asian Pacific American business community.

National Latina Business Women Association. 11664 National Blvd., Ste. 283, Los Angeles, CA 90064. Phone: 888-MY-NLBWA; Email: info@nlbwa.org • URL: http://nlbwa.org • Strives to promote, develop, and support the growth of Latina business owners and professionals. Seeks to create networking and mentoring opportunities for members.

National Nurses in Business Association. 8941 Atlanta Ave., Ste. 202, Huntington Beach, CA 92646. Phone: 877-353-8888 • URL: http://www.nnba.net • Promotes, supports, educates, and provides a comprehensive network for nurse entrepreneurs.

NBFI and Modaraba Association of Pakistan. 602, Progressive Ctr., 30-A, Blk. 6, PEHCS, Shahrah-e-Faisal, Karachi 75400, Pakistan. Phone: 92 21 34389774; Fax: 92 21 34389775; Email: association@nbfi-modaraba.com.pk • URL: http://www.nbfi-modaraba.com.pk • Seeks to promote the Islamic way of business. Encourages public awareness of the role of modaraba in financing. Conducts surveys and analysis on the Islamic modes of business and finance. Safeguards and protects the interests of members.

Netherlands Society for Industry and Trade. Jan Van Nassaustraat 75, NL-2596 BP The Hague, Netherlands. Phone: 31 70 3141940; Fax: 31 70 3247515; Email: info@de-maatschappij.nl • URL: http://www.de-maatschappij.nl • Association of businesses and industries in the Netherlands. Promotes trade and investment. Conducts research.

North American Association of Inventory Services. PO Box 120145, Saint Paul, MN 55112. • URL: http://www.naais.com • Represents Independent inventory services; individuals interested in the inventory industry; individuals outside the industry who have performed notable service. Promotes activities aimed at enabling the inventory service to operate efficiently and maintain high standards of conduct. Provides a clearinghouse and medium for the benefit of owners of businesses and shops involving the utilization and maintenance of product inventories. Considers and deals with problems of operation and management, such as those associated with customer accounts and employment. Disseminates business information on the inventory service industry. Maintains speakers' bureau; compiles statistics.

North American Trailer Dealers Association. 111 2nd Ave. NE, Unit 1405, Saint Petersburg, FL 33701-3480. Phone: (727)360-0304; Fax: (727)231-8356; Email: info@natda.org • URL: http://natda.org • Supports the light and medium duty trailer dealers industry. Promotes financial strength, professional credibility and industry recognition for trailer dealers and manufacturers throughout the United States. Provides trailer dealers with benefits, programs and education.

Parachute Industry Association. 3833 W Oakton St., Skokie, IL 60076-3429. Phone: (847)674-9742; Fax: (847)674-9743 • URL: http://www.pia.com • Represents companies and individuals united by a common desire to improve business opportunities in the parachute industry. Develops technical, service and operating standards for parachute equipment, skydiving safety, and related aviation topics.

Personal Injury Lawyers Marketing and Management Association. 607 Briarwood Dr., Ste. 4, Myrtle Beach, SC 29572. Phone: 800-497-1890 or (843)361-1700; Fax: (866)859-8126; Email: info@pilmma.org • URL: http://www.pilmma.org • Represents personal injury lawyers and disability attorneys. Provides members with the necessary tools, information and education to help grow and manage a successful contingency-based injury and disability law practice. Seeks to fulfill the marketing and management needs of members by granting access to sources of credible information and educational events.

Polish Private Equity Association. ul. E Plater 53, 31 pietro, 00-113 Warsaw, Poland. Phone: 48 22 4588430; Fax: 48 22 4588555; Email: psik@psik.org.pl • URL: http://www.ppea.org.pl • Promotes and develops the private equity and venture capital industry in Poland. Represents the interests of the Polish private equity and venture capital community in Poland and abroad. Keeps members informed about significant initiatives and proposed changes to the legal, tax and regulatory environment.

Private Equity CFO Association. c/o RBS Citizens, 28 State St., 14th Fl., Boston, MA 02109. • URL: http://www.privateequitycfo.org • Provides networking opportunities for members to share best practices. Responds to and addresses industry and professional issues of current interest. Develops programs that will provide education to association members. Improves and strengthens the flow of information among members.

Product Development and Management Association. 330 N Wabash Ave., Ste. 2000, Chicago, IL 60611. Phone: 800-232-5241 or (312)321-5145; Fax: (312)673-6885; Email: pdma@pdma.org • URL: http://www.pdma.org • Managers working in product innovation; teachers and researchers in the areas of product innovation management, product planning and development, and new product marketing; government regulators and facilitators involved in the product development process; product innovation consultants; market research firms; new product institutes; advertising agencies and media; testing companies; trade associations. Promotes improved product innovation management by drawing upon members' resources. Encourages research designed to make product innovation management more effective and efficient; Provides forum for the exchange of ideas and findings among universities, industry, government and related sectors.

Productivity Association of Pakistan. Natl. Productivity Organization, Ministry of Industries, Software Technology Park, 2nd Fl., Constitution Ave., Islamabad, Pakistan. Phone: 92 51 2823304 or 92 51 2823305; Fax: 92 51 2823309; Email: info@npo.gov.pk • URL: http://www.npo.gov.pk/productivity-association • Seeks to promote and increase productivity by utilizing the knowledge, experience, expertise and resources of members. Aims to strengthen networking activities with public and private sector organizations. Provides a platform for the exchange of information and knowledge that are of strategic importance to research and development.

Professional Decorative Painters Association. PO Box 13427, Denver, CO 80201-3427. Email: admin@pdpa.org • URL: http://www.pdpa.org • Promotes the advancement of professional decorative painting worldwide. Provides a forum for the industry's stakeholders, craftspersons, students, and manufacturers to improve the level of practice and relationship design in the field. Offers resources to foster growth and professionalism within the industry.

Qatari Businessmen Association. PO Box 24475, Doha, Qatar. Phone: 974 443 53 120; Fax: 974 443 53 834; Email: qba@qataribusinessmen.org • URL: http://www.qataribusinessmen.org • Seeks to strengthen Qatar's business and economic growth. Supports and enhances the role of the private sector in the economy. Promotes private sectors' activities and establishes a channel of communication among Qatari businessmen. Acts as a catalyst for the promotion of diversified investment flows, modern entrepreneurial spirit and corporate development in Qatar.

Restaurant Facility Management Association. 5600 Tennyson Pkwy., Ste. 280, Plano, TX 75024. Phone: (972)805-0905; Fax: (972)805-0906; Email: tracy@rfmaonline.com • URL: http://www.rfmaonline.com • Aims to promote the advancement of the restaurant facility management profession. Maintains professional and ethical standards among members. Provides networking to share knowledge and exchange information.

Retail Energy Supply Association. PO Box 6089, Harrisburg, PA 17112. Phone: (717)566-5405; Email: tmccormick@resausa.org • URL: http://www.resausa.org • Represents the interests of retail energy suppliers. Promotes the development and furthering of retail energy markets in the United States. Sponsors social and networking opportunities for members.

Russian Association of Business Education. Kronstadt Blvd. St., d. 37 B, Ste. 140, 125499 Moscow, Russia. Phone: 7 499 9439302; Fax: 7 499 9439309; Email: office@rabe.ru • URL: http://www.rabe.ru • Aims to unite universities, institutes, business schools and other training centers in the field of business education. Trains, retrains and upgrades the qualifications of personnel engaged in developing Russian business. Participates in the elaboration of the strategy of business education development in Russia and CIS.

Russian Venture Capital Association. ORm. 209, Bldg. 12B, prospekt Engelsa 27, 194156 Saint Petersburg, Russia. Phone: 7 812 3266180; Fax: 7 812 3266180; Email: rvca@rvca.ru • URL: http://www.rvca.ru • Promotes the development of the venture capital industry in Russia. Seeks to create a positive political and entrepreneurial environment for investment activities. Represents members' interests at the government level and in financial and industrial markets within the country and abroad.

Security Analysis and Risk Management Association. PO Box 100284, Arlington, VA 22210. Phone: (703)635-7906; Fax: (703)635-7935; Email: info@sarma.org • URL: http://sarma.org • Aims to further the development, standardization and professionalization of the security analysis and risk management discipline. Provides leadership, education and certification for security analysis and risk management professionals. Serves as a forum to share information, ideas and methodologies to improve the development and application of the security analysis and risk management profession.

Self Storage Association of the United Kingdom. Priestley House, The Gullet, Nantwich CW5 5SZ, United Kingdom. Phone: 44 1270 623150; Email: admin@ssauk.com • URL: http://www.ssauk.com • Encourages members, of the Self Storage Industry, to operate their storage facilities to a recommended minimum standard. Encourages prospective self-storage operators to carry out a full research of the Industry before opening their facilities. Preserves high standards of conduct in its members and in the industry. Promotes the industry to the general public.

Shop, Distributive, and Allied Employees' Association. 53 Queen St., Level 6, Melbourne, VIC 3000, Australia. Phone: 61 3 86117000; Fax: 61 3 86117099 • URL: http://www.sda.org.au • Shop-workers in the retail and fast food industries. Promotes equal opportunity and equal treatment of all members regardless of race, creed, disability, sexual preference, or gender. Works to improve the terms and conditions of members' employment and to protect the interests of members.

Singapore Productivity Association. 11 Eunos Rd. 8, No. 08-01, Singapore 408601, Singapore. Phone: 65

62783344; Fax: 65 62725095; Email: customersvc@spa.org.sg • URL: http://www.spa.org.sg • Promotes the active involvement of organizations and individuals in the productivity movement. Encourages the spread of productivity and techniques.

Singapore Venture Capital and Private Equity Association. 14 Robinson Rd., No. 07-02A, Far East Finance Bldg., Singapore 048545, Singapore. Phone: 65 6 2247001; Fax: 65 6 2246772; Email: info@svca.org.sg • URL: http://www.svca.org.sg • Promotes, develops, and maintains local venture capital and private equity industry as a source of equity finance. Represents the local venture capital industry in dealing with parties from other countries. Fosters interaction among members, investors, and investees.

Slovak Venture Capital Association. Stefanikova 6a, 811 05 Bratislava, Slovakia. Phone: 421 2 754414356; Fax: 421 2 754431180; Email: slovca@slovca.sk • URL: http://www.slovca.sk • Provides information for people seeking capital for new and existing enterprises. Represents the interests of members before the government and other related institutions/agencies. Encourages the highest standards of business practice.

Small Firms Association. Confederation House, 84-86 Lower Baggot St., Dublin 2, Dublin, Ireland. Phone: 353 1 6051500 or 353 1 6051602; Fax: 353 1 353 1 6381602; Email: info@sfa.ie • URL: http://www.sfa.ie • Represents the small enterprises in Ireland. Provides economic, commercial, employee relations and social affairs advice and assistance.

South African Venture Capital and Private Equity Association. PO Box 1140, Houghton 2041, South Africa. Phone: 27 11 2680041; Fax: 27 11 2680527; Email: info@savca.co.za • URL: http://www.savca.co.za • Promotes the venture capital and private equity profession in Southern Africa. Develops and stimulates professional and transactional venture capital and private equity investments.

Southeastern Fisheries Association. 1118-B Thomasville Rd., Tallahassee, FL 32303. Phone: (850)224-0612; Fax: (850)222-3663; Email: info@sfaonline.org • URL: http://www.sfaonline.org/ • Producers, distributors and suppliers of seafood in the South Atlantic and Gulf of Mexico areas. Disseminates information on legislation, both proposed and implemented, that affects fishermen in that area. Promotes and represents commercial fishermen's interests in legislative, industrial and environmental matters. Provides HAACP training onsite.

Southwest Case Research Association. Augusta State University, Knox School of Accountancy, Hull College of Business, 2500 Walton Way, Augusta, GA 30904-2200. Phone: (706)667-4541 • URL: http://www.swcrahome.org • Promotes research, writing, and publication of decision-based cases for graduate and undergraduate business studies.

Sudanese Chambers of Industries Association. PO Box 2565, Khartoum, Sudan. Phone: 249 1 83471717; Fax: 249 1 83471720; Email: sec.general@sudanindustry.org • URL: http://sudanindustry.org • Represents businessmen from the private industrial sector. Participates in trade agreements, workers' legislation and decision making in issues regarding the industry as well as the economy of Sudan. Encourages local and foreign investment in the industrial sector.

Sustainable Food Trade Association. 49 Race St., New Castle, VA 24127-6397. Phone: (413)624-6678; Email: info@sustainablefoodtrade.org • URL: http://www.sustainablefoodtrade.org • Works to foster sustainable business practices in the organic food trade. Collaborates with businesses in the organic and natural foods trade to align their day-to-day business practices with sustainability principles. Provides education, research, and networking for industry leaders to create opportunities for cross-supply chain innovation and best practices.

Swedish Business Association of Singapore. No. 05-01 Triple One Somerset, 111 Somerset Rd., Singapore 238164, Singapore. Phone: 65 67345009; Email: swedbiz@singnet.com.sg • URL: http://www.sbas.org.sg • Aims to promote the development of commerce between Singapore and Sweden.

Sweet and Fortified Wine Association. PO Box 193, Applegate, CA 95703. Phone: (916)258-7115; Email: sweetandfortified@sbcglobal.net • URL: http://sweetandfortifiedwine.org • Aims to expand and develop the market for sweet and fortified wines. Provides a forum for industry partners and the general public to share ideas and information on sweet and fortified wines. Advocates for responsible consumption of alcoholic beverages.

Swiss Business Association Singapore. c/o Embassy of Switzerland, 1, Swiss Club Link, Singapore 288162, Singapore. Phone: 65 67220799 • URL: http://www.swissbusiness.org.sg • Assists Swiss companies established in Singapore in conducting, sponsoring or promoting any activity that will benefit its members. Promotes the interests of members related to trade. Encourages the growth of the Swiss trade by promoting investment, finance, commerce and industry.

Swiss Malaysian Business Association. c/o Embassy of Switzerland, 16 Persiaran Madge, 55000 Kuala Lumpur, Malaysia. Phone: 60 3 21629889; Fax: 60 3 21418410; Email: info@smba.org.my • URL: http://www.myswiss.org • Promotes and fosters bilateral trade, services and investment between Switzerland and Malaysia. Assists potential new Swiss companies in establishing their headquarters in Malaysia. Maintains and improves close trading, commercial and other links between Malaysia and Switzerland. Provides a forum for members in exchanging information and identifying and discussing issues of common interests regarding economic, industrial and commercial objectives.

Taipei Business Association in Singapore. No. 06-07 SCCCI Bldg., 47 Hill St., Singapore 179365, Singapore. Phone: 65 63383916; Fax: 65 63383930; Email: tpebiz@singnet.com.sg • URL: http://www.tbas.org.sg.

Taiwan Private Equity and Venture Capital Association. Rm. 133, 10th Fl., No. 133, Sect. C, Minsheng E Rd., Songshan Dist., Taipei 105, Taiwan. Phone: 886 2 25450075; Fax: 886 2 25452752; Email: public@tvca.org.tw • URL: http://www.tvca.org.tw • Promotes awareness of the venture capital industry in Taiwan and its importance to the economy. Provides networking opportunity among members. Acts as a liaison between members and the government in order to update members of relevant investment regulations. Establishes professional venture capital information center in Taiwan in order to provide members with relevant local and international industry information. Promotes relevant business laws and regulations and economic policies.

TechAssure Association. 1550 17th St., Ste. 600, Denver, CO 80202. Phone: (888)208-8670 • Provides training and education services for risk management professionals that specialize in technology, life sciences and digital media industries. Works with insurance companies to customize policy forms and to improve the underwriting process. Encourages members to share best practices and to discuss ideas and experiences.

Thai Venture Capital Association. 19/1 Bldg. 2, King Chamnan-aksorn, Phaholyothin Rd., Phayathai, Bangkok 10400, Thailand. Phone: 66 2 6617898; Fax: 66 2 6617899; Email: tvca@venturecapital.or.th • URL: http://www.venturecapital.or.th • Promotes venture capital and private equity businesses in Thailand. Supports and assists members in all problems related to venture capital businesses, including negotiations with any foreign parties. Promotes closer working relationships among members in order to exchange ideas and opinions regarding technical knowledge, news, economic research and financial information.

Total Attorneys. 25 E Washington St., Ste. 510, Chicago, IL 60602. Phone: 877-349-1307; Email: solutions@totalattorneys.com • URL: http://www.totalattorneys.com • Focuses on the advancement of attorneys, paralegals and other legal support staff. Offers solo practitioners and small law firms the tools, training and network needed to collaborate with peers, connect with experts and find better work-life balance. Coordinates workshops and conferences, educational resources, legal tools, affinity partnerships and community forums.

Turnaround Management Association. 150 N Wacker Dr., Ste. 1900, Chicago, IL 60606. Phone: (312)578-6900; Fax: (312)578-8336; Email: info@turnaround.org • URL: http://www.turnaround.org/Default.aspx • Practitioners (interim managers, consultants, corporate managers and professional advisors), academics, students, attorneys and judges, commercial lenders and legislative personnel. Promotes the image and credibility of the turnaround profession; fosters professional development and networking opportunities for turnaround executives; serves as a clearinghouse of information and research pertinent to the profession. Conducts networking forums; offers educational and credentialing programs.

UNIMA. 10, Cours Aristide Briand, BP 402, F-08107 Charleville-Mezieres, France. Phone: 33 324 328563; Fax: 33 324 327692; Email: sgi@unima.org • URL: http://www.unima.org/en/home • Agricultural contractors, farm workers, farmers, farm equipment manufacturers, and other providers of support and services to agricultural industries. Seeks to advance the interests of agribusinesses. Represents members' commercial and regulatory interests at the national level.

Women Entrepreneurs of Canada. 720 Spadina Ave., Ste. 202, Toronto, ON, Canada M5S 2T9. Phone: 866-207-4439 or (416)921-5050; Fax: (416)929-5256; Email: wec@wec.ca • URL: http://www.wec.ca • Addresses the need of women entrepreneurs and supports their growth and development. Provides meaningful networking opportunities to connect with peers as well as the larger business community, government and the international business community. Builds entrepreneurship acumen and business leadership capacity.

World Energy Cities Partnership. 901 Bagby, Houston, TX 77002. Phone: (832)393-0829; Email: matthew.shailer@houstontx.gov • URL: http://www.energycities.org • Collaborates and assists cities around the world to support the local energy sectors. Encourages exchange of petroleum industry knowledge and economic and infrastructure development strategies. Provides a network of industry support services and resources.

ASSOCIATIONS, INTERNATIONAL

See INTERNATIONAL AGENCIES

ASTRONAUTICS

See ROCKET INDUSTRY

ATHLETIC GOODS

See SPORTING GOODS INDUSTRY

ATLASES

See MAPS

ATOMIC POWER

See NUCLEAR ENERGY

ATTORNEYS

See LAWYERS

AUCTIONS

DIRECTORIES

Real Estate Auctioneers Directory. InfoGroup Inc. • Annual. Number of listings: 11,136. Entries include: Name, address, phone, size of advertisement, name of owner or manager, number of employees, year first in "Yellow Pages." Compiled from telephone company "Yellow Pages," nationwide.

PRICE SOURCES

Book Auction Records. RoweCom UK Ltd. • Annual. $150.00.

TRADE/PROFESSIONAL ASSOCIATIONS

Industrial Auctioneers Association. 3213 Ayr Ln., Dresher, PA 19025. Phone: 800-805-8359 or (215)366-5450; Fax: (215)657-1964; Email: info@industrialauctioneers.org • URL: http://www.industrialauctioneers.org • Represents industrial machinery and equipment auctioneers. Promotes the use of auction sales in idle industrial equipment. Maintains ethical and professional standards among member auctioneers.

Livestock Marketing Association. 10510 NW Ambassador Dr., Kansas City, MO 64153. Phone: 800-821-2048 • URL: http://www.lmaweb.com • Livestock marketing businesses and livestock dealers. Sponsors annual World Livestock Auctioneer Championships. Offers management and promotional services.

National Auctioneers Association. 8880 Ballentine St., Overland Park, KS 66214. Phone: (913)541-8084; Fax: (913)894-5281 or (913)548-0932; Email: support@auctioneers.org • URL: http://www.auctioneers.org • Professional auctioneers. Provides continuing education classes for auctioneers, promotes use of the auction method of marketing in both the private and public sectors. Encourages the highest ethical standards for the profession.

National Auto Auction Association. 5320 Spectrum Dr., Ste. D, Frederick, MD 21703. Phone: (301)696-0400; Fax: (301)631-1359; Email: naaa@naaa.com • URL: http://www.naaa.com • Owners/operators of wholesale automobile and truck auctions; associate members are car and truck manufacturers, insurers of checks and titles, car and truck rental companies, publishers of auto price guide books, and others connected with the industry. Maintains hall of fame.

AUDIO EQUIPMENT INDUSTRY

See HIGH FIDELITY/STEREO

AUDIOVISUAL AIDS IN EDUCATION

See also AUDIOVISUAL AIDS IN INDUSTRY

ALMANACS AND YEARBOOKS

Educational Media and Technology Yearbook. Libraries Unlimited. • Annual. $80 print.

BIBLIOGRAPHIES

Films and Audiovisual Information. U. S. Government Printing Office. • Annual. Free. Issued by the Superintendent of Documents. A list of government publications on motion picture and audiovisual topics. Formerly *Motion Pictures, Films and Audiovisual Information*. (Subject Bibliography No. 73.).

CD-ROM DATABASES

ERIC SilverPlatter. U.S. Department of Education Institute of Education Sciences Education Resources Information Center. • Opinion papers, evaluations, speeches.

DIRECTORIES

AV Market Place: The Complete Business Directory of Audio, Audio Visual, Computer Systems, Film, Video, and Programming, with Industry Yellow Pages. Information Today, Inc. • Annual. $279.50 Individuals list price. Provides information on "more than 7,500 companies that create, apply, or distribute AV equipment and services for business, education, science, and government." Multimedia, virtual reality, presentation software, and interactive video are among the categories. Formerly published by R. R. Bowker.

Film and Video Finder. National Information Center for Educational Media. Plexus Publishing Inc. • Biennial. Contains 675,000 listings of film and video educational, technical and vocational children's programs and literary materials.

Index to AV Producers and Distributors. National Information Center for Educational Media. Plexus Publishing Inc. • Biennial. $89.00. A directory listing about 23,300 producers and distributors of all types of audiovisual educational materials.

ONLINE DATABASES

A-V Online. National Information Center for Educational Media. • Provides online descriptions of non-print educational materials for all levels, kindergarten to graduate school. Includes all types of audio, film, and video media. Updated quarterly. Inquire as to online cost and availability.

ERIC. U.S. Department of Education Institute of Education Sciences Educational Resources Information Center. • Funded by the U.S. Department of Education, Institute of Education Sciences (formerly Office of Educational Research and Improvement). Provides access to more than one million online records covering education-related journal and report literature, 1966 to date. Updating is monthly. Inquire as to online cost and availability.

PERIODICALS AND NEWSLETTERS

Educational Marketer: The Educational Publishing Industry's Voice of Authority Since 1968. SIMBA Information Inc. • Biweekly. $695 Individuals Online download. Edited for suppliers of educational materials to schools and colleges at all levels. Covers print and electronic publishing, software, audiovisual items, and multimedia. Includes corporate news and educational statistics.

Educational Technology Research and Development. Association for Educational Communications and Technology. • Bimonthly. Focuses entirely on research and development in educational technology.

Multimedia Schools: A Practical Journal of Technology for Education including Multimedia, CD-ROM, Online and Internet and Hardware in K-12. Information Today, Inc. • Six times a year. $39.95 per year. Edited for school librarians, media center directors, computer coordinators, and others concerned with educational multimedia. Coverage includes the use of CD-ROM sources, the Internet, online services, and library technology.

TechTrends: For Leaders in Education and Training. Association for Educational Communications and Technology. • Bimonthly. $65.00 per year.

TRADE/PROFESSIONAL ASSOCIATIONS

Association for Educational Communications and Technology. 320 W 8th St., Ste. 101, Bloomington, IN 47404. Phone: 877-677-2328 or (812)335-7675; Fax: (812)335-7678; Email: aect@aect.org • URL: http://www.aect.org/newsite • Instructional technology professionals. Provides leadership in educational communications and technology by linking professionals holding a common interest in the use of educational technology and its application of the learning process.

AUDIOVISUAL AIDS IN INDUSTRY

See also AUDIOVISUAL AIDS IN EDUCATION

BIBLIOGRAPHIES

Films and Audiovisual Information. U. S. Government Printing Office. • Annual. Free. Issued by the Superintendent of Documents. A list of government publications on motion picture and audiovisual topics. Formerly *Motion Pictures, Films and Audiovisual Information*. (Subject Bibliography No. 73.).

DIRECTORIES

AV Market Place: The Complete Business Directory of Audio, Audio Visual, Computer Systems, Film, Video, and Programming, with Industry Yellow Pages. Information Today, Inc. • Annual. $279.50 Individuals list price. Provides information on "more than 7,500 companies that create, apply, or distribute AV equipment and services for business, education, science, and government." Multimedia, virtual reality, presentation software, and interactive video are among the categories. Formerly published by R. R. Bowker.

ONLINE DATABASES

ERIC. U.S. Department of Education Institute of Education Sciences Educational Resources Information Center. • Funded by the U.S. Department of Education, Institute of Education Sciences (formerly Office of Educational Research and Improvement). Provides access to more than one million online records covering education-related journal and report literature, 1966 to date. Updating is monthly. Inquire as to online cost and availability.

PERIODICALS AND NEWSLETTERS

Harvard Management Communication Letter. Harvard Business School Publishing. • Description: Provides information and techniques for managers on effective communication.

Presentations: Technology and Techniques for Effective Communication. Nielsen Business Media Inc. • Monthly. Free to qualified personnel; others, $69.00 per year. Covers the use of presentation hardware and software, including audiovisual equipment and computerized display systems. Includes an annual *Buyers Guide to Presentation Products*.

Video Librarian: The Video Review Magazine. Video Librarian. • Bimonthly. $64. Edited for public and school libraries. Each issue includes reviews of hundreds of video DVDs or cassettes, in various subject areas.

TRADE/PROFESSIONAL ASSOCIATIONS

Communications Media Management Association. 20423 State Rd. 7, Ste. F6-491, Boca Raton, FL 33498. Phone: (561)477-8100 • URL: http://cmma.org • Professional association of managers of communications media departments of business, education, or government. Aims to provide networking and educational opportunities for communications media managers that build peer professional relationships, facilitate leadership development, deepen managerial skills, expand technical knowledge, and develop skills in business strategy.

For publishers' addresses, refer to SOURCES CITED section at the back of the book.

AUDIOVISUAL EQUIPMENT INDUSTRY

BIBLIOGRAPHIES

Films and Audiovisual Information. U. S. Government Printing Office. • Annual. Free. Issued by the Superintendent of Documents. A list of government publications on motion picture and audiovisual topics. Formerly *Motion Pictures, Films and Audiovisual Information*. (Subject Bibliography No. 73.).

DIRECTORIES

AV Market Place: The Complete Business Directory of Audio, Audio Visual, Computer Systems, Film, Video, and Programming, with Industry Yellow Pages. Information Today, Inc. • Annual. $279.50 Individuals list price. Provides information on "more than 7,500 companies that create, apply, or distribute AV equipment and services for business, education, science, and government." Multimedia, virtual reality, presentation software, and interactive video are among the categories. Formerly published by R. R. Bowker.

AV Presentation--Buyer's Guide. Cygnus Business Media Inc. • Annual. $6. Covers: lists of film and slide laboratory services and manufacturers of media production and presentation equipment and audiovisual supplies. Entries include: Company name, address, product or service.

Entertainment Sourcebook: An Insider's Guide on Where to Find Everything. Applause Theatre & Cinema Books. • Annual. $45.00. Compiled by the Association of Theatrical Artists and Craftspeople (www.entertainmentsourcebook.com/ATAC.htm). Lists more than 5,000 sources of theatrical and entertainment supplies and services, such as props, costumes, publicity agencies, scenic shops, amusement park equipment, audio/video products, balloons, wigs, make-up, magic supplies, etc.

Library Journal Sourcebook: The Reference For Library Products & Services. Reed Elsevier Group plc Reed Business Information. • Annual. Publication includes: List of over 600 suppliers of products and services used by libraries from abstracting to word processing equipment. Entries include: Company name, address, phone, list of products or services. Complete listings for more than 100 architectural firms; Disaster planning for librarians.

PERIODICALS AND NEWSLETTERS

Media and Methods: Educational Products, Technologies and Programs for Schools and Universities. American Society of Educators. • 5/year. $35 /year. Dedicated to reporting on the latest advancements in the field of education.

Presentations: Technology and Techniques for Effective Communication. Nielsen Business Media Inc. • Monthly. Free to qualified personnel; others, $69.00 per year. Covers the use of presentation hardware and software, including audiovisual equipment and computerized display systems. Includes an annual *Buyers Guide to Presentation Products*.

TRADE/PROFESSIONAL ASSOCIATIONS

Association of Theatrical Artists and Craftspeople. 48 Fairway St., Bloomfield, NJ 07003-5515. Phone: (212)234-9001 • URL: http://www.atacbiz.com • Members are artists and craftspeople working in theatre, film, TV, and advertising. Areas of expertise include props, costumes, millinery, puppetry, display, and special effects.

AUDITING

See also ACCOUNTING; CERTIFIED PUBLIC ACCOUNTANTS; COST ACCOUNTING; INTERNAL AUDITING

ABSTRACTS AND INDEXES

Accounting and Tax Index. ProQuest L.L.C. • Quarterly. Indexes accounting, auditing, and taxation literature appearing in journals, books, pamphlets, conference proceedings, and newsletters.

Accounting Articles. Wolters Kluwer Law & Business CCH. • Monthly. $624. Covers accounting news.

DIRECTORIES

America's Corporate Finance Directory. LexisNexis. • Annual. $1,399 Individuals print. Covers: Financial personnel and outside financial services relationships of 5,000 leading United States corporations and their wholly-owned United States subsidiaries. Entries include: Company name, address, phone, fax, telex, e-mail addresses, stock exchange information, earnings, total assets, size of pension/profit-sharing fund portfolio, number of employees, description of business, wholly-owned U.S. Subsidiaries of parent company; name and title of key executives; outside suppliers of financial services.

Who Audits the UK?. Public Relations Consultants Association. • Irregular. $46. Covers: Information on the auditing of 2,000 companies and organizations in the UK. Entries include: Company name, address, phone.

HANDBOOKS AND MANUALS

Applying GAAP and GAAS. Matthew Bender and Company Inc. • $898 Print. In-depth explanations of generally accepted accounting principles (GAAP) and generally accepted auditing standards (GAAS).

GAAS Guide. Larry P. Bailey. Aspen Publishers, Inc. • Annual. $235. Describes standards, practices, and procedures.

Practitioner's Guide to GAAS. John Wiley & Sons Inc. • Annual. $105 paperback. Covers GAAS: Generally Accepted Auditing Standards, promulgated by the American Institute of Certified Public Accountants. (Includes CD-ROM.).

SEC Accounting Rules. Wolters Kluwer Law & Business CCH. • $448.00. Looseleaf service.

ONLINE DATABASES

Accounting and Tax Database. ProQuest L.L.C. • Provides indexing and abstracting of the literature of accounting, taxation, and financial management, 1971 to date. Updating is weekly. Especially covers accounting, auditing, banking, bankruptcy, employee compensation and benefits, cash management, financial planning, and credit. Inquire as to online cost and availability.

OTHER SOURCES

Auditing Research Monographs. American Institute of Certified Public Accountants. • Irregular. Price varies.

Financial Accounting Series. Financial Accounting Standards Board. • Monthly. Price on application.

PERIODICALS AND NEWSLETTERS

Internal Auditor. Institute of Internal Auditors. • Bimonthly. $75 U.S. and Canada print and online. Internal auditing.

Journal of Accounting, Auditing and Finance. New York University Vincent C. Ross Institute of Accounting Research. Greenwood Publishing Group Inc. • Quarterly. Individuals, $70.00 per year; institutions, $165.00 per year.

TRADE/PROFESSIONAL ASSOCIATIONS

American Institute of Certified Public Accountants. 1211 Avenue of the Americas, New York, NY 10036-8775. Phone: 888-777-7077 or (212)596-6200; Fax: (212)596-6213; Email: service@aicpa.org • URL: http://www.aicpa.org • Professional society of accountants certified by the states and territories. Responsibilities include establishing auditing and reporting standards; influencing the development of financial accounting standards underlying the presentation of U.S. corporate financial statements; preparing and grading the national Uniform CPA Examination for the state licensing bodies. Conducts research and continuing education programs and oversight of practice. Maintains over 100 committees including Accounting Standards, Accounting and Review Services, AICPA Effective Legislation Political Action, Auditing Standards, Taxation, Consulting Services, Professional Ethics, Quality Review, Women and Family Issues, and Information Technology.

Association of British Certification Bodies. c/o Trevor Nash, Chief Executive, PO Box 836, Bedford MK45 9DR, United Kingdom. Phone: 44 1525 630679 • URL: http://www.abcb.org.uk • Independent accredited certification bodies who undertake impartial certification of quality and environmental management systems, products, and personnel. Aims to provide a forum for the discussion and formulation of policy on matters of common concern; to represent the collective interests of members and, where consistent with such interests, those of individual members, in appropriate quarters; and to adopt, if thought fit, a code of professional practice in certification matters.

European Organisation of Supreme Audit Institutions. c/o Ramon Alvarez de Miranda, Secretary General, Fuencarral 81, 28004 Madrid, Spain. Phone: 34 91 446 04 66; Fax: 34 91 593 38 94; Email: eurosai@tcu.es • URL: http://www.eurosai.org • Promotes professional and technical understanding of audit and public finance; works to secure unification of terminology in the field of audit of public finance.

AUDITING, INTERNAL

See INTERNAL AUDITING

AUTHORITIES

See CONSULTANTS

AUTHORS

See WRITERS AND WRITING

AUTOMATED TELLER MACHINES (ATM)

See BANK AUTOMATION

AUTOMATIC CONTROL EQUIPMENT

See SCIENTIFIC APPARATUS AND INSTRUMENT INDUSTRIES

AUTOMATIC IDENTIFICATION SYSTEMS

ABSTRACTS AND INDEXES

Applied Science and Technology Index. EBSCO Publishing Inc. • 11/year. Indexes a wide variety of English language technical, industrial, and engineering periodicals.

Computer and Information Systems Abstracts Journal: An Abstract Journal Pertaining to the Theory, Design, Fabrication and Application of Computer and Information Systems. CSA. • Monthly. $1,750 per year.

Computer Science Index. EBSCO Publishing Inc. • Quarterly. $245 per year. Contains brief abstracts of book and periodical literature covering all phases of computing, including approximately 70 specific application areas.

NTIS Alerts: Computers, Control & Information Theory. U.S. Department of Commerce National Technical Information Service. • Biweekly. $130 per year. Covers computer hardware, software, control systems, pattern recognition, image processing, and related subjects.

CD-ROM DATABASES

Applied Science and Technology Abstracts. EBSCO Publishing Inc. • Citations for more than 700 prominent scientific, technical, engineering, and industrial periodicals.

DIRECTORIES

Frontline Solutions Buyer's Guide. Advanstar Communications. • Annual. $34.95 plus $3.50 shipping. Publication includes: List of manufacturers, suppliers, consultants, value added resellers, and dealers/distributors of automatic identification and data capture software, technology, equipment, and products for bar code, biometric identification, electronic data interchange, machine vision, magnetic stripe, optical character recognition, radio frequency data communications, radio frequency identification, smart cards, and voice data entry; also includes related organizations, and sources for industry standards. Entries include: Company name, address, phone, e-mail, web address, products or services.

Manufacturing Systems: Buyers Guide. Reed Elsevier Group plc Reed Business Information. • Annual. Price on application. Contains information on companies manufacturing or supplying materials handling systems, CAD/CAM systems, specialized software for manufacturing, programmable controllers, machine vision systems, and automatic identification systems.

ONLINE DATABASES

Applied Science and Technology Index Online. H.W. Wilson Co. • Provides online indexing of 500 major scientific, technical, industrial, and engineering periodicals. Time period is 1983 to date. Monthly updates. Inquire as to online cost and availability.

PERIODICALS AND NEWSLETTERS

Card Technology. SourceMedia Inc. • Monthly. $79.00 per year. Covers advanced technology for credit, debit, and other cards. Topics include smart cards, optical recognition, and card design.

Item Processing Report. Access Intelligence L.L.C. • Description: Monitors developments in the processing of remittances and checks, including image processing, optical character recognition, check truncation, hardware, and software. **Remarks:** Absorbed The Powell Report, 1992.

Sensors: Your Resource for Sensing, Communications, and Control. Advanstar Communications. • Monthly. $70.00 per year. Edited for design, production, and manufacturing engineers involved with sensing systems. Emphasis is on emerging technology.

Supply Chain Systems: The Resource for Supply Chain Automation. Helmers Publishing, Inc. • Monthly. Free to qualified personnel; others, $55.00 per year. Covers trends in automatic identification technology and management. Formerly *ID Systems7*.

TRADE/PROFESSIONAL ASSOCIATIONS

AIM Global. One Landmark N, 20399 Rte. 19, Ste. 203, Cranberry Township, PA 16066. Phone: (724)742-4473; Fax: (724)742-4476; Email: info@aim-na.org • URL: http://www.aimglobal.org • Serves as a trade association for the automatic identification data captures technology industry.

AUTOMATIC TRANSLATING

See MACHINE TRANSLATING

AUTOMATION

See also COMPUTERS; CONTROL EQUIPMENT INDUSTRY; LINEAR PROGRAMMING; MACHINE VISION; ONLINE INFORMATION SYSTEMS; OPERATIONS RESEARCH; ROBOTS

ABSTRACTS AND INDEXES

Applied Science and Technology Index. EBSCO Publishing Inc. • 11/year. Indexes a wide variety of English language technical, industrial, and engineering periodicals.

Internet and Personal Computing Abstracts (print edition). EBSCO Publishing Inc. • Quarterly. $269.00 per year, including cumulative index. Provides more than 10,000 abstracts annually from both trade and academic publications. Covers computer hardware, software, product reviews, Web topics, e-commerce, networks, corporate news, security, and related topics. Formerly *Microcomputer Abstracts*.

Key Abstracts: Factory Automation. Institution of Engineering and Technology. • Monthly. $1,138. Provides international coverage of journal and proceedings literature, including publications on CAD/CAM, materials handling, robotics, and factory management.

NTIS Alerts: Manufacturing Technology. U.S. Department of Commerce National Technical Information Service. • Biweekly. $130 per year. Covers computer-aided design and manufacturing (CAD/CAM), engineering materials, quality control, machine tools, robots, lasers, productivity, and related subjects.

BIBLIOGRAPHIES

Automation. U. S. Government Printing Office. • Annual. Free. Issued by the Superintendent of Documents. A list of government publications on automation, computers, and related topics. Formerly *Computers and Data Processing*. (Subject Bibliography No. 51.).

DIRECTORIES

Assembly Buyers Guide. Reed Elsevier Group plc Reed Business Information. • Annual. $68.00. Lists manufacturers and suppliers of equipment relating to assembly automation, fasteners, adhesives, robotics, and power tools.

ONLINE DATABASES

Computer Database. Cengage Learning Inc. • Provides one year of full-text online for 150 leading computer-related publications. Also includes 70,000 product specifications and brief profiles of 13,000 computer product vendors and manufacturers. Inquire as to prices and availability.

INSPEC. Institution of Electrical Engineers. • Provides online citations, with abstracts, to the world literature of electrical engineering, electronics, optoelectronics, telecommunications, industrial controls, instrumentation, computer technology, information technology, and physics. Coverage includes more than 4,000 technical and scientific journals from 1969 to date, with weekly updating. (INSPEC is Information Services in Physics, Electronics, and Computing.) Inquire as to online cost and availability.

OTHER SOURCES

Annual Reviews in Control. Elsevier. • Annual. $807 Institutions print only.

PERIODICALS AND NEWSLETTERS

Advanced Manufacturing Technology: Monthly Report. Technical Insights. • Monthly. $695 Institutions. Covers technological developments relating to robotics, computer graphics, automation, computer-integrated manufacturing, and machining.

Information Week: Business Innovation Powered by Technology. UBM L.L.C. • Weekly. $199.00 per year. The magazine for information systems management.

Sensors: Your Resource for Sensing, Communications, and Control. Advanstar Communications. • Monthly. $70.00 per year. Edited for design, production, and manufacturing engineers involved with sensing systems. Emphasis is on emerging technology.

RESEARCH CENTERS AND INSTITUTES

Industrial Relations Research Institute. University of Wisconsin-Madison, c, Madison, WI 53706. Phone: (608)262-1300; Fax: (608)265-4591; Email: irri@mhub.facstaff.wisc.edu • URL: http://www.wisc.edu.

TRADE/PROFESSIONAL ASSOCIATIONS

Society of Manufacturing Engineers - Computer and Automated Systems Techincal Group. 1 SME Dr., Dearborn, MI 48121. Phone: 800-733-4763 or (313)425-3000; Fax: (313)425-3400; Email: service@sme.org • URL: http://www.arcat.com/arcatcos/cos37/arc37031.html • Sponsored by the Society of Manufacturing Engineers. Formerly Computer and Automated Systems Association.

AUTOMATION, BANK

See BANK AUTOMATION

AUTOMATION, LIBRARY

See LIBRARY AUTOMATION

AUTOMATION, OFFICE

See OFFICE AUTOMATION

AUTOMATONS

See ROBOTS

AUTOMOBILE ACCESSORIES INDUSTRY

See AUTOMOBILE EQUIPMENT INDUSTRY

AUTOMOBILE ACCIDENTS

See TRAFFIC ACCIDENTS AND TRAFFIC SAFETY

AUTOMOBILE BATTERIES

See BATTERY INDUSTRY

AUTOMOBILE DEALERS

See also AUTOMOTIVE INDUSTRY; USED CAR INDUSTRY

DIRECTORIES

NAFA Annual Reference Book. NAFA Fleet Management Association. • Online. Automobile manufacturers' sales and leasing representatives throughout the country.

FINANCIAL RATIOS

Annual Statement Studies. Risk Management Association. • Annual. Compiled from over 280,000 financial statements.

Annual Statement Studies: Industry Default Prob-

abilities and Cash Flow Measures. Risk Management Association. • Annual. $405 Nonmembers. Serves as a companion volume to the original *Annual Statement Studies.* Gives probability of default estimates on a percentage scale for more than 450 industries. Includes changes in position year-by-year for eight financial statement line items and provides percentage measures of cash flow.

Industry Norms and Key Business Ratios. Dun & Bradstreet Inc. • Annual. Five volumes. Covers over 800 kinds of businesses, arranged by Standard Industrial Classification number. More detailed editions covering longer periods of time are also available.

HANDBOOKS AND MANUALS

Used Car Sales. Entrepreneur Press. • Looseleaf. $59.50. A practical guide to getting started in the business of selling used cars. Covers profit potential, start-up costs, market size evaluation, owner's time required, site selection, lease negotiation, pricing, accounting, advertising, etc. (Start-Up Business Guide No. E2330.).

INTERNET DATABASES

Advance Monthly Retail Trade Report. U. S. Census Bureau. Phone: 800-541-8345 or (301)457-4100 or (301)763-2713; Fax: (301)457-1296 or (301)457-3842; Email: naics@census.gov • URL: http://www.census.gov/epcd/www/naicstab.htm • Web pages provide monthly sales figures for a wide range of retail businesses. Advance, preliminary, and final statistics are provided for the latest month available in each case, with a previous-year comparison. Updates are monthly.

PERIODICALS AND NEWSLETTERS

Chilton's Automotive Marketing: A Monthly Publication for the Retail Jobber and Distributor of Automotive Aftermarket. Reed Elsevier Group plc Reed Business Information. • Monthly. Free to qualified personnel; others, $48.00 per year. Includes marketing of automobile batteries. Formerly *Automotive Aftermarket News.*

Used Car Dealer. National Independent Automobile Dealers Association. • Monthly. $80 /year for nonmembers. Association magazine for dealers who buy and sell used cars.

STATISTICS SOURCES

Annual Benchmark Report for Retail Trade and Food Services. A Detailed Summary of Retail Sales, Purchases, Accounts Receivable, Inventories, and Food Service Sales. U. S. Government Printing Office. • Annual. $13.00. Issued by the U.S. Census Bureau. Provides detailed annual and monthly retail statistics for the most recent 10 years. Includes data for various kinds of retail outlets, including automobiles, furniture, appliances, building supplies, grocery stores, drug stores, gasoline stations, clothing, sporting goods, department stores, and restaurants.

U.S. Industry and Trade Outlook. U.S. Department of Commerce National Technical Information Service. • Annual. Produced by the International Trade Administration, U.S. Department of Commerce, in a "public-private" partnership with DRI/McGraw-Hill and Standard & Poor's. Provides basic data, outlook for the current year, and "Long-Term Prospects" (five-year projections) for a wide variety of products and services. Includes high technology industries. Formerly *U.S. Industrial Outlook.*

TRADE/PROFESSIONAL ASSOCIATIONS

National Association of Minority Automobile Dealers. 9745 Lottsford Rd., Ste. 150, Largo, MD 20774. Phone: (301)306-1614; Fax: (301)306-1493 • URL: http://www.namad.org • Automobile dealers. Acts as liaison between membership, the federal government, the community, and industry representatives; seeks to better the business conditions of its members on an ongoing basis. Serves as a confidential spokesperson for dealers. Offers business analysis, financial counseling, and short- and long-term management planning. Conducts research programs; compiles statistics.

National Automobile Dealers Association. 8400 Westpark Dr., McLean, VA 22102. Phone: 800-252-6232 or (703)821-7000; Fax: (703)821-7234; Email: help@nada.org • URL: http://www.nada.org • Franchised new car and truck dealers. Provides representation for franchised new car and truck dealers in the areas of government, industry, and public affairs. Offers management services and retirement and insurance programs to member dealers. Maintains National Automobile Dealers Charitable Foundation.

National Independent Automobile Dealers Association. 2521 Brown Blvd., Arlington, TX 76006. Phone: 800-682-3837 or (817)640-3838 or (434)983-2073; Fax: (817)649-5866; Email: info@niada.com • URL: http://www.niada.com • Individuals, companies, or corporations licensed by their states as dealers to buy and sell used motor vehicles; associate members are businesses related to or associated with the buying or selling of motor vehicles. Gathers and disseminates information relative to the used car industry; represents used car dealers before regulatory and legislative bodies; provides educational and other programs to help used car dealers understand their responsibilities; works for the betterment of the automobile industry. Works closely with local and state independent automobile dealers' associations and others concerning dealers and the public. Maintains code of fair dealing for members. Conducts seminars, meetings, and professional training programs. Maintains speakers' bureau, services for children, and charitable programs. Sponsors competitions; compiles statistics.

AUTOMOBILE EQUIPMENT INDUSTRY

See also AUTOMOBILE DEALERS; AUTOMOTIVE INDUSTRY

DIRECTORIES

Automobile Parts Used & Rebuilt Directory. InfoGroup Inc. • Annual. Number of listings: 11,939. Entries include: Name, address, phone, size of advertisement, name of owner or manager, number of employees, year first in "Yellow Pages." Compiled from telephone company "Yellow Pages," nationwide.

Automotive Parts: Industry Sector Profile. Philippine-German Export Development Project Philippine Bureau of Export Trade Promotion. • Publication includes: Companies exporting automotive parts from the Philippines. Entries include: Company name, address, phone, fax, name and title of contact, type of business, year established, subsidiary and branch names and locations, financial data, number of employees, government registrations, professional memberships, bank references, supply capability, export experience, business plan. Principal content of publication is an overview of the business environment and automotive parts industry in the Philippines.

Directory of American Manufacturers & Exporters of Autoparts & Accessories. EXIM Infotek Private Ltd. • $50 Individuals. Covers: e1850 Entries include: Company name, postal address, city, country, telephone, fax, e-mail and websites, contact person, designation, and product details.

Directory of Chinese Manufacturers & Exporters of Autoparts and Accessories. EXIM Infotek Private Ltd. • $20 Individuals. Covers: 190 Chinese manufacturers and exporters of auto accessories, auto fittings, auto lamps, auto parts, auto safety glass, automobile accessories, automobile electric appliances, automobile glass, automobile halogen lamps, automobile lights, automobile locks, automobile parts, automobile spare parts, automobile switches, automobile wipers, automotive glass, automotive parts, brake drums and hubs, brake shoes, brakes, car accessories, car audio devices, car parts, car speakers, clutch covers, clutch discs, gaskets, indicator lights, motor vehicle accessories, plastic autoparts, radiators, sealing products, shock absorbers, spare parts, transmission equipment, vehicle accessories, vehicle fittings, vehicle parts, and wheels. Entries include: Company name, postal address, city, country, phone, fax, e-mail and websites, contact person, designation, and product details.

Directory of Japanese Manufacturers & Exporters of Autoparts & Accessories. EXIM Infotek Private Ltd. • $35 Individuals. Covers: 530 Japanese manufacturers and exporters of accelerator pedals, clutch pedals, alternators, auto accessories, auto doors, automobile parts and equipment, automobile switches, automotive interior products, automotive lamp accessories, automotive lighting supplies, head lamps, horns, ignition coils, joints-universal, light alloy wheels, motor vehicle parts and supplies, radiators, rear-view mirrors, sealed beam units, seat adjusters, signal and indicator lamps, spare parts, steering columns, steering gears, steering wheels, transmission equipment, transmission parts, truck and bus accessories, truck parts and supplies, used auto parts, used automobile engine and body parts, used automobile parts and accessories, used car parts, used light trucks parts, used motor spare parts, used rims, used spare parts, wheels, window regulators, wiper motors, and wiring harnesses. Entries include: Company name, postal address, city, country, telephone, fax, e-mail and websites, contact person, designation, and product details.

Directory of South Korean Manufacturers & Exporters of Autoparts & Accessories. EXIM Infotek Private Ltd. • $30 Individuals. Covers: 400 South Korean manufacturers and exporters of alternators, auto parts, auto spare parts, automobiles relay, automotive accessories, automotive lighting equipment, automotive plastic parts, axles-rear, axles-front (beam/drive), airbags, bars-automotive, brake systems, bulbs-auto, bumpers-plastic, cables-speed meter, caps-wheel, car rear view systems, clutch systems, couplings and clutches, cylinder head gaskets, disc brakes, hardware for motorcars, head lamps, horns-automotive, hydraulic shock absorbers, industrial trailer/truck parts/accessories, joints-universal, liners and pads-brake, motor vehicle accessories, motor vehicle body components and spare parts, motor vehicle transmission parts, radiators, rods-connecting, seats-automotive, shafts-axle, shafts-cam, shafts-crank, signal and indicator lamps, spare parts, springs/shock absorbers, steering and suspension parts, steering wheels, suspension parts, transmission parts, used auto parts, vehicle brake parts, vehicle control instruments and panels, vehicle electrical and electronic equipment, wheels and wheel rims, window regulators, wiper arms, and yokes-automotive. Entries include: Company name, postal address, city, country, telephone, fax, e-mail and websites, contact person, designation, and product details.

Directory of Taiwanese Manufacturers & Exporters of Autoparts & Accessories. EXIM Infotek Private Ltd. • $50 Individuals. Covers: 890 Taiwanese manufacturers & exporters of auto accessories, auto electrical parts, auto lamps, auto parts, auto parts & accessories, auto spare parts, automobile parts, automotive lighting equipment, automotive parts, automotive plastic parts, brake shoes, brass silencers, car alarm systems, car mats, couplings, couplings & clutches, hardware for motorcars, head lamps, hose clamps, hydraulic shock absorbers, industrial trailer/truck parts/accessories, locking devices for cars, motor vehicle accessories, motor vehicle body components & spare parts, motor vehicle transmission parts, socket hoses for trucks, springs/shock absorbers, steering & suspension parts, truck parts, v belts, vehicle brake parts, vehicle control instruments & panels, vehicle electrical & electronic equipment, vehicle ventilation/heating & air conditioning systems, wheels & wheel rims, windshield wiper blades. Entries include: Company name, postal address, city, country, telephone, fax, e-mail & websites, contact person, designation, products detail.

The International Directory of Importers--Automotive Equipment, Parts & Accessories Importers. Interdata. • $320 Individuals print edition. Covers: 6,400 international firms importing automotive equipment, parts & accessories. Entries include: Company name and address, contact person, email, number of employees, year established, phone and telefaxes, business activity, bank references, as well as a listing of automotive equipment, parts & accessories currently being imported.

Plunkett's Automobile Industry Almanac. Plunkett Research Ltd. • $349.99 Individuals print + online; one-year subscription. Covers: 300 leading companies in the automotive industry. Entries include: Name, address, phone, fax, and key executives. Also includes analysis and information on trends, technology, and statistics in the field.

Racing Car Equipment (Manufacturers) Directory. InfoGroup Inc. • Annual. Number of listings: 6,655. Entries include: Name, address, phone, size of advertisement, name of owner or manager, number of employees, year first in "Yellow Pages." Compiled from telephone company "Yellow Pages," nationwide.

FINANCIAL RATIOS

Industry Norms and Key Business Ratios. Dun & Bradstreet Inc. • Annual. Five volumes. Covers over 800 kinds of businesses, arranged by Standard Industrial Classification number. More detailed editions covering longer periods of time are also available.

ONLINE DATABASES

Ward's AutoInfoBank. Ward's Communications. • Provides weekly, monthly, quarterly, and annual statistical data from 1980 to date for U. S. and imported cars and trucks. Covers production, shipments, sales, inventories, optional equipment, etc. Updating varies by series. Inquire as to online cost and availability.

PERIODICALS AND NEWSLETTERS

Brake and Frontend: The Complete Undercar Service Magazine. Babcox. • Monthly. $64.00 per year.

Chilton's Automotive Marketing: A Monthly Publication for the Retail Jobber and Distributor of Automotive Aftermarket. Reed Elsevier Group plc Reed Business Information. • Monthly. Free to qualified personnel; others, $48.00 per year. Includes marketing of automobile batteries. Formerly *Automotive Aftermarket News.*

SEMA News. Specialty Equipment Market Association. • Monthly. Description: Covers the automotive specialty, performance equipment, and accessory sectors. Recurring features include news of government and legislative actions, new products, international markets, and member and Association activities.

PRICE SOURCES

Car Stereo. Orion Research Corp. • Annual. $144 Individuals. Quotes retail and wholesale prices of used stereo sound equipment for automobiles. Original list prices and years of manufacture are also shown.

STATISTICS SOURCES

Standard & Poor's Industry Surveys. Standard & Poor's Financial Services L.L.C. • Semiannual. $1,800.00. Two looseleaf volumes. Includes monthly *Supplements.* Provides detailed, individual surveys of 52 major industry groups. Each survey is revised on a semiannual basis. Also includes "Monthly Investment Review" (industry group investment analysis) and monthly "Trends & Projections" (economic analysis).

U.S. Industry and Trade Outlook. U.S. Department of Commerce National Technical Information Service. • Annual. Produced by the International Trade Administration, U.S. Department of Commerce, in a "public-private" partnership with DRI/McGraw-Hill and Standard & Poor's. Provides basic data, outlook for the current year, and "Long-Term Prospects" (five-year projections) for a wide variety of products and services. Includes high technology industries. Formerly *U.S. Industrial Outlook.*

TRADE/PROFESSIONAL ASSOCIATIONS

Automotive Warehouse Distributors Association. 7101 Wisconsin Ave., Ste. 1300, Bethesda, MD 20814-3415. Phone: (301)654-6664; Fax: (301)654-3299; Email: info@autocare.org • URL: http://www.autocare.org • Warehouse distributors of automotive parts and supplies; manufacturers of automotive parts and suppliers; jobbers, business services, major program groups.

Motor and Equipment Manufacturers Association. 10 Laboratory Dr., Research Triangle Park, NC 27709. Phone: (919)549-4800; Fax: (919)406-1465; Email: info@mema.org • URL: http://www.mema.org • Manufacturers of automotive and heavy-duty original equipment and aftermarket components, maintenance equipment, chemicals, accessories, refinishing supplies, tools, and service equipment united for research into all aspects of the automotive and heavy-duty markets. Provides manufacturer-oriented services and programs including marketing consultation for the automotive industry; federal and state legal, safety, and legislative representation and consultation; personnel services; manpower development workshops; international information.

Transmission Rebuilders Network International. 6501 E Greenway Pkwy., Ste. 103/298, Scottsdale, AZ 85254-2065. Phone: 888-582-8764; Email: info@trannybuilder.com • URL: http://www.trannybuilder.com • Advances the science of rebuilding automatic transmissions and the art of managing a transmission shop. Serves as a forum for the members to share and exchange ideas on automatic transmissions. Provides training, support and technical information based on the needs, trends and opportunities of the transmission/powertrain industry.

AUTOMOBILE INDUSTRY

See AUTOMOTIVE INDUSTRY

AUTOMOBILE INSURANCE

See also ACCIDENT INSURANCE; CASUALTY INSURANCE

ABSTRACTS AND INDEXES

Insurance Periodicals Index. Specials Libraries Association, Insurance and Employees Benefits Div. NILS Publishing Co. • Annual. $250.00. Compiled by the Insurance and Employee Benefits Div., Special Libraries Association. A yearly index of over 15,000 articles from about 35 insurance periodicals. Arrangement is by subject, with an index to authors.

BIBLIOGRAPHIES

Insurance and Employee Benefits Literature. Special Libraries Association. • Bimonthly. $15.00 per year. Lists a wide variety of literature in all branches of the insurance industry. Includes annotations.

INTERNET DATABASES

Free Insurance Advice. InsWeb, Inc. 2868 Prospect Park Dr., Ste. 650, Rancho Cordova, CA 95670. Phone: (916)853-3300; Fax: (916)853-3300; Email: customercare@insweb.com • URL: http://www.insweb.com • Web site offers a wide variety of advice and information on automobile, life, health, and "other" insurance. Includes glossaries of insurance terms, Standard & Poor's ratings of individual insurance companies, and "Financial Needs Estimators." Searching is available. Fees: Free.

ONLINE DATABASES

I.I.I. Data Base Search. Insurance Information Institute. • Provides online citations and abstracts of insurance-related literature in magazines, newspapers, trade journals, and books. Emphasis is on property and casualty insurance issues, including highway safety, product safety, and environmental liability. Inquire as to online cost and availability.

OTHER SOURCES

Automobile Liability Insurance. 3d. Irvin E. Schermer and William J. Schermer. Thomson West. • Seminannual. $501.00. Four looseleaf volumes.

The Law of Liability Insurance. Matthew Bender and Company Inc. • $395. Five looseleaf volumes. Periodic supplementation. Explains the terms and phases essential for a general understanding of liability insurance, and discusses injuries to both persons and property.

PERIODICALS AND NEWSLETTERS

New York No-Fault Arbitration Reports. American Arbitration Association. • Description: Addresses developing laws under the no-fault law in the state of New York. Summarizes awards rendered under state-sponsored arbitration.

STATISTICS SOURCES

Property-Casualty Insurance Facts. Insurance Information Institute. • Annual. $22.50. Formerly *Insurance Facts.*

TRADE/PROFESSIONAL ASSOCIATIONS

American Insurance Alliance. PO Box 7105, Sterling Heights, MI 48311-7105. Phone: 855-242-4321; Email: cstonehill@allianceai.org • URL: http://www.americaninsurancealliance.com.

AUTOMOBILE LAWS

See MOTOR VEHICLE LAW AND REGULATION

AUTOMOBILE LEASE AND RENTAL SERVICES

DIRECTORIES

Plunkett's Airline, Hotel, and Travel Industry Almanac. Plunkett Research Ltd. • Annual. $349.99. Contains profiles of 300 leading companies, including airlines, hotels, travel agencies, theme parks, cruise lines, casinos, and car rental companies.

FINANCIAL RATIOS

Annual Statement Studies. Risk Management Association. • Annual. Compiled from over 280,000 financial statements.

Annual Statement Studies: Industry Default Probabilities and Cash Flow Measures. Risk Management Association. • Annual. $405 Nonmembers. Serves as a companion volume to the original *Annual Statement Studies.* Gives probability of default estimates on a percentage scale for more than 450 industries. Includes changes in position year-by-year for eight financial statement line items and provides percentage measures of cash flow.

HANDBOOKS AND MANUALS

CCH Guide to Car, Travel, Entertainment, and Home Office Deductions. Wolters Kluwer Law & Business CCH. • Annual. Explains how to claim maximum tax deductions for common business expenses. Includes automobile depreciation tables, lease value tables, worksheets, and examples of filled-in tax forms.

Used-Car Rental Agency. Entrepreneur Press. • Looseleaf. $59.50. A practical guide to starting a used-car rental business. Covers profit potential, start-up costs, market size evaluation, owner's time required, site selection, lease negotiation pricing, accounting, advertising, promotion, etc. (Start-Up Business Guide No. E1108.).

Vehicle Leasing. Entrepreneur Press. • Looseleaf. $59.50. A practical guide to starting an automobile leasing business. Covers profit potential, start-up costs, market size evaluation, owner's time required, site selection, lease negotiation, pricing, accounting, advertising, promotion, etc. (Start-Up Business Guide No. E2329.).

AUTOMOBILE LICENSES

See MOTOR VEHICLE LAW AND REGULATION

AUTOMOBILE PARTS INDUSTRY

See AUTOMOBILE EQUIPMENT INDUSTRY

AUTOMOBILE RENTAL SERVICES

See AUTOMOBILE LEASE AND RENTAL SERVICES

AUTOMOBILE REPAIR INDUSTRY

ABSTRACTS AND INDEXES

Business Periodicals Index Retrospective. EBSCO Publishing Inc. • 11/year. Quarterly and annual cumulations.

CD-ROM DATABASES

ABI/INFORM. ProQuest L.L.C. • Monthly. Provides CD-ROM indexing and abstracting of worldwide business literature. Archival discs are available from 1971. Formerly *ABI/INFORM OnDisc*.

Business Abstracts with Full Text. EBSCO Publishing Inc. • Includes full text articles from more than 460 business publications from 1982 to present. Indexing for nearly 880 publications.

DIRECTORIES

Directory of Japanese Manufacturers & Exporters of Automotive Service & Repair Equipment. EXIM Infotek Private Ltd. • $10 Individuals. Covers: 60 Japanese manufacturers and exporters of automotive emission analysis systems, automotive service equipment, car care tools, grinding wheels, lubricants, and lubricating equipments. Entries include: Company name, postal address, city, country, phone, fax, e-mail and websites, contact person, designation, and product details.

Directory of Taiwanese Manufacturers & Exporters of Automotive Service & Repair Equipment. EXIM Infotek Private Ltd. • $10 Individuals. Covers: 70 Taiwanese manufacturers and exporters of garage jacks, mechanical lubrication tools, motor vehicle testing equipment, vehicle service and repair equipment. Entries include: Company name, postal address, city, country, phone, fax, e-mail and websites, contact person, designation, and product details.

Fleet Owner Specs and Buyers' Directory. Primedia Business Magazines and Media. • Annual. $5.00. Lists of manufacturers of equipment and materials used in the operation, management, and maintenance of truck and bus fleets.

ONLINE DATABASES

Wilson Business Abstracts Online. H.W. Wilson Co. • Indexes and abstracts 600 major business periodicals, plus the *Wall Street Journal* and the business section of the *New York Times*. Indexing is from 1982, abstracting from 1990, with the two newspapers included from 1993. Updated weekly. Inquire as to online cost and availability. (*Business Periodicals Index* without abstracts is also available online.).

PERIODICALS AND NEWSLETTERS

Fleet Owner. Primedia Business Magazines and Media. • Monthly. $45.00 per year.

Motor Age: For the Professional Automotive Import and Domestic Service Industry. Reed Elsevier Group plc Reed Business Information. • Monthly. $49.00 per year. Published for independent automotive repair shops and gasoline service stations.

MOTOR: Covering the World of Automotive Service. Hearst Business Publishing Inc. • Monthly. Edited for professional automobile and light-truck mechanics. Includes industry news and market trends.

TRADE/PROFESSIONAL ASSOCIATIONS

Automotive Service Association. 8190 Precinct Line Rd., Ste. 100, Colleyville, TX 76034-7675. Phone: 800-272-7467 or (817)514-2900; Fax: (817)514-0770; Email: asainfo@asashop.org • URL: http://www.asashop.org • Automotive service businesses including body, paint, and trim shops, engine rebuilders, radiator shops, brake and wheel alignment services, transmission shops, tune-up services, and air conditioning services; associate members are manufacturers and wholesalers of automotive parts, and the trade press. Represents independent business owners and managers before private agencies and national and state legislative bodies. Promotes confidence between consumer and the automotive service industry, safety inspection of motor vehicles, and better highways.

Automotive Warehouse Distributors Association. 7101 Wisconsin Ave., Ste. 1300, Bethesda, MD 20814-3415. Phone: (301)654-6664; Fax: (301)654-3299; Email: info@autocare.org • URL: http://www.autocare.org • Warehouse distributors of automotive parts and supplies; manufacturers of automotive parts and suppliers; jobbers, business services, major program groups.

Collision Industry Electronic Commerce Association. 3149 Dundee Rd., No. 181, Northbrook, IL 60062-2402. Phone: (847)498-6945; Fax: (847)897-2094 • URL: http://cieca.com • Aims to facilitate electronic commerce within the collision industry. Works to provide a forum and methods to develop and maintain objective and uniform electronic commerce standards and guidelines. Encourages and supports open competition and free choice for the mutual benefit of all parties.

National Institute for Automotive Service Excellence. 101 Blue Seal Dr. SE, Ste. 101, Leesburg, VA 20175. Phone: 877-346-9327 or (703)669-6600; Fax: (703)669-6127; Email: asehelp@ase.com • URL: http://www.ase.com • A public interest organization which promotes high standards in automotive service and repair. Encourages effective training programs for automobile mechanics/technicians. Affiliated with National Automotive Technicians Education Foundation.

AUTOMOBILE ROAD GUIDES

See MAPS

AUTOMOBILE SERVICE STATIONS

See GASOLINE SERVICE STATIONS

AUTOMOBILE TELEPHONES

See MOBILE TELEPHONE INDUSTRY

AUTOMOBILES

See also AUTOMOTIVE INDUSTRY; FOREIGN AUTOMOBILES; USED CAR INDUSTRY

CD-ROM DATABASES

OECD Statistical Compendium. Organization for Economic Cooperation and Development. • Semiannual. $1,905.00 per year for 1 to 10 users. CD-ROM contains more than 730,000 monthly, quarterly, and annual time series for OECD countries, 1960 to date. Includes fully searchable data on agriculture, food, economic indicators, national accounts, employment, energy, finance, industry, technology, and foreign trade. Results can be displayed in various forms.

Sourcebooks America CD-ROM. CACI Marketing Systems. • Annual. $1,250.00. Provides the CD-ROM version of *The Sourcebook of ZIP Code Demographics: Census Edition* and *The Sourcebook of County Demographics: Census Edition*.

DIRECTORIES

Automobile Telephones Directory. InfoGroup Inc. • Annual. Number of listings: 16,202. Entries include: Name, address, phone, size of advertisement, name of owner or manager, number of employees, year first in "Yellow Pages." Compiled from telephone company "Yellow Pages," nationwide.

International Directory of Commercial Vehicles. Vogt-Schild AG, Druck & Verlag. • Annual. $40. Covers: Manufacturers of light commercial vehicles, municipal vehicles, trucks, small buses, all-wheel drive vehicles, special vehicles, body and trailer manufacturing, and accessories worldwide. Entries include: Manufacturer name, address, phone, technical data.

HANDBOOKS AND MANUALS

CCH Guide to Car, Travel, Entertainment, and Home Office Deductions. Wolters Kluwer Law & Business CCH. • Annual. Explains how to claim maximum tax deductions for common business expenses. Includes automobile depreciation tables, lease value tables, worksheets, and examples of filled-in tax forms.

INTERNET DATABASES

Business 2.0 Web Guide to the Best Business Links. Business 2.0 Media Inc. Phone: (415)293-4800; Email: support@business2.com • URL: http://www.business2.com/webguide • Web site presents an extensive, searchable directory of links to "the best, most informative, and authoritative web pages." Twenty main categories cover business, finance, career, company information, people, and technology topics, with thousands of subtopics, all linking to Web sites recommended by experienced business researchers. Fees: Free.

Fedstats. Federal Interagency Council on Statistical Policy. Phone: (202)395-7254 • URL: http://www.fedstats.gov • Web site features an efficient search facility for full-text statistics produced by more than 100 federal agencies, including the Census Bureau, the Bureau of Economic Analysis, and the Bureau of Labor Statistics. Boolean searches can be made within one agency or for all agencies combined. Links are offered to international statistical bureaus, including the UN, IMF, OECD, UNESCO, Eurostat, and 20 individual countries. Fees: Free.

FreeLunch.com. Economy.com, Inc. Phone: (610)696-8700; Fax: (610)696-1678 • URL: http://www.freelunch.com • Web site provides free access to more than 200 million economic and financial data series, covering industry, demographics, labor markets, prices, retail sales, government spending, trade, interest rates, housing starts, the stock market, etc. Data is available in either chart or table form. Searching is offered. Free, but registration required. Economy.com, Inc. also offers fee-based economic analysis at *The Dismal Scientist* site (www.dismal.com).

ONLINE DATABASES

Ward's AutoInfoBank. Ward's Communications. • Provides weekly, monthly, quarterly, and annual statistical data from 1980 to date for U. S. and imported cars and trucks. Covers production, shipments, sales, inventories, optional equipment, etc. Updating varies by series. Inquire as to online cost and availability.

PERIODICALS AND NEWSLETTERS

Car and Driver. Hachette Filipacchi Media U.S., Inc. • Monthly. $11.97 per year.

Motor Trend. PRIMEDIA Inc. • Monthly. $10 Individuals 12 issues. Informs and entertains with features on the testing of both domestic and import cars, car care, motor sports coverage, sneak peeks at future vehicles, and auto-industry news.

Special Interest Autos. Watering Inc., Special Interest Publications. • Bimonthly. $19.95 per year.

PRICE SOURCES

Edmund's New Cars. Edmund Publications Corp. • Quarterly. $39.96 Individuals. Wholesale and retail prices for all American and import models and accessories. Includes federal crash reports, leasing facts, and accident report forms. Formerly *Edmund's New Car Prices*.

NADA Appraisal Guides. National Automobile Dealers Association. • Prices and frequencies vary. Guides to prices of used cars, old used cars, motorcycles, mobile homes, recreational vehicles, and mopeds.

STATISTICS SOURCES

Survey of Current Business. U. S. Government Printing Office. • Published by Bureau of Economic Analysis, U. S. Department of Commerce. Presents a wide variety of business and economic data.

AUTOMOBILES, USED

See USED CAR INDUSTRY

AUTOMOTIVE INDUSTRY

See also AUTOMOBILES; FOREIGN AUTOMOBILES; USED CAR INDUSTRY

ABSTRACTS AND INDEXES

Engineering Index Monthly: Abstracting and Indexing Services Covering Sources ofthe World's Engineering Literature. Engineering Information Inc. • Monthly. Institutions, $5,279.00 per year. Provides indexing and abstracting of the world's engineering and technical literature.

ALMANACS AND YEARBOOKS

Automotive News Market Data Book. Crain Communications Inc. • Semiannual. $19.95. Directory of automotive vendors and worldwide vehicle manufacturing. Formerly *Automotive News Almanac*.

Ward's Automotive Yearbook. Ward's Communications. • Annual. $570 Single issue 2010 edition. Comprehensive statistical information on automotive production, sales, truck data and suppliers. Included with subscription to *Ward's Automotive Reports*.

CD-ROM DATABASES

OECD Statistical Compendium. Organization for Economic Cooperation and Development. • Semiannual. $1,905.00 per year for 1 to 10 users. CD-ROM contains more than 730,000 monthly, quarterly, and annual time series for OECD countries, 1960 to date. Includes fully searchable data on agriculture, food, economic indicators, national accounts, employment, energy, finance, industry, technology, and foreign trade. Results can be displayed in various forms.

DIRECTORIES

Aligning & Wheel Service Directory. InfoGroup Inc. • Annual. Number of listings: 11,406. Entries include: Name, address, phone, size of advertisement, name of owner or manager, number of employees, year first in "Yellow Pages." Compiled from telephone company "Yellow Pages," nationwide.

All India Directory/Database of Automobile Components/Parts Manufacturers, Exporters, Dealers, Suppliers. NIIR Project Consultancy Services. • $250 Individuals CD-ROM. Covers: 11,000 automobile components/parts manufacturers and exporters, dealers, suppliers in India. Entries include: Company name, addresses, pin, city, phone, mobile (wherever available), fax (wherever available), e-mail (wherever available), website (wherever available), products details.

Asia Pacific Autos Directory. Business Monitor International Ltd. • $975 Individuals CD. Covers: 1,612 top autos executives on 519 leading automotive companies from China, Hong Kong, India, Indonesia, Malaysia, Pakistan, Philippines, Singapore, Taiwan, Thailand, and Vietnam. Entries include: Parent company head offices; full company name and address; telephone, fax, email, and website address; senior contact personnel; full description of company activity; company profile; nationality; and ownership status and parentage.

Automatic Merchandiser--Blue Book Buyer's Guide Issue. Cygnus Business Media Inc. • Annual. Publication includes: Suppliers of products, services, and equipment to the merchandise vending, contract foodservice, and office coffee service industries. Entries include: Company name, address, phone, names of executives, trade and brand names, and products or services offered.

Automobile Racing Directory. InfoGroup Inc. • Annual. Number of listings: 2,233. Entries include: Name, address, phone, size of advertisement, name of owner or manager, number of employees, year first in "Yellow Pages." Compiled from telephone company "Yellow Pages," nationwide.

Automobile Window Tinting Directory. InfoGroup Inc. • Annual. Number of listings: 6,032. Entries include: Name, address, phone, size of advertisement, name of owner or manager, number of employees, year first in "Yellow Pages." Compiled from telephone company "Yellow Pages," nationwide.

Directory of American Manufacturers & Exporters of Automobiles & Vehicles. EXIM Infotek Private Ltd. • $20 Individuals. Covers: 200 American manufacturers and exporters of armored vehicles, articulated dump vehicles, automobiles, fire trucks, heavy duty trucks, heavy trucks, industrial trucks, military truck bodies and utility trailers, military trucks, platform trucks, roll off containers, tilt trucks, trailers and tank trucks, truck beds, truck bodies, trucks-commercial, truck frame beam punch lines, truck mounted equipment, truck wheel covers and accessories, and trucks. Entries include: Company name, postal address, city, country, phone, fax, e-mail and websites, contact person, designation, and product details.

Directory of American Manufacturers & Exporters of Automotive Service & Repair Equipment. EXIM Infotek Private Ltd. • $5 Individuals. Covers: 40 American manufacturers and exporters of analyzers-engine, auto test equipment, automotive analyzers, automotive hand tools, automotive tools, small engine maintenance instruments, and specialty heavy transmission rebuilding hand tools. Entries include: Company name, postal address, city, country, phone, fax, e-mail and websites, contact person, designation, and products detail.

Directory of Japanese Manufacturers & Exporters of Automobiles & Vehicles. EXIM Infotek Private Ltd. • $65 Individuals. Covers: 1,570 Japanese manufacturers and exporters of automobiles, buses, cars, motor vehicles, reconditioned cars, trailers, transport equipment, used buses, used cargo trucks, used cars, used commercial vehicles, used mini buses, used motor vehicles, used passenger cars, used trucks, used vans, used vehicles, used vehicles and spare parts, used wagons, vehicles, and wagons for hotel and restaurants. Entries include: Company name, postal address, city, country, phone, fax, e-mail and websites, contact person, designation, and product details.

Directory of South Korean Manufacturers & Exporters of Automobiles & Vehicles. EXIM Infotek Private Ltd. • $5 Individuals. Covers: 20 South Korean manufacturers and exporters of automobile body builders, automobiles, buses and trucks, buses, cars, tractors/trucks/trailers-industrial, truck and lorry trailers, trucks/lorries, used cars, used trucks, used vehicles, and vehicles-special purpose. Entries include: Company name, postal address, city, country, phone, fax, e-mail and websites, contact person, designation, and product details.

Directory of South Korean Manufacturers & Exporters of Automotive Service & Repair Equipment. EXIM Infotek Private Ltd. • $5 Individuals. Covers: 30 South Korean manufacturers and exporters of grills-radiator, mechanical lubrication tools, motor vehicle testing equipment, vehicle service and repair equipment. Entries include: Company name, postal address, city, country, phone, fax, e-mail and websites, contact person, designation, and product details.

Directory of Taiwanese Manufacturers & Exporters of Automobiles & Vehicles. EXIM Infotek Private Ltd. • $5 Individuals. Covers: 40 Taiwanese manufacturers and exporters of automobile body builders, tractors/trucks/trailers-industrial, truck and lorry trailers, trucks/lorries, and vehicles-special purpose. Entries include: Company name, postal address, city, country, phone, fax, e-mail and websites, contact person, designation, and product details.

Emerging Europe Autos Directory. Business Monitor International Ltd. • $895 Individuals. Covers: 1,275 top autos executives on 443 leading automotive companies from Bosnia-Herzegovina, Bulgaria, Croatia, the Czech Republic, Estonia, Hungary, Latvia, Lithuania, Macedonia, Poland, Romania, Russia, Serbia, Slovakia, Slovenia and the Ukraine. Entries include: parent company head offices, full company name, address, phone and fax numbers, email and website address, senior contact personnel, company description and profile, nationality, and ownership status.

Latin America and Caribbean Autos Directory. Business Monitor International Ltd. • $975 Individuals CD. Covers: 1,145 top autos executives on 374 leading automotive companies from Argentina, Brazil, Chile, Colombia, Mexico, Peru, Venezuela,

For publishers' addresses, refer to SOURCES CITED section at the back of the book.

Anguilla, Antigua & Barbuda, Aruba, the Bahamas, Barbados, Bermuda, British Virgin Islands, Cayman Islands, Cuba, Dominica, Dominican Rep. French Guiana, Grenada, Guadeloupe, Guyana, Haiti, Jamaica, Martinique, Montserrat, Netherland Antilles, Puerto Rico, St Kitts, St Lucia, St Vincent, Suriname, Trinidad & Tobago, Turks & Caicos and US Virgin Islands. Entries include: parent company head offices, full company name, address, phone and fax numbers, email and website address, senior contact personnel, company description and profile, nationality, and ownership status.

Middle East and Africa Autos Directory. Business Monitor International Ltd. • $995 Individuals CD. Covers: 1,483 top autos executives on 445 leading automotive companies from Algeria, Bahrain, Botswana, Egypt, Iran, Jordan, Kuwait, Lebanon, Libya, Morocco, Mozambique, Namibia, Oman, Qatar, Saudi Arabia, South Africa, Syria, Tunisia, Turkey, United Arab Emirates, Yemen, Zambia and Zimbabwe. Entries include: Parent company head offices, full company name, address, phone and fax numbers, email and website address, senior contact personnel, company description and profile, nationality, and ownership status.

Plunkett's Automobile Industry Almanac. Plunkett Research Ltd. • $349.99 Individuals print + online: one-year subscription. Covers: 300 leading companies in the automotive industry. Entries include: Name, address, phone, fax, and key executives. Also includes analysis and information on trends, technology, and statistics in the field.

Undercar Digest--Buyer's Guide Issue: The Sourcebook. MD Publications Inc. • Annual. $10 Individuals. Publication includes: List of automotive aftermarket manufacturers and suppliers of mufflers, exhaust pipes, brakes, chassis, steering, suspension, driveline, shop equipment and tools, and other products. Entries include: Company name, address, phone, fax, name and title of contact, products.

E-BOOKS

Encyclopedia of American Industries. Cengage Learning Inc. • 2011. $807.00. 6th edition. Three volumes. Volume one is Manufacturing Industries and volume two is Service and Non-Manufacturing Industries. Provides the history, development, and recent status of approximately 1,000 industries. Includes statistical graphs, with industry and general indexes. Also available as eBook.

FINANCIAL RATIOS

Annual Statement Studies. Risk Management Association. • Annual. Compiled from over 280,000 financial statements.

Annual Statement Studies: Industry Default Probabilities and Cash Flow Measures. Risk Management Association. • Annual. $405 Nonmembers. Serves as a companion volume to the original *Annual Statement Studies*. Gives probability of default estimates on a percentage scale for more than 450 industries. Includes changes in position year-by-year for eight financial statement line items and provides percentage measures of cash flow.

Industry Norms and Key Business Ratios. Dun & Bradstreet Inc. • Annual. Five volumes. Covers over 800 kinds of businesses, arranged by Standard Industrial Classification number. More detailed editions covering longer periods of time are also available.

HANDBOOKS AND MANUALS

SAE Handbook. Society of Automotive Engineers. • Annual. $425.00. Three volumes. Contains standards, recommended practices and information reports on ground vehicle design, manufacturing, testing and performance.

INTERNET DATABASES

Business 2.0 Web Guide to the Best Business Links. Business 2.0 Media Inc. Phone: (415)293-4800: Email: support@business2.com • URL: http://www.business2.com/webguide • Web site presents an extensive, searchable directory of links to "the best, most informative, and authoritative web pages." Twenty main categories cover business, finance, career, company information, people, and technology topics, with thousands of subtopics, all linking to Web sites recommended by experienced business researchers. Fees: Free.

Fedstats. Federal Interagency Council on Statistical Policy. Phone: (202)395-7254 • URL: http://www.fedstats.gov • Web site features an efficient search facility for full-text statistics produced by more than 100 federal agencies, including the Census Bureau, the Bureau of Economic Analysis, and the Bureau of Labor Statistics. Boolean searches can be made within one agency or for all agencies combined. Links are offered to international statistical bureaus, including the UN, IMF, OECD, UNESCO, Eurostat, and 20 individual countries. Fees: Free.

FreeLunch.com. Economy.com, Inc. Phone: (610)696-8700; Fax: (610)696-1678 • URL: http://www.freelunch.com • Web site provides free access to more than 200 million economic and financial data series, covering industry, demographics, labor markets, prices, retail sales, government spending, trade, interest rates, housing starts, the stock market, etc. Data is available in either chart or table form. Searching is offered. Free, but registration required. Economy.com, Inc. also offers fee-based economic analysis at *The Dismal Scientist* site (www.dismal.com).

ONLINE DATABASES

Alternative Fuel Vehicle Businesses in the World. Momentum Technologies L.L.C. • Contains detailed directory listings and contact information for dozens of businesses involved with alternative fuel vehicles in operation throughout the world. Includes business name, address, phone number, fax number, e-mail address, and web site address. Includes brief descriptions of product lines, services offered, and business type. Covers manufacturers, wholesale and retail suppliers, system design businesses, system installers, nonprofit organizations, trade organizations, and more.

Hybrid Electric Vehicle Businesses in the World. Momentum Technologies L.L.C. • Contains directory listings and contact information for more than 60 businesses involved with hybrid electric vehicles and related automotive areas throughout the world. Includes business name, address, phone number, fax number, e-mail address, and web site address. Includes brief descriptions of product lines, services offered, and business type. Covers businesses concerned with vehicles with hybrid power systems, such as electric power and traditional gasoline fuel. Includes manufacturers, component makers, wholesalers, retailers, component installers, and more. Searchable by location, business type, company name, and keyword.

Ward's AutoInfoBank. Ward's Communications. • Provides weekly, monthly, quarterly, and annual statistical data from 1980 to date for U. S. and imported cars and trucks. Covers production, shipments, sales, inventories, optional equipment, etc. Updating varies by series. Inquire as to online cost and availability.

PERIODICALS AND NEWSLETTERS

In Car Business. Vehicle Security News Ltd. • Semimonthly. $21 Individuals. Professional magazine covering automobile audio and security.

Road & Track. Hearst Magazines. • Monthly. $15 Individuals. Automotive magazine.

Ward's Automotive Reports. Ward's Communications. • Description: Reports "vital statistical information and exclusive news of critical interest" to the automotive industry. **Remarks:** Subscription includes Ward's Automotive Yearbook. Ward's Communications, Inc. is a subsidiary of Intertec Publishing Corp.

PRICE SOURCES

Automotive Market Report. Automotive Auction Publishing Inc. • Biweekly. $130.00 Per Year. Current wholesale values of used vehicles.

STATISTICS SOURCES

American Trucking Trends. American Trucking Associations, Trucking Information Services, Inc. • Annual. $95.00 for members. $200.00 for nonmembers.

Standard & Poor's Industry Surveys. Standard & Poor's Financial Services L.L.C. • Semiannual. $1,800.00. Two looseleaf volumes. Includes monthly *Supplements*. Provides detailed, individual surveys of 52 major industry groups. Each survey is revised on a semiannual basis. Also includes "Monthly Investment Review" (industry group investment analysis) and monthly "Trends & Projections" (economic analysis).

Statistics of Income: Corporation Income Tax Returns. U.S. Internal Revenue Service. U. S. Government Printing Office. • Annual.

Survey of Current Business. U. S. Government Printing Office. • Published by Bureau of Economic Analysis, U. S. Department of Commerce. Presents a wide variety of business and economic data.

United States Census of Manufactures. U.S. Department of Commerce U.S. Census Bureau. • Quinquennial. Results presented in reports, tape, CD-ROM, and Diskette files.

TRADE/PROFESSIONAL ASSOCIATIONS

ASM International. 9639 Kinsman Rd., Materials Park, OH 44073-0002. Phone: 800-336-5152 or (440)338-5151; Email: memberservicecenter@asminternational.org • URL: http://www.asminternational.org • Metallurgists, materials engineers, executives in materials producing and consuming industries; teachers and students. Disseminates technical information about the manufacture, use, and treatment of engineered materials. Offers in-plant, home study, and intensive courses through Materials Engineering Institute.

Auto Suppliers Benchmarking Association. 4606 FM 1960 W, Ste. 250, Houston, TX 77069-9949. Phone: (281)440-5044; Fax: (281)440-6677 • URL: http://www.asbabenchmarking.com • Automotive supplier firms with an interest in benchmarking. Promotes the use of benchmarking, wherein businesses compare their processes with those of their competitors, as a means of improving corporate efficiency and profitability. Facilitates exchange of information among members; conducts target operations, procurement, development, and maintenance studies; identifies model business practices.

Automotive Engine Rebuilders Association. 500 Coventry Ln., Ste. 180, Crystal Lake, IL 60014. Phone: 888-326-2372 or (815)526-7600; Fax: (815)526-7601; Email: info@aera.org • URL: http://www.aera.org • Wholesalers of automotive replacement parts and equipment with machine shop operations; associate members are suppliers of parts, equipment, tools and services to the rebuilder members. Acts as clearinghouse for automotive jobber machine shop information.

Automotive Trade Association Executives. 8400 Westpark Dr., McLean, VA 22102. Phone: (703)821-7072; Fax: (703)556-8581 • URL: http://www.atae.info • Executives of state and local automotive dealer associations.

Automotive Warehouse Distributors Association. 7101 Wisconsin Ave., Ste. 1300, Bethesda, MD 20814-3415. Phone: (301)654-6664; Fax: (301)654-3299; Email: info@autocare.org • URL: http://www.autocare.org • Warehouse distributors of automotive parts and supplies; manufacturers of automotive parts and suppliers; jobbers, business services, major program groups.

Global Automotive Management Council. 5305 Plymouth Rd., Ann Arbor, MI 48105. Phone: (734)997-9249; Fax: (734)997-9443; Email: info@gamcinc.com • URL: http://gamcinc.com • Represents senior executives from the global automotive industry. Promotes the globalization of automotive industries through meetings, seminars and educational forums. Provides educational and networking opportunities for senior executives.

Japan Auto Parts Industries Association. Jidosha Buhin Kaikan, 5th Fl., 1-16-15 Takanawa, Minato-ku, Tokyo, Tokyo 108-0074, Japan. Phone: 81 3 34454211; Fax: 81 3 34475372; Email: info@japia.or.jp • URL: http://www.japia.or.jp • Manufacturers of automotive parts and components; suppliers to the automotive parts industry. Seeks to improve the business climate for members. Facilitates exchange of information among members and between members and related international organizations and overseas manufacturing concerns. Gathers technical and economic data of interest to members.

AV EQUIPMENT INDUSTRY

See AUDIOVISUAL EQUIPMENT INDUSTRY

AVIATION, BUSINESS

See BUSINESS AVIATION

AVIATION ELECTRONICS

See AVIONICS

AVIATION INDUSTRY

See also AEROSPACE INDUSTRY; AIRLINE INDUSTRY; AIRPLANE INDUSTRY; BUSINESS AVIATION

BIBLIOGRAPHIES

Aviation. U. S. Government Printing Office. • Annual. Free. Lists government publications. (GPO Subject Bibliography Number 18).

DIRECTORIES

Air Freight Directory. Air Cargo Inc. • Bimonthly. $34.50 single copy. Publication includes: Directory of more than 500 motor carriers contracting with Air Cargo, Inc. for delivery and pick up of freight. Air Cargo is a ground service specialist organization jointly owned by 18 major air carriers. Entries include: Airport city and code, firm name, address, phone, and services offered. Principal content of publication is chart of service points and rates.

Atlantic Region Aviation Business Directory. Martin Charlton Communications Inc. • Annual. $7.50. Covers companies involved in or serving the aviation industry in New Brunswick, Newfoundland, Nova Scotia, and Prince Edward Island, Canada.

Business Commercial Aviation Planning & Purchasing Handbook. Aviation Week Group. • Monthly. Directory of airframe and avionics manufacturers, and suppliers of related products and services.

National Agricultural Aviation Association--Membership Directory. National Agricultural Aviation Association. • Annual. Covers: Nearly 1300 executives, pilots, and supplier companies engaged primarily in aerial application. Entries include: For chapter and supplier company members--Name, spouse's name, company name, address, phone.

National Air Transportation Association--Aviation Resource and Membership Directory. National Air Transportation Association. • Annual. $50 Nonmembers. Covers: More than 1,000 regular, associate, and affiliate members; regular members include airport service organizations, air taxi operators, and commuter airlines. Entries include: Company name, address, phone, fax number, name and title of contact.

National Business Aircraft Association--Membership Directory. National Business Aviation Association. • Periodic.

FINANCIAL RATIOS

Industry Norms and Key Business Ratios. Dun & Bradstreet Inc. • Annual. Five volumes. Covers over 800 kinds of businesses, arranged by Standard Industrial Classification number. More detailed editions covering longer periods of time are also available.

GENERAL WORKS

Business Air Today: The Premiere Source for Corporate Aviation Acquisitions. Heartland Communications Group Inc. • Monthly. $19.95 Individuals. Source for corporate aircraft and services.

OTHER SOURCES

Aviation Law Reports. Wolters Kluwer Law & Business CCH. • Semimonthly. Four looseleaf volumes covering aviation law.

Jane's All the World's Aircraft. Jane's Information Group, Inc. • Annual. $630.00; CD-ROM edition, $1,455.00; online edition, $1,566.00; microfiche edition, $3,075.00. Lists civil and military aircraft, helicopters, airships, and aero engines.

PERIODICALS AND NEWSLETTERS

AIAA Journal. American Institute of Aeronautics and Astronautics. • Monthly. $80 Members /year for members in the U.S.; print and online. Technical journal providing original archival research papers on new theoretical developments and/or experimental results in the fields of aeronautics and astronautics. For research-oriented readers.

Air Transport World. Intertec Publishing. • Monthly. $89 Individuals print and online. Includes supplement *World Airline Reports.*

European Business Air News. Stansted News Ltd. • Professional publication for business aircraft owners and operators in Europe.

Global Business Jet: The News Magazine For Intercontinental Business Jet Owners. Stansted News Ltd. • Monthly. Professional magazine for owners and operators of long-range business jets worldwide.

Human Factors and Aviation Medicine. Flight Safety Foundation. • Bimonthly. $120 Members. Contains information important to the training and performance of all aviation professionals.

The ICAO Journal. International Civil Aviation Organization. • Bimonthly. $10 Single issue. Contains concise account of the activities of the International Civil Aviation Organization and features additional information of interest to Contracting States and the international aeronautical world.

Which Airline & Business Travel Update. BMI Publications Ltd. • Semiannual. Consumer magazine covering airline services for business travelers.

RESEARCH CENTERS AND INSTITUTES

Flight Mechanics Laboratory. Texas A & M University, 701 HR Bright Bldg., College Station, TX 77843-3141. Phone: (979)862-1749; Fax: (979)845-6051; Email: saric@tamu.edu • URL: http://flight.tamu.edu.

Joint Institute for Advancement of Flight Sciences. 725 23rd St. NW, 227 Hunting Ave., Washington, DC 20052. Phone: (202)994-6080; Fax: (202)994-3394; Email: jiafs@seas.gwu.edu • Conducts research in aeronautics, astronautics, and acoustics (flight-produced noise).

Ohio University - Avionics Engineering Center. Russ College of Engineering and Technology, 131 McFarland Avionics Bldg., Athens, OH 45701. Phone: (740)593-1534 or (740)597-2657; Email: avionics@ohio.edu • URL: http://www.ohio.edu/avionics • Aeronautical electronics, including studies on aircraft navigational aids, propagation of very high frequency omnirange signals, weather radar systems, radio frequency interference, global positioning satellite (GPS) navigation, instrument landing system (ILS) technology, microwave landing system (MLS) technology, Loran-C navigation, navigation system air analyses, predictions of VHF communications coverage, datalink testing and analysis, UAVs, synthetic vision display research, and specialized computer equipment for flight data collection.

STATISTICS SOURCES

Aerospace Facts and Figures. Aerospace Industries Association of America. • Annual. $35 Individuals. Includes financial data for the aerospace industries.

Air Transport. Airlines for America. • Annual. $20. Airline industry information.

TRADE/PROFESSIONAL ASSOCIATIONS

Aviation Development Council. 141-07 20th Ave., Ste. 404, Whitestone, NY 11357. Phone: (718)746-0212; Fax: (718)746-1006; Email: root@aviationdevelopmentcouncil.org • URL: http://www.aviationdevelopmentcouncil.org • U.S. and foreign scheduled air carriers serving the New York-New Jersey metropolitan area; Port Authority of New York and New Jersey; Allied Pilots Association; and Air Line Pilots Association, International. Aims to explore, evaluate, and recommend to the proper authorities measures in various fields that will afford possible relief to people affected by noise of aircraft. Initiates public information on significant developments in the metropolitan area. Compiles runway analysis data on New York City area airports. Administers industry-funded outreach programs designed to encourage local purchasing; administers "crime and security watch" programs for JFK, LGA & EWR.

Aviation Distributors and Manufacturers Association. 100 N 20th St., Ste. 400, Philadelphia, PA 19103-1462. Phone: (215)320-3872; Fax: (215)564-2175; Email: adma@fernley.com • URL: http://www.adma.org • Wholesalers and manufacturers of general aviation aircraft parts, supplies and equipment. Strives to further the development of the aviation marketplace through the services and products produced and distributed by members.

National Aeronautic Association. Reagan Washington National Airport, Hangar 7, Ste. 202, Washington, DC 20001-6015. Phone: 800-644-9777 or (703)416-4888; Fax: (703)416-4877; Email: admin@naa.aero • URL: http://naa.aero • Persons interested in the progress and development of American general and military aviation. Supervises sporting aviation competitions and official world records in aeronautics and astronautics, model flying, gliding, soaring, parachuting, hang gliding, ballooning and helicopters.

National Air Transportation Association. 4226 King St., Alexandria, VA 22302. Phone: 800-808-6282 or (703)845-9000; Fax: (703)845-8176 • URL: http://www.nata.aero • Represents the interests of aviation businesses nationwide. Provides vital aviation services to the airlines, the military, and business/corporate/individual aircraft owners and operators; services includes fueling, maintenance, and flight instruction.

National Association of State Aviation Officials. Washington National Airport, Hangar 7, Ste. 218, Washington, DC 20001. Phone: (703)417-1883; Email: info@nasao.org • URL: http://www.nasao.

org • Represents state aeronautics commissions or departments (including those in Guam and Puerto Rico) that promote, administer, and regulate aviation, and seek uniform aviation laws. Sponsors National Association of State Aviation Officials Center for Aviation Research and Education.

Parachute Industry Association. 3833 W Oakton St., Skokie, IL 60076-3429. Phone: (847)674-9742; Fax: (847)674-9743 • URL: http://www.pia.com • Represents companies and individuals united by a common desire to improve business opportunities in the parachute industry. Develops technical, service and operating standards for parachute equipment, skydiving safety, and related aviation topics.

AVIONICS

See also ELECTRONICS INDUSTRY

ABSTRACTS AND INDEXES

Applied Science and Technology Index. EBSCO Publishing Inc. • 11/year. Indexes a wide variety of English language technical, industrial, and engineering periodicals.

Science Citation Index. Thomson Reuters Intellectual Property and Science. • Weekly. Includes *Source Index*, *Citation Index*, *Permuterm Subject Index*, and *Corporate Index*. Provides researchers, administrators, faculty, and students with quick, powerful access to the bibliographic and citation information they need to find research data, analyze trends, journals and researchers, and share their findings.

CD-ROM DATABASES

Science Citation Index. Thomson Reuters Intellectual Property and Science. • Weekly. Includes *Source Index*, *Citation Index*, *Permuterm Subject Index*, and *Corporate Index*. Provides researchers, administrators, faculty, and students with quick, powerful access to the bibliographic and citation information they need to find research data, analyze trends, journals and researchers, and share their findings.

DIRECTORIES

Business Commercial Aviation Planning & Purchasing Handbook. Aviation Week Group. • Monthly. Directory of airframe and avionics manufacturers, and suppliers of related products and services.

ONLINE DATABASES

Aerospace America Magazine. American Institute of Aeronautics and Astronautics. • Monthly. $200 Institutions non member, domestic. Covers aeronautics and space technology with special attention to aerospace defense, design, and electronics.

Aerospace Database. American Institute of Aeronautics and Astronautics. • Contains abstracts of literature covering all aspects of the aerospace and aircraft industry 1983 to date. Monthly updates. Inquire as to online cost and availability.

INSPEC. Institution of Electrical Engineers. • Provides online citations, with abstracts, to the world literature of electrical engineering, electronics, optoelectronics, telecommunications, industrial controls, instrumentation, computer technology, information technology, and physics. Coverage includes more than 4,000 technical and scientific journals from 1969 to date, with weekly updating. (INSPEC is Information Services in Physics, Electronics, and Computing.) Inquire as to online cost and availability.

PERIODICALS AND NEWSLETTERS

Aerospace America Magazine. American Institute of Aeronautics and Astronautics. • Monthly. $200 Institutions non member, domestic. Covers aeronautics and space technology with special attention to aerospace defense, design, and electronics.

Aerospace Engineering Magazine. Society of Automotive Engineers. • Monthly. $66.00 per year. Provides technical information that can be used in the design of new and improved aerospace systems.

Defense Electronics. RentPath Inc. • Monthly.

Flight International. Reed Business Information Ltd. • Weekly. $140.00 per year. Technical aerospace coverage.

Professional Pilot Magazine. Queensmith Communications Corp. • Monthly. $50 Individuals. Edited for career pilots in all areas of aviation: airline, corporate, charter, and military. Includes flying technique, avionics, navigation, accident analysis, career planning, corporate profiles, and business aviation news.

RESEARCH CENTERS AND INSTITUTES

Ohio University - Avionics Engineering Center. Russ College of Engineering and Technology, 131 McFarland Avionics Bldg., Athens, OH 45701. Phone: (740)593-1534 or (740)597-2657; Email: avionics@ohio.edu • URL: http://www.ohio.edu/avionics • Aeronautical electronics, including studies on aircraft navigational aids, propagation of very high frequency omnirange signals, weather radar systems, radio frequency interference, global positioning satellite (GPS) navigation, instrument landing system (ILS) technology, microwave landing system (MLS) technology, Loran-C navigation, navigation system air analyses, predictions of VHF communications coverage, datalink testing and analysis, UAVs, synthetic vision display research, and specialized computer equipment for flight data collection.

TRADE/PROFESSIONAL ASSOCIATIONS

American Institute of Aeronautics and Astronautics. 1801 Alexander Bell Dr., Ste. 500, Reston, VA 20191-4344. Phone: 800-639-2422 or (703)264-7500; Fax: (703)264-7551; Email: custserv@aiaa.org • URL: http://www.aiaa.org • Represents scientists and engineers in the field of aeronautics and astronautics. Facilitates interchange of technological information through publications and technical meetings in order to foster overall technical progress in the field and increase the professional competence of members. Operates Public Policy program to provide federal decision-makers with the technical information and policy guidance needed to make effective policy on aerospace issues. Public Policy program activities include congressional testimony, position papers, section public policy activities, and workshops. Offers placement assistance; compiles statistics; offers educational programs. Provides abstracting services through its AIAA Access.

Aviation Distributors and Manufacturers Association. 100 N 20th St., Ste. 400, Philadelphia, PA 19103-1462. Phone: (215)320-3872; Fax: (215)564-2175; Email: adma@fernley.com • URL: http://www.adma.org • Wholesalers and manufacturers of general aviation aircraft parts, supplies and equipment. Strives to further the development of the aviation marketplace through the services and products produced and distributed by members.

Avionics Maintenance Conference. Aeronautical Radio, Inc., 2551 Riva Rd., Annapolis, MD 21401. Phone: (410)266-2008; Fax: (410)266-2047; Email: sbuckwal@arinc.com • URL: http://www.aviation-ia.com/amc • Avionics maintenance professionals from commercial airlines, airframe manufacturers, avionics suppliers, and government organizations. Seeks to improve safety and reliability and reduce the costs of operating and supporting avionics equipment. Contributes to reduce the growth of avionics maintenance costs per flight hour despite growth in avionics capital costs. Conducts projects such as: the establishment of a standard language source document for writing automatic test programs; definition of an economic alternative to costly dedicated automatic test systems provided by manufacturers; development of an industry standard for automated preparation of test software; specification of documentation standards for software-based avionics; coordination of technical training needs for maintenance; and development of voluntary standards for the avionics industry.

AWARDS

See CONTESTS, PRIZES, AND AWARDS

B

BABY CLOTHES

See CHILDREN'S APPAREL INDUSTRY

BABY SITTING

See also DAY CARE CENTERS

ONLINE DATABASES

ERIC. U.S. Department of Education Institute of Education Sciences Educational Resources Information Center. • Funded by the U.S. Department of Education, Institute of Education Sciences (formerly Office of Educational Research and Improvement). Provides access to more than one million online records covering education-related journal and report literature, 1966 to date. Updating is monthly. Inquire as to online cost and availability.

BAG INDUSTRY

See PAPER BAG INDUSTRY

BAKING INDUSTRY

See also FOOD INDUSTRY; SNACK FOOD INDUSTRY

ABSTRACTS AND INDEXES

Flour Milling and Baking Abstracts. CCFAA Technology Ltd. • Bimonthly. Members, $275.00 per year; non-members, $325.00 per year. Includes print and online editions.

Food Science and Technology Abstracts. Ovid Technologies Inc. • Monthly. $1,780.00 per year. Provides worldwide coverage of the literature of food technology and food production.

Foods Adlibra: Key to the World's Food Literature. General Mills, Inc. Foods Adlibra Publications. • Semimonthly. $240.00 per year. Provides journal citations and abstracts to the literature of food technology and packaging.

DIRECTORIES

Baking/Snack Directory & Buyer's Guide. Sosland Publishing Co. • Annual. $205 Individuals S&H for ea. additional copy is $2 reg., $16 prior. Covers: Wholesale bakers of bread, cake, cookies, crackers, pasta; manufacturers of snack foods, mixes, and frozen dough; licensors of proprietary brands; manufacturers of equipment and products and suppliers of services used in wholesale baking. For bakers--Company name, address, phone, principal headquarters and plant personnel, principal products, sales volume, production method, and number of employees. For manufacturers--Company name, address, phone, name and title of contact. Entries include: Company name, address, phone, executive name.

Directory of American Manufacturers & Exporters of Confectionery & Bakery Products. EXIM Infotek Private Ltd. • $10 Individuals. Covers: 90 American manufacturers & exporters of baked foods, boxed chocolates, bubble gum, buttercrunch, candy, cheesecake & carrot cake, chewing gum base, chocolate coatings, chocolates, confectionery items, cookies, fruit snacks & fruit rolls, fudge making, hard candy, ingredients & chocolate products, jelly beans, marshmallows, peanuts. Entries include: Company name, postal address, city, country, phone, fax, e-mail & websites, contact person, designation, products detail.

Directory of Chinese Manufacturers & Exporters of Confectionery and Bakery Products. EXIM Infotek Private Ltd. • $5 Individuals. Covers: 20 Chinese manufacturers and exporters of biscuits/crackers, cakes and pastries, candy, fried peanuts, instant noodles, and vinegar. Entries include: Company name, postal address, city, country, phone, fax, e-mail and websites, contact person, designation, and product details.

Directory of Japanese Manufacturers & Exporters of Confectionery & Bakery Products. EXIM Infotek Private Ltd. • $5 Individuals. Covers: 20 Japanese manufacturers and exporters of biscuits/crackers, confectionery, and vinegar. Entries include: Company name, postal address, city, country, phone, fax, e-mail and websites, contact person, designation, and product details.

Directory of South Korean Manufacturers & Exporters of Confectionery & Bakery Products. EXIM Infotek Private Ltd. • $10 Individuals. Covers: 80 South Korean manufacturers and exporters of biscuits/crackers, bread/cakes and pastry, noodles-instant, soups and extracts, sugar confectionery, and vinegar and sauce. Entries include: Company name, postal address, city, country, phone, fax, e-mail and websites, contact person, designation, and product details.

Directory of Taiwanese Manufacturers & Exporters of Confectionery & Bakery Products. EXIM Infotek Private Ltd. • $10 Individuals. Covers: 80 Taiwanese manufacturers and exporters of biscuits/crackers, bread/cakes and pastry, fruit-candied, instant porridge, noodles-instant, soups and extracts, sugar confectionery, vinegar and sauce. Entries include: Company name, postal address, city, country, phone, fax, e-mail and websites, contact person, designation, and product details.

Major Food and Drink Companies of the World. Cengage Learning Inc. • 12th edition. eBook. Published by Graham & Whiteside. Contains profiles and trade names for more than 9,200 important food and beverage companies in various countries. In addition to foods, includes both alcoholic and nonalcoholic drink products.

Plunkett's Food Industry Almanac. Plunkett Research Ltd. • $349.99 Individuals print + online. Covers: 340 leading companies in the global food industry. Entries include: Name, address, phone, fax, and key executives. Also includes analysis and information on trends, technology, and statistics in the field.

World Food Marketing Directory. Euromonitor International Business Reference Div. • $475 Individuals. Covers: Over 2,000 retailers and wholesalers, 1,500 manufacturers, over 2,000 international and European organizations, statistical agencies, trade journals and associations, databases, and trade fairs in the grocery and food industries worldwide. Entries include: Company name, address, phone, telex, names of parent company and subsidiaries, number of employees, financial data, products and brand names handled; retailers and wholesalers include type of outlet, names and titles of key personnel.

FINANCIAL RATIOS

Annual Statement Studies. Risk Management Association. • Annual. Compiled from over 280,000 financial statements.

Annual Statement Studies: Industry Default Probabilities and Cash Flow Measures. Risk Management Association. • Annual. $405 Nonmembers. Serves as a companion volume to the original *Annual Statement Studies*. Gives probability of default estimates on a percentage scale for more than 450 industries. Includes changes in position year-by-year for eight financial statement line items and provides percentage measures of cash flow.

Industry Norms and Key Business Ratios. Dun & Bradstreet Inc. • Annual. Five volumes. Covers over 800 kinds of businesses, arranged by Standard Industrial Classification number. More detailed editions covering longer periods of time are also available.

HANDBOOKS AND MANUALS

Bakery. Entrepreneur Press. • Looseleaf. $59.50. A practical guide to starting a retail bakery. Covers profit potential, start-up costs, market size evaluation, owner's time required, site selection, lease negotiation, pricing, accounting, advertising, promotion, etc. (Start-Up Business Guide No. E1158.).

Pizzeria. Entrepreneur Press. • Looseleaf. $59.50. A practical guide to starting a pizza shop. Covers profit potential, start-up costs, market size evaluation, owner's time required, site selection, lease negotiation, pricing, accounting, advertising, promotion, etc. (Start-Up Business Guide No. E1006.).

ONLINE DATABASES

Food Science and Technology Abstracts (online). IFIS North American Desk. • Produced by International Food Information Service. Provides about 500,000 online citations, with abstracts, to the international literature of food science, technology, commodities, engineering, and processing. Approximately 2,000 periodicals are covered. Time period is 1969 to date, with monthly updates. Inquire as to online cost and availability.

OTHER SOURCES

American Society of Baking Proceedings. American Society of Baking. • Annual. Membership.

PERIODICALS AND NEWSLETTERS

Deli News. Delicatessen Council of Southern California, Inc. Pacific Rim Publishing Co. • Monthly. $25.00 per year. Includes product news and comment related to cheeses, lunch meats, packaged fresh meats, kosher foods, gourmet-specialty items, and bakery products.

Fancy Food and Culinary Products. Talcott Communications Corp. • Monthly. $34.00 per year. Emphasizes new specialty food products and the business management aspects of the specialty food and confection industries. Includes special issues on wine, cheese, candy, "upscale" cookware, and gifts. Formerly (Fancy Foods).

Food Distribution Magazine. Phoenix Media Network Inc. • Monthly. $49.00 per year. Edited for marketers and buyers of domestic and imported, specialty or gourmet food products, including ethnic foods, seasonings, and bakery items.

Gourmet Retailer. Nielsen Business Media Inc. • Monthly. Free to qualified personnel; others, $75.00 per year. Covers upscale food and housewares, including confectionery items, bakery operations, and coffee.

Reference Source. Sosland Publishing Co. • Annual. $45.00 per year. A statistical reference manual and specification guide for wholesale baking.

Snack Food and Wholesale Bakery: The Magazine That Defines the Snack Food Industry. BNP Media. • Monthly. Monthly. Free to qualified personnel; others, $85.06 per year. Provides information for producers of pretzels, potato chips, cookies, crackers, nuts, and other snack foods. Includes *Annual Buyers Guide* and *State of Industry Report.*

Specialty Baker's Voice. Specialty Bakery Owners of America. • Monthly. $25.00 per year.

PRICE SOURCES

PPI Detailed Report. Periodical covering business. Bureau of Labor Statistics, U.S. Department of Labor. U. S. Government Printing Office. • Monthly. $55 Individuals.

RESEARCH CENTERS AND INSTITUTES

Quality Bakers of America Cooperative Laboratory. 1275 Glenlivet Dr., Ste. 100, Allentown, PA 18106. Phone: (203)531-7100; Fax: (203)531-1406; Email: info@qba.com • URL: http://www.qba.com.

STATISTICS SOURCES

United States Census of Manufactures. U.S. Department of Commerce U.S. Census Bureau. • Quinquennial. Results presented in reports, tape, CD-ROM, and Diskette files.

U.S. Industry and Trade Outlook. U.S. Department of Commerce National Technical Information Service. • Annual. Produced by the International Trade Administration, U.S. Department of Commerce, in a "public-private" partnership with DRI/McGraw-Hill and Standard & Poor's. Provides basic data, outlook for the current year, and "Long-Term Prospects" (five-year projections) for a wide variety of products and services. Includes high technology industries. Formerly *U.S. Industrial Outlook.*

TRADE/PROFESSIONAL ASSOCIATIONS

American Institute of Baking. 1213 Bakers Way, Manhattan, KS 66505-3999. Phone: 800-633-5137 or (785)537-4750; Fax: (785)537-1493; Email: info@aibonline.org • URL: http://www.aibonline.org • Nutrition, including effects of ingredients, processing, and baked products on physiological responses in humans; and cereal science, particularly applied technology. Contract research projects include performance characteristics of new and improved ingredients for the baking industry and product and process development utilizing laboratory and pilot bakeries.

American Society of Baking. 7809 N Chestnut Ave., Kansas City, MO 64119. Phone: 800-713-0462; Fax: (888)315-2612; Email: info@asbe.org • URL: http://www.asbe.org • Professional organization of persons engaged in bakery production; chemists, production supervisors, engineers, technicians, and others from allied fields. Maintains information service and library references to baking and related subjects.

Bakery Equipment Manufacturers and Allieds. 10740 Nall Ave., Ste. 230, Overland Park, KS 66211. Phone: (913)338-1300; Fax: (913)338-1327; Email: info@bema.org • URL: http://www.bema.org.

Baking Industry Sanitation Standards Committee. PO Box 3999, Manhattan, KS 66505-3999. Phone: 866-342-4772 or (785)537-4750; Fax: (785)537-1493; Email: bissc@bissc.org • URL: http://www.bissc.org • Industry association representing 120 bakery equipment manufacturers. Seeks to establish standards of sanitation in bakery food processing equipment. Receives advisory assistance from national and international public health and food sanitation groups. Develops and publishes sanitation standards for the baking industry. Offers an equipment certification program for bakery equipment conforming to standards (annual).

Retail Bakers of America. 15941 Harlem Ave., No. 347, Tinley Park, IL 60477. Phone: 800-638-0924; Email: info@rbanet.com • URL: http://www.retailbakersofamerica.org • Independent and in-store bakeries, food service, specialty bakeries, suppliers of ingredients, tools and equipment; other. Provides information, management, production, merchandising and small business services.

BALANCE OF PAYMENTS

See also FOREIGN TRADE

CD-ROM DATABASES

EconLit. Ovid Technologies Inc. • Updated monthly. Lists journal articles, book reviews, disserations of economic literature. Over 1,400 journals covered.

Global Trade Atlas. Global Trade Information Services Inc. • Subscription fees are tailored. Provides government statistics on trade between the U. S. and each of more than 80 countries. Includes import-export data, trade balances, product information, market share, price data, etc.

OECD Statistical Compendium. Organization for Economic Cooperation and Development. • Semiannual. $1,905.00 per year for 1 to 10 users. CD-ROM contains more than 730,000 monthly, quarterly, and annual time series for OECD countries, 1960 to date. Includes fully searchable data on agriculture, food, economic indicators, national accounts, employment, energy, finance, industry, technology, and foreign trade. Results can be displayed in various forms.

INTERNET DATABASES

Business 2.0 Web Guide to the Best Business Links. Business 2.0 Media Inc. Phone: (415)293-4800; Email: support@business2.com • URL: http://www.business2.com/webguide • Web site presents an extensive, searchable directory of links to "the best, most informative, and authoritative web pages." Twenty main categories cover business, finance, career, company information, people, and technology topics, with thousands of subtopics, all linking to Web sites recommended by experienced business researchers. Fees: Free.

Fedstats. Federal Interagency Council on Statistical Policy. Phone: (202)395-7254 • URL: http://www.fedstats.gov • Web site features an efficient search facility for full-text statistics produced by more than 100 federal agencies, including the Census Bureau, the Bureau of Economic Analysis, and the Bureau of Labor Statistics. Boolean searches can be made within one agency or for all agencies combined. Links are offered to international statistical bureaus, including the UN, IMF, OECD, UNESCO, Eurostat, and 20 individual countries. Fees: Free.

FreeLunch.com. Economy.com, Inc. Phone: (610)696-8700; Fax: (610)696-1678 • URL: http://www.freelunch.com • Web site provides free access to more than 200 million economic and financial data series, covering industry, demographics, labor markets, prices, retail sales, government spending, trade, interest rates, housing starts, the stock market, etc. Data is available in either chart or table form. Searching is offered. Free, but registration required. Economy.com, Inc. also offers fee-based economic analysis at *The Dismal Scientist* site (www.dismal.com).

ONLINE DATABASES

Balance of Payments Statistics. International Monetary Fund. • Time series compiled by IMF, mid-1960's to present. Inquire as to online cost and availability.

PERIODICALS AND NEWSLETTERS

IMF Survey. International Monetary Fund. • Description: Timely news on topics of general interest in the fields of international finance, country economics, trade, and commodities. Contains information on the IMF's activities, including press releases, major management speeches, and lending activity data rates.

International Monetary Fund Staff Papers. International Monetary Fund, Publication Services. • Quarterly. Individuals, $56.00 per year; students, $28.00 per year. Contains studies by IMF staff members on balance of payments, foreign exchange, fiscal policy, and related topics. Formerly *International Monetary Fund Staff Papers.*

STATISTICS SOURCES

Statistical Yearbook. United Nations Publications. • Annual. $125.00. Contains statistics for about 200 countries on a wide variety of economic, industrial, and demographic topics. Compiled by United Nations Statistical Office.

Survey of Current Business. U. S. Government Printing Office. • Published by Bureau of Economic Analysis, U. S. Department of Commerce. Presents a wide variety of business and economic data.

BALL BEARINGS

See BEARINGS AND BALL BEARINGS

BALL POINT PENS

See WRITING INSTRUMENTS

BANANA INDUSTRY

See also FRUIT INDUSTRY

DIRECTORIES

Major Food and Drink Companies of the World. Cengage Learning Inc. • 12th edition. eBook. Published by Graham & Whiteside. Contains profiles and trade names for more than 9,200 important food and beverage companies in various countries. In addition to foods, includes both alcoholic and nonalcoholic drink products.

INTERNET DATABASES

USDA. U.S. National Institute of Standards and Technology. 100 Bureau Dr., Gaithersburg, MD 20899-1070. Phone: 800-877-8339 or (301)975-6478 or (202)720-2791; Fax: (301)975-8295; Email: inquiries@nist.gov • URL: http://www.nist.gov • The USDA home page has six sections: News and Information; What's New; About USDA; Agencies; Opportunities; Search and Help. Keyword searching is offered from the USDA home page and from various individual agency home pages. Agencies are the Economic Research Service, Agricultural Marketing Service, National Agricultural Statistics Service, National Agricultural Library, and about 12 others. Updating varies. Fees: Free.

ONLINE DATABASES

Agricola. U.S. National Agricultural Library World List of Agricultural Serials. • Covers worldwide agricultural literature. Over 3.3 million citations, 1970 to present, with monthly updates. Inquire as to online cost and availability.

Food Science and Technology Abstracts (online). IFIS North American Desk. • Produced by International Food Information Service. Provides about 500,000 online citations, with abstracts, to the international literature of food science, technology, commodities, engineering, and processing. Approximately 2,000 periodicals are covered. Time period is 1969 to date, with monthly updates. Inquire as to online cost and availability.

PRICE SOURCES

PPI Detailed Report. Periodical covering business. Bureau of Labor Statistics, U.S. Department of Labor. U. S. Government Printing Office. • Monthly. $55 Individuals.

RESEARCH CENTERS AND INSTITUTES

College of Tropical Agriculture and Human Resources. University of Hawaii at Manoa, 2515 Campus Rd., Miller Hall 110, Honolulu, HI 96822. Phone: (808)956-8234; Fax: (808)956-9105; Email: gallom@ctahr.hawaii.edu • URL: http://www.ctahr.hawaii.edu • Concerned with the production and marketing of tropical food and ornamental plant products, including pineapples, bananas, coffee, and macadamia nuts.

STATISTICS SOURCES

Agricultural Statistics. U.S. Department of Agriculture National Agricultural Statistics Service. • Annual. $46 Individuals. Provides a wide variety of statistical data relating to agricultural production, supplies, consumption, prices/price-supports, foreign trade, costs, and returns, as well as farm labor, loans, income, and population. In many cases, historical data is shown annually for 10 years. In addition to farm data, includes detailed fishery statistics.

BANK ACCOUNTING

INTERNET DATABASES

Rutgers Accounting Web. Rutgers University Accounting Research Center. Phone: (973)353-5172; Fax: (973)353-1283 • URL: http://www.rutgers.edu/accounting • RAW Web site provides extensive links to sources of national and international accounting information, such as the Big Six accounting firms, the Financial Accounting Standards Board (FASB), SEC filings (EDGAR), journals, publishers, software, the International Accounting Network, and "Internet's largest list of accounting firms in USA." Searching is offered. Fees: Free.

PERIODICALS AND NEWSLETTERS

Journal of Bank Cost and Management Accounting. Association for Management Information in Financial Services. • 3/year.

TRADE/PROFESSIONAL ASSOCIATIONS

Association for Management Information in Financial Services. 14247 Saffron Cir., Carmel, IN 46032. Phone: (317)815-5857; Email: ami2@amifs.org • URL: http://www.amifs.org • Members are financial institution employees interested in management accounting and cost analysis.

Bank Administration Institute. 115 S La Salle St., Ste. 3300, Chicago, IL 60603-3801. Phone: 800-375-5543; Fax: (312)683-2373; Email: info@bai.org • URL: http://www.bai.org • Works to improve the competitive position of banking companies through strategic research and educational offerings.

BANK AUTOMATION

ABSTRACTS AND INDEXES

Business Periodicals Index Retrospective. EBSCO Publishing Inc. • 11/year. Quarterly and annual cumulations.

PERIODICALS AND NEWSLETTERS

Card Technology. SourceMedia Inc. • Monthly. $79.00 per year. Covers advanced technology for credit, debit, and other cards. Topics include smart cards, optical recognition, and card design.

Corporate EFT Report. Phillips International, Inc. • Biweekly. $695.00 per year. Newsletter on subject of electronic funds transfer.

Item Processing Report. Access Intelligence L.L.C. • Description: Monitors developments in the processing of remittances and checks, including image processing, optical character recognition, check truncation, hardware, and software. **Remarks:** Absorbed The Powell Report, 1992.

U.S. Banker. SourceMedia Inc. • Monthly. $65.00 per year. Edited for bank executives and managers. Covers a wide variety of banking and financial topics.

WebFinance. SourceMedia Inc. • Semimonthly. $995.00 per year. Newsletter (also available online at www.webfinance.net). Covers the Internet-based provision of online financial services by banks, online brokers, mutual funds, and insurance companies. Provides news stories, analysis, and descriptions of useful resources.

STATISTICS SOURCES

Statistical Information on the Financial Services Industry. American Bankers Association. • Annual. Members, $150.00; non-members, $275.00. Presents a wide variety of data relating to banking and financial services, including consumer economics, personal finance, credit, government loans, capital markets, and international banking.

TRADE/PROFESSIONAL ASSOCIATIONS

Association for Financial Technology. 34 N High St., New Albany, OH 43054-8507. Phone: (614)895-1208; Fax: (614)895-3466; Email: aft@aftweb.com • URL: http://www.aftweb.com/aws/AFT/pt/sp/home_page • Concerned with bank computer technology.

Bank Administration Institute - Operations and Technology Commission. 115 S LaSalle St., Ste. 3300, Chicago, IL 60603-3801. Phone: 800-224-9889 or (312)653-2464; Fax: (312)683-2373; Email: info@bai.org • URL: http://www.bai.org.

Electronic Funds Transfer Association. 4000 Legato Rd., Ste. 1100, Fairfax, VA 22033. Phone: (571)318-5556; Fax: (571)318-5557; Email: dennisambach@efta.org • URL: http://www.efta.org • Financial institutions, credit card companies, ATM owners, networks and processors, hardware and software manufacturers and e-commerce companies dedicated to the advancement of electronic payment systems and commerce.

Financial and Security Products Association. 1024 Mebane Oaks Rd., No. 273, Mebane, NC 27302. Phone: 800-843-6082 or (919)648-0664; Fax: (919)648-0670 • URL: http://fspa1.com • Formerly National Independent Bank Equipment and Systems Association.

NACHA: The Electronic Payments Association. 13450 Sunrise Valley Dr., Ste. 100, Herndon, VA 20171. Phone: (703)561-1100; Fax: (703)787-0996; Email: abuse@nacha.org • URL: http://www.nacha.org • Automated Clearing House (ACH) association. Provides an interregional exchange for electronic debits and credits among ACHs and to establish and administer nationwide standards and operating rules for ACHs. Conducts national seminars and conferences on ACH operations and products; sponsors annual Payments and Electronic Commerce Institute; sponsors Accredited ACH Professional program. Sponsors national marketing campaign; compiles statistics.

BANK CREDIT

See BANK LOANS

BANK DEPOSITS

See also BANKS AND BANKING

ABSTRACTS AND INDEXES

Accounting and Tax Index. ProQuest L.L.C. • Quarterly. Indexes accounting, auditing, and taxation literature appearing in journals, books, pamphlets, conference proceedings, and newsletters.

PERIODICALS AND NEWSLETTERS

Jumbo Rate News. BauerFinancial Inc. • Description: Reports on high-yielding, insured Jumbo CD (Certificate of Deposit) rates nationwide. Analyzes each institution by current credit-worthiness, and lists current assets and capital ratios. Provides phone numbers, contacts, methods of computation, and information on how interest is paid. Also contains financial news, insights, and commentary of interest to Jumbo CD investors. Recurring features include editorials and news of interest.

STATISTICS SOURCES

Aggregate Reserves of Depository Institutions and the Monetary Base. U.S. Federal Reserve System Board of Governors Publications Services. • Weekly. $20 Individuals.

Statistical Information on the Financial Services Industry. American Bankers Association. • Annual. Members, $150.00; non-members, $275.00. Presents a wide variety of data relating to banking and financial services, including consumer economics, personal finance, credit, government loans, capital markets, and international banking.

BANK FAILURES

ABSTRACTS AND INDEXES

Business Periodicals Index Retrospective. EBSCO Publishing Inc. • 11/year. Quarterly and annual cumulations.

CD-ROM DATABASES

ABI/INFORM. ProQuest L.L.C. • Monthly. Provides CD-ROM indexing and abstracting of worldwide business literature. Archival discs are available from 1971. Formerly *ABI/INFORM OnDisc.*

Applied Science & Business Periodicals Retrospective. EBSCO Publishing Inc. • Includes citations for more than 3 million articles detailing events, issues, and trends in business and industry.

PAIS International. ProQuest L.L.C. • Monthly. $1,995.00 per year. Contains over 650,000 citations to the literature of contemporary social, political, and economic issues.

ONLINE DATABASES

American Banker Full Text. American Banker-Bond Buyer, Database Services. • Provides complete text online of the daily *American Banker*. Inquire as to cost and availability.

Banking Information Source. ProQuest L.L.C. • Provides indexing and abstracting of periodical and other literature from 1982 to date, with weekly updates. Covers the financial services industry: banks, savings institutions, investment houses, credit unions, insurance companies, and real estate organizations. Emphasis is on marketing and management. Inquire as to online cost and availability. (Formerly *FINIS: Financial Industry Information Service*.).

Wilson Business Abstracts Online. H.W. Wilson Co. • Indexes and abstracts 600 major business periodicals, plus the *Wall Street Journal* and the business section of the *New York Times*. Indexing is from 1982, abstracting from 1990, with the two newspapers included from 1993. Updated weekly. Inquire as to online cost and availability. (*Business Periodicals Index* without abstracts is also available online.).

OTHER SOURCES

Bank and Lender Litigation Reporter: The Nationwide Litigation Report of Failed National and State Banks and Savings and Loan Associations, including FDIC and FSLIC Complaints and Related Actions Among Shareholders, Officers, Directors, Ins. Andrews Publications. • Semimonthly. $875.00 per year. Newsletter. Provides summaries of significant litigation and regulatory agency complaints. Formerly *Lender Liability Litigation Reporter*.

PERIODICALS AND NEWSLETTERS

American Banker: The Financial Services Daily. SourceMedia Inc. • Daily. $895.00 per year. Provides news of banking, investment products, mortgages, credit unions, finance, bank technology, and legal developments.

Troubled and Problematic Bank and Thrift Report. BauerFinancial Inc. • Quarterly. $225.00 per year. Newsletter provides information on seriously undercapitalized ("Troubled") banks and savings institutions, as defined by a federal Prompt Corrective Action Rule. "Problematic" banks and thrifts are those meeting regulatory capital levels, but showing negative trends.

U.S. Banker. SourceMedia Inc. • Monthly. $65.00 per year. Edited for bank executives and managers. Covers a wide variety of banking and financial topics.

RESEARCH CENTERS AND INSTITUTES

Boston University - Center for Finance, Law and Policy. 53 Bay State Rd., 1st Fl., Boston, MA 02215. Phone: 888-285-7003 or (617)353-3023; Fax: (617)353-2444; Email: ckhurley@bu.edu • URL: http://www.bu.edu/bucflp • Research fields include banking law, regulation of depository institutions, and deposit insurance.

Financial Institutions and Markets Research Center. c/o Ravi Jagannathan, Director, Kellogg School of Management, Northwestern University, 2001 Sheridan Rd., Jacobs Ctr., Rm. 4213, Evanston, IL 60208. Phone: (847)491-8338; Fax: (847)491-5719 • URL: http://www.kellogg.northwestern.edu/research/fimrc/index.htm • Does research in the management and public regulation of financial institutions. A unit of the J. L. Kellogg Graduate School of Management.

TRADE/PROFESSIONAL ASSOCIATIONS

American Council of State Savings Supervisors. 1129 20th St. NW, 9th Fl., Washington, DC 20036. Phone: (202)728-5757 or (703)669-5440; Fax: (703)669-5441 • URL: http://www.acsss.org • Members are state savings and loan supervisors. Includes a Joint Committee on Examinations and Education.

Conference of State Bank Supervisors. 1129 20th St. NW, 9th Fl., Washington, DC 20036. Phone: (202)296-2840; Fax: (202)296-1928 • URL: http://www.csbs.org/Pages/default.aspx • Members are state officials responsible for supervision of state-chartered banking institutions.

BANK FINANCE

See BANK LOANS

BANK LAW

See BANKING LAW AND REGULATION

BANK LOANS

See also COMMERCIAL LENDING; CONSUMER CREDIT

ABSTRACTS AND INDEXES

Business Periodicals Index Retrospective. EBSCO Publishing Inc. • 11/year. Quarterly and annual cumulations.

CD-ROM DATABASES

OECD Statistical Compendium. Organization for Economic Cooperation and Development. • Semiannual. $1,905.00 per year for 1 to 10 users. CD-ROM contains more than 730,000 monthly, quarterly, and annual time series for OECD countries, 1960 to date. Includes fully searchable data on agriculture, food, economic indicators, national accounts, employment, energy, finance, industry, technology, and foreign trade. Results can be displayed in various forms.

DIRECTORIES

Business Capital Sources. International Wealth Success, Inc. • Annual. $20 Individuals. Covers: About 1,500 banks, insurance and mortgage companies, commercial finance, leasing, and venture capital firms that lend money for business investment. Entries include: Company or institution name, address, phone.

HANDBOOKS AND MANUALS

SBA Loan Guide. Entrepreneur Meida, Inc. • Looseleaf. $59.50. A practical guide to obtaining loans through the Small Business Administration. (Start-Up Business Guide No. E1315.).

INTERNET DATABASES

BanxQuote Banking, Mortgage, and Finance Center. BanxQuote, Inc. Phone: (914)722-1600; Fax: (914)722-6630; Email: info@banx.com • URL: http://www.banx.com • Daily. Web site quotes interest rates paid by banks around the country on various savings products, as well as rates paid by consumers for automobile loans, mortgages, credit cards, home equity loans, and personal loans. Also provided: stock quotes, indexes, stock options, futures trading data, economic indicators, and links to many other financial sites.

Business 2.0 Web Guide to the Best Business Links. Business 2.0 Media Inc. Phone: (415)293-4800; Email: support@business2.com • URL: http://www.business2.com/webguide • Web site presents an extensive, searchable directory of links to "the best, most informative, and authoritative web pages." Twenty main categories cover business, finance, career, company information, people, and technology topics, with thousands of subtopics, all linking to Web sites recommended by experienced business researchers. Fees: Free.

Fedstats. Federal Interagency Council on Statistical Policy. Phone: (202)395-7254 • URL: http://www.fedstats.gov • Web site features an efficient search facility for full-text statistics produced by more than 100 federal agencies, including the Census Bureau, the Bureau of Economic Analysis, and the Bureau of Labor Statistics. Boolean searches can be made within one agency or for all agencies combined. Links are offered to international statistical bureaus, including the UN, IMF, OECD, UNESCO, Eurostat, and 20 individual countries. Fees: Free.

FreeLunch.com. Economy.com, Inc. Phone: (610)696-8700; Fax: (610)696-1678 • URL: http://www.freelunch.com • Web site provides free access to more than 200 million economic and financial data series, covering industry, demographics, labor markets, prices, retail sales, government spending, trade, interest rates, housing starts, the stock market, etc. Data is available in either chart or table form. Searching is offered. Free, but registration required. Economy.com, Inc. also offers fee-based economic analysis at *The Dismal Scientist* site (www.dismal.com).

OTHER SOURCES

Bank and Lender Litigation Reporter: The Nationwide Litigation Report of Failed National and State Banks and Savings and Loan Associations, including FDIC and FSLIC Complaints and Related Actions Among Shareholders, Officers, Directors, Ins. Andrews Publications. • Semimonthly. $875.00 per year. Newsletter. Provides summaries of significant litigation and regulatory agency complaints. Formerly *Lender Liability Litigation Reporter*.

Country Finance. The Economist Intelligence Unit. • Annual $425.00 per year. Discusses banking and financial conditions in each of 47 countries. Includes foreign exchange regulations, the currency outlook, sources of capital, financing techniques, and tax considerations.

PERIODICALS AND NEWSLETTERS

Bank Loan Report. IDD Enterprises L.P. • Description: Discusses banking loans and transactions made by large corporations. Recurring features include a column titled Term Sheets.

Consumer Credit and Truth-in-Lending Compliance Report. Thomson RIA. • Monthly. $183.75 per year. Newsletter. Focuses on the latest regulatory rulings and findings involving consumer lending and credit activity. Incorporates (Consumer Lending Report).

Grant's Interest Rate Observer. Grant's Financial Publishing Inc. • Biweekly. $1,025 Individuals. Newsletter containing detailed analysis of money-related topics, including interest rate trends, global credit markets, fixed-income investments, bank loan policies, and international money markets.

International Bank Credit Analyst. BCA Publications Ltd. • Monthly. $795.00 per year. "A monthly forecast and analysis of currency movements, interest rates, and stock market developments in the principal countries, based on a continuous appraisal of money and credit trends worldwide." Includes many charts and graphs providing international coverage of money, credit, and securities.

Lender Liability Law Report. Thomson RIA. • Description: Discusses the impact of relevant cases and legislation on lenders and spotlights legal landmines which lenders may encounter. Recurring features include summaries of recent cases and avoidance techniques.

STATISTICS SOURCES

Statistical Information on the Financial Services Industry. American Bankers Association. • Annual. Members, $150.00; non-members, $275.00. Presents a wide variety of data relating to banking and financial services, including consumer economics, personal finance, credit, government loans, capital markets, and international banking.

Survey of Current Business. U. S. Government Printing Office. • Published by Bureau of Economic Analysis, U. S. Department of Commerce. Presents a wide variety of business and economic data.

TRADE/PROFESSIONAL ASSOCIATIONS

Credit Research Foundation. 1812 Baltimore Blvd., Ste. H, Westminster, MD 21157. Phone: (443)821-3000; Fax: (443)821-3627 • URL: http://www.crfonline.org • Represents credit, financial, and working capital executives of manufacturing and banking concerns. Aims to create a better understanding of the impact of credit on the economy. Plans, supervises, and administers research and educational programs. Conducts surveys on economic conditions, trends, policies, practices, theory, systems, and methodology. Sponsors formal educational programs in credit and financial management. Maintains library on credit, collections, and management.

Risk Management Association. 1801 Market St., Ste. 300, Philadelphia, PA 19103-1613. Phone: (215)446-4000; Fax: (215)446-4101; Email: rmaar@rmahq.org • URL: http://www.rmahq.org • Commercial and savings banks, and savings and loan, and other financial services companies. Conducts research and professional development activities in areas of loan administration, asset management, and commercial lending and credit to increase professionalism.

BANK MANAGEMENT

See also BANKS AND BANKING

ABSTRACTS AND INDEXES

Business Periodicals Index Retrospective. EBSCO Publishing Inc. • 11/year. Quarterly and annual cumulations.

BIBLIOGRAPHIES

Financial Institutions. U. S. Government Printing Office. • Annual. Free. Lists government publications. Formerly *Banks and Banking*. GPO Subject Bibliography No. 128.

BIOGRAPHICAL SOURCES

Who's Who in Finance and Business. Marquis Who's Who L.L.C. • Biennial. $349 Individuals. Provides over 21,000 concise biographies of business leaders in all fields.

DIRECTORIES

Who's Who in Finance and Business. Marquis Who's Who L.L.C. • Biennial. $349 Individuals. Provides over 21,000 concise biographies of business leaders in all fields.

HANDBOOKS AND MANUALS

Bank CEO's Operating and Management Desk Reference. SourceMedia Inc. • $395.00. Two looseleaf volumes. Periodic updates available. Provides up-to-date information and advice on all areas of bank management. (A Sheshunoff publication.).

Banking Crimes: Fraud, Money Laundering & Embezzlement. John K. Villa. Thomson West. • $369.60 Full Set. Covers fraud and embezzlement.

Trust Department Administration and Operations. Matthew Bender and Company Inc. • Semiannual. $726 Individuals Book or Electronic version. Covers every aspect of setting up a trust department, day-to-day administration, asset management, operations, marketing, and internal management. A procedural manual, training guide and idea source.

ONLINE DATABASES

American Banker Full Text. American Banker-Bond Buyer, Database Services. • Provides complete text online of the daily *American Banker*. Inquire as to cost and availability.

Banking Information Source. ProQuest L.L.C. • Provides indexing and abstracting of periodical and other literature from 1982 to date, with weekly updates. Covers the financial services industry: banks, savings institutions, investment houses, credit unions, insurance companies, and real estate organizations. Emphasis is on marketing and management. Inquire as to online cost and availability. (Formerly *FINIS: Financial Industry Information Service*.).

PERIODICALS AND NEWSLETTERS

ABA Banking Journal. American Bankers Association. Member Communications. Simmons-Boardman Books Inc. • Monthly. Monthly. Free to qualified personnel.

American Banker: The Financial Services Daily. SourceMedia Inc. • Daily. $895.00 per year. Provides news of banking, investment products, mortgages, credit unions, finance, bank technology, and legal developments.

The Community Bank President. Siefer Consultants Inc. • Monthly. $329.00 per year.

Fee Income Growth Strategies. Siefer Consultants Inc. • Description: Discusses the role of fees and service charges for money orders, cashier's checks, nonsufficient funds, loans, automatic teller machine cards, and other ancillary services in the profitability of financial institutions.

Operations Alert. America's Community Bankers. • Description: Reviews recent regulatory and product developments that affect community bank operations.

U.S. Banker. SourceMedia Inc. • Monthly. $65.00 per year. Edited for bank executives and managers. Covers a wide variety of banking and financial topics.

RESEARCH CENTERS AND INSTITUTES

Financial Institutions and Markets Research Center. c/o Ravi Jagannathan, Director, Kellogg School of Management, Northwestern University, 2001 Sheridan Rd., Jacobs Ctr., Rm. 4213, Evanston, IL 60208. Phone: (847)491-8338; Fax: (847)491-5719 • URL: http://www.kellogg.northwestern.edu/research/fimrc/index.htm • Does research in the management and public regulation of financial institutions. A unit of the J. L. Kellogg Graduate School of Management.

TRADE/PROFESSIONAL ASSOCIATIONS

Bank Administration Institute. 115 S La Salle St., Ste. 3300, Chicago, IL 60603-3801. Phone: 800-375-5543; Fax: (312)683-2373; Email: info@bai.org • URL: http://www.bai.org • Works to improve the competitive position of banking companies through strategic research and educational offerings.

National Bankers Association. 1513 P St. NW, Washington, DC 20005. Phone: (202)588-5432; Fax: (202)588-5443; Email: execdesk@nationalbankers.org • URL: http://www.nationalbankers.org • Minority banking institutions owned by minority individuals and institutions. Serves as an advocate for the minority banking industry. Organizes banking services, government relations, marketing, scholarship, and technical assistance programs. Offers placement services; compiles statistics.

BANK MARKETING

ABSTRACTS AND INDEXES

Business Periodicals Index Retrospective. EBSCO Publishing Inc. • 11/year. Quarterly and annual cumulations.

ONLINE DATABASES

Banking Information Source. ProQuest L.L.C. • Provides indexing and abstracting of periodical and other literature from 1982 to date, with weekly updates. Covers the financial services industry: banks, savings institutions, investment houses, credit unions, insurance companies, and real estate organizations. Emphasis is on marketing and management. Inquire as to online cost and availability. (Formerly *FINIS: Financial Industry Information Service*.).

OTHER SOURCES

Home Banking Report. Jupitermedia Corp. • Annual. $695.00. Market research report. Covers banking from home by phone or online, with projections of growth in future years.

PERIODICALS AND NEWSLETTERS

American Banker: The Financial Services Daily. SourceMedia Inc. • Daily. $895.00 per year. Provides news of banking, investment products, mortgages, credit unions, finance, bank technology, and legal developments.

Bank Investment Consultant: Sales Strategies for the Financial Adviser. SourceMedia Inc. • Monthly. Controlled circulation. Covers sales and marketing techniques for bank investment and asset management divisions. Formerly *Bank Investment Marketing*.

International Journal of Bank Marketing. Emerald Group Publishing Inc. • Seven times a year. $12,519.00 per year.

U.S. Banker. SourceMedia Inc. • Monthly. $65.00 per year. Edited for bank executives and managers. Covers a wide variety of banking and financial topics.

TRADE/PROFESSIONAL ASSOCIATIONS

American Bankers Association. 1120 Connecticut Ave. NW, Washington, DC 20036. Phone: 800-226-5377 or (202)663-5268; Fax: (202)828-5053; Email: custserv@aba.com • URL: http://www.aba.com • Members are principally commercial banks and trust companies; combined assets of members represent approximately 90% of the U.S. banking industry; approximately 94% of members are community banks with less than $500 million in assets. Seeks to enhance the role of commercial bankers as preeminent providers of financial services through communications, research, legal action, lobbying of federal legislative and regulatory bodies, and education and training programs. Serves as spokesperson for the banking industry; facilitates exchange of information among members. Maintains the American Institute of Banking, an industry-sponsored adult education program. Conducts educational and training programs for bank employees and officers through a wide range of banking schools and national conferences. Maintains liaison with federal bank regulators; lobbies Congress on issues affecting commercial banks; testifies before congressional committees; represents members in U.S. postal rate proceedings. Serves as secretariat of the International Monetary Conference and the Financial Institutions Committee for the American National Standards Institute. Files briefs and lawsuits in major court cases affecting the industry. Conducts teleconferences with state banking associations on such issues as regulatory compliance; works to build consensus and coordinate activities of leading bank and financial service trade groups. Provides services to members including: public advocacy; news media contact; insurance program providing directors and officers with liability coverage, financial institution bond, and trust errors and omissions coverage; research service operated through ABA Center for Banking Information; fingerprint set processing in conjunction with the Federal Bureau of Investigation; discounts on operational and income-producing projects through the Corporation for American Banking. Conducts conferences, forums, and workshops covering subjects such as small business, consumer credit, agricultural and community banking, trust management, bank operations, and automation. Sponsors ABA Educational Foundation and the Personal Economics Program, which educates schoolchildren and the community on banking, economics, and personal finance.

BANK RESERVES

See also BANKS AND BANKING

CD-ROM DATABASES

CreditDisk 2.0. Fitch. • Price and frequency on application. CD-ROM provides credit research and ratings on individual banks throughout the world, with Internet updating. Includes graphic displays of rating histories and financial ratios.

INTERNET DATABASES

Federal Reserve Board Publications and Education Resources. Board of Governors of the Federal Reserve System. Phone: (202)452-3000; Fax: (202)452-3819 • URL: http://www.federalreserve.gov/publications.htm • Web site provides access to statistics, surveys, and research from the Federal Reserve Board. *Federal Reserve Bulletin* articles are available as abstracts or full text (PDF) currently or from six-year archives. The link "Statistics: Releases and Historical Data" offers daily, weekly, monthly, quarterly, and annual data in great detail for interest rates, foreign exchange, consumer credit, money stock measures, industrial production indexes, bank reserves, and other items. Historical tabulations are available for various time periods. Free.

STATISTICS SOURCES

Statistical Information on the Financial Services Industry. American Bankers Association. • Annual. Members, $150.00; non-members, $275.00. Presents a wide variety of data relating to banking and financial services, including consumer economics, personal finance, credit, government loans, capital markets, and international banking.

BANK TECHNOLOGY

See BANK AUTOMATION

BANK TELLER MACHINES

See BANK AUTOMATION

BANKING LAW AND REGULATION

ABSTRACTS AND INDEXES

Business Periodicals Index Retrospective. EBSCO Publishing Inc. • 11/year. Quarterly and annual cumulations.

Index to Legal Periodicals and Books. H.W. Wilson Co. • Monthly. $490.00 per year. Quarterly and annual cumulations.

ALMANACS AND YEARBOOKS

Securities, Commodities, and Federal Banking: 1999 in Review. Wolters Kluwer Law & Business CCH. • Irregular. $57.00. Summarizes the year's significant legal and regulatory developments.

BIBLIOGRAPHIES

Financial Institutions. U. S. Government Printing Office. • Annual. Free. Lists government publications. Formerly *Banks and Banking*. GPO Subject Bibliography No. 128.

DIRECTORIES

Lawyer's Register International by Specialties and Fields of Law Including a Directory of Corporate Counsel. Lawyer's Register Publishing Co. • Annual. $359 Individuals. Referral source for law firms.

HANDBOOKS AND MANUALS

U.S. Master Bank Tax Guide. Wolters Kluwer Law & Business CCH. • Annual. $389.95 Individuals book-softcover. Summarizes and explains federal tax rules affecting financial institutions.

INTERNET DATABASES

Lexis.com Research System. Lexis-Nexis Group. Phone: 800-227-4908 or (937)865-6800; Fax: (937)865-6909; Email: webmaster@prod.lexis-nexis.com • URL: http://www.nexis.com • Fee-based Web site offers extensive searching of a wide variety of legal sources. Additional features include Daily Opinion Service, lexis.com Bookstore, Career Center, CLE Center, Law Schools, and Practice Pages ("Pages specific to areas of specialty").

PERIODICALS AND NEWSLETTERS

International Financial Law Review. American Educational Systems. • Monthly. $750.00 per year. Includes print and online editions.

RESEARCH CENTERS AND INSTITUTES

Boston University - Center for Finance, Law and Policy. 53 Bay State Rd., 1st Fl., Boston, MA 02215. Phone: 888-285-7003 or (617)353-3023; Fax: (617)353-2444; Email: ckhurley@bu.edu • URL: http://www.bu.edu/bucflp • Research fields include banking law, regulation of depository institutions, and deposit insurance.

Center for Study of Responsive Law. PO Box 19367, Washington, DC 20036. Phone: (202)387-8030; Fax: (202)234-5176 • URL: http://csrl.org • A consumer-oriented research group.

Financial Institutions and Markets Research Center. c/o Ravi Jagannathan, Director, Kellogg School of Management, Northwestern University, 2001 Sheridan Rd., Jacobs Ctr., Rm. 4213, Evanston, IL 60208. Phone: (847)491-8338; Fax: (847)491-5719 • URL: http://www.kellogg.northwestern.edu/research/fimrc/index.htm • Does research in the management and public regulation of financial institutions. A unit of the J. L. Kellogg Graduate School of Management.

University of Pennsylvania - The Wharton School - Rodney L. White Center for Financial Research. 3254 Steinberg Hall-Dietrich Hall, Philadelphia, PA 19104-6367. Phone: (215)898-7616; Fax: (215)573-8084; Email: rlwctr@finance.wharton.upenn.edu • URL: http://rodneywhitecenter.wharton.upenn.edu • Research areas include financial management, money markets, real estate finance, and international finance.

TRADE/PROFESSIONAL ASSOCIATIONS

Conference of State Bank Supervisors. 1129 20th St. NW, 9th Fl., Washington, DC 20036. Phone: (202)296-2840; Fax: (202)296-1928 • URL: http://www.csbs.org/Pages/default.aspx • Members are state officials responsible for supervision of state-chartered banking institutions.

BANKRUPTCY

See also BUSINESS FAILURES; BUSINESS LAW

ABSTRACTS AND INDEXES

Accounting and Tax Index. ProQuest L.L.C. • Quarterly. Indexes accounting, auditing, and taxation literature appearing in journals, books, pamphlets, conference proceedings, and newsletters.

Current Law Index. Cengage Learning Inc. • $1,332 Individuals. Monthly. $1269.00 per year. Produced in cooperation with the American Association of Law Libraries. Indexes more than 900 law journals, legal newspapers, and specialty publications from the U.S., Canada, U.K., Ireland, Australia, and New Zealand.

Index to Legal Periodicals and Books. H.W. Wilson Co. • Monthly. $490.00 per year. Quarterly and annual cumulations.

ALMANACS AND YEARBOOKS

American Law Yearbook. Cengage Learning Inc. • $308 Individuals. Annual. $280.00. Serves as a yearly supplement to *West's Encyclopedia of American Lawa*. Describes new legal developments in many subject areas.

Bankruptcy Yearbook & Almanac. New Generation Research Inc. • Annual. $295. Contains updated information on US Bankruptcy Court data.

CD-ROM DATABASES

Authority Collier Bankruptcy Library. Matthew Bender and Company Inc. • Periodic revisions. Price on request. CD-ROM contains updated full text of *Collier on Bankruptcy* and 13 other Collier publications. Various aspects of bankruptcy are covered, including attorney compensation, proceedings, farm insolvencies, real estate failures, family law, taxation, and business workouts.

Index to Legal Periodicals and Books. EBSCO Publishing Inc. • Contains indexing of more than 1,400 English language legal periodicals from 1981 to date and 2,500 books.

DIRECTORIES

National Directory of Corporate Distress Specialists. Lustig Data Research Inc. • Annual. $245. Covers: 1,830 organizations and over 4,000 professionals providing 20 types of services in bankruptcies, workouts, turnarounds, and distressed securities investing, including attorneys, accountants, crisis managers, financial advisors, turnaround consultants, valuation experts, financing sources, investors, in-house workout officers, appraisers, auctioneers, liquidators, PR/crisis communications experts, real estate managers, etc. Entries include: Organization name, address, phone, fax, toll-free phone, year founded, parent company, department name, other offices, staff size, size of cases, types of representations, geographical area served, industry specializations, services offered, institutional clients, transaction history, party represented, key personnel, titles.

ENCYCLOPEDIAS AND DICTIONARIES

West's Encyclopedia of American Law. Cengage Learning Inc. • 2004. eBook. Second edition. Covers a wide variety of legal topics for the general reader. Inquire for pricing.

GENERAL WORKS

Bankruptcy Law Fundamentals. Thomson West. • Annual. $412.30 Individuals book - softbound. Looseleaf service.

HANDBOOKS AND MANUALS

Business Taxpayer Information Publications. U. S. Government Printing Office. • Annual. $66 U.S. Looseleaf. Two volumes, consisting of *Circular E, Employer's Tax Guide* and *Employer's Supplemental Tax Guide*. Issued by the Internal Revenue Service (http://www.irs.ustreas.gov). Includes a variety of business-related tax information, including withholding tables, tax calendars, self-employment issues, partnership matters,

For publishers' addresses, refer to SOURCES CITED section at the back of the book.

corporation topics, depreciation, and bankruptcy.

INTERNET DATABASES

Lexis.com Research System. Lexis-Nexis Group. Phone: 800-227-4908 or (937)865-6800; Fax: (937)865-6909; Email: webmaster@prod.lexis-nexis.com • URL: http://www.nexis.com • Fee-based Web site offers extensive searching of a wide variety of legal sources. Additional features include Daily Opinion Service, lexis.com Bookstore, Career Center, CLE Center, Law Schools, and Practice Pages ("Pages specific to areas of specialty").

ONLINE DATABASES

Accounting and Tax Database. ProQuest L.L.C. • Provides indexing and abstracting of the literature of accounting, taxation, and financial management, 1971 to date. Updating is weekly. Especially covers accounting, auditing, banking, bankruptcy, employee compensation and benefits, cash management, financial planning, and credit. Inquire as to online cost and availability.

OTHER SOURCES

Bankruptcy Law Reports. Wolters Kluwer Law & Business CCH. • Biweekly. $1,150.00 per year. Three looseleaf volumes.

PERIODICALS AND NEWSLETTERS

American Bankruptcy Law Journal. National Conference of Bankruptcy Judges. • Quarterly. $45 Individuals /year for new lawyers (less than two years in practice). Peer-reviewed journal focusing on bankruptcy law and related subjects.

The Bankruptcy Strategist. Law Journal Newsletter. • $510. Reports on substantive legal developments and successful strategy decisions by bankruptcy attorneys. Recurring features include a calendar of upcoming seminars.

Chapter 11 Update: Monitors All Major Developments in Today's Corporate Bankruptcies and Examines Pertinent Court Decisions Related to Chapter 11 Filings. Andrews Publications. • Semimonthly. $500.00 per year. Newsletter on corporate Chapter 11 bankruptcy filings.

Collections and Credit Risk: The Authority for Commercial and Consumer Credit Professionals. SourceMedia Inc. • Monthly. $95.00 per year. Contains articles on the technology and business management of credit and collection functions. Includes coverage of bad debts, bankruptcy, and credit risk management.

Credit Risk Management. Phillips International, Inc. • Biweekly. $695.00 per year. Newsletter on consumer credit, including delinquency aspects.

Insolvency Law & Practice. LexisNexis Butterworths Tolley. • Bimonthly. $181.00 per year. United Kingdom emphasis.

Norton Bankruptcy Law Adviser. William L. Norton, Jr. Thomson West. • Monthly. $598 Individuals.

STATISTICS SOURCES

Weekly Business Failures. Dun & Bradstreet Inc. • Weekly. $445.00 per year.

TRADE/PROFESSIONAL ASSOCIATIONS

Association of Insolvency and Restructuring Advisors. 221 Stewart Ave., Ste. 207, Medford, OR 97501. Phone: (541)858-1665; Fax: (541)858-9187; Email: aira@aira.org • URL: http://www.aira.org • Certified and licensed public accountants, attorneys, examiners, trustees and receivers. Seeks to define and develop the accountant's role provided by the Bankruptcy Reform Act of 1978 and to improve accounting skills used in insolvency cases. Promotes the primary role of creditors in insolvency situations and the enforcement of ethical standards of practice. Seeks to develop judicial reporting standards for insolvency and provide technical, analytical and accounting skills necessary in insolvent situations. Works to educate others in the field of the role of the accountant in order to foster better working relationships. Provides information about legislative issues that affect members and testifies before legislative bodies. Offers technical referral service. Administers the Certified Insolvency and Restructuring Advisor (CIRA) program.

Insol International. 6 - 7 Queen St., 5th Fl., London EC4N 1SP, United Kingdom. Phone: 44 20 79296679 or 44 20 72483333; Fax: 44 20 79296678 or 44 20 72483384 • URL: http://www.insol.org • Organizations representing 7,300 insolvency practitioners from 62 countries worldwide. Seeks international professional recognition of insolvency practitioners. Works to improve communication and cooperation among members; facilitates the exchange of information; establishes working committees to examine international issues of insolvency practice. Is developing a bibliographic database of insolvency publications.

National Conference of Bankruptcy Judges. c/o Jeanne Sleeper, 954 La Mirada St., Laguna Beach, CA 92651-3751. Phone: (949)497-3673; Fax: (949)497-2523 • URL: http://www.ncbj.org • Represents active and former bankruptcy judges. Promotes improvements in law practice and administration of justice in U.S. bankruptcy courts; encourages uniformity in the administration of estates in bankruptcy.

BANKS AND BANKING

ABSTRACTS AND INDEXES

Business Periodicals Index Retrospective. EBSCO Publishing Inc. • 11/year. Quarterly and annual cumulations.

NTIS Alerts: Business & Economics. U.S. Department of Commerce National Technical Information Service. • Biweekly. $130 per year. Covers consumer affairs, minority enterprises, marketing and economics, international commerce, banking, and finance.

World Banking Abstracts. Institution of European Finance. John Wiley & Sons Inc. Wiley-Blackwell. • Bimonthly. Provides worldwide coverage of articles appearing in over 400 financial publications.

ALMANACS AND YEARBOOKS

Bankers' Almanac. Reed Business Information. • Semiannual. $1,170.00. Six volumes. Lists more than 27,000 financial institutions; international coverage. Formerly *Bankers' Almanac and Yearbook.*

BIBLIOGRAPHIES

FED in Print: Economics and Banking Topics. Federal Reserve Bank of Philadelphia. • Semiannual. Free. Business and banking topics.

BIOGRAPHICAL SOURCES

Who's Who in Finance and Business. Marquis Who's Who L.L.C. • Biennial. $349 Individuals. Provides over 21,000 concise biographies of business leaders in all fields.

CD-ROM DATABASES

Business Abstracts with Full Text. EBSCO Publishing Inc. • Includes full text articles from more than 460 business publications from 1982 to present. Indexing for nearly 880 publications.

CreditDisk 2.0. Fitch. • Price and frequency on application. CD-ROM provides credit research and ratings on individual banks throughout the world, with Internet updating. Includes graphic displays of rating histories and financial ratios.

OECD Statistical Compendium. Organization for Economic Cooperation and Development. • Semiannual. $1,905.00 per year for 1 to 10 users. CD-ROM contains more than 730,000 monthly, quarterly, and annual time series for OECD countries, 1960 to date. Includes fully searchable data on agriculture, food, economic indicators, national accounts, employment, energy, finance, industry, technology, and foreign trade. Results can be displayed in various forms.

DIRECTORIES

American Banker--Top World Banks by Deposits and Assets. American Banker/Bond Buyer Inc. • Annual. $25. Publication includes: List of 500 largest banks in the world by assets with total deposits and deposit rank; also, the risk-based capital position of the 100 largest banking companies in the world as measured by total assets. Entries include: Bank name, headquarters, rankings by assets and amount of deposits and assets for two previous years.

American Bankers Association Directory of Trust Banking. Accuity Inc. • Annual. $575 Individuals. Covers: Approximately 3,000 financial institutions in the U.S. that are involved in trust banking. Database includes: Number of accounts under management by type for the past year and three year compounded growth. Entries include: Name, address, phone, fax, key trust officials with title and functional responsibility, personal and employee benefit assets for the two most current years along with a three year compounded growth rate.

America's Corporate Finance Directory. LexisNexis. • Annual. $1,399 Individuals print. Covers: Financial personnel and outside financial services relationships of 5,000 leading United States corporations and their wholly-owned United States subsidiaries. Entries include: Company name, address, phone, fax, telex, e-mail addresses, stock exchange information, earnings, total assets, size of pension/profit-sharing fund portfolio, number of employees, description of business, wholly-owned U.S. Subsidiaries of parent company; name and title of key executives; outside suppliers of financial services.

Annual Report of the Bank Commissioner of the State of Maryland. Maryland Department of Labor, Licensing and Regulation. • Biennial. Covers: State-chartered banks and credit unions in Maryland. Entries include: Financial institution name, address, phone, fax, names and titles of key personnel, financial data.

The Bank Directory. Accuity Inc. • Semiannual. $1,670 Individuals. Covers: In five volumes, about 11,000 banks and 50,000 branches of United States banks, and 60,000 foreign banks and branches engaged in foreign banking; Federal Reserve system and other United States government and state government banking agencies; 500 largest North American and International commercial banks; paper and automated clearinghouses. Volumes 1 and 2 contain North American listings; volumes 3 and 4, international listings (also cited as 'Thomson International Bank Directory; volume 5, Worldwide Correspondents Guide containing key correspondent data to facilitate funds transfer. Database includes: Bank operations information, asset ranking in state and country, bank routing numbers in numeric sequence, discontinued or changed bank names in geographical sequence. Entries include: For domestic banks--Bank name, address, phone, telex, cable, date established, routing number, charter type, bank holding company affiliation, memberships in Federal Reserve System and other banking organizations, principal officers by function performed, principal correspondent banks, and key financial data (deposits, etc.). For international banks--Bank name, address, phone, fax, telex, cable, SWIFT address, transit or sort codes within home country, ownership, financial data, names and titles of key personnel, branch locations. For branches--Bank name, address, phone, charter type, ownership and other details comparable to domestic bank listings.

BIN Number Directory of All Visa/Mastercard Issu-

ing Banks. Fraud and Theft Information Bureau. • Annual. $1,175 Individuals postpaid print edition. Covers: About 30,000 banks worldwide issuing Visa and Mastercard credit cards. Entries include: Name of issuing bank, bank identification number, address, phone. BIN numbers, the digits on credit cards that identify a credit card holder's issuing bank are also called prefix numbers and ISO numbers. Directory is used by merchants to prevent fraud by verifying that customer is actually the cardholder.

Compact Disc of the National Bank of Belgium. Banque Nationale de Belgique S.A. • Quarterly. $284.94 CD-ROM. CD-ROM. Database covers: About 260,000 Belgian companies. Database includes: Company name, address, national number, financial data, activity, juridical form, and juridical situation.

Directory of Trust Banking. Thomson Financial Publishing. • Annual. $344.00. Contains profiles of bank affiliated trust companies, independent trust companies, trust investment advisors, and trust fund managers. Provides contact information for professional personnel at more than 3,000 banking and other financial institutions.

Financial Yellow Book: Who's Who at the Leading U. S. Financial Institutions. Leadership Directories Inc. • Semiannual. $465. Gives the names and titles of over 28,000 key executives in financial institutions. Includes the areas of banking, investment, money management, and insurance. Five indexes are provided: institution, executive name, geographic by state, financial service segment, and parent company.

Germany's Top 300. Frankfurter Allgemeine Zeitung GmbH. • Annual. $595. Covers: Germany's top 300 corporations, banks, and insurance companies; corporations are ranked based on their turnover; banks are ranked according to business volume; insurance companies are ranked according to premium income. Entries include: Company name, address, phone, fax ranking, products and activities, Standard Industrial Classification (SIC) codes, names of key management personnel, number of employees, turnover, pre-tax profit, net profit, cash flow, assets, investments, cash reserves, shareholders, investor relations, dividend, and high/low share price.

Global Central Banks Directory. International Business Publications, USA. • $99.95 Individuals paperback. Covers: Central banks for over 150 countries.

Global Chambers of Commerce Directory. International Business Publications, USA. • $99.95 Individuals paperback. Covers: Approximately 3,000 U.S. Local chambers of commerce interested in international trade.

Golden States Financial Directory. Accuity Inc. • Semiannual. $540 Individuals. Holding companies, head offices and branches of all commercial banks, savings and loans, and credit unions with assets over $5 million in Alaska, Arizona, California, Colorado, Hawaii, Idaho, Montana, New Mexico, Oregon, Utah, Washington, and Wyoming.

Green Book. Independent Bankers Association of Texas. • Covers: Banks and loan institutions in Texas.

LaSalle Bank Guide: Major Publicly Held Corporations and Financial Institutions Headquartered in Illinois. Scholl Corporate Guides. • Annual. $29.95 Single issue. Covers: Approximately 232 major publicly held corporations and financial institutions headquartered in Illinois. Database includes: List of companies ranked by revenue and assets; (NAICS) code listings; list of changes from previous edition. Entries include: Company name, headquarters location and phone, brief description of product lines and organizational structure, names of outside directors, names and titles of key personnel; consolidated balance sheet in abbreviated form, consolidated income statement; number of employees, date of annual meeting, stockholder information.

Major Financial Institutions of the World. Cengage Learning Inc. • $1,460 Individuals. 2012. 16th edition. eBook. Published by Graham & Whiteside. Contains detailed information on more than 10,000 important financial institutions in various countries. Includes banks, investment companies, and insurance companies.

Plunkett's Financial Services Industry Almanac: The Only Complete Guide to the Technologies and Companies Changing the Way the World Banks, Invest and Borrows. Plunkett Research Ltd. • Annual. $249.99 plus $9.50 shipping (includes CD-ROM). Covers: 500 of the largest investment, banking, and financial companies. Entries include: Firm name, address, phone, fax; description; and leading executives with their titles, addresses, phone numbers, E-mail addresses, Web sites, and fax numbers.

Southwestern Financial Directory: 11th Fed, Dallas. Accuity Inc. • Semiannual. $400 Individuals. Holding companies, head offices and branches of every commercial bank, Savings & Loan, and credit union over $5 million in the states of Arkansas, Louisiana, New Mexico, Oklahoma, and Texas.

State of Washington Supervisor of Banking--Annual Report. Division of Banking Washington State Department of Financial Institutions. • Covers: About 100 state-chartered commercial banks and trust companies, savings banks, and alien banks. Database includes: Composite financial statements for each type of institution, and changes of location for banks, trust companies, and consumer loan offices. Entries include: For banks and trust companies--total assets, deposits.

Thomson World Bank Directory: International Edition. Accuity Inc. • Annual. $685 Individuals. Covers: Over 10,000 international banks and their branches in around 200 countries around the globe, including the top 1,000 U.S. Banks. Entries include: Institution name, address, phone, fax, key banking officers by functional title, directors, data established, expanded statement of condition, including a profit and loss account and historic performance ratios.

Top 500 MBS Investors. Inside Mortgage Finance Publications Inc. • $500. Database covers: The top 500 thrift, commercial bank, and federal credit unions in terms of their mortgage-related securities holdings. Entries include: Name, address, phone.

Walker's Manual of Community Bank Stocks. Walker's Manual Inc. • $95. Covers 502 community banks in the United States--community banks are financed with less than $10 million and usually serve a limited geographic area.

Who Owns What in World Banking. Public Relations Consultants Association. • Biennial. $350 airmail postpaid. Covers: about 225 leading multinational and consortium banks and their subsidiaries and affiliated banks. Entries include: Name of bank, location, financial data, percentage held by parent company, subsidiaries and affiliates and whether they are domestic or international.

Who's Who in Asian Banking & Finance. Bibliotheque: Worldwide. • Annual. $210 plus $7.50 shipping. Covers: 1,851 prominent and influential bankers and investors and 1,552 banks and financial institutions in Asia. Entries include: For individuals--Name, address, phone, fax, current job title and function, other professional, educational, and personal background details. For companies--Name, address, phone, fax, names and titles of key personnel.

Who's Who in Finance and Business. Marquis Who's Who L.L.C. • Biennial. $349 Individuals. Provides over 21,000 concise biographies of business leaders in all fields.

ENCYCLOPEDIAS AND DICTIONARIES

Encyclopedia of American Business. Cengage Learning Inc. • 2013. eBook. 2 volumes. 800 essays. A guide to the nuts and bolts of business jargon. Difficult ideas are explained in straightforward language to help non-specialists, students, and general readers understand the complex and sometimes confusing concepts and terms that are used in business. Five general areas of business are covered: accounting, banking, finance, marketing, and management.

Encyclopedia of Business and Finance. Cengage Learning Inc. • 2014. $485. 3rd edition. Two volumes. Published by Macmillan Reference USA. Contains articles on accounting, business administration, banking, finance, management information systems, and marketing.

GENERAL WORKS

Accounting and Business Research. Routledge. • 6/year. $137 Individuals print. Publication for the banking, finance, and accounting industries.

Business Opportunities Journal. Business Service Corp. • Monthly. Newspaper covering businesses for sale.

HANDBOOKS AND MANUALS

Moody's Bank and Finance Manual. Mergent. • Annual. $1,750 Four volumes. Includes biweekly supplements in *Moody's Bank and Finance News Report*.

INTERNET DATABASES

The Bauer Group: Reporting On and Analyzing the Performance of U. S. Banks, Thrifts, and Credit Unions. Bauer Financial Reports, Inc. Phone: 800-388-6686 or (305)445-9500; Fax: (305)445-6775 or (800)230-9569 • URL: http://www.bauerfinancial.com • Web site provides ratings (0 to 5 stars) of individual banks and credit unions, based on capital ratios and other financial criteria. Online searching for bank or credit union names is offered. Fees: Free.

Business 2.0 Web Guide to the Best Business Links. Business 2.0 Media Inc. Phone: (415)293-4800; Email: support@business2.com • URL: http://www.business2.com/webguide • Web site presents an extensive, searchable directory of links to "the best, most informative, and authoritative web pages." Twenty main categories cover business, finance, career, company information, people, and technology topics, with thousands of subtopics, all linking to Web sites recommended by experienced business researchers. Fees: Free.

Factiva. Dow Jones Reuters Business Interactive, LLC. Phone: 800-369-7466 or (609)452-1511; Fax: (609)520-5770; Email: solutions@factiva.com • URL: http://www.factiva.com • Fee-based Web site provides "global news and business information through Web sites and content integration solutions." Includes Dow Jones and Reuters newswires, The Wall Street Journal, and more than 7,000 other sources of current news, historical articles, market research reports, and investment analysis. Content includes 96 major U. S. newspapers, 900 non-English sources, trade publications, media transcripts, country profiles, news photos, etc.

Federal Reserve Board Publications and Education Resources. Board of Governors of the Federal Reserve System. Phone: (202)452-3000; Fax: (202)452-3819 • URL: http://www.federalreserve.gov/publications.htm • Web site provides access to statistics, surveys, and research from the Federal Reserve Board. *Federal Reserve Bulletin* articles are available as abstracts or full text (PDF) currently or from six-year archives. The link "Statistics: Releases and Historical Data" offers daily, weekly, monthly, quarterly, and annual data in great detail for interest rates, foreign exchange, consumer credit, money

For publishers' addresses, refer to SOURCES CITED section at the back of the book.

stock measures, industrial production indexes, bank reserves, and other items. Historical tabulations are available for various time periods. Free.

Fedstats. Federal Interagency Council on Statistical Policy. Phone: (202)395-7254 • URL: http://www.fedstats.gov • Web site features an efficient search facility for full-text statistics produced by more than 100 federal agencies, including the Census Bureau, the Bureau of Economic Analysis, and the Bureau of Labor Statistics. Boolean searches can be made within one agency or for all agencies combined. Links are offered to international statistical bureaus, including the UN, IMF, OECD, UNESCO, Eurostat, and 20 individual countries. Fees: Free.

FreeLunch.com. Economy.com, Inc. Phone: (610)696-8700; Fax: (610)696-1678 • URL: http://www.freelunch.com • Web site provides free access to more than 200 million economic and financial data series, covering industry, demographics, labor markets, prices, retail sales, government spending, trade, interest rates, housing starts, the stock market, etc. Data is available in either chart or table form. Searching is offered. Free, but registration required. Economy.com, Inc. also offers fee-based economic analysis at *The Dismal Scientist* site (www.dismal.com).

Gateway to the European Union. European Union. Email: pressoffice@eurostat.cec.be • URL: http://www.europa.eu.int • Web site provides access to a wide variety of EU information, including statistics (Eurostat), news, policies, publications, key issues, and official exchange rates for the euro. Includes links to the European Central Bank, the European Investment Bank, and other institutions. Fees: Free.

Nexis.com. Lexis-Nexis Group. Phone: 800-227-4908 or (937)865-6800; Fax: (937)865-6909; Email: webmaster@prod.lexis-nexis.com • URL: http://www.nexis.com • Fee-based Web site offers searching of about 2.8 billion documents in some 30,000 news, business, and legal information sources. Features include a subject directory covering 1,200 topics in 34 categories and a Company Dossier containing information on more than 500,000 public and private companies. Boolean searching is offered.

ONLINE DATABASES

American Banker Full Text. American Banker-Bond Buyer. Database Services. • Provides complete text online of the daily *American Banker*. Inquire as to cost and availability.

Banking Information Source. ProQuest L.L.C. • Provides indexing and abstracting of periodical and other literature from 1982 to date, with weekly updates. Covers the financial services industry: banks, savings institutions, investment houses, credit unions, insurance companies, and real estate organizations. Emphasis is on marketing and management. Inquire as to online cost and availability. (Formerly *FINIS: Financial Industry Information Service*.).

Wilson Business Abstracts Online. H.W. Wilson Co. • Indexes and abstracts 600 major business periodicals, plus the *Wall Street Journal* and the business section of the *New York Times*. Indexing is from 1982, abstracting from 1990, with the two newspapers included from 1993. Updated weekly. Inquire as to online cost and availability. (*Business Periodicals Index* without abstracts is also available online.).

OTHER SOURCES

BNA's Banking Report: Legal and Regulatory Developments in the Financial Services Industry. Bloomberg BNA. • Weekly. $1,221.00 per year. Two looseleaf volumes. Emphasis on federal regulations.

PERIODICALS AND NEWSLETTERS

ABA Banking Journal. American Bankers Association, Member Communications. Simmons-Boardman Books Inc. • Monthly. Monthly. Free to qualified personnel.

American Banker: The Financial Services Daily. SourceMedia Inc. • Daily. $895.00 per year. Provides news of banking, investment products, mortgages, credit unions, finance, bank technology, and legal developments.

Banker News. American Bankers Association. • Biweekly. $48 Members.

Business Finance. Intertec Publishing. • Quarterly. $39 Individuals. Magazine reporting on key financial issues, strategies, trends and technologies, significant to senior finance executives.

Business Money. Business Money Ltd. • Monthly. £149 Individuals single copy print, online and app. Professional magazine covering finance, business banking, and related topics.

Central Banking: Policy, Markets, Supervision. European Business Publications Inc. • Quarterly. $260.00 per year, including annual *Central Banking Directory*. Published in England by Central Banking Publications. Reports and comments on the activities of central banks around the world. Also provides discussions of the International Monetary Fund (IMF), the Organization for Economic Cooperation and Development (OECD), the Bank for International Settlements (BIS), and the World Bank.

Financial Markets, Institutions, and Instruments. New York University, Salomon Center. Blackwell Publishing Inc. • Five times a year. Institutions, $338.00 per year. Includes online edition. Edited to "bridge the gap between the academic and professional finance communities." Special fifth issue each year provides surveys of developments in four areas: money and banking, derivative securities, corporate finance, and fixed-income securities.

Guide to Banks and Thrifts: A Quarterly Compilation of Financial Institutions Ratings and Analysis. Weiss Research Inc. • Quarterly. $438.00 per year. Emphasis is on rating of financial safety and relative risk. Includes annual summary.

Hindu Business Line. Kasturi & Sons Ltd. • Daily. Rs 1,496 Individuals all days. Newspaper covering business, economics, banks and banking.

Jumbo Rate News. BauerFinancial Inc. • Description: Reports on high-yielding, insured Jumbo CD (Certificate of Deposit) rates nationwide. Analyzes each institution by current credit-worthiness, and lists current assets and capital ratios. Provides phone numbers, contacts, methods of computation, and information on how interest is paid. Also contains financial news, insights, and commentary of interest to Jumbo CD investors. Recurring features include editorials and news of interest.

One Hundred Highest Yields. Bankrate Inc. • Weekly. $124.00 per year. Newsletter. List CD's and money markets offered by federally insured banks. National coverage.

Recommended Bank and Thrift Report. BauerFinancial Inc. • Quarterly. $585.00 per year. Newsletter provides information on "safe, financially sound" commercial banks, savings banks, and savings and loan institutions. Various factors are considered, including tangible capital ratios and total risk-based capital ratios. (Six regional editions are also available at $150.00 per edition per year.).

Safe Money Report. Weiss Research Inc. • Monthly. $99.00 per year. Newsletter. Provides financial advice and current safety ratings of various banks, savings and loan companies, insurance companies, and securities dealers.

Treasury Manager's Report: Strategic Information for the Financial Executive. Access Intelligence L.L.C. • Biweekly. $630.00. Newsletter reporting on legal developments affecting the operations of banks, savings institutions, and other financial service organizations. Formerly *Financial Services Law Report*.

Troubled and Problematic Bank and Thrift Report. BauerFinancial Inc. • Quarterly. $225.00 per year. Newsletter provides information on seriously undercapitalized ("Troubled") banks and savings institutions, as defined by a federal Prompt Corrective Action Rule. "Problematic" banks and thrifts are those meeting regulatory capital levels, but showing negative trends.

U.S. Banker. SourceMedia Inc. • Monthly. $65.00 per year. Edited for bank executives and managers. Covers a wide variety of banking and financial topics.

RESEARCH CENTERS AND INSTITUTES

American Institute for Economic Research. 250 Division St., Great Barrington, MA 01230-1000. Phone: 888-528-1216; Fax: (413)528-0103; Email: info@aier.org • URL: http://www.aier.org • Through research and publications, provides "information on economic and financial subjects that is useful and completely independent of special interests." Sponsors a fellowship program for graduate study of economics at the institute and in absentia.

University of Cyprus - Center for Banking and Financial Research. School of Economics & Management, Nicosia 1678, Cyprus. Phone: 357 2 2892496; Fax: 357 2 2892421; Email: hermes@ucy.ac.cy • URL: http://www.ucy.ac.cy/hermes/en • Computational finance and economics.

STATISTICS SOURCES

Ranking the Banks. American Banker/Bond Buyer Inc. • Annual. Price on application. Ranks domestic and foreign banks by 75 financial parameters.

Standard & Poor's Industry Surveys. Standard & Poor's Financial Services L.L.C. • Semiannual. $1,800.00. Two looseleaf volumes. Includes monthly *Supplements*. Provides detailed, individual surveys of 52 major industry groups. Each survey is revised on a semiannual basis. Also includes "Monthly Investment Review" (industry group investment analysis) and monthly "Trends & Projections" (economic analysis).

Statistical Information on the Financial Services Industry. American Bankers Association. • Annual. Members, $150.00; non-members, $275.00. Presents a wide variety of data relating to banking and financial services, including consumer economics, personal finance, credit, government loans, capital markets, and international banking.

Survey of Current Business. U. S. Government Printing Office. • Published by Bureau of Economic Analysis, U. S. Department of Commerce. Presents a wide variety of business and economic data.

TRADE/PROFESSIONAL ASSOCIATIONS

Asian Clearing Union. 47, 7th Negarestan Alley, Pasdaran Ave., Tehran, Iran. Phone: 98 21 2842076 or 98 21 2854509; Fax: 98 21 2847677; Email: acusecret@cbi.ir • URL: http://www.asianclearingunion.org • Central banks, monetary authorities, and treasuries of Asian countries. Works to economize on the use of exchange reserves; promotes shifting of national banking services to domestic banks; seeks to enhance economic, financial, and commercial cooperation among Asian nations. Provides short-term credit facilities.

Bankers' Association for Finance and Trade. 1120 Connecticut Ave. NW, Washington, DC 20036. Phone: (202)663-7575; Fax: (202)663-5538; Email: info@baft-ifsa.com • URL: http://www.baft-ifsa.com • Formerly Bankers' Association for Foreign Trade.

Bretton Woods Committee. 1726 M St. NW, Ste. 200, Washington, DC 20036. Phone: (202)331-1616; Fax: (202)785-9423; Email: info@brettonwoods.org • URL: http://www.brettonwoods.org • Corporate CEOs, university administrators, former government officials, state governors, association and trade union executives, and bankers.

Seeks to inform and educate the public regarding the activities of the World Bank, International Monetary Fund, and other Multinational Development Banks (MDB). Promotes U.S. participation in MDBs.

Community Development Bankers Association. 1444 Eye St., Ste. 201, Washington, DC 20005. Phone: (202)689-8935; Email: info@cdbanks.org • URL: http://www.cdbanks.org • Represents the interests of the community development bank sector. Educates policy makers on how to deliver credit and financial services to low and moderate income communities.

Consumer Bankers Association. 1225 Eye St. NW, Ste. 550, Washington, DC 20005. Phone: (202)552-6382 or (202)552-6363; Fax: (703)528-1290; Email: jpike@cbanet.org • URL: http://www.cbanet.org • Federally insured deposit-taking institutions. Sponsors Graduate School of Retail Bank Management at the university of Virginia.

Financial Services Round Table. 1001 Pennsylvania Ave. NW, Ste. 500 S, Washington, DC 20004. Phone: (202)289-4322; Fax: (202)628-2507; Email: info@fsroundtable.org • URL: http://fsroundtable.org • Companies registered with the Federal Reserve Board under the Bank Holding Company Act of 1956.

Mortgage Bankers Association. 1919 M St. NW, 5th Fl., Washington, DC 20036. Phone: 800-793-6222 or (202)557-2700; Email: membership@mba.org • URL: http://www.mbaa.org • Principal lending and investor interests in the mortgage finance field, including mortgage banking firms, commercial banks, life insurance companies, title companies, and savings and loan associations. Seeks to improve methods of originating, servicing, and marketing loans of residential and income-producing properties through industry education and cooperation with federal agencies and the Congress. Holds clinics on all aspects of the mortgage finance business. Sponsors School of Mortgage Banking, and correspondence courses and web-based training on mortgage subjects for member personnel. Collects statistics and conducts research on the industry.

Society of Medical Banking Excellence. The Medical Banking Project, 401 Pond View Ct., Franklin, TN 37064. Phone: (615)794-2009; Fax: (615)468-7606; Email: info@mbproject.org • Seeks to advance the creation of digital infrastructures to be used to test and implement EDI processing techniques and analytics in medical payment channels.

BARBER AND BEAUTY SHOPS

See also COSMETICS INDUSTRY

DIRECTORIES

American Salon's Green Book. Advanstar Communications Inc. • Annual. $225 Individuals. Covers: about 1,300 manufacturers of supplies and equipment for salons and spas; 130 manufacturers' representatives; 3,200 distributors; employment agencies, show management companies, and related trade organizations. Entries include: For manufacturers and agents--Company name, address, phone, names of principal executives, products available. For distributors--Company name, address, phone, branches, name of owner or president, number of sales representatives, trade association affiliation, Metropolitan Statistical Area (MSA) in which located. For representatives--Company name, address, phone, territory covered.

Hairstyling Services Directory. InfoGroup Inc. • Annual. Number of listings: 230,354. Entries include: Name, address, phone, size of advertisement, name of owner or manager, number of employees, year first in "Yellow Pages." Compiled from telephone company "Yellow Pages," nationwide.

FINANCIAL RATIOS

Annual Statement Studies. Risk Management Association. • Annual. Compiled from over 280,000 financial statements.

Annual Statement Studies: Industry Default Probabilities and Cash Flow Measures. Risk Management Association. • Annual. $405 Nonmembers. Serves as a companion volume to the original *Annual Statement Studies.* Gives probability of default estimates on a percentage scale for more than 450 industries. Includes changes in position year-by-year for eight financial statement line items and provides percentage measures of cash flow.

PERIODICALS AND NEWSLETTERS

Hairdressers' Journal International. Reed Business Information Ltd. • Weekly. Contains latest styling techniques and fashions, product features, a celebrity style feature and the latest hairdressing industry news.

Modern Salon Magazine. Vance Publishing Corp. • Monthly. The constant leader and voice of the salon industry since 1915, providing peer-based education, inspiration and collaboration for salon professionals.

STATISTICS SOURCES

United States Census of Service Industries. U.S. Department of Commerce U.S. Census Bureau. • Quinquennial. Various reports available.

TRADE/PROFESSIONAL ASSOCIATIONS

Beauty and Barber Supply Institute. 11811 N Tatum Blvd., No. 1085, Phoenix, AZ 85028-1625. Phone: 800-468-2274 or (602)404-1800; Fax: (602)404-8900; Email: denise@bbsi.org • URL: http://www.beautyweb.com/beauty_associations.htm#BBSI.

National Hair Society. 39252 Winchester Rd., No. 107-383, Murrieta, CA 92563. Phone: (619)928-9750; Email: hsimon@nationalhairjournal.com • URL: http://www.nationalhairsociety.org • Represents hair management professionals. Offers information, education and networking pathways. Provides cross-marketing opportunities, seminars and workshops.

BARLEY INDUSTRY

See AGRICULTURE

BARRELS

See COOPERAGE INDUSTRY

BARTER AND COUNTERTRADE

PERIODICALS AND NEWSLETTERS

Countertrade and Offset. CTO Data Services. • Semimonthly. $1,194 /year. Intelligence on reciprocal international trade and unconventional trade finance. Covers developments and trends in the directory publishing industry, including publisher profiles, start-ups, corporate acquisitions, and business opportunities. Includes *Directory of Countertrade Services.* Formerly *Countertrade Outlook.*

Trade Channel. Trade Channel Europe. • Monthly. Features export "offers" and import "wants." Worldwide coverage. Technical products and consumer products. Formerly *Export Channel.*

BATTERY INDUSTRY

ABSTRACTS AND INDEXES

Applied Science and Technology Index. EBSCO Publishing Inc. • 11/year. Indexes a wide variety of English language technical, industrial, and engineering periodicals.

Current Contents: Engineering, Computing and Technology. Thomson Reuters Intellectual Property and Science. • Weekly. $730 per year. Reproductions of contents pages of technical journals. Includes *Author Index, Address Directory, Current Book Contents,* and *Title Word Index.* Formerly *Current Contents: Engineering, Technology and Applied Sciences.*

NTIS Alerts: Energy. U.S. Department of Commerce National Technical Information Service. • Biweekly. $130 per year. Covers electric power, batteries, fuels, geothermal energy, heating/cooling systems, nuclear technology, solar energy, energy policy, and related subjects.

DIRECTORIES

Directory of American Manufacturers & Exporters of Batteries & Accumulators. EXIM Infotek Private Ltd. • $20 Individuals. Covers: 200 American manufacturers and exporters of aircraft batteries, automotive batteries, batteries, batteries-deep cycle, batteries-dry cell, batteries-electric storage, batteries-lead acid, batteries-lithium, batteries-military specifications, batteries-nickel cadmium, batteries-sealed lead acid, batteries-solar, batteries-storage, batteries-wet and sealed, battery cables, battery chargers, battery packs and chargers, battery testers, commercial and industrial batteries, marine batteries, primary batteries, rechargeable batteries, and truck batteries. Entries include: Company name, postal address, city, country, phone, fax, e-mail and websites, contact person, designation, and product details.

Directory of Chinese Manufacturers & Exporters of Batteries & Accumulators. EXIM Infotek Private Ltd. • $10 Individuals. Covers: 110 Chinese manufacturers and exporters of accumulator cells, batteries, batteries for ups, batteries-rechargeable, batteries-storage, battery chargers, batteries for vehicles, dry batteries, lead acid batteries. Entries include: Company name, postal address, city, country, phone, fax, e-mail and websites, contact person, designation, products detail.

Directory of Japanese Manufacturers & Exporters of Batteries & Accumulators. EXIM Infotek Private Ltd. • $5 Individuals. Covers: 20 Japanese manufacturers and exporters of batteries and accumulators, batteries, and battery chargers. Entries include: Company name, postal address, city, country, phone, fax, e-mail and websites, contact person, designation, and product details.

Directory of South Korean Manufacturers & Exporters of Batteries & Accumulators. EXIM Infotek Private Ltd. • $10 Individuals. Covers: 90 South Korean manufacturers & exporters of automotive batteries, batteries & accumulators, battery, ups & battery chargers. Entries include: Company name, postal address, city, country, phone, fax, e-mail & websites, contact person, designation, products detail.

Directory of Taiwanese Manufacturers & Exporters of Batteries & Accumulators. EXIM Infotek Private Ltd. • $25 Individuals. Covers: 290 Taiwanese manufacturers and exporters of batteries and accumulators, batteries for ups, battery back-up sirens, mobility small scooter (battery operated), ups and battery chargers. Entries include: Company name, postal address, city, country, phone, fax, e-mail and websites, contact person, designation, and product details.

E-BOOKS

Macmillan Encyclopedia of Energy. Cengage Learning Inc. • 2003. eBook. Published by Macmillan Reference USA. Covers the business, technology, and history of a wide variety of energy sources. Inquire as to price and availability.

ONLINE DATABASES

Applied Science and Technology Index Online. H.W. Wilson Co. • Provides online indexing of 500 major scientific, technical, industrial, and engineering periodicals. Time period is 1983 to date. Monthly updates. Inquire as to online cost and availability.

Thomas Register Online. Thomas Publishing Company L.L.C. • Provides concise information on approximately 194,000 U. S. companies, mainly manufacturers, with over 50,000 product classifications. Indexes over 115,000 trade names. Information is updated semiannually. Inquire as to online cost and availability.

OTHER SOURCES

Major Energy Companies of the World. Cengage Learning Inc. • Annual. $1,460 Individuals. 2008. 12th edition. eBook. Published by Graham & Whiteside. Contains detailed information on more than 4,850 important energy companies in various countries. Industries include electricity generation, coal, natural gas, nuclear energy, petroleum, fuel distribution, and equipment for energy production.

PERIODICALS AND NEWSLETTERS

Advanced Battery Technology. Seven Mountains Scientific Inc. • Monthly. $165 Individuals. Provides technical and marketing information for the international battery industry.

Aftermarket Business. Advanstar Communications. • Monthly. $48 Individuals. Automobile aftermarket, including batteries.

Chilton's Automotive Marketing: A Monthly Publication for the Retail Jobber and Distributor of Automotive Aftermarket. Reed Elsevier Group plc Reed Business Information. • Monthly. Free to qualified personnel; others, $48.00 per year. Includes marketing of automobile batteries. Formerly *Automotive Aftermarket News.*

Industrial Equipment News. Thomas Publishing Company L.L.C. • Monthly. Contains new product information for manufacturing industries.

New Equipment Digest. Intertec Publishing. • Monthly. Magazine (tabloid) showcasing new or improved equipment, products, materials, and components. Formerly *Material Handling Engineering.*

New Equipment Reporter: New Products Industrial News. DeRoche Publications. • Monthly. Controlled circulation.

RESEARCH CENTERS AND INSTITUTES

Electrochemical Analysis and Diagnostic Laboratory. Argonne National Laboratory, 9700 S Cass Ave., Lemont, IL 60439-4803. Phone: (630)252-2000; Fax: (630)252-4176; Email: bloom@cmt.anl.gov • URL: http://www.anl.gov.

TRADE/PROFESSIONAL ASSOCIATIONS

Automotive Warehouse Distributors Association. 7101 Wisconsin Ave., Ste. 1300, Bethesda, MD 20814-3415. Phone: (301)654-6664; Fax: (301)654-3299; Email: info@autocare.org • URL: http://www.autocare.org • Warehouse distributors of automotive parts and supplies; manufacturers of automotive parts and suppliers; jobbers, business services, major program groups.

Battery Council International. 401 N Michigan Ave., 24th Fl., Chicago, IL 60611-4227. Phone: (312)644-6610; Fax: (312)527-6640; Email: info@batterycouncil.org • URL: http://batterycouncil.org • Manufacturers, suppliers of materials and national distributors of lead-acid storage batteries. Recommends industry standards; compiles statistics.

Battery Recycling Association of North America. 12505 N Main St., Ste. 212, Rancho Cucamonga, CA 91739. • URL: http://www.brana-online.org • Represents companies that handle, recycle, transport and manage portable power batteries. Seeks to establish guidance and training on the proper methods and regulations governing the safe handling of batteries. Fosters dialogue with battery handlers, recyclers, manufacturers and the regulatory community.

BAUXITE

See MINES AND MINERAL RESOURCES

BAZAARS

See FAIRS

BEARINGS AND BALL BEARINGS

See also ENGINES

ABSTRACTS AND INDEXES

Applied Science and Technology Index. EBSCO Publishing Inc. • 11/year. Indexes a wide variety of English language technical, industrial, and engineering periodicals.

DIRECTORIES

Directory of American Manufacturers & Exporters of Bearings. EXIM Infotek Private Ltd. • $20 Individuals. Covers: 280 American manufacturers and exporters of air bearings, antifriction bearings, automotive bearings, ball bearings, bearingsmetal, bearing pads, bearing parts-ball and roller, bearings-jewel, bearings, bearings-acid and corrosion resistant, bearings-air, bearings-aircraft, bearings-instrument, bearings-non metallic, bearings-self lubricating, bearings-sleeve, bearings-thrust, bronze bearings, carbide bearings, carbon-graphite bearings, conveyor bearings, cylindrical bearings, engine bearings, linear bearings, linear motion bearings, magnetic bearings, miniature bearings, needle bearings, pillow block bearings, precision ball bearings, radial ball bearings, roller bearings, self aligning bearings, semi-precise bearings, slide bearings, specialty bearings, spherical bearings, stainless steel bearings, tapered roller bearings, water lubricated bearings. Entries include: Company name, postal address, city, country, telephone, fax, e-mail and websites, contact person, designation, and product details.

Directory of Chinese Manufacturers & Exporters of Bearings. EXIM Infotek Private Ltd. • $10 Individuals. Covers: 60 Chinese manufacturers and exporters of ball bearings, bearings, needles and rollers, cylindrical roller bearings, engine bearings, needle bearings, needle roller bearings, roller bearings, sliding bearings, spherical roller bearings, steel balls, and tapered roller bearings. Entries include: Company name, postal address, city, country, phone, fax, e-mail and websites, contact person, designation, and product details.

Directory of Japanese Manufacturers & Exporters of Bearings. EXIM Infotek Private Ltd. • $10 Individuals. Covers: 60 Japanese manufacturers and exporters of ball bearings, ball screws, balls for bearings, bearing parts, bearing units, bearings, bushings, clutch release bearings, cylindrical roller bearings, engine bearings, linear motion rolling guide units and bearings, needle roller bearings, roller bearings, rollers for bearings, slide bearing and processing materials, spherical roller bearings, and tapered roller bearings. Entries include: Company name, postal address, city, country, phone, fax, e-mail and websites, contact person, designation, and product details.

Directory of South Korean Manufacturers & Exporters of Bearings. EXIM Infotek Private Ltd. • $10 Individuals. Covers: 50 South Korean manufacturers and exporters of bearing and bushing-metal, bearings-ball, needle and roller, cap-bearings, clutch release bearings, plain bearings, plumber and pillow blocks/bushing, and roller bearings. Entries include: Company name, postal address, city, country, phone, fax, e-mail and websites, contact person, designation, and product details.

Directory of Taiwanese Manufacturers & Exporters of Bearings. EXIM Infotek Private Ltd. • $10 Individuals. Covers: 110 Taiwanese manufacturers and exporters of balls, bearings-ball, needle and roller, plain bearings, plumber and pillow blocks/bushing. Entries include: Company name, postal address, city, country, phone, fax, e-mail and websites, contact person, designation, products detail.

Dun's Industrial Guide: The Metalworking Directory. Dun & Bradstreet Inc. • Annual. Libraries, $485; commercial institutions, $795.00. Lease basis. Three volumes. Lists about 65,000 U. S. manufacturing plants using metal and suppliers of metalworking equipment and materials. Includes names and titles of key personnel. Products, purchases, and processes are indicated.

INTERNET DATABASES

Manufacturing Profiles. U. S. Bureau of the Census. Phone: (301)763-4636 or (301)763-4100; Fax: (301)763-4794; Email: webmaster@census.gov • URL: http://www.census.gov/prod/www/abs/mfg-prof.html • The Census Bureau makes available free on PDF (Portable Document Format) an annual consolidation of the entire Current Industrial Report series, presenting "all the data compiled." Contains statistics on production, shipments, inventories, consumption, exports, imports, and orders for a wide variety of manufactured products.

ONLINE DATABASES

Applied Science and Technology Index Online. H.W. Wilson Co. • Provides online indexing of 500 major scientific, technical, industrial, and engineering periodicals. Time period is 1983 to date. Monthly updates. Inquire as to online cost and availability.

STATISTICS SOURCES

U.S. Industry and Trade Outlook. U.S. Department of Commerce National Technical Information Service. • Annual. Produced by the International Trade Administration, U.S. Department of Commerce, in a "public-private" partnership with DRI/McGraw-Hill and Standard & Poor's. Provides basic data, outlook for the current year, and "Long-Term Prospects" (five-year projections) for a wide variety of products and services. Includes high technology industries. Formerly *U.S. Industrial Outlook.*

TRADE/PROFESSIONAL ASSOCIATIONS

Bearing Specialists Association. 800 Roosevelt Rd., Bldg. C, Ste. 312, Glen Ellyn, IL 60137. Phone: (630)858-3838; Fax: (630)790-3095; Email: info@bsahome.org • URL: http://www.bsahome.org • Distributors of anti-friction bearings. Promotes networking and knowledge sharing and promotes the sale of bearings through authorized distributors.

BEAUTY SHOPS AND BARBER SHOPS

See BARBER AND BEAUTY SHOPS

BEDDING INDUSTRY

See FURNITURE INDUSTRY

BEE INDUSTRY

See HONEY INDUSTRY

BEEF INDUSTRY

See CATTLE INDUSTRY

BEER INDUSTRY

See BREWING INDUSTRY

BEETS AND BEET SUGAR INDUSTRY

See SUGAR INDUSTRY

BENEFITS, EMPLOYEE

See EMPLOYEE BENEFIT PLANS

BEQUESTS

See WILLS

BERYLLIUM INDUSTRY

See METAL INDUSTRY

BETTER BUSINESS BUREAUS

See also CONSUMER EDUCATION

DIRECTORIES

Better Business Bureau--Directory & Consumer Guide. Better Business Bureau of Metropolitan Toronto. • Covers: about 7,000 member companies and over 500,000 homes in metropolitan Toronto, Ontario. Entries include: Company name, address, phone, products and services.

TRADE/PROFESSIONAL ASSOCIATIONS

Better Business Bureau - Wise Giving Alliance. 3033 Wilson Blvd., Ste. 600, Arlington, VA 22201. Phone: (703)276-0100; Fax: (703)525-8277; Email: info@bbb.org • URL: http://www.bbb.org • Supported by companies and local Better Business Bureaus operated autonomously in the United States and Puerto Rico, which are in turn supported by 270,000 local business members. Seeks to promote and foster the highest ethical relationship between businesses and the public through voluntary self-regulation, consumer and business education, and service excellence. Provides support to local Better Business Bureaus. Administers the advertising industry's self-regulatory program that monitors and investigates the truth and accuracy of national advertising claims; monitors and pre-screens advertising directed towards children. Develops information on national charitable organizations and whether they meet voluntary ethical standards for soliciting organizations. Provides information to help consumers and businesses make informed purchasing decisions and avoid costly scams and frauds; and settles consumer complaints through arbitration and other means. Operates BBB AUTO LINE, a national mediation and arbitration service providing an independent forum to resolve consumer complaints involving 32 participating auto manufacturers; Local Better Business Bureaus respond to more than 23 million requests for service annually, fielding 20 million pre-purchase inquiries and 3 million complaints.

BEVERAGE INDUSTRY

See also BREWING INDUSTRY; DISTILLING INDUSTRY; SOFT DRINK INDUSTRY

ABSTRACTS AND INDEXES

Food Science and Technology Abstracts. Ovid Technologies Inc. • Monthly. $1,780.00 per year. Provides worldwide coverage of the literature of food technology and food production.

Foods Adlibra: Key to the World's Food Literature. General Mills, Inc. Foods Adlibra Publications. • Semimonthly. $240.00 per year. Provides journal citations and abstracts to the literature of food technology and packaging.

DIRECTORIES

Beverage Marketing Directory. Beverage Marketing Corp. • Annual. $995 Individuals print. Covers: Over 25,500 beer wholesalers, wine and spirits wholesalers, soft drink bottlers and franchisors, breweries, wineries, distilleries, alcoholic beverage importers, bottled water companies; and trade associations, government agencies, micro breweries, juice, coffee, tea, milk companies, and others concerned with the beverage and bottling industries; coverage includes Canada. Entries include: Beverage and bottling company listings contain company name, address, phone, names of key executives, number of employees, brand names, and other information, including number of franchisees, number of delivery trucks, sales volume. Suppliers and related companies and organizations listings include similar but less detailed information.

Coffee Shops Directory. InfoGroup Inc. • Annual. Number of listings: 7,515. Entries include: Name, address, phone, size of advertisement, name of owner or manager, number of employees, year first in "Yellow Pages." Compiled from telephone company "Yellow Pages," nationwide.

Directory of Asian Importers of Juices and Soft Drinks. EXIM Infotek Private Ltd. • $750 Individuals. Covers: 410 Asian importers of beverages, concentrated juices, pure water, drinks and cakes, energy drinks, fruit and vegetable concentrates, fruit and vegetable juices, fruit drinks, fruit flavored drinks, fruit pulp, fruit syrups, lychee juice concentrate, malted food drinks, mango-purees, mineral water, non-alcoholic beverages, orange juice, pine pulp, puree, and softdrinks. Entries include: Company name, postal address, telephone, fax, e-mail, website, contact person, designation, and product details.

Directory of Australia and New Zealand Importers of Alcoholic Beverages, Wines. EXIM Infotek Private Ltd. • $250 Individuals. Covers: 70 Australian and New Zealand importers of alcohol, alcoholic beverages, beer, ale, champagne, Corona beer, distilled spirits, French wine, gin, grape wine, liquors, malt beer, rum, sparkling wine, vodka, and whisky. Entries include: Company name, postal address, telephone, fax, e-mail, website, contact person, designation, and product details.

Directory of British Importers of Alcoholic Beverages and Wines. EXIM Infotek Private Ltd. • $250 Individuals. Covers: 60 British importers of alcohol, beer, ale, beverages, champagne, distilled spirits, spirits, whisky, wine, and alcoholic beverages. Entries include: Company name, postal address, telephone, fax, e-mail, website, contact person, designation, and product details.

Directory of British Importers of Juices and Soft Drinks. EXIM Infotek Private Ltd. • $200 Individuals. Covers: 45 British importers of coca-cola, fruit and vegetable juices, mineral water, non-alcoholic beverages, and soft drinks. Entries include: Company name, postal address, telephone, fax, e-mail, website, contact person, designation, and product details.

Directory of Chinese Manufacturers and Exporters of Alcoholic Beverages, Wines. EXIM Infotek Private Ltd. • $200 Individuals. Covers: 60 Chinese manufacturers and exporters of beer, beverages, dry red wine, fruit wine, grape wine, and liquor. Entries include: Company name, postal address, telephone, fax, e-mail, website, contact person, designation, and product details.

Directory of French Importers of Juices and Soft Drinks. EXIM Infotek Private Ltd. • $150 Individuals. Covers: 20 French importers of fruit and vegetable juices, mineral water, non-alcoholic beverages, and soft drinks. Entries include: Company name, postal address, telephone, fax, e-mail, website, contact person, designation, and product details.

Directory of German Importers of Alcoholic Beverages and Wines. EXIM Infotek Private Ltd. • Covers: 50 German importers of alcoholic beverages, beer, ale, distilled spirits, rum, whisky, wine, and alcoholic beverages. Entries include: Company name, postal address, telephone, fax, e-mail, website, contact person, designation, and product details.

Directory of Japanese Importers of Alcoholic Beverages and Wines. EXIM Infotek Private Ltd. • $500 Individuals. Covers: 250 Japanese importers of alcoholic beverages, barley malt, beer and ale, bourbon, brandy, distilled spirits, hard liquor, soft liquor, whisky, wine, and alcoholic beverages. Entries include: Company name, postal address, telephone, fax, e-mail, website, contact person, designation, and product details.

Directory of Japanese Importers of Juices and Soft Drinks. EXIM Infotek Private Ltd. • $400 Individuals. Covers: 180 Japanese importers of beverages, concentrated fruit juices, vegetable juices, fruit puree, mineral water, non-alcoholic beverages, and soft drinks. Entries include: Company name, postal address, telephone, fax, e-mail, website, contact person, designation, and product details.

Directory of Japanese Manufacturers and Exporters of Alcoholic Beverages and Wines. EXIM Infotek Private Ltd. • Covers: 30 Japanese manufacturers and exporters of beer, beverages, liquor, sake plum wine, and wine. Entries include: Company name, postal address, telephone, fax, e-mail, website, contact person, designation, and product details.

Directory of South Korean Manufacturers and Exporters of Alcoholic Beverages and Wines. EXIM Infotek Private Ltd. • Covers: 20 South Korean manufacturers and exporters of alcoholic spirits, beer, fermented cider, grape wine, whisky, bourbon, and wine (non-grape). Entries include: Company name, postal address, telephone, fax, e-mail, website, contact person, designation, and product details.

Emerging Europe Food and Drink Directory. Business Monitor International Ltd. • $895 Individuals. Covers: 1,577 top food and drink executives on 559 leading food and drink companies from Emerging Europe. Entries include: parent company head offices, full company name, address, phone and fax numbers, email and website address, senior contact personnel, company description and profile, nationality, and ownership status.

Espresso and Espresso Bars Directory. InfoGroup Inc. • Annual. Number of listings: 1,696. Entries include: Name, address, phone, size of advertisement, name of owner or manager, number of employees, year first in "Yellow Pages." Compiled from telephone company "Yellow Pages," nationwide.

European Drinks Marketing Directory. Euromonitor International Business Reference Div. • Irregular Biennial. $215. Covers: The European drinks industry, including marketing, retailers, wholesalers, leading companies, market trends, and industry details. Entries include: Name, address, phone, fax, telex.

European Union--Food and Drinks Directory. Trade Publishing Resources. • Covers: 100,000 brand names, 29,000 executives, and 16,000 companies engaged in importing, wholesaling, and retailing of food and drinks.

Food Chemicals News Directory. Food Chemical News. CRC Press. • Semiannual. $497.00. Over 2,000 subsidiaries belonging to nearly 250 corporate parents plus an additional 3,000 independent processors. Formerly *Hereld's 1,500.*

The International Directory of Importers - Food & Beverage Importers. Interdata. • $320 Individuals print. Covers: 7,300 international firms importing food and beverage. Entries include: Company name and address, contact person, email, number of employees, year established, phone and telefaxes, business activity, bank references, as well as a listing of food and beverage currently being imported.

Kompass Agribusiness, Food, and Beverage. APN News & Media Group Ltd. APN Business Information Group. • Annual. $85. Covers: Agricultural food and beverage companies and their products and services.

Major Food and Drink Companies of the World. Cengage Learning Inc. • 12th edition. eBook. Published by Graham & Whiteside. Contains profiles and trade names for more than 9,200 important food and beverage companies in various countries. In addition to foods, includes both alcoholic and nonalcoholic drink products.

The Mardek Guide to the UK's Top Food & Drink Suppliers. William Reed Publishing Ltd. • Annual. $295. Covers: 260 leading companies and over 100 major subsidiaries of food and drink manufacturers in the United Kingdom. Entries include: Corporate structure, company activities, personnel, products, brands, new product launches, turnover/pre-tax profit--up to the last three year, mergers, acquisitions and disposals.

Middle East and Africa Food and Drink Directory. Business Monitor International Ltd. • $995 Individuals CD. Covers: 1,553 top food and drink executives on 459 leading food and drink companies from Middle East and Africa. Entries include: Parent company head offices, full company name, address, phone and fax numbers, email and website address, senior contact personnel, company description and profile, nationality, and ownership status.

FINANCIAL RATIOS

Industry Norms and Key Business Ratios. Dun & Bradstreet Inc. • Annual. Five volumes. Covers over 800 kinds of businesses, arranged by Standard Industrial Classification number. More detailed editions covering longer periods of time are also available.

ONLINE DATABASES

Food Science and Technology Abstracts (online). IFIS North American Desk. • Produced by International Food Information Service. Provides about 500,000 online citations, with abstracts, to the international literature of food science, technology, commodities, engineering, and processing. Approximately 2,000 periodicals are covered. Time period is 1969 to date, with monthly updates. Inquire as to online cost and availability.

PERIODICALS AND NEWSLETTERS

Advertising Age: The International Newspaper of Marketing. Crain Communications Inc. • Weekly. $178.50 Individuals. Includes supplement *Creativity.*

Food Distribution Magazine. Phoenix Media Network Inc. • Monthly. $49.00 per year. Edited for marketers and buyers of domestic and imported, specialty or gourmet food products, including ethnic foods, seasonings, and bakery items.

Soft Drink Letter. Whitaker Newsletters Inc. • Description: Covers news pertaining to the beverage industry with emphasis on soft drinks, mixers, and bottled water. Includes reports on new products and federal/state regulations, interviews with leading industry executives, marketing trends, and advertising and marketing research.

Wisconsin Beverage Business. Illinois Beverage Media Inc. • Monthly. $15 Individuals. Trade magazine for the bar and package beverage alcohol industry.

PRICE SOURCES

Beverage Industry News. BIN Publications. • Monthly. $49 Individuals. Magazine for the alcoholic beverages retail trade. Incorporates *Beverage Industry News Merchandiser.*

Beverage Media. Beverage Network. Beverage Media Group. • Monthly. $78 Individuals. Wholesale prices.

PPI Detailed Report. Periodical covering business. Bureau of Labor Statistics, U.S. Department of Labor. U. S. Government Printing Office. • Monthly. $55 Individuals.

STATISTICS SOURCES

Standard & Poor's Industry Surveys. Standard & Poor's Financial Services L.L.C. • Semiannual. $1,800.00. Two looseleaf volumes. Includes monthly *Supplements.* Provides detailed, individual surveys of 52 major industry groups. Each survey is revised on a semiannual basis. Also includes "Monthly Investment Review" (industry group investment analysis) and monthly "Trends & Projections" (economic analysis).

United States Census of Manufactures. U.S. Department of Commerce U.S. Census Bureau. • Quinquennial. Results presented in reports, tape, CD-ROM, and Diskette files.

U.S. Industry and Trade Outlook. U.S. Department of Commerce National Technical Information Service. • Annual. Produced by the International Trade Administration, U.S. Department of Commerce, in a "public-private" partnership with DRI/McGraw-Hill and Standard & Poor's. Provides basic data, outlook for the current year, and "Long-Term Prospects" (five-year projections) for a wide variety of products and services. Includes high technology industries. Formerly *U.S. Industrial Outlook.*

TRADE/PROFESSIONAL ASSOCIATIONS

American Beverage Association. 1101 16th St. NW, Washington, DC 20036. Phone: (202)463-6732 or (202)463-6770; Fax: (202)659-5349; Email: info@ameribev.org • URL: http://www.ameribev.org • Active members are bottlers and distributors of soft drinks and franchise companies; associate members are suppliers of materials and services. Conducts government affairs activities on the national and state levels, discussion of industry problems, and general improvement of operating procedures. Conducts research on beverage laws.

BIBLIOGRAPHY

See also BOOK CATALOGS; BUSINESS LITERATURE

ABSTRACTS AND INDEXES

Bibliographic Index: A Subject List of Bibliographies in English and Foreign Languages. H.W. Wilson Co. • Three times a year. Third issues cumulates all three issues. Price varies.

CD-ROM DATABASES

LISA Plus. Cambridge Scientific Abstracts L.P. • Quarterly. $2,000 per year. CD-ROM version of Library Information and Science Abstracts, providing abstracting and indexing of the world's library and information science literature, 1969 to date. Contains more than 180,000 citations.

DIRECTORIES

Biographical Dictionary of American Business Leaders. Greenwood Electronic Media. • $183.95 hardcover. Covers: In four volumes, over 1,100 American business people from early merchants and farmers through contemporary leaders. Entries include: Name, date and place of birth, summary of subject's business activities and historical significance, ethnic background, religion.

ONLINE DATABASES

Books in Print Online. Bowker Electronic Publishing. • The online version of *Books in Print, Forthcoming Books, Paperbound Books in Print* and other Bowker bibliographic publications: lists the books of over 50,000 U.S. publishers. Includes books recently declared out-of-print. Updated monthly. Inquire as to online cost and availability.

PERIODICALS AND NEWSLETTERS

Bulletin of Bibliography. Greenwood Publishing Group Inc. • Quarterly. $125.00 per year.

Research Strategies: A Journal of Library Concepts and Instruction. Elsevier. • Quarterly. Individuals, $76.00 per year; institutions, $152.00 per year. Edited for librarians involved in bibliographic or library instruction.

TRADE/PROFESSIONAL ASSOCIATIONS

Bibliographical Society of America. PO Box 1537, Lenox Hill Sta., New York, NY 10021. Phone: (212)452-2710; Fax: (212)452-2710; Email: bsa@bibsocamer.org • URL: http://www.bibsocamer.org • Scholars, collectors, librarians, rare book dealers, and others interested in books and descriptive bibliography. Promotes bibliographical research and issues bibliographical publications. Maintains Fellowship Program which supports bibliography inquiries and research in the history of publishing and book trades.

Bibliographical Society of the University of Virginia. PO Box 400152, Charlottesville, VA 22904. Phone: (434)924-7013; Fax: (434)924-1431; Email: bibsoc@virginia.edu • URL: http://www.bsuva.org.

BICYCLE INDUSTRY

DIRECTORIES

Directory of Chinese Manufacturers & Exporters of Bicycles, Parts & Accessories. EXIM Infotek Private Ltd. • $5 Individuals. Covers: 25 Chinese manufacturers and exporters of bicycle frames, bicycle lamps, bicycle parts, bicycles, electric bicycles, and sprockets. Entries include: Company name, postal address, city, country, phone, fax, e-mail and websites, contact person, designation, and product details.

Directory of South Korean Manufacturers & Exporters of Bicycles, Parts & Accessories. EXIM Infotek Private Ltd. • $5 Individuals. Covers: 30 South Korean manufacturers and exporters of bicycle parts and accessories, bicycles and exercisers, flywheels. Entries include: Company name, postal address, city, country, phone, fax, e-mail and websites, contact person, designation, and product details.

Directory of Taiwanese Manufacturers & Exporters of Bicycles, Parts & Accessories. EXIM Infotek Private Ltd. • $45 Individuals. Covers: 770 Taiwanese manufacturers and exporters of bicycle accessories, bicycle parts and accessories, bicycles and exercisers, and electric powered wheelchairs. Entries include: Company name, postal address, city, country, phone, fax, e-mail and websites, contact person, designation, and product details.

The International Directory of Importers--Bicycles, Mopeds and Motorcycles Importers. Interdata. • $200 Individuals print. Covers: 800 international firms importing bicycles, mopeds and motorcycles. Entries include: Company name and address, contact person, email, number of employees, year established, phone and telefaxes, business activity, bank references, as well as a listing of bicycles, mopeds and motorcycles currently being imported.

PERIODICALS AND NEWSLETTERS

American Bicyclist. Willow Publishing Co. • Monthly. Free to qualified personnel; others, $35.00 per year. Trade journal edited for bicycle retailers and wholesalers. Includes product reviews.

Outspokin'. National Bicycle Dealers Association. • 10/year. Description: Offers bicycle retailing and management tips, and provides consumer survey results. Recurring features include Association and industry news.

RESEARCH CENTERS AND INSTITUTES

Human Power, Biochemechanics, and Robotics Laboratory. Cornell University, Dept. of Theoretical and Applied Mechanics, 306 Kimball Hall, Ithaca, NY 14853-1503. Phone: (607)255-7108; Fax: (607)255-2011; Email: ruina@cornell.edu • URL: http://ruina.tam.cornell.edu/ • Conducts research relating to human muscle-powered machines, such as bicycles and rowers.

STATISTICS SOURCES

United States Census of Manufactures. U.S. Department of Commerce U.S. Census Bureau. • Quinquennial. Results presented in reports, tape, CD-ROM, and Diskette files.

U.S. Industry and Trade Outlook. U.S. Department of Commerce National Technical Information Service. • Annual. Produced by the International Trade Administration, U.S. Department of Commerce, in a "public-private" partnership with DRI/McGraw-Hill and Standard & Poor's. Provides basic data, outlook for the current year, and "Long-Term Prospects" (five-year projections) for a wide variety of products and services. Includes high technology industries. Formerly *U.S. Industrial Outlook*.

TRADE/PROFESSIONAL ASSOCIATIONS

Bicycle Product Suppliers Association. 740 34th St., Boulder, CO 80303. Phone: (303)442-2466; Fax: (303)552-2060 • URL: http://bpsa.org • Wholesalers of bicycles, bicycle parts, and accessories; vendor members are manufacturers and suppliers. Affiliate members supply services and products to bicycle retailers. Offers educational programs; compiles statistics and safety information.

National Bicycle Dealers Association. 3176 Pullman St., No. 117, Costa Mesa, CA 92626. Phone: (949)722-6909; Email: info@nbda.com • URL: http://nbda.com • Represents independent retail dealers who sell and service bicycles. Sponsors workshops and provides programs.

BILLBOARDS

See OUTDOOR ADVERTISING

BINDING OF BOOKS

See BOOKBINDING

BIOENGINEERING

See BIOTECHNOLOGY

BIOGRAPHY

ABSTRACTS AND INDEXES

Biography and Genealogy Master Index (BGMI). Cengage Learning Inc. • $1,894 Individuals. Annual. $1,284.00. Two volumes. $642.00 per volume. Previous editions available. Provides coverage of contemporary and historcial figures. Also available online.

Biography Index. H.W. Wilson Co. • Quarterly. $280.00 per year. Annual and biennial cumulations.

Index to Marquis Who's Who Publications. Marquis Who's Who L.L.C. • Annual. $159. A combined index to current editions of most Marquis Who's Who publications. Contains over 320,000 entries.

BIOGRAPHICAL SOURCES

Almanac of Famous People. Cengage Learning Inc. • $308 Individuals. 2011. $280.00. 10th edition. Contains about 30,000 short biographies, with bibliographic citations. Chronological, geographic, and occupational indexes. Formerly *Biography Almanac*.

American Men & Women of Science (AMWS). Cengage Learning Inc. • 2013. $1508.00. 31st edition. Over 135,000 scientists active in the physical, biological, mathematical, computer science and engineering fields in the United States and Canada.

Canadian Who's Who. University of Toronto Press Inc. • Annual. $185.00. Provides concise biographical information in English and French on 15,000 prominent Canadians.

Current Biography Illustrated. EBSCO Publishing Inc. • Offers the content of the printed monthly magazine *Current Biography*.

Directory of American Scholars. Cengage Learning Inc. • $928. Volumes one to volume five, $212.00; volume six, $72.00. Provides biographical information and publication history for more than 24,000 scholars in the humanities.

Directory of Directors. Financial Post Datagroup. • Annual. $175.00. Provides brief biographical information on 16,000 directors and key officers of Canadian companies who are also Canadian residents.

International Who's Who. Taylor & Francis Group. • Annual. £490.00. Includes print and online editions. Published by Europa Publications (www.europapublications.com). Contains brief biographical information on important people in many different countries.

Newsmakers. Cengage Learning Inc. • Annual. $314 Individuals. Four softbound issues and one hardbound annual. Biographical information on individuals currently in the news. Includes photographs. Formerly *Contemporary Newsmakers*. eBook also available. Contact for pricing.

Who's Who Among African Americans. Cengage Learning Inc. • Annual. Includes biographical details on over 20,000 notable African Americans. eBook also available. Contact for pricing.

Who's Who: An Annual Biographical Dictionary. St. Martin's Press. • Annual. $330.00. Over 29,000 prominent individuals worldwide, but with emphasis on the United Kingdom.

Who's Who in America. Marquis Who's Who L.L.C. • Annual. $789.00. Two volumes. Contains over 90,000 concise biographies, with a Geographic/Professional Index.

Who's Who in Finance and Business. Marquis Who's Who L.L.C. • Biennial. $349 Individuals. Provides over 21,000 concise biographies of business leaders in all fields.

Who's Who in Science and Engineering. Marquis Who's Who L.L.C. • Biennial. $249.00. Provides concise biographical information on 33,545 prominent engineers and scientists. International coverage, with geographical and professional indexes.

Who's Who in the World. Marquis Who's Who L.L.C. • Annual. $324.00. Provides biographical profiles of about 35,000 prominent individuals. International coverage.

Who's Who of American Women. Marquis Who's Who L.L.C. • Biennial. $305.00. Provides over 30,444 biographical profiles of important women, including individuals prominent in business, finance, and industry.

CD-ROM DATABASES

Biography Index. EBSCO Publishing Inc. • Coverage from 1946 to present. Over 1 million article and book citations.

Complete Marquis Who's Who. Marquis Who's Who, Reed Reference Publishing. • Frequency and price on application. Contains CD-ROM biographical profiles of over 800,000 notable individuals. Includes *Who's Who in America*, *Who Was Who in America*, and 14 regional and professonal directories.

OECD Statistical Compendium. Organization for Economic Cooperation and Development. • Semiannual. $1,905.00 per year for 1 to 10 users. CD-ROM contains more than 730,000 monthly, quarterly, and annual time series for OECD countries, 1960 to date. Includes fully searchable data on agriculture, food, economic indicators, national accounts, employment, energy, finance, industry, technology, and foreign trade. Results can be displayed in various forms.

DIRECTORIES

Who's Who in Finance and Business. Marquis Who's Who L.L.C. • Biennial. $349 Individuals. Provides over 21,000 concise biographies of business leaders in all fields.

INTERNET DATABASES

Business 2.0 Web Guide to the Best Business Links. Business 2.0 Media Inc. Phone: (415)293-4800; Email: support@business2.com • URL: http://www.business2.com/webguide • Web site presents an extensive, searchable directory of links to "the best, most informative, and authoritative web pages." Twenty main categories cover business, finance, career, company information, people, and technology topics, with thousands of subtopics, all linking to Web sites recommended by experienced business researchers. Fees: Free.

ONLINE DATABASES

Biography Index Online. H.W. Wilson Co. • An index to biographies appearing in periodicals, newspapers, current books, and other sources. Covers 1984 to date. Inquire as to online cost and availability.

PERIODICALS AND NEWSLETTERS

The New York Times Biographical Service. ProQuest L.L.C. • Monthly. Price on application. Looseleaf service.

TRADE/PROFESSIONAL ASSOCIATIONS

New York Genealogical and Biographical Society. 36 W 44th St., 7th Fl., Ste. 711, New York, NY 10036-8105. Phone: (212)755-8532; Fax: (212)754-4218; Email: pcampbell@nygbs.org • URL: http://www.newyorkfamilyhistory.org • Collects, preserves, and makes available to the public, information relating to genealogy, biography, and history, especially of the state of New York.

BIOTECHNOLOGY

See also GENETIC ENGINEERING

ABSTRACTS AND INDEXES

Agricultural and Environmental Biotechnology Abstracts. Cambridge Scientific Abstracts L.P. • Monthly. $345 Individuals. Scientific journal covering agricultural and environmental biotechnology. Formerly *Biotechnology Research Abstracts*.

Applied Science and Technology Index. EBSCO Publishing Inc. • 11/year. Indexes a wide variety of English language technical, industrial, and engineering periodicals.

BioCommerce Abstracts. PharmaBooks. •

Semimonthly. $996.00 per year. Quarterly cumulation. Includes CD-Rom. Emphasis is on commercial biotechnology.

Current Biotechnology Abstracts. DECHEMA. • Monthly. $1,229.00 per year. Reports on the latest scientific, technical and commercial advances in the field of technology.

Current Contents: Engineering, Computing and Technology. Thomson Reuters Intellectual Property and Science. • Weekly. $730 per year. Reproductions of contents pages of technical journals. Includes *Author Index, Address Directory, Current Book Contents,* and *Title Word Index.* Formerly *Current Contents: Engineering, Technology and Applied Sciences.*

Excerpta Medica: Biophysics, Bioengineering, and Medical Instrumentation. Elsevier. • $7,353 Institutions print journal. 16 times a year. Institutions, $2,859 per year. Section 27 of *Excerpta Medica.*

Index Medicus. U.S. National Library of Medicine. U. S. Government Printing Office. • Monthly. $522 Individuals. Bibliographic listing of references to current articles from approximately 3,000 of the world's biomedical journals.

NTIS Alerts: Biomedical Technology & Human Factor Engineering. U.S. Department of Commerce National Technical Information Service. • Biweekly. $130 per year. Covers biotechnology, ergonomics, bionics, artificial intelligence, prosthetics, and related subjects.

Science Citation Index. Thomson Reuters Intellectual Property and Science. • Weekly. Includes *Source Index, Citation Index, Permuterm Subject Index,* and *Corporate Index.* Provides researchers, administrators, faculty, and students with quick, powerful access to the bibliographic and citation information they need to find research data, analyze trends, journals and researchers, and share their findings.

ALMANACS AND YEARBOOKS

Annual Review of Biophysics. Annual Reviews. • Annual. $99 Individuals online only.

BIBLIOGRAPHIES

Reference Reviews. Information Today, Inc. • Eight times a year. Price on application. Published in London by Aslib: The Association for Information Management. Incorporates *Aslib Book Guide.*

BIOGRAPHICAL SOURCES

Who's Who in Science and Engineering. Marquis Who's Who L.L.C. • Biennial. $249.00. Provides concise biographical information on 33,545 prominent engineers and scientists. International coverage, with geographical and professional indexes.

CD-ROM DATABASES

Biological & Agricultural Index Plus. EBSCO Publishing Inc. • Full text of literature in biology and agriculture. Also includes podcasts, indexing and abstracts.

Biotechnology Abstracts on CD-ROM. Thomson Derwent, Inc. • Quarterly. Price on application. Provides CD-ROM indexing and abstracting of the world's biotechnology journal literature since 1982, including genetic engineering topics.

Science Citation Index. Thomson Reuters Intellectual Property and Science. • Weekly. Includes *Source Index, Citation Index, Permuterm Subject Index,* and *Corporate Index.* Provides researchers, administrators, faculty, and students with quick, powerful access to the bibliographic and citation information they need to find research data, analyze trends, journals and researchers, and share their findings.

DIRECTORIES

Biometric Information Directory. Grey House Publishing. • $225 Individuals softcover. Covers: 700+ manufacturers and service providers in the biometrics industry, including finger, voice, face, hand, signature, iris, vein and palm identification systems. Includes information resources such as organizations, trade & educational associations, publications, conferences, trade shows and expositions worldwide. Entries include: Name, address, phone, fax, email, website, key executives, company size and a detailed, indexed description of their product line.

California Bioscience Directory. San Diego Regional Chamber of Commerce. • $345 Members. Covers: 1,700 California companies and over 6,000 key managers in biotechnology, biomedical, pharmaceutical, bioresearch, and medical device firms.

Genetic Engineering and Biotechnology Firms Worldwide Directory. Mega-Type Publishing. • Annual. $299.00. About 6,000 firms, including major firms with biotechnology divisions as well as small independent firms.

Israel Agro and Biotechnology Industry Export-Import Directory. International Business Publications, USA. • Annual. $99.95 Individuals hardcover, e-book, CD-ROM. Covers: Information on strategic economic, investment, export-import, and business opportunities. Contains important export-import, government, and business contacts. Ultimate directory for conducting export-import operations in the country.

Major Pharmaceutical & Biotechnology Companies of the World. Cengage Learning Inc. • Contains directory information on more than 4070 of the world's largest pharmaceutical companies, providing essential business profiles of the international leaders in the industry.

Medical Research Centres: A World Directory of Organizations and Programmes. Informa Group PLC. • Biennial. $470.00. Two volumes. Contains profiles of more than 7,000 medical research facilities around the world. Includes medical, dental, nursing, pharmaceutical, psychiatric, and surgical research centers.

Plunkett's Biotech and Genetics Industry Almanac. Plunkett Research Ltd. • Annual. $349.99 Individuals. Provides detailed profiles of 400 leading biotech corporations. Includes information on current trends and research in the field of biotechnology/genetics.

INTERNET DATABASES

National Library of Medicine. National Institutes of Health. 9000 Rockville Pke., Bethesda, MD 20892. Phone: (301)496-4000; Email: nihinfo@od.nih.gov • URL: http://www.nih.gov • NLM Web site offers free access through MEDLINE ("PubMed") to about nine million references to articles appearing in some 4,000 biomedical journals, with abstracts. Search interfaces range from "simple keywords to advanced Boolean expressions." The NLM site offers many links to other sources of biomedical and technical information (the National Center for Biotechnology Information, for example). Fees: Free.

ONLINE DATABASES

Applied Science and Technology Index Online. H.W. Wilson Co. • Provides online indexing of 500 major scientific, technical, industrial, and engineering periodicals. Time period is 1983 to date. Monthly updates. Inquire as to online cost and availability.

Biological Sciences Database. Cambridge Scientific Abstracts L.P. • Includes online versions of *Biotechnology Research Abstracts, Entomology Abstracts, Genetics Abstracts,* and about 20 other abstract collections. Time period is 1978 to date, with monthly updates. Inquire as to online cost and availability.

Biomass Energy System Businesses in the World. Momentum Technologies L.L.C. • Contains directory listings for more than 500 biomass energy system businesses in operation throughout the world. Includes business name, address, phone number, fax number, e-mail address, and web site address. Provides brief descriptions of product lines, services offered, and business type. Includes information on manufacturers, component makers, wholesalers, retailers, system designers, system installers, architectural services, trade associations, and more. Searchable by location, business type, business name, and keyword.

Derwent Biotechnology Abstracts. Derwent Information Ltd. • Provides indexing and abstracting of the world's biotechnology journal literature since 1982, including genetic engineering topics. Monthly updates. Inquire as to online cost and availability.

F-D-C Reports. Elsevier Business Intelligence. • An online version of "The Gray Sheet" (medical devices), "The Pink Sheet" (pharmaceuticals), "The Rose Sheet" (cosmetics), "The Blue Sheet" (biomedical), and "The Tan Sheet" (nonprescription). Contains full-text information on legal, technical, corporate, financial, and marketing developments from 1987 to date, with weekly updates. Inquire as to online cost and availability.

OTHER SOURCES

Biotechnology and the Law. Iver P. Cooper. Thomson West. • Annual. $424.50. Three looseleaf volumes.

PERIODICALS AND NEWSLETTERS

Biotech Business Week. NewsRX. • Weekly. $2,295 Other countries. Publication that provides news and information from pharmaceutical and biotechnology companies, with a focus on business trends and analysis.

Genetic Engineering News: The Information Source of the Biotechnology Industry. Mary Ann Liebert, Inc. • $666 Individuals. Newsletter. Business and financial coverage.

Genetic Technology News. John Wiley & Sons Inc. • Description: Informs corporate development and research managers of advances in genetic engineering with applications in medical, agricultural, chemical, food, and other businesses. Covers areas such as recombinant DNA, monoclonal antibodies, and interferon. Recurring features include news of research, company reports, a calendar of events, and supplements titled Market Forecasts, Patent Update, and Strategic Partners. **Remarks:** Also available as part of Biotechnology Information Package, which includes Industrial Bioprocessing (see separate listings).

Health News Daily. Elsevier Business Intelligence. • Description: Tracks developments in health care policy, legislation and regulation, insurance, pharmaceuticals, delivery, manufacturing, technology and treatment, funding, and research.

Health Policy and Biomedical Research: The Blue Sheet. Elsevier Business Intelligence. • 51 times a year. $716.00 per year. Newsletter. Emphasis is on news of medical research agencies and institutions, especially the National Institutes of Health (NIH).

IEEE Pulse. IEEE - Communications Society. • Bimonthly. Published for biomedical engineers.

Journal of Biotechnology. Elsevier. • Provides a medium for the rapid publication of both full-length articles and short communications on novel and innovative aspects of biotechnology.

Journal of Crop Improvement. The Haworth Press Inc. • 6/year. $396 Individuals online. Topics include plant biotechnology, plant genetics, crop productivity, quality, safety, pest control, and environmental concerns. Formerly *Journal of Crop Production.*

McGraw-Hill's Biotechnology Newswatch. McGraw Hill Financial Inc. • Semimonthly. Price on application. Newsletter.

The Pink Sheet: Prescription Pharmaceuticals and

Biotechnology. Elsevier Business Intelligence. • 51 times a year. Institutions, $1,431.00 per year. Newsletter covering business and regulatory developments affecting the pharmaceutical and biotechnology industries. Provides information on generic drug approvals and includes a drug sector stock index.

RESEARCH CENTERS AND INSTITUTES

Laboratory of Electronics. Rockefeller University, 1230 York Ave., New York, NY 10065. Phone: (212)327-8000; Fax: (212)327-7613; Email: ros@rockvax.rockefeller.edu • URL: http://www.rockefeller.edu • Studies the application of computer engineering and electronics to biomedicine.

Massachusetts Institute of Technology - Laser Biomedical Research Center. GR Harrison Spectroscopy Laboratory, 6-205, 77 Massachusetts Ave., Cambridge, MA 02139. Phone: (617)253-8418 or (617)253-7700; Fax: (617)253-4513; Email: rrdasari@mit.edu • URL: http://web.mit.edu/spectroscopy/facilities/lbrc.html • Concerned with the medical use of lasers.

Mayo Biomedical Imaging Resource. Mayo Clinic, 200 First St. SW, Rochester, MN 55905. Phone: (507)284-2511; Fax: (507)284-0161; Email: rar@mayo.edu • URL: http://www.mayoclinic.org • Develops three-dimensional medical imaging systems and software.

Salk Institute for Biological Studies. 10010 N Torrey Pines Rd., La Jolla, CA 92037. Phone: (858)453-4100; Fax: (858)453-8534 or (858)552-8534; Email: wrbrody@salk.edu • URL: http://www.salk.edu • Cellular and molecular biology and neuroscience with particular emphasis on cancer, molecular genetics, tumor virology, reproductive biology, neurobiology, neuroendocrinology, growth control, prebiotic chemistry, and neurotransmitter/neuroreceptor structure and function; research aimed toward the discovery of cause, prevention, control, and cure of disease.

University of California, Los Angeles - Molecular Biology Institute. Paul D. Boyer Hall, Box 951570, 611 Charles E Young Dr. E, Los Angeles, CA 90095-1570. Phone: (310)825-1018; Fax: (310)206-7286; Email: arispe@mcdb.ucla.edu • URL: http://www.mbi.ucla.edu • Supports, encourages, and facilitates university-wide research and training in molecular biology, with emphasis on molecular genetics; protein and nucleic acid synthesis, properties, and function; cell biology; molecular medicine.

STATISTICS SOURCES

Standard & Poor's Industry Surveys. Standard & Poor's Financial Services L.L.C. • Semiannual. $1,800.00. Two looseleaf volumes. Includes monthly *Supplements*. Provides detailed, individual surveys of 52 major industry groups. Each survey is revised on a semiannual basis. Also includes "Monthly Investment Review" (industry group investment analysis) and monthly "Trends & Projections" (economic analysis).

TRADE/PROFESSIONAL ASSOCIATIONS

American Institute for Medical and Biological Engineering. 1701 K St. NW, Ste. 510, Washington, DC 20006. Phone: (202)496-9660; Email: info@aimbe.org • URL: http://www.aimbe.org • Represents individuals with an interest in medical and biological engineering. Fosters exchange of ideas and information among members; works to establish a clear identity for the field and improve public awareness of members' activities; serves as liaison between members and government agencies. Conducts educational programs; promotes public interest in science and science education.

American Institute of Biological Sciences. 1444 I St. NW, Ste. 200, Washington, DC 20005. Phone: 800-992-2427 or (202)628-1500; Fax: (202)628-1509 • URL: http://www.aibs.org.

Biomedical Engineering Society. 8201 Corporate Dr., Ste. 1125, Landover, MD 20785-2224. Phone: 877-871-2637 or (301)459-1999; Fax: (301)459-2444 • URL: http://www.bmes.org • Biomedical, chemical, electrical, civil, agricultural and mechanical engineers, physicians, managers, and university professors representing all fields of biomedical engineering; students and corporations. Encourages the development, dissemination, integration, and utilization of knowledge in biomedical engineering.

Biotechnology Industry Organization. 1201 Maryland Ave. SW, Ste. 900, Washington, DC 20024. Phone: (202)962-9200; Fax: (202)488-6301; Email: info@bio.org • URL: http://www.bio.org • Represents biotechnology companies, academic institutions, state biotechnology centers and related organizations in all 50 U.S. states and 33 other nations. Members are involved in the research and development of healthcare, agricultural, industrial and environmental biotechnology products.

BIRTH CERTIFICATES

See VITAL STATISTICS

BIRTHS AND DEATHS

See VITAL STATISTICS

BITUMINOUS COAL

See COAL INDUSTRY

BLACK BUSINESS

See MINORITY BUSINESS

BLACK CONSUMERS

See MINORITY MARKETS

BLACK NEWSPAPERS

See MINORITY NEWSPAPERS

BLOOD PRESSURE

See HYPERTENSION

BLUE COLLAR WORKERS

See LABOR

BLUE SKY LAW

See SECURITIES LAW AND REGULATION

BOARDING SCHOOLS

See PRIVATE SCHOOLS

BOARDS OF DIRECTORS

See CORPORATE DIRECTORS AND OFFICERS

BOARDS OF TRADE

See CHAMBERS OF COMMERCE

BOAT INDUSTRY

See also MARINAS; SHIPS, SHIPPING AND SHIPBUILDING

ALMANACS AND YEARBOOKS

Pacific Boating Almanac. ProStar Publications, Inc. • Annual. $24.95 Individuals. Three volumes. Volume one, *Pacific Northwest*; volume two, *Northern California and the Delta*; volume three *Southern California and Mexico*. Lists over 3,000 marine facilities serving recreational boating.

DIRECTORIES

Atlantic Boating Almanac. Atlantic Boating Almanac. • Annual. $24.95 Individuals. Covers: Listings on coast piloting, electronics, GPS by Gordon West, first aid, weather, facilities and fuel docks. There are four separate regional editions: Florida & Bahamas; North & South Carolina and Georgia; Massachusetts, Rhode Island, Connecticut and Long Island; and Maine, New Hampshire & Massachusetts. Database includes: Tide and current tables; maps and fishing charts; navigation and star charts; first aid; US coast pilot.

Canoes Directory. InfoGroup Inc. • Annual. Number of listings: 1,783. Entries include: Name, address, phone, size of advertisement, name of owner or manager, number of employees, year first in "Yellow Pages." Compiled from telephone company "Yellow Pages," nationwide.

Charter Boats Directory. InfoGroup Inc. • Annual. Number of listings: 5,435. Entries include: Name, address, phone, size of advertisement, name of owner or manager, number of employees, year first in "Yellow Pages." Compiled from telephone company "Yellow Pages," nationwide.

Directory of American Manufacturers & Exporters of Marine & Boating Equipment & Supplies. EXIM Infotek Private Ltd. • $25 Individuals. Covers: 330 American manufacturers and exporters of aluminum work boats, anchors, boat engines, boat ladders and accessories, boat windshields, boats, buoy and open link chains, capstans, diesel and electric, environmental samplers and equipment, fiberglass boats and houseboats, floodlights, junction boxes, keel coolers, marine accessories, marine barges, marine coatings, marine diesel engines, marine electronics, marine engines, marine engines-gasoline, marine equipment and spare parts, marine equipment and supplies, marine furniture, marine hardware, marine instruments, marine parts, marine portlights, marine propellers, marine propulsion units, marine pumps, marine safety equipment, marine suppliers and repair, marine windows, marine-engines, nautical instruments, nautical products, navigation equipment, navigation instruments, navigation systems, oceanographic instruments, outboard motors, plumbing fittings, power supplies, propellers, rollers, satcom systems, shipboard wire and cables, spot lights, starters, steering components, surface air supply dive systems, tachometers, tug boats, water makers and radios, water samplers and plankton nets, windlasses, wire ropes. Entries include: Company name, postal address, city, country, telephone, fax, e-mail and websites, contact person, designation, and product details.

Directory of Japanese Manufacturers & Exporters of Marine & Boating Equipment & Supplies. EXIM Infotek Private Ltd. • $10 Individuals. Covers: 70 Japanese manufacturers and exporters of boat accessories, boats, fishing boat, marine engine spare parts, marine equipment and supplies, marine radios, naval stores products, ships, and used marine engines. Entries include: Company name, postal address, city, country, phone, fax, e-mail and websites, contact person, designation, and product details.

Directory of South Korean Manufacturers & Exporters of Marine & Boating Equipment & Supplies.

EXIM Infotek Private Ltd. • $5 Individuals. Covers: 40 South Korean manufacturers and exporters of boat parts and accessories, coastal vessels, control and navigational instruments-ship, equipment/ signals for ships/boats, marine propulsion units, radar and navigation systems/equipment-marine, yacht and pleasure craft. Entries include: Company name, postal address, city, country, phone, fax, e-mail and websites, contact person, designation, and product details.

Directory of Taiwanese Manufacturers & Exporters of Marine & Boating Equipment & Supplies. EXIM Infotek Private Ltd. • $10 Individuals. Covers: 120 Taiwanese manufacturers and exporters of boat parts and accessories, coastal vessels, control and navigational instruments-ship, equipment/signals for ships/boats, marine propulsion units, radar and navigation systems/equipment-marine, submersible vessels and equipment, yacht and pleasure craft. Entries include: Company name, postal address, city, country, phone, fax, e-mail and websites, contact person, designation, products detail.

The International Directory of Importers - Marine & Boating Equipment Supplies Importers. Interdata. • $260 Individuals print. Covers: 3,100 international firms importing marine & boating equipment and supplies. Entries include: Company name and address, contact person, email, number of employees, year established, phone and telefaxes, business activity, bank references, as well as a listing of marine & boating equipment and supplies currently being imported.

FINANCIAL RATIOS

Annual Statement Studies. Risk Management Association. • Annual. Compiled from over 280,000 financial statements.

Annual Statement Studies: Industry Default Probabilities and Cash Flow Measures. Risk Management Association. • Annual. $405 Nonmembers. Serves as a companion volume to the original *Annual Statement Studies*. Gives probability of default estimates on a percentage scale for more than 450 industries. Includes changes in position year-by-year for eight financial statement line items and provides percentage measures of cash flow.

PERIODICALS AND NEWSLETTERS

Boat and Motor Dealer: Business Solutions for the Boating Trade. Preston Publications Inc. • $75 Individuals. Magazine for boat, motor, and accessory dealers.

Boating Business. Formula Publications. • Bimonthly. Magazine for manufacturers, distributors, dealers, boatyards, and marinas serving the recreational marine industry.

Commercial Fisheries News. Compass Publications, Fisheries Division. • Monthly. $21.95 print only. Covers the commercial fishing industry in New England. Includes news of marine technology, boatbuilding, fish and lobster prices, business trends, government regulation, and other topics.

Marine Business Journal: The Voice of the Marine Industries. Marine Business Journal Inc. • Bimonthly. $30 Other countries. Trade magazine.

Vapor Trail's Boating News and International Yachting and Cruiser and Manufacturers Report. Gemini Productions, Ltd. • Monthly. $24.00 per year.

Workboat. Diversified Business Communications Inc. • Monthly. Provides in-depth reporting on topics including offshore services, shipbuilding and repair, port security, marine electronics, environmental regulations and more.

PRICE SOURCES

BUC Used Boat Price Guide. BUC International Corp. • Semiannual. $172.95 Individuals. Current market price for about 3,500 manufacturers of outboard, inboard, outdrives, sailboats, houseboats, and custom boats as well as approximately 20 manufacturers of boat trailers. In three volumes--Volume 1 covers 1994-2003; volume 2 covers 1982-1993; volume 3 covers 1905-1981. Formerly *Older Boat Price Guide*.

NADA Marine Appraisal Guide. National Automobile Dealers Association. N.A.D.A. Appraisal Guides. • 3/year. $140 Individuals.

STATISTICS SOURCES

U.S. Industry and Trade Outlook. U.S. Department of Commerce National Technical Information Service. • Annual. Produced by the International Trade Administration, U.S. Department of Commerce, in a "public-private" partnership with DRI/ McGraw-Hill and Standard & Poor's. Provides basic data, outlook for the current year, and "Long-Term Prospects" (five-year projections) for a wide variety of products and services. Includes high technology industries. Formerly *U.S. Industrial Outlook*.

TRADE/PROFESSIONAL ASSOCIATIONS

Boat Owners Association of the United States. 880 S Pickett St., Alexandria, VA 22304-4606. Phone: 800-395-2628; Email: mail@boatus.com • URL: http://www.boatus.com • Absorbed American Yachtmen's Association.

National Marine Representatives Association. PO Box 360, Gurnee, IL 60031. Phone: (847)662-3167; Fax: (847)336-7126; Email: info@nmraonline.org • URL: http://www.nmraonline.org • Works to serve the marine industry independent sales representatives and the manufacturers selling through representatives. Serves as industry voice, networking tool and information source promoting benefits of utilizing independent marine representatives for sales. Aims to assist manufacturers find the right marine sales reps for product lines.

BOILERS

See HEATING AND VENTILATION

BONDS

See also GOVERNMENT BONDS; MUNICIPAL BONDS

CD-ROM DATABASES

OECD Statistical Compendium. Organization for Economic Cooperation and Development. • Semiannual. $1,905.00 per year for 1 to 10 users. CD-ROM contains more than 730,000 monthly, quarterly, and annual time series for OECD countries, 1960 to date. Includes fully searchable data on agriculture, food, economic indicators, national accounts, employment, energy, finance, industry, technology, and foreign trade. Results can be displayed in various forms.

DIRECTORIES

Mergent Municipal and Government Manual. Mergent Inc. • Covers all U.S. taxing jurisdictions and agencies with total long-term rated debt of $25,000,000 or over.

Stocks, Bonds, Options & Derivatives: Symbol Book. American Stock Exchange Inc. • Quarterly. $8 per edition. Covers: Ticker symbols, corporate names, cusip numbers, and other information on stocks, bonds, options, and derivative products listed on the American Stock Exchange.

INTERNET DATABASES

Bondtalk.com: Live Talk & Analysis on the Bond Market & the Economy. Miller Tabak & Co., LLC. Phone: (212)370-0040; Email: acrescenzi@bondtalk.com • URL: http://www.bondtalk.com • Web site provides extensive, free data on the fixed income securities market, including individual bond prices, yields, interest rates, Federal Reserve information, charts, bond market news, and economic analysis. Also offered on a fee basis is "Bondtalkpro.com: The New and Enhanced Service for Market Professionals.".

Business 2.0 Web Guide to the Best Business Links. Business 2.0 Media Inc. Phone: (415)293-4800; Email: support@business2.com • URL: http://www.business2.com/webguide • Web site presents an extensive, searchable directory of links to "the best, most informative, and authoritative web pages." Twenty main categories cover business, finance, career, company information, people, and technology topics, with thousands of subtopics, all linking to Web sites recommended by experienced business researchers. Fees: Free.

Factiva. Dow Jones Reuters Business Interactive, LLC. Phone: 800-369-7466 or (609)452-1511; Fax: (609)520-5770; Email: solutions@factiva.com • URL: http://www.factiva.com • Fee-based Web site provides "global news and business information through Web sites and content integration solutions." Includes Dow Jones and Reuters newswires, The Wall Street Journal, and more than 7,000 other sources of current news, historical articles, market research reports, and investment analysis. Content includes 96 major U. S. newspapers, 900 non-English sources, trade publications, media transcripts, country profiles, news photos, etc.

Federal Reserve Board Publications and Education Resources. Board of Governors of the Federal Reserve System. Phone: (202)452-3000; Fax: (202)452-3819 • URL: http://www.federalreserve.gov/publications.htm • Web site provides access to statistics, surveys, and research from the Federal Reserve Board. *Federal Reserve Bulletin* articles are available as abstracts or full text (PDF) currently or from six-year archives. The link "Statistics: Releases and Historical Data" offers daily, weekly, monthly, quarterly, and annual data in great detail for interest rates, foreign exchange, consumer credit, money stock measures, industrial production indexes, bank reserves, and other items. Historical tabulations are available for various time periods. Free.

Fedstats. Federal Interagency Council on Statistical Policy. Phone: (202)395-7254 • URL: http://www.fedstats.gov • Web site features an efficient search facility for full-text statistics produced by more than 100 federal agencies, including the Census Bureau, the Bureau of Economic Analysis, and the Bureau of Labor Statistics. Boolean searches can be made within one agency or for all agencies combined. Links are offered to international statistical bureaus, including the UN, IMF, OECD, UNESCO, Eurostat, and 20 individual countries. Fees: Free.

FreeLunch.com. Economy.com, Inc. Phone: (610)696-8700; Fax: (610)696-1678 • URL: http://www.freelunch.com • Web site provides free access to more than 200 million economic and financial data series, covering industry, demographics, labor markets, prices, retail sales, government spending, trade, interest rates, housing starts, the stock market, etc. Data is available in either chart or table form. Searching is offered. Free, but registration required. Economy.com, Inc. also offers fee-based economic analysis at *The Dismal Scientist* site (www.dismal.com).

Nexis.com. Lexis-Nexis Group. Phone: 800-227-4908 or (937)865-6800; Fax: (937)865-6909; Email: webmaster@prod.lexis-nexis.com • URL: http://www.nexis.com • Fee-based Web site offers searching of about 2.8 billion documents in some 30,000 news, business, and legal information sources. Features include a subject directory covering 1,200 topics in 34 categories and a Company Dossier containing information on more than 500,000 public and private companies. Boolean searching is offered.

U.S. Securities and Exchange Commission. 100 F St. NE, Washington, DC 20549. Phone: 800-732-0330 or (202)942-8088; Fax: (202)942-9634; Email: webmaster@sec.gov • URL: http://www.sec.gov • SEC Web site offers free access through EDGAR to text of official corporate filings, such as annual reports (10-K), quarterly reports (10-Q), and proxies. (EDGAR is "Electronic Data Gathering, Analysis, and Retrieval System.") An example is given of how to obtain executive compensation data from proxies. Text of the daily *SEC News Digest* is offered, as are links to other government sites, non-government market regulators, and U. S. stock exchanges. Search facilities are extensive. Fees: Free.

Wall Street Journal Interactive Edition. Dow Jones & Co., Inc. 1211 Avenue of the Americas, New York, NY 10036. Phone: 800-369-5663; Email: service@dowjones.com • URL: http://new.dowjones.com • Fee-based Web site providing online searching of worldwide information from *The Wall Street Journal*. Includes "Company Snapshots," "The Journal's Greatest Hits," "Index to Market Data," "Journal Links," etc. Financial price quotes are available. Fees: $49.00 per year; $29.00 per year to print subscribers.

ONLINE DATABASES

EdgarPlus: SEC Basic Filings. Thomson Reuters Markets. • Online service provides full text of about 60,000 documents that have been filed with the U.S. Securities and Exchange Commission, 1987 to date, with daily updates. Filings include 6-K, 8-K, 10-K, 10-C, 10-Q, 20-F, and proxy statements. Inquire as to online cost and availability.

Fitch Ratings Delivery Service. Fitch. • Daily. Provides online delivery of Fitch financial ratings in three sectors: "Corporate Finance" (corporate bonds, insurance companies), "Structured Finance" (asset-backed securities), and "U.S. Public Finance" (municipal bonds).

Value Line Convertible Data Base. Value Line Inc. • Provides online data for about 600 convertible bonds and other convertible securities: price, yield, premium, issue size, liquidity, and maturity. Information is current, with weekly updates. Inquire as to online cost and availability.

OTHER SOURCES

Fitch Insights. Fitch Investors Service, Inc. • Biweekly. $1,040.00 per year. Includes bond rating actions and explanation of actions. Provides commentary and Fitch's view of the financial markets.

PERIODICALS AND NEWSLETTERS

Emerging Markets Debt Report. SourceMedia Inc. • Weekly. $895.00 per year. Newsletter. Provides information on new and prospective sovereign and corporate bond issues from developing countries. Includes an emerging market bond index and pricing data.

Financial Markets, Institutions, and Instruments. New York University, Salomon Center. Blackwell Publishing Inc. • Five times a year. Institutions, $338.00 per year. Includes online edition. Edited to "bridge the gap between the academic and professional finance communities." Special fifth issue each year provides surveys of developments in four areas: money and banking, derivative securities, corporate finance, and fixed-income securities.

The Financial Post: Canadian's Business Voice. Financial Post Datagroup. • Daily. $200.00 per year. Provides Canadian business, economic, financial, and investment news. Features extensive price quotes from all major Canadian markets: stocks, bonds, mutual funds, commodities, and currencies. Supplement available: *Financial Post 500*. Includes annual supplement.

Financial Times (London). The Financial Times, Inc. • Daily, except Sunday. $572.88 per year. An international business and financial newspaper, featuring news from London, Paris, Frankfurt, New York, and Tokyo. Includes worldwide stock and bond market data, commodity market data, and monetary/currency exchange information.

Grant's Interest Rate Observer. Grant's Financial Publishing Inc. • Biweekly. $1,025 Individuals. Newsletter containing detailed analysis of money-related topics, including interest rate trends, global credit markets, fixed-income investments, bank loan policies, and international money markets.

Investor's Business Daily. Investor's Business Daily, Inc. • Daily. $329 Individuals print. Business and financial newspaper.

Mergent Bond Record and Annual Bond Record. Mergent Inc. • Monthly. Formerly *Moody's Bond Record and Annual Bond Record*. Provides the most complete and accurate coverage available on corporate, government, municipal, industrial development/environmental control revenue and international bonds.

Moody's Bond Survey. Moody's Investors Service Inc. • Weekly (Mon.). Description: Presents statistical information and analysis of corporate, municipal, government, federal agency, and international bonds, preferred stock, and commercial paper. Includes ratings changes and withdrawals, calendars of recent and prospective bond offerings, and Moody's bond and preferred stock yield averages.

Private Placement Letter: The Weekly for Privately Placed Fixed-Income Securities. SourceMedia Inc. • Weekly. $1,495 per year. Newsletter. Provides information on private financing of debt and convertible securities.

Richard C. Young's Intelligence Report. Access Intelligence L.L.C. • Description: Provides information for "serious, conservative investors (buy and hold as opposed to active traders)." Features investing advice and recommendations for best funds, stocks, and bonds for current or retirement income.

Standard and Poor's Bond Guide. Standard & Poor's Financial Services L.L.C. • Monthly. $239.00 per year.

Standard and Poor's Ratings Handbook. Standard & Poor's Financial Services L.L.C. • Monthly. $275.00 per year. Newsletter. Provides news and analysis of international credit markets, including information on new bond issues. Formerly *Credit Week International Ratings*.

Standard and Poor's Semi-Weekly Called Bond Record. Standard & Poor's Financial Services L.L.C. • Semiweekly. $1,175.00 per year.

PRICE SOURCES

National Bond Summary. OTC Markets Group Inc. • Monthly, with semiannual cumulations. $504.00 per year. Includes price quotes for both active and inactive issues, with transfer agents, market makers (brokers), capital changes, name changes, and other corporate information. Formerly published by the National Quotation Bureau.

STATISTICS SOURCES

Stocks, Bonds, Bills, and Inflation Classic Yearbook. Ibbotson Associates. • Annual. $185. Provides detailed data from 1926 to the present on inflation and the returns from various kinds of financial investments, such as small-cap stocks and long-term government bonds.

Survey of Current Business. U. S. Government Printing Office. • Published by Bureau of Economic Analysis, U. S. Department of Commerce. Presents a wide variety of business and economic data.

BONDS, GOVERNMENT

See GOVERNMENT BONDS

BONDS, JUNK

See JUNK BOND FINANCING

BONDS, MUNICIPAL

See MUNICIPAL BONDS

BOOK CATALOGS

See also BIBLIOGRAPHY; BUSINESS LITERATURE

BIBLIOGRAPHIES

American Book Publishing Record: Arranged by Dewey Decimal Classification and Indexed by Author, Title, and Subject. R.R. Bowker L.L.C. • Monthly. $365 Individuals Annual. Offers access to the newest cataloging records from the Library of Congress.

American Reference Books Annual. Bohdan S. Wynar, editor. Libraries Unlimited. • Annual. $155 Individuals Hardcover. Provides librarians with insightful, critical reviews of all reference resources released in 2013 as well as some from 2012 and 2014.

Books in Print. R.R. Bowker L.L.C. • Combines the trusted and authoritative source of bibliographic information with powerful search, discovery and collection development tools designed specifically to streamline the book discovery and acquisition process.

Forthcoming Books. R.R. Bowker L.L.C. • Quarterly. $375 Individuals Annual. Reference database listing forthcoming publications and new issues, editions, or volumes of previously published books or serials. Supplement to *Books in Print*.

Subject Guide to Books in Print. Grey House Publishing. • Annual. $880. Six volumes.

CD-ROM DATABASES

LISA Plus. Cambridge Scientific Abstracts L.P. • Quarterly. $2,000 per year. CD-ROM version of Library Information and Science Abstracts, providing abstracting and indexing of the world's library and information science literature, 1969 to date. Contains more than 180,000 citations.

INTERNET DATABASES

Publishers' Catalogues Home Page. EBSCO Publishing Inc. 10 Estes St., Ipswich, MA 01938-2106. Phone: 800-653-2726 or (978)356-6500; Fax: (978)356-6565; Email: information@ebscohost.com • URL: http://www.ebscohost.com • Provides links to the Web home pages of about 1,700 U. S. publishers (including about 80 University presses) and publishers in 48 foreign countries. "International/Multinational Publishers" are included, such as the International Monetary Fund, the World Bank, and the World Trade Organization. Publishers are arranged in convenient alphabetical lists. Searching is offered. Fees: Free.

PERIODICALS AND NEWSLETTERS

Publishers Weekly: The International News Magazine of Book Publishing. Reed Elsevier Group plc Reed Business Information. • Weekly. $20.95 print and online; monthly. The international news magazine of book publishing.

BOOK COLLECTING

See also BIBLIOGRAPHY

PRICE SOURCES

American Book Prices Current. Bancroft-Parkman Inc. • Annual. $119.95 Individuals.

Bookman's Price Index. Cengage Learning Inc. • An index to rare and antiquarian books offered for sale in the catalogs of 100-200 book dealers in the U.S., Canada, and the British Isles. Approx. 15,000 tites listed per volume. 2013. Volumes 92-97. $686.00.

TRADE/PROFESSIONAL ASSOCIATIONS

Antiquarian Booksellers Association of America. 20 W 44th St., Ste. 507, New York, NY 10036-6604. Phone: (212)944-8291; Fax: (212)944-8293 • URL: http://www.abaa.org • Dealers and appraisers of fine, rare and out-of-print books, manuscripts, and related materials. Sponsors two annual regional international book fairs and four biennial regional international book fairs. Promotes ethical standards in the industry. Sponsors educational programs for members, librarians, archivists, and the public. Administers the Antiquarian Booksellers' Benevolent Fund.

Bibliographical Society of America. PO Box 1537, Lenox Hill Sta., New York, NY 10021. Phone: (212)452-2710; Fax: (212)452-2710; Email: bsa@bibsocamer.org • URL: http://www.bibsocamer.org • Scholars, collectors, librarians, rare book dealers, and others interested in books and descriptive bibliography. Promotes bibliographical research and issues bibliographical publications. Maintains Fellowship Program which supports bibliography inquiries and research in the history of publishing and book trades.

BOOK INDUSTRY

See also BIBLIOGRAPHY; BOOK COLLECTING; BOOKSELLING; PAPERBOUND BOOK INDUSTRY; PUBLISHING INDUSTRY

ALMANACS AND YEARBOOKS

The Library and Book Trade Almanac. Information Today, Inc. • $209 Individuals Hardbound. Reviews key trends and events and provides basic statistical information. Includes financial averages: library expenditures, salaries, and book prices. Contains lists of "best books, literary prizes, winners, and bestsellers." Formerly published by R. R. Bowker.

BIBLIOGRAPHIES

American Book Publishing Record: Arranged by Dewey Decimal Classification and Indexed by Author, Title, and Subject. R.R. Bowker L.L.C. • Monthly. $365 Individuals Annual. Offers access to the newest cataloging records from the Library of Congress.

CD-ROM DATABASES

LISA Plus. Cambridge Scientific Abstracts L.P. • Quarterly. $2,000 per year. CD-ROM version of Library Information and Science Abstracts, providing abstracting and indexing of the world's library and information science literature, 1969 to date. Contains more than 180,000 citations.

DIRECTORIES

American Book Trade Directory (ABD). Information Today, Inc. • Annual. $379.50 Individuals softbound. Covers: Nearly 20,000 retail and antiquarian book dealers, plus 1,200 book and magazine wholesalers, distributors, and jobbers-in all 50 states and U.S. territories. Also included are sections of auctioneers of literary property, exporters/importers, booktrade associations, foreign language book dealers, book and literary appraisers, and rental library chains. Entries include: Bookstore name, address, phone, owner or manager, types and subjects of books stocked, specialty, sidelines, year established, SAN (Standard Address Number), number of volumes stocked, square footage.

International Literary Market Place: The Directory of the International Book Publishing Industry. Information Today, Inc. • Annual. $299 Individuals softbound. Covers more than 180 countries. Listings include publishers, literary agents, major booksellers, book clubs, literary prizes, distributors, trade associations, etc. Formerly published by R. R. Bowker.

Literary Market Place: The Directory of the American Book Publishing Industry. Information Today, Inc. • Annual. $399 Individuals 2-volume set/softbound plus $25 shipping/handling. Listings include publishers, agents, ad agencies, associations, distributors, events, key executives, services, and suppliers (50 directory sections in all). Formerly published by R. R. Bowker.

Philadelphia Business Journal--Book of Business Lists Issue. Philadelphia Business Journal. • Annual. $65 Individuals print edition. Publication includes: About 89 ranked lists (about 25 names per list) of major public and private businesses and organizations, including banks, brokers, construction companies, hospitals, schools, child-care centers, law firms, hotels, apartment complexes, office parks, architects, ad agencies, and employers in the Philadelphia area. Entries include: For organizations and institutions--Name, location, type of business or service, key personnel, financial facts.

Publishers Directory. Cengage Learning Inc. • Annual. $756 Individuals print. Contains detailed information on more than 30,000 U.S. and Canadian publishers as well as small, independent presses.

Publishers' International ISBN Directory. Walter de Gruyter GmbH & Co. KG. • Annual. Covers: About 620,000 publishers in the United States and 200 other countries, of which about 555,000 have been assigned International Standard Book Numbers (ISBNs) by one of 140 ISBN Group Agencies. Entries include: For publishers--Name, address, phone, fax, telex, e-mail, ISBN, group, and prefix numbers. For agencies--Name, address, phone, fax, e-mail, group number, names and titles of key personnel in charge of ISBN matters. Publication is a merger of "International ISBN Publishers' Directory" and "Publishers' International Directory.".

The Stock Exchange of Hong Kong--Fact Book. The Stock Exchange of Hong Kong Corporate Communications Department. • Annual. Publication includes: List of companies listed on the Stock Exchange of Hong Kong. Principal content of publication is stock price index movement, trading value and volume, market capitalization, dividend yields and P/E ratios, and listed companies' activities and statistical records. Principal content of publication is a picture of the Hong Kong stock market for the year.

The Times 1,000: The Indispensable Annual Review of the World's Leading Industrial and Financial Companies. Times Books Ltd. • Annual. $32.50. Covers: 1,000 leading companies in the United Kingdom; 1,000 leading companies in Europe; leading firms in the United States, Canada, Australia, South Africa, Ireland, Hong Kong, and Japan. Entries include: For all companies--Company name and address. For British firms--Company name, names of chairman and managing director, sales, profits, capital, number of employees, and ranks and ratios. Listings for other firms vary in detail.

Writer's Guide to Book Editors, Publishers, and Literary Agents, Who They Are, What They Want, and How to Win Them Over. Prima Publishing Inc. • Annual. $27.95; with CD-ROM, $49.95. Directory for authors includes information on publishers' response times and pay rates.

FINANCIAL RATIOS

Annual Statement Studies. Risk Management Association. • Annual. Compiled from over 280,000 financial statements.

Annual Statement Studies: Industry Default Probabilities and Cash Flow Measures. Risk Management Association. • Annual. $405 Nonmembers. Serves as a companion volume to the original *Annual Statement Studies*. Gives probability of default estimates on a percentage scale for more than 450 industries. Includes changes in position year-by-year for eight financial statement line items and provides percentage measures of cash flow.

HANDBOOKS AND MANUALS

ABA Book Buyer's Handbook. American Booksellers Association. • Annual. Available electronically to members. Includes trade terms, discount informatio, return policies, and imprint listings.

INTERNET DATABASES

Publishers' Catalogues Home Page. EBSCO Publishing Inc. 10 Estes St., Ipswich, MA 01938-2106. Phone: 800-653-2726 or (978)356-6500; Fax: (978)356-6565; Email: information@ebscohost.com • URL: http://www.ebscohost.com • Provides links to the Web home pages of about 1,700 U. S. publishers (including about 80 University presses) and publishers in 48 foreign countries. "International/Multinational Publishers" are included, such as the International Monetary Fund, the World Bank, and the World Trade Organization. Publishers are arranged in convenient alphabetical lists. Searching is offered. Fees: Free.

ONLINE DATABASES

Business Periodicals Index Retrospective™: 1913-1982. EBSCO Publishing Inc. • Contains citations to more than 2.5 million articles and book reviews in more than 1000 general business periodicals and trade journals.

PERIODICALS AND NEWSLETTERS

Advertising Age: The International Newspaper of Marketing. Crain Communications Inc. • Weekly. $178.50 Individuals. Includes supplement *Creativity*.

Book Business. North American Publishing Co. • Magazine publishing information about book production and manufacturing.

Publishers Weekly: The International News Magazine of Book Publishing. Reed Elsevier Group plc Reed Business Information. • Weekly. $20.95 print and online; monthly. The international news magazine of book publishing.

PRICE SOURCES

American Book Prices Current. Bancroft-Parkman Inc. • Annual. $119.95 Individuals.

STATISTICS SOURCES

U.S. Industry and Trade Outlook. U.S. Department of Commerce National Technical Information Service. • Annual. Produced by the International Trade Administration, U.S. Department of Commerce, in a "public-private" partnership with DRI/McGraw-Hill and Standard & Poor's. Provides basic data, outlook for the current year, and "Long-Term Prospects" (five-year projections) for a wide variety of products and services. Includes high technology industries. Formerly *U.S. Industrial Outlook*.

TRADE/PROFESSIONAL ASSOCIATIONS

Association of American Publishers. 71 5th Ave., 2nd Fl., New York, NY 10003-3004. Phone: (212)255-0200; Fax: (212)255-7007; Email: info@publishers.org • URL: http://www.publishers.org • Represents the major commercial publishers in the United States as well as smaller and non-profit publishers, university presses and scholarly societies. Helps in the protection of intellectual property rights in all media. Promotes reading and literacy and the freedom to publish at home and abroad. Conducts seminars and workshops on various publishing topics including rights and permission, sales, and educational publishing. Compiles statistics.

Book Industry Study Group. 145 W 45th St., Ste. 601, New York, NY 10036. Phone: (646)336-7141; Fax: (646)336-6214; Email: info@bisg.org • URL: http://www.bisg.org • Represents publishers, manufacturers, suppliers, wholesalers, retailers, librarians, and other engaged in the business of print and electronic media.

Book Manufacturers' Institute. Two Armand Beach

Dr., Ste. 1B, Palm Coast, FL 32137-2612. Phone: (386)986-4552; Fax: (386)986-4553; Email: info@bmibook.com • URL: http://www.bmibook.com • Represents the trade association for manufacturers of books.

BOOK REVIEWS

ABSTRACTS AND INDEXES

Book Review Digest: An Index to Reviews of Current Books. H.W. Wilson Co. • 10 times a year. Quarterly and annual cumulation. Price varies.

Book Review Index (BRI). Cengage Learning Inc. • $591 paperback. Three-issue subscription. An index to reviews appearing in hundreds of periodicals. Back volumes available.

Children's Book Review Index. Cengage Learning Inc. • $308 Individuals. Annual. $280.00. Back volumes available. Contains more than 25,000 review citations on books for children through age 10.

BIBLIOGRAPHIES

American Reference Books Annual. Bohdan S. Wynar, editor. Libraries Unlimited. • Annual. $155 Individuals Hardcover. Provides librarians with insightful, critical reviews of all reference resources released in 2013 as well as some from 2012 and 2014.

Booklist. Library and Information Technology Association. • Biweekly. $147.50 U.S. and Canada /year. Reviews library materials for school and public libraries. Incorporates *Reference Books Bulletin.*

Reference Books Bulletin: A Compilation of Evaluations. Mary Ellen Quinn, editor. Library and Information Technology Association. • *Booklist.*

PERIODICALS AND NEWSLETTERS

Choice Magazine: Current Reviews for Academic Libraries. Association of College Research Libraries. Library and Information Technology Association. • Monthly. $415. A publication of the Association of College and Research Libraries. Contains book reviews, primarily for college and university libraries.

New York Times Book Review. The New York Times Co. • Weekly. $54.60 Individuals.

Reference and User Services Quarterly. Reference and User Services Association of the American Library Association. • Quarterly. $65 Nonmembers /year. In addition to articles, includes reviews of databases, reference books, and library professional material. Formerly *RQ.*

BOOK STORES

See BOOKSELLING

BOOKBINDING

CD-ROM DATABASES

LISA Plus. Cambridge Scientific Abstracts L.P. • Quarterly. $2,000 per year. CD-ROM version of Library Information and Science Abstracts, providing abstracting and indexing of the world's library and information science literature, 1969 to date. Contains more than 180,000 citations.

FINANCIAL RATIOS

Annual Statement Studies. Risk Management Association. • Annual. Compiled from over 280,000 financial statements.

Annual Statement Studies: Industry Default Probabilities and Cash Flow Measures. Risk Management Association. • Annual. $405 Nonmembers. Serves as a companion volume to the original *Annual Statement Studies.* Gives probability of default estimates on a percentage scale for more than 450 industries. Includes changes in position year-by-year for eight financial statement line items and provides percentage measures of cash flow.

PERIODICALS AND NEWSLETTERS

Shelflife. Library Binding Council. • Quarterly. $29 Individuals.

TRADE/PROFESSIONAL ASSOCIATIONS

Binding Industries Association International. 200 Deer Run Rd., Sewickley, PA 15143. Phone: (317)347-2665; Fax: (317)347-2666; Email: printing@printing.org • URL: http://www.printing.org/bia • Formerly Binding Industries of America.

Library Binding Council. 4440 PGA Blvd., Ste. 600, Palm Beach Gardens, FL 33410. Phone: 800-837-7321 or (561)745-6821 • URL: http://www.lbibinders.org • Firms and certified library binders doing library binding in accordance with LBI Standard for Library Binding, including rebinding of worn volumes, prebinding of new volumes, initial hardcover binding of periodicals, and other binding principally for libraries and schools; associate members are suppliers and manufacturers of library binding materials and equipment. Certifies qualified binding companies after examination of work and investigation of experience, insurance for protection of customers' property, and examination of bank and library references. Conducts research on materials used in library binding. Conducts statistical surveys of unit production, operating statement data, and wage data.

BOOKKEEPING

See ACCOUNTING

BOOKSELLER'S CATALOGS

See BOOK CATALOGS

BOOKSELLING

See also BIBLIOGRAPHY; BOOK COLLECTING; BOOK INDUSTRY

BIBLIOGRAPHIES

American Book Publishing Record: Arranged by Dewey Decimal Classification and Indexed by Author, Title, and Subject. R.R. Bowker L.L.C. • Monthly. $365 Individuals Annual. Offers access to the newest cataloging records from the Library of Congress.

DIRECTORIES

American Book Trade Directory (ABD). Information Today, Inc. • Annual. $379.50 Individuals softbound. Covers: Nearly 20,000 retail and antiquarian book dealers, plus 1,200 book and magazine wholesalers, distributors, and jobbers-in all 50 states and U.S. territories. Also included are sections of auctioneers of literary property, exporters/importers, booktrade associations, foreign language book dealers, book and literary appraisers, and rental library chains. Entries include: Bookstore name, address, phone, owner or manager, types and subjects of books stocked, specialty, sidelines, year established, SAN (Standard Address Number), number of volumes stocked, square footage.

FINANCIAL RATIOS

Annual Statement Studies. Risk Management Association. • Annual. Compiled from over 280,000 financial statements.

Annual Statement Studies: Industry Default Probabilities and Cash Flow Measures. Risk Management Association. • Annual. $405 Nonmembers. Serves as a companion volume to the original *Annual Statement Studies.* Gives probability of default estimates on a percentage scale for more than 450 industries. Includes changes in position year-by-year for eight financial statement line items and provides percentage measures of cash flow.

HANDBOOKS AND MANUALS

ABA Book Buyer's Handbook. American Booksellers Association. • Annual. Available electronically to members. Includes trade terms, discount informatio, return policies, and imprint listings.

Used Book Store. Entrepreneur Press. • Looseleaf. $59.50. A practical guide to starting a used book store. Covers profit potential, start-up costs, market size evaluation, owner's time required, site selection, lease negotiation, pricing, accounting, advertising, promotion, etc. (Start-Up Business Guide No. E1117.).

INTERNET DATABASES

Advance Monthly Retail Trade Report. U. S. Census Bureau. Phone: 800-541-8345 or (301)457-4100 or (301)763-2713; Fax: (301)457-1296 or (301)457-3842; Email: naics@census.gov • URL: http://www.census.gov/epcd/www/naicstab.htm • Web pages provide monthly sales figures for a wide range of retail businesses. Advance, preliminary, and final statistics are provided for the latest month available in each case, with a previous-year comparison. Updates are monthly.

BookWeb. American Booksellers Association. 333 Westchester Ave., Ste. S202, White Plains, NY 10604. Phone: 800-637-0037 or (914)417-4013; Fax: (914)406-7500; Email: info@bookweb.org • URL: http://www.bookweb.org • Web site provides descriptions of more than 4,500 independent bookstores, searchable by name, specialty, or zip code. Fees: Free.

PERIODICALS AND NEWSLETTERS

CBA Marketplace. Christian Booksellers Association. CBA Service Corp. • Monthly. $49.95 per year. Edited for religious book stores. Formerly *Bookstore Journal.*

Publishers Weekly: The International News Magazine of Book Publishing. Reed Elsevier Group plc Reed Business Information. • Weekly. $20.95 print and online; monthly. The international news magazine of book publishing.

PRICE SOURCES

American Book Prices Current. Bancroft-Parkman Inc. • Annual. $119.95 Individuals.

Bookman's Price Index. Cengage Learning Inc. • An index to rare and antiquarian books offered for sale in the catalogs of 100-200 book dealers in the U.S., Canada, and the British Isles. Approx. 15,000 tites listed per volume. 2013. Volumes 92-97. $686.00.

STATISTICS SOURCES

Annual Benchmark Report for Retail Trade and Food Services..A Detailed Summary of Retail Sales, Purchases, Accounts Receivable, Inventories, and Food Service Sales. U. S. Government Printing Office. • Annual. $13.00. Issued by the U.S. Census Bureau. Provides detailed annual and monthly retail statistics for the most recent 10 years. Includes data for various kinds of retail outlets, including automobiles, furniture, appliances, building supplies, grocery stores, drug stores, gasoline stations, clothing, sporting goods, department stores, and restaurants.

United States Census of Retail Trade. U.S. Department of Commerce U.S. Census Bureau. • Quinquennial.

TRADE/PROFESSIONAL ASSOCIATIONS

Antiquarian Booksellers Association of America. 20 W 44th St., Ste. 507, New York, NY 10036-6604. Phone: (212)944-8291; Fax: (212)944-8293 • URL: http://www.abaa.org • Dealers and appraisers of fine, rare and out-of-print books, manuscripts, and related materials. Sponsors two annual regional international book fairs and four biennial regional international book fairs. Promotes ethical standards in the industry. Sponsors educational programs for members, librarians, archivists, and the public. Administers the Antiquarian Booksellers' Benevolent Fund.

CBA: The Association for Christian Retail. 9240 Explorer Dr., Ste. 200, Colorado Springs, CO 80920. Phone: 800-252-1950 or (719)265-9895; Fax: (719)272-3508; Email: info@cbaonline.org • URL: http://www.cbaonline.org • Serves as trade association for retail stores selling Christian books, Bibles, gifts, and Sunday school and church supplies. Compiles statistics; conducts specialized education programs.

Mountains and Plains Independent Booksellers Association. 3278 Big Spruce Way, Park City, UT 84098. Phone: (435)649-6079; Fax: (435)649-6105; Email: info@mountainsplains.org • URL: http://www.mountainsplains.org • Supports independent bookstores; promotes literacy and defends freedom of speech and of the press.

BOOTS AND SHOES

See SHOE INDUSTRY

BORING MACHINERY

See MACHINERY

BOTANY, ECONOMIC

See ECONOMIC BOTANY

BOTTLED WATER INDUSTRY

See WATER SUPPLY

BOX INDUSTRY

See also PAPER BOX AND PAPER CONTAINER INDUSTRIES

DIRECTORIES

Directory of European Importers of Gears & Boxes. EXIM Infotek Private Ltd. • $10 Individuals. Covers: 90 European importers of gears and boxes. Entries include: Company name, postal address, telephone, fax, e-mail, website, contact person, designation, and product details.

Paperboard Packaging Council Member Directory. Paperboard Packaging Council. • Annual.

FINANCIAL RATIOS

Annual Statement Studies. Risk Management Association. • Annual. Compiled from over 280,000 financial statements.

Annual Statement Studies: Industry Default Probabilities and Cash Flow Measures. Risk Management Association. • Annual. $405 Nonmembers. Serves as a companion volume to the original *Annual Statement Studies.* Gives probability of default estimates on a percentage scale for more than 450 industries. Includes changes in position year-by-year for eight financial statement line items and provides percentage measures of cash flow.

PERIODICALS AND NEWSLETTERS

Paperboard Packaging Worldwide. Advanstar Communications. • Monthly. $39.00 per year.

PRICE SOURCES

PPI Detailed Report. Periodical covering business. Bureau of Labor Statistics, U.S. Department of Labor. U. S. Government Printing Office. • Monthly. $55 Individuals.

STATISTICS SOURCES

United States Census of Manufactures. U.S. Department of Commerce U.S. Census Bureau. • Quinquennial. Results presented in reports, tape, CD-ROM, and Diskette files.

TRADE/PROFESSIONAL ASSOCIATIONS

Pacific Coast Paper Box Manufacturers' Association. 201 N Union St., Ste. 220, Alexandria, VA 22314. Phone: (703)836-3300; Fax: (703)836-3290; Email: ben@paperbox.org • URL: http://www.paper-world.com/firmeninfo.php?sprache=uk&menue=10&keyfirma=1697536 • Represents folding carton and rigid carton manufacturers. Furthers the success and development of paperboard packaging in the territory west of the Rocky Mountains. Offers statistical, and labor data summary programs for members. Conducts technical and production seminars and employee training in plant and equipment operations. Sponsors student design-school competition.

BOXES, PAPER

See PAPER BOX AND PAPER CONTAINER INDUSTRIES

BRAINSTORMING

See CREATIVITY

BRANCH STORES

See CHAIN STORES

BRAND AWARENESS STUDIES

See MARKET RESEARCH

BRAND NAMES

See TRADEMARKS AND TRADE NAMES

BREAD INDUSTRY

See BAKING INDUSTRY

BREWING INDUSTRY

See also BEVERAGE INDUSTRY; DISTILLING INDUSTRY

ALMANACS AND YEARBOOKS

Brewers Almanac. Beer Institute. • Annual. $170. Provides a wealth of information and statistics covering the beer industry.

The U.S. Beer Market: Impact Databank Review and Forecast. M. Shanken Communications Inc. • Annual. Price varies. Includes industry commentary and statistics.

CD-ROM DATABASES

OECD Statistical Compendium. Organization for Economic Cooperation and Development. • Semiannual. $1,905.00 per year for 1 to 10 users. CD-ROM contains more than 730,000 monthly, quarterly, and annual time series for OECD countries, 1960 to date. Includes fully searchable data on agriculture, food, economic indicators, national accounts, employment, energy, finance, industry, technology, and foreign trade. Results can be displayed in various forms.

DIRECTORIES

Major Food and Drink Companies of the World. Cengage Learning Inc. • 12th edition. eBook. Published by Graham & Whiteside. Contains profiles and trade names for more than 9,200 important food and beverage companies in various countries. In addition to foods, includes both alcoholic and nonalcoholic drink products.

INTERNET DATABASES

Business 2.0 Web Guide to the Best Business Links. Business 2.0 Media Inc. Phone: (415)293-4800; Email: support@business2.com • URL: http://www.business2.com/webguide • Web site presents an extensive, searchable directory of links to "the best, most informative, and authoritative web pages." Twenty main categories cover business, finance, career, company information, people, and technology topics, with thousands of subtopics, all linking to Web sites recommended by experienced business researchers. Fees: Free.

Fedstats. Federal Interagency Council on Statistical Policy. Phone: (202)395-7254 • URL: http://www.fedstats.gov • Web site features an efficient search facility for full-text statistics produced by more than 100 federal agencies, including the Census Bureau, the Bureau of Economic Analysis, and the Bureau of Labor Statistics. Boolean searches can be made within one agency or for all agencies combined. Links are offered to international statistical bureaus, including the UN, IMF, OECD, UNESCO, Eurostat, and 20 individual countries. Fees: Free.

FreeLunch.com. Economy.com, Inc. Phone: (610)696-8700; Fax: (610)696-1678 • URL: http://www.freelunch.com • Web site provides free access to more than 200 million economic and financial data series, covering industry, demographics, labor markets, prices, retail sales, government spending, trade, interest rates, housing starts, the stock market, etc. Data is available in either chart or table form. Searching is offered. Free, but registration required. Economy.com, Inc. also offers fee-based economic analysis at *The Dismal Scientist* site (www.dismal.com).

OTHER SOURCES

Liquor Control Law Reporter. Wolters Kluwer Law & Business CCH. • Biweekly. Federal and state regulation and taxation of alcoholic beverages.

PERIODICALS AND NEWSLETTERS

American Brewer: The Business of Beer. American Brewer. • $50 Individuals. Business magazine aimed primarily at small and medium-sized breweries in the U.S. and Canada.

Brewers Digest. Siebel Publishing Co., Inc. • Monthly. $25.00 per year. Covers all aspects of brewing. Annual *Buyers' Guide* and *Directory* available.

Brewing and Distilling International. Brewery Traders Publications, Ltd. • Monthly. $82.00 per year.

Impact: U.S. News and Research for the Wine, Spirits, and Beer Industries. M. Shanken Communications Inc. • Semimonthly. $375.00 per year. Newsletter covering the marketing, economic, and financial aspects of alcoholic beverages.

MBAA Technical Quarterly. Master Brewers Association of the Americas. • Quarterly. $60 for nonmembers in the brewing industry. Technical brewing magazine.

Modern Brewery Age. Business Journals Inc. • Bimonthly. $125 Individuals. Magazine for the wholesale and brewing industry.

PRICE SOURCES

Beverage Media. Beverage Network. Beverage Media Group. • Monthly. $78 Individuals. Wholesale prices.

Feedstuffs. Miller Publishing Co. • Weekly. $144 Individuals.

RESEARCH CENTERS AND INSTITUTES

Cereal Crops Research Unit U.S. Department of Agricultural Research Service. 502 N Walnut St., Madison, WI 53726. Phone: (608)262-0377; Fax: (608)890-0306; Email: cynthia.henson@ars.usda.gov • URL: http://www.ars.usda.gov.

STATISTICS SOURCES

Standard & Poor's Industry Surveys. Standard & Poor's Financial Services L.L.C. • Semiannual. $1,800.00. Two looseleaf volumes. Includes monthly *Supplements*. Provides detailed, individual surveys of 52 major industry groups. Each survey is revised on a semiannual basis. Also includes "Monthly Investment Review" (industry group investment analysis) and monthly "Trends & Projections" (economic analysis).

Survey of Current Business. U. S. Government Printing Office. • Published by Bureau of Economic Analysis, U. S. Department of Commerce. Presents a wide variety of business and economic data.

TRADE/PROFESSIONAL ASSOCIATIONS

American Society of Brewing Chemists. 3340 Pilot Knob Rd., Saint Paul, MN 55121-2097. Phone: (651)454-7250; Fax: (651)454-0766; Email: asbc@scisoc.org • URL: http://www.asbcnet.org • Serves as professional organization of chemists in brewing and malting industries. Develops standard methods of analysis for raw materials, supplies, and products of brewing, malting, and related industries. Provides professional development resources to members through publications, continuing education courses.

Beer Institute. 122 C St., Ste. 350, Washington, DC 20001-2109. Phone: (202)737-2337; Fax: (202)737-7004; Email: info@beerinstitute.org • URL: http://www.beerinstitute.org • Brewers, importers, and suppliers to the industry. Committed to the development of public policy and to the values of civic duty and personal responsibility.

Brewers Association. 1327 Spruce St., Boulder, CO 80302-5006. Phone: 888-822-6273 or (303)447-0816; Email: info@brewersassociation.org • URL: http://www.brewersassociation.org • Represents micro and regional brewers of beer. Aims to promote and protect American Craft Beer and American Craft Brewers and the community of brewing enthusiasts.

Brewery and Soft Drink Conference. 25 Louisiana Ave. NW, Washington, DC 20001-2130. Phone: (202)624-6800; Fax: (202)624-8137; Email: brewery@teamster.org • URL: http://www.teamster.org/content/brewery-soft-drink-conference • Promotes the interests of brewery and soft drink workers in the United States and Canada.

Master Brewers Association of the Americas. 3340 Pilot Knob Rd., Saint Paul, MN 55121. Phone: (651)454-7250; Fax: (651)454-0766; Email: mbaa@mbaa.com • URL: http://www.mbaa.com • Formerly Master Brewers Association of America.

National Beer Wholesalers Association. 1101 King St., Ste. 600, Alexandria, VA 22314-2944. Phone: 800-300-6417 or (703)683-4300; Fax: (703)683-8965; Email: info@nbwa.org • URL: http://www.nbwa.org • Independent wholesalers of malt beverages and affiliates of the malt beverage industry. Conducts specialized education programs.

BRIBES AND PAYOFFS

See BUSINESS ETHICS

BROKERS, STOCK

See STOCK BROKERS

BUDGET, FEDERAL

See FEDERAL BUDGET

BUDGETING, BUSINESS

ABSTRACTS AND INDEXES

Accounting and Tax Index. ProQuest L.L.C. • Quarterly. Indexes accounting, auditing, and taxation literature appearing in journals, books, pamphlets, conference proceedings, and newsletters.

PERIODICALS AND NEWSLETTERS

Strategic Finance. Institute of Management Accountants. • Monthly. $220 Nonmembers. Provides articles on corporate finance, cost control, cash flow, budgeting, corporate taxes, and other financial management topics.

Successful Cost Control Strategies for CEOs, Managers, and Administrators. Siefer Consultants Inc. • Monthly. $279.00 per year. Newsletter. Provides a variety of ideas on business budgeting and controlling company expenses. Formerly *Employee Cost Control Strategies for CEOs, Managers, and Administrators*.

TRADE/PROFESSIONAL ASSOCIATIONS

National Association of State Budget Officers. Hall of the States Bldg., 444 N Capitol St. NW, Ste. 642, Washington, DC 20001-1556. Phone: (202)624-5382 or (202)624-8804; Fax: (202)624-7745; Email: nasbo-direct@nasbo.org • URL: http://www.nasbo.org • Budget directors, their deputies, and superior officers of the states and territories. Seeks to encourage study and research in state budgeting and promote cooperation and efficiency in budget programs. Conducts budget and legislative briefing every spring and four to five educational seminars each year.

BUDGETING, PERSONAL

See PERSONAL FINANCE

BUILDING AND LOAN ASSOCIATIONS

See SAVINGS AND LOAN ASSOCIATIONS

BUILDING CONTRACTS

See also BUILDING INDUSTRY; CONTRACTS

ABSTRACTS AND INDEXES

Current Law Index. Cengage Learning Inc. • $1,332 Individuals. Monthly. $1269.00 per year. Produced in cooperation with the American Association of Law Libraries. Indexes more than 900 law journals, legal newspapers, and specialty publications from the U.S., Canada, U.K., Ireland, Australia, and New Zealand.

DIRECTORIES

ENR Top 400 Construction Contractors. McGraw Hill Financial Inc. • Annual. Lists 400 United States contractors receiving largest dollar volume of contracts in preceding calendar year.

FindContractors.com. Associated Builders and Contractors, Inc. • Online member directory.

INTERNET DATABASES

Lexis.com Research System. Lexis-Nexis Group. Phone: 800-227-4908 or (937)865-6800; Fax: (937)865-6909; Email: webmaster@prod.lexis-nexis.com • URL: http://www.nexis.com • Fee-based Web site offers extensive searching of a wide variety of legal sources. Additional features include Daily Opinion Service, lexis.com Bookstore, Career Center, CLE Center, Law Schools, and Practice Pages ("Pages specific to areas of specialty").

OTHER SOURCES

Forms and Agreements for Architects, Engineers and Contractors. Albert Dib. Thomson West. • $2,687.25 full set. Three times a year. Five looseleaf volume. Covers evaluation of construction documents and alternative clauses. Includes pleadings for litigation and resolving of claims. (Real Property Law Series).

Government Contracts Reports. Wolters Kluwer Law & Business CCH. • Weekly. $2,600.00 per year. 10 looseleaf volumes. Laws and regulations affecting government contracts.

PERIODICALS AND NEWSLETTERS

ASA Today. American Subcontractors Association. • Weekly. Weekly. $40.00 per year.

Constructor: The Management Magazine of the Construction Industry. Associated General Contractors of America. AGC Information, Inc. • Monthly. Members, $15.00 per year; non-members, $250.00 per year. Includes *Directory*.

Government Contractor. West DC Editorial. • Weekly. $1,700 Individuals.

TRADE/PROFESSIONAL ASSOCIATIONS

American Institute of Constructors. 700 N Fairfax St., Ste. 510, Alexandria, VA 22314. Phone: (703)683-4999; Fax: (571)527-3105; Email: info@professionalconstructor.org • URL: http://www.professionalconstructor.org • Professionals engaged in construction practice, education, and research. Serves as the certifying body for the professional constructor. Promotes the study and advances the practice of construction. Facilitates the exchange of information and ideas relating to construction.

American Subcontractors Association. 1004 Duke St., Alexandria, VA 22314. Phone: (703)684-3450; Fax: (703)836-3482; Email: asaoffice@asa-hq.com • URL: http://www.asaonline.com • Construction subcontractors of trades and specialties such as foundations, concrete, masonry, steel, mechanical, drywall, electrical, painting, plastering, roofing and acoustical. Formed to deal with issues common to subcontractors. Works with other segments of the construction industry in promoting ethical practices, beneficial legislation and education of construction subcontractors and suppliers. Manages the Foundation of the American Subcontractors Association (FASA).

Associated Builders and Contractors. 440 1st St. NW, Ste. 200, Washington, DC 20001. Email: gotquestions@abc.org • URL: http://www.abc.org • Construction contractors, subcontractors, suppliers and associates. Aims to foster and perpetuate the principles of rewarding construction workers and management on the basis of merit. Sponsors management education programs and craft training; also sponsors apprenticeship and skill training programs. Disseminates technological and labor relations information.

Associated General Contractors of America. 2300 Wilson Blvd., Ste. 400, Arlington, VA 22201. Phone: 800-242-1767 or (703)548-3118 or (703)837-5319; Fax: (703)548-3119 or (703)837-5407; Email: info@agc.org • URL: http://www.agc.org • General construction contractors; subcontractors; industry suppliers; service firms. Provides market services through its divisions. Conducts special conferences and seminars designed specifically for construction firms. Compiles statistics on job accidents reported by member firms. Maintains 65 committees, including joint cooperative committees with other associations and liaison committees with federal agencies.

Associated Specialty Contractors. 3 Bethesda Metro Ctr., Ste. 1100, Bethesda, MD 20814. Email: dgw@

necanet.org • URL: http://www.assoc-spec-con.org • Works to promote efficient management and productivity. Coordinates the work of specialized branches of the industry in management information, research, public information, government relations and construction relations. Serves as a liaison among specialty trade associations in the areas of public relations, government relations, and with other organizations. Seeks to avoid unnecessary duplication of effort and expense or conflicting programs among affiliates. Identifies areas of interest and problems shared by members, and develops positions and approaches on such problems.

BUILDING EQUIPMENT

See CONSTRUCTION EQUIPMENT

BUILDING ESTIMATING

See ESTIMATING

BUILDING INDUSTRY

See also APARTMENT HOUSES; ARCHITECTURE; BUILDING MATERIALS INDUSTRY; CONSTRUCTION EQUIPMENT; DOOR INDUSTRY; ELECTRICAL CONSTRUCTION INDUSTRY; ESTIMATING; HOME IMPROVEMENT INDUSTRY; OFFICE BUILDINGS; PREFABRICATED HOUSE INDUSTRY

ABSTRACTS AND INDEXES

Applied Science and Technology Index. EBSCO Publishing Inc. • 11/year. Indexes a wide variety of English language technical, industrial, and engineering periodicals.

NTIS Alerts: Building Industry Technology. U.S. Department of Commerce National Technical Information Service. • Biweekly. $130 per year. Covers architecture, construction management, building materials, maintenance, furnishings, and related subjects.

CD-ROM DATABASES

OECD Statistical Compendium. Organization for Economic Cooperation and Development. • Semiannual. $1,905.00 per year for 1 to 10 users. CD-ROM contains more than 730,000 monthly, quarterly, and annual time series for OECD countries, 1960 to date. Includes fully searchable data on agriculture, food, economic indicators, national accounts, employment, energy, finance, industry, technology, and foreign trade. Results can be displayed in various forms.

DIRECTORIES

Building Industry--Slovakia. I.S.M.C. Information Systems and Marketing Contacts Ltd. • $65. Covers: Companies in the building industry in the Slovak Republic and their suppliers.

Building Officials and Code Administrators International-Membership Directory. • Annual. $16. 00. Approximately 14,000 construction code officials, architects, engineers, trade associations, and manufacturers.

Building Supply Home Centers--Buyers Guide Issue. Reed Elsevier Group plc Reed Business Information. • Annual. $30. Covers: U.S. manufacturers of building supply materials and products. Entries include: Company name and address, trade and brand names, list of products.

Construction Consultants Directory. InfoGroup Inc. • Annual. Number of listings: 734. Entries include: Name, address, phone, size of advertisement, name of owner or manager, number of employees, year first in "Yellow Pages." Compiled from telephone company "Yellow Pages," nationwide.

FindContractors.com. Associated Builders and Contractors, Inc. • Online member directory.

International Construction Directory. Dataguide Inc. • Irregular. Covers: Approximately 3,550 companies engaged in the construction of buildings, roads, public works, and industrial plants; international coverage. Database includes: Rankings of top 1,000 companies by revenue and by number of employees. Entries include: Company name, address, phone, fax, mailing address, telex, principal officers, number of employees, financial data, business activity, year established, stock exchange listing.

The International Directory of Importers--Construction and Building Equipment Importers. Interdata. • $260 Individuals print. Covers: 3,100 international firms importing construction and building equipment. Entries include: Company name and address, contact person, email, number of employees, year established, phone and telefaxes, business activity, bank references, as well as a listing of construction and building equipment currently being imported.

Malaysia Builders Directory. Marshall Cavendish Business Information Private Ltd. • S$40 Individuals local, foreign and other countries. Covers: building contractors & consultants, architects, engineers, property developers, quantity surveyors, and construction equipment and suppliers. Entries include: contact information, brand names, products and services, certified companies, trade associations and professional bodies.

Masonry Buyer's Guide. Mason Contractors Association of America. • Lists manufacturers or suppliers of products and services related to masonry construction.

Professional Builder--Annual Report of Housing's Giants. Reed Elsevier Group plc Reed Business Information. • Annual. Publication includes: list of top 400 firms that started and closed the greatest number of housing construction units in the preceding year. Entries include: Company name, city, state, housing revenues, total revenues, units started, units sold.

ProSales Buyer's Guide. DoveTale Publishers. • Annual. Price on application. A directory of equipment for professional builders.

Tools of the Trade Annual Buyers Guide. DoveTale Publishers. • Annual. Price on application. A directory of tools for the construction industry.

E-BOOKS

Encyclopedia of American Industries. Cengage Learning Inc. • 2011. $807.00. 6th edition. Three volumes. Volume one is Manufacturing Industries and volume two is Service and Non-Manufacturing Industries. Provides the history, development, and recent status of approximately 1,000 industries. Includes statistical graphs, with industry and general indexes. Also available as eBook.

FINANCIAL RATIOS

Construction Industry Annual Financial Survey. Construction Financial Management Association. • Annual. $262. Contains key financial ratios for various kinds and sizes of construction contractors.

INTERNET DATABASES

Business 2.0 Web Guide to the Best Business Links. Business 2.0 Media Inc. Phone: (415)293-4800; Email: support@business2.com • URL: http://www.business2.com/webguide • Web site presents an extensive, searchable directory of links to "the best, most informative, and authoritative web pages." Twenty main categories cover business, finance, career, company information, people, and technology topics, with thousands of subtopics, all linking to Web sites recommended by experienced business researchers. Fees: Free.

Fedstats. Federal Interagency Council on Statistical Policy. Phone: (202)395-7254 • URL: http://www.fedstats.gov • Web site features an efficient search facility for full-text statistics produced by more than 100 federal agencies, including the Census Bureau, the Bureau of Economic Analysis, and the Bureau of Labor Statistics. Boolean searches can be made within one agency or for all agencies combined. Links are offered to international statistical bureaus, including the UN, IMF, OECD, UNESCO, Eurostat, and 20 individual countries. Fees: Free.

FreeLunch.com. Economy.com, Inc. Phone: (610)696-8700; Fax: (610)696-1678 • URL: http://www.freelunch.com • Web site provides free access to more than 200 million economic and financial data series, covering industry, demographics, labor markets, prices, retail sales, government spending, trade, interest rates, housing starts, the stock market, etc. Data is available in either chart or table form. Searching is offered. Free, but registration required. Economy.com, Inc. also offers fee-based economic analysis at *The Dismal Scientist* site (www.dismal.com).

OTHER SOURCES

Construction Law. Matthew Bender and Company Inc. • $1,844. Eight volumes. Periodic supplementation available. Edited for lawyers who prepare construction contracts or engage in construction dispute litigation.

Forms and Agreements for Architects, Engineers and Contractors. Albert Dib. Thomson West. • $2,687.25 full set. Three times a year. Five looseleaf volume. Covers evaluation of construction documents and alternative clauses. Includes pleadings for litigation and resolving of claims. (Real Property Law Series).

International Code Council, Uniform Building Code. International Conference of Building Officials. • Triennial. Two volumes. Members, $144. 55; non-members, $180.70. (International Conference of Building Officials. Uniform Building Code).

PERIODICALS AND NEWSLETTERS

Builder: The Voice of America's Housing Industry. Finance and Housing Policy Div. DoveTale Publishers. • Monthly. $29.95 per year. Covers the home building and remodeling industry in general, including design, construction, and marketing.

Building Design and Construction: The Magazine for the Building Team. Reed Elsevier Group plc Reed Business Information. • Monthly. $119.00 per year. For non-residential building owners, contractors, engineers and architects.

Buildings: The Source for Facilities Decision-Makers. Stamats Communications Inc. • Monthly. $70.00 per year. Serves professional building ownership/management organizations.

CFMA Building Profits. Construction Financial Management Association. • Bimonthly. Covers the financial side of the construction industry.

Commercial Building: Tranforming Plans into Buildings. Stamats Communications Inc. • Bimonthly. $48.00 per year. Edited for building contractors, engineers, and architects. Includes special features on new products, climate control, plumbing, and vertical transportation.

Construction Law Digest. Matthew Bender and Company Inc. • $852. Provides practical information on emerging legal trends, issues, and court decisions relevant to the construction industry.

Construction Specifier: For Commercial and Industrial Construction. Construction Specifications Institute. • Monthly. Free to members; non-members, $36.00 per year; libraries, $30.00 per year. Technical aspects of the construction industry.

Custom Builder: The Business Magazine for Builders of Premier Homes. Willows Publishing Group Inc. • Bimonthly. $23. Magazine reporting on energy efficiency and quality home construction.

Design Cost Data. DC & D Technologies Inc. • Bimonthly. $149 U.S. /year plus online access to archive. Provides a preliminary cost estimating system for architects, contractors, builders, and developers, utilizing historical data. Includes case studies of actual costs. Formerly *Design Cost and Data.*

ENR: Connecting the Industry Worldwide. McGraw Hill Financial Inc. • Weekly. $74.00 per year.

Professional Builder: Small Builders and Contractors Business Magazine. Reed Elsevier Group plc Reed Business Information. • 11 times a year. $39.00 per year. Provides price and market forecasts on industrial products, components and materials. Office products, business systems and transportation. Includes supplement Luxury Homes. Formerly *Professional Builder and Remodeler.*

ProSales: For Dealers and Distributors Serving the Professional Contractor. DoveTale Publishers. • Includes special feature issues on selling, credit, financing, and the marketing of power tools.

PRICE SOURCES

Building Construction Cost Data. RSMeans. • Annual. $194.95 Individuals. Lists over 20,000 entries for estimating.

Labor Rates for the Construction Industry. RSMeans. • Annual. $424.95 Individuals.

Means Construction Cost Indexes. RSMeans. • Quarterly. $362 Individuals.

RESEARCH CENTERS AND INSTITUTES

Hong Kong Polytechnic University - Research Center for Construction and Real Estate Economics. Department of Bldg. & Real Estate, Hung Hom, Kowloon, Hong Kong, China. Phone: 86 852 27665821; Fax: 86 852 27645131; Email: bskwwong@polyu.edu.uk • URL: http://www.bre.polyu.edu.hk/rccree/index.htm • Construction and real estate economics.

STATISTICS SOURCES

Standard & Poor's Industry Surveys. Standard & Poor's Financial Services L.L.C. • Semiannual. $1,800.00. Two looseleaf volumes. Includes monthly *Supplements.* Provides detailed, individual surveys of 52 major industry groups. Each survey is revised on a semiannual basis. Also includes "Monthly Investment Review" (industry group investment analysis) and monthly "Trends & Projections" (economic analysis).

Survey of Current Business. U. S. Government Printing Office. • Published by Bureau of Economic Analysis, U. S. Department of Commerce. Presents a wide variety of business and economic data.

United States Census of Construction Industries. U.S. Department of Commerce U.S. Census Bureau. • Quinquennial. Results presented in reports, tape, and CD-ROM files.

Value of Construction Put in Place. U.S. Bureau of the Census. U. S. Government Printing Office. • Monthly.

TRADE/PROFESSIONAL ASSOCIATIONS

AFL-CIO - Building and Construction Trades Department. 815 16th St., Ste. 600, Washington, DC 20006. Phone: (202)347-1461; Fax: (202)628-0724; Email: insulatorslocal78@aol.com • URL: http://www.bctd.org • Federation of labor unions in the construction industry including asbestos workers, bricklayers, masons, plasterers, carpenters, electrical workers, elevator constructors, operating engineers, granite cutters, hood carriers, common laborers, ironworkers, carpet, tile and stone workers, painters, decorators, paperhangers, plumbers, steamfitters, roofers, boilermakers, lathers, sheet metal workers, and other related trades. Maintains liaison with Center to Protect Workers Rights that provides independent research and support.

Association of Equipment Manufacturers. 6737 W Washington St., Ste. 2400, Milwaukee, WI 53214-5647. Phone: 866-AEM-0442 or (414)272-0943; Fax: (414)272-1170; Email: aem@aem.org • URL: http://www.aem.org • Provides business development services on a global basis for companies that manufacture equipment, products and services used worldwide in the agricultural, construction, industrial, mining, forestry, and utility fields.

Construction Financial Management Association. 100 Village Blvd., Ste. 200, Princeton, NJ 08540. Phone: 888-421-9996 or (609)452-8000; Fax: (609)452-0474; Email: sbinstock@cfma.org • URL: http://www.cfma.org • Contractors, subcontractors, architects, real estate developers and engineers; associate members are equipment and material suppliers, accountants, lawyers, bankers and others involved with the financial management of the construction industry. Provides a forum for the exchange of ideas; coordinates educational programs dedicated to improving the professional standards of financial management in the construction industry. Offers expanded national programs, technical assistance and industry representation. Conducts research programs; maintains speakers' bureau and placement service; compiles statistics.

Construction Management Association of America. 7926 Jones Branch Dr., Ste. 800, McLean, VA 22102. Phone: (703)356-2622; Fax: (703)356-6388; Email: info@cmaanet.org • URL: http://cmaanet.org • Promotes the growth and development of construction management as a professional service; encourages high professional standards. Conducts conferences and forums on construction management topics. Sponsors a professional certification program.

Federation of Industries Products Systems and Services for Construction. Via Brenta, 13, I-00198 Rome, Italy. Phone: 39 6 8555203; Fax: 39 6 8559860; Email: finco@fincoweb.org • URL: http://www.fincoweb.org • Promotes the products systems and services used by the construction industries.

International Code Council. 500 New Jersey Ave. NW, 6th Fl., Washington, DC 20001-2070. Phone: 888-422-7233 or (202)370-1800; Fax: (202)783-2348; Email: carecenter@iccsafe.org • URL: http://www.iccsafe.org • Formerly Building Officials Conference of America.

National Association of Home Builders - Systems Builder Council. 1201 15th St. NW, Washington, DC 20005. Phone: 800-368-5242 or (202)266-8200; Fax: (202)266-8400 • URL: http://www.nahb.org/reference_list.aspx?sectionID=815 • Formerly Home Manufacturers Councils of NAHB.

National Association of the Remodeling Industry. PO Box 4250, Des Plaines, IL 60016. Phone: (847)298-9200; Fax: (847)298-9225; Email: info@nari.org • URL: http://www.nari.org • Represents remodeling contractors, manufacturers of remodeling/building products, lending institutions and wholesalers and distributors. Promotes the common business interests of those engaged in the home improvement and remodeling industries. Encourages ethical conduct, good business practices and professionalism in the remodeling industry. Conducts seminars, workshops and promotional programs and has developed an extensive certification program. Local chapters monitor legislations and regulations affecting the industry.

National Association of Women in Construction. 327 S Adams St., Fort Worth, TX 76104. Phone: 800-552-3506 or (817)877-5551; Fax: (817)877-0324; Email: nawic@nawic.org • URL: http://www.nawic.org • Seeks to enhance the success of women in the construction industry.

BUILDING LOANS

See MORTGAGES

BUILDING MAINTENANCE

See MAINTENANCE OF BUILDINGS

BUILDING MANAGEMENT

See PROPERTY MANAGEMENT

BUILDING MATERIALS INDUSTRY

CD-ROM DATABASES

OECD Statistical Compendium. Organization for Economic Cooperation and Development. • Semiannual. $1,905.00 per year for 1 to 10 users. CD-ROM contains more than 730,000 monthly, quarterly, and annual time series for OECD countries, 1960 to date. Includes fully searchable data on agriculture, food, economic indicators, national accounts, employment, energy, finance, industry, technology, and foreign trade. Results can be displayed in various forms.

DIRECTORIES

International Code Council Membership directory. International Code Council. • Annual. Price on application.

The International Directory of Importers--Building and Construction Materials and Supplies Importers. Interdata. • $320 Individuals print. Covers: 6,400 international firms importing building, construction materials and supplies. Entries include: Company name and address, contact person, email, number of employees, year established, phone and telefaxes, business activity, bank references, as well as a listing of building, construction materials and supplies currently being imported.

Remodeling--Product Guide. DoveTale Publishers. • Annual. $10. Publication includes: List of more than 2,000 manufacturers and suppliers serving the remodeling contracting industry; list of industry-related associations. Entries include: For manufacturers and suppliers--Company name, address, phone, name and title of contact, product line, geographical area served. For associations--Association name, address, phone, director.

FINANCIAL RATIOS

Annual Statement Studies. Risk Management Association. • Annual. Compiled from over 280,000 financial statements.

Annual Statement Studies: Industry Default Probabilities and Cash Flow Measures. Risk Management Association. • Annual. $405 Nonmembers. Serves as a companion volume to the original *Annual Statement Studies.* Gives probability of default estimates on a percentage scale for more than 450 industries. Includes changes in position year-by-year for eight financial statement line items and provides percentage measures of cash flow.

INTERNET DATABASES

Advance Monthly Retail Trade Report. U. S. Census Bureau. Phone: 800-541-8345 or (301)457-4100 or (301)763-2713; Fax: (301)457-1296 or (301)457-3842; Email: naics@census.gov • URL: http://www.census.gov/epcd/www/naicstab.htm • Web pages provide monthly sales figures for a wide range of retail businesses. Advance, preliminary, and final statistics are provided for the latest month available in each case, with a previous-year comparison. Updates are monthly.

Business 2.0 Web Guide to the Best Business Links. Business 2.0 Media Inc. Phone: (415)293-4800; Email: support@business2.com • URL: http://www.business2.com/webguide • Web site presents an extensive, searchable directory of links to "the best, most informative, and authoritative web pages."

Twenty main categories cover business, finance, career, company information, people, and technology topics, with thousands of subtopics, all linking to Web sites recommended by experienced business researchers. Fees: Free.

Fedstats. Federal Interagency Council on Statistical Policy. Phone: (202)395-7254 • URL: http://www.fedstats.gov • Web site features an efficient search facility for full-text statistics produced by more than 100 federal agencies, including the Census Bureau, the Bureau of Economic Analysis, and the Bureau of Labor Statistics. Boolean searches can be made within one agency or for all agencies combined. Links are offered to international statistical bureaus, including the UN, IMF, OECD, UNESCO, Eurostat, and 20 individual countries. Fees: Free.

FreeLunch.com. Economy.com, Inc. Phone: (610)696-8700; Fax: (610)696-1678 • URL: http://www.freelunch.com • Web site provides free access to more than 200 million economic and financial data series, covering industry, demographics, labor markets, prices, retail sales, government spending, trade, interest rates, housing starts, the stock market, etc. Data is available in either chart or table form. Searching is offered. Free, but registration required. Economy.com, Inc. also offers fee-based economic analysis at *The Dismal Scientist* site (www.dismal.com).

PERIODICALS AND NEWSLETTERS

Building Material Dealer. National Lumber and Building Material Dealers Association. • Monthly. $48.00 per year. Includes special feature issues on hand and power tools, lumber, roofing, kitchens, flooring, windows and doors, and insulation. Formerly *Builder Material Retailer*.

HQ: Good Design is Good Business. McGraw-Hill Inc. • Quarterly. Design magazine for C-level executives, building owners and developers, and design and construction professionals.

National Home Center News: News and Analysis for the Home Improvement, Building Material Industry. Lebhar-Friedman Inc. • 22 times a year. $99.00 per year. Includes special feature issues on hardware and tools, building materials, millwork, electrical supplies, lighting, and kitchens.

U.S. Glass, Metal, and Glazing. AutoGlass Repair and Replacement Key Communications Inc. • Monthly. $35.00 per year. Edited for glass fabricators, glaziers, distributors, and retailers. Special feature issues are devoted to architectural glass, mirror glass, windows, storefronts, hardware, machinery, sealants, and adhesives. Regular topics include automobile glass and fenestration (window design and placement).

PRICE SOURCES

PPI Detailed Report. Periodical covering business. Bureau of Labor Statistics, U.S. Department of Labor. U. S. Government Printing Office. • Monthly. $55 Individuals.

RESEARCH CENTERS AND INSTITUTES

NAHB Home Innovation Research Labs. 400 Prince George's Blvd., Upper Marlboro, MD 20774. Phone: 800-638-8556 or (301)249-4000; Fax: (301)430-6180 • URL: http://www.homeinnovation.com.

STATISTICS SOURCES

Annual Benchmark Report for Retail Trade and Food Services..A Detailed Summary of Retail Sales, Purchases, Accounts Receivable, Inventories, and Food Service Sales. U. S. Government Printing Office. • Annual. $13.00. Issued by the U.S. Census Bureau. Provides detailed annual and monthly retail statistics for the most recent 10 years. Includes data for various kinds of retail outlets, including automobiles, furniture, appliances, building supplies, grocery stores, drug stores, gasoline stations, clothing, sporting goods, department stores, and restaurants.

Survey of Current Business. U. S. Government Printing Office. • Published by Bureau of Economic Analysis, U. S. Department of Commerce. Presents a wide variety of business and economic data.

TRADE/PROFESSIONAL ASSOCIATIONS

National Lumber and Building Material Dealers Association. 2025 M St. NW, Ste. 800, Washington, DC 20036-3309. Phone: (202)367-1169; Fax: (202)367-2169; Email: info@dealer.org • URL: http://www.dealer.org • Formerly National Retail Lumber Dealers Association.

North American Building Material Distribution Association. 330 N Wabash Ave., Ste. 2000, Chicago, IL 60611. Phone: 888-747-7862 or (312)321-6845; Fax: (312)644-0310; Email: info@nbmda.org • URL: http://www.nbmda.org • Formerly National Building Material Distributors Association.

BUILDING REPAIR AND RECONSTRUCTION

See HOME IMPROVEMENT INDUSTRY

BUILDING RESEARCH

See also ARCHITECTURE; BUILDING INDUSTRY; BUSINESS RESEARCH

RESEARCH CENTERS AND INSTITUTES

Centre for Building Science - University of Toronto Department of Civil Engineering. 35 St. George St., Toronto, ON, Canada M5S 1A4. Phone: (416)978-6813; Fax: (416)978-6813 • URL: http://www.civ.utoronto.ca.

NAHB Home Innovation Research Labs. 400 Prince George's Blvd., Upper Marlboro, MD 20774. Phone: 800-638-8556 or (301)249-4000; Fax: (301)430-6180 • URL: http://www.homeinnovation.com.

TRADE/PROFESSIONAL ASSOCIATIONS

International Code Council. 500 New Jersey Ave. NW, 6th Fl., Washington, DC 20001-2070. Phone: 888-422-7233 or (202)370-1800; Fax: (202)783-2348; Email: carecenter@iccsafe.org • URL: http://www.iccsafe.org • Formerly Building Officials Conference of America.

BUILDING STONE

See QUARRYING

BUILDING SUPPLY INDUSTRY

See BUILDING MATERIALS INDUSTRY

BUILDINGS, PREFABRICATED

See PREFABRICATED HOUSE INDUSTRY

BUILDINGS, RESIDENTIAL

See HOUSING

BULLION

See MONEY

BUREAUCRACY

See also GOVERNMENT EMPLOYEES

ABSTRACTS AND INDEXES

Business Periodicals Index Retrospective. EBSCO Publishing Inc. • 11/year. Quarterly and annual cumulations.

BIBLIOGRAPHIES

Census of Governments: Subject Bibliography No. 156. U. S. Government Printing Office. • Annual. Free. Lists government publications.

Intergovernmental Relations. U. S. Government Printing Office. • Annual. Free. Lists government publications. (Subject Bibliography 211.).

CD-ROM DATABASES

Newspaper Abstracts Ondisc. ProQuest L.L.C. • Monthly. $2,950.00 per year (covers 1989 to date; archival discs are available for 1985-88). Provides cover-to-cover CD-ROM indexing and abstracting of 19 major newspapers, including the *New York Times*, *Wall Street Journal*, *Washington Post*, *Chicago Tribune*, and *Los Angeles Times*.

DIRECTORIES

Carroll's Federal & Federal Regional Directory. Caroll Publishing. • Semiannual. $500 Individuals. Lists more than 23,000 U. S. government officials throughout the country, including military installations.

Carroll's Federal Directory. Caroll Publishing. • $550 Single issue 4 issues per year. Covers approximately 37,000 executive managers in federal government offices in Washington, DC, including executive, congressional and judicial branches; members of Congress and Congressional committees and staff.

Carroll's Federal Regional Directory. Caroll Publishing. • Annual. $500 Individuals. Covers: Over 32,000 officials in federal congressional, judicial, and executive branch departments and agencies outside the District of Columbia. Database includes: Regional maps showing states covered in each federal region and Federal Information Centers. Entries include: Organization or agency name; names, addresses, and phone numbers of key personnel.

Federal Regional Yellow Book: Who's Who in the Federal Government's Departments, Agencies, Military Installations, and Service Academies Outside of Washington, DC. Leadership Directories Inc. • Semiannual. $465 Individuals annual. Lists over 35,000 federal officials and support staff at 8,000 regional offices.

Federal Staff Directory: With Biographical Information on Executive Staff Personnel. CQ Press. • Three times a year. $259.00 per year. Single copies, $149.00. Lists 35,000 staff members of federal departments and agencies, with biographies of 3,200 key executives. Includes keyword and name indexes.

Government Phone Book USA: Your Comprehensive Guide to Federal, State, County, and Local Government Offices in the United States. Omnigraphics Inc. • Annual. $265.00. Contains more than 270,000 listings of federal, state, county, and local government offices and personnel, including legislatures. Formerly *Government Directory of Addresses and Phone Numbers*.

United States Government Manual. Office of the Federal Register. • Annual. $29 Individuals. Provides information on the agencies of the executive, judicial, and legislative branches of the Federal government. Contains a section on terminated or transferred agencies. Database includes: Includes boards, commissions, committees and quasi-official agencies and organizations in which US participates.

OTHER SOURCES

Government Employee Relations Report. Bloomberg BNA. • Weekly. $1,144.00 per year.

Three looseleaf volumes. Concerned with labor relations in the public sector.

PERIODICALS AND NEWSLETTERS

Administration and Society. Pine Forge Press. • 9/year. $1,546 Institutions print. Scholarly journal concerned with public administration and the effects of bureaucracy.

The Federal Manager. Federal Managers Association. • Quarterly. Covers management and legislative issues in the government that affect federal managers. Formerly *Federal Managers Quarterly*.

Government Computer News: The Newspaper Serving Computer Users Throughout the Federal Government. Business Information, Inc..

Government Executive: Federal Government's Business Magazine. National Journal Group Inc. • Monthly. $48 Individuals. Includes management of computerized information systems in the federal government.

Legal Times: Law and Lobbying in the Nation's Capital. ALM Media Properties LLC. • Weekly. $318.00 per year. Published in Washington, DC. Provides news relating to lawyers and the federal government. Special features cover a variety of topics relating to law firm administration.

Public Administration Review (PAR). American Society for Public Administration. • Bimonthly. $539 Institutions U.S., print + online. Serves governmental administrators, public officials, educators, research workers, and others interested in the public management profession. Includes online edition.

The Public Manager: The Journal for Practitioners. Bureaucrat, Inc. • Quarterly. $39 Members print and online. Formerly *Bureaucrat*.

TRADE/PROFESSIONAL ASSOCIATIONS

American Society for Public Administration. 1301 Pennsylvania Ave. NW, Ste. 700, Washington, DC 20004-1716. Phone: (202)393-7878; Fax: (202)638-4952; Email: info@aspanet.org • URL: http://www.aspanet.org/public • Promotes excellence in public service, including government, non-profit and private sectors, and academic community.

BUREAUS OF BUSINESS RESEARCH

See BUSINESS RESEARCH; ECONOMIC RESEARCH

BURGLAR ALARMS

See ELECTRONIC SECURITY SYSTEMS

BURLAP INDUSTRY

See also JUTE INDUSTRY

ABSTRACTS AND INDEXES

Textile Technology Index™. EBSCO Publishing Inc. • Monthly. $545 Individuals. Includes indexing and abstracts for more than 470 periodicals.

ALMANACS AND YEARBOOKS

CRB Commodity Yearbook. Commodity Research Bureau. CRB. • Annual. $179 plus $10.00 shipping cost. The single most comprehensive source of commodity and futures market information available.

DIRECTORIES

Directory of Taiwanese Manufacturers & Exporters of Jute, Hemp, Sisal, Burlap & Its Products. EXIM Infotek Private Ltd. • $10 Individuals. Covers: 60 Taiwanese manufacturers and exporters of canvas and duck, canvas and duck products. Entries include: Company name, postal address, city, country, phone, fax, e-mail and websites, contact person, designation, and product details.

Directory of 20 South Korean Manufacturers & Exporters of Jute, Hemp, Sisal, Burlap & Its Products. EXIM Infotek Private Ltd. • $5 Individuals. Covers: 20 South Korean manufacturers and exporters of canvas and duck, canvas and duck products. Entries include: Company name, postal address, city, country, phone, fax, e-mail and websites, contact person, designation, and product details.

ONLINE DATABASES

Agricola. U.S. National Agricultural Library World List of Agricultural Serials. • Covers worldwide agricultural literature. Over 3.3 million citations, 1970 to present, with monthly updates. Inquire as to online cost and availability.

Textile Technology Index™. EBSCO Publishing Inc. • Monthly. $545 Individuals. Includes indexing and abstracts for more than 470 periodicals.

World Textiles. Elsevier. • Provides abstracting and indexing from 1970 of worldwide textile literature (periodicals, books, pamphlets, and reports). Includes U. S., European, and British patent information. Updating is monthly. Inquire as to online cost and availability.

PRICE SOURCES

PPI Detailed Report. Periodical covering business. Bureau of Labor Statistics, U.S. Department of Labor. U. S. Government Printing Office. • Monthly. $55 Individuals.

BUSES

See MOTOR BUSES

BUSINESS

See also ADMINISTRATION; CORPORATIONS; ECONOMICS; EXECUTIVES; INDUSTRY; INTERNATIONAL BUSINESS

ABSTRACTS AND INDEXES

Business Periodicals Index Retrospective. EBSCO Publishing Inc. • 11/year. Quarterly and annual cumulations.

CBER-LIED Report on Housing-Market Conditions; Southern Nevada Business Confidence Index. University of Nevada, Las Vegas Center for Business and Economic Research. • Quarterly.

NTIS Alerts: Business & Economics. U.S. Department of Commerce National Technical Information Service. • Biweekly. $130 per year. Covers consumer affairs, minority enterprises, marketing and economics, international commerce, banking, and finance.

Social Sciences Citation Index. Thomson Reuters Corp. • Weekly. Product is accessed via *Web of Science*.

ALMANACS AND YEARBOOKS

Information Please Business Almanac and Desk Reference. Information Please L.L.C. • Annual. $21.95.

BIOGRAPHICAL SOURCES

Who's Who in Finance and Business. Marquis Who's Who L.L.C. • Biennial. $349 Individuals. Provides over 21,000 concise biographies of business leaders in all fields.

CD-ROM DATABASES

ABI/INFORM. ProQuest L.L.C. • Monthly. Provides CD-ROM indexing and abstracting of worldwide business literature. Archival discs are available from 1971. Formerly *ABI/INFORM OnDisc*.

Business Abstracts with Full Text. EBSCO Publishing Inc. • Includes full text articles from more than 460 business publications from 1982 to present. Indexing for nearly 880 publications.

Canada Greater Montreal Business CD-ROM. Manufacturers' News Inc. • Contains detailed directory information on companies in and around Montreal, Quebec. Covers more than 22,100 companies and provides information on nearly 29,200 executives and key decision-makers.

Canada Greater Vancouver Business CD-ROM. Manufacturers' News Inc. • Contains detailed directory information on more than 18,600 companies in and around Vancouver, British Columbia.

D & B Business Locator. Dun & Bradstreet Inc. • Quarterly. $2,495.00 per year. CD-ROM provides concise information on more than 10 million U. S. companies or businesses. Includes data on number of employees.

OECD Statistical Compendium. Organization for Economic Cooperation and Development. • Semiannual. $1,905.00 per year for 1 to 10 users. CD-ROM contains more than 730,000 monthly, quarterly, and annual time series for OECD countries, 1960 to date. Includes fully searchable data on agriculture, food, economic indicators, national accounts, employment, energy, finance, industry, technology, and foreign trade. Results can be displayed in various forms.

Social Sciences Citation Index. Thomson Reuters Corp. • Weekly. Product is accessed via *Web of Science*.

DIRECTORIES

Addison County Business Directory & Community Profile. Addison County Chamber of Commerce. • Description: Serves as a resource guide for businesses and individuals that are relocating to Addison County, Vermont, and surrounding areas. Covers: over 500 member businesses, and local government officials in Addison County, Vermont. Entries include: For businesses--Name, address, phone, business description, name and title of contact, fax, e-mail and URL addresses. For government officials--Name, business office address, phone, hours of operation.

Afghanistan Investment and Business Guide. International Business Publications, USA. • Annual. $99.95 Individuals hardcover. Covers: Strategic and business information, contacts, regulations and more.

Alameda County Business Directory. Rich's Business Directories Inc. • $199 Individuals online. Contains directory information for more than 3700 companies and 12,000 contacts in Alameda County, California.

Albuquerque Economic Development Business Directory. Albuquerque Economic Development Inc. • Covers: Business resources in the Albuquerque, New Mexico, metropolitan area. Includes list of categories with links and a searchable database. Entries include: Name, address, phone, fax, URL, map link.

Albuquerque Women in Business Directory. Duval Publications Inc. • Annual. Covers approximately 400 women business executives and owners in the Albuquerque, New Mexico area. Informative articles, government resources, related women's resources and organizations.

Algeria Business Directory. Business Guide. • $150 download. Covers: 10,000 business listings including wholesalers, importers, retailers, business houses, and agents in Algeria.

Algeria Investment and Business Guide. International Business Publications, USA. • $99.95 Individuals hardcover. Covers: Basic information on economy, export-import and investment climate, opportunities, industrial development, banking, and government. Entries include: Important business contacts and business travel.

American Big Businesses Directory. InfoGroup Inc. • Annual. $295. Covers: 218,000 U.S. businesses with more than 100 employees, and 500,000 key executives and directors. CD-ROM version contains 160,000 top firms and 431,000 key executives. Entries include: Name, address, phone, names and titles of key personnel, number of employees, sales volume, Standard Industrial Classification (SIC) codes, subsidiaries and parent company names, stock exchanges on which traded.

American Business Database. Mailer's Software. • Covers: More than 1.2 million listings of all the companies and organizations in the U.S. that possess their own unique ZIP Plus 4 code. Entries include: Company name, phone, complete mailing address with ZIP Plus 4 and Carrier Route Codes; state and county FIPS Codes; Standard Industrial Classification (SIC) code.

American Business Leaders from Colonial Times to the Present. ABC-Clio Inc. • $175 Individuals print. Covers: The last three centuries of visionary figures in American business.

American Library Association Guide to Information Access. Library and Information Technology Association. • $18.95. Publication includes: List of reference sources for areas including business and finance, consumer information, education, jobs and careers, and science and technology. Principal content of publication is a guide to general research methods.

American Manufacturers Directory. InfoGroup Inc. • Annual. $295. Covers: more than 150,000 manufacturing companies with 20 or more employees. CD-ROM version lists all 531,000 U.S. manufacturers, in all employee size ranges. Entries include: Company name, address, phone, contact name, Standard Industrial Classification (SIC) codes, number of employees, sales volume code, credit rating scores.

America's Corporate Families. Dun & Bradstreet Inc. • Annual. Covers approximately 12,700 U.S. corporations. Ultimate companies must meet all of the following criteria for inclusion: two or more business locations, 250 or more employees at that location or in excess of $25 million in sales volume or a tangible net worth greater than $500,000, and controlling interest in one or more subsidiary company.

Andorra Offshore Investment and Business Guide. International Business Publications, USA. • $99.95 Individuals hardcover. Covers: Information on conducting business and investment activity in the country with offshore status.

Angel Capital: How to Raise Early-Stage Private Equity Financing. John Wiley & Sons Inc. • $85 Individuals hardcover. Covers: How to find investors and take control of the private placement process; alternative capital resources.

Angola Business Directory. Business Guide. • $25 download. Covers: Over 7,300 business listings including wholesalers, importers, retailers, business houses, and agents in Angola.

Angola Industrial and Business Directory. International Business Publications, USA. • $99.95 Individuals hardcover. Covers: Strategic and practical economic and business information. Entries include: Business contacts for conducting business activity in the country.

Angola Investment and Business Guide. International Business Publications, USA. • $99.95 Individuals hardcover. Covers: Basic information on economy, export-import and investment climate, regulations, industrial development, banking, opportunities and government. Entries include: Business contacts and business travel.

Ann Arbor Area Chamber of Commerce--Business Directory. Ann Arbor/Ypsilanti Regional Chamber. • Covers: Member companies in Ann Arbor, Michigan. Entries include: Name of firm, address, phone, number of employees, line of business, names and titles of key personnel, products or services.

Annuaire des Entreprises et Organismes d'Outre-Mer l'Afrique Noire Francophone. Rene Moreux et Cie. • Biennial. $715 payment must accompany order. Covers: about 10,000 national and multinational companies in or related to Benin, Burundi, Central African Empire, Chad, Congo, Gabon, Guinea, Ivory Coast, Malagasy Republic, Mali, Mauritania, Niger, Rwanda, Senegal, Togo, Cameroon, Upper Volta, Zaire, and the French overseas departments and territories. Includes banking and other financial institutions, chambers of commerce, government agencies, and associations. Entries include: Company name, address, capital, line of business, names and titles of key personnel, year established, products, branch offices, associated companies in France.

Arab-British Trade Directory. Arab-British Chamber of Commerce. • $6 Other countries additional copy. Covers: Over 5,000 UK and Arab companies from the manufacturing, trading, services, and financial sectors. Entries include: Contact details of companies from joint Arab-Foreign chambers around the world.

Argentina Government and Business Contacts Handbook. International Business Publications, USA. • $99.95 Individuals hardcopy, E-book and CD-ROM. Covers: Strategic government and business information, export-import activity in the country, investment, business contacts and regulations.

Argentina Industrial and Business Directory. International Business Publications, USA. • Annual. $99.95 Individuals hardcover. Covers: Detailed information on investment, export-import business opportunities, foreign economic assistance projects, government and business contacts.

Armenia Government and Business Contacts Handbook. International Business Publications, USA. • $99.95 Individuals hardcopy, E-book and CD-ROM. Covers: Strategic government and business information, export-import activity in the country, investment, business contacts and regulations.

Asian Business League of San Francisco Membership Directory. Asian Business League of San Francisco. • Includes contact information for both Asian-Pacific Americans and non-Asian Pacific Americans with an interest in expanding leadership skills.

Athens Area Chamber of Commerce Membership Directory. Athens Area Chamber of Commerce. • Lists member businesses in Athens, Georgia. Publication includes directory details for largest employers, retail centers, chamber member realtors and banks.

Atlanta Business Chronicle's Book of Lists. Metro Atlanta Chamber of Commerce. • $49.95 Individuals. Lists companies in the Atlanta business community, including sections on business and industry, business services, commercial real estate, education and human resources, finance, general interests, healthcare, hospitality and travel, marketing, residential real estate and technology sections. Entries include name, address, phone, fax, facts and figures, and detailed information.

Australia Government and Business Contacts Handbook. International Business Publications, USA. • $99.95 Individuals hardcopy, E-book and CD-ROM. Covers: Strategic government and business information, export-import activity in the country, investment, business contacts and regulations.

Australia Industrial and Business Directory. International Business Publications, USA. • Annual. $99.95 Individuals hardcover. Covers: Strategic industrial, investment, and business contacts for conducting export-import and investment activity in the country.

Australia Investment and Business Guide. International Business Publications, USA. • $99.95 Individuals hardcover. Covers: Basic information on economy and government, export-import activity and investment climate, regulations and industrial development, and banking. Entries include: Important business contacts and business travel.

Austria Industrial and Business Directory. International Business Publications, USA. • Annual. $99.95 Individuals hardcover. Covers: Detailed information on investment, export-import business opportunities, foreign economic assistance projects, government and business contacts.

Awards, Honors, and Prizes: An International Directory of Awards and Their Donors Recognizing Achievement in Advertising, Architecture, Arts and Humanities, Business and Finance. Cengage Learning Inc. • Annual. $898 Individuals set series (3 volumes). Volume 1 covers more than 21,6000 awards given by organizations in the U.S. and Canada, in recognition of achievement, and major competitive prizes, some fellowships are also described; Volume 2 contains approximately 12,500 international awards.

Azerbaijan Government and Business Contacts Handbook. International Business Publications, USA. • $99.95 Individuals hardcopy, E-book and CD-ROM. Covers: Strategic government and business information, export-import activity in the country, investment, business contacts and regulations.

Azerbaijan Investment and Business Guide. International Business Publications, USA. • $99.95 Individuals hardcover. Covers: Strategic and practical information on economy, export-import and investment climate, regulations and industrial development, banking, and government. Entries include: Important business contacts and business travel.

Bahrain Golden Key Directory. International Institute of Trade Relation Promotion, Trade Information Centre of Iran. • £100 Individuals. Covers: 4,879 companies in Bahrain. Entries include: Company name, address, telephone, fax, e-mail, products, services, Managing Director, and business activities.

Bahrain Investment & Business Guide. International Business Publications, USA. • $99.95 Individuals hardcover. Covers: Major investment, strategic business opportunities and basic information on economy, export-import, industrial development, banking and government. Entries include: Business contacts and business travel.

Baltimore Business Journal--Book of Lists. Baltimore Business Journal. • $60 print only. Covers: Major companies, foundations, government officials, utilities, newspapers, radio and television stations, airlines, hospitals, financial institutions, shopping centers, resorts, and prominent individuals in the Baltimore, Maryland area. Entries include: Company, organization, or individual name, address, phone, name and title of contact.

Bangladesh Government and Business Contacts Handbook. International Business Publications, USA. • $99.95 Individuals hardcopy, E-book and CD-ROM. Covers: Strategic government and business information, export-import activity in the country, investment, business contacts and regulations.

Bangladesh Industrial and Business Directory.

International Business Publications, USA. • Annual. $99.95 Individuals hardcover. Covers: Strategic industrial, investment and business contacts for conducting export-import and investment activity in the country.

Bangladesh Investment and Business Guide. International Business Publications, USA. • $99.95 Individuals hardcover. Covers: Practical and strategic information on economy, export-import activity, investment climate, regulations and industrial development, banking, and government. Entries include: Business contacts and business travel.

Bartercard National Directory. Bartercard International. • 3/year. Covers: 23,000 businesses in Australia and over 55,000 businesses around the world. Entries include: Detailed contact information.

The Basic Business Library. Greenwood Publishing Group Inc. • Lists current business resources and essays on topics in business librarianship.

Belarus Industrial and Business Directory. International Business Publications, USA. • Annual. $99.95 Individuals hardcover. Covers: Strategic industrial, investment and business contacts for conducting export-import and investment activity in the country.

Belgium Industrial and Business Directory. International Business Publications, USA. • Annual. $99.95 Individuals hardcover. Covers: Detailed information on investment, export-import business opportunities, foreign economic assistance projects, government and business contacts.

Belize Investment & Business Guide. International Business Publications, USA. • $99.95 Individuals hardcover. Covers: Strategic business information, export-import activity in the state, regulations and industrial development, banking, government, and opportunities. Entries include: Guides for conducting investment and business contacts.

Benin Business Directory. Business Guide. • $150 download. Covers: 4,400 business listings including wholesalers, importers, retailers, business houses, and agents in Benin.

Bermuda Business Directory. Bermuda Directories Ltd. • Covers: Listings of businesses in Bermuda including insurance, banking and legal services, local events, sightseeing, shopping, dining, and restaurants. Entries include: Company name, contact information, and e-mail address.

Better Business Bureau of New Jersey Consumer Guide. Better Business Bureau of New Jersey. • Annual.

Big Business in Metro Detroit. Detroit Regional Chamber. • Covers: More than 1,500 businesses and agencies which represent the largest employers in Metro Detroit, Michigan. Entries include: Company name, address, phone, SIC code, fax, product description, e-mail, and website.

Biographical Dictionary of American Business Leaders. Greenwood Electronic Media. • $183.95 hardcover. Covers: In four volumes, over 1,100 American business people from early merchants and farmers through contemporary leaders. Entries include: Name, date and place of birth, summary of subject's business activities and historical significance, ethnic background, religion.

Blowing Rock Chamber of Commerce--Chamber Businesses. Blowing Rock Chamber of Commerce. • Annual. Listing of businesses in Blowing Rock, North Carolina.

Bolivia Industrial and Business Directory. International Business Publications, USA. • Annual. $99.95 Individuals hardcover. Covers: Strategic industrial, investment and business contacts for conducting export-import and investment activity in the country.

B.O.S.S.: A Supplier Directory for Doing Business in Canada. International Press Publications Inc. • Annual. $200. Canadian suppliers and products.

Braby's Durban Business Directory. A.C. Braby (Pty) Ltd. • Covers: Businesses in Durban, South Africa. Entries include: Contact information and maps.

Braby's Mpumalanga Business Directory. A.C. Braby (Pty) Ltd. • Annual. $75. Covers: Businesses in South Africa's Lowveld region. Entries include: Contact information.

Braby's Pretoria Business Directory. A.C. Braby (Pty) Ltd. • Covers: Businesses in Pretoria, South Africa. Entries include: Contact information and maps.

Braby's SADC Directory. A.C. Braby (Pty) Ltd. • Annual. $420 2 volume set. Covers: about 875,000 businesses in South Africa, Angola, Botswana, Lesotho, Malawi, Mauritius, Mozambique, Namibia, Swaziland, Tanzania, Zambia, Zimbabwe. Also includes foreign firms represented in South Africa and South African firms represented outside South Africa. Entries include: Company name, address, phone, telex, other details.

Brazil Industrial and Business Directory. International Business Publications, USA. • Annual. $99.95 Individuals hardcopy. Covers: Strategic industrial, investment and business contacts for conducting export-import and investment activity in the country.

Brookline Business Directory. Brookline Chamber of Commerce. • Covers: Approximately 700 businesses in Brookline, Massachusetts; 30 area restaurants; schools, neighborhood associations, and other community resources. Entries include: For businesses and institutions--Company or organization name, address, phone. For restaurants--Name, address, phone, hours of operation, type of cuisine, credit cards accepted, etc.

Burkina Faso Business Directory. Business Guide. • $150 download. Covers: 3,600 business listings including wholesalers, importers, retailers, business houses, and agents in Burkina Faso.

Burundi Business Directory. Business Guide. • $150 download. Covers: 2,300 business listings including wholesalers, importers, retailers, and business houses in Burundi.

BUSINESS. BUSINESS Datenbanken GmbH. • Monthly. Database covers: About 35,000 manufacturers, importers and exporters, research establishments, chambers of commerce, trade promotion agencies, banks and investment companies offering or seeking business opportunities worldwide. Database includes: Name of company, address, type of opportunity or business, product and country codes.

Business. Georgetown Chamber of Commerce.

Business. Palm City Chamber of Commerce. • Monthly.

Business and Community Directory. Waterville Area Chamber of Commerce. • Quarterly.

Business and Financial News Media. Larriston Communications. • Annual. $99 book. Covers: over 300 daily newspapers with at least 50,000 in circulation and a business or finance correspondent; television stations and all-news radio stations in the largest 40 markets; periodicals of general or business and finance interest; syndicated business and financial columnists and newswriters; news and wire services; and free-lance writers whose specialties include business and financial topics. Entries include: Outlet name, address, phone, names and titles of contacts who cover business, finance, or economic news; news services used; circulation or audience figures.

Business and Industry Directory. Lebanon Area Chamber of Commerce. • Periodic.

Business and Industry Directory. Asheville Area Chamber of Commerce. • Periodic. $40 Members online.

Business and Information Directory. Buena Vista Area Chamber of Commerce. • Annual. Covers business in Buena Vista, CO.

Business & Legal CD-ROMs in Print. Mecklermedia Corp. • Annual. $55. Covers: Approximately 600 business and legal CD-ROMs. Entries include: Title, producer name, address, phone.

Business and Professional Directory. Cedar Rapids Metro Economic Alliance. • Annual. $30 for nonmembers.

Business and Professional Organizations Directory. Nashville Area Chamber of Commerce. • $25 Members. Covers 300 business and professional organizations in 10-county Nashville Metropolitan area.

Business and the Environment: A Resource Guide. Island Press-Center For Resource Economics. • Publication includes: List of approximately 185 business and environmental educators working to intergrate environmental issues into management research, education, and practices. Entries include: Name, address, phone, affiliation, publications, courses taught, research activity, education, employment.

Business Atlanta--Hotel and Meeting Services Guide Issue. Primedia Business. • Annual. $6.50 postpaid. Covers over 150 hotels in and around the metropolitan Atlanta area, and nearly 200 Atlanta companies providing convention services.

Business Consultants Directory. InfoGroup Inc. • Annual. Number of listings: 12,750 (U.S. edition); 1,667 (Canadian edition). Entries include: Company or individual name, address, and phone (including area code), size of advertisement, year first in "Yellow Pages," name of owner or manager, number of employees. Compiled from telephone company "Yellow Pages," nationwide.

Business Council of Fairfield County--Fairfield County Business Directory. Business Council of Fairfield County. • Covers: Approximately 2,100 non-retail companies and service firms in Fairfield County, Connecticut. Entries include: Company name, address, phone, fax, names & titles of key employees, website, company description, number of employees, annual sales, Standard Industrial Classification (SIC) code code(s).

Business Database Finder. The Information Advisor. • Annual. $99. Covers: Business databases and online hosts. Database includes: Comparative charts/tables showing features and costs of databases. Entries include: Name of database, description of product/service.

Business Directory. Millbrae Chamber of Commerce. • Annual.

Business Directory. Anchor Point Chamber of Commerce. • Periodic. $100 for nonmembers.

Business Directory. Chico Chamber of Commerce. • Annual.

Business Directory and Community Guide. Brea Chamber of Commerce. • Annual.

Business Directory and Community Profile. Renton Chamber of Commerce. • Annual.

Business Directory & Community Profile. Southwest King County Chamber of Commerce. • Annual.

Business Directory of South India: Andhra Pradesh, Karnataka, Kerala, Tamil Nadu. NIIR Project Consultancy Services. • $200 Individuals CD-ROM. Covers: 31,000 South India companies. Entries include: Contact person, profile, address, city, pin, state, phone, fax, e-mail (wherever available) and website (wherever available).

Business Directory of the Parry Sound Area. Parry Sound Area Chamber of Commerce. • Covers businesses in Parry Sound, Ontario, Canada. Entries include contact details.

Business Finland. Helsinki Media. • Annual. Publication includes: Lists of 250 major exporters and the 50 largest business groups in Finland. Principal content of publication is information on Finnish business and economic issues. Entries include: Company or organization name, address, phone, name and title of contact, number of employees, financial data, description, Standard Industrial Classification (SIC) code.

Business Hellas. Trade Publishing Resources. • Provides information on Greek companies covering all sectors of business and economy, manufacturing, and trade services.

Business History Conference--Membership Directory. Business History Conference. • Quadrennial. $25. Lists 500 Business History Conference members.

Business in the Arab World. National United States-Arab Chamber of Commerce. • $2 /profile. Contains series of business profiles with regulations, procedures, and contacts for each Arab country.

Business Information Desk Reference: Where to Find Answers to Business Questions. Macmillan Creative Services. • $20 paper. Covers: Approximately 1,000 print materials, online databases, federal agencies, private organizations and other information sources covering 24 business areas.

The Business Information Report. Dun & Bradstreet Inc. • Continuous. Database covers: More than 9 million public and private U.S. Companies. Database includes: Company name, address, history, financial and sales data, number of employees, selling terms, products/services.

Business Information Sources. Hoover's Inc. • $39. 95. Covers: Sources of business information, including books, periodicals, CD-ROMs, and online databases.

Business Phone Directory. Quincy Valley Chamber of Commerce. • Annual.

Business Referral. Palm Springs Chamber of Commerce. • Annual. Covers businesses in the Palm Springs, CA area.

Business Resource Directory. Plano Chamber of Commerce. • Annual. Contains directory of all members listed by alpha and category.

Business Resource Directory. Escondido Chamber of Commerce. • Annual.

Business Services Directory. German American Chamber of Commerce. • $10. Covers: Member firms which provide business, engineering, research, accounting, technical, marketing, and personnel management consulting services. Entries include: Company name, address, phone, fax, contact, number of employees, geographical location, foreign language capabilities, activities, history.

The Businessman's Guide to Southern Africa. Safto. • Covers: Travel information for countries in South Africa, including, Botswana, Lesotho, Malawi, Mozambique, Namibia, South Africa, Swaziland, Zambia, and Zimbabwe. Entries include: Country name, climate, geography, industries and trade, finance, economy, excise and customs duties.

Buyers Directory of the Former Soviet Union: Medical Equipment & Pharmaceutical Products. Flegon Press. • $55. Covers: Health authorities and other medical organizations of the former Soviet Union responsible for medical supplies in health-care institutions. Entries include: Name, address, phone.

Cabell's Directory of Publishing Opportunities in Management. Cabell Publishing Inc. • Irregular. $244.95 Individuals. Covers: Over 1,180 scholarly periodicals in management. Entries include: Publication name, address, subject interests, editorial guidelines and style, submission procedures, audience and circulation of the publication, and reviewer acceptance rate data.

California Business Register. Harris InfoSource. • Annual. $355 Individuals print. Profiles 56,750 top manufacturers, wholesalers, high-tech, and software companies in the state and lists the names and titles of more than 135,000 CEOs, owners, and key executives. Ninety-two percent of the companies are privately held. The listings include company name and address; telephone, fax, and toll-free numbers; Web site email addresses; number of employees; annual sales; products and services; SIC codes; export/ import indicators; and primary bank.

Camara de Comercio Luso-Britanica Directory. British-Portuguese Chamber of Commerce. • Annual. $30 Nonmembers. Covers: Portuguese and United Kingdom economic, financial, and trade matters. Entries include: Organization name, address, phone, fax.

Cambodia Investment & Business Guide. International Business Publications, USA. • $99.95 Individuals hardcopy. Covers: Information on economy, business, export-import and investment climate, regulations and industrial development, banking, government, and opportunities. Entries include: Important business contacts and business travel.

Cameroon Business Directory. Business Guide. • $150 download. Covers: 4,300 business listings including wholesalers, importers, retailers, business houses, and agents in Cameroon.

Cameroon Industrial and Business Directory. International Business Publications, USA. • $99.95 Individuals hardcover. Covers: Strategic and practical economic and business information. Entries include: Business contacts for conducting business activity in the country.

Canada Golden Key Directory. International Institute of Trade Relation Promotion, Trade Information Centre of Iran. • £60 Individuals. Covers: 8,000 companies in Canada. Entries include: Company name, address, telephone, fax, e-mail, products, services, Managing Director, and business activities.

Canada Government and Business Contacts Handbook. International Business Publications, USA. • $99.95 Individuals hardcopy. E-book and CD-ROM. Covers: Strategic government and business information, export-import activity in the country, investment, business contacts and regulations.

Canada Industrial and Business Directory. International Business Publications, USA. • Annual. $99.95 Individuals hardcopy. Covers: Detailed information on investment, export-import business opportunities, foreign economic assistance projects, government and business contacts.

Canadian Aboriginal Business and Communities Directory: British Columbia. Indiana Marketing. • C$74.95 Individuals plus $12.95 for shipping and handling. Aboriginal companies and organizations in British Columbia, Canada.

Careers in Focus--Business. InfoBase Holdings Inc. • $35 Individuals hardcover. Covers: An overview of business, followed by a selection of jobs profiled in detail, including the nature of the job, earnings, prospects for employment, what kind of training and skills it requires, and sources for further information.

Careers in Focus--Business Managers. InfoBase Holdings Inc. • $35 Individuals hardcover. Covers: An overview of business managers, followed by a selection of jobs profiled in detail, including the nature of the job, earnings, prospects for employment, what kind of training and skills it requires, and sources for further information. Database includes: Black and white photographs.

Caribbean Basin Investment and Business Guide. International Business Publications, USA. • $99.95 Individuals hardcopy, e-book, CD-ROM. Covers: Strategic and basic business information, export-import activity, regulations and industrial development, banking, government, and opportunities. Entries include: Important business contacts and business travel.

Cary Chamber of Commerce Member Directory. Cary Chamber of Commerce. • Covers chamber member businesses employing more than 100 people. Entries include company name, address, phone, fax, website, headquarters location, description of business.

Chad Business Directory. Business Guide. • $150 download. Covers: 3,600 business listings including wholesalers, importers, retailers, business houses, and agents in Chad.

Chamber of Commerce of the Bellmores Business and Professional Directory. Chamber of Commerce of the Bellmores. • Covers: All current members.

Chamber South Business Directory. Image Factory. • Covers: about 4,400 member businesses, organizations, and other community resources in South Dade County, Florida. Entries include: Company name, address, phone, contact name and fax.

Chile Industrial and Business Directory. International Business Publications, USA. • Annual. $99.95 Individuals hardcopy, e-book, CD-ROM. Covers: Strategic industrial, investment and business contacts for conducting export-import and investment activity in the country.

Chile Investment and Business Guide. International Business Publications, USA. • $99.95 Individuals hardcopy, e-book, CD-ROM. Covers: Strategic information on economy, export-import, business and investment climate, regulations and industrial development, banking, and government. Entries include: Important business contacts and business travel.

The China Commercial Relations Directory. American Chamber of Commerce in Hong Kong. • Biennial. $215 Nonmembers. Covers: Approximately 230 top China trade and service companies in Hong Kong; 115 companies in the PRC. Entries include: Addresses, names and titles of key personnel.

China Investment and Business Guide. International Business Publications, USA. • $99.95 Individuals hardcopy, e-book, CD-ROM. Covers: Basic information on economy, export-import and investment climate, regulations, industrial development, opportunities, banking, and government. Entries include: Important business contacts and business travel.

China Investment Atlas. American Chamber of Commerce in Hong Kong. • $622 Nonmembers. Covers: 600 of China's leading listed companies. Database includes: Charts.

Chugiak-Eagle River Business & Service Directory. Chugiak-Eagle River Chamber of Commerce.

Cincinnati U.S.A. Business Connections Directory. Greater Cincinnati Chamber of Commerce. • Annual.

CLA Business Directory. Country Land and Business Association. • Covers: 250 business organizations, owners of land, and properties in rural England and Wales. Entries include: Company name, address, contact information, and e-mail.

Colombia Government and Business Contacts Handbook. International Business Publications, USA. • $99.95 Individuals hardcopy. E-book and CD-ROM. Covers: Strategic government and business information, export-import activity in the country, investment, business contacts and regulations.

Colombia Investment and Business Guide. International Business Publications, USA. • $99.95 Individuals hardcopy, e-book, CD-ROM. Covers: Information on economy, export-import and investment climate, regulations and industrial development, banking, and government. Entries include: Important business contacts and business travel.

Colorado Investment and Business Guide. International Business Publications, USA. • $99.95 Individuals hardcopy, e-book, CD-ROM. Covers: State economy, business, investment and export-import opportunities, government structure, mineral resources, technology, and government. Entries include: Political and business contacts.

Colstrip Chamber of Commerce--Business Directory. Colstrip Chamber of Commerce. • Covers businesses in Colstrip, Montana.

Commerce Directory of Costa Rica. Mercadeo Profesional, S.A. • Annual. Covers: Member businesses and non-members of Chamber of Commerce of Costa Rica.

Community Business Directory. Bellbrook - Sugarcreek Area Chamber of Commerce. • Annual.

Community Guide & Business Directory. Southern Berkshire Chamber of Commerce. • Contains directory of members and community guide/relocation informational publication.

Congo Business Directory. Business Guide. • $150 download. Covers: 1,600 business listings including wholesalers, importers, retailers, business houses, and agents in Congo.

Connecticut Investment and Business Guide. International Business Publications, USA. • $99.95 Individuals. Covers: Strategic and business information, contacts, regulations and more.

Contra Costa County Business Directory. Rich's Business Directories Inc. • $199 Individuals online. Entries include: Company name, address, phone, fax, year established, branch or headquarters, SIC code, and product type.

Cordele-Crisp Chamber of Commerce--Business Directory. Cordele-Crisp Chamber of Commerce. • Annual. Covers businesses and firms in Crisp County.

Costa Rica Investment and Business Guide. International Business Publications, USA. • $99.95 Individuals hardcopy, e-book, CD-ROM. Covers: Strategic and business information, business contacts, and business travel. Entries include: Basic information on economy, business, export-import and investment climate, opportunities, and regulations.

Cote d'Ivoire Investment and Business Guide. International Business Publications, USA. • $99.95 Individuals hardcopy, e-book, CD-ROM. Covers: Basic information on economy, export-import and investment climate, regulations and industrial development, banking, and government. Entries include: Important business contacts and business travel.

Crawley Business Guide and Directory. Crawley Borough Council. • Covers businesses in Crawley, United Kingdom.

Croatia Investment and Business Guide. International Business Publications, USA. • $99.95 Individuals hardcopy, e-book, CD-ROM. Covers: Strategic business information, export-import activity, regulations and industrial development, banking, government, and opportunities. Entries include: Important business contacts and business travel.

Croner's A-Z of Business Information Sources. Wolters Kluwer Ltd. • Annual. $71.50 includes first year's updates & shipping. Covers: Organizations, publications, and other sources of business information in the United Kingdom from abrasives to zinc and the aerospace industry to wire products. Entries include: Name, address, phone, telex, contact name, brief description.

Cross-Reference Christian Business Directory. Cross-Reference Christian Business Directory. • Annual. Covers christ-centered businesses.

CSR Professional Services Directory. Dunstan Publishing. • $65 Individuals. Covers: 675 service providers including consultants, academic institutions, rating agencies, ethical auditors, training providers, and research organizations. Entries include: Contact information and services they provide.

Cuba Investment and Business Guide. International Business Publications, USA. • $99.95 Individuals hardcopy, e-book, CD-ROM. Covers: Strategic and business information, contacts, regulations and more.

Czech Republic Business Services Providers Leads. Business Information Agency Inc. PlanetInform. • Monthly. $109 Individuals mailing list. Covers Czech companies and all sub-industries that provide various services to commercial businesses, establishments, and organizations, including consulting, advertising and marketing services, and facilities maintenance.

Czech Republic Government and Business Contacts Handbook: Trade, Investment & Business Development Contacts. International Business Publications, USA. • Annual. $99.95 Individuals hardcopy, E-book and CD-ROM. Covers: Strategic government and business information, export-import activity in the country, investment, business contacts and regulations.

D & B Business Register: Edinburgh. Dun & Bradstreet (UK) Ltd. • Local businesses in Edinburgh, Scotland including commercial and manufacturing companies, public and social sector services, shops and retail outlets, pubs, restaurants, entertainment outlets, schools, and education facilities.

D & B Business Register: London - Western Central, Eastern Central, East, North. Dun & Bradstreet (UK) Ltd. • £270 Individuals. Local businesses in Western Central, Eastern Central, East, and North London including commercial and manufacturing companies, public and social sector services, shops and retail outlets, pubs, restaurants, entertainment outlets, schools, and education facilities.

D & B Business Register: North of Scotland. Dun & Bradstreet (UK) Ltd. • £270 Individuals. Local businesses in North of Scotland including commercial and manufacturing companies, public and social sector services, shops and retail outlets, pubs, restaurants, entertainment outlets, schools, and education facilities.

D & B Business Register: South of Scotland. Dun & Bradstreet (UK) Ltd. • £270 Individuals. Local businesses in South of Scotland including commercial and manufacturing companies, public and social sector services, shops and retail outlets, pubs, restaurants, entertainment outlets, schools, and education facilities.

D & B-Dun's Market Identifiers. Dun & Bradstreet Inc. • Quarterly. Covers 7.5 million public and private companies with at least five employees or $1 million in sales.

Dalton's Baltimore/Washington Metropolitan Directory of Business/Industry. Dalton Directory. • Covers: over 8,500 companies in the Baltimore and Washington, D.C. metropolitan area, including manufacturers, law firms, hospitals, hotels, schools and colleges, accounting firms, etc. Entries include: Company name, address, phone, fax, names and titles of key personnel, number of employees, Standard Industrial Classification (SIC) code, product/service.

Dana Point Official Visitors Guide & Business Directory. Dana Point Chamber of Commerce. • Covers businesses in Dana Point, California.

Data Sources for Business and Market Analysis. Hoover's Inc. • $54.95. Covers: Sources of business information from providers including the federal government, regional and local governments, foreign sources, universities, research centers, and professional and trade associations.

Database of World Wide General Traders. NIIR Project Consultancy Services. • $200 Individuals CD-ROM. Covers: Worldwide general traders (exporters and importers). Entries include: Company name, postal address, city, state, pin code, phone, fax and email (2,100,000+).

Decatur Business Association--Membership Directory. Decatur Business Association. • Covers businesses, professionals, financial institutions, art groups, associated agencies and organizations, and private individuals engaged in doing business in Decatur.

Decatur Chamber of Commerce Business Directory. Greater Decatur Chamber of Commerce. • Covers chamber members. Entries include name, address, phone.

Denmark Industrial and Business Directory. International Business Publications, USA. • Annual. $99.95 Individuals hardcopy, e-book, CD-ROM. Covers: Detailed information on investment, export-import business opportunities, foreign economic assistance projects, government and business contacts.

Denmark Investment and Business Guide. International Business Publications, USA. • $99.95 Individuals hardcopy, e-book, CD-ROM. Covers: Basic information on economy, export-import and investment climate, regulations and industrial development, banking, and government. Entries include: Important business contacts and business travel.

Dennis Business Directory and Visitor Guide. Dennis Chamber of Commerce. • Publication includes: List of about 250 member businesses in the Dennis, Massachusetts, area; list of 40 area accessories. Entries include: For businesses--Company name, address, phone. For accommodations--Hotel or inn name, address, phone, number of rooms, credit cards accepted, price range, operating season, whether handicapped access and other facilities are available. Principal content of publication is suggested routes for touring the area, descriptions of nearby attractions, etc.

Developing Business in Eastern Europe. Intervisual Advertising Ltd. • Monthly. Covers: Eastern European industries. Entries include: Company name, address, phone, fax, geographical area served, subsidiary and branch names and locations, description of product/services provided.

DIALOG Business Connection. The Dialog Corp. • Continuous. Database covers: 10,000,000 private and public companies in the United States; over 1,000,000 companies in Canada and Europe. Database includes: Company name, address, phone, corporate affiliations, key officers, names of directors, products or services, revenue, sales volume, market share, financial information, number of employees, merger activities, new equipment or facility purchases. This online service provides access to 25 databases already available on DIALOG as individual files, including "D&B--Dun's Market Identifiers," "D&B--Dun's Financial Records," "Disclosure," "Media General Databank," and "BusinessWire." The database provides the ability to conduct corporate intelligence, financial screening, and sales prospecting; to locate information on products and markets; to gain access to the latest news; and to set up an electronic clipping service.

Directories in Print. Cengage Learning Inc. • Annual. $1,009 Individuals. Provides profiles of more than 17,000 directories published worldwide. eBook also available.

Directory of Business Information. John Wiley and Sons Inc. Technical Insights. • $290 Individuals. Covers: Over 10,000 sources of business information, including publications, associations, companies, government offices, and libraries.

The Directory of Business Information Resources.

Grey House Publishing. • Annual. $195 Libraries Softcover. Provides contact names as well as editorial and advertising personnel, phone and fax numbers, description, frequency, pricing information, industry's associations, newsletters, magazines, trade shows, directories, databases and industry websites of 21,000 businesses.

Directory of Business Opportunities. Todd Publications. • Annual. $15. Covers: Hundreds of business opportunities, new products, franchises, dealerships and investment opportunities, including import/export deals and wholesale merchandising. Entries include: Contact name, address, phone.

The Directory of Business to Business Catalogs. Grey House Publishing. • Annual. $450 Libraries softcover. More than 5,000 suppliers of business products, including computers, laboratory supplies, office products, office design, marketing resources, safety equipment, landscaping firms, maintenance supplies, building construction, and others.

Directory of Chartered Accountants in Business. Institute of Chartered Accountants in Australia. • Annual. $35. Covers business members in Australia and overseas.

Directory of International Chambers of Commerce in the World. EXIM Infotek Private Ltd. • $55 Individuals. Covers: 1,000 international chambers of commerce. Entries include: Company name, postal address, telephone, fax, e-mail, website, contact person, designation, and product details.

Djibouti Business Directory. Business Guide. • $150 Individuals Soft copy. Covers: 1,500 business listings including wholesalers, importers, retailers, business houses, and agents in Djibouti.

Doing Business in Beijing. China Knowledge Press. • $49.95 Individuals. Covers: Information on Beijing's vital economic statistics, trends, business opportunities, and many more. Entries include: Contact information of government departments, embassies, courier services, executive search firms, and banks.

Doing Business in Emerging Europe. Palgrave Macmillan. • £110 Individuals Hardback. Publication includes: Additional details about conducting business in each country featured. Entries include: Name, address, phone, fax, and URL. Principal content of publication is practical information about doing business in twelve countries in eastern Europe: Belarus, Croatia, the Czech Republic, Estonia, Hungary, Latvia, Lithuania, Poland, Slovakia, Slovenia, Turkey, and Ukraine.

Doing Business in Memphis. Doing Business in Memphis. • Covers: Over 10,000 Memphis, Tennessee companies, and 25,000 contact names. Entries include: Company name, address, phone, fax, toll-free number, Standard Industrial Classification (SIC) code, names and titles of key personnel, number of employees, descriptions of product/service, product/service provided, e-mail addresses, website, square footage.

Doing Business in Memphis: A Directory of Business and Industry. Doing Business in Memphis. • Biennial. $199.95 plus $18.50 tax and $6 shipping. Over 10,000 Memphis, Tennessee companies, and 25,000 contact names.

Doing Business in Shanghai. China Knowledge Press. • $49.95 Individuals. Covers: Information on Shanghai's vital economic statistics, trends, business opportunities, and many more. Entries include: Contact information of service-related organizations and government bodies, trade fairs, history, geography, and political system.

Doing Business in Today's Hong Kong. American Chamber of Commerce in Hong Kong. • Publication includes: In an appendix lists of business organizations in Hong Kong, including quality and standards organizations, government agencies, chambers of commerce, and industry-specific associations. Entries include: Organization name, address, phone, fax, telex. Principal content of publication is information on investment, business, sales and manufacturing trade, real estate, and the electronics industry in Hong Kong.

Doing Business with China. Kogan Page US. • Publication includes: List of helpful business contacts in China. Entries include: Name, address, phone, fax. Principal content of publication is extensive general and business information about China.

Dominica Investment and Business Guide. International Business Publications, USA. • $99.95 Individuals hardcopy, e-book, CD-ROM. Covers: Strategic information on economy, business, export-import and investment climate, regulations and industrial development, banking, government, and opportunities. Entries include: Important business contacts and business travel.

Dominican Republic Industrial and Business Directory. International Business Publications, USA. • Annual. $99.95 Individuals hardcopy, e-book, CD-ROM. Covers: Strategic industrial, investment and business contacts for conducting export-import and investment activity in the country. Contains strategic practical economic and business information.

Dubai Industrial and Business Directory. International Business Publications, USA. • $99.95 Individuals hardcopy, e-book, CD-ROM. Covers: Strategic investment and business contacts for conducting export-import activity in the country. Entries include: Strategic economic and business information.

Dubai Investment and Business Guide. International Business Publications, USA. • Annual. $99.95 Individuals hardcopy, e-book, CD-ROM. Covers: Detailed information on investment, business opportunities, foreign economic assistance projects, government and business contacts and more. An ultimate guide for starting and conducting a successful business in the country.

Dun & Bradstreet State Sales Guide. Dun & Bradstreet Inc. • Quarterly. $69 Available only to Dun & Bradstreet Credit Services customers. Covers: all businesses in each state that are included in Dun & Bradstreet's national "Reference Book of American Business." A separate "State Sales Guide" is published for each state and the District of Columbia. Entries include: Company name, phone, D&B credit rating, branches, primary Standard Industrial Classification (SIC) code, year established; indicators note new businesses and those with ratings changes.

Dun's Asia Pacific Key Business Enterprises. Dun & Bradstreet Inc. • Annual. Covers 30,000 leading companies in 14 Pacific Rim countries whose annual sales are $10 million and who have 500 or more employees.

Dun's Business Update. Dun & Bradstreet Inc. • Biweekly. Database covers: more than 600,000 business establishments in the U.S. Database includes: Company name, address, phone, line of business, chief executive officer, number of employees, corporation affiliation, company status, sales.

DunsPrint Worldwide. Dun & Bradstreet Inc. • Continuous. Database covers: Approximately 16 million companies worldwide. Database includes: Company name, address, phone, legal structure, products and services, SIC code, number of employees, branch offices, officer name, parent and subsidiary companies, company history, operation summary, legal suits against company, financial data, stock issues, projected sales, payment history, DUNS number.

DunsScope. Dun & Bradstreet France S.A. • Daily. Database covers: Approximately 2 million French businesses and 18 million businesses in other countries. Database includes: Company name, address, phone, legal structure, products/services, SIC code, number of employees, officer name and title, parent and subsidiary companies, branch offices, company history, operations summary, legal suits against company, financial data, stock issues and mergers, dividends, review of payment history, credit rating, company's bank.

East European Business Handbook. Euromonitor International Business Reference Div. • $190. Publication includes: List of sources of information on doing business in eastern Europe. Principal content of publication is a guide in identifying market opportunities in eastern Europe.

EC-EDI Solution Provider Directory. Vantage Point & Associates Inc. • Covers: 300 EC/EDI vendors serving business to business (B2B) and healthcare industries.

Ecuador Investment and Business Guide. International Business Publications, USA. • $99.95 Individuals hardcopy, e-book, CD-ROM. Covers: Strategic information on economy, business, export-import and investment climate, regulations and industrial development, banking, government, and opportunities. Entries include: Important business contacts and business travel.

Edmonds Chamber of Commerce Preferred Business Directory. Greater Edmonds Chamber of Commerce. • Annual. Covers member businesses in Edmonds, Washington. Entries include contact details.

Egypt Business Directory. Business Guide. • $150 Individuals Soft copy. Covers: 65,000 business listings including wholesalers, importers, retailers, business houses, and agents in Egypt.

Egypt Golden Key Directory. International Institute of Trade Relation Promotion, Trade Information Centre of Iran. • £100 Individuals. Covers: 51,901 companies in Egypt. Entries include: Company name, address, telephone, fax, products, services, managing director, and business activities.

Egypt Industrial and Business Directory. International Business Publications, USA. • Annual. $99.95 Individuals paperback, e-book, CD-ROM. Covers: Strategic industrial, investment and business contacts for conducting export-import and investment activity in the country.

Egypt Investment and Business Guide. International Business Publications, USA. • $99.95 Individuals hardcover, e-book, CD-ROM. Covers: Strategic and business information, contacts, regulations and more.

850 Key Decision Makers of Listed Companies in Hong Kong. Asian Market Information & Analysis Centre. • Covers: 850 businesses with over 50 employees in Hong Kong. Entries include: Company name, Website, contact address, phone, fax, e-mail, contact person, and job title.

El Salvador Investment and Business Guide. International Business Publications, USA. • $99.95 Individuals hardcover, e-book, CD-ROM. Covers: Basic information on economy, export-import and investment climate, regulations and industrial development, banking, and government. Entries include: Important business contacts and business travel.

Encyclopedia of Business Information Sources. Cengage Learning Inc. • Annual. $626 Individuals. Contains bibliographic information on more than 35,000 live, print, and electronic sources of information covering more than 1,100 subjects of interest to business personnel. Includes abstracts and indexes, almanacs and yearbooks, bibliographies, online databases, research centers and institutes, and more. Available as eBook.

Eritrea Investment and Business Guide. International Business Publications, USA. • $99.95 Individuals hardcopy, e-book, CD-ROM. Covers:

Strategic business information, export-import activity, regulations and industrial development, banking, government, and opportunities. Entries include: Guides for conducting investment and business contacts.

Estonia Government and Business Contacts Handbook. International Business Publications, USA. • $99.95 Individuals hardcopy, E-book and CD-ROM. Covers: Strategic government and business information, export-import activity in the country, investment, business contacts and regulations.

Estonia Industrial and Business Directory. International Business Publications, USA. • Annual. $99.95 Individuals paperback, e-book, CD-ROM. Covers: Strategic industrial, investment and business contacts for conducting export-import and investment activity in the country. Contains strategic practical economic and business information.

Ethiopia Business Directory. Business Guide. • $150 Individuals Soft copy. Covers: 9,000 business listings including wholesalers, importers, retailers, business houses, and agents in Ethiopia.

European Business Association--Membership Directory. European Business Association. • Annual. Features profiles of member businesses. Entries include: Company contact information.

European Directory of Business Information Libraries. Euromonitor International Business Reference Div. • Irregular. $650. Covers: More than 2,000 European business libraries and services. Entries include: location, accessibility, fees, stock, and subject area.

Fair Oaks Business Directory. Fair Oaks Chamber of Commerce. • Annual.

Fairfax County Business Database. Fairfax County Economic Development Authority. • Description: Database cover approximately 7,000 Fairfax County-located businesses, including high-tech firms, financial and legal firms, retail, and personal services. Government agencies are not included. Entries include: Company name, address, phone, fax, e-mail (if available), name and title of contact; number of employees, occupied space in square feet, and geographical submarket of county. Formerly available in print edition; latest edition 1990.

FCCIA Directory. Union des Chambers de Commerce et d'Industrie Francaises a l'Etranger. • $45 Individuals available in French version only. Covers: 107 Chambers of Commerce and industry in Europe, Africa, Middle East, North America, South America, Asia, and Oceania. Entries include: Contact information and name of staff in 77 countries.

Financing Opportunities for New Hampshire-Based Businesses. Office of Economic Initiatives. • Covers: sources of financial assistance for businesses in New Hampshire, including federal, state, and local government agencies, nonprofit organizations, and venture capital firms. Entries include: Name, address, phone, description of activities.

Find A Christian Business. Initiate Media Ltd. • Annual. $29.95 Individuals. Covers: Service providers and businesses owned and managed by Christians in New Zealand.

Finland Government and Business Contacts Handbook. International Business Publications, USA. • $99.95 Individuals. Covers: Strategic government and business information, export-import activity in the country, investment, business contacts and regulations.

Florida's Gold Coast Business & Employer's Directory: Palm Beach, Ft. Lauderdale, Miami. Silver Reede Services. • Covers: Approximately 1,000 manufacturers, banks, hospitals, retailers, resorts, real estate development firms, and other corporate organizations employing 20 or more people in the metropolitan Palm Beach, Ft. Lauderdale, and Miami, Florida areas. Entries include: Company or organization name, address, phone, name and title of contact, number of employees, description of products, services, or projects, and Standard Industrial Classification (SIC) code (where appropriate).

Florida's Gulf Coast Business and Employers Directory: Tampa, Clearwater, St. Petersburg. Silver Reede Services. • Covers: manufacturers, banks, hospitals, retailers, resorts, real estate development firms, and other corporate organizations employing 20 or more people, in the Tampa/Clearwater/St. Petersburg, Florida area. Entries include: Company or organization name, address, phone, name and title of contact, number of employees, description of products, services, or projects, Standard Industrial Classification (SIC) code (where appropriate).

France Business Directory, Database. NIIR Project Consultancy Services. • $100 Individuals CD-ROM. Covers: 40,000 categorized listings of French business companies. Entries include: Company name, phone, fax, email, website address, details of business/services provided.

France Government and Business Contacts Handbook. International Business Publications, USA. • $99.95 Individuals. Covers: Strategic government and business information, export-import activity in the country, investment, business contacts and regulations.

France Industrial and Business Directory. International Business Publications, USA. • Annual. $99.95 Individuals hardcopy, e-book, CD-ROM. Covers: Detailed information on investment, export-import business opportunities, foreign economic assistance projects, government and business contacts.

France Investment and Business Guide. International Business Publications, USA. • $99.95 Individuals hardcover, e-book, CD-ROM. Covers: Basic information on economy, export-import activity and investment climate, regulations and industrial development, banking, and government. Entries include: Important business contacts and business travel.

Gardena Valley Business Directory. Gardena Valley Chamber of Commerce. • Covers: About 500 member industrial, commercial, and service firms in the Gardena, California area. Entries include: Company name, address, phone, line of business, contact name.

Gardena Valley Chamber of Commerce Business Directory. Gardena Valley Chamber of Commerce. • Annual.

Gauteng Business Directory. Intratex Holdings. • Covers: Businesses in the Rand/Pretoria area. Entries include: Company name, address, phone.

General Trade Index & Business Guide. Business Foundation Company Ltd. • Annual. $135. Publication includes: More than 3,500 public and private Polish companies seeking foreign joint ventures or foreign trade opportunities. Entries include: Company name, address, phone. Principal content of publication is information on doing business and living in Poland.

Georgia Republic Business and Industrial Directory. International Business Publications, USA. • Annual. $99.95 Individuals hardcover, e-book, CD-ROM. Covers: Strategic industrial, investment and business contacts for conducting export-import and investment activity in the country.

German Business CD-ROM. Datamedia GmbH. • Description: CD-ROM. Database covers: approximately 1.8 businesses in Germany. Entries include: Company name, address, phone, fax, classification information.

Germany Government and Business Contacts Handbook. International Business Publications, USA. • $99.95 Individuals. Covers: Strategic government and business information, export-import activity in the country, investment, business contacts and regulations.

Germany Industrial and Business Directory. International Business Publications, USA. • Annual. $99.95 Individuals hardcover, e-book, CD-ROM. Covers: Strategic industrial, investment and business contacts for conducting export-import and investment activity in the country.

Grand Junction Area Chamber of Commerce--Business Directory. Grand Junction Area Chamber of Commerce. • Covers businesses in Grand Junction, Colorado.

Greater Bowie Chamber of Commerce--Business Directory. Greater Bowie Chamber of Commerce. • Annual. Covers businesses in Greater Bowie, Maryland.

Greater Calgary & Edmonton Business. Scott's Directories. • Annual. $209 Individuals CD-ROM, pinpointer. Covers: 15,400+ manufacturers, manufacturers' sales offices, wholesalers, wholesale agents, and distributors operating in Greater Calgary and Edmonton along with 28,900+ business contact names. Entries include: Company name, address, phone, fax, names and titles of key personnel, number of employees, parent companies, SIC, product, year established.

Greater Dover Chamber of Commerce Business Directory. Greater Dover Chamber of Commerce. • Covers: Member businesses in New Hampshire. Entries include: Company name, address, phone, name of contact, category of product or service.

Greater Hermiston Chamber of Commerce--Member Business Directory. Greater Hermiston Chamber of Commerce. • Covers businesses in Hermiston, Oregon.

Greater Kendall Business Association--Member Directory. Greater Kendall Business Association. • Lists business members in Miami, Florida.

Greater Madison Area Christian Business Directory. Red Letter Publishing. • Covers: Businesses, churches, organizations, and schools in Madison, Wisconsin. Entries include: Company or organization name, address, e-mail, website, contact person, and hours of operation.

Greater Omaha Area Christian Business Directory. Red Letter Publishing. • Businesses, churches, organizations, and schools in Greater Omaha Area.

Greater Seattle & Eastside Christian Business Directory. Red Letter Publishing. • Businesses, churches, organizations, and schools in Greater Seattle and Eastside, Washington.

Greater Topeka Christian Business Directory. Red Letter Publishing. • Businesses, churches, organizations, and schools in Greater Topeka, Kansas.

Greater Tucson Christian Business Directory. Red Letter Publishing. • Businesses, churches, organizations, and schools in Greater Tucson, Arizona.

Greater Vancouver Business. Scott's Directories. • Annual. $299 Individuals CD-ROM, pinpointer. Covers: 17,900+ manufacturers, manufacturers' sales offices, wholesalers, wholesale agents, and distributors operating in Vancouver, Port Coquitlam, Surrey, North Vancouver, Langley, Burnaby, Maple Ridge, Victoria and capital region along with 28,200+ business contact names. Entries include: Company name, address, phone, fax, names and titles of key personnel, number of employees, parent companies, SIC, product, year established.

Greater Windham Chamber of Commerce--Annual Business and Pleasure Guide. Sebago Lakes Region Chamber of Commerce. • Annual. Covers: Attractions for business or pleasure in Windham, Maine.

Greece Industrial and Business Directory. International Business Publications, USA. • Annual. $99.95 Individuals hardcopy, e-book, CD-ROM. Covers: Strategic industrial, investment and business contacts for conducting export-import and investment activity in the country. Contains strategic, practical economic and business information.

Greek Financial Directory. ICAP AE. • Annual. Covers: Over 20,000 companies operating in Greece; volume 1 includes manufacturing firms; volume 2 includes trading firms (representatives, importers, distributors, and exporters), foreign firms represented in Greece, and tradenames; volume 3 includes service rendering firms and firms related to the tourism industry; volume 4 includes alphabetical index of all listed firms; volume 5 includes statistics on Greek firms. Entries include: Company name, address, phone, fax, telex, year established, names and titles of key personnel, line of business, products/services, trademarks, number of employees, foreign firms represented, financial data for two prior years.

Guelph Business Directory. City of Guelph Guelph Economic Development. • $30 Individuals print version. Covers 1,100 businesses in the city of Guelph.

Guide to American Directories. Todd Publications. • Biennial. $125.00. Provides more than 11,000 listings with descriptions, prices, etc.

Guide to Business Information on Central and Eastern Europe. Taylor & Francis Ltd. • $98.95 Individuals Paperback. Covers: Twelve countries of Central and Eastern Europe. Entries include: Country overview; current developments; company name, address, phone, fax; names and titles of key personnel; industries and services; legislation; and organizations.

Guide to Business Information on Russia, the NIS, and the Baltic States. Taylor & Francis Ltd. • $104.95 Individuals Paperback. Covers: Fifteen countries of Russia, the NIS, and the Baltic States. Entries include: Current developments; company name, address, phone, fax; industries and services; legislation; and organizations.

Hampshire Business Directory. Hampshire County Council. • Covers 6,000 Hampshire-based companies and business contacts within and outside Hampshire County.

Hanover Association of Business and Chamber of Commerce--Business Directory. Hanover Association of Business and Chamber of Commerce. • Annual. List of businesses in Hanover. Also provides information for companies and families moving to Hanover county and the town of Ashland.

Havre de Grace Chamber of Commerce Directory and Business Guide. Havre de Grace Chamber of Commerce. • Annual. Covers: List of members and information on the area's history.

Headquarters USA: A Directory of Contact Information for Headquarters and Other Central Offices of Major Businesses and Organizations Nationwide. Omnigraphics Inc. • $195 Individuals Hardcover - Web price. Two volumes. Volume one is alphabetical by name of business or organization. Volume two is classified by subject. Includes more than 112,000 businesses, organizations, agencies, institutions, and "high-profile" individuals. Listings include addresses, telephone numbers, fax numbers, and toll-free numbers and Web addresses where available. Formerly *Business Phone Book USA.*

Hobart Business Directory. Hobart Chamber of Commerce. • Covers: More than 450 businesses and professionals in Hobart, Indiana; 65 clubs and organizations; schools and day care centers, local government officials and boards, churches, etc. Entries include: Company, institution, or organization name, address, phone, name of contact; government boards also include meeting days and times or office hours.

Holden's Annual Directory 1811. S&N British Data Archive Ltd. • £16.95 Individuals. Database covers: Professions, trades, and residents in London and other towns in Great Britain. Entries include: Name and address.

Hollywood Financial Directory. Hollywood Creative Directory. • Annual. $49.50. Covers: Over 600 entertainment-related companies and their corporate, financial, legal, and business affairs staff. Entries include: Name, address, phone, names and titles of key personnel, subsidiary and branch names and locations, description, company type.

Hong Kong Classified Business Telephone Directory. Hong Kong Telephone Company Ltd. • Covers: Company listings for Hong Kong businesses.

Hoover's Handbook of World Business. Dun & Bradstreet Inc. Hoover's Inc. • Annual. $225 Individuals Hardcover. Covers: Hundreds of companies headquartered outside the U.S., including many with substantial activity in the U.S.; global enterprises, businesses that dominate their respective industries, and representative companies from all major industries. Entries include: Company name, overview, history, exchange and stock symbols, fiscal year-end date, names and titles of key personnel, name of auditors, number of employees, headquarters address, phone, fax, description of where the company does business, specific products/services/brand names produced, key competitors, 10 years of key financial data.

How to Start, Run, and Stay in Business: The Nuts-and-Bolts Guide to Turning Your Business Dream into a Reality. John Wiley & Sons Inc. • $20 Individuals paperback. Covers: Every aspect of starting and running a business.

Howick, Lidgetton, Merrivale, Mpophomeni Directory. A.C. Braby (Pty) Ltd. • Annual. Covers: Businesses in Howick, Lidgetton, Merrivale, and Mpophomeni. Database includes: Maps. Entries include: Company name, address, phone, and descriptive text.

Hungary Government and Business Contacts Handbook: Trade, Investment & Business Development Contacts. International Business Publications, USA. • $99.95 Individuals hardcopy. Covers: Strategic government and business information, export-import activity in the country, investment, business contacts and regulations.

Hungary Investment and Business Guide. International Business Publications, USA. • $99.95 Individuals hardcopy, e-book, CD-ROM. Covers: Strategic and business information, contacts, regulations, etc. Entries include: Business contacts and business travel.

India Government and Business Contacts Handbook. International Business Publications, USA. • $99.95 Individuals hardcopy, e-book, CD-ROM. Covers: Strategic government and business information, export-import activity in the country, investment, business contacts and regulations.

India Investment and Business Guide. International Business Publications, USA. • $99.95 Individuals hardcopy, e-book, CD-ROM. Covers: Strategic and business information, contacts, regulations and more.

Indian Industrial & Business Register: All India Industrial & Commercial Directory. NIIR Project Consultancy Services. • $350 Individuals CD-ROM. Covers: Indian industrial and business register. Entries include: Addresses, product details, e-mail, websites, phone and fax nos.

Indonesia Industrial and Business Directory. International Business Publications, USA. • $99.95 Individuals hardcopy, e-book, CD-ROM. Covers: Strategic investment, industrial and business contacts for conducting investment and export-import activity in the country.

Industry Business. Upper Sandusky Area Chamber of Commerce. • Periodic.

Inside U.S. Business: A Concise Encyclopedia of Leading Industries. QSU Publishing. • Irregular. $65. List of largest companies and leading firms in major industries in the U.S.

Iran Business Database. Faust Information GmbH. • $539 Individuals CD-ROM. Covers 30,000 companies in Iran.

Iran Golden Key Directory. International Institute of Trade Relation Promotion, Trade Information Centre of Iran. • £100 Individuals CD version. Covers: 19,000 companies in Iran. Entries include: Company name, telephone, fax, e-mail, Managing Director, date established, number of employees, and business date.

Iran Industrial and Business Directory. International Business Publications, USA. • Annual. $99.95 Individuals hardcopy, e-book, CD-ROM. Covers: Strategic industrial, investment and business contacts for conducting export-import and investment activity in the country.

Iran Investment and Business Guide. International Business Publications, USA. • $99.95 Individuals hardcopy, e-book, CD-ROM. Covers: Basic information on economy, export-import and investment climate, regulations and industrial development, banking, and government. Entries include: Business contacts and business travel.

Iraq Industrial and Business Directory. International Business Publications, USA. • Annual. $99.95 Individuals hardcopy, e-book, CD-ROM. Covers: Strategic industrial, investment and business contacts for conducting export-import and investment activity in the country. Contains strategic practical economic and business information.

Ireland Government and Business Contacts Handbook. International Business Publications, USA. • $99.95 Individuals hardcopy, e-book, CD-ROM. Covers: Strategic government and business information, export-import activity in the country, investment, business contacts and regulations.

Ireland Industrial and Business Directory. International Business Publications, USA. • Annual. $99.95 Individuals hardcover, e-book, CD-ROM. Covers: Strategic industrial, investment and business contacts for conducting export-import and investment activity in the country. Contains strategic practical economic and business information.

Irwin Business and Investment Almanac. QSU Publishing. • Annual. $75. Publication includes: Lists of online databases and their producers; executive search firms, accounting firms, and advertising agencies. Principal content of publication is review of significant business and finance events and statistical data for the year covered. Database includes: Major and group stock market averages, reviews of major futures markets and charts for futures-traded commodities, expanded coverage of foreign business and investment activity.

Israel Business Services Providers Leads. Business Information Agency Inc. PlanetInform. • Monthly. $98 Individuals mailing list. Covers Israeli companies and all sub-industries that provide services to commercial businesses, establishments, and organizations, including consulting, advertising and marketing services, and facilities maintenance.

Italy Business Services Providers Leads. Business Information Agency Inc. PlanetInform. • Monthly. $181 Individuals mailing list. Covers Italian companies and all sub-industries that provide various services to commercial businesses, establishments, and organizations, including consulting, advertising and marketing services, and facilities maintenance.

Italy Industrial and Business Directory. International Business Publications, USA. • Annual. $99.95 Individuals hardcover, e-book, CD-ROM. Covers: Strategic industrial, investment and business contacts for conducting export-import and investment activity in the country. Contains strategic, practical economic and business information.

Italy Investment and Business Guide. International Business Publications, USA. • $99.95 Individuals hardcopy, e-book, CD-ROM. Covers: Basic information on economy, export-import and investment climate, regulations and industrial development, banking, and government. Entries include: Business contacts and business travel.

Jamaica Hills Association--Business Directory. Jamaica Hills Association. • Covers entrepreneurs, businesses, and artists in Jamaica Plain, Massachusetts.

Japan Business Directory, Database. NIIR Project Consultancy Services. • $100 Individuals CD-ROM. Covers: 12,800 categorized listings of Japanese business companies. Entries include: Company name, phone, fax, email, website address, details of business/services provided.

Japan Government and Business Contacts Handbook. International Business Publications, USA. • $99.95 Individuals hardcopy, e-book, CD-ROM. Covers: Strategic government and business information, export-import activity in the country, investment, business contacts and regulations.

Japan Industrial and Business Directory. International Business Publications, USA. • $99.95 Individuals hardcopy, e-book, CD-ROM. Covers: Customs, trade regulations and procedures.

Japan Investment and Business Guide. International Business Publications, USA. • $99.95 Individuals hardcopy, e-book, CD-ROM. Covers: Strategic information on economy, business, export-import and investment climate, regulations and industrial development, banking, government, and opportunities. Entries include: Important business contacts and business travel.

Jordan Golden Key Directory. International Institute of Trade Relation Promotion, Trade Information Centre of Iran. • £100 Individuals. Covers: 29,424 companies in Jordan. Entries include: Company name, address, telephone, fax, products, services, Managing Director, and business activities.

Katy Business Association--Directory. Katy Business Association. • List of businesses in Katy, Texas.

Kawana Waters Chamber of Commerce and Industry--Business Directory. Kawana Waters Chamber of Commerce and Industry Inc. • Annual. Covers businesses in Kawana, Queensland, Australia.

Kazakhstan Government and Business Contacts Handbook. International Business Publications, USA. • $99.95 Individuals hardcopy, e-book, CD-ROM. Covers: Strategic government and business information, export-import activity in the country, investment, business contacts and regulations.

Kearsarge Area Chamber of Commerce--Business Directory. Kearsarge Area Chamber of Commerce. • Covers businesses in Kearsarge Area, New Hampshire.

Kelly's Post Office--London Business Directory. Reed Business Information. • Covers: 96,000 London businesses, 70,000 streets with postal district name, 21,000 buildings, local and regional government offices and officials, public bodies and societies, and professional firms. Entries include: Company name, address, phone, government official name, position, title.

Kenya Business Directory. Business Guide. • $250 Individuals Soft copy. Covers: 48,000 business listings including wholesalers, importers, retailers, business houses, and agents in Kenya.

Kenya Industrial and Business Directory. International Business Publications, USA. • Annual. $99.95 Individuals hardcopy, e-book, CD-ROM. Covers: Strategic industrial, investment and business contacts for conducting export-import and investment activity in the country. Contains strategic practical economic and business information.

Kompass. AffarsData. • Quarterly. Database covers: Approximately 400,000 manufacturers and distributors of approximately 70,000 products and services in Sweden, Norway, Denmark, Germany, United Kingdom, Switzerland, Netherlands, Belgium, Luxemberg, France, Spain, Italy, and Finland. Database includes: Company name, address, phone, products and services, turnover, share capital, year of establishment, export areas, and managing director.

Korea Business Directory, Database. NIIR Project Consultancy Services. • $100 Individuals CD-ROM. Covers: 85,000 categorized listings of Korean business companies. Entries include: Company name, phone, fax, email, website address, details of business/services provided.

Korea South Government and Business Contacts Handbook: Trade, Investment & Business Development Contacts. International Business Publications, USA. • $99.95 Individuals hardcopy. Covers: Strategic government and business information, export-import activity in the country, investment, business contacts and regulations.

Kuwait Golden Key Directory. International Institute of Trade Relation Promotion, Trade Information Centre of Iran. • £100 Individuals. Covers: 22,064 companies in Kuwait. Entries include: Company name, address, telephone, fax, e-mail, products, services, Managing Director, and business activities.

Kwazulu/Natal Business Register. Intratex Holdings. • Covers: businesses in the Kwazulu/Natal area. Entries include: Company name, address, phone.

Kyrgyzstan Government and Business Contacts Handbook. International Business Publications, USA. • $99.95 Individuals hardcopy, e-book, CD-ROM. Covers: Strategic government and business information, export-import activity in the country, investment, business contacts and regulations.

Kyrgyzstan Industrial and Business Directory. International Business Publications, USA. • Annual. $99.95 Individuals hardcopy, e-book, CD-ROM. Covers: Strategic industrial, investment and business contacts for conducting export-import and investment activity in the country.

Labuan Offshore Investment & Business Guide. International Business Publications, USA. • $99.95 Individuals hardcopy, e-book, CD-ROM. Covers: Basic information on economy, export-import and investment climate, regulations and industrial development, banking, and government. Entries include: Important business contacts and business travel.

LaPorte Business Resource Guide. Greater La Porte Chamber of Commerce. • Annual. Covers businesses, professional firms, and individuals in La Porte, IN.

Las Vegas Christian Business Directory. Red Letter Publishing. • Businesses, churches, organizations, and schools in Las Vegas, Nevada.

Latin American Environmental Directory. Business Publishers Inc. • Annual. $179. Covers: Associations, corporations, embassies, consulates, legal specialists, U.S. registered foreign agents, and research centers located in Latin America involved in the environmental community. Entries include: Organization name, address, phone, fax, telex, key officers, SIC codes.

Latvia Business Services Providers Leads. Business Information Agency Inc. PlanetInform. • Monthly. $67 Individuals mailing list. Covers Latvian companies and all sub-industries that provide various services to commercial businesses, establishments, and organizations, including consulting, advertising and marketing services, and facilities maintenance.

Latvia Industrial and Business Directory. International Business Publications, USA. • Annual. $99.95 Individuals hardcopy, e-book, CD-ROM. Covers: Strategic industrial, investment and business contacts for conducting export-import and investment activity in the country.

Latvia Investment and Business Guide. International Business Publications, USA. • $99.95 Individuals hardcopy, e-book, CD-ROM. Covers: Basic information on economy, export-import and investment climate, regulations and industrial development, banking, and government. Entries include: Business contacts and business travel.

Lebanon Golden Key Directory. International Institute of Trade Relation Promotion, Trade Information Centre of Iran. • £100 Individuals. Covers: 14,209 companies in Lebanon. Entries include: Company name, address, telephone, fax, products, services, Managing Director, and business activities.

Lehigh Valley Metro Business Directory. Dalton Directory. • Covers: Approximately 5,000 companies in the Pennsylvania counties of Lehigh, Berks, Lancaster, and Northampton; includes manufacturers, banks, law firms, hospitals, schools and colleges, hotels, etc. Entries include: Company name, address, phone, fax, telex, names and titles of key personnel, number of employees, Standard Industrial Classification (SIC) code, product/service.

Libya Business Directory. Business Guide. • $150 Individuals Soft copy. Covers: 1,800 business listings including wholesalers, importers, retailers, business houses, and agents in Libya.

Liechtenstein Industrial and Business Directory. International Business Publications, USA. • Annual. $99.95 Individuals hardcover, e-book, CD-ROM. Covers: Strategic industrial, investment and business contacts for conducting export-import and investment activity in the country.

Lincoln Christian Business Directory. Red Letter Publishing. • Businesses, churches, organizations, and schools in Lincoln, Nebraska.

Lithuania Industrial and Business Directory. International Business Publications, USA. • Annual. $99.95 Individuals hardcover, e-book, CD-ROM. Covers: Strategic industrial, investment and business contacts for conducting export-import and investment activity in the country.

London Business School: A SourceGuide to European Company Information. Cengage Learning Inc. • $108. Over 1,000 business information resources in 18 European countries, including trade councils, government agencies, directories, databases, newspapers, newsletters, and other media.

Luxembourg Industrial and Business Directory. International Business Publications, USA. • Annual. $99.95 Individuals paperback, e-book, CD-ROM. Covers: Strategic industrial, investment and business contacts for conducting export-import and investment activity in the country. Contains strategic, practical economic and business information.

Macao Government and Business Contacts Handbook. International Business Publications, USA. • $99.95 Individuals hardcopy, e-book, CD-ROM. Covers: Strategic government and business information, export-import activity in the country, investment, business contacts and regulations.

Madagascar Business Directory. Business Guide. • $150 Individuals Soft copy. Covers: 14,000 business listings including wholesalers, importers, retailers, business houses, and agents in Madagascar.

The Maine Business and Professional Directory. Tower Publishing Co. • Annual. $115 Individuals.

For publishers' addresses, refer to SOURCES CITED section at the back of the book.

42,588 Maine professional and industrial firms.

Malaysia Government and Business Contacts Handbook. International Business Publications, USA. • $99.95 Individuals hardcopy, e-book, CD-ROM. Covers: Strategic government and business information, export-import activity in the country, investment, business contacts and regulations.

Malaysia Industrial and Business Directory. International Business Publications, USA. • $99.95 Individuals hardcopy, e-book, CD-ROM. Covers: Customs, trade regulations and procedures.

Mali Business Directory. Business Guide. • $150 Individuals. Covers: 2,000 business listings including wholesalers, importers, retailers, business houses, and agents in Mali.

Malibu Business and Community Directory. Malibu Chamber of Commerce. • Covers businesses and communities in Malibu, California.

Manager's Handbook: Everything You Need to Know about How Business and Management Work. Pearson Learning Group. • $24.95. Publication includes: Business directory representing key areas of management in Canada and the United States. Principal content of publication is reference guide for new and experienced managers.

Marconi's International Register. Telegraphic Cable & Radio Registrations Inc. • Annual. $150 payment with order. Covers: 45,000 firms worldwide which do business internationally. Entries include: Company name, address, phone, fax, e-mail and URL addresses, brief description of business or legal specialty, names of officers and partners.

MarketPlace. Dun and Bradstreet Sales and Marketing Solutions. • Quarterly. $850 list price. Database covers: Over 11 million U.S. businesses. Database includes: four quarterly updates of databases and software along with 1000 meter credits. Entries include: Company name, address, phone, name and title of contact, type of business, annual sales, number of employees, year founded, type of site, ownership, Standard Industrial Classification (SIC) code, DUNS number, latitude/longitude, firmographic and industry specific data.

The Massachusetts Business and Professional Directory. Tower Publishing Co. • Annual. $125 Individuals softcover. 25,000 Massachusetts professional and industrial firms with 20 or more employees.

Mauritius Industrial and Business Directory. International Business Publications, USA. • Annual. $99.95 Individuals hardcopy, e-book, CD-ROM. Covers: Strategic industrial, investment and business contacts for conducting export-import and investment activity in the country.

Membership Directory and Business Guide for Huntsville and Madison County. Chamber of Commerce of Huntsville/Madison County. • Covers 2,100 businesses in Huntsville and Madison county.

Membership Directory and Business Resource Guide. West Shore Chamber of Commerce. • Annual.

Metro Orlando International Business Directory. Greater Orlando Chamber of Commerce. • Covers: about 400 central Florida, manufacturers, distributors, services, and support organizations involved in world trade. Entries include: Company name, address, phone, fax, telex, name of contact, product, and countries where the company does business.

Metroplex Business Directory--Dallas Area. Business Marketing Source. • Covers: over 88,000 businesses in the Dallas, Texas area. Entries include: Company name, address, phone, names and titles of key personnel, number of employees, description, product/service, Standard Industrial Classification (SIC) code.

Metroplex Business Directory--Tarrant Area. Business Marketing Source. • Annual. Covers: Approximately 47,500 businesses in Tarrant Area, Texas. Entries include: Company name, address, phone, names and titles of key personnel, number of employees, description of product/service, Standard Industrial Classification (SIC) code.

Mexican Buyers Guide. Auto Care Association. • $50 Members. Covers: Approximately 450 dealers, distributors and wholesalers in Mexico interested in U.S. products. Entries include: Name, address, phone of companies, name and title of contact, names and titles of key personnel, type of business, company histories and geographical area served.

Mexico Government and Business Contacts Handbook. International Business Publications, USA. • $99.95 Individuals hardcopy, e-book, CD-ROM. Covers: Strategic government and business information, export-import activity in the country, investment, business contacts and regulations.

Mexico Investment and Business Guide. International Business Publications, USA. • $99.95 Individuals hardcopy, e-book, CD-ROM. Covers: Strategic information on economy, business, export-import and investment climate, regulations and industrial development, banking, government, and opportunities. Entries include: Important business contacts and business travel.

Mill Valley Business Directory. Mill Valley Chamber of Commerce. • Covers: Businesses, information centers, and conferences in Mill Valley, CA.

Milwaukee Christian Business Directory. Red Letter Publishing. • Businesses, churches, organizations, and schools in Milwaukee, Wisconsin.

Moldova Government and Business Contacts Handbook. International Business Publications, USA. • $99.95 Individuals hardcopy, e-book, CD-ROM. Covers: Strategic government and business information, export-import activity in the country, investment, business contacts and regulations.

Moldova Industrial and Business Directory. International Business Publications, USA. • Annual. $99.95 Individuals hardcopy, e-book, CD-ROM. Covers: Strategic industrial, investment and business contacts for conducting export-import and investment activity in the country. Contains strategic practical economic and business information.

Mongolia Industrial and Business Directory. International Business Publications, USA. • $99.95 Individuals hardcopy, e-book, CD-ROM. Covers: Strategic and practical economic and business information. Entries include: Business contacts for conducting business activity in the country.

Moorpark Chamber of Commerce--Business Directory. Moorpark Chamber of Commerce. • Annual. Business organizations in Moorpark, California.

Morocco Business Directory. Business Guide. • $250 Individuals. Covers: Over 245,000 business listings including wholesalers, importers, retailers, business houses, and agents in Morocco.

Morocco Investment and Business Guide. International Business Publications, USA. • $99.95 Individuals hardcopy, e-book, CD-ROM. Covers: Strategic information on economy, business, export-import and investment climate, opportunities, industrial development, banking and government. Entries include: Business contacts and business travel.

Moscow City Investment and Business Guide. International Business Publications, USA. • Annual. $99.95 Individuals hardcopy, e-book, CD-ROM. Covers: Strategic and business information, contacts, regulations and more. An ultimate guide for conducting investment, export-import activity in the Moscow City.

Moving a Business to Stow. Stow-Munroe Falls Chamber of Commerce.

Namibia Industrial and Business Directory. International Business Publications, USA. • Annual. $99.95 Individuals hardcopy, e-book, CD-ROM. Covers: Strategic industrial, investment and business contacts for conducting export-import and investment activity in the country. Contains strategic practical economic and business information.

Nashville Business Journal--Book of Lists. Nashville Business Journals. • $65 print only. Covers: About 700 major companies, foundations, government officials, utilities, news papers, radio and television stations, airlines, hospitals, financial institutions, shopping centers, resorts, and prominent individuals in the Nashville, Tennessee area. Entries include: Company, organization, or individual name, address, phone, names and titles of key personnel, financial data, products or services.

National Directory of Woman-Owned Business Firms. Business Research Services Inc. • Annual. $295 Individuals paperback. Covers more than 28,000 entries with up to 17 points of data about each firm. Each business listing is arranged first by SIC code and business description, then alphabetically by state, city and company name within the SIC category.

Netherlands Business Services Providers Leads. Business Information Agency Inc. PlanetInform. • Monthly. $231 Individuals mailing list. Covers Netherlands' companies and all sub-industries that provide various services to commercial businesses, establishments, and organizations, including consulting, advertising and marketing services, and facilities maintenance.

Netherlands Government and Business Contacts Handbook. International Business Publications, USA. • $99.95 Individuals hardcopy, e-book, CD-ROM. Covers: Strategic government and business information, export-import activity in the country, investment, business contacts and regulations.

Netherlands Industrial and Business Directory. International Business Publications, USA. • Annual. $99.95 Individuals hardcover, e-book, CD-ROM. Covers: Detailed information on investment, export-import business opportunities, foreign economic assistance projects, government and business contacts.

New Bern Area Guide and Business. New Bern Area Chamber of Commerce. • Annual. Covers businesses in New Bern/Craven County, NC.

New Caledonia Industrial and Business Directory. International Business Publications, USA. • Annual. $99.95 Individuals hardcopy, e-book, CD-ROM. Covers: Strategic industrial, investment and business contacts for conducting export-import and investment activity in the country. Contains strategic, practical economic and business information.

The New Hampshire Business and Professional Directory. Tower Publishing Co. • Annual. $95 Individuals plus $7 shipping fee per book. 27,409 New Hampshire professional and industrial firms.

New Zealand Government and Business Contacts Handbook. International Business Publications, USA. • $99.95 Individuals hardcopy, e-book, CD-ROM. Covers: Strategic government and business information, export-import activity in the country, investment, business contacts and regulations.

New Zealand Industrial and Business Directory. International Business Publications, USA. • Annual. $99.95 Individuals hardcopy, e-book, CD-ROM. Covers: Strategic industrial, investment and business contacts for conducting export-import and investment activity in the country.

Newcomer's Guide and Business Directory. Greater Summerville/Dorchester County Chamber of Commerce. • Annual. $20 /issue.

Nigeria Business Directory. Business Guide. • $250 Individuals. Covers: 47,500 business listings including wholesalers, importers, retailers, business houses, and agents in Nigeria.

Nigeria Industrial and Business Directory. International Business Publications, USA. • Annual. $99.95 Individuals hardcover. Covers: Strategic industrial, investment and business contacts for conducting export-import and investment activity in the country.

Nisku Business Directory. Nisku Business Association. • Annual. $30 Nonmembers book or CD. Lists companies located in Nisku Business Park and Edmonton International Airport.

Northeast Texas Buyers Guide to Minority Business. Dallas/Fort Worth Minority Business Development Council. • Annual. Covers about 730 private firms offering professional, commercial, and industrial products and services, and in which more than 50% of company ownership is held by minority group members.

Northern California Business Directory. Harris InfoSource. • $198 Members. Covers manufacturers, wholesalers and service businesses in the 45 counties north of San Luis Obispo, California. Entries include: Company profile, owners, names and titles of key personnel.

Northern California Business Directory and Buyers Guide. Harris InfoSource. • Covers: 23,540 businesses in Northern California. Entries include: Company name, address, county, phone, fax, web site address (on CD-ROM only), number of employees, names and titles of key executives, plant size, year established, parent company, annual sales, import/export information, Standard Industrial Classification (SIC) code, and product description.

Northern Colorado Christian Business Directory. Red Letter Publishing. • Businesses, churches, organizations, and schools in Northern Colorado.

Northern Kentucky Business Directory. Christian Blue Pages. • Annual. Christian-owned business enterprises in Northern Kentucky.

Northern Saskatchewan Business Directory. Economic Development Commission. • Covers businesses, services, and goods in Saskatchewan's Northern Administration District.

Northwest Manitoba Business Directory. Northwest Manitoba Business Directory. • Business directory covering businesses in Manitoba.

Novi Chamber of Commerce--Business Directory. Novi Chamber of Commerce. • Annual. Covers: Member businesses in Novi, Michigan.

Oakdale Business and Professional Association--Directory of Members. Oakdale Business and Professional Association. • List of business members in Oakdale, Minnesota.

Oman Golden Key Directory. International Institute of Trade Relation Promotion, Trade Information Centre of Iran. • £100 Individuals. Covers: 7,685 companies in Oman. Entries include: Company name, address, telephone, fax, products, services, Managing Director, and business activities.

Online Business Link. InfoGroup Inc. • Monthly. Database covers: More than 14 million United States businesses listed in "Yellow Pages" phone books nationwide, 551,000 manufacturers, and 4.3 million high-income consumers. Database includes: For businesses--Company name, address, phone, Standard Industrial Classification (SIC) code, brand and speciality information. For manufacturers--Company name, address, phone, name and title of chief officer, number of employees, sales volume, Standard Industrial Classification (SIC) code. For consumers--Name, address, phone, whether under or over 50 years of age. For company profiles--Company name, address, phone, Standard Industrial Classification (SIC) code, "Yellow Pages" category, as size, year listing first appeared in "Yellow Pages" (tracking began in 1985), franchise, brand or professional speciality. Business listings only were previously available under the title "Instant Yellow Page Service." A print version is available for each of the business categories listed in the "Yellow Pages" (use "Yellow Pages" categories to locate separate entries).

Opening a Business in Stow. Stow-Munroe Falls Chamber of Commerce.

Orange County Business and Industrial Directory. Orange County Business Council. • Number of listings: 5,000. Entries include: Company name, address, phone, names and titles of key personnel, line of business, number of employees.

Orange County, New York Business Directory and Buyer's Guide. Centers Composition. • Number of listings: 11,000. Entries include: Company name, address, phone, name and title of contact, number of employees, type of business, product or service.

Osceola County Manufacturers/Industrial Business Directory. Osceola Economic Alliance. • Annual. Covers: Information on all Osceola County, Michigan, businesses.

Owen's Worldwide Africa Business Directory. Owen's Worldtrade Ltd. • Annual. $87.50. Covers: 12,000 manufacturers, importers, exporters; and travel, finance, transport other service firms; and government agencies and associations concerned with international trade in 21 African countries: Botswana, Burundi, Cameroon, Djibouti, Ethiopia, Gabon, Ivory Coast, Kenya, Liberia, Malawi, Nigeria, Rwanda, Senegal, Seychelles, Sierra Leone, Somalia, Sudan, Tanzania, Togo, Uganda, and Zimbabwe. Database includes: For each country, detailed information covering climate, currency, language, government, business days and hours, economy customs, etc. Entries include: Company or organization name, address, phone, telex, cable address; product, service, or line of business; some listings also include name of parent company.

Panama Government and Business Contacts Handbook. International Business Publications, USA. • $99.95 Individuals hardcopy, e-book, CD-ROM. Covers: Strategic government and business information, export-import activity in the country, investment, business contacts and regulations.

Panama Industrial and Business Directory. International Business Publications, USA. • Annual. $99.95 Individuals hardcopy, e-book, CD-ROM. Covers: Strategic industrial, investment and business contacts for conducting export-import and investment activity in the country.

Panama Investment and Business Guide. International Business Publications, USA. • $99.95 Individuals hardcopy, e-book, CD-ROM. Covers: Strategic information on economy, business, export-import and investment climate, regulations and industrial development, banking, government, and opportunities. Entries include: Important business contacts and business travel.

Peru Government and Business Contacts Handbook. International Business Publications, USA. • $99.95 Individuals hardcopy, e-book, CD-ROM. Covers: Strategic government and business information, export-import activity in the country, investment, business contacts and regulations.

Peru Industrial and Business Directory. International Business Publications, USA. • Annual. $99.95 Individuals hardcopy, e-book, CD-ROM. Covers: Strategic industrial, investment and business contacts for conducting export-import and investment activity in the country. Contains strategic, practical economic and business information.

Peru Investment and Business Guide. International Business Publications, USA. • Annual. $99.95 Individuals hardcopy, e-book, CD-ROM. Covers: Strategic and business information, contacts, regulations and more. An ultimate guide for conducting investment, export-import activity in the country.

Philippine-European Business Directory. European Chamber of Commerce of the Philippines. • 2,600 PHP Nonmembers hard copy. Covers: 750 European business in the Philippines. Entries include: Contact details of each member.

Philippines Government and Business Contacts Handbook. International Business Publications, USA. • $99.95 Individuals hardcopy, e-book, CD-ROM. Covers: Strategic government and business information, export-import activity in the country, investment, business contacts and regulations.

Philippines Industrial and Business Directory. International Business Publications, USA. • Annual. $99.95 Individuals hardcopy, e-book, CD-ROM. Covers: Strategic industrial, investment and business contacts for conducting export-import and investment activity in the country.

Philippines Investment and Business Guide. International Business Publications, USA. • $99.95 Individuals hardcopy, e-book, CD-ROM. Covers: Basic information on economy, export-import and investment climate, regulations and industrial development, banking, and government. Entries include: Important business contacts and business travel.

Poland Government and Business Contacts Handbook. International Business Publications, USA. • $99.95 Individuals hardcopy, e-book, CD-ROM. Covers: Strategic government and business information, export-import activity in the country, investment, business contacts and regulations.

Poland Investment and Business Guide. International Business Publications, USA. • $99.95 Individuals hardcopy, e-book, CD-ROM. Covers: Strategic information on economy, business, export-import and investment climate, opportunities, industrial development, banking and government. Entries include: Business contacts and business travel.

Portugal Business Services Providers Leads. Business Information Agency Inc. PlanetInform. • Monthly. $113 Individuals mailing list. Covers Portuguese companies and all sub-industries that provide services to commercial businesses, establishments, and organizations, including consulting, advertising and marketing services, and facilities maintenance.

Portugal Government and Business Contacts Handbook. International Business Publications, USA. • Annual. $99.95 Individuals hardcopy, e-book, CD-ROM. Covers: Information on strategic economic, investment, export-import, and business opportunities. Contains important export-import, government, and business contacts. Ultimate directory for conducting export-import operations in the country.

Portugal Investment and Business Guide. International Business Publications, USA. • $99.95 Individuals hardcopy, e-book, CD-ROM. Covers: Strategic information on economy, business, export-import and investment climate, opportunities, industrial development, banking and government. Entries include: Business contacts and business travel.

Products and Services to China. Intervisual Advertising Ltd. • Covers: Industries in China and Hong Kong. Database includes: Product/service, name, tradename. Entries include: Company name, location, phone, geographical area served, subsidiary and branch names and locations, description of product/services.

Q Pages: WA Gay and Lesbian Business Directory. Q Pages. • Gay and Lesbian-owned businesses in Western Australia.

Qatar Golden Key Directory. International Institute of Trade Relation Promotion, Trade Information Centre of Iran. • £100 Individuals. Covers: 10,256 companies in Qatar. Entries include: Company name, address, telephone, fax, products, services, Managing Director, and business activities.

Racine/Kenosha Christian Business Directory. Red

For publishers' addresses, refer to SOURCES CITED section at the back of the book.

Letter Publishing. • Businesses, churches, organizations, and schools in Racine and Kenosha, Wisconsin.

Reference Book of Manufacturers. Dun & Bradstreet Inc. • Semiannual. Covers: over 400,000 U.S. manufacturers. Entries include: Company name, address, phone, line of business, branch offices, number of employees, year established, DUNS number, D&B credit rating.

Regional Business Directory. Business Service Div. Birmingham Area Chamber of Commerce. • Covers: Approximately 4,000 businesses that are members of the area Chamber of Commerce. Entries include: Company name, address, phone, name and title of contact.

Romania Investment and Business Guide. International Business Publications, USA. • $99.95 Individuals hardcopy, e-book, CD-ROM. Covers: Detailed information on investment, export-import business opportunities, foreign economic assistance projects, government and business contacts.

Rowlett Business Directory. Business Directories of Texas. • List of businesses in Rowlett, Texas.

Russia Industrial and Business Directory. International Business Publications, USA. • Annual. $99.95 Individuals hardcopy, e-book, CD-ROM. Covers: Strategic industrial, investment and business contacts for conducting export-import and investment activity in the country.

Russia Investment and Business Guide. International Business Publications, USA. • $99.95 Individuals hardcopy, e-book, CD-ROM. Covers: Basic information on economy, export-import and investment climate, regulations and industrial development, banking, and government. Entries include: Important business contacts and business travel.

Russian Business White & Yellow Pages. European Business Publications Inc. • Covers: More than 25,000 major business companies, industrial enterprises and banks in Moscow, St. Petersburg and all 87 provinces of Russia and Worldwide. White Pages include Russian Federal Government information and contacts. Entries include: Name, address, phone, fax, line of business and product information.

Rwanda Investment and Business Guide. International Business Publications, USA. • $99.95 Individuals hardcopy, e-book, CD-ROM. Covers: Strategic information on economy, business, export-import and investment climate, regulations and industrial development, banking, government, and opportunities. Entries include: Important business contacts and business travel.

St. Agnes Traders Business Directory. StAgnes-Traders.com. • Covers: Businesses in Cornish village including the surrounding areas of Porthtowan, Mount Hawke, Blackwater, and Mithian.

St. George Area Chamber of Commerce Business Directory. St. George Area Chamber of Commerce. • Covers businesses, attractions, and history of the St. George, Utah, area.

St. John's Board of Trade Business Directory. St. John's Board of Trade. • Annual. 900 business organizations in Newfoundland and Labrador.

St. Petersburg Business Guide. Arguments and Facts Media Ltd. • Covers: Government agencies and companies of interest to individuals and firms conducting business in St. Petersburg, Russia: includes state and local government authorities, business organizations, financial and commercial services, consulting and legal services, customs offices, communications and transport services, advertising agencies, security firms, recruitment services, training specialists, and mass media outlets. Entries include: In general, agency or company name, address, phone, fax, description.

St. Petersburg (Russia) Investment and Business Guide. International Business Publications, USA. • Annual. $99.95 Individuals hardcopy, e-book, CD-ROM. Covers: Strategic and business information, contacts, regulations and more. An ultimate guide for conducting investment, export-import activity in the country.

Salem Area Chamber of Commerce Business Directory and Resource Guide. Salem Area Chamber of Commerce. • Annual. Covers 1,250 businesses and organizations in Salem, OR.

San Diego County Business Directory. Harris InfoSource. • Annual. $115 Individuals. Covers: Approximately 24,700 manufacturers, wholesalers, and service companies in San Diego County, California. Includes names of key executives. Entries include: Company name, address, parent name/location, telephone, fax and 800 numbers, Web site address (on CD-ROM only), number of employees, year established, annual revenue, plant size, business description, Standard Industrial Classification (SIC) codes, executive names/titles, public ownership, legal structure, import/export designators, female/minority ownership, and Thomas Guide Page and Grid Number.

San Francisco Bay Area Silicon Valley International Business Directory. San Francisco Chamber of Commerce. • $45 Members. Covers international businesses based in the San Francisco Bay/Silicon Valley area. Entries include contact details, parent companies, products and services.

San Francisco County Business Directory. Rich's Business Directories Inc. • $215 Individuals. Covers: 3,911 firms in San Francisco County. Entries include: Company name, address, phone, fax, year established, branch or headquarters, SIC code, and product type.

San Marcos Chamber of Commerce Business & Relocation Directory. San Marcos Chamber of Commerce. • Annual. $5.

San Mateo County Business Directory. Rich's Business Directories Inc. • $199 Individuals online. Covers: 2,963 firms in San Mateo County. Entries include: Company name, address, phone, fax, year established, branch or headquarters, SIC code, and product type.

Sanger District Chamber of Commerce--Business Directory. Sanger District Chamber of Commerce. • Biennial. Covers 225 business organizations in Sanger, California.

Santa Clara County Business Directory. Rich's Business Directories Inc. • $219 Individuals online. Covers: 5,745 firms in Santa Clara County. Entries include: Company name, address, phone, fax, year established, branch or headquarters, SIC code, and product type.

Santa Monica Chamber of Commerce Business Profile and Membership Directory. Santa Monica Chamber of Commerce. • Annual. Covers: Member businesses in Santa Monica, California.

Saudi Arabia Golden Key Directory. International Institute of Trade Relation Promotion, Trade Information Centre of Iran. • £100 Individuals. Covers: 37,309 companies in Saudi Arabia. Entries include: Company name, address, telephone, fax, products, services, Managing Director, and business activities.

Saudi Arabia Industrial and Business Directory. International Business Publications, USA. • Annual. $99.95 Individuals hardcopy, e-book, CD-ROM. Covers: Strategic industrial, investment and business contacts for conducting export-import and investment activity in the country.

Saudi Arabia Investment and Business Guide. International Business Publications, USA. • $99.95 Individuals hardcopy, e-book, CD-ROM. Covers: Strategic information on economy, business, export-import and investment climate, regulations and industrial development, banking, government, and opportunities. Entries include: Important business contacts and business travel.

School Business Affairs--Association of School Business Officials Official Membership Directory Issue. Association of School Business Officials International.

Scott's Business Suite. Scott's Directories. • $1,449 Individuals CD-ROM, pinpointer. Covers: 134,200+ manufacturers, manufacturers' sales offices, wholesalers, wholesale agents, and distributors operating in Greater Montreal, North and South Shore, Ontario, Greater Calgary, Edmonton and Greater Vancouver along with 245,000+ business contact names. Entries include: Company name, address, phone, fax, names and titles of key personnel, number of employees, parent companies, SIC, product, year established.

Scotts Valley Business Today. Scotts Valley Chamber of Commerce. • Monthly.

Sharjah Commercial Directory. Express Print Publishers. • Covers: Commercial industries in Sharjah. Entries include: Name, address, phone, fax.

Shingle Springs/Cameron Park Chamber of Commerce Business Directory. Shingle Springs/Cameron Park Chamber of Commerce. • Complete business listings, shopping information, and history of the Shingle Springs and Cameron Park areas of California.

Shoals Chamber of Commerce--Membership Directory and Business Reference Guide. Shoals Chamber of Commerce. • Annual. Covers 1,400 business organizations in Florence, Alabama.

Sierra Leone Investment and Business Guide. International Business Publications, USA. • $99.95 Individuals hardcopy, e-book, CD-ROM. Covers: Guide for conducting business activity in the country. Entries include: Important business information, business travel, and contacts.

Singapore Business Services. International Enterprise Singapore. • Annual.

Singapore Government and Business Contacts Handbook. International Business Publications, USA. • $99.95 Individuals hardcopy, e-book, CD-ROM. Covers: Strategic government and business information, export-import activity in the country, investment, business contacts and regulations.

Singapore Investment & Business Guide. International Business Publications, USA. • $99.95 Individuals hardcopy, e-book, CD-ROM. Covers: Basic information on economy, export-import and investment climate, regulations and industrial development, banking, and government. Entries include: Important business contacts and business travel.

Sioux Falls Christian Business Directory. Red Letter Publishing. • Businesses, churches, organizations, and schools in Sioux Falls, South Dakota.

Skagway Business Directory. Skagway Chamber of Commerce. • Annual. Covers: Comprehensive listing of area businesses.

SMI and SME Business Directory: The Official Business Directory of SMI Association of Malaysia. Tourism Publications Corporation Sdn. Bhd. • $69.90 Individuals. Aims to develop the potential of SMIs/SMEs and to enable them to evolve according to the demands of the new economy.

Solomon Islands Investment and Business Guide. International Business Publications, USA. • $99.95 Individuals hardcopy, e-book, CD-ROM. Covers: Strategic and business information, contacts, regulations and more. An ultimate guide for conducting investment, export-import activity in the country.

Somerset County Chamber of Commerce Business Directory. Somerset County Chamber of Commerce. • Covers: Area businesses.

SourceGuide to Management Information. London Business School Information Service. • $50. Covers: Sources of published and unpublished information on management issues available worldwide, including journals, databases and other electronic sources, abstracting and indexing services, reference works, academic working papers, and other relevant materials. Entries include: Source name, address, phone, description.

Sources of Free Business Information. Kogan Page, Limited. • Irregular. $12.95 hardback. Covers: Free business information and how to obtain it, including taxation, business finance, grants and incentives, exporting and overseas business, general economic and business information, small business advice, legal matters, computers, and investment. Entries include: Providers of information name, address, phone.

South Africa Business Directory. Business Guide. • $250 Individuals. Covers: 32,600 business listings including wholesalers, importers, retailers, business houses, and agents in South Africa.

South Africa Industrial and Business Directory. International Business Publications, USA. • Annual. $99.95 Individuals hardcopy, e-book, CD-ROM. Covers: Strategic industrial, investment and business contacts for conducting export-import and investment activity in the country.

South Carolina Investment and Business Guide. International Business Publications, USA. • $99.95 Individuals hardcopy, e-book, CD-ROM. Covers: Strategic and business information, contacts, regulations and more. An ultimate guide for conducting investment, export-import activity in the country.

South Sound Christian Business Directory. Red Letter Publishing. • Businesses, churches, organizations, and schools in Seattle South Sound.

Southern California Business Directory. Harris InfoSource. • Profiles 32,000 top companies in the 13 Southern California counties and lists the names and titles of 81,412 CEOs, owners, and key executives. The listings include company name and address; telephone, fax, and toll-free numbers; Web site email addresses; number of employees; annual sales; products and services; SIC codes; export/import indicators; and primary bank.

Southern California Business Directory and Buyers Guide. Dun & Bradstreet Inc. • Annual. $220 Individuals. Covers: 174,700 Southern California businesses. Database includes: Statistical data, trade show calendar. Entries include: Company name, address, county, phone, fax, number of employees, names and titles of key executives, plant size, year established, parent company, annual sales, import/export information, Standard Industrial Classification (SIC) code, and product description.

Spain Government and Business Contacts Handbook. International Business Publications, USA. • $99.95 Individuals hardcopy, e-book, CD-ROM. Covers: Strategic government and business information, export-import activity in the country, investment, business contacts and regulations.

Spain Industrial and Business Directory. International Business Publications, USA. • Annual. $99.95 Individuals hardcopy, e-book, CD-ROM. Covers: Strategic industrial, investment and business contacts for conducting export-import and investment activity in the country.

Sparks Chamber of Commerce--Business Directory. Sparks Chamber of Commerce. • Covers 1,500 business members in Spark, Nevada.

Springfield and Urbana Business Directory. Christian Blue Pages. • Annual. Christian-owned business enterprises in Springfield and Urbana area, Ohio.

Springfield Christian Business Directory. Red Letter Publishing. • Businesses, churches, organizations, and schools in Springfield, Illinois.

Starting an Online Business for Dummies. John Wiley & Sons Inc. • $24.99 Individuals paperback. Covers: Information needed to get an online business off the ground: identifying a market need, choosing a Web hosting service, securing transactions, and attracting customers.

State and Business in Russia. Maximov Publications. • Semiannual. Updated twice per year. Covers nearly 100,000 figures in Russian government and business. Available in multiple formats.

Stow-Munroe Falls Chamber of Commerce Member Business Directory. Stow-Munroe Falls Chamber of Commerce.

Strathalbyn District Commerce Association--Business Directory. Strathalbyn District Commerce Association. • Covers local businesses in Strathalbyn, South Australia.

Sudan Business Directory. Business Guide. • $150 Individuals. Covers: 1,200 business listings including wholesalers, importers, retailers, business houses, and agents in Sudan.

Swansea Business Directory. Burrows Publishing Ltd. • $27 Individuals with CD-ROM. Covers over 2,000 local companies trading in the city and county of Swansea, U.K.

Sweden Government and Business Contacts Handbook: Trade, Investment & Business Development Contacts. International Business Publications, USA. • $99.95 Individuals hardcopy,e-book,cd-rom. Covers: Strategic government and business information, export-import activity in the country, investment, business contacts and regulations.

Sweden Industrial and Business Directory. International Business Publications, USA. • Annual. $99.95 Individuals hardcopy, e-book, CD-ROM. Covers: Strategic industrial, investment and business contacts for conducting export-import and investment activity in the country. Contains strategic, practical economic and business information.

Switzerland Industrial and Business Directory. International Business Publications, USA. • Annual. $99.95 Individuals hardcopy, e-book, CD-ROM. Covers: Strategic industrial, investment and business contacts for conducting export-import and investment activity in the country.

Syria Golden Key Directory. International Institute of Trade Relation Promotion, Trade Information Centre of Iran. • £100 Individuals. Covers: 27,614 companies in Syria. Entries include: Company name, address, telephone, fax, products, services, Managing Director, and business activities.

Tacoma-Pierce County Business Directory. Tacoma-Pierce County Chamber of Commerce. • Annual. $19.95 for nonmembers.

Taiwan Government and Business Contacts Handbook. International Business Publications, USA. • $99.95 Individuals hardcopy, e-book, CD-ROM. Covers: Strategic government and business information, export-import activity in the country, investment, business contacts and regulations.

Taiwan Industrial and Business Directory. International Business Publications, USA. • Annual. $99.95 Individuals hardcopy, e-book, CD-ROM. Covers: Strategic industrial, investment and business contacts for conducting export-import and investment activity in the country.

Tajikistan Industrial and Business Directory. International Business Publications, USA. • Annual. $99.95 Individuals hardcopy, e-book, CD-ROM. Covers: Strategic industrial, investment and business contacts for conducting export-import and investment activity in the country.

Tanzania Business Directory. Business Guide. • $250 Individuals. Covers: 23,000 business listings including wholesalers, importers, retailers, business houses, and agents in Tanzania.

Tanzania Investment and Business Guide. International Business Publications, USA. • $99.95 Individuals hardcopy, e-book, CD-ROM. Covers: Strategic information on economy, opportunities, export-import and investment climate, regulations and industrial development, banking, and government. Entries include: Business contacts and business travel.

Thailand Investment and Business Guide. International Business Publications, USA. • $99.95 Individuals hardcopy, e-book, CD-ROM. Covers: Basic information on economy, export-import and investment climate, regulations and industrial development, banking, and government. Entries include: Important business contacts and business travel.

Tianjin Yellow Pages: Commercial/Industrial Directory. China Yellow Pages Directories Co. • $65. Covers: over 20,000 companies in the Tianjin area. Database includes: Investment information. Entries include: Company, name, address, phone.

Toll-Free Phone Book USA: A Directory of Toll-Free Numbers for Businesses and Organizations Nationwide. Omnigraphics Inc. • Annual. $175 Individuals softcover. Approximately 45,000 toll-free numbers for major companies, associations, educational institutions, travel providers, and government agencies in the U.S.

Top Careers for Business Graduates. InfoBase Holdings Inc. • $14.95 Individuals Paperback. Covers: What it takes to transform a major in business into a job that pays well, is expected to grow, offers a sense of security and opportunity for advancement, and is likely to provide a sense of job satisfaction.

Trade Directory of Nigeria. World Trade Center of Nigeria. • Triennial. Covers: Trade-related information for import/export companies, manufacturers, government representatives, lawyers, accountants, and interested individuals in Nigeria.

Trade Directory of Yugoslavia. Privredni Pregled. • Annual. $150. Covers: Trading and manufacturing entities and products, chambers of commerce, and other economic organizations. Entries include: Name, address, phone, products.

The Training Manager's Yearbook. AP Information Services Ltd. • Annual. £239 Individuals /year. Covers: Training managers in 8,750 organizations in the United Kingdom; profiles of over 4,500 suppliers and advisors to training managers in the United Kingdom. Entries include: For organizations--Name, address, phone, fax, e-mail, contact, history, names and titles of key personnel.

Tri-Cities Christian Business Directory. Red Letter Publishing. • Businesses, churches, organizations, and schools in Tri-Cities, Washington.

Triangle Business Journal's Book of Lists. Greater Raleigh Chamber of Commerce. • $45 Members. Provides 25 listings for 75 different business sectors in Raleigh and Durham area including advertising agencies, architects, banks, real estate agencies, hotels, accountants, and golf courses.

Trinidad and Tobago Investment and Business Guide. International Business Publications, USA. • $99.95 Individuals hardcopy, E-book and CD-ROM. Covers: Strategic and information on economy, business, export-import activity, investment climate, opportunities, industrial development, banking and government. Entries include: Business contacts, regulations, etc.

Tulsa Chamber Membership Directory. • Covers Tulsa Metro Chamber of Commerce membership roster.

Turkey Government and Business Contacts Handbook. International Business Publications, USA. • $99.95 Individuals hardcopy, e-book, CD-ROM. Covers: Strategic government and business information, export-import activity in the country, investment, business contacts and regulations.

For publishers' addresses, refer to SOURCES CITED section at the back of the book.

Turkey Investment and Business Guide. International Business Publications, USA. • $99.95 Individuals hardcopy, E-book and CD-ROM. Covers: Detailed information on investment, export-import business opportunities, foreign economic assistance projects, government and business contacts.

Turkish Business Directory. London Business Guide. • Covers: 25,000 companies and businesses in United Kingdom and Europe.

Turkmenistan Government and Business Contacts Handbook. International Business Publications, USA. • $99.95 Individuals hardcopy, e-book, CD-ROM. Covers: Strategic government and business information, export-import activity in the country, investment, business contacts and regulations.

TwinWest Chamber of Commerce--Membership Directory & Business Guide. TwinWest Chamber of Commerce. • Annual. Cvers 1,000 businesses and industries ranging from nationally and internationally renowned corporations and industrially driven manufacturers, to home-based businesses and companies involved in the service and professional sectors.

Tyne & Wear Chamber Regional Business Directory. Ten Alps Publishing. • Covers: businesses in Tyne and Wear, England. Entries include: Company name, address, phone, telex, fax, description of products or services.

UAE Golden Key Directory. International Institute of Trade Relation Promotion, Trade Information Centre of Iran. • £100 Individuals. Covers: 237,564 companies in United Arab Emirates. Entries include: Company name, address, telephone, fax, products, services, managing director, and business activities.

Uganda Business Directory. Business Guide. • $250 Individuals. Covers: 11,000 business listings including wholesalers, importers, retailers, business houses, and agents in Uganda.

Ukraine Government and Business Contacts Handbook. International Business Publications, USA. • Annual. $99.95 Individuals hardcopy, E-book and CD-ROM. Covers: Strategic industrial, investment and business contacts for conducting export-import and investment activity in the country.

United Arab Emirates Government and Business Contacts Handbook. International Business Publications, USA. • $99.95 Individuals hardcopy, e-book, CD-ROM. Covers: Strategic government and business information, export-import activity in the country, investment, business contacts and regulations.

United Arab Emirates Industrial and Business Directory. International Business Publications, USA. • Annual. $99.95 Individuals hardcopy, E-book and CD-ROM. Covers: Strategic industrial, investment and business contacts for conducting export-import and investment activity in the country.

United States Industrial and Business Directory. International Business Publications, USA. • Annual. $99.95 Individuals hardcopy, E-book and CD-ROM. Covers: Detailed information on investment, export-import business opportunities, foreign economic assistance projects, government and business contacts.

Uruguay Government and Business Contacts Handbook. International Business Publications, USA. • Annual. $99.95 Individuals hardcopy, e-book, CD-ROM. Covers: Strategic government and business information, export-import activity in the country, investment, business contacts and regulations.

Uruguay Industrial and Business Directory. International Business Publications, USA. • Annual. $99.95 Individuals hardcopy, E-book and CD-ROM. Covers: Strategic industrial, investment and business contacts for conducting export-import and investment activity in the country.

Uruguay Investment & Business Guide. International Business Publications, USA. • $99.95 Individuals hardcopy, E-book and CD-ROM. Covers: Strategic information on economy, business, export-import and investment climate, regulations and industrial development, banking, government, and opportunities. Entries include: Important business contacts and business travel.

USA/France Business and Culture Update. Integrated Information Technologies. • Monthly. $190 per year (12 issues). Publication includes: List of organizations or sources providing information to businesses wishing to enter markets in France. Entries include: Name, address, phone, fax, description of products/services offered. Principal content of publication is a newsletter providing general information on the French business and cultural climate.

USACC Business Directory. Unites States-Azerbaijan Chamber of Commerce. • Annual. $50 Nonmembers. Covers: Government, business, and international organizations in the United States and Azerbaijan. Entries include: Contact information.

Uzbekistan Government and Business Contacts Handbook. International Business Publications, USA. • $99.95 Individuals hardcopy, e-book, CD-ROM. Covers: Strategic government and business information, export-import activity in the country, investment, business contacts and regulations.

Uzbekistan Industrial and Business Directory. International Business Publications, USA. • $99.95 Individuals hardcopy, E-book and CD-ROM. Covers: Strategic and practical economic and business information. Entries include: Business contacts for conducting business activity in the country.

Vendor Guide: How to Do Business with the States. National Association of State Procurement Officials. • Annual. $60.

Venezuela Industrial and Business Directory. International Business Publications, USA. • Annual. $99.95 Individuals hardcopy, E-book and CD-ROM. Covers: Strategic industrial, investment and business contacts for conducting export-import and investment activity in the country.

Vermont Business Phone Book. Manufacturers' News Inc. • Covers: about 850 industrial firms in Vermont. Entries include: Company name, address, phone, number of employees, name of chief executive officer, products imported and exported.

Vero Beach Christian Business Association--Directory. Vero Beach Christian Business Association. • Covers Christian business leaders in Vero Beach, Florida.

Vietnam Investment and Business Guide. International Business Publications, USA. • $99.95 Individuals hardcopy, E-book and CD-ROM. Covers: Strategic and business information, contacts, regulations and more. An ultimate guide for conducting investment, export-import activity in the country.

Virginia Peninsula Regional Business Directory. Virginia Peninsula Chamber of Commerce. • Annual. $25 Individuals. Covers: Over 2,500 business leaders and chamber members.

Wabash Business Directory. Wabash Area Chamber of Commerce. • Covers businesses and industrial businesses in Wabash, Indiana. Entries include contact details.

Wallis & Futuna Investment & Business Guide. International Business Publications, USA. • $99.95 Individuals hardcopy, E-book and CD-ROM. Covers: Basic information on economy, export-import and investment climate, regulations and industrial development, banking, and government. Entries include: Important business contacts and business travel.

Ward's Business Directory of U.S. Private and Public Companies. Cengage Learning Inc. • Annual. $3,627 Individuals five-volume set. Eight volumes. Ward's contains basic information on about 115,000 business firms, of which 90 percent are private companies. Volumes available individually.

Warner Business Association--Business Directory. Warner Business Association. • List of businesses, artists, and artisans in Warner, New Hampshire.

The Waterlow Stock Exchange Yearbook. Macmillan Publishers Ltd. • Annual. $400 Individuals. Covers: firms whose stock is traded on the London Stock Exchange; worldwide coverage. Entries include: Company name, address, registrars, directors, auditors, bankers, date registered on the exchange, line of business, capital, loan capital, additional financial data.

West Lincoln Business Directory. West Lincoln Chamber of Commerce. • Covers 1,200 businesses in West Lincoln, Canada.

Western Cape Business Register. Intratex Holdings. • Covers: businesses and residences in the Cape Peninsula area of South Africa. Entries include: Company or personal name, address, phone.

Which European Database?. K.G. Saur Verlag KG. • Annual. $299 plus $15.00 shipping. Publication includes: List of leading business databases available throughout Europe. Entries include: Database name, description.

Who Knows What: The Essential Business Resource Book. Henry Holt and Co. • $45. Covers: Approximately 5,500 businesses, special libraries, government agencies, and other organizations in the U.S. that have access to information in over 500 business-related subject areas. Entries include: Company or organization name, address, phone, fax, name and title of contact, description of services and projects.

Who's Who in Alexandria Business. Alexandria Chamber of Commerce. • Annual. Covers businesses in Alexandria, Virginia.

Who's Who in Athens Magazine. Image Marketing Inc. • Semiannual. Covers: Individuals and businesses in Athens, AL.

Who's Who in Business. Bixby Metro Chamber of Commerce. • Annual. $20 for nonmembers. Covers businesses in Marion County, FL.

Who's Who in Finance and Business. Marquis Who's Who L.L.C. • Biennial. $349 Individuals. Provides over 21,000 concise biographies of business leaders in all fields.

Who's Who of European Business and Industry. Triumph Books Inc. • Covers: over 9,500 European business executives (volume 1) and over 1,400 companies (volume 2). Entries include: For executives--Name, biographical data. For companies--Name, address, phone, profile.

Wichita Christian Business Directory. Red Letter Publishing. • Businesses, churches, organizations, schools and professionals in Wichita, Kansas.

Will County Business Directory. Manufacturers' News Inc. • Biennial. $41. Approximately 1,212 manufacturing and related service companies in Will County, Illinois.

Wilton Manors Business Association--Directory. Wilton Manors Business Association. • Covers 200 businesses in Wilton Manors.

The Woman's Consultants Directory. CAE Consultants Inc. • Annual. $75. Covers: About 3,000 women consultants in every line of business. Entries include: Consultant name, address, phone, fax, line of business, description.

Working Solo: The Real Guide to Freedom & Financial Success with Your Own Business, 2nd Edition. Portico Press. • $21.95 Individuals paperback. Covers: Over 1,000 solo business opportunities, as well as a resource section on publications, organizations, and other essential contacts for solo professionals.

World Database of Business Information Sources on the Internet. Euromonitor International Business Reference Div. • $690. Covers: Over 35,000 business information sources worldwide, including 12,000 organizations, 13,000 publications, 2,000 exhibitions, and 700 online databases. Entries include: Source name, contact information, description.

Wytheville Chamber of Commerce Business Directory. Wytheville-Wythe-Bland Chamber of Commerce. • Covers: List of members. Entries include: name, address, phone.

Wytheville-Wythe-Bland Chamber of Commerce Business Directory. Wytheville-Wythe-Bland Chamber of Commerce. • Annual. Contains complete list of member's addresses and phone numbers.

Xiamen Yellow Pages: Commercial/Industrial Directory. China Yellow Pages Directories Co. • Annual. $65. Covers: over 15,000 companies in the Xiamen area. Database includes: Investment information. Entries include: Company name, address, phone, fax, postal code.

Yancey County Business Directory. Yancey County/ Burnsville Chamber of Commerce. • Periodic.

Yellow Pages Moscow. Deutsche Telekom Medien GmbH. • Annual. Covers: Approximately 70,000 commercial telephone subscribers in Moscow. Entries include: Name, address, phone, product/ service.

York County Regional Chamber of Commerce Business Directory. York County Regional Chamber of Commerce. • Covers: Information on all York County, New York, businesses.

Yugoslavia (Serbia) Government and Business Contacts Handbook. International Business Publications, USA. • Annual. $99.95 Individuals hardcopy, e-book, CD-ROM. Covers: Strategic government and business information, export-import activity in the country, investment, business contacts and regulations.

Yugoslavia (Serbia) Industrial and Business Directory. International Business Publications, USA. • Annual. $99.95 Individuals hardcopy, E-book and CD-ROM. Covers: Strategic industrial, investment and business contacts for conducting export-import and investment activity in the country.

E-BOOKS

The American Beauty Industry Encyclopedia. Cengage Learning Inc. • 2011. eBook. Published by Greenwood Publishing Group. Focuses exclusively on the many aspects of the American beauty industry, covering both its diverse origins and its global reach.

Business Data Communications and Networking: A Research Perspective. Cengage Learning Inc..

Green Technologies and Business Practices: An IT Approach. Cengage Learning Inc. • 2012. eBook. Published by IGI Global. An international platform that brings together academics, researchers, lecturers, policy makers, practitioners, and persons in decision-making positions from all backgrounds who ultimately share new theories, research findings and case studies, together enhancing understanding and collaboration of green issues in business and the role of information technologies and also analyze recent developments in theory and practice.

How to Value and Sell Your Business. Cengage Learning Inc. • 2009. eBook. Published by Kogan Page. Provides in-depth commentary and advice on the valuation and sale of a small- to medium-sized business, developing an exit strategy, tax and legal issues, marketing your business, managing the sale process, etc, in order to ensure maximum profit.

Information Communication Technology Standardization for E-Business Sectors: Integrating Supply and Demand Factors. Cengage Learning Inc. • Published by Information Science Reference. Explores aspects affecting the nature, relevance, and quality of standards, and the impact they have on businesses.

SAGE Sourcebook of Modern Biomedical Devices Business Environments in a Global Market. Cengage Learning Inc. • 2007. eBook. Published by Sage Publications. A source of information that presents and quantifies the commercial success of numerous types of biomedical devices available in the global market.

Selected Readings on Information Technology and Business Systems Management. Cengage Learning Inc. • 2009. eBook. Published by Information Science Reference. Focuses on key issues concerning technology in business. Contains selected readings in areas such as e-business, mobile marketing, and information resources management.

ENCYCLOPEDIAS AND DICTIONARIES

Blackwell Encyclopedia of Management. John Wiley & Sons Inc. Scientific, Technical, Medical, and Scholarly Div. (Wiley-Blackwell). • 2010. eBook. 2nd edition. Published by John Wiley & Sons. Divided into 12 individual subject volumes and an index. Volumes provide clear, concise, expert definitions and explanations of the key concepts in each area.

Encyclopedia of American Business. Cengage Learning Inc. • 2013. eBook. 2 volumes. 800 essays. A guide to the nuts and bolts of business jargon. Difficult ideas are explained in straightforward language to help non-specialists, students, and general readers understand the complex and sometimes confusing concepts and terms that are used in business. Five general areas of business are covered: accounting, banking, finance, marketing, and management.

Encyclopedia of Business and Finance. Cengage Learning Inc. • 2014. $485. 3rd edition. Two volumes. Published by Macmillan Reference USA. Contains articles on accounting, business administration, banking, finance, management information systems, and marketing.

Encyclopedia of Global Brands. Cengage Learning Inc. • 2013. $735. 2 volumes. Contains 270 entries, written in case-study style, that highlight details including how a product originated and was first marketed, how it developed commercially and how it fares today compared with its competitors and its own history. eBook available. Contact for pricing.

Encyclopedia of Networked and Virtual Organizations. Cengage Learning Inc. • Documents 249 of the most relevant contributions authored by over 400 of the world's leading experts to the introduction of networked, dynamic, agile, and virtual organizational models; definitions; taxonomies; opportunities; and reference models and architectures.

GENERAL WORKS

Alexandria Chamber of Commerce. • Promotes business and community development in Alexandria, VA.

Barbados Chamber of Commerce and Industry. • Businesses, business and trade promotion organizations, and individuals with an interest in promoting trade and commerce in Barbados. Seeks to improve domestic business conditions and increase foreign trade. Facilitates communication among members; functions as liaison between members and government agencies and international business organizations. Gathers and disseminates business and trade information; compiles statistics. Administers Duty Free Scheme in Barbados.

African Business. IC Publications Ltd. • Monthly. £40 Individuals U.K.. Business publication.

African Journal of Business and Economic Research. Adonis & Abbey Publishers Ltd. • £200 Institutions print. Peer-reviewed journal covering theoretical and empirical research of business and economy of Africa.

Agribusiness Connections. Agribusiness Association of Australia. • Peer-reviewed journal dealing with resource management and economic issues in the food and fibre sectors.

American Journal of Business (AJB). Ball State University. • Semiannual. $25 Individuals. Journal informing business professionals about recent research developments and their practical implications.

Annual Business and Pleasure Guide. Sebago Lakes Region Chamber of Commerce. • Annual. Covers businesses in Windham and the Sebago Lake Region.

Applied Stochastic Models in Business and Industry. John Wiley & Sons Inc. • Bimonthly. $2,744 Institutions, other countries print only. Journal covering applications and problem-solving techniques of applied probability and data analysis.

Baltimore Business Journal. American City Business Journal. • Weekly. $88 Individuals print + online. Newspaper reporting Baltimore business news.

Barbados Business Directory. Barbados Chamber of Commerce and Industry. • Biennial. Serves as a concise business reference.

Basic Business Essentials: Concepts and Tools. American CPE Inc. • Contains detailed training information covering fundamental topics in business and business management.

Brampton Business Times. Metroland Media Group. • Community business-to-business newspaper.

Business. Albany Area Chamber of Commerce - Georgia. • Bimonthly. $50 Nonmembers /year. Contains chamber activities and items of interest to businesses.

Business. Corona Del Mar Chamber of Commerce.

Business and Economic Forecasting Unit Annual reports. Monash University Business and Economic Forecasting Unit.

Business and Professional Directory. Chamber of Commerce of the Bellmores. • Annual. Journal containing listings of all current members of the Chamber of Commerce of The Bellmores area, NY.

Business Cards Tomorrow. BCT International Inc..

The Business Connection. Garner Chamber of Commerce. • Monthly. Contains member and community news, information on upcoming Chamber and Town of Garner events and meetings.

Business Focus. Bunbury Chamber of Commerce and Industries. • Contains articles and reports about the Bunbury Chamber of Commerce and Industries organization's works and accomplishments.

Business Herald. K.G.P. Nayar. • Monthly. $32.50. Journal on business management.

Business in Russia. Business in Russia. • Monthly. $197. Journal covering business and economics.

Business India Intelligence. The Economist Intelligence Unit. • Provides news on political, economic, and legal developments throughout the region, including business and e-business news; regulatory changes; distribution, human resources, market-entry strategies and regulatory development issues; economic and political risk analysis; company case studies; business intelligence.

Business Ireland. Dublin Chamber of Commerce. • Quarterly. Covers all areas of interest for business within the Dublin region.

The Business Journal. The Business Journal. • Weekly. $49 Individuals electronic. Journal covering business interests.

Business Ledger. Ledger Publishing Co. • $45 Individuals. Regional business newspaper covering DuPage, Northwest Cook County and the Fox Valley.

Business Link. Delano Chamber of Commerce.

The Business Link. Union County Chamber of Commerce. • Bimonthly. Provides updates on Chamber and member activities and events.

Business Matters. Chapel Hill - Carrboro Chamber of Commerce. • Bimonthly. Provides weekly events, government updates, and chamber news.

Business News. Bainbridge Island Chamber of Commerce. • Monthly. Includes issues about the business community and information about the chamber.

Business/Offices Services Guide. Business in Vancouver Media Group. • List of office supply firms in British Columbia.

Business Outlook. Costa Mesa Chamber of Commerce. • Periodic.

Business Owner. Business Technology Association. • Bimonthly. Delivers valuable information containing ideas, advisories, case studies and reports provided for members.

Business Russia. The Economist Intelligence Unit. • Provides news on political, economic, and legal developments throughout the region, including business and e-business news: regulatory changes: distribution, human resources, market-entry strategies and regulatory development issues: political and economic risk analysis: company case studies: business intelligence.

Business Services. S1 Corp. • Offers applications and solutions for customer education and support services.

Business to Business. Angola Area Chamber of Commerce. • Monthly. Includes information about Geneva business community.

Business Today. Chapel Hill - Carrboro Chamber of Commerce. • Monthly. Contains member profile, articles for small business and information about the community.

Business Update. Arlington Chamber of Commerce. • Monthly.

Business Ventures. Business Service Corp. • Monthly. Journal covering franchising, real estate, and investments. Also lists businesses for sale by owner.

Business Woman. Business and Professional Women's Foundation. • Quarterly Periodic. $12 /year. Features articles reflecting member's concerns including issues affecting working women.

Business World. ABP Pvt. Limited Publication. • Weekly. Journal on business and economics.

BusinessLinks. Pittsburgh Airport Area Chamber of Commerce. • Monthly. Contains information and updates on the latest issues, newest members, upcoming events, sponsorship, and recognition opportunities.

Cape of Good Hope Business Guide. Cape Town Regional Chamber of Commerce and Industry. • Annual. Contains business information.

Carpinteria Valley Business. Carpinteria Valley Chamber of Commerce. • Monthly.

Choosing the Right Business Entity. American CPE Inc. • Contains detailed training information covering methods and factors involved in selecting the most advantageous type of business entity for a new venture.

Columbus Business Journal. Columbus Business Journal. • Monthly. $12. Business tabloid.

The Complete Guide to Buying a Business. Nolo. • Contains information and forms for purchasing a business in the United States.

Covina Business. Covina Chamber of Commerce. • 10/year.

Creating Excellence: Vermont's Journal for people in growing businesses. New World Publishing Inc. • Bimonthly. $12. Magazine featuring successful Vermont business people and emphasizing personal development.

Culver City Business. Culver City Chamber of Commerce. • Monthly.

Cupertino Business. Cupertino Chamber of Commerce. • Monthly. $1.25 /issue.

Dearborn Business Journal. Dearborn Chamber of Commerce. • Monthly. Magazine containing news about Dearborn businesses and information about Dearborn Chamber of Commerce events and activities.

Duarte Business. Duarte Chamber of Commerce. • Biennial.

Dynamic Business. SMC Business Councils. • Bimonthly.

E-Business Institute Reports. University of Wisconsin—Madison E-Business Institute.

The Eco-antique and Retro Guide: Supporting Local Businesses--Promoting Source Reduction and Energy Conservation--Helping Our Communities. Ariela Press. • $1 from publisher. Covers Oregon stores and other organizations that recycle, recondition, or resell, and/or promote the use of recycled materials.

EMECA Review of Business. European Major Exhibition Centres Association. • Annual.

Everett Business Journal. The Wenatchee Business Journal Inc. • Monthly. Publication covering local business issues.

Financial Concepts and Tools for Business Management. American CPE Inc. • Contains detailed training information covering basic financial concepts and their use in business management settings.

Fort Bend Business Journal. Carter Publications Inc. • Monthly. $35 Individuals. Journal highlighting business in the Fort Bend community.

Georgia Business and Economic Conditions. University of Georgia Selig Center for Economic Growth. • Bimonthly Quarterly.

Getting Cash Out of Your Business. American CPE Inc. • Contains detailed training information covering methods of minimizing tax burdens and maximizing owner benefits and opportunities to draw cash from businesses.

Hatboro Online Business Directory. Greater Hatboro Chamber of Commerce. • $170 /year for members. Highlights participating businesses and services in the Greater Hatboro area.

Hong Kong for the Business Visitor. Hong Kong Trade Development Council. • Annual. Journal of travel, tourism, business and economics.

ie: The Business of International Events. International Festivals and Events Association. • Quarterly. $50 for nonmembers. Includes industry updates, trends and issues.

In Business for Yourself. Nashville Area Chamber of Commerce. • List of businesses located in Nashville, TN.

Incorporate Your Business. Nolo. • Contains information on establishing a corporation in each state.

Indian Management: Business and Management. Vinod Shanbhag. • Monthly. $112. Management publication.

International Journal of Business Communication (IJBC). Association for Business Communication. • Quarterly. $497 Institutions online only. Journal focusing on professional business communication.

Journal of Behavioral Studies in Business (JBSB). Academic and Business Research Institute. • Journal containing manuscripts of behavioral studies in business related disciplines.

Journal of Business and Psychology. Business Psychology Research Institute. Springer Science-Business Media LLC. • Quarterly. $614 Institutions print. An international outlet publishing high quality research designed to advance organizational science and practice.

Journal of Business Case Studies (JBCS). The Clute Institute for Academic Research. • Monthly. $495 Institutions. Journal containing case studies for use in business and economics courses.

Journal of Business Logistics. Council of Supply Chain Management Professionals. • Quarterly. $88 Individuals print + online. Provides a forum for the dissemination of thoughts, research, and practices within the logistics and supply chain arenas. Features articles in subject areas which have significant current impact on thought and practice in logistics and supply chain management.

The Journal of Business Valuation. Thomson Reuters Canada Ltd. • Annual. $52.52 Individuals. Journal including papers presented at the Business Valuation Conference in Canada.

Journal of Enterprise Business Intelligence Systems. IBIMA Publishing. • Peer-reviewed journal featuring the latest research and practices in enterprise business intelligence systems.

Journal of Family Business Management. Emerald Group Publishing Ltd. • Peer-reviewed journal publishing research on all aspects of family business management.

Journal of Integrated Business Decisions. IBIMA Publishing. • Peer-reviewed journal publishing research in business decision-making practices.

Journal of Media Business Studies. Joenkoeping International Business School, Media Management and Transformation Centre. • Quarterly. $65 Individuals. Peer-reviewed journal devoted to research on business aspects of media including strategic, organizational, financial, marketing, and entrepreneurial issues and practices.

Journal of Nature-Inspired Business Computing. IBIMA Publishing. • Peer-reviewed journal focusing on nature-inspired computing for businesses.

Kyle Area Chamber of Commerce Business Directory and Guidebook. Kyle Area Chamber of Commerce and Visitors' Bureau. • Biennial. Covers businesses in the city of Kyle.

The Lincoln Business Journal. Midlands Business Journal Publications. • Semimonthly. $53.50 Individuals. Business publication covering regional business and government issues in Lincoln, Nebraska.

Lithuania Business Services Providers Leads. Business Information Agency Inc. PlanetInform. • Monthly. $67 Individuals mailing list. Covers Lithuanian companies and all sub-industries that provide various services to commercial businesses, establishments, and organizations, including consulting, advertising and marketing services, and facilities maintenance.

Main Line Chamber of Commerce--Membership Directory and Business Resource Guide. Main Line Chamber of Commerce. • Annual. $10 Members. Covers bsinesses in Chester, Delaware, and Montgomery counties, PA.

Metro Business Review. Metro Business Review. • Monthly. Professional journal covering local business.

Mid-Atlantic Journal of Business. Seton Hall University - W. Paul Stillman School of Business. • Biweekly. $39.95 Individuals print & online. Scholarly business journal for researchers and professionals.

The Mountain/Plains Business Journal. Midlands

Business Journal Publications. • Business publication covering regional business issues in Nebraska, Colorado, Iowa, Missouri, Kansas, Oklahoma, South Dakota, and Minnesota.

North Mobile Business. Saraland Area Chamber of Commerce. • Biennial. Lists businesses in Saraland/North Mobile, AL.

North Shore Business Journal. North Shore Chamber of Commerce. • Monthly. Includes information, updates of the chamber's events and other articles concerning North Shore Chamber of Commerce.

Patuxtent Business Review. Patuxent Publishing Co. • Monthly. Business newspaper covering Howard County and Laurel, MD.

Philippine Review of Economics and Business. University of the Philippines College of Business Administration. • Semiannual. Journal covering research work and articles about Philippine economic and business conditions.

Planning Guide. Ypsilanti Convention and Visitors Bureau. • Annual. Contains a resource guide for meetings.

Poland Business Services Providers Leads. Business Information Agency Inc. PlanetInform. • Monthly. $160 Individuals mailing list. Covers Polish companies and all sub-industries that provide various services to commercial businesses, establishments, and organizations, including consulting, advertising and marketing services, and facilities maintenance.

Prague Business Journal. New World Publishing Inc. • Weekly. $100 Individuals. English language business publication.

Redmond Business. Greater Redmond Chamber of Commerce. • Monthly. Includes topical articles of issues affecting Redmond business community and information on sponsorship/promotional opportunities.

Richmond Business Directory. City of Richmond Business and Development Division. • Lists resident businesses with valid business license.

Romania Business Services Providers Leads. Business Information Agency Inc. PlanetInform. • Monthly. $84 Individuals mailing list. Covers Romanian companies and all sub-industries that provide various services to commercial businesses, establishments, and organizations, including consulting, advertising and marketing services, and facilities maintenance.

Savannah Business Journal. Savannah Business Journal. • Monthly. $15 Individuals. Business journal.

The Small Business Resource Guide. National Black Chamber of Commerce.

Southern Ulster County Chamber of Commerce Business Directory. Southern Ulster County Chamber of Commerce. • Annual. Covers bsinesses and local organizations in southern Ulster County, NY.

Survey of Current Business. Bureau of Economic Analysis Office of Regional Economic Accounts. • Monthly.

Thai-American Business (T-AB). American Chamber of Commerce in Thailand. • Annual. Business and Economics journal.

The Tri-County Business Advocate. Arcade Area Chamber of Commerce. • Quarterly. Contains latest news and events about Arcade Area Chamber of Commerce.

U.S. Japan Business News. U.S. Japan Business News. • Weekly. $78 Individuals. Japanese language business newspaper.

What to Buy for Business. Dagens Industri. • Monthly. General business publication.

White Paper on American Business in China. American Chamber of Commerce - People's Republic of China. • Annual.

Who's Who Greater Norwalk Business Directory. Greater Norwalk Chamber of Commerce. • Annual. $525 Individuals employees. Businesses, community phone numbers, and regional information about the greater Norwalk, CT area.

Working Papers of the College of Business and Economics. University of Kentucky Center for Business and Economic Research.

Yonsei Business Review. Yonsei University Industrial Management Research Centre. • Semiannual. $8,000. Business and economics journal.

HANDBOOKS AND MANUALS

Business Taxation Manual. Business SA. • $418 Nonmembers. Contains information on taxation obligations for businesses.

The Company Secretary's Handbook. Cengage Learning Inc. • Published by Kogan Page. A practical guide that will help newly appointed company secretaries do their job efficiently and comply with company law. Covers the formation of companies, corporate governance and day-to-day administration, keeping the statutory records, annual routines and dissolution. It also includes useful addresses and examples of all the necessary official documentation.

Gulf Business Development Handbook. National United States-Arab Chamber of Commerce. • $5 for members. Includes public and private trade resources.

Metrowest Business Review: Metropolitan Boston's Business Magazine. • Monthly. Magazine serving the business and professional community throughout the western suburbs of Boston.

World Directory of Business Websites. Euromonitor P.L.C. • A handbook of consumer market size data. It provides volume and value sales statistics (1999-2004) for more than 330 consumer products from 13 European countries.

INTERNET DATABASES

Bureau of Economic Analysis. U. S. Department of Commerce, Bureau of Economic Analysis. Phone: (202)606-9900; Fax: (202)606-5310; Email: webmaster@bea.doc.gov • URL: http://www.bea.doc.gov • Web site includes "News Release Information" covering national, regional, and international economic estimates from the BEA. Highlights of releases appear online the same day, complete text and tables appear the next day. "Recent News Releases" section provides titles for past nine months, with links. "BEA Data and Methodology" includes "Frequently Requested NIPA Data" (national income and product accounts, such as gross domestic product and personal income). Other statistics are available. Fees: Free.

Business 2.0 Web Guide to the Best Business Links. Business 2.0 Media Inc. Phone: (415)293-4800; Email: support@business2.com • URL: http://www.business2.com/webguide • Web site presents an extensive, searchable directory of links to "the best, most informative, and authoritative web pages." Twenty main categories cover business, finance, career, company information, people, and technology topics, with thousands of subtopics, all linking to Web sites recommended by experienced business researchers. Fees: Free.

Business Week Online. McGraw-Hill. Phone: (212)512-2511; Fax: (684)842-6101 • URL: http://www.businessweek.com • Web site provides complete contents of current issue of *Business Week* plus "BW Daily" with additonal business news, financial market quotes, and corporate information from Standard & Poor's. Includes various features, such as "Banking Center" with mortgage and interest data, and "Interactive Computer Buying Guide." The "Business Week Archive" is fully searchable back to 1996.

Commerce Business Daily Desktop (CBD). Information Systems and Services Inc. 8601 Georgia Ave., Ste. 708, Silver Spring, MD 20910-3439. Phone: (301)588-3800; Fax: (301)588-3986; Email: info@issinet.com • URL: http://www.issinet.com • Software package that provides download and query access to the Commerce Business Daily database.

Factiva. Dow Jones Reuters Business Interactive, LLC. Phone: 800-369-7466 or (609)452-1511; Fax: (609)520-5770; Email: solutions@factiva.com • URL: http://www.factiva.com • Fee-based Web site provides "global news and business information through Web sites and content integration solutions." Includes Dow Jones and Reuters newswires, The Wall Street Journal, and more than 7,000 other sources of current news, historical articles, market research reports, and investment analysis. Content includes 96 major U. S. newspapers, 900 non-English sources, trade publications, media transcripts, country profiles, news photos, etc.

Fedstats. Federal Interagency Council on Statistical Policy. Phone: (202)395-7254 • URL: http://www.fedstats.gov • Web site features an efficient search facility for full-text statistics produced by more than 100 federal agencies, including the Census Bureau, the Bureau of Economic Analysis, and the Bureau of Labor Statistics. Boolean searches can be made within one agency or for all agencies combined. Links are offered to international statistical bureaus, including the UN, IMF, OECD, UNESCO, Eurostat, and 20 individual countries. Fees: Free.

FreeLunch.com. Economy.com, Inc. Phone: (610)696-8700; Fax: (610)696-1678 • URL: http://www.freelunch.com • Web site provides free access to more than 200 million economic and financial data series, covering industry, demographics, labor markets, prices, retail sales, government spending, trade, interest rates, housing starts, the stock market, etc. Data is available in either chart or table form. Searching is offered. Free, but registration required. Economy.com, Inc. also offers fee-based economic analysis at *The Dismal Scientist* site (www.dismal.com).

InSite 2. Intelligence Data/Thomson Financial. Phone: 800-654-0393 or (617)856-1890; Fax: (617)737-3182; Email: intelligence.data@tfn.com • URL: http://www.insite2.gale.com/ • Fee-based Web site consolidates information in a "Base Pack" consisting of Business InSite, Market InSite, and Company InSite. Optional databases are Consumer InSite, Health and Wellness InSite, Newsletter InSite, and Computer InSite. Includes fulltext content from more than 2,500 trade publications, journals, newsletters, newspapers, analyst reports, and other sources. Continuous updating. Formerly produced by The Gale Group.

Nexis.com. Lexis-Nexis Group. Phone: 800-227-4908 or (937)865-6800; Fax: (937)865-6909; Email: webmaster@prod.lexis-nexis.com • URL: http://www.nexis.com • Fee-based Web site offers searching of about 2.8 billion documents in some 30,000 news, business, and legal information sources. Features include a subject directory covering 1,200 topics in 34 categories and a Company Dossier containing information on more than 500,000 public and private companies. Boolean searching is offered.

1997 NAICS and 1987 SIC Correspondence Tables. U. S. Census Bureau. Phone: 800-541-8345 or (301)457-4100 or (301)763-2713; Fax: (301)457-1296 or (301)457-3842; Email: naics@census.gov • URL: http://www.census.gov/epcd/www/naicstab.htm • Web site provides detailed tables for converting four-digit Standard Industrial Classification (SIC) numbers to the six-digit North American Industrial Classification System (NAICS) or vice versa: "1987 SIC Matched to 1997 NAICS" or "1997 NAICS Matched to 1987 SIC." Fees: Free.

Switchboard. Switchboard, Inc. Phone: (508)898-8000; Fax: (508)898-1755; Email: webmaster@switchboard.com • URL: http://www.switchboard.com • Web site provides telephone numbers and street addresses for more than 100 million business locations and residences in the U. S. Broad industry categories are available. Fees: Free.

U.S. Business Advisor. Small Business Administration. Phone: (202)205-6600; Fax: (202)205-7064 • URL: http://www.sba.gov • Web site provides "a one-stop electronic link to all the information and services government provides for the business community." Covers about 60 federal agencies that exist to assist or regulate business. Detailed information is provided on financial assistance, workplace issues, taxes, regulations, international trade, and other business topics. Searching is offered. Fees: Free.

Wall Street Journal Interactive Edition. Dow Jones & Co., Inc. 1211 Avenue of the Americas, New York, NY 10036. Phone: 800-369-5663; Email: service@dowjones.com • URL: http://new.dowjones.com • Fee-based Web site providing online searching of worldwide information from *The Wall Street Journal*. Includes "Company Snapshots," "The Journal's Greatest Hits," "Index to Market Data," "Journal Links," etc. Financial price quotes are available. Fees: $49.00 per year; $29.00 per year to print subscribers.

WilsonWeb Periodicals Databases. H.W. Wilson Co. 950 University Ave., Bronx, NY 10452-4224. Phone: 800-367-6770 or (718)588-8400 or (718)558-8400; Fax: (718)590-1617 or (800)590-1617; Email: custserv@hwwilson.com • URL: http://www.hwwilson.com • Web sites provide fee-based access to *Wilson Business Full Text, Applied Science & Technology Full Text, Biological & Agricultural Index, Library Literature & Information Science Full Text*, and *Readers' Guide Full Text, Mega Edition*. Daily updates.

ONLINE DATABASES

Albany Business Review. American City Business Journals, Inc. • $86 Individuals print + online. Contains the full text of The Business Review, a local business tabloid covering news in the Albany, New York, area.

Alberta & Saskatchewan Business. Scott's Directories. • Contains information on more than 41,000 individuals at more than 26,000 companies in the areas of Alberta and Saskatchewan, Canada.

American Business Lists—Online. InfoUSA. • Allows subscribers to access three databases containing directory information: 1) U.S. Businesses—contains 10 million listings for U.S. businesses. 2) Canadian Business Listings—contains 1.1 million listings for Canadian businesses. 3) Residential Listings - U.S. The databases can be used as a source for new sales leads, market planning, direct mail lists, telemarketing, distribution analysis, and locating suppliers.

Business & Company ASAP. Cengage Learning Inc. • Provides business and company information including 200,000 company directory listings, the complete text of PR Newswire releases for the preceding 30 days, and articles from leading business and industry publications. Includes more than 1300 indexed and 800 full-text periodical titles and over 200,000 combined directory listings, including the Graham & Whiteside international company directories.

Business & Management Practices™. Cengage Learning Inc. • Focuses on the processes, methods, and strategies of managing a business. Includes information on business planning, decision making, and management issues.

Business, Economics and Theory Collection. Cengage Learning Inc. • Contains the full-text of more than 7 million articles from 450 academic journals and magazines on all aspects of business and economics. Also offers feeds of videos from Forbes.com that contain business news coverage and interviews with CEOs and entrepreneurs.

Business Franchise Guide. Wolters Kluwer Law & Business CCH. • Contains extensive legal and regulatory information related to all aspects of business franchising.

Business Insights. ProQuest LLC. • Dtabase of market research reports based on primary research, data houses, consultancy and author research, and trade/industry associations, from Reuters Business Insight. The reports contain data on e-commerce, consumer goods, energy, financial services, healthcare, technology, and human resources. Users can analyze consumer and business-to-business purchasing attitudes in e-commerce, find advice on individual issues in niche healthcare markets and the technological revolution, and read interviews with oil, gas, electricity, and renewable energy industry executives, among other things.

Business U.K. NewsBank Inc. • Contains the full-text of business-related journals, magazines, newspapers, newsletters, wire services, trade publications, and other publications from the United Kingdom.

BusinessAnalystCrossing.com. • Offers business analyst job listings. Includes entry level business analyst, technical and business analyst jobs.

Canadian Business. Rogers Communications Inc. • Contains the full text of the Canadian publication, *Canadian Business* magazine.

Canadian Business Directory. Infogroup Inc. infoUSA Inc. • Contains contact information for more than 1.2 million Canadian business establishments. Includes address, telephone number, employment data, key contact and title, primary Standard Industrial Classification (SIC) code, yellow pages and brand/trade name information, actual and estimated financial data, and corporate linkages.

Dow Jones News Service. Dow Jones and Co., Inc. • Full text and edited news stories and articles on business affairs. Inquire as to online cost and availability.

EIU: Business Newsletters. The Economist Intelligence Unit Ltd. • Offers access to a variety of business journals in electronic form. Coverage extends from January 2001 to the present, and the database is updated weekly with new records. The journals covered include: CFO magazine, The Economist, The Journal of Commerce, and Roll Call, among others. The publications covered in this database offer international coverage of business issues, news, and information, and government activities in the U.S. and U.K. Subject areas include the arts, banking and capital markets, economic trends, politics, science, technology, transportation, international political issues, environmental issues, government, investment, and privatization.

Environmental Business Journal. Environmental Business International Inc. • Contains the complete text of *Environmental Business Journal*, a monthly newsletter covering business-related information on the environmental industry.

Gale Digital Archives. Cengage Learning Inc. • Provides ownership of archival content from Gale proprietary data, including the following databases: *Associations Unlimited, Biography and Genealogy Master Index, Biography Resource Center, Contemporary Authors, Dictionary of Literary Biography, History Resource Center, Literature Resource Center, The Times Digital Archive*, the *Times Literary Supplement Centenary Digital Archive*, and *Ward's Business Directory*.

Greater Montreal Business. Scott's Directories. • Contains information on more than 40,000 individuals at more than 21,000 companies in greater Montreal, Quebec, Canada.

Greater Toronto & Golden Horseshoe Business. Scott's Directories. • Contains information on more than 84,000 individuals at more than 50,000 companies in greater Toronto and the Golden Horseshoe area of Ontario, Canada.

National Business Directory. Scott's Directories. • Contains information on more than 308,000 individuals at more than 191,000 companies in Canada.

NYU Stern School of Business. • Office of Career Development section of website provides career resources for business graduates, along with resume databases arranged by classes. Many resources restricted to Stern students and alumni.

Ontario Business. Scott's Directories. • Contains information on more than 130,000 individuals at more than 79,000 companies in Ontario, Canada.

Quebec Business. Scott's Directories. • Contains information on more than 74,000 individuals at more than 42,000 Quebec companies.

Thomas Register Online. Thomas Publishing Company L.L.C. • Provides concise information on approximately 194,000 U. S. companies, mainly manufacturers, with over 50,000 product classifications. Indexes over 115,000 trade names. Information is updated semiannually. Inquire as to online cost and availability.

Westlaw Business Law Practitioner. Thomson Reuters Westlaw. • Contains comprehensive and current online resources, by practice and jurisdiction, for legal research in business and commercial pursuits.

Wilson Business Abstracts Online. H.W. Wilson Co. • Indexes and abstracts 600 major business periodicals, plus the *Wall Street Journal* and the business section of the *New York Times*. Indexing is from 1982, abstracting from 1990, with the two newspapers included from 1993. Updated weekly. Inquire as to online cost and availability. (*Business Periodicals Index* without abstracts is also available online.).

OTHER SOURCES

Business Organizations with Tax Planning. Zolman Cavitch, editor. Matthew Bender and Company Inc. • Quarterly. $6,433 book. Periodic supplementation. In-depth analytical coverage of corporation law and all relevant aspects of federal corporation taxation.

Business Rankings Annual (BRA). Cengage Learning Inc. • Annual. $584 Individuals. A guide to lists and rankings appearing in major business publications. The top ten names are listed in each case.

Business Strategies. Wolters Kluwer Law & Business CCH. • Semimonthly. $795.00 per year. Four looseleaf volumes. Semimonthly updates. Legal, tax, and accounting aspects of business planning and decision-making. Provides information on start-ups, forms of ownership (partnerships, corporations), failing businesses, reorganizations, acquisitions, and so forth. Includes *Business Strategies Bulletin*, a monthly newsletter.

PERIODICALS AND NEWSLETTERS

Abacus: A Journal of Accounting, Finance and Business Studies. John Wiley & Sons Inc. Wiley-Blackwell. • Quarterly. $597 Institutions Australia & New Zealand, print and online. Journal covering academic and professional aspects of accounting, finance and business.

African Review of Business and Technology. Alain Charles Publishing Ltd. • Magazine covering technology and business information about Africa.

Alberta Business. Alberta Business. • Monthly. Regional business magazine.

Australian Business News. NSW Business Chamber. • Bimonthly. A$7 for nonmembers.

Barron's: The Dow Jones Business and Financial Weekly. Dow Jones & Co., Inc. • Weekly (Mon.). $100.94 Individuals. Business and finance magazine.

bII BUSINESS. British Institute of Innkeeping. • 10/ year. Contains articles on licensing reform, smoking, qualifications and training.

Blair Business Mirror. Blair County Chamber of Commerce. • Monthly. Features chamber news, stories of chamber members and notices of upcoming programs and events.

Blue Ridge Business Journal. Blue Ridge Business. • Monthly. $22 Individuals. Tabloid covering business news about Henderson, Transylvania, and Buncombe counties.

Boston Business Journal. American City Business Journals. • Weekly. $102 Individuals print and online. Business newspaper specializing in local and regional business for upper management and CEO's of large and mid-sized businesses.

Business Advocate. Escondido Chamber of Commerce. • Monthly.

Business Agenda. Top of Virginia Regional Chamber. • Monthly.

Business and Professional Women. Canadian Federation of Business and Professional Women's Clubs. • Quarterly. C$4 for nonmembers.

Business & Society. Pine Forge Press. • Bimonthly. $790 Institutions combined (print & e-access). Peer-reviewed journal on business and society. Sponsored by the International Association for Business and Society.

Business Computer Report. Lawrence Oakly. • Monthly. $99 Individuals. Reviews business applications software and hardware for IBM and compatible computers.

Business Confidence Report. Economic Policy Research Center. • Annual.

Business Connections. Centralia-Chehalis Chamber of Commerce. • Monthly.

Business Day. BDFM Publishers Ltd. • Daily. R 1,700 Individuals. Business newspaper.

Business Development News. World Teleport Association. • Bimonthly. Contains information on business opportunities in the teleport industry.

Business Development News. Lancaster Chamber of Commerce and Industry. • Monthly.

Business Digest of Lower Fairfield County. Newfield Communications Inc. • Monthly. Regional business magazine.

Business Edge. Business Edge, Inc. • Semimonthly. $96 Individuals. Magazine covering Canada's local business scenes.

Business Ethics: The Magazine of Corporate Responsibility. Business Ethics. • Quarterly. Business newsletter.

Business Executive. Advantage Canada Inc. • Monthly. $28 Canada plus GST. Business magazine for southern and southwestern Ontario, Canada.

Business First of Buffalo: Western New York's Business Newspaper. American City Business Journals, Inc. • Weekly. $100 Individuals. Business Newspaper.

Business Futures. University of Stellenbosch Institute for Futures Research. • Annual.

Business guide. National Institutes of Health Office of Administration Office of Acquisition Management and Policy.

Business Horizons. Vermont Businesses for Social Responsibility. • Semiannual.

Business Information Center Newsletter. University of Richmond Business Information Center.

Business Insider. Cerritos Chamber of Commerce. • Monthly.

Business Link. Central California Hispanic Chamber of Commerce. • Monthly.

Business Luxembourg. International City Magazines S.A.R.L. • Business magazine.

Business Media Matters. Association of Business Information & Media Companies. • Monthly.

Business Month: The Magazine of Corporate Management. Goldhirsh Group. • Monthly. Magazine for business executives.

Business Monthly. American Chamber of Commerce in Egypt. • Monthly.

Business News. Porterville Chamber of Commerce. • Monthly.

Business News. Bainbridge Island Chamber of Commerce. • Monthly. Includes issues about the business community and information about the chamber.

Business News. American Chamber of Commerce of El Salvador. • Quarterly. Informs, educates and promotes member businesses.

Business News Alaska. Petroleum Newspapers of Alaska L.L.C.

Business News and Views. Battle Ground Chamber of Commerce. • Monthly.

Business News, Business Agenda, Programs and Services. Campbell County Chamber of Commerce. • Monthly.

Business NH Magazine. Millyard Communication Inc. • Monthly. $53 Individuals cover price. Business Magazine.

Business Products Industry Report. Independent Office Products and Furniture Dealers Association. • Semimonthly. $95 Nonmembers. Magazine serving the business products industry.

Business Pulse. Council of EU Chambers of Commerce in India. • Quarterly.

Business Standards. BSI Business Information. • Quarterly.

Business Traveller. BRT Reise Publishing GmbH. • Bimonthly. Consumer magazine covering business travel.

Business 2.0. Time Inc. • General business magazine emphasizing ideas, insight, and innovation.

Business Update. Kinston-Lenoir County Chamber of Commerce. • Monthly.

Business Valuation Review. American Society of Appraisers. • Quarterly. $45 Members. Journal containing topics regarding professional practice of appraising various business interests.

Business Week. McGraw Hill Financial Inc. • Weekly. $45.97 per year. Last volume is a double issue.

Business Week--1,000 Issue. The McGraw-Hill Companies Inc. • Annual. List of 1,000 U.S. Corporations by market value in all business, industrial, and financial categories, with financial results from preceding year and extensive analytical text.

Business West. Hagen Marketing & Communication. • Quarterly. $20 Individuals. Magazine featuring Pacific Rim business news for Californians.

Business Wise. New Bern Area Chamber of Commerce. • Monthly. Magazine highlighting news and information about the New Bern Area and Havelock Chambers of Commerce.

Business World. BusinessWorld Publishing Corp. • Daily. Business and financial newspaper.

CA Magazine: Leading Figures in Business. Institute of Chartered Accountants of Scotland. • Monthly. £45 Individuals. Professional journal covering business, finance, management and accountancy of the Institute of Chartered Accountants of Scotland.

Canadian Business. Canadian Business Media. • Biweekly. $20 per year. Edited for corporate managers and executives, this is a major periodical in Canada covering a variety of business, economic, and financial topics. Emphasis is on the top 500 Canadian corporations.

Cape Business News. Cape Business News. • Monthly. R 172 Individuals print. Business newspaper.

Caspian Business News. Caspian Business News. • Weekly. Local business newspaper.

Catalogue & E-business. Catalogue & e-business. • Monthly. £65 Individuals. Trade magazine covering catalog, mail order, and electronic commerce.

Chamber Business Monthly. South Snohomish County Chamber of Commerce. • Monthly.

Chamber Business Update. Greenville - Pitt County Chamber of Commerce. • Monthly.

Chamber News: A Focus on Business. East Providence Area Chamber of Commerce. • Quarterly.

Charleston Regional Business Journal. SC Biz News. • Contains the full text of Charleston Regional Business Journal, a business tabloid covering the Charleston, South Carolina and surrounding region.

Charlotte Business Journal. American City Business Journals, Inc. • Weekly. $92 Individuals print + online. Newspaper for the business community of Charlotte and the surrounding thirteen-county area.

Chemical Business. Colour Publications Private Ltd. • Weekly Monthly. Technical journal.

Chicago Business. Chicago Business. • Semimonthly. $15 Individuals. Collegiate business school publication.

Christian Business Men's Committee of U.S.A.--Contact Quarterly. Christian Business Men's Connection. • Quarterly. $12.95 /year for nonmembers.

Cincinnati Business Courier. American City Business Journals, Inc. • Contains the full text of Cincinnati Business Courier, a business tabloid covering Cincinnati, Ohio.

Club Business Quarterly. Boys and Girls Clubs. • Quarterly.

Columbus Business First. American City Business Journals, Inc. • Contains the full text of Columbus Business First, a business tabloid covering Columbus, Ohio.

Commerce Business Daily. U. S. Government Printing Office. • Daily. $275 Individuals. Publication listing U.S. and foreign government procurements and contract awards.

Commerce News: Reaching Edmonton's Entire Business Community. Edmonton Chamber of Commerce. • Monthly. Commerce News. Magazine (tabloid) for Edmonton's business community.

Commercial and Financial Chronicle. William B. Dana Co. • Weekly. $140.00. per year.

Crain's Chicago Business. Crain Communications Inc. • Weekly. $99 Individuals print & online. Newspaper covering news stories about various aspects of business and labor activity in the Chicago market.

Crain's Detroit Business. Crain Communications Inc. • Weekly (Mon.). $59 Individuals print edition. Local business tabloid covering Wayne, Macomb, Oakland, Livingston, and Washtenaw counties.

Daily Report for Executives. Bloomberg BNA. • Daily. Covers legal, regulatory, economic, and tax developments affecting corporations.

Dallas Business Journal. American City Business Journals, Inc. • Weekly. $95 Individuals print + online. Metro business journal.

Dayton Business Journal. American City Business Journals, Inc. • Contains the full text of Dayton Business Journal, a business tabloid covering Dayton, Ohio.

Edmonton and Homersham Commerce & Industry: Report on Business. Edmonton and Homersham

Commerce & Industry. • Monthly. $5. Business newspaper.

Essential Business Guide. National Federation of Meat and Food Traders. • £20 /copy for nonmembers.

Europe Business Review. First Charlton Communications Proprietary Ltd. • Quarterly. General business publication.

CampdenFB. Campden Publishing Ltd. • Quarterly. $415. Magazine featuring home-based family businesses.

Family Business Magazine. Canadian Association of Family Enterprise. • Quarterly.

Fast Company: How Smart Business Works. Fast Company, Inc. • Monthly. $12.00 per year. Covers business management, with emphasis on creativity, leadership, innovation, career advancement, teamwork, the global economy, and the "new workplace.".

First Alaskans: A Statewide Magazine of Business and Culture. Alaska Newspapers Inc. • Quarterly. $16 Individuals. Consumer magazine covering business and culture in Alaska.

Florida Business. Business Journal Publishing Co. • Monthly. $36 Institutions. Regional business journal.

Focus on Business. Elk Grove Chamber of Commerce. • Quarterly.

Forbes. Forbes Inc. • Biweekly. $29.99 Individuals. Magazine reporting on industry, business and finance management.

Fortune India: Indian Magazine for Business, Finance and Investment. Fortune Publications Private Ltd. • Biweekly. Rs 555 Individuals. Trade publication on premier business, finance and investment.

Fortune Magazine. Time Inc., Business Information Group. • Biweekly. $19.99 all access. Edited for top executives and upper-level managers.

Fremont Business Review. Fremont Chamber of Commerce. • Monthly. Includes promotional articles and meeting information.

Global Business and Economics Review. Inderscience Enterprises Limited. • €520 Individuals print or online. Peer-reviewed journal focusing on the discussion and analysis of advanced concepts, initial treatments, and fundamental research in all fields of business and economics.

Global Business and Finance Review. Global Business and Finance Review. • Semiannual. $50 Individuals. The GBFR is a referred journal specializing in global business and finance.

Green Channel Business. Indo-American Chamber of Commerce. • Monthly.

The Halton Business Journal. The Halton Business Journal. • Monthly. $24. Regional business magazine.

Harvard Business Review. Harvard University, Graduate School of Business Administration. Harvard Business School Publishing. • 10/year.

Harvard Business Review. Harvard Business Review Press. • Monthly. $89 U.S.. Magazine for business executives.

Hindu Business Line. Kasturi & Sons Ltd. • Daily. Rs 1,496 Individuals all days. Newspaper covering business, economics, banks and banking.

Hudson Valley Business Journal. The Hudson Valley Business Journal. • Semiweekly. $20 Individuals. Business and financial newspaper.

In Business for Business. Bethlehem Chamber of Commerce. • Monthly.

Indo-US Business. Indo-American Chamber of Commerce. • Monthly.

IndustryWeek: The Management Resource. Penton Media Inc. • Monthly. Edited for industrial and business managers. Covers organizational and technological developments affecting industrial management.

Inside Business. Great Lakes Publishing Co. • Monthly. Publication covering general business issues.

Insider--The Business Magazine of North London. Atom Publishing Ltd. • Quarterly. $2 Single issue. Trade magazine covering local business news and issues.

International Journal of Business Communication. Association for Business Communication. • Quarterly. Includes empirical and theoretically conceptual research results in business communication.

Issaquah! Chamber Business News. Greater Issaquah Chamber of Commerce. • Monthly.

It's Your Business. Marlborough Regional Chamber of Commerce. • Monthly. Contains latest information and events of Marlborough Regional Chamber of Commerce.

J@pan Inc Magazine: Business Technology People. Japan Incorporated Communications K.K. • Monthly. English language magazine covering business and technology in Japan for professionals worldwide.

Journal of Applied Research for Business Instruction. Association for Research in Business Education - Delta Pi Epsilon. • Quarterly. $15 /year. Includes research articles to improve instruction in all business disciplines.

The Journal of Business. The University of Chicago Press, Journals Div. • Quarterly. Individuals, $31.00 per year; institutions, $125.00 per year; students, $25.00 per year.

Journal of Business and Psychology. Business Psychology Research Institute. Springer Science-Business Media LLC. • Quarterly. $614 Institutions print. An international outlet publishing high quality research designed to advance organizational science and practice.

Journal of Business Strategies. Gibson D. Lewis Center for Business and Economic Research. • Semiannual. $45 Individuals domestic. Periodical covering issues in business.

Journal of EU Research in Business. IBIMA Publishing. • Peer-reviewed journal publishing information on research management and new ideas regarding the economics in Europe.

Journal of International Business Studies (JIBS). Academy of International Business. • 9/year. $498 Institutions in U.S. (print only). Publishes academic papers of significant interest that contribute to the theoretical basis of business and management studies.

Journal of Internet and e-Business Studies. IBIMA Publishing. • Peer-reviewed journal publishing research, analyses, case studies and reviews relating to internet and electronic business.

Kansas City Business Journal. American City Business Journal. • Weekly Weekly (Fri.). $50 Individuals print and digital - 52 weeks. Local business newspaper.

The Kiplinger Letter. Kiplinger Washington Editors Inc. • Description: Provides information on current events and future outlook in business, economics, legislation, politics, finance, labor, and other topics of interest to business professionals.

Latin Business Association Business Journal. Latin Business Association. • Weekly. $129.95 Individuals 52 issues. Journal providing comprehensive data and statistics on top-ranked Los Angeles companies across all industries.

Latin Business Association Business Newsletter. Latin Business Association. • Monthly.

Lehigh Valley Business Digest: The Newspaper in Business FOR Business. Business Digest Inc. • Monthly. $25. Tabloid devoted to small- and medium-sized businesses in Lehigh Valley.

The Los Angeles Business Journal. The Los Angeles Business Journal. • Weekly (Mon.). $129.95 Individuals. Newspaper (tabloid) covering local business news, business trends, executive profiles, and information for the Los Angeles area executive.

Louisville Business First: The Weekly Business Newspaper of Greater Louisville. American City Business Journals, Inc. • Weekly. $80 Individuals. Weekly Business Newspaper.

Luxembourg Business Journal. Luxembourg American Chamber of Commerce. • Contains organization's activities, member news and developments in the economic relations between the Grand Duchy and North America.

Matthews Business News. Matthews Chamber of Commerce. • Monthly.

Metrosouth Business Review: Metropolitan Boston's Business Magazine. • Monthly. Magazine serving the business and professional community throughout the southern suburbs of Boston.

Michiana Business. Indiana University South Bend Judd Leighton School of Business and Economics Bureau of Business and Economic Research. • Quarterly.

Mid-Missouri Business. Network Publishing Corp. • Monthly. $14.98 Individuals. Journal providing business information on central Missouri.

Minimize the Impact of Stress Claims on Your Business. Chamber of Commerce and Industry Queensland. • A$29.95 for members.

Mississauga Business Times. Metroland News. • Monthly. Regional business magazine.

National Business News Bulletin. Brotherhood of Working Farriers Association. • Periodic. Includes business news for trade, letters, and calendar of events.

New England Business. New England Business Corp. • Monthly. $29.95 Individuals. Business magazine.

New Jersey Business. New Jersey Business & Industry Association. • $24 Individuals /year.

Northern Business Journal. Northern Business Journal. • Magazine presenting business articles related to northeastern Ontario, Canada.

The Northern Colorado Business Report. The Northern Colorado Business Report. • Biweekly. $44.97 Individuals. Business newspaper.

Observer of Business and Politics. Anthony Jasudasan. • Daily. Newspaper focusing on business and economics.

Osceola Business Journal. St. Cloud Greater Osceola Chamber of Commerce. • Monthly.

Ottawa Business Journal (OBJ). InBusiness Media Network Inc. • Weekly (Mon.). $84.75 Individuals HST included. Local business magazine.

Peninsula Business Journal. Olympic View Publishing L.L.C. • Monthly. $9. Business journal serving Jefferson and Clallam Counties.

The Perspective: Main Street Perspective (Business in the Southwest). Cheallaigh Shamrock. • Biweekly. Magazine.

Prairie Business Magazine. Forum Communications Co. • Magazine featuring business people and companies from North Dakota, Minnesota and South Dakota.

Project Bait Business Magazine. Black Awareness in Television.

Russian Nuclear Industry Business Opportunities Handbook. International Business Publications, USA. • $99.95 Individuals. Strategic and business information on Russian nuclear industry, research on nuclear reactors, and contact information for major industrial and research facilities.

St. Louis Business Journal. American City Business Journals, Inc. • Weekly. $89 Individuals print + online. Business newspaper.

St. Louis ComputerUser: A Business to Business Computing Publication. Creative Publications Ltd. • Monthly. $12 Individuals. A business publication on computers and office technology.

San Diego Business Journal. San Diego Business Journal. • Weekly (Mon.). $99 Individuals. Metropolitan business newspaper specializing in investigative and enterprise reporting on San Diego County businesses and related issues.

San Francisco Business Times. American City Business Journals, Inc. • Contains the full text of San Francisco Business Times, a business tabloid covering the San Francisco, California, area.

Saudi Arabia Business Week. Saudi Arabia Business Week. • Weekly. Business and economics magazine.

Security Director News: Business News for Security Practitioners. HME News. • Monthly. Magazine for professional leaders in the security industry.

South Carolina Business Journal. South Carolina Chamber of Commerce. • Monthly. $25. Business newspaper.

Strictly Business. Tuscarawas County Chamber of Commerce. • Quarterly. $5.

Survey of Business. University of Tennessee College of Business Administration. • Quarterly. Magazine for Tennessee business professionals about current economic and socio-economic trends in the state.

Texas Business Magazine. • Monthly. Magazine on Texas industry, commerce, and finance.

Toronto Business Journal. Toronto Business Journal. • Weekly. $93 By mail. Newspaper covering local business.

Tucson Business Digest. Thompson Publications Ltd. • Monthly. $24 Individuals. Business magazine covers news and information for the Tucson business community.

Tunnel Business Magazine: Covering the North American Tunneling Market. Benjamin Media Inc. • $99 Other countries. Magazine featuring tunnel construction and engineering in North America.

University District Business News. Greater University Chamber of Commerce. • Monthly.

University of Calcutta Business Studies. University of Calcutta. • Semiannual. $20. Publication on business and economic studies.

Up Here Business. Up Here Publishing. • Monthly. $28.29 Individuals canada, digital subscription. Magazine featuring Northern Canada's business community.

Uptown San Diego Examiner: Business News. Uptown Examiner Group. • Semiweekly (Wed. and Fri.). $35 Individuals. Community newspaper.

Vermont Business. Vermont Chamber of Commerce. • Annual.

Waste Business West. CHMM Inc. • Bimonthly. Magazine for waste-industry.

Women in Business. Ogden/Weber Chamber of Commerce. • Quarterly.

Women in Business. The ABWA Company Inc. • Bimonthly. Women's business magazine.

RESEARCH CENTERS AND INSTITUTES

Auburn University at Montgomery - Center for Business. 7515 Halcyon Summit Dr., Ste. 305, Montgomery, AL 36117. Phone: (334)244-3700; Fax: (334)244-3718; Email: cforehand@cbed.aum.edu • URL: http://www.cbed.aum.edu • Economic impact studies, revenue forecasting, market research, equipment use and need analysis, management, and personnel research.

Bernard Baruch College of City University of New York - Center for the Study of Business and Government. 1 Bernard Baruch Way, New York, NY 10010-5518. Phone: (646)312-3540; Email: june.oneill@baruch.cuny.edu • URL: http://zicklin.baruch.cuny.edu/centers/csbg • Economic, social, and public policy issues, including regulation of banks and of capital markets, labor market patterns and the impact of government policies on them, differences and change in the incomes of demographic groups and regions with emphasis on New York and related government policies, urban problems and governmental solutions, particularly as related to New York City, and economic analysis of social issues, such as poverty, crime, and health.

Board of Research. Babson College, 204 Babson, Babson Park, MA 02457-0310. Phone: (781)235-1200; Fax: (718)239-6416; Email: chern@babson.edu • URL: http://www.babson.edu/bor • Research areas include management, entrepreneurial characteristics, and multi-product inventory analysis.

Columbia University - Columbia Center for Excellence in E-Business. Corporate & Foundation Relations, Columbia Business School, 33 W 60th St., 7th Fl., New York, NY 10023-7905. Phone: (212)854-3427; Fax: (212)678-0825; Email: ejj3@columbia.edu • URL: http://www4.gsb.columbia.edu/cebiz • Business, information technology, and e-commerce.

De La Salle University - Ramon V. del Rosario College of Business - Center for Business and Economics Research and Development. 2401 Taft Ave., Manila 1004, Philippines. Phone: 63 2 3030869; Fax: 63 2 5219094; Email: cbedean@dlsu.edu.ph • URL: http://www.dlsu.edu.ph/research/centers/cberd/default.asp • Business education, entrepreneurship, and administrative policy.

Harvard University - John F. Kennedy School of Government - Mossavar-Rahmani Center for Business and Government. Weil Hall, 79 John F. Kennedy St., Cambridge, MA 02138. Phone: (617)495-1110; Fax: (617)495-5821; Email: mrcbg@hks.harvard.edu • URL: http://www.hks.harvard.edu/centers/mrcbg • Governmental regulations, focusing on energy and environmental industries, Asia programs, international trade, corporate social responsibility and collaborative governance.

Middle Tennessee State University - Business and Economic Research Center. 1301 E Main St., Murfreesboro, TN 37132-0001. Phone: (615)898-2300 or (615)898-2610; Fax: (615)898-5045; Email: dpenn@mtsu.edu • URL: http://www.mtsu.edu • Various fields within business and economics.

Troy State University - Center for Business and Economic Services. Sorrell College of Business, Troy, AL 36082. Phone: (334)670-3524; Fax: (334)670-3636; Email: jkervin@trojan.troyst.edu • URL: http://troy.troy.edu/cbes/index.html • Business and economics, including feasibility studies, market research, economic projections, cost analyses, accounting and budgeting models, and similar projects.

University of Hong Kong - Hong Kong Institute of Economics and Business Strategy. Faculty of Business & Economics, Pokfulam Rd., Hong Kong, China. Phone: 86 852 25489300; Fax: 86 852 25483223; Email: info@hiebs.hku.hk • URL: http://www.hiebs.hku.hk • Economic policy and business strategy in Hong Kong and its role in China and the Asia-Pacific region.

University of Idaho - Center for Business Development and Entrepreneurship. College of Business & Economics, Moscow, ID 83844-3161. Phone: 800-960-3033; Fax: (208)885-8939; Email: dansmith@uidaho.edu • URL: http://www.cbehome.uidaho.edu/default.aspx?pid=32593 • Business and economics, including studies on market and labor force, regional economics.

West Virginia University - College of Business and Economics - Center for Chinese Business. PO Box 6025, Morgantown, WV 26506-6025. Phone: (304)293-7885; Fax: (304)293-3274 • URL: http://www.be.wvu.edu/chinese_business • Emerging market economy in China.

STATISTICS SOURCES

Manufacturing & Distribution USA. Cengage Learning Inc. • Biennial. $631 Individuals three-volume set. 2012. 7th edition. eBook. Three volumes. Presents statistics and projections relating to economic activity in more than 600 business classifications.

Statistical Abstract of the United States. U. S. Government Printing Office. • Annual. $44.00. Issued by the U. S. Bureau of the Census.

Survey of Current Business. U. S. Government Printing Office. • Published by Bureau of Economic Analysis, U. S. Department of Commerce. Presents a wide variety of business and economic data.

TRADE/PROFESSIONAL ASSOCIATIONS

Alpha Beta Gamma International. 75 Grasslands Rd., Valhalla, NY 10595. Phone: (914)606-6877; Fax: (914)606-6481; Email: ceo@abg.org • URL: http://www.abg.org • Honor Society - Business. Students enrolled at accredited two-year community, technical, and junior colleges in North America; also initiates distinguished International business persons and academics as honorary members. Sponsors training sessions and cultural and college activities. Maintains speakers' bureau.

Alpha Iota Sorority. 3219 SE 18th Ct., Des Moines, IA 50320-1901. Phone: (515)282-4896; Email: clmekus@aol.com • URL: http://www.alphaiota.org • Honorary sorority - business. Helps each member to become a better businesswoman through development of self-confidence, leadership and awareness of responsibility to herself and her community.

Alpha Kappa Psi. 7801 E 88th St., Indianapolis, IN 46256-1233. Phone: (317)872-1553; Fax: (317)872-1567; Email: mail@akpsi.org • URL: http://www.akpsi.org • Professional fraternity - business administration. Conducts educational and charitable programs. Focuses on leadership development.

American Business Council of Pakistan. F-30, Block-7, K.D.A., Scheme No. 5, Kehkashan, Clifton, Karachi, Pakistan. Phone: 92 21 5877351 or 92 21 5877390; Fax: 92 21 5877391; Email: abcpak@cyber.net.pk • URL: http://www.abcpk.org.pk • Promotes private American business efforts in Pakistan and friendly relations between Americans and Pakistani nationals. Provides information on the business climate and development and trade issues in Pakistan.

American Business Women's Association. 11050 Roe Ave., Ste. 200, Overland Park, KS 66211. Phone: 800-228-0007; Fax: (913)660-0101; Email: webmail@abwa.org • URL: http://www.abwa.org • Women in business, including women owning or operating their own businesses, women in professions and women employed in any level of government, education, or retailing, manufacturing and service companies. Provides opportunities for businesswomen to help themselves and others grow personally and professionally through leadership, education, networking support and national recognition. Offers leadership training, business skills training and business education; special membership options for retired businesswomen and the Company Connection for business owners, a resume service, credit card and programs, various travel and insurance benefits. Sponsors American Business Women's Day and National Convention and regional conferences held annually.

American Businesspersons Association. Hillsboro Executive Center North, 350 Fairway Dr., Ste. 107, Deerfield Beach, FL 33441-1834. Phone: 800-221-2168; Fax: (954)571-8582; Email: membership@assnservices.com • URL: http://www.aba-assn.com

For publishers' addresses, refer to SOURCES CITED section at the back of the book.

• Owners of businesses and individuals in executive, managerial, and sales capacities. Provides substantial discounts, affordable insurance, products and other special services to members.

American Management Association. 1601 Broadway, New York, NY 10019-7420. Phone: 877-566-9441 or (212)586-8100 or (518)891-5510; Fax: (212)903-8168 or (518)891-0368; Email: customerservice@amanet.org • URL: http://www.amanet.org • Provides educational forums worldwide where members and their colleagues learn superior, practical business skills and explore best practices of world-class organizations through interaction with each other and expert faculty practitioners. Maintains a publishing program providing tools individuals use to extend learning beyond the classroom in a process of life-long professional growth and development through education.

Argentine Chamber of Limited Companies. Libertad 1340, PB, C1016ABB Buenos Aires, Argentina. Phone: 54 11 40107701; Email: camaradesociedades@camaradesociedades.com • URL: http://www.camaradesociedades.com • Represents members of Chamber of Limited Companies in Argentina.

Asian Business League of San Francisco. PO Box 191345, San Francisco, CA 94119-1345. Phone: (415)670-9022; Email: info@ablsf.org • URL: http://www.ablsf.org • Seeks to promote and further the success of Asian Americans in business. Provides its members with seminars and opportunities to meet with other business leaders in the community, to participate in the advocacy to issues important to Asian Americans and to learn and share pertinent information about the current economic and business climate on both local and international level.

Association of Business Process Management Professionals. 1000 Westgate Dr., Ste. 252, Saint Paul, MN 55114. Phone: (651)288-3420; Fax: (651)290-2266; Email: president@abpmp.org • URL: http://www.abpmp.org • Fosters the advancement of business process management concepts and its practices. Seeks to develop a common body of knowledge in business process management. Provides educational and networking activities for the continuing education of its members and their professional colleagues.

Association of European Businesses. Krasnoproletarskaya ul 16, Bldg. 3, entrance 8, 4th Fl., 127473 Moscow, Russia. Phone: 7 495 2342764; Fax: 7 495 2342807; Email: info@aebrus.ru • URL: http://www.aebrus.ru • Represents and promotes the interests of European companies conducting business in the Russian Federation.

Association of Ghana Industries. Trade Fair Centre, 2nd Fl., Addison House, Accra, Ghana. Phone: 233 21 779023 or 233 21 779024; Fax: 233 21 773143 or 233 21 763383; Email: agi@agighana.org • URL: http://www.agighana.org • Voluntary business association, providing policy advocacy and advisory services, market development/market clinic, industrial sub-contracting, management training, business plan preparation, export market promotion, information gathering, analysis and dissemination, media planning and events management, and networking.

Bahrain Management Society. PO Box 3268, Manama, Bahrain. Phone: 973 17827676; Fax: 973 17827678; Email: admin@bms.org.bh • URL: http://www.bms.org.bh • Promotes best practices and standards of professionalism in management. Fosters research pertaining to all aspects of management. Aims to strengthen ties with other related organizations for the purpose of developing a better understanding of all concepts in management.

Beta Pi Sigma Sorority. 256 Waterville St., San Francisco, CA 94124. Email: bpssi@betapisigmasorority.org • URL: http://betapisigmasorority.org • Business and professional sorority. Conducts civic, cultural, charitable, and educational projects. Cooperates with the Close Up Foundation on the Program for Older Americans. Offers tutoring services. Youth programs partnerships with schools, book donation programs (schools and libraries), and youth programs.

Business Architects Association. 727 S Dearborn St., Ste. 710, Chicago, IL 60605-3826. Email: info@businessarchitects.org • URL: http://www.businessarchitectsassociation.org • Aims to promote and advance the business architecture profession through education, research, and application of methodologies. Provides educational and networking opportunities for the continuing education of members. Offers professional training and certification programs.

Business Council. 1901 Pennsylvania Ave., NW Ste. 701, Washington, DC 20006. Phone: (202)298-7650; Fax: (202)785-0296 • URL: http://www.thebusinesscouncil.org • Represents business executives. Aims to serve the national interest, with the primary objectives of developing a constructive point of view on matters of public policy affecting the business interests of the country and by providing a medium for a better understanding of government problems by business. Members are former and present chief executive officers of corporations.

Business Council of Australia. GPO Box 1472, Melbourne, VIC 3001, Australia. Phone: 61 3 86642664; Fax: 61 3 86642666 • URL: http://www.bca.com.au • Businesses and trade organizations. Promotes establishment of a national economic climate conducive to business growth. Represents members' interests before government agencies, trade organizations, and the public.

Business Council of Papua New Guinea. PO Box 404, Konedobu, Papua New Guinea. Phone: 675 3200700; Fax: 675 3200701; Email: executive@bcpng.org.pg • URL: http://www.bcpng.org.pg • Represents the interests of the private sector to the government and public institutions. Promotes the importance and role of economic growth, freedom and enterprise. Fosters dialogue and debate between the public sector, the private sector and academia.

Business for Social Responsibility. 88 Kearny St., 12th Fl., San Francisco, CA 94108. Phone: (415)984-3200; Fax: (415)984-3201; Email: connect@bsr.org • URL: http://www.bsr.org • Large, small, and medium-sized businesses. Promotes responsible business behavior and serves as a resource to companies striving to make ethical business decisions.

Business Industry Promotion Association of Pakistan. 455 Shadman 1, Lahore, Pakistan. Phone: 92 42 7581288; Fax: 92 42 7581288; Email: bipap@brain.net.pk • Seeks to integrate the activities of professionals in the fields of trade, industry, manufacturing, exporting, engineering, investment, finance and general services. Facilitates cooperation and networking among business professionals.

Business Network International - Suriname. Verl Hoogestraat No. 1, Paramaribo, Suriname. Phone: 597 424354 • URL: http://www.bnisuriname.com • Seeks to increase business opportunities for members. Encourages members to share ideas, contacts and business referrals. Fosters and develops personal relationships with other qualified business professionals.

Business NZ. Level 6, Lumley House, 3-11 Hunter St., Wellington 6011, New Zealand. Phone: 64 4 4966555; Fax: 64 4 4966550; Email: info@businessnz.org.nz • URL: http://www.businessnz.org.nz • Advocacy body working to maintain a favorable business climate and reasonable conditions of employment in New Zealand. Facilitates communication and cooperation among members.

Business Retention and Expansion International. PO Box 3212, Bismarck, ND 58502-3212. Email: brei@brei.org • URL: http://www.brei.org • Promotes business retention and expansion as a fundamental strategy for economic sustainability and growth. Provides leadership resources, education and networking opportunities in business retention and expansion. Fosters communication and collaboration among members.

Camara de Comercio Argentino-Brasilena. Montevideo 770-12 Piso, 1019 Buenos Aires, Argentina. Phone: 54 11 48114503; Email: institucionales@cambras.org.ar • URL: http://www.cambras.org.ar • Represents business and commerce in Argentina.

Camara de Comercio e Industria de Trenque Lauquen. Bvard. Villegas 150, 6400 Buenos Aires, Argentina. Phone: 54 2392412000 or 54 2392431672; Fax: 54 2392430414; Email: info@lacamaradetrenque.com.ar • URL: http://www.tlauquen.com.ar • Represents business in Argentina.

Camara de Comercio Exterior de Rosario. 1868 Cordoba St., 1st Fl., 2000 Rosario, Argentina. Phone: 54 341 4257147; Fax: 54 341 4257486; Email: ccer@commerce.com.ar • URL: http://www.commerce.com.ar • Promotes international trade for export and import businesses in the Rosario region of Argentina.

Camara de Comercio Exterior de Salta. Alvarado 51, 4400 Salta, Argentina. Phone: 54 387 4311003; Fax: 54 387 4225293 • URL: http://www.camcomexsalta.com.ar • Represents businesses in the Salta region of Argentina.

Camara de Comercio, Industria Y Servicios de Carlos Casares. Avda. San Martin 318, B6530 Carlos Casares, Argentina. Fax: 54 2395451022 • URL: http://www.camaracarloscasares.com.ar • Promotes business and industry in the Carlos Casares region of Argentina.

Camara de Comercio Italiana de Rosario. Cordoba 1868, 2000 Rosario, Argentina. Phone: 54 341 4266789 or 54 341 4245691; Email: info@italrosario.com • URL: http://www.italrosario.com/ • Represent Italian business interests in Rosario, Argentina.

Camara de Comercio Sueco Argentina. Carlos Pellegrini 833, Buenos Aires, Argentina. Phone: 54 11 43428867; Fax: 54 11 43428867; Email: info@ccsa.com.ar • URL: http://www.ccsa.com.ar • Represents businesses in Argentina.

Camara de Industria y Comercio de Matanza. Cal. Entre Rios 3026, San Justo, 1754 Buenos Aires, Argentina. Phone: 54 11 46511830; Fax: 54 11 46511830; Email: info@cicm.com.ar • URL: http://www.cicm.com.ar • Represents business in Argentina.

Camara Empresaria Parque Industrial de Pilar. Ruta 8, km. 60, Parque Industrial Pilar, Calle Del Canal Nro. 1758, 1629 Buenos Aires, Argentina. Phone: 54 230 4491994 or 54 230 4491892; Email: info@cepip.org.ar • URL: http://www.cepip.org.ar • Represents businesses in Argentina.

Canadian Capital Markets Association. 85 Richmond St. W, Toronto, ON, Canada M5H 2C9. Phone: (416)410-1050; Email: info@ccma-acmc.ca • URL: http://www.ccma-acmc.ca • Enhances the competitiveness of the Canadian capital markets through a forum of industry experts who provide leadership and direction to the investment community. Promotes straight-through processing strategies that reduce ongoing errors and processing costs. Addresses the massive changes occurring in global securities markets such as increased on and off exchange securities trading volumes and volatility due in part to the growth of on-line trading.

Canadian Council of Chief Executives. 99 Bank St., Ste. 1001, Ottawa, ON, Canada K1P 6B9. Phone: (613)238-3727; Fax: (613)238-3247; Email: info@ceocouncil.ca • URL: http://www.ceocouncil.ca •

Businesses and trade organizations. Promotes a healthy national economy. Conducts research; lobbies for legislation favorable to business; represents members' interests.

Canadian Federation of Independent Business. 401-4141 Yonge St., Toronto, ON, Canada M2P 2A6. Phone: 888-234-2232 or (416)222-8022; Fax: (416)222-6103; Email: cfib@cfib.ca • URL: http://www.cfib-fcei.ca/english/index.html • Independent businesses. Promotes economic well-being of members and seeks to maintain a healthy domestic business climate. Represents members' interests before government agencies, labor and industrial organizations, and the public.

China Business Council for Sustainable Development. A6 Huixin E St., Chaoyang District, Beijing 100029, China. Phone: 86 10 69166788; Fax: 86 10 69196630; Email: info@cbcsd.org.cn • URL: http://www.cbcsd.org.cn • Provides a platform for exchange and cooperation among Chinese and foreign enterprises, government and social communities. Shares information, experiences and best practices in the field of sustainable development. Improves understanding and performance in environment health safety, corporate social responsibility and climate change.

Chinese Finance Association. Church Street Station, New York, NY 10008. • URL: http://www.tcfaglobal.org • Promotes Chinese finance, business, economy, financial institutions and financial markets.

College of Performance Management. 101 S Whiting St., Ste. 320, Alexandria, VA 22304. Phone: (703)370-7885; Fax: (703)370-1757 • URL: http://www.mycpm.org • Serves as a forum for the exchange of information on project management and performance measurement in business. Conducts educational programs.

Community College Business Officers. 3 Boar's Head Ln., Ste. B, Charlottesville, VA 22903-4604. Phone: (434)293-2825; Fax: (434)245-8453; Email: info@ccbo.org • URL: http://www.ccbo.org • Represents business officers. Works to support business officers.

Community Managers International Association. PO Box 848, Dana Point, CA 92629-0848. Phone: (949)940-9263; Email: cmiamanager@gmail.com • URL: http://www.cmiamanager.org • Aims to promote the community management profession. Provides an environment for the exchange of ideas among members. Collaborates with other national and state organizations. Sponsors seminars and workshops.

Coordinating Committee of Agriculture, Commercial, Industrial and Financial Associations. Route 6, 9-21, Zone 4, Level 9, 01004 Guatemala City, Guatemala. Phone: 502 2201-0000; Email: unice@cacif.org.gt • URL: http://www.cacif.org.gt.

Delta Mu Delta Honor Society. 9217 Broadway Ave., Brookfield, IL 60513-1251. Phone: 866-789-7067 or (708)485-8494; Fax: (708)221-6183; Email: dmd@dmd-ntl.org • URL: http://deltamudelta.org • Serves as honor society for business administration.

Eta Phi Beta. 19983 Livernois Ave., Detroit, MI 48221-1299. Phone: (313)862-0600; Fax: (313)862-6245; Email: contact@etaphibetasorority.com • URL: http://www.etaphibetasorority.com • Professional sorority - business. Conducts national projects concerning retarded citizens and retarded children. Conducts leadership and career programs and seminars; sponsors competitions. Operates speakers' bureau; provides children's services; maintains charitable program.

European Business Angel Network. Rue de la Science 14B, B-1040 Brussels, Belgium. Phone: 32 2 626 20 60; Fax: 32 2 626 20 69; Email: info@eban.org • URL: http://www.eban.org • Encourages exchange of experience among business angels networks. Promotes recognition of business angels networks. Works to create and develop a positive environment for business angels' activities.

Foundation for Student Communication. 48 University Pl., Princeton, NJ 08544. Phone: (609)258-1111; Fax: (609)258-1222; Email: info@businesstoday.org • URL: http://www.businesstoday.org • Student subscribers and conference participants who desire to promote communication among students and businesspersons. Sponsors student/business forums.

Franco-Argentina Chamber of Commerce and Industry. Av. Libertador 498, 17e etage, C1001AAO Buenos Aires, Argentina. Phone: 54 11 43101000; Fax: 54 11 43101021; Email: ccifa@ccifa.com.ar • URL: http://www.ccifa.com.ar • Promotes business and trade between Argentine and French companies.

Future Business Leaders of America - Phi Beta Lambda. 1912 Association Dr., Reston, VA 20191-1591. Phone: 800-325-2946; Fax: (866)500-5610; Email: general@fbla.org • URL: http://www.fbla-pbl.org • Maintains 4 divisions: Future Business Leaders of America for high school students preparing for business and related careers; Phi Beta Lambda for post-secondary and college men and women enrolled in business or teacher education programs; Professional Division for business persons FBLA - parents and teachers; Middle Level for students in junior high schools. Sponsors educational program and National Student Award program based on national competition for members.

Green Partners. • URL: http://www.greenpartnersllc.com • Represents the interests of businesses that are committed to protect the environment. Promotes environmentally an "green" concept to the business sectors. Educates businesses on ways to be environmentally friendly through classes, on-site inspections and mentorship.

Iota Phi Lambda. 1015 15th St. NW, Ste. 1110, Washington, DC 20005. Phone: (202)462-4682; Email: iotahq@verizon.net • URL: http://iota1929.org • Business and professional civic sorority. Seeks to: develop leadership expertise among business and professional women; promote increased interest in business education among high school and college girls through planned programs and scholarships; encourage the development of personalities for all areas of leadership through provision of educational opportunities; establish and promote civic and social service activities for youth and adults. Conducts children's services and tutoring sessions. Maintains small library. Provides educational, tutorial, senior citizen, and health programs.

Latin Business Association. 120 S San Pedro St., Ste. 530, Los Angeles, CA 90012. Phone: (213)628-8510; Fax: (213)628-8519 • URL: http://www.lbausa.com • Latino business owners and corporations. Assists Latino business owners to develop their businesses.

Moscow International Business Association. Office 505, Ilyinka d.5/2, 109012 Moscow, Russia. Phone: 7 495 6200130; Fax: 7 495 6200552; Email: miba@mibas.ru • URL: http://www.mibas.ru • Strives to create an environment for Russian and foreign businessmen operating in Moscow. Boosts the Russian economy by helping businessmen engaged in productive endeavors.

Movement of French Businesses. 55 Ave. Bosquet, F-75330 Paris, France. Phone: 33 1 53591919; Fax: 33 1 45512044 • URL: http://archive.medef.com/main/core.php • Promotes French businesses.

National Aboriginal Capital Corporation Association. 75 Albert St., Ste. 908, Ottawa, ON, Canada K1P 5E7. Phone: (613)688-0894; Fax: (613)688-0895 • URL: http://www.nacca.net • Assists Aboriginal Financial Institutions (AFIs) in promoting the growth and development of Aboriginal businesses. Provides products and services to AFIs and Aboriginal-focused organizations including institutional capacity-building, training, access to capital, advocacy, partnerships, and member services with quality and accountability.

National Business Incubation Association. 340 W State St., Unit 25, Athens, OH 45701-1565. Phone: (740)593-4331; Fax: (740)593-1996; Email: info@nbia.org • URL: http://www.nbia.org • Incubator developers and managers; corporate joint venture partners, venture capital investors; economic development professionals. (Incubators are business assistance programs providing business consulting services and financing assistance to start-up and fledgling companies.) Helps newly formed businesses to succeed. Educates businesses and investors on incubator benefits; offers specialized training in incubator formation and management. Conducts research and referral services; compiles statistics; maintains speakers' bureau; publishes information relevant to business incubation and growing companies.

National Business Initiative. Bldg. D, 3rd Fl., 32 Princess of Wales Terr., Sunnyside Office Park, Johannesburg 2193, South Africa. Phone: 27 11 5446000; Fax: 27 11 4842754; Email: info@nbi.org.za • URL: http://www.nbi.org.za • Businesses. Promotes creation and maintenance of a social and economic climate conducive to the domestic development of South Africa. Conducts and assists programs in areas including education, economic growth and equity, enterprise, local government capacity building and transformation and public/private partnerships.

National Business Officers Association. 1400 L St. NW, Ste. 850, Washington, DC 20005. Phone: (202)407-7140 or (202)407-7141; Fax: (202)354-4944; Email: jeff.shields@nboa.net • URL: http://www.nboa.net • Independent school business officers. Helps members streamline business and strategic operations.

National Nurses in Business Association. 8941 Atlanta Ave., Ste. 202, Huntington Beach, CA 92646. Phone: 877-353-8888 • URL: http://www.nnba.net • Promotes, supports, educates, and provides a comprehensive network for nurse entrepreneurs.

National Society of Hispanic MBAs. 450 E John Carpenter Fwy., Irving, TX 75062. Phone: 877-467-4622 or (214)596-9338; Fax: (214)596-9325 • URL: http://www.nshmba.org • Hispanic MBA professional business network dedicated to economic and philanthropic advancement.

Phi Chi Theta. 1508 E Beltline Rd., Ste. 104, Carrollton, TX 75006. Phone: (972)245-7202; Email: executivedirector@phichitheta.org • URL: http://www.phichitheta.org • Co-ed professional fraternity - business and economics. Maintains hall of fame; sponsors educational programs.

Phi Gamma Nu. 6745 Cheryl Ann Dr., Seven Hills, OH 44131-3720. Phone: (216)524-0019; Email: pgnexecutivedirector@gmail.com • URL: http://www.phigammanu.com • Professional fraternity - business administration and economics.

Phi Theta Pi. 6552 Bradford Dr., West Des Moines, IA 50266-2308. Phone: (515)440-2045 or (515)271-1540; Email: ptpfrat@mchsi.com • URL: http://www.phithetapi.org • Honorary fraternity of businessmen and women (includes faculty members).

Polish-U.S. Business Council. Chamber of Commerce of the United States, 1615 H St. NW, Washington, DC 20062-2000. Phone: 800-638-6582 or (202)659-6000; Email: press@uschamber.com • URL: http://www.uschamber.com • U.S. corporations involved in industry, agriculture, or services. Seeks to expand trade between the U.S. and Poland.

For publishers' addresses, refer to SOURCES CITED section at the back of the book.

and to encourage investment in Poland by U.S. firms.

Portuguese Confederation of Business and Services. Av. Dom Vasco da Gama 29, P-1449-032 Lisbon, Portugal. Phone: 351 21 3031380 or 351 21 3929990; Fax: 351 21 3031401; Email: ccp@ccp.pt • URL: http://www.ccp.pt • Aims to strengthen the capacity of action of the industry.

Qatari Businessmen Association. PO Box 24475, Doha, Qatar. Phone: 974 443 53 120; Fax: 974 443 53 834; Email: qba@qataribusinessmen.org • URL: http://www.qataribusinessmen.org • Seeks to strengthen Qatar's business and economic growth. Supports and enhances the role of the private sector in the economy. Promotes private sectors' activities and establishes a channel of communication among Qatari businessmen. Acts as a catalyst for the promotion of diversified investment flows, modern entrepreneurial spirit and corporate development in Qatar.

Rwanda Private Sector Federation. PO Box 319, Kigali, Rwanda. Phone: 250 570650; Email: info@rpsf.org.rw • URL: http://www.psf.org.rw • Promotes and protects the interests of the Rwandan business community through lobbying and advocacy. Provides business development services that lead to sustainable economic growth and development. Facilitates a dialogue with the government on matters related to the improvement of business.

Sigma Iota Epsilon. c/o Dr. G. James Francis, President, Colorado State University, 213 Rockwell Hall, Fort Collins, CO 80523. Phone: (970)491-6265 or (970)491-7200; Fax: (970)491-3522; Email: jim.francis@business.colostate.edu • URL: http://www.sienational.com • Honorary and professional fraternity for students in all management concentrations (business, construction management, etc.) Provides competitions, educational and charitable programs, and speakers' bureau on a local level. Student division of the Academy of Management.

Spanish Confederation of Business Organisations. Calle Diego de Leon, 50, E-28006 Madrid, Spain. Phone: 34 91 5663400; Fax: 34 91 5622562; Email: ceoe@ceoe.es • URL: http://www.ceoe.es • Represents the Spanish business community in all sectors, including agriculture, industry and services.

Swiss-Argentine Chamber of Commerce. Av. Leandro N Alem 1074, Piso 10, C1001AAS Buenos Aires, Argentina. Phone: 54 11 43117187; Email: info@suiza.org.ar • URL: http://www.suiza.org.ar/select_lang.php • Promotes businesses between Argentina and Switzerland.

Swiss Business Association Singapore. c/o Embassy of Switzerland, 1, Swiss Club Link, Singapore 288162, Singapore. Phone: 65 67220799 • URL: http://www.swissbusiness.org.sg • Assists Swiss companies established in Singapore in conducting, sponsoring or promoting any activity that will benefit its members. Promotes the interests of members related to trade. Encourages the growth of the Swiss trade by promoting investment, finance, commerce and industry.

Swiss Malaysian Business Association. c/o Embassy of Switzerland, 16 Persiaran Madge, 55000 Kuala Lumpur, Malaysia. Phone: 60 3 21629889; Fax: 60 3 21418410; Email: info@smba.org.my • URL: http://www.myswiss.org • Promotes and fosters bilateral trade, services and investment between Switzerland and Malaysia. Assists potential new Swiss companies in establishing their headquarters in Malaysia. Maintains and improves close trading, commercial and other links between Malaysia and Switzerland. Provides a forum for members in exchanging information and identifying and discussing issues of common interests regarding economic, industrial and commercial objectives.

Yemeni Businessmen Club. PO Box 15539, Sana'a, Yemen. Phone: 967 1 440360 or 967 1 444910; Fax: 967 1 440207; Email: ybc-yemen@yemen.net.ye • URL: http://www.ybc-yemen.com • Seeks to strengthen links between members and to develop their institutions and contribute to the overall development process. Implements programs and activities by trust and a spirit of cooperation. Works to strengthen links between members.

BUSINESS ADMINISTRATION

See ADMINISTRATION

BUSINESS AIRPLANES

See BUSINESS AVIATION

BUSINESS AND GOVERNMENT

See REGULATION OF INDUSTRY

BUSINESS AND PROFESSIONAL WOMEN

See EMPLOYMENT OF WOMEN

BUSINESS AND SOCIETY

See SOCIAL RESPONSIBILITY

BUSINESS APPRAISAL

See VALUATION

BUSINESS ARCHIVES

See RECORDS MANAGEMENT

BUSINESS AVIATION

See also AVIATION INDUSTRY

ABSTRACTS AND INDEXES

Business Periodicals Index Retrospective. EBSCO Publishing Inc. • 11/year. Quarterly and annual cumulations.

BIBLIOGRAPHIES

Aviation. U. S. Government Printing Office. • Annual. Free. Lists government publications. (GPO Subject Bibliography Number 18).

DIRECTORIES

ABD--Aviation Buyer's Directory. Air Service Directory Inc. • Quarterly. Covers: aircraft, parts, and equipment manufacturers and dealers, and service firms in the aviation industry. Entries include: Company name, address, phone.

Airport/Facility Directory. U.S. National Ocean Service. • Covers: Non-military airports in the continental United States; separate volumes cover the southeast, northeast, northwest, east central, north central, southwest, and south central states (including Puerto Rico and the Virgin Islands). Entries include: Airport name, location, weather service phone number, control center frequencies, and information concerning navigational and other aids and systems.

Jet and PropJet Business Aircraft Directory. Avcom International Inc. • Annual. $26.95. Owners of business jet and turboprop aircraft. Worldwide coverage. Formerly *Propjet.*

OTHER SOURCES

Aviation Law Reports. Wolters Kluwer Law & Business CCH. • Semimonthly. Four looseleaf volumes covering aviation law.

PERIODICALS AND NEWSLETTERS

A/C Flyer: Best Read Resale Magazine Worldwide. McGraw Hill Financial Inc. • Monthly. Individuals $49.00 per year; students, $28.00 per year. Lists used airplanes for sale by dealers, brokers, and private owners. Provides news and trends relating to the aircraft resale industry. Special issues include "Product & Service Buyer's Guide" and "Dealer/Broker Directory.".

Business and Commercial Aviation. McGraw-Hill Aviation Week Group. • Monthly. $52.00 per year. Supplement available: *Annual Planning Purchasing Handbook.*

FAA Aviation News. Federal Aviation Administration. U. S. Government Printing Office. • Bimonthly. $28.00. per year. Designed to help airmen become safer pilots. Includes updates on major rule changes and proposals.

Flying. Bonnier Corp. • Monthly. $14 Individuals print. General aviation magazine. Includes three *Special Issues.* Price on application.

General Aviation News. Flyer Media Inc. • Semimonthly. $29.95 Individuals 1 year. General aviation newspaper (tabloid) for aircraft pilots and owners.

Professional Pilot Magazine. Queensmith Communications Corp. • Monthly. $50 Individuals. Edited for career pilots in all areas of aviation: airline, corporate, charter, and military. Includes flying technique, avionics, navigation, accident analysis, career planning, corporate profiles, and business aviation news.

Trade-a-Plane. • 36 issues per year. $36.00 per year. Subject matter is aircraft for sale or trade.

RESEARCH CENTERS AND INSTITUTES

Ohio Aerospace Institute. 22800 Cedar Point Rd., Cleveland, OH 44142. Phone: (440)962-3000; Fax: (216)962-3120 or (440)962-3120; Email: info@oai.org • URL: http://www.oai.org • Aerospace-related research, education, and technology transfers. Formerly Ohio Aerospace Institute.

STATISTICS SOURCES

Air Transport. Airlines for America. • Annual. $20. Airline industry information.

TRADE/PROFESSIONAL ASSOCIATIONS

National Business Aviation Association. 1200 G St. NW, Ste. 1100, Washington, DC 20005-3830. Phone: (202)783-9000; Fax: (202)331-8364; Email: info@nbaa.org • URL: http://www.nbaa.org • Companies owning and operating aircraft for business use, suppliers, and maintenance and air fleet service companies. Compiles statistics; provides literature for researchers and students.

BUSINESS BROKERS

See BUSINESS ENTERPRISES, SALE OF

BUSINESS BUDGETING

See BUDGETING, BUSINESS

BUSINESS CHOICE

See OCCUPATIONS

BUSINESS CONDITIONS

See also BANKRUPTCY; BUSINESS CYCLES; BUSINESS FORECASTING

ALMANACS AND YEARBOOKS

Political Risk Yearbook. The PRS Group Inc. • Annual. Each volume covers a separate region of the world and assesses economic and political conditions as they relate to the risk of doing business.

CD-ROM DATABASES

Newspaper Abstracts Ondisc. ProQuest L.L.C. • Monthly. $2,950.00 per year (covers 1989 to date; archival discs are available for 1985-88). Provides cover-to-cover CD-ROM indexing and abstracting of 19 major newspapers, including the *New York Times, Wall Street Journal, Washington Post, Chicago Tribune,* and *Los Angeles Times.*

OECD Statistical Compendium. Organization for Economic Cooperation and Development. • Semiannual. $1,905.00 per year for 1 to 10 users. CD-ROM contains more than 730,000 monthly, quarterly, and annual time series for OECD countries, 1960 to date. Includes fully searchable data on agriculture, food, economic indicators, national accounts, employment, energy, finance, industry, technology, and foreign trade. Results can be displayed in various forms.

ENCYCLOPEDIAS AND DICTIONARIES

The Way We Work: An Encyclopedia of Business Culture. Cengage Learning Inc. • 2010. eBook. Published by Greenwood Publishing Group. Explores in over 150 A-Z entries, the origins and impact of the concepts, ideas, fads and themes that have become part of the business vernacular, shedding light on the dynamic ways in which business and society both influence and reflect each other.

INTERNET DATABASES

Business 2.0 Web Guide to the Best Business Links. Business 2.0 Media Inc. Phone: (415)293-4800; Email: support@business2.com • URL: http://www.business2.com/webguide • Web site presents an extensive, searchable directory of links to "the best, most informative, and authoritative web pages." Twenty main categories cover business, finance, career, company information, people, and technology topics, with thousands of subtopics, all linking to Web sites recommended by experienced business researchers. Fees: Free.

Factiva. Dow Jones Reuters Business Interactive, LLC. Phone: 800-369-7466 or (609)452-1511; Fax: (609)520-5770; Email: solutions@factiva.com • URL: http://www.factiva.com • Fee-based Web site provides "global news and business information through Web sites and content integration solutions." Includes Dow Jones and Reuters newswires, The Wall Street Journal, and more than 7,000 other sources of current news, historical articles, market research reports, and investment analysis. Content includes 96 major U. S. newspapers, 900 non-English sources, trade publications, media transcripts, country profiles, news photos, etc.

Fedstats. Federal Interagency Council on Statistical Policy. Phone: (202)395-7254 • URL: http://www.fedstats.gov • Web site features an efficient search facility for full-text statistics produced by more than 100 federal agencies, including the Census Bureau, the Bureau of Economic Analysis, and the Bureau of Labor Statistics. Boolean searches can be made within one agency or for all agencies combined. Links are offered to international statistical bureaus, including the UN, IMF, OECD, UNESCO, Eurostat, and 20 individual countries. Fees: Free.

FreeLunch.com. Economy.com, Inc. Phone: (610)696-8700; Fax: (610)696-1678 • URL: http://www.freelunch.com • Web site provides free access to more than 200 million economic and financial data series, covering industry, demographics, labor markets, prices, retail sales, government spending, trade, interest rates, housing starts, the stock market, etc. Data is available in either chart or table form. Searching is offered. Free, but registration required. Economy.com, Inc. also offers fee-based economic analysis at *The Dismal Scientist* site (www.dismal.com).

Nexis.com. Lexis-Nexis Group. Phone: 800-227-4908 or (937)865-6800; Fax: (937)865-6909; Email: webmaster@prod.lexis-nexis.com • URL: http://www.nexis.com • Fee-based Web site offers searching of about 2.8 billion documents in some 30,000 news, business, and legal information sources. Features include a subject directory covering 1,200 topics in 34 categories and a Company Dossier containing information on more than 500,000 public and private companies. Boolean searching is offered.

Summary of Commentary on Current Economic Conditions by Federal Reserve District. Board of Governors of the Federal Reserve System. Phone: (202)452-3000; Fax: (202)452-3819 • URL: http://www.federalreserve.gov/publications.htm • 8/year. Free Web site provides current "anecdotal information" eight times a year on economic conditions within each of the 12 Federal Reserve Districts, plus an extensive national *Summary.* Text is based on the opinions of bank officials, business executives, economists, financial market experts, and others. Typically contains views of consumer spending, manufacturing, services, credit, employment, prices, wages, and the economy in general. Usually referred to as the Beige Book.

ONLINE DATABASES

Country Report Services. The PRS Group Inc. • Provides full text of reports describing the business risks and opportunities currently existing in more than 150 countries of the world. Contains a wide variety of statistics and forecasts relating to economics political and social conditions. Also includes demographics, tax, and currency information. Updated monthly. Inquire as to online cost and availability.

OTHER SOURCES

Consensus Forecasts: A Worldwide Survey. Consensus Economics Inc. • Monthly. Provides a survey of more than 200 "prominent"financial and economic forecasters, covering 20 major countries. Two-year forecasts for each country include future growth, inflation, interest rates, and exchange rates. Each issue contains analysis of business conditions in various countries.

World Economic and Social Survey: Trends and Policies in the World Economy. United Nations Publications. • Annual. $55.00. Includes discussion and "an extensive statistical annex of economic, trade, and financial indicators, incorporating current data and forecasts.".

World Economic Situation and Prospects. United Nations Publications. • Annual. $42 Individuals print. Serves as a supplement and update to the UN *World Economic and Social Survey.*

PERIODICALS AND NEWSLETTERS

Economic Perspectives. Federal Reserve Bank of Chicago. • Quarterly. Contains in-depth articles reporting on the Bank's economic research.

Federal Reserve Bank of Atlanta: Economic Review. Federal Reserve Bank of Atlanta. • Quarterly. Free.

Federal Reserve Bank of Dallas: Southwest Economy Economic Review. Federal Reserve Bank of Dallas. • Quarterly. Economic banking review.

Federal Reserve Bank of Kansas City. Federal Reserve Bank of Kansas City. • Quarterly. Free.

Federal Reserve Bank of Minneapolis: Quarterly Review. Federal Reserve Bank of Minneapolis, Research Department. • Quarterly. Free.

Federal Reserve Bank of New York: Economic Policy Review. Federal Reserve Bank of New York, Public Information Office. • Quarterly. Free.

Federal Reserve Bank of Philadelphia: Business Review. Federal Reserve Bank of Philadelphia, Research Dept. • Quarterly. Free. Contains articles on current topics in economics, finance, and banking.

Federal Reserve Bank of Richmond: Economic Quarterly. Federal Reserve Bank of Richmond - Research Department. • Quarterly. Free. Formerly *Federal Reserve Bank of Richmond: Economic Review.*

Federal Reserve Bank of Saint Louis: Review. Federal Reserve Bank of Saint Louis. • Quarterly. Bimonthly. Free.

Federal Reserve Bank of San Francisco Economic Letter. Federal Reserve Bank of San Francisco. Economic Letter. • 38 times a year. Free. Formerly *Federal Reserve Bank of San Francisco: Weekly Letter.*

Federal Reserve Bank of San Francisco: Economic Review. Federal Reserve Bank of San Francisco. • Annual. Free.

First Alaskans: A Statewide Magazine of Business and Culture. Alaska Newspapers Inc. • Quarterly. $16 Individuals. Consumer magazine covering business and culture in Alaska.

The Levy Institute Forecast. Forecasting Center Jerome Levy Economics Institute. • Description: Provides analyses and forecasts of U.S. business conditions. Reports on production, sales, inflation, corporate profits, and interest rates.

Ragan's Annual Report Review. Lawrence Ragan Communications Inc. • Description: Provides business trends, tips, and tactics.

Research Reports. American Institute for Economic Research. • Contains two or more current economic events in each issue.

STATISTICS SOURCES

OECD Economic Outlook. Organisation for Economic Co-operation and Development Publications and Information Center. • Semiannual. Price on application. $95.00 per year. Contains a wide range of economic and monetary data relating to the member countries of the Organization for Economic Cooperation and Development. Includes about 100 statistical tables and graphs, with 24-month forecasts for each of the OECD countries. Provides extensive review and analysis of recent economic trends.

OECD Economic Survey of the United States. Organisation for Economic Co-operation and Development Publications and Information Center. • Annual. €60.00.

OECD Economic Surveys. Organisation for Economic Co-operation and Development Publications and Information Center. • Annual. $26.00 each. These are separate, yearly reviews for each of the economies of the industrialized nations that comprise the OECD. Each edition includes forecasts, analyses, and detailed statistical tables for the country being surveyed. (The combined series, one annual volume for each nation, is available at $485.00.).

Standard & Poor's Industry Surveys. Standard & Poor's Financial Services L.L.C. • Semiannual. $1,800.00. Two looseleaf volumes. Includes monthly *Supplements.* Provides detailed, individual surveys of 52 major industry groups. Each survey is revised on a semiannual basis. Also includes "Monthly Investment Review" (industry group investment analysis) and monthly "Trends & Projections" (economic analysis).

Survey of Current Business. U. S. Government Printing Office. • Published by Bureau of Economic Analysis, U. S. Department of Commerce. Presents a wide variety of business and economic data.

World Economic Factbook. Cengage Learning Inc. • Annual. $475 Individuals E-book. Published by Euromonitor International. Presents key economic facts and figures for each of 204 countries worldwide, including details of chief industries, export-import trade, currency, political risk, household expenditures, and the economic situation in general.

World Economic Prospects. Cengage Learning Inc. • 2010. $650.00. 8th edition. Published by Euromonitor International. Ranks countries by specific economic characteristics, such as gross domestic product (GDP) per capita and short term growth prospects. Discusses the economic situation, prospects, and market potential of each of the countries.

TRADE/PROFESSIONAL ASSOCIATIONS

Local Initiatives Support Corporation. 501 7th Ave., New York, NY 10018-5903. Phone: (212)455-9800; Fax: (212)682-5929; Email: info@lisc.org • URL: http://www.lisc.org • Seeks to help independent community-based organizations in deteriorated areas to improve local, physical, and economic conditions while strengthening their own management and financial capabilities. Matches funds contributed by local corporations and foundations with those provided by national donors and investors; offers loans and grants to local organizations and projects. Administers national community development loan programs in cooperation with major financial institutions.

BUSINESS CONSOLIDATION

See MERGERS AND ACQUISITIONS

BUSINESS CORRESPONDENCE

See also COMMUNICATION; REPORT WRITING

E-BOOKS

Business and Technical Communication: An Annotated Guide to Sources, Skills, and Strategies. Cengage Learning Inc. • 2007. eBook. Includes research sources, an annotated bibliography of how-to information, and detailed indexes to identify the most relevant items in aiding business and technical communication.

PERIODICALS AND NEWSLETTERS

Harvard Management Communication Letter. Harvard Business School Publishing. • Description: Provides information and techniques for managers on effective communication.

RESEARCH CENTERS AND INSTITUTES

Aarhus University - School of Business and Social Sciences - Department of Business Communication - Center for Corporate Communication. Fuglesangs Allè 4, DK-8210 Aarhus, Denmark. Phone: 45 89486268; Fax: 45 86150188 • URL: http://bcom.au.dk/research/academicareas/ccc • Business communications, including management communication, market communication, corporate communication, public relations, internal communication, business journalism, etc.

BUSINESS CYCLES

See also BUSINESS CONDITIONS; BUSINESS FORECASTING; BUSINESS RESEARCH

CD-ROM DATABASES

OECD Statistical Compendium. Organization for Economic Cooperation and Development. • Semiannual. $1,905.00 per year for 1 to 10 users. CD-ROM contains more than 730,000 monthly, quarterly, and annual time series for OECD countries, 1960 to date. Includes fully searchable data on agriculture, food, economic indicators, national accounts, employment, energy, finance, industry, technology, and foreign trade. Results can be displayed in various forms.

E-BOOKS

Continuous Computing Technologies for Enhancing Business Continuity. Cengage Learning Inc. • 2009. eBook. Provides an explanation of business continuity, business continuity management, and continuous computing technologies. Covers topics such as clustering technologies, fault tolerance, and technologies for reducing downtime.

E-Business Process Management: Technologies and Solutions. Cengage Learning Inc. • 2007. eBook. Explores supply chain management by providing examples of integrated framework for global SCM, novel ways of improving flexibility, responsiveness and competitiveness via strategic IT alliances among channel members in a supply chain network, and techniques that might facilitate improved strategic decision-making in a SCM environment.

ENCYCLOPEDIAS AND DICTIONARIES

Encyclopedia of the Great Depression. Cengage Learning Inc. • $465 Individuals. Covers about two decades of U.S. economic history, from the farm crisis of the mid-1920s, through the gradual recovery of the 1930s, to the beginning of World War II. (Macmillan Reference USA imprint). eBook also available.

GENERAL WORKS

Great Depression and New Deal Reference Library. Cengage Learning Inc. • 2003. $236.00. Four volumes. Published by UXL. Includes Great Depression and New Deal: Almanac; Great Depression and New Deal: Biographies and Great Depression and New Deal: Primary Sources. Also available as eBook.

INTERNET DATABASES

Business 2.0 Web Guide to the Best Business Links. Business 2.0 Media Inc. Phone: (415)293-4800; Email: support@business2.com • URL: http://www.business2.com/webguide • Web site presents an extensive, searchable directory of links to "the best, most informative, and authoritative web pages." Twenty main categories cover business, finance, career, company information, people, and technology topics, with thousands of subtopics, all linking to Web sites recommended by experienced business researchers. Fees: Free.

Fedstats. Federal Interagency Council on Statistical Policy. Phone: (202)395-7254 • URL: http://www.fedstats.gov • Web site features an efficient search facility for full-text statistics produced by more than 100 federal agencies, including the Census Bureau, the Bureau of Economic Analysis, and the Bureau of Labor Statistics. Boolean searches can be made within one agency or for all agencies combined. Links are offered to international statistical bureaus, including the UN, IMF, OECD, UNESCO, Eurostat, and 20 individual countries. Fees: Free.

FreeLunch.com. Economy.com, Inc. Phone: (610)696-8700; Fax: (610)696-1678 • URL: http://www.freelunch.com • Web site provides free access to more than 200 million economic and financial data series, covering industry, demographics, labor markets, prices, retail sales, government spending, trade, interest rates, housing starts, the stock market, etc. Data is available in either chart or table form. Searching is offered. Free, but registration required. Economy.com, Inc. also offers fee-based economic analysis at *The Dismal Scientist* site (www.dismal.com).

PERIODICALS AND NEWSLETTERS

Cycle Projections. Foundation for the Study of Cycles Inc. • Monthly. Includes trend projections for stocks, commodities, real estate, and the economy. Short, intermediate, and long-term cycles are covered.

Trading Cycles. R.E. Andrews, editor. Andrews Publications, Inc. • Monthly. $97.99 per year. Newsletter. Technical investment newsletter. Formerly *Andrews Trading Cycles.*

STATISTICS SOURCES

The AIER Chart Book. AIER Research Staff. American Institute for Economic Research. • Annual. $4 Individuals. A compact compilation of long-range charts ("Purchasing Power of the Dollar," for example, goes back to 1780) covering various aspects of the U. S. economy. Includes inflation, interest rates, debt, gold, taxation, stock prices, etc. (Economic Education Bulletin.).

Survey of Current Business. U. S. Government Printing Office. • Published by Bureau of Economic Analysis, U. S. Department of Commerce. Presents a wide variety of business and economic data.

BUSINESS DEPRESSIONS

See BUSINESS CYCLES

BUSINESS DIRECTORIES

See also CATALOGS AND DIRECTORIES

BUSINESS DIRECTORIES, GENERAL

HANDBOOKS AND MANUALS

International Business Handbook. Chamber of Commerce and Industry Queensland.

BUSINESS ECONOMICS

ABSTRACTS AND INDEXES

Business Periodicals Index Retrospective. EBSCO Publishing Inc. • 11/year. Quarterly and annual cumulations.

CD-ROM DATABASES

EconLit. Ovid Technologies Inc. • Updated monthly. Lists journal articles, book reviews, disserations of economic literature. Over 1,400 journals covered.

DIRECTORIES

Business Economics--Membership Directory Issue. National Association for Business Economics. • Annual. $125 electronic with membership. List of about 3,000 association members, including students.

Institute of Business Appraisers--Directory. Institute of Business Appraisers. • $20 Members. Listing of members and certified business appraisers.

National Association for Business Economics Membership Directory. National Association for Business Economics. • Annual. Membership.

National Association for Business Economics--Membership Directory. National Association for Business Economics. • Annual. Covers about 3,600 members internationally.

Russia: Political and Economic Analysis and Business Directory. Chamber World Network. • $29.95. Publication includes: Directories of organizations, companies, and other agencies in or doing business in Russia, including Russian companies, joint ventures, firms from outside Russia accredited to do business there, banks, insurance companies, consulates and embassies, hotels. Database includes:

Essays and tables on the economic and legal structure of Russia, including summaries of Russian law, statistics, and surveys of future trends. Entries include: For companies--Name, address, phone, annual sales, number of employees, products.

E-BOOKS

Business and Technology in China. Cengage Learning Inc. • 2011. eBook. Explores the inner workings of China's business world, highlighting the country's attempts to develop the scientific and technological base for a greener economic model.

The Growing Business Handbook. Cengage Learning Inc. • 2010. eBook. 12th edition. Published by Kogan Page. Focuses on key issues such as funding, innovation, customer service, business technology and international expansion. Includes case studies from top companies.

21st Century Economics: A Reference Handbook. Cengage Learning Inc. • 2010. eBook. Published by Sage Publications. Covers traditional economic theory as well as challenges that face the nation in an economy with unemployment issues, failures of major businesses and industries, and continued dependence on oil with its wildly fluctuating prices.

ENCYCLOPEDIAS AND DICTIONARIES

Encyclopedia of Management (EoM). Cengage Learning Inc. • $434 Individuals. 2012. 7th Edition. Contains 316 essays on business management topics. eBook available. Inquire for pricing.

Historical Encyclopedia of American Business. Cengage Learning Inc. • 2009. eBook. Published by Salem Press. Long overviews on different sectors of the economy, such as agriculture and banking; individual industries such as advertising and electronics; and general topics such as business cycles, labor strikes and outsourcing. There are also overviews on broad legal topics such as antitrust legislation, bankruptcy laws and patent laws.

GENERAL WORKS

ADB Business Opportunities. Asian Development Bank. • Monthly. Publication covering economic development.

Business and Economic Forecasting Unit Working papers. Monash University Business and Economic Forecasting Unit.

Business History Studies. KK Roy Ltd. • Quarterly. $460. Journal on business and economics.

Cost of Doing Business Report. American Rental Association. • $650 Nonmembers.

Economic and business reports. University of Nebraska—Lincoln Bureau of Business Research. • Monthly.

International Business & Economics Research Journal (IBER). The Clute Institute for Academic Research. • Monthly. $495 Institutions. Applied business research magazine.

New Mexico Business Current Economic Report. University of New Mexico Bureau of Business and Economic Research. • Monthly. $25 1 year.

ONLINE DATABASES

Business & Management Practices™. Cengage Learning Inc. • Focuses on the processes, methods, and strategies of managing a business. Includes information on business planning, decision making, and management issues.

Wilson Business Abstracts Online. H.W. Wilson Co. • Indexes and abstracts 600 major business periodicals, plus the *Wall Street Journal* and the business section of the *New York Times*. Indexing is from 1982, abstracting from 1990, with the two newspapers included from 1993. Updated weekly. Inquire as to online cost and availability. (*Business Periodicals Index* without abstracts is also available online.).

PERIODICALS AND NEWSLETTERS

Asia Pacific Business Review. Routledge Journals Taylor & Francis Group. • $154 Individuals print only. Journal covering the origins of national economic success.

Business Analyst. University of Delhi, New Delhi. • Semiannual. $300. Periodical focusing on business economics analysis.

Business Economics: Designed to Serve the Needs of People Who Use Economics in Their Work. National Association for Business Economics. • Quarterly. Quarterly. $85.00 per year. Features articles on applied economics.

Business History Review. Harvard Business School. • Quarterly. $70 Individuals. A scholarly journal that seeks to publish articles with rigorous primary research that addresses major topics of debate, offers comparative perspectives, and contributes to the broadening of the subject.

Challenge: The Magazine of Economic Affairs. M.E. Sharpe Inc. • 6/year. $72 Individuals print only. A nontechnical journal on current economic policy and economic trends.

The Economist. The Economist Intelligence Unit. • 190 ₱ Individuals Print and Digital per week.

Fortune Magazine. Time Inc., Business Information Group. • Biweekly. $19.99 all access. Edited for top executives and upper-level managers.

Harvard Business Review. Harvard University, Graduate School of Business Administration. Harvard Business School Publishing. • 10/year.

Institute of Business Appraisers--Newsletter. Institute of Business Appraisers. • Quarterly. Covers association and industry news.

International Business: Your Passport to the Global Marketplace. American International Publishing. • Monthly. $48 Individuals. Magazine for senior managers of U.S. Based mid-market multi-national companies seeking to gor internationally through export/import, joint ventures, acquisitions or relocation/expansion.

The Journal of Business. The University of Chicago Press, Journals Div. • Quarterly. Individuals, $31.00 per year; institutions, $125.00 per year; students, $25.00 per year.

MIT Sloan Management Review. Sloan Management Review Association. Massachusetts Institute of Technology Department of Urban Studies and Planning Community Innovators Lab. • Quarterly. $69. A business journal that bridges the gap between management research and practice.

NABE News. National Association for Business Economics. • Quarterly. Description: Concerned with business economics. Serves this professional Association of persons employed by private, institutional, or government concerns in the area of business-related economic analysis. Recurring features include results of the NABE quarterly outlook survey, featured articles of timely interest, reviews of seminars and annual meetings, news from local chapters and roundtables, and personal notes.

Quarterly Journal of Finance and Accounting. University of Nebraska at Lincoln College of Business Administration.

The Quarterly Review of Economics and Finance. JAI Press. • Quarterly. $142 Individuals. Publishes high quality manuscripts that cover topics in the areas of economics, financial economics and finance.

TRADE/PROFESSIONAL ASSOCIATIONS

Association of Danish Business Economists. PO Box 2043, 1012 Copenhagen, Denmark. Phone: 45 33141446; Fax: 45 33141149; Email: info@c3.dk • URL: http://www.c3.dk • Business administration alumni of Danish schools and universities. Sponsors educational courses, seminars, and forums; conducts research programs. Operates placement service.

National Association for Business Economics. 1920 L St. NW, Ste. 300, Washington, DC 20036. Phone: (202)463-6223; Fax: (202)463-6239; Email: nabe@nabe.com • URL: http://www.nabe.com • Formerly National Association of Business Economists.

National Black Chamber of Commerce. 4400 Jenifer St. NW, Ste. 331, Washington, DC 20015-2133. Phone: (202)466-6888; Fax: (202)466-4918; Email: info@nationalbcc.org • URL: http://www.nationalbcc.org • Works for the issues of economics and entrepreneurship in the African-American community.

BUSINESS EDUCATION

See also ADULT EDUCATION; COLLEGES AND UNIVERSITIES; GRADUATE WORK IN UNIVERSITIES; VOCATIONAL EDUCATION

ABSTRACTS AND INDEXES

Current Index to Journals in Education (CIJE). Oryx Press. • Monthly. $245.00 per year. Semiannual cumulations, $475.00.

Education Index. H.W. Wilson Co. • 10 times a year. Quarterly and annual cumulations. Price varies.

Educational Administration Abstracts. Pine Forge Press. • Quarterly. $722 Institutions.

ALMANACS AND YEARBOOKS

National Business Education Yearbook. National Business Education Association. • Annual. $40 Individuals. Written by business education professionals with expertise in this ever-changing field. Refereed publication examines topical business education-related subjects.

BIOGRAPHICAL SOURCES

Who's Who in American Education. Marquis Who's Who L.L.C. • Biennial. $159.95. Contains over 27,000 concise biographies of teachers, administrators, and other individuals involved in all levels of American education.

CD-ROM DATABASES

Education Index Retrospective: 1929-1983. EBSCO Publishing Inc. • Provides indexing of education-related literature from 1983 to date.

ERIC SilverPlatter. U.S. Department of Education Institute of Education Sciences Education Resources Information Center. • Opinion papers, evaluations, speeches.

OECD Statistical Compendium. Organization for Economic Cooperation and Development. • Semiannual. $1,905.00 per year for 1 to 10 users. CD-ROM contains more than 730,000 monthly, quarterly, and annual time series for OECD countries, 1960 to date. Includes fully searchable data on agriculture, food, economic indicators, national accounts, employment, energy, finance, industry, technology, and foreign trade. Results can be displayed in various forms.

DIRECTORIES

American Universities and Colleges. American Council on Education USA. Walter de Gruyter Inc. • Quadrennial. $249.50. Two volumes. Produced in collaboration with the American Council on Education. Provides full descriptions of more than 1,900 institutions of higher learning, including details of graduate and professional programs.

Barron's Guide to Graduate Business Schools. Barron's Educational Series Inc. • Biennial. Contains profiles of more than 600 business schools offering graduate business degrees in the U. S. and Canada. Includes advice on choosing a school.

Business Education Forum--Professional Leadership Roster Issue. National Business Education

For publishers' addresses, refer to SOURCES CITED section at the back of the book.

Association. • Quarterly. Publication includes: List of key personnel in business education, including officers of national, regional, and state associations and state and local supervisory personnel in business education. Entries include: Institution or association name, names of officers and board members, addresses, phone, and Internet address.

Business Education Index. Delta Pi Epsilon Inc. • Annual. $25. Publication includes: List of selected periodicals and yearbooks which have published articles on business education in the previous year. Entries include: Publication acronym, full name, editor, address. Principal content of publication is an index of articles and authors.

BusinessWeek Guide to the Best Business Schools. The McGraw-Hill Companies Inc. • Covers: The top 25 business schools and 25 runners-up, ranked by recent graduates and corporate recruiters. Entries include: School contact information; tips on GMAT prep courses; free application software.

Careers and the MBA. Bob Adams Inc. • $12.95. Publication includes: List of over 200 companies that employ people with Master of Business Administration degrees. Database includes: Feature articles, career biographies, company profiles and industry reports for major industries. Entries include: For companies--Name, address, phone, name of contact person or office, description of company, possible positions open, and when to contact about them. For recruiters--Name, address.

Company Profiles for Students. Cengage Learning Inc. • $338 print. Covers approximately 280 most studied companies. Entries include company logos, illustrations, ticker symbol, market share, etc.

Guide to East European Business Education. Imec Publishing. • Covers: Institutions offering business education in Eastern Europe. Entries include: Name, address, phone, year founded, organizations represented, funding sources, main areas of activity, type of students, faculty information.

ISWorld Net Faculty Directory. MIS Research Center. • Database covers: college-level teachers of subjects related to management information systems and technology. Database includes: Faculty name, school, address, office phone, research and teaching areas, highest degree.

Job Training & Vocational Rehabilitation Services Directory. InfoGroup Inc. • Annual. Number of listings: 1,605. Entries include: Name, address, phone, size of advertisement, name of owner or manager, number of employees, year first in "Yellow Pages." Compiled from telephone company "Yellow Pages," nationwide.

Peterson's Guide to Graduate Programs in Business, Education, Health, and Law. Peterson's. • Annual. $38.47 Individuals. Covers colleges and universities in the United States and Canada that offer more than 16,800 accredited graduate programs in business, education, health, and law.

Peterson's Guide to MBA Programs: The Most Comprehensive Guide to U.S., Canadian, & International Business Schools. Peterson's. • $28.35 Individuals softcover. Covers: Over 4,000 U.S. accredited MBA programs worldwide. Entries include: Program name, address, phone.

Wall Street Journal Guide to the Top Business Schools. Simon and Schuster Inc. • Annual. $11.99. Rankings are based on surveys of recruiters of MBA graduates. Includes detailed descriptions of the leading U.S. business schools and information for applicants.

Who's Who in International Business Education and Research. Edward Elgar Publishing Inc. • $256.50 Individuals hardbound. Covers: 150 individuals in international business education and research. Entries include: Biographical data and professional data, career summary, URL.

E-BOOKS

The College Blue Book. Cengage Learning Inc. • Annual. $572 Individuals. Published by Macmillan Reference USA. Provides detailed information on programs, degrees, and financial aid sources in the U.S. and Canada.

Corporate Disasters: What Went Wrong and Why. Cengage Learning Inc. • Covers corporate misdeeds and mistakes in business. Published June 2012. Available in print ($483) and eBook.

GENERAL WORKS

Basic Business Essentials: Concepts and Tools. American CPE Inc. • Contains detailed training information covering fundamental topics in business and business management.

Focus on Business Education. STBED. • $39 Individuals. Publication covering business education.

How to Organize and Run a Small Business. American CPE Inc. • Contains detailed training information covering the basics of creating, organizing, and running a small business.

Journal of Behavioral Studies in Business (JBSB). Academic and Business Research Institute. • Journal containing manuscripts of behavioral studies in business related disciplines.

Journal of Business Ethics Education. Dienas Zurnali. • $490 Institutions library - hard copy. Journal assisting educators by providing conceptual tools managers needed to make choices those are ethically responsible and culturally sensitive as well as technically sound.

Journal of Education for Business. Routledge. • 8/year. $227 Institutions online only. Journal for business teachers, featuring business fundamentals, career and distributive education, consumer economics, management and trends in communications, information systems, and knowledge systems for business.

Legal Environments of Business. American CPE Inc. • Contains detailed training information covering legal structures and environments in which businesses operate in the United States.

101 Business Problems: Diagnosis and Remedy. American CPE Inc. • Contains detailed training information covering causes and solutions to more than 100 common business problems.

Who's Who in International Business Education and Research. Edward Elgar Publishing Inc. • $256.50 Individuals hardbound. Covers: 150 individuals in international business education and research. Entries include: Biographical data and professional data, career summary, URL.

INTERNET DATABASES

Business 2.0 Web Guide to the Best Business Links. Business 2.0 Media Inc. Phone: (415)293-4800; Email: support@business2.com • URL: http://www.business2.com/webguide • Web site presents an extensive, searchable directory of links to "the best, most informative, and authoritative web pages." Twenty main categories cover business, finance, career, company information, people, and technology topics, with thousands of subtopics, all linking to Web sites recommended by experienced business researchers. Fees: Free.

ONLINE DATABASES

ERIC. U.S. Department of Education Institute of Education Sciences Educational Resources Information Center. • Funded by the U.S. Department of Education, Institute of Education Sciences (formerly Office of Educational Research and Improvement). Provides access to more than one million online records covering education-related journal and report literature, 1966 to date. Updating is monthly. Inquire as to online cost and availability.

PERIODICALS AND NEWSLETTERS

BizEd: The Leading Voice of Business Education. Association to Advance Collegiate Schools of Business. • Bimonthly. $35 Individuals. Magazine covering trends in business education.

Business Education Forum. National Business Education Association. • Four times a year. Libraries, $70.00 per year. Includes *Yearbook* and *Keying In*, a newsletter.

Business Teacher Education Journal. National Association for Business Teacher Education. • Annual. $20 Members. Provides information on business education including curriculum and instructional implications, internships, and technologies.

Education Business. Public Sector Publishing Ltd. • Bimonthly. Magazine featuring administrative and commercial issues affecting education.

International Review for Business Education. International Society for Business Education. • Semiannual. $36.00 per year. Text in English, French, German, Italian, and Spanish.

Resources in Education. Educational Resources Information Center. U. S. Government Printing Office. • Monthly. Reports on educational research.

Teaching Business & Economics. Economics and Business Education Association. • 3/year. Publication covering business education.

RESEARCH CENTERS AND INSTITUTES

Center for Financial Responsibility. Texas Tech University, Lubbock, TX 79409-11210. Phone: (806)742-5050; Fax: (806)742-5033 • URL: http://www.depts.ttu.edu/cfr • Research areas include financial preparation for retirement, financial education, determinants of financial satisfaction, risk tolerance, and the career preparation of retirement industry professionals.

East Tennessee State University - Tennessee Small Business Development Center. College of Business & Technology, 2109 W Market St., Johnson City, TN 37604. Phone: (423)439-8505; Fax: (423)439-8506; Email: bjustice@mail.tsbdc.org • URL: http://www.tsbdc.org • Small business assistance in the areas of business plans and strategies, financial forecasts, feasibility studies, financial statement analysis, credit establishment and collection policies, inventory control analysis, marketing plans, accounting and record-keeping systems, licenses, permits, tax authorities, organizational structure, management succession, professional development, and buying and selling.

Georgia Institute of Technology - Tennenbaum Institute. Centergy Bldg., Ste. 600, 75 5th St. NW, Atlanta, GA 30338. Phone: (404)385-6013; Fax: (404)385-6127; Email: ron.johnson@gatech.edu • URL: http://www.ti.gatech.edu • Fundamental changes of private and public sector enterprises.

University of Maryland at College Park - Center for Global Business Education. 2410 Van Munching Hall, Robert H. Smith School of Business, College Park, MD 20742-1815. Phone: (301)405-0200; Fax: (301)314-9526; Email: lbarnard@rhsmith.umd.edu • URL: http://www.rhsmith.umd.edu/global • Global business and management.

University of Maryland at College Park - International Communications and Negotiations Simulations. 0145 Tydings Hall, Department of Government & Politics, College Park, MD 20742. Phone: (301)405-4172; Fax: (301)314-9301; Email: dfridl@umd.edu • URL: http://www.icons.umd.edu • Focuses on the critical connections between international issues and the perspectives that different cultures bring to negotiations. Also teaches cross cultural negotiation and develops international economic, environmental, and political scenarios/ curriculum materials for university and high school students.

University of Nebraska—Omaha - Nebraska Business Development Center. Mammel Hall, Ste. 200, College of Business Administration, 6708 Pine St., Omaha, NE 68182. Phone: (402)554-2521; Fax: (402)554-3473; Email: rbernier@unomaha.edu • URL: http://nbdc.unomaha.edu • Sustainable development, technology commercialization, management education, market research, marketing plans, strategic planning, financial planning, cash flow budgeting, capital budgeting, loan packaging, and rural development.

University of Warwick - Centre for Education and Industry. CEDAR, Rm. WE145, Coventry CV4 7AL, United Kingdom. Phone: 44 24 76523909; Fax: 44 24 76524472; Email: geoff.lindsay@warwick.ac.uk • URL: http://www2.warwick.ac.uk/fac/soc/cei • Advisory teaching and consultation in national and international education in business partnership and collaboration.

STATISTICS SOURCES

Occupational Projections and Training Data. U. S. Government Printing Office. • Biennial. $31.50. Issued by Bureau of Labor Statistics, U. S. Department of Labor. Contains projections of employment change and job openings over the next 15 years for about 500 specific occupations. Also includes the number of associate, bachelor's, master's, doctoral, and professional degrees awarded in a recent year for about 900 specific fields of study.

TRADE/PROFESSIONAL ASSOCIATIONS

Academy of Management. PO Box 3020, Briarcliff Manor, NY 10510-8020. Phone: (914)923-2607; Fax: (914)923-2615; Email: membership@aom.org • URL: http://www.aom.org • Professors in accredited universities and colleges who teach management; selected business executives who have made significant written contributions to the literature in the field of management and organization. Offers placement service.

Accounting and Finance Benchmarking Consortium. 4606 FM 1960 W, Ste. 250, Houston, TX 77069-9949. Phone: (281)440-5044 • URL: http://www.afbc.org • Accounting and finance managers of corporations with an interest in benchmarking. Promotes the use of benchmarking, wherein businesses compare their processes with those of their competitors, as a means of improving corporate efficiency and profitability. Facilitates exchange of information among members; conducts target operations, procurement, development, and maintenance studies; identifies model business practices.

AIESEC Alumni International. Ave. de Tervuren 300, B-1150 Brussels, Belgium. Email: info@aiesec-alumni.org • URL: http://www.aiesec-alumni.org • Alumni of the International Association of Students in Economics and Management. Promotes excellence in the study and practice of economics. Facilitates exchange of information among members; sponsors social programs.

Alliance of Merger and Acquisition Advisors. 200 E Randolph St., 24th Fl., Chicago, IL 60601. Phone: 877-844-2535; Fax: (312)729-9800; Email: info@amaaonline.org • URL: http://www.amaaonline.com • Serves the educational and resource needs of mergers and acquisitions professionals. Helps members improve their level of knowledge to better market and deliver their advisory services. Maintains the highest recognized standards of professional excellence for corporate advisory and transaction services.

American Escrow Association. 211 N Union St., Ste. 100, Alexandria, VA 22314. Phone: (703)519-1240; Email: hq@a-e-a.org • URL: http://www.a-e-a.org • Furthers the education and professionalism of the escrow industry. Enhances the education of escrow/settlement professionals. Increases the public knowledge and understanding of escrow and closing services. Coordinates legislative efforts throughout the United States.

American Indian Business Leaders. Gallagher Business Bldg., Ste. 366, Missoula, MT 59812. Phone: 877-245-2425; Fax: (406)243-2086 • URL: http://www.aibl.org • Provides a support system for American Indian students interested in learning the skills necessary to acquire a job, design their own business, raise capital, and network with successful American Indian business people. Provides career development opportunities for members as well as opportunities to develop strong work ethics and gain professional experience.

American Management Association. 1601 Broadway, New York, NY 10019-7420. Phone: 877-566-9441 or (212)586-8100 or (518)891-5510; Fax: (212)903-8168 or (518)891-0368; Email: customerservice@amanet.org • URL: http://www.amanet.org • Provides educational forums worldwide where members and their colleagues learn superior, practical business skills and explore best practices of world-class organizations through interaction with each other and expert faculty practitioners. Maintains a publishing program providing tools individuals use to extend learning beyond the classroom in a process of life-long professional growth and development through education.

American Society for Competitiveness. 664 Pratt Dr., 304 Eberly, IUP, Indiana, PA 15705. Phone: (724)357-5928; Fax: (724)357-7768; Email: office.asc2@gmail.com • URL: http://www.eberly.iup.edu/ASCWeb • Seeks to foster education and knowledge in subjects related to competitiveness by: facilitating exchange of information and ideas among educators, policy makers, and business people, and by encouraging and assisting research activities which advance knowledge of competitiveness practices and increase the available body of teaching and practice materials. Seeks to serve the needs of entrepreneurial scholars and intellectual managers. Specifically through its conferences and publications, intends to effectively serve the needs of academicians interested in the practical application of organizational theory and practicing managers interested in the intellectual development of the discipline.

America's Edge. 1212 New York Ave. NW, Ste. 300, Washington, DC 20005-3988. Phone: (202)408-9284 • URL: http://www.americasedge.org • Encourages business leaders to support education policies and initiatives aimed at providing all Americans the skills and knowledge essential for success in a competitive global marketplace. Facilitates exchange of information on best practices in business advocacy and support for education reform. Supports legislative changes in public policy and programs that will help build a qualified workforce.

Asset Based Finance Association. 3rd Fl., 20 Hill Rise, Surrey, Richmond TW10 6UA, United Kingdom. Phone: 44 20 8332 9955; Fax: 44 20 8332 2585 • URL: http://www.abfa.org.uk • Brokers, business agents, and factors in the United Kingdom. Promotes and protects members' interests in the fields of factoring and invoice discounting. Conducts educational and research programs. Maintains a code of conduct; fosters the advancement of knowledge and experience; awards diplomas to students. Disseminates information; compiles statistics.

Association for Research in Business Education - Delta Pi Epsilon. 1914 Association Dr., Reston, VA 20191-1596. Phone: (703)860-8300 or (703)620-4483 • URL: http://www.dpe.org • Professional society - men and women, business education.

Association of MBAs. 25 Hosier Ln., London EC1A 9LQ, United Kingdom. Phone: 44 20 72462686 or 44 20 72462691; Fax: 44 20 72462687; Email: info@mbaworld.com • URL: http://www.mbaworld.com • Consists of students and graduates of Association of MBAs-approved MBA programmes, business schools, companies and organizations who share the objectives of the Association and who wish to contribute towards them. Seeks to enhance quality in management and provide a unique network of contracts for members. Provides a range of services including a membership book, networking/educational events, career opportunities, accreditation of MBA programmes, salary research, administration of a preferential rate MBA loan scheme for students of accredited programmes and an MBA information service.

Association of Small and Medium Enterprises. 167 Jalan Bukit Merah, Tower 4, No.03-13, Singapore 150167, Singapore. Phone: 65 65130388; Fax: 65 65130399; Email: enquiries@edc-asme.sg • URL: http://www.asme.org.sg • Seeks to bring together entrepreneurs of various industries and service sectors for information exchange; promotes relationship between various national interest bodies; provides continuous business education and training; fosters entrepreneurship networking both locally and internationally; works toward the institutionalization of ASME as a business association network body.

Association to Advance Collegiate Schools of Business. 77 S Harbour Island Blvd., Ste. 750, Tampa, FL 33602. Phone: (813)769-6500; Fax: (813)769-6559; Email: events@aacsb.edu • URL: http://www.aacsb.edu • Represents educational institutions, businesses, and other entities devoted to the advancement of management education. Works to advance quality management education worldwide through accreditation.

Auto Suppliers Benchmarking Association. 4606 FM 1960 W, Ste. 250, Houston, TX 77069-9949. Phone: (281)440-5044; Fax: (281)440-6677 • URL: http://www.asbabenchmarking.com • Automotive supplier firms with an interest in benchmarking. Promotes the use of benchmarking, wherein businesses compare their processes with those of their competitors, as a means of improving corporate efficiency and profitability. Facilitates exchange of information among members; conducts target operations, procurement, development, and maintenance studies; identifies model business practices.

Beta Gamma Sigma. 125 Weldon Pkwy., Maryland Heights, MO 63043. Phone: 800-337-4677 or (314)432-5650; Fax: (314)432-7083; Email: bgshonors@betagammasigma.org • URL: http://www.betagammasigma.org • International honor society. For students in business and management at business programs accredited by AACSB International. Supports the advancement of business thought and practice to encourage lifelong learning.

Beta Gamma Sigma Alumni. PO Box 297-006, Brooklyn, NY 11229-7006. • URL: http://www.bgs-nyc.org • Alumni members of the collegiate national honor society Beta Gamma Sigma. Promotes excellence in business education, ethics, and scholastic achievement and recognition. Local New York chapter.

Beyster Institute. 9500 Gilman Dr. Otterson Hall S, Fourth Fl., La Jolla, CA 92093-0553. Phone: (858)246-0654; Email: beysterinfo@rady.ucsd.edu • URL: http://beysterinstitute.ucsd.edu • Helps business leaders build successful companies worldwide through training, education and outreach. Serves entrepreneurs by teaching them how to be effective managers and showing them how employee ownership can be adapted to fit their individual companies.

BPM-Focus. 3640-B3 N Federal Hwy., No. 421, Lighthouse Point, FL 33064. Phone: (954)688-4922; Fax: (954)758-7219; Email: info@bpmfocus.org • URL: http://www.bpmfocus.org • Identifies and clarifies issues that are common to users of workflow, electronic commerce, knowledge

For publishers' addresses, refer to SOURCES CITED section at the back of the book.

management and those who are in the process of reengineering their organizations.

Business Educators Australasia. Carringbush Business Ctre., 134-136 Cambridge St., Ste. 201, Level 2, Collingwood, VIC 3066, Australia. Phone: 61 3 94199622; Fax: 61 3 94191205 • URL: http://www.bea.asn.au • Promotes and represents business educators in Australasia.

Business-Higher Education Forum. 2025 M St. NW, Ste. 800, Washington, DC 20036-2422. Phone: (202)367-1189; Fax: (202)367-2269; Email: info@bhef.com • URL: http://www.bhef.com • Board chairmen and chief executive officers of Fortune 500 corporations; presidents and chancellors of universities and colleges. Addresses issues of interest to American business and higher education institutions such as: tax incentives for university research; worker training and retraining; new links between industry and academia; innovative methods of corporate support for higher education. Seeks to expand public awareness of the concerns of business and academic leaders and to influence policymaking affecting those concerns; to enhance relationships between corporate America and institutions of higher learning. Provides interchange between the business and academic communities. Has recently completed several studies on competitiveness; believes that improving the ability of American industry and workers to compete is essential to all other economic and societal goals. Organizes special task forces for in-depth studies on special issues. Disseminates reports and recommendations to policymakers in the public and private sector.

Business Modeling and Integration Domain Task Force. Object Management Group, 109 Highland Ave., Needham, MA 02494. Phone: (781)444-0404; Fax: (781)444-0320; Email: info@omg.org • URL: http://bmi.omg.org • Aims to empower all companies, across all industries, to develop and operate business processes that span multiple applications and business partners, behind the firewall and over the Internet.

Business Volunteers Unlimited. 1300 E 9th St., Ste. 1805, Cleveland, OH 44114-1509. Phone: (216)736-7711; Fax: (216)736-7710; Email: bvu@bvuvolunteers.org • URL: http://www.bvuvolunteers.org • Works to promote effective volunteerism and strong leadership. Provides consulting, education and volunteer referral services to nonprofit and businesses. Trains business executives for leadership roles on nonprofit boards.

CARTHA. 33 Buchanan Ct., Iowa City, IA 52246. Phone: (319)248-9625; Email: cartha.global@gmail.com • URL: http://www.cartha.org • Aims to strengthen academic-practitioner partnerships. Seeks to train, build and empower networks of professionals. Enhances the positive impact of technological and social innovations in the lives of individuals. Provides education, training and professional development programs.

Central and East European Management Development Association. Presernova cesta 33, 4260 Bled, Slovenia. Phone: 386 4 5792505 or 386 4 5792570; Email: info@ceeman.org • URL: http://www.ceeman.org • Specialists in business education and management personnel in commercial business, industry, professional, and technical fields from 42 countries. Seeks to improve the quality of management education throughout central and Eastern Europe. Provides a forum for discussion and exchange among individuals teaching, practicing, or studying management; provides IQA accreditation.

Central Asian Foundation for Management Development. Abai Ave., No. 52, 480008 Almaty, Kazakhstan. Phone: 7 3272 423545; Fax: 7 3272 509228; Email: caman@iab.almaty.kz • URL: http://caman-kz.euro.ru • Aims to promote formation and development of business education in the region. Promotes management and management education development and improvement in the Central Asian region.

Chartered Alternative Investment Analyst Association. 100 University Dr., Amherst, MA 01002-2357. Phone: (413)253-7373; Fax: (413)253-4494; Email: info@caia.org • URL: http://caia.org • Seeks to establish the Chartered Alternative Investment Analyst designation as the educational standard for the alternative investment industry. Advocates for high standards of professional conduct in the field of alternative investment analysis. Promotes professional development through continuous education. Facilitates communication among industry professionals.

ChristianTrade Association International. PO Box 62187, Colorado Springs, CO 80962-2187. Phone: (719)432-8428; Email: info@christiantrade.com • URL: http://www.ctaintl.org • Forms, develops and recognizes national organizations committed to the growth of the Christian trade. Encourages the industry to grow based on fairness, equally accessible markets, and a biblical model. Facilitates networking and sharing of ideas publishes directory. Designs and develops training programs leading to professional excellence for participants in the Christian trade.

Confederation of Norwegian Enterprise. Naeringslivets Hus, Middelthuns gate 27, Majorstuen, N-0303 Oslo, Norway. Phone: 47 23 088000; Fax: 47 23 088001 • URL: http://www.nho.no • Promotes the interests of Norwegian companies as regards to exports and internationalization. Provides information on EU matters relevant for the business community.

Council for Ethical Leadership. 1 College and Main, Columbus, OH 43209. Phone: (614)236-7222 • URL: http://www.businessethics.org • Leaders in business, education, and the professions. Seeks to "strengthen the ethical fabric of business and economic life." Facilitates the development of international networks of businesspeople interested in economic ethics; sponsors educational programs and develops and distributes educational materials; advises and supports communities wishing to implement character educational programs; makes available consulting services.

Council for Hospitality Management Education. University of Bournemouth, Dorset House, Talbot Campus, Fern Barrow, Dorset, Poole BH12 5BB, United Kingdom. • URL: http://www.chme.co.uk • Universities and colleges which offer degree and/or HND courses in hospitality management. Represents member institutions' interests in the field of hospitality management education at HE level, EC, government, industry and professional levels. Promotes hospitality management education in general, as well as specialist levels, e.g. industrial placement, research, access to courses, etc.

Delta Sigma Pi. 330 S Campus Ave., Oxford, OH 45056-2405. Phone: (513)523-1907; Fax: (513)523-7292; Email: centraloffice@dspnet.org • URL: http://www.dspnet.org • Professional fraternity - commerce and business administration. Operates Delta Sigma Pi Leadership Foundation. Maintains museum; sponsors competitions; offers computerized services; compiles statistics. Provides educational and career assistance.

Economics, Business and Enterprise Association. Adur Business Ctre., Little High St., Shoreham-by-Sea BN43 5EG, United Kingdom. Phone: 44 1273 467542; Email: office@ebea.org.uk • URL: http://www.ebea.org.uk/home • Teachers of economics, business studies and related subjects in schools and colleges. Represents teachers of economics, business studies and related subjects in schools and colleges throughout the UK and provides its members with the professional support they need in the classroom. Aims to encourage and promote the teaching and study of economics and related subjects within a broadly based curriculum.

European Foundation for Management Development. Rue Gachard 88, 1050 Brussels, Belgium. Phone: 32 2 6290810; Fax: 32 2 6290811 • URL: http://www.efmd.org • Corporations, educational institutions, employers associations, management consultants, and individuals in 45 countries with an interest in management development, training, and education. Seeks to identify, research, and address leading management development issues. Fosters development of professional competence of those responsible for management development within companies and educational institutions; promotes education, development, and research in the field through working groups, seminars and conferences. Strives to organize effective interaction among all those involved in the management development process.

Expediting Management Association. c/o Patricia Murphy, Executive Administrator, 534 Bridlecreek Green SW, Calgary, AB, Canada T2Y 3P2. Phone: (403)201-6401; Fax: (403)201-6402 • URL: http://www.expedite.org • Expediting managers; associate members are organizations, firms, and other individuals involved in the profession. (Expeditors work to ensure the efficient delivery of goods and services within or between businesses.) Promotes high professional and ethical standards in expediting. Conducts training programs, seminars, and workshops. Certifies expediting managers and associates; offers courses. Conducts on-site programs for corporations and groups.

Finance Project. 1150 18th St. NW, Ste. 325, Washington, DC 20036-3856. Phone: (202)628-4200; Fax: (202)628-1293; Email: info@financeproject.org • URL: http://www.financeproject.org • Develops and disseminates information, knowledge, tools, technical assistance for improved policies, programs, financing strategies that will benefit children, families and communities.

Graduate Management Association of Australia. PO Box 6328, Melbourne, VIC 8008, Australia. Phone: 61 3 95363109; Fax: 61 3 95253656; Email: service@gmaa.com.au • URL: http://www.gmaa.asn.au • Promotes the standing graduate schools and postgraduate management. Enhances the value of graduate management qualifications. Contributes to the development of Australia and its managerial resources. Provides a forum for the interaction of members and students from various management schools. Pursues the regular exchange of ideas and knowledge between members and leaders in industry and management education.

INJAZ Bahrain. Manama Ctr. Entrance 3, 4th Fl., office 606/607, Government Rd., Manama, Bahrain. Phone: 973 17225050; Fax: 973 17225052; Email: websmaster@injazbh.org • URL: http://injazbh.org • Aims to educate and inspire young people to value enterprise, business and economics to improve the quality of their lives. Teaches economics, entrepreneurship and financial literacy, focusing on the importance of market-driven economies. Encourages students to apply lessons into action, and learn the value of contributing to their communities.

Institute of Commercial Management. ICM House, Castleman Way, Hampshire, Ringwood BH24 3BA, United Kingdom. Phone: 44 1202 490555; Email: info@icm.education • URL: http://icm.education • Serves as a UK Examining and Awarding body for business and management students. Seeks to provide a range of high quality global education, training, and consulting services which raise performance standards for business and enhances the professional status of individuals. Offers a number of certified programs to meet special training needs.

Institute of Directors - Zimbabwe. 1 Grantchester

Close, Northwood, Mt. Pleasant, Harare, Zimbabwe. Phone: 263 4 301866 or 263 4 301136 • URL: http://www.iodzim.com • Individuals employed as directors either in a managerial or administrative capacity or as a non-executive director by corporations in Zimbabwe. Promotes the interests of domestic businesses; works to develop management techniques particularly suited to local needs. Facilitates communication among members. Conducts research and educational programs.

International Association for Business and Society. IABS Philosophy Dr. Center, Charlottesville, VA 22906-7147. Phone: 800-444-2419 or (434)220-3300; Fax: (434)220-3301 • URL: http://www.iabs.net • Seeks to provide an international forum for discussion and scholarship regarding social, business and public policy issues.

International Contact Center Benchmarking Consortium. The Benchmarking Network, 4606 FM 1960 W, Ste. 250, Houston, TX 77069-9949. Phone: (281)440-5044; Fax: (281)440-6677; Email: info@iccbc.org • URL: http://www.iccbc.org • Corporations that manage call centers. Promotes the use of benchmarking, wherein businesses compare their processes with those of their competitors, as a means of improving corporate efficiency and profitability. Facilitates exchange of information among members; conducts target operations, procurement, development, and maintenance studies; identifies model business practices.

International PEN - Writers in Prison Committee. Brownlow House, 50/51 High Holborn, London WC1V 6ER, United Kingdom. Phone: 44 20 74050338; Fax: 44 20 74050339; Email: info@pen-international.org • URL: http://www.pen-international.org • Serves as a key resource for the writing instruments industry. Provides leadership and direction for its members by staying at the forefront of trends, education, and technology in order to promote and procure the future of writing instrument development and distribution. Offers strategic analysis of manufacturer and retail marketing efforts.

International Society for Business Education. 21 Russell Rd., Wellesley, MA 02482. Phone: (781)237-3035; Email: msherry@massasoit.mass.edu • URL: http://www.isbeusa.org • Educators involved in business education; heads of in-company training institutions; firms; schools and universities at various levels. Aims to promote the international exchange of ideas and experiences in business education and to further the education of teachers in business fields. Organizes courses in economic and business education. New members must join National Business Education Association before joining ISBE.

Irish Business and Employers' Confederation. Confederation House, 84-86 Lower Baggot St., Dublin IRL-2, Dublin, Ireland. Phone: 353 1 6051500; Fax: 353 1 6381500; Email: info@ibec.ie • URL: http://www.ibec.ie • Firms: industrial, commercial, and public sector firms that manufacture products or provide services. Promotes the growth and development of Irish industry and commercial activity. Advises the government and represents interests of industry on relevant legislative issues. Maintains the Irish Business Bureau in conjunction with Irish Business and Employers Confederation and the Chambers of Commerce of Ireland. Develops public awareness of the role of industry in national development through press, radio, television, and public meetings. Monitors technological developments; compiles statistics; provides advice and assistance to members; maintains speakers' bureau.

Italian Private Equity and Venture Capital Association. Via Pietro Mascagni n. 7, I-20122 Milan, Italy. Phone: 39 2 7607531; Fax: 39 2 76398044; Email: info@aifi.it • URL: http://www.aifi.it • Lobbies in the legislative and institutional process. Organizes symposia and seminars, educational programs and supports research activities.

Japan Management Association. Convention Div., 3-1-22 Shiba-koen, Minato-ku, Tokyo 105-8522, Japan. Phone: 81 3 34346211 or 81 334 341246; Fax: 81 3 34341087 or 81 334 340269; Email: global@jma.or.jp • URL: http://www.jma.or.jp • Japanese corporations and individuals. Management education organization working to develop and conduct public business education and training programs including seminars, conferences, symposia, and overseas study tours. Makes available correspondence courses, audiovisual and computer-assisted instruction programs, in-company training programs, and cruise seminars. Conducts research and disseminates information on topics including white-collar productivity in Japan, creativity development in business and industry, and globally oriented management reform. Maintains liaison with similar organizations worldwide. Organizes conferences and exhibitions for trade associations. Maintains 14 interdisciplinary divisions and 13 supporting departments. Provides management consulting service; operates speakers' bureau.

JumpStart Coalition for Personal Financial Literacy. 919 18th St. NW, Ste. 300, Washington, DC 20006. Phone: 888-45-EDUCATE; Fax: (202)223-0321 • URL: http://www.jumpstartcoalition.org • Aims to improve the financial literacy of kindergarten through college-age youth. Seeks to prepare youth for life-long, successful financial decision-making. Provides advocacy, research, standards, and educational resources.

Junior Achievement. 1 Education Way, Colorado Springs, CO 80906. Phone: (719)540-8000; Fax: (719)540-6299; Email: newmedia@ja.org • URL: http://www.juniorachievement.org/web/ja-usa/home • Aims to educate students in grades K-12 about entrepreneurship, work readiness, and financial literacy through experiential, hands-on programs. Helps prepare young people for the "real world" by showing them how to generate wealth and effectively manage it, how to create jobs which make their communities more robust, and how to apply entrepreneurial thinking to the workplace. Encourages students to apply lessons into action, and learn the value of contributing to their communities.

Junior Achievement China. Bldg. 5, Ste. 201, Unit 5, Julong Garden, 68 Xinzhongjie, Dongcheng District, Beijing 100027, Hebei, China. Phone: 86 10 65515235; Fax: 86 10 65527850; Email: beijing@jachina.org • URL: http://www.jachina.org • Educates young people to value free enterprise, business and economics. Serves as a catalyst for character, creativity and leadership development of young people. Implements principle-centered, interactive business and economic education programs.

Junior Achievement Ireland. 8 Longford Pl., Monkstown, Dublin, Dublin, Ireland. Phone: 353 1 2366644; Fax: 353 1 2803758; Email: info@jai.ie • URL: http://www.juniorachievement.ie • Aims to build a bridge between classroom and workplace. Provides young people the opportunity to participate in educational programs. Recruits persons who are qualified to teach students about business.

Junior Achievement of Canada. 1 Eva Rd., Ste. 218, Toronto, ON, Canada M9C 4Z5. Phone: 800-265-0699 or (416)622-4602; Fax: (416)622-6861 • URL: http://jacan.org • Works to help young Canadians discover leadership, entrepreneurial and workforce readiness skills to achieve highest potential as citizens for the global community.

Junior Achievement Russia. Leninsky Prospekt, 113/1 Park Pl., 3rd Fl., Ste. B-301, 117 198 Moscow, Russia. Phone: 7 95 9565810; Fax: 7 95 9565246; Email: ja-russia@inbox.ru • URL: http://www.ja-russia.ru • Promotes the growth and development of business and economic educational programs for youth. Establishes partnerships between business and educational communities.

Junior Achievement Tajikistan. 169, Lenina St., Sughd, 735700 Khujand, Tajikistan. Phone: 992 927777917; Email: ja-tajikistan@mail.ru • URL: http://www.ja-ap.org • Aims to educate and inspire young people to value free enterprise and understand the mechanisms of market economy. Facilitates innovative teaching methods of business and economics. Fosters a spirit of entrepreneurship among young people.

Medical Spa Society. 60 E 56th St., 2nd Fl., New York, NY 10022. Phone: 888-MED-ISPA or (212)688-5882; Email: coordinator@medicalspasociety.com • URL: http://www.medicalspasociety.com • Seeks to raise and uphold the level of professionalism practiced throughout the medical spa industry. Promotes education, communication and standards of excellence for the medical spa profession. Encourages exchange of information and ideas that will further enhance the image and credibility of the medical spa industry.

My Own Business, Inc. 13181 Crossroads Pkwy. N, Ste. 190, City of Industry, CA 91746. Phone: (562)463-1800; Fax: (562)463-1802; Email: support@myownbusiness.org • URL: http://www.myownbusiness.org • Educates small business owners by providing free coursework. Develops, produces, implements, updates and markets educational offerings through multiple delivery channels. Seeks to expand collaborations with companies, schools, the community and other institutions. Works to support the vital social and economic contributions of small businesses by nurturing entrepreneurship and helping individuals build their own business.

National Association for Business Teacher Education. 1914 Association Dr., Reston, VA 20191-1596. Phone: (703)860-8300; Fax: (703)620-4483; Email: nbea@nbea.org • URL: http://www.nabte.org • An institutional division of National Business Education Association. Represents colleges and universities with programs for the education of business teachers. Works to improve and advance business teacher education. Operates Business Education Research Foundation.

National Association for Community College Entrepreneurship. Bldg. 101-R, 1 Federal St., Springfield, MA 01105. Phone: (413)306-3131; Fax: (413)755-6101; Email: wolpert@nacce.com • URL: http://www.nacce.com • Establishes entrepreneurship education as a core offering to foster economic development through community colleges. Focuses on increasing economic development through entrepreneurship education and student business incubation at the community college level.

National Association of Blessed Billionaires. Presbyterian Church of Mt. Vernon, 199 N Columbus Ave., Mount Vernon, NY 10553. Phone: (914)633-4417 or (347)933-3000; Email: nabb10m@aol.com • URL: http://blessedbillionaires.org • Aims to build self-esteem and good moral character among young people. Helps young men and women gain the skills they need to become successful and responsible adults. Provides a vehicle for inner-city youth to learn about and participate in the competitive market through leadership and entrepreneurial training. Conducts training on all aspects of business and money management.

National Association of Health and Educational Facilities Finance Authorities. PO Box 906, Oakhurst, NJ 07755. Phone: 888-414-5713; Fax: (888)414-5713 • URL: http://www.naheffa.com • Serves the common interests and improves effectiveness of member authorities through communication, education, and advocacy, with emphasis on issues which directly influence the availability of or access to tax-exempt financing for healthcare facilities.

National Association of Supervisor of Business Education. c/o Melissa Scott, Treasurer, 9890 S Maryland Pkwy., Ste. 221, Las Vegas, NV 89183. Phone: (702)486-6625 or (303)982-6654; Fax: (702)668-4321 • URL: http://www.nasbe.us • Acts as a representative voice for local supervisors of business and office education programs in public and private schools. Supports programs and activities in cooperation with the American Vocational Association and other business education organizations.

National Association of Women MBAs. Rice University, PO Box 2932, Houston, TX 77251-2932. Email: philana.kiely@mbawomen.org • URL: http://www.mbawomen.org • Provides networking opportunities for its members. Increases communication among graduate business schools regarding their initiatives to educate and support women in business.

National Business Education Association. 1914 Association Dr., Reston, VA 20191-1596. Phone: (703)860-8300; Fax: (703)620-4483; Email: nbea@nbea.org • URL: http://www.nbea.org • Teachers of business subjects in secondary and postsecondary schools and colleges; administrators and research workers in business education; businesspersons interested in business education; teachers in educational institutions training business teachers; high school and college students preparing for careers in business.

National Center on Nonprofit Enterprise. 205 S Patrick St., Alexandria, VA 22314. Phone: (703)548-7978 or (757)214-5084; Fax: (501)637-2807; Email: richard@nationalcne.org • URL: http://www.nationalcne.org • Represents academic researchers, business leaders, consultants and non-profit practitioners supporting a comprehensive program of educational activities and services addressing economic and business decision-making issues facing the non-profit sector.

Network for Teaching Entrepreneurship. 120 Wall St., 18th Fl., New York, NY 10005. • URL: http://www.nfte.com • Devoted to teaching entrepreneurship education to low-income young people, ages 11 through 18.

New Zealand Institute of Management. Level 7, Lumley House, 3-11 Hunter St., Wellington 6140, New Zealand. Phone: 64 4 4958300; Email: enquiries@nzim.co.nz • URL: http://www.nzim.co.nz • Managers and managerial personnel. Promotes improved management of businesses in New Zealand. Conducts continuing professional education programs; maintains information center.

Organization for Entrepreneurial Development. 25 Pine St., Ste. 9, Rockaway, NJ 07866. Phone: 800-767-0999; Fax: (973)784-1099; Email: questions@oedglobal.org • URL: http://www.oedglobal.org • Offers educational and training programs that are focused on the entrepreneurial community. Collaborates with educators and educational institutions for the improvement of entrepreneurial skills and knowledge. Seeks to solicit the help and support of the business community at large in aiding the entrepreneurial community.

Pi Omega Pi. Box 9730, Mississippi State, MS 39762. Phone: (662)325-7528; Fax: (662)325-1837; Email: cforde@colled.msstate.edu • URL: http://catpages.nwmissouri.edu/m/oisbe/piomegapi • Purpose Honor society - men and women, business education.

Private Equity CFO Association. c/o RBS Citizens, 28 State St., 14th Fl., Boston, MA 02109. • URL: http://www.privateequitycfo.org • Provides networking opportunities for members to share best practices. Responds to and addresses industry and professional issues of current interest. Develops programs that will provide education to association members. Improves and strengthens the flow of information among members.

Pro Mujer. 253 W 35th St., 11th Fl., New York, NY 10001. Phone: (646)626-7000; Fax: (212)904-1038; Email: communications@promujer.org • URL: http://promujer.org • Establishes microfinance organizations that provide financial and human development services for women. Provides business training and healthcare support.

Professional Scripophily Trade Association. PO Box 223795, Chantilly, VA 20153. Phone: 888-786-2576 or (703)579-4209; Fax: (703)995-4422; Email: bob@psta.com • URL: http://www.psta.com • Promotes the study and collection of scripophily for collectors, researchers, and for the interpretation and preservation of financial history. Helps support educational projects, programs, and seminars to help collectors and the general public gain a better understanding of scripophily, finance and business history.

Professional Women Controllers. PO Box 23924, Washington, DC 20024. Email: info@pwcinc.org • URL: http://www.pwcinc.org • Women controllers. Promotes the advancement of women within the financial industry. Represents members' interests; facilitates networking among women controllers; and makes available educational programs.

Russian Association of Business Education. Kronstadt Blvd. St., d. 37 B, Ste. 140, 125499 Moscow, Russia. Phone: 7 499 9439302; Fax: 7 499 9439309; Email: office@rabe.ru • URL: http://www.rabe.ru • Aims to unite universities, institutes, business schools and other training centers in the field of business education. Trains, retrains and upgrades the qualifications of personnel engaged in developing Russian business. Participates in the elaboration of the strategy of business education development in Russia and CIS.

Seton Hill University's E-magnify. Seton Hill University, 1 Seton Hill Dr., 3rd Fl., Administration Bldg., Greensburg, PA 15601. Phone: (724)830-4625; Fax: (724)834-7131; Email: info@e-magnify.com • URL: http://www.e-magnify.com • Promotes women and business ownership. Offers a variety of entrepreneurial resources, educational programs, advocacy initiatives and networking opportunities to women entrepreneurs. Works "to strengthen the economic impact of women business owners as a collective force and to advance their growth through innovative programming in entrepreneurship and new venture creation." Provides support, education and encouragement essential for the continued growth of women-owned businesses through its services.

Social Venture Network. PO Box 29221, San Francisco, CA 94129-0221. Phone: (415)561-6501; Fax: (415)561-6435; Email: svn@svn.org • URL: http://www.svn.org • Aims to build a just and sustainable world through business. Promotes new models and leadership for socially and environmentally sustainable business through initiatives, information services and forums.

Society of Quantitative Analysts. PO Box 6, Rutledge, MO 63563. Phone: 800-918-7930; Email: sqa@sqa-us.org • URL: http://www.sqa-us.org • Works for the application of new and innovative techniques in finance, with particular emphasis on the use of quantitative techniques in investment and risk management. Sponsors a half-day program in the fall and a Fuzzy Day seminar in the spring on an exploratory topic.

Strategic Planning Society. New Bond House, 124 New Bond St., London W1S 1DX, United Kingdom. Phone: 44 845 0563663; Email: members@sps.org.uk • URL: http://www.sps.org.uk • Corporations, educational institutions, and small companies and firms; executives, planners, government officials, and interested individuals. Promotes strategic planning in private, public, and governmental organizations. Seeks to: create and maintain networks for decision makers and planners; develop improved techniques for strategic planning; provide resources of knowledge and experience to aid businesses with planning problems; address political, economic, and social issues facing planners. Has established special interest and regional groups. Maintains Speaker's Bureau.

Team Success. 5050 Laguna Blvd., Ste. 112-415, Elk Grove, CA 95758-4151. Phone: (916)629-4229; Email: admin@teamsuccessinc.com • URL: http://www.teamsuccessinc.org • Promotes the education and improvement of youth throughout the United States. Seeks to improve the social development, life skills, employability, social skills and entrepreneurship abilities of youth. Assists the community by providing business related workshops, mentoring and job assistance.

U.S. Council of Better Business Bureaus. 3033 Wilson Blvd., Ste. 600, Arlington, VA 22201. Phone: (703)276-0100 • URL: http://www.bbb.org • Promotes ethical relationships between businesses and the public through self-regulation, consumer and business education, and service excellence.

Young Women Social Entrepreneurs. 6006 Colton Blvd., Oakland, CA 94611. Phone: (415)378-4417; Email: sara@ywse.org • URL: http://www.ywse.org • Serves women, primarily ages 25-40, with socially conscious agenda who are founders and leaders within businesses, non-profits, and government organizations. Aims to promote young women entrepreneurs by providing training and development, access to resources, and networking opportunities.

Youth Venture. 1700 N Moore St., Ste. 2000, Arlington, VA 22209. Phone: (703)527-8300; Fax: (703)527-8383; Email: yvinfo@youthventure.org • URL: http://www.youthventure.org • Works to empower young people to create and launch their own enterprises in order to take greater responsibility for their lives and communities.

BUSINESS ENTERPRISES, SALE OF

See also SMALL BUSINESS

ABSTRACTS AND INDEXES

Business Periodicals Index Retrospective. EBSCO Publishing Inc. • 11/year. Quarterly and annual cumulations.

Index to Legal Periodicals and Books. H.W. Wilson Co. • Monthly. $490.00 per year. Quarterly and annual cumulations.

CD-ROM DATABASES

ABI/INFORM. ProQuest L.L.C. • Monthly. Provides CD-ROM indexing and abstracting of worldwide business literature. Archival discs are available from 1971. Formerly *ABI/INFORM OnDisc*.

Business Abstracts with Full Text. EBSCO Publishing Inc. • Includes full text articles from more than 460 business publications from 1982 to present. Indexing for nearly 880 publications.

Index to Legal Periodicals and Books. EBSCO Publishing Inc. • Contains indexing of more than 1,400 English language legal periodicals from 1981 to date and 2,500 books.

DIRECTORIES

Business Brokers Directory. InfoGroup Inc. • Annual. Number of listings: 3,487. Entries include: Name, address, phone (including area code), size of advertisement, year first in "Yellow Pages," name of owner or manager, number of employees. Compiled from telephone company "Yellow Pages," nationwide.

Directory of Buyout Financing Sources. Buyout Publications, Inc. • Annual. $445 plus $9.00 shipping. Covers: over 1,000 sources of acquisition financing, including banks, asset-based lenders, small business investment companies, insurance companies, and venture capital firms. Entries include: Company name, address, phone, E-mail, URL, names and titles of key personnel, financial data, type of company and size requirements, underwriting criteria, equity requirements, post-closing role, information required, response time, sample transactions. Also promoted under title 'Financing Sourcebook for Buyouts & Acquisitions.'.

ONLINE DATABASES

Wilson Business Abstracts Online. H.W. Wilson Co. • Indexes and abstracts 600 major business periodicals, plus the *Wall Street Journal* and the business section of the *New York Times*. Indexing is from 1982, abstracting from 1990, with the two newspapers included from 1993. Updated weekly. Inquire as to online cost and availability. (*Business Periodicals Index* without abstracts is also available online.).

BUSINESS ETHICS

See also SOCIAL RESPONSIBILITY

DIRECTORIES

Business and the Environment: A Resource Guide. Island Press-Center For Resource Economics. • Publication includes: List of approximately 185 business and environmental educators working to intergrate environmental issues into management research, education, and practices. Entries include: Name, address, phone, affiliation, publications, courses taught, research activity, education, employment.

E-BOOKS

Essential Managers: Ethical Business. Cengage Learning Inc. • 2010. eBook. Published by Dorling Kindersley US. Goal of this book is to teach you how to improve your bottom line and employee morale while listening to your conscience.

Ethical Issues in E-Business: Models and Frameworks. Cengage Learning Inc. • 2012. eBook. Published by IGI Global. Offers a diverse and global perspective concerning the ethical consequences of e-business transactions, e-commerce applications, and technological advancements in secure online use.

ENCYCLOPEDIAS AND DICTIONARIES

Encyclopedia of Business Ethics and Society. Cengage Learning Inc. • 2007. eBook. 5 volumes. Spans the relationships among business, ethics, and society by including more than 800 entries that feature broad coverage of corporate social responsibility, the obligation of companies to various stakeholder groups, the contribution of business to society and culture, and the relationship between organizations and the quality of the environment.

Encyclopedia of Management (EoM). Cengage Learning Inc. • $434 Individuals. 2012. 7th Edition. Contains 316 essays on business management topics. eBook available. Inquire for pricing.

GENERAL WORKS

Business Ethics Quarterly. Philosophy Documentation Center. • Quarterly. $185 Institutions. Peer-reviewed scholarly journal covering business ethics studies.

Journal of Academic and Business Ethics (JABE). Academic and Business Research Institute. • Journal containing information on the ethical issues of business and education.

HANDBOOKS AND MANUALS

ABA/BNA Lawyer's Manual on Professional Conduct. Bloomberg BNA. • Updated monthly. Available via print and web. Covers American Bar Association's model rules governing ethical practice of law.

PERIODICALS AND NEWSLETTERS

Business and Society: A Journal of Interdisciplinary Exploration. International Association for Business and Society Research Committee. Pine Forge Press. • Quarterly. $402.00 per year.

Journal of Business Ethics. European Business Ethics Network. • Annual.

RESEARCH CENTERS AND INSTITUTES

Australian Catholic University - Centre for Research into Ethics and Decision-Making in Organisations. 24 Brunswick St., Locked Bag 4115, Fitzroy, VIC 3065, Australia. Phone: 61 3 99533270; Email: j.little@patrick.acu.edu.au • URL: http://www.acu.edu.au/research/Research_Centres_and_Flagships/credo • Values, policies, decision-making, and ethics in an organization.

San Jose State University - Institute for Social Responsibility, Ethics, and Education. 1 Washington Sq., San Jose, CA 95192-0096. Phone: (408)924-5563; Fax: (408)924-4527; Email: lawrence.quill@sjsu.edu • URL: http://www.sjsu.edu/isree • Social responsibility, including professional and business ethics.

University of Pittsburgh - Business, Government, and Society Research Institute. School of Business, Mervis Hall, Pittsburgh, PA 15260. Phone: (412)648-1555; Fax: (412)648-1693; Email: mitnick@pitt.edu.

University of St. Gallen - Institute for Business Ethics. Tannenstrasse 19, CH-9000 Saint Gallen, Switzerland. Phone: 41 71 2242644; Fax: 41 71 2242881; Email: ethik@unisg.ch • URL: http://www.iwe.unisg.ch • Economic ethics, including normative fundamentals of economics as a scientific discipline, crisis reflection of economics in industrial societies, business ethics, political philosophy, and sociology.

University of Stellenbosch - Faculty of Arts and Social Sciences - Department of Philosophy - Center for Applied Ethics. Private Bag X1, Matieland 7602, South Africa. Phone: 27 21 8082055; Fax: 27 21 8083556 • URL: http://sun025.sun.ac.za/portal/page/portal/Arts/Departments/philosophy/cae • Bioethics, environmental and business ethics.

STATISTICS SOURCES

Business Ethics Survey. Paul & Co. • Annual. $99.95. Published by the Society for Human Resource Management (www.shrm.org). Provides benchmarks, with trends in business ethics data since 1997.

TRADE/PROFESSIONAL ASSOCIATIONS

American Indian Business Leaders. Gallagher Business Bldg., Ste. 366, Missoula, MT 59812. Phone: 877-245-2425; Fax: (406)243-2086 • URL: http://www.aibl.org • Provides a support system for American Indian students interested in learning the skills necessary to acquire a job, design their own business, raise capital, and network with successful American Indian business people. Provides career development opportunities for members as well as opportunities to develop strong work ethics and gain professional experience.

Business Ethics Forum. 905 Main St., Houston, TX 77002-6408. Email: info@businessethicsforum.net • URL: http://businessethicsforum.net • Aims to develop partnerships among peer executives. Fosters philosophically sound and actionable frameworks for the ethical and effective management of organizations. Facilitates information exchange regarding research and activities in business ethics.

BVI Association of Compliance Officers. Road Town, Tortola, British Virgin Islands. • URL: http://www.bviaco.com • Promotes the role and importance of compliance in the British Virgin Islands. Encourages education, training and standards of practice within the BVI financial industry. Provides a forum for the exchange of ideas among members.

Coalition Against Counterfeiting and Piracy. US Chamber of Commerce, Global Intellectual Property Center, 1615 H St. NW, Washington, DC 20062-0001. Phone: (202)463-5601; Fax: (202)463-3114; Email: gipc@uschamber.com • URL: http://www.theglobalipcenter.com/index.php/cacp • Aims to fight the threat of counterfeiting and piracy to the economy, jobs, consumer health and safety. Strives to increase understanding of the negative impact of counterfeiting and piracy. Seeks to find real solutions by working with government, industry, opinion leaders, the media and consumers.

Conference Board - Europe. Chaussee de la Hulpe 178, 6th Fl., B-1170 Brussels, Belgium. Phone: 32 2 675 5405; Email: brussels@conferenceboard.org • URL: http://www.conference-board.org • Promotes management and the marketplace to help businesses strengthen their performance and better serve society. Conducts research, makes forecasts, assesses trends, publishes information and analysis, and brings executives together for exchange of ideas.

Council for Ethical Leadership. 1 College and Main, Columbus, OH 43209. Phone: (614)236-7222 • URL: http://www.businessethics.org • Leaders in business, education, and the professions. Seeks to "strengthen the ethical fabric of business and economic life." Facilitates the development of international networks of businesspeople interested in economic ethics; sponsors educational programs and develops and distributes educational materials; advises and supports communities wishing to implement character educational programs; makes available consulting services.

Ethics and Compliance Officer Association. 411 Waverley Oaks Rd., Ste. 324, Waltham, MA 02452-8420. Phone: (781)647-9333; Fax: (781)647-9399; Email: membership@theecoa.org • URL: http://www.theecoa.org • Managers of ethics, compliance, and business conduct programs. Offers educational business ethics and compliance programs; conducts national research; and provides free job-listing service.

Ethics Resource Center. 2345 Crystal Dr., Ste. 201, Arlington, VA 22202-4807. Phone: 800-777-1285 or (703)647-2185; Fax: (703)647-2180; Email: ethics@ethics.org • URL: http://www.ethics.org • Seeks to serve as a catalyst to improve the ethical practices of individuals and organizations from the classroom to the boardroom. Fulfills its mission through three distinct areas of expertise: as a leader in the fields of organizational/business ethics consulting; as a provider and facilitator of character education programs; and as an ethics information clearinghouse.

European Association of Consultants to and about Not-For-Profit Organisations. Sarphatistraat 370 B22, NL-1018 GW Amsterdam, Netherlands. Phone: 49 30 4053 6845; Fax: 49 30 4053 6846; Email: info@euconsult.org • URL: http://www.euconsult.org • Provides international forum for consultants to the not-for-profit sector. Encourages and stimulates ethical and professional behavior and collaboration. Develops the technical and business skills of members.

European Business Ethics Network. c/o Mario Silar, Secretary, C/Elizmendi 31, Bajo B, Sarriguren, 31621 Navarra, Spain. Email: secretariat@eben-net.org • URL: http://www.eben-net.org • Supports research centers in Europe researching business ethics issues.

Gibraltar Association of Compliance Officers. PO Box 1493, Gibraltar, Gibraltar. Phone: 350 200 74518; Email: info@gaco.gi • URL: http://www.

gaco.gi • Represents and protects the interests of compliance officers. Seeks to promote the exchange of views and the professional development of officers engaged in the performance of a compliance function within the Gibraltar Finance Centre.

International Association of Financial Executives Institutes. 1003 Pasong Tamo Tower, 10th Fl., 2210 Don Chino Roces Ave., Makati City 1231, Philippines. Phone: 63 2 7280315 • URL: http://www.iafei.org • Seeks to build and improve mutual understanding internationally among financial executives through the exchange of financial information, experience, and ideas. Provides a basis for international cooperation among financial executives towards making financial systems and regulations more uniform, compatible, and harmonious worldwide. Promotes ethical considerations in the practice of financial management throughout the world.

International Christian Union of Business Executives. c/o Pierre Lecocq, President, 15-25 Blvd. de l'Amiral Bruix, F-75016 Paris, France. Phone: 33 1 56022121; Fax: 33 1 4526 • URL: http://www.uniapac.org • National Christian employers' associations in 29 countries. Works to promote Christian ethics and sound economic policies in both business and social sectors. Serves as liaison between members and Christian associations with common goals. Conducts biennial symposium.

National Association of Commercial Finance Brokers. Hamilton House, 1 Temple Ave., London EC4Y 0HA, United Kingdom. Phone: 44 20 74892056; Email: admin@nacfb.org.uk • URL: http://www.nacfb.org • Seeks to protect consumer from fraud and malpractice in the commercial finance industry. Raises professional standards of commercial finance brokers. Provides training, education and information.

National Association of Settlement Purchasers. c/o Susan Barnes, Association Administrator, 720 Collier Dr., Dixon, CA 95620. Phone: (707)888-2647; Email: susan@barnescompany.com • URL: http://www.nasp-usa.com • Finance companies that purchase structured settlements from individuals for a lump sum (structured settlements are received by individuals as redress for personal injury or other liability). Seeks to insure ethical practice in the trading of structured settlements; promotes advancement of the structured settlement purchasing industry. Serves as a clearinghouse on the purchase of structured settlements; lobbies for reform of regulations governing the trade in structured settlements.

Transparency, Consciousness and Citizenship. CLN 202, Bloco B, Sala 101, 70832-525 Brasilia, DF, Brazil. Phone: 55613218085; Fax: 55 55613216333; Email: mail@tcc-brasil.org.br • URL: http://www.tcc-brasil.org.br • Corporations, organizations, and individuals interested in reducing fraud and corruption in international business transactions. Seeks to: raise public awareness of anticorruption measures; influence legislation regulating international business transactions. Formulates standards of integrity to govern international business dealings; maintains network of businesses agreeing to adhere to these standards. Conducts anticorruption and antifraud programs. Sponsors research and educational activities.

Transparency International Anti-corruption Center. Aygestan 9th St., House 6, 0025 Yerevan, Armenia. Phone: 374 2 10569910 or 374 2 10553069; Fax: 374 2 10571399; Email: info@transparency.am • URL: http://transparency.am • Represents corporations, organizations and individuals interested in reducing fraud and corruption in international business transactions. Raises public awareness of anticorruption measures and influences legislation regulating international business transactions. Formulates standards of integrity to govern international business dealings. Conducts anticorruption and antifraud programs.

Transparency International - Argentina. Piedras 547, 1070 Buenos Aires, Argentina. Phone: 54 11 43314925; Fax: 54 11 43314925; Email: comunicacion@poderciudadano.org • URL: http://www.poderciudadano.org.ar • Corporations, organizations, and individuals interested in reducing fraud and corruption in international business transactions. Seeks to raise public awareness of anticorruption measures and influence legislation regulating international business transactions. Formulates standards of integrity to govern international business dealings and maintains network of businesses agreeing to adhere to these standards. Conducts anticorruption and antifraud programs. Sponsors research and educational activities.

Transparency International - Australia. PO Box 41, Melbourne, VIC 3130, Australia. Phone: 61 3 98770369; Fax: 61 3 98771628; Email: tioz@transparency.org.au • URL: http://www.transparency.org.au • Corporations, organizations, and individuals interested in reducing fraud and corruption in international business transactions. Seeks to: raise public awareness of anticorruption measures; influence legislation regulating international business transactions. Formulates standards of integrity to govern international business dealings; maintains network of businesses agreeing to adhere to these standards. Conducts anticorruption and antifraud programs. Sponsors research and educational activities.

Transparency International - Azerbaijan. Jafar Jabbarli St. 16, Apt. 7, AZ1001 Baku, Azerbaijan. Phone: 994 12 4978170; Fax: 994 12 5962038; Email: info@transparency.az • URL: http://transparency.az • Represents corporations, organizations and individuals interested in reducing fraud and corruption in international business transactions. Raises public awareness of anticorruption measures and influences legislation regulating international business transactions. Formulates standards of integrity to govern international business dealings. Conducts anticorruption and antifraud programs.

Transparency International - Bangladesh. House 141, Blk. E, Rd. 12, Banani, Dhaka 1213, Bangladesh. Phone: 880 2 9887884 or 880 2 8826036; Fax: 880 2 9884811; Email: info@ti-bangladesh.org • URL: http://www.ti-bangladesh.org • Corporations, organizations, and individuals interested in reducing fraud and corruption in international business transactions. Seeks to: raise public awareness of anticorruption measures; influence legislation regulating international business transactions. Formulates standards of integrity to govern international business dealings; maintains network of businesses agreeing to adhere to these standards. Conducts anticorruption and antifraud programs. Sponsors research and educational activities.

Transparency International - Bosnia and Herzegovina. Gajeva 2, 78000 Banja Luka, Bosnia and Herzegovina. Phone: 387 51 216928; Fax: 387 51 216369; Email: info@ti-bih.org • URL: http://www.ti-bih.org • Represents corporations, organizations and individuals interested in reducing fraud and corruption in international business transactions. Raises public awareness of anticorruption measures and influences legislation regulating international business transactions. Formulates standards of integrity to govern international business dealings. Conducts anticorruption and antifraud programs.

Transparency International - Brazil. Rua Francisco Leitao 339, cj 122, 05414-025 Sao Paulo, SP, Brazil. Phone: 55 11 30623436; Fax: 55 11 30623436; Email: tbrasil@transparencia.org.br • URL: http://www.transparencia.org.br • Represents corporations, organizations and individuals interested in reducing fraud and corruption in international business transactions. Raises public awareness of anticorruption measures and influences legislation regulating international business transactions. Formulates standards of integrity to govern international business dealings. Conducts anticorruption and antifraud programs.

Transparency International - Brussels. E Jacqmainlaan 135, B-1000 Brussels, Belgium. Phone: 32 2 5090031; Email: info@transparencybelgium.be • URL: http://www.transparencybelgium.be • Corporations, organizations, and individuals interested in reducing fraud and corruption in international business transactions. Seeks to raise public awareness of anticorruption measures and influence legislation regulating international business transactions. Formulates standards of integrity to govern international business dealings and maintains network of businesses agreeing to adhere to these standards. Conducts anticorruption and antifraud programs. Sponsors research and educational activities.

Transparency International - Bulgaria. PO Box 72, Sofia, Bulgaria. Phone: 359 2 9867713 or 359 2 9867920; Fax: 359 2 9867834; Email: mbox@transparency.bg • URL: http://www.transparency.bg • Represents corporations, organizations and individuals interested in reducing fraud and corruption in international business transactions. Raises public awareness of anti-corruption measures and influences legislation regulating international business transactions. Formulates standards of integrity to govern international business dealings. Conducts anti-corruption and anti-fraud programs.

Transparency International - Burundi. c/o ABUCO, Ave. du 28 Novembre, No. 4611/C, Bujumbura, Burundi. Phone: 257 237686; Email: abuco@ymail.com • URL: http://www.burunditransparence.org • Aims to promote good governance and fight against corruption. Seeks to raise public awareness of anticorruption measures and influence legislation regulating international business transactions. Formulates standards of integrity to govern international business dealings.

Transparency International - Cameroon. Nouvelle Route Bastos, rue 1.839, Yaounde, Cameroon. Phone: 237 33156378; Email: transparency@ti-cameroon.org • URL: http://www.ti-cameroon.org • Aims to promote good governance and fight against corruption. Works with coalitions of individuals and organizations to prevent corruption and reform the systems. Fosters dialogue with the government and companies.

Transparency International - Canada. Business Ethics Office - N211, Schulich School of Business, York University, 4700 Keele St., Toronto, ON, Canada M3J 1P3. Phone: (416)488-3939; Fax: (416)483-5128; Email: ti-can@transparency.ca • URL: http://www.transparency.ca • Represents corporations, organizations and individuals interested in reducing fraud and corruption in international business transactions. Raises public awareness of anticorruption measures and influences legislation regulating international business transactions. Formulates standards of integrity to govern international business dealings. Conducts anticorruption and antifraud programs.

Transparency International - Chile. Avda. Providencia 1017, Providencia, Santiago, Chile. Phone: 56 2 2364507; Fax: 56 2 2364507; Email: chiletransparente@chiletransparente.cl • URL: http://www.chiletransparente.cl • Represents corporations, organizations and individuals interested in reducing fraud and corruption in international business transactions. Raises public awareness of anticorruption measures and influences legislation regulating international business transactions. Formulates standards of integrity to govern international business dealings. Conducts anticorruption and antifraud programs.

Transparency International - Colombia. Carrera 45, No. 93-61, Barrio la Castellana, Bogota, Colombia. Phone: 57 1 6100822; Fax: 57 1 6373603; Email: transparencia@transparenciacolombia.org.co • URL: http://www.transparency.org/whoweare/contact#O_nc_colombia • Represents corporations, organizations and individuals interested in reducing fraud and corruption in international business transactions. Raises public awareness of anticorruption measures and influences legislation regulating international business transactions. Formulates standards of integrity to govern international business dealings. Conducts anticorruption and antifraud programs.

Transparency International - Costa Rica. 800 metros oeste del Restaurante Tony Romas, Urbanizacion Trejos Montealegre, San Jose, Costa Rica. Phone: 506 40340929; Email: crintegra@gmail.com • URL: http://www.transparency.org/whoweare/contact#O_nc_costarica • Represents corporations, organizations and individuals interested in reducing fraud and corruption in international business transactions. Raises public awareness of anti-corruption measures and influences legislation regulating international business transactions. Formulates standards of integrity to govern international business dealings. Conducts anti-corruption and antifraud programs.

Transparency International - Croatia. Ilica 35, CT-10000 Zagreb, Croatia. Phone: 385 1 4830653; Fax: 385 1 4830654; Email: ti-croatia@transparency.hr • URL: http://www.transparency.hr • Represents corporations, organizations and individuals interested in reducing fraud and corruption in international business transactions. Raises public awareness of anticorruption measures and influences legislation regulating international business transactions. Formulates standards of integrity to govern international business dealings. Conducts anticorruption and antifraud programs.

Transparency International - Czech Republic. Sokolovska 260/143, CZ-180 00 Prague, Czech Republic. Phone: 420 2 24240895 or 420 2 24240897; Email: info@transparency.cz • URL: http://www.transparency.cz • Represents corporations, organizations and individuals interested in reducing fraud and corruption in international business transactions. Raises public awareness of anticorruption measures and influences legislation regulating international business transactions. Formulates standards of integrity to govern international business dealings. Conducts anticorruption and antifraud programs.

Transparency International - Denmark. c/o Mellemfolkeligt Samvirke, Faelledvej 12, DK-2200 Copenhagen, Denmark. Email: sekretariatet@transparency.dk • URL: http://transparency.dk • Represents corporations, organizations and individuals interested in reducing fraud and corruption in international business transactions. Raises public awareness of anti-corruption measures and influences legislation regulating international business transactions. Formulates standards of integrity to govern international business dealings. Conducts anti-corruption and antifraud programs.

Transparency International - Dominican Republic. Calle Wenceslao Alvarez, No. 8, Santo Domingo, Dominican Republic. Phone: (809)685-6200; Fax: (809)685-6631; Email: info@pciudadana.org • URL: http://www.pciudadana.org • Aims to promote good governance and fight against corruption. Seeks to raise public awareness of anti-corruption measures and influence legislation regulating international business transactions. Formulates standards of integrity to govern international business dealings.

Transparency International - Estonia. Telliskivi 60a, 10412 Tallinn, Estonia. Phone: 372 56678118; Email: info@transparency.ee • URL: http://www.transparency.ee • Seeks to highlight the appearance of corruption in the public and private sector. Strengthens cooperation between the institutions and private persons concerned with the fight against corruption. Analyzes the risks of corruption and proposes legislative amendments related to transparency, accountability and corruption.

Transparency International - Ethiopia. PO Box 27847, Addis Ababa, Ethiopia. Phone: 251 11 6621596 or 251 11 6555508 • URL: http://transparencyethiopia.org • Aims to promote good governance and fight against corruption. Seeks to raise public awareness of anti-corruption measures and influence legislation regulating international business transactions. Formulates standards of integrity to govern international business dealings.

Transparency International - Fiji. 72 Pratt St., Suva, Fiji. Phone: 679 3304702; Fax: 679 3303533; Email: oa@transparencyfiji.org • URL: http://www.transparencyfiji.org • Represents corporations, organizations and individuals interested in reducing fraud and corruption in international business transactions. Raises public awareness of anticorruption measures and influences legislation regulating international business transactions. Formulates standards of integrity to govern international business dealings. Conducts anticorruption and antifraud programs.

Transparency International - France. 14, passage Dubail, F-75010 Paris, France. Phone: 33 1 84169565; Email: contact@transparence-france.org • URL: http://www.transparence-france.org • Represents corporations, organizations and individuals interested in reducing fraud and corruption in international business transactions. Raises public awareness of anti-corruption measures and influences legislation regulating international business transactions. Formulates standards of integrity to govern international business dealings. Conducts anti-corruption and antifraud programs.

Transparency International - Georgia. 26, Rustaveli Ave., 0108 Tbilisi, Republic of Georgia. Phone: 995 32 2921403; Fax: 995 32 2920251; Email: info@transparency.ge • URL: http://www.transparency.ge • Represents corporations, organizations and individuals interested in reducing fraud and corruption in international business transactions. Raises public awareness of anti-corruption measures and influences legislation regulating international business transactions. Formulates standards of integrity to govern international business dealings. Conducts anti-corruption and antifraud programs.

Transparency International - Greece. Thetidos 4, GR-11528 Athens, Greece. Phone: 30 210 7224940; Fax: 30 210 7224947; Email: tihellas@otenet.gr • URL: http://www.transparency.gr • Represents corporations, organizations and individuals interested in reducing fraud and corruption in international business transactions. Raises public awareness of anticorruption measures and influences legislation regulating international business transactions. Formulates standards of integrity to govern international business dealings. Conducts anticorruption and antifraud programs.

Transparency International - Haiti. PO Box 16136, Petionville, Haiti. Phone: 509 37017089; Fax: 509 25137089; Email: heritagehaiti@yahoo.com • URL: http://www.transparency.org • Aims to promote good governance and fight against corruption. Seeks to raise public awareness of anti-corruption measures and influence legislation regulating international business transactions. Formulates standards of integrity to govern international business dealings.

Transparency International - Hungary. Falk Miksa u. 30th 4th em. 2, 1055 Budapest, Hungary. Phone: 36 1 2699534; Fax: 36 1 2699535; Email: info@transparency.hu • URL: http://www.transparency.org • Represents corporations, organizations and individuals interested in reducing fraud and corruption in international business transactions. Raises public awareness of anti-corruption measures and influences legislation regulating international business transactions. Formulates standards of integrity to govern international business dealings. Conducts anti-corruption and anti-fraud programs.

Transparency International - India. Qr.No.- 4, Lajpat Bhawan, Lajpat Nagar - IV, New Delhi 110 024, Delhi, India. Phone: 91 11 26460826; Fax: 91 11 26460824; Email: tiindia.newdelhi@gmail.com • URL: http://www.transparencyindia.org • Represents corporations, organizations and individuals interested in reducing fraud and corruption in international business transactions. Raises public awareness of anticorruption measures and influences legislation regulating international business transactions. Formulates standards of integrity to govern international business dealings. Conducts anticorruption and antifraud programs.

Transparency International - Indonesia. Jl. Senayan Bawah No. 17, 12180 Jakarta, Indonesia. Phone: 62 21 7208515; Fax: 62 21 7267815; Email: info@ti.or.id • URL: http://www.transparency.org • Represents corporations, organizations and individuals interested in reducing fraud and corruption in international business transactions. Raises public awareness of anticorruption measures and influences legislation regulating international business transactions. Formulates standards of integrity to govern international business dealings. Conducts anticorruption and antifraud programs.

Transparency International - Initiative Madagascar. Lot 11 M 98 B, Antsakaviro, Antananarivo 101, Madagascar. Phone: 261 2 2265357; Email: transparency.mg@moov.mg • URL: http://www.transparency.org/whoweare/contact/org/nc_madagascar • Represents corporations, organizations and individuals interested in reducing fraud and corruption in international business transactions. Raises public awareness of anticorruption measures and influences legislation regulating international business transactions. Formulates standards of integrity to govern international business dealings. Conducts anticorruption and antifraud programs.

Transparency International - Ireland. The Capel Bldg., Ste. 109, Dublin 7, Dublin, Ireland. Phone: 353 1 8719433; Email: info@transparency.ie • URL: http://transparency.ie • Aims to promote good governance and fight against corruption. Seeks to raise public awareness of anti-corruption measures and influence legislation regulating international business transactions. Provides anti-corruption tools, strategies and programs.

Transparency International - Israel. PO Box 39874, IL-61398 Tel Aviv, Israel. Phone: 972 3 6409176; Fax: 972 3 6409176; Email: shvil@ti-israel.org • URL: http://www.ti-israel.org • Represents corporations, organizations and individuals interested in reducing fraud and corruption in international business transactions. Raises public awareness of anticorruption measures and influences legislation regulating international business transactions. Formulates standards of integrity to govern international business dealings. Conducts anticorruption and antifraud programs.

Transparency International - Italy. Via Zamagna 19, I-20148 Milan, Italy. Phone: 39 2 40093560; Fax: 39 2 406829; Email: info@transparency.it • URL: http://www.transparency.org • Represents corporations, organizations and individuals interested in reducing fraud and corruption in international business transactions. Raises public awareness of anticorruption measures and influences legislation regulating international business transactions. Formulates standards of integrity to govern international business dealings. Conducts anticorruption and antifraud programs.

Transparency International - Kazakhstan. Karasai

Batyr 85, 4th Fl., Office 41, 050026 Almaty, Kazakhstan. Phone: 7 327 2726981; Fax: 7 327 2726981 • URL: http://www.transparencykazakhstan.org • Represents corporations, organizations and individuals interested in reducing fraud and corruption in international business transactions. Raises public awareness of anticorruption measures and influences legislation regulating international business transactions. Formulates standards of integrity to govern international business dealings. Conducts anticorruption and antifraud programs.

Transparency International - Kenya. ACK Garden House, 3rd Fl., Wing D, 1st Ngong Ave. off Bishops Rd., Nairobi, Kenya. Phone: 254 2 2727763 or 254 2 2730324; Fax: 254 2 2729530; Email: transparency@tikenya.org • URL: http://www.tikenya.org • Represents corporations, organizations and individuals interested in reducing fraud and corruption in international business transactions. Raises public awareness of anticorruption measures and influences legislation regulating international business transactions. Formulates standards of integrity to govern international business dealings. Conducts anticorruption and antifraud programs.

Transparency International - Korea. 1006 Pierson Bldg., 89-27 Sinmunno 2-ga, Jongno-Gu, Seoul 110-762, South Korea. Phone: 82 2 7176211; Fax: 82 2 7176210; Email: ti@ti.or.kr • URL: http://ti.or.kr/xe • Represents corporations, organizations and individuals interested in reducing fraud and corruption in international business transactions. Raises public awareness of anti-corruption measures and influences legislation regulating international business transactions. Formulates standards of integrity to govern international business dealings. Conducts anti-corruption and antifraud programs.

Transparency International - Lithuania. Didzioji St. 5, LT-01128 Vilnius, Lithuania. Phone: 370 5 2126951; Fax: 370 5 2121687; Email: info@transparency.lt • URL: http://www.transparency.org • Represents corporations, organizations and individuals interested in reducing fraud and corruption in international business transactions. Raises public awareness of anticorruption measures and influences legislation regulating international business transactions. Formulates standards of integrity to govern international business dealings. Conducts anticorruption and antifraud programs.

Transparency International - Malaysia. Wisma Pantai, Plz. Pantai, Ste. B-11-1, No. 5 Jalan 4/83A, Off Jalan Pantai Baru, 59200 Kuala Lumpur, Malaysia. Phone: 60 3 22840630; Fax: 60 3 22840690; Email: admin@transparency.org.my • URL: http://www.transparency.org • Represents corporations, organizations and individuals interested in reducing fraud and corruption in international business transactions. Raises public awareness of anticorruption measures and influences legislation regulating international business transactions. Formulates standards of integrity to govern international business dealings. Conducts anticorruption and antifraud programs.

Transparency International - Moldova. 98, 31-August 1989 St., Rm. 205, MD-2004 Chisinau, Moldova. Phone: 373 2 2203484 or 373 2 2203485; Fax: 373 2 2237876; Email: office@transparency.md • URL: http://www.transparency.md • Represents corporations, organizations and individuals interested in reducing fraud and corruption in international business transactions. Raises public awareness of anticorruption measures and influences legislation regulating international business transactions. Formulates standards of integrity to govern international business dealings. Conducts anticorruption and antifraud programs.

Transparency International - Mongolia. Bldg. of Zorig Foundation, 2nd Fl., Peace Ave. 17, Sukhbaataar District, Ulan Bator, Mongolia. Phone: 976 1 70154250; Fax: 976 1 70154250 • URL: http://www.transparency.org/country#MNG_Chapter • Represents corporations, organizations and individuals interested in reducing fraud and corruption in international business transactions. Raises public awareness of anticorruption measures and influences legislation regulating international business transactions. Formulates standards of integrity to govern international business dealings. Conducts anticorruption and antifraud programs.

Transparency International - Nepal. Newplaza, Pulalisadak, Kathmandu, Nepal. Phone: 977 1 436462 or 977 1 420412; Email: trans@tinepal.org • URL: http://www.tinepal.org • Represents corporations, organizations and individuals interested in reducing fraud and corruption in international business transactions. Raises public awareness of anticorruption measures and influences legislation regulating international business transactions. Formulates standards of integrity to govern international business dealings. Conducts anticorruption and antifraud programs.

Transparency International - New Zealand. Lambton Quay, Wellington, New Zealand. Email: mpetrie@ihug.co.nz • URL: http://www.transparency.org/whoweare/contact#O_nc_newzealand • Represents corporations, organizations and individuals interested in reducing fraud and corruption in international business transactions. Raises public awareness of anti-corruption measures and influences legislation regulating international business transactions. Formulates standards of integrity to govern international business dealings. Conducts anti-corruption and antifraud programs.

Transparency International - Nigeria. No. 11B Otukpo St., Gimbiya St., Area 11, Off Onitsha Crescent, Garki, Abuja, Nigeria. Email: info@ti-nigeria.org • URL: http://www.transparency.org/content/view/full/337/(filter)/n • Represents corporations, organizations and individuals interested in reducing fraud and corruption in international business transactions. Raises public awareness of anticorruption measures and influences legislation regulating international business transactions. Formulates standards of integrity to govern international business dealings. Conducts anticorruption and antifraud programs.

Transparency International - Pakistan. 5-C, 2nd Fl., Khayaban-e-Ittehad, Phase VII, D.H.A., Karachi, Pakistan. Phone: 92 21 5390408 or 92 21 5390409; Fax: 92 21 5390410; Email: ti.pakistan@gmail.com • URL: http://www.transparency.org.pk • Aims to raise public awareness of the effects of bribery and corruption. Encourages the government, government departments, municipalities, civic agencies and private-sector organizations to establish and implement laws, policies and anti-corruption programs. Enhances public transparency and accountability in administrative, financial and business transactions.

Transparency International - Papua New Guinea. PO Box 591, Port Moresby, Papua New Guinea. Phone: 675 3202188; Fax: 675 3202189 • URL: http://www.transparencypng.org.pg • Aims to combat corruption. Promotes openness, honesty and accountability in public and private dealings. Encourages research and analysis of the extent and effect of corruption in Papua New Guinea. Raises awareness of the presence and adverse effects of dishonest and corrupt practices.

Transparency International - Philippine Chapter. Philippine International Convention Center, Rm. S-370, CCP Complex, Pasay City 1000, Philippines. Phone: 63 2 5529188; Fax: 63 2 5529188; Email: transparencyinternational_ph@yahoo.com • URL: http://www.transparency.org • Represents corporations, organizations and individuals interested in reducing fraud and corruption in international business transactions. Raises public awareness of anticorruption measures and influences legislation regulating international business transactions. Formulates standards of integrity to govern international business dealings. Conducts anticorruption and antifraud programs.

Transparency International - Poland. ul. Ordynacka 9, pok. 33, 00-364 Warsaw, Poland. Phone: 48 22 8289243; Email: ti@transparency.pl • URL: http://www.transparency.pl • Represents corporations, organizations and individuals interested in reducing fraud and corruption in international business transactions. Raises public awareness of anticorruption measures and influences legislation regulating international business transactions. Formulates standards of integrity to govern international business dealings. Conducts anticorruption and antifraud programs.

Transparency International - Romania. 21 Nicolae Balcescu Blvd., 2nd Fl., Sector 1, 010044 Bucharest, Romania. Phone: 40 21 3177170; Fax: 40 21 3177172; Email: office@ransparency.org.ro • URL: http://www.transparency.org.ro • Represents corporations, organizations and individuals interested in reducing fraud and corruption in international business transactions. Raises public awareness of anticorruption measures and influences legislation regulating international business transactions. Formulates standards of integrity to govern international business dealings. Conducts anticorruption and antifraud programs.

Transparency International - Russia. Nikoloyamskaya ul. 6, 109240 Moscow, Russia. Phone: 7 95 9150019; Fax: 7 95 9150019; Email: info@transparency.org.ru • URL: http://www.transparency.org.ru • Represents corporations, organizations and individuals interested in reducing fraud and corruption in international business transactions. Raises public awareness of anticorruption measures and influences legislation regulating international business transactions. Formulates standards of integrity to govern international business dealings. Conducts anticorruption and antifraud programs.

Transparency International - Slovakia. Bajkalska 25, 827 18 Bratislava, Slovakia. Phone: 421 2 53417207; Fax: 421 2 53417207; Email: tis@transparency.sk • URL: http://www.transparency.sk • Represents corporations, organizations and individuals interested in reducing fraud and corruption in international business transactions. Raises public awareness of anticorruption measures and influences legislation regulating international business transactions. Formulates standards of integrity to govern international business dealings. Conducts anticorruption and antifraud programs.

Transparency International - Solomon Islands. PO Box 1665, Honiara, Solomon Islands. Email: tsi@solomon.com.sb • URL: http://www.transparency.org • Aims to promote good governance and fight against corruption. Seeks to raise public awareness of anti-corruption measures and influence legislation regulating international business transactions. Formulates standards of integrity to govern international business dealings.

Transparency International - South Africa. Methodist House, 114 Rissik St., Braamfontein 2017, South Africa. Phone: 27 11 4037746; Fax: 27 11 4034966 • URL: http://www.tisa.org.za • Corporations, organizations, and individuals interested in reducing fraud and corruption in international business transactions. Seeks to raise public awareness of anticorruption measures and to influence legislation regulating international business transactions. Formulates standards of integrity to govern international business dealings; maintains network of businesses agreeing to adhere to these standards. Conducts anticorruption and antifraud programs. Sponsors research and educational activities.

Transparency International - Sri Lanka. No. 6, 37th

Ln., Off Queens Rd., Colombo 3, Sri Lanka. Fax: 94 112 506419; Email: tisl@tisrilanka.org • URL: http://www.tisrilanka.org • Represents corporations, organizations and individuals interested in reducing fraud and corruption in international business transactions. Raises public awareness of anticorruption measures and influences legislation regulating international business transactions. Formulates standards of integrity to govern international business dealings. Conducts anticorruption and antifraud programs.

Transparency International - Sweden. Linnegatan 14, 6 tr, S-114 47 Stockholm, Sweden. Phone: 46 8 7914040; Email: info@transparency-se.org • URL: http://www.transparency-se.org • Represents corporations, organizations and individuals interested in reducing fraud and corruption in international business transactions. Raises public awareness of anti-corruption measures and influences legislation regulating international business transactions. Formulates standards of integrity to govern international business dealings. Conducts anti-corruption and antifraud programs.

Transparency International - Switzerland. Schanzeneckstrasse 25, Postfach 8509, CH-3001 Bern, Switzerland. Phone: 41 31 3823550; Fax: 41 31 3825044; Email: info@transparency.ch • URL: http://www.transparency.ch/de/index.php?navid=1 • Corporations, organizations, and individuals interested in reducing fraud and corruption in international business transactions. Seeks to raise public awareness of anti-corruption measures and to influence legislation regulating international business transactions. Formulates standards of integrity to govern international business dealings; maintains network of businesses agreeing to adhere to these standards. Conducts anti-corruption and antifraud programs. Sponsors research and educational activities.

Transparency International - Taiwan. PO Box 6-16 Mucha, Taipei 11699, Taiwan. Phone: 886 2 22362204; Fax: 886 2 22363325; Email: tict@tict.org.tw • URL: http://www.transparency.org • Represents corporations, organizations and individuals interested in reducing fraud and corruption in international business transactions. Raises public awareness of anticorruption measures and influences legislation regulating international business transactions. Formulates standards of integrity to govern international business dealings. Conducts anticorruption and antifraud programs.

Transparency International - Thailand. Centre for Philanthropy and Civil Society, 118 Seri-Thai Rd., Bankapi, Bangkok 10240, Thailand. Phone: 66 2 3777206; Fax: 66 2 3747399 • URL: http://www.transparency-thailand.org • Represents corporations, organizations, and individuals interested in reducing fraud and corruption in international business transactions. Seeks to raise public awareness of anticorruption measures and influence legislation regulating international business transactions. Formulates standards of integrity to govern international business dealings and maintains network of businesses agreeing to adhere to these standards. Conducts anticorruption and antifraud programs. Sponsors research and educational activities.

Transparency International - Turkey. Niyazi Bey Apt., No. 30, D:5 Sisli, Istanbul, Turkey. Phone: 90 212 240 52 81; Fax: 90 212 240 52 81; Email: info@seffaflik.org • URL: http://www.seffaflik.org/index_en.asp • Corporations, individuals, organizations interested in reducing fraud and corruption in Turkish government, business and society. Seeks to raise public awareness of anticorruption measures and to influence legislation regulating transparency and good governance. Formulates standards of integrity in all sectors; maintains network of businesses agreeing to adhere to these standards. Conducts anticorruption and antifraud programs. Sponsors research and educational activities.

Transparency International - Uganda. Plot 3 Martyrs Ln., Ntinda, Kampala, Uganda. Phone: 256 414 255836; Fax: 256 414 341546; Email: info@tiuganda.org • URL: http://tiuganda.org • Aims to promote good governance and fight against corruption. Seeks to raise public awareness of anti-corruption measures and influence legislation regulating international business transactions. Formulates standards of integrity to govern international business dealings.

Transparency International - UK. 32-36 Loman St., London SE1 0EH, United Kingdom. Phone: 44 20 7922-7906; Email: info@transparency.org.uk • URL: http://www.transparency.org.uk • Corporations, organizations, and individuals interested in reducing corruption in international business transactions. Eliminates corruption, particularly its corrosive impact on development in poorer countries and corruption's role in worsening poverty, increasing political instability and undermining the rule of law and democracy. Aims to encourage business to adopt commercial practices that are ethical. Formulates standards of integrity to govern international business dealings; maintains network of businesses agreeing to adhere to these standards. Priority areas are: construction and engineering sector; corruption in the official arms trade; money laundering in the UK; transparency in the extractive industries and reform of the UK law of corruption. Conducts anticorruption programs. Undertakes research and educational activities.

Transparency International - Ukraine. 17, Egorova St., Off. 4, 25006 Kirovograd, Ukraine. Phone: 380 522 272754; Fax: 380 522 321553; Email: info@ti-ukraine.org • URL: http://www.transparency.org • Represents corporations, organizations and individuals interested in reducing fraud and corruption in international business transactions. Raises public awareness of anti-corruption measures and influences legislation regulating international business transactions. Formulates standards of integrity to govern international business dealings. Conducts anti-corruption and antifraud programs.

Transparency International - Vanuatu. PO Box 355, Port Vila, Vanuatu. Phone: 678 25715; Fax: 678 25716; Email: transparency@vanuatu.com.vu • URL: http://www.transparencyvanuatu.org • Represents corporations, organizations and individuals interested in reducing fraud and corruption in international business transactions. Raises public awareness of anticorruption measures and influences legislation regulating international business transactions. Formulates standards of integrity to govern international business dealings. Conducts anticorruption and antifraud programs.

Transparency International - Zambia. Stand No. 3880, Kwacha Rd., Olympia Park, Lusaka, Zambia. Phone: 260 1 290080; Fax: 260 1 293649; Email: tizambia@zamnet.zm • URL: http://www.transparency.org/whoweare/contact#O_nc_zambia • Represents corporations, organizations and individuals interested in reducing fraud and corruption in international business transactions. Raises public awareness of anti-corruption measures and influences legislation regulating international business transactions. Formulates standards of integrity to govern international business dealings. Conducts anti-corruption and antifraud programs.

Transparency International - Zimbabwe. 96 Central Ave., Causeway, Harare, Zimbabwe. Phone: 263 4 793246 or 263 4 793277; Email: tiz@transparency.org.zw • URL: http://www.transparency.org.zw • Corporations, organizations, and individuals interested in reducing fraud and corruption in international business transactions. Seeks to raise public awareness of anti-corruption measures and influence legislation regulating international business transactions. Formulates standards of integrity to govern international business dealings and maintains network of businesses agreeing to adhere to these standards. Conducts anti-corruption and antifraud programs. Sponsors research and educational activities.

Transparency Maldives. MF Bldg., 7th Fl., Chaandhanee Magu, Male, Maldives. Phone: 960 3304017; Fax: 960 3006062; Email: office@transparencymaldives.org • URL: http://www.transparencymaldives.org • Promotes collaboration, awareness and other initiatives to improve governance and eliminate corruption. Encourages discussion on transparency, accountability and the fight against corruption. Seeks to engage stakeholders from all sectors to raise awareness on corruption.

Transparency Mauritius. TN Tower, 6th Fl., St. Georges St., Port Louis, Mauritius. Phone: 230 2130796; Fax: 230 2130795; Email: transparency.mauritius@gmail.com • URL: http://www.transparency.org • Represents corporations, organizations and individuals interested in reducing fraud and corruption in international business transactions. Raises public awareness of anti-corruption measures and influences legislation regulating international business transactions. Formulates standards of integrity to govern international business dealings. Conducts anti-corruption and antifraud programs.

U.S. Council of Better Business Bureaus. 3033 Wilson Blvd., Ste. 600, Arlington, VA 22201. Phone: (703)276-0100 • URL: http://www.bbb.org • Promotes ethical relationships between businesses and the public through self-regulation, consumer and business education, and service excellence.

BUSINESS FAILURES

See also BANK FAILURES; BANKRUPTCY

ABSTRACTS AND INDEXES

Business Periodicals Index Retrospective. EBSCO Publishing Inc. • 11/year. Quarterly and annual cumulations.

CD-ROM DATABASES

Authority Collier Bankruptcy Library. Matthew Bender and Company Inc. • Periodic revisions. Price on request. CD-ROM contains updated full text of *Collier on Bankruptcy* and 13 other Collier publications. Various aspects of bankruptcy are covered, including attorney compensation, proceedings, farm insolvencies, real estate failures, family law, taxation, and business workouts.

OECD Statistical Compendium. Organization for Economic Cooperation and Development. • Semiannual. $1,905.00 per year for 1 to 10 users. CD-ROM contains more than 730,000 monthly, quarterly, and annual time series for OECD countries, 1960 to date. Includes fully searchable data on agriculture, food, economic indicators, national accounts, employment, energy, finance, industry, technology, and foreign trade. Results can be displayed in various forms.

E-BOOKS

Corporate Disasters: What Went Wrong and Why. Cengage Learning Inc. • Covers corporate misdeeds and mistakes in business. Published June 2012. Available in print ($483) and eBook.

INTERNET DATABASES

Business 2.0 Web Guide to the Best Business Links. Business 2.0 Media Inc. Phone: (415)293-4800; Email: support@business2.com • URL: http://www.business2.com/webguide • Web site presents an extensive, searchable directory of links to "the best, most informative, and authoritative web pages." Twenty main categories cover business, finance, career, company information, people, and technol-

For publishers' addresses, refer to SOURCES CITED section at the back of the book.

ogy topics, with thousands of subtopics, all linking to Web sites recommended by experienced business researchers. Fees: Free.

Fedstats. Federal Interagency Council on Statistical Policy. Phone: (202)395-7254 • URL: http://www.fedstats.gov • Web site features an efficient search facility for full-text statistics produced by more than 100 federal agencies, including the Census Bureau, the Bureau of Economic Analysis, and the Bureau of Labor Statistics. Boolean searches can be made within one agency or for all agencies combined. Links are offered to international statistical bureaus, including the UN, IMF, OECD, UNESCO, Eurostat, and 20 individual countries. Fees: Free.

FreeLunch.com. Economy.com, Inc. Phone: (610)696-8700; Fax: (610)696-1678 • URL: http://www.freelunch.com • Web site provides free access to more than than 200 million economic and financial data series, covering industry, demographics, labor markets, prices, retail sales, government spending, trade, interest rates, housing starts, the stock market, etc. Data is available in either chart or table form. Searching is offered. Free, but registration required. Economy.com, Inc. also offers fee-based economic analysis at *The Dismal Scientist* site (www.dismal.com).

OTHER SOURCES

Business Strategies. Wolters Kluwer Law & Business CCH. • Semimonthly. $795.00 per year. Four looseleaf volumes. Semimonthly updates. Legal, tax, and accounting aspects of business planning and decision-making. Provides information on start-ups, forms of ownership (partnerships, corporations), failing businesses, reorganizations, acquisitions, and so forth. Includes *Business Strategies Bulletin*, a monthly newsletter.

PERIODICALS AND NEWSLETTERS

Insolvency Law & Practice. LexisNexis Butterworths Tolley. • Bimonthly. $181.00 per year. United Kingdom emphasis.

STATISTICS SOURCES

Quarterly Analysis of Failures. Dun & Bradstreet Inc. • Quarterly. $20.00.

Standard & Poor's Statistical Service. Current Statistics. Standard & Poor's Financial Services L.L.C. • Monthly. $688.00 per year. Includes 10 *Basic Statistics* sections, *Current Statistics Supplements* and *Annual Security Price Index Record.*

Survey of Current Business. U. S. Government Printing Office. • Published by Bureau of Economic Analysis, U. S. Department of Commerce. Presents a wide variety of business and economic data.

Weekly Business Failures. Dun & Bradstreet Inc. • Weekly. $445.00 per year.

TRADE/PROFESSIONAL ASSOCIATIONS

Institute for Turnaround. Juxon House, 2nd Fl., 100 St. Paul's Churchyard, London EC4M 8BU, United Kingdom. Phone: 44 20 3102 7710; Fax: 44 20 3102 7301; Email: info@instituteforturnaround.com • URL: http://www.instituteforturnaround.com • Raises the profile of turnaround professionals and its culture. Encourages intervention into underperforming businesses. Promotes turnaround knowledge among business community. Encourages high standards of ethics, behavior and quality of turnaround practitioners.

BUSINESS FILMS

See AUDIOVISUAL AIDS IN INDUSTRY

BUSINESS FORECASTING

See also BUSINESS CYCLES; BUSINESS STATISTICS; ECONOMIC POLICY

BIBLIOGRAPHIES

Future Survey Annual: A Guide to the Recent Literature of Trends, Forecasts, and Policy Proposals. World Future Society. • Annual. $35.00.

E-BOOKS

Enterprise Business Modeling, Optimization Techniques, and Flexible Information Systems. Cengage Learning Inc. • 2013. eBook. Provides research on the intersections of business modeling, information systems, and optimization techniques. These various business models and structuring methods are proposed to provide ideas, methods, and points of view for managers, practitioners, entrepreneurs, and researchers on how to improve business processes.

Handbook of Ontologies for Business Interaction. Cengage Learning Inc. • 2008. eBook. Published by Information Science Reference. Documents high-quality research addressing ontological issues that are relevant to the modeling of enterprises and information systems in general and business processes in particular covering both static and dynamic aspects of structural concepts.

ONLINE DATABASES

MarkIntel. Thomson Financial. • Provides the current full text online of more than 50,000 market research reports covering 54 industries, from 85 leading research firms worldwide. Reports include extensive forecasts and market analysis. Inquire as to online cost and availability.

OTHER SOURCES

Consensus Forecasts: A Worldwide Survey. Consensus Economics Inc. • Monthly. Provides a survey of more than 200 "prominent"financial and economic forecasters, covering 20 major countries. Two-year forecasts for each country include future growth, inflation, interest rates, and exchange rates. Each issue contains analysis of business conditions in various countries.

PERIODICALS AND NEWSLETTERS

Argentina Business Forecast Report. Telecommunications Insight. • Quarterly. $1,195 Individuals Single User. Business forecast report for Argentina.

Brazil Business Forecast Report. Telecommunications Insight. • Quarterly. $1,195 Individuals Single user. Business forecast report for Brazil.

Chile Business Forecast Report. Telecommunications Insight. • Quarterly. $1,195 Individuals Single user. Business forecast report for Chile.

China Business Forecast Report. Telecommunications Insight. • Quarterly. $1,195 Individuals single user. Business forecast reports.

Colombia Business Forecast Report. Telecommunications Insight. • Quarterly. $1,195 Individuals Single user. Business forecast report for Colombia.

Egypt Business Forecast Report. Telecommunications Insight. • Quarterly. $1,195 Individuals Single user. Business forecast report for Egypt.

Family Business Advisor. Family Enterprise Publishers. • Monthly. Covers business management, family relations, and asset protection. Addresses succession planning, estate planning, conflict management, compensation, family meetings, strategic planning, and board composition. Recurring features include news of research.

Hungary Business Forecast Report. Telecommunications Insight. • Quarterly. $1,195 Individuals Single user. Business forecast report for Hungary.

Indonesia Business Forecast Report. Telecommunications Insight. • Quarterly. $1,195 Individuals Single user. Business forecasting reports for Indonesia.

International Economic Scoreboard. The Conference Board. • Description: Provides current data on the business outlook in 11 major industrial countries: Australia, Canada, France, West Germany, Italy, Japan, Korea, New Zealand, Taiwan, the United Kingdom, and the U.S. **Remarks:** A source for additional information on this indicator system and its uses is available at the Center for International Business Cycle Research, Columbia University Business School.

Iran Business Forecast Report. Telecommunications Insight. • Quarterly. $1,195 Individuals Single user. Business forecast report for Iran.

Malaysia Business Forecast Report. Telecommunications Insight. • Quarterly. $1,195 Individuals Single user. Business forecast reports for Malaysia.

Mexico Business Forecast Report. Telecommunications Insight. • Quarterly. $1,195 Individuals Single user. Business forecast report for Mexico.

Peru Business Forecast Report. Telecommunications Insight. • Quarterly. $1,195 Individuals Single user. Business forecast report for Peru.

Philippines Business Forecast Report. Telecommunications Insight. • Quarterly. $1,195 Individuals Single user. Business forecasting reports for the Phillipines.

Poland Business Forecast Report. Telecommunications Insight. • Quarterly. $1,195 Individuals Single user. Business forecast report for Poland.

Russia Business Forecast Report. Telecommunications Insight. • Quarterly. $1,195 Individuals Single user. Business forecast report for Russia.

Saudi Arabia Business Forecast Report. Telecommunications Insight. • Quarterly. $1,195 Individuals Single user. Business forecast report for Saudi Arabia.

South Africa Business Forecast Report. Telecommunications Insight. • Quarterly. $1,195 Individuals Single user. Business forecast report for South Africa.

Technological Forecasting and Social Change: An International Journal of the Dragon Project. Elsevier. • Nine times a year. Individuals, $131.00 per year; institutions, $839.00 per year.

Thailand Business Forecast Report. Telecommunications Insight. • Quarterly. $1,195 Individuals Single user. Business forecasting report for Thailand.

The Trends Journal: The Authority on Trends Management. Gerald Celente, editor. Trends Research Institute. • Quarterly. $185.00 per year. Newsletter. Provides forecasts on a wide variety of economic, social, and political topics. Includes "Hot Trends to Watch.".

Turkey Business Forecast Report. Telecommunications Insight. • Quarterly. $1,195 Individuals Single user. Business forecast report for Turkey.

United Arab Emirates Business Forecast Report. Telecommunications Insight. • Quarterly. $1,195 Individuals Single user. Business forecast report for the United Arab Emirates.

Vietnam Business Forecast Report. Telecommunications Insight. • Quarterly. $1,195 Individuals Single user. Business forecast report for Vietnam.

RESEARCH CENTERS AND INSTITUTES

Georgia State University - Economic Forecasting Center. PO Box 3988, Atlanta, GA 30302-3988. Phone: (404)413-7260; Fax: (404)413-7264; Email: rdhawan@gsu.edu • URL: http://efc.robinson.gsu.edu • Concerned with national and regional economic analysis and forecasting.

University of California, Los Angeles - Anderson Forecast. Gold Hall, Ste. B302, 110 Westwood Plz., Los Angeles, CA 90095. Phone: (310)825-1623; Fax: (310)206-9940; Email: eleamer@anderson.ucla.edu • URL: http://uclaforecast.com • Development and continuous revision of complex econometric models for the U.S., California, and subregions of the state, using these models to project short-run and long-range forecasts and to conduct impact studies, including evaluating the effects of alternative governmental policies. Provides econometric model for California to on-line users through a time-sharing firm.

STATISTICS SOURCES

Economic Outlook Statistics. • Includes country and global forecasts of over 170 economic and business variables. Actual data is shown for two years, with forecasts up to ten years.

U.S. Survey of Business Expectations. Dun & Bradstreet Inc. • Quarterly. $40. A survey of 3,000 U. S. business executives as to their expectations for next quarter's sales, profits, prices, inventories, employment, exports, and new orders.

TRADE/PROFESSIONAL ASSOCIATIONS

Renewable Natural Resources Foundation. 5430 Grosvenor Ln., Bethesda, MD 20814-2142. Phone: (301)493-9101; Email: info@rnrf.org • URL: http://www.rnrf.org • Members are American Fisheries Society, American Geophysical Union, American Meteorological Society, American Society of Agronomy, American Society of Civil Engineers, Society of Landscape Architects, American Society for Photogrammetry and Remote Sensing, American Water Resources Association, Association of American Geographers, Humane Society of the United States, Society for Range Management, Society of Wood Science and Technology, Society of Environmental Toxicology and Chemistry, Soil and Water Conservation Society, Universities Council on Water Resources, and Wildlife Society. Concerned with renewable natural resources subjects and public policy alternatives. Develops 35-acre, forested Renewable Natural Resources Center, an office-park complex for natural resources and other nonprofit organizations.

BUSINESS FORMS

See FORMS AND BLANKS

BUSINESS GIFTS

See GIFT BUSINESS

BUSINESS HISTORY

ALMANACS AND YEARBOOKS

Development of the Industrial U.S. Reference Library. Cengage Learning Inc. • 2005. $236. 4 volumes. Traces the influence of the British Industrial Revolution on America and other nations and discusses such potent forces as advances in transportation and communication, inventions that transformed manufacturing and agriculture, the growth of trade and much more. eBook available. Contact for pricing.

DIRECTORIES

Academy of Accounting Historians--Membership Directory. Academy of Accounting Historians. • Annual. Covers: over 900 member individuals and organizations concerned with accounting and business history. Entries include: Member name, address, phone, and fax.

Historical Dictionary of Aid and Development Organizations. The Scarecrow Press Inc. • $55 Individuals Hardback. Covers: Major organizations involved in the post-WWII economic development.

International Directory of Company Histories. St. James Press. • $343 Individuals. Multi-volume work that covers histories of companies that are a leading influence in a particular industry or geographic location. eBook available. Contact for pricing.

Report on Business Corporate Database. Globe Information Services Info Globe Online. • Weekly. Database covers: Current and historical information on over 3,000 Canadian companies, taken from their quarterly and annual reports. Database includes: Company name, address, phone, description of business, financial data, officers, general corporate information.

E-BOOKS

Advice from the Presidents: The Student's Guide to Reaching the Top in Business and Politics. Cengage Learning Inc. • 2010. eBook. Author details 2 years of research examining the lives of nearly 200 presidential candidates to make up the advice offerec in this work.

Corporate Disasters: What Went Wrong and Why. Cengage Learning Inc. • Covers corporate misdeeds and mistakes in business. Published June 2012. Available in print ($483) and eBook.

Encyclopedia of American Industries. Cengage Learning Inc. • 2011. $807.00. 6th edition. Three volumes. Volume one is Manufacturing Industries and volume two is Service and Non-Manufacturing Industries. Provides the history, development, and recent status of approximately 1,000 industries. Includes statistical graphs, with industry and general indexes. Also available as eBook.

ENCYCLOPEDIAS AND DICTIONARIES

Encyclopedia of Management (EoM). Cengage Learning Inc. • $434 Individuals. 2012. 7th Edition. Contains 316 essays on business management topics. eBook available. Inquire for pricing.

Encyclopedia of the Great Depression. Cengage Learning Inc. • $465 Individuals. Covers about two decades of U.S. economic history, from the farm crisis of the mid-1920s, through the gradual recovery of the 1930s, to the beginning of World War II. (Macmillan Reference USA imprint). eBook also available.

Evolution of Modern Business Series. Cengage Learning Inc. • Contains in-depth surveys on business trends and waves of industrial progress. Offers a critical look at the practices and evolution of the business world. Series includes: Curtiss-Wright, History of Black Business in America, Incorporating Women, and The Invisible Fuel: A History of Natural Gas in America. Volumes available individually.

Gale Encyclopedia of U.S. Economic History. Cengage Learning Inc. • 2003. eBook. Contains about 1,000 alphabetically arranged entries. Includes industry profiles, biographies, social issue profiles, geographic profiles, and chronological tables. Inquire as to price and availability.

GENERAL WORKS

Computer Sciences: Macmillan Science Library. Cengage Learning Inc. • $690 Individuals. 2013. $629.00. Presents a general and historical review of the impact of computers on modern society. Includes biographical information and multidisciplinary examples. Macmillan Reference USA imprint. eBook also available.

Great Depression and New Deal Reference Library. Cengage Learning Inc. • 2003. $236.00. Four volumes. Published by UXL. Includes Great Depression and New Deal: Almanac; Great Depression and New Deal: Biographies and Great Depression and New Deal: Primary Sources. Also available as eBook.

Industrial Revolution Reference Library. Cengage Learning Inc. • 2003. $247. Three volumes. Individual volumes are available. Includes *Industrial Revolution: Almanac; Industrial Revolution: Biographies* and *Industrial Revolution: Primary Sources.* (UXL imprint).

OTHER SOURCES

Botswick Company Business Records. Cengage Learning Inc.

Goldsmiths' Kress Library of Economic Literature: A Consolidated Guide to the Microfilm Collection, 1976-1983. Primary Source Microfilm. • $1,200.00. Four volumes. Individual volumes, $300.00. An estimated 60,000 titles on 1,500 reels of microfilm (or fiche).

PERIODICALS AND NEWSLETTERS

Business History. Frank Cass Publishers. • Quarterly. Institutions, $382.00 per year. Includes print and online editions.

Business History Review. Harvard Business School. • Quarterly. $70 Individuals. A scholarly journal that seeks to publish articles with rigorous primary research that addresses major topics of debate, offers comparative perspectives, and contributes to the broadening of the subject.

Explorations in Economic History. Elsevier. • Quarterly. Individuals, $214.00 per year; institutions, $439.00 per year.

Financial History: Chronicling the History of America's Capital Markets. Museum of American Finance. • Quarterly. Membership. Contains articles on early stock and bond markets and trading in the U. S., with photographs and other illustrations. Current trading in rare and unusual, obsolete stock and bond certificates is featured. Formerly *Friends of Financial History.*

RESEARCH CENTERS AND INSTITUTES

Duke University - David M. Rubenstein Rare Book and Manuscript Library - John W. Hartman Center for Sales, Advertising and Marketing History. PO Box 90185, Durham, NC 27708-0185. Phone: (919)660-5827; Fax: (919)660-5934; Email: hartman-center@duke.edu • URL: http://library.duke.edu/rubenstein/hartman • Concerned with the study of the roles of sales, advertising, and marketing in society.

London School of Economics and Political Science - Business History Unit. Houghton St., London WC2A 2AE, United Kingdom. Phone: 44 20 79557073; Email: t.r.gourvish@lse.ac.uk • URL: http://www.lse.ac.uk/economicHistory/BHU/Home.aspx • Business history, focusing on economic, social and political issues.

University of Newcastle upon Tyne - Cultures, Imperialism and Accounting Practice Research Group. Ridley Bldg., Business School, Newcastle upon Tyne NE1 7RU, United Kingdom. Phone: 44 191 2227586; Email: s.s.k.davie@newcastle.ac.uk • URL: http://www.ncl.ac.uk/niassh/ciap/index.htm • History of accounting across cultures and its relation to economics, politics, and society.

University of Reading - Centre for International Business History. Henley Business School, Whiteknights, Reading RG6 6UD, United Kingdom. Phone: 44 118 3785435; Fax: 44 118 3784029; Email: p.m.scott@henley.ac.uk • URL: http://www.henley.reading.ac.uk/research/research-centres/the-centre-for-international-business-history • Empirical research on the past of business to concepts and theories developed in economics, management, and other disciplines.

TRADE/PROFESSIONAL ASSOCIATIONS

Business History Conference. c/o Hagley Museum and Library, PO Box 3630, Wilmington, DE 19807-0630. Phone: (302)658-2400; Fax: (302)655-3188 • URL: http://www.thebhc.org • Business historians and economic historians (most are from the academic community but a number of business firms are represented through their corporate historians). Brings together persons who are active historians of American and international business, with interests ranging from writing biographies of businessmen and histories of firms to the application of economic theory to analysis of the evolution of American business.

Economic History Association. University of

Arizona. Dept. of Economics. McClelland Hall. 401GG. Tucson. AZ 85721-0108. Phone: (520)621-4421; Fax: (520)621-8450 • URL: http://eh.net/eha • Represents scholars, teachers and students of economic history.

European Business History Association. Gesellschaft fur Unternehmensgeschichte e.V., Sophienstr. 44. D-60487 Frankfurt am Main. Germany. Phone: 49 69 97203314; Fax: 49 69 97203357 • URL: http://www.ebha.org • Promotes research on all aspects of European business and management history.

Professional Scripophily Trade Association. PO Box 223795. Chantilly. VA 20153. Phone: 888-786-2576 or (703)579-4209; Fax: (703)995-4422; Email: bob@psta.com • URL: http://www.psta.com • Promotes the study and collection of scripophily for collectors, researchers, and for the interpretation and preservation of financial history. Helps support educational projects, programs, and seminars to help collectors and the general public gain a better understanding of scripophily, finance and business history.

BUSINESS INDICATORS

See ECONOMIC INDICATORS

BUSINESS INFORMATION SOURCES

See INFORMATION SOURCES

BUSINESS INNOVATION

See also BUSINESS START-UP PLANS AND PROPOSALS; NEW PRODUCTS; RESEARCH AND DEVELOPMENT

ABSTRACTS AND INDEXES

Business Periodicals Index Retrospective. EBSCO Publishing Inc. • 11/year. Quarterly and annual cumulations.

DIRECTORIES

World Buyers' Guide to Unusual & Innovative Products. Emir Publications. • Biennial. $20. Covers: manufacturers and suppliers of unusual merchandise worldwide for mail order dealers, gift stores, novelty dealers, catalog businesses, importers, and opportunity seekers. Entries include: Name of firm, address, cable address, telex, fax, products.

E-BOOKS

Business Information Systems: Concepts, Methodologies, Tools and Applications. Cengage Learning Inc. • 2011. eBook. Offers a complete view of current business information systems within organizations and the advancements that technology has provided to the business community, including how technological advancements have revolutionized financial transactions, management infrastructure, and knowledge workers.

Handbook of Research in Mobile Business: Technical, Methodological, and Social Perspectives. Cengage Learning Inc. • 2011. eBook. 2 volumes. 2nd edition. Published by Information Science Reference. Provides research and scientific findings in the constantly expanding field of mobile business. 63 chapters.

Handbook of Research on Business Social Networking: Organizational, Managerial, and Technological Dimensions. Cengage Learning Inc. • 2012. eBook. Published by IGI Global. Investigates the beginning of social networks and provides perspectives on how they can enhance business, covering discussions on the main issues, challenges, opportunities, and trends related to the range of new developments and applications in business social networking.

Handbook of Research on Serious Games as Educational, Business and Research Tools. Cengage Learning Inc. • 2012. eBook. Published by IGI Global. Collects research on the most recent technological developments in all fields of knowledge or disciplines of computer games development, including planning, design, development, marketing, business management, users and behavior.

Mass Customization Information Systems in Business. Cengage Learning Inc. • 2007. eBook. Published by Information Science Reference. Describes original, innovative works on IT systems for mass customization, and provides a multitude of solutions, tools, concepts and successful realizations of IT systems for mass customization.

ENCYCLOPEDIAS AND DICTIONARIES

Innovation Masters: History's Best Examples of Business Transformation. Cengage Learning Inc. • $483 print only. Covers the best examples of successful businesses and/or business people that have incorporated or developed a new product, service or technology that help to reinvent or revolutionize their business and/or industry.

GENERAL WORKS

International Journal of Business Process Integration & Management (IJBPIM). Inderscience Publishers. • €494 Individuals print or online only for 1 user. Journal covering the emerging business process modeling, simulation, integration and management using emerging technologies.

Journal of Innovation and Business Best Practices (JIBBP). IBIMA Publishing. • Peer-reviewed journal focusing on business innovation and best practices.

ONLINE DATABASES

Wilson Business Abstracts Online. H.W. Wilson Co. • Indexes and abstracts 600 major business periodicals, plus the *Wall Street Journal* and the business section of the *New York Times*. Indexing is from 1982, abstracting from 1990, with the two newspapers included from 1993. Updated weekly. Inquire as to online cost and availability. (*Business Periodicals Index* without abstracts is also available online.).

OTHER SOURCES

Joint Ventures. Glasser LegalWorks. • Looseleaf. $225.00, including CD-ROM version. Periodic Supplementation. Includes explanations of legal procedures for joint ventures, with annotated forms. (Emerging Growth Companies Series.).

PERIODICALS AND NEWSLETTERS

Business 2.0. Time Inc. • General business magazine emphasizing ideas, insight, and innovation.

Fast Company: How Smart Business Works. Fast Company, Inc. • Monthly. $12.00 per year. Covers business management, with emphasis on creativity, leadership, innovation, career advancement, teamwork, the global economy, and the "new workplace.".

RESEARCH CENTERS AND INSTITUTES

Aalborg University - Department of Business and Management - Innovation, Knowledge and Economic Dynamics Research Group. Fibigerstraede 11. DK-9220 Alborg. Denmark. Phone: 45 99408235; Email: ike-secr@business.aau.dk • URL: http://www.ike.aau.dk • Economic, technical and institutional changes, especially economic evolutionary modeling, theory of the firm, national systems of innovation, international trade and competitiveness, and the interplay between economic and ecological issues.

Mack Center for Technological Innovation. University of Pennsylvania. 1050 Steinberg Hall-Dietrich Hall. 3620 Locust Walk. Philadelphia. PA 19104. Phone: (215)898-2104; Fax: (215)573-2129; Email: mackcenter@wharton.upenn.edu • URL: http://www.mackcenter.wharton.upenn.edu • Conducts research related to international business. Formerly Huntsman Center for Global Competition and Innovation.

Texas Tech University - Center for Healthcare Innovation, Education and Research. Rawls College of Business Administration. Lubbock. TX 79409. Phone: (806)742-1236; Fax: (806)742-3434; Email: tim.huerta@ttu.edu • URL: http://chier.ba.ttu.edu/index.asp • Interdisciplinary approaches to studying healthcare safety issues and addition of electronic medical records.

TRADE/PROFESSIONAL ASSOCIATIONS

BC Innovation Council. 1188 W Georgia St., 9th Fl., Vancouver. BC. Canada V6E 4A2. Phone: 800-665-7222 or (604)683-2724; Fax: (604)683-6567; Email: info@bcic.ca • URL: http://www.bcic.ca • Provides support and access to companies and institutions by using research results, development projects and programs to further enhance in creating innovations.

European Business and Innovation Centre Network. Ave. de Tervueren 168. B-1150 Brussels. Belgium. Phone: 32 2 772 89 00; Fax: 32 2 772 9574; Email: info@ebn.eu • URL: http://www.ebn.be • Promotes business innovation and the entrepreneurial spirit in Europe.

National Productivity and Competitiveness Council. 4th Fl. Alexander House. Cybercity. Ebene City. Mauritius. Phone: 230 4677700; Fax: 230 4673838; Email: natpro@intnet.mu • URL: http://www.npccmauritius.com • Generating consensus and building innovation capacity to move to a higher growth path. Hosts seminars and assemblies.

United Kingdom Science Park Association. Chesterford Research Park. Little Chesterford. Essex. Saffron Walden CB10 1XL. United Kingdom. Phone: 44 1799 532050; Fax: 44 1799 532049; Email: info@ukspa.org.uk • URL: http://www.ukspa.org.uk • Supports and encourages the startup, incubation and development of innovation led, high growth, knowledge-based businesses. Provides opportunity for larger and international businesses to develop specific and close interactions with a particular centre of knowledge creation for mutual benefit.

Villgro. 3rd Flr., IIT Madras Research Park. Kanagam Rd., Taramani. Chennai 600113. Tamil Nadu. India. Phone: 91 44 66630400; Email: info@villgro.org • URL: http://www.villgro.org • Promotes the spirit of innovation; encourages experimentation, nurtures the creativity of rural innovators.

BUSINESS INTELLIGENCE

See COMPETITIVE INTELLIGENCE

BUSINESS, INTERNATIONAL

See INTERNATIONAL BUSINESS

BUSINESS INTERRUPTION INSURANCE

See also INSURANCE

PERIODICALS AND NEWSLETTERS

Business Insurance: News Magazine for Corporate Risk, Employee Benefit and Financial Executives. Crain Communications Inc. • Weekly. $95.00 per year. Covers a wide variety of business insurance topics, including risk management, employee benefits, workers compensation, marine insurance, and casualty insurance.

BUSINESS JOURNALISM

See also FARM JOURNALS; HOUSE ORGANS; TRADE JOURNALS

DIRECTORIES

Editor & Publisher Market Guide. Editor and Publisher Company Inc. • Annual. $150 Individuals. Market data for more than 1,600 cities and 3,096 counties.

Grey House Directory of Special Issues: A Guide to Business Magazines. Grey House Publishing. • $175 Softcover. Covers: 4,000 business magazines with special issues as well as industry-specific magazines targeting researchers. Entries include: Publisher name, address, phone, fax, e-mail, brief description of content or audience.

Plymouth County Business Review. Plymouth County Development Council. • Semiannual. $2 Free to qualified subscribers. Trade business review covering regional business trends and stories.

Professional Freelance Writers Directory. National Writers Association. • Annual. Database covers: About 200 professional members selected from the club's membership on the basis of significant articles or books, or production of plays or movies. Entries include: Name, address, phone (home and business numbers), special fields of writing competence, titles of books published by royalty firms, mention of contributions to specific magazines, journals, newspapers or anthologies, recent awards received, relevant activities and skills (photography, etc.).

Writer's Market: Where & How to Sell What You Write. North Light Books. • Annual. $19.79 Individuals paperback. Covers: Over 3,500 buyers of books, articles, short stories, plays, gags, verse, fillers, and other original written material. Includes book and periodical publishers, greeting card publishers, play producers and publishers, audiovisual material producers, syndicates, and contests and awards. Database includes: Interviews with editors and writers and advice on writing, freelancing, and marketing. Entries include: Name and address of buyer, phone, payment rates, editorial requirements, reporting time, how to break in.

GENERAL WORKS

Branson Business Journal. Branson Business Journal. • $16.50 Individuals per year. Publication focusing on business issues.

Burbank Business Journal. Burbank Chamber of Commerce. • Monthly. Contains a variety of articles about business, chamber members and the community at large.

Charleston Regional Business Journal. Setcom Inc. • Biweekly. $99 Individuals /year. Local business journal.

Construction Executive: The Magazine for the Business of Construction. Associated Builders and Contractors. • Monthly. $15 Members. Magazine for contractors and subcontractors. Includes articles on national and regional construction news, construction management, project case histories, new products, building design, and legislative and regulatory updates.

Greater Hartford Business Review. Middlesex Magazine & Business Review. • Monthly. Business journal.

Meadow's Greater New York Business. Meadow Publications Inc. • Quarterly. Magazine covering a variety of business topics concerning New York and suburban New York businesses.

Middlesex Magazine & Business Review. Middlesex Magazine & Business Review. • Monthly. $20. Business journal/Consumer Mag.

South Shore Business Journal. Mariner Newspapers. • Monthly. Tabloid covering business news in Plymouth and Norfolk counties.

Triad Business News. Triad Business News. • Weekly. $36. Business publication.

ONLINE DATABASES

Bloomberg BusinessWeek. Bloomberg L.P. • Contains the complete text (including images) of *Bloomberg BusinessWeek*, a business and industry news magazine. Covers finance, labor and production, corporate news and investment policies, and the effects of legislative and regulatory developments on commerce. Includes analyses of the economic outlook. Provides daily business briefings, market news, investing coverage, and other business information. Provides information on global business, technology, small business, investing, and electronic commerce. Offers reviews of hundreds of business books, including sample chapters. Provides data on the best business schools and provides coverage of work and career issues. Allows users to search back issues of the magazine.

PERIODICALS AND NEWSLETTERS

Agribusiness Worldwide. Keller International Publishing L.L.C. • Bimonthly. $30 Individuals. Trade magazine for those involved in agriculture and livestock development in Asia, Africa, Latin America, and the Middle East. Subjects covered include agricultural production, financing, marketing, and handling.

Art Calendar: The Business Magazine for Visual Artists. Art Calendar. • Monthly. $37 Individuals. Business magazine for visual artists.

Boulder County Business Report (BCBR). Boulder County Business Report. • Biweekly. $44.97 Individuals. Local business newspaper.

Business. Chamber of Commerce and Industry of Tirana. • Monthly. Contains information on business and economics.

Business Alabama. PMT Publishing Company Inc. • Monthly. $22.95 Individuals. Magazine for owners, managers, and presidents of companies covering issues and people in business in Alabama.

Business China. The Economist Intelligence Unit. • Provides news on political, economic, and legal developments throughout the region, including business and e-business news; regulatory changes; distribution, human resources, market-entry strategies and regulatory development issues; company case studies; business intelligence.

Business Development News. World Teleport Association. • Bimonthly. Contains information on business opportunities in the teleport industry.

Business Digest of Central Massachusetts. Business Digest of Central Massachusetts. • Bimonthly. $17 Individuals.

The Business Examiner. Business Examiner Newspaper Group. • Biweekly. $50 Individuals. Local business newspaper.

Business India. Business India Group of Publications. • Biweekly. Periodical covering business news.

The Business Journal: Monthly Business Magazine. Lee Enterprises Inc. • Monthly. Local business editorial.

Business Month. Central Pennsylvania Publishing Co. • Monthly. $15. Community newspaper.

Business Monthly. • Monthly. $9 Individuals. Local business newspaper.

Business News: North of Scotland. North of Scotland Publications. • Monthly. $15 Individuals. Business newspaper.

The Business News: The Miami Valley's Business and Financial News Journal. ACBJ Business Publications. • Weekly. $50 Individuals. Newsmagazine containing information for business owners and company leaders in the Dayton, OH area.

Business Report. 10 Publishing. • Monthly. $22.50 Individuals. Professional business newspaper.

The Business Times of Western Colorado. The Business Times of Western Colorado. • Biweekly. $24.95 Individuals 26 issues. Newspaper covering local business.

Business Today. Living Media India Ltd. • Biweekly. Periodical covering business news.

Business Week. The McGraw-Hill Companies Inc. • Weekly. $5 Individuals 12 issues. Magazine providing business news and intelligence for executives.

Business Woman. Business Women's Committee of Armenia. • Periodic. Armenian and Russian language newspaper covering women in business.

Charitable Business Magazine: Canada's Non-Profit Management Magazine. Momentum Media Management. • Bimonthly. $15. Magazine for Canadian executives, administrators, purchasing and operations personnel at charitable and non-profit organizations.

The Costco Connection: A Lifestyle Magazine for Small Business. BPA International. • Monthly. Magazine serving small businesses who are members of Costco Wholesale.

Crain's Small Business. Crain Communications Inc. • Monthly. Tabloid covering topics of interest for companies with under 100 employees.

The Daily Record: Business and Legal News of Maryland. The Daily Record CPN. • Mon.-Sat. $269 Individuals print and online. Daily Business Newspaper reporting news and features on business, real estate, technology, healthcare and law.

Denver Business. Tall Oaks Publishing Inc. • Monthly. $24 Individuals. Consumer business magazine serving metropolitan Denver.

Export-Import News: International Business and Economics Fortnightly. India - International News Service. • Biweekly. $500. Periodical covering international business news.

The Finger Lakes Business Almanac: Your Window into Finger Lakes Businesses and Their Concerns. OnPoint Publishing. • Biweekly. $38.75 local annual. Tabloid containing news about business and the economy in the northeast Finger Lakes.

GSA Business. GSA Business. • Biweekly. $49.95 Individuals /year. Local business newspaper.

HME News: The Business Newspaper for Home Medical Equipment Providers. HME News. • Monthly. Business newspaper for home medical equipment providers. Editorial coverage focuses on industry news, mergers and acquisitions, governmental and regulatory impact on the HME industry, as well as product reviews and industry trend coverage.

Iceland Business. Iceland Review. • Magazine covering business in Iceland.

In Business: Dane County's Business Magazine. Business Information L.L.C. • Monthly. $28 Individuals. Local business magazine.

Indonesia Business Weekly. PT. Jurnalindo Aksara Grafika. • Weekly. Business magazine.

Ingram's: Kansas City's Business Magazine. Show-Me Publishing Inc. • Monthly. $44.95 Individuals. Business and lifestyle magazine covering Lawrence, Topeka, Overland Park, KS, and Kansas City and St. Joseph, MO.

Jacksonville Business Journal. The Business Journals. • $92 Individuals print and online. Local business news coverage.

Journal of Asia-Pacific Business. Routledge Journals Taylor & Francis Group. • Quarterly. $405 Institutions online only. Journal featuring managerially oriented as well as academic articles centered on the Asia-Pacific region.

Journal of Business Strategy. Emerald Group Publishing Ltd. • Bimonthly. Business magazine.

Journal of East-West Business. Routledge Journals Taylor & Francis Group. • Quarterly. $530 Institutions online only. Journal dealing with contemporary and emerging topics of business studies, strategies, development, and practice relating to Eastern Europe and Asia.

Marketplace Magazine: Northeast Wisconsin's Business Magazine. Marketplace Magazine. • Semimonthly. $48. Business magazine (tabloid).

METROBusiness Magazine: The Entrepreneurial Spirit of Metropolitan Boston. METROBusiness Magazine. • Bimonthly. $18. Magazine serving the business and professional community in metropolitan Boston.

Metropolitan Toronto Business Journal. The Toronto Region Board of Trade. • Magazine serving the greater Toronto business community.

Minnesota Business. Tiger Oak Publications Inc. • Business magazine.

My Business. Hammock Inc. • Bimonthly. Business magazine.

Nashville Business Journal. American City Business Journals, Inc. • Weekly. $91 Individuals print and digital. Regional business newspaper.

New England Business. New England Business Corp. • Monthly. $29.95 Individuals. Business magazine.

Pacific Magazine with Islands Business. PacificBasin Communications. • Monthly. $15 Individuals. Magazine covering business in Hawaii.

Pork: The Business Magazine for Professional Pork Producers. Vance Publishing Corp. • Monthly. $50 Individuals. Magazine on pork production and marketing.

Real Business. Caspian Publishing. • Monthly. £40 Individuals. Professional magazine covering business.

Rocky Mountain Business Journal. Rocky Mountain Business Journal. • Weekly (Mon.). $26 Individuals. Metro business journal.

Route 422 Business Advisor. TriCounty Area Chamber of Commerce. • Monthly. Magazine containing topics of interest to the business community of the Pottstown, PA area.

School Business Magazine: Canada's Education Management Magazine. Momentum Media Management. • Bimonthly. $15. Magazine for Canadian educators, executives, administrators, transportation, and operations personnel at schools, boards, colleges, and universities.

Seattle Business Monthly. Tiger Oak Publications Inc. • Monthly. Business magazine.

Small Business Exchange. Canadian Auto Review. • Semimonthly. $92.50 -220. Trade newspaper.

South East Business. Evegate Publishing Ltd. • Monthly. £40 Individuals. Professional magazine covering local business news.

South Florida Business Journal. The Business Journals. • $91 Individuals. Newspaper covering business in Miami, Fort Lauderdale, and West Palm Beach.

Stanford Business. Stanford University Stanford Graduate School of Business. • Quarterly. $10 U.S. and Canada. Magazine for business school alumni.

Teleconferencing Business Magazine: Annual Directory of Teleconferencing Products & Services. Business Teleconferencing. • Annual. $36. Magazine for news on the industry of teleconferencing.

Thunder Bay Business. North Superior Publishing Inc. • Monthly. Trade magazine.

Total Quality Management & Business Excellence. Routledge. • Monthly. $929 Individuals print only. Peer-reviewed journal general business publication.

Wichita Business Journal. The Business Journals. • Weekly. $91 Individuals /year, print and online. Business newspaper.

RESEARCH CENTERS AND INSTITUTES

Aarhus University - School of Business and Social Sciences - Department of Business Communication - Center for Corporate Communication. Fuglesangs Allè 4, DK-8210 Aarhus, Denmark. Phone: 45 89486268; Fax: 45 86150188 • URL: http://bcom.au.dk/research/academicareas/ccc • Business communications, including management communication, market communication, corporate communication, public relations, internal communication, business journalism, etc.

TRADE/PROFESSIONAL ASSOCIATIONS

American Society of Business Publications Editors. 214 N Hale St., Wheaton, IL 60187. Phone: (603)510-4588; Fax: (603)510-4501; Email: info@asbpe.org • URL: http://www.asbpe.org.

BUSINESS LAW

ABSTRACTS AND INDEXES

Current Law Index. Cengage Learning Inc. • $1,332 Individuals. Monthly. $1269.00 per year. Produced in cooperation with the American Association of Law Libraries. Indexes more than 900 law journals, legal newspapers, and specialty publications from the U.S., Canada, U.K., Ireland, Australia, and New Zealand.

Index to Legal Periodicals and Books. H.W. Wilson Co. • Monthly. $490.00 per year. Quarterly and annual cumulations.

ALMANACS AND YEARBOOKS

American Law Yearbook. Cengage Learning Inc. • $308 Individuals. Annual. $280.00. Serves as a yearly supplement to *West's Encyclopedia of American Lawa.* Describes new legal developments in many subject areas.

CD-ROM DATABASES

Authority Computer and Telecommunications Law Library. Matthew Bender and Company Inc. • Quarterly. Price on request. Full text CD-ROM provides cases, analysis, sample agreements, and other information relating to computer law, telecommunications regulation (cable, broadcasting, satellite, Internet), international computer law, and computer contracts.

Index to Legal Periodicals and Books. EBSCO Publishing Inc. • Contains indexing of more than 1,400 English language legal periodicals from 1981 to date and 2,500 books.

DIRECTORIES

Afghanistan Business Law Handbook. International Business Publications, USA. • $99.95 Individuals hardcover. Covers: Information on basic business legislation, laws and climate, export-import regulations, and contacts.

Antilles (Netherlands) Business Law Handbook. International Business Publications, USA. • $99.95 Individuals hardcopy, E-book and CD-ROM. Covers: Basic information on business laws and legislations, export-import regulations, business climate and contacts.

Australia Business Law Handbook. International Business Publications, USA. • $99.95 Individuals hardcopy, e-book, CD-ROM. Covers: Basic information on business laws and legislations, export-import regulations, business climate and contacts.

Brazil Business Law Handbook. International Business Publications, USA. • Annual. $99.95 Individuals hardcover. Covers: Information on basic business legislation, laws, business climate, and contacts.

Burundi Business Law Handbook. International Business Publications, USA. • $99.95 Individuals hardcopy. Covers: Information on basic business legislation, laws and climate, export-import regulations, and contacts.

Business and Legal Forms for Authors and Self-publishers. Allworth Press. • $24.99 Single issue paperback. Publication includes: Contact information for volunteer lawyers for the arts. Principal content of publication is instruction and use of business and legal forms for authors and self-publishers.

Business Litigation Database. Trans Union Credit Information Co. • Continuous. Database covers: 8 million court records on companies from New York and New Jersey, including suits, judgments, satisfactions, bankruptcies, forecloseures (for New Jersey only), and federal, state, and city tax liens. Entries include: Defendant name and address, plaintiff name and address, court of filing, filing date, docket number, dollar amount of action, type of action.

Cambodia Business Law Handbook. International Business Publications, USA. • $99.95 Individuals hardcopy. Covers: Information on basic business legislation, laws, business climate, export-import regulations, taxation, banking and contacts.

Cameroon Business Law Handbook. International Business Publications, USA. • $99.95 Individuals hardcopy. Covers: Information on basic business legislation, laws and climate, export-import regulations, and contacts.

Cape Verde Business Law Handbook. International Business Publications, USA. • $99.95 Individuals hardcopy, e-book, CD-ROM. Covers: Information on basic business legislation, laws and climate, export-import regulations, and contacts.

Cayman Islands Business Law Handbook. International Business Publications, USA. • $99.95 Individuals hardcopy, E-book and CD-ROM. Covers: Basic information on business laws and legislations, export-import regulations, business climate and contacts.

Chile Business Law Handbook. International Business Publications, USA. • $99.95 Individuals hardcopy, E-book and CD-ROM. Covers: Basic information on business laws and legislations, export-import regulations, business climate and contacts.

China Business Law Handbook. International Business Publications, USA. • $99.95 Individuals hardcopy, e-book, CD-ROM. Covers: Information on basic business legislation, laws, business climate, foreign investments, export-import regulations, and contacts.

Commercial Bar Association Directory. Wiley Chancery. • Annual. $25. Covers: Over 700 barristers in the U.K. specializing in corporate and commercial law; includes chamber and individual members. Entries include: Chamber name, address, phone, fax, principal fields of work; associated barristers, with name, date of birth, date of call, Queen's counsel, inn, academic and professional qualifications, pubications, languages spoken.

Congo Business Law Handbook. International Business Publications, USA. • $99.95 Individuals hardcopy, e-book, CD-ROM. Covers: Information on basic business legislation, laws, business climate, export-import regulations, and contacts.

Croatia Business Law Handbook. International Business Publications, USA. • $99.95 Individuals hardcopy, e-book, CD-ROM. Covers: Basic information on business, export-import regulations, and contacts.

Cyprus Business Law Handbook. International Business Publications, USA. • $99.95 Individuals hardcopy, e-book, CD-ROM. Covers: Basic information on business, laws, export-import, regulations, and contacts.

Dubai Business Law Handbook. International Business Publications, USA. • $99.95 Individuals hardcopy, e-book, CD-ROM. Covers: Basic information on business, laws, export-import, business climate, regulations, and contacts.

Ecuador Business Law Handbook. International Business Publications, USA. • $99.95 Individuals hardcopy, e-book, CD-ROM. Covers: Business laws and climate, export-import regulations, investment, tax, and contacts.

Egypt Business Law Handbook. International Business Publications, USA. • $99.95 Individuals hardcopy, e-book, CD-ROM. Covers: Information on basic business legislation, property rights, laws, business climate, export-import regulations, taxation, banking and contacts.

Equatorial Guinea Business Law Handbook. International Business Publications, USA. • $99.95 Individuals hardcopy, e-book, CD-ROM. Covers: Basic information on business, laws, export-import, business climate, regulations, and contacts.

Eritrea Business Law Handbook. International Business Publications, USA. • $99.95 Individuals hardcopy, E-book and CD-ROM. Covers: Basic business laws and legislations, export-import regulations, business climate and contacts.

Estonia Business Law Handbook. International Business Publications, USA. • $99.95 Individuals hardcopy, e-book, CD-ROM. Covers: Basic information on business, laws, export-import, investment, tax, regulations, and contacts.

Gabon Business Law Handbook. International Business Publications, USA. • $99.95 Individuals hardcopy, E-book and CD-ROM. Covers: Basic business laws and legislations, export-import regulations, business climate and contacts.

Gambia Business Law Handbook. International Business Publications, USA. • $99.95 Individuals hardcover, e-book, CD-ROM. Covers: Information on basic business legislation, laws and climate, export-import regulations, and contacts.

Georgia (Republic) Business Law Handbook. International Business Publications, USA. • $99.95 Individuals hardcover, e-book, CD-ROM. Covers: Information on basic business legislation, laws, business climate, foreign investments, export-import regulations, and contacts.

Greece Business Law Handbook. International Business Publications, USA. • $99.95 Individuals hardcover, e-book, CD-ROM. Covers: Information on business laws and climate, investment, tax, export-import regulations, and contacts.

Guinea-Bissau Business Law Handbook. International Business Publications, USA. • $99.95 Individuals hardcopy, E-book and CD-ROM. Covers: Basic business laws and legislations, export-import regulations, business climate and contacts.

Guinea Business Law Handbook. International Business Publications, USA. • $99.95 Individuals hardcopy, e-book, CD-ROM. Covers: Basic information on business laws and legislations, export-import regulations, business climate and contacts.

Guyana Business Law Handbook. International Business Publications, USA. • $99.95 Individuals hardcopy, E-book and CD-ROM. Covers: Basic information on business laws and legislations, export-import regulations, business climate and contacts.

India Business Law Handbook. International Business Publications, USA. • $99.95 Individuals hardcopy, e-book, CD-ROM. Covers: Information on basic business legislation, laws and climate, export-import regulations, and contacts.

Iran Business Law Handbook. International Business Publications, USA. • $99.95 Individuals hardcover, e-book, CD-ROM. Covers: Information on basic business legislation, laws, business climate, export-import regulations and contacts.

Iraq Business Law Handbook. International Business Publications, USA. • $99.95 Individuals hardcopy, e-book, CD-ROM. Covers: Information on basic business legislation, laws and climate, export-import regulations, and contacts.

Israel Business Law Handbook. International Business Publications, USA. • $99.95 Individuals hardcover, e-book, CD-ROM. Covers: Information on basic business legislation, laws, business climate, export-import regulations, and contacts.

Italy Business Law Handbook. International Business Publications, USA. • $99.95 Individuals hardcover, e-book, CD-ROM. Covers: Information on basic business legislation, laws and climate, export-import regulations, and contacts.

Jordan Business Law Handbook. International Business Publications, USA. • $99.95 Individuals hardcopy, E-book and CD-ROM. Covers: Basic business laws and legislations, export-import regulations, business climate and contacts.

Kazakhstan Business Law Handbook. International Business Publications, USA. • $99.95 Individuals hardcopy, E-book and CD-ROM. Covers: Basic information on business laws and legislations, export-import regulations, business climate and contacts.

Kenya Business Law Handbook. International Business Publications, USA. • $99.95 Individuals hardcopy, e-book, CD-ROM. Covers: Information on basic business legislation, laws and climate, export-import regulations, and contacts.

Korea North Business Law Handbook. International Business Publications, USA. • $99.95 Individuals hardcopy, e-book, CD-ROM. Covers: Information on basic business legislation, laws, business climate, and contacts.

Korea South Business Law Handbook. International Business Publications, USA. • $99.95 Individuals hardcopy, e-book, CD-ROM. Covers: Information on basic business legislation, laws and climate, export-import regulations, and contacts.

Kuwait Business Law Handbook. International Business Publications, USA. • $99.95 Individuals hardcopy, e-book, CD-ROM. Covers: Information on basic business legislation, laws, business climate, export-import regulations, and contacts.

Kyrgyzstan Business Law Handbook. International Business Publications, USA. • $99.95 Individuals hardcopy, e-book, CD-ROM. Covers: Business climate and legislation, laws, export-import regulations affecting business and contacts.

Laos Business Law Handbook. International Business Publications, USA. • $99.95 Individuals hardcopy, e-book, CD-ROM. Covers: Information on basic business legislation, laws and climate, export-import regulations, and contacts.

Luxembourg Business Law Handbook. International Business Publications, USA. • $99.95 Individuals hardcopy, e-book, CD-ROM. Covers: Information on basic business legislation, laws and regulations affecting business and foreign investments, property rights, taxation and banking.

Malaysia Business Law Handbook. International Business Publications, USA. • $99.95 Individuals hardcopy, e-book, CD-ROM. Covers: Information on basic business legislation, laws, business climate, export-import regulations, and contacts.

Mexico Business Law Handbook. International Business Publications, USA. • $99.95 Individuals hardcopy, e-book, CD-ROM. Covers: Information on basic business legislation, laws, export-import regulations, and contacts.

Mozambique Business Law Handbook. International Business Publications, USA. • $99.95 Individuals hardcover, e-book, CD-ROM. Covers: Information on basic business legislation, laws, business climate, export-import regulations, and contacts.

Nauru Business Law Handbook. International Business Publications, USA. • $99.95 Individuals hardcopy, E-book and CD-ROM. Covers: Basic information on business laws and legislations, export-import regulations, business climate and contacts.

Nicaragua Business Law Handbook. International Business Publications, USA. • $99.95 Individuals hardcopy, e-book, CD-ROM. Covers: Information on basic business legislation, laws, business climate, foreign investments, export-import regulations, and contacts.

Paraguay Business Law Handbook. International Business Publications, USA. • $99.95 Individuals hardcopy, e-book, CD-ROM. Covers: Information on basic business legislation, laws, business climate, export-import regulations, and contacts.

Peru Business Law Handbook. International Business Publications, USA. • $99.95 Individuals hardcopy, e-book, CD-ROM. Covers: Information on basic business legislation, laws, business climate, export-import regulations, and contacts.

Philippines Business Law Handbook. International Business Publications, USA. • $99.95 Individuals hardcopy, e-book, CD-ROM. Covers: Information on basic business legislation, laws and regulations affecting business, and contacts.

Portugal Business Law Handbook. International Business Publications, USA. • $99.95 Individuals hardcopy, e-book, CD-ROM. Covers: Information on basic business legislation, investment, tax, laws, export-import regulations, and contacts.

Russia Business Law Handbook. International Business Publications, USA. • $99.95 Individuals hardcopy, e-book, CD-ROM. Covers: Information on business laws and climate, legislation, export-import regulations, and contacts.

Saudi Arabia Business Law Handbook. International Business Publications, USA. • $99.95 Individuals hardcopy, e-book, CD-ROM. Covers: Basic information on business laws and legislations, export-import regulations, business climate and contacts.

Senegal Business Law Handbook. International Business Publications, USA. • $99.95 Individuals hardcopy, e-book, CD-ROM. Covers: Information on basic business legislation, laws and regulations affecting business, business climate and contacts.

Seychelles Business Law Handbook. International Business Publications, USA. • $99.95 Individuals hardcopy, e-book, CD-ROM. Covers: Information on basic business legislation, property rights, laws, business climate, export-import regulations, taxation, banking and contacts.

Solomon Islands Business Law Handbook. International Business Publications, USA. • $99.95 Individuals hardcopy, e-book, CD-ROM. Covers: Information on basic business legislation, laws, business climate, export-import regulations, and contacts.

Somalia Business Law Handbook. International Business Publications, USA. • $99.95 Individuals hardcopy, e-book, CD-ROM. Covers: Information on basic business legislation, laws and climate, export-import regulations, and contacts.

Spain Business Law Handbook. International Business Publications, USA. • $99.95 Individuals hardcopy, e-book, CD-ROM. Covers: Information on basic business legislation, tax, investment, laws, export-import regulations, and contacts.

Sweden Business Law Handbook. International Business Publications, USA. • $99.95 Individuals hardcopy, e-book, CD-ROM. Covers: Information on business laws and climate, investment, tax, export-import regulations, and contacts.

Syria Business Law Handbook. International Business Publications, USA. • $149.95 Individuals. Covers: Basic information on business, laws, export-import, business climate, regulations, and contacts.

Tanzania Business Law Handbook. International Business Publications, USA. • $99.95 Individuals hardcopy, e-book, CD-ROM. Covers: Basic information on business, laws, export-import, business climate, regulations, and contacts.

Thailand Business Law Handbook. International Business Publications, USA. • $99.95 Individuals hardcopy, e-book, CD-ROM. Covers: Information on business laws and regulations, business, investments, tax and contacts.

Tonga Business Law Handbook. International Business Publications, USA. • $99.95 Individuals hardcopy, E-book and CD-ROM. Covers: Basic information on business laws and legislations, export-import regulations, business climate and contacts.

Venezuela Business Law Handbook. International Business Publications, USA. • $99.95 Individuals hardcopy, e-book, CD-ROM. Covers: Basic information on business laws and legislations, export-import regulations, business climate and contacts.

Vietnam Business Law Handbook. International Business Publications, USA. • $99.95 Individuals hardcopy, E-book and CD-ROM. Covers: Information on basic business legislation, laws, business climate, export-import regulations, taxation, banking and contacts.

Western Sahara Business Law Handbook. International Business Publications, USA. • $99.95 Individuals hardcopy, E-book and CD-ROM. Covers: Information on business laws and climate, legislation, export-import regulations, and contacts.

Yemen Business Law Handbook. International Business Publications, USA. • $99.95 Individuals hardcopy, E-book and CD-ROM. Covers: Information on basic business legislation, laws and climate, export-import regulations, and contacts.

E-BOOKS

Cyberlaw for Global E-business: Finance, Payment and Dispute Resolution. Cengage Learning Inc. • 2009. eBook. Examines cyberlaw discussions worldwide on topics such as cybercrime and risk management, comparative electronic trading systems of securities, digital currency regulation, jurisdiction and consumer protection in cross-border markets, and case law on international bank transfers.

Starting a Successful Business. Cengage Learning Inc. • 2009. eBook. Published by Kogan Page. Covers topics such as franchises, marketing, publicity, e-business, financial management, business law, recruitment, taxation, insurance, business planning and development.

ENCYCLOPEDIAS AND DICTIONARIES

Dictionary of Commercial, Financial and Legal Terms in Two Languages. Adler's Foreign Books Inc. • Two volumes. Vol. A, $179.50; vol. B $179. 50. Text in English and German.

GENERAL WORKS

ALI-ABA Business Law Course Materials Journal. ALI-ABA Continuing Professional Education. • Bimonthly. $40 /year. Provides articles from ALI-ABA continuing education course books.

American Business Law Journal. Academy of Legal Studies in Business. • Quarterly. $852 Institutions print & online. Journal focusing on a range of topics related to business law.

Annotated Business Agreements. Thomson Reuters Canada Ltd. • Contains information on business agreement law in Canada. Includes precedents for the most common types of business organization agreements, such as shareholders' agreements, partnership agreements, and other related agreements.

Berkeley Business Law Journal.

Border Business Review. University of Texas at El Paso Institute for Policy and Economic Development. • Quarterly.

Business Law Journal.

Business Voice. New Jersey Business & Industry Association. • Monthly. Updates legislation and member services.

Duquesne Business Law Journal.

European Legal Business. Legalese Ltd. • Bimonthly. $195 Individuals. Journal covering the European legal market.

Hastings Business Law Journal. University of California Hastings College of the Law.

Latin American Law and Business Report. Prentice Hall Press. • Monthly. $345 Individuals. Journal covering current business and legal developments and practices in Latin America.

Northwestern Journal of International Law & Business. Northwestern University School of Law Office of Legal Publications. • 3/year. $40 Individuals. Journal covering business law issues worldwide.

Pacific McGeorge Global Business and Development Law Journal. University of the Pacific McGeorge School of Law.

Stanford Journal of Law, Business and Finance.

the Journal of Business, Entrepreneurship, and the Law.

HANDBOOKS AND MANUALS

Gale Business Insights Handbook Of. Cengage Learning Inc. • $627 Individuals. Examines the questions "What is social media marketing" and "How can it be used in my business?".

Lawrence's Anderson on the Uniform Commercial Code. Lary Lawrence. Thomson West. • $4,807 Individuals Book - Hardbound - Full Set. Provides article-by-article analysis of the UCC.

Manual of Credit and Commercial Laws. National Association of Credit Management. National Association of Credit Management. • Annual. $69.95 Individuals. Provides information for credit professionals. Formerly *Credit Manual of Commercial Laws.*

Warren's Forms of Agreements. Matthew Bender and Company Inc. • Biennial. $2,368 print. 8-volume set. A compact source of forms that business transaction lawyers are most frequently asked to document.

INTERNET DATABASES

Factiva. Dow Jones Reuters Business Interactive, LLC. Phone: 800-369-7466 or (609)452-1511; Fax: (609)520-5770; Email: solutions@factiva.com • URL: http://www.factiva.com • Fee-based Web site provides "global news and business information through Web sites and content integration solutions." Includes Dow Jones and Reuters newswires, The Wall Street Journal, and more than 7,000 other sources of current news, historical articles, market research reports, and investment analysis. Content includes 96 major U. S. newspapers, 900 non-English sources, trade publications, media transcripts, country profiles, news photos, etc.

Lexis.com Research System. Lexis-Nexis Group. Phone: 800-227-4908 or (937)865-6800; Fax: (937)865-6909; Email: webmaster@prod.lexis-nexis.com • URL: http://www.nexis.com • Fee-based Web site offers extensive searching of a wide variety of legal sources. Additional features include Daily Opinion Service, lexis.com Bookstore, Career Center, CLE Center, Law Schools, and Practice Pages ("Pages specific to areas of specialty").

Nexis.com. Lexis-Nexis Group. Phone: 800-227-4908 or (937)865-6800; Fax: (937)865-6909; Email: webmaster@prod.lexis-nexis.com • URL: http://www.nexis.com • Fee-based Web site offers searching of about 2.8 billion documents in some 30,000 news, business, and legal information sources. Features include a subject directory covering 1,200 topics in 34 categories and a Company Dossier containing information on more than 500,000 public and private companies. Boolean searching is offered.

www.BusinessLaw.gov. U.S. Small Business Administration. 409 3rd St. SW, Washington, DC 20416. Phone: 800-827-5722 or (202)205-8800 • URL: http://www.sba.gov • Web site provides information on legal and regulatory issues for small businesses. It offers access to critical information on topics from advertising to zoning, including laws on hiring and managing employees. The site allows businesses to apply for licenses or permits, e-file tax returns, and confer with other business owners.

ONLINE DATABASES

Access Business News. NewsBank Inc. • Contains the full-text of current and archived editions of approximately 200 business and law journals, local and regional news weeklies, and other news sources across North America.

RICO Business Disputes Guide. Wolters Kluwer Law & Business CCH. • Contains information on pending U.S. Supreme Court RICO cases, as well as pending federal and state legislation.

Westlaw Business Law Practitioner. Thomson Reuters Westlaw. • Contains comprehensive and current online resources, by practice and jurisdiction, for legal research in business and commercial pursuits.

OTHER SOURCES

Business Law Monographs. Matthew Bender and Company Inc. • Quarterly. $3,645 book. Intended for in-house and outside corporate counsel. Each monograph concentrates on a particular subject.

Forms of Business Agreements and Resolutions-Annotated, Tax Tested. Prentice Hall PTR. • Three looseleaf volumes. Periodic supplementation. Price on application.

Joint Ventures. Glasser LegalWorks. • Looseleaf. $225.00, including CD-ROM version. Periodic Supplementation. Includes explanations of legal procedures for joint ventures, with annotated forms. (Emerging Growth Companies Series.).

Quicken Business Law Partner. Broderbund and The Learning Co. • A computer software program that is capable of preparing up to 59 legal documents. The program allows the user to enter information either through the Interview method—in which documents are created based on answers to questions—or the typical Fill-in-the-Blank format. Quicken Business Law Partner prepares documents in 12 different categories, including Personal Information; Powers of Attorney; Consumer Letters; Credit Letters; Government Letters; Other Letters; Corporate Forms; Employment Forms; Small Claims Forms; Business Forms; Financial Forms; and Real Estate Forms. Business Law Partner is available on diskette or CD-ROM.

PERIODICALS AND NEWSLETTERS

The Business Lawyer. American Bar Association. • Quarterly. $65 Individuals. Law journal.

Corporate and Business Law Journal. National Centre for Corporate Law and Policy Research. • Semiannual. $44 Individuals. Law periodical.

Federal Register. Office of the Federal Register. U. S. Government Printing Office. • Daily except Saturday and Sunday. $764.00 per year. Publishes regulations and legal notices issued by federal agencies, including executive orders and presidential proclamations. Issued by the National Archives and Records Administration (www.nara.gov).

UCC Bulletin. Thomson West. • Monthly. $560.00 per year. Newsletter. Includes case summaries of recent UCC decisions.

RESEARCH CENTERS AND INSTITUTES

Alabama Law Institute. Law Center, Rm. 326, Tuscaloosa, AL 35486-0013. Phone: (205)348-7411; Fax: (205)348-8411 • URL: http://ali.state.al.us • Statutes of Alabama, including studies of existing laws with systematic revision of laws to be proposed to Alabama legislature. Conducts investigations into state tax structure, evidence, criminal law, business law, probate law, real property, and family law. Develops manuals for legislators, county commissioners, tax assessors and collectors, and other governmental offices.

TRADE/PROFESSIONAL ASSOCIATIONS

Commercial Law League of America. 205 N Michigan Ave., Ste. 2212, Chicago, IL 60601. Phone: 800-978-2552 or (312)240-1400; Fax: (312)240-1408; Email: info@clla.org • URL: http://www.clla.org • Represents lawyers and other professionals engaged in bankruptcy and other commercial law areas; commercial collection agencies; law list publishers. Elevates the standards and improve the practice of commercial law. Promotes uniformity of legislation in matters affecting commercial law. Conducts educational programs on legal topics and issues of public interest at regional and national meetings. Maintains speakers' bureau and over 40 special and standing committees covering areas of commercial law including Bankruptcy and Uniform Commercial Code.

BUSINESS LETTERS

See BUSINESS CORRESPONDENCE

BUSINESS LIBRARIES

See SPECIAL LIBRARIES

BUSINESS LITERATURE

See also BUSINESS; BUSINESS HISTORY; BUSINESS RESEARCH; ECONOMIC RESEARCH; GOVERNMENT PUBLICATIONS

ABSTRACTS AND INDEXES

Business Periodicals Index Retrospective. EBSCO Publishing Inc. • 11/year. Quarterly and annual cumulations.

BIBLIOGRAPHIES

U.S. Government Information for Business. U. S. Government Printing Office. • Annual. Free. A selected list of currently available publications, periodicals, and electronic products on business, trade, labor, federal regulations, economics, and other topics. Also known as *Business Catalog.*

DIRECTORIES

World Directory of Trade and Business Journals. Euromonitor International Business Reference Div. • $590. Covers: international consumer and industrial trade journals. Entries include: title, publisher address, coverage, language, frequency, readership, cost, and circulation.

INTERNET DATABASES

EBSCO Information Services. EBSCO Publishing Inc. 10 Estes St., Ipswich, MA 01938-2106. Phone: 800-653-2726 or (978)356-6500; Fax: (978)356-6565; Email: information@ebscohost.com • URL: http://www.ebscohost.com • Fee-based Web site providing Internet access to a wide variety of databases, including business-related material. Full text is available for many periodical titles, with daily updates. Fees: Apply.

InSite 2. Intelligence Data/Thomson Financial. Phone: 800-654-0393 or (617)856-1890; Fax: (617)737-3182; Email: intelligence.data@tfn.com • URL: http://www.insite2.gale.com/ • Fee-based Web site consolidates information in a "Base Pack" consisting of Business InSite, Market InSite, and Company InSite. Optional databases are Consumer InSite, Health and Wellness InSite, Newsletter InSite, and Computer InSite. Includes fulltext content from more than 2,500 trade publications, journals, newsletters, newspapers, analyst reports, and other sources. Continuous updating. Formerly produced by The Gale Group.

ProQuest. ProQuest L.L.C. 789 E Eisenhower Pkwy., Ann Arbor, MI 48106-1346. Phone: 800-521-0600 or (734)761-4700; Fax: (734)662-4554; Email: info@proquest.com • URL: http://www.proquest.com • Fee-based Web site providing Internet access to more than 3,000 periodicals, newspapers, and other publications. Many items are available full-text, with daily updates. Includes extensive corporate and financial information. Fees: Apply.

PERIODICALS AND NEWSLETTERS

Business and Finance Division Bulletin. Special Libraries Association. • Quarterly. $12.00 per year.

Business Information Alert: Sources, Strategies and Signposts for Information Professionals. Alert Publications Inc. • 10 times per year. Libraries, $162.00 per year. Newsletter for business librarians and information specialists.

The Information Report. Washington Researchers Ltd. • Description: Contains 40-140 items in each issue identifying little-known sources of information. Lists and describes directories, special libraries, booklets, seminars, studies, and other research sources available on markets, competition, federal regulation, and economic conditions. Covers government as well as corporate sources, trade, and professional organizations.

SI: Special Issues. Trip Wyckoff, editor. Hoover's Inc. • Bimonthly. $149.95 per year. Newsletter. Serves as a supplement to *Directory of Business Periodical Special Issues.* Provides information on trade journal special issues and editorial calendars.

BUSINESS LOANS

See BANK LOANS

BUSINESS MACHINES

See OFFICE EQUIPMENT AND SUPPLIES

BUSINESS MARKETING

See INDUSTRIAL MARKETING

BUSINESS MATHEMATICS

See also STATISTICAL METHODS

CD-ROM DATABASES

MathSciNet. American Mathematical Society. • Electronic resource with citations, abstracts, and reviews to the literature of mathematics, statistics, and computer science, 1940 to date.

PERIODICALS AND NEWSLETTERS

Mathematical Finance: An International Journal of Mathematics, Statistics, and Financial Economics. Blackwell Publishing Inc. • Quarterly. $1,453 Institutions print only. Covers the use of sophisticated mathematical tools in financial research and practice.

RESEARCH CENTERS AND INSTITUTES

Center for Mathematical Studies in Economics and Management Science. Northwestern University, 580 Leverone Hall, 2001 Sheridan Rd., Evanston, IL 60208-2014. Phone: (847)491-3527; Fax: (847)491-2530; Email: cms-ems@kellogg.northwestern.edu • URL: http://www.kellogg.northwestern.edu/research/math.

BUSINESS MERGERS

See MERGERS AND ACQUISITIONS

BUSINESS MORALE

See HUMAN RELATIONS

BUSINESS ORGANIZATION AND ADMINISTRATION

See INDUSTRIAL MANAGEMENT

BUSINESS PERIODICALS

See TRADE JOURNALS

BUSINESS PROPOSALS

See BUSINESS START-UP PLANS AND PROPOSALS

BUSINESS PSYCHOLOGY

See INDUSTRIAL PSYCHOLOGY

BUSINESS RATIOS

See FINANCIAL RATIOS

BUSINESS RECORDS MANAGEMENT

See RECORDS MANAGEMENT

BUSINESS RESEARCH

See also BUREAUS OF BUSINESS RESEARCH; BUSINESS LITERATURE; COMPETITIVE INTELLIGENCE; ECONOMIC RESEARCH

BIBLIOGRAPHIES

Business Research Handbook: Methods and Sources for Lawyers and Business Professionals. Kathy E. Shimpock. Wolters Kluwer Law and Business. • Semiannual. $859 Individuals Looseleaf. Provides detailed advice on how to find business information. Describes a wide variety of data sources, both private and government.

CD-ROM DATABASES

Business Marketing CD. Herold Business Data GmbH. • Contains information on 320,000 Austrian companies. The database is available on CD-ROM. It supports such marketing activities as mailings and customer identification.

OECD Statistical Compendium. Organization for Economic Cooperation and Development. • Semiannual. $1,905.00 per year for 1 to 10 users. CD-ROM contains more than 730,000 monthly, quarterly, and annual time series for OECD countries, 1960 to date. Includes fully searchable data on agriculture, food, economic indicators, national accounts, employment, energy, finance, industry, technology, and foreign trade. Results can be displayed in various forms.

16 Million Businesses Phone Book. Info U.S.A. • Contains business information and phone numbers of U.S. and Canada businesses. Cross-referenced to search for company name or contact information. The database is available on CD-ROM.

Time Table of Business, Politics and Media. Etronica. • A computer-readable database containing more than 6200 stories tracing the quest for wealth, power, and knowledge through history from the Trojan Horse to Desert Storm. Entries feature voiceover narration providing a political context, pictures, graphics and animations, zoom-in maps, bibliographic references, pertinent quotes, portraits, and portions of significant documents.

DIRECTORIES

Association for University Business and Economic Research--Membership Directory. Association for University Business and Economic Research. • Annual. $10. Covers: member institutions in the United States and abroad with centers, bureaus, departments, etc., concerned with business and economic research. Entries include: Name of bureau, center, etc., sponsoring institution name, address, phone, names and titles of director and staff, publications and frequency.

British Business in China Directory. British Chamber of Commerce in Hong Kong. • Annual. Provides full details of all British chamber members across Hong Kong, Macao and Guangdong.

Business and Economics Research Directory. Routledge Reference. • £495 Individuals hardback. Covers: Approximately 1,500 institutes concerned with business and economics research worldwide. Entries include: Organization name, address, phone, fax, e-mail address, names and titles of key personnel, foundation date, description of activities, publications with frequencies.

Business Researchers Network. Penny Hill Press. • Monthly. $195 per year. Publication includes: Listing of sources of critical data and insights on foreign competition, political risks, and new export markets. Entries include: Name, address, phone, description of information available.

California Business Register. Harris InfoSource. • Annual. $355 Individuals print. Profiles 56,750 top manufacturers, wholesalers, high-tech, and software companies in the state and lists the names and titles of more than 135,000 CEOs, owners, and key executives. Ninety-two percent of the companies are privately held. The listings include company name and address; telephone, fax, and toll-free numbers; Web site email addresses; number of employees; annual sales; products and services; SIC codes; export/import indicators; and primary bank.

Croatia Business Services Providers Leads. Business Information Agency Inc. PlanetInform. • Monthly. $50 Individuals mailing list. Covers: Croatian companies and all sub-industries that provide various services to commercial businesses, establishments, and organizations, including consulting, advertising and marketing services, and facilities maintenance.

D & B Business Rankings. Dun & Bradstreet Inc. • Annual. Covers more than 25,000 leading U.S. public and private businesses.

Directory of Special Libraries and Information Centers. Cengage Learning Inc. • Annual. $966 Individuals. 2010. 38th edition. eBook. Provides detailed contact and descriptive information on subject-specific resource collections maintained by government agencies, businesses, publishers, educational and nonprofit organizations, and associations worldwide.

Doing Business in Washington Country. Portland General Electric Co. • $20 plus $3.00 shipping. Covers government agencies, schools and universities, utilities, economic development organizations, financing sources, parks and recreation, social services, arts and cultural agencies, business services, waste disposal and recycling services, and other agencies and organizations in Washington County, Oregon.

The European Association for Business Research. European Association for Business Research, Planning, and Development in the Chemical Industry. • Annual. Includes memebers of the European Association for Business Research.

Indonesia Yellow Pages Business Directory. Faust Information GmbH. • Contains comprehensive business and directory information on companies in Indonesia. Includes information on more than 470,000 companies in 3000 industries and classifications. Provides data such as company name, mailing address, phone and fax numbers, e-mail address, web site address, names of contact persons, and more. Where available, includes information on product lines, services offered, and number of employees, plus financial data, brand names, company location, company background, and more. Includes keyword search functions. Allows export of data for use in spreadsheets, mailing programs, and other applications.

International Business Information on the Web: Searcher Magazine's Guide to Sites and Strategies for Global Business Research. Information Today, Inc. • $29.95. Lists directories, search engines, banks, financial institutions, news sources, government contacts, chambers of commerce, and other country-specific information. Covers: Approximately 1,000 Web sites related to international business research including general business sites in the United States and worldwide. Publication includes: URLs. Entries include: Information regarding each site.

New Jersey Business and Agency TTY/TDD Directory. Scotch Plains Lions Club. • Annual. Covers more than 300 New Jersey businesses, government agencies, police departments, services for the handicapped (including qualified interpreters for the deaf), associations, schools, libraries, churches, and medical facilities equipped with devices which make them accessible by telephone to the hearing- and speech-impaired.

Plunkett's Engineering and Research Industry Almanac: The Only Complete Guide to the Business of Research, Development, and Engineering. Plunkett Research Ltd. • Annual. $349.99 Individuals eBook, print and CD-ROM. Covers 500 of the largest companies involved in research, engineering and development in the biotech, electronics, aerospace and infotech industries.

Portugal Business Services Providers Leads. Business Information Agency Inc. PlanetInform. • Monthly. $113 Individuals mailing list. Covers Portuguese companies and all sub-industries that provide services to commercial businesses, establishments, and organizations, including consulting, advertising and marketing services, and facilities maintenance.

Research Centers Directory. Cengage Learning Inc. • Annual. $1,071 Individuals paperback. 2012. 42nd edition. Covers university, government, and other nonprofit research organizations established on a permanent basis to carry on continuing research programs in all areas of study; includes research institutes, laboratories, experiment stations, research parks, technology transfer centers, and other facilities and activities; coverage includes Canada. eBook also available.

Who's Who in International Business Education and Research. Edward Elgar Publishing Inc. • $256.50 Individuals hardbound. Covers: 150 individuals in international business education and research. Entries include: Biographical data and professional data, career summary, URL.

Wollombi Valley--Business Directory. Greater Wollombi Communities Alliance Inc. • Covers businesses in Wollombi Valley Region.

E-BOOKS

Branding Your Business. Cengage Learning Inc. • 2010. eBook. Details what a brand is and what it is not, how to conduct a 'DIY' brand audit and how to use marketing NLP and psychology principles to create a powerful brand.

Business Applications and Computational Intelligence. Cengage Learning Inc. • 2005. eBook. Addresses the need for a compact overview of the diversity of applications in a number of business disciplines, and consists of chapters written by leading international researchers. Chapters cover most fields of business, including: marketing, data mining, e-commerce, production and operations, finance, decision-making, and general management.

Contemporary Chief Information Officers: Management Experiences. Cengage Learning Inc. • 2007. eBook. Published by Information Science Reference. Explores the experiences of contemporary Chief Information Officers in the United States, Taiwan, and New Zealand, who agreed to participate and to be identified by name and company.

Entrepreneur's Showcase: Market Research for Small Businesses and the Woman Entrepreneur's Guide to Financing a Business. Cengage Learning Inc. • 2006. eBook. Published by Know!Books Press. Provides information on multiple aspects of entrepreneurship, focusing on market research for small business as well as on more gender-specific topics involved in starting a business.

Handbook of Research on Serious Games as Educational, Business and Research Tools. Cengage Learning Inc. • 2012. eBook. Published by IGI Global. Collects research on the most recent technological developments in all fields of knowledge or disciplines of computer games development, including planning, design, development, marketing, business management, users and behavior.

Handbook of Research on Virtual Workplaces and the New Nature of Business Practices. Cengage Learning Inc. • 2008. eBook. Published by Information Science Reference. Compiles authoritative research from 51 scholars from 17 countries, covering the issues surrounding the influx of information technology to the office environment, from choice and effective use of technologies to necessary participants in the virtual workplace.

Knowledge Management Strategies for Business Development. Cengage Learning Inc. • Published by IGI Global. Addresses the relevance of knowledge management strategies for the advancement of organizations worldwide. Supplies business practitioners, academicians, and researchers with comprehensive tools to systematically guide through a process that focuses on data gathering, analysis, and decision making.

21st Century Management: A Reference Handbook. Cengage Learning Inc. • 2008. eBook. Published by Sage Pubications. Highlights the topics, issues, questions and debates that any student obtaining a degree in the field of management must master to be effective in today's business world.

ENCYCLOPEDIAS AND DICTIONARIES

Business Leader Profiles for Students. Cengage Learning Inc. • $193 Individuals. Focuses on an additional 100 new business leaders to those listed in volume 1 and 25 updated profles from the first volume. Biographical profiles range from 1,250 to 2,500 words in length.

Encyclopedia of Products & Industries - Manufacturing (EPIM). Cengage Learning Inc. • $978 Individuals. 2007. 2 volumes. Designed to assist college students who need to research products and the relationships between products and their industries. Includes tables, charts, and statistics. eBook available. Inquire for pricing.

Historical Encyclopedia of American Business. Cengage Learning Inc. • 2009. eBook. Published by Salem Press. Long overviews on different sectors of the economy, such as agriculture and banking; individual industries such as advertising and electronics; and general topics such as business cycles, labor strikes and outsourcing. There are also overviews on broad legal topics such as antitrust legislation, bankruptcy laws and patent laws.

The Way We Work: An Encyclopedia of Business Culture. Cengage Learning Inc. • 2010. eBook. Published by Greenwood Publishing Group. Explores in over 150 A-Z entries, the origins and impact of the concepts, ideas, fads and themes that have become part of the business vernacular, shedding light on the dynamic ways in which business and society both influence and reflect each other.

GENERAL WORKS

American Journal of Business (AJB). Ball State University. • Semiannual. $25 Individuals. Journal informing business professionals about recent research developments and their practical implications.

Business & Legal Reports (BLR). Business & Legal Resources, Inc. • A multimedia publisher that specializes in reporting government regulatory developments to business and providing practical compliance advice.

Business Asia. The Economist Intelligence Unit. • Provides news on political, economic, and legal developments throughout the region, including business and e-business news; regulatory changes; distribution, human resources, market-entry strategies and regulatory development issues; economic and political risk analysis; company case studies; business intelligence.

Business Eastern Europe. The Economist Intelligence Unit. • Provides news on political, economic, and legal developments throughout the region, including business and e-business news; regulatory changes; distribution, human resources, market-entry strategies and regulatory development issues; economic and political risk analysis; company case studies; business intelligence.

Business Ireland. Dublin Chamber of Commerce. • Quarterly. Covers all areas of interest for business within the Dublin region.

Business Journal. American Chamber of Commerce of the Philippines. • Monthly. $220 overseas. Contains business updates, corporate information and current trends in the different industries within the Philippines.

Business Middle East. The Economist Intelligence Unit. • Provides news on political, economic, and legal developments throughout the region, including business and e-business news; regulatory changes; distribution, human resources, market-entry strategies and regulatory development issues; economic and political risk analysis; company case studies; business intelligence.

Business Panama. American Chamber of Commerce and Industry of Panama. • Monthly. Covers timely news items, interviews, and business-related developments both within Panama and in the Americas.

Business Suite. S1 Corp. • Provides solutions for business interaction with small to medium-sized companies.

Canada Business Database. The Data Supplier. • Contains contact information for more than 2.7 million companies in Canada. Includes business name, full contact information, and type of business.

Canada Business Email Database. The Data Supplier. • Contains e-mail addresses for more than 360,000 business contacts in Canada. Also includes contact name, business name, address, telephone and fax numbers, and Web site.

CBMC Contact Quarterly: The Magazine for Business Today. Christian Business Men's Committee of USA. • Quarterly. $12.95 Individuals. Trade magazine of the Christian Business Men's Committee of USA covering Christian business issues.

China Business Database. The Data Supplier. • Contains contact information for more than 500,000 manufacturers in China. Covers approximately 50,000 manufacturers in the automobile, motor, and machinery industry; 55,000 in the shoes, watch, bags, toys, and sports industry; 70,000 in the textiles, clothing, fabrics, garments, and fashion industry; 55,000 in the electrical, electronics, computers, and digital entertainment industry; 75,000 in the furniture, appliance, arts, jewelry, stationery, and crafts industry; and 90,000 in the chemicals, plastics, ceramics, metals, petroleum, and leather industry. Includes business name and full contact information.

France Business Database. The Data Supplier. • Contains contact information for more than 136,000 companies in France. Includes business name, full contact information, e-mail addresses, and Web site.

Germany Business Database. The Data Supplier. • Contains contact information for more than 136,000 companies in Germany. Includes business name, full contact information, e-mail addresses, Web site, and contacts.

India Business Database. The Data Supplier. • Contains contact information for more than 256,000 manufacturers in India. Includes business name, full contact information, e-mail addresses, and Web site.

Indonesia Business Database. The Data Supplier. • Contains contact information for more than 230,537 companies in Indonesia. Includes business name, full contact information, e-mail addresses, Web site.

International Journal of Business and Systems Research (IJBSR). Inderscience Publishers. • €494 Individuals print or online only for 1 user. Journal covering advances in business & systems research.

Italy Business Database. The Data Supplier. • Contains contact information for more than 80,000 companies in Italy. Includes business name, full contact information, e-mail addresses, Web site, and contacts.

Journal of African Research in Business and Technology (JARBT). IBIMA Publishing. • Peer-reviewed journal covering business and technology research in Africa.

Research Journal of Business Management. Academic Journals Inc. • Peer-reviewed journal covering research in business management.

Tests: A Comprehensive Reference for Assessments in Psychology, Education and Business. Pro-Ed Inc. • Irregular. $108 Individuals Hardcover. Covers over 200 publishers of over 2,000 psychological, educational, aptitude, and business tests.

USA Business Database. The Data Supplier. • Contains contact information for more than 13.6 million companies in the United States. Includes business name, full contact information, NAICS/SIC codes, year founded, number of employees, annual sales, parent and subsidiary companies, and other data.

USA Business Email Database. The Data Supplier. • Contains e-mail addresses for more than 4 million companies in the United States. Also includes business name, address, telephone and fax numbers, Web site, and category/SIC.

Who's Who in International Business Education and Research. Edward Elgar Publishing Inc. • $256.50 Individuals hardbound. Covers: 150 individuals in international business education and research. Entries include: Biographical data and professional data, career summary, URL.

Worldwide Business Contact Name Email Database. The Data Supplier. • Contains e-mail addresses for more than 2.8 million business contacts around the world. Also includes contact name, business name, address, telephone and fax numbers, and Web site.

HANDBOOKS AND MANUALS

Gale Business Insights Handbook Of. Cengage Learning Inc. • $627 Individuals. Examines the questions "What is social media marketing" and "How can it be used in my business?".

INTERNET DATABASES

Business Job Finder. Ohio State University Department of Finance. Max M. Fisher College of Business, 700 Fisher Hall, 2100 Neil Ave., Columbus, OH 43210. Phone: (614)292-5026 • URL: http://www.fisher.osu.edu • Internet site containing information on jobs in the business sector, primarily in accounting, finance, and consulting. Links to many corporations who hire extensively in this area are included for those wishing to make contacts and/or mail out resumes. Detailed information on job search aids and employer profiles are provided with job areas broken down into subject.

Business 2.0 Web Guide to the Best Business Links. Business 2.0 Media Inc. Phone: (415)293-4800; Email: support@business2.com • URL: http://www.business2.com/webguide • Web site presents an extensive, searchable directory of links to "the best, most informative, and authoritative web pages." Twenty main categories cover business, finance, career, company information, people, and technology topics, with thousands of subtopics, all linking to Web sites recommended by experienced business researchers. Fees: Free.

FedWorld: A Program of the United States Department of Commerce. National Technical Information Service. Phone: 800-553-NTIS or (703)605-6000; Fax: (703)605-6900; Email: webmaster@fedworld.gov • URL: http://www.fedworld.gov • Web site offers "a comprehensive central access point for searching, locating, ordering, and acquiring government and business information." Emphasis is on searching the Web pages, databases, and government reports of a wide variety of federal agencies. Fees: Free.

Find a Business. Switchboard Inc. 120 Flanders Rd., Westborough, MA 01581. Phone: (508)898-1122; Fax: (508)870-2000 • URL: http://www.switchboard.com • Offers a solution to find business information on merchants with a web presence. Switchboard provides web generated leads to businesses providing services and technologies which utilize the Internet to facilitate commerce.

FirstGov: Your First Click to the U. S. Government. General Services Administration. Phone: 800-333-4636 or (202)501-0705; Email: public.affairs@gsa.gov • URL: http://www.gsa.gov • Free Web site provides extensive links to federal agencies covering a wide variety of topics, such as agriculture, business, consumer safety, education, the environment, government jobs, grants, health, social security, statistics sources, taxes, technology, travel, and world affairs. Also provides links to federal forms, including IRS tax forms. Searching is offered, both keyword and advanced.

ONLINE DATABASES

American Business Directory. ProQuest LLC. • Quarterly. An electronic directory of more than 9 million businesses currently operating in the U.S. It is produced by InfoUSA, and lists companies with all available contact information and SIC (Standard Industrial Classification) codes, yellow pages information, trade and financial data, as well as corporate linkages on more than 10 million U.S. business establishments. Public companies, private companies, small businesses, government agencies, professionals, and schools are among the types of entities listed. Descriptions of brand names and franchises are included with many SIC codes. Contact information includes addresses, telephone numbers, employment data, key contact and title. Print sources, telephone interviews, and companies' annual reports are used in gathering the data in this database. Among the print sources are more than 5,000 yellow-page books.

American Business Lists—Online. InfoUSA. • Allows subscribers to access three databases containing directory information: 1) U.S. Businesses—contains 10 million listings for U.S. businesses. 2) Canadian Business Listings—contains 1.1 million listings for Canadian businesses. 3) Residential Listings - U.S. The databases can be used as a source for new sales leads, market planning, direct mail lists, telemarketing, distribution analysis, and locating suppliers.

Business & Industry™. Cengage Learning Inc. • A multi-industry business database with a strong global focus on company, product and industry information.

Business Insights: Essentials (BI:E). Cengage Learning Inc. • Formerly Business & Company Resource Center. Contact for pricing. Contains in-depth, searchable information on U.S. and International businesses, industries, and products.

Business News. MDExpress CEOExpress Co. • Business News provides links for business oriented news sources, such as the Wall Street Journal.

Business Periodicals Index Retrospective™*: 1913-1982*. EBSCO Publishing Inc. • Contains citations to more than 2.5 million articles and book reviews in more than 1000 general business periodicals and trade journals.

Business Wire. Business Wire. • Contains more than 1.4 million records that make up the complete text of press releases from public and private companies and other organizations, such as hospitals and universities.

Gale Business Insights: Global. Cengage Learning Inc. • Contains broad yet detailed coverage of international business. Includes case studies, full-text articles, and data sets coupled with authoritative references and tools for analysis. Features topic overviews, interactive rankings and statistics, company histories and market share data, global industry research reports, hundreds of economic and business indicators, case studies, and full-text articles from academic journals, business periodicals, newswires, and other media outlets.

Gale Digital Archives. Cengage Learning Inc. • Provides ownership of archival content from Gale proprietary data, including the following databases: *Associations Unlimited*, *Biography and Genealogy Master Index*, *Biography Resource Center*, *Contemporary Authors*, *Dictionary of Literary Biography*, *History Resource Center*, *Literature Resource Center*, *The Times Digital Archive*, the *Times Literary Supplement Centenary Digital Archive*, and *Ward's Business Directory*.

Gale Directory Library. Cengage Learning Inc. • Contains the full-text of more than 40 directories published by Gale. Offers search and export features. Customizable. Contact for pricing.

General BusinessFile ASAP. Cengage Learning Inc. • A fully international database designed to provide users with access to 200,000 company profiles: more than 50,000 full-text Investext reports; late-breaking news and event coverage on companies, industries, products, and executives; and the latest in business theory, economics, and favored practices.

TableBase™. Cengage Learning Inc. • Contains tabular data on companies, industries, products, and demographics on more than 90 global industries.

Warshaw Collection of Business Americana, ca. 1724-1977. Smithsonian Institution National Museum of American History Archives Center. • Contains bibliographic and cataloguing references to items from the Warshaw Collection of Business Americana held in the collections of the Smithsonian Institution's National Museum of American History.

Worldwide Business Database. The Data Supplier. • Contains contact information for more than 32.6 million companies around the world. Includes business name, full contact information, year founded, number of employees, products and services, type of business, income, and other data.

PERIODICALS AND NEWSLETTERS

The Information Advisor: Tips and Techniques for Smart Information Users. MarketResearch.com. • Monthly. $159.00 per year. Newsletter. Evaluates and discusses online, CD-ROM, and published sources of business, financial, and market research information.

The Information Advisor's Guide to Internet Research. Information Today, Inc. • 10/year. $199.95 U.S. One year subscription. Evaluates free and low-cost websites.

International Journal of Economics and Business Modeling. Bioinfo Publications. • Peer-reviewed journal publishing information in areas of business modeling, management and applied research.

Journal of Business and Finance Librarianship. The Haworth Press Inc. • Quarterly. $165.00 per year.

The Journal of Research Administration. Society of Research Administrators International. • Publishes articles dedicated to the education and the professional development of research administrators. Also serves to provide articles covering the changing research environment worldwide, and to highlight quality and innovation in research administration. Quarterly. Members, $35.00 per year; non-members, $45.00 per year. Formerly *SRA Journal*.

RESEARCH CENTERS AND INSTITUTES

Australian Catholic University - Centre for Research into Ethics and Decision-Making in Organisations. 24 Brunswick St., Locked Bag 4115, Fitzroy, VIC 3065, Australia. Phone: 61 3 99533270; Email: j.little@patrick.acu.edu.au • URL: http://www.acu.edu.au/research/Research_Centres_and_Flagships/credo • Values, policies, decision-making, and ethics in an organization.

Ball State University - Bureau of Business Research. Whitinger Business Bldg., Rm. 149, 2000 W University Ave., Muncie, IN 47306. Phone: (765)285-5926; Fax: (765)285-8024; Email: mhicks@bsu.edu • URL: http://cms.bsu.edu/Academics/CentersandInstitutes/BBR.aspx • Business and economics, including special studies designed to contribute to policy research, economic development and growth of eastern/central Indiana. Compiles and disseminates current economic and business data.

Carnegie Mellon University - Center for Analytical Research in Technology. 5000 Forbes Ave., Tepper School of Business, Pittsburgh, PA 15213. Phone: (412)268-6903; Fax: (412)268-7357; Email: holgers@andrew.cmu.edu • URL: http://www.tepper.cmu.edu/faculty-research/research-centers/center-for-analyticalresearch-in-technology-cart/index.aspx • Business and technology.

Chuo University - Institute of Business Research. 742-1 Higashinakano, Hachioji-shi, Tokyo 192-0393, Japan. Phone: 81 3 426743272; Fax: 81 3 426743278; Email: kigyoken@tamajs.chuo-u.ac.jp • URL: http://www2.chuo-u.ac.jp/ipcs/kigyoeng.htm • Management science, accounting, commerce, marketing, banking, and business economics. Institute also conducts comparative studies of businesses and corporations.

Dundalk Institute of Technology - Centre for Entrepreneurship Research. Dublin Rd., Dundalk, Louth, Ireland. Phone: 353 42 9370200; Fax: 353 42 9370201; Email: info@dkit.ie • URL: http://ww2.dkit.ie/research/research_centres/cer • Entrepreneurship, on a regional, national, and international basis.

Fort Lewis College - Office of Business and Economic Research. 1000 Rim Dr., Durango, CO 81301. Phone: (970)247-7296; Fax: (970)247-7205; Email: sonora_t@fortlewis.edu • URL: http://www.fortlewis.edu/ober/Home.aspx • Economics and local economic conditions.

Georgia Institute of Technology - Tennenbaum Institute. Centergy Bldg., Ste. 600, 75 5th St. NW, Atlanta, GA 30338. Phone: (404)385-6013; Fax: (404)385-6127; Email: ron.johnson@gatech.edu • URL: http://www.ti.gatech.edu • Fundamental changes of private and public sector enterprises.

Massey University - New Zealand Centre for Small and Medium Enterprise Research. Private Box 756, Wellington, New Zealand. Phone: 64 4 8015799; Fax: 64 4 8020290; Email: d.deakins@massey.ac.nz • URL: http://www.massey.ac.nz/massey/learning/departments/centres-research/new-zealand-centre-for-sme-research/nzsmerc.cfm • Micro-enterprises, small enterprises, and medium enterprises.

Midwestern State University - Bureau of Business and Government Research. Dillard College of Business Administration, 3410 Taft Blvd., Wichita Falls, TX 76308. Phone: (940)397-4722; Fax: (940)397-4693; Email: john.martinez@mwsu.edu • URL: http://www.mwsu.edu/academics/business • North Texas and southwest U.S. economic and business research.

Mississippi State University - Division of Business Research. 240 Darden/McCool Hall, Mississippi State, MS 39762-5288. Phone: (662)325-3817; Fax: (662)325-8686; Email: jspencer@cobilan.msstate.edu • Business and economic affairs with particular reference to Mississippi. Serves as an information, advisory, and consulting agency on special research projects for local, state, and national governments and business.

Radboud University Nijmegen - Faculty of Law - Business and Law Research Center. Thomas van Aquinostraat 8, NL-6500 Nijmegen, Netherlands. Phone: 31 24 3615565; Fax: 31 24 3615662; Email: oor@jur.ru.nl • URL: http://www.ru.nl/law/businessandlawresearchcentre • Business and law.

Turku School of Economics and Business Administration - Business Research and Development Center. PO Box 110, FIN-20521 Turku, Finland. Phone: 358 2 4814548; Fax: 358 2 4814268; Email: antti.paasio@tse.fi • URL: http://www.tukkk.fi/brdc/default.asp • Economy, business, small business, management, entrepreneurship, communications, marketing and development.

University of Alabama - Culverhouse College of Commerce and Business Administration - Center for Business and Economic Research. Box 870221, Tuscaloosa, AL 35487. Phone: (205)348-6191; Fax: (205)348-2951; Email: uacber@cba.ua.edu • URL: http://www.cber.cba.ua.edu • Business and economics, revenue forecasting, and employment in Alabama; estimates of population in Alabama counties; and investigations of state and regional economies. Engaged in construction and maintenance of annual econometric model for the state.

University of Alabama - Enterprise Integration Laboratory. Culverhouse College of Commerce & Business Administration, Tuscaloosa, AL 35487-0226. Phone: (205)348-5525; Fax: (205)348-6327; Email: dhale@cba.ua.edu • URL: http://old.cba.ua.edu/mis/research/eil • Sharing, managing, controlling, and coordinating business data, work practices, and networks.

University of Arizona - Eller College of Management - Economic and Business Research Center. McClelland Hall, Rm. 103, 1130 Helen St., Tucson, AZ 85721-0108. Phone: (520)621-2155 or

(520)621-2109; Fax: (520)621-2150; Email: ebrlib@eller.arizona.edu • URL: http://ebr.eller.arizona.edu • Regional economic forecasting, economic data collection and analysis, econometric and input-output impact models, policy-analytic studies, and international economic research. Assists individuals and groups interested in Arizona economy and aids public and private organizations with their research and planning activities.

University of California, Berkeley - Institute of Business and Economic Research. 371 Stephens Hall, Haas School of Business, UCB MC 1922, Berkeley, CA 94720-1922. Phone: (510)642-1922; Fax: (510)642-5018 or (510)642-1420; Email: iber@haas.berkeley.edu • URL: http://iber.berkeley.edu • Research fields are business administration, economics, finance, real estate, and international development.

University of Edinburgh - Arts and Humanities Research Council - Research Centre for Studies in Intellectual Property and Technology Law. School of Law, Old College, S Bridge, Edinburgh EH8 9YL, United Kingdom. Phone: 44 131 6502014; Fax: 44 131 6506317; Email: itandip@ed.ac.uk • URL: http://www.law.ed.ac.uk/ahrc/aboutus.aspx • Intellectual property, copyright, patents, technology, commerce, society, information technology, genetics, and medical jurisprudence and ethics.

University of Exeter - Business School - Centre for Innovation and Service Research. Streatham Ct., Rennes Dr., Exeter EX4 4PU, United Kingdom. Phone: 44 1392 722557; Fax: 44 1392 723210 • URL: http://business-school.exeter.ac.uk/research/areas/centres/isr • Design, analysis and management of business processes, including the analysis of process flows, capacity, resource utilization, and throughput analyses.

University of Illinois at Urbana-Champaign - Bureau of Economic and Business Research. 430 Wohlers Hall, Office of Research, College of Business, 1206 S 6th St., Champaign, IL 61820. Phone: (217)333-2330; Fax: (217)333-7410; Email: lhuff@uiuc.edu • URL: http://business.illinois.edu/research • Economics and business, including studies in business expectations, health economics, forecasting and planning, innovation, entrepreneurship, consumer behavior, poverty problems, small business operations and problems, investment and growth, productivity, research methodology, organizational behavior, and international business and banking.

University of Missouri—Columbia - Business Research and Information Development Group. 410 S 6th St., 200 Engineering N, Columbia, MO 65211. Phone: (573)882-8855; Fax: (573)884-4297; Email: schmidtdc@missouri.edu • URL: http://www.bridg.org • Entrepreneurship, small business development and growth.

University of Montana - Bureau of Business and Economic Research. Gallagher Business Bldg., 32 Campus Dr., Rm. 6840, Missoula, MT 59812-6840. Phone: (406)243-4831 or (406)243-5113; Fax: (406)243-2086 or (406)248-2086 • URL: http://www.bber.umt.edu • Business, economics, and other social sciences, including regional economic analysis and forecasting emphasizing Montana and the northern Rocky Mountain region, forest industry analysis and data collection, survey research, and public opinion surveys. Provides Montana business community with statistical data and interpretation and disseminates general information on economic conditions and prospects in the state.

University of Navarra - International Research Center on Organizations. IESE Business School, Camino del Cerro del Águila, 3, E-28023 Madrid, Spain. Phone: 34 91 2113000; Fax: 34 91 3572913; Email: info@iese.edu • URL: http://www.iese.edu/en/Research/CentersandChairs/Centers/IRCO/Homeirco/IRCOInternationalResearchCenterforOrganizations.asp • Business, strategic management of human resources in organizations, management models, international human relations, and leadership and motivation.

University of New Orleans - Division of Business and Economic Research. 315 Kirshman Hall, College of Business Administration, 2000 Lakeshore Dr., New Orleans, LA 70148. Phone: (504)280-6240; Fax: (504)280-6094; Email: jspeyrer@uno.edu • URL: http://www.uno.edu/coba/DBER/index.aspx • Business, economic, and demographic characteristics and trends at local, state, and national levels. Also studies local economic forecasting and tourism.

University of Newcastle upon Tyne - Cultures, Imperialism and Accounting Practice Research Group. Ridley Bldg., Business School, Newcastle upon Tyne NE1 7RU, United Kingdom. Phone: 44 191 2227586; Email: s.s.k.davie@newcastle.ac.uk • URL: http://www.ncl.ac.uk/niassh/ciap/index.htm • History of accounting across cultures and its relation to economics, politics, and society.

University of Oxford - Department of Education - Centre on Skills, Knowledge and Organisational Performance. 15 Norham Gardens, Oxford OX2 6PY, United Kingdom. Phone: 44 1865 611030; Fax: 44 1865 611031; Email: skope@education.ox.ac.uk • URL: http://www.skope.ox.ac.uk • Link between acquisition and use of skills and knowledge, product market strategies, and economic development.

University of Reading - Centre for International Business History. Henley Business School, Whiteknights, Reading RG6 6UD, United Kingdom. Phone: 44 118 3785435; Fax: 44 118 3784029; Email: p.m.scott@henley.ac.uk • URL: http://www.henley.reading.ac.uk/research/research-centres/the-centre-for-international-business-history • Empirical research on the past of business to concepts and theories developed in economics, management, and other disciplines.

University of Rhode Island - Research Center in Business and Economics. College of Business Administration, 7 Lippitt Rd., Kingston, RI 02881. Phone: (401)874-2549; Fax: (401)874-4825; Email: rcbe@etal.uri.edu • URL: http://www.cba.uri.edu/research/rcbe/ • Services research activities of faculty members of the College in fields of accounting, business law, economics, finance, insurance, management, marketing, and quantitative analysis. Conducts survey research, economic analyses, and business-related research projects on a contract basis.

Western Washington University - Center for Economic and Business Research. Parks Hall 326, MS 9074, College of Business & Economics, 516 High St., Bellingham, WA 98225. Phone: (360)650-3909; Fax: (360)650-7688; Email: hart.hodges@wwu.edu • URL: http://www.cbe.wwu.edu/cebr/index.shtml • Acts as grant agent for the College of Business and Economics and contracts research for the local area.

TRADE/PROFESSIONAL ASSOCIATIONS

American Society for Competitiveness. 664 Pratt Dr., 304 Eberly, IUP, Indiana, PA 15705. Phone: (724)357-5928; Fax: (724)357-7768; Email: office.asc2@gmail.com • URL: http://www.eberly.iup.edu/ASCWeb • Seeks to foster education and knowledge in subjects related to competitiveness by: facilitating exchange of information and ideas among educators, policy makers, and business people, and by encouraging and assisting research activities which advance knowledge of competitiveness practices and increase the available body of teaching and practice materials. Seeks to serve the needs of entrepreneurial scholars and intellectual managers. Specifically through its conferences and publications, intends to effectively serve the needs of academicians interested in the practical application of organizational theory and practicing managers interested in the intellectual development of the discipline.

Canada's Venture Capital and Private Equity Association. 1201-372 Bay St., Toronto, ON, Canada M5H 2W9. Phone: (416)487-0519; Fax: (416)487-5899; Email: cvca@cvca.ca • URL: http://www.cvca.ca • Ventures and risks capital companies. Promotes economic growth through provision of capital to emerging businesses. Conducts research; facilitates exchange of information among members; represents the venture capital industry before government agencies, industrial and financial organizations, and the public.

European Business Ethics Network. c/o Mario Silar, Secretary, C/Elizmendi 31, Bajo B, Sarriguren, 31621 Navarra, Spain. Email: secretariat@eben-net.org • URL: http://www.eben-net.org • Supports research centers in Europe researching business ethics issues.

European Money and Finance Forum. c/o Oesterreichische Nationalbank, Otto Wagner-Platz 3, A-1090 Vienna, Austria. Phone: 43 1 404207206; Fax: 43 1 404207298; Email: suerf@oenb.at • URL: http://www.suerf.org • Represents academics, bank economists, and interested individuals in 37 countries. Develops contacts among members in order to discuss monetary and financial questions. Sponsors research in monetary, economic, and financial areas. Aims to create an active network between professional economists, financial practitioners, central bankers and academics for the analysis and mutual understanding of monetary and financial issues. Sponsors conferences, seminars, workshops and lectures. Publishes study volumes each year.

International Association for Chinese Management Research. Kogod School of Business, 4400 Massachusetts Ave. NW, Washington, DC 20016. Phone: (316)978-6788; Fax: (316)978-3349; Email: iacmrus@gmail.com • URL: http://www.iacmr.org • Promotes scholarly studies of organization and management of firms in the Chinese context. Fosters the development of management research capabilities in and on China. Facilitates international collaboration between management researchers from around the globe.

Italian Private Equity and Venture Capital Association. Via Pietro Mascagni n. 7, I-20122 Milan, Italy. Phone: 39 2 7607531; Fax: 39 2 76398044; Email: info@aifi.it • URL: http://www.aifi.it • Lobbies in the legislative and institutional process. Organizes symposia and seminars, educational programs and supports research activities.

National Association for Business Economics. 1920 L St. NW, Ste. 300, Washington, DC 20036. Phone: (202)463-6223; Fax: (202)463-6239; Email: nabe@nabe.com • URL: http://www.nabe.com • Formerly National Association of Business Economists.

National Bureau of Certified Consultants. c/o Peter A. Land Associates, Inc., 4210 Lomac St., Montgomery, AL 36106. Phone: (334)271-2639 • URL: http://www.peteland.com/cpcm.htm • Promotes adherence to high standards of ethics and practice in the field of management consulting. Works to improve management consulting curricula.

National Productivity Council. Utpadakta Bhavan, 5-6 Institutional Area, Lodhi Rd., New Delhi 110 003, Delhi, India. Phone: 91 11 24690331; Fax: 91 11 24615002; Email: npcinfo@npcindia.gov.in • URL: http://www.npcindia.gov.in • Represents professionals in the field of productivity. Promotes increased efficiency in all aspects of Indian economic activity. Conducts research, gathers and disseminates information.

Outsourcing Institute. 6800 Jericho Tpke., Ste. 120W, Syosset, NY 11791. Phone: (516)279-6850;

Email: info@outsourcing.com • URL: http://www.outsourcing.com • Represents corporations making use of outside resources and services. Serves as a clearinghouse on the strategic use of outside resources. Conducts research, executive events, publications and educational programs.

Southwest Case Research Association. Augusta State University, Knox School of Accountancy, Hull College of Business, 2500 Walton Way, Augusta, GA 30904-2200. Phone: (706)667-4541 • URL: http://www.swcrahome.org • Promotes research, writing, and publication of decision-based cases for graduate and undergraduate business studies.

Workflow Management Coalition. 759 CJC Hwy., Ste. No. 363, Cohasset, MA 02025-2115. Phone: (781)719-9209; Fax: (781)735-0491; Email: nathaniel@wfmc.org • URL: http://www.wfmc.org • Represents adopters, developers, consultants, analysts, university and research groups engaged in workflow and Business Process Management (BPM). Seeks to expand the BPM market by promoting the business value of process management. Strives to decrease the risk of using BPM and workflow products through interoperability standards.

BUSINESS RESPONSIBILITY

See SOCIAL RESPONSIBILITY

BUSINESS SCHOOLS

See BUSINESS EDUCATION

BUSINESS, SMALL

See SMALL BUSINESS

BUSINESS START-UP PLANS AND PROPOSALS

See also BUSINESS INNOVATION; VENTURE CAPITAL

ABSTRACTS AND INDEXES

Business Periodicals Index Retrospective. EBSCO Publishing Inc. • 11/year. Quarterly and annual cumulations.

DIRECTORIES

Free Help from Uncle Sam to Start Your Own Business. Puma Publishing Co. • Irregular. $15.95 plus $3.00 shipping. Covers: over 100 federal programs that provide loans, services, and information to businesses. Entries include: Program name, agency name, address, phone, name of contact.

How to Start a Business in Alabama. Entrepreneur Press. • $24.95 Individuals paperback. Entries include: Detailed information on mailing addresses, Internet addresses, and telephone numbers of federal, state, local and private agencies.

How to Start a Business in Alaska. Entrepreneur Press. • Annual. $24.95 Individuals paperback. Entries include: Detailed information on mailing addresses, Internet addresses, and telephone numbers of federal, state, local and private agencies.

How to Start a Business in Arkansas. Entrepreneur Press. • Annual. $24.95 Individuals paperback. Entries include: Detailed information on mailing addresses, Internet addresses, and telephone numbers of federal, state, local and private agencies.

How to Start a Business in Delaware. Entrepreneur Press. • Annual. $24.95 Individuals paperback. Entries include: Detailed information on mailing addresses, Internet addresses, and telephone numbers of federal, state, local and private agencies.

How to Start a Business in District of Columbia. Entrepreneur Press. • Annual. $24.95 Individuals paperback. Entries include: Detailed information on mailing addresses, Internet addresses, and telephone numbers of federal, state, local and private agencies.

How to Start a Business in Idaho. Entrepreneur Press. • Annual. $24.95 Individuals paperback. Entries include: Detailed information on mailing addresses, Internet addresses, and telephone numbers of federal, state, local and private agencies.

How to Start a Business in Iowa. Entrepreneur Press. • $24.95 Individuals paperback. Entries include: Detailed information on mailing addresses, Internet addresses, and telephone numbers of federal, state, local and private agencies.

How to Start a Business in Kansas. Entrepreneur Press. • Annual. $24.95 Individuals paperback. Entries include: Detailed information on mailing addresses, Internet addresses, and telephone numbers of federal, state, local and private agencies.

How to Start a Business in Kentucky. Entrepreneur Press. • Annual. $24.95 Individuals paperback. Entries include: Detailed information on mailing addresses, Internet addresses, and telephone numbers of federal, state, local and private agencies.

How to Start a Business in Louisiana. Entrepreneur Press. • Annual. $24.95 Individuals paperback. Entries include: Detailed information on mailing addresses, Internet addresses, and telephone numbers of federal, state, local and private agencies.

How to Start a Business in Maine. Entrepreneur Press. • Annual. $24.95 Individuals paperback. Entries include: Detailed information on mailing addresses, Internet addresses, and telephone numbers of federal, state, local and private agencies.

How to Start a Business in Mississippi. Entrepreneur Press. • Annual. $24.95 Individuals paperback. Entries include: Detailed information on mailing addresses, Internet addresses, and telephone numbers of federal, state, local and private agencies.

How to Start a Business in Montana. Entrepreneur Press. • $24.95 Individuals paperback. Entries include: Detailed information on mailing addresses, Internet addresses, and telephone numbers of federal, state, local and private agencies.

How to Start a Business in Nebraska. Entrepreneur Press. • Annual. $24.95 Individuals paperback. Entries include: Detailed information on mailing addresses, Internet addresses, and telephone numbers of federal, state, local and private agencies.

How to Start a Business in Nevada. Entrepreneur Press. • Annual. $24.95 Individuals paperback. Entries include: Detailed information on mailing addresses, Internet addresses, and telephone numbers of federal, state, local and private agencies.

How to Start a Business in New Mexico. Entrepreneur Press. • Annual. $24.95 Individuals paperback. Entries include: Detailed information on mailing addresses, Internet addresses, and telephone numbers of federal, state, local and private agencies.

How to Start a Business in New York City. Entrepreneur Press. • Annual. $24.95 Individuals paperback. Entries include: Detailed information on mailing addresses, Internet addresses, and telephone numbers of federal, state, local and private agencies.

How to Start a Business in North Dakota. Entrepreneur Press. • $24.95 Individuals paperback. Entries include: Detailed information on mailing addresses, Internet addresses, and telephone numbers of federal, state, local and private agencies.

How to Start a Business in Oklahoma. Entrepreneur Press. • Annual. $24.95 Individuals paperback. Entries include: Detailed information on mailing addresses, Internet addresses, and telephone numbers of federal, state, local and private agencies.

How to Start a Business in Rhode Island. Entrepreneur Press. • Annual. $24.95 Individuals paperback. Entries include: Detailed information on mailing addresses, Internet addresses, and telephone numbers of federal, state, local and private agencies.

How to Start a Business in South Dakota. Entrepreneur Press. • Annual. $24.95 Individuals paperback. Entries include: Detailed information on mailing addresses, Internet addresses, and telephone numbers of federal, state, local and private agencies.

How to Start a Business in Utah. Entrepreneur Press. • Annual. $24.95 Individuals paperback. Entries include: Detailed information on mailing addresses, Internet addresses, and telephone numbers of federal, state, local and private agencies.

How to Start a Business in Vermont. Entrepreneur Press. • Annual. $24.95 Individuals paperback. Entries include: Detailed information on mailing addresses, Internet addresses, and telephone numbers of federal, state, local and private agencies.

How to Start a Business in West Virginia. Entrepreneur Press. • Annual. $24.95 Individuals paperback. Entries include: Detailed information on mailing addresses, Internet addresses, and telephone numbers of federal, state, local and private agencies.

How to Start a Business in Wyoming. Entrepreneur Press. • Annual. $24.95 Individuals paperback. Entries include: Detailed information on mailing addresses, Internet addresses, and telephone numbers of federal, state, local and private agencies.

How to Start, Run, and Stay in Business: The Nuts-and-Bolts Guide to Turning Your Business Dream into a Reality. John Wiley & Sons Inc. • $20 Individuals paperback. Covers: Every aspect of starting and running a business.

New Business Survival Package. Greater Orlando Chamber of Commerce. • Annual. $49.99. Covers: taxing, licensing, registration, and zoning authorities and other contacts of interest to those starting new businesses in the Florida counties of Seminole, Orange, and Osceola. Database includes: Advice on starting a new business. Entries include: Agency name, address, phone.

Starting an Online Business for Dummies. John Wiley & Sons Inc. • $24.99 Individuals paperback. Covers: Information needed to get an online business off the ground: identifying a market need, choosing a Web hosting service, securing transactions, and attracting customers.

E-BOOKS

Entrepreneur's Showcase: Market Research for Small Businesses and the Woman Entrepreneur's Guide to Financing a Business. Cengage Learning Inc. • 2006. eBook. Published by Know!Books Press. Provides information on multiple aspects of entrepreneurship, focusing on market research for small business as well as on more gender-specific topics involved in starting a business.

How to Prepare a Business Plan. Cengage Learning Inc. • 2009. eBook. 5th edition. Published by Kogan Page. Offers advice on writing a business plan, producing cash flow forecasts, planning the borrowing and expanding the business.

Start Up and Run Your Own Business. Cengage Learning Inc. • 2010. eBook. Published by Kogan Page. Offers a complete information resource for those looking to set up their own business, including raising finance, taxation, IT, market research and employment issues.

Starting a Business from Home. Cengage Learning Inc. • 2009. eBook. Published by Kogan Page. Offers information about running a profitable and successful business from your own home with particular emphasis on opportunities provided by the internet.

Starting a Successful Business. Cengage Learning Inc. • 2009. eBook. Published by Kogan Page. Covers topics such as franchises, marketing, publicity, e-business, financial management, business law, recruitment, taxation, insurance, business planning and development.

ENCYCLOPEDIAS AND DICTIONARIES

Encyclopedia of Small Business. Cengage Learning Inc. • $763 Individuals. 2010. $696.00. 4th edition. Two volumes. Contains about 600 informative entries on a wide variety of topics affecting small business. Arrangement is alphabetical. eBook also available. Inquire for pricing.

GENERAL WORKS

Homemade Money: How to Select, Start, Manage, Market and Multiply the Profits of a Business at Home. Rowman and Littlefield Publishers Inc. • $24.95 Individuals book 1 and 2. Provides information on beginning and developing a home-based business.

International Business. Chamber of Commerce and Industry Queensland. • A$55.45. Contains guidelines to become a successful international business.

The Omaha Business Journal. Midlands Business Journal Publications. • Monthly. Business publication covering local start-ups and entrepreneurs.

Preparing an Entrepreneurial Business Plan. American CPE Inc. • Contains detailed training and instructional information on preparing and writing entrepreneurial business plans for beginning businesses. Offers insight and guidance on the process of writing the business plan, what a business plan accomplishes for start-up entrepreneurs, and how business plans can be helpful at all stages in the business life cycle. Covers topics such as the definition of a business plan, what goes into a business plan, meshing the entrepreneurial process and business planning, preparing the first draft of the plan, financing a business, redrafting and revising business plans, reaching the final draft, and more. Offers self-paced courseware and learning materials designed to enhance users' skills, interpersonal development, and professional abilities.

HANDBOOKS AND MANUALS

Business Plans Handbook. Cengage Learning Inc. • Annual. $243 Individuals. Contains examples of detailed plans for starting or developing various kinds of businesses. Categories within plans include statement of purpose, market description, personnel requirements, financial needs, etc.

Start-Up Business Guides. Entrepreneur Press. • Looseleaf. $59.50 each. Practical guides to starting a wide variety of small businesses.

Writing Effective Business Plans. Entrepreneur Press. • Looseleaf. $49.50. A step-by-step guide. Includes a sample business plan.

INTERNET DATABASES

U.S. Business Advisor. Small Business Administration. Phone: (202)205-6600; Fax: (202)205-7064 • URL: http://www.sba.gov • Web site provides "a one-stop electronic link to all the information and services government provides for the business community." Covers about 60 federal agencies that exist to assist or regulate business. Detailed information is provided on financial assistance, workplace issues, taxes, regulations, international trade, and other business topics. Searching is offered. Fees: Free.

ONLINE DATABASES

Wilson Business Abstracts Online. H.W. Wilson Co. • Indexes and abstracts 600 major business periodicals, plus the *Wall Street Journal* and the business section of the *New York Times.* Indexing is from 1982, abstracting from 1990, with the two newspapers included from 1993. Updated weekly. Inquire as to online cost and availability. (*Business Periodicals Index* without abstracts is also available online.).

OTHER SOURCES

Formation and Financing of Emerging Companies. Daniel E. O'Connor and others. Glasser LegalWorks. • $499 Individuals Binder/Looseleaf (Full set). Periodic Supplementation. Covers incorporation, bylaws, indemnification, intellectual property, financing sources, venture capital, due diligence, bridge loans, investor rights, compliance, and other legal issues associated with company formation. (Emerging Growth Companies Series.).

How to Write a Business Plan. American Management Association Extension Institute. • Looseleaf. $159.00. Self-study course. Emphasis is on practical explanations, examples, and problem solving. Quizzes and a case study are included.

Start-Up and Emerging Companies: Planning, Financing, and Operating the Successful Business, with Forms on Disk. ALM Media Properties LLC. • $925 print + online + ebook. Covers a wide variety of business and legal topics relating to new enterprises. Provides information on venture financing, formation of corporations, tax laws, limited liability companies, employee benefits, contracts, and accounting. Includes a CD-ROM containing more than 75 sample legal forms, clauses, agreements, organizational resolutions, and checklists. (Law Journal Press).

PERIODICALS AND NEWSLETTERS

Business Start-Ups: Smart Ideas for Your Small Business. Entrepreneur Press. • Monthly. $14.97 per year. Provides advice for starting a small business. Includes business trends, new technology, E-commerce, and case histories ("real-life stories").

Small Business Opportunities. Harris Publications Inc. • Monthly. Source for entrepreneurs and small business owners.

RESEARCH CENTERS AND INSTITUTES

New York University - Berkley Center for Entrepreneurial Studies. NYU Stern School of Business, Ste. 7-150, KMC, 44 W 4th St., New York, NY 10012. Phone: (212)998-0070; Fax: (212)995-4211; Email: jeffrey.carr@stern.nyu.edu • URL: http://w4.stern.nyu.edu/berkley • Factors that promote entrepreneurship and lead to the creation of new wealth and business revenues; business venturing within established firms. Topics include the major pitfalls and obstacles to start-ups, securing of venture capital, psychology and sociology of entrepreneurship, valuation and management of new ventures, technological innovation and new product development, emerging and creative industries, and cross-cultural environments that stimulate entrepreneurship.

Stockholm School of Economics - Center for Entrepreneurship and Business Creation. Saltmätargatan 13-17, SE-113 83 Stockholm, Sweden. Phone: 46 8 7369355; Email: info@hhs.se • URL: http://www.hhs.se/cebc/Pages/default.aspx • Entrepreneurship, business creation, and economic change.

TRADE/PROFESSIONAL ASSOCIATIONS

Association of Proposal Management Professionals. PO Box 77272, Washington, DC 20013-8272. Phone: (202)450-2549; Email: rick.harris@apmp.org • URL: http://www.apmp.org • Proposal managers, proposal planners, proposal writers, consultants, desktop publishers and marketing managers. Encourages unity and cooperation among industry professionals. Seeks to broaden member knowledge and skills through developmental, educational and social activities. Maintains speakers' bureau. Provides current information and developments in the field.

Japan Business Incubation Association. Shiba-Koen, Minato-ku 3-5-8 Kikai, Tokyo 105 0011, Japan. Phone: 81 50 36021751; Email: reception@jbia.jp • URL: http://jbia.jp • Promotes new business creation in local communities and encourages the exchange of information among major international organizations. Conducts studies and makes proposals on new business creation and implements training programs for incubation managers. Provides consulting support, implementation, and policy proposals related to business incubation.

United Kingdom Science Park Association. Chesterford Research Park, Little Chesterford, Essex, Saffron Walden CB10 1XL, United Kingdom. Phone: 44 1799 532050; Fax: 44 1799 532049; Email: info@ukspa.org.uk • URL: http://www.ukspa.org.uk • Supports and encourages the startup, incubation and development of innovation led, high growth, knowledge-based businesses. Provides opportunity for larger and international businesses to develop specific and close interactions with a particular centre of knowledge creation for mutual benefit.

BUSINESS STATISTICS

See also ECONOMIC STATISTICS; MARKET STATISTICS; STATISTICAL METHODS

ABSTRACTS AND INDEXES

Current Index to Statistics: Applications, Methods, and Theory. American Statistical Association. • Annual. An index to journal articles on statistical applications and methodology.

ALMANACS AND YEARBOOKS

National Accounts Statistics: Main Aggregates and Detailed Tables. United Nations Publications. • Annual.

BIBLIOGRAPHIES

Statistics Sources. Cengage Learning Inc. • $874 Individuals. 2012. $836.00. 37th edition. Lists sources of statistical information for more than 20,000 topics.

CD-ROM DATABASES

OECD Statistical Compendium. Organization for Economic Cooperation and Development. • Semiannual. $1,905.00 per year for 1 to 10 users. CD-ROM contains more than 730,000 monthly, quarterly, and annual time series for OECD countries, 1960 to date. Includes fully searchable data on agriculture, food, economic indicators, national accounts, employment, energy, finance, industry, technology, and foreign trade. Results can be displayed in various forms.

DIRECTORIES

IAL Directory of European Industrial and Business Market Reports. IAL Consultants. • Irregular. $250 postpaid. Covers: publishers and producers of market reports, statistical summaries, and other data; includes government and non-government organizations, libraries, press, and international sources in Europe, including the socialist states of Eastern Europe. Entries include: Publisher name and address, title and subject of report, language, number of pages, price.

Intercompany Relations on Charts. Hoppenstedt Produktinformationen GmbH. • Shows in chart form the economic and financial relations between 700 parent companies from all over the world and their 90,000 subsidiaries.

GENERAL WORKS

Boston Business Journal--Book of Lists. Boston Business Journal. • Annual. $75 Institutions print. Covers 'Top 25' financial institutions, computer companies, law firms, insurance companies, advertising firms, architectural firms, and other companies and organizations in the Boston, Massachusetts area.

San Francisco Business Times--Book of Lists. San Francisco Business Times. • Annual. $70 Individuals print. A compilation of lists of the top 25

companies in various industries in the Bay Area.

INTERNET DATABASES

Business 2.0 Web Guide to the Best Business Links. Business 2.0 Media Inc. Phone: (415)293-4800; Email: support@business2.com • URL: http://www.business2.com/webguide • Web site presents an extensive, searchable directory of links to "the best, most informative, and authoritative web pages." Twenty main categories cover business, finance, career, company information, people, and technology topics, with thousands of subtopics, all linking to Web sites recommended by experienced business researchers. Fees: Free.

Federal Reserve Board Publications and Education Resources. Board of Governors of the Federal Reserve System. Phone: (202)452-3000; Fax: (202)452-3819 • URL: http://www.federalreserve.gov/publications.htm • Web site provides access to statistics, surveys, and research from the Federal Reserve Board. *Federal Reserve Bulletin* articles are available as abstracts or full text (PDF) currently or from six-year archives. The link "Statistics: Releases and Historical Data" offers daily, weekly, monthly, quarterly, and annual data in great detail for interest rates, foreign exchange, consumer credit, money stock measures, industrial production indexes, bank reserves, and other items. Historical tabulations are available for various time periods. Free.

Fedstats. Federal Interagency Council on Statistical Policy. Phone: (202)395-7254 • URL: http://www.fedstats.gov • Web site features an efficient search facility for full-text statistics produced by more than 100 federal agencies, including the Census Bureau, the Bureau of Economic Analysis, and the Bureau of Labor Statistics. Boolean searches can be made within one agency or for all agencies combined. Links are offered to international statistical bureaus, including the UN, IMF, OECD, UNESCO, Eurostat, and 20 individual countries. Fees: Free.

FedWorld: A Program of the United States Department of Commerce. National Technical Information Service. Phone: 800-553-NTIS or (703)605-6000; Fax: (703)605-6900; Email: webmaster@fedworld.gov • URL: http://www.fedworld.gov • Web site offers "a comprehensive central access point for searching, locating, ordering, and acquiring government and business information." Emphasis is on searching the Web pages, databases, and government reports of a wide variety of federal agencies. Fees: Free.

FirstGov: Your First Click to the U. S. Government. General Services Administration. Phone: 800-333-4636 or (202)501-0705; Email: public.affairs@gsa.gov • URL: http://www.gsa.gov • Free Web site provides extensive links to federal agencies covering a wide variety of topics, such as agriculture, business, consumer safety, education, the environment, government jobs, grants, health, social security, statistics sources, taxes, technology, travel, and world affairs. Also provides links to federal forms, including IRS tax forms. Searching is offered, both keyword and advanced.

FreeLunch.com. Economy.com, Inc. Phone: (610)696-8700; Fax: (610)696-1678 • URL: http://www.freelunch.com • Web site provides free access to more than 200 million economic and financial data series, covering industry, demographics, labor markets, prices, retail sales, government spending, trade, interest rates, housing starts, the stock market, etc. Data is available in either chart or table form. Searching is offered. Free, but registration required. Economy.com, Inc. also offers fee-based economic analysis at *The Dismal Scientist* site (www.dismal.com).

InSite 2. Intelligence Data/Thomson Financial. Phone: 800-654-0393 or (617)856-1890; Fax: (617)737-3182; Email: intelligence.data@tfn.com • URL: http://www.insite2.gale.com/ • Fee-based Web site consolidates information in a "Base Pack" consisting of Business InSite, Market InSite, and Company InSite. Optional databases are Consumer InSite, Health and Wellness InSite, Newsletter InSite, and Computer InSite. Includes fulltext content from more than 2,500 trade publications, journals, newsletters, newspapers, analyst reports, and other sources. Continuous updating. Formerly produced by The Gale Group.

U.S. Census Bureau: The Official Statistics. U. S. Bureau of the Census. Phone: (301)763-4636 or (301)763-4100; Fax: (301)763-4794; Email: webmaster@census.gov • URL: http://www.census.gov/prod/www/abs/mfg-prof.html • Web site is "Your Source for Social, Demographic, and Economic Information." Contains "Current U. S. Population Count," "Current Economic Indicators," and a wide variety of data under "Other Official Statistics." Keyword searching is provided. Fees: Free.

ONLINE DATABASES

Industry Insider. Thomson Financial. • Contains full-text online industry research reports from more than 200 leading trade associations, covering 50 specific industries. Reports include extensive statistics and market research data. Inquire as to online cost and availability.

OTHER SOURCES

Business Rankings Annual (BRA). Cengage Learning Inc. • Annual. $584 Individuals. A guide to lists and rankings appearing in major business publications. The top ten names are listed in each case.

PERIODICALS AND NEWSLETTERS

Business Week--1,000 Issue. The McGraw-Hill Companies Inc. • Annual. List of 1,000 U.S. Corporations by market value in all business, industrial, and financial categories, with financial results from preceding year and extensive analytical text.

JASA. American Statistical Association. • Quarterly. $652 Individuals. Statistics information.

Journal of Business and Economic Statistics. American Statistical Association. • Quarterly. $62 for members. Emphasis is on statistical measurement and applications for business and economics.

STATISTICS SOURCES

Statistical Abstract of the United States. U. S. Government Printing Office. • Annual. $44.00. Issued by the U. S. Bureau of the Census.

Survey of Current Business. U. S. Government Printing Office. • Published by Bureau of Economic Analysis. U. S. Department of Commerce. Presents a wide variety of business and economic data.

TRADE/PROFESSIONAL ASSOCIATIONS

American Statistical Association. 732 N Washington St., Alexandria, VA 22314-1943. Phone: 888-231-3473 or (703)684-1221; Fax: (703)684-2037; Email: asainfo@amstat.org • URL: http://www.amstat.org • Professional society of persons interested in the theory, methodology, and application of statistics to all fields of human endeavor.

Centre for Interfirm Comparison. Wintex House, 4 Easton Lane Business Park, Easton Ln., Hants, Winchester SO23 7RQ, United Kingdom. Phone: 44 1962 844144; Fax: 44 1962 843180; Email: enquiries@cifc.co.uk • URL: http://www.cifc.co.uk • Provides expertise in performance measurement and financial control of companies and other organizations. Services include interfirm comparison; benchmarking; development of performance indicators; surveys, statistics and business information; and training in these topics.

Econometric Society. New York University, Department of Economics, 19 W 4th St., 6th Fl., New York, NY 10012. Phone: (212)998-3820; Fax: (212)995-4487; Email: sashi@econometricsociety.org • URL: http://www.econometricsociety.org • Economists, statisticians, and mathematicians. Promotes studies that are directed towards unification of the theoretical and empirical approaches to economic problems and advancement of economic theory in its relation to statistics and mathematics.

BUSINESS STRATEGY

See also PLANNING

ABSTRACTS AND INDEXES

Business Periodicals Index Retrospective. EBSCO Publishing Inc. • 11/year. Quarterly and annual cumulations.

DIRECTORIES

Austria Export-Import Trade and Business Directory. International Business Publications, USA. • $99.95 Individuals. Contains information on strategic economic, investment, export-import, and business opportunities and contact numbers.

Azerbaijan Export-Import Trade and Business Directory. International Business Publications, USA. • $99.95 Individuals. Contains information on strategic economic, investment, export-import, and business opportunities and contact numbers.

E-BOOKS

Adaptive Technologies and Business Integration: Social, Managerial, and Organizational Dimensions. Cengage Learning Inc. • 2007. eBook. Provides an authoritative review of both intra-organizational and inter-organizational aspects in business integration, including: managerial and organizational integration, social integration, and technology integration, along with the resources to accomplish this competitive advantage.

Agent Systems in Electronic Business. Cengage Learning Inc. • 2008. eBook. Agent technologies are believed to be one of the most promising tools to conduct business via networks and the Web in an autonomous, intelligent, and efficient way. The ever-expanding application of business automation necessitates clarification of the methods and techniques of agent-based electronic business systems.

Business Dynamics in Information Technology. Cengage Learning Inc. • 2007. eBook. Presents business-technology alignment processes, business-technology interaction processes, and business-technology decision processes, serving the purpose of helping the reader study information technology from a dynamic, rather than a static, perspective.

Business Information Systems: Concepts, Methodologies, Tools and Applications. Cengage Learning Inc. • 2011. eBook. Offers a complete view of current business information systems within organizations and the advancements that technology has provided to the business community, including how technological advancements have revolutionized financial transactions, management infrastructure, and knowledge workers.

Business-Oriented Enterprise Integration for Organizational Agility. Cengage Learning Inc..

Business Web Strategy: Design, Alignment, and Application. Cengage Learning Inc. • 2009. eBook. Published by Information Science Reference. Addresses the gap in business Web strategy through a collection of concentrated managerial issues, gathering the latest theoretical frameworks, case studies, and research pertaining to maximizing the power of the Web.

CIO and Corporate Strategic Management: Changing Role of CIO to CEO. Cengage Learning Inc. • Published by Information Science Reference. Provides analysis within theoretical frameworks and consulting recommendations, and starts with the demand side of CEO successions, specifically highlighting approaches in IT foundations, e-business development and IT sourcing decisions.

Co-Engineering Applications and Adaptive Business Technologies in Practice: Enterprise Service Ontologies, Models, and Frameworks. Cengage Learning Inc. • 2009. eBook. Provides knowledge that forms the basis for successful co-engineering of the adaptive complex enterprise for services delivery.

Continuous Computing Technologies for Enhancing Business Continuity. Cengage Learning Inc. • 2009. eBook. Provides an explanation of business continuity, business continuity management, and continuous computing technologies. Covers topics such as clustering technologies, fault tolerance, and technologies for reducing downtime.

Different Thinking. Cengage Learning Inc. • 2009. eBook. Published by Kogan Page. Presents practical tools and strategies your company can use to help you drastically increase productivity and earning power. The authors show you how you can question your strategies, create new markets, give your products a radical makeover, and invent innovative new price and profit models to give you a competitive advantage over your rivals.

E-Business Innovation and Process Management. Cengage Learning Inc. • 2007. eBook. Provides researchers and practitioners with information on recent advances and developments in emerging e-business models and technologies. This book covers a variety of topics, such as e-business models, e-business strategies, online consumer behavior, e-business process modeling and practices, electronic communication adoption and service provider strategies, privacy policies, and implementation issues.

E-Business Models, Services and Communications. Cengage Learning Inc. • 2008. eBook. Provides researchers and practitioners with valuable information on recent advances and developments in emerging e-business models and technologies.

E-Logistics and E-Supply Chain Management: Applications for Evolving Business. Cengage Learning Inc. • 2013. eBook. Explores the creation of integrated supply chains, the developments of virtual business, and the processes of re-engineering for business development.

E-Supply Chain Technologies and Management. Cengage Learning Inc. • 2007. eBook. Explores concepts, models, and IT infrastructures of the e-supply chain, and develops a broad understanding of issues pertaining to the use of emerging technologies and their impact on supply chain flexibility and management.

Effective Web Presence Solutions for Small Businesses: Strategies for Successful Implementation. Cengage Learning Inc. • 2009. eBook. Provides small businesses with a holistic approach to implementing their Web presence through identification of Web site content that matches their business strategy.

Enterprise Business Modeling, Optimization Techniques, and Flexible Information Systems. Cengage Learning Inc. • 2013. eBook. Provides research on the intersections of business modeling, information systems, and optimization techniques. These various business models and structuring methods are proposed to provide ideas, methods, and points of view for managers, practitioners, entrepreneurs, and researchers on how to improve business processes.

Enterprise Information Systems for Business Integration in SMEs: Technological, Organizational, and Social Dimensions. Cengage Learning Inc. • 2010. eBook. Covers the main issues, challenges, opportunities, and trends related to the impact of IT on every part of organizational and inter-organizational environments.

Entrepreneurship and Innovations in E-Business: An Integrative Perspective. Cengage Learning Inc. • 2006. eBook. Published by Information Science Reference. Develops and explores theoretical constructs and the working concepts of e-entrepreneurship and e-innovation through comprehensive and collective studies conducted by a number of researchers and practitioners with e-business and management expertise.

Fashion Supply Chain Management: Industry and Business Analysis. Cengage Learning Inc. • 2012. eBook. Published by IGI Global. Covers quantitative research on Fashion Supply Chain Management (FSCM) and exploratory studies on emerging supply chain management issues in the fashion industry.

The Growing Business Handbook. Cengage Learning Inc. • 2010. eBook. 12th edition. Published by Kogan Page. Focuses on key issues such as funding, innovation, customer service, business technology and international expansion. Includes case studies from top companies.

Handbook of Ontologies for Business Interaction. Cengage Learning Inc. • 2008. eBook. Published by Information Science Reference. Documents high-quality research addressing ontological issues that are relevant to the modeling of enterprises and information systems in general and business processes in particular covering both static and dynamic aspects of structural concepts.

Handbook of Research on E-Business Standards and Protocols: Documents, Data and Advanced Web Technologies. Cengage Learning Inc. • 2012. eBook. Published by IGI Global. Contains an overview of new achievements in the field of e-business standards and protocols, offers in-depth analysis of and research on the development and deployment of cutting-edge applications, and provides insight into future trends.

High Performance Business Strategy. Cengage Learning Inc. • 2009. eBook. Published by Kogan Page. Designed to help senior management analyse the weak points in a business and focus HR on transforming problem areas by maximizing staff and business performance.

HR Strategy for the High Performing Business. Cengage Learning Inc. • 2009. eBook. Published by Kogan Page. Designed to help senior management analyze the weak points in their business and focus HR on transforming problem areas by maximizing staff and business performance.

Knowledge Ecology in Global Business: Managing Intellectual Capital. Cengage Learning Inc. • Published by Information Science Reference. Provides ideas on how intellectual capital through emerging technologies can support business performance. Covers topics such as competitive strategy, human resource management, and organizational learning.

Knowledge Management Strategies for Business Development. Cengage Learning Inc. • Published by IGI Global. Addresses the relevance of knowledge management strategies for the advancement of organizations worldwide. Supplies business practitioners, academicians, and researchers with comprehensive tools to systematically guide through a process that focuses on data gathering, analysis, and decision making.

Mind the Gaps: Singapore Business in China. Cengage Learning Inc. • 2009. eBook. Published by Institute of Southeast Asian Studies. Provides analysis on how to be successful in China, especially for Singapore businessmen.

Reference Modeling for Business Systems Analysis. Cengage Learning Inc. • 2007. eBook. Published by Information Science Reference. Covers all aspects of reference modeling, and provides foundations for model-driven systems development.

Starting a Successful Business. Cengage Learning Inc. • 2009. eBook. Published by Kogan Page. Covers topics such as franchises, marketing, publicity, e-business, financial management, business law, recruitment, taxation, insurance, business planning and development.

ENCYCLOPEDIAS AND DICTIONARIES

Encyclopedia of Emerging Markets. Cengage Learning Inc. • Covers emerging markets and industry profiles in 33 nations worldwide. Available in print ($549) and eBook. Published June 2013.

GENERAL WORKS

Enterprise Development and Microfinance Journal. Practical Action. • Quarterly. $104 Other countries print. Journal covering small enterprise development.

International Journal of Business Process Integration & Management (IJBPIM). Inderscience Publishers. • €494 Individuals print or online only for 1 user. Journal covering the emerging business process modeling, simulation, integration and management using emerging technologies.

International Journal of Strategic Business Alliances (IJSBA). Inderscience Enterprises Limited. • Quarterly. €520 Individuals print. Peer-reviewed journal covering strategic alliances in businesses.

INTERNET DATABASES

Intelligence Data. Thomson Financial. Phone: 800-654-0393; Fax: (617)824-2477 • URL: http://www.intelligencedata.com • Fee-based Web site provides a wide variety of information relating to competitive intelligence, strategic planning, business development, mergers, acquisitions, sales, and marketing. "Intelliscope" feature offers searching of other Thomson units, such as Investext, MarkIntel, InSite 2, and Industry Insider. Weekly updating.

ONLINE DATABASES

Wilson Business Abstracts Online. H.W. Wilson Co. • Indexes and abstracts 600 major business periodicals, plus the *Wall Street Journal* and the business section of the *New York Times*. Indexing is from 1982, abstracting from 1990, with the two newspapers included from 1993. Updated weekly. Inquire as to online cost and availability. (*Business Periodicals Index* without abstracts is also available online.).

PERIODICALS AND NEWSLETTERS

Business Performance Management. Intertec Publishing. • Magazine for business managers. Covers organizing, automating, and analyzing of business methodologies and processes.

Daily Report for Executives. Bloomberg BNA. • Daily. Covers legal, regulatory, economic, and tax developments affecting corporations.

Distribution Business. UK Transport Press Ltd. • Monthly. $75 Individuals. Business to business magazine covering logistics and distribution.

Family Business Advisor. Family Enterprise Publishers. • Monthly. Covers business management, family relations, and asset protection. Addresses succession planning, estate planning, conflict management, compensation, family meetings, strategic planning, and board composition. Recurring features include news of research.

The Grower: Profitable Business Strategies for Fruit and Vegetable Growers. Vance Publishing Corp. • Monthly. $45 Individuals. Magazine providing management information for the commercial fruit and vegetable producer with emphasis on management, industry trends, effective marketing, chemicals, and legislative and regulatory environments.

International Journal of Disaster Recovery and Business Continuity. Science and Engineering Research Support Society. • Annual. Peer-reviewed journal focusing on research related to disaster recovery and business continuity technology and applications.

Journal of Business Strategy. SourceMedia Inc. • Bimonthly. $98.00 per year. Covers managememt planning techniques and corporate strategy for senior executives.

Journal of East-West Business. Routledge Journals Taylor & Francis Group. • Quarterly. $530 Institutions online only. Journal dealing with contemporary and emerging topics of business studies, strategies, development, and practice relating to Eastern Europe and Asia.

The Small Business Advisor. Small Business Advisors Inc. • Monthly. $45 print or soft copy. Seeks to help emerging growth companies increase profits. Considers small business issues, including marketing sales, finance, taxes, organizing, competition, management, and human resources. Recurring features include letters to the editor, interviews, and columns titled Info Bank, In the Mail Box, Taxes, Human Resources, Marketing, Insurance, and Law. Remarks: Publication suspended in 1980; resumed publication Fall 1993.

Strategic Management Journal. John Wiley and Sons, Inc., Journals Div. • $2,992 Institutions. Original refereed material concerned with all aspects of strategic management. Devoted to the development and improvement of both theory and practice. Provides international coverage.

Strategize Magazine: tomorrow's ideas for today's business. Avenir Publishing Inc. • Bimonthly. Magazine for business improvement and innovation.

strategy business. • Quarterly. $38.00 per year.

RESEARCH CENTERS AND INSTITUTES

Strategic Planning Institute. PO Box 447, Newton Center, MA 02459-0004. Phone: (617)491-9200; Fax: (617)491-9200 or (617)491-1634; Email: spi@pimsonline.com • URL: http://www.pimsonline.com/ • Conducts research in business information and strategy.

University of Exeter - Business School - Centre for Innovation and Service Research. Streatham Ct., Rennes Dr., Exeter EX4 4PU, United Kingdom. Phone: 44 1392 722557; Fax: 44 1392 723210 • URL: http://business-school.exeter.ac.uk/research/areas/centres/isr • Design, analysis and management of business processes, including the analysis of process flows, capacity, resource utilization, and throughput analyses.

University of Minnesota - Hubert H. Humphrey Institute of Public Affairs. 301 19th Ave. S, Minneapolis, MN 55455. Phone: (612)625-0669 or (612)626-8910; Fax: (612)625-3513 or (612)626-6351; Email: jbatwood@umn.edu • URL: http://www.hhh.umn.edu • Studies strategic management in both the private and the public sectors.

TRADE/PROFESSIONAL ASSOCIATIONS

Institute for Turnaround. Juxon House, 2nd Fl., 100 St. Paul's Churchyard, London EC4M 8BU, United Kingdom. Phone: 44 20 3102 7710; Fax: 44 20 3102 7301; Email: info@instituteforturnaround.com • URL: http://www.instituteforturnaround.com • Raises the profile of turnaround professionals and its culture. Encourages intervention into underperforming businesses. Promotes turnaround knowledge among business community. Encourages high standards of ethics, behavior and quality of turnaround practitioners.

Strategic Planning Society. New Bond House, 124 New Bond St., London W1S 1DX, United Kingdom. Phone: 44 845 0563663; Email: members@sps.org.uk • URL: http://www.sps.org.uk • Corporations, educational institutions, and small companies and firms; executives, planners, government officials, and interested individuals. Promotes strategic planning in private, public, and governmental organizations. Seeks to: create and maintain networks for decision makers and planners; develop improved techniques for strategic planning; provide resources of knowledge and experience to aid businesses with planning problems; address political, economic, and social issues facing planners. Has established special interest and regional groups. Maintains Speaker's Bureau.

Competitiveness Review: An International Business Journal. Emerald Group Publishing Ltd. Howard House, Wagon Ln., Bingley BD16 1WA, United Kingdom. Phone: 44 1274 777 700; Fax: 44 1274 785 201 • URL: http://www.emeraldinsight.com • Semiannual. Professional journal covering business and competitiveness worldwide.

BUSINESS TO BUSINESS MARKETING

See INDUSTRIAL MARKETING

BUSINESS TRAVEL

See also AIR TRAVEL; TRAVEL INDUSTRY

ABSTRACTS AND INDEXES

Business Periodicals Index Retrospective. EBSCO Publishing Inc. • 11/year. Quarterly and annual cumulations.

Leisure, Recreation and Tourism Abstracts. CABI Publishing North America. • Quarterly. Members, $280.00 per year; Institutions, $610.00 per year. Includes single site internet access. Provides coverage of the worldwide literature of travel, recreation, sports, and the hospitality industry.

Readers' Guide to Periodical Literature. EBSCO Publishing Inc. • Provides indexing for over 400 periodicals dating back to 1983.

BIBLIOGRAPHIES

Travel and Tourism. U. S. Government Printing Office. • Annual. Free. Issued by the Superintendent of Documents. A list of government publications on the travel industry and tourism. Formerly *Mass Transit, Travel and Tourism.* (Subject Bibliography No. 302.).

CD-ROM DATABASES

Readers' Guide to Periodical Literature. EBSCO Publishing Inc. • Provides indexing for over 400 periodicals dating back to 1983.

GENERAL WORKS

Business Travel Almanac. Pearson Education Inc. • $23.99 Individuals print. List of travel advice, reference material, directory information and city guides.

HANDBOOKS AND MANUALS

CCH Guide to Car, Travel, Entertainment, and Home Office Deductions. Wolters Kluwer Law & Business CCH. • Annual. Explains how to claim maximum tax deductions for common business expenses. Includes automobile depreciation tables, lease value tables, worksheets, and examples of filled-in tax forms.

Health Information for International Travel. U.S. Dept. of Health and Human Services - Centers for Disease Control and Prefabricated. • Annual. $38. Produced by the Centers for Disease Control and Prevention (CDC). Primarily edited for "healthcare providers who administer pre- and post-travel counseling and care." Also serves as a reference for airlines, cruise lines, and the travel industry in general. Covers such items as injuries during travel, motion sickness, disabilities, vaccines, insect repellents, and travel with children. Sometimes known as "The Yellow Book.".

ONLINE DATABASES

Wilson Business Abstracts Online. H.W. Wilson Co. • Indexes and abstracts 600 major business periodicals, plus the *Wall Street Journal* and the business section of the *New York Times*. Indexing is from 1982, abstracting from 1990, with the two newspapers included from 1993. Updated weekly. Inquire as to online cost and availability. (*Business Periodicals Index* without abstracts is also available online.).

PERIODICALS AND NEWSLETTERS

Business Travel News: News and Ideas for Business Travel Management. Nielsen Business Media Inc. • Monthly. $119.00 per year. Includes annual directory of travel sources. Formerly *Corporate Travel.*

Frequent Flyer: For Business People Who Must Travel. Official Airline Guides. • Monthly. $89.00 per year to individuals. Also known as *OAG Frequent Flyer.* Edited for business travelers. Contains news of frequent flyer programs, airport developments, airline services, and business travel trends. Available only with *OAG Flight Guide.*

Front Row Advisor: Business and First Class Air Travel and the Alluring World of Free Upgrades. Diversified Specialties Inc. • Bimonthly. $145.00 per year. Newsletter. Contains information on opportunities provided by airlines to upgrade coach seats to business class, including frequent flyer upgrades.

Inside Flyer. • Monthly. $36.00 per year. Newsletter. Provides information relating to frequent flyer awards and air travel.

Newsline: Research News from the U. S. Travel Data Center. U.S. National Research Council. • Monthly. $55.00 per year. Newsletter. Covers trends in the U. S. travel industry.

Runzheimer Mobility Report. Runzheimer International. • Monthly. $295.00 per year. Newsletter on the control of business travel costs.

Summary of Health Information for International Travel. U.S. Department of Health and Human Services. • Biweekly. Formerly *Weekly Summary of Health Information for International Travel.*

Travel Manager's Executive Briefing. American Business Publishing C/0 Health Resources Publishing. • Description: Follows developments in the field of travel and expense cost control. Recurring features include news of discounted air fares, car rentals, and hotel bills; case histories of other companies cutting costs; travel alternatives, phone savings, planning for meetings; and trends in government legislation affecting business travel costs.

Travel Weekly. Northstar Travel Media L.L.C. • Weekly. $266.00 per year. Includes cruise guides, a weekly "Business Travel Update," and special issues devoted to particular destinations and areas. Edited mainly for travel agents and tour operators.

STATISTICS SOURCES

Outlook for Travel and Tourism. U.S. Travel Association. • Annual. Members, $100.00; non-members, $175.00. Contains forecasts of the performance of the U. S. travel industry, including air travel, business travel, recreation (attractions), and accomodations.

Summary of International Travel to the United States. International Trade Administration, Tourism Industries. U.S. Department of Commerce. • Monthly. Quarterly and annual versions available. Provides statistics on air travel to the U.S. from 90 countries. Formerly *Summary and Analysis of International Travel to the United States.*

Survey of Business Travelers. U.S. Travel Association. • Biennial. Members, $100.00 per year; non-members, $175.00 per year.

TRADE/PROFESSIONAL ASSOCIATIONS

National Association of Business Travel Agents. 3699 Wilshire Blvd., Ste. 700, Los Angeles, CA 90010-2726. Phone: (213)382-3335 • Members specialize in corporate and business travel services.

BUSINESS VALUATION

See VALUATION

BUTANE

See PROPANE AND BUTANE GAS INDUSTRY

BUTCHER SHOPS

See MEAT INDUSTRY

BUTTER INDUSTRY

See DAIRY INDUSTRY

BUYING

See PURCHASING

BUYING A BUSINESS

See BUSINESS ENTERPRISES, SALE OF

BUYING POWER

See PURCHASING POWER

BUYOUTS, LEVERAGED

See LEVERAGED BUYOUTS

BY-PRODUCTS

See WASTE PRODUCTS

C

CABLE TELEVISION INDUSTRY

See also TELEVISION BROADCASTING INDUSTRY

ABSTRACTS AND INDEXES

Business Periodicals Index Retrospective. EBSCO Publishing Inc. • 11/year. Quarterly and annual cumulations.

DIRECTORIES

Burrelle's Media Directory: Broadcast Media. BurrellesLuce. • Annual. $550.00. Approximately 48,000 print and electronic media in North America. Provides detailed descriptions, including programming and key personnel.

Cable Television Directory. InfoGroup Inc. • Annual. Number of listings: 9,002. Entries include: Name, address, phone, size of advertisement, name of owner or manager, number of employees, year first in "Yellow Pages." Compiled from telephone company "Yellow Pages," nationwide.

Cable TV Facts. Cabletelevision Advertising Bureau. • Annual. $50 Members. Publication includes: List of ad-supported cable networks. Principal content of publication is discussion of the growth of the cable television industry, changes in viewership, marketing, and research trends. Covers demographic information, audience ratings, cable penetration, regional sports and news networks, major market inter-connects.

Cable TV Financial Databook. SNL Kagan. • Annual. $595. Publication includes: Lists of 100 top multiple system cable TV operators, 100 top single cable TV systems, top publicly-owned cable TV equipment suppliers, financial institutions active in cable TV financing, venture capitalists in the field, and appraisers, brokers, and consultants, Telcos in cable, High-Speed access rollouts, digital cable. Entries include: For leading operators--Name, total subscribers, homes passed, homes under franchise, plant miles, names of key personnel; ranked in separate lists by total revenues. For equipment suppliers--Name, product supplied, operating statistics from annual report. For single systems--Name, address, total subscribers, name of general manager. Principal content of publication is financial and statistical data on cable television companies, securities, accounting, etc.

SRDS Interactive Advertising Source. Kantar Media SRDS. • Quarterly. $569.00 per year. Provides descriptive profiles, rates, audience, personnel, etc., for producers of various forms of interactive or multimedia advertising: online/Internet, CD-ROM, interactive TV, interactive cable, interactive telephone, interactive kiosk, and others.

ONLINE DATABASES

ERIC. U.S. Department of Education Institute of Education Sciences Educational Resources Information Center. • Funded by the U.S. Department of Education, Institute of Education Sciences (formerly Office of Educational Research and Improvement). Provides access to more than one million online records covering education-related journal and report literature, 1966 to date. Updating is monthly. Inquire as to online cost and availability.

OTHER SOURCES

Telecommunications Regulation: Cable, Broadcasting, Satellite, and the Internet. Matthew Bender and Company Inc. • Semiannual. $1,747. Four looseleaf volumes. Covers local, state, and federal regulation, with emphasis on the Telecommunications Act of 1996. Includes regulation of television, telephone, cable, satellite, computer communication, and online services. Formerly *Cable Television Law*.

PERIODICALS AND NEWSLETTERS

Broadband Technology: Newsletter on Technical Advances, Construction of New Systms and Rebuild of Existing Systems. Paul Kagan Associates, Inc. • Monthly. $895.00 per year. Newsletter. Contains news of cable TV technical advances. Formerly (Cable TV Technology).

Broadcasting and Cable. NewBay Media, LLC. • 51 times a year. $179.00 per year; includes print and online editions. Formerly *Broadcasting*.

Cable TV Investor: Newsletter on Investments in Cable TV Systems and Publicly Held Cable TV Stocks. Paul Kagan Associates, Inc. • Monthly. $995.00 per year.

Cable TV Programming: Newsletter on Programs for Pay Cable TV and Analysis of Basic Cable Networks. Paul Kagan Associates, Inc. • Monthly. $895.00 per year.

Communications Daily: The Authoritative News Service of Electronic Communications. Warren Communications News Inc. • Covers telecommunications, including the telephone industry, broadcasting, cable TV, satellites, data communications, and electronic publishing. Features corporate and industry news.

The Hollywood Reporter. • Daily. $199.00 per year. Covers the latest news in film, TV, cable, multimedia, music, and theatre. Includes box office grosses and entertainment industry financial data.

Multichannel News. Reed Elsevier Group plc Reed Business Information. • 51 times a year. $139.00 per year. Covers the business, programming, market and technology concerns of cable television operators and their suppliers.

Television Digest with Consumer Electronics. Warren Communications News Inc. • Weekly. $944.00 per year. Newsletter featuring new consumer entertainment products utilizing electronics. Also covers the television broadcasting and cable TV industries, with corporate and industry news.

Television Week. Crain Communications Inc. • Weekly. $119.00 per year. Formerly *Electronic Media*.

STATISTICS SOURCES

Standard & Poor's Industry Surveys. Standard & Poor's Financial Services L.L.C. • Semiannual. $1,800.00. Two looseleaf volumes. Includes monthly *Supplements*. Provides detailed, individual surveys of 52 major industry groups. Each survey is revised on a semiannual basis. Also includes "Monthly Investment Review" (industry group investment analysis) and monthly "Trends & Projections" (economic analysis).

Television and Cable Factbook. Warren Communications News Inc. • Annual. $595. Commercial and noncommercial television stations and networks.

U.S. Industry and Trade Outlook. U.S. Department of Commerce National Technical Information Service. • Annual. Produced by the International Trade Administration, U.S. Department of Commerce, in a "public-private" partnership with DRI/McGraw-Hill and Standard & Poor's. Provides basic data, outlook for the current year, and "Long-Term Prospects" (five-year projections) for a wide variety of products and services. Includes high technology industries. Formerly *U.S. Industrial Outlook*.

TRADE/PROFESSIONAL ASSOCIATIONS

Cabletelevision Advertising Bureau. 830 3rd Ave., 2nd Fl., New York, NY 10022. Phone: (212)508-1200; Fax: (212)832-3268; Email: chuckt@cabletvadbureau.com • URL: http://www.thecab.tv • Ad-supported cable networks. Provides marketing and advertising support to members and promotes the use of cable by advertisers and ad agencies locally, regionally, and nationally.

CTAM: Cable and Telecommunications Association for Marketing. 120 Waterfront St., Ste. 200, Oxon Hill, MD 20745. Phone: (301)485-8900; Fax: (301)560-4964; Email: info@ctam.com • URL: http://www.ctam.com • Formerly CTAM, The Marketing Society for Cable and Telecommunications Industry.

Jones NCTI. 9697 E Mineral Ave., Centennial, CO 80112. Phone: 866-575-7206 or (303)797-9393; Fax: (303)797-9394; Email: info@jonesncti.com • URL: http://www.jonesncti.com.

National Cable and Telecommunications Association. 25 Massachusetts Ave. NW, Ste. 100,

Washington, DC 20001. Phone: (202)222-2300; Email: webmaster@ncta.com • URL: http://www.ncta.com • Affiliated with Motion Pictute Association of America. Formerly National Cable Television Association.

CAFETERIAS

See RESTAURANTS, LUNCHROOMS, ETC.

CAFETERIAS, EMPLOYEE

See EMPLOYEE LUNCHROOMS AND CAFETERIAS

CALENDAR

See CHRONOLOGY

CAMCORDERS

See VIDEO RECORDING INDUSTRY

CAMERA INDUSTRY

See also PHOTOGRAPHIC INDUSTRY

FINANCIAL RATIOS

Annual Statement Studies. Risk Management Association. • Annual. Compiled from over 280,000 financial statements.

Annual Statement Studies: Industry Default Probabilities and Cash Flow Measures. Risk Management Association. • Annual. $405 Nonmembers. Serves as a companion volume to the original *Annual Statement Studies.* Gives probability of default estimates on a percentage scale for more than 450 industries. Includes changes in position year-by-year for eight financial statement line items and provides percentage measures of cash flow.

Cost of Doing Business Survey. Professional School Photographers Association International. • Biennial. $99. Emphasis is on photographic retailing.

PERIODICALS AND NEWSLETTERS

Japan Camera Trade News: Monthly Information on Photographic Products, Optical Instruments and Accessories. K. Eda, editor. Genyosha Publications Inc. • Monthly. $130.00 per year. Information on the photographic industry worldwide. Text in English.

PRICE SOURCES

Camera. Orion Research Corp. • Annual. $144 Individuals. Quotes retail and wholesale prices of used cameras and equipment. Original list prices and years of manufacture are also shown.

STATISTICS SOURCES

United States Census of Manufactures. U.S. Department of Commerce U.S. Census Bureau. • Quinquennial. Results presented in reports, tape, CD-ROM, and Diskette files.

U.S. Industry and Trade Outlook. U.S. Department of Commerce National Technical Information Service. • Annual. Produced by the International Trade Administration, U.S. Department of Commerce, in a "public-private" partnership with DRI/McGraw-Hill and Standard & Poor's. Provides basic data, outlook for the current year, and "Long-Term Prospects" (five-year projections) for a wide variety of products and services. Includes high technology industries. Formerly *U.S. Industrial Outlook.*

TRADE/PROFESSIONAL ASSOCIATIONS

International Imaging Industry Association. 2001 L St., NW Ste. 700, Washington, DC 20036-4928. Phone: 800-272-6657 or (202)371-0101; Fax: (202)728-9614; Email: help@computer.org • URL: http://www.ieee.org • Develops and promotes the adoption of open industry standards, addressing environmental issues and providing a voice for the industry that will benefit all users. Promotes environment, health and safety concerns; works with various government agencies including the EPA, TSA, and WTO to ensure the best interests of the imaging industry are represented.

National Association of Photo Equipment Technicians. c/o Worldwide Community of Imaging Associations, 2282 Springport Rd., Ste. F, Jackson, MI 49202. Phone: 800-762-9287 or (517)788-8100; Fax: (517)788-8371 • URL: http://www.pmai.org/napet • Affiliated with Photo Marketing Association International.

Photoimaging Manufacturers and Distributors Association. 7600 Jericho Tpke., Ste. 301, Woodbury, NY 11797. Phone: (516)802-0895; Fax: (516)364-0140 • URL: http://www.pmda.com • Formerly Photographic Manufacturers and Distributors Association.

CAMPER INDUSTRY

See RECREATIONAL VEHICLE INDUSTRY

CAMPING INDUSTRY

See RECREATION INDUSTRY

CANADIAN MARKETS

ABSTRACTS AND INDEXES

F & S Index: International. Cengage Learning Inc. • $2,659 Individuals. Monthly. $2,532.00 per year, including quarterly and annual cumulations. Provides annotated citations to marketing, business, financial, and industrial literature. Coverage of international business activity includes trade journals, financial magazines, business newspapers, and special reports. Areas included are Asia, Latin America, Africa, the Middle East, Oceania, and Canada.

ALMANACS AND YEARBOOKS

Canadian Almanac and Directory. Micromedia ProQuest. • Annual. $269.00. Contains general information and statistical data relating to Canada and provides information on about 60,000 Canadian agencies, associations, institutions, museums, libraries, etc.

BIOGRAPHICAL SOURCES

Canadian Who's Who. University of Toronto Press Inc. • Annual. $185.00. Provides concise biographical information in English and French on 15,000 prominent Canadians.

Directory of Directors. Financial Post Datagroup. • Annual. $175.00. Provides brief biographical information on 16,000 directors and key officers of Canadian companies who are also Canadian residents.

CD-ROM DATABASES

Canada Greater Montreal Business CD-ROM. Manufacturers' News Inc. • Contains detailed directory information on companies in and around Montreal, Quebec. Covers more than 22,100 companies and provides information on nearly 29,200 executives and key decision-makers.

Canada Greater Vancouver Business CD-ROM. Manufacturers' News Inc. • Contains detailed directory information on more than 18,600 companies in and around Vancouver, British Columbia.

Canada Year Book. Statistics Canada, Publications Division. • Annual. Available via HTML or PDF.

DIRECTORIES

B.O.S.S.: A Supplier Directory for Doing Business in Canada. International Press Publications Inc. • Annual. $200. Canadian suppliers and products.

Bottin Touristique du Quebec. Quebec Dans Le Monde. • Annual. $51.95 Individuals. Covers: Approximately 800 business, cultural and recreational travel agencies and agents in Quebec. Entries include: Company name, address, phone, fax, agent name, address, phone, fax, activities.

Canadian Aboriginal Business and Communities Directory: British Columbia. Indiana Marketing. • C$74.95 Individuals plus $12.95 for shipping and handling. Aboriginal companies and organizations in British Columbia, Canada.

Canadian Directory of Shopping Centres. Rogers Publishing Ltd. • Annual Periodic. $1,125 1-year online subscription plus 3-volume print set. (Eastern Canada and Western Canada). Describes about 2,200 shopping centers and malls, including those under development.

Directory of Retail Chains in Canada. Rogers Publishing Ltd. • Annual Monthly. $1,399 print and online. Provides detailed information on approximately 2,500 retail chains of all sizes in Canada.

Frasers Canadian Trade Directory. Rogers Publishing Ltd. • Annual. $220 Individuals print/CDR combo; includes s&h; PST and GST extra. Covers: over 42,000 manufacturers and distributors and over 14,000 foreign companies with Canadian representatives. Entries include: Company name, address. Products are included for manufacturers; name and address of Canadian representative is included for foreign firms.

Hoover's Handbook of World Business. Dun & Bradstreet Inc. Hoover's Inc. • Annual. $225 Individuals Hardcover. Covers: Hundreds of companies headquartered outside the U.S., including many with substantial activity in the U.S.; global enterprises, businesses that dominate their respective industries, and representative companies from all major industries. Entries include: Company name, overview, history, exchange and stock symbols, fiscal year-end date, names and titles of key personnel, name of auditors, number of employees, headquarters address, phone, fax, description of where the company does business, specific products/services/brand names produced, key competitors, 10 years of key financial data.

International Media Guide: Business/Professional Publications: The Americas. Kantar Media SRDS. • $553 Individuals online; 1 year. Describes over 4,400 trade publications from North, South, and Central America, with advertising rates and circulation data.

Northwest Manitoba Business Directory. Northwest Manitoba Business Directory. • Business directory covering businesses in Manitoba.

INTERNET DATABASES

CANOE: Canadian Online Explorer. Canoe Limited Partnership. Phone: (416)947-2154; Fax: (416)947-2209 • URL: http://www.canoe.ca • Web site provides a wide variety of Canadian news and information, including business and financial data. Includes "Money," "Your Investment," "Technology," and "Stock Quotes." Allows keyword searching, with links to many other sites. Daily updating. Fees: Free.

The Financial Post. National Post Online. Phone: 800-805-1184 or (244)383-2300; Fax: (416)383-2443 • URL: http://www.nationalpost.com/financialpost/ • Provides a broad range of Canadian business news online, with daily updates. Includes news, opinion, and special reports, as well as "Investing," "Money Rates," "Market Watch," and "Daily Mutual Funds." Allows advanced searching

(Boolean operators), with links to various other sites. Fees: Free.

Globeandmail.com:. Bell Globemedia Publishing, Inc. Phone: 800-268-9128 or (416)585-5000; Fax: (416)585-5249 • URL: http://www.globeandmail.ca • Web site provides access to selected sections of *The Globe and Mail.* Includes current news, national issues, career information, "Report on Business," and other topics. Keyword searching is offered for "a seven-day archive of the portion of the *Globe and Mail* that we publish online." Daily updates. Fees: free.

Statistics Canada!. Statistics Canada. 150 Tunney's Pasture Driveway, Ottawa, ON, Canada K1A 0T6. Phone: 800-263-1136; Email: infostats@statcan.gc.ca • URL: http://www.statcan.gc.ca • Web site in English and French provides basic statistical information relating to economic and social conditions in Canada: "The Land," "The People," "The Economy," "The State." Includes daily news, latest indicators, products and services, and links to other sites. Keyword searching is provided. Fees: Free.

TAXNET.PRO. Carswell. Phone: 800-387-5164 or (416)609-3800; Fax: (416)298-5082; Email: orders@carswell.com • URL: http://www.carswell.com/taxnetpro.asp • Fee-based Web site provides complete coverage of Canadian tax law and regulation, including income tax, provincial taxes, accounting, and payrolls. Daily updates. Base price varies according to product.

ONLINE DATABASES

Canadian Business. Rogers Communications Inc. • Contains the full text of the Canadian publication, *Canadian Business* magazine.

Canadian Business and Current Affairs Fulltext. Micromedia ProQuest. • Provides full-text of eight Canadian daily newspapers and more than 480 Canadian business magazines and trade journals. Indexing is 1982 to date, with selected full text from 1993. Updates are twice a month. Inquire as to online cost and availability.

CANSIM Time Series Database. Statistics Canada, Statistical Reference Center. • Daily. CANSIM is the Canadian Socio-Economic Information Management System. Contains more than 700,000 statistical time series relating to Canadian business, industry, trade, economics, finance, labor, health, welfare, and demographics. Time period is mainly 1946 to date, with daily updating. Inquire as to online cost and availability.

CNW Group. CNW Group Ltd. • Provides the complete online text of currrent press releases from more than 5,000 Canadian companies, institutions, and government agencies, including stock exchanges and the Ontario Securities Commission. Emphasis is on mining, petroleum, technology, and pharmaceuticals. Time span is 1996 to date, with daily updates. Inquire as to online cost and availability.

CPI.Q. Cengage Learning Inc. • Electronic version of the *Canadian Periodical Index.* Provides citations from 1988 to date for English and French language periodicals. Indexing from 1980 to present. Inquire as to price and availability.

PERIODICALS AND NEWSLETTERS

Canadian Business. Canadian Business Media. • Biweekly. $20 per year. Edited for corporate managers and executives, this is a major periodical in Canada covering a variety of business, economic, and financial topics. Emphasis is on the top 500 Canadian corporations.

The Financial Post: Canadian's Business Voice. Financial Post Datagroup. • Daily. $200.00 per year. Provides Canadian business, economic, financial, and investment news. Features extensive price quotes from all major Canadian markets: stocks, bonds, mutual funds, commodities, and currencies. Supplement available: *Financial Post 500.* Includes annual supplement.

Globe and Mail Report on Business. Globe and Mail Publishing. • Daily. Controlled circulation. Provides general coverage of business activity in Canada, with emphasis on the economy, foreign trade, technology, and personal finance.

RESEARCH CENTERS AND INSTITUTES

Conference Board of Canada. 255 Smyth Rd., Ottawa, ON, Canada K1H 8M7. Phone: 866-711-2262 or (613)526-3280; Fax: (613)526-4857; Email: contactcboc@conferenceboard.ca • URL: http://www.conferenceboard.ca • Research areas include economics, finance, international business, and consumer buying intentions.

Statistics Canada. 150 Tunney's Pasture Driveway, Ottawa, ON, Canada K1A 0T6. Phone: 800-263-1136; Email: infostats@statcan.gc.ca • URL: http://www.statcan.gc.ca • Issues compilations of census data and other facts relating to Canadian business, finance, industry, economics, and society in general. Statistics Canada is the country's national statistical agency, required to collect data according to the Statistics Act.

University of Maine - Canadian-American Center. 154 College Ave., Orono, ME 04473. Phone: (207)581-4220; Fax: (207)581-4223; Email: hornsby@maine.edu • URL: http://www.umaine.edu/canam/ • Research areas include Canadian-American business, economics, and trade.

University of Vermont - Canadian Studies Program. Wheeler House, Rm. 309, 94 University Pl., Burlington, VT 05405. Phone: (802)656-8451 or (802)656-1096; Fax: (802)656-8518; Email: paul.martin@uvm.edu • URL: http://www.uvm.edu/global/canadian • Research areas include Canadian corporate strategies, telecommunications, and natural resources.

Western Washington University - Center for Canadian-American Studies. Canada House 201, 516 High St., Bellingham, WA 98225-9110. Phone: (360)650-3728 or (360)650-3000; Fax: (360)650-3995; Email: donald.alper@wwu.edu • URL: http://www.wwu.edu/canam • Research areas include Canadian business and economics.

STATISTICS SOURCES

Provincial Outlook. Conference Board of Canada. • Quarterly. Free to members; non-members, $2,500.00 per year. Contains detailed forecasts of economic conditions in each of the Canadian provinces.

TRADE/PROFESSIONAL ASSOCIATIONS

Canada-United States Business Association. 2000 Town Center Ste. 1800, Southfield, MI 48075. Email: info@cusbaonline.com • URL: http://www.canadainternational.gc.ca/detroit/commerce_can/ba-ab.aspx?lang=eng • Consists of supporters of business such as labor, banking, consulting, government, and academia. Promotes stronger business and trading lineages between the U.S. and Canada by providing a forum to exchange information and ideas and to build relationships. Conducts educational programs; maintains speakers' bureau, panels, and special events.

Canadian-American Business Council. 1900 K St. NW, Ste. 100, Washington, DC 20006. Phone: (202)496-7906; Fax: (202)496-7756; Email: info@cabc.co • URL: http://cabc.co • Individuals, corporations, institutions and organizations with an interest in trade between the United States and Canada. Promotes free trade. Gathers and disseminates information; maintains speakers' bureau.

Canadian Federation of Independent Business. 401-4141 Yonge St., Toronto, ON, Canada M2P 2A6. Phone: 888-234-2232 or (416)222-8022; Fax: (416)222-6103; Email: cfib@cfib.ca • URL: http://www.cfib-fcei.ca/english/index.html • Independent businesses. Promotes economic well-being of members and seeks to maintain a healthy domestic business climate. Represents members' interests before government agencies, labor and industrial organizations, and the public.

Canadian Manufacturers and Exporters. 1 Nicholas St., Ste. 1500, Ottawa, ON, Canada K1N 7B7. Phone: (613)238-8888; Fax: (613)563-9218 • URL: http://www.cme-mec.ca • Formerly Alliance of Manufacturers and Exporters of Canada.

I.E. Canada. PO Box 189 Sta., Don Mills, ON, Canada M3C 2S2. Phone: (416)595-5333; Fax: (416)595-8226; Email: info@iecanada.com • URL: http://www.iecanada.com • Individuals and firms with an interest in Canada's international trade. Promotes increased participation by Canada in the global economy; seeks to maintain a business climate conducive to increased international trade. Represents members' interests before government agencies; prepares model trade programs, regulations, and policies. Provides advice and assistance to members; serves as a clearinghouse on international trade.

Seeds of Diversity Canada. PO Box 36, Sta. Q, Toronto, ON, Canada M4T 2L7. Phone: 866-509-7333 or (905)372-8983; Email: mail@seeds.ca • URL: http://www.seeds.ca • Promotes biodiversity of food crops through conservation, documentation, and use of open-pollinated plants. Teaches and encourages seed-saving of vegetables, fruits, and grains suitable for the diverse climates of Canada through magazines, member seed exchange, presentations, publications, and exhibits.

CANDY INDUSTRY

See also CHOCOLATE INDUSTRY; COCOA INDUSTRY

ABSTRACTS AND INDEXES

Food Science and Technology Abstracts. Ovid Technologies Inc. • Monthly. $1,780.00 per year. Provides worldwide coverage of the literature of food technology and food production.

Foods Adlibra: Key to the World's Food Literature. General Mills, Inc. Foods Adlibra Publications. • Semimonthly. $240.00 per year. Provides journal citations and abstracts to the literature of food technology and packaging.

DIRECTORIES

Food Chemicals News Directory. Food Chemical News. CRC Press. • Semiannual. $497.00. Over 2,000 subsidiaries belonging to nearly 250 corporate parents plus an additional 3,000 independent processors. Formerly *Hereld's 1,500.*

Major Food and Drink Companies of the World. Cengage Learning Inc. • 12th edition. eBook. Published by Graham & Whiteside. Contains profiles and trade names for more than 9,200 important food and beverage companies in various countries. In addition to foods, includes both alcoholic and nonalcoholic drink products.

FINANCIAL RATIOS

Annual Statement Studies. Risk Management Association. • Annual. Compiled from over 280,000 financial statements.

Annual Statement Studies: Industry Default Probabilities and Cash Flow Measures. Risk Management Association. • Annual. $405 Nonmembers. Serves as a companion volume to the original *Annual Statement Studies.* Gives probability of default estimates on a percentage scale for more than 450 industries. Includes changes in position year-by-year for eight financial statement line items and provides percentage measures of cash flow.

INTERNET DATABASES

Manufacturing Profiles. U. S. Bureau of the Census. Phone: (301)763-4636 or (301)763-4100; Fax:

(301)763-4794; Email: webmaster@census.gov • URL: http://www.census.gov/prod/www/abs/mfg-prof.html • The Census Bureau makes available free on PDF (Portable Document Format) an annual consolidation of the entire Current Industrial Report series, presenting "all the data compiled." Contains statistics on production, shipments, inventories, consumption, exports, imports, and orders for a wide variety of manufactured products.

ONLINE DATABASES

Food Science and Technology Abstracts (online). IFIS North American Desk. • Produced by International Food Information Service. Provides about 500,000 online citations, with abstracts, to the international literature of food science, technology, commodities, engineering, and processing. Approximately 2,000 periodicals are covered. Time period is 1969 to date, with monthly updates. Inquire as to online cost and availability.

OTHER SOURCES

The Candy Dish. National Candy Brokers and Salesmen's Association. • Monthly. Price on application. Provides industry news and event information for candy brokers and distributors.

NCBA Membership Roster. National Candy Brokers Association. • Annual. $25.00. Lists broker, manufacturer, and distributor members of the National Candy Brokers Association.

PERIODICALS AND NEWSLETTERS

Candy Industry: The Global Magazine of Chocolate and Confectionery. BNP Media. • Monthly.

Confectioner: The Magazine. BNP Media. • Bimonthly. $70.17 per year. Covers a wide variety of topics relating to the distribution and retailing of candy and snacks.

Convenience Distribution. American Wholesale Marketers Association. • Weekly. $36 Nonmembers print and online (U.S.). *Distribution Channels.* Official magazine of the American Wholesale Marketers Association (AWMA), owned and published by AWMA.

Fancy Food and Culinary Products. Talcott Communications Corp. • Monthly. $34.00 per year. Emphasizes new specialty food products and the business management aspects of the specialty food and confection industries. Includes special issues on wine, cheese, candy, "upscale" cookware, and gifts. Formerly (Fancy Foods).

Gourmet Retailer. Nielsen Business Media Inc. • Monthly. Free to qualified personnel; others, $75.00 per year. Covers upscale food and housewares, including confectionery items, bakery operations, and coffee.

Spotlight. World Affairs Council of Northern California. • Description: Includes one major and 30-40 brief annotated reviews of books on international relations, world politics, and economics. Includes transcripts of council programs.

PRICE SOURCES

PPI Detailed Report. Periodical covering business. Bureau of Labor Statistics, U.S. Department of Labor. U. S. Government Printing Office. • Monthly. $55 Individuals.

STATISTICS SOURCES

United States Census of Manufactures. U.S. Department of Commerce U.S. Census Bureau. • Quinquennial. Results presented in reports, tape, CD-ROM, and Diskette files.

U.S. Industry and Trade Outlook. U.S. Department of Commerce National Technical Information Service. • Annual. Produced by the International Trade Administration, U.S. Department of Commerce, in a "public-private" partnership with DRI/McGraw-Hill and Standard & Poor's. Provides basic data, outlook for the current year, and "Long-Term Prospects" (five-year projections) for a wide variety of products and services. Includes high technology industries. Formerly *U.S. Industrial Outlook.*

TRADE/PROFESSIONAL ASSOCIATIONS

American Wholesale Marketers Association. 2750 Prosperity Ave., Ste. 530, Fairfax, VA 22031. Phone: 800-482-2962; Fax: (703)573-5738 • URL: http://www.awmanet.org • Represents the interests of distributors of convenience-related products. Its members include wholesalers, retailers, manufacturers, brokers and allied organizations from across the U.S. and abroad. Programs include strong legislative representation in Washington and a broad spectrum of targeted education, business and information services. Sponsors the country's largest show for candy and convenience related products in conjunction with its semi-annual convention.

Bakery, Confectionery, Tobacco Workers and Grain Millers International Union. 10401 Connecticut Ave., Kensington, MD 20895. Phone: (301)933-8600; Fax: (301)946-8452; Email: bctgmwebmaster@bctgm.org • URL: http://www.bctgm.org • Formerly Bakery, Confectionery and Tobacco Workers International Union.

National Confectioners Association of the U.S. 1101 30th St. NW, Ste. 200, Washington, DC 20007. Phone: (202)534-1440; Fax: (202)337-0637; Email: info@candyusa.org • URL: http://www.candyusa.com/ • Affiliated with American Cocoa Research Institute and the Chocolate Manufacturers Associations of the U.S.A.

National Confectionery Sales Association. Spitfire House, 3135 Berea Rd., Cleveland, OH 44111. Phone: (216)631-8200; Fax: (216)631-8210; Email: info@candyhalloffame.org • URL: http://www.candyhalloffame.org • Salespersons, brokers, sales managers, wholesalers, and manufacturers in the candy industry. Maintains Candy Hall of Fame.

Retail Confectioners International. 2053 S Waverly, Ste. C, Springfield, MO 65804. Phone: 800-545-5381; Email: info@retailconfectioners.org • URL: http://www.retailconfectioners.org • Manufacturing retail confectioners who make and sell their own candies through directly-owned retail candy shops; associates are suppliers to the industry. Provides education, promotion and legislative and information service. Monitors legislative activities that affect the industry at state and national levels. Holds comprehensive two-week course and one-week specialized course on retail candy making biennially.

CANNED BEVERAGES

See BEVERAGE INDUSTRY

CANNED FOOD INDUSTRY

See also FISH INDUSTRY; FOOD INDUSTRY; FROZEN FOOD INDUSTRY

ABSTRACTS AND INDEXES

Food Science and Technology Abstracts. Ovid Technologies Inc. • Monthly. $1,780.00 per year. Provides worldwide coverage of the literature of food technology and food production.

Foods Adlibra: Key to the World's Food Literature. General Mills, Inc. Foods Adlibra Publications. • Semimonthly. $240.00 per year. Provides journal citations and abstracts to the literature of food technology and packaging.

ALMANACS AND YEARBOOKS

Almanac of the Canning, Freezing, Preserving Industries. Food Institute. • Annual. $110 Individuals Hard Copy mail delivery or pdf email from publisher. Contains U.S. food laws and regulations and detailed production statistics.

DIRECTORIES

Major Food and Drink Companies of the World. Cengage Learning Inc. • 12th edition. eBook. Published by Graham & Whiteside. Contains profiles and trade names for more than 9,200 important food and beverage companies in various countries. In addition to foods, includes both alcoholic and nonalcoholic drink products.

Plunkett's Food Industry Almanac. Plunkett Research Ltd. • $349.99 Individuals print + online. Covers: 340 leading companies in the global food industry. Entries include: Name, address, phone, fax, and key executives. Also includes analysis and information on trends, technology, and statistics in the field.

World Food Marketing Directory. Euromonitor International Business Reference Div. • $475 Individuals. Covers: Over 2,000 retailers and wholesalers, 1,500 manufacturers, over 2,000 international and European organizations, statistical agencies, trade journals and associations, databases, and trade fairs in the grocery and food industries worldwide. Entries include: Company name, address, phone, telex, names of parent company and subsidiaries, number of employees, financial data, products and brand names handled; retailers and wholesalers include type of outlet, names and titles of key personnel.

INTERNET DATABASES

USDA. U.S. National Institute of Standards and Technology. 100 Bureau Dr., Gaithersburg, MD 20899-1070. Phone: 800-877-8339 or (301)975-6478 or (202)720-2791; Fax: (301)975-8295; Email: inquiries@nist.gov • URL: http://www.nist.gov • The USDA home page has six sections: News and Information; What's New; About USDA; Agencies; Opportunities; Search and Help. Keyword searching is offered from the USDA home page and from various individual agency home pages. Agencies are the Economic Research Service, Agricultural Marketing Service, National Agricultural Statistics Service, National Agricultural Library, and about 12 others. Updating varies. Fees: Free.

ONLINE DATABASES

Food Science and Technology Abstracts (online). IFIS North American Desk. • Produced by International Food Information Service. Provides about 500,000 online citations, with abstracts, to the international literature of food science, technology, commodities, engineering, and processing. Approximately 2,000 periodicals are covered. Time period is 1969 to date, with monthly updates. Inquire as to online cost and availability.

PERIODICALS AND NEWSLETTERS

Food Production-Management: Monthly Publication of the Canning, Glass-Packing, As eptic, and Frozen Food Industry. CTI Publications Inc. • Monthly. $35.00 per year.

Prepared Foods. BNP Media. • Monthly. Edited for food manufacturing management, marketing, and operations personnel.

PRICE SOURCES

Supermarket News: The Industry's Weekly Newspaper. Fairchild Publications. • Weekly. Individuals, $196.00 per year; retailers, $45.00 per year; manufacturers, $89.00 per year.

STATISTICS SOURCES

Agricultural Statistics. U.S. Department of Agriculture National Agricultural Statistics Service. • Annual. $46 Individuals. Provides a wide variety of statistical data relating to agricultural production, supplies, consumption, prices/price-supports, foreign trade, costs, and returns, as well as farm labor, loans, income, and population. In many cases, historical data is shown annually for 10 years. In addition to farm data, includes detailed fishery statistics.

United States Census of Manufactures. U.S. Department of Commerce U.S. Census Bureau. • Quinquennial. Results presented in reports, tape, CD-ROM, and Diskette files.

CANVASSING

See DIRECT MARKETING

CAPITAL EQUIPMENT

See INDUSTRIAL EQUIPMENT INDUSTRY

CAPITAL GAINS TAX

See also TAXATION

ABSTRACTS AND INDEXES

Accounting and Tax Index. ProQuest L.L.C. • Quarterly. Indexes accounting, auditing, and taxation literature appearing in journals, books, pamphlets, conference proceedings, and newsletters.

INTERNET DATABASES

Internal Revenue Service IRS.gov. Internal Revenue Service. Phone: 800-829-1040 or (202)622-5000; Fax: (202)622-5844 • URL: http://www.irs.gov • Web site provides a wide variety of tax information, including IRS forms and publications. Searching is available. Fees: Free.

ONLINE DATABASES

Accounting and Tax Database. ProQuest L.L.C. • Provides indexing and abstracting of the literature of accounting, taxation, and financial management, 1971 to date. Updating is weekly. Especially covers accounting, auditing, banking, bankruptcy, employee compensation and benefits, cash management, financial planning, and credit. Inquire as to online cost and availability.

OTHER SOURCES

Taxation of Securities Transactions. Matthew Bender and Company Inc. • Semiannual. $653. Looseleaf service. Covers taxation of a wide variety of securities transactions, including those involving stocks, bonds, options, short sales, new issues, mutual funds, dividend distributions, foreign securities, and annuities.

PERIODICALS AND NEWSLETTERS

National Tax Journal. National Tax Association-Tax Institute of America. • Quarterly. Membership. Topics of current interest in the field of taxation and public finance in the U.S. and foreign countries.

RESEARCH CENTERS AND INSTITUTES

Harvard Law School International Tax Program. Harvard Law School, 1563 Massachusetts Ave., 1563 Massachusetts Ave., Cambridge, MA 02138. Phone: (617)495-3100 or (617)495-4406; Fax: (617)495-1110; Email: sfs@law.harvard.edu • URL: http://www.law.harvard.edu/programs/index.html • Studies the worldwide problems of taxation, including tax law and tax administration.

STATISTICS SOURCES

Statistics of Income Bulletin. U. S. Government Printing Office. • Quarterly. $44. Current data compiled from tax returns relating to income, assets, and expenses of individuals and businesses. (U. S. Internal Revenue Service.).

TRADE/PROFESSIONAL ASSOCIATIONS

Citizens for a Sound Economy. 1250 H St. NW, Ste. 700, Washington, DC 20005-3908. Phone: 888-564-6273 or (202)783-3870 or (202)942-7649; Fax: (202)783-4687; Email: cse@cse.org • URL: http://www.cse.org • Absorbed Council for a Competitive Economy and Tax Foundation.

CAPITAL, VENTURE

See VENTURE CAPITAL

CAR PHONES

See MOBILE TELEPHONE INDUSTRY

CARBONATED BEVERAGES

See BEVERAGE INDUSTRY

CARDS, GREETING

See GREETING CARD INDUSTRY

CAREER PLANNING

See VOCATIONAL GUIDANCE

CARIBBEAN AREA

See LATIN AMERICAN MARKETS

CARPENTRY

See also HOME IMPROVEMENT INDUSTRY; WOODWORKING INDUSTRIES

DIRECTORIES

Wood Digest-Showcase. Cygnus Business Media Inc. • Monthly. Publication includes: List of suppliers of materials, machinery, tools, and services for woodworking, cabinetry, casegoods, and furniture manufacturing processes (SIC 24, 25, 37, and 39). Entries include: Company name, phone number, photograph of product, services.

FINANCIAL RATIOS

Annual Statement Studies. Risk Management Association. • Annual. Compiled from over 280,000 financial statements.

Annual Statement Studies: Industry Default Probabilities and Cash Flow Measures. Risk Management Association. • Annual. $405 Nonmembers. Serves as a companion volume to the original *Annual Statement Studies.* Gives probability of default estimates on a percentage scale for more than 450 industries. Includes changes in position year-by-year for eight financial statement line items and provides percentage measures of cash flow.

PERIODICALS AND NEWSLETTERS

The Carpenter. United Brotherhood of Carpenters and Joiners of America. • Bimonthly.

CARPET CLEANING INDUSTRY

See CLEANING INDUSTRY

CARTOGRAPHY

See MAPS

CARWASH INDUSTRY

PERIODICALS AND NEWSLETTERS

American Clean Car. Crain Communications Inc. • Bimonthly. $135.00 per year. Provides articles on new products and management for the carwash industry.

Professional Carwashing and Detailing. National Trade Publications Inc. • Monthly. Edited for owners, operators, and managers of automatic carwashes, custom hand carwash facilities, detail shops, and coin-operated, self-service carwashes.

TRADE/PROFESSIONAL ASSOCIATIONS

Car Wash Owners and Suppliers Association. 1822 South St., Racine, WI 53404. Phone: (262)639-2289; Fax: (262)639-4393 • Formerly Car Wash Manufacturers and Suppliers Association.

CASE STUDIES

E-BOOKS

CaseBase: Case Studies in Global Business. Cengage Learning Inc. • Details business case studies; focused on worldwide emerging markets and industries. Available in print ($218) and eBook. Second volume published June 2012.

GENERAL WORKS

IBIMA Business Review (IBIMABR). IBIMA Publishing. • Peer-reviewed journal publishing case studies for business organizations.

Journal of Case Research in Business and Economics (JCRBE). Academic and Business Research Institute. • Journal containing case studies on business related issues.

PERIODICALS AND NEWSLETTERS

Journal of Internet and e-Business Studies. IBIMA Publishing. • Peer-reviewed journal publishing research, analyses, case studies and reviews relating to internet and electronic business.

CASH FLOW AND CASH MANAGEMENT

ABSTRACTS AND INDEXES

Accounting and Tax Index. ProQuest L.L.C. • Quarterly. Indexes accounting, auditing, and taxation literature appearing in journals, books, pamphlets, conference proceedings, and newsletters.

ONLINE DATABASES

Accounting and Tax Database. ProQuest L.L.C. • Provides indexing and abstracting of the literature of accounting, taxation, and financial management, 1971 to date. Updating is weekly. Especially covers accounting, auditing, banking, bankruptcy, employee compensation and benefits, cash management, financial planning, and credit. Inquire as to online cost and availability.

OTHER SOURCES

Planning Cash Flow. American Management Association Extension Institute. • Looseleaf. $139.00. Self-study course. Emphasis is on practical explanations, examples, and problem solving. Quizzes and a case study are included.

PERIODICALS AND NEWSLETTERS

AFP Exchange. Association for Financial Professionals. • Bimonthly. $90 for nonmembers. Treasury and finance newsletter.

Strategic Finance. Institute of Management Accountants. • Monthly. $220 Nonmembers. Provides articles on corporate finance, cost control, cash flow, budgeting, corporate taxes, and other financial management topics.

Successful Cost Control Strategies for CEOs, Managers, and Administrators. Siefer Consultants Inc. • Monthly. $279.00 per year. Newsletter. Provides a variety of ideas on business budgeting and controlling company expenses. Formerly *Employee Cost Control Strategies for CEOs, Managers, and Administrators.*

CASINOS

See GAMBLING INDUSTRY

CASKS

See COOPERAGE INDUSTRY

CASTING

See FOUNDRIES

CASTOR BEAN INDUSTRY

See OIL AND FATS INDUSTRY

CASUALTY INSURANCE

See also ACCIDENT INSURANCE

ABSTRACTS AND INDEXES

Insurance Periodicals Index. Specials Libraries Association, Insurance and Employees Benefits Div. NILS Publishing Co. • Annual. $250.00. Compiled by the Insurance and Employee Benefits Div., Special Libraries Association. A yearly index of over 15,000 articles from about 35 insurance periodicals. Arrangement is by subject, with an index to authors.

ALMANACS AND YEARBOOKS

Casualty Actuarial Society Yearbook and Proceedings. Casualty Actuarial Society. • Annual. $40. Approximately 2,500 actuaries working in insurance other than life insurance.

BIBLIOGRAPHIES

Insurance and Employee Benefits Literature. Special Libraries Association. • Bimonthly. $15.00 per year. Lists a wide variety of literature in all branches of the insurance industry. Includes annotations.

ONLINE DATABASES

I.I.I. Data Base Search. Insurance Information Institute. • Provides online citations and abstracts of insurance-related literature in magazines, newspapers, trade journals, and books. Emphasis is on property and casualty insurance issues, including highway safety, product safety, and environmental liability. Inquire as to online cost and availability.

OTHER SOURCES

Best's Insurance Reports: Property-Casualty. A.M. Best Company Inc. • Annual. $750.00. Guide to over 3,200 major property/casualty companies.

BestWeek: Insurance News and Analysis. A.M. Best Company Inc. • Weekly. $495.00 per year. Newsletter. Focuses on key areas of the insurance industry.

Casualty Insurance Claims: Coverage-Investigation-Law. Pat Magarick and Ken Brownlee. Thomson West. • $917 full set. Insurance claim and law information.

Fire and Casualty Insurance Law Reports. Wolters Kluwer Law & Business CCH. • $870.00 per year. Looseleaf service. Semimonthly updates.

PERIODICALS AND NEWSLETTERS

Business Insurance: News Magazine for Corporate Risk, Employee Benefit and Financial Executives. Crain Communications Inc. • Weekly. $95.00 per year. Covers a wide variety of business insurance topics, including risk management, employee benefits, workers compensation, marine insurance, and casualty insurance.

Chartered Property and Casualty Underwriters eJournal. Society of Chartered Property and Casualty Underwriters. • Monthly. Published by the Chartered Property and Casualty Underwriters Society (CPCU). Edited for professional insurance underwriters and agents.

Fire, Casualty and Surety Bulletin. • Monthly. $420.00 per year. Five looseleaf volumes.

Guide to Property and Casualty Insurers: A Quarterly Compilation of Insurance Company Ratings and Analysis. Weiss Research Inc. • Quarterly. $499. Emphasis is on rating of financial safety and relative risk. Includes annual summary.

Insurance and Technology. UBM L.L.C. • Monthly. $65.00 per year. Covers information technology and systems management as applied to the operation of life, health, casualty, and property insurance companies.

National Underwriter, Property and Casualty Edition. • Weekly. $92.00 per year.

Risk Management. Risk and Insurance Management Society. Risk and Insurance Management Society. • 10/year. $115 Individuals. Magazine featuring analysis, insight, and news for corporate risk managers.

RESEARCH CENTERS AND INSTITUTES

University of Pennsylvania - S.S. Huebner Foundation. 3000 Steinberg Hall-Dietrich Hall, 3620 Locust Walk, Philadelphia, PA 19104-6302. Phone: (215)898-9631; Fax: (215)573-2218; Email: huebner_foundation@wharton.upenn.edu • URL: http://www.huebnergeneva.org/huebner • Awards grants for research in various areas of insurance.

STATISTICS SOURCES

Property-Casualty Insurance Facts. Insurance Information Institute. • Annual. $22.50. Formerly *Insurance Facts.*

Standard & Poor's Industry Surveys. Standard & Poor's Financial Services L.L.C. • Semiannual. $1,800.00. Two looseleaf volumes. Includes monthly *Supplements.* Provides detailed, individual surveys of 52 major industry groups. Each survey is revised on a semiannual basis. Also includes "Monthly Investment Review" (industry group investment analysis) and monthly "Trends & Projections" (economic analysis).

TRADE/PROFESSIONAL ASSOCIATIONS

American Insurance Association. 2101 L St. NW, Ste. 400, Washington, DC 20037. Phone: (202)828-7100; Fax: (202)293-1219 • URL: http://www.aiadc.org/aiapub • Represents companies providing property and casualty insurance and suretyship. Monitors and reports on economic, political, and social trends; serves as a clearinghouse for ideas, advice, and technical information. Represents members' interests before state and federal legislative and regulatory bodies; coordinates members' litigation.

Casualty Actuarial Society. 4350 N Fairfax Dr., Ste. 250, Arlington, VA 22203. Phone: (703)276-3100; Fax: (703)276-3108; Email: office@casact.org • URL: http://www.casact.org • Professional society of property/casualty actuaries. Seeks to advance the body of knowledge of actuarial science applied to property, casualty and similar risk exposures, to maintain qualification standards, promote high standards of conduct and competence, and increase awareness of actuarial science. Examinations required for membership.

CPCU Society. 720 Providence Rd., Malvern, PA 19355-0709. Phone: 800-932-2728; Fax: (610)251-2780; Email: membercenter@cpcusociety.org • URL: http://www.cpcusociety.org • Serves as a professional society of individuals who have passed national examinations of the American Institute for Chartered Property Casualty Underwriters, have 3 years of work experience, have agreed to be bound by a code of ethics, and have been awarded CPCU designation. Promotes education, research, social responsibility, and professionalism in the field. Holds seminars, symposia, and workshops.

National Association of Professional Insurance Agents. 400 N Washington St., Alexandria, VA 22314. Phone: (703)836-9340; Fax: (703)836-1279; Email: web@pianet.org • URL: http://www.pianet.com • Members are independent agents in various fields of insurance. Formerly National Association of Mutual Insurance Agents.

CATALOGS AND DIRECTORIES

See also ASSOCIATIONS; BOOK CATALOGS

BIBLIOGRAPHIES

Books in Print. R.R. Bowker L.L.C. • Combines the trusted and authoritative source of bibliographic information with powerful search, discovery and collection development tools designed specifically to streamline the book discovery and acquisition process.

CD-ROM DATABASES

MediaFinder. Oxbridge Communications Inc. • $1,295 per year. Online database with 77,000 magazines, catalogs, newspapers, and journals.

DIRECTORIES

A-Z Credit Directory. Legal & Commercial State Services Ltd. • Annual. Covers: Over 30,000 credit records of companies and individuals in the Republic of Ireland. Entries include: Company or personal name and address.

Academy of Accounting Historians--Membership Directory. Academy of Accounting Historians. • Annual. Covers: over 900 member individuals and organizations concerned with accounting and business history. Entries include: Member name, address, phone, and fax.

Academy of International Business--Membership Directory. Academy of International Business. • Covers: About 3,068 members. Entries include: Name, address, phone, fax, Bitnet, discipline.

Access Nippon: How to Succeed in Japan. Hoover's Inc. • Annual. $34.95 plus $3.50 shipping. Covers: Brief profiles of 498 companies and 493 of their affiliates in Japan. Database includes: Overview of major industries & trends; Japan business practices/regulations; listing of major trade shows to be held in Japan; business travel guide; information on hotels, transportation, emergency services, etc. Entries include: Company headquarters, address, phone, date established, capital maintained, number of employees, financial data, product/service.

Accounting and Bookkeeping General Services Directory. InfoGroup Inc. • Annual. Number of listings: 27,213. Entries include: Name, address, phone, size of advertisement, name of owner or manager, number of employees, year first in "Yellow Pages." Compiled from telephone company "Yellow Pages," nationwide.

Accounting and Bookkeeping Systems (Wholesale) Directory. InfoGroup Inc. • Annual. Number of listings: 547. Entries include: Name, address, phone, size of advertisement, name of owner or manager, number of employees, year first in "Yellow Pages." Compiled from telephone company "Yellow Pages," nationwide.

Accounts Receivable (Financing) Directory. InfoGroup Inc. • Annual. Number of listings: 19,980. Entries include: Name, address, phone, size of advertisement, name of owner or manager, number of employees, year first in "Yellow Pages." Compiled from telephone company "Yellow Pages," nationwide.

Active Real Estate Lenders. Todd Publications. • Biennial. $35. Covers: 2,500 banks, finance companies, mortgage lenders, real estate investment trusts, brokers, and other firms offering real estate investment money.

Addison County Business Directory & Community Profile. Addison County Chamber of Commerce. • Description: Serves as a resource guide for businesses and individuals that are relocating to Addison County, Vermont, and surrounding areas. Covers: over 500 member businesses, and local government officials in Addison County, Vermont. Entries include: For businesses--Name, address, phone, business description, name and title of contact, fax, e-mail and URL addresses. For government officials--Name, business office address, phone, hours of operation.

Addressing & Letter Service Directory. InfoGroup Inc. • Annual. Number of listings: 8,077. Entries include: Name, address, phone, size of advertisement, name of owner or manager, number of employees, year first in "Yellow Pages." Compiled from telephone company "Yellow Pages," nationwide.

ADFIAP Factbook. Association of Development Financing Institutions in Asia and the Pacific. • 64. $10 postpaid. Covers: about 80 member institutions in Asia-Pacific whose main purpose is to provide capital for industrial development. Entries include: Institution name, address, phone.

Adjusters Directory. InfoGroup Inc. • Annual. Number of listings: 5,785. Entries include: Name, address, phone, size of advertisement, name of owner or manager, number of employees, year first in "Yellow Pages." Compiled from telephone company "Yellow Pages," nationwide.

Adjustment & Collection Services Directory. InfoGroup Inc. • Annual. Number of listings: 7,138. Entries include: Name, address, phone, size of advertisement, name of owner or manager, number of employees, year first in "Yellow Pages." Compiled from telephone company "Yellow Pages," nationwide.

Advance Payment Directory. InfoGroup Inc. • Annual. Number of listings: 14,867. Entries include: Name, address, phone, size of advertisement, name of owner or manager, number of employees, year first in "Yellow Pages." Compiled from telephone company "Yellow Pages," nationwide.

Advertiser's Yearbook. Oekonomisk Literatur Norge A/S. • Annual. $780. Covers: Advertising agencies in Norway. Entries include: Company name, address, phone, fax, management/ad/text, list of customers, special services, number of employees, share capital, sales.

Advertising Companies Contact Lists. Sheila Greco Associates L.L.C. • $65. Consists of 3 individually-priced lists covering advertising companies in the U.S. Each list features details for one company and includes global headquarter name, address, phone, fax, U.S. headquarter phone number, URL, company description, ticker symbol, revenues reported, industry type, key executive names and titles. All lists downloadable via PDF format.

Advertising Consultants Directory. InfoGroup Inc. • Annual. Number of listings: 51,839. Entries include: Name, address, phone, size of advertisement, name of owner or manager, number of employees, year first in "Yellow Pages." Compiled from telephone company "Yellow Pages," nationwide.

Advertising--Displays Directory. InfoGroup Inc. • Annual. Number of listings: 4,029. Entries include: Name, address, phone, size of advertisement, name of owner or manager, number of employees, year first in "Yellow Pages." Compiled from telephone company "Yellow Pages," nationwide.

Advertising (Promotional) Directory. InfoGroup Inc. • Annual. Number of listings: 6,226. Entries include: Name, address, phone, size of advertisement, name of owner or manager, number of employees, year first in "Yellow Pages." Compiled from telephone company "Yellow Pages," nationwide.

Advertising (Signs) Directory. InfoGroup Inc. • Annual. Number of listings: 28,945. Entries include: Name, address, phone, size of advertisement, name of owner or manager, number of employees, year first in "Yellow Pages." Compiled from telephone company "Yellow Pages," nationwide.

AEDC Resource Directory. American Economic Development Council. • Annual. Covers: Approximately 2,800 member industrial and economic development managers, including executive directors of chambers of commerce; federal, state, and regional industrial organizations; transportation agencies, utility companies, banks, and others who promote economic and industrial development. Entries include: Name, title, affiliation, address, phone, fax, email, and web, as well as practice speciality.

Aerospace Consultants Directory. InfoGroup Inc. • Annual. Number of listings: 10,653. Entries include: Name, address, phone, size of advertisement, name of owner or manager, number of employees, year first in "Yellow Pages." Compiled from telephone company "Yellow Pages," nationwide.

Africa-North America Business Register. KWL Associates. • Annual. $70 postpaid. Covers: African, Canadian, and U.S. business organizations involved in import/export trade inquiries. Database includes: Trade statistics and demographic data; list of trade associations, chambers of commerce, foreign trade representatives, government agencies, calendar of trade events. Entries include: Company name, address, phone, names and titles of key personnel, product/service, banking references, subsidiaries, annual revenue.

African International Business Directory of Importers. Coble International. • $285 print or CD-ROM. Covers: 9,000 importers from 42 countries in Africa. Entries include: Name, address, phone, fax, primary contact person, list of products, e-mail addresses, and Web site.

African Publishers Network Consultants Register. Bellagio Publishing Network. • Covers: 66 publishing consultants in Africa with specializations in bookselling, children's books, copyright, design, distribution, electronic publishing, finance, editing, librarianship, management, marketing, printing, production, training, scholarly publishing, translation, and writing.

African Telecommunications Directory. Information Gatekeepers Inc. • $495 Individuals. Publication includes: Lists of service providers and equipment providers in 36 African countries in the fields of fiber optics, optical networks, WDM, ADSL, ATM, Internet, high-speed local area networks, wireless, and the emerging telecom markets.

Afro-Brazilian Organization Directory. Universal Publishers Inc. • Covers: Listings of Black entities and organizations in Brazil.

Agricultural and Mineral Commodities Year Book. Routledge Reference. • $420 Individuals Hardback. Publication includes: List of international commodity organizations. Entries include: Name, address, phone, fax, e-mail, URL, publications, name of the chairperson, and description. Principal content of publication is a gathering of information about 40 commodities traded internationally, including barley, phosphates, soybeans, wool, zinc, lead, and natural gas.

Agricultural Producers Directory. InfoGroup Inc. • Annual. Number of listings: 22,572. Entries include: Name, address, phone, size of advertisement, name of owner or manager, number of employees, year first in "Yellow Pages." Compiled from telephone company "Yellow Pages," nationwide.

Agronomists Directory. InfoGroup Inc. • Annual. Number of listings: 1,029. Entries include: Name, address, phone, size of advertisement, name of owner or manager, number of employees, year first in "Yellow Pages." Compiled from telephone company "Yellow Pages," nationwide.

The AI Week Directory. R.R. Bowker L.L.C. • Irregular. $99. Covers: The US and international artificial intelligence community and related businesses. Entries include: Company name, size, and financial status; names of key personnel; products and services.

Air Compressors Directory. InfoGroup Inc. • Annual. Number of listings: 3,405. Entries include: Name, address, phone, size of advertisement, name of owner or manager, number of employees, year first in "Yellow Pages." Compiled from telephone company "Yellow Pages," nationwide.

Air Conditioning & Heating & Refrigeration Equipment Directory. InfoGroup Inc. • Annual. Number of listings: 689. Entries include: Name, address, phone, size of advertisement, name of owner or manager, number of employees, year first in "Yellow Pages." Compiled from telephone company "Yellow Pages," nationwide.

Air Duct Cleaning Directory. InfoGroup Inc. • Annual. Number of listings: 2,109. Entries include: Name, address, phone, size of advertisement, name of owner or manager, number of employees, year first in "Yellow Pages." Compiled from telephone company "Yellow Pages," nationwide.

Aircraft Parts & Auxiliary Equipment NEC Directory. InfoGroup Inc. • Annual. Number of listings: 1,412. Entries include: Name, address, phone, size of advertisement, name of owner or manager, number of employees, year first in "Yellow Pages." Compiled from telephone company "Yellow Pages," nationwide.

Airfinance Annual. Euromoney Institutional Investor P.L.C. • Annual. $450 Individuals. Covers: About 1,200 banks, finance houses, insurers, consultants, brokers, legal consultants, accountants, and leasing companies serving the aviation industry worldwide. Entries include: Company name, address, phone, e-mail, contact, key personnel, servicers provided, branch office names and locations.

Al-Batinah Tourist Guide. Oman Chamber of Commerce and Industry. • Provides information and data on tourist sites, locations, services, and facilities they offer in Batinah Region. Entries include: Names and addresses of travel and tourism organizations and companies.

Alabama Business Directory. InfoGroup Inc. • Annual. Covers: 184,277 businesses in Alabama. Entries include: Company name, address, phone, number of employees, name of owner or manager, sales volume. Compiled from telephone company "Yellow Pages," statewide. All states covered (see separate entries).

Alabama Industrial Directory. Alabama Development Office Alabama Center for Commerce. • Biennial. $75 Individuals print. Covers: More than 6,000 industrial companies in Alabama. Entries include: Company name, address, phone, fax number, e-mail and website addresses, NAICS code, name and title of principal executive, name and address of parent company, number of employees, product or service provided, Standard Industrial Classification (SIC) code, year established.

Alameda County Business Directory. Rich's Business Directories Inc. • $199 Individuals online. Contains directory information for more than 3700 companies and 12,000 contacts in Alameda County, California.

Alarm Systems Directory. InfoGroup Inc. • Annual. Number of listings: 11,847. Entries include: Name, address, phone, size of advertisement, name of owner or manager, number of employees, year first in "Yellow Pages." Compiled from telephone company "Yellow Pages," nationwide.

Alaska Business License Directory. Alaska Department of Community and Economic Development. • Covers: Approx. 70,000 businesses licensed by the state of Alaska. Entries include: Company name, address, name of owner, license number, line of business.

Alaska Industrial Directory. Harris InfoSource. • Annual. $495 Individuals Online. Covers: 6,200 manufacturing companies in Alaska. Database includes: Statistical data, trade show calendar. Entries include: Company name, address, county, phone, fax, web site address (on CD-ROM only), number of employees, names and titles of key executives, plant size, year established, parent company, annual sales, import/export information, Standard Industrial Classification (SIC) code, and product description.

Alberta Business Directory. InfoGroup Inc. • Annual. Covers: 122,660 businesses in Alberta, Canada. Entries include: Company name, address, phone, number of employees, name of owner or manager, sales volume. Compiled from telephone company "Yellow Pages," statewide (see separate entry).

Albuquerque Economic Development Business Directory. Albuquerque Economic Development Inc. • Covers: Business resources in the Albuquerque, New Mexico, metropolitan area. Includes list of categories with links and a searchable database. Entries include: Name, address, phone, fax, URL, map link.

Algeria Business Directory. Business Guide. • $150 download. Covers: 10,000 business listings including wholesalers, importers, retailers, business houses, and agents in Algeria.

Aligning & Wheel Service Directory. InfoGroup Inc. • Annual. Number of listings: 11,406. Entries include: Name, address, phone, size of advertisement, name of owner or manager, number of employees, year first in "Yellow Pages." Compiled from telephone company "Yellow Pages," nationwide.

All India Directory/Database of Automobile Components/Parts Manufacturers, Exporters, Dealers, Suppliers. NIIR Project Consultancy Services. • $250 Individuals CD-ROM. Covers: 11,000 automobile components/parts manufacturers and exporters, dealers, suppliers in India. Entries include: Company name, addresses, pin, city, phone, mobile (wherever available), fax (wherever available), e-mail (wherever available), website (wherever available), products details.

All India Manufacturers & Exporters of Herbal Products. NIIR Project Consultancy Services. • $200 Individuals CD-ROM. Covers: 2,500+ manufacturers and exporters of herbal products in India. Entries include: Name of company, address, city, phone (wherever available), fax (wherever available), e-mail (wherever available), activities (wherever available).

All India Textile Exporters and Manufacturers. NIIR Project Consultancy Services. • $100 Individuals CD-ROM. Covers: 4,000 textile exporters and manufacturers in India. Entries include: Company name, contact person name, email (wherever available).

All Ordinaries Index Companies Handbook. Australian Stock Exchange Ltd. Exchange Centre. • $29.95 plus $10.00 postage and handling. Covers: approximately 314 companies that comprise the Australian All Ordinaries Index as of September of the year issued, plus Health-Biotechnology and Telecommunications Index companies that are not included in the All Ordinaries Companies Index. Entries include: Company name, address, phone, names and titles of key personnel, key business summary, financial data, description of product/service, list of major shareholders, share price chart.

Alteration Contractors Directory. InfoGroup Inc. • Annual. Number of listings: 22,248. Entries include: Name, address, phone, size of advertisement, name of owner or manager, number of employees, year first in "Yellow Pages." Compiled from telephone company "Yellow Pages," nationwide.

Alternative Energy Directory & Handbook. Grey House Publishing. • $165 Individuals softcover. Covers: Alternative energy sources including hydro, wind, solar, coal, natural gas and atomic energy sources. Includes information on associations, magazines, trade shows and vendors.

AmCham Yearbook. American Chamber of Commerce for Brazil - Sao Paulo. • Annual. $250 Individuals for associates. Covers: More than 5,400 corporate members of the American Chamber of Commerce for Brazil.

American and Common Market Club Directory. American and Common Market Club. • Annual. Entries include: name, address, phone, fax.

American Banker--Top World Banks by Deposits and Assets. American Banker/Bond Buyer Inc. • Annual. $25. Publication includes: List of 500 largest banks in the world by assets with total deposits and deposit rank; also, the risk-based capital position of the 100 largest banking companies in the world as measured by total assets. Entries include: Bank name, headquarters, rankings by assets and amount of deposits and assets for two previous years.

American Bankers Association Directory of Trust Banking. Accuity Inc. • Annual. $575 Individuals. Covers: Approximately 3,000 financial institutions in the U.S. that are involved in trust banking. Database includes: Number of accounts under management by type for the past year and three year compounded growth. Entries include: Name, address, phone, fax, key trust officials with title and functional responsibility, personal and employee benefit assets for the two most current years along with a three year compounded growth rate.

American Business Directory for the USSR. Amtorg Trading Corp. • Publication consists of paid advertisements and business reply cards from U.S. companies wishing to do business with the U.S.S.R.

American Business in China. Caravel Inc. • Annual. $99 print edition. Publication includes: More than 1,000 U.S. firms with offices in China and Hong Kong, including Beijing, Shanghai, and Guangzhou. Database includes: Exporting to China; Marketing, Advertising and Exhibiting in China; China's major cites for foreign investments. Entries include: Company name, address, phone, fax; websites and e-mail addresses, name of contact for both U.S. Headquarters and China branch offices; and products or services provided.

American Business Leaders from Colonial Times to the Present. ABC-Clio Inc. • $175 Individuals print. Covers: The last three centuries of visionary figures in American business.

American Companies: A Guide to Sources of Information. CBD Research Ltd. • Biennial. £78 Individuals. Covers: Business information sources from over 50 countries in North, South, and Central America and the Caribbean. Entries include: For companies--company name, address, phone, fax, telex, year established, description, countries of specialization, branch offices, and languages spoken; for publications--title, publisher, address, telephone, fax, telex, year first published, frequency; latest edition, price, page count, description, company information, types of indexes, languages, and formats available.

American Companies Directory. NIIR Project Consultancy Services. • $200 Individuals CD-ROM. Covers: 1.5 million American companies. Entries include: Company name, email, phone, fax, email, websites and SIC code.

American Companies' Hong Kong Agents and Distributors. American Chamber of Commerce in Hong Kong. • $500 Nonmembers. Covers: Over 1,000 U.S. companies represented by 120 agents and distributors from Hong Kong.

American Companies in Brazil. U.S. Chamber of Commerce. • $75 plus $4.00 shipping. Covers: U.S. subsidiary and affiliate companies in Brazil. Entries include: Company name, address, phone.

American Incomes: Demographics of Who Has Money. New Strategist Publications Inc. • $138 Individuals hardcover. Publication includes: List of telephone numbers for agencies involved in economic information gathering. Principal content of publication is household income, women's and discretionary income, and wealth and poverty.

American Stock Exchange Guide. Wolters Kluwer Law & Business CCH. • Annual. $896 Individuals print. Covers: About 1,275 member companies listed as traders with the American Stock Exchange, and exchange and floor officials. Entries include: Company name, address, date admitted, names of representatives.

American Subsidiaries and Affiliates of French Firms. French Embassy Trade Office. • $125. Covers: French firms and their American subsidiaries. Database includes: Address, telephone and fax of french parent company. Entries include: firm address, telephone and fax numbers, activity.

America's Best Midsized Companies. Financial World Publishing. • Annual. $1.95. Entries include: Company name, address, phone.

America's International Trade: A Reference Handbook. ABC-Clio Inc. • $45 Individuals print. Covers: The importance of international trade to the American economy and the influence it has on American businesses. Publication includes: List of organizations relevant to America and international trade, such as the World Bank. Entries include: Contact data. Principal content of publication is a discussion of international trade and the American economy and businesses and international trade agreement.

The Americas Review: The Economic and Business Report. Kogan Page, Limited. • £50 Individuals. Covers: about 200 United States manufacturers and remanufacturers; includes facts on suppliers, country profiles, business guides, and directories for areas of North, Central, and South America, and all the Caribbean states and South Atlantic. Entries include: Heads of States, currencies, official languages, capital city, population, GNP, inflation, oil revenues, exports/imports, country profile, information for international visitors, name, address, phone of hotels, chambers of commerce, airlines, banks, government ministries and industrial associations.

Angel Capital: How to Raise Early-Stage Private Equity Financing. John Wiley & Sons Inc. • $85 Individuals hardcover. Covers: How to find investors and take control of the private placement process; alternative capital resources.

Angola Business Directory. Business Guide. • $25 download. Covers: Over 7,300 business listings including wholesalers, importers, retailers, business houses, and agents in Angola.

Angola Industrial and Business Directory. International Business Publications, USA. • $99.95 Individuals hardcover. Covers: Strategic and practical economic and business information. Entries include: Business contacts for conducting business activity in the country.

Ankara Chamber of Industry Export Catalogue. Ankara Chamber of Industry. • Irregular. $5. Covers: Manufacturing and exporting companies associated with the Ankara Chamber of Industry. Entries include: Names, addresses, and products.

Ann Arbor Area Chamber of Commerce--Business

Directory. Ann Arbor/Ypsilanti Regional Chamber. • Covers: Member companies in Ann Arbor, Michigan. Entries include: Name of firm, address, phone, number of employees, line of business, names and titles of key personnel, products or services.

Annuaire Bureautique--Informatique. Alphamedian Louis Johanet. • Annual. Covers: manufacturers and suppliers of office machinery in France.

Annuaire des Entreprises et Organismes d'Outre-Mer l'Afrique Noire Francophone. Rene Moreux et Cie. • Biennial. $715 payment must accompany order. Covers: about 10,000 national and multinational companies in or related to Benin, Burundi, Central African Empire, Chad, Congo, Gabon, Guinea, Ivory Coast, Malagasy Republic, Mali, Mauritania, Niger, Rwanda, Senegal, Togo, Cameroon, Upper Volta, Zaire, and the French overseas departments and territories. Includes banking and other financial institutions, chambers of commerce, government agencies, and associations. Entries include: Company name, address, capital, line of business, names and titles of key personnel, year established, products, branch offices, associated companies in France.

Annuaire National de Fournisseurs des Administrations Francaises. Editions le Fil d'Ariane. • Annual. Covers: Over 2,00 industrial firms and merchant and service companies which are the main suppliers to the French Civil Service. Entries include: Company name, address, phone, fax, telex number, data on clients.

Answering Bureaus Directory. InfoGroup Inc. • Annual. Number of listings: 5,102. Entries include: Name, address, phone, size of advertisement, name of owner or manager, number of employees, year first in "Yellow Pages." Compiled from telephone company "Yellow Pages," nationwide.

Antenna Industry Directory and Buyers Guide. Webcom Communications Corp. • $195 Individuals hardcopy. Covers: Over 2,000 antenna designers, manufacturers, distributors, installers, suppliers, consultants, government agencies and information sources worldwide. Entries include: Company name, address, phone, fax, email, website address, executive names and titles, year founded, sales, company description, and antenna types offered.

Arab-British Trade Directory. Arab-British Chamber of Commerce. • $6 Other countries additional copy. Covers: Over 5,000 UK and Arab companies from the manufacturing, trading, services, and financial sectors. Entries include: Contact details of companies from joint Arab-Foreign chambers around the world.

Area Development Sites & Facility Planning--Industrial Development Directory of Canada Issue. Halcyon Business Publications Inc. • Annual. $25. Publication includes: List of industrial development organizations at provincial and municipal levels. Entries include: Name, address, phone, and name and title of contact.

Argentina Company Handbook. Hoover's Inc. • Annual. $49.95. Covers: 32 of Argentina's major public companies. Database includes: Information on Argentina's economy, the securities market, the stock exchange, and the rules governing foreign investments in the Argentina capital markets. Entries include: Name, address, phone, fax, year established, stock ticker symbol, names and titles of key personnel, number of employees, number of stockholders, company history, financial data, names of major stockholders, affiliated companies.

Argentina Government and Business Contacts Handbook. International Business Publications, USA. • $99.95 Individuals hardcopy, E-book and CD-ROM. Covers: Strategic government and business information, export-import activity in the country, investment, business contacts and regulations.

Argentina Industrial and Business Directory. International Business Publications, USA. • Annual. $99.95 Individuals hardcover. Covers: Detailed information on investment, export-import business opportunities, foreign economic assistance projects, government and business contacts.

Arkansas Business Directory. InfoGroup Inc. • Annual. $450. Covers: 126,071 businesses in Arkanasas. Entries include: Company name, address, phone, number of employees, name of owner or manager, sales volume. Compiled from telephone company "Yellow Pages," statewide. All states covered (see separate entries).

Arkansas Export Directory. Arkansas Economic Development Commission. • Annual. Covers: Products produced by Arkansas firms who export or are seeking to develop export sales. Entries include: Company name, address, phone.

Arkansas Manufacturing Directory. Arkansas Industrial Development Foundation. • Annual. $75 pre-payment required. Covers: about 2,800 firms in Arkansas. Entries include: Company name, address, phone, names of principal executives, number of employees, list of products or services, Standard Industrial Classification (SIC) codes, whether company exports, name of parent company if firm is a subsidiary.

Armenia Government and Business Contacts Handbook. International Business Publications, USA. • $99.95 Individuals hardcopy, E-book and CD-ROM. Covers: Strategic government and business information, export-import activity in the country, investment, business contacts and regulations.

Asia: A Directory and Sourcebook. Euromonitor International Business Reference Div. • Irregular. $430. Publication includes: Regional overview, major companies, information sources statistical datafile. Entries include: Name of organization, firm, or agency, address, statistical data, purpose or service.

The Asia and Pacific Review: The Economic and Business Report. Kogan Page, Limited. • Covers: Key facts, indicators, country profile, business guide and directory for 60 countries in Asia and the Pacific. Database includes: Charts, tables and maps. Entries include: Heads of States, currencies, official languages, capital city, population, GNP, inflation, oil revenues, exports/imports, country profile, information for international visitors, name, address, phone of hotels, chambers of commerce, airlines, banks, government ministries and associations.

Asia Corporate Profile and National Finance. Dataline Asia-Pacific Ltd. • Annual. $70. Covers: about 1,900 companies in Asia; includes list of the 500 largest companies. Entries include: Company name, address, phone, fax, telex, names and titles of key personnel, number of employees, financial data.

Asia Pacific Autos Directory. Business Monitor International Ltd. • $975 Individuals CD. Covers: 1,612 top autos executives on 519 leading automotive companies from China, Hong Kong, India, Indonesia, Malaysia, Pakistan, Philippines, Singapore, Taiwan, Thailand, and Vietnam. Entries include: Parent company head offices; full company name and address; telephone, fax, email, and website address; senior contact personnel; full description of company activity; company profile; nationality; and ownership status and parentage.

Asia Pacific Food and Drink Directory. Business Monitor International Ltd. • $895 Individuals CD. Covers: 2,022 top food and drink executives on 688 leading food and drink companies from Asia Pacific. Entries include: Company name and address; phone, fax, email and website address; senior contact personnel; full description of company activity; local company profile; nationality; and ownership status and parentage.

Asia-Pacific International Business Directory of Importers. Coble International. • $455 print or CD-ROM. Covers: 32,000 importers from South Korea, Australia, Philippines, New Zealand, India, Vietnam, Sri Lanka, Japan, Kazakhstan, Malaysia, Pakistan, Singapore, Indonesia, Mauritius, South Pacific Islands, Mongolia, Hong Kong, Taiwan, Thailand, China, and Uzbekistan. Entries include: Name, address, phone, fax, primary contact person, list of products, e-mail addresses, and Web site.

Asia Pacific Oil and Gas Directory. Business Monitor International Ltd. • $895 Individuals. Covers: 1,329 top oil and gas executives on 445 leading oil and gas companies from Asia Pacific. Entries include: Company name and address; phone, fax, email and website address; senior contact personnel; full description of company activity; local company profile; nationality; and ownership status and parentage.

Asia Pacific Pharmaceuticals and Healthcare Directory. Business Monitor International Ltd. • $895 Individuals. Covers: 3,353 top pharmaceutical executives at 1,120 leading pharmaceutical companies from China, Hong Kong, India, Indonesia, Malaysia, the Philippines, Singapore, South Korea, Taiwan, Thailand and Vietnam. Entries include: Company name and address; phone, fax, email and website address; senior contact personnel; full description of company activity; local company profile; nationality; and ownership status and parentage.

Asia Pacific Telecommunications Directory. Business Monitor International Ltd. • $895 Individuals. Covers: 2,438 top telecommunications executives at 893 leading telecommunications companies from Asia Pacific. Entries include: company name and address; phone, fax, email and website address; senior contact personnel; full description of company activity; local company profile; nationality; and ownership status and parentage.

Asian and Australasian Companies: A Guide to Sources of Information. CBD Research Ltd. • $160 Individuals. Covers: Over 2,000 company information sources for the 69 countries in the Far East and Australasian organizations responsible for registering business enterprises; stock exchanges; credit reporting and business information services; publishers of business and finance publications. Entries include: Generally, company, agency, or organization name, address, phone, telex, date founded, type of company, method of selection. For publications--Title, English translation (if necessary), publisher name, address, phone, and telex; description of contents, date of publication or frequency, language, price, size.

Asian Business League of San Francisco Membership Directory. Asian Business League of San Francisco. • Includes contact information for both Asian-Pacific Americans and non-Asian Pacific Americans with an interest in expanding leadership skills.

Asian Company Handbook. Toyo Keizai Inc. • $65. Covers: Approximately 1,060 companies listed on the stock exchanges of Hong Kong, Indonesia, Malaysia, the Republic of Korea, Singapore, Taiwan, and Thailand. Entries include: Company name, address, phone, fax, geographical area served, financial data, subsidiary and branch names and locations, stock price information, description of product/service, stock price charts.

Asian Directory of Trade & Business Associations. Asia Pacific Infoserv. • $245 Individuals book only. Covers: Trade associations and service sectors in every Asia Pacific country. Entries include: Association name, address, telephone number, fax number, e-mail, year of establishment, President and General

Secretary, number of members, memberships of international associations, and field of activity.

Asian Finance Directory. Mead Ventures Inc. • $195. Covers: about 400 Asian financial companies, banks, securities firms, venture capitalists, and real estate financers in the United States. Entries include: Company name, address, phone, telex, fax, names and titles of key personnel, number of employees, geographical area served, financial data, local offices, subsidiaries or parent companies, description of services provided, and description of projects.

Assisted Living and Elder Care Directory. InfoGroup Inc. • Annual. Number of listings: 14,305. Entries include: Name, address, phone, size of advertisement, name of owner or manager, number of employees, year first in "Yellow Pages." Compiled from telephone company "Yellow Pages," nationwide.

Association for University Business and Economic Research--Membership Directory. Association for University Business and Economic Research. • Annual. $10. Covers: member institutions in the United States and abroad with centers, bureaus, departments, etc., concerned with business and economic research. Entries include: Name of bureau, center, etc., sponsoring institution name, address, phone, names and titles of director and staff, publications and frequency.

Association of Thai Industries--Industrial Directory. Business Company Ltd. • Biennial. $350. Covers: 827 manufacturers, wholesalers, and distributors in Thailand. Entries include: Company name, address, phone, telex, and names of directors and officials.

AT&T Easylink Services--Electronic Messaging Directory & Buyers Guide. AT&T National Toll-Free Directory. • Irregular. $30. Covers: about 200,000 AT&T customers with Easylink and Telex I/II numbers. Entries include: Company name, city, state, Telex I/II, or Easylink number and answerback.

Athens Area Chamber of Commerce Membership Directory. Athens Area Chamber of Commerce. • Lists member businesses in Athens, Georgia. Publication includes directory details for largest employers, retail centers, chamber member realtors and banks.

Atlanta Business Chronicle's Book of Lists. Metro Atlanta Chamber of Commerce. • $49.95 Individuals. Lists companies in the Atlanta business community, including sections on business and industry, business services, commercial real estate, education and human resources, finance, general interests, healthcare, hospitality and travel, marketing, residential real estate and technology sections. Entries include name, address, phone, fax, facts and figures, and detailed information.

Atlanta Larger Employers. Metro Atlanta Chamber of Commerce. • Biennial. $5 plus $2 shipping. Covers: Approximately 600 companies in the metropolitan Atlanta, Georgia, area that employ 300 or more. Entries include: Company name, address, phone, Standard Industrial Classification (SIC) code.

Australia Business Directory. INFOT Inc. • $64.60 Individuals. Covers: 96,347 companies, importers, and exporters from Australia. Entries include: Company name, email and website addresses, telephone and fax number, and business description.

Australia Business Law Handbook. International Business Publications, USA. • $99.95 Individuals hardcopy, e-book, CD-ROM. Covers: Basic information on business laws and legislations, export-import regulations, business climate and contacts.

Australia Government and Business Contacts Handbook. International Business Publications, USA. • $99.95 Individuals hardcopy, E-book and CD-ROM. Covers: Strategic government and business information, export-import activity in the country, investment, business contacts and regulations.

Australia Industrial and Business Directory. International Business Publications, USA. • Annual. $99.95 Individuals hardcover. Covers: Strategic industrial, investment, and business contacts for conducting export-import and investment activity in the country.

Australian Company Handbook. Hoover's Inc. • $49.95. Covers: 300 Australian companies listed on the All Ordinaries Index and 300 other leading Australian companies not included on the index. Entries include: Company name, address, phone, fax, description.

Australian Health and Medical Industry. APN News & Media Group Ltd. APN Business Information Group. • Annual. Covers: Australian companies involved in the medical and health industry and interested in exporting their products and services.

Australian Hospitality Directory. Associated Media Group. • Annual. Provides business information on transport, food service, entertainment, equipment and supplies, education and management, furniture, bedding, and lighting.

Australian Key Business Directory. Dun & Bradstreet (Australia) Proprietary Ltd. • Covers: Leading companies in Australia whose annual sales are $10 million and who have 500 or more employees. Entries include: Company name, address, phone, fax, telex, number of employees, import/export designation, primary and secondary Standard Industrial Classification (SIC) codes, sales volume.

Australian Newsagent & Stationer Buyer's Guide. Thorpe-Bowker. • Annual. $45. Covers: manufacturers and suppliers of office supplies in Australia; some foreign office supply manufacturers with their Australian agents; related organizations in Australia. Entries include: Manufacturer, supplier, agent, or organization name, address, phone.

Australian Public Companies Guide. Schwartz & Wilkinson Publishers PLC. • Annual. $395. Covers: 12,000 companies on the Australian Stock Exchange. Entries include: Company name, address, phone, telex, names of directors, financial data.

Australian Scientific and Laboratory Exports. Peter Isaacson Publications. • Annual. $80. Covers: Scientific and medical products and services available for export from Australia.

Australia's Top 100. Australian Stock Exchange Ltd. Exchange Centre. • Annual. $20 plus 10 dollars shipping. Covers: top 100 listed companies on the Australian Stock Exchange ranked by market capitalization. Entries include: Company name, address, phone, fax, telex, names and titles of key personnel, financial data, company history, description of products and activities.

Austria Industrial and Business Directory. International Business Publications, USA. • Annual. $99.95 Individuals hardcover. Covers: Detailed information on investment, export-import business opportunities, foreign economic assistance projects, government and business contacts.

Austrian Commercial Directory. Jupiter Verlagsgesellschaft mbH. • Annual. Covers: 120,000 Austrian industrial, trading, and service firms. Entries include: Company name, address, phone, fax, telex, products, names of owners, board members, directors, and other key personnel.

Automatic Merchandising Machine Operation Directory. InfoGroup Inc. • Annual. Number of listings: 11,954. Entries include: Name, address, phone, size of advertisement, name of owner or manager, number of employees, year first in "Yellow Pages." Compiled from telephone company "Yellow Pages," nationwide.

Automobile Parts Used & Rebuilt Directory. InfoGroup Inc. • Annual. Number of listings: 11,939. Entries include: Name, address, phone, size of advertisement, name of owner or manager, number of employees, year first in "Yellow Pages." Compiled from telephone company "Yellow Pages," nationwide.

Automobile Racing Directory. InfoGroup Inc. • Annual. Number of listings: 2,233. Entries include: Name, address, phone, size of advertisement, name of owner or manager, number of employees, year first in "Yellow Pages." Compiled from telephone company "Yellow Pages," nationwide.

Automobile Telephones Directory. InfoGroup Inc. • Annual. Number of listings: 16,202. Entries include: Name, address, phone, size of advertisement, name of owner or manager, number of employees, year first in "Yellow Pages." Compiled from telephone company "Yellow Pages," nationwide.

Automobile Window Tinting Directory. InfoGroup Inc. • Annual. Number of listings: 6,032. Entries include: Name, address, phone, size of advertisement, name of owner or manager, number of employees, year first in "Yellow Pages." Compiled from telephone company "Yellow Pages," nationwide.

Automotive Parts: Industry Sector Profile. Philippine-German Export Development Project Philippine Bureau of Export Trade Promotion. • Publication includes: Companies exporting automotive parts from the Philippines. Entries include: Company name, address, phone, fax, name and title of contact, type of business, year established, subsidiary and branch names and locations, financial data, number of employees, government registrations, professional memberships, bank references, supply capability, export experience, business plan. Principal content of publication is an overview of the business environment and automotive parts industry in the Philippines.

Awards Directory. InfoGroup Inc. • Annual. Number of listings: 7,623. Entries include: Name, address, phone, size of advertisement, name of owner or manager, number of employees, year first in "Yellow Pages." Compiled from telephone company "Yellow Pages," nationwide.

Azerbaijan Government and Business Contacts Handbook. International Business Publications, USA. • $99.95 Individuals hardcopy, E-book and CD-ROM. Covers: Strategic government and business information, export-import activity in the country, investment, business contacts and regulations.

Bahamas Chamber of Commerce--Annual Chamber Directory. Bahamas Chamber of Commerce. • Annual. $8. Entries include: name, address, phone, fax.

Bahrain Golden Key Directory. International Institute of Trade Relation Promotion, Trade Information Centre of Iran. • £100 Individuals. Covers: 4,879 companies in Bahrain. Entries include: Company name, address, telephone, fax, e-mail, products, services, Managing Director, and business activities.

Balconies Directory. InfoGroup Inc. • Annual. Number of listings: 2,199. Entries include: Name, address, phone, size of advertisement, name of owner or manager, number of employees, year first in "Yellow Pages." Compiled from telephone company "Yellow Pages," nationwide.

Balloons--Manned--Directory. InfoGroup Inc. • Annual. Number of listings: 604. Entries include: Name, address, phone, size of advertisement, name of owner or manager, number of employees, year first in "Yellow Pages." Compiled from telephone company "Yellow Pages," nationwide.

Baltimore Business Journal--Book of Lists. Baltimore Business Journal. • $60 print only. Covers: Major companies, foundations, government officials, utilities, newspapers, radio and television stations, airlines, hospitals, financial institutions, shopping centers, resorts, and prominent individuals in the Baltimore, Maryland area. Entries include: Company, organization, or individual name, address, phone, name and title of contact.

Bangladesh Government and Business Contacts Handbook. International Business Publications, USA. • $99.95 Individuals hardcopy, E-book and CD-ROM. Covers: Strategic government and business information, export-import activity in the country, investment, business contacts and regulations.

Bangladesh Industrial and Business Directory. International Business Publications, USA. • Annual. $99.95 Individuals hardcover. Covers: Strategic industrial, investment and business contacts for conducting export-import and investment activity in the country.

Bartercard National Directory. Bartercard International. • 3/year. Covers: 23,000 businesses in Australia and over 55,000 businesses around the world. Entries include: Detailed contact information.

Baseball Batting Ranges Directory. InfoGroup Inc. • Annual. Number of listings: 1,050. Entries include: Name, address, phone, size of advertisement, name of owner or manager, number of employees, year first in "Yellow Pages." Compiled from telephone company "Yellow Pages," nationwide.

The Basic Business Library. Greenwood Publishing Group Inc. • Lists current business resources and essays on topics in business librarianship.

Basic Guide to Exporting. Todd Publications. • Quadrennial. $20. Covers: Sources for aid in understanding foreign business practices, government regulations, taxes, and currency. Database includes: How to evaluate a product or service's overseas potential; how to make contacts and sell overseas; how to handle financing; and how to get paid.

Bay Area Employer Directory. James R. Albin. • Annual. $99.95. Covers: over 2,000 employers in the San Francisco Bay Area each having 100 or more employees; includes both private and government employers. Entries include: Firm name, address, phone, year established, type of business or activity, number of employees, sales, names and titles of local chief executive and personnel manager.

BDO Stoy Hayward Guide to Venture & Buy-Out Capital. BDO Stoy Hayward. • Annual. Covers: about 170 companies and agencies with funds available for new ventures. Entries include: Agency or company name, address, phone, description of services, financial data, funds available for venture and capital development.

Belarus Industrial and Business Directory. International Business Publications, USA. • Annual. $99.95 Individuals hardcover. Covers: Strategic industrial, investment and business contacts for conducting export-import and investment activity in the country.

Belfast Business Network. Century Newspapers Ltd. • $12.50. Covers: 13,500 business companies in Belfast. Entries include: Company name, address, phone, fax.

Belgium Industrial and Business Directory. International Business Publications, USA. • Annual. $99.95 Individuals hardcover. Covers: Detailed information on investment, export-import business opportunities, foreign economic assistance projects, government and business contacts.

Belgium-Luxembourg Chamber of Commerce in Hong Kong--Directory. Belgium-Luxembourg Chamber of Commerce in Hong Kong. • Covers: Member organizations involved in developing two-way trade between Belgium - Luxembourg and Hong Kong.

Benin Business Directory. Business Guide. • $150 download. Covers: 4,400 business listings including wholesalers, importers, retailers, business houses, and agents in Benin.

Bergano's Worldwide Register of Distributors. Bergano Book Co. • Irregular. $125. Covers: Approximately 4,000 importing firms and distributors; international coverage. Entries include: Company name, address, phone, fax, name and title of contact, year established, number of employees, goods imported.

Bermuda Business Directory. Bermuda Directories Ltd. • Covers: Listings of businesses in Bermuda including insurance, banking and legal services, local events, sightseeing, shopping, dining, and restaurants. Entries include: Company name, contact information, and e-mail address.

Best of British. Jordans Ltd. • Annual. $225 for four volume set. Covers: in four volumes, 20,000 leading companies in the United Kingdom; 5,000 per volume. Entries include: Company name, registered office address, chief executive, financial data for previous three years, business description.

Better Business Bureau--Directory & Consumer Guide. Better Business Bureau of Metropolitan Toronto. • Covers: about 7,000 member companies and over 500,000 homes in metropolitan Toronto, Ontario. Entries include: Company name, address, phone, products and services.

Bibliography: A Guide to Development Research Resources. Bentz Whaley Flessner. • Annual. Covers: Online services, Internet sites, listservs, and other resources of interest to business prospectors. Entries include: Company name, address, phone, fax, e-mail, Web address, name and title of contact, biographical data, description of services/projects.

Big Business in Metro Detroit. Detroit Regional Chamber. • Covers: More than 1,500 businesses and agencies which represent the largest employers in Metro Detroit, Michigan. Entries include: Company name, address, phone, SIC code, fax, product description, e-mail, and website.

Binley's Directory of NHS Estates & Facilities Management. Beachwood House Publishing Ltd. • Annual. £150 Individuals online version. Covers: 5,178 named personnel, located at 575 separate NHS sites. Entries include: Name, address, phone and fax numbers, email and website address.

Binley's Directory of NHS Management. Beachwood House Publishing Ltd. • Annual. £250 Individuals online version. Covers: Over 30,649 named personnel working at NHS organizations throughout the U.K. from chief executives and medical directors to estates managers, IT managers, and suppliers and purchasing managers. Database includes: Maps. Entries include: Organization name, address, NHS code, phone and fax numbers, email and website address.

Biomass Industry Profile Directory. DIANE Publishing Co. • $40 Individuals Paperback. Publication includes: Lists of all businesses and agencies involved in biomass energy in the Western United States.

Biometric Information Directory. Grey House Publishing. • $225 Individuals softcover. Covers: 700+ manufacturers and service providers in the biometrics industry, including finger, voice, face, hand, signature, iris, vein and palm identification systems. Includes information resources such as organizations, trade & educational associations, publications, conferences, trade shows and expositions worldwide. Entries include: Name, address, phone, fax, email, website, key executives, company size and a detailed, indexed description of their product line.

Birmingham and Solihull Business Guide and Directory. Kemps Publishing Ltd. • Annual. Covers: Chamber of Commerce listings in Birmingham and Solihull, Great Britain. Entries include: Name, address, phone, fax.

Birmingham Area Industrial Directory. Birmingham Regional Chamber of Commerce. • Biennial. $55 Members. Covers: about 2,800 manufacturing establishments in 21 counties of Alabama including maps. Features pinpointer county maps. Entries include: Company name, address, phone, name of principal executive, number of employees, product/service, SIC numbers.

Birmingham Chamber of Commerce--Prospect List. Birmingham Regional Chamber of Commerce. • Covers: 4,000 prospect companies for the Birmingham Chamber of Commerce. Entries include: Name, address, phone, fax.

BizEkon News--Soviet Business Directory. RIA Novosti Russian News & Information Agency. • Quarterly. Covers: over 2,500 companies in the Commonwealth of Independent States that have contracts abroad. Database includes: Company name, address, phone, fax, telex, names and titles of key personnel, banker, number of employees, production data, legal status, production program, list of products.

Black Enterprise--Black Engineering Firms Issue. Earl Graves Publishing Co. • Irregular. $3.50. Covers: U.S. companies owned or controlled by African Americans. Entries include: Name, address, phone.

Blinds-Venetian & Vertical- Retail Directory. InfoGroup Inc. • Annual. Number of listings: 8,244. Entries include: Name, address, phone, size of advertisement, name of owner or manager, number of employees, year first in "Yellow Pages." Compiled from telephone company "Yellow Pages," nationwide.

Blowing Rock Chamber of Commerce--Chamber Businesses. Blowing Rock Chamber of Commerce. • Annual. Listing of businesses in Blowing Rock, North Carolina.

Blue Book of the East--Asia, Africa, Middle East and Far East Directory. Indian Export Trade Journal. • Biennial. $750. Covers: Trade and industry in Asia, Africa, the Middle East and Far East.

Boat Appraisers Directory. InfoGroup Inc. • Annual. Number of listings: 17,331. Entries include: Name, address, phone, size of advertisement, name of owner or manager, number of employees, year first in "Yellow Pages." Compiled from telephone company "Yellow Pages," nationwide.

Bolivia--American Chamber of Commerce--Membership Directory. U.S. Chamber of Commerce. • Annual. Covers: American and Bolivian companies and individuals interested in the development of trade within and between the two countries. Entries include: For firms--Company name, address, phone, fax, telex, cable address, names and titles of key personnel, line of business, subsidiary and branch names and locations, locations of plants or branch offices, product/service information. For individuals--Name, title, affiliation, address. Plus details on Bolivia's investment climate, economic indicators, new land reform laws, and trade agreement obligations.

Bolivia Industrial and Business Directory. International Business Publications, USA. • Annual. $99.95 Individuals hardcover. Covers: Strategic industrial, investment and business contacts for conducting export-import and investment activity in the country.

The Book of Lists. • Annual. $125 Individuals Zip file download. Covers: Leading employers and private companies located in Orange County, California. Entries include: Company name, address, phone, names and titles of key personnel; product/service, financial data, number of employees.

Books--Publishing & Printing Directory. InfoGroup Inc. • Annual. Number of listings: 1,224. Entries include: Name, address, phone, size of advertisement, name of owner or manager, number of employees, year first in "Yellow Pages." Compiled from telephone company "Yellow Pages," nationwide.

Bowdens International Directory. Cision Canada Inc. • $275 Individuals per year (book). Covers daily and community newspapers, periodicals, radio and television broadcasting stations, and cable television systems; network television personnel, wire service offices, and other media in Canada.

BPIA Directory and Buyer's Guide. Independent Office Products and Furniture Dealers Association. • Annual. $100 payment must accompany order. Covers: Approximately 3,000 manufacturers, wholesalers, retailers, and sales and marketing representatives in the office products industry. Entries include: Company name, address, phone, principal executives, number of employees, branch stores, and products or services.

BPO, Call Center IT, Telecom, Computer Software & Hardware Companies Database, Directory of India. NIIR Project Consultancy Services. • $200 Individuals CD-ROM. Covers: BPO, call center, telecom, computer software and hardware companies in India. Entries include: Name of companies, address, city, pin code, phone, fax, 2,250 e-mail, 2,350 website and contact person with designation.

Braby's Durban Business Directory. A.C. Braby (Pty) Ltd. • Covers: Businesses in Durban, South Africa. Entries include: Contact information and maps.

Braby's Mpumalanga Business Directory. A.C. Braby (Pty) Ltd. • Annual. $75. Covers: Businesses in South Africa's Lowveld region. Entries include: Contact information.

Braby's Pretoria Business Directory. A.C. Braby (Pty) Ltd. • Covers: Businesses in Pretoria, South Africa. Entries include: Contact information and maps.

Braby's SADC Directory. A.C. Braby (Pty) Ltd. • Annual. $420 2 volume set. Covers: about 875,000 businesses in South Africa, Angola, Botswana, Lesotho, Malawi, Mauritius, Mozambique, Namibia, Swaziland, Tanzania, Zambia, Zimbabwe. Also includes foreign firms represented in South Africa and South African firms represented outside South Africa. Entries include: Company name, address, phone, telex, other details.

Braby's Zambia Trade Directory. A.C. Braby (Pty) Ltd. • Annual. $100. Covers: Businesses in Zambia. Database includes: Maps. Entries include: Contact information.

Brazil Business Directory. INFOT Inc. • Annual. $67.15 CD-ROM; additional $65 for MS Access format. Covers: 329,752 companies, from Brazil. Entries include: company name, email and website addresses, telephone and fax number, and business description.

Brazil Company Handbook. Hoover's Inc. • Annual. $74.95 Individuals tradepaper. Covers: About 72 of Brazil's largest public companies. Database includes: Profile of Brazil's economy, international trade, and investment climate; data on stock exchanges. Entries include: Company name, address, phone, fax, year established, stock ticker symbol, names and titles of key personnel, number of employees, number of stockholders, bank references, auditor, company history, financial data, markets and competition, raw materials used and sources, names of major stockholders, affiliated companies.

Brazil Dez Mil. Dun & Bradstreet Inc. • Biennial. Covers: 10,000 of the largest companies in Brazil. Entries include: Company name, address, phone, fax, telex, sales volume, Standard Industrial Classification (SIC) code, names and titles of key personnel, number of employees, import/export designation.

Brazil Industrial and Business Directory. International Business Publications, USA. • Annual. $99.95 Individuals hardcopy. Covers: Strategic industrial, investment and business contacts for conducting export-import and investment activity in the country.

Brazilian-American Who's Who. Brazilian-American Chamber of Commerce. • Irregular. $55. Covers: more than 1,300 firms, subsidiaries, and affiliates operating and/or having interests in both the United States and Brazil. Entries include: Company name, address, names and titles of key personnel.

Bremer Geschafts-Adressbuch. Carl Ed. Schuenemann KG. • Annual. Covers: about 20,000 businesses in the state of Bremen, Germany. Entries include: Company name, address, phone.

Brick Walkways & Patios Directory. InfoGroup Inc. • Annual. Number of listings: 13,770. Entries include: Name, address, phone, size of advertisement, name of owner or manager, number of employees, year first in "Yellow Pages." Compiled from telephone company "Yellow Pages," nationwide.

Bricker's International Directory: Long-Term University-Based Executive Programs. Peterson's. • Annual. Covers: Several hundred residential management development programs at academic institutions in the United States and abroad. Criteria for listing include that program must be residential, at least one week in length, in English, not introductory in content, and with emphasis on "strategic" issues and functions covering a wide range of organizations. Entries include: Name of program; sponsoring institution; location, dates, and duration of program; tuition fees; curriculum content; modes of instruction; size of classes; information on participants; living accommodations; faculty; special features; official contact.

Bridal Consultants Directory. InfoGroup Inc. • Annual. Number of listings: 6,167. Entries include: Name, address, phone, size of advertisement, name of owner or manager, number of employees, year first in "Yellow Pages." Compiled from telephone company "Yellow Pages," nationwide.

British Business Rankings. Dun & Bradstreet Inc. • Covers: 5,000 key British companies. Entries include: Company name, address, phone, telex, TWX, sales volume, number of employees, SIC codes.

British Firms in Germany. British Chamber of Commerce in Germany. • $200. Covers: companies in the Federal Republic of Germany which are subsidiaries of or otherwise affiliated with United Kingdom firms. Entries include: German company name and address, name and address of British affiliate or owner, code indicating products.

Brookline Business Directory. Brookline Chamber of Commerce. • Covers: Approximately 700 businesses in Brookline, Massachusetts; 30 area restaurants; schools, neighborhood associations, and other community resources. Entries include: For businesses and institutions--Company or organization name, address, phone. For restaurants--Name, address, phone, hours of operation, type of cuisine, credit cards accepted, etc.

Brunei Yearbook. Forward Media Sdn Bhd. • Information on Brunei companies, products and services. Entries include: Company name, address, phone and fax numbers, company's main business activities, names of top executives, e-mail and website addresses.

BTA Membership Directory. Business Technology Association. • Annual. $125 for members. Publication includes: List of 3,000 retailers and 500 manufacturers of typewriters, calculators, word processors, computers, dictation equipment, copying machines, mailing equipment, network equipment, and other office machines. Entries include: Company name, address, phone, fax, e-mail, website, names of executives; dealer listings include codes showing products handled.

Building & Loan Associations Directory. InfoGroup Inc. • Annual. Number of listings: 11,966. Entries include: Name, address, phone, size of advertisement, name of owner or manager, number of employees, year first in "Yellow Pages." Compiled from telephone company "Yellow Pages," nationwide.

Building Industry--Slovakia. I.S.M.C. Information Systems and Marketing Contacts Ltd. • $65. Covers: Companies in the building industry in the Slovak Republic and their suppliers.

Building Supply Home Centers--Buyers Guide Issue. Reed Elsevier Group plc Reed Business Information. • Annual. $30. Covers: U.S. manufacturers of building supply materials and products. Entries include: Company name and address, trade and brand names, list of products.

Bulgarian Trade Directory. Bulgarian Chamber of Commerce and Industry. • Annual. €35 Individuals EU member. Covers: 2,000 export/import companies and 120 economic committees and ministries in Bulgaria. Entries include: Name, address, phone, description of activities.

Burkina Faso Business Directory. Business Guide. • $150 download. Covers: 3,600 business listings including wholesalers, importers, retailers, business houses, and agents in Burkina Faso.

Burundi Business Directory. Business Guide. • $150 download. Covers: 2,300 business listings including wholesalers, importers, retailers, and business houses in Burundi.

Busconi's Worldwide Importers Directory. Small Business Publications. • Irregular. $100. Covers: Importers of Indian products, engineering goods, chemicals, pharmaceuticals, electronics, electrical goods, foodstuffs, handicrafts, jewelry, leather products, medicinal plants, spices, ready-made garments. Entries include: Contact details.

Business and Economics Research Directory. Routledge Reference. • £495 Individuals hardback. Covers: Approximately 1,500 institutes concerned with business and economics research worldwide. Entries include: Organization name, address, phone, fax, e-mail address, names and titles of key personnel, foundation date, description of activities, publications with frequencies.

Business and Financial News Media. Larriston Communications. • Annual. $99 book. Covers: over 300 daily newspapers with at least 50,000 in circulation and a business or finance correspondent; television stations and all-news radio stations in the largest 40 markets; periodicals of general or business and finance interest; syndicated business and financial columnists and newswriters; news and wire services; and free-lance writers whose specialties include business and financial topics. Entries include: Outlet name, address, phone, names and titles of contacts who cover business, finance, or economic news; news services used; circulation or audience figures.

Business and the Environment: A Resource Guide. Island Press-Center For Resource Economics. • Publication includes: List of approximately 185 business and environmental educators working to intergrate environmental issues into management research, education, and practices. Entries include: Name, address, phone, affiliation, publications, courses taught, research activity, education, employment.

Business Consultants Directory. InfoGroup Inc. • Annual. Number of listings: 12,750 (U.S. edition);

For publishers' addresses, refer to SOURCES CITED section at the back of the book.

1,667 (Canadian edition). Entries include: Company or individual name, address, and phone (including area code), size of advertisement, year first in "Yellow Pages," name of owner or manager, number of employees. Compiled from telephone company "Yellow Pages," nationwide.

Business Contacts in Finland. Larenco Oy. • Annual. Covers: Approximately 200 Finnish companies interested in foreign trade. Entries include: Name, address, phone, fax, list of products exported/imported, geographical area served.

Business Council of Fairfield County--Fairfield County Business Directory. Business Council of Fairfield County. • Covers: Approximately 2,100 non-retail companies and service firms in Fairfield County, Connecticut. Entries include: Company name, address, phone, fax, names & titles of key employees, website, company description, number of employees, annual sales, Standard Industrial Classification (SIC) code code(s).

Business Directory of Macedonia. Balkanika Publishing and Marketing Ltd. • Covers: Institutions and companies in the Republic of Macedonia. Entries include: Institution/company name, address, phone, fax, description, e-mail, and website.

Business Directory of South India: Andhra Pradesh, Karnataka, Kerala, Tamil Nadu. NIIR Project Consultancy Services. • $200 Individuals CD-ROM. Covers: 31,000 South India companies. Entries include: Contact person, profile, address, city, pin, state, phone, fax, e-mail (wherever available) and website (wherever available).

Business Directory of the Parry Sound Area. Parry Sound Area Chamber of Commerce. • Covers businesses in Parry Sound, Ontario, Canada. Entries include contact details.

Business Directory of United Kingdom. INFOT Inc. • $51 CD-ROM. Covers: 67,281 companies from United Kingdom, importers, and exporters. Entries include: Email and website addresses, telephone and fax number, and business titles and descriptions.

Business Education Index. Delta Pi Epsilon Inc. • Annual. $25. Publication includes: List of selected periodicals and yearbooks which have published articles on business education in the previous year. Entries include: Publication acronym, full name, editor, address. Principal content of publication is an index of articles and authors.

Business Europe: The Essential Guide to Who's Who and What's What in Europe. Macmillan Publishers Ltd. • $14.99. Covers: Businesses in Europe, encompassing service industries, wholesale and retail trades, professions, and trade unions. Entries include: Name, address, phone.

Business Forms & Systems (Wholesale) Directory. InfoGroup Inc. • Annual. Number of listings: 7,565. Entries include: Company name, address, phone (including area code), size of advertisement, year first in "Yellow Pages," name of owner or manager, number of employees. Compiled from telephone company "Yellow Pages," nationwide.

Business Forms, Labels & Systems--Who's Who of Manufacturers and Suppliers. North American Publishing Co. • Annual. Covers: More than 800 manufacturers of business forms, labels, and related products, and 500 suppliers of equipment and paper used to manufacture business forms. Entries include: Company name, address, phone, fax, toll-free number, company profile.

Business Foundation Book: General Trade Index & Business Guide--Poland. Business Foundation Company Ltd. • Annual. $90 plus $40.00 shipping. Covers: Approximately 3,500 Polish businesses and firms seeking foreign cooperation and trade with the West. Database includes: General information on Polish industry and trade, including the Polish economy, business and labor law, finance, taxation, import/export regulations, and laws pertaining to foreign investment and business. Entries include: Abbreviated trade names; firm name, address, phone, fax, telex; year established; name and title of contact and languages spoken; line of business; proposed fields of cooperation or goods sought; number of employees; financial data.

Business Guide Central--East Europe. Overseas-Post-Organisation. • Annual. $30. Publication includes: Businesses and organizations in the Baltic States, Bulgaria, Czech Republic, Hungary, Poland, Romania, Slovakia, Belarus, Moldova, Russia, and Ukraine. Entries include: Name, address, phone, telex. Principal content of publication is general business information for each country or region.

Business Hellas. Trade Publishing Resources. • Provides information on Greek companies covering all sectors of business and economy, manufacturing, and trade services.

Business Incubators of North America. National Business Incubation Association. • Biennial. $10 Members. Covers: approximately 800 facilities that house small businesses in the beginning stage of development; coverage includes Canada and Mexico. Entries include: Facility name, address, phone, fax, e-mail; name and title of contact; type of incubator; year opened; sponsorship; square footage; number of clients; incubator sponsor information.

Business Schools Directory. InfoGroup Inc. • Annual. Number of listings: 5,329. Entries include: Name, address, phone, size of advertisement, name of owner or manager, number of employees, year first in "Yellow Pages." Compiled from telephone company "Yellow Pages," nationwide.

Business Services Directory. German American Chamber of Commerce. • $10. Covers: Member firms which provide business, engineering, research, accounting, technical, marketing, and personnel management consulting services. Entries include: Company name, address, phone, fax, contact, number of employees, geographical location, foreign language capabilities, activities, history.

The Business Who's Who of Australia. Dun & Bradstreet (Australia) Proprietary Ltd. • Daily (eve.). $2,292.95 Individuals 2004 volume 1, price includes GST. Covers: In two volumes, over 40,029 business and associations. Volume 1 covers larger companies; volume 2 covers medium-sized companies. Database includes: Industry statistics. Entries include: Company name, address, names and locations of branches and names of subsidiary and associated companies, names and titles of directors and key personnel, number of employees, capital, annual sales, firms represented, banking firm, products and services, trade names, brief description of activities.

Businessdele. Helsinki Media. • Annual. Covers: Businesses, government offices, and public institutions in Finland. Entries include: Entity name, address, phone, telex number, cable address, product/service.

Businessman's Directory of the Republic of China. Taiwan Enterprise Press Ltd. • Annual. $75 airmail postpaid. Covers: Taiwan manufacturers, exporters, importers, and services.

The Businessman's Guide to Southern Africa. Safto. • Covers: Travel information for countries in South Africa, including, Botswana, Lesotho, Malawi, Mozambique, Namibia, South Africa, Swaziland, Zambia, and Zimbabwe. Entries include: Country name, climate, geography, industries and trade, finance, economy, excise and customs duties.

BusinessWeek Guide to the Best Business Schools. The McGraw-Hill Companies Inc. • Covers: The top 25 business schools and 25 runners-up, ranked by recent graduates and corporate recruiters. Entries include: School contact information; tips on GMAT prep courses; free application software.

Buyers Directory of the Former Soviet Union: Medical Equipment & Pharmaceutical Products. Flegon Press. • $55. Covers: Health authorities and other medical organizations of the former Soviet Union responsible for medical supplies in health-care institutions. Entries include: Name, address, phone.

Buyer's Guide for Morocco. Annuaire de l'Acheteur. • $100 Out of country. Covers: Commercial, industrial and service companies in Morocco. Entries include: Company name, address, phone, product/service, trade name.

The Buyouts Directory of Mergers & Acquisition Intermediaries. Securities Data Publishing. • Annual. $195. Covers: 600 U.S. and Canadian business brokers, as well as other merger and acquisition intermediaries. Database includes: Five articles explaining the role of acquisition intermediaries. Entries include: Company name, address, phone, profiles of commercial, merchant and investment banks.

Cabell's Directory of Publishing Opportunities in Economics and Finance. Cabell Publishing Inc. • Irregular. Covers: Over 860 scholarly periodicals in economics and finance. Entries include: Publication name, address, subject interests, editorial guidelines and style, submission procedures, audience and circulation of the publication, and reviewer acceptance rate data.

Cabell's Directory of Publishing Opportunities in Management. Cabell Publishing Inc. • Irregular. $244.95 Individuals. Covers: Over 1,180 scholarly periodicals in management. Entries include: Publication name, address, subject interests, editorial guidelines and style, submission procedures, audience and circulation of the publication, and reviewer acceptance rate data.

Cable Television Directory. InfoGroup Inc. • Annual. Number of listings: 9,002. Entries include: Name, address, phone, size of advertisement, name of owner or manager, number of employees, year first in "Yellow Pages." Compiled from telephone company "Yellow Pages," nationwide.

Cable TV Financial Databook. SNL Kagan. • Annual. $595. Publication includes: Lists of 100 top multiple system cable TV operators, 100 top single cable TV systems, top publicly-owned cable TV equipment suppliers, financial institutions active in cable TV financing, venture capitalists in the field, and appraisers, brokers, and consultants. Telcos in cable. High-Speed access rollouts, digital cable. Entries include: For leading operators--Name, total subscribers, homes passed, homes under franchise, plant miles, names of key personnel; ranked in separate lists by total revenues. For equipment suppliers--Name, product supplied, operating statistics from annual report. For single systems--Name, address, total subscribers, name of general manager. Principal content of publication is financial and statistical data on cable television companies, securities, accounting, etc.

California Bioscience Directory. San Diego Regional Chamber of Commerce. • $345 Members. Covers: 1,700 California companies and over 6,000 key managers in biotechnology, biomedical, pharmaceutical, bioresearch, and medical device firms.

California Business Register. Harris InfoSource. • Annual. $355 Individuals print. Profiles 56,750 top manufacturers, wholesalers, high-tech, and software companies in the state and lists the names and titles of more than 135,000 CEOs, owners, and key executives. Ninety-two percent of the companies are privately held. The listings include company name and address; telephone, fax, and toll-free numbers; Web site email addresses; number of employees; annual sales; products and services; SIC codes; export/import indicators; and primary bank.

California International Trade Register. Harris

InfoSource. • Annual. $155. Covers: 15,656 California international trade companies. Entries include: Company name, address, county, phone, fax, web site address (on CD-ROM only), number of employees, names and titles of key executives, plant size, year established, parent company, annual sales, import/export information, Standard Industrial Classification (SIC) code, and product description.

California Manufacturers Register: 2008 Edition. San Francisco Chamber of Commerce. • Annual. $259 Nonmembers (with book and Read only CD-ROM). Covers: 34,000 manufacturing firms which are members of the California Manufacturers Association. Entries include: Contact details.

Camara de Comercio Luso-Britanica Directory. British-Portuguese Chamber of Commerce. • Annual. $30 Nonmembers. Covers: Portuguese and United Kingdom economic, financial, and trade matters. Entries include: Organization name, address, phone, fax.

Cameras Directory--Retail Companies. InfoGroup Inc. • Annual. Number of listings: 5,303. Entries include: Name, address, phone, size of advertisement, name of owner or manager, number of employees, year first in "Yellow Pages." Compiled from telephone company "Yellow Pages," nationwide.

Cameroon Business Directory. Business Guide. • $150 download. Covers: 4,300 business listings including wholesalers, importers, retailers, business houses, and agents in Cameroon.

Cameroon Industrial and Business Directory. International Business Publications, USA. • $99.95 Individuals hardcover. Covers: Strategic and practical economic and business information. Entries include: Business contacts for conducting business activity in the country.

Canada Golden Key Directory. International Institute of Trade Relation Promotion, Trade Information Centre of Iran. • £60 Individuals. Covers: 8,000 companies in Canada. Entries include: Company name, address, telephone, fax, e-mail, products, services, Managing Director, and business activities.

Canada Government and Business Contacts Handbook. International Business Publications, USA. • $99.95 Individuals hardcopy, E-book and CD-ROM. Covers: Strategic government and business information, export-import activity in the country, investment, business contacts and regulations.

Canada Industrial and Business Directory. International Business Publications, USA. • Annual. $99.95 Individuals hardcopy. Covers: Detailed information on investment, export-import business opportunities, foreign economic assistance projects, government and business contacts.

Canadian National Business Directory. Todd Publications. • $250. Covers: 200,000 businesses, including tradeshows, exhibitions, and meetings. Database includes: Glossary of Internet terms; list of products and services online. Entries include: Address and phone number.

Canoes Directory. InfoGroup Inc. • Annual. Number of listings: 1,783. Entries include: Name, address, phone, size of advertisement, name of owner or manager, number of employees, year first in "Yellow Pages." Compiled from telephone company "Yellow Pages," nationwide.

Car Washing & Polishing Directory. InfoGroup Inc. • Annual. Number of listings: 18,030. Entries include: Name, address, phone, size of advertisement, name of owner or manager, number of employees, year first in "Yellow Pages." Compiled from telephone company "Yellow Pages," nationwide.

Card Security & Fraud Prevention Sourcebook. Thomson Financial Inc. • Annual. $245 Individuals. Covers: Credit card, debit card, and internet security products and services. Entries include: Company name, product name, profile.

Cards--Baseball Directory. InfoGroup Inc. • Annual. Number of listings: 4,538. Entries include: Name, address, phone, size of advertisement, name of owner or manager, number of employees, year first in "Yellow Pages." Compiled from telephone company "Yellow Pages," nationwide.

Careers and the MBA. Bob Adams Inc. • $12.95. Publication includes: List of over 200 companies that employ people with Master of Business Administration degrees. Database includes: Feature articles, career biographies, company profiles and industry reports for major industries. Entries include: For companies--Name, address, phone, name of contact person or office, description of company, possible positions open, and when to contact about them. For recruiters--Name, address.

Careers in Focus--Business. InfoBase Holdings Inc. • $35 Individuals hardcover. Covers: An overview of business, followed by a selection of jobs profiled in detail, including the nature of the job, earnings, prospects for employment, what kind of training and skills it requires, and sources for further information.

Caribbean Basin Investment and Business Guide. International Business Publications, USA. • $99.95 Individuals hardcopy, e-book, CD-ROM. Covers: Strategic and basic business information, export-import activity, regulations and industrial development, banking, government, and opportunities. Entries include: Important business contacts and business travel.

Caribbean Countries Mineral Industry Handbook. International Business Publications, USA. • $99.95 Individuals hardcopy, E-book and CD-ROM. Covers: strategic information and contacts on mining and mineral industry of the Caribbean countries.

The Caricom Exporter: A Comprehensive Buyers' Guide to Caribbean Products and Services. Caribbean Imprint Directory Service. • Annual. $50. Covers: 1,600 listings of Caribbean products and services. Database includes: A separate listing of service companies, maps, and facts-at-a-glance for each country. Entries include: Exporter name, address, telephone number, fax number, telex number, name of contact, product brand name, banker name, plant location, size of firm.

Carrageenan/Seaweeds: Industry Sector Profile. Philippine-German Export Development Project Philippine Bureau of Export Trade Promotion. • Publication includes: Companies exporting seaweed from the Philippines. Entries include: Company name, address, phone, fax, name and title of contact, type of business, year established, subsidiary and branch names and locations, financial data, number of employees, government registrations, professional memberships, bank references, supply capability, export experience, business plan. Principal content of publication is an overview of the business environment and seaweed industry in the Philippines.

Carry Out Food Service Directory. InfoGroup Inc. • Annual. Number of listings: 28,970. Entries include: Name, address, phone, size of advertisement, name of owner or manager, number of employees, year first in "Yellow Pages." Compiled from telephone company "Yellow Pages," nationwide.

Carson City Area Chamber of Commerce--Membership Business Directory. Carson City Area Chamber of Commerce. • Covers: Approximately 850 community profile and business listing member businesses in the greater Carson City, Nevada area. Entries include: Company name, address, phone, name and title of contact, products and services.

Cary Chamber of Commerce Member Directory. Cary Chamber of Commerce. • Covers chamber member businesses employing more than 100 people. Entries include company name, address, phone, fax, website, headquarters location, description of business.

Cash Registers and Supplies-Wholesale Directory. InfoGroup Inc. • Annual. Number of listings: 2,539. Entries include: Name, address, phone (including area code), size of advertisement, year first in "Yellow Pages," name of owner or manager, number of employees. Compiled from telephone company "Yellow Pages," nationwide.

Casinos Directory. InfoGroup Inc. • Annual. Number of listings: 1,792. Entries include: Name, address, phone, size of advertisement, name of owner or manager, number of employees, year first in "Yellow Pages." Compiled from telephone company "Yellow Pages," nationwide.

Cataloging Handbook H4/H8 Commercial and Government Entity. Defense Logistics Service Center U.S. Defense Logistics Agency. • Bimonthly. $40 per year (S/N 008-007-80003-5). Covers: about 92,000 companies, primarily manufacturers, that produce or maintain design control for products cataloged by federal government agencies. Entries include: Company name, address, five-digit Federal Supply Code for Manufacturers, and letter code indicating active or inactive status or other attributes; some listings include previous company name, previous location, or other information.

Catalogue of Firms in Slovakia. I.S.M.C. Information Systems and Marketing Contacts Ltd. • Annual. $65. Covers: Over 50,000 firms in Slovakia with a list of 50,000 goods. Entries include: Company contact information, economic data.

Catalogue of Firms in the Czech Republic. I.S.M.C. Information Systems and Marketing Contacts Ltd. • Annual. $84. Covers: Over 50,000 firms located in the Czech Republic, as well as a list of 30,000 goods. Entries include: Company contact information, economic data.

Catalogue of Manufacturers and Exporters. Durban Regional Chamber of Business. • Publication includes: Company listings of manufacturing members that do business with Africa in the following categories: basic metal, chemicals, clothing, food and beverages, furniture, hair care products, hardware, household, and investment, among others. Entries include: Company name, address, phone, fax. Principal content of publication is advertisements.

Catawba County Chamber of Commerce--Membership Directory/Relocation Guide. Catawba County Chamber of Commerce. • Covers: Chamber members. Entries include: Contact details.

Cats Boarding Directory. InfoGroup Inc. • Annual. Number of listings: 9,391. Entries include: Name, address, phone, size of advertisement, name of owner or manager, number of employees, year first in "Yellow Pages." Compiled from telephone company "Yellow Pages," nationwide.

CBI European Business Handbook. Kogan Page, Limited. • $35. Publication includes: A business directory of 27 countries in Europe. Principal content of publication is an analysis of economic, business, and industrial prospects in Europe.

CCBC--Membership Directory. Canada-China Business Council. • Annual. Covers: 200 Canadian companies in China. Entries include: Company profile.

CD-MAIL: The address database for mailings. Wer liefert was GmbH. • Semiannual. $1,200. Covers: Approximately 184,000 companies in Germany, Austria, Switzerland, Belgium, Luxembourg, and the Netherlands. Entries include: Name, address, phone, fax, names and titles of key personnel, description of product/service.

Central Africa Business Directory. A.C. Braby (Pty) Ltd. • Annual. $35. Covers: Businesses in Botswana, Lesotho, Mauritius, Malawi, Mozambique, Reunion,

For publishers' addresses, refer to SOURCES CITED section at the back of the book.

Seychelles, South West Africa, Swaziland, Zambia, and Zimbabwe. Entries include: Company name, address, phone, type of business.

Chad Business Directory. Business Guide. • $150 download. Covers: 3,600 business listings including wholesalers, importers, retailers, business houses, and agents in Chad.

Chamber of Commerce of Hawaii--Business Networking Directory. Chamber of Commerce of Hawaii. • Covers: Approximately 2,000 member businesses in Hawaii; approximately 20 associate regional and ethnic chambers of commerce and affiliate organizations. Entries include: Firm name; address; phone; e-mail; website; name, and title of key contact.

Chamber of Commerce of the Bellmores Business and Professional Directory. Chamber of Commerce of the Bellmores. • Covers: All current members.

Chamber South Business Directory. Image Factory. • Covers: about 4,400 member businesses, organizations, and other community resources in South Dade County, Florida. Entries include: Company name, address, phone, contact name and fax.

Charter Boats Directory. InfoGroup Inc. • Annual. Number of listings: 5,435. Entries include: Name, address, phone, size of advertisement, name of owner or manager, number of employees, year first in "Yellow Pages." Compiled from telephone company "Yellow Pages," nationwide.

Chemicals, Plastics & Rubber Yearbook. George Warman Publications Ltd. • Biennial. $45. Covers: Chemical, plastics and rubber products, manufacturers, associations, and colleges/universities in South Africa. Entries include: Company name, address, phone, brand name, specifications, statistics, services, suppliers of machinery and instrumentation.

Chicago Area Business Directory. InfoGroup Inc. • Annual. $495. Number of listings: 314,000. Entries include: Company name, address, phone, number of employees, name of owner or manager, annual sales. Compiled from telephone company "Yellow Pages," statewide.

Child Therapists Directory. InfoGroup Inc. • Annual. Number of listings: 41,340. Entries include: Name, address, phone, size of advertisement, name of owner or manager, number of employees, year first in "Yellow Pages." Compiled from telephone company "Yellow Pages," nationwide.

Chile Industrial and Business Directory. International Business Publications, USA. • Annual. $99.95 Individuals hardcopy, e-book, CD-ROM. Covers: Strategic industrial, investment and business contacts for conducting export-import and investment activity in the country.

Chile Investment and Business Guide. International Business Publications, USA. • $99.95 Individuals hardcopy, e-book, CD-ROM. Covers: Strategic information on economy, export-import, business and investment climate, regulations and industrial development, banking, and government. Entries include: Important business contacts and business travel.

China and Venture Capital & Private Equity Directory 500. Zero2IPO. • Annual. $455 Individuals. Covers: 600 institutions specializing in venture capital and private equity investment in China. Entries include: Company contact information, executive team, criteria for investment, cases of investment, and amount of capital under the management.

China Business Directory. China Business Information Center. • Annual. $239. More than 25,000 companies in the People's Republic of China, excluding Taiwan and Hong Kong, with assets over $1.5 million.

China Business Guide. American Chamber of Commerce in Hong Kong. • $40 Individuals. Covers: Companies engaged in business and trade in China. Database includes: Statistics, charts.

The China Commercial Relations Directory. American Chamber of Commerce in Hong Kong. • Biennial. $215 Nonmembers. Covers: Approximately 230 top China trade and service companies in Hong Kong; 115 companies in the PRC. Entries include: Addresses, names and titles of key personnel.

China Investment and Business Guide. International Business Publications, USA. • $99.95 Individuals hardcopy, e-book, CD-ROM. Covers: Basic information on economy, export-import and investment climate, regulations, industrial development, opportunities, banking, and government. Entries include: Important business contacts and business travel.

China Investment Atlas. American Chamber of Commerce in Hong Kong. • $622 Nonmembers. Covers: 600 of China's leading listed companies. Database includes: Charts.

China Logistics Directory. SinoMedia Ltd. • $80 Individuals book. Covers: 2,300 logistics companies operating in China across 12 industry sectors including airlines, airport, harbor & station operators, associations & consultants, construction companies, express forwarders, IT resources, land transportation, logistics equipment suppliers, logistics industrial parks, logistics services (custom brokers, air carriers and service companies), non-vessel operating common carriers, shipping companies, warehousing, third party logistics & supply chain solution. Entries include: English and Chinese names, address, headquarters location, phone and faxes, emails, key contact individuals, website.

China Product Handbook. Chis Info-Consultants Company Ltd. • $300 Individuals. Covers: 20,000 famous enterprises in China, including machinery, electric, electronic, light, textile, chemical, and pharmaceutical industries. Entries include: Enterprise name, address, phone, fax, director, major products.

China Stock Directory. China Economic Review. • $75 Individuals. Covers: 1,800 mainland-listed companies on the Shanghai and Shenzhen markets. Publication includes: Information about a company history, business operations, share price range, shareholders, key executives, contact details, complete financials top shareholders, their share types and percentage stakes.

Chinese Business in America. Caravel Inc. • Annual. $88 Individuals. Publication includes: Approximately 2,900 major ethnic Chinese enterprises in the U.S. Entries include: Contact name, address, phone, fax, websites, products/services imported/exported. Principal content of publication is is a how-to on establishing a new business in the U. S; marketing and sourcing in the U.S.

Cinemas Directory. InfoGroup Inc. • Annual. Number of listings: 9,544. Entries include: Name, address, phone, size of advertisement, name of owner or manager, number of employees, year first in "Yellow Pages." Compiled from telephone company "Yellow Pages," nationwide.

CINFOLINK Directory of Information Services and the Internet in China. CINFOLINK Services. • Biennial. $20 U.S. plus airmail postage within North America $2.50. Covers: nearly 400 electronic databases and information networks, approximately 225 related publication and information sources (including associations, research institutes of the Chinese Academy of Sciences, universities and colleges, and libraries), and 150 current Internet sources in China and Hong Kong. Entries include: For database services--Name, description, type of data, language, size, updating frequency, timespan; producer name and address; contact name, phone, fax; other formats, subject(s), status, price, etc. For publication sources--Name, address, phone, fax, titles produced, description.

Civil Defense Agencies Directory. InfoGroup Inc. • Annual. Number of listings: 1,516. Entries include: Name, address, phone, size of advertisement, name of owner or manager, number of employees, year first in "Yellow Pages." Compiled from telephone company "Yellow Pages," nationwide.

CLA Business Directory. Country Land and Business Association. • Covers: 250 business organizations, owners of land, and properties in rural England and Wales. Entries include: Company name, address, contact information, and e-mail.

Classified Business Directory of the State of Connecticut: Buyer's Blue Book. Connecticut Directory Company Inc. • Annual. $66.95. Covers: manufacturers, banks, schools, service companies, distributors, wholesalers, restaurants, and hotels in Connecticut and surrounding states. All listings are paid. Entries include: Company, name, address, phone. No sales in Connecticut except to libraries.

Classified Directory of Products & Services. SMC Business Councils. • Biennial. Covers: over 5,000 small business concerns in central and western Pennsylvania. Entries include: Company name, address, phone, e-mail address, URL, contact name, description of products or services provided, Standard Industrial Classification (SIC) code.

Cleaning-House and Office-Directory. InfoGroup Inc. • Annual. Number of listings: 37,431. Entries include: Name, address, phone, size of advertisement, name of owner or manager, number of employees, year first in "Yellow Pages." Compiled from telephone company "Yellow Pages," nationwide.

Clothes & Accessories (Women) Wholesale Directory. InfoGroup Inc. • Annual. Number of listings: 4,468. Entries include: Name, address, phone, size of advertisement, name of owner or manager, number of employees, year first in "Yellow Pages." Compiled from telephone company "Yellow Pages," nationwide.

Co-op America's National Green Pages: A Directory of Products and Services for People and the Planet. Green America. • Annual. Covers: 3,000 businesses and nonprofit organizations in the U.S. that produce environmentally benign products such as non-toxic household products, plant based paints, cruelty free body care products, organic foods, and energy saving devices. Also companies that offer socially responsible financial services. Database includes: List of producers of home-based crafts businesses and Native American-made products. Entries include: Company or organization name, address, phone, product/service, e-mail and web addresses.

Coal Preparation Directory & Handbook. • Annual. $95 Individuals Softcover. Covers: Suppliers and manufacturers of coal preparation equipment and services in the U.S.

Coalition for Minority Business Development Resource Directory. Indianapolis Chamber of Commerce. • Annual. $25 Nonmembers. Covers: Agencies and organizations in Indiana devoted to aiding minority-owned businesses and entrepreneurs. Entries include: Organization name, address, phone.

Coffee Shops Directory. InfoGroup Inc. • Annual. Number of listings: 7,515. Entries include: Name, address, phone, size of advertisement, name of owner or manager, number of employees, year first in "Yellow Pages." Compiled from telephone company "Yellow Pages," nationwide.

Collections Agency Directory. InfoGroup Inc. • Annual. Number of listings: 7,183. Entries include: Name, address, phone, size of advertisement, name of owner or manager, number of employees, year first in "Yellow Pages." Compiled from telephone company "Yellow Pages," nationwide.

Colombia Government and Business Contacts Handbook. International Business Publications, USA. • $99.95 Individuals hardcopy, E-book and CD-ROM. Covers: Strategic government and business information, export-import activity in the country, investment, business contacts and regulations.

Colombian Business Guide. Asesorias Finanzas Ltda. • Annual. $30. Covers: Colombia businesses, foreign investment, import and export credit, main imports, export products, chambers of commerce, mining, livestock, and Colombian enterprise abroad.

Colombian Exportable Offer. The Export Promotion Fund, Proexpo. • Covers: Manufacturers, distributors, and wholesalers in Colombia. Entries include: Contact information.

Commerce Directory of Costa Rica. Mercadeo Profesional, S.A. • Annual. Covers: Member businesses and non-members of Chamber of Commerce of Costa Rica.

Commercial and Industrial Directory. Impresos Litograficos de Centro America. • Annual. $15. Covers: Commercial and industrial manufacturers, wholesalers, and distributors in El Salvador. Entries include: Company name, address, phone, telex, names of directors, type of company.

Commercial and Industrial Directory of Switzerland. Mosse Adress AG. • Annual. $901 Individuals. Covers: 300,000 industrial, trade, and export businesses and services in Switzerland. Entries include: Company name, address, phone.

Commercial & Industrial Register of Southern Africa. A.C. Braby (Pty) Ltd. • Annual. $120 payment must accompany order. Covers: businesses in southern Africa. Database includes: Maps, list of PO Box renters. Entries include: Company name, address, phone.

Commercial Bar Association Directory. Wiley Chancery. • Annual. $25. Covers: Over 700 barristers in the U.K. specializing in corporate and commercial law; includes chamber and individual members. Entries include: Chamber name, address, phone, fax, principal fields of work; associated barristers, with name, date of birth, date of call, Queen's counsel, inn, academic and professional qualifications, pubications, languages spoken.

Company Handbook--Hong Kong. Reference Press Inc. • Semiannual. $44.95 per issue, plus $3.50 shipping. Covers: about 400 companies in Hong Kong; 200 are profiled in detail. Entries include: Company name, address, phone, fax, description, major shareholders and officers, financial data; detailed entries include financial data for previous five years, commentary on recent performance and trends, and share prices for the previous year. Published in Hong Kong by Corporate International Ltd.

Company Handbook Spain: The Maxwell Espinosa Shareholders Directory. S.p.A. • Annual. $84.95 plus $3.50 shipping. Covers: 2,000 corporations in Spain. Entries include: Company name, address, phone, fax, names and titles of key personnel, major shareholders, line of business, sales for previous year and preceding four years, number of employees, names of advertising agency, attorneys, auditors, banks, and investment relations director.

Company Information. Bowker Ltd. • Biennial. $199 plus $15.00 shipping. Covers: Sources of company information in the United Kingdom, including print, online, and CD-ROM data sources, and organizations.

Company Profiles for Students. Cengage Learning Inc. • $338 print. Covers approximately 280 most studied companies. Entries include company logos, illustrations, ticker symbol, market share, etc.

Comprehensive Directory of Mexican Importers. Todd Publications. • Biennial. $75. Covers: More than 2,700 Mexican importers.

Computers & Office Equipment Importers & Buyers Directory. BD International. • $132 Individuals. Covers: 8,000 importers, buyers, wholesalers, and distributors of computers and office equipment. Entries include: Name, address, phone, fax, contact person, nature of business, website, and e-mail.

Computers-Dealers (Used) Directory. InfoGroup Inc. • Annual. Number of listings: 2,336. Entries include: Name, address, phone, size of advertisement, name of owner or manager, number of employees, year first in "Yellow Pages." Compiled from telephone company "Yellow Pages," nationwide.

Confederation of Zimbabwe Industries: Register & Buyers Guide--Brand Names, Manufacturers, Products. Thomson Publications. • Annual. $115 please inquire. Covers: Commercial enterprises and members of the Confederation of Zimbabwe Industries. Entries include: Company name, address, phone, member name, address.

Congo Business Directory. Business Guide. • $150 download. Covers: 1,600 business listings including wholesalers, importers, retailers, business houses, and agents in Congo.

Connecticut Investment and Business Guide. International Business Publications, USA. • $99.95 Individuals. Covers: Strategic and business information, contacts, regulations and more.

Construction Consultants Directory. InfoGroup Inc. • Annual. Number of listings: 734. Entries include: Name, address, phone, size of advertisement, name of owner or manager, number of employees, year first in "Yellow Pages." Compiled from telephone company "Yellow Pages," nationwide.

Consultants (Tax) Directory. InfoGroup Inc. • Annual. Number of listings: 63,898. Entries include: Name, address, phone, size of advertisement, name of owner or manager, number of employees, year first in "Yellow Pages." Compiled from telephone company "Yellow Pages," nationwide.

Contact Peru. American Chamber of Commerce of Peru. • Quarterly. Covers: Member companies and American Chambers of Commerce in Latin America. Entries include: Company name, address, phone, telex.

Contacts for Kuwaiti Contracting. International Executive Reports. • $195. Covers: business contacts in Kuwait, including Kuwaiti federal and state government agencies; U.S. Defense Reconstruction Assistance Office; Kuwaiti importers, agents, banks, airlines, and hotels; and U.S., British, and German firms actively doing business in Kuwait. Entries include: Name, address.

Contemporary Entrepreneurs. Omnigraphics Inc. • Irregular. $95. Covers: Approximately 74 companies often cited as successful and the entrepreneurs who founded them. Entries include: Entrepreneur's name, year of birth, marital status, number of children, type of venture; venture's address, phone, founding, incorporation, revenues, number of employees, original investment, net worth; text describing the history, growth, and vision of the company and entrepreneurial lessons.

Contra Costa County Business Directory. Rich's Business Directories Inc. • $199 Individuals online. Entries include: Company name, address, phone, fax, year established, branch or headquarters, SIC code, and product type.

Convalescent Homes Directory. InfoGroup Inc. • Annual. Number of listings: 2,178. Entries include: Name, address, phone, size of advertisement, name of owner or manager, number of employees, year first in "Yellow Pages." Compiled from telephone company "Yellow Pages," nationwide.

Copying & Duplicating Machine & Supplies Directory. InfoGroup Inc. • Annual. Number of listings: 10,350. Entries include: Name, address, phone (including area code), size of advertisement, year first in "Yellow Pages." Coding indicates brands carried, specialties, or franchises held. Franchise editions also available. Compiled from telephone company "Yellow Pages," nationwide.

Copying & Duplicating Service Directory. InfoGroup Inc. • Annual. Number of listings: 20,946. Entries include: Company name, address, phone (including area code), size of advertisement, year first in "Yellow Pages," name of owner or manager, number of employees. Compiled from telephone company "Yellow Pages," nationwide.

Corporate Affiliations. LexisNexis. • Annual. $2,395 8 volume set. Covers: Business and financial information on approximately 3,800 U.S. parent companies and 44,500 subsidiaries, divisions, and affiliates worldwide, as well as 140,000 key executives. Entries include: Sales, assets, liabilities, ownership percentage.

Corporate Affiliations Plus. LexisNexis. • Quarterly. $2,595 Individuals 12 month single-user license (database). CD-ROM. Covers corporate statistics and current financial information on over 30,000 domestic and foreign parent companies and their 145,000 subsidiaries, as well as 306,000 key executives. Entries include: Sales, assets, liabilities, ownership percentage.

The Corporate Directory of U.S. Public Companies. Grey House Publishing. • Annual. Covers: More than 11,000 publicly held corporations traded on the New York or American exchanges, NASDAQ, or other over-the-counter markets. Includes foreign companies filing American Depositary Receipts. Database includes: List of acronyms and common terms. Entries include: Company name, address, phone, stock data, business description, primary and additional Standard Industrial Classification (SIC) code, major subsidiaries, officers, directors, owners, and financial data.

Corporate Finance Sourcebook: The Guide to Major Capital Investment Sources and Related Financial Services. LexisNexis. • Annual. $695 Individuals list price. Covers: Securities research analysts; major private lenders; investment banking firms; commercial banks; United States-based foreign banks; commercial finance firms; leasing companies; foreign investment bankers in the United States; pension managers; banks that offer master trusts; cash managers; business insurance brokers; business real estate specialists; lists about 3,500 firms; 14,500 key financial experts. Entries include: All entries include firm name, address, phone, e-mail, and names and titles of officers, contacts, or specialists in corporate finance. Additional details are given as appropriate, including names of major clients, number of companies served, services, total assets, branch locations, years in business.

Corporate 500: Directory of Corporate Philanthropy. Public Management Institute. • Annual. $375 plus $10.00 shipping. Covers: 554 major corporations with philanthropic programs. Entries include: Corporation name, corporate foundation name (if applicable), address, philanthropic interests and priorities, policy statement, contribution committee members, financial profile, activities eligible for funding, contact person, sample grants, application procedures, analysis of giving patterns.

Corporate Giving Directory. Information Today, Inc. • Annual. $699.50 Individuals softbound; plus $20 shipping and handling. Covers: Top 1,000 major corporation- and company-sponsored foundations and direct-giving programs. Database includes: Apendix to abridged entries of more than 2,000 additional funders. Entries include: Giving program's sponsoring company name, address, phone, fax, e-mail, website; names and biographies of living officers, and contact person; grants data, including types, average amounts, sample grants; application procedures; analysis of giving priorities; and information on the company, including products, Fortune rank, sales, ticker symbol/stock exchange information, operating locations, number of employees, information on employee-matching gifts (including restrictions and ratio), and nonmonetary support.

Corporate Giving Yellow Pages: Guide to Corporate Giving Contacts. Taft Group. • $99. Covers: more than 3,500 corporate contact persons with information on corporate charitable giving. Entries include: Company name, address, phone, fax, name and title of contact, name of company foundation (if any).

The Corporate Handbook. Riddell Information Services Proprietary Ltd. • Annual. $145. Covers: over 400 corporate service agencies, consultancies, and suppliers in Australia. Database includes: Articles on how to identify and select appropriate companies; overviews of industry categories. Entries include: Company name, address, phone, fax, names and titles of key personnel, qualifications and experience, description of services, recent clients and projects, fee structure information, financial data.

Corporate Report Fact Book. City Media Inc. • Annual. $147. Covers: about 320 public corporations in the Ninth Federal Reserve District (Minnesota, North and South Dakota, Montana, upper Michigan, and northwestern Wisconsin) having stock actively traded; 1,550 privately owned companies with over 50 employees; 650 regional operations with over 50 employees, 115 non-profit corporations; 600 top executives in businesses of the upper Midwest. Entries include: For public companies--Company name, address, phone, fax; names of officers, directors, and major shareholders; profile, two-year balance sheet and five-year earnings history; recent events, recent four quarters results; number of employees, number of stockholders; general counsel, auditors; state and year of incorporation, transfer agent and registrar, subsidiaries, SIC codes. For private and nonprofit companies and regional operations--Name, address, phone, fax, names of principal executives; revenue (if provided), description of business, number of employees, corporate affiliations, year established. For top executives--Name, title, affiliation, office address and phone, date and place of birth; personal, education, and career data; awards, activities, memberships.

Cosmetology Schools Directory. InfoGroup Inc. • Annual. Number of listings: 2,069. Entries include: Name, address, phone, size of advertisement, name of owner or manager, number of employees, year first in "Yellow Pages." Compiled from telephone company "Yellow Pages," nationwide.

Costume Jewelry: Industry Sector Profile. Philippine-German Export Development Project Philippine Bureau of Export Trade Promotion. • Publication includes: Companies exporting costume jewelry from the Philippines. Entries include: Company name, address, phone, fax, name and title of contact, type of business, year established, subsidiary and branch names and locations, financial data, number of employees, government registrations, professional memberships, bank references, supply capability, export experience, business plan. Principal content of publication is an overview of the business environment and costume jewelry industry in the Philippines.

Cotton Council International Buyers' Guide. Cotton Council International. • Covers: Exporters of U.S. raw cotton. Entries include: Company name, addresses of exporting companies, production and ginning seasons, and official U.S. cotton standards, packaging, and transportation data.

Craighead's International Business, Travel, and Relocation Guide to 84 Countries. Cengage Learning Inc. • $775 Individuals hardcover. Publication includes: List of Web sites for children's organizations, spousal employment, telephones/ telecommunications, visa requirements, and more. Principal content of publication is detailed information on relocating or traveling to foreign countries.

Crawford's Directory of City Connections. AP Information Services Ltd. • $325. Covers: Approximately 3,500 private and public sector companies in the U.K., as well as advisers to the financial sector, including stockholders, solicitors, auditors, and insurance advisers. Entries include: Name, address, phone, names and titles of key personnel.

Crescenta Valley Chamber of Commerce Business Directory. Crescenta Valley Chamber of Commerce. • Covers: Member companies and organizations in La Crescenta, La Canada, Montrose, Sunland, and Tujunga, California. Entries include: Company or organization name, address, phone.

Croner's A-Z of Business Information Sources. Wolters Kluwer Ltd. • Annual. $71.50 includes first year's updates & shipping. Covers: Organizations, publications, and other sources of business information in the United Kingdom from abrasives to zinc and the aerospace industry to wire products. Entries include: Name, address, phone, telex, contact name, brief description.

CSR Professional Services Directory. Dunstan Publishing. • $65 Individuals. Covers: 675 service providers including consultants, academic institutions, rating agencies, ethical auditors, training providers, and research organizations. Entries include: Contact information and services they provide.

Current Directory of International Chambers of Commerce and Industry. Current Pacific Ltd. • $150 Individuals. Covers: More than 4,000 international chambers of commerce and industry selected from major cities in more than 165 countries in territories in the world.

Cyberstocks: An Investors Guide to Internet Companies. Hoover's Inc. • $24.95. Covers: Companies involved in the Internet industry. Entries include: Name, address, phone.

Czech Republic Government and Business Contacts Handbook: Trade, Investment & Business Development Contacts. International Business Publications, USA. • Annual. $99.95 Individuals hardcopy, E-book and CD-ROM. Covers: Strategic government and business information, export-import activity in the country, investment, business contacts and regulations.

D & B Directory of Service Companies. Dun & Bradstreet Inc. • Annual. Covers: 50,000 U.S. businesses in the service sector, private and public, including accounting, auditing and bookkeeping, advertising and public relations, architecture and engineering, consumer services, executive search, health, hospitality, management consulting, motion pictures, repair, research, social services, and law. Entries include: DUNS number, company name, address, phone, year started, state of incorporation, sales volume, number of employees, primary and secondary Standard Industrial Classification (SIC) codes, names and titles of key personnel, principal bank, stock exchange symbol, accounting firm, line of business, trade name.

D & B Europa Directory. Dun & Bradstreet Inc. • Annual. $650 commercial. Covers: more than 62,000 leading manufacturers, distributors, finance, and service companies in 20 European countries. Database includes: Ranking of top 5,000 companies based on sales and number of employees,top 500 banks based on assets, top companies by main business activity. Entries include: DUNS number, company name, address, phone, fax, year established, line of business, primary and secondary Standard Industrial Classification (SIC) codes, company number (may be the V.A.T. number needed for export sales invoices), import/export designation, bankers' details, percentage of annual sales which go to export.

D & B Million Dollar Directory. Dun & Bradstreet Inc. • Annual. Covers 1,600,000 public and private businesses with either a net worth of $500,000 or more, 250 or more employees at that location, or $25,000,000 or more in sales volume; includes industrial corporations, utilities, transportation companies, bank and trust companies, stock brokers, mutual and stock insurance companies, wholesalers, retailers, and domestic subsidiaries of foreign corporations.

D & B Million Dollar Directory--Top 50,000 Companies. Dun & Bradstreet Inc. • Annual. $500 commercially. 50,000 top corporations, utilities, transportation companies, bank and trust companies, stock brokers, mutual and stock insurance companies, wholesalers, retailers, and domestic subsidiaries of foreign corporations; business must have 250 or more employees at main location, or have at least $25 million in sales volume.

Dafsaliens Database of Ownership Links--France. Dafsaliens. • Monthly. Covers: More than 120,000 companies worldwide. Entries include: Company names, registration number, form of incorporation, addresses, telephone, fax, description of business, shareholders subsidiaries and cross holdings, and financial data. CD-ROM includes historical data to trace changing structures and current and former directors and officers.

Dakhiliya Region Tourist Guide. Oman Chamber of Commerce and Industry. • Provides information and data on tourist sites, locations, services in Dakhiliya Region. Entries include: Names and addresses of travel and tourism organizations and companies.

Dalton's Baltimore/Washington Metropolitan Directory of Business/Industry. Dalton Directory. • Covers: over 8,500 companies in the Baltimore and Washington, D.C. metropolitan area, including manufacturers, law firms, hospitals, hotels, schools and colleges, accounting firms, etc. Entries include: Company name, address, phone, fax, names and titles of key personnel, number of employees, Standard Industrial Classification (SIC) code, product/service.

Das Grosse Einkaufs 1x1 der Deutschen Wirtschaft: Band 3: Deutsche Wirtschafts-Standorte. Deutscher Adressbuch-Verlag fur Wirtschaft und Verkehr GmbH. • Annual. $200 prepaid. Covers: federal and state govermental agencies of the Federal Republic of Germany; approximately 220,000 German industrial, retail, wholesale, and service companies; national and regional trade organizations. Database includes: List of place names with former names and geographical location; maps. Entries include: Agency, organization, or company name, address, phone; headquarters office location for branch companies.

Data, Where It Is and How to Get It: Directory of Business, Environment and Energy Data Sources. Coleman/Morse. • $24.95. Covers: Over 2,500 sources of information produced by the U.S. government on business, environmental and energy activities; includes experts, federal departments and agencies, data centers, and user groups. Entries include: Data sources for agriculture, banking and finance, international trade, demographics, employment, prices, income, and rural development.

Database, Directory of MNCs Companies in India. NIIR Project Consultancy Services. • $100 U.S. CD-ROM. Covers: Multinational companies in India. Entries include: Name, address, country of origin, phone, fax, e-mail, website, CEO name.

Datalink Regional Business Directory. Datatech Communications Inc. • Covers: More than 180,000 companies in New York, Vermont, New Hampshire, Maine, Massachusetts, Rhode Island, Maryland, Connecticut, and New Jersey. Entries include: Company name, address, phone, fax, 800 numbers, URL, e-mail.

Datatech Communications Business Directory. Datatech Communications Inc. • Covers: More than 160,000 companies throughout the U.S. Entries include: Company name, address, phone, fax, 800 numbers, URL, e-mail.

Decatur Chamber of Commerce Business Directory. Greater Decatur Chamber of Commerce. • Covers chamber members. Entries include name, address, phone.

Decorators Directory. InfoGroup Inc. • Annual. Number of listings: 33,751. Entries include: Name, address, phone, size of advertisement, name of owner or manager, number of employees, year first in "Yellow Pages." Compiled from telephone company "Yellow Pages," nationwide.

Definitive Directory of Competitive Telecommunications Service Providers. Advanstar Communications Inc. • Annual. $275 Nonmembers plus $6 shipping. Covers: Hundreds of new and existing competitive telecommunications service providers. Entries include: Name, address, phone, fax, statistical data, company profiles, market research on revenues, services, operating territories.

Delaware Agricultural Trade Directory. Delaware Department of Agriculture. • Irregular. Covers: about 300 producers, processors, and distributors of agricultural products in Delaware; includes exporters. Entries include: Company name, address, phone, type of product or service, quantity, variety, other information.

Delaware Directory of Commerce and Industry. Delaware State Chamber of Commerce Inc. • Periodic Annual. $50 Members per additional copy for members. Covers: About 5,000 manufacturers, retailers, wholesalers, and service establishments. Entries include: Name, address, phone, name, address, phone, name and title of contact, list of products or services.

Denmark Industrial and Business Directory. International Business Publications, USA. • Annual. $99.95 Individuals hardcopy, e-book, CD-ROM. Covers: Detailed information on investment, export-import business opportunities, foreign economic assistance projects, government and business contacts.

Denmark's 10,000 Largest Companies. William Snyder Publishing Associates. • Annual. $175 plus 30 pounds shipping. Covers: 10,000 "leading" (by turnover) companies in Denmark. Database includes: Table of companies ranked by common currency listing sales figures, percentage growth indicators, profitability, capital structure, number of employees, year established. Entries include: In an index--Company name, address, phone, turnover, profit, number of employees.

Dennis Business Directory and Visitor Guide. Dennis Chamber of Commerce. • Publication includes: List of about 250 member businesses in the Dennis, Massachusetts, area; list of 40 area accessories. Entries include: For businesses--Company name, address, phone. For accommodations--Hotel or inn name, address, phone, number of rooms, credit cards accepted, price range, operating season, whether handicapped access and other facilities are available. Principal content of publication is suggested routes for touring the area, descriptions of nearby attractions, etc.

Denton's Directories. Denton's Directories Ltd. • Annual. $11. Covers: Local businesses and community services in various British towns; separate volumes cover Bath, Calne/Lyneham, Chippenham/Corsham, Cirencester, Devizes, Keynsham/Saltford, Malmesbury/Tetbury, Marlborough/Hungerford, Melksham, Shaftesbury/Gillingham/Mere, Sherborne/Milborne Port, Trowbridge/Bradford on Avon, Warminster, Westbury, Bridport, Dorchester, Wootton, and Bassett. Entries include: Company name, address, phone.

Department of Trade and Industry--The Single Market: Guide to Sources of Advice. Department of Trade and Industry. • Covers: Organizations providing information on business and trade in the European Community, including representative organizations, research and technology organizations, chambers of commerce, public sector advisers, and language advisers. Entries include: For representative organizations and research and technology organizations--Name, address, phone, name and title of contact, sectors covered, restrictions on service, type of information offered, European links. For others--Name, address, phone, type of information offered.

Desktop Publishing Directory. InfoGroup Inc. • Annual. Number of listings: 5,952. Entries include: Name, address, phone, size of advertisement, name of owner or manager, number of employees, year first in "Yellow Pages." Compiled from telephone company "Yellow Pages," nationwide.

Developing Business in Eastern Europe. Intervisual Advertising Ltd. • Monthly. Covers: Eastern European industries. Entries include: Company name, address, phone, fax, geographical area served, subsidiary and branch names and locations, description of product/services provided.

The Development Directory: A Guide to the International Development Community in the U.S. and Canada. Omnigraphics Inc. • Irregular. $110. Covers: over 1,000 organizations and individuals involved in economic and social development worldwide. Entries include: For organizations--Name, address, phone, fax, telex, size of community, statement of purpose, geographical areas of interest or activity, names and titles of key personnel, publications, financial data. For individuals--Name, position or title, address, phone, affiliation, degrees, publications, experience, subjects, geographic areas, background comments.

Dial-A-Fax Business Directory: World's Largest Resources of Fax Services. Dial-A-Fax Directories Corp. • $289 plus 4.95 postage. Database covers: Approximately 1,400,000 companies in the United States. Entries include: Name, city, state, phone, fax, Standard Industrial Classification (SIC) code.

Dictating Machines & Supplies Wholesale Directory. InfoGroup Inc. • Updated continuously; printed on request. Number of listings: 585. Entries include: Name, address, phone, size of advertisement, name of owner or manager, number of employees, year first in "Yellow Pages." Compiled from telephone company "Yellow Pages," nationwide.

Dictionary of International Trade. Reference Press Inc. • $16.45. Covers: More than 4,000 entries concerning international trade, including 200 trade groups, 750 acronyms and abbreviations, 180 country codes, 300 city codes, currencies for 200 countries, and a source guide for 125 publications. Database includes: Regional maps of the world. Entries include: For trade groups--name, address, phone, fax.

Directory for Setting Up Enterprises in Japan. • Covers: Approximately 700 companies in Japan that offer market research, direct investment planning, and incorporation and other professional services. Entries include: Name, address, phone, fax, profile, services offered, and contact persons/divisions.

Directory of Affiliates & Offices of Japanese Firms in USA & Canada. Want Publishing Co. • Irregular. $190. Covers: over 6,000 Japanese-affiliated or owned firms in the U.S. and Canada.

Directory of African Importers of Construction Machinery and Equipment. EXIM Infotek Private Ltd. • Covers: 120 African importers of caterpillar, concrete mixers, construction and building equipment, construction machinery, earthmoving equipment, excavating equipment, mixers and pavers, stone crusher, and street maintenance equipment. Entries include: Company name, postal address, telephone, fax, e-mail, website, contact person, designation, and product details.

Directory of African Importers of Dyes, Colors, and Pigments. EXIM Infotek Private Ltd. • $250 Individuals. Covers: 90 African importers of textiles chemical, dye, colors, pigments, intermediates, dyestuff, and printing ink. Entries include: Company name, postal address, telephone, fax, e-mail, website, contact person, designation, and product details.

Directory of African Importers of Energy and Power Equipment. EXIM Infotek Private Ltd. • $150 Individuals. Covers: 30 African importers of power transmission equipment and supplies, solar energy equipment, solar panels, solar water heaters, and wind energy equipment. Entries include: Company name, postal address, telephone, fax, e-mail, website, contact person, designation, and product details.

Directory of African Importers of Environment Protection and Pollution Control Equipment. EXIM Infotek Private Ltd. • $200 Individuals. Covers: 40 African importers of pollution control equipment, wastewater treatment, water treatment, and purifying equipment. Entries include: Company name, postal address, telephone, fax, e-mail, website, contact person, designation, and product details.

Directory of African Importers of Fibre Products. EXIM Infotek Private Ltd. • $150 Individuals. Covers: 35 African importers of fiberglass cloth and products, fiberglass resins, fiber products, and synthetic fiber. Entries include: Company name, postal address, telephone, fax, e-mail, website, contact person, designation, and product details.

Directory of African Importers of Fire Fighting Equipment & Supplies. EXIM Infotek Private Ltd. • Covers: 35 African importers of fire fighting equipment. Entries include: Company name, postal address, telephone, fax, e-mail, website, contact person, designation, and product details.

Directory of African Importers of Fodder and Animal Foodstuffs. EXIM Infotek Private Ltd. • $250 Individuals. Covers: 70 African importers of animal foodstuff additives, animal foodstuff, feed additives, fodder, cereals, livestock breeding supplies, and oats. Entries include: Company name, postal address, telephone, fax, e-mail, website, contact person, designation, and product details.

Directory of African Importers of Food Additives and Aromatics. EXIM Infotek Private Ltd. • $150 Individuals. Covers: 40 African importers of aromatic chemicals, bakery and pastry ingredients, food additives, food colors, food colouring, fragrances, flavors, and yeast. Entries include: Company name, postal address, telephone, fax, e-mail, website, contact person, designation, and product details.

Directory of African Importers of Handkerchives, Scarves and Neckwears. EXIM Infotek Private Ltd. • $150 Individuals. Covers: 20 African importers of handkerchieves, scarves, neckwear, and neckties.

Directory of African Importers of Laboratory & Scientific Instruments & Supplies. EXIM Infotek Private Ltd. • Covers: 250 African importers of binoculars, microscopes, telescopes, laboratory and scientific glass, laboratory and scientific instruments, laboratory chemicals, laboratory equipment, laboratory glassware, laboratory reagents, magnifiers, scientific equipment, and testing equipment.

For publishers' addresses, refer to SOURCES CITED section at the back of the book.

Entries include: Company name, postal address, telephone, fax, e-mail, website, contact person, designation, and product details.

Directory of African Importers of Lumber, Timber, Plywood and Hardboards. EXIM Infotek Private Ltd. • $300 Individuals. Covers: 70 African importers of doors and windows, formica sheets, gypsum board and sheetrock, hardboard and particle board, laminates (wood), hardwood lumber, softwood lumber, timber, plywood, medium-density fiberboard, millwork (wooden), veneer, special decorative plywood, poles, pilings and logs, sawn timber, saw and saw blades, and wood. Entries include: Company name, postal address, telephone, fax, e-mail, website, contact person, designation, and product details.

Directory of African Importers of Machinery for Paper & Pulp Industry. EXIM Infotek Private Ltd. • Covers: 20 African importers of envelope making machinery, exercise book making machinery, paper making machinery and toilet paper making machines. Entries include: Company name, postal address, telephone, fax, e-mail, website, contact person, designation, and product details.

Directory of African Importers of Material Handling Equipment & Supplies. EXIM Infotek Private Ltd. • $250 Individuals. Covers: 60 African importers of conveyors, cranes and hoists, elevators and lifts, forklifts, lifting machinery and equipment, liquid handling equipment, loading and unloading equipment, material handling systems for garment industries, and monorail materials handling equipment. Entries include: Company name, postal address, telephone, fax, e-mail, website, contact person, designation, and product details.

Directory of African Importers of Motors and Motor Parts--Electric. EXIM Infotek Private Ltd. • $250 Individuals. Covers: 50 African importers of AC and DC motors, electric motors and spares, motor equipment, and motor parts. Entries include: Company name, postal address, telephone, fax, e-mail, website, contact person, designation, and product details.

Directory of African Importers of Photographic Equipment and Supplies. EXIM Infotek Private Ltd. • $300 Individuals. Covers: 95 African importers of cameras and videos, lens and accessories, photographic chemicals, motion picture and theater equipment, digital camera, microfilm and blueprint equipment, photographic equipment and supplies, photographic goods, photographic materials and hardware, photographic processing supplies, and video cameras. Entries include: Company name, postal address, telephone, fax, e-mail, website, contact person, designation, and product details.

Directory of African Importers of Plastic Scrap and Raw Materials. EXIM Infotek Private Ltd. • $300 Individuals. Covers: 90 African importers of plastic raw materials, plastic scrap and waste, polyethylene raw materials, PVC compounds, low-density polyethylene (LDPE) raw material, PF raw materials, molding powder, polester chips raw materials, PP/PVC/PE raw materials, PVC resins raw materials, and plasticizers. Entries include: Company name, postal address, telephone, fax, e-mail, website, contact person, designation, and product details.

Directory of African Importers of Sewing Machines and Parts. EXIM Infotek Private Ltd. • $250 Individuals. Covers: 80 African importers of embroidery machine, garment industry machinery and equipment, industrial sewing machine and parts, and pleating machine. Entries include: Company name, postal address, telephone, fax, e-mail, website, contact person, designation, and product details.

Directory of African Importers of Sporting Goods. EXIM Infotek Private Ltd. • $350 Individuals. Covers: 125 African importers of diving equipment, golf equipment and supplies, scuba and diving equipment and supply, sports equipment, sporting goods and toys, tennis and badminton equipment and supplies, and watersports equipment. Entries include: Company name, postal address, telephone, fax, e-mail, website, contact person, designation, and product details.

Directory of African Importers of Telephone Instruments and Accessories. EXIM Infotek Private Ltd. • $400 Individuals. Covers: 120 African Importers of mobile phone, cordless telephone, fax machine, GSM cellular handset, GSM mobile phone, headphone, mobile accessories, telefax equipment, telephone equipment, and telephone systems. Entries include: Company name, postal address, telephone, fax, e-mail, website, contact person, designation, and product details.

Directory of African Importers of Yarns and Threads. EXIM Infotek Private Ltd. • $300 Individuals. Covers: 90 African importers of acrylic yarn, cotton yarn and thread, embroidery threads, polyester yarn, sewing threads, synthetic yarns and thread, and wool yarn. Entries include: Company name, postal address, telephone, fax, e-mail, website, contact person, designation, and product details.

Directory of American Agribusiness. Agricultural Resources & Communications Inc. • $64.95. Covers: Over 7,200 leading companies in agricultural chemicals, implements, seed, grain, feed, food processing, animal health and services, including public relations and consulting in 27 different types of agribusinesses in the U.S. Entries include: Company name, address, phone, fax, type of business, key company contacts.

Directory of American Business in Hong Kong. GTE Directories Ltd. • $20. Covers: American companies, their agents, and distributors in Hong Kong; US State and Port of Authority representatives in Hong Kong; products and service of the American Consulate General in Hong Kong.

Directory of American Business in South China. American Chamber of Commerce in Hong Kong. • Covers: Over 900 American companies that have regional headquarters or representative offices in Hong Kong.

Directory of American Companies Operating in Mexico. American Chamber of Commerce of Mexico - Mexico City. • Biennial. Covers: over 2,500 United States commercial and investment companies with operations in Mexico, and the 2,500 Mexican companies that represent them in Mexico. Entries include: For United States companies--Name, address, phone, fax, contact person, products, names of Mexican firm with which associated, type of affiliation. For Mexican companies--Name, address, phone, fax, contact person, products, sales, name of United States company.

Directory of American Companies Overseas. Overseas Employment Services. • Annual. $15. Covers: Approximately 250 American companies that have branch plants or offices outside the U.S. Entries include: Company name, address, geographical area served, and product/service.

Directory of American Manufacturers & Exporters of Adhesive, Glues & Sealants. EXIM Infotek Private Ltd. • $30 Individuals. Covers: 390 American manufacturers and exporters of adhesive applicators, adhesive chemicals, adhesive fastening systems, adhesive paper rolls, adhesive products, adhesives, adhesives for duct insulation, adhesives for leather and rubber, adhesives-bonding, adhesives-bushing, adhesives-canvas, adhesives-ceramic, adhesives-concrete, adhesives-cyanocrylates, adhesives-electrical, adhesives-electrically conductive, adhesives-epoxy, adhesives-gasket, adhesives-gasoline resistant, adhesives-glass block, adhesives-graphite, adhesives-grinding and polishing wheel, adhesives-heat seal, adhesives-hot melt, adhesives-latex, adhesives-leather, adhesives-linoleum, adhesives-metal, adhesives-oil resistant, adhesives-paper, adhesives-patching and repair, adhesives-plastic, adhesives-pressure sensitive products, adhesives-raw materials, adhesives-resin, adhesives-structural laminating, adhesives-textile bonding, adhesives-therosetting and thermoplastic, adhesives-ultra violet curing, adhesives-urethane, adhesives-vinyl, adhesives-water resistant, adhesives-waterproofing, adhesives-wood and plywood, aerosol, animal glue, carpet and ceramic flooring, carton sealing adhesives, cyanoacrylates, cyanocrylate adhesives, epoxy, epoxy adhesives, epoxy solvent, eva and polyamide based adhesives for product assembly, floor covering installation adhesives, flooring adhesives, fluid applied roofing, glue, glue-bookbinders, glue-casein, heat seal adhesives, high temp adhesives, hot melt adhesives, industry adhesives, packaging adhesive, polishing wheel and belt inorganic adhesives, polyurethane adhesives, potting compounds, precision torque strength sealing, sealants, structural adhesives, stuffing box sealant, threadlocking and retaining anaerobic, tire sealants, white glue, wire self adhesive backed clips, and woodworking adhesive. Entries include: Company name, postal address, city, country, telephone, fax, e-mail and websites, contact person, designation, and product details.

Directory of American Manufacturers & Exporters of Agro Chemicals. EXIM Infotek Private Ltd. • $10 Individuals. Covers: 50 American manufacturers and exporters of agricultural chemicals, agricultural deodorants for swine and manure, biochemicals, fungicides, insecticides, pesticides, and phosphatic chemicals. Entries include: Company name, postal address, city, country, phone, fax, e-mail and websites, contact person, designation, and product details.

Directory of American Manufacturers & Exporters of Automobiles & Vehicles. EXIM Infotek Private Ltd. • $20 Individuals. Covers: 200 American manufacturers and exporters of armored vehicles, articulated dump vehicles, automobiles, fire trucks, heavy duty trucks, heavy trucks, industrial trucks, military truck bodies and utility trailers, military trucks, platform trucks, roll off containers, tilt trucks, trailers and tank trucks, truck beds, truck bodies, trucks-commercial, truck frame beam punch lines, truck mounted equipment, truck wheel covers and accessories, and trucks. Entries include: Company name, postal address, city, country, phone, fax, e-mail and websites, contact person, designation, and product details.

Directory of American Manufacturers & Exporters of Automotive Service & Repair Equipment. EXIM Infotek Private Ltd. • $5 Individuals. Covers: 40 American manufacturers and exporters of analyzers-engine, auto test equipment, automotive analyzers, automotive hand tools, automotive tools, small engine maintenance instruments, and specialty heavy transmission rebuilding hand tools. Entries include: Company name, postal address, city, country, phone, fax, e-mail and websites, contact person, designation, and products detail.

Directory of American Manufacturers & Exporters of Autoparts & Accessories. EXIM Infotek Private Ltd. • $50 Individuals. Covers: 850 American manufacturers and exporters of air fitting and tubing brakes, alternators, asbestos gaskets, assemblies, automatic transmission parts, automotive accessories, automotive axle components, automotive cable, automotive components, automotive composite transmission filters, automotive exhaust systems, automotive gaskets, automotive ignition wire sets, automotive mirrors, automotive parts, automotive parts and accessories, automotive parts and supplies, automotive parts-clutch plates, automotive parts-mufflers, automotive parts-spark plugs, automotive parts-starters and alternators, automotive relays, automotive replacement bushings, automotive replacement parts, automotive service tools, automotive spare parts and assemblies, automotive steering components, automotive transmission and friction parts, automotive transmission components, axle scale systems, axles, brake, brake drum, brake pads, brake shoes, camshafts, car care products, cargo truck, cars and light trucks superchargers, clutches, couplings, custom wheels, disc brakes for cars, felt gaskets, fifth wheels, flat gaskets, fork lift truck attachments, fuel filters, fuel system components, gasket materials, gaskets, gaskets and sealing for the automotive industry, heavy duty truck and trailer parts, horns, hubs, hydraulic equipment, hydraulic tailgates and inserts, industrial gaskets, light truck and van accessories, mobile home tires and wheels, molded gaskets, molded rubber gaskets, non-asbestos gaskets, non-metallic gasket material, plastic gaskets, powder metal products, radiators, replacement parts, replacement parts and accessories, seat belts, seat covers, shock absorbers, silicone gaskets, suspension/chassis components, Teflon encapsuled gaskets, Teflon gaskets, top gaskets, transmission, transmission and parts, transmission components, truck and automotive parts, truck clutches, truck dump bodies, truck equipment, truck parts, truck parts and equipment, truck parts and suppliers, truck replacement parts, truck tool boxes and rubber mats, truck wheel lifts, v bowl rings, vehicular lighting equipment, viton gaskets, wheels, and windshields.e1 American manufacturers and exporters of air fitting and tubing brakes, alternators, asbestos gaskets, assemblies, automatic transmission parts, automotive accessories, automotive axle components, automotive cable, automotive components, automotive composite transmission filters, automotive exhaust systems, automotive gaskets, automotive ignition wire sets, automotive mirrors, automotive parts, automotive parts and accessories, automotive parts and supplies, automotive parts-clutch plates, automotive parts-mufflers, automotive parts-spark plugs, automotive parts-starters and alternators, automotive relays, automotive replacement bushings, automotive replacement parts, automotive service tools, automotive spare parts and assemblies, automotive steering components, automotive transmission and friction parts, automotive transmission components, axle scale systems, axles, brake, brake drum, brake pads, brake shoes, camshafts, car care products, cargo truck, cars and light trucks superchargers, clutches, couplings, custom wheels, disc brakes for cars, felt gaskets, fifth wheels, flat gaskets, fork lift truck attachments, fuel filters, fuel system components, gasket materials, gaskets, gaskets and sealing for the automotive industry, heavy duty truck and trailer parts, horns, hubs, hydraulic equipment, hydraulic tailgates and inserts, industrial gaskets, light truck and van accessories, mobile home tires and wheels, molded gaskets, molded rubber gaskets, non-asbestos gaskets, non-metallic gasket material, plastic gaskets, powder metal products, radiators, replacement parts, replacement parts and accessories, seat belts, seat covers, shock absorbers, silicone gaskets, suspension/chassis components, Teflon encapsuled gaskets, Teflon gaskets, top gaskets, transmission, transmission and parts, transmission components, truck and automotive parts, truck clutches, truck dump bodies, truck equipment, truck parts, truck parts and equipment, truck parts and suppliers, truck replacement parts, truck tool boxes and rubber mats, truck wheel lifts, v bowl rings, vehicular lighting equipment, viton gaskets, wheels, and windshields. Entries include: Company name, postal address, city, country, telephone, fax, e-mail and websites, contact person, designation, and product details.

Directory of American Manufacturers & Exporters of Batteries & Accumulators. EXIM Infotek Private Ltd. • $20 Individuals. Covers: 200 American manufacturers and exporters of aircraft batteries, automotive batteries, batteries, batteries-deep cycle, batteries-dry cell, batteries-electric storage, batteries-lead acid, batteries-lithium, batteries-military specifications, batteries-nickel cadmium, batteries-sealed lead acid, batteries-solar, batteries-storage, batteries-wet and sealed, battery cables, battery chargers, battery packs and chargers, battery testers, commercial and industrial batteries, marine batteries, primary batteries, rechargeable batteries, and truck batteries. Entries include: Company name, postal address, city, country, phone, fax, e-mail and websites, contact person, designation, and product details.

Directory of American Manufacturers & Exporters of Bearings. EXIM Infotek Private Ltd. • $20 Individuals. Covers: 280 American manufacturers and exporters of air bearings, antifriction bearings, automotive bearings, ball bearings, bearingsmetal, bearing pads, bearing parts-ball and roller, bearings-jewel, bearings, bearings-acid and corrosion resistant, bearings-air, bearings-aircraft, bearings-instrument, bearings-non metallic, bearings-self lubricating, bearings-sleeve, bearings-thrust, bronze bearings, carbide bearings, carbon-graphite bearings, conveyor bearings, cylindrical bearings, engine bearings, linear bearings, linear motion bearings, magnetic bearings, miniature bearings, needle bearings, pillow block bearings, precision ball bearings, radial ball bearings, roller bearings, self aligning bearings, semi-precise bearings, slide bearings, specialty bearings, spherical bearings, stainless steel bearings, tapered roller bearings, water lubricated bearings. Entries include: Company name, postal address, city, country, telephone, fax, e-mail and websites, contact person, designation, and product details.

Directory of American Manufacturers & Exporters of Beauty Supplies, Cosmetics, Perfumes & Toiletries. EXIM Infotek Private Ltd. • $20 Individuals. Covers: 200 American manufacturers and exporters of aloe vera products, bath products, beauty care products, beauty creams, blackhead removers, body lotions, cosmetic bags, cosmetic brushes, cosmetic chemicals, cosmetic pencils, cosmetic plastic containers, cosmetics, cosmetics raw materials, eyeliners, face make-up, facial sponges, hair conditioners, hair gels, Halloween accessories, health care, herbal products, lip glosses, lip care products, lipstick, mascara, mouthwash, nail care products, nail polish, oral hygiene products, perfumes, personal care products, scalp conditioners, shampoos, skin care creams and lotions, skin care products, sun care products, toiletries, and toothpaste. Entries include: Company name, postal address, city, country, phone, fax, e-mail and websites, contact person, designation, and product details.

Directory of American Manufacturers and Exporters of Boiler and Boiler Parts. EXIM Infotek Private Ltd. • Covers: 100 American manufacturers and exporters of boilers, gas boilers, oil boilers, hot water boilers, packaged steam and hot water boilers, steam and hot water boilers. Entries include: Company name, postal address, telephone, fax, e-mail, website, contact person, designation, and product details.

Directory of American Manufacturers & Exporters of Chemicals & Allied Products. EXIM Infotek Private Ltd. • $40 Individuals. Covers: 680 American manufacturers and exporters of aerosol chemicals, aircraft cleaning chemicals, allied accessories, analytical chemicals, automotive chemicals, boiler chemicals, chemicals for x-ray processing, chemical intermediates, chemical raw materials, chemical sprayers, chemicals, chemicals for laboratory, chlorine chemicals, construction chemicals, dry chemicals, electronic chemicals, electroplating chemicals, fertilizer chemicals, fine chemicals, germicides, household chemicals, hydrogen peroxide, industrial chemicals, inorganic chemicals, laboratory chemicals, leather chemicals, liquid chemicals, lubricant chemicals, magnesium chloride, metal working chemicals, natural chemicals, organic chemicals, paint chemicals, paper chemicals, pharmaceutical and cosmetic industry chemicals, pharmaceutical chemicals, plastic chemicals, polymer chemicals, polyurethane foam chemicals, reagent chemicals, resins, rubber chemicals, sodium bisulfite chemicals, sodium silico fluoride, solvent chemicals, specialty chemicals, specialty cleaning chemicals, starches, textile chemicals, water softeners, water treatment, water treatment chemicals, and zinc dies casting. Entries include: company name, postal address, city, country, telephone, fax, e-mail and websites, contact person, designation, and product details.

Directory of American Manufacturers & Exporters of Confectionery & Bakery Products. EXIM Infotek Private Ltd. • $10 Individuals. Covers: 90 American manufacturers & exporters of baked foods, boxed chocolates, bubble gum, buttercrunch, candy, cheesecake & carrot cake, chewing gum base, chocolate coatings, chocolates, confectionery items, cookies, fruit snacks & fruit rolls, fudge making, hard candy, ingredients & chocolate products, jelly beans, marshmallows, peanuts. Entries include: Company name, postal address, city, country, phone, fax, e-mail & websites, contact person, designation, products detail.

Directory of American Manufacturers & Exporters of Dyes, Colours, Pigments & Intermediates. EXIM Infotek Private Ltd. • $20 Individuals. Covers: 200 American manufacturers and exporters of color concentrates, colors and pigments, colors and pigments-dispersions and flushes, concentrates-colors and pigments, dies, dispersions, dye and pigment intermediates, dyes, dyes and dyestuffs, flushed color and presscakes, intermediates, leather dyes, organic and inorganic dyes, organic and inorganic pigments, organic pigments for printing inks, pigment dispersions, pigment preparations, pigments, pigments and colors-brick, pigments and colors-ceramic and glass, pigments and colors-dry and dispersed, pigments and colors-paint, pigments and colors-rubber, plastic dyes, plastic industry colorants and additives, rust remover, textile dyestuffs, and water colors. Entries include: Company name, postal address, city, country, phone, fax, e-mail and websites, contact person, designation, and product details.

Directory of American Manufacturers & Exporters of Electronic Equipment. EXIM Infotek Private Ltd. • $250 Individuals. Covers: 90 American manufacturers and exporters of semiconductor materials, semiconductor processing equipment, and semiconductors. Entries include: Company name, postal address, telephone, fax, e-mail, website, contact person, designation, and product details.

Directory of American Manufacturers and Exporters of Energy and Power Equipment. EXIM Infotek Private Ltd. • $200 Individuals. Covers: 50 American manufacturers and exporters of solar control film, power systems and components, battery-free solar equipment, solar battery charge regulators, solar control equipment, solar electric (photovoltaics), solar energy equipment, solar modules, solar panels, and solar photovoltics. Entries include: Company name, postal address, telephone, fax, e-mail, website, contact person, designation, and product details.

Directory of American Manufacturers & Exporters of Engines & Engine Parts. EXIM Infotek Private Ltd. • $20 Individuals. Covers: 240 American manufacturers and exporters of auto engines, automobile engines, automotive and truck engines, automotive engines, boiler and air conditioning tow-

For publishers' addresses, refer to SOURCES CITED section at the back of the book.

ers and engines, car engines, crankshafts, cylinders, cylinder sleeves, diesel engine parts, diesel engine parts and accessories, diesel engines, engines, engine aircraft modifications, engine parts, engine treatments, engines-gasoline, exhaust system parts, gasoline and diesel engines, gasoline engines, heavy duty diesel engines, industrial diesel engines, injectors, internal combustion engines, natural gas engines, piston automotive and light truck applications, piston pins, piston rings, piston-compressors, piston-engines, pistons, replacement parts for heavy duty diesel engines, steam engines, stern drive and inboard engines, timing components, truck engines, and turbine engines. Entries include: Company name, postal address, city, country, telephone, fax, e-mail and websites, contact person, designation, and product details.

Directory of American Manufacturers and Exporters of Environment and Pollution Control Equipment. EXIM Infotek Private Ltd. • $650 Individuals. Covers: 340 American manufacturers and exporters of air filtration and cleaning equipment, environmental control and monitoring equipment, environmental products, gas absorbers, lease environmental instrument systems, oil and water separators, oil boom accessories, pollution control equipment and systems, pollution sampling equipment, portable water treatment plants, reverse osmosis, distillation water purifying equipment, waste heat recovery equipment, water pollution control equipment, water treatment equipment, water treatment for PH reduction utilizing carbon dioxide, water treatment plants and engineering services, and water treatment including ozone technology. Entries include: Company name, postal address, telephone, fax, e-mail, website, contact person, designation, and product details.

Directory of American Manufacturers & Exporters of Essential Oils. EXIM Infotek Private Ltd. • $10 Individuals. Covers: 90 American manufacturers & exporters of essential oil of peppermint & spearmint, essential oils, fragrance, massage oils. Entries include: Company name, postal address, city, country, phone, fax, e-mail & websites, contact person, designation, products detail.

Directory of American Manufacturers & Exporters of Filters & Strainers--Industrial. EXIM Infotek Private Ltd. • $30 Individuals. Covers: 400 American manufacturers and exporters of air filters, ceramic and iodine portable camping filters, cloth filters, compressed-air filters, cooling towers water filter systems, counter-top and under counter filters, filter media, filter pads, filter paper, filter systems and pumps, filters, fire restoration, interference filters, media filters, sand filters and replacement filter elements, screens, water filters for commercial, consumer water filters for home, business and restaurant, water filtration equipment, water filters, water filtration and purification conditioning, water filtration and purification equipment, water filtration and purification ultraviolet, water filtration equipment, water filtration treatment, water filtration and purification equipment, water purification and treatment systems, and water purifiers. Entries include: Company name, postal address, city, country, telephone, fax, e-mail and websites, contact person, designation, and product details.

Directory of American Manufacturers & Exporters of Fire Fighting Equipment & Supplies. EXIM Infotek Private Ltd. • Covers: 250 American manufacturers and exporters of airflame, fire alarms, detectors and holder releases, fire doors, fireproof, electric valves, electronic burglary equipment, fire alarm control equipment, extinguishers and cabinets, fire apparatus, residential fire alarm, fire fighting clothing, fire fighting equipment and supplies, gloves, pumps, nozzles, reels, adapters, fire protective coatings, fire rescue blankets, fire retardant products for fabrics, paper, wood and paint, fire sprinklers, fire suppression equipment, industrial foam fire, retardant coatings and mastics, life safety systems, pumpers, rated and non-rated doors, single and double jacket, smoke detectors, smoke vents, sprinkler systems, water tankers, wireless commercial and residential burglar alarm.

Directory of American Manufacturers & Exporters of Food Additives & Aromatic Chemicals. EXIM Infotek Private Ltd. • $5 Individuals. Covers: 20 American manufacturers and exporters of aroma chemicals and chemicals for food and beverage. Entries include: Company name, postal address, city, country, phone, fax, e-mail and websites, contact person, designation, and product details.

Directory of American Manufacturers & Exporters of Furniture--All Types. EXIM Infotek Private Ltd. • $25 Individuals. Covers: 330 American manufacturers and exporters of bed frames, bed liners, bedroom furniture, bookcases, chairs, church furniture, commercial furniture, computer furniture, computer tables, custom upholstered wood furniture, decorative furniture, dining room furniture, dining tables, edge-glued furniture panels, fine home theater furniture, finished furniture, folding chairs, folding tables, furniture, furniture and supplies, furniture parts, garden furniture, hardwood furniture, hotel furniture, institution furniture, metal furniture, motel furniture, occasional furniture, occasional tables, office furniture and accessories, outdoor furniture, residential furniture, restaurant furniture, safes, school furniture, steel furniture, steel shelving, unfinished wood furniture, upholstered furniture, vault doors, wood library furniture, wrought iron furniture. Entries include: Company name, postal address, city, country, telephone, fax, e-mail and websites, contact person, designation, and product details.

Directory of American Manufacturers & Exporters of Gears & Gears Boxes. EXIM Infotek Private Ltd. • $15 Individuals. Covers: 150 American manufacturers and exporters of custom gears, gear boxes, gears, gears-bevel, gears-helical, gears-helical and worm, gears-instruments, gears-master, gears-miter, gears-pinions, gears-plastic, gears-precision, gears-racks, gears-speed reducers, gears-spiral bevel, gears-splines, gears-sprocket, gears-spur, gears-straight and spiral bevel, gears-worms, and zerol and hypoid gears. Entries include: Company name, postal address, city, country, phone, fax, e-mail and websites, contact person, designation, and product details.

Directory of American Manufacturers & Exporters of Giftware & Novelties. EXIM Infotek Private Ltd. • $10 Individuals. Covers: 50 American manufacturers and exporters of ceramic mugs with logos, gift items, gift wrap, novelties, silverplate halloware and giftware cutlery. Entries include: Company name, postal address, city, country, phone, fax, e-mail and websites, contact person, designation, and product details.

Directory of American Manufacturers & Exporters of Gold & Silvery Jewelry. EXIM Infotek Private Ltd. • $5 Individuals. Covers: 20 American manufacturers and exporters of gold, gold jewelry, silver, and silver jewelry. Entries include: Company name, postal address, city, country, phone, fax, e-mail and websites, contact person, designation, and product details.

Directory of American Manufacturers & Exporters of Handtools. EXIM Infotek Private Ltd. • $30 Individuals. Covers: 400 American manufacturers and exporters of copper and aluminum press sleeve swagers, cutting tools, diamond saw blades, fixtures tools, flange spreaders, grinder tools, grooving and proofing tools, hacksaw, hand tools-electric and air, hand tools-files, hand tools-hammers, hand tools-modeling, hand tools-pillers, hand tools-power, hand tools, hand tools-shovels, hand tools-utica, hand tools-wrenches, high speed steel, hydraulic maintenance tools, jewelry, landscaping tools, miniature tools, non-sparking safety tools, nut splitters, pneumatic tools, pocket knives, power tool accessories, precision miniature tools, precision tools, reamers, rivet setting machines, safety tools, screwdrivers, serrated blades, sheet metal hand tools, sledges, pry bars and railroad track tools, socket sets, special tools-custom, special tools, tool holders, tooling, tools, torque tools, torque wrenches, tube tools, wire tools, and wrenches. Entries include: Company name, postal address, city, country, telephone, fax, e-mail and websites, contact person, designation, and product details.

Directory of American Manufacturers & Exporters of Hardwares--All Types. EXIM Infotek Private Ltd. • $15 Individuals. Covers: 170 American manufacturers and exporters of builders' hardware, cabinet hardware, cabinet locks, door hardware, door hardware locks, door locks, electrical hardware, electronic hardware, furniture hardware, granite blocks and panels, hardware, hinges, industrial hardware, luggage hardware, metal and plastic adjustable hand levers, padlocks, panels, patch panels, structural and decorative panels, and wall panels. Entries include: Company name, postal address, city, country, phone, fax, e-mail and websites, contact person, designation, and product details.

Directory of American Manufacturers & Exporters of Home Furnishing Materials. EXIM Infotek Private Ltd. • $5 Individuals. Covers: 40 American manufacturers and exporters of bedspreads and sleeping bags, cleaners, cushion grips, doors, earring cushions and accessories, home furnishings, pillows, table cloths, vacuum cleaners, and wooden bedroom. Entries include: Company name, postal address, city, country, phone, fax, e-mail and websites, contact person, designation, and product details.

Directory of American Manufacturers & Exporters of Houseware, Kitchenware & Tableware. EXIM Infotek Private Ltd. • $10 Individuals. Covers: 90 American manufacturers & exporters of brooms, cleaning materials, coasters, cutlery, dinnerware, flatware cutlery, gas stoves, holloware cutlery, household brooms, household cutlery, housewares, kitchen cutlery, knife sets, knives, plastic cups, plastic cutlery, plastic disposable cutlery, professional cutlery, scissors & knives, stainless steel cutlery, stainless steel flatware cutlery. Entries include: Company name, postal address, city, country, phone, fax, e-mail & websites, contact person, designation, products detail.

Directory of American Manufacturers & Exporters of Imitation & Fashion Jewellery. EXIM Infotek Private Ltd. • $10 Individuals. Covers: 80 American manufacturers and exporters of bracelets, costume jewelry, custom jewelry, diamond cabbing and polishing equipment, earrings, fashion jewelry, hair pins, jewelry casting investments, jewelry chains, jewelry findings, jewelry tools, and necklaces. Entries include: Company name, postal address, city, country, phone, fax, e-mail and websites, contact person, designation, and product details.

Directory of American Manufacturers & Exporters of Lighting Fixtures, Lamps & Accessories. EXIM Infotek Private Ltd. • $25 Individuals. Covers: 320 American manufacturers and exporters of architectural lighting/dimming equipment, ballasts and fixture lamps, black light lamps, emergency lighting equipment, fixtures, fixtures-lamps, flash lamps, flashlights, floor lamps, fluorescent fixtures and supplies, fluorescent lamp ballasts, fluorescent lighting fixtures, fluorescent tubes, fuel lamps, H.I.D. lamps, halogen lamps, hand lamps, high intensity lamps, incandescent lamps, indoor/outdoor lighting equipment, lamp parts, lamp shades, lamp sockets, lamps, lamps-electric, lamps-fluorescent, lamps-germicidal, light bulbs, lights for nightclubs and discotheques, lighting control equipment for theatrical, lighting equipment and supplies, lighting fixture glassware, lighting fixtures, lighting systems, low voltage lighting, portable lamps, searchlights, solar lighting, solar rail and bus waiting station lights, solar-electric lighting, store display fixtures, table lamps. Entries include: Company name, postal address, city, country, telephone, fax, e-mail and websites, contact person, designation, and product details.

Directory of American Manufacturers & Exporters of Machinery for Chemicals & Pharma Industry. EXIM Infotek Private Ltd. • $10 Individuals. Covers: 60 American manufacturers and exporters of chemical process equipment, petroleum chemical processing equipment. Entries include: Company name, postal address, city, country, phone, fax, e-mail and websites, contact person, designation, and product details.

Directory of American Manufacturers & Exporters of Machinery for Rubber Industry. EXIM Infotek Private Ltd. • Covers: 25 American manufacturers and exporters of machinery for rubber, tire retreading equipment and supplies, tire spreaders, and inspection machines. Entries include: Company name, postal address, telephone, fax, e-mail, website, contact person, designation, and product details.

Directory of American Manufacturers & Exporters of Machinery for Textile & Knitting Industry. EXIM Infotek Private Ltd. • $10 Individuals. Covers: 110 American manufacturers & exporters of dyeing machinery, knitting & braiding machinery, manmade fiber toe cutters, textile & printing machinery, textile machinery, weaving machinery. Entries include: Company name, postal address, city, country, phone, fax, e-mail & websites, contact person, designation, products detail.

Directory of American Manufacturers & Exporters of Marine & Boating Equipment & Supplies. EXIM Infotek Private Ltd. • $25 Individuals. Covers: 330 American manufacturers and exporters of aluminum work boats, anchors, boat engines, boat ladders and accessories, boat windshields, boats, buoy and open link chains, capstans, diesel and electric, environmental samplers and equipment, fiberglass boats and houseboats, floodlights, junction boxes, keel coolers, marine accessories, marine barges, marine coatings, marine diesel engines, marine electronics, marine engines, marine engines-gasoline, marine equipment and spare parts, marine equipment and supplies, marine furniture, marine hardware, marine instruments, marine parts, marine portlights, marine propellers, marine propulsion units, marine pumps, marine safety equipment, marine suppliers and repair, marine windows, marine-engines, nautical instruments, nautical products, navigation equipment, navigation instruments, navigation systems, oceanographic instruments, outboard motors, plumbing fittings, power supplies, propellers, rollers, satcom systems, shipboard wire and cables, spot lights, starters, steering components, surface air supply dive systems, tachometers, tug boats, water makers and radios, water samplers and plankton nets, windlasses, wire ropes. Entries include: Company name, postal address, city, country, telephone, fax, e-mail and websites, contact person, designation, and product details.

Directory of American Manufacturers & Exporters of Material Handling Equipment. EXIM Infotek Private Ltd. • $850 Individuals. Covers: 480 American manufacturers and exporters of airport baggage handling equipment, bag openers, bulk bag loading and unloading equipment, bulk handling systems, bulk materials handling equipment, carts, chain and cable conveyors, conveyor chains, conveyor bands, conveyor systems, cranes, endless conveyor belts, forklift trucks, hand trucks, hoists, hydraulic cranes, lift trucks, liquid handling products, lumber materials handling equipment, material handling booms, mining and construction equipment, non-powered materials handling equipment, pallet racks, platforms, pneumatic conveying systems, restraint equipment, turntables, weigh belt feeders, winches, and hoists.

Directory of American Manufacturers & Exporters of Minerals. EXIM Infotek Private Ltd. • $10 Individuals. Covers: 70 American manufacturers and exporters of calcium carbonate, carbonate magnesium, crushed lime, dolomitic quicklime, high calcium lime, hydrated lime, lime and limestone, magnesia chemicals, magnesium, mica, minerals, oxide magnesium, pulverized lime, quartz, stearate magnesium, and talc. Entries include: Company name, postal address, city, country, phone, fax, e-mail and websites, contact person, designation, and product details.

Directory of American Manufacturers and Exporters of Motors and Motor Parts--Electric. EXIM Infotek Private Ltd. • Covers: 230 American manufacturers and exporters of AC and DC motors, brushless motors, air motors, electric motors, fractional horsepower motors, gear motors, hydraulic motor, integral horsepower motors, miniature motors, permanent magnet motors, servo motor, springs motors, stepping motors, stepper motors, sub-fractional horsepower motors, and submersible motors. Entries include: Company name, postal address, telephone, fax, e-mail, website, contact person, designation, and product details.

Directory of American Manufacturers & Exporters of Nuts, Bolts, Screws & Fasteners. EXIM Infotek Private Ltd. • $20 Individuals. Covers: 260 American manufacturers & exporters of belt fasteners, bolts, captive screws, clevis pins, electronic & electrical enclosure closing systems, fasteners, fasteners for electronics & aerospace, fasteners-aluminum steel, fasteners-automotive, fasteners-industrial, fasteners-military specialties, fasteners-nylon, fasteners-plastic, fasteners-specialty, fasteners-spring steel, fasteners-stainless steel, fasteners-textiles, hand adjusting & fastening components, hex head bolts, marine snap fasteners, metric fasteners, military snap fasteners, nuts, nuts & bolts, pins, plastic fasteners, plastic snap fasteners, precision fasteners for military & commercial aircraft, quarter-turn fasteners, rivets, screws, self-locking nuts, special threaded & non-threaded fasteners, staples, threaded inserts & related high-tech fasteners. Entries include: Company name, postal address, city, country, telephone, fax, e-mail & websites, contact person, designation, products detail.

Directory of American Manufacturers & Exporters of Paints, Varnishes & Allied Products. EXIM Infotek Private Ltd. • $30 Individuals. Covers: 450 American manufacturers and exporters of abrasion resistant coatings, agricultural/horticultural foliar applied coatings, anodizing, anti-slip paints and coatings, buffing compound applicators, chartek intumescant epoxy for structural steel, coatings, coatings and coating materials, coatings-abrasion resistant, coatings-anti- graffiti, coatings-anti-skid, coatings-asphalt, coatings-ceramic, coatings-corrosion resistant, coatings-floor, coatings-heat resistant, coatings-metal, coatings-metallic, coatings-pipeline, coatings-ultraviolet, corrosion resistant, corrosion resistant coatings, custom coatings, decorative coatings, easels, electrically conductive coatings, encapsulating resins, epoxy coatings, flexible bright metallic coatings for auto wheels, trims, high performance coatings, industrial coatings, lacquers coatings, military specification coatings, optical coatings, paint brushes, paints, paper coatings, permanent protective coatings, pipe coatings, plastic coatings, polyester coatings, polyester resins and coatings, polyurethane coatings, primers coatings, refractory coatings, self locking coating for screws and studs, solvents, urethane coatings, waterproof, waterproofing coatings, wear and corrosion resistant, and wood coatings. Entries include: Company name, postal address, city, country, telephone, fax, e-mail and websites, contact person, designation, and product details.

Directory of American Manufacturers & Exporters of Paper & Paper Products. EXIM Infotek Private Ltd. • $5 Individuals. Covers: 40 American manufacturers and exporters of bags-paper lined, carbon papers, collect and process paper for recycling, computer paper products, fax paper, paper, and white paper recycling. Entries include: Company name, postal address, city, country, phone, fax, e-mail and websites, contact person, designation, and product details.

Directory of American Manufacturers & Exporters of Petroleum Products. EXIM Infotek Private Ltd. • $10 Individuals. Covers: 120 American manufacturers & exporters of additives for engines, brake & transmission fluid, gas, gear lubricants, hydraulic oils, industrial oil, lubricants, lubricating oil & greases, oils-cutting & drawing, oils-hardening, tempering & quenching, petroleum & chemical industry, synthetic oil, water soluble oils. Entries include: Company name, postal address, city, country, phone, fax, e-mail & websites, contact person, designation, products detail.

Directory of American Manufacturers & Exporters of Pharmaceutical Products. EXIM Infotek Private Ltd. • $5 Individuals. Covers: 30 American manufacturers and exporters of animal health products, dental medicaments, dental pharmaceuticals, generic pharmaceuticals, nuclear medicine, pharmaceuticals. Entries include: Company name, postal address, city, country, phone, fax, e-mail and websites, contact person, designation, and product details.

Directory of American Manufacturers and Exporters of Restaurant, Hotel and Catering Equipment and Supplies. EXIM Infotek Private Ltd. • Covers: 120 American manufacturers and exporters of beverage dispensers and equipment for hotels and restaurants. Entries include: Company name, postal address, telephone, fax, e-mail, website, contact person, designation, and product details.

Directory of American Manufacturers & Exporters of Seeds & Bulbs--Flowers & Vegetables. EXIM Infotek Private Ltd. • $10 Individuals. Covers: 80 American manufacturers and exporters of agricultural vegetable seeds, alfalfa seeds, cotton seeds, edible seeds, field seeds, flower seeds, forage seeds, grass seeds, hybrid sunflower seeds, livestock forage, rice seeds, seeds, sorghum seeds, soybeans seeds, sunflower seeds, turf seeds, vegetable seeds, and wheat seeds. Entries include: Company name, postal address, city, country, phone, fax, e-mail and websites, contact person, designation, and product details.

Directory of American Manufacturers & Exporters of Soap, Detergent & Cleaning Supplies. EXIM Infotek Private Ltd. • $5 Individuals. Covers: 40 American manufacturers and exporters of carpet cleaning chemicals, cleaning chemicals, detergents, and detergents-chemicals. Entries include: Company name, postal address, city, country, phone, fax, e-mail and websites, contact person, designation, and product details.

Directory of American Manufacturers & Exporters of Stationery Articles & Education Supplies. EXIM Infotek Private Ltd. • $15 Individuals. Covers: 180 American manufacturers and exporters of address books, air brush colors, appointment books, ball pens, ball point pens, artists' brush, card and passport cases, clip boards, desk pads and accessories, desk pens, desk sets, desk top accessories, envelopes, felt tip, files, filing folders, fluorescent, hobby brushes, ink, letter openers, markers, nibs, organizers, paper clips, parker pens, pencils, lead and mechanical pencils, non-mechanical pencils, steel pens, refills, rulers, scrapbooks, stationery products, stationery specialties, stationery supplies, stencil, and writing instruments. Entries include: Company name, postal address, telephone, fax, e-mail, website, contact person, designation, and product details.

Directory of American Manufacturers & Exporters of Tobacco & Tobacco Products. EXIM Infotek Private Ltd. • Covers: 20 American manufacturers and exporters of cigarettes. Entries include: Company name, postal address, telephone, fax, e-mail, website, contact person, designation, and product details.

Directory of American Manufacturers & Exporters of Toys & Games. EXIM Infotek Private Ltd. • $15 Individuals. Covers: 170 American manufacturers and exporters of arts and craft kits, baby cribs, balloons, carnival toys, children's toys, coin operated games, dolls, educational toys, games, infant toys, inflatable, joke novelties, juvenile furniture, kite reels, magic tricks, outdoor games, outdoor toys, pedal cars, plastic playing cards, plastic toys, playing cards and children's games, plush toys, pools, preschool toys, puzzles, ride-on toys, slot machines, sports memorabilia, stuffed toys, toy parts-plastic, toys, toys and games, and video games. Entries include: Company name, postal address, city, country, phone, fax, e-mail and websites, contact person, designation, and product details.

Directory of American Manufacturers & Exporters of Tractors, Parts & Accessories. EXIM Infotek Private Ltd. • $5 Individuals. Covers: 25 American manufacturers and exporters of agricultural tractors and spare parts, farm tractors, tractor parts, and tractors. Entries include: Company name, postal address, city, country, phone, fax, e-mail and websites, contact person, designation, and product details.

Directory of American Manufacturers & Exporters of Tyres & Tubes. EXIM Infotek Private Ltd. • $10 Individuals. Covers: 70 American manufacturers and exporters of tire repair materials, tires, tires and tubes, and tires for trucks and heavy equipment. Entries include: Company name, postal address, city, country, phone, fax, e-mail and websites, contact person, designation, and product details.

Directory of American Manufacturers & Exporters of Waste Disposal & Recycling Equipment. EXIM Infotek Private Ltd. • Covers: 340 American manufacturers and exporters of advanced wash recycling systems, balers and recycling equipment, baling presses, compactors, decontamination waste disposable systems, garbage disposers, glass and can crushers, hazardous materials, hazardous waste disposal system, food waste disposers, indoor and outdoor steel and fiberglass receptacles, modern gas chlorinators, recycled wood and paper waste and fiber materials, recycling center equipment, aluminum can densors and flattener, sewage treatment systems, shredders, solid waste disposable systems, stump and wood waste disposable equipment, tire shredders, trash compactors, waste handling equipment, wastewater reclamation equipment, wastewater treatment systems, and wood waste recycling equipment.

Directory of American Manufacturers & Exporters of Wax & Wax Products. EXIM Infotek Private Ltd. • $10 Individuals. Covers: 100 American manufacturers and exporters of car waxes, dental waxes, floor finishes wax, microcrystalline waxes, synthetic waxes, wax, waxes and polishes, wax floors. Entries include: Company name, postal address, city, country, phone, fax, e-mail and websites, contact person, designation, products detail.

Directory of American Manufacturers & Exporters of Wire, Chain & Wire Products. EXIM Infotek Private Ltd. • $5 Individuals. Covers: 20 American manufacturers and exporters of cables-mechanical, silver wire, steel wire rope, and wires. Entries include: Company name, postal address, city, country, phone, fax, e-mail and websites, contact person, designation, and product details.

Directory of American Manufacturers & Exporters of Wires & Cables--Electrical. EXIM Infotek Private Ltd. • Covers: 280 American manufacturers and exporters of assemblies coaxial cables, bonding and grounding cables, booster cables, cable accessories, cable assemblies, coaxial cable, electrical cables, electronic cables, fiber optic cables, triaxial cables, twisted pair cables, conduits electrical cables, copper cable, electric cables, electrical wire, high temperature wire and cables, high temperature wires, magnet insulated wires, public utility electrical cables, PVC coaxial cables, retractile cables, teflon cables, teflon insulated wires, high voltage wire, insulated wire, and wire-plastic coated. Entries include: Company name, postal address, telephone, fax, e-mail, website, contact person, designation, and product details.

Directory of American Manufacturers and Exporters of Woodworking Equipment and Tools. EXIM Infotek Private Ltd. • Covers: 240 American manufacturers and exporters of automatic saws and circular, band sawing machine, band saw, band saw blades, belt conveyors, circular cold sawing machine, circular saw blades for wood, circular saw, compass saw, cut off saw, forestry equipment, high speed saw, lumber, machinery for woodworking industry, panel saw, plywood, reciprocating saw, resaw, sabre saw, saw blades, saw mill, saw mill machinery, saws woodworking, chain saw and parts, portable saws, round hole saw, slitting and slotting saw, stackers, trimmers, wood machinery, and woodworking accessories. Entries include: Company name, postal address, telephone, fax, e-mail, website, contact person, designation, and product details.

Directory of American Manufacturers & Exporters of Yarns & Threads. EXIM Infotek Private Ltd. • $10 Individuals. Covers: 80 American manufacturers and exporters of bleaching and space dyeing yarns, carpet yarns, cotton yarns, synthetic yarns, textile yarn, woolen yarns, and yarns. Entries include: Company name, postal address, city, country, phone, fax, e-mail and websites, contact person, designation, and product details.

Directory of American Manufacturers & Exporters of Zippers, Garment & Shoe Accessories. EXIM Infotek Private Ltd. • $5 Individuals. Covers: 40 American manufacturers and exporters of bar code labels, belts-buckles, buckles, buttons, metal snap fasteners, metal zippers, nylon molded zippers, and zippers. Entries include: Company name, postal address, city, country, phone, fax, e-mail and websites, contact person, designation, and product details.

Directory of Argentine Exporters and Importers. Telmo G. Mirat. • Annual. $100 postpaid. Covers: 3,250 manufacturers, importers, and exporters in Argentina, and companies and organizations providing products and services to international traders. Entries include: Organization name, address, phone, telex, fax, description of product/service, and Brussels tariff number.

Directory of Arizona Exporters. Arizona Commerce Authority. • Annual. Covers: Arizona enterprises currently involved in international trade. Entries include: Company name, address, phone, fax, e-mail, names of principal executive, and international marketing contact, number of employees, products or services, date established, current or planned export regions.

Directory of Asian Importers of Audio Visual Training Equipment and Projectors. EXIM Infotek Private Ltd. • $300 Individuals. Covers: 60 Asian importers of audio, audio visual equipment, audio visual training equipment, LCD projector, projectors, project equipment, slides, and slide projectors. Entries include: Company name, postal address, telephone, fax, e-mail, website, contact person, designation, and product details.

Directory of Asian Importers of Biological Products. EXIM Infotek Private Ltd. • $250 Individuals. Covers: 20 Asian importers of biological products and molecular biology. Entries include: Company name, postal address, telephone, fax, e-mail, website, contact person, designation, and product details.

Directory of Asian Importers of Boiler and Boiler Parts. EXIM Infotek Private Ltd. • Covers: 120 Asian importers of boiler machinery, boilers, boilers and parts, boiler fittings, gas boiler, hot water boilers, and steam boilers. Entries include: Company name, postal address, telephone, fax, e-mail, website, contact person, designation, and product details.

Directory of Asian Importers of Calendars, Greeting, Prints and Lithographs. EXIM Infotek Private Ltd. • $300 Individuals. Covers: 105 Asian importers of calendars, greeting cards, postcards, diaries, posters, prints, lithographs, etching, serigraphs, original painting, smart cards, vinyl flooring, visiting cards, and wedding cards. Entries include: Company name, postal address, telephone, fax, e-mail, website, contact person, designation, and product details.

Directory of Asian Importers of Dyes, Colors, and Pigments. EXIM Infotek Private Ltd. • $950 Individuals. Covers: 580 Asian importers of acrylic color, activated carbon, auxiliaries, candle additives, dye and scent, chemical for textile, chemical intermediates, dye for leather industry, dye for textile industry, colors and pigments, dyestuff, dyestuff intermediates, fluorescent pigments, ink, leather chemicals, phthalic anhydride, resin for printing ink, synthetic organic dyestuff, textile auxiliaries, textile chemicals, textile dye, and washing chemicals. Entries include: Company name, postal address, telephone, fax, e-mail, website, contact person, designation, and product details.

Directory of Asian Importers of Energy and Power Equipment. EXIM Infotek Private Ltd. • Covers: 130 Asian importers of high voltage equipment and component, nuclear equipment and materials, power equipment, power generation projects, power plants, power transmission component, power transmission equipment and supplies, power transmission products, solar cells, solar charge controller and modules, solar energy equipment, wind energy equipment, and transmission and allied equipment. Entries include: Company name, postal address, telephone, fax, e-mail, website, contact person, designation, and product details.

Directory of Asian Importers of Environment Protection and Pollution Control Equipment. EXIM Infotek Private Ltd. • Covers: 230 Asian importers of air cleaner, dust collectors, dust extractor systems, environment equipment, environment protection equipment, environmental monitoring equipment, environmentally conserving or improving products, noise control equipment, ozone generators, pollution control equipment, sewage treatment, water purification equipment, water treatment, water treatment equipment, water treatment plants, and purifying equipment. Entries include: Company name, postal address, telephone, fax, e-mail, website, contact person, designation, and product details.

Directory of Asian Importers of Fibre Products. EXIM Infotek Private Ltd. • $500 Individuals. Covers: 190 Asian importers of acrylic fiber, carbon fiber, fiberglass materials, fiber waste, fiberglass, fiberglass cloth, fiberglass products and cloth, fiber products, fiber materials, fiberglass chopped strands, fiberglass products, high-density fiberboard, natural fiber, optic fiber, polyester fiber, polyester staple fiber, polynosic staple fiber, synthetic fiber, viscose fiber, viscose rayon staple fiber, and vulcanized fiber. Entries include: Company name, postal address, telephone, fax, e-mail, website, contact person, designation, and product details.

Directory of Asian Importers of Fire Fighting Equipment & Supplies. EXIM Infotek Private Ltd. • $500 Individuals. Covers: 250 Asian importers of automatic fire alarm systems, CO2 gas and extinguishers, fire alarm and detection systems, fire alarm equipment, fire alarm panels, fire blankets, fire detection products, fire fighting equipment, fire fighting supplies, fire hose reel, hydrant and sprinkler systems, fire hose systems, fire hydrants, fire panels, fire protective clothing, fire resistant products, fire sensors and components, fire suppression systems, firefighting vehicles and accessories, flame detectors, optical smoke detector, security and fire fighting equipment, smoke detection systems, and smoke detectors. Entries include: Company name, postal address, telephone, fax, e-mail, website, contact person, designation, and product details.

Directory of Asian Importers of Fodder and Animal Foodstuffs. EXIM Infotek Private Ltd. • $450 Individuals. Covers: 210 Asian importers of alfalfa, alfalfa hay cubes, animal and foodstuff aditives, animal feeds, feed additives, animal food, cottonseed meal, feeder calves, fodder, cereals, and livestock breeding supplies, livestock products, and whey. Entries include: Company name, postal address, telephone, fax, e-mail, website, contact person, designation, and product details.

Directory of Asian Importers of Food Additives and Aromatics. EXIM Infotek Private Ltd. • $750 Individuals. Covers: 410 Asian importers of agar, agar-agar, aromatic chemicals, chemical for food, essence, flavor and fragrance chemicals, flavoring materials, flavoring essence, food additives, food colors, food flavors, food ingredients, food raw materials, fragrances, fruit powder, natural coloring matters, oleoresin, raw material for flavors, raw materials for food colors, tapioca starch, vanillin (pollar BR), whey powder, xylitol, and yeasts. Entries include: Company name, postal address, telephone, fax, e-mail, website, contact person, designation, and product details.

Directory of Asian Importers of Handkerchives, Scarves and Neckwears. EXIM Infotek Private Ltd. • $350 Individuals. Covers: 130 Asian importers of clothing accessories, ties, scarves, corsage, handkerchieves, neckwear, mufflers, necktie, pashmina shawls, silk neckties, silk scarves, and stoles. Entries include: Company name, postal address, telephone, fax, e-mail, website, contact person, designation, and product details.

Directory of Asian Importers of Heaters and Heating Equipment. EXIM Infotek Private Ltd. • Covers: 120 Asian importers of electric heaters for industry, heat detectors, heat exchangers, heaters, heating and ventilation equipment, heating elements and spare parts, heating equipment, solar energy heating products, solar water systems, thermic fluid heaters, waste heat recovery systems, and water heaters. Entries include: Company name, postal address, telephone, fax, e-mail, website, contact person, designation, and product details.

Directory of Asian Importers of Honey and Syrup. EXIM Infotek Private Ltd. • $150 Individuals. Covers: 35 Asian importers of honey, syrups, and honey products. Entries include: Company name, postal address, telephone, fax, e-mail, website, contact person, designation, and product details.

Directory of Asian Importers of Juices and Soft Drinks. EXIM Infotek Private Ltd. • $750 Individuals. Covers: 410 Asian importers of beverages, concentrated juices, pure water, drinks and cakes, energy drinks, fruit and vegetable concentrates, fruit and vegetable juices, fruit drinks, fruit flavored drinks, fruit pulp, fruit syrups, lychee juice concentrate, malted food drinks, mango-purees, mineral water, non-alcoholic beverages, orange juice, pine pulp, puree, and softdrinks. Entries include: Company name, postal address, telephone, fax, e-mail, website, contact person, designation, and product details.

Directory of Asian Importers of Laboratory & Scientific Instruments and Supplies. EXIM Infotek Private Ltd. • $1,400 Individuals. Covers: 620 Asian importers of analysis equipment, analytical instruments, anatomical models, binoculars, microscopes, telescopes, biotechnology instruments, borosilicate glass tubing, educational scientific equipment, electrical test equipment, glass tubular vial and ampoules, gyrocompass, laboratory equipment, laboratory and scientific glass, laboratory supplies, laboratory glassware, laboratory instruments, laboratory reagents, non-contact infrared thermometers, non-destructive testing equipment, radiology equipment, scientific instruments, testing and measuring equipment, testing instruments, testing machines, thermometers, and barometers. Entries include: Company name, postal address, telephone, fax, e-mail, website, contact person, designation, and product details.

Directory of Asian Importers of Material Handling Equipment & Supplies. EXIM Infotek Private Ltd. • Covers: 300 Asian importers of aerial lifts and platforms, backhoe loaders, chain hoist, conveying machine, conveyor systems, crane equipment, hoists, crawler crane, electric hoist, elevator lifts, elevators, escalators, forklift parts and accessories, hand pallet truck, hoisting blocks chipping machine and spares, liebherr tower cranes, liquid handling equipment, loaders, loading and unloading equipment, materials handling containers and equipment materials handling and lifting system, mobile cranes, monorail materials handling equipment, pallet truck, pulley, roller chain, used conveyor belts, used excavators, used forklift, wheel loaders, and winch. Entries include: Company name, postal address, telephone, fax, e-mail, website, contact person, designation, and product details.

Directory of Asian Importers of Military & Police Equipment & Supplies. EXIM Infotek Private Ltd. • $250 Individuals. Covers: 70 Asian importers of ammunition, military clothing, military electronic equipment, military equipment and supplies, military surplus goods, police equipment, surplus military equipment and supplies, and traffic control systems. Entries include: Company name, postal address, telephone, fax, e-mail, website, contact person, designation, and product details.

Directory of Asian Importers of Minerals. EXIM Infotek Private Ltd. • $800 Individuals. Covers: 370 Asian importers of acid phosphoric mineral, bauxite, borax, carbon and graphite products, copper mineral, crucibles made of alumina or quartz, faucets, ferrites, flourspar, fossils, graphite, gypsum, industrial minerals, iron ore, iron oxide, lead, limestone, magnesium oxide, manganese ore, metals and minerals, mica, mineral oil, mineral products and raw materials, mineral raw materials, ores, phosphoric acid, rare earth minerals, rare metal minerals, rare metals, rock phosphate, silica sand, soil, sulfur, zinc, zircon sand, zirconic, and zirconium sand. Entries include: Company name, postal address, telephone, fax, e-mail, website, contact person, designation, and product details.

Directory of Asian Importers of Motors and Motor Parts--Electric. EXIM Infotek Private Ltd. • Covers: 150 Asian importers of DC motors, Eddy current variable speed motors, electric motor control, electric motors, geared motors, induction motors, motor equipment and parts, motor graders, motor parts and accessories, motor starters, pump and motor accessories, servo motors and controllers. Entries include: Company name, postal address, telephone, fax, e-mail, website, contact person, designation, and product details.

Directory of Asian Importers of Photographic Equipment and Supplies. EXIM Infotek Private Ltd. • $500 Individuals. Covers: 170 Asian importers of cameras, lens and accessories, photographic chemicals, motion picture and theater equipment, colored film, black and white film, digital camera, plate and photographic papers, graphic films, microfilm and blueprint equipment, motion picture films, photo film, photo finishing equipment, photo finishing paper and chemicals, photographic equipment, photographic goods, photographic materials, photographic paper, and tripod. Entries include: Company name, postal address, telephone, fax, e-mail, website, contact person, designation, and product details.

Directory of Asian Importers of Refrigeration Equipment and Supplies. EXIM Infotek Private Ltd. • $400 Individuals. Covers: 180 Asian importers of air cooled water chillers, centrifugal chillers, chest freezers, cold rooms, cooling towers, deep freezers, freezers, ice cream display, refrigeration and air conditioning equipment, refrigeration parts and supplies, refrigeration spare parts, refrigeration and air conditioning servicing accessories, commercial refrigeration, and industrial refrigeration. Entries include: Company name, postal address, telephone, fax, e-mail, website, contact person, designation, and product details.

Directory of Asian Importers of Restaurant, Hotel and Catering Equipment. EXIM Infotek Private Ltd. • $250 Individuals. Covers: 70 Asian importers of catering equipment, catering supplies, commercial kitchen equipment, cooking equipment (patio and outdoors), food service equipment, food waste disposer, hotel and restaurant equipment, hotel amenity goods, hotel equipment and supplies, microwave equipment and component, hotel and catering service requisites. Entries include: Company name, postal address, telephone, fax, e-mail, website, contact person, designation, and product details.

Directory of Asian Importers of Sewing Machines and Parts. EXIM Infotek Private Ltd. • $450 Individuals. Covers: 125 Asian importers of embroidery machinery, garment industry equipment and accessories, household sewing machine, industrial sewing machine, industrial sewing machine parts, new and reconditioned sewing machine, sewing machine and spare parts, sewing machine repairs, domestic sewing machine, sewing needles, stitch machine, and used embroidery machine. Entries include: Company name, postal address, telephone, fax, e-mail, website, contact person, designation, and product details.

Directory of Asian Importers of Sporting Goods. EXIM Infotek Private Ltd. • $1,050 Individuals. Covers: 460 Asian importers of badminton, badminton rackets, baseball and golf caps, baseball supplies, basketball, billiard game table and equipment, billiard pool equipment, bowling equipment and supplies, cricket and hockey goods, firearms, football tools, golf accessories, golf ball, golf carts, golf club and bags, hobby and do-it-yourself articles, leisure and sports goods, playground equipment, equipment for sauna, spa, and swimming pool, shuttlecocks, ski equipment and supplies, snow sports goods, sports bags, sports wear, sports gloves, stadium equipment, table tennis equipment and accessories, tennis equipment and supplies, tennis rackets, volley balls, water sports equipment and supplies, windsurfing and surfing products.

Directory of Asian Importers of Telephone Instruments and Accessories. EXIM Infotek Private Ltd. • $600 Individuals. Covers: 300 Asian importers of caller ID telephone instruments, CDMA phone, cellular phone accessories and parts, cordless telephone, EPABX systems, GSM mobile phone, handphone accessories, headphone, intercom systems, microphone, microwave components, PABX and intercom equipment, pager alphanumberic, pagers, beepers, telefax equipment, telephone accessories, telephone answering equipment, telephone electronic components, telephone (cables), and used cellular phone. Entries include: Company name, postal address, telephone, fax, e-mail, website, contact person, designation, and product details.

Directory of Asian Importers of Waste Disposal & Recycling Equipment. EXIM Infotek Private Ltd. • $300 Individuals. Covers: 100 Asian importers of compactors, garbage disposals and compactors, incinerators, incubators, sand and recycles use, sewage systems, syringe and needle destroyers, waste disposal equipment, waste management, waste recycling equipment, waste water treatment equipment, and water treatment systems. Entries include: Company name, postal address, telephone, fax, e-mail, website, contact person, designation, and product details.

Directory of Asian Importers of Wires & Cables--Electrical. EXIM Infotek Private Ltd. • Covers: 190 Asian importers of cables, cables and accessories, copper winding wires, copper wires, electric cables, electrical cable, electrical wires, enameled copper wires, instrumentation cables, power cables, power cords, speaker AV cable, thermocouple wire, and wiring accessories. Entries include: Company name, postal address, telephone, fax, e-mail, website, contact person, designation, and product details.

Directory of Asian Importers of Yarns and Threads. EXIM Infotek Private Ltd. • $950 Individuals. Covers: 580 Asian importers of 100% cotton yarn for weaving cotton, acetate filament yarn, acrylic yarn, acrylic yarn carded and dyed, carpet yarn, cotton yarn and thread, dupion silk yarn, fancy yarns, fibers and yarns, filament yarn, jute yarn, knitting yarn, linen yarn, man-made fiber, man-made yarn, metallic yarn and thread, nylon filament yarn, nylon thread, nylon yarn, polyester filament yarn, polyester yarn, polypropylene yarn, raw silk yarn, rayon yarn, sewing threads, silk yarn and thread, spun silk yarn, stitching thread, synthetic yarn and thread, viscose filament yarn, viscose rayon filament yarn, viscose yarn, wool yarn, yarn twister, and yarn waste. Entries include: Company name, postal address, telephone, fax, e-mail, website, contact person, designation, and product details.

Directory of Australia and New Zealand Importers of Alcoholic Beverages, Wines. EXIM Infotek Private Ltd. • $250 Individuals. Covers: 70 Australian and New Zealand importers of alcohol, alcoholic beverages, beer, ale, champagne, Corona beer, distilled spirits, French wine, gin, grape wine, liquors, malt beer, rum, sparkling wine, vodka, and whisky. Entries include: Company name, postal address, telephone, fax, e-mail, website, contact person, designation, and product details.

Directory of Australia and New Zealand Importers of Calendars. EXIM Infotek Private Ltd. • $150 Individuals. Covers: 20 Australian and New Zealand importers of calendars, greeting cards, postcards, cards, morals, posters, prints, lithographs and etching. Entries include: Company name, postal address, telephone, fax, e-mail, website, contact person, designation, and product details.

Directory of Australia and New Zealand Importers of Carpets, Durries, Floor Coverings. EXIM Infotek Private Ltd. • $150 Individuals. Covers: 30 Australian and New Zealand importers of carpets, rugs, designer rugs, floor coverings, hand knotted rugs, hand tufted rugs, handloomed wool rugs, handmade carpets, handmade woollen rugs, linoleum (vinyl), mats (grass, rattan, bamboo, cotton), and rubber floor coverings. Entries include: Company name, postal address, telephone, fax, e-mail, website, contact person, designation, and product details.

Directory of Australia and New Zealand Importers of Computer Hardware, Peripherals. EXIM Infotek Private Ltd. • $250 Individuals. Covers: 75 Australian and New Zealand importers of compact disc, compressor parts, computer and computer accessories, computer components, computer consumables, computer driven routing systems, computer equipment and supplies, computer hardware, computer keyboards, computer networking hardware, computer parts, computer peripherals, printers, Dell P3 notebooks, dot matrix printers, DVR capture cards, graphic cards, imaging products, ink jet cartridges, ink jet printers, ink jet refill, laptop, laser printers, memories, modems-fax and data, monitors, motherboard, mouse pads, netservers, network equipment, and printing devices. Entries include: Company name, postal address, telephone, fax, e-mail, website, contact person, designation, and product details.

Directory of Australia and New Zealand Importers of Computer Software. EXIM Infotek Private Ltd. • $150 Individuals. Covers: 30 Australian and New Zealand importers of architech design software, business software, computer software, geographic information systems technologies, LAN/network hardware and software, mapping software, and software for garment industry. Entries include: Company name, postal address, telephone, fax, e-mail, website, contact person, designation, and product details.

Directory of Australia and New Zealand Importers of Construction Machinery and Equipment. EXIM Infotek Private Ltd. • $150 Individuals. Covers: 25 Australian and New Zealand importers of bulldozers, concrete machinery, concrete paving plant, concrete product plant, construction and building equipment, construction machinery, earthmoving equipment and machinery, excavating equipment, excavator parts, hot mix asphalt plant, hydraulic brake parts, parts for excavators and dozers, road construction machinery, scale model and construction kit, street maintenance equipment, and used construction equipment. Entries include: Company name, postal address, telephone, fax, e-mail, website, contact person, designation, and product details.

Directory of Australia and New Zealand Importers of Energy and Power Equipment. EXIM Infotek Private Ltd. • $150 Individuals. Covers: 20 Australian and New Zealand importers of energy conservation products, industrial power system, industrial transmission products, power transmission equipment supplies, power transmission products, solar cells, solar charge controller and modules, solar energy equipment, solar pool heating, transmission and allied equipment. Entries include: Company name, postal address, telephone, fax, e-mail, website, contact person, designation, and product details.

Directory of Australia and New Zealand Importers of Fibre and Fibre Products. EXIM Infotek Private Ltd. • $150 Individuals. Covers: 20 Australian and New Zealand importers of acrylic fibers, fiber glass grating, fiber optic cables, fiber glass, fiber glass products and cloth, fiber glass chopped strands, fiber glass products, microfibers, PU fiber glass, staple fibers, synthetic fibers, and viscose fiber. Entries include: Company name, postal address, telephone, fax, e-mail, website, contact person, designation, and product details.

Directory of Australia & New Zealand Importers of Fire Fighting Equipment & Supplies. EXIM Infotek Private Ltd. • $150 Individuals. Covers: 20 Australian and New Zealand importers of CO2 gas and extinguishers, electrical fire stopping and protection systems, fire alarm, fire detection for smoke, flame, heat, and gas, fire detection products, fire extinguishers, fire fighting equipment, fire fighting supplies, fire hoses, fire panels, fire proofing chemicals, fire protection equipment, fire rescue equipment, firefighting powders and foams, paramedic and trauma products, fire rescue tools, flame detection instruments, flame protection products, monitors (foam/water), and pressure protection products. Entries include: Company name, postal address, telephone, fax, e-mail, website, contact person, designation, and product details.

Directory of Australia and New Zealand Importers of Food Additives and Aromatic Chemicals. EXIM Infotek Private Ltd. • $150 Individuals. Covers: 30 Australian and New Zealand importers of bakery raw materials, baking improvers, carbohydrates derivatives, citrates, essence, flavor and fragrance chemicals, flavors, flower essences, food additives, food colors, food chemicals, food colors, food ingredients, fragrances, industrial food flavors, and industrial food ingredients. Entries include: Company name, postal address, telephone, fax, e-mail, website, contact person, designation, and product details.

Directory of Australia and New Zealand Importers of Gold and Silver Jewellery. EXIM Infotek Private Ltd. • $150 Individuals. Covers: 20 Australian and New Zealand importers of bracelet, gold, silver jewelry, gold and silver leaf mirrors, jewelry parts and components. Entries include: Company name, postal address, telephone, fax, e-mail, website, contact person, designation, and product details.

Directory of Australia & New Zealand Importers of Herbs & Herbal Medicine Products. EXIM Infotek Private Ltd. • $150 Individuals. Covers: 20 Australian and New Zealand importers of Chinese herbal products, Chinese herbs, Chinese medicines, herb extracts, herb seeds, herbal cosmetics, herbal extracts, herbal medicine, herbal powders, herbal products, herbal remedies, herbal tea, herbs, legumes, medicinal herb and botanicals, natural and herbal medicines, natural cosmetic ingredients, and natural health. Entries include: Company name, postal address, telephone, fax, e-mail, website, contact person, designation, and product details.

Directory of Australia and New Zealand Importers of Lumber, Timber, Plywood and Hardwood. EXIM Infotek Private Ltd. • $150 Individuals. Covers: 40 Australian and New Zealand importers of board, construction plywood, decorative plywood, doors and windows, hardboard and particleboard, hardwood flooring, floor tiles, laminates, hardwood lumber, softwood lumber, marine plywood, medium-density fiberboards, millwork (wooden), plywood, veneer, poles, pilings and logs, sawn lumber, teak, timber, timber products, timberland products, and wood. Entries include: Company name, postal address, telephone, fax, e-mail, website, contact person, designation, and product details.

Directory of Australia & New Zealand Importers of Material Handling Equipment. EXIM Infotek Private Ltd. • $150 Individuals. Covers: 35 Australian and New Zealand importers of chain hoist, chip conveyer, conveyor products, conveyor systems, crane equipment, cranes and hoists, electric hoist, elevators lifts, escalators, forklifts, forklift parts and accessories, forklift trucks, freight and shipping containers, grain handling equipment, hand trolleys, industrial brake equipment, lifting equipment, liquid handling equipment, loaders, loading and unloading equipment, materials handling equipment and hardware, monorail materials handling equipment, pulley, and winches. Entries include: Company name, postal address, telephone, fax, e-mail, website, contact person, designation, and product details.

Directory of Australia & New Zealand Importers of Paper & Paper Products. EXIM Infotek Private Ltd.

• $150 Individuals. Covers: 30 Australian and New Zealand importers of cardboard vases, coated paper, colored copy paper, construction paper in rolls, graphic papers, greaseproof paper, kraft paper, label papers, newsprint paper, paper products, paper bags, paper cups and plates, paper napkins, paper waste, photocopy paper, printing paper, recycled paper, rice paper, specialty papers, tissue paper products, and toilet paper rolls. Entries include: Company name, postal address, telephone, fax, e-mail, website, contact person, designation, and product details.

Directory of Australia and New Zealand Importers of Photographic Equipment. EXIM Infotek Private Ltd. • $150 Individuals. Covers: 20 Australian and New Zealand importers of camera bags and cases, camera lenses, photographic chemicals, motion picture and theater equipment, digital camera, film, plate and photographic papers, infrared cameras, infrared camera accessories, photo film, photo process equipment, photographic equipment and supplies. Entries include: Company name, postal address, telephone, fax, e-mail, website, contact person, designation, and product details.

Directory of Australia and New Zealand Importers of Plastic Scrap and Raw Materials. EXIM Infotek Private Ltd. • $5 Individuals. Covers: 20 Australian and New Zealand importers of fiberglass resins, high-density polyethylene (HDPE), HMS scrap, industrial polyurethane, nylon resin, plastic raw materials, plastic scrap and waste, poly propylene, polyethylene resin, polymers, polyurethane chemicals, polyurethane form, polyurethane products, and polypropylene raw materials. Entries include: Company name, postal address, telephone, fax, e-mail, website, contact person, designation, and product details.

Directory of Australia & New Zealand Importers of Sporting Goods. EXIM Infotek Private Ltd. • $300 Individuals. Covers: 95 Australian and New Zealand importers of adventure sporting goods, baseball supplies, basketball equipment, beach accessories, firearms, footballs, golf ball, golf carts, golf course accessories, golf equipment, golf tools, handballs, hobby and do-it-yourself articles, judo accessories, motorcycle boots, mountaineering equipment and supplies, net balls, rugby balls, skates and accessories, ski equipment, ski gloves, ski sports goods, snow sports goods, snowboards, soccer balls, sports bags, sports gloves, sports water equipment, string for rackets, surfing products, volley balls, water sports equipment and supplies, wind surfing accessories and equipment, winter sports equipment and goods.

Directory of Australia and New Zealand Importers of Telephone Instruments and Accessories. EXIM Infotek Private Ltd. • $150 Individuals. Covers: 20 Australian and New Zealand importers of cellular phone accessories and parts, cellular phone camera lens, EPABX systems, GSM phones, handphone accessories, intercom systems, microphones, microwave components, pagers, beepers, telephone headsets, telephone systems, and used mobile phones. Entries include: Company name, postal address, telephone, fax, e-mail, website, contact person, designation, and product details.

Directory of Australia and New Zealand Importers of Woodworking Equipment and Tools. EXIM Infotek Private Ltd. • $150 Individuals. Covers: 30 Australian and New Zealand importers of band saw and blades, chain saw, circular saw, dimension saw, forestry equipment, hydraulic chain saw, new and reconditioned woodworking machine, saw blades, saw mill equipment, wood chipping machine, woodworking equipment, woodworking machine and accessories, and woodworking tools. Entries include: Company name, postal address, telephone, fax, e-mail, website, contact person, designation, and product details.

Directory of Australia and New Zealand Importers of Yarns and Threads. EXIM Infotek Private Ltd. • $150 Individuals. Covers: 25 Australian and New Zealand importers of cotton yarn, embroidery thread, filament yarn, industrial filament yarn, knitting yarn, metallic yarn and thread, polyster yarn, sewing threads, silk yarn and thread, synthetic yarn and thread, textile fibers, wool yarn, and worsted weaving yarn. Entries include: Company name, postal address, telephone, fax, e-mail, website, contact person, designation, and product details.

Directory of Automated Criminal Justice Information Systems. U.S. Bureau of Justice Statistics. • $60. Covers: Over 1,870 computerized information systems serving over 700 police, courts, state and local government judicial and correctional agencies. Entries include: Description of system or agency; acronym; type of system; functions; hardware and software configuration; function names, addresses, and phone numbers of agency contact.

Directory of Belgian Importers of American Products. American Chamber of Commerce in Belgium. • Annual. $125. Covers: 1,000 Belgian importers and distributors and 3,000 U.S. exporters of U.S. products in Belgium. Entries include: Company name, address, phone, fax, executives, products.

Directory of Belgian Research Centers with Libraries or Documentation Services. National Center for Scientific & Technical Documentation Royal Library. • Annual. $1,000. Covers: 1,090 research centers, including universities and companies, in Belgium. Entries include: Center name, address, phone, databases, uses of information.

Directory of Belgium Importers of Computer Hardware and Peripherals. EXIM Infotek Private Ltd. • $300 Individuals. Covers: 110 Belgium importers of computer equipment and supplies, computer peripherals, computer supplies, computers and components, LAN/network hardware and software, and laser printers. Entries include: Company name, postal address, telephone, fax, e-mail, website, contact person, designation, and product details.

Directory of Belgium Importers of Computer Software. EXIM Infotek Private Ltd. • $150 Individuals. Covers: 35 Belgium importers of computer software. Entries include: Company name, postal address, telephone, fax, e-mail, website, contact person, designation, and product details.

Directory of Belgium Importers of Construction Machinery and Equipment. EXIM Infotek Private Ltd. • Covers: 30 Belgium importers of construction, building equipment and parts, earthmoving equipment, excavating equipment, industrial and construction vehicles, scale model and construction kit, and street maintenance equipment. Entries include: Company name, postal address, telephone, fax, e-mail, website, contact person, designation, and product details.

Directory of Belgium Importers of Laboratory & Scientific Instruments & Supplies. EXIM Infotek Private Ltd. • $250 Individuals. Covers: 50 Belgium importers of binoculars, microscopes, telescopes, scientific and laboratory instrument, and testing equipment. Entries include: Company name, postal address, telephone, fax, e-mail, website, contact person, designation, and product details.

Directory of Belgium Importers of Lumber, Timber, Plywood and Hardboards. EXIM Infotek Private Ltd. • $150 Individuals. Covers: 25 Belgium importers of doors, windows, hardwood flooring, floor tiles, hardwood lumber, softwood lumber, plywood, veneer, poles, wood, pilings and logs. Entries include: Company name, postal address, telephone, fax, e-mail, website, contact person, designation, and product details.

Directory of Belgium Importers of Materials Handling Equipment. EXIM Infotek Private Ltd. • $150 Individuals. Covers: 35 companies in Belgium that import conveyors, cranes and hoisting equipment, fork lifts, liquid handling equipment, loading and unloading equipment, materials handling equipment and parts, winches, and pulleys. Entries include: Company name, postal address, telephone, fax, e-mail, website, contact person, designation, and product details.

Directory of Blue Chip Companies. InfoGroup Inc. • Entries include: Company name, address, phone, name and title of chief executive, Standard Industrial Classification (SIC) codes, code indicating annual sales and number of employees.

Directory of British Footwear Exporters. British Footwear Association. • Biennial. Covers: Manufacturers of footwear who export products. Entries include: Company name, address, phone, telex, trade name.

Directory of British Importers of Alcoholic Beverages and Wines. EXIM Infotek Private Ltd. • $250 Individuals. Covers: 60 British importers of alcohol, beer, ale, beverages, champagne, distilled spirits, spirits, whisky, wine, and alcoholic beverages. Entries include: Company name, postal address, telephone, fax, e-mail, website, contact person, designation, and product details.

Directory of British Importers of Carpets, Durries and Floor Coverings. EXIM Infotek Private Ltd. • $200 Individuals. Covers: 25 British importers of carpets, rugs, oriental carpets, oriental rugs, and vinyl floorings. Entries include: Company name, postal address, telephone, fax, e-mail, website, contact person, designation, and product details.

Directory of British Importers of Computer Hardwares and Peripherals. EXIM Infotek Private Ltd. • $300 Individuals. Covers: 95 British importers of computer equipment and supplies, computer hardware, computer monitors, computer parts, computer peripherals, computer supplies, computers, computer components, inkjet cartridges, LAN/network hardware and software, and laser printers. Entries include: Company name, postal address, telephone, fax, e-mail, website, contact person, designation, and product details.

Directory of British Importers of Construction Machinery and Equipment. EXIM Infotek Private Ltd. • $150 Individuals. Covers: 30 British importers of construction, building equipment and parts, excavating equipment, scale model and construction kit. Entries include: Company name, postal address, telephone, fax, e-mail, website, contact person, designation, and product details.

Directory of British Importers of Environmental Protection and Pollution Control Equipment. EXIM Infotek Private Ltd. • $150 Individuals. Covers: 40 British importers of environmental protection equipment, pollution control equipment, water treatment, and purifying equipment. Entries include: Company name, postal address, telephone, fax, e-mail, website, contact person, designation, and product details.

Directory of British Importers of Juices and Soft Drinks. EXIM Infotek Private Ltd. • $200 Individuals. Covers: 45 British importers of coca-cola, fruit and vegetable juices, mineral water, non-alcoholic beverages, and soft drinks. Entries include: Company name, postal address, telephone, fax, e-mail, website, contact person, designation, and product details.

Directory of British Importers of Laboratory & Scientific Instruments & Supplies. EXIM Infotek Private Ltd. • $300 Individuals. Covers: 120 British importers of binoculars, microscopes, telescopes, laboratory and scientific glass, scientific and laboratory instrument, and testing equipment. Entries include: Company name, postal address, telephone, fax, e-mail, website, contact person, designation, and product details.

For publishers' addresses, refer to SOURCES CITED section at the back of the book.

Directory of British Importers of Lumber, Timber, Plywood and Hardboards. EXIM Infotek Private Ltd. • $250 Individuals. Covers: 80 British importers of doors, windows, hardboard, particleboard, hardwood flooring, floor tiles, wood laminates, lumber, timber, plywood, hardwood lumber, softwood lumber, plywood, veneer, poles, pilings and logs. Entries include: Company name, postal address, telephone, fax, e-mail, website, contact person, designation, and product details.

Directory of British Importers of Material Handling Equipment. EXIM Infotek Private Ltd. • $200 Individuals. Covers: 45 British importers of conveyors, cranes and hoisting equipment, elevators lifts, forklifts, liquid handling equipment, loading and unloading equipment, materials handling equipment and parts, monorail materials handling equipment, winches, and pulleys. Entries include: Company name, postal address, telephone, fax, e-mail, website, contact person, designation, and product details.

Directory of British Importers of Restaurant, Hotel and Catering Equipment. EXIM Infotek Private Ltd. • Covers: 25 British importers of catering equipment and supplies, cooking equipment (patio and outdoors), microwave equipment and component, restaurant and hotel equipment. Entries include: Company name, postal address, telephone, fax, e-mail, website, contact person, designation, and product details.

Directory of British Importers of Woodenware & Wooden Products. EXIM Infotek Private Ltd. • Covers: 30 British importers of baskets and basket ware, wooden millwork, and wooden products. Entries include: Company name, postal address, telephone, fax, e-mail, website, contact person, designation, and product details.

Directory of British Importers of Yarns and Threads. EXIM Infotek Private Ltd. • $150 Individuals. Covers: 20 British importers of yarn and thread, cotton yarn and thread, synthetic yarn and thread. Entries include: Company name, postal address, telephone, fax, e-mail, website, contact person, designation, and product details.

Directory of Business Information. John Wiley and Sons Inc. Technical Insights. • $290 Individuals. Covers: Over 10,000 sources of business information, including publications, associations, companies, government offices, and libraries.

The Directory of Business Information Resources. Grey House Publishing. • Annual. $195 Libraries Softcover. Provides contact names as well as editorial and advertising personnel, phone and fax numbers, description, frequency, pricing information, industry's associations, newsletters, magazines, trade shows, directories, databases and industry websites of 21,000 businesses.

Directory of Business Opportunities. Todd Publications. • Annual. $15. Covers: Hundreds of business opportunities, new products, franchises, dealerships and investment opportunities, including import/export deals and wholesale merchandising. Entries include: Contact name, address, phone.

Directory of Business/Trade/Professional Associations, Chambers of Commerce and Industrial Development Authorities. West Virginia Chamber of Commerce. • Biennial. $5 Individuals. Covers: About 50 chambers of commerce, 95 chamber and association executives, 50 trade associations, and about 50 development authority offices. Entries include: For chambers, associations, and development offices--Name, address, phone, names and titles of key officials. For chamber and association executives--Name, address, phone, name of affiliated chamber or association, title.

Directory of Buyout Financing Sources. Buyout Publications, Inc. • Annual. $445 plus $9.00 shipping. Covers: over 1,000 sources of acquisition financing, including banks, asset-based lenders, small business investment companies, insurance companies, and venture capital firms. Entries include: Company name, address, phone, E-mail, URL, names and titles of key personnel, financial data, type of company and size requirements, underwriting criteria, equity requirements, post-closing role, information required, response time, sample transactions. Also promoted under title 'Financing Sourcebook for Buyouts & Acquisitions.'.

Directory of California Agricultural Exporters. • Biennial. $50. Covers: Approximately 1,600 California companies in the growing, processing, and trading of food and fiber products in the worldwide market. Entries include: Company name, address, phone, fax, E-mail/web address, name and title of contact, number of employees, year established, products grown, processed, or traded, names and titles of key personnel, type of company.

Directory of California Technology Companies. San Francisco Chamber of Commerce. • $161 Members. Covers: 12,000 California-based technology manufacturers, wholesalers, and software and service companies working in fields such as research and development, aerospace, software, biotech, aerospace and others. Entries include: Contact details.

Directory of California Wholesalers and Service Companies. Harris InfoSource. • Annual. $210 Individuals hardcover. Covers: Approximately 225,200 wholesalers, distributors, and other service firms in California. Includes key executives. Database includes: Statistical data, trade show calendar. Entries include: Company name, address, parent name/location, telephone, fax and 800 numbers, web site address (on CD-ROM only), number of employees, year established, annual revenue, plant size, business description, Standard Industrial Classification (SIC) code, executive names/titles, public ownership, legal structure, import/export designators, and female/minority ownership.

Directory of Canadian Companies Overseas. Overseas Employment Services. • Annual. $15 postpaid. Covers: about 250 Canadian companies and professional firms with branch plants or offices outside of Canada and the U.S. Entries include: Company name, address, geographical area served, product/service.

Directory of Canadian Information Sources. Browning Associates. • Covers: approximately 1,500 directories, market surveys, trade guides, association publications, and special periodical issues that are sources of Canadian information. Entries include: Publication title, publisher name, address, phone, frequency, price, scope of coverage, description of contents and arrangement, whether advertising is accepted, other details.

Directory of Caribbean Importers. Caribbean Export Development Agency. • $15. Covers: Companies importing goods in the Carribean business community. Database includes: Profiles of sixteen Caribbean countries. Entries include: Name, address, phone, products imported.

Directory of Central Atlantic States Manufacturers. George D. Hall Company Inc. • Biennial. $83 plus $4.90 shipping (1994 edition). Covers: about 18,000 companies in Maryland, Delaware, Virginia, West Virginia, North Carolina, and South Carolina. Entries include: Company name, address, phone, name of principal executive, number of employees, products or services, Standard Industrial Classification (SIC) code.

Directory of CEOs. IBCON S.A. • Irregular. $458 Individuals. Covers: 14,640 companies incorporated in Mexico City. Entries include: Name and position of top executive, company name, address, phone, fax, industry code.

Directory of Certified Business Counselors. Institute of Certified Business Counselors. • Irregular. Covers: 160 member counselors, brokers, and attorneys qualified to act as advisors for persons with business problems. Entries include: Name, address, phone, business specialty.

Directory of Chinese and Foreign Industrial and Commercial Enterprises Special Issue on Chemicals and Petroleum. Xinhua Publishing House. • $30. Covers: industrial and commercial petroleum and chemical companies worldwide. Database includes: Statistics on China's chemical export. Entries include: Company name, address, phone, telex, names and titles of key personnel, registered capital, export data, and description.

Directory of Chinese and Foreign Management and Sales Personnel. Standards Press of China. • Biennial. $30. Covers: 8,700 companies, organizations, and individuals in business, industry, and other professionals. Entries include: Name, address, phone, telex, name and title of contact, names and titles of key personnel, geographical area covered, description of activities.

Directory of Chinese Importers of Chemicals & Allied Products. EXIM Infotek Private Ltd. • Covers: 900 Chinese importers of acetic anhydride, acetone, acids, chemical and allied products, chemical products, chemical raw materials, glycerin, industrial chemicals, liquid chemicals, molybdenum concentrate, naphthalene, organic chemicals, oxalic acid, plastic chemicals, potassium hydroxide, reagents, resins and gums, specialty chemicals, tetra ethyl lead, and toluene. Entries include: Company name, postal address, telephone, fax, e-mail, website, contact person, designation, and product details.

Directory of Chinese Importers of Fibre Products. EXIM Infotek Private Ltd. • $150 Individuals. Covers: 20 Chinese importers of fibers, high-density fiberboard, optic fibers, polyester staple fibers, and synthetic fibers. Entries include: Company name, postal address, telephone, fax, e-mail, website, contact person, designation, and product details.

Directory of Chinese Importers of Leather, Hides, Skins & Furs. EXIM Infotek Private Ltd. • Covers: 30 Chinese importers of cow leathers, hides, skins and fur, leather, mink and fox tails, pig skins, scrap sheep, and fox skin. Entries include: Company name, postal address, telephone, fax, e-mail, website, contact person, designation, and product details.

Directory of Chinese Importers of Lumber, Timber, Plywood and Hardboards. EXIM Infotek Private Ltd. • $150 Individuals. Covers: 30 Chinese importers of beechwood lumber, hardwood lumber, softwood lumber, plywood, veneer, poles, pilings and logs, sawn timber, and wood. Entries include: Company name, postal address, telephone, fax, e-mail, website, contact person, designation, and product details.

Directory of Chinese Importers of Minerals. EXIM Infotek Private Ltd. • $150 Individuals. Covers: 25 Chinese importers of copper mineral, iron ore, iron oxide, metals, and minerals. Entries include: Company name, postal address, telephone, fax, e-mail, website, contact person, designation, and product details.

Directory of Chinese Importers of Packaging Materials & Supplies. EXIM Infotek Private Ltd. • Covers: 35 Chinese importers of bopp film, cardboard, packaging materials, and wrapping paper. Entries include: Company name, postal address, telephone, fax, e-mail, website, contact person, designation, and product details.

Directory of Chinese Importers of Paper & Paper Products. EXIM Infotek Private Ltd. • $150 Individuals. Covers: 40 Chinese importers of newsprint, paper, wood pulp, paper products, paper waste, printing paper, pulp, and specialty paper. Entries include: Company name, postal address, telephone, fax, e-mail, website, contact person, designation, and product details.

Directory of Chinese Importers of Plastic Scrap and Raw Materials. EXIM Infotek Private Ltd. • $200 Individuals. Covers: 60 Chinese importers of ABS scrap, high-density polyethylene (HDPE), pet bottle scrap in flakes and PVC waste, plastic raw materials, plastic resins, plastic scrap and waste, plastic additives, and polypropylene. Entries include: Company name, postal address, telephone, fax, e-mail, website, contact person, designation, and product details.

Directory of Chinese Manufacturers & Exporters of Adhesive, Glues, Sealants. EXIM Infotek Private Ltd. • $10 Individuals. Covers: 50 Chinese manufacturers and exporters of adhesive products, adhesives, bone glue, epoxy resins, glue, glue products, hot melt adhesives, polyurethane adhesive, and sealing materials. Entries include: Company name, postal address, city, country, phone, fax, e-mail and websites, contact person, designation, and product details.

Directory of Chinese Manufacturers & Exporters of Agro Chemicals, Fertilizers, Pesticides, Insecticides. EXIM Infotek Private Ltd. • $20 Individuals. Covers: 210 Chinese manufacturers and exporters of agricultural chemical products, agricultural chemicals, agrochemicals, biochemical products, biological pesticides, bio-pesticides, chemical fertilizers, farm chemicals, fertilizers, herbicides, insecticide, nitrogen fertilizer, pesticide intermediates, pesticides, and phosphate fertilizers. Entries include: Company name, postal address, city, country, phone, fax, e-mail and websites, contact person, designation, and product details.

Directory of Chinese Manufacturers & Exporters of Agro Commodities. EXIM Infotek Private Ltd. • $10 Individuals. Covers: 80 Chinese manufacturers and exporters of agricultural products, beans, broad beans, buckwheat, farm products, grains, maize, rice, soy beans, sugar, and wheats. Entries include: Company name, postal address, city, country, phone, fax, e-mail and websites, contact person, designation, and product details.

Directory of Chinese Manufacturers and Exporters of Alcoholic Beverages, Wines. EXIM Infotek Private Ltd. • $200 Individuals. Covers: 60 Chinese manufacturers and exporters of beer, beverages, dry red wine, fruit wine, grape wine, and liquor. Entries include: Company name, postal address, telephone, fax, e-mail, website, contact person, designation, and product details.

Directory of Chinese Manufacturers & Exporters of Autoparts and Accessories. EXIM Infotek Private Ltd. • $20 Individuals. Covers: 190 Chinese manufacturers and exporters of auto accessories, auto fittings, auto lamps, auto parts, auto safety glass, automobile accessories, automobile electric appliances, automobile glass, automobile halogen lamps, automobile lights, automobile locks, automobile parts, automobile spare parts, automobile switches, automobile wipers, automotive glass, automotive parts, brake drums and hubs, brake shoes, brakes, car accessories, car audio devices, car parts, car speakers, clutch covers, clutch discs, gaskets, indicator lights, motor vehicle accessories, plastic autoparts, radiators, sealing products, shock absorbers, spare parts, transmission equipment, vehicle accessories, vehicle fittings, vehicle parts, and wheels. Entries include: Company name, postal address, city, country, phone, fax, e-mail and websites, contact person, designation, and product details.

Directory of Chinese Manufacturers & Exporters of Batteries & Accumulators. EXIM Infotek Private Ltd. • $10 Individuals. Covers: 110 Chinese manufacturers and exporters of accumulator cells, batteries, batteries for ups, batteries-rechargeable, batteries-storage, battery chargers, batteries for vehicles, dry batteries, lead acid batteries. Entries include: Company name, postal address, city, country, phone, fax, e-mail and websites, contact person, designation, products detail.

Directory of Chinese Manufacturers & Exporters of Bearings. EXIM Infotek Private Ltd. • $10 Individuals. Covers: 60 Chinese manufacturers and exporters of ball bearings, bearings, needles and rollers, cylindrical roller bearings, engine bearings, needle bearings, needle roller bearings, roller bearings, sliding bearings, spherical roller bearings, steel balls, and tapered roller bearings. Entries include: Company name, postal address, city, country, phone, fax, e-mail and websites, contact person, designation, and product details.

Directory of Chinese Manufacturers & Exporters of Beauty Supplies, Cosmetics, Perfumes, Toiletries. EXIM Infotek Private Ltd. • $10 Individuals. Covers: 80 Chinese manufacturers and exporters of bathing products, beauty products, brushes-cosmetics, cosmetic accessories, cosmetic brushes, cosmetics, eyebrow pencils, eyeshadow pencil, fragrances, hair brushes, lipstick, manicure sets, perfume, perfume bottles, perfumes, shampoo, skin care products, talcum, and talcum powder. Entries include: Company name, postal address, city, country, phone, fax, e-mail and websites, contact person, designation, and product details.

Directory of Chinese Manufacturers & Exporters of Bicycles, Parts & Accessories. EXIM Infotek Private Ltd. • $5 Individuals. Covers: 25 Chinese manufacturers and exporters of bicycle frames, bicycle lamps, bicycle parts, bicycles, electric bicycles, and sprockets. Entries include: Company name, postal address, city, country, phone, fax, e-mail and websites, contact person, designation, and product details.

Directory of Chinese Manufacturers & Exporters of Candles & Candle Products. EXIM Infotek Private Ltd. • $5 Individuals. Covers: 35 Chinese manufacturers and exporters of candle holders, candle lamps, candles, craft candles. Entries include: Company name, postal address, city, country, phone, fax, e-mail and websites, contact person, designation, and product details.

Directory of Chinese Manufacturers & Exporters of Carpets, Durries, Floor Coverings. EXIM Infotek Private Ltd. • $10 Individuals. Covers: 50 Chinese manufacturers and exporters of carpets, PVC floor tiles, PVC tiles, rugs, silk carpets, and woolen carpets. Entries include: Company name, postal address, city, country, phone, fax, e-mail and websites, contact person, designation, and product details.

Directory of Chinese Manufacturers & Exporters of Castings and Forgings. EXIM Infotek Private Ltd. • $15 Individuals. Covers: 130 Chinese manufacturers and exporters of cast iron, cast iron fittings, cast iron pipes, cast iron products, cast steel products, casting, casting-iron, castings, die casting mould, die castings, forging, forging parts, grey cast iron, iron casting, manhole covers, nodular cast iron, precision castings, steel castings. Entries include: Company name, postal address, city, country, phone, fax, e-mail & websites, contact person, designation, products detail.

Directory of Chinese Manufacturers & Exporters of Chemicals & Allied Products. EXIM Infotek Private Ltd. • $50 Individuals. Covers: 900 Chinese manufacturers & exporters of acids, acrylic acid, activated carbon, activated carbon fiber, activated carbon products, alkali, allyl chloride, ammonia, ammonium bicarbonate, ammonium carbonate, ammonium chloride, ammonium hydrogen carbonate, ammonium nitrate, ammonium paratungstate, ammonium persulphate, ammonium phosphate, ammonium sulphate, ammonium thiocyanate, antimony potassium tartrate, antioxidants, barium carbonate, barium hydroxide, barium nitrate, barium salts, barium sulfates, benzene, benzoic acid, benzotriazole, benzotri-fluoride, boric acid, calcium carbide, calcium chloride, calcium citrate, calcium hydroxide, calcium nitrite, calcium superphosphate, carbon additives, carbon black, carbon block, catalysts, caustic soda, chemical & allied products, chemical additives, chemical assistants, chemical fiber, chemical industrial materials, chemical industrial products, chemical materials, chemical products, chemical raw materials & products, chemical reagent, chemicals, chemicals for cosmetics/perfumery/detergent/soaps, chemicals for textiles, chemistry reagents, chlorinated polyethylene, chlorine, chlorine alkali, chlorine dioxide, chlorine-liquefied, chondroitin sulfate, chromic acid, citric acid, coatings, dicalcium phosphate, dicyandiamide, dsd acid, fine chemical products, fine chemicals, formic acid, hydrochloric acid, hydrofluoric acid, hydrogen peroxide, industrial chemicals, inorganic acids & anhydrides, inorganic chemicals, inorganic products, l-cysteic acid, liquid chemicals, methanol, molybdenum chemical products, mono ammonium phosphate, naphthenic acid, natural resins & pithces, nitrate, nitric acid, nitrobenzene, nitrofurazone, nitromethane, organic chemical material, organic chemicals, organic products, organo pophasphorus, oxalic acid, paper making chemicals, petrochemical products, p-fluoro benzaldehyde, phosphate chemicals, potassium, potassium bicarbonate, potassium carbonate, potassium chloride, potassium hydroxide, potassium nitrate, potassium permaganate, potassium persulfate, potassium sulfate, raw material for chemicals, raw material for cosmetic, refined chemical products, sebacic acid, silicon, soda, soda ash, sodium acetate, sodium alginate, sodium bicarbonate, sodium bromate, sodium carnllite, sodium chlorate, sodium citrate, sodium cyanide, sodium fluoride, sodium hydrosulfite, sodium hydroxide, sodium magnesium chlorophyllin, sodium nitrate, sodium silicate, sodium sulphate, sodium tartrate, sodium thiocyanate, stearic acids, sulfuric acid, sulphur, sulphur black, sulphuric acids, synthetic ammonia, synthetic chemicals, tannic acid, tartaric acid, water treatment chemicals, zirconium chemicals. Entries include: Company name, postal address, city, country, telephone, fax, e-mail & websites, contact person, designation, products detail.

Directory of Chinese Manufacturers & Exporters of Confectionery and Bakery Products. EXIM Infotek Private Ltd. • $5 Individuals. Covers: 20 Chinese manufacturers and exporters of biscuits/crackers, cakes and pastries, candy, fried peanuts, instant noodles, and vinegar. Entries include: Company name, postal address, city, country, phone, fax, e-mail and websites, contact person, designation, and product details.

Directory of Chinese Manufacturers and Exporters of Construction Machinery and Equipment. EXIM Infotek Private Ltd. • $150 Individuals. Covers: 30 Chinese manufacturers and exporters of building machinery, construction equipment, construction machinery, crusher, dust collectors, and mixers. Entries include: Company name, postal address, telephone, fax, e-mail, website, contact person, designation, and product details.

Directory of Chinese Manufacturers & Exporters of Cotton, Silk, Wool Raw and Waste. EXIM Infotek Private Ltd. • $10 Individuals. Covers: 50 Chinese manufacturers and exporters of cotton, cotton products, cotton pulp, goat's wool, mulberry silk, wool, wool and wool products. Entries include: Company name, postal address, city, country, phone, fax, e-mail and websites, contact person, designation, and product details.

Directory of Chinese Manufacturers & Exporters of Dyes, Colors, Pigments, Intermediates. EXIM Infotek Private Ltd. • $25 Individuals. Covers: 290 Chinese manufacturers and exporters of acid dyestuffs, auxiliaries, auxiliary materials, cationic dyestuff, chemical dyes, chemical intermediates, disperse dyes, dye intermediates, dyeing materials, dyes, dyes intermediates, dyes-red base, dyestuff, dyes-vet, fluorescent brightener series, fluorescent pigment products, fluorescent whitening, inorganic pigments, intermediate for dyestuffs, intermediates, intermediates-various, iron oxide pigments, iron oxide yellow, organic intermediates, organic pigments, pigment intermediates, pigments, pigments-natural, plastic dyes, reactive dyes, vat dyes. Entries include: Company name, postal address, city, country, phone, fax, e-mail and websites, contact person, designation, and product details.

Directory of Chinese Manufacturers & Exporters of Electronic Equipment & Supplies. EXIM Infotek Private Ltd. • Covers: 90 Chinese manufacturers and exporters of electronic devices, electronic equipment, electronic instrument, oscilloscope, and television transmission equipment. Entries include: Company name, postal address, telephone, fax, e-mail, website, contact person, designation, and product details.

Directory of Chinese Manufacturers & Exporters of Engines & Engine Parts. EXIM Infotek Private Ltd. • $5 Individuals. Covers: 35 Chinese manufacturers and exporters of diesel engines, engine beds-ordinary, engine parts and accessories, engines, inlet valves, piston rings, pistons, spark plugs. Entries include: Company name, postal address, city, country, phone, fax, e-mail and websites, contact person, designation, and product details.

Directory of Chinese Manufacturers & Exporters of Fire Fighting Equipment & Supplies. EXIM Infotek Private Ltd. • Covers: 20 Chinese manufacturers and exporters of fire alarm systems, fire extinguishing systems, fire fighting equipment, fire proof materials, fire protection equipment, fireclay bricks, and flame retardant. Entries include: Company name, postal address, telephone, fax, e-mail, website, contact person, designation, and product details.

Directory of Chinese Manufacturers & Exporters of Flowers, Plants & Trees, Seeds & Bulbs. EXIM Infotek Private Ltd. • $5 Individuals. Covers: 35 Chinese manufacturers and exporters of artificial flowers, artificial plants, asparagus, flower plants, flowers-cut, flowers-dried, flowers-manmade, flowers-various, lotus roots, ornamental plants, plants, plants-natural, potpourri, roses. Entries include: Company name, postal address, city, country, phone, fax, e-mail and websites, contact person, designation, and product details.

Directory of Chinese Manufacturers & Exporters of Food Additives & Aromatic Chemicals. EXIM Infotek Private Ltd. • $5 Individuals. Covers: 40 Chinese manufacturers and exporters of essence, flavors, food additives, food flavor, food ingredients, and yeast. Entries include: Company name, postal address, city, country, phone, fax, e-mail and websites, contact person, designation, and product details.

Directory of Chinese Manufacturers & Exporters of Fruits & Vegetables. EXIM Infotek Private Ltd. • $15 Individuals. Covers: 150 Chinese manufacturers and exporters of apples, bamboo shoots, canned fruits, canned mushrooms, canned pineapples, carrots, cherries, dehydrated vegetables, dried carrots, dried mushrooms, dried vegetables, frozen bamboo shoots, frozen carrots, frozen fruits, frozen vegetables, fruit, garlic, garlic sprouts, ginger, grapes, green beans, vermicelli, green vegetables, lychee, mushrooms, mushrooms and fungi, onion slices, onions, onions-Chinese, oranges, pea pods, salted vegetables, strawberries, vegetable products, vegetables, and vegetables-canned. Entries include: Company name, postal address, city, country, phone, fax, e-mail and websites, contact person, designation, and product details.

Directory of Chinese Manufacturers & Exporters of Furniture--All Types. EXIM Infotek Private Ltd. • $15 Individuals. Covers: 170 Chinese manufacturers and exporters of aluminum chairs, bamboo furniture, beach chairs, beds, benches, cabinets, chairs, Chinese antique furniture, coffee tables, dinner tables, foldable chairs, furniture-domestic, furniture-garden, furniture-hotel/restaurant/bar, furniture-kitchen, furniture-office, furniture, furniture-antique, furniture-outdoor, metal furniture, plastic chairs, plastic tables, racks and fittings, sofas, steel furniture, steel tube furniture, tables, wood furniture, and wooden furniture. Entries include: Company name, postal address, city, country, phone, fax, e-mail and websites, contact person, designation, and product details.

Directory of Chinese Manufacturers & Exporters of Garden Tools, Equipment & Supplies. EXIM Infotek Private Ltd. • $5 Individuals. Covers: 20 Chinese manufacturers and exporters of garden decorations, garden products, garden tools, and garden tools-all kinds. Entries include: Company name, postal address, city, country, phone, fax, e-mail and websites, contact person, designation, and product details.

Directory of Chinese Manufacturers & Exporters of Giftwares & Novelties. EXIM Infotek Private Ltd. • $10 Individuals. Covers: 90 Chinese manufacturers & exporters of Christmas articles, Christmas gifts, gifts, giftware, key chain, novelty, photo frames, picture frames, plastic photo frames, premiums, promotional items, souvenirs. Entries include: Company name, postal address, city, country, phone, fax, e-mail & websites, contact person, designation, products detail.

Directory of Chinese Manufacturers & Exporters of Glassware, Chinaware, Ceramicware & Porcelainware. EXIM Infotek Private Ltd. • $10 Individuals. Covers: 100 Chinese manufacturers and exporters of artistic porcelain, ashtrays, ceramic pots, ceramic tea sets, ceramics household, Chinaware, daily use porcelain, glass art decoration, glass candle holders, glass chimneys, glass vases, glassware, porcelain and ceramic products-commercial/industrial, porcelain dolls, porcelains, porcelainware, pottery, white porcelainware. Entries include: Company name, postal address, city, country, phone, fax, e-mail and websites, contact person, designation, products detail.

Directory of Chinese Manufacturers & Exporters of Handicrafts & Decorative Items. EXIM Infotek Private Ltd. • $25 Individuals. Covers: 310 Chinese manufacturers and exporters of antiques, arts and crafts, art decoration, artware, building decoration materials, carvings, Christmas decorations, Christmas items, Christmas tree ornaments, Christmas tree sets, crafts, craft clocks, craft products, craft works, decoration items, decorative products, figurines, folk crafts, Halloween decorations, handicrafts, hanging decorations, hanging objects, hanging pictures, metal crafts, oil paintings, sculptures, tombstones, tourist articles, vases. Entries include: Company name, postal address, city, country, phone, fax, e-mail and websites, contact person, designation, and product details.

Directory of Chinese Manufacturers & Exporters of Handkerchieves, Scarves & Neckwear. EXIM Infotek Private Ltd. • $10 Individuals. Covers: 60 Chinese manufacturers and exporters of bows and ties, cashmere scarves, neckties/scarves, scarves, shawls, silk ties, textile accessories, and ties. Entries include: Company name, postal address, city, country, phone, fax, e-mail and websites, contact person, designation, and product details.

Directory of Chinese Manufacturers & Exporters of Handtools. EXIM Infotek Private Ltd. • $10 Individuals. Covers: 70 Chinese manufacturers and exporters of air tools, electric power tools, hammers, hand tools, hardware tools, pliers/clamps and similar tools, screwdrivers, tool cabinets, tool cases, and tools. Entries include: Company name, postal address, city, country, phone, fax, e-mail and websites, contact person, designation, and product details.

Directory of Chinese Manufacturers & Exporters of Hardwares--All Types. EXIM Infotek Private Ltd. • $20 Individuals. Covers: 200 Chinese manufacturers and exporters of abrasive materials, abrasive paper, abrasives products, brackets, brass locks, clamps, clips, decorations-indoor, door closers, door locks, fittings, flanges, hardware, hardware fittings, hardware minerals, hardware products, hardware tools, hinges, locks, locksets, pad locks, panels, and pins. Entries include: Company name, postal address, city, country, phone, fax, e-mail and websites, contact person, designation, and product details.

Directory of Chinese Manufacturers & Exporters of Hats & Headwears. EXIM Infotek Private Ltd. • $10 Individuals. Covers: 70 Chinese manufacturers and exporters of baseball caps, caps, hats, headwear, knitted hats, sports caps, and straw hats. Entries include: Company name, postal address, city, country, phone, fax, e-mail and websites, contact person, designation, and product details.

Directory of Chinese Manufacturers & Exporters of Heaters & Heating Equipment. EXIM Infotek Private Ltd. • Covers: 30 Chinese manufacturers and exporters of electric water heaters, electrical heaters, heat exchangers, heaters, plate heat exchanger, solar energy water heaters, solar water heaters, and water heaters. Entries include: Company name, postal address, telephone, fax, e-mail, website, contact person, designation, and product details.

Directory of Chinese Manufacturers & Exporters of Herbs & Herbal Medicine Products. EXIM Infotek Private Ltd. • $10 Individuals. Covers: 110 Chinese manufacturers & exporters of biological medicine, botanical extracts, burdock, Chinese herbs, Chinese medicine, Chinese medicine-traditional, ginseng, herbal extracts, herbal medicines, herbs, natural plant extracts. Entries include: Company name, postal address, city, country, phone, fax, e-mail & websites, contact person, designation, products detail.

Directory of Chinese Manufacturers & Exporters of Home Furnishing Materials. EXIM Infotek Private Ltd. • $15 Individuals. Covers: 170 Chinese manufacturers and exporters of baby quilts, bath towels, beach towels, bed cloths, bed covers, bed sheets, bedding products, bedroom articles, blankets, curtains, cushion covers, cushions, doormats, down quilts, face towels, home decorations, home textiles, household textiles, kitchen towels, linen clothing, mats, mattresses, cushions and pillows, pillowcases, pillows, PVC table cloths, quilt cases, quilts, sanitary towels and baby napkins, shower curtains, silk towels, sleeping bags, table cloths, textiles-household, towels-jacquard bath, towels-plain bath, towels, and woolen blankets. Entries include: Company name, postal address, city, country, phone, fax, e-mail and websites, contact person, designation, and product details.

Directory of Chinese Manufacturers & Exporters of Houseware, Kitchenware & Tableware. EXIM Infotek Private Ltd. • $20 Individuals. Covers: 210 Chinese manufacturers and exporters of aluminum utensils, beer mugs, bottle openers, bowls, brooms and brushes for domestic use, brushes, choppers, chopsticks, coffee and tea sets, coffee mugs, coffee pots, combs, cooking utensils, cookwares, cups, cutlery, daily use goods, dinnerware, electric mosquito killer series, flasks, gas lighters, gas stoves, hangers, household goods, household plastic products, household utensils, housewares, ice cream spoons, kitchen articles-metal, kitchen products, kitchen tools, kitchen utensils, kitchenware, knives-metal, mugs, plastic household goods, plastic products for daily use, pressure cookers, scissors, stainless steel cookware sets, stainless steel kitchenware, stainless steel knives, stainless steel tableware, stainless steel utensils, tableware, trays, utensils, and vacuum flasks. Entries include: Company name, postal address, city, country, telephone, fax, e-mail and websites, contact person, designation, and product details.

Directory of Chinese Manufacturers & Exporters of Imitation & Fashion Jewelry. EXIM Infotek Private Ltd. • $10 Individuals. Covers: 70 Chinese manufacturers and exporters of bangles, beads, bracelets, brooches, buckles, costume accessories, costume jewelry, costumes, earrings, fashion accessories, glass beads, glass ornaments, hair accessories, hair clips, hair pins, imitation jewelry, jewelry, jewelry boxes, necklaces, ornament chains, ornaments, pendants, and synthetic diamonds. Entries include: Company name, postal address, city, country, phone, fax, e-mail and websites, contact person, designation, and product details.

Directory of Chinese Manufacturers & Exporters of Laces, Ribbons & Embroidery Products. EXIM Infotek Private Ltd. • $10 Individuals. Covers: 50 Chinese manufacturers & exporters of badges, embroidery-all types, embroideries, embroidery products, garlands, laces, ribbons. Entries include: Company name, postal address, city, country, phone, fax, e-mail & websites, contact person, designation, products detail.

Directory of Chinese Manufacturers & Exporters of Leather Products. EXIM Infotek Private Ltd. • $15 Individuals. Covers: 170 Chinese manufacturers and exporters of artificial leather products, bags, fashion bags, fur clothing & products, fur products, hand bags, leather articles, leather bags, leather belts, leather cases, leather clothing, leather garments, leather goods, leather jackets, leather products, leather purses, leather waist belts, purses, sheep and lamb skin leather products, and wallets. Entries include: Company name, postal address, city, country, phone, fax, e-mail and website, contact person, designation, and product details.

Directory of Chinese Manufacturers & Exporters of Lighting Fixtures, Lamps & Accessories. EXIM Infotek Private Ltd. • $20 Individuals. Covers: 190 Chinese manufacturers and exporters of bulbs, ceramic lamps, Christmas lights, compact fluorescent lamps, decorative lights, electric bulbs, electric lamps, electric lighting, emergency lighting, energy saving lamps, energy saving tubes, flashlights, floodlights, floor lamps, fluorescent lamps, garden lamps, glass lighting products, halogen lamps, lampholders, lamps, lanterns, lighting, lighting appliances, lighting electric appliances, lighting equipment, lighting fixtures, lighting products, metal halide lamps and ballast, neon lamps, rope lights, solar lights, solar powered lights, solar warning lights, spotlights, table lamps, and tungsten lamps. Entries include: Company name, postal address, city, country, phone, fax, e-mail and websites, contact person, designation, and product details.

Directory of Chinese Manufacturers & Exporters of Machinery for Chemical & Pharmaceutical Industry. EXIM Infotek Private Ltd. • $5 Individuals. Covers: 40 Chinese manufacturers and exporters of auxiliary equipments, chemical equipment, chemical industrial equipment, chemical industries machinery, chemical machinery, chemical process equipment, essence/perfume production plant equipment, pharmaceutical machinery, pharmacy equipments, and pharmacy machinery. Entries include: Company name, postal address, city, country, phone, fax, e-mail and websites, contact person, designation, and product details.

Directory of Chinese Manufacturers & Exporters of Machinery for Textile & Knitting Industry. EXIM Infotek Private Ltd. • $5 Individuals. Covers: 40 Chinese manufacturers and exporters of arrow-shaft looms, drying machines, knitting machines, textile machinery, and textile machinery parts. Entries include: Company name, postal address, city, country, phone, fax, e-mail and websites, contact person, designation, and product details.

Directory of Chinese Manufacturers & Exporters of Material Handling Equipment. EXIM Infotek Private Ltd. • $150 Individuals. Covers: 40 Chinese manufacturers and exporters of conveyors, cranes, electric hoist, elevators, escalators, forklift trucks, hand trucks, handling tools, hoisting machine, lifting equipment, lifts, materials handling equipment, pallets, containers, and pulleys. Entries include: Company name, postal address, telephone, fax, e-mail, website, contact person, designation, and product details.

Directory of Chinese Manufacturers & Exporters of Meat & Meat Products. EXIM Infotek Private Ltd. • $5 Individuals. Covers: 30 Chinese manufacturers and exporters of chicken meat, crabs and crabmeat, frozen beef, lean meat products, meat, meat and meat products, pork meat, walnut meat. Entries include: Company name, postal address, city, country, phone, fax, e-mail and websites, contact person, designation, and product details.

Directory of Chinese Manufacturers & Exporters of Minerals. EXIM Infotek Private Ltd. • $15 Individuals. Covers: 170 Chinese manufacturers and exporters of alumina products, carbon graphite, dolomite, faucet, feldspar, graphite, graphite-natural, iron oxide red, magnesium sulphate, mica and mecanite products, mineral products, minerals, natural quartz powder, non-metallic minerals, phosphate, phosphoric acid, phosphorous acid, phosphorous yellow, phosphorus products, quartz, rare earths, rare metals, and sulphate. Entries include: Company name, postal address, city, country, phone, fax, e-mail and websites, contact person, designation, and product details.

Directory of Chinese Manufacturers & Exporters of Motorcycles, Parts & Accessories. EXIM Infotek Private Ltd. • $10 Individuals. Covers: 50 Chinese manufacturers and exporters of bikes, motor bike accessories, motorcycle bulbs, motorcycle fittings, motorcycle locks, motorcycle parts, motorcycle starting motors, motorcycles, and scooters. Entries include: Company name, postal address, city, country, phone, fax, e-mail and websites, contact person, designation, and product details.

Directory of Chinese Manufacturers and Exporters of Motors and Motor Parts--Electric. EXIM Infotek Private Ltd. • $200 Individuals. Covers: 50 Chinese manufacturers and exporters of DC motors, electric motors, induction motors, motorcycle parts and accessories, AC motors, and sewing machine motors. Entries include: Company name, postal address, telephone, fax, e-mail, website, contact person, designation, and product details.

Directory of Chinese Manufacturers & Exporters of Nuts & Dried Fruits. EXIM Infotek Private Ltd. • $5 Individuals. Covers: 30 Chinese manufacturers and exporters of chestnuts, dried fruits, dry fruits, nuts-dried, peanut kernels, walnuts. Entries include: Company name, postal address, city, country, phone, fax, e-mail and websites, contact person, designation, and product details.

Directory of Chinese Manufacturers & Exporters of Nuts, Bolts, Screws & Fasteners. EXIM Infotek Private Ltd. • $5 Individuals. Covers: 40 Chinese manufacturers and exporters of bolts, chestnut kernels, fasteners, nuts and bolts, rivets, screws, slide fasteners, and washers. Entries include: Company name, postal address, city, country, phone, fax, e-mail and websites, contact person, designation, and product details.

Directory of Chinese Manufacturers & Exporters of Oil & Fats--Cooking & Vegetable. EXIM Infotek Private Ltd. • $5 Individuals. Covers: 30 Chinese manufacturers and exporters of cooking oil, edible oil, oils and fats-edible, peanut oil, pine oils, rapeseed, soybean oil, vegetable oil. Entries include: Company name, postal address, city, country, phone, fax, e-mail and websites, contact person, designation, and product details.

Directory of Chinese Manufacturers & Exporters of Paints, Varnishes & Allied Products. EXIM Infotek Private Ltd. • $10 Individuals. Covers: 70 Chinese manufacturers and exporters of absorbent resin, coating materials, coating raw materials, coating-automobiles, coating-fire proof, coating-water proof, lacquer, latex paints, paint, paint brushes, paint mixers, paint rollers, paints, polyester paints, polyurethane resins, powder coatings, and wall paints. Entries include: Company name, postal address, city, country, phone, fax, e-mail and websites, contact person, designation, and product details.

Directory of Chinese Manufacturers & Exporters of Paper & Paper Products. EXIM Infotek Private Ltd. • $10 Individuals. Covers: 60 Chinese manufacturers and exporters of cardboard, disposable paper products, craft paper tapes, napkins, paper, paper products, paper pulp, paperboard, and tissue papers. Entries include: Company name, postal address, city, country, phone, fax, e-mail and websites, contact person, designation, and product details.

Directory of Chinese Manufacturers & Exporters of Petroleum Products. EXIM Infotek Private Ltd. • $10 Individuals. Covers: 50 Chinese manufacturers and exporters of coal tar, fuel, lubricating oil, natural gases, petrochemicals, petroleum chemicals, and petroleum products. Entries include: Company name, postal address, city, country, phone, fax, e-mail and websites, contact person, designation, and product details.

Directory of Chinese Manufacturers & Exporters of Pharmaceutical Products. EXIM Infotek Private Ltd. • $25 Individuals. Covers: 330 Chinese manufacturers and exporters of antibiotics, biopharmaceuticals, bulk drugs, capsules, drugs, eye drops, intermediate for medicines, medicaments, medicines, medicines for animals, paracetamol, pharmaceutical materials, pharmaceutical products, pharmaceuticals, veterinary medicines. Entries include: Company name, postal address, city, country, phone, fax, e-mail and websites, contact person, designation, and product details.

Directory of Chinese Manufacturers & Exporters of Pharmaceutical Raw Materials. EXIM Infotek Private Ltd. • $10 Individuals. Covers: 80 Chinese manufacturers and exporters of amino-acid, enzymes, medicine industrial chemicals, pharmaceutical chemicals, pharmaceutical intermediates, pharmaceutical raw material, raw material for medicines, and vitamins/hormones and organ extracts. Entries include: Company name, postal address, city, country, phone, fax, e-mail and websites, contact person, designation, and product details.

Directory of Chinese Manufacturers & Exporters of Readymade Garments. EXIM Infotek Private Ltd. • $40 Individuals. Covers: 580 Chinese manufacturers and exporters of apparel, aprons, baby clothing, blouses, boxer shorts, cardigans, cashmere sweaters, casual and leisurewear, children's wear, clothing, coats, cotton garments, cotton knitwear, cotton shirts, cotton t-shirts, cowboy leisure clothes, denimwears, down garments, dress, fashionable garments, fashionable ladies garments, garments, handkerchiefs, handmade clothings, hosiery, jackets, jeans, jogging suits, kimono dresses, knitted children's tights, knitted garments, knitted goods, knitting garments, knitting products, knitwear, knitwear-children, ladies fashionable garments, ladies wear, men's suits, night wears, nylon garments, outerwears, overcoats, pajamas, pants, plastic clothes, polo t-shirts, readymade garments for men/

boys, shirts, shorts, silk garments, silk knitted garments, silk knitted products, skirts, sleepwears, sleeveless garments, sportswear, suits, surgical gowns, sweaters, swim and beach wear, textile clothings, tracksuits, trousers, t-shirts, uniforms, winter wears, woolen garments, woolen sweaters, working clothes, workwear, woven and knitted garments, woven and knitted shirts, and woven garments. Entries include: Company name, postal address, city, country, telephone, fax, e-mail and websites, contact person, designation, and product details.

Directory of Chinese Manufacturers & Exporters of Seafood & Fish. EXIM Infotek Private Ltd. • $10 Individuals. Covers: 50 Chinese manufacturers and exporters of Alaska pollack fillets, asparagus-frozen, canned asparagus, fish, fish fillets, frozen cooked crawfish, frozen fillets, frozen fish, frozen octopus, frozen seafood products, marine products, scallops, seafood, seaweed, shrimps and prawns. Entries include: Company name, postal address, city, country, phone, fax, e-mail and websites, contact person, designation, and product details.

Directory of Chinese Manufacturers & Exporters of Shoes & Footwears. EXIM Infotek Private Ltd. • $20 Individuals. Covers: 260 Chinese manufacturers and exporters of baby shoes, boots-rubber, boots, canvas shoes, casual shoes, children's shoes, footwear, jogging shoes, ladies leather shoes, leather shoes, plastic sandals, plastic slippers, up shoes, rubber boots, rubber shoes, sandals, school shoes, shoes, slippers, snow boots. Entries include: Company name, postal address, city, country, phone, fax, e-mail and websites, contact person, designation, and product details.

Directory of Chinese Manufacturers & Exporters of Soap, Detergent & Cleaning Supplies. EXIM Infotek Private Ltd. • $5 Individuals. Covers: 25 Chinese manufacturers and exporters of cleaning products, detergent liquid, detergent powder, detergents, soap, synthetic detergent. Entries include: Company name, postal address, city, country, phone, fax, e-mail and websites, contact person, designation, and product details.

Directory of Chinese Manufacturers & Exporters of Spices, Seasonings & Flavorings. EXIM Infotek Private Ltd. • $5 Individuals. Covers: 30 Chinese manufacturers and exporters of chili, dried chili, dried ginger, garlic powder, pepper, salt, seasonings, spices. Entries include: Company name, postal address, city, country, phone, fax, e-mail and websites, contact person, designation, and product details.

Directory of Chinese Manufacturers & Exporters of Sporting Goods. EXIM Infotek Private Ltd. • Covers: 170 Chinese manufacturers and exporters of athletic sports equipment, badminton rackets, basket balls, bowling equipment, camping goods, fishing accessories, fishing nets, fishing tackle, football, golf accessories, golf carts and vans, golf goods, gymnasium and exercise equipment, handball, leisure goods, mountaineering products, outdoor products, ruck sack, shuttle cock, skate scooters, sporting goods, sports bags, sports equipment, sports goods, sports shoes, sports suits, sportswear, tennis rackets, and volleyball. Entries include: Company name, postal address, telephone, fax, e-mail, website, contact person, designation, and product details.

Directory of Chinese Manufacturers & Exporters of Tea & Coffee. EXIM Infotek Private Ltd. • $10 Individuals. Covers: 50 Chinese manufacturers and exporters of black tea, Chinese tea, coffee, green tea, jasmine tea, oolong tea, and organic tea. Entries include: Company name, postal address, city, country, phone, fax, e-mail and websites, contact person, designation, and product details.

Directory of Chinese Manufacturers & Exporters of Textiles & Fabrics. EXIM Infotek Private Ltd. • $30 Individuals. Covers: 380 Chinese manufacturers and exporters of acrylic fabric, cloth, cotton fabrics, cotton textiles, dyed fabrics, fabrics-blended, fabrics-grey, fabrics, fabrics for industrial use, fabrics-denim, fabrics-silk, garment fabrics, industrial cloths, jacquard fabrics, knitted fabrics, linens, non-woven fabrics, polyester cloth, polyester fabrics, printed fabrics, pure silk, rayon products, silk, silk products, silk velvet, spinning fabrics, synthetic textiles, textile fabrics, textile materials, textile products, textile raw material and products, textiles, textiles accessories, tricot fabrics, woolen fabric garments, woolen fabrics, worsted fabrics, and woven fabrics. Entries include: Company name, postal address, city, country, phone, fax, e-mail and websites, contact person, designation, and product details.

Directory of Chinese Manufacturers & Exporters of Toys & Games. EXIM Infotek Private Ltd. • $20 Individuals. Covers: 240 Chinese manufacturers and exporters of baby care products, baby carriages, baby products, baby strollers, babyware, chess sets, child bicycles, children's toys, children's vehicles, cloth toys, craft toys, dolls, electric toys, electrical toys (a/c), electronic toys, firecrackers, fireworks, games, masks, plastic toys, playing cards, plush toys, porcelain toys, remote control toys, rubber toys, stuffed toys, toy fireworks, toy guns, toys, toy parts, toys-intelligent-adults, waterguns, wooden puzzles, and wooden toys. Entries include: Company name, postal address, city, country, phone, fax, e-mail and websites, contact person, designation, and product details.

Directory of Chinese Manufacturers & Exporters of Travel & Luggage Accessories. EXIM Infotek Private Ltd. • $10 Individuals. Covers: 60 Chinese manufacturers and exporters of briefcases, hardside luggage, leather briefcases, luggage carts, luggage, suitcases, suitcase accessories, travel bags, and travel goods. Entries include: Company name, postal address, city, country, phone, fax, e-mail and websites, contact person, designation, and product details.

Directory of Chinese Manufacturers & Exporters of Tyres & Tubes. EXIM Infotek Private Ltd. • $10 Individuals. Covers: 60 Chinese manufacturers and exporters of automobile tires and tubes, inner tubes for tires, rubber tires and tubes, tires and tubes, tires for truck, vehicle tires and inner tubes. Entries include: Company name, postal address, city, country, phone, fax, e-mail and websites, contact person, designation, and product details.

Directory of Chinese Manufacturers & Exporters of Undergarments. EXIM Infotek Private Ltd. • $10 Individuals. Covers: 50 Chinese manufacturers and exporters of briefs, socks, sport socks, stockings, underwear, and underwear-ladies. Entries include: Company name, postal address, city, country, phone, fax, e-mail and websites, contact person, designation, and product details.

Directory of Chinese Manufacturers & Exporters of Watches & Clocks. EXIM Infotek Private Ltd. • $10 Individuals. Covers: 50 Chinese manufacturers and exporters of alarm clocks, clocks, electronic quartz clocks, electronic watches, quartz clock LCD clocks, quartz clocks, quartz watches, table clocks, wall clock, and watches. Entries include: Company name, postal address, city, country, phone, fax, e-mail and websites, contact person, designation, and product details.

Directory of Chinese Manufacturers & Exporters of Wire, Chain & Wire Products. EXIM Infotek Private Ltd. • $10 Individuals. Covers: 90 Chinese manufacturers & exporters of anchors, barbed wire, brass wire mesh, chains, copper wires, galvanized iron wires, hexagonal wire mesh, hexagonal wire netting, iron wire, mesh products, metal wire mesh, metal wires, pet chains, roller chains, steel wire, welded wire mesh, wire, wire harness, wire mesh, wire netting, wire products, wire rack & accessories, wire rope, wire rope clips. Entries include: Company name, postal address, city, country, phone, fax, e-mail & websites, contact person, designation, products detail.

Directory of Chinese Manufacturers & Exporters of Woodenware & Wooden Products. EXIM Infotek Private Ltd. • $15 Individuals. Covers: 160 Chinese manufacturers and exporters of bamboo basketry, bamboo crafts, bamboo curtains, bamboo decorations, bamboo floorings, bamboo handicraft products, bamboo mats, bamboo products, bamboo tableware, baskets-various, cane and wicker products, carvings and marquetry-wooden, rattan products, wicker products, willow baskets, willow products, wood and wood articles, wood products, wooden baskets, wooden boxes, wooden crafts, wooden decorations, wooden floorings, wooden gifts, wooden handicraft products, wooden products, and woodenware. Entries include: Company name, postal address, city, country, phone, fax, e-mail and websites, contact person, designation, and product details.

Directory of Chinese Manufacturers and Exporters of Woodworking Equipment and Tools. EXIM Infotek Private Ltd. • Covers: 20 Chinese manufacturers and exporters of hacksaw blades, saw blades, saw cutting machinery, sawing machine, wood working machine, and wood working tools. Entries include: Company name, postal address, telephone, fax, e-mail, website, contact person, designation, and product details.

Directory of Chinese Manufacturers & Exporters of Yarns & Threads. EXIM Infotek Private Ltd. • $10 Individuals. Covers: 80 Chinese manufacturers and exporters of cashmere yarn, chenille yarn, cotton yarn, embroidery thread, knitting yarn, linen yarns, metallic yarns, polyester filaments, polyester thread, polyester yarn, sewing thread, thread, viscose filament yarns, yarn products, yarns, and yarns-blended. Entries include: Company name, postal address, city, country, phone, fax, e-mail and websites, contact person, designation, and product details.

Directory of Chinese Manufacturers & Exporters of Zipper, Garment & Shoe Accessories. EXIM Infotek Private Ltd. • $10 Individuals. Covers: 80 Chinese manufacturers and exporters of apparel accessories, belt buckles, buttons, buttons-resin, clothing accessories, fashion garment accessories, garment accessories, hooks, lining cloths, metal buckles, metal zippers, needles, plastic zipper, sewing kits, sewing needles, tailoring accessories, zipper products, and zippers. Entries include: Company name, postal address, city, country, phone, fax, e-mail and websites, contact person, designation, and product details.

Directory of Colorado Manufacturers. University of Colorado at Boulder Leeds School of Business Business Research Division. • $100 Individuals book; plus tax. Covers: 6,000 manufacturing firms in Colorado. Entries include: Company name, mailing address, plant address, phone, Standard Metropolitan Statistical Area (SMSA), names and titles of executives, date founded, distribution area, approximate employment, products or services.

Directory of Colorado Manufacturers--Information, Science, & Technology. University of Colorado at Boulder Leeds School of Business Business Research Division. • $25 clearance price. Covers: More than 1,600 Colorado manufacturers in the information, science and technology fields. Entries include: Plant address, mailing address, telephone number, e-mail, Web address, names and titles of key personnel, NAICS code numbers, number of employees, branch and subsidiary details, area of distribution.

Directory of Companies. IBCON S.A. • Irregular. $473 Individuals. Covers: 14,640 companies that are SA corporations located in Mexico City. Entries include: Company name, address, phone, fax, industry code, Producing, Distributing, Servicing initials, name and position of the top executive.

Directory of Companies, Board Members and Directors. Dicodi S.A. • Annual. Covers: 25,000 companies and 80,000 board members in Spain. Entries include: Company name, address, phone, director names.

Directory of Companies by Quarters. IBCON S.A. • Irregular. $473 Individuals. Covers: 14,041 companies incorporated in Mexico City. Entries include: Company name, address, phone, fax; industry code; Producing, Distributing, or Servicing initials, name and position of the top executive.

Directory of Computer and Point-of-Sale Systems for Office Products and Furniture Dealers. Independent Office Products and Furniture Dealers Association. • Irregular. $60. Covers: Approximately 45 manufacturers and distributors of computer, point-of-sale, and contract furniture systems for the office products industry. Entries include: Company name, address, phone, description of product or service.

Directory of Consulting Offices in Arab Countries. Arab Industrial Development and Metrology Organization League of Arab States. • Irregular.

Directory of Cordoba Exporters. Imagen S.A. • Covers: Products exported from Cordoba. Entries include: Product name, company name.

Directory of Corporate and Foundation Givers. Taft Group. • $270. Covers: 8,000 private foundations, corporate foundations, and companies that give money to nonprofit organizations. Entries include: Foundation name, sponsoring company name, address, phone, fax, e-mail, URL, contact name; financial summary, including assets and amounts given for up to previous three years; Employer Identification Number; summary of contributions, including typical recipients, grant types, nonmonetary support types, geographic distribution; names and titles of key personnel; application procedures; grants summary including total grants, highest grant, typical grant range, and list of recent grants, giving amounts and names of recipients.

Directory of Corporate and Foundation Grants. Taft Group. • $155. Covers: in two sections; Section 1 lists over 95,000 grants and their recipients. Section 2 lists over 5,500 corporate and foundation grantmakers. Entries include: Section 1--Recipient category, location, name of recipient, amount of grant, grant description, name of corporate or foundation grantmaker. Section 2--Foundation/company name, location, grants data, alpha record of grants.

Directory of Corporate Name Changes. The Scarecrow Press Inc. • $104 Individuals Hardback. Lists names by which corporations have been known, including original and current names. Entries include: Name, preceding and succeeding names, year changed, original name (if the name listed isn't the original).

Directory of Corporations and Corporate Officers. DAFSA. • Annual. Covers: 13,000 corporation board members and 1,200 companies on the stock exchange in France. Entries include: For members--Name, address, positions held, responsibilities. For companies--Company name, address, phone, line of business, executives, shareholders, subsidiaries, financial data.

Directory of Danish Importers of Computer Hardwares and Peripherals. EXIM Infotek Private Ltd. • $250 Individuals. Covers: 70 Danish importers of computer equipment and supplies, computer peripherals, computer supplies, computer components, LAN/network hardware and software. Entries include: Company name, postal address, telephone, fax, e-mail, website, contact person, designation, and product details.

Directory of Danish Importers of Construction Machinery and Equipment. EXIM Infotek Private Ltd. • $150 Individuals. Covers: 20 Danish importers of construction, building equipment and parts, industrial and construction vehicles, and snow removal equipment. Entries include: Company name, postal address, telephone, fax, e-mail, website, contact person, designation, and product details.

Directory of Danish Importers of Office Equipment & Supplies. EXIM Infotek Private Ltd. • $10 Individuals. Covers: 50 Danish importers of accounting and bookkeeping equipment, addressing and mailing equipment, banking equipment and supplies, calculators, cash registers, copying machines and supplies, fax and duplicating papers, office equipment and supplies, office machines, time recorders and timers, and typewriters. Entries include: Company name, postal address, telephone, fax, e-mail, website, contact person, designation, and product details.

Directory of Development Research and Training Institutes in Africa. Organisation for Economic Co-operation and Development Washington Center. • Irregular. $40. Covers: Nearly 500 organizations engaged in research and training in the fields of economic and social development in Africa. Entries include: Name of organization, address, phone, telex, cable address, name of director, number of professional staff, year established, research and training activities, other activities, periodicals, library facilities, computer facilities, and conference facilities.

Directory of Development Research and Training Institutes in Europe. OECD Publishing. • Irregular. $70 Individuals. Covers: Approximately 540 organizations and institutes in Europe engaged in research and training in the fields of development policy, international relations, foreign aid, industry, rural development, social change, environmental protection, and other economic and social issues. Entries include: Institution name, address, phone, fax, telex, cable address, name of director, number of professional staff, year established, research and training activities, other activities, periodicals, library facilities, computer facilities, and conference facilities.

Directory of Development Research and Training Institutes in Latin America. OECD Publishing. • Irregular. $27. Covers: 122 Latin American organizations in 19 countries of South and Central America engaged in research and training in the fields of economic and social development. Entries include: Name of institution, address, phone, telex, cable address, name of director, number of professional staff, year established, research and training activities, other activities, periodicals, library facilities, computer facilities, and conference facilities.

Directory of Directors. Reed Business Information. • Annual. $275 plus 7.50 pounds shipping; 15 pounds overseas. Covers: Approximately 50,000 directors of the top 15,000 public and private corporations in the United Kingdom. Entries include: Name, address, phone, fax, title and/or profession, list of companies of which a director, code indicating business interest.

Directory of East European Businesses. Mercury Books Gold Arrow Publications Ltd. • $74.95 plus $3.50 shipping. Covers: 2,000 leading manufacturing and engineering companies in Albania, Bulgaria, the Commonwealth of Independent States, eastern Germany, Hungary, Poland, Romania, and Czechoslovakia and Yugoslavia (prior to their separations). Entries include: Company name, address, phone, fax, telex, name and title of contact, line of business, sales, profits.

Directory of EC Industry Information Sources. Macmillan Publishers Ltd. Nature Publishing Group. • $105 plus $6.00 postage. Covers: Organizations and individuals in the European Communities responsible for specific industrial information, including finding business partners, business start-ups, lobbying, electronic information services, and statistics.

Directory of Economic Development Organizations in Oregon. Council for Economic Development in Oregon. • Irregular. $25. Covers: public and private organizations concerned with economic development in Oregon; includes federal, state, and local governmental agencies. Entries include: Organization or agency name, address, phone, name and title of contact, geographic territory covered.

Directory of European Importers of Biological Products. EXIM Infotek Private Ltd. • $15 Individuals. Covers: 50 European importers of biological products. Entries include: Company name, postal address, telephone, fax, e-mail, website, contact person, designation, and product details.

Directory of European Importers of Fodder & Animal Foodstuffs. EXIM Infotek Private Ltd. • $20 Individuals. Covers: 270 European importers of animal food meals, animal foodstuff additives, feed additives, fodder, livestock breeding supplies, and oats. Entries include: Company name, postal address, telephone, fax, e-mail, website, contact person, designation, and product details.

Directory of European Importers of Gears & Boxes. EXIM Infotek Private Ltd. • $10 Individuals. Covers: 90 European importers of gears and boxes. Entries include: Company name, postal address, telephone, fax, e-mail, website, contact person, designation, and product details.

Directory of European Importers of Heaters and Heating Equipment. EXIM Infotek Private Ltd. • Covers: 270 European importers of air heaters, copper tubes for central heating, heat exchangers, heating equipment, heating household application of iron and steel (non-electric), heating systems, and water heaters. Entries include: Company name, postal address, telephone, fax, e-mail, website, contact person, designation, and product details.

Directory of European Importers of Hoses & Fittings. EXIM Infotek Private Ltd. • Covers: 40 European importers of hoses, hose fittings, and adaptors. Entries include: Company name, postal address, telephone, fax, e-mail, website, contact person, designation, and product details.

Directory of European Importers of Laboratory & Scientific Instruments & Supplies. EXIM Infotek Private Ltd. • Covers: 1,300 European importers of binoculars, microscopes, telescopes, evaporators, laboratory and scientific glass, laboratory diagnostic equipment and supplies, laboratory instruments, reagents for laboratories, scientific instrument, and testing equipment. Entries include: Company name, postal address, telephone, fax, e-mail, website, contact person, designation, and product details.

Directory of European Importers of Lumber, Timber, Plywood and Hardboards. EXIM Infotek Private Ltd. • $950 Individuals. Covers: 580 European importers of coniferous raw wood, doors and windows, glued timber, gypsum board and sheetrock, hardboard and particleboard, hardwood flooring and tiles, hardwood lumber, hardwood, laminates, wood laminates, lumber goods, timber and plywood, softwood lumber, oak flooring, oak sheets, parquet, particle boards, pinewood, planed wood, plywood and veneer, poles, pilings and logs, round logs, sawdust, softwood, solid wood, teak and mahogany wood, teak logs, veneering wood, wood particle slabs, wood sawn, and wooden moldings. Entries include: Company name, postal address, telephone, fax, e-mail, website, contact person, designation, and product details.

Directory of European Importers of Machinery for Glass and Ceramic Industry. EXIM Infotek Private Ltd. • $150 Individuals. Covers: 20 European importers of ceramic industry equipment and supplies, glass making machinery and equipment.

Entries include: Company name, postal address, telephone, fax, e-mail, website, contact person, designation, and product details.

Directory of European Importers of Machinery for Rubber Industry. EXIM Infotek Private Ltd. • Covers: 35 European importers of industrial equipment tires and rubber industry equipment and supplies. Entries include: Company name, postal address, telephone, fax, e-mail, website, contact person, designation, and product details.

Directory of European Importers of Material Handling Equipment & Supplies. EXIM Infotek Private Ltd. • Covers: 450 European importers of conveyors, cranes and hoisting equipment, elevating work platforms, elevators lifts, elevators, lifts and escalators, forklifts, handling equipment, lifting and hoisting tools, lifting equipment, liquid handling equipment, loading and unloading equipment, material handling systems for garment industries, monorail materials handling equipment, winches, and pulleys. Entries include: Company name, postal address, telephone, fax, e-mail, website, contact person, designation, and product details.

Directory of European Importers of Motors and Motor Parts--Electric. EXIM Infotek Private Ltd. • Covers: 160 European importers of electric motor, gas fuel equipment for motor vehicle, and motor equipment and parts. Entries include: Company name, postal address, telephone, fax, e-mail, website, contact person, designation, and product details.

Directory of European Importers of Paper & Paper Products. EXIM Infotek Private Ltd. • Covers: 480 European importers of coated paper, envelopes, handmade paper and products, newsprint, office goods of paper and cardboard, office papers, paper and paper products, wood pulp, paper bags, paper cups and plates, paper waste, photographic paper, printing paper, sanitary and toilet paper goods, sanitary napkins, specialty papers, sugarcane paper, tissue paper, and wrapping articles. Entries include: Company name, postal address, telephone, fax, e-mail, website, contact person, designation, and product details.

Directory of European Importers of Photographic Equipment and Supplies. EXIM Infotek Private Ltd. • $600 Individuals. Covers: 300 European importers of cameras, lens and accessories, photographic chemicals, motion picture and theater equipment, digital still camera, film, plates and photographic papers, microfilm and blueprint equipment, motion picture films, photo films, photo processing and developing equipment, photocameras, photographic chemicals and papers, photographic equipment and supplies, photographic films for offset reproduction, photographic processing equipment, and thermographic camera. Entries include: Company name, postal address, telephone, fax, e-mail, website, contact person, designation, and product details.

Directory of European Importers of Plastic Scrap and Raw Materials. EXIM Infotek Private Ltd. • $550 Individuals. Covers: 260 European importers of acrylic polymers, fiberglass resins, low-density polyethylene (LDPE), pet scrap and waste, plastic granules, plastic raw materials, plastic scrap and waste, polymer and plastic raw materials, polymers for textile and plastic, polypropylene, polyvinyl chloride, polypropylene raw material, ABS/PC and pet raw materials, HDPE and pet raw materials, PVC raw materials, and reagents. Entries include: Company name, postal address, telephone, fax, e-mail, website, contact person, designation, and product details.

Directory of European Importers of Sewing Machines & Parts. EXIM Infotek Private Ltd. • $10 Individuals. Covers: 60 European importers of industrial sewing machines and parts, knitting equipment parts and articles, knitting machine needles, and sewing machine needles. Entries include: Company name, postal address, telephone, fax, e-mail, website, contact person, designation, and product details.

Directory of European Importers of Soap, Detergent and Cleaning Supplies. EXIM Infotek Private Ltd. • $400 Individuals. Covers: 170 European importers of cleaning products, cleaning supplies, soap, detergents, household cleaning products, preparations for soap, and bleach. Entries include: Company name, postal address, telephone, fax, e-mail, website, contact person, designation, and product details.

Directory of European Importers of Sporting Goods. EXIM Infotek Private Ltd. • $1,350 Individuals. Covers: 610 European importers of balls, baseball supplies, billiard pool equipment and supplies, bowling equipment and supplies, climbing equipment and supplies, footwear, golf equipment and supplies, hiking accessories, uniforms and accessories, mountaineering equipment and supplies, playground equipment, scuba and diving equipment and supply, ski equipment and supplies, ski bindings, snow sports goods, snowmobiles and accessories, soccer training ball, sporting goods and toys, sporting guns and rifles, sports bags, sports gloves, sports inventory, stadium equipment, surfboards, tennis and badminton equipment and supplies, water ski equipment and supplies, water sports equipment and supplies, windsurfing accessories, windsurfing equipment and supplies, and wintersports goods.

Directory of European Importers of Telephone Instruments and Accessories. EXIM Infotek Private Ltd. • $600 Individuals. Covers: 320 European importers of cellular phone, mobile phone accessories, faces for mobile phone, GSM cellular phone, microphone, headphone, wireless phone, Nokia phone, pagers, beepers, telefax equipment, telephone answering equipment, telephone housing, telephonic switching apparatus, wires and cables. Entries include: Company name, postal address, telephone, fax, e-mail, website, contact person, designation, and product details.

Directory of European Importers of Vending and Coin Operated Machines. EXIM Infotek Private Ltd. • $200 Individuals. Covers: 60 European importers of vending and coin operated machine. Entries include: Company name, postal address, telephone, fax, e-mail, website, contact person, designation, and product details.

Directory of European Importers of Wax & Wax Products. EXIM Infotek Private Ltd. • Covers: 50 European importers of paraffin, paraffin waxes, polishes and creams. Entries include: Company name, postal address, telephone, fax, e-mail, website, contact person, designation, and product details.

Directory of European Importers of Welding Equipment and Supplies. EXIM Infotek Private Ltd. • $350 Individuals. Covers: 130 European importers of arc welding equipment, electrodes, soldering equipment, welding equipment, and welding supplies. Entries include: Company name, postal address, telephone, fax, e-mail, website, contact person, designation, and product details.

Directory of European Importers of Wires & Cables--Electrical. EXIM Infotek Private Ltd. • Covers: 170 European importers of wires and cables. Entries include: Company name, postal address, telephone, fax, e-mail, website, contact person, designation, and product details.

Directory of European Importers of Woodworking Equipment & Tools. EXIM Infotek Private Ltd. • Covers: 160 European importers of bamboo, rattan, wicker products, baskets and basket ware, caskets, desks, logs moldings, wooden millwork, oak strips, planks, raw wood, sculptures, wood panels, wood slabs, wooden handicrafts, wooden bedroom furniture, wooden materials, wooden products and woodenware. Entries include: Company name, postal address, telephone, fax, e-mail, website, contact person, designation, and product details.

Directory of European Importers of Yarns and Threads. EXIM Infotek Private Ltd. • $550 Individuals. Covers: 190 European importers of 100% cotton yarn, acrylic yarn, cotton sewing thread, cotton yarn and thread, embroidery thread, flax yarn, nylon filaments, polyester textured yarn, silk yarn and thread, synthetic elementary filament yarn, synthetic yarn and thread, textured yarn of polymers, twists, wool yarn, and yarn waste. Entries include: Company name, postal address, telephone, fax, e-mail, website, contact person, designation, and product details.

Directory of European Information Brokers and Consultants. Information Marketmakers Ltd. • Annual. $59. Covers: information systems brokers and consultants in Europe. Entries include: Company name, address, phone, name and title of contact, names and titles of key personnel, subject expertise, and description of products and services.

Directory of Exporting Industrialists. Istanbul Chamber of Industry. • Annual. $8 Restricted circulation. Covers: Approximately 700 exporting industrialist members of the Istanbul Chamber of Industry. Entries include: Company name, address, phone, telex number: Standard Industrial Classification (SIC) code; export amounts; description of products/services offered.

Directory of Fisheries of the Former Soviet Union. Flegon Press. • $100. Covers: Fisheries of the former USSR, including production associations, research and design institutes, nautical and fishery schools, shipyards, fishing gear factories, netting mills, fish processing and breeding plants, fish farms, and retail fish vendors among others. Entries include: Name, address, phone, telex, managing personnel.

Directory of Florida Industries. Florida Chamber of Commerce. • Annual. Covers: About 15,300 manufacturing, mining, and processing concerns with 4 or more employees. Entries include: Company name, address, phone, names of principal executives, number of employees, products or services, Standard Industrial Classification (SIC) numbers, whether firm imports or exports.

Directory of Foreign Buyers, Importers of Food and Agro Based Products. NIIR Project Consultancy Services. • $100 Individuals CD-ROM. Covers: 1,000 buyers/importers of food and agro-based products, processed food, additives and ingredients. Entries include: Company name, full postal address, phone, fax, email (wherever available), website address (wherever available).

Directory of Foreign Firms Operating in the United States. Uniworld Business Publications Inc. • Biennial. $350 Individuals hardcover plus s&h. Covers: Approximately 4,900 firms in 86 countries that own or have substantial investments in about 18,250 U.S. Companies. Entries include: Company name, address, phone, fax, name of chief executive officer, number of employees, annual sales, web address, product or service; affiliated U.S. company name, address, phone, fax, name of chief executive, number of employees, product or service, percent foreign-owned. Separate country editions are also available.

Directory of Foreign Investors That Invest in U.S.A. Property and Real Estate. Communication Network International Inc. • Biennial. $650. Covers: more than 3,500 investors. Entries include: Personal name, address; United States representative name, address, phone; approximate dollar amount of U.S. investments.

Directory of Foreign Manufacturers in the United States. Georgia State University Business Press. • Biennial. $195 payment must accompany orders from individuals. Covers: over 7,300 United States manufacturing, mining, and petroleum companies, and the over 6,800 firms abroad that own them. Entries include: Company name, address, phone, fax, products or services, Standard Industrial Classification (SIC) codes, parent company name and address.

Directory of French Importers of Advertising and Display Articles and Supplies. EXIM Infotek Private Ltd. • $150 Individuals. Covers: 35 French importers of advertising articles, displays, flags, banners, and signs. Entries include: Company name, postal address, telephone, fax, e-mail, website, contact person, designation, and product details.

Directory of French Importers of Computer Hardwares and Peripherals. EXIM Infotek Private Ltd. • $400 Individuals. Covers: 150 French importers of computer equipment and supplies, computer peripherals, computer components, LAN/network hardware and software, and laser printers. Entries include: Company name, postal address, telephone, fax, e-mail, website, contact person, designation, and product details.

Directory of French Importers of Computer Softwares. EXIM Infotek Private Ltd. • $150 Individuals. Covers: 40 French importers of computer software. Entries include: Company name, postal address, telephone, fax, e-mail, website, contact person, designation, and product details.

Directory of French Importers of Construction Machinery and Equipment. EXIM Infotek Private Ltd. • $150 Individuals. Covers: 40 French importers of construction, building equipment and parts, excavating equipment, industrial and construction vehicles, scale model and construction kit, and street maintenance equipment. Entries include: Company name, postal address, telephone, fax, e-mail, website, contact person, designation, and product details.

Directory of French Importers of Environmental and Pollution Control Equipment. EXIM Infotek Private Ltd. • Covers: 30 French importers of environmental protection equipment, pollution control equipment, water treatment, and purifying equipment. Entries include: Company name, postal address, telephone, fax, e-mail, website, contact person, designation, and product details.

Directory of French Importers of Juices and Soft Drinks. EXIM Infotek Private Ltd. • $150 Individuals. Covers: 20 French importers of fruit and vegetable juices, mineral water, non-alcoholic beverages, and soft drinks. Entries include: Company name, postal address, telephone, fax, e-mail, website, contact person, designation, and product details.

Directory of French Importers of Laboratory & Scientific Instruments & Supplies. EXIM Infotek Private Ltd. • Covers: 110 French importers of binoculars, microscopes, binoculars, telescopes, scientific and laboratory instruments, and testing equipment. Entries include: Company name, postal address, telephone, fax, e-mail, website, contact person, designation, and product details.

Directory of French Importers of Lumber, Timber, Plywood and Hardboards. EXIM Infotek Private Ltd. • $200 Individuals. Covers: 60 French importers of doors, windows, hardboard and particleboard, hardwood flooring, floor tiles, wood laminates, lumber goods, lumber, timber, plywood, hardwood lumber, softwood lumber, plywood, veneer, poles, wood, pilings and logs. Entries include: Company name, postal address, telephone, fax, e-mail, website, contact person, designation, and product details.

Directory of French Importers of Material Handling Equipment. EXIM Infotek Private Ltd. • $250 Individuals. Covers: 70 French importers of conveyors, cranes and hoisting equipment, elevators lifts, forklifts, liquid handling equipment, loading and unloading equipment, materials handling equipment and parts, winches, and pulleys. Entries include: Company name, postal address, telephone, fax, e-mail, website, contact person, designation, and product details.

Directory of French Importers of Photographic Equipment and Supplies. EXIM Infotek Private Ltd. • $150 Individuals. Covers: 25 French importers of cameras, lenses and accessories, photographic chemicals motion picture and theater equipment, film, plate photographic papers, microfilm and blueprint equipment, photo processing and developing equipment, photographic equipment and supplies. Entries include: Company name, postal address, telephone, fax, e-mail, website, contact person, designation, and product details.

Directory of French Importers of Plastics Scrap and Raw Materials. EXIM Infotek Private Ltd. • $150 Individuals. Covers: 20 French importers of plastic raw materials and reagents. Entries include: Company name, postal address, telephone, fax, e-mail, website, contact person, designation, and product details.

Directory of French Importers of Refrigeration Equipment and Supplies. EXIM Infotek Private Ltd. • Covers: 20 French importers of freezers, refrigerators, and refrigeration equipment. Entries include: Company name, postal address, telephone, fax, e-mail, website, contact person, designation, and product details.

Directory of French Importers of Soap, Detergents and Cleaning Supplies. EXIM Infotek Private Ltd. • $150 Individuals. Covers: 25 French importers of cleaning supplies, soap, and detergent. Entries include: Company name, postal address, telephone, fax, e-mail, website, contact person, designation, and product details.

Directory of French Importers of Sporting Goods. EXIM Infotek Private Ltd. • $250 Individuals. Covers: 80 French importers of firearms, golf equipment and supplies, playground equipment, scuba and diving equipment and supply, ski equipment and supplies, sporting goods and toys, sporting goods, tennis and badminton equipment and supplies, water sports equipment and supplies. Entries include: Company name, postal address, telephone, fax, e-mail, website, contact person, designation, and product details.

Directory of Fund Raising and Nonprofit Management Consultants. Taft Group. • $49. Covers: 1,500 consultants and training organizations for nonprofit groups. Entries include: Organization name, address, phone, fax, year founded, publications and videos, partners or executives, description of service.

Directory of German Importers of Alcoholic Beverages and Wines. EXIM Infotek Private Ltd. • Covers: 50 German importers of alcoholic beverages, beer, ale, distilled spirits, rum, whisky, wine, and alcoholic beverages. Entries include: Company name, postal address, telephone, fax, e-mail, website, contact person, designation, and product details.

Directory of German Importers of Carpets, Durries and Floor Coverings. EXIM Infotek Private Ltd. • $200 Individuals. Covers: 20 German importers of carpets, rugs, coir mats, coir mattings, floor coverings, and oriental rugs. Entries include: Company name, postal address, telephone, fax, e-mail, website, contact person, designation, and product details.

Directory of German Importers of Computer Hardwares and Peripherals. EXIM Infotek Private Ltd. • $250 Individuals. Covers: 70 German importers of CD-ROM, computer equipment and supplies, computer peripherals, computer components, LAN/network hardware and software, toner, and cartridges. Entries include: Company name, postal address, telephone, fax, e-mail, website, contact person, designation, and product details.

Directory of German Importers of Computer Softwares. EXIM Infotek Private Ltd. • $150 Individuals. Covers: 30 German importers of CAD software and computer software. Entries include: Company name, postal address, telephone, fax, e-mail, website, contact person, designation, and product details.

Directory of German Importers of Laboratory & Scientific Instruments & Supplies. EXIM Infotek Private Ltd. • $250 Individuals. Covers: 50 German importers of binoculars, microscopes, telescopes, scientific and laboratory instrument, and testing equipment. Entries include: Company name, postal address, telephone, fax, e-mail, website, contact person, designation, and product details.

Directory of German Importers of Lumber, Timber, Plywood and Hardboards. EXIM Infotek Private Ltd. • $250 Individuals. Covers: 60 German importers of doors, windows, glued timber, hardboard, particleboard, hardwood flooring, floor tiles, laminates, wood laminates, lumber, timber, plywood, hardwood lumber, softwood lumber, parquet, pine wood, planed wood, veneer, poles, pilings and logs, round logs, softwood, solid wood, wood, and wooden moldings. Entries include: Company name, postal address, telephone, fax, e-mail, website, contact person, designation, and product details.

Directory of German Importers of Photographic Equipment and Supplies. EXIM Infotek Private Ltd. • $150 Individuals. Covers: 25 German importers of cameras, lens and accessories, motion picture and theater equipment, film, plate and photographic papers, photographic equipment and supplies. Entries include: Company name, postal address, telephone, fax, e-mail, website, contact person, designation, and product details.

Directory of German Importers of Sporting Goods. EXIM Infotek Private Ltd. • Covers: 40 German importers of golf equipment and supplies, mountaineering equipment and supplies, scuba and diving equipment and supply, ski equipment and supplies, sporting goods and toys, sporting goods, tennis and badminton equipment and supplies, water ski equipment and supplies, and water sports equipment and supplies. Entries include: Company name, postal address, telephone, fax, e-mail, website, contact person, designation, and product details.

Directory of German Importers of Telephone Instruments and Accessories. EXIM Infotek Private Ltd. • $200 Individuals. Covers: 40 German importers of mobile phone, cellular phone accessories, microphone, Nokia phone, telefax equipment, and telephone answering equipment. Entries include: Company name, postal address, telephone, fax, e-mail, website, contact person, designation, and product details.

Directory of Global eCommerce Companies. Nandini Institute of Chemical Industries. • $50. Covers: List of names and addresses of eCommerce companies.

Directory of Hong Kong Traders. Hong Kong Productivity Council. • $380 pick up at HKPC Office. Covers: major traders in Hong Kong, over 8,000 products, and 7,000 brand names. Entries include: Companies--name, address, phone, fax, number of employees, sales turnover, major products, and brand names.

Directory of ICT Companies in Mauritius. National Computer Board. • Annual. Covers: 300 companies operating in the ICT sector in Mauritius in a wide range of activities including software development, call centre, BPO, web-enabled activities, training, hardware assembly and sales, networking and other support services. Entries include: Company name, address, phone, fax, e-mail, website, directors, contact person, number of employees, company profile, competencies, export markets, products, and services.

Directory of Importers. IBCON S.A. • Irregular. $488 Individuals. 2,284 Mexican companies importing at least $1,000,000 a year, for their own supplies or commercial distribution with executive in charge of imports.

Directory of Incorporated (Registered) Companies in Nigeria. ICIC Ltd. • Biennial. $50. Covers: Companies from 1912 to present in Nigeria. Entries include: Company name, address.

Directory of Indian Importers of Computer Softwares. EXIM Infotek Private Ltd. • $150 Individuals. Covers: 30 Indian importers of computer software and LAN/network hardware. Entries include: Company name, postal address, telephone, fax, e-mail, website, contact person, designation, and product details.

Directory of Indian Importers of Construction Machinery and Equipment. EXIM Infotek Private Ltd. • $200 Individuals. Covers: 50 Indian importers of construction and building equipment, construction machinery, earthmoving spare parts, excavating equipment, spare parts for earthmoving machinery, and spare parts for heavy construction machine. Entries include: Company name, postal address, telephone, fax, e-mail, website, contact person, designation, and product details.

Directory of Indian Importers of Dyes, Colors, and Pigments. EXIM Infotek Private Ltd. • $350 Individuals. Covers: 80 Indian importers of activated carbon, dye, dye intermediates, colors, pigments, dyestuff, ink, and leather chemicals. Entries include: Company name, postal address, telephone, fax, e-mail, website, contact person, designation, and product details.

Directory of Indian Importers of Fibre Products. EXIM Infotek Private Ltd. • $200 Individuals. Covers: 45 Indian importers of acrylic fiber, fiber waste, fiberglass, fiberglass cloth, fiberglass products, staple fiber, and synthetic fiber. Entries include: Company name, postal address, telephone, fax, e-mail, website, contact person, designation, and product details.

Directory of Indian Importers of Fire Fighting Equipment & Supplies. EXIM Infotek Private Ltd. • Covers: 20 Indian importers of fire alarm panels, fire alarm systems, fire detection systems, fire extinguishers, fire fighting equipment, and fire hydrants. Entries include: Company name, postal address, telephone, fax, e-mail, website, contact person, designation, and product details.

Directory of Indian Importers of Food Additives and Aromatics. EXIM Infotek Private Ltd. • $5 Individuals. Covers: 40 Indian importers of aroma chemicals, flavors, food additives, food colors, fragrances, and vanillin (pollar Br). Entries include: Company name, postal address, telephone, fax, e-mail, website, contact person, designation, and product details.

Directory of Indian Importers of Heaters and Heating Equipment. EXIM Infotek Private Ltd. • Covers: 20 Indian importers of heat exchangers, heaters, and heating equipment. Entries include: Company name, postal address, telephone, fax, e-mail, website, contact person, designation, and product details.

Directory of Indian Importers of Herbs & Herbal Medicine Products. EXIM Infotek Private Ltd. • $200 Individuals. Covers: 30 Indian importers of herbs, legumes, medicinal herbs, and botanicals. Entries include: Company name, postal address, telephone, fax, e-mail, website, contact person, designation, and product details.

Directory of Indian Importers of Laboratory & Scientific Instruments & Supplies. EXIM Infotek Private Ltd. • $300 Individuals. Covers: 120 Indian importers of binoculars, microscope, telescopes, borosilicate glass tubing, educational scientific equipment, laboratory equipment, laboratory glassware, laboratory instruments, scientific instruments, testing and measuring equipment, testing instruments, thermometers, and barometers. Entries include: Company name, postal address, telephone, fax, e-mail, website, contact person, designation, and product details.

Directory of Indian Importers of Lumber, Timber, Plywood and Hardboards. EXIM Infotek Private Ltd. • $250 Individuals. Covers: 80 Indian importers of gypsum board, hard boards, wood laminates, logs, hardwood lumber, softwood lumber, particle boards, plywood, veneer, poles, pilings and logs, sheetrock, spruce logs, teak wood, timber, timber logs, veneer sheets, and wood. Entries include: Company name, postal address, telephone, fax, e-mail, website, contact person, designation, and product details.

Directory of Indian Importers of Material Handling Equipment & Supplies. EXIM Infotek Private Ltd. • $150 Individuals. Covers: 20 Indian importers of loading equipment, unloading equipment, and materials handling equipment. Entries include: Company name, postal address, telephone, fax, e-mail, website, contact person, designation, and product details.

Directory of Indian Importers of Minerals. EXIM Infotek Private Ltd. • Covers: 80 Indian Importers of borax, graphite, iron ore, lead, mica, mineral oil, minerals, ores, sulfur, zinc, and zirconium sand. Entries include: Company name, postal address, telephone, fax, e-mail, website, contact person, designation, and product details.

Directory of Indian Importers of Paper & Paper Products. EXIM Infotek Private Ltd. • $450 Individuals. Covers: 200 Indian importers of absorbent tissue, art paper, base paper, coated paper, decorative paper, kraft paper, newsprints paper, paper and paper boards, paper products, wood pulp, paper bags, paper waste, printing paper, sanitary and toilet paper goods, sanitary napkins, specialty paper, thermal paper reels for fax, and tissue paper. Entries include: Company name, postal address, telephone, fax, e-mail, website, contact person, designation, and product details.

Directory of Indian Importers of Plastic Scrap and Raw Materials. EXIM Infotek Private Ltd. • $600 Individuals. Covers: 200 Indian importers of ABS scrap, acrylamide, butyl acrylate, granules, HD, high-density polyethylene (HDPE), HDPE granules, HMS scrap, low-density polyethylene (LDPE), LDPE granules, linear low-density polyethylene (LLDPE), master batches, plastic granules, plastic raw materials, plastic scrap and waste, polycarbonate, polypropylene, polymers, polypropylene scraps, polypropylene granules, polyurethane chemicals, polyurethane resin, polyvinyl alcohol, polytetrafluoroethylene (PTFE) products, PVC compound, PVC resin, raw materials, and styrene monomer. Entries include: Company name, postal address, telephone, fax, e-mail, website, contact person, designation, and product details.

Directory of Indian Importers of Wax & Wax Products. EXIM Infotek Private Ltd. • Covers: 30 Indian importers of micro waxes, paraffin waxes, polishes and creams, and slack waxes. Entries include: Company name, postal address, telephone, fax, e-mail, website, contact person, designation, and product details.

Directory of Indian Importers of Wires & Cables--Electrical. EXIM Infotek Private Ltd. • Covers: 40 Indian importers of cables, copper wires, power cords, thermocouple wire, and wires and cables. Entries include: Company name, postal address, telephone, fax, e-mail, website, contact person, designation, and product details.

Directory of Indian Importers of Yarns and Threads. EXIM Infotek Private Ltd. • $400 Individuals. Covers: 90 Indian importers of cotton yarn, dupion silk yarn, fibers, yarns, filament yarn, man-made yarn, metallic yarn and thread, nylon yarn, polyester yarn, raw silk yarn, sewing threads, silk yarn and thread, synthetic yarn and thread, viscose yarn, wool yarn, and yarn waste. Entries include: Company name, postal address, telephone, fax, e-mail, website, contact person, designation, and product details.

Directory of Industrial Suppliers. Hong Kong Productivity Council. • Annual. $280 pick up at HKPC Office. Covers: Over 3,000 industrial suppliers in Hong Kong as well as their operations in Mainland China. Entries include: Name, address, phone, fax, e-mail, URL, number of employees, turnover, and products/brand names.

Directory of International Benefits. AP Information Services Ltd. • Irregular. $78.50 bpd. Publication includes: List of private organizations worldwide providing information on international employee benefits, including actuarial benefits, insurance companies and associations, benefit consultants, publishing companies, property managers, and accounting, communication, and legal firms. Database includes: Statistics on education, working population, economics, business, and benefit surveys. Entries include: Company name, address, phone, contact person, fax, telex, parent and subsidiary companies.

Directory of International Buyers. Auto Care Association. • Annual. $70. Covers: 650 foreign firms that attended the association's annual show. Entries include: Company name, address, name and title of contact, type of buyer.

Directory of International Chambers of Commerce in the World. EXIM Infotek Private Ltd. • $55 Individuals. Covers: 1,000 international chambers of commerce. Entries include: Company name, postal address, telephone, fax, e-mail, website, contact person, designation, and product details.

Directory of International Corporate Giving in America and Abroad. Taft Group. • $215. Covers: 443 foreign-owned companies that support nonprofit organizations in the U.S., and 170 U.S. companies that support organizations overseas. Entries include: Corporation name, foundation name; name, title, and phone of contact; location of U.S. headquarters, number of employees, total foundation assets, name and address of overseas parent company; summary of grant support, including amounts given, geographical area and types of activities preferred, and recently funded programs.

Directory of International Sources of Business Information. Pearson Education Ltd. • Annual. $85. Covers: Sources of business information worldwide, including business information brokers, Euro-Info centers, banks, stockbrokers, associations, embassies and councils, market research organizations, economic and statistical organizations, publishers, publications, online databases, and United Kingdom packet switching exchanges. Entries include: For business information brokers and Euro-Info centers--Name, address, phone, fax, host and databases accessed, subject areas covered, languages spoken, description of services offered. For banks, stockbrokers, associations, embassies and councils, market research organizations, economic and statistical organizations, and publications--Name, address, phone. For online databases--Name, address, phone, host. For United Kingdom packet switching exchanges--Phone. For publishers--Name, address, phone, fax, telex.

Directory of International Trade & Industrial Association in the World. EXIM Infotek Private Ltd. • Covers: 2,150 international trade and industrial associations. Entries include: Company name, postal address, telephone, fax, e-mail, website, contact person, designation, and product details.

Directory of Japanese-Affiliated Companies in the USA and Canada. • Covers: Over 5,000 Japanese-affiliated companies operating in the United States or Canada. Entries include: Name, address, phone, fax, year of establishment, capital, annual sales, managing directors, and main products/services.

Directory of Japanese-Affiliated Companies in USA & Canada. Database S.L. • Biennial. $260. Covers: Approximately 8,200 Japanese-affiliated companies operating in North America. Entries include: Company name, address, phone, status, type of business, product/service, names and titles of key personnel, Japanese parent company.

Directory of Japanese Giving. Corporate Citizen. • $190. Covers: Approximately 190 Japanese firms that participate in philanthropic activities in the U.S. Entries include: Company; name, address, phone; telex, names and titles of key personnel; description of policies, programs, and foundations; history of giving and volunteer activities in the U.S.; U.S. nonprofit organizations funded, geographical area served.

Directory of Japanese Importers of Alcoholic Beverages and Wines. EXIM Infotek Private Ltd. • $500 Individuals. Covers: 250 Japanese importers of alcoholic beverages, barley malt, beer and ale, bourbon, brandy, distilled spirits, hard liquor, soft liquor, whisky, wine, and alcoholic beverages. Entries include: Company name, postal address, telephone, fax, e-mail, website, contact person, designation, and product details.

Directory of Japanese Importers of Camping and Backpacking Equipments and Supplies. EXIM Infotek Private Ltd. • $150 Individuals. Covers: 40 Japanese importers of camping and backpacking equipment, camping goods, mountaineering equipment, and outdoor goods. Entries include: Company name, postal address, telephone, fax, e-mail, website, contact person, designation, and product details.

Directory of Japanese Importers of Carpets, Durries, Rugs and Floor Coverings. EXIM Infotek Private Ltd. • $250 Individuals. Covers: 80 Japanese importers of carpets, rugs, floor coverings, flooring goods, and mats. Entries include: Company name, postal address, telephone, fax, e-mail, website, contact person, designation, and product details.

Directory of Japanese Importers of Computer Hardwares and Peripherals. EXIM Infotek Private Ltd. • $350 Individuals. Covers: 125 Japanese importers of bar coding equipment, compact disc, computers, computer accessories, computer components, computer equipment and supplies, computer hardware, computer peripherals, computer supplies, printers, information processing equipment and peripherals, ink jet printers, laser printers, LCD monitor, monitors, personal computers, and scanners. Entries include: Company name, postal address, telephone, fax, e-mail, website, contact person, designation, and product details.

Directory of Japanese Importers of Computer Softwares. EXIM Infotek Private Ltd. • $200 Individuals. Covers: 55 Japanese importers of computer software and internet technology. Entries include: Company name, postal address, telephone, fax, e-mail, website, contact person, designation, and product details.

Directory of Japanese Importers of Construction Machinery and Equipment. EXIM Infotek Private Ltd. • $250 Individuals. Covers: 80 Japanese importers of construction and building equipment, construction machinery, mixers and pavers, road rollers, scale model and construction kit, shovels, street maintenance equipment, and used construction equipment. Entries include: Company name, postal address, telephone, fax, e-mail, website, contact person, designation, and product details.

Directory of Japanese Importers of Dyes, Colors, Pigments and Intermediates. EXIM Infotek Private Ltd. • $300 Individuals. Covers: 100 Japanese importers of activated carbon, chemical intermediates, dyes, colors, pigments, dyestuff, dyestuff intermediates, ink, pigment colors and metallic, and printing ink. Entries include: Company name, postal address, telephone, fax, e-mail, website, contact person, designation, and product details.

Directory of Japanese Importers of Environment and Pollution Control Equipment. EXIM Infotek Private Ltd. • $200 Individuals. Covers: 45 Japanese importers of dust collectors, environmental equipment, environmental protection equipment, environmentally conserving or improving products, noise control equipment, pollution control equipment, water purification equipment, water treatment, water treatment equipment, and purifying equipment. Entries include: Company name, postal address, telephone, fax, e-mail, website, contact person, designation, and product details.

Directory of Japanese Importers of Fibre and Fibre Products. EXIM Infotek Private Ltd. • $200 Individuals. Covers: 40 Japanese importers of fiber glass cloth, fiber products, glass fibers, natural fiber, and synthetic fiber. Entries include: Company name, postal address, telephone, fax, e-mail, website, contact person, designation, and product details.

Directory of Japanese Importers of Fishing & Hunting Equipment & Supplies. EXIM Infotek Private Ltd. • Covers: 35 Japanese importers of fishing and hunting equipment, fishing supplies, fishing nets and floats, and fishing tackles. Entries include: Company name, postal address, telephone, fax, e-mail, website, contact person, designation, and product details.

Directory of Japanese Importers of Fodder and Animal Foodstuffs. EXIM Infotek Private Ltd. • $200 Individuals. Covers: Japanese importers of animal foodstuff, food additives, feeder calves, fodder, cereals, and livestock products. Entries include: Company name, postal address, telephone, fax, e-mail, website, contact person, designation, and product details.

Directory of Japanese Importers of Food Additives and Aromatic Chemicals. EXIM Infotek Private Ltd. • $350 Individuals. Covers: 145 Japanese importers of agar-agar, aromatic chemicals, essence, food additives, food colors, food flavors, food ingredients, fragrances, natural coloring matters, raw materials for food colors, and yeasts. Entries include: Company name, postal address, telephone, fax, e-mail, website, contact person, designation, and product details.

Directory of Japanese Importers of Heaters and Heating Equipment. EXIM Infotek Private Ltd. • Covers: 35 Japanese importers of heat exchangers, heaters, and heating equipment. Entries include: Company name, postal address, telephone, fax, e-mail, website, contact person, designation, and product details.

Directory of Japanese Importers of Juices and Soft Drinks. EXIM Infotek Private Ltd. • $400 Individuals. Covers: 180 Japanese importers of beverages, concentrated fruit juices, vegetable juices, fruit puree, mineral water, non-alcoholic beverages, and soft drinks. Entries include: Company name, postal address, telephone, fax, e-mail, website, contact person, designation, and product details.

Directory of Japanese Importers of Laboratory & Scientific Instruments & Supplies. EXIM Infotek Private Ltd. • $450 Individuals. Covers: 200 Japanese importers of analytical instruments, binoculars, microscopes, telescopes, laboratory and scientific glass, laboratory instruments, laboratory reagents, scientific and laboratory equipment, scientific instruments, testing and measuring equipment, testing instruments, testing machines, thermometers, and barometers. Entries include: Company name, postal address, telephone, fax, e-mail, website, contact person, designation, and product details.

Directory of Japanese Importers of Lumber, Timber, Plywood and Hardboards. EXIM Infotek Private Ltd. • $650 Individuals. Covers: 340 Japanese importers of bamboo shoots, bamboo and rattan (raw), doors and door frames, windows, gypsum board, hardboard, particleboard, hardwood flooring, floor tiles, hardwood products, laminated lumber, wood laminates, logs, lumber, hardwood lumber, softwood lumber, timber, plywood, medicament plywood, millwork (wooden), veneer, poles, pilings and logs, rattans, sandalwood, sawn goods, sawn timber, sheetrock, teak wood, timber, wood, wood housing products, woodchips, and wooden doors. Entries include: Company name, postal address, telephone, fax, e-mail, website, contact person, designation, and product details.

Directory of Japanese Importers of Material Handling Equipment. EXIM Infotek Private Ltd. • $150 Individuals. Covers: 40 Japanese importers of conveying machine, conveyors, cranes and hoists, elevators lifts, elevators, lifts and escalators, forklifts, loading and unloading equipment, materials handling equipment and parts. Entries include: Company name, postal address, telephone, fax, e-mail, website, contact person, designation, and product details.

Directory of Japanese Importers of Minerals. EXIM Infotek Private Ltd. • Covers: 150 Japanese importers of carbon and graphite products, crucibles made of alumina or quartz, graphite, gypsum, iron ore, limestone, manganese ore, mica, mineral oil, mineral products and raw materials, minerals, ores, rare metal minerals, silica sand, soil, sulfur, and zinc. Entries include: Company name, postal address, telephone, fax, e-mail, website, contact person, designation, and product details.

Directory of Japanese Importers of Paper & Paper Products. EXIM Infotek Private Ltd. • Covers: 120 Japanese importers of base paper for coatings, corrugated paper, foreign paper, kraft paper, paper and paper boards, paper products, wood pulp, paper bags, paper boards, paper lantern, paper napkins, paper pulp products article, paperboards, printing paper, pulp, screen paper, special paper, specialty paper, tissue paper, and waste paper. Entries include: Company name, postal address, telephone, fax, e-mail, website, contact person, designation, and product details.

Directory of Japanese Importers of Plastic Scrap and Raw Materials. EXIM Infotek Private Ltd. • $200 Individuals. Covers: 30 Japanese importers of plastic raw materials, plastic resins, plasticizers, plastics, and plastic additives. Entries include: Company name, postal address, telephone, fax, e-mail, website, contact person, designation, and product details.

Directory of Japanese Importers of Soap, Detergents and Cleaning Supplies. EXIM Infotek Private Ltd. • $200 Individuals. Covers: 60 Japanese importers of cleaning supplies, detergent, soap chip, soap, toiletry and bathroom preparations. Entries include: Company name, postal address, telephone, fax, e-mail, website, contact person, designation, and product details.

Directory of Japanese Importers of Woodenware & Wooden Products. EXIM Infotek Private Ltd. • Covers: 270 Japanese importers of bamboo products, bamboo, rattan and wicker products, bamboo/rattan/wicker products, baskets, baskets and basket ware, chopsticks, folding fan, lacquer ware, rattan baskets, rattan products, softwood products, wood and wooden products, wood articles, wood products, wood pulp products, wooden articles, wooden decoration goods, wooden housing components, wooden interior goods, wooden kitchenware, wooden pallets, wooden products, wooden products, wooden tableware, wooden tray, woodenware, and woodworks. Entries include: Company name, postal address, telephone, fax, e-mail, website, contact

For publishers' addresses, refer to SOURCES CITED section at the back of the book.

person, designation, and product details.

Directory of Japanese Importers of Yarns and Threads. EXIM Infotek Private Ltd. • $250 Individuals. Covers: 75 Japanese importers of yarns and thread, cotton yarn and thread, silk yarn and thread, synthetic yarn and thread, and yarn twister. Entries include: Company name, postal address, telephone, fax, e-mail, website, contact person, designation, and product details.

Directory of Japanese Manufacturers & Exporters of Adhesive, Glues & Sealants. EXIM Infotek Private Ltd. • $5 Individuals. Covers: 20 Japanese manufacturers & exporters of adhesives, epoxy resins, glue, plastic adhesives. Entries include: Company name, postal address, city, country, phone, fax, e-mail & websites, contact person, designation, products detail.

Directory of Japanese Manufacturers and Exporters of Alcoholic Beverages and Wines. EXIM Infotek Private Ltd. • Covers: 30 Japanese manufacturers and exporters of beer, beverages, liquor, sake plum wine, and wine. Entries include: Company name, postal address, telephone, fax, e-mail, website, contact person, designation, and product details.

Directory of Japanese Manufacturers & Exporters of Automobiles & Vehicles. EXIM Infotek Private Ltd. • $65 Individuals. Covers: 1,570 Japanese manufacturers and exporters of automobiles, buses, cars, motor vehicles, reconditioned cars, trailers, transport equipment, used buses, used cargo trucks, used cars, used commercial vehicles, used mini buses, used motor vehicles, used passenger cars, used trucks, used vans, used vehicles, used vehicles and spare parts, used wagons, vehicles, and wagons for hotel and restaurants. Entries include: Company name, postal address, city, country, phone, fax, e-mail and websites, contact person, designation, and product details.

Directory of Japanese Manufacturers & Exporters of Automotive Service & Repair Equipment. EXIM Infotek Private Ltd. • $10 Individuals. Covers: 60 Japanese manufacturers and exporters of automotive emission analysis systems, automotive service equipment, car care tools, grinding wheels, lubricants, and lubricating equipments. Entries include: Company name, postal address, city, country, phone, fax, e-mail and websites, contact person, designation, and product details.

Directory of Japanese Manufacturers & Exporters of Autoparts & Accessories. EXIM Infotek Private Ltd. • $35 Individuals. Covers: 530 Japanese manufacturers and exporters of accelerator pedals, clutch pedals, alternators, auto accessories, auto doors, automobile parts and equipment, automobile switches, automotive interior products, automotive lamp accessories, automotive lighting supplies, head lamps, horns, ignition coils, joints-universal, light alloy wheels, motor vehicle parts and supplies, radiators, rear-view mirrors, sealed beam units, seat adjusters, signal and indicator lamps, spare parts, steering columns, steering gears, steering wheels, transmission equipment, transmission parts, truck and bus accessories, truck parts and supplies, used auto parts, used automobile engine and body parts, used automobile parts and accessories, used car parts, used light trucks parts, used motor spare parts, used rims, used spare parts, wheels, window regulators, wiper motors, and wiring harnesses. Entries include: Company name, postal address, city, country, telephone, fax, e-mail and websites, contact person, designation, and product details.

Directory of Japanese Manufacturers & Exporters of Batteries & Accumulators. EXIM Infotek Private Ltd. • $5 Individuals. Covers: 20 Japanese manufacturers and exporters of batteries and accumulators, batteries, and battery chargers. Entries include: Company name, postal address, city, country, phone, fax, e-mail and websites, contact person, designation, and product details.

Directory of Japanese Manufacturers & Exporters of Bearings. EXIM Infotek Private Ltd. • $10 Individuals. Covers: 60 Japanese manufacturers and exporters of ball bearings, ball screws, balls for bearings, bearing parts, bearing units, bearings, bushings, clutch release bearings, cylindrical roller bearings, engine bearings, linear motion rolling guide units and bearings, needle roller bearings, roller bearings, rollers for bearings, slide bearing and processing materials, spherical roller bearings, and tapered roller bearings. Entries include: Company name, postal address, city, country, phone, fax, e-mail and websites, contact person, designation, and product details.

Directory of Japanese Manufacturers & Exporters of Beauty Supplies, Cosmetics, Perfumes & Toiletries. EXIM Infotek Private Ltd. • $10 Individuals. Covers: 120 Japanese manufacturers & exporters of air fresheners, cosmetics, fragrances, hand sprayers, perfumes. Entries include: Company name, postal address, city, country, phone, fax, e-mail & websites, contact person, designation, products detail.

Directory of Japanese Manufacturers & Exporters of Confectionery & Bakery Products. EXIM Infotek Private Ltd. • $5 Individuals. Covers: 20 Japanese manufacturers and exporters of biscuits/crackers, confectionery, and vinegar. Entries include: Company name, postal address, city, country, phone, fax, e-mail and websites, contact person, designation, and product details.

Directory of Japanese Manufacturers and Exporters of Construction Machinery and Equipment. EXIM Infotek Private Ltd. • $1,000 Individuals. Covers: 610 Japanese manufacturers and exporters of building machinery, bulldozers (new and used), construction equipment and spare parts, crushers, dust collectors, excavators (new and used), land machinery, mixers and pavers, used concrete mixer trucks, used cranes, used crawler cranes, used crawler dump, used crawler loader, used dump trucks, used earthmoving equipment, used heavy equipment, used hydraulic excavators and truck cranes, used loaders, used mechanical truck cranes, used mini-excavators, used mixer truck, used motor grader, used road rollers, used rough terrain cranes, used tire shovels, used truck crane, used vibratory road rollers, and used wheel loaders. Entries include: Company name, postal address, telephone, fax, e-mail, website, contact person, designation, and product details.

Directory of Japanese Manufacturers & Exporters of Cotton, Silk, Wool Raw & Waste. EXIM Infotek Private Ltd. • $5 Individuals. Covers: 20 Japanese manufacturers and exporters of cotton, cotton products, felt, wool and wool products. Entries include: Company name, postal address, city, country, phone, fax, e-mail and websites, contact person, designation, and product details.

Directory of Japanese Manufacturers & Exporters of Dyes, Colours, Pigments & Intermediates. EXIM Infotek Private Ltd. • $5 Individuals. Covers: 30 Japanese manufacturers and exporters of dyes, inks, pigments. Entries include: Company name, postal address, city, country, phone, fax, e-mail and websites, contact person, designation, and product details.

Directory of Japanese Manufacturers & Exporters of Electronic Equipment & Supplies. EXIM Infotek Private Ltd. • Covers: 20 Japanese manufacturers and exporters of electronic devices, electronic equipment, electronic instrument, and semiconductor equipment. Entries include: Company name, postal address, telephone, fax, e-mail, website, contact person, designation, and product details.

Directory of Japanese Manufacturers & Exporters of Engines & Engine Parts. EXIM Infotek Private Ltd. • $15 Individuals. Covers: 130 Japanese manufacturers and exporters of diesel engines, diesel engine parts, electric equipment for diesel engines, engine parts and accessories, engine valves, engines, internal combustion engines, oil seals, parts for internal combustion engines, piston pin bushings, pistons, plugs, spark plugs, used car engines, used diesel engines, used engines and body parts, used gasoline engines, and used truck engines. Entries include: Company name, postal address, city, country, phone, fax, e-mail and websites, contact person, designation, and product details.

Directory of Japanese Manufacturers and Exporters of Environment and Pollution Control Equipment. EXIM Infotek Private Ltd. • Covers: 20 Japanese manufacturers and exporters of air pollution systems, environmental equipment, evaporators, ion exchange equipment, and pollution control equipment. Entries include: Company name, postal address, telephone, fax, e-mail, website, contact person, designation, and product details.

Directory of Japanese Manufacturers & Exporters of Food Additives & Aromatic Chemicals. EXIM Infotek Private Ltd. • $5 Individuals. Covers: 30 Japanese manufacturers and exporters of aromatic chemicals, dairy farming products, food additives, food flavoring. Entries include: Company name, postal address, city, country, phone, fax, e-mail and websites, contact person, designation, and product details.

Directory of Japanese Manufacturers & Exporters of Furniture--All Types. EXIM Infotek Private Ltd. • $5 Individuals. Covers: 20 Japanese manufacturers and exporters of furniture, safes and strong boxes, showcases, steel furniture, upholstered furniture, and wooden furniture. Entries include: Company name, postal address, city, country, phone, fax, e-mail and websites, contact person, designation, and product details.

Directory of Japanese Manufacturers & Exporters of Gemstones & Diamonds. EXIM Infotek Private Ltd. • $5 Individuals. Covers: 30 Japanese manufacturers and exporters of crystal, cultured pearls, diamonds, natural pearls, precious stones. Entries include: Company name, postal address, city, country, phone, fax, e-mail and websites, contact person, designation, and product details.

Directory of Japanese Manufacturers & Exporters of Giftware & Novelties. EXIM Infotek Private Ltd. • $5 Individuals. Covers: 30 Japanese manufacturers and exporters of gift items, gifts, giftware, souvenirs, trophies/ceremonial plates. Entries include: Company name, postal address, city, country, phone, fax, e-mail and websites, contact person, designation, and product details.

Directory of Japanese Manufacturers & Exporters of Handicrafts & Decorative Items. EXIM Infotek Private Ltd. • $5 Individuals. Covers: 20 Japanese manufacturers and exporters of art and crafts, art handicrafts, Christmas decorations, Christmas goods, folk crafts, handicrafts, and vases. Entries include: Company name, postal address, city, country, phone, fax, e-mail and websites, contact person, designation, and product details.

Directory of Japanese Manufacturers & Exporters of Handtools. EXIM Infotek Private Ltd. • $10 Individuals. Covers: 60 Japanese manufacturers and exporters of air tools, hand tools, tools, and turning tools. Entries include: Company name, postal address, city, country, phone, fax, e-mail and websites, contact person, designation, and product details.

Directory of Japanese Manufacturers & Exporters of Hardwares--All Types. EXIM Infotek Private Ltd. • $5 Individuals. Covers: 40 Japanese manufacturers and exporters of builders' hardware, casters, door handles, door locks, door operators, fittings, pins, and springs. Entries include: Company name, postal address, city, country, phone, fax, e-mail and websites, contact person, designation, and product details.

Directory of Japanese Manufacturers & Exporters of Herbs & Herbal Medicine Products. EXIM Infotek Private Ltd. • $5 Individuals. Covers: 20 Japanese manufacturers and exporters of agricultural medicines, and herbal medicines. Entries include: Company name, postal address, city, country, phone, fax, e-mail and websites, contact person, designation, and product details.

Directory of Japanese Manufacturers & Exporters of Home Furnishing Materials. EXIM Infotek Private Ltd. • $5 Individuals. Covers: 20 Japanese manufacturers and exporters of curtains, interior goods for housing, venetian blinds, and wallpaper. Entries include: Company name, postal address, city, country, phone, fax, e-mail and websites, contact person, designation, and product details.

Directory of Japanese Manufacturers & Exporters of Houseware, Kitchenware & Tableware. EXIM Infotek Private Ltd. • $10 Individuals. Covers: 110 Japanese manufacturers & exporters of combs, cutlery, daily use goods, gas utensils, home accessories, housing components for various system equipment, kitchen utensils, kitchenware, knives, scissors, tableware. Entries include: Company name, postal address, city, country, phone, fax, e-mail & websites, contact person, designation, products detail.

Directory of Japanese Manufacturers & Exporters of Imitation & Fashion Jewellery. EXIM Infotek Private Ltd. • $5 Individuals. Covers: 30 Japanese manufacturers and exporters of costume accessories, fancy goods, hair accessories, imitation jewelry, imitation pearls, personal accessories, personal ornaments. Entries include: Company name, postal address, city, country, phone, fax, e-mail and websites, contact person, designation, and product details.

Directory of Japanese Manufacturers & Exporters of Leather, Hides, Skins & Furs. EXIM Infotek Private Ltd. • $5 Individuals. Covers: 20 Japanese manufacturers and exporters of artificial fur, leather, rabbit fur and skin, raw hide leather, raw hide skins (fresh, salted), raw skins, and synthetic leather. Entries include: Company name, postal address, city, country, phone, fax, e-mail and websites, contact person, designation, and product details.

Directory of Japanese Manufacturers & Exporters of Leather Products. EXIM Infotek Private Ltd. • $5 Individuals. Covers: 20 Japanese manufacturers and exporters of bags, hand bags, leather goods, and leather products. Entries include: Company name, postal address, city, country, phone, fax, e-mail and websites, contact person, designation, and product details.

Directory of Japanese Manufacturers & Exporters of Lighting Fixtures, Lamps & Accessories. EXIM Infotek Private Ltd. • $5 Individuals. Covers: 30 Japanese manufacturers and exporters of fog lamps, halogen lamps, incandescent lamps, lamps, lighting fixtures-glass, lighting fixtures, lighting fixtures and parts, mercury lamps. Entries include: Company name, postal address, city, country, phone, fax, e-mail and websites, contact person, designation, and product details.

Directory of Japanese Manufacturers & Exporters of Machinery for Chemicals & Pharma Industry. EXIM Infotek Private Ltd. • $5 Individuals. Covers: 20 Japanese manufacturers and exporters of chemical equipment, chemical industrial equipment, chemical industries machinery, chemical machinery, chemical plant equipment, and pharmaceutical plant equipment. Entries include: Company name, postal address, city, country, phone, fax, e-mail and websites, contact person, designation, and product details.

Directory of Japanese Manufacturers & Exporters of Machinery for Textile & Knitting Industry. EXIM Infotek Private Ltd. • $5 Individuals. Covers: 20 Japanese manufacturers and exporters of dyeing machines, knitting machines, knitting needles, spindle machines, textile machinery, and textile machinery parts. Entries include: Company name, postal address, city, country, phone, fax, e-mail and websites, contact person, designation, and product details.

Directory of Japanese Manufacturers & Exporters of Marine & Boating Equipment & Supplies. EXIM Infotek Private Ltd. • $10 Individuals. Covers: 70 Japanese manufacturers and exporters of boat accessories, boats, fishing boat, marine engine spare parts, marine equipment and supplies, marine radios, naval stores products, ships, and used marine engines. Entries include: Company name, postal address, city, country, phone, fax, e-mail and websites, contact person, designation, and product details.

Directory of Japanese Manufacturers & Exporters of Material Handling Equipment. EXIM Infotek Private Ltd. • $250 Individuals. Covers: 80 Japanese manufacturers and exporters of conveying machines, conveyors, cranes, escalators, forklifts, hand trolleys, hand trucks, materials handling equipment, used forklift trucks, and warehousing equipment. Entries include: Company name, postal address, telephone, fax, e-mail, website, contact person, designation, and product details.

Directory of Japanese Manufacturers & Exporters of Meat Products. EXIM Infotek Private Ltd. • $5 Individuals. Covers: 20 Japanese manufacturers and exporters of fresh and frozen meat, meat, salmon, and salmon products. Entries include: Company name, postal address, city, country, phone, fax, e-mail and websites, contact person, designation, and product details.

Directory of Japanese Manufacturers & Exporters of Minerals. EXIM Infotek Private Ltd. • $5 Individuals. Covers: 20 Japanese manufacturers and exporters of graphite, limestones, mineral products, phosphate, and rare metals. Entries include: Company name, postal address, city, country, phone, fax, e-mail and websites, contact person, designation, and product details.

Directory of Japanese Manufacturers & Exporters of Motorcycles, Parts & Accessories. EXIM Infotek Private Ltd. • $20 Individuals. Covers: 280 Japanese manufacturers and exporters of motorcycle parts, motorcycles, motorcycles and accessories, used motorcycles and parts, used scooters. Entries include: Company name, postal address, city, country, phone, fax, e-mail and websites, contact person, designation, and product details.

Directory of Japanese Manufacturers and Exporters of Motors and Motor Parts--Electric. EXIM Infotek Private Ltd. • Covers: 20 Japanese manufacturers and exporters of DC motors, electric motors, motorcycle parts and accessories, starter motors, and stepping motors. Entries include: Company name, postal address, telephone, fax, e-mail, website, contact person, designation, and product details.

Directory of Japanese Manufacturers & Exporters of Nuts, Bolts, Screws & Fasteners. EXIM Infotek Private Ltd. • $5 Individuals. Covers: 20 Japanese manufacturers and exporters of bifurcated rivets, bolts and nuts, bolts, fasteners, hexagon socket button head cap screws, hexagon socket cap screws, hexagon socket flat cap screws, hexagon socket set screws, industrial fasteners, rivets, screws, socket cap screws, tubular rivets, washers, and wood screws. Entries include: Company name, postal address, city, country, phone, fax, e-mail and websites, contact person, designation, and product details.

Directory of Japanese Manufacturers & Exporters of Paints, Varnishes & Allied Products. EXIM Infotek Private Ltd. • $5 Individuals. Covers: 20 Japanese manufacturers and exporters of paint, paints, polyurethane resin coatings, powder coatings, and synthetic resins for paint. Entries include: Company name, postal address, city, country, phone, fax, e-mail and websites, contact person, designation, and product details.

Directory of Japanese Manufacturers & Exporters of Paper & Paper Products. EXIM Infotek Private Ltd. • $10 Individuals. Covers: 50 Japanese manufacturers and exporters of copying paper, corrugated paper and board, decorative laminating paper, foreign paper, craft paper, paper, paper cups, paper napkins, paper pulp products articles, paperboard, plain paper for copying machines, printing paper, pulp, screen paper, sensitized paper for blue printing machines, special paper, stencil paper, thermal paper, and wood pulp. Entries include: Company name, postal address, city, country, phone, fax, e-mail and websites, contact person, designation, and product details.

Directory of Japanese Manufacturers & Exporters of Petroleum Products. EXIM Infotek Private Ltd. • $5 Individuals. Covers: 20 Japanese manufacturers and exporters of fuel, mineral oils and greases, petrochemical industries, petroleum hydrocarbon resins, petroleum products, and petroleum utensils. Entries include: Company name, postal address, city, country, phone, fax, e-mail and websites, contact person, designation, and product details.

Directory of Japanese Manufacturers & Exporters of Pharmaceutical Products. EXIM Infotek Private Ltd. • $10 Individuals. Covers: 120 Japanese manufacturers & exporters of hygienic-pharmaceutical goods, medicaments, medicines, pharmaceutical materials, pharmaceuticals. Entries include: Company name, postal address, city, country, phone, fax, e-mail & websites, contact person, designation, products detail.

Directory of Japanese Manufacturers & Exporters of Readymade Garments. EXIM Infotek Private Ltd. • $10 Individuals. Covers: 50 Japanese manufacturers and exporters of baby clothing, blouses, garments, mufflers, pajamas, regulators, scarfs, shirts, sweaters, and used clothing. Entries include: Company name, postal address, city, country, phone, fax, e-mail and websites, contact person, designation, and product details.

Directory of Japanese Manufacturers and Exporters of Refrigeration Equipment and Supplies. EXIM Infotek Private Ltd. • Covers: 20 Japanese manufacturers and exporters of fluorocarbon refrigerants, refrigeration equipment, and used refrigerators. Entries include: Company name, postal address, telephone, fax, e-mail, website, contact person, designation, and product details.

Directory of Japanese Manufacturers & Exporters of Spices, Seasoning & Flavourings. EXIM Infotek Private Ltd. • $5 Individuals. Covers: 20 Japanese manufacturers and exporters of seasonings. Entries include: Company name, postal address, city, country, phone, fax, e-mail and websites, contact person, designation, and product details.

Directory of Japanese Manufacturers & Exporters of Sporting Goods. EXIM Infotek Private Ltd. • Covers: 30 Japanese manufacturers and exporters of fishing nets, fishing nets and floats, golf bags, leisure goods, ski carrier and roof racks, sporting goods, sports goods, sports shoes, and sportswear. Entries include: Company name, postal address, telephone, fax, e-mail, website, contact person, designation, and product details.

Directory of Japanese Manufacturers & Exporters of Textile & Fabrics. EXIM Infotek Private Ltd. • $10 Individuals. Covers: 80 Japanese manufacturers and exporters of chenille, clothing and textile products, cords and tassels, core fabrics, dyed fabrics, fabrics, knitted fabrics, net and tulle, non woven fabrics, PTFE coated glass fiber fabrics, silk, silk products, textile and its articles, textile piece goods, textile products, textiles, and woven fabrics. Entries include: Company name, postal address, city, country, phone, fax, e-mail and websites, contact person, designation, and product details.

For publishers' addresses, refer to SOURCES CITED section at the back of the book.

Directory of Japanese Manufacturers & Exporters of Toys & Games. EXIM Infotek Private Ltd. • $10 Individuals. Covers: 80 Japanese manufacturers and exporters of baby chairs, battery operated toys, board games, cloth toys, dolls, educational toys, electronic toys, games, general toys, hobbies, hobby crafts, inflatable vinyl toys, jigsaw puzzles, metal and plastic toys, plastic toys, pre-school toys, puzzles, radio controlled cars, ride on toys, shadow masks, stuffed toys, stuffed animals, toys, trading cards, vehicles for children, and wooden toys. Entries include: Company name, postal address, city, country, phone, fax, e-mail and websites, contact person, designation, and product details.

Directory of Japanese Manufacturers & Exporters of Tractors, Parts & Accessories. EXIM Infotek Private Ltd. • $5 Individuals. Covers: 30 Japanese manufacturers and exporters of used agricultural tractor, used farm tractors, used tractors. Entries include: Company name, postal address, city, country, phone, fax, e-mail and websites, contact person, designation, and product details.

Directory of Japanese Manufacturers & Exporters of Tyres & Tubes. EXIM Infotek Private Ltd. • $10 Individuals. Covers: 70 Japanese manufacturers and exporters of automobile tires and tubes, rubber tires and tubes, tires, tires and tubes, tires-used, used truck tires, and used tires. Entries include: Company name, postal address, city, country, phone, fax, e-mail and websites, contact person, designation, and product details.

Directory of Japanese Manufacturers & Exporters of Watches & Clocks. EXIM Infotek Private Ltd. • $5 Individuals. Covers: 20 Japanese manufacturers and exporters of clocks, watch bands and straps, and watches. Entries include: Company name, postal address, city, country, phone, fax, e-mail and websites, contact person, designation, and product details.

Directory of Japanese Manufacturers & Exporters of Wire, Chain & Wire Products. EXIM Infotek Private Ltd. • $5 Individuals. Covers: 40 Japanese manufacturers and exporters of chain and chain block, chains, steel wire, wire, wire netting, and wire products. Entries include: Company name, postal address, city, country, phone, fax, e-mail and websites, contact person, designation, and product details.

Directory of Japanese Manufacturers & Exporters of Wires & Cables--Electrical. EXIM Infotek Private Ltd. • $200 Individuals. Covers: 50 Japanese manufacturers and exporters of arc welding machinery and equipment, electrodes, resistance welding machines, used welder, welding machinery, and welding rods. Entries include: Company name, postal address, telephone, fax, e-mail, website, contact person, designation, and product details.

Directory of Japanese Manufacturers and Exporters of Woodworking Equipment and Tools. EXIM Infotek Private Ltd. • Covers: 20 Japanese manufacturers and exporters of band saw blades, band sawing machine, circle saw, plywood machinery, wood processing machinery, and wood working machine. Entries include: Company name, postal address, telephone, fax, e-mail, website, contact person, designation, and product details.

Directory of Kansas Manufacturers and Products. Kansas Department of Commerce & Housing. • Biennial. $50. Covers: Approximately 2,500 manufacturers in Kansas. Entries include: Company name, address, phone, fax, name of principal executive, products or services, codes for number of employees.

Directory of Linkage Industries. Hong Kong Productivity Council. • Annual. $220 pick up at HKPC Office. Covers: Major jobshops and suppliers in the metal industry in Hong Kong as well as their operations in Mainland China including mold and tool making, surface finishing, industrial machinery repair and maintenance, and hot and cold working and metal machinery.

Directory of Louisiana Manufacturers. Dun & Bradstreet Inc. • Annual. Covers: Over 6,500 manufacturing companies in Louisiana. Database includes: Statistical data, trade show calendar. Entries include: Company name, address, county, phone, fax, number of employees, names and titles of key executives, plant size, year established, parent company, annual sales, import and export information, Standard Industrial Classification (SIC) code, and product description.

Directory of Major Manufacturers of T&D Equipment. NRG Expert. • Covers: More than 1,500 international manufacturers of equipment used in the power sector, including switchgear, HV transformers, insulated cables, uninsulated lines, insulators, bushings, and fittings. Entries include: Company name, address, telephone and fax numbers.

Directory of Manufacturers of Pressure-Sensitive Tape, Label Stock, and Other Coated Products. Satas & Associates. • $99. Covers: 92 manufacturers of specialized coated tapes and labeling products. Entries include: Company name, address, phone, product/service.

Directory of Mexican Corporations. IBCON S.A. • Irregular. $488 Individuals. 1,621 Mexican corporations selling at least $10,000,000 a year.

Directory of Middle East Importers of Boiler and Boiler Parts. EXIM Infotek Private Ltd. • $200 Individuals. Covers: 50 Middle East importers of boilers and parts, oil/gas/electric boilers, and pressure vessels. Entries include: Company name, postal address, telephone, fax, e-mail, website, contact person, designation, and product details.

Directory of Middle East Importers of Calendars, Greeting, Prints and Lithographs. EXIM Infotek Private Ltd. • $200 Individuals. Covers: 55 Middle East importers of calendars, greeting cards, postcards, Christmas cards, greeting cards, morals, pictures, etchings, posters, prints, and lithographs. Entries include: Company name, postal address, telephone, fax, e-mail, website, contact person, designation, and product details.

Directory of Middle East Importers of Dyes, Colors, and Pigments. EXIM Infotek Private Ltd. • $250 Individuals. Covers: 80 Middle East importers of carbon black, dyes, colors, pigments, and dyestuff. Entries include: Company name, postal address, telephone, fax, e-mail, website, contact person, designation, and product details.

Directory of Middle East Importers of Energy and Power Equipment. EXIM Infotek Private Ltd. • $300 Individuals. Covers: 100 Middle East importers of alternative energy equipment, nuclear equipment and material, power generation equipment, power transmission equipment and supplies, solar energy equipment, wind energy equipment, and transmission and allied equipment. Entries include: Company name, postal address, telephone, fax, e-mail, website, contact person, designation, and product details.

Directory of Middle East Importers of Environment Protection and Pollution Control Equipment. EXIM Infotek Private Ltd. • Covers: 200 Middle East importers of environmental protection equipment, garbage disposals and compactors, pollution control equipment, water purification equipment, and water treatment equipment. Entries include: Company name, postal address, telephone, fax, e-mail, website, contact person, designation, and product details.

Directory of Middle East Importers of Fibre and Fibre Products. EXIM Infotek Private Ltd. • $300 Individuals. Covers: 100 Middle East importers of acrylic fibers, fiber optic equipment, fiber glass, fiber glass cloth and products, fiber products, glass fibers, polyester fibers, polyester staple fibers, synthetic fibers, and viscose fibers. Entries include: Company name, postal address, telephone, fax, e-mail, website, contact person, designation, and product details.

Directory of Middle East Importers of Fire Fighting Equipment & Supplies. EXIM Infotek Private Ltd. • Covers: 200 Middle East importers of fire alarm equipment and fire fighting equipment. Entries include: Company name, postal address, telephone, fax, e-mail, website, contact person, designation, and product details.

Directory of Middle East Importers of Fodder and Animal Foodstuffs. EXIM Infotek Private Ltd. • $400 Individuals. Covers: 170 Middle East importers of animal and poultry fodder, animal feeds, animal feed additives, animal feed ingredients, animal food, animal foodstuff additives, fodder, cereals, and livestock breeding supplies. Entries include: Company name, postal address, telephone, fax, e-mail, website, contact person, designation, and product details.

Directory of Middle East Importers of Food Additives and Aromatics. EXIM Infotek Private Ltd. • $250 Individuals. Covers: 90 Middle East importers of additives, aromatic chemicals, artificial sweeteners, food additives, food colors, food chemicals, margarine, and yeast. Entries include: Company name, postal address, telephone, fax, e-mail, website, contact person, designation, and product details.

Directory of Middle East Importers of Handkerchives, Scarves and Neckwears. EXIM Infotek Private Ltd. • $150 Individuals. Covers: 20 Middle East importers of handkerchieves, scarves, and neckwear.

Directory of Middle East Importers of Heaters and Heating Equipment. EXIM Infotek Private Ltd. • Covers: 130 Middle East importers of central heating plants and equipment, heat exchangers, and heaters. Entries include: Company name, postal address, telephone, fax, e-mail, website, contact person, designation, and product details.

Directory of Middle East Importers of Herbs & Herbal Medicine Products. EXIM Infotek Private Ltd. • Covers: 20 Middle East importers of medicinal herbs and botanicals. Entries include: Company name, postal address, telephone, fax, e-mail, website, contact person, designation, and product details.

Directory of Middle East Importers of Honey and Syrup. EXIM Infotek Private Ltd. • $150 Individuals. Covers: 20 Middle East importers of honey and syrups. Entries include: Company name, postal address, telephone, fax, e-mail, website, contact person, designation, and product details.

Directory of Middle East Importers of Laboratory & Scientific Instruments & Supplies. EXIM Infotek Private Ltd. • Covers: 510 Middle East importers of analysis equipment, binoculars, microscopes, telescopes, laboratory and scientific glass ware, laboratory and scientific instruments, laboratory equipment, material testing equipment, microscopes, scientific and laboratory instruments, scientific equipment, scientific instruments, soil testing equipment, and testing equipment. Entries include: Company name, postal address, telephone, fax, e-mail, website, contact person, designation, and product details.

Directory of Middle East Importers of Lumber, Timber, Plywood and Hardboards. EXIM Infotek Private Ltd. • $500 Individuals. Covers: 260 Middle East importers of blockboard and hardboard, doors and windows, formica, gypsum boards, hardboard and particle board, hardwood flooring and floor tiles, laminates, hardwood lumber, softwood lumber, timber, plywood, medium-density fiberboard, millwork (wooden), veneer, poles, pilings and logs, and sawdust. Entries include: Company name, postal address, telephone, fax, e-mail, website, contact person, designation, and product details.

Directory of Middle East Importers of Machinery for Glass and Ceramic Industry. EXIM Infotek Private Ltd. • $150 Individuals. Covers: 20 Middle East importers of ceramic industry equipment, ceramic industry supplies, glass making machinery and equipment. Entries include: Company name, postal address, telephone, fax, e-mail, website, contact person, designation, and product details.

Directory of Middle East Importers of Machinery for Paper & Pulp Industry. EXIM Infotek Private Ltd. • Covers: 30 Middle East importers of paper bag manufacturing machinery and paper making machinery. Entries include: Company name, postal address, telephone, fax, e-mail, website, contact person, designation, and product details.

Directory of Middle East Importers of Material Handling Equipment & Supplies. EXIM Infotek Private Ltd. • Covers: 320 Middle East importers of conveying equipment and supplies, conveyors, crane overload indicators, cranes and hoists, elevators and lifts, escalators, forklifts, electric and hydraulic lifts, liquid handling equipment, loading and unloading equipment, materials handling systems for garment industries, monorail materials handling equipment, road construction handling equipment, winches, and pulleys. Entries include: Company name, postal address, telephone, fax, e-mail, website, contact person, designation, and product details.

Directory of Middle East Importers of Military & Police Equipment & Supplies. EXIM Infotek Private Ltd. • $200 Individuals. Covers: 45 Middle East importers of ammunition, military electronic equipment, military equipment and supplies, police equipment, surplus military equipment and supplies, traffic control systems and equipment. Entries include: Company name, postal address, telephone, fax, e-mail, website, contact person, designation, and product details.

Directory of Middle East Importers of Minerals. EXIM Infotek Private Ltd. • $250 Individuals. Covers: 60 Middle East importers of aluminum alloy ingot, clay, lead, mica, minerals, ores, titanium dioxide, zinc, zinc concentrate, zinc ingot, and zinc ingueat. Entries include: Company name, postal address, telephone, fax, e-mail, website, contact person, designation, and product details.

Directory of Middle East Importers of Motors and Motor Parts--Electric. EXIM Infotek Private Ltd. • Covers: 170 Middle East importers of electric motors, motor equipment and parts, motor oil, and outboard motor. Entries include: Company name, postal address, telephone, fax, e-mail, website, contact person, designation, and product details.

Directory of Middle East Importers of Photographic Equipment and Supplies. EXIM Infotek Private Ltd. • $350 Individuals. Covers: 130 Middle East importers of cameras, lens and accessories, photographic chemicals, motion picture and theater equipment, cinematographic equipment and accessories, film, microfilm and blueprint equipment, motion picture film, photo processing and developing equipment, photographic apparatus and accessories, and photographic equipment. Entries include: Company name, postal address, telephone, fax, e-mail, website, contact person, designation, and product details.

Directory of Middle East Importers of Plastic Scrap and Raw Materials. EXIM Infotek Private Ltd. • $450 Individuals. Covers: 180 Middle East importers of fiberglass resins, high-density polyethylene (HDPE), LDPE scrap, phenol formaldehyde resin, plastic materials, plastic raw materials, plastic scrap and waste, polyester powder, polymer, polypropylene, PVC (granule), and waste plastic. Entries include: Company name, postal address, telephone, fax, e-mail, website, contact person, designation, and product details.

Directory of Middle East Importers of Restaurant, Hotel and Catering Equipment. EXIM Infotek Private Ltd. • Covers: 160 Middle East importers of catering equipment, cooking ranges and oven, restaurant and hotel equipment. Entries include: Company name, postal address, telephone, fax, e-mail, website, contact person, designation, and product details.

Directory of Middle East Importers of Sewing Machines and Parts. EXIM Infotek Private Ltd. • $250 Individuals. Covers: 70 Middle East importers of embroidery machinery, garment industry equipment, industrial sewing machine and parts, new and used industrial sewing machine and spare parts, and domestic sewing machine. Entries include: Company name, postal address, telephone, fax, e-mail, website, contact person, designation, and product details.

Directory of Middle East Importers of Soap, Detergent and Cleaning Supplies. EXIM Infotek Private Ltd. • $450 Individuals. Covers: 180 Middle East importers of cleaning supplies, soap, detergent, disinfectant products, polishes and cleansing materials, and bleach. Entries include: Company name, postal address, telephone, fax, e-mail, website, contact person, designation, and product details.

Directory of Middle East Importers of Sporting Goods. EXIM Infotek Private Ltd. • Covers: 280 Middle East importers of billiard, pool equipment and supplies, bowling equipment and supplies, diving equipment, firearms, golf equipment and supplies, hiking accessories, mountain climbing equipment, playground equipment, ski boots, skiing accessories, sporting goods and toys, sporting goods, sporting guns and cartridges, sports goods, stadium equipment, tennis and badminton equipment and supplies, turf maintenance equipment, water ski equipment and supplies, water sports equipment and supplies, and windsurfing goods. Entries include: Company name, postal address, telephone, fax, e-mail, website, contact person, designation, and product details.

Directory of Middle East Importers of Telephone Instruments and Accessories. EXIM Infotek Private Ltd. • $350 Individuals. Covers: 110 Middle East importers of mobile phone, microphone, mobile accessories, pagers, beepers, telefax equipment, telephone control unit, and telephone index. Entries include: Company name, postal address, telephone, fax, e-mail, website, contact person, designation, and product details.

Directory of Middle East Importers of Waste Disposal & Recycling Equipment. EXIM Infotek Private Ltd. • Covers: 55 Middle East importers of sewage equipment, waste disposal equipment, and waste recycling equipment. Entries include: Company name, postal address, telephone, fax, e-mail, website, contact person, designation, and product details.

Directory of Middle East Importers of Wax & Wax Products. EXIM Infotek Private Ltd. • Covers: 40 Middle East importers of paraffin, paraffin waxes, polishes and creams. Entries include: Company name, postal address, telephone, fax, e-mail, website, contact person, designation, and product details.

Directory of Middle East Importers of Welding Equipment and Supplies. EXIM Infotek Private Ltd. • $350 Individuals. Covers: 140 Middle East importers of electrodes, soldering equipment, soldering supplies, welding equipment, welding products, and welding supplies. Entries include: Company name, postal address, telephone, fax, e-mail, website, contact person, designation, and product details.

Directory of Middle East Importers of Wires & Cables--Electrical. EXIM Infotek Private Ltd. • Covers: 180 Middle East importers of cable equipment, cables, copper cable and accessories, copper wire, electrical cables, electrical wires, and power cables. Entries include: Company name, postal address, telephone, fax, e-mail, website, contact person, designation, and product details.

Directory of Middle East Importers of Woodenware & Wood Products. EXIM Infotek Private Ltd. • Covers: 40 Middle East importers of baskets and basket ware, wooden poles, wooden products, and wooden screws. Entries include: Company name, postal address, telephone, fax, e-mail, website, contact person, designation, and product details.

Directory of Middle East Importers of Yarns and Threads. EXIM Infotek Private Ltd. • $500 Individuals. Covers: 200 Middle East importers of acetate yarns, cotton yarn and thread, elastic yarn, metallic yarn and thread, nylon filament yarn, nylon yarn, polyester yarn, sewing thread, silk yarns, sisal yarns and ropes, synthetic yarn and thread, viscose yarns, and wool yarn. Entries include: Company name, postal address, telephone, fax, e-mail, website, contact person, designation, and product details.

Directory of Minority & Women-Owned Businesses. Business Service Div. Birmingham Area Chamber of Commerce. • Covers: Approximately 1,200 businesses in Birmingham, Alabama, that are owned by women or minorities. Entries include: Company name, address, phone, name and title of contact, Standard Industrial Classification (SIC) code.

Directory of Multinationals. Macmillan Publishers Ltd. Nature Publishing Group. • Irregular. $595 plus s/h. Approximately 450 multinational corporations with sales of $1 billion during 1996 and significant foreign investments.

Directory of North American Importers of Calendars, Greeting, Prints and Lithographs. EXIM Infotek Private Ltd. • $300 Individuals. Covers: 110 North American importers of art prints, cards, calendars, greeting cards, postcards, pictures, posters, prints, lithograph and etching, printing and graphic arts. Entries include: Company name, postal address, telephone, fax, e-mail, website, contact person, designation, and product details.

Directory of North American Importers of Camping and Backpacking Equipment and Supplies. EXIM Infotek Private Ltd. • $300 Individuals. Covers: 100 North American importers of awnings, backpack, backsacks, backpacking equipment and supplies, camping equipment, outdoor recreational equipment and tents. Entries include: Company name, postal address, telephone, fax, e-mail, website, contact person, designation, and product details.

Directory of North American Importers of Dyes, Colors, and Pigments. EXIM Infotek Private Ltd. • $250 Individuals. Covers: 50 North American importers of chemical intermediates, dyes, colors, pigments, and dyestuff. Entries include: Company name, postal address, telephone, fax, e-mail, website, contact person, designation, and product details.

Directory of North American Importers of Energy and Power Equipment. EXIM Infotek Private Ltd. • Covers: 100 North American importers of alternative energy equipment, power supply system, power transmission component, power transmission equipment and supplies, solar cell products, solar energy equipment, and wind energy equipment. Entries include: Company name, postal address, telephone, fax, e-mail, website, contact person, designation, and product details.

Directory of North American Importers of Environment Protection and Pollution Control Equipment. EXIM Infotek Private Ltd. • $200 Individuals. Covers: 50 North American importers of environmental protection equipment, pollution control equipment, water purification equipment, water treatment, and purifying equipment. Entries include: Company name, postal address, telephone, fax, e-mail, website, contact person, designation, and product details.

Directory of North American Importers of Fodder and Animal Foodstuffs. EXIM Infotek Private Ltd. • $150 Individuals. Covers: 40 North American importers of animal feed, animal food, animal foodstuff additives, animal foodstuff, feed additives, fodder, cereals, and livestock breeding supplies. Entries include: Company name, postal address, telephone, fax, e-mail, website, contact person, designation, and product details.

Directory of North American Importers of Food Additives and Aromatics. EXIM Infotek Private Ltd. • $250 Individuals. Covers: 80 North American importers of aromatic chemicals, aromatics, baking ingredients, citric acid, flavor ingredients, flavoring extracts, food additives, food colors, food ingredients, food preparations, fragrances, preservatives, and starches. Entries include: Company name, postal address, telephone, fax, e-mail, website, contact person, designation, and product details.

Directory of North American Importers of Handkerchives, Scarves and Neckwears. EXIM Infotek Private Ltd. • $250 Individuals. Covers: 60 North American importers of bows, handkerchieves, scarves, neckwear, mufflers, napkins, neckties, pashmina shawls, silk scarves, and wool shawls. Entries include: Company name, postal address, telephone, fax, e-mail, website, contact person, designation, and product details.

Directory of North American Importers of Heaters and Heating Equipment. EXIM Infotek Private Ltd. • $300 Individuals. Covers: 120 North American importers of heat exchangers, heating and ventilation equipment, and heating elements. Entries include: Company name, postal address, telephone, fax, e-mail, website, contact person, designation, and product details.

Directory of North American Importers of Herbs & Herbal Medicine Products. EXIM Infotek Private Ltd. • $300 Individuals. Covers: 60 North American importers of ayurvedic medicines, ayurvedic products, botanicals, bulk herbs, Chinese herbs, crude botanical drugs, ginseng, herb products, herb seeds, herbal cosmetics, herbal extracts, herbal products, herbal tea, herbicides, herbs, medicinal herbs, and botanical. Entries include: Company name, postal address, telephone, fax, e-mail, website, contact person, designation, and product details.

Directory of North American Importers of Honey and Syrup. EXIM Infotek Private Ltd. • $150 Individuals. Covers: 25 North American importers of cinnamon honey, honey, and syrup. Entries include: Company name, postal address, telephone, fax, e-mail, website, contact person, designation, and product details.

Directory of North American Importers of Laboratory & Scientific Instruments and Supplies. EXIM Infotek Private Ltd. • Covers: 150 North American importers of binoculars, microscope, telescopes, laboratory equipment, laboratory and scientific glass, laboratory apparatus, magnifiers, microscope accessories, microscopes, scientific instruments, soil testing equipment, and testing equipment. Entries include: Company name, postal address, telephone, fax, e-mail, website, contact person, designation, and product details.

Directory of North American Importers of Lumber, Timber, Plywood and Hardboards. EXIM Infotek Private Ltd. • $700 Individuals. Covers: 350 North American importers of bamboo and rattan raw, doors, windows, exotic wood, forestry products, gypsum board and sheetrock, hardboard, particleboard, hardwood, hardwood flooring, hardwood floor tiles, lumber, laminates (wood), lumber (hardwood), lumber (softwood), lumber products, lumber timber and plywood, mahogany, millwork (wooden), oak vanities, plywood, veneer, poles, pilings and logs, rattan, teakwood, timber, tropical hardwood, and wicker. Entries include: Company name, postal address, telephone, fax, e-mail, website, contact person, designation, and product details.

Directory of North American Importers of Material Handling Equipment & Supplies. EXIM Infotek Private Ltd. • Covers: 120 North American importers of cargo handling equipment, conveyors, cranes and hoists, elevators and lifts, forklift parts, liquid handling equipment and supplies, loading and unloading equipment, materials handling equipment and parts, and winches. Entries include: Company name, postal address, telephone, fax, e-mail, website, contact person, designation, and product details.

Directory of North American Importers of Minerals. EXIM Infotek Private Ltd. • $200 Individuals. Covers: 50 North American importers of alabaster, clay, graphite, industrial minerals, limestone, magnesium, mica, minerals, and ores. Entries include: Company name, postal address, telephone, fax, e-mail, website, contact person, designation, and product details.

Directory of North American Importers of Oil Seeds. EXIM Infotek Private Ltd. • Covers: 30 North American importers of mustard, oil seeds, peanut, sesame seeds, soybeans, and sunflower seeds. Entries include: Company name, postal address, telephone, fax, e-mail, website, contact person, designation, and product details.

Directory of North American Importers of Paper & Paper Products. EXIM Infotek Private Ltd. • Covers: 210 North American importers of copier paper, decorative paper, fax and duplicating paper, gift wrap, gold foil paper, handmade paper, handmade paper materials, kraft paper, newsprint, paper and paper products, wood pulp, paper bags, paper cups, paper goods, paper napkins, paper plates, paper waste, printing paper, recycled paper, sanitary and toilet paper goods, specialty paper, and tissue paper. Entries include: Company name, postal address, telephone, fax, e-mail, website, contact person, designation, and product details.

Directory of North American Importers of Photographic Equipment and Supplies. EXIM Infotek Private Ltd. • $300 Individuals. Covers: 130 North American importers of camera film, cameras, lens and accessories, motion picture and theater equipment, digital camera, disposable flash camera, film, plates and photographic papers, graphic art supplies, graphic arts equipment, microfilm equipment, motion picture film, photographic equipment and supplies, photographic goods, photographic papers, photographic products, professional motion picture equipment, and slide projectors. Entries include: Company name, postal address, telephone, fax, e-mail, website, contact person, designation, and product details.

Directory of North American Importers of Plastic Scrap and Raw Materials. EXIM Infotek Private Ltd. • $250 Individuals. Covers: 80 North American importers of high-density polyethylene (HDPE), low-density polyethylene (LDPE), phenolic, plastic raw materials, plastic resins, plastic scrap and waste, polyester, polyvinyl alcohol, and polypropylene (PP). Entries include: Company name, postal address, telephone, fax, e-mail, website, contact person, designation, and product details.

Directory of North American Importers of Refrigeration Equipment and Supplies. EXIM Infotek Private Ltd. • $300 Individuals. Covers: 110 North American importers of freezer, refrigeration and air conditioning equipment, and refrigerator parts. Entries include: Company name, postal address, telephone, fax, e-mail, website, contact person, designation, and product details.

Directory of North American Importers of Restaurant, Hotel and Catering Equipment. EXIM Infotek Private Ltd. • $250 Individuals. Covers: 80 North American importers of bar supplies, barbecue, catering equipment and supplies, cooking equipment (patio and outdoors), cooking range and oven, food service components, painted serving trays, restaurant equipment, restaurant supplies, hotel equipment and supplies, tray and chafing dishes, wine baskets and racks. Entries include: Company name, postal address, telephone, fax, e-mail, website, contact person, designation, and product details.

Directory of North American Importers of Sewing Machines and Parts. EXIM Infotek Private Ltd. • $250 Individuals. Covers: 60 North American importers of embroidery machinery, industrial sewing machine and parts, sewing machine and sewing accessories, domestic sewing machine, and sewing machine needles. Entries include: Company name, postal address, telephone, fax, e-mail, website, contact person, designation, and product details.

Directory of North American Importers of Soap, Detergent and Cleaning Supplies. EXIM Infotek Private Ltd. • $350 Individuals. Covers: 140 North American importers of antiseptics, disinfectant soap, cleaning supplies, detergent, shampoo, toilet and bathroom preparations. Entries include: Company name, postal address, telephone, fax, e-mail, website, contact person, designation, and product details.

Directory of North American Importers of Sporting Goods. EXIM Infotek Private Ltd. • Covers: 440 North American importers of baseball caps, baseball supplies, billiard, pool equipment and supplies, climbing equipment, climbing gear, exercise equipment, firearms, golf ball, golf caps, golf cart accessories, golf course accessories and tools, golf equipment and supplies, martial arts supplies, medals, mountain climbing equipment, playground equipment, polo seats, scuba and diving equipment, skateboards and accessories, ski equipment and supplies, snowboard, soccer balls, soccer equipment, soccer games, sport bags, sporting goods, toys, sports bags, sports footwear, tennis and badminton equipment, trekking wear, water ski equipment and supplies, water sports equipment and supplies, and windsurfing accessories.

Directory of North American Importers of Telephone Instruments and Accessories. EXIM Infotek Private Ltd. • $300 Individuals. Covers: 100 North American importers of beepers, cellular accessories, cellular mobile phone, cellular phone, cordless telephone, GSM phones, headphone, microphone, Nokia phone, pagers, telephone accessories, telephone answering equipment, telephone equipment, and used cellphone. Entries include: Company name, postal address, telephone, fax, e-mail, website, contact person, designation, and product details.

Directory of North American Importers of Wires & Cables--Electrical. EXIM Infotek Private Ltd. • $200 Individuals. Covers: 60 American and Canadian importers for wires, cables, electrical cables, electrical wires, extension cords, and combination wires. Entries include: Company name, postal address, telephone, fax, e-mail, website, contact person, designation, and product details.

Directory of North American Importers of Yarns and Threads. EXIM Infotek Private Ltd. • $300 Individuals. Covers: 100 North American importers of acrylic yarn, cotton yarn, embroidery thread, filament yarn, metallic yarn, polyester yarn, sewing thread, silk yarn and thread, synthetic yarn, thread, viscose, wool yarn, cotton, and silk. Entries include: Company name, postal address, telephone, fax, e-mail, website, contact person, designation, and product details.

Directory of North Carolina Manufacturing Firms:

Federal ID 56-1611-847. Harris InfoSource. • Annual. $70 payment must accompany order. Covers: Approximately 7,200 manufacturers in North Carolina. Entries include: Company name, address, names and titles of principal executives, names and address of parent company, geographical area served, Standard Industrial Classification (SIC) code, product/service provided, number of employees, year established.

Directory of Packaging and Allied Industries. NIIR Project Consultancy Services. • $100 Individuals. Covers: 1,000 companies/industries (manufacturers and suppliers) of packaging industries, packaging raw material, packaging machineries in India. Entries include: Company name, full postal address, phone, fax, email (wherever available), website address (wherever available).

Directory of Plastics Industry. Hong Kong Productivity Council. • Annual. $300 pick up at HKPC office. Covers: Over 3,000 companies from plastic manufacturers in Hong Kong as well as their operations in mainland China. Entries include: Name, address, phone, fax, e-mail, URL, number of employees, turnover, and products/name brands.

Directory of Printing and Allied Industries. NIIR Project Consultancy Services. • $100 Individuals CD-ROM. Covers: 1,000 companies/industries (manufacturers and suppliers), printing inks, printing machineries, printing raw material in India. Entries include: Company name, full postal address, phone, fax, email (wherever available), website address (wherever available).

Directory of Private Sector Services to Cities. Texas Municipal League. • Annual. $10. Covers: about 300 firms providing services to city governments in Texas, including attorneys, accountants, architects, auditors, construction managers, engineers, inspectors, real estate appraisers and counselors, and water resource and supply companies. Entries include: Firm name, address, phone, name and title of contact, services, geographical area served.

Directory of Public Companies in Canada. Micromedia ProQuest. • Irregular. $125. Covers: over 3,500 public companies in Canada. Database includes: Citations of recent newspaper articles in a Corporate News Index. Entries include: Company name, address, phone, fax, names and titles of key personnel, date and location of incorporation, ticker symbols, auditor, financial data, history.

Directory of Registered Belgian Entrepreneurs and Companies. Cite Administrative de l'Etat. • Annual. Covers: Companies in Belgium. Entries include: Company name, address, phone, registration number, line of business, number of employees, business code.

Directory of Rhode Island Manufacturers. Rhode Island Economic Development Corporation. • Annual. Covers: 2800 manufacturers in Rhode Island. Entries include: Company name, address, phone, product/service, name and title of contact, number of employees, parent company, and estimated sales.

Directory of SAARC Importers of Construction Machinery and Equipment. EXIM Infotek Private Ltd. • $300 Individuals. Covers: 80 companies in member countries of the South Asian Association for Regional Cooperation (SAARC) that import asphalt mixing plants, asphalt paving equipment, bulldozers, chip spreaders, road sweepers, concrete breakers, chipping hammer, concrete machinery and mixer, concrete production equipment, construction equipment and spare parts, dumpers, earthmoving equipment, excavating equipment, heavy construction machinery, hoists for construction, hydraulic concrete mixer, mixers and pavers, plate compactors, prime movers, rammers, road rollers, used construction machinery, used hydraulic truck mounted cranes, vibrators, and vibrating and pneumatic rollers. Entries include: Company name, postal address, telephone, fax, e-mail, website, contact person, designation, and product details.

Directory of SAARC Importers of Dyes, Colors, Pigments and Intermediates. EXIM Infotek Private Ltd. • $350 Individuals. Covers: 80 SAARC countries importers of acrylic color, activated carbon, auxiliaries, chemical for pashmina, dye intermediates, dye, colors, pigments, dyestuff, fabric colors, ink, leather chemicals, leather dyestuff and chemicals, phthalic anhydride, pigment emulsions, printing ink, textile auxiliaries, textile chemicals, textile dye, textile binder, and washing chemicals. Entries include: Company name, postal address, telephone, fax, e-mail, website, contact person, designation, and product details.

Directory of SAARC Importers of Environment Protection and Pollution Control Equipment. EXIM Infotek Private Ltd. • Covers: 20 companies in member countries of the South Asian Association for Regional Cooperation (SAARC) that import carbon dioxide and kitchen hood flooring systems, deionizers, environmental control equipment, environmental noise monitor, pollution control equipment, sewage cleaning equipment, sewage treatment, water purification equipment, water treatment equipment and plants. Entries include: Company name, postal address, telephone, fax, e-mail, website, contact person, designation, and product details.

Directory of SAARC Importers of Fibre and Fibre Products. EXIM Infotek Private Ltd. • $150 Individuals. Covers: 20 SAARC Countries importers of acrylic fiber, carbon fiber, fiber glass materials, fiber glass products and cloth, fiber rods and sheets, Mexican fiber, mineral fiber board, natural fiber, palmyra fiber, polyester fiber, polyester staple fiber, staple fiber, synthetic fiber, viscose fiber, and vulcanized fiber. Entries include: Company name, postal address, telephone, fax, e-mail, website, contact person, designation, and product details.

Directory of SAARC Importers of Fire Fighting Equipment & Supplies. EXIM Infotek Private Ltd. • Covers: 40 companies in member countries of the South Asian Association for Regional Cooperation (SAARC) that import fire and safety instruments, fire alarm systems, fire clothing and equipment, fire demonstration and training, fire detection and alarm systems, fire detection products, fire doors and panic hardware, fire extinguishers, fire fighting equipment, fire hose reel, hydrant and sprinkler systems, fire hose systems, fire rated shutters, fire resistant products, fire trucks and sewerage equipment, fire vehicles and accessories, firefighting uniforms, helmet, emblems, badges, tarpaulins, foam extinguishers, and smoke detection systems. Entries include: Company name, postal address, telephone, fax, e-mail, website, contact person, designation, and product details.

Directory of SAARC Importers of Hardwares--All Types. EXIM Infotek Private Ltd. • Covers: 90 companies in member countries of the South Asian Association for Regional Cooperation (SAARC) that import abrasives, anchors, blades, brass ball knob, brass collars, knobs for brass beds, brass fittings, brass hardware, builder's hardware, cabinet hardware, castor wheel, ceiling fittings, coated abrasives, curtain fittings, curtain rails, door accessories, door closers, door fittings, door handles, door locks, emery paper, furniture hardware and parts, general hardware, hardware merchants, hinges, hooded ball casters, hooks, lipped channel, cylinder lock, locks for homes and hotels, magnet catches, nails, overhead sliding door systems, pantry cupboards fittings, railings, roller doors, roller shutter spring, sand paper, spring, flat washers, taper lock bushes, tug pins, twin wheel casters, vibrator roller, water sand paper, zigzag, and engineering tools.

Directory of SAARC Importers of Lumber, Timber, Plywood and Hardboards. EXIM Infotek Private Ltd. • $200 Individuals. Covers: 60 SAARC countries importers of artificial timber, bio-fold doors, windows, board, ebonite rods and sheets, false ceiling board, formica, gypsum board, hard boards, particleboard, laminated boards, laminated wooden boards, doors, windows, laminated decorative-sheets, laminates, hardwood lumber, softwood lumber, medium-density fiberboards, particle boards, plywood, veneer, doors, plywood sheets, sawn goods, sliding doors, straw boards, swing door, teak wood, timber, timber products, white boards, window shutters, window type, and wood. Entries include: Company name, postal address, telephone, fax, e-mail, website, contact person, designation, and product details.

Directory of SAARC Importers of Material Handling Equipment. EXIM Infotek Private Ltd. • Covers: 45 companies in member countries of the South Asian Association for Regional Cooperation (SAARC) that import backhoe loaders, cargo hooks, cement factory chains, chain for conveyors, container handling equipment, conveyors, crane lorries, cranes and hoists, crawler crane, electric chain block, elevators lifts, escalators, forklift parts and accessories, hand pallet truck, hoisting blocks chipping machine and spares, electrical and manual hoists, hydraulic excavators, loaders, loading and unloading equipment, materials handling containers and equipment, material handling systems, material lifting system, mobile cranes, mop carts, pallet truck, pulley, roller and accumulating conveyors, rough terrain crane, and wheel loaders. Entries include: Company name, postal address, telephone, fax, e-mail, website, contact person, designation, and product details.

Directory of SAARC Importers of Minerals. EXIM Infotek Private Ltd. • Covers: 20 companies in member countries of the South Asian Association for Regional Cooperation (SAARC) that import borax, faucets, graphite, gypsum, lead, magnesium oxide, manganese ore, mica, mineral products, rock phosphate, silica base, soil, sulfur, and zinc. Entries include: Company name, postal address, telephone, fax, e-mail, website, contact person, designation, and product details.

Directory of SAARC Importers of Motors and Motor Parts--Electric. EXIM Infotek Private Ltd. • $200 Individuals. Covers: 40 companies in member countries of the South Asian Association for Regional Cooperation (SAARC) that import agitators and geared motors, Eddy current variable speed motors, electric motor control, flange mounted motors, geared and variable speed geared motors, speed controllers, induction motors, motorboard, motor graders, motor parts and accessories, motor starters, single wiper motor, swing motors, variable speed motors, and vertical deep tubewell motor. Entries include: Company name, postal address, telephone, fax, e-mail, website, contact person, designation, and product details.

Directory of SAARC Importers of Plastic Scrap and Raw Materials. EXIM Infotek Private Ltd. • $300 Individuals. Covers: 95 SAARC Countries importers of ABS scrap, acrylic thickener, granules, high-density polyethylene (HDPE), HDPE film grade granules, low-density polyethylene (LDPE), linear low density polythylene (LLDPE), pet resin, plastic granules, plastic molding compounds, plastic raw materials and semi-finished products, plastic scrap and waste, polycarbonate, polyethylene granules, polypropylene and waste, polyvinyl alcohol, PP and PE resins for rope making, PP granules, PVC compound, PVC resin, PVC scrap, raw materials for polyurethane form, raw materials for printed laminate, soft PVC scrap, and transparent PVC scrap. Entries include: Company name, postal address, telephone, fax, e-mail, website, contact person, designation, and product details.

Directory of SAARC Importers of Sewing Machines and Parts. EXIM Infotek Private Ltd. • $200 Individuals. Covers: 55 SAARC countries importers of buttonholer and button covering machine, compact fusing press M/C, embroidery machinery, garment industry equipment and accessories, household sewing machine and parts, sewing machine equipment, sewing machine repairs, domestic and industrial sewing machine, sewing needles, stitch machine, thread trimmers, used embroidery machine, and used schiffli embroidery. Entries include: Company name, postal address, telephone, fax, e-mail, website, contact person, designation, and product details.

Directory of SAARC Importers of Sporting Goods. EXIM Infotek Private Ltd. • Covers: 50 companies in member countries of the South Asian Association for Regional Cooperation (SAARC) that import cricket and hockey goods, rafting equipment, equipment for sauna, spa, swimming pool, shuttlecocks, sporting goods, sports gloves, swimming accessories, tennis and badminton equipment and supplies, tennis balls, and trekking equipment. Entries include: Company name, postal address, telephone, fax, e-mail, website, contact person, designation, and product details.

Directory of SAARC Importers of Telephone Instruments and Accessories. EXIM Infotek Private Ltd. • $200 Individuals. Covers: 55 SAARC Countries importers of cellular phone accessories and parts, cordless telephone, digital telephone systems, EPABX systems, headphone, intercom systems, PABX and intercom equipment, pagers, beepers, telecommunication products, telefax equipment, telephone accessories, telephone answering equipment, telephone (cables), used auto phone set, and VHF/SSB radio telephone. Entries include: Company name, postal address, telephone, fax, e-mail, website, contact person, designation, and product details.

Directory of SAARC Importers of Welding Equipments and Supplies. EXIM Infotek Private Ltd. • $150 Individuals. Covers: 30 SAARC Countries importers of crush electrodes, ferrosillicon and graphite electrodes, M.S. welding rods, soldering and earthing materials, welding equipment, welding electrodes, welding gases, welding generators, welding machine and materials, welding products, welding rods, and welding supplies. Entries include: Company name, postal address, telephone, fax, e-mail, website, contact person, designation, and product details.

Directory of SAARC Importers of Wire & Cables--Electrical. EXIM Infotek Private Ltd. • Covers: 25 companies in member countries of the South Asian Association for Regional Cooperation (SAARC) that import armored cables, armored jelly filled cables, bare wires, cables and accessories, coaxial cables, copper winding wires, copper wires, enamel and cotton insulated winding wires, enameled copper wires, instrumentation cables, internal cables, non-armored SF cables, overhead cables, plastic coated wire products, power cables, PVC flexible flat cables, PVC insulated automobile cables and battery cables, and wiring accessories. Entries include: Company name, postal address, telephone, fax, e-mail, website, contact person, designation, and product details.

Directory of SAARC Importers of Zipper and Garment Accessories. EXIM Infotek Private Ltd. • $250 Individuals. Covers: 90 SAARC Countries importers of badges and crests, buckles, buttons, eyelets, fusing multiflexible, garment accessories, labels (textile), ladies garment accessories, leather hardware, needles, sewing notions/zippers/buttons, shirt clips, stitching needles, and zipper. Entries include: Company name, postal address, telephone, fax, e-mail, website, contact person, designation, and product details.

Directory of St. Petersburg Free-Zone Region. Flegon Press. • $75 postpaid. Covers: import-export enterprises in St. Petersburg (formerly Leningrad) and surrounding areas in Russia. Entries include: Enterprise name, address, phone, telex, names and titles of key personnel.

Directory of Scottish Grant Making Trusts. Scottish Council for Voluntary Organisations. • Irregular. $9.50 Members. Number of listings: 524. Entries include: Company name, address, phone, grant name and subject, requirements, recipients.

Directory of Service Companies. Dun & Bradstreet Inc. • Annual. Covers: Management consulting services; executive search services; public relations, engineering, and architectural services; business services; accounting, auditing, and bookkeeping services; consumer services; health services; legal services; social services; research services; repair services; and hospitality, motion picture, amusement, and recreation services.

Directory of Service, Industrial and Foreign Trading Companies in Egypt. International Trade Consulting Co. • $45. Covers: Companies in Egypt. Entries include: Company name, address, phone.

Directory of Services to Exporters. IBCON S.A. • Irregular. $283 Individuals. Covers: 654 companies, associations and government agencies, located in Mexico City, that offer a variety of services needed by exporters.

Directory of South American Importers of Calendars, Greeting, Prints and Lithographs. EXIM Infotek Private Ltd. • $150 Individuals. Covers: 30 South American importers of calendars, greeting cards, postcards, prints, lithographs, and etchings. Entries include: Company name, postal address, telephone, fax, e-mail, website, contact person, designation, and product details.

Directory of South American Importers of Construction Machinery and Equipment. EXIM Infotek Private Ltd. • $550 Individuals. Covers: 260 South American importers of building and construction materials, concrete production equipment, construction and building equipment, construction machinery, excavating equipment, mixers and pavers, new parquet machinery, scale models and construction kit, street maintenance equipment, and used construction equipment. Entries include: Company name, postal address, telephone, fax, e-mail, website, contact person, designation, and product details.

Directory of South American Importers of Dyes, Colors, and Pigments. EXIM Infotek Private Ltd. • $300 Individuals. Covers: 100 South American importers of dye, colors, pigments, and food colors. Entries include: Company name, postal address, telephone, fax, e-mail, website, contact person, designation, and product details.

Directory of South American Importers of Energy and Power Equipment. EXIM Infotek Private Ltd. • $250 Individuals. Covers: 70 South American importers of power transmission equipment and supplies, solar energy equipment, wind energy equipment, transmission and allied equipment. Entries include: Company name, postal address, telephone, fax, e-mail, website, contact person, designation, and product details.

Directory of South American Importers of Environment Protection and Pollution Control Equipment. EXIM Infotek Private Ltd. • $200 Individuals. Covers: 80 South American importers of environmental protection equipment, pollution control equipment, water treatment, and purifying equipment. Entries include: Company name, postal address, telephone, fax, e-mail, website, contact person, designation, and product details.

Directory of South American Importers of Fibre and Fibre Products. EXIM Infotek Private Ltd. • $200 Individuals. Covers: 30 South American importers of fiberboard products, fiber glass cloth and products, fiber products, glass fiber, and synthetic fiber. Entries include: Company name, postal address, telephone, fax, e-mail, website, contact person, designation, and product details.

Directory of South American Importers of Fire Fighting Equipment. EXIM Infotek Private Ltd. • Covers: 40 South American importers of fire fighting equipment. Entries include: Company name, postal address, telephone, fax, e-mail, website, contact person, designation, and product details.

Directory of South American Importers of Fodder and Animal Foodstuffs. EXIM Infotek Private Ltd. • $300 Individuals. Covers: 140 South American importers of animal food, animal foodstuff additives, fodder, livestock breeding supplies, oats, and sorghum. Entries include: Company name, postal address, telephone, fax, e-mail, website, contact person, designation, and product details.

Directory of South American Importers of Furnaces and Ovens--Industrial. EXIM Infotek Private Ltd. • $150 Individuals. Covers: 20 South American importers of industrial furnaces and oven. Entries include: Company name, postal address, telephone, fax, e-mail, website, contact person, designation, and product details.

Directory of South American Importers of Hardwares--All Types. EXIM Infotek Private Ltd. • $35 Individuals. Covers: 500 South American importers of abrasives, builders hardware, casters, furniture hardware and parts, and locks. Entries include: Company name, postal address, telephone, fax, e-mail, website, contact person, designation, and product details.

Directory of South American Importers of Heaters and Heating Equipment. EXIM Infotek Private Ltd. • Covers: 50 South American importers of heat exchangers and heating equipment. Entries include: Company name, postal address, telephone, fax, e-mail, website, contact person, designation, and product details.

Directory of South American Importers of Laboratory & Scientific Instruments & Supplies. EXIM Infotek Private Ltd. • Covers: 480 South American importers of binoculars, microscopes, telescopes, laboratory and scientific instruments, laboratory articles and equipment, laboratory glassware, laboratory products, and testing equipment. Entries include: Company name, postal address, telephone, fax, e-mail, website, contact person, designation, and product details.

Directory of South American Importers of Lumber, Timber, Plywood and Hardboards. EXIM Infotek Private Ltd. • $400 Individuals. Covers: 200 South American importers of doors and windows, gypsum boards, hardboard and particle board, hardwood flooring and floor tiles, laminates (wood), hardwood lumber, softwood lumber, timber, plywood, millwork (wooden), veneer, poles, pilings and logs. Entries include: Company name, postal address, telephone, fax, e-mail, website, contact person, designation, and product details.

Directory of South American Importers of Machinery for Paper & Pulp Industry. EXIM Infotek Private Ltd. • Covers: 40 South American importers of paper and pulp mill machinery and equipment and paper making machinery. Entries include: Company name, postal address, telephone, fax, e-mail, website, contact person, designation, and product details.

Directory of South American Importers of Material Handling Equipment & Supplies. EXIM Infotek Private Ltd. • Covers: 140 South American importers of conveyors, cranes and hoists, elevator parts, elevators and lifts, escalators, forklifts, loading and unloading equipment, materials handling equipment and parts, monorail material handling equipment, winches, and pulleys. Entries include: Company name, postal address, telephone, fax, e-mail, website, contact person, designation, and product details.

Directory of South American Importers of Motors and Motor Parts--Electric. EXIM Infotek Private Ltd. • $250 Individuals. Covers: 80 South American importers of electric motors, motor equipment, and motor parts. Entries include: Company name, postal address, telephone, fax, e-mail, website, contact person, designation, and product details.

Directory of South American Importers of Petroleum Products. EXIM Infotek Private Ltd. • $350 Individuals. Covers: 120 South American importers of crude oil, fuel products, hydraulic fluid, lubricants, oil, grease and petroleum products, propane gas, and specialty lubricants. Entries include: Company name, postal address, telephone, fax, e-mail, website, contact person, designation, and product details.

Directory of South American Importers of Photographic Equipment and Supplies. EXIM Infotek Private Ltd. • $350 Individuals. Covers: 130 South American importers of cameras, lens and accessories, cinema, motion picture equipment, theater equipment and supplies, film, plates and photographic papers, microfilm and blueprint equipment, photographic equipment and supplies, and photographic processing equipment. Entries include: Company name, postal address, telephone, fax, e-mail, website, contact person, designation, and product details.

Directory of South American Importers of Plastic Scrap and Raw Materials. EXIM Infotek Private Ltd. • $300 Individuals. Covers: 110 South American importers of pet resins, plastic raw materials, plastic scrap and waste, polyester resins, and PVC compounds. Entries include: Company name, postal address, telephone, fax, e-mail, website, contact person, designation, and product details.

Directory of South American Importers of Restaurant, Hotel and Catering Equipment. EXIM Infotek Private Ltd. • Covers: 100 South American importers of catering equipment, cooking equipment (patio and outdoors), cooking range and oven, fast food equipment, restaurant and hotel equipment. Entries include: Company name, postal address, telephone, fax, e-mail, website, contact person, designation, and product details.

Directory of South American Importers of Sewing Machines and Parts. EXIM Infotek Private Ltd. • $350 Individuals. Covers: 110 South American importers of garment industry equipment, sewing machine and parts (domestic and industrial), and sewing machine needles. Entries include: Company name, postal address, telephone, fax, e-mail, website, contact person, designation, and product details.

Directory of South American Importers of Sporting Goods. EXIM Infotek Private Ltd. • Covers: 140 South American importers of bowling equipment and supplies, fire arms, golf equipment and supplies, hiking accessories, mountaineering equipment and supplies, play ground equipment, riding accessories, skating equipment, ski boots, skiing accessories, sporting goods and toys, sporting goods, tennis and badminton equipment and supplies, and water sports equipment and supplies. Entries include: Company name, postal address, telephone, fax, e-mail, website, contact person, designation, and product details.

Directory of South American Importers of Telephone Instruments and Accessories. EXIM Infotek Private Ltd. • $300 Individuals. Covers: 110 South American importers of mobile phone, mobile phone accessories, microphone, headphone, pagers, telecommunication equipment, telefax equipment, and telephone equipment. Entries include: Company name, postal address, telephone, fax, e-mail, website, contact person, designation, and product details.

Directory of South American Importers of Vending and Coin Operated Machines. EXIM Infotek Private Ltd. • $150 Individuals. Covers: 20 South American importers of vending and coin operated machinery. Entries include: Company name, postal address, telephone, fax, e-mail, website, contact person, designation, and product details.

Directory of South American Importers of Waste Disposal & Recycling Equipment. EXIM Infotek Private Ltd. • Covers: 40 South American importers of garbage disposals and compactors, waste disposal equipment, and waste recycling equipment. Entries include: Company name, postal address, telephone, fax, e-mail, website, contact person, designation, and product details.

Directory of South American Importers of Wax & Wax Products. EXIM Infotek Private Ltd. • Covers: 20 South American importers of paraffin waxes, polishes and creams. Entries include: Company name, postal address, telephone, fax, e-mail, website, contact person, designation, and product details.

Directory of South American Importers of Yarns and Threads. EXIM Infotek Private Ltd. • $250 Individuals. Covers: 100 South American importers of cotton yarn and thread, embroidery threads, metallic yarn and thread, nylon yarn for carpets, polyester yarn, sewing thread, synthetic yarns and thread, and wool yarn. Entries include: Company name, postal address, telephone, fax, e-mail, website, contact person, designation, and product details.

Directory of South Korean Manufacturers & Exporters of Adhesive, Glues & Sealants. EXIM Infotek Private Ltd. • $5 Individuals. Covers: 30 South Korean manufacturers and exporters of processed rubber-solution and adhesives, synthetic adhesives. Entries include: Company name, postal address, city, country, phone, fax, e-mail and websites, contact person, designation, and product details.

Directory of South Korean Manufacturers & Exporters of Agro Chemicals. EXIM Infotek Private Ltd. • $5 Individuals. Covers: 20 South Korean manufacturers and exporters of fertilizers, fungicides/insecticides/bactericides, and herbicides/plant growth control substances. Entries include: Company name, postal address, city, country, phone, fax, e-mail and websites, contact person, designation, and product details.

Directory of South Korean Manufacturers and Exporters of Alcoholic Beverages and Wines. EXIM Infotek Private Ltd. • Covers: 20 South Korean manufacturers and exporters of alcoholic spirits, beer, fermented cider, grape wine, whisky, bourbon, and wine (non-grape). Entries include: Company name, postal address, telephone, fax, e-mail, website, contact person, designation, and product details.

Directory of South Korean Manufacturers & Exporters of Automobiles & Vehicles. EXIM Infotek Private Ltd. • $5 Individuals. Covers: 20 South Korean manufacturers and exporters of automobile body builders, automobiles, buses and trucks, buses, cars, tractors/trucks/trailers-industrial, truck and lorry trailers, trucks/lorries, used cars, used trucks, used vehicles, and vehicles-special purpose. Entries include: Company name, postal address, city, country, phone, fax, e-mail and websites, contact person, designation, and product details.

Directory of South Korean Manufacturers & Exporters of Automotive Service & Repair Equipment. EXIM Infotek Private Ltd. • $5 Individuals. Covers: 30 South Korean manufacturers and exporters of grills-radiator, mechanical lubrication tools, motor vehicle testing equipment, vehicle service and repair equipment. Entries include: Company name, postal address, city, country, phone, fax, e-mail and websites, contact person, designation, and product details.

Directory of South Korean Manufacturers & Exporters of Autoparts & Accessories. EXIM Infotek Private Ltd. • $30 Individuals. Covers: 400 South Korean manufacturers and exporters of alternators, auto parts, auto spare parts, automobiles relay, automotive accessories, automotive lighting equipment, automotive plastic parts, axles-rear, axles-front (beam/drive), airbags, bars-automotive, brake systems, bulbs-auto, bumpers-plastic, cables-speed meter, caps-wheel, car rear view systems, clutch systems, couplings and clutches, cylinder head gaskets, disc brakes, hardware for motorcars, head lamps, horns-automotive, hydraulic shock absorbers, industrial trailer/truck parts/accessories, joints-universal, liners and pads-brake, motor vehicle accessories, motor vehicle body components and spare parts, motor vehicle transmission parts, radiators, rods-connecting, seats-automotive, shafts-axle, shafts-cam, shafts-crank, signal and indicator lamps, spare parts, springs/shock absorbers, steering and suspension parts, steering wheels, suspension parts, transmission parts, used auto parts, vehicle brake parts, vehicle control instruments and panels, vehicle electrical and electronic equipment, wheels and wheel rims, window regulators, wiper arms, and yokes-automotive. Entries include: Company name, postal address, city, country, telephone, fax, e-mail and websites, contact person, designation, and product details.

Directory of South Korean Manufacturers & Exporters of Batteries & Accumulators. EXIM Infotek Private Ltd. • $10 Individuals. Covers: 90 South Korean manufacturers & exporters of automotive batteries, batteries & accumulators, battery, ups & battery chargers. Entries include: Company name, postal address, city, country, phone, fax, e-mail & websites, contact person, designation, products detail.

Directory of South Korean Manufacturers & Exporters of Bearings. EXIM Infotek Private Ltd. • $10 Individuals. Covers: 50 South Korean manufacturers and exporters of bearing and bushing-metal, bearings-ball, needle and roller, cap-bearings, clutch release bearings, plain bearings, plumber and pillow blocks/bushing, and roller bearings. Entries include: Company name, postal address, city, country, phone, fax, e-mail and websites, contact person, designation, and product details.

Directory of South Korean Manufacturers & Exporters of Beauty Supplies, Cosmetics, Perfumes & Toiletries. EXIM Infotek Private Ltd. • $5 Individuals. Covers: 40 South Korean manufacturers and exporters of air fresheners, cosmetic brushes, cosmetic/hair/skin and dental products, cosmetics, hair brushes, hair combs, hand mirrors, manicure sets, nail clippers, and perfume. Entries include: Company name, postal address, city, country, phone, fax, e-mail and websites, contact person, designation, and product details.

Directory of South Korean Manufacturers & Exporters of Bicycles, Parts & Accessories. EXIM Infotek Private Ltd. • $5 Individuals. Covers: 30 South Korean manufacturers and exporters of bicycle parts and accessories, bicycles and exercisers, flywheels. Entries include: Company name, postal address, city, country, phone, fax, e-mail and websites, contact person, designation, and product details.

Directory of South Korean Manufacturers and Exporters of Boiler and Boiler Parts. EXIM Infotek Private Ltd. • Covers: 20 South Korean manufacturers and exporters of boilers and accessories, industrial steam boilers and accessories. Entries include: Company name, postal address, telephone, fax, e-mail, website, contact person, designation, and product details.

Directory of South Korean Manufacturers & Export-

ers of Castings & Forgings. EXIM Infotek Private Ltd. • $10 Individuals. Covers: 80 South Korean manufacturers and exporters of casting, casting-aluminum and zinc, forging, iron castings, and steel castings. Entries include: Company name, postal address, city, country, phone, fax, e-mail and websites, contact person, designation, and product details.

Directory of South Korean Manufacturers & Exporters of Chemicals & Allied Products. EXIM Infotek Private Ltd. • $25 Individuals. Covers: 350 South Korean manufacturers and exporters of acid coolers, alcohols and epoxides, amines, artificial resins, barium/boron/bromine/hydrogen compounds, base materials for non-metallic elements, calcium-strontium and thallium compounds, carbohydrates/proteins and enzymes, carbon based materials and products, catalysts, chemicals for basic metal industries, chemicals for building materials, chemicals for cosmetics/perfumery/detergent/soaps, chemicals for electrical/electronic industries, chemicals for laboratory and microbiology, chemicals for leather and fur tanning extract, chemicals for lubricants and waxes, chemicals for metal surface treatment, chemicals for metal welding/soldering fluxes, chemicals for paint/lacquer/varnish, chemicals for paper making/printing/photography, chemicals for plastic/rubber/ceramic, chemicals for unspecified uses, chemicals for water treatment, chemotherapeutic agents, compressed and liquefied gases/chemicals for refrigeration, detergents/cleansers and bleaching agents, disinfections and indoor deodorants, esters/acetates/ethyls and methyls, explosives, hydrocarbons and halcarbons, inorganic acids and anhydrides, inorganic alkalis-hydroxides, miscellaneous organic chemicals, natural resins and pitches, organic acids and anhydrides, phosphorus/sulphur/carbon/silicon and cassium compounds, polyphenols/ethers/aldehydes/ketones, potassium and ammonium compounds, pyrotechnic products, soaps/fatty-acid based detergents, sodium compounds. Entries include: Company name, postal address, city, country, telephone, fax, e-mail and websites, contact person, designation, and product details.

Directory of South Korean Manufacturers & Exporters of Confectionery & Bakery Products. EXIM Infotek Private Ltd. • $10 Individuals. Covers: 80 South Korean manufacturers and exporters of biscuits/crackers, bread/cakes and pastry, noodles-instant, soups and extracts, sugar confectionery, and vinegar and sauce. Entries include: Company name, postal address, city, country, phone, fax, e-mail and websites, contact person, designation, and product details.

Directory of South Korean Manufacturers and Exporters of Construction Machinery and Equipment. EXIM Infotek Private Ltd. • $250 Individuals. Covers: 90 South Korean manufacturers and exporters of asphalt mixing plant, bridge and tunnel construction machinery, building machinery, cement production plant, cement and plaster making plant, clay tile and brick production plant, concrete elements production plant, concrete making machinery, construction equipment, cranes and construction platforms, earthmoving and road making machinery, harbor and canal construction machinery, heavy mechanical handling equipment, road maintenance machinery, road rollers, scaffoldings and ladders, used construction equipment, and used cranes. Entries include: Company name, postal address, telephone, fax, e-mail, website, contact person, designation, and product details.

Directory of South Korean Manufacturers & Exporters of Cotton, Silk, Wool Raw & Waste. EXIM Infotek Private Ltd. • $5 Individuals. Covers: 40 South Korean manufacturers and exporters of raw cotton and vegetable textile fiber, raw wool and other animal fibers, silkworms and silkworm cocoons. Entries include: Company name, postal address, city, country, phone, fax, e-mail and websites, contact person, designation, and product details.

Directory of South Korean Manufacturers & Exporters of Dairy Products. EXIM Infotek Private Ltd. • $5 Individuals. Covers: 20 South Korean manufacturers and exporters of goat and sheep cheese, ice cream and sorbet, milk and milk products, and milk-condensed/dried. Entries include: Company name, postal address, city, country, phone, fax, e-mail and websites, contact person, designation, and product details.

Directory of South Korean Manufacturers & Exporters of Dyes, Colours, Pigments & Intermediates. EXIM Infotek Private Ltd. • $10 Individuals. Covers: 90 South Korean manufacturers & exporters of chemicals for textiles, colorants for leather/rubber/plastic & cosmetics, dyes-synthetic, pigments-natural, pigments-synthetic, textile coatings. Entries include: Company name, postal address, city, country, phone, fax, e-mail & websites, contact person, designation, products detail.

Directory of South Korean Manufacturers and Exporters of Energy and Power Equipment. EXIM Infotek Private Ltd. • Covers: 30 South Korean manufacturers and exporters of nuclear engineering plants, nuclear protection and detection instruments, power distribution equipment for various uses, power relays, and solar energy equipment. Entries include: Company name, postal address, telephone, fax, e-mail, website, contact person, designation, and product details.

Directory of South Korean Manufacturers & Exporters of Engines & Engine Parts. EXIM Infotek Private Ltd. • $15 Individuals. Covers: 140 South Korean manufacturers and exporters of engine components/spare parts, engine parts and accessories, gaskets-various, internal combustion engines, pin-pistons, piston engines, piston brakes, used engines. Entries include: Company name, postal address, city, country, phone, fax, e-mail and websites, contact person, designation and product details.

Directory of South Korean Manufacturers and Exporters of Environment and Pollution Control Equipment. EXIM Infotek Private Ltd. • $200 Individuals. Covers: 60 South Korean manufacturers and exporters of air pollution control equipment, air cleaner, noise pollution control equipment, water and sewage treatment plant. Entries include: Company name, postal address, telephone, fax, e-mail, website, contact person, designation, and product details.

Directory of South Korean Manufacturers & Exporters of Filters & Strainers--Industrial. EXIM Infotek Private Ltd. • $10 Individuals. Covers: 50 South Korean manufacturers and exporters of bolting and filter cloths/gauzes, filters, filters and strainers for processing industries, filters and strainers-metal, line filters, and water and waste water filters. Entries include: Company name, postal address, city, country, phone, fax, e-mail and websites, contact person, designation, and product details.

Directory of South Korean Manufacturers & Exporters of Fire Fighting Equipment & Supplies. EXIM Infotek Private Ltd. • Covers: 30 South Korean manufacturers and exporters of fire fighting equipment. Entries include: Company name, postal address, telephone, fax, e-mail, website, contact person, designation, and product details.

Directory of South Korean Manufacturers & Exporters of Furniture--All Types. EXIM Infotek Private Ltd. • $15 Individuals. Covers: 140 South Korean manufacturers and exporters of arm-rockers, furniture and fittings for shops/stores, furniture for manufactured products, furniture/racking-industrial/lab, furniture-children, furniture-domestic, furniture-garden, furniture-hospital, furniture-hotel/restaurant/bar, furniture-kitchen, furniture-office, furniture-public places, furniture-school, furniture-ships, furniture-upholstered, knockdown furniture, metal cabinets, small furniture articles. Entries include: Company name, postal address, city, country, phone, fax, e-mail and websites, contact person, designation and product details.

Directory of South Korean Manufacturers & Exporters of Gears & Gears Boxes. EXIM Infotek Private Ltd. • $5 Individuals. Covers: 20 South Korean manufacturers and exporters of gear boxes and gears. Entries include: Company name, postal address, city, country, phone, fax, e-mail and websites, contact person, designation, and product details.

Directory of South Korean Manufacturers & Exporters of Gemstones & Diamonds. EXIM Infotek Private Ltd. • $5 Individuals. Covers: 20 South Korean manufacturers and exporters of colored precious stones-polished, diamond-polished, diamonds-rough, ivory/coral/pearl articles, and rough colored precious stones. Entries include: Company name, postal address, city, country, phone, fax, e-mail and websites, contact person, designation, and product details.

Directory of South Korean Manufacturers & Exporters of Giftware & Novelties. EXIM Infotek Private Ltd. • $5 Individuals. Covers: 40 South Korean manufacturers and exporters of albums and files, coins/medals/decorations and badges, key holders, medals, photo albums, photo frames, promotional giftware, and trophies/ceremonial plates. Entries include: Company name, postal address, city, country, phone, fax, e-mail and websites, contact person, designation, and product details.

Directory of South Korean Manufacturers & Exporters of Glass, China, Ceramic & Porcelainware. EXIM Infotek Private Ltd. • $150 Individuals. Covers: 40 South Korean manufacturers and exporters of glass tableware, glassware, handmade glassware, porcelain and ceramic products, pottery, Chinaware, and shaped glass products. Entries include: Company name, postal address, telephone, fax, e-mail, website, contact person, designation, and product details.

Directory of South Korean Manufacturers & Exporters of Handtools. EXIM Infotek Private Ltd. • $10 Individuals. Covers: 70 South Korean manufacturers and exporters of box-tool, builders tools, carbide tools, chisels/taps/dies and similar tools, electric and electro-magnetic tools, hammers/mallets and similar tools, metal hand and diamond tools, pliers/clamps and similar tools, roofers and decorators tools, and screwdrivers/wrenches. Entries include: Company name, postal address, city, country, phone, fax, e-mail and websites, contact person, designation, and product details.

Directory of South Korean Manufacturers & Exporters of Hardwares--All Types. EXIM Infotek Private Ltd. • $15 Individuals. Covers: 160 South Korean manufacturers and exporters of abrasive coated products, abrasive paper, brackets, clips, frame-doors (channel), haberdashery metalware, hinge-doors/trunks/hoods, ironmongery and hardware, ironmongery and hardware for furniture, locksmith articles, metal fittings, metal smallwares for various uses, nails/tacks/spikes/staples-metal, paint brushes and rollers, pins, and springs-various types. Entries include: Company name, postal address, city, country, phone, fax, e-mail and websites, contact person, designation, and product details.

Directory of South Korean Manufacturers & Exporters of Health Care Products & Foods. EXIM Infotek Private Ltd. • Covers: 20 South Korean manufacturers and exporters of health and diet products. Entries include: Company name, postal address, telephone, fax, e-mail, website, contact person, designation, and product details.

Directory of South Korean Manufacturers & Exporters of Heaters & Heating Equipment. EXIM Infotek Private Ltd. • $350 Individuals. Covers: 130 South Korean manufacturers and exporters of air and gas heaters, central heating equipment, central heating systems, driers, drying plants, electric heating equipment, heat exchangers, heaters, and heating machine. Entries include: Company name, postal address, telephone, fax, e-mail, website, contact person, designation, and product details.

Directory of South Korean Manufacturers & Exporters of Herbs & Herbal Medicine Products. EXIM Infotek Private Ltd. • $5 Individuals. Covers: 30 South Korean manufacturers and exporters of Chinese medical preparations, herb plants, herbal medicines. Entries include: Company name, postal address, city, country, phone, fax, e-mail and websites, contact person, designation, and product details.

Directory of South Korean Manufacturers & Exporters of Home Furnishing Materials. EXIM Infotek Private Ltd. • $10 Individuals. Covers: 50 South Korean manufacturers and exporters of blankets, household linen and soft furnishings, mattresses, cushions and pillows, sanitary towels and baby napkins, and tapestries. Entries include: Company name, postal address, city, country, phone, fax, e-mail and websites, contact person, designation, and product details.

Directory of South Korean Manufacturers & Exporters of Imitation & Fashion Jewellery. EXIM Infotek Private Ltd. • $15 Individuals. Covers: 150 South Korean manufacturers and exporters of bracelets, buckles, ladies belts, costume jewelry, cuff links, custom jewelry, earrings, fashion goods, fashion jewelry, hair bands, hair ornaments, hair pins, imitation jewelry, jewelry, necklaces, synthetic diamonds, synthetic jewels for watches, and tie pins. Entries include: Company name, postal address, city, country, phone, fax, e-mail and websites, contact person, designation, and product details.

Directory of South Korean Manufacturers & Exporters of Laces, Ribbons & Embroidery Products. EXIM Infotek Private Ltd. • $10 Individuals. Covers: 50 South Korean manufacturers and exporters of badges, embroidery-all types, embroidery/lace mending services, embroidery-hand made, lace, lace-machine made, ribbons, ribbons and tapes for industrial use, ribbons and tapes-non industrial, and trimmings/cordings/braids and fringes. Entries include: Company name, postal address, city, country, phone, fax, e-mail and websites, contact person, designation, and product details.

Directory of South Korean Manufacturers & Exporters of Leather, Hides, Skins & Furs. EXIM Infotek Private Ltd. • $10 Individuals. Covers: 110 South Korean manufacturers & exporters of leather-reconstituted, leather-processed, PVC leathercloth, sheep & goat skins, sheep & lamb skins, skins, hides & leather, swine skins/leather. Entries include: Company name, postal address, city, country, phone, fax, e-mail & websites, contact person, designation, products detail.

Directory of South Korean Manufacturers & Exporters of Leather Products. EXIM Infotek Private Ltd. • $15 Individuals. Covers: 130 South Korean manufacturers and exporters of bags, cases and covers of leather, fancy leather goods, fur clothing and products, leather airbags/sportbags, leather clothing, leather goods for industrial use and leather waist belts. Entries include: Company name, postal address, city, country, phone, fax, e-mail and websites, contact person, designation, and product details.

Directory of South Korean Manufacturers & Exporters of Lighting Fixtures, Lamps & Accessories. EXIM Infotek Private Ltd. • $10 Individuals. Covers: 90 South Korean manufacturers & exporters of aluminum flashlights, bulbs-halogen, discharge & special purpose lamps, electric lamp components, filament lamps-all types, fluorescent lamps, halogen lamps, indoor electric lighting equipment, lamp accessories & parts, lamp-combination, lamps, lamp various, lighting appliances-non electric, lighting equipment-outdoor, matches, pilot lamps, portable electric lamps & accessories, sub-miniature lamps. Entries include: Company name, postal address, city, country, phone, fax, e-mail & websites, contact person, designation, products detail.

Directory of South Korean Manufacturers & Exporters of Machinery for Chemicals & Pharma Industry. EXIM Infotek Private Ltd. • $10 Individuals. Covers: 60 South Korean manufacturers and exporters of crushers/pulverizers for chemical industries, dryers/evaporators/crystallizers for chemical industries, electrochemical and electrolytic plant equipment, electroplating plant machinery, glycerine production plant machinery, heaters/boilers/distillers for chemical industries, organic chemical production plant equipment, paint/varnish/enamel/ink production plant equipment, pharmaceutical/cosmetic production plant equipment, reactors for chemical industry, screeners/mixers/centrifuges for chemical industry, and technical gas production plant equipment. Entries include: Company name, postal address, city, country, phone, fax, e-mail and websites, contact person, designation, and product details.

Directory of South Korean Manufacturers & Exporters of Machinery for Leather & Shoe Industry. EXIM Infotek Private Ltd. • $5 Individuals. Covers: 20 South Korean manufacturers and exporters of boot and shoe making machinery/equipment, leather working and saddlery making equipment. Entries include: Company name, postal address, city, country, phone, fax, e-mail and websites, contact person, designation, and product details.

Directory of South Korean Manufacturers & Exporters of Machinery for Paper & Pulp Industry. EXIM Infotek Private Ltd. • $5 Individuals. Covers: 30 South Korean manufacturers and exporters of cardboard finishing/forming/cutting machinery/equipment, cardboard making machinery/equipment, paper finishing/converting machinery/equipment, paper making plant equipment, pulp and cellulose production plant equipment. Entries include: Company name, postal address, city, country, phone, fax, e-mail and websites, contact person, designation, and product details.

Directory of South Korean Manufacturers & Exporters of Machinery for Textile and Knitting Industry. EXIM Infotek Private Ltd. • $15 Individuals. Covers: 150 South Korean manufacturers and exporters of beam brakes and discs for textile machinery, belts/hoses/webbing-textile, bobbins for textile industry, carpet and tapestry looms, cotton preparation machinery and equipment, felt and non-woven fabric making machinery, knitting machinery and attachments, lace and net making machinery, man-made fiber production and processing plants, ribbon and trim making machinery, silk and schappe preparation machinery and equipment, sleeves and strips for spinning mills, textile dyeing and boiling machinery/equipment, textile finishing machinery and equipment, textile machinery, textile machinery parts, textile printing machinery and equipment, textile printings, textile spinning and twisting machinery, textile washing/mercerizing machinery and equipment, textile waste processing, textile waste processing machinery and equipment, textile weaving machinery parts/accessories, textile weaving machinery/looms, textile winding and reeling machinery, weaving machines, yarn preparation machinery/equipment, and yarn tensioners. Entries include: Company name, postal address, city, country, telephone, fax, e-mail and websites, contact person, designation, and product details.

Directory of South Korean Manufacturers & Exporters of Marine & Boating Equipment & Supplies. EXIM Infotek Private Ltd. • $5 Individuals. Covers: 40 South Korean manufacturers and exporters of boat parts and accessories, coastal vessels, control and navigational instruments-ship, equipment/signals for ships/boats, marine propulsion units, radar and navigation systems/equipment-marine, yacht and pleasure craft. Entries include: Company name, postal address, city, country, phone, fax, e-mail and websites, contact person, designation, and product details.

Directory of South Korean Manufacturers & Exporters of Material Handling Equipment. EXIM Infotek Private Ltd. • $400 Individuals. Covers: 170 South Korean manufacturers and exporters of automated handling and storage equipment, barrows, trolleys, carts, conveyors and elevators, cranes, hoists, winches, forklift trucks, handling equipment parts and accessories, ice crushers, lifts, mobile cranes, overhead conveyors, pallets and containers, pneumatic handling equipment, pulleys, and cable wheels. Entries include: Company name, postal address, telephone, fax, e-mail, website, contact person, designation, and product details.

Directory of South Korean Manufacturers & Exporters of Meat & Meat Products. EXIM Infotek Private Ltd. • $5 Individuals. Covers: 20 South Korean manufacturers and exporters of meat and game-processed/preserved, meat and meat products, meat-dried, and sausage casings. Entries include: Company name, postal address, city, country, phone, fax, e-mail and websites, contact person, designation, and product details.

Directory of South Korean Manufacturers & Exporters of Minerals. EXIM Infotek Private Ltd. • $10 Individuals. Covers: 70 South Korean manufacturers and exporters of clays, graphite and clay bonded graphite products, graphite-natural, gypsum and anhydrite, gypsum/plaster and lime, gypsum/plaster and stucco products, limestones, magnesium minerals, mica and mecanite products, quartz and silica electro thermic products, quartzite of crystal, silicon minerals, slate products, and steatite and pyrophillite. Entries include: Company name, postal address, city, country, phone, fax, e-mail and websites, contact person, designation, and product details.

Directory of South Korean Manufacturers and Exporters of Motors and Motor Parts--Electric. EXIM Infotek Private Ltd. • $250 Individuals. Covers: 70 South Korean manufacturers and exporters of motorcycles and mopeds. Entries include: Company name, postal address, telephone, fax, e-mail, website, contact person, designation, and product details.

Directory of South Korean Manufacturers & Exporters of Nuts, Bolts, Screws & Fasteners. EXIM Infotek Private Ltd. • $10 Individuals. Covers: 50 South Korean manufacturers and exporters of bolts and nuts, nails, fasteners-metal, metal nuts/bolts/washers, metal rivets, metal screws/bolts/nuts, and screws-metal. Entries include: Company name, postal address, city, country, phone, fax, e-mail and websites, contact person, designation, and product details.

Directory of South Korean Manufacturers & Exporters of Oil & Fats--Cooking & Vegetable. EXIM Infotek Private Ltd. • $5 Individuals. Covers: 20 South Korean manufacturers and exporters of oils and fats-edible. Entries include: Company name, postal address, city, country, phone, fax, e-mail and websites, contact person, designation, and product details.

Directory of South Korean Manufacturers & Exporters of Paints, Varnishes & Allied Products. EXIM Infotek Private Ltd. • $5 Individuals. Covers: 40 South Korean manufacturers and exporters of anti-corrosion products, lacquers and paints-primers, varnishes and stains-distempers, and vitreous colors/enamels and glazes. Entries include: Company name, postal address, city, country, phone, fax, e-mail and websites, contact person, designation, and product details.

Directory of South Korean Manufacturers & Exporters of Paper & Paper Products. EXIM Infotek

Private Ltd. • $20 Individuals. Covers: 280 South Korean manufacturers and exporters of base and backing paper, cardboard, cardboard/corrugated-packaging, coated and laminated paper/board, corrugated paper and board, paper and cardboard tubes, paper and paper rolls for technical use, paper and paper rolls printed for writing/technical, paper article-diecut/embossed, paper packaging/bags and sacks, photographic paper/board/film, printing and drawing paper/board, pulp mechanical and chemicals, reinforced cardboard and vulcanized fiber products, reinforced cardboard products, tissue paper and cellulose wadding, wallpaper and paper backed wallcoverings, wrapping/crepe paper. Entries include: Company name, postal address, city, country, phone, fax, e-mail and websites, contact person, designation, and product details.

Directory of South Korean Manufacturers & Exporters of Petroleum Products. EXIM Infotek Private Ltd. • $10 Individuals. Covers: 60 South Korean manufacturers and exporters of mineral oils and greases, natural oils and greases for technical use, petroleum products/fuels and lubricants, solvents-petroleum based, tar and bituminous products, tar and resin distillation products. Entries include: Company name, postal address, city, country, phone, fax, e-mail and websites, contact person, designation, and product details.

Directory of South Korean Manufacturers & Exporters of Pharmaceutical Products. EXIM Infotek Private Ltd. • $10 Individuals. Covers: 120 South Korean manufacturers & exporters of antibiotics, microencapsulated pharmaceuticals, ophthalmic preparations, pharmaceutical preparations for cardio-vascular, pharmaceutical preparations, veterinary preparations-general, vitamin preparations. Entries include: Company name, postal address, city, country, phone, fax, e-mail & websites, contact person, designation, products detail.

Directory of South Korean Manufacturers & Exporters of Pharmaceutical Raw Materials. EXIM Infotek Private Ltd. • $5 Individuals. Covers: 20 South Korean manufacturers and exporters of gelatins for pharmaceuticals, hypodermoclysis and phleboclysis solutions, pharmaceutical base and suppository compounds, vitamins/hormones and organ extracts. Entries include: Company name, postal address, city, country, phone, fax, e-mail and websites, contact person, designation, and product details.

Directory of South Korean Manufacturers & Exporters of Plastics & Plastic Products. EXIM Infotek Private Ltd. • $600 Individuals. Covers: 300 South Korean manufacturers and exporters of doors, windows, skylights, glass fiber reinforced plastic products, haberdasher articles, laminating roll film, offlets drain channels, plastic articles for shops, plastic films, plastic injection molding products, plastic laminated sheets, plastic products for agricultural industry, building industry, chemical industry, pharmaceutical industry, cosmetic industry, electrical and electronics industry, mechanical engineering industry, optical and photographic industry, surgical and orthopedic use, textile industry, food and beverage industry; plastic semi-finished products-bars/rods/shapes, plastic semi-finished products-plates/sheets/film/tape, plastic-injection molding, polyester film, and sponges.

Directory of South Korean Manufacturers & Exporters of Readymade Garments. EXIM Infotek Private Ltd. • $30 Individuals. Covers: 400 South Korean manufacturers and exporters of casual and leisurewear, clothing and accessories-rubber, garments, handkerchiefs, hosiery, knitwear, ladies blouses, mufflers, protective work clothing, readymade for infants, readymade for ladies/girls, readymade garment for men/boy, scarves, shirts-all types, sundries, swim and beach wear, uniforms and professional clothing, and waterproof garments. Entries include: Company name, postal address, city, country, phone, fax, e-mail and websites, contact person, designation, and product details.

Directory of South Korean Manufacturers & Exporters of Safety & Security Equipment & Supplies. EXIM Infotek Private Ltd. • Covers: 40 South Korean manufacturers and exporters of alarms, intruder detection systems, protection and life saving equipment, signaling and alarm equipment, video doorphones, and video security systems. Entries include: Company name, postal address, telephone, fax, e-mail, website, contact person, designation, and product details.

Directory of South Korean Manufacturers & Exporters of Sea Food & Fish. EXIM Infotek Private Ltd. • $400 Individuals. Covers: 160 South Korean manufacturers and exporters of crustaceans, fish and shelfish by-products, fish roes, fish (canned/bottled), fish, processed fish, saltwater fish, frozen sea food products, marine algae and plankton, mollusks, shelfish and seaweed (canned/bottled), shrimps and prawns. Entries include: Company name, postal address, telephone, fax, e-mail, website, contact person, designation, and product details.

Directory of South Korean Manufacturers & Exporters of Shoes & Footwears. EXIM Infotek Private Ltd. • $10 Individuals. Covers: 90 South Korean manufacturers & exporters of boots-rubber, footwear soles/components, footwear-industrial/protective, footwear-sports, footwear-standard. Entries include: Company name, postal address, city, country, phone, fax, e-mail & websites, contact person, designation, products detail.

Directory of South Korean Manufacturers & Exporters of Sporting Goods. EXIM Infotek Private Ltd. • $250 Individuals. Covers: 90 South Korean manufacturers and exporters of ball sports equipment, billiard table sets/cues, camping equipment, fishing tackle, golf carts and van, golf club and badminton shafts, gymnasium and exercise equipment, sports equipment, winter and mountaineering sports equipment. Entries include: Company name, postal address, telephone, fax, e-mail, website, contact person, designation, and product details.

Directory of South Korean Manufacturers & Exporters of Stationery Articles & Education Supplies. EXIM Infotek Private Ltd. • $250 Individuals. Covers: 70 South Korean manufacturers and exporters of drawing and mathematical instruments, filing systems, inks and artists colors, pencil cases, pens, pencils, rubber stamps and pads, staplers, stationeries, stationery and greeting cards, stationery articles, writing and drawing equipment. Entries include: Company name, postal address, telephone, fax, e-mail, website, contact person, designation, and product details.

Directory of South Korean Manufacturers & Exporters of Textile & Fabrics. EXIM Infotek Private Ltd. • $30 Individuals. Covers: 390 South Korean manufacturers and exporters of dyeing and finishing for fabrics and textile goods, fabric-cotton for furnishing, fabrics for industrial use, fabrics-cotton, fabrics-hemp/jute/paper, fabric-silk, fabrics-knitted, fabrics-linen, fabrics-manmade fiber, fabrics-non woven, felts/felted fabrics, net and tulle, textiles, velvet items, wadding and flock textile for industrial use, and woolen fabrics. Entries include: Company name, postal address, city, country, phone, fax, e-mail and websites, contact person, designation, and product details.

Directory of South Korean Manufacturers & Exporters of Toys & Games. EXIM Infotek Private Ltd. • $10 Individuals. Covers: 90 South Korean manufacturers & exporters of animal toys, dolls & puppets, model aircrafts, musical articles & toys, party & educational games, plush toys, stuffed toys, toys & games-electric/electronic, toys & games-mechanical, toys & games-plastic, toys & games-rubber, toys & games-wooden. Entries include: Company name, postal address, city, country, phone, fax, e-mail & websites, contact person, designation, products detail.

Directory of South Korean Manufacturers & Exporters of Travel & Luggage Accessories. EXIM Infotek Private Ltd. • $10 Individuals. Covers: 70 South Korean manufacturers and exporters of leather travel goods/handbags, umbrellas and walking sticks. Entries include: Company name, postal address, city, country, phone, fax, e-mail and websites, contact person, designation, and product details.

Directory of South Korean Manufacturers & Exporters of Tyres & Tubes. EXIM Infotek Private Ltd. • $5 Individuals. Covers: 20 South Korean manufacturers and exporters of tires-remolded, vehicle tires and inner tubes. Entries include: Company name, postal address, city, country, phone, fax, e-mail and websites, contact person, designation, and product details.

Directory of South Korean Manufacturers & Exporters of Undergarments. EXIM Infotek Private Ltd. • $10 Individuals. Covers: 60 South Korean manufacturers and exporters of lingerie/corsetry, nightwear, underwear, and stockings. Entries include: Company name, postal address, city, country, phone, fax, e-mail and websites, contact person, designation, and product details.

Directory of South Korean Manufacturers & Exporters of Ventilation Equipment. EXIM Infotek Private Ltd. • $250 Individuals. Covers: 80 South Korean manufacturers and exporters of blowers and ventilators, dust and fume collectors, fans and blowers. Entries include: Company name, postal address, telephone, fax, e-mail, website, contact person, designation, and product details.

Directory of South Korean Manufacturers & Exporters of Watches & Clocks. EXIM Infotek Private Ltd. • $10 Individuals. Covers: 60 South Korean manufacturers and exporters of clocks and clock parts, timing mechanisms, watch bracelets/straps, watch/clock and instrument parts, watch/clock and instrument springs, watches, wrist and pocket watches. Entries include: Company name, postal address, city, country, phone, fax, e-mail and websites, contact person, designation, and product details.

Directory of South Korean Manufacturers & Exporters of Wire, Chain & Wire Products. EXIM Infotek Private Ltd. • $15 Individuals. Covers: 140 South Korean manufacturers and exporters of chains/chain slings/grips-metal, chain-tire, ferrous wires, fine bare-copper wire, metal cables/cords/ropes, metal fencing and barbed wire, metal gauze/cloth/netting, wire goods-metal. Entries include: Company name, postal address, city, country, phone, fax, e-mail and websites, contact person, designation, and product details.

Directory of South Korean Manufacturers & Exporters of Wires & Cables--Electrical. EXIM Infotek Private Ltd. • $300 Individuals. Covers: 120 South Korean manufacturers and exporters of cable-battery, cable-control, cable-high tension, cables, electric wires/cables-non insulated, lead wires, power cable, power wires/cables-insulated, power-line cable and wire fittings, phone wires, wires and cables for electronics, and telecom wires and cables. Entries include: Company name, postal address, telephone, fax, e-mail, website, contact person, designation, and product details.

Directory of South Korean Manufacturers & Exporters of Woodenware & Wood Products. EXIM Infotek Private Ltd. • $5 Individuals. Covers: 40 South Korean manufacturers and exporters of cane and wicker products, carvings and marquetry-wooden, ladders-wooden, molding and frames-wooden, wooden cases/boxes, wooden decorative cases/boxes, wooden products for industrial use, and wooden products for non-industrial use. Entries include: Company name, postal address, city, country, phone, fax, e-mail and websites, contact person, designation, and product details.

Directory of South Korean Manufacturers and Exporters of Woodworking Equipment and Tools. EXIM Infotek Private Ltd. • $150 Individuals. Covers: 40 South Korean manufacturers and exporters of sawing and cutting tools, folding saw, tools for wood working machinery, wood boring and mortising machine, wood conditioning and surface treatment equipment, wood deforming machine, wood joining machine, wood milling and molding machine, wood sanding machine, wood sawing machine, wood turning lathes, wooden picture frame making machinery, and woodworking tools. Entries include: Company name, postal address, telephone, fax, e-mail, website, contact person, designation, and product details.

Directory of South Korean Manufacturers & Exporters of Yarns & Threads. EXIM Infotek Private Ltd. • $25 Individuals. Covers: 310 South Korean manufacturers and exporters of cotton yarn, dyeing and finishing for textile fiber/yarn, sewing and embroidery thread, textile fiber-manmade, yarn and twists-silk, yarn and twists-manmade fiber, yarns and twists-vegetable fibers, yarns and twists-wool/hair. Entries include: Company name, postal address, city, country, phone, fax, e-mail and websites, contact person, designation, and product details.

Directory of State Level Enterprises in China. Han Ying Shan Research Inc. • Irregular. $165. Covers: 1,064 "first or second grade enterprises" in China. Entries include: Company name, address, phone, telex, name and title of contact, number of employees, geographical area served, financial data, names and titles of key personnel, description of product/service.

Directory of Taiwanese Manufacturers & Exporters of Adhesive, Glues & Sealants. EXIM Infotek Private Ltd. • $20 Individuals. Covers: 190 Taiwanese manufacturers and exporters of adhesives-instant settings, adhesive packing materials, glue, processed rubber-solution and adhesives, and synthetic adhesives. Entries include: Company name, postal address, city, country, phone, fax, e-mail and websites, contact person, designation, and product details.

Directory of Taiwanese Manufacturers & Exporters of Agro Chemicals. EXIM Infotek Private Ltd. • $10 Individuals. Covers: 50 Taiwanese manufacturers and exporters of agrochemicals, fertilizers, fungicides/insecticides/bactericides destroyers, and herbicides/plant growth control substances. Entries include: Company name, postal address, city, country, phone, fax, e-mail and websites, contact person, designation, and product details.

Directory of Taiwanese Manufacturers & Exporters of Automobiles & Vehicles. EXIM Infotek Private Ltd. • $5 Individuals. Covers: 40 Taiwanese manufacturers and exporters of automobile body builders, tractors/trucks/trailers-industrial, truck and lorry trailers, trucks/lorries, and vehicles-special purpose. Entries include: Company name, postal address, city, country, phone, fax, e-mail and websites, contact person, designation, and product details.

Directory of Taiwanese Manufacturers & Exporters of Automotive Service & Repair Equipment. EXIM Infotek Private Ltd. • $10 Individuals. Covers: 70 Taiwanese manufacturers and exporters of garage jacks, mechanical lubrication tools, motor vehicle testing equipment, vehicle service and repair equipment. Entries include: Company name, postal address, city, country, phone, fax, e-mail and websites, contact person, designation, and product details.

Directory of Taiwanese Manufacturers & Exporters of Autoparts & Accessories. EXIM Infotek Private Ltd. • $50 Individuals. Covers: 890 Taiwanese manufacturers & exporters of auto accessories, auto electrical parts, auto lamps, auto parts, auto parts & accessories, auto spare parts, automobile parts, automotive lighting equipment, automotive parts, automotive plastic parts, brake shoes, brass silencers, car alarm systems, car mats, couplings, couplings & clutches, hardware for motorcars, head lamps, hose clamps, hydraulic shock absorbers, industrial trailer/truck parts/accessories, locking devices for cars, motor vehicle accessories, motor vehicle body components & spare parts, motor vehicle transmission parts, socket hoses for trucks, springs/shock absorbers, steering & suspension parts, truck parts, v belts, vehicle brake parts, vehicle control instruments & panels, vehicle electrical & electronic equipment, vehicle ventilation/heating & air conditioning systems, wheels & wheel rims, windshield wiper blades. Entries include: Company name, postal address, city, country, telephone, fax, e-mail & websites, contact person, designation, products detail.

Directory of Taiwanese Manufacturers & Exporters of Batteries & Accumulators. EXIM Infotek Private Ltd. • $25 Individuals. Covers: 290 Taiwanese manufacturers and exporters of batteries and accumulators, batteries for ups, battery back-up sirens, mobility small scooter (battery operated), ups and battery chargers. Entries include: Company name, postal address, city, country, phone, fax, e-mail and websites, contact person, designation, and product details.

Directory of Taiwanese Manufacturers & Exporters of Bearings. EXIM Infotek Private Ltd. • $10 Individuals. Covers: 110 Taiwanese manufacturers and exporters of balls, bearings-ball, needle and roller, plain bearings, plumber and pillow blocks/bushing. Entries include: Company name, postal address, city, country, phone, fax, e-mail and websites, contact person, designation, products detail.

Directory of Taiwanese Manufacturers & Exporters of Beauty Supplies, Cosmetics, Perfumes & Toiletries. EXIM Infotek Private Ltd. • $15 Individuals. Covers: 140 Taiwanese manufacturers and exporters of air fresheners, body glitter gel, cosmetic accessories, cosmetic brushes, cosmetic/hair/skin and dental products, cosmetics, cosmetics accessories, eye liner, eye pencil, eyebrow needles, eyebrow pencils, eyelash stick, eyelash wave lotion kit, eyelets, eyeshadow pencil, face foundation, fragrance bottles, hair brushes, hair combs, hair steamers, lip pens, lipstick, lipstick cases, lipstick containers, make-up kits, mascara, nail polish, perfume, perfume atomizers, perfume bottles, perfumes, shampoo. Entries include: Company name, postal address, city, country, phone, fax, e-mail and websites, contact person, designation and product details.

Directory of Taiwanese Manufacturers & Exporters of Bicycles, Parts & Accessories. EXIM Infotek Private Ltd. • $45 Individuals. Covers: 770 Taiwanese manufacturers and exporters of bicycle accessories, bicycle parts and accessories, bicycles and exercisers, and electric powered wheelchairs. Entries include: Company name, postal address, city, country, phone, fax, e-mail and websites, contact person, designation, and product details.

Directory of Taiwanese Manufacturers & Exporters of Carpets, Durries, Rugs & Floor Coverings. EXIM Infotek Private Ltd. • $5 Individuals. Covers: 20 Taiwanese manufacturers and exporters of carpets and rugs. Entries include: Company name, postal address, city, country, phone, fax, e-mail and websites, contact person, designation, and product details.

Directory of Taiwanese Manufacturers & Exporters of Castings & Forgings. EXIM Infotek Private Ltd. • $15 Individuals. Covers: 170 Taiwanese manufacturers and exporters of casting, iron castings, and steel castings. Entries include: Company name, postal address, city, country, phone, fax, e-mail and websites, contact person, designation, and product details.

Directory of Taiwanese Manufacturers & Exporters of Chemicals & Allied Products. EXIM Infotek Private Ltd. • $30 Individuals. Covers: 380 Taiwanese manufacturers and exporters of alcohols and epoxides, amines, artificial resins, barium/boron/bromine/hydrogen compounds, calcium-strontium and thallium compounds, carbohydrates/proteins and enzymes, carbon based materials and products, chemicals, chemicals for basic metal industries, chemicals for building materials, chemicals for cosmetics/perfumery/detergent/soaps, chemicals for electrical/electronic industries, chemicals for laboratory and microbiology, chemicals for leather and fur tanning extract, chemicals for lubricants and waxes, chemicals for metal welding/soldering fluxes, chemicals for mining/oil extraction, chemicals for paint/lacquer/varnish, chemicals for paper making/printing/photography, chemicals for plastic/rubber/ceramic, chemicals for unspecified uses, chemicals for water treatment, chemotherapeutic agents, compact & conventional detergent powder, compressed and liquefied gases/chem for refrigeration, detergents/cleansers and bleaching agents, dish wash detergent, disinfections and indoor deodorants, esters/acetates/ethyls and methyls, explosives, hydrocarbons and halcarbons, inorganic acids and anhydrides, inorganic alkalis-hydroxides, liquid bleaching agent, misc. organic chemicals, natural resins and pitches, organic acids and anhydrides, phosphorus/sulphur/carbon/silicon and cassium compounds, polyphenols/ethers/aldehydes/ketones, potash vats, potassium and ammonium compounds, soaps/fatty-acid based detergents, and sodium compounds. Entries include: Company name, postal address, city, country, telephone, fax, e-mail and websites, contact person, designation, and product details.

Directory of Taiwanese Manufacturers & Exporters of Confectionery & Bakery Products. EXIM Infotek Private Ltd. • $10 Individuals. Covers: 80 Taiwanese manufacturers and exporters of biscuits/crackers, bread/cakes and pastry, fruit-candied, instant porridge, noodles-instant, soups and extracts, sugar confectionery, vinegar and sauce. Entries include: Company name, postal address, city, country, phone, fax, e-mail and websites, contact person, designation, and product details.

Directory of Taiwanese Manufacturers and Exporters of Construction Machinery and Equipment. EXIM Infotek Private Ltd. • $350 Individuals. Covers: 150 Taiwanese manufacturers and exporters of bridge and tunnel construction machinery, building machinery and equipment, cement production plant, cement and plaster making plant, clay tile and brick production plant, concrete elements production plant, concrete making machinery, cranes and construction platform, crushing machinery, earth-moving and road making machinery, harbor and canal construction machinery, heavy mechanical handling equipment, mixers, railway track construction machinery, road rollers, scaffoldings and ladders. Entries include: Company name, postal address, telephone, fax, e-mail, website, contact person, designation, and product details.

Directory of Taiwanese Manufacturers & Exporters of Cotton, Silk, Wool Raw & Waste. EXIM Infotek Private Ltd. • $5 Individuals. Covers: 20 Taiwanese manufacturers and exporters of raw cotton and vegetable textile fiber, raw wool and other animal fibers. Entries include: Company name, postal address, city, country, phone, fax, e-mail and websites, contact person, designation, and product details.

Directory of Taiwanese Manufacturers & Exporters of Dyes, Colours, Pigments & Intermediates. EXIM Infotek Private Ltd. • $10 Individuals. Covers: 90 Taiwanese manufacturers & exporters of chemicals for textiles, colorants for leather/rubber/plastic & cosmetics, dyes, dyes-synthetic, pigments-natural, pigments-synthetic, textile coatings. Entries include:

For publishers' addresses, refer to SOURCES CITED section at the back of the book.

Company name, postal address, city, country, phone, fax, e-mail & websites, contact person, designation, products detail.

Directory of Taiwanese Manufacturers and Exporters of Energy and Power Equipment. EXIM Infotek Private Ltd. • $250 Individuals. Covers: 80 Taiwanese manufacturers and exporters of fuel and elements for nuclear energy industry, nuclear engineering plants, nuclear protection and detection instruments, nuclear reactors, power distribution equipment for various uses, and solar energy equipment. Entries include: Company name, postal address, telephone, fax, e-mail, website, contact person, designation, and product details.

Directory of Taiwanese Manufacturers & Exporters of Engines & Engine Parts. EXIM Infotek Private Ltd. • $15 Individuals. Covers: 130 Taiwanese manufacturers and exporters of engine components/spare parts, internal combustion engines, oil seals, pistons and plugs. Entries include: Company name, postal address, city, country, phone, fax, e-mail and websites, contact person, designation and product details.

Directory of Taiwanese Manufacturers and Exporters of Environment and Pollution Control Equipment. EXIM Infotek Private Ltd. • $400 Individuals. Covers: 160 Taiwanese manufacturers and exporters of air pollution control equipment, noise pollution control equipment, water and sewage treatment plant. Entries include: Company name, postal address, telephone, fax, e-mail, website, contact person, designation, and product details.

Directory of Taiwanese Manufacturers & Exporters of Filters & Strainers--Industrial. EXIM Infotek Private Ltd. • $10 Individuals. Covers: 80 Taiwanese manufacturers and exporters of bolting and filter cloths/gauzes, filters and strainers for processing industries, filters and strainers-metal, glue for air filters, and water and waste water filters. Entries include: Company name, postal address, city, country, phone, fax, e-mail and websites, contact person, designation, products detail.

Directory of Taiwanese Manufacturers & Exporters of Fire Fighting Equipment & Supplies. EXIM Infotek Private Ltd. • Covers: 30 Taiwanese manufacturers and exporters of fire extinguishing systems and fire fighting equipment. Entries include: Company name, postal address, telephone, fax, e-mail, website, contact person, designation, and product details.

Directory of Taiwanese Manufacturers & Exporters of Fishing & Hunting Equipment & Supplies. EXIM Infotek Private Ltd. • $250 Individuals. Covers: 70 Taiwanese manufacturers and exporters of fish farming equipment, fishing lure, knotted nets, and nettings. Entries include: Company name, postal address, telephone, fax, e-mail, website, contact person, designation, and product details.

Directory of Taiwanese Manufacturers & Exporters of Food Additives & Aromatic Chemicals. EXIM Infotek Private Ltd. • $5 Individuals. Covers: 40 Taiwanese manufacturers and exporters of aromo compounds, chemicals for food and beverages, colorants for food and beverages, and natural additives for the food and beverages. Entries include: Company name, postal address, city, country, phone, fax, e-mail and websites, contact person, designation, and product details.

Directory of Taiwanese Manufacturers & Exporters of Furniture--All Types. EXIM Infotek Private Ltd. • $40 Individuals. Covers: 690 Taiwanese manufacturers and exporters of bamboo furniture, chairs, flexible shelving systems, furniture and fittings for shops/stores, furniture fittings, furniture for manufactured products, furniture/racking-industrial/lab, furniture-cane and wicker, furniture-children, furniture-domestic, furniture-garden, furniture-hospital, furniture-hotel/restaurant/bar, furniture-institutional, furniture-kitchen, furniture-office, furniture-public places, furniture-school, furniture-upholstered, knockdown furniture, leisure folding chairs, metal cabinets, small furniture articles, store fixtures, walking cane chairs, and wooden furniture. Entries include: Company name, postal address, city, country, phone, fax, e-mail and websites, contact person, designation, and product details.

Directory of Taiwanese Manufacturers & Exporters of Garden Tools, Equipment & Supplies. EXIM Infotek Private Ltd. • $10 Individuals. Covers: 70 Taiwanese manufacturers and exporters of garden irrigation accessories, garden tools, and garden tools-all kinds. Entries include: Company name, postal address, city, country, phone, fax, e-mail and websites, contact person, designation, and product details.

Directory of Taiwanese Manufacturers & Exporters of Gears & Gears Boxes. EXIM Infotek Private Ltd. • $10 Individuals. Covers: 70 Taiwanese manufacturers and exporters of gears, worm gear reducers.

Directory of Taiwanese Manufacturers & Exporters of Giftware & Novelties. EXIM Infotek Private Ltd. • $20 Individuals. Covers: 250 Taiwanese manufacturers and exporters of albums and files, ceramic faucet accessories, coins/medals/decorations and badges, enamel badges, gift articles, gift sets, gifts, key chains, key holders, kitchen utensils, medals, novelty glasses, photo frames, promotional giftware, religious festive seasonal gifts, solid brass quick release key chains, souvenirs, trophies/ceremonial plates. Entries include: Company name, postal address, city, country, phone, fax, e-mail and websites, contact person, designation, and product details.

Directory of Taiwanese Manufacturers & Exporters of Handicrafts & Decorative Items. EXIM Infotek Private Ltd. • $10 Individuals. Covers: 120 Taiwanese manufacturers and exporters of bronze/copper/brass and wrought iron artistic goods, candle holders, Christmas tree ornaments, Christmas tree sets, fancy metal boxes, festival articles and decorations, handicrafts, religious articles-Buddhist/Hindu, religious articles-Christian, religious articles-Jewish. Entries include: Company name, postal address, city, country, phone, fax, e-mail and websites, contact person, designation, products detail.

Directory of Taiwanese Manufacturers & Exporters of Handkerchieves, Scarves & Neckwares. EXIM Infotek Private Ltd. • $5 Individuals. Covers: 20 Taiwanese manufacturers & exporters of neckties/scarves. Entries include: Company name, postal address, city, country, phone, fax, e-mail & websites, contact person, designation, products detail.

Directory of Taiwanese Manufacturers & Exporters of Handtools. EXIM Infotek Private Ltd. • $35 Individuals. Covers: 510 Taiwanese manufacturers and exporters of builders tools, carbide tools, chisels/taps/dies and similar tools, electric and electro-magnetic tools, files/rasps and similar tools, hammers/mallets and similar tools, hand tools, handy sealer, metal hand and diamond tools, multipurpose tools, pliers/clamps and similar tools, roofers and decorators tools, screwdrivers/wrenches, tagging guns, tool cases, and tools for powerline maintenance. Entries include: Company name, postal address, city, country, phone, fax, e-mail and websites, contact person, designation, and product details.

Directory of Taiwanese Manufacturers & Exporters of Hardwares--All Types. EXIM Infotek Private Ltd. • $40 Individuals. Covers: 650 Taiwanese manufacturers and exporters of abrasive coated products, abrasive media, blind rivets, brass hardware, brass knobs and pulls, brass padlocks, builders' hardware, building hardware, cabinet hardware, cam locks, casters, ceramic cabinet hardware, door edge guards, door fittings, door handles, door hardware, door knob/lever handles, door locks, d-rings, furniture hardware, furniture lock sets, haberdashery metalware, home hardwares, ironmongery and hardware, ironmongery and hardware for furniture, key lock switches, locking handles, locks, locks for luggage and bags, locksmith articles, luggage hardware and accessories, metal fittings, metal smallwares for various uses, nails/tacks/spikes/staples-metal, pad locks, paint brushes and rollers, pins, plastic foot studs, plastic handles w/loops, roller strips, screen door hardware, sliders, springs, and stainless steel hardware. Entries include: Company name, postal address, city, country, telephone, fax, e-mail and websites, contact person, designation, and product details.

Directory of Taiwanese Manufacturers & Exporters of Hats & Headwears. EXIM Infotek Private Ltd. • $10 Individuals. Covers: 120 Taiwanese manufacturers and exporters of caps, hats, hats and headwear, shower caps. Entries include: Company name, postal address, city, country, phone, fax, e-mail and websites, contact person, designation, products detail.

Directory of Taiwanese Manufacturers & Exporters of Heaters & Heating Equipment. EXIM Infotek Private Ltd. • $450 Individuals. Covers: 200 Taiwanese manufacturers and exporters of central heating systems, driers, drying plants, electric heating equipment, heat exchanger, heating elements and accessories, heating machine, high frequency induction heating machine, and water heaters. Entries include: Company name, postal address, telephone, fax, e-mail, website, contact person, designation, and product details.

Directory of Taiwanese Manufacturers & Exporters of Herbs & Herbal Medicine Products. EXIM Infotek Private Ltd. • $15 Individuals. Covers: 160 Taiwanese manufacturers and exporters of Chinese medical preparations, and herbal medicines. Entries include: Company name, postal address, city, country, phone, fax, e-mail and websites, contact person, designation, and product details.

Directory of Taiwanese Manufacturers & Exporters of Home Furnishing Materials. EXIM Infotek Private Ltd. • $15 Individuals. Covers: 140 Taiwanese manufacturers and exporters of bathroom mats, crochet lace table cloths, curtains, curtain blinds, door curtains, household linens and soft furnishings, mattresses, cushions and pillows, sanitary towels and baby napkins, shower curtain cloths, table cloths, table lamps, vertical blinds, vinyl placemats, vinyl table cloths, and window curtains. Entries include: Company name, postal address, city, country, phone, fax, e-mail and websites, contact person, designation, and product details.

Directory of Taiwanese Manufacturers & Exporters of Houseware, Kitchenware & Tableware. EXIM Infotek Private Ltd. • $30 Individuals. Covers: 470 Taiwanese manufacturers and exporters of baskets-plastic, brooms and brushes for domestic use, cloth hangers-plastic, cutlery, decorative plastic articles, domestic articles-metal, fashion acrylic houseware, gold-plated/silverplated and pewterware, hangers, household cutlery-metal, household plastic products, kitchen articles/tableware-plastic, kitchen articles-metal, knife, knives-metal, plastic houseware, scissors, and scissors for cloth or paper cutting. Entries include: Company name, postal address, city, country, phone, fax, e-mail and websites, contact person, designation, and product details.

Directory of Taiwanese Manufacturers & Exporters of Imitation & Fashion Jewellery. EXIM Infotek Private Ltd. • $10 Individuals. Covers: 90 Taiwanese manufacturers & exporters of bracelets, buckles, costume jewelry, cuff links, earrings, fashion goods, fashion metal accessories, hair bands, hair clips, hair ornaments, imitation jewelry, jewelry, necklaces, synthetic jewels for watches, theatrical masks for arts, craft & festivals, tie pins. Entries include: Company name, postal address, city, country, phone, fax, e-mail & websites, contact person, designation, products detail.

Directory of Taiwanese Manufacturers & Exporters of Jute, Hemp, Sisal, Burlap & Its Products. EXIM Infotek Private Ltd. • $10 Individuals. Covers: 60 Taiwanese manufacturers and exporters of canvas and duck, canvas and duck products. Entries include: Company name, postal address, city, country, phone, fax, e-mail and websites, contact person, designation, and product details.

Directory of Taiwanese Manufacturers & Exporters of Laces, Ribbons & Embroidery Products. EXIM Infotek Private Ltd. • $15 Individuals. Covers: 180 Taiwanese manufacturers and exporters of badges, decorative trim, embroidery-all types, embroidered emblems, embroideries, embroidery, embroidery emblems, embroidery-hand made, flower tapes, lace and embroidery, lace-hand made, lace-machine made, ribbons, ribbons and tapes for industrial use, ribbons and tapes-non industrial, trimmings/cordings/braids and fringes, and woven ribbon. Entries include: Company name, postal address, city, country, phone, fax, e-mail and websites, contact person, designation, and product details.

Directory of Taiwanese Manufacturers & Exporters of Leather, Hides, Skins & Furs. EXIM Infotek Private Ltd. • $20 Individuals. Covers: 190 Taiwanese manufacturers and exporters of leather-reconstituted, leather-processed, PVC leathercloth, PVC sponge leather, sheep and goat skins, sheep and lamb skins, skins, hides and leather, and swine skins/leather. Entries include: Company name, postal address, city, country, phone, fax, e-mail and websites, contact person, designation, and product details.

Directory of Taiwanese Manufacturers & Exporters of Leather Products. EXIM Infotek Private Ltd. • $20 Individuals. Covers: 280 Taiwanese manufacturers and exporters of bags, cases and covers of leather, fancy leather goods, fur clothing and products, leather airbags/sportbags, leather clothing, leather goods for industrial use, leather purses, leather waist belts. Entries include: Company name, postal address, city, country, phone, fax, e-mail and websites, contact person, designation, and product details.

Directory of Taiwanese Manufacturers & Exporters of Lighting Fixtures, Lamps & Accessories. EXIM Infotek Private Ltd. • $30 Individuals. Covers: 450 Taiwanese manufacturers and exporters of bulbs, decoration bulbs, discharge and special purpose lamps, electric lamp components, filament lamps-all types, flash light, fluorescent lamps, fog lamps, halogen lamps, indoor electric lighting equipment, laser lights, lighting equipment-outdoor, miniature lamps, portable electric lamps and accessories, and turning lamps. Entries include: Company name, postal address, city, country, phone, fax, e-mail and websites, contact person, designation, and product details.

Directory of Taiwanese Manufacturers & Exporters of Machinery for Chemicals & Pharma Industry. EXIM Infotek Private Ltd. • $25 Individuals. Covers: 290 Taiwanese manufacturers and exporters of crushers/pulverizers for chemical industries, dryers/evaporators/crystallizers for chemical industries, electrochemical and electrolytic plant equipment, electroplating plant machinery, essence/perfume production plant equipment, explosive/match production plant equipment, fertilizer production plant equipment, glue/gelatin making plant equipment, heaters/boilers/distillers for chemical industries, inorganic chemical production plant equipment, organic chemical production plant equipment, paint/varnish/enamel/ink production plant equipment, pharmaceutical/cosmetic production plant equipment, reactors for chemical industry, screeners/mixers/centrifuges for chemical industry, soap making equipment, technical gas production plant equipment. Entries include: Company name, postal address, city, country, phone, fax, e-mail and websites, contact person, designation, and product details.

Directory of Taiwanese Manufacturers & Exporters of Machinery for Leather & Shoe Industry. EXIM Infotek Private Ltd. • $10 Individuals. Covers: 100 Taiwanese manufacturers and exporters of boot and shoe making machinery/equipment, leather working and saddlery making/equipment, shoe industry equipment, tannery machinery and equipment. Entries include: Company name, postal address, city, country, phone, fax, e-mail and websites, contact person, designation, products detail.

Directory of Taiwanese Manufacturers & Exporters of Machinery for Paper & Pulp Industry. EXIM Infotek Private Ltd. • $10 Individuals. Covers: 120 Taiwanese manufacturers and exporters of cardboard finishing/forming/cutting machinery/equipment, cardboard making machinery/equipment, paper finishing/converting machinery/equipment, paper making plant equipment, pulp and cellulose production plant equipment. Entries include: Company name, postal address, city, country, phone, fax, e-mail and websites, contact person, designation, products detail.

Directory of Taiwanese Manufacturers & Exporters of Machinery for Rubber Industry. EXIM Infotek Private Ltd. • $250 Individuals. Covers: 80 Taiwanese manufacturers and exporters of bicycle tire building machine, raw rubber processing and vulcanizing machine and equipment, rubber injection molding machine, rubber products, and tire making machinery. Entries include: Company name, postal address, telephone, fax, e-mail, website, contact person, designation, and product details.

Directory of Taiwanese Manufacturers & Exporters of Machinery for Textile & Knitting Industry. EXIM Infotek Private Ltd. • $30 Individuals. Covers: 400 Taiwanese manufacturers and exporters of automatic mini thread winders, beam brakes and discs for textile machinery, belts/hoses/webbing-textile, bobbins for textile industry, carpet and tapestry looms, cone type automatic cross cone winders, cordage/rope/twine and braid production machinery, cotton preparation machinery and equipment, cotton wool and surgical dressing making machinery/equipment, felt and non woven fabric making machinery, hemp/flex fiber preparation machinery and equipment, knitting machinery and attachments, lace and net making machinery, manmade fiber production and processing plants, mattress and upholstery making machinery/equipment, parts for textile machinery, ribbon and trimming making machinery, sleeves and strips for spinning mills, textile calendaring machinery and equipment, textile cleaning spray guns, textile coating machinery and equipment, textile dyeing and boiling machinery/equipment, textile finishing machinery and equipment, textile printing machinery and equipment, textile printings, textile spinning and twisting machinery, textile spinning/twisting/winding/reeling machine parts, textile steaming/conditioning/folding/shearing machinery, textile washing/mercerizing machinery and equipment, textile waste processing machinery and equipment, textile weaving machinery parts/accessories, textile weaving machinery/looms, textile winding and reeling machinery, thread and high speed drum winders, universal type multipurpose combiner and thread winders, washing machines for textile industry, weaving machinery for metal thread, wool carding and combing machinery and equipment, yarn preparation machinery/equipment, and yarn tensioners. Entries include: Company name, postal address, city, country, telephone, fax, e-mail and websites, contact person, designation, and product details.

Directory of Taiwanese Manufacturers & Exporters of Marine & Boating Equipment & Supplies. EXIM Infotek Private Ltd. • $10 Individuals. Covers: 120 Taiwanese manufacturers and exporters of boat parts and accessories, coastal vessels, control and navigational instruments-ship, equipment/signals for ships/boats, marine propulsion units, radar and navigation systems/equipment-marine, submersible vessels and equipment, yacht and pleasure craft. Entries include: Company name, postal address, city, country, phone, fax, e-mail and websites, contact person, designation, products detail.

Directory of Taiwanese Manufacturers & Exporters of Material Handling Equipment. EXIM Infotek Private Ltd. • $750 Individuals. Covers: 400 Taiwanese manufacturers and exporters of automated handling storage equipment, barrows, trolleys, carts, conveyors, elevators, cranes, hoists, winches, forklift trucks, handling equipment parts and accessories, hydraulic dump hoists, lifts, elevators, mobile cranes, overhead conveyors, pallets and containers, pneumatic handling equipment, pulleys, and cable wheels. Entries include: Company name, postal address, telephone, fax, e-mail, website, contact person, designation, and product details.

Directory of Taiwanese Manufacturers & Exporters of Meat & Meat Products. EXIM Infotek Private Ltd. • $5 Individuals. Covers: 30 Taiwanese manufacturers and exporters of meat and game-processed/preserved, meat and meat products, meat-dried. Entries include: Company name, postal address, city, country, phone, fax, e-mail and websites, contact person, designation, and product details.

Directory of Taiwanese Manufacturers & Exporters of Minerals. EXIM Infotek Private Ltd. • $5 Individuals. Covers: 30 Taiwanese manufacturers and exporters of clays, gypsum/plaster and stucco products, limestones, magnesium minerals, mica and mecanite products, quartz and silica electro thermic products, quartzite of crystal, silicon minerals, slate products. Entries include: Company name, postal address, city, country, phone, fax, e-mail and websites, contact person, designation, and product details.

Directory of Taiwanese Manufacturers & Exporters of Motorcycles, Parts & Accessories. EXIM Infotek Private Ltd. • $10 Individuals. Covers: 50 Taiwanese manufacturers and exporters of motorcycle mirrors, motorcycle parts, motorcycles and mopeds. Entries include: Company name, postal address, city, country, phone, fax, e-mail and websites, contact person, designation, and product details.

Directory of Taiwanese Manufacturers and Exporters of Motors and Motor Parts--Electric. EXIM Infotek Private Ltd. • $650 Individuals. Covers: 340 Taiwanese manufacturers and exporters of electric motors below 1hp, electric motors over 1hp, explosion proof motors, motorcycle parts and accessories. Entries include: Company name, postal address, telephone, fax, e-mail, website, contact person, designation, and product details.

Directory of Taiwanese Manufacturers & Exporters of Nuts, Bolts, Screws & Fasteners. EXIM Infotek Private Ltd. • $20 Individuals. Covers: 260 Taiwanese manufacturers and exporters of bolts and nuts, bolts, fasteners, fasteners-metal, metal nuts/bolts/washers, metal rivets, metal screws/bolts/nuts, rivet nuts, rivets, screws, screws-metal, self-drilling screws, special screws and nuts, washers. Entries include: Company name, postal address, city, country, phone, fax, e-mail and websites, contact person, designation, and product details.

Directory of Taiwanese Manufacturers & Exporters of Oil & Fats--Cooking & Vegetable. EXIM Infotek Private Ltd. • $5 Individuals. Covers: 20 South Korean manufacturers and exporters of oils and fats-edible. Entries include: Company name, postal address, city, country, phone, fax, e-mail and websites, contact person, designation, and product details.

Directory of Taiwanese Manufacturers & Exporters

For publishers' addresses, refer to SOURCES CITED section at the back of the book.

of Paints, Varnishes & Allied Products. EXIM Infotek Private Ltd. • $10 Individuals. Covers: 60 Taiwanese manufacturers and exporters of anti-corrosion products, lacquers and paints-primers, mastics/putties and sealing compounds, varnishes and stains-distempers, and vitreous colors/enamels and glazes. Entries include: Company name, postal address, city, country, phone, fax, e-mail and websites, contact person, designation, and product details.

Directory of Taiwanese Manufacturers & Exporters of Paper & Paper Products. EXIM Infotek Private Ltd. • $20 Individuals. Covers: 240 Taiwanese manufacturers and exporters of base and backing paper, cardboard, cardboard articles-diecut/embossed, cardboard/corrugated-packaging, coated and laminated paper/board, corrugated paper and board, heat transfer printing paper, paper and cardboard tubes, paper and paper rolls for technical use, paper and paper rolls printed for writing/technical, paper articles-diecut/embossed, paper packaging/bags and sacks, printing and drawing paper/board, pulp mechanical and chemicals, recycled paper pulp, reinforced cardboard products, tissue paper and cellulose wadding, wallpaper and paper backed wallcoverings, and wrapping/crepe paper. Entries include: Company name, postal address, city, country, phone, fax, e-mail and websites, contact person, designation, and product details.

Directory of Taiwanese Manufacturers & Exporters of Petroleum Products. EXIM Infotek Private Ltd. • $10 Individuals. Covers: 50 Taiwanese manufacturers and exporters of mineral oils and greases, natural gases, natural oils and greases for technical use, petroleum products/fuels and lubricants, tar and bituminous products, and tar and resin distillation products. Entries include: Company name, postal address, city, country, phone, fax, e-mail and websites, contact person, designation, products detail.

Directory of Taiwanese Manufacturers & Exporters of Pharmaceutical Products. EXIM Infotek Private Ltd. • $20 Individuals. Covers: 250 Taiwanese manufacturers and exporters of antibiotics, microencapsulated pharmaceuticals, ophthalmic preparations, pharmaceutical preparations for cardiovascular, pharmaceutical preparations, veterinary preparations-general, vitamin preparations. Entries include: Company name, postal address, city, country, phone, fax, e-mail and websites, contact person, designation, and product details.

Directory of Taiwanese Manufacturers & Exporters of Pharmaceutical Raw Materials. EXIM Infotek Private Ltd. • $20 Individuals. Covers: 190 Taiwanese manufacturers and exporters of gelatins for pharmaceuticals, hypodermoclysis and phleboclysis solution, pharmaceutical base and suppository compounds, vitamins/hormones and organ extracts. Entries include: Company name, postal address, city, country, phone, fax, e-mail and websites, contact person, designation, and product details.

Directory of Taiwanese Manufacturers & Exporters of Railway Equipment & Supplies. EXIM Infotek Private Ltd. • $5 Individuals. Covers: 20 Taiwanese manufacturers and exporters of locomotives/railcars and tramcars, railway equipments, railways and tram carriage/wagons. Entries include: Company name, postal address, city, country, phone, fax, e-mail and websites, contact person, designation, and product details.

Directory of Taiwanese Manufacturers & Exporters of Readymade Garments. EXIM Infotek Private Ltd. • $45 Individuals. Covers: 710 Taiwanese manufacturers and exporters of casual and leisurewear, clothing and accessories-rubber, dressing gowns, hosiery, knitwear, ladies blouses, protective work clothing, readymade for infants, readymade for ladies/girls, readymade for men/boys, reflective jackets, shirts-all types, swim and beach wear, uniforms and professional clothing, and waterproof garments. Entries include: Company name, postal address, city, country, phone, fax, e-mail and websites, contact person, designation, and product details.

Directory of Taiwanese Manufacturers and Exporters of Restaurant, Hotel and Catering Equipment. EXIM Infotek Private Ltd. • $150 Individuals. Covers: 30 Taiwanese manufacturers and exporters of catering machinery and equipment. Entries include: Company name, postal address, telephone, fax, e-mail, website, contact person, designation, and product details.

Directory of Taiwanese Manufacturers & Exporters of Shoes & Footwears. EXIM Infotek Private Ltd. • $30 Individuals. Covers: 430 Taiwanese manufacturers and exporters of baby shoes, footwear soles/components, footwear-industrial/protective, footwear-sports, footwear-standard, footwear-wooden, shoes, and shoes materials. Entries include: Company name, postal address, city, country, phone, fax, e-mail and websites, contact person, designation, and product details.

Directory of Taiwanese Manufacturers & Exporters of Sporting Goods. EXIM Infotek Private Ltd. • $1,200 Individuals. Covers: 830 Taiwanese manufacturers and exporters of athletic sports equipment, ball sports equipment, billiard equipment, billiard table sets and cues, camping equipment, camping goods, fishing tackle, golf carts and vans, golf club and badminton shafts, golf putter, gymnasium and exercise equipment, martial arts, sports equipment, water sports equipment, and winter and mountaineering sports equipment. Entries include: Company name, postal address, telephone, fax, e-mail, website, contact person, designation, and product details.

Directory of Taiwanese Manufacturers & Exporters of Tea & Coffee. EXIM Infotek Private Ltd. • $5 Individuals. Covers: 20 Taiwanese manufacturers and exporters of Chinese tea, cocoa and chocolate products, coffee and coffee substitutes. Entries include: Company name, postal address, city, country, phone, fax, e-mail and websites, contact person, designation, and product details.

Directory of Taiwanese Manufacturers & Exporters of Textile & Fabrics. EXIM Infotek Private Ltd. • $30 Individuals. Covers: 410 Taiwanese manufacturers and exporters of clothing and textile products, cotton fabrics, dyeing and finishing for fabrics and textile goods, fabric-cotton for furnishing, fabrics, fabrics for industrial use, fabrics-cotton, fabrics-hemp/jute/paper, fabric-silk, fabrics-knitted, fabrics-linen, fabrics-manmade fiber, fabrics-non woven, felts/felted fabrics, garment fabrics, knitted fabrics, knitted fabrics-pile/plush, net and tulle, non woven fabrics, polyester cloth, reflective fabrics, textiles, wadding and flock textiles for industrial use, and woolen fabrics. Entries include: Company name, postal address, city, country, phone, fax, e-mail and websites, contact person, designation, and product details.

Directory of Taiwanese Manufacturers & Exporters of Toys & Games. EXIM Infotek Private Ltd. • $40 Individuals. Covers: 670 Taiwanese manufacturers and exporters of aircraft models, baby buggies, baby carriages, baby music potties, baby prams and cycles, baby tricycles and bicycles, baby walkers, cots, cradles and prams, dart game sets, dolls and puppets, educational toys, jumping balls, model aircrafts, music planes, musical articles and toys, party and educational games, plastic sporting games, puzzles/jigsaw puzzles, stuffed toys, talking planes, toys, toys and games-electric/electronic, toys and games-mechanical, toys and games-plastic, toys and games-rubber, toys and games-wooden, and video game machines. Entries include: Company name, postal address, city, country, phone, fax, e-mail and websites, contact person, designation, and product details.

Directory of Taiwanese Manufacturers & Exporters of Travel & Luggage Accessories. EXIM Infotek Private Ltd. • $30 Individuals. Covers: 370 Taiwanese manufacturers and exporters of all kinds of umbrellas, leather travel goods/handbags, luggage carts, travel bags, umbrellas and walking sticks. Entries include: Company name, postal address, city, country, phone, fax, e-mail and websites, contact person, designation, and product details.

Directory of Taiwanese Manufacturers & Exporters of Tyres & Tubes. EXIM Infotek Private Ltd. • $10 Individuals. Covers: 110 Taiwanese manufacturers & exporters of tire repair materials, tires, tires-remolded, vehicle tires & inner tubes. Entries include: Company name, postal address, city, country, phone, fax, e-mail & websites, contact person, designation, products detail.

Directory of Taiwanese Manufacturers & Exporters of Undergarments. EXIM Infotek Private Ltd. • $10 Individuals. Covers: 50 Taiwanese manufacturers and exporters of brassieres/panties, lingerie/corsetry and nightwear, pantyhose, socks, underwear-men, and underwear-stockings. Entries include: Company name, postal address, city, country, phone, fax, e-mail and websites, contact person, designation, and product details.

Directory of Taiwanese Manufacturers and Exporters of Waste Disposal and Recycling Equipment. EXIM Infotek Private Ltd. • $250 Individuals. Covers: 70 Taiwanese manufacturers and exporters of domestic refuse and waste incinerators. Entries include: Company name, postal address, telephone, fax, e-mail, website, contact person, designation, and product details.

Directory of Taiwanese Manufacturers & Exporters of Watches & Clocks. EXIM Infotek Private Ltd. • $20 Individuals. Covers: 220 Taiwanese manufacturers and exporters of blank movements for quartz watches, clocks, clocks and clock parts, meters-time interval, table clocks, timing mechanisms, watch bracelets/straps, watch/clock and instrument parts, watch/clock and instrument springs, watches, wrist and pocket watches. Entries include: Company name, postal address, city, country, phone, fax, e-mail and websites, contact person, designation, product details.

Directory of Taiwanese Manufacturers & Exporters of Wire, Chain & Wire Products. EXIM Infotek Private Ltd. • $20 Individuals. Covers: 260 Taiwanese manufacturers and exporters of chains, chains/chain slings/grips-metal, ferrous wires, fine bare-copper wire, galvanized steel wire rope, metal cables/cords/ropes, metal fencing and barbed wire, metal gauze/cloth/netting, stainless steel wire rope, steel wire-zinc coated strands, wire goods-metal, wire products, wire racks and accessories. Entries include: Company name, postal address, city, country, phone, fax, e-mail and websites, contact person, designation, and product details.

Directory of Taiwanese Manufacturers and Exporters of Woodworking Equipment and Tools. EXIM Infotek Private Ltd. • Covers: 290 Taiwanese manufacturers and exporters of ancillary equipment for wood working machine, multi-operational wood working machine, sawing and cutting tools, timber preparing machinery and equipment, tools for wood working machinery, wood boring and mortising machine, wood conditioning treatment equipment, wood deforming machine, wood joining machine, wood milling and molding machine, wood planning machine, wood sanding machine, wood sawing machine, wood turning lathes, portable wood working machine, wooden picture frame making machinery, woodworking machinery, and woodworking tools. Entries include: Company name, postal address, telephone, fax, e-mail, website, contact person, designation, and product details.

Directory of Taiwanese Manufacturers & Exporters

of Yarns & Threads. EXIM Infotek Private Ltd. • $20 Individuals. Covers: 270 Taiwanese manufacturers and exporters of cotton yarn, dying and finishing for textile fiber/yarn, reflective filaments, sewing and embroidery thread, textile fiber-manmade, thread, yarn and twist-silk, yarn and twists-manmade fiber, yarns and twists-vegetable fibers, yarns and twists-wool/hair. Entries include: Company name, postal address, city, country, phone, fax, e-mail and websites, contact person, designation, and product details.

Directory of Taiwanese Manufacturers & Exporters of Zippers, Garment & Shoe Accessories. EXIM Infotek Private Ltd. • $15 Individuals. Covers: 140 Taiwanese manufacturers and exporters of apparel accessories, belt buckles, buttons, elastic band accessories, elastic braid, elastic cords, elastic ribbons, elastic yarn and fabrics, eyelets, garment accessories, hooks, loop fasteners, metal buttons, patches, plastic buckles, sewing kits, sewing notions, shoe buckles, woven labels, zipper products, and zippers. Entries include: Company name, postal address, city, country, phone, fax, e-mail and websites, contact person, designation, and product details.

Directory of Taiwan's Leading Exporters. China Economic News Service. • Annual. $90. Covers: 6,000 suppliers of machinery, toys, giftware, stationery, jewelry, sporting goods, leather goods, footwear, bicycles, automobiles, hardware, building materials, electronics, computers, textiles, furniture, and lighting.

Directory of Texas Manufacturers. University of Texas at Austin IC2 Institute Bureau of Business Research. • Annual. $139. Covers: more than 17,000 manufacturers in Texas and Texarkana, Arkansas; includes Standard Industrial Classification (SIC) manufacturing codes, products. Entries include: Company name, address, phone, toll-free number, fax number, geographical territory covered, form of company organization, number of employees, products, sales volume, SIC code. Updated monthly by "Texas Industrial Expansion" (see separate entry).

Directory of the Coal Industry of the Former Soviet Union. Flegon Press. • $150. Covers: Over 450 coal mines and companies associated with the industry of the former Soviet Union, including collieries, machinery manufacturing, equipment repair, and associations. Database includes: Full coal specifications and import requests. Entries include: Company national, telex, and names of managing personnel.

Directory of the Russian Far East. Flegon Press. • Irregular. $99. Covers: Industry in the Far East of Russia. Entries include: Company name and location, manager name, phone, telex, number of employees, products, and import/export details.

Directory of Top Computer Executives. Applied Computer Research Inc. • Semiannual. $345 Individuals single volume, per issue. Covers: In three volumes, over 65,000 U.S. and Canadian executives with major information technology or communications responsibilities in over 35,500 U.S. and Canadian companies. Database includes: Listings of manufacturer and model numbers of systems that are installed at each company. Entries include: Company name, address, phone, subsidiary and/or division names, major systems installed, names and titles of top information system executives, number of IT employees, number of PCs, and web address.

The Directory of Toronto Recruiters. Continental Records Company Ltd. • Annual. $49.95 Individuals plus express post shipping cost and GST. Covers: More than 1,200 recruiting firms in the Toronto, Canada area. Entries include: Firm name, address, phone, fax, e-mail, URL, name and title of contact, and industry and professional specialties.

Directory of Training. Training Information Network Ltd. • Annual. $170 Set. A three-volume set: "Directory of Computer Training" lists 5,000 computer courses from over 500 training companies; "Directory of Management Training" describes more than 5,000 management and supervisory courses; and "Directory of Multi-Media Training" lists 2,000 computer-based, interactive video, self-study, and other training packages; coverage includes the United Kingdom. Database includes: Lists of consultants, training venues, training associations, and sources of training advice; glossaries. Entries include: Company or institute name, address, phone, contact name, company profile; title, cost, duration, frequency, and location of each course offered.

Directory of Training Programmes. Gower Publishing Australia Proprietary Ltd. • Annual. $275 postpaid. Covers: Approximately 700 organizations and other institutions in Australia that provide management training programs. Entries include: Organization name, address, phone, fax, name and title of contact, geographical area served, description of programs offered.

Directory of 20 South Korean Manufacturers & Exporters of Jute, Hemp, Sisal, Burlap & Its Products. EXIM Infotek Private Ltd. • $5 Individuals. Covers: 20 South Korean manufacturers and exporters of canvas and duck, canvas and duck products. Entries include: Company name, postal address, city, country, phone, fax, e-mail and websites, contact person, designation, and product details.

Directory of 2,500 Active Real-Estate Lenders. International Wealth Success Inc. • Annual. $25 Individuals. Covers: About 2,500 financial institutions that actively lend money for real estate investments and purchases. Entries include: Company name, address.

Directory of UK Exporters. Hemming Information Services. • $275 plus $9.00 shipping. Covers: 10,500 manufacturing exporters. Entries include: Named export contact, products, countries of destination, tonnage shipped and turnover.

Directory of U.S. Agricultural Cooperative Exporters: SR21. U.S. Department of Agriculture. • Covers: 102 U.S. agricultural cooperatives that export or have the capability of exporting commodities to foreign countries. Entries include: Cooperative name, address, phone, name and title of contact, commodities available, communications numbers.

Directory of U.S. Companies Doing Business in Central and Eastern Europe and the Commonwealth of Independent States. Wetherby International Co. • Quarterly. $25 postpaid. Covers: over 500 U.S. firms with operations in the Commonwealth of Independent States and Central and Eastern Europe; sources of assistance for U.S. business at the Commerce Department. Entries include: Company or agency name, address, phone, type of activity.

Directory of U.S. Importers. Journal of Commerce Group. • Annual. $2,750 Master Edition CD. Covers: 32,000 importers in the United States. Database includes: Lists of world ports and international banks; trade commissions, consulates, embassies, and foreign trade zones; guide to operations of the U.S. Customs Service and company name. Entries include: Company name, address, phone, fax, names and titles of key personnel, SIC code, commodities imported, import country, U.S. port of entry, tonnage and volume indicators.

Directory of U.S. Meat Suppliers. United States Meat Export Federation. • Annual. Covers: U.S. packers, processors, purveyors, and exporters of red meat and red meat products. Directory is included with payment of membership dues.

Directory of Vendors. IBCON S.A. • Irregular. $473 Individuals. Covers: 14,640 companies that are SA corporations located in Mexico City. Entries include: Company name, address, phone, fax, industry code, Producing, Distributing, Servicing initials, name and position of the top executive.

Directory of Washington, DC Chief Executive Officers. Labor Market Information and Research Division District of Columbia Department of Employment Services. • Annual. Covers: 200 large nongovernmental companies in the District of Columbia, selected on the basis of number of employees. Entries include: Company name, name of chief executive officer, address and the telephone numbers.

Directory of Websites for International Jobs. Development Concepts Inc. • $19.95 Individuals. Covers: 1,400 websites.

Directory of White & Yellow Goods Manufacturers in India. Steel Guru. • $250 Individuals additional fee for delivery of CD or printed form. Covers: 56 white and yellow goods manufacturers in India. Entries include: Company name, address, telephone number, mobile number, fax number, and e-mail address.

Directory of Wholesale Printing & Office Supplies Sources. Gordon Press Publishers. • Irregular. $260. 95.

The Directory of World Industrial & Commercial Organizations: China, Mainland Volume. Economic Management Publishing House. • $195. Covers: About 4,000 major import and export businesses in mainland China. Database includes: An introduction to China's economic situation, trade control, regulation, investment policy, exchange control, banking services, insurance, China's Coastal Open Areas, major economic management organizations, major chambers of commerce. Entries include: Company name, address, phone, fax, scope of business.

Directory of World Trade Center & Trade Points. EXIM Infotek Private Ltd. • Covers: 280 World Trade Centers and trade points. Entries include: Company name, postal address, telephone, fax, e-mail, website, contact person, designation, and product details.

Directory of Worldwide Export-Import Promotion Center. EXIM Infotek Private Ltd. • Covers: 550 export and import promotion centers worldwide. Entries include: Company name, postal address, telephone, fax, e-mail, website, contact person, designation, and product details.

Dirigeants and Cadres. Editus S.A.R.L. • Annual. Covers: 4,500 executives in the commerce trade and industry in Luxembourg. Entries include: Names and addresses.

Djibouti Business Directory. Business Guide. • $150 Individuals Soft copy. Covers: 1,500 business listings including wholesalers, importers, retailers, business houses, and agents in Djibouti.

DMA's Who's Who in Hong Kong Trading Industries. Asian Market Information & Analysis Centre. • Covers: 1,500 companies in Hong Kong's trading industries. Entries include: Company name, website; contact address, phone, fax, and e-mail; contact person, job title, and e-mail address.

Doing Business in Beijing. China Knowledge Press. • $49.95 Individuals. Covers: Information on Beijing's vital economic statistics, trends, business opportunities, and many more. Entries include: Contact information of government departments, embassies, courier services, executive search firms, and banks.

Doing Business in Memphis. Doing Business in Memphis. • Covers: Over 10,000 Memphis, Tennessee companies, and 25,000 contact names. Entries include: Company name, address, phone, fax, toll-free number, Standard Industrial Classification (SIC) code, names and titles of key personnel, number of employees, descriptions of product/service, product/service provided, e-mail addresses, website, square footage.

Doing Business in Shanghai. China Knowledge

Press. • $49.95 Individuals. Covers: Information on Shanghai's vital economic statistics, trends, business opportunities, and many more. Entries include: Contact information of service-related organizations and government bodies, trade fairs, history, geography, and political system.

Doing Business in Today's Hong Kong. American Chamber of Commerce in Hong Kong. • Publication includes: In an appendix lists of business organizations in Hong Kong, including quality and standards organizations, government agencies, chambers of commerce, and industry-specific associations. Entries include: Organization name, address, phone, fax, telex. Principal content of publication is information on investment, business, sales and manufacturing trade, real estate, and the electronics industry in Hong Kong.

Dominican Republic--American Chamber of Commerce--Membership Directory. U.S. Chamber of Commerce. • Covers: American and Dominican Republic companies and individuals interested in the development of trade within and between the two countries. Entries include: For firms--Company name, address, phone, fax, telex, cable address, names and titles of key personnel, line of business, subsidiary and branch names and locations, locations of plants or branch offices, product/service information. For individuals--Name, title, affiliation, address.

Dominican Republic Industrial and Business Directory. International Business Publications, USA. • Annual. $99.95 Individuals hardcopy, e-book, CD-ROM. Covers: Strategic industrial, investment and business contacts for conducting export-import and investment activity in the country. Contains strategic practical economic and business information.

The Dow Jones Guide to the World Stock Market. Reference Press Inc. • Annual. $39.95. Covers: 2,600 companies in 20 countries that form the Dow Jones World Stock Index. Database includes: A ranking of the companies listed by country, market value, industry, and other factors. Entries include: Company name, address, phone, description, main lines of business, history, sales, earnings, dividends, and financial performance.

Downstate Illinois Business Directory. InfoGroup Inc. • Annual. $415. Number of listings: 188,000. Entries include: Company name, address, phone (including area code). Compiled from telephone company "Yellow Pages," statewide.

Dry Cleaners Directory. InfoGroup Inc. • Annual. Number of listings: 50,053. Entries include: Name, address, phone, size of advertisement, name of owner or manager, number of employees, year first in "Yellow Pages." Compiled from telephone company "Yellow Pages," nationwide.

Dubai Industrial and Business Directory. International Business Publications, USA. • $99.95 Individuals hardcopy, e-book, CD-ROM. Covers: Strategic investment and business contacts for conducting export-import activity in the country. Entries include: Strategic economic and business information.

Dun & Bradstreet Reference Book of American Businesses. Dun & Bradstreet Inc. • Covers: more than 3 million large and small, public and private U.S. companies. Entries include: Company name and phone, branch offices, D&B credit rating, Standard Industrial Classification (SIC) code, new business and rating change indicators, year established, finansial data.

Dun & Bradstreet Regional Business Directories. Dun & Bradstreet Inc. • Annual. Covers: Top 20,000 businesses in one of 54 metropolitan areas in the U.S. Entries include: Company name, address, phone, trade name, Dun & Bradstreet D-U-N-S number, line of business, Standard Industrial Classification (SIC) code, sales volume names and titles of key personnel, number of employees, number of employees at location, parent company, year established, stock exchange symbol, indication of public or private ownership.

Dun & Bradstreet State Sales Guide. Dun & Bradstreet Inc. • Quarterly. $69 Available only to Dun & Bradstreet Credit Services customers. Covers: all businesses in each state that are included in Dun & Bradstreet's national "Reference Book of American Business." A separate "State Sales Guide" is published for each state and the District of Columbia. Entries include: Company name, phone, D&B credit rating, branches, primary Standard Industrial Classification (SIC) code, year established; indicators note new businesses and those with ratings changes.

Dun & Bradstreet 25,000 Series Directory. Dun & Bradstreet Inc. • Annual. $250 per volume. Covers: In three separate volumes, top 25,000 businesses, based on number of employees, for the Asia Pacific, Latin America, and Western Europe. Entries include: Company name, address, phone, fax, telex, Dun & Bradstreet D-U-N-S number, Standard Industrial Classification (SIC) code, name of CEO, number of employees, import/export designation, ownership date.

Dun's Electronic Business Directory. Dun & Bradstreet Inc. • Quarterly. Database covers: about 9 million U.S. financial services, professionals, hospitals and other medical facilities, wholesalers, retailers, construction firms, business services, government agencies, manufacturers, agriculture and mining companies, transportation firms, and utilities. Database includes: For businesses--Name, address, phone, county, Standard Industrial Classification (SIC) code, description of business, population of city, number of employees, type of advertising in yellow pages, whether a company, a corporation, or an individual.

Dun's 15,000 Largest Companies--Belgium. Dun & Bradstreet Inc. • Covers: 15,000 industrial, trading, banking, insurance, and service companies in Belgium. Entries include: Company name, address, phone, fax, telex, equity capital, number of employees, primary and secondary Standard Industrial Classification (SIC) codes, profit/loss ratios, export percentages.

Dun's 15,000 Largest Companies--Portugal. Dun & Bradstreet Inc. • Covers: 15,000 industrial, trading, banking, insurance, and service companies in Portugal. Entries include: Company name, address, phone, fax, telex, equity capital, number of employees, primary and secondary Standard Industrial Classification (SIC) codes, profit/loss ratios, export percentages.

Dun's 15,000 Largest Companies--Spain. Dun & Bradstreet Inc. • Covers: 15,000 industrial, trading, banking, insurance, and service companies in Spain. Entries include: Company name, address, phone, fax, telex, equity capital, number of employees, primary and secondary Standard Industrial Classification (SIC) codes, profit/loss ratios, export percentages.

Dun's 50,000--Spain's Largest Companies. Dun & Bradstreet Inc. • Annual. £438. Covers: 50,000 of the largest marketing companies in Spain. Entries include: Company name, address, operation information, key marketing information, key financial information.

Dun's Guide to Israel. Dun & Bradstreet Inc. • Covers: over 10,000 leading companies in Israel. Entries include: Company name, address, phone, fax, product exported, names and titles of key personnel, Standard Industrial Classification (SIC) code, number of employees, sales volume.

Dun's Key Decision-Makers in Hong Kong. Dun & Bradstreet Inc. • Quarterly. HK$3,850 Individuals. Covers: 10,000 directors and senior executives from leading businesses in Hong Kong. Entries include: D&B D-U-N-S number, company name, address, phone, fax, descriptive line of business, SIC codes, presence in People's Republic of China, number of employees, multiple executive names and titles, year started.

Dun's Regional Business Directory. Dun & Bradstreet Inc. • Annual. $495 commercial. Covers: in regional three-volume sets, approximately 20,000 companies employing 10 or more persons in each of 52 metropolitan areas. Database includes: Marketing advice. Entries include: DUNS number, company name, address, phone, number of employees, parent company, year established, primary and secondary Standard Industrial Classification (SIC) codes, names and titles of key personnel, sales volume, number of employees, stock exchange symbol.

Dun's Regional Directory of Service Companies--Canada. Dun & Bradstreet Inc. • Covers: more than 10,000 service enterprises in Canada with eight or more employees and from Standard Industrial Classification (SIC) codes 07, 47, 60-80, and 82-89. Entries include: Company name, address, phone, SIC codes, parent company, number of employees, names and titles of key personnel, DUNS number.

Duplicating Machines & Supplies-Wholesalers Directory. InfoGroup Inc. • Updated continuously; printed on request. Number of listings: 560. Entries include: Name, address, phone (including area code), size of advertisement, year first in "Yellow Pages," name or owner or manager, number of employees. Compiled from telephone company "Yellow Pages," nationwide.

Durban Regional Chamber of Business--Directory. Durban Regional Chamber of Business. • Covers: about 7,500 businesses in the Durban, South Africa area; welfare organizations in Natal and businesses outside Natal (associate members). Entries include: Company name, address, phone, telex, fax, products or services.

Durham Business Directory & Consumers' Guide. Lloyd Local Directory Div. Lloyd Publications of Canada. • Annual. $40. Covers: 12,000 businesses, professions, services, institutions, and government office within the Durham region of Ontario. Entries include: Company name, address, phone, subsidiary and branch names and locations, product/service.

Dutch Chamber of Commerce--Business Directory. Dutch Chamber of Commerce. • Annual. Covers: 480 individual members representing 180 companies in Hong Kong and mainland China.

DVD Replication Directory. Corbell Publishing Co. • Annual. $457 Individuals plus 40 shipping. Covers: Over 100 video duplicators in the U.S. and Canada. Database includes: Statistics. Entries include: Name, address, phone, fax, url, e-mail address, names and titles of key personnel, financial data, types of accounts, geographical area served, number of employees, formats duplicated, other services offered.

East European Business Information. Headland Press. • Annual. $99. Covers: Organizations providing commercial and industrial information in Eastern Europe, including information on joint ventures, banking, legislation, and marketing. Entries include: Name, address, phone.

East Midlands Chambers of Commerce Business Directory. Kemps Publishing Ltd. • Annual. Covers: Chamber of Commerce listings in East Midlands, Great Britain. Entries include: Name, address, phone, fax.

The East-West Business Directory. Duncan Publishing. • Irregular. $65 plus $3.50 shipping. Covers: Approximately 863 companies that have central and eastern European capital participation, located in over 20 European and North American countries, Australia, and Japan. Database includes: Lists (with addrs.) of official Eastern bloc trade missions and commercial, shipping, banking, airline, and tourist offices in the OECD countries, and an overview of investment activities of Soviet and eastern European state ent. Entries include: Company name, address, phone, telex, name and title of principal executive, number of employees, financial information, ownership structure, statistical data, products or services.

Eastern Europe: A Directory and Sourcebook. Euromonitor International Business Reference Div. • $440. Publication includes: Lists of publishers of private research, journals and newsletters, online databases, consultants, and abstracts and indexes providing information on eastern Europe. Database includes: Economic and demographic data, analysis of business practices, markets, investment opportunities, and rankings.

EC-EDI Solution Provider Directory. Vantage Point & Associates Inc. • Covers: 300 EC/EDI vendors serving business to business (B2B) and healthcare industries.

Economic Guide--Tunisia. Information Economique Africaine. • Biennial. $50. Covers: Industrial, commercial and agricultural entities in Tunisia. Entries include: Company name, address, phone.

Economic World Directory of Japanese Companies in the U.S.A. Economic Salon Ltd. • Biennial. $300. Covers: about 850 companies in the United States that are subsidiaries, divisions, etc., of Japanese parent firms. Entries include: United States company name, address, phone; branch facilities, addresses, and phone numbers; financial data, type of business, names of executives, number of Japanese and United States employees, history, current company information, and similar but less extensive data on parent company.

Edmonds Chamber of Commerce Preferred Business Directory. Greater Edmonds Chamber of Commerce. • Annual. Covers member businesses in Edmonds, Washington. Entries include contact details.

Educators' Guide to Corporate Support. Information Interface Institute. • $375 per year. Covers: Approximately 450 corporations, 300 associations, 200 government agencies, and 100 foundations that provide support to educational concerns. Entries include: Sponsoring organization name, address, phone, programs and teaching aids, contact person, geographic preferences for funding, program preferences, and grade levels supported.

Egypt Business Directory. Business Guide. • $150 Individuals Soft copy. Covers: 65,000 business listings including wholesalers, importers, retailers, business houses, and agents in Egypt.

Egypt Golden Key Directory. International Institute of Trade Relation Promotion, Trade Information Centre of Iran. • £100 Individuals. Covers: 51,901 companies in Egypt. Entries include: Company name, address, telephone, fax, products, services, managing director, and business activities.

Egypt Industrial and Business Directory. International Business Publications, USA. • Annual. $99.95 Individuals paperback, e-book, CD-ROM. Covers: Strategic industrial, investment and business contacts for conducting export-import and investment activity in the country.

850 Key Decision Makers of Listed Companies in Hong Kong. Asian Market Information & Analysis Centre. • Covers: 850 businesses with over 50 employees in Hong Kong. Entries include: Company name, Website, contact address, phone, fax, e-mail, contact person, and job title.

El Salvador--American Chamber of Commerce--Membership Directory. U.S. Chamber of Commerce. • Annual. $100 Nonmembers for investment. Covers: Companies in the U.S. and El Salvador and individuals interested in the development of trade, labor law, investment regulations, economic trends, and foreign policy within and between the two countries. Entries include: For firms--Company, name, address, phone, fax, telex, cable address, names and titles of key personnel, line of business, subsidiary and branch names and locations, locations of plants or branch offices, product/service information. For individuals--Name, title, affiliation, address.

Electric Appliances Major Repair & Parts Directory. InfoGroup Inc. • Annual. Number of listings: 13,612. Entries include: Name, address, phone, size of advertisement, name of owner or manager, number of employees, year first in "Yellow Pages." Compiled from telephone company "Yellow Pages," nationwide.

Electronic Equipment & Supplies--Retail Directory. InfoGroup Inc. • Annual. Number of listings: 13,108. Entries include: Name, address, phone, size of advertisement, name of owner or manager, number of employees, year first in "Yellow Pages." Compiled from telephone company "Yellow Pages," nationwide.

The Electronic Industry Sector in Switzerland. AT Zeitschriftenverlag. • Covers: Computer and electronics companies and products in Switzerland and Liechtenstein. Entries include: Company name, address, phone, product description.

Electronics: Industry Sector Profile. Philippine-German Export Development Project Philippine Bureau of Export Trade Promotion. • Publication includes: Companies exporting electronics from the Philippines. Entries include: Company name, address, phone, fax, name and title of contact, type of business, year established, subsidiary and branch names and locations, financial data, number of employees, government registrations, professional memberships, bank references, supply capability, export experience, business plan. Principal content of publication is an overview of the business environment and electronics industry in the Philippines.

Elsevier Manufacturing and Processing Data Base Directory. Reed Elsevier Group plc Reed Business Information. • Annual. $599. Covers: the manufacturing/processing industry. Entries include: Individual name and title and/or function, company or facility name, address, phone, Standard Industrial Classification (SIC) code, number of employees.

Emerging Europe Autos Directory. Business Monitor International Ltd. • $895 Individuals. Covers: 1,275 top autos executives on 443 leading automotive companies from Bosnia-Herzegovina, Bulgaria, Croatia, the Czech Republic, Estonia, Hungary, Latvia, Lithuania, Macedonia, Poland, Romania, Russia, Serbia, Slovakia, Slovenia and the Ukraine. Entries include: parent company head offices, full company name, address, phone and fax numbers, email and website address, senior contact personnel, company description and profile, nationality, and ownership status.

Emerging Europe Food and Drink Directory. Business Monitor International Ltd. • $895 Individuals. Covers: 1,577 top food and drink executives on 559 leading food and drink companies from Emerging Europe. Entries include: parent company head offices, full company name, address, phone and fax numbers, email and website address, senior contact personnel, company description and profile, nationality, and ownership status.

Emerging Europe Oil and Gas Directory. Business Monitor International Ltd. • $895 Individuals. Covers: 698 top oil and gas executives on 234 leading oil and gas companies from Emerging Europe. Entries include: Parent company head offices, full company name, address, phone and fax numbers, email and website address, senior oil and gas contact personnel, company description and profile, nationality, and ownership status.

Emerging Europe Pharmaceuticals and Healthcare Directory. Business Monitor International Ltd. • $895 Individuals. Covers: 2,212 top pharmaceutical executives at 794 leading pharmaceutical companies from Bosnia, Bulgaria, Croatia, the Czech Republic, Estonia, Hungary, Latvia, Lithuania, Macedonia, Poland, Romania, Russia, Serbia, Slovakia, Slovenia and the Ukraine. Entries include: Parent company head offices, full company name, address, phone and fax numbers, email and website address, senior contact personnel, company description and profile, nationality, and ownership status.

Emerging Europe Telecommunications Directory. Business Monitor International Ltd. • $895 Individuals. Covers: 1,333 top telecommunications executives at 445 leading telecommunications companies from Emerging Europe. Entries include: parent company head offices, full company name, address, phone and fax numbers, email and website address, senior contact personnel, company description and profile, nationality, and ownership status.

Employer Directory for the United States. James R. Albin. • Annual. $99.95. Covers: Approximately 2,000 corporations in the U.S. with more than 500 employees, including all Double Fortune and Forbes 500 companies. Entries include: Company name, address, phone, fax, telex, names and titles of key personnel, number of employees, financial data, description.

EMPRESAS. Brazilian Institute for Information in Science and Technology. • Monthly. Database covers: companies that sell publicly available software programs. Entries include: Name of firm, address, phone, telex, products and services.

Encyclopedia of Chinese-Foreign Joint Ventures, Contractual Joint Ventures, Foreign-Funded Enterprises. Jinghua Publishing House. • $300. Covers: Approximately 30,000 Chinese-foreign joint ventures, contractual joint ventures, and foreign-funded enterprises. Database includes: An introduction to China's laws, regulations, and rules related to Chinese-foreign joint ventures, contractual joint ventures, and foreign-funded enterprises. Entries include: Contact information.

Enterprise: Greater Portland Business Directory. Tower Publishing Co. • Annual. $47.50. Covers: more than 7,000 companies in the Portland, Maine metropolitan area. Entries include: Company name, address, phone, fax, names and titles of contact and key personnel, number of employees, product or service, year established.

The Entrepreneur's Sourcebook. Todd Publications. • $25. Covers: 7,000 organizations, publications, companies, and consultants that provide advice to entrepreneurs and small business owners. Database includes: List of more than 500 books, videos, CDs, and audiocassettes. Entries include: Name, address, phone, fax.

ERISA Top 25,000 Companies: The Red Book of Pension Funds, National Edition. Dun & Bradstreet Inc. • Annual. Covers: 25,000 companies with the largest combined sum of the assets in their pension plans. Entries include: Company name, address, phone, number of employees, total net plan assets, number and type of plans, names and titles of key personnel.

Espresso and Espresso Bars Directory. InfoGroup Inc. • Annual. Number of listings: 1,696. Entries include: Name, address, phone, size of advertisement, name of owner or manager, number of employees, year first in "Yellow Pages." Compiled from telephone company "Yellow Pages," nationwide.

Essex Business Directory. Burrows Publishing Ltd. • Covers: Over 10,000 businesses in Essex. Entries include: Name, address, phone, fax, e-mail, website, key organization contact, year of establishment, size of company, turnover, and a brief description of company activity.

ESSOR. Union Francaise d'Annuaires Professionnels. • Annual. Covers: more than 200,000 French companies involved in industry and services. Entries include: Company name, address, phone, fax, telex, names and titles of key personnel, line of business, number of employees, registered capital, sales, product descriptions, legal and administrative information.

Estonia Government and Business Contacts Handbook. International Business Publications, USA. • $99.95 Individuals hardcopy, E-book and CD-ROM. Covers: Strategic government and business information, export-import activity in the country, investment, business contacts and regulations.

Estonia Industrial and Business Directory. International Business Publications, USA. • Annual. $99.95 Individuals paperback, e-book, CD-ROM. Covers: Strategic industrial, investment and business contacts for conducting export-import and investment activity in the country. Contains strategic practical economic and business information.

Ethiopia Business Directory. Business Guide. • $150 Individuals Soft copy. Covers: 9,000 business listings including wholesalers, importers, retailers, business houses, and agents in Ethiopia.

The Euromoney Syndicated Lending Handbook. Euromoney Institutional Investor P.L.C. • Annual. $195 Individuals. Covers: Contact details for 307 relevant personnel in banks, law firms, rating agencies, and associations involved in syndicated lending worldwide. Entries include: Company name, address, phone, fax, e-mail address, Web site, telex number, and names and titles of key personnel.

Europa--Key European Enterprises. AP Information Services Ltd. • $600 Individuals. Covers: Over 50,000 leading European companies. Entries include: Statistical profiles and geographical information.

European Business Association--Membership Directory. European Business Association. • Annual. Features profiles of member businesses. Entries include: Company contact information.

European Business Information Sourcebook. Headland Press. • Annual. $139. Covers: Sources of European business information, including databanks, online services, market research firms, sources of official statistics, business research services, libraries, directories, magazines, and newspapers. Entries include: Name, address, phone, fax.

European Business Top 1000. European Business Press Group N.V. • Annual. $398. Covers: About 1,500 companies in 19 European countries ranked according to financial success; approximately 4,000 company executives. Database includes: Private corporations, government and union controlled enterprises, non-European multinational companies consolidated at the European level, mergers, acquisitions. Entries include: Company name, address, phone, fax, names and titles of key personnel, gross and net profit, number of employees, depreciation, equity, cash flow, affiliations.

European Cooler Company Directory. Zenith International Ltd. • $823 Individuals hard copy. Covers: active cooler distributors in the markets of West and East Europe. Entries include: company name, address, telephone number, fax number, website, email, company ownership, number of employees, subsidiaries, company activities, and names and job titles of senior management.

European Development Directory. Euromonitor International Business Reference Div. • Irregular. $335. Covers: over 700 government agencies, banks, and other organizations in Europe that administer business development grants and related financial aid. Database includes: List of available grants and funding opportunities, with contact information. Entries include: Organization or agency name, address, phone, fax, names and titles of key personnel, description.

European Directory of Business Information Libraries. Euromonitor International Business Reference Div. • Irregular. $650. Covers: More than 2,000 European business libraries and services. Entries include: location, accessibility, fees, stock, and subject area.

European Directory of Financial Information Sources. Euromonitor International Business Reference Div. • $160. Covers: Sources of financial information for companies in Europe, including official sources and publications, libraries, information services, banks and other financial institutions, accountancy firms and tax advisors, stockbrokers, stock exchanges, databases, indexes, abstracts, banking journals, and European business contacts. Entries include: Name, address, phone, fax, year founded.

European Directory of Management Consultants. AP Information Services Ltd. • Biennial. $130. Covers: Approximately 3,500 management consultancy firms in varying areas of activity and industry in Europe. Entries include: Company name, address, phone, fax, managing director, principal consultants, business contacts, year established, number of consulting staff, financial data, geographical area served, languages, locations of branch offices, description of activities, industry area expertise, major clients, professional memberships.

European Federation of Management Consultants Associations--European Directory: European Directory of Management Consultants. European Federation of Management Consultants Associations. • Covers: 22 associations plus members. Entries include: Name, address, phone, fax; activities; date established; number of consultants.

European International Business Academy--Membership Directory. European International Business Academy. • Covers: 300 individuals involved in international business.

The European Market for High Voltage Switchgear. ABS Publications. • $800. Covers: European manufacturers of high voltage switchgear (greater than 1kV). Entries include: Utility statistics, company profiles, trade production and market data for both supply and demand.

European Markets: A Guide to Company and Industry Information Sources. MarketResearch.com. • Irregular. $335. Covers: sources worldwide of information on European companies. Entries include: Source name, contact name, address, phone, fax, telex.

European Regional Incentives. Bowker-Saur. • Annual. $85. Directory and review of regional grants and other aid available for industrial and business expansion or relocation from European Community member state governments and Sweden. Entries include: Program title, organization name, address, phone, name and title of contact, description of program, type of incentives (grant, loan, tax concession, etc.), application procedure, selection procedure, eligibility requirements, legislative authority, maximum and average awards.

European Sources of Scientific and Technical Information. Cartermill International. • Irregular. $225. Covers: over 1,500 patents and standards offices, national offices of information, and organizations active in scientific fields in Europe, including former Soviet bloc nations. Provides English-language version of foreign terminology. Entries include: Organization name, address, phone, fax, e-mail and website addresses, year founded, name of contact, parent company, subject(s) covered, publications, library facilities, and information, consulting, and training services.

European Union--Food and Drinks Directory. Trade Publishing Resources. • Covers: 100,000 brand names, 29,000 executives, and 16,000 companies engaged in importing, wholesaling, and retailing of food and drinks.

European Valves for Control, Isolation and Safety. Roles & Associates Ltd. • Irregular. $96. Covers: suppliers of valves, actuators, auxiliary equipment, piping and connectors in Europe. Entries include: Company name, address, phone, descriptions of services, products provided.

European Venture Capital Association--Yearbook. KPMG L.L.P. (U.K.). • Annual. Covers: about 175 member companies that provide venture capital funding and services; 10 national venture capital associations in Europe. Database includes: Report and statistics on the venture capital industry in Europe. Entries include: For companies--Name, address, phone, telex, name of chief executive, type of firm, minimum and preferred investment amounts, type of financing, industry and geographical preferences, contact names. For associations--Name, address, phone, telex, contact name.

Europe's 15,000 Largest Companies. GAP Books. • Annual. £415 Individuals hardcover. Covers: 8,000 leading industrial companies, 2,500 trading companies, 350 banks, 350 transportation firms, 200 insurance firms, 100 hotels and restaurants, 150 advertising agencies; and 250 other firms; also includes ranked lists (without extensive data) of 125 largest money losers, 500 most profitable firms, 250 most profitable firms using profits as percentage of sales. Entries include: Company name, headquarters, contact, International Standard Industrial Classification (ISIC) code, sales, rank, number of employees and shareholders, profit, sales per employee, and other operating ratios. Headings are in English, German, and French.

Europe's Major and Medium Sized Companies Directory. Euromonitor International Business Reference Div. • Irregular. $990. Covers: 12,000 companies headquartered in eastern and western Europe. Database includes: Ranked lists of companies. Entries include: Company name, address, phone, fax, telex, type of company, ownership, major subsidiaries, names and titles of key personnel, products, outlets, number of employees, sales, recent company developments.

Europe's Medium Sized Companies Directory. Euromonitor International Business Reference Div. • $550 Individuals. Covers: More than 4,000 medium-sized companies in Europe. Entries include: Company name, address, phone, fax, contact experts.

Europe's Top 1,000 Food & Drink Companies. Datamonitor. • $995. Covers: 1,000 leading food and drink companies in Europe. Entries include: Company name, address, phone, telex, names and titles of key personnel, number of employees; financial data, product/service, Standard Industrial Classification (SIC) code, production locations.

Expatriate's Guide to Savings & Investments. Public Relations Consultants Association. • Biennial. $20. Covers: Over 400 investment funds and their management companies situated outside of the United Kingdom. Entries include: Name, address, phone, fax, names and titles of key personnel, procedures, policy, financial data.

Export and Import Directory of Peru. Association of Peruvian Exporters. • Annual. $60. Covers: Exporters, importers, and export service firms in Peru.

Export--Buyers Guide Issue. Johnston International Publishing Corp. • Annual. $10. Publication includes: About 250 manufacturers and exporters of hardware, air conditioning and refrigeration equipment, garden supplies, sporting goods, automotive accessories, and building products. Limited to advertisers. Entries include: Company name, address, phone, telex, names of contacts.

Export Denmark. Kongeriget Danmarks Handels-Kalender. • Annual. Covers: 10,000 exporters in Denmark. Entries include: Company name, address, phone, telex number, products, trade names.

Export Mail-Order. Todd Publications. • Biennial. $20. Covers: Suppliers, overseas firms seeking exports, firms serving as export management companies, and other information to aid in choosing products to export.

Exporter Directory. People Publishing Ltd. • Annual. Covers: 2,000 export companies in New Zealand seeking overseas contacts and clients.

Extel Handbook of Market Leaders. Extel Financial Ltd. • Semiannual. $90. Covers: Major quoted companies. Entries include: Adress, phone, name of chairman, financial data.

Eyeglasses Directory. InfoGroup Inc. • Annual. Number of listings: 18,811. Entries include: Name, address, phone, size of advertisement, name of owner or manager, number of employees, year first in "Yellow Pages." Compiled from telephone company "Yellow Pages," nationwide.

Facial Skin Care Directory. InfoGroup Inc. • Annual. Number of listings: 11,460. Entries include: Name, address, phone, size of advertisement, name of owner or manager, number of employees, year first in "Yellow Pages." Compiled from telephone company "Yellow Pages," nationwide.

Facilities Design & Management--Directory Issue. Bpi Communications Inc. • $10. Publication includes: List of about 2,000 suppliers of office furnishings, equipment, services; professional associations. Entries include: For suppliers--Company name, address, phone, products or services. For associations--Name, address.

Facilities Design & Management--Directory of Consultants & Service Firms Issue. Bpi Communications Inc. • Annual. $7. Publication includes: Listing of firms offering products, services, and consulting services to facilities designers and managers.

Family Clothing Stores Directory. InfoGroup Inc. • Annual. Number of listings: 22,853. Entries include: Name, address, phone, size of advertisement, name of owner or manager, number of employees, year first in "Yellow Pages." Compiled from telephone company "Yellow Pages," nationwide.

Faulkner & Gray's European Business Directory. Thomson Financial Inc. • Annual. $295. Covers: over 2,000 attorneys, accountants, consultants, search firms, translators, shippers, commercial and investment banks, and industry leaders in Europe and the U.S. interested in or presently doing business in Europe. Database includes: Profiles of 40 countries. Entries include: Company or personal name, address, phone, telex, name and title of contact, subsidiary and branch names and locations, description of service.

FCCIA Directory. Union des Chambers de Commerce et d'Industrie Francaises a I'Etranger. • $45 Individuals available in French version only. Covers: 107 Chambers of Commerce and industry in Europe, Africa, Middle East, North America, South America, Asia, and Oceania. Entries include: Contact information and name of staff in 77 countries.

Field Trade Directory of Peru. Field Servicio de Informaciones del Peru. • Annual. $65. Covers: 7,000 Peruvian importers, factories, exporters, wholesalers, retailers, and more than 1,000 business activities. Database includes: Information on hotels, restaurants, and general information on selling, buying, and information sources in Peru. Entries include: Name, address, phone, cable, telex, manager name.

Financial Annual Registrars Service. Extel Financial Ltd. • Annual. $110. Covers: United Kingdom companies listed on one of the UK stock exchanges. Entries include: Company name, registrar's name, address, phone, fax, telex, types of stocks and shares, nominal value.

Financial Post Corporate Surveys. Financial Post DataGroup. • Database covers: 6,300 Canadian public companies and 19,000 defunct companies. Includes financial and operational information, key events, and key executives.

Financial Review of Alien Insurers. National Association of Insurance Commissioners. • Annual. $275 per year, including updates; payment with order. Covers: alien insurance companies operating in the United States market. Entries include: Company name, address, balance sheet, operating statement, financial statement with notes, and names of auditors; description of trust account with location, valuation, and expiration date.

Financing Manufacturing Efficiency and Growth: A Manufacturer's Guide to State & Federal Resources. Northeast-Midwest Institute. • Triennial. $36. Covers: federal and state government programs in business development, finance, targeted development, infrastructure, cooperative research and technology centers, trade, training, tax incentive, and similar activities. Entries include: For federal agencies--Agency or unit name, address, description of program with objectives, funding, eligible applicants, eligible activities, requirements, funding cycle, and examples of past recipients. For state agencies--Agency name, address, phone, description of program, requirements, case studies.

Financing Opportunities for New Hampshire-Based Businesses. Office of Economic Initiatives. • Covers: sources of financial assistance for businesses in New Hampshire, including federal, state, and local government agencies, nonprofit organizations, and venture capital firms. Entries include: Name, address, phone, description of activities.

Find A Christian Business. Initiate Media Ltd. • Annual. $29.95 Individuals. Covers: Service providers and businesses owned and managed by Christians in New Zealand.

Finland Government and Business Contacts Handbook. International Business Publications, USA. • $99.95 Individuals. Covers: Strategic government and business information, export-import activity in the country, investment, business contacts and regulations.

Finnish Trade. Federation of Finnish Trade and Commerce. • Annual. Covers: Member firms of the Federation of Finnish Commerce and Trade. Entries include: Company name, address, phone, fax, telex.

Firms Headquartered in Kansas. Kansas Department of Commerce - Office of Minority and Women Business Development. • Annual. $5. Covers: 400 firms headquartered in Kansas. Entries include: For companies--Name, address, phone, principal officials, sales, number of employees, products.

Fish (Tropical) Dealers Directory. InfoGroup Inc. • Annual. Number of listings: 2,236. Entries include: Name, address, phone, size of advertisement, name of owner or manager, number of employees, year first in "Yellow Pages." Compiled from telephone company "Yellow Pages," nationwide.

Fitness Centers Directory. InfoGroup Inc. • Annual. Number of listings: 17,012. Entries include: Name, address, phone, size of advertisement, name of owner or manager, number of employees, year first in "Yellow Pages." Compiled from telephone company "Yellow Pages," nationwide.

500 Contractors Receiving the Largest Dollar Volume of Prime Contract Awards for RDT&E. U.S. Department of Defense. • Annual. Covers the 500 largest contractors (including business, nonprofit organizations, foreign contractors, and government agencies) that received the largest dollar volume of prime contract awards over $25,000 for military research, development, test, and evaluation projects.

The 5,000 Largest French Companies. Le Nouvel Economiste. • Annual. Covers: 5,000 leading companies in France. Entries include: Company name, address, phone.

Florida Industries Guide. Industries Guides Inc. • Biennial. $95. Number of listings: 10,000. Entries include: Company name, address, phone, name of contact, products or services, number of employees, sic codes, fax and 800 numbers.

Florida Trend--Directory of Public Companies Issue. Trend Book Div. • Annual. $3.95. Publication includes: List of 250 publicly owned companies headquartered in Florida. Entries include: Name, address, phone, name of chief executive, financial keys, product or service.

Florida's Gold Coast Business & Employer's Directory: Palm Beach, Ft. Lauderdale, Miami. Silver Reede Services. • Covers: Approximately 1,000 manufacturers, banks, hospitals, retailers, resorts, real estate development firms, and other corporate organizations employing 20 or more people in the metropolitan Palm Beach, Ft. Lauderdale, and Miami, Florida areas. Entries include: Company or organization name, address, phone, name and title of contact, number of employees, description of products, services, or projects, and Standard Industrial Classification (SIC) code (where appropriate).

Florida's Gulf Coast Business and Employers Directory: Tampa, Clearwater, St. Petersburg. Silver Reede Services. • Covers: manufacturers, banks, hospitals, retailers, resorts, real estate development firms, and other corporate organizations employing 20 or more people, in the Tampa/Clearwater/St. Petersburg, Florida area. Entries include: Company or organization name, address, phone, name and title of contact, number of employees, description of products, services, or projects, Standard Industrial Classification (SIC) code (where appropriate).

The Fono Directory. CMP Information Ltd. • $66. Covers: Radio, record labels, television stations, artist management, and retail organizations in Europe including the United Kingdom and Ireland for those interested in the music industry. Entries include: Name, address, phone, fax.

Food Business Mergers & Acquisitions. Food Institute. • Annual. $295 Individuals print version and disk. Covers: Companies involved in food industry company mergers or take-overs, including import-export, banking, and advertising firms. Database includes: Ratings and financial information for selected firms from Moody's Investors Service. Entries include: Acquiring company name, location; acquired company name, location, products, number of units or stores.

Food Industry--Slovakia. I.S.M.C. Information Systems and Marketing Contacts Ltd. • $65. Covers: Companies in the food industry in Slovakia, including suppliers of technologies for food processing and packaging.

Foreign Companies in Asia Yearbook. Business Monitor International Ltd. • $5,445 Individuals 40% discount. Covers: 49,270 senior executive contacts on 16,775 foreign company subsidiaries across 32 industry sectors in Asia. Entries include: full company name, address, phone and fax numbers, email and web addresses, and key contact names and titles.

Foreign Subsidiaries in Michigan. Global Business Development. • Irregular. Covers: over 930 Michigan subsidiaries of companies from outside the U.S. Entries include: Subsidiary company name, address; parent company name, address; product/service, type of establishment in Michigan.

Fortune Directory. Fortune Directories. • Annual. $25 payment with order. Covers: combined, in a fall reprint, 500 largest United States industrial corporations (published in an April issue each year) and the Service 500 (published in a June issue). The Service 500 comprises 100-company rankings of each of the largest diversified service, and commercial banking companies, and 50-company rankings each of the largest, diversified financial, savings institutions, life insurance, retailing, transportation, and utility companies. Database includes: Various other rankings by different measures. Entries include: Company name, address, headquarters city, sales, assets, net income, market value, comparative earnings per share for ten years, names and titles of key personnel, phone, and various other statistical and financial information.

Fortune Directory of United States Corporations. Time Inc. • Annual. $25. Publication includes: The top 500 firms in the U.S. Entries include: Company name, address, headquarters address, financial data.

Foundation Directory. Foundation Center. • Annual. $215 Individuals main. Over 10,000 of the largest foundations in the United States, all having $1.3 million or more in assets or awarding $400,000 or more in grants in a recent year.

Foundations of the 1990s: A Directory of Newly Established Foundations. • $150 plus shipping cost. Covers: Over 9,000 independent, community, and corporate foundations incorporated since 1989. Entries include: Foundation name, address, phone, name and title of contact, names of trustees and officers, application procedures, financial data, grant-making interests and giving limitations, and grant descriptions.

France Environment. Editions Louis Johanet. • Annual. Covers: 8,000 office machinery and supply manufacturers, wholesalers, and distributors in France. Entries include: Company name, address, phone, telex number.

France Government and Business Contacts Handbook. International Business Publications, USA. • $99.95 Individuals. Covers: Strategic government and business information, export-import activity in the country, investment, business contacts and regulations.

France Industrial and Business Directory. International Business Publications, USA. • Annual. $99.95 Individuals hardcopy, e-book, CD-ROM. Covers: Detailed information on investment, export-import business opportunities, foreign economic assistance projects, government and business contacts.

France 30,000. Dun & Bradstreet France S.A. • Annual. Covers: 30,000 companies in France. Entries include: Company name, address, phone, date founded, number of employees, key personnel, capital, turnover, affiliations.

Free Money from the Federal Government for Small Businesses and Entrepreneurs. John Wiley and Sons Inc. Technical Insights. • $18.95 Individuals. Covers: Approximately 1,500 grants and funding programs from 52 government agencies. Database includes: Bibliography. Entries include: Program name, description, contact information.

Free State Directory. A.C. Braby (Pty) Ltd. • Annual. R 100. Covers: businesses in Free State province of South Africa. Entries include: Company name, address, phone, fax, descriptive text.

Fremont Chamber of Commerce--Community Profile and Business Directory. Fremont Chamber of Commerce. • Annual. Covers: Listing of member businesses. Entries include: name, address, phone, fax.

French Companies and their Partners Abroad. DAFSA. • Annual. Covers: 80,000 French companies in France and abroad. Entries include: Company name, address, phone, ownership connections, subsidiaries, ownership percentages.

French Company Handbook. International Herald Tribune. • Annual. $50. Covers: 120 major French companies included in the SBF 120 Index, plus other important bond issuers. Entries include: Company name, address, phone, fax, telex, names of principal officials, description of business, background, sales breakdown, major known shareholders and percentages of stock held, subsidiaries and holdings (with brief details on each), international activities, key recent developments, investments, and financial data for five years.

Futons Directory. InfoGroup Inc. • Annual. Number of listings: 1,793. Entries include: Name, address, phone, size of advertisement, name of owner or manager, number of employees, year first in "Yellow Pages." Compiled from telephone company "Yellow Pages," nationwide.

Gale Directory of Databases (GDD). Cengage Learning Inc. • Semiannual. $723 Individuals in 6 volumes. Offers comprehensive coverage of the electronic database industry with profiles for more than 15,000 databases and more than 3,000 producers, online services, and vendors.

Gardena Valley Business Directory. Gardena Valley Chamber of Commerce. • Covers: About 500 member industrial, commercial, and service firms in the Gardena, California area. Entries include: Company name, address, phone, line of business, contact name.

Gardeners Directory. InfoGroup Inc. • Annual. Number of listings: 33,994. Entries include: Name, address, phone, size of advertisement, name of owner or manager, number of employees, year first in "Yellow Pages." Compiled from telephone company "Yellow Pages," nationwide.

Gauteng Business Directory. Intratex Holdings. • Covers: Businesses in the Rand/Pretoria area. Entries include: Company name, address, phone.

General Merchandise--Wholesale Directory. InfoGroup Inc. • Annual. Number of listings: 1,045. Entries include: Name, address, phone, size of advertisement, name of owner or manager, number of employees, year first in "Yellow Pages." Compiled from telephone company "Yellow Pages," nationwide.

General Trade Index & Business Guide. Business Foundation Company Ltd. • Annual. $135. Publication includes: More than 3,500 public and private Polish companies seeking foreign joint ventures or foreign trade opportunities. Entries include: Company name, address, phone. Principal content of publication is information on doing business and living in Poland.

George D. Hall's Directory of New England Manufacturers. George D. Hall Company Inc. • $128 plus $4.95 shipping. Covers: about 21,000 manufacturers in Connecticut, Maine, Massachusetts, New Hampshire, Rhode Island, and Vermont. Entries include: For manufacturers--company name, address, phone, names of principal executives, Standard Industrial Classification (SIC) code, product/service, number of employees, whether firm exports or imports. For banks--Name, address, phone, names of principal executives, service, number of employees.

Georgia Business Directory. InfoGroup Inc. • Annual. $520 both print & CD-ROM. Covers: 346,843 businesses in Georgia. Entries include: Company name, address, phone, number of employees, name of owner or manager, sales volume. Compiled from telephone company "Yellow Pages," statewide. All states covered (see separate entries).

Georgia Industries Guide. Industries Guides Inc. • $95. Covers: Approximately 9,000 manufacturers in Georgia. Entries include: Company name, address, phone.

Georgia Manufacturing Directory. Georgia Chamber of Commerce. • Annual. $99.95 book; payment must accompany order. Covers: about 9,400 firms manufacturing products within Standard Industrial Classification (SIC) codes 20-39. Entries include: Company name, address, phone, names of principal executives, number of men and women employees, products or services, 4-digit SIC numbers, date established, market served, e-mail and web addresses.

Georgia Republic Business and Industrial Directory. International Business Publications, USA. • Annual. $99.95 Individuals hardcover, e-book, CD-ROM. Covers: Strategic industrial, investment and business contacts for conducting export-import and investment activity in the country.

Geriatric Care Directory. InfoGroup Inc. • Annual. Number of listings: 5,059. Entries include: Name, address, phone, size of advertisement, name of owner or manager, number of employees, year first in "Yellow Pages." Compiled from telephone company "Yellow Pages," nationwide.

German Business CD-ROM. Datamedia GmbH. • Description: CD-ROM. Database covers: approximately 1.8 businesses in Germany. Entries include: Company name, address, phone, fax, classification information.

German Canadian Business and Trade Directory. German Canadian and Trade Publication. • Covers: Companies in all business sectors. Entries include: Multinational corporations, public institutions, professional associations, and importer/exporter.

German Chamber of Commerce in China--Membership Directory. German Industry & Commerce Company Ltd. • 1,200 ¥ Nonmembers. Number of listings: 1,800. Entries include: Company name, address, e-mail, phone, and fax numbers.

Germany Government and Business Contacts Handbook. International Business Publications, USA. • $99.95 Individuals. Covers: Strategic government and business information, export-import activity in the country, investment, business contacts and regulations.

Germany Industrial and Business Directory. International Business Publications, USA. • Annual. $99.95 Individuals hardcover, e-book, CD-ROM. Covers: Strategic industrial, investment and business contacts for conducting export-import and investment activity in the country.

Germany's Top 300. Frankfurter Allgemeine Zeitung GmbH. • Annual. $595. Covers: Germany's top 300 corporations, banks, and insurance companies; corporations are ranked based on their turnover; banks are ranked according to business volume; insurance companies are ranked according to premium income. Entries include: Company name, address, phone, fax ranking, products and activities, Standard Industrial Classification (SIC) codes, names of key management personnel, number of employees, turnover, pre-tax profit, net profit, cash flow, assets, investments, cash reserves, shareholders, investor relations, dividend, and high/low share price.

Gevers International Consultants. Gevers International Consultants. • Annual. $75 Individuals. Covers: 10,000 consulting firms, including accountants, property consultants, lawyers, management consultants, and tax consultants in 124 countries. Entries include: Company name, address, phone, telex number, description, associate firms, language, clients, countries covered.

Gibaud Directory--Industrial, Commercial and Trade Enterprises. Annuaire Gibaud. • Annual. Covers: 27,000 industrial, commercial and trade enterprises in France. Entries include: Company name, address, phone, name and title of contact, year established, number of employees, subsidiaries, manager name, product/service.

Gids bij de Officiele Prijscourant van de Amsterdamse Effectenbeurs. Uitgeverij J. H. de Bussy B.V. • Annual. $195. Covers: companies listed on the Amsterdam Stock Exchange. Database includes: Information on shares, bonds, warrants, etc. Entries include: Company name, address, financial data.

Giftwares--Manufacturers Directory. InfoGroup Inc. • Annual. Number of listings: 1,180. Entries include: Name, address, phone, size of advertisement, name of owner or manager, number of employees, year first in "Yellow Pages." Compiled from telephone company "Yellow Pages," nationwide.

Glasses Directory--Sun & Ski. InfoGroup Inc. • Annual. Number of listings: 3,278. Entries include: Name, address, phone, size of advertisement, name of owner or manager, number of employees, year first in "Yellow Pages." Compiled from telephone company "Yellow Pages," nationwide.

Glassware (Collectible) Directory. InfoGroup Inc. • Annual. Number of listings: 12,366. Entries include: Name, address, phone, size of advertisement, name of owner or manager, number of employees, year first in "Yellow Pages." Compiled from telephone company "Yellow Pages," nationwide.

Global Business and Industrial Directories Publishers Directory. International Business Publications, USA. • $99.95 Individuals. Covers: Largest business and industrial directories publishers worldwide.

Global Business Associations. International Business Publications, USA. • Covers: Approximately 1,000 largest business associations in over 100 countries.

Global Business Contacts Directory. International Business Publications, USA. • $99.95 Individuals. Covers: Major business and government contacts in over 100 countries.

Global Business Directory. INFOT Inc. • $51.85 CD-ROM. Covers: 801,813 major global companies, businesses and services, suppliers, manufacturers, buyers, agents, importers, exporters, and organizations by industry. Entries include: Email and website addresses, telephone and fax number, and business titles and descriptions.

Global Central Banks Directory. International Business Publications, USA. • $99.95 Individuals paperback. Covers: Central banks for over 150 countries.

Global Chambers of Commerce Directory. International Business Publications, USA. • $99.95 Individuals paperback. Covers: Approximately 3,000 U.S. Local chambers of commerce interested in international trade.

The Global Directory of Financial Information Vendors. QSU Publishing. • $95. Covers: On-line financial services vendors and their operating systems. Database includes: Geographic market information and principal applications.

Global Economic, Financial, and Development Organizations Directory. International Business Publications, USA. • $99.95 Individuals paperback. Covers: International economic development agencies and organizations in over 100 countries.

Global Foreign Trade Barriers to U.S. Products and Services Exports Handbook. International Business Publications, USA. • $99.95 Individuals paperback. Covers: Foreign trade barriers to the U.S. Products and services exports to various countries.

Global Investment Funds Directory. International Business Publications, USA. • $99.95 Individuals paperback. Covers: Major investment funds interested in international ventures.

Global Offshore Business and Investment Contacts Handbook. International Business Publications, USA. • Annual. $99.95. Covers: Business and investment contacts in 33 offshore countries and territories. Entries include: Contact details.

Global Offshore Business Laws and Regulations Handbook. International Business Publications, USA. • Annual. $99.95. Covers: Business laws and regulations for conducting business in 33 offshore countries and territories.

Global Offshore Investment and Business Guide. International Business Publications, USA. • $99.95 Individuals paperback. Comprehensive guide for conducting offshore business.

Global Offshore Tax Guide. International Business Publications, USA. • Annual. $99.95. Covers: Tax regulations guidelines for 33 offshore countries and territories.

Global Pere Investors Directory. PEI London. • $1,195 Individuals. Covers: 1,200 institutions investing in unlisted real estate funds. Entries include: Contact information.

Global Tax Guide Handbook. International Business Publications, USA. • $149. Basic tax guide for over 80 countries.

Global Top 1,000 Bakery Companies. Datamonitor. • $995. Covers: 1,000 leading international bakery companies. Entries include: Company name, address, phone, telex, names and titles of key personnel, number of employees; financial data, product/service, Standard Industrial Classification (SIC) code, production locations.

Global Top 1,000 Canned Food Companies. Datamonitor. • $995. Covers: 1,000 leading international canned food companies. Entries include: Company name, address, phone, telex, names and titles of key personnel, number of employees; financial data, product/service, Standard Industrial Classification (SIC) code, production locations.

Global Top 1,000 Confectionery Companies. Datamonitor. • $995. Covers: 1,000 leading international confectionery companies. Entries include: Company name, address, phone, telex, names and titles of key personnel, number of employees; financial data, product/service, Standard Industrial Classification (SIC) code, production locations.

Global Top 1,000 Dairy Companies. Datamonitor. • $995. Covers: 1,000 leading international dairy companies. Entries include: Company name, address, phone, telex, names and titles of key personnel, number of employees; financial data, product/service, Standard Industrial Classification (SIC) code, production locations.

Global Top 1,000 Frozen Food Companies. Datamonitor. • $995. Covers: 1,000 leading international frozen food companies. Entries include: Company name, address, phone, telex, names and titles of key personnel, number of employees; financial data, product/service, Standard Industrial Classification (SIC) code, production locations.

Global Top 1,000 Ready Meals Companies. Datamonitor. • $995. Covers: 1,000 leading international companies that provide ready meals. Entries include: Company name, address, phone, telex, names and titles of key personnel, number of employees; financial data, product/service, Standard Industrial Classification (SIC) code, production locations.

Global Trade & Business Show Directory. International Business Publications, USA. • $99.95 Individuals paperback. Covers: Approximately 1,000 largest trade, business, and professional shows and exhibitions in the U.S. and other countries.

Global Trade Leads. INFOT Inc. • $114.75 CD-ROM; additional $150 for MS Access format. Covers: More than 493,448 suppliers & buyers active in major online market places. Entries include: Email and website addresses, telephone and fax number, and business titles and descriptions.

Global Trade Review Directory. Exporta Publishing & Events Ltd. • Annual. £125 Individuals non-subscribers. Covers: 450 service providers to global trade, commodity, and export finance markets. Entries include: Company contact information.

Global U.S. Economic Assistance Guide. International Business Publications, USA. • $99.95. Covers: Information on U.S. economic assistance worldwide.

Global World Trade Centers Directory. International Business Publications, USA. • $99.95 Individuals paperback. Covers: World Trade Centers located in over 100 countries.

The Globe and Mail Report on Business: Canada Company Handbook. Globe Interactive. • Annual. $49.95. Covers: over 400 Canadian companies. Entries include: Company name, address, phone, line of business, names and titles of key personnel, financial data including balance sheets, stock ratios and prices, and debts, rankings by profit, revenues, and assets, description of activities, stock exchange symbols.

Glues Directory--Wholesalers. InfoGroup Inc. • Annual. Number of listings: 916. Entries include: Name, address, phone, size of advertisement, name of owner or manager, number of employees, year first in "Yellow Pages." Compiled from telephone company "Yellow Pages," nationwide.

Gold Book of Venture Capital Firms. Todd Publications. • $75. Covers: 869 venture capital firms in 37 specialties. Database includes: Introduction on working with venture capital firms. Entries include: Firm name, names and titles of key personnel, specialty, preferred stage of financing.

Golf Cars & Carts Dealers. InfoGroup Inc. • Annual. Number of listings: 1,507. Entries include: Name, address, phone, size of advertisement, name of owner or manager, number of employees, year first in "Yellow Pages." Compiled from telephone company "Yellow Pages," nationwide.

Goods and Services--Firm Directory. International Bureau for Information and Telecommunications. • Annual. $17. Covers: 5,000 leading and active companies in the Moscow region and their products and services. Entries include: Company name, address, phone, products or services provided.

Government Product News--Buyers Guide for Office Equipment Issue. Intertec Publishing. • Annual. $5. Publication includes: List of over 1,000 manufacturers of office equipment. Entries include: Company name, address, phone, name and title of contact.

Gown--Rental and Sales Directory. InfoGroup Inc. • Annual. Number of listings: 8,328. Entries include: Name, address, phone, size of advertisement, name of owner or manager, number of employees, year first in "Yellow Pages." Compiled from telephone company "Yellow Pages," nationwide.

Gravel Directory--Wholesalers. InfoGroup Inc. • Annual. Number of listings: 12,943. Entries include: Name, address, phone, size of advertisement, name of owner or manager, number of employees, year first in "Yellow Pages." Compiled from telephone company "Yellow Pages," nationwide.

Great Big Book of Business Lists. Entrepreneur Press. • $34.95 Individuals paperback. Covers: Approximately 10,000 listings of business information. Entries include: Business' contact information.

Greater Calgary & Edmonton Business. Scott's Directories. • Annual. $209 Individuals CD-ROM, pinpointer. Covers: 15,400+ manufacturers, manufacturers' sales offices, wholesalers, wholesale agents, and distributors operating in Greater Calgary and Edmonton along with 28,900+ business contact names. Entries include: Company name, address, phone, fax, names and titles of key personnel, number of employees, parent companies, SIC, product, year established.

Greater Cincinnati Chamber of Commerce--Cincinnati USA Business Connections Directory. Greater Cincinnati Chamber of Commerce. • Covers: Over 5,000 member firms in the Greater Cincinnati area (Hamilton, Clermont, Butler, Brown, and Warren counties in Ohio; Boone, Campbell, Grant, Gallatin, Pendleton, and Kenton counties in Kentucky; Dearborn and Ohio counties in Indiana). Entries include: Company name, address, phone, market area, names and titles of principal executives, number of employees, product/service, Standard Industrial Classification (SIC) code, date established, whether firm imports or exports, branches, parent company, annual sales, whether publicly or privately held.

Greater Dover Chamber of Commerce Business Directory. Greater Dover Chamber of Commerce. • Covers: Member businesses in New Hampshire. Entries include: Company name, address, phone, name of contact, category of product or service.

Greater San Diego Chamber of Commerce Business Referral Directory. San Diego Regional Chamber of Commerce. • Covers: Approximately 4,500 member businesses in San Diego, California. Entries include: Company name, address, phone, name and title of contact, products or services.

Greater Vancouver Business. Scott's Directories. • Annual. $299 Individuals CD-ROM, pinpointer. Covers: 17,900+ manufacturers, manufacturers' sales offices, wholesalers, wholesale agents, and distributors operating in Vancouver, Port Coquitlam, Surrey, North Vancouver, Langley, Burnaby, Maple Ridge, Victoria and capital region along with 28,200+ business contact names. Entries include: Company name, address, phone, fax, names and titles of key personnel, number of employees, parent companies, SIC, product, year established.

The Greater Washington Board of Trade--Membership Directory. Greater Washington Board of Trade. • Annual. $150. Covers: Over 900 member firms in the greater Washington, DC, metropolitan area. Entries include: Organization name, address, phone, name of key executive, type of organization, Standard Industrial Classification (SIC) code.

Greater Windham Chamber of Commerce--Annual Business and Pleasure Guide. Sebago Lakes Region Chamber of Commerce. • Annual. Covers: Attractions for business or pleasure in Windham, Maine.

Greece Industrial and Business Directory. International Business Publications, USA. • Annual. $99.95 Individuals hardcopy, e-book, CD-ROM. Covers: Strategic industrial, investment and business contacts for conducting export-import and investment activity in the country. Contains strategic, practical economic and business information.

Greek Exporters. European P.L.C. • Provides specific proposals of co-operation between Greek companies and their counterparts within the Eastern European, Balkans and N.I.S. countries. Covers: Greek export companies in Eastern Europe, Balkans, and N.I.S.

Greek Financial Directory. ICAP AE. • Annual. Covers: Over 20,000 companies operating in Greece; volume 1 includes manufacturing firms; volume 2 includes trading firms (representatives, importers, distributors, and exporters), foreign firms represented in Greece, and tradenames; volume 3 includes service rendering firms and firms related to the tourism industry; volume 4 includes alphabetical index of all listed firms; volume 5 includes statistics on Greek firms. Entries include: Company name, address, phone, fax, telex, year established, names and titles of key personnel, line of business, products/services, trademarks, number of employees, foreign firms represented, financial data for two prior years.

Green Book. Independent Bankers Association of Texas. • Covers: Banks and loan institutions in Texas.

Grey House Directory of Special Issues: A Guide to Business Magazines. Grey House Publishing. • $175 Softcover. Covers: 4,000 business magazines with special issues as well as industry-specific magazines targeting researchers. Entries include: Publisher name, address, phone, fax, e-mail, brief description of content or audience.

Grills--Gas & Electric--Parts Directory. InfoGroup Inc. • Annual. Number of listings: 2,171. Entries include: Name, address, phone, size of advertisement, name of owner or manager, number of employees, year first in "Yellow Pages." Compiled from telephone company "Yellow Pages," nationwide.

Grooming Directory--Pets. InfoGroup Inc. • Annual. Number of listings: 21,803. Entries include: Name, address, phone, size of advertisement, name of owner or manager, number of employees, year first in "Yellow Pages." Compiled from telephone company "Yellow Pages," nationwide.

Growth Companies Register. Financial Publishing Ltd. • Annual. $175. Covers: Private companies in Britain with profits of 50,000 or more. Entries include: Financial data, company profile, name of company directors, SIC codes, addresses.

The Guardian Guide to the UK's Top Companies. Hoover's Inc. • Annual. $49.95. Covers: 150 top British business companies. Database includes: Five years of detailed financial data. Entries include: Company name, address, phone, top officers and directors, information on board compensation, major subsidiaries; information on donations, history, policies and outlook for the future.

Guia Senior. Guia Senior. • Covers: Argentina's national government, provincial government, diplomatic corps, foreign diplomatic corps, armed forces, political groups, banks, saving banks, loan companies, stocks, investment, credit companies, financial associations, insurance companies, stock exchange, and advertising agencies.

The Guide: A Practical Handbook of Marketing Research Sources in the United Kingdom and Western Europe. Key Note Publications Ltd. • $165. Covers: Sources of marketing research in the United Kingdom and Western Europe, including business information sources, market research sources, advertising organizations, periodicals, newspapers, magazines, official statistical sources, online databases, and libraries. Entries include: For databases--Database name, host, producer, contents, frequency of updates. For others--Name, address, phone, fax, description.

Guide to American Directories. Todd Publications. • Biennial. $125.00. Provides more than 11,000 listings with descriptions, prices, etc.

Guide to Business and Real Estate Loan Sources. International Wealth Success, Inc. • Annual. $25 Individuals. Covers: Several hundred financial institutions that lend money for real estate investment. Entries include: Institution name, address, phone.

Guide to Business Information on Central and Eastern Europe. Taylor & Francis Ltd. • $98.95 Individuals Paperback. Covers: Twelve countries of Central and Eastern Europe. Entries include: Country overview; current developments; company name, address, phone, fax; names and titles of key personnel; industries and services; legislation; and organizations.

Guide to Business Information on Russia, the NIS, and the Baltic States. Taylor & Francis Ltd. • $104.95 Individuals Paperback. Covers: Fifteen countries of Russia, the NIS, and the Baltic States. Entries include: Current developments; company name, address, phone, fax; industries and services; legislation; and organizations.

Guide to Centres of International Document Delivery. International Federation of Library Associations and Institutions - Offices for UAP and International Lending. • $20. Covers: Centers of copying and document delivery, including some commercial suppliers, in nearly 190 countries. Entries include: details of major collections and union catalogues; postal address, phone, fax and e-mail address; types of forms accepted; charges; method of payment; restrictions.

A Guide to China's New and High-Tech Development Zone Enterprises. Social Sciences Documentation Publishing House. • $75. Covers: 5,000 high-tech enterprises in China. Entries include: Contact information, administrative person, revenues, fixed assets, number of employees, product names.

Guide to Credit Cards on the Internet. Thomson Financial Inc. • Annual. $235 Individuals. Covers: Credit card issuers and credit card related web sites. Entries include: Product/service name, web site address.

Guide to East European Business Education. Imec Publishing. • Covers: Institutions offering business education in Eastern Europe. Entries include: Name, address, phone, year founded, organizations represented, funding sources, main areas of activity, type of students, faculty information.

Guide to Grants for Business. Associated Management Services Ltd. • Annual. $39.50. Covers: Sources of grants in the European Community and the United Kingdom, including national and local government sources, job centers, environmental organizations, energy efficiency organizations, and loan guarantee schemes. Entries include: For national and local government sources--Name, address, phone, fax, name and title of contact. For others--Name, address, phone, fax, name and title of contact, benefits, amount available, description.

Guide to Montana's Economic Development and Community Development Programs. Economic Development Div. Montana Department of Commerce. • Covers: 28 state and local government agencies that offer economic development programs. Entries include: Program name, sponsoring agency name, address, phone.

Guide to the Canadian Financial Services Industry. Globe Interactive. • Annual. $349.99. Covers: over 800 financial service companies operating in Canada. Database includes: Executive listings with biographical information; lists of government agencies which deal with the financial services industry, industry associations, and top accounting firms in Canada. Entries include: Company name, address, phone, company officers and directors, regional offices, total assets, revenue, net income, number of branches, number of employees, Canadian Standard Industrial Classification.

Gulf Coast Industrial Atlas/Directory. Industrial Info Resources Inc. • Continuous. Covers: about 2,400 heavy industrial plants (including refineries, steel mills, power plants, pulp and paper mills, terminals, docks, storage saltdomes, gas processing plants, chemical plants) and 4,800 management contacts in Florida, Alabama, Mississippi, Louisiana, and Texas. Database includes: Wall maps from Laredo, Texas to St. Marks, Florida. Entries include: For plants--Company or plant name, mailing address, street address, phone, fax, names of plant manager and purchasing agent. For engineering and service companies--Name, address, phone, fax, line of business, description of company.

Hair Removing Services Directory. InfoGroup Inc. • Annual. Number of listings: 4,169. Entries include: Name, address, phone, size of advertisement, name of owner or manager, number of employees, year first in "Yellow Pages." Compiled from telephone company "Yellow Pages," nationwide.

Hairstyling Services Directory. InfoGroup Inc. •

Annual. Number of listings: 230,354. Entries include: Name, address, phone, size of advertisement, name of owner or manager, number of employees, year first in "Yellow Pages." Compiled from telephone company "Yellow Pages," nationwide.

Handbook of NASDAQ Stocks. Mergent Inc. • Quarterly. $105 Individuals. Covers: Over 600 corporations whose stocks are among the most actively traded in dollar volume on the Nasdaq market. Entries include: Company name, address, phone, names and titles of key personnel, product/service, number of employees, detailed financial data, analysis of stock performance and trends, trading volume, per share earnings and yields, and other stock performance evaluations.

Handbook of Rupee Companies. Colombo Brokers Association. • Annual. $30. Covers: Companies registered in Sri Lanka and quoted on the share market.

Handicraft Supplies Directory. InfoGroup Inc. • Annual. Number of listings: 9,320. Entries include: Name, address, phone, size of advertisement, name of owner or manager, number of employees, year first in "Yellow Pages." Compiled from telephone company "Yellow Pages," nationwide.

Harris County Business Guide. Business Extension Bureau Inc. • Biennial. $150 Individuals Hardcopies. Covers: 70,000 industrial, service, retail, wholesale, and professional firms in Harris County, Texas. Database includes: List of 110,000 top executives, includes phone numbers. Entries include: Company name, mailing and street addresses, phone, names and titles of key personnel, number of employees, product or service, years in business, URLs for about 40 percent of companies.

Harris Minnesota Directory of Manufacturers. Dun & Bradstreet Inc. • Annual. Covers: over 11,500 manufacturers in Minnesota. Entries include: Company name, address, key executives, annual sales, phone, fax, toll-free number, number of employees, date established, Standard Industrial Classification (SIC) codes, list of products, international trade, and plant square footage.

Hart's Oil and Gas Finance Sourcebook. Hart Energy. • Annual. $495 Individuals. Covers: More than 3,500 oil and gas companies in eight categories: drilling risk capital, reserve purchasers, downstream risk capital, financial institutions, and intermediaries. Entries include: Company name, address, phone, fax, telex, e-mail address, website, names and titles of key personnel, geographic and operating preferences, deal criteria, total assets, recent deal history, number of wells owned and/or participating in, total annual production figures, primary contact for proposals, proposal turn around time.

Havre de Grace Chamber of Commerce Directory and Business Guide. Havre de Grace Chamber of Commerce. • Annual. Covers: List of members and information on the area's history.

Hawaii Business Abroad. Hawaii Department of Business, Economic Development, and Tourism Research and Economic Analysis Division. • Irregular. Covers: approximately 400 Hawaiian firms that export, import, maintain overseas offices, or have business activities in foreign countries. Entries include: Company name, address, phone, fax, telex, name of contact, cable address, line of business, year established, number of employees, locations of overseas offices, description of overseas activities, parent company name and address (if any), names of countries with which business is done.

Hawaii Industrial Directory. Harris InfoSource. • Annual. $495 Individuals Online. Covers: 9,400 manufacturing companies in Hawaii. Entries include: Company name, address, phone, fax, web site address (on CD-ROM only), toll-free, names and titles of key personnel, number of employees, geographical area served, financial data, descriptions of product/service, Standard Industrial Classification (SIC) code, year established, annual revenues, plant size, legal structure, export/import information.

Headquarters USA. Omnigraphics Inc. • Annual. $210 Individuals web price. Covers: Approximately 110,000 U.S. Businesses, federal, state, and local government offices, banks, colleges and universities, associations, labor unions, political organizations, newspapers, magazines, TV and radio stations, foundations, postal and shipping services, hospitals, office equipment suppliers, airlines, hotels and motels, profiles of top cities, accountants, law firms, computer firms, foreign corporations, overseas trade contacts, and other professional services. Also covers Internet access providers; Internet mailing lists, publications, and sources; freenets. Personal names now included. Entries include: Company, organization, agency, or firm name, address, phone, fax, website addresses as available, and toll-free phone.

Health & Beauty Aids--Retail Directory. InfoGroup Inc. • Annual. Number of listings: 18,716. Entries include: Name, address, phone, size of advertisement, name of owner or manager, number of employees, year first in "Yellow Pages." Compiled from telephone company "Yellow Pages," nationwide.

Heating Equipment--Manufacturers Directory. InfoGroup Inc. • Annual. Number of listings: 1,419. Entries include: Name, address, phone, size of advertisement, name of owner or manager, number of employees, year first in "Yellow Pages." Compiled from telephone company "Yellow Pages," nationwide.

Historical Dictionary of Aid and Development Organizations. The Scarecrow Press Inc. • $55 Individuals Hardback. Covers: Major organizations involved in the post-WWII economic development.

Hobart Business Directory. Hobart Chamber of Commerce. • Covers: More than 450 businesses and professionals in Hobart, Indiana; 65 clubs and organizations; schools and day care centers, local government officials and boards, churches, etc. Entries include: Company, institution, or organization name, address, phone, name of contact; government boards also include meeting days and times or office hours.

Hollis Sponsorship & Donations Yearbook. Hobsons PLC. • Annual. £145 Individuals. Covers: Companies in the United Kingdom offering commercial sponsorships and donations to arts, charity, educational, media, and sports organizations; organizations looking for sponsorships and donations; sponsorship consultants; providers of services such as speakers, caterers, lawyers, insurance, and suppliers of promotional merchandise. Over 3,000 companies and organizations are listed. Entries include: Company or organization name, address, phone, fax, name and title of contact; sponsors list projects sponsored, sponsorship budget and date set, preferred areas of support, total donations; organizations seeking sponsors list projects needing aid, amount of funding required, benefits to the sponsoring company; consultants list number of employees, main interests.

Hollywood Financial Directory. Hollywood Creative Directory. • Annual. $49.50. Covers: Over 600 entertainment-related companies and their corporate, financial, legal, and business affairs staff. Entries include: Name, address, phone, names and titles of key personnel, subsidiary and branch names and locations, description, company type.

Holo-Pack Holo-Print Guidebook and Business Directory: 2nd Edition. Smithers Pira. • $47.50 Individuals. Covers: Organizations around the world which supply holograms or holographic products and services.

Home Decorating Services Directory. InfoGroup Inc. • Annual. Number of listings: 33,751. Entries include: Name, address, phone, size of advertisement, name of owner or manager, number of employees, year first in "Yellow Pages." Compiled from telephone company "Yellow Pages," nationwide.

Home Design and Planning Service Directory. InfoGroup Inc. • Annual. Number of listings: 3,518. Entries include: Name, address, phone, size of advertisement, name of owner or manager, number of employees, year first in "Yellow Pages." Compiled from telephone company "Yellow Pages," nationwide.

Home Improvements Directory. InfoGroup Inc. • Annual. Number of listings: 43,179. Entries include: Name, address, phone, size of advertisement, name of owner or manager, number of employees, year first in "Yellow Pages." Compiled from telephone company "Yellow Pages," nationwide.

Homes for the Aged Directory. InfoGroup Inc. • Annual. Number of listings: 5,059. Entries include: Name, address, phone, size of advertisement, name of owner or manager, number of employees, year first in "Yellow Pages." Compiled from telephone company "Yellow Pages," nationwide.

Homes--Nursing--Directory. InfoGroup Inc. • Annual. Number of listings: 22,509. Entries include: Name, address, phone, size of advertisement, name of owner or manager, number of employees, year first in "Yellow Pages." Compiled from telephone company "Yellow Pages," nationwide.

Hong Kong Classified Business Telephone Directory. Hong Kong Telephone Company Ltd. • Covers: Company listings for Hong Kong businesses.

Hong Kong Commercial/Industrial Guide. GTE Directories Ltd. • $30. Covers: over 200,000 suppliers of 2,000 products and services in Hong Kong; banks, importers and exporters. Entries include: Company name, address, phone, telex, fax.

Hong Kong Importer Directory. Biz Focus Company Ltd. • $240 Individuals. Covers: 4,972 importers with various product categories. Entries include: Company name, contact person, contact address, telephone number, fax number, e-mail, URL, and import products.

Hong Kong Importers List. INFOT Inc. • $80.75 CD-ROM; additional $119 for MS Access format. Covers: 15,826 selected importers and buyers from Hong Kong and P.R. China. Entries include: Company name, contact person, physical addresses, email and website addresses, telephone and fax number, and business description.

Hong Kong Public Companies. Data Base Asia Ltd. • Irregular. $700. Covers: Investing in 245 local and 15 overseas companies of the Hong Kong Stock Exchange. Entries include: Company name, details, history, balance sheet.

Hoover's Guide to the Top New York Companies. Hoover's Inc. • Annual. $24.95 plus $3.50 shipping. Covers: 1,390 leading public and private companies located in New York City. Entries include: Company name, address, phone, fax, web sites, names and titles of key personnel, industry, stock symbols, sales, number of employees.

Hoover's Guide to the Top Texas Companies: The Ultimate Guide to Texas. Hoover's Inc. • Biennial. $24.95 plus $3.50 shipping. Covers: 850 private and public companies in Texas. The 55 largest companies; another 70 selected firms are described in detail. Database includes: Lists of the top 500 companies ranked by sales and the 50 fastest-growing companies; overview of the Texas economy and business environment. Entries include: For the 30 largest firms--Company name, address, phone, fax, overview of operations and strategies, history, financial data for previous 10 years, names and titles of key personnel, products/services/brand names. For selected firms--Company name, address, phone, fax, names and titles of key personnel, line of business, stock symbols, sales, number of employees. Less detail is given for the remaining firms.

Hoover's Handbook of American Business. Dun & Bradstreet Inc. Hoover's Inc. • Annual. $245 Individuals hardcover. Provides detailed profiles of more than 750 large public and private companies, including history, executives, brand names, key competitors, and up to 10 years of financial data. Includes indexes by industry, location, executive name, company name, and brand name.

Hoover's Handbook of Private Companies: Profiles of Major U.S. Private Enterprises. Hoover's Inc. • Annual. $215 Individuals hardcover. Covers: 900 privately held companies and other enterprises; 250 firms are covered in detail. Entries include: Company name, address, phone, fax, brief overview of operations, products, competitors, names and titles of key personnel, sales, number of employees; detailed entries add in-depth profile of operations and strategies, financial data for preceding 10 years.

Hoover's Handbook of World Business. Dun & Bradstreet Inc. Hoover's Inc. • Annual. $225 Individuals Hardcover. Covers: Hundreds of companies headquartered outside the U.S., including many with substantial activity in the U.S.; global enterprises, businesses that dominate their respective industries, and representative companies from all major industries. Entries include: Company name, overview, history, exchange and stock symbols, fiscal year-end date, names and titles of key personnel, name of auditors, number of employees, headquarters address, phone, fax, description of where the company does business, specific products/services/brand names produced, key competitors, 10 years of key financial data.

Hoover's Masterlist of Latin American Companies. Hoover's Inc. • $79.95 Book. Covers: 2,500 profiles of the largest public and private companies in Latin America. Database includes: All financial information converted to U.S. dollars. Entries include: Headquarters, address, phone, fax, key officers, industry description, sales figures, employment data.

Hoover's Masterlist of Major Asian Companies. Hoover's Inc. • $79.95. Covers: More than 3,000 companies in 10 Asian countries. Entries include: Name, address, phone, fax, names and titles of key personnel, financial data, employment data, description of industry.

Hoover's Masterlist of Major European Companies. Hoover's Inc. • $79.95 Book. Covers: 2,500 profiles of the largest public and private companies in Western Europe, including Greece and Turkey, plus all companies on the major European stock indexes. Database includes: All financial information converted to U.S. dollars. Entries include: Headquarters, address, phone, fax, key officers, industry description, sales figures, employment data.

Hoover's MasterList of Major U.S. Companies. Hoover's Inc. • $320 Individuals hardcover. Covers: Over 10,000 of the largest public and private companies in the U.S. Entries include: Company name, address, phone, fax, web site addresses, names and titles of key personnel, company overview, stock symbols, net income, market value, sales and employment data, fiscal year end.

Horse Riding & Rentals Directory. InfoGroup Inc. • Annual. Number of listings: 6968. Entries include: Name, address, phone, size of advertisement, name of owner or manager, number of employees, year first in "Yellow Pages." Compiled from telephone company "Yellow Pages," nationwide.

Hospitals Directory. InfoGroup Inc. • Annual. Number of listings: 13,914. Entries include: Name, address, phone, size of advertisement, name of owner or manager, number of employees, year first in "Yellow Pages." Compiled from telephone company "Yellow Pages," nationwide.

Hospodarsky Almanach. CompAlmanach spol S.R.O. • Annual. $110. Covers: Approximately 20,000 Czech companies in commerce, industry, service, and trading. Entries include: Company name, address, phone, fax, founding date, capital, name of general manager, board, owner, turnover rate, number in trade register, languages for correspondence, banking-relations, number of employees, countries of import, countries of export, branches, mechanical equipment, production lines.

Hotel Directory and Travel Guide. Radius, the Global Travel Co. • $1,475 U.S. 1/8 page. Covers: nearly 9,000 hotels in 135 countries offering 'preferred rates'; international coverage. Entries include: Hotel name, address, phone, regular rate for single room, preferred rate for single and double rooms, facilities, amenities, city and county travel information, and maps.

House Furnishings Directory--Retail. InfoGroup Inc. • Annual. Number of listings: 2,728. Entries include: Name, address, phone, size of advertisement, name of owner or manager, number of employees, year first in "Yellow Pages." Compiled from telephone company "Yellow Pages," nationwide.

Houseboats Directory--Rentals. InfoGroup Inc. • Annual. Number of listings: 5274. Entries include: Name, address, phone, size of advertisement, name of owner or manager, number of employees, year first in "Yellow Pages." Compiled from telephone company "Yellow Pages," nationwide.

Household Appliances (Major) Directory--Dealers. InfoGroup Inc. • Annual. Number of listings: 21,271. Entries include: Name, address, phone, size of advertisement, name of owner or manager, number of employees, year first in "Yellow Pages." Compiled from telephone company "Yellow Pages," nationwide.

Houston International Business Directory. Houston Chamber of Commerce. • Annual. $20 Individuals MBS. Covers: More than 3,300 U.S. and foreign companies involved in international business activities in Houston, Texas. Entries include: Company name, address, phone, principal executives, type of business, imports/exports.

Houston 1000 Corporate Directory. • $115 Members plus $3.00 shipping and handling. Covers: 7,000 major businesses in the Houston area. Entries include: Company name, address, phone, fax, type of business, names and titles of key officers and personnel, number of employoess.

How to Find Business Intelligence in Washington. MarketResearch.com. • $295 payment with order. Covers: over 500 government libraries, archives, offices, agencies, statistical centers, and other sources of publications, market studies, statistical summaries, and census data. Entries include: Office, agency, or organization name, address, phone, description of information, price (if any).

How to Find Information about Companies. MarketResearch.com. • Annual. $395 per volume. Covers: in Part 1, over 9,000 sources of corporate intelligence, including federal, state, and local repositories of company filings, individual industry experts, published sources, databases, CD-ROM products, and corporate research services. Entries include: Source name, address, phone, contact name, description. Parts 2 and 3 provide guidelines for company research.

How to Find Information about Private Companies. MarketResearch.com. • Irregular. $59. Covers: Organizations, publications, and individuals that collect information on private companies. Database includes: Corporate research tips. Entries include: Name, address, phone.

Howick, Lidgetton, Merrivale, Mpophomeni Directory. A.C. Braby (Pty) Ltd. • Annual. Covers: Businesses in Howick, Lidgetton, Merrivale, and Mpophomeni. Database includes: Maps. Entries include: Company name, address, phone, and descriptive text.

Hungary Government and Business Contacts Handbook: Trade, Investment & Business Development Contacts. International Business Publications, USA. • $99.95 Individuals hardcopy. Covers: Strategic government and business information, export-import activity in the country, investment, business contacts and regulations.

IAL Directory of European Industrial and Business Market Reports. IAL Consultants. • Irregular. $250 postpaid. Covers: publishers and producers of market reports, statistical summaries, and other data; includes government and non-government organizations, libraries, press, and international sources in Europe, including the socialist states of Eastern Europe. Entries include: Publisher name and address, title and subject of report, language, number of pages, price.

ICC UK Company Directory. ICC Information Ltd. • Weekly. Database covers: approximately 3.83 million registered companies in England, Wales, Scotland, and Northern Ireland. Contains a record for each company included on the Index of Companies maintained by the official Companies Registration office in the UK. Also incorporates companies that have been dissolved since 1968.

Idaho Manufacturers Directory and Industrial Database. Manufacturers' News Inc. • Annual. $89 Individuals print. Covers: 2,560 manufacturers in Idaho. Entries include: Company name, address, phone, names and titles of key personnel, year established, number of employees, plant square footage, services, Standard Industry Classification (SIC) code, parent and subsidiary company information, type of in-house computer system, URL, e-mail address.

Illinois Industries Guide. Industries Guides Inc. • $95. Covers: Approximately 20,000 manufacturers in Illinois. Entries include: Company name, address, phone.

Illinois Manufacturers Directory. Manufacturers' News Inc. • Annual. $211 Individuals print; plus shipping and handling. Covers: 19,423 manufacturers and 61,317 executives in Illinois. Entries include: Company name, address, phone, titles and functions of key personnel, year established, number of employees, plant square footage, services, Standard Industrial Classification (SIC) code, parent and subsidiary company information, type of in-house computer system, fax, web address, e-mail address.

Illinois Services Directory. Manufacturers' News Inc. • Annual. $209 Individuals Print (Hardcover); plus Shipping and Handling. Covers: Over 26,548 wholesalers, jobbers, contractors, retailers, services, and 76,898 executives in Illinois. Entries include: Company name, address, phone; names, titles, and functions of key personnel; year established, number of employees, office square footage, services, Standard Industrial Classification (SIC) code, net worth, parent company and subsidiary company information, type of in-house computer system, email address, fax, web address.

Imports and Exports of the Republic of China and Taiwan. Taiwan External Trade Development Council. • Annual. $150. Covers import commodities whose import value exceeds $200,000 (U.S. funds) annually.

Income Tax Service Directory. InfoGroup Inc. • Annual. Number of listings: 63,898. Entries include: Name, address, phone, size of advertisement, name of owner or manager, number of employees, year first in "Yellow Pages." Compiled from telephone company "Yellow Pages," nationwide.

India Government and Business Contacts Handbook. International Business Publications, USA. • $99.95 Individuals hardcopy, e-book, CD-ROM. Covers: Strategic government and business information, export-import activity in the country, investment, business contacts and regulations.

The Indian Export Directory. Indian Export Trade Journal. • Annual. $120. Covers: Indian manufacturers, exporters, importers, foreign firms interested in trade with India, world chambers of commerce, trade associations, and products. Entries include: Company name, address, phone, telex, cable.

Indian Export Yearbook. M/S Sales Overseas. • Annual. $80. Covers: Importers, exporters, manufacturers, Indian agents, foreign trade statistics, Indian economy, events, government trade offices, export firms, information for tourists; exporters and importers trading with SAARC countries (Bangladesh, Bhutan, Maldives, Nepal, Pakistan, and Sri Lanka). Entries include: Contact information.

Indian Handicrafts Directory: Exporters & Manufacturers. NIIR Project Consultancy Services. • $200 Individuals CD-ROM. Covers: 1,850+ exporters and manufacturers of handicrafts in India. Entries include: Company name, full address, city, state, pin code, phone, fax, e-mail (wherever available), website (wherever available), product, contact person.

Indian Industrial & Business Register: All India Industrial & Commercial Directory. NIIR Project Consultancy Services. • $350 Individuals CD-ROM. Covers: Indian industrial and business register. Entries include: Addresses, product details, e-mail, websites, phone and fax nos.

Indiana Chamber of Commerce--Business Directory & Resource Guide. Indiana Chamber of Commerce. • Covers: Approximately 5,000 member businesses; state agencies and institutions that offer business assistance services in Indiana. Entries include: For agencies and institutions--Name, address, phone, description of services. For businesses--Business name, address, phone, name and title of contact, products or services.

Indiana Financial Institutions Directory. Indiana Bankers Association. • $35 Members. Covers: State and federal agencies associated with the financial institutions industry. Entries include: Name, address, phone, officers and directors of every Indiana bank, savings and loan and credit union, plus listings of officers, directors, total assets, deposits, correspondent banks, counties and population.

Indonesia Industrial and Business Directory. International Business Publications, USA. • $99.95 Individuals hardcopy, e-book, CD-ROM. Covers: Strategic investment, industrial and business contacts for conducting investment and export-import activity in the country.

Indonesian Business Directory. PT Sumber Daya Multimedia. • $30. Database covers: 94,000 Indonesian importers, exporters, and other businesses. Entries include: Contact information, industry, and description of products and services.

Industrial and Corporate Services Directory. Durham Region Economic Development and Tourism Department. • Covers: Lists of industrial and corporate businesses located in Durham region.

Industrial & Service Contacts in Ex-Soviet Union Area Republics. MZM Publications Publishing Promotion Co. • Irregular. Entries include: Company name, address, phone, telex.

Industrial & Technology-Based Firms Directory. Charleston Metro Chamber of Commerce. • $150 Members. Covers: 1,500 plus manufacturing, distribution, and technology-based firms operating in the tri-county area. Technology-based firms included are not only from certain manufacturing sectors but also from the information technology, engineering, biotech, research and development, and other sciences sectors. Entries include: Company name, address, county, phone, web site if known, NAICS code, number of local employees, primary products or services, year established locally, and names of the top officer on site, human resource representative and purchasing agent where applicable.

Industrial/Commercial Directory of Peru. Confederacion Nacional de Comerciantes. • Annual. $50. Covers: Industrial and commercial firms in Peru. Entries include: Name, address, phone, telex, products, services.

Industrial Directory of Colombia Guide. Legis Ltda. • Annual. $18. Covers: Manufacturers, distributors, and services in Colombia. Entries include: Name, address, phone, telex.

Industrial Directory of Israel. Dun & Bradstreet Israel Ltd. • Irregular. $48. Covers: Local industries in Israel. Entries include: Address, telephone, annual sales, names and titles of key personnel, products, exports.

Industridata: AA Enterprises. Mercametrica Ediciones S.A. • Annual. $550 Individuals. Covers: Over 1,700 industrial, commercial, and services companies in Mexico with 251 to 500 employees. Includes banks and insurance companies. Companion volume of 'Industridata: AAA Enterprises' (see separate entry). Information from both titles is listed by postal code in 'Industridata by Zip Codes.' Entries include: Company name, location, phone, fax, telex, days and hours of operation, main products and brands, number of employees, sales, installed capacity and output for previous four years, government and foreign ownership, year established, names and titles of key personnel.

L'Industrie Luxenbourgeoise. Federation Des Industries Luxembourgeois. • Annual. Covers: Approximately 320 of Luxembourg's industries. Entries include: Company name, address, phone, telex number, names and titles of key personnel, number of employees, financial data, description of services and products provided.

Industry--New and Expanding. Alabama Development Office Alabama Center for Commerce. • Annual. Covers: List of industrial companies announcing plans to locate or expand facilities in Alabama. Entries include: Company name, location, products or services, amount of capital investment, number of jobs created.

Inform Katalog. Inform Katalog Spol. S.R.O. • Annual. $190. Covers: Approximately 20,000 Czech companies. Entries include: Business information.

Inform Katalog Business Directory. Inform Katalog Spol. S.R.O. • Annual. Covers: Approved contacts for 60,000 Czech companies. Entries include: Business contact information.

Inform Katalog Export Import. Inform Katalog Spol. S.R.O. • Annual. Covers: More than 4,000 of the leading Czech exporters and importers classified by commodities.

Inform Katalog Slovakia. Inform Katalog Slovakia Ltd. • Annual. $88. Covers: 6,000 companies in Slovakia. Entries include: Detailed business information.

Inform Slovenskych Podnikov. Inform Katalog Slovakia Ltd. • Annual. $26. Covers: 15,000 business contacts at Slovakian companies classified in detail by area of activity.

Infotel--The Electronic Directory of Companies from Romania. Chamber of Commerce and Industry of Romania. • Covers: More than 500,00 Romanian companies. Entries include: Company name, headquarters address, telephone and fax number, registration, statistical and fiscal codes, profile, equity, shareholders, number of employees, gross profit.

Initiative Europe. ICC Online Services Div. ICC Information Group Ltd. • Monthly. Covers: Small- and medium-sized businesses in Europe seeking international joint venture, partnership, and licensing agreements.

Inside Japanese Support. Taft Group. • Annual. $199. Covers: 340 U.S. subsidiaries of Japanese firms and 40 Japan-based foundations awarding grants in the United States. Entries include: Company name, address, phone, name and title of contact, application information, program descriptions, recent grants, U.S. operating locations; Japanese parent company name, address, and financial information. Graphs and essay entitled "The Current Status of Japanese Foundations" comprise Section 1; directory information is in Section 2.

Insiders' Chronicle. American Banker Newsletters. • Covers: publicly held companies in whose securities there has been significant buying or selling by executive officers, directors, and those who hold 10% or more of its shares. Database includes: Market news, quotations, and statistics. Entries include: Company name, name and title of person involved, number of shares held, number of shares bought or sold, price per share, date of transaction.

Institute of Management Consultants--Management Consultants Resource Guide. Institute of Management Consultants USA. • Database covers: 2,800 individuals who practice management consulting as individuals or members of firms worldwide. Database includes: Name, firm, address, phone; fax; email; website; areas of competence for certified management consultants.

Insurance Companies' Directory List of Mortgage Directors. Communication Network International Inc. • Irregular. $350. Covers: 170 mortgage officers of major insurance companies that make real estate mortgages and related investments. Entries include: Company name, address, phone, name and title of mortgage officer.

Intellectual Property World Directory. World Bureau L.L.C. • Annual. Covers: Patent, trademark, and copyright agencies and officials in over 100 countries. Entries include: Name, address, phone, fax, and e-mail address of officials responsible for intellectual property issues. Also includes statistics, reports, full cabinets, embassies, and organizational charts.

Inter-Corporate Ownership. Industrial Organization and Finance Div. Statistics Canada. • Biennial. $350 plus shipping charges for outside country. Covers: 72,000 Canadian corporations with ownership links to one or more other corporations. Entries include: Parent corporation and subsidiaries, site of control, Canadian domicile, Standard Industrial Classification (SIC) code, etc.

Inter Region. Editus S.A.R.L. • Annual. Covers: the top 15,000 companies in the European area of Saar-Lor-Lux including: south Belgium, Saarland, Trier, Grand Duchy of Luxembourg and French region Lorraine. Entries include: Company name, address, phone, fax, number of employees, financial data, names and titles of key personnel and line of business, trademarks.

International Business and Trade Directories. Grey House Publishing. • $225 Individuals softcover. Covers: Approximately 8,000 directories concerned with international business and trade. Entries include: Directory title, publisher name, address, phone, fax, description of directory, ISBN, size, price, frequency, editor, U.S. Distributor.

International Business in South Africa. Investor Responsibility Research Center Institute. • Annual. $500. Covers: about 600 non-U.S. companies with business links to South Africa. Database includes:

Lists of companies that do business in South Africa but do not own any assets there; companies with "non equity" links to South Africa. Entries include: Name and address of parent company, line of business, names and locations of South African subsidiaries, number of employees, policies. Companies based in the United States are listed in "U.S. Business in South Africa" (see separate entry). Updated monthly for "South Africa Review Service" subscribers.

International Business Information on the Web: Searcher Magazine's Guide to Sites and Strategies for Global Business Research. Information Today, Inc. • $29.95. Lists directories, search engines, banks, financial institutions, news sources, government contacts, chambers of commerce, and other country-specific information. Covers: Approximately 1,000 Web sites related to international business research including general business sites in the United States and worldwide. Publication includes: URLs. Entries include: Information regarding each site.

International Business Lawyers Index/Industrial Property/Chambers of Commerce. Datapress Ltd. • Biennial. $35. Covers: 10,000 business lawyers, 10,000 chambers of commerce and industry, 2,000 official industrial property agencies, and 110 state property agencies for 140 countries. Entries include: Name, address, phone, telex numbers.

International Construction Directory. Dataguide Inc. • Irregular. Covers: Approximately 3,550 companies engaged in the construction of buildings, roads, public works, and industrial plants; international coverage. Database includes: Rankings of top 1,000 companies by revenue and by number of employees. Entries include: Company name, address, phone, fax, mailing address, telex, principal officers, number of employees, financial data, business activity, year established, stock exchange listing.

International Corporate Yellow Book. Leadership Directories Inc. • Semiannual. $170 per year. Covers: leading corporations outside of the United States. Entries include: Company name, address, phone, fax, telex, description of activities, assets or revenue, names and titles of key personnel, names and affiliations of board members; name, address, phone, fax and names and titles of key personnel for subsidiaries.

International Dallas. Dallas Regional Chamber. • Annual. $20 Members. Covers: Listings of over 1,500 international businesses in the Dallas/Ft. Worth area, including importers, exporters, foreign-owned companies, plus trade statistics and a guide to exporting. Entries include: Company name, address, phone, fax; description; product codes; local executives; parent company.

International Directory for Selling Military Products and Services. DIANE Publishing Co. • $50 Individuals Paperback. Covers: Procurement policies and procedures for 13 European countries plus Australia, Canada, Egypt and Israel. Entries include: Points of contact, getting started, access to technical documents, procurement methods, types of contracts, contract provisions, pre-award surveys, classified information, restrictions on foreign competition, contract administration.

International Directory of Business Information Sources and Services. Routledge Reference. • $240. Covers: over 4,500 chambers of commerce, government agencies, foreign trade promotion agencies, associations, research organizations, business libraries, and other sources of business information in 50 countries. Entries include: Agency name, address, phone, fax, names and titles of key personnel, name and title of contact, description.

International Directory of Commercial Vehicles. Vogt-Schild AG, Druck & Verlag. • Annual. $40. Covers: Manufacturers of light commercial vehicles, municipal vehicles, trucks, small buses, all-wheel drive vehicles, special vehicles, body and trailer manufacturing, and accessories worldwide. Entries include: Manufacturer name, address, phone, technical data.

International Directory of Company Histories. St. James Press. • $343 Individuals. Multi-volume work that covers histories of companies that are a leading influence in a particular industry or geographic location. eBook available. Contact for pricing.

International Directory of Corporate Affiliations: Public and Private Companies. LexisNexis. • $540. Covers: Approximately 1,500 U.S. and approximately 1,600 non-U.S. parent companies and their approximately 30,000 subsidiaries. Entries include: Name, address, phone, description of activities.

International Directory of Importers--Africa. Croner Publications Inc. • Irregular. $225. Covers: 10,000 importers in 40 countries in Africa. Entries include: Company name, address, phone.

The International Directory of Importers - Africa. Interdata. • $250 By mail print. Covers: 9,000 firms importing in 44 African countries a broad variety of products from abrasives to zippers. Entries include: Company name and address, contact person, email, number of employees, year established, phone and telefaxes, business activity, bank references, as well as a detailed listing of products imported.

The International Directory of Importers - Agricultural Machinery & Implements Importers. Interdata. • $220 Individuals print. Covers: 2,300 international firms importing agricultural equipment. Entries include: Company name and address, contact person, email, number of employees, year established, phone and telefaxes, business activity, bank references, as well as a listing of agricultural machinery & implements currently being imported.

The International Directory of Importers--Aircraft and Aviation Equipment and Accessories Importers. Interdata. • $200 Individuals print. Covers: 500 international firms importing aircraft and aviation equipment and accessories. Entries include: Company name and address, contact person, email, number of employees, year established, phone and telefaxes, business activity, bank references, as well as listing of aircraft equipment currently being imported.

The International Directory of Importers - Apparel & Clothing Importers. Interdata. • $320 Individuals print. Covers: 5,600 international firms importing apparel and clothing. Entries include: Company name and address, contact person, email, number of employees, year established, phone and telefaxes, business activity, bank references, as well as a listing of apparel and clothing currently being imported.

The International Directory of Importers - Asia/Pacific. Interdata. • $385 U.S. print edition. Covers: 32,000 firms importing in 22 Asian countries a broad variety of products from abrasives to zippers. Entries include: Company name and address, contact person, email, number of employees, year established, phone and telefaxes, business activity, bank references, as well as a detailed listing of products imported.

International Directory of Importers--Asia/Pacific. Croner Publications Inc. • Irregular. $350. Covers: 30,000 importers in Australia, Hong Kong, Indonesia, Japan, Malaysia, New Zealand, Pakistan, Philippines, Singapore, South Korea, Sri Lanka, Taiwan, and Thailand. Entries include: Company name, address, phone.

The International Directory of Importers--Automotive Equipment, Parts & Accessories Importers. Interdata. • $320 Individuals print edition. Covers: 6,400 international firms importing automotive equipment, parts & accessories. Entries include: Company name and address, contact person, email, number of employees, year established, phone and telefaxes, business activity, bank references, as well as a listing of automotive equipment, parts & accessories currently being imported.

The International Directory of Importers - Beauty Supplies, Cosmetic and Toiletries Importers. Interdata. • $295 Individuals print. Covers: 4,100 international firms importing beauty supplies, cosmetics and toiletries. Entries include: Company name and address, contact person, email, number of employees, year established, phone and telefaxes, business activity, bank references, as well as a listing of beauty supplies, cosmetics and toiletries currently being imported.

The International Directory of Importers--Bicycles, Mopeds and Motorcycles Importers. Interdata. • $200 Individuals print. Covers: 800 international firms importing bicycles, mopeds and motorcycles. Entries include: Company name and address, contact person, email, number of employees, year established, phone and telefaxes, business activity, bank references, as well as a listing of bicycles, mopeds and motorcycles currently being imported.

The International Directory of Importers--Building and Construction Materials and Supplies Importers. Interdata. • $320 Individuals print. Covers: 6,400 international firms importing building, construction materials and supplies. Entries include: Company name and address, contact person, email, number of employees, year established, phone and telefaxes, business activity, bank references, as well as a listing of building, construction materials and supplies currently being imported.

The International Directory of Importers--Chemicals and Allied Products Importers. Interdata. • Annual. $320 Individuals print. Covers: 6,200 international firms importing chemicals and allied products. Entries include: Company name and address, contact person, email, number of employees, year established, phone and telefaxes, business activity, bank references, as well as a listing of chemicals and allied products currently being imported.

The International Directory of Importers--Communications Equipment Importers. Interdata. • $295 Individuals print. Covers: 4,000 international firms importing communications equipment. Entries include: Company name and address, contact person, email, number of employees, year established, phone and telefaxes, business activity, bank references, as well as a listing of communications equipment currently being imported.

The International Directory of Importers--Computers and Data Processing Equipment Importers. Interdata. • $320 Individuals print. Covers: 7,100 international firms importing computers and data processing equipment. Entries include: Company name and address, contact person, email, number of employees, year established, phone and telefaxes, business activity, bank references, as well as a listing of computers and data processing equipment currently being imported.

The International Directory of Importers--Construction and Building Equipment Importers. Interdata. • $260 Individuals print. Covers: 3,100 international firms importing construction and building equipment. Entries include: Company name and address, contact person, email, number of employees, year established, phone and telefaxes, business activity, bank references, as well as a listing of construction and building equipment currently being imported.

The International Directory of Importers - Consumer Electronics, Audio/Video, TV's and CD's Importers. Interdata. • $295 Individuals printed edition. Covers: 4,000 international firms importing consumer electronics, audio/video, TV's and CD's. Entries include: Company name and address, contact person, email, number of employees, year established, phone and telefaxes, business activity, bank references, as well as a listing of consumer electronics, audio/video, TV's and CD's currently being imported.

The International Directory of Importers--Control Equipment and Switches Importers. Interdata. • $200 Individuals print. Covers: 1,400 international firms importing control equipment and switches. Entries include: Company name and address, contact person, email, number of employees, year established, phone and telefaxes, business activity, bank references, as well as a listing of control equipment and switches currently being imported.

The International Directory of Importers--Drugs and Pharmaceuticals Importers. Interdata. • Annual. $260 Individuals print. Covers: 2,900 international firms importing drugs and pharmaceuticals. Entries include: Company name and address, contact person, email, number of employees, year established, phone and telefaxes, business activity, bank references, as well as a listing of drugs and pharmaceuticals currently being imported.

The International Directory of Importers--Electrical Equipment and Supplies Importers. Interdata. • $295 Individuals print edition. Covers: 4,900 international firms importing electrical equipment and supplies. Entries include: Company name and address, contact person, email, number of employees, year established, phone and telefaxes, business activity, bank references, as well as a listing of electrical equipment and supplies currently being imported.

The International Directory of Importers--Electronic and Computer Components and Parts Importers. Interdata. • $320 Individuals print. Covers: 7,000 international firms importing electronic and computer components and parts. Entries include: Company name and address, contact person, email, number of employees, year established, phone and telefaxes, business activity, bank references, as well as a listing of electronic and computer components and parts currently being imported.

The International Directory of Importers--Environmental Protection Equipment Importers. Interdata. • $200 Individuals print. Covers: 1,100 international firms importing environmental protection equipment. Entries include: Company name and address, contact person, email, number of employees, year established, phone and telefaxes, business activity, bank references, as well as a listing of environmental protection equipment currently being imported.

International Directory of Importers--Europe. Croner Publications Inc. • Irregular. $450. Covers: 54,000 importers in Austria, Belgium, Denmark, France, Holland, Italy, Norway, Spain, Sweden, Switzerland, United Kingdom, and West Germany. Entries include: Company name, address, phone.

The International Directory of Importers - Europe. Interdata. • $485 Individuals regular mail. Covers: 54,000 firms importing in 35 European countries a broad variety of products from abrasives to zippers. Entries include: Company name and address, contact person, email, number of employees, year established, phone and telefaxes, business activity, bank references, as well as a detailed listing of products imported.

The International Directory of Importers - Floor Coverings, Carpets and Rugs Importers. Interdata. • $200 Individuals print. Covers: 1,000 international firms importing floor coverings, carpets and rugs. Entries include: Company name and address, contact person, email, number of employees, year established, phone and telefaxes, business activity, bank references, as well as a listing of floor coverings, carpets and rugs currently being imported.

The International Directory of Importers - Food & Beverage Importers. Interdata. • $320 Individuals print. Covers: 7,300 international firms importing food and beverage. Entries include: Company name and address, contact person, email, number of employees, year established, phone and telefaxes, business activity, bank references, as well as a listing of food and beverage currently being imported.

The International Directory of Importers - Furniture and Home Furnishings Importers. Interdata. • $320 Individuals print. Covers: 5,100 international firms importing furniture and home furnishings. Entries include: Company name and address, contact person, email, number of employees, year established, phone and telefaxes, business activity, bank references, as well as a listing of furniture and home furnishings currently being imported.

The International Directory of Importers - Garden, Lawn and Patio Equipment and Supplies Importers. Interdata. • $295 Individuals print edition. Covers: 3,800 international firms importing garden, lawn, patio equipment and supplies. Entries include: Company name and address, contact person, email, number of employees, year established, phone and telefaxes, business activity, bank references, as well as a listing of garden, lawn, patio equipment and supplies currently being imported.

The International Directory of Importers - Hand Tools and Power Tools Importers. Interdata. • $260 Individuals print. Covers: 3,000 international firms importing hand tools and power tools. Entries include: Company name and address, contact person, email, number of employees, year established, phone and telefaxes, business activity, bank references, as well as a listing of hand tools and power tools currently being imported.

The International Directory of Importers - Household and Kitchen Appliances Importers. Interdata. • $220 Individuals print. Covers: 2,300 international firms importing household and kitchen appliances. Entries include: Company name and address, contact person, email, number of employees, year established, phone and telefaxes, business activity, bank references, as well as a listing of household and kitchen appliances currently being imported.

The International Directory of Importers - Housewares and Home Accessories Importers. Interdata. • $320 Individuals print. Covers: 6,200 international firms importing housewares and home accessories. Entries include: Company name and address, contact person, email, number of employees, year established, phone and telefaxes, business activity, bank references, as well as a listing of housewares and home accessories currently being imported.

The International Directory of Importers - Jewelry and Costume Jewelry Importers. Interdata. • $220 Individuals print. Covers: 2,100 international firms importing jewelry and costume jewelry. Entries include: Company name and address, contact person, email, number of employees, year established, phone and telefaxes, business activity, bank references, as well as a listing of jewelry and costume jewelry currently being imported.

The International Directory of Importers - Kitchenware, Tableware and Glassware Importers. Interdata. • $220 Individuals print. Covers: 3,000 international firms importing kitchenware, tableware and glassware. Entries include: Company name and address, contact person, email, number of employees, year established, phone and telefaxes, business activity, bank references, as well as a listing of kitchenware, tableware and glassware currently being imported.

The International Directory of Importers - Leather Goods, Footwear and Travel Accessories Importers. Interdata. • $260 Individuals print edition. Covers: 3,200 international firms importing leather goods, footwear and travel accessories. Entries include: Company name and address, contact person, email, number of employees, year established, phone and telefaxes, business activity, bank references, as well as a listing of leather goods, footwear and travel accessories currently being imported.

The International Directory of Importers - Lighting Equipment, Lamps and Accessories Importers. Interdata. • Annual. $220 Individuals print. Covers: 2,500 international firms importing lighting equipment, lamps and accessories. Entries include: Company name and address, contact person, email, number of employees, year established, phone and telefaxes, business activity, bank references, as well as a listing of lighting equipment, lamps and accessories currently being imported.

The International Directory of Importers--Machine Tools and Accessories Importers. Interdata. • $220 Individuals print. Covers: 1,900 international firms importing machine tools and accessories. Entries include: Company name and address, contact person, email, number of employees, year established, phone and telefaxes, business activity, bank references, as well as a listing of machine tools and accessories currently being imported.

The International Directory of Importers - Marine & Boating Equipment Supplies Importers. Interdata. • $260 Individuals print. Covers: 3,100 international firms importing marine & boating equipment and supplies. Entries include: Company name and address, contact person, email, number of employees, year established, phone and telefaxes, business activity, bank references, as well as a listing of marine & boating equipment and supplies currently being imported.

The International Directory of Importers - Measuring Equipment and Scales Importers. Interdata. • $220 Individuals print version. Covers: 1,900 international firms importing measuring equipment and scales. Entries include: Company name and address, contact person, email, number of employees, year established, phone and telefaxes, business activity, bank references, as well as a listing of measuring equipment and scales currently being imported.

International Directory of Importers--Medical, Hospital, and Surgical Equipment and Supplies. International Directory of Importers. • Annual. $295 Individuals print. Covers: 5,000 worldwide manufacturers, importers, and firms trading in medical, hospital, and surgical equipment and supplies. Entries include: Company name, address, phone, fax, email address when available, importing manager, year established.

The International Directory of Importers - Medical, Hospital and Surgical Equipment and Supplies Importers. Interdata. • $295 Individuals print. Covers: 4,400 international firms importing medical, hospital and surgical equipment and supplies. Entries include: Company name and address, contact person, email, number of employees, year established, phone and telefaxes, business activity, bank references, as well as a listing of medical, hospital and surgical equipment and supplies currently being imported.

The International Directory of Importers - Middle East. Interdata. • $250 Individuals print. Covers: 13,000 firms importing in 14 Middle East countries a broad variety of products from abrasives to zippers. Entries include: Company name and address, contact person, email, number of employees, year established, phone and telefaxes, business activity, bank references, as well as a detailed listing of products imported.

International Directory of Importers--Middle East. Croner Publications Inc. • Irregular. $225. Covers: 14,000 importers in Bahrain, Egypt, Iran, Iraq, Israel, Jordan, Kuwait, Lebanon, Oman, Qatar, Saudi Arabia, Syria, United Arab Emirates, and

North/South Yemen. Entries include: Company name, address, phone.

The International Directory of Importers - North America. Interdata. • $250 Individuals print. Covers: 19,000 firms importing in North America a broad variety of products from abrasives to zippers. Entries include: Company name and address, contact person, email, number of employees, year established, phone and telefaxes, business activity, bank references, as well as a detailed listing of products imported.

International Directory of Importers--North America. Croner Publications Inc. • Irregular. $225. Covers: 20,000 importers in the United States and Canada. Entries include: Company name, address, phone.

The International Directory of Importers - Office Equipment, Stationery and Supplies Importers. Interdata. • Annual. $320 Individuals print. Covers: 7,100 international firms importing office equipment, stationery and supplies. Entries include: Company name and address, contact person, email, number of employees, year established, phone and telefaxes, business activity, bank references, as well as a listing of office equipment, stationery and supplies currently being imported.

The International Directory of Importers - Optical Goods & Instruments Importers. Interdata. • $220 Individuals print. Covers: 2,100 international firms importing optical goods and instruments. Entries include: Company name and address, contact person, email, number of employees, year established, phone and telefaxes, business activity, bank references, as well as a listing of optical goods and instruments currently being imported.

The International Directory of Importers - Paper, Paper Goods and Stationery Products Importers. Interdata. • $295 Individuals print version. Covers: 4,400 international firms importing paper, paper goods and stationery products. Entries include: Company name and address, contact person, email, number of employees, year established, phone and telefaxes, business activity, bank references, as well as a listing of paper, paper goods and stationery products currently being imported.

The International Directory of Importers--Photographic Equipment and Supplies Importers. Interdata. • $200 Individuals print version. Covers: 1,700 international firms importing photographic equipment and supplies. Entries include: Company name and address, contact person, email, number of employees, year established, phone and telefaxes, business activity, bank references, as well as a listing of photographic equipment and supplies currently being imported.

The International Directory of Importers--Plastics & Plastic Products Importers. Interdata. • $295 Individuals print. Covers: 4,400 international firms importing plastics and plastic products. Entries include: Company name and address, contact person, email, number of employees, year established, phone and telefaxes, business activity, bank references, as well as a listing of plastics and plastic products currently being imported.

The International Directory of Importers--Plumbing, Sanitary Ware, Pipes & Fittings Importers. Interdata. • $260 Individuals print. Covers: 3,700 international firms importing plumbing, sanitary ware, pipes and fittings. Entries include: Company name and address, contact person, email, number of employees, year established, phone and telefaxes, business activity, bank references, as well as a listing of plumbing, sanitary ware, pipes and fittings currently being imported.

The International Directory of Importers--Printing and Graphic Arts Equipment and Supplies Importers. Interdata. • $220 Individuals print. Covers: 2,500 international firms importing printing and graphic arts equipment and supplies. Entries include: Company name and address, contact person, email, number of employees, year established, phone and telefaxes, business activity, bank references, as well as a listing of printing and graphic arts equipment and supplies currently being imported.

The International Directory of Importers--Pumps & Compressors Importers. Interdata. • $220 Individuals print. Covers: 2,200 international firms importing pumps and compressors. Entries include: Company name and address, contact person, email, number of employees, year established, phone and telefaxes, business activity, bank references, as well as a listing of pumps and compressors currently being imported.

The International Directory of Importers - Refrigeration, Ventilation and Heating Equipment Importers. Interdata. • $260 Individuals print. Covers: 3,300 international firms importing refrigeration, ventilation and heating equipment. Entries include: Company name and address, contact person, email, number of employees, year established, phone and telefaxes, business activity, bank references, as well as a listing of refrigeration, ventilation and heating equipment currently being imported.

The International Directory of Importers--Safety, Security and Fire Fighting Equipment Importers. Interdata. • $260 Individuals print edition. Covers: 3,300 international firms importing safety, security and fire fighting equipment. Entries include: Company name and address, contact person, email, number of employees, year established, phone and telefaxes, business activity, bank references, as well as a listing of safety, security and fire fighting equipment currently being imported.

The International Directory of Importers--Screws, Nuts, Bolts and Fasteners Importers. Interdata. • $200 Individuals print. Covers: 900 international firms importing screws, nuts, bolts and fasteners. Entries include: Company name and address, contact person, email, number of employees, year established, phone and telefaxes, business activity, bank references, as well as a listing of screws, nuts, bolts and fasteners currently being imported.

The International Directory of Importers - South America. Interdata. • $250 Individuals print edition. Covers: 23,000 firms importing in 27 South American countries a broad variety of products from abrasives to zippers. Entries include: Company name and address, contact person, e-mail address, number of employees, year established, phone and telefaxes, business activity, bank references, as well as a detailed listing of products imported.

The International Directory of Importers--Sporting Goods and Toys Importers. Interdata. • Annual. $295 Individuals print. Covers: 4,700 international firms importing sporting goods and toys. Entries include: Company name and address, contact person, email, number of employees, year established, phone and telefaxes, business activity, bank references, as well as a listing of sporting goods and toys currently being imported.

The International Directory of Importers--Textiles & Fabrics Importers. Interdata. • $260 Individuals print. Covers: 3,600 international firms importing textiles and fabrics. Entries include: Company name and address, contact person, email, number of employees, year established, phone and telefaxes, business activity, bank references, as well as a listing of textiles and fabrics currently being imported.

The International Directory of Importers--Tires and Tubes Importers: Auto, Cycle, Truck. Interdata. • $200 Individuals print. Covers: 1,300 international firms importing tires and tubes (auto/cycle/truck). Entries include: Company name and address, contact person, email, number of employees, year established, phone and telefaxes, business activity, bank references, as well as a listing of tires and tubes (auto/cycle/truck) currently being imported.

The International Directory of Importers - Watches and Clocks Importers. Interdata. • $200 Individuals print. Covers: 1,000 international firms importing watches and clocks. Entries include: Company name and address, contact person, email, number of employees, year established, phone and telefaxes, business activity, bank references, as well as a listing of watches and clocks currently being imported.

International Directory of Importers--Welding and Soldering Equipment Importers. Interdata. • Annual. $200 Individuals print. Covers: 700 international firms importing welding and soldering equipment. Entries include: Company name and address, contact person, email, number of employees, year established, phone and telefaxes, business activity, bank references, as well as a listing of welding and soldering equipment currently being imported.

The International Directory of Importers - Woodworking Equipment and Tools Importers. Interdata. • $200 Individuals print edition. Covers: 1,800 international firms importing woodworking equipment and tools. Entries include: Company name and address, contact person, email, number of employees, year established, phone and telefaxes, business activity, bank references, as well as a listing of woodworking equipment and tools currently being imported.

International Directory of Marketing Information Sources. Euromonitor International Business Reference Div. • Irregular. $650. Covers: Marketing sources in major non-European industrialized countries. Entries include: Over 6,000 contacts, services, and publications.

International Intertrade Index of New Imported Products. International Intertrade Index. • Monthly. $45 per year. Covers: manufacturers of new products that are announced at foreign trade fairs and available to United States importers. Entries include: Company name, address, description of new products, and prices. Subscription includes "Foreign Trade Fairs" newsletter.

International M & A Review. Euromoney Institutional Investor P.L.C. • $375 Individuals. Covers: Merger and acquisition advising companies in Europe and U.S. Database includes: Country profiles and reviews of mergers and acquisitions by industry. Entries include: Name, address, phone, fax, names and titles of key personnel, year founded, description of business activities.

International Plastics Directory. Verlag fur Internationale Wirtschaftsliteratur Ltd. • 64. $600. Covers: Plastics producers and processors worldwide. Entries include: Company name, address, phone, description, production line, trademarks, number of machines, associated companies.

International Trade Directory. Indian Export Trade Journal. • Biennial. $50. Covers: Importers, exporters, shipping, clearing agents, banks, and chambers of commerce in 150 countries. Entries include: Contact information.

International Trade Directory for Dayton, Ohio. Dayton Area Chamber of Commerce. • Biennial. $25 Members. Covers: International firms importing and exporting in Dayton. Entries include: Company name, address, phone.

International Trade Directory of Contacts/Sources/Services. Hilary House Publishers Inc. • Biennial. $120 plus $5.00 shipping. Covers: more than 14,800 U.S. organizations and key executives in 26 international business categories. Entries include: Company or personal name, address, phone, name and title of contact, service provided.

Internet Access Providers: An International Resource Directory. Mecklermedia Corp. • $30. Covers: 150 private companies, electronic bulletin board systems, and regional networks that offer dial-in access to the Internet. Entries include: Description.

Internet Resources and Services for International Business: A Global Guide. Greenwood Electronic Media. • $82.95 Single issue Paperback. Covers: More than 2,500 business-related Web sites, most of which are government and university sites, international. Entries include: Web site, content.

Internet Resources and Services for International Marketing and Advertising: A Global Guide. Greenwood Electronic Media. • $75 Individuals hardcover. Covers: Over 2,000 Web sites with information pertaining to marketing and advertising in more than 150 countries.

Internet Service Providers Directory (ISP). Info-Group Inc. • Annual. Number of listings: 27,032. Entries include: Name, address, phone, size of advertisement, name of owner or manager, number of employees, year first in "Yellow Pages." Compiled from telephone company "Yellow Pages," nationwide.

Investment Blue Book. Securities Investigations Inc. • Irregular. $145. Covers: 6,000 brokers and dealers in tax shelter plans; 2,000 sponsors of tax shelter product and suppliers of services to the industry. Entries include: Company name, address, phone, toll-free, phone, fax, name of contact.

Investment Opportunities in China: Chemical Industry. Pasha Publications. • $255. Covers: Approximately 530 Chinese projects in the chemical industry seeking international offshore capital investments. Entries include: Project name, address, phone, cable number; name and title of contact; financial data; description of project.

IOMA Business Directory. Institute of Management & Administration Inc. • Covers: Business Web sites. Entries include: Web links.

Iran Golden Key Directory. International Institute of Trade Relation Promotion, Trade Information Centre of Iran. • £100 Individuals CD version. Covers: 19,000 companies in Iran. Entries include: Company name, telephone, fax, e-mail, Managing Director, date established, number of employees, and business date.

Iran Industrial and Business Directory. International Business Publications, USA. • Annual. $99.95 Individuals hardcopy, e-book, CD-ROM. Covers: Strategic industrial, investment and business contacts for conducting export-import and investment activity in the country.

Iraq Industrial and Business Directory. International Business Publications, USA. • Annual. $99.95 Individuals hardcopy, e-book, CD-ROM. Covers: Strategic industrial, investment and business contacts for conducting export-import and investment activity in the country. Contains strategic practical economic and business information.

Ireland Government and Business Contacts Handbook. International Business Publications, USA. • $99.95 Individuals hardcopy, e-book, CD-ROM. Covers: Strategic government and business information, export-import activity in the country, investment, business contacts and regulations.

Ireland Industrial and Business Directory. International Business Publications, USA. • Annual. $99.95 Individuals hardcover, e-book, CD-ROM. Covers: Strategic industrial, investment and business contacts for conducting export-import and investment activity in the country. Contains strategic practical economic and business information.

Iron and Steel International Directory. DMG World Media. • Annual. $48. Covers: Plant and equipment manufacturers in the steel industry, worldwide. Entries include: Company name, address, phone, fax, product/service provided.

Irwin Business and Investment Almanac. QSU Publishing. • Annual. $75. Publication includes: Lists of online databases and their producers; executive search firms, accounting firms, and advertising agencies. Principal content of publication is review of significant business and finance events and statistical data for the year covered. Database includes: Major and group stock market averages, reviews of major futures markets and charts for futures-traded commodities, expanded coverage of foreign business and investment activity.

Isle of Man: General Information Factfile. Commercial Development Div. The Treasury Isle of Man Government. • Annual. Covers: financial institutions, insurance companies, real estate agencies, legal and accounting firms, shipowners, manufacturer, and other service trades on the Isle of Man; government service agencies. Database includes: Summaries of economic activity and opportunity; government policies regarding trade and industry; information on education and social issues. Entries include: Company or agency name, address, phone; shipowners and stockbrokers also include telex and fax numbers; financial institutions and real estate agencies include names of contact or other key personnel; banks and insurance companies include branch office and subsidiary names, addresses, and phone numbers.

Israel Agro and Biotechnology Industry Export-Import Directory. International Business Publications, USA. • Annual. $99.95 Individuals hardcover, e-book, CD-ROM. Covers: Information on strategic economic, investment, export-import, and business opportunities. Contains important export-import, government, and business contacts. Ultimate directory for conducting export-import operations in the country.

Israel Business & Government Directory. Jerusalem Marketing Group. • Semiannual. $39. Covers: over 750 persons active in national government, local municipalities, foreign embassies and consulates, political parties, government companies, and major business organizations and associations in Israel. Entries include: Organization or company name, address, phone, fax, name and title of contact, names and titles of key personnel, number of employees, financial data.

Israel IT and Telecommunication Industry Export-Import Directory. International Business Publications, USA. • Annual. $99.95 Individuals hardcover, e-book, CD-ROM. Covers: Major investment, export-import and other strategic business opportunities, contacts, and basic information for conducting business in the country.

IT Legal Guide. VNU Business Publications Ltd. • Annual. $45 plus 4 postage. Covers: More than 400 manufacturers, distributors, and consultants in the United Kingdom specializing with information on 300 technology products and services for the legal profession. Database includes: List of pertinent information sources. Entries include: Name, address, phone, fax, description of products/services.

The IT Locator. Information Resource Group. • Monthly. Covers: computer installations in the following states: Connecticut, the District of Columbia, Georgia, Illinois, Maryland, Massachusetts, Michigan, Missouri, Minnesota, New Jersey, New York, Ohio, Pennsylvania, Texas, Wisconsin, Colorado, Florida, North Carolina, South Carolina, Iowa, Indiana, Kansas, Tennessee, California, Arizona, Washington, and Oregon; separate edition available on a lease basis for each region. Entries include: Company name, address, phone, names and titles of key personnel in data processing and management information systems, hardware systems and software utilized.

Italy Business Directory (ITBD). INFOT Inc. • $55.25 CD-ROM. Covers: 80,063 major industries from Italy and related regions. Entries include: Contact person, physical addresses, email and website addresses, telephone and fax number, and business description.

Italy Industrial and Business Directory. International Business Publications, USA. • Annual. $99.95 Individuals hardcover, e-book, CD-ROM. Covers: Strategic industrial, investment and business contacts for conducting export-import and investment activity in the country. Contains strategic, practical economic and business information.

IVCI Directory of Domestic and International Venture Groups. International Venture Capital Institute Inc. Baxter Associates Inc. • Annual. $9.95 per issue. Covers: over 200 venture capital clubs; international coverage. Entries include: Organization name, address, phone, name and title of contact.

IVCI Directory of Venture Capital Seed and Early-Stage Funds. International Venture Capital Institute Inc. Baxter Associates Inc. • Covers: Over 225 venture capital firms which do seed and/or early-stage joint ventures. Entries include: Contact information.

J W Business International: International Business Communications Directory. Telex-Verlag Jaeger + Waldmann GmbH. • Annual. $210. Covers: Approximately 2,000,000 companies on fax and telex worldwide in all trades and industries classified by products and services within 43 main groups. Entries include: Company name, address, fax and telex numbers; subsidiary and branch names and locations.

J W CD-ROM Fax Directory. Telex-Verlag Jaeger + Waldmann GmbH. • Annual. $690. Covers: Nearly 95,000 Canadian businesses and other institutions and organizations owning fax machines. Also includes some listings for North and South America, Asia, Africa, and Australia. Entries include: Company or organization name, address, phone, fax, telex, and information on product/service, J+W trade codes.

Japan Electronics Buyers' Guide. Dempa Publications Inc. • Annual. $220. Covers: manufacturers of electronic equipment and components in Japan, and import-export firms and agents dealing in those products. Entries include: For manufacturers and traders--Company name, address, phone, fax, branches, names and titles of president and key sales executives, establishment, capital, sales, number of employees, products, trade names, percentage of sales in export, main factory. For agents--Company name, address, phone, companies represented.

Japan Government and Business Contacts Handbook. International Business Publications, USA. • $99.95 Individuals hardcopy, e-book, CD-ROM. Covers: Strategic government and business information, export-import activity in the country, investment, business contacts and regulations.

Japan Industrial and Business Directory. International Business Publications, USA. • $99.95 Individuals hardcopy, e-book, CD-ROM. Covers: Customs, trade regulations and procedures.

Japanese-Affiliated Companies in U.S.A. and Canada. Japan External Trade Organization. • Biennial. Covers: 9,870 Japanese firms, restaurants, and various information sources. Database includes: Area maps. Entries include: Company name, address, phone, fax, line of business, parent company, executive officers, year established.

Japanese Business in Britain. Culver Financial Surveys. • Annual. $100 2000 edition. Covers: Approximately 550 Japanese-owned, United Kingdom-registered limited companies. Entries include: Company name, address, names and titles of key personnel, number of employees, financial data, subsidiary and branch names and locations, description, ownership information, sales and profits data.

Japanese Companies in the UK. Jordans Ltd. • Annual. $195. Covers: Top 180 Japanese companies in the United Kingdom. Entries include: Company name, address, phone, contact name, description of business.

Japanese Investment in U.S. and Canadian Real Estate Directory. Mead Ventures Inc. • Annual. $295. Covers: about 550 Japanese investors, brokers, lenders, consultants, and developers in the United States and Canada; and about 275 companies in Japan. Entries include: Company name, address, phone, fax, telex, name and title of contact, geographical area served, services provided and description of projects and services.

Japanese Overseas Investments. Toyo Keizai Inc. • $550. Covers: over 13,000 Japanese affiliate and subsidiary companies operating in over 100 countries. Entries include: Company name, address, phone, capital and business lines, product/service.

Jewelers Directory--Supplies. InfoGroup Inc. • Annual. Number of listings: 594. Entries include: Name, address, phone, size of advertisement, name of owner or manager, number of employees, year first in "Yellow Pages." Compiled from telephone company "Yellow Pages," nationwide.

Jiu Jitsu Instruction Directory. InfoGroup Inc. • Annual. Number of listings: 5,198. Entries include: Name, address, phone, size of advertisement, name of owner or manager, number of employees, year first in "Yellow Pages." Compiled from telephone company "Yellow Pages," nationwide.

Job Seeker's Guide to 1000 Top Employers. Visible Ink Press. • $22.95. Covers: 1,000 large or prominent private and public companies in the U.S. Entries include: Company name, address, phone, fax, year founded, type of company, stock exchanges on which traded, stock symbol, description, locations of operating units, subsidiaries and affiliated companies, corporate officers, financial data, number of employees, human resources contact, job application procedures.

Job Training & Vocational Rehabilitation Services Directory. InfoGroup Inc. • Annual. Number of listings: 1,605. Entries include: Name, address, phone, size of advertisement, name of owner or manager, number of employees, year first in "Yellow Pages." Compiled from telephone company "Yellow Pages," nationwide.

Jobson's Yearbook of Public Companies. Dun & Bradstreet (Australia) Proprietary Ltd. • Daily (eve.). $520 Individuals. Database covers: All companies (about 1,400) listed on the Industrial Boards of the Australian and New Zealand stock exchanges; includes mining and petroleum industries. Database includes: Information on money market companies, trust companies, and stockbrokers, ranking of top 100 companies by revenue and profit. Entries include: Company name, address, phone, fax; DUNS number; subsidiaries; associated companies; names and titles of key personnel; branch office locations; share register; home exchange subsidiaries; voting rights; auditors; bankers; solicitors; financial data; major shareholder; history; operations, and ACN number.

Joint Venture Directory of the New Independent States. Triumph Books Inc. • $295 payment must accompany order. Covers: about 2,650 firms in the Commonwealth of Independent States that are joint ventures between CIS companies and foreign firms. Entries include: Company name, address, phone, fax, telex, name and title of contact, product or service, names of domestic and foreign partners, capitalization, number of employees, date registered, objectives.

Joint Venture Partner Search Directory. Michigan Department of Agriculture. • Irregular. $15. Covers: more than 200 Michigan companies interested in forming international partnerships. Entries include: Company name, address, phone, Standard Industrial Classification (SIC) code, annual sales (if available), number of employees, geographical areas in which interested in conducting business.

Jordan Golden Key Directory. International Institute of Trade Relation Promotion, Trade Information Centre of Iran. • £100 Individuals. Covers: 29,424 companies in Jordan. Entries include: Company name, address, telephone, fax, products, services, Managing Director, and business activities.

Juke Boxes Wholesalers Directory. InfoGroup Inc. • Annual. Number of listings: 1,002. Entries include: Name, address, phone, size of advertisement, name of owner or manager, number of employees, year first in "Yellow Pages." Compiled from telephone company "Yellow Pages," nationwide.

Juvenile Joys--Toys and Games of the Philippines. Philippine-German Export Development Project Philippine Bureau of Export Trade Promotion. • $350. Publication includes: List of almost 60 manufacturers and exporters of toys in the Philippines; also lists 25 overseas trade posts. Entries include: Company name, address, phone, telex, name and title of contact. Principal content of publication is a catalog of toys exported from the Philippines.

Kansas Directory of Manufacturers and Products. Wichita Eagle. • Biennial. $50. Covers: Approximately 2,400 manufacturers in Kansas; includes Standard Industrial Classification (SIC) code 02, 07, 13, 14, 20, 22-39, and 49. Entries include: Company name, address, phone, telex, names and titles of key personnel, number of employees, description of products, Standard Industrial Classification (SIC) code.

Kansas International Trade Resource Directory. Kansas Department of Commerce - Office of Minority and Women Business Development. • Annual. Covers: Agencies and organizations in Kansas that provide international trade information. Entries include: Agency or organization name, address, phone, telex, name and title of contact, description of services.

Kansas Manufacturers Register. Harris InfoSource. • Annual. $145 Individuals All-Businesses Price. Covers: Over 4,900 manufacturers in Kansas. Entries include: Company name, address, phone, fax, toll-free numbers, names and titles of key personnel, number of employees, annual sales, square feet, Standard Industrial Classification (SIC) codes, products produced, year established, foreign trade, and headquarters information.

Kansas Manufacturing Firms in Export. Kansas Department of Commerce - Office of Minority and Women Business Development. • Biennial. Covers: nearly 1,000 Kansas companies in major groups 20 through 39 of the Standard Industrial Classification (SIC). Entries include: Company name, address, phone, name of principal executive, parent or subsidiary company, number of employees, products or services.

Kazakhstan Government and Business Contacts Handbook. International Business Publications, USA. • $99.95 Individuals hardcopy, e-book, CD-ROM. Covers: Strategic government and business information, export-import activity in the country, investment, business contacts and regulations.

Kazakhstan Health Care Directory. Flegon Press. • $100. Covers: Health care organizations, schools, provides, trade unions, and departments of health in the republic of Kazakhstan of the former Soviet Union. Entries include: Name, address, phone, fax, contact person.

Kazakhstan Trade Directory. Flegon Press. • $200 Complete set. Covers: Business contacts from all industrial branches and government offices, including Agriculture, Fisheries, Health Care, Science and Tourism, in Kazakhstan, the richest republic of the former Soviet Union. Database includes: Over 1,000 trade propositions and requests for partnerships. Entries include: For contacts--name, address, phone; for producers--name, address, phone, fax, telex, directors' name, output/import needs, requests for partnership.

Kelly's Industrial Directory Book. Reed Business Information. • Annual. Directory of over 94,600 U.K. industrial companies.

Kelly's Industrial Directory--CD. Reed Business Information. • Annual. Database of UK industrial companies. Database covers: 200,000 companies under 17,000 headings.

Kelly's Post Office--London Business Directory. Reed Business Information. • Covers: 96,000 London businesses, 70,000 streets with postal district name, 21,000 buildings, local and regional government offices and officials, public bodies and societies, and professional firms. Entries include: Company name, address, phone, government official name, position, title.

Kentucky Directory of Manufacturers. Kentucky Cabinet for Economic Development. • Annual. $87. Covers: Approximately 5,900 manufacturing firms in Kentucky. Entries include: Company name, address, phone, names of principal executives, number of employees, products or services, date established, parent company (with name and address).

Kenya Business Directory. Business Guide. • $250 Individuals Soft copy. Covers: 48,000 business listings including wholesalers, importers, retailers, business houses, and agents in Kenya.

Kenya Industrial and Business Directory. International Business Publications, USA. • Annual. $99.95 Individuals hardcopy, e-book, CD-ROM. Covers: Strategic industrial, investment and business contacts for conducting export-import and investment activity in the country. Contains strategic practical economic and business information.

Key Business Directory--Latin America. Dun & Bradstreet Inc. • Covers: Leading companies in Latin America whose annual sales are $10 million and who have 500 or more employees. Entries include: Company name, address, phone, fax, telex, number of employees, import/export designation, primary and secondary Standard Industrial Classification (SIC) codes, sales volume.

Key Business Directory of Indonesia/Thailand. Dun & Bradstreet Inc. • Covers: Approximately 1,500 public and private companies in Indonesia and Thailand; Indonesian companies listed have an annual turnover of over 10 billion Rupiah and more than 50 employees; Thai companies listed have an annual turnover of over 150 Baht and more than 50 employees.

Key Business Directory of Malaysia. Dun & Bradstreet Inc. • Covers: 1,500 public and private companies in Malaysia, each with an annual turnover of $18 million and over 50 employees.

Key Business Directory of Singapore. Dun & Bradstreet Inc. • Covers: leading companies in Singapore. Database includes: Directory of company directors. Entries include: Company name, address, phone, fax, line of business, sales volume, industry designation, names and titles of key personnel, year established, number of employees, import/export designation, accountants and bankers.

Kitchen Cabinets & Equipment Directory--Household. InfoGroup Inc. • Annual. Number of listings: 17,583. Entries include: Name, address, phone, size of advertisement, name of owner or manager, number of employees, year first in "Yellow Pages." Compiled from telephone company "Yellow Pages," natyonwide.

Kompass. Kompass Deutschland Verlags- und Vertriebsgesellschaft, mbH. • Annual. $88. Covers: German products and companies specializing in coal extraction, ore mining, quarries, cement industry, glass and ceramics.

Kompass Agribusiness, Food, and Beverage. APN News & Media Group Ltd. APN Business Information Group. • Annual. $85. Covers: Agricultural food and beverage companies and their products and services.

Kompass (Branchenauszuge)--Chemische Industrie. Kompass Deutschland Verlags- und Vertriebsgesellschaft, mbH. • Annual. $98. Covers: Chemical industry profiles and products in Germany for purchasers and marketers.

Kompass Canada. Micromedia ProQuest. • Irregular. $399 plus 9.95 shipping. Covers: Approximately 30,000 Canadian companies. Entries include: Company name, address, phone, fax, senior executives, statement of activities, financial information, number of employees, parent and affiliated companies, date established.

Kompass Croatia Direct. Promar Ltd. • Annual. $100. Covers: 19,000 companies in Croatia. Entries include: Company name and address, directors and management, turnover, trade marks, employment, complete product list according to Kompass classification.

Kompass Croatia--Register. Promar Ltd. • Annual. $1,700. Covers: More than 19,000 Croatian companies with a complete product list of 58,000 products and services classified according to Kompass. Entries include: Company name and address, directors and management, turnover rate, employment.

Kompass Deutschland: Jahrbuch der Deutschen Wirtschaft. Kompass Deutschland Verlags- und Vertriebsgesellschaft, mbH. • Annual. Covers: Major German manufacturers, distributors, and service companies linked to 40,000 products and services. Database includes: Glossary. Entries include: Company name, address, phone, telex, names and titles of key personnel, bank, key to product and service listings, year established, symbols indicating whether company is a manufacturer, wholesaler, or agent, and whether it imports and exports, turnover, number of employees, shareholders; reference to dot-chart index.

Kompass--Diamonds. Kompass Belgium Products. • Annual. Covers: All Belgian diamond cutters/merchants.

Kompass International. Kompass France. • Annual. Covers: Over 1,500,000 commercial and industrial firms worldwide; over 500,000 prominent business and industry professionals in 64 countries.

Kompass New Zealand. Reg Birchfield. • Annual. $350 plus GST. Covers: 12,000 organizations classified by the products and services they offer. Entries include: Company name, address, phone, fax, contact person, key personnel, directors, number of employees, turnover, paid capital, banks, date established, description of activity, products and services classification, brand names, export markets.

Kompass Philippines. Croner Publications Inc. • Annual. $225. Covers: 5,000 companies and 15,000 products in 400 categories of industry and commerce in the Philippines.

Kompass Professionnel Chimie--Plastiques. Kompass France. • Annual. Covers: French chemical industry companies. Entries include: Company name, activity, products, services, decision makers and their functions, key figures.

Kompass Register United Kingdom. Reed Business Information. • Annual. Covers: In 3 volumes, information on over 45,000 industrial and commercial companies in UK. Financial data. Entries include: Company name, address, phone, fax, product, trade name.

Kompass Sweden. Kompass Sverige AB Ett foretag inom Bonnier Affarsinformation. • Annual. $289. Covers: 12,000 industrial and commercial firms, including wholesalers, manufacturers, importers/exporters, and distributors, in Sweden. Entries include: Company name, address, phone, line of business, product/service.

Kontaks Philippines. Massmark Philippines Publishers. • Biennial. $950. Covers: Members of Chambers of Commerce, including those in industry, manufacturing, exporting, importing, distributing, dealers, wholesalers, retailers, trade entities, banking investments, finance, real estate, housing, tourism, health industries, and consumer groups.

Korea South Government and Business Contacts Handbook: Trade, Investment & Business Development Contacts. International Business Publications, USA. • $99.95 Individuals hardcopy. Covers: Strategic government and business information, export-import activity in the country, investment, business contacts and regulations.

Korean Importers Association Directory. Korean Importers Association. • Annual. $12. Covers: 3,600 Korean companies. Entries include: Company name, address, phone, telex, name of official, items traded, suppliers.

Korean Trade Directory. Korean Foreign Trade Association. • Annual. Covers: Exporters, importers, commodities, and foreign firms established in Korea, including airline offices, marine insurance companies, shipping firms, and trade associations. Database includes: Details on trade and investment laws and regulations. Entries include: Company name, address, phone, telex, names and titles of key personnel.

Kraks Industrial and Commercial Directory of Denmark. Kraks Forlag A.S. • Annual. $2,765. Covers: 73,400 industrial and commercial firms in Denmark; 94,000 companies in the Register of Limited Liability Companies, the Insurance Register, and Trade Register in Denmark; public authorities, institutions, libraries, churches, hospitals, museums, schools, universities, and societies in Denmark. Entries include: Organization name, address, phone, product/service (where applicable).

Kuwait Golden Key Directory. International Institute of Trade Relation Promotion, Trade Information Centre of Iran. • £100 Individuals. Covers: 22,064 companies in Kuwait. Entries include: Company name, address, telephone, fax, e-mail, products, services, Managing Director, and business activities.

Kwazulu/Natal Business Register. Intratex Holdings. • Covers: businesses in the Kwazulu/Natal area. Entries include: Company name, address, phone.

Kyrgyzstan Government and Business Contacts Handbook. International Business Publications, USA. • $99.95 Individuals hardcopy, e-book, CD-ROM. Covers: Strategic government and business information, export-import activity in the country, investment, business contacts and regulations.

Kyrgyzstan Industrial and Business Directory. International Business Publications, USA. • Annual. $99.95 Individuals hardcopy, e-book, CD-ROM. Covers: Strategic industrial, investment and business contacts for conducting export-import and investment activity in the country.

Labels Directory. InfoGroup Inc. • Updated continuously; printed on request. Number of listings: 1,730. Entries include: Name, address, phone, size of advertisement, name of owner or manager, number of employees, year first in "Yellow Pages." Compiled from telephone company "Yellow Pages," nationwide.

Labels--Paper Directory. InfoGroup Inc. • Annual. Number of listings: 1,366. Entries include: Name, address, phone, size of advertisement, name of owner or manager, number of employees, year first in "Yellow Pages." Compiled from telephone company "Yellow Pages," nationwide.

Lacrosse Equipment & Suppliers Directory. InfoGroup Inc. • Annual. Number of listings: 22,706. Entries include: Name, address, phone, size of advertisement, name of owner or manager, number of employees, year first in "Yellow Pages." Compiled from telephone company "Yellow Pages," nationwide.

The Largest Companies in Norway. Okonomisk litteratur Norge A.S. • Annual. $1,300. Covers: 10,000 of the largest industrial companies, trading companies, banks, shipping companies, insurance companies, hotels, restaurants, travel agencies, advertising agencies, insurance companies, and consultant companies in Norway. Entries include: Company name, address, phone, telex number.

Largest Employers Directory. Greater San Antonio Chamber of Commerce. • Annual. $75 Nonmembers CD/email. Covers: About 1,700 manufacturing and nonmanufacturing firms in the San Antonio metropolitan statistical area: manufacturing firms each have at least 25 employees, nonmanufacturing firms have at least 50 employees. Entries include: Company name, address, phone; names and titles of key personnel, number of employees, year established, description of service, marketing area, and Standard Industrial Classification (SIC) code.

Las Vegas Chamber of Commerce--Business Directory. Las Vegas Metro Chamber of Commerce. • Covers: Businesses in Las Vegas, Nevada, who are chamber members. Entries include: Company name, address, phone, contact name.

LaSalle Bank Guide: Major Publicly Held Corporations and Financial Institutions Headquartered in Illinois. Scholl Corporate Guides. • Annual. $29.95 Single issue. Covers: Approximately 232 major publicly held corporations and financial institutions headquartered in Illinois. Database includes: List of companies ranked by revenue and assets; (NAICS) code listings; list of changes from previous edition. Entries include: Company name, headquarters location and phone, brief description of product lines and organizational structure, names of outside directors, names and titles of key personnel; consolidated balance sheet in abbreviated form, consolidated income statement; number of employees, date of annual meeting, stockholder information.

Latin America and Caribbean Autos Directory. Business Monitor International Ltd. • $975 Individuals CD. Covers: 1,145 top autos executives on 374 leading automotive companies from Argentina, Brazil, Chile, Colombia, Mexico, Peru, Venezuela, Anguilla, Antigua & Barbuda, Aruba, the Bahamas, Barbados, Bermuda, British Virgin Islands, Cayman Islands, Cuba, Dominica, Dominican Rep, French Guiana, Grenada, Guadeloupe, Guyana, Haiti, Jamaica, Martinique, Montserrat, Netherland Antilles, Puerto Rico, St Kitts, St Lucia, St Vincent, Suriname, Trinidad & Tobago, Turks & Caicos and US Virgin Islands. Entries include: parent company head offices, full company name, address, phone and fax numbers, email and website address, senior contact personnel, company description and profile, nationality, and ownership status.

Latin America and Caribbean Food and Drink Directory. Business Monitor International Ltd. • $975 Individuals CD. Covers: 1,642 top food and drink executives on 550 leading food and drink companies from Latin America and Caribbean. Entries include: parent company head offices, full company name, address, phone and fax numbers, email and website address, senior contact personnel, company description and profile, nationality, and ownership status.

Latin America & Caribbean Oil and Gas Directory. Business Monitor International Ltd. • $995 Individuals CD. Covers: 828 top oil and gas executives on 309 leading oil and gas companies from Latin America. Entries include: parent company head offices, full company name, address, phone and fax numbers, email and website address, senior contact personnel, company description and profile, nationality, and ownership status.

Latin America and Caribbean Pharmaceuticals and Healthcare Directory. Business Monitor International Ltd. • $995 Individuals CD. Covers: 1,908 top pharmaceutical executives at 598 leading pharmaceutical companies from Argentina, Brazil, Chile, Colombia, Mexico, Peru, Venezuela and the Caribbean. Entries include: parent company head offices, full company name, address, phone and fax numbers, email and website address, senior contact personnel, company description and profile, nationality, and ownership status.

Latin America and Caribbean Telecommunications Directory. Business Monitor International Ltd. • $995 Individuals CD. Covers: 2,506 top telecommunications executives at 808 leading telecommunications companies from Latin America and Caribbean. Entries include: parent company head offices, full company name, address, phone and fax numbers, email and website address, senior contact personnel, company description and profile, nationality, and ownership status.

Latin American Environmental Directory. Business Publishers Inc. • Annual. $179. Covers: Associations, corporations, embassies, consulates, legal specialists, U.S. registered foreign agents, and research centers located in Latin America involved in the environmental community. Entries include: Organization name, address, phone, fax, telex, key officers, SIC codes.

Latin American Import-Export Directory. International Trade Council. • Annual. Covers: 24,500 importing and exporting companies in Argentina, Bolivia, Brazil, Chile, Panama, Paraguay, Peru, Uruguay, Venezuela, Colombia, Costa Rica, Ecuador, El Salvador, Guatemala, Honduras, Mexico, Nicaragua, and the Dominican Republic; lists top companies in Latin American markets.

Latin American Markets: A Guide to Company and Information Sources. MarketResearch.com. • Irregular. $335. Covers: sources of information on businesses in Central America, South America, and the Caribbean. Entries include: Source name, address, phone, fax, names and titles of key personnel.

Latin American Product Guide. Todd Publications. • $125. Covers: Over 10,000 exporters from 18 Latin American countries.

Latvia Industrial and Business Directory. International Business Publications, USA. • Annual. $99.95 Individuals hardcopy, e-book, CD-ROM. Covers: Strategic industrial, investment and business contacts for conducting export-import and investment activity in the country.

Leading Employers of the New Hampshire & Southern Maine Seacoast. Greater Portsmouth Chamber of Commerce. • Biennial. $10. Covers: Approximately 200 companies in the Portsmouth, New Hampshire area (including part of southern Maine) that employ over 25 people. Entries include: Company name, address, phone, name and title of contact, number of employees, products or services provided.

Leather Goods Directory--Wholesalers. InfoGroup Inc. • Annual. Number of listings: 690. Entries include: Name, address, phone, size of advertisement, name of owner or manager, number of employees, year first in "Yellow Pages." Compiled from telephone company "Yellow Pages," nationwide.

Lebanese Industrial and Commercial Directory. Publitec Publications. • Annual. $120. Covers: Industrial and commercial companies in Lebanon. Entries include: Contact information.

Lebanon Golden Key Directory. International Institute of Trade Relation Promotion, Trade Information Centre of Iran. • £100 Individuals. Covers: 14,209 companies in Lebanon. Entries include: Company name, address, telephone, fax, products, services, Managing Director, and business activities.

Lehigh Valley Metro Business Directory. Dalton Directory. • Covers: Approximately 5,000 companies in the Pennsylvania counties of Lehigh, Berks, Lancaster, and Northampton; includes manufacturers, banks, law firms, hospitals, schools and colleges, hotels, etc. Entries include: Company name, address, phone, fax, telex, names and titles of key personnel, number of employees, Standard Industrial Classification (SIC) code, product/service.

Lewiston Chamber Business Directory. Lewiston Chamber of Commerce. • Covers: About 600 manufacturing and service companies in the Lewiston area. Entries include: Name, address, phone, fax, contact person.

LGBT Friendly Directory. VCS Gay Pride Rockland. • Covers: Businesses, services, and community organizations. Entries include: Company name, address, contact information, e-mail, and website.

Library Journal: Reference: Print, CD-ROM, Online (year). Reed Elsevier Group plc Reed Business Information. • Annual. Issued in November as a supplement to *Library Journal*. Lists new and updated reference material, including general and trade print titles, directories, annuals, CD-ROM titles, and online sources. Includes material from more than 200 publishers, arranged by company name, with an index by subject.

Library Journal Sourcebook: The Reference For Library Products & Services. Reed Elsevier Group plc Reed Business Information. • Annual. Publication includes: List of over 600 suppliers of products and services used by libraries from abstracting to word processing equipment. Entries include: Company name, address, phone, list of products or services. Complete listings for more than 100 architectural firms; Disaster planning for librarians.

Libya Business Directory. Business Guide. • $150 Individuals Soft copy. Covers: 1,800 business listings including wholesalers, importers, retailers, business houses, and agents in Libya.

Liechtenstein Industrial and Business Directory. International Business Publications, USA. • Annual. $99.95 Individuals hardcover, e-book, CD-ROM. Covers: Strategic industrial, investment and business contacts for conducting export-import and investment activity in the country.

Listed Companies in Finland. Kansallis-Osake-Pankki Sijoitustutkimus/Investment Research. • Annual. $545. Covers: all Finnish companys listed on the Helsinki Stock Exchange. Database includes: Charts and tables summarizing developments such as income statements, balance sheet, financial ratios, and per-share ratios. Entries include: Company name, address, phone, year established, line of business, subsidiary and branch names and locations, names and titles of key personnel, number of shareholders, financial data.

Lithuania Industrial and Business Directory. International Business Publications, USA. • Annual. $99.95 Individuals hardcover, e-book, CD-ROM. Covers: Strategic industrial, investment and business contacts for conducting export-import and investment activity in the country.

The Little Green Book--Business Directory for the Polish Community. AdMark Graphics Inc. • Annual. Covers: over 3,000 businesses of interest to the Polish communities of New York, New Jersey, Connecticut, Pennsylvania, and Massachusetts. Entries include: Company name, address, phone, subsidiary and branch names and locations, description of product/service.

Lobbyists Directory. InfoGroup Inc. • Annual. Number of listings: 1,107. Entries include: Name, address, phone, size of advertisement, name of owner or manager, number of employees, year first in "Yellow Pages." Compiled from telephone company "Yellow Pages," nationwide.

Locaguide: Locaguide du BTP et de la Manutention. Societe technique d'Editions pour l'Entreprise. • Annual. €23. Covers: 1,000 French companies. Entries include: Company name, address, phone, fax, telex, names and titles of key personnel, product/service provided.

Logos of America's Fastest Growing Corporations. Hoover's Inc. • $39.95. Covers: Over 500 logotypes, trademarks, and symbols from growing U.S. companies.

Logos of America's Largest Corporations. Hoover's Inc. • $39.95. Covers: Over 500 logotypes, trademarks, and symbols of U.S. companies.

Logos of Major World Corporations. Hoover's Inc. • $39.95. Covers: Over 500 logotypes, trademarks, and symbols of international companies.

Long Distance Telephone Services Directory. InfoGroup Inc. • Annual. Number of listings: 2,403. Entries include: Name, address, phone, size of advertisement, name of owner or manager, number of employees, year first in "Yellow Pages." Compiled from telephone company "Yellow Pages," nationwide.

Louisiana Business Directory. InfoGroup Inc. • Annual. $795 for both print & CD-ROM. Covers: 184,886 businesses in Louisiana. Entries include: Company name, address, phone, number of employees, standard industrial classification (sic) code, line of business, name of owner or manager, sales volume, credit ratings. Compiled from telephone company 'Yellow Pages,' statewide. All states covered independently (see separate entries).

Luxembourg Industrial and Business Directory. International Business Publications, USA. • Annual. $99.95 Individuals paperback, e-book, CD-ROM. Covers: Strategic industrial, investment and business contacts for conducting export-import and investment activity in the country. Contains strategic, practical economic and business information.

Macao Government and Business Contacts Handbook. International Business Publications, USA. • $99.95 Individuals hardcopy, e-book, CD-ROM. Covers: Strategic government and business information, export-import activity in the country, investment, business contacts and regulations.

Macmillan Directory of Multinationals. Palgrave Macmillan. • Biennial. $295 plus 9 for shipping. Covers over 400 multinational industrial companies with consolidated sales of over $1 billion.

MacRae's Blue Book. MacRae's Blue Book. • Annual. Covers: about 50,000 manufacturing firms. Entries include: Company name, address, products or services, phone, email and URL addresses.

Madagascar Business Directory. Business Guide. • $150 Individuals Soft copy. Covers: 14,000 business listings including wholesalers, importers, retailers, business houses, and agents in Madagascar.

Made in Greece. Trade Publishing Resources. • Covers: Greek companies engaged in establishing trade and business relations in 155 countries.

Made in Malta. Malta External Trade Corp. • Annual. Covers: Over 850 manufacturing companies and service providers in Malta. Entries include: Company name, address, phone, fax, name and title of contact, number of employees, product/services, company logo.

Magicians Directory. InfoGroup Inc. • Annual. Number of listings: 1,133. Entries include: Name, address, phone, size of advertisement, name of owner or manager, number of employees, year first in "Yellow Pages." Compiled from telephone company "Yellow Pages," nationwide.

Maine Manufacturers Register and Industrial

Database. Manufacturers' News Inc. • Annual. $92 Individuals print. Covers: 2,683 manufacturers in Maine. Entries include: Company name, address, phone, names and titles of key personnel, year established, number of employees, plant square footage, services, Standard Industry Classification (SIC) code, parent and subsidiary company information, type of in-house computer system, URL, e-mail address.

Maine Manufacturing Directory. Tower Publishing Co. • Annual. $55 Individuals. Covers: Approximately 1,584 manufacturers and processors in Maine. Entries include: Company name, address, phone, fax, toll-free phone, e-mail and web addresses, names and titles of principal officers, number of employees, product or service, Standard Industrial Classification (SIC) code, parent company (if applicable), sales revenue, import/export data.

Major and Medium-Sized Companies in the Czech Republic. Hoppenstedt Produktinformationen GmbH. • Annual. €195. Covers: over 18,000 companies in the Czech Republic. Entries include: Name, address, phone, fax, management, production or services, number of employees, turnover (revenue), and capital.

The Major Companies Guide: The Charitable and Community Support of the UK's Leading Companies. The Directory of Social Change. • Biennial. $16.95. Covers: about 400 companies in the United Kingdom with 160 millions Ls in cash donations and 100 millions Ls in community contributions. Entries include: Company name, address, phone, names and titles of key personnel, financial data, amount of donations annually, donation policy and practice, number of employees, employee involvement, branch office or subsidiary names, descriptions of product/service, type of business, community support programs.

Major Companies in China. Hoppenstedt Produktinformationen GmbH. • $520. Covers: 10,000 major companies in China. Entries include: Name, address, phone, fax, range of products or services, import and export, revenue, number of employees, and joint ventures.

Major Companies in Southeast Asia. Euromonitor International Business Reference Div. • $550 Individuals. Covers: Nearly 2,000 companies in Brunei, Hong Kong, Indonesia, Malaysia, the Philippines, Singapore, South Korea, Taiwan, and Thailand. Entries include: Company name, address, phone, fax, type of business, ownership, subsidiaries, key personnel, products and brands, main operations, outlets and trading names, number of employees, turnover, pre-tax profit, sales, background information.

Major Companies in the Netherlands. Netherlands-British Chamber of Commerce. • Biennial. $10. Covers: Businesses in the Netherlands. Entries include: Company name, address, phone, telex, directors.

Major Companies of Latin America and the Caribbean. Cengage Learning Inc. • $1,275. Includes more than 8,650 major companies in Latin America and more than 1,100 leading Caribbean firms.

Major Companies of Slovakia. I.S.M.C. Information Systems and Marketing Contacts Ltd. • Annual. $164. Covers: The most important companies in the Slovak Republic. Entries include: Detailed business information and data.

Major Companies of the Arab World. Cengage Learning Inc. • Annual. $1,480 Individuals. Published by Graham & Whiteside Ltd. Coverage of the world's largest companies in the Arab world. Includes names of senior executives, contact information, and financial information.

Major Companies of Turkey Directory. Poyraz Publications A.S. • Annual. $50. Covers: 2,500 companies, products, and industries in Turkey. Entries include: Company name, address, phone, telex, names and titles of key personnel, products, and trade names.

Major Employers in Metropolitan Chicago. Chicagoland Chamber of Commerce. • Biennial. $55. Covers: over 2,000 firms employing at least 250 employees in their Chicago area plants and offices; also listed are subsidiaries, affiliates, and divisions. Entries include: Company name, address, phone, names of major officers; line of business and Standard Industrial Classification (SIC) code; coding to indicate number of employees and whether manufacturer or non-manufacturer.

Major Firms in Czech Republic. I.S.M.C. Information Systems and Marketing Contacts Ltd. • Annual. $164. Covers: Significant business firms in Czech Republic. Entries include: Detailed business information.

Major French Companies. DAFSA. • Annual. Covers: Companies with shares traded on the stock exchange in France. Entries include: Company name, address, phone, officers, directors, executives, banking information, financial institutions, broker-trading.

Major Market Share Companies. Euromonitor International Business Reference Div. • $1,295 Individuals hard copy mail delivery. Covers: List of top national and regional companies in the Americas, Asia-Pacific, Europe, and South Africa across 15 consumer sectors. Entries include: Company name, address, phone; company share; leading brands; and merger and acquisition information.

Major Telecommunications Companies of Europe. Graham & Whiteside. • Annual. $245 softback. Covers: Over 1,500 telecommunications companies in Austria, Belgium, Bulgaria, Croatia, Cyprus, Czech Republic, Denmark, Eire, Estonian Republic, Finland, France, Germany, Greece, Hungary, Israel, Italy, Latvian Republic, Lithuanian Republic, Luxembourg, Netherlands, Norway, Poland, Portugal, Romania, Slovakia, Slovenia, Spain, Sweden, Switzerland, and the United Kingdom involved in the telecommunications industry, including telecommunications companies, equipment suppliers, and Internet companies. Entries include: Company name, address, phone and names and titles of key personnel.

Major Telecommunications Companies of the Far East & Australasia. Graham & Whiteside. • Annual. $245 softback. Covers: Over 1,000 telecommunications companies in Australia, Brunei, Cambodia, China, Hong Kong, Indonesia, Japan, Laos, Malaysia, New Zealand, Philippines, Singapore, South Korea, Taiwan, Thailand, and Vietnam involved in the telecommunications industry, including telecommunications companies, equipment suppliers, and Internet companies. Entries include: Company name, address, phone and names and titles of key personnel.

Malaysia Builders Directory. Marshall Cavendish Business Information Private Ltd. • S$40 Individuals local, foreign and other countries. Covers: building contractors & consultants, architects, engineers, property developers, quantity surveyors, and construction equipment and suppliers. Entries include: contact information, brand names, products and services, certified companies, trade associations and professional bodies.

Malaysia Exporters of Halal Products and Services Directory. Malaysia External Trade Development Corp. • Covers: 200 exporters of halal products including food and beverages, palm oil products, herbal, cosmetics, and dietary supplements.

Malaysia Exports. Malaysia External Trade Development Corp. • $60 Individuals. Includes manufacturers of a wide range of products in 31 categories that cover the agricultural & food sectors; electrical & electronics; building & construction materials; furniture; automotive components; and other sectors. Covers: 8,000 exporting companies from both manufacturing and exporting sectors.

Malaysia Government and Business Contacts Handbook. International Business Publications, USA. • $99.95 Individuals hardcopy, e-book, CD-ROM. Covers: Strategic government and business information, export-import activity in the country, investment, business contacts and regulations.

Malaysia Industrial and Business Directory. International Business Publications, USA. • $99.95 Individuals hardcopy, e-book, CD-ROM. Covers: Customs, trade regulations and procedures.

Malaysia Logistics Directory (MLD). Marshall Cavendish Business Information Private Ltd. • $30 Individuals local, foreign and other countries. Covers: information and contacts on Malaysian logistics industry, freight forwarders, transport companies, airlines and other cargo related supporting industries.

Malaysia Printing and Supporting Industries Directory (MPSID). Marshall Cavendish Business Information Private Ltd. • $30 Individuals local, foreign and other countries. Covers: information on the printing industry of Malaysia. Entries include: corporate profiles, contact details on printing and publishing companies, equipment, supplies and accessories.

Malaysian German Business. Malaysian-German Chamber of Commerce and Industry. • Annual. RM150 Individuals. Covers: Listings of Malaysian-German business members. Entries include: Members' contact information and activities.

Malaysian-Thai Chamber of Commerce--Handbook and Directory. Malaysian-Thai Chamber of Commerce. • Covers: Malaysian and Thai member companies and individuals.

Mali Business Directory. Business Guide. • $150 Individuals. Covers: 2,000 business listings including wholesalers, importers, retailers, business houses, and agents in Mali.

Malta Export-Import, Economic, Financial, Trade and Industrial Development Handbook. International Business Publications, USA. • $99.95. Covers: Government programs and plans for economic, industrial, and business development in Malta.

Malta Trade Directory. Malta Chamber of Commerce, Enterprise and Industry. • Annual. $10. Covers: Business and professional organizations, drydock facilities, tourist offices, government offices and agencies, and other businesses in Malta; overseas chambers of commerce. Database includes: Economic and trade statistics. Entries include: Company, agency, or organization name, address, phone, name and title of contact, products or services provided.

Management Consultancy. Jordans Ltd. • $50 plus 5 pounds shipping. Covers: management consultants in the United Kingdom. Database includes: Industry market profiles. Entries include: Company name, address, phone, name of chief executive, financial data for previous three years, corporate ownership, shareholder data, and business description.

Management Consultants Directory. InfoGroup Inc. • Annual. Number of listings: 51,839. Entries include: Name, address, phone, size of advertisement, name of owner or manager, number of employees, year first in "Yellow Pages." Compiled from telephone company "Yellow Pages," nationwide.

Management Consulting: A Complete Guide to the Industry, 2nd Edition. John Wiley & Sons Inc. • $60 Individuals hardcover. Covers: Top fifty consulting firms in the nation; complete game plan for novice management consultants trying to break into the business along with expert guidelines for veterans looking to expand their services.

Management Professionals Association--Directory of MPA Members. Management Professionals Association. • Annual. Covers: 26,000 members worldwide. Entries include: Company name, member name and title, address, phone, biographical information.

Management Services and Technical Assistance: Small Business Resource. Metro Atlanta Chamber of Commerce. • $8. Covers: Resources available to small businesses in the metropolitan Atlanta area. Entries include: Organization name, address, phone, description.

Management Training Buyer's Guide. Training Information Network Ltd. • Annual. $25. Covers: Over 600 suppliers of management training courses, consultancy, videos, films, packages, and training aids throughout the United Kingdom. Entries include: Company name, address, phone, fax, name and title of contact, number of employees, geographical area served, branch office or subsidiary names and addresses, description.

Manager's Handbook: Everything You Need to Know about How Business and Management Work. Pearson Learning Group. • $24.95. Publication includes: Business directory representing key areas of management in Canada and the United States. Principal content of publication is reference guide for new and experienced managers.

Manufactured Homes Manufacturers Directory. InfoGroup Inc. • Annual. Number of listings: 2,002. Entries include: Name, address, phone, size of advertisement, name of owner or manager, number of employees, year first in "Yellow Pages." Compiled from telephone company "Yellow Pages," nationwide.

Manufacturer Importers/Exporters. Tower Publishing Co. • $225. Covers: 5,034 manufacturing companies in Maine, Massachusetts, New Hampshire and Vermont which import or export products outside the U.S. Entries include: Company name, address, phone, fax, contact name and title, e-mail, URL, SIC code, type of office, countries to which the company exports.

Marconi's International Register. Telegraphic Cable & Radio Registrations Inc. • Annual. $150 payment with order. Covers: 45,000 firms worldwide which do business internationally. Entries include: Company name, address, phone, fax, e-mail and URL addresses, brief description of business or legal specialty, names of officers and partners.

The Mardek Guide to the UK's Top Food & Drink Suppliers. William Reed Publishing Ltd. • Annual. $295. Covers: 260 leading companies and over 100 major subsidiaries of food and drink manufacturers in the United Kingdom. Entries include: Corporate structure, company activities, personnel, products, brands, new product launches, turnover/pre-tax profit--up to the last three year, mergers, acquisitions and disposals.

Marketing Economics Key Plants: Guide to Industrial Purchasing Power. Marketing Economics Institute Ltd. • Biennial. $136 national edition. Covers: more than 40,000 key manufacturing plants with 100 or more employees (SIC 2011-3999); there are also editions for New England, Middle Atlantic, East North Central, West North Central, South Atlantic, East South Central, West South Central, and Mountain/Pacific regions. Entries include: Company name, address, number of employees, phone, SIC numbers.

The Marketing Guide to Ireland. Dun & Bradstreet International. • Annual. Covers: 4,000 Irish businesses, including 3,000 in the Republic of Ireland and 1,000 in Northern Ireland. Our new section contains exporters and importers. Entries include: Company name, address, phone, fax, name and title of up to 8 contacts, number of employees, line of business, sales turnover, parent company, importer/exporter indicator, year established.

The Marketing Managers Yearbook. AP Information Services Ltd. • Annual. £229 Single issue. Covers: Approximately 10,500 private and public sector companies in the U.K., as well as 6,000 companies providing marketing related products and services, including advertising agencies, public relations firms, consultancies, research experts, hospitality industry companies, media outlets, software producers, professional associations, and other organizations. Database includes: Articles written by marketing professionals; statistical tables; list of forthcoming exhibitions. Entries include: For major companies--Name, address, phone, fax, names and titles of key personnel, number of employees, number of sales employees, line of business, brand/product names, parent company, Standard Industrial Classification (SIC) codes. For service companies--Name, address, phone, fax, year established, name and title of contact, names and titles of key personnel, fields of specialization, number of employees, associated firms, major clients, subsidiary and branch names and locations.

Marketing Surveys Index. Marketing Answers Ltd. • $380 per year. Covers: about 8,000 recently-published market research and business reports from around the world. Entries include: Report title; publisher name, address, phone, fax, e-mail and contact name; countries covered by report, publication date, number of pages, price, description of report.

The Markets Directory. The Markets Directory. • Annual. Database covers: Over 7,000 service organizations implementing marketing research projects for marketing professionals in the U.S. and around the world. Entries include: Company name, address, phone, fax, contact name, line of business, facilities.

Marriage & Family Counselors Directory. InfoGroup Inc. • Annual. Number of listings: 55,129. Entries include: Name, address, phone, size of advertisement, name of owner or manager, number of employees, year first in "Yellow Pages." Compiled from telephone company "Yellow Pages," nationwide.

Massachusetts Manufacturers Register and Industrial Database. Manufacturers' News Inc. • Annual. $141 Individuals print. Covers: 9,577 manufacturers in Massachusetts. Entries include: Company name, address, phone, names and titles of key personnel, year established, number of employees, plant square footage, services, Standard Industry Classification (SIC) code, parent and subsidiary company information, type of in-house computer system, URL, e-mail address.

Massachusetts Service Directory. George D. Hall Company Inc. • $69 plus $4.95 shipping. Covers: over 12,700 non-manufacturing companies with five or more employees. Entries include: Company name, address, phone, names of key executives, number of employees, product or service, Standard Industrial Classification (SIC) code.

Mauritius Industrial and Business Directory. International Business Publications, USA. • Annual. $99.95 Individuals hardcopy, e-book, CD-ROM. Covers: Strategic industrial, investment and business contacts for conducting export-import and investment activity in the country.

MBA Track's Directory of Employers on Diskette. Hoover's Inc. • $99.95. Database covers: 2,500 companies employing the greatest number of MBAs in the U.S. Entries include: Company name, address, phone, fax, human resources director, industry type.

Media Rates & Data. Media-Daten AG. • Biennial. Covers: National and international newspapers, journals, trade press and local Swiss newsletters, radio and television. Entries include: Publications name, address, phone, rates, schedules.

MediaMap/High-Tech Trade Show Report. Cision US Inc. • Annual. $495. Covers: 350 domestic and international high-tech trade shows. Entries include: Name, address, phone, fax; contact persons; show dates, focus and technology profile; exhibitor and attendee figures; attendee demographics; booth space rates.

Medical Quality Management Sourcebook. Thomson Financial Inc. • Annual. $295 Individuals. Covers: Clinical performance measurement and improvement systems, and organizations and individuals involved in patient satisfaction surveys. Database includes: Fact sheets, charts. Entries include: Company and individual name, address, phone, fax.

Medium Companies of Europe. Graham & Trotman Ltd. • Annual. $1,198 for set. Covers: Approximately 8,000 medium-sized companies in western Europe. Entries include: Company name, address, phone, telex, names and titles of key personnel, number of employees, financial data, subsidiary and branch names and locations, product/service. Companion to "Major Companies of Europe" (see separate entry).

The MEED Middle East Financial Directory. EMAP Business International. • Annual. $120. Covers: 4,000 banks and financial institutions in the Middle East. Entries include: Company name, address, phone, telex, financial statistics, branch offices.

Meeting Facilities Directory. InfoGroup Inc. • Annual. Number of listings: 6508. Entries include: Name, address, phone, size of advertisement, name of owner or manager, number of employees, year first in "Yellow Pages." Compiled from telephone company "Yellow Pages," nationwide.

Mergent Industrial Manual and News Reports. Mergent Inc. • Annual. $2,095 including 'News Reports.' Covers: nearly 2,000 companies listed on the New York, American, or regional stock exchanges. Entries include: Company name, headquarters address, phone, names and titles of executive officers and directors, history, Standard Industrial Classification (SIC) code, Moody's rating, and financial and statistical data.

Mergent OTC Industrial Manual. Mergent Inc. • Annual. $1,995 including 'News Reports.' Covers over 2,500 companies whose stock is traded over the counter. Includes biweekly *Moody's OTC Industrial News Report.*

The Merger Yearbook. Cambridge Corp. • Annual. $490 plus $5.00 shipping. Publication includes: About 15,000 mergers and joint ventures announced during preceding year, including lists of largest mergers, firms participating most frequently in acquisitions or joint ventures, active acquirers and divesters, acquisitions by foreign firms, and leveraged buyouts, mergers, and joint ventures in preceding year. Principal content of pubication is information on corporate mergers and acquisitions. Entries include: Company names, locations, and announced terms and prices; many listings include financial or other data.

Metal & Steel Traders of the World. Metal Bulletin Ltd. • Annual. $995 Individuals. Covers: 2,000 steel traders worldwide, including exporters, importers, merchants, producers, sales companies, and agents. Entries include: Company name, address, phone, e-mail and web addresses where possible, executives, date founded, parent and subsidiary companies, products.

Metal Products: Industry Sector Profile. Philippine-German Export Development Project Philippine Bureau of Export Trade Promotion. • Publication includes: Companies exporting metal products from the Philippines. Entries include: Company name, address, phone, fax, name and title of contact, type of business, year established, subsidiary and branch names and locations, financial data, number of employees, government registrations, professional memberships, bank references, supply capability, export experience, business plan. Principal content of publication is an overview of the business environment and metal products industry in the Philippines.

Metro Atlanta Chamber of Commerce--Who's Who in Metro Atlanta Business. Metro Atlanta Chamber of Commerce. • Covers: Over 5,000 member firms in Atlanta, Georgia. Entries include: Company or firm name, address, phone, name of contact, and description of products or services.

Metro Orlando International Business Directory. Greater Orlando Chamber of Commerce. • Covers: about 400 central Florida, manufacturers, distributors, services, and support organizations involved in world trade. Entries include: Company name, address, phone, fax, telex, name of contact, product, and countries where the company does business.

Metroplex Business Directory--Dallas Area. Business Marketing Source. • Covers: over 88,000 businesses in the Dallas, Texas area. Entries include: Company name, address, phone, names and titles of key personnel, number of employees, description, product/service, Standard Industrial Classification (SIC) code.

Metroplex Business Directory--Tarrant Area. Business Marketing Source. • Annual. Covers: Approximately 47,500 businesses in Tarrant Area, Texas. Entries include: Company name, address, phone, names and titles of key personnel, number of employees, description of product/service, Standard Industrial Classification (SIC) code.

Metropolitan Atlanta Manufacturing Directory. Metro Atlanta Chamber of Commerce. • Biennial. $30 Members only available in PDF document sent via email. Covers: About 4,000 firms with Standard Industrial Classification (SIC) codes 20-39 in the Atlanta metropolitan area. Entries include: Company name, address, phone, names of principal executives, number of employees, product or service provided, SIC code, date established, market served.

Mexican Buyers Guide. Auto Care Association. • $50 Members. Covers: Approximately 450 dealers, distributors and wholesalers in Mexico interested in U.S. products. Entries include: Name, address, phone of companies, name and title of contact, names and titles of key personnel, type of business, company histories and geographical area served.

Mexican Product Guide. Todd Publications. • Biennial. $125. Covers: Over 5,000 Mexican importers and exporters. Entries include: Company name, address, phone, fax, telex.

Mexico Company Handbook. Hoover's Inc. • Annual. $49.95 plus $4.50 shipping. Covers: about 70 of Mexico's largest public companies and 8 mutual funds and investment advisors. Database includes: Profile of the Mexican economy, international trade, and investment climate; data on stock exchanges, investment advisors, and money managers. Entries include: Company name, address, phone, fax, year established, stock ticker symbol, names and titles of key personnel, number of employees, number of stockholders, bank references, auditor, company history, financial data, markets and competition, raw materials used and sources, names of major stockholders, affiliated companies.

Mexico Government and Business Contacts Handbook. International Business Publications, USA. • $99.95 Individuals hardcopy, e-book, CD-ROM. Covers: Strategic government and business information, export-import activity in the country, investment, business contacts and regulations.

Michigan Business Directory. InfoGroup Inc. • Annual. $795 for both print & CD-ROM. Covers: 416,857 businesses in Michigan. Entries include: Company name, address, phone, number of employees, name of owner or manager, sales volume. Compiled from telephone company 'Yellow Pages,' statewide. All states covered independently (see separate entries).

Michigan Centennial Business Directory. Historical Society of Michigan. • Irregular. Covers: over 500 firms that have been operating continuously in Michigan for at least 100 years; also includes list of about 15 business archives. Database includes: Map of Michigan. Entries include: For firms--Firm name, address, phone, date founded, name and title of chief executive officer. For archives--Facility name, address, date established, description of holdings.

Michigan Exporters of Wood Products. Forest Management Division of the Michigan Dept. of Natural Resources. • Irregular. Covers: Approximately 500 sawmills and manufacturers in Michigan that want to become involved in or are currently exporting their wood products. Entries include: Company name, address, phone, fax, telex, name and title of contact, number of employees, annual amount of wood purchased, principal products manufactured, species or material used, equipment, services, and specialty.

Michigan Industrial Directory. Dun & Bradstreet Inc. • Annual. Covers: 20,100 Michigan manufacturing companies. Database includes: Statistical data, trade show calendar. Entries include: Company name, address, county, phone, fax, number of employees, names and titles of key executives, plant size, year established, parent company, annual sales, import and export information, Standard Industrial Classification (SIC) code, and product description.

Middle East and Africa Autos Directory. Business Monitor International Ltd. • $995 Individuals CD. Covers: 1,483 top autos executives on 445 leading automotive companies from Algeria, Bahrain, Botswana, Egypt, Iran, Jordan, Kuwait, Lebanon, Libya, Morocco, Mozambique, Namibia, Oman, Qatar, Saudi Arabia, South Africa, Syria, Tunisia, Turkey, United Arab Emirates, Yemen, Zambia and Zimbabwe. Entries include: Parent company head offices, full company name, address, phone and fax numbers, email and website address, senior contact personnel, company description and profile, nationality, and ownership status.

Middle East and Africa Food and Drink Directory. Business Monitor International Ltd. • $995 Individuals CD. Covers: 1,553 top food and drink executives on 459 leading food and drink companies from Middle East and Africa. Entries include: Parent company head offices, full company name, address, phone and fax numbers, email and website address, senior contact personnel, company description and profile, nationality, and ownership status.

Middle East and Africa Oil and Gas Directory. Business Monitor International Ltd. • $975 Individuals CD. Covers: 1,126 top oil and gas executives on 424 leading oil and gas companies from Middle East and Africa. Entries include: Parent company head offices, full company name, address, phone and fax numbers, email and website address, senior contact personnel, company description and profile, nationality, and ownership status.

Middle East and Africa Pharmaceuticals and Healthcare Directory. Business Monitor International Ltd. • $975 Individuals CD. Covers: 2,032 top pharmaceutical executives on 615 leading pharmaceutical companies from Algeria, Bahrain, Botswana, Egypt, Greece, Iran, Jordan, Kuwait, Lebanon, Libya, Morocco, Mozambique, Namibia, Oman, Qatar, Saudi Arabia, South Africa, Syria, Tunisia, Turkey, UAE, Yemen, Zambia and Zimbabwe. Entries include: Parent company head offices, full company name, address, phone and fax numbers, email and website address, senior contact personnel, company description and profile, nationality, and ownership status.

Middle East and Africa Telecommunications Directory. Business Monitor International Ltd. • $995 Individuals CD. Covers: 1,402 top telecommunications executives on 450 leading telecommunications companies from Middle East and Africa. Entries include: Parent company head offices, full company name, address, phone and fax numbers, email and website address, senior contact personnel, company description and profile, nationality, and ownership status.

Middle East and World Food Directory: An Essential Food Industry Resource. CPH World Media s.a.r.l. • Covers: Major organizations participating in the food, beverage, packaging and catering industries in the Middle East and worldwide. Also includes a country report describing market needs, export-import figures, and forecasts of how these industries will develop.

Middle East Countries Mineral Industry Handbook. International Business Publications, USA. • $99.95 Individuals hardcopy, e-book, CD-ROM. Covers: Strategic information and contacts on mining resources and mineral industry on Middle East Countries.

Middle East (Gulf) Business Directory. NIIR Project Consultancy Services. • $100 Individuals CD-ROM. Covers: 20,000+ Middle East businesses. Entries include: Company name, full postal address, phone, fax, e-mail address (wherever available), website address (wherever available) as well as a listing of activities involved in or products dealt with.

Midwest Stock Exchange Guide. Wolters Kluwer Law & Business CCH. • Annual. $395 per year. Covers: members, associate members, and member organizations. Database includes: List of stocks and bonds traded on the exchange, arranged alphabetically by name of issuing company, trading code, trading post, and par value; rules of exchange. Entries include: Name, affiliation, address, date of admission to exchange.

Milk Producers Directory. InfoGroup Inc. • Annual. Number of listings: 1,964. Entries include: Name, address, phone, size of advertisement, name of owner or manager, number of employees, year first in "Yellow Pages." Compiled from telephone company "Yellow Pages," nationwide.

Milking Machines--Wholesalers Directory. InfoGroup Inc. • Annual. Number of listings: 956. Entries include: Name, address, phone, size of advertisement, name of owner or manager, number of employees, year first in "Yellow Pages." Compiled from telephone company "Yellow Pages," nationwide.

Minnesota Industries Guide. Industries Guides Inc. • $95. Covers: Approximately 10,000 manufacturers in Minnesota. Entries include: Company name, address, phone.

Minority and Women-Owned Business Resource Guide. Dallas Regional Chamber. • Annual. $15 Members. Covers: Minority and women-owned businesses in the greater Dallas area. Entries include: Company name, address, phone; business classification.

Mississippi Business Directory. InfoGroup Inc. • Annual. $795 for both print & CD-ROM. Covers: 114,788 businesses in Mississippi. Entries include: Company name, address, phone, number of employees, name of owner or manager, sales volume. Compiled from telephone company 'Yellow Pages,' statewide. All states covered independently (see separate entries).

Mitchell Guide to New Jersey Foundations, Corporations and Their Managers. Littman Associates. • Biennial. $135 postpaid; payment with order. Approximately 450 private foundations with minimum assets of $150,000 and grants in excess of

$15,000 per year, and about 700 businesses in New Jersey with over 300 employees.

Moldova Government and Business Contacts Handbook. International Business Publications, USA. • $99.95 Individuals hardcopy, e-book, CD-ROM. Covers: Strategic government and business information, export-import activity in the country, investment, business contacts and regulations.

Moldova Industrial and Business Directory. International Business Publications, USA. • Annual. $99.95 Individuals hardcopy, e-book, CD-ROM. Covers: Strategic industrial, investment and business contacts for conducting export-import and investment activity in the country. Contains strategic practical economic and business information.

The Money Source Book. Business Information Network Inc. • Annual. $24.95. Covers: Approximately 1,800 traditional and non-traditional sources of business capital, with emphasis on the south-central U.S. Entries include: Company or organization name, address, phone, name and title of contact, geographical area served, financial data, subsidiary and branch names and locations, eligibility requirements, prior 12 month loan/investment history, required client (customer) profiles.

Money Sources for Small Business--How You Can Find Private, State, Federal, and Corporate Financing. Puma Publishing Co. • $19.95. Covers: sources of financing for small businesses. Entries include: Company or organization name, address, phone, name and title of contact, geographical area served, financial data.

Mongolia Industrial and Business Directory. International Business Publications, USA. • $99.95 Individuals hardcopy, e-book, CD-ROM. Covers: Strategic and practical economic and business information. Entries include: Business contacts for conducting business activity in the country.

Montana Business Directory. InfoGroup Inc. • Annual. $375 both print & CD-ROM. Covers: 58,819 businesses in Montana. Entries include: Company name, address, phone, number of employees, name of owner or manager, sales volume. Compiled from telephone company "Yellow Pages," statewide. All states covered (see separate entries).

Montana Manufacturers Directory. Montana Department of Commerce Office of Trade and International Relations. • $50. Covers: Approximately 1,900 manufacturing firms in Montana. Entries include: Company name, address, phone, name of principal executive, number of employees, products or service provided.

Moody's Corporate Profiles. Moody's Investors Service Inc. • Weekly. Database covers: more than 5,000 publicly held companies listed on the New York Stock Exchange or the American Stock Exchange or NMS companies traded on the National Association of Securities Dealers Automated Quotations. Database includes: Company name, address, phone, D-U-N-S number, Moody's number, stock exchange, ticker symbol, primary and secondary Standard Industrial Classification (SIC) codes and industries; line of business analysis, annual earnings and dividends per share and other financial and stock trading data for five-year period.

Morocco Business Directory. Business Guide. • $250 Individuals. Covers: Over 245,000 business listings including wholesalers, importers, retailers, business houses, and agents in Morocco.

Mortgage Banking Sourcebook. Mortgage Bankers Association. • $40 plus $4.95 shipping. Covers: federal, state, and private agencies and associations involved in the real estate finance industry. Database includes: Information on the mortgage banking industry, including sources of relevant information on regulations, legislation, tax & accounting procedures; definitions of industry jargon; educational programs; statistics & forecasts. Entries include: Organization name, address, phone, websites and fax numbers.

Movers Directory. InfoGroup Inc. • Annual. Number of listings: 15,712. Entries include: Name, address, phone, size of advertisement, name of owner or manager, number of employees, year first in "Yellow Pages." Compiled from telephone company "Yellow Pages," nationwide.

Multinational Companies in Argentina. Business Monitor International Ltd. • Annual. $995 Individuals CD-ROM. Covers: 4,470 senior executive contacts on 1,650 leading US, European and Asian multinational companies across 34 industry sectors in Argentina. Entries include: Full company name, address, phone and fax numbers, email and web addresses, and key contact names and titles.

Multinational Companies in Bahrain. Business Monitor International Ltd. • Annual. $995 Individuals CD-ROM. Covers: 2,040 senior executive contacts on 640 leading US, European and Asian multinational companies across 34 industry sectors in Bahrain. Entries include: Full company name, address, phone and fax numbers, email and web addresses, and key contact names and titles.

Multinational Companies in Brazil. Business Monitor International Ltd. • Annual. $995 Individuals CD-ROM. Covers: 9,520 senior executive contacts on 3,880 leading US, European and Asian multinational companies across 34 industry sectors in Brazil. Entries include: Full company name, address, phone and fax numbers, email and web addresses, and key contact names and titles.

Multinational Companies in Chile. Business Monitor International Ltd. • Annual. $995 Individuals CD-ROM. Covers: 3,530 senior executive contacts on 1,080 leading US, European and Asian multinational companies across 34 industry sectors in Chile. Entries include: Full company name, address, phone and fax numbers, email and web addresses, and key contact names and titles.

Multinational Companies in Colombia. Business Monitor International Ltd. • Annual. $995 Individuals CD-ROM. Covers: 2,200 senior executive contacts on 830 leading US, European and Asian multinational companies across 34 industry sectors in Colombia. Entries include: Full company name, address, phone and fax numbers, email and web addresses, and key contact names and titles.

Multinational Companies in Egypt. Business Monitor International Ltd. • Annual. $995 Individuals CD-ROM. Covers: 4,630 senior executive contacts on 1,520 leading US, European and Asian multinational companies across 37 industry sectors in Egypt. Entries include: full company name, address, phone and fax numbers, email and web addresses, and key contact names and titles.

Multinational Companies in Estonia. Business Monitor International Ltd. • Annual. $995 Individuals CD-ROM. Covers: 1,310 senior executive contacts on 400 leading US, European and Asian multinational companies across 34 industry sectors in Estonia. Entries include: Full company name, address, phone and fax numbers, email and web addresses, and key contact names and titles.

Multinational Companies in Greece. Business Monitor International Ltd. • Annual. $1,660 Individuals CD-ROM. Covers: 5,330 senior executive contacts on 2,070 leading US, European and Asian multinational companies across 34 industry sectors in Greece. Entries include: Full company name, address, phone and fax numbers, email and web addresses, and key contact names and titles.

Multinational Companies in Hungary. Business Monitor International Ltd. • Annual. $1,660 Individuals CD-ROM. Covers: 4,630 senior executive contacts on 1,450 leading US, European and Asian multinational companies 34 industry sectors in Hungary. Entries include: Full company name, address, phone and fax numbers, email and web addresses, and key contact names and titles.

Multinational Companies in Iran. Business Monitor International Ltd. • Annual. $995 Individuals CD-ROM. Covers: 2,910 senior executive contacts on 1,940 leading US, European and Asian multinational companies across 34 industry sectors in Iran. Entries include: Full company name, address, phone and fax numbers, email and web addresses, and key contact names and titles.

Multinational Companies in Jordan, Lebanon & Syria. Business Monitor International Ltd. • Annual. $1,110 Individuals. Covers: 3,860 senior executive contacts on 1,150 foreign company subsidiaries across 34 industry sectors in Jordan, Lebanon, and Syria. Entries include: Full company name, address, phone and fax numbers, email and web addresses, and key contact names and titles.

Multinational Companies in Kuwait. Business Monitor International Ltd. • $995 Individuals. Covers: 2,110 senior executive contacts on 610 leading US, European and Asian multinational companies across 34 industry sectors in Kuwait. Entries include: Full company name, address, phone and fax numbers, email and web addresses, and key contact names and titles.

Multinational Companies in Latvia. Business Monitor International Ltd. • Annual. $995 Individuals. Covers: 1,340 senior executive contacts on 460 leading US, European and Asian multinational companies across 34 industry sectors in Latvia. Entries include: Full company name, address, phone and fax numbers, email and web addresses, and key contact names and titles.

Multinational Companies in Lithuania. Business Monitor International Ltd. • Annual. $995 Individuals. Covers: 1,000 senior executive contacts on 450 leading US, European and Asian multinational companies across 34 industry sectors in Lithuania. Entries include: Full company name, address, phone and fax numbers, email and web addresses, and key contact names and titles.

Multinational Companies in Macedonia. Business Monitor International Ltd. • Annual. $1,110 Individuals USA. Covers: 900 senior executive contacts on 290 leading US, European and Asian multinational companies across 34 industry sectors in Macedonia. Entries include: Full company name, address, phone and fax numbers, email and web addresses, and key contact names and titles.

Multinational Companies in Mexico. Business Monitor International Ltd. • Annual. $995 Individuals. Covers: 5,990 senior executive contacts on 2,030 leading US, European and Asian multinational companies across 34 industry sectors in Mexico. Entries include: Full company name, address, phone and fax numbers, email and web addresses, and key contact names and titles.

Multinational Companies in Peru. Business Monitor International Ltd. • Annual. $995 Individuals. Covers: 2,260 senior executive contacts on 720 leading US, European and Asian multinational companies across 37 industry sectors in Peru. Entries include: Full company name, address, phone and fax numbers, email and web addresses, and key contact names and titles.

Multinational Companies in Poland. Business Monitor International Ltd. • Annual. $1,660 Individuals. Covers: 5,340 senior executive contacts on 2,030 leading US, European and Asian multinational companies across 37 industry sectors in Poland. Entries include: Full company name, address, phone and fax numbers, email and web addresses, and key contact names and titles.

Multinational Companies in Qatar. Business Monitor International Ltd. • Annual. $995 Individuals. Covers: 1,690 senior executive contacts on 640 leading US, European and Asian multinational across 34 industry sectors in Qatar. Entries include: Full company name, address, phone and fax numbers, email and web addresses, and key contact names and titles.

Multinational Companies in Romania. Business Monitor International Ltd. • Annual. $1,110 Individuals. Covers: 3,190 senior executive contacts on 1,190 leading US, European and Asian multinational companies across 34 industry sectors in Romania. Entries include: Full company name, address, phone and fax numbers, email and web addresses, and key contact names and titles.

Multinational Companies in Russia. Business Monitor International Ltd. • Annual. $1,660 Individuals. Covers: 6,150 senior executive contacts on 2,560 leading US, European and Asian multinational companies across 34 industry sectors in Russia. Entries include: Full company name, address, phone and fax numbers, email and web addresses, and key contact names and titles.

Multinational Companies in Saudi Arabia. Business Monitor International Ltd. • Annual. $1,660 Individuals. Covers: 6,730 senior executive contacts on 1,650 leading US, European and Asian multinational companies across 34 industry sectors in Saudi Arabia. Entries include: Full company name, address, phone and fax numbers, email and web addresses, and key contact names and titles.

Multinational Companies in Serbia. Business Monitor International Ltd. • Annual. $1,110 Individuals. Covers: 2,230 senior executive contacts on 760 leading US, European and Asian multinational companies across 34 industry sectors in Serbia. Entries include: Full company name, address, phone and fax numbers, email and web addresses, and key contact names and titles.

Multinational Companies in Slovakia. Business Monitor International Ltd. • Annual. $995 Individuals. Covers: 2,610 senior executive contacts on 830 leading US, European and Asian multinational companies across 34 industry sectors in Slovakia. Entries include: Full company name, address, phone and fax numbers, email and web addresses, and key contact names and titles.

Multinational Companies in Slovenia. Business Monitor International Ltd. • Annual. $1,110 Individuals. Covers: 2,290 senior executive contacts on 620 leading US, European and Asian multinational companies across 34 industry sectors in Slovenia. Entries include: Full company name, address, phone and fax numbers, email and web addresses, and key contact names and titles.

Multinational Companies in Southern Africa. Business Monitor International Ltd. • Annual. $1,110 Individuals. Covers: 2,960 senior executive contacts on 1,890 leading US, European and Asian multinational companies across 34 industry sectors in Southern Africa. Entries include: Full company name, address, phone and fax numbers, email and web addresses, and key contact names and titles.

Multinational Companies in the Caribbean. Business Monitor International Ltd. • Annual. $995 Individuals CDR. Covers: 7,000 senior executive contacts on 2,120 leading US, European and Asian multinational companies across 34 industry sectors in the Caribbean. Entries include: full company name, address, phone and fax numbers, email and web addresses, and key contact names and titles.

Multinational Companies in the Philippines: Yearbook 2010. Business Monitor International Ltd. • $995 Individuals CD. Covers: 4,910 senior executive contacts at 1,220 leading US, European and Asian multinational companies across 34 industry sectors in the Philippines. Entries include: Name, location, description, phone, ownership status and parentage.

Multinational Companies in the UAE. Business Monitor International Ltd. • Annual. $2,215 Individuals. Covers: 12,010 senior executive contacts on 3,970 leading US, European and Asian multinational companies across 34 industry sectors in United Arab Emirates. Entries include: Full company name, address, phone and fax numbers, email and web addresses, and key contact names and titles.

Multinational Companies in Turkey. Business Monitor International Ltd. • Annual. $1,660 Individuals. Covers: 5,960 senior executive contacts on 2,150 leading US, European and Asian multinational companies across 34 industry sectors in Turkey. Entries include: Full company name, address, phone and fax numbers, email and web addresses, and key contact names and titles.

Multinational Companies in Ukraine. Business Monitor International Ltd. • Annual. $1,110 Individuals. Covers: 2,420 senior executive contacts on 850 leading US, European and Asian multinational companies across 34 industry sectors in Ukraine. Entries include: Full company name, address, phone and fax numbers, email and web addresses, and key contact names and titles.

Multinational Companies in Venezuela. Business Monitor International Ltd. • Annual. $1,150 Individuals. Covers: 1,658 senior executive contacts on 568 foreign company subsidiaries across 34 industry sectors in Venezuela. Entries include: Full company name, address, phone and fax numbers, email and web addresses, and key contact names and titles.

Multinational Food & Drink Companies in Emerging Europe Directory. Aroq Ltd. • $577.46 with CD-ROM. Covers: 1,577 decision makers and 559 multinational food and drink companies in Europe.

Municipal Year Book. Hemming Information Services. • Annual. Covers: local authorities, central government, agencies and officials of the United Kingdom; associations, development organizations, libraries, museums, and other local authorities. Entries include: Name of authority or governing agency, address, phone, fax, names of elected councillors, officers, names and titles of key personnel, contacts, population, and pay.

The Music Week International Directory. CMP Information Ltd. • Annual. $80. Covers: Music companies worldwide operating in over 20 sectors including record companies, distributors, publishers, manufacturers, promoters, and studios. Entries include: Name, address, phone, fax, e-mail address, and URL.

MZM World Business Directory. MZM Publications Publishing Promotion Co. • Irregular. $154 plus airmail. Covers: companies in 33 post-socialist countries involved in international trade and business: Albania, Armenia, Azerbaijan, Bosnia & Herzegovina, Bulgaria, Belorus, China, Croatia, Cuba, Czech Republic, Slovakia, Estonia, Georgia, former East Germany, Hungary, Kazakhstan, Kirghizia, Latvia, Lithuania, North Korea, Macedonia, Moldova, Mongolia, Poland, Romania, Russia, Kaliningrad Province of Russia, Slovenia, Tadzhikistan, Turkmenistan, Ukraine, Uzbekistan, Vietnam, and Yugoslavia. Entries include: Company name, address, phone, fax, telex, number of employees, year established, subsidiary companies, description.

NAFTA Register. Global Contact Inc. • Annual. Covers: Companies within the NAFTA region interested in exporting their products/services. Entries include: Company name, address, phone, fax, e-mail and Internet addresses, name and title of contact, list of products/services offered.

Namibia Business Directory. A.C. Braby (Pty) Ltd. • Annual. Covers: Businesses in Namibia. Entries include: Company name, address, phone.

Namibia Industrial and Business Directory. International Business Publications, USA. • Annual. $99.95 Individuals hardcopy, e-book, CD-ROM. Covers: Strategic industrial, investment and business contacts for conducting export-import and investment activity in the country. Contains strategic practical economic and business information.

Namibia Trade Directory. Namibia Trade Directory. • Covers: Trade and industries in Namibia. Entries include: Addresses and contact persons.

NAN-Directorio Nacional Negocio a Negocio. Yell Publicidad S.A. • Annual. Covers: Approximately 230,000 business firms whose main activity is sales of products or services to the business to business sector in Spain.

NASDAQ BX Guide. Wolters Kluwer Law & Business CCH. • Annual. Covers: Members and member organizations, constitution & rules of the Exchange. Database includes: List of stocks and bonds admitted to trading on the exchange, arranged alphabetically by name of issuing company, and including description and class of stock or bond, trading code, trading post, and par value. Entries include: Name, affiliation, address, date of admission to exchange.

NASDAQ PHLX Guide. Wolters Kluwer Law & Business CCH. • Annual. $794 Individuals print. Covers: Members, associate members, and member organizations of the stock exchange in Philadelphia, Pennsylvania. Database includes: Directory and Constitution rules published for the Exchange. Entries include: Name, affiliation, address, date of admission to exchange.

Nashville Business Journal--Book of Lists. Nashville Business Journals. • $65 print only. Covers: About 700 major companies, foundations, government officials, utilities, news papers, radio and television stations, airlines, hospitals, financial institutions, shopping centers, resorts, and prominent individuals in the Nashville, Tennessee area. Entries include: Company, organization, or individual name, address, phone, names and titles of key personnel, financial data, products or services.

The National Directory of Catalogs. Oxbridge Communications Inc. • Annual. $995 Individuals print version. Describes over 12,000 United States and Canadian catalogs within 78 subject areas.

National Directory of Corporate Distress Specialists. Lustig Data Research Inc. • Annual. $245. Covers: 1,830 organizations and over 4,000 professionals providing 20 types of services in bankruptcies, workouts, turnarounds, and distressed securities investing, including attorneys, accountants, crisis managers, financial advisors, turnaround consultants, valuation experts, financing sources, investors, in-house workout officers, appraisers, auctioneers, liquidators, PR/crisis communications experts, real estate managers, etc. Entries include: Organization name, address, phone, fax, toll-free phone, year founded, parent company, department name, other offices, staff size, size of cases, types of representations, geographical area served, industry specializations, services offered, institutional clients, transaction history, party represented, key personnel, titles.

National Directory of Corporate Giving. • Annual. $195 Individuals. Provides information on nearly 4,400 company-sponsored foundations and corporate giving programs.

National Directory of Corporate Public Affairs. Columbia Books and Information Services. • Annual. $249 Individuals. Covers: About 17,000 corporations that have PACs foundations or other public affairs activities; over 14,000 corporate public affairs personnel. Database includes: List of contract lobbyists serving corporations at the state level; membership directory of the Public Affairs Council. Entries include: Company name, headquarters address, Washington, DC, address (if any), names of political action committees, PAC funds contributed, names of principal recipients;

For publishers' addresses, refer to SOURCES CITED section at the back of the book.

name of corporate foundation; total grants per year, assets; giving priorities; names and titles of public affairs personnel. For personnel--Name, title, affiliation, address, phone; if a lobbyist, where registered.

National Directory of Pension Funds That Invest in Real Estate Investments and Mortgages. Communication Network International Inc. • Irregular. $750 payment must accompany order. Covers: 1,300 pension funds. Entries include: Fund name, manager's name, address, phone, amount of investment.

National Distributors Select. Scott's Directories. • Annual. $224.75 Profiler (additional). Covers: Over 59,000 wholesalers, distributors, and wholesale agents of industrial products across Canada. Entries include: 34,500 company name, address, phone, description, brand names carried.

The National Managed Care Leadership Directory. HealthQuest Publishers from MCOL. • $249 Individuals print. Covers: 844 companies and 7,020 executive listings in the managed care industry including health plans, provider networks, PBMs, administrative organizations (quality improvement organizations, utilizations and disease management organizations, and TPAs) and specialty organizations (dental, vision and behavioral).

National Real Estate Investor Sourcebook. Primedia Business. • Annual. $79.95 payment must accompany order. List of about 7,000 companies and individuals in 18 real estate fields, including appraisers; asset managers; builders, contractors, and developers; communication services; corporate real estate managers; environmental consultants; equity investors; financial services; hospitality services; institutional advisors; pension funds; property managers; real estate brokers, agents, consultants, and counselors; software products and services; title insurance companies; related associations; and others.

The National Register of Fashion Accessories. Marche Publishing. • $200 Individuals print. Covers: Apparel accessory companies in the United States. Entries include: company name, address, phone, fax and toll free numbers, website and email addresses, officers, year established, brands, and affiliates.

The National Register of Independent Sales Reps--Apparel and Accessories. Marche Publishing. • $250 Individuals print. Covers: 1,200 representatives throughout the United States and Canada. Entries include: Company name, address, phone and fax numbers, email address, year established, lines of business, origin of companies, and quote from reps.

National Services Directory. Dun & Bradstreet Inc. • $495. Covers: Approximately 20,000 service companies in Canada. Entries include: Name, address, phone, fax.

National Verticals. Scott's Directories. • $1,395 Individuals CD-ROM (food and beverage) prospector. Covers: Canadian industry-specific contacts and company profiles. Entries include: Complete business name, names and titles of executives and decision-makers, mailing and location addresses, phone and faxes, corporate email, products and/or services offered, annual estimated gross sales, year established, number of employees, ISO registration, North American industry classification standard (NAICS) codes, web site address.

Nations of the World: A Political, Economic and Business Handbook. Grey House Publishing. • Annual. $180 Individuals softcover. Covers: Political, economic and business information for 231 nations and self-governing territories around the world. Database includes: Five regional chapters. Entries include: Key facts, political and economic issues, country profile, business information, maps, demographics, GDP figures, climate, chambers of commerce, media, travel information, and contact information for government offices.

Netherlands Government and Business Contacts Handbook. International Business Publications, USA. • $99.95 Individuals hardcopy, e-book, CD-ROM. Covers: Strategic government and business information, export-import activity in the country, investment, business contacts and regulations.

Netherlands Industrial and Business Directory. International Business Publications, USA. • Annual. $99.95 Individuals hardcover, e-book, CD-ROM. Covers: Detailed information on investment, export-import business opportunities, foreign economic assistance projects, government and business contacts.

Nevada Manufacturers Directory and Industrial Database. Manufacturers' News Inc. • Annual. $86 Individuals print. Covers: 2,104 manufacturers in Nevada. Entries include: Company name, address, phone, names and titles of key personnel, year established, number of employees, plant square footage, services, Standard Industry Classification (SIC) code, parent and subsidiary company information, type of in-house computer system, URL, e-mail address.

New Business Survival Package. Greater Orlando Chamber of Commerce. • Annual. $49.99. Covers: taxing, licensing, registration, and zoning authorities and other contacts of interest to those starting new businesses in the Florida counties of Seminole, Orange, and Osceola. Database includes: Advice on starting a new business. Entries include: Agency name, address, phone.

New Caledonia Industrial and Business Directory. International Business Publications, USA. • Annual. $99.95 Individuals hardcopy, e-book, CD-ROM. Covers: Strategic industrial, investment and business contacts for conducting export-import and investment activity in the country. Contains strategic, practical economic and business information.

New Hampshire Manufacturers Register and Industrial Database. Manufacturers' News Inc. • Annual. $93 Individuals print. Covers: 2,963 manufacturers in New Hampshire. Entries include: Company name, address, phone, names and titles of key personnel, year established, number of employees, plant square footage, services, Standard Industry Classification (SIC) code, parent and subsidiary company information, type of in-house computer system, URL, e-mail address.

New Industries and Plant Expansions Reported in Wisconsin. Wisconsin Department of Development Bureau of Information Services. • Annual. Covers: plant additions, new plants, branch plants, and relocated plants announced during the year to be built in Wisconsin; about 300 projects in recent edition. Entries include: Company name, city of new or expanded construction, type of project, square footage, type of facility (plant, office, etc.), number of workers to be added, product or service.

New Jersey Business Source Book. Research Communications. • Annual. $495 Individuals book with CD. Covers: Sources of New Jersey business information, including 555 of the state's top employers, 798 trade and professional associations, and 170 NJ chambers of commerce. Database includes: Information on services available to the New Jersey business community and New Jersey web sites. Entries include: For companies--Name, address, phone, e-mail, URL, description names and titles of key personnel. For associations--Name, address, phone, number of members. For chambers of commerce--Name, address, phone, fax, e-mail.

The New Jersey Corporate Guide. Business Journal of New Jersey. • Annual. Covers: Approximately 1,000 of the largest public and private companies, financial institutions, leading firms in New Jersey and important out-of-state companies whose major operations are located in New Jersey. Entries include: Name, address, phone, fax, parent company, number of employees, sales volume, year founded, names and titles of executives. Public companies also include--5-year income statement, names and titles of officers and directors, subsidiaries, name of trade exchange and symbol, auditors, and number of shareholders.

New Mexico International Trade Directory. Proparaguay. • Annual. $10. Covers: about 511 New Mexico firms seeking international trade. Database includes: Exportable products list. Entries include: Name of firm, address, phone, number of employees, name of contact, Standard Industrial Classification (SIC) code, product or service provided.

New York Stock Exchange Guide. Commerce Clearing House Inc. • Monthly. $485 per year, postpaid; payment with order. Covers: about 1,380 member companies listed as traders with the New York Stock Exchange, and exchange and floor officials. Entries include: Company name, address, date admitted, representatives.

New Zealand Government and Business Contacts Handbook. International Business Publications, USA. • $99.95 Individuals hardcopy, e-book, CD-ROM. Covers: Strategic government and business information, export-import activity in the country, investment, business contacts and regulations.

New Zealand Industrial and Business Directory. International Business Publications, USA. • Annual. $99.95 Individuals hardcopy, e-book, CD-ROM. Covers: Strategic industrial, investment and business contacts for conducting export-import and investment activity in the country.

Newbuildings Register. IHS Global Ltd. Lloyd's Register--Fairplay Ltd. • Monthly. $2,850 Individuals CD-ROM. Covers: Shipowners and builders of new commercial ships. Entries include: Name, address, phone.

NFT Directory & Buying Guide. BNP Media. • Annual. $35 Individuals. Covers: Floor covering manufacturers, distributors, retail groups and franchises, installation and technical training schools, sales agents, and products.

NHMA Export Interest Directory. International Housewares Association. • Covers: Approximately 300 member manufacturers that export housewares and small appliances. Products listed are at least 51% manufactured in the U.S. Entries include: Company name, address, phone, telex, fax, name and title of contact, geographical area served, products.

Nigeria Business Directory. Business Guide. • $250 Individuals. Covers: 47,500 business listings including wholesalers, importers, retailers, business houses, and agents in Nigeria.

Nigeria Industrial and Business Directory. International Business Publications, USA. • Annual. $99.95 Individuals hardcover. Covers: Strategic industrial, investment and business contacts for conducting export-import and investment activity in the country.

Nigerian Directory of Directors. Asoms Biblio-Info Consult Publishers. • $5 Nigerian naira. Covers: directors of business firms in Nigeria. Entries include: Name of official, address, firm(s) for which a director.

Non-Profit Organizations Directory. InfoGroup Inc. • Annual. Number of listings: 80,335. Entries include: Name, address, phone, size of advertisement, name of owner or manager, number of employees, year first in "Yellow Pages." Compiled from telephone company "Yellow Pages," nationwide.

Nonprofit Management Resources Directory. Global Ties U.S. • Covers: Nonprofit organizations. Entries include: Name, address, phone, fax, email, and website address.

Nordic Stock Guide. Delphi Economics AB. • $34.95 plus $3.50 shipping. Covers: nearly 250 public companies in Denmark, Finland, Norway, and Sweden. Database includes: Interest rate histories, exchange rates, and commodities prices for each country. Entries include: Company name, address, phone, names and titles of key personnel, overview of company operations, stock and financial data for previous six years.

North American Companies Manufacturing in Scotland. Scottish Enterprise. • Covers: about 200 North American-owned companies in Scotland. Entries include: Company name, address, phone, telex, name and title of contact, number of employees, description of services.

North American Directory of U.S. Importers and Canadian Importers. Coble International. • $285 print or CD-ROM. Covers: 19,000 importers in Canada and in the United States. Entries include: Name, address, phone, fax, primary contact person, list of products, e-mail addresses, and Web site.

North Carolina Business Directory. InfoGroup Inc. • Annual. $795 for both print & CD-ROM. Covers: 359,291 businesses in North Carolina. Entries include: Company name, address, phone, number of employees, name of owner or manager, sales volume. Compiled from telephone company 'Yellow Pages,' statewide. All states covered (see separate entries).

North Carolina/South Carolina Industries Guide. Industries Guides Inc. • $95. Covers: Approximately 14,000 manufacturers in North Carolina and South Carolina. Entries include: Company name, address, phone.

Northern California Business Directory. Harris InfoSource. • $198 Members. Covers manufacturers, wholesalers and service businesses in the 45 counties north of San Luis Obispo, California. Entries include: Company profile, owners, names and titles of key personnel.

Northern California Business Directory and Buyers Guide. Harris InfoSource. • Covers: 23,540 businesses in Northern California. Entries include: Company name, address, county, phone, fax, web site address (on CD-ROM only), number of employees, names and titles of key executives, plant size, year established, parent company, annual sales, import/export information, Standard Industrial Classification (SIC) code, and product description.

Northern California High Technology. Rich's Business Directories Inc. • $935 Individuals database download. Covers: Over 9,104 high technology firms in Northern California. Publication includes: Over 38,839 contact names. Entries include: Company name, address, web address, stock symbol, headquarters, year established, product type.

Northern Ireland Trade Directory. Industrial Development Board for Northern Ireland Her Majesty's Stationary Office. • Annual. $33. Covers: Approximately 5,200 manufacturing companies in Northern Ireland. Entries include: Company name, address, phone, telex, name and title of contact, number of employees, description of product/service.

Northwest Native American Business Directory. ONABEN - Native American Business Network. • $19.95 Individuals. Covers: 350 native businesses, casinos, tribes, Native American chambers, and business associations in the Northwest.

Norway Exports--Products and Services for Development. The Export Council of Norway. • Biennial. Covers: Products and services exported in Norway in a variety of lines of business, including financial and banking services, construction, mining, electricity, manufacturing and metals, electronics, training, surveying and mapping, wood processing, water supply and electricity. Entries include: Company name, address, phone, telex number, product/service.

Norway's Top 10,000 Companies. Dun & Bradstreet Inc. • Covers: Approximately 15,000 companies in Norway. Entries include: Company name, address, phone, fax, telex, sales volume, rank, profit, SIC code, principal officer name and title, number of employees, export designation, equity capital.

Novi Chamber of Commerce--Business Directory. Novi Chamber of Commerce. • Annual. Covers: Member businesses in Novi, Michigan.

Oesterreich's Ten Thousand Groesste Unternehmen. D & B - Schimmelpfeng Gesellschaft GmbH. • Annual. $525. Covers: 11,000 Austrian companies. Entries include: Company name, address, phone, names and titles of key personnel, year founded, line of business, name and location of parent company, number of employees, year founded, SIC numbers, and sales volumes.

Oferta Exportable del Sector Textil de la Confeccion, Colombia. The Export Promotion Fund, Proexpo. • Covers: Textiles and clothing manufacturers in Columbia. Entries include: Company name, address, phone, number of employees, type of product exported, export capacity, name of contact person.

Office--Czech Republic. I.S.M.C. Information Systems and Marketing Contacts Ltd. • $75. Covers: Companies in the office furnishment and office equipment industries in the Czech Republic.

Office Equipment, Stationery & Supplies, Packaging Importer Directory. Biz Focus Company Ltd. • $320 Individuals. Covers: 8,596 importers of accounting and invoicing machine, calculating machine, packaging and bottling machinery accessories, mailing and postal machinery and equipment, office machinery and equipment, and plastic articles for office use. Entries include: Company name, contact person, contact address, telephone number, fax number, e-mail, URL, and import products.

Office Products Dealer--Product Buying Guide and Industry Directory Issue. Hitchcock Publishing Co. • Annual. $15 plus $3.00 shipping. Publication includes: Lists of manufacturers, wholesalers, and distributors of furniture, machines, computer and word processing systems, and office products and equipment; manufacturers' representatives, and national industry associations that serve retail office products dealers.

Office Products Representatives Alliance--Membership Directory. Office Products Representatives Alliance. • Annual. $50 Nonmembers. Covers: nearly 120 independent office product and office furniture distribution firms. Entries include: Firm name, address, phone, product and service provided.

Office Supplies Directory. InfoGroup Inc. • Annual. Lists companies that offer office supplies and equipment.

Official E-mail and Fax Directory. Todd Publications. • $150. Covers: 160,000 contacts at 50,000 U.S. companies, government agencies, and public and private institutions; includes manufacturers, professional service firms, media and publishing agencies, consultants, financial institutions, and government offices. Entries include: e-mail addresses.

Official Export and Import Directory of Costa Rica. Mercadeo Profesional, S.A. • Annual. Covers: Export and import companies in Costa Rica.

Ohio Industrial Directory. Harris InfoSource. • Annual. $220 Individuals manufacturing price. Covers: 22,900 Ohio manufacturing companies. Database includes: Statistical data, trade show calendar. Entries include: Company name, address, county, phone, fax, number of employees, names and titles of key executives, plant size, year established, parent company, annual sales, import/export information, Standard Industrial Classification (SIC) code, and product description.

Ohio Industries Guide. Industries Guides Inc. • $95. Covers: Approximately 20,000 manufacturers in Ohio. Entries include: Company name, address, phone.

Ohio Roster. Edward Howard & Co. • $12. Covers: the 200 largest manufacturers, retailers, service companies, transportation firms, public utilities, and financial institutions headquartered in Ohio whose stock is publicly traded. Database includes: Lists of the top 20 firms by revenue, assets, net income, and biggest sales gain. Entries include: Firm name, location, total revenues, net income, total assets, earnings per share, stock exchange on which traded.

Oklahoma Business Directory. InfoGroup Inc. • Annual. $795 for both print & CD-ROM. Covers: 163,042 businesses in Oklahoma. Entries include: Company name, address, phone, number of employees, name of owner or manager, sales volume. Compiled from telephone company 'Yellow Pages,' statewide. All states covered (see separate entries).

Oklahoma Directory of Manufacturers and Processors. Dun & Bradstreet Inc. • Annual. $100 Individuals. Covers: 5,000 Oklahoma manufacturers (Standard Industrial Classification (SIC) codes 20-39). Entries include: Company name, address, phone, fax, name of principal executive, employment number, date established, Standard Industrial Classification (SIC) codes, list of products or services.

Oman Chamber of Commerce and Industry--Industrial Directory. Oman Chamber of Commerce and Industry. • Provides data on companies and industrial enterprises in the Sultanate and supporting institutions to invest in the industrial sector, investment incentives and facilities as well as available investment opportunities in all areas of economic activity.

Oman Golden Key Directory. International Institute of Trade Relation Promotion, Trade Information Centre of Iran. • £100 Individuals. Covers: 7,685 companies in Oman. Entries include: Company name, address, telephone, fax, products, services, Managing Director, and business activities.

Oman Trade Directory. Oman Chamber of Commerce and Industry. • Provides information about companies and economic institutions in Oman.

100 Great Businesses and the Minds Behind Them. Bolinda Publishing. • NZ$39.95 Individuals. Covers: Entrepreneurs and their collection of stories from Australia and around the world.

1,000 China Leading Enterprises. China Statistics Publishing House. • $200. Covers: 1,000 leading companies in China. Entries include: Company name and address, director, economic types, and sponsor unit, main economic indicators.

OPAC Directory: An Annual Guide to Internet-Accessible Online Public Access Catalogs. Mecklermedia Corp. • Annual. $70. Covers: Approximately 1,000 online public access catalogs (OPACs) and other locally mounted databases form hundreds of libraries worldwide. Database includes: Accessing Online Bibliographic Databases--annotated entries on over 700 Internet-accessible OPACs worldwide. Entries include: Description, access, search methods.

Optical Goods Manufacturers Directory. InfoGroup Inc. • Annual. Number of listings: 1,197. Entries include: Name, address, phone, size of advertisement, name of owner or manager, number of employees, year first in "Yellow Pages." Compiled from telephone company "Yellow Pages," nationwide.

Orange County Business and Industrial Directory. Orange County Business Council. • Number of listings: 5,000. Entries include: Company name, address, phone, names and titles of key personnel, line of business, number of employees.

Orange County, New York Business Directory and Buyer's Guide. Centers Composition. • Number of listings: 11,000. Entries include: Company name, address, phone, name and title of contact, number of employees, type of business, product or service.

Oregon Manufacturers Directory and Industrial Database. Manufacturers' News Inc. • Annual. $114 Individuals print. Covers: 6,835 manufacturers in Oregon. Entries include: Company name, address, phone, names and titles of key personnel, year established, number of employees, plant square footage, services, Standard Industry Classification (SIC) code, parent and subsidiary company information, type of in-house computer system, URL, e-mail address.

Oregon Manufacturers Register. Harris InfoSource. • Annual. Covers: Approximately 8,400 manufacturers plus key executives in Oregon. Entries include: Company, address, parent name/location, telephone, fax and 800 numbers, Web site address (on CD-ROM only), number of employees, year established, annual revenue, plant size, business description, Standard Industrial Classification (SIC) codes, executive names/titles, public ownership, legal structure, import/export designators, female/minority ownership.

Orient Trade Directory. Selective Books International. • $19.95 Individuals. Covers: Suppliers of over 4,000 products in Japan, Korea, Malaysia, China, India, Thailand, Indonesia and Singapore. Entries include: Photos, names, addresses, phones and fax.

Orion Blue Book--Copier. Orion Research Corp. • Annual. $130 Individuals hardbound or CD. Publication includes: List of manufacturers of copiers and other office equipment. Entries include: Company name, address, phone. Principal content of publication is a listing of 3,091 office equipment products with the original retail value, value paid to customer on trade-in when in mint condition, and average value paid to customer on trade-in.

Osceola County Manufacturers/Industrial Business Directory. Osceola Economic Alliance. • Annual. Covers: Information on all Osceola County, Michigan, businesses.

Outdoor Advertising Directory. InfoGroup Inc. • Annual. Number of listings: 2,647. Entries include: Name, address, phone, size of advertisement, name of owner or manager, number of employees, year first in "Yellow Pages." Compiled from telephone company "Yellow Pages," nationwide.

Overseas and European Companies Manufacturing in Scotland. Scottish Enterprise. • Covers: over 130 foreign owned companies, excluding North American owned, located in Scotland. Entries include: Company name, address, phone, telex, name and title of contact, number of employees, geographical area covered, description of services.

Overseas Companies in Ireland. Industrial Development Agency of Ireland. • Updated continuously; printed on request. Computer printout. About 1,000 overseas manufacturers and international service companies with operations in Ireland. Entries include: Name and address of parent company; name, address, phone of Irish filial company, description of product or service specialty.

Owen's Worldwide Africa Business Directory. Owen's Worldtrade Ltd. • Annual. $87.50. Covers: 12,000 manufacturers, importers, exporters; and travel, finance, transport other service firms; and government agencies and associations concerned with international trade in 21 African countries: Botswana, Burundi, Cameroon, Djibouti, Ethiopia, Gabon, Ivory Coast, Kenya, Liberia, Malawi, Nigeria, Rwanda, Senegal, Seychelles, Sierra Leone, Somalia, Sudan, Tanzania, Togo, Uganda, and Zimbabwe. Database includes: For each country, detailed information covering climate, currency, language, government, business days and hours, economy customs, etc. Entries include: Company or organization name, address, phone, telex, cable address; product, service, or line of business; some listings also include name of parent company.

Owners and Officers of Private Companies. Taft Group. • Annual. $320. Covers over 128,000 key executives who own and operate America's 48,000 private companies with annual sales over $3 million.

Pakistan Export-Import and Business Directory. International Business Publications, USA. • $99.95 Individuals paperback. Covers: Information on strategic economic, investment, export-import, and business opportunities. Contains important export-import, government, and business contacts and more.

Panama Annual Directory. U.S. Chamber of Commerce. • Annual. $40 Individuals. Covers: 350 member companies of AmCham Panama. Entries include: Company name, address, phone.

Panama Government and Business Contacts Handbook. International Business Publications, USA. • $99.95 Individuals hardcopy, e-book, CD-ROM. Covers: Strategic government and business information, export-import activity in the country, investment, business contacts and regulations.

Panama Industrial and Business Directory. International Business Publications, USA. • Annual. $99.95 Individuals hardcopy, e-book, CD-ROM. Covers: Strategic industrial, investment and business contacts for conducting export-import and investment activity in the country.

Paper Manufacturers Directory. InfoGroup Inc. • Annual. Number of listings: 1,832. Entries include: Name, address, phone, size of advertisement, name of owner or manager, number of employees, year first in "Yellow Pages." Compiled from telephone company "Yellow Pages," nationwide.

Paper Shredding Machines Directory. InfoGroup Inc. • Updated continuously; printed on request. Number of listings: 700. Entries include: Name, address, phone, size of advertisement, name of owner or manager, number of employees, year first in "Yellow Pages." Compiled from telephone company "Yellow Pages," nationwide.

Partnership Houston: Membership Directory and Resource Guide. Greater Houston Partnership. • Annual. $40 Nonmembers print. Covers: Over 1,700 member firms in the Houston, Texas area. Entries include: Firm name, address, phone, URL, name and title of contact, product or service provided, number of employees, line of business.

PC Register. IHS Global Ltd. Lloyd's Register--Fairplay Ltd. • $7,600 Individuals CD-ROM; single user; quarterly updates. Covers: Shipbuilder and owner information for over 170,000 vessels of 100 GT and above. Entries include: Name, address, phone.

PennSuburban Chamber of Commerce--Membership Directory. PennSuburban Chamber of Commerce. • Annual. Covers: Over 900 member businesses and industries in Montgomery, Bucks, and Chester counties in Pennsylvania. Entries include: Company name, address, phone, names and titles of key personnel, number of employees, product or service provided.

Pennsylvania Industrial Directory. Dun & Bradstreet Inc. • Annual. Covers: 22,600 manufacturing establishments in Pennsylvania. Database includes: Statistical data and trade show calendar. Entries include: Company name, address, county, phone, toll-free number, number of employees, names and titles of key executives, plant size, year established, parent company, annual sales, import/export information, SIC code, and product description.

Pennsylvania Industries Guide. Industries Guides Inc. • $95. Covers: Approximately 17,000 manufacturers in Pennsylvania. Entries include: Company name, address, phone.

Pension World--Real Estate Portfolio Manager Directory Issue. Primedia Business. • Annual. $19.95 payment must accompany order. List of about 100 firms each currently managing real estate investments totalling at least $10 million for pension funds.

Perishable Products Export Control Board--Export Directory. Perishable Products Export Council Board. • Provides information and statistics of South African perishable export products.

Personen-Compass. Compass-Verlag. • Annual. $1,250. Covers: over 19,000 principal executives of major Austrian companies. Entries include: Name, address, affiliations.

Peru Government and Business Contacts Handbook. International Business Publications, USA. • $99.95 Individuals hardcopy, e-book, CD-ROM. Covers: Strategic government and business information, export-import activity in the country, investment, business contacts and regulations.

Peru Industrial and Business Directory. International Business Publications, USA. • Annual. $99.95 Individuals hardcopy, e-book, CD-ROM. Covers: Strategic industrial, investment and business contacts for conducting export-import and investment activity in the country. Contains strategic, practical economic and business information.

Pet Hospitals and Clinics Directory. InfoGroup Inc. • Annual. Number of listings: 14,050. Entries include: Name, address, phone, size of advertisement, name of owner or manager, number of employees, year first in "Yellow Pages." Compiled from telephone company "Yellow Pages," nationwide.

Peterson's Guide to MBA Programs: The Most Comprehensive Guide to U.S., Canadian, & International Business Schools. Peterson's. • $28.35 Individuals softcover. Covers: Over 4,000 U.S. accredited MBA programs worldwide. Entries include: Program name, address, phone.

Pharmaceutical Strategic Alliances: The Complete Drug and Biotech Alliances Reference Guide. Windhover Information Inc. • Annual. $2,495 Single issue volume XVII (print). Covers: Pharmaceutical industry strategic alliances, including joint ventures, research and development collaborations, marketing/licensing agreements, and equity investments. Entries include: Company name, address, phone, names and titles of key personnel, financial data, description of transaction, terms, valuations, product information including therapeutic categories, clinical phase of development, geographic marketing rights, statistical charts.

Philippine-European Business Directory. European Chamber of Commerce of the Philippines. • 2,600 PHP Nonmembers hard copy. Covers: 750 European business in the Philippines. Entries include: Contact details of each member.

Philippines Business Directory. Philippine Editors and Publishers. • Annual. $75. Covers: 15,000 business and trade organizations, professional associations, civic groups, manufacturers, wholesalers, and distributors. Entries include: name, address, phone, telex.

Philippines Government and Business Contacts Handbook. International Business Publications, USA. • $99.95 Individuals hardcopy, e-book, CD-ROM. Covers: Strategic government and business information, export-import activity in the country, investment, business contacts and regulations.

Philippines Industrial and Business Directory. International Business Publications, USA. • Annual. $99.95 Individuals hardcopy, e-book, CD-ROM. Covers: Strategic industrial, investment and business contacts for conducting export-import and investment activity in the country.

Phone Communication Services Directory. Info-Group Inc. • Annual. Number of listings: 5473. Entries include: Name, address, phone, size of advertisement, name of owner or manager, number of employees, year first in "Yellow Pages." Compiled from telephone company "Yellow Pages," nationwide.

Photo Copying Directory. InfoGroup Inc. • Annual. Number of listings: 20,946. Entries include: Name, address, phone (including area code), size of advertisement, year first in "Yellow Pages," name of owner or manager, number of employees. Compiled from telephone company "Yellow Pages," nationwide.

Plunkett's Companion to the Almanac of American Employers: Mid-Size Firms. Plunkett Research Ltd. • Annual. $349.99 Individuals Printed Almanac & Online Tools. Covers: Approximately 500 rapidly growing mid-sized firms, defined as between 150 and 2,300 employees. Entries include: Name, address, phone, fax, and key executives.

Plunkett's Consulting Industry Almanac. Plunkett Research Ltd. • $349.99 Individuals pint + online. Covers: Leading companies that provide consulting in areas including marketing, technology, management, manufacturing, and health care. Entries include: Name, address, phone, fax, and key executives. Also includes analysis and information on trends, technology, and statistics in the field.

Plunkett's Financial Services Industry Almanac: The Only Complete Guide to the Technologies and Companies Changing the Way the World Banks, Invest and Borrows. Plunkett Research Ltd. • Annual. $249.99 plus $9.50 shipping (includes CD-ROM). Covers: 500 of the largest investment, banking, and financial companies. Entries include: Firm name, address, phone, fax; description; and leading executives with their titles, addresses, phone numbers, E-mail addresses, Web sites, and fax numbers.

Plunkett's Retail Industry Almanac: Complete Profiles on the Retail 500: The Leading Firms in Retail Stores, Services, Catalogs, and On-Line Sales. Plunkett Research Ltd. • Annual. $349.99 Individuals print. Covers: 500 of the largest retail stores, services, catalogs, and on-line sales companies. Entries include: Firm name, address, phone, fax; description; and leading executives with their titles, addresses, phone numbers, fax numbers, E-mail addresses, and Web sites.

Poland Government and Business Contacts Handbook. International Business Publications, USA. • $99.95 Individuals hardcopy, e-book, CD-ROM. Covers: Strategic government and business information, export-import activity in the country, investment, business contacts and regulations.

Polish Business Directory. Branzowy Katalog Firm-Ravi Sp. • Annual. Covers: More than 3,000 companies in Poland. Entries include: Company name, address, phone, name and title of contact, product/service.

Polish Business Directory for Beginners. MZM Publications Publishing Promotion Co. • $43 plus s&h. Covers: Polish commercial and diplomatic offices, hotels, publications, central institutions and organizations, advertising and marketing agencies, courts, banks, learning institutions, offices to rent, travel services and other services.

Polish Industry Directory. Branzowy Katalog Firm-Ravi Sp. • Annual. Covers: More than 10,000 companies in Poland, including leading Polish importers/exporters. Entries include: Company name, address, phone, product/service.

Pool Table Equipment and Supplies Directory. Info-Group Inc. • Annual. Number of listings: 22,706. Entries include: Name, address, phone, size of advertisement, name of owner or manager, number of employees, year first in "Yellow Pages." Compiled from telephone company "Yellow Pages," nationwide.

Ports and Terminals Guide. IHS Global Ltd. Lloyd's Register--Fairplay Ltd. • Biennial. $895 Individuals. Covers: Over 23,000 ports and service providers and details on over 10,000 ports. Also includes port conditions and news and ship index of 58,000 vessels. Database includes: Over 4,000 plans, maps, and port photographs. Entries include: For ports and service providers--Name, address, phone; for ports--location, general overview, load line zone, and maximum vessel size.

Portugal Government and Business Contacts Handbook. International Business Publications, USA. • Annual. $99.95 Individuals hardcopy, e-book, CD-ROM. Covers: Information on strategic economic, investment, export-import, and business opportunities. Contains important export-import, government, and business contacts. Ultimate directory for conducting export-import operations in the country.

Power Companies Directory. InfoGroup Inc. • Annual. Number of listings: 6,906. Entries include: Name, address, phone, size of advertisement, name of owner or manager, number of employees, year first in "Yellow Pages." Compiled from telephone company "Yellow Pages," nationwide.

Pratt's Guide to Venture Capital Sources. Greenwood Electronic Media. • Annual. $249. Covers: Approximately 800 venture capital firms, principally in the United States; small business investment corporations (SBICs); corporate venture groups; and selected consultants and "deal men"; separate section for providers of professional services to venture capitalists. Database includes: Articles on raising venture capital. Entries include: Company name, address, phone, names of executives, investment preferences, and industry preferences.

President's Club! Presidents of Computer and Telecommunications Companies Directory. Ex-IBM Corp. • $95 per issue. Covers: over 2,200 presidents of companies, organizations, or associations involved in the computer and telecommunications industries. Entries include: Company, organization, or association name, president's name, address, and phone.

Probe Directory of Foreign Direct Investment in the United States. Probe International. • Triennial. $250. Covers: over 1,500 affiliate firms in the United States which are partially or totally owned by over 800 Japanese companies. Entries include: For U.S. companies--Company name, address, phone, subsidiary names, name of executive officer, foreign investor's name, line of business/product. For foreign investors--Company name, address, names of U.S. affiliates.

Process Industry Directory. Telmo G. Mirat. • Annual. $95. Covers: Argentine manufacturers, importers, and exporters of raw materials, industrial chemicals, and products for the process industry.

Product Safety Consultants Directory. InfoGroup Inc. • Annual. Number of listings: 2,727. Entries include: Name, address, phone, size of advertisement, name of owner or manager, number of employees, year first in "Yellow Pages." Compiled from telephone company "Yellow Pages," nationwide.

Production and Consumption. Produccion y Consumo SACEFI. • Annual. $100. Covers: Manufacturers and distributors of Argentine and foreign products, including factories, workshops, services, trademarks, transport, automotive, nautics, seacraft, and chambers of commerce. Entries include: Contact information.

Products and Services to China. Intervisual Advertising Ltd. • Covers: Industries in China and Hong Kong. Database includes: Product/service, name, tradename. Entries include: Company name, location, phone, geographical area served, subsidiary and branch names and locations, description of product/services.

Professional Consulting Services: Industry Sector Profile. Philippine-German Export Development Project Philippine Bureau of Export Trade Promotion. • Publication includes: Companies exporting professional consulting services from the Philippines. Entries include: Company name, address, phone, fax, name and title of contact, type of business, year established, subsidiary and branch names and locations, financial data, number of employees, government registrations, professional memberships, bank references, supply capability, export experience, business plan. Principal content of publication is an overview of the business environment and professional consulting services industry in the Philippines.

Professional Financial Planning Directory. Info-Group Inc. • Annual. Number of listings: 14,191. Entries include: Name, address, phone, size of advertisement, name of owner or manager, number of employees, year first in "Yellow Pages." Compiled from telephone company "Yellow Pages," nationwide.

Profile's Stock Exchange Handbook. Profile Media. • Quarterly. R 155 Individuals. Covers: About 650 companies whose stock is traded on the Johannesburg, South Africa, stock exchange. Entries include: Company name, address, names and titles of key personnel, line of business, names of associated and subsidiary companies, capital, dates of dividend payments, five-year financial data, five-year comparison of high and low share prices and volumes traded.

Project Finance Yearbook. Euromoney Institutional Investor P.L.C. • $375 Individuals. Contains innovative project finance modelling, case studies of recent ground-breaking projects, advice on managing both country and project risk, legal and contractual problems and how they were solved. Covers: Approximately 3,000 companies involved in project finance worldwide. Entries include: Name, address, phone, fax, e-mail, names and titles of key personnel.

Provincial/Territorial Directories. A.C. Braby (Pty) Ltd. • Annual. $35 Botswana ed. Covers: Business listings in South Africa. Entries include: Company name, address, phone, telex number.

Public Companies. InfoGroup Inc. • Number of listings: 9,084. Entries include: Company name, address, phone, names and titles of key personnel, stock exchange symbol, Standard Industrial Classification (SIC) codes, annual sales, number of employees.

Publishers-Directory & Guide Directory. Info-Group Inc. • Updated continuously; printed on request. Number of listings: 1,792. Entries include: Name, address, phone, size of advertisement, name of owner or manager, number of employees, year first in "Yellow Pages." Compiled from telephone company "Yellow Pages," nationwide.

Purchasing People in Major Corporations. Diversity Information Resources. • Annual. $175 Individuals /year (print and online). Covers: Information regarding Diversity Information Resources. Lists corporate purchasing locations; listings include name of minority business program administrator, if that position exists.

Qatar Golden Key Directory. International Institute of Trade Relation Promotion, Trade Information Centre of Iran. • £100 Individuals. Covers: 10,256 companies in Qatar. Entries include: Company name, address, telephone, fax, products, services, Managing Director, and business activities.

Quarterly Report on Companies whose Stocks are

For publishers' addresses, refer to SOURCES CITED section at the back of the book.

Quoted on the Stock Markets. Bolsas de Comercio de Madrid, Bilbao, Barcelona, Valencia. • Quarterly. Covers: Companies on the stock exchange in Spain. Entries include: Company name, address, phone, financial and economic data.

Qui Deade. Bottin S.A. • Annual. Covers: 200,000 commercial and industrial entities and 4,000 products and services in France. Entries include: Company name, address, phone, product/service.

Quoted Companies on the Brussels and Antwerp Stock Exchange. DAFSA - Belgique S.A. • Annual. Covers: Companies with shares traded on the Antwerp and Brussels stock exchanges. Entries include: Company name, address, phone, officers, directors, executives, banks, brokers.

R & S Annual Directory. Ricerche e Studi S.p.A. Mediobanca. • Annual. €150 Individuals European countries. Covers: Nearly 10,000 businesses forming part of 180 groups representing over a third of Italy's manufacturing industry. Database includes: Italian-English glossary. Entries include: Group name, address, phone, directors, details of shareholders, products, market shares, production facilities, sales and employees, financial data.

Racine Area Manufacturers Directory. • Annual. Covers: About 400 manufacturers in the Racine, Wisconsin, area. Entries include: Company name, address, phone, name of principal executive, number of employees, product or service provided, fax, and e-mail.

Racing Car Equipment (Manufacturers) Directory. InfoGroup Inc. • Annual. Number of listings: 6,655. Entries include: Name, address, phone, size of advertisement, name of owner or manager, number of employees, year first in "Yellow Pages." Compiled from telephone company "Yellow Pages," nationwide.

The Rauch Guide to the US Cosmetics and Toiletries Industry. Impact Marketing Consultants Inc. • $895. Covers: Structure and current market information on cosmetics and toiletries industry.

Real Estate Advertisers Directory. InfoGroup Inc. • Annual. Number of listings: 7,204. Entries include: Name, address, phone, size of advertisement, name of owner or manager, number of employees, year first in "Yellow Pages." Compiled from telephone company "Yellow Pages," nationwide.

Real Estate Auctioneers Directory. InfoGroup Inc. • Annual. Number of listings: 11,136. Entries include: Name, address, phone, size of advertisement, name of owner or manager, number of employees, year first in "Yellow Pages." Compiled from telephone company "Yellow Pages," nationwide.

Real Estate Loans Directory. InfoGroup Inc. • Annual. Number of listings: 74,550. Entries include: Name, address, phone, size of advertisement, name of owner or manager, number of employees, year first in "Yellow Pages." Compiled from telephone company "Yellow Pages," nationwide.

Reference Book of Manufacturers. Dun & Bradstreet Inc. • Semiannual. Covers: over 400,000 U.S. manufacturers. Entries include: Company name, address, phone, line of business, branch offices, number of employees, year established, DUNS number, D&B credit rating.

Regional Business Directory. Business Service Div. Birmingham Area Chamber of Commerce. • Covers: Approximately 4,000 businesses that are members of the area Chamber of Commerce. Entries include: Company name, address, phone, name and title of contact.

Regional Industrial Buying Guide Series. Thomas Regional Directory Company Inc. • Annual. Guides to manufacturers of industrial products within regions of a state or within contiguous portions of two or three states; the "Greater Allegheny Regional Industrial Buying Guide," for example, covers western Pennsylvania, northern West Virginia, and eastern Ohio. Guides also include listings for related industrial services, such as trucking, maintenance services, etc., and distributors and manufacturers' representatives. Guides now available cover eastern and western New England, greater New York City, upstate New York, northern New Jersey, greater Delaware Valley, greater Allegheny Valley, "Capital Cities" (Washington, DC, eastern Maryland, Delaware, eastern Virginia), north central tri-state area (Wisconsin/Illinois/Indiana), southern Michigan, northern Ohio, the Ohio Valley, north Texas/Oklahoma, Texas Gulf, North and South Carolina; northern California and southern California. Each includes 15,000-40,000 listings. Entries include: Company name, address, phone; product/service.

Register of Arab Importers and Traders. The Amalgamated Press. • Biennial. $150. Publication includes: Arab importers, exporters, distributors, wholesalers, agents, products, services, chambers of commerce, import/export trade associations, state trading organizations, boards of trade, consulates, embassies, high commissions, banks, hotels, travel, shipping and insurance companies, newspapers. Entries include: Company or organization name, address, phone. Principal content of publication is Geography, ports, econtomy, trade and travel in Algeria, Bahrain, Egypt, Iraq, Jordan, Kuwait, Lebanon, Libya, Mauritania, Morocco, Oman, Qatar, Saudi Arabia, Somalia, Sudan, Syria, Tunisia, United Arab Emirates, and Yemen.

Register of Development Research Projects in Latin America. OECD Publishing. • Irregular. $75. Covers: 1,304 development research projects in 16 Latin American countries concerned with economic and social development, including economic policy, institutional framework, demography, labor, culture, and education. Entries include: Project title, institution name and address, researcher names, financial sponsor names and addresses, dates, description of project, planned output.

Rest of the World Food Companies. Datamonitor. • $995. Covers: Food companies in countries outside of Europe, Asia, and the U.S. Entries include: Company name, address, phone, telex, names and titles of key personnel; number of employees; financial data, product/service, Standard Industrial Classification (SIC) code, production locations.

Rest of the World Toiletry Index. Datamonitor. • $995. Covers: Companies involved in the toiletry and cosmetics industry in nations outside of Asia and North, Central, and South America. Entries include: Company name, address, phone, telex, names and titles of key personnel, number of employees; financial data, product/service, Standard Industrial Classification (SIC) code, production locations.

Retail Shops Directory. InfoGroup Inc. • Annual. Number of listings: 7,325. Entries include: Name, address, phone, size of advertisement, name of owner or manager, number of employees, year first in "Yellow Pages." Compiled from telephone company "Yellow Pages," nationwide.

Roller Rinks Directory. InfoGroup Inc. • Annual. Number of listings: 2,944. Entries include: Name, address, phone, size of advertisement, name of owner or manager, number of employees, year first in "Yellow Pages." Compiled from telephone company "Yellow Pages," nationwide.

The Romanian Business Directory. Topaz General Activities S.R.L. • Annual. $20. Covers: The most active companies and operators in the Romanian market, along with products and services. Entries include: Company business information.

Roofing Service Consultants Directory. InfoGroup Inc. • Annual. Number of listings: 1,225. Entries include: Name, address, phone, size of advertisement, name of owner or manager, number of employees, year first in "Yellow Pages." Compiled from telephone company "Yellow Pages," nationwide.

Russia/CIS Exporters-Importers Directory. Business Information Agency Inc. PlanetInform. • Annual. $149 Individuals Paperback (plus shipping charge). Covers: 5,936 representatives of foreign firms and joint-venture companies in Russia. Entries include: Company name, location, detailed contact information, type of business, SIC codes, number of employees, year founded, legal status, and subsidiary indicators.

Russia Defense Industry Directory. International Business Publications, USA. • $99.95 Individuals hardcopy, e-book, CD-ROM. Covers: Strategic and practical information on government, national security, army, foreign and domestic politics, conflicts, relations with the US, international activity, economy, technology, mineral resources, culture, traditions, government and business contacts.

Russia Industrial and Business Directory. International Business Publications, USA. • Annual. $99.95 Individuals hardcopy, e-book, CD-ROM. Covers: Strategic industrial, investment and business contacts for conducting export-import and investment activity in the country.

Russia: Political and Economic Analysis and Business Directory. Chamber World Network. • $29.95. Publication includes: Directories of organizations, companies, and other agencies in or doing business in Russia, including Russian companies, joint ventures, firms from outside Russia accredited to do business there, banks, insurance companies, consulates and embassies, hotels. Database includes: Essays and tables on the economic and legal structure of Russia, including summaries of Russian law, statistics, and surveys of future trends. Entries include: For companies--Name, address, phone, annual sales, number of employees, products.

Russian Business White & Yellow Pages. European Business Publications Inc. • Covers: More than 25,000 major business companies, industrial enterprises and banks in Moscow, St. Petersburg and all 87 provinces of Russia and Worldwide. White Pages include Russian Federal Government information and contacts. Entries include: Name, address, phone, fax, line of business and product information.

Russian Encyclopedia of Information and Telecommunications: Information on Information. International Bureau for Information and Telecommunications. • $30. Covers: Approximately 1,500 organizations, 2,500 managers and senior employees in information and telecommunications in Russia. Also includes detailed descriptions of 1,700 electronic databases, 150 telecommunication networks, hosts, and their information resource. Entries include: Company, organization or personal name, address, phone, e-mail, website address, names and titles of key personnel, biographical data for individuals, number of employees, financial data, branch office or subsidiary names and addresses, products or services provided, key data, title of database.

Russian Exporters and Importers--Firm Directory. International Bureau for Information and Telecommunications. • Annual. $25. Covers: 4,300 leading Russian companies trading on the international market and their exports and imports product range. Entries include: Company name, address, phone, fax, geographical area served, products or services provided.

St. Agnes Traders Business Directory. StAgnes-Traders.com. • Covers: Businesses in Cornish village including the surrounding areas of Porthtowan, Mount Hawke, Blackwater, and Mithian.

St. George Area Chamber of Commerce Business Directory. St. George Area Chamber of Commerce.

• Covers businesses, attractions, and history of the St. George, Utah, area.

St. Paul Area Chamber of Commerce--Membership Directory and Business Resource Guide. Saint Paul Area Chamber of Commerce. • Annual. Covers: 2,100 members of the St. Paul Area Chamber of Commerce. Entries include: Company name, address, phone, name of principal executive, product or service provided, website address, e-mail address.

St. Petersburg Business Guide. Arguments and Facts Media Ltd. • Covers: Government agencies and companies of interest to individuals and firms conducting business in St. Petersburg, Russia; includes state and local government authorities, business organizations, financial and commercial services, consulting and legal services, customs offices, communications and transport services, advertising agencies, security firms, recruitment services, training specialists, and mass media outlets. Entries include: In general, agency or company name, address, phone, fax, description.

San Diego County Business Directory. Harris InfoSource. • Annual. $115 Individuals. Covers: Approximately 24,700 manufacturers, wholesalers, and service companies in San Diego County, California. Includes names of key executives. Entries include: Company name, address, parent name/location, telephone, fax and 800 numbers, Web site address (on CD-ROM only), number of employees, year established, annual revenue, plant size, business description, Standard Industrial Classification (SIC) codes, executive names/titles, public ownership, legal structure, import/export designators, female/minority ownership, and Thomas Guide Page and Grid Number.

San Francisco Bay Area Silicon Valley International Business Directory. San Francisco Chamber of Commerce. • $45 Members. Covers international businesses based in the San Francisco Bay/Silicon Valley area. Entries include contact details, parent companies, products and services.

San Francisco Business--Top 51 Public Companies Issue. San Francisco Chamber of Commerce. • Annual. $3 payment with order. Publication includes: List of 51 leading San Francisco Bay area public corporations (selected on the basis of sales). Entries include: Company name, address, phone, name of chief executive officer, current and prior year's rankings, line of business, sales, net assets, net income, net worth, number of employees.

San Francisco County Business Directory. Rich's Business Directories Inc. • $215 Individuals. Covers: 3,911 firms in San Francisco County. Entries include: Company name, address, phone, fax, year established, branch or headquarters, SIC code, and product type.

San Mateo County Business Directory. Rich's Business Directories Inc. • $199 Individuals online. Covers: 2,963 firms in San Mateo County. Entries include: Company name, address, phone, fax, year established, branch or headquarters, SIC code, and product type.

Santa Clara County Business Directory. Rich's Business Directories Inc. • $219 Individuals online. Covers: 5,745 firms in Santa Clara County. Entries include: Company name, address, phone, fax, year established, branch or headquarters, SIC code, and product type.

Santa Monica Chamber of Commerce Business Profile and Membership Directory. Santa Monica Chamber of Commerce. • Annual. Covers: Member businesses in Santa Monica, California.

Sao Paulo Year Book: Amcham Yearbook Directory. American Chamber of Commerce for Brazil - Sao Paulo. • Annual. $500 Members. Covers: 5,450 member American and Brazilian firms and 20,000 individual members interested in developing trade and investment within and between the two countries; other American chambers of commerce, American organizations in Sao Paulo, government agencies, institutions, and associations. Database includes: Glossary of product terms in Portuguese; section on Brazilian business and economics; statistics. Entries include: For firms--Company name, address, phone, telex, fax, names and titles of key personnel, product/service, export and domestic sales, net worth, number of employees, registered capital, branches, affiliates abroad. For individual members--Name, title, company name, phone, home or office address, telex. For others--Name, address, phone.

Saudi Arabia Golden Key Directory. International Institute of Trade Relation Promotion, Trade Information Centre of Iran. • £100 Individuals. Covers: 37,309 companies in Saudi Arabia. Entries include: Company name, address, telephone, fax, products, services, Managing Director, and business activities.

Saudi Arabia Industrial and Business Directory. International Business Publications, USA. • Annual. $99.95 Individuals hardcopy, e-book, CD-ROM. Covers: Strategic industrial, investment and business contacts for conducting export-import and investment activity in the country.

Saudi Industrial Development Fund--National Industries Directory. Saudi Industrial Development Fund. • Covers: More than 2000 industrial plants in Saudi Arabia. Entries include: Name, address, phone, fax.

Savings Institutions--Top 200. Savings & Commerce Bankers-America. • Annual. $5. Covers: 200 leading savings institutions as determined by their assets and savings. Entries include: Contact information.

SBIC Directory and Handbook of Small Business Finance. International Wealth Success Inc. • Annual. $15 payment with order. Covers: over 400 small business investment companies (SBIC's) that lend money for periods from 5 to 20 years to small businesses. Entries include: Company name, address, amount and type of financing.

Schools (Dancing) Directory. InfoGroup Inc. • Annual. Number of listings: 14,474. Entries include: Name, address, phone, size of advertisement, name of owner or manager, number of employees, year first in "Yellow Pages." Compiled from telephone company "Yellow Pages," nationwide.

Scotland's Top 500 Companies. Jordans Ltd. • Annual. $55. Covers: Companies in Scotland. Entries include: Company name, address, phone, fax, type of activity, chief executives, sales figures, capital, profits, net cash flow.

Scott's Business Suite. Scott's Directories. • $1,449 Individuals CD-ROM, pinpointer. Covers: 134,200+ manufacturers, manufacturers' sales offices, wholesalers, wholesale agents, and distributors operating in Greater Montreal, North and South Shore, Ontario, Greater Calgary, Edmonton and Greater Vancouver along with 245,000+ business contact names. Entries include: Company name, address, phone, fax, names and titles of key personnel, number of employees, parent companies, SIC, product, year established.

Scott's Custom Solutions. Scott's Directories. • Covers: Details for 175,000+ companies and 275,000+ business contact names can be provided customized as per client requirements on the basis of specific geographies, specific products or services, specific job functions, size demographics. Entries include: Company name, address, phone, fax, names and titles of key personnel, number of employees, parent companies, SIC, product, year established.

Scott's Directories: Greater Montreal and Laval Business Directory. Scott's Directories. • Annual. $229 Individuals. Covers: More than 18,000 manufacturers, distributors, wholesalers, manufacturers' representatives, contractors, transportation companies, financial institutions; legal, engineering, and architectural firms; real estate brokers, retail main offices, and special services related to industry in Montreal. Entries include: Name, postal code, phone, fax, executive names and titles, type of business or product produced, North American Standard Industrial Classification (NAICS) code, number of employees; code indicating line of business; year established.

Sea-web Directory. IHS Global Ltd. Lloyd's Register--Fairplay Ltd. • $1,175 Individuals Online. Covers: Over entries including 178,000 companies in the shipping industry, 129,000 ship operators details and 52,000 contact names. Maritime organizations, ship brokers, marine insurance companies, and maritime schools are among the groups included. Entries include: Name, address, phone, fax.

Security Systems Directory. InfoGroup Inc. • Annual. Number of listings: 2,295. Entries include: Name, address, phone, size of advertisement, name of owner or manager, number of employees, year first in "Yellow Pages." Compiled from telephone company "Yellow Pages," nationwide.

Sell's Products and Services Directory. Miller Freeman UK Ltd. • Annual. $99 print. Covers: Approximately 60,000 firms in United Kingdom and Ireland, including over 8,900 suppliers of health care products, equipment, and services in the United Kingdom and industry associations. Entries include: Company name, address, phone, fax, telex, description of product/service, names and titles of key personnel.

Sell's Scottish Directory. Miller Freeman UK Ltd. • Annual. $30. Covers: 8,000 industrial and commercial firms in Scotland, including firms int he North Sea oil industry. Entries include: Company name, address, phone, telex number, type of business.

Services et Expertise--Conseil du Quebec. Quebec Dans Le Monde. • Biennial. $63.95 Individuals. Covers: Approximately 1,600 organizations and consultants who provide business counsel. Entries include: name, address, phone.

Shanghai Yellow Pages: Commercial/Industrial Directory. China Yellow Pages Directories Co. • Annual. $65. Covers: over 30,000 companies in Shanghai. Database includes: Lists of trade contacts in Hong Kong, Taiwan, Macau, and Singapore. Entries include: Company name, address, phone, fax, postal code.

Sharjah Commercial Directory. Express Print Publishers. • Covers: Commercial industries in Sharjah. Entries include: Name, address, phone, fax.

Sharjah Industrial Products Directory. Express Print Publishers. • Covers: Manufacturing firms operating in United Arab Emirates. Entries include: Company address, executives, and activities.

Shenzhen Yellow Pages: Commercial/Industrial Directory. China Yellow Pages Directories Co. • Annual. $65. Covers: over 20,000 Shenzhen companies. Database includes: Guide to investment in the Shenzhen area. Entries include: Company name, address, phone, fax, postal codes.

Shingle Springs/Cameron Park Chamber of Commerce Business Directory. Shingle Springs/Cameron Park Chamber of Commerce. • Complete business listings, shopping information, and history of the Shingle Springs and Cameron Park areas of California.

Short Courses and Seminars--The Who's Who of Training in Canada. Development Publications Inc. • Semiannual. $59. Covers: more than 3,000 business and management courses, seminars, and workshops offered in Canada on subjects such as accounting, communications, conflict management, human relations, and supervisory development.

Each issue lists programs for the following six months. Entries include: Name of program, sponsors, location, date, fees.

Sibbald Guide to Every Public and the Top 100 Private Companies in Missouri. Acorn Press Inc. • Annual. $80 per year, plus $5.00 shipping; payment must accompany order. Covers: 205 public and privately-held corporations and financial institutions in Missouri. Entries include: Company name, address, phone; brief company history and description, names and titles of officers and directors; return on beginning equity, return on sales/revenues; condensed balance sheet, income statement for past five years, auditors, transfer agent, legal counsel, stock exchange.

Sibbald Guide to the Texas Top 250 Public Companies and Top 250 Private Companies. Acorn Press Inc. • Annual. $102.50 per year, plus $5.00 shipping; payment must accompany order. Covers: 500 public and privately-held corporations and financial institutions in Texas. Entries include: Company name, address, phone; brief company history and description, names and titles of officers and directors; return on beginning equity, return on sales/revenues; condensed balance sheet, income statement for past five years, auditors, transfer agent, legal counsel, stock exchange.

SIBD--The Business Directory for the Soviet Region. FYI Information Resources for a Changing World. • Annual. $240 plus $10.00 shipping. Covers: Approximately 6,500 independent, cooperative, and private business organizations from industry, agriculture, and service sectors in the 15 republics of the former Soviet Union. Database includes: List of 500 largest enterprises. Entries include: Company or organization name, address, phone, telex, names and titles of key personnel, number of employees, geographical area served, financial data, subsidiary and branch names and locations, description of product/service.

Signal Magazine--AFCEA Source Book Issue. • Annual. Publication includes: List of member companies concerned with communications, design, production, maintenance and operation of communications, electronics, command and control, computers, intelligence systems and imagery. Entries include: Company name, address, phone, names and titles of key personnel, financial keys, trade and brand names, products or services, affiliations, description of organizational purpose, objectives.

Singapore Electronics Industry Directory. Marshall Cavendish Business Information Private Ltd. • $50 Individuals local. Covers: information on electronics manufacturers, traders, distributors, suppliers, and international purchasing offices. Entries include: corporate profiles, company listings and contacts.

Singapore Electronics Trade Directory. International Enterprise Singapore. • Annual. $140 Individuals Print and CD. Covers: Information and contacts of numerous manufacturers, traders, and other supporting service providers in the electronics industry.

Singapore Exchange--Companies Handbook. Singapore Exchange Ltd. • Semiannual. $400 per year. Covers: companies whose stock is traded on the Singapore Exchange. Entries include: Company name, address, names and titles of key personnel, capital, history, line of business, products, three year comparison of financial data.

Singapore Government and Business Contacts Handbook. International Business Publications, USA. • $99.95 Individuals hardcopy, e-book, CD-ROM. Covers: Strategic government and business information, export-import activity in the country, investment, business contacts and regulations.

Singapore International Chamber of Commerce. Singapore International Chamber of Commerce. • Annual. $15 Nonmembers. Covers: Singapore Chamber of Commerce members. Entries include: Members' addresses and their type of business.

Singapore International 100 Ranking. International Enterprise Singapore. • S$30.60 local. Covers: Singapore's top 100 companies with largest revenue contributions from the markets of Africa, Americas, China, Europe, India, Middle East, North Asia, Oceania, Southeast Asia. Entries include: top 100 companies ranked by overseas revenue, top 10 companies ranked by market, and corporate profiles.

Site Selection and Industrial Development--Geo-Political Index Issue. Conway Data Inc. • Annual. $20 plus $2.00 shipping. Publication includes: List of state, county, and local governmental agencies which negotiate and administer inducements to industrial firms to locate new offices, plants, warehouses, or other facilities within their jurisdiction. Database includes: Tabulations of incentives, financing plans, etc., offered by state and local agencies. Entries include: Agency name, address, phone, name of principal executive, and indication of special services and incentives.

Site Selection--Geo-Economic Index Issue. Conway Data Inc. • $20 plus $2.00 shipping. Publication includes: List of area development bodies, including state development agencies, city and county development offices, urban renewal agencies, port and airport agencies, railroads, utilities, banks, chambers of commerce, etc.; coverage includes Canada and over 50 other countries. Entries include: Group name, phone, name of contact.

Skagway Business Directory. Skagway Chamber of Commerce. • Annual. Covers: Comprehensive listing of area businesses.

SLAM--Trade Yearbook of Africa. SLAM Trade Year Book of Africa. • Annual. $60. Covers: Approximately 400,000 industrial and commercial companies in Africa. Entries include: Company name, address, phone, line of business, product/service, trademarks.

Small Business Investment Company Directory and Handbook. International Wealth Success Inc. • $20 Individuals. Gives tips from the U.S. Small Business Administration (SBA) on obtaining financing and on small business financial management and explains how SBICs work. Covers: Over 400 small business investment companies interested in investing in various businesses.

Small Business Reference Guide. Bluechip Books. • Irregular. $14.95. Covers: over 350 firms, associations, and government agencies offering products and services of assistance to small businesses. Entries include: Organization name, address, phone; most listings also include description of services, products, or activities.

Small Business Sources of Capital Handbook. Metro Atlanta Chamber of Commerce. • $8. Covers: Sources of capital available to small businesses in the metropolitan Atlanta area. Entries include: Source name, address, phone, description.

Smart/Utilize Catalog Index. Property Management Systems Corp. • Bimonthly. Database covers: about 20,000 manufacturers of over 250,000 models of electronic, computer, office, and machine tool equipment; limited international coverage. Database includes: Company name, address, phone, subsidiary and branch names and locations, description of products with model number and performance specifications, trade/brand names, merger/buyout audit trail.

SMI and SME Business Directory: The Official Business Directory of SMI Association of Malaysia. Tourism Publications Corporation Sdn. Bhd. • $69.90 Individuals. Aims to develop the potential of SMIs/SMEs and to enable them to evolve according to the demands of the new economy.

Somalia--Productive Sectors of the Economy. Indigo Publications. • Irregular. $500. Covers: Major companies in Somalia, including government services, state and private entities. Entries include: Company name, address, phone, managers, production figures.

Somerset County Chamber of Commerce Business Directory. Somerset County Chamber of Commerce. • Covers: Area businesses.

Sonoma County International Trade Directory. Sonoma County Economic Development Board. • Irregular. $5 plus $2.00 shipping. Covers: Approximately 100 government agencies, banks, foreign consulates, and international chambers of commerce located in Sonoma County, California that provide international trade assistance. Database includes: Publications on the topic, guide to overseas communications, pertinent government regulations. Entries include: Company or organization name, address, phone, names and titles of key personnel.

The Sourcebook of Franchise Opportunities. QSU Publishing. • Annual. $35. Covers: Over 3,000 franchising opportunities. Entries include: Franchisor name, address, phone, and profiles are included for approximately 1,000.

SourceGuide to Management Information. London Business School Information Service. • $50. Covers: Sources of published and unpublished information on management issues available worldwide, including journals, databases and other electronic sources, abstracting and indexing services, reference works, academic working papers, and other relevant materials. Entries include: Source name, address, phone, description.

SourceGuide to Market Share and Business Ranking Tables. London Business School Information Service. • $100. Covers: Key U.K., Pan European, and international business ranking and market share information published in 1989 or later and available in U.K. commercial libraries; includines newspapers, journals, directories, and databases. Entries include: Source name, address, phone, description.

South Africa Business Directory. Business Guide. • $250 Individuals. Covers: 32,600 business listings including wholesalers, importers, retailers, business houses, and agents in South Africa.

South Africa Industrial and Business Directory. International Business Publications, USA. • Annual. $99.95 Individuals hardcopy, e-book, CD-ROM. Covers: Strategic industrial, investment and business contacts for conducting export-import and investment activity in the country.

South Africa National Classified Directory. A.C. Braby (Pty) Ltd. • Annual. Covers: Government and businesses in South Africa. Database includes: Maps.

South America: A Directory and Sourcebook. Euromonitor International Business Reference Div. • $390. Covers: major companies in South America; international and national organizations and statistical agencies, trade journals, electronic databases, consultants, market research firms, research centers, trade associations, trade unions, libraries, and other information sources. Database includes: Overview and statistical tables summarizing the economies of South America and the individual countries. Entries include: For companies--Name, address, phone, fax, telex, line of business, chief executive, number of employees, sales, products, outlets. For others--Organization name or publication title, address, phone, telex, fax, names and titles of key personnel, description of activities or contents.

South America Mineral Industry Handbook. International Business Publications, USA. • $99.95 Individuals hardcopy, e-book, CD-ROM. Covers: Strategic information and contacts on mining resources and mineral industry on South America.

South Carolina Business Directory. InfoGroup Inc. • Annual. $795 for both print & CD-ROM. Covers: 172,002 businesses in South Carolina. Entries include: Company name, address, phone, number of employees, name of owner or manager, sales volume. Compiled from telephone company 'Yellow Pages,' statewide. All states covered (see separate entries).

South Carolina Chamber of Commerce Business Directory & Resource Guide. South Carolina Chamber of Commerce. • Covers: Member businesses, chambers of commerce, and professional and trade associations in South Carolina.

South Carolina Industrial Directory. South Carolina Department of Commerce. • Annual. Covers: nearly 4,000 industrial companies throughout South Carolina. Entries include: Company name, address, phone, parent company (if applicable), plant address, names of principal executives, whether firm exports or imports, number of employees, product or service provided, Standard Industrial Classification (SIC) code, NAICS code, email, and web addresses.

South-Central American International Business Directory of Importers. Coble International. • $285 print or CD-ROM. Covers: 23,000 importers from the West Indies, Nicaragua, Mexico, Honduras, Guyana, El Salvador, Uruguay, Paraguay, Brazil, Guatemala, Belize, Colombia, Costa Rica, Puerto Rico, Dominican Republic, Chile, Haiti, Bahamas, Jamaica, Panama, Peru, Bolivia, Ecuador, Venezuela and Argentina. Entries include: Name, address, phone, fax, primary contact person, list of products, e-mail addresses, and Web site.

South Central High Technology Firms. Rich's Business Directories Inc. • $199 Individuals 1 year premium online. Covers: Approximately 2,221 high tech research, manufacturing, and development firms in south central United States (Arkansas, Louisiana, and Oklahoma). Entries include: Company name, address, phone, names and titles of key personnel, year established, number of employees, type of ownership, annual sales volume, product service provided, SIC code.

Southern California Business Directory and Buyers Guide. Dun & Bradstreet Inc. • Annual. $220 Individuals. Covers: 174,700 Southern California businesses. Database includes: Statistical data, trade show calendar. Entries include: Company name, address, county, phone, fax, number of employees, names and titles of key executives, plant size, year established, parent company, annual sales, import/export information, Standard Industrial Classification (SIC) code, and product description.

Soviet Trade Directory. Flegon Press. • $200. Covers: Over 20,000 listings of ex-Soviet plants, factories, and enterprises in all branches of industry. Entries include: Company name and address.

Spain: A Directory and Sourcebook. Euromonitor International Business Reference Div. • $390. Publication includes: Lists of major companies and sources of information regarding to consumer markets in Spain. Database includes: Statistics. Entries include: Company or organization name, address, phone, telex, names and titles of key personnel, description. Principal content of publication is an overview of issues affecting Spain.

Spain Government and Business Contacts Handbook. International Business Publications, USA. • $99.95 Individuals hardcopy, e-book, CD-ROM. Covers: Strategic government and business information, export-import activity in the country, investment, business contacts and regulations.

Spain Industrial and Business Directory. International Business Publications, USA. • Annual. $99.95 Individuals hardcopy, e-book, CD-ROM. Covers: Strategic industrial, investment and business contacts for conducting export-import and investment activity in the country.

Spain-Portugal Mergers and Acquisitions Directory. S.p.A. • Biennial. Covers: 200 banks, brokers, auditors, lawyers of the mergers and acquisitions sector with the names of the principals in Spain and Portugal. Entries include: Company name, names and titles of key personnel, number of employees, financial data, branch office name and address, description, services provided.

Spain's 30,000 Top Companies. Dun & Bradstreet Inc. • Annual. $385. 15,000 companies in Spain with annual sales of at least $500,000.

Spanish-American Commercial Directory. IBAR. • Triennial. $60. Covers: More than 350,000 businesses in Spain, Portugal, and Latin-American countries, as well as companies in African, Asia, Australia, Canada, and Europe interested in conducting business with Latin-American countries. Entries include: Company name, address, phone.

Spanish Business Directory. INFOT Inc. • $72.25 CD-ROM; additional $125 for MS Access format. Covers: 86,807 selected businesses from the Spanish-speaking countries. Entries include: Name, physical address, email and website addresses, telephone and fax number, business description etc.

Standard & Poor's Corporation Records. Standard & Poor's Financial Services L.L.C. • Covers: Over 12,000 publicly-owned companies. Entries include: Corporation name, address, detailed descriptions of background, financial structure, and securities.

Standard & Poor's 500 Directory. Index Products & Services Standard & Poor's Corp. • Annual. Covers: The 500 companies included in the Standard & Poor's 500 Stock Index. Database includes: Derivative product information including futures, options, options on futures. Entries include: Company name, address, phone, fax, profile.

Standard & Poor's MarketScope. Standard & Poor's Financial Services L.L.C. • Daily. Covers: Over 7,000 companies in the 'Reference Section' of Standard and Poors database, incoluding all NYSE and ASE listed companies and 3,500 NASDAQ listed companies. Database covers: Over 7,000 companies in the 'Reference Section' of Standard and Poors database, including all NYSE and ASE listed companies and 3,500 NASDAQ listed companies. Database includes: Company name, phone, background information, current and historical financial information, earnings and dividend projections (for 1,1 00 major companies). No addresses or locations are given."Action Section," which details financial investment information, including stock market commentaries, company news and analyses, specific buy and sell recommendations on stocks, interest, and exchange rate information.

Standard & Poor's Register of Corporations, Directors and Executives. Standard & Poor's Financial Services L.L.C. • Annual. Covers: over 55,000 public and privately held corporations in the United States, including names and titles of over 400,000 officials (Volume 1); 70,000 biographies of directors and executives (Volume 2). Database includes: In Volume 3, lists of new executives, new companies, a corporate "Family Tree," Standard & Poor's 500 composite stock indices, and obituaries. Entries include: For companies--Name, address, phone, names of principal executives and accountants; primary bank, primary law firm, number of employees, estimated annual sales, outside directors, Standard Industrial Classification (SIC) code, product or service provided. For directors and executives--Name, home and principal business addresses, date and place of birth, fraternal organization memberships, business affiliations.

Standard Directory of Advertisers: The Advertiser Red Book. LexisNexis. • Annual. $1,399 Individuals classified 2010. Covers over 14,000 U.S. and Canadian companies that place over $200,000 worth of national and/or regional advertising.

State and Business in Russia. Maximov Publications. • Semiannual. Updated twice per year. Covers nearly 100,000 figures in Russian government and business. Available in multiple formats.

State of Washington Supervisor of Banking--Annual Report. Division of Banking Washington State Department of Financial Institutions. • Covers: About 100 state-chartered commercial banks and trust companies, savings banks, and alien banks. Database includes: Composite financial statements for each type of institution, and changes of location for banks, trust companies, and consumer loan offices. Entries include: For banks and trust companies--total assets, deposits.

State-Owned Companies in Finland. Advisory Committee on State-Owned Cos. • Annual. Covers: about 13 government-owned manufacturing companies in Finland. Entries include: Company name, address, phone, telex, names and titles of key personnel, number of employees, financial data, subsidiary and branch names and locations.

The States and Small Business: A Directory of Programs and Activities. U.S. Small Business Administration - Office of Advocacy. • Irregular. $21. Covers: over 750 state government small business offices, legislative committees, small business conferences. Entries include: Agency name, address, phone; name and title of contact; description of activities; summary of small business legislation, etc.

Stock Brokers Bible: Directory of Public Companies. Wall Street Financial Services Inc. • Semiannual. $28.95. Covers: about 9,000 publicly traded companies in the U.S.; major broker dealers, mutual funds, and trusts. Entries include: Company name, address, phone, Standard Industrial Classification (SIC) code, exchange on which company is traded, ticker symbol.

The Stock Exchange of Hong Kong--List of Exchange Participants and Holders of Stock Exchange Trading Rights. The Stock Exchange of Hong Kong Corporate Communications Department. • Quarterly. $134. Covers: Hong Kong stock exchange, including lists of exchange participants, holders of stock exchange trading rights, dealing directors, options exchange participants, and registered branch offices. Entries include: Name, address, phone.

Stocks, Bonds, Options & Derivatives: Symbol Book. American Stock Exchange Inc. • Quarterly. $8 per edition. Covers: Ticker symbols, corporate names, cusip numbers, and other information on stocks, bonds, options, and derivative products listed on the American Stock Exchange.

Subsidiaries of German Firms in the U.S. German American Chamber of Commerce. • Annual. $100 Members. Covers: Over 3,500 German firms and subsidiaries in the U.S. Entries include: Name, address, phone, and telex of American firm; name and address of German parent company; percentage of German participation; number of employees; type of company (manufacturer, sales agent, etc.); and products.

Sudan Business Directory. Business Guide. • $150 Individuals. Covers: 1,200 business listings including wholesalers, importers, retailers, business houses, and agents in Sudan.

Sultanate of Oman Telephone Directory. Tele-Gulf Directory Publication WLL. • Annual. Covers: businesses in Oman; separate editions in English and Arabic. Entries include: Company name, address, phone.

Sunday Telegraph Business Finance Directory. Graham & Trotman Ltd. • Annual. $219. Covers: 900 institutions providing financial services for businesses and sources of financial advice. Entries include: Institution name, address, phone, telex number, contact name, requirements, conditions.

For publishers' addresses, refer to SOURCES CITED section at the back of the book.

Surface Coating Resin Index. European Resin Manufacturers' Association. • Triennial. $5. Covers: Manufacturers, products and trade names of surface coating resins in the United Kingdom. Entries include: Manufacturer name, address, phone, products, trade names.

Survey of Industries in Texarkana--Arkansas/Texas. Texarkana Chamber of Commerce. • Quarterly. $2. Covers: Approximately 120 Texarkana manufacturers, processors, and sales agencies. Entries include: Company name, address, phone, number of employees, name of contact person, and products/ services.

Survey of Pharmaceutical Enterprises in China. Xinhua Publishing House. • $30. Covers: pharmaceutical companies in China. Entries include: Company name, address, description, including product information and management.

Sveriges Handelskalender. Telenor Foretagsinformation, AB. • Annual. $960. Covers: Approximately 16,000 commercial companies in Sweden. Entries include: Company name, address, phone, business data.

Sweden Government and Business Contacts Handbook: Trade, Investment & Business Development Contacts. International Business Publications, USA. • $99.95 Individuals hardcopy,e-book,cd-rom. Covers: Strategic government and business information, export-import activity in the country, investment, business contacts and regulations.

Sweden Industrial and Business Directory. International Business Publications, USA. • Annual. $99.95 Individuals hardcopy, e-book, CD-ROM. Covers: Strategic industrial, investment and business contacts for conducting export-import and investment activity in the country. Contains strategic, practical economic and business information.

Swedish Chamber of Commerce--Trade Directory. Swedish Chamber of Commerce. • Annual. Covers: 400 member companies representing Swedish, British and European companies.

Swedish Industrial Directory. Sveriges Industrieforbund. • Annual. $400. Covers: Manufacturing companies in Sweden. Entries include: Manufacturer name, address, phone.

Swedish Related Companies in the United States. Swedish-American Chamber of Commerce. • Annual. $24.90 Members. Covers: Swedish-related companies in the U.S. and their parent companies; lists more than 700 companies in the US; chambers of commerce, trade offices, embassies and consulates, information offices, and tourist offices. Entries include: Name of parent company, address, phone, telex, fax, name of United States subsidiary, address, phone, name and title of key executive, products.

Swiss Foundry and Metalworks. Verlag fur Internationale Wirtschaftsliteratur Ltd. • Biennial. $60. Covers: Manufacturers, associations, and importers in the metal, iron, foundry and metal working industries. Entries include: Company or association name, address, phone.

Switzerland Industrial and Business Directory. International Business Publications, USA. • Annual. $99.95 Individuals hardcopy, e-book, CD-ROM. Covers: Strategic industrial, investment and business contacts for conducting export-import and investment activity in the country.

Syria Golden Key Directory. International Institute of Trade Relation Promotion, Trade Information Centre of Iran. • £100 Individuals. Covers: 27,614 companies in Syria. Entries include: Company name, address, telephone, fax, products, services, Managing Director, and business activities.

Taiwan Government and Business Contacts Handbook. International Business Publications, USA. • $99.95 Individuals hardcopy, e-book, CD-ROM. Covers: Strategic government and business information, export-import activity in the country, investment, business contacts and regulations.

Taiwan Industrial and Business Directory. International Business Publications, USA. • Annual. $99.95 Individuals hardcopy, e-book, CD-ROM. Covers: Strategic industrial, investment and business contacts for conducting export-import and investment activity in the country.

Taiwan Industrial Pages. INFOT Inc. • $46.75 CD-ROM; additional $167.50 for MS Access format. Covers: 100,882 Taiwan manufacturers, factories, plants, exporters, and importers. Entries include: Email and website addresses, telephone and fax number, business titles, address, number of employees, capital, and industry.

Taiwan Product Guide. Todd Publications. • Biennial. $125. Covers: More than 6,000 Taiwan exporters. Database includes: Taiwan government agencies and essential services available. Entries include: Company name, address, phone, fax, telex.

Tajikistan Industrial and Business Directory. International Business Publications, USA. • Annual. $99.95 Individuals hardcopy, e-book, CD-ROM. Covers: Strategic industrial, investment and business contacts for conducting export-import and investment activity in the country.

Taking Stocks: A Snapshot of Portland Metro-Area Public Companies. The Business Journal. • Annual. Covers: About 75 public firms that are either based in Portland, Oregon, or have a strong presence there. Entries include: Firm address, phone, names, and titles of executive officers, board of directors, products or services, significant stockholders, financial data.

Tanzania Business Directory. Business Guide. • $250 Individuals. Covers: 23,000 business listings including wholesalers, importers, retailers, business houses, and agents in Tanzania.

Taylors Corporate Birmingham & West Midlands. Vincent Taylor & Co. • Annual. $20. Covers: Approximately 800 major companies in Birmingham and the West Midlands of England. Entries include: Company name, address, phone, names and titles of key personnel, number of employees, geographical area served, financial data, description of services, products provided.

Taylors Corporate North of England. Vincent Taylor & Co. • Annual. $20. Covers: Approximately 800 major companies and agencies in the North of England. Entries include: Company name, address, phone, names and titles of key personnel, number of employees, geographical area served, financial data, description of services, products provided.

Taylors Corporate Scotland. Vincent Taylor & Co. • Annual. $20. Covers: Approximately 850 major company entities and government agencies involved in the development of business in Scotland. Entries include: Company name, address, phone, names and titles of key personnel, number of employees, geographical area served, financial data, description of services, products provided.

Taylors Corporate South Africa. Vincent Taylor & Co. • Annual. $120. Covers: Approximately 400 companies and agencies involved in the development of business in South Africa. Entries include: Company name, address, phone, names and titles of key personnel, number of employees, geographical area served, financial data, description of services, products provided.

Technical Services in the United Kingdom. Financial Times Healthcare. • Irregular. $400. Covers: 2,000 public and private companies offering technical services and facilities for hire in the United Kingdom. Entries include: Company name, address, phone, type of service, facilities.

Telecommunications Export Guide. North American Telecommunications Association. • Irregular. $103. Publication includes: List of about 135 foreign telecommunications agencies, and federal and state government agencies concerned with exports in the United States, including Department of Commerce district offices, port authorities, and small business administration field offices. Entries include: For foreign agencies--Name of the official telecommunications agency, address, U.S. representative, customs requirements, type of electrical current, technical data and statistics. For U.S. agencies--Name, address.

Tennessee Business Services Directory. Nashville Area Chamber of Commerce. • $121 Members. Covers: 7,500 Tennessee businesses in the service industry with 20 employees and in the restaurant industry with 50 employees. Entries include: Name, address, phone, and fax.

Texas Industrial Expansion. University of Texas at Austin IC2 Institute Bureau of Business Research. • Monthly. $60. Covers: New and expanding manufacturing facilities in Texas in Standard Industrial Classifications (SIC) 1321, 1477, 2011-3999, 4911. Entries include: Company name, address, phone, name of principal executive square footage and cost of project when available, number of employees, products or services.

Textile Month. Reed Business Information. • Biennial. $4. Covers: United Kingdom companies representing overseas manufacturers of textile machinery. Entries include: Company name, address, phone, telex, key personnel, overseas contacts, types of machinery handled.

Thai Business Groups: A Unique Guide to Who Owns What. Brooker Group Public Company Ltd. • Annual. $340 Individuals. Covers: 150 top family business groups in Thailand. Entries include: Contact addresses, key executives of major companies, history and background of the top Thailand business families.

Thailand Export-Import Yellow Pages. Teleinfo Media Company Ltd. • Covers: Updated information for exporters and importers in Thailand. Entries include: Company information and contact details.

Thailand Investment: A Directory of Companies Promoted by the Board of Investment. Cosmic Group of Cos. • Annual. $60 plus shipping charges. Covers: Approximately 3,600 companies in Thailand that are promoted by the Thailand Board of Investment. Database includes: Information on doing business in Thailand. Entries include: Company name, address, phone.

Thailand Product Guide. Todd Publications. • $95. Covers: Over 1,500 Thailand exporters. Entries include: Company name, address, phone, fax, telex.

Thailand Showcase: A Buyers' Guide. Cosmic Group of Cos. • Annual. $48 plus shipping charges. Covers: More than 3,000 companies in Thailand engaged in exporting their goods. Database includes: Overview of the Thailand economy. Entries include: Company name, address, phone.

Thailand: The MFC Investment Handbook. Hoover's Inc. • Annual. $46.95 plus $3.50 shipping. Covers: over 340 companies listed on the Stock Exchange of Thailand; 23 unit trusts. Entries include: Company name, address, phone, fax, stock symbol, company overview, price per share, trading volume, net income, capital, financial ratios, foreign holdings, limits on foreign ownership, list of major shareholders, names and titles of key personnel.

Thomas Register of American Manufacturers. Thomas Publishing Company L.L.C. • Annual. More than 168,000 manufacturing firms are listed in this 34 volume set. Volumes 1-23 list the firms under 68,000 product headings. Thomas Register is enhanced with over 8,000 manufacturers' catalogs and is available in print, CD-ROM, DVD or online. Logistics Guide, a reference manual for freight and shipping sourcing.

Thornton Guide to Hong Kong Companies. Hoover's Inc. • Semiannual. $69.95. Covers: More than 500 companies in Hong Kong. Database includes: Introduction to the Hong Kong capital market. Entries include: Name, address, phone, fax, stock codes and sector of business, board of directors, major shareholders, financial data, description of business activities.

Thornton Guide to the Companies of Singapore and Malaysia. Hoover's Inc. • Semiannual. $69.95. Covers: Nearly 250 companies in Singapore and nearly 500 companies in Malaysia. Database includes: Overview of the Stock Exchange of Singapore and the Kuala Lumpur Stock Exchange. Entries include: Name, address, phone, fax, stock codes and sector of business, board of directors, major shareholders, financial data, description of business activities.

3W Register of Chinese Business. 3W International Digital Publishing. • Biennial. $298. Covers: Approximately 31,000 Chinese companies in a variety of industries, including textile and garment, electronics and computer, mechanical and metallurgical, chemical and materials, construction and construction materials, service, wholesale trade and food, and agriculture, engineering, and management service. Entries include: Company name, address, phone, fax, telex, cable number, names and titles of key personnel, ownership information, financial data, date founded, number of employees, stock availability, imports, exports, product/service, Standard Industrial Classification (SIC) codes.

The Thunderbird Guide to International Business Resources on the World Wide Web. Wiley Publishing Group. • $57.95 Individuals Paperback. Covers: Web sites for political and economic developments that affect trade worldwide. Derived from a study by Dean's Global Information and Technology at Thunderbird (American Graduate School of International Management). Entries include: country, category (country information, business, business topics, government resources, information providers), title, URL, and description.

Tianjin Yellow Pages: Commercial/Industrial Directory. China Yellow Pages Directories Co. • $65. Covers: over 20,000 companies in the Tianjin area. Database includes: Investment information. Entries include: Company, name, address, phone.

Today's Top 100 Service Providers. Coordinated Service Inc. • $99. Covers: The top 100 customer service providers in the U.S. Entries include: Company name, address, phone, fax, contacts, years in business, equipment serviced, geographical locations covered, other services offered.

Top Careers for Business Graduates. InfoBase Holdings Inc. • $14.95 Individuals Paperback. Covers: What it takes to transform a major in business into a job that pays well, is expected to grow, offers a sense of security and opportunity for advancement, and is likely to provide a sense of job satisfaction.

Top Global 500 Companies in China. SinoMedia Ltd. • Annual. $200 Individuals. Covers: 500 companies in China including 4,500 contacts, 4,400 offices and 1,700 email addresses. Entries include: Manager's names, telephone, profiles of the top global 50 enterprises.

Top 1,000 Food & Drink Companies in Asia-Pacific. Datamonitor. • $995. Covers: 1,000 leading food and drink companies in Asia and the Pacific. Entries include: Company name, address, phone, telex, names and titles of key personnel, number of employees; financial data, product/service, Standard Industrial Classification (SIC) code, production locations.

Top 1,000 Food & Drink Companies in Latin America. Datamonitor. • $995. Covers: 1,000 leading food and drink companies in Latin America. Entries include: Company name, address, phone, telex, names and titles of key personnel, number of employees; financial data, product/service, Standard Industrial Classification (SIC) code, production locations.

Top 1,000 Food & Drink Companies in the U.S. Datamonitor. • $995. Covers: 1,000 leading food and drink companies in the U.S. Entries include: Company name, address, phone, telex, names and titles of key personnel, number of employees; financial data, product/service, Standard Industrial Classification (SIC) code, production locations.

Top 1000 Performing Companies in Asia Pacific. Dun & Bradstreet Singapore Pte. Ltd. • $299.60 local. Covers: top 1000 performing companies in Asia Pacific, profiles of the Local top 50 companies, and payment trend analysis in the Asia Pacific region.

Top Romanian Companies. Chamber of Commerce and Industry of Romania. • Annual. $20. Covers: 600 of the most efficient Romanian companies ranked by size, field of activity, turnover rate, profit margin, development effort, and turnover per employee. Entries include: Company name, address, profile, contact person.

Top 22,000 Businesses in the People's Republic of China. China Books. • $360 cloth. Covers: Leading 22,000 businesses in China, including manufacturing, foods, apparel, paper, chemicals, and real estate industries. Entries include: Name, address, phone, executive names, number of employees, profits.

Toy Trader Year Book. Turret-Wheatland Ltd. • Annual. Covers: Toy and toy supplier manufacturers, importers, wholesalers, retailers, and agents in the U.K. Entries include: Company name, address, phone, products, brand names.

Trade Directory for Istanbul. Istanbul Chamber of Commerce. • Annual. Covers: Exporters, importers, commission agents, and building contractors in Istanbul.

Trade Directory of Nigeria. World Trade Center of Nigeria. • Triennial. Covers: Trade-related information for import/export companies, manufacturers, government representatives, lawyers, accountants, and interested individuals in Nigeria.

Trade Directory of the Former Soviet Union. Flegon Press. • Biennial. $300. Covers: over 60,000 plants, factories, and other companies in all branches of industry in the former Soviet Union. Entries include: Company name, address, phone, telex, subsidiary and branch names and locations, description of product/service, number of employees.

Trade Directory of Western Sweden. Goteborg and Western Sweden Chamber of Commerce. • Biennial. $300. Covers: Companies, wholesalers, importers/ exporters, and manufacturers in Goteborg and the western Sweden Chamber of Commerce area. Entries include: Company name, address, phone, telex number, line of business.

Trade Directory of Yugoslavia. Privredni Pregled. • Annual. $150. Covers: Trading and manufacturing entities and products, chambers of commerce, and other economic organizations. Entries include: Name, address, phone, products.

Trade Unions of the World. Cengage Learning Inc. • $160 Individuals. Covers trade union centers, international affiliations of trade unions, and major organizations outside of the trade union centers.

Trado Asian & African Directory. Trado Publications Private Ltd. • Annual. $115 airmail postpaid. Covers: manufacturers, exporters, and importers in Bahrain, Bangladesh, Canary Islands, Cyprus, Ethiopia, Hong Kong, India, Iran, Iraq, Japan, Jordan, Kenya, Kuwait, Liberia, Libya, Malta, Malawi, Mauritius, Nigeria, Philippines, Saudi Arabia, Sierra Leone, Singapore, Malaysia, Somalia, South Yemen, Sri Lanka, Sudan, Syria, Tanzania, Thailand, United Arab Emirates, and Zambia.

The Training Manager's Yearbook. AP Information Services Ltd. • Annual. £239 Individuals /year. Covers: Training managers in 8,750 organizations in the United Kingdom; profiles of over 4,500 suppliers and advisors to training managers in the United Kingdom. Entries include: For organizations--Name, address, phone, fax, e-mail, contact, history, names and titles of key personnel.

Transkei Business Directory. A.C. Braby (Pty) Ltd. • Annual. R 30 payment must accompany order. Covers: businesses in Transkei. Entries include: Company name, address, phone.

Transnational Corporations and Labor: A Directory of Resources. WorldViews. • $12.95 plus $2.00 shipping. Covers: sources for books, periodicals, pamphlets, audiovisuals, and other educational resources on transnational corporations and labor issues; names of resources with annotations and ordering information. Entries include: Organization name, address, phone, titles of print and audio/ visual material. Part of a 10 volume series (updated in "Third World Resources"), each volume covering single region or issue.

Tri-State Directory of Export Management and Trading Companies. National Association of Export Cos. • Irregular. $20 Nonmembers. Covers: 700 export management and trading companies in Connecticut, New Jersey, and New York who are National Association of Export Companies (NEXCO) members. Entries include: Company name, address, phone, fax, contact name, product specialty.

Trinidad & Tobago--American Chamber of Commerce--Membership Directory. U.S. Chamber of Commerce. • Annual. $80 Individuals. Covers: Companies in the U.S. and Trinidad and Tobago and individuals interested in the development of trade within and between the two countries. Entries include: For firms--Company name, address, phone, fax, telex, cable address, names and titles of key personnel, line of business, subsidiary and branch names and locations, locations of plants or branch offices, product/service information. For individuals--Name, title, affiliation, address.

Tulsa Chamber Membership Directory. • Covers Tulsa Metro Chamber of Commerce membership roster.

Tulsa Metropolitan Chamber Business Directory and Buyer's Guide. Mary Brett & Associates/Image Publishing. • Covers: about 3,500 companies; federal, state, and local government agencies and officials, schools, and associations in the greater Tulsa, Oklahoma area. Entries include: Company, institution, organization, or individual name, address, phone.

Turkey Government and Business Contacts Handbook. International Business Publications, USA. • $99.95 Individuals hardcopy, e-book, CD-ROM. Covers: Strategic government and business information, export-import activity in the country, investment, business contacts and regulations.

Turkey Industry and Trade Directory. AGT Research Development & Information Corporation Inonu Caddesi. • Annual. $112. Covers: 14,500 producers, marketers, foreign trade investment service companies, representatives, authorized sellers, and wholesalers in Turkey.

Turkish Business Directory. London Business Guide. • Covers: 25,000 companies and businesses in United Kingdom and Europe.

Turkmenistan Government and Business Contacts Handbook. International Business Publications, USA. • $99.95 Individuals hardcopy, e-book, CD-ROM. Covers: Strategic government and business information, export-import activity in the country, investment, business contacts and regulations.

Turnkey Offers from India. EEPC India. • Biennial.

For publishers' addresses, refer to SOURCES CITED section at the back of the book.

Covers: Companies in India involved in international projects.

The 2,000 Top Spanish Companies. Fomento de la Produccion. • Annual. $15. Covers: 2,000 leading companies in Spain. Entries include: Company name, address, phone, telex number, sales, ranking.

Tyne & Wear Chamber Regional Business Directory. Ten Alps Publishing. • Covers: businesses in Tyne and Wear, England. Entries include: Company name, address, phone, telex, fax, description of products or services.

UAE Commercial Directory. Federation of UAE Chamber of Commerce & Industry. • Annual. Provides information on UAE diplomatic missions abroad, Chambers of Commerce and Industry, and lists of business establishments. Entries include: Addresses of government institutions.

UAE Golden Key Directory. International Institute of Trade Relation Promotion, Trade Information Centre of Iran. • £100 Individuals. Covers: 237,564 companies in United Arab Emirates. Entries include: Company name, address, telephone, fax, products, services, managing director, and business activities.

UAE Industrial Directory. Federation of UAE Chamber of Commerce & Industry. • Aims to widen the industrial channels and provide all the available services in order to help industrialists, business men and investors in different fields and to consolidate trust and provide suitable ambience for cooperation between industrialists and consumers. Covers: Industrial firms and companies operating in UAE. Entries include: Company name and address.

Uganda Business Directory. Business Guide. • $250 Individuals. Covers: 11,000 business listings including wholesalers, importers, retailers, business houses, and agents in Uganda.

U.K. Directory of Talent Management. Executive Grapevine International Ltd. • $239 Individuals. Covers: 700 top U.K. executive recruitment and interim management providers and over 3,000 consultant biographies. Entries include: Company profile, consultant biographies, salary range of assignments, function, fees, and major clients.

The UK/USA Investment Directory & Business Resource. BritishAmerican Business Inc. of New York and London. • Biennial. $149. Covers: Over 6,000 British and American companies and their approximately 4,000 subsidiaries in the United Kingdom and the United States. Entries include: Parent company name, address, phone, fax; name of British subsidiary in the United States, address, phone, fax; percentage of business British or American owned, number of staff, product or service provided, Standard Industrial Classification (SIC) code.

Ukraine Top 100 Exporters. IIA Sistema-Reserve. • Annual. $75. Covers: 100 exporting companies in Ukraine, with partial listing for approximately 20 other exporting companies. Entries include: Company name, address, phone, fax, telex, names and titles of key personnel, number of employees, financial data, description of product/service, import purchases planned.

UNCTAD Handbook of Statistics. United Nations Conference on Trade and Development. • $130 Individuals Book with CD-Rom. Database covers: Statistical data relevant to the analysis of international trade, investment and development, for individual countries and for economic and trade groupings. It presents reference statistics on international merchandise trade, trade and commodity price indices, structure of international trade by region, structure of international trade by product, international trade in services, international finance, indicators of development, special studies.

United Arab Emirates Government and Business Contacts Handbook. International Business Publications, USA. • $99.95 Individuals hardcopy, e-book, CD-ROM. Covers: Strategic government and business information, export-import activity in the country, investment, business contacts and regulations.

United Arab Emirates Industrial and Business Directory. International Business Publications, USA. • Annual. $99.95 Individuals hardcopy, E-book and CD-ROM. Covers: Strategic industrial, investment and business contacts for conducting export-import and investment activity in the country.

United Kingdom Business Finance Directory. Graham & Trotman Ltd. • Annual. $265. Covers: 1,500 financial institutions, banks, insurance companies, accountants, investment brokers, and job hunters in the United Kingdom. Entries include: Company name, address, phone, fax, telex number.

United Kingdom's 10,000 Largest Companies. William Snyder Publishing Associates. • Annual. $250. Covers: top 10,000 companies in the United Kingdom, ranked by turnover. Database includes: Financial and statistical business information on each company. Entries include: Company name, address, phone, name of director, number of employees, financial data, year established, International Standard Industrial Classification (ISIC) code, parent company.

U.S.-China Business Services Directory. U.S.-China Business Council. • Irregular. $35. Covers: more than 900 companies in the U. S., Hong Kong, and China providing business services to China, such as consulting firms, architectural and construction engineering firms, freight forwarding companies, and law firms. Entries include: Company name, address, phone, telex, name and title of contact, subsidiary and branch names and locations, description of products or services.

U.S. Export Directory. Reed Business Information. • Annual. $235. Covers: Exporting companies in the U.S. Entries include: Company name, address, telecommunication information, overseas agents and subsidiaries.

U.S. Firms in Germany. German American Chamber of Commerce. • Annual. $100. Covers: Over 700 U.S. companies located in Germany. Entries include: Company name, address, phone in Germany, company name, address, phone of their American parent company.

United States Foreign Trade Sanctions Handbook. International Business Publications, USA. • $99.95 Individuals paperback. Covers: United States trade sanctions for selected countries.

U.S. Importers Product Guide. Todd Publications. • Biennial. $195. Covers: Approximately 10,000 United States import companies. Entries include: Name, address, phone, fax, name and title of contact, description of product/service.

United States Industrial and Business Directory. International Business Publications, USA. • Annual. $99.95 Individuals hardcopy, E-book and CD-ROM. Covers: Detailed information on investment, export-import business opportunities, foreign economic assistance projects, government and business contacts.

U.S. Industrial Directory. Reed. • Annual. $179 per set. Publication consists of three volumes, of which the "Telephone/Address Section" provides name, address, phone, fax, local sales offices and distributors for over 52,000 companies. Other volumes comprise the "Product Sections," with listings of suppliers categorized by product and service.

U.S. Industrial Outlook: An Almanac of Industry, Technology, and Services. Reference Press Inc. • Annual. $27.95. Covers: Nearly 200 service and manufacturing industries. Database includes: Tables, rankings, forecasts, projections. Entries include: Description.

U.S. Investments in Germany: A Listing of American Subsidiaries in Germany. American Chamber of Commerce in Germany. • €150 Individuals print. Covers: Approximately 3,000 German subsidiaries of U.S. Firms. Entries include: Company address, management details, and SIC code.

U.S. List. American Chamber of Commerce in Austria. • Biennial. €80 Members. Covers: About 360 U.S. subsidiaries and affiliated companies located in Austria. Entries include: U.S. Parent company name and address, Austrian subsidiary or affiliated company name, address, phone, fax, managing director, line of business, e-mail, Internet-homepage address, kind of relationship.

U.S. 1 Business Directory: Your Source for Business in Central New Jersey. U.S. 1 Publishing Corp. • Annual. $18.95. Covers: Approximately 5,500 business to business listings in 212 categories in such areas as computer science, pharmaceuticals, R & D, architecture, advertising agencies, accounting, law firms, warehouses, consultants in the central New Jersey area. Entries include: Company name, address, phone, fax, number of employees, financial data, descriptions of product/service, e-mail, home page addresses, year founded, and revenue range.

Uruguay Government and Business Contacts Handbook. International Business Publications, USA. • Annual. $99.95 Individuals hardcopy, e-book, CD-ROM. Covers: Strategic government and business information, export-import activity in the country, investment, business contacts and regulations.

Uruguay Industrial and Business Directory. International Business Publications, USA. • Annual. $99.95 Individuals hardcopy, E-book and CD-ROM. Covers: Strategic industrial, investment and business contacts for conducting export-import and investment activity in the country.

USA Food Manufacturers Directory. Business Information Agency Inc. PlanetInform. • Annual. $149 Individuals Hard copy or PDF. Covers: 2,500 American food manufacturers of meat and meat products, bakery, beverages, and dairy products, along with 1,000 food manufacturers in Asia and Europe. Entries include: Company name, location, industry description, manufacturing indicator, contact information, SIC codes, number of employees, type of business, year founded, legal status, and subsidiary indicators.

USA/France Business and Culture Update. Integrated Information Technologies. • Monthly. $190 per year (12 issues). Publication includes: List of organizations or sources providing information to businesses wishing to enter markets in France. Entries include: Name, address, phone, fax, description of products/services offered. Principal content of publication is a newsletter providing general information on the French business and cultural climate.

USA Major Manufacturers Directory. Business Information Agency Inc. PlanetInform. • Annual. $199 Individuals Hard copy or PDF. Covers: 4,000 industrial and consumer product manufacturers in the U.S.A. Entries include: Company name, location, contact information, SIC codes, number of employees, type of business, year founded, legal status, and subsidiary indicators.

USACC Business Directory. Unites States-Azerbaijan Chamber of Commerce. • Annual. $50 Nonmembers. Covers: Government, business, and international organizations in the United States and Azerbaijan. Entries include: Contact information.

Utah Major Employers Guide. • Biennial. $50 Individuals for investors. Covers: More than 900 companies in 29 counties in Utah that have 100 or more full-time employees. Entries include: Company name, address, phone, fax, contact names, names and titles of key personnel, year established, type of operation, Standard Industrial Classification (SIC) code, product/service, county, number of full-time employees, website addresses.

Utah Manufacturers Directory and Industrial Database. Manufacturers' News Inc. • Annual. $102 Individuals print. Covers: 4,504 manufacturers in Utah. Entries include: Company name, address, phone, names and titles of key personnel, year established, number of employees, plant square footage, services, Standard Industry Classification (SIC) code, parent and subsidiary company information, type of in-house computer system, URL, e-mail address.

Uzbekistan Government and Business Contacts Handbook. International Business Publications, USA. • $99.95 Individuals hardcopy, e-book, CD-ROM. Covers: Strategic government and business information, export-import activity in the country, investment, business contacts and regulations.

Uzbekistan Industrial and Business Directory. International Business Publications, USA. • $99.95 Individuals hardcopy, E-book and CD-ROM. Covers: Strategic and practical economic and business information. Entries include: Business contacts for conducting business activity in the country.

Vankirk's International Venture Capital Directory. Online Publishing Inc. • Semiannual. $245. Covers: more than 350 companies and organizations providing capital to business ventures outside the U.S. Database includes: Articles on working with venture capitalists, trends and statistics, and how to develop an effective business plan; glossary. Entries include: Organization name, address, phone, fax, names and titles of key personnel, preferred stage of funding; preferred industries, geographic preference, minimum and maximum amounts invested, preferred size of investment, total capital under management, current activity level, total of recently made investments, compensation method, type of organization, year founded, staff size, trade association memberships, affiliated organizations and funds; corporate description.

Vankirk's Venture Capital Directory. Online Publishing Inc. • Semiannual. $245. Covers: over 1,000 sources of venture capital in the U.S. Database includes: Articles on working with venture capitalists, venture capital trends, and developing a business plan; statistics. Entries include: Organization name, address, phone, fax, name and title of contact, preferred stage of funding (start-up, acquisition, leveraged buyout, etc.), industry preference, geographic preference (mid-Atlantic, U.S., global, etc.), type of investments (debt, equity, etc), minimum and maximum initial investments, preferred size of investment, amount of capital under management, current activity level, total value of recent investments, compensation method, type of organization, year founded, number of employees, trade association memberships, affiliated organizations and funds, description.

Vankirk's Venture Capital Investments Profiled. Online Publishing Inc. • Semiannual. $245. Covers: more than 1,200 investments made by over 110 venture capital firms. Database includes: Statistics; glossary. Entries include: Investing firm name, address, phone, fax, names and titles of key personnel; recipient firm's name, location, description of product or service, amount of funding provided, stage of funding; industry, type of investment (debt, equity, etc.).

Vault Guide to the Top Business Services Employers. Vault.com Inc. • $19.95 Individuals Online. Covers: Top business service companies in United States. Entries include: Company name, contact person, location, address, phone and fax numbers, zip code, statistics, hiring process and email.

Venezuela Business Law Handbook. International Business Publications, USA. • $99.95 Individuals hardcopy, e-book, CD-ROM. Covers: Basic information on business laws and legislations, export-import regulations, business climate and contacts.

Venezuela Company Handbook. Hoover's Inc. • $29.95 plus $3.50 shipping. Covers: major Venezuelan companies listed on the Caracas Stock Exchange. Database includes: Profile of Venezuela's economy, including information on privatization and accounting rules. Entries include: Company name, address, phone, fax, year established, stock ticker symbol, names and titles of key personnel, number of employees, number of stockholders, bank references, auditor, company history, financial data, markets and competition, raw materials used and sources, names of major stockholders, affiliated companies.

Venezuela Industrial and Business Directory. International Business Publications, USA. • Annual. $99.95 Individuals hardcopy, E-book and CD-ROM. Covers: Strategic industrial, investment and business contacts for conducting export-import and investment activity in the country.

The Venture Capital Directory on CD-ROM. Infon Corp. • Covers: over 500 venture capital firms and over 2,000 investors. Entries include: venture capital firms--investment size, location, and industry; investors--education and experience.

Venture Capital Report Guide to Venture Capital in Europe. Pitman Publishing. • $125. Covers: over 500 European venture capital firms, companies supplying funds for research and development, banks with venture capital divisions, organizations disbursing government funds, and venture capital associations. Entries include: Company profile, size of investment, industry and geographic preferences, number of executives, time-table for investments, fees. Covers 960.

Vermont Business Phone Book. Manufacturers' News Inc. • Covers: about 850 industrial firms in Vermont. Entries include: Company name, address, phone, number of employees, name of chief executive officer, products imported and exported.

Vermont Manufacturers Register and Industrial Database. Manufacturers' News Inc. • Annual. $82 Individuals print. Covers: 1,698 manufacturers in Vermont. Entries include: Company name, address, phone, names and titles of key personnel, year established, number of employees, plant square footage, services, Standard Industry Classification (SIC) code, parent and subsidiary company information, type of in-house computer system, URL, e-mail address.

Vietnam: Business Opportunities and Risks. China Books. • A$5. Publication includes: Business contacts in Vietnam. Database includes: Maps, charts, and a bibliography. Entries include: Name, address, phone. Principal content of publication is information on the business environment, forms of foreign investment, laws, taxes, and investment regulations in Vietnam.

Virginia Business Directory. InfoGroup Inc. • Annual. $795 for both print & CD-ROM. Covers: 297,373 businesses in Virginia. Entries include: Company name, address, phone, number of employees, name of owner or manager, sales volume. Compiled from telephone company 'Yellow Pages,' statewide. All states covered (see separate entries).

Virginia Industrial Directory. Florida Chamber of Commerce. • Annual. $105 Members. Covers: over 6,000 manufacturing and mining firms. Entries include: Company name, address, phone, names and titles of key personnel, number of employees, product/service provided, headquarters address (if different). Separate list of firms with foreign affiliations gives parent company, country, and product only.

Virginia Peninsula Regional Business Directory. Virginia Peninsula Chamber of Commerce. • Annual. $25 Individuals. Covers: Over 2,500 business leaders and chamber members.

Wabash Business Directory. Wabash Area Chamber of Commerce. • Covers businesses and industrial businesses in Wabash, Indiana. Entries include contact details.

Wales Business Directory. Kemps Publishing Ltd. • Annual. $18. Covers: Members of the Chambers of Commerce of Cardiff, Chester, North Wales, Neath, Newport, Gwent, Port Talbot, and Swansea and local businesses. Entries include: Company name, address, phone, member name.

Walker's Manual of Community Bank Stocks. Walker's Manual Inc. • $95. Covers 502 community banks in the United States--community banks are financed with less than $10 million and usually serve a limited geographic area.

Walker's Manual of Western Corporations. Walker's Manual Inc. • Annual. $380 base edition. Covers: over 1,500 publicly owned corporations headquartered in Alaska, Arizona, California, Colorado, Hawaii, Idaho, Montana, Nevada, New Mexico, Oregon, Utah, Washington, and Wyoming. Entries include: Company name, address, phone, description of business; names of executives and directors with shareholdings of each; number of employees, brand names or product lines, financial data and common share data covering five years, capitalization, number of shareholders, sales and management statements, income and balance sheet information for five years.

Washington Manufacturers Directory and Industrial Database. Manufacturers' News Inc. • Annual. $118 Individuals print. Covers: 7,834 manufacturers in Washington State. Entries include: Company name, address, phone, names and titles of key personnel, year established, number of employees, plant square footage, services, Standard Industry Classification (SIC) code, parent and subsidiary company information, type of in-house computer system, URL, e-mail address.

Washington Manufacturers Register. Harris InfoSource. • Annual. Covers: 12,600 manufacturers in Washington state, plus names of key executives. Entries include: Company name, address, parent name/location, telephone, fax and 800 numbers, Web site address (on CD-ROM only), number of employees, year established, annual revenue, plant size, business description, Standard Industrial Classification (SIC) codes, executive names/titles, public ownership, legal structure, import/export designators, female/minority ownership.

The Waterlow Stock Exchange Yearbook. Macmillan Publishers Ltd. • Annual. $400 Individuals. Covers: firms whose stock is traded on the London Stock Exchange; worldwide coverage. Entries include: Company name, address, registrars, directors, auditors, bankers, date registered on the exchange, line of business, capital, loan capital, additional financial data.

Web Site Source Book: A Guide to Major U.S. Businesses, Organizations, Agencies, Institutions, and Other Information Resources on the World Wide Web. Omnigraphics Inc. • Annual. $185 Individuals paperback. Covers: Over 99,000 websites for businesses, organizations, agencies, and institutions. Entries include: Name, address, phone, fax, toll-free phone number, and URL addresses.

Western Cape Business Register. Intratex Holdings. • Covers: businesses and residences in the Cape Peninsula area of South Africa. Entries include: Company or personal name, address, phone.

Western European Countries Mineral Industry Handbook. International Business Publications, USA. • $99.95 Individuals Hardbound. Covers: strategic information and contacts on mining and mineral industry of the Western European countries.

Western Lumber Export Buyers Guide. Western

Wood Products Association. • Annual. Covers: Approximately 75 producers of softwood lumber products for overseas markets. Entries include: Company name, address, phone, telex, name and title of contact, subsidiary and branch names and locations, description of products and services.

Western States Exporters and Importers Database. Harris InfoSource. • $445. Covers: 11,500 exporting and 5,000 importing companies in Alaska, Arizona, California, Colorado, Hawaii, Idaho, Montana, New Mexico, Nevada, Oregon, Utah, Washington, and Wyoming. Entries include: Company name, address, phone, fax, toll-free, names and titles of key personnel, number of employees, geographical area served, financial data, descriptions of product/ service, Standard Industrial Classification (SIC) code, year established, annual revenues, plant size, legal structure, export/import information.

Western Union Directory and Buyer's Guide. Western Union Directory Services. • Publication includes: Yellow Pages Buyers' Guide list of businesses under classified business headings. Entries include: Company name, address, phone, telex, and EasyLink numbers. Principal content of publication is a listing of more than 200,000 US subscribers to Western Union Telex, EasyLink, and Worldcom; 60,000 subscribers in Canada and Mexico.

Which European Database?. K.G. Saur Verlag KG. • Annual. $299 plus $15.00 shipping. Publication includes: List of leading business databases available throughout Europe. Entries include: Database name, description.

Who Audits the UK?. Public Relations Consultants Association. • Irregular. $46. Covers: Information on the auditing of 2,000 companies and organizations in the UK. Entries include: Company name, address, phone.

Who Belongs to Whom: Capital Links in German Companies. Commerzbank AG. • Semiannual. Covers: about 11,000 German companies and their domestic and foreign shareholders. Database includes: Glossary of German technical terms, translated in English, French, Italian, and Spanish. Entries include: Company name, trade or industry code number, capital, names of principal shareholders, partners, investors, and percentage of stock owned.

Who Knows About Foreign Industries and Markets. MarketResearch.com. • Annual. $85. Covers: 2,500 U.S. experts and authorities on international trade. Entries include: Name and telephone number.

Who Knows What: The Essential Business Resource Book. Henry Holt and Co. • $45. Covers: Approximately 5,500 businesses, special libraries, government agencies, and other organizations in the U.S. that have access to information in over 500 business-related subject areas. Entries include: Company or organization name, address, phone, fax, name and title of contact, description of services and projects.

Who Knows Who: Networking through Corporate Boards. Who Knows Who Publishers. • Annual. $165. Publication includes: List of over 1,000 companies noted by either Fortune magazine or Forbes magazine, or both; over 120 major foundations. Entries include: Company or foundation name, address, phone, boards of directors. Principal content of publication is lists of the companies and their boards of directors showing relationships among the companies by showing which of the board members sit on several of the companies' boards, i.e. interlocking directorates.

Who Owns Corporate America. Taft Group. • Annual. $285. Covers: nearly 75,000 officers, directors, and 10% principal stockholders who own securities registered with the Securities and Exchange Commission. Entries include: Name, company, stock symbol, number of shares held, date of last stock transaction, class of security held, type of ownership, relationship of stockholder to the company, market value of holdings.

Who Owns What in World Banking. Public Relations Consultants Association. • Biennial. $350 airmail postpaid. Covers: about 225 leading multinational and consortium banks and their subsidiaries and affiliated banks. Entries include: Name of bank, location, financial data, percentage held by parent company, subsidiaries and affiliates and whether they are domestic or international.

Who Owns Whom--North America. Dun & Bradstreet Inc. • Annual. Covers: Parent companies located in the U.S., Canada, South America, and the West Indies and their foreign and domestic subsidiaries; 66,000 parent companies, 200,000 subsidiaries. Parents with international investments only are shown in the United States section. Entries include: Parent company name, address, phone, industrial classification, direct subsidiary names, and country of incorporation.

Who's Who Among Business Printing Independents. Print Services and Distribution Association. • Annual. Covers: about 2,400 member independent manufacturers and distributors of business forms; coverage is international. Database includes: Calendar of events; description of events and seminars. Entries include: Company name, address, phone, names of executives, financial keys, branch offices or subsidiaries, member services.

Who's Who in Asian Banking & Finance. Bibliotheque: Worldwide. • Annual. $210 plus $7.50 shipping. Covers: 1,851 prominent and influential bankers and investors and 1,552 banks and financial institutions in Asia. Entries include: For individuals--Name, address, phone, fax, current job title and function, other professional, educational, and personal background details. For companies--Name, address, phone, fax, names and titles of key personnel.

Who's Who in Athens Magazine. Image Marketing Inc. • Semiannual. Covers: Individuals and businesses in Athens, AL.

Who's Who in British Economics: A Directory of Economists in Higher Education, Business and Government. Edward Elgar Publishing Inc. • £106.20 Individuals hardback. Covers: Professional economists in the United Kingdom. Entries include: Name, address, biographical data, select bibliography of works, description of main area of work.

Who's Who in Canadian Business. University of Toronto Press Inc. • Annual. $192.95 Individuals plus shipping charges. Covers: About 5,400 corporate and entrepreneurial leaders, each with a detailed biography and contact information. Biographies include such information as current employment, address, education, career history, publications, favorite charities and honors. Entries include: Name, degree(s), position, and title; office address, phone, fax, e-mail, and URL; personal, education, and career data; memberships, affiliations, and other interests.

Who's Who in Export. Indian Export Trade Journal. • Biennial. $25.

Who's Who in International Business Education and Research. Edward Elgar Publishing Inc. • $256.50 Individuals hardbound. Covers: 150 individuals in international business education and research. Entries include: Biographical data and professional data, career summary, URL.

Who's Who in Metro Atlanta Business: Membership Directory & Buyers Guide. Metro Atlanta Chamber of Commerce. • Annual. $35 Individuals. Covers: Over 7,000 member firms. Database includes: Chamber of commerce history, business facts and figures, annual report and initiatives for Metro Atlanta Chamber. Entries include: Company name, line of business, address, phone, names of key personnel and their URL addresses.

Who's Who of European Business and Industry. Triumph Books Inc. • Covers: over 9,500 European business executives (volume 1) and over 1,400 companies (volume 2). Entries include: For executives--Name, biographical data. For companies--Name, address, phone, profile.

The Wilson Guide to Internet Experts. H.W. Wilson Co. • $54.99. Covers: Noted authorities in the Internet industry. Entries include: Biographical details, office address and phone number, e-mail and Web site addresses, current projects, specialties.

Wisconsin Business Directory. InfoGroup Inc. • Annual. $520 both print & CD-ROM. Covers: 256,558 businesses in Wisconsin. Entries include: Company name, address, phone, number of employees, name of owner or manager, sales volume. Compiled from telephone company "Yellow Pages," statewide. All states covered (see separate entries).

Wisconsin Business Services Directory. WMC Foundation. • Annual. $199 Individuals. Covers: Over 10,700 business service companies with 25 or more employees in Wisconsin. Entries include: Company name, address, phone, fax, number of employees, SIC codes, names and titles of key personnel, services offered, product descriptions, ownership status, import/export activity, parent company.

Wisconsin Exporters' Directory. Wisconsin Department of Commerce. • Irregular. Covers: about 1,400 Wisconsin firms that export or are interested in exporting. Entries include: Company name, address, telex, names and titles of key personnel, product and service, Standard Industrial Classification (SIC) code.

Wisconsin Industries Guide. Industries Guides Inc. • $95. Covers: Approximately 10,000 manufacturers in Wisconsin. Entries include: Company name, address, phone.

Wisconsin Manufacturers Directory. WMC Foundation. • Annual. $177 Individuals. Covers: Approximately 12,300 manufacturers in Wisconsin. Entries include: Company name, address, phone, fax, number of employees, SIC codes, names and titles of key personnel, import/export activity, product descriptions, ownership status, parent company.

Wisconsin Services Directory. Harris InfoSource. • Annual. $98 members/libraries. Covers: 16,000 business service companies in Wisconsin and over 24,000 key contact personnel. Entries include: Company name, address, phone, fax, name and title of contact, names and titles of key personnel, number of employees, geographical area served, financial data, subsidiary and branch names and locations, product/service, Standard Industrial Classification (SIC) code, computer used, year established, import/export information, web and e-mail address, first month of fiscal year, export countries.

WISE International Business Directory. World Institute of Scientology Enterprises. • Covers: Business people who use L. Ron Hubbard management technology. Entries include: Contact information.

The Woman's Consultants Directory. CAE Consultants Inc. • Annual. $75. Covers: About 3,000 women consultants in every line of business. Entries include: Consultant name, address, phone, fax, line of business, description.

Women Directors of the Top Corporate 1,000. National Women's Economic Alliance Foundation. • Annual. $100. Covers: about 600 women serving on the boards of Fortune 1,000 corporations; compiled from surveys of Fortune 500 Industrial and Fortune 500 Service corporations and the Corporate Yellow Book. Entries include: Name, title, company name, address, corporate boards on which serves.

Wood & Wood Products--Laminating Users Guide Issue. Laminating Materials Association. • Annual. Publication includes: List of approximately 150 manufacturers and importers of decorative overlays, wood substrates, adhesives, laminating equipment, and laminated products. Entries include: Company name, address, phone, name and title of contact.

Working Solo: The Real Guide to Freedom & Financial Success with Your Own Business, 2nd Edition. Portico Press. • $21.95 Individuals paperback. Covers: Over 1,000 solo business opportunities, as well as a resource section on publications, organizations, and other essential contacts for solo professionals.

World Business Directory. NIIR Project Consultancy Services. • $200 Individuals CD-ROM. Covers: More than 300,000 worldwide businesses. Entries include: Company name, postal address, city, state, pin code, phone, fax and the emails.

World Buyers' Guide to Unusual & Innovative Products. Emir Publications. • Biennial. $20. Covers: manufacturers and suppliers of unusual merchandise worldwide for mail order dealers, gift stores, novelty dealers, catalog businesses, importers, and opportunity seekers. Entries include: Name of firm, address, cable address, telex, fax, products.

World Database of Consumer Brands and Their Owners. Euromonitor International Business Reference Div. • Annual. $995. Covers: Descriptive information on the owning companies of approximately 56,000 brands across 1,000 consumer sectors in 85 countries.

World Databases in Company Information. K.G. Saur Verlag KG. • Covers: Electronically published databases and their vendors, worldwide.

World Directory of Business Information Sources. Euromonitor International Business Reference Div. • $700 Individuals U.S.D. Covers: National and international Web sites of interest to business researchers, provided by trade associations, magazines, government agencies, private research firms and others.

World Directory of Clothing, Garments and Apparel Importers. World-Wide Market-Link. • Irregular. $35. Covers: 1,500 apparel importers in 27 countries. Entries include: Company name, address, phone, products.

World Directory of Cosmetics, Beauty Supplies, and Toiletries Importers. World-Wide Market-Link. • Irregular. $35. Covers: 800 importers and wholesaler of cosmetics, beauty supplies an toiletries in 30 countries. Entries include: Company name, address, phone, products.

World Directory of Hides, Skins & Raw Leather Importers. World-Wide Market-Link. • Irregular. $35. Covers: 400 leather importers and wholesalers in the U.S. and Canada, the United Kingdom, Australia, Austria, Belgium, Denmark, Finland, France, West Germany, Greece, Holland, Italy, Israel, Japan, Spain, Sweden, and Switzerland. Entries include: Company name, address, phone, products handled.

World Directory of Industrial Information Sources. United Nations Publications. • $40 Individuals. Covers: Industrial information sources for the most appropriate sources of technology and equipment. It contains profiles of information providers such as information and documentation centers, banks, training institutes, development agencies and manufacturers associations that are prepared to provide entrepreneurs in developing countries with answers to their industrial needs.

World Directory of Marketing Information Sources. Euromonitor International Business Reference Div. • Irregular. $590. Covers: 6,000 market research organizations, libraries and information services, information databases, business and marketing associations, business and marketing journals, statistical offices, chambers of commerce, embassies, and foreign trade departments in Europe. Entries include: Organization, agency, or association name, contact name and address, type of data offered, publications.

World Directory of Non-Official Statistical Sources. Euromonitor International Business Reference Div. • $750 Individuals U.S.D. Covers: Over 2,800 titles, serials, and statistical data services produced by associations, business schools, trade journals, market research companies, banks, insurance companies, employers' organizations, and building societies in the world. Entries include: Source title, publisher or producer name, address, phone, fax, description.

World Directory of Toys & Games. World-Wide Market-Link. • Irregular. $35. Covers: 1,700 toy and game importers and wholesalers in 60 countries. Entries include: Company name, address, phone.

World Directory of Trade and Business Association. Euromonitor Publications Ltd. • $750 Individuals. Covers: publication and membership details of each association. Entries include: full contact details of trade and business associations world wide.

World Directory of Trade and Business Journals. Euromonitor International Business Reference Div. • $590. Covers: international consumer and industrial trade journals. Entries include: title, publisher address, coverage, language, frequency, readership, cost, and circulation.

World Directory of Trade Promotion Organizations and Other Foreign Trade Bodies. International Trade Centre. • Annual. $50 Free to developing countries/economies in transition. Covers: over 1,200 international trade promotion organizations and other foreign trade bodies involved in international trade, including ministries, trade promotion organizations, import promotion offices, chambers of commerce in principal business centers and/or federations of chambers of commerce, trade associations, operational trade pointes, and selected regional and inter-regional organizations. Entries include: Organization name, address, phone, fax, telex, e-mail, URL, and codes description of services provided when available.

World Financial System. Financial Times Healthcare. • Irregular. $165. Publication includes: Descriptions of 56 international economic organizations, including monetary, developmental, trade, and petroleum organizations. Database includes: Essays on international monetary relations from 1944 to 1992, including summaries of events, conferences, and important documents. Entries include: Name, address, name of chief executive, background, functions, member countries, structure, operations, description of activities, conferences, etc.

World Leading Global Brand Owners. Euromonitor International Business Reference Div. • $1,495 Individuals Hardcopy. Covers: Profiles of the top 200 multinationals worldwide operating in key consumer markets. Entries include: Detailed corporate and financial information and analysis, information on the global market share and significant subsidiaries, strengths, weaknesses, opportunities and threats, main brands, product range, and full operational data.

World M&A Network. NVST Inc. • Monthly Quarterly. $395 U.S.. Lists companies for sale, companies seeking to purchase other companies, and sources of acquisition financing.

World Market Share Reporter. Cengage Learning Inc. • $572 Individuals. Compilation of global market share data from periodical literature. Covers nearly 1,670 entries in 360 geographic worldwide locations of companies and products and services.

World of Information Business & Economic Europe Review. Kogan Page, Limited. • Covers: Tourist and business information, including airlines, banks, hotels, ministries and associations in Europe. Entries include: Address.

World Trade Almanac. Hoover's Inc. • $86.95. Publication includes: Lists of embassies and consulates, trade organizations, chambers of commerce, world trade centers, industrial associations, trade fair sponsors, domestic and international banks, and major business service providers for 120 countries of the world. Entries include: Name, address, phone. Principal content of publication is country profiles.

World Trade Association International Business Directory. San Francisco Chamber of Commerce. • Annual. $12.50. Covers: Members of the San Francisco Chamber of Commerce engaged in import or export activities. Entries include: Company name, address, phone, commodities, countries imported from or exported to, services.

The World Trade System. Cartermill International. • $165. Publication includes: List of national and international trade organizations. Entries include: Organization name, address, phone, contact information. Principal content of publication is information on and analysis of world trade activity.

World Wide Importers Register International Buyers Directory. NIIR Project Consultancy Services. • $250 Individuals. Covers: 45,000 entries of importing firms in Europe, America, Middle East, Asia/Pacific, South/Central America and Africa. Entries include: Indian missions/embassies, e-mail, phone, fax and complete address to facilitate exporters.

The World's Major Companies. Euromonitor International Business Reference Div. • $550. Covers: Approximately 4,000 major multinational companies. Entries include: Company name, address, phone, telex, names and titles of key personnel, number of employees, financial data, subsidiary and branch names and locations, description.

Worldwide Magnetics Industry Directory. Webcom Communications Corp. • $195 Individuals hardcopy. Covers: 2,400 companies that manufacture, distribute, and assemble materials and equipment in the magnetic industry worldwide. Includes industry-wide listing of magnetic manufacturers and distributors as well as suppliers of parts, components, systems and supplies used in the manufacture and aftermarket service of the magnet and materials industry. Information on over 4,800 personnel involved in the industry.

Worldwide Tradeshow Schedule. Glahe International, Inc. • Covers: Approximately 200 international trade fairs in all major industrial sectors worldwide. Entries include: Organization name, address, phone, telex, name and title of contact, description of event.

Wyoming Business Directory. InfoGroup Inc. • Annual. $375 both print & CD-ROM. Covers: 33,514 businesses in Wyoming. Entries include: Company name, address, phone, number of employees, name of owner or manager, sales volume. Compiled from telephone company "Yellow Pages," statewide. All states covered (see separate entries).

Wyoming Directory of Manufacturing and Mining. Wyoming Business Council. • Biennial. $15. Covers: About 790 companies in mining and manufacturing; state and local organizations and government agencies that provide business assistance. Entries include: For businesses--Name of firm, address, phone, name of key executive, product or activity, parent company (if any), codes for number of employees and geographic scope, Standard Industrial Classification (SIC) code. For organizations and agencies--Name of agency or organization, address, phone, contact name or official.

Wytheville Chamber of Commerce Business Directory. Wytheville-Wythe-Bland Chamber of

Commerce. • Covers: List of members. Entries include: name, address, phone.

Xiamen Yellow Pages: Commercial/Industrial Directory. China Yellow Pages Directories Co. • Annual. $65. Covers: over 15,000 companies in the Xiamen area. Database includes: Investment information. Entries include: Company name, address, phone, fax, postal code.

Yearbook of the Athens Stock Exchange. Athens Stock Exchange. • Annual. €20 plus postage. Covers: About 196 companies quoted on the Athens Stock Exchange; list of stockbrokers. Database includes: List of business loans available, with description and financial data; financial statistics. Entries include: For companies--Name, address, phone, telex, year established, year first listed, line of business, number of shareholders, board of directors, number of employees, financial data. For brokers--Name, address, phone.

Yearbook of the Lebanese Joint-Stock Companies. Publitec Publications. • Annual. $120. Covers: Lebanese and foreign companies operating in Lebanon, including companies working in the fields of insurance, banking, commerce, industry, real estate, transport, finance, holdings, and offshore. Entries include: Contact information.

Yearbook of the Lebanese Limited Liability Companies. Publitec Publications. • Annual. $120. Covers: Lebanese limited liability companies, including insurance companies, commerce, industry, real estate, transport, and finance. Entries include: Contact information.

Yellow Pages Industry Sourcebook. Communications Trends Inc. • Annual. $295. Publication includes: Company listings. Entries include: Company name, address, phone, description, officer names, financial data, key customers, national accounts.

Yellow Pages Moscow. Deutsche Telekom Medien GmbH. • Annual. Covers: Approximately 70,000 commercial telephone subscribers in Moscow. Entries include: Name, address, phone, product/service.

York County Regional Chamber of Commerce Business Directory. York County Regional Chamber of Commerce. • Covers: Information on all York County, New York, businesses.

Yritys-Suomi CD. Helsinki Media. • Biennial. Database covers: Information on 170,000 companies from other Blue Book directories.

Yugoslavia Export-Import Directory. Yugoslaviapublic. • Annual. Covers: Foreign trade organizations, products, services in Yugoslavia. Entries include: Name, address, phone.

Yugoslavia (Serbia) Government and Business Contacts Handbook. International Business Publications, USA. • Annual. $99.95 Individuals hardcopy, e-book, CD-ROM. Covers: Strategic government and business information, export-import activity in the country, investment, business contacts and regulations.

Yugoslavia (Serbia) Industrial and Business Directory. International Business Publications, USA. • Annual. $99.95 Individuals hardcopy, E-book and CD-ROM. Covers: Strategic industrial, investment and business contacts for conducting export-import and investment activity in the country.

Yunnan Yellow Pages. China Yellow Pages Directories Co. • Annual. Covers: Over 20,000 companies in Yunnan Province, Taiwan. Database includes: An investment guide containing Yunnan's policies, rules and procedures for investment plus a compilation of product and service advertisements. Entries include: Company name, address, phone.

GENERAL WORKS

Who's Who in International Business Education and Research. Edward Elgar Publishing Inc. • $256.50 Individuals hardbound. Covers: 150 individuals in international business education and research. Entries include: Biographical data and professional data, career summary, URL.

HANDBOOKS AND MANUALS

Mergent OTC Industrial Manual. Mergent Inc. • Annual. $1,995 including 'News Reports.' Covers over 2,500 companies whose stock is traded over the counter. Includes biweekly *Moody's OTC Industrial News Report*.

ONLINE DATABASES

Books in Print Online. Bowker Electronic Publishing. • The online version of *Books in Print*, *Forthcoming Books*, *Paperbound Books in Print* and other Bowker bibliographic publications: lists the books of over 50,000 U.S. publishers. Includes books recently declared out-of-print. Updated monthly. Inquire as to online cost and availability.

Business Insights: Essentials (BI:E). Cengage Learning Inc. • Formerly Business & Company Resource Center. Contact for pricing. Contains in-depth, searchable information on U.S. and International businesses, industries, and products.

PERIODICALS AND NEWSLETTERS

Catalog Age. PRIMEDIA Business Magazine and Media. • 13 times a year. Free to qualified personnel; others, $85.00 per year. Edited for catalog marketing and management personnel.

CSM. CSM Marketing, Inc. • Monthly. $30.00 per year. Formerly *Catalog Showroom Merchandiser*.

Direct Marketing News. Haymarket Media Group Ltd. • Monthly. $148 U.S. /year. Includes special feature issues on catalog marketing, telephone marketing, database marketing, and fundraising. Includes monthly supplements, *DM News International*, *DRTV News*, and *TeleServices*.

The SIMBA Report on Directory Publishing. SIMBA Information Inc. • Monthly. Newsletter.

STATISTICS SOURCES

World Market Share Reporter. Cengage Learning Inc. • $572 Individuals. Compilation of global market share data from periodical literature. Covers nearly 1,670 entries in 360 geographic worldwide locations of companies and products and services.

TRADE/PROFESSIONAL ASSOCIATIONS

Association of Directory Publishers. 116 Cass St., Traverse City, MI 49685. Phone: 800-267-9002; Fax: (231)486-2182; Email: hq@adp.org • URL: http://www.adp.org • Represents publishers of printed and electronic telephone, city, and special interest directories.

National Catalog Managers Association. Automotive Aftermarket Industry Association, 7101 Wisconsin Ave., Ste. 1300, Bethesda, MD 20814-3415. Phone: (301)654-6664; Fax: (301)654-3299; Email: ncma@aftermarket.org • URL: http://www.autocare.org/SegmentsDetail.aspx?id=594&gmssopc=1 • Individuals actively engaged in the management, preparation, production, and distribution of automotive product catalogs. Purposes are to: exchange practical and useful ideas in the creation, compilation, production and distribution of catalogs; raise standards of catalogs in automotive and related industries; create a better understanding of the current developments in the field of graphics; establish a professional and fraternal relationship with colleagues; improve professional recognition of the catalog specialist; promote high standards of ethics in the cataloging industry. Operates placement service.

CATERERS AND CATERING

See also HOTEL AND MOTEL INDUSTRY; RESTAURANTS, LUNCHROOMS, ETC.

PERIODICALS AND NEWSLETTERS

Catering Industry Employee. Hotel Employees and Restaurant Employees International Union. • Quarterly. $5.00.

Chef. Aktiebolaget Electrolux. • Monthly. $24.00 per year. Edited for executive chefs, food and beverage directors, caterers, banquet and club managers, and others responsible for food buying and food service. Special coverage of regional foods is provided.

TRADE/PROFESSIONAL ASSOCIATIONS

Convenience Caterers and Food Manufacturers Association. 1205 Spartan Dr., Madison Heights, MI 48071. Phone: (248)982-5379; Email: ccfma@ymail.com • URL: http://www.mobilecaterers.com • Firms and corporations engaged in the mobile catering business and in any other business catering to industrial feeding by mobile equipment; associate members are suppliers and manufacturers. Deals with common intra-industry problems through exchange of ideas, advice on legal problems, and safety standards and licensing regulations.

CATTLE INDUSTRY

See also DAIRY INDUSTRY; LIVESTOCK INDUSTRY

CD-ROM DATABASES

OECD Statistical Compendium. Organization for Economic Cooperation and Development. • Semiannual. $1,905.00 per year for 1 to 10 users. CD-ROM contains more than 730,000 monthly, quarterly, and annual time series for OECD countries, 1960 to date. Includes fully searchable data on agriculture, food, economic indicators, national accounts, employment, energy, finance, industry, technology, and foreign trade. Results can be displayed in various forms.

FINANCIAL RATIOS

Annual Statement Studies. Risk Management Association. • Annual. Compiled from over 280,000 financial statements.

Annual Statement Studies: Industry Default Probabilities and Cash Flow Measures. Risk Management Association. • Annual. $405 Nonmembers. Serves as a companion volume to the original *Annual Statement Studies*. Gives probability of default estimates on a percentage scale for more than 450 industries. Includes changes in position year-by-year for eight financial statement line items and provides percentage measures of cash flow.

INTERNET DATABASES

BEEF. National Cattlemen's Beef Association. Phone: (303)694-0305; Fax: (303)694-2851; Email: cows@beef.org • URL: http://www.beef.org • Web site provides detailed information from the "Cattle and Beef Handbook," including "Beef Economics" (production, sales, consumption, retail value, foreign competition, etc.). Text of monthly newsletter is also available: "The Beef Brief-Issues & Trends in the Cattle Industry." Keyword searching is offered. Fees: Free.

Business 2.0 Web Guide to the Best Business Links. Business 2.0 Media Inc. Phone: (415)293-4800; Email: support@business2.com • URL: http://www.business2.com/webguide • Web site presents an extensive, searchable directory of links to "the best, most informative, and authoritative web pages." Twenty main categories cover business, finance, career, company information, people, and technology topics, with thousands of subtopics, all linking to Web sites recommended by experienced business researchers. Fees: Free.

Fedstats. Federal Interagency Council on Statistical Policy. Phone: (202)395-7254 • URL: http://www.fedstats.gov • Web site features an efficient search facility for full-text statistics produced by more than 100 federal agencies, including the Census Bureau, the Bureau of Economic Analysis, and the Bureau of Labor Statistics. Boolean searches can be made within one agency or for all agencies combined. Links are offered to international statistical bureaus, including the UN, IMF, OECD, UNESCO, Eurostat, and 20 individual countries. Fees: Free.

FreeLunch.com. Economy.com, Inc. Phone: (610)696-8700; Fax: (610)696-1678 • URL: http://www.freelunch.com • Web site provides free access to more than 200 million economic and financial data series, covering industry, demographics, labor markets, prices, retail sales, government spending, trade, interest rates, housing starts, the stock market, etc. Data is available in either chart or table form. Searching is offered. Free, but registration required. Economy.com, Inc. also offers fee-based economic analysis at *The Dismal Scientist* site (www.dismal.com).

USDA. U.S. National Institute of Standards and Technology. 100 Bureau Dr., Gaithersburg, MD 20899-1070. Phone: 800-877-8339 or (301)975-6478 or (202)720-2791; Fax: (301)975-8295; Email: inquiries@nist.gov • URL: http://www.nist.gov • The USDA home page has six sections: News and Information; What's New; About USDA; Agencies; Opportunities; Search and Help. Keyword searching is offered from the USDA home page and from various individual agency home pages. Agencies are the Economic Research Service, Agricultural Marketing Service, National Agricultural Statistics Service, National Agricultural Library, and about 12 others. Updating varies. Fees: Free.

PERIODICALS AND NEWSLETTERS

Cattleman. Texas and Southwestern Cattle Raisers Association. • Monthly. $40 per year.

PRICE SOURCES

The National Provisioner: Serving Meat, Poultry, and Seafood Processors. BNP Media. • Monthly. $85.04 Individuals. *Buyer's Guide* available. Meat, poultry and seafood newsletter.

RESEARCH CENTERS AND INSTITUTES

Economic Research Service - Cattle and Beef. 355 E St. SW, Washington, DC 20024-3221. Phone: 800-999-6779 or (202)694-5183; Email: kmathews@ers.usda.gov • URL: http://ers.usda.gov/topics/animal-products/cattle-beef.aspx#.U5Eq73I2aDg • Market analysis and research on the U.S. cattle and beef sectors, including domestic supply and utilization, live cattle and retail beef prices, and international trade.

Montana State University, Bozeman - College of Agriculture - Montana Agricultural Experiment Station. 202 Linfield Hall, Bozeman, MT 59717. Phone: (406)994-3681; Fax: (406)994-6579 • URL: http://ag.montana.edu/maes.htm • Biological, physical, and social sciences as applied to agriculture, including research in agronomy, plant genetics and breeding, plant pathology, animal science, plant breeding and genetics, veterinary medicine, entomology, environmental sciences, microbiology, biochemistry, agricultural engineering, molecular biology, economics, and sociology.

Pennsylvania State University - Beef Cattle and Sheep Research Center. 324 Henning Bldg., University Park, PA 16802. Phone: (814)865-5893; Fax: (814)863-6042; Email: rswope@das.psu.edu • URL: http://www.das.cas.psu.edu/ • Animal science, including breeding selection, nutrition, and physiology of beef cattle and sheep; pasture management and intensive rotational grazing practices.

STATISTICS SOURCES

Agricultural Statistics. U.S. Department of Agriculture National Agricultural Statistics Service. • Annual. $46 Individuals. Provides a wide variety of statistical data relating to agricultural production, supplies, consumption, prices/price-supports, foreign trade, costs, and returns, as well as farm labor, loans, income, and population. In many cases, historical data is shown annually for 10 years. In addition to farm data, includes detailed fishery statistics.

Survey of Current Business. U. S. Government Printing Office. • Published by Bureau of Economic Analysis, U. S. Department of Commerce. Presents a wide variety of business and economic data.

TRADE/PROFESSIONAL ASSOCIATIONS

Fullblood Simmental Fleckvieh Federation. PO Box 321, Cisco, TX 76437. Phone: 855-353-2584; Fax: (855)638-2582; Email: info@fleckvieh.com • URL: http://www.fleckvieh.com • Aims to develop and promote Fullblood Simmental and Fullblood Fleckvieh cattle. Seeks to educate beef producers on the economic traits of Fullblood Simmental and Fullblood Fleckvieh cattle. Strives to promote the use of Fullblood Simmental and Fullblood Fleckvieh beef cattle genetics and to preserve and market the breeds in North America and worldwide to both purebred and commercial beef producers.

Livestock Marketing Association. 10510 NW Ambassador Dr., Kansas City, MO 64153. Phone: 800-821-2048 • URL: http://www.lmaweb.com • Livestock marketing businesses and livestock dealers. Sponsors annual World Livestock Auctioneer Championships. Offers management and promotional services.

National Cattlemen's Beef Association. 9110 E Nichols Ave., Ste. 300, Centennial, CO 80112. Phone: (303)694-0305; Fax: (303)694-2851; Email: information@beef.org • URL: http://www.beefusa.org • Represents 149 organizations of livestock marketers, growers, meat packers, food retailers, and food service firms. Conducts extensive program of promotion, education and information about beef, veal, and associated meat products. Conducts projects such as recipe testing and development, food demonstrations, food photography, educational service to colleges, experimental meat cutting methods, merchandising programs, and preparation of materials for newspapers, magazines, radio, and television.

CATV

See CABLE TELEVISION INDUSTRY

CELLULAR TELEPHONES

See MOBILE TELEPHONE INDUSTRY

CEMENT INDUSTRY

See also CONCRETE INDUSTRY

CD-ROM DATABASES

OECD Statistical Compendium. Organization for Economic Cooperation and Development. • Semiannual. $1,905.00 per year for 1 to 10 users. CD-ROM contains more than 730,000 monthly, quarterly, and annual time series for OECD countries, 1960 to date. Includes fully searchable data on agriculture, food, economic indicators, national accounts, employment, energy, finance, industry, technology, and foreign trade. Results can be displayed in various forms.

DIRECTORIES

American Cement Directory. Bradley Pulverizer Co. • Annual. $90 U.S. and Canada Postpaid. Covers: Approximately 100 cement manufacturing companies in the United States, Canada, Mexico, Central and South America. Entries include: Company Name, address, phone, fax, names of principal executives, capacity, capitalization, brand names and process, plant locations.

Directory of Asian Importers of Machinery for Rubber Industry. EXIM Infotek Private Ltd. • Covers: 30 Asian importers of rubber industry equipment and supplies and rubber processing machinery. Entries include: Company name, postal address, telephone, fax, e-mail, website, contact person, designation, and product details.

Directory of Asian Importers of Wax & Wax Products. EXIM Infotek Private Ltd. • Covers: 90 Asian importers of micro waxes, normal paraffin, paraffin waxes, polishes and creams, and slack waxes. Entries include: Company name, postal address, telephone, fax, e-mail, website, contact person, designation, and product details.

Directory of European Importers of Energy and Power Equipment. EXIM Infotek Private Ltd. • Covers: 180 European importers of alternative energy equipment, energy saving equipment, nuclear equipment and materials, power transmission component, power transmission equipment and supplies, power transmission equipment, solar energy equipment, and wind energy equipment. Entries include: Company name, postal address, telephone, fax, e-mail, website, contact person, designation, and product details.

Directory of Japanese Importers of Handkerchieves, Scarves and Neckwears. EXIM Infotek Private Ltd. • $250 Individuals. Covers: 90 Japanese importers of clothing accessories, ties, scarves, handkerchieves, neckwear, mufflers, and silk neckties. Entries include: Company name, postal address, telephone, fax, e-mail, website, contact person, designation, and product details.

Kompass. Kompass Deutschland Verlags- und Vertriebsgesellschaft, mbH. • Annual. $88. Covers: German products and companies specializing in coal extraction, ore mining, quarries, cement industry, glass and ceramics.

INTERNET DATABASES

Business 2.0 Web Guide to the Best Business Links. Business 2.0 Media Inc. Phone: (415)293-4800; Email: support@business2.com • URL: http://www.business2.com/webguide • Web site presents an extensive, searchable directory of links to "the best, most informative, and authoritative web pages." Twenty main categories cover business, finance, career, company information, people, and technology topics, with thousands of subtopics, all linking to Web sites recommended by experienced business researchers. Fees: Free.

Fedstats. Federal Interagency Council on Statistical Policy. Phone: (202)395-7254 • URL: http://www.fedstats.gov • Web site features an efficient search facility for full-text statistics produced by more than 100 federal agencies, including the Census Bureau, the Bureau of Economic Analysis, and the Bureau of Labor Statistics. Boolean searches can be made within one agency or for all agencies combined. Links are offered to international statistical bureaus, including the UN, IMF, OECD, UNESCO, Eurostat, and 20 individual countries. Fees: Free.

FreeLunch.com. Economy.com, Inc. Phone: (610)696-8700; Fax: (610)696-1678 • URL: http://www.freelunch.com • Web site provides free access to more than 200 million economic and financial data series, covering industry, demographics, labor markets, prices, retail sales, government spending, trade, interest rates, housing starts, the stock market, etc. Data is available in either chart or table form. Searching is offered. Free, but registration required. Economy.com, Inc. also offers fee-based economic analysis at *The Dismal Scientist* site (www.dismal.com).

PERIODICALS AND NEWSLETTERS

Cement and Concrete Research. Elsevier. • Monthly. $3,893 Institutions. Covers information regarding on cement, cement composites, concrete and other allied materials that incorporate cement.

Pit and Quarry. Advanstar Communications. • Monthly. Covers crushed stone, sand and gravel, etc.

Quarry Management: The Monthly Journal for the Quarrying, Asphalt, Concrete and Recycling Industries. QMJ Publishing Ltd. • Monthly. £45 Individuals. Covers the latest news, issues, developments and advances in the quarry products sector.

Rock Products: The Aggregate Industry's Journal of Applied Technology. Primedia Business Magazines and Media. • Monthly. $56.00 per year.

RESEARCH CENTERS AND INSTITUTES

University of Illinois at Urbana-Champaign - Center for Cement Composite Materials. 2129 Newmark Civil Engineering Laboratory, 205 Mathews Ave., Urbana, IL 61801. Phone: (217)333-2544 or (217)333-6900; Fax: (217)265-8040; Email: lstruble@uiuc.edu • URL: http://ccm.cee.uiuc.edu • Concrete, cement, and their constituent materials, including comprehensive interdisciplinary studies of advanced cement-based materials. Center works with high-performance materials such as DSP cements, MDF cements, and magnesium phosphate cements. Expertise includes electron microscopy, rheology, computer-based modeling, fracture, cement chemistry, and microstructure characterization.

STATISTICS SOURCES

Survey of Current Business. U. S. Government Printing Office. • Published by Bureau of Economic Analysis, U. S. Department of Commerce. Presents a wide variety of business and economic data.

United States Census of Manufactures. U.S. Department of Commerce U.S. Census Bureau. • Quinquennial. Results presented in reports, tape, CD-ROM, and Diskette files.

TRADE/PROFESSIONAL ASSOCIATIONS

International Brotherhood of Boilermakers. 753 State Ave., Ste. 570, Kansas City, KS 66101. Phone: (913)371-2640 or (913)342-2100; Fax: (913)281-8101 or (913)281-8104; Email: ipjones@boilermakers.org • URL: http://www.boilermakers.org • Affiliated with International Brotherhood of Boilermakers, Iron Ship Builders, Blacksmiths, Forgers and Helpers.

Operative Plasterers and Cement Masons International Association. 11720 Beltsville Dr., Ste. 700, Beltsville, MD 20705. Phone: (301)623-1000; Fax: (301)623-1032; Email: opcmiaintl@opcmia.org • URL: http://www.opcmia.org.

Portland Cement Association. 5420 Old Orchard Rd., Skokie, IL 60077-1083. Phone: 800-868-6733 or (847)966-6200 or (202)408-9494; Fax: (847)966-8389; Email: info@cement.org • URL: http://www.cement.org • Companies in the U.S. and Canada. Seeks to improve and extend the uses of Portland cement and concrete through market promotion, research and development, educational programs, and representation with governmental entities. Conducts research on concrete technology and durability; concrete pavement design; load-bearing capacities, field performance, and fire resistance of concrete; transportation, building, and structural uses of concrete. Operates Construction Technology Laboratories, which conducts research and technical services in construction materials, products, and applications. Sponsors a public affairs program in Washington, DC.

CEMETERIES

See FUNERAL HOMES AND DIRECTORS

CENSUS REPORTS

See also GOVERNMENT PUBLICATIONS; POPULATION

BIBLIOGRAPHIES

Monthly Product Announcement. U. S. Bureau of the Census. • Monthly. Lists Census Bureau publications and products that became available during the previous month.

U.S. Census Bureau Catalog and Guide. U. S. Government Printing Office. • Annual. Lists publications and electronic media products currently available from the U. S. Bureau of the Census, along with some out of print items. Includes comprehensive title and subject indexes. Formerly *Bureau of the Census Catalog.*

CD-ROM DATABASES

OECD Statistical Compendium. Organization for Economic Cooperation and Development. • Semiannual. $1,905.00 per year for 1 to 10 users. CD-ROM contains more than 730,000 monthly, quarterly, and annual time series for OECD countries, 1960 to date. Includes fully searchable data on agriculture, food, economic indicators, national accounts, employment, energy, finance, industry, technology, and foreign trade. Results can be displayed in various forms.

Sourcebooks America CD-ROM. CACI Marketing Systems. • Annual. $1,250.00. Provides the CD-ROM version of *The Sourcebook of ZIP Code Demographics: Census Edition* and *The Sourcebook of County Demographics: Census Edition.*

INTERNET DATABASES

Business 2.0 Web Guide to the Best Business Links. Business 2.0 Media Inc. Phone: (415)293-4800; Email: support@business2.com • URL: http://www.business2.com/webguide • Web site presents an extensive, searchable directory of links to "the best, most informative, and authoritative web pages." Twenty main categories cover business, finance, career, company information, people, and technology topics, with thousands of subtopics, all linking to Web sites recommended by experienced business researchers. Fees: Free.

Fedstats. Federal Interagency Council on Statistical Policy. Phone: (202)395-7254 • URL: http://www.fedstats.gov • Web site features an efficient search facility for full-text statistics produced by more than 100 federal agencies, including the Census Bureau, the Bureau of Economic Analysis, and the Bureau of Labor Statistics. Boolean searches can be made within one agency or for all agencies combined. Links are offered to international statistical bureaus, including the UN, IMF, OECD, UNESCO, Eurostat, and 20 individual countries. Fees: Free.

FreeLunch.com. Economy.com, Inc. Phone: (610)696-8700; Fax: (610)696-1678 • URL: http://www.freelunch.com • Web site provides free access to more than 200 million economic and financial data series, covering industry, demographics, labor markets, prices, retail sales, government spending, trade, interest rates, housing starts, the stock market, etc. Data is available in either chart or table form. Searching is offered. Free, but registration required. Economy.com, Inc. also offers fee-based economic analysis at *The Dismal Scientist* site (www.dismal.com).

1997 NAICS and 1987 SIC Correspondence Tables. U. S. Census Bureau. Phone: 800-541-8345 or (301)457-4100 or (301)763-2713; Fax: (301)457-1296 or (301)457-3842; Email: naics@census.gov • URL: http://www.census.gov/epcd/www/naicstab.htm • Web site provides detailed tables for converting four-digit Standard Industrial Classification (SIC) numbers to the six-digit North American Industrial Classification System (NAICS) or vice versa: "1987 SIC Matched to 1997 NAICS" or "1997 NAICS Matched to 1987 SIC." Fees: Free.

PERIODICALS AND NEWSLETTERS

Population and Development Review. Blackwell Publishing Inc. • Quarterly. $64. Includes print and online editions. *Supplement* available. Text in English; summaries in English, French and Spanish.

Population Bulletin. Population Reference Bureau. • Quarterly. $3.50 Single issue. Covers population issues, country/regional studies, and health issues.

RESEARCH CENTERS AND INSTITUTES

University of Alabama - Alabama State Data Center. Box 870221, Tuscaloosa, AL 35487-0221. Phone: (205)348-6191; Email: asdc@cba.ua.edu • URL: http://cber.cba.ua.edu/asdc • Makes census data (1980-) available for research and other uses at the University and throughout the state. Maintains both census and other varied technical documentation.

STATISTICS SOURCES

Statistical Abstract of the United States. U. S. Government Printing Office. • Annual. $44.00. Issued by the U. S. Bureau of the Census.

United States Census of Agriculture. U.S. Department of Agriculture National Agricultural Statistics Service. • Quinquennial. Provides uniform, comprehensive farming and ranching operations data for every U.S. state and county, including production expenses, market value of products, and operator characteristics.

United States Census of Construction Industries. U.S. Department of Commerce U.S. Census Bureau. • Quinquennial. Results presented in reports, tape, and CD-ROM files.

United States Census of Governments. Bureau of the Census, U.S. Department of Commerce. U. S. Government Printing Office. • Quinquennial.

United States Census of Manufactures. U.S. Department of Commerce U.S. Census Bureau. • Quinquennial. Results presented in reports, tape, CD-ROM, and Diskette files.

United States Census of Mineral Industries. Bureau of the Census, U.S. Department of Commerce. U. S. Government Printing Office. • Quinquennial.

United States Census of Population and Housing. Bureau of the Census, U.S. Department of Commerce. U. S. Government Printing Office. • Quinquennial.

United States Census of Retail Trade. U.S. Department of Commerce U.S. Census Bureau. • Quinquennial.

United States Census of Service Industries. U.S. Department of Commerce U.S. Census Bureau. • Quinquennial. Various reports available.

United States Census of Transportation. Bureau of the Census, U.S. Department of Commerce. U. S. Government Printing Office. • Quinquennial.

United States Census of Wholesale Trade. Bureau of the Census, U.S. Department of Commerce. U. S. Government Printing Office. • Quinquennial.

TRADE/PROFESSIONAL ASSOCIATIONS

Population Association of America. 8630 Fenton St., Ste. 722, Silver Spring, MD 20910-3812. Phone: (301)565-6710; Fax: (301)565-7850; Email: lmbrown@popassoc.org • URL: http://www.populationassociation.org • Individuals interested in demography and its scientific aspects.

Population Council. 1 Dag Hammarskjold Plz., New York, NY 10017. Phone: 877-339-0500 or (212)339-0500 or (212)237-9434; Fax: (212)755-6052; Email: pubinfo@popcouncil.org • URL: http://www.popcouncil.org • Seeks to improve the well-being and reproductive health of current and future generations around the world. Helps achieve a humane, equitable, and sustainable balance between people and resources. Conducts research in three areas: HIV and AIDS; poverty, gender, and youth; and reproductive health.

Population Reference Bureau. 1875 Connecticut Ave. NW, Ste. 520, Washington, DC 20009-5728. Phone: 800-877-9881; Fax: (202)328-3937; Email: popref@prb.org • URL: http://www.prb.org • Gathers, interprets, and disseminates information on the facts and implications of national and world population trends.

CENTRAL AMERICA

See LATIN AMERICAN MARKETS

CERAMIC TILE INDUSTRY

See TILE INDUSTRY

CERAMICS INDUSTRY

See also CLAY INDUSTRY; POTTERY INDUSTRY

ABSTRACTS AND INDEXES

Applied Science and Technology Index. EBSCO Publishing Inc. • 11/year. Indexes a wide variety of English language technical, industrial, and engineering periodicals.

Ceramics Abstracts/World Ceramics Abstracts. American Ceramic Society. Cambridge Scientific Abstracts L.P. • Monthly. Provide international coverage of the ceramics industry.

Engineered Materials Abstracts. Cambridge Information Group. • Monthly. $995.00 per year. Provides citations to the technical and engineering literature of plastic, ceramic, and composite materials.

NTIS Alerts: Materials Sciences. U.S. Department of Commerce National Technical Information Service. • Biweekly. $130 per year. Covers ceramics, glass, coatings, composite materials, alloys, plastics, wood, paper, adhesives, fibers, lubricants, and related subjects.

CD-ROM DATABASES

METADEX Materials Collection: Metals-Polymers-Ceramics. Cambridge Scientific Abstracts L.P. • Quarterly. Provides CD-ROM citations to the worldwide literature of materials science and metallurgy. Corresponds to *Metals Abstracts, Alloys Index, Steels Alert, Nonferrous Alert, Polymers/Ceramics/Composites Alert,* and *Engineered Materials Abstracts*. (Formerly produced by ASM International.).

DIRECTORIES

Directory of European Importers of Machinery for Glass and Ceramic Industry. EXIM Infotek Private Ltd. • $150 Individuals. Covers: 20 European importers of ceramic industry equipment and supplies, glass making machinery and equipment. Entries include: Company name, postal address, telephone, fax, e-mail, website, contact person, designation, and product details.

Kompass. Kompass Deutschland Verlags- und Vertriebsgesellschaft, mbH. • Annual. $88. Covers: German products and companies specializing in coal extraction, ore mining, quarries, cement industry, glass and ceramics.

ONLINE DATABASES

Applied Science and Technology Index Online. H.W. Wilson Co. • Provides online indexing of 500 major scientific, technical, industrial, and engineering periodicals. Time period is 1983 to date. Monthly updates. Inquire as to online cost and availability.

Engineered Materials Abstracts (online). Cambridge Scientific Abstracts L.P. • Provides online citations to the technical and engineering literature of plastic, ceramic, and composite materials. Time period is 1986 to date, with monthly updates. (Formerly produced by ASM International.) Inquire as to online cost and availability.

PERIODICALS AND NEWSLETTERS

American Ceramic Society Bulletin. American Ceramic Society. • 9/year. $95 U.S. and Canada nonmembers. Contains items of interest to the ceramics community, and provides current information on R&D, technology, manufacturing, engineered ceramics, fuel cells, nanotechnology, glass, refractories, environmental concerns, whitewares, etc. Bulletin publishes "the Glass Researcher" as a quarterly feature section. The December issue of Bulletin includes ceramic Source, an annual buyer's guide.

American Ceramic Society Journal. American Ceramic Society. • Monthly. Members, $150.00 per year; non-members, $750.00 per year. Includes subscription to *Ceramic Bulletin and Abstracts*.

Ceramic Industries International. Turret Group Ltd. • Bimonthly. $94.00. per year.

Ceramic Industry: The Magazine for Refractories, Traditional and Advanced Ceramic Manufacturers. BNP Media. • Monthly. Includes *Data Buyers Guide, Materials Handbook, Economic Forecast*, and *Giants in Ceramic*.

Ceramics Monthly. American Ceramic Society. • $34.95 Individuals. Consumer magazine containing ceramic art and craft. Features articles on ceramic artists, exhibitions, production processes, critical commentary, book and video reviews, clay and glaze recipes, and kiln designs.

High-Tech Materials Alert: Advanced Materials: Their Uses and Manufacture. Technical Insights. • Monthly. Institutions, $695.00 per year. Newsletter on technical developments relating to high-performance materials, including metals and ceramics. Includes market forecasts.

RESEARCH CENTERS AND INSTITUTES

Massachusetts Institute of Technology - Materials Processing Center. 77 Massachusetts Ave., Cambridge, MA 02139-4301. Phone: (617)253-5179; Fax: (617)258-6900; Email: cthomp@mit.edu • URL: http://mpc-web.mit.edu • Conducts processing, engineering, and economic research in ferrous and nonferrous metals, ceramics, polymers, photonic materials, superconductors, welding, composite materials, and other materials.

STATISTICS SOURCES

Refractories. U. S. Bureau of the Census. • Annual. Provides data on value of manufacturers' shipments, quantity, exports, imports, etc. (Current Industrial Reports, MA-32C.).

TRADE/PROFESSIONAL ASSOCIATIONS

American Ceramic Society. 600 N Cleveland Ave., Ste. 210, Westerville, OH 43082. Phone: 866-721-3322 or (240)646-7054; Fax: (204)396-5637; Email: customerservice@ceramics.org • URL: http://www.ceramics.org • Formerly National Institute of Ceramic Engineers.

CEREAL INDUSTRY

See GRAIN INDUSTRY

CERTIFIED PUBLIC ACCOUNTANTS

See also ACCOUNTING; WOMEN ACCOUNTANTS

ABSTRACTS AND INDEXES

Accounting and Tax Index. ProQuest L.L.C. • Quarterly. Indexes accounting, auditing, and taxation literature appearing in journals, books, pamphlets, conference proceedings, and newsletters.

Accounting Articles. Wolters Kluwer Law & Business CCH. • Monthly. $624. Covers accounting news.

CD-ROM DATABASES

The Tax Directory. Tax Analysts. • Quarterly. $499 Individuals both volumes, web, CD or print. Updated quarterly on CD-ROM and in print; updated continually online. Covering federal, state, and international tax officials, tax practitioners, and corporate tax executives.

DIRECTORIES

Emerson's Directory of Leading U.S. Accounting Firms. Emerson Co. • Biennial. $195.00. Provides information on 500 major CPA firms.

The Tax Directory. Tax Analysts. • Quarterly. $499 Individuals both volumes, web, CD or print. Updated quarterly on CD-ROM and in print; updated continually online. Covering federal, state, and international tax officials, tax practitioners, and corporate tax executives.

HANDBOOKS AND MANUALS

Accountant's Business Manual. American Institute of Certified Public Accountants. • $198.75. Looseleaf. Two volumes. Semiannual updates. Covers a wide variety of topics relating to financial and accounting management, including types of ownership, business planning, financing, cash management, valuation, retirement plans, estate planning, workers' compensation, unemployment insurance, social security, and employee benefits management.

Accountants' Liability. Practising Law Institute. • $335 free shipping. Covers all aspects of accountants' professional liability issues, including depositions and court cases.

INTERNET DATABASES

Rutgers Accounting Web. Rutgers University Accounting Research Center. Phone: (973)353-5172; Fax: (973)353-1283 • URL: http://www.rutgers.edu/accounting • RAW Web site provides extensive links to sources of national and international accounting information, such as the Big Six accounting firms, the Financial Accounting Standards Board (FASB), SEC filings (EDGAR), journals, publishers, software, the International Accounting Network, and "Internet's largest list of accounting firms in USA." Searching is offered. Fees: Free.

OTHER SOURCES

Andrews' Professional Liability Litigation Reporter. Andrews Publications. • Monthly. $550.00 per year. Provides reports on lawsuits against attorneys, accountants, and investment professionals.

PERIODICALS AND NEWSLETTERS

The CPA Journal. New York State Society of Certified Public Accountants. • Monthly. $150 Individuals U.S.. Provides analysis, perspective, and debate on the issues affecting the financial world.

CPA Managing Partner Report: Management News for Accounting Executives. Strafford Publications Inc. • Monthly. $396.00 per year. Newsletter. Covers practice management and professional relationships.

Journal of Accountancy. American Institute of Certified Public Accountants. • Monthly. $75 Individuals. Accounting journal.

Main Street Practitioner. National Society of Accountants. • Bimonthly. For accounting and tax practitioners.

The Practical Accountant: Providing the Competitive Edge. SourceMedia Inc. • Monthly. $65.00 per year. Covers tax planning, financial planning, practice management, client relationships, and related topics.

Public Accounting Report: Competitive Intelligence for Accounting Firms. Strafford Publications Inc. • Presents news and trends affecting the accounting profession.

Tax Practice. Tax Analysts. • Weekly. $199.00 per year. Newsletter. Covers news affecting tax practitioners and litigators, with emphasis on federal court decisions, rules and regulations, and tax petitions. Provides a guide to Internal Revenue Service audit issues.

RESEARCH CENTERS AND INSTITUTES

Accounting Research Program. UCLA Anderson School of Management, 110 Westwood Plz., Los Angeles, CA 90095-1481. Phone: (310)206-8711; Fax: (310)825-3165 • URL: http://www.anderson.ucla.edu.

STATISTICS SOURCES

U.S. Industry and Trade Outlook. U.S. Department of Commerce National Technical Information Service. • Annual. Produced by the International Trade Administration, U.S. Department of Commerce, in a "public-private" partnership with DRI/McGraw-Hill and Standard & Poor's. Provides basic data, outlook for the current year, and "Long-Term Prospects" (five-year projections) for a wide variety of products and services. Includes high technology industries. Formerly *U.S. Industrial Outlook.*

TRADE/PROFESSIONAL ASSOCIATIONS

American Institute of Certified Public Accountants. 1211 Avenue of the Americas, New York, NY 10036-8775. Phone: 888-777-7077 or (212)596-6200; Fax: (212)596-6213; Email: service@aicpa.org • URL: http://www.aicpa.org • Professional society of accountants certified by the states and territories. Responsibilities include establishing auditing and reporting standards; influencing the development of financial accounting standards underlying the presentation of U.S. corporate financial statements; preparing and grading the national Uniform CPA Examination for the state licensing bodies. Conducts research and continuing education programs and oversight of practice. Maintains over 100 committees including Accounting Standards, Accounting and Review Services, AICPA Effective Legislation Political Action, Auditing Standards, Taxation, Consulting Services, Professional Ethics, Quality Review, Women and Family Issues, and Information Technology.

American Woman's Society of Certified Public Accountants. 136 S Keowee St., Dayton, OH 45402. Phone: 800-297-2721 or (937)222-1872; Fax: (937)222-5794; Email: info@awscpa.org • URL: http://www.awscpa.org • Citizens who hold Certified Public Accountant certificates as well as those who have passed the CPA examination but do not have certificates. Works to improve the status of professional women and to make the business community aware of the professional capabilities of the woman CPA. Conducts semiannual statistical survey of members; offers specialized education and research programs.

National Association of State Boards of Accountancy. 150 4th Ave. N, Ste. 700, Nashville, TN 37219-2417. Phone: 866-MY-NASBA or (615)880-4200; Fax: (615)880-4290; Email: cbtcpa@nasba.org • URL: http://nasba.org • Formerly Association of Certified Public Accountants.

National Society of Accountants. 1010 N Fairfax St., Alexandria, VA 22314. Phone: 800-966-6679 or (703)549-6400; Fax: (703)549-2984; Email: members@nsacct.org • URL: http://www.nsacct.org • Formerly *National Society of Public Accountants.*

CHAIN STORES

See also DISCOUNT HOUSES; DRUG STORES; FRANCHISES; RETAIL TRADE

CD-ROM DATABASES

OECD Statistical Compendium. Organization for Economic Cooperation and Development. • Semiannual. $1,905.00 per year for 1 to 10 users. CD-ROM contains more than 730,000 monthly, quarterly, and annual time series for OECD countries, 1960 to date. Includes fully searchable data on agriculture, food, economic indicators, national accounts, employment, energy, finance, industry, technology, and foreign trade. Results can be displayed in various forms.

DIRECTORIES

Directory of Retail Chains in Canada. Rogers Publishing Ltd. • Annual Monthly. $1,399 print and online. Provides detailed information on approximately 2,500 retail chains of all sizes in Canada.

Discount Store News - Top Chains. Lebhar-Friedman Inc. • Annual. $79.00.

National Association of Chain Drug Stores - Communications Directory. National Association of Chain Drug Stores. • Annual. Membership. About 150 chain drug retailers and their 31,000 individual pharmacies; 900 supplier companies; state boards of pharmacy, pharmaceutical and retail associations, colleges of pharmacy; drug trade associations.

Subsidiaries of German Firms in the U.S. German American Chamber of Commerce. • Annual. $100 Members. Covers: Over 3,500 German firms and subsidiaries in the U.S. Entries include: Name, address, phone, and telex of American firm; name and address of German parent company; percentage of German participation; number of employees; type of company (manufacturer, sales agent, etc.); and products.

INTERNET DATABASES

Business 2.0 Web Guide to the Best Business Links. Business 2.0 Media Inc. Phone: (415)293-4800; Email: support@business2.com • URL: http://www.business2.com/webguide • Web site presents an extensive, searchable directory of links to "the best, most informative, and authoritative web pages." Twenty main categories cover business, finance, career, company information, people, and technology topics, with thousands of subtopics, all linking to Web sites recommended by experienced business researchers. Fees: Free.

Fedstats. Federal Interagency Council on Statistical Policy. Phone: (202)395-7254 • URL: http://www.fedstats.gov • Web site features an efficient search facility for full-text statistics produced by more than 100 federal agencies, including the Census Bureau, the Bureau of Economic Analysis, and the Bureau of Labor Statistics. Boolean searches can be made within one agency or for all agencies combined. Links are offered to international statistical bureaus, including the UN, IMF, OECD, UNESCO, Eurostat, and 20 individual countries. Fees: Free.

FreeLunch.com. Economy.com, Inc. Phone: (610)696-8700; Fax: (610)696-1678 • URL: http://www.freelunch.com • Web site provides free access to more than 200 million economic and financial data series, covering industry, demographics, labor markets, prices, retail sales, government spending, trade, interest rates, housing starts, the stock market, etc. Data is available in either chart or table form. Searching is offered. Free, but registration required. Economy.com, Inc. also offers fee-based economic analysis at *The Dismal Scientist* site (www.dismal.com).

PERIODICALS AND NEWSLETTERS

Chain Drug Review: The Reporter for the Chain Drug Store Industry. Racher Press Inc. • $199 Institutions. Covers news and trends of concern to the chain drug store industry. Includes special articles on OTC (over-the-counter) drugs.

Chain Store Age: The NewsMagazine for Retail Executives. Lebhar-Friedman Inc. • 9/year. Formerly *Chain Store Age Executive with Shopping Center Age.*

Drug Topics. Thomson Medical Economics. • Monthly. Edited for retail pharmacists, hospital pharmacists, pharmacy chain store executives, wholesalers, buyers, and others concerned with drug dispensing and drug store management. Provides information on new products, including personal care items and cosmetics.

Franchising World. International Franchise Association. • Monthly. $50 Individuals. Trade magazine covering topics of interest to franchise company executives and the business world. Formerly *Franchising Opportunities.*

Retail Pharmacy Management. McMahon Group. • Monthly. $60.00 per year. Featues include product news for pharmacists and financial news for chain store executives. Formerly *Retail Pharmacy Management News.*

Retailing Today: The Newspaper of Discount Retailing; The News Source for Power Retailing. Lebhar-Friedman Inc. • Semimonthly. $119 Individuals. Retailing business industry news and information.

Stores. National Retail Federation. NRF Enterprises Inc. • Monthly. Offers an insider's view of the entire retail industry by featuring the latest trends, hottest ideas, current technologies and consumer attitudes.

Value Retail News: The Journal of Outlet and Off-Price Retail and Development. Off-Price Specialists, Inc. Value Retail News. • Monthly. $99 Members. Provides news of the off-price and outlet store industry. Emphasis is on real estate for outlet store centers.

RESEARCH CENTERS AND INSTITUTES

Northwestern University - Center for Retail Management. Kellogg School of Management, 2001 Sheridan Rd., Evanston, IL 60208. Phone: (847)467-3600; Fax: (847)467-3620; Email: r-blattberg@kellogg.northwestern.edu • URL: http://www.kellogg.northwestern.edu/research/retail/ • Conducts research related to retail marketing and management.

Texas A&M University - Center for Retailing Studies. Wehner Bldg., Ste. 201, Mays Business School, 4112 TAMU, College Station, TX 77843-4112. Phone: (979)845-0325; Fax: (979)845-5117 or (979)845-5230; Email: c-bridges@mays.tamu.edu • URL: http://www.crstamu.org • Research areas include retailing issues and consumer economics.

STATISTICS SOURCES

Survey of Current Business. U. S. Government Printing Office. • Published by Bureau of Economic Analysis, U. S. Department of Commerce. Presents a wide variety of business and economic data.

TRADE/PROFESSIONAL ASSOCIATIONS

CIES, The Food Business Forum. 8455 Colesville Rd., Ste. 705, Silver Spring, MD 20910-3318. Phone: (301)563-3383; Fax: (301)563-3386; Email: washington@theconsumergoodsforum.com • URL: http://www.ciesnet.com • Membership in 44 countries includes: food industry chain store firms with combined outlets of over 100,000; associations; firms supplying articles and services to chain food stores. Fosters cooperation between chain store organizations and their suppliers. Serves as a liaison between members. Assists in the exchange of trainees among member firms. Conducts studies on methods, technical progress, and the growth rate of chain store organizations throughout the world.

National Association of Chain Drug Stores. 1776 Wilson Blvd., Ste. 200, Arlington, VA 22209. Phone: (703)549-3001; Fax: (703)836-4869; Email: contactus@nacds.org • URL: http://www.nacds.org • Represents the concerns of community pharmacies in Washington, in state capitals, and across the country. Members are more than 210 chain community pharmacy companies. Collectively, community pharmacy comprises the largest component of pharmacy practice with over 107,000 FTE pharmacists.

CHAMBERS OF COMMERCE

DIRECTORIES

Athens Area Chamber of Commerce Membership Directory. Athens Area Chamber of Commerce. • Lists member businesses in Athens, Georgia. Publication includes directory details for largest employers, retail centers, chamber member realtors and banks.

Atlanta Business Chronicle's Book of Lists. Metro Atlanta Chamber of Commerce. • $49.95 Individuals. Lists companies in the Atlanta business community, including sections on business and industry, business services, commercial real estate, education and human resources, finance, general interests, healthcare, hospitality and travel, marketing, residential real estate and technology sections. Entries include name, address, phone, fax, facts and figures, and detailed information.

Austria in U.S.A. American Chamber of Commerce in Austria. • Periodic. €150 Members. Covers: 550 Austrian companies with U.S. Subsidiaries, branch offices, associates, joint ventures, or representations in the U.S.; American representations and Austrian-American organizations in Austria, Austrian representations in the U.S., American Chambers of Commerce in Europe, and the representation of American states in Europe. Entries include: For companies--Name, address, phone; name, address, phone of U.S. Affiliated company; name of the Austrian company's general manager; a brief description of the U.S. Company; type of business and nature of relationship.

Big Business in Metro Detroit. Detroit Regional Chamber. • Covers: More than 1,500 businesses and agencies which represent the largest employers in Metro Detroit, Michigan. Entries include: Company name, address, phone, SIC code, fax, product description, e-mail, and website.

Birmingham and Solihull Business Guide and Directory. Kemps Publishing Ltd. • Annual. Covers: Chamber of Commerce listings in Birmingham and Solihull, Great Britain. Entries include: Name, address, phone, fax.

Blowing Rock Chamber of Commerce--Chamber Businesses. Blowing Rock Chamber of Commerce. • Annual. Listing of businesses in Blowing Rock, North Carolina.

Bolivia--American Chamber of Commerce--Membership Directory. U.S. Chamber of Commerce. • Annual. Covers: American and Bolivian companies and individuals interested in the development of trade within and between the two countries. Entries include: For firms--Company name, address, phone, fax, telex, cable address, names and titles of key personnel, line of business, subsidiary and branch names and locations, locations of plants or branch offices, product/service information. For individuals--Name, title, affiliation, address. Plus details on Bolivia's investment climate, economic indicators, new land reform laws, and trade agreement obligations.

Business and Information Directory. Buena Vista Area Chamber of Commerce. • Annual. Covers business in Buena Vista, CO.

Business and Professional Organizations Directory. Nashville Area Chamber of Commerce. • $25 Members. Covers 300 business and professional organizations in 10-county Nashville Metropolitan area.

Business Directory. Cerritos Chamber of Commerce. • Annual.

Business Directory. Arcadia Chamber of Commerce. • Biennial.

Business Directory of the Parry Sound Area. Parry Sound Area Chamber of Commerce. • Covers businesses in Parry Sound, Ontario, Canada. Entries include contact details.

Business News. DeSoto Chamber of Commerce. • Monthly.

Business Referral. Palm Springs Chamber of Commerce. • Annual. Covers businesses in the Palm Springs, CA area.

Business Reporter. Atascadero Chamber of Commerce. • 11/year.

Carson City Area Chamber of Commerce--Membership Business Directory. Carson City Area Chamber of Commerce. • Covers: Approximately 850 community profile and business listing member businesses in the greater Carson City, Nevada area. Entries include: Company name, address, phone, name and title of contact, products and services.

Cary Chamber of Commerce Member Directory. Cary Chamber of Commerce. • Covers chamber member businesses employing more than 100 people. Entries include company name, address, phone, fax, website, headquarters location, description of business.

Chamber of Commerce of Hawaii--Business Networking Directory. Chamber of Commerce of Hawaii. • Covers: Approximately 2,000 member businesses in Hawaii; approximately 20 associate regional and ethnic chambers of commerce and affiliate organizations. Entries include: Firm name; address; phone; e-mail; website; name, and title of key contact.

Chamber of Commerce of the Bellmores Business and Professional Directory. Chamber of Commerce of the Bellmores. • Covers: All current members.

Crescenta Valley Chamber of Commerce Business Directory. Crescenta Valley Chamber of Commerce. • Covers: Member companies and organizations in La Crescenta, La Canada, Montrose, Sunland, and Tujunga, California. Entries include: Company or organization name, address, phone.

Decatur Chamber of Commerce Business Directory. Greater Decatur Chamber of Commerce. • Covers chamber members. Entries include name, address, phone.

Delaware Directory of Commerce and Industry. Delaware State Chamber of Commerce Inc. • Periodic Annual. $50 Members per additional copy for members. Covers: About 5,000 manufacturers, retailers, wholesalers, and service establishments. Entries include: Name, address, phone, name, address, phone, name and title of contact, list of products or services.

Dominican Republic--American Chamber of Commerce--Membership Directory. U.S. Chamber of Commerce. • Covers: American and Dominican Republic companies and individuals interested in the development of trade within and between the two countries. Entries include: For firms--Company name, address, phone, fax, telex, cable address, names and titles of key personnel, line of business, subsidiary and branch names and locations, locations of plants or branch offices, product/service information. For individuals--Name, title, affiliation, address.

Dublin Business. Dublin Chamber of Commerce. • Quarterly.

Durban Regional Chamber of Business--Directory. Durban Regional Chamber of Business. • Covers: about 7,500 businesses in the Durban, South Africa area; welfare organizations in Natal and businesses outside Natal (associate members). Entries include: Company name, address, phone, telex, fax, products or services.

East Midlands Chambers of Commerce Business Directory. Kemps Publishing Ltd. • Annual. Covers: Chamber of Commerce listings in East Midlands, Great Britain. Entries include: Name, address, phone, fax.

Edmonds Chamber of Commerce Preferred Business Directory. Greater Edmonds Chamber of Commerce. • Annual. Covers member businesses in Edmonds, Washington. Entries include contact details.

El Salvador--American Chamber of Commerce--Membership Directory. U.S. Chamber of Commerce. • Annual. $100 Nonmembers for investment. Covers: Companies in the U.S. and El Salvador and individuals interested in the development of trade, labor law, investment regulations, economic trends, and foreign policy within and between the two countries. Entries include: For firms--Company, name, address, phone, fax, telex, cable address, names and titles of key personnel, line of business, subsidiary and branch names and locations, locations of plants or branch offices, product/service information. For individuals--Name, title, affiliation, address.

Greater Cincinnati Chamber of Commerce--Cincinnati USA Business Connections Directory. Greater Cincinnati Chamber of Commerce. • Covers: Over 5,000 member firms in the Greater Cincinnati area (Hamilton, Clermont, Butler, Brown, and Warren counties in Ohio; Boone, Campbell, Grant, Gallatin, Pendleton, and Kenton counties in Kentucky; Dearborn and Ohio counties in Indiana). Entries include: Company name, address, phone, market area, names and titles of principal executives, number of employees, product/service, Standard Industrial Classification (SIC) code, date established, whether firm imports or exports, branches, parent company, annual sales, whether publicly or privately held.

Greater Dover Chamber of Commerce Business Directory. Greater Dover Chamber of Commerce. • Covers: Member businesses in New Hampshire. Entries include: Company name, address, phone, name of contact, category of product or service.

Greater San Diego Chamber of Commerce Business Referral Directory. San Diego Regional Chamber of Commerce. • Covers: Approximately 4,500 member businesses in San Diego, California. Entries include: Company name, address, phone, name and title of contact, products or services.

Greater Windham Chamber of Commerce--Annual Business and Pleasure Guide. Sebago Lakes Region Chamber of Commerce. • Annual. Covers: Attractions for business or pleasure in Windham, Maine.

Havre de Grace Chamber of Commerce Directory and Business Guide. Havre de Grace Chamber of Commerce. • Annual. Covers: List of members and information on the area's history.

Indiana Chamber of Commerce--Business Directory & Resource Guide. Indiana Chamber of Commerce. • Covers: Approximately 5,000 member businesses; state agencies and institutions that offer business assistance services in Indiana. Entries include: For agencies and institutions--Name, address, phone, description of services. For businesses--Business name, address, phone, name and title of contact, products or services.

Indo-German Business Directory. Indo-German Chamber of Commerce. • Rs 1,500 for nonmembers. Includes profiles of more than 6500 members of the Indo-German Chamber of Commerce.

International Business Lawyers Index/Industrial Property/Chambers of Commerce. Datapress Ltd. • Biennial. $35. Covers: 10,000 business lawyers, 10,000 chambers of commerce and industry, 2,000 official industrial property agencies, and 110 state property agencies for 140 countries. Entries include: Name, address, phone, telex numbers.

LaPorte Business Resource Guide. Greater La Porte Chamber of Commerce. • Annual. Covers businesses, professional firms, and individuals in La Porte, IN.

Las Vegas Chamber of Commerce--Business Directory. Las Vegas Metro Chamber of Commerce. • Covers: Businesses in Las Vegas, Nevada, who are chamber members. Entries include: Company name, address, phone, contact name.

Lewiston Chamber Business Directory. Lewiston Chamber of Commerce. • Covers: About 600 manufacturing and service companies in the Lewiston area. Entries include: Name, address, phone, fax, contact person.

Membership Directory and Business Guide for Huntsville and Madison County. Chamber of Commerce of Huntsville/Madison County. • Covers 2,100 businesses in Huntsville and Madison county.

Metro Atlanta Chamber of Commerce--Who's Who in Metro Atlanta Business. Metro Atlanta Chamber of Commerce. • Covers: Over 5,000 member firms in Atlanta, Georgia. Entries include: Company or firm name, address, phone, name of contact, and description of products or services.

Mill Valley Business Directory. Mill Valley Chamber of Commerce. • Covers: Businesses, information centers, and conferences in Mill Valley, CA.

Monterey Peninsula Chamber of Commerce--Membership Directory & Business Referral Guide. Monterey Peninsula Chamber of Commerce. • Annual. Contains business organizations and members of the association.

Moorpark Chamber of Commerce--Business Directory. Moorpark Chamber of Commerce. • Annual. Business organizations in Moorpark, California.

New Bern Area Guide and Business. New Bern Area Chamber of Commerce. • Annual. Covers businesses in New Bern/Craven County, NC.

Northern California Business Directory. Harris InfoSource. • $198 Members. Covers manufacturers, wholesalers and service businesses in the 45 counties north of San Luis Obispo, California. Entries include: Company profile, owners, names and titles of key personnel.

Novi Chamber of Commerce--Business Directory. Novi Chamber of Commerce. • Annual. Covers: Member businesses in Novi, Michigan.

Palos Verdes Peninsula Chamber of Commerce and Visitors' Center--Business Directory and Community Guide. Palos Verdes Peninsula Chamber of Commerce and Visitors' Center. • Business organizations in Palos Verdes Hills, California.

PennSuburban Chamber of Commerce--Membership Directory. PennSuburban Chamber of Commerce. • Annual. Covers: Over 900 member businesses and industries in Montgomery, Bucks, and Chester counties in Pennsylvania. Entries include: Company name, address, phone, names and titles of key personnel, number of employees, product or service provided.

Regional Business Directory. Business Service Div. Birmingham Area Chamber of Commerce. • Covers: Approximately 4,000 businesses that are members of the area Chamber of Commerce. Entries include: Company name, address, phone, name and title of contact.

St. George Area Chamber of Commerce Business Directory. St. George Area Chamber of Commerce. • Covers businesses, attractions, and history of the St. George, Utah, area.

St. Paul Area Chamber of Commerce--Membership Directory and Business Resource Guide. Saint Paul Area Chamber of Commerce. • Annual. Covers: 2,100 members of the St. Paul Area Chamber of Commerce. Entries include: Company name, address, phone, name of principal executive, product or service provided, website address, e-mail address.

Salem Area Chamber of Commerce Business Directory and Resource Guide. Salem Area Chamber of Commerce. • Annual. Covers 1,250 businesses and organizations in Salem, OR.

San Francisco Bay Area Silicon Valley International Business Directory. San Francisco Chamber of Commerce. • $45 Members. Covers international businesses based in the San Francisco Bay/Silicon Valley area. Entries include contact details, parent companies, products and services.

Shingle Springs/Cameron Park Chamber of Commerce Business Directory. Shingle Springs/ Cameron Park Chamber of Commerce. • Complete business listings, shopping information, and history of the Shingle Springs and Cameron Park areas of California.

Singapore International Chamber of Commerce. Singapore International Chamber of Commerce. • Annual. $15 Nonmembers. Covers: Singapore Chamber of Commerce members. Entries include: Members' addresses and their type of business.

Skagway Business Directory. Skagway Chamber of Commerce. • Annual. Covers: Comprehensive listing of area businesses.

Somerset County Chamber of Commerce Business Directory. Somerset County Chamber of Commerce. • Covers: Area businesses.

South Carolina Chamber of Commerce Business Directory & Resource Guide. South Carolina Chamber of Commerce. • Covers: Member businesses, chambers of commerce, and professional and trade associations in South Carolina.

Swansea Business Directory. Burrows Publishing Ltd. • $27 Individuals with CD-ROM. Covers over 2,000 local companies trading in the city and county of Swansea, U.K.

Trinidad & Tobago--American Chamber of Commerce--Membership Directory. U.S. Chamber of Commerce. • Annual. $80 Individuals. Covers: Companies in the U.S. and Trinidad and Tobago and individuals interested in the development of trade within and between the two countries. Entries include: For firms--Company name, address, phone, fax, telex, cable address, names and titles of key personnel, line of business, subsidiary and branch names and locations, locations of plants or branch offices, product/service information. For individuals--Name, title, affiliation, address.

Tulsa Chamber Membership Directory. • Covers Tulsa Metro Chamber of Commerce membership roster.

Tulsa Metropolitan Chamber Business Directory and Buyer's Guide. Mary Brett & Associates/Image Publishing. • Covers: about 3,500 companies; federal, state, and local government agencies and officials, schools, and associations in the greater Tulsa, Oklahoma area. Entries include: Company, institution, organization, or individual name, address, phone.

TwinWest Chamber of Commerce--Membership Directory & Business Guide. TwinWest Chamber of Commerce. • Annual. Cvers 1,000 businesses and industries ranging from nationally and internationally renowned corporations and industrially driven manufacturers, to home-based businesses and companies involved in the service and professional sectors.

Tyne & Wear Chamber Regional Business Directory. Ten Alps Publishing. • Covers: businesses in Tyne and Wear, England. Entries include: Company name, address, phone, telex, fax, description of products or services.

Wabash Business Directory. Wabash Area Chamber of Commerce. • Covers businesses and industrial businesses in Wabash, Indiana. Entries include contact details.

Who's Who in Business. Bixby Metro Chamber of Commerce. • Annual. $20 for nonmembers. Covers businesses in Marion County, FL.

World Chamber of Commerce Directory. • Annual. $50.00.

Wytheville Chamber of Commerce Business Directory. Wytheville-Wythe-Bland Chamber of Commerce. • Covers: List of members. Entries include: name, address, phone.

York County Regional Chamber of Commerce Business Directory. York County Regional Chamber of Commerce. • Covers: Information on all York County, New York, businesses.

GENERAL WORKS

Barbados Chamber of Commerce and Industry. • Businesses, business and trade promotion organizations, and individuals with an interest in promoting trade and commerce in Barbados. Seeks to improve domestic business conditions and increase foreign trade. Facilitates communication among members; functions as liaison between members and government agencies and international business organizations. Gathers and disseminates business and trade information; compiles statistics. Administers Duty Free Scheme in Barbados.

All About Folsom Business. Folsom Chamber of Commerce. • Monthly. Contains updates on current and upcoming events and new members.

Annual Business and Pleasure Guide. Sebago Lakes Region Chamber of Commerce. • Annual. Covers businesses in Windham and the Sebago Lake Region.

Area Business Councils/Small Business Update. Greater San Antonio Chamber of Commerce. • Weekly.

Barbados Business Directory. Barbados Chamber of Commerce and Industry. • Biennial. Serves as a concise business reference.

Batavia Business. Batavia Chamber of Commerce. • Monthly. Contains information on businesses in Batavia.

Business. Albany Area Chamber of Commerce - Georgia. • Bimonthly. $50 Nonmembers /year. Contains chamber activities and items of interest to businesses.

Business Connection. Russellville Chamber of Commerce. • Quarterly.

Business Focus. Bunbury Chamber of Commerce and Industries. • Contains articles and reports about the Bunbury Chamber of Commerce and Industries organization's works and accomplishments.

Business Guide to Trinidad & Tobago. American Chamber of Commerce of Trinidad and Tobago. • Biennial. $50. Contains market entry information for foreign companies doing business in Trinidad and Tobago.

The Business Link. Union County Chamber of Commerce. • Bimonthly. Provides updates on Chamber and member activities and events.

Business Matters. Chapel Hill - Carrboro Chamber of Commerce. • Bimonthly. Provides weekly events, government updates, and chamber news.

Business News. Bainbridge Island Chamber of Commerce. • Monthly. Includes issues about the business community and information about the chamber.

Downey Business. Downey Chamber of Commerce. • Monthly. Features updates on chamber activities, future events and business community news.

Hatboro Online Business Directory. Greater Hatboro Chamber of Commerce. • $170 /year for members. Highlights participating businesses and services in the Greater Hatboro area.

In Business for Yourself. Nashville Area Chamber of Commerce. • List of businesses located in Nashville, TN.

Kyle Area Chamber of Commerce Business Directory and Guidebook. Kyle Area Chamber of Commerce and Visitors' Bureau. • Biennial. Covers businesses in the city of Kyle.

Main Line Chamber of Commerce--Membership Directory and Business Resource Guide. Main Line Chamber of Commerce. • Annual. $10 Members.

Covers bsinesses in Chester, Delaware, and Montgomery counties, PA.

North Houston Greenspoint Business. Houston Intercontinental Chamber of Commerce. • Annual. Includes information on member firms.

North Mobile Business. Saraland Area Chamber of Commerce. • Biennial. Lists businesses in Saraland/ North Mobile, AL.

North Shore Business Journal. North Shore Chamber of Commerce. • Monthly. Includes information, updates of the chamber's events and other articles concerning North Shore Chamber of Commerce.

Richmond Business Directory. City of Richmond Business and Development Division. • Lists resident businesses with valid business license.

Southern Ulster County Chamber of Commerce Business Directory. Southern Ulster County Chamber of Commerce. • Annual. Covers bsinesses and local organizations in southern Ulster County, NY.

The Tri-County Business Advocate. Arcade Area Chamber of Commerce. • Quarterly. Contains latest news and events about Arcade Area Chamber of Commerce.

Voice of Business. Mesquite Chamber of Commerce and Convention and Visitors Bureau.

Who's Who Greater Norwalk Business Directory. Greater Norwalk Chamber of Commerce. • Annual. $525 Individuals employees. Businesses, community phone numbers, and regional information about the greater Norwalk, CT area.

PERIODICALS AND NEWSLETTERS

Anaheim Business Advocate. Anaheim Chamber of Commerce. • Monthly.

The Business Advisor. South Metro Regional Chamber of Commerce. • Monthly. South Metro Regional Chamber news and information.

Business News. Bainbridge Island Chamber of Commerce. • Monthly. Includes issues about the business community and information about the chamber.

Business Notes. Tallmadge Chamber of Commerce. • Monthly. Includes reports and other artcles concerning Tallmadge Chamber of Commerce.

Carlsbad Business Journal. Carlsbad Chamber of Commerce. • Monthly.

Chamber Business Monthly. South Snohomish County Chamber of Commerce. • Monthly.

Commerce News: Reaching Edmonton's Entire Business Community. Edmonton Chamber of Commerce. • Monthly. Commerce News. Magazine (tabloid) for Edmonton's business community.

TRADE/PROFESSIONAL ASSOCIATIONS

ACT and Region Chamber of Commerce and Industry. 12a Thesiger Ct., Canberra, ACT 2600, Australia. Phone: 61 2 62835200; Fax: 61 2 62822436; Email: chamber@actchamber.com.au • URL: http://www.actchamber.com.au • Represents businesses in the Australian Capital Territory of Australia.

American Chamber of Commerce Executives. 1330 Braddock Pl., Ste. 300, Alexandria, VA 22314. Phone: 888-577-9883 or (703)998-0072; Email: hero@acce.org • URL: http://www.acce.org • Professional society of chamber of commerce executives and staff members.

American Chamber of Commerce in Lithuania. Konstitucijos 7, 10th Fl., LT-09308 Vilnius, Lithuania. Phone: 370 5 2611181; Email: acc@iti.lt • URL: http://www.amcham.lt • American, international, and Lithuanian corporations; interested organizations and individuals. Promotes members' common business interests. Strives to improve business climate in Lithuania. Provides referral service for new members; consults on investment and business environment.

American Chamber of Commerce in Moldova. 45 B, Puskin St., 3rd Fl., MD-2005 Chisinau, Moldova. Phone: 373 22 211781; Fax: 373 22 211782; Email: info@amcham.md • URL: http://www.amcham.md • Open to all business leaders with a common interest in improving the business climate in Moldova and increasing foreign trade and investment with Moldova. Promotes American trade and investment in Moldova and works with the Moldovan government and business leaders to foster a more favorable business climate in Moldova for foreign trade and investment.

American Chamber of Commerce in the Kyrgyz Republic. Office No. 123, 191 Abdrakhmanov Str., 720011 Bishkek, Kyrgyzstan. Phone: 996 312 623389; Fax: 996 312 623406; Email: memberservices@amcham.kg • URL: http://www.amcham.kg • Represents foreign and local companies. Fosters a favorable business climate for local and foreign companies by promoting members' businesses and lobbying for their interests. Works on different areas such as corruption fighting, business services and attraction of foreign investment.

American Chamber of Commerce to the European Union. Ave. des Arts/Kunstlaan 53, B-1000 Brussels, Belgium. Phone: 32 2 5136892; Fax: 32 2 5137928; Email: info@amchameu.eu • URL: http://www.amchameu.eu • Works to represent the companies of American parentage committed to Europe towards the institutions and governments of the European Union. Helps improve the business and investment climate in Europe. Facilitates the resolution of EU - US issues that impact business and plays a role in creating better understanding of EU and US positions on business matters.

Argentina Israel Chamber of Commerce. Phone: 54 11 43726273; Email: info@ccai.com.ar • URL: http://www.ccai.com.ar • Promotes trade between Argentina and Israel.

Argentine-American Chamber of Commerce. 150 E 58th St., New York, NY 10155. Phone: (212)698-2238; Fax: (212)698-1144; Email: info@argentinechamber.org • URL: http://www.argentinechamber.org • Promotes business and trade between Argentina and the United States.

Associated Chambers of Commerce and Industry of India. Corporate Office, 5, Sardar Patel Marg, Chanakyapuri, New Delhi 110 021, Delhi, India. Phone: 91 11 46550555; Fax: 91 11 23017008; Email: assocham@nic.in • URL: http://www.assocham.org • Corporations, chambers of commerce, and business and trade organizations. Promotes increased international trade involving India. Works to ensure a domestic political and business climate conducive to trade; gathers and disseminates economic information.

Bunbury Chamber of Commerce and Industries. 15 Stirling St., Bunbury, WA 6230, Australia. Phone: 61 97912292; Fax: 61 97916646; Email: ceo@bcci.asn.au • URL: http://www.bunburycci.com.au • Represents business and industry in the South West region of Western Australia.

Business SA. 136 Greenhill Rd., Adelaide, SA 5061, Australia. Phone: 61 8 83000000; Fax: 61 8 83000001; Email: accoutsquery@business-sa.com • URL: http://business-sa.com • Represents businesses in South Australia; provides services to businesses and employers, including management of export transactions.

Cairns Chamber of Commerce. Ste. M2a, Mezzanine Level, The Pier, Pier Point Rd., Cairns, QLD 4870, Australia. Phone: 61 7 40311838; Fax: 61 7 40310883; Email: info@cairnschamber.com.au • URL: http://www.cairnschamber.com.au • Represents business in the Cairns region. Provides statistical and business advice. Works to attract investment and business relocation to the area. Provides trade and export support.

Camara de Comercio de la Republica de Cuba. Calle 21 esq. a Calle A, No. 661, Vedado, Havana, Cuba. Phone: 53 7 833-8040; Fax: 53 7 838-1324; Email: ccicuba@camara.com.cu • URL: http://www.camaracuba.cu • Represents trade, industry, finance, transport, insurance and all sectors of international businesses. Shapes policies and raises awareness of international business concerns. Fosters networking and cooperation among members.

China Environment Chamber of Commerce. 4 Districts Anhuili, 15th China Minmetals Tower, Rm. 1315, Chaoyang District, Beijing 100029, China. Phone: 86 10 84640865; Fax: 86 10 84649343; Email: cesia@cesia.org • URL: http://www.cecc-china.org • Aims to promote the sustainable development of China's environmental industry. Provides a platform for its members to share information and experience and discuss critical issues regarding environmental technology and policy.

Coffs Harbour Chamber of Commerce and Industry. The Promenade, 321 Harbour Dr., Coffs Harbour, NSW 2450, Australia. Phone: 61 2 66514101; Fax: 61 2 66514081; Email: info@coffschamber.com.au • URL: http://www.coffschamber.com.au • Represents the local interests of small, medium sized, and multinational organizations throughout the Coffs Harbour region.

Geelong Chamber of Commerce. 10 Moorabool St., Geelong, VIC 3220, Australia. Phone: 61 3 52222234; Fax: 61 3 52222235 • URL: http://www.geelongchamber.com.au • Represents businesses in Geelong and the Surfcoast region of Australia.

Hong Kong General Chamber of Commerce. 22nd Fl., United Ctr., 95 Queensway, Hong Kong, Hong Kong, China. Phone: 852 52 99229 or 852 28231236; Fax: 852 5279843; Email: chamber@chamber.org.hk • URL: http://www.chamber.org.hk/en/index.aspx • Businesses and industries that operates in Hong Kong. Seeks to protect and develop a trading climate conducive to members' interests; promotes investment in Hong Kong businesses. Facilitates international trade by: issuing certificates of origin for goods produced in Hong Kong; disseminating information about business, trade, and industrial opportunities in Hong Kong. Represents members' interests before government bodies; acts as a forum for exchange of information among members; informs members about proposed legislation of interest to the business community. Facilitates meetings between members and business visitors.

Kingdom Chamber of Commerce. 383 Kings Hwy. N, Ste. 201, Cherry Hill, NJ 08034. Phone: (856)414-0818; Fax: (856)414-6140; Email: partnerservices@kingdomchamberofcommerce.org • URL: http://www.kingdomchamberofcommerce.org • Christians who own and operate their own businesses; other Christian professionals. Seeks to: identify members in the Christian community; encourage fellowship and cooperation among members, ministries, and other organizations.

National United States-Arab Chamber of Commerce. 1023 15th St. NW, Ste. 400, Washington, DC 20005. Phone: (202)289-5920; Fax: (202)289-5938; Email: info@nusacc.org • URL: http://www.nusacc.org • Individuals, companies, corporations, and associations interested in commercial trade relations with the Arab world. Promotes business between the United States and the Arab world; encourages policies that promote better commercial relations. Conducts research and information services on commercial opportunities, export regulations, and conditions that affect the trade and investment climate. Sponsors trade delegations; holds seminars, conferences, and training sessions; acts as a central information center. Maintains relations with U.S. and Arab governments and agencies to develop, monitor, and recommend relevant legislation.

SwissCham Australia. 46 Market St., Ste. 303, Sydney, NSW 2000, Australia. Phone: 61 2 92621511; Fax: 61 2 92901928 • URL: http://www.swisscham.com.au • Represents Swiss business interests in Australia.

Tasmanian Chamber of Commerce and Industry. 309 Liverpool St., Hobart, TAS 7000, Australia. Phone: 61 3 62363600; Fax: 61 3 62311278; Email: admin@tcci.com.au • URL: http://www.tcci.com.au • Represents businesses in Tasmania, Australia.

U.S. Chamber of Commerce. 1615 H St. NW, Washington, DC 20062-2000. Phone: 800-638-6582 or (202)463-5500 or (202)659-6000; Fax: (202)463-3129; Email: foundation@uschamber.com • URL: http://www.uschambersmallbusinessnation.com • National federation of business organizations and companies. Membership includes chambers of commerce, trade and professional associations, and companies. Determines and makes known to the government the recommendations of the business community on national issues and problems affecting the economy and the future of the country. Works to advance human progress through an economic, political, and social system based on individual freedom and initiative. Informs, trains, equips, and encourages members to participate in policy-making at federal, state, and local levels and in legislative and political action at the national level. Produces First Business, a daily business-oriented news broadcast; and It's Your Business, a weekly television debate program. Operates the American Business Network (BizNet), through which the group maintains a video production studio to produce and syndicate programs. Conducts continuing education program for business executives, including satellite seminars and Institutes for Organization Management (courses to improve management skills of chamber of commerce and association executives). Maintains speakers' bureau; compiles statistics; conducts research programs.

United States Christian Chamber of Commerce. 2201 Main St., Ste. 400, Dallas, TX 75201-4418. Phone: (214)801-5419 • URL: http://www.usccc1.org • Represents Christian-led businesses, churches, ministry and para-church organizations, schools and individuals. Promotes Christian business ownership and organizational leadership in the United States of America. Fosters the development of biblically-based operating standards for Christian-led businesses, churches, schools and ministries.

Venezuelan-American Chamber of Commerce and Industry. PO Box 5181, Caracas 1010-A, Venezuela. Phone: 58 212 2630833; Fax: 58 212 2631829 • URL: http://www.venamcham.org • Promotes business and commercial relations between the U.S. and Venezuela. Represents members' interests in areas of public policies and legislation. Strives to create a climate favorable to the growth of companies in Venezuela.

Victorian Employers' Chamber of Commerce and Industry. 486 Albert St., Melbourne, VIC 3002, Australia. Phone: 61 3 86625333; Fax: 61 3 86625462; Email: vecci@vecci.org.au • URL: http://www.vecci.org.au • Represents businesses in Victoria, Australia.

Zurich Chamber of Commerce. Selnaustrasse 32, CH-8022 Zurich, Switzerland. Phone: 41 44 2174050 or 41 44 2174040; Fax: 41 44 2174051; Email: direktion@zurichcci.ch • URL: http://www.zurichcci.ch • Keeps members up-to-date on economically relevant political and legal issues. Collects opinions during hearings on the drafting of new laws. Maintains documentation to provide economic information, informs members about import regulations, and provides educational courses on international trading formalities. Represents Swiss interests abroad, particularly in the International Chamber.

CHARITABLE TRUSTS

See FOUNDATIONS

CHARITY

See PHILANTHROPY

CHARTS

See GRAPHS AND CHARTS

CHEESE INDUSTRY

See also DAIRY INDUSTRY

ABSTRACTS AND INDEXES

Food Science and Technology Abstracts. Ovid Technologies Inc. • Monthly. $1,780.00 per year. Provides worldwide coverage of the literature of food technology and food production.

Foods Adlibra: Key to the World's Food Literature. General Mills, Inc. Foods Adlibra Publications. • Semimonthly. $240.00 per year. Provides journal citations and abstracts to the literature of food technology and packaging.

ALMANACS AND YEARBOOKS

CRB Commodity Yearbook. Commodity Research Bureau. CRB. • Annual. $179 plus $10.00 shipping cost. The single most comprehensive source of commodity and futures market information available.

DIRECTORIES

Major Food and Drink Companies of the World. Cengage Learning Inc. • 12th edition. eBook. Published by Graham & Whiteside. Contains profiles and trade names for more than 9,200 important food and beverage companies in various countries. In addition to foods, includes both alcoholic and nonalcoholic drink products.

INTERNET DATABASES

USDA. U.S. National Institute of Standards and Technology. 100 Bureau Dr., Gaithersburg, MD 20899-1070. Phone: 800-877-8339 or (301)975-6478 or (202)720-2791; Fax: (301)975-8295; Email: inquiries@nist.gov • URL: http://www.nist.gov • The USDA home page has six sections: News and Information; What's New; About USDA; Agencies; Opportunities; Search and Help. Keyword searching is offered from the USDA home page and from various individual agency home pages. Agencies are the Economic Research Service, Agricultural Marketing Service, National Agricultural Statistics Service, National Agricultural Library, and about 12 others. Updating varies. Fees: Free.

ONLINE DATABASES

Food Science and Technology Abstracts (online). IFIS North American Desk. • Produced by International Food Information Service. Provides about 500,000 online citations, with abstracts, to the international literature of food science, technology, commodities, engineering, and processing. Approximately 2,000 periodicals are covered. Time period is 1969 to date, with monthly updates. Inquire as to online cost and availability.

PERIODICALS AND NEWSLETTERS

Cheese Importers Association of America Bulletin. Cheese Importers Association of America. • Irregular.

Cheese Market News. Quarne Publishing L.L.C. • Weekly. $135 print and online. Covers market trends, legislation, and new products.

Cheese Market News: The Weekly Newspaper of the Nation's Cheese and Dairy-Deli Business. Quarne Publishing L.L.C. • Weekly (Fri.). $145 U.S. 2nd class. Newspaper (tabloid) covering the cheese manufacturing and marketing business.

Cheese Reporter. Dick Groves, editor. Cheese Reporter Publishing Company Inc. • Weekly. $140. Reports technology, production, sales, merchandising, promotion, research and general industry news of and pertaining to the manufacture and marketing of cheese.

Dairy Foods. BNP Media. • Monthly. Provides broad coverage of new developments in the dairy industry, including cheese and ice cream products.

Deli News. Delicatessen Council of Southern California, Inc. Pacific Rim Publishing Co. • Monthly. $25.00 per year. Includes product news and comment related to cheeses, lunch meats, packaged fresh meats, kosher foods, gourmet-specialty items, and bakery products.

Fancy Food and Culinary Products. Talcott Communications Corp. • Monthly. $34.00 per year. Emphasizes new specialty food products and the business management aspects of the specialty food and confection industries. Includes special issues on wine, cheese, candy, "upscale" cookware, and gifts. Formerly (Fancy Foods).

Food Distribution Magazine. Phoenix Media Network Inc. • Monthly. $49.00 per year. Edited for marketers and buyers of domestic and imported, specialty or gourmet food products, including ethnic foods, seasonings, and bakery items.

PRICE SOURCES

Dairy Market Statistics. U.S. Department of Agriculture - Agricultural Marketing Service. • Annual.

STATISTICS SOURCES

Agricultural Statistics. U.S. Department of Agriculture National Agricultural Statistics Service. • Annual. $46 Individuals. Provides a wide variety of statistical data relating to agricultural production, supplies, consumption, prices/price-supports, foreign trade, costs, and returns, as well as farm labor, loans, income, and population. In many cases, historical data is shown annually for 10 years. In addition to farm data, includes detailed fishery statistics.

TRADE/PROFESSIONAL ASSOCIATIONS

Cheese Importers Association of America. 204 E St. NE, Washington, DC 20002. Phone: (202)547-0899; Fax: (202)547-6348; Email: info@theciaa.org • URL: http://www.theciaa.org • Represents importers, brokers, steamship lines, warehousemen, and firms interested in the importation of cheese.

National Cheese Institute. International Dairy Foods Association, 1250 H St. NW, Ste. 900, Washington, DC 20005-3952. Phone: (202)737-4332; Fax: (202)331-7820 • URL: http://www.idfa.org/about-idfa/boards-committees/national-cheese-institute • Represents manufacturers, processors, marketers, assemblers, and distributors of cheese and cheese products; advocates before government and regulatory bodies on behalf of members.

CHEMICAL ENGINEERING

See also CHEMICAL INDUSTRIES

ABSTRACTS AND INDEXES

Applied Science and Technology Index. EBSCO Publishing Inc. • 11/year. Indexes a wide variety of English language technical, industrial, and engineering periodicals.

Chemical Abstracts. American Chemical Society Chemical Abstracts Service. • Available via CAS' electronic products including SciFinder and STN.

Engineering Index Monthly: Abstracting and Indexing Services Covering Sources ofthe World's Engineering Literature. Engineering Information Inc. • Monthly. Institutions, $5,279.00 per year. Provides indexing and abstracting of the world's engineering and technical literature.

ALMANACS AND YEARBOOKS

Advances in Chemical Engineering. Elsevier. • $260 Individuals. Provides information on modeling of complex chemical systems. Multiple volumes available. Contact for pricing.

BIOGRAPHICAL SOURCES

Who's Who in Science and Engineering. Marquis Who's Who L.L.C. • Biennial. $249.00. Provides concise biographical information on 33,545 prominent engineers and scientists. International coverage, with geographical and professional indexes.

DIRECTORIES

Plunkett's Engineering and Research Industry Almanac. Plunkett Research Ltd. • Annual. $349.99. Contains detailed profiles of major engineering and technology corporations. Includes CD-ROM.

ONLINE DATABASES

Applied Science and Technology Index Online. H.W. Wilson Co. • Provides online indexing of 500 major scientific, technical, industrial, and engineering periodicals. Time period is 1983 to date. Monthly updates. Inquire as to online cost and availability.

CA Search. American Chemical Society Chemical Abstracts Service. • Guide to chemical literature, 1967 to present. Inquire as to online cost and availability.

Current Contents Connect. Thomson Reuters Intellectual Property and Science. • Provides online abstracts of articles listed in the tables of contents of about 7,500 journals. Coverage is very broad, including science, social science, life science, technology, engineering, industry, agriculture, the environment, economics, and arts and humanities. Time period is two years, with weekly updates. Inquire as to online cost and availability.

PERIODICALS AND NEWSLETTERS

AIChe Journal. Center for Chemical Process Safety. • Monthly. $105 Members. Devoted to research and technological developments in chemical engineering and allied fields. Available online.

CEC Communications. Taylor & Francis. • Monthly. $6,593 Institutions. Formerly *Chemical Engineering Communications.*

Chemical Engineering. Chemical Week Associates. • Monthly. $299.97 print or online. Includes annual *Chemical Engineering Buyers Guide.*

Chemical Engineering Progress. Center for Chemical Process Safety. • Monthly. $170 Nonmembers in North America. Covers current advances and trends in the chemical process and related industries. Supplement available *AICh Extra.*

Industrial & Engineering Chemistry Research. American Chemical Society. • Semimonthly. $2,388 Institutions. Magazine on industrial and engineering chemistry. Formerly *Industrial and Engineering Chemistry Product Research and Development.*

PRICE SOURCES

Chemical & Engineering News. American Chemical Society. • Weekly Annual. $265 Nonmembers print, North America. Magazine on chemical and engineering news.

RESEARCH CENTERS AND INSTITUTES

Alberta Innovates Technology Futures. 250 Karl Clark Rd., Edmonton, AB, Canada T6N 1E4. Phone: 800-661-2000 or (780)450-5111; Fax: (780)450-5333; Email: referral@albertainnovates.ca • URL: http://www.albertatechfutures.ca • Development and commercialization technologies that provide solutions to the petroleum, energy and environment, and bio and industrial sectors.

TRADE/PROFESSIONAL ASSOCIATIONS

American Chemical Society. 1155 16th St. NW, Washington, DC 20036. Phone: 800-227-5558 or (202)872-4600; Email: help@acs.org • URL: http://www.acs.org • Scientific and educational society of chemists and chemical engineers. Conducts: studies and surveys; special programs for disadvantaged persons; legislation monitoring, analysis, and reporting; courses for graduate chemists and chemical engineers; radio and television programming. Offers career guidance counseling; administers the Petroleum Research Fund and other grants and fellowship programs. Operates Employment Clearing Houses. Compiles statistics. Maintains speakers' bureau and 33 divisions.

Association of Consulting Chemists and Chemical Engineers. PO Box 902, Murray Hill, NJ 07974-0902. Phone: (908)464-3182 or (973)729-6671; Fax: (908)464-3182 or (973)729-7088; Email: accce@chemconsult.org • URL: http://www.chemconsult.org • Serves the chemical and related industries through its expertise on a wide variety of technical and business knowledge. Provides experienced counseling for new members.

Center for Chemical Process Safety. 3 Park Ave., 19th Fl., New York, NY 10016-5991. Phone: 800-242-4363 or (646)495-1370 or (646)495-1371; Fax: (646)495-1504 or (203)775-5177; Email: ccps@aiche.org • URL: http://www.aiche.org/ccps • Chemical and hydrocarbon manufacturers; engineering firms. Purpose is to study process safety issues in the chemical and hydrocarbon industries and publish and disseminate the results. Is concerned with safety in the manufacture, handling, and storage of toxic and reactive materials and those scientific and engineering practices that can prevent episodic events involving the release of potentially hazardous materials. Conducts research on hazard evaluation procedures, bulk storage and handling of toxic or reactive materials, plant operating procedures, safety training, and dispersion modeling. Seeks to enhance the personal, professional, and technical development of engineers in process plant safety.

CHEMICAL INDUSTRIES

See also AGRICULTURAL CHEMICALS; FERTILIZER INDUSTRY; PLASTICS INDUSTRY

ABSTRACTS AND INDEXES

Applied Science and Technology Index. EBSCO Publishing Inc. • 11/year. Indexes a wide variety of English language technical, industrial, and engineering periodicals.

Chemical Abstracts. American Chemical Society Chemical Abstracts Service. • Available via CAS' electronic products including SciFinder and STN.

CD-ROM DATABASES

Hazardous Substances Data Bank. SilverPlatter Information Inc. • Provides CD-ROM information on hazardous substances, including 140,000 chemicals in the *Registry of Toxic Effects of Chemical Substances* and 60,000 materials covered by the *Toxic Substances Control Act Initial Inventory.*

OECD Statistical Compendium. Organization for Economic Cooperation and Development. • Semiannual. $1,905.00 per year for 1 to 10 users. CD-ROM contains more than 730,000 monthly, quarterly, and annual time series for OECD countries, 1960 to date. Includes fully searchable data on agriculture, food, economic indicators, national accounts, employment, energy, finance, industry, technology, and foreign trade. Results can be displayed in various forms.

DIRECTORIES

Chemicals, Plastics & Rubber Yearbook. George Warman Publications Ltd. • Biennial. $45. Covers: Chemical, plastics and rubber products, manufacturers, associations, and colleges/universities in South Africa. Entries include: Company name, address, phone, brand name, specifications, statistics, services, suppliers of machinery and instrumentation.

Directory of American Manufacturers & Exporters of Chemicals & Allied Products. EXIM Infotek Private Ltd. • $40 Individuals. Covers: 680 American manufacturers and exporters of aerosol chemicals, aircraft cleaning chemicals, allied accessories, analytical chemicals, automotive chemicals, boiler chemicals, chemicals for x-ray processing, chemical intermediates, chemical raw materials, chemical sprayers, chemicals, chemicals for laboratory, chlorine chemicals, construction chemicals, dry chemicals, electronic chemicals, electroplating chemicals, fertilizer chemicals, fine chemicals, germicides, household chemicals, hydrogen peroxide, industrial chemicals, inorganic chemicals, laboratory chemicals, leather chemicals, liquid chemicals, lubricant chemicals, magnesium chloride, metal working chemicals, natural chemicals, organic chemicals, paint chemicals, paper chemicals, pharmaceutical and cosmetic industry chemicals, pharmaceutical chemicals, plastic chemicals, polymer chemicals, polyurethane foam chemicals, reagent chemicals, resins, rubber chemicals, sodium bisulfite chemicals, sodium silico fluoride, solvent chemicals, specialty chemicals, specialty cleaning chemicals, starches, textile chemicals, water softeners, water treatment, water treatment chemicals, and zinc dies casting. Entries include: company name, postal address, city, country, telephone, fax, e-mail and websites, contact person, designation, and product details.

Directory of Chinese Importers of Chemicals & Allied Products. EXIM Infotek Private Ltd. • Covers: 900 Chinese importers of acetic anhydride, acetone, acids, chemical and allied products, chemical products, chemical raw materials, glycerin, industrial chemicals, liquid chemicals, molybdenum concentrate, naphthalene, organic chemicals, oxalic acid, plastic chemicals, potassium hydroxide, reagents, resins and gums, specialty chemicals, tetra ethyl lead, and toluene. Entries include: Company name, postal address, telephone, fax, e-mail, website, contact person, designation, and product details.

Directory of Chinese Manufacturers & Exporters of Chemicals & Allied Products. EXIM Infotek Private Ltd. • $50 Individuals. Covers: 900 Chinese manufacturers & exporters of acids, acrylic acid, activated carbon, activated carbon fiber, activated carbon products, alkali, allyl chloride, ammonia, ammonium bicarbonate, ammonium carbonate, ammonium chloride, ammonium hydrogen carbonate, ammonium nitrate, ammonium paratungstate, ammonium persulphate, ammonium phosphate, ammonium sulphate, ammonium thiocyanate, antimony potassium tartrate, antioxidants, barium carbonate, barium hydroxide, barium nitrate, barium salts, barium sulfates, benzene, benzoic acid, benzotriazole, benzotri-fluoride, boric acid, calcium carbide, calcium chloride, calcium citrate, calcium hydroxide, calcium nitrite, calcium superphosphate, carbon additives, carbon black, carbon block, catalysts, caustic soda, chemical & allied products, chemical additives, chemical assistants, chemical fiber, chemical industrial materials, chemical industrial products, chemical materials, chemical products, chemical raw materials & products, chemical reagent, chemicals, chemicals for cosmetics/perfumery/detergent/soaps, chemicals for textiles, chemistry reagents, chlorinated polyethylene, chlorine, chlorine alkali, chlorine dioxide, chlorine-liquefied, chondroitin sulfate, chromic acid, citric acid, coatings, dicalcium phosphate, dicyandiamide, dsd acid, fine chemical products, fine chemicals, formic acid, hydrochloric acid, hydrofluoric acid, hydrogen peroxide, industrial chemicals, inorganic acids & anhydrides, inorganic chemicals, inorganic products, l-cysteic acid, liquid chemicals, methanol, molybdenum chemical products, mono ammonium phosphate, naphthenic acid, natural resins & pithces, nitrate, nitric acid, nitrobenzene, nitrofurazone, nitromethane, organic chemical material, organic chemicals, organic products, organo pophasphorus, oxalic acid, paper making chemicals, petrochemical products, p-fluoro benzaldehyde, phosphate chemicals, potassium, potassium bicarbonate, potassium carbonate, potassium chloride, potassium hydroxide, potassium nitrate, potassium permaganate, potassium persulfate, potassium sulfate, raw material for chemicals, raw material for cosmetic, refined chemical products, sebacic acid, silicon, soda, soda ash, sodium acetate, sodium alginate, sodium bicarbonate, sodium bromate, sodium carnllite, sodium chlorate, sodium citrate, sodium cyanide, sodium fluoride, sodium hydrosulfite, sodium hydroxide, sodium magnesium chlorophyllin, sodium nitrate, sodium silicate, sodium sulphate, sodium tartrate, sodium thiocyanate, stearic acids, sulfuric acid, sulphur, sulphur black, sulphuric acids, synthetic ammonia, synthetic chemicals, tannic acid, tartaric acid, water treatment chemicals, zirconium chemicals. Entries include: Company name, postal address, city, country, telephone, fax, e-mail & websites, contact person, designation, products detail.

Directory of Chinese Manufacturers & Exporters of Machinery for Chemical & Pharmaceutical Industry. EXIM Infotek Private Ltd. • $5 Individuals. Covers: 40 Chinese manufacturers and exporters of auxiliary equipments, chemical equipment, chemical industrial equipment, chemical industries machinery, chemical machinery, chemical process equipment, essence/perfume production plant equipment, pharmaceutical machinery, pharmacy equipments, and pharmacy machinery. Entries include: Company name, postal address, city, country, phone, fax, e-mail and websites, contact person, designation, and product details.

Directory of Japanese Manufacturers & Exporters of Machinery for Chemicals & Pharma Industry. EXIM Infotek Private Ltd. • $5 Individuals. Covers: 20 Japanese manufacturers and exporters of chemical equipment, chemical industrial equipment, chemical industries machinery, chemical machinery, chemical plant equipment, and pharmaceutical plant equipment. Entries include: Company name, postal address, city, country, phone, fax, e-mail and websites, contact person, designation, and product details.

Directory of South Korean Manufacturers & Exporters of Chemicals & Allied Products. EXIM Infotek Private Ltd. • $25 Individuals. Covers: 350 South Korean manufacturers and exporters of acid coolers, alcohols and epoxides, amines, artificial resins, barium/boron/bromine/hydrogen compounds, base materials for non-metallic elements, calcium-strontium and thallium compounds, carbohydrates/proteins and enzymes, carbon based materials and products, catalysts, chemicals for basic metal industries, chemicals for building materials, chemicals for cosmetics/perfumery/detergent/soaps, chemicals for electrical/electronic industries, chemicals for laboratory and microbiology, chemicals for leather and fur tanning extract, chemicals for lubricants and waxes, chemicals for metal surface treatment, chemicals for metal welding/soldering fluxes, chemicals for paint/lacquer/varnish, chemicals for paper making/printing/photography, chemicals for plastic/rubber/ceramic, chemicals for unspecified uses, chemicals for water treatment, chemotherapeutic agents, compressed and liquefied gases/chemicals for refrigeration, detergents/cleansers and bleaching agents, disinfections and indoor deodorants, esters/acetates/ethyls and methyls, explosives, hydrocarbons and halcarbons, inorganic acids and anhydrides, inorganic alkalis-hydroxides, miscellaneous organic chemicals, natural resins and pitches, organic acids and anhydrides, phosphorus/sulphur/carbon/silicon and cassium compounds, polyphenols/ethers/aldehydes/ketones, potassium and ammonium compounds, pyrotechnic products, soaps/fatty-acid based detergents, sodium compounds. Entries include: Company name, postal address, city, country, telephone, fax, e-mail and websites, contact person, designation, and product details.

Directory of Taiwanese Manufacturers & Exporters of Chemicals & Allied Products. EXIM Infotek Private Ltd. • $30 Individuals. Covers: 380 Taiwanese manufacturers and exporters of alcohols and epoxides, amines, artificial resins, barium/boron/bromine/hydrogen compounds, calcium-strontium and thallium compounds, carbohydrates/proteins and enzymes, carbon based materials and products, chemicals, chemicals for basic metal industries, chemicals for building materials, chemicals for cosmetics/perfumery/detergent/soaps, chemicals for electrical/electronic industries, chemicals for laboratory and microbiology, chemicals for leather and fur tanning extract, chemicals for lubricants and waxes, chemicals for metal welding/soldering fluxes, chemicals for mining/oil extraction, chemicals for paint/lacquer/varnish, chemicals for paper making/printing/photography, chemicals for plastic/rubber/ceramic, chemicals for unspecified uses, chemicals for water treatment, chemotherapeutic agents, compact & conventional detergent powder, compressed and liquefied gases/chem for refrigeration, detergents/cleansers and bleaching agents, dish wash detergent, disinfections and indoor deodorants, esters/acetates/ethyls and methyls, explosives, hydrocarbons and halcarbons, inorganic acids and anhydrides, inorganic alkalis-hydroxides, liquid bleaching agent, misc. organic chemicals, natural resins and pitches, organic acids and anhydrides, phosphorus/sulphur/carbon/silicon and cassium compounds, polyphenols/ethers/aldehydes/ketones, potash vats, potassium and ammonium compounds, soaps/fatty-acid based detergents, and sodium compounds. Entries include: Company name, postal address, city, country, telephone, fax, e-mail and websites, contact person, designation, and product details.

Directory of Taiwanese Manufacturers & Exporters of Machinery for Chemicals & Pharma Industry. EXIM Infotek Private Ltd. • $25 Individuals. Covers: 290 Taiwanese manufacturers and exporters of crushers/pulverizers for chemical industries, dryers/evaporators/crystallizers for chemical industries, electrochemical and electrolytic plant equipment, electroplating plant machinery, essence/perfume production plant equipment, explosive/match production plant equipment, fertilizer production plant equipment, glue/gelatin making plant equipment, heaters/boilers/distillers for chemical industries, inorganic chemical production plant equipment, organic chemical production plant equipment, paint/varnish/enamel/ink production plant equipment, pharmaceutical/cosmetic production plant equipment, reactors for chemical industry, screeners/mixers/centrifuges for chemical industry, soap making equipment, technical gas production plant equipment. Entries include: Company name, postal address, city, country, phone, fax, e-mail and websites, contact person, designation, and product details.

The International Directory of Importers--Chemicals and Allied Products Importers. Interdata. • Annual. $320 Individuals print. Covers: 6,200 international firms importing chemicals and allied products. Entries include: Company name and address, contact person, email, number of employees, year established, phone and telefaxes, business activity, bank references, as well as a listing of chemicals and allied products currently being imported.

Investment Opportunities in China: Chemical Industry. Pasha Publications. • $255. Covers: Approximately 530 Chinese projects in the chemical industry seeking international offshore capital investments. Entries include: Project name, address, phone, cable number; name and title of contact; financial data; description of project.

Kompass (Branchenauszuge)--Chemische Industrie. Kompass Deutschland Verlags- und Vertriebsgesellschaft, mbH. • Annual. $98. Covers: Chemical industry profiles and products in Germany for purchasers and marketers.

Kompass Professionnel Chimie--Plastiques. Kompass France. • Annual. Covers: French chemical industry companies. Entries include: Company name, activity, products, services, decision makers and their functions, key figures.

Major Chemical and Petrochemical Companies of the World. Cengage Learning Inc. • Annual. $1,460 Individuals. 2008. 12th edition. eBook. Published by Graham & Whiteside. Contains profiles of more than 8,500 important chemical and petrochemical companies in various countries. Subject areas include general chemicals, specialty chemicals, agricultural chemicals, petrochemicals, industrial gases, and fertilizers.

McCutcheon's Functional Materials Volumes 2. Manufacturing Confectioner Publishing Corp. • Edited for product development, quality control and research and development chemists.

McCutcheon's Volume 1: Emulsifiers and Detergents. Manufacturing Confectioner Publishing Corp. • Two volumes. International coverage.

E-BOOKS

Encyclopedia of American Industries. Cengage Learning Inc. • 2011. $807.00. 6th edition. Three volumes. Volume one is Manufacturing Industries and volume two is Service and Non-Manufacturing Industries. Provides the history, development, and recent status of approximately 1,000 industries. Includes statistical graphs, with industry and general indexes. Also available as eBook.

FINANCIAL RATIOS

Annual Statement Studies. Risk Management Association. • Annual. Compiled from over 280,000 financial statements.

Annual Statement Studies: Industry Default Probabilities and Cash Flow Measures. Risk Management Association. • Annual. $405 Nonmembers. Serves as a companion volume to the original *Annual Statement Studies.* Gives probability of default estimates on a percentage scale for more than 450 industries. Includes changes in position year-by-year for eight financial statement line items and provides percentage measures of cash flow.

Quarterly Financial Report for Manufacturing, Mining, Trade, and Selected Service Industries. U.S. Federal Trade Commission and U.S. Securities and Exchange Commission. U.S. Census Bureau Foreign Trade Division. • Quarterly. Quarterly. Report on financial results of U.S. corporations.

GENERAL WORKS

Guide to Products and Services of Small Chemical Businesses. Division of Small Chemical Businesses. • Includes information for small chemical businesses.

INTERNET DATABASES

Business 2.0 Web Guide to the Best Business Links. Business 2.0 Media Inc. Phone: (415)293-4800; Email: support@business2.com • URL: http://www.business2.com/webguide • Web site presents an extensive, searchable directory of links to "the best, most informative, and authoritative web pages." Twenty main categories cover business, finance, career, company information, people, and technology topics, with thousands of subtopics, all linking to Web sites recommended by experienced business researchers. Fees: Free.

Fedstats. Federal Interagency Council on Statistical Policy. Phone: (202)395-7254 • URL: http://www.fedstats.gov • Web site features an efficient search facility for full-text statistics produced by more than 100 federal agencies, including the Census Bureau, the Bureau of Economic Analysis, and the Bureau of Labor Statistics. Boolean searches can be made within one agency or for all agencies combined. Links are offered to international statistical bureaus, including the UN, IMF, OECD, UNESCO, Eurostat, and 20 individual countries. Fees: Free.

FreeLunch.com. Economy.com, Inc. Phone: (610)696-8700; Fax: (610)696-1678 • URL: http://www.freelunch.com • Web site provides free access to more than 200 million economic and financial data series, covering industry, demographics, labor markets, prices, retail sales, government spending, trade, interest rates, housing starts, the stock market, etc. Data is available in either chart or table form. Searching is offered. Free, but registration required. Economy.com, Inc. also offers fee-based economic analysis at *The Dismal Scientist* site (www.dismal.com).

Manufacturing Profiles. U. S. Bureau of the Census. Phone: (301)763-4636 or (301)763-4100; Fax: (301)763-4794; Email: webmaster@census.gov • URL: http://www.census.gov/prod/www/abs/mfg-prof.html • The Census Bureau makes available free on PDF (Portable Document Format) an annual consolidation of the entire Current Industrial Report series, presenting "all the data compiled." Contains statistics on production, shipments, inventories, consumption, exports, imports, and orders for a wide variety of manufactured products.

ONLINE DATABASES

CA Search. American Chemical Society Chemical Abstracts Service. • Guide to chemical literature, 1967 to present. Inquire as to online cost and availability.

OTHER SOURCES

Chemical Regulation Reporter: A Weekly Review of Activity Affecting Chemical Users and Manufacturers. Bloomberg BNA. • Weekly. $2,226 per year. Looseleaf service.

PERIODICALS AND NEWSLETTERS

Chemical Business. Colour Publications Private Ltd. • Weekly Monthly. Technical journal.

Chemical Processing. Putman Media Inc. • Monthly.

Chemical Week. Chemical Week Associates. • 49 times a year. $139.00 per year. Includes annual *Buyers' Guide.*

PetroChemical News: A Weekly News Service in English Devoted to the Worldwide Petrochemical Industry. William F. Bland Co. • Weekly. $897. Report of current and significant news about the petrochemical business worldwide.

Today's Chemist at Work. American Chemical Society. • Monthly. Institutions, $200.00 per year; others, price on application. Provide pracrtical information for chemists on day-to-day operations. Product coverage includes chemicals, equipment, apparatus, instruments, and supplies.

PRICE SOURCES

Chemical & Engineering News. American Chemical Society. • Weekly Annual. $265 Nonmembers print, North America. Magazine on chemical and engineering news.

STATISTICS SOURCES

Annual Review of the Chemical Industry. United Nations Publications. • Annual. $100.00.

Standard & Poor's Industry Surveys. Standard & Poor's Financial Services L.L.C. • Semiannual. $1,800.00. Two looseleaf volumes. Includes monthly *Supplements.* Provides detailed, individual surveys of 52 major industry groups. Each survey is revised on a semiannual basis. Also includes "Monthly Investment Review" (industry group investment analysis) and monthly "Trends & Projections" (economic analysis).

Survey of Current Business. U. S. Government Printing Office. • Published by Bureau of Economic Analysis, U. S. Department of Commerce. Presents a wide variety of business and economic data.

Synthetic Organic Chemicals: United States Production and Sales. International Trade Commission. U. S. Government Printing Office. • Annual.

United States Census of Manufactures. U.S. Department of Commerce U.S. Census Bureau. • Quinquennial. Results presented in reports, tape, CD-ROM, and Diskette files.

TRADE/PROFESSIONAL ASSOCIATIONS

American Chemical Society. 1155 16th St. NW, Washington, DC 20036. Phone: 800-227-5558 or (202)872-4600; Email: help@acs.org • URL: http://www.acs.org • Scientific and educational society of chemists and chemical engineers. Conducts: studies and surveys; special programs for disadvantaged persons; legislation monitoring, analysis, and reporting; courses for graduate chemists and chemical engineers; radio and television programming. Offers career guidance counseling; administers the Petroleum Research Fund and other grants and fellowship programs. Operates Employment Clearing Houses. Compiles statistics. Maintains speakers' bureau and 33 divisions.

American Chemistry Council. 700 2nd St. NE, Washington, DC 20002. Phone: (202)249-7000; Fax: (202)249-6100 • URL: http://www.americanchemistry.com • Represents the leading companies engaged in the business of chemistry. Members apply the science of chemistry to make innovative products and services that make people's lives "better, healthier and safer." Improves environmental, health and safety performance through "Responsible Care"(R), common sense advocacy designed to address major public policy issues and health and environmental research and product testing.

Association of Consulting Chemists and Chemical Engineers. PO Box 902, Murray Hill, NJ 07974-0902. Phone: (908)464-3182 or (973)729-6671; Fax: (908)464-3182 or (973)729-7088; Email: accce@chemconsult.org • URL: http://www.chemconsult.org • Serves the chemical and related industries through its expertise on a wide variety of technical and business knowledge. Provides experienced counseling for new members.

Commercial Development and Marketing Association. Product Development and Management Association, 401 N Michigan Ave., Ste. 2200, Chicago, IL 60611. Phone: 800-232-5241 or (312)321-5145; Fax: (312)673-6885; Email: cdma@pdma.org • URL: http://www.pdma.org/p/cm/ld/fid=78 • Formerly Commercial Chemical Development Association.

Consumer Specialty Products Association. 1667 K St. NW, Ste. 300, Washington, DC 20006. Phone: (202)872-8110; Fax: (202)223-2636 • URL: http://www.cspa.org • Formerly National Association Insecticide and Disinfectant Manufacturers.

National Association of Chemical Distributors. 1560 Wilson Blvd., Ste. 1100, Arlington, VA 22209. Phone: (703)527-6223; Fax: (703)527-7747; Email: nacdpublicaffairs@nacd.com • URL: http://www.nacd.com • Represents chemical distributor companies that purchase and take title of chemical products from manufacturers. Promotes professionalism in the chemical distribution industry.

National Chemical Credit Association. 1100 Main St., Buffalo, NY 14209-2356. Phone: (716)887-9547; Fax: (716)878-0479 • URL: http://www.ncca1.org/document_1.html • Represents chemical companies. Aims to facilitate the exchange of commercial credit information among leaders of the chemical industry, as well as provide continual professional education to its members. Sponsors monthly educational programs at divisional meetings.

CHEMICAL LABORATORIES

See LABORATORIES

CHEMICAL MARKETING

ABSTRACTS AND INDEXES

Business Periodicals Index Retrospective. EBSCO Publishing Inc. • 11/year. Quarterly and annual cumulations.

ONLINE DATABASES

Wilson Business Abstracts Online. H.W. Wilson Co. • Indexes and abstracts 600 major business periodicals, plus the *Wall Street Journal* and the business section of the *New York Times.* Indexing is from 1982, abstracting from 1990, with the two newspapers included from 1993. Updated weekly. Inquire as to online cost and availability. (*Business Periodicals Index* without abstracts is also available online.).

PERIODICALS AND NEWSLETTERS

Chemical Week. Chemical Week Associates. • 49 times a year. $139.00 per year. Includes annual *Buyers' Guide.*

STATISTICS SOURCES

Annual Bulletin of Trade in Chemical Products. Economic Commission for Europe. United Nations Publications. • Annual. $47.00.

Synthetic Organic Chemicals: United States Production and Sales. International Trade Commission. U. S. Government Printing Office. • Annual.

TRADE/PROFESSIONAL ASSOCIATIONS

American Chemical Society. 1155 16th St. NW, Washington, DC 20036. Phone: 800-227-5558 or (202)872-4600; Email: help@acs.org • URL: http://www.acs.org • Scientific and educational society of chemists and chemical engineers. Conducts: studies and surveys; special programs for disadvantaged persons; legislation monitoring, analysis, and reporting; courses for graduate chemists and chemical engineers; radio and television programming. Offers career guidance counseling; administers the Petroleum Research Fund and other grants and fellowship programs. Operates Employment Clearing Houses. Compiles statistics. Maintains speakers' bureau and 33 divisions.

American Chemistry Council. 700 2nd St. NE, Washington, DC 20002. Phone: (202)249-7000; Fax: (202)249-6100 • URL: http://www.americanchemistry.com • Represents the leading companies engaged in the business of chemistry. Members apply the science of chemistry to make innovative products and services that make people's lives "better, healthier and safer." Improves environmental, health and safety performance through "Responsible Care"(R), common sense advocacy designed to address major public policy issues and health and environmental research and product testing.

National Association of Chemical Distributors. 1560 Wilson Blvd., Ste. 1100, Arlington, VA 22209. Phone: (703)527-6223; Fax: (703)527-7747; Email: nacdpublicaffairs@nacd.com • URL: http://www.nacd.com • Represents chemical distributor companies that purchase and take title of chemical products from manufacturers. Promotes professionalism in the chemical distribution industry.

CHILD CARE

See DAY CARE CENTERS

CHILD LABOR

See also LABOR; LABOR LAW AND REGULATION

TRADE/PROFESSIONAL ASSOCIATIONS

National Child Labor Committee. 1501 Broadway, Ste. 1908, New York, NY 10036. Phone: (212)840-1801; Fax: (212)768-0963; Email: nclckapow@aol.com • URL: http://www.nationalchildlabor.org • Parent organization of National Committee on Employment of Youth and National Committee on the Education of Migrant Children. Provides direct and technical assistance to programs on youth-related issues, particularly education, job training, and employment.

National Youth Employment Coalition. 1836 Jefferson Pl. NW, Washington, DC 20036. Phone: (202)659-1064; Fax: (202)659-0399; Email: nyec@nyec.org • URL: http://www.nyec.org • A network of over 180 community-based organizations, research organizations, public interest groups, policy analysis organizations, and others dedicated to promoting improved policies and practices related to youth employment/development, to help youth succeed in becoming lifelong learners, productive workers and self-sufficient citizens.

CHILD MARKET

See YOUTH MARKET

CHILDREN'S APPAREL INDUSTRY

See also CLOTHING INDUSTRY

DIRECTORIES

Directory of Apparel Specialty Stores. Chain Store Guide. • Annual. $495 Individuals Directory. Covers 4,700 apparel and sporting goods specialty stores in the United States and Canada, operating more than 80,000 stores. Include company name, phone and fax numbers, company e-mail and web addresses and other information.

FINANCIAL RATIOS

Annual Statement Studies. Risk Management Association. • Annual. Compiled from over 280,000 financial statements.

Annual Statement Studies: Industry Default Probabilities and Cash Flow Measures. Risk Management Association. • Annual. $405 Nonmembers. Serves as a companion volume to the original *Annual Statement Studies.* Gives probability of default estimates on a percentage scale for more than 450 industries. Includes changes in position year-by-year for eight financial statement line items and provides percentage measures of cash flow.

INTERNET DATABASES

Manufacturing Profiles. U. S. Bureau of the Census. Phone: (301)763-4636 or (301)763-4100; Fax: (301)763-4794; Email: webmaster@census.gov • URL: http://www.census.gov/prod/www/abs/mfg-prof.html • The Census Bureau makes available free on PDF (Portable Document Format) an annual consolidation of the entire Current Industrial Report series, presenting "all the data compiled." Contains statistics on production, shipments, inventories, consumption, exports, imports, and orders for a wide variety of manufactured products.

PERIODICALS AND NEWSLETTERS

Baby Shop: The Business Magazine for Independent Juvenile Product Retailers. Spindle Publishing Company Inc. • Semiannual. Magazine providing relevant articles and resources that help maternity retailers better manage their stores.

Earnshaw's Infants, Girls and Boys Wear Review - Children's Wear Directory. Earnshaw Publications Inc. • Annual. Controlled circulation.

Tobe Report. Tobe Associates Inc. • Monthly. Edited for fashion retailers. Provides detailed information and analysis relating to current trends in the women's, children's, and men's apparel and accessories markets.

CHINA

See ASIAN MARKETS

CHINAWARE

See TABLEWARE

CHLORINE INDUSTRY

See CHEMICAL INDUSTRIES

CHOCOLATE INDUSTRY

See also CANDY INDUSTRY; COCOA INDUSTRY

ABSTRACTS AND INDEXES

Food Science and Technology Abstracts. Ovid Technologies Inc. • Monthly. $1,780.00 per year. Provides worldwide coverage of the literature of food technology and food production.

Foods Adlibra: Key to the World's Food Literature. General Mills, Inc. Foods Adlibra Publications. • Semimonthly. $240.00 per year. Provides journal citations and abstracts to the literature of food technology and packaging.

DIRECTORIES

Major Food and Drink Companies of the World. Cengage Learning Inc. • 12th edition. eBook. Published by Graham & Whiteside. Contains profiles and trade names for more than 9,200 important food and beverage companies in various countries. In addition to foods, includes both alcoholic and nonalcoholic drink products.

ONLINE DATABASES

Food Science and Technology Abstracts (online). IFIS North American Desk. • Produced by International Food Information Service. Provides about 500,000 online citations, with abstracts, to the international literature of food science, technology, commodities, engineering, and processing. Approximately 2,000 periodicals are covered. Time period is 1969 to date, with monthly updates. Inquire as to online cost and availability.

STATISTICS SOURCES

Statistical Bulletin of the International Office of Cocoa, Chocolate and Sugar Confectionary. International Confectionery Association. • Annual.

TRADE/PROFESSIONAL ASSOCIATIONS

Cocoa Merchants' Association of America. 55 E 52nd St., 40th Flr., New York, NY 10055. Phone: (212)748-4193; Email: cmaa@cocoamerchants.com • URL: http://www.cocoamerchants.com • Dealers and importers of raw cocoa beans and cocoa products. Provides arbitration in contract disputes. Maintains speakers' bureau and a voluntary warehouse inspection program; conducts traffic and orientation seminars; compiles statistics.

National Confectioners Association. 1101 30th St. NW, Ste. 200, Washington, DC 20007. Phone: (202)534-1440; Fax: (202)337-0637; Email: info@candyusa.org • URL: http://www.candyusa.com • Formerly Association of Cocoa and Chocolate Manufacturers of the U.S.

World Cocoa Foundation. 1411 K St. NW, Ste. 502, Washington, DC 20005. Phone: (202)737-7870; Fax: (202)737-7832; Email: wcf@worldcocoa.org • URL: http://www.worldcocoafoundation.org • Supported by manufacturers of cocoa and chocolate products. Encourages educational and research projects in the cultivation of more cacao of better quality; strives to improve economic conditions of cacao farmers by increasing yields on farms and reducing the per unit production cost. Projects include: research on life history and control of insects attacking cacao; studies on principal cacao diseases; germ plasma assembly and testing; breeding for yield and disease resistance; and physiology. Sponsors exchanges of personnel and training fellowships. Disseminates information.

CHRISTMAS CARDS

See GREETING CARD INDUSTRY

CHROMIUM INDUSTRY

See METAL INDUSTRY

CHRONOLOGY

See also ANNIVERSARIES AND HOLIDAYS

ALMANACS AND YEARBOOKS

The Annual Register: A Record of World Events. ProQuest L.L.C. • Annual. Contains yearly British and world events.

ENCYCLOPEDIAS AND DICTIONARIES

Gale Encyclopedia of U.S. Economic History. Cengage Learning Inc. • 2003. eBook. Contains about 1,000 alphabetically arranged entries. Includes industry profiles, biographies, social issue profiles, geographic profiles, and chronological tables. Inquire as to price and availability.

CIGAR AND CIGARETTE INDUSTRY

See also SMOKING POLICY; TOBACCO AND TOBACCO INDUSTRY

ALMANACS AND YEARBOOKS

Tobacco Retailers Almanac. International Premium Cigar and Pipe Retailers. • Annual. Lists virtually every tobacco related product available (including cigars, cigarettes, pipes, tobacco, lighters and gift items).

CD-ROM DATABASES

OECD Statistical Compendium. Organization for Economic Cooperation and Development. • Semiannual. $1,905.00 per year for 1 to 10 users. CD-ROM contains more than 730,000 monthly, quarterly, and annual time series for OECD countries, 1960 to date. Includes fully searchable data on agriculture, food, economic indicators, national accounts, employment, energy, finance, industry, technology, and foreign trade. Results can be displayed in various forms.

INTERNET DATABASES

Business 2.0 Web Guide to the Best Business Links. Business 2.0 Media Inc. Phone: (415)293-4800; Email: support@business2.com • URL: http://www.business2.com/webguide • Web site presents an extensive, searchable directory of links to "the best, most informative, and authoritative web pages." Twenty main categories cover business, finance, career, company information, people, and technology topics, with thousands of subtopics, all linking to Web sites recommended by experienced business researchers. Fees: Free.

Fedstats. Federal Interagency Council on Statistical Policy. Phone: (202)395-7254 • URL: http://www.fedstats.gov • Web site features an efficient search facility for full-text statistics produced by more than 100 federal agencies, including the Census Bureau, the Bureau of Economic Analysis, and the Bureau of Labor Statistics. Boolean searches can be made within one agency or for all agencies combined. Links are offered to international statistical bureaus, including the UN, IMF, OECD, UNESCO, Eurostat, and 20 individual countries. Fees: Free.

FreeLunch.com. Economy.com, Inc. Phone: (610)696-8700; Fax: (610)696-1678 • URL: http://www.freelunch.com • Web site provides free access to more than 200 million economic and financial data series, covering industry, demographics, labor markets, prices, retail sales, government spending, trade, interest rates, housing starts, the stock market, etc. Data is available in either chart or table form. Searching is offered. Free, but registration required. Economy.com, Inc. also offers fee-based economic analysis at *The Dismal Scientist* site (www.dismal.com).

ONLINE DATABASES

Agricola. U.S. National Agricultural Library World List of Agricultural Serials. • Covers worldwide agricultural literature. Over 3.3 million citations, 1970 to present, with monthly updates. Inquire as to online cost and availability.

OTHER SOURCES

Westlaw Journal Tobacco Industry. Thomson Reuters Westlaw. • $2,988.96. Reports on major lawsuits brought against tobacco companies.

PERIODICALS AND NEWSLETTERS

Smokeshop. • Bimonthly. $24.00 per year.

TMA Tobacco Tax Guide: Summaries of Key Provisions of Tobacco Tax Laws, All Tobacco Products, All States. Tobacco Merchants Association of the U.S. • Looseleaf service. Members, $750.00 per year; non-members, $2,250.00 per year. Quarterly updates.

Tobacco-Cigarette News. International Press Cutting Service. • Weekly. $85.00 per year. Formerly *Tobacco News.*

PRICE SOURCES

Tobacco Market Review. U.S. Department of Agriculture - Agricultural Marketing Service. • Annual.

RESEARCH CENTERS AND INSTITUTES

Lower Coastal Plain Research Station/Cunningham Research Station. c/o Phillip Winslow, Manager, North Carolina Dept. of Agricultural and Consumer Services, 200 Cunningham Rd., Kinston, NC 28501-1700. Phone: (252)527-3579; Fax: (252)527-2036; Email: lowercoastal.resst@ncmail.net • URL: http://www.ncagr.com.

North Carolina Department of Agriculture and Consumer Services - Border Belt Tobacco Research Station. N Carolina State University, 86 Border Belt Dr., Whiteville, NC 28472-6828. Phone: (910)648-4703; Fax: (910)648-4858; Email: BorderBelt.ResSt@ncagr.gov • URL: http://www.ncagr.gov/research/bbtrs.htm • Tobacco breeding, variety testing, insect control, plant phenology, plant growth regulators, residues, plant physiology, fertilization, and methods development. Also studies corn, soybeans, and peanuts.

University of Kentucky - College of Agriculture, Food and Environment - Kentucky Tobacco Research and Development Center. Cooper & University Drs., Lexington, KY 40546-0236. Phone: (859)257-5798; Fax: (859)323-1077; Email: ochamb@uky.edu • URL: http://www2.ca.uky.edu/ktrdc/index.html • Application of biotechnology for the development of new crops based on tobacco and other plants. Development of new medicinal and industrial applications for plant natural products. Development of new crops from native plants and adaptation of existing crops for more efficient production of plant-made pharmaceuticals, plant-made industrial products, and plant natural products.

STATISTICS SOURCES

Standard & Poor's Industry Surveys. Standard & Poor's Financial Services L.L.C. • Semiannual. $1,800.00. Two looseleaf volumes. Includes monthly *Supplements.* Provides detailed, individual surveys of 52 major industry groups. Each survey is revised on a semiannual basis. Also includes "Monthly Investment Review" (industry group investment analysis) and monthly "Trends & Projections" (economic analysis).

Survey of Current Business. U. S. Government Printing Office. • Published by Bureau of Economic Analysis, U. S. Department of Commerce. Presents a wide variety of business and economic data.

TRADE/PROFESSIONAL ASSOCIATIONS

American Wholesale Marketers Association. 2750 Prosperity Ave., Ste. 530, Fairfax, VA 22031. Phone: 800-482-2962; Fax: (703)573-5738 • URL: http://www.awmanet.org • Represents the interests of distributors of convenience-related products. Its members include wholesalers, retailers, manufacturers, brokers and allied organizations from across the U.S. and abroad. Programs include strong legislative representation in Washington and a broad spectrum of targeted education, business and information services. Sponsors the country's largest show for candy and convenience related products in conjunction with its semi-annual convention.

Cigar Association of America. 1100 G St. NW, Ste. 1050, Washington, DC 20005-7405. Phone: (202)223-8204; Fax: (202)833-0379 • URL: http://www.cigarassociation.org.

International Premium Cigar and Pipe Retailers. No. 4 Bradley Park Ct., Ste. 2-H, Columbus, GA 31904-3637. Phone: (706)494-1143; Fax: (706)494-1893; Email: info@ipcpr.org • URL: http://www.ipcpr.org • Formerly Retail Tobacco Dealers of America.

Retail, Wholesale and Department Store Union. 30 E 29th St., New York, NY 10016. Phone: (212)684-5300; Fax: (212)779-2809; Email: info@rwdsu.org • URL: http://www.rwdsu.info • Represents workers throughout the United States and Canada. Works in a wide variety of occupations that range from food processing, retail, manufacturing, service and healthcare.

CIGARETTE INDUSTRY

See CIGAR AND CIGARETTE INDUSTRY

CINEMA

See MOTION PICTURE THEATERS

CINEMATOGRAPHY

See MOTION PICTURE PHOTOGRAPHY

CIRCULATION MANAGEMENT (PUBLISHING)

See also PERIODICALS

HANDBOOKS AND MANUALS

Grossman on Circulation. Gordon W. Grossman. Penton. • Annual. $99.95. Covers magazine circulation management and marketing, with emphasis on circulaton incentives, such as free-issue offers, sweepstakes, premiums, "freemiums," and professional courtesy offers. Includes examples of promotions used by consumer and trade publications.

PERIODICALS AND NEWSLETTERS

Circulation Management. Media Central. • Monthly. $39.00 per year. Edited for circulation professionals in the magazine and newsletter publishing industry. Covers marketing, planning, promotion, management, budgeting, and related topics.

TRADE/PROFESSIONAL ASSOCIATIONS

Audit Bureau of Circulations. 48 W Seegers Rd., Arlington Heights, IL 60005-3913. Phone: (224)366-6939 or (224)366-6500; Fax: (224)366-6949; Email: service@accessabc.com • URL: http://www.accessabc.com • Verifies newspaper and periodical circulation statements. Includes a Business Publications Industry Committee and a Magazine Directors Advisory Committee.

BPA Worldwide. 100 Beard Sawmill Rd., 6th Fl., Shelton, CT 06484. Phone: (203)447-2800; Fax: (203)447-2900; Email: ghansen@bpaww.com • URL: http://www.bpaww.com • Verifies business and consumer periodical circulation statements. Includes a Circulation Managers Committee. Formerly Business Publications Audit of Circulation.

Direct Marketing Association. 1120 Ave. of the Americas, New York, NY 10036-6700. Phone: (212)768-7277; Fax: (212)302-6714; Email: info@the-dma.org • URL: http://www.thedma.org • A division of the Direct Marketing Association. Members include publishers and circulation directors.

MPA - The Association of Magazine Media. 757 3rd Ave., 11th Fl., New York, NY 10017. Phone: (212)872-3700 or (212)872-3745; Email: mpa@magazine.org • URL: http://www.magazine.org • Members are publishers of consumer and other periodicals. Affiliated with American Society of Magazine Editors; Media Credit Association; Publishers Information Bureau. Formerly Magazine Publishers Association.

CITIES AND TOWNS

See also MUNICIPAL GOVERNMENT; URBAN DEVELOPMENT

ABSTRACTS AND INDEXES

PAIS International. ProQuest L.L.C. • Monthly. $850.00 per year; cumulations three times a year. Provides topical citations to the worldwide literature of public affairs, economics, demographics, sociology, and trade. Text in English; indexed materials in English, French, German, Italian, Portuguese and Spanish.

Readers' Guide to Periodical Literature. EBSCO Publishing Inc. • Provides indexing for over 400 periodicals dating back to 1983.

Sage Public Administration Abstracts. EBSCO Publishing Inc. • Titles include Journal of Public

Economics, Public Administration, and Public Administratioin Review.

Social Sciences Citation Index. Thomson Reuters Corp. • Weekly. Product is accessed via *Web of Science*.

Social Sciences Index Retrospective: 1907-1983. EBSCO Publishing Inc. • Indexing for 1,000,000 articles. Coverage includes international index and social sciences and humanities index.

Urban Studies Abstracts. EBSCO Publishing Inc. • Quarterly. $967 Institutions print only. Coverage includes community development, urban affairs, urban history.

CD-ROM DATABASES

Newspaper Abstracts Ondisc. ProQuest L.L.C. • Monthly. $2,950.00 per year (covers 1989 to date; archival discs are available for 1985-88). Provides cover-to-cover CD-ROM indexing and abstracting of 19 major newspapers, including the *New York Times, Wall Street Journal, Washington Post, Chicago Tribune*, and *Los Angeles Times*.

PAIS International. ProQuest L.L.C. • Monthly. $1,995.00 per year. Contains over 650,000 citations to the literature of contemporary social, political, and economic issues.

Readers' Guide to Periodical Literature. EBSCO Publishing Inc. • Provides indexing for over 400 periodicals dating back to 1983.

Social Sciences Abstracts. EBSCO Publishing Inc. • Provides indexing from 1983 and abstracting from 1994 of more than 750 periodicals covering economics, area studies, community health, public administration, public welfare, urban studies, and many other topics related to the social sciences.

Social Sciences Citation Index. Thomson Reuters Corp. • Weekly. Product is accessed via *Web of Science*.

Sourcebooks America CD-ROM. CACI Marketing Systems. • Annual. $1,250.00. Provides the CD-ROM version of *The Sourcebook of ZIP Code Demographics: Census Edition* and *The Sourcebook of County Demographics: Census Edition*.

DIRECTORIES

Carroll's Municipal/County Directory. Caroll Publishing. • Semiannual. $500 Individuals. Provides listings of about 90,000 city, town, and county officials in the U. S.

Carroll's Municipal Directory. Caroll Publishing. • Annual. $500 Individuals. Covers: About 51,000 officials in more than 7,900 cities towns and villages: includes top elected council or elected board members. Entries include: Name, county name, locator phone, address, population; officials' names, titles, addresses, and phone numbers.

Municipal Yellow Book: Who's Who in the Leading City and County Governments and Local Authorities. Leadership Directories Inc. • Annual. $465 /year. Lists approximately 30,000 key personnel in city and county departments, agencies, subdivisions, and branches.

E-BOOKS

Cities of the World. Cengage Learning Inc. • 2003. 6th edition. eBook. Detailed information is provided for more than 3,400 cities in 177 countries (excluding U.S.) Includes maps and photographs. Based in U.S. State Department reports. Available as eBook.

INTERNET DATABASES

U.S. Census Bureau: The Official Statistics. U. S. Bureau of the Census. Phone: (301)763-4636 or (301)763-4100; Fax: (301)763-4794; Email: webmaster@census.gov • URL: http://www.census.gov/prod/www/abs/mfg-prof.html • Web site is "Your Source for Social, Demographic, and Economic Information." Contains "Current U. S. Population Count," "Current Economic Indicators," and a wide variety of data under "Other Official Statistics." Keyword searching is provided. Fees: Free.

ONLINE DATABASES

Wilson Social Sciences Abstracts Online. H.W. Wilson Co. • Provides online abstracting and indexing of more than 500 periodicals covering area studies, community health, public administration, public welfare, urban studies, and many other social science topics. Time period is 1994 to date for abstracts and 1983 to date for indexing, with updates weekly. Inquire as to online cost and availability.

PERIODICALS AND NEWSLETTERS

American City and County: Administration, Engineering and Operations in Relation to Local Government. RentPath Inc. • Monthly. Free to qualified personnel. Edited for mayors, city managers, and other local officials. Emphasis is on equipment and basic services.

Downtown Idea Exchange: Essential Information for Downtown Research and Development Center. Downtown Research and Development Center. Alexander Communications Group Inc. • Monthly. $227 Individuals. Newsletter for those concerned with central business districts. Provides news and other information on planning, development, parking, mass transit, traffic, funding, and other topics.

Greenville Business Magazine (GBM). Integrated Media Publishing. • Monthly. $23.95 Individuals. Magazine featuring Greenville businesses and communities.

ICMA Newsletter. International City/County Management Association. • Description: Discusses local government, professional management, and federal regulation. Publishes news of Association activities. Recurring features include news of members; reports of publications, educational workshops, positions open in public management; and two main supplements titled Nuts & Bolts and ICMA University.

Nation's Cities Weekly. National League of Cities. • Weekly. $96 Nonmembers. Description: Presents news on the latest developments in Congress, the White House, federal agencies, and other public interest groups which may affect the nation's cities.

RESEARCH CENTERS AND INSTITUTES

University of California, Berkeley - Institute of Urban and Regional Development. 316 Wurster Hall, MC 1870, Berkeley, CA 94720-1870. Phone: (510)642-4874; Fax: (510)643-9576; Email: iurd@berkeley.edu • URL: http://iurd.berkeley.edu • Research topics include the effects of changing economic trends in urban areas.

University of Louisville - Department of Urban and Public Affairs - Urban Studies Institute. 426 W Bloom St., Louisville, KY 40208. Phone: (502)852-2435; Fax: (502)852-7386; Email: upa@louisville.edu • URL: http://usi.louisville.edu • Social policy and economics.

STATISTICS SOURCES

America's Top Rated Cities: A Statistical Handbook. Grey House Publishing. • Annual. $250.00. Four volumes. $75.00 per volume. Each volume covers major cities in a region of the U. S.: Eastern, Southern, Central, and Western. City statistics cover the "Business Environment" (finances, employment, taxes, utilities, etc.) and the "Living Environment" (cost of living, housing, education, health care, climate, etc.).

America's Top-Rated Smaller Cities: A Statistical Handbook. Grey House Publishing. • Biennial. $225 Individuals. Provides detailed profiles of 60 smaller U. S. cities ranging in population from 25,000 to 100,000. Includes data on cost of living, employment, income, taxes, climate, media, and many other factors.

Cities of the United States. Cengage Learning Inc. • $731 Individuals per volume. Four regional volumes. $218.00 per volume. Detailed information is provided on U.S. cities. Includes economic data, climate, geography, government, and history, with maps and photographs.

Statistical Abstract of the United States. U. S. Government Printing Office. • Annual. $44.00. Issued by the U. S. Bureau of the Census.

ULI Market Profiles: North America. Urban Land Institute. • Annual. Members, $249.95; nonmembers, $299.95. Provides real estate marketing data for residential, retail, office, and industrial sectors. Covers 76 U. S. metropolitan areas and 13 major foreign metropolitan areas.

TRADE/PROFESSIONAL ASSOCIATIONS

International Downtown Association. 1025 Thomas Jefferson St. NW, Ste. 500W, Washington, DC 20007. Phone: (202)393-6801; Fax: (202)393-6869; Email: question@ida-downtown.org • URL: http://www.ida-downtown.org • Represents vital and livable urban centers. Works to build partnerships that anchor the well-being of towns, cities and regions throughout the world.

National Association of Towns and Townships. 1130 Connecticut Ave. NW, Ste. 300, Washington, DC 20036. Phone: 866-830-0008 or (202)454-3954 or (202)454-3950; Fax: (202)331-1598; Email: jimo@tfgnet.com • URL: http://www.natat.org • Provides technical and other assistance to officials of small communities.

National League of Cities. 1301 Pennsylvania Ave. NW, Ste. 550, Washington, DC 20004-1747. Phone: 877-827-2385 or (202)626-3000; Email: memberservices@nlc.org • URL: http://www.nlc.org • Formerly American Municipal Association.

CITIZENSHIP

See also CIVIL RIGHTS

PERIODICALS AND NEWSLETTERS

Presidential Studies Quarterly. Center for the Study of the Presidency. Pine Forge Press. • Quarterly. $559 Institutions print and online. Offers articles, features, review essays, and book reviews covering US Presidency.

TRADE/PROFESSIONAL ASSOCIATIONS

Center for the Study of the Presidency and Congress. 1020 19th St. NW, Ste. 250, Washington, DC 20010. Phone: (202)872-9800; Fax: (202)872-9811; Email: email@thepresidency.org • URL: http://www.thepresidency.org • Counsels the White House and Executive Branch on policy issues critical to strengthening presidential leadership and improving executive-congressional relations. Formerly Library of Presidential Papers.

National Conference on Citizenship. 1100 17th St. NW, 12th Fl., Washington, DC 20036. Phone: (202)601-7096; Email: info@ncoc.net • URL: http://www.ncoc.net • Promotes citizenship activities and spirit of cooperation on part of all citizens. Leads annual Citizenship Day on September 17 to recognize youth reaching voting age and salutes foreign-born receiving citizenship through naturalization.

National Immigration Forum. 50 F St. NW, Ste. 300, Washington, DC 20001-1552. Phone: (202)347-0040; Fax: (202)347-0058 or (202)544-0004; Email: info@immigrationforum.org • URL: http://www.immigrationforum.org • Dedicated to extending and defending America's tradition as a nation of immigrants. Supports the reunification of families, the rescue and resettlement of refugees fleeing persecution, and the equitable treatment of immigrants under the law. Encourages immigrants to become U.S. citizens and promote cooperation and understanding between immigrants and other Americans.

CITRUS FRUIT INDUSTRY

ABSTRACTS AND INDEXES

Food Science and Technology Abstracts. Ovid Technologies Inc. • Monthly. $1,780.00 per year. Provides worldwide coverage of the literature of food technology and food production.

Foods Adlibra: Key to the World's Food Literature. General Mills, Inc. Foods Adlibra Publications. • Semimonthly. $240.00 per year. Provides journal citations and abstracts to the literature of food technology and packaging.

DIRECTORIES

Major Food and Drink Companies of the World. Cengage Learning Inc. • 12th edition. eBook. Published by Graham & Whiteside. Contains profiles and trade names for more than 9,200 important food and beverage companies in various countries. In addition to foods, includes both alcoholic and nonalcoholic drink products.

FINANCIAL RATIOS

Annual Statement Studies. Risk Management Association. • Annual. Compiled from over 280,000 financial statements.

Annual Statement Studies: Industry Default Probabilities and Cash Flow Measures. Risk Management Association. • Annual. $405 Nonmembers. Serves as a companion volume to the original *Annual Statement Studies.* Gives probability of default estimates on a percentage scale for more than 450 industries. Includes changes in position year-by-year for eight financial statement line items and provides percentage measures of cash flow.

INTERNET DATABASES

USDA. U.S. National Institute of Standards and Technology. 100 Bureau Dr., Gaithersburg, MD 20899-1070. Phone: 800-877-8339 or (301)975-6478 or (202)720-2791; Fax: (301)975-8295; Email: inquiries@nist.gov • URL: http://www.nist.gov • The USDA home page has six sections: News and Information; What's New; About USDA; Agencies; Opportunities; Search and Help. Keyword searching is offered from the USDA home page and from various individual agency home pages. Agencies are the Economic Research Service, Agricultural Marketing Service, National Agricultural Statistics Service, National Agricultural Library, and about 12 others. Updating varies. Fees: Free.

ONLINE DATABASES

Agricola. U.S. National Agricultural Library World List of Agricultural Serials. • Covers worldwide agricultural literature. Over 3.3 million citations, 1970 to present, with monthly updates. Inquire as to online cost and availability.

Food Science and Technology Abstracts (online). IFIS North American Desk. • Produced by International Food Information Service. Provides about 500,000 online citations, with abstracts, to the international literature of food science, technology, commodities, engineering, and processing. Approximately 2,000 periodicals are covered. Time period is 1969 to date, with monthly updates. Inquire as to online cost and availability.

PERIODICALS AND NEWSLETTERS

Citrograph: Magazine of the Citrus Industry. Agricultural Publishing Co. • Monthly. $19.95 per year. Gives produce growing tips.

Citrus Industry Magazine. Associated Publications Corp. • Monthly. $24 per year. Gives food growing tips.

Triangle. Florida Citrus Mutual. • Description: Contains items of interest to citrus growers, including statistical data, market information, ongoing scientific research, and action by various government agencies. Recurring features include weather forecasts, market information, production statistics, news of research, a calendar of events, and reports of meetings.

PRICE SOURCES

California Farmer: The Business Magazine for Commercial Agriculture. Farm Progress Companies Inc. • $23.95 Individuals. Three editions: Northern, Southern and Central Valley.

Supermarket News: The Industry's Weekly Newspaper. Fairchild Publications. • Weekly. Individuals, $196.00 per year; retailers, $45.00 per year; manufacturers, $89.00 per year.

RESEARCH CENTERS AND INSTITUTES

New South Wales Department of Primary Industries - Orange Agricultural Institute. Forest Rd., Orange, NSW 2800, Australia. Phone: 61 2 63913800; Fax: 61 2 63913899; Email: david.michalk@dpi.nsw.gov.au • URL: http://www.dpi.nsw.gov.au/research/centres/orange • Animal health, including infectious and toxicity diseases; animal production, including sheep genetics, wool production, and vertebrate pests; plant production, including weed control and ecology, crops, pastures, and horticulture; agricultural scientific collections; plant protection, including entomology and plant pathology; biometrics; and economics.

STATISTICS SOURCES

Agricultural Statistics. U.S. Department of Agriculture National Agricultural Statistics Service. • Annual. $46 Individuals. Provides a wide variety of statistical data relating to agricultural production, supplies, consumption, prices/price-supports, foreign trade, costs, and returns, as well as farm labor, loans, income, and population. In many cases, historical data is shown annually for 10 years. In addition to farm data, includes detailed fishery statistics.

United States Census of Agriculture. U.S. Department of Agriculture National Agricultural Statistics Service. • Quinquennial. Provides uniform, comprehensive farming and ranching operations data for every U.S. state and county, including production expenses, market value of products, and operator characteristics.

CITY ATTORNEYS

See MUNICIPAL GOVERNMENT

CITY CLERKS

See MUNICIPAL GOVERNMENT

CITY FINANCE

See MUNICIPAL FINANCE

CITY GOVERNMENT

See MUNICIPAL GOVERNMENT

CITY PLANNING

See also REGIONAL PLANNING; URBAN DEVELOPMENT; ZONING

ABSTRACTS AND INDEXES

Art Index. EBSCO Publishing Inc. • Quarterly. Annual cumulations. Price varies. Subject and author index to periodicals in art, architecture, industrial design, city planning, photography, and various related topics.

Journal of Planning Literature. Ohio State University, Dept. of City and Regional Planning. Pine Forge Press. • Quarterly. $1,380 Institutions Print and E-access. Provides reviews and abstracts of city and regional planning lierature.

Social Sciences Citation Index. Thomson Reuters Corp. • Weekly. Product is accessed via *Web of Science.*

Social Sciences Index Retrospective: 1907-1983. EBSCO Publishing Inc. • Indexing for 1,000,000 articles. Coverage includes international index and social sciences and humanities index.

CD-ROM DATABASES

Social Sciences Abstracts. EBSCO Publishing Inc. • Provides indexing from 1983 and abstracting from 1994 of more than 750 periodicals covering economics, area studies, community health, public administration, public welfare, urban studies, and many other topics related to the social sciences.

Social Sciences Citation Index. Thomson Reuters Corp. • Weekly. Product is accessed via *Web of Science.*

HANDBOOKS AND MANUALS

Progress in Planning. Elsevier. • Eight times a year. $755.00 per year.

Zoning and Planning Deskbook, 2d. Katherine Kmiec Turner and Douglas W. Kmiec, authors. Thomson West. • Annual. $530.60 book - softbound; full set. Emphasis is on legal issues. Examines the latest developments in land use control, discussing procedural and substantive considerations, remedies, strategies, and state and federal litigation.

Zoning and Planning Law Handbook. Patricia Salkin. Thomson West. • Annual. $601.30. Assembles the insights and guidance offered by the country's leading authorities in zoning law, land use planning, and conservation.

ONLINE DATABASES

Art Index Online. H.W. Wilson Co. • Indexes a wide variety of art-related periodicals, 1984 to date. Monthly updates. Inquire as to online cost and availability.

Wilson Social Sciences Abstracts Online. H.W. Wilson Co. • Provides online abstracting and indexing of more than 500 periodicals covering area studies, community health, public administration, public welfare, urban studies, and many other social science topics. Time period is 1994 to date for abstracts and 1983 to date for indexing, with updates weekly. Inquire as to online cost and availability.

OTHER SOURCES

American Land Planning Law. John Taylor and Norma Williams. Thomson West. • $1,058 Individuals full set. Examines the changing priorities in zoning and land use practices, focusing on the relationship between private activity and governmental power, and analyzing over 15,000 cases from all 50 states.

PERIODICALS AND NEWSLETTERS

Greenville Business Magazine (GBM). Integrated Media Publishing. • Monthly. $23.95 Individuals. Magazine featuring Greenville businesses and communities.

Planning. American Planning Association. • Monthly. $85 Nonmembers.

Planning and Zoning News. Planning & Zoning Center Inc. • Monthly. $185 per year. Newsletter on planning and zoning issues in the United States.

Urban Land: News and Trends in Land Development. Urban Land Institute. • Monthly.

RESEARCH CENTERS AND INSTITUTES

Center for Urban and Regional Studies. University of North Carolina at Chapel Hill. 108 Battle Ln., Chapel Hill, NC 27599-3410. Phone: (919)962-3074 or (919)962-3077; Fax: (919)962-2518; Email: brohe@unc.edu • URL: http://curs.unc.edu •

Founded by the Institute for Research in Social Science of the University of North Carolina to facilitate research in urban and regional affairs. Center is concerned with: the investigation of underlying processes responsible for rapid growth and change in the urban scene; the study of problems and issues associated with these processes; the development of systems for the stimulation of urban processes so that policy and program alternatives for achieving local objectives can be tested and their implications studied before putting them into effect. Current research projects include: studies of urban and regional problems such as housing and community development; coastal zone management; flood hazard management; land use management; urban growth management; water source protection in urbanizing watersheds, brown fields' redevelopment, sustainable development and poverty and equity issues.

Cornell University - Program in International Studies in Planning. 106 W Sibley Hall, Ithaca, NY 14853-3901. Phone: (607)255-4331 or (607)255-4613; Fax: (607)255-1971; Email: wwg1@cornell.edu • URL: http://aap.cornell.edu/crp/programs/grad/internation-studies.cfm • Research activities are related to international urban and regional planning, with emphasis on developing areas.

TRADE/PROFESSIONAL ASSOCIATIONS

National Association of Housing and Redevelopment Officials. 630 Eye St. NW, Washington, DC 20001-3736. Phone: 877-866-2476 or (202)289-3500; Fax: (202)289-8181; Email: nahro@nahro.org • URL: http://www.nahro.org • Formerly National Association of Housing Officials.

National Community Development Association. 522 21st St. NW, No. 120, Washington, DC 20006-5012. Phone: (202)293-7587; Fax: (202)887-5546 • URL: http://www.ncdaonline.org • Represents community development program directors. Supports the interests of Community Development Block Grant Programs as well as other community and economic development issues; disseminates information; operates workshops on various aspects of housing, economic, and community development.

CIVIL ENGINEERING

ABSTRACTS AND INDEXES

Applied Science and Technology Index. EBSCO Publishing Inc. • 11/year. Indexes a wide variety of English language technical, industrial, and engineering periodicals.

Engineering Index Monthly: Abstracting and Indexing Services Covering Sources ofthe World's Engineering Literature. Engineering Information Inc. • Monthly. Institutions, $5,279.00 per year. Provides indexing and abstracting of the world's engineering and technical literature.

Fluid Abstracts: Civil Engineering. Elsevier. • Monthly. $3,804 Institutions print. Monthly. Institutions, $1,709.00 per year. Includes annual cumulation. Includes the literature of coastal structures. Published in England by Elsevier Science Publishing Ltd. Formerly *Civil Engineering Hydraulics Abstracts.*

ONLINE DATABASES

Applied Science and Technology Index Online. H.W. Wilson Co. • Provides online indexing of 500 major scientific, technical, industrial, and engineering periodicals. Time period is 1983 to date. Monthly updates. Inquire as to online cost and availability.

Civil Engineering Database. Architectural Engineering Institute of ASCE. • Provides abstracts of the U. S. and international literature of civil engineering, 1975 to date. Inquire as to online cost and availability.

TRIS: Transportation Research Information Service. The National Academies National Research Council. • Contains abstracts and citations to a wide range of transportation literature, 1968 to present, with monthly updates. Includes references to the literature of air transportation, highways, ships and shipping, railroads, trucking, and urban mass transportation. Formerly *TRIS-ON-LINE.* Inquire as to online cost and availability.

OTHER SOURCES

American Society of Civil Engineers: Transactions. Architectural Engineering Institute of ASCE. • $422 Nonmembers. Publication for civil engineers.

Forms and Agreements for Architects, Engineers and Contractors. Albert Dib. Thomson West. • $2,687.25 full set. Three times a year. Five looseleaf volume. Covers evaluation of construction documents and alternative clauses. Includes pleadings for litigation and resolving of claims. (Real Property Law Series).

PERIODICALS AND NEWSLETTERS

Civil Engineering: Engineered Design and Construction. Architectural Engineering Institute of ASCE. • Monthly. $160.00 per year.

ENR: Connecting the Industry Worldwide. McGraw Hill Financial Inc. • Weekly. $74.00 per year.

RESEARCH CENTERS AND INSTITUTES

Engineering Dean's Office. University of California at Berkeley. 320 McLaughlin Hall, Berkeley, CA 94720-1700. Phone: (510)642-5771; Fax: (510)642-9178; Email: sastry@coe.berkeley.edu • URL: http://www.coe.berkeley.edu • Research fields include civil, electrical, industrial, mechanical, and other types of engineering.

TRADE/PROFESSIONAL ASSOCIATIONS

Architectural Engineering Institute of ASCE. 1801 Alexander Bell Dr., Reston, VA 20191-4400. Phone: 800-548-2723; Email: aei@asce.org • URL: http://www.asce.org/aei • Seeks to advance the state-of-the-art and state-of-the-practice of the building industry worldwide by facilitating effective and timely technology transfer. Provides a multidisciplinary forum for building industry professionals to examine technical, scientific and professional issues of common interest.

Geosynthetics Materials Association. c/o Industrial Fabrics Association International, 1801 County Rd. B W, Roseville, MN 55113-4061. Phone: 800-225-4324 or (651)222-2508; Fax: (651)631-9334; Email: generalinfo@ifai.com • URL: http://www.ifai.com/groups/gma • Represents members of the geosynthetics industry including manufacturers, testing firms and service companies. Aims to promote the acceptance and use of geosynthetic materials in a variety of applications. Provides resources and offers networking opportunities among members.

CIVIL RIGHTS

See also CITIZENSHIP; HUMAN RELATIONS

ABSTRACTS AND INDEXES

Current Law Index. Cengage Learning Inc. • $1,332 Individuals. Monthly. $1269.00 per year. Produced in cooperation with the American Association of Law Libraries. Indexes more than 900 law journals, legal newspapers, and specialty publications from the U.S., Canada, U.K., Ireland, Australia, and New Zealand.

Social Sciences Citation Index. Thomson Reuters Corp. • Weekly. Product is accessed via *Web of Science.*

Social Sciences Index Retrospective: 1907-1983. EBSCO Publishing Inc. • Indexing for 1,000,000 articles. Coverage includes international index and social sciences and humanities index.

ALMANACS AND YEARBOOKS

World Labour Report. International Labour Office. • Irregular. Price varies. International coverage. Reviews significant recent events and labor policy developments in the following areas: employment, human rights, labor relations, and working conditions.

CD-ROM DATABASES

Social Sciences Abstracts. EBSCO Publishing Inc. • Provides indexing from 1983 and abstracting from 1994 of more than 750 periodicals covering economics, area studies, community health, public administration, public welfare, urban studies, and many other topics related to the social sciences.

Social Sciences Citation Index. Thomson Reuters Corp. • Weekly. Product is accessed via *Web of Science.*

DIRECTORIES

Human Rights Organizations and Periodicals Directory. Meiklejohn Civil Liberties Institute. • Quadrennial Biennial. $150 Individuals per year. Over 1,200 United States organiations and periodicals dedicated to improving human rights.

ENCYCLOPEDIAS AND DICTIONARIES

Encyclopedia of Crime and Justice. Cengage Learning Inc. • 2001. $737. 2nd edition. 4 volumes. Published by Macmillan Reference USA. Contains extensive information on a wide variety of topics pertaining to crime, criminology, social issues, and the courts. Also available as eBook.

HANDBOOKS AND MANUALS

Women and the Law. Carol H. Lefcourt, editor. Thomson West. • Annual. $691.60 Individuals book - softbound. Covers such topics as employment discrimination, pay equity (comparable worth), sexual harassment in the workplace, property rights, and child custody issues.

INTERNET DATABASES

Lexis.com Research System. Lexis-Nexis Group. Phone: 800-227-4908 or (937)865-6800; Fax: (937)865-6909; Email: webmaster@prod.lexis-nexis.com • URL: http://www.nexis.com • Fee-based Web site offers extensive searching of a wide variety of legal sources. Additional features include Daily Opinion Service, lexis.com Bookstore, Career Center, CLE Center, Law Schools, and Practice Pages ("Pages specific to areas of specialty").

ONLINE DATABASES

Wilson Social Sciences Abstracts Online. H.W. Wilson Co. • Provides online abstracting and indexing of more than 500 periodicals covering area studies, community health, public administration, public welfare, urban studies, and many other social science topics. Time period is 1994 to date for abstracts and 1983 to date for indexing, with updates weekly. Inquire as to online cost and availability.

OTHER SOURCES

Civil Rights Actions. Matthew Bender and Company Inc. • $2,492 book. Seven looseleaf volumes. Periodic supplementation. Contains legal analysis of civil rights activities.

Government Discrimination: Equal Protection Law and Litigation. James A. Kushner. Thomson West. • Semiannual. $708.75 full set. Covers discrimination in employment, housing, and other areas by local, state, and federal offices or agencies. (Civil Rights Series).

Housing Discrimination: Law and Litigation. Robert G. Schwemm. Thomson West. • Annual. $593 full set. Covers provisions of the Fair Housing Act and related topics.

PERIODICALS AND NEWSLETTERS

Civil Rights: State Capitals. Wakeman/Walworth Inc. • 50 times a year. $245.00 per year; print and online editions, $350.00 per year. Newsletter. Includes coverage of state affirmative action programs. Formerly *From the State Capitals: Civil Rights*.

CORE Magazine. Congress of Racial Equality. CORE Publications. • Quarterly. $10.00 per year.

Police Misconduct and Civil Rights Law Report. National Lawyers Guild. Thomson West. • Bimonthly. $297. Provides expert analysis ot the most current developments in police misconduct and civil rights law.

RESEARCH CENTERS AND INSTITUTES

Center for National Policy. 1250 I St. NW, Ste. 500, Washington, DC 20005. Phone: (202)216-9723; Email: info@trumancnp.org • URL: http://cnponline.org • Promotes open discussion of the fundamentals of American public policy, including understanding of the substance of issues, determination of individual and common interests, and assessment of the attitudes, values and opinions of the public.

State University of New York at Buffalo - Buffalo Human Rights Center. 710 John Lord O'Brian Hall, School of Law, North Campus, Buffalo, NY 14260-1100. Phone: (716)645-2257; Email: buffalohrc@gmail.com • URL: http://wings.buffalo.edu/law/BHRC • Human rights issues around the globe. The group focuses primarily on economic, cultural and social rights, as well as the relationships between labor, trade, and human rights.

TRADE/PROFESSIONAL ASSOCIATIONS

Afghan Peace and Democracy Act. 220 St. 9, District 4, Taimani, Kabul, Afghanistan. Email: info@afghanact.org • URL: http://www.alternatives.ca/en/about-us • Enhances the role of civil society organizations. Helps the NGOs in advocating peace and democracy in Afghanistan. Provides direct support and collaboration to Afghan NGOs and civil societies.

American Civil Liberties Union. 125 Broad St., 18th Fl., New York, NY 10004. Phone: (212)549-2500; Email: media@aclu.org • URL: http://www.aclu.org • Champions the rights set forth in the Bill of Rights of the U.S. Constitution: freedom of speech, press, assembly, and religion; due process of law and fair trial; equality before the law regardless of race, color, sexual orientation, national origin, political opinion, or religious belief. Conducts activities including litigation, advocacy, and public education. Sponsors litigation projects on topics such as women's rights, gay and lesbian rights, and children's rights.

Leadership Conference on Civil and Human Rights. 1629 K St. NW, 10th Fl., Washington, DC 20006-1602. Phone: (202)466-3311; Fax: (202)466-3434 • URL: http://www.civilrights.org • Formerly Civil Rights Mobilization.

National Association for the Advancement of Colored People. 4805 Mt. Hope Dr., Baltimore, MD 21215. Phone: 877-NAACP-98 or (410)580-5777 or (410)580-5110; Email: actso@naacpnet.org • URL: http://www.naacp.org • Persons "of all races and religions" who believe in the objectives and methods of the NAACP. Works to achieve equal rights through the democratic process and eliminate racial prejudice by removing racial discrimination in housing, employment, voting, schools, the courts, transportation, recreation, prisons, and business enterprises. Offers referral services, tutorials, job referrals, and day care. Sponsors seminars; maintains law library. Sponsors the NAACP National Housing Corporation to assist in the development of low and moderate income housing for families. Compiles statistics.

National Urban League. 120 Wall St., New York, NY 10005. Phone: (212)558-5300; Fax: (212)344-5332; Email: info@nul.org • URL: http://nul.iamempowered.com • Voluntary nonpartisan community service agency of civic, professional, business, labor, and religious leaders with a staff of trained social workers and other professionals. Aims to eliminate racial segregation and discrimination in the United States and to achieve parity for blacks and other minorities in every phase of American life. Works to eliminate institutional racism and to provide direct service to minorities in the areas of employment, housing, education, social welfare, health, family planning, mental retardation, law and consumer affairs, youth and student affairs, labor affairs, veterans' affairs, and community and minority business development. Maintains research department in Washington, DC.

CIVIL SERVICE

See also GOVERNMENT EMPLOYEES

ABSTRACTS AND INDEXES

Social Sciences Citation Index. Thomson Reuters Corp. • Weekly. Product is accessed via *Web of Science*.

Social Sciences Index Retrospective: 1907-1983. EBSCO Publishing Inc. • Indexing for 1,000,000 articles. Coverage includes international index and social sciences and humanities index.

ALMANACS AND YEARBOOKS

Federal Employees Almanac. 1105 Media Inc. • Annual. $20.95 print. Comprehensive guide for federal employees.

CD-ROM DATABASES

Social Sciences Abstracts. EBSCO Publishing Inc. • Provides indexing from 1983 and abstracting from 1994 of more than 750 periodicals covering economics, area studies, community health, public administration, public welfare, urban studies, and many other topics related to the social sciences.

Social Sciences Citation Index. Thomson Reuters Corp. • Weekly. Product is accessed via *Web of Science*.

ONLINE DATABASES

Wilson Social Sciences Abstracts Online. H.W. Wilson Co. • Provides online abstracting and indexing of more than 500 periodicals covering area studies, community health, public administration, public welfare, urban studies, and many other social science topics. Time period is 1994 to date for abstracts and 1983 to date for indexing, with updates weekly. Inquire as to online cost and availability.

OTHER SOURCES

Carroll's Federal Organization Charts. Caroll Publishing. • 8/year. $1,650 Individuals. Provides 200 large, fold-out paper charts showing personnel relationships in 2,100 federal departments and agencies. Charts are also available online and on CD-ROM.

PERIODICALS AND NEWSLETTERS

Federal Human Resources Week: News, Strategies and Best Practices for the HR Professional. LRP Publications Library. • 48 times a year. $350.00 per year. Newsletter. Covers federal personnel issues, including legislation, benefits, budgets, and downsizing.

Federal Times. Gannett Government Media Corp. • Weekly (Mon.). Federal bureaucracy; technology in government.

Public Personnel Management. International Personnel Management Association. • Quarterly. $273 Institutions. Contains trends, case studies, and the latest research by top human resource scholars and industry experts.

CLAY INDUSTRY

See also CERAMICS INDUSTRY; POTTERY INDUSTRY

CD-ROM DATABASES

OECD Statistical Compendium. Organization for Economic Cooperation and Development. • Semiannual. $1,905.00 per year for 1 to 10 users. CD-ROM contains more than 730,000 monthly, quarterly, and annual time series for OECD countries, 1960 to date. Includes fully searchable data on agriculture, food, economic indicators, national accounts, employment, energy, finance, industry, technology, and foreign trade. Results can be displayed in various forms.

INTERNET DATABASES

Business 2.0 Web Guide to the Best Business Links. Business 2.0 Media Inc. Phone: (415)293-4800; Email: support@business2.com • URL: http://www.business2.com/webguide • Web site presents an extensive, searchable directory of links to "the best, most informative, and authoritative web pages." Twenty main categories cover business, finance, career, company information, people, and technology topics, with thousands of subtopics, all linking to Web sites recommended by experienced business researchers. Fees: Free.

Fedstats. Federal Interagency Council on Statistical Policy. Phone: (202)395-7254 • URL: http://www.fedstats.gov • Web site features an efficient search facility for full-text statistics produced by more than 100 federal agencies, including the Census Bureau, the Bureau of Economic Analysis, and the Bureau of Labor Statistics. Boolean searches can be made within one agency or for all agencies combined. Links are offered to international statistical bureaus, including the UN, IMF, OECD, UNESCO, Eurostat, and 20 individual countries. Fees: Free.

FreeLunch.com. Economy.com, Inc. Phone: (610)696-8700; Fax: (610)696-1678 • URL: http://www.freelunch.com • Web site provides free access to more than 200 million economic and financial data series, covering industry, demographics, labor markets, prices, retail sales, government spending, trade, interest rates, housing starts, the stock market, etc. Data is available in either chart or table form. Searching is offered. Free, but registration required. Economy.com, Inc. also offers fee-based economic analysis at *The Dismal Scientist* site (www.dismal.com).

Manufacturing Profiles. U. S. Bureau of the Census. Phone: (301)763-4636 or (301)763-4100; Fax: (301)763-4794; Email: webmaster@census.gov • URL: http://www.census.gov/prod/www/abs/mfg-prof.html • The Census Bureau makes available free on PDF (Portable Document Format) an annual consolidation of the entire Current Industrial Report series, presenting "all the data compiled." Contains statistics on production, shipments, inventories, consumption, exports, imports, and orders for a wide variety of manufactured products.

PERIODICALS AND NEWSLETTERS

Clays and Clay Minerals. Clay Minerals Society. • Bimonthly. $510 Institutions.

STATISTICS SOURCES

Survey of Current Business. U. S. Government Printing Office. • Published by Bureau of Economic Analysis, U. S. Department of Commerce. Presents a wide variety of business and economic data.

United States Census of Mineral Industries. Bureau of the Census, U.S. Department of Commerce. U. S. Government Printing Office. • Quinquennial.

TRADE/PROFESSIONAL ASSOCIATIONS

Brick Industry Association. 1850 Centennial Park Dr., Ste. 301, Reston, VA 20191. Phone: (703)620-0010; Fax: (703)620-3928; Email: brickinfo@bia.org • URL: http://www.gobrick.com • Manufacturers and distributors of clay brick. Promotes clay brick with the goal of increasing its market share.

Clay Minerals Society. 3635 Concorde Pkwy., Ste.

500, Chantilly, VA 20151-1110. Phone: (703)652-9960; Fax: (703)652-9951; Email: cms@clays.org • URL: http://www.clays.org • Professionals concerned with clay mineralogy and technology in industry, university research, and government. Includes students of mineralogy, geology, soil science, astronomy, physics, geochemistry, and engineering, and representatives of such firms as oil companies, instrument makers, and clay mining companies. Seeks to stimulate research and disseminate information relating to all aspects of clay science and technology. Provides a forum for exchange of information and ideas. Maintains quantities of Source and Special Clays at the Source Clays Repository.

CLEANING COMPOSITIONS

See CLEANING PRODUCTS INDUSTRY

CLEANING INDUSTRY

See also LAUNDRY INDUSTRY

ABSTRACTS AND INDEXES

Textile Technology Index™. EBSCO Publishing Inc. • Monthly. $545 Individuals. Includes indexing and abstracts for more than 470 periodicals.

DIRECTORIES

Association for Linen Management Membership Directory. Association for Linen Management. • Annual. $150.00. Lists managers of in-house laundries for institutions, hotels, schools, etc.

Cleaning-House and Office-Directory. InfoGroup Inc. • Annual. Number of listings: 37,431. Entries include: Name, address, phone, size of advertisement, name of owner or manager, number of employees, year first in "Yellow Pages." Compiled from telephone company "Yellow Pages," nationwide.

Dry Cleaners Directory. InfoGroup Inc. • Annual. Number of listings: 50,053. Entries include: Name, address, phone, size of advertisement, name of owner or manager, number of employees, year first in "Yellow Pages." Compiled from telephone company "Yellow Pages," nationwide.

FINANCIAL RATIOS

Annual Statement Studies. Risk Management Association. • Annual. Compiled from over 280,000 financial statements.

Annual Statement Studies: Industry Default Probabilities and Cash Flow Measures. Risk Management Association. • Annual. $405 Nonmembers. Serves as a companion volume to the original *Annual Statement Studies*. Gives probability of default estimates on a percentage scale for more than 450 industries. Includes changes in position year-by-year for eight financial statement line items and provides percentage measures of cash flow.

ONLINE DATABASES

Textile Technology Index™. EBSCO Publishing Inc. • Monthly. $545 Individuals. Includes indexing and abstracts for more than 470 periodicals.

PERIODICALS AND NEWSLETTERS

American Coin-Op: The Magazine for Coin-Operated Laundry and Drycleaning Businessmen. Crain Communications Inc. • Monthly. Free.

American Drycleaner. Crain Communications Inc. • Monthly. Free.

Cleaning Business: Published Monthly for the Self-Employed Cleaning and Maintenance Professionals. William R. Griffin, Publisher. • Monthly. $20. Formerly *Service Business*.

Drycleaners News. Zackin Publications Inc. • Monthly. $36.00.

Industrial Launderer. Uniform and Textile Service Association. • Monthly. $100.00 per year.

STATISTICS SOURCES

United States Census of Service Industries. U.S. Department of Commerce U.S. Census Bureau. • Quinquennial. Various reports available.

TRADE/PROFESSIONAL ASSOCIATIONS

Association for Linen Management. 2161 Lexington Rd., Ste. 2, Richmond, KY 40475. Phone: 800-669-0863 or (859)624-0177; Fax: (859)624-3580 • URL: http://www.almnet.org • Formerly National Assoiciation of Institutional Laundry Managers.

Association of Residential Cleaning Services International. c/o Ernie Hartong, 7870 Olentangy River Rd., Ste. 301, Columbus, OH 43235. Phone: (614)547-0887; Fax: (614)505-7136; Email: chris@arcsi.org • URL: http://www.arcsi.org • Represents residential cleaning service owners and professionals. Advances and improves the residential cleaning industry. Shares knowledge and information to ensure the growth and development of cleaning service businesses.

Coin Laundry Association. 1 S 660 Midwest Rd., Ste. 205, Oakbrook Terrace, IL 60181. Phone: 800-570-5629 or (630)953-7920; Fax: (630)953-7925; Email: info@coinlaundry.org • URL: http://coinlaundry.org • Manufacturers of equipment or supplies used in self-service (coin-operated) laundry or dry cleaning establishments; distributors of equipment services and supplies; owners and operators of self-service laundry and/or dry cleaning stores. Compiles statistics.

International Janitorial Cleaning Services Association. 2011 Oak St., Wyandotte, MI 48192. Phone: (734)252-6189; Email: info@ijcsa.com • URL: http://www.ijcsanetwork.com • Represents the interests of the janitorial industry. Promotes professionalism and ethics in the janitorial and cleaning services field. Provides training and education for cleaning professionals.

Multi-Housing Laundry Association. 1500 Sunday Dr., Ste. 102, Raleigh, NC 27607. Phone: (919)861-5579; Fax: (919)787-4916; Email: nshore@mla-online.com • URL: http://www.mla-online.com • Operating and supplier companies. Strives to provide tenants with professionally operated laundry facilities. Sponsors annual convention and trade show.

National Cleaners Association. 252 W 29th St., New York, NY 10001-5271. Phone: 800-888-1622 or (212)967-3002; Fax: (212)967-2240; Email: info@nca-i.com • URL: http://www.nca-i.com • Members are dry cleaning establishments.

CLEANING PRODUCTS INDUSTRY

ABSTRACTS AND INDEXES

Applied Science and Technology Index. EBSCO Publishing Inc. • 11/year. Indexes a wide variety of English language technical, industrial, and engineering periodicals.

DIRECTORIES

Directory of American Manufacturers & Exporters of Soap, Detergent & Cleaning Supplies. EXIM Infotek Private Ltd. • $5 Individuals. Covers: 40 American manufacturers and exporters of carpet cleaning chemicals, cleaning chemicals, detergents, and detergents-chemicals. Entries include: Company name, postal address, city, country, phone, fax, e-mail and websites, contact person, designation, and product details.

Directory of Chinese Manufacturers & Exporters of Soap, Detergent & Cleaning Supplies. EXIM Infotek Private Ltd. • $5 Individuals. Covers: 25 Chinese manufacturers and exporters of cleaning products, detergent liquid, detergent powder, detergents, soap, synthetic detergent. Entries include: Company name, postal address, city, country, phone, fax, e-mail and websites, contact person, designation, and product details.

Directory of European Importers of Soap, Detergent and Cleaning Supplies. EXIM Infotek Private Ltd. • $400 Individuals. Covers: 170 European importers of cleaning products, cleaning supplies, soap, detergents, household cleaning products, preparations for soap, and bleach. Entries include: Company name, postal address, telephone, fax, e-mail, website, contact person, designation, and product details.

Directory of French Importers of Soap, Detergents and Cleaning Supplies. EXIM Infotek Private Ltd. • $150 Individuals. Covers: 25 French importers of cleaning supplies, soap, and detergent. Entries include: Company name, postal address, telephone, fax, e-mail, website, contact person, designation, and product details.

Directory of Japanese Importers of Soap, Detergents and Cleaning Supplies. EXIM Infotek Private Ltd. • $200 Individuals. Covers: 60 Japanese importers of cleaning supplies, detergent, soap chip, soap, toiletry and bathroom preparations. Entries include: Company name, postal address, telephone, fax, e-mail, website, contact person, designation, and product details.

Directory of Middle East Importers of Soap, Detergent and Cleaning Supplies. EXIM Infotek Private Ltd. • $450 Individuals. Covers: 180 Middle East importers of cleaning supplies, soap, detergent, disinfectant products, polishes and cleansing materials, and bleach. Entries include: Company name, postal address, telephone, fax, e-mail, website, contact person, designation, and product details.

Directory of North American Importers of Soap, Detergent and Cleaning Supplies. EXIM Infotek Private Ltd. • $350 Individuals. Covers: 140 North American importers of antiseptics, disinfectant soap, cleaning supplies, detergent, shampoo, toilet and bathroom preparations. Entries include: Company name, postal address, telephone, fax, e-mail, website, contact person, designation, and product details.

Household and Personal Products Industry Buyers Guide. Rodman Publications. • Annual. Lists of suppliers to manufacturers of cosmetics, toiletries, soaps, detergents, and related household and personal products.

Household and Personal Products Industry Contract Manufacturing/Private Label Directory. Rodman Publications. • Annual. Provides information for about 450 companies offering private label or contract packaged household and personal care products, such as detergents, cosmetics, polishes, insecticides, and various aerosol items.

McCutcheon's Functional Materials Volumes 2. Manufacturing Confectioner Publishing Corp. • Edited for product development, quality control and research and development chemists.

McCutcheon's Volume 1: Emulsifiers and Detergents. Manufacturing Confectioner Publishing Corp. • Two volumes. International coverage.

FINANCIAL RATIOS

Annual Statement Studies. Risk Management Association. • Annual. Compiled from over 280,000 financial statements.

Annual Statement Studies: Industry Default Probabilities and Cash Flow Measures. Risk Management Association. • Annual. $405 Nonmembers. Serves as a companion volume to the original *Annual Statement Studies*. Gives probability of default estimates on a percentage scale for more than 450 industries. Includes changes in position year-by-year for eight financial statement line items and provides percentage measures of cash flow.

ONLINE DATABASES

CA Search. American Chemical Society Chemical Abstracts Service. • Guide to chemical literature, 1967 to present. Inquire as to online cost and availability.

PERIODICALS AND NEWSLETTERS

Household and Personal Products Industry: The Magazine for the Detergent, Soap, Cosmetic and Toiletry, Wax, Polish and Aerosol Industries. Rodman Publications. • Monthly. Covers marketing, packaging, production, technical innovations, private label developments, and aerosol packaging for soap, detergents, cosmetics, insecticides, and a variety of other household products.

ISSA Today. International Sanitary Supply Association. • Bimonthly. $20. Covers industry trends, certifications, and technologies to ever-changing legislation, business advice, and how-to applications.

Soap and Cosmetics. Cygnus Business Media. • Monthly. $60.00 per year. Formerly *Soap, Cosmetics, Chemical Specialties.*

PRICE SOURCES

Chemical & Engineering News. American Chemical Society. • Weekly Annual. $265 Nonmembers print, North America. Magazine on chemical and engineering news.

STATISTICS SOURCES

U.S. Industry and Trade Outlook. U.S. Department of Commerce National Technical Information Service. • Annual. Produced by the International Trade Administration, U.S. Department of Commerce, in a "public-private" partnership with DRI/McGraw-Hill and Standard & Poor's. Provides basic data, outlook for the current year, and "Long-Term Prospects" (five-year projections) for a wide variety of products and services. Includes high technology industries. Formerly *U.S. Industrial Outlook.*

TRADE/PROFESSIONAL ASSOCIATIONS

International Housewares Association. 6400 Shafer Ct., Ste. 650, Rosemont, IL 60018. Phone: (847)292-4200; Fax: (847)292-4211 • URL: http://www.housewares.org • Manufacturers and distributors of housewares and small appliances. Conducts annual market research survey of the housewares industry. Manages the international housewares show.

CLIMATE

See also TRAVEL INDUSTRY; WEATHER AND WEATHER FORECASTING

ABSTRACTS AND INDEXES

Meteorological & Geoastrophysical Abstracts (MGA). American Meteorological Society. American Meteorological Society. • Monthly. $1,605 print. Journal presenting abstrcts of current world literature in meteorology, climatology, aeronomy, planetary atmospheres, solar-terrestrial relations, hydrology, oceanography, glaciology.

E-BOOKS

Weather Almanac. Cengage Learning Inc. • 2004. eBook. 11th edition. Weather records for 108 major U.S. cities and a climatic overview of the country. Contact for pricing.

PERIODICALS AND NEWSLETTERS

International Journal of Climatology. Royal Meteorological Society. John Wiley and Sons, Inc., Journals Div. • 15 times a year. $1,065.00 per year; institutions, $2,135.00 per year. Published in England by John Wiley and Sons Ltd.

RESEARCH CENTERS AND INSTITUTES

Atmospheric Sciences Research Center - University of Albany, State University of New York. 251 Fuller Rd., Albany, NY 12203. Phone: (518)437-8754 or (518)437-8705; Fax: (518)437-8758; Email: info@asrc.cestm.albany.edu • URL: http://www.asrc.cestm.albany.edu.

University of Wisconsin - Madison - Center for Climatic Research. 1225 W Dayton St., Madison, WI 53706-1695. Phone: (608)262-2839; Fax: (608)263-4190; Email: jww@geography.wisc.edu • URL: http://ccr.aos.wisc.edu.

TRADE/PROFESSIONAL ASSOCIATIONS

American Meteorological Society. 45 Beacon St., Boston, MA 02108-3693. Phone: (617)227-2425 or (617)227-2426; Fax: (617)742-8718; Email: amsinfo@ametsoc.org • URL: http://www.ametsoc.org • Professional meteorologists, oceanographers, and hydrologists; interested students and nonprofessionals. Develops and disseminates information on the atmospheric and related oceanic and hydrospheric sciences; seeks to advance professional applications. Activities include guidance service, scholarship programs, career information, certification of consulting meteorologists, and a seal of approval program to recognize competence in radio and television weathercasting. Issues statements of policy to assist public understanding on subjects such as weather modification, forecasting, tornadoes, hurricanes, flash floods, and meteorological satellites. Provides abstracting services. Prepares educational films, filmstrips, and slides for a new curriculum in meteorology at the ninth grade level. Issues monthly announcements of job openings for meteorologists.

Asia Pacific Network for Global Change Research. East Bldg., 4th Fl., 1-5-2 Wakinohama Kaigan Dori, Chuo-ku, Kobe, Hyogo 651 0073, Japan. Phone: 81 78 2308017; Fax: 81 78 2308018; Email: info@apn-gcr.org • URL: http://www.apn-gcr.org • Promotes, encourages and supports research activities on long-term global changes in climate, ocean and terrestrial systems, and on related physical, chemical, biological and socio-economic processes. Fosters global environmental change research in the Asia-Pacific region; increases developing country participation in research; strengthens interactions between the science community and policy makers. Cooperates closely with various scientific programmers and other networks.

Climate Action Network Australia. Level 1, 1 Smail St., Ultimo, NSW 2007, Australia. Phone: 61 2 82021248 • URL: http://www.cana.net.au • Increases understanding and the causes of climate change. Encourages governments, businesses and individuals to undertake actions to reduce greenhouse gas emissions. Promotes energy efficiency, renewable energy and sustainable transport and protects the natural ecosystem of Australia.

Climate Action Network Europe. Rue d'Edimbourg 26, B-1050 Brussels, Belgium. Phone: 32 2 8944670; Email: info@climnet.org • URL: http://www.climnet.org • European nongovernmental organizations with an interest in global climate and climatic change. Advocates a commitment to a 20% decrease in carbon dioxide emissions by the industrialized countries of the world over the next ten years. Gathers and disseminates information on greenhouse gases and global warming; works to increase public awareness of the implications of global climatic change.

Climate Group. 145 W 58th St., Ste. 2a, New York, NY 10019. Phone: (646)233-0550; Email: info@theclimategroup.org • URL: http://www.theclimategroup.org • Advances business and government leadership on climate change. Creates international effort to stop climate change. Works to accelerate international action on global warming. Promotes profitability and competitiveness among the government, business and non-profit sectors.

International Association for Urban Climate. School of Geography, Planning and Environment Policy, Newman Bldg., Belfield, Dublin 4, Dublin, Ireland. Phone: 353 1 7168229; Email: gerald.mills@ucd.ie • URL: http://www.urban-climate.org • Represents professionals in the fields of climatology and meteorology. Promotes and facilitates the study of urban climate, urban ecosystems and urban air quality.

United Nations Framework Convention on Climate Change. PO Box 260124, D-53153 Bonn, Germany. Phone: 49 228 8151000; Fax: 49 228 8151999; Email: secretariat@unfccc.int • URL: http://unfccc.int/2860.php • Member countries united to stabilize greenhouse gas concentrations in the atmosphere at a level that would prevent dangerous anthropogenic interference with the climate system. Works to achieve this goal within a time-frame sufficient to allow ecosystems to adapt naturally to climate change, to ensure that food production is not threatened, and to enable economic development to proceed in a sustainable manner.

University of Victoria - Centre for Global Studies - Canadian Institute for Climate Studies. 3800 Finnerty Rd., Sedgewick Bldg., Sta. C173, Victoria, BC, Canada V8P 1A1. Phone: (250)721-8800; Fax: (250)472-4830 • URL: http://www.uvic.ca/research/centres/globalstudies • Corporations, societies, companies, universities, government departments, and individuals with an interest in climate. Seeks to further the understanding of the climate system, its variability, and potential for change and the application of that understanding to decision-making, both in the public and private sectors. Manages climate related research initiatives; provides advice and consultation to those whose decisions are sensitive to variations in climate; and provides climate scenario data, maps, and background materials.

CLINICAL LABORATORY INDUSTRY

DIRECTORIES

AHA Integrated Delivery Network Directory: U.S. Health Care Systems, Networks, and Alliances. American Hospital Association. • Annual. $250.00. Provides information about a wide variety of U.S. health care groups and affiliations, including hospitals, nursing homes, rehabilitation centers, psychiatric facilities, home health care agencies, clinical laboratories, outpatient facilities, and diagnostic imaging centers. Includes names of more than 8,000 key executives.

FINANCIAL RATIOS

Annual Statement Studies. Risk Management Association. • Annual. Compiled from over 280,000 financial statements.

Annual Statement Studies: Industry Default Probabilities and Cash Flow Measures. Risk Management Association. • Annual. $405 Nonmembers. Serves as a companion volume to the original *Annual Statement Studies.* Gives probability of default estimates on a percentage scale for more than 450 industries. Includes changes in position year-by-year for eight financial statement line items and provides percentage measures of cash flow.

Industry Norms and Key Business Ratios. Dun & Bradstreet Inc. • Annual. Five volumes. Covers over 800 kinds of businesses, arranged by Standard Industrial Classification number. More detailed editions covering longer periods of time are also available.

PERIODICALS AND NEWSLETTERS

Clinical Leadership and Management Review. Clinical Laboratory Management Association. Lippincott Williams & Wilkins. • *Clinical Laboratory Management Review.*

MLO. Thomson Medical Economics. • Monthly. Covers management, regulatory, and technical top-

For publishers' addresses, refer to SOURCES CITED section at the back of the book.

ics for clinical laboratory administrators.

TRADE/PROFESSIONAL ASSOCIATIONS

American Clinical Laboratory Association. 1100 New York Ave. NW, Ste. 725 W, Washington, DC 20005. Phone: (202)637-9466; Fax: (202)637-2050; Email: info@clinical-labs.org • URL: http://www.acla.com • Corporations, partnerships, or individuals owning or controlling one or more independent clinical laboratory facilities operating for a profit and licensed under the Clinical Laboratories Improvement Act of 1967 or the Clinical Laboratories Improvement Amendment of 1988, or accredited by the Medicare program. Promotes the development of uniformly high quality laboratory testing; eliminates the present inequalities in the standards applied to different segments of the clinical laboratory market; discourages the enactment of restrictive legislative or regulatory policies that may impede the free flow of commerce or operate to the detriment of the public. Examines federal and state health care and laboratory regulatory and legislative proposals and submits comments and opinions to the appropriate agencies or legislative bodies.

American Society for Clinical Laboratory Science. 1861 International Dr., Ste. 200, McLean, VA 22102. Phone: (571)748-3770; Email: ascls@ascls.org • URL: http://www.ascls.org • Seeks to promote high standards in clincal laboratory methods. Formerly American Society for Medical Technology.

Clinical and Laboratory Standards Institute. 940 W Valley Rd., Ste. 2500, Wayne, PA 19087. Phone: 877-447-1888 or (610)688-0100; Fax: (610)688-0700; Email: customerservice@clsi.org • URL: http://www.clsi.org • Government agencies, professional societies, clinical laboratories, and industrial firms with interests in medical testing. Purposes are to promote the development of national and international standards for medical testing and to provide a consensus mechanism for defining and resolving problems that influence the quality and cost of healthcare work performed.

Clinical Laboratory Management Association. 330 N Wabash Ave., Ste. 2000, Chicago, IL 60611. Phone: (312)321-5111; Fax: (312)673-6927; Email: info@clma.org • URL: http://www.clma.org • Individuals holding managerial or supervisory positions with clinical laboratories; persons engaged in education of such individuals; manufacturers or distributors of equipment or services to clinical laboratories. Objectives are: to enhance management skills and promote more efficient and productive department operations; to further exchange of professional knowledge, new technology, and colleague experience; to encourage cooperation among those engaged in management or supervisory functions. Activities include: workshops, seminars, and expositions; dissemination of information about legislation and other topics.

CLIPPING SERVICES

See also NEWSPAPERS; PERIODICALS

ABSTRACTS AND INDEXES

Vertical File Index: Guide to Pamphlets and References to Current Topics. H.W. Wilson Co. • 11 times a year. $115.00 per year. A subject and title index to selected pamphlet material.

ALMANACS AND YEARBOOKS

Editor & Publisher International Yearbook: Encyclopedia of the Newspaper Industry. Editor and Publisher Company Inc. • Annual. $150.00. Daily and Sunday newspapers in the United States and Canada.

OTHER SOURCES

Bacon's Newspaper and Magazine Directories. Cision US Inc. • Annual. $325.00 per year. Two volumes: Magazines and Newspapers. Covers print media in the United States and Canada. Formerly *Bacon's Publicity Checker.*

CLOCK AND WATCH INDUSTRY

See also JEWELRY BUSINESS

DIRECTORIES

Directory of Chinese Manufacturers & Exporters of Watches & Clocks. EXIM Infotek Private Ltd. • $10 Individuals. Covers: 50 Chinese manufacturers and exporters of alarm clocks, clocks, electronic quartz clocks, electronic watches, quartz clock LCD clocks, quartz clocks, quartz watches, table clocks, wall clock, and watches. Entries include: Company name, postal address, city, country, phone, fax, e-mail and websites, contact person, designation, and product details.

Directory of Japanese Manufacturers & Exporters of Watches & Clocks. EXIM Infotek Private Ltd. • $5 Individuals. Covers: 20 Japanese manufacturers and exporters of clocks, watch bands and straps, and watches. Entries include: Company name, postal address, city, country, phone, fax, e-mail and websites, contact person, designation, and product details.

Directory of South Korean Manufacturers & Exporters of Watches & Clocks. EXIM Infotek Private Ltd. • $10 Individuals. Covers: 60 South Korean manufacturers and exporters of clocks and clock parts, timing mechanisms, watch bracelets/straps, watch/clock and instrument parts, watch/clock and instrument springs, watches, wrist and pocket watches. Entries include: Company name, postal address, city, country, phone, fax, e-mail and websites, contact person, designation, and product details.

Directory of Taiwanese Manufacturers & Exporters of Watches & Clocks. EXIM Infotek Private Ltd. • $20 Individuals. Covers: 220 Taiwanese manufacturers and exporters of blank movements for quartz watches, clocks, clocks and clock parts, meters-time interval, table clocks, timing mechanisms, watch bracelets/straps, watch/clock and instrument parts, watch/clock and instrument springs, watches, wrist and pocket watches. Entries include: Company name, postal address, city, country, phone, fax, e-mail and websites, contact person, designation, product details.

The International Directory of Importers - Watches and Clocks Importers. Interdata. • $200 Individuals print. Covers: 1,000 international firms importing watches and clocks. Entries include: Company name and address, contact person, email, number of employees, year established, phone and telefaxes, business activity, bank references, as well as a listing of watches and clocks currently being imported.

HANDBOOKS AND MANUALS

The Watch Repairer's Manual. Henry B. Fried. American Watchmakers-Clockmakers Institute. • $35.00. 1986. Fourth revised edition.

PERIODICALS AND NEWSLETTERS

Journal Suisse d'Horlogerie et de Bijouterie Internationale. Editions Scriptar S.A. • Six times a year. $95.00. Text in English, French and German. Formery J S H- Journal Suisse d'Horlogerie e de Bijouterie Internationale.

Modern Jeweler. Cygnus Business Media. • Monthly. $60.00 per year. Edited for retail jewelers. Covers the merchandising of jewelry, gems, and watches. Supersedes in part *Modern Jeweler.*

National Jeweler. Nielsen Business Media Inc. • Bimonthly. $65.00 per year. For jewelry retailers.

CLOSED-END FUNDS

See also INVESTMENT COMPANIES

ALMANACS AND YEARBOOKS

Investment Company Yearbook. Thomson Financial Inc. • Annual. $310.00. Provides an "entire history of recent events in the mutual funds industry," with emphasis on changes during the past year. About 100 pages are devoted to general information and advice for fund investors. Includes 600 full-page profiles of popular mutual funds, with brief descriptions of 10,000 others, plus 7,000 variable annuities and 500 closed-end funds. Contains a glossary of technical terms, a Web site index, and an overall book index. Also known as *Wiesenberger Investment Companies Yearbook.*

INTERNET DATABASES

ETF Connect. Nuveen Investments. Phone: 800-257-8787 • URL: http://www.etfconnect.com • Free Web site makes available extensive, searchable information on individual closed-end investment funds, preferred share funds, and exchange-traded index funds. Information on a particular fund is available by name or as part of a classification (high yield, investment grade, municipal, emerging markets, global equity, etc.). Fund charts are available for various time periods, as is data concerning premiums or discounts, dividends, annualized total return, credit quality, "Top 10 Holdings," and so forth.

Factiva. Dow Jones Reuters Business Interactive, LLC. Phone: 800-369-7466 or (609)452-1511; Fax: (609)520-5770; Email: solutions@factiva.com • URL: http://www.factiva.com • Fee-based Web site provides "global news and business information through Web sites and content integration solutions." Includes Dow Jones and Reuters newswires, The Wall Street Journal, and more than 7,000 other sources of current news, historical articles, market research reports, and investment analysis. Content includes 96 major U. S. newspapers, 900 non-English sources, trade publications, media transcripts, country profiles, news photos, etc.

Nexis.com. Lexis-Nexis Group. Phone: 800-227-4908 or (937)865-6800; Fax: (937)865-6909; Email: webmaster@prod.lexis-nexis.com • URL: http://www.nexis.com • Fee-based Web site offers searching of about 2.8 billion documents in some 30,000 news, business, and legal information sources. Features include a subject directory covering 1,200 topics in 34 categories and a Company Dossier containing information on more than 500,000 public and private companies. Boolean searching is offered.

U.S. Securities and Exchange Commission. 100 F St. NE, Washington, DC 20549. Phone: 800-732-0330 or (202)942-8088; Fax: (202)942-9634; Email: webmaster@sec.gov • URL: http://www.sec.gov • SEC Web site offers free access through EDGAR to text of official corporate filings, such as annual reports (10-K), quarterly reports (10-Q), and proxies. (EDGAR is "Electronic Data Gathering, Analysis, and Retrieval System.") An example is given of how to obtain executive compensation data from proxies. Text of the daily *SEC News Digest* is offered, as are links to other government sites, non-government market regulators, and U. S. stock exchanges. Search facilities are extensive. Fees: Free.

Wall Street Journal Interactive Edition. Dow Jones & Co., Inc. 1211 Avenue of the Americas, New York, NY 10036. Phone: 800-369-5663; Email: service@dowjones.com • URL: http://new.dowjones.com • Fee-based Web site providing online searching of worldwide information from *The Wall Street Journal.* Includes "Company Snapshots," "The Journal's Greatest Hits," "Index to Market Data," "Journal Links," etc. Financial price quotes are available. Fees: $49.00 per year; $29.00 per year to print subscribers.

OTHER SOURCES

Fund Governance: Legal Duties of Investment Company Directors. ALM Media Properties LLC. • $580 print and online + ebook. Covers the legal obligations of directors of mutual funds and closed-end funds. (Law Journal Press).

PERIODICALS AND NEWSLETTERS

The Investor's Guide to Closed-End Funds. Thomas J. Herzfeld Advisors Inc. • Monthly. $475.00 per year. Looseleaf service. Provides detailed information on closed-end investment funds, including charts and recommendations.

Mutual Funds Update. Thomson Financial Inc. • Monthly. $325.00 per year. Provides recent performance information and statistics for approximately 10,000 mutual funds and closed-end funds as compiled from the CDA/Wiesenberger database. Includes commentary and analysis relating to the mutual fund industry. Information is provided on new funds, name changes, mergers, and liquidations.

CLOSELY HELD CORPORATIONS

See also PRIVATE COMPANIES

ABSTRACTS AND INDEXES

Business Periodicals Index Retrospective. EBSCO Publishing Inc. • 11/year. Quarterly and annual cumulations.

DIRECTORIES

Thai Business Groups: A Unique Guide to Who Owns What. Brooker Group Public Company Ltd. • Annual. $340 Individuals. Covers: 150 top family business groups in Thailand. Entries include: Contact addresses, key executives of major companies, history and background of the top Thailand business families.

INTERNET DATABASES

Lexis.com Research System. Lexis-Nexis Group. Phone: 800-227-4908 or (937)865-6800; Fax: (937)865-6909; Email: webmaster@prod.lexis-nexis.com • URL: http://www.nexis.com • Fee-based Web site offers extensive searching of a wide variety of legal sources. Additional features include Daily Opinion Service, lexis.com Bookstore, Career Center, CLE Center, Law Schools, and Practice Pages ("Pages specific to areas of specialty").

ONLINE DATABASES

Wilson Business Abstracts Online. H.W. Wilson Co. • Indexes and abstracts 600 major business periodicals, plus the *Wall Street Journal* and the business section of the *New York Times*. Indexing is from 1982, abstracting from 1990, with the two newspapers included from 1993. Updated weekly. Inquire as to online cost and availability. (*Business Periodicals Index* without abstracts is also available online.).

PERIODICALS AND NEWSLETTERS

Inc.: The Magazine for Growing Companies. INC. • 10/year. $10 U.S. /year for two subscription. Edited for small office and home businesses with one to 25 employees. Covers management, office technology, and lifestyle. Incorporates *Self-Employed Professional*.

TRADE/PROFESSIONAL ASSOCIATIONS

International Association of Women in Family Enterprises. 1906 Vista Del Lago Dr., No. L-119, Valley Springs, CA 95252. Phone: (209)772-9200 or (209)772-2810; Fax: (209)772-2810; Email: info@iawife.com • URL: http://www.iawife.com • Aims to support women who are building and growing family businesses. Offers opportunities to help members become successful in family enterprises. Provides support, education and networking among members.

CLOTHING, CHILDREN'S

See CHILDREN'S APPAREL INDUSTRY

CLOTHING INDUSTRY

See also CHILDREN'S APPAREL INDUSTRY; FASHION INDUSTRY; MEN'S CLOTHING INDUSTRY; TAILORING; WOMEN'S APPAREL

ABSTRACTS AND INDEXES

Textile Technology Index™. EBSCO Publishing Inc. • Monthly. $545 Individuals. Includes indexing and abstracts for more than 470 periodicals.

CD-ROM DATABASES

OECD Statistical Compendium. Organization for Economic Cooperation and Development. • Semiannual. $1,905.00 per year for 1 to 10 users. CD-ROM contains more than 730,000 monthly, quarterly, and annual time series for OECD countries, 1960 to date. Includes fully searchable data on agriculture, food, economic indicators, national accounts, employment, energy, finance, industry, technology, and foreign trade. Results can be displayed in various forms.

DIRECTORIES

American Apparel Producers' Network--Directory for Sourcing Apparel. American Apparel Producers' Network. • Annual. Covers: Over 300 member contractors, manufacturers, and suppliers in the apparel industry. Entries include: Firm name, address, phone, names and titles of key personnel, apparel and services provided.

Directory of Chinese Manufacturers & Exporters of Handkerchieves, Scarves & Neckwear. EXIM Infotek Private Ltd. • $10 Individuals. Covers: 60 Chinese manufacturers and exporters of bows and ties, cashmere scarves, neckties/scarves, scarves, shawls, silk ties, textile accessories, and ties. Entries include: Company name, postal address, city, country, phone, fax, e-mail and websites, contact person, designation, and product details.

Directory of Chinese Manufacturers & Exporters of Hats & Headwears. EXIM Infotek Private Ltd. • $10 Individuals. Covers: 70 Chinese manufacturers and exporters of baseball caps, caps, hats, headwear, knitted hats, sports caps, and straw hats. Entries include: Company name, postal address, city, country, phone, fax, e-mail and websites, contact person, designation, and product details.

Directory of Chinese Manufacturers & Exporters of Readymade Garments. EXIM Infotek Private Ltd. • $40 Individuals. Covers: 580 Chinese manufacturers and exporters of apparel, aprons, baby clothing, blouses, boxer shorts, cardigans, cashmere sweaters, casual and leisurewear, children's wear, clothing, coats, cotton garments, cotton knitwear, cotton shirts, cotton t-shirts, cowboy leisure clothes, denimwears, down garments, dress, fashionable garments, fashionable ladies garments, garments, handkerchiefs, handmade clothings, hosiery, jackets, jeans, jogging suits, kimono dresses, knitted children's tights, knitted garments, knitted goods, knitting garments, knitting products, knitwear, knitwear-children, ladies fashionable garments, ladies wear, men's suits, night wears, nylon garments, outerwears, overcoats, pajamas, pants, plastic clothes, polo t-shirts, readymade garments for men/boys, shirts, shorts, silk garments, silk knitted garments, silk knitted products, skirts, sleepwears, sleeveless garments, sportswear, suits, surgical gowns, sweaters, swim and beach wear, textile clothings, tracksuits, trousers, t-shirts, uniforms, winter wears, woolen garments, woolen sweaters, working clothes, workwear, woven and knitted garments, woven and knitted shirts, and woven garments. Entries include: Company name, postal address, city, country, telephone, fax, e-mail and websites, contact person, designation, and product details.

Directory of Chinese Manufacturers & Exporters of Undergarments. EXIM Infotek Private Ltd. • $10 Individuals. Covers: 50 Chinese manufacturers and exporters of briefs, socks, sport socks, stockings, underwear, and underwear-ladies. Entries include: Company name, postal address, city, country, phone, fax, e-mail and websites, contact person, designation, and product details.

Directory of Japanese Manufacturers & Exporters of Readymade Garments. EXIM Infotek Private Ltd. • $10 Individuals. Covers: 50 Japanese manufacturers and exporters of baby clothing, blouses, garments, mufflers, pajamas, regulators, scarfs, shirts, sweaters, and used clothing. Entries include: Company name, postal address, city, country, phone, fax, e-mail and websites, contact person, designation, and product details.

Directory of South Korean Manufacturers & Exporters of Readymade Garments. EXIM Infotek Private Ltd. • $30 Individuals. Covers: 400 South Korean manufacturers and exporters of casual and leisurewear, clothing and accessories-rubber, garments, handkerchiefs, hosiery, knitwear, ladies blouses, mufflers, protective work clothing, readymade for infants, readymade for ladies/girls, readymade garment for men/boy, scarves, shirts-all types, sundries, swim and beach wear, uniforms and professional clothing, and waterproof garments. Entries include: Company name, postal address, city, country, phone, fax, e-mail and websites, contact person, designation, and product details.

Directory of South Korean Manufacturers & Exporters of Undergarments. EXIM Infotek Private Ltd. • $10 Individuals. Covers: 60 South Korean manufacturers and exporters of lingerie/corsetry, nightwear, underwear, and stockings. Entries include: Company name, postal address, city, country, phone, fax, e-mail and websites, contact person, designation, and product details.

Directory of Taiwanese Manufacturers & Exporters of Hats & Headwears. EXIM Infotek Private Ltd. • $10 Individuals. Covers: 120 Taiwanese manufacturers and exporters of caps, hats, hats and headwear, shower caps. Entries include: Company name, postal address, city, country, phone, fax, e-mail and websites, contact person, designation, products detail.

Directory of Taiwanese Manufacturers & Exporters of Readymade Garments. EXIM Infotek Private Ltd. • $45 Individuals. Covers: 710 Taiwanese manufacturers and exporters of casual and leisurewear, clothing and accessories-rubber, dressing gowns, hosiery, knitwear, ladies blouses, protective work clothing, readymade for infants, readymade for ladies/girls, readymade for men/boys, reflective jackets, shirts-all types, swim and beach wear, uniforms and professional clothing, and waterproof garments. Entries include: Company name, postal address, city, country, phone, fax, e-mail and websites, contact person, designation, and product details.

Directory of Taiwanese Manufacturers & Exporters of Undergarments. EXIM Infotek Private Ltd. • $10 Individuals. Covers: 50 Taiwanese manufacturers and exporters of brassieres/panties, lingerie/corsetry and nightwear, pantyhose, socks, underwear-men, and underwear-stockings. Entries include: Company name, postal address, city, country, phone, fax, e-mail and websites, contact person, designation, and product details.

Family Clothing Stores Directory. InfoGroup Inc. • Annual. Number of listings: 22,853. Entries include: Name, address, phone, size of advertisement, name of owner or manager, number of employees, year first in "Yellow Pages." Compiled from telephone company "Yellow Pages," nationwide.

Gown--Rental and Sales Directory. InfoGroup Inc. • Annual. Number of listings: 8,328. Entries include: Name, address, phone, size of advertisement, name of owner or manager, number of employees, year first in "Yellow Pages." Compiled from telephone company "Yellow Pages," nationwide.

The International Directory of Importers - Apparel & Clothing Importers. Interdata. • $320 Individuals print. Covers: 5,600 international firms importing apparel and clothing. Entries include: Company name and address, contact person, email, number of employees, year established, phone and telefaxes, business activity, bank references, as well as a listing of apparel and clothing currently being imported.

International Textile & Apparel Association--Membership Directory. International Textile and Apparel Association. • Irregular. Covers: About 1,000 college professors of clothing and textile studies. Entries include: Name, address, phone, academic credentials.

Oferta Exportable del Sector Textil de la Confeccion, Colombia. The Export Promotion Fund, Proexpo. • Covers: Textiles and clothing manufacturers in Columbia. Entries include: Company name, address, phone, number of employees, type of product exported, export capacity, name of contact person.

World Directory of Clothing, Garments and Apparel Importers. World-Wide Market-Link. • Irregular. $35. Covers: 1,500 apparel importers in 27 countries. Entries include: Company name, address, phone, products.

INTERNET DATABASES

Advance Monthly Retail Trade Report. U. S. Census Bureau. Phone: 800-541-8345 or (301)457-4100 or (301)763-2713; Fax: (301)457-1296 or (301)457-3842; Email: naics@census.gov • URL: http://www.census.gov/epcd/www/naicstab.htm • Web pages provide monthly sales figures for a wide range of retail businesses. Advance, preliminary, and final statistics are provided for the latest month available in each case, with a previous-year comparison. Updates are monthly.

Business 2.0 Web Guide to the Best Business Links. Business 2.0 Media Inc. Phone: (415)293-4800; Email: support@business2.com • URL: http://www.business2.com/webguide • Web site presents an extensive, searchable directory of links to "the best, most informative, and authoritative web pages." Twenty main categories cover business, finance, career, company information, people, and technology topics, with thousands of subtopics, all linking to Web sites recommended by experienced business researchers. Fees: Free.

Fedstats. Federal Interagency Council on Statistical Policy. Phone: (202)395-7254 • URL: http://www.fedstats.gov • Web site features an efficient search facility for full-text statistics produced by more than 100 federal agencies, including the Census Bureau, the Bureau of Economic Analysis, and the Bureau of Labor Statistics. Boolean searches can be made within one agency or for all agencies combined. Links are offered to international statistical bureaus, including the UN, IMF, OECD, UNESCO, Eurostat, and 20 individual countries. Fees: Free.

FreeLunch.com. Economy.com, Inc. Phone: (610)696-8700; Fax: (610)696-1678 • URL: http://www.freelunch.com • Web site provides free access to more than 200 million economic and financial data series, covering industry, demographics, labor markets, prices, retail sales, government spending, trade, interest rates, housing starts, the stock market, etc. Data is available in either chart or table form. Searching is offered. Free, but registration required. Economy.com, Inc. also offers fee-based economic analysis at *The Dismal Scientist* site (www.dismal.com).

Manufacturing Profiles. U. S. Bureau of the Census. Phone: (301)763-4636 or (301)763-4100; Fax: (301)763-4794; Email: webmaster@census.gov • URL: http://www.census.gov/prod/www/abs/mfg-prof.html • The Census Bureau makes available free on PDF (Portable Document Format) an annual consolidation of the entire Current Industrial Report series, presenting "all the data compiled." Contains statistics on production, shipments, inventories, consumption, exports, imports, and orders for a wide variety of manufactured products.

ONLINE DATABASES

Textile Technology Index™. EBSCO Publishing Inc. • Monthly. $545 Individuals. Includes indexing and abstracts for more than 470 periodicals.

World Textiles. Elsevier. • Provides abstracting and indexing from 1970 of worldwide textile literature (periodicals, books, pamphlets, and reports). Includes U. S., European, and British patent information. Updating is monthly. Inquire as to online cost and availability.

PERIODICALS AND NEWSLETTERS

Textile Hi-Lights. American Textile Manufacturers Institute. • Quarterly. $125.00 per year. Monthly *Supplements.*

Textile World. Biilian Publishing Inc. • Monthly. Free to qualified personnel.

RESEARCH CENTERS AND INSTITUTES

Textile Materials Technology. Philadelphia University, 4201 Henry Ave., Philadelphia, PA 19144. Phone: (215)951-2700; Fax: (215)951-2651; Email: admissions@philau.edu • URL: http://www.philau.edu/textilemat • Many research areas, including industrial and nonwoven textiles.

STATISTICS SOURCES

Annual Benchmark Report for Retail Trade and Food Services..A Detailed Summary of Retail Sales, Purchases, Accounts Receivable, Inventories, and Food Service Sales. U. S. Government Printing Office. • Annual. $13.00. Issued by the U.S. Census Bureau. Provides detailed annual and monthly retail statistics for the most recent 10 years. Includes data for various kinds of retail outlets, including automobiles, furniture, appliances, building supplies, grocery stores, drug stores, gasoline stations, clothing, sporting goods, department stores, and restaurants.

Standard & Poor's Industry Surveys. Standard & Poor's Financial Services L.L.C. • Semiannual. $1,800.00. Two looseleaf volumes. Includes monthly *Supplements.* Provides detailed, individual surveys of 52 major industry groups. Each survey is revised on a semiannual basis. Also includes "Monthly Investment Review" (industry group investment analysis) and monthly "Trends & Projections" (economic analysis).

Survey of Current Business. U. S. Government Printing Office. • Published by Bureau of Economic Analysis, U. S. Department of Commerce. Presents a wide variety of business and economic data.

TRADE/PROFESSIONAL ASSOCIATIONS

Clothing Manufacturers Association of the U.S.A. 730 Broadway, 10th Fl., New York, NY 10003. Phone: (212)529-0823; Fax: (212)529-1739 or (212)529-1443; Email: kaplancma730@hotmail.com.

CLOTHING, MEN'S

See MEN'S CLOTHING INDUSTRY

CLOTHING, WOMEN'S

See WOMEN'S APPAREL

CLUBS

See also ASSOCIATIONS; WOMEN'S CLUBS

ALMANACS AND YEARBOOKS

CMAA Yearbook. Club Managers Association of America. • Annual. Membership directory.

DIRECTORIES

Washington: A Comprehensive Directory of the Key Institutions and Leaders in th e National Capitol Area. Columbia Books Inc. • Annual. $149.00. Provides information on about 5,000 Washington, DC key businesses, government offices, non-profit organizations, and cultural institutions, with the names of about 25,000 principal executives. Includes Washington media, law offices, foundations, labor unions, international organizations, clubs, etc.

FINANCIAL RATIOS

Annual Statement Studies. Risk Management Association. • Annual. Compiled from over 280,000 financial statements.

Annual Statement Studies: Industry Default Probabilities and Cash Flow Measures. Risk Management Association. • Annual. $405 Nonmembers. Serves as a companion volume to the original *Annual Statement Studies.* Gives probability of default estimates on a percentage scale for more than 450 industries. Includes changes in position year-by-year for eight financial statement line items and provides percentage measures of cash flow.

HANDBOOKS AND MANUALS

Federal Taxes and the Private Club. PKF International. • Annual. $25.00. Provides a summary of tax issues affecting private clubs.

PERIODICALS AND NEWSLETTERS

Bottomline. Hospitality Financial and Technology Professionals. • Bimonthly. Free to members, educational institutions and libraries; non-members, $50.00 per year. Contains articles on accounting, finance, information technology, and management for hotels, resorts, casinos, clubs, and other hospitality businesses.

Club Director. National Club Association. • Quarterly. Magazine for directors, owners and managers of private clubs.

Club Management: The Resource for Successful Club Operations. Club Managers Association of America. Finan Publishing. • Bimonthly. $21.95 per year.

GFWC Clubwoman: Magazine of the General Federation of Women's Club. General Federation of Women's Clubs. • Bimonthly. $6 Individuals.

Hospitality Technology: Guiding High-Growth Businesses to Best-Choice IT Solutions. Edgell Communications Inc. • 10/year. Covers information technology, computer communications, and software for foodservice and lodging enterprises.

STATISTICS SOURCES

Profiles of Success. International Health, Racquet and Sportsclub Association. • Annual. Members, $249.95; non-members, $499.95. Provides detailed financial statistics for commercial health clubs, sports clubs, and gyms.

TRADE/PROFESSIONAL ASSOCIATIONS

Club Managers Association of America. 1733 King St., Alexandria, VA 22314. Phone: (703)739-9500; Fax: (703)739-0124 • URL: http://www.cmaa.org • Professional managers and assistant managers of private golf, yacht, athletic, city, country, luncheon, university, and military clubs. Encourages education and advancement of members and promotes efficient and successful club operations. Provides reprints of articles on club management. Supports courses in club management. Compiles statistics;

maintains management referral service.

National Club Association. 1201 15th St. NW, Ste. 450, Washington, DC 20005. Phone: 800-625-6221 or (202)822-9822; Fax: (202)822-9808; Email: info@nationalclub.org • URL: http://www.nationalclub.org • Represents the business and legal interests of private clubs. Analyzes proposed laws and regulations affecting clubs; compiles statistics and economic data; drafts model legislation; and acts as a general center of information about club matters.

CLUBS, WOMEN'S

See WOMEN'S CLUBS

COAL GASIFICATION

See ENERGY SOURCES

COAL INDUSTRY

See also COKE INDUSTRY; ENERGY SOURCES

ALMANACS AND YEARBOOKS

CRB Commodity Yearbook. Commodity Research Bureau. CRB. • Annual. $179 plus $10.00 shipping cost. The single most comprehensive source of commodity and futures market information available.

UK Coal. Organisation for Economic Co-operation and Development Publications and Information Center. • Annual. $200. A yearly report on world coal market trends and prospects.

BIBLIOGRAPHIES

Coal Industry. Charles Kernot. American Educational Systems. • $710.00. Looseleaf service. Periodic supplementation.

CD-ROM DATABASES

OECD Statistical Compendium. Organization for Economic Cooperation and Development. • Semiannual. $1,905.00 per year for 1 to 10 users. CD-ROM contains more than 730,000 monthly, quarterly, and annual time series for OECD countries, 1960 to date. Includes fully searchable data on agriculture, food, economic indicators, national accounts, employment, energy, finance, industry, technology, and foreign trade. Results can be displayed in various forms.

DIRECTORIES

Coal Preparation Directory & Handbook. • Annual. $95 Individuals Softcover. Covers: Suppliers and manufacturers of coal preparation equipment and services in the U.S.

FINANCIAL RATIOS

Annual Statement Studies. Risk Management Association. • Annual. Compiled from over 280,000 financial statements.

Annual Statement Studies: Industry Default Probabilities and Cash Flow Measures. Risk Management Association. • Annual. $405 Nonmembers. Serves as a companion volume to the original *Annual Statement Studies*. Gives probability of default estimates on a percentage scale for more than 450 industries. Includes changes in position year-by-year for eight financial statement line items and provides percentage measures of cash flow.

INTERNET DATABASES

Business 2.0 Web Guide to the Best Business Links. Business 2.0 Media Inc. Phone: (415)293-4800; Email: support@business2.com • URL: http://www.business2.com/webguide • Web site presents an extensive, searchable directory of links to "the best, most informative, and authoritative web pages." Twenty main categories cover business, finance, career, company information, people, and technology topics, with thousands of subtopics, all linking to Web sites recommended by experienced business researchers. Fees: Free.

Fedstats. Federal Interagency Council on Statistical Policy. Phone: (202)395-7254 • URL: http://www.fedstats.gov • Web site features an efficient search facility for full-text statistics produced by more than 100 federal agencies, including the Census Bureau, the Bureau of Economic Analysis, and the Bureau of Labor Statistics. Boolean searches can be made within one agency or for all agencies combined. Links are offered to international statistical bureaus, including the UN, IMF, OECD, UNESCO, Eurostat, and 20 individual countries. Fees: Free.

FreeLunch.com. Economy.com, Inc. Phone: (610)696-8700; Fax: (610)696-1678 • URL: http://www.freelunch.com • Web site provides free access to more than 200 million economic and financial data series, covering industry, demographics, labor markets, prices, retail sales, government spending, trade, interest rates, housing starts, the stock market, etc. Data is available in either chart or table form. Searching is offered. Free, but registration required. Economy.com, Inc. also offers fee-based economic analysis at *The Dismal Scientist* site (www.dismal.com).

NMA. National Mining Association. Phone: (202)463-2600; Fax: (202)463-2666 • URL: http://www.nma.org • Web site provides information on the U. S. coal and mineral industries. Includes "Salient Statistics of the Mining Industry," showing a wide variety of annual data (six years) for coal and non-fuel minerals. Publications of the National Mining Association are described and links are provided to other sites. (National Mining Association formerly known as National Coal Association.) Fees: Free.

PERIODICALS AND NEWSLETTERS

Coal Leader: Coal's National Newspaper. Coal, Inc. • Monthly. $18.00 per year. Formerly *National Coal Leader*.

Energy & Fuels. American Chemical Society. • Bimonthly. $1,537 Institutions. An interdisciplinary technical journal covering non-nuclear energy sources: petroleum, gas, synthetic fuels, etc.

Mining Week. National Mining Association. • Weekly. Covers legislative, business, research, and other developments of interest to the mining industry.

Power Generation Technology and Markets. Pasha Publishing Inc. • Weekly. $790.00 per year. Newsletter. Formerly *Coal and Synfuels Technology*.

PRICE SOURCES

Energy Prices and Taxes. International Energy Agency. Organisation for Economic Co-operation and Development Publications and Information Center. • Quarterly. $385 Individuals. Compiled by the International Energy Agency. Provides data on prices and taxation of petroleum products, natural gas, coal, and electricity. Diskette edition, $800.00. (Published in Paris).

RESEARCH CENTERS AND INSTITUTES

University of Kentucky - Center for Applied Energy Research. 2540 Research Park Dr., Lexington, KY 40511-8479. Phone: (859)257-0305; Fax: (859)257-0220; Email: rodney.andrews@uky.edu • URL: http://www.caer.uky.edua • Technical and environmental problems related to the use of coal for energy. Other areas of study include synthetic fuels and alternative energies such as biomass and solid waste conversion. Conducts joint research projects with coal companies, utilities, high technology industries, and government agencies to help bring new developments into practical application.

STATISTICS SOURCES

Annual Energy Outlook, with Projections to (year). U. S. Government Printing Office. • Annual. $39.00. Issued by the Energy Information Administration, U. S. Department of Energy (www.eia.doe.gov). Contains detailed statistics and 20-year projections for electricity, oil, natural gas, coal, and renewable energy. Text provides extensive discussion of energy issues and "Market Trends.".

Annual Energy Review. U. S. Government Printing Office. • Annual. $59.00. Issued by the Energy Information Administration, Office of Energy Markets and End Use, U. S. Department of Energy. Presents long-term historical as well as recent data on production, consumption, stocks, imports, exports, and prices of the principal energy commodities in the U. S.

Coal Information. Organization for Economic Cooperation and Development. • Annual. €165. Presents comprehensive data from the International Energy Agency (IEA) on the world coal market, including supply, demand, production, trade, and prices. In addition to coal itself, provides country-specific data on coal-fired power stations and coal-related environmental issues.

Quarterly Coal Report. Energy Information Administration, U.S. Department of Energy. U. S. Government Printing Office. • Quarterly. $30.00 per year. Annual summary.

Quarterly Mining Review. National Mining Association. • Quarterly. $300.00 per year. Contains detailed data on production, shipments, consumption, stockpiles, and trade for coal and various minerals. (Publisher formerly National Coal Association.).

Steam Electric Market Analysis. National Mining Association. • Monthly. Free to members; non-members, $300.00 per year. Covers 400 major electric power plants, with detailed data on coal consumption and stockpiles. Shows percent of power generated by fuel type. (Publisher formerly National Coal Association.).

Survey of Current Business. U. S. Government Printing Office. • Published by Bureau of Economic Analysis, U. S. Department of Commerce. Presents a wide variety of business and economic data.

United States Census of Mineral Industries. Bureau of the Census, U.S. Department of Commerce. U. S. Government Printing Office. • Quinquennial.

TRADE/PROFESSIONAL ASSOCIATIONS

National Mining Association. 101 Constitution Ave. NW, Ste. 500 E, Washington, DC 20001-2133. Phone: (202)463-2600 or (202)463-2639; Fax: (202)463-2666 • URL: http://www.nma.org • Producers and sellers of coal and hardrock minerals, equipment manufacturers, distributors, equipment suppliers, other energy suppliers, consultants, utility companies, and coal transporters. Serves as liaison between the industry and federal government agencies. Keeps members informed of legislative and regulatory actions. Works with industry, consumers, and government agencies on mining industry issues. Seeks improved conditions for export of steam and metallurgical coal. Collects, analyzes, and distributes industry statistics; makes special studies of competitive fuels, coal and metal markets, production and consumption forecasts, and industry planning.

COAL MINING INDUSTRY

See COAL INDUSTRY

COAL TAR PRODUCTS

See CHEMICAL INDUSTRIES

COAST GUARD

PERIODICALS AND NEWSLETTERS

The Coast Guard Reservist. U.S. Department of Homeland Security U.S. Coast Guard. • Monthly.

Ocean Navigator: Marine Navigation and Ocean Voyaging. Navigator Publishing L.L.C. • Bimonthly. $27.95 per year.

COATINGS, INDUSTRIAL

See INDUSTRIAL COATINGS

COBALT INDUSTRY

See METAL INDUSTRY

COCOA INDUSTRY

See also CHOCOLATE INDUSTRY

ALMANACS AND YEARBOOKS

CRB Commodity Yearbook. Commodity Research Bureau. CRB. • Annual. $179 plus $10.00 shipping cost. The single most comprehensive source of commodity and futures market information available.

DIRECTORIES

Major Food and Drink Companies of the World. Cengage Learning Inc. • 12th edition. eBook. Published by Graham & Whiteside. Contains profiles and trade names for more than 9,200 important food and beverage companies in various countries. In addition to foods, includes both alcoholic and nonalcoholic drink products.

ONLINE DATABASES

Food Science and Technology Abstracts (online). IFIS North American Desk. • Produced by International Food Information Service. Provides about 500,000 online citations, with abstracts, to the international literature of food science, technology, commodities, engineering, and processing. Approximately 2,000 periodicals are covered. Time period is 1969 to date, with monthly updates. Inquire as to online cost and availability.

PERIODICALS AND NEWSLETTERS

Coffee and Cocoa International. DMG World Media Ltd. • Seven times a year. $124.00 per year.

PRICE SOURCES

The New York Times. Gannett Co., Inc. • Mon.-Sun. (morn.). $5.85 Individuals. Provides personal finance expertise.

TRADE/PROFESSIONAL ASSOCIATIONS

Cocoa Merchants' Association of America. 55 E 52nd St., 40th Flr., New York, NY 10055. Phone: (212)748-4193; Email: cmaa@cocoamerchants.com • URL: http://www.cocoamerchants.com • Dealers and importers of raw cocoa beans and cocoa products. Provides arbitration in contract disputes. Maintains speakers' bureau and a voluntary warehouse inspection program; conducts traffic and orientation seminars; compiles statistics.

World Cocoa Foundation. 1411 K St. NW, Ste. 502, Washington, DC 20005. Phone: (202)737-7870; Fax: (202)737-7832; Email: wcf@worldcocoa.org • URL: http://www.worldcocoafoundation.org • Supported by manufacturers of cocoa and chocolate products. Encourages educational and research projects in the cultivation of more cacao of better quality; strives to improve economic conditions of cacao farmers by increasing yields on farms and reducing the per unit production cost. Projects include: research on life history and control of insects attacking cacao; studies on principal cacao diseases; germ plasma assembly and testing; breeding for yield and disease resistance; and physiology. Sponsors exchanges of personnel and training fellowships. Disseminates information.

COCONUT OIL INDUSTRY

See OIL AND FATS INDUSTRY

COFFEE INDUSTRY

See also TEA INDUSTRY

ALMANACS AND YEARBOOKS

CRB Commodity Yearbook. Commodity Research Bureau. CRB. • Annual. $179 plus $10.00 shipping cost. The single most comprehensive source of commodity and futures market information available.

DIRECTORIES

Directory of Chinese Manufacturers & Exporters of Tea & Coffee. EXIM Infotek Private Ltd. • $10 Individuals. Covers: 50 Chinese manufacturers and exporters of black tea, Chinese tea, coffee, green tea, jasmine tea, oolong tea, and organic tea. Entries include: Company name, postal address, city, country, phone, fax, e-mail and websites, contact person, designation, and product details.

Directory of Taiwanese Manufacturers & Exporters of Tea & Coffee. EXIM Infotek Private Ltd. • $5 Individuals. Covers: 20 Taiwanese manufacturers and exporters of Chinese tea, cocoa and chocolate products, coffee and coffee substitutes. Entries include: Company name, postal address, city, country, phone, fax, e-mail and websites, contact person, designation, and product details.

INTERNET DATABASES

USDA. U.S. National Institute of Standards and Technology. 100 Bureau Dr., Gaithersburg, MD 20899-1070. Phone: 800-877-8339 or (301)975-6478 or (202)720-2791; Fax: (301)975-8295; Email: inquiries@nist.gov • URL: http://www.nist.gov • The USDA home page has six sections: News and Information; What's New; About USDA; Agencies; Opportunities; Search and Help. Keyword searching is offered from the USDA home page and from various individual agency home pages. Agencies are the Economic Research Service, Agricultural Marketing Service, National Agricultural Statistics Service, National Agricultural Library, and about 12 others. Updating varies. Fees: Free.

OTHER SOURCES

International Coffee Organization.

PERIODICALS AND NEWSLETTERS

Coffee and Cocoa International. DMG World Media Ltd. • Seven times a year. $124.00 per year.

Coffee Intelligence. Coffee Publications. • Monthly. $95.00 per year. Provides trade information for the coffee industry.

The Coffee Reporter. National Coffee Association of U.S.A. • Weekly.

Fancy Food and Culinary Products. Talcott Communications Corp. • Monthly. $34.00 per year. Emphasizes new specialty food products and the business management aspects of the specialty food and confection industries. Includes special issues on wine, cheese, candy, "upscale" cookware, and gifts. Formerly (Fancy Foods).

Gourmet Retailer. Nielsen Business Media Inc. • Monthly. Free to qualified personnel; others, $75.00 per year. Covers upscale food and housewares, including confectionery items, bakery operations, and coffee.

Specialty Coffee Retailer: The Coffee Business Monthly. RCM Enterprises Inc. • Monthly. $5 Single issue. Magazine reporting on new products, equipment, trends and management techniques for retail specialty coffee businesses.

Tea and Coffee Trade Journal. Lockwood Publications Inc. • Monthly. $49 Individuals. Current trends in coffee roasting and tea packing industry.

PRICE SOURCES

Supermarket News: The Industry's Weekly Newspaper. Fairchild Publications. • Weekly. Individuals. $196.00 per year; retailers, $45.00 per year; manufacturers, $89.00 per year.

RESEARCH CENTERS AND INSTITUTES

College of Tropical Agriculture and Human Resources. University of Hawaii at Manoa, 2515 Campus Rd., Miller Hall 110, Honolulu, HI 96822. Phone: (808)956-8234; Fax: (808)956-9105; Email: gallom@ctahr.hawaii.edu • URL: http://www.ctahr.hawaii.edu • Concerned with the production and marketing of tropical food and ornamental plant products, including pineapples, bananas, coffee, and macadamia nuts.

STATISTICS SOURCES

Agricultural Statistics. U.S. Department of Agriculture National Agricultural Statistics Service. • Annual. $46 Individuals. Provides a wide variety of statistical data relating to agricultural production, supplies, consumption, prices/price-supports, foreign trade, costs, and returns, as well as farm labor, loans, income, and population. In many cases, historical data is shown annually for 10 years. In addition to farm data, includes detailed fishery statistics.

TRADE/PROFESSIONAL ASSOCIATIONS

National Coffee Association of U.S.A. 45 Broadway, Ste. 1140, New York, NY 10006. Phone: (212)766-4007; Fax: (212)766-5815; Email: info@ncausa.org • URL: http://www.ncausa.org • Formerly Associated Coffee Industries of America.

COGENERATION OF ENERGY

CD-ROM DATABASES

Environment Abstracts on CD-ROM. University Publications of America. • Quarterly. $1,295.00 per year. Contains the following CD-ROM databases: *Environment Abstracts*, *Energy Abstracts*, and *Acid Rain Abstracts*. Length of coverage varies.

DIRECTORIES

Energy User News: Energy Technology Buyers Guide. BNP Media. • Annual. $10.00. List of about 400 manufacturers, manufacturers' representatives, dealers, and distributors of energy management equipment. *Annual Review* and *Forecast* issue.

PERIODICALS AND NEWSLETTERS

Alternative Energy Retailer. Zackin Publications Inc. • Monthly. $32.00 per year.

Global Power Report: An Exclusive Biweekly Covering the Cogeneration and Small Power Market. Platts Global Energy. • Biweekly. $1,165.00 per year. Newsletter. Covers industry trends, new projects, new contracts, rate changes, and regulations, with emphasis on the Federal Energy Regulatory Commission (FERC). Formerly *Cogeneration Report.*

Independent Energy: The Power Industry's Business Magazine. PennWell Corp., Industrial Div. • 10 times a year. $127.00 per year. Covers non-utility electric power plants (cogeneration) and other alternative sources of electric energy.

Journal of Energy Engineering: The International Journal. Architectural Engineering Institute of ASCE. • Quarterly. $350 Individuals Online only. Contains reports on the development of scientific and engineering knowledge in the planning, management, and generation of electrical power.

Power. The McGraw-Hill Companies Inc. • Description: Covers design, operation, construction, and maintenance of power plants for utilities, process industries, and manufacturers.

Private Power Executive. Pequot Publishing Inc. • Bimonthly. $90.00 per year. Covers private power (non-utility) enterprises, including cogeneration projects and industrial self-generation.

RESEARCH CENTERS AND INSTITUTES

University of Hawaii at Manoa - Hawaii Natural Energy Institute. 1680 E West Rd., Post 109, Honolulu, HI 96822. Phone: (808)956-8890; Fax: (808)956-2336; Email: hnei@hawaii.edu • URL: http://www.hnei.hawaii.edu • Research areas include geothermal, wind, solar, hydroelectric, and other energy sources.

STATISTICS SOURCES

Annual Energy Outlook, with Projections to (year). U. S. Government Printing Office. • Annual. $39.00. Issued by the Energy Information Administration, U. S. Department of Energy (www.eia.doe.gov). Contains detailed statistics and 20-year projections for electricity, oil, natural gas, coal, and renewable energy. Text provides extensive discussion of energy issues and "Market Trends.".

TRADE/PROFESSIONAL ASSOCIATIONS

American Wind Energy Association. 1501 M St. NW, Ste. 1000, Washington, DC 20005. Phone: (202)383-2500 or (202)383-2557; Fax: (202)383-2505; Email: windmail@awea.org • URL: http://www.awea.org • Wind energy equipment manufacturers; project developers and dealers; individuals from industry, government, and academia; interested others. Works to: advance the art and science of using energy from the wind for human purposes; encourage the use of wind turbines and wind power plants as alternatives to current energy systems that depend on depletable fuels; facilitate the widespread use of wind as a renewable, non-polluting energy source by fostering communication within the field of wind energy and between the technical community and the public. Provides federal and state legislators with information on wind as an energy source; offers consultation to federal, state, and local government and private industry. Promotes exportation of U.S. manufactured wind energy equipment.

Association of Energy Engineers. 4025 Pleasantdale Rd., Ste. 420, Atlanta, GA 30340. Phone: (770)447-5083; Fax: (770)446-3969; Email: info@aeecenter.org • URL: http://www.aeecenter.org • Members are engineers and other professionals concerned with energy management and cogeneration.

Electric Power Supply Association. 1401 New York Ave. NW, Ste. 1230, Washington, DC 20005-2110. Phone: (202)628-8200; Fax: (202)628-8260 • URL: http://www.epsa.org • Represents competitive power suppliers, including generators and power marketers. Provides reliable, competitively priced electricity from environmentally responsible facilities serving global power markets. Seeks to bring the benefits of competition to all power customers.

COIN MACHINES

See VENDING MACHINES

COINS AS AN INVESTMENT

ALMANACS AND YEARBOOKS

Coin Yearbook. British Royal Mint. • Annual. $15.95.

DIRECTORIES

Stamp Exchangers Directory. Levine Publications. • Annual. $35. Covers: over 1000 people who are interested in exchanging stamps, coins, and other collectibles with Americans; international coverage. Entries include: Name, address, item collected.

PERIODICALS AND NEWSLETTERS

Coin World: World's 1 Publication for Coin Collectors. • Weekly. $19.99 Individuals. Newspaper for coin collectors.

Coinage. Miller Magazines Inc. • Monthly. $18.95.

Coins. Krause Publications Inc. • Monthly. $56.98 per year.

Numismatic News: The Complete Information Source for Coin Collectors. Krause Publications Inc. • Weekly. $32.00 per year.

PRICE SOURCES

Coin Prices: Complete Guide to U.S. Coin Values. Krause Publications Inc. • Bimonthly. $18.98 Individuals. Gives current values of U. S. coins.

TRADE/PROFESSIONAL ASSOCIATIONS

American Numismatic Association. 818 N Cascade Ave., Colorado Springs, CO 80903-3208. Phone: 800-367-9723 or (719)632-2646 or (719)482-9821; Fax: (719)634-4085; Email: ana@money.org • URL: http://www.money.org • Collectors of coins, medals, tokens, and paper money. Promotes the study, research, and publication of articles on coins, coinage, and history of money. Sponsors correspondence courses; conducts research. Maintains museum, archive, authentication service for coins, and hall of fame. Sponsors National Coin Week; operates speakers' bureau.

American Numismatic Society. 75 Varick St., 11th Fl., New York, NY 10013. Phone: (212)571-4470; Fax: (212)571-4479; Email: meadows@numismatics.org • URL: http://www.numismatics.org • Collectors and others interested in coins, medals, and related materials. Advances numismatic knowledge as it relates to history, art, archaeology, and economics by collecting coins, medals, tokens, decorations, and paper money. Maintains only museum devoted entirely to numismatics. Presents annual Graduate Fellowship in Numismatics. Sponsors Graduate Seminar in Numismatics, a nine-week individual study program for ten students.

Numismatics International. PO Box 570842, Dallas, TX 75357-0842. • URL: http://www.numis.org • Numismatists, coin dealers, students, and numismatic authors in 35 countries. Works to: encourage and promote the science of numismatics; cultivate fraternal relations among collectors and numismatic students; encourage new collectors and foster the interest of youth in numismatics; stimulate and advance affiliations among collectors and kindred organizations; acquire, share, and disseminate numismatic knowledge including cultural and historical information on coins. Sponsors periodic lectures. Maintains coin collection.

Professional Numismatists Guild. 28441 Rancho California Rd., Ste. 106, Temecula, CA 92590-3618. Phone: 800-375-4653 or (951)587-8300; Fax: (951)587-8301; Email: info@pngdealers.com • URL: http://www.pngdealers.com • Represents coin dealers who have been involved full-time in the profession for at least five years. Establishes, promotes, and defends ethics in the hobby of numismatics.

COKE INDUSTRY

See also COAL INDUSTRY

ALMANACS AND YEARBOOKS

CRB Commodity Yearbook. Commodity Research Bureau. CRB. • Annual. $179 plus $10.00 shipping cost. The single most comprehensive source of commodity and futures market information available.

DIRECTORIES

Kompass. Kompass Deutschland Verlags- und Vertriebsgesellschaft, mbH. • Annual. $88. Covers: German products and companies specializing in coal extraction, ore mining, quarries, cement industry, glass and ceramics.

STATISTICS SOURCES

American Iron and Steel Annual Statistical Report. American Iron and Steel Institute. • Annual. $100 Individuals.

Quarterly Coal Report. Energy Information Administration, U.S. Department of Energy. U. S. Government Printing Office. • Quarterly. $30.00 per year. Annual summary.

TRADE/PROFESSIONAL ASSOCIATIONS

American Coke and Coal Chemicals Institute. 25 Massachusetts Ave. NW, Ste. 800, Washington, DC 20001. Phone: (202)452-7198; Fax: (202)463-6573; Email: information@accci.org • URL: http://www.accci.org • Producers of oven coke and coal chemicals; producers of metallurgical coal; tar distillers; producers of chemicals and suppliers to the industry.

COLLECTING OF ACCOUNTS

See also CREDIT

DIRECTORIES

Adjustment & Collection Services Directory. InfoGroup Inc. • Annual. Number of listings: 7,138. Entries include: Name, address, phone, size of advertisement, name of owner or manager, number of employees, year first in "Yellow Pages." Compiled from telephone company "Yellow Pages," nationwide.

Collections Agency Directory. InfoGroup Inc. • Annual. Number of listings: 7,183. Entries include: Name, address, phone, size of advertisement, name of owner or manager, number of employees, year first in "Yellow Pages." Compiled from telephone company "Yellow Pages," nationwide.

FINANCIAL RATIOS

Annual Statement Studies. Risk Management Association. • Annual. Compiled from over 280,000 financial statements.

Annual Statement Studies: Industry Default Probabilities and Cash Flow Measures. Risk Management Association. • Annual. $405 Nonmembers. Serves as a companion volume to the original *Annual Statement Studies*. Gives probability of default estimates on a percentage scale for more than 450 industries. Includes changes in position year-by-year for eight financial statement line items and provides percentage measures of cash flow.

PERIODICALS AND NEWSLETTERS

Collections and Credit Risk: The Authority for Commercial and Consumer Credit Professionals. SourceMedia Inc. • Monthly. $95.00 per year. Contains articles on the technology and business management of credit and collection functions. Includes coverage of bad debts, bankruptcy, and credit risk management.

Collector. ACA International. • Monthly. $70 Nonmembers per year. Provides news and education in the field of credit and collections.

TRADE/PROFESSIONAL ASSOCIATIONS

ACA International. 4040 W 70th St., Minneapolis, MN 55435. Phone: (952)926-6547; Email: aca@acainternational.org • URL: http://www.acainternational.org • Formerly American Collectors Association.

American Fair Credit Council. 100 W Cypress Creek Rd., Ste. 700, Fort Lauderdale, FL 33309. Phone: 888-657-8272; Fax: (954)343-6960; Email: info@americanfaircreditcouncil.org • URL: http://www.americanfaircreditcouncil.org • Promotes good practice in the debt settlement industry. Protects the interests of consumer debtors. Advances the application of consumer protection, principals in marketing, sales, and fulfillment of debt settlement services.

COLLECTIVE BARGAINING

See also ARBITRATION; LABOR UNIONS

DIRECTORIES

International Centre for Settlement of Investment Disputes - Annual Report. International Centre for Settlement of Investment Disputes. • Annual. Contains an overview of the activities during the past ICSID fiscal year.

LERA Membership Directory. Labor and Employment Relations Associations. • Quadrennial. $10 print only. About 3,200 business people, union leaders, government officials, lawyers, arbitrators, academics, consultants, and others interested in labor relations.

PERIODICALS AND NEWSLETTERS

Dispute Resolution Journal. American Arbitration Association. • Quarterly. $55 /year for nonmembers. Professional journal covering topics on dispute resolution. Formerly *Arbitration Journal.*

Labor Relations Bulletin. Aspen Publishers Inc. • Description: Provides information and insight to management and labor officials to help them avoid or resolve conflicts. Recurring features include reports on current developments in labor law and relations, discipline and grievance cases based on actual arbitration, a question and answer column on labor and employment relations, and a column titled Reflections of an Arbitrator, offering the insight and experience of prominent national arbitrators.

Summary of Labor Arbitration Awards. American Arbitration Association. • Monthly. Periodical covering private sector arbitration decisions and collective bargaining issues.

Union Labor Report. Bloomberg BNA. • Biweekly. Description: Covers legal, legislative, and regulatory developments and trends affecting management and labor in the workplace.

RESEARCH CENTERS AND INSTITUTES

University of Alabama at Birmingham - Center for Labor Education and Research. 1044 11th St. S., Birmingham, AL 35294-4500. Phone: (205)934-2101 or (205)856-8030; Fax: (205)975-5087 or (205)856-8044; Email: csturgis@uab.edu • URL: http://www.jeffstateonline.com/clear • Labor issues, including studies on collective bargaining, arbitration, occupational safety and health, confined space rescue, labor law, trade union organization and administration, and workplace topics of individual faculty interest.

TRADE/PROFESSIONAL ASSOCIATIONS

National Academy of Arbitrators. NAA Operations Ctr., Ste. 412, 1 N Main St., Cortland, NY 13045. Phone: 888-317-1729 or (607)756-8363; Email: naa@naarb.org • URL: http://www.naarb.org • Labor-management arbitrators. Works to improve general understanding of the nature and use of arbitration as a means of settling labor disputes. Conducts research and educational programs.

COLLEGE AND SCHOOL NEWSPAPERS

See also NEWSPAPERS

CD-ROM DATABASES

MediaFinder. Oxbridge Communications Inc. • $1,295 per year. Online database with 77,000 magazines, catalogs, newspapers, and journals.

DIRECTORIES

Burrelle's Media Directory: Newspapers and Related Media. BurrellesLuce. • Annual. $550.00. *Daily Newspapers* volume lists more than 2,200 daily publications in the U. S., Canada, and Mexico. *Non-Daily Newspapers* volume lists more than 10,400 items published no more than three times a week. Provides detailed descriptions, including key personnel.

PERIODICALS AND NEWSLETTERS

College Media Review. College Media Association. • Quarterly Periodic. $15 /year. Contains aricles on advising collegiate media in print, broadcast and electronic forms.

Columbia Journalism Review. Columbia University, Graduate School of Journalism. • Bimonthly. Critical review of news media.

Quill and Scroll. International Honorary Society for High School Journalists. Quill and Scroll Society. • Quarterly. $17 /year. Devoted exclusively to the field of high school publications.

TRADE/PROFESSIONAL ASSOCIATIONS

Associated Collegiate Press. University of Minnesota, 2221 University Ave. SE, Ste. 121, Minneapolis, MN 55414. Phone: (612)625-8335; Fax: (612)605-0072; Email: info@studentpress.org • URL: http://www.studentpress.org/acp • Conducts annual critique of newspapers and annual critique of magazines and yearbooks. Sponsors competitions.

College Media Association. 2301 Vanderbilt Pl., VU Sta. B 35166, Nashville, TN 37235. Phone: (415)338-3134 or (615)322-6610; Fax: (901)678-4798; Email: rsplbrgr@memphis.edu • URL: http://www.collegemedia.org • Formerly National Council of College Publications Advisers.

Columbia Scholastic Press Association. Columbia University, Mail Code 5711, New York, NY 10027-6902. Phone: (212)854-9400; Fax: (212)854-9401; Email: cspa@columbia.edu • URL: http://www.columbia.edu/cu/cspa • Newspapers, magazines, and yearbooks and online student media issued by schools from junior high school level through college and university, with the majority being from secondary schools. Works to promote student writing through the medium of the school publication. Improves publications in all phases. Offers critiques for each regular member. Compiles statistics. Provides consultation and referral services to student publications.

National Scholastic Press Association. University of Minnesota, 2221 University Ave. SE, Ste. 121, Minneapolis, MN 55414-3074. Phone: (612)625-8335; Fax: (612)605-0072 or (612)626-0720; Email: info@studentpress.org • URL: http://www.studentpress.org/nspa • Represents publishers of high school newspapers, yearbooks, and magazines. Offers critical services for newspapers, yearbooks, and magazines.

Quill and Scroll Society. University of Iowa, 100 Adler Journalism Bldg., Iowa City, IA 52242. Phone: (319)335-3457; Fax: (319)335-3989; Email: quill-scroll@uiowa.edu • URL: http://www.uiowa.edu • Honor Society high school journalism students recommended for membership by their schools. Seeks to reward individual achievements and to encourage individual initiative in high school journalism, creative writing, and allied fields. Provides information to editors, staffs, and advisers on all phases of publication work and supports news media evaluation service. Promotes research and conducts surveys through Quill and Scroll Foundation.

COLLEGE AND UNIVERSITY LIBRARIES

ABSTRACTS AND INDEXES

Library Literature and Information Science Index. H.W. Wilson Co. • Quarterly. Annual cumulation. Price varies.

ALMANACS AND YEARBOOKS

The Library and Book Trade Almanac. Information Today, Inc. • $209 Individuals Hardbound. Reviews key trends and events and provides basic statistical information. Includes financial averages: library expenditures, salaries, and book prices. Contains lists of "best books, literary prizes, winners, and bestsellers." Formerly published by R. R. Bowker.

CD-ROM DATABASES

ERIC SilverPlatter. U.S. Department of Education Institute of Education Sciences Education Resources Information Center. • Opinion papers, evaluations, speeches.

LISA Plus. Cambridge Scientific Abstracts L.P. • Quarterly. $2,000 per year. CD-ROM version of Library Information and Science Abstracts, providing abstracting and indexing of the world's library and information science literature, 1969 to date. Contains more than 180,000 citations.

WILSONDISC: Library Literature and Information Science Index. H.W. Wilson Co. • Quarterly. Includes unlimited access to the online version of *Library Literature.* Provides CD-ROM indexing of about 400 periodicals, covering a wide range of topics having to do with libraries, library management, and the information industry.

DIRECTORIES

American Library Directory (ALD). Information Today, Inc. • Annual. $369.50 Individuals hardbound; plus $25 shipping and handling. Covers: Over 36,000 U.S. and Canadian academic, public, county, provincial, and regional libraries; library systems; medical, law, and other special libraries; and libraries for the blind and physically handicapped. Separate section lists over 350 library networks and consortia and 220 accredited and unaccredited library school programs. Entries include: For libraries--Name, supporting or affiliated institution or firm name, address, phone, fax, electronic mail address, Standard Address Number (SANs), names of librarian and department heads, income, collection size, special collections, computer hardware, automated functions, and type of catalog. For library systems--Name, location. For library schools--Name, address, phone, fax, electronic mail address, director, type of training and degrees, admission requirements, tuition, faculty size. For networks and consortia--Name, address, phone, names of affiliates, name of director, function.

ONLINE DATABASES

American Library Directory Online. Information Today, Inc. • Provides information on more than 30,000 public, college, and special libraries in the U.S. and Canada, with annual updates. Includes library networks, consortia, organizations, and schools. Inquire as to online cost and availability.

ERIC. U.S. Department of Education Institute of Education Sciences Educational Resources Information Center. • Funded by the U.S. Department of Education, Institute of Education Sciences (formerly Office of Educational Research and Improvement). Provides access to more than one million online records covering education-related journal and report literature, 1966 to date. Updating is monthly. Inquire as to online cost and availability.

PERIODICALS AND NEWSLETTERS

Choice Magazine: Current Reviews for Academic Libraries. Association of College Research Libraries. Library and Information Technology

Association. • Monthly. $415. A publication of the Association of College and Research Libraries. Contains book reviews, primarily for college and university libraries.

College and Research Libraries. Association of College and Research Libraries. • Bimonthly. $53 Nonmembers 1 year. Magazine reporting news, trends, and research of interest to academic library professionals.

College and Undergraduate Libraries. The Haworth Press Inc. • Semiannual. $105.00 per year. A practical journal dealing with everyday library problems.

Community and Junior College Libraries: The Journal for Learning Resources Centers. The Haworth Press Inc. • Quarterly. $85.00 per year.

Focus: On the Center for Research Libraries. Center for Research Libraries. • Bimonthly. Free. Newsletter. Provides news of Center activites.

The Journal of Academic Librarianship: Articles, Features, and Book Reviews for the Academic Library Professional. Elsevier. • $472 Institutions. Bimonthly. Qualified personnel.

TRADE/PROFESSIONAL ASSOCIATIONS

Association of College and Research Libraries. 50 E Huron St., Chicago, IL 60611. Phone: 800-545-2433 or (312)280-2523; Fax: (312)280-2520; Email: acrl@ala.org • URL: http://www.ala.org/acrl • A division of the American Library Association. Academic and research librarians seeking to improve the quality of service in academic libraries; promotes the professional and career development of academic and research librarians; represent the interests and support the programs of academic and research libraries. Operates placement services; sponsors specialized education and research grants and programs; gathers, compiles, and disseminates statistics. Establishes and adopts standards; maintains publishing program; offers professional development courses.

Association of Research Libraries. 21 Dupont Cir. NW, Ste. 800, Washington, DC 20036-1543. Phone: (202)296-2296; Fax: (202)872-0884; Email: webmgr@arl.org • URL: http://www.arl.org • Aims to influence the changing environment of scholarly communication and the public policies that affect research libraries and the diverse communities they serve. Pursues this mission by advancing the goals of its member research libraries, providing leadership in public and information policy to the scholarly and higher education communities, fostering the exchange of ideas and expertise, facilitating the emergence of new roles for research libraries, and shaping a future environment that leverages its interests with those of allied organizations.

COLLEGE DEGREES

See ACADEMIC DEGREES

COLLEGE ENROLLMENT

See also COLLEGE ENTRANCE REQUIREMENTS; COLLEGES AND UNIVERSITIES

DIRECTORIES

American Universities and Colleges. American Council on Education USA. Walter de Gruyter Inc. • Quadrennial. $249.50. Two volumes. Produced in collaboration with the American Council on Education. Provides full descriptions of more than 1,900 institutions of higher learning, including details of graduate and professional programs.

ONLINE DATABASES

ERIC. U.S. Department of Education Institute of Education Sciences Educational Resources Information Center. • Funded by the U.S. Department of Education, Institute of Education Sciences (formerly Office of Educational Research and Improvement). Provides access to more than one million online records covering education-related journal and report literature, 1966 to date. Updating is monthly. Inquire as to online cost and availability.

STATISTICS SOURCES

Occupational Projections and Training Data. U. S. Government Printing Office. • Biennial. $31.50. Issued by Bureau of Labor Statistics, U. S. Department of Labor. Contains projections of employment change and job openings over the next 15 years for about 500 specific occupations. Also includes the number of associate, bachelor's, master's, doctoral, and professional degrees awarded in a recent year for about 900 specific fields of study.

COLLEGE ENTRANCE REQUIREMENTS

See also COLLEGE ENROLLMENT; COLLEGES AND UNIVERSITIES; GRADUATE WORK IN UNIVERSITIES

ONLINE DATABASES

ERIC. U.S. Department of Education Institute of Education Sciences Educational Resources Information Center. • Funded by the U.S. Department of Education, Institute of Education Sciences (formerly Office of Educational Research and Improvement). Provides access to more than one million online records covering education-related journal and report literature, 1966 to date. Updating is monthly. Inquire as to online cost and availability.

PERIODICALS AND NEWSLETTERS

College Board Review. The College Board. • 3/year. $30 /year. Connects students to success and opportunity in college.

TRADE/PROFESSIONAL ASSOCIATIONS

ACT Inc. 500 ACT Dr., Iowa City, IA 52243-0168. Phone: (319)337-1000; Fax: (319)339-3020 • URL: http://www.act.org.

The College Board. 45 Columbus Ave., New York, NY 10023-6917. Phone: (212)713-8000; Email: aces@info.collegeboard.org • URL: http://www.collegeboard.org • Represents the schools, colleges, universities, and other educational organizations that seek to connect members to success and opportunity. Serves students, parents, high schools, and colleges through major programs and services in college admission, guidance, assessment, financial aid, enrollment, and teaching and learning.

Educational Testing Service. 225 Phillips Blvd., Ewing, NJ 08628. Phone: (609)921-9000; Fax: (609)734-5410 • URL: http://www.ets.org • Educational measurement and research organization, founded by merger of the testing activities of American Council on Education, Carnegie Foundation for the Advancement of Teaching, and The College Board. Provides tests and related services for schools, colleges, governmental agencies, and the professions; offers advisory services in the sound application of measurement techniques and materials; conducts educational, psychological, and measurement research. Offers a summer program in educational testing for scholars and educators from other countries, continuing education programs, and measurement, evaluation, and other instructional activities.

National Association for College Admission Counseling. 1050 N Highland St., Ste. 400, Arlington, VA 22201-2197. Phone: 800-822-6285 or (703)836-2222; Fax: (703)243-9375; Email: info@nacacnet.org • URL: http://www.nacacnet.org • Formerly National Association of College Admissions Counselors.

COLLEGE FACULTIES

BIOGRAPHICAL SOURCES

Directory of American Scholars. Cengage Learning Inc. • $928. Volumes one to volume five, $212.00; volume six, $72.00. Provides biographical information and publication history for more than 24,000 scholars in the humanities.

Who's Who in American Education. Marquis Who's Who L.L.C. • Biennial. $159.95. Contains over 27,000 concise biographies of teachers, administrators, and other individuals involved in all levels of American education.

DIRECTORIES

Fulbright Scholar Program Grants for U.S. Faculty and Professionals. Council for International Exchange of Scholars. • Annual. Lists about 800 grants available for postdoctoral university lecturing and advanced research by American citizens in more than 140 countries.

ISWorld Net Faculty Directory. MIS Research Center. • Database covers: college-level teachers of subjects related to management information systems and technology. Database includes: Faculty name, school, address, office phone, research and teaching areas, highest degree.

ONLINE DATABASES

ERIC. U.S. Department of Education Institute of Education Sciences Educational Resources Information Center. • Funded by the U.S. Department of Education, Institute of Education Sciences (formerly Office of Educational Research and Improvement). Provides access to more than one million online records covering education-related journal and report literature, 1966 to date. Updating is monthly. Inquire as to online cost and availability.

PERIODICALS AND NEWSLETTERS

ACADEME. American Association of University Professors. • Bimonthly. $85 Nonmembers /year; individual; domestic. Explores developments in higher education from the perspective of faculty members.

College Teaching: International Quarterly Journal. Helen Dwight Reid Educational Foundation. Taylor & Francis Group Heldref Publications. • Quarterly. $73 Individuals print and onlione. Practical ideas, successful methods, and new programs for faculty development.

STATISTICS SOURCES

The Annual Report on the Economic Status of the Profession. American Association of University Professors. • Special annual issue of *ACADEME.*

COLLEGE INSTRUCTORS AND PROFESSORS

See COLLEGE FACULTIES

COLLEGE LIBRARIES

See COLLEGE AND UNIVERSITY LIBRARIES

COLLEGE NEWSPAPERS

See COLLEGE AND SCHOOL NEWSPAPERS

COLLEGE PLACEMENT BUREAUS

TRADE/PROFESSIONAL ASSOCIATIONS

National Student Employment Association. c/o June Hagler, Office Manager, 715 Northhill Dr., Richardson, TX 75080. Phone: (972)690-8772; Fax: (972)767-5131; Email: nsea@nsea.info • URL: http://www.nsea.info • Directors, coordinators, and senior staff personnel of postsecondary educational institutions, including proprietary schools and corporate human resource directors, who are involved in student employment, internships, cooperative and experiential education, federal work-study, job location and development, and student placement. Answers problems associated with the management of student employment programs. Provides financial support for students in higher education. Creates and conducts training and professional development programs for higher education student employment professionals. Sponsors State Work Study Clearinghouse on state sponsored student employment programs. Compiles statistics. Conducts research programs. Provides legislative updates on current issues.

COLLEGE PRESIDENTS

See also COLLEGES AND UNIVERSITIES

BIOGRAPHICAL SOURCES

Who's Who in American Education. Marquis Who's Who L.L.C. • Biennial. $159.95. Contains over 27,000 concise biographies of teachers, administrators, and other individuals involved in all levels of American education.

PERIODICALS AND NEWSLETTERS

For Your Information. Western New York Library Resources Council. • Bimonthly. Free.

TRADE/PROFESSIONAL ASSOCIATIONS

American Council on Education. 1 Dupont Cir. NW, Washington, DC 20036. Phone: (202)939-9300 or (202)939-9420; Email: membership@ace.nche.edu • URL: http://www.acenet.edu • A council of colleges and universities, educational organizations, and affiliates. Represents accredited, degree-granting postsecondary institutions directly or through national and regional higher education associations; advocates on their behalf before congress, the federal government, and federal and state courts. Advances education and educational methods through comprehensive voluntary action on the part of American educational associations, organizations, and institutions. Serves as an advocate for adult education and nationally administers the GED high school equivalency exam. Provides college credit equivalency evaluations for courses taught outside the traditional campus classroom by corporations and the military. Maintains numerous commissions, committees, and councils.

Association of American Universities. 1200 New York Ave. NW, Ste. 550, Washington, DC 20005. Phone: (202)408-7500; Fax: (202)408-8184 • URL: http://www.aau.edu • Executive heads of universities; membership is determined by appraisal of breadth and quality of a university's research and education efforts. Conducts activities to encourage cooperative consideration of major issues concerning research universities, and to enable members to communicate effectively with the federal government.

COLLEGE PUBLISHERS

See UNIVERSITY PRESSES

COLLEGE STORES

See also BOOKSELLING; DEPARTMENT STORES; RETAIL TRADE

PERIODICALS AND NEWSLETTERS

The College Store. The College Store. • Bimonthly. $66 Members. Books and college supplies magazine. Formerly *College Store Journal*.

College Store Executive. Executive Business Media Inc. • 10/year.

TRADE/PROFESSIONAL ASSOCIATIONS

National Association of College Auxiliary Services. 3 Boar's Head Ln., Ste B, Charlottesville, VA 22903. Phone: (434)245-8425; Fax: (434)245-8453; Email: info@nacas.org • URL: http://www.nacas.org • Formerly Association of College Auxiliary Services.

National Association of College Stores. 500 E Lorain St., Oberlin, OH 44074. Phone: 800-622-7498 or (440)775-7777; Fax: (440)775-4769; Email: webteam@nacs.org • URL: http://www.nacs.org • Formerly College Bookstore Association.

COLLEGE TEACHERS

See COLLEGE FACULTIES

COLLEGES AND UNIVERSITIES

See also COLLEGE ENROLLMENT; COLLEGE ENTRANCE REQUIREMENTS; COLLEGE FACULTIES; COLLEGE PRESIDENTS; GRADUATE WORK IN UNIVERSITIES; SCHOLARSHIPS AND STUDENT AID

ABSTRACTS AND INDEXES

Current Index to Journals in Education (CIJE). Oryx Press. • Monthly. $245.00 per year. Semiannual cumulations, $475.00.

Education Index. H.W. Wilson Co. • 10 times a year. Quarterly and annual cumulations. Price varies.

Educational Administration Abstracts. Pine Forge Press. • Quarterly. $722 Institutions.

Index of Majors. College Board Publications. • Annual. $22.95.

CD-ROM DATABASES

Education Index Retrospective: 1929-1983. EBSCO Publishing Inc. • Provides indexing of education-related literature from 1983 to date.

ERIC SilverPlatter. U.S. Department of Education Institute of Education Sciences Education Resources Information Center. • Opinion papers, evaluations, speeches.

DIRECTORIES

American Universities and Colleges. American Council on Education USA. Walter de Gruyter Inc. • Quadrennial. $249.50. Two volumes. Produced in collaboration with the American Council on Education. Provides full descriptions of more than 1,900 institutions of higher learning, including details of graduate and professional programs.

BusinessWeek Guide to the Best Business Schools. The McGraw-Hill Companies Inc. • Covers: The top 25 business schools and 25 runners-up, ranked by recent graduates and corporate recruiters. Entries include: School contact information; tips on GMAT prep courses; free application software.

The Europa World of Learning. Routledge. • Annual. $1,500 Individuals hardback. Covers about 33,000 colleges, libraries, museums, learned societies, academies, and research institutions throughout the world. Edited by Europa Publications.

Peterson's Guide to Graduate Programs in Business, Education, Health, and Law. Peterson's. • Annual. $38.47 Individuals. Covers colleges and universities in the United States and Canada that offer more than 16,800 accredited graduate programs in business, education, health, and law.

E-BOOKS

The College Blue Book. Cengage Learning Inc. • Annual. $572 Individuals. Published by Macmillan Reference USA. Provides detailed information on programs, degrees, and financial aid sources in the U.S. and Canada.

INTERNET DATABASES

U.S. Census Bureau: The Official Statistics. U. S. Bureau of the Census. Phone: (301)763-4636 or (301)763-4100; Fax: (301)763-4794; Email: webmaster@census.gov • URL: http://www.census.gov/prod/www/abs/mfg-prof.html • Web site is "Your Source for Social, Demographic, and Economic Information." Contains "Current U. S. Population Count," "Current Economic Indicators," and a wide variety of data under "Other Official Statistics." Keyword searching is provided. Fees: Free.

ONLINE DATABASES

Education Index Online. H.W. Wilson Co. • Indexes a wide variety of periodicals related to schools, colleges, and education. 1984 to date. Monthly updates. Inquire as to online cost and availability.

ERIC. U.S. Department of Education Institute of Education Sciences Educational Resources Information Center. • Funded by the U.S. Department of Education, Institute of Education Sciences (formerly Office of Educational Research and Improvement). Provides access to more than one million online records covering education-related journal and report literature, 1966 to date. Updating is monthly. Inquire as to online cost and availability.

PERIODICALS AND NEWSLETTERS

Change: The Magazine of Higher Learning. American Association of Higher Education. Taylor & Francis Group Heldref Publications. • 6/year. $70 Individuals print and online. Contains issues regarding the implications of educational programs, policies and practices.

The Chronicle of Higher Education. The Chronicle of Higher Education. • Weekly. $89 Individuals. Includes *Almanac*. Provides news, book reviews and job listings for college professors and administrators.

College and University. American Association of Collegiate Registrars and Admissions Officers. • Quarterly. $80 Individuals non-member. Addresses issues in higher education; looks at new procedures, policies, technology; reviews new publications.

Community College Journal. American Association of Community Colleges. • Bimonthly. $36 Members. Highlights field research, outstanding programs, college leaders, and membership activities. Formerly *Community, Technical and Junior College Journal*.

Community College Week: The Independent Voice Serving Community, Technical and Junior Colleges. Cox, Matthews and Associates Inc. • Biweekly. $52. Covers a wide variety of current topics relating to the administration and operation of community colleges.

Higher Education and National Affairs. American Council on Education. • Biweekly.

New Directions for Higher Education. Jossey-Bass. • $402 Institutions print + online. Quarterly. Institutions, $311.00 per year; with online edition, $375.00 per year. Sample issue free to librarians.

The Presidency: The Magazine for Higher Education Leaders. American Council on Education. • Quarterly. $70 Other countries. Magazine publishes articles on issues affecting higher education leadership; provides a forum for the presentation of ideas and information for college and university presidents. Formerly *Educational Record*.

Resources in Education. Educational Resources Information Center. U. S. Government Printing

Office. • Monthly. Reports on educational research.

Stanford Business. Stanford University Stanford Graduate School of Business. • Quarterly. $10 U.S. and Canada. Magazine for business school alumni.

University Business: Solutions for Today's Higher Education. Educational Media L.L.C. • 10 times a year. $60.00 per year. Edited for college administrators, including managers of business services, finance, computing, and telecommunications. Includes information on relevant technological advances.

RESEARCH CENTERS AND INSTITUTES

Acton Institute for the Study of Religion and Liberty - Center for Academic Research. 98 E Fulton St., Grand Rapids, MI 49503. Phone: 800-345-2286 or (616)454-3080; Fax: (616)454-9454; Email: info@acton.org • URL: http://www.acton.org/index/research • Generating new economic models synthesizing free market economic theory and the central tenets of Christian social thought, morality and the free market, welfare reform, poverty and development, and other methodological and moral considerations.

Pennsylvania State University - Center for the Study of Higher Education. 400 Rackley Bldg., University Park, PA 16802-3202. Phone: (814)865-9756 or (814)865-6346; Fax: (814)865-3638; Email: cshe@psu.edu • URL: http://www.ed.psu.edu/educ/cshe • Policy analysis of major trends, issues, and practices in higher education at the institutional, state, regional, and national levels. Research initiatives include postsecondary teaching, learning assessment, program review and evaluation, the impact of college on students, strategic and regional planning, organizational cultures, business-industry relationships with colleges and universities, and international higher education. Encourages interdisciplinary studies.

STATISTICS SOURCES

School Enrollment, Social and Economic Characteristics of Students. U. S. Government Printing Office. • Annual. $2.50. Issued by the U. S. Bureau of the Census. Presents detailed tabulations of data on school enrollment of the civilian noninstitutional population three years old and over. Covers nursery school, kindergarten, elementary school, high school, college, and graduate school. Information is provided on age, race, sex, family income, marital status, employment, and other characteristics.

Statistical Abstract of the United States. U. S. Government Printing Office. • Annual. $44.00. Issued by the U. S. Bureau of the Census.

TRADE/PROFESSIONAL ASSOCIATIONS

Academy of International Business. Michigan State University, The Eli Broad College of Business, 645 N Shaw Ln., Rm. 7, East Lansing, MI 48824-1121. Phone: (517)432-1452; Fax: (517)432-1009; Email: aib@aib.msu.edu • URL: http://aib.msu.edu • Consists primarily of university professors, doctoral students, researchers, writers, consultants, executives, and policy setters in the international business/trade research and education fields. Facilitates information exchange among people in academia, business, and government and encourages research activities that advance the knowledge of international business operations and increase the available body of teaching materials. Compiles an inventory of collegiate courses in international business, a survey of research projects, and statistics.

Academy of Management. PO Box 3020, Briarcliff Manor, NY 10510-8020. Phone: (914)923-2607; Fax: (914)923-2615; Email: membership@aom.org • URL: http://www.aom.org • Professors in accredited universities and colleges who teach management; selected business executives who have made significant written contributions to the literature in the field of management and organization. Offers placement service.

Alpha Beta Gamma International. 75 Grasslands Rd., Valhalla, NY 10595. Phone: (914)606-6877; Fax: (914)606-6481; Email: ceo@abg.org • URL: http://www.abg.org • Honor Society - Business. Students enrolled at accredited two-year community, technical, and junior colleges in North America; also initiates distinguished International business persons and academics as honorary members. Sponsors training sessions and cultural and college activities. Maintains speakers' bureau.

Alpha Iota Delta. University of Detroit Mercy, 4001 W McNichols Rd., Detroit, MI 48221. Phone: (313)993-1219; Fax: (313)993-1052; Email: ulfertgw@udmercy.edu • URL: http://www.alphaiotadelta.com • Serves as honor society for men and women in decision sciences and information systems.

American Council on Education. 1 Dupont Cir. NW, Washington, DC 20036. Phone: (202)939-9300 or (202)939-9420; Email: membership@ace.nche.edu • URL: http://www.acenet.edu • A council of colleges and universities, educational organizations, and affiliates. Represents accredited, degree-granting postsecondary institutions directly or through national and regional higher education associations; advocates on their behalf before congress, the federal government, and federal and state courts. Advances education and educational methods through comprehensive voluntary action on the part of American educational associations, organizations, and institutions. Serves as an advocate for adult education and nationally administers the GED high school equivalency exam. Provides college credit equivalency evaluations for courses taught outside the traditional campus classroom by corporations and the military. Maintains numerous commissions, committees, and councils.

Association of American Colleges and Universities. 1818 R St. NW, Washington, DC 20009. Phone: 800-297-3775 or (202)387-3760; Fax: (202)265-9532 • URL: http://www.aacu.org • Advances and strengthens liberal learning for all students, regardless of academic specialization or intended career. Functions as a catalyst and facilitator, forging links among presidents, administrators, and faculty members who are engaged in institutional and curricular planning. Aims to reinforce the collective commitment to liberal education at both the national and local levels and to help individual institutions keep the quality of student learning at the core of their work as they evolve to meet new economic and social challenges.

Association of American Universities. 1200 New York Ave. NW, Ste. 550, Washington, DC 20005. Phone: (202)408-7500; Fax: (202)408-8184 • URL: http://www.aau.edu • Executive heads of universities; membership is determined by appraisal of breadth and quality of a university's research and education efforts. Conducts activities to encourage cooperative consideration of major issues concerning research universities, and to enable members to communicate effectively with the federal government.

Association of American University Presses. 28 W 36th St., Ste. 602, New York, NY 10018. Phone: (212)989-1010; Fax: (212)989-0275 or (212)989-0975; Email: info@aaupnet.org • URL: http://www.aaupnet.org • Helps university presses do their work more economically, creatively, and effectively through its own activities in education-training, fundraising and development, statistical research and analysis, and community and institutional relations.

Association of Governing Boards of Universities and Colleges. 1133 20th St. NW, Ste. 300, Washington, DC 20036-3475. Phone: (202)296-8400; Fax: (202)223-7053; Email: membership@agb.org • URL: http://www.agb.org • Members are governing boards of public and private 2- and 4-year colleges and universities; constituents include regents, trustees, presidents, and other high-level administrators of colleges and universities. Addresses the problems and responsibilities of trusteeship in all sectors of higher education and the relationships of trustees and regents to the president, the faculty, and the student body. Operates Zwingle Resource Center; conducts the National Conference on Trusteeship. Conducts research programs and the Robert L. Gale Fund for the Study of Trusteeship.

Association of Graduate Schools. 1200 New York Ave. NW, Ste. 550, Washington, DC 20005. Phone: (202)408-7500; Fax: (202)408-8184 • Deans of graduate studies in the 61 universities comprising the Association of American Universities. Works to consider matters of common interest relating to graduate study and research.

Beta Gamma Sigma Alumni. PO Box 297-006, Brooklyn, NY 11229-7006. • URL: http://www.bgs-nyc.org • Alumni members of the collegiate national honor society Beta Gamma Sigma. Promotes excellence in business education, ethics, and scholastic achievement and recognition. Local New York chapter.

Business-Higher Education Forum. 2025 M St. NW, Ste. 800, Washington, DC 20036-2422. Phone: (202)367-1189; Fax: (202)367-2269; Email: info@bhef.com • URL: http://www.bhef.com • Board chairmen and chief executive officers of Fortune 500 corporations; presidents and chancellors of universities and colleges. Addresses issues of interest to American business and higher education institutions such as: tax incentives for university research; worker training and retraining; new links between industry and academia; innovative methods of corporate support for higher education. Seeks to expand public awareness of the concerns of business and academic leaders and to influence policy-making affecting those concerns; to enhance relationships between corporate America and institutions of higher learning. Provides interchange between the business and academic communities. Has recently completed several studies on competitiveness; believes that improving the ability of American industry and workers to compete is essential to all other economic and societal goals. Organizes special task forces for in-depth studies on special issues. Disseminates reports and recommendations to policymakers in the public and private sector.

The College Board. 45 Columbus Ave., New York, NY 10023-6917. Phone: (212)713-8000; Email: aces@info.collegeboard.org • URL: http://www.collegeboard.org • Represents the schools, colleges, universities, and other educational organizations that seek to connect members to success and opportunity. Serves students, parents, high schools, and colleges through major programs and services in college admission, guidance, assessment, financial aid, enrollment, and teaching and learning.

Council for Advancement and Support of Education. 1307 New York Ave. NW, Ste. 1000, Washington, DC 20005-4701. Phone: 800-554-8536 or (202)328-2273 or (202)478-5673; Fax: (202)387-4973; Email: membersupportcenter@case.org • URL: http://www.case.org • Formerly American College Public Relations Association.

Council for Hospitality Management Education. University of Bournemouth, Dorset House, Talbot Campus, Fern Barrow, Dorset, Poole BH12 5BB, United Kingdom. • URL: http://www.chme.co.uk • Universities and colleges which offer degree and/or HND courses in hospitality management. Represents member institutions' interests in the field of hospitality management education at HE level, EC, government, industry and professional levels. Promotes hospitality management education in general, as well as specialist levels, e.g. industrial placement, research, access to courses, etc.

Council of Graduate Schools. 1 Dupont Cir. NW, Ste. 230, Washington, DC 20036. Phone: (202)223-3791; Fax: (202)331-7157; Email: general_inquiries@cgs.nche.edu • URL: http://www.cgsnet.org • Formerly Council of Graduate Schools in the United States.

Foundation for Student Communication. 48 University Pl., Princeton, NJ 08544. Phone: (609)258-1111; Fax: (609)258-1222; Email: info@businesstoday.org • URL: http://www.businesstoday.org • Student subscribers and conference participants who desire to promote communication among students and businesspersons. Sponsors student/business forums.

Graduate Management Admission Council. 11921 Freedom Dr., Ste. 300, Reston, VA 20190. Phone: 866-505-6559 or (703)668-9600; Fax: (703)668-9601; Email: customercare@gmac.com • URL: http://www.gmac.com • Graduate schools of management and business administration. Works to establish criteria for use in admission to graduate management programs. Provides professional development for academic administrators and seminars for admissions officers. Maintains Graduate Management Admission Search Service, a program that provides institutions with the names of qualified students with desirable characteristics. Employs Educational Testing Service to develop and administer the Graduate Management Admission Test. Conducts research on student selection issues and political and social issues related to graduate management education.

National Association for Community College Entrepreneurship. Bldg. 101-R, 1 Federal St., Springfield, MA 01105. Phone: (413)306-3131; Fax: (413)755-6101; Email: wolpert@nacce.com • URL: http://www.nacce.com • Establishes entrepreneurship education as a core offering to foster economic development through community colleges. Focuses on increasing economic development through entrepreneurship education and student business incubation at the community college level.

Nonprofit Academic Centers Council. 2121 Euclid Ave., Cleveland, OH 44115-2214. Phone: (216)687-9221 • URL: http://nonprofit-academic-centers-council.org • Provides leadership to strengthen existing centers and supports the establishment of new centers. Fosters collaboration among programs and centers. Develops creative approaches to researcher-practitioner collaborations.

COLOR IN INDUSTRY

See also ART IN INDUSTRY

ONLINE DATABASES

CA Search. American Chemical Society Chemical Abstracts Service. • Guide to chemical literature, 1967 to present. Inquire as to online cost and availability.

PERIODICALS AND NEWSLETTERS

Chromatographia: An International Journal for Rapid Communication in Chromatography and Associated Techniques. Elsevier. • Text in English; summaries in English, French and German.

Color Publishing. PennWell Corp., Advanced Technology Div. • Bimonthly. $29.70 per year.

Color Research and Application. John Wiley & Sons Inc. • Bimonthly. $2,208 Institutions print and online. Covers reports on science, technology and application of color in business, art, design, education and industry.

RESEARCH CENTERS AND INSTITUTES

Center for Imaging Science. Rochester Institute of Technology, 54 Lomb Memorial Dr., Rochester, NY 14623. Phone: (585)475-5994; Fax: (585)475-5988; Email: contactus@cis.rit.edu • URL: http://www.cis.rit.edu • Activities include research in color science and digital image processing.

Rensselaer Polytechnic Institute. Rensselaer Union, 110 8th St., Troy, NY 12180-3590. Phone: (518)276-6000 or (518)276-6344; Fax: (518)276-8728 or (518)276-4887; Email: ads@poly.rpi.edu • URL: http://www.rpi.edu • Serves as a conduit for research interactions between Rensselaer Polytechnic Institute and private companies.

TRADE/PROFESSIONAL ASSOCIATIONS

Color Association of the United States. 33 Whitehall St., Ste. M3, New York, NY 10004. Phone: (212)947-7774; Fax: (212)757-4557; Email: info@colorassociation.com • URL: http://www.colorassociation.com • Formerly The Textile Color Card Association of America.

Color Marketing Group. 1908 Mt. Vernon Ave., Alexandria, VA 22301. Phone: (703)329-8500 or (703)647-4729; Fax: (703)329-0155 or (703)535-3190; Email: sgriffis@colormarketing.org • URL: http://www.colormarketing.org • International group of professionals who forecast colors for consumer and contract markets. Examines color as it applies to the profitable marketing of products and services. Provides a forum for the exchange of ideas for all phases of color marketing, including styling, design, trends, merchandising, sales, education and research.

Color Pigments Manufacturers Association. 300 N Washington St., Ste. 105, Alexandria, VA 22314. Phone: (703)684-4044 or (202)465-4900; Fax: (202)465-4905 or (703)684-1795; Email: cpma@cpma.com • URL: http://www.pigments.org/cms/ • Manufacturers of inorganic and organic color pigments. Disseminates technical, regulatory, and legislative information on laboratory testing, toxicity, and subjects of general interest to manufacturers of pigments.

Optical Society of America. 2010 Massachusetts Ave. NW, Washington, DC 20036-1023. Phone: 800-766-405A or (202)223-8130; Fax: (202)223-1096; Email: info@osa.org • URL: http://www.osa.org • Persons interested in any branch of optics: research, instruction, optical applications, manufacture, distribution of optical equipment, and physiological optics. Sponsors topical meetings.

COLOR PHOTOGRAPHY

See PHOTOGRAPHIC INDUSTRY

COLOR TELEVISION

See TELEVISION APPARATUS INDUSTRY

COLUMNISTS

See WRITERS AND WRITING

COMMERCIAL ART

See also ART IN INDUSTRY; CREATIVITY; DESIGN IN INDUSTRY; GRAPHIC ARTS INDUSTRY

ABSTRACTS AND INDEXES

Art Index. EBSCO Publishing Inc. • Quarterly. Annual cumulations. Price varies. Subject and author index to periodicals in art, architecture, industrial design, city planning, photography, and various related topics.

ALMANACS AND YEARBOOKS

Art Directors Annual. Art Directors Club. • Annual. $70.00. Formerly *Annual of Advertising, Editorial and Television Art and Design with the Annual Copy Awards*.

Graphis Design Annual. Graphis Inc. • Annual. $120 Hardcover. Text in English, French, and German.

CD-ROM DATABASES

Art Index. EBSCO Publishing Inc. • Indexing for over 600 periodicals and 13,000 art dissertations.

ONLINE DATABASES

Art Index Online. H.W. Wilson Co. • Indexes a wide variety of art-related periodicals, 1984 to date. Monthly updates. Inquire as to online cost and availability.

PERIODICALS AND NEWSLETTERS

Graphic Design: U.S.A. Kaye Publishing Corp. • Monthly. $60.00.

Graphis: International Journal of Visual Communication. Graphis Inc. • Bimonthly. $90.00 per year. Text in English, French and German.

RESEARCH CENTERS AND INSTITUTES

Rochester Institute of Technology - Chester F. Carlson Center for Imaging Science. 54 Lomb Memorial Dr., Rochester, NY 14623. Phone: (585)475-5944; Fax: (585)475-5988; Email: baum@cis.rit.edu • URL: http://www.cis.rit.edu • Imaging sciences, including remote sensing, digital image processing, color science, optics, medical diagnostic imaging, visual perception, sensor development, printing technology, and astronomical imaging.

TRADE/PROFESSIONAL ASSOCIATIONS

Art Directors Club. 106 W 29th St., New York, NY 10001. Phone: (212)643-1440; Fax: (212)643-4266; Email: info@adcglobal.org • URL: http://www.adcglobal.org • Art directors of advertising magazines and agencies, visual information specialists, and graphic designers; associate members are artists, cinematographers, photographers, copywriters, educators, journalists, and critics. Promotes and stimulates interest in the practice of art direction. Sponsors Annual Exhibition of Advertising, Editorial and Television Art and Design; International Traveling Exhibition. Provides educational, professional, and entertainment programs; on-premise art exhibitions; portfolio review program. Conducts panels for students and faculty.

COMMERCIAL AVIATION

See BUSINESS AVIATION

COMMERCIAL CODE

See BUSINESS LAW

COMMERCIAL CORRESPONDENCE

See BUSINESS CORRESPONDENCE

COMMERCIAL CREDIT

See COMMERCIAL LENDING

COMMERCIAL EDUCATION

See BUSINESS EDUCATION

COMMERCIAL FINANCE COMPANIES

See FINANCE COMPANIES

COMMERCIAL LAW AND REGULATION

See BUSINESS LAW

COMMERCIAL LENDING

See also BANK LOANS

ABSTRACTS AND INDEXES

Business Periodicals Index Retrospective. EBSCO Publishing Inc. • 11/year. Quarterly and annual cumulations.

DIRECTORIES

Directory of 2,500 Active Real-Estate Lenders. International Wealth Success Inc. • Annual. $25 Individuals. Covers: About 2,500 financial institutions that actively lend money for real estate investments and purchases. Entries include: Company name, address.

The Euromoney Syndicated Lending Handbook. Euromoney Institutional Investor P.L.C. • Annual. $195 Individuals. Covers: Contact details for 307 relevant personnel in banks, law firms, rating agencies, and associations involved in syndicated lending worldwide. Entries include: Company name, address, phone, fax, e-mail address, Web site, telex number, and names and titles of key personnel.

Real Estate Loans Directory. InfoGroup Inc. • Annual. Number of listings: 74,550. Entries include: Name, address, phone, size of advertisement, name of owner or manager, number of employees, year first in "Yellow Pages." Compiled from telephone company "Yellow Pages," nationwide.

HANDBOOKS AND MANUALS

Manual of Credit and Commercial Laws. National Association of Credit Management. National Association of Credit Management. • Annual. $69.95 Individuals. Provides information for credit professionals. Formerly *Credit Manual of Commercial Laws.*

ONLINE DATABASES

TRW Business Credit Profiles. Experian Information Solutions Inc. • Provides credit history (trade payments, payment trends, payment totals, payment history, etc.) for public and private U. S. companies. Key facts and banking information are also given. Updates are weekly. Inquire as to online cost and availability.

Wilson Business Abstracts Online. H.W. Wilson Co. • Indexes and abstracts 600 major business periodicals, plus the *Wall Street Journal* and the business section of the *New York Times.* Indexing is from 1982, abstracting from 1990, with the two newspapers included from 1993. Updated weekly. Inquire as to online cost and availability. (*Business Periodicals Index* without abstracts is also available online.).

OTHER SOURCES

Bank and Lender Litigation Reporter: The Nationwide Litigation Report of Failed National and State Banks and Savings and Loan Associations, including FDIC and FSLIC Complaints and Related Actions Among Shareholders, Officers, Directors, Ins. Andrews Publications. • Semimonthly. $875.00 per year. Newsletter. Provides summaries of significant litigation and regulatory agency complaints. Formerly *Lender Liability Litigation Reporter.*

PERIODICALS AND NEWSLETTERS

Lender Liability Law Report. Thomson RIA. • Description: Discusses the impact of relevant cases and legislation on lenders and spotlights legal landmines which lenders may encounter. Recurring features include summaries of recent cases and avoidance techniques.

TRADE/PROFESSIONAL ASSOCIATIONS

National Chemical Credit Association. 1100 Main St., Buffalo, NY 14209-2356. Phone: (716)887-9547; Fax: (716)878-0479 • URL: http://www.nccal.org/document_1.html • Represents chemical companies. Aims to facilitate the exchange of commercial credit information among leaders of the chemical industry, as well as provide continual professional education to its members. Sponsors monthly educational programs at divisional meetings.

Risk Management Association. 1801 Market St., Ste. 300, Philadelphia, PA 19103-1613. Phone: (215)446-4000; Fax: (215)446-4101; Email: rmaar@rmahq.org • URL: http://www.rmahq.org • Commercial and savings banks, and savings and loan, and other financial services companies. Conducts research and professional development activities in areas of loan administration, asset management, and commercial lending and credit to increase professionalism.

COMMERCIAL PHOTOGRAPHY

See also PHOTOGRAPHIC INDUSTRY

ABSTRACTS AND INDEXES

Art Index. EBSCO Publishing Inc. • Quarterly. Annual cumulations. Price varies. Subject and author index to periodicals in art, architecture, industrial design, city planning, photography, and various related topics.

DIRECTORIES

American Society of Media Photographers--Membership Directory. American Society of Media Photographers. • Covers: 5,000 professional photographers for publications. Entries include: Name, address, phone, fax, e-mail address, specialty.

FINANCIAL RATIOS

Annual Statement Studies. Risk Management Association. • Annual. Compiled from over 280,000 financial statements.

Annual Statement Studies: Industry Default Probabilities and Cash Flow Measures. Risk Management Association. • Annual. $405 Nonmembers. Serves as a companion volume to the original *Annual Statement Studies.* Gives probability of default estimates on a percentage scale for more than 450 industries. Includes changes in position year-by-year for eight financial statement line items and provides percentage measures of cash flow.

ONLINE DATABASES

Art Index Online. H.W. Wilson Co. • Indexes a wide variety of art-related periodicals, 1984 to date. Monthly updates. Inquire as to online cost and availability.

PERIODICALS AND NEWSLETTERS

News Photographer: Dedicated to the Service and Advancement of News Photography. National Press Photographers Association. • Monthly. $48.00 per year.

Professional Photographer. Professional Photographers of America. • Monthly. $27.00 per year.

Studio Photography and Design. Cygnus Business Media Inc. • Monthly. Free to qualified personnel; others, $60.00 per year. Incorporates *Commercial Image.*

TRADE/PROFESSIONAL ASSOCIATIONS

American Society of Media Photographers. 150 N 2nd St., Philadelphia, PA 19106-1912. Phone: (215)451-2767; Fax: (215)451-0880; Email: info@asmp.org • URL: http://www.asmp.org • Professional society of freelance photographers. Works to evolve trade practices for photographers in communications fields. Provides business information to photographers and their potential clients; promotes ethics and rights of members. Holds educational programs and seminars. Compiles statistics.

National Press Photographers Association. 3200 Croasdaile Dr., Ste. 306, Durham, NC 27705-2588. Phone: (919)383-7246; Fax: (919)383-7261; Email: info@nppa.org • URL: http://www.nppa.org • Professional news photographers and others whose occupation has a direct professional relationship with photojournalism, the art of news communication by photographic image through publication, television film, or theater screen. Sponsors annual television-news film workshop and annual cross-country (five locations) short course. Conducts annual competition for news photos and for television-news film, and monthly contest for still clipping and television-news film.

COMMERCIAL REAL ESTATE

See INDUSTRIAL REAL ESTATE

COMMERCIAL STATISTICS

See BUSINESS STATISTICS

COMMODITIES

See also COMMODITY FUTURES TRADING

ALMANACS AND YEARBOOKS

Commodity Market Review. Bernan Associates. • Biennial. $45. Published by the Food and Agriculture Organization of the United Nations (FAO). Reviews the global outlook for over 20 specific commodities.

CRB Commodity Yearbook. Commodity Research Bureau. CRB. • Annual. $179 plus $10.00 shipping cost. The single most comprehensive source of commodity and futures market information available.

Securities, Commodities, and Federal Banking: 1999 in Review. Wolters Kluwer Law & Business CCH. • Irregular. $57.00. Summarizes the year's significant legal and regulatory developments.

UNCTAD Commodity Yearbook. United Nations Conference on Trade and Development. United Nations Publications. • Contains statistics on trade, production and consumption of commodities, as well as special tables showing the most important exporting and importing countries.

CD-ROM DATABASES

World Trade Analyzer. Statistics Canada, International Trade Division. • $4,000. Annual. CD-ROM provides 20 years of export-import data for 800 commodities traded by the 180 member countries of the United Nations.

DIRECTORIES

Commodity Price Statistics. United Nations Publications. • Database covers: Free-market prices and price indices for selected commodities that concern commodity-dependant countries. Price indices are provided for commodity groups (including food, tropical beverages, vegetable oilseeds and oils, agricultural raw materials, minerals, ores and metals), and for all groups in current dollars and SDRs.

INTERNET DATABASES

USDA. U.S. National Institute of Standards and Technology. 100 Bureau Dr., Gaithersburg, MD

For publishers' addresses, refer to SOURCES CITED section at the back of the book.

20899-1070. Phone: 800-877-8339 or (301)975-6478 or (202)720-2791; Fax: (301)975-8295; Email: inquiries@nist.gov • URL: http://www.nist.gov • The USDA home page has six sections: News and Information; What's New; About USDA; Agencies; Opportunities; Search and Help. Keyword searching is offered from the USDA home page and from various individual agency home pages. Agencies are the Economic Research Service, Agricultural Marketing Service, National Agricultural Statistics Service, National Agricultural Library, and about 12 others. Updating varies. Fees: Free.

ONLINE DATABASES

CAB Abstracts. CABI. • Contains 46 specialized abstract collections covering over 10,000 journals and monographs in the areas of agriculture, horticulture, forest products, farm products, nutrition, dairy science, poultry, grains, animal health, entomology, etc. Time period is 1972 to date, with monthly updates. Inquire as to online cost and availability. *CAB Abstracts on CD-ROM* also available, with annual updating.

PERIODICALS AND NEWSLETTERS

Financial Times (London). The Financial Times, Inc. • Daily, except Sunday. $572.88 per year. An international business and financial newspaper, featuring news from London, Paris, Frankfurt, New York, and Tokyo. Includes worldwide stock and bond market data, commodity market data, and monetary/currency exchange information.

PRICE SOURCES

CRB Commodity Index Report. Commodity Research Bureau. • $795.00 per year. Coverage of all Commodity Research Bureau indexes in tabular and graphical format.

Monthly Commodity Price Bulletin. United Nations Publications. • Monthly. $125.00 per year. Provides monthly average prices for the previous 12 months for a wide variety of commodities traded internationally.

PPI Detailed Report. Periodical covering business. Bureau of Labor Statistics, U.S. Department of Labor. U. S. Government Printing Office. • Monthly. $55 Individuals.

Wholesale Commodity Report. The Financial Times, Inc. • Weekly.

STATISTICS SOURCES

Agricultural Statistics. U.S. Department of Agriculture National Agricultural Statistics Service. • Annual. $46 Individuals. Provides a wide variety of statistical data relating to agricultural production, supplies, consumption, prices/price-supports, foreign trade, costs, and returns, as well as farm labor, loans, income, and population. In many cases, historical data is shown annually for 10 years. In addition to farm data, includes detailed fishery statistics.

Statistical Yearbook. United Nations Publications. • Annual. $125.00. Contains statistics for about 200 countries on a wide variety of economic, industrial, and demographic topics. Compiled by United Nations Statistical Office.

COMMODITY EXCHANGES

See COMMODITY FUTURES TRADING

COMMODITY FUTURES TRADING

ALMANACS AND YEARBOOKS

Commodity Trading Guide. Commodity Research Bureau. • Annual. Serves as a concise "Almanac, Encyclopedia, Yearbook, and Calendar for the Futures Market." Includes many price charts, tables, government report dates, contract specifications, and price outlooks.

CRB Commodity Yearbook. Commodity Research Bureau. CRB. • Annual. $179 plus $10.00 shipping cost. The single most comprehensive source of commodity and futures market information available.

DIRECTORIES

Futures Magazine SourceBook: The Most Complete List of Exchanges, Companies, Regulators, Organizations, etc., Offering Products and Services to the Futures and Options Industry. Futures Magazine Inc. • Annual. $19.50. Provides information on commodity futures brokers, trading method services, publications, and other items of interest to futures traders and money managers.

Handbook of World Stock and Commodity Exchanges. Blackwell Publishing Inc. • Annual. $265.00. Provides detailed information on over 200 stock and commodity exchanges in more than 50 countries.

HANDBOOKS AND MANUALS

Money Manager's Compliance Guide. Thompson Publishing Group Inc. • $739.00 per year. Two looseleaf volumes. Monthly updates and newletters. Edited for investment advisers and investment companies to help them be in compliance with governmental regulations, including SEC rules, restrictions based on the Employee Retirement Income Security Act (ERISA), and regulations issued by the Commodity Futures Trading Commission (CFTC).

National Futures Association Manual. National Futures Association. • Quarterly. Price on application. Looseleaf service. Rules and regulations concerning commodity futures trading.

INTERNET DATABASES

BanxQuote Banking, Mortgage, and Finance Center. BanxQuote, Inc. Phone: (914)722-1600; Fax: (914)722-6630; Email: info@banx.com • URL: http://www.banx.com • Daily. Web site quotes interest rates paid by banks around the country on various savings products, as well as rates paid by consumers for automobile loans, mortgages, credit cards, home equity loans, and personal loans. Also provided: stock quotes, indexes, stock options, futures trading data, economic indicators, and links to many other financial sites.

Chicago Board of Trade: The World's Leading Futures Exchange. Chicago Board of Trade. Phone: (312)535-3500; Fax: (312)341-3392; Email: comments@cbot.com • URL: http://www.cbot.com • Web site provides a wide variety of statistics, commentary, charts, and news relating to both agricultural and financial futures trading. For example, Web page "MarketPlex: Information MarketPlace to the World" offers prices & volume, contract specifications & margins, government reports, etc. Searching is available, with daily updates for current data. Fees: Mostly free (some specialized services are fee-based).

CRB Market Overview. Commodity Research Bureau. Phone: 800-621-5271 or (312)554-8456; Fax: (312)939-4135; Email: info@crbtrader.com • URL: http://www.crbtrader.com/data/ • Web site provides free, detailed, current price quotes for about 100 futures contracts, covering Currencies, Energies, Financials, Grains, Meats, Metals, "Softs" (orange juice, coffee, etc.) and stock price indexes. Includes contract specifications and detailed prices of options on futures.

Factiva. Dow Jones Reuters Business Interactive, LLC. Phone: 800-369-7466 or (609)452-1511; Fax: (609)520-5770; Email: solutions@factiva.com • URL: http://www.factiva.com • Fee-based Web site provides "global news and business information through Web sites and content integration solutions." Includes Dow Jones and Reuters newswires, The Wall Street Journal, and more than 7,000 other sources of current news, historical articles, market research reports, and investment analysis. Content includes 96 major U. S. newspapers, 900 non-English sources, trade publications, media transcripts, country profiles, news photos, etc.

Futures Online. Futures Magazine Inc. Phone: (312)846-4600; Fax: (312)846-4638 • URL: http://www.futuresmag.com • Web site presents updates of *Futures* magazine and links to other futures-related sites.

Nexis.com. Lexis-Nexis Group. Phone: 800-227-4908 or (937)865-6800; Fax: (937)865-6909; Email: webmaster@prod.lexis-nexis.com • URL: http://www.nexis.com • Fee-based Web site offers searching of about 2.8 billion documents in some 30,000 news, business, and legal information sources. Features include a subject directory covering 1,200 topics in 34 categories and a Company Dossier containing information on more than 500,000 public and private companies. Boolean searching is offered.

Wall Street Journal Interactive Edition. Dow Jones & Co., Inc. 1211 Avenue of the Americas, New York, NY 10036. Phone: 800-369-5663; Email: service@dowjones.com • URL: http://new.dowjones.com • Fee-based Web site providing online searching of worldwide information from *The Wall Street Journal*. Includes "Company Snapshots," "The Journal's Greatest Hits," "Index to Market Data," "Journal Links," etc. Financial price quotes are available. Fees: $49.00 per year; $29.00 per year to print subscribers.

OTHER SOURCES

Westlaw Journal Securities Litigation & Regulation. Thomson Reuters Westlaw. • $3,563.52 full set. Provides coverage of shareholder lawsuits against public companies.

PERIODICALS AND NEWSLETTERS

Consensus: National Futures and Financial Weekly. Consensus Inc. • Weekly. $365.00 per year. Newspaper. Contains news, statistics, and special reports relating to agricultural, industrial, and financial futures markets. Features daily basis price charts, reprints of market advice, and "The Consensus Index of Bullish Market Opinion" (charts show percent bullish of advisors for various futures).

The Financial Post: Canadian's Business Voice. Financial Post Datagroup. • Daily. $200.00 per year. Provides Canadian business, economic, financial, and investment news. Features extensive price quotes from all major Canadian markets: stocks, bonds, mutual funds, commodities, and currencies. Supplement available: *Financial Post 500*. Includes annual supplement.

Futures Market Service. Commodity Research Bureau. • Weekly. $155 Individuals.

Futures: News, Analysis, and Strategies for Futures, Options, and Derivatives Traders. Futures Magazine Inc. • Monthly. $39 Individuals. Edited for institutional money managers and traders, brokers, risk managers, and individual investors or speculators. Includes special feature issues on interest rates, technical indicators, currencies, charts, precious metals, hedge funds, and derivatives. Supplements available.

SFO: Stocks, Futures & Options. W and A Publishing. • Subtitle: *Official Journal for Personal Investing in Stocks, Futures, and Options*. Covers mainly speculative techniques for stocks, commodity futures, financial futures, stock index futures, foreign exchange, short selling, and various kinds of options.

PRICE SOURCES

CRB Commodity Index Report. Commodity Research Bureau. • $795.00 per year. Coverage of all Commodity Research Bureau indexes in tabular and graphical format.

CRB Futures Perspective: Agricultural Edition. Commodity Research Bureau. • Weekly. $230.00 per year. Service provides comprehensive price charts for more than 20 agricultural commodity futures, from cocoa to wheat (includes lumber). Also provides technical analysis of price movements and market commentary. Formerly part of *CRB Futures Chart Service.*

STATISTICS SOURCES

Statistical Annual: Grains, Options on Agricultural Futures. Chicago Board of Trade. • Annual. Includes historical data on Wheat Futures, Options on Wheat Futures, Corn Futures, Options on Corn Futures, Oats Futures, Soybean Futures, Options on Soybean Futures, Soybean Oil Futures, Soybean Meal Futures.

Statistical Annual: Interest Rates, Metals, Stock Indices, Options on Financial Futures, Options on Metals Futures. Chicago Board of Trade. • Annual. Includes historical data on GNMA CDR Futures, Cash-Settled GNMA Futures, U. S. Treasury Bond Futures, U. S. Treasury Note Futures, Options on Treasury Note Futures, NASDAQ-100 Futures, Major Market Index Futures, Major Market Index MAXI Futures, Municipal Bond Index Futures, 1,000-Ounce Silver Futures, Options on Silver Futures, and Kilo Gold Futures.

TRADE/PROFESSIONAL ASSOCIATIONS

National Futures Association. 300 S Riverside Plz., No. 1800, Chicago, IL 60606-6615. Phone: 800-621-3570 or (312)781-1300 or (312)781-1410; Fax: (312)781-1467; Email: information@nfa.futures.org • URL: http://www.nfa.futures.org • Futures commission merchants; commodity trading advisors; commodity pool operators; brokers and their associated persons. Works to: strengthen and expand industry self-regulation to include all segments of the futures industry; provide uniform standards to eliminate duplication of effort and conflict; remove unnecessary regulatory constraints to aid effective regulation. Conducts member qualification screening, financial surveillance, and registration. Monitors and enforces customer protection rules and uniform business standards. Maintains information center. Arbitrates customer disputes; audits non-exchange member FCM's.

COMMON MARKET

See EUROPEAN MARKETS

COMMUNICATION

See also BUSINESS CORRESPONDENCE; BUSINESS JOURNALISM; COMMUNICATION SYSTEMS; COMMUNICATIONS SATELLITES; COMPUTER COMMUNICATIONS; CORPORATION REPORTS; TELECOMMUNICATIONS

ABSTRACTS AND INDEXES

Communication Abstracts: An International Information Service. Pine Forge Press. • Bimonthly. Institutions, $1,150.00 per year. Provides broad coverage of the literature of communications, including broadcasting and advertising.

Psychological Abstracts. American Psychological Association. • Monthly. Members, $815.00 per year; individuals and institutions, $1,207.00 per year. Covers the international literature of psychology and the behavioral sciences. Includes journals, technical reports, dissertations, and other sources.

Social Sciences Citation Index. Thomson Reuters Corp. • Weekly. Product is accessed via *Web of Science.*

Social Sciences Index Retrospective: 1907-1983. EBSCO Publishing Inc. • Indexing for 1,000,000 articles. Coverage includes international index and social sciences and humanities index.

ALMANACS AND YEARBOOKS

Communication Yearbook. International Communication Association. • Annual. Literature reviews and essays.

CD-ROM DATABASES

Business Abstracts with Full Text. EBSCO Publishing Inc. • Includes full text articles from more than 460 business publications from 1982 to present. Indexing for nearly 880 publications.

Social Sciences Abstracts. EBSCO Publishing Inc. • Provides indexing from 1983 and abstracting from 1994 of more than 750 periodicals covering economics, area studies, community health, public administration, public welfare, urban studies, and many other topics related to the social sciences.

Social Sciences Citation Index. Thomson Reuters Corp. • Weekly. Product is accessed via *Web of Science.*

DIRECTORIES

Datatech Communications Business Directory. Datatech Communications Inc. • Covers: More than 160,000 companies throughout the U.S. Entries include: Company name, address, phone, fax, 800 numbers, URL, e-mail.

Directory of ICT Companies in Mauritius. National Computer Board. • Annual. Covers: 300 companies operating in the ICT sector in Mauritius in a wide range of activities including software development, call centre, BPO, web-enabled activities, training, hardware assembly and sales, networking and other support services. Entries include: Company name, address, phone, fax, e-mail, website, directors, contact person, number of employees, company profile, competencies, export markets, products, and services.

International Communications and Business Database on CD-ROM. Jaeger and Waldmann. • Annual. $440. Covers: Extensive list of companies located in approximately 220 countries. Entries include: Company name, address, phone; products and services; various data.

National E-mail and Fax Directory. Cengage Learning Inc. • Annual. $265 Individuals. 2009. 23rd edition. A comprehensive "one stop" source of information on contact information -- fax numbers, e-mail addresses, voice telephone numbers, and mailing addresses. Coverage spans over 151,000 major businesses, agencies and organizations in the United States.

Signal Magazine--AFCEA Source Book Issue. • Annual. Publication includes: List of member companies concerned with communications, design, production, maintenance and operation of communications, electronics, command and control, computers, intelligence systems and imagery. Entries include: Company name, address, phone, names and titles of key personnel, financial keys, trade and brand names, products or services, affiliations, description of organizational purpose, objectives.

E-BOOKS

Business and Technical Communication: An Annotated Guide to Sources, Skills, and Strategies. Cengage Learning Inc. • 2007. eBook. Includes research sources, an annotated bibliography of how-to information, and detailed indexes to identify the most relevant items in aiding business and technical communication.

Business Data Communications and Networking: A Research Perspective. Cengage Learning Inc..

ENCYCLOPEDIAS AND DICTIONARIES

Encyclopedia of Communication and Information. Cengage Learning Inc. • 2003. eBook. Published by Macmillan Reference USA. Provides an overview of universal modes of communication. Inquire about price and availability.

GENERAL WORKS

Business Communications Made Simple. Butterworth-Heinemann. • Date not set. Price on application.

International Journal of Business Communication (IJBC). Association for Business Communication. • Quarterly. $497 Institutions online only. Journal focusing on professional business communication.

HANDBOOKS AND MANUALS

Personnel Management: Communications. Prentice Hall PTR. • Looseleaf. Periodic supplementation. Price on application. Includes how to write effectively and how to prepare employee publications.

ONLINE DATABASES

Wilson Business Abstracts Online. H.W. Wilson Co. • Indexes and abstracts 600 major business periodicals, plus the *Wall Street Journal* and the business section of the *New York Times.* Indexing is from 1982, abstracting from 1990, with the two newspapers included from 1993. Updated weekly. Inquire as to online cost and availability. (*Business Periodicals Index* without abstracts is also available online.).

Wilson Social Sciences Abstracts Online. H.W. Wilson Co. • Provides online abstracting and indexing of more than 500 periodicals covering area studies, community health, public administration, public welfare, urban studies, and many other social science topics. Time period is 1994 to date for abstracts and 1983 to date for indexing, with updates weekly. Inquire as to online cost and availability.

PERIODICALS AND NEWSLETTERS

Business and Professional Communication Quarterly (BPCQ). Association for Business Communication. • Quarterly. $497 Institutions online only. Features articles about teaching and writing course outlines. Description of training programs, problems, solutions, etc. Includes *Journal of Business Communication.*

Business Communications Review. Key3Media Group, Inc. • Monthly. $45.00 per year. Edited for communications managers in large end-user companies and institutions. Includes special feature issues on intranets and network management.

Communication Briefings: A Monthly Idea Source for Decision Makers. Briefings Publishing Group. • Monthly. $97. Presents useful ideas for communication, public relations, customer service, human resources, and employee training.

Communication Research. Pine Forge Press. • Bimonthly. Contains articles that explore the processes, antecedents, and consequences of communication in a broad range of societal systems.

Communication World: The Magazine for Communication Professionals. International Association of Business Communicators. • Emphasis is on public relations, media relations, corporate communication, and writing.

Communications News. Nelson Publishing Inc. • Monthly.

Communications News: Solutions for Today's Networking Decision Managers. Nelson Publishing Inc. • Monthly. Free to qualified personnel; others, $84.00 per year. Includes coverage of "Internetworking" and "Intrenetworking." Emphasis is on emerging telecommunications technologies.

Harvard Management Communication Letter. Harvard Business School Publishing. • Description: Provides information and techniques for managers on effective communication.

Homeland Security and Defense: Weekly Intelligence for the Global Homeland Security and Defense Community. Aviation Week Business Intelligence Services. • Weekly. $595.00 per year. Newsletter. Emphasis is on airline and airport programs (federal, state, and local). Also covers counterterrorism, protection of military units, Department of Homeland Security activities, industrial security, communications equipment, and other topics related to homeland security.

Human Communication Research. International Communication Association. Oxford University Press, Journals. • A scholarly journal of interpersonal communication.

International Journal of Business Communication. Association for Business Communication. • Quarterly. Includes empirical and theoretically conceptual research results in business communication.

9-1-1 Magazine: Public Safety Communications and Response. Official Publications Inc. • Bimonthly. $29.95 per year. Covers technical information and applications for public safety communications personnel.

Presentations: Technology and Techniques for Effective Communication. Nielsen Business Media Inc. • Monthly. Free to qualified personnel; others, $69.00 per year. Covers the use of presentation hardware and software, including audiovisual equipment and computerized display systems. Includes an annual *Buyers Guide to Presentation Products*.

The Successful Benefits Communicator. Lawrence Ragan Communications Inc. • Description: Offers ideas, techniques, and tips for those who communicate benefits information.

RESEARCH CENTERS AND INSTITUTES

Aarhus University - School of Business and Social Sciences - Department of Business Communication - Center for Corporate Communication. Fuglesangs Allè 4, DK-8210 Aarhus, Denmark. Phone: 45 89486268; Fax: 45 86150188 • URL: http://bcom.au.dk/research/academicareas/ccc • Business communications, including management communication, market communication, corporate communication, public relations, internal communication, business journalism, etc.

Agency for Healthcare Research and Quality - Office of Communications and Knowledge Transfer. 540 Gaither Rd., Rockville, MD 20850-6649. Phone: (301)427-1364; Fax: (301)427-1873; Email: howard.holland@ahrq.hhs.gov • URL: http://www.ahrq.gov/cpi/centers/ockt/index.html • Disseminates health services research and other initiatives to the health care industry, health care providers, consumers and patients, policy makers, research, and the media with particular emphasis on communicating agency initiatives in the ways each of these constituencies are most interested and are likely to lead to behavior change.

East-West Center. 1601 E West Rd., Honolulu, HI 96848-1601. Phone: (808)944-7111; Fax: (808)944-7376 • URL: http://www.eastwestcenter.org • Established by congress as a national education and research organization to promote US-Asia-Pacific relations and understanding through cooperative study, training and research. Assists in "building an Asia Pacific community in which the United States is a natural, valued and leading partner." Provides awards annually to scholars, researchers, graduate students, and professionals in business and government. Holds seminars and workshops in conjunction with long-term research projects and research grants. Education and dialogue programs seek to prepare Americans for an era in which the Asia-Pacific region is vastly more important to the United States.

University of Calgary - Institute of Professional Communication. Social Sciences 110, 2500 University Dr. NW, Calgary, AB, Canada T2N 1N4. Phone: (403)220-7255; Fax: (403)220-6716; Email: cmsopcza@ucalgary.ca • URL: http://www.ipc.ucalgary.ca/ • Professional communication.

STATISTICS SOURCES

AM/FM Broadcast Financial Data/TV Broadcast Financial Data. U.S. Federal Communications Commission. • Annual. Free.

TRADE/PROFESSIONAL ASSOCIATIONS

Association for Business Communication. 181 Turner St. NW, Blacksburg, VA 24061. Phone: (540)231-8460 or (540)231-1939; Email: abcoffice@businesscommunication.org • URL: http://www.businesscommunication.org • College teachers of business communication; management consultants in business communications; training directors and correspondence supervisors of business firms, direct mail copywriters, public relations writers, and others interested in communication for business.

Corporate Speech Pathology Network. 10 Glenlake Pkwy., Ste. 130, Atlanta, GA 30328. Phone: (678)592-0052 • URL: http://www.corspan.org • Represents the interests of corporate speech pathologists and other individuals and corporations exploring speech training. Seeks to promote and improve speech in the business and corporate settings. Encourages members to share information and ideas.

Electronic Industry Citizenship Coalition. 1155 15th St. NW, Ste. 500, Washington, DC 20005. Email: info@eicc.info • URL: http://www.eicc.info • Represents global ICT companies and their suppliers. Aims to promote a common code of conduct for the electronics, information and communications technology (ICT) industry. Works to improve environmental and worker conditions.

Foundation for Student Communication. 48 University Pl., Princeton, NJ 08544. Phone: (609)258-1111; Fax: (609)258-1222; Email: info@businesstoday.org • URL: http://www.businesstoday.org • Student subscribers and conference participants who desire to promote communication among students and businesspersons. Sponsors student/business forums.

International Ombudsman Association. 111 Deer Lake Rd., Ste. 100, Deerfield, IL 60015. Phone: (847)509-7991; Fax: (847)480-9282; Email: info@ombudsassociation.org • URL: http://www.ombudsassociation.org/home.aspx • Individuals actively engaged in the practice of organizational ombudsmanry, as designated neutrals. Works to enhance the quality and value of the ombudsman function by: establishing and communicating appropriate standards of excellence for the profession; developing and disseminating ethical guidelines for organizational ombudspeople; training new and experienced ombuds practitioners in complaint handling skills and principles of effective practice; communicating the latest developments of the profession; and fostering appropriate forums to share common interests and strengthen skills.

Italian American Alliance for Business and Technology. 535 Griswold, Ste. 1844, Detroit, MI 48226. Phone: (248)227-6143; Email: info@iaabt.org • URL: http://iaabt.org • Serves the needs of Italian industrial companies wanting to do business in the United States and U.S. industrial companies seeking to do business in Italy. Promotes the technological, scientific, research and development, design and manufacturing capabilities of member companies. Fosters business opportunities and facilitates exchange of ideas among its members.

Medical Spa Society. 60 E 56th St., 2nd Fl., New York, NY 10022. Phone: 888-MED-ISPA or (212)688-5882; Email: coordinator@medicalspasociety.com • URL: http://www.medicalspasociety.com • Seeks to raise and uphold the level of professionalism practiced throughout the medical spa industry. Promotes education, communication and standards of excellence for the medical spa profession. Encourages exchange of information and ideas that will further enhance the image and credibility of the medical spa industry.

TechAmerica. 1001 19th St. N, 20th Fl., Arlington, VA 22209. Phone: (202)682-9110; Fax: (202)682-9111; Email: database@techamerica.org • URL: http://www.techamerica.org • A division of the Information Technology Association of America; software companies involved in the development or marketing of software for personal, midrange, and mainframe computers. Promotes the software industry and addresses specific problems of the industry. Represents the industry before various governmental units; provides educational programs to members; conducts research and makes available legal services. Develops standards.

COMMUNICATION, COMPUTER

See COMPUTER COMMUNICATIONS

COMMUNICATION, MASS

See MASS MEDIA

COMMUNICATION SYSTEMS

See also COMPUTERS; TELECOMMUNICATIONS

ABSTRACTS AND INDEXES

Electronics and Communications Abstracts Journal: Comprehensive Coverage of Essential Scientific Literature. CSA. • Monthly. $1,665.00 per year. Includes print and online editions.

ALMANACS AND YEARBOOKS

OECD Communications Outlook. Organisation for Economic Co-operation and Development Publications and Information Center. • Biennial. Provides international coverage of yearly telecommunications activity. Includes charts, graphs, and maps.

CD-ROM DATABASES

Datapro on CD-ROM: Communications Analyst. Gartner Inc. • Monthly. Price on application. Provides detailed information on products and services for communications systems, including local area networks and voice systems.

DIRECTORIES

The International Directory of Importers--Communications Equipment Importers. Interdata. • $295 Individuals print. Covers: 4,000 international firms importing communications equipment. Entries include: Company name and address, contact person, email, number of employees, year established, phone and telefaxes, business activity, bank references, as well as a listing of communications equipment currently being imported.

Major Information Technology Companies of the World. Cengage Learning Inc. • Annual. $1,460 Individuals. 2008. 11th edition. eBook. Published by Graham & Whiteside. Contains profiles of more than 8,250 leading information technology companies in various countries.

Plunkett's E-Commerce and Internet Business Almanac. Plunkett Research Ltd. • Annual. $349.99. Contains detailed profiles of 250 large companies engaged in various areas of Internet commerce, including e-business Web sites, communications equipment manufacturers, and Internet service providers. Includes CD-ROM.

Telecommunications Directory. Cengage Learning Inc. • Annual. $993 Individuals. Two volumes: North America and International. Cover national and international voice and data communications networks, electronic mail services, teleconferencing facilities and services, facsimile services, Internet access providers, videotex and teletext operations, transactional services, local area networks, audiotex services, microwave systems/networkers, satellite facilities, and others involved in telecommunications, including related consultants, advertisers/ marketers; associations, regulatory bodies, and publishers. Available as eBook.

Telehealth Buyer's Guide. Miller Freeman Inc. • Annual. $10.00. Lists sources of telecommunications and information technology products and services for the health care industry.

ONLINE DATABASES

INSPEC. Institution of Electrical Engineers. • Provides online citations, with abstracts, to the world literature of electrical engineering, electronics, optoelectronics, telecommunications, industrial controls, instrumentation, computer technology, information technology, and physics. Coverage includes more than 4,000 technical and scientific journals from 1969 to date, with weekly updating. (INSPEC is Information Services in Physics, Electronics, and Computing.) Inquire as to online cost and availability.

PERIODICALS AND NEWSLETTERS

C E D: The Premier Magazine of Technology. Reed Elsevier Group plc Reed Business Information. • 10/ year. Formerly *Communications Engineering and Design*.

Call Center. UBM L.L.C. • Monthly. Free to qualified personnel. Emphasis is on telemarketing, selling, and customer service. Includes articles on communication technology. Formerly *Call Center Solutions*.

CC News: The Business Newspaper for Call Center and Customer Care Professionals. HME News. • Monthly. Free to qualified personnel; others, $60.00 per year. Includes news of call center technical developments.

IEEE Transactions on Communications. IEEE - Communications Society. • Monthly. $108 print only.

Poptronics. Gernsback Publications, Inc. • Monthly. $19.99 per year. Incorporates *Electronics Now*.

RCR Wireless News: The Newspaper for the Wireless Communications Industry. Crain Communications. • Weekly. $64.00 per year. Covers news of the wireless communications industry, including business and financial developments. Formerly *RCR*.

Telecommunications Reports. • Twice monthly. $2,039.00 per year.

Telecons. Applied Business Telecommunications. • Bimonthly. $30.00 per year. Topics include teleconferencing, videoconferencing, distance learning, telemedicine, and telecommuting.

RESEARCH CENTERS AND INSTITUTES

Massachusetts Institute of Technology - Laboratory for Information and Decision Systems. 77 Massachusetts Ave., Rm. 32-D608, Cambridge, MA 02139. Phone: (617)253-2142; Fax: (617)253-3578; Email: willsky@mit.edu • URL: http://lids.mit.edu • Research areas include data communication networks and fiber optic networks.

Stanford University - Space, Telecommunications and Radioscience Laboratory. David Packard Electrical & Engineering Bldg., Rm. 356, Department of Electrical Engineering, 350 Serra Mall, Stanford, CA 94305-9515. Phone: (650)723-4994; Fax: (650)723-9251; Email: inan@nova.stanford.edu • URL: http://nova.stanford.edu • Radio and radar astronomy, ionospheric physics, high frequency and very low frequency (whistler) propagation, tropospheric sensing and propagation, communication satellite system analysis, telecommunications, environmental monitoring oceanscatter, computer simulation of propagation, satellite measurements, planetary exploration, space plasma physics, signal processing, and telescience.

TRADE/PROFESSIONAL ASSOCIATIONS

AFCEA International. 4400 Fair Lakes Ct., Fairfax, VA 22033. Phone: 800-336-4583 or (703)631-6100; Fax: (703)631-6169; Email: info@afcea.org • URL: http://www.afcea.org • Serves as a bridge between government requirements and industry capabilities. Represents top government, industry, and military professionals in the fields of communications, intelligence, information systems, imaging, and multimedia. Aims for the continuing education of its members and for peace through civil government effectiveness and military and industrial preparedness. Supports global security by providing an ethical environment encouraging a close cooperative relationship among civil government agencies, the military and industry.

COMMUNICATIONS SATELLITES

See also TELECOMMUNICATIONS

ABSTRACTS AND INDEXES

NTIS Alerts: Communication. U.S. Department of Commerce National Technical Information Service. • Biweekly. $130 Individuals per year; domestic/ foreign. Covers common carriers, satellites, radio/TV equipment, telecommunication regulations, and related subjects.

DIRECTORIES

International Satellite Directory: A Complete Guide to the Satellite Communications Industry. SatNews Publishers. • Annual. $495 plus shipping and handling. Lists over 25,000 satellite operators, common carriers, earth stations, manufacturers, associations, etc.

Major Telecommunications Companies of the World. Cengage Learning Inc. • Annual. $1,360 Individuals. Published by Graham & Whiteside. Contains detailed information and trade names for more than 5,950 important telecommunications companies in various countries.

OTHER SOURCES

Telecommunications Regulation: Cable, Broadcasting, Satellite, and the Internet. Matthew Bender and Company Inc. • Semiannual. $1,747. Four looseleaf volumes. Covers local, state, and federal regulation, with emphasis on the Telecommunications Act of 1996. Includes regulation of television, telephone, cable, satellite, computer communication, and online services. Formerly *Cable Television Law*.

PERIODICALS AND NEWSLETTERS

Communications Daily: The Authoritative News Service of Electronic Communications. Warren Communications News Inc. • Covers telecommunications, including the telephone industry, broadcasting, cable TV, satellites, data communications, and electronic publishing. Features corporate and industry news.

Satellite News: The Monthly Newsletter Covering Management, Marketing Technology and Regulation. Access Intelligence L.L.C. • 50 times a year. $1,097.00 per year. Newsletter. Covers business applications in space, including remote sensing and satellites. Incorporates (Space Business News).

Satellite Week. Warren Communications News Inc. • Weekly. Covers satellite broadcasting, telecommunications, and the industrialization of space.

Via Satellite. Access Intelligence L.L.C. • Monthly. $49 Individuals. Covers the communications satellite industry.

RESEARCH CENTERS AND INSTITUTES

Massachusetts Institute of Technology - Kavli Institute for Astrophysics and Space Research. 77 Massachusetts Ave., 37-241, Cambridge, MA 02139. Phone: (617)253-7501; Fax: (617)253-3111; Email: jhewitt@mit.edu • URL: http://space.mit.edu • Space sciences, including theoretical astrophysics. Experimental studies include X-ray astronomy, gravitational waves, interplanetary plasmas, optical and infrared astronomy, very-long-baseline interferometry, synthetic aperture radar, human/machine system interaction, response of human systems to zero-gravity environment, and space environmental studies.

Space Institute - University of Tennessee. B.H. Goethert Pky;, MS01, Tullahoma, TN 37388-9700. Phone: (931)393-7213; Fax: (931)393-7211; Email: tmccay@utsi.edu • URL: http://www.utsi.edu.

Stanford University - Space, Telecommunications and Radioscience Laboratory. David Packard Electrical & Engineering Bldg., Rm. 356, Department of Electrical Engineering, 350 Serra Mall, Stanford, CA 94305-9515. Phone: (650)723-4994; Fax: (650)723-9251; Email: inan@nova.stanford.edu • URL: http://nova.stanford.edu • Radio and radar astronomy, ionospheric physics, high frequency and very low frequency (whistler) propagation, tropospheric sensing and propagation, communication satellite system analysis, telecommunications, environmental monitoring oceanscatter, computer simulation of propagation, satellite measurements, planetary exploration, space plasma physics, signal processing, and telescience.

University of Texas at Austin - Applied Research Laboratories. PO Box 8029, Austin, TX 78713-8029. Phone: (512)835-3200; Fax: (512)835-3259; Email: webcontactUs@arlut.utexas.edu • URL: http://www.arlut.utexas.edu • Sonar systems, underwater acoustics, satellite tracking, high accuracy positioning using satellite systems, industrial acoustics, biomedical acoustics, network security, information assurance, digital communications, electromagnetic security systems.

STATISTICS SOURCES

U.S. Industry and Trade Outlook. U.S. Department of Commerce National Technical Information Service. • Annual. Produced by the International Trade Administration, U.S. Department of Commerce, in a "public-private" partnership with DRI/ McGraw-Hill and Standard & Poor's. Provides basic data, outlook for the current year, and "Long-Term Prospects" (five-year projections) for a wide variety of products and services. Includes high technology industries. Formerly *U.S. Industrial Outlook*.

COMMUNITY ANTENNA TELEVISION

See CABLE TELEVISION INDUSTRY

COMMUNITY CHESTS

See COMMUNITY FUNDS

COMMUNITY COLLEGES

See JUNIOR COLLEGES

COMMUNITY DEVELOPMENT

See also PLANNING; URBAN DEVELOPMENT

ABSTRACTS AND INDEXES

Social Sciences Citation Index. Thomson Reuters Corp. • Weekly. Product is accessed via *Web of Science.*

Social Sciences Index Retrospective: 1907-1983. EBSCO Publishing Inc. • Indexing for 1,000,000 articles. Coverage includes international index and social sciences and humanities index.

CD-ROM DATABASES

Social Sciences Abstracts. EBSCO Publishing Inc. • Provides indexing from 1983 and abstracting from 1994 of more than 750 periodicals covering economics, area studies, community health, public administration, public welfare, urban studies, and many other topics related to the social sciences.

Social Sciences Citation Index. Thomson Reuters Corp. • Weekly. Product is accessed via *Web of Science.*

HANDBOOKS AND MANUALS

Zoning and Planning Law Handbook. Patricia Salkin. Thomson West. • Annual. $601.30. Assembles the insights and guidance offered by the country's leading authorities in zoning law, land use planning, and conservation.

ONLINE DATABASES

Wilson Social Sciences Abstracts Online. H.W. Wilson Co. • Provides online abstracting and indexing of more than 500 periodicals covering area studies, community health, public administration, public welfare, urban studies, and many other social science topics. Time period is 1994 to date for abstracts and 1983 to date for indexing, with updates weekly. Inquire as to online cost and availability.

OTHER SOURCES

American Land Planning Law. John Taylor and Norma Williams. Thomson West. • $1,058 Individuals full set. Examines the changing priorities in zoning and land use practices, focusing on the relationship between private activity and governmental power, and analyzing over 15,000 cases from all 50 states.

PERIODICALS AND NEWSLETTERS

Community Development Digest: Semi-Monthly Report on Development, Planning, Infrastructure Financing. Community Services Development, Inc. CD Publications. • $362 6 months, print and online. Contains authoritative reports on the Community Development Block Grant program (CDBG).

RESEARCH CENTERS AND INSTITUTES

Institute of Cultural Affairs. 4750 N Sheridan Rd., Chicago, IL 60640. Phone: (773)769-6363; Fax: (773)944-1582; Email: chicago@ica-usa.org • URL: http://www.ica-usa.org • U.S. branch of the Institute of Cultural Affairs International. Global research, training, and demonstration group concerned with the human factor in world development. Activities are based on the belief that effective human development must be initiated on the local level. Major training and demonstration programs include community development and facilitation services and training programs in 35 nations.

Irish Agriculture and Food Development Authority - Rural Economy Research Centre. Teagasc, Athenry 4, Galway, Ireland. Phone: 353 59 9170200; Fax: 353 59 9182097; Email: cathal.odonoghue@teagasc.ie • URL: http://www.agresearch.teagasc.ie/rerc • Agricultural economics, production economics, agricultural policy, and rural development.

National Institute of Food and Agriculture - Rural and Community Development Program. Waterfront Ctr., 800 9th St. SW, Washington, DC 20024. Phone: (202)401-2185; Fax: (202)730-9366; Email: phipple@nifa.usda.gov • URL: http://www.csrees.usda.gov/ruralcommunitydevelopment.cfm • Economic and rural community development.

STATISTICS SOURCES

Agriculture Fact Book. U. S. Government Printing Office. • Annual. $26 Individuals. Issued by the Office of Communications, U. S. Department of Agriculture. Includes data on U. S. agriculture, farmers, food, nutrition, and rural America. Programs of the Department of Agriculture in six areas are described: rural economic development, foreign trade, nutrition, the environment, inspection, and education.

TRADE/PROFESSIONAL ASSOCIATIONS

Agricultural Development Initiatives. PO Box 50006, Nashville, TN 37205. Phone: (615)599-2015; Email: adi@onepost.net • URL: http://www.agri-develop.org • Aims to serve rural households by teaching them sustainable agriculture. Encourages enterprise development among local entrepreneurs toward the end goal of financial freedom. Facilitates the transfer of appropriate technology to local agricultural enterprises.

Community Associations Institute. 6402 Arlington Blvd., Ste. 500, Falls Church, VA 22042. Phone: 888-224-4321 or (703)970-9220; Fax: (703)970-9558; Email: cai-info@caionline.org • URL: http://www.caionline.org • Condominium and homeowner associations, cooperatives, and association-governed planned communities of all sizes and architectural types; community or property managers and management firms; individual homeowners; community association managers and management firms; public officials; and lawyers, accountants, engineers, reserve specialists, builder/developers and other providers of professional services and products for CAs. Seeks to educate and represent America's 250,000 residential condominium, cooperative and homeowner associations and related professionals and service providers. Aims to foster vibrant, responsive, competent community associations that promote harmony, community and responsible leadership.

Community Development Bankers Association. 1444 Eye St., Ste. 201, Washington, DC 20005. Phone: (202)689-8935; Email: info@cdbanks.org • URL: http://www.cdbanks.org • Represents the interests of the community development bank sector. Educates policy makers on how to deliver credit and financial services to low and moderate income communities.

Community Development Society. 17 S High St., Ste. 200, Columbus, OH 43215. Phone: (614)221-1900; Fax: (614)221-1989; Email: cds@assnoffices.com • URL: http://www.comm-dev.org • Professionals and practitioners in community development: international, national, state, and local groups interested in community development efforts. Provides a forum for exchange of ideas and experiences; disseminates information to the public; advocates excellence in community programs, scholarship, and research; promotes citizen participation as essential to effective community development. Sponsors educational programs.

Geode Resource, Conservation, and Development. 308 N 3rd St., Burlington, IA 52601. Phone: (319)752-6395; Fax: (319)752-0106 • URL: http://geodercd.org • Provides rural development services in natural resources in such areas as water quality, crop diversification, grant writing, community facilities or services, and planning resource economic development projects for an administration cost.

Mananga Management Centre. PO Box 5100, Mbabane, Swaziland. Email: info@mananga.sz • URL: http://www.mananga.sz • Development organizations and individuals with an interest in development issues. Promotes more effective management of development projects. Sponsors training courses for development administrators; initiates programs in areas including agricultural development, women's rights, rural development, environmental protection, water supply and sanitation, and vocational education.

National Alliance of Craftsmen Associations. 816 Camaron St., Ste. 212, San Antonio, TX 78212. Phone: (210)271-9100; Fax: (210)212-9250 • Works to create and promote community empowerment, sustainability and growth through the development of employment, economic and educational opportunities in blighted communities. Concentrates on the barriers that perpetuate the underutilized, underemployed, unemployed, unskilled and underskilled community. Aims to build a stronger and healthier country one community at a time.

Rising Tide Capital. 334 Martin Luther King Dr., Jersey City, NJ 07305. Phone: (201)432-4316; Fax: (201)432-3504; Email: info@risingtidecapital.org • URL: http://risingtidecapital.org • Strives to assist entrepreneurs and communities to build tough businesses that transform lives, strengthen families and create vibrant, sustainable neighborhoods. Works to build a replicable model for high-quality entrepreneurial development services that can be locally adopted in low-wealth communities and used as a catalyst for social and economic empowerment. Connects entrepreneurs to appropriate business financing.

COMMUNITY FUNDS

See also FUND-RAISING

STATISTICS SOURCES

United Way Annual Report. United Way Worldwide. • Annual.

TRADE/PROFESSIONAL ASSOCIATIONS

Association of Fundraising Professionals. 4300 Wilson Blvd., Ste. 300, Arlington, VA 22203. Phone: 800-666-3863 or (703)684-0410; Fax: (703)684-0540; Email: afp@afpnet.org • URL: http://www.afpnet.org • Formerly National Society of Fundraising Executives.

COMMUNITY PLANNING

See CITY PLANNING

COMMUNITY RELATIONS

See also SOCIAL RESPONSIBILITY

ABSTRACTS AND INDEXES

Business Periodicals Index Retrospective. EBSCO Publishing Inc. • 11/year. Quarterly and annual cumulations.

Readers' Guide to Periodical Literature. EBSCO Publishing Inc. • Provides indexing for over 400 periodicals dating back to 1983.

Social Sciences Citation Index. Thomson Reuters Corp. • Weekly. Product is accessed via *Web of Science.*

Social Sciences Index Retrospective: 1907-1983. EBSCO Publishing Inc. • Indexing for 1,000,000 articles. Coverage includes international index and social sciences and humanities index.

CD-ROM DATABASES

Newspaper Abstracts Ondisc. ProQuest L.L.C. • Monthly. $2,950.00 per year (covers 1989 to date; archival discs are available for 1985-88). Provides cover-to-cover CD-ROM indexing and abstracting of 19 major newspapers, including the *New York Times, Wall Street Journal, Washington Post, Chicago Tribune,* and *Los Angeles Times.*

Readers' Guide to Periodical Literature. EBSCO Publishing Inc. • Provides indexing for over 400 periodicals dating back to 1983.

Social Sciences Abstracts. EBSCO Publishing Inc. • Provides indexing from 1983 and abstracting from 1994 of more than 750 periodicals covering economics, area studies, community health, public administration, public welfare, urban studies, and many other topics related to the social sciences.

Social Sciences Citation Index. Thomson Reuters Corp. • Weekly. Product is accessed via *Web of Science*.

ONLINE DATABASES

Wilson Business Abstracts Online. H.W. Wilson Co. • Indexes and abstracts 600 major business periodicals, plus the *Wall Street Journal* and the business section of the *New York Times*. Indexing is from 1982, abstracting from 1990, with the two newspapers included from 1993. Updated weekly. Inquire as to online cost and availability. (*Business Periodicals Index* without abstracts is also available online.).

Wilson Social Sciences Abstracts Online. H.W. Wilson Co. • Provides online abstracting and indexing of more than 500 periodicals covering area studies, community health, public administration, public welfare, urban studies, and many other social science topics. Time period is 1994 to date for abstracts and 1983 to date for indexing, with updates weekly. Inquire as to online cost and availability.

PERIODICALS AND NEWSLETTERS

Corporate Public Issues and Their Management: The Executive Systems Approach to Public Policy Formation. Issue Action Publications Inc. • Monthly. $195. Covers the approach to public policy creation.

RESEARCH CENTERS AND INSTITUTES

Boston College - Center for Corporate Citizenship. Carroll School of Management, 55 Lee Rd., Chestnut Hill, MA 02467-3942. Phone: (617)552-4545; Fax: (617)552-8499; Email: kv.smith@bc.edu • URL: http://www.bcccc.net • Areas of study include corporate images within local communities, corporate community relations, social vision, and philanthropy. Formerly Center for Corporate Community Relations.

University of Colorado at Denver - Center for Nonprofit Leadership and Research. PO Box 173364, Denver, CO 80217-3364. Phone: (303)352-3800 or (303)315-2089; Fax: (303)315-2229; Email: lisa.carlson@cudenver.edu • URL: http://www.ucdenver.edu/about/centers-institutes/Pages/default.aspx • Conducts research on public sector issues. Provides leadership training for public, private, and nonprofit managers, offers facilitation and technical assistance services.

COMMUNITY SHOPPING CENTERS

See SHOPPING CENTERS

COMMUTER AIRLINES

See AIRLINE INDUSTRY

COMPACT DISCS

See OPTICAL DISK STORAGE DEVICES

COMPANY ANNIVERSARIES

See ANNIVERSARIES AND HOLIDAYS

COMPANY HISTORIES

See BUSINESS HISTORY

COMPENSATION OF EMPLOYEES

See WAGES AND SALARIES

COMPENSATION OF EXECUTIVES

See EXECUTIVE COMPENSATION

COMPETITIVE INTELLIGENCE

See also BUSINESS RESEARCH

DIRECTORIES

KMWorld Buyer's Guide. Knowledge Asset Media Inc. • Semiannual. $2,395 (Basic Corporate Profile Package) One Issue — Spring 2014 Edition PLUS 6 Months Online. Controlled circulation as part of *KMWorld*. Contains corporate and product profiles related to various aspects of knowledge management and information systems. (Knowledge Asset Media is a an affiliate of Information Today, Inc.).

E-BOOKS

Adaptive Technologies and Business Integration: Social, Managerial, and Organizational Dimensions. Cengage Learning Inc. • 2007. eBook. Provides an authoritative review of both intra-organizational and inter-organizational aspects in business integration, including: managerial and organizational integration, social integration, and technology integration, along with the resources to accomplish this competitive advantage.

INTERNET DATABASES

Competitive Intelligence Guide. Fuld & Co. Phone: (617)492-5900; Fax: (617)492-7108; Email: info@fuld.com • URL: http://www.fuld.com • Web site includes "Intelligence Index" (links to Internet sites), "Strategic Intelligence Organizer" (game-board format), "Intelligence Pyramid"(graphics), "Thoughtleaders" (expert commentary), "Intelligence System Evaluator" (interactive questionnaire), and "Reference Resource" (book excerpts from *New Competitor Intelligence*). Fees: information provided by Web site is free, but Fuld & Co. offers fee-based research and consulting services.

EBSCO Information Services. EBSCO Publishing Inc. 10 Estes St., Ipswich, MA 01938-2106. Phone: 800-653-2726 or (978)356-6500; Fax: (978)356-6565; Email: information@ebscohost.com • URL: http://www.ebscohost.com • Fee-based Web site providing Internet access to a wide variety of databases, including business-related material. Full text is available for many periodical titles, with daily updates. Fees: Apply.

Ebusiness Forum: Global Business Intelligence for the Digital Age. Economist Intelligence Unit (EIU), Economist Group. Phone: 800-938-4685 or (212)554-0600; Fax: (212)586-0248; Email: newyork@eiu.com • URL: http://www.ebusinessforum.com • Web site provides information relating to multinational business, with an emphasis on activities in specific countries. Includes rankings of countries for "e-business readiness," additional data on the political, economic, and business environment in 180 nations ("Doing Business in" and "Today's News Analysis.") Fees: Free, but registration is required for access to all content. Daily updates.

Factiva. Dow Jones Reuters Business Interactive, LLC. Phone: 800-369-7466 or (609)452-1511; Fax: (609)520-5770; Email: solutions@factiva.com • URL: http://www.factiva.com • Fee-based Web site provides "global news and business information through Web sites and content integration solutions." Includes Dow Jones and Reuters newswires, The Wall Street Journal, and more than 7,000 other sources of current news, historical articles, market research reports, and investment analysis. Content includes 96 major U. S. newspapers, 900 non-English sources, trade publications, media transcripts, country profiles, news photos, etc.

InSite 2. Intelligence Data/Thomson Financial. Phone: 800-654-0393 or (617)856-1890; Fax: (617)737-3182; Email: intelligence.data@tfn.com • URL: http://www.insite2.gale.com/ • Fee-based Web site consolidates information in a "Base Pack" consisting of Business InSite, Market InSite, and Company InSite. Optional databases are Consumer InSite, Health and Wellness InSite, Newsletter InSite, and Computer InSite. Includes fulltext content from more than 2,500 trade publications, journals, newsletters, newspapers, analyst reports, and other sources. Continuous updating. Formerly produced by The Gale Group.

Intelligence Data. Thomson Financial. Phone: 800-654-0393; Fax: (617)824-2477 • URL: http://www.intelligencedata.com • Fee-based Web site provides a wide variety of information relating to competitive intelligence, strategic planning, business development, mergers, acquisitions, sales, and marketing. "Intelliscope" feature offers searching of other Thomson units, such as Investext, MarkIntel, InSite 2, and Industry Insider. Weekly updating.

Nexis.com. Lexis-Nexis Group. Phone: 800-227-4908 or (937)865-6800; Fax: (937)865-6909; Email: webmaster@prod.lexis-nexis.com • URL: http://www.nexis.com • Fee-based Web site offers searching of about 2.8 billion documents in some 30,000 news, business, and legal information sources. Features include a subject directory covering 1,200 topics in 34 categories and a Company Dossier containing information on more than 500,000 public and private companies. Boolean searching is offered.

ProQuest. ProQuest L.L.C. 789 E Eisenhower Pkwy., Ann Arbor, MI 48106-1346. Phone: 800-521-0600 or (734)761-4700; Fax: (734)662-4554; Email: info@proquest.com • URL: http://www.proquest.com • Fee-based Web site providing Internet access to more than 3,000 periodicals, newspapers, and other publications. Many items are available full-text, with daily updates. Includes extensive corporate and financial information. Fees: Apply.

PERIODICALS AND NEWSLETTERS

DM Review: The Premier Publication for Business Intelligence and Analytics. SourceMedia Inc. • Monthly. $49.00 per year. Edited for corporate executives and information technology personnel. Covers data management, business intelligence, data warehousing, systems management, data integration, knowledge management, data mining, and related topics.

strategy business. • Quarterly. $38.00 per year.

RESEARCH CENTERS AND INSTITUTES

Asian Institute of Management Policy Center. Eugenio Lopez Foundation Bldg., 3rd Fl., 123 Paseo de Roxas, Makati City 1260, Philippines. Phone: 63 2 8924011; Fax: 63 2 4039498; Email: policycenter@aim.edu • URL: http://policy.aim.edu • Business competitiveness, especially involving globalization, technological advances, and economic opportunities.

COMPOSITE MATERIALS

See also MATERIALS

ABSTRACTS AND INDEXES

Applied Science and Technology Index. EBSCO Publishing Inc. • 11/year. Indexes a wide variety of

English language technical, industrial, and engineering periodicals.

Engineered Materials Abstracts. Cambridge Information Group. • Monthly. $995.00 per year. Provides citations to the technical and engineering literature of plastic, ceramic, and composite materials.

Engineering Index Monthly: Abstracting and Indexing Services Covering Sources ofthe World's Engineering Literature. Engineering Information Inc. • Monthly. Institutions, $5,279.00 per year. Provides indexing and abstracting of the world's engineering and technical literature.

Key Abstracts: Advanced Materials. Institution of Engineering and Technology. • $790 per year. Provides international coverage of journal and proceedings literature, including publications on ceramics and composite materials.

NTIS Alerts: Manufacturing Technology. U.S. Department of Commerce National Technical Information Service. • Biweekly. $130 per year. Covers computer-aided design and manufacturing (CAD/CAM), engineering materials, quality control, machine tools, robots, lasers, productivity, and related subjects.

NTIS Alerts: Materials Sciences. U.S. Department of Commerce National Technical Information Service. • Biweekly. $130 per year. Covers ceramics, glass, coatings, composite materials, alloys, plastics, wood, paper, adhesives, fibers, lubricants, and related subjects.

CD-ROM DATABASES

Applied Science and Technology Abstracts. EBSCO Publishing Inc. • Citations for more than 700 prominent scientific, technical, engineering, and industrial periodicals.

Materials Science Citation Index. Thomson Reuters Intellectual Property & Science. • Contains citations and abstracts, providing international coverage of materials science journals.

METADEX Materials Collection: Metals-Polymers-Ceramics. Cambridge Scientific Abstracts L.P. • Quarterly. Provides CD-ROM citations to the worldwide literature of materials science and metallurgy. Corresponds to *Metals Abstracts, Alloys Index, Steels Alert, Nonferrous Alert, Polymers/Ceramics/Composites Alert*, and *Engineered Materials Abstracts*. (Formerly produced by ASM International.).

ONLINE DATABASES

Applied Science and Technology Index Online. H.W. Wilson Co. • Provides online indexing of 500 major scientific, technical, industrial, and engineering periodicals. Time period is 1983 to date. Monthly updates. Inquire as to online cost and availability.

Current Contents Connect. Thomson Reuters Intellectual Property and Science. • Provides online abstracts of articles listed in the tables of contents of about 7,500 journals. Coverage is very broad, including science, social science, life science, technology, engineering, industry, agriculture, the environment, economics, and arts and humanities. Time period is two years, with weekly updates. Inquire as to online cost and availability.

Engineered Materials Abstracts (online). Cambridge Scientific Abstracts L.P. • Provides online citations to the technical and engineering literature of plastic, ceramic, and composite materials. Time period is 1986 to date, with monthly updates. (Formerly produced by ASM International.) Inquire as to online cost and availability.

PERIODICALS AND NEWSLETTERS

Advanced Composites Monthly. Composite Market Reports Inc. • Description: Covers advanced composite materials processes and markets in the aerospace industry worldwide. "Prepared for engineering, program, and manufacturing management at primes and their subcontractors where aerospace components made of high-performance composite materials are designed, fabricated, or assembled." Discusses subcontract opportunities of interest to U.S., Canadian, and overseas aerospace companies. Recurring features include a calendar of events, reports of meetings, interviews, news of research, and application case histories.

The Composites and Adhesives Newsletter. T/C Press. • Quarterly. $190.00. Presents news of the composite materials and adhesives industries, with particular coverage of new products and applications.

High-Tech Materials Alert: Advanced Materials: Their Uses and Manufacture. Technical Insights. • Monthly. Institutions, $695.00 per year. Newsletter on technical developments relating to high-performance materials, including metals and ceramics. Includes market forecasts.

International Materials Review. ASM International. • $1,801 Nonmembers online. Bimonthly. Provides technical and research coverage of metals, alloys, and advanced materials. Formerly *International Metals Review*.

Journal of Advanced Materials. Society for the Advancement of Material and Process Engineering. • Quarterly. Individuals, $60.00 per year; institutions, $150.00 per year. Contains technical and research articles. Formerly *SAMPE Quarterly*.

SAMPE Journal. Society for the Advancement of Material and Process Engineering. • Bimonthly. $125 Individuals print and online. Magazine covering materials and process engineering.

RESEARCH CENTERS AND INSTITUTES

Composite Materials Research Group. University of Wyoming, Department of Mechanical Engineering, 1000 E University Ave., Laramie, WY 82071. Phone: (307)766-2122; Fax: (307)766-2695; Email: me.info@uwyo.edu • URL: http://www.uwyo.edu/mechanical/facilities/compositematerials.

Massachusetts Institute of Technology - Materials Processing Center. 77 Massachusetts Ave., Cambridge, MA 02139-4301. Phone: (617)253-5179; Fax: (617)258-6900; Email: cthomp@mit.edu • URL: http://mpc-web.mit.edu • Conducts processing, engineering, and economic research in ferrous and nonferrous metals, ceramics, polymers, photonic materials, superconductors, welding, composite materials, and other materials.

Michigan State University - Composite Materials and Structures Center. 2100 Engineering Bldg., East Lansing, MI 48824-1226. Phone: (517)353-5466 or (517)353-4696; Fax: (517)432-1634; Email: rich@egr.msu.edu • URL: http://www.egr.msu.edu/cmsc/ • Studies polymer, metal, and ceramic based composites.

University of Delaware - Center for Composite Materials. 202 Composites Manufacturing Science Lab, Newark, DE 19716-3144. Phone: (302)831-8149; Fax: (302)831-8525; Email: gillespie@udel.edu • URL: http://www.ccm.udel.edu • Development of core competencies in composites science and engineering, including textile preforming, liquid molding (resin transfer molding, vacuum-assisted resin infusion), thermoplastic processing, joining, interphase science, sensing and control, multifunctional materials, cost modeling, and application of composites to civil infrastructure. Major programs include a national testbed for intelligent VARTM processing.

TRADE/PROFESSIONAL ASSOCIATIONS

ASM International. 9639 Kinsman Rd., Materials Park, OH 44073-0002. Phone: 800-336-5152 or (440)338-5151; Email: memberservicecenter@asminternational.org • URL: http://www.asminternational.org • Metallurgists, materials engineers, executives in materials producing and consuming industries; teachers and students. Disseminates technical information about the manufacture, use, and treatment of engineered materials. Offers in-plant, home study, and intensive courses through Materials Engineering Institute.

Composites Manufacturing Association. 1 SME Dr., Dearborn, MI 48121. Phone: 800-733-4763 or (313)271-1500; Fax: (313)271-2861; Email: service@sme.org • URL: http://www.sme.org • Members are composites manufacturing professionals and students.

Materials Research Society. 506 Keystone Dr., Warrendale, PA 15086-7573. Phone: (724)779-3003 or (724)779-3004; Fax: (724)779-8313; Email: info@mrs.org • URL: http://www.mrs.org • Represents the interests of materials researchers from academia, industry, and government that promotes communication for the advancement of interdisciplinary materials research to improve the quality of life. Fosters interaction among researchers working on different classes of inorganic and organic materials and to promote interdisciplinary basic research on materials. Provides forum for industry, government, and university cooperation; conducts technical conferences, tutorial lectures. Maintains speakers' bureau.

COMPRESSORS

See PUMPS AND COMPRESSORS

COMPTROLLERS

See CORPORATE DIRECTORS AND OFFICERS

COMPUTER ACCESSORIES

See COMPUTER PERIPHERALS AND ACCESSORIES

COMPUTER-AIDED DESIGN AND MANUFACTURING (CAD/CAM)

See also COMPUTER GRAPHICS

ABSTRACTS AND INDEXES

Applied Science and Technology Index. EBSCO Publishing Inc. • 11/year. Indexes a wide variety of English language technical, industrial, and engineering periodicals.

Key Abstracts: Factory Automation. Institution of Engineering and Technology. • Monthly. $1,138. Provides international coverage of journal and proceedings literature, including publications on CAD/CAM, materials handling, robotics, and factory management.

NTIS Alerts: Manufacturing Technology. U.S. Department of Commerce National Technical Information Service. • Biweekly. $130 per year. Covers computer-aided design and manufacturing (CAD/CAM), engineering materials, quality control, machine tools, robots, lasers, productivity, and related subjects.

Science Citation Index. Thomson Reuters Intellectual Property and Science. • Weekly. Includes *Source Index, Citation Index, Permuterm Subject Index*, and *Corporate Index*. Provides researchers, administrators, faculty, and students with quick, powerful access to the bibliographic and citation information they need to find research data, analyze trends, journals and researchers, and share their findings.

CD-ROM DATABASES

Science Citation Index. Thomson Reuters Intellectual Property and Science. • Weekly. Includes

Source Index, Citation Index, Permuterm Subject Index, and *Corporate Index*. Provides researchers, administrators, faculty, and students with quick, powerful access to the bibliographic and citation information they need to find research data, analyze trends, journals and researchers, and share their findings.

DIRECTORIES

Manufacturing Systems: Buyers Guide. Reed Elsevier Group plc Reed Business Information. • Annual. Price on application. Contains information on companies manufacturing or supplying materials handling systems, CAD/CAM systems, specialized software for manufacturing, programmable controllers, machine vision systems, and automatic identification systems.

Modern Machine Shop. Gardner Business Media, Inc. • Monthly. $89 Individuals. Lists products and services for the metalworking industry. Formerly *Modern Machine Shop CNC and Software Guide*.

PERIODICALS AND NEWSLETTERS

ACM Transactions on Graphics. Association for Computing Machinery. • Bimonthly. $41 Members.

Commline. Numeridex Inc. • Bimonthly. Free to qualified personnel; others, $20.00 per year. Emphasizes NC/CNC (numerically controlled and computer numerically controlled machinery).

Computer-Aided Engineering; Data Base Applications in Design and Manufacturing. Penton Media Inc. • Quarterly. $55.00 per year.

IEEE Computer Graphics and Applications. Institute of Electrical and Electronics Engineers. • Bimonthly. $39 print only. Covers a variety of topics catering to both computer graphics practitioners and researchers.

IEEE Transactions on Visualization and Computer Graphics. IEEE - Communications Society. • Monthly. Contains research on subjects related to computer graphics and visualization techniques, systems, software, hardware, and user interface issues.

Modern Machine Shop. Gardner Business Media, Inc. • Monthly. $89 Individuals. Lists products and services for the metalworking industry. Formerly *Modern Machine Shop CNC and Software Guide*.

RESEARCH CENTERS AND INSTITUTES

Advanced Manufacturing Engineering Institute. University of Hartford, College of Engineering, Technology, and Architecture, 200 Bloomfield Ave., West Hartford, CT 06117. Phone: 800-678-4844 or (860)768-4112; Fax: (860)768-5073; Email: shetty@mail.hartford.edu.

Computer Network Center. Purdue University at Indianapolis, 799 W Michigan St., ET 003, Indianapolis, IN 46202-5160. Phone: (317)274-0814; Fax: (317)274-4567; Email: cnchelp@iupui.edu • URL: http://et.engr.iupui.edu/sites/cnc/index.php.

Massachusetts Institute of Technology - Laboratory for Manufacturing and Productivity. 77 Massachusetts Ave., Rm. 35-231, Cambridge, MA 02139. Phone: (617)253-1759 or (617)452-2395; Email: jchun@mit.edu • URL: http://web.mit.edu/lmp • Photovoltaics, nano manufacturing development such as micro-fluidic devices, environmentally-benign manufacturing, axiomatic design theory, precision motion control, discrete die forming, precision machine design, droplet-based manufacturing, semiconductor manufacturing processes, design and operation of manufacturing systems, data and model integration, rapid autonomous machining, and three-dimensional printing.

Techsolve Inc. 6705 Steger Dr., Cincinnati, OH 45237. Phone: 800-345-4482 or (513)948-2000; Fax: (513)948-2109 or (800)345-4482; Email: perkins@techsolve.org • URL: http://www.techsolve.org • Fields of research include quality improvement, computer-aided design, artificial intelligence, and employee training.

STATISTICS SOURCES

U.S. Industry and Trade Outlook. U.S. Department of Commerce National Technical Information Service. • Annual. Produced by the International Trade Administration, U.S. Department of Commerce, in a "public-private" partnership with DRI/McGraw-Hill and Standard & Poor's. Provides basic data, outlook for the current year, and "Long-Term Prospects" (five-year projections) for a wide variety of products and services. Includes high technology industries. Formerly *U.S. Industrial Outlook*.

TRADE/PROFESSIONAL ASSOCIATIONS

Society of Manufacturing Engineers - Computer and Automated Systems Techincal Group. 1 SME Dr., Dearborn, MI 48121. Phone: 800-733-4763 or (313)425-3000; Fax: (313)425-3400; Email: service@sme.org • URL: http://www.arcat.com/arcatcos/cos37/arc37031.html • Sponsored by the Society of Manufacturing Engineers. Formerly Computer and Automated Systems Association.

COMPUTER ANIMATION

See also VIRTUAL REALITY

ABSTRACTS AND INDEXES

Internet and Personal Computing Abstracts (print edition). EBSCO Publishing Inc. • Quarterly. $269.00 per year, including cumulative index. Provides more than 10,000 abstracts annually from both trade and academic publications. Covers computer hardware, software, product reviews, Web topics, e-commerce, networks, corporate news, security, and related topics. Formerly *Microcomputer Abstracts*.

ALMANACS AND YEARBOOKS

Computer Animation Proceedings. Institute of Electrical and Electronic Engineers. • Annual. $110.00.

E-BOOKS

Handbook of Research on Serious Games as Educational, Business and Research Tools. Cengage Learning Inc. • 2012. eBook. Published by IGI Global. Collects research on the most recent technological developments in all fields of knowledge or disciplines of computer games development, including planning, design, development, marketing, business management, users and behavior.

INTERNET DATABASES

Wired News. Lycos Inc. 400-2 Totten Pond Rd., Waltham, MA 02451-2053. Phone: (781)370-2700 or (415)276-8400; Fax: (781)370-2600 or (415)276-8500; Email: press@lycos.com • URL: http://www.lycos.com • Provides summaries and full-text of "Top Stories" relating to the Internet, computers, multimedia, telecommunications, and the electronic information industry in general. These news stories are placed in the broad categories of Politics, Business, Culture, and Technology. Affiliated with *Wired* magazine. Fees: Free.

ONLINE DATABASES

Computer Database. Cengage Learning Inc. • Provides one year of full-text online for 150 leading computer-related publications. Also includes 70,000 product specifications and brief profiles of 13,000 computer product vendors and manufacturers. Inquire as to prices and availability.

PERIODICALS AND NEWSLETTERS

DV Magazine. UBM L.L.C. • Monthly. Edited for producers and creators of digital media. Includes topics relating to video, audio, animation, multimedia, interactive design, and special effects. Covers both hardware and software, with product reviews. Formerly *Digital Video Magazine*.

SHOOT: The Leading Newsweekly for Commercial Production and Postproduction. Nielsen Business Media Inc. • Weekly. $125 /year. Covers animation, music, sound design, computer graphics, visual effects, cinematography, and other aspects of television and motion picture production, with emphasis on TV commercials.

RESEARCH CENTERS AND INSTITUTES

Computer Graphics Laboratory. New York Institute of Technology, Fine Arts, Old Westbury, NY 11568. Phone: (516)686-7542; Fax: (516)686-7428; Email: pvoci@nyit.edu • URL: http://www.nyit.edu • Research areas include computer graphics, computer animation, and digital sound.

UCLA Film and Television Archive-Research and Study Center. University of California, Los Angeles, 46 Powell Library, Los Angeles, CA 90095. Phone: (310)206-5388; Fax: (310)206-5392; Email: arsc@cinema.ucla.edu • URL: http://www.cinema.ucla.edu • Research areas include animation.

U.S. Department of Energy - Office of Energy Efficiency and Renewable Energy - Industrial Technologies Program - Industrial Assessment Center. School of Engineering, San Francisco State University, 1600 Holloway Ave., San Francisco, CA 94132. Phone: (415)338-6218 or (415)338-7736; Fax: (415)338-3086; Email: iac@sfsu.edu • URL: http://www.sfsu.edu/iac • Research areas include multimedia, computerized experimental arts processes, and digital sound.

COMPUTER BULLETIN BOARDS

See COMPUTER COMMUNICATIONS

COMPUTER COMMUNICATIONS

See also INTERNET; LOCAL AREA NETWORKS; MICROCOMPUTERS AND MINICOMPUTERS; ONLINE INFORMATION SYSTEMS; TELECOMMUNICATIONS; TELECOMMUTING

ABSTRACTS AND INDEXES

Applied Science and Technology Index. EBSCO Publishing Inc. • 11/year. Indexes a wide variety of English language technical, industrial, and engineering periodicals.

Business Periodicals Index Retrospective. EBSCO Publishing Inc. • 11/year. Quarterly and annual cumulations.

Communication Abstracts: An International Information Service. Pine Forge Press. • Bimonthly. Institutions, $1,150.00 per year. Provides broad coverage of the literature of communications, including broadcasting and advertising.

Computer and Information Systems Abstracts Journal: An Abstract Journal Pertaining to the Theory, Design, Fabrication and Application of Computer and Information Systems. CSA. • Monthly. $1,750 per year.

Computer Science Index. EBSCO Publishing Inc. • Quarterly. $245 per year. Contains brief abstracts of book and periodical literature covering all phases of computing, including approximately 70 specific application areas.

Current Contents: Engineering, Computing and Technology. Thomson Reuters Intellectual Property and Science. • Weekly. $730 per year. Reproductions of contents pages of technical journals. Includes *Author Index, Address Directory, Current*

Book Contents, and *Title Word Index*. Formerly *Current Contents: Engineering, Technology and Applied Sciences*.

Electronics and Communications Abstracts Journal: Comprehensive Coverage of Essential Scientific Literature. CSA. • Monthly. $1,665.00 per year. Includes print and online editions.

Inspec Direct. Institution of Engineering and Technology. • Monthly. $2,400 per year. Section C of *Science Abstracts*.

Key Abstracts: Computer Communications and Storage. Institution of Engineering and Technology. • Monthly. $1,138. Provides international coverage of journal and proceedings literature, including material on optical disks and networks.

Science Citation Index. Thomson Reuters Intellectual Property and Science. • Weekly. Includes *Source Index*, *Citation Index*, *Permuterm Subject Index*; and *Corporate Index*. Provides researchers, administrators, faculty, and students with quick, powerful access to the bibliographic and citation information they need to find research data, analyze trends, journals and researchers, and share their findings.

CD-ROM DATABASES

Authority Computer and Telecommunications Law Library. Matthew Bender and Company Inc. • Quarterly. Price on request. Full text CD-ROM provides cases, analysis, sample agreements, and other information relating to computer law, telecommunications regulation (cable, broadcasting, satellite, Internet), international computer law, and computer contracts.

Science Citation Index. Thomson Reuters Intellectual Property and Science. • Weekly. Includes *Source Index*, *Citation Index*, *Permuterm Subject Index*, and *Corporate Index*. Provides researchers, administrators, faculty, and students with quick, powerful access to the bibliographic and citation information they need to find research data, analyze trends, journals and researchers, and share their findings.

DIRECTORIES

The Annual Directory of the Information Industry Association. Software and Information Industry Association. • Annual. Members, $75.00; non-members, $125.00.

Major Information Technology Companies of the World. Cengage Learning Inc. • Annual. $1,460 Individuals. 2008. 11th edition. eBook. Published by Graham & Whiteside. Contains profiles of more than 8,250 leading information technology companies in various countries.

Major Telecommunications Companies of the World. Cengage Learning Inc. • Annual. $1,360 Individuals. Published by Graham & Whiteside. Contains detailed information and trade names for more than 5,950 important telecommunications companies in various countries.

Plunkett's E-Commerce and Internet Business Almanac. Plunkett Research Ltd. • Annual. $349.99. Contains detailed profiles of 250 large companies engaged in various areas of Internet commerce, including e-business Web sites, communications equipment manufacturers, and Internet service providers. Includes CD-ROM.

Telecommunications Directory. Cengage Learning Inc. • Annual. $993 Individuals. Two volumes: North America and International. Cover national and international voice and data communications networks, electronic mail services, teleconferencing facilities and services, facsimile services, Internet access providers, videotex and teletext operations, transactional services, local area networks, audiotex services, microwave systems/networkers, satellite facilities, and others involved in telecommunications, including related consultants, advertisers/marketers; associations, regulatory bodies, and publishers. Available as eBook.

E-BOOKS

Handbook of Research on Business Social Networking: Organizational, Managerial, and Technological Dimensions. Cengage Learning Inc. • 2012. eBook. Published by IGI Global. Investigates the beginning of social networks and provides perspectives on how they can enhance business, covering discussions on the main issues, challenges, opportunities, and trends related to the range of new developments and applications in business social networking.

ENCYCLOPEDIAS AND DICTIONARIES

Encyclopedia of Communication and Information. Cengage Learning Inc. • 2003. eBook. Published by Macmillan Reference USA. Provides an overview of universal modes of communication. Inquire about price and availability.

Encyclopedia of Networked and Virtual Organizations. Cengage Learning Inc. • Documents 249 of the most relevant contributions authored by over 400 of the world's leading experts to the introduction of networked, dynamic, agile, and virtual organizational models; definitions; taxonomies; opportunities; and reference models and architectures.

INTERNET DATABASES

eBusiness. KANA Software Inc. 840 W California Ave., Ste. 100, Sunnyvale, CA 94086. Phone: 800-737-738 or (650)614-8300; Fax: (408)736-7613; Email: info@kana.com • URL: http://www.kana.com • A Web-based framework for enabling and managing personalized interactions, collaborations, and transactions with customers, partners or employees.

InfoTech Trends. Data Analysis Group. Phone: (925)462-1202; Fax: (925)462-1225; Email: support@infotechtrends.com • URL: http://www.infotechtrends.com • Web site provides both free and fee-based market research data on the information technology industry, including computers, peripherals, telecommunications, the Internet, software, CD-ROM/DVD, e-commerce, and workstations. Fees: Free for current (most recent year) data; more extensive information has various fee structures. Formerly *Computer Industry Forecasts*.

ONLINE DATABASES

Applied Science and Technology Index Online. H.W. Wilson Co. • Provides online indexing of 500 major scientific, technical, industrial, and engineering periodicals. Time period is 1983 to date. Monthly updates. Inquire as to online cost and availability.

INSPEC. Institution of Electrical Engineers. • Provides online citations, with abstracts, to the world literature of electrical engineering, electronics, optoelectronics, telecommunications, industrial controls, instrumentation, computer technology, information technology, and physics. Coverage includes more than 4,000 technical and scientific journals from 1969 to date, with weekly updating. (INSPEC is Information Services in Physics, Electronics, and Computing.) Inquire as to online cost and availability.

Wilson Business Abstracts Online. H.W. Wilson Co. • Indexes and abstracts 600 major business periodicals, plus the *Wall Street Journal* and the business section of the *New York Times*. Indexing is from 1982, abstracting from 1990, with the two newspapers included from 1993. Updated weekly. Inquire as to online cost and availability. (*Business Periodicals Index* without abstracts is also available online.).

PERIODICALS AND NEWSLETTERS

Business Communications Review. Key3Media Group, Inc. • Monthly. $45.00 per year. Edited for communications managers in large end-user companies and institutions. Includes special feature issues on intranets and network management.

CIO: The Magazine for Chief Information Officers. CXO Media Inc. • Monthly. $129 per year. Edited for chief information officers. Includes a monthly "Web Business" section (incorporates the former *WebMaster* periodical) and a monthly "Enterprise" section for other company executives.

Communications News. Nelson Publishing Inc. • Monthly.

Communications News: Solutions for Today's Networking Decision Managers. Nelson Publishing Inc. • Monthly. Free to qualified personnel; others, $84.00 per year. Includes coverage of "Internetworking" and "Intrenetworking." Emphasis is on emerging telecommunications technologies.

Computer Communication Review. Association for Computing Machinery - Special Interest Group on Management of Data. • Quarterly. Contains articles on topics within the SIG's field of interest.

Computerworld: Newsweekly for Information Technology Leaders. ComputerWorld Inc. • Weekly. $190.00 per year.

Electronic Messaging News: Strategies, Applications, and Standards. Access Intelligence L.L.C. • Biweekly. $597.00 per year. Newsletter.

Handheld Computing: The Number One Guide to Handheld Devices. Mobile Media Group. • 9/year. Covers handheld devices for consumers, including PDAs, cell phones, digital cameras, MP3 players, tablet PCs, accessories, and software. Includes product reviews.

IEEE Communications Magazine. IEEE - Communications Society. • Monthly. Covers all areas of communications such as lightwave telecommunications, high-speed data communications, personal communications systems (PCS), ISDN, and more.

Information Processing and Management: An International Journal. Elsevier. • $327 Individuals. Bimonthly. Qualified personnel, $301.00 per year; institutions, $1,196.00 per year. Text in English, French, German and Italian.

Information Today: The Newspaper for Users and Producers of Electronic Information Services. Information Today, Inc. • 11 times a year. $68.95 per year.

Insurance Networking: Strategies and Solutions for Electronic Commerce. SourceMedia Inc. • 10 times a year. Price on application. Covers information technology for the insurance industry, with emphasis on computer communications and the Internet.

Interactive Marketing and P R News: News and Practical Advice on Using Interactive Advertising and Marketing to Sell Your Products. Access Intelligence L.L.C. • Biweekly. $495.00 per year. Newsletter. Provides information and guidance on merchandising via CD-ROM ("multimedia catalogs"), the Internet, and interactive TV. Topics include "cybermoney," addresses for e-mail marketing, "virtual malls," and other interactive subjects. Formerly *Interactive Marketing News*.

International Journal of Communication Systems. John Wiley and Sons, Inc., Journals Div. • Monthly. $3,378 Institutions. Published in England by John Wiley and Sons Ltd. Formerly *International Journal of Digital and Analog Communication Systems*.

Laptop Magazine. Bedford Communications Inc. • Monthly. Consumer magazine containing articles and product reviews for notebook/laptop computers, handheld computers, tablet devices, cell phones, digital cameras, and other consumer electronic products.

Mobile PC. Future Network USA. • Monthly. $20.00 per year. Provides information and detailed product reviews for consumers. Covers notebook/laptop computers, personal digital assistants

(PDAs), wireless network equipment, cell phones, digital cameras, and other electronic products.

NetMag: Strategies and Solutions for the Network Professional. UBM L.L.C. • 13 times a year. Free to qualified personnel. Incorporates *Data Communications.*

Network Computing: Computing in a Network Environment. UBM L.L.C. • Semimonthly. Free to qualified personnel.

Network: Strategies and Solutions for the Network Professional. UBM L.L.C. • 13 times a year. Free to qualified personnel. Covers network products and peripherals for computer professionals. Includes annual network managers salary survey and annual directory issue. Formerly *LAN: The Network Solutions Magazine.*

Network World: The Newsweekly of Enterprise Network Computing. Network World Inc. • Weekly. $129.00 per year. Includes special feature issues on enterprise Internets, network operating systems, network management, high-speed modems, LAN management systems, and Internet access providers.

Telematics and Informatics: An International Journal on Telecommunications and Internet Technology. Elsevier. • Four times a year. Institutions, $938.00 per year.

Wireless Data News. Access Intelligence L.L.C. • Description: Provides analysis of technology, applications, marketing, and competition in the mobile communications industry. Scope is international. Recurring features include news of research.

RESEARCH CENTERS AND INSTITUTES

Massachusetts Institute of Technology - Laboratory for Information and Decision Systems. 77 Massachusetts Ave., Rm. 32-D608, Cambridge, MA 02139. Phone: (617)253-2142; Fax: (617)253-3578; Email: willsky@mit.edu • URL: http://lids.mit.edu • Research areas include data communication networks and fiber optic networks.

University of Southern California - Information Sciences Institute. 4676 Admiralty Way, Ste. 1001, Marina del Rey, CA 90292. Phone: (310)822-1511; Fax: (310)823-6714; Email: vcomms@usc.edu • URL: http://www.isi.edu/home • Research fields include online information and computer science, with emphasis on the World Wide Web.

STATISTICS SOURCES

Standard & Poor's Industry Surveys. Standard & Poor's Financial Services L.L.C. • Semiannual. $1,800.00. Two looseleaf volumes. Includes monthly *Supplements.* Provides detailed, individual surveys of 52 major industry groups. Each survey is revised on a semiannual basis. Also includes "Monthly Investment Review" (industry group investment analysis) and monthly "Trends & Projections" (economic analysis).

TRADE/PROFESSIONAL ASSOCIATIONS

Computer and Communications Industry Association. 900 17th St. NW, Ste. 1100, Washington, DC 20006. Phone: (202)783-0070; Fax: (202)783-0534; Email: info@ccianet.org • URL: http://www.ccianet.org • Formerly Computer Industry Association.

Electronic Frontier Foundation. 815 Eddy St., San Francisco, CA 94109. Phone: (415)436-9333; Fax: (415)436-9993; Email: info@eff.org • URL: http://www.eff.org • Promotes the creation of legal and structural approaches to help ease the assimilation of new technologies by society. Seeks to: help policymakers develop a better understanding of issues underlying telecommunications; increase public understanding of the opportunities and challenges posed by computing and telecommunications fields. Fosters awareness of civil liberties issues arising from the advancements in new computer-based communications media and supports litigation to preserve, protect, and extend First Amendment rights in computing and telecommunications technology. Maintains speakers' bureau; conducts educational programs. Encourages and supports the development of tools to endow non-technical users with access to computer-based telecommunications.

COMPUTER CRIME AND SECURITY

ABSTRACTS AND INDEXES

Applied Science and Technology Index. EBSCO Publishing Inc. • 11/year. Indexes a wide variety of English language technical, industrial, and engineering periodicals.

Business Periodicals Index Retrospective. EBSCO Publishing Inc. • 11/year. Quarterly and annual cumulations.

Computer and Information Systems Abstracts Journal: An Abstract Journal Pertaining to the Theory, Design, Fabrication and Application of Computer and Information Systems. CSA. • Monthly. $1,750 per year.

Computer Science Index. EBSCO Publishing Inc. • Quarterly. $245 per year. Contains brief abstracts of book and periodical literature covering all phases of computing, including approximately 70 specific application areas.

Current Contents: Engineering, Computing and Technology. Thomson Reuters Intellectual Property and Science. • Weekly. $730 per year. Reproductions of contents pages of technical journals. Includes *Author Index, Address Directory, Current Book Contents,* and *Title Word Index.* Formerly *Current Contents: Engineering, Technology and Applied Sciences.*

Inspec Direct. Institution of Engineering and Technology. • Monthly. $2,400 per year. Section C of *Science Abstracts.*

CD-ROM DATABASES

Authority Computer and Telecommunications Law Library. Matthew Bender and Company Inc. • Quarterly. Price on request. Full text CD-ROM provides cases, analysis, sample agreements, and other information relating to computer law, telecommunications regulation (cable, broadcasting, satellite, Internet), international computer law, and computer contracts.

OECD Statistical Compendium. Organization for Economic Cooperation and Development. • Semiannual. $1,905.00 per year for 1 to 10 users. CD-ROM contains more than 730,000 monthly, quarterly, and annual time series for OECD countries, 1960 to date. Includes fully searchable data on agriculture, food, economic indicators, national accounts, employment, energy, finance, industry, technology, and foreign trade. Results can be displayed in various forms.

HANDBOOKS AND MANUALS

Trade Secret Protection in an Information Age. Gale R. Peterson. Glasser LegalWorks. • Looseleaf. $149.00, including sample forms on disk. Periodic supplementation available. Covers trade secret law relating to computer software, online databases, and multimedia products. Explanations are based on more than 1,000 legal cases. Sample forms on disk include work-for-hire examples and covenants not to compete.

INTERNET DATABASES

Business 2.0 Web Guide to the Best Business Links. Business 2.0 Media Inc. Phone: (415)293-4800; Email: support@business2.com • URL: http://www.business2.com/webguide • Web site presents an extensive, searchable directory of links to "the best, most informative, and authoritative web pages." Twenty main categories cover business, finance, career, company information, people, and technology topics, with thousands of subtopics, all linking to Web sites recommended by experienced business researchers. Fees: Free.

ONLINE DATABASES

Applied Science and Technology Index Online. H.W. Wilson Co. • Provides online indexing of 500 major scientific, technical, industrial, and engineering periodicals. Time period is 1983 to date. Monthly updates. Inquire as to online cost and availability.

Wilson Business Abstracts Online. H.W. Wilson Co. • Indexes and abstracts 600 major business periodicals, plus the *Wall Street Journal* and the business section of the *New York Times.* Indexing is from 1982, abstracting from 1990, with the two newspapers included from 1993. Updated weekly. Inquire as to online cost and availability. (*Business Periodicals Index* without abstracts is also available online.).

OTHER SOURCES

White Collar Crime: Business and Regulatory Offenses. ALM Media Properties LLC. • $740 print + online + ebook. Covers such legal matters as criminal tax cases, securities fraud, computer crime, mail fraud, bank embezzlement, criminal antitrust activities, extortion, perjury, the criminal liability of corporations, and RICO (Racketeer Influenced and Corrupt Organization Act). (Law Journal Press).

PERIODICALS AND NEWSLETTERS

Computer Fraud and Security. Elsevier. • Monthly. Formerly *Computer Fraud and Security Bulletin.*

Computers and Security: The International Source of Innovation for the Information Security and IT Audit Professional. Computer Security. Elsevier. • Eight times a year. Institutions, $760.00 per year.

CSO: The Resource for Security Executives. CXO Media Inc. • 10/year. $70 U.S. and Canada. Edited for corporate chief security officers (CSOs). Covers a wide variety of business security issues, including computer security, identity theft, spam, physical security, loss prevention, risk management, privacy, and investigations.

EDP Weekly: The Leading Weekly Computer News Summary. Computer Age and EDP News Services. • Weekly. $495.00 per year. Newsletter. Summarizes news from all areas of the computer and microcomputer industries.

FBI Law Enforcement Bulletin. U. S. Government Printing Office. • Monthly. $36.00 per year. Issued by Federal Bureau of Investigation, U. S. Department of Justice. Contains articles on a wide variety of law enforcement and crime topics, including computer-related crime.

IEEE Security & Privacy. IEEE - Computer Society. • Bimonthly. $19.95 Nonmembers online. Emphasis is on computer and netwoek security for large systems.

Information Systems Security. Auerbach Publications. • Quarterly. $175 Individuals. Journal provides standards, guidelines, and techniques for creating more secure, less vulnerable information systems. Formerly *Journal of Information Systems Security.*

Journal of Computer Security. Sushil Jajodia and Jonathan K. Millen, editors. IOS Press, Inc. • Bimonthly. $1,330 Institutions. Contains research and development results of lasting significance in the theory, design, implementation, analysis, and application of secure computer systems.

Security Management. ASIS International. • Monthly. $60 Nonmembers print and online. Included in membership. Articles cover the protection of corporate assets, including personnel property and information security.

Security: The Magazine for Buyers of Security Products, Systems and Service. BNP Media. • Monthly. Security industry news and trends.

TRADE/PROFESSIONAL ASSOCIATIONS

ASIS International. 1625 Prince St., Alexandria, VA 22314. Phone: (703)519-6200; Fax: (703)519-6299; Email: asis@asisonline.org • URL: http://www.asisonline.org/Pages/default.aspx • ASIS is the world's largest organization dedicated to security professionals. Presents seminars and exhibits and offers a variety of educational programs on security issues in a number of fields including communications.

COMPUTER DEALERS

See COMPUTER RETAILING

COMPUTER GRAPHICS

See also COMPUTER ANIMATION

ABSTRACTS AND INDEXES

Computer Science Index. EBSCO Publishing Inc. • Quarterly. $245 per year. Contains brief abstracts of book and periodical literature covering all phases of computing, including approximately 70 specific application areas.

PERIODICALS AND NEWSLETTERS

ACM Transactions on Graphics. Association for Computing Machinery. • Bimonthly. $41 Members.

Advanced Manufacturing Technology: Monthly Report. Technical Insights. • Monthly. $695 Institutions. Covers technological developments relating to robotics, computer graphics, automation, computer-integrated manufacturing, and machining.

Computer Graphics. Special Interest Group on Computer Graphics. Association for Computing Machinery. • Quarterly. Members, $59.00 per year; non-members, $95.00 per year; students, $50.00 per year.

Computer Graphics World. PennWell Publishing Co., Advanced Technology Div. • Bimonthly. $68.

Computers and Graphics: International Journal of Systems Applications in Computer Graphics. Elsevier. • 8/year. Contains information on research and applications of computer graphics (CG) techniques.

Engineering Design Graphics Journal. American Society for Engineering Education. • Three times a year. Free to members; Non-members, $24.00 per year. Concerned with engineering graphics, computer graphics, geometric modeling, computer-aided drafting, etc.

IEEE Computer Graphics and Applications. Institute of Electrical and Electronics Engineers. • Bimonthly. $39 print only. Covers a variety of topics catering to both computer graphics practitioners and researchers.

IEEE Transactions on Visualization and Computer Graphics. IEEE - Communications Society. • Monthly. Contains research on subjects related to computer graphics and visualization techniques, systems, software, hardware, and user interface issues.

IMAGES. IMAGE Society. • Semiannual. $25. Newsletter Provides news of virtual reality developments and the IMAGE Society.

The Magazine for Electronic Publishing Professionals. Publish Media. • Monthly. $39.90 per year. Edited for professional publishers, graphic designers, and industry service providers. Covers new products and emerging technologies for the electronic publishing industry.

SHOOT: The Leading Newsweekly for Commercial Production and Postproduction. Nielsen Business Media Inc. • Weekly. $125 /year. Covers animation, music, sound design, computer graphics, visual effects, cinematography, and other aspects of television and motion picture production, with emphasis on TV commercials.

Step-By-Step Electronic Design: The How-To Newsletter for Electronic Designers. Dynamic Graphics Inc. • Monthly. $48.00 per year.

Step Inside Design: The World of Design from Inside Out. Dynamic Graphics Inc. • Bimonthly. $42.00 per year. Formerly *Step-by-Step Graphics*.

RESEARCH CENTERS AND INSTITUTES

Computer Graphics Laboratory. New York Institute of Technology, Fine Arts, Old Westbury, NY 11568. Phone: (516)686-7542; Fax: (516)686-7428; Email: pvoci@nyit.edu • URL: http://www.nyit.edu • Research areas include computer graphics, computer animation, and digital sound.

University of Illinois at Chicago - Electronic Visualization Laboratory. Department of Computer Science, Rm. 1120, MC 152, 851 S Morgan St., Chicago, IL 60607-7053. Phone: (312)996-3002; Fax: (312)413-7585; Email: spiff@uic.edu • URL: http://www.evl.uic.edu • Research areas include computer graphics, virtual reality, multimedia, and interactive techniques.

Worcester Polytechnic Institute - Department of Computer Science - Image Science Research Group. 100 Institute Rd., Worcester, MA 01609-2280. Phone: (508)831-5671 or (508)831-5357; Fax: (508)831-5776; Email: matt@wpi.edu • URL: http://web.cs.wpi.edu/Research/isrg/ • Areas of research include image processing, computer graphics, and computational vision.

COMPUTER IMAGING

See DOCUMENT IMAGING

COMPUTER LAW

ABSTRACTS AND INDEXES

Computer Science Index. EBSCO Publishing Inc. • Quarterly. $245 per year. Contains brief abstracts of book and periodical literature covering all phases of computing, including approximately 70 specific application areas.

Current Law Index. Cengage Learning Inc. • $1,332 Individuals. Monthly. $1269.00 per year. Produced in cooperation with the American Association of Law Libraries. Indexes more than 900 law journals, legal newspapers, and specialty publications from the U.S., Canada, U.K., Ireland, Australia, and New Zealand.

Index to Legal Periodicals and Books. H.W. Wilson Co. • Monthly. $490.00 per year. Quarterly and annual cumulations.

CD-ROM DATABASES

Authority Computer and Telecommunications Law Library. Matthew Bender and Company Inc. • Quarterly. Price on request. Full text CD-ROM provides cases, analysis, sample agreements, and other information relating to computer law, telecommunications regulation (cable, broadcasting, satellite, Internet), international computer law, and computer contracts.

Authority Intellectual Property Library. Matthew Bender and Company Inc. • Quarterly. Price on request. CD-ROM contains updated full text of *Intellectual Property Counseling and Litigation, Computer Law, International Computer Law, Nimmer on Copyright, Milgrim on Trade Secrets, Patent Litigation, Patent Licensing Transactions, Trademark Protection and Practice*, and other Matthew Bender publications relating to the law of intellectual property.

Index to Legal Periodicals and Books. EBSCO Publishing Inc. • Contains indexing of more than 1,400 English language legal periodicals from 1981 to date and 2,500 books.

DIRECTORIES

Lawyer's Register International by Specialties and Fields of Law Including a Directory of Corporate Counsel. Lawyer's Register Publishing Co. • Annual. $359 Individuals. Referral source for law firms.

INTERNET DATABASES

Lexis.com Research System. Lexis-Nexis Group. Phone: 800-227-4908 or (937)865-6800; Fax: (937)865-6909; Email: webmaster@prod.lexis-nexis.com • URL: http://www.nexis.com • Fee-based Web site offers extensive searching of a wide variety of legal sources. Additional features include Daily Opinion Service, lexis.com Bookstore, Career Center, CLE Center, Law Schools, and Practice Pages ("Pages specific to areas of specialty").

ONLINE DATABASES

LegalTrac. Cengage Learning Inc. • Online database. Provides indexing for approximately 875 titles of periodical literature relating to legal matters from 1980 to date. Corresponds to online *Legal Resource Index*. Inquire as to price and availability.

OTHER SOURCES

E-Commerce and Internet Law: Treatise with Forms. Ian C. Ballon. Glasser LegalWorks. • $1,479 Individuals Binder/Looseleaf (Full Set). Periodic supplementation. Analyzes Internet legalities, including litigious matters relating to downloading, streaming, music, video, content aggregation, domain names, chatrooms, and search engines. Includes forms, contracts, checklists, sample pleadings, and an extensive glossary.

Guide to Computer Law. Wolters Kluwer Law & Business CCH. • Monthly. Computer and internet law.

PERIODICALS AND NEWSLETTERS

Computer Law Reporter: A Monthly Journal of Computer Law and Practice, Intellectual Property, Copyright and Trademark Law. Computer Law Reporter. • Monthly. $3,475. Contains reports on legal developments affecting high technology industries.

Computer Law Strategist. ALM Media Properties LLC. • Monthly. $265.00 per year. Newsletter.

Technology Law Alert: Monthly Newsletter Covering Computer-Related Law and Tax Issues. Roditti Reports Corp. • Monthly. $297.00 per year. Newsletter. Formerly *Computer Law and Tax Report*.

RESEARCH CENTERS AND INSTITUTES

Arizona State University - Sandra Day O'Connor College of Law - Center for Law, Science and Innovation. Armstrong Hall, 1100 S McAllister Ave., Tempe, AZ 85287. Phone: (480)965-6181 • URL: http://www.law.asu.edu/lsi • Studies the development of legal frameworks for new technologies and advancing the use of science in legal decision making.

TRADE/PROFESSIONAL ASSOCIATIONS

International Technology Law Association. 401 Edgewater Pl., Ste. 600, Wakefield, MA 01880. Phone: (781)876-8877; Fax: (781)224-1239; Email: office@itechlaw.org • URL: http://www.itechlaw.org • Lawyers, law students, and others interested in legal problems related to computer-communications technology. Aids in: contracting for computer-communications goods and services; perfecting and protecting proprietary rights chiefly in software; and taxing computer-communications goods, services, and transactions, and liability for acquisition and use of computer-communications goods and services. Provides specialized educational programs; and offers limited placement service. Holds Annual Computer Law Update.

COMPUTER OUTPUT MICROFILM (COM)

See MICROFORMS

COMPUTER PERIPHERALS AND ACCESSORIES

See also MICROCOMPUTERS AND MINICOMPUTERS

ABSTRACTS AND INDEXES

Applied Science and Technology Index. EBSCO Publishing Inc. • 11/year. Indexes a wide variety of English language technical, industrial, and engineering periodicals.

Business Periodicals Index Retrospective. EBSCO Publishing Inc. • 11/year. Quarterly and annual cumulations.

Computer and Information Systems Abstracts Journal: An Abstract Journal Pertaining to the Theory, Design, Fabrication and Application of Computer and Information Systems. CSA. • Monthly. $1,750 per year.

Computer Science Index. EBSCO Publishing Inc. • Quarterly. $245 per year. Contains brief abstracts of book and periodical literature covering all phases of computing, including approximately 70 specific application areas.

Inspec Direct. Institution of Engineering and Technology. • Monthly. $2,400 per year. Section C of *Science Abstracts*.

CD-ROM DATABASES

Datapro on CD-ROM: Computer Systems Hardware and Software. Gartner Inc. • Monthly. Price on application. CD-ROM provides product specifications, product reports, user surveys, and market forecasts for a wide range of computer hardware and software.

DIRECTORIES

Directory of Belgium Importers of Computer Hardware and Peripherals. EXIM Infotek Private Ltd. • $300 Individuals. Covers: 110 Belgium importers of computer equipment and supplies, computer peripherals, computer supplies, computers and components, LAN/network hardware and software, and laser printers. Entries include: Company name, postal address, telephone, fax, e-mail, website, contact person, designation, and product details.

FINANCIAL RATIOS

Industry Norms and Key Business Ratios. Dun & Bradstreet Inc. • Annual. Five volumes. Covers over 800 kinds of businesses, arranged by Standard Industrial Classification number. More detailed editions covering longer periods of time are also available.

INTERNET DATABASES

InfoTech Trends. Data Analysis Group. Phone: (925)462-1202; Fax: (925)462-1225; Email: support@infotechtrends.com • URL: http://www.infotechtrends.com • Web site provides both free and fee-based market research data on the information technology industry, including computers, peripherals, telecommunications, the Internet, software, CD-ROM/DVD, e-commerce, and workstations. Fees: Free for current (most recent year) data; more extensive information has various fee structures. Formerly *Computer Industry Forecasts*.

ONLINE DATABASES

Applied Science and Technology Index Online. H.W. Wilson Co. • Provides online indexing of 500 major scientific, technical, industrial, and engineering periodicals. Time period is 1983 to date. Monthly updates. Inquire as to online cost and availability.

Wilson Business Abstracts Online. H.W. Wilson Co. • Indexes and abstracts 600 major business periodicals, plus the *Wall Street Journal* and the business section of the *New York Times*. Indexing is from 1982, abstracting from 1990, with the two newspapers included from 1993. Updated weekly. Inquire as to online cost and availability. (*Business Periodicals Index* without abstracts is also available online.).

PERIODICALS AND NEWSLETTERS

EDP Weekly: The Leading Weekly Computer News Summary. Computer Age and EDP News Services. • Weekly. $495.00 per year. Newsletter. Summarizes news from all areas of the computer and microcomputer industries.

Interactive Home: Consumer Technology Monthly. Jupiter Communications. • Monthly. $625.00 per year; with online edition, $725.00 per year. Newsletter on devices to bring the Internet into the average American home. Covers TV set-top boxes, game devices, telephones with display screens, handheld computer communication devices, the usual PCs, etc.

Network: Strategies and Solutions for the Network Professional. UBM L.L.C. • 13 times a year. Free to qualified personnel. Covers network products and peripherals for computer professionals. Includes annual network managers salary survey and annual directory issue. Formerly *LAN: The Network Solutions Magazine*.

Presentations: Technology and Techniques for Effective Communication. Nielsen Business Media Inc. • Monthly. Free to qualified personnel; others, $69.00 per year. Covers the use of presentation hardware and software, including audiovisual equipment and computerized display systems. Includes an annual *Buyers Guide to Presentation Products*.

RESEARCH CENTERS AND INSTITUTES

Carnegie Mellon Research Institute-The Robotics Institute. 5000 Forbes Ave., Pittsburgh, PA 15213. Phone: (412)268-3818; Fax: (412)268-6436; Email: robotics@ri.cmu.edu • URL: http://www.ri.cmu.edu • Multidisciplinary research activities include expert systems applications, minicomputer and microcomputer systems design, genetic engineering, and transportation systems analysis.

Columbia University - Center for Advanced Information Management. 650 W 168th St., Black Bldg. - 130, New York, NY 10032. Phone: (212)305-2944 or (212)305-5334; Fax: (212)305-0196 or (212)305-3302; Email: tomaselli@cat.columbia.edu • URL: http://www.cat.columbia.edu • Biomedical informatics, computer science, computational and systems biology, biomedical imaging.

STATISTICS SOURCES

Standard & Poor's Industry Surveys. Standard & Poor's Financial Services L.L.C. • Semiannual. $1,800.00. Two looseleaf volumes. Includes monthly *Supplements*. Provides detailed, individual surveys of 52 major industry groups. Each survey is revised on a semiannual basis. Also includes "Monthly Investment Review" (industry group investment analysis) and monthly "Trends & Projections" (economic analysis).

TRADE/PROFESSIONAL ASSOCIATIONS

Computing Technology Industry Association. 3500 Lacey Rd., Ste. 100, Downers Grove, IL 60515. Phone: (630)678-8300; Fax: (630)678-8384; Email: membership@comptia.org • URL: http://www.comptia.org • Trade association of more than 19,000 companies and professional IT members in the rapidly converging computing and communications market. Has members in more than 89 countries and provides a unified voice for the industry in the areas of e-commerce standards, vendor-neutral certification, service metrics, public policy and workforce development. Serves as information clearinghouse and resource for the industry; sponsors educational programs.

COMPUTER PROGRAMMING

See COMPUTER SOFTWARE INDUSTRY

COMPUTER RESELLERS

See COMPUTER RETAILING

COMPUTER RETAILING

DIRECTORIES

Computers-Dealers (Used) Directory. InfoGroup Inc. • Annual. Number of listings: 2,336. Entries include: Name, address, phone, size of advertisement, name of owner or manager, number of employees, year first in "Yellow Pages." Compiled from telephone company "Yellow Pages," nationwide.

Plunkett's E-Commerce & Internet Business Almanac: Your Reference Source to All Facets of the Internet Business. Plunkett Research Ltd. • Biennial. $349.99 Individuals ebook, print and CD-ROM. Covers 400 of the largest companies working in all facets of e-commerce and Internet business, including Internet service providers, Web site operators, equipment and others.

Plunkett's Retail Industry Almanac: Complete Profiles on the Retail 500: The Leading Firms in Retail Stores, Services, Catalogs, and On-Line Sales. Plunkett Research Ltd. • Annual. $349.99 Individuals print. Covers: 500 of the largest retail stores, services, catalogs, and on-line sales companies. Entries include: Firm name, address, phone, fax; description; and leading executives with their titles, addresses, phone numbers, fax numbers, E-mail addresses, and Web sites.

FINANCIAL RATIOS

Annual Statement Studies. Risk Management Association. • Annual. Compiled from over 280,000 financial statements.

Annual Statement Studies: Industry Default Probabilities and Cash Flow Measures. Risk Management Association. • Annual. $405 Nonmembers. Serves as a companion volume to the original *Annual Statement Studies*. Gives probability of default estimates on a percentage scale for more than 450 industries. Includes changes in position year-by-year for eight financial statement line items and provides percentage measures of cash flow.

HANDBOOKS AND MANUALS

Software Store. Entrepreneur Press. • Looseleaf. $59.50. A practical guide to opening a computer software retail establishment. Covers profit potential, start-up costs, market size evaluation, owner's time required, site selection, lease negotiation, pricing, accounting, advertising, promotion, etc. (Start-Up Business Guide No. E1261.).

INTERNET DATABASES

Advance Monthly Retail Trade Report. U. S. Census Bureau. Phone: 800-541-8345 or (301)457-4100 or (301)763-2713; Fax: (301)457-1296 or (301)457-3842; Email: naics@census.gov • URL: http://www.census.gov/epcd/www/naicstab.htm • Web pages provide monthly sales figures for a wide range of retail businesses. Advance, preliminary, and final statistics are provided for the latest month available in each case, with a previous-year comparison. Updates are monthly.

PERIODICALS AND NEWSLETTERS

Computer Shopper: The Computer Magazine for Direct Buyers. Media Inc. • Nationwide marketplace for computer equipment.

CRN: The Newsweekly for Builders of Technology Solutions. CMP Worldwide Media Networks. • Monthly. Incorporates *Computer Reseller Sources and Macintosh News.* Formerly *Computer Retailer News.*

STATISTICS SOURCES

Annual Benchmark Report for Retail Trade and Food Services..A Detailed Summary of Retail Sales, Purchases, Accounts Receivable, Inventories, and Food Service Sales. U. S. Government Printing Office. • Annual. $13.00. Issued by the U.S. Census Bureau. Provides detailed annual and monthly retail statistics for the most recent 10 years. Includes data for various kinds of retail outlets, including automobiles, furniture, appliances, building supplies, grocery stores, drug stores, gasoline stations, clothing, sporting goods, department stores, and restaurants.

TRADE/PROFESSIONAL ASSOCIATIONS

Computing Technology Industry Association. 3500 Lacey Rd., Ste. 100, Downers Grove, IL 60515. Phone: (630)678-8300; Fax: (630)678-8384; Email: membership@comptia.org • URL: http://www.comptia.org • Trade association of more than 19,000 companies and professional IT members in the rapidly converging computing and communications market. Has members in more than 89 countries and provides a unified voice for the industry in the areas of e-commerce standards, vendor-neutral certification, service metrics, public policy and workforce development. Serves as information clearinghouse and resource for the industry; sponsors educational programs.

COMPUTER SECURITY

See COMPUTER CRIME AND SECURITY

COMPUTER SOFTWARE INDUSTRY

See also COMPUTERS; MICROCOMPUTERS AND MINICOMPUTERS; UNIX

ABSTRACTS AND INDEXES

Computer Science Index. EBSCO Publishing Inc. • Quarterly. $245 per year. Contains brief abstracts of book and periodical literature covering all phases of computing, including approximately 70 specific application areas.

Internet and Personal Computing Abstracts (print edition). EBSCO Publishing Inc. • Quarterly. $269.00 per year, including cumulative index. Provides more than 10,000 abstracts annually from both trade and academic publications. Covers computer hardware, software, product reviews, Web topics, e-commerce, networks, corporate news, security, and related topics. Formerly *Microcomputer Abstracts.*

Key Abstracts: Software Engineering. Institution of Engineering and Technology. • Monthly. $1,138. Provides international coverage of journal and proceedings literature.

CD-ROM DATABASES

Datapro on CD-ROM: Computer Systems Hardware and Software. Gartner Inc. • Monthly. Price on application. CD-ROM provides product specifications, product reports, user surveys, and market forecasts for a wide range of computer hardware and software.

Datapro Software Finder. Gartner Inc. • Quarterly. $1,770.00 per year. CD-ROM provides detailed information on more than 18,000 software products for a wide variety of computers, personal to mainframe. Covers software for 130 types of business, finance, and industry. (Editions limited to either microcomputer or mainframe software are available at $995.00 per year.).

OECD Statistical Compendium. Organization for Economic Cooperation and Development. • Semiannual. $1,905.00 per year for 1 to 10 users. CD-ROM contains more than 730,000 monthly, quarterly, and annual time series for OECD countries, 1960 to date. Includes fully searchable data on agriculture, food, economic indicators, national accounts, employment, energy, finance, industry, technology, and foreign trade. Results can be displayed in various forms.

DIRECTORIES

BPO, Call Center IT, Telecom, Computer Software & Hardware Companies Database, Directory of India. NIIR Project Consultancy Services. • $200 Individuals CD-ROM. Covers: BPO, call center, telecom, computer software and hardware companies in India. Entries include: Name of companies, address, city, pin code, phone, fax, 2,250 e-mail, 2,350 website and contact person with designation.

Directory of Australia and New Zealand Importers of Computer Software. EXIM Infotek Private Ltd. • $150 Individuals. Covers: 30 Australian and New Zealand importers of architech design software, business software, computer software, geographic information systems technologies, LAN/network hardware and software, mapping software, and software for garment industry. Entries include: Company name, postal address, telephone, fax, e-mail, website, contact person, designation, and product details.

Directory of Belgium Importers of Computer Software. EXIM Infotek Private Ltd. • $150 Individuals. Covers: 35 Belgium importers of computer software. Entries include: Company name, postal address, telephone, fax, e-mail, website, contact person, designation, and product details.

Directory of French Importers of Computer Softwares. EXIM Infotek Private Ltd. • $150 Individuals. Covers: 40 French importers of computer software. Entries include: Company name, postal address, telephone, fax, e-mail, website, contact person, designation, and product details.

Directory of German Importers of Computer Softwares. EXIM Infotek Private Ltd. • $150 Individuals. Covers: 30 German importers of CAD software and computer software. Entries include: Company name, postal address, telephone, fax, e-mail, website, contact person, designation, and product details.

Directory of Indian Importers of Computer Softwares. EXIM Infotek Private Ltd. • $150 Individuals. Covers: 30 Indian importers of computer software and LAN/network hardware. Entries include: Company name, postal address, telephone, fax, e-mail, website, contact person, designation, and product details.

Directory of Japanese Importers of Computer Softwares. EXIM Infotek Private Ltd. • $200 Individuals. Covers: 55 Japanese importers of computer software and internet technology. Entries include: Company name, postal address, telephone, fax, e-mail, website, contact person, designation, and product details.

Music Technology Buyer's Guide. United Entertainment Media. • $6.95. Annual. Lists more than 4,000 hardware and software music production products from 350 manufacturers. Includes synthesizers, MIDI hardware and software, mixers, microphones, music notation software, etc. Produced by the editorial staffs of *Keyboard* and *EQ* magazines.

GENERAL WORKS

Business Services. S1 Corp. • Offers applications and solutions for customer education and support services.

Journal of Business Process Oriented Software Engineering. IBIMA Publishing. • Peer-reviewed journal covering the area of business software engineering.

INTERNET DATABASES

Business 2.0 Web Guide to the Best Business Links. Business 2.0 Media Inc. Phone: (415)293-4800; Email: support@business2.com • URL: http://www.business2.com/webguide • Web site presents an extensive, searchable directory of links to "the best, most informative, and authoritative web pages." Twenty main categories cover business, finance, career, company information, people, and technology topics, with thousands of subtopics, all linking to Web sites recommended by experienced business researchers. Fees: Free.

InfoTech Trends. Data Analysis Group. Phone: (925)462-1202; Fax: (925)462-1225; Email: support@infotechtrends.com • URL: http://www.infotechtrends.com • Web site provides both free and fee-based market research data on the information technology industry, including computers, peripherals, telecommunications, the Internet, software, CD-ROM/DVD, e-commerce, and workstations. Fees: Free for current (most recent year) data; more extensive information has various fee structures. Formerly *Computer Industry Forecasts.*

Wired News. Lycos Inc. 400-2 Totten Pond Rd., Waltham, MA 02451-2053. Phone: (781)370-2700 or (415)276-8400; Fax: (781)370-2600 or (415)276-8500; Email: press@lycos.com • URL: http://www.lycos.com • Provides summaries and full-text of "Top Stories" relating to the Internet, computers, multimedia, telecommunications, and the electronic information industry in general. These news stories are placed in the broad categories of Politics, Business, Culture, and Technology. Affiliated with *Wired* magazine. Fees: Free.

ONLINE DATABASES

Computer Database. Cengage Learning Inc. • Provides one year of full-text online for 150 leading computer-related publications. Also includes 70,000 product specifications and brief profiles of 13,000 computer product vendors and manufacturers. Inquire as to prices and availability.

OTHER SOURCES

Keyboard: The World's Leading Music Technology Magazine. United Entertainment Media. • Monthly. $25.95 per year. Emphasis is on recording systems, keyboard technique, and computer-assisted music (MIDI) systems.

PERIODICALS AND NEWSLETTERS

Business Computer Report. Lawrence Oakly. • Monthly. $99 Individuals. Reviews business applications software and hardware for IBM and compatible computers.

Computer Languages, Systems and Structures. Elsevier. • Quarterly. Contains papers on all aspects of the design, implementation and use of programming languages, from theory to practice.

Computerworld: Newsweekly for Information Technology Leaders. ComputerWorld Inc. • Weekly. $190.00 per year.

Dr. Dobb's Journal: Software Tools for the Professional Programmer. UBM L.L.C. • Monthly. $34.95 per year. A technical publication covering software development, languages, operating systems, and applications.

IEEE Software. Institute of Electrical and Electronic

Engineers. • Bimonthly. Covers software engineering, technology, and development. Affiliated with the Institute of Electrical and Electronics Engineers.

InfoWorld: Defining Technology for Business. InfoWorld Publishing. • Weekly. $195.00 per year. For personal computing professionals.

Insurance and Technology. UBM L.L.C. • Monthly. $65.00 per year. Covers information technology and systems management as applied to the operation of life, health, casualty, and property insurance companies.

MSDN Magazine. UBM L.L.C. • Monthly. $25 U.S. 1-year subscription (online). Produced for professional software developers using Windows, MS-DOS, Visual Basic, and other Microsoft Corporation products. Incorporates *Microsoft Internet Developer.*

Network Computing: Computing in a Network Environment. UBM L.L.C. • Semimonthly. Free to qualified personnel.

Soft-Letter: Trends and Strategies in Software Publishing. UCG Technologies. • Monthly. $399 Individuals 1 year. Newsletter on the software industry, including new technology and financial aspects.

Software Development. Miller Freeman Inc. • Monthly. $39.00 per year. Edited for professional software developers and managers.

Software Digest: The Independent Comparative Ratings Report for PC and LAN Software. NSTL. • 12 times a year. $450.00 per year. Critical evaluations of personal computer software.

Software Economics Letter: Maximizing Your Return on Corporate Software. Computer Economics Inc. • Monthly. $395.00 per year. Newsletter for information systems managers. Contains data on business software trends, vendor licensing policies, and other corporate software management issues.

Software Magazine. Wiesner Publishing, Inc. • Monthly. Free to qualified personnel; others, $42.00 per year.

Telematics and Informatics: An International Journal on Telecommunications and Internet Technology. Elsevier. • Four times a year. Institutions, $938.00 per year.

STATISTICS SOURCES

Standard & Poor's Industry Surveys. Standard & Poor's Financial Services L.L.C. • Semiannual. $1,800.00. Two looseleaf volumes. Includes monthly *Supplements.* Provides detailed, individual surveys of 52 major industry groups. Each survey is revised on a semiannual basis. Also includes "Monthly Investment Review" (industry group investment analysis) and monthly "Trends & Projections" (economic analysis).

U.S. Industry and Trade Outlook. U.S. Department of Commerce National Technical Information Service. • Annual. Produced by the International Trade Administration, U.S. Department of Commerce, in a "public-private" partnership with DRI/McGraw-Hill and Standard & Poor's. Provides basic data, outlook for the current year, and "Long-Term Prospects" (five-year projections) for a wide variety of products and services. Includes high technology industries. Formerly *U.S. Industrial Outlook.*

COMPUTER STORES

See COMPUTER RETAILING

COMPUTER VIRUSES

See COMPUTER CRIME AND SECURITY

COMPUTER VISION

See MACHINE VISION

COMPUTERIZED TRANSLATION

See MACHINE TRANSLATING

COMPUTERS

See also AUTOMATION; COMMUNICATION SYSTEMS; COMPUTER SOFTWARE INDUSTRY; LINEAR PROGRAMMING; MICROCOMPUTERS AND MINICOMPUTERS; OPERATIONS RESEARCH; PORTABLE COMPUTERS

ABSTRACTS AND INDEXES

Applied Science and Technology Index. EBSCO Publishing Inc. • 11/year. Indexes a wide variety of English language technical, industrial, and engineering periodicals.

Computer Abstracts. Emerald Group Publishing Inc. • Bimonthly. $4,739.

Computer and Information Systems Abstracts Journal: An Abstract Journal Pertaining to the Theory, Design, Fabrication and Application of Computer and Information Systems. CSA. • Monthly. $1,750 per year.

Computer Science Index. EBSCO Publishing Inc. • Quarterly. $245 per year. Contains brief abstracts of book and periodical literature covering all phases of computing, including approximately 70 specific application areas.

Computing Reviews. Association for Computing Machinery. • Price varies. New reviews published daily.

Internet and Personal Computing Abstracts (print edition). EBSCO Publishing Inc. • Quarterly. $269.00 per year, including cumulative index. Provides more than 10,000 abstracts annually from both trade and academic publications. Covers computer hardware, software, product reviews, Web topics, e-commerce, networks, corporate news, security, and related topics. Formerly *Microcomputer Abstracts.*

NTIS Alerts: Computers, Control & Information Theory. U.S. Department of Commerce National Technical Information Service. • Biweekly. $130 per year. Covers computer hardware, software, control systems, pattern recognition, image processing, and related subjects.

ALMANACS AND YEARBOOKS

Advances in Computers. Elsevier. • $182 Individuals. Coverage of innovations in computer hardware, software, theory, design, and applications. Contact for pricing.

Information Technology Outlook. Organisation for Economic Co-operation and Development Publications and Information Center. • Biennial. A review of recent developments in international markets for computer hardware, software, and services. Also examines current legal provisions for information systems security and privacy in OECD countries.

BIBLIOGRAPHIES

ACM Electronic Guide to Computing Literature: Bibliographic Listing, Author Index, Keyword Index, Category Index, Proper Noun Subject Index, Reviewer Index, Source Index. Association for Computing Machinery. • Quarterly. Members, $175. 00; non-members, $499.00 per year. A comprehensive guide to each year's computer literature (books, proceedings, journals, etc.), with an emphasis on technical material. Indexed by author, keyword, category, proper noun, reviewer, and source. Formerly *A C M Guide to Computing Literature.*

Automation. U. S. Government Printing Office. • Annual. Free. Issued by the Superintendent of Documents. A list of government publications on automation, computers, and related topics. Formerly *Computers and Data Processing.* (Subject Bibliography No. 51.).

IEEE Products and Publications Bulletin. IEEE - Communications Society. • Quarterly. Free. Provides information on all IEEE journals, proceedings, and other publications. Formerly *IEEE Publications Bulletin.*

Reference Reviews. Information Today, Inc. • Eight times a year. Price on application. Published in London by Aslib: The Association for Information Management. Incorporates *Aslib Book Guide.*

BIOGRAPHICAL SOURCES

Who's Who in Science and Engineering. Marquis Who's Who L.L.C. • Biennial. $249.00. Provides concise biographical information on 33,545 prominent engineers and scientists. International coverage, with geographical and professional indexes.

CD-ROM DATABASES

Business Abstracts with Full Text. EBSCO Publishing Inc. • Includes full text articles from more than 460 business publications from 1982 to present. Indexing for nearly 880 publications.

Datapro on CD-ROM: Computer Systems Hardware and Software. Gartner Inc. • Monthly. Price on application. CD-ROM provides product specifications, product reports, user surveys, and market forecasts for a wide range of computer hardware and software.

MathSciNet. American Mathematical Society. • Electronic resource with citations, abstracts, and reviews to the literature of mathematics, statistics, and computer science, 1940 to date.

DIRECTORIES

Computer Industry Almanac. Computer Industry Almanac Inc. • Annual. $53 Individuals paperback. Covers: Over 3,000 firms involved in the computer industry in the U.S. Database includes: Lists of firms in various categories; industry overview; lists of trade shows, associations, publications, market research companies, high-tech PR companies. Entries include: Company Name, address, phone, fax, products, sales, number of employees, names and titles of key personnel, e-mail addresses, websites.

Computers & Office Equipment Importers & Buyers Directory. BD International. • $132 Individuals. Covers: 8,000 importers, buyers, wholesalers, and distributors of computers and office equipment. Entries include: Name, address, phone, fax, contact person, nature of business, website, and e-mail.

Directory of Australia and New Zealand Importers of Computer Hardware, Peripherals. EXIM Infotek Private Ltd. • $250 Individuals. Covers: 75 Australian and New Zealand importers of compact disc, compressor parts, computer and computer accessories, computer components, computer consumables, computer driven routing systems, computer equipment and supplies, computer hardware, computer keyboards, computer networking hardware, computer parts, computer peripherals, printers, Dell P3 notebooks, dot matrix printers, DVR capture cards, graphic cards, imaging products, ink jet cartridges, ink jet printers, ink jet refill, laptop, laser printers, memories, modems-fax and data, monitors, motherboard, mouse pads, net-servers, network equipment, and printing devices. Entries include: Company name, postal address, telephone, fax, e-mail, website, contact person, designation, and product details.

Directory of Belgium Importers of Computer Hardware and Peripherals. EXIM Infotek Private Ltd. • $300 Individuals. Covers: 110 Belgium importers of computer equipment and supplies, computer peripherals, computer supplies, computers and components, LAN/network hardware and software, and laser printers. Entries include: Company name, postal address, telephone, fax, e-mail, website, contact person, designation, and product details.

Directory of British Importers of Computer Hardwares and Peripherals. EXIM Infotek Private Ltd. • $300 Individuals. Covers: 95 British importers of computer equipment and supplies, computer hardware, computer monitors, computer parts, computer peripherals, computer supplies, computers, computer components, inkjet cartridges, LAN/network hardware and software, and laser printers. Entries include: Company name, postal address, telephone, fax, e-mail, website, contact person, designation, and product details.

Directory of Computer and Point-of-Sale Systems for Office Products and Furniture Dealers. Independent Office Products and Furniture Dealers Association. • Irregular. $60. Covers: Approximately 45 manufacturers and distributors of computer, point-of-sale, and contract furniture systems for the office products industry. Entries include: Company name, address, phone, description of product or service.

Directory of Danish Importers of Computer Hardwares and Peripherals. EXIM Infotek Private Ltd. • $250 Individuals. Covers: 70 Danish importers of computer equipment and supplies, computer peripherals, computer supplies, computer components, LAN/network hardware and software. Entries include: Company name, postal address, telephone, fax, e-mail, website, contact person, designation, and product details.

Directory of French Importers of Computer Hardwares and Peripherals. EXIM Infotek Private Ltd. • $400 Individuals. Covers: 150 French importers of computer equipment and supplies, computer peripherals, computer components, LAN/network hardware and software, and laser printers. Entries include: Company name, postal address, telephone, fax, e-mail, website, contact person, designation, and product details.

Directory of German Importers of Computer Hardwares and Peripherals. EXIM Infotek Private Ltd. • $250 Individuals. Covers: 70 German importers of CD-ROM, computer equipment and supplies, computer peripherals, computer components, LAN/network hardware and software, toner, and cartridges. Entries include: Company name, postal address, telephone, fax, e-mail, website, contact person, designation, and product details.

Directory of Japanese Importers of Computer Hardwares and Peripherals. EXIM Infotek Private Ltd. • $350 Individuals. Covers: 125 Japanese importers of bar coding equipment, compact disc, computers, computer accessories, computer components, computer equipment and supplies, computer hardware, computer peripherals, computer supplies, printers, information processing equipment and peripherals, ink jet printers, laser printers, LCD monitor, monitors, personal computers, and scanners. Entries include: Company name, postal address, telephone, fax, e-mail, website, contact person, designation, and product details.

The International Directory of Importers--Computers and Data Processing Equipment Importers. Interdata. • $320 Individuals print. Covers: 7,100 international firms importing computers and data processing equipment. Entries include: Company name and address, contact person, email, number of employees, year established, phone and telefaxes, business activity, bank references, as well as a listing of computers and data processing equipment currently being imported.

The International Directory of Importers--Electronic and Computer Components and Parts Importers. Interdata. • $320 Individuals print. Covers: 7,000 international firms importing electronic and computer components and parts. Entries include: Company name and address, contact person, email, number of employees, year established, phone and telefaxes, business activity, bank references, as well as a listing of electronic and computer components and parts currently being imported.

President's Club! Presidents of Computer and Telecommunications Companies Directory. Ex-IBM Corp. • $95 per issue. Covers: over 2,200 presidents of companies, organizations, or associations involved in the computer and telecommunications industries. Entries include: Company, organization, or association name, president's name, address, and phone.

ENCYCLOPEDIAS AND DICTIONARIES

Encyclopedia of Computer Science and Technology. Taylor & Francis Online. • Dates vary. 45 volumes. $8,775.00. $195.00 per volume. Contains scholarly articles written by computer experts. Includes bibliographies.

GENERAL WORKS

Computer Sciences: Macmillan Science Library. Cengage Learning Inc. • $690 Individuals. 2013. $629.00. Presents a general and historical review of the impact of computers on modern society. Includes biographical information and multidisciplinary examples. Macmillan Reference USA imprint. eBook also available.

Journal of Enterprise Business Intelligence Systems. IBIMA Publishing. • Peer-reviewed journal featuring the latest research and practices in enterprise business intelligence systems.

Journal of Nature-Inspired Business Computing. IBIMA Publishing. • Peer-reviewed journal focusing on nature-inspired computing for businesses.

INTERNET DATABASES

InfoTech Trends. Data Analysis Group. Phone: (925)462-1202; Fax: (925)462-1225; Email: support@infotechtrends.com • URL: http://www.infotechtrends.com • Web site provides both free and fee-based market research data on the information technology industry, including computers, peripherals, telecommunications, the Internet, software, CD-ROM/DVD, e-commerce, and workstations. Fees: Free for current (most recent year) data; more extensive information has various fee structures. Formerly *Computer Industry Forecasts*.

Manufacturing Profiles. U. S. Bureau of the Census. Phone: (301)763-4636 or (301)763-4100; Fax: (301)763-4794; Email: webmaster@census.gov • URL: http://www.census.gov/prod/www/abs/mfg-prof.html • The Census Bureau makes available free on PDF (Portable Document Format) an annual consolidation of the entire Current Industrial Report series, presenting "all the data compiled." Contains statistics on production, shipments, inventories, consumption, exports, imports, and orders for a wide variety of manufactured products.

Wired News. Lycos Inc. 400-2 Totten Pond Rd., Waltham, MA 02451-2053. Phone: (781)370-2700 or (415)276-8400; Fax: (781)370-2600 or (415)276-8500; Email: press@lycos.com • URL: http://www.lycos.com • Provides summaries and full-text of "Top Stories" relating to the Internet, computers, multimedia, telecommunications, and the electronic information industry in general. These news stories are placed in the broad categories of Politics, Business, Culture, and Technology. Affiliated with *Wired* magazine. Fees: Free.

ONLINE DATABASES

Applied Science and Technology Index Online. H.W. Wilson Co. • Provides online indexing of 500 major scientific, technical, industrial, and engineering periodicals. Time period is 1983 to date. Monthly updates. Inquire as to online cost and availability.

Computer and Electronic Component Businesses in the World. Momentum Technologies L.L.C. • Contains directory listings for more than 170 businesses throughout the world that manufacture or sell computer components and electronic parts. Includes business name, address, phone number, fax number, e-mail address, and web site address. Provides brief descriptions of product lines, services offered, and business type. Includes information on manufacturers, component makers, wholesalers, retailers, system designers, system installers, trade associations, and more. Searchable by location, business type, company name, and keyword.

Computer Database. Cengage Learning Inc. • Provides one year of full-text online for 150 leading computer-related publications. Also includes 70,000 product specifications and brief profiles of 13,000 computer product vendors and manufacturers. Inquire as to prices and availability.

INSPEC. Institution of Electrical Engineers. • Provides online citations, with abstracts, to the world literature of electrical engineering, electronics, optoelectronics, telecommunications, industrial controls, instrumentation, computer technology, information technology, and physics. Coverage includes more than 4,000 technical and scientific journals from 1969 to date, with weekly updating. (INSPEC is Information Services in Physics, Electronics, and Computing.) Inquire as to online cost and availability.

Wilson Business Abstracts Online. H.W. Wilson Co. • Indexes and abstracts 600 major business periodicals, plus the *Wall Street Journal* and the business section of the *New York Times*. Indexing is from 1982, abstracting from 1990, with the two newspapers included from 1993. Updated weekly. Inquire as to online cost and availability. (*Business Periodicals Index* without abstracts is also available online.).

OTHER SOURCES

Survey of Advanced Technology: A Strategic Analysis of Today's Leading-edge Information Technologies. I.T. Works. • Annual. $795.00. Surveys the corporate use (or neglect) of advanced computer technology. Topics include major technology trends and emerging technologies.

PERIODICALS AND NEWSLETTERS

ACM Computing Surveys: The Survey and Tutorial Journal of the ACM. Association for Computing Machinery. • Quarterly. $26 Members.

CIO: The Magazine for Chief Information Officers. CXO Media Inc. • Monthly. $129 per year. Edited for chief information officers. Includes a monthly "Web Business" section (incorporates the former *WebMaster* periodical) and a monthly "Enterprise" section for other company executives.

Computer. Institute of Electrical and Electronic Engineers. • Monthly. Covers all aspects of computer science.

Computer Economics Networking Strategies Report: Advising IT Decision Maker ractices and Current Trends. Computer Economics Inc. • Monthly. $395.00 per year. Newsletter. Edited for information technology managers. Covers news and trends relating to a variety of corporate computer network and management information systems topics. Emphasis is on costs. Formerly *Intranet and Networking Strategies Report*.

Computer Economics Report: The Financial Advisor of Data Processing Users. Computer Economics Inc. • Monthly. $695. Newsletter on lease/purchase decisions, prices, discounts, residual value forecasts, personnel allocation, cost control, and other corporate computer topics. Edited for information technology (IT) executives.

Computer Letter: Business Issues in Technology. Technologic Partners. • 40 times a year. $695.00 per year. Newsletter. Computer industry newsletter with emphasis on information for investors.

Computer Shopper: The Computer Magazine for Direct Buyers. Media Inc. • Nationwide marketplace for computer equipment.

Computerworld: Newsweekly for Information Technology Leaders. ComputerWorld Inc. • Weekly. $190.00 per year.

CRN: The Newsweekly for Builders of Technology Solutions. CMP Worldwide Media Networks. • Monthly. Incorporates *Computer Reseller Sources and Macintosh News.* Formerly *Computer Retailer News.*

IBM Journal of Research and Development. International Business Machines Corp. • Bimonthly. Contains work of authors in the science, technology and engineering of information systems.

Information Processing and Management: An International Journal. Elsevier. • $327 Individuals. Bimonthly. Qualified personnel, $301.00 per year; institutions, $1,196.00 per year. Text in English, French, German and Italian.

Information Retrieval and Library Automation. Lomond Publications. • Monthly. $75.00 per year. Summarizes research events and literature worldwide.

International Spectrum: The Businessperson's Computer Magazine. IDBMA Inc. • Bimonthly. $40 Individuals. News magazine for the computer industry focusing on the PICK/UNIX/DOS-based computer operating environment.

IT Cost Management Strategies: The Planning Assistant for IT Directors. Computer Economics Inc. • Monthly. $495.00 per year. Newsletter for information technology professionals. Covers data processing costs, budgeting, financial management, and related topics.

Network Computing: Computing in a Network Environment. UBM L.L.C. • Semimonthly. Free to qualified personnel.

PCResource: The Hands-On Guide to Business and Personal Productivity. IDG Communications Inc. • Monthly. Educational magazine for home and small business users of personal computers.

St. Louis ComputerUser: A Business to Business Computing Publication. Creative Publications Ltd. • Monthly. $12 Individuals. A business publication on computers and office technology.

Smart Computing. Sandhills Publishing Co. • Monthly. $29.00 per year. Provides basic computer advice "in plain English." Includes reviews of hardware and software.

PRICE SOURCES

Computer Price Guide: The Blue Book of Used IBM Computer Prices. Computer Economics Inc. • Quarterly. $140.00 per year. Provides average prices of used IBM computer equipment, including "complete lists of obsolete IBM equipment." Includes a newsletter on trends in the used computer market. Edited for dealers, leasing firms, and business computer buyers.

RESEARCH CENTERS AND INSTITUTES

International Data Corp. 5 Speen St., Ste. 1, Framingham, MA 01701-4674. Phone: 800-343-4935 or (508)872-8200; Fax: (508)935-4015 or (508)935-4271; Email: idcinfo@idc.com • URL: http://www.idc.com • Private research firm specializing in market research related to computers, multimedia, and telecommunications.

Massachusetts Institute of Technology - Computer Science and Artificial Intelligence Laboratory. The Stata Ctr., Bldg. 32, 32 Vassar St., Cambridge, MA 02139. Phone: (617)253-5851; Fax: (617)258-8682; Email: rus@csail.mit.edu • URL: http://www.csail.mit.edu • Research is in four areas: Intelligent Systems; Parallel Systems; Systems, Languages, and Networks; and Theory. Emphasis is on the application of online computing.

Stanford University - Center for Integrated Systems. Paul G. Allen Bldg., MS 4070, 420 Via Palou Mall, Stanford, CA 94305-4070. Phone: (650)725-3621; Fax: (650)725-0991; Email: rdasher@cis.stanford.edu • URL: http://cis.stanford.edu • Research programs include manufacturing science, design science, computer architecture, semiconductor technology, and telecommunications.

STATISTICS SOURCES

Standard & Poor's Industry Surveys. Standard & Poor's Financial Services L.L.C. • Semiannual. $1,800.00. Two looseleaf volumes. Includes monthly *Supplements.* Provides detailed, individual surveys of 52 major industry groups. Each survey is revised on a semiannual basis. Also includes "Monthly Investment Review" (industry group investment analysis) and monthly "Trends & Projections" (economic analysis).

U.S. Industry and Trade Outlook. U.S. Department of Commerce National Technical Information Service. • Annual. Produced by the International Trade Administration, U.S. Department of Commerce, in a "public-private" partnership with DRI/McGraw-Hill and Standard & Poor's. Provides basic data, outlook for the current year, and "Long-Term Prospects" (five-year projections) for a wide variety of products and services. Includes high technology industries. Formerly *U.S. Industrial Outlook.*

TRADE/PROFESSIONAL ASSOCIATIONS

AFCOM. 9100 Chester Towne Centre Rd., West Chester, OH 45069. Phone: (714)643-8110 or (714)997-7966; Fax: (714)997-9743; Email: membership@afcom.com • URL: http://www.afcom.com • Data center, networking and enterprise systems management professionals from medium and large scale mainframe, midrange and client/server data centers worldwide. Works to meet the professional needs of the enterprise system management community. Provides information and support through educational events, research and assistance hotlines, and surveys.

Association for Computing Machinery. 2 Penn Plz., Ste. 701, New York, NY 10121-0701. Phone: 800-342-6626 or (212)626-0500 or (212)869-7440; Fax: (212)944-1318; Email: acmhelp@acm.org • URL: http://www.acm.org • Includes many Special Interest Groups.

Association of Information Technology Professionals. 15000 Commerce Parkway, Ste. C, Mount Laurel, NJ 08054. Phone: 800-224-9371; Fax: (856)439-0525; Email: aitp_hq@aitp.org • URL: http://www.aitp.org • Managerial personnel, staff, educators, and individuals interested in the management of information resources. Founder of the Certificate in Data Processing examination program, now administered by an intersociety organization. Maintains Legislative Communications Network. Professional education programs include EDP-oriented business and management principles self-study courses and a series of videotaped management development seminars. Sponsors student organizations around the country interested in information technology and encourages members to serve as counselors for the Scout computer merit badge. Conducts research projects, including a business information systems curriculum for two- and four-year colleges.

Society of Manufacturing Engineers - Computer and Automated Systems Techincal Group. 1 SME Dr., Dearborn, MI 48121. Phone: 800-733-4763 or (313)425-3000; Fax: (313)425-3400; Email: service@sme.org • URL: http://www.arcat.com/arcatcos/cos37/arc37031.html • Sponsored by the Society of Manufacturing Engineers. Formerly Computer and Automated Systems Association.

COMPUTERS, HOME

See MICROCOMPUTERS AND MINICOMPUTERS

COMPUTERS IN ACCOUNTING

ABSTRACTS AND INDEXES

Accounting and Tax Index. ProQuest L.L.C. • Quarterly. Indexes accounting, auditing, and taxation literature appearing in journals, books, pamphlets, conference proceedings, and newsletters.

Accounting Articles. Wolters Kluwer Law & Business CCH. • Monthly. $624. Covers accounting news.

Business Periodicals Index Retrospective. EBSCO Publishing Inc. • 11/year. Quarterly and annual cumulations.

Computer Science Index. EBSCO Publishing Inc. • Quarterly. $245 per year. Contains brief abstracts of book and periodical literature covering all phases of computing, including approximately 70 specific application areas.

Key Abstracts: Business Automation. Institution of Engineering and Technology. • Monthly. $1,138. Provides international coverage of journal and proceedings literature.

CD-ROM DATABASES

ABI/INFORM. ProQuest L.L.C. • Monthly. Provides CD-ROM indexing and abstracting of worldwide business literature. Archival discs are available from 1971. Formerly *ABI/INFORM OnDisc.*

Applied Science & Business Periodicals Retrospective. EBSCO Publishing Inc. • Includes citations for more than 3 million articles detailing events, issues, and trends in business and industry.

INTERNET DATABASES

Rutgers Accounting Web. Rutgers University Accounting Research Center. Phone: (973)353-5172; Fax: (973)353-1283 • URL: http://www.rutgers.edu/accounting • RAW Web site provides extensive links to sources of national and international accounting information, such as the Big Six accounting firms, the Financial Accounting Standards Board (FASB), SEC filings (EDGAR), journals, publishers, software, the International Accounting Network, and "Internet's largest list of accounting firms in USA." Searching is offered. Fees: Free.

ONLINE DATABASES

Wilson Business Abstracts Online. H.W. Wilson Co. • Indexes and abstracts 600 major business periodicals, plus the *Wall Street Journal* and the business section of the *New York Times.* Indexing is from 1982, abstracting from 1990, with the two newspapers included from 1993. Updated weekly. Inquire as to online cost and availability. (*Business Periodicals Index* without abstracts is also available online.).

PERIODICALS AND NEWSLETTERS

Accounting Technology: Turning Technology into Business Know How. SourceMedia Inc. • 11 times a year. $61.00 per year. Provides advice and information on computers and software for the accounting profession. Formerly *Computers in Accounting.*

CPA Practice Advisor. Cygnus Business Media. • Provides articles and reviews relating to computer technology and software for accountants.

CPA Technology and Internet Tax Advisor. Wolters Kluwer Law and Business. • Monthly. $261.00 per year. Newsletter. Describes hardware and software products and makes recommendations. Formerly *CPA Technology and Internet Advisor.*

Quantum PC Report for CPAs. QNet. • Monthly. $235.00 per year. Newsletter on personal computer software and hardware for the accounting profession.

RESEARCH CENTERS AND INSTITUTES

Accounting Research Program. UCLA Anderson School of Management. 110 Westwood Plz., Los

Angeles, CA 90095-1481. Phone: (310)206-8711; Fax: (310)825-3165 • URL: http://www.anderson.ucla.edu.

TRADE/PROFESSIONAL ASSOCIATIONS

American Institute of Certified Public Accountants. 1211 Avenue of the Americas, New York, NY 10036-8775. Phone: 888-777-7077 or (212)596-6200; Fax: (212)596-6213; Email: service@aicpa.org • URL: http://www.aicpa.org • Professional society of accountants certified by the states and territories. Responsibilities include establishing auditing and reporting standards; influencing the development of financial accounting standards underlying the presentation of U.S. corporate financial statements; preparing and grading the national Uniform CPA Examination for the state licensing bodies. Conducts research and continuing education programs and oversight of practice. Maintains over 100 committees including Accounting Standards, Accounting and Review Services, AICPA Effective Legislation Political Action, Auditing Standards, Taxation, Consulting Services, Professional Ethics, Quality Review, Women and Family Issues, and Information Technology.

Association for Accounting Administration. 136 S Keowee St., Dayton, OH 45402. Phone: (937)222-0030; Fax: (937)222-5794; Email: aaainfo@cpaadmin.org • URL: http://www.cpaadmin.org • Members are accounting and office systems executives.

COMPUTERS IN EDUCATION

See also MICROCOMPUTERS AND MINICOMPUTERS

ABSTRACTS AND INDEXES

Computer Science Index. EBSCO Publishing Inc. • Quarterly. $245 per year. Contains brief abstracts of book and periodical literature covering all phases of computing, including approximately 70 specific application areas.

ALMANACS AND YEARBOOKS

Educational Media and Technology Yearbook. Libraries Unlimited. • Annual. $80 print.

GENERAL WORKS

Computers in Education Today. Steven L. Mandell. Thomson West. • $52.00. Date not set.

ONLINE DATABASES

Education Index Online. H.W. Wilson Co. • Indexes a wide variety of periodicals related to schools, colleges, and education, 1984 to date. Monthly updates. Inquire as to online cost and availability.

PERIODICALS AND NEWSLETTERS

Computers in the Schools: The Interdisciplinary Journal of Practice, Theory, and Applied Research. The Haworth Press Inc. • Quarterly. $450.00 per year. Includes print and online editions.

Education Technology News: Insiders Guide to Multimedia in the K-12 Classroom. Business Publishers Inc. • Biweekly. $357.00 per year. Looseleaf service. Formerly *Education Computer News*.

Electronic Learning. Scholastic Inc. • Eight times a year. $19.95 per year. Includes classroom applications for computers. For teachers of grades K-12.

Mathematics and Computer Education. George M. Miller, editor. MATYC Journal, Inc. • Quarterly. $36 U.S.. Articles for high school and college teachers.

Multimedia Schools: A Practical Journal of Technology for Education including Multimedia, CD-ROM, Online and Internet and Hardware in K-12. Information Today, Inc. • Six times a year. $39.95 per year. Edited for school librarians, media center directors, computer coordinators, and others concerned with educational multimedia. Coverage includes the use of CD-ROM sources, the Internet, online services, and library technology.

T H E Journal. Ed Warnshuis Ltd. • 11 times a year. $29.00 per year. For educators of all levels.

Technology and Learning: The Leading Magazine of Electronic Education. UBM L.L.C. • Eight times a year. $29.95 per year. Covers all levels of computer/electronic education, from elementary to college. Formerly *Classroom Computer Learning*.

University Business: Solutions for Today's Higher Education. Educational Media L.L.C. • 10 times a year. $60.00 per year. Edited for college administrators, including managers of business services, finance, computing, and telecommunications. Includes information on relevant technological advances.

RESEARCH CENTERS AND INSTITUTES

Instructional Technology Center. University of Delaware, College of Education, 305 Willard Hall, Newark, DE 19716. Phone: (302)831-2394; Fax: (302)831-4110; Email: fth@udel.edu • URL: http://www.udel.edu.

COMPUTERS IN FINANCE

ABSTRACTS AND INDEXES

Business Periodicals Index Retrospective. EBSCO Publishing Inc. • 11/year. Quarterly and annual cumulations.

Computer Science Index. EBSCO Publishing Inc. • Quarterly. $245 per year. Contains brief abstracts of book and periodical literature covering all phases of computing, including approximately 70 specific application areas.

CD-ROM DATABASES

ABI/INFORM. ProQuest L.L.C. • Monthly. Provides CD-ROM indexing and abstracting of worldwide business literature. Archival discs are available from 1971. Formerly *ABI/INFORM OnDisc*.

Applied Science & Business Periodicals Retrospective. EBSCO Publishing Inc. • Includes citations for more than 3 million articles detailing events, issues, and trends in business and industry.

DIRECTORIES

Futures Magazine SourceBook: The Most Complete List of Exchanges, Companies, Regulators, Organizations, etc., Offering Products and Services to the Futures and Options Industry. Futures Magazine Inc. • Annual. $19.50. Provides information on commodity futures brokers, trading method services, publications, and other items of interest to futures traders and money managers.

INTERNET DATABASES

Futures Online. Futures Magazine Inc. Phone: (312)846-4600; Fax: (312)846-4638 • URL: http://www.futuresmag.com • Web site presents updates of *Futures* magazine and links to other futures-related sites.

ONLINE DATABASES

Banking Information Source. ProQuest L.L.C. • Provides indexing and abstracting of periodical and other literature from 1982 to date, with weekly updates. Covers the financial services industry: banks, savings institutions, investment houses, credit unions, insurance companies, and real estate organizations. Emphasis is on marketing and management. Inquire as to online cost and availability. (Formerly *FINIS: Financial Industry Information Service*.).

Wilson Business Abstracts Online. H.W. Wilson Co. • Indexes and abstracts 600 major business periodicals, plus the *Wall Street Journal* and the business section of the *New York Times*. Indexing is from 1982, abstracting from 1990, with the two newspapers included from 1993. Updated weekly. Inquire as to online cost and availability. (*Business Periodicals Index* without abstracts is also available online.).

PERIODICALS AND NEWSLETTERS

American Banker: The Financial Services Daily. SourceMedia Inc. • Daily. $895.00 per year. Provides news of banking, investment products, mortgages, credit unions, finance, bank technology, and legal developments.

Securities Technology Monitor. SourceMedia Inc. • Newsletter covers securities dealing and processing, including regulatory compliance, shareholder services, human resources, transaction clearing, and technology.

U.S. Banker. SourceMedia Inc. • Monthly. $65.00 per year. Edited for bank executives and managers. Covers a wide variety of banking and financial topics.

WebFinance. SourceMedia Inc. • Semimonthly. $995.00 per year. Newsletter (also available online at www.webfinance.net). Covers the Internet-based provision of online financial services by banks, online brokers, mutual funds, and insurance companies. Provides news stories, analysis, and descriptions of useful resources.

Windows in Financial Services. • Quarterly. $39.00 per year. Covers information technology applications and products for Microsoft Windows users in the financial sector.

COMPUTERS IN GOVERNMENT

ABSTRACTS AND INDEXES

Computer Science Index. EBSCO Publishing Inc. • Quarterly. $245 per year. Contains brief abstracts of book and periodical literature covering all phases of computing, including approximately 70 specific application areas.

Sage Public Administration Abstracts. EBSCO Publishing Inc. • Titles include Journal of Public Economics, Public Administration, and Public Administratioin Review.

CD-ROM DATABASES

NTIS Database. Ovid Technologies Inc. • Quarterly. $2,850.00 per year. Guide to over 2 million bibliographic entries. Compiled by the U.S. National Technical Information Service.

PAIS International. ProQuest L.L.C. • Monthly. $1,995.00 per year. Contains over 650,000 citations to the literature of contemporary social, political, and economic issues.

DIRECTORIES

Directory of Automated Criminal Justice Information Systems. U.S. Bureau of Justice Statistics. • $60. Covers: Over 1,870 computerized information systems serving over 700 police, courts, state and local government judicial and correctional agencies. Entries include: Description of system or agency; acronym; type of system; functions; hardware and software configuration; function names, addresses, and phone numbers of agency contact.

PERIODICALS AND NEWSLETTERS

Federal Computer Week: The Newspaper for the Government Systems Community. FCW Government Technology Group. • 41 times a year. $95.00 per year.

Governing: The States and Localities. • Monthly. $39.95 per year. Edited for state and local government officials. Covers finance, office management, computers, telecommunications, environmental concerns, etc.

Government Computer News: The Newspaper Serving Computer Users Throughout the Federal Government. Business Information, Inc..

Government Executive: Federal Government's Business Magazine. National Journal Group Inc. • Monthly. $48 Individuals. Includes management of computerized information systems in the federal government.

Government Technology: Solutions for State and Local Government in the Information Age. e.Republic Inc. • Monthly.

COMPUTERS IN INVESTING

See COMPUTERS IN FINANCE

COMPUTERS, PERSONAL

See MICROCOMPUTERS AND MINICOMPUTERS

COMPUTERS, PORTABLE

See PORTABLE COMPUTERS

CONCESSIONS

See also FAIRS; FRANCHISES

TRADE/PROFESSIONAL ASSOCIATIONS

National Association of Concessionaires. 180 N Michigan Ave., Ste. 2215, Chicago, IL 60601. Phone: (312)236-3858; Fax: (312)236-7809; Email: info@naconline.org • URL: http://www.naconline.org • Formerly Popcorn and Concessions Association.

National Park Hospitality Association. 1200 G St. NW, Ste. 650, Washington, DC 20005. Phone: (202)682-9530; Fax: (202)682-9529 • URL: http://parkpartners.org • Represents private concessionaires operating in the U.S. national parks. Acts as liaison between members and the National Park Service and Congress.

CONCILIATION, INDUSTRIAL

See ARBITRATION

CONCRETE INDUSTRY

See also BUILDING INDUSTRY; CEMENT INDUSTRY

ALMANACS AND YEARBOOKS

The Concrete Yearbook. EMAP Construction Ltd. • Annual. $100.00.

DIRECTORIES

Masonry Buyer's Guide. Mason Contractors Association of America. • Lists manufacturers or suppliers of products and services related to masonry construction.

FINANCIAL RATIOS

Annual Statement Studies. Risk Management Association. • Annual. Compiled from over 280,000 financial statements.

Annual Statement Studies: Industry Default Probabilities and Cash Flow Measures. Risk Management Association. • Annual. $405 Nonmembers. Serves as a companion volume to the original *Annual Statement Studies*. Gives probability of default estimates on a percentage scale for more than 450 industries. Includes changes in position year-by-year for eight financial statement line items and provides percentage measures of cash flow.

HANDBOOKS AND MANUALS

ACI Manual of Concrete Practice. American Concrete Institute. • $846.50 Nonmembers Print (7 Volume Set). Contains all of the widely used ACI concrete and masonry code requirements, specifications, guides and reports.

PERIODICALS AND NEWSLETTERS

Concrete International. American Concrete Institute. • Monthly. $126.00 per year. Covers practical technology, industry news, and business management relating to the concrete construction industry.

The Concrete Producer. DoveTale Publishers. • Monthly. $27 Individuals. Covers the production and marketing of various concrete products, including precast and prestressed concrete. Formerly *Aberdeen's Concrete Trader*.

Concrete Products. Primedia Business Magazines and Media. • Monthly. $61.00 per year. Free to qualified personnel; others, $61.00 per year.

RESEARCH CENTERS AND INSTITUTES

University of Illinois at Urbana-Champaign - Center for Cement Composite Materials. 2129 Newmark Civil Engineering Laboratory, 205 Mathews Ave., Urbana, IL 61801. Phone: (217)333-2544 or (217)333-6900; Fax: (217)265-8040; Email: lstruble@uiuc.edu • URL: http://ccm.cee.uiuc.edu • Concrete, cement, and their constituent materials, including comprehensive interdisciplinary studies of advanced cement-based materials. Center works with high-performance materials such as DSP cements, MDF cements, and magnesium phosphate cements. Expertise includes electron microscopy, rheology, computer-based modeling, fracture, cement chemistry, and microstructure characterization.

TRADE/PROFESSIONAL ASSOCIATIONS

American Concrete Institute. 38800 Country Club Dr., Farmington Hills, MI 48331-3439. Phone: (248)848-3700; Fax: (248)848-3701; Email: ann.daugherty@acifoundation.org • URL: http://www.concrete.org • Technical and educational society of engineers, architects, contractors, educators, and others interested in improving techniques of design construction and maintenance of concrete products and structures. Offers certification program.

National Concrete Masonry Association. 13750 Sunrise Valley Dr., Herndon, VA 20171. Phone: (703)713-1900; Fax: (703)713-1910; Email: info@ncma.org • URL: http://www.ncma.org • Manufacturers of concrete masonry units (concrete blocks), segmental retaining wall units and paving block; associate members are machinery, cement and aggregate manufacturers. Conducts testing and research on masonry units and masonry assemblies. Compiles statistics.

National Ready Mixed Concrete Association. 900 Spring St., Silver Spring, MD 20910. Phone: (240)485-1139 • URL: http://www.nrmca.org • Concrete plant manufacturers. Develops engineering standards with a view toward simplification and standardization of sizes, capacities, and other criteria associated with the manufacture of concrete plants. Performs services leading to higher quality concrete plant equipment.

CONDIMENTS INDUSTRY

See SPICE INDUSTRY

CONDOMINIUMS

See also APARTMENT HOUSES; HOUSING; REAL ESTATE BUSINESS

CD-ROM DATABASES

Sourcebooks America CD-ROM. CACI Marketing Systems. • Annual. $1,250.00. Provides the CD-ROM version of *The Sourcebook of ZIP Code Demographics: Census Edition* and *The Sourcebook of County Demographics: Census Edition*.

PERIODICALS AND NEWSLETTERS

CondoBusiness. MediaEdge Inc. • Monthly. $55.00 per year. Covers condominum development and administration industries.

Mortgage and Real Estate Executives Report. Thomson West. • Source of ideas and new updates. Covers the latest opportunities and developments.

STATISTICS SOURCES

American Housing Survey for the United States in (year). U. S. Government Printing Office. • Biennial. $51.00. Issued by the U. S. Census Bureau (www.census.gov). Covers both owner-occupied and renter-occupied housing. Includes data on such factors as condition of building, type of mortgage, utility costs, and housing occupied by minorities. (Current Housing Reports, H150.).

TRADE/PROFESSIONAL ASSOCIATIONS

Community Associations Institute. 6402 Arlington Blvd., Ste. 500, Falls Church, VA 22042. Phone: 888-224-4321 or (703)970-9220; Fax: (703)970-9558; Email: cai-info@caionline.org • URL: http://www.caionline.org • Condominium and homeowner associations, cooperatives, and association-governed planned communities of all sizes and architectural types; community or property managers and management firms; individual homeowners; community association managers and management firms; public officials; and lawyers, accountants, engineers, reserve specialists, builder/developers and other providers of professional services and products for CAs. Seeks to educate and represent America's 250,000 residential condominium, cooperative and homeowner associations and related professionals and service providers. Aims to foster vibrant, responsive, competent community associations that promote harmony, community and responsible leadership.

National Association of Realtors. 430 N Michigan Ave., Chicago, IL 60611-4087. Phone: 800-874-6500; Email: infocentral@realtors.org • URL: http://www.realtor.org • Federation of 54 state and territory associations and 1,860 local real estate boards whose members are real estate brokers and agents; terms are registered by the association in the U.S. Patent and Trademark Office and in the states. Promotes education, high professional standards and modern techniques in specialized real estate work such as brokerage, appraisal, property management, land development, industrial real estate, farm brokerage and counseling. Conducts research programs.

CONFECTIONERY INDUSTRY

See CANDY INDUSTRY

CONFERENCE MANAGEMENT

See MEETING MANAGEMENT

CONFERENCES, WORKSHOPS, AND SEMINARS

See also CONVENTIONS; SALES CONVENTIONS

DIRECTORIES

Directory of Festivals, Schools and Workshops. Chamber Music America. • Annual. Covers: over

150 chamber music workshops and schools for students, young professionals, and adult amateurs; international listings. Entries include: Name, location or address, description of program and participants sought, procedure for auditions, type of accommodations and recreational facilities, dates, age requirements, and fees as of spring 2000.

Directory of Training. Training Information Network Ltd. • Annual. $170 Set. A three-volume set: "Directory of Computer Training" lists 5,000 computer courses from over 500 training companies; "Directory of Management Training" describes more than 5,000 management and supervisory courses; and "Directory of Multi-Media Training" lists 2,000 computer-based, interactive video, self-study, and other training packages; coverage includes the United Kingdom. Database includes: Lists of consultants, training venues, training associations, and sources of training advice; glossaries. Entries include: Company or institute name, address, phone, contact name, company profile; title, cost, duration, frequency, and location of each course offered.

Instrumentalist--Directory of Summer Music Camps, Clinics, and Workshops Issue. Instrumentalist Co. • Annual. Publication includes: List of nearly 250 summer music camps, clinics, and workshops in the United States; limited Canadian and foreign coverage. Entries include: Camp name, location, name of director, opening and closing dates, tuition fees, courses offered.

Short Courses and Seminars--The Who's Who of Training in Canada. Development Publications Inc. • Semiannual. $59. Covers: more than 3,000 business and management courses, seminars, and workshops offered in Canada on subjects such as accounting, communications, conflict management, human relations, and supervisory development. Each issue lists programs for the following six months. Entries include: Name of program, sponsors, location, date, fees.

Trade Shows Worldwide. Cengage Learning Inc. • 2013. $645.00. 31st edition. Provides detailed information from over 75 countries on more than 10,000 trade shows and exhibitions. Separate sections are provided for trade shows/exhibitions, for sponsors/organizers, and for services, facilities, and information sources. Indexing is by date, location, subject, name, and keyword.

HANDBOOKS AND MANUALS

Seminar Promoting. Entrepreneur Press. • Looseleaf. $59.50. A practical guide to starting a seminar promotion business. Covers profit potential, start-up costs, market size evaluation, owner's time required, site selection, pricing, accounting, advertising, promotion, etc. (Start-Up Business Guide No. E1071.).

INTERNET DATABASES

Trade Show Center. Global Sources/Trade Media Holdings Ltd. Phone: (656)574-2800; Email: service@globalsources.com • URL: http://www.globalsources.com/TRADESHW/TRDSHFRM.HTM • Free Web site provides current, detailed information on more than 1,000 major trade shows worldwide, including events in the U. S., but with an emphasis on "Asia and Greater China." Searching is offered by product, supplier, country, and month of year. Includes links to "Trade Information.".

PERIODICALS AND NEWSLETTERS

The Meeting Professional. Meeting Professionals International. • Monthly. $99 Nonmembers. Published for professionals in the meeting and convention industry. Contains news, features, and how-to's for domestic and international meetings management. Formerly *Meeting Manager*.

Scientific Meetings. Scientific Meetings Publications. • Quarterly. $85.00 per year. Provides information on forthcoming scientific, technical, medical, health, engineering and management meetings held throughout the world.

TRADE/PROFESSIONAL ASSOCIATIONS

Association of Danish Business Economists. PO Box 2043, 1012 Copenhagen, Denmark. Phone: 45 33141446; Fax: 45 33141149; Email: info@c3.dk • URL: http://www.c3.dk • Business administration alumni of Danish schools and universities. Sponsors educational courses, seminars, and forums; conducts research programs. Operates placement service.

CARTHA. 33 Buchanan Ct., Iowa City, IA 52246. Phone: (319)248-9625; Email: cartha.global@gmail.com • URL: http://www.cartha.org • Aims to strengthen academic-practitioner partnerships. Seeks to train, build and empower networks of professionals. Enhances the positive impact of technological and social innovations in the lives of individuals. Provides education, training and professional development programs.

Estonian Business Association. Sadama 5/7, EE-10111 Tallinn, Estonia. Email: esea@esea.ee • URL: http://www.esea.ee • Fosters active business community in the country. Develops cooperation with foreign business associations. Keeps its members updated through local and international seminars and workshops. Meets with state authorities to advance the organization's interests.

European Money and Finance Forum. c/o Oesterreichische Nationalbank, Otto Wagner-Platz 3, A-1090 Vienna, Austria. Phone: 43 1 404207206; Fax: 43 1 404207298; Email: suerf@oenb.at • URL: http://www.suerf.org • Represents academics, bank economists, and interested individuals in 37 countries. Develops contacts among members in order to discuss monetary and financial questions. Sponsors research in monetary, economic, and financial areas. Aims to create an active network between professional economists, financial practitioners, central bankers and academics for the analysis and mutual understanding of monetary and financial issues. Sponsors conferences, seminars, workshops and lectures. Publishes study volumes each year.

Finance and Leasing Association. Imperial House, 2nd Fl., 15-19 Kingsway, London WC2B 6UN, United Kingdom. Phone: 44 20 78366511; Fax: 44 20 74209600; Email: info@fla.org.uk • URL: http://www.financeleasingassociation.co.uk • Trade association representing the UK asset, consumer, and motor finance sectors. Provides high-level representation and lobbying at both national and EU levels, supported by technical information and industry statistics. Complies with the association's code of conduct, which is supported by their conciliation and arbitration schemes. Provides a focus and forum for the industry, and has a high level of member involvement in its many working groups. Organizes conferences, workshops, and training courses.

Institute of Directors - England. 116 Pall Mall, London SW1Y 5ED, United Kingdom. Phone: 44 20 77668866; Fax: 44 20 77668833; Email: enquiries@iod.com • URL: http://www.iod.com/Home • Represents company directors and other people holding a similar position in industry, commerce, the professions or government organizations. Aims to advance company directors' interests and foster free enterprise. Includes services to members: branch network, professional development activities and conferences, information and advisory services. Provides meeting rooms and restaurant facilities to its members.

Japan Management Association. Convention Div., 3-1-22 Shiba-koen, Minato-ku, Tokyo 105-8522, Japan. Phone: 81 3 34346211 or 81 334 341246; Fax: 81 3 34341087 or 81 334 340269; Email: global@jma.or.jp • URL: http://www.jma.or.jp • Japanese corporations and individuals. Management education organization working to develop and conduct public business education and training programs including seminars, conferences, symposia, and overseas study tours. Makes available correspondence courses, audiovisual and computer-assisted instruction programs, in-company training programs, and cruise seminars. Conducts research and disseminates information on topics including white-collar productivity in Japan, creativity development in business and industry, and globally oriented management reform. Maintains liaison with similar organizations worldwide. Organizes conferences and exhibitions for trade associations. Maintains 14 interdisciplinary divisions and 13 supporting departments. Provides management consulting service; operates speakers' bureau.

Paraguayan Industrial Union. Av. Sacramento 945, Asuncion, Paraguay. Phone: 595 21 606988 • URL: http://www.uip.org.py • Promotes the economic and social development of Paraguay. Organizes conference and seminars.

CONGLOMERATES

See CORPORATIONS

CONGRESS

See UNITED STATES CONGRESS

CONSERVATION

See NATURAL RESOURCES

CONSTRUCTION CONTRACTS

See BUILDING CONTRACTS

CONSTRUCTION, ELECTRICAL

See ELECTRICAL CONSTRUCTION INDUSTRY

CONSTRUCTION EQUIPMENT

See also BUILDING INDUSTRY; CIVIL ENGINEERING; HOUSING

DIRECTORIES

ProSales Buyer's Guide. DoveTale Publishers. • Annual. Price on application. A directory of equipment for professional builders.

Tools of the Trade Annual Buyers Guide. DoveTale Publishers. • Annual. Price on application. A directory of tools for the construction industry.

FINANCIAL RATIOS

Annual Statement Studies. Risk Management Association. • Annual. Compiled from over 280,000 financial statements.

Annual Statement Studies: Industry Default Probabilities and Cash Flow Measures. Risk Management Association. • Annual. $405 Nonmembers. Serves as a companion volume to the original *Annual Statement Studies*. Gives probability of default estimates on a percentage scale for more than 450 industries. Includes changes in position year-by-year for eight financial statement line items and provides percentage measures of cash flow.

GENERAL WORKS

Cost of Doing Business. Associated Equipment Distributors. • Annual. $595 Members nonparticipants. For construction equipment distributors covering business costs, sales, and financial data.

INTERNET DATABASES

Manufacturing Profiles. U. S. Bureau of the Census. Phone: (301)763-4636 or (301)763-4100; Fax: (301)763-4794; Email: webmaster@census.gov • URL: http://www.census.gov/prod/www/abs/mfg-prof.html • The Census Bureau makes available free on PDF (Portable Document Format) an annual consolidation of the entire Current Industrial Report series, presenting "all the data compiled." Contains statistics on production, shipments, inventories, consumption, exports, imports, and orders for a wide variety of manufactured products.

PERIODICALS AND NEWSLETTERS

Building Business & Apartment Management. Home Builders Association of Southeastern Michigan. • Monthly. $48 Individuals. Construction and apartment industry magazine.

Construction Equipment Distribution. Associated Equipment Distributors. • Monthly. Members, $20.00 per year; non-members, $40.00 per year.

Construction Equipment Operation and Maintenance. Construction Publications Inc. • Bimonthly. $12.00 per year. Information for users of construction equipment and industry news.

Equipment Today. Cygnus Business Media Inc. • Monthly. $65 Individuals. Includes annual *Product* issue.

STATISTICS SOURCES

U.S. Industry and Trade Outlook. U.S. Department of Commerce National Technical Information Service. • Annual. Produced by the International Trade Administration, U.S. Department of Commerce, in a "public-private" partnership with DRI/McGraw-Hill and Standard & Poor's. Provides basic data, outlook for the current year, and "Long-Term Prospects" (five-year projections) for a wide variety of products and services. Includes high technology industries. Formerly *U.S. Industrial Outlook*.

TRADE/PROFESSIONAL ASSOCIATIONS

Associated Equipment Distributors. 600 22nd St., Ste. 220, Oak Brook, IL 60523. Phone: 800-388-0650 or (630)574-0650; Fax: (630)574-0132; Email: info@aednet.org • URL: http://www.aednet.org • Represents distributors and manufacturers of agriculture, and construction, mining, logging, forestry, public works and road maintenance equipment in the U.S., Canada, and overseas. Includes activities such as industry information and statistics, educational programs on customer service, financial management, rental management, sales management, and service and parts management program for younger executives. Maintains Washington, DC office. Oversees AED Foundation which offers industry educational programs and career/vocational services. Offers group and business insurance to members; conducts ongoing industry relations program with construction equipment manufacturers and users.

Association of Equipment Manufacturers. 6737 W Washington St., Ste. 2400, Milwaukee, WI 53214-5647. Phone: 866-AEM-0442 or (414)272-0943; Fax: (414)272-1170; Email: aem@aem.org • URL: http://www.aem.org • Provides business development services on a global basis for companies that manufacture equipment, products and services used worldwide in the agricultural, construction, industrial, mining, forestry, and utility fields.

CONSTRUCTION ESTIMATING

See ESTIMATING

CONSTRUCTION INDUSTRIES, ELECTRICAL

See ELECTRICAL CONSTRUCTION INDUSTRY

CONSTRUCTION INDUSTRY

See BUILDING INDUSTRY

CONSULAR SERVICE

See DIPLOMATIC AND CONSULAR SERVICE

CONSULTANTS

See also ENGINEERING CONSULTANTS; MANAGEMENT CONSULTANTS

DIRECTORIES

Bridal Consultants Directory. InfoGroup Inc. • Annual. Number of listings: 6,167. Entries include: Name, address, phone, size of advertisement, name of owner or manager, number of employees, year first in "Yellow Pages." Compiled from telephone company "Yellow Pages," nationwide.

Consultants & Consulting Organizations Directory (CCOD). Cengage Learning Inc. • Annual. $1,455 Individuals paperback. 2014. 39th edition. Over 26,000 firms, individuals, and organizations active in consulting. eBook available.

Consultants (Tax) Directory. InfoGroup Inc. • Annual. Number of listings: 63,898. Entries include: Name, address, phone, size of advertisement, name of owner or manager, number of employees, year first in "Yellow Pages." Compiled from telephone company "Yellow Pages," nationwide.

Directory of Consulting Offices in Arab Countries. Arab Industrial Development and Metrology Organization League of Arab States. • Irregular.

Directory of European Information Brokers and Consultants. Information Marketmakers Ltd. • Annual. $59. Covers: information systems brokers and consultants in Europe. Entries include: Company name, address, phone, name and title of contact, names and titles of key personnel, subject expertise, and description of products and services.

The Expert Marketplace. Dun & Bradstreet Inc. • Database covers: More than 200,000 business consulting firms, business case studies and business improvement articles. Entries include: Consulting firm name, address, phone, fax, services, areas of expertise, executive name and title, staff, e-mail address, client list.

Facilities Design & Management--Directory of Consultants & Service Firms Issue. Bpi Communications Inc. • Annual. $7. Publication includes: Listing of firms offering products, services, and consulting services to facilities designers and managers.

Gevers International Consultants. Gevers International Consultants. • Annual. $75 Individuals. Covers: 10,000 consulting firms, including accountants, property consultants, lawyers, management consultants, and tax consultants in 124 countries. Entries include: Company name, address, phone, telex number, description, associate firms, language, clients, countries covered.

National Directory of Corporate Distress Specialists. Lustig Data Research Inc. • Annual. $245. Covers: 1,830 organizations and over 4,000 professionals providing 20 types of services in bankruptcies, workouts, turnarounds, and distressed securities investing, including attorneys, accountants, crisis managers, financial advisors, turnaround consultants, valuation experts, financing sources, investors, in-house workout officers, appraisers, auctioneers, liquidators, PR/crisis communications experts, real estate managers, etc. Entries include: Organization name, address, phone, fax, toll-free phone, year founded, parent company, department name, other offices, staff size, size of cases, types of representations, geographical area served, industry specializations, services offered, institutional clients, transaction history, party represented, key personnel, titles.

Nelson Information's Directory of Pension Fund Consultants. Nelson Information. • Annual. $995. Covers the pension plan sponsor industry. More than 325 worldwide consulting firms are described. Formerly *Nelson's Guide to Pension Fund Consultants*.

Plunkett's Consulting Industry Almanac. Plunkett Research Ltd. • $349.99 Individuals pint + online. Covers: Leading companies that provide consulting in areas including marketing, technology, management, manufacturing, and health care. Entries include: Name, address, phone, fax, and key executives. Also includes analysis and information on trends, technology, and statistics in the field.

Professional Consulting Services: Industry Sector Profile. Philippine-German Export Development Project Philippine Bureau of Export Trade Promotion. • Publication includes: Companies exporting professional consulting services from the Philippines. Entries include: Company name, address, phone, fax, name and title of contact, type of business, year established, subsidiary and branch names and locations, financial data, number of employees, government registrations, professional memberships, bank references, supply capability, export experience, business plan. Principal content of publication is an overview of the business environment and professional consulting services industry in the Philippines.

Qualitative Research Consultants Association--Membership Directory. Qualitative Research Consultants Association. • Annual. Covers: About 600 qualitative market and social researchers and consultants. Entries include: Company name, address, phone, name of contact, specialties, areas.

Services et Expertise--Conseil du Quebec. Quebec Dans Le Monde. • Biennial. $63.95 Individuals. Covers: Approximately 1,600 organizations and consultants who provide business counsel. Entries include: name, address, phone.

INTERNET DATABASES

FindLaw: Internet Legal Resources. FindLaw. 610 Opperman Dr., Eagan, MN 55123. Phone: 800-455-4565 or (408)524-4799 or (650)940-4300; Fax: (800)392-6206 or (408)524-4798; Email: findlawexperience@thomsonreuters.com • URL: http://www.findlaw.com • Web site provides a wide variety of information and links relating to laws, law schools, professional development, lawyers, the U. S. Supreme Court, consultants (experts), law reviews, legal news, etc. Online searching is provided. Fees: Free.

PERIODICALS AND NEWSLETTERS

Consultants News: Independent Commentary on Management Consulting Since 1970. Kennedy Information Inc. • Monthly. $295.00 per year. Newsletter. News and ideas for management consultants.

TRADE/PROFESSIONAL ASSOCIATIONS

APQC. 123 N Post Oak Ln., Houston, TX 77024. Phone: 800-776-9676 or (713)681-4020; Fax: (713)681-8578; Email: apqcinfo@apqc.org • URL: http://www.apqc.org • Resource for process and performance improvement. Helps organizations adapt to rapidly changing environments, build new and better ways to work, and succeed in a competitive marketplace. Focuses on productivity, knowledge management, benchmarking, and quality improvement initiatives. Works with member organizations to identify best practices, discover effective methods of improvement, broadly disseminate findings, and connect individuals with one another and the knowledge and tools they need to succeed. Serves approximately 500 organizations worldwide in all sectors of business, education, and government.

Association of Proposal Management Professionals. PO Box 77272, Washington, DC 20013-8272. Phone: (202)450-2549; Email: rick.harris@apmp.org • URL: http://www.apmp.org • Proposal managers, proposal planners, proposal writers, consultants, desktop publishers and marketing managers. Encourages unity and cooperation among industry professionals. Seeks to broaden member knowledge and skills through developmental, educational and social activities. Maintains speakers' bureau. Provides current information and developments in the field.

BPM-Focus. 3640-B3 N Federal Hwy., No. 421, Lighthouse Point, FL 33064. Phone: (954)688-4922; Fax: (954)758-7219; Email: info@bpmfocus.org • URL: http://www.bpmfocus.org • Identifies and clarifies issues that are common to users of workflow, electronic commerce, knowledge management and those who are in the process of re-engineering their organizations.

Consultants Association for the Natural Products Industry. PO Box 4014, Clovis, CA 93613-4014. Phone: (559)325-7192; Email: info@cani-consultants.org • URL: http://www.cani-consultants.org • Works to enhance the growth and integrity of the natural products industry. Offers professional services to help manufacturers, distributors, retailers, and non-profit organizations thrive in the nutraceutical marketplace. Promotes education and ethical standards for the improvement of manufacturing, distribution, marketing and advertising to help the industry develop safe and beneficial products for the public.

Council for Ethical Leadership. 1 College and Main, Columbus, OH 43209. Phone: (614)236-7222 • URL: http://www.businessethics.org • Leaders in business, education, and the professions. Seeks to "strengthen the ethical fabric of business and economic life." Facilitates the development of international networks of businesspeople interested in economic ethics; sponsors educational programs and develops and distributes educational materials; advises and supports communities wishing to implement character educational programs; makes available consulting services.

Information Technology Alliance. 23940 N 73rd Pl., Scottsdale, AZ 85255. Phone: (480)515-2003; Fax: (602)294-2399 • URL: http://www.italliance.com • Represents mid-market technology professionals, consultants, and product/service providers in North America. Aims to create a community where members share information and build relationships that improve the way they do business with their clients. Protects the quality of the profession and promotes public welfare.

MRA - The Management Association. N19 W24400 Riverwood Dr., Waukesha, WI 53188. Phone: 800-488-4845 or (262)523-9090; Email: businesssolutions@mranet.org • URL: http://www.mranet.org • Aims to maximize performance of organizations and employees. Provides information and communications, training, transactional HR solutions, and high-level business and human resource consulting; members range in size from two employees to 10,000 and represent manufacturing service, healthcare, and finance.

National Alliance of Independent Crop Consultants. 349 E Nolley Dr., Collierville, TN 38017. Phone: (901)861-0511; Fax: (901)861-0512; Email: jonesnaicc@aol.com • URL: http://www.naicc.org • Independent crop consultants and contract researchers united to promote agriculture and professionalism in the field. Seeks to: assist in the formation of state and national policies relating to agricultural production and of crop management philosophies; support agricultural crop producers by the most ecologically sound, environmentally safe, and economical means. Encourages members to expand their knowledge concerning crop management practices and techniques; participates in research in this area. Provides assistance in the formation of state and regional consultant organizations; offers referral system for members. Compiles statistics; sponsors educational programs.

National Association of Real Estate Consultants. 404 4th Ave., Lewiston, ID 83501. Phone: (208)746-7963; Fax: (208)746-4760 • URL: http://www.narec.com • Works to assist real estate professionals in reframing their focus as real estate consultants to better meet the needs of today's savvy consumer. Helps promote alternative or fee-for-service real estate business models.

National Business Incubation Association. 340 W State St., Unit 25, Athens, OH 45701-1565. Phone: (740)593-4331; Fax: (740)593-1996; Email: info@nbia.org • URL: http://www.nbia.org • Incubator developers and managers; corporate joint venture partners, venture capital investors; economic development professionals. (Incubators are business assistance programs providing business consulting services and financing assistance to start-up and fledgling companies.) Helps newly formed businesses to succeed. Educates businesses and investors on incubator benefits; offers specialized training in incubator formation and management. Conducts research and referral services; compiles statistics; maintains speakers' bureau; publishes information relevant to business incubation and growing companies.

Turnaround Management Association. 150 N Wacker Dr., Ste. 1900, Chicago, IL 60606. Phone: (312)578-6900; Fax: (312)578-8336; Email: info@turnaround.org • URL: http://www.turnaround.org/Default.aspx • Practitioners (interim managers, consultants, corporate managers and professional advisors), academics, students, attorneys and judges, commercial lenders and legislative personnel. Promotes the image and credibility of the turnaround profession; fosters professional development and networking opportunities for turnaround executives; serves as a clearinghouse of information and research pertinent to the profession. Conducts networking forums; offers educational and credentialing programs.

CONSULTANTS, ENGINEERING

See ENGINEERING CONSULTANTS

CONSULTANTS, MANAGEMENT

See MANAGEMENT CONSULTANTS

CONSUMER AFFAIRS

ABSTRACTS AND INDEXES

Business Periodicals Index Retrospective. EBSCO Publishing Inc. • 11/year. Quarterly and annual cumulations.

NTIS Alerts: Business & Economics. U.S. Department of Commerce National Technical Information Service. • Biweekly. $130 per year. Covers consumer affairs, minority enterprises, marketing and economics, international commerce, banking, and finance.

Readers' Guide to Periodical Literature. EBSCO Publishing Inc. • Provides indexing for over 400 periodicals dating back to 1983.

CD-ROM DATABASES

Newspaper Abstracts Ondisc. ProQuest L.L.C. • Monthly. $2,950.00 per year (covers 1989 to date; archival discs are available for 1985-88). Provides cover-to-cover CD-ROM indexing and abstracting of 19 major newspapers, including the *New York Times*, *Wall Street Journal*, *Washington Post*, *Chicago Tribune*, and *Los Angeles Times*.

Readers' Guide to Periodical Literature. EBSCO Publishing Inc. • Provides indexing for over 400 periodicals dating back to 1983.

ONLINE DATABASES

Wilson Business Abstracts Online. H.W. Wilson Co. • Indexes and abstracts 600 major business periodicals, plus the *Wall Street Journal* and the business section of the *New York Times*. Indexing is from 1982, abstracting from 1990, with the two newspapers included from 1993. Updated weekly. Inquire as to online cost and availability. (*Business Periodicals Index* without abstracts is also available online.).

RESEARCH CENTERS AND INSTITUTES

American Council on Consumer Awareness, Inc. 1251 Kent St., St. Paul, MN 55117-4263. Phone: (651)489-2835; Fax: (651)489-5650; Email: bennerassociates@aol.com.

Center for Consumer Research. University of Florida, Gainesville, FL 32611-7150. Phone: (352)392-2397; Fax: (352)392-2086; Email: joel.cohen@cba.ufl.edu • URL: http://www.cba.ufl.edu/.

Consumer Research Center. The Conference Board, 845 3rd Ave., New York, NY 10022. Phone: (212)339-0232; Fax: (212)836-9754; Email: crc@conference-board.org • URL: http://www.conference-board.org/economics/crc.cfm • Conducts research on the consumer market, including elderly and working women segments.

TRADE/PROFESSIONAL ASSOCIATIONS

American Council on Consumer Interests. PO Box 2528, Tarpon Springs, FL 34688-2528. Phone: (727)493-2131 • URL: http://www.consumerinterests.org • Formerly Council on Consumer Information.

Consumer Federation of America. 1620 I St. NW, Ste. 200, Washington, DC 20006. Phone: (202)387-6121 or (202)737-0766; Email: cfa@consumerfed.org • URL: http://www.consumerfed.org • Members are national, regional, state, and local consumer groups. Absorbed Electric Consumers Information Committee.

National Consumers League. 1701 K St. NW, Ste. 1200, Washington, DC 20006. Phone: (202)835-3323; Fax: (202)835-0747; Email: info@nclnet.org • URL: http://www.nclnet.org • Identifies, protects, represents, and advances the economic and social interests of consumers and workers. Addresses issues including healthcare, food and drug safety, and consumer fraud. Promotes fairness and safety at the marketplace and in the workplace. Coordinates the Alliance Against Fraud in Telemarketing and the Child Labor Coalition. Administers the National Fraud Information Center and Internet Fraud Watch.

Public Citizen. 1600 20th St. NW, Washington, DC 20009-1001. Phone: (202)588-1000; Email: member@citizen.org • URL: http://www.citizen.org • Formed by Ralph Nader to support the work of citizen advocates. Areas of focus include: consumer rights in the marketplace, safe products, a healthful environment and workplace, clean and safe energy sources, corporate and government accountability, and citizen empowerment. Methods for change include lobbying, litigation, monitoring government agencies, research, and public education including special reports, periodicals, expert testimony, and news media coverage. Acquires funding primarily through direct mail and also through payment for publications and court awards.

CONSUMER ATTITUDES

See CONSUMER SURVEYS

CONSUMER BUYING POWER

See also PURCHASING POWER

E-BOOKS

American Buyers: Demographics of Shopping. Cengage Learning Inc. • 2010. eBook. Published by New Strategist Publications. While most businesses have a feel for what is happening in their own establishment, this work lets them see the big picture beyond their walls or web site. Its weekly and quarterly data show you how many households buy certain products and services and how much buyers pay for them, all broken down by demographics.

TRADE/PROFESSIONAL ASSOCIATIONS

Buying Influence. 801 W 47th St., Ste. 110, Country Club Plz., Kansas City, MO 64112. Phone: (816)931-7896; Email: info@buyinginfluence.com • Seeks to help consumers harness their buying power so that corporations make more socially responsible business decisions. Conducts corporate reviews of publicly-traded companies. Provides a forum for online discussions of issues concerning consumers and businesses.

CONSUMER CREDIT

See also CREDIT

CD-ROM DATABASES

OECD Statistical Compendium. Organization for Economic Cooperation and Development. • Semiannual. $1,905.00 per year for 1 to 10 users. CD-ROM contains more than 730,000 monthly, quarterly, and annual time series for OECD countries, 1960 to date. Includes fully searchable data on agriculture, food, economic indicators, national accounts, employment, energy, finance, industry, technology, and foreign trade. Results can be displayed in various forms.

DIRECTORIES

Card Security & Fraud Prevention Sourcebook. Thomson Financial Inc. • Annual. $245 Individuals. Covers: Credit card, debit card, and internet security products and services. Entries include: Company name, product name, profile.

Guide to Credit Cards on the Internet. Thomson Financial Inc. • Annual. $235 Individuals. Covers: Credit card issuers and credit card related web sites. Entries include: Product/service name, web site address.

FINANCIAL RATIOS

Annual Statement Studies. Risk Management Association. • Annual. Compiled from over 280,000 financial statements.

Annual Statement Studies: Industry Default Probabilities and Cash Flow Measures. Risk Management Association. • Annual. $405 Nonmembers. Serves as a companion volume to the original *Annual Statement Studies*. Gives probability of default estimates on a percentage scale for more than 450 industries. Includes changes in position year-by-year for eight financial statement line items and provides percentage measures of cash flow.

INTERNET DATABASES

BanxQuote Banking, Mortgage, and Finance Center. BanxQuote, Inc. Phone: (914)722-1600; Fax: (914)722-6630; Email: info@banx.com • URL: http://www.banx.com • Daily. Web site quotes interest rates paid by banks around the country on various savings products, as well as rates paid by consumers for automobile loans, mortgages, credit cards, home equity loans, and personal loans. Also provided: stock quotes, indexes, stock options, futures trading data, economic indicators, and links to many other financial sites.

Business 2.0 Web Guide to the Best Business Links. Business 2.0 Media Inc. Phone: (415)293-4800; Email: support@business2.com • URL: http://www.business2.com/webguide • Web site presents an extensive, searchable directory of links to "the best, most informative, and authoritative web pages." Twenty main categories cover business, finance, career, company information, people, and technology topics, with thousands of subtopics, all linking to Web sites recommended by experienced business researchers. Fees: Free.

Federal Reserve Board Publications and Education Resources. Board of Governors of the Federal Reserve System. Phone: (202)452-3000; Fax: (202)452-3819 • URL: http://www.federalreserve.gov/publications.htm • Web site provides access to statistics, surveys, and research from the Federal Reserve Board. *Federal Reserve Bulletin* articles are available as abstracts or full text (PDF) currently or from six-year archives. The link "Statistics: Releases and Historical Data" offers daily, weekly, monthly, quarterly, and annual data in great detail for interest rates, foreign exchange, consumer credit, money stock measures, industrial production indexes, bank reserves, and other items. Historical tabulations are available for various time periods. Free.

Fedstats. Federal Interagency Council on Statistical Policy. Phone: (202)395-7254 • URL: http://www.fedstats.gov • Web site features an efficient search facility for full-text statistics produced by more than 100 federal agencies, including the Census Bureau, the Bureau of Economic Analysis, and the Bureau of Labor Statistics. Boolean searches can be made within one agency or for all agencies combined. Links are offered to international statistical bureaus, including the UN, IMF, OECD, UNESCO, Eurostat, and 20 individual countries. Fees: Free.

FreeLunch.com. Economy.com, Inc. Phone: (610)696-8700; Fax: (610)696-1678 • URL: http://www.freelunch.com • Web site provides free access to more than 200 million economic and financial data series, covering industry, demographics, labor markets, prices, retail sales, government spending, trade, interest rates, housing starts, the stock market, etc. Data is available in either chart or table form. Searching is offered. Free, but registration required. Economy.com, Inc. also offers fee-based economic analysis at *The Dismal Scientist* site (www.dismal.com).

ONLINE DATABASES

Banking Information Source. ProQuest L.L.C. • Provides indexing and abstracting of periodical and other literature from 1982 to date, with weekly updates. Covers the financial services industry: banks, savings institutions, investment houses, credit unions, insurance companies, and real estate organizations. Emphasis is on marketing and management. Inquire as to online cost and availability. (Formerly *FINIS: Financial Industry Information Service*.).

PERIODICALS AND NEWSLETTERS

American Banker: The Financial Services Daily. SourceMedia Inc. • Daily. $895.00 per year. Provides news of banking, investment products, mortgages, credit unions, finance, bank technology, and legal developments.

Business Credit. National Association of Credit Management. • 9/year. $54 U.S.. Formerly *Credit and Financial Management*. Covers business and trade credit as well as risk management.

Consumer Credit and Truth-in-Lending Compliance Report. Thomson RIA. • Monthly. $183.75 per year. Newsletter. Focuses on the latest regulatory rulings and findings involving consumer lending and credit activity. Incorporates (Consumer Lending Report).

Credit Risk Management. Phillips International, Inc. • Biweekly. $695.00 per year. Newsletter on consumer credit, including delinquency aspects.

U.S. Banker. SourceMedia Inc. • Monthly. $65.00 per year. Edited for bank executives and managers. Covers a wide variety of banking and financial topics.

STATISTICS SOURCES

Statistical Information on the Financial Services Industry. American Bankers Association. • Annual. Members, $150.00; non-members, $275.00. Presents a wide variety of data relating to banking and financial services, including consumer economics, personal finance, credit, government loans, capital markets, and international banking.

Survey of Current Business. U. S. Government Printing Office. • Published by Bureau of Economic Analysis, U. S. Department of Commerce. Presents a wide variety of business and economic data.

TRADE/PROFESSIONAL ASSOCIATIONS

American Fair Credit Council. 100 W Cypress Creek Rd., Ste. 700, Fort Lauderdale, FL 33309. Phone: 888-657-8272; Fax: (954)343-6960; Email: info@americanfaircreditcouncil.org • URL: http://www.americanfaircreditcouncil.org • Promotes good practice in the debt settlement industry. Protects the interests of consumer debtors. Advances the application of consumer protection, principals in marketing, sales, and fulfillment of debt settlement services.

American Financial Services Association. 919 18th St. NW, Ste. 300, Washington, DC 20006. Email: info@afsamail.org • URL: http://www.afsaonline.org • Represents companies whose business is primarily direct credit lending to consumers and/or the purchase of sales finance paper on consumer goods. Has members that have insurance and retail subsidiaries; some are themselves subsidiaries of highly diversified parent corporations. Encourages the business of financing individuals and families for necessary and useful purposes at reasonable charges, including interest; promotes consumer understanding of basic money management principles as well as constructive uses of consumer credit. Includes educational services such as films, textbooks and study units for the classroom and budgeting guides for individuals and families. Compiles statistical reports; offers seminars.

Clearpoint Financial Solutions. 8000 Franklin Farms Dr., Richmond, VA 23229-5004. Phone: 877-422-9040; Fax: (804)526-8271; Email: customer.service@clearpointccs.org • URL: http://www.clearpointfinancialsolutions.org • Provides consumer credit counseling services to all consumers in need. Strives to increase financial literacy.

Consumer Credit Industry Association. 6300 Powers Ferry Rd., Ste. 600-286, Atlanta, GA 30339. Phone: (678)858-4001; Email: sjcipinko@cciaonline.com • URL: http://www.cciaonline.com • Insurance companies underwriting consumer credit insurance in areas of life insurance, accident and health insurance, and property insurance.

Consumer Credit Trade Association. The Wave, Ste. 4, 1 View Croft Rd., Shipley BD17 7DU, United Kingdom. Phone: 44 127 4714959; Fax: 44 845 2571199 • URL: http://www.ccta.co.uk • Credit grantors of many types who offer credit to consumers. Includes finance companies, retailers, some building societies, other lenders and suppliers of ancillary services. Represents to government, the media and EC authorities the interests of companies providing and operating credit, leasing and rental facilities. Offers a range of services to members including advice, courses and seminars, standard agreement forms, Short Guides on legislation, magazine and discussion groups and forums.

Consumer Data Industry Association. 1090 Vermont Ave. NW, Ste. 200, Washington, DC 20005-4905. Phone: (202)371-0910; Fax: (202)371-0134; Email: cdia@cdiaonline.org • URL: http://www.cdiaonline.org • Serves as international association of credit reporting and collection service offices. Maintains hall of fame and biographical archives; conducts specialized educational programs. Offers computerized services and compiles statistics.

National Foundation for Credit Counseling. 2000 M St. NW, Ste. 505, Washington, DC 20036. Phone: (202)677-4300 • URL: http://www.nfcc.org • Supersedes Retail Credit Institute of America.

CONSUMER ECONOMICS

See also CONSUMER EDUCATION; ECONOMIC RESEARCH; MARKET RESEARCH

CD-ROM DATABASES

EconLit. Ovid Technologies Inc. • Updated monthly. Lists journal articles, book reviews, disserations of economic literature. Over 1,400 journals covered.

OECD Statistical Compendium. Organization for Economic Cooperation and Development. • Semiannual. $1,905.00 per year for 1 to 10 users. CD-ROM contains more than 730,000 monthly, quarterly, and annual time series for OECD countries, 1960 to date. Includes fully searchable data on agriculture, food, economic indicators, national accounts, employment, energy, finance, industry, technology, and foreign trade. Results can be displayed in various forms.

DIRECTORIES

Consumer Spain. Euromonitor International Business Reference Div. • Irregular. $575. Publication includes: Lists of 100 Spanish companies and retailers. Database includes: List of sources of information on Spain. Entries include: Company name, address, phone, brand and product information, market shares, sales and profits. Principal content of publication is business briefings and analysis of Spain's consumer markets.

Consumer USA: 2010. Euromonitor International Business Reference Div. • Annual. $995 Individuals U.S.D. An analytical overview of the U.S. market. Provides historic and forecast volume and value sales statistics on over 330 consumer product sectors. Database includes: Company and brand share data.

East European Business Handbook. Euromonitor International Business Reference Div. • $190. Publication includes: List of sources of information on doing business in eastern Europe. Principal content of publication is a guide in identifying market opportunities in eastern Europe.

INTERNET DATABASES

Bureau of Economic Analysis. U. S. Department of Commerce, Bureau of Economic Analysis. Phone: (202)606-9900; Fax: (202)606-5310; Email: webmaster@bea.doc.gov • URL: http://www.bea.doc.gov • Web site includes "News Release Information" covering national, regional, and international economic estimates from the BEA. Highlights of releases appear online the same day, complete text and tables appear the next day. "Recent News Releases" section provides titles for past nine months, with links. "BEA Data and Methodology" includes "Frequently Requested NIPA Data" (national income and product accounts, such as gross domestic product and personal income). Other statistics are available. Fees: Free.

Business 2.0 Web Guide to the Best Business Links. Business 2.0 Media Inc. Phone: (415)293-4800; Email: support@business2.com • URL: http://www.business2.com/webguide • Web site presents an extensive, searchable directory of links to "the best, most informative, and authoritative web pages." Twenty main categories cover business, finance, career, company information, people, and technology topics, with thousands of subtopics, all linking to Web sites recommended by experienced business researchers. Fees: Free.

Fedstats. Federal Interagency Council on Statistical Policy. Phone: (202)395-7254 • URL: http://www.fedstats.gov • Web site features an efficient search facility for full-text statistics produced by more than 100 federal agencies, including the Census Bureau, the Bureau of Economic Analysis, and the Bureau of Labor Statistics. Boolean searches can be made within one agency or for all agencies combined. Links are offered to international statistical bureaus, including the UN, IMF, OECD, UNESCO, Eurostat, and 20 individual countries. Fees: Free.

FreeLunch.com. Economy.com, Inc. Phone: (610)696-8700; Fax: (610)696-1678 • URL: http://www.freelunch.com • Web site provides free access to more than 200 million economic and financial data series, covering industry, demographics, labor markets, prices, retail sales, government spending, trade, interest rates, housing starts, the stock market, etc. Data is available in either chart or table form. Searching is offered. Free, but registration required. Economy.com, Inc. also offers fee-based economic analysis at *The Dismal Scientist* site (www.dismal.com).

PERIODICALS AND NEWSLETTERS

American Demographics: Consumer Trends for Business Leaders. Media Central. • Monthly. $58.00 per year.

Family Economics and Nutrition Review. U. S. Government Printing Office. • Semi-annual. $13.00 per year. Issued by the Consumer and Food Economics Institute, U. S. Department of Agriculture. Provides articles on consumer expenditures and budgeting for food, clothing, housing, energy, education, etc.

STATISTICS SOURCES

Statistical Information on the Financial Services Industry. American Bankers Association. • Annual. Members, $150.00; non-members, $275.00. Presents a wide variety of data relating to banking and financial services, including consumer economics, personal finance, credit, government loans, capital markets, and international banking.

CONSUMER EDUCATION

See also BETTER BUSINESS BUREAUS; CONSUMER ECONOMICS

CD-ROM DATABASES

Consumer Health Complete. EBSCO Publishing Inc. • Full text of more than 250 health references, health diagrams, videos, pamphlets.

PERIODICALS AND NEWSLETTERS

Consumer Reports. Consumers Union of United States. • Monthly. $30 Individuals. Magazine featuring analyses and investigative reporting of products. Includes *Annual Buying Guide*.

Consumer's Research Magazine: Analyzing Consumer Issues. Consumers' Research. • Monthly. $24.00 per year.

FDA Consumer. U. S. Government Printing Office. • Bimonthly. $14.00 per year. Issued by the U. S. Food and Drug Administration. Provides consumer information about FDA regulations and product safety.

TRADE/PROFESSIONAL ASSOCIATIONS

Alliance Credit Counseling. 15720 John J. Delaney Dr., Ste. 575, Charlotte, NC 28277. Phone: 888-594-9554 or (704)341-1010; Fax: (704)540-5495; Email: service@knowdebt.org • URL: http://www.knowdebt.org • Provides help and hope through personalized education, counseling and support programs that seek to reduce and avoid the burdens of financial crisis, debt stress, bankruptcy and consequences. Provides empowerment to the public through charitable education programs of financial literacy, money management, credit management and debt reduction. Offers services of financial counseling, education and debt management.

American Council on Consumer Interests. PO Box 2528, Tarpon Springs, FL 34688-2528. Phone: (727)493-2131 • URL: http://www.consumerinterests.org • Formerly Council on Consumer Information.

American Escrow Association. 211 N Union St., Ste. 100, Alexandria, VA 22314. Phone: (703)519-1240; Email: hq@a-e-a.org • URL: http://www.a-e-a.org • Furthers the education and professionalism of the escrow industry. Enhances the education of escrow/settlement professionals. Increases the public knowledge and understanding of escrow and closing services. Coordinates legislative efforts throughout the United States.

Buying Influence. 801 W 47th St., Ste. 110, Country Club Plz., Kansas City, MO 64112. Phone: (816)931-7896; Email: info@buyinginfluence.com • Seeks to help consumers harness their buying power so that corporations make more socially responsible business decisions. Conducts corporate reviews of publicly-traded companies. Provides a forum for online discussions of issues concerning consumers and businesses.

Clearpoint Financial Solutions. 8000 Franklin Farms Dr., Richmond, VA 23229-5004. Phone: 877-422-9040; Fax: (804)526-8271; Email: customer.service@clearpointccs.org • URL: http://www.clearpointfinancialsolutions.org • Provides consumer credit counseling services to all consumers in need. Strives to increase financial literacy.

Consumer Credit Trade Association. The Wave, Ste. 4, 1 View Croft Rd., Shipley BD17 7DU, United Kingdom. Phone: 44 127 4714959; Fax: 44 845 2571199 • URL: http://www.ccta.co.uk • Credit grantors of many types who offer credit to consumers. Includes finance companies, retailers, some building societies, other lenders and suppliers of ancillary services. Represents to government, the media and EC authorities the interests of companies providing and operating credit, leasing and rental facilities. Offers a range of services to members including advice, courses and seminars, standard agreement forms, Short Guides on legislation, magazine and discussion groups and forums.

Consumer Federation of America. 1620 I St. NW, Ste. 200, Washington, DC 20006. Phone: (202)387-6121 or (202)737-0766; Email: cfa@consumerfed.org • URL: http://www.consumerfed.org • Members are national, regional, state, and local consumer groups. Absorbed Electric Consumers Information Committee.

Consumers Education and Protective Association International. 6048 Ogontz Ave., Philadelphia, PA 19141-1347. Phone: (215)424-1441; Fax: (215)424-8045.

Institute of Consumer Financial Education. PO Box 34070, San Diego, CA 92163-4070. Phone: (619)239-1401; Fax: (619)923-3284; Email: info@icfe.info • URL: http://www.financial-education-icfe.org • Aims to encourage Americans to improve spending, saving, investing, insuring, and financial planning habits to lessen their dependence on Social Security, welfare, or other individuals. Provides financial education courses to junior high and high school. Maintains a resource section of videos, books and home study courses in personal finance.

Irish Business and Employers' Confederation. Confederation House, 84-86 Lower Baggot St., Dublin IRL-2, Dublin, Ireland. Phone: 353 1 6051500; Fax: 353 1 6381500; Email: info@ibec.ie • URL: http://www.ibec.ie • Firms: industrial, commercial, and public sector firms that manufacture products or provide services. Promotes the growth and development of Irish industry and commercial activity. Advises the government and represents interests of industry on relevant legislative issues. Maintains the Irish Business Bureau in conjunction with Irish Business and Employers Confederation and the Chambers of Commerce of Ireland. Develops public awareness of the role of industry in national development through press, radio, television, and public meetings. Monitors technological developments; compiles statistics; provides advice and assistance to members; maintains speakers' bureau.

National Association for Moisture Management. 76 D St., Hull, MA 02045. Phone: (781)925-0354; Fax: (781)925-0650 • URL: http://na4mm.com • Educates and protects the consumer from problems associated with moisture. Works with state, federal and local officials to develop standards and practices in the moisture management industry. Offers continuing education programs for moisture management professionals.

National Consumers League. 1701 K St. NW, Ste. 1200, Washington, DC 20006. Phone: (202)835-3323; Fax: (202)835-0747; Email: info@nclnet.org • URL: http://www.nclnet.org • Identifies, protects, represents, and advances the economic and social interests of consumers and workers. Addresses issues including healthcare, food and drug safety, and consumer fraud. Promotes fairness and safety at the marketplace and in the workplace. Coordinates the Alliance Against Fraud in Telemarketing and the Child Labor Coalition. Administers the National Fraud Information Center and Internet Fraud Watch.

CONSUMER ELECTRONICS

See also ELECTRIC APPLIANCE INDUSTRY

ABSTRACTS AND INDEXES

Readers' Guide to Periodical Literature. EBSCO Publishing Inc. • Provides indexing for over 400 periodicals dating back to 1983.

CD-ROM DATABASES

Readers' Guide to Periodical Literature. EBSCO Publishing Inc. • Provides indexing for over 400 periodicals dating back to 1983.

DIRECTORIES

Household Appliances (Major) Directory--Dealers. InfoGroup Inc. • Annual. Number of listings: 21,271. Entries include: Name, address, phone, size of advertisement, name of owner or manager, number of employees, year first in "Yellow Pages." Compiled from telephone company "Yellow Pages," nationwide.

The International Directory of Importers - Consumer Electronics, Audio/Video, TV's and CD's Importers. Interdata. • $295 Individuals printed edition. Covers: 4,000 international firms importing consumer electronics, audio/video, TV's and CD's. Entries include: Company name and address, contact person, email, number of employees, year established, phone and telefaxes, business activity, bank references, as well as a listing of consumer electronics, audio/video, TV's and CD's currently being imported.

FINANCIAL RATIOS

Industry Norms and Key Business Ratios. Dun & Bradstreet Inc. • Annual. Five volumes. Covers over 800 kinds of businesses, arranged by Standard Industrial Classification number. More detailed editions covering longer periods of time are also available.

INTERNET DATABASES

Advance Monthly Retail Trade Report. U. S. Census Bureau. Phone: 800-541-8345 or (301)457-4100 or (301)763-2713; Fax: (301)457-1296 or (301)457-3842; Email: naics@census.gov • URL: http://www.census.gov/epcd/www/naicstab.htm • Web pages provide monthly sales figures for a wide range of retail businesses. Advance, preliminary, and final statistics are provided for the latest month available in each case, with a previous-year comparison. Updates are monthly.

Manufacturing Profiles. U. S. Bureau of the Census. Phone: (301)763-4636 or (301)763-4100; Fax: (301)763-4794; Email: webmaster@census.gov • URL: http://www.census.gov/prod/www/abs/mfg-prof.html • The Census Bureau makes available free on PDF (Portable Document Format) an annual consolidation of the entire Current Industrial Report series, presenting "all the data compiled." Contains statistics on production, shipments, inventories, consumption, exports, imports, and orders for a wide variety of manufactured products.

PERIODICALS AND NEWSLETTERS

Dealerscope: Product and Strategy for Consumer Technology Retailing. North American Publishing Co. • Monthly. $79 /year. Formerly *Dealerscope Consumer Electronices Marketplace.* Provides product information and valuable strategy for consumer technology retailers.

Handheld Computing: The Number One Guide to Handheld Devices. Mobile Media Group. • 9/year. Covers handheld devices for consumers, including PDAs, cell phones, digital cameras, MP3 players, tablet PCs, accessories, and software. Includes product reviews.

Laptop Magazine. Bedford Communications Inc. • Monthly. Consumer magazine containing articles and product reviews for notebook/laptop computers, handheld computers, tablet devices, cell phones, digital cameras, and other consumer electronic products.

Mobile PC. Future Network USA. • Monthly. $20.00 per year. Provides information and detailed product reviews for consumers. Covers notebook/laptop computers, personal digital assistants (PDAs), wireless network equipment, cell phones, digital cameras, and other electronic products.

T W I C E: This Week in Consumer Electronics. Reed Elsevier Group plc Reed Business Information. • 29 times a year. $129.90 per year. Contains marketing and manufacturing news relating to a wide variety of consumer electronic products, including video, audio, telephone, and home office equipment.

Television Digest with Consumer Electronics. Warren Communications News Inc. • Weekly. $944.00 per year. Newsletter featuring new consumer entertainment products utilizing electronics. Also covers the television broadcasting and cable TV industries, with corporate and industry news.

PRICE SOURCES

Audio. Orion Research Corp. • Annual. $179 Individuals. Quotes retail and wholesale prices of used audio equipment. Original list prices and years of manufacture are also shown.

Video and Television. Orion Research Corp. • Annual. $144 Individuals. Quotes retail and wholesale prices of used video and TV equipment. Original list prices and years of manufacture are also shown.

STATISTICS SOURCES

Annual Benchmark Report for Retail Trade and Food Services..A Detailed Summary of Retail Sales, Purchases, Accounts Receivable, Inventories, and Food Service Sales. U. S. Government Printing Office. • Annual. $13.00. Issued by the U.S. Census Bureau. Provides detailed annual and monthly retail statistics for the most recent 10 years. Includes data for various kinds of retail outlets, including automobiles, furniture, appliances, building supplies, grocery stores, drug stores, gasoline stations, clothing, sporting goods, department stores, and restaurants.

Standard & Poor's Industry Surveys. Standard & Poor's Financial Services L.L.C. • Semiannual. $1,800.00. Two looseleaf volumes. Includes monthly *Supplements.* Provides detailed, individual surveys of 52 major industry groups. Each survey is revised on a semiannual basis. Also includes "Monthly Investment Review" (industry group investment analysis) and monthly "Trends & Projections" (economic analysis).

U.S. Industry and Trade Outlook. U.S. Department of Commerce National Technical Information Service. • Annual. Produced by the International Trade Administration, U.S. Department of Commerce, in a "public-private" partnership with DRI/McGraw-Hill and Standard & Poor's. Provides basic data, outlook for the current year, and "Long-Term Prospects" (five-year projections) for a wide variety of products and services. Includes high technology industries. Formerly *U.S. Industrial Outlook.*

TRADE/PROFESSIONAL ASSOCIATIONS

Consumer Electronics Association. 1919 S Eads St., Arlington, VA 22202. Phone: 866-858-1555 or (703)907-7600 or (703)907-7650; Fax: (703)907-7675 or (630)953-8957; Email: info@ce.org • URL: http://www.ce.org • Manufacturers of consumer technology and electronics products. Strives to aid members in growth through connections, education, exposure, and by providing information. Hosts workshops and educational programs.

Electronics Representatives Association. 309 W Washington St., Ste. 500, Chicago, IL 60606. Phone: (312)419-1432 or (312)559-3050; Fax: (312)419-1660; Email: info@era.org • URL: http://www.era.org • Professional field sales organizations selling components and materials; computer, instrumentation and data communications products; audiovisual, security, land/mobile communications and commercial sound components and consumer products to the electronics industry. Sponsors insurance programs and educational conference for members.

LCD TV Association. 16055 SW Walker Rd., Ste. 264, Beaverton, OR 97006-4942. Phone: (215)206-6506; Email: membership@lcdtvassociation.org • URL: http://www.lcdtvassociation.org • Aims to help the LCD TV supply chain and retail channel as well as the end customer. Creates and promotes new features and functions for the industry. Provides methods to improve members' products and services.

CONSUMER FINANCE COMPANIES

See FINANCE COMPANIES

CONSUMER LOANS

See CONSUMER CREDIT

CONSUMER PRICE INDEXES

CD-ROM DATABASES

OECD Statistical Compendium. Organization for Economic Cooperation and Development. • Semiannual. $1,905.00 per year for 1 to 10 users. CD-ROM contains more than 730,000 monthly, quarterly, and annual time series for OECD countries, 1960 to date. Includes fully searchable data on agriculture, food, economic indicators, national accounts, employment, energy, finance, industry, technology, and foreign trade. Results can be displayed in various forms.

INTERNET DATABASES

Business 2.0 Web Guide to the Best Business Links. Business 2.0 Media Inc. Phone: (415)293-4800; Email: support@business2.com • URL: http://www.business2.com/webguide • Web site presents an extensive, searchable directory of links to "the best, most informative, and authoritative web pages." Twenty main categories cover business, finance, career, company information, people, and technology topics, with thousands of subtopics, all linking to Web sites recommended by experienced business researchers. Fees: Free.

Fedstats. Federal Interagency Council on Statistical Policy. Phone: (202)395-7254 • URL: http://www.fedstats.gov • Web site features an efficient search facility for full-text statistics produced by more than 100 federal agencies, including the Census Bureau, the Bureau of Economic Analysis, and the Bureau of Labor Statistics. Boolean searches can be made within one agency or for all agencies combined. Links are offered to international statistical bureaus, including the UN, IMF, OECD, UNESCO, Eurostat, and 20 individual countries. Fees: Free.

FreeLunch.com. Economy.com, Inc. Phone: (610)696-8700; Fax: (610)696-1678 • URL: http://www.freelunch.com • Web site provides free access to more than 200 million economic and financial data series, covering industry, demographics, labor markets, prices, retail sales, government spending, trade, interest rates, housing starts, the stock market, etc. Data is available in either chart or table form. Searching is offered. Free, but registration required. Economy.com, Inc. also offers fee-based economic analysis at *The Dismal Scientist* site (www.dismal.com).

PRICE SOURCES

CPI Detailed Report: Consumer Price Index. U. S. Government Printing Office. • Monthly. $45 Individuals. Cost of living data.

STATISTICS SOURCES

ACCRA Cost of Living Index. Council for Community and Economic Research. • Quarterly. $165 Individuals. Compares price levels for 280-310 U.S. cities.

Bulletin of Labour Statistics: Supplementing the Annual Data Presented in the Year Book of Labour Statistics. International Labor Ofice. • Quarterly. $84.00 per year. Includes five Supplements. A supplement to *Yearbook of Labour Statistics*. Provides current labor and price index statistics for over 130 countries. Generally includes data for the most recent four years. Text in English, French and Spanish.

Prices and Earnings Around the Globe. Union Bank of Switzerland. • Triennial. Free. Published in Zurich. Compares prices and purchasing power in 48 major cities of the world. Wages and hours are also compared.

Report on the American Workforce. U. S. Government Printing Office. • Annual. Issued by the U. S. Department of Labor (www.dol.gov). Appendix contains tabular statistics, including employment, unemployment, price indexes, consumer expenditures, employee benefits (retirement, insurance, vacation, etc.), wages, productivity, hours of work, and occupational injuries. Annual figures are shown for up to 50 years.

Survey of Current Business. U. S. Government Printing Office. • Published by Bureau of Economic Analysis, U. S. Department of Commerce. Presents a wide variety of business and economic data.

United States Department of State Indexes of Living Costs Abroad, Quarters Allowances, and Hardship Differentials. U. S. Government Printing Office. • Quarterly. Provides data on the difference in living costs between Washington, DC and each of 160 foreign cities.

CONSUMER RESEARCH

See CONSUMER ECONOMICS

CONSUMER SURVEYS

See also MARKET RESEARCH

ALMANACS AND YEARBOOKS

Research Alert Yearbook: Vital Facts on Consumer Behavior and Attitudes. EPM Communications Inc. • Annual. $349 Individuals Single user (PDF) or Print. Provides summaries of consumer market research from the newsletters *Research Alert, Youth Markets Alert*, and *Minority Markets Alert*. Includes tables, charts, graphs, and textual summaries for 41 subject categories. Sources include reports, studies, polls, and focus groups.

DIRECTORIES

Findex: The Worldwide Directory of Market Research Reports, Studies, and Surveys. MarketResearch.com. • Annual. Provides brief annotations of market research reports and related publications from about 1,000 publishers, arranged by topic. Back of book includes Report Titles by Publisher, Publishers/Distributors Directory, Subject Index, Geography Index, and Company Index. (Formerly published by Cambridge Information Group.).

GreenBook. New York American Marketing Association. • Annual. Contains information on companies offering focus group facilities, including recruiting, moderating, and transcription services.

GreenBook Worldwide Directory of Marketing Research Companies and Services. New York AMA - Green Book. • Annual. Contains information in 300 categories on more than 2,500 market research companies, consultants, field services, computer services, survey research companies, etc. Indexed by specialty, industry, company, computer program, and personnel. Available online. Formerly *Greenbook Worldwide International Directory of Marketing Research Companies and Services*.

Medical Quality Management Sourcebook. Thomson Financial Inc. • Annual. $295 Individuals. Covers: Clinical performance measurement and improvement systems, and organizations and individuals involved in patient satisfaction surveys. Database includes: Fact sheets, charts. Entries include: Company and individual name, address, phone, fax.

INTERNET DATABASES

Summary of Commentary on Current Economic Conditions by Federal Reserve District. Board of Governors of the Federal Reserve System. Phone: (202)452-3000; Fax: (202)452-3819 • URL: http://www.federalreserve.gov/publications.htm • 8/year. Free Web site provides current "anecdotal information" eight times a year on economic conditions within each of the 12 Federal Reserve Districts, plus an extensive national *Summary*. Text is based on the opinions of bank officials, business executives, economists, financial market experts, and others. Typically contains views of consumer spending, manufacturing, services, credit, employment, prices, wages, and the economy in general. Usually referred to as the Beige Book.

PERIODICALS AND NEWSLETTERS

Public Pulse: Roper's Authoritative Report on What Americans are Thinking, Doing, and Buying. GfK SE. • Monthly. $297.00. Newsletter. Contains news of surveys of American attitudes, values, and behavior. Each issue includes a research supplement giving "complete facts and figures behind each survey question.".

Research Alert: A Bi-Weekly Report of Consumer Marketing Studies. EPM Communications Inc. • Biweekly. $389 /year. Provides descriptions (abstracts) of new, consumer market research reports from private, government, and academic sources. Includes sample charts and tables.

TRADE/PROFESSIONAL ASSOCIATIONS

National Council on Public Polls. 1425 Broad St., Ste. 7, Clifton, NJ 07013. Phone: 800-786-8000 or (973)857-8500; Fax: (973)857-8578; Email: info@ncpp.org • URL: http://www.ncpp.org • Members are public opinion polling organizations.

CONSUMERS' COOPERATIVE SOCIETIES

See COOPERATIVES

CONSUMERS' LEAGUES

See COOPERATIVES

CONSUMERS, MATURE

See MATURE CONSUMER MARKET

CONSUMERS' PRODUCTS RESEARCH

See QUALITY OF PRODUCTS

CONTACT LENS AND INTRAOCULAR LENS INDUSTRIES

See also OPHTHALMIC INDUSTRY

ABSTRACTS AND INDEXES

Index Medicus. U.S. National Library of Medicine. U. S. Government Printing Office. • Monthly. $522 Individuals. Bibliographic listing of references to current articles from approximately 3,000 of the world's biomedical journals.

BIBLIOGRAPHIES

Medical & Health Care Books & Serials in Print. Grey House Publishing. • $645 Individuals Hardcover. Provides immediate access to the highly specialized publishing activity in the health sciences and allied health fields.

DIRECTORIES

Contact Lens Manufacturers Association--Member Directory. Contact Lens Manufacturers Association. • Annual. Number of listings: 130. Entries include: Company name, address, phone, name and title of contact.

HANDBOOKS AND MANUALS

Physicians' Desk Reference for Ophthalmology. Medical Economics Co. • Annual. $49.95. Provides detailed descriptions of ophthalmological instrumentation, equipment, supplies, lenses, and prescription drugs. Indexed by manufacturer, product name, product category, active drug ingredient, and instrumentation. Editorial discussion is included.

ONLINE DATABASES

Embase. Elsevier. • Worldwide medical literature, 1974 to present. Weekly updates. Inquire as to online cost and availability.

PERIODICALS AND NEWSLETTERS

Eye and Contact Lens: Science and Clinical Practices. University of Texas, Dept. of Ophthalmology. Lippincott Williams & Wilkins. • 6/year. $237 Individuals. Formerly *The CLAO Journal*.

International Contact Lens Clinic. Elsevier. • Bimonthly. Individuals, $139.00 per year; institutions, $272.00 per year.

Ocular Surgery News. SLACK Inc. • Biweekly. Individuals, $472.00 per year; institutions, $599.00 per year. Formerly *IOL & Ocular Surgery News*.

TRADE/PROFESSIONAL ASSOCIATIONS

American Optometric Association - Contact Lens and Cornea Section. 243 N Lindbergh Blvd., 1st Fl., Saint Louis, MO 63141-7881. Phone: 800-365-2219; Fax: (314)991-4101; Email: clcs@aoa.org • URL: http://www.aoa.org • Members are optometrists, students of optometry and paraoptometric assistants and technicians. Formerly American Optical Association.

American Society of Cataract and Refractive Surgery. 4000 Legato Rd., Ste. 700, Fairfax, VA 22033. Phone: (703)591-2220; Fax: (703)591-0614 • URL: http://www.ascrs.org • Affiliated with American Medical Association and American Society Ophthalmic Administrators.

Contact Lens Association of Ophthalmologists. 4000 Legato Rd., Ste. 700, Fairfax, VA 22033-9937. Phone: 855-264-8818 or (703)788-5799; Fax: (703)434-3003; Email: eyes@clao.org • URL: http://www.clao.org • Affiliated with American Academy of Ophthalmology, American Medical Association and American National Standards Institute.

Contact Lens Manufacturers Association. PO Box 29398, Lincoln, NE 68529. Phone: 800-344-9060 or (402)465-4122; Fax: (402)465-4187 • URL: http://www.clma.net • Represents contact lens laboratories, material, solution and equipment manufacturers in the United States and abroad. Aims to increase awareness and utilization of custom-manufactured contact lenses.

Contact Lens Society of America. 491A Carlisle Dr., Herndon, VA 20170. Phone: 800-296-9776 or (703)437-5100; Fax: (703)437-0727; Email: clsa@clsa.info • URL: http://www.clsa.info • Contact lens fitters; manufacturers of products associated with contact lenses. Aims to share knowledge of contact lens technology and to foster the growth and ability of the contact lens technician throughout the world. Conducts activities such as: developing improvements in instrumentation, fitting procedures, and manufacturing processes; providing a national public relations medium through which information is disseminated to governmental agencies, legislative bodies, and other professional groups. Provides Home Study Course of Contact Lens Fitters. Operates speakers' bureau.

CONTAINER INDUSTRY

See also COOPERAGE INDUSTRY; GLASS CONTAINER INDUSTRY; PAPER BAG INDUSTRY; PAPER BOX AND PAPER CONTAINER INDUSTRIES

CD-ROM DATABASES

OECD Statistical Compendium. Organization for Economic Cooperation and Development. • Semiannual. $1,905.00 per year for 1 to 10 users. CD-ROM contains more than 730,000 monthly, quarterly, and annual time series for OECD countries, 1960 to date. Includes fully searchable data on agriculture, food, economic indicators, national accounts, employment, energy, finance, industry, technology, and foreign trade. Results can be displayed in various forms.

DIRECTORIES

European Cooler Company Directory. Zenith International Ltd. • $823 Individuals hard copy. Covers: active cooler distributors in the markets of West and East Europe. Entries include: company name, address, telephone number, fax number, website, email, company ownership, number of employees, subsidiaries, company activities, and names and job titles of senior management.

FINANCIAL RATIOS

Annual Statement Studies. Risk Management Association. • Annual. Compiled from over 280,000 financial statements.

Annual Statement Studies: Industry Default Probabilities and Cash Flow Measures. Risk Management Association. • Annual. $405 Nonmembers. Serves as a companion volume to the original *Annual Statement Studies*. Gives probability of default estimates on a percentage scale for more than 450 industries. Includes changes in position year-by-year for eight financial statement line items and provides percentage measures of cash flow.

INTERNET DATABASES

Business 2.0 Web Guide to the Best Business Links. Business 2.0 Media Inc. Phone: (415)293-4800; Email: support@business2.com • URL: http://www.business2.com/webguide • Web site presents an extensive, searchable directory of links to "the best, most informative, and authoritative web pages." Twenty main categories cover business, finance, career, company information, people, and technology topics, with thousands of subtopics, all linking to Web sites recommended by experienced business researchers. Fees: Free.

Fedstats. Federal Interagency Council on Statistical Policy. Phone: (202)395-7254 • URL: http://www.fedstats.gov • Web site features an efficient search facility for full-text statistics produced by more than 100 federal agencies, including the Census Bureau, the Bureau of Economic Analysis, and the Bureau of Labor Statistics. Boolean searches can be made within one agency or for all agencies combined. Links are offered to international statistical bureaus, including the UN, IMF, OECD, UNESCO, Eurostat, and 20 individual countries. Fees: Free.

FreeLunch.com. Economy.com, Inc. Phone: (610)696-8700; Fax: (610)696-1678 • URL: http://www.freelunch.com • Web site provides free access to more than 200 million economic and financial data series, covering industry, demographics, labor markets, prices, retail sales, government spending, trade, interest rates, housing starts, the stock market, etc. Data is available in either chart or table form. Searching is offered. Free, but registration required. Economy.com, Inc. also offers fee-based economic analysis at *The Dismal Scientist* site (www.dismal.com).

Manufacturing Profiles. U. S. Bureau of the Census. Phone: (301)763-4636 or (301)763-4100; Fax: (301)763-4794; Email: webmaster@census.gov • URL: http://www.census.gov/prod/www/abs/mfg-prof.html • The Census Bureau makes available free on PDF (Portable Document Format) an annual consolidation of the entire Current Industrial Report series, presenting "all the data compiled." Contains statistics on production, shipments, inventories, consumption, exports, imports, and orders for a wide variety of manufactured products.

PERIODICALS AND NEWSLETTERS

Packaging Digest. Reed Elsevier Group plc Reed Business Information. • 13 times a year. $119.90 per year.

PRICE SOURCES

Official Board Markets: "The Yellow Sheet". Mark Arzoumanian. Advanstar Communications. • Weekly. $160.00 per year. Covers the corrugated container, folding carton, rigid box and waste paper industries.

STATISTICS SOURCES

American Iron and Steel Annual Statistical Report. American Iron and Steel Institute. • Annual. $100 Individuals.

Survey of Current Business. U. S. Government Printing Office. • Published by Bureau of Economic Analysis, U. S. Department of Commerce. Presents a wide variety of business and economic data.

TRADE/PROFESSIONAL ASSOCIATIONS

Associated Cooperage Industries of America. 10001 Taylorsville Rd., Ste. 201, Louisville, KY 40299-3116. Phone: (502)261-2242; Fax: (502)261-9425; Email: acia@att.net • URL: http://www.acia.net • Serves as contact point for members; disseminates information about the wooden barrel, with emphasis on white oak; promotes the common interest of those in the industry.

Can Manufacturers Institute. 1730 Rhode Island Island Ave. NW, Ste. 1000, Washington, DC 20036. Phone: (202)232-4677; Fax: (202)232-5756 • URL: http://www.cancentral.com • Represents can makers and can industry suppliers. Aims to foster the prosperity of the industry and bring value to its members in a cost effective way.

Containerization and Intermodal Institute. PO Box 836, West Caldwell, NJ 07006. Phone: (201)226-0160 or (973)226-0160; Fax: (201)364-1212; Email: info@containerization.org • URL: http://www.containerization.org • Formerly Containerization Institute.

CONTESTS, PRIZES, AND AWARDS

DIRECTORIES

Awards, Honors & Prizes. Cengage Learning Inc. • 2014. $898.00. Two volumes. 35th edition. Comprises awards given in virtually every field. Domestic volume, $477.00. International volume, $520.00.

PERIODICALS AND NEWSLETTERS

Potentials: Ideas and Products that Motivate. Nielsen Business Media Inc. • Monthly. $59.00 per year. Covers incentives, premiums, awards, and gifts as related to promotional activities. Formerly *Potentials in Marketing*.

PROMO: Promotion Marketing Worldwide. Primedia Business Magazines and Media. • Monthly. $65.00 per year. Edited for companies and agencies that utilize couponing, point-of-purchase advertising, special events, games, contests, premiums, product samples, and other unique promotional items.

TRADE/PROFESSIONAL ASSOCIATIONS

Awards and Recognition Association. 8735 W Higgins Rd., Ste. 300, Chicago, IL 60631. Phone: 800-344-2148 or (847)375-4800; Fax: (847)375-6480 or (888)374-7257; Email: info@ara.org • URL: http://www.ara.org • Awards and recognition industry retailers and suppliers. Advances the business growth of recognition specialists.

CONTRACTIONS

See ABBREVIATIONS

CONTRACTORS, ELECTRICAL

See ELECTRICAL CONSTRUCTION INDUSTRY

CONTRACTS

See also BUILDING CONTRACTS; GOVERNMENT CONTRACTS

ABSTRACTS AND INDEXES

Current Law Index. Cengage Learning Inc. • $1,332 Individuals. Monthly. $1269.00 per year. Produced in cooperation with the American Association of Law Libraries. Indexes more than 900 law journals, legal newspapers, and specialty publications from the U.S., Canada, U.K., Ireland, Australia, and New Zealand.

Index to Legal Periodicals and Books. H.W. Wilson Co. • Monthly. $490.00 per year. Quarterly and annual cumulations.

ALMANACS AND YEARBOOKS

American Law Yearbook. Cengage Learning Inc. • $308 Individuals. Annual. $280.00. Serves as a yearly supplement to *West's Encyclopedia of American Lawa.* Describes new legal developments in many subject areas.

CD-ROM DATABASES

Index to Legal Periodicals and Books. EBSCO Publishing Inc. • Contains indexing of more than 1,400 English language legal periodicals from 1981 to date and 2,500 books.

DIRECTORIES

500 Contractors Receiving the Largest Dollar Volume of Prime Contract Awards for RDT&E. U.S. Department of Defense. • Annual. Covers the 500 largest contractors (including business, nonprofit organizations, foreign contractors, and government agencies) that received the largest dollar volume of prime contract awards over $25,000 for military research, development, test, and evaluation projects.

ENCYCLOPEDIAS AND DICTIONARIES

West's Encyclopedia of American Law. Cengage Learning Inc. • 2004. eBook. Second edition. Covers a wide variety of legal topics for the general reader. Inquire for pricing.

HANDBOOKS AND MANUALS

Williston on Contracts. Richard A. Lord. Thomson West. • $3,224.20 Full Set. Encyclopedic coverage of contract law.

INTERNET DATABASES

Lexis.com Research System. Lexis-Nexis Group. Phone: 800-227-4908 or (937)865-6800; Fax: (937)865-6909; Email: webmaster@prod.lexis-nexis.com • URL: http://www.nexis.com • Fee-based Web site offers extensive searching of a wide variety of legal sources. Additional features include Daily Opinion Service, lexis.com Bookstore, Career Center, CLE Center, Law Schools, and Practice Pages ("Pages specific to areas of specialty").

OTHER SOURCES

Government Contracts Reports. Wolters Kluwer Law & Business CCH. • Weekly. $2,600.00 per year. 10 looseleaf volumes. Laws and regulations affecting government contracts.

PERIODICALS AND NEWSLETTERS

Contract Management. National Contract Management Association. • Monthly. $158 Individuals nonmembers. Trade magazine for contract management professionals.

TRADE/PROFESSIONAL ASSOCIATIONS

National Contract Management Association. 21740 Beaumeade Cir., Ste. 125, Ashburn, VA 20147. Phone: 800-344-8096 or (571)382-0082 or (703)448-9231; Fax: (703)448-0939; Email: wearelistening@ncmahq.org • URL: http://www.ncmahq.org • Professional individuals concerned with administration, procurement, acquisition, negotiation and management of contracts and subcontracts. Works for the education, improvement and professional development of members and nonmembers through national and chapter programs, symposia and educational materials. Offers certification in Contract Management (CPCM, CFCM, and CCCM) designations as well as a credential program. Operates speakers' bureau.

CONTRACTS, GOVERNMENT

See GOVERNMENT CONTRACTS

CONTROL EQUIPMENT INDUSTRY

See also AUTOMATION; FLUIDICS INDUSTRY

ABSTRACTS AND INDEXES

Applied Science and Technology Index. EBSCO Publishing Inc. • 11/year. Indexes a wide variety of English language technical, industrial, and engineering periodicals.

Engineering Index Monthly: Abstracting and Indexing Services Covering Sources ofthe World's Engineering Literature. Engineering Information Inc. • Monthly. Institutions, $5,279.00 per year. Provides indexing and abstracting of the world's engineering and technical literature.

Key Abstracts: Machine Vision. Institution of Engineering and Technology. • Monthly. $1,138. Provides international coverage of journal and proceedings literature on optical noncontact sensing.

Key Abstracts: Robotics and Control. Institution of Engineering and Technology. • Monthly. $1,138. Provides international coverage of journal and proceedings literature.

NTIS Alerts: Computers, Control & Information Theory. U.S. Department of Commerce National Technical Information Service. • Biweekly. $130 per year. Covers computer hardware, software, control systems, pattern recognition, image processing, and related subjects.

Science Citation Index. Thomson Reuters Intellectual Property and Science. • Weekly. Includes *Source Index, Citation Index, Permuterm Subject Index,* and *Corporate Index.* Provides researchers, administrators, faculty, and students with quick, powerful access to the bibliographic and citation information they need to find research data, analyze trends, journals and researchers, and share their findings.

CD-ROM DATABASES

Science Citation Index. Thomson Reuters Intellectual Property and Science. • Weekly. Includes *Source Index, Citation Index, Permuterm Subject Index,* and *Corporate Index.* Provides researchers, administrators, faculty, and students with quick, powerful access to the bibliographic and citation information they need to find research data, analyze trends, journals and researchers, and share their findings.

DIRECTORIES

Frontline Solutions Buyer's Guide. Advanstar Communications. • Annual. $34.95 plus $3.50 shipping. Publication includes: List of manufacturers, suppliers, consultants, value added resellers, and dealers/distributors of automatic identification and data capture software, technology, equipment, and products for bar code, biometric identification, electronic data interchange, machine vision, magnetic stripe, optical character recognition, radio frequency data communications, radio frequency identification, smart cards, and voice data entry; also includes related organizations, and sources for industry standards. Entries include: Company name, address, phone, e-mail, web address, products or services.

The International Directory of Importers--Control Equipment and Switches Importers. Interdata. • $200 Individuals print. Covers: 1,400 international firms importing control equipment and switches. Entries include: Company name and address, contact person, email, number of employees, year established, phone and telefaxes, business activity, bank references, as well as a listing of control equipment and switches currently being imported.

ISA Directory of Automation. International Society of Automation. • Over 2,400 manufacturers of control and instrumentation equipment, over 1,000 manufacturers' representatives, and several hundred service companies; coverage includes Canada.

Manufacturing Systems: Buyers Guide. Reed Elsevier Group plc Reed Business Information. • Annual. Price on application. Contains information on companies manufacturing or supplying materials handling systems, CAD/CAM systems, specialized software for manufacturing, programmable controllers, machine vision systems, and automatic identification systems.

FINANCIAL RATIOS

Industry Norms and Key Business Ratios. Dun & Bradstreet Inc. • Annual. Five volumes. Covers over 800 kinds of businesses, arranged by Standard Industrial Classification number. More detailed editions covering longer periods of time are also available.

INTERNET DATABASES

Manufacturing Profiles. U. S. Bureau of the Census. Phone: (301)763-4636 or (301)763-4100; Fax: (301)763-4794; Email: webmaster@census.gov • URL: http://www.census.gov/prod/www/abs/mfg-prof.html • The Census Bureau makes available free on PDF (Portable Document Format) an annual consolidation of the entire Current Industrial Report series, presenting "all the data compiled." Contains statistics on production, shipments, inventories, consumption, exports, imports, and orders for a wide variety of manufactured products.

ONLINE DATABASES

FLUIDEX. Elsevier. • Produced in the Netherlands by Elsevier Science B.V. Provides indexing and abstracting of the international literature of fluid engineering and technology, 1973 to date, with monthly updates. Also known as *Fluid Engineering Abstracts.* Inquire as to online cost and availability.

INSPEC. Institution of Electrical Engineers. • Provides online citations, with abstracts, to the world literature of electrical engineering, electronics, optoelectronics, telecommunications, industrial controls, instrumentation, computer technology, information technology, and physics. Coverage includes more than 4,000 technical and scientific journals from 1969 to date, with weekly updating. (INSPEC is Information Services in Physics, Electronics, and Computing.) Inquire as to online cost and availability.

Thomas Register Online. Thomas Publishing Company L.L.C. • Provides concise information on approximately 194,000 U. S. companies, mainly manufacturers, with over 50,000 product classifications. Indexes over 115,000 trade names. Information is updated semiannually. Inquire as to online cost and availability.

PERIODICALS AND NEWSLETTERS

Control Engineering: Covering Control, Instrumentation and Automation Systems

Worldwide. Reed Elsevier Group plc Reed Business Information. • Monthly. $109.90 per year.

IEEE Industry Applications Magazine. IEEE - Communications Society. • Bimonthly. Covers new industrial applications of power conversion, drives, lighting, and control. Emphasis is on the petroleum, chemical, rubber, plastics, textile, and mining industries.

Instrumentation and Automation News: Instruments, Controls, Manufacturing Software, Electronic and Mechanical Components. Reed Elsevier Group plc Reed Business Information. • Monthly. $61.90 per year.

INTECH: The International Journal of Instrumentation and Control. ISA Services Inc. • Monthly. $72.00 per year.

Measurements and Control. Measurements and Data Corp. • Bimonthly. $24.00 per year. Supplement available: *M & C: Measurement and Control News*.

Processing. Putman Media Inc. • 14 times a year. $54.00 per year. Emphasis is on descriptions of new products for all areas of industrial processing, including valves, controls, filters, pumps, compressors, fluidics, and instrumentation.

Sensor Technology: A Monthly Intgelligence Service. Technical Insights. • Monthly. Institutions, $685.00 per year. Newsletter on technological developments relating to industrial sensors and process control.

Sensors: Your Resource for Sensing, Communications, and Control. Advanstar Communications. • Monthly. $70.00 per year. Edited for design, production, and manufacturing engineers involved with sensing systems. Emphasis is on emerging technology.

Test and Measurement World: The Magazine for Quality in Electronics. Reed Electronics Group. • 15 times a year. $93.99 per year.

STATISTICS SOURCES

U.S. Industry and Trade Outlook. U.S. Department of Commerce National Technical Information Service. • Annual. Produced by the International Trade Administration, U.S. Department of Commerce, in a "public-private" partnership with DRI/McGraw-Hill and Standard & Poor's. Provides basic data, outlook for the current year, and "Long-Term Prospects" (five-year projections) for a wide variety of products and services. Includes high technology industries. Formerly *U.S. Industrial Outlook*.

TRADE/PROFESSIONAL ASSOCIATIONS

Process Equipment Manufacturers Association. 201 Park Washington Ct., Falls Church, VA 22046-4527. Phone: (703)538-1796; Email: info@pemanet.org • URL: http://www.pemanet.org • Represents North American process equipment companies. Maintains an organization of capital equipment manufacturers. Provides a social/business base where members can meet to share and exchange views on common interests.

CONTROLLERS

See CORPORATE DIRECTORS AND OFFICERS

CONVENIENCE STORES

ABSTRACTS AND INDEXES

Business Periodicals Index Retrospective. EBSCO Publishing Inc. • 11/year. Quarterly and annual cumulations.

CD-ROM DATABASES

ABI/INFORM. ProQuest L.L.C. • Monthly. Provides CD-ROM indexing and abstracting of worldwide business literature. Archival discs are available from 1971. Formerly *ABI/INFORM OnDisc*.

Business Abstracts with Full Text. EBSCO Publishing Inc. • Includes full text articles from more than 460 business publications from 1982 to present. Indexing for nearly 880 publications.

ONLINE DATABASES

Wilson Business Abstracts Online. H.W. Wilson Co. • Indexes and abstracts 600 major business periodicals, plus the *Wall Street Journal* and the business section of the *New York Times*. Indexing is from 1982, abstracting from 1990, with the two newspapers included from 1993. Updated weekly. Inquire as to online cost and availability. (*Business Periodicals Index* without abstracts is also available online.).

PERIODICALS AND NEWSLETTERS

Convenience Store Decisions. Donohue-Meehan Publishing Co. • Monthly. $60.00 per year. Edited for headquarters and regional management personnel of convenience store chains.

Convenience Store News: The Information Source for the Industry. Nielsen Business Media Inc. • 15 times a year. Free to qualified personnel; others, $89.00 per year. Contains news of industry trends and merchandising techniques.

CSP: The Magazine for C-Store People. CSP Information Group. • Monthly. Emphasizes the influence of people (both store personnel and consumers) on the C-store industry.

Oil Express: Inside Report on Trends in Petroleum Marketing Without the Influence of Advertising. UCG Holdings L.P. • 50 times a year. $337.00 per year. Newsletter. Provides news of trends in petroleum marketing and convenience store operations. Includes *U.S. Oil Week's Price Monitor* (petroleum product prices) and *C-Store Digest* (news concerning convenience stores operated by the major oil companies) and *Fuel Oil Update*. Formerly *U.S. Oil Week*.

RESEARCH CENTERS AND INSTITUTES

Northwestern University - Center for Retail Management. Kellogg School of Management, 2001 Sheridan Rd., Evanston, IL 60208. Phone: (847)467-3600; Fax: (847)467-3620; Email: r-blattberg@kellogg.northwestern.edu • URL: http://www.kellogg.northwestern.edu/research/retail/ • Conducts research related to retail marketing and management.

Texas A&M University - Center for Retailing Studies. Wehner Bldg., Ste. 201, Mays Business School, 4112 TAMU, College Station, TX 77843-4112. Phone: (979)845-0325; Fax: (979)845-5117 or (979)845-5230; Email: c-bridges@mays.tamu.edu • URL: http://www.crstamu.org • Research areas include retailing issues and consumer economics.

TRADE/PROFESSIONAL ASSOCIATIONS

National Association of Convenience Stores. 1600 Duke St., 7th Fl., Alexandria, VA 22314. Phone: 800-966-6227 or (703)684-3600; Fax: (703)836-4564; Email: nacs@nacsonline.com • URL: http://www.nacsonline.com • Members are small retail stores that sell a variety of food and nonfood items and that usually have extended hours of opening.

CONVENTION MANAGEMENT

See MEETING MANAGEMENT

CONVENTIONS

See also CONFERENCES, WORKSHOPS, AND SEMINARS; SALES CONVENTIONS; TRADE SHOWS

DIRECTORIES

The HCEA Directory of Healthcare Meetings and Conventions. Healthcare Convention and Exhibitors Association. • Annual. $345 Nonmembers. Lists more than 6,000 health care meetings, most of which have an exhibit program. Formerly *Handbook-A Directory of Health Care Meetings and Conventions*.

Trade Shows Worldwide. Cengage Learning Inc. • 2013. $645.00. 31st edition. Provides detailed information from over 75 countries on more than 10,000 trade shows and exhibitions. Separate sections are provided for trade shows/exhibitions, for sponsors/organizers, and for services, facilities, and information sources. Indexing is by date, location, subject, name, and keyword.

INTERNET DATABASES

Trade Show Center. Global Sources/Trade Media Holdings Ltd. Phone: (656)574-2800; Email: service@globalsources.com • URL: http://www.globalsources.com/TRADESHW/TRDSHFRM.HTM • Free Web site provides current, detailed information on more than 1,000 major trade shows worldwide, including events in the U. S., but with an emphasis on "Asia and Greater China." Searching is offered by product, supplier, country, and month of year. Includes links to "Trade Information.".

ONLINE DATABASES

Conference Papers Index. Cambridge Scientific Abstracts L.P. • Bimonthly. Citations to scientific and technical papers presented at meetings, 1973 to present. Inquire as to online cost and availability.

PERIODICALS AND NEWSLETTERS

Scientific Meetings. Scientific Meetings Publications. • Quarterly. $85.00 per year. Provides information on forthcoming scientific, technical, medical, health, engineering and management meetings held throughout the world.

Successful Meetings: The Authority on Meetings and Incentive Travel Management. Nielsen Business Media Inc. • Monthly. Monthly. $79.00 per year.

TRADE/PROFESSIONAL ASSOCIATIONS

Professional Convention Management Association. 35 E Wacker Dr., Ste. 500, Chicago, IL 60601-2105. Phone: 877-827-7262 or (312)423-7262; Fax: (312)423-7222; Email: deborah.sexton@pcma.org • URL: http://www.pcma.org • Represents the interests of meeting management executives from associations, non-profit organizations, corporations, independent meeting planning companies, and multi-management firms who recognize the importance of meetings to their organization. Provides education, research and advocacy to advance the meetings and hospitality industry. Empowers members with the tools they need to succeed as meeting professionals and to promote the value of the industry to their organizations and the general public.

Religious Conference Management Association. 7702 Woodland Dr., Ste. 120, Indianapolis, IN 46278. Phone: (317)632-1888; Fax: (317)632-7909 • URL: http://www.rcmaweb.org.

CONVERTIBILITY OF CURRENCY

See FOREIGN EXCHANGE

CONVERTIBLE SECURITIES

See also SECURITIES

INTERNET DATABASES

Factiva. Dow Jones Reuters Business Interactive, LLC. Phone: 800-369-7466 or (609)452-1511; Fax:

(609)520-5770; Email: solutions@factiva.com • URL: http://www.factiva.com • Fee-based Web site provides "global news and business information through Web sites and content integration solutions." Includes Dow Jones and Reuters newswires, The Wall Street Journal, and more than 7,000 other sources of current news, historical articles, market research reports, and investment analysis. Content includes 96 major U. S. newspapers, 900 non-English sources, trade publications, media transcripts, country profiles, news photos, etc.

Nexis.com. Lexis-Nexis Group. Phone: 800-227-4908 or (937)865-6800; Fax: (937)865-6909; Email: webmaster@prod.lexis-nexis.com • URL: http://www.nexis.com • Fee-based Web site offers searching of about 2.8 billion documents in some 30,000 news, business, and legal information sources. Features include a subject directory covering 1,200 topics in 34 categories and a Company Dossier containing information on more than 500,000 public and private companies. Boolean searching is offered.

U.S. Securities and Exchange Commission. 100 F St. NE, Washington, DC 20549. Phone: 800-732-0330 or (202)942-8088; Fax: (202)942-9634; Email: webmaster@sec.gov • URL: http://www.sec.gov • SEC Web site offers free access through EDGAR to text of official corporate filings, such as annual reports (10-K), quarterly reports (10-Q), and proxies. (EDGAR is "Electronic Data Gathering, Analysis, and Retrieval System.") An example is given of how to obtain executive compensation data from proxies. Text of the daily *SEC News Digest* is offered, as are links to other government sites, non-government market regulators, and U. S. stock exchanges. Search facilities are extensive. Fees: Free.

Wall Street Journal Interactive Edition. Dow Jones & Co., Inc. 1211 Avenue of the Americas, New York, NY 10036. Phone: 800-369-5663; Email: service@dowjones.com • URL: http://new.dowjones.com • Fee-based Web site providing online searching of worldwide information from *The Wall Street Journal*. Includes "Company Snapshots," "The Journal's Greatest Hits," "Index to Market Data," "Journal Links," etc. Financial price quotes are available. Fees: $49.00 per year; $29.00 per year to print subscribers.

ONLINE DATABASES

EdgarPlus: SEC Basic Filings. Thomson Reuters Markets. • Online service provides full text of about 60,000 documents that have been filed with the U.S. Securities and Exchange Commission, 1987 to date, with daily updates. Filings include 6-K, 8-K, 10-K, 10-C, 10-Q, 20-F, and proxy statements. Inquire as to online cost and availability.

Value Line Convertible Data Base. Value Line Inc. • Provides online data for about 600 convertible bonds and other convertible securities: price, yield, premium, issue size, liquidity, and maturity. Information is current, with weekly updates. Inquire as to online cost and availability.

PERIODICALS AND NEWSLETTERS

Private Placement Letter: The Weekly for Privately Placed Fixed-Income Securities. SourceMedia Inc. • Weekly. $1,495 per year. Newsletter. Provides information on private financing of debt and convertible securities.

CONVEYING MACHINERY

See also MACHINERY; MATERIALS HANDLING

DIRECTORIES

Modern Materials Handling Casebook Directory. Reed Elsevier Group plc Reed Business Information. • Annual. Lists about 2,300 manufacturers of equipment and supplies in the materials handling industry. Supplement to *Modern Materials Handling*.

PERIODICALS AND NEWSLETTERS

Material Handling Management: Educating Industry on Product Handling, Flow Strategies, and Automation Technology. Penton Media Inc. • 13 times a year. Free to qualified personnel; others, $50.00 per year. Formerly *Material Handling Engineering*.

Modern Materials Handling. Reed Elsevier Group plc Reed Business Information. • 14 times a year. $99.90 per year. For managers and engineers who buy or specify equipment used to move, store, control and protect products throughout the manufacturing and warehousing cycles. Includes *Casebook Directory* and *Planning Guide*. Also includes *ADC News and Solutions*.

On the Mhove. Material Handling Industry. • Quarterly. Free. Formerly *MHI News*.

PHL Bulletin. National Institute of Packaging, Handling and Logistics Engineers. • 6/year.

TRADE/PROFESSIONAL ASSOCIATIONS

Association of Professional Material Handling Consultants. 8720 Red Oak Blvd., Ste. 201, Charlotte, NC 28217-3992. Phone: (704)676-1190; Fax: (704)676-1199; Email: jworoniecki@mhi.org • URL: http://www.mhi.org/apmhc • Professional and independent material handling consultants; individuals who perform similar functions within multi-plant corporations. Promotes the art and science of material handling; aims to elevate the profession of the material handling consultant and establishes codes of ethics, conduct and qualifications. Develops, maintains and enforces rigorous membership requirements and high standards of ethical professional practice which will make membership in the association a recognized mark of experience, stability, competence, reliability and character.

Conveyor Equipment Manufacturers Association. 5672 Strand Ct., Ste. 2, Naples, FL 34110. Phone: (239)514-3441; Fax: (239)514-3470 • URL: http://www.cemanet.org • Manufacturers and engineers of conveyors and conveying systems and portable and stationary machinery used in the transportation of raw materials and finished products in warehouses and on assembly line operations. Aims to standardize design, manufacture and application of conveying machinery and component parts.

Material Handling Equipment Distributors Association. 201 US Hwy. 45, Vernon Hills, IL 60061-2398. Phone: (847)680-3500; Fax: (847)362-6989; Email: connect@mheda.org • URL: http://www.mheda.org • Distributors and manufacturers of material handling equipment. Aims to improve the proficiency of independent material handling distributors.

Material Handling Industry. 8720 Red Oak Blvd., Ste. 201, Charlotte, NC 28217-3996. Phone: 800-345-1815 or (704)676-1190; Fax: (704)676-1199; Email: jnofsinger@mhia.org • URL: http://www.mhia.org • Formerly Material Handling Industry.

COOKING UTENSILS

See HOUSEWARES INDUSTRY

COOKWARE

See HOUSEWARES INDUSTRY

COOPERAGE INDUSTRY

See also CONTAINER INDUSTRY

TRADE/PROFESSIONAL ASSOCIATIONS

Associated Cooperage Industries of America. 10001 Taylorsville Rd., Ste. 201, Louisville, KY 40299-3116. Phone: (502)261-2242; Fax: (502)261-9425; Email: acia@att.net • URL: http://www.acia.net • Serves as contact point for members; disseminates information about the wooden barrel, with emphasis on white oak; promotes the common interest of those in the industry.

COOPERATIVE ADVERTISING

ABSTRACTS AND INDEXES

Business Periodicals Index Retrospective. EBSCO Publishing Inc. • 11/year. Quarterly and annual cumulations.

DIRECTORIES

RAB Co-op Directory. Radio Advertising Bureau. • Annual. Database covers: Over 5,000 manufacturers that provide cooperative allowances for radio advertising. Database includes: Company name, address, name of contact, phone, fax, allowance, accrual rate, whether plan is administered by distributor, and expiration dates.

ONLINE DATABASES

Wilson Business Abstracts Online. H.W. Wilson Co. • Indexes and abstracts 600 major business periodicals, plus the *Wall Street Journal* and the business section of the *New York Times*. Indexing is from 1982, abstracting from 1990, with the two newspapers included from 1993. Updated weekly. Inquire as to online cost and availability. (*Business Periodicals Index* without abstracts is also available online.).

STATISTICS SOURCES

Radio Facts: The Voice of Urban Culture. RadioMan Publishing Inc. • Annual. $50.00.

TRADE/PROFESSIONAL ASSOCIATIONS

Radio Advertising Bureau. 1320 Greenway Dr., Ste. 500, Irving, TX 75038-2587. Phone: 800-232-3131 or (972)753-6786 or (516)753-6782; Fax: (972)753-6727 or (212)753-6727; Email: efarber@rab.com • URL: http://www.rab.com • Includes radio stations, radio networks, station sales representatives, and allied industry services, such as producers, research firms, schools, and consultants. Calls on advertisers and agencies to promote the sale of radio time as an advertising medium. Sponsors program to increase professionalism of radio salespeople, awarding Certified Radio Marketing Consultant designation to those who pass examination. Sponsors regional marketing conferences. Conducts extensive research program into all phases of radio sales. Issues reports on use of radio by national, regional, and local advertisers. Speaks before conventions and groups to explain benefits of radio advertising. Sponsors Radio Creative Fund. Compiles statistics.

COOPERATIVE AGRICULTURE

See COOPERATIVES

COOPERATIVE MOVEMENT

See COOPERATIVES

COOPERATIVES

DIRECTORIES

Directory of Wholesale Grocers. Chain Store Guide. • Annual. $327.00. Online edition, $747.00. Profiles over 1,100 cooperatives, voluntaries, non-sponsoring wholesalers, cash and carry warehouses, and nearly 220 service merchandisers. Covers United States and Canada.

PERIODICALS AND NEWSLETTERS

CHF Newsbriefs. Global Communities. • Description: Seeks to "help families throughout the world by focusing on the development of communities, habitat, and finance.".

Communities: Journal of Cooperative Living. Fellowship for Intentional Communities. • Quarterly. Contains information, issues, stories, and ideas about intentional communities in North America from urban co-ops to cohousing groups to ecovillages to rural communes.

Cooperative Housing Bulletin. National Association of Housing Cooperatives. • Quarterly. $75 per year. Includes *Cooperative Housing Journal*.

Rural Cooperatives. Rural Business Cooperative Service Cooperative Services Program. • Bimonthly. Issued by the U.S. Department of Agriculture. Contains articles on cooperatives in rural America. Formerly *Farmer Cooperatives*.

RESEARCH CENTERS AND INSTITUTES

Cornell University - Cornell Cooperative Extension. Kennedy Hall, Box 26, Ithaca, NY 14853. Phone: (607)255-0789 or (607)255-2237; Fax: (607)255-0788; Email: ck236@cornell.edu • URL: http://cce.cornell.edu/Pages/Default.aspx • Coordinates campus research with needs of residents of the State of New York. Activities focus on five broad areas, including children, youth and family well-being; community and economic vitality; environmental and natural resource enhancement; agricultural and food systems sustainability; and nutrition, health and safety.

University of California Cooperative Extension, Riverside County. 21150 Box Springs Rd., Ste. 202, Moreno Valley, CA 92557-8718. Phone: (951)683-6491; Fax: (951)788-2615; Email: ceriverside@ucdavis.edu • URL: http://ceriverside.ucanr.edu • Agriculture, food safety, food preservation, consumer economics, and human nutrition. Provides assistance in the development and dissemination of information about the public's supply of food and fiber and seeks to educate the public on the wide use of natural resources.

University of Wisconsin—Madison - Center for Cooperatives. 427 Lorch St., Madison, WI 53706-1503. Phone: (608)262-3981; Fax: (608)262-3251; Email: hueth@wisc.edu • URL: http://www.uwcc.wisc.edu • Cooperative action to meet the economic and social needs of people.

TRADE/PROFESSIONAL ASSOCIATIONS

National Cooperative Business Association. 1401 New York Ave. NW, Ste. 1100, Washington, DC 20005. Phone: (202)638-6222; Fax: (202)638-1374 • URL: http://www.ncba.coop • Local, state, regional and national cooperative business organizations including farm supply, agricultural marketing, insurance, banking, housing, health care, consumer goods and services, student, worker, fishery and other cooperatives. Represents, strengthens and expands cooperative businesses. Programs include: supporting the development of cooperative businesses in the U.S.; developing and providing technical assistance to cooperatives in developing nations; representing American cooperatives in Washington, DC and abroad; promoting and developing commercial relations among the world's cooperatives. Supports the Cooperative Hall of Fame and the Cooperative Development Foundation.

National Rural Utilities Cooperative Finance Corp. 20701 Cooperative Way, Dulles, VA 20166. Phone: 800-424-2954 or (703)709-6700 or (703)467-1800; Fax: (703)467-5175; Email: publicrelations@nrucfc.coop • URL: http://www.nrucfc.coop.

COPIERS

See COPYING MACHINE INDUSTRY

COPPER INDUSTRY

See also METAL INDUSTRY; MINES AND MINERAL RESOURCES

ALMANACS AND YEARBOOKS

CRB Commodity Yearbook. Commodity Research Bureau. CRB. • Annual. $179 plus $10.00 shipping cost. The single most comprehensive source of commodity and futures market information available.

CD-ROM DATABASES

METADEX Materials Collection: Metals-Polymers-Ceramics. Cambridge Scientific Abstracts L.P. • Quarterly. Provides CD-ROM citations to the worldwide literature of materials science and metallurgy. Corresponds to *Metals Abstracts, Alloys Index, Steels Alert, Nonferrous Alert, Polymers/Ceramics/Composites Alert*, and *Engineered Materials Abstracts*. (Formerly produced by ASM International.).

PERIODICALS AND NEWSLETTERS

Oil Daily: Daily Newspaper of the Petroleum Industry. Energy Intelligence Group. • Daily. Email, $1,595.00 per year; fax, $2,395.00 per year, online, $1,495.00 per year. Newspaper for the petroleum industry.

33 Metalproducing: For Primary Producers of Steel, Aluminum, and Copper-Base Alloys. Penton Media Inc. • Monthly. $65.00 per year. Covers metal production technology and methods and industry news. Includes a bimonthly *Nonferrous Supplement*.

PRICE SOURCES

Chemical & Engineering News. American Chemical Society. • Weekly Annual. $265 Nonmembers print, North America. Magazine on chemical and engineering news.

The New York Times. Gannett Co., Inc. • Mon.-Sun. (morn.). $5.85 Individuals. Provides personal finance expertise.

Platt's Metals Week. Platts Global Energy. • Weekly. $770 Individuals.

STATISTICS SOURCES

Non-Ferrous Metal Data Yearbook. American Bureau of Metal Statistics. • Annual. $405.00. Provides worldwide data on approximately about 200 statistical tables covering many nonferrous metals. Includes production, consumption, inventories, exports, imports, and other data.

Standard & Poor's Industry Surveys. Standard & Poor's Financial Services L.L.C. • Semiannual. $1,800.00. Two looseleaf volumes. Includes monthly *Supplements*. Provides detailed, individual surveys of 52 major industry groups. Each survey is revised on a semiannual basis. Also includes "Monthly Investment Review" (industry group investment analysis) and monthly "Trends & Projections" (economic analysis).

United States Census of Mineral Industries. Bureau of the Census, U.S. Department of Commerce. U. S. Government Printing Office. • Quinquennial.

U.S. Industry and Trade Outlook. U.S. Department of Commerce National Technical Information Service. • Annual. Produced by the International Trade Administration, U.S. Department of Commerce, in a "public-private" partnership with DRI/McGraw-Hill and Standard & Poor's. Provides basic data, outlook for the current year, and "Long-Term Prospects" (five-year projections) for a wide variety of products and services. Includes high technology industries. Formerly *U.S. Industrial Outlook*.

TRADE/PROFESSIONAL ASSOCIATIONS

Copper and Brass Fabricators Council. 3050 K St. NW, Ste. 400, Washington, DC 20007-5108. Phone: (202)833-8575; Fax: (202)342-8451 • URL: http://www.cbfc.us • Formerly Copper and Brass Fabricators Foreign Trade Association.

Copper and Brass Servicenter Association. 6734 W 121st St., Overland Park, KS 66209. Phone: (913)396-0697; Fax: (913)345-1006; Email: cbsahq@copper-brass.org • URL: http://www.copper-brass.org • Represents wholesalers of copper and brass sheet, tubing, pipe, and related products; supplier members are copper mills, metal strip platters and re-rollers. Compiles statistics.

Copper Development Association. 260 Madison Ave., New York, NY 10016-2401. Phone: (212)251-7200; Fax: (212)251-7234; Email: questions@copperalliance.us • URL: http://www.copper.org • Represents U.S. and foreign copper mining, smelting and refining companies, U.S. fabricating companies such as brass and wire mills, foundries, and ingot makers. Seeks to expand the uses and applications and to broaden the markets of copper and copper products. Functions in groups or divisions corresponding to principal market areas such as transportation, building construction, electrical and electronic products, industrial machinery and equipment, and consumer and general products. Provides technical service to users of copper and copper alloy products. Has industrywide responsibility for market statistics and research. Maintains 10 field offices in the U.S.

Non-Ferrous Metals Producers Committee. 2030 M St. NW, Ste. 800, Washington, DC 20036. Phone: (202)466-7720; Fax: (202)466-2710 • URL: http://www.arcat.com/arcatcos/cos37/arc37679.cfm • Represents domestic copper, lead, and zinc producers. Promotes the interests of copper, lead, and zinc mining and metal industries in the U.S. with emphasis on tariffs, laws, regulations, and government policies affecting international trade and foreign imports.

COPYING MACHINE INDUSTRY

DIRECTORIES

Copying & Duplicating Machine & Supplies Directory. InfoGroup Inc. • Annual. Number of listings: 10,350. Entries include: Name, address, phone (including area code), size of advertisement, year first in "Yellow Pages." Coding indicates brands carried, specialties, or franchises held. Franchise editions also available. Compiled from telephone company "Yellow Pages," nationwide.

Copying & Duplicating Service Directory. InfoGroup Inc. • Annual. Number of listings: 20,946. Entries include: Company name, address, phone (including area code), size of advertisement, year first in "Yellow Pages," name of owner or manager, number of employees. Compiled from telephone company "Yellow Pages," nationwide.

Duplicating Machines & Supplies-Wholesalers Directory. InfoGroup Inc. • Updated continuously; printed on request. Number of listings: 560. Entries include: Name, address, phone (including area code), size of advertisement, year first in "Yellow Pages," name or owner or manager, number of employees. Compiled from telephone company "Yellow Pages," nationwide.

Photo Copying Directory. InfoGroup Inc. • Annual. Number of listings: 20,946. Entries include: Name, address, phone (including area code), size of advertisement, year first in "Yellow Pages," name of owner or manager, number of employees. Compiled from telephone company "Yellow Pages," nationwide.

PERIODICALS AND NEWSLETTERS

Digital Information Network. Buyers Laboratory L.L.C. • Monthly. $725.00 per year. Newsletter. Information on the copier industry, including test reports on individual machines.

COPYRIGHT

ABSTRACTS AND INDEXES

Current Law Index. Cengage Learning Inc. • $1,332 Individuals. Monthly. $1269.00 per year. Produced in cooperation with the American Association of Law Libraries. Indexes more than 900 law journals, legal newspapers, and specialty publications from the U.S., Canada, U.K., Ireland, Australia, and New Zealand.

Library Literature and Information Science Index. H.W. Wilson Co. • Quarterly. Annual cumulation. Price varies.

CD-ROM DATABASES

Authority Intellectual Property Library. Matthew Bender and Company Inc. • Quarterly. Price on request. CD-ROM contains updated full text of *Intellectual Property Counseling and Litigation, Computer Law, International Computer Law, Nimmer on Copyright, Milgrim on Trade Secrets, Patent Litigation, Patent Licensing Transactions, Trademark Protection and Practice,* and other Matthew Bender publications relating to the law of intellectual property.

WILSONDISC: Library Literature and Information Science Index. H.W. Wilson Co. • Quarterly. Includes unlimited access to the online version of *Library Literature.* Provides CD-ROM indexing of about 400 periodicals, covering a wide range of topics having to do with libraries, library management, and the information industry.

HANDBOOKS AND MANUALS

Intellectual Property Primary Law Sourcebook. Matthew Bender and Company Inc. • $175 print only. Provides federal copyright, patent, and trademark statutes, as well as the Leahy-Smith America Invents Act.

Nimmer on Copyright. David Nimmer. Matthew Bender and Company Inc. • $3,087 book. 10 looseleaf volumes. Periodic supplementation. Analytical and practical guide on the law of literary, musical, and artistic proprerty.

Protecting Trade Secrets, Patents, Copyrights, and Trademarks. Robert C. Dorr and Christopher H. Munch. Aspen Publishers, Inc. • $165.00. Looseleaf service.

INTERNET DATABASES

Lexis.com Research System. Lexis-Nexis Group. Phone: 800-227-4908 or (937)865-6800; Fax: (937)865-6909; Email: webmaster@prod.lexis-nexis.com • URL: http://www.nexis.com • Fee-based Web site offers extensive searching of a wide variety of legal sources. Additional features include Daily Opinion Service, lexis.com Bookstore, Career Center, CLE Center, Law Schools, and Practice Pages ("Pages specific to areas of specialty").

ONLINE DATABASES

U.S. Copyrights. DIALOG. • Provides access to registration details for all active copyright registrations on file at the U. S. Copyright Office since 1978. Contains information on initial registration, renewal, assignments, and ownership status. Weekly updates. Inquire as to online cost and availability.

OTHER SOURCES

Catalog of Copyright Entries. U.S. Library of Congress, Copyright Office. U. S. Government Printing Office. • Frequency and prices vary.

Cyberlaw: Intellectual Property in the Digital Millennium. ALM Media Properties LLC. • $530 per year. A basic guide to copyright as applied to the Internet and other electronic sources. (Law Journal Press).

Intellectual Property and Antitrust Law. William C. Holmes. Thomson West. • Semiannual. $1,347 full set. Includes patent, trademark, and copyright practices.

Lindey on Entertainment, Publishing and the Arts. Alexander Lindey, editor. Thomson West. • $1,582.86 Full Set. Provides basic forms, applicable law, and guidance.

PERIODICALS AND NEWSLETTERS

Copyright Bulletin: Quarterly Review. Bernan Associates. • Quarterly. Available online only.

Copyright Society of the United States of America Journal. Copyright Society of the U.S.A. • Quarterly. Individuals, $125.00 per year; nonprofit organizations, $50.00 per year; corporations, $500.00 per year.

Information Outlook: The Monthly Magazine of the Special Libraries Association. Special Libraries Association. • Monthly. $65.00 per year. Topics include information technology, the Internet, copyright, research techniques, library management, and professional development. Replaces *Special Libraries* and *SpeciaList.*

Intellectual Property Today. • Monthly. $96.00 per year. Covers legal developments in copyright, patents, trademarks, and licensing. Emphasizes the effect of new technology on intellectual property. Formerly *Law Works.*

TRADE/PROFESSIONAL ASSOCIATIONS

Copyright Clearance Center. 222 Rosewood Dr., No. 910, Danvers, MA 01923-4510. Phone: (978)750-8400; Fax: (508)741-2318 or (978)646-8600; Email: info@copyright.com • URL: http://www.copyright.com • Facilitates compliance with U.S. copyright law. Provides licensing systems for the reproduction and distribution of copyrighted materials in print and electronic formats throughout the world. Manages rights relating to over 1.75 million works and represents more than 9600 publishers and hundreds of thousands of authors and other creators, directly or through their representatives.

Copyright Society of the U.S.A. 1 East 53rd St., 8th Fl., New York, NY 10022. • URL: http://www.csusa.org • Lawyers and laymen; libraries, universities, publishers, and firms interested in the protection and study of rights in music, literature, art, motion pictures, and other forms of intellectual property. Promotes research in the field of copyright; encourages study of economic and technological aspects of copyright by those who deal with problems of communication, book publishing, motion picture production, and television and radio broadcasting. Seeks better understanding among students and scholars of copyright in foreign countries, to lay a foundation for development of international copyright. Co-sponsors (with New York University School of Law) the Walter J. Derenberg Copyright and Trademark Library, which includes foreign periodicals dealing with literary and artistic property and related fields. Sponsors symposia and lectures on copyright. Encourages study of copyright in U.S. law schools.

COPYWRITING

See ADVERTISING COPY

CORDAGE INDUSTRY

See ROPE AND TWINE INDUSTRY

CORN INDUSTRY

See also FEED AND FEEDSTUFFS INDUSTRY

ABSTRACTS AND INDEXES

Field Crop Abstracts. CABI Publishing North America. • Monthly. Published in England by CABI Publishing, formerly Commonwealth Agricultural Bureaux.

Maize Abstracts. CABI Publishing North America. • Bimonthly. $840.00 per year. Published in England by CABI Publishing. Provides worldwide coverage of the literature.

ALMANACS AND YEARBOOKS

Corn Annual. Corn Refiners Association. • Annual. Annual.

CRB Commodity Yearbook. Commodity Research Bureau. CRB. • Annual. $179 plus $10.00 shipping cost. The single most comprehensive source of commodity and futures market information available.

CD-ROM DATABASES

OECD Statistical Compendium. Organization for Economic Cooperation and Development. • Semiannual. $1,905.00 per year for 1 to 10 users. CD-ROM contains more than 730,000 monthly, quarterly, and annual time series for OECD countries, 1960 to date. Includes fully searchable data on agriculture, food, economic indicators, national accounts, employment, energy, finance, industry, technology, and foreign trade. Results can be displayed in various forms.

DIRECTORIES

American Vegetable Grower--Source Book. Meister Media Worldwide. • Annual. Publication includes: Lists of suppliers of agricultural chemicals and manufacturers and suppliers of other agricultural products, equipment, and services including packaging equipment, transportation services, direct marketing suppliers, plants and seeds, etc. Entries include: Company name, address, phone, fax, e-mail.

Major Food and Drink Companies of the World. Cengage Learning Inc. • 12th edition. eBook. Published by Graham & Whiteside. Contains profiles and trade names for more than 9,200 important food and beverage companies in various countries. In addition to foods, includes both alcoholic and nonalcoholic drink products.

INTERNET DATABASES

Business 2.0 Web Guide to the Best Business Links. Business 2.0 Media Inc. Phone: (415)293-4800; Email: support@business2.com • URL: http://www.business2.com/webguide • Web site presents an extensive, searchable directory of links to "the best, most informative, and authoritative web pages." Twenty main categories cover business, finance, career, company information, people, and technology topics, with thousands of subtopics, all linking to Web sites recommended by experienced business researchers. Fees: Free.

Fedstats. Federal Interagency Council on Statistical Policy. Phone: (202)395-7254 • URL: http://www.fedstats.gov • Web site features an efficient search facility for full-text statistics produced by more than 100 federal agencies, including the Census Bureau, the Bureau of Economic Analysis, and the Bureau of Labor Statistics. Boolean searches can be made within one agency or for all agencies combined. Links are offered to international statistical bureaus, including the UN, IMF, OECD, UNESCO, Eurostat, and 20 individual countries. Fees: Free.

FreeLunch.com. Economy.com, Inc. Phone: (610)696-8700; Fax: (610)696-1678 • URL: http://www.freelunch.com • Web site provides free access to more than 200 million economic and financial data series, covering industry, demographics, labor markets, prices, retail sales, government spending, trade, interest rates, housing starts, the stock market, etc. Data is available in either chart or table form. Searching is offered. Free, but registration required.

Economy.com, Inc. also offers fee-based economic analysis at *The Dismal Scientist* site (www.dismal.com).

USDA. U.S. National Institute of Standards and Technology. 100 Bureau Dr., Gaithersburg, MD 20899-1070. Phone: 800-877-8339 or (301)975-6478 or (202)720-2791; Fax: (301)975-8295; Email: inquiries@nist.gov • URL: http://www.nist.gov • The USDA home page has six sections: News and Information; What's New; About USDA; Agencies; Opportunities; Search and Help. Keyword searching is offered from the USDA home page and from various individual agency home pages. Agencies are the Economic Research Service, Agricultural Marketing Service, National Agricultural Statistics Service, National Agricultural Library, and about 12 others. Updating varies. Fees: Free.

ONLINE DATABASES

CAB Abstracts. CABI. • Contains 46 specialized abstract collections covering over 10,000 journals and monographs in the areas of agriculture, horticulture, forest products, farm products, nutrition, dairy science, poultry, grains, animal health, entomology, etc. Time period is 1972 to date, with monthly updates. Inquire as to online cost and availability. *CAB Abstracts on CD-ROM* also available, with annual updating.

Food Science and Technology Abstracts (online). IFIS North American Desk. • Produced by International Food Information Service. Provides about 500,000 online citations, with abstracts, to the international literature of food science, technology, commodities, engineering, and processing. Approximately 2,000 periodicals are covered. Time period is 1969 to date, with monthly updates. Inquire as to online cost and availability.

PRICE SOURCES

Agricultural Letter. Federal Reserve Bank of Chicago. • Quarterly. Looseleaf service.

The New York Times. Gannett Co., Inc. • Mon.-Sun. (morn.). $5.85 Individuals. Provides personal finance expertise.

RESEARCH CENTERS AND INSTITUTES

University of California - California Agricultural Experiment Station. 1111 Franklin St., Rm. 6402, Oakland, CA 94607-5200. Phone: (510)987-0036 or (510)987-0060; Fax: (510)465-2659 or (510)451-2317; Email: steve.nation@ucop.edu • URL: http://ucanr.org/AES.shtml • Plant and animal biology, agricultural engineering and economics, soils, and water, including basic and applied studies directed toward solving problems of agriculture involved in production, storage, and transportation of over 300 commodities produced in California. Studies problems relating to forestry, human welfare and nutrition, pest management, mosquito control, and outdoor recreation. Operates on a statewide basis, with main units on Berkeley, Davis, and Riverside campuses of the University and ten research and extension centers throughout the state.

University of Nebraska—Lincoln - Agricultural Research Division. 207 Agricultural Hall, Lincoln, NE 68583-0704. Phone: (402)472-2045; Fax: (402)472-9071; Email: aclutter2@unl.edu.

STATISTICS SOURCES

Agricultural Statistics. U.S. Department of Agriculture National Agricultural Statistics Service. • Annual. $46 Individuals. Provides a wide variety of statistical data relating to agricultural production, supplies, consumption, prices/price-supports, foreign trade, costs, and returns, as well as farm labor, loans, income, and population. In many cases, historical data is shown annually for 10 years. In addition to farm data, includes detailed fishery statistics.

Statistical Annual: Grains, Options on Agricultural Futures. Chicago Board of Trade. • Annual. Includes historical data on Wheat Futures, Options on Wheat Futures, Corn Futures, Options on Corn Futures, Oats Futures, Soybean Futures, Options on Soybean Futures, Soybean Oil Futures, Soybean Meal Futures.

Survey of Current Business. U. S. Government Printing Office. • Published by Bureau of Economic Analysis, U. S. Department of Commerce. Presents a wide variety of business and economic data.

United States Census of Agriculture. U.S. Department of Agriculture National Agricultural Statistics Service. • Quinquennial. Provides uniform, comprehensive farming and ranching operations data for every U.S. state and county, including production expenses, market value of products, and operator characteristics.

TRADE/PROFESSIONAL ASSOCIATIONS

Corn Refiners Association. 1701 Pennsylvania Ave. NW, Ste. 950, Washington, DC 20006. Phone: (202)331-1634 or (202)534-3494; Fax: (202)331-2054; Email: comments@corn.org • URL: http://www.corn.org • Corn refining firms that manufacture corn starches, sugars, syrups, oils, feed and alcohol by wet process.

National Corn Growers Association. 632 Cepi Dr., Chesterfield, MO 63005-1221. Phone: (636)733-9004; Fax: (636)733-9005; Email: corninfo@ncga.com • URL: http://www.ncga.com/home • Growers of corn. Furthers the use, proper marketing, legislative position, and efficient production of corn. Conducts research and educational programs. Sponsors National Yield Contest; compiles statistics.

CORPORATE ACQUISITIONS AND MERGERS

See MERGERS AND ACQUISITIONS

CORPORATE CULTURE

ABSTRACTS AND INDEXES

Business Periodicals Index Retrospective. EBSCO Publishing Inc. • 11/year. Quarterly and annual cumulations.

ONLINE DATABASES

Wilson Business Abstracts Online. H.W. Wilson Co. • Indexes and abstracts 600 major business periodicals, plus the *Wall Street Journal* and the business section of the *New York Times*. Indexing is from 1982, abstracting from 1990, with the two newspapers included from 1993. Updated weekly. Inquire as to online cost and availability. (*Business Periodicals Index* without abstracts is also available online.).

PERIODICALS AND NEWSLETTERS

Chief Executive Magazine. Chief Executive Group, LLC. • Monthly. $99 per year.

Corporate Public Issues and Their Management: The Executive Systems Approach to Public Policy Formation. Issue Action Publications Inc. • Monthly. $195. Covers the approach to public policy creation.

Fortune Magazine. Time Inc., Business Information Group. • Biweekly. $19.99 all access. Edited for top executives and upper-level managers.

Harvard Business Review. Harvard University, Graduate School of Business Administration. Harvard Business School Publishing. • 10/year.

RESEARCH CENTERS AND INSTITUTES

University of Pittsburgh - Business, Government, and Society Research Institute. School of Business, Mervis Hall, Pittsburgh, PA 15260. Phone: (412)648-1555; Fax: (412)648-1693; Email: mitnick@pitt.edu.

CORPORATE DIRECTORS AND OFFICERS

See also EXECUTIVES

BIOGRAPHICAL SOURCES

Newsmakers. Cengage Learning Inc. • Annual. $314 Individuals. Four softbound issues and one hardbound annual. Biographical information on individuals currently in the news. Includes photographs. Formerly *Contemporary Newsmakers*. eBook also available. Contact for pricing.

Who's Who in Finance and Business. Marquis Who's Who L.L.C. • Biennial. $349 Individuals. Provides over 21,000 concise biographies of business leaders in all fields.

CD-ROM DATABASES

Standard & Poor's Corporations. Dialog OnDisc. • Monthly. Price on application. Produced by Standard & Poor's. Contains three CD-ROM files: Executives, Private Companies, and Public Companies, providing detailed information on more than 70,000 business executives, 55,000 private companies, and 12,000 publicly-traded corporations.

DIRECTORIES

Canadian Federal Corporations and Directors. Postmedia Network Inc. • Monthly. Covers: About 400,000 federally incorporated Canadian companies. Database includes: Company name, address, date incorporated, parent or subsidiary companies, financial data for two years, names and home addresses of directors.

DASH: Directors and Shareholdings. Bureau van Dijk S.A. • Database covers: One million limited companies and two million directors combined with details on individual and corporate shareholders in the United Kingdom. Entries include: Company name, address, phone, fax, activity, employee range, legal form, status, capital, turnover, holding companies and corporate shareholders; director name, date of birth, address, marital status, nationality, occupation, qualification, appointment date.

Directory of Companies, Board Members and Directors. Dicodi S.A. • Annual. Covers: 25,000 companies and 80,000 board members in Spain. Entries include: Company name, address, phone, director names.

Directory of Corporations and Corporate Officers. DAFSA. • Annual. Covers: 13,000 corporation board members and 1,200 companies on the stock exchange in France. Entries include: For members--Name, address, positions held, responsibilities. For companies--Company name, address, phone, line of business, executives, shareholders, subsidiaries, financial data.

Directory of Directors. Reed Business Information. • Annual. $275 plus 7.50 pounds shipping; 15 pounds overseas. Covers: Approximately 50,000 directors of the top 15,000 public and private corporations in the United Kingdom. Entries include: Name, address, phone, fax, title and/or profession, list of companies of which a director, code indicating business interest.

Nigerian Directory of Directors. Asoms Biblio-Info Consult Publishers. • $5 Nigerian naira. Covers: directors of business firms in Nigeria. Entries include: Name of official, address, firm(s) for which a director.

Owners and Officers of Private Companies. Taft Group. • Annual. $320. Covers over 128,000 key executives who own and operate America's 48,000 private companies with annual sales over $3 million.

Reference Book of Corporate Managements. • Annual. Libraries, $650.00 per year; others, $795.00 per year. Lease basis. Management executives at over 12,000 leading United States companies.

Standard & Poor's Register of Corporations, Direc-

tors and Executives. Standard & Poor's Financial Services L.L.C. • Annual. Covers: over 55,000 public and privately held corporations in the United States, including names and titles of over 400,000 officials (Volume 1); 70,000 biographies of directors and executives (Volume 2). Database includes: In Volume 3, lists of new executives, new companies, a corporate "Family Tree," Standard & Poor's 500 composite stock indices, and obituaries. Entries include: For companies--Name, address, phone, names of principal executives and accountants; primary bank, primary law firm, number of employees, estimated annual sales, outside directors, Standard Industrial Classification (SIC) code, product or service provided. For directors and executives--Name, home and principal business addresses, date and place of birth, fraternal organization memberships, business affiliations.

Who Owns Corporate America. Taft Group. • Annual. $285. Covers: nearly 75,000 officers, directors, and 10% principal stockholders who own securities registered with the Securities and Exchange Commission. Entries include: Name, company, stock symbol, number of shares held, date of last stock transaction, class of security held, type of ownership, relationship of stockholder to the company, market value of holdings.

Who's Who in Finance and Business. Marquis Who's Who L.L.C. • Biennial. $349 Individuals. Provides over 21,000 concise biographies of business leaders in all fields.

HANDBOOKS AND MANUALS

Responsibilities of Corporate Officers and Directors Under Federal Securities Law. Wolters Kluwer Law & Business CCH. • Annual. $132 paperback. Includes discussions of indemnification, "D & O" insurance, corporate governance, and insider liability.

OTHER SOURCES

Directors and Officers Liability: Prevention, Insurance, and Indemnification. ALM Media Properties LLC. • $530 per year. Covers the legal risks faced by corporate directors and officers. (Law Journal Press).

Fund Governance: Legal Duties of Investment Company Directors. ALM Media Properties LLC. • $580 print and online + ebook. Covers the legal obligations of directors of mutual funds and closed-end funds. (Law Journal Press).

PERIODICALS AND NEWSLETTERS

Corporate Board Member: The Magazine for Directors of Public Companies. Board Member Inc. • Quarterly. $115.00 per year. Edited for board members of publicly traded corporations. Includes such topics as liability, executive compensation, mergers, corporate administration, and management succession.

Corporate Controller. Thomson RIA. • $420. Bimonthly.

D & O Advisor: Risk Management for Directors and Officers. ALM Media Properties LLC. • Quarterly. $125.00 per year. Covers a wide range of legal topics of concern to corporate boards and key executives.

Forbes. Forbes Inc. • Biweekly. $29.99 Individuals. Magazine reporting on industry, business and finance management.

Fortune Magazine. Time Inc., Business Information Group. • Biweekly. $19.99 all access. Edited for top executives and upper-level managers.

RESEARCH CENTERS AND INSTITUTES

Financial Executives Research Foundation. Financial Executives International. 1250 Headquarters Plz., West Tower, 7th Fl., Morristown, NJ 07960. Phone: (973)765-1000; Fax: (973)765-1018; Email: mhollein@financialexecutives.org • URL: http://www.financialexecutives.org • Publishes research in business management, with emphasis on corporate financial management issues. Maintains inquiry services.

TRADE/PROFESSIONAL ASSOCIATIONS

American Management Association. 1601 Broadway, New York, NY 10019-7420. Phone: 877-566-9441 or (212)586-8100 or (518)891-5510; Fax: (212)903-8168 or (518)891-0368; Email: customerservice@amanet.org • URL: http://www.amanet.org • Provides educational forums worldwide where members and their colleagues learn superior, practical business skills and explore best practices of world-class organizations through interaction with each other and expert faculty practitioners. Maintains a publishing program providing tools individuals use to extend learning beyond the classroom in a process of life-long professional growth and development through education.

Association for Corporate Growth - Toronto Chapter. 720 Spadina Ave., Ste. 202, Toronto, ON, Canada M5S 2T9. Phone: (416)868-1881; Fax: (416)391-3633; Email: acgtoronto@acg.org • URL: http://www.acg.org/toronto • Professionals with a leadership role in strategic corporate growth. Seeks to facilitate the professional advancement of members, and the practice of corporate growth management. Fosters communication and cooperation among members; conducts continuing professional education programs.

Association of AE Business Leaders. 948 Capp St., San Francisco, CA 94110-3911. Phone: (415)713-5379; Email: events@aebl.org • URL: http://www.aebl.org • Individuals responsible for any or all aspects of business management in a professional design firm. Aims to improve the effectiveness of professional design firms through the growth and development of business management skills. Seeks to: provide a forum for the exchange of ideas and information and discussion and resolution of common problems and issues; establish guidelines for approaches to common management concerns; initiate and maintain professional relationships among members; improve recognition and practice of management as a science in professional design firms; advance and improve reputable service to clients; offer a variety of comprehensive educational programs and opportunities. Maintains speakers' bureau and placement service. Holds seminars. Conducts surveys and research programs. Compiles statistics.

Association of Corporate Treasurers of Southern Africa. PO Box 5853, Cresta 2118, South Africa. Phone: 27 11 4821512; Fax: 27 11 4821996 • URL: http://www.actsa.org.za • Provides a forum for the promotion of the common interests of corporate treasurers in Southern Africa. Provides learning and networking opportunities for its members.

Association of Corporate Treasurers Singapore. Block 51, Telok Blangah Dr., No. 06-142, Singapore 100051, Singapore. • URL: http://www.act.org.sg • Provides a platform for the exchange of ideas and information relating to treasury. Enhances treasury management skills through training and education. Facilitates a platform for dialogue between the industry and the government. Promotes the growth of the treasury profession to help Singapore develop into a financial hub in the region.

Cayman Islands Directors Association. George Town, Grand Cayman, Cayman Islands. Phone: (345)945-0012; Fax: (345)947-7328 • URL: http://www.cida2008.com • Represents individuals who hold office as directors of one or more Cayman Islands registered companies. Promotes and safeguards the interests of directors of Cayman Islands registered companies. Maintains code of conduct and best practice among members to ensure corporate governance.

Corporate Responsibility Association. 123 S Broad St., Ste. 1930, Philadelphia, PA 19109. Phone: (215)606-9520; Fax: (267)800-2701 • URL: http://www.croassociation.org • Seeks to advance the corporate responsibility officers (CRO) community and its role within corporations. Strengthens the community of practice across all corporate responsibility disciplines. Establishes professional development and certification programs for corporate responsibility officers.

Corporate Speech Pathology Network. 10 Glenlake Pkwy., Ste. 130, Atlanta, GA 30328. Phone: (678)592-0052 • URL: http://www.corspan.org • Represents the interests of corporate speech pathologists and other individuals and corporations exploring speech training. Seeks to promote and improve speech in the business and corporate settings. Encourages members to share information and ideas.

Dutch Association of Corporate Treasurers. PO Box 279, 1400 AG Bussum, Netherlands. Phone: 31 35 6954101; Fax: 31 35 6945045 • URL: http://www.dact.nl • Represents the Dutch treasury community. Promotes the development of treasury in The Netherlands.

Institute of Directors - England. 116 Pall Mall, London SW1Y 5ED, United Kingdom. Phone: 44 20 77668866; Fax: 44 20 77668833; Email: enquiries@iod.com • URL: http://www.iod.com/Home • Represents company directors and other people holding a similar position in industry, commerce, the professions or government organizations. Aims to advance company directors' interests and foster free enterprise. Includes services to members: branch network, professional development activities and conferences, information and advisory services. Provides meeting rooms and restaurant facilities to its members.

Institute of Directors in Ireland. Europa House, Harcourt St., Dublin 2, Dublin, Ireland. Phone: 353 1 4110010; Fax: 353 1 4110090; Email: info@iodireland.ie • URL: http://www.iodireland.ie • Provides a forum for the exchange of ideas and information, encourages members to improve the standards and performance as directors and represents the views of business leaders to government and other associations. Supports the provision of a wealth-creating environment in Ireland.

International Association of CFOs and Corporate Treasurers China. c/o Mr. Francis Ho, CLP Holdings, Group Treasury Dept., 147 Argyle St., Mongkok, Kowloon, Hong Kong, China. • URL: http://www.iacctchina.com • Promotes the development of professional corporate treasury practice in China. Fosters exchange and sharing among a network of corporate treasurers and CFOs in both mainland Chinese. Supports financial reforms in China by developing a platform for dialogue between members and financial regulators.

National Association of Corporate Directors. 2001 Pennsylvania Ave. NW, Ste. 500, Washington, DC 20006. Phone: (202)775-0509; Fax: (202)775-4857; Email: join@nacdonline.org • URL: http://www.nacdonline.org • Corporate directors and boards of directors; chief executive officers, presidents, accountants, lawyers, consultants, and other executives are members. Conducts research, surveys, and seminars.

Society of Corporate Secretaries and Governance Professionals. 240 W 35th St., Ste. 400, New York, NY 10001. Phone: (212)681-2000; Fax: (212)681-2005 • URL: http://www.governanceprofessionals.org • Corporate secretaries, assistant secretaries, officers and executives of corporations and others interested in corporate practices and procedures. Conducts surveys and research. Sponsors educational programs for members. Maintains a central information and reference service.

CORPORATE FINANCE

See also FINANCE; FINANCIAL MANAGEMENT

ABSTRACTS AND INDEXES

Business Periodicals Index Retrospective. EBSCO Publishing Inc. • 11/year. Quarterly and annual cumulations.

CD-ROM DATABASES

ABI/INFORM. ProQuest L.L.C. • Monthly. Provides CD-ROM indexing and abstracting of worldwide business literature. Archival discs are available from 1971. Formerly *ABI/INFORM OnDisc*.

Applied Science & Business Periodicals Retrospective. EBSCO Publishing Inc. • Includes citations for more than 3 million articles detailing events, issues, and trends in business and industry.

Buyout Financing Sources/M & A Intermediaries. SourceMedia Inc. • Annual. $895.00. Provides the CD-ROM combination of *Directory of Buyout Financing Sources* and *Directory of M & A Intermediaries*. Contains information on more than 1,000 financing sources (banks, insurance companies, venture capital firms, etc.) and 850 intermediaries (corporate acquirers, valuation firms, lawyers, accountants, etc.). Also includes back issues of *Buyouts Newsletter* and *Mergers & Acquisitions Report*. Fully searchable.

Compact D/SEC. Thomson Reuters Corp. • Monthly. Provides 200 financial data items for 12,000 U. S. publicly-held corporations filing reports with the Securities and Exchange Commission. Includes company profiles.

DIRECTORIES

America's Corporate Finance Directory. LexisNexis. • Annual. $1,399 Individuals print. Covers: Financial personnel and outside financial services relationships of 5,000 leading United States corporations and their wholly-owned United States subsidiaries. Entries include: Company name, address, phone, fax, telex, e-mail addresses, stock exchange information, earnings, total assets, size of pension/profit-sharing fund portfolio, number of employees, description of business, wholly-owned U.S. Subsidiaries of parent company; name and title of key executives; outside suppliers of financial services.

Corporate Finance Sourcebook: The Guide to Major Capital Investment Sources and Related Financial Services. LexisNexis. • Annual. $695 Individuals list price. Covers: Securities research analysts; major private lenders; investment banking firms; commercial banks; United States-based foreign banks; commercial finance firms; leasing companies; foreign investment bankers in the United States; pension managers; banks that offer master trusts; cash managers; business insurance brokers; business real estate specialists; lists about 3,500 firms; 14,500 key financial experts. Entries include: All entries include firm name, address, phone, e-mail, and names and titles of officers, contacts, or specialists in corporate finance. Additional details are given as appropriate, including names of major clients, number of companies served, services, total assets, branch locations, years in business.

French Companies Full Financials. RENCOM S&W. • Monthly. Database covers: Over 100,000 French companies in various sectors of industry and commerce. Entries include: Name, address, phone, senior management personnel, legal status, year founded, line of business, products, financial information.

INFOTRADE Belgian Company Financial Data. INFOTRADE N.V. • Daily. Database covers: More than 1,000,000 descriptive and financial profiles of Belgian companies and private businesses. Entries include: Company name, address, name and title of contact; commercial registration numbers; date and form of incorporation; bank accounts; association memberships; principal language; number of employees; names of management personnel; activities and products; trademarks; trading partners; financial statements for the most recent three years.

Major Financial Institutions of the World. Cengage Learning Inc. • $1,460 Individuals. 2012. 16th edition. eBook. Published by Graham & Whiteside. Contains detailed information on more than 10,000 important financial institutions in various countries. Includes banks, investment companies, and insurance companies.

Zacks Analyst Directory. Zacks Investment Research Inc. • Updated daily. Lists stockbroker investment analysts and gives the names of major U.S. corporations covered by those analysts.

Zacks Analyst Guide. Zacks Investment Research Inc. • Ranks analysts within more than 70 industry groups.

HANDBOOKS AND MANUALS

SEC Handbook: Rules and Forms for Financial Statements and Related Disclosures. Wolters Kluwer Law & Business CCH. • Annual. $59.00. Contains full text of rules and requirements set by the Securities and Exchange Commisssion for preparation of corporate financial statements.

INTERNET DATABASES

Mergent Online. Mergent Inc. 580 Kingsley Park Dr., Fort Mill, SC 29715. Phone: 800-937-1398 or (704)527-2700 or (704)559-7601; Fax: (704)559-6837 or (704)559-6960; Email: customerservice@mergent.com • URL: http://www.mergent.com • Fee-based Web site provides detailed information on 20,000 publicly-owned companies in 100 foreign countries, as well as more than 10,000 corporations listed on the New York Stock Exchange, American Stock Exchange, NASDAQ, and U.S. regional exchanges. Searching is offered on many financial variables and text fields. Weekly updating. Formerly *FIS Online*.

U.S. Securities and Exchange Commission. 100 F St. NE, Washington, DC 20549. Phone: 800-732-0330 or (202)942-8088; Fax: (202)942-9634; Email: webmaster@sec.gov • URL: http://www.sec.gov • SEC Web site offers free access through EDGAR to text of official corporate filings, such as annual reports (10-K), quarterly reports (10-Q), and proxies. (EDGAR is "Electronic Data Gathering, Analysis, and Retrieval System.") An example is given of how to obtain executive compensation data from proxies. Text of the daily *SEC News Digest* is offered, as are links to other government sites, non-government market regulators, and U. S. stock exchanges. Search facilities are extensive. Fees: Free.

ONLINE DATABASES

Banking Information Source. ProQuest L.L.C. • Provides indexing and abstracting of periodical and other literature from 1982 to date, with weekly updates. Covers the financial services industry: banks, savings institutions, investment houses, credit unions, insurance companies, and real estate organizations. Emphasis is on marketing and management. Inquire as to online cost and availability. (Formerly *FINIS: Financial Industry Information Service*.).

First Call Consensus Earnings Estimates. Thomson Financial Inc. • Online service provides corporate earnings estimates for more than 2,500 U. S. companies, based on data from leading brokerage firms. Weekly updates. Inquire as to online cost and availability.

Fitch Ratings Delivery Service. Fitch. • Daily. Provides online delivery of Fitch financial ratings in three sectors: "Corporate Finance" (corporate bonds, insurance companies), "Structured Finance" (asset-backed securities), and "U.S. Public Finance" (municipal bonds).

Wilson Business Abstracts Online. H.W. Wilson Co. • Indexes and abstracts 600 major business periodicals, plus the *Wall Street Journal* and the business section of the *New York Times*. Indexing is from 1982, abstracting from 1990, with the two newspapers included from 1993. Updated weekly. Inquire as to online cost and availability. (*Business Periodicals Index* without abstracts is also available online.).

Zacks Earnings Estimates. Zacks Investment Research Inc. • Provides online earnings projections for about 6,000 U. S. corporations, based on investment analysts' reports. Data is mainly from 200 major brokerage firms. Time span varies according to online provider, with daily or weekly updates. Inquire as to online cost and availability.

OTHER SOURCES

Finance and Accounting for Nonfinancial Managers. American Management Association Extension Institute. • $19.95. Looseleaf. Self-study course. Emphasis is on practical explanations, examples, and problem solving. Quizzes and a case study are included.

Financial Accounting Series. Financial Accounting Standards Board. • Monthly. Price on application.

Formation and Financing of Emerging Companies. Daniel E. O'Connor and others. Glasser LegalWorks. • $499 Individuals Binder/Looseleaf (Full set). Periodic Supplementation. Covers incorporation, bylaws, indemnification, intellectual property, financing sources, venture capital, due diligence, bridge loans, investor rights, compliance, and other legal issues associated with company formation. (Emerging Growth Companies Series.).

Managing Financial Risk with Forwards, Futures, Options, and Swaps. American Management Association Extension Institute. • Looseleaf. $159.00. Self-study course. Emphasis is on practical explanations, examples, and problem solving. Quizzes and a case study are included.

PERIODICALS AND NEWSLETTERS

American Banker: The Financial Services Daily. SourceMedia Inc. • Daily. $895.00 per year. Provides news of banking, investment products, mortgages, credit unions, finance, bank technology, and legal developments.

Bank Loan Report. IDD Enterprises L.P. • Description: Discusses banking loans and transactions made by large corporations. Recurring features include a column titled Term Sheets.

Business Finance. Penton. • Monthly. $59.00 per year. Covers trends in finance, technology, and economics for corporate financial executives.

CFO: The Magazine for Senior Financial Executives. CFO Publishing Corp. • Monthly.

Corporate Financing Week: The Newsweekly of Corporate Finance, Investment Banking and M and A. Institutional Investor Inc. Journals Group. • Weekly. $2,550.00 per year. Includes print and online editions. Newsletter for corporate finance officers. Emphasis is on debt and equity financing, mergers, leveraged buyouts, investment banking, and venture capital.

Financial Markets, Institutions, and Instruments. New York University, Salomon Center. Blackwell Publishing Inc. • Five times a year. Institutions, $338.00 per year. Includes online edition. Edited to "bridge the gap between the academic and professional finance communities." Special fifth issue each year provides surveys of developments in four areas: money and banking, derivative securities, corporate finance, and fixed-income securities.

Private Placement Letter: The Weekly for Privately Placed Fixed-Income Securities. SourceMedia Inc. •

For publishers' addresses, refer to SOURCES CITED section at the back of the book.

Weekly. $1,495 per year. Newsletter. Provides information on private financing of debt and convertible securities.

Strategic Finance. Institute of Management Accountants. • Monthly. $220 Nonmembers. Provides articles on corporate finance, cost control, cash flow, budgeting, corporate taxes, and other financial management topics.

U.S. Banker. SourceMedia Inc. • Monthly. $65.00 per year. Edited for bank executives and managers. Covers a wide variety of banking and financial topics.

RESEARCH CENTERS AND INSTITUTES

Princeton University - Bendheim Center for Finance. Department of Economics, 26 Prospect Ave., Princeton, NJ 08540-5296. Phone: (609)258-0770; Fax: (609)258-0771; Email: jessicab@princeton.edu • URL: http://www.princeton.edu/bcf • Research areas include securities markets, portfolio analysis, credit markets, and corporate finance. Emphasis is on quantitative and mathematical perspectives.

University of California, Los Angeles - Richard S. Ziman Center for Real Estate. Gold Hall, Ste. B100, 110 Westwood Plz., Los Angeles, CA 90095-1481. Phone: (310)206-9424 or (213)825-3977; Fax: (310)267-5391 or (310)206-5455; Email: stuart.gabriel@anderson.ucla.edu • URL: http://www.anderson.ucla.edu/centers/ziman • Secondary mortgage markets, housing finance, growth management, infrastructure, corporate finance issues, and development industry.

University of Virginia - McIntire School of Commerce Foundation - Center for Growth Enterprises. 125 Ruppel Dr., Charlottesville, VA 22903. Phone: (434)924-7063 • URL: http://www.commerce.virginia.edu/centers/growthenterprises/Pages/default.aspx • Strategic, finance, and management issues associated with growth companies, including closely held firms, venture capital/private equity, mature industries, real estate/asset-intensive firms, and non-financial performance measures.

STATISTICS SOURCES

Standard & Poor's Stock Reports: NASDAQ and Regional Exchanges. Standard & Poor's Financial Services L.L.C. • Irregular. $1,100.00 per year. Looseleaf service. Provides two pages of financial details and other information for each corporation included.

Standard & Poor's Stock Reports: New York Stock Exchange. Standard & Poor's Financial Services L.L.C. • Irregular. $1,295.00 per year. Looseleaf service. Provides two pages of financial details and other information for each corporation with stock listed on the N. Y. Stock Exchange.

TRADE/PROFESSIONAL ASSOCIATIONS

Association of Chinese Finance Professionals. 240 Hazelwood Ave., San Francisco, CA 94127. Email: acfp_us@yahoo.com • URL: http://www.acfp.net • Promotes cooperation between U.S. and China in the fields of commercial and investment banking, asset management, insurance, corporate finance, financial planning and financial software. Provides a forum for finance professionals to exchange ideas and discuss experiences.

Association of Corporate Treasurers. 51 Moorgate, London EC2R 6BH, United Kingdom. Phone: 44 20 7847 2540; Fax: 44 20 7374 8744; Email: enquiries@treasurers.co.uk • URL: http://www.treasurers.org • Professional body supporting those working in treasury, risk and corporate finance in the international marketplace. Promotes the study and best practice of finance and treasury management; offers education and examination, conferences, publications and training for financial professionals.

Dutch Corporate Finance Association. Koopvaardijweg 2, 4906 CV Oosterhout, Netherlands. Email: secretariaat@dcfa.nl • URL: http://www.dcfa.nl • Represents the interests of financial professionals. Facilitates sharing of knowledge and information among members. Creates a platform for managers within the financial sector.

National Association of Corporate Treasurers. 12100 Sunset Hills Rd., Ste. 130, Reston, VA 20190. Phone: (703)437-4377; Fax: (703)435-4390; Email: nact@nact.org • URL: http://www.nact.org • Members are corporate financial executives.

CORPORATE FORMATION

See INCORPORATION

CORPORATE GIVING

See PHILANTHROPY

CORPORATE HISTORIES

See BUSINESS HISTORY

CORPORATE IMAGE

ABSTRACTS AND INDEXES

Business Periodicals Index Retrospective. EBSCO Publishing Inc. • 11/year. Quarterly and annual cumulations.

PAIS International. ProQuest L.L.C. • Monthly. $850.00 per year; cumulations three times a year. Provides topical citations to the worldwide literature of public affairs, economics, demographics, sociology, and trade. Text in English; indexed materials in English, French, German, Italian, Portuguese and Spanish.

CD-ROM DATABASES

ABI/INFORM. ProQuest L.L.C. • Monthly. Provides CD-ROM indexing and abstracting of worldwide business literature. Archival discs are available from 1971. Formerly *ABI/INFORM OnDisc*.

Business Abstracts with Full Text. EBSCO Publishing Inc. • Includes full text articles from more than 460 business publications from 1982 to present. Indexing for nearly 880 publications.

PAIS International. ProQuest L.L.C. • Monthly. $1,995.00 per year. Contains over 650,000 citations to the literature of contemporary social, political, and economic issues.

ONLINE DATABASES

Wilson Business Abstracts Online. H.W. Wilson Co. • Indexes and abstracts 600 major business periodicals, plus the *Wall Street Journal* and the business section of the *New York Times*. Indexing is from 1982, abstracting from 1990, with the two newspapers included from 1993. Updated weekly. Inquire as to online cost and availability. (*Business Periodicals Index* without abstracts is also available online.).

RESEARCH CENTERS AND INSTITUTES

Boston College - Center for Corporate Citizenship. Carroll School of Management, 55 Lee Rd., Chestnut Hill, MA 02467-3942. Phone: (617)552-4545; Fax: (617)552-8499; Email: kv.smith@bc.edu • URL: http://www.bcccc.net • Areas of study include corporate images within local communities, corporate community relations, social vision, and philanthropy. Formerly Center for Corporate Community Relations.

TRADE/PROFESSIONAL ASSOCIATIONS

Public Relations Society of America. 33 Maiden Ln., 11th Fl., New York, NY 10038-5150. Phone: (212)460-1400; Fax: (212)995-0757 or (212)995-5024; Email: hq@prsa.org • URL: http://www.prsa.org • Absorbed American Public Relations Association and National Communication Council for Human Services.

CORPORATE INCOME TAX

See also TAXATION

ABSTRACTS AND INDEXES

Accounting and Tax Index. ProQuest L.L.C. • Quarterly. Indexes accounting, auditing, and taxation literature appearing in journals, books, pamphlets, conference proceedings, and newsletters.

CD-ROM DATABASES

Authority Tax and Estate Planning Library. Matthew Bender and Company Inc. • Periodic revisions. Price on request. CD contains updated full text of *Bender's Payroll Tax Guide, Depreciation Handbook, Federal Income Taxation of Corporations, Tax Planning for Corporations, Modern Estate Planning, Planning for Large Estates, Murphy's Will Clauses, Tax & Estate Planning for the Elderly*, and 12 other Matthew Bender publications. The Internal Revenue Code is also included.

Federal Tax Products. U. S. Government Printing Office. • Annual. $27.00. CD-ROM issued by the Internal Revenue Service (www.irs.treas.gov/forms_pubs/). Provides current tax forms, instructions, and publications. Also includes older tax forms beginning with 1991.

OECD Statistical Compendium. Organization for Economic Cooperation and Development. • Semiannual. $1,905.00 per year for 1 to 10 users. CD-ROM contains more than 730,000 monthly, quarterly, and annual time series for OECD countries, 1960 to date. Includes fully searchable data on agriculture, food, economic indicators, national accounts, employment, energy, finance, industry, technology, and foreign trade. Results can be displayed in various forms.

The Tax Directory. Tax Analysts. • Quarterly. $499 Individuals both volumes, web, CD or print. Updated quarterly on CD-ROM and in print; updated continually online. Covering federal, state, and international tax officials, tax practitioners, and corporate tax executives.

DIRECTORIES

The Tax Directory. Tax Analysts. • Quarterly. $499 Individuals both volumes, web, CD or print. Updated quarterly on CD-ROM and in print; updated continually online. Covering federal, state, and international tax officials, tax practitioners, and corporate tax executives.

HANDBOOKS AND MANUALS

Business Taxpayer Information Publications. U. S. Government Printing Office. • Annual. $66 U.S. Looseleaf. Two volumes, consisting of *Circular E, Employer's Tax Guide* and *Employer's Supplemental Tax Guide*. Issued by the Internal Revenue Service (http://www.irs.ustreas.gov). Includes a variety of business-related tax information, including withholding tables, tax calendars, self-employment issues, partnership matters, corporation topics, depreciation, and bankruptcy.

Tax Planning for Corporations and Shareholders: Forms. Matthew Bender and Company Inc. • Annual. $422 Individuals Book or electronic version. Includes expertly crafted forms for such transactions as forming a new corporation, S corporation elections and revocations, and more.

U.S. Master Multistate Corporate Tax Guide. Wolters Kluwer Law & Business CCH. • Annual. $136.75 Quantiy: 1 - 4. Provides corporate income tax information for 47 states, New York City, and the District of Columbia.

INTERNET DATABASES

Business 2.0 Web Guide to the Best Business Links. Business 2.0 Media Inc. Phone: (415)293-4800; Email: support@business2.com • URL: http://www.business2.com/webguide • Web site presents an extensive, searchable directory of links to "the best, most informative, and authoritative web pages." Twenty main categories cover business, finance, career, company information, people, and technology topics, with thousands of subtopics, all linking to Web sites recommended by experienced business researchers. Fees: Free.

CCH Essentials: An Internet Tax Research and Primary Source Library. CCH, Inc. Phone: 800-248-3248 or (773)866-6000; Fax: (773)866-3608 or (800)224-8299; Email: cust_serv@cch.com • URL: http://tax.cch.com/essentials • Fee-based Web site provides full-text coverage of federal tax law and regulations, including rulings, procedures, tax court decisions, and IRS publications, announcements, notices, and penalties. Includes explanation, analysis, tax planning guides, and a daily tax news service. Searching is offered, including citation search.

Court Filings. ProQuest LLC. 2250 Perimeter Park Dr., Ste. 300, Morrisville, NC 27560. Phone: 800-334-2564 or (919)804-6400; Fax: (919)804-6410; Email: contact@dialog.com • URL: http://www.dialog.com • The three main sections of Tax Analysts home page are "Tax News" (Today's Tax News, Feature of the Week, Tax Snapshots, Tax Calendar); "Products & Services" (Product Catalog, Press Releases); and "Public Interest" (Discussion Groups, Tax Clinic, Tax History Project). Fees: Free for coverage of current tax events; fee-based for comprehensive information. Daily updating.

Factiva. Dow Jones Reuters Business Interactive, LLC. Phone: 800-369-7466 or (609)452-1511; Fax: (609)520-5770; Email: solutions@factiva.com • URL: http://www.factiva.com • Fee-based Web site provides "global news and business information through Web sites and content integration solutions." Includes Dow Jones and Reuters newswires, The Wall Street Journal, and more than 7,000 other sources of current news, historical articles, market research reports, and investment analysis. Content includes 96 major U. S. newspapers, 900 non-English sources, trade publications, media transcripts, country profiles, news photos, etc.

Fedstats. Federal Interagency Council on Statistical Policy. Phone: (202)395-7254 • URL: http://www.fedstats.gov • Web site features an efficient search facility for full-text statistics produced by more than 100 federal agencies, including the Census Bureau, the Bureau of Economic Analysis, and the Bureau of Labor Statistics. Boolean searches can be made within one agency or for all agencies combined. Links are offered to international statistical bureaus, including the UN, IMF, OECD, UNESCO, Eurostat, and 20 individual countries. Fees: Free.

FreeLunch.com. Economy.com, Inc. Phone: (610)696-8700; Fax: (610)696-1678 • URL: http://www.freelunch.com • Web site provides free access to more than 200 million economic and financial data series, covering industry, demographics, labor markets, prices, retail sales, government spending, trade, interest rates, housing starts, the stock market, etc. Data is available in either chart or table form. Searching is offered. Free, but registration required. Economy.com, Inc. also offers fee-based economic analysis at *The Dismal Scientist* site (www.dismal.com).

Internal Revenue Service IRS.gov. Internal Revenue Service. Phone: 800-829-1040 or (202)622-5000; Fax: (202)622-5844 • URL: http://www.irs.gov • Web site provides a wide variety of tax information, including IRS forms and publications. Searching is available. Fees: Free.

Nexis.com. Lexis-Nexis Group. Phone: 800-227-4908 or (937)865-6800; Fax: (937)865-6909; Email: webmaster@prod.lexis-nexis.com • URL: http://www.nexis.com • Fee-based Web site offers searching of about 2.8 billion documents in some 30,000 news, business, and legal information sources. Features include a subject directory covering 1,200 topics in 34 categories and a Company Dossier containing information on more than 500,000 public and private companies. Boolean searching is offered.

Rutgers Accounting Web. Rutgers University Accounting Research Center. Phone: (973)353-5172; Fax: (973)353-1283 • URL: http://www.rutgers.edu/accounting • RAW Web site provides extensive links to sources of national and international accounting information, such as the Big Six accounting firms, the Financial Accounting Standards Board (FASB), SEC filings (EDGAR), journals, publishers, software, the International Accounting Network, and "Internet's largest list of accounting firms in USA." Searching is offered. Fees: Free.

ONLINE DATABASES

Accounting and Tax Database. ProQuest L.L.C. • Provides indexing and abstracting of the literature of accounting, taxation, and financial management, 1971 to date. Updating is weekly. Especially covers accounting, auditing, banking, bankruptcy, employee compensation and benefits, cash management, financial planning, and credit. Inquire as to online cost and availability.

OTHER SOURCES

Capital Changes Reports. Wolters Kluwer Law & Business CCH. • Weekly. $1,395.00. Six looseleaf volumes. Arranged alphabetically by company. This service presents a chronological capital history that includes reorganizations, mergers and consolidations. Recent actions are found in Volume One - "New Matters.".

Manufacturers' Tax Alert. Wolters Kluwer Law & Business CCH. • Monthly $297.00 per year. Newsletter. Covers the major tax issues affecting manufacturing companies. Includes current developments in various kind of federal, state, and international taxes: sales, use, franchise, property, and corporate income.

Reproducible Copies of Federal Tax Forms and Instructions. U. S. Government Printing Office. • Annual. $64 U.S. Looseleaf. Two looseleaf volumes issued by the Internal Revenue Service (www.irs.gov). "Contains the most frequently requested tax forms and instructions," prepared especially for libraries.

PERIODICALS AND NEWSLETTERS

Highlights and Documents. Tax Analysts. • Daily. $2,599.95 Individuals. Provides daily coverage of IRS, congressional, judicial, state, and international tax developments. Includes abstracts and citations for "all tax documents released within the previous 24 to 48 hours." Annual compilation available *Highlights and Documents on Microfiche.*

Strategic Finance. Institute of Management Accountants. • Monthly. $220 Nonmembers. Provides articles on corporate finance, cost control, cash flow, budgeting, corporate taxes, and other financial management topics.

Tax Notes: The Weekly Tax Service. Tax Analysts. • Weekly. Weekly. $1,699.00 per year. Includes an *Annual* and compilations of previous years. Newsletter. Covers "tax news from all federal sources," including congressional committees, tax courts, and the Internal Revenue Service. Each issue contains "summaries of every document that pertains to federal tax law," with citations. Commentary is provided.

Tax Practice. Tax Analysts. • Weekly. $199.00 per year. Newsletter. Covers news affecting tax practitioners and litigators, with emphasis on federal court decisions, rules and regulations, and tax petitions. Provides a guide to Internal Revenue Service audit issues.

STATISTICS SOURCES

Statistics of Income Bulletin. U. S. Government Printing Office. • Quarterly. $44. Current data compiled from tax returns relating to income, assets, and expenses of individuals and businesses. (U. S. Internal Revenue Service.).

Statistics of Income: Corporation Income Tax Returns. U.S. Internal Revenue Service. U. S. Government Printing Office. • Annual.

Survey of Current Business. U. S. Government Printing Office. • Published by Bureau of Economic Analysis, U. S. Department of Commerce. Presents a wide variety of business and economic data.

CORPORATE PLANNING

See PLANNING

CORPORATE REAL ESTATE

See INDUSTRIAL REAL ESTATE

CORPORATE RESPONSIBILITY

See SOCIAL RESPONSIBILITY

CORPORATION LAW AND REGULATION

See also ADMINISTRATIVE LAW AND REGULATION; BUSINESS LAW; INCORPORATION

ABSTRACTS AND INDEXES

Current Law Index. Cengage Learning Inc. • $1,332 Individuals. Monthly. $1269.00 per year. Produced in cooperation with the American Association of Law Libraries. Indexes more than 900 law journals, legal newspapers, and specialty publications from the U.S., Canada, U.K., Ireland, Australia, and New Zealand.

Index to Legal Periodicals and Books. H.W. Wilson Co. • Monthly. $490.00 per year. Quarterly and annual cumulations.

ALMANACS AND YEARBOOKS

American Law Yearbook. Cengage Learning Inc. • $308 Individuals. Annual. $280.00. Serves as a yearly supplement to *West's Encyclopedia of American Lawa.* Describes new legal developments in many subject areas.

CD-ROM DATABASES

Index to Legal Periodicals and Books. EBSCO Publishing Inc. • Contains indexing of more than 1,400 English language legal periodicals from 1981 to date and 2,500 books.

ENCYCLOPEDIAS AND DICTIONARIES

Encyclopedia of White-Collar & Corporate Crime. Cengage Learning Inc. • 2 volumes. More than 500 entries. This work gathers history, definitions, examples, investigation, prosecution, assessments, challenges, and projections into one definitive reference work on the topic.

West's Encyclopedia of American Law. Cengage Learning Inc. • 2004. eBook. Second edition. Covers a wide variety of legal topics for the general reader. Inquire for pricing.

INTERNET DATABASES

Lexis.com Research System. Lexis-Nexis Group. Phone: 800-227-4908 or (937)865-6800; Fax: (937)865-6909; Email: webmaster@prod.lexis-nexis.com • URL: http://www.nexis.com • Fee-based Web site offers extensive searching of a wide variety of legal sources. Additional features include Daily Opinion Service, lexis.com Bookstore, Career Center, CLE Center, Law Schools, and Practice Pages ("Pages specific to areas of specialty").

OTHER SOURCES

Business Law Monographs. Matthew Bender and Company Inc. • Quarterly. $3,645 book. Intended for in-house and outside corporate counsel. Each monograph concentrates on a particular subject.

Fletcher Corporation Forms Annotated. Thomson West. • Annual. $5,220 hardbound (full set). Cover all aspects of corporate law.

Going Private. ALM Media Properties LLC. • $560 print + online + ebook. Discusses the legal ramifications of a publicly-owned company "going private" by way of a sale, leveraged buyout, reverse stock split, or merger. (Law Journal Press).

PERIODICALS AND NEWSLETTERS

Corporate Counselor. ALM Media Properties LLC. • Monthly. $459 /year. Covers issues involved with managing the legal department of a corporation, including relations with outside counsel. (A Law Journal Newsletter, formerly published by Leader Publications).

D & O Advisor: Risk Management for Directors and Officers. ALM Media Properties LLC. • Quarterly. $125.00 per year. Covers a wide range of legal topics of concern to corporate boards and key executives.

Daily Report for Executives. Bloomberg BNA. • Daily. Covers legal, regulatory, economic, and tax developments affecting corporations.

Federal Register. Office of the Federal Register. U. S. Government Printing Office. • Daily except Saturday and Sunday. $764.00 per year. Publishes regulations and legal notices issued by federal agencies, including executive orders and presidential proclamations. Issued by the National Archives and Records Administration (www.nara.gov).

Securities and Federal Corporate Law Report. Thomson West. • Features articles on securities and corporate law topics, providing highlights of significant cases, administrative policy, staff guidelines, and other important news and trends.

Securities Regulation & Law Report. Bloomberg BNA. • Weekly. Reports on developments in the regulation of securities and futures trading.

TRADE/PROFESSIONAL ASSOCIATIONS

U.S. Council of Better Business Bureaus. 3033 Wilson Blvd., Ste. 600, Arlington, VA 22201. Phone: (703)276-0100 • URL: http://www.bbb.org • Promotes ethical relationships between businesses and the public through self-regulation, consumer and business education, and service excellence.

CORPORATION REPORTS

See also BUSINESS JOURNALISM; COMMUNICATION

CD-ROM DATABASES

Compact D/SEC. Thomson Reuters Corp. • Monthly. Provides 200 financial data items for 12,000 U. S. publicly-held corporations filing reports with the Securities and Exchange Commission. Includes company profiles.

DIRECTORIES

ADVERTISE. Deutscher Sparkassenverlag GmbH. • Weekly. Database covers: Worldwide cooperative venture offers and requests, covering product import and export, technology transfer, joint ventures, and related ventures. Emphasis is on opportunities for small and medium-sized European companies. Entries include: Company name, address, phone; company profile; descriptors and codes for products and services; type of cooperation sought; dates of entry and validity.

BISNES Plus. INFOTRADE N.V. • Daily. Database covers: Financial and descriptive information on more than one million Belgian companies and private businesses. Entries include: Name, address, name and title of contact, commercial registration numbers, data and form of incorporation, bank accounts, association memberships, principal language, number of employees, names of management personnel, activities and products, trademarks, trading partners, financial statements for the most recent three years.

Bullseye Ownership Report. CDA/Equity Intelligence. • Weekly. $800. Covers: over 1,300 institutions that have filed statements of company ownership with the Securities and Exchange Commission, including 13D and 13G five-percent beneficial ownership, 14D-1 tender offers, 13(f) institutional common stock holdings, 13(f) institutional convertible holdings, U.S. investment company holdings, foreign investment company holdings. Entries include: Company name, value held, change in shares, going back five consecutive quarters, money center, turnover, investment style, type of institute, investment discretion, voting authority, filing date and percent of shares outstanding.

Financial Post Corporate Surveys. Financial Post DataGroup. • Database covers: 6,300 Canadian public companies and 19,000 defunct companies. Includes financial and operational information, key events, and key executives.

INFOTRADE Belgian Company Financial Data. INFOTRADE N.V. • Daily. Database covers: More than 1,000,000 descriptive and financial profiles of Belgian companies and private businesses. Entries include: Company name, address, name and title of contact; commercial registration numbers; date and form of incorporation; bank accounts; association memberships; principal language; number of employees; names of management personnel; activities and products; trademarks; trading partners; financial statements for the most recent three years.

Marketing Surveys Index. Marketing Answers Ltd. • $380 per year. Covers: about 8,000 recently-published market research and business reports from around the world. Entries include: Report title; publisher name, address, phone, fax, e-mail and contact name; countries covered by report, publication date, number of pages, price, description of report.

Professional Builder--Annual Report of Housing's Giants. Reed Elsevier Group plc Reed Business Information. • Annual. Publication includes: list of top 400 firms that started and closed the greatest number of housing construction units in the preceding year. Entries include: Company name, city, state, housing revenues, total revenues, units started, units sold.

REACH: Review and Analysis of Companies in Holland. Bureau van Dijk S.A. • Bimonthly. Database covers: 150,000 company reports, including top 7,000 companies in Holland. Entries include: Company name, address, phone, fax, company history, description, historical annual accounts, financial ratios, directors and officers, names of holdings and subsidiaries, stock data.

The Weekly Corporate Growth Report. NVST Inc. • Weekly. Publication includes: Current acquisition and merger transactions. Entries include: Buyer and seller names and locations, annual sales and net income for each, seller's net worth and price-earnings ratio, and purchase price, including terms and various ratios.

HANDBOOKS AND MANUALS

Not-for-Profit Entities - Best Practices in Presentation and Disclosure. American Institute of Certified Public Accountants. • $86.25 Nonmembers Print/Online. Provides preparers and auditors with the tools they need to work through the process of creating and verifying the format and accuracy of their company or clients' financial statements.

SEC Financial Reporting: Annual Reports to Shareholders, Form 10-K, and Quarterly Financial Reporting. Matthew Bender and Company Inc. • Annual. $254.00. Looseleaf service. Coverage of aspects of financial reporting with GAAP disclosure and Regulation S-X preparation Step-by-step procedures for preparing information for Form 10-K and annual shareholders reports.

SEC Handbook: Rules and Forms for Financial Statements and Related Disclosures. Wolters Kluwer Law & Business CCH. • Annual. $59.00. Contains full text of rules and requirements set by the Securities and Exchange Commisssion for preparation of corporate financial statements.

INTERNET DATABASES

Factiva. Dow Jones Reuters Business Interactive, LLC. Phone: 800-369-7466 or (609)452-1511; Fax: (609)520-5770; Email: solutions@factiva.com • URL: http://www.factiva.com • Fee-based Web site provides "global news and business information through Web sites and content integration solutions." Includes Dow Jones and Reuters newswires, The Wall Street Journal, and more than 7,000 other sources of current news, historical articles, market research reports, and investment analysis. Content includes 96 major U. S. newspapers, 900 non-English sources, trade publications, media transcripts, country profiles, news photos, etc.

Nexis.com. Lexis-Nexis Group. Phone: 800-227-4908 or (937)865-6800; Fax: (937)865-6909; Email: webmaster@prod.lexis-nexis.com • URL: http://www.nexis.com • Fee-based Web site offers searching of about 2.8 billion documents in some 30,000 news, business, and legal information sources. Features include a subject directory covering 1,200 topics in 34 categories and a Company Dossier containing information on more than 500,000 public and private companies. Boolean searching is offered.

Wall Street Journal Interactive Edition. Dow Jones & Co., Inc. 1211 Avenue of the Americas, New York, NY 10036. Phone: 800-369-5663; Email: service@dowjones.com • URL: http://new.dowjones.com • Fee-based Web site providing online searching of worldwide information from *The Wall Street Journal.* Includes "Company Snapshots," "The Journal's Greatest Hits," "Index to Market Data," "Journal Links," etc. Financial price quotes are available. Fees: $49.00 per year; $29.00 per year to print subscribers.

ONLINE DATABASES

Compustat. Standard and Poor's. • Financial data on publicly held U.S. and some foreign corporations; data held for 20 years. Inquire as to online cost and availability.

EdgarPlus: SEC Basic Filings. Thomson Reuters Markets. • Online service provides full text of about 60,000 documents that have been filed with the U.S. Securities and Exchange Commission, 1987 to date, with daily updates. Filings include 6-K, 8-K, 10-K, 10-C, 10-Q, 20-F, and proxy statements. Inquire as to online cost and availability.

First Call Consensus Earnings Estimates. Thomson Financial Inc. • Online service provides corporate earnings estimates for more than 2,500 U. S. companies, based on data from leading brokerage firms. Weekly updates. Inquire as to online cost and availability.

PERIODICALS AND NEWSLETTERS

Ragan's Annual Report Review. Lawrence Ragan Communications Inc. • Description: Provides business trends, tips, and tactics.

STATISTICS SOURCES

Standard & Poor's Stock Reports: NASDAQ and Regional Exchanges. Standard & Poor's Financial Services L.L.C. • Irregular. $1,100.00 per year. Looseleaf service. Provides two pages of financial details and other information for each corporation included.

Standard & Poor's Stock Reports: New York Stock Exchange. Standard & Poor's Financial Services L.L.C. • Irregular. $1,295.00 per year. Looseleaf service. Provides two pages of financial details and other information for each corporation with stock listed on the N. Y. Stock Exchange.

CORPORATIONS

See also MULTINATIONAL CORPORATIONS

CD-ROM DATABASES

Business Abstracts with Full Text. EBSCO Publishing Inc. • Includes full text articles from more than 460 business publications from 1982 to present. Indexing for nearly 880 publications.

InvesText. Thomson Financial. • Monthly. Contains full text on CD-ROM of investment research reports from about 630 sources, including leading brokers and investment bankers. Reports are available on both U. S. and international publicly traded corporations. Separate industry reports cover more than 50 industries. Time span is 1982 to date.

OECD Statistical Compendium. Organization for Economic Cooperation and Development. • Semiannual. $1,905.00 per year for 1 to 10 users. CD-ROM contains more than 730,000 monthly, quarterly, and annual time series for OECD countries, 1960 to date. Includes fully searchable data on agriculture, food, economic indicators, national accounts, employment, energy, finance, industry, technology, and foreign trade. Results can be displayed in various forms.

Standard & Poor's Corporations. Dialog OnDisc. • Monthly. Price on application. Produced by Standard & Poor's. Contains three CD-ROM files: Executives, Private Companies, and Public Companies, providing detailed information on more than 70,000 business executives, 55,000 private companies, and 12,000 publicly-traded corporations.

DIRECTORIES

ABC/Dienstverleners. ABC Business Directories BV. • Quarterly. Database covers: 24,000 Dutch service companies, including accounting firms, law firms, car leasing firms, audiovisual consultants, transport companies, advertising agencies, hotels, and restaurants. Entries include: Company name, address, phone, fax, telex; executive names; capital; bank affiliation; year founded; number of employees; product information.

ABC Netherlands. ABC voor Handel en Industries C.V. • Quarterly. Database covers: 120,000 profiles of Dutch companies in all lines of business. Entries include: Company name, address, management, products, number of employees, sales, founding year, parent companies, subsidiaries, branches and offices abroad, export/import activities.

ABC voor Handel en Industrie. ABC voor Handel en Industries C.V. • Quarterly. Database covers: Approximately 120,000 profiles of Dutch manufacturers, importers, import agents and service providers and their products/services; also includes some 46,000 foreign houses' representatives in Holland. Entries include: Company name, address, phone, fax, telex; executive names; capital; bank affiliation; year founded; number of employees.

Access Nippon: How to Succeed in Japan. Hoover's Inc. • Annual. $34.95 plus $3.50 shipping. Covers: Brief profiles of 498 companies and 493 of their affiliates in Japan. Database includes: Overview of major industries & trends; Japan business practices/regulations; listing of major trade shows to be held in Japan; business travel guide; information on hotels, transportation, emergency services, etc. Entries include: Company headquarters, address, phone, date established, capital maintained, number of employees, financial data, product/service.

Advertiser's Yearbook. Oekonomisk Literatur Norge A/S. • Annual. $780. Covers: Advertising agencies in Norway. Entries include: Company name, address, phone, fax, management/ad/text, list of customers, special services, number of employees, share capital, sales.

Air Compressors Directory. InfoGroup Inc. • Annual. Number of listings: 3,405. Entries include: Name, address, phone, size of advertisement, name of owner or manager, number of employees, year first in "Yellow Pages." Compiled from telephone company "Yellow Pages," nationwide.

Air Duct Cleaning Directory. InfoGroup Inc. • Annual. Number of listings: 2,109. Entries include: Name, address, phone, size of advertisement, name of owner or manager, number of employees, year first in "Yellow Pages." Compiled from telephone company "Yellow Pages," nationwide.

Alabama Business Directory. InfoGroup Inc. • Annual. Covers: 184,277 businesses in Alabama. Entries include: Company name, address, phone, number of employees, name of owner or manager, sales volume. Compiled from telephone company "Yellow Pages," statewide. All states covered (see separate entries).

Alaska Business License Directory. Alaska Department of Community and Economic Development. • Covers: Approx. 70,000 businesses licensed by the state of Alaska. Entries include: Company name, address, name of owner, license number, line of business.

Alberta Business Directory. InfoGroup Inc. • Annual. Covers: 122,660 businesses in Alberta, Canada. Entries include: Company name, address, phone, number of employees, name of owner or manager, sales volume. Compiled from telephone company "Yellow Pages," statewide (see separate entry).

All Ordinaries Index Companies Handbook. Australian Stock Exchange Ltd. Exchange Centre. • $29.95 plus $10.00 postage and handling. Covers: approximately 314 companies that comprise the Australian All Ordinaries Index as of September of the year issued, plus Health-Biotechnology and Telecommunications Index companies that are not included in the All Ordinaries Companies Index. Entries include: Company name, address, phone, names and titles of key personnel, key business summary, financial data, description of product/service, list of major shareholders, share price chart.

AmCham Yearbook. American Chamber of Commerce for Brazil - Sao Paulo. • Annual. $250 Individuals for associates. Covers: More than 5,400 corporate members of the American Chamber of Commerce for Brazil.

American Big Businesses Directory. InfoGroup Inc. • Annual. $295. Covers: 218,000 U.S. businesses with more than 100 employees, and 500,000 key executives and directors. CD-ROM version contains 160,000 top firms and 431,000 key executives. Entries include: Name, address, phone, names and titles of key personnel, number of employees, sales volume, Standard Industrial Classification (SIC) codes, subsidiaries and parent company names, stock exchanges on which traded.

American Companies: A Guide to Sources of Information. CBD Research Ltd. • Biennial. £78 Individuals. Covers: Business information sources from over 50 countries in North, South, and Central America and the Caribbean. Entries include: For companies--company name, address, phone, fax, telex, year established, description, countries of specialization, branch offices, and languages spoken; for publications--title, publisher, address, telephone, fax, telex, year first published, frequency; latest edition, price, page count, description, company information, types of indexes, languages, and formats available.

American Companies Directory. NIIR Project Consultancy Services. • $200 Individuals CD-ROM. Covers: 1.5 million American companies. Entries include: Company name, email, phone, fax, email, websites and SIC code.

American Companies in Brazil. U.S. Chamber of Commerce. • $75 plus $4.00 shipping. Covers: U.S. subsidiary and affiliate companies in Brazil. Entries include: Company name, address, phone.

American Manufacturers Directory. InfoGroup Inc. • Annual. $295. Covers: more than 150,000 manufacturing companies with 20 or more employees. CD-ROM version lists all 531,000 U.S. manufacturers, in all employee size ranges. Entries include: Company name, address, phone, contact name, Standard Industrial Classification (SIC) codes, number of employees, sales volume code, credit rating scores.

American Subsidiaries and Affiliates of French Firms. French Embassy Trade Office. • $125. Covers: French firms and their American subsidiaries. Database includes: Address, telephone and fax of french parent company. Entries include: firm address, telephone and fax numbers, activity.

America's Best Midsized Companies. Financial World Publishing. • Annual. $1.95. Entries include: Company name, address, phone.

Analyse Major Databases from European Sources. Bureau van Dijk S.A. • Annual. Covers: 150,000 of the top companies in Europe. Entries include: Company name, address, phone, fax, telex; date of incorporation.

Analysis. FT Analysis. • Daily. Database covers: all U.K. publicly quoted and Unlisted Securities Market (USM) companies. Database includes: Company name, address, phone, principal activities, names and titles of key personnel, business history, major holdings, capital structure, and share prices, key ratios, dividend data, balance sheets, and profit and loss summaries for the most recent five years. Also includes complete text of recent company announcements filed with the London Stock Exchange, complete text of more than 7,000 stockbroker research reports, and complete text of U.K. annual reports.

Annuaire National de Fournisseurs des Administrations Francaises. Editions le Fil d'Ariane. • Annual. Covers: Over 2,00 industrial firms and merchant and service companies which are the main suppliers to the French Civil Service. Entries include: Company name, address, phone, fax, telex number, data on clients.

Argentina Company Handbook. Hoover's Inc. • Annual. $49.95. Covers: 32 of Argentina's major public companies. Database includes: Information on Argentina's economy, the securities market, the stock exchange, and the rules governing foreign investments in the Argentina capital markets. Entries include: Name, address, phone, fax, year established, stock ticker symbol, names and titles of key personnel, number of employees, number of stockholders, company history, financial data, names of major stockholders, affiliated companies.

Arkansas Business Directory. InfoGroup Inc. • Annual. $450. Covers: 126,071 businesses in Arkanasas. Entries include: Company name, address, phone, number of employees, name of owner or manager, sales volume. Compiled from telephone company "Yellow Pages," statewide. All states covered (see separate entries).

Asia: A Directory and Sourcebook. Euromonitor

International Business Reference Div. • Irregular. $430. Publication includes: Regional overview, major companies, information sources statistical datafile. Entries include: Name of organization, firm, or agency, address, statistical data, purpose or service.

Asia Corporate Profile and National Finance. Dataline Asia-Pacific Ltd. • Annual. $70. Covers: about 1,900 companies in Asia; includes list of the 500 largest companies. Entries include: Company name, address, phone, fax, telex, names and titles of key personnel, number of employees, financial data.

Asian and Australasian Companies: A Guide to Sources of Information. CBD Research Ltd. • $160 Individuals. Covers: Over 2,000 company information sources for the 69 countries in the Far East and Australasian organizations responsible for registering business enterprises; stock exchanges; credit reporting and business information services; publishers of business and finance publications. Entries include: Generally, company, agency, or organization name, address, phone, telex, date founded, type of company, method of selection. For publications--Title, English translation (if necessary), publisher name, address, phone, and telex; description of contents, date of publication or frequency, language, price, size.

Asian Company Handbook. Toyo Keizai Inc. • $65. Covers: Approximately 1,060 companies listed on the stock exchanges of Hong Kong, Indonesia, Malaysia, the Republic of Korea, Singapore, Taiwan, and Thailand. Entries include: Company name, address, phone, fax, geographical area served, financial data, subsidiary and branch names and locations, stock price information, description of product/service, stock price charts.

Asian Company Profiles. Asian Company Profiles Ltd. • Bimonthly. Database covers: over 500,000 Asian-based companies (including companies in China, Malaysia, Singapore, Indonesia, Korea, Hong Kong, Philippines, Thailand, Vietnam, Australia, New Zealand, Laos, Cambodia, Taiwan, and Papua New Guinea). Database includes: Company name, address, phone, fax, E-mail, products, Standard Industrial Classification (SIC) codes and Harmonized codes, year established, number of employees, issued capital, names and titles of key personnel, company type, subsidiaries and affiliates, organizational chart, factory description and size, product descriptions, related companies, financial data, importers' agencies, trade statistics. Expanded coverage to include companies of other Asian nations is planned.

ASTREE: L'Annuaire Commercial Electronique. Bureau van Dijk S.A. • Quarterly. Database covers: Company reports on 800,000 French companies. Entries include: Company name, address, date of incorporation, company type, type of activity, managers, turnover, export, profit, shareholders' funds, debt, number of employees, shareholders, and subsidiaries.

Atlanta Larger Employers. Metro Atlanta Chamber of Commerce. • Biennial. $5 plus $2 shipping. Covers: Approximately 600 companies in the metropolitan Atlanta, Georgia, area that employ 300 or more. Entries include: Company name, address, phone, Standard Industrial Classification (SIC) code.

ATTILA Business Database. Ost-West Direkt Werbegesellschaft mbH. • Quarterly. Database covers: over 2.6 million companies in Bulgaria, Poland, the Czech Republic, Hungary, Lithuania, and the Slovak Republic. Database includes: Company name, address, phone, fax, legal status, ownership, foundation date/capital, registration court, governmental district, contact person, number of employees, products, line of business.

Australia Business Directory. INFOT Inc. • $64.60 Individuals. Covers: 96,347 companies, importers, and exporters from Australia. Entries include: Company name, email and website addresses, telephone and fax number, and business description.

Australian Company Handbook. Hoover's Inc. • $49.95. Covers: 300 Australian companies listed on the All Ordinaries Index and 300 other leading Australian companies not included on the index. Entries include: Company name, address, phone, fax, description.

Australian Key Business Directory. Dun & Bradstreet (Australia) Proprietary Ltd. • Covers: Leading companies in Australia whose annual sales are $10 million and who have 500 or more employees. Entries include: Company name, address, phone, fax, telex, number of employees, import/export designation, primary and secondary Standard Industrial Classification (SIC) codes, sales volume.

Australian Public Companies Guide. Schwartz & Wilkinson Publishers PLC. • Annual. $395. Covers: 12,000 companies on the Australian Stock Exchange. Entries include: Company name, address, phone, telex, names of directors, financial data.

Australia's Top 100. Australian Stock Exchange Ltd. Exchange Centre. • Annual. $20 plus 10 dollars shipping. Covers: top 100 listed companies on the Australian Stock Exchange ranked by market capitalization. Entries include: Company name, address, phone, fax, telex, names and titles of key personnel, financial data, company history, description of products and activities.

Austria in U.S.A. American Chamber of Commerce in Austria. • Periodic. €150 Members. Covers: 550 Austrian companies with U.S. Subsidiaries, branch offices, associates, joint ventures, or representations in the U.S.; American representations and Austrian-American organizations in Austria, Austrian representations in the U.S., American Chambers of Commerce in Europe, and the representation of American states in Europe. Entries include: For companies--Name, address, phone; name, address, phone of U.S. Affiliated company; name of the Austrian company's general manager; a brief description of the U.S. Company; type of business and nature of relationship.

Austrian Commercial Directory. Jupiter Verlagsgesellschaft mbH. • Annual. Covers: 120,000 Austrian industrial, trading, and service firms. Entries include: Company name, address, phone, fax, telex, products, names of owners, board members, directors, and other key personnel.

Austrian Companies Database. Hoppenstedt Produktinformationen GmbH. • Semiannual. €2,318. Database covers: 15,000 major companies (or those which bill at least 70 million annually and/or have at least 100 employees) and 55,000 business executives in Austria. Entries include: Name, address, phone, fax, management names, range of products or services, number of employees, revenue and equity.

Bahamas Chamber of Commerce--Annual Chamber Directory. Bahamas Chamber of Commerce. • Annual. $8. Entries include: name, address, phone, fax.

Bay Area Employer Directory. James R. Albin. • Annual. $99.95. Covers: over 2,000 employers in the San Francisco Bay Area each having 100 or more employees; includes both private and government employers. Entries include: Firm name, address, phone, year established, type of business or activity, number of employees, sales, names and titles of local chief executive and personnel manager.

Belfast Business Network. Century Newspapers Ltd. • $12.50. Covers: 13,500 business companies in Belfast. Entries include: Company name, address, phone, fax.

Best of British. Jordans Ltd. • Annual. $225 for four volume set. Covers: in four volumes, 20,000 leading companies in the United Kingdom; 5,000 per volume. Entries include: Company name, registered office address, chief executive, financial data for previous three years, business description.

BISNES Plus. INFOTRADE N.V. • Daily. Database covers: Financial and descriptive information on more than one million Belgian companies and private businesses. Entries include: Name, address, name and title of contact, commercial registration numbers, data and form of incorporation, bank accounts, association memberships, principal language, number of employees, names of management personnel, activities and products, trademarks, trading partners, financial statements for the most recent three years.

BizEkon News--Soviet Business Directory. RIA Novosti Russian News & Information Agency. • Quarterly. Covers: over 2,500 companies in the Commonwealth of Independent States that have contracts abroad. Database includes: Company name, address, phone, fax, telex, names and titles of key personnel, banker, number of employees, production data, legal status, production program, list of products.

Bottin Entreprises. Bottin S.A. • Annual. Database covers: about 100,000 French companies. Database includes: Company name, address, phone, telex, type of business, capital, legal incorporation, formal structure, branches or other locations, if any; some include names of directors, financial turnover (period specified), number of employees.

Braby's Zambia Trade Directory. A.C. Braby (Pty) Ltd. • Annual. $100. Covers: Businesses in Zambia. Database includes: Maps. Entries include: Contact information.

Brazil Business Directory. INFOT Inc. • Annual. $67.15 CD-ROM; additional $65 for MS Access format. Covers: 329,752 companies, from Brazil. Entries include: company name, email and website addresses, telephone and fax number, and business description.

Brazil Company Handbook. Hoover's Inc. • Annual. $74.95 Individuals tradepaper. Covers: About 72 of Brazil's largest public companies. Database includes: Profile of Brazil's economy, international trade, and investment climate; data on stock exchanges. Entries include: Company name, address, phone, fax, year established, stock ticker symbol, names and titles of key personnel, number of employees, number of stockholders, bank references, auditor, company history, financial data, markets and competition, raw materials used and sources, names of major stockholders, affiliated companies.

Brazil Dez Mil. Dun & Bradstreet Inc. • Biennial. Covers: 10,000 of the largest companies in Brazil. Entries include: Company name, address, phone, fax, telex, sales volume, Standard Industrial Classification (SIC) code, names and titles of key personnel, number of employees, import/export designation.

Brazilian-American Who's Who. Brazilian-American Chamber of Commerce. • Irregular. $55. Covers: more than 1,300 firms, subsidiaries, and affiliates operating and/or having interests in both the United States and Brazil. Entries include: Company name, address, names and titles of key personnel.

Bremer Geschafts-Adressbuch. Carl Ed. Schuenemann KG. • Annual. Covers: about 20,000 businesses in the state of Bremen, Germany. Entries include: Company name, address, phone.

British Export Interactive Website. Reed Business Information. • Database covers: 17,000 companies in the United Kingdom, as well as the products and services they actively export. Database includes: Full electronic commerce.

British Firms in Germany. British Chamber of Commerce in Germany. • $200. Covers: companies in the Federal Republic of Germany which are subsidiaries of or otherwise affiliated with United Kingdom firms. Entries include: German company name and address, name and address of British affiliate or owner, code indicating products.

Browning Database Review. Browning Associates. • Irregular. $50 payment with order. Covers: over 125 databases providing Canadian business information. Entries include: Database name and acronym, content, scope, time span, frequency of update, size, percentage of Canadian content, connect rates and requirements; name, address, and phone of producer and of the Canadian and/or United States distributor.

Brunei Yearbook. Forward Media Sdn Bhd. • Information on Brunei companies, products and services. Entries include: Company name, address, phone and fax numbers, company's main business activities, names of top executives, e-mail and website addresses.

Bulgarian Trade Directory. Bulgarian Chamber of Commerce and Industry. • Annual. €35 Individuals EU member. Covers: 2,000 export/import companies and 120 economic committees and ministries in Bulgaria. Entries include: Name, address, phone, description of activities.

Bullseye Ownership Report. CDA/Equity Intelligence. • Weekly. $800. Covers: over 1,300 institutions that have filed statements of company ownership with the Securities and Exchange Commission, including 13D and 13G five-percent beneficial ownership, 14D-1 tender offers, 13(f) institutional common stock holdings, 13(f) institutional convertible holdings, U.S. investment company holdings, foreign investment company holdings. Entries include: Company name, value held, change in shares, going back five consecutive quarters, money center, turnover, investment style, type of institute, investment discretion, voting authority, filing date and percent of shares outstanding.

Business Contacts in Finland. Larenco Oy. • Annual. Covers: Approximately 200 Finnish companies interested in foreign trade. Entries include: Name, address, phone, fax, list of products exported/imported, geographical area served.

Business Directory of Macedonia. Balkanika Publishing and Marketing Ltd. • Covers: Institutions and companies in the Republic of Macedonia. Entries include: Institution/company name, address, phone, fax, description, e-mail, and website.

Business Directory of United Kingdom. INFOT Inc. • $51 CD-ROM. Covers: 67,281 companies from United Kingdom, importers, and exporters. Entries include: Email and website addresses, telephone and fax number, and business titles and descriptions.

Business Europe: The Essential Guide to Who's Who and What's What in Europe. Macmillan Publishers Ltd. • $14.99. Covers: Businesses in Europe, encompassing service industries, wholesale and retail trades, professions, and trade unions. Entries include: Name, address, phone.

Business Foundation Book: General Trade Index & Business Guide--Poland. Business Foundation Company Ltd. • Annual. $90 plus $40.00 shipping. Covers: Approximately 3,500 Polish businesses and firms seeking foreign cooperation and trade with the West. Database includes: General information on Polish industry and trade, including the Polish economy, business and labor law, finance, taxation, import/export regulations, and laws pertaining to foreign investment and business. Entries include: Abbreviated trade names; firm name, address, phone, fax, telex; year established; name and title of contact and languages spoken; line of business; proposed fields of cooperation or goods sought; number of employees; financial data.

Business Guide Central--East Europe. Overseas-Post-Organisation. • Annual. $30. Publication includes: Businesses and organizations in the Baltic States, Bulgaria, Czech Republic, Hungary, Poland, Romania, Slovakia, Belarus, Moldova, Russia, and Ukraine. Entries include: Name, address, phone, telex. Principal content of publication is general business information for each country or region.

The Business Who's Who of Australia. Dun & Bradstreet (Australia) Proprietary Ltd. • Daily (eve.). $2,292.95 Individuals 2004 volume 1, price includes GST. Covers: In two volumes, over 40,029 business and associations. Volume 1 covers larger companies; volume 2 covers medium-sized companies. Database includes: Industry statistics. Entries include: Company name, address, names and locations of branches and names of subsidiary and associated companies, names and titles of directors and key personnel, number of employees, capital, annual sales, firms represented, banking firm, products and services, trade names, brief description of activities.

Businessdele. Helsinki Media. • Annual. Covers: Businesses, government offices, and public institutions in Finland. Entries include: Entity name, address, phone, telex number, cable address, product/service.

Buyer's Guide for Morocco. Annuaire de l'Acheteur. • $100 Out of country. Covers: Commercial, industrial and service companies in Morocco. Entries include: Company name, address, phone, product/service, trade name.

Camerdata. Camerdata S.A. • Monthly. Database covers: Approximately 2 million Spanish business firms. Database includes: Company name, address, number of employees, sector of activity.

Canadian Federal Corporations and Directors. Postmedia Network Inc. • Monthly. Covers: About 400,000 federally incorporated Canadian companies. Database includes: Company name, address, date incorporated, parent or subsidiary companies, financial data for two years, names and home addresses of directors.

Canadian Financial Database. Globe Interactive. • Database covers: about 500 of the leading Canadian corporations. Database includes: Company name, address, phone, names and titles of key personnel, financial data.

Canadian National Business Directory. Todd Publications. • $250. Covers: 200,000 businesses, including tradeshows, exhibitions, and meetings. Database includes: Glossary of Internet terms; list of products and services online. Entries include: Address and phone number.

Cataloging Handbook H4/H8 Commercial and Government Entity. Defense Logistics Service Center U.S. Defense Logistics Agency. • Bimonthly. $40 per year (S/N 008-007-80003-5). Covers: about 92,000 companies, primarily manufacturers, that produce or maintain design control for products cataloged by federal government agencies. Entries include: Company name, address, five-digit Federal Supply Code for Manufacturers, and letter code indicating active or inactive status or other attributes; some listings include previous company name, previous location, or other information.

Catalogue of Firms in Slovakia. I.S.M.C. Information Systems and Marketing Contacts Ltd. • Annual. $65. Covers: Over 50,000 firms in Slovakia with a list of 50,000 goods. Entries include: Company contact information, economic data.

Catalogue of Firms in the Czech Republic. I.S.M.C. Information Systems and Marketing Contacts Ltd. • Annual. $84. Covers: Over 50,000 firms located in the Czech Republic, as well as a list of 30,000 goods. Entries include: Company contact information, economic data.

CBI European Business Handbook. Kogan Page, Limited. • $35. Publication includes: A business directory of 27 countries in Europe. Principal content of publication is an analysis of economic, business, and industrial prospects in Europe.

CCBC--Membership Directory. Canada-China Business Council. • Annual. Covers: 200 Canadian companies in China. Entries include: Company profile.

CCN Business Information Database. CCN Business Information Ltd. • Continuous. Database covers: Approximately 3 million companies in the U.K. Database includes: Company name, address, phone, registration number, date and legal form of incorporation, holding company, directors, auditor, number of employees, prinicpal activities, financial data.

CD-MAIL: The address database for mailings. Wer liefert was GmbH. • Semiannual. $1,200. Covers: Approximately 184,000 companies in Germany, Austria, Switzerland, Belgium, Luxembourg, and the Netherlands. Entries include: Name, address, phone, fax, names and titles of key personnel, description of product/service.

CD-ROM EEKOD. Promar Ltd. • Annual. $2,500. Covers: More than 246,500 company profiles in Eastern Europe, including Austria, Czech Republic, Croatia, Latvia, Lithuania, Hungary, Poland, Slovenia, Azerbaidjan, Slovakia, Belarus, Estonia, Romania, Moldavia, Russia, Ukraine, and Yugoslavia.

Central Africa Business Directory. A.C. Braby (Pty) Ltd. • Annual. $35. Covers: Businesses in Botswana, Lesotho, Mauritius, Malawi, Mozambique, Reunion, Seychelles, South West Africa, Swaziland, Zambia, and Zimbabwe. Entries include: Company name, address, phone, type of business.

Chicago Area Business Directory. InfoGroup Inc. • Annual. $495. Number of listings: 314,000. Entries include: Company name, address, phone, number of employees, name of owner or manager, annual sales. Compiled from telephone company "Yellow Pages," statewide.

China Business Directory. China Business Information Center. • Annual. $239. More than 25,000 companies in the People's Republic of China, excluding Taiwan and Hong Kong, with assets over $1.5 million.

China Business Guide. American Chamber of Commerce in Hong Kong. • $40 Individuals. Covers: Companies engaged in business and trade in China. Database includes: Statistics, charts.

The China Commercial Relations Directory. American Chamber of Commerce in Hong Kong. • Biennial. $215 Nonmembers. Covers: Approximately 230 top China trade and service companies in Hong Kong; 115 companies in the PRC. Entries include: Addresses, names and titles of key personnel.

China Logistics Directory. SinoMedia Ltd. • $80 Individuals book. Covers: 2,300 logistics companies operating in China across 12 industry sectors including airlines, airport, harbor & station operators, associations & consultants, construction companies, express forwarders, IT resources, land transportation, logistics equipment suppliers, logistics industrial parks, logistics services (custom brokers, air carriers and service companies), non-vessel operating common carriers, shipping companies, warehousing, third party logistics & supply chain solution. Entries include: English and Chinese names, address, headquarters location, phone and faxes, emails, key contact individuals, website.

China Stock Directory. China Economic Review. • $75 Individuals. Covers: 1,800 mainland-listed companies on the Shanghai and Shenzhen markets. Publication includes: Information about a company history, business operations, share price range, shareholders, key executives, contact details, complete financials top shareholders, their share types and percentage stakes.

China's Machine & Electric Enterprises and Products Database. Computing Center of the Ministry of Foreign Trade and Economic Cooperation. • $1,600. Database covers: 100,000 Chinese machine and electric companies. Entries include: Contact information, office hours, executives, bankers, number of employees, contact person, registered capital, sales, list of products.

Chinese Business in America. Caravel Inc. • Annual. $88 Individuals. Publication includes: Approximately 2,900 major ethnic Chinese enterprises in the U.S. Entries include: Contact name, address, phone, fax, websites, products/services imported/exported. Principal content of publication is is a how-to on establishing a new business in the U. S: marketing and sourcing in the U.S.

CIS-States Companies. COMMIT GmbH. • Quarterly. Database covers: companies in the nations of the Commonwealth of Independent States. Database includes: Company name, address, legal status, products, number of employees.

Classified Business Directory of the State of Connecticut: Buyer's Blue Book. Connecticut Directory Company Inc. • Annual. $66.95. Covers: manufacturers, banks, schools, service companies, distributors, wholesalers, restaurants, and hotels in Connecticut and surrounding states. All listings are paid. Entries include: Company, name, address, phone. No sales in Connecticut except to libraries.

Colombian Business Guide. Asesorias Finanzas Ltda. • Annual. $30. Covers: Colombia businesses, foreign investment, import and export credit, main imports, export products, chambers of commerce, mining, livestock, and Colombian enterprise abroad.

Commercial & Industrial Register of Southern Africa. A.C. Braby (Pty) Ltd. • Annual. $120 payment must accompany order. Covers: businesses in southern Africa. Database includes: Maps, list of PO Box renters. Entries include: Company name, address, phone.

Compact Disc Monaci. Guida Monaci S.p.A. • Semiannual. Covers: 110,000 companies and agencies of the public and private sector in Italy, along with 200,000 business professionals. Entries include: For individuals--Name, address, position, qualifications.

Companies in Greenland at Randburg. Randburg.com. • Database covers: Companies in Greenland. Entries include: Company name, address, phone, fax, description.

Company Handbook--Hong Kong. Reference Press Inc. • Semiannual. $44.95 per issue, plus $3.50 shipping. Covers: about 400 companies in Hong Kong; 200 are profiled in detail. Entries include: Company name, address, phone, fax, description, major shareholders and officers, financial data; detailed entries include financial data for previous five years, commentary on recent performance and trends, and share prices for the previous year. Published in Hong Kong by Corporate International Ltd.

Company Handbook Spain: The Maxwell Espinosa Shareholders Directory. S.p.A. • Annual. $84.95 plus $3.50 shipping. Covers: 2,000 corporations in Spain. Entries include: Company name, address, phone, fax, names and titles of key personnel, major shareholders, line of business, sales for previous year and preceding four years, number of employees, names of advertising agency, attorneys, auditors, banks, and investment relations director.

Confederation of Zimbabwe Industries: Register & Buyers Guide--Brand Names, Manufacturers, Products. Thomson Publications. • Annual. $115 please inquire. Covers: Commercial enterprises and members of the Confederation of Zimbabwe Industries. Entries include: Company name, address, phone, member name, address.

Consumer Spain. Euromonitor International Business Reference Div. • Irregular. $575. Publication includes: Lists of 100 Spanish companies and retailers. Database includes: List of sources of information on Spain. Entries include: Company name, address, phone, brand and product information, market shares, sales and profits. Principal content of publication is business briefings and analysis of Spain's consumer markets.

Contact Peru. American Chamber of Commerce of Peru. • Quarterly. Covers: Member companies and American Chambers of Commerce in Latin America. Entries include: Company name, address, phone, telex.

Corporate Affiliations. LexisNexis. • Annual. $2,395 8 volume set. Covers: Business and financial information on approximately 3,800 U.S. parent companies and 44,500 subsidiaries, divisions, and affiliates worldwide, as well as 140,000 key executives. Entries include: Sales, assets, liabilities, ownership percentage.

Corporate Finance Sourcebook: The Guide to Major Capital Investment Sources and Related Financial Services. LexisNexis. • Annual. $695 Individuals list price. Covers: Securities research analysts; major private lenders; investment banking firms; commercial banks; United States-based foreign banks; commercial finance firms; leasing companies; foreign investment bankers in the United States; pension managers; banks that offer master trusts; cash managers; business insurance brokers; business real estate specialists; lists about 3,500 firms; 14,500 key financial experts. Entries include: All entries include firm name, address, phone, e-mail, and names and titles of officers, contacts, or specialists in corporate finance. Additional details are given as appropriate, including names of major clients, number of companies served, services, total assets, branch locations, years in business.

Corporate 500: Directory of Corporate Philanthropy. Public Management Institute. • Annual. $375 plus $10.00 shipping. Covers: 554 major corporations with philanthropic programs. Entries include: Corporation name, corporate foundation name (if applicable), address, philanthropic interests and priorities, policy statement, contribution committee members, financial profile, activities eligible for funding, contact person, sample grants, application procedures, analysis of giving patterns.

Corporate Giving Directory. Information Today, Inc. • Annual. $699.50 Individuals softbound; plus $20 shipping and handling. Covers: Top 1,000 major corporation- and company-sponsored foundations and direct-giving programs. Database includes: Appendix to abridged entries of more than 2,000 additional funders. Entries include: Giving program's sponsoring company name, address, phone, fax, e-mail, website; names and biographies of living officers, and contact person; grants data, including types, average amounts, sample grants; application procedures; analysis of giving priorities; and information on the company, including products, Fortune rank, sales, ticker symbol/stock exchange information, operating locations, number of employees, information on employee-matching gifts (including restrictions and ratio), and nonmonetary support.

Corporate Giving Yellow Pages: Guide to Corporate Giving Contacts. Taft Group. • $99. Covers: more than 3,500 corporate contact persons with information on corporate charitable giving. Entries include: Company name, address, phone, fax, name and title of contact, name of company foundation (if any).

Corporate Philanthropy in New England. Development and Technical Assistance Center Inc. • Irregular. $80 Connecticut. Corporations in New England that have gross sales of over $10 million or at least 200 employees and an office in the state and that have given grants or have other funding programs; separate editions available for Connecticut, Maine, New Hampshire, Rhode Island, and Vermont.

Corporate Report Fact Book. City Media Inc. • Annual. $147. Covers: about 320 public corporations in the Ninth Federal Reserve District (Minnesota, North and South Dakota, Montana, upper Michigan, and northwestern Wisconsin) having stock actively traded; 1,550 privately owned companies with over 50 employees; 650 regional operations with over 50 employees, 115 non-profit corporations; 600 top executives in businesses of the upper Midwest. Entries include: For public companies--Company name, address, phone, fax; names of officers, directors, and major shareholders; profile, two-year balance sheet and five-year earnings history; recent events, recent four quarters results; number of employees, number of stockholders; general counsel, auditors; state and year of incorporation, transfer agent and registrar, subsidiaries, SIC codes. For private and nonprofit companies and regional operations--Name, address, phone, fax, names of principal executives; revenue (if provided), description of business, number of employees, corporate affiliations, year established. For top executives--Name, title, affiliation, office address and phone, date and place of birth; personal, education, and career data; awards, activities, memberships.

Crawford's Directory of City Connections. AP Information Services Ltd. • $325. Covers: Approximately 3,500 private and public sector companies in the U.K., as well as advisers to the financial sector, including stockholders, solicitors, auditors, and insurance advisers. Entries include: Name, address, phone, names and titles of key personnel.

Creditreform-Datenbank. Verband der Vereine Creditreform e.V. • Daily. Database covers: Credit information on more than 3,100,000 million joint stock and individual trading companies in Austria and Germany. Entries include: Company name, address, legal form, dates of formation or reformation, capital, partners, number of employees, product line, financial indicators covering capital, obligations, annual income, property and equipment, warehouse stocks, loan payment record, liabilities, credit rating, biographical information on company principal officials.

D & B Million Dollar Directory. Dun & Bradstreet Inc. • Annual. Covers 1,600,000 public and private businesses with either a net worth of $500,000 or more, 250 or more employees at that location, or $25,000,000 or more in sales volume; includes industrial corporations, utilities, transportation companies, bank and trust companies, stock brokers, mutual and stock insurance companies, wholesalers, retailers, and domestic subsidiaries of foreign corporations.

D & B Million Dollar Directory--Top 50,000 Companies. Dun & Bradstreet Inc. • Annual. $500 commercially. 50,000 top corporations, utilities, transportation companies, bank and trust companies, stock brokers, mutual and stock insurance companies, wholesalers, retailers, and domestic subsidiaries of foreign corporations; business must have 250 or more employees at main location, or have at least $25 million in sales volume.

Dafsaliens Database of Ownership Links--France. Dafsaliens. • Monthly. Covers: More than 120,000 companies worldwide. Entries include: Company names, registration number, form of incorporation, addresses, telephone, fax, description of business, shareholders subsidiaries and cross holdings, and financial data. CD-ROM includes historical data to trace changing structures and current and former directors and officers.

Das Grosse Einkaufs 1x1 der Deutschen Wirtschaft: Band 3: Deutsche Wirtschafts-Standorte. Deutscher Adressbuch-Verlag fur Wirtschaft und Verkehr GmbH. • Annual. $200 prepaid. Covers: federal and state govermental agencies of the Federal Republic of Germany; approximately 220,000 German industrial, retail, wholesale, and service companies; national and regional trade organizations. Database includes: List of place names with former names and geographical location; maps. Entries include: Agency, organization, or company name, address, phone; headquarters office location for branch companies.

DASH: Directors and Shareholdings. Bureau van Dijk S.A. • Database covers: One million limited companies and two million directors combined with details on individual and corporate shareholders in the United Kingdom. Entries include: Company name, address, phone, fax, activity, employee range, legal form, status, capital, turnover, holding companies and corporate shareholders; director name, date of birth, address, marital status, nationality, occupation, qualification, appointment date.

Datalink Regional Business Directory. Datatech Communications Inc. • Covers: More than 180,000 companies in New York, Vermont, New Hampshire, Maine, Massachusetts, Rhode Island, Maryland, Connecticut, and New Jersey. Entries include: Company name, address, phone, fax, 800 numbers, URL, e-mail.

Delaware Directory of Commerce and Industry. Delaware State Chamber of Commerce Inc. • Periodic Annual. $50 Members per additional copy for members. Covers: About 5,000 manufacturers, retailers, wholesalers, and service establishments. Entries include: Name, address, phone, name, address, phone, name and title of contact, list of products or services.

Denmark's 10,000 Largest Companies. William Snyder Publishing Associates. • Annual. $175 plus 30 pounds shipping. Covers: 10,000 "leading" (by turnover) companies in Denmark. Database includes: Table of companies ranked by common currency listing sales figures, percentage growth indicators, profitability, capital structure, number of employees, year established. Entries include: In an index--Company name, address, phone, turnover, profit, number of employees.

Denton's Directories. Denton's Directories Ltd. • Annual. $11. Covers: Local businesses and community services in various British towns; separate volumes cover Bath, Calne/Lyneham, Chippenham/Corsham, Cirencester, Devizes, Keynsham/Saltford, Malmesbury/Tetbury, Marlborough/Hungerford, Melksham, Shaftesbury/Gillingham/Mere, Sherborne/Milborne Port, Trowbridge/Bradford on Avon, Warminster, Westbury, Bridport, Dorchester, Wootton, and Bassett. Entries include: Company name, address, phone.

Der Runde Herold. Herold Business Data GmbH. • Annual. Database covers: Approximately 225,000 Austrian companies. Entries include: Company name, address, phone, type of business, region, and postal code. For the 10,000 largest companies, includes turnover figures, number of employees, and key personnel.

Directory of Affiliates & Offices of Japanese Firms in USA & Canada. Want Publishing Co. • Irregular. $190. Covers: over 6,000 Japanese-affiliated or owned firms in the U.S. and Canada.

Directory of American Business in Hong Kong. GTE Directories Ltd. • $20. Covers: American companies, their agents, and distributors in Hong Kong; US State and Port of Authority representatives in Hong Kong; products and service of the American Consulate General in Hong Kong.

Directory of American Business in South China. American Chamber of Commerce in Hong Kong. • Covers: Over 900 American companies that have regional headquarters or representative offices in Hong Kong.

Directory of American Companies Operating in Mexico. American Chamber of Commerce of Mexico - Mexico City. • Biennial. Covers: over 2,500 United States commercial and investment companies with operations in Mexico, and the 2,500 Mexican companies that represent them in Mexico. Entries include: For United States companies--Name, address, phone, fax, contact person, products, names of Mexican firm with which associated, type of affiliation. For Mexican companies--Name, address, phone, fax, contact person, products, sales, name of United States company.

Directory of American Companies Overseas. Overseas Employment Services. • Annual. $15. Covers: Approximately 250 American companies that have branch plants or offices outside the U.S. Entries include: Company name, address, geographical area served, and product/service.

Directory of American Manufacturers & Exporters of Wax & Wax Products. EXIM Infotek Private Ltd. • $10 Individuals. Covers: 100 American manufacturers and exporters of car waxes, dental waxes, floor finishes wax, microcrystalline waxes, synthetic waxes, wax, waxes and polishes, wax floors. Entries include: Company name, postal address, city, country, phone, fax, e-mail and websites, contact person, designation, products detail.

Directory of Belgian Importers of American Products. American Chamber of Commerce in Belgium. • Annual. $125. Covers: 1,000 Belgian importers and distributors and 3,000 U.S. exporters of U.S. products in Belgium. Entries include: Company name, address, phone, fax, executives, products.

Directory of Canadian Companies Overseas. Overseas Employment Services. • Annual. $15 postpaid. Covers: about 250 Canadian companies and professional firms with branch plants or offices outside of Canada and the U.S. Entries include: Company name, address, geographical area served, product/service.

Directory of CEOs. IBCON S.A. • Irregular. $458 Individuals. Covers: 14,640 companies incorporated in Mexico City. Entries include: Name and position of top executive, company name, address, phone, fax, industry code.

Directory of China Address--China Enterprises and Institutes Volume. Xinhua Publishing House. • $160. Covers: More than 80,000 enterprises and institutes in over 300 cities, districts, and countries of China. Entries include: Contact information, business scope, products.

Directory of Chinese and Foreign Management and Sales Personnel. Standards Press of China. • Biennial. $30. Covers: 8,700 companies, organizations, and individuals in business, industry, and other professionals. Entries include: Name, address, phone, telex, name and title of contact, names and titles of key personnel, geographical area covered, description of activities.

Directory of Companies. IBCON S.A. • Irregular. $473 Individuals. Covers: 14,640 companies that are SA corporations located in Mexico City. Entries include: Company name, address, phone, fax, industry code, Producing, Distributing, Servicing initials, name and position of the top executive.

Directory of Companies, Board Members and Directors. Dicodi S.A. • Annual. Covers: 25,000 companies and 80,000 board members in Spain. Entries include: Company name, address, phone, director names.

Directory of Companies by Quarters. IBCON S.A. • Irregular. $473 Individuals. Covers: 14,041 companies incorporated in Mexico City. Entries include: Company name, address, phone, fax; industry code; Producing, Distributing, or Servicing initials, name and position of the top executive.

Directory of Corporate Name Changes. The Scarecrow Press Inc. • $104 Individuals Hardback. Lists names by which corporations have been known, including original and current names. Entries include: Name, preceding and succeeding names, year changed, original name (if the name listed isn't the original).

Directory of Corporations and Corporate Officers. DAFSA. • Annual. Covers: 13,000 corporation board members and 1,200 companies on the stock exchange in France. Entries include: For members--Name, address, positions held, responsibilities. For companies--Company name, address, phone, line of business, executives, shareholders, subsidiaries, financial data.

Directory of East European Businesses. Mercury Books Gold Arrow Publications Ltd. • $74.95 plus $3.50 shipping. Covers: 2,000 leading manufacturing and engineering companies in Albania, Bulgaria, the Commonwealth of Independent States, eastern Germany, Hungary, Poland, Romania, and Czechoslovakia and Yugoslavia (prior to their separations). Entries include: Company name, address, phone, fax, telex, name and title of contact, line of business, sales, profits.

Directory of Foreign Firms Operating in the United States. Uniworld Business Publications Inc. • Biennial. $350 Individuals hardcover plus s&h. Covers: Approximately 4,900 firms in 86 countries that own or have substantial investments in about 18,250 U.S. Companies. Entries include: Company name, address, phone, fax, name of chief executive officer, number of employees, annual sales, web address, product or service; affiliated U.S. company name, address, phone, fax, name of chief executive, number of employees, product or service, percent foreign-owned. Separate country editions are also available.

Directory of Incorporated (Registered) Companies in Nigeria. ICIC Ltd. • Biennial. $50. Covers: Companies from 1912 to present in Nigeria. Entries include: Company name, address.

Directory of Japanese-Affiliated Companies in the USA and Canada. • Covers: Over 5,000 Japanese-affiliated companies operating in the United States or Canada. Entries include: Name, address, phone, fax, year of establishment, capital, annual sales, managing directors, and main products/services.

Directory of Japanese-Affiliated Companies in USA & Canada. Database S.L. • Biennial. $260. Covers: Approximately 8,200 Japanese-affiliated companies operating in North America. Entries include: Company name, address, phone, status, type of business, product/service, names and titles of key personnel, Japanese parent company.

Directory of Japanese Giving. Corporate Citizen. • $190. Covers: Approximately 190 Japanese firms that participate in philanthropic activities in the U.S. Entries include: Company; name, address, phone; telex, names and titles of key personnel; description of policies, programs, and foundations; history of giving and volunteer activities in the U.S.; U.S. nonprofit organizations funded, geographical area served.

Directory of Mexican Corporations. IBCON S.A. • Irregular. $488 Individuals. 1,621 Mexican corporations selling at least $10,000,000 a year.

Directory of Registered Belgian Entrepreneurs and Companies. Cite Administrative de l'Etat. • Annual. Covers: Companies in Belgium. Entries include: Company name, address, phone, registration number, line of business, number of employees, business code.

Directory of Scottish Grant Making Trusts. Scottish

For publishers' addresses, refer to SOURCES CITED section at the back of the book.

Council for Voluntary Organisations. • Irregular. $9.50 Members. Number of listings: 524. Entries include: Company name, address, phone, grant name and subject, requirements, recipients.

Directory of Service, Industrial and Foreign Trading Companies in Egypt. International Trade Consulting Co. • $45. Covers: Companies in Egypt. Entries include: Company name, address, phone.

Directory of State Level Enterprises in China. Han Ying Shan Research Inc. • Irregular. $165. Covers: 1,064 "first or second grade enterprises" in China. Entries include: Company name, address, phone, telex, name and title of contact, number of employees, geographical area served, financial data, names and titles of key personnel, description of product/service.

Directory of the Russian Far East. Flegon Press. • Irregular. $99. Covers: Industry in the Far East of Russia. Entries include: Company name and location, manager name, phone, telex, number of employees, products, and import/export details.

Directory of U.S. Companies Doing Business in Central and Eastern Europe and the Commonwealth of Independent States. Wetherby International Co. • Quarterly. $25 postpaid. Covers: over 500 U.S. firms with operations in the Commonwealth of Independent States and Central and Eastern Europe; sources of assistance for U.S. business at the Commerce Department. Entries include: Company or agency name, address, phone, type of activity.

Directory of Washington, DC Chief Executive Officers. Labor Market Information and Research Division District of Columbia Department of Employment Services. • Annual. Covers: 200 large nongovernmental companies in the District of Columbia, selected on the basis of number of employees. Entries include: Company name, name of chief executive officer, address and the telephone numbers.

The Directory of World Industrial & Commercial Organizations: China, Mainland Volume. Economic Management Publishing House. • $195. Covers: About 4,000 major import and export businesses in mainland China. Database includes: An introduction to China's economic situation, trade control, regulation, investment policy, exchange control, banking services, insurance, China's Coastal Open Areas, major economic management organizations, major chambers of commerce. Entries include: Company name, address, phone, fax, scope of business.

Disclosure SEC Database. Disclosure Inc. • Weekly. Database covers: Approximately 11,000 public companies that have at least 500 shareholders of one class of stock and a minimum of five million dollars in assets, and have filed a 10K, 20F, or Registration Statement with the Securities and Exchange Commission within the preceding 18 months. Database includes: Company name, address, phone, names and titles of key personnel and directors, state in which incorporated; Standard Industrial Classification (SIC) code; Fortune, Forbes, CUSIP, DUNS numbers; auditors, subsidiaries; annual and quarterly balance sheets and income statements; five-year financial summary; sources and uses of funds, price/earnings data, stock transfer agent, text of management discussion and President's letter, and other information. Institutional holdings, 5% ownership holdings, and ownership by insiders for 5,000 companies are reported in "Disclosure/ Spectrum Ownership," updated quarterly; detailed data list of specific institutions and individuals, their relationship to the company, their holdings, and their most recent trades. Full text of documents available in print and on microfiche.

Downstate Illinois Business Directory. InfoGroup Inc. • Annual. $415. Number of listings: 188,000. Entries include: Company name, address, phone (including area code). Compiled from telephone company "Yellow Pages," statewide.

Dun & Bradstreet Germany. Dun & Bradstreet Inc. • €70 Individuals. Database covers: Over 160 million companies in Germany. Database includes: Company name, address, phone, names and titles of key personnel, number of employees, turnover, financial data, SIC code.

Dun & Bradstreet Italy. CRIBIS D & B Ltd. • Database covers: Approximately 473,000 companies in Italy. Database includes: Company name, address, names and titles of key personnel, number of employees, turnover, financial data, line of business, SIC code.

Dun & Bradstreet Reference Book of American Businesses. Dun & Bradstreet Inc. • Covers: more than 3 million large and small, public and private U.S. companies. Entries include: Company name and phone, branch offices, D&B credit rating, Standard Industrial Classification (SIC) code, new business and rating change indicators, year established, finansial data.

Dun & Bradstreet Regional Business Directories. Dun & Bradstreet Inc. • Annual. Covers: Top 20,000 businesses in one of 54 metropolitan areas in the U.S. Entries include: Company name, address, phone, trade name, Dun & Bradstreet D-U-N-S number, line of business, Standard Industrial Classification (SIC) code, sales volume names and titles of key personnel, number of employees, number of employees at location, parent company, year established, stock exchange symbol, indication of public or private ownership.

Dun & Bradstreet Swiss Company Information. Dun & Bradstreet AG. • Monthly. Database covers: more than 180,000 businesses in Switzerland and Liechtenstein. Database includes: Company name, address, phone, headquarter and subsidiary, name and title of contact, year founded, SIC code, business activities, number of employees, senior executive name, sales volume, accounting and banking firm, DUNS number.

Dun & Bradstreet 25,000 Series Directory. Dun & Bradstreet Inc. • Annual. $250 per volume. Covers: In three separate volumes, top 25,000 businesses, based on number of employees, for the Asia Pacific, Latin America, and Western Europe. Entries include: Company name, address, phone, fax, telex, Dun & Bradstreet D-U-N-S number, Standard Industrial Classification (SIC) code, name of CEO, number of employees, import/export designation, ownership date.

Dundsdata. Dun & Bradstreet France S.A. • Database covers: more than 9 million European businesses, with emphasis on France. Database includes: Company name, address, product trade name, capital, net value, financial data, affiliates and subsidiaries, principal directors.

Dun's 15,000 Largest Companies--Belgium. Dun & Bradstreet Inc. • Covers: 15,000 industrial, trading, banking, insurance, and service companies in Belgium. Entries include: Company name, address, phone, fax, telex, equity capital, number of employees, primary and secondary Standard Industrial Classification (SIC) codes, profit/loss ratios, export percentages.

Dun's 15,000 Largest Companies--Portugal. Dun & Bradstreet Inc. • Covers: 15,000 industrial, trading, banking, insurance, and service companies in Portugal. Entries include: Company name, address, phone, fax, telex, equity capital, number of employees, primary and secondary Standard Industrial Classification (SIC) codes, profit/loss ratios, export percentages.

Dun's 15,000 Largest Companies--Spain. Dun & Bradstreet Inc. • Covers: 15,000 industrial, trading, banking, insurance, and service companies in Spain. Entries include: Company name, address, phone, fax, telex, equity capital, number of employees, primary and secondary Standard Industrial Classification (SIC) codes, profit/loss ratios, export percentages.

Dun's 50,000--Spain's Largest Companies. Dun & Bradstreet Inc. • Annual. £438. Covers: 50,000 of the largest marketing companies in Spain. Entries include: Company name, address, operation information, key marketing information, key financial information.

Dun's Guide to Israel. Dun & Bradstreet Inc. • Covers: over 10,000 leading companies in Israel. Entries include: Company name, address, phone, fax, product exported, names and titles of key personnel, Standard Industrial Classification (SIC) code, number of employees, sales volume.

Dun's Regional Directory of Service Companies--Canada. Dun & Bradstreet Inc. • Covers: more than 10,000 service enterprises in Canada with eight or more employees and from Standard Industrial Classification (SIC) codes 07, 47, 60-80, and 82-89. Entries include: Company name, address, phone, SIC codes, parent company, number of employees, names and titles of key personnel, DUNS number.

Dunsmarketing. Dun & Bradstreet France S.A. • Database covers: over 240,000 French companies with more than 10 employees or annual turnover exceeding 10 million French Francs. Database includes: Company name, address, phone, year founded, executive officer name and title, number of employees, sector of activity, SIC code, business and import/export volume, affiliate and subsidiary companies, financial data.

The East-West Business Directory. Duncan Publishing. • Irregular. $65 plus $3.50 shipping. Covers: Approximately 863 companies that have central and eastern European capital participation, located in over 20 European and North American countries, Australia, and Japan. Database includes: Lists (with addrs.) of official Eastern bloc trade missions and commercial, shipping, banking, airline, and tourist offices in the OECD countries, and an overview of investment activities of Soviet and eastern European state ent. Entries include: Company name, address, phone, telex, name and title of principal executive, number of employees, financial information, ownership structure, statistical data, products or services.

Economic World Directory of Japanese Companies in the U.S.A. Economic Salon Ltd. • Biennial. $300. Covers: about 850 companies in the United States that are subsidiaries, divisions, etc., of Japanese parent firms. Entries include: United States company name, address, phone; branch facilities, addresses, and phone numbers; financial data, type of business, names of executives, number of Japanese and United States employees, history, current company information, and similar but less extensive data on parent company.

EEKOD--East European Kompass on Disc. Kompass Deutschland Verlags- und Vertriebsgesellschaft, mbH. • €1,789.52 Individuals includes print, data export, and 1 update. Covers: Approximately 464,498 East European company profiles, including Austria, Azerbaidjan, Belarus, Boznia-Herzegovina, Bulgaria, Croatia, Czech Republic, Estonia, Hungary, Latvia, Lithuania, Moldavia, Poland, Romania, Russia, Slovakia, Slovenia, Ukraina, and Yugoslavia.

The Electronic Industry Sector in Switzerland. AT Zeitschriftenverlag. • Covers: Computer and electronics companies and products in Switzerland and Liechtenstein. Entries include: Company name, address, phone, product description.

EMMA: Easy Mailing and Marketing Applications. Bureau van Dijk S.A. • Quarterly. Database covers: More than 1,000,000 companies in the United Kingdom. Entries include: Company name, address, date of incorporation, company type, activity, directors, holding companies, turnover, net assets, pre-tax profit, number of employees.

EMPRESAS. Brazilian Institute for Information in Science and Technology. • Monthly. Database covers: companies that sell publicly available software programs. Entries include: Name of firm, address, phone, telex, products and services.

Enterprise: Greater Portland Business Directory. Tower Publishing Co. • Annual. $47.50. Covers: more than 7,000 companies in the Portland, Maine metropolitan area. Entries include: Company name, address, phone, fax, names and titles of contact and key personnel, number of employees, product or service, year established.

Essex Business Directory. Burrows Publishing Ltd. • Covers: Over 10,000 businesses in Essex. Entries include: Name, address, phone, fax, e-mail, website, key organization contact, year of establishment, size of company, turnover, and a brief description of company activity.

ESSOR. Union Francaise d'Annuaires Professionnels. • Annual. Covers: more than 200,000 French companies involved in industry and services. Entries include: Company name, address, phone, fax, telex, names and titles of key personnel, line of business, number of employees, registered capital, sales, product descriptions, legal and administrative information.

Europa--Key European Enterprises. AP Information Services Ltd. • $600 Individuals. Covers: Over 50,000 leading European companies. Entries include: Statistical profiles and geographical information.

European Business Top 1000. European Business Press Group N.V. • Annual. $398. Covers: About 1,500 companies in 19 European countries ranked according to financial success; approximately 4,000 company executives. Database includes: Private corporations, government and union controlled enterprises, non-European multinational companies consolidated at the European level, mergers, acquisitions. Entries include: Company name, address, phone, fax, names and titles of key personnel, gross and net profit, number of employees, depreciation, equity, cash flow, affiliations.

European Markets: A Guide to Company and Industry Information Sources. MarketResearch.com. • Irregular. $335. Covers: sources worldwide of information on European companies. Entries include: Source name, contact name, address, phone, fax, telex.

Europe's 15,000 Largest Companies. GAP Books. • Annual. £415 Individuals hardcover. Covers: 8,000 leading industrial companies, 2,500 trading companies, 350 banks, 350 transportation firms, 200 insurance firms, 100 hotels and restaurants, 150 advertising agencies; and 250 other firms; also includes ranked lists (without extensive data) of 125 largest money losers, 500 most profitable firms, 250 most profitable firms using profits as percentage of sales. Entries include: Company name, headquarters, contact, International Standard Industrial Classification (ISIC) code, sales, rank, number of employees and shareholders, profit, sales per employee, and other operating ratios. Headings are in English, German, and French.

Europe's Major and Medium Sized Companies Directory. Euromonitor International Business Reference Div. • Irregular. $990. Covers: 12,000 companies headquartered in eastern and western Europe. Database includes: Ranked lists of companies. Entries include: Company name, address, phone, fax, telex, type of company, ownership, major subsidiaries, names and titles of key personnel, products, outlets, number of employees, sales, recent company developments.

Europe's Medium Sized Companies Directory. Euromonitor International Business Reference Div. • $550 Individuals. Covers: More than 4,000 medium-sized companies in Europe. Entries include: Company name, address, phone, fax, contact experts.

Euroretailnet. Corporate Intelligence Group. • Database covers: Approximately 3,000 retailers in 17 European countries, including U.S. and Japanese companies doing business in Europe. Entries include: Company name, address, phone, fax, names and titles of key personnel, geographical area served; number of employees, financial data, subsidiary and branch names and locations; description; promotional activity; distribution system; information technology utilized.

Expansion Management--Atlas/Guide Issue: The Resource Manual for Companies on the Move. Intertec Publishing. • Annual. $10 for just Atlas issue. Publication includes: List of companies and agencies providing assistance to expanding or relocating businesses, including state and city departments of commerce, public and private economic development agencies, financial institutions, consultants, utility companies, and other professionals. Entries include: Company name, address, phone, fax, name and title of contact.

Extel Handbook of Market Leaders. Extel Financial Ltd. • Semiannual. $90. Covers: Major quoted companies. Entries include: Adress, phone, name of chairman, financial data.

Family Tree. Dun & Bradstreet Inc. • Continuous. Database covers: About 200,000 corporations and their subsidiaries and branch companies. Database includes: Company name, address, phone, corporate standing (whether parent or holding company, subsidiary, or other), Standard Industrial Classification (SIC) code, names and titles of key personnel, sales volume, financial information, Dun & Bradstreet rating.

The Fax Banque. InterCom Projects Ltd. • Quarterly. Diskette. Covers: Over 16,000 businesses in Central America and Miami, Florida. Entries include: Company name, address, phone, fax, description of commercial activity.

Field Trade Directory of Peru. Field Servicio de Informaciones del Peru. • Annual. $65. Covers: 7,000 Peruvian importers, factories, exporters, wholesalers, retailers, and more than 1,000 business activities. Database includes: Information on hotels, restaurants, and general information on selling, buying, and information sources in Peru. Entries include: Name, address, phone, cable, telex, manager name.

Financial Annual Registrars Service. Extel Financial Ltd. • Annual. $110. Covers: United Kingdom companies listed on one of the UK stock exchanges. Entries include: Company name, registrar's name, address, phone, fax, telex, types of stocks and shares, nominal value.

Financial Post Corporate Surveys. Financial Post DataGroup. • Database covers: 6,300 Canadian public companies and 19,000 defunct companies. Includes financial and operational information, key events, and key executives.

Finnish Export Companies. FINPRO. • Database covers: over 2,500 Finnish export companies. Database includes: Company name, address, names and titles of key personnel, products.

Finnish Trade. Federation of Finnish Trade and Commerce. • Annual. Covers: Member firms of the Federation of Finnish Commerce and Trade. Entries include: Company name, address, phone, fax, telex.

Firms Headquartered in Kansas. Kansas Department of Commerce - Office of Minority and Women Business Development. • Annual. $5. Covers: 400 firms headquartered in Kansas. Entries include: For companies--Name, address, phone, principal officials, sales, number of employees, products.

The 5,000 Largest French Companies. Le Nouvel Economiste. • Annual. Covers: 5,000 leading companies in France. Entries include: Company name, address, phone.

Florida Trend--Directory of Public Companies Issue. Trend Book Div. • Annual. $3.95. Publication includes: List of 250 publicly owned companies headquartered in Florida. Entries include: Name, address, phone, name of chief executive, financial keys, product or service.

Forbes--The Forbes International 500 Issue. Forbes Inc. • Annual. Publication includes: 500 largest foreign corporations, 50 largest corporations in the world. Entries include: For foreign companies--Company name, revenue, net income, assets, market value of common stock, location of corporate headquarters, number of employees.

Foreign Companies in Asia Yearbook. Business Monitor International Ltd. • $5,445 Individuals 40% discount. Covers: 49,270 senior executive contacts on 16,775 foreign company subsidiaries across 32 industry sectors in Asia. Entries include: full company name, address, phone and fax numbers, email and web addresses, and key contact names and titles.

Fortune Directory. Fortune Directories. • Annual. $25 payment with order. Covers: combined, in a fall reprint, 500 largest United States industrial corporations (published in an April issue each year) and the Service 500 (published in a June issue). The Service 500 comprises 100-company rankings of each of the largest diversified service, and commercial banking companies, and 50-company rankings each of the largest, diversified financial, savings institutions, life insurance, retailing, transportation, and utility companies. Database includes: Various other rankings by different measures. Entries include: Company name, address, headquarters city, sales, assets, net income, market value, comparative earnings per share for ten years, names and titles of key personnel, phone, and various other statistical and financial information.

Fortune Directory of United States Corporations. Time Inc. • Annual. $25. Publication includes: The top 500 firms in the U.S. Entries include: Company name, address, headquarters address, financial data.

FP500 Database. International Press Publications Inc. • $139 Individuals for subscribers of National Post. Publication includes: Company contact information, revenue, assets, net income, return on investment capital and officer information. Principal content of publication is 1,000 Canadian corporations, including Canada's top 500 private and public companies plus 300 additional corporations.

France 30,000. Dun & Bradstreet France S.A. • Annual. Covers: 30,000 companies in France. Entries include: Company name, address, phone, date founded, number of employees, key personnel, capital, turnover, affiliations.

Free State Directory. A.C. Braby (Pty) Ltd. • Annual. R 100. Covers: businesses in Free State province of South Africa. Entries include: Company name, address, phone, fax, descriptive text.

French Companies and their Partners Abroad. DAFSA. • Annual. Covers: 80,000 French companies in France and abroad. Entries include: Company name, address, phone, ownership connections, subsidiaries, ownership percentages.

French Companies Full Financials. RENCOM S&W. • Monthly. Database covers: Over 100,000 French companies in various sectors of industry and commerce. Entries include: Name, address, phone, senior management personnel, legal status, year founded, line of business, products, financial information.

French Company Handbook. International Herald Tribune. • Annual. $50. Covers: 120 major French companies included in the SBF 120 Index, plus other important bond issuers. Entries include:

For publishers' addresses, refer to SOURCES CITED section at the back of the book.

Company name, address, phone, fax, telex, names of principal officials, description of business, background, sales breakdown, major known shareholders and percentages of stock held, subsidiaries and holdings (with brief details on each), international activities, key recent developments, investments, and financial data for five years.

Georgia Business Directory. InfoGroup Inc. • Annual. $520 both print & CD-ROM. Covers: 346,843 businesses in Georgia. Entries include: Company name, address, phone, number of employees, name of owner or manager, sales volume. Compiled from telephone company "Yellow Pages," statewide. All states covered (see separate entries).

German Chamber of Commerce in China--Membership Directory. German Industry & Commerce Company Ltd. • 1,200 ¥ Nonmembers. Number of listings: 1,800. Entries include: Company name, address, e-mail, phone, and fax numbers.

Germany's Top 300. Frankfurter Allgemeine Zeitung GmbH. • Annual. $595. Covers: Germany's top 300 corporations, banks, and insurance companies; corporations are ranked based on their turnover; banks are ranked according to business volume; insurance companies are ranked according to premium income. Entries include: Company name, address, phone, fax ranking, products and activities, Standard Industrial Classification (SIC) codes, names of key management personnel, number of employees, turnover, pre-tax profit, net profit, cash flow, assets, investments, cash reserves, shareholders, investor relations, dividend, and high/low share price.

Gibaud Directory--Industrial, Commercial and Trade Enterprises. Annuaire Gibaud. • Annual. Covers: 27,000 industrial, commercial and trade enterprises in France. Entries include: Company name, address, phone, name and title of contact, year established, number of employees, subsidiaries, manager name, product/service.

Gids bij de Officiele Prijscourant van de Amsterdamse Effectenbeurs. Uitgeverij J. H. de Bussy B.V. • Annual. $195. Covers: companies listed on the Amsterdam Stock Exchange. Database includes: Information on shares, bonds, warrants, etc. Entries include: Company name, address, financial data.

Giftwares--Manufacturers Directory. InfoGroup Inc. • Annual. Number of listings: 1,180. Entries include: Name, address, phone, size of advertisement, name of owner or manager, number of employees, year first in "Yellow Pages." Compiled from telephone company "Yellow Pages," nationwide.

Glasses Directory--Sun & Ski. InfoGroup Inc. • Annual. Number of listings: 3,278. Entries include: Name, address, phone, size of advertisement, name of owner or manager, number of employees, year first in "Yellow Pages." Compiled from telephone company "Yellow Pages," nationwide.

Glasses Directory--Wholesale. InfoGroup Inc. • Annual. Number of listings: 2,221. Entries include: Name, address, phone, size of advertisement, name of owner or manager, number of employees, year first in "Yellow Pages." Compiled from telephone company "Yellow Pages," nationwide.

Global Business Directory. INFOT Inc. • $51.85 CD-ROM. Covers: 801,813 major global companies, businesses and services, suppliers, manufacturers, buyers, agents, importers, exporters, and organizations by industry. Entries include: Email and website addresses, telephone and fax number, and business titles and descriptions.

The Globe and Mail Report on Business: Canada Company Handbook. Globe Interactive. • Annual. $49.95. Covers: over 400 Canadian companies. Entries include: Company name, address, phone, line of business, names and titles of key personnel, financial data including balance sheets, stock ratios and prices, and debts, rankings by profit, revenues, and assets, description of activities, stock exchange symbols.

Golf Cars & Carts Dealers. InfoGroup Inc. • Annual. Number of listings: 1,507. Entries include: Name, address, phone, size of advertisement, name of owner or manager, number of employees, year first in "Yellow Pages." Compiled from telephone company "Yellow Pages," nationwide.

Goods and Services--Firm Directory. International Bureau for Information and Telecommunications. • Annual. $17. Covers: 5,000 leading and active companies in the Moscow region and their products and services. Entries include: Company name, address, phone, products or services provided.

Great Big Book of Business Lists. Entrepreneur Press. • $34.95 Individuals paperback. Covers: Approximately 10,000 listings of business information. Entries include: Business' contact information.

The Greater Washington Board of Trade--Membership Directory. Greater Washington Board of Trade. • Annual. $150. Covers: Over 900 member firms in the greater Washington, DC, metropolitan area. Entries include: Organization name, address, phone, name of key executive, type of organization, Standard Industrial Classification (SIC) code.

Grills--Gas & Electric--Parts Directory. InfoGroup Inc. • Annual. Number of listings: 2,171. Entries include: Name, address, phone, size of advertisement, name of owner or manager, number of employees, year first in "Yellow Pages." Compiled from telephone company "Yellow Pages," nationwide.

Grooming Directory--Pets. InfoGroup Inc. • Annual. Number of listings: 21,803. Entries include: Name, address, phone, size of advertisement, name of owner or manager, number of employees, year first in "Yellow Pages." Compiled from telephone company "Yellow Pages," nationwide.

The Guardian Guide to the UK's Top Companies. Hoover's Inc. • Annual. $49.95. Covers: 150 top British business companies. Database includes: Five years of detailed financial data. Entries include: Company name, address, phone, top officers and directors, information on board compensation, major subsidiaries; information on donations, history, policies and outlook for the future.

Guia Senior. Guia Senior. • Covers: Argentina's national government, provincial government, diplomatic corps, foreign diplomatic corps, armed forces, political groups, banks, saving banks, loan companies, stocks, investment, credit companies, financial associations, insurance companies, stock exchange, and advertising agencies.

Guide to UK Company Giving. The Directory of Social Change. • Biennial. $75 Individuals. Covers: Over 600 largest corporate donors in the United Kingdom. Entries include: Company name, address, phone, name and title of contact, financial data, including donation figures (additional information given for companies donating in excess of 500 million Ls per year).

Handbook of Rupee Companies. Colombo Brokers Association. • Annual. $30. Covers: Companies registered in Sri Lanka and quoted on the share market.

Harris County Business Guide. Business Extension Bureau Inc. • Biennial. $150 Individuals Hardcopies. Covers: 70,000 industrial, service, retail, wholesale, and professional firms in Harris County, Texas. Database includes: List of 110,000 top executives, includes phone numbers. Entries include: Company name, mailing and street addresses, phone, names and titles of key personnel, number of employees, product or service, years in business, URLs for about 40 percent of companies.

Hawaii Business Abroad. Hawaii Department of Business, Economic Development, and Tourism Research and Economic Analysis Division. • Irregular. Covers: approximately 400 Hawaiian firms that export, import, maintain overseas offices, or have business activities in foreign countries. Entries include: Company name, address, phone, fax, telex, name of contact, cable address, line of business, year established, number of employees, locations of overseas offices, description of overseas activities, parent company name and address (if any), names of countries with which business is done.

Headquarters USA. Omnigraphics Inc. • Annual. $210 Individuals web price. Covers: Approximately 110,000 U.S. Businesses, federal, state, and local government offices, banks, colleges and universities, associations, labor unions, political organizations, newspapers, magazines, TV and radio stations, foundations, postal and shipping services, hospitals, office equipment suppliers, airlines, hotels and motels, profiles of top cities, accountants, law firms, computer firms, foreign corporations, overseas trade contacts, and other professional services. Also covers Internet access providers; Internet mailing lists, publications, and sources; freenets. Personal names now included. Entries include: Company, organization, agency, or firm name, address, phone, fax, website addresses as available, and toll-free phone.

Headquarters USA: A Directory of Contact Information for Headquarters and Other Central Offices of Major Businesses and Organizations Nationwide. Omnigraphics Inc. • $195 Individuals Hardcover - Web price. Two volumes. Volume one is alphabetical by name of business or organization. Volume two is classified by subject. Includes more than 112,000 businesses, organizations, agencies, institutions, and "high-profile" individuals. Listings include addresses, telephone numbers, fax numbers, and toll-free numbers and Web addresses where available. Formerly *Business Phone Book USA*.

Hong Kong Public Companies. Data Base Asia Ltd. • Irregular. $700. Covers: Investing in 245 local and 15 overseas companies of the Hong Kong Stock Exchange. Entries include: Company name, details, history, balance sheet.

Hoover's Company Capsules on CD-ROM. Hoover's Inc. • Quarterly. $399.95. CD-ROM contains information on approximately 11,000 U.S. companies and over 30,000 CEOs and CFOs. Database includes: Built-in mailing label capability. Entries include: Company name, address, phone, fax, operations overview, web site address, CEO, CFO, sales, employment size, ticker symbol, stock exchange, industry, fiscal year end.

Hoover's Company Profiles on CD-ROM. Hoover's Inc. • Quarterly. $324.95 per year. CD-ROM. Contains over 1,200 in-depth company profiles and approximately 200 detailed industry profiles of U.S., international, and private companies. Database includes: 200 industry profiles from the U.S. Department of Commerce. Entries include: Operations, strategies, histories, products and brand names, officers, competitors, locations, and financial informtion.

Hoover's Guide to the Top New York Companies. Hoover's Inc. • Annual. $24.95 plus $3.50 shipping. Covers: 1,390 leading public and private companies located in New York City. Entries include: Company name, address, phone, fax, web sites, names and titles of key personnel, industry, stock symbols, sales, number of employees.

Hoover's Guide to the Top Texas Companies: The Ultimate Guide to Texas. Hoover's Inc. • Biennial. $24.95 plus $3.50 shipping. Covers: 850 private and public companies in Texas. The 55 largest companies; another 70 selected firms are described in detail. Database includes: Lists of the top 500 companies ranked by sales and the 50 fastest-growing companies; overview of the Texas economy and business environment. Entries include: For the 30 largest firms--Company name, address, phone, fax, overview of operations and strategies, history, financial data for previous 10 years, names and titles of key personnel, products/services/brand names. For selected firms--Company name, address, phone, fax, names and titles of key personnel, line of business, stock symbols, sales, number of employees. Less detail is given for the remaining firms.

Hoover's Handbook of American Business. Dun & Bradstreet Inc. Hoover's Inc. • Annual. $245 Individuals hardcover. Provides detailed profiles of more than 750 large public and private companies, including history, executives, brand names, key competitors, and up to 10 years of financial data. Includes indexes by industry, location, executive name, company name, and brand name.

Hoover's Handbook of Emerging Companies. Dun & Bradstreet Inc. Hoover's Inc. • Annual. $213. Contains detailed profiles of 600 rapidly growing corporations. Includes indexes by industry, location, executive name, company name, and brand name.

Hoover's Handbook of Private Companies: Profiles of Major U.S. Private Enterprises. Hoover's Inc. • Annual. $215 Individuals hardcover. Covers: 900 privately held companies and other enterprises; 250 firms are covered in detail. Entries include: Company name, address, phone, fax, brief overview of operations, products, competitors, names and titles of key personnel, sales, number of employees; detailed entries add in-depth profile of operations and strategies, financial data for preceding 10 years.

Hoover's Masterlist of Latin American Companies. Hoover's Inc. • $79.95 Book. Covers: 2,500 profiles of the largest public and private companies in Latin America. Database includes: All financial information converted to U.S. dollars. Entries include: Headquarters, address, phone, fax, key officers, industry description, sales figures, employment data.

Hoover's Masterlist of Major Asian Companies. Hoover's Inc. • $79.95. Covers: More than 3,000 companies in 10 Asian countries. Entries include: Name, address, phone, fax, names and titles of key personnel, financial data, employment data, description of industry.

Hoover's Masterlist of Major European Companies. Hoover's Inc. • $79.95 Book. Covers: 2,500 profiles of the largest public and private companies in Western Europe, including Greece and Turkey, plus all companies on the major European stock indexes. Database includes: All financial information converted to U.S. dollars. Entries include: Headquarters, address, phone, fax, key officers, industry description, sales figures, employment data.

Hoover's MasterList of Major U.S. Companies. Hoover's Inc. • $320 Individuals hardcover. Covers: Over 10,000 of the largest public and private companies in the U.S. Entries include: Company name, address, phone, fax, web site addresses, names and titles of key personnel, company overview, stock symbols, net income, market value, sales and employment data, fiscal year end.

Horse Riding & Rentals Directory. InfoGroup Inc. • Annual. Number of listings: 6968. Entries include: Name, address, phone, size of advertisement, name of owner or manager, number of employees, year first in "Yellow Pages." Compiled from telephone company "Yellow Pages," nationwide.

Hospodarsky Almanach. CompAlmanach spol S.R.O. • Annual. $110. Covers: Approximately 20,000 Czech companies in commerce, industry, service, and trading. Entries include: Company name, address, phone, fax, founding date, capital, name of general manager, board, owner, turnover rate, number in trade register, languages for correspondence, banking-relations, number of employees, countries of import, countries of export, branches, mechanical equipment, production lines.

Houston 1000 Corporate Directory. • $115 Members plus $3.00 shipping and handling. Covers: 7,000 major businesses in the Houston area. Entries include: Company name, address, phone, fax, type of business, names and titles of key officers and personnel, number of employess.

How to Find Information about Companies. MarketResearch.com. • Annual. $395 per volume. Covers: in Part 1, over 9,000 sources of corporate intelligence, including federal, state, and local repositories of company filings, individual industry experts, published sources, databases, CD-ROM products, and corporate research services. Entries include: Source name, address, phone, contact name, description. Parts 2 and 3 provide guidelines for company research.

Hungarian Companies. S2UV Rt. Computing and Management Services. • Continuous. Database covers: Approximately 30,000 companies in Hungary. Database includes: Company name, address, phone, management, official tax and company registration numbers, industry activity codes, year founded, number of employees.

ICC UK Company Directory. ICC Information Ltd. • Weekly. Database covers: approximately 3.83 million registered companies in England, Wales, Scotland, and Northern Ireland. Contains a record for each company included on the Index of Companies maintained by the official Companies Registration office in the UK. Also incorporates companies that have been dissolved since 1968.

ICC UK Company Financial Database. Dun & Bradstreet U.K. ICC Information. • Weekly. Database covers: Comprehensive analysis on 2.2 million companies with limited liability in the UK--large, medium, and small, quoted and non-quoted, public and private, from all sectors on industry and commerce. Provides data for all types of company research, providing extended profit and loss accounts and balance sheet information, new cash flow items, together with new auditors' qualification reference data, comprehensive business ratios, industrial comparisons, growth rates, and an improved credit rating system. Access to complete database of U.K. Directors with over 5 million directorships covered exact images of alt company accounts and annual returns.

Indonesian Business Directory. PT Sumber Daya Multimedia. • $30. Database covers: 94,000 Indonesian importers, exporters, and other businesses. Entries include: Contact information, industry, and description of products and services.

Industrial and Corporate Services Directory. Durham Region Economic Development and Tourism Department. • Covers: Lists of industrial and corporate businesses located in Durham region.

Industrial/Commercial Directory of Peru. Confederacion Nacional de Comerciantes. • Annual. $50. Covers: Industrial and commercial firms in Peru. Entries include: Name, address, phone, telex, products, services.

Industrial Market Location. Market Location Ltd. • Database covers: about 150,000 manufacturing and distribution firms and commercial businesses in the United Kingdom. Database includes: Company name, address, phone, names and titles of key personnel, number of employees, description of product/service, Standard Industrial Classification (SIC) code.

Industridata: AA Enterprises. Mercametrica Ediciones S.A. • Annual. $550 Individuals. Covers: Over 1,700 industrial, commercial, and services companies in Mexico with 251 to 500 employees. Includes banks and insurance companies. Companion volume of 'Industridata: AAA Enterprises' (see separate entry). Information from both titles is listed by postal code in 'Industridata by Zip Codes.' Entries include: Company name, location, phone, fax, telex, days and hours of operation, main products and brands, number of employees, sales, installed capacity and output for previous four years, government and foreign ownership, year established, names and titles of key personnel.

Inform Katalog. Inform Katalog Spol. S.R.O. • Annual. $190. Covers: Approximately 20,000 Czech companies. Entries include: Business information.

Inform Katalog Business Directory. Inform Katalog Spol. S.R.O. • Annual. Covers: Approved contacts for 60,000 Czech companies. Entries include: Business contact information.

Inform Katalog Slovakia. Inform Katalog Slovakia Ltd. • Annual. $88. Covers: 6,000 companies in Slovakia. Entries include: Detailed business information.

Inform Slovenskych Podnikov. Inform Katalog Slovakia Ltd. • Annual. $26. Covers: 15,000 business contacts at Slovakian companies classified in detail by area of activity.

Infotel--The Electronic Directory of Companies from Romania. Chamber of Commerce and Industry of Romania. • Covers: More than 500,00 Romanian companies. Entries include: Company name, headquarters address, telephone and fax number, registration, statistical and fiscal codes, profile, equity, shareholders, number of employees, gross profit.

Initiative Europe. ICC Online Services Div. ICC Information Group Ltd. • Monthly. Covers: Small- and medium-sized businesses in Europe seeking international joint venture, partnership, and licensing agreements.

Insiders' Chronicle. American Banker Newsletters. • Covers: publicly held companies in whose securities there has been significant buying or selling by executive officers, directors, and those who hold 10% or more of its shares. Database includes: Market news, quotations, and statistics. Entries include: Company name, name and title of person involved, number of shares held, number of shares bought or sold, price per share, date of transaction.

Inter-Corporate Ownership. Industrial Organization and Finance Div. Statistics Canada. • Biennial. $350 plus shipping charges for outside country. Covers: 72,000 Canadian corporations with ownership links to one or more other corporations. Entries include: Parent corporation and subsidiaries, site of control, Canadian domicile, Standard Industrial Classification (SIC) code, etc.

Inter Region. Editus S.A.R.L. • Annual. Covers: the top 15,000 companies in the European area of Saar-Lor-Lux including: south Belgium, Saarland, Trier, Grand Duchy of Luxembourg and French region Lorraine. Entries include: Company name, address, phone, fax, number of employees, financial data, names and titles of key personnel and line of business, trademarks.

International Corporate Yellow Book. Leadership Directories Inc. • Semiannual. $170 per year. Covers: leading corporations outside of the United States. Entries include: Company name, address, phone, fax, telex, description of activities, assets or revenue, names and titles of key personnel, names and affiliations of board members; name, address, phone, fax and names and titles of key personnel for subsidiaries.

International Directory of Company Histories. St. James Press. • $343 Individuals. Multi-volume work that covers histories of companies that are a leading influence in a particular industry or geographic location. eBook available. Contact for pricing.

International Directory of Corporate Affiliations: Public and Private Companies. LexisNexis. • $540. Covers: Approximately 1,500 U.S. and approximately 1,600 non-U.S. parent companies and

For publishers' addresses, refer to SOURCES CITED section at the back of the book.

their approximately 30,000 subsidiaries. Entries include: Name, address, phone, description of activities.

International M & A Review. Euromoney Institutional Investor P.L.C. • $375 Individuals. Covers: Merger and acquisition advising companies in Europe and U.S. Database includes: Country profiles and reviews of mergers and acquisitions by industry. Entries include: Name, address, phone, fax, names and titles of key personnel, year founded, description of business activities.

Isle of Man: General Information Factfile. Commercial Development Div. The Treasury Isle of Man Government. • Annual. Covers: financial institutions, insurance companies, real estate agencies, legal and accounting firms, shipowners, manufacturer, and other service trades on the Isle of Man; government service agencies. Database includes: Summaries of economic activity and opportunity; government policies regarding trade and industry; information on education and social issues. Entries include: Company or agency name, address, phone; shipowners and stockbrokers also include telex and fax numbers; financial institutions and real estate agencies include names of contact or other key personnel; banks and insurance companies include branch office and subsidiary names, addresses, and phone numbers.

Israel Business & Government Directory. Jerusalem Marketing Group. • Semiannual. $39. Covers: over 750 persons active in national government, local municipalities, foreign embassies and consulates, political parties, government companies, and major business organizations and associations in Israel. Entries include: Organization or company name, address, phone, fax, name and title of contact, names and titles of key personnel, number of employees, financial data.

ITALI. SEAT. • Monthly. Database covers: Over 260,000 Italian companies in all lines of business.

Italy Business Directory (ITBD). INFOT Inc. • $55.25 CD-ROM. Covers: 80,063 major industries from Italy and related regions. Entries include: Contact person, physical addresses, email and website addresses, telephone and fax number, and business description.

Japanese-Affiliated Companies in U.S.A. and Canada. Japan External Trade Organization. • Biennial. Covers: 9,870 Japanese firms, restaurants, and various information sources. Database includes: Area maps. Entries include: Company name, address, phone, fax, line of business, parent company, executive officers, year established.

Japanese Business in Britain. Culver Financial Surveys. • Annual. $100 2000 edition. Covers: Approximately 550 Japanese-owned, United Kingdom-registered limited companies. Entries include: Company name, address, names and titles of key personnel, number of employees, financial data, subsidiary and branch names and locations, description, ownership information, sales and profits data.

Japanese Companies in the UK. Jordans Ltd. • Annual. $195. Covers: Top 180 Japanese companies in the United Kingdom. Entries include: Company name, address, phone, contact name, description of business.

Job Seeker's Guide to 1000 Top Employers. Visible Ink Press. • $22.95. Covers: 1,000 large or prominent private and public companies in the U.S. Entries include: Company name, address, phone, fax, year founded, type of company, stock exchanges on which traded, stock symbol, description, locations of operating units, subsidiaries and affiliated companies, corporate officers, financial data, number of employees, human resources contact, job application procedures.

Jobson's Yearbook of Public Companies. Dun & Bradstreet (Australia) Proprietary Ltd. • Daily (eve.). $520 Individuals. Database covers: All companies (about 1,400) listed on the Industrial Boards of the Australian and New Zealand stock exchanges; includes mining and petroleum industries. Database includes: Information on money market companies, trust companies, and stockbrokers, ranking of top 100 companies by revenue and profit. Entries include: Company name, address, phone, fax; DUNS number; subsidiaries; associated companies; names and titles of key personnel; branch office locations; share register; home exchange subsidiaries; voting rights; auditors; bankers; solicitors; financial data; major shareholder; history; operations, and ACN number.

Kelly's Industrial Directory Book. Reed Business Information. • Annual. Directory of over 94,600 U.K. industrial companies.

Kelly's Industrial Directory--CD. Reed Business Information. • Annual. Database of UK industrial companies. Database covers: 200,000 companies under 17,000 headings.

Key British Enterprises Financial Performance. Dun & Bradstreet Inc. • Monthly. Database covers: Approximately 50,000 of the largest companies in the United Kingdom. Database includes: Company name, address, director name, parent company, product trade name, annual and export sales, number of employees, export markets, trade description, trade awards, Companies Registration Office number, pre-tax profit, net worth, total assets, current assets, current liabilities, working capital, long-term debt, return on capital, profit margin, current ratio, profit per employee, U.S. and U.K. SIC code.

Key Business Directory--Latin America. Dun & Bradstreet Inc. • Covers: Leading companies in Latin America whose annual sales are $10 million and who have 500 or more employees. Entries include: Company name, address, phone, fax, telex, number of employees, import/export designation, primary and secondary Standard Industrial Classification (SIC) codes, sales volume.

Key Business Directory of Indonesia/Thailand. Dun & Bradstreet Inc. • Covers: Approximately 1,500 public and private companies in Indonesia and Thailand; Indonesian companies listed have an annual turnover of over 10 billion Rupiah and more than 50 employees; Thai companies listed have an annual turnover of over 150 Baht and more than 50 employees.

Key Business Directory of Malaysia. Dun & Bradstreet Inc. • Covers: 1,500 public and private companies in Malaysia, each with an annual turnover of $18 million and over 50 employees.

Key Business Directory of Singapore. Dun & Bradstreet Inc. • Covers: leading companies in Singapore. Database includes: Directory of company directors. Entries include: Company name, address, phone, fax, line of business, sales volume, industry designation, names and titles of key personnel, year established, number of employees, import/export designation, accountants and bankers.

Kompass Asia/Pacific. Kompass International Management Corp. • Annual. Database covers: over 260,000 Asian and Pacific companies in Japan, Korea, Hong Kong, Taiwan, China, Singapore, Malaysia, Thailand, Indonesia, Philippines, Brunei/Darussalem, India, Australia, and New Zealand. Database includes: Company name, address, phone, names and titles of key personnel, foreign trade status, number of employees, languages spoken, business descriptions, industry and product listings.

Kompass-Benelux. Kompass Belgium Products. • Database covers: 50,000 companies in the Benelux countries, which includes Belgium, the Netherlands, and Luxembourg. Entries include: Company name, address, product list, directors and management, turnover, number of employees.

Kompass Canada. Micromedia ProQuest. • Irregular. $399 plus 9.95 shipping. Covers: Approximately 30,000 Canadian companies. Entries include: Company name, address, phone, fax, senior executives, statement of activities, financial information, number of employees, parent and affiliated companies, date established.

Kompass Croatia Direct. Promar Ltd. • Annual. $100. Covers: 19,000 companies in Croatia. Entries include: Company name and address, directors and management, turnover, trade marks, employment, complete product list according to Kompass classification.

Kompass Croatia--Register. Promar Ltd. • Annual. $1,700. Covers: More than 19,000 Croatian companies with a complete product list of 58,000 products and services classified according to Kompass. Entries include: Company name and address, directors and management, turnover rate, employment.

Kompass Deutschland: Jahrbuch der Deutschen Wirtschaft. Kompass Deutschland Verlags- und Vertriebsgesellschaft, mbH. • Annual. Covers: Major German manufacturers, distributors, and service companies linked to 40,000 products and services. Database includes: Glossary. Entries include: Company name, address, phone, telex, names and titles of key personnel, bank, key to product and service listings, year established, symbols indicating whether company is a manufacturer, wholesaler, or agent, and whether it imports and exports, turnover, number of employees, shareholders; reference to dot-chart index.

Kompass International. Kompass France. • Annual. Covers: Over 1,500,000 commercial and industrial firms worldwide; over 500,000 prominent business and industry professionals in 64 countries.

Kompass Philippines. Croner Publications Inc. • Annual. $225. Covers: 5,000 companies and 15,000 products in 400 categories of industry and commerce in the Philippines.

Kompass Poland. EUROSTART Sp. z o.o. • Semiannual. Database covers: 25,000 Polish companies. Entries include: Company name, address, name and title of contact; general manager's name; rate of turnover; employment information; details of products and services offered.

Kompass Register United Kingdom. Reed Business Information. • Annual. Covers: In 3 volumes, information on over 45,000 industrial and commercial companies in UK. Financial data. Entries include: Company name, address, phone, fax, product, trade name.

Kompass Sweden. Kompass Sverige AB Ett foretag inom Bonnier Affarsinformation. • Annual. $289. Covers: 12,000 industrial and commercial firms, including wholesalers, manufacturers, importers/exporters, and distributors, in Sweden. Entries include: Company name, address, phone, line of business, product/service.

Kontaks Philippines. Massmark Philippines Publishers. • Biennial. $950. Covers: Members of Chambers of Commerce, including those in industry, manufacturing, exporting, importing, distributing, dealers, wholesalers, retailers, trade entities, banking investments, finance, real estate, housing, tourism, health industries, and consumer groups.

KOOPERACJA. EUROSTART Sp. z o.o. • Semiannual. Database covers: small and medium-sized businesses in Poland. Database includes: Company name, address, phone, line of business, products.

Korean Importers Association Directory. Korean Importers Association. • Annual. $12. Covers: 3,600 Korean companies. Entries include: Company name, address, phone, telex, name of official, items traded, suppliers.

Large Employers of Metro St. Louis. St. Louis Regional Chamber & Growth Association. •

Biennial. $50. Covers: 700 business firms employing 200 persons or more in the City of St. Louis, six Missouri counties (Franklin, Jefferson, Lincoln, St. Charles, St. Louis, and Warren), and five Illinois counties (Clinton, Jersey, Madison, Monroe, and St. Clair); includes companies that are not members of the association. Entries include: Company name, address, phone, fax, names of principal executives, Standard Industrial Classification (SIC) code, type of business, year established, number of employees, product or service.

The Largest Companies in Norway. Okonomisk litteratur Norge A.S. • Annual. $1,300. Covers: 10,000 of the largest industrial companies, trading companies, banks, shipping companies, insurance companies, hotels, restaurants, travel agencies, advertising agencies, insurance companies, and consultant companies in Norway. Entries include: Company name, address, phone, telex number.

Largest Employers Directory. Greater San Antonio Chamber of Commerce. • Annual. $75 Nonmembers CD/email. Covers: About 1,700 manufacturing and nonmanufacturing firms in the San Antonio metropolitan statistical area; manufacturing firms each have at least 25 employees, nonmanufacturing firms have at least 50 employees. Entries include: Company name, address, phone; names and titles of key personnel, number of employees, year established, description of service, marketing area, and Standard Industrial Classification (SIC) code.

LaSalle Bank Guide: Major Publicly Held Corporations and Financial Institutions Headquartered in Illinois. Scholl Corporate Guides. • Annual. $29.95 Single issue. Covers: Approximately 232 major publicly held corporations and financial institutions headquartered in Illinois. Database includes: List of companies ranked by revenue and assets; (NAICS) code listings; list of changes from previous edition. Entries include: Company name, headquarters location and phone, brief description of product lines and organizational structure, names of outside directors, names and titles of key personnel; consolidated balance sheet in abbreviated form, consolidated income statement; number of employees, date of annual meeting, stockholder information.

Leading Employers of the New Hampshire & Southern Maine Seacoast. Greater Portsmouth Chamber of Commerce. • Biennial. $10. Covers: Approximately 200 companies in the Portsmouth, New Hampshire area (including part of southern Maine) that employ over 25 people. Entries include: Company name, address, phone, name and title of contact, number of employees, products or services provided.

Lebanese Industrial and Commercial Directory. Publitec Publications. • Annual. $120. Covers: Industrial and commercial companies in Lebanon. Entries include: Contact information.

Les Pages Pro. Bureau van Dijk S.A. • Annual. Database covers: Business to business directory of France Telecom with more than 300,000 subscribers. Entries include: Name, SIRET identification number, telephone number, type of number, full address, activity, employee range.

Listed Companies in Finland. Kansallis-Osake-Pankki Sijoitustutkimus/Investment Research. • Annual. $545. Covers: all Finnish companys listed on the Helsinki Stock Exchange. Database includes: Charts and tables summarizing developments such as income statements, balance sheet, financial ratios, and per-share ratios. Entries include: Company name, address, phone, year established, line of business, subsidiary and branch names and locations, names and titles of key personnel, number of shareholders, financial data.

Lithuanian Companies. Litauisches Informationsinstitut. • Quarterly. Database covers: companies in Lithuania. Database includes: Company name, address, legal status, products, number of employees.

Locaguide: Locaguide du BTP et de la Manutention. Societe technique d'Editions pour l'Entreprise. • Annual. €23. Covers: 1,000 French companies. Entries include: Company name, address, phone, fax, telex, names and titles of key personnel, product/service provided.

Logos of America's Fastest Growing Corporations. Hoover's Inc. • $39.95. Covers: Over 500 logotypes, trademarks, and symbols from growing U.S. companies.

Logos of America's Largest Corporations. Hoover's Inc. • $39.95. Covers: Over 500 logotypes, trademarks, and symbols of U.S. companies.

Logos of Major World Corporations. Hoover's Inc. • $39.95. Covers: Over 500 logotypes, trademarks, and symbols of international companies.

Los Angeles Business Journal--Book of Lists. LABJ Inc. • Annual. $395. Covers: major companies, foundations, government officials, utilities, newspapers, radio and television stations, airlines, hospitals, financial institutions, shopping centers, resorts, and prominent individuals in Los Angeles County, California. Incorporates information in "Los Angeles Business Journal--Consultants Directory," now discontinued.

Louisiana Business Directory. InfoGroup Inc. • Annual. $795 for both print & CD-ROM. Covers: 184,886 businesses in Louisiana. Entries include: Company name, address, phone, number of employees, standard industrial classification (sic) code, line of business, name of owner or manager, sales volume, credit ratings. Compiled from telephone company 'Yellow Pages,' statewide. All states covered independently (see separate entries).

Major and Medium-Sized Companies in the Czech Republic. Hoppenstedt Produktinformationen GmbH. • Annual. €195. Covers: over 18,000 companies in the Czech Republic. Entries include: Name, address, phone, fax, management, production or services, number of employees, turnover (revenue), and capital.

The Major Companies Guide: The Charitable and Community Support of the UK's Leading Companies. The Directory of Social Change. • Biennial. $16.95. Covers: about 400 companies in the United Kingdom with 160 millions Ls in cash donations and 100 millions Ls in community contributions. Entries include: Company name, address, phone, names and titles of key personnel, financial data, amount of donations annually, donation policy and practice, number of employees, employee involvement, branch office or subsidiary names, descriptions of product/service, type of business, community support programs.

Major Companies in China. Hoppenstedt Produktinformationen GmbH. • $520. Covers: 10,000 major companies in China. Entries include: Name, address, phone, fax, range of products or services, import and export, revenue, number of employees, and joint ventures.

Major Companies in Southeast Asia. Euromonitor International Business Reference Div. • $550 Individuals. Covers: Nearly 2,000 companies in Brunei, Hong Kong, Indonesia, Malaysia, the Philippines, Singapore, South Korea, Taiwan, and Thailand. Entries include: Company name, address, phone, fax, type of business, ownership, subsidiaries, key personnel, products and brands, main operations, outlets and trading names, number of employees, turnover, pre-tax profit, sales, background information.

Major Companies in the Netherlands. Netherlands-British Chamber of Commerce. • Biennial. $10. Covers: Businesses in the Netherlands. Entries include: Company name, address, phone, telex, directors.

Major Companies of Latin America and the Caribbean. Cengage Learning Inc. • $1,275. Includes more than 8,650 major companies in Latin America and more than 1,100 leading Caribbean firms.

Major Companies of Slovakia. I.S.M.C. Information Systems and Marketing Contacts Ltd. • Annual. $164. Covers: The most important companies in the Slovak Republic. Entries include: Detailed business information and data.

Major Companies of the Arab World. Cengage Learning Inc. • Annual. $1,480 Individuals. Published by Graham & Whiteside Ltd. Coverage of the world's largest companies in the Arab world. Includes names of senior executives, contact information, and financial information.

Major Companies of Turkey Directory. Poyraz Publications A.S. • Annual. $50. Covers: 2,500 companies, products, and industries in Turkey. Entries include: Company name, address, phone, telex, names and titles of key personnel, products, and trade names.

Major Companies on CD-ROM. Graham & Whiteside. • $7,845 Individuals individual countries sold separately; inquire for. Database covers: 55,000 companies outside North America, including Europe, the Far East and Australia, Middle East, Africa, Latin America, Central Europe, Eastern Europe, the CIS, and Southwest Asia. Entries include: Company name, address, phone, fax, number of employees, sales, assets, profits, date established, SIC codes, parent and subsidiary companies, name and title of contact.

Major Employers in Metropolitan Chicago. Chicagoland Chamber of Commerce. • Biennial. $55. Covers: over 2,000 firms employing at least 250 employees in their Chicago area plants and offices; also listed are subsidiaries, affiliates, and divisions. Entries include: Company name, address, phone, names of major officers; line of business and Standard Industrial Classification (SIC) code; coding to indicate number of employees and whether manufacturer or non-manufacturer.

Major Firms in Czech Republic. I.S.M.C. Information Systems and Marketing Contacts Ltd. • Annual. $164. Covers: Significant business firms in Czech Republic. Entries include: Detailed business information.

Major French Companies. DAFSA. • Annual. Covers: Companies with shares traded on the stock exchange in France. Entries include: Company name, address, phone, officers, directors, executives, banking information, financial institutions, broker-trading.

Major Market Share Companies. Euromonitor International Business Reference Div. • $1,295 Individuals hard copy mail delivery. Covers: List of top national and regional companies in the Americas, Asia-Pacific, Europe, and South Africa across 15 consumer sectors. Entries include: Company name, address, phone; company share; leading brands; and merger and acquisition information.

Malta Trade Directory. Malta Chamber of Commerce, Enterprise and Industry. • Annual. $10. Covers: Business and professional organizations, drydock facilities, tourist offices, government offices and agencies, and other businesses in Malta; overseas chambers of commerce. Database includes: Economic and trade statistics. Entries include: Company, agency, or organization name, address, phone, name and title of contact, products or services provided.

Marketing Address Data. Herold Business Data GmbH. • Annual. Database covers: More than 246,000 businesses in Austria. Entries include: Company name, address, phone, fax, line of business.

The Marketing Guide to Ireland. Dun & Bradstreet International. • Annual. Covers: 4,000 Irish businesses, including 3,000 in the Republic of Ireland and 1,000 in Northern Ireland. Our new section contains exporters and importers. Entries include: Company name, address, phone, fax, name and title of up to 8 contacts, number of employees, line of business, sales turnover, parent company, importer/exporter indicator, year established.

The Marketing Managers Yearbook. AP Information Services Ltd. • Annual. £229 Single issue. Covers: Approximately 10,500 private and public sector companies in the U.K., as well as 6,000 companies providing marketing related products and services, including advertising agencies, public relations firms, consultancies, research experts, hospitality industry companies, media outlets, software producers, professional associations, and other organizations. Database includes: Articles written by marketing professionals; statistical tables; list of forthcoming exhibitions. Entries include: For major companies--Name, address, phone, fax, names and titles of key personnel, number of employees, number of sales employees, line of business, brand/product names, parent company, Standard Industrial Classification (SIC) codes. For service companies--Name, address, phone, fax, year established, name and title of contact, names and titles of key personnel, fields of specialization, number of employees, associated firms, major clients, subsidiary and branch names and locations.

MARKUS: Marketinguntersuchungen. Bureau van Dijk S.A. • Quarterly. Database covers: More than 900,000 German and Austrian companies. Entries include: Company name, address, date of incorporation, company type, register number, managers, shareholders, banks, WZ activity codes, trade description, number of employees, turnover, shareholders' funds.

Massachusetts Service Directory. George D. Hall Company Inc. • $69 plus $4.95 shipping. Covers: over 12,700 non-manufacturing companies with five or more employees. Entries include: Company name, address, phone, names of key executives, number of employees, product or service, Standard Industrial Classification (SIC) code.

MASTER: Marketing Strategy and Efficient Research. Bureau van Dijk S.A. • Quarterly. Database covers: More than 700,000 companies and business entities in Belgium. Entries include: Company name, address, date of incorporation, company type, activity, management, turnover, shareholders' funds, profit, debt, number of employees.

Mexico Company Handbook. Hoover's Inc. • Annual. $49.95 plus $4.50 shipping. Covers: about 70 of Mexico's largest public companies and 8 mutual funds and investment advisors. Database includes: Profile of the Mexican economy, international trade, and investment climate; data on stock exchanges, investment advisors, and money managers. Entries include: Company name, address, phone, fax, year established, stock ticker symbol, names and titles of key personnel, number of employees, number of stockholders, bank references, auditor, company history, financial data, markets and competition, raw materials used and sources, names of major stockholders, affiliated companies.

Michigan Business Directory. InfoGroup Inc. • Annual. $795 for both print & CD-ROM. Covers: 416,857 businesses in Michigan. Entries include: Company name, address, phone, number of employees, name of owner or manager, sales volume. Compiled from telephone company 'Yellow Pages,' statewide. All states covered independently (see separate entries).

Michigan Centennial Business Directory. Historical Society of Michigan. • Irregular. Covers: over 500 firms that have been operating continuously in Michigan for at least 100 years; also includes list of about 15 business archives. Database includes: Map of Michigan. Entries include: For firms--Firm name, address, phone, date founded, name and title of chief executive officer. For archives--Facility name, address, date established, description of holdings.

Microcosm. Dun & Bradstreet Inc. • Microfiche. Covers: Over 150 separate editions list companies in local business areas throughout the U.S. Entries include: Company name, address, phone, number of employees, Standard Industrial Classification (SIC) code, sales volume, principal officer name and title, DUNS number.

Middle East (Gulf) Business Directory. NIIR Project Consultancy Services. • $100 Individuals CD-ROM. Covers: 20,000+ Middle East businesses. Entries include: Company name, full postal address, phone, fax, e-mail address (wherever available), website address (wherever available) as well as a listing of activities involved in or products dealt with.

Mississippi Business Directory. InfoGroup Inc. • Annual. $795 for both print & CD-ROM. Covers: 114,788 businesses in Mississippi. Entries include: Company name, address, phone, number of employees, name of owner or manager, sales volume. Compiled from telephone company 'Yellow Pages,' statewide. All states covered independently (see separate entries).

Mitchell Guide to New Jersey Foundations, Corporations and Their Managers. Littman Associates. • Biennial. $135 postpaid; payment with order. Approximately 450 private foundations with minimum assets of $150,000 and grants in excess of $15,000 per year, and about 700 businesses in New Jersey with over 300 employees.

Montana Business Directory. InfoGroup Inc. • Annual. $375 both print & CD-ROM. Covers: 58,819 businesses in Montana. Entries include: Company name, address, phone, number of employees, name of owner or manager, sales volume. Compiled from telephone company "Yellow Pages," statewide. All states covered (see separate entries).

Moody's Corporate Profiles. Moody's Investors Service Inc. • Weekly. Database covers: more than 5,000 publicly held companies listed on the New York Stock Exchange or the American Stock Exchange or NMS companies traded on the National Association of Securities Dealers Automated Quotations. Database includes: Company name, address, phone, D-U-N-S number, Moody's number, stock exchange, ticker symbol, primary and secondary Standard Industrial Classification (SIC) codes and industries; line of business analysis, annual earnings and dividends per share and other financial and stock trading data for five-year period.

MZM World Business Directory. MZM Publications Publishing Promotion Co. • Irregular. $154 plus airmail. Covers: companies in 33 post-socialist countries involved in international trade and business: Albania, Armenia, Azerbaijan, Bosnia & Herzegovina, Bulgaria, Belorus, China, Croatia, Cuba, Czech Republic, Slovakia, Estonia, Georgia, former East Germany, Hungary, Kazakhstan, Kirghizia, Latvia, Lithuania, North Korea, Macedonia, Moldova, Mongolia, Poland, Romania, Russia, Kaliningrad Province of Russia, Slovenia, Tadzhikistan, Turkmenistan, Ukraine, Uzbekistan, Vietnam, and Yugoslavia. Entries include: Company name, address, phone, fax, telex, number of employees, year established, subsidiary companies, description.

Namibia Business Directory. A.C. Braby (Pty) Ltd. • Annual. Covers: Businesses in Namibia. Entries include: Company name, address, phone.

NAN-Directorio Nacional Negocio a Negocio. Yell Publicidad S.A. • Annual. Covers: Approximately 230,000 business firms whose main activity is sales of products or services to the business to business sector in Spain.

National Directory of Corporate Giving. • Annual. $195 Individuals. Provides information on nearly 4,400 company-sponsored foundations and corporate giving programs.

National Directory of Corporate Public Affairs. Columbia Books and Information Services. • Annual. $249 Individuals. Covers: About 17,000 corporations that have PACs foundations or other public affairs activities; over 14,000 corporate public affairs personnel. Database includes: List of contract lobbyists serving corporations at the state level; membership directory of the Public Affairs Council. Entries include: Company name, headquarters address, Washington, DC, address (if any), names of political action committees, PAC funds contributed, names of principal recipients; name of corporate foundation; total grants per year, assets; giving priorities; names and titles of public affairs personnel. For personnel--Name, title, affiliation, address, phone; if a lobbyist, where registered.

National Real Estate Investor Sourcebook. Primedia Business. • Annual. $79.95 payment must accompany order. List of about 7,000 companies and individuals in 18 real estate fields, including appraisers; asset managers; builders, contractors, and developers; communication services; corporate real estate managers; environmental consultants; equity investors; financial services; hospitality services; institutional advisors; pension funds; property managers; real estate brokers, agents, consultants, and counselors; software products and services; title insurance companies; related associations; and others.

National Verticals. Scott's Directories. • $1,395 Individuals CD-ROM (food and beverage) prospector. Covers: Canadian industry-specific contacts and company profiles. Entries include: Complete business name, names and titles of executives and decision-makers, mailing and location addresses, phone and faxes, corporate email, products and/or services offered, annual estimated gross sales, year established, number of employees, ISO registration, North American industry classification standard (NAICS) codes, web site address.

The New Jersey Corporate Guide. Business Journal of New Jersey. • Annual. Covers: Approximately 1,000 of the largest public and private companies, financial institutions, leading firms in New Jersey and important out-of-state companies whose major operations are located in New Jersey. Entries include: Name, address, phone, fax, parent company, number of employees, sales volume, year founded, names and titles of executives. Public companies also include--5-year income statement, names and titles of officers and directors, subsidiaries, name of trade exchange and symbol, auditors, and number of shareholders.

Nordic Stock Guide. Delphi Economics AB. • $34.95 plus $3.50 shipping. Covers: nearly 250 public companies in Denmark, Finland, Norway, and Sweden. Database includes: Interest rate histories, exchange rates, and commodities prices for each country. Entries include: Company name, address, phone, names and titles of key personnel, overview of company operations, stock and financial data for previous six years.

North American Companies Manufacturing in Scotland. Scottish Enterprise. • Covers: about 200 North American-owned companies in Scotland. Entries include: Company name, address, phone, telex, name and title of contact, number of employees, description of services.

North Carolina Business Directory. InfoGroup Inc. • Annual. $795 for both print & CD-ROM. Covers: 359,291 businesses in North Carolina. Entries include: Company name, address, phone, number of employees, name of owner or manager, sales volume. Compiled from telephone company 'Yellow Pages,' statewide. All states covered (see separate entries).

Northern Ireland Trade Directory. Industrial Development Board for Northern Ireland Her Majesty's Stationary Office. • Annual. $33. Covers: Approximately 5,200 manufacturing companies in Northern Ireland. Entries include: Company name, address, phone, telex, name and title of contact, number of employees, description of product/service.

Norway's Top 10,000 Companies. Dun & Bradstreet Inc. • Covers: Approximately 15,000 companies in Norway. Entries include: Company name, address, phone, fax, telex, sales volume, rank, profit, SIC code, principal officer name and title, number of employees, export designation, equity capital.

OCREFO Creditreform Companies. Verband der Vereine Creditreform e.V. • Quarterly. Database covers: over 20,000 profiles of companies registered in the new German states. Database includes: Company name, address, phone, legal status, year founded, registration data, owner, capital, management description, industry classification code, number of employees, annual sales.

Oesterreich's Ten Thousand Groesste Unternehmen. D & B - Schimmelpfeng Gesellschaft GmbH. • Annual. $525. Covers: 11,000 Austrian companies. Entries include: Company name, address, phone, names and titles of key personnel, year founded, line of business, name and location of parent company, number of employees, year founded, SIC numbers, and sales volumes.

OFERES. Instituto Espanol de Comercio Exterior. • Weekly. Database covers: Approximately 100,000 export companies in Spain. Database includes: Company name, address, phone, fax, number of employees, export representative, languages, activity, current annual and total export volume, product sector, trademarks and brand names, trade partners.

Official E-mail and Fax Directory. Todd Publications. • $150. Covers: 160,000 contacts at 50,000 U.S. companies, government agencies, and public and private institutions; includes manufacturers, professional service firms, media and publishing agencies, consultants, financial institutions, and government offices. Entries include: e-mail addresses.

Ohio Roster. Edward Howard & Co. • $12. Covers: the 200 largest manufacturers, retailers, service companies, transportation firms, public utilities, and financial institutions headquartered in Ohio whose stock is publicly traded. Database includes: Lists of the top 20 firms by revenue, assets, net income, and biggest sales gain. Entries include: Firm name, location, total revenues, net income, total assets, earnings per share, stock exchange on which traded.

Oklahoma Business Directory. InfoGroup Inc. • Annual. $795 for both print & CD-ROM. Covers: 163,042 businesses in Oklahoma. Entries include: Company name, address, phone, number of employees, name of owner or manager, sales volume. Compiled from telephone company 'Yellow Pages,' statewide. All states covered (see separate entries).

1,000 China Leading Enterprises. China Statistics Publishing House. • $200. Covers: 1,000 leading companies in China. Entries include: Company name and address, director, economic types, and sponsor unit, main economic indicators.

Overseas and European Companies Manufacturing in Scotland. Scottish Enterprise. • Covers: over 130 foreign owned companies, excluding North American owned, located in Scotland. Entries include: Company name, address, phone, telex, name and title of contact, number of employees, geographical area covered, description of services.

Overseas Companies in Ireland. Industrial Development Agency of Ireland. • Updated continuously; printed on request. Computer printout. About 1,000 overseas manufacturers and international service companies with operations in Ireland. Entries include: Name and address of parent company; name, address, phone of Irish filial company, description of product or service specialty.

OZ on Disc--Top 25,000. Read Only Memory Proprietary Ltd. • Quarterly. $4,950 per year. CD-ROM. Covers over 25,000 companies in Australia. Entries include: Company name, address, phone, fax, names and titles of key personnel, number of employees, Standard Industrial Classification (SIC) codes and descriptions, gross sales, related companies, banker.

Panama Annual Directory. U.S. Chamber of Commerce. • Annual. $40 Individuals. Covers: 350 member companies of AmCham Panama. Entries include: Company name, address, phone.

Partnership Houston: Membership Directory and Resource Guide. Greater Houston Partnership. • Annual. $40 Nonmembers print. Covers: Over 1,700 member firms in the Houston, Texas area. Entries include: Firm name, address, phone, URL, name and title of contact, product or service provided, number of employees, line of business.

PennSuburban Chamber of Commerce--Membership Directory. PennSuburban Chamber of Commerce. • Annual. Covers: Over 900 member businesses and industries in Montgomery, Bucks, and Chester counties in Pennsylvania. Entries include: Company name, address, phone, names and titles of key personnel, number of employees, product or service provided.

Personen-Compass. Compass-Verlag. • Annual. $1,250. Covers: over 19,000 principal executives of major Austrian companies. Entries include: Name, address, affiliations.

Philadelphia Business Journal--Book of Business Lists Issue. Philadelphia Business Journal. • Annual. $65 Individuals print edition. Publication includes: About 89 ranked lists (about 25 names per list) of major public and private businesses and organizations, including banks, brokers, construction companies, hospitals, schools, child-care centers, law firms, hotels, apartment complexes, office parks, architects, ad agencies, and employers in the Philadelphia area. Entries include: For organizations and institutions--Name, location, type of business or service, key personnel, financial facts.

Philippines Business Directory. Philippine Editors and Publishers. • Annual. $75. Covers: 15,000 business and trade organizations, professional associations, civic groups, manufacturers, wholesalers, and distributors. Entries include: name, address, phone, telex.

Plunkett's Companion to the Almanac of American Employers: Mid-Size Firms. Plunkett Research Ltd. • Annual. $349.99 Individuals Printed Almanac & Online Tools. Covers: Approximately 500 rapidly growing mid-sized firms, defined as between 150 and 2,300 employees. Entries include: Name, address, phone, fax, and key executives.

Polish Business Directory. Branzowy Katalog Firm-Ravi Sp. • Annual. Covers: More than 3,000 companies in Poland. Entries include: Company name, address, phone, name and title of contact, product/service.

Polish Companies. Informationsvermittlungsagentur Waldemar Kubanski. • Quarterly. Database covers: Polish companies. Entries include: Company name, address, phone, fax, industrial sector, legal status.

Polish Industry Directory. Branzowy Katalog Firm-Ravi Sp. • Annual. Covers: More than 10,000 companies in Poland, including leading Polish importers/exporters. Entries include: Company name, address, phone, product/service.

Power Companies Directory. InfoGroup Inc. • Annual. Number of listings: 6,906. Entries include: Name, address, phone, size of advertisement, name of owner or manager, number of employees, year first in "Yellow Pages." Compiled from telephone company "Yellow Pages," nationwide.

ProFile Canada. Micromedia ProQuest. • Quarterly. Database covers: Approximately 17,000 Canadian companies and organizations. Entries include: Legal company name, trade name, address, phone, fax, e-mail, URL, number of employees, benefits, pension information, and number of branches. Some listings include sales range, size of customer base, Standard Industrial Classification (SIC) code, import/export activity, Canadian Business 500 ranking, Financial Post 500 ranking, and key personnel.

Provincial/Territorial Directories. A.C. Braby (Pty) Ltd. • Annual. $35 Botswana ed.. Covers: Business listings in South Africa. Entries include: Company name, address, phone, telex number.

Purchasing People in Major Corporations. Diversity Information Resources. • Annual. $175 Individuals /year (print and online). Covers: Information regarding Diversity Information Resources. Lists corporate purchasing locations; listings include name of minority business program administrator, if that position exists.

Quarterly Report on Companies whose Stocks are Quoted on the Stock Markets. Bolsas de Comercio de Madrid, Bilbao, Barcelona, Valencia. • Quarterly. Covers: Companies on the stock exchange in Spain. Entries include: Company name, address, phone, financial and economic data.

Qui Deade. Bottin S.A. • Annual. Covers: 200,000 commercial and industrial entities and 4,000 products and services in France. Entries include: Company name, address, phone, product/service.

Quoted Companies on the Brussels and Antwerp Stock Exchange. DAFSA - Belgique S.A. • Annual. Covers: Companies with shares traded on the Antwerp and Brussels stock exchanges. Entries include: Company name, address, phone, officers, directors, executives, banks, brokers.

R & S Annual Directory. Ricerche e Studi S.p.A. Mediobanca. • Annual. €150 Individuals European countries. Covers: Nearly 10,000 businesses forming part of 180 groups representing over a third of Italy's manufacturing industry. Database includes: Italian-English glossary. Entries include: Group name, address, phone, directors, details of shareholders, products, market shares, production facilities, sales and employees, financial data.

Reference Book of Corporate Managements. • Annual. Libraries, $650.00 per year; others, $795.00 per year. Lease basis. Management executives at over 12,000 leading United States companies.

Report on Business Corporate Database. Globe Information Services Info Globe Online. • Weekly. Database covers: Current and historical information on over 3,000 Canadian companies, taken from their quarterly and annual reports. Database includes: Company name, address, phone, description of business, financial data, officers, general corporate information.

Researching Company Financial Information. MarketResearch.com. • $59 Individuals. Helps readers learn how to research and understand financial data from companies, as well as compile in-depth financial data on competitors in order to get a better picture of the competition. Publication includes: A directory of corporate financial info sources.

The Romanian Business Directory. Topaz General Activities S.R.L. • Annual. $20. Covers: The most active companies and operators in the Romanian market, along with products and services. Entries include: Company business information.

Russia: Political and Economic Analysis and Business Directory. Chamber World Network. • $29.95.

Publication includes: Directories of organizations, companies, and other agencies in or doing business in Russia, including Russian companies, joint ventures, firms from outside Russia accredited to do business there, banks, insurance companies, consulates and embassies, hotels. Database includes: Essays and tables on the economic and legal structure of Russia, including summaries of Russian law, statistics, and surveys of future trends. Entries include: For companies--Name, address, phone, annual sales, number of employees, products.

San Francisco Business--Top 51 Public Companies Issue. San Francisco Chamber of Commerce. • Annual. $3 payment with order. Publication includes: List of 51 leading San Francisco Bay area public corporations (selected on the basis of sales). Entries include: Company name, address, phone, name of chief executive officer, current and prior year's rankings, line of business, sales, net assets, net income, net worth, number of employees.

SANI. CERVED S.p.A. • Daily. Database covers: about 4 million Italian industrial, commercial, agricultural, and trade companies. Database includes: Company name, address, date and type of incorporation, incorporation capital, product/service, names and titles of key personnel. CERVED stands for Centri Elettronici Reteconnessi Valutazione Elaborazione Dati.

Scotland's Top 500 Companies. Jordans Ltd. • Annual. $55. Covers: Companies in Scotland. Entries include: Company name, address, phone, fax, type of activity, chief executives, sales figures, capital, profits, net cash flow.

Scott's Custom Solutions. Scott's Directories. • Covers: Details for 175,000+ companies and 275,000+ business contact names can be provided customized as per client requirements on the basis of specific geographies, specific products or services, specific job functions, size demographics. Entries include: Company name, address, phone, fax, names and titles of key personnel, number of employees, parent companies, SIC, product, year established.

Scott's Directories: Greater Montreal and Laval Business Directory. Scott's Directories. • Annual. $229 Individuals. Covers: More than 18,000 manufacturers, distributors, wholesalers, manufacturers' representatives, contractors, transportation companies, financial institutions; legal, engineering, and architectural firms; real estate brokers, retail main offices, and special services related to industry in Montreal. Entries include: Name, postal code, phone, fax, executive names and titles, type of business or product produced, North American Standard Industrial Classification (NAICS) code, number of employees; code indicating line of business; year established.

Seibt - Umwelttechnikprodukte: Buyer's Guide for Environmental Technology. Seibt Verlag GmbH. • Semiannual. €33. Database covers: German manufacturers, wholesalers, importers, exporters, and service firms that supply products for industry and international trade; German companies involved in the manufacturing and supply of medical and pharmaceutical equipment and supplies.

Sell's Scottish Directory. Miller Freeman UK Ltd. • Annual. $30. Covers: 8,000 industrial and commercial firms in Scotland, including firms int he North Sea oil industry. Entries include: Company name, address, phone, telex number, type of business.

Sharjah Industrial Products Directory. Express Print Publishers. • Covers: Manufacturing firms operating in United Arab Emirates. Entries include: Company address, executives, and activities.

Sibbald Guide to Every Public and the Top 100 Private Companies in Missouri. Acorn Press Inc. • Annual. $80 per year, plus $5.00 shipping; payment must accompany order. Covers: 205 public and privately-held corporations and financial institutions in Missouri. Entries include: Company name, address, phone; brief company history and description, names and titles of officers and directors; return on beginning equity, return on sales/revenues; condensed balance sheet, income statement for past five years, auditors, transfer agent, legal counsel, stock exchange.

Sibbald Guide to the Texas Top 250 Public Companies and Top 250 Private Companies. Acorn Press Inc. • Annual. $102.50 per year, plus $5.00 shipping; payment must accompany order. Covers: 500 public and privately-held corporations and financial institutions in Texas. Entries include: Company name, address, phone; brief company history and description, names and titles of officers and directors; return on beginning equity, return on sales/revenues; condensed balance sheet, income statement for past five years, auditors, transfer agent, legal counsel, stock exchange.

SIBD--The Business Directory for the Soviet Region. FYI Information Resources for a Changing World. • Annual. $240 plus $10.00 shipping. Covers: Approximately 6,500 independent, cooperative, and private business organizations from industry, agriculture, and service sectors in the 15 republics of the former Soviet Union. Database includes: List of 500 largest enterprises. Entries include: Company or organization name, address, phone, telex, names and titles of key personnel, number of employees, geographical area served, financial data, subsidiary and branch names and locations, description of product/service.

Singapore Exchange--Companies Handbook. Singapore Exchange Ltd. • Semiannual. $400 per year. Covers: companies whose stock is traded on the Singapore Exchange. Entries include: Company name, address, names and titles of key personnel, capital, history, line of business, products, three year comparison of financial data.

Singapore International Chamber of Commerce. Singapore International Chamber of Commerce. • Annual. $15 Nonmembers. Covers: Singapore Chamber of Commerce members. Entries include: Members' addresses and their type of business.

Singapore International 100 Ranking. International Enterprise Singapore. • S$30.60 local. Covers: Singapore's top 100 companies with largest revenue contributions from the markets of Africa, Americas, China, Europe, India, Middle East, North Asia, Oceania, Southeast Asia. Entries include: top 100 companies ranked by overseas revenue, top 10 companies ranked by market, and corporate profiles.

SIRENE. France Institut National de la Statistique et des Etudes Economiques. • Daily. Database covers: Approximately 2.5 million French industrial and commercial firms. Entries include: Firm name, address, type of incorporation, national identification code, sector of activity, number of salaried employees, quarterly business volume.

SLAM--Trade Yearbook of Africa. SLAM Trade Year Book of Africa. • Annual. $60. Covers: Approximately 400,000 industrial and commercial companies in Africa. Entries include: Company name, address, phone, line of business, product/service, trademarks.

Somalia--Productive Sectors of the Economy. Indigo Publications. • Irregular. $500. Covers: Major companies in Somalia, including government services, state and private entities. Entries include: Company name, address, phone, managers, production figures.

SourceGuide to Market Share and Business Ranking Tables. London Business School Information Service. • $100. Covers: Key U.K., Pan European, and international business ranking and market share information published in 1989 or later and available in U.K. commercial libraries; includines newspapers, journals, directories, and databases. Entries include: Source name, address, phone, description.

South Africa National Classified Directory. A.C. Braby (Pty) Ltd. • Annual. Covers: Government and businesses in South Africa. Database includes: Maps.

South America: A Directory and Sourcebook. Euromonitor International Business Reference Div. • $390. Covers: major companies in South America; international and national organizations and statistical agencies, trade journals, electronic databases, consultants, market research firms, research centers, trade associations, trade unions, libraries, and other information sources. Database includes: Overview and statistical tables summarizing the economies of South America and the individual countries. Entries include: For companies--Name, address, phone, fax, telex, line of business, chief executive, number of employees, sales, products, outlets. For others--Organization name or publication title, address, phone, telex, fax, names and titles of key personnel, description of activities or contents.

South Carolina Business Directory. InfoGroup Inc. • Annual. $795 for both print & CD-ROM. Covers: 172,002 businesses in South Carolina. Entries include: Company name, address, phone, number of employees, name of owner or manager, sales volume. Compiled from telephone company 'Yellow Pages,' statewide. All states covered (see separate entries).

Southern California Business Directory and Buyers Guide. Dun & Bradstreet Inc. • Annual. $220 Individuals. Covers: 174,700 Southern California businesses. Database includes: Statistical data, trade show calendar. Entries include: Company name, address, county, phone, fax, number of employees, names and titles of key executives, plant size, year established, parent company, annual sales, import/export information, Standard Industrial Classification (SIC) code, and product description.

Spain: A Directory and Sourcebook. Euromonitor International Business Reference Div. • $390. Publication includes: Lists of major companies and sources of information regarding to consumer markets in Spain. Database includes: Statistics. Entries include: Company or organization name, address, phone, telex, names and titles of key personnel, description. Principal content of publication is an overview of issues affecting Spain.

Spain's 30,000 Top Companies. Dun & Bradstreet Inc. • Annual. $385. 15,000 companies in Spain with annual sales of at least $500,000.

Spanish-American Commercial Directory. IBAR. • Triennial. $60. Covers: More than 350,000 businesses in Spain, Portugal, and Latin-American countries, as well as companies in African, Asia, Australia, Canada, and Europe interested in conducting business with Latin-American countries. Entries include: Company name, address, phone.

Spanish Business Directory. INFOT Inc. • $72.25 CD-ROM; additional $125 for MS Access format. Covers: 86,807 selected businesses from the Spanish-speaking countries. Entries include: Name, physical address, email and website addresses, telephone and fax number, business description etc.

Standard & Poor's Corporation Records. Standard & Poor's Financial Services L.L.C. • Covers: Over 12,000 publicly-owned companies. Entries include: Corporation name, address, detailed descriptions of background, financial structure, and securities.

Standard & Poor's MarketScope. Standard & Poor's Financial Services L.L.C. • Daily. Covers: Over 7,000 companies in the 'Reference Section' of Standard and Poors database, incoluding all NYSE and ASE listed companies and 3,500 NASDAQ listed companies. Database covers: Over 7,000 companies in the 'Reference Section' of Standard and Poors database, including all NYSE and ASE listed companies and 3,500 NASDAQ listed companies. Database includes: Company name, phone, background information, current and historical financial information, earnings and dividend projections (for 1,1 00 major companies). No addresses or locations are given."Action Section," which details financial investment information, including stock market commentaries, company news and analyses, specific buy and sell recommendations on stocks, interest, and exchange rate information.

Standard & Poor's Register of Corporations, Directors and Executives. Standard & Poor's Financial Services L.L.C. • Annual. Covers: over 55,000 public and privately held corporations in the United States, including names and titles of over 400,000 officials (Volume 1); 70,000 biographies of directors and executives (Volume 2). Database includes: In Volume 3, lists of new executives, new companies, a corporate "Family Tree," Standard & Poor's 500 composite stock indices, and obituaries. Entries include: For companies--Name, address, phone, names of principal executives and accountants; primary bank, primary law firm, number of employees, estimated annual sales, outside directors, Standard Industrial Classification (SIC) code, product or service provided. For directors and executives--Name, home and principal business addresses, date and place of birth, fraternal organization memberships, business affiliations.

State-Owned Companies in Finland. Advisory Committee on State-Owned Cos. • Annual. Covers: about 13 government-owned manufacturing companies in Finland. Entries include: Company name, address, phone, telex, names and titles of key personnel, number of employees, financial data, subsidiary and branch names and locations.

Stock Brokers Bible: Directory of Public Companies. Wall Street Financial Services Inc. • Semiannual. $28.95. Covers: about 9,000 publicly traded companies in the U.S.; major broker dealers, mutual funds, and trusts. Entries include: Company name, address, phone, Standard Industrial Classification (SIC) code, exchange on which company is traded, ticker symbol.

The Stock Exchange of Hong Kong--Fact Book. The Stock Exchange of Hong Kong Corporate Communications Department. • Annual. Publication includes: List of companies listed on the Stock Exchange of Hong Kong. Principal content of publication is stock price index movement, trading value and volume, market capitalization, dividend yields and P/E ratios, and listed companies' activities and statistical records. Principal content of publication is a picture of the Hong Kong stock market for the year.

STOR-TELE. AffarsData. • Database covers: Approximately 100,000 Swedish companies. Database includes: Company name, address, phone, products and services.

Sultanate of Oman Telephone Directory. Tele-Gulf Directory Publication WLL. • Annual. Covers: businesses in Oman; separate editions in English and Arabic. Entries include: Company name, address, phone.

Sveriges Handelskalender. Telenor Foretagsinformation, AB. • Annual. $960. Covers: Approximately 16,000 commercial companies in Sweden. Entries include: Company name, address, phone, business data.

Swedish Chamber of Commerce--Trade Directory. Swedish Chamber of Commerce. • Annual. Covers: 400 member companies representing Swedish, British and European companies.

Taking Stocks: A Snapshot of Portland Metro-Area Public Companies. The Business Journal. • Annual. Covers: About 75 public firms that are either based in Portland, Oregon, or have a strong presence there. Entries include: Firm address, phone, names, and titles of executive officers, board of directors, products or services, significant stockholders, financial data.

Taylors Corporate Birmingham & West Midlands. Vincent Taylor & Co. • Annual. $20. Covers: Approximately 800 major companies in Birmingham and the West Midlands of England. Entries include: Company name, address, phone, names and titles of key personnel, number of employees, geographical area served, financial data, description of services, products provided.

Taylors Corporate North of England. Vincent Taylor & Co. • Annual. $20. Covers: Approximately 800 major companies and agencies in the North of England. Entries include: Company name, address, phone, names and titles of key personnel, number of employees, geographical area served, financial data, description of services, products provided.

Taylors Corporate Scotland. Vincent Taylor & Co. • Annual. $20. Covers: Approximately 850 major company entities and government agencies involved in the development of business in Scotland. Entries include: Company name, address, phone, names and titles of key personnel, number of employees, geographical area served, financial data, description of services, products provided.

Taylors Corporate South Africa. Vincent Taylor & Co. • Annual. $120. Covers: Approximately 400 companies and agencies involved in the development of business in South Africa. Entries include: Company name, address, phone, names and titles of key personnel, number of employees, geographical area served, financial data, description of services, products provided.

Technical Services in the United Kingdom. Financial Times Healthcare. • Irregular. $400. Covers: 2,000 public and private companies offering technical services and facilities for hire in the United Kingdom. Entries include: Company name, address, phone, type of service, facilities.

Tennessee Business Services Directory. Nashville Area Chamber of Commerce. • $121 Members. Covers: 7,500 Tennessee businesses in the service industry with 20 employees and in the restaurant industry with 50 employees. Entries include: Name, address, phone, and fax.

Thai Business Groups: A Unique Guide to Who Owns What. Brooker Group Public Company Ltd. • Annual. $340 Individuals. Covers: 150 top family business groups in Thailand. Entries include: Contact addresses, key executives of major companies, history and background of the top Thailand business families.

Thailand Investment: A Directory of Companies Promoted by the Board of Investment. Cosmic Group of Cos. • Annual. $60 plus shipping charges. Covers: Approximately 3,600 companies in Thailand that are promoted by the Thailand Board of Investment. Database includes: Information on doing business in Thailand. Entries include: Company name, address, phone.

Thailand Showcase: A Buyers' Guide. Cosmic Group of Cos. • Annual. $48 plus shipping charges. Covers: More than 3,000 companies in Thailand engaged in exporting their goods. Database includes: Overview of the Thailand economy. Entries include: Company name, address, phone.

Thailand: The MFC Investment Handbook. Hoover's Inc. • Annual. $46.95 plus $3.50 shipping. Covers: over 340 companies listed on the Stock Exchange of Thailand; 23 unit trusts. Entries include: Company name, address, phone, fax, stock symbol, company overview, price per share, trading volume, net income, capital, financial ratios, foreign holdings, limits on foreign ownership, list of major shareholders, names and titles of key personnel.

Thornton Guide to Hong Kong Companies. Hoover's Inc. • Semiannual. $69.95. Covers: More than 500 companies in Hong Kong. Database includes: Introduction to the Hong Kong capital market. Entries include: Name, address, phone, fax, stock codes and sector of business, board of directors, major shareholders, financial data, description of business activities.

Thornton Guide to the Companies of Singapore and Malaysia. Hoover's Inc. • Semiannual. $69.95. Covers: Nearly 250 companies in Singapore and nearly 500 companies in Malaysia. Database includes: Overview of the Stock Exchange of Singapore and the Kuala Lumpur Stock Exchange. Entries include: Name, address, phone, fax, stock codes and sector of business, board of directors, major shareholders, financial data, description of business activities.

3W Register of Chinese Business. 3W International Digital Publishing. • Biennial. $298. Covers: Approximately 31,000 Chinese companies in a variety of industries, including textile and garment, electronics and computer, mechanical and metallurgical, chemical and materials, construction and construction materials, service, wholesale trade and food, and agriculture, engineering, and management service. Entries include: Company name, address, phone, fax, telex, cable number, names and titles of key personnel, ownership information, financial data, date founded, number of employees, stock availability, imports, exports, product/service, Standard Industrial Classification (SIC) codes.

The Times 1,000: The Indispensable Annual Review of the World's Leading Industrial and Financial Companies. Times Books Ltd. • Annual. $32.50. Covers: 1,000 leading companies in the United Kingdom; 1,000 leading companies in Europe; leading firms in the United States, Canada, Australia, South Africa, Ireland, Hong Kong, and Japan. Entries include: For all companies--Company name and address. For British firms--Company name, names of chairman and managing director, sales, profits, capital, number of employees, and ranks and ratios. Listings for other firms vary in detail.

Today's Top 100 Service Providers. Coordinated Service Inc. • $99. Covers: The top 100 customer service providers in the U.S. Entries include: Company name, address, phone, fax, contacts, years in business, equipment serviced, geographical locations covered, other services offered.

Top European Companies Database. European Business Press Group N.V. • Annual. Diskette. Covers 500 major companies in Europe. Entries include: Company name, address, phone, names and titles of key personnel, financial data.

Top Global 500 Companies in China. SinoMedia Ltd. • Annual. $200 Individuals. Covers: 500 companies in China including 4,500 contacts, 4,400 offices and 1,700 email addresses. Entries include: Manager's names, telephone, profiles of the top global 50 enterprises.

Top 900 Blue Chip Indian Companies Database. NIIR Project Consultancy Services. • $200 Individuals CD-ROM. Covers: 900 Blue chip Indian companies. Entries include: Company name, name of CEO, postal address, city, state, pin code, phone, fax and the stock exchanges on which they are listed.

Top 1000 Performing Companies in Asia Pacific. Dun & Bradstreet Singapore Pte. Ltd. • $299.60 local. Covers: top 1000 performing companies in Asia Pacific, profiles of the Local top 50 companies, and payment trend analysis in the Asia Pacific region.

Top Romanian Companies. Chamber of Commerce and Industry of Romania. • Annual. $20. Covers: 600 of the most efficient Romanian companies ranked by size, field of activity, turnover rate, profit margin, development effort, and turnover per employee. Entries include: Company name, address, profile, contact person.

Top 22,000 Businesses in the People's Republic of China. China Books. • $360 cloth. Covers: Leading 22,000 businesses in China, including manufacturing, foods, apparel, paper, chemicals, and real estate industries. Entries include: Name, address, phone, executive names, number of employees, profits.

Toyo Keizai Company Information. Toyo Keizai Inc. • Daily. Database covers: Japanese companies.

Trade Directory of Western Sweden. Goteborg and Western Sweden Chamber of Commerce. • Biennial. $300. Covers: Companies, wholesalers, importers/exporters, and manufacturers in Goteborg and the western Sweden Chamber of Commerce area. Entries include: Company name, address, phone, telex number, line of business.

Transkei Business Directory. A.C. Braby (Pty) Ltd. • Annual. R 30 payment must accompany order. Covers: businesses in Transkei. Entries include: Company name, address, phone.

Transnational Corporations and Labor: A Directory of Resources. WorldViews. • $12.95 plus $2.00 shipping. Covers: sources for books, periodicals, pamphlets, audiovisuals, and other educational resources on transnational corporations and labor issues; names of resources with annotations and ordering information. Entries include: Organization name, address, phone, titles of print and audio/visual material. Part of a 10 volume series (updated in "Third World Resources"), each volume covering single region or issue.

Turnkey Offers from India. EEPC India. • Biennial. Covers: Companies in India involved in international projects.

The 2,000 Top Spanish Companies. Fomento de la Produccion. • Annual. $15. Covers: 2,000 leading companies in Spain. Entries include: Company name, address, phone, telex number, sales, ranking.

The UK/USA Investment Directory & Business Resource. BritishAmerican Business Inc. of New York and London. • Biennial. $149. Covers: Over 6,000 British and American companies and their approximately 4,000 subsidiaries in the United Kingdom and the United States. Entries include: Parent company name, address, phone, fax; name of British subsidiary in the United States, address, phone, fax; percentage of business British or American owned, number of staff, product or service provided, Standard Industrial Classification (SIC) code.

United Kingdom's 10,000 Largest Companies. William Snyder Publishing Associates. • Annual. $250. Covers: top 10,000 companies in the United Kingdom, ranked by turnover. Database includes: Financial and statistical business information on each company. Entries include: Company name, address, phone, name of director, number of employees, financial data, year established, International Standard Industrial Classification (ISIC) code, parent company.

U.S.-China Business Services Directory. U.S.-China Business Council. • Irregular. $35. Covers: more than 900 companies in the U. S., Hong Kong, and China providing business services to China, such as consulting firms, architectural and construction engineering firms, freight forwarding companies, and law firms. Entries include: Company name, address, phone, telex, name and title of contact, subsidiary and branch names and locations, description of products or services.

U.S. Firms in Germany. German American Chamber of Commerce. • Annual. $100. Covers: Over 700 U.S. companies located in Germany. Entries include: Company name, address, phone in Germany, company name, address, phone of their American parent company.

U.S. List. American Chamber of Commerce in Austria. • Biennial. €80 Members. Covers: About 360 U.S. subsidiaries and affiliated companies located in Austria. Entries include: U.S. Parent company name and address, Austrian subsidiary or affiliated company name, address, phone, fax, managing director, line of business, e-mail, Internet-homepage address, kind of relationship.

U.S. 1 Business Directory: Your Source for Business in Central New Jersey. U.S. 1 Publishing Corp. • Annual. $18.95. Covers: Approximately 5,500 business to business listings in 212 categories in such areas as computer science, pharmaceuticals, R & D, architecture, advertising agencies, accounting, law firms, warehouses, consultants in the central New Jersey area. Entries include: Company name, address, phone, fax, number of employees, financial data, descriptions of product/service, e-mail, home page addresses, year founded, and revenue range.

Utah Major Employers Guide. • Biennial. $50 Individuals for investors. Covers: More than 900 companies in 29 counties in Utah that have 100 or more full-time employees. Entries include: Company name, address, phone, fax, contact names, names and titles of key personnel, year established, type of operation, Standard Industrial Classification (SIC) code, product/service, county, number of full-time employees, website addresses.

Vault Guide to the Top Business Services Employers. Vault.com Inc. • $19.95 Individuals Online. Covers: Top business service companies in United States. Entries include: Company name, contact person, location, address, phone and fax numbers, zip code, statistics, hiring process and email.

VenCap Data Quest. Reference Press Inc. • $89.95 Eastern version. Diskette. Contains over 750 venture capital firms in the eastern and western U.S. Entries include: Company name, address, phone, fax, officers, partners, type of fund, number of years providing funding, dollars under management, industries covered and geographical preferences, preferred low- and high-average investments, preferred maturity stages, and product description of portfolio companies.

Venezuela Company Handbook. Hoover's Inc. • $29.95 plus $3.50 shipping. Covers: major Venezuelan companies listed on the Caracas Stock Exchange. Database includes: Profile of Venezuela's economy, including information on privatization and accounting rules. Entries include: Company name, address, phone, fax, year established, stock ticker symbol, names and titles of key personnel, number of employees, number of stockholders, bank references, auditor, company history, financial data, markets and competition, raw materials used and sources, names of major stockholders, affiliated companies.

Virginia Business Directory. InfoGroup Inc. • Annual. $795 for both print & CD-ROM. Covers: 297,373 businesses in Virginia. Entries include: Company name, address, phone, number of employees, name of owner or manager, sales volume. Compiled from telephone company 'Yellow Pages,' statewide. All states covered (see separate entries).

Wales Business Directory. Kemps Publishing Ltd. • Annual. $18. Covers: Members of the Chambers of Commerce of Cardiff, Chester, North Wales, Neath, Newport, Gwent, Port Talbot, and Swansea and local businesses. Entries include: Company name, address, phone, member name.

Walker's Manual of Western Corporations. Walker's Manual Inc. • Annual. $380 base edition. Covers: over 1,500 publicly owned corporations headquartered in Alaska, Arizona, California, Colorado, Hawaii, Idaho, Montana, Nevada, New Mexico, Oregon, Utah, Washington, and Wyoming. Entries include: Company name, address, phone, description of business; names of executives and directors with shareholdings of each; number of employees, brand names or product lines, financial data and common share data covering five years, capitalization, number of shareholders, sales and management statements, income and balance sheet information for five years.

Ward's Business Directory of U.S. Private and Public Companies. Cengage Learning Inc. • Annual. $3,627 Individuals five-volume set. Eight volumes. Ward's contains basic information on about 115,000 business firms, of which 90 percent are private companies. Volumes available individually.

Wer Liefert Was? Central Europe: Business-to-Business Directory. Wer liefert was GmbH. • Annual. Database covers: Over 45,000 companies in the Czech Republic, Slovenia, Slovakia, and Croatia. Entries include: Name, address, phone, fax, description of products/services offered.

Who Belongs to Whom: Capital Links in German Companies. Commerzbank AG. • Semiannual. Covers: about 11,000 German companies and their domestic and foreign shareholders. Database includes: Glossary of German technical terms, translated in English, French, Italian, and Spanish. Entries include: Company name, trade or industry code number, capital, names of principal shareholders, partners, investors, and percentage of stock owned.

Who Knows Who: Networking through Corporate Boards. Who Knows Who Publishers. • Annual. $165. Publication includes: List of over 1,000 companies noted by either Fortune magazine or Forbes magazine, or both; over 120 major foundations. Entries include: Company or foundation name, address, phone, boards of directors. Principal content of publication is lists of the companies and their boards of directors showing relationships among the companies by showing which of the board members sit on several of the companies' boards, i.e. interlocking directorates.

Who Owns Whom--North America. Dun & Bradstreet Inc. • Annual. Covers: Parent companies located in the U.S., Canada, South America, and the West Indies and their foreign and domestic subsidiaries; 66,000 parent companies, 200,000 subsidiaries. Parents with international investments only are shown in the United States section. Entries include: Parent company name, address, phone, industrial classification, direct subsidiary names, and country of incorporation.

Who's Who in Canadian Business. University of Toronto Press Inc. • Annual. $192.95 Individuals plus shipping charges. Covers: About 5,400 corporate and entrepreneurial leaders, each with a detailed biography and contact information. Biographies include such information as current employment, address, education, career history, publications, favorite charities and honors. Entries include: Name, degree(s), position, and title; office address, phone, fax, e-mail, and URL; personal, education, and career data; memberships, affiliations, and other interests.

Who's Who in Metro Atlanta Business: Membership Directory & Buyers Guide. Metro Atlanta Chamber of Commerce. • Annual. $35 Individuals. Covers: Over 7,000 member firms. Database includes: Chamber of commerce history, business facts and figures, annual report and initiatives for Metro Atlanta Chamber. Entries include: Company name, line of business, address, phone, names of key personnel and their URL addresses.

Wisconsin Business Directory. InfoGroup Inc. • Annual. $520 both print & CD-ROM. Covers: 256,558 businesses in Wisconsin. Entries include: Company name, address, phone, number of employees, name of owner or manager, sales volume. Compiled from telephone company "Yellow Pages," statewide. All states covered (see separate entries).

Wisconsin Business Services Directory. WMC Foundation. • Annual. $199 Individuals. Covers: Over 10,700 business service companies with 25 or more employees in Wisconsin. Entries include: Company name, address, phone, fax, number of employees, SIC codes, names and titles of key personnel, services offered, product descriptions, ownership status, import/export activity, parent company.

Wisconsin Services Directory. Harris InfoSource. • Annual. $98 members/libraries. Covers: 16,000 business service companies in Wisconsin and over 24,000 key contact personnel. Entries include: Company name, address, phone, fax, name and title of contact, names and titles of key personnel, number of employees, geographical area served, financial data, subsidiary and branch names and locations, product/service, Standard Industrial Classification (SIC) code, computer used, year established, import/export information, web and e-mail address, first month of fiscal year, export countries.

World Business Directory. NIIR Project Consultancy Services. • $200 Individuals CD-ROM. Covers: More than 300,000 worldwide businesses. Entries include: Company name, postal address, city, state, pin code, phone, fax and the emails.

World Market Share Reporter. Cengage Learning Inc. • $572 Individuals. Compilation of global market share data from periodical literature. Covers nearly 1,670 entries in 360 geographic worldwide locations of companies and products and services.

The World's Major Companies. Euromonitor International Business Reference Div. • $550. Covers: Approximately 4,000 major multinational companies. Entries include: Company name, address, phone, telex, names and titles of key personnel, number of employees, financial data, subsidiary and branch names and locations, description.

Wyoming Business Directory. InfoGroup Inc. • Annual. $375 both print & CD-ROM. Covers: 33,514 businesses in Wyoming. Entries include: Company name, address, phone, number of employees, name of owner or manager, sales volume. Compiled from telephone company "Yellow Pages," statewide. All states covered (see separate entries).

Yearbook of the Athens Stock Exchange. Athens Stock Exchange. • Annual. €20 plus postage. Covers: About 196 companies quoted on the Athens Stock Exchange; list of stockbrokers. Database includes: List of business loans available, with description and financial data; financial statistics. Entries include: For companies--Name, address, phone, telex, year established, year first listed, line of business, number of shareholders, board of directors, number of employees, financial data. For brokers--Name, address, phone.

Yearbook of the Lebanese Limited Liability Companies. Publitec Publications. • Annual. $120. Covers: Lebanese limited liability companies, including insurance companies, commerce, industry, real estate, transport, and finance. Entries include: Contact information.

Yritys-Suomi CD. Helsinki Media. • Biennial. Database covers: Information on 170,000 companies from other Blue Book directories.

Yunnan Yellow Pages. China Yellow Pages Directories Co. • Annual. Covers: Over 20,000 companies in Yunnan Province, Taiwan. Database includes: An investment guide containing Yunnan's policies, rules and procedures for investment plus a compilation of product and service advertisements. Entries include: Company name, address, phone.

FINANCIAL RATIOS

Quarterly Financial Report for Manufacturing, Mining, Trade, and Selected Service Industries. U.S. Federal Trade Commission and U.S. Securities and Exchange Commission. U.S. Census Bureau Foreign Trade Division. • Quarterly. Quarterly. Report on financial results of U.S. corporations.

GENERAL WORKS

The Complete Guide to Buying a Business. Nolo. • Contains information and forms for purchasing a business in the United States.

Incorporate Your Business. Nolo. • Contains information on establishing a corporation in each state.

INTERNET DATABASES

Business 2.0 Web Guide to the Best Business Links. Business 2.0 Media Inc. Phone: (415)293-4800; Email: support@business2.com • URL: http://www.business2.com/webguide • Web site presents an extensive, searchable directory of links to "the best, most informative, and authoritative web pages." Twenty main categories cover business, finance, career, company information, people, and technology topics, with thousands of subtopics, all linking to Web sites recommended by experienced business researchers. Fees: Free.

Business Week Online. McGraw-Hill. Phone: (212)512-2511; Fax: (684)842-6101 • URL: http://www.businessweek.com • Web site provides complete contents of current issue of *Business Week* plus "BW Daily" with additonal business news, financial market quotes, and corporate information from Standard & Poor's. Includes various features, such as "Banking Center" with mortgage and interest data, and "Interactive Computer Buying Guide." The "Business Week Archive" is fully searchable back to 1996.

EBSCO Information Services. EBSCO Publishing Inc. 10 Estes St., Ipswich, MA 01938-2106. Phone: 800-653-2726 or (978)356-6500; Fax: (978)356-6565; Email: information@ebscohost.com • URL: http://www.ebscohost.com • Fee-based Web site providing Internet access to a wide variety of databases, including business-related material. Full text is available for many periodical titles, with daily updates. Fees: Apply.

Factiva. Dow Jones Reuters Business Interactive, LLC. Phone: 800-369-7466 or (609)452-1511; Fax: (609)520-5770; Email: solutions@factiva.com • URL: http://www.factiva.com • Fee-based Web site provides "global news and business information through Web sites and content integration solutions." Includes Dow Jones and Reuters newswires, The Wall Street Journal, and more than 7,000 other sources of current news, historical articles, market research reports, and investment analysis. Content includes 96 major U. S. newspapers, 900 non-English sources, trade publications, media transcripts, country profiles, news photos, etc.

Hoover's Online. Hoover's Inc. 5800 Airport Blvd., Austin, TX 78752-4204. Phone: 866-443-3939 or (512)374-4500 or (866)281-5969; Fax: (512)374-4501; Email: salesteam@hoovers.com • URL: http://www.hoovers.com • Web site provides stock quotes, lists of companies, and a variety of business information at no charge. In-depth company profiles are available.

InSite 2. Intelligence Data/Thomson Financial. Phone: 800-654-0393 or (617)856-1890; Fax: (617)737-3182; Email: intelligence.data@tfn.com • URL: http://www.insite2.gale.com/ • Fee-based Web site consolidates information in a "Base Pack" consisting of Business InSite, Market InSite, and Company InSite. Optional databases are Consumer InSite, Health and Wellness InSite, Newsletter InSite, and Computer InSite. Includes fulltext content from more than 2,500 trade publications, journals, newsletters, newspapers, analyst reports, and other sources. Continuous updating. Formerly produced by The Gale Group.

Mergent Online. Mergent Inc. 580 Kingsley Park Dr., Fort Mill, SC 29715. Phone: 800-937-1398 or (704)527-2700 or (704)559-7601; Fax: (704)559-6837 or (704)559-6960; Email: customerservice@mergent.com • URL: http://www.mergent.com • Fee-based Web site provides detailed information on 20,000 publicly-owned companies in 100 foreign countries, as well as more than 10,000 corporations listed on the New York Stock Exchange, American Stock Exchange, NASDAQ, and U.S. regional exchanges. Searching is offered on many financial variables and text fields. Weekly updating. Formerly *FIS Online*.

Nexis.com. Lexis-Nexis Group. Phone: 800-227-4908 or (937)865-6800; Fax: (937)865-6909; Email: webmaster@prod.lexis-nexis.com • URL: http://www.nexis.com • Fee-based Web site offers searching of about 2.8 billion documents in some 30,000 news, business, and legal information sources. Features include a subject directory covering 1,200 topics in 34 categories and a Company Dossier containing information on more than 500,000 public and private companies. Boolean searching is offered.

ProQuest. ProQuest L.L.C. 789 E Eisenhower Pkwy., Ann Arbor, MI 48106-1346. Phone: 800-521-0600 or (734)761-4700; Fax: (734)662-4554; Email: info@proquest.com • URL: http://www.proquest.com • Fee-based Web site providing Internet access to more than 3,000 periodicals, newspapers, and other publications. Many items are available full-text, with daily updates. Includes extensive corporate and financial information. Fees: Apply.

Switchboard. Switchboard, Inc. Phone: (508)898-8000; Fax: (508)898-1755; Email: webmaster@switchboard.com • URL: http://www.switchboard.com • Web site provides telephone numbers and street addresses for more than 100 million business locations and residences in the U. S. Broad industry categories are available. Fees: Free.

ONLINE DATABASES

Business & Company ASAP. Cengage Learning Inc. • Provides business and company information including 200,000 company directory listings, the complete text of PR Newswire releases for the preceding 30 days, and articles from leading business and industry publications. Includes more than 1300 indexed and 800 full-text periodical titles and over 200,000 combined directory listings, including the Graham & Whiteside international company directories.

Business Insights: Essentials (BI:E). Cengage Learning Inc. • Formerly Business & Company Resource Center. Contact for pricing. Contains in-depth, searchable information on U.S. and International businesses, industries, and products.

Dow Jones News Service. Dow Jones and Co., Inc. • Full text and edited news stories and articles on business affairs. Inquire as to online cost and availability.

InvesText. Thomson Financial. • Provides full text online of investment research reports from more than 600 sources, including leading brokers and investment bankers. Reports are available on approximately 60,000 U. S. and international corporations. Separate industry reports cover 54 industries. Time span is 1982 to date, with daily updates. Inquire as to online cost and availability.

Wilson Business Abstracts Online. H.W. Wilson Co. • Indexes and abstracts 600 major business periodicals, plus the *Wall Street Journal* and the business section of the *New York Times*. Indexing is from 1982, abstracting from 1990, with the two newspapers included from 1993. Updated weekly. Inquire as to online cost and availability. (*Business Periodicals Index* without abstracts is also available online.).

OTHER SOURCES

Business Organizations with Tax Planning. Zolman Cavitch, editor. Matthew Bender and Company Inc. • Quarterly. $6,433 book. Periodic supplementation.

For publishers' addresses, refer to SOURCES CITED section at the back of the book.

In-depth analytical coverage of corporation law and all relevant aspects of federal corporation taxation.

Business Rankings Annual (BRA). Cengage Learning Inc. • Annual. $584 Individuals. A guide to lists and rankings appearing in major business publications. The top ten names are listed in each case.

Business Strategies. Wolters Kluwer Law & Business CCH. • Semimonthly. $795.00 per year. Four looseleaf volumes. Semimonthly updates. Legal, tax, and accounting aspects of business planning and decision-making. Provides information on start-ups, forms of ownership (partnerships, corporations), failing businesses, reorganizations, acquisitions, and so forth. Includes *Business Strategies Bulletin*, a monthly newsletter.

PERIODICALS AND NEWSLETTERS

Forbes. Forbes Inc. • Biweekly. $29.99 Individuals. Magazine reporting on industry, business and finance management.

Fortune Magazine. Time Inc., Business Information Group. • Biweekly. $19.99 all access. Edited for top executives and upper-level managers.

Standard & Poor's SmallCap 600 Guide. McGraw Hill Financial Inc. • Monthly. $24.95. Contains detailed profiles of the companies included in Standard & Poor's SmallCap 600 Index of stock prices. Includes income and balance sheet data for up to 10 years, with growth and stability rankings for 600 small capitalization corporations.

RESEARCH CENTERS AND INSTITUTES

University of Pittsburgh - Business, Government, and Society Research Institute. School of Business, Mervis Hall, Pittsburgh, PA 15260. Phone: (412)648-1555; Fax: (412)648-1693; Email: mitnick@pitt.edu.

STATISTICS SOURCES

Statistics of Income: Corporation Income Tax Returns. U.S. Internal Revenue Service. U. S. Government Printing Office. • Annual.

World Market Share Reporter. Cengage Learning Inc. • $572 Individuals. Compilation of global market share data from periodical literature. Covers nearly 1,670 entries in 360 geographic worldwide locations of companies and products and services.

TRADE/PROFESSIONAL ASSOCIATIONS

Association for Corporate Growth. 125 S Wacker Dr., Ste. 3100, Chicago, IL 60606. Phone: 877-358-2220 • URL: http://www.acg.org • Aims to drive middle market growth. Represents 14,000 members who are investors, lenders, advisors and leaders of more than 20,000 middle-market companies. Provides networking, resources and research.

National Rural Utilities Cooperative Finance Corp. 20701 Cooperative Way, Dulles, VA 20166. Phone: 800-424-2954 or (703)709-6700 or (703)467-1800; Fax: (703)467-5175; Email: publicrelations@nrucfc.coop • URL: http://www.nrucfc.coop.

Society of Corporate Secretaries and Governance Professionals. 240 W 35th St., Ste. 400, New York, NY 10001. Phone: (212)681-2000; Fax: (212)681-2005 • URL: http://www.governanceprofessionals.org • Corporate secretaries, assistant secretaries, officers and executives of corporations and others interested in corporate practices and procedures. Conducts surveys and research. Sponsors educational programs for members. Maintains a central information and reference service.

CORPORATIONS, MULTINATIONAL

See MULTINATIONAL CORPORATIONS

CORPORATIONS, PROFESSIONAL

See PROFESSIONAL CORPORATIONS

CORRECTIONAL INSTITUTIONS

See LAW ENFORCEMENT INDUSTRIES

CORRESPONDENCE

See BUSINESS CORRESPONDENCE

CORRESPONDENCE SCHOOLS AND COURSES

See also ADULT EDUCATION

PERIODICALS AND NEWSLETTERS

DETC News. Distance Education and Training Council. • Semiannual. Description: Discusses issues pertaining to distance study education and reports activities of the Council. Recurring features include news of research, book reviews, news of members, and a calendar of events.

TRADE/PROFESSIONAL ASSOCIATIONS

Distance Education and Training Council. 1601 18th St. NW, Ste. 2, Washington, DC 20009. Phone: (202)234-5100; Fax: (202)332-1386; Email: info@detc.org • URL: http://www.detc.org • Formerly National Home Study Council.

CORROSION CONTROL INDUSTRY

See INDUSTRIAL COATINGS

ABSTRACTS AND INDEXES

Corrosion Abstracts: Abstracts of the World's Literature on Corrosion and Corrosion Mitigation. National Association of Corrosion Engineers. CSA. • Monthly. $240 Individuals per year. Includes print and online editions. Provides abstracts of the worldwide literature of corrosion and corrosion control. Also available on CD-ROM.

PERIODICALS AND NEWSLETTERS

Corrosion: Journal of Science and Engineering. National Association of Corrosion Engineers. NACE International: The Corrosion Society. • Monthly. Individuals, $160.00 per year; institutions, $290.00 per year. Covers corrosion control science, theory, engineering, and practice.

Materials Performance: Articles on Corrosion Science and Engineering Solutions for Corrosion Problems. National Association of Corrosion Engineers. NACE International: The Corrosion Society. • Monthly. $115 Nonmembers 1-year subscription. Covers the protection and performance of materials in corrosive environments. Includes information on new materials and industrial coatings.

RESEARCH CENTERS AND INSTITUTES

Center for Applied Thermodynamics Studies. University of Idaho, Dept. of Mechanical Engineering, 875 Perimeter Dr., MS 0902, Moscow, ID 83844-0902. Phone: (208)885-6779; Fax: (208)885-9031 • URL: http://www.uidaho.edu/engr/me/research/centersandinstitutes.

Ohio State University - Fontana Corrosion Center. 477 Watts Hall, 2041 College Rd., Columbus, OH 43210. Phone: (614)292-9857; Fax: (614)292-9857; Email: frankel.10@osu.edu • URL: http://www.matsceng.ohio-state.edu/frankel/FCC • Research areas include metal coatings and corrosion of alloys.

University of Minnesota - Corrosion Research Center. 112 Amundson Hall, 421 Washington Ave., Minneapolis, MN 55455. Phone: (612)625-0014 or (612)625-1313; Fax: (612)626-7246; Email: dshores@umn.edu • URL: http://www.cems.umn.edu/research/crc • Research areas include the effect of corrosion on high technology materials and devices.

TRADE/PROFESSIONAL ASSOCIATIONS

NACE International: The Corrosion Society. 1440 S Creek Dr., Houston, TX 77084-4906. Phone: 800-797-6223 or (281)228-6200 or (281)228-6223; Fax: (281)228-6300; Email: firstservice@nace.org • URL: http://www.nace.org • Serves as professional technical society dedicated to reducing the economic impact of corrosion, promoting public safety, and protecting the environment by advancing the knowledge of corrosion engineering and science. Conducts programs for technical training, sponsors technical conferences, and produces standards, publications, and software. Maintains certification program for engineers, technicians, and coating inspectors.

National Association for Surface Finishing. 1155 15th St. NW, Ste. 500, Washington, DC 20005. Phone: (202)457-8404 or (703)887-7235; Fax: (202)530-0659; Email: passante@nasf.org • URL: http://www.nasf.org • Members are management personnel of metal and plastic finishing companies. Finishing includes plating, coating, polishing, rust-proofing, and other processes.

CORRUGATED PAPERBOARD

See PAPERBOARD AND PAPERBOARD PACKAGING INDUSTRIES

COSMETICS INDUSTRY

See also BARBER AND BEAUTY SHOPS; PERFUME INDUSTRY

DIRECTORIES

Cosmetics & Toiletries--Cosmetic Bench Reference. • Annual. $199 Individuals. Publication includes: List of cosmetic ingredient suppliers. Entries include: Supplier name, address, phone, fax, chemicals, trade names. Principal content of publication is data on cosmetic ingredients, with label names, trade names, functions, EINECS, INCI names, and CAS numbers.

Cosmetology Schools Directory. InfoGroup Inc. • Annual. Number of listings: 2,069. Entries include: Name, address, phone, size of advertisement, name of owner or manager, number of employees, year first in "Yellow Pages." Compiled from telephone company "Yellow Pages," nationwide.

Directory of American Manufacturers & Exporters of Beauty Supplies, Cosmetics, Perfumes & Toiletries. EXIM Infotek Private Ltd. • $20 Individuals. Covers: 200 American manufacturers and exporters of aloe vera products, bath products, beauty care products, beauty creams, blackhead removers, body lotions, cosmetic bags, cosmetic brushes, cosmetic chemicals, cosmetic pencils, cosmetic plastic containers, cosmetics, cosmetics raw materials, eyeliners, face make-up, facial sponges, hair conditioners, hair gels, Halloween accessories, health care, herbal products, lip glosses, lip care products, lipstick, mascara, mouthwash, nail care products, nail polish, oral hygiene products, perfumes, personal care products, scalp conditioners, shampoos, skin care creams and lotions, skin care products, sun care products, toiletries, and toothpaste. Entries include: Company name, postal address, city, country, phone, fax, e-mail and websites, contact person, designation, and product details.

Directory of Chinese Manufacturers & Exporters of Beauty Supplies, Cosmetics, Perfumes, Toiletries. EXIM Infotek Private Ltd. • $10 Individuals. Covers: 80 Chinese manufacturers and exporters of bathing products, beauty products, brushes-cosmetics, cosmetic accessories, cosmetic brushes, cosmetics, eyebrow pencils, eyeshadow pencil, fragrances, hair brushes, lipstick, manicure sets, perfume, perfume bottles, perfumes, shampoo, skin care products, talcum, and talcum powder. Entries include: Company name, postal address, city, country, phone, fax, e-mail and websites, contact person, designation, and product details.

Directory of Japanese Manufacturers & Exporters of Beauty Supplies, Cosmetics, Perfumes & Toiletries. EXIM Infotek Private Ltd. • $10 Individuals. Covers: 120 Japanese manufacturers & exporters of air fresheners, cosmetics, fragrances, hand sprayers, perfumes. Entries include: Company name, postal address, city, country, phone, fax, e-mail & websites, contact person, designation, products detail.

Directory of South Korean Manufacturers & Exporters of Beauty Supplies, Cosmetics, Perfumes & Toiletries. EXIM Infotek Private Ltd. • $5 Individuals. Covers: 40 South Korean manufacturers and exporters of air fresheners, cosmetic brushes, cosmetic/hair/skin and dental products, cosmetics, hair brushes, hair combs, hand mirrors, manicure sets, nail clippers, and perfume. Entries include: Company name, postal address, city, country, phone, fax, e-mail and websites, contact person, designation, and product details.

Directory of Taiwanese Manufacturers & Exporters of Beauty Supplies, Cosmetics, Perfumes & Toiletries. EXIM Infotek Private Ltd. • $15 Individuals. Covers: 140 Taiwanese manufacturers and exporters of air fresheners, body glitter gel, cosmetic accessories, cosmetic brushes, cosmetic/hair/skin and dental products, cosmetics, cosmetics accessories, eye liner, eye pencil, eyebrow needles, eyebrow pencils, eyelash stick, eyelash wave lotion kit, eyelets, eyeshadow pencil, face foundation, fragrance bottles, hair brushes, hair combs, hair steamers, lip pens, lipstick, lipstick cases, lipstick containers, make-up kits, mascara, nail polish, perfume, perfume atomizers, perfume bottles, perfumes, shampoo. Entries include: Company name, postal address, city, country, phone, fax, e-mail and websites, contact person, designation and product details.

Household and Personal Products Industry Buyers Guide. Rodman Publications. • Annual. Lists of suppliers to manufacturers of cosmetics, toiletries, soaps, detergents, and related household and personal products.

Household and Personal Products Industry Contract Manufacturing/Private Label Directory. Rodman Publications. • Annual. Provides information for about 450 companies offering private label or contract packaged household and personal care products, such as detergents, cosmetics, polishes, insecticides, and various aerosol items.

The International Directory of Importers - Beauty Supplies, Cosmetic and Toiletries Importers. Interdata. • $295 Individuals print. Covers: 4,100 international firms importing beauty supplies, cosmetics and toiletries. Entries include: Company name and address, contact person, email, number of employees, year established, phone and telefaxes, business activity, bank references, as well as a listing of beauty supplies, cosmetics and toiletries currently being imported.

The Rauch Guide to the US Cosmetics and Toiletries Industry. Impact Marketing Consultants Inc. • $895. Covers: Structure and current market information on cosmetics and toiletries industry.

Rest of the World Toiletry Index. Datamonitor. • $995. Covers: Companies involved in the toiletry and cosmetics industry in nations outside of Asia and North, Central, and South America. Entries include: Company name, address, phone, telex, names and titles of key personnel, number of employees; financial data, product/service, Standard Industrial Classification (SIC) code, production locations.

Who's Who Membership Directory. Personal Care Product Council. • Annual. Available on website. Lists 600 member companies, with key personnel, products, and services.

World Cosmetics and Toiletries Marketing Directory. Cengage Learning Inc. • 2010. $475.00. 6th edition. Published by Euromonitor. Provides detailed descriptions of the world's cosmetics and toiletries companies. Includes consumers market research data.

World Directory of Cosmetics, Beauty Supplies, and Toiletries Importers. World-Wide Market-Link. • Irregular. $35. Covers: 800 importers and wholesaler of cosmetics, beauty supplies an toiletries in 30 countries. Entries include: Company name, address, phone, products.

E-BOOKS

The American Beauty Industry Encyclopedia. Cengage Learning Inc. • 2011. eBook. Published by Greenwood Publishing Group. Focuses exclusively on the many aspects of the American beauty industry, covering both its diverse origins and its global reach.

FINANCIAL RATIOS

Annual Statement Studies. Risk Management Association. • Annual. Compiled from over 280,000 financial statements.

Annual Statement Studies: Industry Default Probabilities and Cash Flow Measures. Risk Management Association. • Annual. $405 Nonmembers. Serves as a companion volume to the original *Annual Statement Studies*. Gives probability of default estimates on a percentage scale for more than 450 industries. Includes changes in position year-by-year for eight financial statement line items and provides percentage measures of cash flow.

OTHER SOURCES

Food Law Reports. Wolters Kluwer Law & Business CCH. • Weekly. $1,459.00 per year. Six looseleaf volumes. Covers regulation of adulteration, packaging, labeling, and additives. Formerly *Food Drug Cosmetic Law Reports.*

PERIODICALS AND NEWSLETTERS

Beauty Store Business. Creative Age Publications Inc. • Monthly. Business magazine for beauty industry professionals and beauty store owners.

Cosmetic World News: The International News Magazine of the Perfumery, Cosmetic s and Toiletries Industry. World News Publications. • Bimonthly. $192.00 per year.

Cosmetics and Toiletries: The International Journal of Cosmetic Technology. Allured Business Media. • $98 U.S..

Drug Topics. Thomson Medical Economics. • Monthly. Edited for retail pharmacists, hospital pharmacists, pharmacy chain store executives, wholesalers, buyers, and others concerned with drug dispensing and drug store management. Provides information on new products, including personal care items and cosmetics.

Executive Update. Personal Care Product Council. • Monthly newsletter for members.

Global Cosmetic Industry: The Business Magazine for the Global Beauty Industry. Allured Business Media. • 9/year. Trade publication covering the cosmetics industry worldwide.

Household and Personal Products Industry: The Magazine for the Detergent, Soap, Cosmetic and Toiletry, Wax, Polish and Aerosol Industries. Rodman Publications. • Monthly. Covers marketing, packaging, production, technical innovations, private label developments, and aerosol packaging for soap, detergents, cosmetics, insecticides, and a variety of other household products.

The Rose Sheet: Toiletries, Fragrances and Skin Care. Elsevier Business Intelligence. • 51 times a year. $1,910.00 online only. Newsletter. Provides industry news, regulatory news, market data, and a "Weekly Trademark Review" for the cosmetics industry.

Soap and Cosmetics. Cygnus Business Media. • Monthly. $60.00 per year. Formerly *Soap, Cosmetics, Chemical Specialties.*

STATISTICS SOURCES

U.S. Industry and Trade Outlook. U.S. Department of Commerce National Technical Information Service. • Annual. Produced by the International Trade Administration, U.S. Department of Commerce, in a "public-private" partnership with DRI/McGraw-Hill and Standard & Poor's. Provides basic data, outlook for the current year, and "Long-Term Prospects" (five-year projections) for a wide variety of products and services. Includes high technology industries. Formerly *U.S. Industrial Outlook.*

TRADE/PROFESSIONAL ASSOCIATIONS

National Beauty Culturists' League. 25 Logan Cir. NW, Washington, DC 20005-3725. Phone: (202)332-2695; Fax: (202)332-0940; Email: nbcl@bellsouth.net • URL: http://www.nbcl.org • Beauticians, cosmetologists, and beauty products manufacturers. Encourages standardized, scientific, and approved methods of hair, scalp, and skin treatments. Offers scholarships and plans to establish a research center. Sponsors: National Institute of Cosmetology, a training course in operating and designing and business techniques. Maintains hall of fame; conducts research program.

National - Interstate Council of State Boards of Cosmetology. c/o Debra Norton, Coordinator, 7622 Briarwood Cir., Little Rock, AR 72205. Phone: (501)227-8262; Fax: (501)227-8212 • URL: http://www.nictesting.org • Persons commissioned by 50 state governments as administrators of cosmetology laws and examiners of applicants for licenses to practice cosmetology.

Personal Care Products Council. 1620 L St. NW, Ste. 1200, Washington, DC 20036. Phone: (202)331-1770; Fax: (202)331-1969 • URL: http://www.personalcarecouncil.org • Formerly Cosmetic, Toiletry and Fragrance Association.

COST ACCOUNTING

See also ACCOUNTING; COST CONTROL

ABSTRACTS AND INDEXES

Accounting Articles. Wolters Kluwer Law & Business CCH. • Monthly. $624. Covers accounting news.

Business Periodicals Index Retrospective. EBSCO Publishing Inc. • 11/year. Quarterly and annual cumulations.

FINANCIAL RATIOS

Income and Fees of Accountants in Public Practice. National Society of Accountants. • Contains info on fees charged for tax and accounting services by geography. Members, $49.00; non-members, $125.00.

INTERNET DATABASES

Rutgers Accounting Web. Rutgers University Accounting Research Center. Phone: (973)353-5172;

Fax: (973)353-1283 • URL: http://www.rutgers.edu/accounting • RAW Web site provides extensive links to sources of national and international accounting information, such as the Big Six accounting firms, the Financial Accounting Standards Board (FASB), SEC filings (EDGAR), journals, publishers, software, the International Accounting Network, and "Internet's largest list of accounting firms in USA." Searching is offered. Fees: Free.

ONLINE DATABASES

Wilson Business Abstracts Online. H.W. Wilson Co. • Indexes and abstracts 600 major business periodicals, plus the *Wall Street Journal* and the business section of the *New York Times*. Indexing is from 1982, abstracting from 1990, with the two newspapers included from 1993. Updated weekly. Inquire as to online cost and availability. (*Business Periodicals Index* without abstracts is also available online.).

PERIODICALS AND NEWSLETTERS

Journal of Bank Cost and Management Accounting. Association for Management Information in Financial Services. • 3/year.

Management for Strategic Business Ideas. Society of Management Accountants of Canada. • 10 times a year. $60.00 per year. Text in English and French.

RESEARCH CENTERS AND INSTITUTES

Agency for Healthcare Research and Quality - Center for Financing, Access, and Cost Trends. John M. Eisenberg Bldg., 540 Gaither Rd., Rockville, MD 20850. Phone: (301)427-1104; Fax: (301)427-1276; Email: joel.cohen@ahrq.hhs.gov • URL: http://www.ahrq.gov/about/cfact • Cost and financing of health care and access to health care services and related trends. Develops data sets to support policy and behavioral research and analyses.

TRADE/PROFESSIONAL ASSOCIATIONS

American Institute of Certified Public Accountants. 1211 Avenue of the Americas, New York, NY 10036-8775. Phone: 888-777-7077 or (212)596-6200; Fax: (212)596-6213; Email: service@aicpa.org • URL: http://www.aicpa.org • Professional society of accountants certified by the states and territories. Responsibilities include establishing auditing and reporting standards; influencing the development of financial accounting standards underlying the presentation of U.S. corporate financial statements; preparing and grading the national Uniform CPA Examination for the state licensing bodies. Conducts research and continuing education programs and oversight of practice. Maintains over 100 committees including Accounting Standards, Accounting and Review Services, AICPA Effective Legislation Political Action, Auditing Standards, Taxation, Consulting Services, Professional Ethics, Quality Review, Women and Family Issues, and Information Technology.

Association for Management Information in Financial Services. 14247 Saffron Cir., Carmel, IN 46032. Phone: (317)815-5857; Email: ami2@amifs.org • URL: http://www.amifs.org • Members are financial institution employees interested in management accounting and cost analysis.

Institute of Management Accountants. Cost Management Group. 10 Paragon Dr., Ste. 1, Montvale, NJ 07645-1718. Phone: 800-638-4427 or (201)573-9000; Fax: (201)474-1600; Email: ima@imanet.org • URL: http://www.imanet.org • A group within the Institute of Management Accountants. Seeks to improve the quality of corporate cost management systems. Educates business professionals about decision-making and productivity improvement. Provides a means of exchanging opinions and experiences about cost management systems. Conducts surveys; compiles statistics.

COST CONTROL

See also COST ACCOUNTING

CD-ROM DATABASES

Authority Health Care Law Library. Matthew Bender and Company Inc. • Periodic updates. Price on request. Full text CD-ROM provides legal information, case law, and analysis relating to health care facilities, health insurance, longterm care, Medigap, and Medicare.

OTHER SOURCES

AACE International. Transactions of the Annual Meetings. American Assoiciation of Cost Engineers. AACE International. • Annual. Price varies. Contains texts of papers presented at AACE meetings.

PERIODICALS AND NEWSLETTERS

IT Cost Management Strategies: The Planning Assistant for IT Directors. Computer Economics Inc. • Monthly. $495.00 per year. Newsletter for information technology professionals. Covers data processing costs, budgeting, financial management, and related topics.

Strategic Finance. Institute of Management Accountants. • Monthly. $220 Nonmembers. Provides articles on corporate finance, cost control, cash flow, budgeting, corporate taxes, and other financial management topics.

Successful Cost Control Strategies for CEOs, Managers, and Administrators. Siefer Consultants Inc. • Monthly. $279.00 per year. Newsletter. Provides a variety of ideas on business budgeting and controlling company expenses. Formerly *Employee Cost Control Strategies for CEOs, Managers, and Administrators*.

COST OF LIVING INDEXES

See CONSUMER PRICE INDEXES

COSTUME JEWELRY

See JEWELRY BUSINESS

COTTON INDUSTRY

See also TEXTILE INDUSTRY

ABSTRACTS AND INDEXES

Textile Technology Index™. EBSCO Publishing Inc. • Monthly. $545 Individuals. Includes indexing and abstracts for more than 470 periodicals.

CD-ROM DATABASES

OECD Statistical Compendium. Organization for Economic Cooperation and Development. • Semiannual. $1,905.00 per year for 1 to 10 users. CD-ROM contains more than 730,000 monthly, quarterly, and annual time series for OECD countries, 1960 to date. Includes fully searchable data on agriculture, food, economic indicators, national accounts, employment, energy, finance, industry, technology, and foreign trade. Results can be displayed in various forms.

DIRECTORIES

Cotton Council International Buyers' Guide. Cotton Council International. • Covers: Exporters of U.S. raw cotton. Entries include: Company name, addresses of exporting companies, production and ginning seasons, and official U.S. cotton standards, packaging, and transportation data.

Directory of Chinese Manufacturers & Exporters of Cotton, Silk, Wool Raw and Waste. EXIM Infotek Private Ltd. • $10 Individuals. Covers: 50 Chinese manufacturers and exporters of cotton, cotton products, cotton pulp, goat's wool, mulberry silk, wool, wool and wool products. Entries include: Company name, postal address, city, country, phone, fax, e-mail and websites, contact person, designation, and product details.

INTERNET DATABASES

Business 2.0 Web Guide to the Best Business Links. Business 2.0 Media Inc. Phone: (415)293-4800; Email: support@business2.com • URL: http://www.business2.com/webguide • Web site presents an extensive, searchable directory of links to "the best, most informative, and authoritative web pages." Twenty main categories cover business, finance, career, company information, people, and technology topics, with thousands of subtopics, all linking to Web sites recommended by experienced business researchers. Fees: Free.

Fedstats. Federal Interagency Council on Statistical Policy. Phone: (202)395-7254 • URL: http://www.fedstats.gov • Web site features an efficient search facility for full-text statistics produced by more than 100 federal agencies, including the Census Bureau, the Bureau of Economic Analysis, and the Bureau of Labor Statistics. Boolean searches can be made within one agency or for all agencies combined. Links are offered to international statistical bureaus, including the UN, IMF, OECD, UNESCO, Eurostat, and 20 individual countries. Fees: Free.

FreeLunch.com. Economy.com, Inc. Phone: (610)696-8700; Fax: (610)696-1678 • URL: http://www.freelunch.com • Web site provides free access to more than 200 million economic and financial data series, covering industry, demographics, labor markets, prices, retail sales, government spending, trade, interest rates, housing starts, the stock market, etc. Data is available in either chart or table form. Searching is offered. Free, but registration required. Economy.com, Inc. also offers fee-based economic analysis at *The Dismal Scientist* site (www.dismal.com).

Manufacturing Profiles. U. S. Bureau of the Census. Phone: (301)763-4636 or (301)763-4100; Fax: (301)763-4794; Email: webmaster@census.gov • URL: http://www.census.gov/prod/www/abs/mfg-prof.html • The Census Bureau makes available free on PDF (Portable Document Format) an annual consolidation of the entire Current Industrial Report series, presenting "all the data compiled." Contains statistics on production, shipments, inventories, consumption, exports, imports, and orders for a wide variety of manufactured products.

USDA. U.S. National Institute of Standards and Technology. 100 Bureau Dr., Gaithersburg, MD 20899-1070. Phone: 800-877-8339 or (301)975-6478 or (202)720-2791; Fax: (301)975-8295; Email: inquiries@nist.gov • URL: http://www.nist.gov • The USDA home page has six sections: News and Information; What's New; About USDA; Agencies; Opportunities; Search and Help. Keyword searching is offered from the USDA home page and from various individual agency home pages. Agencies are the Economic Research Service, Agricultural Marketing Service, National Agricultural Statistics Service, National Agricultural Library, and about 12 others. Updating varies. Fees: Free.

ONLINE DATABASES

Textile Technology Index™. EBSCO Publishing Inc. • Monthly. $545 Individuals. Includes indexing and abstracts for more than 470 periodicals.

World Textiles. Elsevier. • Provides abstracting and indexing from 1970 of worldwide textile literature (periodicals, books, pamphlets, and reports). Includes U. S., European, and British patent information. Updating is monthly. Inquire as to online cost and availability.

PERIODICALS AND NEWSLETTERS

Cotton Digest International. Cotton Digest Co., Inc. • Monthly. $40. Textiles and Cotton merchandising magazine. Exports & Imports-Domestic & foreign.

Cotton Farming. One Grower Publishing L.L.C. • Monthly. $40 Individuals.

Cotton Grower. Meister Media Worldwide. • Monthly.

Journal of Natural Fibers. The Haworth Press Inc. • Quarterly. $400.00 per year to libraries; $45.00 per year to individuals. Covers applications, technology, research, and world markets relating to fibers from silk, wool, cotton, flax, hemp, jute, etc. Previously *Natural Fibres*, published annually.

PRICE SOURCES

Cotton Price Statistics. U.S. Department of Agriculture. • Annual.

The New York Times. Gannett Co., Inc. • Mon.-Sun. (morn.). $5.85 Individuals. Provides personal finance expertise.

Weekly Board of Trade, Cotton Exchange. New York Cotton Exchange. • Weekly. $100.00 per year.

RESEARCH CENTERS AND INSTITUTES

Institute of Textile Technology. College of Textiles, Box 8301, N Carolina State University, 2401 Research Dr., Raleigh, NC 27695-8301. Phone: (919)513-7583; Fax: (888)348-3512; Email: wgoneal@itt.edu • URL: http://www.itt.edu • Textile materials, processes, and technology, with an emphasis on processing, instrumentation, statistical quality control, and testing of raw materials and finished products. Special attention given to yarn manufacture, carding, finishing operations, operations research applications, computer applications to manufacturing, techniques for evaluation of fiber quality, chemical treatment of raw materials, mechanical blending of fibers, environmental and energy conservation, methods of improving fabric finishes, applications of statistical methods, simulation, expert systems, processing, and interrelation of production, costs, and quality in yarn and fabric manufacture.

University of Florida - Tropical Research and Education Center. 18905 SW 280th St., Homestead, FL 33031. Phone: (305)246-7000; Fax: (305)246-7003; Email: hom@gnv.ifas.ufl.edu • URL: http://trec.ifas.ufl.edu • Production of tropical and subtropical fruits and winter-grown vegetables, including studies in horticulture, pathology, entomology, plant breeding, soils, irrigation, plant nutrition, and tissue culture.

STATISTICS SOURCES

Agricultural Statistics. U.S. Department of Agriculture National Agricultural Statistics Service. • Annual. $46 Individuals. Provides a wide variety of statistical data relating to agricultural production, supplies, consumption, prices/price-supports, foreign trade, costs, and returns, as well as farm labor, loans, income, and population. In many cases, historical data is shown annually for 10 years. In addition to farm data, includes detailed fishery statistics.

Quality of Cotton Report. Agricultural Marketing Service. U.S. Department of Agriculture. • Weekly.

Survey of Current Business. U. S. Government Printing Office. • Published by Bureau of Economic Analysis, U. S. Department of Commerce. Presents a wide variety of business and economic data.

United States Census of Agriculture. U.S. Department of Agriculture National Agricultural Statistics Service. • Quinquennial. Provides uniform, comprehensive farming and ranching operations data for every U.S. state and county, including production expenses, market value of products, and operator characteristics.

TRADE/PROFESSIONAL ASSOCIATIONS

Cotton Council International. 1521 New Hampshire Ave. NW, Washington, DC 20036. Phone: (202)745-7805; Fax: (202)483-4040; Email: cottonusa@cotton.org • URL: http://www.cottonusa.org • Representatives of all segments of the U.S. cotton industry. Works as an international cotton sales promotion organization cooperating with cotton interests in foreign countries.

Cotton Inc. 6399 Weston Pkwy., Cary, NC 27513. Phone: (919)678-2220; Fax: (919)678-2230; Email: contact@cottoninc.com • URL: http://www.cottoninc.com • Represents cotton producers for research and promotion.

National Cotton Council of America. 7193 Goodlett Farms Pkwy., Cordova, TN 38016. Phone: (901)274-9030; Fax: (901)725-0510 • URL: http://www.cotton.org • Delegates are from 19 cotton producing states.

COTTON TEXTILE INDUSTRY

See TEXTILE INDUSTRY

COTTONSEED OIL INDUSTRY

See OIL AND FATS INDUSTRY

COUNCIL MANAGER PLAN

See MUNICIPAL GOVERNMENT

COUNSELING

See also PERSONNEL MANAGEMENT; VOCATIONAL GUIDANCE

ABSTRACTS AND INDEXES

Psychological Abstracts. American Psychological Association. • Monthly. Members, $815.00 per year; individuals and institutions, $1,207.00 per year. Covers the international literature of psychology and the behavioral sciences. Includes journals, technical reports, dissertations, and other sources.

DIRECTORIES

Marriage & Family Counselors Directory. Info-Group Inc. • Annual. Number of listings: 55,129. Entries include: Name, address, phone, size of advertisement, name of owner or manager, number of employees, year first in "Yellow Pages." Compiled from telephone company "Yellow Pages," nationwide.

ENCYCLOPEDIAS AND DICTIONARIES

Encyclopedia of E-Leadership, Counseling and Training. Cengage Learning Inc. • Offers an in-depth description of key terms and concepts related to different themes, issues, and trends in educational leadership, counseling, and technology integration in modern universities and organizations worldwide.

PERIODICALS AND NEWSLETTERS

Counseling and Values. Association for Spiritual, Ethical and Religious Values in Counseling. American Counseling Association. • Semiannual. $107 Nonmembers print or online. Journal focusing on the role of values and religion in counseling and psychology.

The Counseling Psychologist. Pine Forge Press. • 8/year. £1,194 Institutions print & e-access. Journal for counseling psychologists. Published in association with the Division of Counseling Psychology of the American Psychological Association.

Counseling Services: IACS Newsletter. International Association of Counseling Services. • Three times a year. Membership.

Counselor: The Magazine for Addiction Professionals. Health Communications, Inc. • Bimonthly. $9.95 Individuals /year, online only. Covers both clinical and societal aspects of substance abuse.

Journal of Workplace Behavior Health. The Haworth Press Inc. • Quarterly. $160 Individuals print + online. An academic and practical journal focusing on employee alcoholism and mental health problems. Formerly *Labor-Management Alcoholism Journal.*

RESEARCH CENTERS AND INSTITUTES

Mississippi State University - Bureau of Educational Research and Evaluation. PO Box 9710, Mississippi State, MS 39762. Phone: (662)325-3717; Fax: (662)325-8784; Email: rhr2@colled.msstate.edu • URL: http://www.msstate.edu.

TRADE/PROFESSIONAL ASSOCIATIONS

American Counseling Association. 5999 Stevenson Ave., Alexandria, VA 22304. Phone: 800-347-6647; Fax: (703)823-0252; Email: membership@counseling.org • URL: http://www.counseling.org • Counseling professionals in elementary and secondary schools, higher education, community agencies and organizations, rehabilitation programs, government, industry, business, private practice, career counseling, and mental health counseling. Conducts professional development institutes and provides liability insurance. Maintains Counseling and Human Development Foundation to fund counseling projects.

American Mental Health Counselors Association. 801 N Fairfax St., Ste. 304, Alexandria, VA 22314. Phone: 800-326-2642 or (703)548-6002; Fax: (703)548-4775 • URL: http://www.amhca.org • Professional counselors employed in mental health services; students. Aims to: deliver quality mental health services to children, youth, adults, families, and organizations; improve the availability and quality of counseling services through licensure and certification, training standards, and consumer advocacy. Supports specialty and special interest networks. Fosters communication among members. A division of the American Counseling Association.

American Rehabilitation Counseling Association. c/o Quiteya Walker, President-Elect, Albany State University, College of Education, 504 College Dr., Albany, GA 31705. Phone: (252)744-6297 or (229)430-4783; Fax: (229)430-4993 • URL: http://www.arcaweb.org • A division of the American Counseling Association. Rehabilitation counselors and interested professionals and students. Aims to improve the rehabilitation counseling profession and its services to individuals with disabilities. Promotes high standards in rehabilitation counseling, practice, research, and education. Encourages the exchange of information between rehabilitation professionals and consumer groups. Serves as liaison among members and public and private rehabilitation counselors across the country. Sponsors educational and training programs.

Association of Career Management Consulting Firms International. 204 E St., NE, Washington, DC 20002. Phone: (202)547-6344; Fax: (202)547-6348; Email: acf@acfinternational.org • Firms providing displaced employees who are sponsored by their organization, with counsel and assistance in job searching and the techniques and practices of choosing a career.

COUNTERFEITING

See also CRIME AND CRIMINALS; FORGERIES

DIRECTORIES

Glasses Directory--Wholesale. InfoGroup Inc. • Annual. Number of listings: 2,221. Entries include: Name, address, phone, size of advertisement, name of owner or manager, number of employees, year first in "Yellow Pages." Compiled from telephone company "Yellow Pages," nationwide.

TRADE/PROFESSIONAL ASSOCIATIONS

Coalition Against Counterfeiting and Piracy. US Chamber of Commerce, Global Intellectual Property Center, 1615 H St. NW, Washington, DC 20062-0001. Phone: (202)463-5601; Fax: (202)463-3114; Email: gipc@uschamber.com • URL: http://www.theglobalipcenter.com/index.php/cacp • Aims to fight the threat of counterfeiting and piracy to the economy, jobs, consumer health and safety. Strives to increase understanding of the negative impact of counterfeiting and piracy. Seeks to find real solutions by working with government, industry, opinion leaders, the media and consumers.

COUNTERTRADE

See BARTER AND COUNTERTRADE

COUNTRY CLUBS

See CLUBS

COUNTY FINANCE

See also PUBLIC FINANCE

DIRECTORIES

Mergent Municipal and Government Manual. Mergent Inc. • Covers all U.S. taxing jurisdictions and agencies with total long-term rated debt of $25,000,000 or over.

STATISTICS SOURCES

United States Census of Governments. Bureau of the Census, U.S. Department of Commerce. U. S. Government Printing Office. • Quinquennial.

TRADE/PROFESSIONAL ASSOCIATIONS

Association of Government Accountants. 2208 Mt. Vernon Ave., Alexandria, VA 22301-1314. Phone: 800-AGA-7211 or (703)684-6931; Fax: (703)548-9367; Email: agamembers@agacgfm.org • URL: http://www.agacgfm.org • Members are employed by federal, state, county, and city government agencies. Includes accountants, auditors, budget officers, and other government finance administrators and officials.

National Association of County Collectors, Treasurers and Finance Officers. PO Box 385, Stanton, NE 68779. Phone: (402)439-2223; Fax: (402)439-2262 • URL: http://www.nacctfo.org • Elected and appointed county treasurers, tax collectors and finance officers. Promotes improved and efficient operating and financial procedures in the financial administration of county tax revenue collection.

COUNTY GOVERNMENT

See also MUNICIPAL GOVERNMENT

BIOGRAPHICAL SOURCES

Who's Who in American Politics. Marquis Who's Who L.L.C. • Biennial. $349 Individuals. Contains about 27,000 biographical sketches of local, state, and national elected or appointed individuals.

DIRECTORIES

Carroll's County Directory. Caroll Publishing. • Annual. $500 Individuals 2 issues per year. Covers over 51,000 officials in more than 3,000 counties; includes elected, appointed, and career office holders.

Carroll's Municipal/County Directory. Caroll Publishing. • Semiannual. $500 Individuals. Provides listings of about 90,000 city, town, and county officials in the U. S.

Government Phone Book USA: Your Comprehensive Guide to Federal, State, County, and Local Government Offices in the United States. Omnigraphics Inc. • Annual. $265.00. Contains more than 270,000 listings of federal, state, county, and local government offices and personnel, including legislatures. Formerly *Government Directory of Addresses and Phone Numbers.*

Municipal Yellow Book: Who's Who in the Leading City and County Governments and Local Authorities. Leadership Directories Inc. • Annual. $465 /year. Lists approximately 30,000 key personnel in city and county departments, agencies, subdivisions, and branches.

OTHER SOURCES

Local Government Law. Chester J. Antieau. Matthew Bender and Company Inc. • $2,619 Print. States the principle of law for all types of local governments, and backs those principles with case citations from all jurisdictions. Examines the laws and their impact in three primary cases.

PERIODICALS AND NEWSLETTERS

County News. National Association of Counties. • Semimonthly.

Governing: The States and Localities. • Monthly. $39.95 per year. Edited for state and local government officials. Covers finance, office management, computers, telecommunications, environmental concerns, etc.

Public Risk. Public Risk Management Association. • Monthly. $130 Individuals. Covers risk management for state and local governments, including various kinds of liabilities.

STATISTICS SOURCES

United States Census of Governments. Bureau of the Census, U.S. Department of Commerce. U. S. Government Printing Office. • Quinquennial.

TRADE/PROFESSIONAL ASSOCIATIONS

National Association of Counties. 25 Massachusetts Ave. NW, Ste. 500, Washington, DC 20001. Phone: 888-407-6226 or (202)393-6226; Fax: (202)393-2630; Email: naco@naco.org • URL: http://www.naco.org • Formerly National Association of County Human Services Administrators.

National Association of County Planners. 440 1st St. NW, 8th Fl., Washington, DC 20001. Phone: (202)661-8807; Fax: (202)737-0480; Email: jdavenpo@naco.org • URL: http://www.countyplanning.org • Formerly National Association of County Planning Directors.

Public Risk Management Association. 700 S Washington St., Ste. 218, Alexandria, VA 22314. Phone: (703)528-7701; Fax: (703)739-0200; Email: info@primacentral.org • URL: http://www.primacentral.org • Public agency risk, insurance, human resources, attorneys, and/or safety managers from cities, counties, villages, towns, school boards, and other related areas. Provides an information clearinghouse and communications network for public risk managers to share resources, ideas, and experiences. Offers information on risk, insurance, and safety management. Monitors state and federal legislative actions and court decisions that deal with immunity, tort liability, and intergovernmental risk pools. Maintains library containing current reports from governmental units on their insurance procedures, self-insurance plans, and loss control and safety programs; and copies of policy statements, job descriptions, contractual arrangements, and indemnification clauses.

COUNTY OFFICIALS

See COUNTY GOVERNMENT

COUNTY PLANNING

See REGIONAL PLANNING

COUPONS AND REFUNDS

ABSTRACTS AND INDEXES

Business Periodicals Index Retrospective. EBSCO Publishing Inc. • 11/year. Quarterly and annual cumulations.

CD-ROM DATABASES

Business Abstracts with Full Text. EBSCO Publishing Inc. • Includes full text articles from more than 460 business publications from 1982 to present. Indexing for nearly 880 publications.

ONLINE DATABASES

Wilson Business Abstracts Online. H.W. Wilson Co. • Indexes and abstracts 600 major business periodicals, plus the *Wall Street Journal* and the business section of the *New York Times.* Indexing is from 1982, abstracting from 1990, with the two newspapers included from 1993. Updated weekly. Inquire as to online cost and availability. (*Business Periodicals Index* without abstracts is also available online.).

PERIODICALS AND NEWSLETTERS

Moneytalk. Jean Kwiatowski. • Description: Provides suggestions for saving money through the use of coupons and refund offers. Recurring features include letters to the editor and news of research.

PROMO: Promotion Marketing Worldwide. Primedia Business Magazines and Media. • Monthly. $65.00 per year. Edited for companies and agencies that utilize couponing, point-of-purchase advertising, special events, games, contests, premiums, product samples, and other unique promotional items.

Refundable Bundle. • Bimonthly. $10.00 per year. Newsletter for grocery shoppers. Each issue provides details of new coupon and refund offers.

COURTS

See also LAW; LAWS; LAWYERS

ABSTRACTS AND INDEXES

Current Law Index. Cengage Learning Inc. • $1,332 Individuals. Monthly. $1269.00 per year. Produced in cooperation with the American Association of Law Libraries. Indexes more than 900 law journals, legal newspapers, and specialty publications from the U.S., Canada, U.K., Ireland, Australia, and New Zealand.

Index to Legal Periodicals and Books. H.W. Wilson Co. • Monthly. $490.00 per year. Quarterly and annual cumulations.

ALMANACS AND YEARBOOKS

American Law Yearbook. Cengage Learning Inc. • $308 Individuals. Annual. $280.00. Serves as a yearly supplement to *West's Encyclopedia of American Lawa.* Describes new legal developments in many subject areas.

BIOGRAPHICAL SOURCES

Who's Who in American Law. Marquis Who's Who L.L.C. • Biennial. $345 Individuals. Contains over 23,000 concise biographies of American lawyers, judges, and others in the legal field.

CD-ROM DATABASES

Index to Legal Periodicals and Books. EBSCO Publishing Inc. • Contains indexing of more than

1,400 English language legal periodicals from 1981 to date and 2,500 books.

DIRECTORIES

Carroll's Federal & Federal Regional Directory. Caroll Publishing. • Semiannual. $500 Individuals. Lists more than 23,000 U. S. government officials throughout the country, including military installations.

Carroll's Federal Directory. Caroll Publishing. • $550 Single issue 4 issues per year. Covers approximately 37,000 executive managers in federal government offices in Washington, DC, including executive, congressional and judicial branches; members of Congress and Congressional committees and staff.

Federal-State Court Directory. Leadership Directories Inc. • Annual. $20 Individuals plus S&H. Covers: All federal court judges and clerks of court, and United States attorneys and magistrates, judges; state supreme court chief justices and state court administrators; Supreme Court Chief Justices of Canada and other nations. Database includes: Organization charts for state court systems. Entries include: Judge, clerk, probation office, or magistrate's name, address, phone.

Judicial Staff Directory: With Biographical Information on Judges and Key Court Staff. CQ Press. • Semiannual. $450.00. $225.00 per volume. Lists 33,500 federal court personnel, including 1,900 federal judges and their staffs, including biographies of judges and key executives. Includes maps of court jurisdictions.

Judicial Yellow Book: Who's Who in Federal and State Courts. Leadership Directories Inc. • Semiannual. $465 /year. Lists more than 3,200 judges and staffs in various federal courts and 1,200 judges and staffs in state courts. Includes biographical profiles of judges.

ENCYCLOPEDIAS AND DICTIONARIES

Encyclopedia of Crime and Justice. Cengage Learning Inc. • 2001. $737. 2nd edition. 4 volumes. Published by Macmillan Reference USA. Contains extensive information on a wide variety of topics pertaining to crime, criminology, social issues, and the courts. Also available as eBook.

West's Encyclopedia of American Law. Cengage Learning Inc. • 2004. eBook. Second edition. Covers a wide variety of legal topics for the general reader. Inquire for pricing.

INTERNET DATABASES

Lexis.com Research System. Lexis-Nexis Group. Phone: 800-227-4908 or (937)865-6800; Fax: (937)865-6909; Email: webmaster@prod.lexis-nexis.com • URL: http://www.nexis.com • Fee-based Web site offers extensive searching of a wide variety of legal sources. Additional features include Daily Opinion Service, lexis.com Bookstore, Career Center, CLE Center, Law Schools, and Practice Pages ("Pages specific to areas of specialty").

PERIODICALS AND NEWSLETTERS

Court Review. American Judges Association. National Center for State Courts. • Quarterly. Journal for members of the American Judges Association.

Family Court Review: An Interdisciplinary Journal. Association of Family and Conciliation Courts. Pine Forge Press. • Quarterly. Institutions, $456.00 per year.

United States Law Week: A National Survey of Current Law. Bloomberg BNA. • Weekly. $1,152.00 per year. Covers U.S. Supreme Court proceedings and gives full text of decisions. Also provides detailed reports on important legislative and regulatory actions.

U.S. Supreme Court Bulletin. Wolters Kluwer Law & Business CCH. • Monthly and on each decision day while the Court is in session.

STATISTICS SOURCES

Annual Report of the Director. Administrative Office of the United States Courts. • Annual.

TRADE/PROFESSIONAL ASSOCIATIONS

National Association for Court Management. National Center for State Courts, 300 Newport Ave., Williamsburg, VA 23185-4147. Phone: 800-616-6165 or (757)259-1841; Fax: (757)259-1520; Email: nacm@ncsc.org • URL: http://nacmnet.org • Court management professionals. Aims to foster communication among members. Conducts educational programs.

National Center for State Courts. 300 Newport Ave., Williamsburg, VA 23185. Phone: 800-616-6164 or (757)259-1525 or (757)259-1826; Fax: (757)220-0449; Email: jcochet@ncsc.org • URL: http://www.ncsc.org • Provides assistance to state and local trial and appellate courts in improving their structure and administration. Furnishes consultant services; conducts national studies and projects; acts as a clearinghouse for exchange of information on court problems; coordinates activities of other organizations involved in judicial improvement, providing secretariat services for several. Conducts conferences and training courses. Compiles statistics on state court caseload and administrative operations. Research includes: appellate procedures, pretrial services, court delay, alternatives to incarceration, juvenile justice, rural court services, alternative dispute resolution, jury management, and sentencing and judicial information systems. Offers placement service.

National Council of Juvenile and Family Court Judges. PO Box 8970, Reno, NV 89507-8970. Phone: (775)784-6012; Fax: (775)784-6628; Email: staff@ncjfcj.org • URL: http://www.ncjfcj.org • Judges with juvenile and family court jurisdiction and others with a professional interest in the nation's juvenile justice system. Works to further more effective administration of justice for young people through the improvement of juvenile and family court standards and practices. Sponsors continuing education programs. Compiles and disseminates research data.

CREATIVITY

ABSTRACTS AND INDEXES

Psychological Abstracts. American Psychological Association. • Monthly. Members, $815.00 per year; individuals and institutions, $1,207.00 per year. Covers the international literature of psychology and the behavioral sciences. Includes journals, technical reports, dissertations, and other sources.

ALMANACS AND YEARBOOKS

Creativity. Art Directon Book Company Inc. • Annual. $62.95.

PERIODICALS AND NEWSLETTERS

Business 2.0. Time Inc. • General business magazine emphasizing ideas, insight, and innovation.

Fast Company: How Smart Business Works. Fast Company, Inc. • Monthly. $12.00 per year. Covers business management, with emphasis on creativity, leadership, innovation, career advancement, teamwork, the global economy, and the "new workplace.".

RESEARCH CENTERS AND INSTITUTES

Center for Studies in Creativity - State University of New York College at Buffalo. 1300 Elmwood Ave., Buffalo, NY 14222. Phone: (716)878-6223 or (716)878-4000; Fax: (716)878-4040; Email: createps@buffalostate.edu • URL: http://suny.buffalostate.edu.

TRADE/PROFESSIONAL ASSOCIATIONS

Supporting Emotional Needs of the Gifted. PO Box 488, Poughquag, NY 12570. Phone: (845)797-5054; Fax: (866)728-4990; Email: office@sengifted.org • URL: http://www.sengifted.org.

CREDIT

See also AGRICULTURAL CREDIT; CONSUMER CREDIT; CREDIT INSURANCE; CREDIT MANAGEMENT; FOREIGN CREDIT

CD-ROM DATABASES

Business Abstracts with Full Text. EBSCO Publishing Inc. • Includes full text articles from more than 460 business publications from 1982 to present. Indexing for nearly 880 publications.

CreditDisk 2.0. Fitch. • Price and frequency on application. CD-ROM provides credit research and ratings on individual banks throughout the world, with Internet updating. Includes graphic displays of rating histories and financial ratios.

EconLit. Ovid Technologies Inc. • Updated monthly. Lists journal articles, book reviews, disserations of economic literature. Over 1,400 journals covered.

OECD Statistical Compendium. Organization for Economic Cooperation and Development. • Semiannual. $1,905.00 per year for 1 to 10 users. CD-ROM contains more than 730,000 monthly, quarterly, and annual time series for OECD countries, 1960 to date. Includes fully searchable data on agriculture, food, economic indicators, national accounts, employment, energy, finance, industry, technology, and foreign trade. Results can be displayed in various forms.

DIRECTORIES

A-Z Credit Directory. Legal & Commercial State Services Ltd. • Annual. Covers: Over 30,000 credit records of companies and individuals in the Republic of Ireland. Entries include: Company or personal name and address.

Creditreform-Datenbank. Verband der Vereine Creditreform e.V. • Daily. Database covers: Credit information on more than 3,100,000 million joint stock and individual trading companies in Austria and Germany. Entries include: Company name, address, legal form, dates of formation or reformation, capital, partners, number of employees, product line, financial indicators covering capital, obligations, annual income, property and equipment, warehouse stocks, loan payment record, liabilities, credit rating, biographical information on company principal officials.

SBA Loans: A Step-by-Step Guide. John Wiley & Sons Inc. • $27.95 Individuals paperback. Publication includes: A directory of Small Business Association field offices and a directory of services offered by the SBA. Principal content of publication is Step-by-step information of locating and securing a small business loan, including developing a business plan, researching finance options, recent lending statistics, eligibility requirements and other details.

HANDBOOKS AND MANUALS

Manual of Credit and Commercial Laws. National Association of Credit Management. National Association of Credit Management. • Annual. $69.95 Individuals. Provides information for credit professionals. Formerly *Credit Manual of Commercial Laws*.

INTERNET DATABASES

Business 2.0 Web Guide to the Best Business Links. Business 2.0 Media Inc. Phone: (415)293-4800; Email: support@business2.com • URL: http://www.business2.com/webguide • Web site presents an extensive, searchable directory of links to "the best, most informative, and authoritative web pages." Twenty main categories cover business, finance, career, company information, people, and technol-

ogy topics, with thousands of subtopics, all linking to Web sites recommended by experienced business researchers. Fees: Free.

EBSCO Information Services. EBSCO Publishing Inc. 10 Estes St., Ipswich, MA 01938-2106. Phone: 800-653-2726 or (978)356-6500; Fax: (978)356-6565; Email: information@ebscohost.com • URL: http://www.ebscohost.com • Fee-based Web site providing Internet access to a wide variety of databases, including business-related material. Full text is available for many periodical titles, with daily updates. Fees: Apply.

Fedstats. Federal Interagency Council on Statistical Policy. Phone: (202)395-7254 • URL: http://www.fedstats.gov • Web site features an efficient search facility for full-text statistics produced by more than 100 federal agencies, including the Census Bureau, the Bureau of Economic Analysis, and the Bureau of Labor Statistics. Boolean searches can be made within one agency or for all agencies combined. Links are offered to international statistical bureaus, including the UN, IMF, OECD, UNESCO, Eurostat, and 20 individual countries. Fees: Free.

FreeLunch.com. Economy.com, Inc. Phone: (610)696-8700; Fax: (610)696-1678 • URL: http://www.freelunch.com • Web site provides free access to more than 200 million economic and financial data series, covering industry, demographics, labor markets, prices, retail sales, government spending, trade, interest rates, housing starts, the stock market, etc. Data is available in either chart or table form. Searching is offered. Free, but registration required. Economy.com, Inc. also offers fee-based economic analysis at *The Dismal Scientist* site (www.dismal.com).

InSite 2. Intelligence Data/Thomson Financial. Phone: 800-654-0393 or (617)856-1890; Fax: (617)737-3182; Email: intelligence.data@tfn.com • URL: http://www.insite2.gale.com/ • Fee-based Web site consolidates information in a "Base Pack" consisting of Business InSite, Market InSite, and Company InSite. Optional databases are Consumer InSite, Health and Wellness InSite, Newsletter InSite, and Computer InSite. Includes fulltext content from more than 2,500 trade publications, journals, newsletters, newspapers, analyst reports, and other sources. Continuous updating. Formerly produced by The Gale Group.

ProQuest. ProQuest L.L.C. 789 E Eisenhower Pkwy., Ann Arbor, MI 48106-1346. Phone: 800-521-0600 or (734)761-4700; Fax: (734)662-4554; Email: info@proquest.com • URL: http://www.proquest.com • Fee-based Web site providing Internet access to more than 3,000 periodicals, newspapers, and other publications. Many items are available full-text, with daily updates. Includes extensive corporate and financial information. Fees: Apply.

Summary of Commentary on Current Economic Conditions by Federal Reserve District. Board of Governors of the Federal Reserve System. Phone: (202)452-3000; Fax: (202)452-3819 • URL: http://www.federalreserve.gov/publications.htm • 8/year. Free Web site provides current "anecdotal information" eight times a year on economic conditions within each of the 12 Federal Reserve Districts, plus an extensive national *Summary*. Text is based on the opinions of bank officials, business executives, economists, financial market experts, and others. Typically contains views of consumer spending, manufacturing, services, credit, employment, prices, wages, and the economy in general. Usually referred to as the Beige Book.

ONLINE DATABASES

Accounting and Tax Database. ProQuest L.L.C. • Provides indexing and abstracting of the literature of accounting, taxation, and financial management, 1971 to date. Updating is weekly. Especially covers accounting, auditing, banking, bankruptcy, employee compensation and benefits, cash management, financial planning, and credit. Inquire as to online cost and availability.

Banking Information Source. ProQuest L.L.C. • Provides indexing and abstracting of periodical and other literature from 1982 to date, with weekly updates. Covers the financial services industry: banks, savings institutions, investment houses, credit unions, insurance companies, and real estate organizations. Emphasis is on marketing and management. Inquire as to online cost and availability. (Formerly *FINIS: Financial Industry Information Service.*).

TRW Business Credit Profiles. Experian Information Solutions Inc. • Provides credit history (trade payments, payment trends, payment totals, payment history, etc.) for public and private U. S. companies. Key facts and banking information are also given. Updates are weekly. Inquire as to online cost and availability.

Wilson Business Abstracts Online. H.W. Wilson Co. • Indexes and abstracts 600 major business periodicals, plus the *Wall Street Journal* and the business section of the *New York Times*. Indexing is from 1982, abstracting from 1990, with the two newspapers included from 1993. Updated weekly. Inquire as to online cost and availability. (*Business Periodicals Index* without abstracts is also available online.).

PERIODICALS AND NEWSLETTERS

American Banker: The Financial Services Daily. SourceMedia Inc. • Daily. $895.00 per year. Provides news of banking, investment products, mortgages, credit unions, finance, bank technology, and legal developments.

Credit Executive Letter. American Financial Services Association. • Monthly. Members, $12.00 per year; non-members, $22.00 per year.

Grant's Interest Rate Observer. Grant's Financial Publishing Inc. • Biweekly. $1,025 Individuals. Newsletter containing detailed analysis of money-related topics, including interest rate trends, global credit markets, fixed-income investments, bank loan policies, and international money markets.

International Bank Credit Analyst. BCA Publications Ltd. • Monthly. $795.00 per year. "A monthly forecast and analysis of currency movements, interest rates, and stock market developments in the principal countries, based on a continuous appraisal of money and credit trends worldwide." Includes many charts and graphs providing international coverage of money, credit, and securities.

U.S. Banker. SourceMedia Inc. • Monthly. $65.00 per year. Edited for bank executives and managers. Covers a wide variety of banking and financial topics.

RESEARCH CENTERS AND INSTITUTES

Princeton University - Bendheim Center for Finance. Department of Economics, 26 Prospect Ave., Princeton, NJ 08540-5296. Phone: (609)258-0770; Fax: (609)258-0771; Email: jessicab@princeton.edu • URL: http://www.princeton.edu/bcf • Research areas include securities markets, portfolio analysis, credit markets, and corporate finance. Emphasis is on quantitative and mathematical perspectives.

STATISTICS SOURCES

Statistical Information on the Financial Services Industry. American Bankers Association. • Annual. Members, $150.00; non-members, $275.00. Presents a wide variety of data relating to banking and financial services, including consumer economics, personal finance, credit, government loans, capital markets, and international banking.

Survey of Current Business. U. S. Government Printing Office. • Published by Bureau of Economic Analysis, U. S. Department of Commerce. Presents a wide variety of business and economic data.

TRADE/PROFESSIONAL ASSOCIATIONS

Credit Builders Alliance. 1701 K St. NW, Ste. 1000, Washington, DC 20006. Phone: (202)730-9390; Fax: (202)350-9430; Email: info@creditbuildersalliance.org • URL: http://www.creditbuildersalliance.org • Represents the interests of community lenders including CDFIs, microenterprise and housing development organizations, asset building organizations and community credit unions. Provides assistance to low and moderate income individuals served by non-traditional financial and asset building institutions to build their credit and financial access. Raises awareness to open new credit building opportunities for low-income and underserved populations.

Credit Professionals International. 10726 Manchester Rd., Ste. 210, Saint Louis, MO 63122. Phone: (314)821-9393; Fax: (314)821-7171; Email: creditpro@creditprofessionals.org • URL: http://www.creditprofessionals.org • Represents individuals employed in credit or collection departments of business firms or professional offices. Conducts educational program in credit work. Sponsors Career Club composed of members who have been involved in credit work for at least 25 years.

Forius Business Credit Resources. 8441 Wayzata Blvd., Ste. 270, Golden Valley, MN 55426. Phone: 800-279-6226 or (763)253-4300 • URL: http://www.forius.com • Represents credit executives and owners of distribution and manufacturing companies. Promotes mutually beneficial ideas on credit techniques and methods. Provides a forum for the exchange of credit information.

National Association of Credit Management. 8840 Columbia 100 Pkwy., Columbia, MD 21045-2158. Phone: (410)740-5560; Fax: (410)740-5574; Email: nacm_national@nacm.org • URL: http://www.nacm.org • Formerly National Institute of Credit.

Society of Certified Credit Executives. ACA International, 4040 W 70th St., Minneapolis, MN 55435. Phone: (952)926-6547; Fax: (952)926-1624; Email: aca@acainternational.org • URL: http://www.acainternational.org • A division of the International Credit Association. Credit executives who have been certified through SCCE's professional certification programs. Seeks to improve industry operations while expanding the knowledge of its members. Maintains placement service.

CREDIT, BANK

See BANK LOANS

CREDIT CARD INDUSTRY

ABSTRACTS AND INDEXES

Business Periodicals Index Retrospective. EBSCO Publishing Inc. • 11/year. Quarterly and annual cumulations.

DIRECTORIES

International Association of Financial Crimes Investigators: Membership Directory. International Association of Financial Crimes Investigators. • Annual. About 3,500 firms and individuals engaged in investigation of fraudulent use of credit cards. Formerly *International Association of Credit Card Investigators-Membership Directory.*

Low Rate and No Fee Credit Card List. Bankcard Holders of America. • Quarterly. $4.00 per copy. Lists about 50 banks offering relatively low interest rates and/or no annual fee for credit card accounts. Formerly *Low Interest Rate.*

INTERNET DATABASES

BanxQuote Banking, Mortgage, and Finance Center. BanxQuote, Inc. Phone: (914)722-1600;

Fax: (914)722-6630; Email: info@banx.com • URL: http://www.banx.com • Daily. Web site quotes interest rates paid by banks around the country on various savings products, as well as rates paid by consumers for automobile loans, mortgages, credit cards, home equity loans, and personal loans. Also provided: stock quotes, indexes, stock options, futures trading data, economic indicators, and links to many other financial sites.

ONLINE DATABASES

Wilson Business Abstracts Online. H.W. Wilson Co. • Indexes and abstracts 600 major business periodicals, plus the *Wall Street Journal* and the business section of the *New York Times*. Indexing is from 1982, abstracting from 1990, with the two newspapers included from 1993. Updated weekly. Inquire as to online cost and availability. (*Business Periodicals Index* without abstracts is also available online.).

OTHER SOURCES

Internet Payments Report. Jupitermedia Corp. • Annual. $1,095.00. Market research report. Provides data, comment, and forecasts on the collection of electronic payments ("e-money") for goods and services offered through the Internet.

PERIODICALS AND NEWSLETTERS

Card News: The Executive Report on the Transaction Card Marketplace. Access Intelligence L.L.C. • 25 times per year. $997.00 per year. Newsletter on transaction cards, debit and credit cards, automatic teller machines, etc.

Card Technology. SourceMedia Inc. • Monthly. $79.00 per year. Covers advanced technology for credit, debit, and other cards. Topics include smart cards, optical recognition, and card design.

Credit Card Management: The Magazine of Electronic Payments. SourceMedia Inc. • Monthly. $98.00 per year. Edited for bankers and other managers of electronic payment systems.

Credit Executive Letter. American Financial Services Association. • Monthly. Members, $12.00 per year; non-members, $22.00 per year.

Credit Risk Management. Phillips International, Inc. • Biweekly. $695.00 per year. Newsletter on consumer credit, including delinquency aspects.

Directory of Credit Card Merchant Processors: The Directory of Credit Card & Ecommerce Sources for Small Business. PM Financial Services. • Annual. $10. Credit card merchant processors in the United States.

The Nilson Report. HSN Consultants Inc. • Description: Provides information about the credit card industry.

Online Marketplace. Jupiter Communications. • Description: Keeps abreast of the fast-emerging developments in the digital marketplace and emerging interactive technologies. Reports on players and devices to provide the "inside scoop" on this marketplace. Topics include screen phones, interactive television, and smart cards, to name a few. Recurring features include interviews, and columns titled Tool Watch, Site Watch, and News Digest.

STATISTICS SOURCES

Statistical Information on the Financial Services Industry. American Bankers Association. • Annual. Members, $150.00; non-members, $275.00. Presents a wide variety of data relating to banking and financial services, including consumer economics, personal finance, credit, government loans, capital markets, and international banking.

TRADE/PROFESSIONAL ASSOCIATIONS

American Financial Services Association. 919 18th St. NW, Ste. 300, Washington, DC 20006. Email: info@afsamail.org • URL: http://www.afsaonline.org • Represents companies whose business is primarily direct credit lending to consumers and/or the purchase of sales finance paper on consumer goods. Has members that have insurance and retail subsidiaries; some are themselves subsidiaries of highly diversified parent corporations. Encourages the business of financing individuals and families for necessary and useful purposes at reasonable charges, including interest; promotes consumer understanding of basic money management principles as well as constructive uses of consumer credit. Includes educational services such as films, textbooks and study units for the classroom and budgeting guides for individuals and families. Compiles statistical reports; offers seminars.

CardTrak. 99 Vandebilt Beach Rd., 2nd Fl., Naples, FL 34108. Phone: 800-344-7714; Email: media@cardtrak.com • URL: http://www.cardtrak.com • Promotes the "wise and careful" use of credit cards. A consumer organization.

National Foundation for Credit Counseling. 2000 M St. NW, Ste. 505, Washington, DC 20036. Phone: (202)677-4300 • URL: http://www.nfcc.org • Supersedes Retail Credit Institute of America.

CREDIT, CONSUMER

See CONSUMER CREDIT

CREDIT INSURANCE

See also INSURANCE

TRADE/PROFESSIONAL ASSOCIATIONS

Consumer Credit Industry Association. 6300 Powers Ferry Rd., Ste. 600-286, Atlanta, GA 30339. Phone: (678)858-4001; Email: sjcipinko@cciaonline.com • URL: http://www.cciaonline.com • Insurance companies underwriting consumer credit insurance in areas of life insurance, accident and health insurance, and property insurance.

CREDIT MANAGEMENT

See also CREDIT

PERIODICALS AND NEWSLETTERS

Business Credit. National Association of Credit Management. • 9/year. $54 U.S.. Formerly *Credit and Financial Management*. Covers business and trade credit as well as risk management.

Collections and Credit Risk: The Authority for Commercial and Consumer Credit Professionals. SourceMedia Inc. • Monthly. $95.00 per year. Contains articles on the technology and business management of credit and collection functions. Includes coverage of bad debts, bankruptcy, and credit risk management.

TRADE/PROFESSIONAL ASSOCIATIONS

Advertising Media Credit Executives Association. 24600 Detroit Rd., Ste. 100, Bay Village, OH 44140-0036. Email: amcea@tx.rr.com • URL: http://www.amcea.org • Credit executives for advertising media such as newspapers, magazines, radio, and television. Provides information for exchange of ideas on credit management methods and procedures; encourages study in advanced educational courses in fundamentals, such as business law, finance, banking, accounting, and economics.

Alliance Credit Counseling. 15720 John J. Delaney Dr., Ste. 575, Charlotte, NC 28277. Phone: 888-594-9554 or (704)341-1010; Fax: (704)540-5495; Email: service@knowdebt.org • URL: http://www.knowdebt.org • Provides help and hope through personalized education, counseling and support programs that seek to reduce and avoid the burdens of financial crisis, debt stress, bankruptcy and consequences. Provides empowerment to the public through charitable education programs of financial literacy, money management, credit management and debt reduction. Offers services of financial counseling, education and debt management.

Business Products Credit Association. 607 Westridge Dr., O Fallon, MO 63366-2439. Phone: 888-514-2722 or (360)612-9507 or (636)294-5775; Fax: (636)754-0567; Email: service@bpca.org • URL: http://www.bpca.org • Member-owned credit association serving businesses. Assists members in protecting their accounts receivable. Provides credit reporting services, collection service letters and business alert reports. Conducts educational programs; compiles statistics.

Credit Research Foundation. 1812 Baltimore Blvd., Ste. H, Westminster, MD 21157. Phone: (443)821-3000; Fax: (443)821-3627 • URL: http://www.crfonline.org • Represents credit, financial, and working capital executives of manufacturing and banking concerns. Aims to create a better understanding of the impact of credit on the economy. Plans, supervises, and administers research and educational programs. Conducts surveys on economic conditions, trends, policies, practices, theory, systems, and methodology. Sponsors formal educational programs in credit and financial management. Maintains library on credit, collections, and management.

Institute of Credit Management. Station Rd., The Water Mill, Leicestershire, South Luffenham LE15 8NB, United Kingdom. Phone: 44 1780 722900 or 44 1780 722912; Fax: 44 1780 721333; Email: info@icm.org.uk • URL: http://www.icm.org.uk • Individuals working in credit management and its ancillary services. Serves as the central reference point in the UK on all matters relating to credit management. Raises professional standards through the provision of examinations, seminars, conferences and publications. Courses are offered at local colleges, by the Rapid Results Correspondence College and by distance learning.

International Energy Credit Association. 1500 Commerce Pkwy., Ste. C, Mount Laurel, NJ 08054. Phone: (856)380-6854; Fax: (856)439-0525 • URL: http://www.ieca.net • Credit executives of petroleum and energy related companies and vendors to the field. Conducts educational seminars.

CREDIT UNIONS

See also SAVINGS AND LOAN ASSOCIATIONS

ALMANACS AND YEARBOOKS

Credit Union Report. Credit Union National Association. • Semiannual. Covers credit union leagues, associations, for each of the 50 states and the District of Columbia.

DIRECTORIES

The Credit Union Directory. Accuity Inc. • Semiannual. $600 Individuals. Covers: Approximately 12,000 credit unions and head offices and over 6,000 branches. Entries include: Institution name, address, phone, fax, routing and transit number, managing officer, financial data, charter number, year established, number of members, number of employees.

HANDBOOKS AND MANUALS

National Credit Union Administration Rules and Regulations. U. S. Government Printing Office. • Looseleaf. $130.00 for basic manual, including updates for an indeterminate period. Incorporates all amendments and revisions.

INTERNET DATABASES

The Bauer Group: Reporting On and Analyzing the Performance of U. S. Banks, Thrifts, and Credit

Unions. Bauer Financial Reports, Inc. Phone: 800-388-6686 or (305)445-9500; Fax: (305)445-6775 or (800)230-9569 • URL: http://www.bauerfinancial.com • Web site provides ratings (0 to 5 stars) of individual banks and credit unions, based on capital ratios and other financial criteria. Online searching for bank or credit union names is offered. Fees: Free.

ONLINE DATABASES

Banking Information Source. ProQuest L.L.C. • Provides indexing and abstracting of periodical and other literature from 1982 to date, with weekly updates. Covers the financial services industry: banks, savings institutions, investment houses, credit unions, insurance companies, and real estate organizations. Emphasis is on marketing and management. Inquire as to online cost and availability. (Formerly *FINIS: Financial Industry Information Service*.).

PERIODICALS AND NEWSLETTERS

American Banker: The Financial Services Daily. SourceMedia Inc. • Daily. $895.00 per year. Provides news of banking, investment products, mortgages, credit unions, finance, bank technology, and legal developments.

The CEO Report. UCG Holdings L.P. • Description: Contains information for managers of credit unions.

Credit Union Executive Center. Credit Union National Association, Inc., Communications Div. CUNA Publications. • Formerly CU Executive Journal. Provides detailed information for credit union professionals.

Credit Union Journal: The Nation's Leading Independent Credit Union Newsweekly. SourceMedia Inc. • Weekly. $109.00 per year. Edited for credit union executives. Covers trends and developments in lending, insurance, investments, mortgages, check processing, relevant technology, and other topics.

Credit Union Magazine. Credit Union National Association, Inc. Credit Union National Association. • Monthly. $71 Individuals. News analysis and operational information for credit union management, staff, directors, and committee executives.

CUIS. UCG Holdings L.P. • Biweekly. $277.00 per year. Newsletter. Supplement available *CUIS Special Report*.

U.S. Banker. SourceMedia Inc. • Monthly. $65.00 per year. Edited for bank executives and managers. Covers a wide variety of banking and financial topics.

United States National Credit Union Administration NCUA Quarterly. National Credit Union Administration Office of Small and Disadvantaged Business Utilization.

STATISTICS SOURCES

Statistical Information on the Financial Services Industry. American Bankers Association. • Annual. Members, $150.00; non-members, $275.00. Presents a wide variety of data relating to banking and financial services, including consumer economics, personal finance, credit, government loans, capital markets, and international banking.

U.S. Industry and Trade Outlook. U.S. Department of Commerce National Technical Information Service. • Annual. Produced by the International Trade Administration, U.S. Department of Commerce, in a "public-private" partnership with DRI/McGraw-Hill and Standard & Poor's. Provides basic data, outlook for the current year, and "Long-Term Prospects" (five-year projections) for a wide variety of products and services. Includes high technology industries. Formerly *U.S. Industrial Outlook*.

TRADE/PROFESSIONAL ASSOCIATIONS

Credit Union Executives Society. 5510 Research Park Dr., Madison, WI 53711-5377. Phone: 800-252-2664 or (608)271-2664; Fax: (608)271-2303; Email: cues@cues.org • URL: http://www.cues.org • Advances the professional development of credit union CEOs, senior management and directors. Serves as an international membership association dedicated to the professional development of credit union CEOs, senior management and directors.

Credit Union National Association. 5710 Mineral Point Rd., Madison, WI 53705. Phone: 800-356-9655 or (202)638-5777; Fax: (202)638-7734 or (608)231-4333 • URL: http://www.cuna.org • Serves as trade association serving more than 90% of credit unions in the U.S. through their respective state leagues with a total membership of more than 77 million persons. (A credit union is a member-owned, nonprofit institution formed to encourage saving and to offer low interest loans to members, usually people working for the same employer, belonging to the same association, or living in the same community.) Promotes credit union membership, use of services, and organization of new credit unions. Seeks to perfect credit union laws; aids in the development of new credit union services, including new payment systems techniques; assists in the training of credit union officials and employees; compiles statistics, annually, by state. Offers charitable program.

Defense Credit Union Council. 601 Pennsylvania Ave. NW, South Bldg., Ste. 600, Washington, DC 20004-2601. Phone: (202)638-3950; Fax: (202)638-3410; Email: admin@dcuc.org • URL: http://www.dcuc.org • Credit unions serving Department of Defense military and civilian personnel. Aims to assist credit unions serving DOD personnel with problems peculiar to military installations and personnel, and to maintain close liaison with DOD.

LICU. 1 Credit Union Plz., 24 McKinley Ave., Endicott, NY 13760. Phone: 800-434-1776 or (607)754-7900; Fax: (607)754-9772 • Member credit unions in the U.S. and Canada. Provides a network for information sharing. Compiles statistics.

National Association of Federal Credit Unions. 3138 10th St. N, Arlington, VA 22201-2149. Phone: 800-336-4644; Email: fbecker@nafcu.org • URL: http://www.nafcu.org • Serves as federally-chartered credit unions. Offers legislative and regulatory advocacy, compliance assistance, training and professional development and a range of products. Provides information on the latest industry developments and proposed and final regulations. Represents members' interests before federal regulatory bodies and Congress. Compiles statistics and holds educational conferences.

CRIME AND CRIMINALS

See also COMPUTER CRIME AND SECURITY; COUNTERFEITING; FORGERIES; FRAUD AND EMBEZZLEMENT

ABSTRACTS AND INDEXES

Current Law Index. Cengage Learning Inc. • $1,332 Individuals. Monthly. $1269.00 per year. Produced in cooperation with the American Association of Law Libraries. Indexes more than 900 law journals, legal newspapers, and specialty publications from the U.S., Canada, U.K., Ireland, Australia, and New Zealand.

Index to Legal Periodicals and Books. H.W. Wilson Co. • Monthly. $490.00 per year. Quarterly and annual cumulations.

Social Sciences Citation Index. Thomson Reuters Corp. • Weekly. Product is accessed via *Web of Science*.

Social Sciences Index Retrospective: 1907-1983. EBSCO Publishing Inc. • Indexing for 1,000,000 articles. Coverage includes international index and social sciences and humanities index.

ALMANACS AND YEARBOOKS

American Law Yearbook. Cengage Learning Inc. • $308 Individuals. Annual. $280.00. Serves as a yearly supplement to *West's Encyclopedia of American Lawa*. Describes new legal developments in many subject areas.

CD-ROM DATABASES

Index to Legal Periodicals and Books. EBSCO Publishing Inc. • Contains indexing of more than 1,400 English language legal periodicals from 1981 to date and 2,500 books.

Newspaper Abstracts Ondisc. ProQuest L.L.C. • Monthly. $2,950.00 per year (covers 1989 to date; archival discs are available for 1985-88). Provides cover-to-cover CD-ROM indexing and abstracting of 19 major newspapers, including the *New York Times, Wall Street Journal, Washington Post, Chicago Tribune*, and *Los Angeles Times*.

Social Sciences Abstracts. EBSCO Publishing Inc. • Provides indexing from 1983 and abstracting from 1994 of more than 750 periodicals covering economics, area studies, community health, public administration, public welfare, urban studies, and many other topics related to the social sciences.

Social Sciences Citation Index. Thomson Reuters Corp. • Weekly. Product is accessed via *Web of Science*.

DIRECTORIES

Directory of Automated Criminal Justice Information Systems. U.S. Bureau of Justice Statistics. • $60. Covers: Over 1,870 computerized information systems serving over 700 police, courts, state and local government judicial and correctional agencies. Entries include: Description of system or agency; acronym; type of system; functions; hardware and software configuration; function names, addresses, and phone numbers of agency contact.

E-BOOKS

Social Trends & Indicators USA. Monique D. Magee, editor. Cengage Learning Inc. • Includes data on labor, economics, the health care industry, crime, leisure, population, education, social security, and many other topics. Sources include various government agencies and major publications. Inquire for pricing.

ENCYCLOPEDIAS AND DICTIONARIES

Encyclopedia of Crime and Justice. Cengage Learning Inc. • 2001. $737. 2nd edition. 4 volumes. Published by Macmillan Reference USA. Contains extensive information on a wide variety of topics pertaining to crime, criminology, social issues, and the courts. Also available as eBook.

Encyclopedia of White-Collar & Corporate Crime. Cengage Learning Inc. • 2 volumes. More than 500 entries. This work gathers history, definitions, examples, investigation, prosecution, assessments, challenges, and projections into one definitive reference work on the topic.

West's Encyclopedia of American Law. Cengage Learning Inc. • 2004. eBook. Second edition. Covers a wide variety of legal topics for the general reader. Inquire for pricing.

HANDBOOKS AND MANUALS

Banking Crimes: Fraud, Money Laundering & Embezzlement. John K. Villa. Thomson West. • $369.60 Full Set. Covers fraud and embezzlement.

Private Investigator. Entrepreneur Press. • Looseleaf. $59.50. A practical guide to starting a private investigation agency. Covers profit potential, start-up costs, market size evaluation, pricing, accounting, advertising, promotion, etc. (Start-Up Business Guide No. E1320.).

Securities Crimes. Thomson West. • Annual. $798 full set. Analyzes the enfo of federal securities laws from the viewpoint of the defendant. Discusses

Securities and Exchange Commission (SEC) investigations and federal sentencing guidelines. (Securities Law Series).

INTERNET DATABASES

Lexis.com Research System. Lexis-Nexis Group. Phone: 800-227-4908 or (937)865-6800; Fax: (937)865-6909; Email: webmaster@prod.lexis-nexis.com • URL: http://www.nexis.com • Fee-based Web site offers extensive searching of a wide variety of legal sources. Additional features include Daily Opinion Service, lexis.com Bookstore, Career Center, CLE Center, Law Schools, and Practice Pages ("Pages specific to areas of specialty").

U.S. Census Bureau: The Official Statistics. U. S. Bureau of the Census. Phone: (301)763-4636 or (301)763-4100; Fax: (301)763-4794; Email: webmaster@census.gov • URL: http://www.census.gov/prod/www/abs/mfg-prof.html • Web site is "Your Source for Social, Demographic, and Economic Information." Contains "Current U. S. Population Count," "Current Economic Indicators," and a wide variety of data under "Other Official Statistics." Keyword searching is provided. Fees: Free.

ONLINE DATABASES

Wilson Social Sciences Abstracts Online. H.W. Wilson Co. • Provides online abstracting and indexing of more than 500 periodicals covering area studies, community health, public administration, public welfare, urban studies, and many other social science topics. Time period is 1994 to date for abstracts and 1983 to date for indexing, with updates weekly. Inquire as to online cost and availability.

OTHER SOURCES

White Collar Crime: Business and Regulatory Offenses. ALM Media Properties LLC. • $740 print + online + ebook. Covers such legal matters as criminal tax cases, securities fraud, computer crime, mail fraud, bank embezzlement, criminal antitrust activities, extortion, perjury, the criminal liability of corporations, and RICO (Racketeer Influenced and Corrupt Organization Act). (Law Journal Press).

PERIODICALS AND NEWSLETTERS

Business Crimes Bulletin. ALM Media Properties LLC. • Monthly. $510 per year. Provides news of the "multifaceted world of financial and white collar crime." Covers such items as foreign corrupt practices, mail fraud, money laundering, tax fraud, securities law violations, environmental crime, and antitrust violations. Includes developments in sentencing guidelines for white collar perpetrators. (A Law Journal Newsletter, formerly published by Leader Publications).

Criminal Law Advocacy Reporter. Matthew Bender and Company Inc. • Monthly. $447.00 per year. Newsletter. Analysis of the latest cases and trends in criminal law and procedure.

Criminology: An Interdisciplinary Journal. American Society of Criminology. • Quarterly. $348 Institutions print and online. Focus is on crime and deviant behavior.

FBI Law Enforcement Bulletin. U. S. Government Printing Office. • Monthly. $36.00 per year. Issued by Federal Bureau of Investigation, U. S. Department of Justice. Contains articles on a wide variety of law enforcement and crime topics, including computer-related crime.

Security: The Magazine for Buyers of Security Products, Systems and Service. BNP Media. • Monthly. Security industry news and trends.

RESEARCH CENTERS AND INSTITUTES

National Council on Crime and Delinquency. 1970 Broadway, Ste. 500, Oakland, CA 94612. Phone: 800-306-6223; Email: info@nccdglobal.org • URL: http://nccdglobal.org • Promotes effective, humane, fair and economically sound solutions to family, community, and justice problems. Conducts research, promotes reform initiatives, and seeks to work with individuals, public and private organizations, and the media to prevent and reduce crime and delinquency.

STATISTICS SOURCES

Prisoners in State and Federal Institutions. Bureau of Justice Statistics, U.S. Department of Justice. U. S. Government Printing Office. • Annual.

Sourcebook of Criminal Justice Statistics. U. S. Government Printing Office. • Annual. $56.00. Issued by the Bureau of Justice Statistics, U. S. Department of Justice (www.usdoj.gov/bjs). Contains both crime data and corrections statistics.

Statistical Abstract of the United States. U. S. Government Printing Office. • Annual. $44.00. Issued by the U. S. Bureau of the Census.

Uniform Crime Reports for the United States. Federal Bureau of Investigation, U.S. Department of Justice. U. S. Government Printing Office. • Annual. $45.

Vital Statistics of the United States. Public Health Service, U.S. Dept. of Health and Human Services. Bernan Press. • Biennial. $110.

TRADE/PROFESSIONAL ASSOCIATIONS

American Society of Criminology. 1314 Kinnear Rd., Ste. 212, Columbus, OH 43212-1156. Phone: (614)292-9207; Fax: (614)292-6767; Email: asc@asc41.com • URL: http://www.asc41.com • Formerly Society for the Advancement of Criminology.

CRIME, COMPUTER

See COMPUTER CRIME AND SECURITY

CRITICAL PATH METHOD/PERT (PROGRAM EVALUATION AND REVIEW TECHNIQUE)

PERIODICALS AND NEWSLETTERS

Project Management Journal. Project Management Institute. • 6/year Quarterly. $465 Institutions. Contains technical articles dealing with the interests of the field of project management.

TRADE/PROFESSIONAL ASSOCIATIONS

Project Management Institute. 14 Campus Blvd., Newtown Square, PA 19073-3299. Phone: 855-746-4849 or (610)356-4600; Fax: (610)482-9971; Email: customercare@pmi.org • URL: http://www.pmi.org • Corporations and individuals engaged in the practice of project management; project management students and educators. Seeks to advance the study, teaching and practice of project management. Establishes project management standards; conducts educational and professional certification courses; bestows Project Management Professional credential upon qualified individuals. Offers educational seminars and global congresses.

CROPS

See FARM PRODUCE

CRUISE LINES

See STEAMSHIP LINES

CRYOGENICS

ABSTRACTS AND INDEXES

Applied Science and Technology Index. EBSCO Publishing Inc. • 11/year. Indexes a wide variety of English language technical, industrial, and engineering periodicals.

Current Contents: Engineering, Computing and Technology. Thomson Reuters Intellectual Property and Science. • Weekly. $730 per year. Reproductions of contents pages of technical journals. Includes *Author Index*, *Address Directory*, *Current Book Contents*, and *Title Word Index*. Formerly *Current Contents: Engineering, Technology and Applied Sciences*.

Science Citation Index. Thomson Reuters Intellectual Property and Science. • Weekly. Includes *Source Index*, *Citation Index*, *Permuterm Subject Index*, and *Corporate Index*. Provides researchers, administrators, faculty, and students with quick, powerful access to the bibliographic and citation information they need to find research data, analyze trends, journals and researchers, and share their findings.

ALMANACS AND YEARBOOKS

Advances in Cryogenic Engineering. Cryogenic Engineering Conference. • Biennial. $235 /volume. Includes invited, unsolicited, and government-sponsored research papers in the research areas of superconductors and structural materials for cryogenic applications.

CD-ROM DATABASES

Applied Science and Technology Abstracts. EBSCO Publishing Inc. • Citations for more than 700 prominent scientific, technical, engineering, and industrial periodicals.

Science Citation Index. Thomson Reuters Intellectual Property and Science. • Weekly. Includes *Source Index*, *Citation Index*, *Permuterm Subject Index*, and *Corporate Index*. Provides researchers, administrators, faculty, and students with quick, powerful access to the bibliographic and citation information they need to find research data, analyze trends, journals and researchers, and share their findings.

ONLINE DATABASES

Applied Science and Technology Index Online. H.W. Wilson Co. • Provides online indexing of 500 major scientific, technical, industrial, and engineering periodicals. Time period is 1983 to date. Monthly updates. Inquire as to online cost and availability.

OTHER SOURCES

Superconductor Week: The Newsletter of Record in the Field of Superconductivity. WestTech. • $450 Individuals Internet Only. Covers applications of superconductivity and cryogenics, including new markets and products.

PERIODICALS AND NEWSLETTERS

Cold Facts Newsletter. Cryogenic Society of America. • 5/year. Description: Technical newsletter serving individuals interested in cryogenics and cryobiology.

CryoGas International. J.R. Campbell and Associates Inc. • 11/year. $75 /year (online). Reports on technology market development and new products for the industrial gases and cryogenic equipment industries. Formerly *Cryogenic Information Report*.

Cryogenics. Elsevier. • Monthly. $3,400 Institutions print or online. Journal of low temperature engineering.

RESEARCH CENTERS AND INSTITUTES

Kurata Thermodynamics Laboratory. University of Kansas, Dept. of Chemical and Petroleum Engineering, 2330 Crowell Dr., Lawrence, KS 66047. Phone: (785)864-4965 • URL: http://www2.ku.edu/build/cgi-bin/kurata-thermodynamics-laboratories • Investigates the behavior of various materials over a wide range of temperatures.

Massachusetts Institute of Technology - Research Laboratory of Electronics. 77 Massachusetts Ave.,

Rm. 36-413, Cambridge, MA 02139-4307. Phone: (617)253-2519; Fax: (617)253-1301; Email: hq@rle.mit.edu • URL: http://www.rle.mit.edu/ • Research areas include heat transfer and cryogenics.

Microkelvin Laboratory. c/o Darlene Latimer, Dept. of Physics, 2273 New Physics Bldg., Gainesville, FL 32611. Phone: (352)392-9261; Fax: (352)392-3591 • URL: http://www.phys.ufl.edu/mkelvin • Focuses on electronic behavior changes in metals, insulators, and semiconductors at ultra-low temperatures.

Stanford University - Edward L. Ginzton Laboratory. Spilker Engineering and Applied Sciences, 348 Via Pueblo Mall, Stanford, CA 94305. Phone: (650)724-2765; Fax: (650)725-2533; Email: solgaard@stanford.edu • URL: http://www.stanford.edu/group/ginzton • Research fields include low-temperature physics and superconducting electronics.

Stanford University - W.W. Hansen Experimental Physics Laboratory. 452 Lomita Mall, Stanford, CA 94305-4085. Phone: (650)724-7667; Fax: (650)725-8311; Email: nchristiansen@stanford.edu • URL: http://www.stanford.edu/group/hepl • Conducts large-scale cryogenic research.

Thermophysical Properties Research Laboratory. 3080 Kent Ave., West Lafayette, IN 47906. Phone: (765)463-1581; Fax: (765)463-5235; Email: tprlinqr@tprl.com • URL: http://www.tprl.com • Studies the thermophysical properties of materials from cryogenic to very high temperatures.

TRADE/PROFESSIONAL ASSOCIATIONS

Cryogenic Society of America. 218 Lake St., Oak Park, IL 60302-2609. Phone: (708)383-6220; Fax: (708)383-9337; Email: laurie@cryogenicsociety.org • URL: http://www.cryogenicsociety.org • Seeks to encourage the dissemination of information on low temperature industrial technology. Formerly Helium Society.

CULINARY

OTHER SOURCES

American Culinary Federation. • Aims to promote the culinary profession and provide on-going educational training and networking for members. Provides opportunities for competition, professional recognition, and access to educational forums with other culinary experts at local, regional, national, and international events. Operates the National Apprenticeship Program for Cooks and pastry cooks. Offers programs that address certification of the individual chef's skills, accreditation of culinary programs, apprenticeship of cooks and pastry cooks, professional development, and the fight against childhood hunger.

TRADE/PROFESSIONAL ASSOCIATIONS

United States Personal Chef Association. 7680 Universal Blvd., Ste. 550, Orlando, FL 32819-8959. Phone: 800-995-2138; Email: info@uspca.com • URL: http://www.uspca.com • Promotes the personal chef; committed in advancing the profession of the personal chef as a legitimate career choice in the culinary arts field; ensures the credibility of the personal chef with the industry-wide implementation of Educational Standards of Knowledge.

CULTURE, CORPORATE

See CORPORATE CULTURE

CURRENCY

See also MONEY

CURRENCY CONVERTIBILITY

See FOREIGN EXCHANGE

CURRENCY EXCHANGE RATES

See also FOREIGN EXCHANGE

INTERNET DATABASES

The Financial Post. National Post Online. Phone: 800-805-1184 or (244)383-2300; Fax: (416)383-2443 • URL: http://www.nationalpost.com/financialpost/ • Provides a broad range of Canadian business news online, with daily updates. Includes news, opinion, and special reports, as well as "Investing," "Money Rates," "Market Watch," and "Daily Mutual Funds." Allows advanced searching (Boolean operators), with links to various other sites. Fees: Free.

Financial Times: Where Information Becomes Intelligence. FT Group. Phone: (800)628-8088 • URL: http://www.ft.com • Web site provides extensive data and information relating to international business and finance, with daily updates. Includes Markets Today, Company News, Economic Indicators, Equities, Currencies, Capital Markets, Euro Prices, etc. Fees: Free (registration required).

Gateway to the European Union. European Union. Email: pressoffice@eurostat.cec.be • URL: http://www.europa.eu.int • Web site provides access to a wide variety of EU information, including statistics (Eurostat), news, policies, publications, key issues, and official exchange rates for the euro. Includes links to the European Central Bank, the European Investment Bank, and other institutions. Fees: Free.

PERIODICALS AND NEWSLETTERS

The Financial Post: Canadian's Business Voice. Financial Post Datagroup. • Daily. $200.00 per year. Provides Canadian business, economic, financial, and investment news. Features extensive price quotes from all major Canadian markets: stocks, bonds, mutual funds, commodities, and currencies. Supplement available: *Financial Post 500.* Includes annual supplement.

Financial Times (London). The Financial Times, Inc. • Daily, except Sunday. $572.88 per year. An international business and financial newspaper, featuring news from London, Paris, Frankfurt, New York, and Tokyo. Includes worldwide stock and bond market data, commodity market data, and monetary/currency exchange information.

Financial Times Currency Forecaster: Consensus Forecasts of the Worldwide Currency and Economic Outlook. Briefings Publishing Group. • Monthly. $695.00 per year. Newsletter. Provides forecasts of foreign currency exchange rates and economic conditions. Supplement available: *Mid-Month Global Financial Report.*

International Market Alert. UCG Holdings L.P. • Description: Provides a fax service covering financial markets, world economy developments, foreign exchange, and U.S. interest rates.

World Business Intelligence: Economic & Political Financial Analysts from Rundt's New York. S.J. Rundt & Associates Inc. • $885 Individuals. Magazine featuring information on international trade, country risk analyses, currencies, and political, financial, and economic intelligence. Formerly *Rundt's Weekly Intelligence.*

CURRENT EVENTS

See also CLIPPING SERVICES; NEWSPAPERS; PERIODICALS

ALMANACS AND YEARBOOKS

The Annual Register: A Record of World Events. ProQuest L.L.C. • Annual. Contains yearly British and world events.

The World Almanac and Book of Facts. The World Almanac and Book of Facts. • Annual. $11.95.

BIOGRAPHICAL SOURCES

Newsmakers. Cengage Learning Inc. • Annual. $314 Individuals. Four softbound issues and one hardbound annual. Biographical information on individuals currently in the news. Includes photographs. Formerly *Contemporary Newsmakers.* eBook also available. Contact for pricing.

CD-ROM DATABASES

Newspaper Abstracts Ondisc. ProQuest L.L.C. • Monthly. $2,950.00 per year (covers 1989 to date; archival discs are available for 1985-88). Provides cover-to-cover CD-ROM indexing and abstracting of 19 major newspapers, including the *New York Times, Wall Street Journal, Washington Post, Chicago Tribune,* and *Los Angeles Times.*

INTERNET DATABASES

Globeandmail.com:. Bell Globemedia Publishing, Inc. Phone: 800-268-9128 or (416)585-5000; Fax: (416)585-5249 • URL: http://www.globeandmail.ca • Web site provides access to selected sections of *The Globe and Mail.* Includes current news, national issues, career information, "Report on Business," and other topics. Keyword searching is offered for "a seven-day archive of the portion of the *Globe and Mail* that we publish online." Daily updates. Fees: free.

Law.com: First in Legal News and Information. ALM Media Properties Inc. Phone: 800-888-8300 or (212)779-9200; Fax: (212)481-8110 • URL: http://www.law.com • Web site provides free, law-related, current news (National News Sites and Regional News Sites). Free searching of martindale.com lawyer locator is offered, including lawyer ratings. Fee-based premium services for the legal profession are also available.

PERIODICALS AND NEWSLETTERS

Canadian News Facts: The Indexed Digest of Canadian Current Events. MPL Communications Inc. • Bimonthly. $280.00 per year. Monthly and quarterly indexes. A summary of current events in Canada.

Facts-on-File World News Digest With Index. InfoBase Holdings Inc. • Weekly. $725.00 per year. Looseleaf service.

Intelligence Digest: A Review of World Affairs; International Political, Economic and Strategic Intelligence. Jane's Information Group, Inc. • Weekly. $240.00 per year. Provides political, strategic and economic information. Gives warnings on political trends and current affairs. Published in England.

CURTAIN INDUSTRY

See WINDOW COVERING INDUSTRY

CUSTOMER SERVICE

ABSTRACTS AND INDEXES

Business Periodicals Index Retrospective. EBSCO Publishing Inc. • 11/year. Quarterly and annual cumulations.

Readers' Guide to Periodical Literature. EBSCO Publishing Inc. • Provides indexing for over 400 periodicals dating back to 1983.

CD-ROM DATABASES

Readers' Guide to Periodical Literature. EBSCO Publishing Inc. • Provides indexing for over 400 periodicals dating back to 1983.

ONLINE DATABASES

Wilson Business Abstracts Online. H.W. Wilson Co. • Indexes and abstracts 600 major business periodicals, plus the *Wall Street Journal* and the business section of the *New York Times*. Indexing is from 1982, abstracting from 1990, with the two newspapers included from 1993. Updated weekly. Inquire as to online cost and availability. (*Business Periodicals Index* without abstracts is also available online.).

PERIODICALS AND NEWSLETTERS

Call Center. UBM L.L.C. • Monthly. Free to qualified personnel. Emphasis is on telemarketing, selling, and customer service. Includes articles on communication technology. Formerly *Call Center Solutions*.

CC News: The Business Newspaper for Call Center and Customer Care Professionals. HME News. • Monthly. Free to qualified personnel; others, $60.00 per year. Includes news of call center technical developments.

Communication Briefings: A Monthly Idea Source for Decision Makers. Briefings Publishing Group. • Monthly. $97. Presents useful ideas for communication, public relations, customer service, human resources, and employee training.

RESEARCH CENTERS AND INSTITUTES

Consumers' Checkbook. 1625 K St. NW, 8th Fl., Washington, DC 20006. Phone: 800-213-7283; Email: editors@checkbook.org • URL: http://www.checkbook.org • Evaluates local consumer services and retailers in Washington D.C. and San Francisco metropolitan areas.

TRADE/PROFESSIONAL ASSOCIATIONS

National Retail Federation. 325 7th St. NW, Ste. 1100, Washington, DC 20004. Phone: 800-673-4692 or (202)783-7971 or (202)347-1932; Fax: (202)737-2849; Email: bookinquiries@nrf.com • URL: http://www.nrf.com • Represents state retail associations, several dozen national retail associations, as well as large and small corporate members representing the breadth and diversity of the retail industry's establishment and employees. Conducts informational and educational conferences related to all phases of retailing including financial planning and cash management, taxation, economic forecasting, expense planning, shortage control, credit, electronic data processing, telecommunications, merchandise management, buying, traffic, security, supply, materials handling, store planning and construction, personnel administration, recruitment and training, and advertising and display.

CUSTOMS BROKERS

See also CUSTOMS HOUSE, U.S. CUSTOMS SERVICE; EXPORT-IMPORT TRADE; FOREIGN TRADE

DIRECTORIES

National Customs Brokers and Forwarders Association of America Membership Directory. National Customs Brokers and Forwarders Association of America. • Annual. $55.00. Lists about 600 customs brokers, international air cargo agents, and freight forwarders in the U.S.

PERIODICALS AND NEWSLETTERS

International Trade Reporter Export Reference Manual. Bloomberg BNA. • Biweekly. $874.00 per year. Looseleaf service.

TRADE/PROFESSIONAL ASSOCIATIONS

National Customs Brokers and Forwarders Association of America. 1200 18th St. NW, No. 901, Washington, DC 20036. Phone: (202)466-0222; Fax: (202)466-0226; Email: staff@ncbfaa.org • URL: http://www.ncbfaa.org • Formerly Customs Brokers and Forwarders Association of America.

CUSTOMS HOUSE, U.S. CUSTOMS SERVICE

CD-ROM DATABASES

U.S. Exports of Merchandise. U.S. Bureau of the Census, Foreign Trade Division. • Monthly and quarterly data. Provides export data in the most extensive detail available, including product, quantity, value, shipping weight, country of destination, customs district of exportation, etc.

U.S. Imports of Merchandise. U.S. Bureau of the Census, Foreign Trade Division. • Monthly. $2,400 per year. Provides import data in the most extensive detail available, including product, quantity, value, shipping weight, country of origin, customs district of entry, rate provision, etc.

DIRECTORIES

U.S. Custom House Guide. UBM Global Trade. • Annual. $899 Individuals online access. Publication includes: List of ports having customs facilities, customs officials, port authorities, chambers of commerce, embassies and consulates, foreign trade zones, and other organizations; related trade services. Entries include: For each principal port--Name of organization or agency, address, phone, fax, names and titles of key personnel; description and limitations of port facilities. For service firms--Company name, address, phone, fax. Principal content is U.S. tariff schedules and customs regulations, and a "How to Import" manual.

INTERNET DATABASES

FedWorld: A Program of the United States Department of Commerce. National Technical Information Service. Phone: 800-553-NTIS or (703)605-6000; Fax: (703)605-6900; Email: webmaster@fedworld.gov • URL: http://www.fedworld.gov • Web site offers "a comprehensive central access point for searching, locating, ordering, and acquiring government and business information." Emphasis is on searching the Web pages, databases, and government reports of a wide variety of federal agencies. Fees: Free.

OTHER SOURCES

Customs Law and Administration: Statutes and Treaties. Oceana Publications Inc. • $475.00. Five volumes. Looseleaf service. Periodic supplementation.

TRADE/PROFESSIONAL ASSOCIATIONS

National Treasury Employees Union. 1750 H St. NW, Washington, DC 20006-4600. Phone: (202)572-5500 • URL: http://www.nteu.org • Employees of the federal government. Conducts research and educational training programs. Sponsors Federal Employees Education and Assistance Fund.

CUSTOMS TAX

See TARIFF

CYCLES, BUSINESS

See BUSINESS CYCLES

D

DAIRY INDUSTRY

See also CHEESE INDUSTRY; DAIRY PRODUCTS

ABSTRACTS AND INDEXES

Biological and Agricultural Index. H.W. Wilson Co. • 11 times a year. Annual and quarterly cumulations. Price varies.

Dairy Science Abstracts. CABI Publishing North America. • Monthly. Published in England by CABI Publishing.

DIRECTORIES

Directory of South Korean Manufacturers & Exporters of Dairy Products. EXIM Infotek Private Ltd. • $5 Individuals. Covers: 20 South Korean manufacturers and exporters of goat and sheep cheese, ice cream and sorbet, milk and milk products, and milk-condensed/dried. Entries include: Company name, postal address, city, country, phone, fax, e-mail and websites, contact person, designation, and product details.

ONLINE DATABASES

CAB Abstracts. CABI. • Contains 46 specialized abstract collections covering over 10,000 journals and monographs in the areas of agriculture, horticulture, forest products, farm products, nutrition, dairy science, poultry, grains, animal health, entomology, etc. Time period is 1972 to date, with monthly updates. Inquire as to online cost and availability. *CAB Abstracts on CD-ROM* also available, with annual updating.

PERIODICALS AND NEWSLETTERS

Dairy Foods. BNP Media. • Monthly. Provides broad coverage of new developments in the dairy industry, including cheese and ice cream products.

DFISA Reporter. Dairy and Food Industries Supply Association, Inc. • Monthly. Free. Provides industry and association news to manufacturers of equipment products and services to the dairy and food industry.

International Association of Food Industry Suppliers Reporter. International Association on Food Industry Suppliers. • Monthly. Free.

RESEARCH CENTERS AND INSTITUTES

Utah State University - Department of Animal, Dairy and Veterinary Sciences - Caine Dairy Center. 4300 S Hwy. 91, Wellsville, UT 84339. Phone: (435)245-6067; Fax: (435)245-7680; Email: john.wallentine@usu.edu • URL: http://advs.usu.edu/htm/about-advs/facilities/caine-dairy-farm • Breeding, feeding, physiology, and management of dairy cattle.

Valacta. 555 boul. des Anciens-Combattants, Sainte-Anne-de-Bellevue, QC, Canada H9X 3R4. Phone: (514)459-3030; Fax: (514)459-3020; Email: service.clientele@valacta.com • URL: http://www.valacta.com.

STATISTICS SOURCES

United States Census of Agriculture. U.S. Department of Agriculture National Agricultural Statistics Service. • Quinquennial. Provides uniform, comprehensive farming and ranching operations data for every U.S. state and county, including production expenses, market value of products, and operator characteristics.

TRADE/PROFESSIONAL ASSOCIATIONS

Dairy Management, Inc. 10255 W Higgins Rd., Ste. 900, Rosemont, IL 60018-5616. Phone: 800-853-2479; Fax: (847)627-2077 • URL: http://www.dairy.org • Operates under the auspices of the United Dairy Industry Association. Milk producers, milk dealers, and manufacturers of butter, cheese, ice cream, dairy equipment, and supplies. Conducts programs of nutrition research and nutrition education in the use of milk and its products.

Pakistan Agriculture and Dairy Farmers Association. JK House, 32-W, Susan Rd., Madina Town, Faisalabad, Pakistan. Phone: 92 41 8721956; Fax: 92 41 8712399; Email: info@padfapak.org • URL: http://www.padfapak.org • Represents trade, commerce, industry or services in agriculture and dairy farming in Pakistan. Encourages unity, mutual understanding and high ethical standards among its members. Supports a unified approach of policies affecting the interests of agriculture and dairy farming.

DAIRY PRODUCTS

See also DAIRY INDUSTRY

ABSTRACTS AND INDEXES

Food Science and Technology Abstracts. Ovid Technologies Inc. • Monthly. $1,780.00 per year. Provides worldwide coverage of the literature of food technology and food production.

Foods Adlibra: Key to the World's Food Literature. General Mills, Inc. Foods Adlibra Publications. • Semimonthly. $240.00 per year. Provides journal citations and abstracts to the literature of food technology and packaging.

CD-ROM DATABASES

OECD Statistical Compendium. Organization for Economic Cooperation and Development. • Semiannual. $1,905.00 per year for 1 to 10 users. CD-ROM contains more than 730,000 monthly, quarterly, and annual time series for OECD countries, 1960 to date. Includes fully searchable data on agriculture, food, economic indicators, national accounts, employment, energy, finance, industry, technology, and foreign trade. Results can be displayed in various forms.

DIRECTORIES

Major Food and Drink Companies of the World. Cengage Learning Inc. • 12th edition. eBook. Published by Graham & Whiteside. Contains profiles and trade names for more than 9,200 important food and beverage companies in various countries. In addition to foods, includes both alcoholic and nonalcoholic drink products.

FINANCIAL RATIOS

Annual Statement Studies. Risk Management Association. • Annual. Compiled from over 280,000 financial statements.

Annual Statement Studies: Industry Default Probabilities and Cash Flow Measures. Risk Management Association. • Annual. $405 Nonmembers. Serves as a companion volume to the original *Annual Statement Studies*. Gives probability of default estimates on a percentage scale for more than 450 industries. Includes changes in position year-by-year for eight financial statement line items and provides percentage measures of cash flow.

INTERNET DATABASES

Business 2.0 Web Guide to the Best Business Links. Business 2.0 Media Inc. Phone: (415)293-4800; Email: support@business2.com • URL: http://www.business2.com/webguide • Web site presents an extensive, searchable directory of links to "the best, most informative, and authoritative web pages." Twenty main categories cover business, finance, career, company information, people, and technology topics, with thousands of subtopics, all linking to Web sites recommended by experienced business researchers. Fees: Free.

Fedstats. Federal Interagency Council on Statistical Policy. Phone: (202)395-7254 • URL: http://www.fedstats.gov • Web site features an efficient search facility for full-text statistics produced by more than 100 federal agencies, including the Census Bureau, the Bureau of Economic Analysis, and the Bureau of Labor Statistics. Boolean searches can be made within one agency or for all agencies combined. Links are offered to international statistical bureaus, including the UN, IMF, OECD, UNESCO, Eurostat, and 20 individual countries. Fees: Free.

FreeLunch.com. Economy.com, Inc. Phone: (610)696-8700; Fax: (610)696-1678 • URL: http://www.freelunch.com • Web site provides free access to more than 200 million economic and financial data series, covering industry, demographics, labor markets, prices, retail sales, government spending, trade, interest rates, housing starts, the stock market, etc. Data is available in either chart or table form. Searching is offered. Free, but registration required. Economy.com, Inc. also offers fee-based economic analysis at *The Dismal Scientist* site (www.dismal.com).

USDA. U.S. National Institute of Standards and Technology. 100 Bureau Dr., Gaithersburg, MD 20899-1070. Phone: 800-877-8339 or (301)975-6478 or (202)720-2791; Fax: (301)975-8295; Email: inquiries@nist.gov • URL: http://www.nist.gov • The USDA home page has six sections: News and Information; What's New; About USDA; Agencies; Opportunities; Search and Help. Keyword searching is offered from the USDA home page and from various individual agency home pages. Agencies are the Economic Research Service, Agricultural Marketing Service, National Agricultural Statistics Service, National Agricultural Library, and about 12 others. Updating varies. Fees: Free.

ONLINE DATABASES

Food Science and Technology Abstracts (online). IFIS North American Desk. • Produced by International Food Information Service. Provides about 500,000 online citations, with abstracts, to the international literature of food science, technology, commodities, engineering, and processing. Approximately 2,000 periodicals are covered. Time period is 1969 to date, with monthly updates. Inquire as to online cost and availability.

PERIODICALS AND NEWSLETTERS

Monthly Price Review. Urner Barry Publications Inc. • Description: Provides daily price information and monthly averages on dairy, egg, and poultry products. **Remarks:** Subscription includes a supplement titled Annual Price Review.

PRICE SOURCES

Supermarket News: The Industry's Weekly Newspaper. Fairchild Publications. • Weekly. Individuals, $196.00 per year; retailers, $45.00 per year; manufacturers, $89.00 per year.

STATISTICS SOURCES

Agricultural Statistics. U.S. Department of Agriculture National Agricultural Statistics Service. • Annual. $46 Individuals. Provides a wide variety of statistical data relating to agricultural production, supplies, consumption, prices/price-supports, foreign trade, costs, and returns, as well as farm labor, loans, income, and population. In many cases, historical data is shown annually for 10 years. In addition to farm data, includes detailed fishery statistics.

Survey of Current Business. U. S. Government Printing Office. • Published by Bureau of Economic Analysis, U. S. Department of Commerce. Presents a wide variety of business and economic data.

TRADE/PROFESSIONAL ASSOCIATIONS

Dairy Management, Inc. 10255 W Higgins Rd., Ste. 900, Rosemont, IL 60018-5616. Phone: 800-853-2479; Fax: (847)627-2077 • URL: http://www.dairy.org • Operates under the auspices of the United Dairy Industry Association. Milk producers, milk dealers, and manufacturers of butter, cheese, ice cream, dairy equipment, and supplies. Conducts programs of nutrition research and nutrition education in the use of milk and its products.

Milk Industry Foundation. International Dairy Foods Association, 1250 H St. NW, Ste. 900, Washington, DC 20005. Phone: (202)737-4332; Fax: (202)331-7820 • URL: http://www.idfa.org/about-idfa/boards-committees/milk-industry-foundation • Represents processors of fluid milk and milk products. Advocates before government and regulatory bodies on behalf of members.

National Cheese Institute. International Dairy Foods Association, 1250 H St. NW, Ste. 900, Washington, DC 20005-3952. Phone: (202)737-4332; Fax: (202)331-7820 • URL: http://www.idfa.org/about-idfa/boards-committees/national-cheese-institute • Represents manufacturers, processors, marketers, assemblers, and distributors of cheese and cheese products; advocates before government and regulatory bodies on behalf of members.

DANGEROUS MATERIALS

See HAZARDOUS MATERIALS

DATA BASES, ONLINE

See ONLINE INFORMATION SYSTEMS

DATA COMMUNICATIONS

See COMPUTER COMMUNICATIONS

DATA IDENTIFICATION SYSTEMS, AUTOMATIC

See AUTOMATIC IDENTIFICATION SYSTEMS

DATA SYSTEMS

See SYSTEMS IN MANAGEMENT

DATES (CHRONOLOGY)

See CHRONOLOGY

DAY CARE CENTERS

See also BABY SITTING

FINANCIAL RATIOS

Annual Statement Studies. Risk Management Association. • Annual. Compiled from over 280,000 financial statements.

Annual Statement Studies: Industry Default Probabilities and Cash Flow Measures. Risk Management Association. • Annual. $405 Nonmembers. Serves as a companion volume to the original *Annual Statement Studies*. Gives probability of default estimates on a percentage scale for more than 450 industries. Includes changes in position year-by-year for eight financial statement line items and provides percentage measures of cash flow.

HANDBOOKS AND MANUALS

Senior Day Care Center. Entrepreneur Press. • Looseleaf. $59.50. A practical guide to starting a day care center for older adults (supervised environment for frail individuals). Covers profit potential, start-up costs, market size evaluation, owner's time required, site selection, lease negotiation, pricing, accounting, advertising, promotion, etc. (Start-Up Business Guide No. E1335.).

DDT

See PESTICIDE INDUSTRY

DEATH TAX

See INHERITANCE TAX

DEATHS AND BIRTHS

See VITAL STATISTICS

DEBATES AND DEBATING

See also PUBLIC SPEAKING

TRADE/PROFESSIONAL ASSOCIATIONS

American Forensic Association. PO Box 256, River Falls, WI 54022. Phone: 800-228-5424 or (715)425-3198; Fax: (715)425-9533; Email: amforensicassoc@aol.com • URL: http://www.americanforensics.org • High school and college directors of forensics and debate coaches. Promotes debate and other speech activities. Sponsors annual collegiate National Individual Events Tournament and National Debate Tournament; sells debate ballots; makes studies of professional standards and debate budgets. Supports research grants.

National Forensic League. 125 Watson St., Ripon, WI 54971. Phone: (920)748-6206; Fax: (920)748-9478; Email: nfl@nflonline.org • URL: http://www.nationalforensicleague.org • High school honor society. Promotes the art of debate, oratory, interpretation, and extemporaneous speaking. Conducts educational and outreach programs; maintains speakers' bureau; maintains hall of fame; compiles statistics.

DEBENTURES

See BONDS

DEBT COLLECTION

See COLLECTING OF ACCOUNTS

DEBT, NATIONAL

See NATIONAL DEBT

DECEPTIVE ADVERTISING

See ADVERTISING LAW AND REGULATION

DECISION-MAKING

See also OPERATIONS RESEARCH

ABSTRACTS AND INDEXES

Psychological Abstracts. American Psychological Association. • Monthly. Members, $815.00 per year; individuals and institutions, $1,207.00 per year. Covers the international literature of psychology and the behavioral sciences. Includes journals, technical reports, dissertations, and other sources.

GENERAL WORKS

Journal of Integrated Business Decisions. IBIMA Publishing. • Peer-reviewed journal publishing research in business decision-making practices.

PERIODICALS AND NEWSLETTERS

Communication Briefings: A Monthly Idea Source for Decision Makers. Briefings Publishing Group. • Monthly. $97. Presents useful ideas for communication, public relations, customer service, human resources, and employee training.

RESEARCH CENTERS AND INSTITUTES

Australian Catholic University - Centre for Research into Ethics and Decision-Making in Organisations. 24 Brunswick St., Locked Bag 4115, Fitzroy, VIC

For publishers' addresses, refer to SOURCES CITED section at the back of the book.

3065, Australia. Phone: 61 3 99533270; Email: j.little@patrick.acu.edu.au • URL: http://www.acu.edu.au/research/Research_Centres_and_Flagships/credo • Values, policies, decision-making, and ethics in an organization.

University of Chicago Graduate School of Business - Center for Decision Research. 5807 S Woodlawn Ave., Chicago, IL 60637. Phone: (773)702-4877; Fax: (773)834-9134; Email: vicki.drozd@chicagobooth.edu • URL: http://research.chicagobooth.edu/cdr.

TRADE/PROFESSIONAL ASSOCIATIONS

Decision Sciences Institute. C.T. Bauer College of Business, 334 Melchor Hall, Ste. 325, Houston, TX 77204-6021. Phone: (713)743-4815; Fax: (713)743-8984; Email: info@decisionsciences.org • URL: http://www.decisionsciences.org • Businesspersons and members of business school faculties. Maintains placement service.

Society for Judgment and Decision Making. PO Box 3061110, Tallahassee, FL 32306-1110. Phone: (850)644-8231; Fax: (850)644-8234; Email: gbc@rci.rutgers.edu • URL: http://www.sjdm.org • Individuals interested in the study of decision-making. Promotes research and scholarship in the field. Conducts research and educational programs; gathers and disseminates information. Facilitates cooperation between members and researchers and scholars in related fields.

DECORATION, INTERIOR

See INTERIOR DECORATION

DEDUCTIONS (INCOME TAX)

See INCOME TAX

DEFENSE CONTRACTS

See GOVERNMENT CONTRACTS

DEFENSE INDUSTRIES

See also AEROSPACE INDUSTRY; AVIATION INDUSTRY; GOVERNMENT CONTRACTS; MILITARY MARKET

ABSTRACTS AND INDEXES

Air University Library Index to Military Periodicals. U.S. Air Force. • Quarterly. Annual cumulation.

ALMANACS AND YEARBOOKS

United Nations Disarmament Yearbook. United Nations Publications. • Annual. $55 Individuals.

BIBLIOGRAPHIES

Defense and Security. U. S. Government Printing Office. • Annual. Free. Issued by the Superintendent of Documents. A list of government publications on defense and related topics. Formerly *Defense Supply and Logistics*. (Subject Bibliography No. 153.).

CD-ROM DATABASES

OECD Statistical Compendium. Organization for Economic Cooperation and Development. • Semiannual. $1,905.00 per year for 1 to 10 users. CD-ROM contains more than 730,000 monthly, quarterly, and annual time series for OECD countries, 1960 to date. Includes fully searchable data on agriculture, food, economic indicators, national accounts, employment, energy, finance, industry, technology, and foreign trade. Results can be displayed in various forms.

DIRECTORIES

Civil Defense Agencies Directory. InfoGroup Inc. • Annual. Number of listings: 1,516. Entries include: Name, address, phone, size of advertisement, name of owner or manager, number of employees, year first in "Yellow Pages." Compiled from telephone company "Yellow Pages," nationwide.

Russia Defense Industry Directory. International Business Publications, USA. • $99.95 Individuals hardcopy, e-book, CD-ROM. Covers: Strategic and practical information on government, national security, army, foreign and domestic politics, conflicts, relations with the US, international activity, economy, technology, mineral resources, culture, traditions, government and business contacts.

INTERNET DATABASES

Business 2.0 Web Guide to the Best Business Links. Business 2.0 Media Inc. Phone: (415)293-4800; Email: support@business2.com • URL: http://www.business2.com/webguide • Web site presents an extensive, searchable directory of links to "the best, most informative, and authoritative web pages." Twenty main categories cover business, finance, career, company information, people, and technology topics, with thousands of subtopics, all linking to Web sites recommended by experienced business researchers. Fees: Free.

Fedstats. Federal Interagency Council on Statistical Policy. Phone: (202)395-7254 • URL: http://www.fedstats.gov • Web site features an efficient search facility for full-text statistics produced by more than 100 federal agencies, including the Census Bureau, the Bureau of Economic Analysis, and the Bureau of Labor Statistics. Boolean searches can be made within one agency or for all agencies combined. Links are offered to international statistical bureaus, including the UN, IMF, OECD, UNESCO, Eurostat, and 20 individual countries. Fees: Free.

FreeLunch.com. Economy.com, Inc. Phone: (610)696-8700; Fax: (610)696-1678 • URL: http://www.freelunch.com • Web site provides free access to more than 200 million economic and financial data series, covering industry, demographics, labor markets, prices, retail sales, government spending, trade, interest rates, housing starts, the stock market, etc. Data is available in either chart or table form. Searching is offered. Free, but registration required. Economy.com, Inc. also offers fee-based economic analysis at *The Dismal Scientist* site (www.dismal.com).

ONLINE DATABASES

Aerospace America Magazine. American Institute of Aeronautics and Astronautics. • Monthly. $200 Institutions non member, domestic. Covers aeronautics and space technology with special attention to aerospace defense, design, and electronics.

Aerospace Database. American Institute of Aeronautics and Astronautics. • Contains abstracts of literature covering all aspects of the aerospace and aircraft industry 1983 to date. Monthly updates. Inquire as to online cost and availability.

OTHER SOURCES

Army AL&T: Professional Publication of the AL&T Community. U. S. Government Printing Office. • Quarterly. $21 U.S.. Produced by the U.S. Army Materiel Command (www.amc.army.mil). Reports on Army research, development, and acquisition. Formerly *Army RD&A*.

Carroll's Defense Industry Charts. Caroll Publishing. • Quarterly. $2,100 Individuals. Provides 180 large, fold-out paper charts showing personnel relationships at more than 100 major U. S. defense contractors. Charts are also available online and on CD-ROM.

Government Contract Litigation Reporter: Covers Defense Procurement Fraud Litigation As Well as False Claims Acts (Qui Tam) Litigation. Andrews Publications. • Semimonthly. $875.00 per year. Newsletter. Provides reports on defense procurement fraud lawsuits.

PERIODICALS AND NEWSLETTERS

Aerospace America Magazine. American Institute of Aeronautics and Astronautics. • Monthly. $200 Institutions non member, domestic. Covers aeronautics and space technology with special attention to aerospace defense, design, and electronics.

Air Force Journal of Logistics. U. S. Government Printing Office. • Quarterly. $15.00 per year. Issued by the Air Force Logistics Management Center, Air Force Department, Defense Department. Presents research and information of interest to professional Air Force logisticians.

Defence & Public Service Helicopter. Shephard Press Ltd. • Bi-monthly. $130.00 per year. Provides international coverage of both the public service (police, emergency, etc.) and military helicopter industries and markets. Includes technical, piloting, and safety topics. Formerly *Defence Helicopter*.

Defense Daily Network: The Business Source for Aerospace and Defense. Access Intelligence L.L.C. • Daily. Covers the global defense industry.

Homeland Security and Defense: Weekly Intelligence for the Global Homeland Security and Defense Community. Aviation Week Business Intelligence Services. • Weekly. $595.00 per year. Newsletter. Emphasis is on airline and airport programs (federal, state, and local). Also covers counterterrorism, protection of military units, Department of Homeland Security activities, industrial security, communications equipment, and other topics related to homeland security.

Inside R and D: A Weekly Report on Technical Innovation. Technical Insights. • Weekly. Institutions. $840.00 per year. Concentrates on new and significant developments. Formerly *Technology Transfer Week*.

National Defense Magazine: Business & Technology Journal. National Defense Industrial Association. • Monthly. $40 Individuals. Magazine on the North American Defense Industry.

National Defense: NDIA's Business and Technology Magazine. National Defense Industrial Association. • 10 times a year. $35.00 per year.

RESEARCH CENTERS AND INSTITUTES

Center for Defense Information. 1779 Massachusetts Ave. NW, Washington, DC 20036-2109. Phone: (202)332-0600; Fax: (202)462-4559; Email: info@cdi.org • URL: http://www.cdi.org • Aims to strengthen security through international cooperation; reduced reliance on unilateral military power to resolve conflict; reduced reliance on nuclear weapons; a transformed and reformed military establishment; and prudent oversight of, and spending on, weapons programs. Seeks to contribute alternative views on security to promote wide-ranging discourse and debate. Educates the public and informs policy-makers about issues of security policy, strategy, operations, weapons systems and defense budgeting, and pursues creative solutions to the problems of today and tomorrow. Aims to improve understanding between the United States and key nations on security matters through new media initiatives that inform and educate opinion-makers, policy-makers and the general public. Accepts no government or defense industry funding, and does not hold organizational positions. Believes on the concept that the public and political leaders "can, and will, make wise choices on complex security matters when provided with facts, and practical alternatives."

Pennsylvania State University - Applied Research Laboratory. PO Box 30, State College, PA 16804-0030. Phone: (814)865-6531 or (814)865-6343; Fax: (814)865-3105; Email: lrh3@psu.edu • URL: http://www.arl.psu.edu • Underwater acoustics, noise and vibration control, hydrodynamics and hydroacoustics, propulsors, guidance and control, signal processing, thermal power plants, engineering materials, systems engineering, modeling and simulation, manufacturing science, communications, information, electro-optics, navigation, condition-based maintenance, and visualization.

Stanford University - Structures and Composites Laboratory. William F. Durand Bldg., Rm. 054, Department of Aeronautics and Astronautics, 496 Lomita Mall, Stanford, CA 94305. Phone: (650)723-3524; Fax: (650)725-3377; Email: fkchang@stanford.edu • URL: http://structure.stanford.edu • Flight vehicle structures and composite materials.

STATISTICS SOURCES

Standard & Poor's Industry Surveys. Standard & Poor's Financial Services L.L.C. • Semiannual. $1,800.00. Two looseleaf volumes. Includes monthly *Supplements*. Provides detailed, individual surveys of 52 major industry groups. Each survey is revised on a semiannual basis. Also includes "Monthly Investment Review" (industry group investment analysis) and monthly "Trends & Projections" (economic analysis).

Survey of Current Business. U. S. Government Printing Office. • Published by Bureau of Economic Analysis, U. S. Department of Commerce. Presents a wide variety of business and economic data.

TRADE/PROFESSIONAL ASSOCIATIONS

National Defense Industrial Association. 2111 Wilson Blvd., Ste. 400, Arlington, VA 22201. Phone: (703)522-1820 or (703)247-2548; Email: bprokuski@ndia.org • URL: http://www.ndia.org • Concerned citizens, military and government personnel, and defense-related industry workers interested in industrial preparedness for the national defense of the United States. Operates Technology Services that provides a forum for discussion of defense industry programs and issues. Conducts 55 technical meetings per year.

National Defense Transportation Association. 50 S Pickett St., Ste. 220, Alexandria, VA 22304-7296. Phone: (703)751-5011; Fax: (703)823-8761 • URL: http://www.ndtahq.com • Men and women in the field of transportation, travel logistics and related areas in the Armed Forces, federal government, private industry and the academic sector. Strives to foster a strong and efficient transportation system in support of national defense. Serves as link between government and industry on transportation matters. Operates a job placement service for members.

DEFENSE MARKET

See MILITARY MARKET

DEFICIT, FEDERAL

See NATIONAL DEBT

DEHYDRATED FOODS

See FOOD INDUSTRY

DENTAL SUPPLY INDUSTRY

PERIODICALS AND NEWSLETTERS

AAID Business Bite. American Academy of Implant Dentistry. • AAID's monthly electronic newsletter providing practical practice management information for those involved in implant dentistry.

Dental Lab Products. MEDEC Dental Communications. • Bimonthly. $35.00 per year. Edited for dental laboratory managers. Covers new products and technical developments.

Dental Products Report Europe. MEDEC Dental Communications. • Seven times a year. $40.00 per year. Covers new dental products for the Europea market.

Dental Products Report: Trends in Dentistry. MEDEC Dental Communications. • 11 times a year. $120.00 per year. Provides information on new dental products, technology, and trends in dentistry.

Large Equipment Sales Report. Dental Trade Alliance. • Monthly Quarterly. $7,680 Individuals Monthly. Monthly and quarterly reports and heavy equipment sales.

Proofs: The Magazine of Dental Sales. PennWell Corp., Industrial Div. • Contains information on dental trade shows, dental industry marketing, sales tools, and industry statistics.

STATISTICS SOURCES

U.S. Industry and Trade Outlook. U.S. Department of Commerce National Technical Information Service. • Annual. Produced by the International Trade Administration, U.S. Department of Commerce, in a "public-private" partnership with DRI/McGraw-Hill and Standard & Poor's. Provides basic data, outlook for the current year, and "Long-Term Prospects" (five-year projections) for a wide variety of products and services. Includes high technology industries. Formerly *U.S. Industrial Outlook*.

TRADE/PROFESSIONAL ASSOCIATIONS

American Dental Association. 211 E Chicago Ave., Chicago, IL 60611-2678. Phone: 800-947-4746 or (312)440-2500; Fax: (312)440-3542; Email: berryj@ada.org • URL: http://www.ada.org • Professional society of dentists. Encourages the improvement of the health of the public and promotes the art and science of dentistry in matters of legislation and regulations. Inspects and accredits dental schools and schools for dental hygienists, assistants, and laboratory technicians. Conducts research programs at ADA Foundation Research Institute. Produces dental health education material used in the U.S. Sponsors National Children's Dental Health Month and Give Kids a Smile Day. Compiles statistics on personnel, practice, and dental care needs and attitudes of patients with regard to dental health.

Dental Trade Alliance. 4350 N Fairfax Dr., Ste. 220, Arlington, VA 22203-1673. Phone: (703)379-7755; Fax: (703)931-9429 • URL: http://www.dentaltradealliance.org • Represents dental manufacturers, dental dealers, dental laboratories, dental market service providers and dental publications.

DEPARTMENT STORES

See also CHAIN STORES; MARKETING; RETAIL TRADE

CD-ROM DATABASES

OECD Statistical Compendium. Organization for Economic Cooperation and Development. • Semiannual. $1,905.00 per year for 1 to 10 users. CD-ROM contains more than 730,000 monthly, quarterly, and annual time series for OECD countries, 1960 to date. Includes fully searchable data on agriculture, food, economic indicators, national accounts, employment, energy, finance, industry, technology, and foreign trade. Results can be displayed in various forms.

FINANCIAL RATIOS

Annual Statement Studies. Risk Management Association. • Annual. Compiled from over 280,000 financial statements.

Annual Statement Studies: Industry Default Probabilities and Cash Flow Measures. Risk Management Association. • Annual. $405 Nonmembers. Serves as a companion volume to the original *Annual Statement Studies*. Gives probability of default estimates on a percentage scale for more than 450 industries. Includes changes in position year-by-year for eight financial statement line items and provides percentage measures of cash flow.

INTERNET DATABASES

Advance Monthly Retail Trade Report. U. S. Census Bureau. Phone: 800-541-8345 or (301)457-4100 or (301)763-2713; Fax: (301)457-1296 or (301)457-3842; Email: naics@census.gov • URL: http://www.census.gov/epcd/www/naicstab.htm • Web pages provide monthly sales figures for a wide range of retail businesses. Advance, preliminary, and final statistics are provided for the latest month available in each case, with a previous-year comparison. Updates are monthly.

Business 2.0 Web Guide to the Best Business Links. Business 2.0 Media Inc. Phone: (415)293-4800; Email: support@business2.com • URL: http://www.business2.com/webguide • Web site presents an extensive, searchable directory of links to "the best, most informative, and authoritative web pages." Twenty main categories cover business, finance, career, company information, people, and technology topics, with thousands of subtopics, all linking to Web sites recommended by experienced business researchers. Fees: Free.

Fedstats. Federal Interagency Council on Statistical Policy. Phone: (202)395-7254 • URL: http://www.fedstats.gov • Web site features an efficient search facility for full-text statistics produced by more than 100 federal agencies, including the Census Bureau, the Bureau of Economic Analysis, and the Bureau of Labor Statistics. Boolean searches can be made within one agency or for all agencies combined. Links are offered to international statistical bureaus, including the UN, IMF, OECD, UNESCO, Eurostat, and 20 individual countries. Fees: Free.

FreeLunch.com. Economy.com, Inc. Phone: (610)696-8700; Fax: (610)696-1678 • URL: http://www.freelunch.com • Web site provides free access to more than 200 million economic and financial data series, covering industry, demographics, labor markets, prices, retail sales, government spending, trade, interest rates, housing starts, the stock market, etc. Data is available in either chart or table form. Searching is offered. Free, but registration required. Economy.com, Inc. also offers fee-based economic analysis at *The Dismal Scientist* site (www.dismal.com).

PERIODICALS AND NEWSLETTERS

Chain Store Age: The NewsMagazine for Retail Executives. Lebhar-Friedman Inc. • 9/year. Formerly *Chain Store Age Executive with Shopping Center Age*.

Retailing Today. Robert Kahn and Associates. • Description: Focuses on general merchandise, apparel, furniture, hardware, automotive, and food retailing. Offers "original research, comments on current trends and conditions, recommendations for company policy, and emphasis on ethical conduct in business.".

Stores. National Retail Federation. NRF Enterprises Inc. • Monthly. Offers an insider's view of the entire retail industry by featuring the latest trends, hottest ideas, current technologies and consumer attitudes.

RESEARCH CENTERS AND INSTITUTES

Northwestern University - Center for Retail Management. Kellogg School of Management, 2001 Sheridan Rd., Evanston, IL 60208. Phone: (847)467-3600; Fax: (847)467-3620; Email: r-blattberg@kellogg.northwestern.edu • URL: http://www.kellogg.northwestern.edu/research/retail/ • Conducts research related to retail marketing and management.

Texas A&M University - Center for Retailing

Studies. Wehner Bldg., Ste. 201, Mays Business School, 4112 TAMU, College Station, TX 77843-4112. Phone: (979)845-0325; Fax: (979)845-5117 or (979)845-5230; Email: c-bridges@mays.tamu.edu • URL: http://www.crstamu.org • Research areas include retailing issues and consumer economics.

STATISTICS SOURCES

Annual Benchmark Report for Retail Trade and Food Services..A Detailed Summary of Retail Sales, Purchases, Accounts Receivable, Inventories, and Food Service Sales. U. S. Government Printing Office. • Annual. $13.00. Issued by the U.S. Census Bureau. Provides detailed annual and monthly retail statistics for the most recent 10 years. Includes data for various kinds of retail outlets, including automobiles, furniture, appliances, building supplies, grocery stores, drug stores, gasoline stations, clothing, sporting goods, department stores, and restaurants.

Survey of Current Business. U. S. Government Printing Office. • Published by Bureau of Economic Analysis, U. S. Department of Commerce. Presents a wide variety of business and economic data.

TRADE/PROFESSIONAL ASSOCIATIONS

National Retail Federation. 325 7th St. NW, Ste. 1100, Washington, DC 20004. Phone: 800-673-4692 or (202)783-7971 or (202)347-1932; Fax: (202)737-2849; Email: bookinquiries@nrf.com • URL: http://www.nrf.com • Represents state retail associations, several dozen national retail associations, as well as large and small corporate members representing the breadth and diversity of the retail industry's establishment and employees. Conducts informational and educational conferences related to all phases of retailing including financial planning and cash management, taxation, economic forecasting, expense planning, shortage control, credit, electronic data processing, telecommunications, merchandise management, buying, traffic, security, supply, materials handling, store planning and construction, personnel administration, recruitment and training, and advertising and display.

North American Retail Dealers Association. 222 S Riverside Plz., Ste. 2100, Chicago, IL 60606. Phone: 800-621-0298 or (312)648-0649; Fax: (312)648-1212; Email: nardasvc@narda.com • URL: http://www.narda.com • Firms engaged in the retailing of electronic and electrical devices and components. Promotes and represents members' interests. Makes available services to members including: legal and technical consulting; employee screening; bank card processing; long-distance phone discounts; financial statements analysis; in-store promotion kits; customer check authorization. Advocates for members' interests before federal regulatory bodies; disseminates information on new regulations affecting members. Conducts educational programs.

Retail, Wholesale and Department Store Union. 30 E 29th St., New York, NY 10016. Phone: (212)684-5300; Fax: (212)779-2809; Email: info@rwdsu.org • URL: http://www.rwdsu.info • Represents workers throughout the United States and Canada. Works in a wide variety of occupations that range from food processing, retail, manufacturing, service and healthcare.

DEPRECIATION

See also ACCOUNTING

CD-ROM DATABASES

Authority Tax and Estate Planning Library. Matthew Bender and Company Inc. • Periodic revisions. Price on request. CD contains updated full text of *Bender's Payroll Tax Guide, Depreciation Handbook, Federal Income Taxation of Corporations, Tax Planning for Corporations, Modern Estate Planning, Planning for Large Estates, Murphy's Will Clauses, Tax & Estate Planning for the Elderly,* and 12 other Matthew Bender publications. The Internal Revenue Code is also included.

HANDBOOKS AND MANUALS

Business Taxpayer Information Publications. U. S. Government Printing Office. • Annual. $66 U.S. Looseleaf. Two volumes, consisting of *Circular E, Employer's Tax Guide* and *Employer's Supplemental Tax Guide.* Issued by the Internal Revenue Service (http://www.irs.ustreas.gov). Includes a variety of business-related tax information, including withholding tables, tax calendars, self-employment issues, partnership matters, corporation topics, depreciation, and bankruptcy.

CCH Guide to Car, Travel, Entertainment, and Home Office Deductions. Wolters Kluwer Law & Business CCH. • Annual. Explains how to claim maximum tax deductions for common business expenses. Includes automobile depreciation tables, lease value tables, worksheets, and examples of filled-in tax forms.

U.S. Master Depreciation Guide. Wolters Kluwer Law & Business CCH. • Annual. $97.50 Institutions 1 - 4. Contains explanations of ADR (asset depreciation range), ACRS (accelerated cost recovery system), and MACRS (modified accelerated cost recovery system). Includes the historical background of depreciation.

RESEARCH CENTERS AND INSTITUTES

University of Illinois at Urbana-Champaign - Center for International Education and Research in Accounting. 320 Wohlers Hall, 1206 S 6th St., Champaign, IL 61820. Phone: (217)333-4545; Fax: (217)244-6565; Email: ciera@uiuc.edu • URL: http://www.cba.uiuc.edu.

STATISTICS SOURCES

Statistics of Income: Corporation Income Tax Returns. U.S. Internal Revenue Service. U. S. Government Printing Office. • Annual.

DEPRESSION

See MENTAL HEALTH

DEPRESSIONS, BUSINESS

See BUSINESS CYCLES

DERIVATIVE SECURITIES

DIRECTORIES

Futures Magazine SourceBook: The Most Complete List of Exchanges, Companies, Regulators, Organizations, etc., Offering Products and Services to the Futures and Options Industry. Futures Magazine Inc. • Annual. $19.50. Provides information on commodity futures brokers, trading method services, publications, and other items of interest to futures traders and money managers.

HedgeWorld Annual Compendium: The Hedge Fund Industry's Definitive Reference Guide. HedgeWorld. • Annual. $499.00. Contains profiles of 500 domestic and offshore hedge funds with more than $50 million in assets under management. Includes articles on "The Basics of Investing in Hedge Funds," "Beyond the Basics," and other information.

HedgeWorld Service Provider League Tables & Analyses. HedgeWorld. • Annual. $595.00. Provides quantitative and qualitative information on firms providing services to hedge funds: accountants/auditors, administrators, custodians, legal counsel, and prime brokers. Detailed categories cover banks, clearing services, consultants, derivatives business, investment companies, wealth management services, etc.

INTERNET DATABASES

Derivatives. Imagine Software Inc. 233 Broadway, 17th Fl., New York, NY 10279. Phone: (212)317-7600; Fax: (212)317-7601 • URL: http://www.derivatives.com • Web site mainly promotes proprietary software for the use of derivatives in risk management, but also provides free access to articles on a variety of derivatives-related topics.

Factiva. Dow Jones Reuters Business Interactive, LLC. Phone: 800-369-7466 or (609)452-1511; Fax: (609)520-5770; Email: solutions@factiva.com • URL: http://www.factiva.com • Fee-based Web site provides "global news and business information through Web sites and content integration solutions." Includes Dow Jones and Reuters newswires, The Wall Street Journal, and more than 7,000 other sources of current news, historical articles, market research reports, and investment analysis. Content includes 96 major U. S. newspapers, 900 non-English sources, trade publications, media transcripts, country profiles, news photos, etc.

Futures Online. Futures Magazine Inc. Phone: (312)846-4600; Fax: (312)846-4638 • URL: http://www.futuresmag.com • Web site presents updates of *Futures* magazine and links to other futures-related sites.

Nexis.com. Lexis-Nexis Group. Phone: 800-227-4908 or (937)865-6800; Fax: (937)865-6909; Email: webmaster@prod.lexis-nexis.com • URL: http://www.nexis.com • Fee-based Web site offers searching of about 2.8 billion documents in some 30,000 news, business, and legal information sources. Features include a subject directory covering 1,200 topics in 34 categories and a Company Dossier containing information on more than 500,000 public and private companies. Boolean searching is offered.

U.S. Securities and Exchange Commission. 100 F St. NE, Washington, DC 20549. Phone: 800-732-0330 or (202)942-8088; Fax: (202)942-9634; Email: webmaster@sec.gov • URL: http://www.sec.gov • SEC Web site offers free access through EDGAR to text of official corporate filings, such as annual reports (10-K), quarterly reports (10-Q), and proxies. (EDGAR is "Electronic Data Gathering, Analysis, and Retrieval System.") An example is given of how to obtain executive compensation data from proxies. Text of the daily *SEC News Digest* is offered, as are links to other government sites, non-government market regulators, and U. S. stock exchanges. Search facilities are extensive. Fees: Free.

Wall Street Journal Interactive Edition. Dow Jones & Co., Inc. 1211 Avenue of the Americas, New York, NY 10036. Phone: 800-369-5663; Email: service@dowjones.com • URL: http://new.dowjones.com • Fee-based Web site providing online searching of worldwide information from *The Wall Street Journal.* Includes "Company Snapshots," "The Journal's Greatest Hits," "Index to Market Data," "Journal Links," etc. Financial price quotes are available. Fees: $49.00 per year; $29.00 per year to print subscribers.

ONLINE DATABASES

EdgarPlus: SEC Basic Filings. Thomson Reuters Markets. • Online service provides full text of about 60,000 documents that have been filed with the U.S. Securities and Exchange Commission, 1987 to date, with daily updates. Filings include 6-K, 8-K, 10-K, 10-C, 10-Q, 20-F, and proxy statements. Inquire as to online cost and availability.

PERIODICALS AND NEWSLETTERS

Financial Markets, Institutions, and Instruments. New York University, Salomon Center. Blackwell Publishing Inc. • Five times a year. Institutions, $338.00 per year. Includes online edition. Edited to "bridge the gap between the academic and professional finance communities." Special fifth issue each year provides surveys of developments in four areas:

money and banking, derivative securities, corporate finance, and fixed-income securities.

Futures: News, Analysis, and Strategies for Futures, Options, and Derivatives Traders. Futures Magazine Inc. • Monthly. $39 Individuals. Edited for institutional money managers and traders, brokers, risk managers, and individual investors or speculators. Includes special feature issues on interest rates, technical indicators, currencies, charts, precious metals, hedge funds, and derivatives. Supplements available.

Journal of Derivatives (JOD). Institutional Investor Inc. Journals Group. • Quarterly. $780 /year plus online access to the complete archive of articles. Includes analysis of theoretical models.

SFO: Stocks, Futures & Options. W and A Publishing. • Subtitle: *Official Journal for Personal Investing in Stocks, Futures, and Options.* Covers mainly speculative techniques for stocks, commodity futures, financial futures, stock index futures, foreign exchange, short selling, and various kinds of options.

STATISTICS SOURCES

Statistical Information on the Financial Services Industry. American Bankers Association. • Annual. Members, $150.00; non-members, $275.00. Presents a wide variety of data relating to banking and financial services, including consumer economics, personal finance, credit, government loans, capital markets, and international banking.

TRADE/PROFESSIONAL ASSOCIATIONS

EMTA. 360 Madison Ave., 17th Fl., New York, NY 10017. Phone: (646)289-5410 or (646)289-5414; Fax: (646)289-5429; Email: sortiz@emta.org • URL: http://www.emta.org • Promotes orderly trading markets for emerging market instruments. Formerly Emerging Markets Traders Association.

DESALINATION INDUSTRY

ABSTRACTS AND INDEXES

Applied Science and Technology Index. EBSCO Publishing Inc. • 11/year. Indexes a wide variety of English language technical, industrial, and engineering periodicals.

Current Contents: Engineering, Computing and Technology. Thomson Reuters Intellectual Property and Science. • Weekly. $730 per year. Reproductions of contents pages of technical journals. Includes *Author Index, Address Directory, Current Book Contents,* and *Title Word Index.* Formerly *Current Contents: Engineering, Technology and Applied Sciences.*

Environment Abstracts. University Publications of America. • Monthly. Price varies. Provides multidisciplinary coverage of the world's environmental literature. Incorporates *Acid Rain Abstracts.*

Environment Abstracts Annual: A Guide to the Key Environmental Literature of the Year. University Publications of America. • Annual. $495.00. A yearly cumulation of *Environment Abstracts.*

Oceanic Abstracts. CSA. • Monthly. $1,645.00 per year. Includes print and online editions. Covers oceanography, marine biology, ocean shipping, and a wide range of other marine-related subject areas.

Science Citation Index. Thomson Reuters Intellectual Property and Science. • Weekly. Includes *Source Index, Citation Index, Permuterm Subject Index,* and *Corporate Index.* Provides researchers, administrators, faculty, and students with quick, powerful access to the bibliographic and citation information they need to find research data, analyze trends, journals and researchers, and share their findings.

CD-ROM DATABASES

Applied Science and Technology Abstracts. EBSCO Publishing Inc. • Citations for more than 700 prominent scientific, technical, engineering, and industrial periodicals.

Environment Abstracts on CD-ROM. University Publications of America. • Quarterly. $1,295.00 per year. Contains the following CD-ROM databases: *Environment Abstracts, Energy Abstracts,* and *Acid Rain Abstracts.* Length of coverage varies.

NTIS Database. Ovid Technologies Inc. • Quarterly. $2,850.00 per year. Guide to over 2 million bibliographic entries. Compiled by the U.S. National Technical Information Service.

Science Citation Index. Thomson Reuters Intellectual Property and Science. • Weekly. Includes *Source Index, Citation Index, Permuterm Subject Index,* and *Corporate Index.* Provides researchers, administrators, faculty, and students with quick, powerful access to the bibliographic and citation information they need to find research data, analyze trends, journals and researchers, and share their findings.

ONLINE DATABASES

Applied Science and Technology Index Online. H.W. Wilson Co. • Provides online indexing of 500 major scientific, technical, industrial, and engineering periodicals. Time period is 1983 to date. Monthly updates. Inquire as to online cost and availability.

Aqualine. Cambridge Scientific Abstracts L.P. • Provides online citations and abstracts to a wide variety of literature relating to the aquatic environment, including 400 journals, from 1960 to date. Updating is monthly. Inquire as to online cost and availability.

PERIODICALS AND NEWSLETTERS

Water Desalination Report. Maria C. Smith. • Description: Concentrates on the activities of government and industry worldwide concerning the desalination of seawater and brackish water. Discusses such topics as problems with water supply and reuse, resource planning, and pollution control. Reports on federal budgets, regulation, new and future programs, opportunities in business, and research. Recurring features include book reviews and a schedule of activities.

RESEARCH CENTERS AND INSTITUTES

Pacific International Center for High Technology Research. 1440 Kapiolani Blvd., Ste. 1225, Honolulu, HI 96814. Phone: (808)943-9581; Fax: (808)943-9582; Email: info@pichtr.org • URL: http://www.pichtr.org • Desalination is included as a field of research.

DESIGN IN INDUSTRY

See also ART IN INDUSTRY; ARTS MANAGEMENT; COMMERCIAL ART; GRAPHIC ARTS INDUSTRY; OFFICE DESIGN

ABSTRACTS AND INDEXES

Art Index. EBSCO Publishing Inc. • Quarterly. Annual cumulations. Price varies. Subject and author index to periodicals in art, architecture, industrial design, city planning, photography, and various related topics.

DIRECTORIES

ENR-Top International Design Firms. McGraw Hill Financial Inc. • Annual. $49.95 Individuals. Lists 200 firms. Includes U.S. firms. Formerly *Engineering News Record - Top International Design Firms.*

The Top 500 Design Firms Sourcebook. McGraw Hill Financial Inc. • Annual. Lists 500 leading architectural, engineering and speciality design firms selected on basis of annual billings. Formerly *ENR Directory of Design Firms.*

ONLINE DATABASES

Art Index Online. H.W. Wilson Co. • Indexes a wide variety of art-related periodicals, 1984 to date. Monthly updates. Inquire as to online cost and availability.

PERIODICALS AND NEWSLETTERS

Design Management Journal. Design Management Institute. • 3/year. $29 Nonmembers Print. Covers the management of product-related design. Dedicated to the highest standards of research, scholarship, and education.

Engineering Design Graphics Journal. American Society for Engineering Education. • Three times a year. Free to members; Non-members, $24.00 per year. Concerned with engineering graphics, computer graphics, geometric modeling, computer-aided drafting, etc.

TRADE/PROFESSIONAL ASSOCIATIONS

American Design Drafting Association. 105 E Main St., Newbern, TN 38059. Phone: (731)627-0802; Fax: (731)627-9321; Email: corporate@adda.org • URL: http://www.adda.org • Designers, drafters, drafting managers, chief drafters, supervisors, administrators, instructors, and students of design and drafting. Encourages a continued program of education for self-improvement and professionalism in design and drafting and computer-aided design/drafting. Informs members of effective techniques and materials used in drawings and other graphic presentations. Evaluates curriculum of educational institutions through certification program; sponsors drafter certification program.

American Institute of Building Design. 529 14th St. NW, Ste. 750, Washington, DC 20045. Phone: 800-366-2423; Fax: (866)204-0293 • URL: http://www.aibd.org • Represents professional building designers engaged in the professional practice of designing residential and light commercial buildings. Other membership categories include draftspersons, educators, and students. Corporate members are residential and light commercial building manufacturers. Keeps members informed of techniques and principles of building design; seeks to stimulate public interest in the aesthetic and practical efficiency of building design; engages in legislative activities and lobbying; provides consumer referral service. Aids in the development of better and continuing education. Local groups meet monthly.

Design Management Institute. 38 Chauncy St., Ste. 800, Boston, MA 02111. Phone: (617)338-6380 • URL: http://www.dmi.org • In-house design groups and consultant design firms; individuals involved in the management of designers with in-house corporate design groups or consultant design firms. Aims to share management techniques as applied to design groups, and to facilitate better understanding by business management of the role design can play in achieving business goals. Design disciplines included are: architecture, advertising, communications, exhibit design, graphics, interior design, packaging and product design. Develops and distributes design management education materials. Sponsors seminars for design professionals. Identifies critical areas of design management study; conducts surveys and research on corporate design management. Maintains design management archive. Operates Center for Research, Center for Education, and Center for Design and Management Resources.

DESKTOP PUBLISHING

See also MICROCOMPUTERS AND MINICOMPUTERS; WORD PROCESSING

ABSTRACTS AND INDEXES

Applied Science and Technology Index. EBSCO Publishing Inc. • 11/year. Indexes a wide variety of English language technical, industrial, and engineering periodicals.

Business Periodicals Index Retrospective. EBSCO Publishing Inc. • 11/year. Quarterly and annual cumulations.

Computer and Information Systems Abstracts Journal: An Abstract Journal Pertaining to the Theory, Design, Fabrication and Application of Computer and Information Systems. CSA. • Monthly. $1,750 per year.

Computer Science Index. EBSCO Publishing Inc. • Quarterly. $245 per year. Contains brief abstracts of book and periodical literature covering all phases of computing, including approximately 70 specific application areas.

Current Contents: Engineering, Computing and Technology. Thomson Reuters Intellectual Property and Science. • Weekly. $730 per year. Reproductions of contents pages of technical journals. Includes *Author Index, Address Directory, Current Book Contents*, and *Title Word Index*. Formerly *Current Contents: Engineering, Technology and Applied Sciences*.

Inspec Direct. Institution of Engineering and Technology. • Monthly. $2,400 per year. Section C of *Science Abstracts*.

Internet and Personal Computing Abstracts (print edition). EBSCO Publishing Inc. • Quarterly. $269.00 per year, including cumulative index. Provides more than 10,000 abstracts annually from both trade and academic publications. Covers computer hardware, software, product reviews, Web topics, e-commerce, networks, corporate news, security, and related topics. Formerly *Microcomputer Abstracts*.

DIRECTORIES

Desktop Publishing Directory. InfoGroup Inc. • Annual. Number of listings: 5,952. Entries include: Name, address, phone, size of advertisement, name of owner or manager, number of employees, year first in "Yellow Pages." Compiled from telephone company "Yellow Pages," nationwide.

INTERNET DATABASES

InfoTech Trends. Data Analysis Group. Phone: (925)462-1202; Fax: (925)462-1225; Email: support@infotechtrends.com • URL: http://www.infotechtrends.com • Web site provides both free and fee-based market research data on the information technology industry, including computers, peripherals, telecommunications, the Internet, software, CD-ROM/DVD, e-commerce, and workstations. Fees: Free for current (most recent year) data; more extensive information has various fee structures. Formerly *Computer Industry Forecasts*.

Wired News. Lycos Inc. 400-2 Totten Pond Rd., Waltham, MA 02451-2053. Phone: (781)370-2700 or (415)276-8400; Fax: (781)370-2600 or (415)276-8500; Email: press@lycos.com • URL: http://www.lycos.com • Provides summaries and full-text of "Top Stories" relating to the Internet, computers, multimedia, telecommunications, and the electronic information industry in general. These news stories are placed in the broad categories of Politics, Business, Culture, and Technology. Affiliated with *Wired* magazine. Fees: Free.

ONLINE DATABASES

Applied Science and Technology Index Online. H.W. Wilson Co. • Provides online indexing of 500 major scientific, technical, industrial, and engineering periodicals. Time period is 1983 to date. Monthly updates. Inquire as to online cost and availability.

Computer Database. Cengage Learning Inc. • Provides one year of full-text online for 150 leading computer-related publications. Also includes 70,000 product specifications and brief profiles of 13,000 computer product vendors and manufacturers. Inquire as to prices and availability.

Wilson Business Abstracts Online. H.W. Wilson Co. • Indexes and abstracts 600 major business periodicals, plus the *Wall Street Journal* and the business section of the *New York Times*. Indexing is from 1982, abstracting from 1990, with the two newspapers included from 1993. Updated weekly. Inquire as to online cost and availability. (*Business Periodicals Index* without abstracts is also available online.).

PERIODICALS AND NEWSLETTERS

Digital Imaging: The Magazine for the Imaging Professional. Cygnus Business Media Inc. • Bimonthly. $24.95 per year. Edited for business and professional users of electronic publishing products and services. Topics covered include document imaging, CD-ROM publishing, digital video, and multimedia services. Formerly *Micro Publishing News*.

EDP Weekly: The Leading Weekly Computer News Summary. Computer Age and EDP News Services. • Weekly. $495.00 per year. Newsletter. Summarizes news from all areas of the computer and microcomputer industries.

Innovative Publisher: Publishing Strategies for New Markets. Emmelle Publishing Co., Inc. • Biweekly. $69.00 per year. Provides articles and news on electronic publishing (CD-ROM or online) and desktop publishing.

The Magazine for Electronic Publishing Professionals. Publish Media. • Monthly. $39.90 per year. Edited for professional publishers, graphic designers, and industry service providers. Covers new products and emerging technologies for the electronic publishing industry.

The Page. Skillsoft Ireland Ltd. • Description: Acts as a visual guide to McIntosh computer desktop publishing.

The Seybold Report. Seybold Publications. • Semimonthly. $499 /year. The definitive and independent source of information about the technologies used for publishing and printing.

Step-By-Step Electronic Design: The How-To Newsletter for Electronic Designers. Dynamic Graphics Inc. • Monthly. $48.00 per year.

RESEARCH CENTERS AND INSTITUTES

Rochester Institute of Technology - Chester F. Carlson Center for Imaging Science. 54 Lomb Memorial Dr., Rochester, NY 14623. Phone: (585)475-5944; Fax: (585)475-5988; Email: baum@cis.rit.edu • URL: http://www.cis.rit.edu • Imaging sciences, including remote sensing, digital image processing, color science, optics, medical diagnostic imaging, visual perception, sensor development, printing technology, and astronomical imaging.

DETERGENTS

See CLEANING PRODUCTS INDUSTRY

DEVELOPING AREAS

See also FOREIGN INVESTMENTS

ABSTRACTS AND INDEXES

World Agricultural Economics and Rural Sociology Abstracts (WAERSA). CABI. • Monthly. Print and online available. Published in England by CABI Publishing. Provides worldwide coverage of the literature.

ALMANACS AND YEARBOOKS

World Development Report. World Bank Group. • Annual. Covers history, conditions, and trends relating to economic globalization and localization. Includes selected data from *World Development Indicators* for 132 countries or economies. Key indicators are provided for 78 additional countries or economies.

BIBLIOGRAPHIES

Catalogue of Statistical Materials of Developing Countries. Institute of Developing Economies/Ajia Keizai Kenkyusho. • Semiannual. Price varies. Text in English and Japanese.

CD-ROM DATABASES

International Development Statistics. Organization for Economic Cooperation and Development. • Annual. $71.00. Issued by the OECD Development Assistance Committee. CD-ROM contains data on aid to more than 180 recipient countries, including amount, origin, type, and recipients' external debt.

Kompass Concord CD-ROM. Kompass USA, Inc. • Provides information on more than 105,000 companies in 17 rapidly developing East European countries: Armenia, Azerbaijan, Belarus, Bulgaria, Czech Republic, Estonia, Hungary, Kazakhstan, Kyrgyzstan, Latvia, Lithuania, Moldova, Poland, Romania, Russia, Ukraine, and Uzbekistan. Classification system covers approximately 50,000 products and services.

World Development Report. World Bank Group. • Annual. Covers history, conditions, and trends relating to economic globalization and localization. Includes selected data from *World Development Indicators* for 132 countries or economies. Key indicators are provided for 78 additional countries or economies.

ENCYCLOPEDIAS AND DICTIONARIES

Worldmark Encyclopedia of National Economies. Cengage Learning Inc. • 2002. $572.00. Four volumes. Covers both the current and historical development of the economies of 200 foreign nations. Includes analysis and statistics. Also available as eBook.

GENERAL WORKS

Trade and Employment in Developing Countries. Anne O. Krueger, editor. The University of Chicago Press. • $20 volume 3. 1983. (National Bureau of Economic Research Project Report Series).

INTERNET DATABASES

ETF Connect. Nuveen Investments. Phone: 800-257-8787 • URL: http://www.etfconnect.com • Free Web site makes available extensive, searchable information on individual closed-end investment funds, preferred share funds, and exchange-traded index funds. Information on a particular fund is available by name or as part of a classification (high yield, investment grade, municipal, emerging markets, global equity, etc.). Fund charts are available for various time periods, as is data concerning premiums or discounts, dividends, annualized total return, credit quality, "Top 10 Holdings," and so forth.

OTHER SOURCES

World Migration Report. United Nations Publications. • Annual. $39.00. Analyzes major trends in world migration, including individual country profiles.

PERIODICALS AND NEWSLETTERS

Development Business. United Nations, Department of Public Information. • Semimonthly. $550 Individuals online. Provides leads on contract opportunities worldwide for engineering firms and multinational corporations. Text in English, French, Portuguese, and Spanish.

Emerging Markets Debt Report. SourceMedia Inc. • Weekly. $895.00 per year. Newsletter. Provides information on new and prospective sovereign and corporate bond issues from developing countries. Includes an emerging market bond index and pricing data.

Emerging Markets Finance & Trade. M.E. Sharpe Inc. • Bimonthly. $1,421 Institutions per year, print and online. Provides research papers on developing markets in Europe, Asia, Latin America, the Middle East, and Africa.

Emerging Markets Quarterly. Institutional Investor Inc. Journals Group. • Quarterly. Price on application. Newsletter on financial markets in developing areas, such as Africa, Latin America, Southeast Asia, and Eastern Europe. Topics include institutional investment opportunities and regulatory matters. Formerly *Emerging Markets Weekly*.

RESEARCH CENTERS AND INSTITUTES

Center for International Policy. 2000 M St. NW, Ste. 720, Washington, DC 20036-3327. Phone: (202)232-3317; Fax: (202)232-3440; Email: cip@ciponline.org • URL: http://www.ciponline.org • Research subjects include the International Monetary Fund, the World Bank, and other international financial institutions. Analyzes the impact of policies on social and economic conditions in developing countries.

Cornell University - Program in International Studies in Planning. 106 W Sibley Hall, Ithaca, NY 14853-3901. Phone: (607)255-4331 or (607)255-4613; Fax: (607)255-1971; Email: wwg1@cornell.edu • URL: http://aap.cornell.edu/crp/programs/grad/internation-studies.cfm • Research activities are related to international urban and regional planning, with emphasis on developing areas.

Stanford University - Stanford Center for International Development. Gunn/SIEPR Bldg., 366 Galvez St., Stanford, CA 94305-6015. Phone: (650)725-8730; Fax: (650)725-6069; Email: nhope@stanford.edu • URL: http://scid.stanford.edu • Economic policy problems facing developing countries and countries with economies in transition.

STATISTICS SOURCES

Statistical Yearbook. United Nations Publications. • Annual. $125.00. Contains statistics for about 200 countries on a wide variety of economic, industrial, and demographic topics. Compiled by United Nations Statistical Office.

TRADE/PROFESSIONAL ASSOCIATIONS

Committee for the Economic Growth of Israel. 100 Manpower Pl., Milwaukee, WI 53212. Phone: (414)906-6250; Fax: (414)906-7878 • URL: http://elmerwinter.com • Businessmen and women. Seeks to expand business relationships between Israel and the U.S. by promoting investment and joint venture opportunities for U.S. and Israeli companies. Promotes the exchange of technology, research and development, and products from Israel.

DOCHAS, The Irish Association of Non-Governmental Development Organisations. 1-2 Baggot Ct., Lower Baggot St., Dublin 2, Dublin, Ireland. Phone: 353 1 4053801; Fax: 353 1 4053802 • URL: http://www.dochas.ie • Brings together 38 Irish NGDO involved in development and relief overseas and/or in the provision of development education. Aims to provide a forum for consultation and cooperation between its members and acts as the Irish Assembly of Development and Relief Organisations in relation to the CONCORD - a European Confederation for relief and development.

EnterpriseWorks - Senegal. BP 10251, Dakar, Senegal. Phone: 221 8254523; Email: ewws@sentoo.sn • URL: http://www.angelfire.com/yt2/EnterpriseWorks/english.htm • Works to fight poverty in the developing world through business development programs that allow small agricultural producers and other entrepreneurs to increase productivity and incomes. Pursues sustainable business opportunities. Creates jobs that benefit families, communities and regions.

Executives Without Borders. 281 Summer St., 5th Fl., Boston, MA 02210. Phone: 800-790-6134; Email: contactus@execwb.org • URL: http://www.executiveswithoutborders.org • Encourages businessmen and businesswomen to use their leadership positions to foster the growth of business in developing countries. Provides humanitarian aid to alleviate the effects of natural and economic disasters. Promotes cooperation and works with research institutions to find sustainable business solutions.

International Executive Service Corps. 1900 M St. NW, Ste. 500, Washington, DC 20036. Phone: (202)589-2600; Fax: (202)326-0289; Email: iesc@iesc.org • URL: http://www.iesc.org • Provides technical and managerial assistance to enterprises, organizations and government bodies in emerging democracies and developing countries. Focuses on the knowledge, skill and experience of its 12,000 industry experts. Maintains a network of experts that includes high-level professionals drawn from nearly every area of private enterprise, government and non-governmental organizations; Geekcorps division includes experts in communications and information technology and is committed to closing the digital divide.

National Democratic Institute for International Affairs. 455 Massachusetts Ave. NW, 8th Fl., Washington, DC 20001-2783. Phone: 888-875-2887 or (202)728-5500; Fax: (202)728-5520; Email: contactndi@ndi.org • URL: http://www.ndi.org • Works to strengthen and expand democracy worldwide. Provides practical assistance to civic and political leaders advancing democratic values, practices and institutions. Works with democrats in every region of the world to build political and civic organizations, safeguard elections, and promote citizen participation, openness and accountability in government.

Nonviolent Peaceforce. 425 Oak Grove St., Minneapolis, MN 55403. Phone: (612)871-0005; Fax: (612)871-0006; Email: info@nonviolentpeaceforce.org • URL: http://www.nonviolentpeaceforce.org • Promotes the widespread implementation of effective nonviolent peacemaking in conflict areas around the world. Currently working to create the Nonviolent Peaceforce, an international organization to send hundreds and eventually thousands of trained peacemakers to work in areas of conflict at the invitation of local peacemakers or human rights workers. The Peace Force will be sent to conflict areas to prevent death and destruction, and protect human rights, thus creating the space for local groups to struggle nonviolently, enter into dialogue, and seek peaceful resolution.

Oxfam - America. 226 Causeway St., 5th Fl., Boston, MA 02114. Phone: 800-77-OXFAM or (617)482-1211; Fax: (617)728-2594; Email: info@oxfamamerica.org • URL: http://www.oxfamamerica.org • Autonomous development and disaster assistance organization cooperating in a worldwide network known as Oxfam, a name derived from the Oxford Committee for Famine Relief, which began in England in 1942. Provides funds for self-help projects in the poorer countries of Asia, Africa, and the Americas. Emphasizes promoting economic and food self-reliance. Responds to emergency needs of political and natural disaster refugees by funding food, water resources, and medical aid programs. Supports development programs that address underlying causes of such disasters. Educates U.S. public about root causes of hunger; advocates for policy changes.

PlaNet Finance US. 44 rue de Prony, 75017 Paris, France. Email: contact@planetfinance.org • URL: http://www.planetfinance.org • Works to alleviate poverty through the development of microfinance. Seeks to support and strengthen the capacity of the microfinance sector. Raises public awareness of microfinancing.

DEVELOPMENT, COMMUNITY

See COMMUNITY DEVELOPMENT

DEVELOPMENT CREDIT CORPORATIONS

See CREDIT

DEVELOPMENT, INDUSTRIAL

See INDUSTRIAL DEVELOPMENT

DEVELOPMENT, URBAN

See URBAN DEVELOPMENT

DIAMOND INDUSTRY

See also GEMS AND GEMSTONES; INDUSTRIAL DIAMONDS

ALMANACS AND YEARBOOKS

Diamond Manufacturers & Importers Association of America Yearbook. • Annual.

DIRECTORIES

Directory of South Korean Manufacturers & Exporters of Gemstones & Diamonds. EXIM Infotek Private Ltd. • $5 Individuals. Covers: 20 South Korean manufacturers and exporters of colored precious stones-polished, diamond-polished, diamonds-rough, ivory/coral/pearl articles, and rough colored precious stones. Entries include: Company name, postal address, city, country, phone, fax, e-mail and websites, contact person, designation, and product details.

Jewelers' Circular/Keystone-Jewelers' Directory. Reed Elsevier Group plc Reed Business Information. • About 8,500 manufacturers, importers and wholesale jewelers providing merchandise and supplies to the jewelry retailing industry; and related trade organizations. Included with subscription to *Jewelers' Circular Keystone*.

Kompass--Diamonds. Kompass Belgium Products. • Annual. Covers: All Belgian diamond cutters/merchants.

PERIODICALS AND NEWSLETTERS

Diamond World Review. World Federation of Diamond Bourses. International Diamond Publications, Ltd. • Bimonthly. $78.00 per year. Text in English.

Israel Diamond and Precious Stones. International Diamond Publications, Ltd. • Bimonthly. $78.00 per year. Text in English. Formerly *Israel Diamonds*.

TRADE/PROFESSIONAL ASSOCIATIONS

Diamond Council of America. 3212 W End Ave., Ste. 400, Nashville, TN 37203. Phone: 877-283-5669 or (615)385-5301; Fax: (615)385-4955 • URL: http://www.diamondcouncil.org • Retail jewelry firms and suppliers of gemstones. Firms operating approximately 4900 retail jewelry stores; associated manufacturers and importers. Offers courses in "gemology" and "diamontology" to employees of member firms; bestows titles of Certified Diamontologist and Guild Gemologist upon those completing courses and examinations. Supplies members with advertising and educational materials, sales tools, displays, ad copy, radio and television scripts, and merchandise plans.

Diamond Dealers Club. 580 5th Ave., 10th Fl., New

York, NY 10036. Phone: (212)790-3600; Fax: (212)869-5164 • URL: http://www.nyddc.com • Seeks to foster the interests of the diamond industry, promote equitable trade principles, eliminate abuses and unfair trade practices, disseminate accurate and reliable information concerning the industry, establish uniform business ethics, and cooperate with other persons and organizations for the advancement of the trade. Maintains active trading floor for all categories of wholesale diamonds and offers all members arbitration tribunals for dispute settlement. Operates charitable program.

DIAMONDS, INDUSTRIAL

See INDUSTRIAL DIAMONDS

DICTATING MACHINES

See OFFICE EQUIPMENT AND SUPPLIES

DIE CASTING

See TOOL INDUSTRY

DIESEL ENGINES

See ENGINES

DIET

See also HEALTH FOOD INDUSTRY; HERBS; VITAMINS

ABSTRACTS AND INDEXES

Nutrition Abstracts and Reviews, Series A: Human and Experimental. CABI Publishing North America. • Monthly. Institutions, $1,835.00 per year. Includes single site internet access. Published in England by CABI Publishing. Provides worldwide coverage of the literature.

CD-ROM DATABASES

Consumer Health Complete. EBSCO Publishing Inc. • Full text of more than 250 health references, health diagrams, videos, pamphlets.

ENCYCLOPEDIAS AND DICTIONARIES

Encyclopedia of Food and Culture. Cengage Learning Inc. • 2003. $657.00. Three volumes. Contains 600 articles covering various aspects of food and its place in society, from agronomy to zucchini. Includes illustrations and a detailed index. eBook also available, updated in 2004.

INTERNET DATABASES

National Library of Medicine. National Institutes of Health. 9000 Rockville Pke., Bethesda, MD 20892. Phone: (301)496-4000; Email: nihinfo@od.nih.gov • URL: http://www.nih.gov • NLM Web site offers free access through MEDLINE ("PubMed") to about nine million references to articles appearing in some 4,000 biomedical journals, with abstracts. Search interfaces range from "simple keywords to advanced Boolean expressions." The NLM site offers many links to other sources of biomedical and technical information (the National Center for Biotechnology Information, for example). Fees: Free.

ONLINE DATABASES

CAB Abstracts. CABI. • Contains 46 specialized abstract collections covering over 10,000 journals and monographs in the areas of agriculture, horticulture, forest products, farm products, nutrition, dairy science, poultry, grains, animal health, entomology, etc. Time period is 1972 to date, with monthly updates. Inquire as to online cost and availability. *CAB Abstracts on CD-ROM* also available, with annual updating.

PERIODICALS AND NEWSLETTERS

Family Economics and Nutrition Review. U. S. Government Printing Office. • Semi-annual. $13.00 per year. Issued by the Consumer and Food Economics Institute, U. S. Department of Agriculture. Provides articles on consumer expenditures and budgeting for food, clothing, housing, energy, education, etc.

International Journal for Vitamin and Nutrition Research. Hogrefe & Huber Publishers. • Quarterly. $202.00 per year.

Journal of the Academy of Nutrition and Dietetics. Academy of Nutrition and Dietetics. Elsevier. • Monthly. Individuals, $208.00 per year; institutions, $288.00 per year.

Nutrition Reviews. International Life Science Institute. • Monthly. Individuals, $222.00 per year; institutions, $452.00 per year.

Nutrition Today. Lippincott Williams & Wilkins. • Bimonthly. Individuals, $104.00 per year; institutions, $393.00 per year.

STATISTICS SOURCES

Agriculture Fact Book. U. S. Government Printing Office. • Annual. $26 Individuals. Issued by the Office of Communications, U. S. Department of Agriculture. Includes data on U. S. agriculture, farmers, food, nutrition, and rural America. Programs of the Department of Agriculture in six areas are described: rural economic development, foreign trade, nutrition, the environment, inspection, and education.

TRADE/PROFESSIONAL ASSOCIATIONS

Academy of Nutrition and Dietetics. 120 S Riverside Plaza, Ste. 2000, Chicago, IL 60606-6995. Phone: 800-877-1600 or (312)899-0040; Email: knowledge@eatright.org • URL: http://www.eatright.org • Represents food and nutrition professionals. Promotes nutrition, health and well-being.

American Society for Nutrition. 9650 Rockville Pike, Bethesda, MD 20814-3998. Phone: (301)634-7050 or (301)634-7110; Fax: (301)634-7892 or (301)634-7894; Email: info@nutrition.org • URL: http://www.nutrition.org • Affiliated with American Society for Clinical Nutrition. Formerly American Institute of Nutrition.

Natural Products Association. 1773 T St. NW, Washington, DC 20009. Phone: 800-966-6632 or (202)223-0101; Fax: (202)223-0250; Email: natural@npainfo.org • URL: http://www.npainfo.org • Represents retailers, wholesalers, brokers, distributors and manufacturers of natural, nutritional, dietetic foods, supplements, services and natural body and home care products.

DIGITAL COMPUTERS

See COMPUTERS

DINERS

See RESTAURANTS, LUNCHROOMS, ETC.

DINNERWARE

See TABLEWARE

DIPLOMATIC AND CONSULAR SERVICE

ABSTRACTS AND INDEXES

PAIS International. ProQuest L.L.C. • Monthly. $850.00 per year; cumulations three times a year. Provides topical citations to the worldwide literature of public affairs, economics, demographics, sociology, and trade. Text in English; indexed materials in English, French, German, Italian, Portuguese and Spanish.

ALMANACS AND YEARBOOKS

The Statesman's Yearbook: Statistical and Historical Annual of the States of the World. St. Martin's Press. • Annual. £220 Individuals Hardcover. presents a political, economic and social account of every country of the world together with facts and analysis.

BIBLIOGRAPHIES

Diplomatic Bookshelf and Review. Arthur H. Thrower, Ltd. • Monthly. $4.00 per year.

CD-ROM DATABASES

PAIS International. ProQuest L.L.C. • Monthly. $1,995.00 per year. Contains over 650,000 citations to the literature of contemporary social, political, and economic issues.

DIRECTORIES

Foreign Consular Offices in the United States. U.S. Department of State. U. S. Government Printing Office. • $7.99. Lists foreign consular offices in the U.S.

Foreign Representatives in the U. S. Yellow Book: Who's Who in the U. S. Offices of Foreign Corporations, Foreign Nations, the Foreign Press, and Intergovernmental Organizations. Leadership Directories Inc. • Semiannual. $465 per year. Lists executives located in the U. S. for 1,200 foreign companies, 300 foreign banks and other financial institutions, 175 embassies and consulates, and 375 foreign press outlets. Includes five indexes.

United States Government Manual. Office of the Federal Register. • Annual. $29 Individuals. Provides information on the agencies of the executive, judicial, and legislative branches of the Federal government. Contains a section on terminated or transferred agencies. Database includes: Includes boards, commissions, committees and quasi-official agencies and organizations in which US participates.

PERIODICALS AND NEWSLETTERS

Diplomatic History. Society for Historians of American Foreign Relations. Oxford University Press, Journals. • 5/year. $548 Institutions print & online. The official journal of Society for Historians of American Foreign Relations (SHAFR).

Diplomatic Observer. Institute for International Sociological Research. • Monthly. $16.50 per year.

Diplomatic World Bulletin and Delegates World Bulletin: Dedicated to Serving the United Nations and the International Community. Diplomatic World Bulletin Publications, Inc. • Biweekly. $45.00 per year.

Foreign Service Journal. American Foreign Service Association. • Monthly. $50 Individuals. Written for United States foreign service members.

Society for Historians of American Foreign Relations Newsletter. Society for Historians of American Foreign Relations. • Quarterly. $15.00 per year.

RESEARCH CENTERS AND INSTITUTES

Princeton University - Princeton Institute for International and Regional Studies. Princeton University, 334 Aaron Burr Hall, Princeton, NJ 08544-2001. Phone: (609)258-7497; Fax: (609)258-3988; Email: piirs@princeton.edu • URL: http://www.princeton.edu/piirs • International relations and world politics, including national defense and military policy, foreign policy, diplomacy and international political organization, comparative politics, political, social, and economic modernization, world order studies, U.S.-Japan relations, and economies of developing countries. Furthers research and publication on international relations at the University directed toward development of systematic, disciplined and comprehensive appraisals of varied aspects of international relations and world politics with special emphasis on U.S. foreign policy.

TRADE/PROFESSIONAL ASSOCIATIONS

American Foreign Service Association. 2101 E St. NW, Washington, DC 20037. Phone: 800-704-AFSA or (202)338-4045; Fax: (202)338-6820; Email: afsa@afsa.org • URL: http://www.afsa.org • Associate membership is open to individuals and international organizations and corporations interested in foreign affairs, international trade, and economic policy. Conducts international conferences and symposia; holds monthly speaker programs. Operates the Foreign Service Club; sponsors member insurance programs. Maintains Speakers' Bureau.

Brazilian Government Trade Bureau of the Consulate General of Brazil in New York. 220 E 42nd St., New York, NY 10017-5806. Phone: (917)777-7777; Fax: (212)827-0225; Email: cg.novayork@itamaraty.gov.br • URL: http://novayork.itamaraty.gov.br/en-us • Commercial Office of the Brazil Consulate in New York. Offers online match between Brazilian exporters of goods and services and U.S. importers.

British Trade Office at Consulate-General. 845 3rd Ave., New York, NY 10022. Phone: (212)745-0200; Fax: (212)745-0456 • URL: http://www.gov.uk/government/world/organisations/british-consulate-general-new-york • British government office that promotes trade with the U.S.; assists British companies selling in the U.S.; aids American companies that wish to import goods from or invest in Britain.

DACOR. 1801 F St. NW, Washington, DC 20006. Phone: (202)682-0500; Fax: (202)842-3295; Email: dacor@dacorbacon.org • URL: http://dacorbacon.org • Formerly Retired Foreign Service Officers Association.

DIRECT COSTING

See COST ACCOUNTING

DIRECT MAIL ADVERTISING

See also ADVERTISING; MAIL ORDER BUSINESS; MAILING LISTS

FINANCIAL RATIOS

Annual Statement Studies. Risk Management Association. • Annual. Compiled from over 280,000 financial statements.

Annual Statement Studies: Industry Default Probabilities and Cash Flow Measures. Risk Management Association. • Annual. $405 Nonmembers. Serves as a companion volume to the original *Annual Statement Studies.* Gives probability of default estimates on a percentage scale for more than 450 industries. Includes changes in position year-by-year for eight financial statement line items and provides percentage measures of cash flow.

PERIODICALS AND NEWSLETTERS

Advertising Age: The International Newspaper of Marketing. Crain Communications Inc. • Weekly. $178.50 Individuals. Includes supplement *Creativity.*

Database Marketer. SIMBA Information Inc. • Monthly. $329.00 per year.

Direct Marketing: Using Direct Response Advertising to Enhance Marketing Database. Hoke Communications Inc. • Monthly. $65.00 per year. Direct marketing to consumers and business.

DMA Politically Direct. Direct Marketing Association. • Quarterly. Available in print and digital to members.

Public Affairs Report. University of California, Berkeley Institute of Governmental Studies. • Quarterly. Description: Publishes essays on emerging governmental and public policy issues of significance to public officials and citizens in both California and the nation. Covers such subjects as pollution, politics, finance, transportation, health and housing policy, and California-Mexico trade relations. Recurring features include bibliographies.

Target Marketing: The Leading Magazine for Integrated Database Marketing. North American Publishing Co. • Monthly. $65.00 per year. Dedicated to direct marketing excellence. Formerly *Zip Target Marketing.*

TRADE/PROFESSIONAL ASSOCIATIONS

Direct Marketing Association. 1120 Ave. of the Americas, New York, NY 10036-6700. Phone: (212)768-7277; Fax: (212)302-6714; Email: info@the-dma.org • URL: http://www.thedma.org • A division of the Direct Marketing Association. Members include publishers and circulation directors.

DMA Nonprofit Federation. 1615 L St. NW, Ste. 1100, Washington, DC 20036. Phone: (202)861-2427; Fax: (202)628-4383; Email: aosgood@the-dma.org • URL: http://www.nonprofitfederation.org • Trade and lobbying group for non-profit organizations that use direct and online marketing to raise funds and communicate with members. Sponsors professional development conferences and seminars, lobbies on state and federal legislation, regulation, and standards related to direct marketing and related issues. Provides information about and participants in litigation affecting non-profits. Promotes the overall welfare of non-profits. Represents health care charities, social service agencies, religious groups, colleges and universities and fraternal organizations.

Mailing and Fulfillment Service Association. 1800 Diagonal Rd., Ste. 320, Alexandria, VA 22314-2806. Phone: (703)836-9200; Fax: (703)548-8204; Email: mfsa-mail@mfsanet.org • URL: http://www.mfsanet.org • Formerly Mail Advertising Service Association International.

Marketing EDGE. 1120 Ave. of the Americas, 13th Fl., New York, NY 10036-6700. Phone: (212)768-7277; Fax: (212)790-1561; Email: admin@marketingedge.org • URL: http://www.marketingedge.org • Represents individuals, firms, and organizations interested in furthering college-level education in direct marketing. Functions as the collegiate arm of the direct marketing profession. Sponsors a summer internship, programs for students and professors, and campaign competition for students. Provides educational materials and course outlines to faculty members; arranges for speakers for college classes and clubs. Co-sponsors academic research competitions. Maintains hall of fame.

DIRECT MARKETING

ABSTRACTS AND INDEXES

Business Periodicals Index Retrospective. EBSCO Publishing Inc. • 11/year. Quarterly and annual cumulations.

ONLINE DATABASES

Wilson Business Abstracts Online. H.W. Wilson Co. • Indexes and abstracts 600 major business periodicals, plus the *Wall Street Journal* and the business section of the *New York Times.* Indexing is from 1982, abstracting from 1990, with the two newspapers included from 1993. Updated weekly. Inquire as to online cost and availability. (*Business Periodicals Index* without abstracts is also available online.).

PERIODICALS AND NEWSLETTERS

Catalog Age. PRIMEDIA Business Magazine and Media. • 13 times a year. Free to qualified personnel; others, $85.00 per year. Edited for catalog marketing and management personnel.

Direct. Intertec Publishing. • Provides analysis on direct marketing issues.

Direct Marketing News. Haymarket Media Group Ltd. • Monthly. $148 U.S. /year. Includes special feature issues on catalog marketing, telephone marketing, database marketing, and fundraising. Includes monthly supplements, *DM News International, DRTV News,* and *TeleServices.*

Direct Marketing: Using Direct Response Advertising to Enhance Marketing Database. Hoke Communications Inc. • Monthly. $65.00 per year. Direct marketing to consumers and business.

Direct Selling Association World Federation News. Direct Selling Association. World Federation of Direct Selling Associations. • Quarterly.

TRADE/PROFESSIONAL ASSOCIATIONS

Direct Selling Association. 1667 K St. NW, Ste. 1100, Washington, DC 20006-1660. Phone: (202)452-8866; Fax: (202)452-9010; Email: info@dsa.org • URL: http://www.dsa.org • Manufacturers and distributors selling consumer products through person-to-person sales, by appointment, and through home-party plans. Products include food, gifts, house wares, dietary supplements, cosmetics, apparel, jewelry, decorative accessories, reference books, and telecommunications products and services. Offers specialized education; conducts research programs; compiles statistics. Maintains hall of fame. Sponsors Direct Selling Education Foundation.

Marketing EDGE. 1120 Ave. of the Americas, 13th Fl., New York, NY 10036-6700. Phone: (212)768-7277; Fax: (212)790-1561; Email: admin@marketingedge.org • URL: http://www.marketingedge.org • Represents individuals, firms, and organizations interested in furthering college-level education in direct marketing. Functions as the collegiate arm of the direct marketing profession. Sponsors a summer internship, programs for students and professors, and campaign competition for students. Provides educational materials and course outlines to faculty members; arranges for speakers for college classes and clubs. Co-sponsors academic research competitions. Maintains hall of fame.

DIRECT SELLING

See DIRECT MARKETING

DIRECTORIES

See CATALOGS AND DIRECTORIES

DIRECTORS

See CORPORATE DIRECTORS AND OFFICERS

DISABILITY INSURANCE

See also EMPLOYEE BENEFIT PLANS

ABSTRACTS AND INDEXES

Business Periodicals Index Retrospective. EBSCO Publishing Inc. • 11/year. Quarterly and annual cumulations.

Current Law Index. Cengage Learning Inc. • $1,332 Individuals. Monthly. $1269.00 per year. Produced in cooperation with the American Association of Law Libraries. Indexes more than 900 law journals, legal newspapers, and specialty publications from the U.S., Canada, U.K., Ireland, Australia, and New Zealand.

Index to Legal Periodicals and Books. H.W. Wilson Co. • Monthly. $490.00 per year. Quarterly and annual cumulations.

Insurance Periodicals Index. Specials Libraries Association, Insurance and Employees Benefits Div. NILS Publishing Co. • Annual. $250.00. Compiled by the Insurance and Employee Benefits Div., Special Libraries Association. A yearly index of over 15,000 articles from about 35 insurance periodicals. Arrangement is by subject, with an index to authors.

ALMANACS AND YEARBOOKS

American Law Yearbook. Cengage Learning Inc. • $308 Individuals. Annual. $280.00. Serves as a yearly supplement to *West's Encyclopedia of American Lawa*. Describes new legal developments in many subject areas.

BIBLIOGRAPHIES

Insurance and Employee Benefits Literature. Special Libraries Association. • Bimonthly. $15.00 per year. Lists a wide variety of literature in all branches of the insurance industry. Includes annotations.

CD-ROM DATABASES

Business Abstracts with Full Text. EBSCO Publishing Inc. • Includes full text articles from more than 460 business publications from 1982 to present. Indexing for nearly 880 publications.

Index to Legal Periodicals and Books. EBSCO Publishing Inc. • Contains indexing of more than 1,400 English language legal periodicals from 1981 to date and 2,500 books.

ENCYCLOPEDIAS AND DICTIONARIES

West's Encyclopedia of American Law. Cengage Learning Inc. • 2004. eBook. Second edition. Covers a wide variety of legal topics for the general reader. Inquire for pricing.

HANDBOOKS AND MANUALS

U.S. Master Employee Benefits Guide. Wolters Kluwer Law & Business CCH. • Annual. $102.50 Individuals. Explains federal tax and labor laws relating to health care benefits, disability benefits, workers' compensation, employee assistance plans, etc.

INTERNET DATABASES

Lexis.com Research System. Lexis-Nexis Group. Phone: 800-227-4908 or (937)865-6800; Fax: (937)865-6909; Email: webmaster@prod.lexis-nexis.com • URL: http://www.nexis.com • Fee-based Web site offers extensive searching of a wide variety of legal sources. Additional features include Daily Opinion Service, lexis.com Bookstore, Career Center, CLE Center, Law Schools, and Practice Pages ("Pages specific to areas of specialty").

Social Security Online: The Official Web Site of the Social Security Administration. U. S. Social Security Administration. Phone: 800-772-1213 or (410)965-7700 • URL: http://www.ssa.gov • Web site provides a wide variety of online information relating to social security and Medicare. Topics include benefits, disability, employer wage reporting, personal earnings statements, statistics, government financing, social security law, and public welfare reform legislation.

ONLINE DATABASES

I.I.I. Data Base Search. Insurance Information Institute. • Provides online citations and abstracts of insurance-related literature in magazines, newspapers, trade journals, and books. Emphasis is on property and casualty insurance issues, including highway safety, product safety, and environmental liability. Inquire as to online cost and availability.

Wilson Business Abstracts Online. H.W. Wilson Co. • Indexes and abstracts 600 major business periodicals, plus the *Wall Street Journal* and the business section of the *New York Times*. Indexing is from 1982, abstracting from 1990, with the two newspapers included from 1993. Updated weekly. Inquire as to online cost and availability. (*Business Periodicals Index* without abstracts is also available online.).

PERIODICALS AND NEWSLETTERS

Broker World. Insurance Publications Inc. • Bimonthly. $6.00 per year. Edited for independent insurance agents and brokers. Special feature issue topics include annuities, disability insurance, estate planning, and life insurance.

Health Insurance Underwriter. National Association of Health Underwriters. • Monthly. Includes special feature issues on long-term care insurance, disability insurance, managed health care, and insurance office management.

TRADE/PROFESSIONAL ASSOCIATIONS

National Association of Health Underwriters. 1212 New York Ave. NW, Ste. 1100, Washington, DC 20005. Phone: (202)552-5060; Fax: (202)747-6820; Email: info@nahu.org • URL: http://www.nahu.org • Members are engaged in the sale of health and disability insurance. Formerly International Association of Health Underwriters.

National Association of Insurance and Financial Advisors. 2901 Telestar Ct., Falls Church, VA 22042-1205. Phone: 877-866-2432; Email: membersupport@naifa.org • URL: http://www.naifa.org • Affiliated with Association for Advanced Life Underwriting. Formerly National Association of Life Underwriters.

DISABLED

See HANDICAPPED WORKERS

DISCHARGED SERVICEMEN

See VETERANS

DISCIPLINE OF EMPLOYEES

See EMPLOYEE DISCIPLINE

DISCOUNT HOUSES

See also CHAIN STORES; DEPARTMENT STORES; MARKETING; RETAIL TRADE

DIRECTORIES

Discount Store News - Top Chains. Lebhar-Friedman Inc. • Annual. $79.00.

INTERNET DATABASES

Advance Monthly Retail Trade Report. U. S. Census Bureau. Phone: 800-541-8345 or (301)457-4100 or (301)763-2713; Fax: (301)457-1296 or (301)457-3842; Email: naics@census.gov • URL: http://www.census.gov/epcd/www/naicstab.htm • Web pages provide monthly sales figures for a wide range of retail businesses. Advance, preliminary, and final statistics are provided for the latest month available in each case, with a previous-year comparison. Updates are monthly.

PERIODICALS AND NEWSLETTERS

Chain Store Age: The NewsMagazine for Retail Executives. Lebhar-Friedman Inc. • 9/year. Formerly *Chain Store Age Executive with Shopping Center Age*.

Retailing Today: The Newspaper of Discount Retailing: The News Source for Power Retailing. Lebhar-Friedman Inc. • Semimonthly. $119 Individuals. Retailing business industry news and information.

Value Retail News: The Journal of Outlet and Off-Price Retail and Development. Off-Price Specialists, Inc. Value Retail News. • Monthly. $99 Members. Provides news of the off-price and outlet store industry. Emphasis is on real estate for outlet store centers.

RESEARCH CENTERS AND INSTITUTES

Northwestern University - Center for Retail Management. Kellogg School of Management, 2001 Sheridan Rd., Evanston, IL 60208. Phone: (847)467-3600; Fax: (847)467-3620; Email: r-blattberg@kellogg.northwestern.edu • URL: http://www.kellogg.northwestern.edu/research/retail/ • Conducts research related to retail marketing and management.

Texas A&M University - Center for Retailing Studies. Wehner Bldg., Ste. 201, Mays Business School, 4112 TAMU, College Station, TX 77843-4112. Phone: (979)845-0325; Fax: (979)845-5117 or (979)845-5230; Email: c-bridges@mays.tamu.edu • URL: http://www.crstamu.org • Research areas include retailing issues and consumer economics.

STATISTICS SOURCES

Annual Benchmark Report for Retail Trade and Food Services..A Detailed Summary of Retail Sales, Purchases, Accounts Receivable, Inventories, and Food Service Sales. U. S. Government Printing Office. • Annual. $13.00. Issued by the U.S. Census Bureau. Provides detailed annual and monthly retail statistics for the most recent 10 years. Includes data for various kinds of retail outlets, including automobiles, furniture, appliances, building supplies, grocery stores, drug stores, gasoline stations, clothing, sporting goods, department stores, and restaurants.

TRADE/PROFESSIONAL ASSOCIATIONS

National Association of Wholesaler-Distributors. 1325 G St. NW, Ste. 1000, Washington, DC 20005. Phone: (202)872-0885; Fax: (202)785-0586; Email: naw@naw.org • URL: http://www.naw.org • Formerly National Association of Wholesalers.

DISCRIMINATION IN EMPLOYMENT

See AFFIRMATIVE ACTION PROGRAMS

DISHWARE

See TABLEWARE

DISINFECTION AND DISINFECTANT

See SANITATION INDUSTRY

DISK STORAGE DEVICES, OPTICAL

See OPTICAL DISK STORAGE DEVICES

DISMISSAL OF EMPLOYEES

See also JOB HUNTING; UNEMPLOYMENT

ABSTRACTS AND INDEXES

Business Periodicals Index Retrospective. EBSCO Publishing Inc. • 11/year. Quarterly and annual cumulations.

Current Law Index. Cengage Learning Inc. • $1,332 Individuals. Monthly. $1269.00 per year. Produced in cooperation with the American Association of Law Libraries. Indexes more than 900 law journals, legal newspapers, and specialty publications from the U.S., Canada, U.K., Ireland, Australia, and New Zealand.

Index to Legal Periodicals and Books. H.W. Wilson Co. • Monthly. $490.00 per year. Quarterly and annual cumulations.

ALMANACS AND YEARBOOKS

American Law Yearbook. Cengage Learning Inc. • $308 Individuals. Annual. $280.00. Serves as a yearly supplement to *West's Encyclopedia of American Lawa*. Describes new legal developments in many subject areas.

CD-ROM DATABASES

Index to Legal Periodicals and Books. EBSCO Publishing Inc. • Contains indexing of more than 1,400 English language legal periodicals from 1981 to date and 2,500 books.

ENCYCLOPEDIAS AND DICTIONARIES

West's Encyclopedia of American Law. Cengage Learning Inc. • 2004. eBook. Second edition. Covers a wide variety of legal topics for the general reader. Inquire for pricing.

INTERNET DATABASES

EBSCO Information Services. EBSCO Publishing Inc. 10 Estes St., Ipswich, MA 01938-2106. Phone: 800-653-2726 or (978)356-6500; Fax: (978)356-6565; Email: information@ebscohost.com • URL: http://www.ebscohost.com • Fee-based Web site providing Internet access to a wide variety of databases, including business-related material. Full text is available for many periodical titles, with daily updates. Fees: Apply.

InSite 2. Intelligence Data/Thomson Financial. Phone: 800-654-0393 or (617)856-1890; Fax: (617)737-3182; Email: intelligence.data@tfn.com • URL: http://www.insite2.gale.com/ • Fee-based Web site consolidates information in a "Base Pack" consisting of Business InSite, Market InSite, and Company InSite. Optional databases are Consumer InSite, Health and Wellness InSite, Newsletter InSite, and Computer InSite. Includes fulltext content from more than 2,500 trade publications, journals, newsletters, newspapers, analyst reports, and other sources. Continuous updating. Formerly produced by The Gale Group.

Lexis.com Research System. Lexis-Nexis Group. Phone: 800-227-4908 or (937)865-6800; Fax: (937)865-6909; Email: webmaster@prod.lexis-nexis.com • URL: http://www.nexis.com • Fee-based Web site offers extensive searching of a wide variety of legal sources. Additional features include Daily Opinion Service, lexis.com Bookstore, Career Center, CLE Center, Law Schools, and Practice Pages ("Pages specific to areas of specialty").

ProQuest. ProQuest L.L.C. 789 E Eisenhower Pkwy., Ann Arbor, MI 48106-1346. Phone: 800-521-0600 or (734)761-4700; Fax: (734)662-4554; Email: info@proquest.com • URL: http://www.proquest.com • Fee-based Web site providing Internet access to more than 3,000 periodicals, newspapers, and other publications. Many items are available full-text, with daily updates. Includes extensive corporate and financial information. Fees: Apply.

ONLINE DATABASES

Wilson Business Abstracts Online. H.W. Wilson Co. • Indexes and abstracts 600 major business periodicals, plus the *Wall Street Journal* and the business section of the *New York Times*. Indexing is from 1982, abstracting from 1990, with the two newspapers included from 1993. Updated weekly. Inquire as to online cost and availability. (*Business Periodicals Index* without abstracts is also available online.).

PERIODICALS AND NEWSLETTERS

HR Briefing. Wolters Kluwer Law and Business. • Monthly. $249.00 per year. Newsletter. Provides HR professionals and other business people with concise, up-to-date information on employment practices and trends, with an emphasis on compliance with federal employment laws.

ReCareering Newsletter: An Idea and Resource Guide to Second Career and Relocation Planning. Publications Plus, Inc. • Monthly. $59.00 per year. Edited for "downsized managers, early retirees, and others in career transition after leaving traditional employment." Offers advice on second careers, franchises, starting a business, finances, education, training, skills assessment, and other matters of interest to the newly unemployed.

TRADE/PROFESSIONAL ASSOCIATIONS

Association of Career Management Consulting Firms International. 204 E St., NE, Washington, DC 20002. Phone: (202)547-6344; Fax: (202)547-6348; Email: acf@acfinternational.org • Firms providing displaced employees who are sponsored by their organization, with counsel and assistance in job searching and the techniques and practices of choosing a career.

DISPLAY OF MERCHANDISE

See also POINT-OF-PURCHASE ADVERTISING; TRADE SHOWS

DIRECTORIES

Visual Merchandising & Store Design--Buyers' Guide Issue. ST Media Group International Inc. • Annual. Publication includes: Over 1,300 manufacturers and distributors of retail display equipment and products; nearly 600 store design, lighting, and visual merchandising firms; related trade and professional associations. Database includes: Calendar of events. Entries include: For manufacturers and service firms--Company name, address, phone, name and title of contact, number of employees, sales volume, products. Similar data given for associations.

PERIODICALS AND NEWSLETTERS

Signs of the Times. ST Media Group International Inc. • 13 times a year. For designers and manufacturers of all types of signs. Features how-to-tips.

TRADE/PROFESSIONAL ASSOCIATIONS

Association for Retail Environments. 4651 Sheridan St., Ste. 470, Hollywood, FL 33021. Phone: (954)893-7300; Fax: (954)893-7500; Email: are@retailenvironments.org • URL: http://www.retailenvironments.org • Formerly National Association of Display Industries.

Point-of-Purchase Advertising International. 440 N Wells St., Ste. 740, Chicago, IL 60654. Phone: (312)863-2900; Fax: (312)229-1152; Email: info@popai.de • URL: http://www.popai.com • Producers and suppliers of point-of-purchase advertising signs and displays and national and regional advertisers and retailers interested in use and effectiveness of signs, displays and other point-of-purchase media. Conducts student education programs; maintains speakers' bureau.

DISPOSABLE FABRICS

See NONWOVEN FABRICS INDUSTRY

DISSERTATIONS

ABSTRACTS AND INDEXES

Dissertation Abstracts International. ProQuest L.L.C. • Monthly.

ONLINE DATABASES

Dissertation Abstracts Online. ProQuest L.L.C. • Citations to all dissertations accepted for doctoral degrees by accredited U.S. educational institutions, 1861 to date. Includes British theses, 1988 to date. Inquire as to online cost and availability.

PERIODICALS AND NEWSLETTERS

American Doctoral Dissertations. Association of Research Libraries. ProQuest L.L.C. • Annual. Price on application.

Resources in Education. Educational Resources Information Center. U. S. Government Printing Office. • Monthly. Reports on educational research.

DISTILLING INDUSTRY

See also BEVERAGE INDUSTRY; BREWING INDUSTRY; WINE INDUSTRY

ALMANACS AND YEARBOOKS

The U.S. Beer, Spirits and Wine Market: Impact Databank Market Review and Forecast. M. Shanken Communications Inc. • Annual. Price varies. Includes industry commentary and statistics.

CD-ROM DATABASES

OECD Statistical Compendium. Organization for Economic Cooperation and Development. • Semiannual. $1,905.00 per year for 1 to 10 users. CD-ROM contains more than 730,000 monthly, quarterly, and annual time series for OECD countries, 1960 to date. Includes fully searchable data on agriculture, food, economic indicators, national accounts, employment, energy, finance, industry, technology, and foreign trade. Results can be displayed in various forms.

DIRECTORIES

Beverage Marketing Directory. Beverage Marketing Corp. • Annual. $995 Individuals print. Covers: Over 25,500 beer wholesalers, wine and spirits wholesalers, soft drink bottlers and franchisors, breweries, wineries, distilleries, alcoholic beverage importers, bottled water companies; and trade associations, government agencies, micro breweries, juice, coffee, tea, milk companies, and others concerned with the beverage and bottling industries; coverage includes Canada. Entries include: Beverage and bottling company listings contain company name, address, phone, names of key executives, number of employees, brand names, and other information, including number of franchisees, number of delivery trucks, sales volume. Suppliers and related companies and organizations listings include similar but less detailed information.

Major Food and Drink Companies of the World. Cengage Learning Inc. • 12th edition. eBook. Published by Graham & Whiteside. Contains profiles and trade names for more than 9,200 important food and beverage companies in various countries. In addition to foods, includes both alcoholic and nonalcoholic drink products.

FINANCIAL RATIOS

Annual Statement Studies. Risk Management Association. • Annual. Compiled from over 280,000 financial statements.

Annual Statement Studies: Industry Default Probabilities and Cash Flow Measures. Risk Management Association. • Annual. $405 Nonmembers. Serves as a companion volume to the original *Annual Statement Studies*. Gives probability of default estimates on a percentage scale for more than 450 industries. Includes changes in position year-by-year for eight financial statement line items and provides percentage measures of cash flow.

INTERNET DATABASES

Business 2.0 Web Guide to the Best Business Links. Business 2.0 Media Inc. Phone: (415)293-4800;

Email: support@business2.com • URL: http://www.business2.com/webguide • Web site presents an extensive, searchable directory of links to "the best, most informative, and authoritative web pages." Twenty main categories cover business, finance, career, company information, people, and technology topics, with thousands of subtopics, all linking to Web sites recommended by experienced business researchers. Fees: Free.

Fedstats. Federal Interagency Council on Statistical Policy. Phone: (202)395-7254 • URL: http://www.fedstats.gov • Web site features an efficient search facility for full-text statistics produced by more than 100 federal agencies, including the Census Bureau, the Bureau of Economic Analysis, and the Bureau of Labor Statistics. Boolean searches can be made within one agency or for all agencies combined. Links are offered to international statistical bureaus, including the UN, IMF, OECD, UNESCO, Eurostat, and 20 individual countries. Fees: Free.

FreeLunch.com. Economy.com, Inc. Phone: (610)696-8700; Fax: (610)696-1678 • URL: http://www.freelunch.com • Web site provides free access to more than 200 million economic and financial data series, covering industry, demographics, labor markets, prices, retail sales, government spending, trade, interest rates, housing starts, the stock market, etc. Data is available in either chart or table form. Searching is offered. Free, but registration required. Economy.com, Inc. also offers fee-based economic analysis at *The Dismal Scientist* site (www.dismal.com).

OTHER SOURCES

Liquor Control Law Reporter. Wolters Kluwer Law & Business CCH. • Biweekly. Federal and state regulation and taxation of alcoholic beverages.

PERIODICALS AND NEWSLETTERS

Brewing and Distilling International. Brewery Traders Publications, Ltd. • Monthly. $82.00 per year.

Bureau of Alcohol, Tobacco, and Firearms Quarterly Bulletin. Bureau of Alcohol, Tobacco, and Firearms, U.S. Department of the Treasury. U. S. Government Printing Office. • Quarterly. $25.00 per year. Laws and regulations.

Communications. Master Brewers Association of the Americas. • Bimonthly. Membership.

Impact: U.S. News and Research for the Wine, Spirits, and Beer Industries. M. Shanken Communications Inc. • Semimonthly. $375.00 per year. Newsletter covering the marketing, economic, and financial aspects of alcoholic beverages.

RESEARCH CENTERS AND INSTITUTES

U.S. Department of the Treasury - Alcohol and Tobacco Tax and Trade Bureau - Scientific Services Division - Compliance Laboratory. 490 N Wiget Ln., Walnut Creek, CA 94598. Phone: (513)684-3356; Email: compliance.laboratory@ttb.gov • URL: http://www.ttb.gov/ssd/compliance_monitoring_lab.shtml • Monitoring of regulatory compliance of both beverage and nonbeverage alcohol products.

STATISTICS SOURCES

Standard & Poor's Industry Surveys. Standard & Poor's Financial Services L.L.C. • Semiannual. $1,800.00. Two looseleaf volumes. Includes monthly *Supplements.* Provides detailed, individual surveys of 52 major industry groups. Each survey is revised on a semiannual basis. Also includes "Monthly Investment Review" (industry group investment analysis) and monthly "Trends & Projections" (economic analysis).

Survey of Current Business. U. S. Government Printing Office. • Published by Bureau of Economic Analysis, U. S. Department of Commerce. Presents a wide variety of business and economic data.

TRADE/PROFESSIONAL ASSOCIATIONS

Distilled Spirits Council of the United States. 1250 Eye St. NW, Ste. 400, Washington, DC 20005. Phone: (202)628-3544; Fax: (202)682-8888 • URL: http://www.discus.org • Serves as national trade association of producers and marketers of distilled spirits sold in the U.S. Provides statistical and legal data for industry and the public and serves as public information source; conducts educational programs.

DISTRIBUTION

See also MARKETING; RACK JOBBERS; TRANSPORTATION INDUSTRY; TRUCKING INDUSTRY; WHOLESALE TRADE

ABSTRACTS AND INDEXES

Business Periodicals Index Retrospective. EBSCO Publishing Inc. • 11/year. Quarterly and annual cumulations.

DIRECTORIES

American Wholesalers and Distributors Directory. Cengage Learning Inc. • Annual. $450 Individuals print. Lists more than 27,000 national, regional, state, and local wholesalesrs.

Grocery Headquarters: The Newspaper for the Food Industry. Trend Publishing Inc. • Monthly. $80. Covers the sale and distribution of food products and other items sold in supermarkets and grocery stores. Edited mainly for retailers and wholesalers. Incorporates (Grocery Distribution).

National Distributors Select. Scott's Directories. • Annual. $224.75 Profiler (additional). Covers: Over 59,000 wholesalers, distributors, and wholesale agents of industrial products across Canada. Entries include: 34,500 company name, address, phone, description, brand names carried.

Warehouse Management's Guide to Public Warehousing. Reed Elsevier Group plc Reed Business Information. • Annual. $55.00. List of general merchandise,contract and refrigerated warehouses.

Warehousing Distribution Directory. UBM Global Trade. • Semiannual. Publication includes: List of about 800 warehousing and consolidation companies and firms offering trucking, trailer on flatcar, container on flatcar, and piggyback carrier services. Entries include: Name of firm, address, phone, name and title of contact, services, insurance provided, bank references, territory covered, restrictions, number of staff, and branches or subsidiaries with their locations.

ONLINE DATABASES

Wilson Business Abstracts Online. H.W. Wilson Co. • Indexes and abstracts 600 major business periodicals, plus the *Wall Street Journal* and the business section of the *New York Times.* Indexing is from 1982, abstracting from 1990, with the two newspapers included from 1993. Updated weekly. Inquire as to online cost and availability. (*Business Periodicals Index* without abstracts is also available online.).

OTHER SOURCES

Product Distribution Law Guide. Wolters Kluwer Law & Business CCH. • $199.00. Looseleaf service. Annual updates available. Covers the legal aspects of various methods of product distribution, including franchising.

PERIODICALS AND NEWSLETTERS

B to B: The Magazine for Marketing and E-Commerce Strategists. Crain Communications Inc. • Monthly. $59.00 per year. Formerly *Advertising Age's Business Marketing.*

Chilton's Distribution: The Transportation and Business Logistics Magazine. Reed Elsevier Group plc Reed Business Information. • Monthly. $65.00 per year.

Industrial Distribution: For Industrial Distributors and Their Sales Personnel. Reed Elsevier Group plc Reed Business Information. • Monthly. $109.90 per year.

Transportation and Distribution: Integrating Logistics in Supply Chain Management. Penton Media Inc. • Monthly. Free to qualified personnel; others, $50.00 per year. Essential information on transportation and distribution practices in domestic and international trade.

RESEARCH CENTERS AND INSTITUTES

Indiana State University - Center for Research and Management Services. School of Business, Terre Haute, IN 47809. Phone: (812)237-6311; Fax: (812)237-8720; Email: Bev.Bitzegaio@indstate.edu • URL: http://cms.indstate.edu.

STATISTICS SOURCES

Manufacturing & Distribution USA. Cengage Learning Inc. • Biennial. $631 Individuals three-volume set. 2012. 7th edition. eBook. Three volumes. Presents statistics and projections relating to economic activity in more than 600 business classifications.

TRADE/PROFESSIONAL ASSOCIATIONS

Council of Supply Chain Management Professionals. 333 E Butterfield Rd., Ste. 140, Lombard, IL 60148. Phone: (630)574-0985; Fax: (630)574-0989; Email: membership@cscmp.org • URL: http://www.cscmp.org • Business executives with a professional interest in logistics and physical distribution management; includes members from industrial concerns as well as consultants and educators. Aims to advance and promote the management science of integrating transportation, warehousing, material handling, protective packaging, inventory size and location, and other areas of customer service, to reduce overall costs of selling and marketing while improving competitive status. Conducts research. Compiles bibliography available on website regarding subjects related to logistics issues. Provides employment clearinghouse.

NAED National Education and Research Foundation. 1181 Corporate Lake Dr., Saint Louis, MO 63132-1716. Phone: 888-791-2512 or (314)991-9000; Fax: (314)991-3060 • URL: http://www.naed.org • Established by the National Association of Electrical Distributors to provide electrical distributor and distributor-oriented manufacturers with the opportunity to become better business people by expanding their managerial skills. Designs and conducts seminars, workshops, conferences and home study materials covering all aspects of professional management in the electrical supply industry.

National Association of Wholesaler-Distributors. 1325 G St. NW, Ste. 1000, Washington, DC 20005. Phone: (202)872-0885; Fax: (202)785-0586; Email: naw@naw.org • URL: http://www.naw.org • Formerly National Association of Wholesalers.

Union of Shop, Distributive and Allied Workers. 188 Wilmslow Rd., Manchester M14 6LJ, United Kingdom. Phone: 44 161 2242804 or 44 161 2492400; Fax: 44 161 2572566; Email: enquiries@usdaw.org.uk • URL: http://www.usdaw.org.uk • Shopworkers in the distributive and allied trades. Seeks to improve the terms and conditions and to protect the interests of members. Works to promote equal opportunities and equal treatment for all members and oppose discrimination on grounds of sex, race, ethnic origin, disability, sexual orientation or religion.

DIVIDENDS

See also INVESTMENTS; STOCKS

CD-ROM DATABASES

OECD Statistical Compendium. Organization for Economic Cooperation and Development. •

Semiannual. $1,905.00 per year for 1 to 10 users. CD-ROM contains more than 730,000 monthly, quarterly, and annual time series for OECD countries, 1960 to date. Includes fully searchable data on agriculture, food, economic indicators, national accounts, employment, energy, finance, industry, technology, and foreign trade. Results can be displayed in various forms.

FINANCIAL RATIOS

Quarterly Financial Report for Manufacturing, Mining, Trade, and Selected Service Industries. U.S. Federal Trade Commission and U.S. Securities and Exchange Commission. U.S. Census Bureau Foreign Trade Division. • Quarterly. Quarterly. Report on financial results of U.S. corporations.

HANDBOOKS AND MANUALS

Moody's Dividend Record and Annual Dividend Record. • Semiweekly. $775.00 per year. Includes annual and cumulative supplement. Formerly *Moody's Dividend Record.*

Standard and Poor's Dividend Record. Standard & Poor's Financial Services L.L.C. • Offers detailed data to track and process payments and corporate actions. Covers more than 26,000 equity securities, including an extensive list of more than 16,000 open and closed end funds. Daily. $825.00 per year.

INTERNET DATABASES

Business 2.0 Web Guide to the Best Business Links. Business 2.0 Media Inc. Phone: (415)293-4800; Email: support@business2.com • URL: http://www.business2.com/webguide • Web site presents an extensive, searchable directory of links to "the best, most informative, and authoritative web pages." Twenty main categories cover business, finance, career, company information, people, and technology topics, with thousands of subtopics, all linking to Web sites recommended by experienced business researchers. Fees: Free.

ETF Connect. Nuveen Investments. Phone: 800-257-8787 • URL: http://www.etfconnect.com • Free Web site makes available extensive, searchable information on individual closed-end investment funds, preferred share funds, and exchange-traded index funds. Information on a particular fund is available by name or as part of a classification (high yield, investment grade, municipal, emerging markets, global equity, etc.). Fund charts are available for various time periods, as is data concerning premiums or discounts, dividends, annualized total return, credit quality, "Top 10 Holdings," and so forth.

Fedstats. Federal Interagency Council on Statistical Policy. Phone: (202)395-7254 • URL: http://www.fedstats.gov • Web site features an efficient search facility for full-text statistics produced by more than 100 federal agencies, including the Census Bureau, the Bureau of Economic Analysis, and the Bureau of Labor Statistics. Boolean searches can be made within one agency or for all agencies combined. Links are offered to international statistical bureaus, including the UN, IMF, OECD, UNESCO, Eurostat, and 20 individual countries. Fees: Free.

FreeLunch.com. Economy.com, Inc. Phone: (610)696-8700; Fax: (610)696-1678 • URL: http://www.freelunch.com • Web site provides free access to more than 200 million economic and financial data series, covering industry, demographics, labor markets, prices, retail sales, government spending, trade, interest rates, housing starts, the stock market, etc. Data is available in either chart or table form. Searching is offered. Free, but registration required. Economy.com, Inc. also offers fee-based economic analysis at *The Dismal Scientist* site (www.dismal.com).

ONLINE DATABASES

Dow Jones News Service. Dow Jones and Co., Inc. • Full text and edited news stories and articles on business affairs. Inquire as to online cost and availability.

EdgarPlus: SEC Basic Filings. Thomson Reuters Markets. • Online service provides full text of about 60,000 documents that have been filed with the U.S. Securities and Exchange Commission, 1987 to date, with daily updates. Filings include 6-K, 8-K, 10-K, 10-C, 10-Q, 20-F, and proxy statements. Inquire as to online cost and availability.

OTHER SOURCES

Mergent's Annual Dividend Record. Mergent Inc. • Annual. Provides detailed dividend data, including tax information, for 12,000 stocks and 18,000 mutual funds. Covers the most recent year. Formerly *Moody's Annual Dividend Record.*

PERIODICALS AND NEWSLETTERS

Commercial and Financial Chronicle. William B. Dana Co. • Weekly. $140.00. per year.

DRIP Investor: Your Guide to Buying Stocks Without a Broker. Horizon Publishing Co. • Monthly. $89.00 per year. Newsletter covering the dividend reinvestment plans (DRIPs) of various publicly-owned corporations. Includes model portfolios and *Directory of Dividend Reinvestment Plans.*

Investment Guide (IG). American Investment Services Inc. • Monthly. $59 printed version. Description: Contains analyses of stock market activity and strategies for investment. Recurring features include market statistics, Dow high-yield stock investing.

The Moneypaper. Temper of the Times Communications, Inc. Temper of the Times Communications Inc. • Description: Contains strategies to minimize stock sales costs and articles on investing and market trends. Includes a summary of monthly financial news drawn from over 70 financial publications and advisory services. Recurring features include columns titled Summing Up, Market Outlook, and Stocktrack.

RESEARCH CENTERS AND INSTITUTES

University of Chicago - Booth School of Business - Center for Research in Security Prices. 105 W Adams St., Ste. 1700, Chicago, IL 60603. Phone: (312)263-6400; Fax: (312)263-6430; Email: subscriptions@crsp.chicagobooth.edu • URL: http://www.crsp.com • Historical financial data.

University of Pennsylvania - The Wharton School - Rodney L. White Center for Financial Research. 3254 Steinberg Hall-Dietrich Hall, Philadelphia, PA 19104-6367. Phone: (215)898-7616; Fax: (215)573-8084; Email: rlwctr@finance.wharton.upenn.edu • URL: http://rodneywhitecenter.wharton.upenn.edu • Research areas include financial management, money markets, real estate finance, and international finance.

STATISTICS SOURCES

Survey of Current Business. U. S. Government Printing Office. • Published by Bureau of Economic Analysis, U. S. Department of Commerce. Presents a wide variety of business and economic data.

DIVORCE

See also FAMILY LAW

ABSTRACTS AND INDEXES

Current Law Index. Cengage Learning Inc. • $1,332 Individuals. Monthly. $1269.00 per year. Produced in cooperation with the American Association of Law Libraries. Indexes more than 900 law journals, legal newspapers, and specialty publications from the U.S., Canada, U.K., Ireland, Australia, and New Zealand.

Family Studies Abstracts. EBSCO Publishing Inc. • Subject coverage includes divorce, family therapy, and marriage.

Index to Legal Periodicals and Books. H.W. Wilson Co. • Monthly. $490.00 per year. Quarterly and annual cumulations.

Psychological Abstracts. American Psychological Association. • Monthly. Members, $815.00 per year; individuals and institutions, $1,207.00 per year. Covers the international literature of psychology and the behavioral sciences. Includes journals, technical reports, dissertations, and other sources.

Women Studies Abstracts. Springer ScienceBusiness Media LLC. • Quarterly. Covers significant research in women's studies.

HANDBOOKS AND MANUALS

Negotiating to Settlement in Divorce. Sanford N. Katz, editor. Wolters Kluwer Law and Business. • $75.00. Looseleaf service. Periodic supplementation.

INTERNET DATABASES

Lexis.com Research System. Lexis-Nexis Group. Phone: 800-227-4908 or (937)865-6800; Fax: (937)865-6909; Email: webmaster@prod.lexis-nexis.com • URL: http://www.nexis.com • Fee-based Web site offers extensive searching of a wide variety of legal sources. Additional features include Daily Opinion Service, lexis.com Bookstore, Career Center, CLE Center, Law Schools, and Practice Pages ("Pages specific to areas of specialty").

ONLINE DATABASES

Contemporary Women's Issues. Cengage Learning Inc. • Provides full-text articles online from 150 periodicals and a wide variety of additional sources relating to economic, legal, social, political, education, health, and other women's issues. Time span is 1992 to date. Weekly updates. Inquire as to online cost and availability.

OTHER SOURCES

Divorce, Separation, and the Distribution of Property. ALM Media Properties LLC. • $540 per year. Covers such thorny divorce settlement issues as earning power, stock options, pensions, repayment of student loans, tort claims, closely held businesses, premarital agreement enforcement, and alimony awards. (Law Journal Press).

PERIODICALS AND NEWSLETTERS

Family Advocate. American Bar Association - Family Law Section. • Quarterly. Members $39.50; non-members, $44.50 per year. Practical advice for attorneys practicing family law.

TRADE/PROFESSIONAL ASSOCIATIONS

Association of Divorce Financial Planners. 514 Fourth St., East Northport, NY 11731-2342. Phone: 888-838-7773; Email: adfp@divorceandfinance.org • URL: http://www.divorceandfinance.org • Aims to create awareness of the benefits of divorce financial planning. Provides members with continuing education. Promotes communication, networking and peer review.

DO-IT-YOURSELF

See HOME IMPROVEMENT INDUSTRY

DOCKS

See PORTS

DOCTORS' DEGREES

See ACADEMIC DEGREES

DOCUMENT IMAGING

See also MICROFORMS

ABSTRACTS AND INDEXES

Applied Science and Technology Index. EBSCO Publishing Inc. • 11/year. Indexes a wide variety of English language technical, industrial, and engineering periodicals.

Computer Science Index. EBSCO Publishing Inc. • Quarterly. $245 per year. Contains brief abstracts of book and periodical literature covering all phases of computing, including approximately 70 specific application areas.

F & S Index: United States. Cengage Learning Inc. • $2,659 Individuals. Monthly. $2,532.00 per year, including quarterly and annual cumulations. Provides annotated citations to marketing, business, financial, and industrial literature. Coverage of U.S. business activity includes trade journals, financial magazines, business newspapers, and special reports.

Imaging Abstracts. Royal Photographic Society of Great Britain, Imaging Science and Technology Group. Elsevier. • Bimonthly. $860.00 per year. Formerly *Photographic Abstracts.*

Key Abstracts: Business Automation. Institution of Engineering and Technology. • Monthly. $1,138. Provides international coverage of journal and proceedings literature.

NTIS Alerts: Computers, Control & Information Theory. U.S. Department of Commerce National Technical Information Service. • Biweekly. $130 per year. Covers computer hardware, software, control systems, pattern recognition, image processing, and related subjects.

CD-ROM DATABASES

Applied Science and Technology Abstracts. EBSCO Publishing Inc. • Citations for more than 700 prominent scientific, technical, engineering, and industrial periodicals.

Datapro on CD-ROM: Computer Systems Analyst. Gartner Inc. • Monthly. Price on application. Includes detailed information on specific computer hardware and software products, such as peripherals, security systems, document imaging systems, and UNIX-related products.

DIRECTORIES

KMWorld Buyer's Guide. Knowledge Asset Media Inc. • Semiannual. $2,395 (Basic Corporate Profile Package) One Issue — Spring 2014 Edition PLUS 6 Months Online. Controlled circulation as part of *KMWorld.* Contains corporate and product profiles related to various aspects of knowledge management and information systems. (Knowledge Asset Media is a an affiliate of Information Today, Inc.).

ONLINE DATABASES

Applied Science and Technology Index Online. H.W. Wilson Co. • Provides online indexing of 500 major scientific, technical, industrial, and engineering periodicals. Time period is 1983 to date. Monthly updates. Inquire as to online cost and availability.

PERIODICALS AND NEWSLETTERS

Advanced Imaging: Solutions for the Electronic Imaging Professional. Cygnus Business Media. • Monthly. $60.00 per year Covers document-based imaging technologies, products, systems, and services. Coverage is also devoted to multimedia and electronic printing and publishing.

Digital Imaging: The Magazine for the Imaging Professional. Cygnus Business Media Inc. • Bimonthly. $24.95 per year. Edited for business and professional users of electronic publishing products and services. Topics covered include document imaging, CD-ROM publishing, digital video, and multimedia services. Formerly *Micro Publishing News.*

DOCUMENT. RB Publishing Co. • Monthly Quarterly. Covers document management tools.

IEEE Transactions on Visualization and Computer Graphics. IEEE - Communications Society. • Monthly. Contains research on subjects related to computer graphics and visualization techniques, systems, software, hardware, and user interface issues.

Imaging Business: The Voice of the Document Imaging Channel. Access Intelligence L.L.C. • Monthly. Free to qualified personnel. Edited for resellers of document imaging equipment.

Imaging KM: Creating and Managing the Knowledge-Based Enterprise. Knowledge Management World. • 10 times a year. Free to qualified personnel; others, $48.00 per year. Covers automated and networked document image handling.

Item Processing Report. Access Intelligence L.L.C. • Description: Monitors developments in the processing of remittances and checks, including image processing, optical character recognition, check truncation, hardware, and software. **Remarks:** Absorbed The Powell Report, 1992.

Transform: Reinventing Business with Content and Collaboration Technologies. UBM L.L.C. • Monthly. $25.00 per year. Emphasis is on descriptions of new imaging products. Formerly *Imaging and Document Solutions.*

RESEARCH CENTERS AND INSTITUTES

Carnegie Mellon University - Imaging Systems Laboratory. 5320 Wean Hall, Robotics Department, Pittsburgh, PA 15213. Phone: (412)268-5601 or (412)268-3824; Fax: (412)621-7068 or (412)683-3763; Email: rht@cs.cmu.edu • URL: http://www.cs.cmu.edu/afs/cs.cmu.edu/project/pcvision/www/ • Fields of research include computer vision and document interpretation.

Center for Imaging Science. Rochester Institute of Technology, 54 Lomb Memorial Dr., Rochester, NY 14623. Phone: (585)475-5994; Fax: (585)475-5988; Email: contactus@cis.rit.edu • URL: http://www.cis.rit.edu • Activities include research in color science and digital image processing.

Digital Image Analysis Laboratory. University of Arizona, Dept. of Electrical and Computer Engineering, 1230 E Speedway Blvd., Tucson, AZ 85721. Phone: (520)621-4554; Fax: (520)621-8076; Email: dial@ece.arizona.edu • URL: http://www.ece.arizona.edu • Research fields include image processing, computer vision, and artificial intelligence.

Rochester Institute of Technology - Center for Integrated Manufacturing Studies. Louise M. Slaughter Hall, Bldg. 78, 111 Lomb Memorial Dr., Rochester, NY 14623-5608. Phone: (585)475-5385 or (585)475-5101; Fax: (585)475-5250; Email: info@sustainability.rit.edu • URL: http://www.rit.edu/gis/research-centers/cims • Research areas include electronics, imaging, printing, and publishing.

Worcester Polytechnic Institute - Department of Computer Science - Image Science Research Group. 100 Institute Rd., Worcester, MA 01609-2280. Phone: (508)831-5671 or (508)831-5357; Fax: (508)831-5776; Email: matt@wpi.edu • URL: http://web.cs.wpi.edu/Research/isrg/ • Areas of research include image processing, computer graphics, and computational vision.

TRADE/PROFESSIONAL ASSOCIATIONS

Association for Information and Image Management International. 1100 Wayne Ave., Ste. 1100, Silver Spring, MD 20910. Phone: 800-477-2446 or (301)587-8202; Fax: (301)587-2711; Email: aiim@aiim.org • URL: http://www.aiim.org • Manufacturers, vendors and individual users of information and image management equipment, products and services. Holds special meetings for trade members and companies. Maintains speakers' bureau. Operates resource center. Compiles statistics.

DOCUMENTATION (INFORMATION RETRIEVAL)

See ONLINE INFORMATION SYSTEMS

DOCUMENTS

See GOVERNMENT PUBLICATIONS

DOG FOOD

See PET INDUSTRY

DOMESTIC APPLIANCES

See ELECTRIC APPLIANCE INDUSTRY

DONATIONS, CHARITABLE

See PHILANTHROPY

DOOR INDUSTRY

See also BUILDING INDUSTRY

ABSTRACTS AND INDEXES

NTIS Alerts: Building Industry Technology. U.S. Department of Commerce National Technical Information Service. • Biweekly. $130 per year. Covers architecture, construction management, building materials, maintenance, furnishings, and related subjects.

PERIODICALS AND NEWSLETTERS

Door and Window Retailing. Jervis and Associates. • Bimonthly. $15.00 per year. Edited for door and window retailers. Formerly *Door and Window Business.*

Doors & Hardware. Door and Hardware Institute. • Monthly. $75 Life member. Covers the architectural openings industry.

International Door & Operator Industry. International Door Association. • Bimonthly. Edited for garage door and opener dealers.

TRADE/PROFESSIONAL ASSOCIATIONS

Door and Access Systems Manufacturers Association International. 1300 Sumner Ave., Cleveland, OH 44115-2851. Phone: (216)241-7333; Fax: (216)241-0105; Email: dasma@dasma.com • URL: http://www.dasma.com • Members are manufacturers of "upward-acting" garage doors and related products, both residential and commercial.

Door and Hardware Institute. 14150 Newbrook Dr., Ste. 200, Chantilly, VA 20151-2223. Phone: (703)222-2010; Fax: (703)222-2410; Email: membership@dhi.org • URL: http://www.dhi.org • Commercial distributors, manufacturers and specifiers involved in doors and builders' hardware (locks, door hardware, latches, hinges, and electrified products). Works with architects, contractors, and building owners. Conducts management and technical courses and membership-related surveys. Offers certification program for the Architectural Openings Industry (AHC, CDC).

National Fenestration Rating Council. 6305 Ivy Ln., Ste. 140, Greenbelt, MD 20770. Phone: (301)589-1776 or (785)862-1890; Fax: (301)589-3884; Email: info@nfrc.org • URL: http://www.nfrc.org • Individuals, organizations, and corporations interested in production, regulation, promotion, and development of technology related to fenestration products. Develops national voluntary energy performance rating system for fenestration products;

coordinates certification and labeling activities to ensure uniform rating application. Promotes consumer awareness of fenestration ratings in an effort to encourage informed purchase of windows, doors, and skylights. Conducts efficiency testing. Maintains speakers' bureau; conducts educational and research programs.

Window and Door Manufacturers Association. 2025 M St. NW, Ste. 800, Washington, DC 20036-3309. Phone: (202)367-1157; Email: wdma@wdma.com • URL: http://www.wdma.com • Members are manufacturers of wooden door and window products. Absorbed Ponderosa Pine Woodwork Association. Formerly National Wood Window and Door Association.

DOOR-TO-DOOR SELLING

See DIRECT MARKETING

DOUGLAS FIR

See LUMBER INDUSTRY

DOW THEORY

See also INVESTMENTS; STOCKS

ONLINE DATABASES

Dow Jones News Service. Dow Jones and Co., Inc. • Full text and edited news stories and articles on business affairs. Inquire as to online cost and availability.

PERIODICALS AND NEWSLETTERS

Dow Theory Forecasts. Horizon Publishing Co. • Weekly. Provides information and advice on blue chip and income stocks.

Dow Theory Letters. Dow Theory Letters, Inc. • Triweekly. $300 /year. Newsletter on stock market trends, investing, and economic conditions.

STATISTICS SOURCES

Advance-Decline Album. Dow Theory Letters, Inc. • Annual. Contains one page for each year since 1931. Includes charts of the New York Stock Exchange advance-decline ratio and the Dow Jones industrial average.

DOWNSIZING

See DISMISSAL OF EMPLOYEES

DRAFTING, MECHANICAL

See MECHANICAL DRAWING

DRAPERY INDUSTRY

See WINDOW COVERING INDUSTRY

DRIED FOODS

See FOOD INDUSTRY

DRILLING AND BORING MACHINERY

See MACHINERY

DRINKING AND TRAFFIC ACCIDENTS

See TRAFFIC ACCIDENTS AND TRAFFIC SAFETY

DRIVE-IN AND CURB SERVICES

See RESTAURANTS, LUNCHROOMS, ETC.

DRUG ABUSE AND TRAFFIC

See also ALCOHOLISM; NARCOTICS; PHARMACEUTICAL INDUSTRY

ABSTRACTS AND INDEXES

Excerpta Medica: Drug Dependence, Alcohol Abuse, and Alcoholism. Elsevier. • Bimonthly. Section 40 of *Excerpta Medica.*

ENCYCLOPEDIAS AND DICTIONARIES

American Drug Index. Wolters Kluwer Health. • Annual. $99.95 Individuals. Lists over 20,000 drug entries in dictionary style.

Encyclopedia of Crime and Justice. Cengage Learning Inc. • 2001. $737. 2nd edition. 4 volumes. Published by Macmillan Reference USA. Contains extensive information on a wide variety of topics pertaining to crime, criminology, social issues, and the courts. Also available as eBook.

Encyclopedia of Drugs, Alcohol, and Addictive Behavior. Cengage Learning Inc. • $820 Individuals. 2009. 3rd Edition. eBook. Published by Macmillan Reference USA. Covers the social, economic, political, and medical aspects of addiction. Inquire for price and availability.

GENERAL WORKS

Drugs, Alcohol & Tobacco: Learning About Addictive Behavior. Edited by Rosalyn Carson-Dewitt, M.D. Cengage Learning Inc. • $512. Three volumes. Contains 200 articles on various aspects of addiction. Includes color illustrations, a glossary, and comprehensive indexing. Macmillan Reference USA imprint. eBook also available. Inquire for pricing.

ONLINE DATABASES

Toxline. National Library of Medicine. • Weekly. Abstracting service covering human and animal toxicity studies, 1965 to present (older studies available in *Toxback* file). Weekly updates. Inquire as to online cost and availability.

OTHER SOURCES

World Drug Report. United Nations Publications. • Annual. $60 Individuals print. Issued by the United Nations Office for Drug Control and Crime Prevention. Includes maps, graphs, charts, and tables.

PERIODICALS AND NEWSLETTERS

Contemporary Drug Problems. Federal Legal Publications, Inc. • Quarterly. Individuals, $30.00 per year; institutions, $36.00 per year.

Counselor: The Magazine for Addiction Professionals. Health Communications, Inc. • Bimonthly. $9.95 Individuals /year, online only. Covers both clinical and societal aspects of substance abuse.

Drug and Alcohol Abuse Education. Editorial Resources Inc. • Monthly. $84.00 per year. Newsletter covering education, prevention, and treatment relating to abuse of drugs and alcohol.

International Drug Report. International Narcotic Enforcement Officers Association. • Description: Discusses current trends in narcotic abuse and enforcement, legal decisions concerning drug abuse, and related subjects. Carries news articles, scientific reports, statistics, and agency information. Recurring features include book reviews, notices of meetings, and news from U.S. Customs and the Drug Enforcement Administration.

Journal of Alcohol and Drug Education. American Alcohol and Drug Information Foundation. • Three times a year. $45.00 per year.

A Journal of Ethnicity in Substance Abuse. The Haworth Press Inc. • Quarterly. $380.00 per year. Includes print and online editions. Edited for researchers and practitioners. Covers various areas of susbstance abuse, including alcoholism. Formerly *Drugs and Society.*

Workplace Substance Abuse Advisor. LRP Publications Library. • Description: Reviews federal, state, and local laws and regulations concerning alcohol and drug use, testing, and policies. Discusses significant court decisions. Contains information on the drug enforcement budgets at all levels of government. Examines employee assistance plans and other educational programs designed to help substance abusers.

TRADE/PROFESSIONAL ASSOCIATIONS

APhA Academy of Pharmacy Practice and Management. 2215 Constitution Ave. NW, Washington, DC 20037. Phone: 800-237-APHA or (202)628-4410 or (202)429-7557; Fax: (202)783-2351; Email: infocenter@aphanet.org • URL: http://www.pharmacist.com/apha-appm • Pharmacists concerned with rendering professional services directly to the public, without regard for status of employment or environment of practice. Formerly Academy of Pharmacy Practice and Management.

Drug, Chemical and Associated Technologies Association. One Washington Blvd., Ste. 7, Robbinsville, NJ 08691-3162. Phone: 800-640-3228 or (609)448-1000; Fax: (609)448-1944 • URL: http://www.dcat.org • Formerly Drug, Chemical and Allied Trades Section of the New York Board of Trade.

DRUG INDUSTRY

See PHARMACEUTICAL INDUSTRY

DRUG STORES

See also CHAIN STORES; DISCOUNT HOUSES; PHARMACEUTICAL INDUSTRY

ALMANACS AND YEARBOOKS

Family Almanac. National Association of Retail Druggists. Creative Publishing. • Annual. $4. Formerly *NARD Almanac and Health Guide.*

CD-ROM DATABASES

OECD Statistical Compendium. Organization for Economic Cooperation and Development. • Semiannual. $1,905.00 per year for 1 to 10 users. CD-ROM contains more than 730,000 monthly, quarterly, and annual time series for OECD countries, 1960 to date. Includes fully searchable data on agriculture, food, economic indicators, national accounts, employment, energy, finance, industry, technology, and foreign trade. Results can be displayed in various forms.

INTERNET DATABASES

Advance Monthly Retail Trade Report. U. S. Census Bureau. Phone: 800-541-8345 or (301)457-4100 or (301)763-2713; Fax: (301)457-1296 or (301)457-3842; Email: naics@census.gov • URL: http://www.census.gov/epcd/www/naicstab.htm • Web pages provide monthly sales figures for a wide range of retail businesses. Advance, preliminary, and final statistics are provided for the latest month available in each case, with a previous-year comparison. Updates are monthly.

Business 2.0 Web Guide to the Best Business Links. Business 2.0 Media Inc. Phone: (415)293-4800; Email: support@business2.com • URL: http://www.business2.com/webguide • Web site presents an extensive, searchable directory of links to "the best, most informative, and authoritative web pages."

Twenty main categories cover business, finance, career, company information, people, and technology topics, with thousands of subtopics, all linking to Web sites recommended by experienced business researchers. Fees: Free.

Fedstats. Federal Interagency Council on Statistical Policy. Phone: (202)395-7254 • URL: http://www.fedstats.gov • Web site features an efficient search facility for full-text statistics produced by more than 100 federal agencies, including the Census Bureau, the Bureau of Economic Analysis, and the Bureau of Labor Statistics. Boolean searches can be made within one agency or for all agencies combined. Links are offered to international statistical bureaus, including the UN, IMF, OECD, UNESCO, Eurostat, and 20 individual countries. Fees: Free.

FreeLunch.com. Economy.com, Inc. Phone: (610)696-8700; Fax: (610)696-1678 • URL: http://www.freelunch.com • Web site provides free access to more than 200 million economic and financial data series, covering industry, demographics, labor markets, prices, retail sales, government spending, trade, interest rates, housing starts, the stock market, etc. Data is available in either chart or table form. Searching is offered. Free, but registration required. Economy.com, Inc. also offers fee-based economic analysis at *The Dismal Scientist* site (www.dismal.com).

PERIODICALS AND NEWSLETTERS

Chain Drug Review: The Reporter for the Chain Drug Store Industry. Racher Press Inc. • $199 Institutions. Covers news and trends of concern to the chain drug store industry. Includes special articles on OTC (over-the-counter) drugs.

Community Pharmacist: Meeting the Professional and Educational Needs of Today's Practitioner. ELF Publicatons, Inc. • Bimonthly. $25.00 per year. Edited for retail pharmacists in various settings, whether independent or chain-operated. Covers both pharmaceutical and business topics.

Computertalk: For Contemporary Pharmacy Management. ComputerTalk Associates Inc. • Bimonthly. $50.00 per year. Provides detailed advice and information on computer systems for pharmacies, including a buyers' guide issue.

Drug Store News. Lebhar-Friedman Inc. • Biweekly. Free to qualified personnel; others, $99.00 per year.

Drug Topics. Thomson Medical Economics. • Monthly. Edited for retail pharmacists, hospital pharmacists, pharmacy chain store executives, wholesalers, buyers, and others concerned with drug dispensing and drug store management. Provides information on new products, including personal care items and cosmetics.

The Green Sheet. Elsevier Business Intelligence. • Weekly. $109.00 per year. Newsletter for retailers and wholesalers of pharmaceutical products. Includes pricing developments and new drug announcements.

Pharmacy Times: Practical Information for Today's Pharmacists. Medical World Communications. • Monthly. $57 Individuals per year. Edited for pharmacists. Covers store management, new products, regulations, home health care products, managed care issues, etc.

Retail Pharmacy Management. McMahon Group. • Monthly. $60.00 per year. Featues include product news for pharmacists and financial news for chain store executives. Formerly *Retail Pharmacy Management News.*

U.S. Pharmacist. Jobson Publishing L.L.C. • Monthly. $25 Individuals U.S.. Covers a wide variety of topics for independent, chain store, hospital, and other pharmacists.

RESEARCH CENTERS AND INSTITUTES

University of Mississippi - Center for Pharmaceutical Marketing and Management. Faser Hall Rms. 128-136, School of Pharmacy, University, MS 38677. Phone: (662)915-5352 or (662)915-5948; Fax: (662)915-5262; Email: benb3@olemiss.edu • URL: http://www.pharmacy.olemiss.edu/cpmm • Proprietary and in-house marketing and management studies relating to pharmaceutical products, including formulary decision factors, generic substitution, reimbursement issues, medication compliance and consumer preferences. Conducts mail surveys, telephone interviews, focus groups, internet surveys, consumer reaction panels, and surveys of professionals at national and state meetings.

STATISTICS SOURCES

Annual Benchmark Report for Retail Trade and Food Services..A Detailed Summary of Retail Sales, Purchases, Accounts Receivable, Inventories, and Food Service Sales. U. S. Government Printing Office. • Annual. $13.00. Issued by the U.S. Census Bureau. Provides detailed annual and monthly retail statistics for the most recent 10 years. Includes data for various kinds of retail outlets, including automobiles, furniture, appliances, building supplies, grocery stores, drug stores, gasoline stations, clothing, sporting goods, department stores, and restaurants.

Standard & Poor's Industry Surveys. Standard & Poor's Financial Services L.L.C. • Semiannual. $1,800.00. Two looseleaf volumes. Includes monthly *Supplements.* Provides detailed, individual surveys of 52 major industry groups. Each survey is revised on a semiannual basis. Also includes "Monthly Investment Review" (industry group investment analysis) and monthly "Trends & Projections" (economic analysis).

Survey of Current Business. U. S. Government Printing Office. • Published by Bureau of Economic Analysis, U. S. Department of Commerce. Presents a wide variety of business and economic data.

TRADE/PROFESSIONAL ASSOCIATIONS

APhA Academy of Pharmacy Practice and Management. 2215 Constitution Ave. NW, Washington, DC 20037. Phone: 800-237-APHA or (202)628-4410 or (202)429-7557; Fax: (202)783-2351; Email: infocenter@aphanet.org • URL: http://www.pharmacist.com/apha-appm • Pharmacists concerned with rendering professional services directly to the public, without regard for status of employment or environment of practice. Formerly Academy of Pharmacy Practice and Management.

Healthcare Distribution Management Association. 901 N Glebe Rd., Ste. 1000, Arlington, VA 22203. Phone: (703)787-0000; Fax: (703)812-5282 • URL: http://www.healthcaredistribution.org • Wholesalers and manufacturers of drug and health care products and industry service providers. Seeks to secure safe and effective distribution of healthcare products, create and exchange industry knowledge affecting the future of distribution management, and influence standards and business processes that produce efficient health care commerce. Compiles statistics; sponsors research and specialized education programs.

National Association of Chain Drug Stores. 1776 Wilson Blvd., Ste. 200, Arlington, VA 22209. Phone: (703)549-3001; Fax: (703)836-4869; Email: contactus@nacds.org • URL: http://www.nacds.org • Represents the concerns of community pharmacies in Washington, in state capitals, and across the country. Members are more than 210 chain community pharmacy companies. Collectively, community pharmacy comprises the largest component of pharmacy practice with over 107,000 FTE pharmacists.

DRUGS, GENERIC

See GENERIC DRUG INDUSTRY

DRUGS, NONPRESCRIPTION

See NONPRESCRIPTION DRUG INDUSTRY

DRUNKENNESS

See ALCOHOLISM

DRY CLEANING INDUSTRY

See CLEANING INDUSTRY

DUPLICATING MACHINES

See COPYING MACHINE INDUSTRY

DYES AND DYEING

See also TEXTILE INDUSTRY

ABSTRACTS AND INDEXES

AATCC Review. American Association of Textile Chemists and Colorists. • Monthly. $650 Individuals print + online. Monthly magazine for professionals in the textile wet processing and dyestuff industries. Formerly Textile Chemist and Colorist and American Dyestuff Reporter.

CPI Digest: Key to World Literature Serving the Coatings, Plastics, Fibers, Adhesives, and Related Industries. CPI Information Services. • Monthly. $397.00 per year. Abstracts of business and technical articles for polymer-based, chemical process industries. Includes a monthly list of relevant U. S. patents. International coverage.

DIRECTORIES

Directory of African Importers of Dyes, Colors, and Pigments. EXIM Infotek Private Ltd. • $250 Individuals. Covers: 90 African importers of textiles chemical, dye, colors, pigments, intermediates, dyestuff, and printing ink. Entries include: Company name, postal address, telephone, fax, e-mail, website, contact person, designation, and product details.

Directory of American Manufacturers & Exporters of Dyes, Colours, Pigments & Intermediates. EXIM Infotek Private Ltd. • $20 Individuals. Covers: 200 American manufacturers and exporters of color concentrates, colors and pigments, colors and pigments-dispersions and flushes, concentrates-colors and pigments, dies, dispersions, dye and pigment intermediates, dyes, dyes and dyestuffs, flushed color and presscakes, intermediates, leather dyes, organic and inorganic dyes, organic and inorganic pigments, organic pigments for printing inks, pigment dispersions, pigment preparations, pigments, pigments and colors-brick, pigments and colors-ceramic and glass, pigments and colors-dry and dispersed, pigments and colors-paint, pigments and colors-rubber, plastic dyes, plastic industry colorants and additives, rust remover, textile dyestuffs, and water colors. Entries include: Company name, postal address, city, country, phone, fax, e-mail and websites, contact person, designation, and product details.

Directory of Asian Importers of Dyes, Colors, and Pigments. EXIM Infotek Private Ltd. • $950 Individuals. Covers: 580 Asian importers of acrylic color, activated carbon, auxiliaries, candle additives, dye and scent, chemical for textile, chemical intermediates, dye for leather industry, dye for textile industry, colors and pigments, dyestuff, dyestuff intermediates, fluorescent pigments, ink, leather chemicals, phthalic anhydride, resin for printing ink, synthetic organic dyestuff, textile auxiliaries, textile chemicals, textile dye, and washing chemicals. Entries include: Company name, postal address, telephone, fax, e-mail, website, contact person, designation, and product details.

Directory of Chinese Manufacturers & Exporters of Dyes, Colors, Pigments, Intermediates. EXIM Infotek Private Ltd. • $25 Individuals. Covers: 290 Chinese manufacturers and exporters of acid dyestuffs, auxiliaries, auxiliary materials, cationic dyestuff, chemical dyes, chemical intermediates, disperse dyes, dye intermediates, dyeing materials, dyes, dyes intermediates, dyes-red base, dyestuff, dyes-vet, fluorescent brightener series, fluorescent pigment products, fluorescent whitening, inorganic pigments, intermediate for dyestuffs, intermediates, intermediates-various, iron oxide pigments, iron oxide yellow, organic intermediates, organic pigments, pigment intermediates, pigments, pigments-natural, plastic dyes, reactive dyes, vat dyes. Entries include: Company name, postal address, city, country, phone, fax, e-mail and websites, contact person, designation, and product details.

Directory of Indian Importers of Dyes, Colors, and Pigments. EXIM Infotek Private Ltd. • $350 Individuals. Covers: 80 Indian importers of activated carbon, dye, dye intermediates, colors, pigments, dyestuff, ink, and leather chemicals. Entries include: Company name, postal address, telephone, fax, e-mail, website, contact person, designation, and product details.

Directory of Japanese Importers of Dyes, Colors, Pigments and Intermediates. EXIM Infotek Private Ltd. • $300 Individuals. Covers: 100 Japanese importers of activated carbon, chemical intermediates, dyes, colors, pigments, dyestuff, dyestuff intermediates, ink, pigment colors and metallic, and printing ink. Entries include: Company name, postal address, telephone, fax, e-mail, website, contact person, designation, and product details.

Directory of Japanese Manufacturers & Exporters of Dyes, Colours, Pigments & Intermediates. EXIM Infotek Private Ltd. • $5 Individuals. Covers: 30 Japanese manufacturers and exporters of dyes, inks, pigments. Entries include: Company name, postal address, city, country, phone, fax, e-mail and websites, contact person, designation, and product details.

Directory of Middle East Importers of Dyes, Colors, and Pigments. EXIM Infotek Private Ltd. • $250 Individuals. Covers: 80 Middle East importers of carbon black, dyes, colors, pigments, and dyestuff. Entries include: Company name, postal address, telephone, fax, e-mail, website, contact person, designation, and product details.

Directory of North American Importers of Dyes, Colors, and Pigments. EXIM Infotek Private Ltd. • $250 Individuals. Covers: 50 North American importers of chemical intermediates, dyes, colors, pigments, and dyestuff. Entries include: Company name, postal address, telephone, fax, e-mail, website, contact person, designation, and product details.

Directory of SAARC Importers of Dyes, Colors, Pigments and Intermediates. EXIM Infotek Private Ltd. • $350 Individuals. Covers: 80 SAARC countries importers of acrylic color, activated carbon, auxiliaries, chemical for pashmina, dye intermediates, dye, colors, pigments, dyestuff, fabric colors, ink, leather chemicals, leather dyestuff and chemicals, phthalic anhydride, pigment emulsions, printing ink, textile auxiliaries, textile chemicals, textile dye, textile binder, and washing chemicals. Entries include: Company name, postal address, telephone, fax, e-mail, website, contact person, designation, and product details.

Directory of South American Importers of Dyes, Colors, and Pigments. EXIM Infotek Private Ltd. • $300 Individuals. Covers: 100 South American importers of dye, colors, pigments, and food colors. Entries include: Company name, postal address, telephone, fax, e-mail, website, contact person, designation, and product details.

Directory of South Korean Manufacturers & Exporters of Dyes, Colours, Pigments & Intermediates. EXIM Infotek Private Ltd. • $10 Individuals. Covers: 90 South Korean manufacturers & exporters of chemicals for textiles, colorants for leather/rubber/plastic & cosmetics, dyes-synthetic, pigments-natural, pigments-synthetic, textile coatings. Entries include: Company name, postal address, city, country, phone, fax, e-mail & websites, contact person, designation, products detail.

Directory of Taiwanese Manufacturers & Exporters of Dyes, Colours, Pigments & Intermediates. EXIM Infotek Private Ltd. • $10 Individuals. Covers: 90 Taiwanese manufacturers & exporters of chemicals for textiles, colorants for leather/rubber/plastic & cosmetics, dyes, dyes-synthetic, pigments-natural, pigments-synthetic, textile coatings. Entries include: Company name, postal address, city, country, phone, fax, e-mail & websites, contact person, designation, products detail.

ONLINE DATABASES

CA Search. American Chemical Society Chemical Abstracts Service. • Guide to chemical literature, 1967 to present. Inquire as to online cost and availability.

PERIODICALS AND NEWSLETTERS

International Dyer. World Textile Publications Ltd. • Monthly. $90.00 per year.

International Textile Bulletin: Dyeing-Printing-Finishing Edition. ITS Publishing, International Textile Service. • Quarterly. $170.00 per year. Editions in Chinese, English, French, German, Italian and Spanish.

E

E-COMMERCE

See ELECTRONIC COMMERCE

EATING FACILITIES, EMPLOYEES

See EMPLOYEE LUNCHROOMS AND CAFETERIAS

EATING PLACES

See RESTAURANTS, LUNCHROOMS, ETC.

ECOLOGY

See ENVIRONMENT

ECONOMETRICS

See also ECONOMIC RESEARCH; ECONOMIC STATISTICS; ECONOMICS

CD-ROM DATABASES

EconLit. Ovid Technologies Inc. • Updated monthly. Lists journal articles, book reviews, disserations of economic literature. Over 1,400 journals covered.

PERIODICALS AND NEWSLETTERS

Econometric Theory. Cambridge University Press Journals Dept. • Bimonthly. Individuals, $152.00 per year; institutions, $440.00 per year. Devoted to the advancement of theoretical research in econometrics.

Econometrica. Blackwell Publishing Inc. • $586 Institutions Online only. Bimonthly. Includes print and online editions. Published in England by Basil Blackwell Ltd.

Journal of Applied Econometrics. John Wiley and Sons, Inc., Journals Div. • 7/year. Individuals, $85.00 per year; institutions, $1,050.00 per year.

RESEARCH CENTERS AND INSTITUTES

Bogazici University - Center for Economics and Econometrics. Bebek, TR-34342 Istanbul, Turkey. Phone: 90 212 3956505; Fax: 90 212 2872453; Email: ezran@boun.edu.tr • URL: http://www.cee.boun.edu.tr • Economic issues, electrical energy.

Catholic University of Louvain - Center for Economic Studies. Department of Economics, Naamsestraat 69, B-3000 Louvain, Belgium. Phone: 32 16 326725; Fax: 32 16 326796; Email: erik.buyst@kuleuven.be • URL: http://www.econ.kuleuven.be/research/CES/display.aspx?URL=main • Information, international, monetary, industrial, public, and developmental economics, econometrics, and game theory.

Center for Mathematical Studies in Economics and Management Science. Northwestern University, 580 Leverone Hall, 2001 Sheridan Rd., Evanston, IL 60208-2014. Phone: (847)491-3527; Fax: (847)491-2530; Email: cms-ems@kellogg.northwestern.edu • URL: http://www.kellogg.northwestern.edu/research/math.

TRADE/PROFESSIONAL ASSOCIATIONS

Econometric Society. New York University, Department of Economics, 19 W 4th St., 6th Fl., New York, NY 10012. Phone: (212)998-3820; Fax: (212)995-4487; Email: sashi@econometricsociety.org • URL: http://www.econometricsociety.org • Economists, statisticians, and mathematicians. Promotes studies that are directed towards unification of the theoretical and empirical approaches to economic problems and advancement of economic theory in its relation to statistics and mathematics.

ECONOMIC BOTANY

See also AGRICULTURE

ABSTRACTS AND INDEXES

Biological and Agricultural Index. H.W. Wilson Co. • 11 times a year. Annual and quarterly cumulations. Price varies.

PERIODICALS AND NEWSLETTERS

The Botanical Review: Interpreting Botanical Progress. Society for Economic Botany. New York Botanical Garden Press. • Quarterly. Individuals, $112.00 per year; institutions, $205.00 per year. Reviews articles in all fields of botany.

Economic Botany: Devoted to Applied Botany and Plant Utilization. Society for Economic Botany. New York Botanical Garden Press. • Quarterly. $115 Individuals Electronic only version with E-access to back issues through 1997. Original research and review articles on the uses of plants.

Journal of Crop Improvement. The Haworth Press Inc. • 6/year. $396 Individuals online. Topics include plant biotechnology, plant genetics, crop productivity, quality, safety, pest control, and environmental concerns. Formerly *Journal of Crop Production*.

Plant Science Bulletin. St. Louis Univeristy Department of Biology. • Description: Carries news of this Association of plant scientists, with some issues including brief articles of more general interest in the field. Recurring features include notices of awards, meetings, courses, and study and professional opportunities; annotated lists of botanical books; and book reviews.

TRADE/PROFESSIONAL ASSOCIATIONS

Botanical Society of America. 4475 Castleman Ave., Saint Louis, MO 63166. Phone: (314)577-9566; Fax: (314)577-9515; Email: bsa-manager@botany.org • URL: http://www.botany.org • Professional society of botanists and others interested in plant science. Conducts special research programs.

ECONOMIC CONDITIONS

See BUSINESS CONDITIONS

ECONOMIC CYCLES

See BUSINESS CYCLES

ECONOMIC DEVELOPMENT

See also DEVELOPING AREAS; INDUSTRIAL DEVELOPMENT; URBAN DEVELOPMENT

ABSTRACTS AND INDEXES

PAIS International. ProQuest L.L.C. • Monthly. $850.00 per year; cumulations three times a year. Provides topical citations to the worldwide literature of public affairs, economics, demographics, sociology, and trade. Text in English; indexed materials in English, French, German, Italian, Portuguese and Spanish.

Social Sciences Citation Index. Thomson Reuters Corp. • Weekly. Product is accessed via *Web of Science*.

Social Sciences Index Retrospective: 1907-1983. EBSCO Publishing Inc. • Indexing for 1,000,000 articles. Coverage includes international index and social sciences and humanities index.

ALMANACS AND YEARBOOKS

Trade and Development Report (TDR). United Nations Conference on Trade and Development. • Annual. Yearly overview of trends in international trade, including an analysis of the economic and trade situation in developing countries. Published by the United Nations Conference on Trade and Development (UNCTAD).

CD-ROM DATABASES

International Development Statistics. Organization for Economic Cooperation and Development. • Annual. $71.00. Issued by the OECD Development

Assistance Committee. CD-ROM contains data on aid to more than 180 recipient countries, including amount, origin, type, and recipients' external debt.

PAIS International. ProQuest L.L.C. • Monthly. $1,995.00 per year. Contains over 650,000 citations to the literature of contemporary social, political, and economic issues.

Social Sciences Abstracts. EBSCO Publishing Inc. • Provides indexing from 1983 and abstracting from 1994 of more than 750 periodicals covering economics, area studies, community health, public administration, public welfare, urban studies, and many other topics related to the social sciences.

Social Sciences Citation Index. Thomson Reuters Corp. • Weekly. Product is accessed via *Web of Science*.

DIRECTORIES

Albuquerque Economic Development Business Directory. Albuquerque Economic Development Inc. • Covers: Business resources in the Albuquerque, New Mexico, metropolitan area. Includes list of categories with links and a searchable database. Entries include: Name, address, phone, fax, URL, map link.

Directory of Economic Development Organizations in Oregon. Council for Economic Development in Oregon. • Irregular. $25. Covers: public and private organizations concerned with economic development in Oregon; includes federal, state, and local governmental agencies. Entries include: Organization or agency name, address, phone, name and title of contact, geographic territory covered.

Economic Development Administration--Annual Report. U.S. Economic Development Administration. • Annual. Covers: Recipients of grants, grant supplements, and loan guarantees from the Economic Development Administration under the Public Works and Economic Development Act of 1965. Projects funded include public works, business development, research, planning, and disaster recovery. Entries include: Recipient name, location, date of obligation, funds received by type of assistance, type of project, identification number.

Expansion Management--Atlas/Guide Issue: The Resource Manual for Companies on the Move. Intertec Publishing. • Annual. $10 for just Atlas issue. Publication includes: List of companies and agencies providing assistance to expanding or relocating businesses, including state and city departments of commerce, public and private economic development agencies, financial institutions, consultants, utility companies, and other professionals. Entries include: Company name, address, phone, fax, name and title of contact.

Fairfax County Business Database. Fairfax County Economic Development Authority. • Description: Database cover approximately 7,000 Fairfax County-located businesses, including high-tech firms, financial and legal firms, retail, and personal services. Government agencies are not included. Entries include: Company name, address, phone, fax, e-mail (if available), name and title of contact; number of employees, occupied space in square feet, and geographical submarket of county. Formerly available in print edition; latest edition 1990.

Global Economic, Financial, and Development Organizations Directory. International Business Publications, USA. • $99.95 Individuals paperback. Covers: International economic development agencies and organizations in over 100 countries.

Global U.S. Economic Assistance Guide. International Business Publications, USA. • $99.95. Covers: Information on U.S. economic assistance worldwide.

Guide to Montana's Economic Development and Community Development Programs. Economic Development Div. Montana Department of Commerce. • Covers: 28 state and local government agencies that offer economic development programs. Entries include: Program name, sponsoring agency name, address, phone.

Malta Export-Import, Economic, Financial, Trade and Industrial Development Handbook. International Business Publications, USA. • $99.95. Covers: Government programs and plans for economic, industrial, and business development in Malta.

E-BOOKS

Encyclopedia of American Industries. Cengage Learning Inc. • 2011. $807.00. 6th edition. Three volumes. Volume one is Manufacturing Industries and volume two is Service and Non-Manufacturing Industries. Provides the history, development, and recent status of approximately 1,000 industries. Includes statistical graphs, with industry and general indexes. Also available as eBook.

ENCYCLOPEDIAS AND DICTIONARIES

Worldmark Encyclopedia of National Economies. Cengage Learning Inc. • 2002. $572.00. Four volumes. Covers both the current and historical development of the economies of 200 foreign nations. Includes analysis and statistics. Also available as eBook.

GENERAL WORKS

Economic and Social Survey of Asia and the Pacific. United Nations Publications. • Annual. $85 print. Emphasis is on trends in economic policy and economic development strategies.

ONLINE DATABASES

Wilson Social Sciences Abstracts Online. H.W. Wilson Co. • Provides online abstracting and indexing of more than 500 periodicals covering area studies, community health, public administration, public welfare, urban studies, and many other social science topics. Time period is 1994 to date for abstracts and 1983 to date for indexing, with updates weekly. Inquire as to online cost and availability.

OTHER SOURCES

World Investment Report. United Nations Publications. • Annual. Concerned with foreign direct investment, economic development, regional trends, transnational corporations, and globalization.

PERIODICALS AND NEWSLETTERS

Economic Development and Cultural Change. The University of Chicago Press, Journals Div. • Quarterly. $77 Individuals Print and electronic. Examines the economic and social forces that affect development and the impact of development on culture.

Economic Development Monitor. Whitaker Newsletters Inc. • Biweekly. $247.00 per year. Newsletter. Covers the news of U. S. economic and industrial development, including legislation, regulation, planning, and financing.

Economic Development Quarterly: The Journal of American Revitalization. Pine Forge Press. • Quarterly. $877 Institutions Print & E-access. Bridges the gap between academics, policymakers, and practitioners and links the various economic development communities.

Economic Development Review. International Economic Development Council. • Quarterly. $50.00 per year.

Financial Flows and the Developing Countries. World Bank Group. • Quarterly. $150.00 per year. Concerned mainly with debt, capital markets, and foreign direct investment. Includes statistical tables.

Plants, Sites, and Parks. Reed Elsevier Group plc Reed Business Information. • Seven times a year. Free to qualified personnel; others, $43.90 per year. Covers economic development, site location, industrial parks, and industrial development programs.

RESEARCH CENTERS AND INSTITUTES

Bureau of International Labor Affairs - Office of International Economic Affairs - Foreign Economic Research Division. 200 Constitution Ave. NW, Rm. S-5317, Washington, DC 20210. Phone: (202)693-4887; Fax: (202)693-4851 • URL: http://www.dol.gov/ilab/programs/oiea • Effects of international economic developments, including policies that affect international trade and investment on U.S. workers. Projects have included analysis of: multilateral trade negotiations; effects on U.S. workers of foreign investment and technology transfer by multinational corporations; compensation of earnings losses for workers who are displaced by trade; changing pattern of U.S. comparative advantage in trade; and effects of trade on employment opportunities, by industry and occupational categories.

Center for International Policy. 2000 M St. NW, Ste. 720, Washington, DC 20036-3327. Phone: (202)232-3317; Fax: (202)232-3440; Email: cip@ciponline.org • URL: http://www.ciponline.org • Research subjects include the International Monetary Fund, the World Bank, and other international financial institutions. Analyzes the impact of policies on social and economic conditions in developing countries.

De La Salle University - Ramon V. del Rosario College of Business - Center for Business and Economics Research and Development. 2401 Taft Ave., Manila 1004, Philippines. Phone: 63 2 3030869; Fax: 63 2 5219094; Email: cbedean@dlsu.edu.ph • URL: http://www.dlsu.edu.ph/research/centers/cberd/default.asp • Business education, entrepreneurship, and administrative policy.

Hawaii Department of Business, Economic Development, and Tourism - Research and Economic Analysis Division. No. 1 Capitol District Bldg., 250 S Hotel St., Honolulu, HI 96813. Phone: (808)586-2355 • URL: http://dbedt.hawaii.gov/economic • Business, economic development, tourism.

University of Minnesota, Duluth - Center for Economic Development. 11 E Superior St., Ste. 210, Duluth, MN 55802. Phone: 888-387-4594 or (218)726-7298; Fax: (218)726-6338; Email: umdced@d.umn.edu • URL: http://www.umdced.com • Economic development and innovation, including management training and innovation commercialization.

W.E. Upjohn Institute for Employment Research. 300 S Westnedge Ave., Kalamazoo, MI 49007-4686. Phone: 888-227-8569 or (269)343-5541; Fax: (269)343-7310; Email: communications@upjohn.org • URL: http://www.upjohninstitute.org • Research fields include unemployment, unemployment insurance, worker's compensation, labor productivity, profit sharing, the labor market, economic development, earnings, training, and other areas related to employment.

TRADE/PROFESSIONAL ASSOCIATIONS

Afghanistan Microfinance Association. House No 547 St. 3, Taimani Project, District 4, Kabul, Afghanistan. Phone: 93 799 308876; Email: info@ama.org.af • URL: http://www.ama.org.af • Promotes the microfinance sector of Afghanistan. Seeks to enhance the security measures between microfinance institutions (MFIs) and increase government support in terms of securing microfinance operations. Develops and delivers a number of training modules in local languages to ensure the best use of the training programs by employees of the microfinance sector.

Association of Microfinance Organizations of Tajikistan. 14 Firuz St., 734003 Dushanbe, Tajikistan. Phone: 992 44 6005794; Fax: 992 44 6005793; Email: office@amfot.tj • URL: http://www.amfot.tj • Facilitates the development of the microfinance sector in Tajikistan. Serves as a forum

For publishers' addresses, refer to SOURCES CITED section at the back of the book.

for interrelation and network of microfinance organizations in Tajikistan. Provides professional services for training and consultations and assists in the introduction of national standards of microfinance activity.

Bretton Woods Committee. 1726 M St. NW, Ste. 200, Washington, DC 20036. Phone: (202)331-1616; Fax: (202)785-9423; Email: info@brettonwoods.org • URL: http://www.brettonwoods.org • Corporate CEOs, university administrators, former government officials, state governors, association and trade union executives, and bankers. Seeks to inform and educate the public regarding the activities of the World Bank, International Monetary Fund, and other Multinational Development Banks (MDB). Promotes U.S. participation in MDBs.

China Association of Microfinance. RDI of CASS, Rm. 1343, 5 Jianguomennei St., Beijing 100732, Hebei, China. Phone: 86 10 8519 6476 or 86 10 8519 5660; Fax: 86 10 8519 6476; Email: cam.net@163.com • URL: http://www.chinamfi.net • Represents and supports the microfinance industry. Promotes governmental support and strengthens international cooperation on microfinance. Raises funds for microfinance development and provides financial services to populations living with poverty and low income. Enhances the management capacity of microfinance institutions.

Committee for Economic Development. 2000 L St. NW, Ste. 700, Washington, DC 20036-4915. Phone: 800-676-7353 or (202)296-5860; Fax: (202)223-0776; Email: info@ced.org • URL: http://www.ced.org • Committee conducts research and formulates policy recommendations on national and international economic issues, including education and trade policy.

Committee for the Economic Growth of Israel. 100 Manpower Pl., Milwaukee, WI 53212. Phone: (414)906-6250; Fax: (414)906-7878 • URL: http://elmerwinter.com • Businessmen and women. Seeks to expand business relationships between Israel and the U.S. by promoting investment and joint venture opportunities for U.S. and Israeli companies. Promotes the exchange of technology, research and development, and products from Israel.

DOCHAS, The Irish Association of Non-Governmental Development Organisations. 1-2 Baggot Ct., Lower Baggot St., Dublin 2, Dublin, Ireland. Phone: 353 1 4053801; Fax: 353 1 4053802 • URL: http://www.dochas.ie • Brings together 38 Irish NGDO involved in development and relief overseas and/or in the provision of development education. Aims to provide a forum for consultation and cooperation between its members and acts as the Irish Assembly of Development and Relief Organisations in relation to the CONCORD - a European Confederation for relief and development.

EnterpriseWorks - Senegal. BP 10251, Dakar, Senegal. Phone: 221 8254523; Email: ewws@sentoo.sn • URL: http://www.angelfire.com/yt2/EnterpriseWorks/english.htm • Works to fight poverty in the developing world through business development programs that allow small agricultural producers and other entrepreneurs to increase productivity and incomes. Pursues sustainable business opportunities. Creates jobs that benefit families, communities and regions.

International Economic Alliance. 1 Mifflin Pl., Ste. 400, Cambridge, MA 02138-4946. Phone: (617)418-1981; Fax: (617)812-0499 • URL: http://www.iealliance.org • Aims to further global trade, economic development and advance business relations. Brings together the world's key players and decision-makers (business and government leaders, investors and leading intellectuals) for practical, open, bi-partisan and solution-oriented exchange of ideas. Serves as a source of knowledge, facilitator of relationships, and catalyst for new business opportunities.

International Economic Development Council. 734 15th St. NW, Ste. 900, Washington, DC 20005. Phone: (202)223-7800; Fax: (202)223-4745 • URL: http://www.iedconline.org • Works to help economic development professionals improve the quality of life in their communities. Represents all levels of government, academia, and private industry; provides a broad range of member services including research, advisory services, conferences, professional certification, professional development, publications, legislative tracking and more.

Local Initiatives Support Corporation. 501 7th Ave., New York, NY 10018-5903. Phone: (212)455-9800; Fax: (212)682-5929; Email: info@lisc.org • URL: http://www.lisc.org • Seeks to help independent community-based organizations in deteriorated areas to improve local, physical, and economic conditions while strengthening their own management and financial capabilities. Matches funds contributed by local corporations and foundations with those provided by national donors and investors; offers loans and grants to local organizations and projects. Administers national community development loan programs in cooperation with major financial institutions.

Middle East Investment Initiative. 500 Eighth St. NW, Washington, DC 20004. Phone: (202)799-4345; Fax: (202)799-5000 • URL: http://www.meiinitiative.org • Partners with public and private entities to offer specialized financial products in the Palestinian territories. Helps to revitalize the economy, stimulate economic activity and create jobs in the Middle East. Works to create risk insurance to address movement of products for Palestinian businesses.

National Alliance of Craftsmen Associations. 816 Camaron St., Ste. 212, San Antonio, TX 78212. Phone: (210)271-9100; Fax: (210)212-9250 • Works to create and promote community empowerment, sustainability and growth through the development of employment, economic and educational opportunities in blighted communities. Concentrates on the barriers that perpetuate the underutilized, underemployed, unemployed, unskilled and underskilled community. Aims to build a stronger and healthier country one community at a time.

National Coalition for Capital. 1028 33rd St. NW, Ste. 200, Washington, DC 20007. Phone: (202)337-1661 • URL: http://www.nationalcoalitionforcapital.org • Represents leaders who support economic development and job creation through long-term access to capital for entrepreneurs and emerging companies. Serves as a resource for promising small and emerging companies, entrepreneurs, investors, economic developers and other stakeholders within the nation's emerging investment infrastructure.

Organisation for Economic Co-Operation and Development. 2, rue Andre Pascal, F-75775 Paris, France. Phone: 33 1 45248200; Fax: 1 45248500; Email: webmaster@oecd.org • URL: http://www.oecd.org.

Paraguayan Industrial Union. Av. Sacramento 945, Asuncion, Paraguay. Phone: 595 21 606988 • URL: http://www.uip.org.py • Promotes the economic and social development of Paraguay. Organizes conference and seminars.

PlaNet Finance US. 44 rue de Prony, 75017 Paris, France. Email: contact@planetfinance.org • URL: http://www.planetfinance.org • Works to alleviate poverty through the development of microfinance. Seeks to support and strengthen the capacity of the microfinance sector. Raises public awareness of microfinancing.

Pro Mujer. 253 W 35th St., 11th Fl., New York, NY 10001. Phone: (646)626-7000; Fax: (212)904-1038; Email: communications@promujer.org • URL: http://promujer.org • Establishes microfinance organizations that provide financial and human development services for women. Provides business training and healthcare support.

WAM International: Women Advancing Microfinance. 402 Constitution Ave. NE, Washington, DC 20002. Phone: (202)547-4546; Email: wam.international.president@gmail.com • URL: http://waminternational.org • Promotes the advancement of women working in the microfinance industry. Seeks to extend economic opportunities to women globally and encourages active participation of women in management and governance roles.

ECONOMIC ENTOMOLOGY

See also PESTICIDE INDUSTRY

ABSTRACTS AND INDEXES

Biological and Agricultural Index. H.W. Wilson Co. • 11 times a year. Annual and quarterly cumulations. Price varies.

Review of Agricultural Entomology: Consisting of Abstracts of Reviews of Current Literature on Applied Entomology Throughout the World. CABI Publishing North America. • Monthly. Institutions, $1,505.00 per year. Print and online edition, $1,505.00 per year. Published in England by CABI Publishing. Provides worldwide coverage of the literature. (Formerly *Review of Applied Entomology, Series A: Agricultural.*).

Review of Medical and Veterinary Entomology. CAB International. • Monthly. Provides worldwide coverage of the literature. Formerly *Review of Applied Entomology, Series B: Medical and Veterinary.*

ALMANACS AND YEARBOOKS

Annual Review of Entomology. Annual Reviews. • Annual. $99 Individuals.

CD-ROM DATABASES

AGRICOLA on SilverPlatter. Ovid Technologies Inc. • Updated monthly. Price varies. Produced by the National Agricultural Library. Provides over 4 million citations to the literature of agriculture, agricultural economics, animal sciences, entomology, fertilizer, food, forestry, nutrition, pesticides, plant science, water resources, and other topics.

ONLINE DATABASES

Derwent Crop Protection File. Derwent Information Ltd. • Provides citations to the international journal literature of agricultural chemicals and pesticides from 1968 to date, with updating eight times per year. Formerly *PESTDOC.* Inquire as to online cost and availability.

PERIODICALS AND NEWSLETTERS

American Entomologist. Entomological Society of America. • Quarterly. $122 Institutions agent; print. A quarterly magazine publishing articles and information of general interest to entomologists. Formerly *Entomological Society of America Bulletin.*

Entomological Society of America Annals: Devoted to the Interest of Classical Entomology. Entomological Society of America. • Bimonthly. $384 Institutions Print or Online only - back issue. Contains manuscripts that integrate different areas of insect biology, and address issues that are likely to be of broad relevance to entomologists.

RESEARCH CENTERS AND INSTITUTES

Cattle Fever Tick Research Laboratory. US Department of Agricultural Livestock Insects Laboratory, Rte. 3, Edinburg, TX 78539. Phone: (956)580-7268; Fax: (956)580-7261; Email: ronald.b.davey@aphis.udsa.gov • URL: http://www.aphis.usda.gov.

Cornell University - Toxic Chemicals Laboratory. New York State College of Agriculture, Tower Rd., Ithaca, NY 14853-7401. Phone: (607)255-4538;

Fax: (607)255-0599; Email: djl22@cornell.edu.

Ohio State University - Laboratory for Pest Control Application Technology. Ohio Agricultural Research & Development Ctr., 1680 Madison Ave., Wooster, OH 44691. Phone: (330)263-3931; Fax: (330)263-3686; Email: downer.2@osu.edu • URL: http://www.oardc.ohio-state.edu/lpcat • Conducts pest control research in cooperation with the U. S. Department of Agriculture.

ECONOMIC FORECASTING

See BUSINESS FORECASTING

ECONOMIC GEOLOGY

See also MINES AND MINERAL RESOURCES

PERIODICALS AND NEWSLETTERS

Economic Geology and the Bulletin of the Society of Economic Geologists. Society of Economic Geologist. Economic Geology Publishing Company Inc. • Irregular. Individuals, $75.00 per year; institutions, $145.00 per year.

RESEARCH CENTERS AND INSTITUTES

University of Texas at Austin - Bureau of Economic Geology. 10100 Burnet Rd., Austin, TX 78758-4445. Phone: (512)471-1534; Fax: (512)471-0140; Email: scott.tinker@beg.utexas.edu • URL: http://www.beg.utexas.edu • Energy, the environment, hydrogeology, geologic mapping, and coastal studies.

ECONOMIC HISTORY

See BUSINESS HISTORY

ECONOMIC INDICATORS

ALMANACS AND YEARBOOKS

State of the World (year). Worldwatch Institute. • Annual. $22.00. Provides yearly analysis of factors influencing the global environment.

Vital Signs: The Trends That Are Shaping Our Future (year). Worldwatch Institute. • Annual. $19. 95. Provides access to selected indicators showing social, economic, and environmental trends throughout the world. Includes data relating to food, energy, transportation, finance, population, and other topics.

World Development Report. World Bank Group. • Annual. Covers history, conditions, and trends relating to economic globalization and localization. Includes selected data from *World Development Indicators* for 132 countries or economies. Key indicators are provided for 78 additional countries or economies.

CD-ROM DATABASES

OECD Statistical Compendium. Organization for Economic Cooperation and Development. • Semiannual. $1,905.00 per year for 1 to 10 users. CD-ROM contains more than 730,000 monthly, quarterly, and annual time series for OECD countries, 1960 to date. Includes fully searchable data on agriculture, food, economic indicators, national accounts, employment, energy, finance, industry, technology, and foreign trade. Results can be displayed in various forms.

World Development Report. World Bank Group. • Annual. Covers history, conditions, and trends relating to economic globalization and localization. Includes selected data from *World Development Indicators* for 132 countries or economies. Key indicators are provided for 78 additional countries or economies.

INTERNET DATABASES

BanxQuote Banking, Mortgage, and Finance Center. BanxQuote, Inc. Phone: (914)722-1600; Fax: (914)722-6630; Email: info@banx.com • URL: http://www.banx.com • Daily. Web site quotes interest rates paid by banks around the country on various savings products, as well as rates paid by consumers for automobile loans, mortgages, credit cards, home equity loans, and personal loans. Also provided: stock quotes, indexes, stock options, futures trading data, economic indicators, and links to many other financial sites.

Bondtalk.com: Live Talk & Analysis on the Bond Market & the Economy. Miller Tabak & Co., LLC. Phone: (212)370-0040; Email: acrescenzi@bondtalk.com • URL: http://www.bondtalk.com • Web site provides extensive, free data on the fixed income securities market, including individual bond prices, yields, interest rates, Federal Reserve information, charts, bond market news, and economic analysis. Also offered on a fee basis is "Bondtalkpro.com: The New and Enhanced Service for Market Professionals.".

Bureau of Economic Analysis. U. S. Department of Commerce, Bureau of Economic Analysis. Phone: (202)606-9900; Fax: (202)606-5310; Email: webmaster@bea.doc.gov • URL: http://www.bea.doc.gov • Web site includes "News Release Information" covering national, regional, and international economic estimates from the BEA. Highlights of releases appear online the same day, complete text and tables appear the next day. "Recent News Releases" section provides titles for past nine months, with links. "BEA Data and Methodology" includes "Frequently Requested NIPA Data" (national income and product accounts, such as gross domestic product and personal income). Other statistics are available. Fees: Free.

Business 2.0 Web Guide to the Best Business Links. Business 2.0 Media Inc. Phone: (415)293-4800: Email: support@business2.com • URL: http://www.business2.com/webguide • Web site presents an extensive, searchable directory of links to "the best, most informative, and authoritative web pages." Twenty main categories cover business, finance, career, company information, people, and technology topics, with thousands of subtopics, all linking to Web sites recommended by experienced business researchers. Fees: Free.

Business Week Online. McGraw-Hill. Phone: (212)512-2511; Fax: (684)842-6101 • URL: http://www.businessweek.com • Web site provides complete contents of current issue of *Business Week* plus "BW Daily" with additonal business news, financial market quotes, and corporate information from Standard & Poor's. Includes various features, such as "Banking Center" with mortgage and interest data, and "Interactive Computer Buying Guide." The "Business Week Archive" is fully searchable back to 1996.

Fedstats. Federal Interagency Council on Statistical Policy. Phone: (202)395-7254 • URL: http://www.fedstats.gov • Web site features an efficient search facility for full-text statistics produced by more than 100 federal agencies, including the Census Bureau, the Bureau of Economic Analysis, and the Bureau of Labor Statistics. Boolean searches can be made within one agency or for all agencies combined. Links are offered to international statistical bureaus, including the UN, IMF, OECD, UNESCO, Eurostat, and 20 individual countries. Fees: Free.

FreeLunch.com. Economy.com, Inc. Phone: (610)696-8700; Fax: (610)696-1678 • URL: http://www.freelunch.com • Web site provides free access to more than 200 million economic and financial data series, covering industry, demographics, labor markets, prices, retail sales, government spending, trade, interest rates, housing starts, the stock market, etc. Data is available in either chart or table form. Searching is offered. Free, but registration required. Economy.com, Inc. also offers fee-based economic analysis at *The Dismal Scientist* site (www.dismal.com).

Summary of Commentary on Current Economic Conditions by Federal Reserve District. Board of Governors of the Federal Reserve System. Phone: (202)452-3000; Fax: (202)452-3819 • URL: http://www.federalreserve.gov/publications.htm • 8/year. Free Web site provides current "anecdotal information" eight times a year on economic conditions within each of the 12 Federal Reserve Districts, plus an extensive national *Summary*. Text is based on the opinions of bank officials, business executives, economists, financial market experts, and others. Typically contains views of consumer spending, manufacturing, services, credit, employment, prices, wages, and the economy in general. Usually referred to as the Beige Book.

U.S. Census Bureau: The Official Statistics. U. S. Bureau of the Census. Phone: (301)763-4636 or (301)763-4100; Fax: (301)763-4794; Email: webmaster@census.gov • URL: http://www.census.gov/prod/www/abs/mfg-prof.html • Web site is "Your Source for Social, Demographic, and Economic Information." Contains "Current U. S. Population Count," "Current Economic Indicators," and a wide variety of data under "Other Official Statistics." Keyword searching is provided. Fees: Free.

PERIODICALS AND NEWSLETTERS

Financial Times Currency Forecaster: Consensus Forecasts of the Worldwide Currency and Economic Outlook. Briefings Publishing Group. • Monthly. $695.00 per year. Newsletter. Provides forecasts of foreign currency exchange rates and economic conditions. Supplement available: *Mid-Month Global Financial Report.*

Research Reports. American Institute for Economic Research. • Contains two or more current economic events in each issue.

World Watch: Working for a Sustainable Future. Worldwatch Institute. • Bimonthly. $25.00 per year. Emphasis is on environmental trends, including developments in population growth, climate change, human behavior, the role of government, and other factors.

STATISTICS SOURCES

The AIER Chart Book. AIER Research Staff. American Institute for Economic Research. • Annual. $4 Individuals. A compact compilation of long-range charts ("Purchasing Power of the Dollar," for example, goes back to 1780) covering various aspects of the U. S. economy. Includes inflation, interest rates, debt, gold, taxation, stock prices, etc. (Economic Education Bulletin.).

Survey of Current Business. U. S. Government Printing Office. • Published by Bureau of Economic Analysis, U. S. Department of Commerce. Presents a wide variety of business and economic data.

ECONOMIC PLANNING

See ECONOMIC POLICY

ECONOMIC POLICY

See also ECONOMIC DEVELOPMENT; ECONOMICS

ABSTRACTS AND INDEXES

Social Sciences Citation Index. Thomson Reuters Corp. • Weekly. Product is accessed via *Web of Science.*

Social Sciences Index Retrospective: 1907-1983. EBSCO Publishing Inc. • Indexing for 1,000,000 articles. Coverage includes international index and social sciences and humanities index.

CD-ROM DATABASES

Social Sciences Abstracts. EBSCO Publishing Inc. • Provides indexing from 1983 and abstracting from 1994 of more than 750 periodicals covering economics, area studies, community health, public administration, public welfare, urban studies, and many other topics related to the social sciences.

Social Sciences Citation Index. Thomson Reuters Corp. • Weekly. Product is accessed via *Web of Science*.

INTERNET DATABASES

Factiva. Dow Jones Reuters Business Interactive, LLC. Phone: 800-369-7466 or (609)452-1511; Fax: (609)520-5770; Email: solutions@factiva.com • URL: http://www.factiva.com • Fee-based Web site provides "global news and business information through Web sites and content integration solutions." Includes Dow Jones and Reuters newswires, The Wall Street Journal, and more than 7,000 other sources of current news, historical articles, market research reports, and investment analysis. Content includes 96 major U. S. newspapers, 900 non-English sources, trade publications, media transcripts, country profiles, news photos, etc.

Nexis.com. Lexis-Nexis Group. Phone: 800-227-4908 or (937)865-6800; Fax: (937)865-6909; Email: webmaster@prod.lexis-nexis.com • URL: http://www.nexis.com • Fee-based Web site offers searching of about 2.8 billion documents in some 30,000 news, business, and legal information sources. Features include a subject directory covering 1,200 topics in 34 categories and a Company Dossier containing information on more than 500,000 public and private companies. Boolean searching is offered.

Wall Street Journal Interactive Edition. Dow Jones & Co., Inc. 1211 Avenue of the Americas, New York, NY 10036. Phone: 800-369-5663; Email: service@dowjones.com • URL: http://new.dowjones.com • Fee-based Web site providing online searching of worldwide information from *The Wall Street Journal*. Includes "Company Snapshots," "The Journal's Greatest Hits," "Index to Market Data," "Journal Links," etc. Financial price quotes are available. Fees: $49.00 per year; $29.00 per year to print subscribers.

ONLINE DATABASES

Wilson Social Sciences Abstracts Online. H.W. Wilson Co. • Provides online abstracting and indexing of more than 500 periodicals covering area studies, community health, public administration, public welfare, urban studies, and many other social science topics. Time period is 1994 to date for abstracts and 1983 to date for indexing, with updates weekly. Inquire as to online cost and availability.

PERIODICALS AND NEWSLETTERS

Challenge: The Magazine of Economic Affairs. M.E. Sharpe Inc. • 6/year. $72 Individuals print only. A nontechnical journal on current economic policy and economic trends.

International Monetary Fund Staff Papers. International Monetary Fund, Publication Services. • Quarterly. Individuals, $56.00 per year; students, $28.00 per year. Contains studies by IMF staff members on balance of payments, foreign exchange, fiscal policy, and related topics. Formerly *International Monetary Fund Staff Papers*.

Journal of Economic Perspectives. American Economic Association. • Quarterly. Quarterly. Membership. Emphasis is on the economic analysis of public policy issues.

RESEARCH CENTERS AND INSTITUTES

American Council for Capital Formation Center for Policy Research. 1750 K St. NW, Ste. 400, Washington, DC 20006-2302. Phone: (202)293-5811; Fax: (202)785-8165; Email: info@accf.org • URL: http://www.accf.org/center.php • Economic growth through sound tax, regulatory, and environmental policies, including Individual Retirement Accounts, personal savings, corporate income taxes, consumption taxes, capital gains taxes, estate taxes, international competitiveness, climate policy, investment and economic growth.

Department of Finance Canada - Economic and Fiscal Policy Branch - Economic Studies and Policy Analysis Division - Structural Analysis Section. East Tower, 19th Fl., 140 O'Connor St., Ottawa, ON, Canada K1A 0G5. Phone: (613)992-1573; Fax: (613)943-0938; Email: finpub@fin.gc.ca • URL: http://www.fin.gc.ca/branches-directions/efp-eng.asp#EconomicStudiesandPolicyAnalysisDivision • Economics and policy, focusing on labor economics, public finance, income distribution and educational issues.

London School of Economics and Political Science - Department of International Relations - International Trade Policy Unit. Clement House, Rm. CLM 613, Houghton St., London WC2A 2AE, United Kingdom. Phone: 44 20 79557696; Fax: 44 20 79557980; Email: itpu@lse.ac.uk • URL: http://www.lse.ac.uk/internationalRelations/centresandunits/ITPU/ITPUhome.aspx • Policies and business implications of trade agreements at the multilateral, regional, and national levels.

Monash University - Centre of Policy Studies - Impact Project. Menzies Bldg., 11th Fl., Wellington Rd., Clayton, VIC 3800, Australia. Phone: 61 3 99052398; Fax: 61 3 99052426; Email: philip.adams@buseco.monash.edu.au • URL: http://www.monash.edu.au/policy/ • Economic modelling.

National University of Singapore - Singapore Center for Applied and Policy Economics. Department of Economics, AS2 No. 06-02, 1 Arts Link, Singapore 117570, Singapore. Phone: 65 65166116; Fax: 65 67752646; Email: ecstabey@nus.edu.sg • URL: http://www.fas.nus.edu.sg/ecs/scape • Singapore and Asian macroeconomics and modeling, human resources and labor economics, public economics and social policy, and behavioral and experimental economics.

Stanford University - Stanford Institute for Economic Policy Research. John A. & Cynthia Fry Gunn Bldg., 366 Galvez St., Stanford, CA 94305-6015. Phone: (650)725-1874; Fax: (650)723-8611; Email: shoven@stanford.edu • URL: http://siepr.stanford.edu • Economic policy issues facing the United States and other countries. Research is conducted through three centers and six programs, focusing on such areas as macroeconomics, regulation, energy economics, policy reform in developing countries, economic growth and technology, tax and budget policy, government and finance.

University of Rochester - Bradley Policy Research Center. 305 Schlegel Hall, William E Simon Graduate School of Business, Rochester, NY 14627. Phone: (585)275-3316 or (585)275-2668; Fax: (585)275-0095; Email: sue.north@simon.rochester.edu • URL: http://www.simon.rochester.edu/faculty--research/research-center-and-conferences/bradley-policy-research-center/index.aspx • Corporate control and corporate takeovers are among the research areas covered.

STATISTICS SOURCES

Budget and Economic Outlook: Fiscal Years (10-year period). U. S. Government Printing Office. • Annual. $27. Issued by the Congressional Budget Office (CBO). Reports on fiscal policy and provides baseline projections of federal budget for 10 years. Also offers "impartial analysis with no recommendations.".

TRADE/PROFESSIONAL ASSOCIATIONS

Institute for Economic Analysis. c/o John S. Atlee, President/Director, 360 Mt. Auburn St., Ste. 001, Cambridge, MA 02138. Email: info@iea-macro-economics.org • URL: http://iea-macro-economics.org • Seeks to develop tools for macroeconomic analysis and policy that can maintain stable full employment growth, low inflation, low interest rates and equitable distribution of income and wealth. Integrates GDP and financial accounts for more systematic coordination of monetary and fiscal policy. Focuses on federal monetary policy, federal budget deficit/surplus, social security, consumer credit, and world economic recovery.

ECONOMIC RESEARCH

See also BUREAUS OF BUSINESS RESEARCH

ABSTRACTS AND INDEXES

Social Sciences Citation Index. Thomson Reuters Corp. • Weekly. Product is accessed via *Web of Science*.

Social Sciences Index Retrospective: 1907-1983. EBSCO Publishing Inc. • Indexing for 1,000,000 articles. Coverage includes international index and social sciences and humanities index.

ALMANACS AND YEARBOOKS

Research in Experimental Economics. Elsevier. • Dates vary. $84.00. Nine volumes. Supplement available *An Experiment in Non-Cooperative Oligopoly*.

Research in Law and Economics: A Research Annual. Richard O. Zerbe. Elsevier. • Dates vary. $78.50. 20 volumes. Supplement available. *Economics of Nonproprietary Organizations*.

CD-ROM DATABASES

Social Sciences Abstracts. EBSCO Publishing Inc. • Provides indexing from 1983 and abstracting from 1994 of more than 750 periodicals covering economics, area studies, community health, public administration, public welfare, urban studies, and many other topics related to the social sciences.

Social Sciences Citation Index. Thomson Reuters Corp. • Weekly. Product is accessed via *Web of Science*.

DIRECTORIES

Association for University Business and Economic Research--Membership Directory. Association for University Business and Economic Research. • Annual. $10. Covers: member institutions in the United States and abroad with centers, bureaus, departments, etc., concerned with business and economic research. Entries include: Name of bureau, center, etc., sponsoring institution name, address, phone, names and titles of director and staff, publications and frequency.

Business and Economics Research Directory. Routledge Reference. • £495 Individuals hardback. Covers: Approximately 1,500 institutes concerned with business and economics research worldwide. Entries include: Organization name, address, phone, fax, e-mail address, names and titles of key personnel, foundation date, description of activities, publications with frequencies.

ENCYCLOPEDIAS AND DICTIONARIES

Everyday Finance: Economics, Personal Money Management, and Entrepreneurship. Cengage Learning Inc. • $258 Individuals. 2008. 2 volumes. Contains 300 topical entries that are organized into 3 units: How the Economy Works: Personal Finance: Buying, Borrowing, Saving, and Insuring; and The World of Business. eBook available. Inquire for pricing.

ONLINE DATABASES

Current Contents Connect. Thomson Reuters Intellectual Property and Science. • Provides online abstracts of articles listed in the tables of contents of about 7,500 journals. Coverage is very broad, including science, social science, life science, technology, engineering, industry, agriculture, the environment, economics, and arts and humanities. Time period is two years, with weekly updates. Inquire as to online cost and availability.

Wilson Social Sciences Abstracts Online. H.W. Wilson Co. • Provides online abstracting and indexing of more than 500 periodicals covering area studies, community health, public administration, public welfare, urban studies, and many other social science topics. Time period is 1994 to date for abstracts and 1983 to date for indexing, with updates weekly. Inquire as to online cost and availability.

PERIODICALS AND NEWSLETTERS

Mathematical Finance: An International Journal of Mathematics, Statistics, and Financial Economics. Blackwell Publishing Inc. • Quarterly. $1,453 Institutions print only. Covers the use of sophisticated mathematical tools in financial research and practice.

Research Reports. American Institute for Economic Research. • Contains two or more current economic events in each issue.

Review of Financial Economics. Elsevier. • $623 /year. Publishes original research in finance.

RESEARCH CENTERS AND INSTITUTES

Aalborg University - Department of Business and Management - Innovation, Knowledge and Economic Dynamics Research Group. Fibigerstraede 11, DK-9220 Alborg, Denmark. Phone: 45 99408235; Email: ike-secr@business.aau.dk • URL: http://www.ike.aau.dk • Economic, technical and institutional changes, especially economic evolutionary modeling, theory of the firm, national systems of innovation, international trade and competitiveness, and the interplay between economic and ecological issues.

Aalborg University - Economic Research Group. Department of Economics, Politics & Public Administration, Fibigerstraede 3, DK-9220 Alborg, Denmark. Phone: 45 96358200; Email: cbruun@socsci.auc.dk • URL: http://www.socsci.aau.dk/econ • Macroeconomics, econometrics, computable economics, agent-based computational economics, finance and history of economic thought.

American Council for Capital Formation Center for Policy Research. 1750 K St. NW, Ste. 400, Washington, DC 20006-2302. Phone: (202)293-5811; Fax: (202)785-8165; Email: info@accf.org • URL: http://www.accf.org/center.php • Economic growth through sound tax, regulatory, and environmental policies, including Individual Retirement Accounts, personal savings, corporate income taxes, consumption taxes, capital gains taxes, estate taxes, international competitiveness, climate policy, investment and economic growth.

American Institute for Economic Research. 250 Division St., Great Barrington, MA 01230-1000. Phone: 888-528-1216; Fax: (413)528-0103; Email: info@aier.org • URL: http://www.aier.org • Through research and publications, provides "information on economic and financial subjects that is useful and completely independent of special interests." Sponsors a fellowship program for graduate study of economics at the institute and in absentia.

Bocconi University - Innocenzo Gasparini Institute for Economic Research. Via Röntgen 1, 5th Fl., 20136 Milan, Italy. Phone: 39 2 58363300; Fax: 39 2 58363302; Email: igier@unibocconi.it • URL: http://www.igier.unibocconi.it • Economics, including open economy macroeconomics, financial markets, and politics and economic policy.

Cardiff University - Welsh Economy Research Unit. Aberconway Bldg., Cardiff Business School, Colum Dr., Cardiff CF10 3EU, United Kingdom. Phone: 44 29 20875089; Fax: 44 29 20874419; Email: mundaymc@cf.ac.uk • URL: http://business.cardiff.ac.uk/welsh-economy-research-unit • Economic issues in Wales.

Center for International Private Enterprise - Albanian Center for Economic Research. Perlat Rexhepi St., Bldg. No. 10, 6th Fl., Apt. 64, Tirana, Albania. Phone: 355 4 2225021; Fax: 355 4 2274603; Email: acer@icc-al.org • URL: http://www.acer.org.al • Economic issues, financial and banking systems, development of small and medium enterprises, improvement of local government services, and issues of corruption.

Chapman University - A. Gary Anderson Center for Economic Research. 1 University Dr., Orange, CA 92866. Phone: (714)997-6693; Fax: (714)997-6601; Email: adibi@chapman.edu • URL: http://www.chapman.edu/research-and-institutions/anderson-center/index.aspx • Economics and business in the U.S. and California, as well as in Orange County, Los Angeles County, and the Inland Empire in California.

De La Salle University - Ramon V. del Rosario College of Business - Center for Business and Economics Research and Development. 2401 Taft Ave., Manila 1004, Philippines. Phone: 63 2 3030869; Fax: 63 2 5219094; Email: cbedean@dlsu.edu.ph • URL: http://www.dlsu.edu.ph/research/centers/cberd/default.asp • Business education, entrepreneurship, and administrative policy.

Economic Research Service - Canada Division. 1800 M St. NW, Washington, DC 20036. Phone: 800-999-6779 or (202)694-5227; Email: jwainio@ers.usda.gov • URL: http://www.ers.usda.gov/Briefing/canada/ • Canadian agricultural supply, consumption, and trade, including Canadian policies related to agriculture.

Economic Research Service - Cattle and Beef. 355 E St. SW, Washington, DC 20024-3221. Phone: 800-999-6779 or (202)694-5183; Email: kmathews@ers.usda.gov • URL: http://ers.usda.gov/topics/animal-products/cattle-beef.aspx#.U5Eq73I2aDg • Market analysis and research on the U.S. cattle and beef sectors, including domestic supply and utilization, live cattle and retail beef prices, and international trade.

Hawaii Department of Business, Economic Development, and Tourism - Research and Economic Analysis Division. No. 1 Capitol District Bldg., 250 S Hotel St., Honolulu, HI 96813. Phone: (808)586-2355 • URL: http://dbedt.hawaii.gov/economic • Business, economic development, tourism.

Irish Agriculture and Food Development Authority - Rural Economy Research Centre. Teagasc, Athenry 4, Galway, Ireland. Phone: 353 59 9170200; Fax: 353 59 9182097; Email: cathal.odonoghue@teagasc.ie • URL: http://www.agresearch.teagasc.ie/rerc • Agricultural economics, production economics, agricultural policy, and rural development.

Lahore University of Management Sciences - Center for Management and Economic Research. Scholarship of Arts & Sciences, Department of Economics, Lahore 54792, Pakistan. Phone: 92 42 5722670; Fax: 92 42 5722591; Email: burki@lums.edu.pk • URL: http://www.lums.edu.pk/ • Management and economic issues facing Pakistan and the region.

London School of Economics and Political Science - Centre for Research into Economics and Finance in Southern Africa. Rm. G409, 20 Kingsway, Houghton St., London WC2A 2AE, United Kingdom. Phone: 44 20 79557505; Email: j.leape@lse.ac.uk • URL: http://www.lse.ac.uk/researchAndExpertise/units/CREFSA/home.aspx • Private capital flows in Southern Africa; financial regulation and the development of financial systems in Southern Africa; prospects for regional trade and monetary integration in the SADC.

Mongolian National Chamber of Commerce and Industry - Economic and Market Research Center. Government Bldg. 11, Rm. 711, J. Sambuu St. 11, Ulaanbaatar, Mongolia. Phone: 976 11 327176; Fax: 976 324620; Email: chamber@mongolchamber.mn • URL: http://www.mongolchamber.mn/en/index.php • Economics, market research, trade and business promotion, consultancy, and training.

National Bureau of Economic Research. 1050 Massachusetts Ave., Cambridge, MA 02138-5398. Phone: (617)868-3900 or (617)253-6673; Fax: (617)868-2742; Email: info@nber.org • URL: http://www.nber.org • Conducts analyses of economic issues, including economic growth and fluctuations, productivity, financial institutions, money, international economic problems, taxation, government spending, labor studies, health, and American economic history.

National Institute of Statistics and Economic Studies - Center for Research in Economics and Statistics. 15 Blvd. Gabriel Péri, F-92245 Malakoff, France. Phone: 33 1 41176081; Fax: 33 1 41176029 • URL: http://www.insee.fr/en/insee-statistique-publique/default.asp?page=connaitre/genes.htm • Economic and social modeling; conception and implementation of statistical methods.

Osaka University - Institute of Social and Economic Research. 6-1 Mihogaoka, Ibaraki 567-0047, Japan. Phone: 81 6 68798552; Fax: 81 6 68798584; Email: ogawa@iser.osaka-u.ac.jp • URL: http://www.iser.osaka-u.ac.jp • General economic theory, econometrics, experimental economics, and the Japanese economy.

Pennsylvania State University at Harrisburg - Economic Development Research and Training Center. Church Hall, 777 W Harrisburg Pke., Middletown, PA 17057. Phone: (717)948-6117; Fax: (717)948-6306; Email: edrtc@psu.edu • URL: http://edrtc.hbg.psu.edu • Public policy, community development, economic development, economics, and economic impacts.

Pennsylvania State University - Economic Research Institute of Erie. Sam & Irene Black School of Business, 5091 Station Rd., Erie, PA 16563-1400. Phone: (814)898-7149; Fax: (814)898-6223; Email: k12@psu.edu • URL: http://128.118.18.108 • Erie County, PA regional economy and its linkages to the national economy, including other issues related to local/metro economic development and regional economics.

Pontifical Catholic University of Peru - Center for Social, Economic, Political and Anthropological Research. Av. Universitaria Cdra. 18, San Miguel, Lima 32, Peru. Phone: 51 1 6262000; Fax: 51 1 6262815 • URL: http://cisepa.pucp.edu.pe • Social sciences, economy, sociology, anthropology and political sciences.

Queen's University at Kingston - Institute for Economic Research. Department of Economics, 94 University Ave., Kingston, ON, Canada K7L 3N6. Phone: (613)533-2250; Fax: (613)533-6668; Email: admina@econ.queensu.ca • URL: http://www.econ.queensu.ca • Economics.

Simon Fraser University - Centre for Research in Adaptive Behaviour in Economics. Department of Economics, 8888 University Dr., Burnaby, BC, Canada V5A 1S6. Phone: (604)291-5603; Fax: (604)291-5944; Email: arifovic@sfu.ca • URL: http://www.sfu.ca/crabe • Behavioral economics.

Slovak Academy of Sciences - Institute of Economic Research. Šancová No. 56, 811 05 Bratislava, Slovakia. Phone: 421 2 52498214; Fax: 421 2 52495106; Email: milan.sikula@savba.sk • URL: http://www.ekonom.sav.sk • Macroeconomics, microeconomics, international economics, economic integration into the EU, economic analysis, and economic modeling.

Stanford University - Stanford Institute for Economic Policy Research. John A. & Cynthia Fry Gunn Bldg., 366 Galvez St., Stanford, CA 94305-6015. Phone: (650)725-1874; Fax: (650)723-8611;

For publishers' addresses, refer to SOURCES CITED section at the back of the book.

Email: shoven@stanford.edu • URL: http://siepr.stanford.edu • Economic policy issues facing the United States and other countries. Research is conducted through three centers and six programs, focusing on such areas as macroeconomics, regulation, energy economics, policy reform in developing countries, economic growth and technology, tax and budget policy, government and finance.

Stockholm School of Economics - Economic Research Institute. PO Box 6501, SE-113 83 Stockholm, Sweden. Phone: 46 8 7369000; Fax: 46 8 316270; Email: filip.wijkstrom@hhs.se • URL: http://www.hhs.se/EFI/Pages/default.aspx • Organization and management, economic psychology, marketing, accounting, control and corporate finance, finance, economics, economic statistics, and law.

Tel Aviv University - Eitan Berglas School of Economics - Foerder Institute for Economic Research. Berglas Bldg., Rm. 123, Ramat Aviv, 69978 Tel Aviv, Israel. Phone: 972 3 6409255; Fax: 972 3 6405815; Email: fersht@post.tau.ac.il • URL: http://econ.tau.ac.il/research/foerder.asp?theSubject=research • All fields of economics.

U.S. Small Business Administration - Office of Advocacy - Research and Statistics - Office of Economic Research. 409 3rd St., 7th Fl., Washington, DC 20416. Phone: (202)205-6533 or (202)205-6973; Fax: (202)206-6928 or (202)205-6928; Email: advocacy@sba.gov • URL: http://www.sba.gov/advo/research • Economic research and analysis pertaining to small business economic issues and statistics. Of particular interest are projects that are policy-oriented to develop alternative approaches to solving small business problems. Proposals may be submitted by any individual or firm (including small businesses).

University of Adelaide - South Australian Centre for Economic Studies. Rundle Mall, 3rd Fl., Nexus 10, 10 Pulteney St., Adelaide, SA 5000, Australia. Phone: 61 8 83035555; Fax: 61 8 83034916 • URL: http://www.adelaide.edu.au/saces • Economic issues.

University of Alabama - Culverhouse College of Commerce and Business Administration - Center for Business and Economic Research. Box 870221, Tuscaloosa, AL 35487. Phone: (205)348-6191; Fax: (205)348-2951; Email: uacber@cba.ua.edu • URL: http://www.cber.cba.ua.edu • Business and economics, revenue forecasting, and employment in Alabama; estimates of population in Alabama counties; and investigations of state and regional economies. Engaged in construction and maintenance of annual econometric model for the state.

University of Arizona - Eller College of Management - Economic and Business Research Center. McClelland Hall, Rm. 103, 1130 Helen St., Tucson, AZ 85721-0108. Phone: (520)621-2155 or (520)621-2109; Fax: (520)621-2150; Email: ebrlib@eller.arizona.edu • URL: http://ebr.eller.arizona.edu • Regional economic forecasting, economic data collection and analysis, econometric and input-output impact models, policy-analytic studies, and international economic research. Assists individuals and groups interested in Arizona economy and aids public and private organizations with their research and planning activities.

University of British Columbia - Centre for Labour and Empirical Economic Research. Department of Economics, 997-1873 E Mall, Vancouver, BC, Canada V6T 1Z1. Phone: (604)822-4870; Fax: (604)822-5915; Email: cleer2@interchange.ubc.ca • URL: http://www.econ.ubc.ca/cleer/ • Labor markets and other sectors of the economy.

University of California, Berkeley - Institute of Business and Economic Research. 371 Stephens Hall, Haas School of Business, UCB MC 1922, Berkeley, CA 94720-1922. Phone: (510)642-1922; Fax: (510)642-5018 or (510)642-1420; Email: iber@haas.berkeley.edu • URL: http://iber.berkeley.edu • Research fields are business administration, economics, finance, real estate, and international development.

University of California, Santa Barbara - Institute for Social, Behavioral, and Economic Research - Center on Police Practices and Community. 2201 N Hall, Santa Barbara, CA 93106-2150. Phone: (805)901-4439; Fax: (805)893-7995; Email: mca@coppac.ucsb.edu • URL: http://www.coppac.ucsb.edu/ • Relationships between law enforcement and society.

University of East Anglia - School of Environmental Sciences - Centre for Social and Economic Research on the Global Environment., Norwich NR4 7TJ, United Kingdom. Phone: 44 1603 593224; Fax: 44 1603 591327; Email: i.bateman@uea.ac.uk • URL: http://www.cserge.ac.uk • Environmental issues, including biodiversity, climate change, coastal zone management, environmental resource valuation, sustainable development, tropical forests, waste management and life cycle assessment, and water and wetlands.

University of Essex - Institute for Social and Economic Research - European Centre for Analysis in the Social Sciences. Wivenhoe Park, Colchester CO4 3SQ, United Kingdom. Phone: 44 1206 872957; Fax: 44 1206 873151; Email: stephenj@essex.ac.uk • URL: http://www.iser.essex.ac.uk/research/ecass • European social and economic change.

University of Hong Kong - School of Economics and Finance - Hong Kong Center for Economic Research. Pokfulam Rd., Hong Kong, China. Phone: 86 852 25478313; Fax: 86 852 25486319; Email: hkcer@econ.hku.hk • URL: http://www.hku.hk/hkcer • Economic issues and economic policy.

University of Illinois at Urbana-Champaign - Bureau of Economic and Business Research. 430 Wohlers Hall, Office of Research, College of Business, 1206 S 6th St., Champaign, IL 61820. Phone: (217)333-2330; Fax: (217)333-7410; Email: lhuff@uiuc.edu • URL: http://business.illinois.edu/research • Economics and business, including studies in business expectations, health economics, forecasting and planning, innovation, entrepreneurship, consumer behavior, poverty problems, small business operations and problems, investment and growth, productivity, research methodology, organizational behavior, and international business and banking.

University of Massachusetts at Amherst - Political Economy Research Institute. Gordon Hall, Ste. A, 418 N Pleasant St., Amherst, MA 01002. Phone: (413)545-6355; Fax: (413)577-0261; Email: gepstein@econs.umass.edu • URL: http://www.peri.umass.edu • Human and ecological well-being in both advanced and developing economies. Areas of interest include globalization and macroeconomics, labor markets and living wages; and development, peace building, and the environment.

University of Melbourne - Faculty of Business and Economics - Melbourne Institute of Applied Economic and Social Research. Business and Economics Bldg., Level 5, 111 Barry St., Melbourne, VIC 3010, Australia. Phone: 61 3 83442100; Fax: 61 3 83442111; Email: melb-inst-director@unimelb.edu.au • URL: http://www.melbourneinstitute.com • Economic performance, including business cycles, economic growth, performance and dynamics of Australian enterprises and social economics, including unemployment and labor markets, taxation, welfare, income distribution, poverty, development of social indicators.

University of Montana - Bureau of Business and Economic Research. Gallagher Business Bldg., 32 Campus Dr., Rm. 6840, Missoula, MT 59812-6840. Phone: (406)243-4831 or (406)243-5113; Fax: (406)243-2086 or (406)248-2086 • URL: http://www.bber.umt.edu • Business, economics, and other social sciences, including regional economic analysis and forecasting emphasizing Montana and the northern Rocky Mountain region, forest industry analysis and data collection, survey research, and public opinion surveys. Provides Montana business community with statistical data and interpretation and disseminates general information on economic conditions and prospects in the state.

University of New Orleans - Division of Business and Economic Research. 315 Kirshman Hall, College of Business Administration, 2000 Lakeshore Dr., New Orleans, LA 70148. Phone: (504)280-6240; Fax: (504)280-6094; Email: jspeyrer@uno.edu • URL: http://www.uno.edu/coba/DBER/index.aspx • Business, economic, and demographic characteristics and trends at local, state, and national levels. Also studies local economic forecasting and tourism.

University of Oklahoma - Michael F. Price College of Business - Center for Economic and Management Research. 307 W Brooks, Ste. 4, Norman, OK 73019. Phone: (405)325-3611; Fax: (405)325-7688; Email: pricecollege@ou.edu • URL: http://www.ou.edu/price/cemr.html • Business and economic problems, including studies on business conditions, energy demand, utilization of human resources, economic development, and business trends in the state. Conducts feasibility analyses, market surveys, impact studies, production analyses, socioeconomic statistical analyses and estimates, and compilation and interpretation of economic data. Develops new techniques of data analysis and maintains an extensive database.

University of Oslo - Ragnar Frisch Centre for Economic Research. Gaustadalléen 21, N-0349 Oslo, Norway. Phone: 47 22958810; Fax: 47 22958825; Email: oddbjorn.raaum@frisch.uio.no • URL: http://www.frisch.uio.no/ • Applied economics.

University of Rhode Island - Research Center in Business and Economics. College of Business Administration, 7 Lippitt Rd., Kingston, RI 02881. Phone: (401)874-2549; Fax: (401)874-4825; Email: rcbe@etal.uri.edu • URL: http://www.cba.uri.edu/research/rcbe/ • Services research activities of faculty members of the College in fields of accounting, business law, economics, finance, insurance, management, marketing, and quantitative analysis. Conducts survey research, economic analyses, and business-related research projects on a contract basis.

University of St. Gallen - Swiss Institute for International Economics and Applied Economic Research. Bodanstrasse 8, CH-9000 Saint Gallen, Switzerland. Phone: 41 71 2242340; Fax: 41 71 2242298; Email: gabriela.schmid@unisg.ch • URL: http://www.siaw.unisg.ch • Applied economics, economic policy, and international economics.

Western Washington University - Center for Economic and Business Research. Parks Hall 326, MS 9074, College of Business & Economics, 516 High St., Bellingham, WA 98225. Phone: (360)650-3909; Fax: (360)650-7688; Email: hart.hodges@wwu.edu • URL: http://www.cbe.wwu.edu/cebr/index.shtml • Acts as grant agent for the College of Business and Economics and contracts research for the local area.

Yale University - Cowles Foundation for Research in Economics. PO Box 208281, New Haven, CT 06520-8281. Phone: (203)432-3702; Fax: (203)432-6167; Email: donald.andrews@yale.edu • URL: http://cowles.econ.yale.edu • Development and application of mathematical and statistical methods in economics and related social sciences.

TRADE/PROFESSIONAL ASSOCIATIONS

Institute for Economic Analysis. c/o John S. Atlee, President/Director, 360 Mt. Auburn St., Ste. 001,

Cambridge, MA 02138. Email: info@iea-macro-economics.org • URL: http://iea-macro-economics.org • Seeks to develop tools for macroeconomic analysis and policy that can maintain stable full employment growth, low inflation, low interest rates and equitable distribution of income and wealth. Integrates GDP and financial accounts for more systematic coordination of monetary and fiscal policy. Focuses on federal monetary policy, federal budget deficit/surplus, social security, consumer credit, and world economic recovery.

National Association for Business Economics. 1920 L St. NW, Ste. 300, Washington, DC 20036. Phone: (202)463-6223; Fax: (202)463-6239; Email: nabe@nabe.com • URL: http://www.nabe.com • Formerly National Association of Business Economists.

ECONOMIC RESPONSIBILITY

See SOCIAL RESPONSIBILITY

ECONOMIC STATISTICS

See also BUSINESS STATISTICS; ECONOMETRICS; ECONOMICS; MARKET STATISTICS; STATISTICAL METHODS; STATISTICS SOURCES

ABSTRACTS AND INDEXES

Current Index to Statistics: Applications, Methods, and Theory. American Statistical Association. • Annual. An index to journal articles on statistical applications and methodology.

Social Sciences Citation Index. Thomson Reuters Corp. • Weekly. Product is accessed via *Web of Science.*

Social Sciences Index Retrospective: 1907-1983. EBSCO Publishing Inc. • Indexing for 1,000,000 articles. Coverage includes international index and social sciences and humanities index.

BIBLIOGRAPHIES

Statistics Sources. Cengage Learning Inc. • $874 Individuals. 2012. $836.00. 37th edition. Lists sources of statistical information for more than 20,000 topics.

CD-ROM DATABASES

OECD Statistical Compendium. Organization for Economic Cooperation and Development. • Semiannual. $1,905.00 per year for 1 to 10 users. CD-ROM contains more than 730,000 monthly, quarterly, and annual time series for OECD countries, 1960 to date. Includes fully searchable data on agriculture, food, economic indicators, national accounts, employment, energy, finance, industry, technology, and foreign trade. Results can be displayed in various forms.

Social Sciences Abstracts. EBSCO Publishing Inc. • Provides indexing from 1983 and abstracting from 1994 of more than 750 periodicals covering economics, area studies, community health, public administration, public welfare, urban studies, and many other topics related to the social sciences.

Social Sciences Citation Index. Thomson Reuters Corp. • Weekly. Product is accessed via *Web of Science.*

USA Trade. U.S. Department of Commerce. • Monthly. $650.00 per year. Provides over 150,000 trade-related data series on CD-ROM. Includes full text of many government publications. Specific data is included on national income, labor, price indexes, foreign exchange, technical standards, and international markets. Website address is www.stat-usa.gov/.

DIRECTORIES

American Incomes: Demographics of Who Has Money. New Strategist Publications Inc. • $138 Individuals hardcover. Publication includes: List of telephone numbers for agencies involved in economic information gathering. Principal content of publication is household income, women's and discretionary income, and wealth and poverty.

Commodity Price Statistics. United Nations Publications. • Database covers: Free-market prices and price indices for selected commodities that concern commodity-dependant countries. Price indices are provided for commodity groups (including food, tropical beverages, vegetable oilseeds and oils, agricultural raw materials, minerals, ores and metals), and for all groups in current dollars and SDRs.

The Internet Blue Pages: The Guide to Federal Government Web Sites. Information Today, Inc. • Annual. $34.95. Provides information on more than 1,800 Web sites used by various agencies of the federal government. Includes indexes to agencies and topics. Links to all Web sites listed are available at www.fedweb.com. (CyberAge Books.).

UNCTAD Handbook of Statistics. United Nations Conference on Trade and Development. • $130 Individuals Book with CD-Rom. Database covers: Statistical data relevant to the analysis of international trade, investment and development, for individual countries and for economic and trade groupings. It presents reference statistics on international merchandise trade, trade and commodity price indices, structure of international trade by region, structure of international trade by product, international trade in services, international finance, indicators of development, special studies.

INTERNET DATABASES

Business 2.0 Web Guide to the Best Business Links. Business 2.0 Media Inc. Phone: (415)293-4800; Email: support@business2.com • URL: http://www.business2.com/webguide • Web site presents an extensive, searchable directory of links to "the best, most informative, and authoritative web pages." Twenty main categories cover business, finance, career, company information, people, and technology topics, with thousands of subtopics, all linking to Web sites recommended by experienced business researchers. Fees: Free.

Fedstats. Federal Interagency Council on Statistical Policy. Phone: (202)395-7254 • URL: http://www.fedstats.gov • Web site features an efficient search facility for full-text statistics produced by more than 100 federal agencies, including the Census Bureau, the Bureau of Economic Analysis, and the Bureau of Labor Statistics. Boolean searches can be made within one agency or for all agencies combined. Links are offered to international statistical bureaus, including the UN, IMF, OECD, UNESCO, Eurostat, and 20 individual countries. Fees: Free.

FreeLunch.com. Economy.com, Inc. Phone: (610)696-8700; Fax: (610)696-1678 • URL: http://www.freelunch.com • Web site provides free access to more than 200 million economic and financial data series, covering industry, demographics, labor markets, prices, retail sales, government spending, trade, interest rates, housing starts, the stock market, etc. Data is available in either chart or table form. Searching is offered. Free, but registration required. Economy.com, Inc. also offers fee-based economic analysis at *The Dismal Scientist* site (www.dismal.com).

ONLINE DATABASES

Wilson Social Sciences Abstracts Online. H.W. Wilson Co. • Provides online abstracting and indexing of more than 500 periodicals covering area studies, community health, public administration, public welfare, urban studies, and many other social science topics. Time period is 1994 to date for abstracts and 1983 to date for indexing, with updates weekly. Inquire as to online cost and availability.

PERIODICALS AND NEWSLETTERS

Journal of Business and Economic Statistics. American Statistical Association. • Quarterly. $62 for members. Emphasis is on statistical measurement and applications for business and economics.

RESEARCH CENTERS AND INSTITUTES

U.S. Census Bureau Demographic Programs - Social, Economic and Housing Statistics Division. 4600 Silver Hill Rd., Washington, DC 20233. Phone: (301)763-3234 or (301)763-6443; Email: david.s.johnson@census.gov • URL: http://www.census.gov/newsroom/releases/archives/bios/david_johnson_bio.html • Physical, economic, and social characteristics of housing: household income, poverty, and labor force characteristics, including health insurance coverage. Division collects and analyzes housing data from the Decennial Census of Housing, American Community Survey, American Housing Survey, Quarterly Housing Vacancy Survey, and Survey of Market Absorption, and socioeconomic data from the Decennial Census of Population, American Community Survey, Current Population Survey, and Survey of Income and Program Participation.

STATISTICS SOURCES

OECD Economic Outlook. Organisation for Economic Co-operation and Development Publications and Information Center. • Semiannual. Price on application. $95.00 per year. Contains a wide range of economic and monetary data relating to the member countries of the Organization for Economic Cooperation and Development. Includes about 100 statistical tables and graphs, with 24-month forecasts for each of the OECD countries. Provides extensive review and analysis of recent economic trends.

OECD Economic Survey of the United States. Organisation for Economic Co-operation and Development Publications and Information Center. • Annual. €60.00.

Standard & Poor's Industry Surveys. Standard & Poor's Financial Services L.L.C. • Semiannual. $1,800.00. Two looseleaf volumes. Includes monthly *Supplements.* Provides detailed, individual surveys of 52 major industry groups. Each survey is revised on a semiannual basis. Also includes "Monthly Investment Review" (industry group investment analysis) and monthly "Trends & Projections" (economic analysis).

Statistical Abstract of the United States. U. S. Government Printing Office. • Annual. $44.00. Issued by the U. S. Bureau of the Census.

Statistical Yearbook. United Nations Publications. • Annual. $125.00. Contains statistics for about 200 countries on a wide variety of economic, industrial, and demographic topics. Compiled by United Nations Statistical Office.

World Economic Factbook. Cengage Learning Inc. • Annual. $475 Individuals E-book. Published by Euromonitor International. Presents key economic facts and figures for each of 204 countries worldwide, including details of chief industries, export-import trade, currency, political risk, household expenditures, and the economic situation in general.

World Economic Prospects. Cengage Learning Inc. • 2010. $650.00. 8th edition. Published by Euromonitor International. Ranks countries by specific economic characteristics, such as gross domestic product (GDP) per capita and short term growth prospects. Discusses the economic situation, prospects, and market potential of each of the countries.

TRADE/PROFESSIONAL ASSOCIATIONS

American Statistical Association. 732 N Washington St., Alexandria, VA 22314-1943. Phone: 888-231-3473 or (703)684-1221; Fax: (703)684-2037; Email:

asainfo@amstat.org • URL: http://www.amstat.org • Professional society of persons interested in the theory, methodology, and application of statistics to all fields of human endeavor.

Econometric Society. New York University, Department of Economics, 19 W 4th St., 6th Fl., New York, NY 10012. Phone: (212)998-3820; Fax: (212)995-4487; Email: sashi@econometricsociety.org • URL: http://www.econometricsociety.org • Economists, statisticians, and mathematicians. Promotes studies that are directed towards unification of the theoretical and empirical approaches to economic problems and advancement of economic theory in its relation to statistics and mathematics.

ECONOMICS

See also BUSINESS RESEARCH; ECONOMETRICS

ABSTRACTS AND INDEXES

NTIS Alerts: Business & Economics. U.S. Department of Commerce National Technical Information Service. • Biweekly. $130 per year. Covers consumer affairs, minority enterprises, marketing and economics, international commerce, banking, and finance.

Social Sciences Citation Index. Thomson Reuters Corp. • Weekly. Product is accessed via *Web of Science.*

Social Sciences Index Retrospective: 1907-1983. EBSCO Publishing Inc. • Indexing for 1,000,000 articles. Coverage includes international index and social sciences and humanities index.

CD-ROM DATABASES

EconLit. Ovid Technologies Inc. • Updated monthly. Lists journal articles, book reviews, disserations of economic literature. Over 1,400 journals covered.

Social Sciences Abstracts. EBSCO Publishing Inc. • Provides indexing from 1983 and abstracting from 1994 of more than 750 periodicals covering economics, area studies, community health, public administration, public welfare, urban studies, and many other topics related to the social sciences.

Social Sciences Citation Index. Thomson Reuters Corp. • Weekly. Product is accessed via *Web of Science.*

DIRECTORIES

Cabell's Directory of Publishing Opportunities in Economics and Finance. Cabell Publishing Inc. • Irregular. Covers: Over 860 scholarly periodicals in economics and finance. Entries include: Publication name, address, subject interests, editorial guidelines and style, submission procedures, audience and circulation of the publication, and reviewer acceptance rate data.

Who's Who in British Economics: A Directory of Economists in Higher Education, Business and Government. Edward Elgar Publishing Inc. • £106.20 Individuals hardback. Covers: Professional economists in the United Kingdom. Entries include: Name, address, biographical data, select bibliography of works, description of main area of work.

E-BOOKS

Social Trends & Indicators USA. Monique D. Magee, editor. Cengage Learning Inc. • Includes data on labor, economics, the health care industry, crime, leisure, population, education, social security, and many other topics. Sources include various government agencies and major publications. Inquire for pricing.

21st Century Economics: A Reference Handbook. Cengage Learning Inc. • 2010. eBook. Published by Sage Publications. Covers traditional economic theory as well as challenges that face the nation in an economy with unemployment issues, failures of major businesses and industries, and continued dependence on oil with its wildly fluctuating prices.

ENCYCLOPEDIAS AND DICTIONARIES

Gale Encyclopedia of U.S. Economic History. Cengage Learning Inc. • 2003. eBook. Contains about 1,000 alphabetically arranged entries. Includes industry profiles, biographies, social issue profiles, geographic profiles, and chronological tables. Inquire as to price and availability.

Historical Encyclopedia of American Business. Cengage Learning Inc. • 2009. eBook. Published by Salem Press. Long overviews on different sectors of the economy, such as agriculture and banking; individual industries such as advertising and electronics; and general topics such as business cycles, labor strikes and outsourcing. There are also overviews on broad legal topics such as antitrust legislation, bankruptcy laws and patent laws.

GENERAL WORKS

ADB Business Opportunities. Asian Development Bank. • Monthly. Publication covering economic development.

African Journal of Business and Economic Research. Adonis & Abbey Publishers Ltd. • £200 Institutions print. Peer-reviewed journal covering theoretical and empirical research of business and economy of Africa.

Business I. ITHAKA JSTOR, the Journal Storage Project. • Contains more than 2 million pages from 47 titles in the fields of economics and finance, accounting, labor relations, marketing, management, operations research, and risk assessment.

Business II. ITHAKA JSTOR, the Journal Storage Project. • Contains more than 1.3 million pages from 60 titles in the fields of international business as well as the intersections between economics and law, policy, and psychology.

Business in Russia. Business in Russia. • Monthly. $197. Journal covering business and economics.

Business Venezuela. Venezuelan-American Chamber of Commerce and Industry. • Features in-depth and objective analyses on the changes that are happening in the country's economic, trade and business environment.

Business World. ABP Pvt. Limited Publication. • Weekly. Journal on business and economics.

Hong Kong for the Business Visitor. Hong Kong Trade Development Council. • Annual. Journal of travel, tourism, business and economics.

Journal of Business Case Studies (JBCS). The Clute Institute for Academic Research. • Monthly. $495 Institutions. Journal containing case studies for use in business and economics courses.

Philippine Review of Economics and Business. University of the Philippines College of Business Administration. • Semiannual. Journal covering research work and articles about Philippine economic and business conditions.

Small Business Barometer. Small Business Association of Michigan. • Contains surveys of Michigan business owners and reports on their economic outlook.

Thai-American Business (T-AB). American Chamber of Commerce in Thailand. • Annual. Business and Economics journal.

Yonsei Business Review. Yonsei University Industrial Management Research Centre. • Semiannual. $8,000. Business and economics journal.

ONLINE DATABASES

Business, Economics and Theory Collection. Cengage Learning Inc. • Contains the full-text of more than 7 million articles from 450 academic journals and magazines on all aspects of business and economics. Also offers feeds of videos from Forbes.com that contain business news coverage and interviews with CEOs and entrepreneurs.

Dow Jones News Service. Dow Jones and Co., Inc. • Full text and edited news stories and articles on business affairs. Inquire as to online cost and availability.

Wilson Social Sciences Abstracts Online. H.W. Wilson Co. • Provides online abstracting and indexing of more than 500 periodicals covering area studies, community health, public administration, public welfare, urban studies, and many other social science topics. Time period is 1994 to date for abstracts and 1983 to date for indexing, with updates weekly. Inquire as to online cost and availability.

PERIODICALS AND NEWSLETTERS

American Economic Review. American Economic Association. • Monthly. $455 Individuals print subscription to seven journals. Includes *Journal of Economic Literature* and *Journal of Economic Persepective.*

Econometrica. Blackwell Publishing Inc. • $586 Institutions Online only. Bimonthly. Includes print and online editions. Published in England by Basil Blackwell Ltd.

The Economist. The Economist Intelligence Unit. • 190 ₱ Individuals Print and Digital per week.

German Business Scope. Representative of German Industry and Trade. • A biweekly online publication which describes politico-economic developments in Germany (and the European Union) from the perspective of German industry.

Global Business and Economics Review. Inderscience Enterprises Limited. • €520 Individuals print or online. Peer-reviewed journal focusing on the discussion and analysis of advanced concepts, initial treatments, and fundamental research in all fields of business and economics.

Hindu Business Line. Kasturi & Sons Ltd. • Daily. Rs 1,496 Individuals all days. Newspaper covering business, economics, banks and banking.

International Review of Applied Economics. Routledge. • Quarterly. Individuals, $310.00 per year; institutions, $1,007.00 per year.

Journal of EU Research in Business. IBIMA Publishing. • Peer-reviewed journal publishing information on research management and new ideas regarding the economics in Europe.

Kentucky Business and Economic Outlook Newsletter. University of Kentucky Center for Business and Economic Research. • Quarterly. Contains forecasts for the Kentucky economy as well as other business and economic issues.

Luxembourg Business Journal. Luxembourg American Chamber of Commerce. • Contains organization's activities, member news and developments in the economic relations between the Grand Duchy and North America.

NABE News. National Association for Business Economics. • Quarterly. Description: Concerned with business economics. Serves this professional Association of persons employed by private, institutional, or government concerns in the area of business-related economic analysis. Recurring features include results of the NABE quarterly outlook survey, featured articles of timely interest, reviews of seminars and annual meetings, news from local chapters and roundtables, and personal notes.

Observer of Business and Politics. Anthony Jasudasan. • Daily. Newspaper focusing on business and economics.

Quarterly Journal of Economics. Harvard University, Dept. of Economics. The MIT Press. • Quarterly. $70 Individuals. Covers all aspects of economics.

The Quarterly Review of Economics and Finance. JAI Press. • Quarterly. $142 Individuals. Publishes high quality manuscripts that cover topics in the areas of economics, financial economics and finance.

Review of Economics and Business. Kansai University Press. • Semiannual. Journal covering economics.

Review of Social Economy. Association for Social Economics. Taylor & Francis Ltd. • Quarterly. $152 Individuals Print and Online. Quarterly. Subject matter is concerned with the relationships between social values and economics. Includes articles on income distribution, poverty, labor, and class.

Saudi Arabia Business Week. Saudi Arabia Business Week. • Weekly. Business and economics magazine.

Survey of Business. University of Tennessee College of Business Administration. • Quarterly. Magazine for Tennessee business professionals about current economic and socio-economic trends in the state.

Survey of Current Business. U. S. Government Printing Office. • Monthly. $29 Individuals. Publication containing economic analyses of business.

University of Calcutta Business Studies. University of Calcutta. • Semiannual. $20. Publication on business and economic studies.

RESEARCH CENTERS AND INSTITUTES

American Institute for Economic Research. 250 Division St., Great Barrington, MA 01230-1000. Phone: 888-528-1216; Fax: (413)528-0103; Email: info@aier.org • URL: http://www.aier.org • Through research and publications, provides "information on economic and financial subjects that is useful and completely independent of special interests." Sponsors a fellowship program for graduate study of economics at the institute and in absentia.

Appalachian State University - Center for Economic Research and Policy Analysis. Raley Hall, Rm. 3095, Walker College of Business, Boone, NC 28608. Phone: (828)262-6081; Fax: (828)262-6105; Email: cherrytl@appstate.edu • URL: http://cerpa.appstate.edu • Economics and public policy, focusing on environment and energy, economic development, survey research and experimental methods.

Aston University - Economics and Strategy Group. Aston Business School, Birmingham B4 7ET, United Kingdom. Phone: 44 121 2043038; Email: l.woolley@aston.ac.uk • URL: http://www1.aston.ac.uk/aston-business-school/research/groups/esg • Strategic management, economics, innovation and entrepreneurship, and international business.

Bogazici University - Center for Economics and Econometrics. Bebek, TR-34342 Istanbul, Turkey. Phone: 90 212 3956505; Fax: 90 212 2872453; Email: ezran@boun.edu.tr • URL: http://www.cee.boun.edu.tr • Economic issues, electrical energy.

Brookings Institution - Center on Social Dynamics and Policy. 1775 Massachusetts Ave. NW, Washington, DC 20036. Phone: (202)797-6105; Fax: (202)797-6181; Email: csed@brookings.edu • URL: http://www.brookings.edu/about/centers/dynamics • Economic and social issues.

Bureau of Economic Analysis - Office of Regional Economic Accounts. 1441 L St. NW, Washington, DC 20230. Phone: (202)606-9605 • URL: http://www.bea.gov/regional/index.htm • Analyses of regional (state and metropolitan) economic trends, developing new analysis methods and models, providing regional input-output multipliers, estimating gross state product by industry, publishing periodic regional economic analyses and projections, estimating state and county personal income (annual) and state personal income (quarterly), and estimating earnings and employment by industry for states and counties.

California Institute of Technology - Division of the Humanities and Social Sciences - Laboratory for Experimental Economics and Political Science. 337 Baxter Hall, MC 228-77, Pasadena, CA 91125. Phone: (626)395-4209; Fax: (626)405-9841; Email: cplott@hss.caltech.edu • URL: http://eeps.caltech.edu • Economic and political behavior research, including studies in pricing strategies, competitive bidding and computer-controlled payload management.

Cardiff University - Julian Hodge Institute of Applied Macroeconomics. Aberconway Bldg., Rm. E46, Cardiff CF10 3EU, United Kingdom. Phone: 44 29 20875728; Fax: 44 29 20874419; Email: minfordp@cardiff.ac.uk • URL: http://business.cardiff.ac.uk/julian-hodge-institute-applied-macroeconomics • Behavior of the United Kingdom's economy, as well as its relationship with other economies in Europe.

Catholic University of Louvain - Center for Economic Studies. Department of Economics, Naamsestraat 69, B-3000 Louvain, Belgium. Phone: 32 16 326725; Fax: 32 16 326796; Email: erik.buyst@kuleuven.be • URL: http://www.econ.kuleuven.be/research/CES/display.aspx?URL=main • Information, international, monetary, industrial, public, and developmental economics, econometrics, and game theory.

Centre for History and Economics. King's College, Cambridge CB2 1ST, United Kingdom. Phone: 44 1223 331197; Fax: 44 1223 331198 • URL: http://www.histecon.magd.cam.ac.uk • Encourages participation of economists and historians in continuing efforts to address issues of immediate and practical public importance, such as economic security, poverty and inequality, the integration of national economies, and political and economic nationalism.

Charles University - Institute of Economic Studies. Opletalova 26, CZ-110 00 Prague, Czech Republic. Phone: 420 2 22112330; Fax: 420 2 22112304; Email: gregor@fsv.cuni.cz • URL: http://ies.fsv.cuni.cz/content/tree/index/lang/en • Economics, the economy, the history of economics, corporate finance, banking, and analysis of capital markets.

Chinese Academy of Sciences - Institute of Quantitative and Technical Economics. 5 Jian Guomen St., Beijing 100732, China. Phone: 86 10 65137561; Fax: 86 10 65125895; Email: iqte@iqte.cass.net.cn • URL: http://iqte1.cass.cn/english/home.htm • Quantitative and technical economics, specifically economic system analysis, economic modeling, mathematical economic theory, environment technical economics, resources technical economics, and technical economic theory and methods. Studies include: analysis and forecast of China's economic situation; theory, management, and implications of China's productivity and economic growth; analysis and quantitative study of mechanisms of stable growth of China's economy; China's economic fluctuation; evaluation of comprehensive efficiency of the CIMS project; human resource development; industrial development policies and economic growth; informalization and economic growth; development strategies of the Bohai economic circle; strategies of China's science and technology in the nineties.

Clark University - Institute for Economic Policy Studies. Department of Economics, 950 Main St., Worcester, MA 01610-1477. Phone: (508)793-7227; Fax: (508)793-7708; Email: aott@iespolicy.org • URL: http://www.iespolicy.org • Economic issues and policy options to deal with them.

Columbia University - Asia-Pacific Economic Cooperation Study Center. 2M-9 Uris Hall, 3022 Broadway, New York, NY 10027-7004. Phone: (212)854-3976; Fax: (212)851-9508; Email: aw2040@columbia.edu • URL: http://www7.gsb.columbia.edu/apec • Issues of economic importance for the Asia-Pacific region.

Congressional Budget Office - Macroeconomic Analysis Division. Ford House Office Bldg., 4th Fl., 2nd & D Sts. SW, Washington, DC 20515-6925. Phone: (202)226-2602; Fax: (202)226-2714 • URL: http://www.cbo.gov/about/our-organization-and-people#mad • U.S. economy, prepares projections of future economic conditions, and studies how that future could be affected by different economic developments or policies. The economic projections serve the Senate and House budget committees in developing concurrent resolutions on the budget and the entire Congress as it considers and passes the budget. Division's analyses focus on such issues as inflation, employment, production, incomes, international economic affairs, and credit as well as on the interaction of those issues with the federal budget. Although the Congressional Budget Office does not have its own large-scale econometric model, its forecasts are based on information from major econometric models and other forecasting services that are available commercially, along with the advice of a panel of advisors who represent a wide spectrum of economic views.

Curtin University of Technology - Communication Economics and Electronic Markets Research Centre. Department of Economics, Perth, WA 6845, Australia. Phone: 61 8 92662391; Fax: 61 8 92669460; Email: g.madden@curtin.edu.au • URL: http://business.curtin.edu.au/research/centres_institutions/research_centres/ceem • Communications economics and electronic markets, focusing on legal, sociological, technical and policy aspects of current debate.

Erasmus University of Rotterdam - Erasmus Institute for Philosophy and Economics. EIPE Office, Rm. H5-23, Faculty of Philosophy, 3000 DR Rotterdam, Netherlands. Phone: 31 10 4088967; Fax: 31 10 4089030; Email: vromen@fwb.eur.nl • URL: http://www.eur.nl/fw/english/eipe • Philosophy and methodology of economics.

Federal Trade Commission - Bureau of Economics. 600 Pennsylvania Ave. NW, Washington, DC 20580. Phone: (202)326-3419; Fax: (202)326-2380; Email: mgaynor@ftc.gov • URL: http://www.ftc.gov/about-ftc/bureaus-offices/bureau-economics • Economics of antitrust, consumer protection, and regulation.

Federal University of Santa Catarina - Socio-Economic Center. Campus Universitário - Trindade, 88040-900 Florianópolis, SC, Brazil. Phone: 55 48 33319560; Fax: 55 48 33319585; Email: rcalves@cse.ufsc.br • URL: http://www.cse.ufsc.br/ • Social and economic issues, including the effectiveness of economic policies designed to direct social change.

Fort Lewis College - Office of Business and Economic Research. 1000 Rim Dr., Durango, CO 81301. Phone: (970)247-7296; Fax: (970)247-7205; Email: sonora_t@fortlewis.edu • URL: http://www.fortlewis.edu/ober/Home.aspx • Economics and local economic conditions.

George Mason University - James M. Buchanan Center for Political Economy. MSN 1D3, Fairfax, VA 22030. Phone: (703)993-2330; Fax: (703)993-2323; Email: tcowen@gmu.edu • URL: http://www.gmu.edu/jbc • Interrelationship of politics, law, and the economy.

George Mason University - Interdisciplinary Center for Economic Science. 3330 Washington Blvd., Arlington, VA 22201. Phone: (703)993-4856; Fax: (703)993-4851; Email: dhouser@gmu.edu • URL: http://ices.gmu.edu • Behavioral and neuro-economics, economic systems design, and experimental economics.

Ghent University - Center for Russian International Socio-political and Economic Studies. Tweekerkenstraat 2, 9000 Ghent, Belgium. Phone: 32 9 2643487; Fax: 32 9 2643599; Email: koen.schoors@ugent.be • URL: http://www.ceriseonline.be • Problems of economic transition in former Soviet republics.

Hong Kong Polytechnic University - Research

For publishers' addresses, refer to SOURCES CITED section at the back of the book.

Center for Construction and Real Estate Economics. Department of Bldg. & Real Estate, Hung Hom, Kowloon, Hong Kong, China. Phone: 86 852 27665821; Fax: 86 852 27645131; Email: bskwwong@polyu.edu.uk • URL: http://www.bre.polyu.edu.hk/rccree/index.htm • Construction and real estate economics.

Humboldt University of Berlin - Center for Applied Statistics and Economics. Spandauer Str. 1, 10178 Berlin, Germany. Phone: 49 30 20935630; Fax: 49 30 20935649; Email: stat@wiwi.hu-berlin.de • URL: http://www.case.hu-berlin.de • Statistics and economics.

Hungarian Academy of Sciences - Centre for Economic and Regional Studies - Institute of Economics. Budaörsi út. 45, H-1112 Budapest, Hungary. Phone: 36 1 3092652; Fax: 36 1 3193136; Email: kti.titkarsag@krtk.mta.hu • URL: http://www.econ.core.hu • Economics and applied research on transition to market economy.

Indian Council of Social Science Research - Center for Economic and Social Studies. Begumpet, Hyderabad 500 016, Andhra Pradesh, India. Phone: 91 40 23402789; Fax: 91 40 23406808; Email: manoj@cess.ac.in • URL: http://www.cess.ac.in/cesshome/cessmain.asp • Rural development and poverty; agriculture and food security; irrigation and water management; public finance; demography; health; the environment.

London School of Economics and Political Science - Centre for Economic Performance. Houghton St., London WC2A 2AE, United Kingdom. Phone: 44 20 79557673; Fax: 44 20 74040612; Email: j.vanreenen@lse.ac.uk • URL: http://cep.lse.ac.uk • Economic performance at the level of the company, the nation and the global economy, focusing on links between globalization, technology and institutions, particularly the labor market, education, technology and growth.

Lund University - School of Economics and Management - Center for Economic Demography. Box 7083, SE-220 07 Lund, Sweden. Phone: 46 2220000 • URL: http://www.ed.lu.se • Population and economy.

Maastricht University - Limburg Institute of Financial Economics. PO Box 616, NL-6200 Maastricht, Netherlands. Phone: 31 43 3883838; Fax: 31 43 3884875; Email: p.schotman@berfin.unimaas.nl • URL: http://www.maastrichtuniversity.nl/web/faculties/sbe/theme/researchportal/aboutgsbe/partnerinstitutes/sbeinstitutes.htm • Financial economics, especially exchange rates, microstructure, real estate and corporate bonds. Other research interests include pension funds, term structure modeling, overreaction in stock markets, tail estimation, corporate governance, financial fragility and mortgage pricing.

Macquarie University - Center for Japanese Economic Studies. Faculty of Business & Economics, Sydney, NSW 2109, Australia. Phone: 61 2 98507444; Fax: 61 2 98508586; Email: cfreedma@efs.mq.edu.au • URL: http://www.econ.mq.edu.au/about_economics/centre_for_japanese_economic_studies • Economics, including theoretical and applied macroeconomics and microeconomics, econometrics, economic history, cultural economics, economies in transition, and Japanese economics and finance.

Max Planck Society for the Advancement of Science - Max Planck Institute of Economics. Kahlaische Strasse 10, D-07745 Jena, Germany. Phone: 49 3641 6865; Fax: 49 3641 686990; Email: witt@econ.mpg.de • URL: http://www.mpiew-jena.mpg.de • Changing economic systems and the forces behind those changes.

McMaster University - McMaster Experimental Economics Laboratory. Department of Economics, 1280 Main St. W, Hamilton, ON, Canada L8S 4M4. Phone: (905)525-9140; Fax: (905)521-8232; Email: mestelma@mcmaster.ca • URL: http://socserv.mcmaster.ca/econ/mceel/ • Economics.

McMaster University - Research Institute for Quantitative Studies in Economics and Population. Kenneth Taylor Hall, Rm. 426, 1280 Main St. W, Hamilton, ON, Canada L8S 4M4. Phone: (905)525-9140; Fax: (905)521-8232; Email: qsep@mcmaster.ca • URL: http://socserv.mcmaster.ca/qsep • Broad-based studies in quantitative economics, demography, and related social science areas.

Middle Tennessee State University - Business and Economic Research Center. 1301 E Main St., Murfreesboro, TN 37132-0001. Phone: (615)898-2300 or (615)898-2610; Fax: (615)898-5045; Email: dpenn@mtsu.edu • URL: http://www.mtsu.edu • Various fields within business and economics.

Monash University - Centre of Policy Studies - Impact Project. Menzies Bldg., 11th Fl., Wellington Rd., Clayton, VIC 3800, Australia. Phone: 61 3 99052398; Fax: 61 3 99052426; Email: philip.adams@buseco.monash.edu.au • URL: http://www.monash.edu.au/policy/ • Economic modelling.

National Bureau of Economic Research. 1050 Massachusetts Ave., Cambridge, MA 02138-5398. Phone: (617)868-3900 or (617)253-6673; Fax: (617)868-2742; Email: info@nber.org • URL: http://www.nber.org • Conducts analyses of economic issues, including economic growth and fluctuations, productivity, financial institutions, money, international economic problems, taxation, government spending, labor studies, health, and American economic history.

National Center for Scientific Research - Institute for Research in the Sociology and Economics of Education. University of Bourgogne, Pôle AAFE-Esplanade Erasme, BP 26513, F-21065 Dijon, France. Phone: 33 3 80395450; Fax: 33 3 80395479; Email: jean-francois.giret@u-bourgogne.fr • URL: http://iredu.u-bourgogne.fr • Economy, education and sociology.

National Research Council Italy - Institute for Economic Research on Firms and Growth. Via Bassini, 15, I-20131 Milan, Italy. Phone: 39 2 70643501; Fax: 39 2 23699530 • URL: http://www.ceris.cnr.it • Structural economic dynamics, technological change, and Schumpeterian economics.

National Science Foundation - Directorate for Social, Behavioral, and Economic Sciences - Division of Social and Economic Sciences. 4201 Wilson Blvd., Rm. 995N, Arlington, VA 22230. Phone: (703)292-8760; Fax: (703)292-9068; Email: jmumpowe@nsf.gov • URL: http://www.nsf.gov/div/index.jsp?div=SES • Economics, law and social science, political science, sociology, measurement methods and data improvement, decision, risk, and management science. The goal of the Division is to develop basic scientific knowledge of human social behavior, interaction, and decision-making, and of social and economic systems, organizations, and institutions. The Division also supports research on the human dimensions of global environmental change and research to improve the quality and the accessibility of social and economic data resources. In addition to research proposals, programs within the Division consider proposals for doctoral dissertation support, research conferences, the acquisition of specialized research and computing equipment, group international travel, and data collection.

New York Institute of Technology - Center for Energy, Environment and Economics. Dept. of Energy Management, Harry Schure Hall, Rm. 116, Northern Blvd., Old Westbury, NY 11568-8000. Phone: (516)686-7990 or (516)686-7578; Fax: (516)686-7933; Email: ramundse@nyit.edu • URL: http://www.nyit.edu/engineering/centers/centers_energy_environment_economics • Established by the New York Institute of Technology as a major facility designed to disseminate information and conduct research into energy utilization and conservation, and to assist public, quasi-public, and private sector organizations in the practical use of present and future findings in the energy field. Conducts Master of Science in Energy Management and specialized professional certificate programs through NYIT's School of Engineering and Technology to provide interdisciplinary training in the technological, economic, sociological, and administrative skills required to implement new approaches to energy conversion and utilization.

Northwestern University - Center for Mathematical Studies in Economics and Management Sciences. 580 Leverone Hall, Kellogg School of Management, 2001 Sheridan Rd., Evanston, IL 60208-2014. Phone: (847)491-3527; Fax: (847)491-2530; Email: cms-ems@northwestern.edu • URL: http://www.kellogg.northwestern.edu/research/math • Mathematical economics, mathematical programming, management science, and mathematical theory of economic organizations.

Polish Academy of Sciences - Institute of Economics. Staszic Palace, 72 Nowy Świat St., Rm. 266, 00-330 Warsaw, Poland. Phone: 48 22 6572707; Fax: 48 22 8267254; Email: inepan@inepan.waw.pl • URL: http://www.inepan.waw.pl/en • Economic theory and policy.

Queen's University of Belfast - Finance and Economics Research Group. Management School, Rm. 25. G07, 25 University Sq., Belfast BT7 1NN, United Kingdom. Phone: 44 28 90975126; Email: k.close@qub.ac.uk • URL: http://www.qub-efrg.com • Economic theory; econometrics; labor economics; microstructure finance; international finance; and financial institutions, including nonprofits.

Rice University - Center for Computational Finance and Economic Systems. Department of Statistics, MS-138, Houston, TX 77251-1892. Phone: (713)348-5839; Fax: (713)348-5476; Email: ensor@rice.edu • URL: http://www.cofes.rice.edu • Computational finance and economic systems, including credit risk management, pricing financial derivatives, emerging markets, energy markets, impact of politics on world finance, and risk fundamentals and integration of risk.

Russian Academy of Sciences - Central Economics and Mathematics Institute. 47 Nakhimovsky prospect, 117418 Moscow, Russia. Phone: 7 495 1291011; Fax: 7 495 7189615; Email: director@cemi.rssi.ru • URL: http://www.cemi.rssi.ru/en • Theoretical modeling and the development of mathematical, computer, and empirical methods for the study of the economic transition. Specific areas of research include the theory of the optimal functioning planned economies, the study of scientific-technical progress, methods of evaluating the economic efficiency of capital investment and of the location of manufacturing, the economics of natural resource use, general equilibrium and disequilibrium theory (including the incorporation of issues related to intellectual property), and decision making under uncertainty.

Russian Academy of Sciences - Institute of World Economy and International Relations. 23 Profsoyuznaya St., 117997 Moscow, Russia. Phone: 7 499 1205236; Fax: 7 499 1206575; Email: imemoran@imemo.ru • URL: http://www.imemo.ru • Internationalization of production and capital, foreign trade, international monetary system, external debt, international relations, security and conflict management, arms control and disarmament, and economic political issues in Russia.

Securities and Exchange Commission - Office of Economic Analysis. 100 F St. NE, Washington, DC 20549. Phone: (202)942-8088; Fax: (202)942-9657; Email: help@sec.gov • URL: http://www.sec.gov/

about/economic.shtml • Utilization of economic and empirical analyses in policy formulation, rule adoption, and post-adoption monitoring processes of the Securities and Exchange Commission. Emphasis is on evaluation of the impact of Commission regulations on capital markets and securities markets participants.

Shanghai Academy of Social Sciences - Institute of National Economy. No. 7, Ln. 622, Huaihai Rd., Shanghai 200020, China. Phone: 86 21 53060606; Fax: 86 21 53063256; Email: jjs@sass.org.cn • URL: http://english.sass.org.cn/Institutions/?newsid=003700350039 • Economic issues, industry policy, development studies, regional studies, social issues.

Troy State University - Center for Business and Economic Services. Sorrell College of Business, Troy, AL 36082. Phone: (334)670-3524; Fax: (334)670-3636; Email: jkervin@trojan.troyst.edu • URL: http://troy.troy.edu/cbes/index.html • Business and economics, including feasibility studies, market research, economic projections, cost analyses, accounting and budgeting models, and similar projects.

Universitat Pompeu Fabra - Research Center in Financial Economics and Accounting. Ramon Trias Fargas, 25-27, E-08005 Barcelona, Spain. Phone: 34 93 5421619; Fax: 34 93 5421746; Email: xavier.freixas@upf.edu • URL: http://www.crefc.upf.edu • Financial economics, accounting, and business.

University of Alberta - Institute for Public Economics. 8-14 HM Tory, Department of Economics, Edmonton, AB, Canada T6G 2H4. Phone: (780)492-3406; Fax: (780)492-3300; Email: rascah@ualberta.ca • URL: http://www.ipe.ualberta.ca • Public economics, including the public sector and its influence on the economy and society.

University of Amsterdam - Center for Nonlinear Dynamics in Economics and Finance. Department of Economics & Econometrics, Roetersstraat 11, 1018 Amsterdam, Netherlands. Phone: 31 20 5254217; Fax: 31 20 5254349; Email: c.h.hommes@uva.nl • URL: http://www1.fee.uva.nl/cendef • Nonlinear dynamics in economics and finance.

University of Arkansas at Little Rock - Institute for Economic Advancement. 2801 S University Ave., Little Rock, AR 72204-1099. Phone: (501)569-8519; Fax: (501)569-8538; Email: jlyoungquist@ualr.edu • URL: http://www.aiea.ualr.edu • Business and economics, industrial development, labor statistics, demographics, government and taxes, economic development and U.S. census.

University of Chicago - George J. Stigler Center for the Study of the Economy and the State. Booth School of Business, 5807 S Woodlawn Ave., Chicago, IL 60637. Phone: (773)702-7519; Fax: (773)834-9134; Email: robert.topel@chicagogsb.edu • URL: http://research.chicagobooth.edu/economy • Effects of legal and political institutions on economic activity, including studies on the growth of government, income redistribution policies of governments, and regulation of utilities, insurance, and water resources.

University of Colorado at Boulder - Center for Economic Analysis. Department of Economics, 256 UCB, Boulder, CO 80309-0256. Phone: (303)492-8024; Fax: (303)492-8960; Email: teresa.decandia@colorado.edu • Economics.

University of Colorado at Boulder - Institutions Program. Institute of Behavioral Science Bldg. 2, 487 UCB, Boulder, CO 80309-0487. Phone: (303)492-8147; Fax: (303)492-3609; Email: edward.greenberg@colorado.edu • URL: http://www.colorado.edu/IBS/pec/ • Political economy, class and stratification, structures of international relations, and national, class, and group conflict.

University of Connecticut - Connecticut Center for Economic Analysis. 2100 Hillside Rd., U-1240, Storrs, CT 06269-1240. Phone: (860)486-0614; Fax: (860)486-0889; Email: fred.carstensen@uconn.edu • URL: http://ccea.uconn.edu • Economic analysis, including state and local finance, economic impact, policy analysis, cluster analysis, assessment of fiscal structure, dynamic REMI forecasting, econometrics, bench-marketing, labor, and health economics.

University of Georgia - Selig Center for Economic Growth. c/o Dr. Jeffrey M. Humphreys, Director, 110 E Clayton St., Athens, GA 30602. Phone: (706)542-4085; Email: jhumphre@uga.edu • URL: http://www.terry.uga.edu/about/centers-institutes/selig • Economics and business conditions, including studies of county income, economic forecasting, and gross state product. Conducts statistical studies on Georgia and neighboring states.

University of Graz - Institute of Public Economics. Universitätsstrasse 15/E4, A-8010 Graz, Austria. Phone: 43 316 3803460; Fax: 43 316 3809530; Email: richard.sturn@uni-graz.at • URL: http://www.uni-graz.at/fwiwww/2010/Frontpage/index.html • Economic aspects of cultural policy in Austria.

University of Helsinki - Research Unit of Economic Structures and Growth. Department of Economics, 4th Fl., Faculty of Social Sciences, Arkadiankatu 7 (PL 17), 00014 Helsinki, Finland. Phone: 358 9 19128718; Fax: 358 9 19128742; Email: erkki.koskela@helsinki.fi • URL: http://www.valt.helsinki.fi/raka/about.htm • Economics, including labor, resource and industrial economics and taxation.

University of Hertfordshire - Group for Research in Organisational Evolution. Business School, de Havilland Campus, Hatfield AL10 9AB, United Kingdom. Phone: 44 1707 284800; Fax: 44 1707 284870; Email: g.m.hodgson@herts.ac.uk • URL: http://www.herts.ac.uk/research/ssahri/research-areas/business-management/groe • Institutional economics, including research in subfields such as the economics of property rights and economics and law.

University of Hong Kong - Hong Kong Institute of Economics and Business Strategy. Faculty of Business & Economics, Pokfulam Rd., Hong Kong, China. Phone: 86 852 25489300; Fax: 86 852 25483223; Email: info@hiebs.hku.hk • URL: http://www.hiebs.hku.hk • Economic policy and business strategy in Hong Kong and its role in China and the Asia-Pacific region.

University of Indonesia - Faculty of Economics - Demographic Institute. Gedung A, Lantai 2 & 3, 16424 Depok, Indonesia. Phone: 62 21 7872911; Fax: 62 21 7872909 • URL: http://www.ld-feui.org • Demography, population, and development studies, including fertility, mortality, migration and urbanization, labor-force, health economics, human resources, and the economic environment.

University of Karachi - Applied Economics Research Center. PO Box 8403, Karachi 75270, Pakistan. Phone: 92 21 99261541; Fax: 92 21 99261545; Email: aerc@cyber.net.pk • URL: http://www.aerc.edu.pk • Applied economics, focusing on the areas of urban and regional economics, agriculture, human resource development, poverty, health, public finance, nutrition and environment, and women's issues.

University of Kent at Canterbury - School of Economics - Centre for European, Regional and Transport Economics. Keynes College, Canterbury CT2 7NP, United Kingdom. Phone: 44 1227 823642; Fax: 44 1227 827784 • URL: http://www.kent.ac.uk/economics/research/certe • Economics of Europe and the European Union, particularly on continuing work on aspects of transport and the regional development of the European Union, especially the role of transport infrastructure, building on the success of the Channel Tunnel Research Unit over the period 1986-93.

University of Liège - Center for Social Economy. Bd du Rectorat, 3, Bat B33 Bte 4, 4000 Liège, Belgium. Phone: 32 4 3662751; Fax: 32 4 3662851; Email: j.defourny@ulg.ac.be • URL: http://www.ces.ulg.ac.be • Social economy, focusing on conceptual approaches in industrialized countries, profiles and issues in developing countries, statistics on associations, the volunteer sector, public contracts and North-South relations.

University of Liège - International and Interregional Economics Service. Department of Economics, Blvd. du Rectorat, 7, Batiment B31, bte. 9, B-4000 Liège, Belgium. Phone: 32 4 3662965; Fax: 32 4 3662981; Email: jgazon@ulg.ac.be • URL: http://www.ecoint.hec.ulg.ac.be • Regional and urban economics, real estate, and international economics.

University of Michigan - Research Seminar in Quantitative Economics. Lorch Hall, Rm. M116, Department of Economics, 611 Tappan St., Ann Arbor, MI 48109. Phone: (734)764-2567; Fax: (734)763-1307; Email: rsqe-admin@umich.edu • URL: http://www.rsqe.econ.lsa.umich.edu • Development and application of econometric techniques to matters of public policy, also construction of large economy-wide and state-wide econometric models for forecasting and policy analysis.

University of Missouri—Kansas City - Center for Economic Information. 210 Haag Hall, Department of Economics, 5211 Rockhill Rd., Kansas City, MO 64110. Phone: (816)235-2832; Fax: (816)235-2834; Email: eatonp@umkc.edu • URL: http://cei.umkc.edu • Provides local, regional, and national information and analysis to economic decision-makers in the Kansas City metropolitan area.

University of Oxford - Centre for the Study of African Economies. Department of Economics, Manor Rd., Oxford OX1 3UQ, United Kingdom. Phone: 44 1865 271084; Fax: 44 1865 281447; Email: paul.collier@economics.ox.ac.uk • URL: http://www.csae.ox.ac.uk • African economies, developing economies.

University of Pennsylvania - Center for Analytical Research in Economics and the Social Sciences. 3718 Locust Walk, Philadelphia, PA 19104-6297. Phone: (215)898-5735 • URL: http://economics.sas.upenn.edu/research • Economic theory and related mathematics.

University of Pennsylvania - Leonard Davis Institute of Health Economics. Colonial Penn Ctr., 3641 Locust Walk, Philadelphia, PA 19104-6218. Phone: (215)898-5611 or (215)898-1657; Fax: (215)898-0229; Email: polsky@mail.med.upenn.edu • URL: http://ldi.upenn.edu • Research fields include health care management and cost-quality trade-offs.

University of Pennsylvania - Institute for Law and Economics. 3501 Sansom St., Philadelphia, PA 19104. Phone: (215)898-7719; Fax: (215)573-2025; Email: mwachter@law.upenn.edu • URL: http://www.law.upenn.edu/academics/institutes/ile • Applies economic analysis in law to major policy issues affecting business and government, including economic analysis of common law doctrine, taxation and tax policy, public finance, labor market regulation, antitrust, financial institutions, and commercial law and industrial organization. Jointly conducts programs with the Law and Wharton Schools and the Department of Economics.

University of Stockholm - Institute for International Economic Studies., S-106 91 Stockholm, Sweden. Phone: 46 8 162000; Fax: 46 8 161443; Email: harry.flam@iies.su.se • URL: http://www.iies.su.se • International economics, macroeconomics, public finance, industrial organization.

University of Strathclyde - Fraser of Allander Institute. Sir William Duncan Bldg., 130 Rottenrow,

Glasgow G4 0GE. United Kingdom. Phone: 44 141 5483958; Fax: 44 141 5485776; Email: fraser@strath.ac.uk • URL: http://www.strath.ac.uk/fraser • Scottish economy, including studies in regional economics, input-output analysis, econometric modeling, labor economics, and economic development. Institute's goals include: analysis and forecasting of short-term trends in the Scottish economy; long-term analysis of prospective trends in the Scottish economy (Medium Term Model); applied computable general equilibrium modeling; compilation, updating, and maintenance of the Scottish Economic Data Bank; and portfolio of applied economics research projects.

University of the West Indies - Sir Arthur Lewis Institute of Social and Economic Studies. St. Augustine Campus, Saint Augustine, Trinidad and Tobago. Phone: (868)662-2002; Fax: (868)645-6329; Email: patrick.watson@sta.uwi.edu • URL: http://sta.uwi.edu/salises • Social and economic problems of the Caribbean. Focuses on issues relating to manpower, economic development, political sciences, public administration, migration, demography, women and development, and human resource development.

University of York - Centre for Experimental Economics. Department of Economics & Related Studies, York YO10 5DD, United Kingdom. Phone: 44 1904 433788; Fax: 44 1904 1433759 • URL: http://www.york.ac.uk/economics/research/research-clusters/experimental-economics • Experimental investigations of economic behavior, particularly under risk and uncertainty (both exogenous and endogenous).

Victoria University - Centre for Strategic Economic Studies. PO Box 14428, Melbourne, VIC 8001, Australia. Phone: 61 3 99191340; Fax: 61 3 99191350; Email: bruce.rasmussen@vu.edu.au • URL: http://www.cfses.com • Long term economic, social, and technological issues. Center has 3 prime areas of regional focus: Australia, the OECD countries, and East Asia, with special reference to China and Indonesia. Current programs include Growth Trade and Development; Technology, Innovation, and Industrial Change; Governance and Regional Economics; Sustainable Development and the Environment; and Inequality and Work.

Washington University in St. Louis - Weidenbaum Center on the Economy, Government, and Public Policy. CB 1027, 1 Brookings Dr., Saint Louis, MO 63130-4899. Phone: (314)935-5630; Fax: (314)935-5688; Email: smith@wustl.edu • URL: http://wc.wustl.edu • Effects of public policy on the American business system, including international trade, government regulation of business, federal taxing, and spending, international regulation, capital formation, federal credit activity, and corporate governance.

Worcester Polytechnic Institute - Center for Economic and Policy Dynamics. Department of Social Science & Policy Studies, 100 Institute Rd., Worcester, MA 01609-2280. Phone: (508)831-5583; Fax: (508)831-5896; Email: doyle@wpi.edu • URL: http://www.wpi.edu/Academics/Depts/SSPS/Research/cepd.html • Economics and public policy.

Worcester Polytechnic Institute - Economics, Policy, and Law Research Group. Department of Social Science & Policy Studies, 100 Institute Rd., Worcester, MA 01609-2280. Phone: (508)831-5234; Fax: (508)831-5892; Email: epl@wpi.edu • URL: http://web.cs.wpi.edu/Research/trg/ • Economics, policy, and law.

TRADE/PROFESSIONAL ASSOCIATIONS

AIESEC Alumni International. Ave. de Tervuren 300, B-1150 Brussels, Belgium. Email: info@aiesec-alumni.org • URL: http://www.aiesec-alumni.org • Alumni of the International Association of Students in Economics and Management. Promotes excellence in the study and practice of economics. Facilitates exchange of information among members; sponsors social programs.

American Economic Association. 2014 Broadway, Ste. 305, Nashville, TN 37203. Phone: (615)322-2595; Fax: (615)343-7590; Email: aeainfo@vanderbilt.edu • URL: http://www.aeaweb.org • Educators, business executives, government administrators, journalists, lawyers, and others interested in economics and its application to present-day problems. Encourages historical and statistical research into actual conditions of industrial life and provides a nonpartisan forum for economic discussion.

Econometric Society. New York University, Department of Economics, 19 W 4th St., 6th Fl., New York, NY 10012. Phone: (212)998-3820; Fax: (212)995-4487; Email: sashi@econometricsociety.org • URL: http://www.econometricsociety.org • Economists, statisticians, and mathematicians. Promotes studies that are directed towards unification of the theoretical and empirical approaches to economic problems and advancement of economic theory in its relation to statistics and mathematics.

Economics, Business and Enterprise Association. Adur Business Ctre., Little High St., Shoreham-by-Sea BN43 5EG, United Kingdom. Phone: 44 1273 467542; Email: office@ebea.org.uk • URL: http://www.ebea.org.uk/home • Teachers of economics, business studies and related subjects in schools and colleges. Represents teachers of economics, business studies and related subjects in schools and colleges throughout the UK and provides its members with the professional support they need in the classroom. Aims to encourage and promote the teaching and study of economics and related subjects within a broadly based curriculum.

National Association for Business Economics. 1920 L St. NW, Ste. 300, Washington, DC 20036. Phone: (202)463-6223; Fax: (202)463-6239; Email: nabe@nabe.com • URL: http://www.nabe.com • Formerly National Association of Business Economists.

National Council on Economic Education. 122 E 42nd St., Ste. 2600, New York, NY 10168. Phone: 800-338-1192 or (212)730-7007; Fax: (212)730-1793; Email: customerservice@councilforeconed.org • URL: http://www.councilforeconed.org • Formerly Joint Council in Economic Education.

Phi Chi Theta. 1508 E Beltline Rd., Ste. 104, Carrollton, TX 75006. Phone: (972)245-7202; Email: executivedirector@phichitheta.org • URL: http://www.phichitheta.org • Co-ed professional fraternity - business and economics. Maintains hall of fame; sponsors educational programs.

Phi Gamma Nu. 6745 Cheryl Ann Dr., Seven Hills, OH 44131-3720. Phone: (216)524-0019; Email: pgnexecutivedirector@gmail.com • URL: http://www.phigammanu.com • Professional fraternity - business administration and economics.

Russian Academy of Entrepreneurship. ul. Radio, 14, 105005 Moscow, Russia. Phone: 7 495 6322425 or 7 495 6322426; Email: priem@rusacad.ru • URL: http://www.rusacad.ru • Works to help Russian businesses compete in a market economy. Conducts economic analysis.

ECONOMICS, BUSINESS

See BUSINESS ECONOMICS

ECONOMICS, MATHEMATICAL

See ECONOMETRICS

EDITORS AND EDITING

See also BUSINESS JOURNALISM; HOUSE ORGANS; NEWSPAPERS; PERIODICALS; PUBLISHING INDUSTRY

ALMANACS AND YEARBOOKS

Editor & Publisher International Yearbook: Encyclopedia of the Newspaper Industry. Editor and Publisher Company Inc. • Annual. $150.00. Daily and Sunday newspapers in the United States and Canada.

DIRECTORIES

Editor & Publisher Market Guide. Editor and Publisher Company Inc. • Annual. $150 Individuals. Market data for more than 1,600 cities and 3,096 counties.

Editor and Publisher Syndicate Directory: Annual Directory of Syndicate Services. Editor & Publisher Magazine. • Annual. $28 Individuals. Directory of several hundred syndicates serving newspapers in the United States and abroad with news, columns, features, comic strips, editorial cartoons, etc.

Working Press of the Nation. R.R. Bowker L.L.C. • Annual. $530.00. $295.00 per volume. Three volumes: (1) *Newspaper Directory*; (2) *Magazine and Internal Publications Directory*; (3) *Radio and Television Directory*. Includes names of editors and other personnel.

Writer's Guide to Book Editors, Publishers, and Literary Agents, Who They Are, What They Want, and How to Win Them Over. Prima Publishing Inc. • Annual. $27.95; with CD-ROM, $49.95. Directory for authors includes information on publishers' response times and pay rates.

PERIODICALS AND NEWSLETTERS

American Editor. American Society of News Editors. • Nine times a year. $29.00 per year. Formerly *American Society of Newspaper Editors Bulletin*.

Copy Editor: Language News for the Publishing Profession. McMurry Newsletters. • Bimonthly. Newsletter for professional copy editors and proofreaders. Includes such items as "Top Ten Resources for Copy Editors.".

Editor and Publisher - The Newsmagazine of the Fourth Estate Since 1894. Editor & Publisher Magazine. • Weekly. $79 Individuals Total Access - Print and Digital. Trade journal of the newspaper industry.

Folio: The New Dynamics of Magazine Publishing. Penton. • Monthly. $96.00 per year.

Quill: The Magazine for Journalists. Society of Professional Journalists. • Bimonthly. $75 Individuals.

TRADE/PROFESSIONAL ASSOCIATIONS

American Society of Business Publications Editors. 214 N Hale St., Wheaton, IL 60187. Phone: (603)510-4588; Fax: (603)510-4501; Email: info@asbpe.org • URL: http://www.asbpe.org.

American Society of Magazine Editors. c/o Nina Fortuna, Director, 757 3rd Ave., 11th Fl., New York, NY 10017-2194. Phone: (212)872-3700 or (212)872-3737; Fax: (212)906-0128 • URL: http://www.magazine.org/asme • Represents magazine editors. Sponsors annual editorial internship program for college juniors and the National Magazine Awards.

American Society of News Editors. Missouri School of Journalism, 209 Reynolds Journalism Inst., Columbia, MO 65211. Phone: (573)884-2405 or (703)453-1133 • URL: http://www.asne.org • Consists of leaders of multimedia news organizations, deans and endowed chairs at accredited journalism schools. Focuses on open government and the First Amendment, journalism education, leadership and diversity.

Associated Press Managing Editors. c/o Debra Adams Simmons, President, 1801 Superior Ave., Cleveland, OH 44114. Phone: (216)999-4737 • URL: http://www.apme.com • Represents managing editors or executives on the news or editorial staff of

The Associated Press newspapers. Aims to: advance the journalism profession; examine the news and other services of the Associated Press in order to provide member newspapers with services that best suit their needs; provide a means of cooperation between the management and the editorial representatives of the members of the Associated Press. Maintains committees dealing with newspapers and news services.

EDUCATION

See SCHOOLS

EDUCATION, BUSINESS

See BUSINESS EDUCATION

EDUCATION, COMPUTERS IN

See COMPUTERS IN EDUCATION

EDUCATION, EMPLOYEE

See TRAINING OF EMPLOYEES

EDUCATION, EXECUTIVE

See EXECUTIVE TRAINING AND DEVELOPMENT

EDUCATION, FEDERAL AID

See FEDERAL AID

EDUCATION, HIGHER

See COLLEGES AND UNIVERSITIES

EDUCATION, TECHNICAL

See TECHNICAL EDUCATION

EDUCATION, VOCATIONAL

See VOCATIONAL EDUCATION

EDUCATIONAL FILMS

See AUDIOVISUAL AIDS IN EDUCATION

EFFICIENCY, INDUSTRIAL

See TIME AND MOTION STUDY

EGG INDUSTRY

See POULTRY INDUSTRY

ELECTRIC APPARATUS

See ELECTRICAL EQUIPMENT INDUSTRY

ELECTRIC APPLIANCE INDUSTRY

See also CONSUMER ELECTRONICS

CD-ROM DATABASES

OECD Statistical Compendium. Organization for Economic Cooperation and Development. • Semiannual. $1,905.00 per year for 1 to 10 users. CD-ROM contains more than 730,000 monthly, quarterly, and annual time series for OECD countries, 1960 to date. Includes fully searchable data on agriculture, food, economic indicators, national accounts, employment, energy, finance, industry, technology, and foreign trade. Results can be displayed in various forms.

DIRECTORIES

Directory of White & Yellow Goods Manufacturers in India. Steel Guru. • $250 Individuals additional fee for delivery of CD or printed form. Covers: 56 white and yellow goods manufacturers in India. Entries include: Company name, address, telephone number, mobile number, fax number, and e-mail address.

Electric Appliances Major Repair & Parts Directory. InfoGroup Inc. • Annual. Number of listings: 13,612. Entries include: Name, address, phone, size of advertisement, name of owner or manager, number of employees, year first in "Yellow Pages." Compiled from telephone company "Yellow Pages," nationwide.

The International Directory of Importers - Household and Kitchen Appliances Importers. Interdata. • $220 Individuals print. Covers: 2,300 international firms importing household and kitchen appliances. Entries include: Company name and address, contact person, email, number of employees, year established, phone and telefaxes, business activity, bank references, as well as a listing of household and kitchen appliances currently being imported.

FINANCIAL RATIOS

Annual Statement Studies. Risk Management Association. • Annual. Compiled from over 280,000 financial statements.

Annual Statement Studies: Industry Default Probabilities and Cash Flow Measures. Risk Management Association. • Annual. $405 Nonmembers. Serves as a companion volume to the original *Annual Statement Studies.* Gives probability of default estimates on a percentage scale for more than 450 industries. Includes changes in position year-by-year for eight financial statement line items and provides percentage measures of cash flow.

NARDA's Cost of Doing Business Survey. North American Retail Dealers Association. • $50 Members. Provides insight into revenue and costs, warranty information, expenses, and asset/liability information.

INTERNET DATABASES

Advance Monthly Retail Trade Report. U. S. Census Bureau. Phone: 800-541-8345 or (301)457-4100 or (301)763-2713; Fax: (301)457-1296 or (301)457-3842; Email: naics@census.gov • URL: http://www.census.gov/epcd/www/naicstab.htm • Web pages provide monthly sales figures for a wide range of retail businesses. Advance, preliminary, and final statistics are provided for the latest month available in each case, with a previous-year comparison. Updates are monthly.

Business 2.0 Web Guide to the Best Business Links. Business 2.0 Media Inc. Phone: (415)293-4800; Email: support@business2.com • URL: http://www.business2.com/webguide • Web site presents an extensive, searchable directory of links to "the best, most informative, and authoritative web pages." Twenty main categories cover business, finance, career, company information, people, and technology topics, with thousands of subtopics, all linking to Web sites recommended by experienced business researchers. Fees: Free.

Fedstats. Federal Interagency Council on Statistical Policy. Phone: (202)395-7254 • URL: http://www.fedstats.gov • Web site features an efficient search facility for full-text statistics produced by more than 100 federal agencies, including the Census Bureau, the Bureau of Economic Analysis, and the Bureau of Labor Statistics. Boolean searches can be made within one agency or for all agencies combined. Links are offered to international statistical bureaus, including the UN, IMF, OECD, UNESCO, Eurostat, and 20 individual countries. Fees: Free.

FreeLunch.com. Economy.com, Inc. Phone: (610)696-8700; Fax: (610)696-1678 • URL: http://www.freelunch.com • Web site provides free access to more than 200 million economic and financial data series, covering industry, demographics, labor markets, prices, retail sales, government spending, trade, interest rates, housing starts, the stock market, etc. Data is available in either chart or table form. Searching is offered. Free, but registration required. Economy.com, Inc. also offers fee-based economic analysis at *The Dismal Scientist* site (www.dismal.com).

Manufacturing Profiles. U. S. Bureau of the Census. Phone: (301)763-4636 or (301)763-4100; Fax: (301)763-4794; Email: webmaster@census.gov • URL: http://www.census.gov/prod/www/abs/mfg-prof.html • The Census Bureau makes available free on PDF (Portable Document Format) an annual consolidation of the entire Current Industrial Report series, presenting "all the data compiled." Contains statistics on production, shipments, inventories, consumption, exports, imports, and orders for a wide variety of manufactured products.

PERIODICALS AND NEWSLETTERS

Dealerscope: Product and Strategy for Consumer Technology Retailing. North American Publishing Co. • Monthly. $79 /year. Formerly *Dealerscope Consumer Electronices Marketplace.* Provides product information and valuable strategy for consumer technology retailers.

Product Design and Development. Advantage Business Media L.L.C. • 9/year.

STATISTICS SOURCES

Annual Benchmark Report for Retail Trade and Food Services..A Detailed Summary of Retail Sales, Purchases, Accounts Receivable, Inventories, and Food Service Sales. U. S. Government Printing Office. • Annual. $13.00. Issued by the U.S. Census Bureau. Provides detailed annual and monthly retail statistics for the most recent 10 years. Includes data for various kinds of retail outlets, including automobiles, furniture, appliances, building supplies, grocery stores, drug stores, gasoline stations, clothing, sporting goods, department stores, and restaurants.

Standard & Poor's Industry Surveys. Standard & Poor's Financial Services L.L.C. • Semiannual. $1,800.00. Two looseleaf volumes. Includes monthly *Supplements.* Provides detailed, individual surveys of 52 major industry groups. Each survey is revised on a semiannual basis. Also includes "Monthly Investment Review" (industry group investment analysis) and monthly "Trends & Projections" (economic analysis).

Survey of Current Business. U. S. Government Printing Office. • Published by Bureau of Economic Analysis, U. S. Department of Commerce. Presents a wide variety of business and economic data.

TRADE/PROFESSIONAL ASSOCIATIONS

Appliance Parts Distributors Association. 3621 N Oakley Ave., Chicago, IL 60618. Phone: (773)230-9851; Fax: (888)308-1423 • URL: http://www.apda.

com • Wholesale distributors of appliance parts, supplies and accessories. Promotes the sale of appliance parts through independent parts distributors.

Association of Home Appliance Manufacturers. 1111 19th St. NW, Ste. 402, Washington, DC 20036. Phone: (202)872-5955; Fax: (202)872-9354; Email: info@aham.org • URL: http://www.aham.org • Companies manufacturing major and portable appliances; supplier members provide products and services to the appliance industry. Major areas of activity include: market research and reporting of industry statistics; development of standard methods for measuring appliance performance and certification of certain characteristics of room air conditioners, refrigerators, freezers, humidifiers, dehumidifiers, and room air cleaners; public relations and press relations. Represents the appliance industry before government at the federal, state, and local levels.

International Housewares Association. 6400 Shafer Ct., Ste. 650, Rosemont, IL 60018. Phone: (847)292-4200; Fax: (847)292-4211 • URL: http://www.housewares.org • Manufacturers and distributors of housewares and small appliances. Conducts annual market research survey of the housewares industry. Manages the international housewares show.

North American Retail Dealers Association. 222 S Riverside Plz., Ste. 2100, Chicago, IL 60606. Phone: 800-621-0298 or (312)648-0649; Fax: (312)648-1212; Email: nardasvc@narda.com • URL: http://www.narda.com • Firms engaged in the retailing of electronic and electrical devices and components. Promotes and represents members' interests. Makes available services to members including: legal and technical consulting; employee screening; bank card processing; long-distance phone discounts; financial statements analysis; in-store promotion kits; customer check authorization. Advocates for members' interests before federal regulatory bodies; disseminates information on new regulations affecting members. Conducts educational programs.

ELECTRIC CONTRACTORS

See ELECTRICAL CONSTRUCTION INDUSTRY

ELECTRIC LAMPS

See LIGHTING

ELECTRIC LIGHTING

See LIGHTING

ELECTRIC MOTOR INDUSTRY

See ELECTRICAL EQUIPMENT INDUSTRY

ELECTRIC POWER

See ELECTRIC UTILITIES

ELECTRIC POWER COGENERATION

See COGENERATION OF ENERGY

ELECTRIC POWER PLANTS

See also ELECTRIC UTILITIES; ELECTRICAL EQUIPMENT INDUSTRY; PUBLIC UTILITIES

ABSTRACTS AND INDEXES

Key Abstracts: Computing in Electronics and Power. Institution of Engineering and Technology. • Bimonthly. $1,138. Provides international coverage of journal and proceedings literature.

Key Abstracts: Power Systems and Applications. Institution of Engineering and Technology. • Monthly. $1,138. Provides international coverage of journal and proceedings literature, including publications on electric power apparatus and machines.

DIRECTORIES

Platt's Directory of Electric Power Producers and Distributors. Platts Global Energy. • Annual. $495 hardcopy. Over 3,500 investor-owned, municipal, rural cooperative and government electric utility systems in the U.S. and Canada. Formerly *Directory of Electric Power Producers and Distributors*.

FINANCIAL RATIOS

Annual Statement Studies. Risk Management Association. • Annual. Compiled from over 280,000 financial statements.

Annual Statement Studies: Industry Default Probabilities and Cash Flow Measures. Risk Management Association. • Annual. $405 Nonmembers. Serves as a companion volume to the original *Annual Statement Studies*. Gives probability of default estimates on a percentage scale for more than 450 industries. Includes changes in position year-by-year for eight financial statement line items and provides percentage measures of cash flow.

PERIODICALS AND NEWSLETTERS

Electrial Construction and Maintenance. Penton. • Monthly. Free to qualified personnel; individuals, $30.00 per year; libraries, $25.00 per year.

Global Power Report: An Exclusive Biweekly Covering the Cogeneration and Small Power Market. Platts Global Energy. • Biweekly. $1,165.00 per year. Newsletter. Covers industry trends, new projects, new contracts, rate changes, and regulations, with emphasis on the Federal Energy Regulatory Commission (FERC). Formerly *Cogeneration Report*.

Power Engineering International. PennWell Corp., Industrial Div. • Monthly.

Private Power Executive. Pequot Publishing Inc. • Bimonthly. $90.00 per year. Covers private power (non-utility) enterprises, including cogeneration projects and industrial self-generation.

STATISTICS SOURCES

Coal Information. Organization for Economic Cooperation and Development. • Annual. €165. Presents comprehensive data from the International Energy Agency (IEA) on the world coal market, including supply, demand, production, trade, and prices. In addition to coal itself, provides country-specific data on coal-fired power stations and coal-related environmental issues.

Statistical YearBook of the Electric Power Industry. Edison Electric Institute. • Annual. $550 print or pdf.

Steam Electric Market Analysis. National Mining Association. • Monthly. Free to members; nonmembers, $300.00 per year. Covers 400 major electric power plants, with detailed data on coal consumption and stockpiles. Shows percent of power generated by fuel type. (Publisher formerly National Coal Association.).

TRADE/PROFESSIONAL ASSOCIATIONS

Association of Edison Illuminating Companies. 600 N 18th St. N, Birmingham, AL 35203-2206. Phone: (205)257-2530; Fax: (205)257-2540; Email: aeicdir@bellsouth.net • URL: http://www.aeic.org • Represents the interests of investor-owned public utilities, generating and transmitting or distributing companies.

Association of Energy Engineers. 4025 Pleasantdale Rd., Ste. 420, Atlanta, GA 30340. Phone: (770)447-5083; Fax: (770)446-3969; Email: info@aeecenter.org • URL: http://www.aeecenter.org • Members are engineers and other professionals concerned with energy management and cogeneration.

Edison Electric Institute. 701 Pennsylvania Ave. NW, Washington, DC 20004-2696. Phone: 800-334-5453 or (202)508-5000; Fax: (800)525-5562; Email: eblume@eei.org • URL: http://www.eei.org/Pages/default.aspx • Shareholder-owned electric utility companies operating in the U.S.; international affiliates and associates worldwide.

Electrical Generating Systems Association. 1650 S Dixie Hwy., Ste. 400, Boca Raton, FL 33432-7462. Phone: (561)750-5575; Fax: (561)395-8557; Email: e-mail@egsa.org • URL: http://www.egsa.org • Manufacturers, distributor/dealers, and manufacturers' representatives of devices used to generate electrical power through the use of an internal combustion engine or a gas turbine coupled to a generator. Conducts training programs and publishes material on On-Site Power Generation.

ELECTRIC POWER, RURAL

See RURAL ELECTRIFICATION

ELECTRIC RATES

See also PUBLIC UTILITIES

PERIODICALS AND NEWSLETTERS

Electric Utility Week: The Electric Utility Industry Newsletter. Platts Global Energy. • Weekly. $1,625.00 per year. Newsletter. Formerly *Electric Week*.

ELECTRIC SIGNS

See SIGNS AND SIGN BOARDS

ELECTRIC UTILITIES

See also COGENERATION OF ENERGY; ELECTRIC POWER PLANTS; HYDROELECTRIC INDUSTRY; PUBLIC UTILITIES

ABSTRACTS AND INDEXES

Business Periodicals Index Retrospective. EBSCO Publishing Inc. • 11/year. Quarterly and annual cumulations.

NTIS Alerts: Energy. U.S. Department of Commerce National Technical Information Service. • Biweekly. $130 per year. Covers electric power, batteries, fuels, geothermal energy, heating/cooling systems, nuclear technology, solar energy, energy policy, and related subjects.

CD-ROM DATABASES

OECD Statistical Compendium. Organization for Economic Cooperation and Development. • Semiannual. $1,905.00 per year for 1 to 10 users. CD-ROM contains more than 730,000 monthly, quarterly, and annual time series for OECD countries, 1960 to date. Includes fully searchable data on agriculture, food, economic indicators, national accounts, employment, energy, finance, industry, technology, and foreign trade. Results can be displayed in various forms.

DIRECTORIES

Platt's Directory of Electric Power Producers and Distributors. Platts Global Energy. • Annual. $495 hardcopy. Over 3,500 investor-owned, municipal, rural cooperative and government electric utility systems in the U.S. and Canada. Formerly *Directory of Electric Power Producers and Distributors.*

E-BOOKS

Macmillan Encyclopedia of Energy. Cengage Learning Inc. • 2003. eBook. Published by Macmillan Reference USA. Covers the business, technology, and history of a wide variety of energy sources. Inquire as to price and availability.

HANDBOOKS AND MANUALS

Mergent's Public Utility Manual. Mergent Inc. • Annual. $1,995.00. Updated weekly online. Contains financial and other information concerning publicly-held utility companies (electric, gas, telephone, water).

INTERNET DATABASES

Business 2.0 Web Guide to the Best Business Links. Business 2.0 Media Inc. Phone: (415)293-4800; Email: support@business2.com • URL: http://www.business2.com/webguide • Web site presents an extensive, searchable directory of links to "the best, most informative, and authoritative web pages." Twenty main categories cover business, finance, career, company information, people, and technology topics, with thousands of subtopics, all linking to Web sites recommended by experienced business researchers. Fees: Free.

Fedstats. Federal Interagency Council on Statistical Policy. Phone: (202)395-7254 • URL: http://www.fedstats.gov • Web site features an efficient search facility for full-text statistics produced by more than 100 federal agencies, including the Census Bureau, the Bureau of Economic Analysis, and the Bureau of Labor Statistics. Boolean searches can be made within one agency or for all agencies combined. Links are offered to international statistical bureaus, including the UN, IMF, OECD, UNESCO, Eurostat, and 20 individual countries. Fees: Free.

FreeLunch.com. Economy.com, Inc. Phone: (610)696-8700; Fax: (610)696-1678 • URL: http://www.freelunch.com • Web site provides free access to more than 200 million economic and financial data series, covering industry, demographics, labor markets, prices, retail sales, government spending, trade, interest rates, housing starts, the stock market, etc. Data is available in either chart or table form. Searching is offered. Free, but registration required. Economy.com, Inc. also offers fee-based economic analysis at *The Dismal Scientist* site (www.dismal.com).

OTHER SOURCES

Major Energy Companies of the World. Cengage Learning Inc. • Annual. $1,460 Individuals. 2008. 12th edition. eBook. Published by Graham & Whiteside. Contains detailed information on more than 4,850 important energy companies in various countries. Industries include electricity generation, coal, natural gas, nuclear energy, petroleum, fuel distribution, and equipment for energy production.

Utilities Industry Litigation Reporter: National Coverage of the Many Types of Litigation Stemming From the Transmission and Distribution of Energy By Publicly and Privately Owned Utilities. Andrews Publications. • Monthly. $775.00 per year. Newsletter. Reports on legal cases involving the generation or distribution of energy.

PERIODICALS AND NEWSLETTERS

Electric Perspectives. Edison Electric Institute. • Bimonthly. $100 Nonmembers. Covers business, financial, and operational aspects of the investor-owned electric utility industry. Edited for utility executives and managers.

Electric Utility Week: The Electric Utility Industry Newsletter. Platts Global Energy. • Weekly. $1,625.00 per year. Newsletter. Formerly *Electric Week*.

Electrical Wholesaling. Penton. • Monthly. $20.00 per year.

Electrical World T and D Magazine. Platts Global Energy. • Monthly. Free to qualified personnel. Formerly *Electrical World*.

EPRI Journal. Electric Power Research Institute. • Bimonthly. Free to members; non-members, $29.00 per year.

Public Power. American Public Power Association. • 8/year.

Public Power Weekly. American Public Power Association. • Description: Reports on legislative, regulatory, judicial, and technical developments affecting local and state-owned electric utilities. Recurring features include employment notices and news briefs.

Utility Automation. PennWell Corp., Industrial Div. • 10 times a year. $69.00 per year; schools and public libraries, $10.00 per year. Covers new information technologies for electric utilities, including automated meter reading, distribution management systems, and customer information systems.

PRICE SOURCES

Energy Prices and Taxes. International Energy Agency. Organisation for Economic Co-operation and Development Publications and Information Center. • Quarterly. $385 Individuals. Compiled by the International Energy Agency. Provides data on prices and taxation of petroleum products, natural gas, coal, and electricity. Diskette edition, $800.00. (Published in Paris).

PPI Detailed Report. Periodical covering business. Bureau of Labor Statistics, U.S. Department of Labor. U. S. Government Printing Office. • Monthly. $55 Individuals.

RESEARCH CENTERS AND INSTITUTES

Massachusetts Institute of Technology - Research Laboratory of Electronics. 77 Massachusetts Ave., Rm. 36-413, Cambridge, MA 02139-4307. Phone: (617)253-2519; Fax: (617)253-1301; Email: hq@rle.mit.edu • URL: http://www.rle.mit.edu/ • Research areas include heat transfer and cryogenics.

STATISTICS SOURCES

Annual Energy Outlook, with Projections to (year). U. S. Government Printing Office. • Annual. $39.00. Issued by the Energy Information Administration, U. S. Department of Energy (www.eia.doe.gov). Contains detailed statistics and 20-year projections for electricity, oil, natural gas, coal, and renewable energy. Text provides extensive discussion of energy issues and "Market Trends.".

Annual Energy Review. U. S. Government Printing Office. • Annual. $59.00. Issued by the Energy Information Administration, Office of Energy Markets and End Use, U. S. Department of Energy. Presents long-term historical as well as recent data on production, consumption, stocks, imports, exports, and prices of the principal energy commodities in the U. S.

OECD Nuclear Energy Data. Organization for Economic Cooperation and Development. Organisation for Economic Co-operation and Development Publications and Information Center. • Annual. $58.00. Produced by the OECD Nuclear Energy Agency. Provides a yearly compilation of basic statistics on electricity generation and nuclear power in OECD member countries. Text in English and French.

Standard & Poor's Industry Surveys. Standard & Poor's Financial Services L.L.C. • Semiannual. $1,800.00. Two looseleaf volumes. Includes monthly *Supplements*. Provides detailed, individual surveys of 52 major industry groups. Each survey is revised on a semiannual basis. Also includes "Monthly Investment Review" (industry group investment analysis) and monthly "Trends & Projections" (economic analysis).

Statistical YearBook of the Electric Power Industry. Edison Electric Institute. • Annual. $550 print or pdf.

Steam Electric Market Analysis. National Mining Association. • Monthly. Free to members; non-members, $300.00 per year. Covers 400 major electric power plants, with detailed data on coal consumption and stockpiles. Shows percent of power generated by fuel type. (Publisher formerly National Coal Association.).

Survey of Current Business. U. S. Government Printing Office. • Published by Bureau of Economic Analysis, U. S. Department of Commerce. Presents a wide variety of business and economic data.

TRADE/PROFESSIONAL ASSOCIATIONS

American Public Power Association. 1875 Connecticut Ave. NW, Ste. 1200, Washington, DC 20009-5715. Phone: 800-515-2772 or (202)467-2900; Fax: (202)467-2910; Email: info@publicpower.org • URL: http://www.publicpower.org • Municipally owned electric utilities, public utility districts, state and county-owned electric systems, and rural cooperatives. Conducts research programs; compiles statistics; offers utility education courses; sponsors competitions.

Association of Edison Illuminating Companies. 600 N 18th St. N, Birmingham, AL 35203-2206. Phone: (205)257-2530; Fax: (205)257-2540; Email: aeicdir@bellsouth.net • URL: http://www.aeic.org • Represents the interests of investor-owned public utilities, generating and transmitting or distributing companies.

Edison Electric Institute. 701 Pennsylvania Ave. NW, Washington, DC 20004-2696. Phone: 800-334-5453 or (202)508-5000; Fax: (800)525-5562; Email: eblume@eei.org • URL: http://www.eei.org/Pages/default.aspx • Shareholder-owned electric utility companies operating in the U.S.; international affiliates and associates worldwide.

ELECTRIC WIRE

See WIRE INDUSTRY

ELECTRICAL CONSTRUCTION INDUSTRY

ALMANACS AND YEARBOOKS

EC&M's Electrical Products Yearbook. Penton. • Annual. $10.00.

BIBLIOGRAPHIES

Census of Construction: Subject Bibliography No. 157. U. S. Government Printing Office. • Annual. Free. Lists government publications.

DIRECTORIES

Electrical Construction Materials Directory. Underwriters Laboratories Inc. • Annual. $22 Individuals. Lists construction materials manufacturers authorized to use UL label.

Plastics Recognized Component Directory: Polymeric Materials, Processes, and Systems. Underwriters Laboratories Inc. • Annual. $220 Individuals electronic CD version. Covers: Companies that have qualified to use the UL recognized component marking on or in connection with materials that have been found to be in compliance with UL's requirements. Coverage includes foreign companies that manufacture for distribution in the U.S. Entries include: Company name, city, ZIP code, UL file number, type of product.

FINANCIAL RATIOS

Annual Statement Studies. Risk Management Association. • Annual. Compiled from over 280,000 financial statements.

Annual Statement Studies: Industry Default Probabilities and Cash Flow Measures. Risk Management Association. • Annual. $405 Nonmembers. Serves as a companion volume to the original *An-*

nual Statement Studies. Gives probability of default estimates on a percentage scale for more than 450 industries. Includes changes in position year-by-year for eight financial statement line items and provides percentage measures of cash flow.

Construction Industry Annual Financial Survey. Construction Financial Management Association. • Annual. $262. Contains key financial ratios for various kinds and sizes of construction contractors.

HANDBOOKS AND MANUALS

CEE News Buyers' Guide. Primedia Business Magazines and Media. • Annual. $25.00. List of approximately 1,900 manufacturers of products used in the electrical construction industry; coverage includes Canada.

PERIODICALS AND NEWSLETTERS

Electrial Construction and Maintenance. Penton. • Monthly. Free to qualified personnel; individuals, $30.00 per year; libraries, $25.00 per year.

Electrical Contractor. National Electrical Contractors Association. • Monthly. Serves the field of electrical construction, including inside, line work, lighting, maintenance, control, electrical work, voice/data systems, security, fire and life safety, fiber optics, home and building automation systems, integrated building systems applications and others applicable to the field.

STATISTICS SOURCES

United States Census of Construction Industries. U.S. Department of Commerce U.S. Census Bureau. • Quinquennial. Results presented in reports, tape, and CD-ROM files.

TRADE/PROFESSIONAL ASSOCIATIONS

Joint Industry Board of the Electrical Industry. 158-11 Harry Van Arsdale Jr. Ave., Flushing, NY 11365. Phone: (718)591-2000; Fax: (718)380-7741 • URL: http://www.jibei.org • Concerned with labor-management relations of electrical contractors.

National Electrical Contractors Association. 3 Bethesda Metro Ctr., Ste. 1100, Bethesda, MD 20814. Phone: (301)657-3110; Fax: (301)215-4500 • URL: http://www.necanet.org • Contractors erecting, installing, repairing, servicing, and maintaining electric wiring, equipment, and appliances. Provides management services and labor relations programs for electrical contractors; conducts seminars for contractor sales and training. Conducts research and educational programs; compiles statistics. Sponsors honorary society, the Academy of Electrical Contracting.

Power and Communication Contractors Association. 1908 Mt. Vernon Ave., 2nd Fl., Alexandria, VA 22301. Phone: 800-542-7222 or (703)212-7734; Fax: (703)548-3733; Email: info@pccaweb.org • URL: http://www.pccaweb.org • Contractors engaged in electrical power and communication line construction.

ELECTRICAL ENGINEERING

ABSTRACTS AND INDEXES

Applied Science and Technology Index. EBSCO Publishing Inc. • 11/year. Indexes a wide variety of English language technical, industrial, and engineering periodicals.

Engineering Index Monthly: Abstracting and Indexing Services Covering Sources ofthe World's Engineering Literature. Engineering Information Inc. • Monthly. Institutions, $5,279.00 per year. Provides indexing and abstracting of the world's engineering and technical literature.

BIBLIOGRAPHIES

IEEE Products and Publications Bulletin. IEEE - Communications Society. • Quarterly. Free. Provides information on all IEEE journals, proceedings, and other publications. Formerly *IEEE Publications Bulletin*.

Reference Reviews. Information Today, Inc. • Eight times a year. Price on application. Published in London by Aslib: The Association for Information Management. Incorporates *Aslib Book Guide*.

BIOGRAPHICAL SOURCES

Who's Who in Science and Engineering. Marquis Who's Who L.L.C. • Biennial. $249.00. Provides concise biographical information on 33,545 prominent engineers and scientists. International coverage, with geographical and professional indexes.

DIRECTORIES

IEEE Membership Directory. IEEE - Communications Society. • Annual.

Plunkett's Engineering and Research Industry Almanac. Plunkett Research Ltd. • Annual. $349.99. Contains detailed profiles of major engineering and technology corporations. Includes CD-ROM.

ONLINE DATABASES

Current Contents Connect. Thomson Reuters Intellectual Property and Science. • Provides online abstracts of articles listed in the tables of contents of about 7,500 journals. Coverage is very broad, including science, social science, life science, technology, engineering, industry, agriculture, the environment, economics, and arts and humanities. Time period is two years, with weekly updates. Inquire as to online cost and availability.

INSPEC. Institution of Electrical Engineers. • Provides online citations, with abstracts, to the world literature of electrical engineering, electronics, optoelectronics, telecommunications, industrial controls, instrumentation, computer technology, information technology, and physics. Coverage includes more than 4,000 technical and scientific journals from 1969 to date, with weekly updating. (INSPEC is Information Services in Physics, Electronics, and Computing.) Inquire as to online cost and availability.

PERIODICALS AND NEWSLETTERS

Electronic Engineering Times: The Industry Newspaper for Engineers and Technical Management. UBM L.L.C. • Weekly. Free to qualified personnel; others, $319.00 per year.

IEEE Industry Applications Magazine. IEEE - Communications Society. • Bimonthly. Covers new industrial applications of power conversion, drives, lighting, and control. Emphasis is on the petroleum, chemical, rubber, plastics, textile, and mining industries.

IEEE Proceedings-Circuits, Devices and Systems. IEEE - Communications Society. • Bimonthly. Covers all aspects of circuit theory, design, and implementation.

IEEE Spectrum. IEEE - Communications Society. • Monthly. $19.95 U.S. and Canada print only or digital only. Magazine for the scientific and engineering professional. Provides information on developments and trends in engineering, physics, mathematics, chemistry, medicine/biology, and the nuclear sciences.

RESEARCH CENTERS AND INSTITUTES

Massachusetts Institute of Technology - Research Laboratory of Electronics. 77 Massachusetts Ave., Rm. 36-413, Cambridge, MA 02139-4307. Phone: (617)253-2519; Fax: (617)253-1301; Email: hq@rle.mit.edu • URL: http://www.rle.mit.edu/ • Research areas include heat transfer and cryogenics.

TRADE/PROFESSIONAL ASSOCIATIONS

JEDEC. 3103 N 10th St., Ste. 240-S, Arlington, VA 22201-2107. Phone: (703)907-7515 • URL: http://www.jedec.org • Affiliated with Electronic Industries Alliance. Formerly Joint Electron Device Engineering Council.

ELECTRICAL EQUIPMENT INDUSTRY

See also ELECTRIC APPLIANCE INDUSTRY; ELECTRIC POWER PLANTS

ABSTRACTS AND INDEXES

Applied Science and Technology Index. EBSCO Publishing Inc. • 11/year. Indexes a wide variety of English language technical, industrial, and engineering periodicals.

Business Periodicals Index Retrospective. EBSCO Publishing Inc. • 11/year. Quarterly and annual cumulations.

Key Abstracts: Power Systems and Applications. Institution of Engineering and Technology. • Monthly. $1,138. Provides international coverage of journal and proceedings literature, including publications on electric power apparatus and machines.

DIRECTORIES

Electrical Apparatus: Electromechanical Bench Reference Supplement. Barks Publications Inc. • Monthly. $45 U.S. /year. Included in subscription to Electric Apparatus Magazine. Lists 3,000 manufacturers and distributors of electrical and electronic products. Formerly *Electrical Apparatus Magazine. Electromechanical Bench Reference Book*.

The European Market for High Voltage Switchgear. ABS Publications. • $800. Covers: European manufacturers of high voltage switchgear (greater than 1kV). Entries include: Utility statistics, company profiles, trade production and market data for both supply and demand.

The International Directory of Importers--Electrical Equipment and Supplies Importers. Interdata. • $295 Individuals print edition. Covers: 4,900 international firms importing electrical equipment and supplies. Entries include: Company name and address, contact person, email, number of employees, year established, phone and telefaxes, business activity, bank references, as well as a listing of electrical equipment and supplies currently being imported.

E-BOOKS

Encyclopedia of American Industries. Cengage Learning Inc. • 2011. $807.00. 6th edition. Three volumes. Volume one is Manufacturing Industries and volume two is Service and Non-Manufacturing Industries. Provides the history, development, and recent status of approximately 1,000 industries. Includes statistical graphs, with industry and general indexes. Also available as eBook.

FINANCIAL RATIOS

Annual Statement Studies. Risk Management Association. • Annual. Compiled from over 280,000 financial statements.

Annual Statement Studies: Industry Default Probabilities and Cash Flow Measures. Risk Management Association. • Annual. $405 Nonmembers. Serves as a companion volume to the original *Annual Statement Studies*. Gives probability of default estimates on a percentage scale for more than 450 industries. Includes changes in position year-by-year for eight financial statement line items and provides percentage measures of cash flow.

GENERAL WORKS

Electrical Business. Electric League of the Pacific Northwest. • Monthly.

HANDBOOKS AND MANUALS

CEE News Buyers' Guide. Primedia Business Magazines and Media. • Annual. $25.00. List of approximately 1,900 manufacturers of products used in the electrical construction industry; coverage includes Canada.

INTERNET DATABASES

Manufacturing Profiles. U. S. Bureau of the Census. Phone: (301)763-4636 or (301)763-4100; Fax: (301)763-4794; Email: webmaster@census.gov • URL: http://www.census.gov/prod/www/abs/mfg-prof.html • The Census Bureau makes available free on PDF (Portable Document Format) an annual consolidation of the entire Current Industrial Report series, presenting "all the data compiled." Contains statistics on production, shipments, inventories, consumption, exports, imports, and orders for a wide variety of manufactured products.

ONLINE DATABASES

Thomas Register Online. Thomas Publishing Company L.L.C. • Provides concise information on approximately 194,000 U. S. companies, mainly manufacturers, with over 50,000 product classifications. Indexes over 115,000 trade names. Information is updated semiannually. Inquire as to online cost and availability.

PERIODICALS AND NEWSLETTERS

Canadian Industrial Equipment News: Reader Service On New, Improved and Redesigned Industrial Equipment and Supplies. Scott's Directories. • Monthly. Formerly *Electrical Equipment News*.

Dealerscope: Product and Strategy for Consumer Technology Retailing. North American Publishing Co. • Monthly. $79 /year. Formerly *Dealerscope Consumer Electronices Marketplace*. Provides product information and valuable strategy for consumer technology retailers.

EE Product News. Penton Media Inc. • Monthly. Free to qualified personnel; others, $60.00 per year.

National Home Center News: News and Analysis for the Home Improvement, Building Material Industry. Lebhar-Friedman Inc. • 22 times a year. $99.00 per year. Includes special feature issues on hardware and tools, building materials, millwork, electrical supplies, lighting, and kitchens.

STATISTICS SOURCES

Standard & Poor's Industry Surveys. Standard & Poor's Financial Services L.L.C. • Semiannual. $1,800.00. Two looseleaf volumes. Includes monthly *Supplements*. Provides detailed, individual surveys of 52 major industry groups. Each survey is revised on a semiannual basis. Also includes "Monthly Investment Review" (industry group investment analysis) and monthly "Trends & Projections" (economic analysis).

United States Census of Manufactures. U.S. Department of Commerce U.S. Census Bureau. • Quinquennial. Results presented in reports, tape, CD-ROM, and Diskette files.

U.S. Industry and Trade Outlook. U.S. Department of Commerce National Technical Information Service. • Annual. Produced by the International Trade Administration, U.S. Department of Commerce, in a "public-private" partnership with DRI/McGraw-Hill and Standard & Poor's. Provides basic data, outlook for the current year, and "Long-Term Prospects" (five-year projections) for a wide variety of products and services. Includes high technology industries. Formerly *U.S. Industrial Outlook*.

TRADE/PROFESSIONAL ASSOCIATIONS

Association of Home Appliance Manufacturers. 1111 19th St. NW, Ste. 402, Washington, DC 20036. Phone: (202)872-5955; Fax: (202)872-9354; Email: info@aham.org • URL: http://www.aham.org • Companies manufacturing major and portable appliances; supplier members provide products and services to the appliance industry. Major areas of activity include: market research and reporting of industry statistics; development of standard methods for measuring appliance performance and certification of certain characteristics of room air conditioners, refrigerators, freezers, humidifiers, dehumidifiers, and room air cleaners; public relations and press relations. Represents the appliance industry before government at the federal, state, and local levels.

Electrical Equipment Representatives Association. 638 W 39th St., Kansas City, MO 64111. Phone: (816)561-5323; Fax: (816)561-1249; Email: info@eera.org • URL: http://www.eera.org • Represents sales agents for manufacturers of electrical equipment used by utilities, industrial firms and the government.

Electrical Generating Systems Association. 1650 S Dixie Hwy., Ste. 400, Boca Raton, FL 33432-7462. Phone: (561)750-5575; Fax: (561)395-8557; Email: e-mail@egsa.org • URL: http://www.egsa.org • Manufacturers, distributor/dealers, and manufacturers' representatives of devices used to generate electrical power through the use of an internal combustion engine or a gas turbine coupled to a generator. Conducts training programs and publishes material on On-Site Power Generation.

NAED National Education and Research Foundation. 1181 Corporate Lake Dr., Saint Louis, MO 63132-1716. Phone: 888-791-2512 or (314)991-9000; Fax: (314)991-3060 • URL: http://www.naed.org • Established by the National Association of Electrical Distributors to provide electrical distributor and distributor-oriented manufacturers with the opportunity to become better business people by expanding their managerial skills. Designs and conducts seminars, workshops, conferences and home study materials covering all aspects of professional management in the electrical supply industry.

National Electrical Manufacturers Association. 1300 N 17th St., Ste. 1752, Rosslyn, VA 22209. Phone: (703)841-3200 or (703)841-3272; Email: communications@nema.org • URL: http://www.nema.org • Aims to maintain and improve quality and reliability of products; insure safety standards in manufacture and use of products; organize and act upon members' interests in productivity, competition from overseas suppliers, energy conservation and efficiency, marketing opportunities, economic matters, and product liability. Develops product standards covering such matters as nomenclature, ratings, performance, testing, and dimensions; actively participates in regional and international standards process for electrical products; participates in developing National Electrical Code and National Electrical Safety Codes, and advocates their acceptance by state and local authorities; conducts regulatory and legislative analyses on issues of concern to electrical manufacturers; compiles and issues market data of all kinds, and statistical data on such factors as sales, new orders, unfilled orders, cancellations, production, and inventories.

ELECTRONIC COMMERCE

See also INTERNET

ABSTRACTS AND INDEXES

Internet and Personal Computing Abstracts (print edition). EBSCO Publishing Inc. • Quarterly. $269.00 per year, including cumulative index. Provides more than 10,000 abstracts annually from both trade and academic publications. Covers computer hardware, software, product reviews, Web topics, e-commerce, networks, corporate news, security, and related topics. Formerly *Microcomputer Abstracts*.

CD-ROM DATABASES

OECD Statistical Compendium. Organization for Economic Cooperation and Development. • Semiannual. $1,905.00 per year for 1 to 10 users. CD-ROM contains more than 730,000 monthly, quarterly, and annual time series for OECD countries, 1960 to date. Includes fully searchable data on agriculture, food, economic indicators, national accounts, employment, energy, finance, industry, technology, and foreign trade. Results can be displayed in various forms.

DIRECTORIES

Cyberstocks: An Investors Guide to Internet Companies. Hoover's Inc. • $24.95. Covers: Companies involved in the Internet industry. Entries include: Name, address, phone.

Directory of Global eCommerce Companies. Nandini Institute of Chemical Industries. • $50. Covers: List of names and addresses of eCommerce companies.

Global Trade Leads. INFOT Inc. • $114.75 CD-ROM; additional $150 for MS Access format. Covers: More than 493,448 suppliers & buyers active in major online market places. Entries include: Email and website addresses, telephone and fax number, and business titles and descriptions.

Guide to EU Information Sources on the Internet. Euroconfidentiel S. A. • Annual. $210.00. Contains descriptions of more than 1,700 Web sites providing information relating to the European Union and European commerce and industry. Includes a quarterly e-mail newsletter with new sites and address changes.

Handbook of Internet Stocks. Mergent Inc. • Annual. $19.95. Contains detailed financial information on more than 200 Internet-related corporations, including e-commerce firms and telecommunications hardware manufacturers. Lists and rankings are provided.

KMWorld Buyer's Guide. Knowledge Asset Media Inc. • Semiannual. $2,395 (Basic Corporate Profile Package) One Issue — Spring 2014 Edition PLUS 6 Months Online. Controlled circulation as part of *KMWorld*. Contains corporate and product profiles related to various aspects of knowledge management and information systems. (Knowledge Asset Media is a an affiliate of Information Today, Inc.).

Plunkett's E-Commerce and Internet Business Almanac. Plunkett Research Ltd. • Annual. $349.99. Contains detailed profiles of 250 large companies engaged in various areas of Internet commerce, including e-business Web sites, communications equipment manufacturers, and Internet service providers. Includes CD-ROM.

Plunkett's E-Commerce & Internet Business Almanac: Your Reference Source to All Facets of the Internet Business. Plunkett Research Ltd. • Biennial. $349.99 Individuals ebook, print and CD-ROM. Covers 400 of the largest companies working in all facets of e-commerce and Internet business, including Internet service providers, Web site operators, equipment and others.

Starting an Online Business for Dummies. John Wiley & Sons Inc. • $24.99 Individuals paperback. Covers: Information needed to get an online business off the ground: identifying a market need, choosing a Web hosting service, securing transactions, and attracting customers.

The Wilson Guide to Internet Experts. H.W. Wilson Co. • $54.99. Covers: Noted authorities in the Internet industry. Entries include: Biographical details, office address and phone number, e-mail and Web site addresses, current projects, specialties.

E-BOOKS

Advances in Electronic Marketing. Cengage Learning Inc. • 2006. eBook. Published by Information Science Reference. Examines the challenges that organizations face today within three major themes: the global environment, the strategic/technological realm, and the buyer behavior of online consumers.

Business Applications and Computational

Intelligence. Cengage Learning Inc. • 2005. eBook. Addresses the need for a compact overview of the diversity of applications in a number of business disciplines, and consists of chapters written by leading international researchers. Chapters cover most fields of business, including: marketing, data mining, e-commerce, production and operations, finance, decision-making, and general management.

E-Business Innovation and Process Management. Cengage Learning Inc. • 2007. eBook. Provides researchers and practitioners with information on recent advances and developments in emerging e-business models and technologies. This book covers a variety of topics, such as e-business models, e-business strategies, online consumer behavior, e-business process modeling and practices, electronic communication adoption and service provider strategies, privacy policies, and implementation issues.

E-Business Models, Services and Communications. Cengage Learning Inc. • 2008. eBook. Provides researchers and practitioners with valuable information on recent advances and developments in emerging e-business models and technologies.

E-Marketing in Developed and Developing Countries: Emerging Practices. Cengage Learning Inc. • 2013. eBook. Highlights the strategies and applications used in both developed and developing countries; proving to be beneficial for entrepreneurs, policy makers, researchers, and students wishing to expand their comprehensive knowledge in this field.

Electronic Business: Concepts, Methodologies, Tools, and Applications. Cengage Learning Inc. • 2009. eBook. Contains articles in topic areas such as e-commerce technologies, online marketing, social networking, and virtual business communities.

Emergent Strategies for E-Business Processes, Services and Implications: Advancing Corporate Frameworks. Cengage Learning Inc. • A collection of original, in-depth, and innovative research articles on e-business concepts, models, processes, services, and applications.

Entrepreneurship and Innovations in E-Business: An Integrative Perspective. Cengage Learning Inc. • 2006. eBook. Published by Information Science Reference. Develops and explores theoretical constructs and the working concepts of e-entrepreneurship and e-innovation through comprehensive and collective studies conducted by a number of researchers and practitioners with e-business and management expertise.

Ethical Issues in E-Business: Models and Frameworks. Cengage Learning Inc. • 2012. eBook. Published by IGI Global. Offers a diverse and global perspective concerning the ethical consequences of e-business transactions, e-commerce applications, and technological advancements in secure online use.

Gale E-Commerce Sourcebook. Cengage Learning Inc. • $532 Individuals hardcover. Covers over 4,700 organizations, associations, and agencies related to e-commerce such as Web site designers, government regulatory agencies, publications, and trade shows. Also covers 250 leading e-commerce companies worldwide.

Global Electronic Business Research: Opportunities and Directions. Cengage Learning Inc. • 2006. eBook. Published by Information Science Reference. Encourages researchers and professionals interested in SMEs (small to medium-sized enterprises) and e-commerce to address the next phase in this field. This book points to some of the impending issues concerning e-commerce in SMEs, and highlights the need to do something in order to bridge the existing divide between the two. Global Electronic Business Research raises the importance of addressing the e-commerce phenomenon in SMEs at a global level.

Handbook of Research on E-Business Standards and Protocols: Documents, Data and Advanced Web Technologies. Cengage Learning Inc. • 2012. eBook. Published by IGI Global. Contains an overview of new achievements in the field of e-business standards and protocols, offers in-depth analysis of and research on the development and deployment of cutting-edge applications, and provides insight into future trends.

Semantic Web for Business: Cases and Applications. Cengage Learning Inc. • 2009. eBook. Published by Information Science Reference. Presents cases that illustrate the benefits of semantic seb technologies as applied to e-business and e-commerce scenarios. Covers topics such as business integration, organizational knowledge management, and semantic web services.

Semantic Web Technologies and E-Business: Toward the Integrated Virtual Organization and Business Process Automation. Cengage Learning Inc. • 2007. eBook. Published by Information Science Reference. Presents research related to the application of semantic Web technologies, including semantic service-oriented architecture, semantic content management, and semantic knowledge sharing in e-business processes.

Social Implications and Challenges of E-Business. Cengage Learning Inc. • 2007. eBook. Published by Information Science Reference. Explores the profound social implications and challenges of e-business, investigates how the rapid development of the Internet and e-business shapes, and is shaped, by various social forces; and highlights the enormous difficulties and challenges involved in applying e-business technologies and principles in public services and other non-business activities.

ENCYCLOPEDIAS AND DICTIONARIES

Encyclopedia of E-Commerce, E-Government and Mobile Commerce. Cengage Learning Inc. • 2 volumes. Includes contributions highlighting current concepts, trends, challenges, applications, and dot.com experiences in the field of e-commerce, e-government, and mobile commerce.

Gale Encyclopedia of E-Commerce. Cengage Learning Inc. • $507 Individuals print. Contains about 470 entries covering Web site development, e-commerce financing, advertising, marketing, legal issues, and other topics related to doing business through the Internet. Includes a bibliography.

GENERAL WORKS

Aston Centre for e-Business Research Conference papers. Aston University Aston Centre for e-Business Research.

Aston Centre for e-Business Research Journal articles. Aston University Aston Centre for e-Business Research.

Aston Centre for e-Business Research Research reports. Aston University Aston Centre for e-Business Research.

INTERNET DATABASES

Business 2.0 Web Guide to the Best Business Links. Business 2.0 Media Inc. Phone: (415)293-4800; Email: support@business2.com • URL: http://www.business2.com/webguide • Web site presents an extensive, searchable directory of links to "the best, most informative, and authoritative web pages." Twenty main categories cover business, finance, career, company information, people, and technology topics, with thousands of subtopics, all linking to Web sites recommended by experienced business researchers. Fees: Free.

Ebusiness Forum: Global Business Intelligence for the Digital Age. Economist Intelligence Unit (EIU), Economist Group. Phone: 800-938-4685 or (212)554-0600; Fax: (212)586-0248; Email: newyork@eiu.com • URL: http://www.ebusinessforum.com • Web site provides information relating to multinational business, with an emphasis on activities in specific countries. Includes rankings of countries for "e-business readiness," additional data on the political, economic, and business environment in 180 nations ("Doing Business in" and "Today's News Analysis.") Fees: Free, but registration is required for access to all content. Daily updates.

Factiva. Dow Jones Reuters Business Interactive, LLC. Phone: 800-369-7466 or (609)452-1511; Fax: (609)520-5770; Email: solutions@factiva.com • URL: http://www.factiva.com • Fee-based Web site provides "global news and business information through Web sites and content integration solutions." Includes Dow Jones and Reuters newswires, The Wall Street Journal, and more than 7,000 other sources of current news, historical articles, market research reports, and investment analysis. Content includes 96 major U. S. newspapers, 900 non-English sources, trade publications, media transcripts, country profiles, news photos, etc.

InfoTech Trends. Data Analysis Group. Phone: (925)462-1202; Fax: (925)462-1225; Email: support@infotechtrends.com • URL: http://www.infotechtrends.com • Web site provides both free and fee-based market research data on the information technology industry, including computers, peripherals, telecommunications, the Internet, software, CD-ROM/DVD, e-commerce, and workstations. Fees: Free for current (most recent year) data; more extensive information has various fee structures. Formerly *Computer Industry Forecasts*.

Nexis.com. Lexis-Nexis Group. Phone: 800-227-4908 or (937)865-6800; Fax: (937)865-6909; Email: webmaster@prod.lexis-nexis.com • URL: http://www.nexis.com • Fee-based Web site offers searching of about 2.8 billion documents in some 30,000 news, business, and legal information sources. Features include a subject directory covering 1,200 topics in 34 categories and a Company Dossier containing information on more than 500,000 public and private companies. Boolean searching is offered.

ONLINE DATABASES

Plunkett's E-Commerce & Internet Business Almanac. Plunkett Research Ltd. • Contains comprehensive information on current trends and developments in electronic commerce and Internet business.

OTHER SOURCES

E-Business, Internet, and Online Transactions. Michael L. Taviss and others. Glasser LegalWorks. • Looseleaf. $225.00, including CD-ROM version. Periodic Supplementation. Covers the legal aspects of online content, marketing, advertising, domain names, software licensing, and other Internet issues. Includes many sample forms. (Emerging Growth Companies Series.).

E-Commerce and Internet Law: Treatise with Forms. Ian C. Ballon. Glasser LegalWorks. • $1,479 Individuals Binder/Looseleaf (Full Set). Periodic supplementation. Analyzes Internet legalities, including litigious matters relating to downloading, streaming, music, video, content aggregation, domain names, chatrooms, and search engines. Includes forms, contracts, checklists, sample pleadings, and an extensive glossary.

PERIODICALS AND NEWSLETTERS

E-Commerce Law and Strategy. ALM Media Properties LLC. • Monthly. $505 print and online. Covers electronic commerce contracts, licensing, copyright, fraud, taxation, etc. (A Law Journal Newsletter, formerly published by Leader Publications).

E-Commerce Tax Alert. Wolters Kluwer Law & Business CCH. • Description: Print and online newsletter covering e-commerce taxation issues, including compliance and sourcing, e-cash implications, the Internet tax debate, and other topics.

Electronic Commerce World. SourceMedia Inc. • Monthly. $45.00 per year. Provides practical information on the application of electronic commerce technology. Also covers such items as taxation of e-business, cash management, copyright, and legal issues.

Internet Retailer: E-Business Strategies. Thomson Financial Inc. • 10 times a year. $98.00 per year. Trade journal on the selling of retail merchandise through the Internet. Provides information on pricing, payment systems, order management, fraud, digital imaging, advertising, Web trends, and other topics.

Journal of Internet Commerce. Taylor & Francis Ltd. • Quarterly. $115 Individuals print and online. Presents scholarly articles on marketing and other aspects of electronic commerce.

Journal of Website Promotion: Innovations in Internet Business Research, Theory, and Practice. The Haworth Press Inc. • Semiannual. $250.00 per year to libraries; $45.00 per year to individuals. Presents a scholarly view of such items as spam, banner ads, pop-ups, click rates, and the use of search engines for advertising.

WebFinance. SourceMedia Inc. • Semimonthly. $995.00 per year. Newsletter (also available online at www.webfinance.net). Covers the Internet-based provision of online financial services by banks, online brokers, mutual funds, and insurance companies. Provides news stories, analysis, and descriptions of useful resources.

RESEARCH CENTERS AND INSTITUTES

Columbia University - Columbia Center for Excellence in E-Business. Corporate & Foundation Relations, Columbia Business School, 33 W 60th St., 7th Fl., New York, NY 10023-7905. Phone: (212)854-3427; Fax: (212)678-0825; Email: ejj3@columbia.edu • URL: http://www4.gsb.columbia.edu/cebiz • Business, information technology, and e-commerce.

TRADE/PROFESSIONAL ASSOCIATIONS

Association for Enterprise Information. 2111 Wilson Blvd., Ste. 400, Arlington, VA 22201. Phone: (703)247-9474 or (703)247-2597; Fax: (703)522-3192; Email: dchesebrough@afei.org • URL: http://www.afei.org/Pages/default.aspx • Strives to advance enterprise integration and electronic business practices for industries and governments.

Collision Industry Electronic Commerce Association. 3149 Dundee Rd., No. 181, Northbrook, IL 60062-2402. Phone: (847)498-6945; Fax: (847)897-2094 • URL: http://cieca.com • Aims to facilitate electronic commerce within the collision industry. Works to provide a forum and methods to develop and maintain objective and uniform electronic commerce standards and guidelines. Encourages and supports open competition and free choice for the mutual benefit of all parties.

ELECTRONIC FUNDS TRANSFER SYSTEMS (EFTS)

See also BANK AUTOMATION; BANKS AND BANKING

PERIODICALS AND NEWSLETTERS

Item Processing Report. Access Intelligence L.L.C. • Description: Monitors developments in the processing of remittances and checks, including image processing, optical character recognition, check truncation, hardware, and software. **Remarks:** Absorbed The Powell Report, 1992.

U.S. Banker. SourceMedia Inc. • Monthly. $65.00 per year. Edited for bank executives and managers. Covers a wide variety of banking and financial topics.

ELECTRONIC IMAGING

See COMPUTER IMAGING

ELECTRONIC MAIL

See COMPUTER COMMUNICATIONS

ELECTRONIC OPTICS

See OPTOELECTRONICS

ELECTRONIC PUBLISHING

See also MULTIMEDIA

ABSTRACTS AND INDEXES

Computer Science Index. EBSCO Publishing Inc. • Quarterly. $245 per year. Contains brief abstracts of book and periodical literature covering all phases of computing, including approximately 70 specific application areas.

F & S Index: United States. Cengage Learning Inc. • $2,659 Individuals. Monthly. $2,532.00 per year, including quarterly and annual cumulations. Provides annotated citations to marketing, business, financial, and industrial literature. Coverage of U.S. business activity includes trade journals, financial magazines, business newspapers, and special reports.

Internet and Personal Computing Abstracts (print edition). EBSCO Publishing Inc. • Quarterly. $269.00 per year, including cumulative index. Provides more than 10,000 abstracts annually from both trade and academic publications. Covers computer hardware, software, product reviews, Web topics, e-commerce, networks, corporate news, security, and related topics. Formerly *Microcomputer Abstracts.*

Key Abstracts: Business Automation. Institution of Engineering and Technology. • Monthly. $1,138. Provides international coverage of journal and proceedings literature.

E-BOOKS

Impact of Electronic Publishing: The Future for Libraries and Publishers. David J. Brown. Cengage Learning Inc. • 2009.Published by K.G. Saur. Explains how libraries and publishers navigate significant expansion in electronic publishing. Inquire for pricing.

INTERNET DATABASES

InfoTech Trends. Data Analysis Group. Phone: (925)462-1202; Fax: (925)462-1225; Email: support@infotechtrends.com • URL: http://www.infotechtrends.com • Web site provides both free and fee-based market research data on the information technology industry, including computers, peripherals, telecommunications, the Internet, software, CD-ROM/DVD, e-commerce, and workstations. Fees: Free for current (most recent year) data; more extensive information has various fee structures. Formerly *Computer Industry Forecasts.*

Wired News. Lycos Inc. 400-2 Totten Pond Rd., Waltham, MA 02451-2053. Phone: (781)370-2700 or (415)276-8400; Fax: (781)370-2600 or (415)276-8500; Email: press@lycos.com • URL: http://www.lycos.com • Provides summaries and full-text of "Top Stories" relating to the Internet, computers, multimedia, telecommunications, and the electronic information industry in general. These news stories are placed in the broad categories of Politics, Business, Culture, and Technology. Affiliated with *Wired* magazine. Fees: Free.

ONLINE DATABASES

Computer Database. Cengage Learning Inc. • Provides one year of full-text online for 150 leading computer-related publications. Also includes 70,000 product specifications and brief profiles of 13,000 computer product vendors and manufacturers. Inquire as to prices and availability.

PERIODICALS AND NEWSLETTERS

Advanced Imaging: Solutions for the Electronic Imaging Professional. Cygnus Business Media. • Monthly. $60.00 per year Covers document-based imaging technologies, products, systems, and services. Coverage is also devoted to multimedia and electronic printing and publishing.

Digital Imaging: The Magazine for the Imaging Professional. Cygnus Business Media Inc. • Bimonthly. $24.95 per year. Edited for business and professional users of electronic publishing products and services. Topics covered include document imaging, CD-ROM publishing, digital video, and multimedia services. Formerly *Micro Publishing News.*

EContent: Digital Content Strategies and Resources. Online Inc. • Monthly. $110.00 per year. Emphasis is on the business management and financial aspects of the digital content industry. (Formerly published by Online, Inc.).

Educational Marketer: The Educational Publishing Industry's Voice of Authority Since 1968. SIMBA Information Inc. • Biweekly. $695 Individuals Online download. Edited for suppliers of educational materials to schools and colleges at all levels. Covers print and electronic publishing, software, audiovisual items, and multimedia. Includes corporate news and educational statistics.

Electronic Information Report: Empowering Industry Decision Makers Since 1979. SIMBA Information Inc. • 46 times a year. $649.00 per year. Newsletter. Provides business and financial news and trends for online services, electronic publishing, storage media, multimedia, and voice services. Includes information on relevant IPOs (initial public offerings) and mergers. Formerly *Electronic Information Week.*

Electronic Publishing: For the Business Leaders Who Buy Technology. PennWell Corp., Advanced Technology Div. • Monthly. Free to qualified personnel; others, 55.00 per year. Edited for digital publishing professionals. New products are featured.

eMedia: The Digital Studio Magazine. Online Inc. • Monthly. $98.00 per year. Covers video production equipment, digital video editing, electronic publishing, digital content streaming, encoding, and other topics related to digital content creation and multimedia. (Formerly published by Online, Inc.).

Interactive Content: Consumer Media Strategies Monthly. Jupitermedia Corp. • Monthly. $675.00 per year; with online edition, $775.00 per year. Newsletter. Covers the broad field of providing content (information, news, entertainment) for the Internet/World Wide Web.

The Magazine for Electronic Publishing Professionals. Publish Media. • Monthly. $39.90 per year. Edited for professional publishers, graphic designers, and industry service providers. Covers new products and emerging technologies for the electronic publishing industry.

RESEARCH CENTERS AND INSTITUTES

International Data Corp. 5 Speen St., Ste. 1, Framingham, MA 01701-4674. Phone: 800-343-4935 or (508)872-8200; Fax: (508)935-4015 or (508)935-4271; Email: idcinfo@idc.com • URL: http://www.idc.com • Private research firm specializing in market research related to computers, multimedia, and telecommunications.

Massachusetts Institute of Technology - The Media Laboratory. Bldg. E15, 77 Massachusetts Ave., Cambridge, MA 02139-4307. Phone: (617)253-5960; Fax: (617)258-6264; Email: walter@media.mit.edu • URL: http://www.media.mit.edu • Research areas include electronic publishing, spatial imaging, human-machine interface, computer vision, and advanced television.

Rochester Institute of Technology - Center for Integrated Manufacturing Studies. Louise M. Slaughter Hall, Bldg. 78, 111 Lomb Memorial Dr., Rochester, NY 14623-5608. Phone: (585)475-5385 or (585)475-5101; Fax: (585)475-5250; Email: info@sustainability.rit.edu • URL: http://www.rit.edu/gis/research-centers/cims • Research areas include electronics, imaging, printing, and publishing.

TRADE/PROFESSIONAL ASSOCIATIONS

Digital Screenmedia Association. 13100 Eastpoint Park Blvd., Louisville, KY 40223. Phone: (502)489-3915 or (502)241-7545; Fax: (502)241-2795 • URL: http://www.digitalscreenmedia.org • Promotes the interests and serves the needs of companies engaged in the self-service and kiosk industry. Encourages its members to exercise effective and ethical business practices. Fosters the growth and health of the self-service and kiosk industry.

ELECTRONIC SECURITY SYSTEMS

See also INDUSTRIAL SECURITY PROGRAMS

DIRECTORIES

Alarm Systems Directory. InfoGroup Inc. • Annual. Number of listings: 11,847. Entries include: Name, address, phone, size of advertisement, name of owner or manager, number of employees, year first in "Yellow Pages." Compiled from telephone company "Yellow Pages," nationwide.

Directory of South Korean Manufacturers & Exporters of Safety & Security Equipment & Supplies. EXIM Infotek Private Ltd. • Covers: 40 South Korean manufacturers and exporters of alarms, intruder detection systems, protection and life saving equipment, signaling and alarm equipment, video doorphones, and video security systems. Entries include: Company name, postal address, telephone, fax, e-mail, website, contact person, designation, and product details.

Security Systems Directory. InfoGroup Inc. • Annual. Number of listings: 2,295. Entries include: Name, address, phone, size of advertisement, name of owner or manager, number of employees, year first in "Yellow Pages." Compiled from telephone company "Yellow Pages," nationwide.

PERIODICALS AND NEWSLETTERS

CSO: The Resource for Security Executives. CXO Media Inc. • 10/year. $70 U.S. and Canada. Edited for corporate chief security officers (CSOs). Covers a wide variety of business security issues, including computer security, identity theft, spam, physical security, loss prevention, risk management, privacy, and investigations.

9-1-1 Magazine: Public Safety Communications and Response. Official Publications Inc. • Bimonthly. $29.95 per year. Covers technical information and applications for public safety communications personnel.

Security Distributing and Marketing. BNP Media. • 13 times a year. Covers applications, merchandising, new technology and management.

Security Management. ASIS International. • Monthly. $60 Nonmembers print and online. Included in membership. Articles cover the protection of corporate assets, including personnel property and information security.

Security Systems Administration. Cygnus Business Media Inc. • Monthly. $10.00 per year.

Security: The Magazine for Buyers of Security Products, Systems and Service. BNP Media. • Monthly. Security industry news and trends.

TRADE/PROFESSIONAL ASSOCIATIONS

ASIS International. 1625 Prince St., Alexandria, VA 22314. Phone: (703)519-6200; Fax: (703)519-6299; Email: asis@asisonline.org • URL: http://www.asisonline.org/Pages/default.aspx • ASIS is the world's largest organization dedicated to security professionals. Presents seminars and exhibits and offers a variety of educational programs on security issues in a number of fields including communications.

Automatic Fire Alarm Association. 82 Mill St., Ste. 300, Gahanna, OH 43230. Phone: 844-438-2322 or (614)416-8076; Fax: (614)453-8744; Email: firealarm@afaa.org • URL: http://www.afaa.org • Represents automatic fire detection and fire alarm systems industry. Membership is made up of state and regional member associations, manufacturers, installing distributors, authorities having jurisdiction, and end users. Promotes Life Safety in America through involvement in the codes and standards making process and by providing training seminars on a national basis.

Central Station Alarm Association. 8150 Leesburg Pike, Ste. 700, Vienna, VA 22182-2721. Phone: (703)242-4670; Fax: (703)242-4675; Email: techadmin@csaaintl.org • URL: http://csaaintl.org • Individuals, firms, associations, and burglar and fire alarm corporations engaged primarily in the operation of central station burglar and fire alarm businesses. Aims to foster and improve the relationship between sellers, users, bureaus, and other agencies for the advancement of the central station electrical protection services industry.

Electronic Security Association. 6333 N State Hwy. 161, Ste. 350, Irving, TX 75038-2228. Phone: 888-447-1689 or (972)807-6800 or (214)260-5970; Fax: (972)807-6883 or (214)260-5979; Email: staff@alarm.org • URL: http://www.esaweb.org • Formerly National Burglar and Fire Alarm Association.

ELECTRONICS, AVIATION

See AVIONICS

ELECTRONICS, CONSUMER

See CONSUMER ECONOMICS

ELECTRONICS INDUSTRY

See also AVIONICS; ELECTRICAL ENGINEERING; MEDICAL ELECTRONICS; OPTOELECTRONICS; RADIO EQUIPMENT INDUSTRY; SEMICONDUCTOR INDUSTRY; TELEVISION APPARATUS INDUSTRY

ABSTRACTS AND INDEXES

Applied Science and Technology Index. EBSCO Publishing Inc. • 11/year. Indexes a wide variety of English language technical, industrial, and engineering periodicals.

Electronics and Communications Abstracts Journal: Comprehensive Coverage of Essential Scientific Literature. CSA. • Monthly. $1,665.00 per year. Includes print and online editions.

Key Abstracts: Computing in Electronics and Power. Institution of Engineering and Technology. • Bimonthly. $1,138. Provides international coverage of journal and proceedings literature.

Key Abstracts: Electronic Circuits. Institution of Engineering and Technology. • Monthly. $1,138. Provides international coverage of journal and proceedings literature.

Key Abstracts: Electronic Instrumentation. The Insititution of Engineering and Technology. • Monthly. $1,138. Provides international coverage of journal and proceedings literature. Published in England by the Institution of Electrical Engineers (IEE).

NTIS Alerts: Electrotechnology. U.S. Department of Commerce National Technical Information Service. • Biweekly. $130 per year. Covers electronic components, semiconductors, antennas, circuits, optoelectronic devices, and related subjects.

Solid State and Superconductivity Abstracts. Cambridge Scientific Abstracts L.P. • Monthly. Covers chemistry, physics, metallurgy, resonance, materials, measurement, and superconductivity theories, applications, and problem areas. Formerly *Solid State Abstracts Journal*.

DIRECTORIES

BTA Membership Directory. Business Technology Association. • Annual. $125 for members. Publication includes: List of 3,000 retailers and 500 manufacturers of typewriters, calculators, word processors, computers, dictation equipment, copying machines, mailing equipment, network equipment, and other office machines. Entries include: Company name, address, phone, fax, e-mail, website, names of executives; dealer listings include codes showing products handled.

Directory of American Manufacturers & Exporters of Electronic Equipment. EXIM Infotek Private Ltd. • $250 Individuals. Covers: 90 American manufacturers and exporters of semiconductor materials, semiconductor processing equipment, and semiconductors. Entries include: Company name, postal address, telephone, fax, e-mail, website, contact person, designation, and product details.

Directory of Chinese Manufacturers & Exporters of Electronic Equipment & Supplies. EXIM Infotek Private Ltd. • Covers: 90 Chinese manufacturers and exporters of electronic devices, electronic equipment, electronic instrument, oscilloscope, and television transmission equipment. Entries include: Company name, postal address, telephone, fax, e-mail, website, contact person, designation, and product details.

Directory of Japanese Manufacturers & Exporters of Electronic Equipment & Supplies. EXIM Infotek Private Ltd. • Covers: 20 Japanese manufacturers and exporters of electronic devices, electronic equipment, electronic instrument, and semiconductor equipment. Entries include: Company name, postal address, telephone, fax, e-mail, website, contact person, designation, and product details.

Directory of Taiwanese Manufacturers & Exporters of Sporting Goods. EXIM Infotek Private Ltd. • $1,200 Individuals. Covers: 830 Taiwanese manufacturers and exporters of athletic sports equipment, ball sports equipment, billiard equipment, billiard table sets and cues, camping equipment, camping goods, fishing tackle, golf carts and vans, golf club and badminton shafts, golf putter, gymnasium and exercise equipment, martial arts, sports equipment, water sports equipment, and winter and mountaineering sports equipment. Entries include: Company name, postal address, telephone, fax, e-mail, website, contact person, designation, and product details.

The Electronic Industry Sector in Switzerland. AT Zeitschriftenverlag. • Covers: Computer and electronics companies and products in Switzerland and Liechtenstein. Entries include: Company name, address, phone, product description.

Electronics: Industry Sector Profile. Philippine-German Export Development Project Philippine Bureau of Export Trade Promotion. • Publication includes: Companies exporting electronics from the Philippines. Entries include: Company name, address, phone, fax, name and title of contact, type of business, year established, subsidiary and branch names and locations, financial data, number of employees, government registrations, professional memberships, bank references, supply capability, export experience, business plan. Principal content of publication is an overview of the business environment and electronics industry in the Philippines.

Japan Electronics Buyers' Guide. Dempa Publications Inc. • Annual. $220. Covers: manufacturers of electronic equipment and components in Japan, and import-export firms and agents dealing in those products. Entries include: For manufacturers and traders--Company name, address, phone, fax, branches, names and titles of president and key sales executives, establishment, capital, sales, number of employees, products, trade names, percentage of sales in export, main factory. For agents--Company name, address, phone, companies represented.

Signal Magazine--AFCEA Source Book Issue. • Annual. Publication includes: List of member companies concerned with communications, design, production, maintenance and operation of communications, electronics, command and control, computers, intelligence systems and imagery. Entries include: Company name, address, phone, names and titles of key personnel, financial keys, trade and brand names, products or services, affiliations, description of organizational purpose, objectives.

Singapore Electronics Industry Directory. Marshall Cavendish Business Information Private Ltd. • $50 Individuals local. Covers: information on electronics manufacturers, traders, distributors, suppliers, and international purchasing offices. Entries include: corporate profiles, company listings and contacts.

Singapore Electronics Trade Directory. International Enterprise Singapore. • Annual. $140 Individuals Print and CD. Covers: Information and contacts of numerous manufacturers, traders, and other supporting service providers in the electronics industry.

FINANCIAL RATIOS

Annual Statement Studies. Risk Management Association. • Annual. Compiled from over 280,000 financial statements.

Annual Statement Studies: Industry Default Probabilities and Cash Flow Measures. Risk Management Association. • Annual. $405 Nonmembers. Serves as a companion volume to the original *Annual Statement Studies*. Gives probability of default estimates on a percentage scale for more than 450 industries. Includes changes in position year-by-year for eight financial statement line items and provides percentage measures of cash flow.

INTERNET DATABASES

Manufacturing Profiles. U. S. Bureau of the Census. Phone: (301)763-4636 or (301)763-4100; Fax: (301)763-4794; Email: webmaster@census.gov • URL: http://www.census.gov/prod/www/abs/mfg-prof.html • The Census Bureau makes available free on PDF (Portable Document Format) an annual consolidation of the entire Current Industrial Report series, presenting "all the data compiled." Contains statistics on production, shipments, inventories, consumption, exports, imports, and orders for a wide variety of manufactured products.

ONLINE DATABASES

INSPEC. Institution of Electrical Engineers. • Provides online citations, with abstracts, to the world literature of electrical engineering, electronics, optoelectronics, telecommunications, industrial controls, instrumentation, computer technology, information technology, and physics. Coverage includes more than 4,000 technical and scientific journals from 1969 to date, with weekly updating. (INSPEC is Information Services in Physics, Electronics, and Computing.) Inquire as to online cost and availability.

PERIODICALS AND NEWSLETTERS

Electronic Business: The Management Magazine for the Electronics Industry. Reed Elsevier Group plc Reed Business Information. • Monthly. $100.99 per year. For the non-technical manager and executive in the electronics industry. Offers news, trends, figures and forecasts. Formerly *Electronic Business Today*.

Electronic Design. Penton Media Inc. • Biweekly. Free to qualified personnel; others, $100.00 per year. Provides technical information for U.S. design engineers and managers.

Electronic News. Reed Elsevier Group plc Reed Business Information. • 51 times a year. $119.00 per year. Serves the electronic OEM industry.

Electronic Products: The Engineer's Magazine of Product Technology. Hearst Business Communications, UTP Div. • Monthly. $65.00 per year.

MEEN Diagnostic and Invasive Technology. Reilly Communications Group. • $90 Canada and Mexico. Bimonthly. Free to qualified personnel. Provides medical electronics industry news and new product information. Formerly *Medical Electronics and Equipment News*.

RESEARCH CENTERS AND INSTITUTES

Curtin University of Technology - Communication Economics and Electronic Markets Research Centre. Department of Economics, Perth, WA 6845, Australia. Phone: 61 8 92662391; Fax: 61 8 92669460; Email: g.madden@curtin.edu.au • URL: http://business.curtin.edu.au/research/centres_institutions/research_centres/ceem • Communications economics and electronic markets, focusing on legal, sociological, technical and policy aspects of current debate.

Massachusetts Institute of Technology - Research Laboratory of Electronics. 77 Massachusetts Ave., Rm. 36-413, Cambridge, MA 02139-4307. Phone: (617)253-2519; Fax: (617)253-1301; Email: hq@rle.mit.edu • URL: http://www.rle.mit.edu/ • Research areas include heat transfer and cryogenics.

STATISTICS SOURCES

Semiconductors, Printed Circuit Boards, and Other Electronic Components. U. S. Bureau of the Census. • Annual. Provides data on shipments: value, quantity, imports, and exports. (Current Industrial Reports, MA-36Q.).

Standard & Poor's Industry Surveys. Standard & Poor's Financial Services L.L.C. • Semiannual. $1,800.00. Two looseleaf volumes. Includes monthly *Supplements*. Provides detailed, individual surveys of 52 major industry groups. Each survey is revised on a semiannual basis. Also includes "Monthly Investment Review" (industry group investment analysis) and monthly "Trends & Projections" (economic analysis).

U.S. Industry and Trade Outlook. U.S. Department of Commerce National Technical Information Service. • Annual. Produced by the International Trade Administration, U.S. Department of Commerce, in a "public-private" partnership with DRI/McGraw-Hill and Standard & Poor's. Provides basic data, outlook for the current year, and "Long-Term Prospects" (five-year projections) for a wide variety of products and services. Includes high technology industries. Formerly *U.S. Industrial Outlook*.

TRADE/PROFESSIONAL ASSOCIATIONS

ASM International. 9639 Kinsman Rd., Materials Park, OH 44073-0002. Phone: 800-336-5152 or (440)338-5151; Email: memberservicecenter@asminternational.org • URL: http://www.asminternational.org • Metallurgists, materials engineers, executives in materials producing and consuming industries; teachers and students. Disseminates technical information about the manufacture, use, and treatment of engineered materials. Offers in-plant, home study, and intensive courses through Materials Engineering Institute.

Electronic Components Industry Association. 1111 Alderman Dr., Ste. 400, Alpharetta, GA 30005. Phone: (678)393-9990; Fax: (678)393-9998 • URL: http://www.eciaonline.org • Represents authorized distributors and manufacturers of electronic components. Conducts research. Compiles statistical reports and surveys.

Electronic Industry Citizenship Coalition. 1155 15th St. NW, Ste. 500, Washington, DC 20005. Email: info@eicc.info • URL: http://www.eicc.info • Represents global ICT companies and their suppliers. Aims to promote a common code of conduct for the electronics, information and communications technology (ICT) industry. Works to improve environmental and worker conditions.

Electronics TakeBack Coalition. 4200 Park Blvd. No. 228, Oakland, CA 94602-1312. Phone: (510)614-0110; Email: info@etakeback.org • URL: http://www.electronicstakeback.com • Promotes green design and responsible recycling in the electronics industry. Aims to protect the health and well being of electronics users, workers, and the communities where electronics are produced and discarded. Encourages electronics manufacturers to offer programs to take back and recycle old electronics.

ELECTRONICS, MEDICAL

See MEDICAL ELECTRONICS

ELECTROPLATING

See METAL FINISHING

ELEVATORS

See also BUILDING INDUSTRY

PERIODICALS AND NEWSLETTERS

Commercial Building: Tranforming Plans into Buildings. Stamats Communications Inc. • Bimonthly. $48.00 per year. Edited for building contractors, engineers, and architects. Includes special features on new products, climate control, plumbing, and vertical transportation.

Elevator World. Elevator World. • Monthly. $75 U.S. Print - 1 year. Publishes latest news, newest innovations, imperative safety issues, current code requirements, events coverage and accessibility, legal and maintenance issues.

TRADE/PROFESSIONAL ASSOCIATIONS

ASME International. 2 Park Ave., New York, NY 10016-5990. Phone: 800-843-2763 or (973)882-1170; Fax: (973)882-1717; Email: customercare@asme.org • URL: http://www.asme.org • Technical society of mechanical engineers and students. Conducts research; develops boiler, pressure vessel, and power test codes. Develops safety codes and standards for equipment. Conducts short course programs, and Identifying Research Needs Program. Maintains 19 research committees and 38 divisions.

National Association of Elevator Contractors. 1298 Wellbrook Cir., Conyers, GA 30012. Phone: 800-900-6232 or (770)760-9660; Fax: (770)760-9714; Email: info@naec.org • URL: http://www.naec.org • Contractors who install and service elevators and lift equipment; suppliers of complete elevators and components.

National Elevator Industry. 1677 County, Rte. 64, Salem, NY 12865-0838. Phone: (518)854-3100; Fax: (518)854-3257; Email: info@neii.org • URL: http://www.neii.org • Serves as a trade association of the building transportation industry. Promotes safe building transportation for new and existing products and technologies, and adoption of the current codes by local government agencies.

EMBASSIES

See DIPLOMATIC AND CONSULAR SERVICE

EMBEZZLEMENT

See FRAUD AND EMBEZZLEMENT

EMERGING MARKETS

See DEVELOPING AREAS

EMIGRATION

See IMMIGRATION AND EMIGRATION

EMPLOYEE BENEFIT PLANS

See also FRINGE BENEFITS; PENSIONS; PROFIT SHARING

ABSTRACTS AND INDEXES

Business Periodicals Index Retrospective. EBSCO Publishing Inc. • 11/year. Quarterly and annual cumulations.

Insurance Periodicals Index. Specials Libraries Association, Insurance and Employees Benefits Div. NILS Publishing Co. • Annual. $250.00. Compiled by the Insurance and Employee Benefits Div., Special Libraries Association. A yearly index of over 15,000 articles from about 35 insurance periodicals. Arrangement is by subject, with an index to authors.

BIBLIOGRAPHIES

Insurance and Employee Benefits Literature. Special Libraries Association. • Bimonthly. $15.00 per year. Lists a wide variety of literature in all branches of the insurance industry. Includes annotations.

DIRECTORIES

EBN Benefits Sourcebook. SourceMedia Inc. • Annual. $36.95. Lists vendors of products and services for the employee benefits industry. Includes industry trends and statistics.

HANDBOOKS AND MANUALS

Accountant's Business Manual. American Institute of Certified Public Accountants. • $198.75. Looseleaf. Two volumes. Semiannual updates. Covers a wide variety of topics relating to financial and accounting management, including types of ownership, business planning, financing, cash management, valuation, retirement plans, estate planning, workers' compensation, unemployment insurance, social security, and employee benefits management.

Medicare: Employer Health Plans. Consumer Information Center. • Free. Published by the U. S. Department of Health and Human Services. Explains the special rules that apply to Medicare beneficiaries who have employer group health plan coverage. (Publication No. 520-Y.).

Money Manager's Compliance Guide. Thompson Publishing Group Inc. • $739.00 per year. Two looseleaf volumes. Monthly updates and newletters. Edited for investment advisers and investment companies to help them be in compliance with governmental regulations, including SEC rules, restrictions based on the Employee Retirement Income Security Act (ERISA), and regulations issued by the Commodity Futures Trading Commission (CFTC).

U.S. Master Employee Benefits Guide. Wolters Kluwer Law & Business CCH. • Annual. $102.50 Individuals. Explains federal tax and labor laws relating to health care benefits, disability benefits, workers' compensation, employee assistance plans, etc.

ONLINE DATABASES

Accounting and Tax Database. ProQuest L.L.C. • Provides indexing and abstracting of the literature of accounting, taxation, and financial management, 1971 to date. Updating is weekly. Especially covers accounting, auditing, banking, bankruptcy, employee compensation and benefits, cash management, financial planning, and credit. Inquire as to online cost and availability.

Employee Benefits Infosource. International Foundation of Employee Benefit Plans. • Provides citations and abstracts to the literature of employee benefits, 1986 to present. Monthly updates. Inquire as to online cost and availability.

Wilson Business Abstracts Online. H.W. Wilson Co. • Indexes and abstracts 600 major business periodicals, plus the *Wall Street Journal* and the business section of the *New York Times*. Indexing is from 1982, abstracting from 1990, with the two newspapers included from 1993. Updated weekly. Inquire as to online cost and availability. (*Business Periodicals Index* without abstracts is also available online.).

OTHER SOURCES

Employee Benefits Law: ERISA and Beyond. ALM Media Properties LLC. • $710 two volumes. Explains the rules and regulations put forth by the Employee Retirement Income Security Act. Three federal agencies are involved: the Internal Revenue Service, the Labor Department, and the Pension Benefit Guaranty Corporation. (Law Journal Press).

Employment Forms and Policies. Matthew Bender and Company Inc. • $150 print and e-book. Periodic supplementation available. Contains more than 300 forms, policies, and checklists for use by small or medium-sized businesses. Covers such topics as employee selection, payroll issues, benefits, performance appraisal, dress codes, and employee termination.

Health Care Benefits Law. ALM Media Properties LLC. • $565. Covers the legal compliance aspects of employer health care plans. Includes checklists and sample forms. (Law Journal Press).

PERIODICALS AND NEWSLETTERS

Business Insurance: News Magazine for Corporate Risk, Employee Benefit and Financial Executives. Crain Communications Inc. • Weekly. $95.00 per year. Covers a wide variety of business insurance topics, including risk management, employee benefits, workers compensation, marine insurance, and casualty insurance.

Compensation and Benefits Update. Thomson RIA. • Monthly. $149.00 per year. Provides information on the latest ideas and developments in the field of employee benefits. In-depth exploration of popular benefits programs. Formerly *Benefits and Compensation Update*.

Contingencies: The Magazine of the Actuarial Profession. American Academy of Actuaries. • Bimonthly. $24 Nonmembers. Provides nontechnical articles on the actuarial aspects of insurance, employee benefits, and pensions.

Employee Benefit News: The News Magazine for Employee Benefit Management. SourceMedia Inc. • Monthly. $94.00 per year. Edited for human relations directors and other managers of employee benefits.

Employee Benefit Plan Review. Charles D. Spencer and Associates, Inc. • $395 Individuals. Monthly. Provides a review of recent events affecting the administration of employee benefit programs.

Employee Benefits Journal. International Foundation of Employee Benefit Plans. • Quarterly. $80.00 per year. Selected articles on timely and important benefit subjects.

Human Resource Executive. LRP Publications Library. • 16 times a year. $89.95 per year. Edited for directors of corporate human resource departments. Special issues emphasize training, benefits, retirement planning, recruitment, outplacement, workers' compensation, legal pitfalls, and oes emphasize training, benefits, retirement planning, recruitment, outplacement, workers' compensation, legal pitfalls, and other personnel topics.

IOMA's Report on Defined Contribution Plan Investing. Institute of Management and Administration. • Semimonthly. $1,189.90 per year. Newsletter. Edited for 401(k) and other defined contribution retirement plan managers, sponsors, and service providers. Reports on such items as investment manager performance, guaranteed investment contract (GIC) yields, and asset allocation trends.

Law Firm Partnership and Benefits Report. ALM Media Properties LLC. • Monthly. $499 per year. Covers personnel issues for law firms, including compensation, partnership agreements, malpractice, employment discrimination, training, health insurance, pension plans, and other matters relating to human resources management. (A Law Journal Newsletter, formerly published by Leader Publications).

Pension Plan Guide. Wolters Kluwer Law & Business CCH. • Weekly. $2,225 Individuals CD-ROM. Loose leaf series on pension plans. Formerly *Pension Plan Guide Summary*.

Risk and Insurance. LRP Publications Library. • Monthly. Price on application. Topics include risk management, workers' compensation, reinsurance, employee benefits, and managed care.

The Successful Benefits Communicator. Lawrence Ragan Communications Inc. • Description: Offers ideas, techniques, and tips for those who communicate benefits information.

STATISTICS SOURCES

Benefits Survey. Paul & Co. • Annual. $99.95. Published by the Society for Human Resource Management (www.shrm.org). Provides five-year data, with discussion, for 200 kinds of employee benefits.

Report on the American Workforce. U. S. Government Printing Office. • Annual. Issued by the U. S. Department of Labor (www.dol.gov). Appendix contains tabular statistics, including employment, unemployment, price indexes, consumer expenditures, employee benefits (retirement, insurance, vacation, etc.), wages, productivity, hours of work, and occupational injuries. Annual figures are shown for up to 50 years.

Social Security Bulletin. Social Security Administration. U. S. Government Printing Office. • Quarterly. $27.00 per year. Annual statistical supplement.

TRADE/PROFESSIONAL ASSOCIATIONS

American Benefits Council. 1501 M St. NW, Ste. 600, Washington, DC 20005-1775. Phone: (202)289-6700; Fax: (202)289-4582; Email: info@abcstaff.org • URL: http://www.americanbenefitscouncil.org • Serves as national trade association for companies concerned about federal legislation and regulations affecting all aspects of the employee benefits system. Represents the entire spectrum of the private employee benefits community and sponsors or administers retirement and health plans covering more than one hundred million Americans.

American Society of Pension Professionals and Actuaries. 4245 N Fairfax Dr., Ste. 750, Arlington, VA 22203. Phone: (703)516-9300; Fax: (703)516-9308; Email: customercare@asppa.org • URL: http://www.asppa.org • Members are involved in the pension and insurance aspects of employee benefits. Includes an Insurance and Risk Management Committee, and sponsors an annual 401(k) Workshop.

Council on Employee Benefits. 1501 M St. NW, Ste. 620, Washington, DC 20005. Phone: (202)861-6025; Fax: (202)861-6027 • URL: http://www.ceb.org • Formerly Council on Employee Benefits Plans.

Employers Council on Flexible Compensation. 1444 I St. NW, Ste. 700, Washington, DC 20005-2210. Phone: (202)659-4300; Fax: (202)216-9646 • URL: http://www.ecfc.org • Promotes flexible or "cafeteria" plans for employee compensation and benefits.

EMPLOYEE COUNSELING

See COUNSELING

EMPLOYEE DISCIPLINE

ABSTRACTS AND INDEXES

Business Periodicals Index Retrospective. EBSCO Publishing Inc. • 11/year. Quarterly and annual cumulations.

ONLINE DATABASES

Wilson Business Abstracts Online. H.W. Wilson Co. • Indexes and abstracts 600 major business periodicals, plus the *Wall Street Journal* and the business section of the *New York Times.* Indexing is from 1982, abstracting from 1990, with the two newspapers included from 1993. Updated weekly. Inquire as to online cost and availability. (*Business Periodicals Index* without abstracts is also available online.).

PERIODICALS AND NEWSLETTERS

HR Briefing. Wolters Kluwer Law and Business. • Monthly. $249.00 per year. Newsletter. Provides HR professionals and other business people with concise, up-to-date information on employment practices and trends, with an emphasis on compliance with federal employment laws.

Labor Relations Bulletin. Aspen Publishers Inc. • Description: Provides information and insight to management and labor officials to help them avoid or resolve conflicts. Recurring features include reports on current developments in labor law and relations, discipline and grievance cases based on actual arbitration, a question and answer column on labor and employment relations, and a column titled Reflections of an Arbitrator, offering the insight and experience of prominent national arbitrators.

EMPLOYEE DISMISSAL

See DISMISSAL OF EMPLOYEES

EMPLOYEE EDUCATION

See TRAINING OF EMPLOYEES

EMPLOYEE EFFICIENCY

See TIME AND MOTION STUDY

EMPLOYEE HEALTH PROGRAMS

See EMPLOYEE WELLNESS PROGRAMS

EMPLOYEE LUNCHROOMS AND CAFETERIAS

See also RESTAURANTS, LUNCHROOMS, ETC.

PERIODICALS AND NEWSLETTERS

Chef. Aktiebolaget Electrolux. • Monthly. $24.00 per year. Edited for executive chefs, food and beverage directors, caterers, banquet and club managers, and others responsible for food buying and food service. Special coverage of regional foods is provided.

EMPLOYEE MAGAZINES

See HOUSE ORGANS

EMPLOYEE MANUALS

See PROCEDURE MANUALS

EMPLOYEE PAMPHLETS

See PAMPHLETS

EMPLOYEE PARTICIPATION

See PARTICIPATIVE MANAGEMENT

EMPLOYEE RATING

See RATING OF EMPLOYEES

EMPLOYEE RELOCATION

See RELOCATION OF EMPLOYEES

EMPLOYEE REPRESENTATION IN MANAGEMENT

PERIODICALS AND NEWSLETTERS

New Horizons. Horticultural Research Institute. • Semiannual. Description: Explores research of the science and art of nursery, retail garden center, and landscape plant production, marketing, and care.

TRADE/PROFESSIONAL ASSOCIATIONS

IdeasAmerica. PO Box 210863, Auburn Hills, MI 48321. Phone: (248)961-2674; Fax: (248)253-9252; Email: ia@ideas-america.org • URL: http://www.ideas-america.org • Represents finance, commerce, industry, and government professionals. Dedicated to the worth, contributions, and benefits of employee suggestion systems and other employee involvement processes. Supports communication between employees and employer for the purpose of exchanging ideas.

EMPLOYEE SELECTION

See RECRUITMENT OF PERSONNEL

EMPLOYEE STOCK OWNERSHIP PLANS

ABSTRACTS AND INDEXES

Business Periodicals Index Retrospective. EBSCO Publishing Inc. • 11/year. Quarterly and annual cumulations.

HANDBOOKS AND MANUALS

U.S. Master Pension Guide. Wolters Kluwer Law & Business CCH. • Annual. $99.95 1 - 4 (quantity). Explains IRS rules and regulations applying to 401(k) plans, 403(k) plans, ESOPs (employee stock ownership plans), IRAs, SEPs (simplified employee pension plans), Keogh plans, and nonqualified plans.

ONLINE DATABASES

Wilson Business Abstracts Online. H.W. Wilson Co. • Indexes and abstracts 600 major business periodicals, plus the *Wall Street Journal* and the business section of the *New York Times.* Indexing is from 1982, abstracting from 1990, with the two newspapers included from 1993. Updated weekly. Inquire as to online cost and availability. (*Business Periodicals Index* without abstracts is also available online.).

OTHER SOURCES

Executive Compensation for Emerging Companies. Daniel Niehans and Shawn E. Lampron. Glasser LegalWorks. • $599 Individuals Binder/Looseleaf (Full set). Periodic Supplementation. Covers various aspects of executive compensation, with emphasis on stock option plans and stock ownership. Includes many annotated legal forms. (Emerging Growth Companies Series.).

Executive Stock Options and Stock Appreciation Rights. ALM Media Properties LLC. • $525. Coverage includes non-qualified stock options and incentive stock options. Contains sample forms and documents. (Law Journal Press).

PERIODICALS AND NEWSLETTERS

ESOP Report. ESOP Association. • Monthly. Contains latest regulatory and case law updates, Capitol Hill briefings, technical and managerial advice from ESOP professionals, tips on winning ESOP companies and employee owners plus Association news to keep you in the loop.

TRADE/PROFESSIONAL ASSOCIATIONS

National Center for Employee Ownership. 1736 Franklin St., 8th Fl., Oakland, CA 94612. Phone: (510)208-1300; Fax: (510)272-9510; Email: customerservice@nceo.org • URL: http://www.nceo.org • Association promotes an increased awareness and understanding of employee ownership of companies.

EMPLOYEE SUGGESTIONS

See SUGGESTION SYSTEMS

EMPLOYEE TRAINING

See TRAINING OF EMPLOYEES

EMPLOYEE WELLNESS PROGRAMS

See also HEALTH CARE INDUSTRY

ABSTRACTS AND INDEXES

Excerpta Medica: Occupational Health and Industrial Medicine. Elsevier. • Monthly. Section 35 of *Excerpta Medica.*

DIRECTORIES

Fitness Management Products and Services Source Guide. Leisure Publications Inc. • Annual. $24.00. A directory of more than 1,250 fitness equipment manufacturers and suppliers of services. Includes a glossary of terms related to the fitness industry and employee wellness programs.

GENERAL WORKS

Principles of Health and Hygiene in the Workplace. Timothy J. Key and Michael A. Mueller. Lewis Publishers. • Date not set. $69.95.

PERIODICALS AND NEWSLETTERS

Fitness Management. Leisure Publications Inc. • Monthly. $24.00 per year. Published for owners and managers of physical fitness centers, both commercial and corporate.

For publishers' addresses, refer to SOURCES CITED section at the back of the book.

Job Safety and Health Quarterly. U. S. Government Printing Office. • Quarterly. $17.00 per year. Issued by the Occupational Safety and Health Administration (OSHA). U. S. Department of Labor. Contains articles on employee safety and health, with information on current OSHA activities.

RESEARCH CENTERS AND INSTITUTES

Health Policy Institute. 1200 Pressler St., Houston, TX 77025. Phone: (713)500-9494; Fax: (713)500-9493; Email: Stephen.H.Linder@uth.tmc.edu • URL: http://sph.uth.edu/research/centers/ihp.

National Wellness Institute. PO Box 827, Stevens Point, WI 54481-0827. Phone: 800-243-8694 or (715)342-2969; Fax: (715)342-2979; Email: nwi@nationalwellness.org • URL: http://www.nationalwellness.org • Aims to provide national leadership in the wellness movement; to assist professionals working in health and wellness promotion in all types of settings, and organizations with planning, development, implementation, and evaluation of wellness programs; and to assist in the development of high quality wellness products and services. Acts as clearinghouse on wellness information. Provides consultations; offers professional development conferences. Sponsors National Wellness Association.

University of Texas—Houston Health Science Center - School of Public Health - Center for Health Promotion and Prevention Research. 7000 Fannin, Ste. 2056D, Houston, TX 77030. Phone: (713)500-9609; Fax: (713)500-9602; Email: susan.tortolero@uth.tmc.edu • URL: http://sph.uth.edu/chppr • Fields of study include worksite health promotion. Formerly Center for Health Promotion Research and Development.

TRADE/PROFESSIONAL ASSOCIATIONS

Alliance for Wellness ROI. 390 Main St., Ste. 400, Worcester, MA 01608. Email: info@roiwellness.org • URL: http://www.roiwellness.org • Promotes corporate wellness programs by demonstrating, through an objective Return on Investment (ROI) measurement, that wellness programs are an investment rather than an expense to a company. Conducts research on corporate wellness programs as well as the costs and the Return on Investment by working with epidemiologists, actuaries, consultants, wellness experts, IT professionals and health management professionals.

EMPLOYEES, TEMPORARY

See TEMPORARY EMPLOYEES

EMPLOYMENT

See also JOB HUNTING; LABOR SUPPLY; OCCUPATIONS; UNEMPLOYMENT

ALMANACS AND YEARBOOKS

World Labour Report. International Labour Office. • Irregular. Price varies. International coverage. Reviews significant recent events and labor policy developments in the following areas: employment, human rights, labor relations, and working conditions.

CD-ROM DATABASES

Business Abstracts with Full Text. EBSCO Publishing Inc. • Includes full text articles from more than 460 business publications from 1982 to present. Indexing for nearly 880 publications.

OECD Statistical Compendium. Organization for Economic Cooperation and Development. • Semiannual. $1,905.00 per year for 1 to 10 users. CD-ROM contains more than 730,000 monthly, quarterly, and annual time series for OECD countries, 1960 to date. Includes fully searchable data on agriculture, food, economic indicators, national accounts, employment, energy, finance, industry, technology, and foreign trade. Results can be displayed in various forms.

Sourcebooks America CD-ROM. CACI Marketing Systems. • Annual. $1,250.00. Provides the CD-ROM version of *The Sourcebook of ZIP Code Demographics: Census Edition* and *The Sourcebook of County Demographics: Census Edition.*

DIRECTORIES

Atlanta Larger Employers. Metro Atlanta Chamber of Commerce. • Biennial. $5 plus $2 shipping. Covers: Approximately 600 companies in the metropolitan Atlanta, Georgia, area that employ 300 or more. Entries include: Company name, address, phone, Standard Industrial Classification (SIC) code.

Bay Area Employer Directory. James R. Albin. • Annual. $99.95. Covers: over 2,000 employers in the San Francisco Bay Area each having 100 or more employees; includes both private and government employers. Entries include: Firm name, address, phone, year established, type of business or activity, number of employees, sales, names and titles of local chief executive and personnel manager.

The Book of Lists. • Annual. $125 Individuals Zip file download. Covers: Leading employers and private companies located in Orange County, California. Entries include: Company name, address, phone, names and titles of key personnel; product/service, financial data, number of employees.

Large Employers of Metro St. Louis. St. Louis Regional Chamber & Growth Association. • Biennial. $50. Covers: 700 business firms employing 200 persons or more in the City of St. Louis, six Missouri counties (Franklin, Jefferson, Lincoln, St. Charles, St. Louis, and Warren), and five Illinois counties (Clinton, Jersey, Madison, Monroe, and St. Clair); includes companies that are not members of the association. Entries include: Company name, address, phone, fax, names of principal executives, Standard Industrial Classification (SIC) code, type of business, year established, number of employees, product or service.

Largest Employers Directory. Greater San Antonio Chamber of Commerce. • Annual. $75 Nonmembers CD/email. Covers: About 1,700 manufacturing and nonmanufacturing firms in the San Antonio metropolitan statistical area; manufacturing firms each have at least 25 employees, nonmanufacturing firms have at least 50 employees. Entries include: Company name, address, phone; names and titles of key personnel, number of employees, year established, description of service, marketing area, and Standard Industrial Classification (SIC) code.

Leading Employers of the New Hampshire & Southern Maine Seacoast. Greater Portsmouth Chamber of Commerce. • Biennial. $10. Covers: Approximately 200 companies in the Portsmouth, New Hampshire area (including part of southern Maine) that employ over 25 people. Entries include: Company name, address, phone, name and title of contact, number of employees, products or services provided.

Major Employers in Metropolitan Chicago. Chicagoland Chamber of Commerce. • Biennial. $55. Covers: over 2,000 firms employing at least 250 employees in their Chicago area plants and offices; also listed are subsidiaries, affiliates, and divisions. Entries include: Company name, address, phone, names of major officers; line of business and Standard Industrial Classification (SIC) code; coding to indicate number of employees and whether manufacturer or non-manufacturer.

National Directory of Personnel Service Firms. National Association of Personnel Services. • Annual. Lists over 1,100 member private (for-profit) employment firms.

Net Jobs. Hoover's Inc. • $12.95. Covers: Internet sites and online sources dealing with employment, including resume writing tips, interviewing advice, and classified listings. Entries include: Name, location/host.

On-Line Job Search Companion. Hoover's Inc. • $14.95. Covers: Online sources of employment opportunities. Database includes: Information on selecting a career path. Entries include: Name, location/host.

Plunkett's Companion to the Almanac of American Employers: Mid-Size Firms. Plunkett Research Ltd. • Annual. $349.99 Individuals Printed Almanac & Online Tools. Covers: Approximately 500 rapidly growing mid-sized firms, defined as between 150 and 2,300 employees. Entries include: Name, address, phone, fax, and key executives.

Utah Major Employers Guide. • Biennial. $50 Individuals for investors. Covers: More than 900 companies in 29 counties in Utah that have 100 or more full-time employees. Entries include: Company name, address, phone, fax, contact names, names and titles of key personnel, year established, type of operation, Standard Industrial Classification (SIC) code, product/service, county, number of full-time employees, website addresses.

E-BOOKS

Social Trends & Indicators USA. Monique D. Magee, editor. Cengage Learning Inc. • Includes data on labor, economics, the health care industry, crime, leisure, population, education, social security, and many other topics. Sources include various government agencies and major publications. Inquire for pricing.

GENERAL WORKS

Careers-In-Business. Careers-In-Business, LLC. • Careers-In-Business contains information on employment in the business sector, primarily in accounting, finance and consulting. Links to many corporations who hire extensively in this area are included for those wishing to make contacts and/or mail out resumes. Detailed information on job search aids and employer profiles provided. Links to many other career sites also available, as well as links to career-related books for sale through Amazon.

HANDBOOKS AND MANUALS

Occupational Outlook Handbook. Bureau of Labor Statistics, U.S. Department of Labor. U. S. Government Printing Office. • Biennial. $22 Individuals. Issued as one of the Bureau's Bulletin series and kept up to date by *Occupational Outlook Quarterly.*

INTERNET DATABASES

Bureau of Economic Analysis. U. S. Department of Commerce, Bureau of Economic Analysis. Phone: (202)606-9900; Fax: (202)606-5310; Email: webmaster@bea.doc.gov • URL: http://www.bea.doc.gov • Web site includes "News Release Information" covering national, regional, and international economic estimates from the BEA. Highlights of releases appear online the same day, complete text and tables appear the next day. "Recent News Releases" section provides titles for past nine months, with links. "BEA Data and Methodology" includes "Frequently Requested NIPA Data" (national income and product accounts, such as gross domestic product and personal income). Other statistics are available. Fees: Free.

Business 2.0 Web Guide to the Best Business Links. Business 2.0 Media Inc. Phone: (415)293-4800; Email: support@business2.com • URL: http://www.business2.com/webguide • Web site presents an extensive, searchable directory of links to "the best, most informative, and authoritative web pages." Twenty main categories cover business, finance, career, company information, people, and technology topics, with thousands of subtopics, all linking to Web sites recommended by experienced business researchers. Fees: Free.

Fedstats. Federal Interagency Council on Statistical Policy. Phone: (202)395-7254 • URL: http://www.fedstats.gov • Web site features an efficient search facility for full-text statistics produced by more than 100 federal agencies, including the Census Bureau, the Bureau of Economic Analysis, and the Bureau of Labor Statistics. Boolean searches can be made within one agency or for all agencies combined. Links are offered to international statistical bureaus, including the UN, IMF, OECD, UNESCO, Eurostat, and 20 individual countries. Fees: Free.

FreeLunch.com. Economy.com, Inc. Phone: (610)696-8700; Fax: (610)696-1678 • URL: http://www.freelunch.com • Web site provides free access to more than 200 million economic and financial data series, covering industry, demographics, labor markets, prices, retail sales, government spending, trade, interest rates, housing starts, the stock market, etc. Data is available in either chart or table form. Searching is offered. Free, but registration required. Economy.com, Inc. also offers fee-based economic analysis at *The Dismal Scientist* site (www.dismal.com).

Summary of Commentary on Current Economic Conditions by Federal Reserve District. Board of Governors of the Federal Reserve System. Phone: (202)452-3000; Fax: (202)452-3819 • URL: http://www.federalreserve.gov/publications.htm • 8/year. Free Web site provides current "anecdotal information" eight times a year on economic conditions within each of the 12 Federal Reserve Districts, plus an extensive national *Summary*. Text is based on the opinions of bank officials, business executives, economists, financial market experts, and others. Typically contains views of consumer spending, manufacturing, services, credit, employment, prices, wages, and the economy in general. Usually referred to as the Beige Book.

ONLINE DATABASES

Wilson Business Abstracts Online. H.W. Wilson Co. • Indexes and abstracts 600 major business periodicals, plus the *Wall Street Journal* and the business section of the *New York Times*. Indexing is from 1982, abstracting from 1990, with the two newspapers included from 1993. Updated weekly. Inquire as to online cost and availability. (*Business Periodicals Index* without abstracts is also available online.).

OTHER SOURCES

Business Immigration Law: Strategies for Employing Foreign Nationals. ALM Media Properties LLC. • $540 per year. Provides step-by-step employment procedures relating to the law and regulations of the State Department, the Immigration and Naturalization Service, specific visa programs, and the Labor Department. Includes guidelines and samples of forms. (Law Journal Press).

Employment Forms and Policies. Matthew Bender and Company Inc. • $150 print and e-book. Periodic supplementation available. Contains more than 300 forms, policies, and checklists for use by small or medium-sized businesses. Covers such topics as employee selection, payroll issues, benefits, performance appraisal, dress codes, and employee termination.

Labor Relations. Wolters Kluwer Law & Business CCH. • $2,589.00 per year. Seven looseleaf volumes. Weekly updates. Covers labor relations, wages and hours, state labor laws, and employment practices. Supplement available, *Labor Law Reports*. Summary Newsletter.

PERIODICALS AND NEWSLETTERS

Business Today: Published for Students by Students. Foundation for Student Communication. • 3/year. $3 /issue (for libraries and career service offices). Provides articles on careers, university campuses, and opinions of students. Includes employment listings.

Employment Law Strategist. Law Journal Newsletter. • $439 per year. Covers employment law topics, including immigration laws, repetitive stress claims, workplace violence, liability of actions of intoxicated employees, record keeping, liability for fetal injury, independent contractor, and employee issues. Monthly. 229 individuals electronic edition. Description: Reports on legal strategy and substantive developments in the area of matrimonial law, including such topics as tax considerations, custody, visitation, division of property, and valuation. Recurring features include litigation roundup and a legislative update.

Occupational Outlook Quarterly. U.S. Department of Labor Bureau of Labor Statistics. • Quarterly. $30 Two years. Magazine providing occupational and employment information.

People to People. American Public Power Association. • Description: Reports on public sector labor and personnel issues, especially those concerning the electric utility industry. Summarizes case studies in public labor relations.

Recruiting Trends: The Monthly Newsletter for the Recruiting Executive. Kennedy Information Inc. • Monthly. $179.00 per year.

Working USA: The Journal of Labor and Society. M.E. Sharpe Inc. • Quarterly. $160.00 per year to institutions; $45.00 to individuals. Provides a wide range of material on employment, labor markets, societal issues, and present-day labor unions.

RESEARCH CENTERS AND INSTITUTES

Federal Employment Services - Institute of Employment Research. Regensburger Strasse 104, D-90478 Nuremberg, Germany. Phone: 49 911 1790; Fax: 49 911 1793258; Email: joachim.moeller@iab.de • URL: http://www.iab.de • Situations and trends in the employment market, in general and in relation to various occupations, vocational training opportunities, and economic sectors. Activities include research (in-house and through contracts with other institutions); theoretical and methodological studies; surveys; advisory services in matters of employment policy; and promotion of activities in the field of labor market statistics in the areas of medium and long-term projections related to employment and the labor market; short-term labor market analysis; working-time studies; sociological research; occupational and qualification studies; research in technology and business economics; and work in analytical statistics, econometrics, and regional and international labor market research.

University of Warwick - Warwick Institute for Employment Research. Social Sciences Bldg., Coventry CV4 7AL, United Kingdom. Phone: 44 24 76523284; Email: r.m.lindley@warwick.ac.uk • URL: http://www2.warwick.ac.uk/fac/soc/ier • Economics and social behavior, policy analysis, and forecasting. Subjects of research include: macroeconomic, industrial and spatial aspects of employment determination and their policy implications; economy/labor market relations; labor market behavior and policy; links between labor market and population change, educational developments, and household behavior, and related policy issues; and relevant international comparative studies.

W.E. Upjohn Institute for Employment Research. 300 S Westnedge Ave., Kalamazoo, MI 49007-4686. Phone: 888-227-8569 or (269)343-5541; Fax: (269)343-7310; Email: communications@upjohn.org • URL: http://www.upjohninstitute.org • Research fields include unemployment, unemployment insurance, worker's compensation, labor productivity, profit sharing, the labor market, economic development, earnings, training, and other areas related to employment.

STATISTICS SOURCES

Bulletin of Labour Statistics: Supplementing the Annual Data Presented in the Year Book of Labour Statistics. International Labor Ofice. • Quarterly. $84.00 per year. Includes five Supplements. A supplement to *Yearbook of Labour Statistics*. Provides current labor and price index statistics for over 130 countries. Generally includes data for the most recent four years. Text in English, French and Spanish.

Occupational Projections and Training Data. U. S. Government Printing Office. • Biennial. $31.50. Issued by Bureau of Labor Statistics, U. S. Department of Labor. Contains projections of employment change and job openings over the next 15 years for about 500 specific occupations. Also includes the number of associate, bachelor's, master's, doctoral, and professional degrees awarded in a recent year for about 900 specific fields of study.

Quarterly Labour Force Statistics. Organization for Economic Cooperation and Development. Organisation for Economic Co-operation and Development Publications and Information Center. • Quarterly. $90.00 per year. Provides current data for OECD member countries on population, employment, unemployment, civilian labor force, armed forces, and other labor factors.

Report on the American Workforce. U. S. Government Printing Office. • Annual. Issued by the U. S. Department of Labor (www.dol.gov). Appendix contains tabular statistics, including employment, unemployment, price indexes, consumer expenditures, employee benefits (retirement, insurance, vacation, etc.), wages, productivity, hours of work, and occupational injuries. Annual figures are shown for up to 50 years.

Survey of Current Business. U. S. Government Printing Office. • Published by Bureau of Economic Analysis, U. S. Department of Commerce. Presents a wide variety of business and economic data.

World Employment Report. International Labor Organization. • Contains detailed information on the world employment situation and world employment trends.

TRADE/PROFESSIONAL ASSOCIATIONS

National Association of Personnel Services. 78 Dawson Village Way, Ste. 410-201, Dawsonville, GA 30534. Phone: (706)531-0060; Fax: (866)739-4750 • URL: http://www.naps360.org • Members are private employment agencies. Formerly National Association of Personnel Consultants.

Shop, Distributive, and Allied Employees' Association. 53 Queen St., Level 6, Melbourne, VIC 3000, Australia. Phone: 61 3 86117000; Fax: 61 3 86117099 • URL: http://www.sda.org.au • Shopworkers in the retail and fast food industries. Promotes equal opportunity and equal treatment of all members regardless of race, creed, disability, sexual preference, or gender. Works to improve the terms and conditions of members' employment and to protect the interests of members.

EMPLOYMENT AGENCIES AND SERVICES

See also CIVIL SERVICE; COLLEGE PLACEMENT BUREAUS

DIRECTORIES

Atlanta JobBank: The Job Hunter's Guide to Georgia. Adams Media Corp. • $17.95 Individuals Paperback. Covers: 3,900 employers in the state of Georgia, including Albany, Columbus, Macon, and Savannah. Database includes: Information on the basics of job winning and writing resumes and cover letters; electronic job search information; 330

industry associations; 90 online career resources; 235 employment services. Entries include: Firm or organization name, address, local phone, toll-free phone, fax, description of organization, subsidiaries, other locations, recorded jobline, name and title of contact, typical titles for common positions, educational backgrounds desired, number of employees, benefits offered, training programs, internships, parent company, revenues, e-mail and URL address, projected number of hires.

Boston JobBank: The Job Hunter's Guide to the Bay State. Adams Media Corp. • Annual. $17.95 Individuals Paperback. Covers: Over 7,000 employers in Massachusetts. Database includes: Information on the basics of job winning and writing resumes and cover letters; electronic job search information; 330 industry associations; 90 online career resources; 420 employment services. Entries include: Firm or organization name, address, local phone, toll-free phone, fax, e-mail, URL, recorded jobline, hours, names of management, name and title of contact, titles of common positions, entry-level positions, fringe benefits offered, stock exchange listing, description of organization, subsidiaries, location of headquarters, educational background desired, projected number of hires, training programs, internships, parent company, number of employees, revenues, other U.S. Locations, and international locations.

California Job Journal. California Job Journal. • Weekly. Covers: Employment issues and job openings in California from entry-level to executive positions. Database includes: Career guidance and job search advice. Entries include: Company name, address, phone, type of business, name and title of contact; comprehensive description of position and required skills/background, salary and/or benefits offered.

Carolina JobBank: The Job Hunter's Guide to North and South Carolina. Adams Media Corp. • $12.21 Individuals Paperback. Covers: 4,600 employers in North Carolina and South Carolina. Database includes: Information on the basics of getting a job and writing resumes and cover letters; regional employment outlook; 330 industry associations; 90 online career resources; 280 employment services. Entries include: Firm or organization name, address, local phone, toll-free phone, fax, e-mail, URL, recorded jobline, description of organization, subsidiaries, other locations, hours, names of management, name and title of contact, location of headquarters, typical titles for common positions, educational backgrounds desired, projected number of hires, company benefits, stock exchange listing, training programs and internships, parent company, number of employees, revenues.

Chicago JobBank: The Job Hunter's Guide to Metro Chicago. Adams Media Corp. • Annual. $17.95 Individuals Paperback. Covers: About 5,500 major employers in northern and central Illinois including Aurora, Peoria, Rockford, and Springfield. Database includes: Information on the basics of job winning and writing resumes and cover letters; electronic job search information; 330 industry association; 90 online career resources, 480 employment services. Entries include: Firm or organization name, address, local phone, toll-free phone, fax, e-mail, URL, description of organization, hours, recorded jobline, subsidiaries, names of management, name and title of contact, names of management, headquarters locations, typical titles for entry-level and middle-level positions, educational backgrounds desired, company benefits, stock exchange listing, training programs, internships, parent company, number of employees, revenues, other U.S. Locations, international locations.

Complete Guide to Public Employment. Development Concepts Inc. • Triennial. $19.95 Individuals paper. Publication includes: List of federal, state, and local government agencies and departments, trade and professional associations, contracting and consulting firms, nonprofit organizations, foundations, research organizations, political support groups, and other organizations offering public service career opportunities. Entries include: Organization name, address, phone, name and title of contact. Complete title is "Complete Guide to Public Employment: Opportunities and Strategies with Federal, State, and Local Government;" Trade and Professional Associations; Contracting and Consulting Firms; Foundations; Research Organizations; and Political Support Groups.

Dallas/Ft. Worth JobBank: The Job Hunter's Guide to the Dallas-Fort Worth Metroplex. Adams Media Corp. • Annual. $9 Individuals Paperback. Covers: 4,000 employers in the Dallas/Ft. Worth, Texas, area including Abilene, Amarillo, Arlington, Garland, Irving, Lubbock, Plano. Database includes: Information on the basics of getting a job and writing resumes and cover letters; electronic job search information. Entries include: Firm or organization name, address, local phone, toll-free phone, fax, e-mail, URL, recorded jobline, hours, description of organization, subsidiaries, names of management, name and title of contact, location of headquarters, typical titles for common positions, educational backgrounds desired, company benefits, stock exchange listing, training programs, internships, parent company, number of employees, revenues, projected number of hires.

Denver JobBank: The Job Hunter's Guide to Colorado. Adams Media Corp. • $17.95 Individuals 4 used & new. Covers: 3,500 employers in Denver and the rest of Colorado including Aurora, Boulder, Colorado Springs, Lakewood. Database includes: Information on the basics of job winning and writing resumes and cover letters; searching for a job online; regional employment outlook; 330 industry associations; 90 online career resources; 150 employment services. Entries include: Firm or organization name, address, local phone, toll-free phone, fax, e-mail, URL, description of organization, subsidiaries, other locations, hours, recorded jobline, names of management, name and title of contact, headquarters location, projected number of hires; listings may also include typical titles for common positions, educational backgrounds desired, company benefits, stock exchange listing, training programs, internships, parent company, number of employees, revenues.

Directory of Contract Staffing Firms. C.E. Publications Inc. • Annual. Covers: Nearly 1,300 contract firms actively engaged in the employment of engineering, IT/IS, and technical personnel for 'temporary' contract assignments throughout the world. Entries include: Company name, address, phone, name of contact, email, web address.

Federal Career Opportunities. Federal Research Service Inc. • Biweekly. $195 Individuals 26 issues, 1 year. Covers: More than 3,000 current federal job vacancies in the United States and overseas; includes permanent, part-time, and temporary positions. Entries include: Position title, location, series and grade, job requirements, special forms, announcement number, closing date, application address.

Federal Jobs Digest. Federal Jobs Digest. • $20 Individuals 3 months. Covers: Over 10,000 specific job openings in the federal government in each issue. Vacancies from over 300 Federal Agencies are covered. Entries include: Position name, title, General Schedule (GS) grade, and Wage Grade (WG), closing date for applications, announcement number, application address, phone, and name of contact.

Florida JobBank: The Job Hunter's Guide to the Sunshine State. Adams Media Corp. • $17.95 Individuals payment with order. Covers: 5,500 employers in Florida including Fort Lauderdale, Jacksonville, Miami, Orlando, Tampa. Database includes: Information on the basics of job winning and writing resumes and cover letters; electronic job search information; 330 industry associations; 90 online career resources; 285 employment services. Entries include: Firm or organization name, address, local phone, toll-free phone, fax, e-mail addresses, web addresses, description of organization, subsidiaries, hours, recorded jobline, name and title of contact, headquarters location, typical titles for common positions, educational backgrounds desired, number of projected hires, company benefits, stock exchange listing, training programs, internships, parent company, number of employees, revenues, other U.S. Locations, international locations.

HireDiversity.com. Hispanic Business Inc. • Database covers: Over 95,000 resumes of multicultural professionals and recent college graduates who are seeking employment with Fortune 500 companies; job listings with a large variety of companies. Entries include: Name, address, phone, employment history, salary requirements, level of management experience, education, geographical preference, and language.

Houston JobBank: The Job Hunter's Guide to Houston. Adams Media Corp. • Annual. $17.95 Individuals 3 used & new. Covers: Over 4,000 employers in Houston, Texas and the surrounding areas including Bayton, Beaumont, Galveston, Pasadena. Database includes: Information on the basics of job winning and writing resumes and cover letters; electronic job search information; 330 industry associations; 90 online career resources; 145 employment services. Entries include: Firm or organization name, address, local phone, toll-free phone, fax, recorded jobline, e-mail, URL, hours, name and title of contact; description of organization; headquarters location, subsidiaries, operations at the facility, names of management, typical titles for common positions, educational backgrounds desired, number of projected hires, fringe benefits offered, stock exchange listing, training programs, internships, parent company, number of employees, revenues, other U.S. locations, international locations.

Los Angeles JobBank: The Job Hunter's Guide to Southern California. Adams Media Corp. • Annual. $16.95 Individuals Paperback. Covers: Over 7,900 southern California employers including Orange, Riverside, San Bernardino, San Diego, Santa Barbara and Ventura counties. Database includes: Information on the basics of job winning and writing resumes and cover letters; electronic job search information; 330 industry associations; 90 online career resources; 515 employment services. Entries include: Firm or organization name, address, local phone, toll-free phone, fax, e-mail, URL, recorded jobline, hours, subsidiaries, other locations, names of management, name and title of contact, description of organization, number of employees, headquarters location, typical titles for common positions, educational backgrounds desired, fringe benefits offered, stock exchange listing, training programs, internships, parent company, number of employees, revenues, corporate headquarters, and number of projected hires. Projected hires.

Metropolitan Washington DC JobBank: The Job Hunter's Guide to Washington DC. Adams Media Corp. • $17.95 Individuals Paperback. Covers: 6,900 employers in Washington, D.C., Greater Baltimore, and Northern Virginia. Database includes: Information on the basics of job winning and writing resumes and cover letters; electronic job search information; 330 industry associations; 90 online career resources; 250 employment services. Entries include: Firm or organization name, address, local phone, toll-free phone, fax, recorded jobline, name and title of contact, description of organization, subsidiaries, other locations, names of management, hours, titles for common positions, educational backgrounds desired, company benefits, stock exchange listing, location of headquarters, training programs, internships, parent company, number of employees, revenues, email and URL address, projected number of hires.

National Directory for Employment in Education. American Association for Employment in Education. • Annual. $20 Nonmembers Processing fee $2. Covers: about 600 placement offices maintained by teacher-training institutions and 300 school district personnel officers and/or superintendents responsible for hiring profesional staff. Entries include: Institution name, address, phone, contact name, email address, and website.

National Directory of Personnel Service Firms. National Association of Personnel Services. • Annual. Lists over 1,100 member private (for-profit) employment firms.

National JobBank. Adams Media Corp. • Annual. $475 Individuals payment with order. Covers: Over 20,000 employers nationwide. Entries include: Firm or organization name, address, local phone, toll-free phone, fax, contact name and title, description of organization, headquarters location, names of management, number of employees, other locations, subsidiaries, parent company, projected number of hires, training offered, internships, hours, recorded jobline, typical titles for common positions, educational backgrounds desired, stock exchange (if listed), fringe benefits offered. Several state and regional volumes are available and described separately.

San Francisco Bay Area JobBank: The Job Hunter's Guide to Northern California. Adams Media Corp. • $17.95 Individuals Paperback. Covers: About 5,600 employers in the San Francisco Bay area and the Northern half of California including Oakland, Sacramento, San Jose, and Silicon Valley. Database includes: Information on the basics of job winning and writing resumes and cover letters; electronic job search information; 330 industry associations; 90 online career resources; 350 employment services. Entries include: Firm or organization name, address, local phone, toll-free phone, fax, e-mail, URL, recorded jobline, hours, description of organization, subsidiaries, other locations, number of employees, name and title of contact, headquarters location, typical titles for common positions, educational backgrounds desired, company benefits, stock exchange listing, training programs, internships, parent company, and number of employees, revenues, corporate headquarters, and number of projected hires.

Seattle JobBank: The Job Hunter's Guide to Washington. Adams Media Corp. • $17.95 Individuals Paperback. Covers: About 4,800 employers in Washington state, including Spokane, Tacoma, and Bellevue. Database includes: Information on the basics of job winning and writing resumes and cover letters; regional employment outlook; 330 industry associations; 90 online career resources; 135 employment services. Entries include: Firm or organization name, address, local phone, toll-free phone, fax, e-mail, URL, description of organization, subsidiaries, name and title of contact, headquarters location, recorded jobline, typical titles for common positions, educational backgrounds desired, projected number of hires, company benefits, stock exchange listing, training programs, internships, parent company, number of employees, revenues.

HANDBOOKS AND MANUALS

Temporary Help Service. Entrepreneur Press. • Looseleaf. $59.50. A practical guide to starting an employment agency for temporary workers. Covers profit potential, start-up costs, market size evaluation, owner's time required, site selection, lease negotiation, pricing, accounting, advertising, promotion, etc. (Start-Up Business Guide No. E1189.).

PERIODICALS AND NEWSLETTERS

Recruiting Trends: The Monthly Newsletter for the Recruiting Executive. Kennedy Information Inc. • Monthly. $179.00 per year.

TRADE/PROFESSIONAL ASSOCIATIONS

American Staffing Association. 277 S Washington St., Ste. 200, Alexandria, VA 22314-3675. Phone: (703)253-2020; Fax: (703)253-2053; Email: asa@americanstaffing.net • URL: http://www.americanstaffing.net/index.cfm • Promotes and represents the staffing industry through legal and legislative advocacy, public relations, education, and the establishment of high standards of ethical conduct.

Association of Career Management Consulting Firms International. 204 E St., NE, Washington, DC 20002. Phone: (202)547-6344; Fax: (202)547-6348; Email: acf@acfinternational.org • Firms providing displaced employees who are sponsored by their organization, with counsel and assistance in job searching and the techniques and practices of choosing a career.

Association of Executive Search Consultants. 425 5thAve., 4th Fl., New York, NY 10016. Phone: (212)398-9556; Email: info@bluesteps.com • URL: http://www.aesc.org/eweb/StartPage.aspx • Represents executive search consulting firms worldwide, establishes professional and ethical standards for its members, and serves to broaden public understanding of the executive search process. Specialized form of management consulting, conducted through an exclusive engagement with a client organization.

National Association of Personnel Services. 78 Dawson Village Way, Ste. 410-201, Dawsonville, GA 30534. Phone: (706)531-0060; Fax: (866)739-4750 • URL: http://www.naps360.org • Members are private employment agencies. Formerly National Association of Personnel Consultants.

Opportunities Industrialization Centers of America. 1415 N Broad St., Ste. 227, Philadelphia, PA 19122-3323. Phone: 800-621-4642 or (215)236-4500; Fax: (215)236-7480; Email: info@oicofamerica.org • URL: http://www.oicofamerica.org • Network of employment and training programs. Serves disadvantaged and unskilled workers.

Outsourcing Institute. 6800 Jericho Tpke., Ste. 120W, Syosset, NY 11791. Phone: (516)279-6850; Email: info@outsourcing.com • URL: http://www.outsourcing.com • Represents corporations making use of outside resources and services. Serves as a clearinghouse on the strategic use of outside resources. Conducts research, executive events, publications and educational programs.

EMPLOYMENT IN FOREIGN COUNTRIES

OTHER SOURCES

Foreign Labor Trends. U. S. Government Printing Office. • Irregular (50 to 60 issues per year, each on an individual country). $95.00 per year. Prepared by various American Embassies. Issued by the Bureau of International Labor Affairs, U. S. Department of Labor. Covers labor developments in important foreign countries, including trends in wages, working conditions, labor supply, employment, and unemployment.

PERIODICALS AND NEWSLETTERS

International Employment Hotline. Carlyle Corp. • Monthly. $69 Individuals per 1 year. Description: Covers the latest developments in the international job market. Summarizes hiring cycles of major employers. Lists current overseas job openings by job title, description, employer contact, and address. Recurring features include editorials and news of research.

Transitions Abroad: The Guide to Learning, Living, and Working Overseas. Transitions Abroad Publishing. • Bimonthly. Provides practical information and advice on foreign education and employment. Supplement available *Overseas Travel Planner.*

EMPLOYMENT MANAGEMENT

See PERSONNEL MANAGEMENT

EMPLOYMENT OF OLDER WORKERS

See also EQUAL EMPLOYMENT OPPORTUNITY; RETIREMENT

ENCYCLOPEDIAS AND DICTIONARIES

Encyclopedia of Aging. David J. Ekerdt, editor. Cengage Learning Inc. • $770. Includes articles relating to the financial aspects of aging, such as housing, long-term care insurance, pensions, social security, individual retirement accounts, savings, and retirement planning. eBook also available. Inquire for pricing.

STATISTICS SOURCES

Social Security Bulletin. Social Security Administration. U. S. Government Printing Office. • Quarterly. $27.00 per year. Annual statistical supplement.

EMPLOYMENT OF THE HANDICAPPED

See HANDICAPPED WORKERS

EMPLOYMENT OF WOMEN

See also EQUAL EMPLOYMENT OPPORTUNITY; WOMEN ACCOUNTANTS; WOMEN ENGINEERS; WOMEN IN THE WORK FORCE; WOMEN LAWYERS; WOMEN PHYSICIANS

ABSTRACTS AND INDEXES

Women Studies Abstracts. Springer ScienceBusiness Media LLC. • Quarterly. Covers significant research in women's studies.

BIOGRAPHICAL SOURCES

Who's Who of American Women. Marquis Who's Who L.L.C. • Biennial. $305.00. Provides over 30,444 biographical profiles of important women, including individuals prominent in business, finance, and industry.

DIRECTORIES

Directory of Minority & Women-Owned Businesses. Business Service Div. Birmingham Area Chamber of Commerce. • Covers: Approximately 1,200 businesses in Birmingham, Alabama, that are owned by women or minorities. Entries include: Company name, address, phone, name and title of contact, Standard Industrial Classification (SIC) code.

HANDBOOKS AND MANUALS

Women and the Law. Carol H. Lefcourt, editor. Thomson West. • Annual. $691.60 Individuals book - softbound. Covers such topics as employment discrimination, pay equity (comparable worth), sexual harassment in the workplace, property rights, and child custody issues.

ONLINE DATABASES

Contemporary Women's Issues. Cengage Learning Inc. • Provides full-text articles online from 150 periodicals and a wide variety of additional sources relating to economic, legal, social, political, education, health, and other women's issues. Time span is 1992 to date. Weekly updates. Inquire as to online cost and availability.

OTHER SOURCES

Practical Guide to Equal Employment Opportunity. ALM Media Properties LLC. • $570 two volumes. Serves as a legal manual for EEO compliance. "Volume one analyzes discrimination on the basis of race, religion, sex, age, and physical handicaps including AIDS." Provides information relating to an employer's liability in cases of sexual harassment of employees, including same-sex harassment. Covers affirmative action and reverse discrimination issues. Volume two contains model affirmative action plans, a sample EEO compliance manual, checklists, and other documents. (Law Journal Press).

PERIODICALS AND NEWSLETTERS

AAUW Outlook. AAUW Legal Advocacy Fund. • 3/year. Magazine covering women's concerns including current family, education and legislative issues. Formerly *Graduate Woman.*

Business Woman Magazine. Business and Professional Women/U.S.A. • Monthly. $30 Individuals. Focuses on the activities and interests of working women.

The Equal Employer. Y. S. Publications, Inc. • Biweekly. $245.00 per year. Newsletter on fair employment practices.

Family Relations: State Capitals. Wakeman/Walworth Inc. • 50 times a year. $245.00 per year: print and online editions. $350.00 per year. Newsletter. Formerly *From the State Capitals: Family Relations.*

Feminist Economics. International Association for Feminist Economics. Taylor & Francis Ltd. • Three times a year. Individuals, $68.00 per year: institutions, $184.00 per year. Includes articles on issues relating to the employment and economic opportunities of women.

MS. British American Tobacco Italia S.p.A. • $14.95 Individuals Digital.

National Now Times. National Organization for Women. • Free to members.

New Woman. Endeavour House. • Monthly. $57.00 per year.

Perspective. Magna Publications Inc. • Description: Provides administrators with guidelines for keeping their schools out of court. Examines current trends in law related to higher education, as well as past and future legal issues affecting students, faculty, administrators and the public. Recurring features include columns titled Key Case Review, Follow-Up, Resources, Legislative Note, Outside the Courts, Cross-Examination, and Cases Noted.

RESEARCH CENTERS AND INSTITUTES

Business and Professional Women's Foundation. 1718 M St. NW, No. 148, Washington, DC 20036. Phone: (202)293-1100; Fax: (202)861-0298; Email: foundation@bpwfoundation.org • URL: http://bpwfoundation.org • Formerly National Federation of Business and Professional Women's Clubs.

STATISTICS SOURCES

United States Equal Employment Opportunity Commission Annual Report: Job Patterns for Minorities and Women in Private Industry. U.S. Equal Employment Opportunity Commission. • Annual.

TRADE/PROFESSIONAL ASSOCIATIONS

American Business Women's Association. 11050 Roe Ave., Ste. 200, Overland Park, KS 66211. Phone: 800-228-0007; Fax: (913)660-0101; Email: webmail@abwa.org • URL: http://www.abwa.org • Women in business, including women owning or operating their own businesses, women in professions and women employed in any level of government, education, or retailing, manufacturing and service companies. Provides opportunities for businesswomen to help themselves and others grow personally and professionally through leadership, education, networking support and national recognition. Offers leadership training, business skills training and business education; special membership options for retired businesswomen and the Company Connection for business owners, a resume service, credit card and programs, various travel and insurance benefits. Sponsors American Business Women's Day and National Convention and regional conferences held annually.

Business and Professional Women Australia. Level 1, 613 Centerbury Rd., Melbourne, VIC 3127, Australia. Phone: 61 3 98954487; Fax: 61 3 98980249; Email: bpwaust@bpw.com.au • URL: http://www.bpw.com.au • Provides a forum for businesswomen to establish personal and professional contacts. Seeks to improve the status of working women.

Business and Professional Women International. PO Box 2042, Fitzroy, VIC 3065, Australia. Email: member.services@bpw-international.org • URL: http://www.bpw-international.org • Promotes the status of women worldwide. Seeks to uphold higher business and professional standards.

Business and Professional Women the Netherlands. PO Box 11069, NL-1001 GB Amsterdam, Netherlands. Phone: 31 681544025; Email: secretaris@bpwnl.org • URL: http://www.bpw-europe.org/countries?id=235 • Promotes equal opportunities for women in business, trade, and economic life. Upholds high standards for women in business and service professions. Encourages women and girls to acquire education, occupational training and advanced education.

Business and Professional Women - UK. 74, Fairfield Rise, Essex, Billericay CM12 9NU, United Kingdom. Phone: 44 1277 623867; Email: hq@bpwuk.co.uk • URL: http://www.bpwuk.co.uk • Serves as networking and lobbying organization. Aims to enable business and professional women to achieve in their careers. Encourages women to take an active part in public life and decision making at all levels. Evaluates changing work patterns and press for development in education and training to meet them. Strives to ensure that the same opportunities and facilities are available to both men and women. Undertakes studies of problems common to business and professional women in Europe and worldwide.

Business and Professional Women's Foundation. 1718 M St. NW, No. 148, Washington, DC 20036. Phone: (202)293-1100; Fax: (202)861-0298; Email: foundation@bpwfoundation.org • URL: http://bpwfoundation.org • Formerly National Federation of Business and Professional Women's Clubs.

Catalyst. 120 Wall St., 5th Fl., New York, NY 10005-3904. Phone: (212)514-7600; Fax: (212)514-8470; Email: info@catalyst.org • URL: http://www.catalyst.org • Works to advance women in Business and the professions. Serves as a source of information on women in business for past four decades. Helps companies and women maximize their potential. Holds current statistics, print media, and research materials on issues related to women in business.

Centre for Women in Business. Mt. Saint Vincent University, The Meadows, 2nd Fl., 166 Bedford Hwy., Halifax, NS, Canada B3M 2J6. Phone: 888-776-9022 or (902)457-6449; Fax: (902)443-4687; Email: cwb@msvu.ca • URL: http://www.centreforwomeninbusiness.ca/en/home/default.aspx • Represents women entrepreneurs in Canada.

Coalition of Labor Union Women. 815 16th St. NW, 2nd Fl. S, Washington, DC 20006. Phone: (202)508-6969 or (202)223-8360; Fax: (202)508-6968 or (202)776-0537; Email: ksee@cluw.org • URL: http://www.cluw.org • Aims to: unify all union women in order to determine common problems within unions and deal effectively with objectives; promote unionism and encourage unions to be more aggressive in their efforts to bring unorganized women under collective bargaining agreements; inform members about what can be done within the labor movement to achieve equal opportunity and correct discriminatory job situations; educate and inspire union brothers to help achieve affirmative action in the workplace. Seeks to encourage members through action programs of the coalition to become more active participants in the political and legislative processes of their unions, to seek election to public office or selection for governmental appointive office at local, county, state, and national levels, and to increase their participation in union policymaking. Conducts training programs and project on empowerment of union women. Maintains Coalition of Labor Union Women Center for Education and Research.

National Association for Female Executives. 2 Park Ave., New York, NY 10016. • URL: http://www.nafe.com • Represents and supports professional women and women business owners; provides resources and services through education, networking and public advocacy to empower members to achieve career success and financial security.

National Association of Women Business Owners. 601 Pennsylvania Ave. NW, South Bldg., Ste. 900, Washington, DC 20004. Phone: 800-556-2926; Fax: (202)403-3788; Email: national@nawbo.org • URL: http://www.nawbo.org • Formerly Association of Women Business Owners.

National Association of Women MBAs. Rice University, PO Box 2932, Houston, TX 77251-2932. Email: philana.kiely@mbawomen.org • URL: http://www.mbawomen.org • Provides networking opportunities for its members. Increases communication among graduate business schools regarding their initiatives to educate and support women in business.

National Organization for Women. 1100 H St. NW, Ste. 300, Washington, DC 20005-5488. Phone: (202)628-8669; Fax: (202)785-8576 • URL: http://now.org • Includes men and women seeking equality for women.

National Partnership for Women & Families. 1875 Connecticut Ave. NW, Ste. 650, Washington, DC 20009. Phone: (202)986-2600; Fax: (202)986-2539; Email: info@nationalpartnership.org • URL: http://www.nationalpartnership.org • Formerly Women's Legal Defense Fund.

National Women's Law Center. 11 Dupont Cir. NW, Ste. 800, Washington, DC 20036-1209. Phone: (202)588-5180; Fax: (202)588-5185; Email: info@nwlc.org • URL: http://www.nwlc.org • Uses the law in all its forms: getting new laws on the books; litigating ground-breaking lawsuits all the way to the Supreme Court; and educating the public about how to make the law and public policies work for women and their families. "Takes on the issues that cut to the core of women's and girls' lives" in health, education, employment, and family economic security, with special priority given to the needs of low-income women and their families.

Seton Hill University's E-magnify. Seton Hill University, 1 Seton Hill Dr., 3rd Fl., Administration Bldg., Greensburg, PA 15601. Phone: (724)830-4625; Fax: (724)834-7131; Email: info@e-magnify.com • URL: http://www.e-magnify.com • Promotes women and business ownership. Offers a variety of entrepreneurial resources, educational programs, advocacy initiatives and networking opportunities to women entrepreneurs. Works "to strengthen the economic impact of women business owners as a collective force and to advance their growth through innovative programming in entrepreneurship and new venture creation." Provides support, education and encouragement essential for the continued growth of women-owned businesses through its services.

EMPLOYMENT RESUMES

See JOB RESUMES

EMPLOYMENT SECURITY

See UNEMPLOYMENT INSURANCE

EMPLOYMENT TESTS

See PSYCHOLOGICAL TESTING

ENDOWMENTS

See FOUNDATIONS

ENERGY COGENERATION

See COGENERATION OF ENERGY

ENERGY, GEOTHERMAL

See GEOTHERMAL ENERGY

ENERGY, NUCLEAR

See NUCLEAR ENERGY

ENERGY, SOLAR

See SOLAR ENERGY

ENERGY SOURCES

See also COAL INDUSTRY; ELECTRIC UTILITIES; GEOTHERMAL ENERGY; NATURAL GAS; NUCLEAR ENERGY; PETROLEUM INDUSTRY; SOLAR ENERGY

ABSTRACTS AND INDEXES

Applied Science and Technology Index. EBSCO Publishing Inc. • 11/year. Indexes a wide variety of English language technical, industrial, and engineering periodicals.

NTIS Alerts: Energy. U.S. Department of Commerce National Technical Information Service. • Biweekly. $130 per year. Covers electric power, batteries, fuels, geothermal energy, heating/cooling systems, nuclear technology, solar energy, energy policy, and related subjects.

ALMANACS AND YEARBOOKS

Annual Review of Environment and Resources. Annual Reviews. • Annual. $93 Individuals online only. Focuses on emerging scientific and policy issues at the interface of environment, resource management, and development.

Vital Signs: The Trends That Are Shaping Our Future (year). Worldwatch Institute. • Annual. $19. 95. Provides access to selected indicators showing social, economic, and environmental trends throughout the world. Includes data relating to food, energy, transportation, finance, population, and other topics.

CD-ROM DATABASES

Environment Abstracts on CD-ROM. University Publications of America. • Quarterly. $1,295.00 per year. Contains the following CD-ROM databases: *Environment Abstracts*, *Energy Abstracts*, and *Acid Rain Abstracts*. Length of coverage varies.

OECD Statistical Compendium. Organization for Economic Cooperation and Development. • Semiannual. $1,905.00 per year for 1 to 10 users. CD-ROM contains more than 730,000 monthly, quarterly, and annual time series for OECD countries, 1960 to date. Includes fully searchable data on agriculture, food, economic indicators, national accounts, employment, energy, finance, industry, technology, and foreign trade. Results can be displayed in various forms.

DIRECTORIES

Alternative Energy Directory & Handbook. Grey House Publishing. • $165 Individuals softcover. Covers: Alternative energy sources including hydro, wind, solar, coal, natural gas and atomic energy sources. Includes information on associations, magazines, trade shows and vendors.

Biomass Industry Profile Directory. DIANE Publishing Co. • $40 Individuals Paperback. Publication includes: Lists of all businesses and agencies involved in biomass energy in the Western United States.

Directory of Asian Importers of Energy and Power Equipment. EXIM Infotek Private Ltd. • Covers: 130 Asian importers of high voltage equipment and component, nuclear equipment and materials, power equipment, power generation projects, power plants, power transmission component, power transmission equipment and supplies, power transmission products, solar cells, solar charge controller and modules, solar energy equipment, wind energy equipment, and transmission and allied equipment. Entries include: Company name, postal address, telephone, fax, e-mail, website, contact person, designation, and product details.

Doing Business with the Department of Energy: Directory. U.S. Department of Energy. • Irregular. Covers regional offices and field organizations of the Energy Department, and major contractors for the department.

Institutional Buyers of Energy Stocks. bigdough. com Inc. • Annual. $645.00. Provides detailed profiles 555 institutional buyers of petroleum-related and other energy stocks. Includes names of financial analysts and portfolio managers.

Renewable Energy Businesses in the World. Momentum Technologies L.L.C. • Contains more than 28,734 directory listings and associated contact data for renewable energy businesses and related companies in operation throughout the world. Includes company name, address, telephone number, fax number, e-mail address, and web site address. Provides description of business type, product types, and services provided. Searchable by location, business type, company name, and keyword.

World Energy and Nuclear Directory. Specialist Journals. • Biennial. $385.00. Lists 5,000 public and private, international research and development organizations functioning in a wide variety of areas related to energy.

E-BOOKS

Macmillan Encyclopedia of Energy. Cengage Learning Inc. • 2003. eBook. Published by Macmillan Reference USA. Covers the business, technology, and history of a wide variety of energy sources. Inquire as to price and availability.

INTERNET DATABASES

U.S. Census Bureau: The Official Statistics. U. S. Bureau of the Census. Phone: (301)763-4636 or (301)763-4100; Fax: (301)763-4794; Email: webmaster@census.gov • URL: http://www.census.gov/prod/www/abs/mfg-prof.html • Web site is "Your Source for Social, Demographic, and Economic Information." Contains "Current U. S. Population Count," "Current Economic Indicators," and a wide variety of data under "Other Official Statistics." Keyword searching is provided. Fees: Free.

ONLINE DATABASES

Applied Science and Technology Index Online. H.W. Wilson Co. • Provides online indexing of 500 major scientific, technical, industrial, and engineering periodicals. Time period is 1983 to date. Monthly updates. Inquire as to online cost and availability.

Hybrid Electric Vehicle Businesses in the World. Momentum Technologies L.L.C. • Contains directory listings and contact information for more than 60 businesses involved with hybrid electric vehicles and related automotive areas throughout the world. Includes business name, address, phone number, fax number, e-mail address, and web site address. Includes brief descriptions of product lines, services offered, and business type. Covers businesses concerned with vehicles with hybrid power systems, such as electric power and traditional gasoline fuel. Includes manufacturers, component makers, wholesalers, retailers, component installers, and more. Searchable by location, business type, company name, and keyword.

Photovoltaic Module Retail Businesses in the World. Momentum Technologies L.L.C. • Contains 811 directory listings of retail businesses throughout the world that supply photovoltaic modules and associated energy equipment. Includes business name, address, phone number, fax number, e-mail address, and web site address. Includes brief descriptions of product lines, services offered, and business type. Provides keyword search functions.

Wind Energy Businesses in the World. Momentum Technologies L.L.C. • Contains directory listings and contact information for more than 2600 businesses involved with wind energy and related subjects throughout the world. Includes business name, address, phone number, fax number, e-mail address, and web site address. Includes brief descriptions of product lines, services offered, and business type. Covers manufacturers, wholesalers, retailers, installers, and more. Searchable by location, business type, company name, and keyword.

OTHER SOURCES

Major Energy Companies of the World. Cengage Learning Inc. • Annual. $1,460 Individuals. 2008. 12th edition. eBook. Published by Graham & Whiteside. Contains detailed information on more than 4,850 important energy companies in various countries. Industries include electricity generation, coal, natural gas, nuclear energy, petroleum, fuel distribution, and equipment for energy production.

PERIODICALS AND NEWSLETTERS

DOE This Month. U. S. Government Printing Office. • Monthly. $22 per year. Describes the U.S. Department of Energy's research and development activities and DOE publications. Includes information on nuclear energy, renewable energy sources, and synthetic fuels.

Energy & Fuels. American Chemical Society. • Bimonthly. $1,537 Institutions. An interdisciplinary technical journal covering non-nuclear energy sources: petroleum, gas, synthetic fuels, etc.

Energy Compass. Energy Intelligence Group. • Description: Focuses on worldwide geopolitical developments and their impact on the oil industry. Also includes marketing and trading information, political risk assessment, and current events and trends. **Remarks:** Available via fax, e-mail, or online.

Energy Magazine. Business Communications Co., Inc. • Quarterly. Quarterly. $395.00 per year.

Energy Sources: Recovery, Utilization, and Environmental Effects. Taylor & Francis Ltd. • Monthly. Individuals, $498.00 per year; institutions, $1,325.00 per year.

Independent Energy: The Power Industry's Business Magazine. PennWell Corp., Industrial Div. • 10 times a year. $127.00 per year. Covers non-utility electric power plants (cogeneration) and other alternative sources of electric energy.

International Journal of Energy Research. John Wiley and Sons, Inc., Journals Div. • 15 times a year. Individuals, $2,685.00 per year; institutions, $3,500.00 per year. Published in England by John Wiley & Sons Ltd.

Journal of Energy Engineering: The International Journal. Architectural Engineering Institute of ASCE. • Quarterly. $350 Individuals Online only. Contains reports on the development of scientific and engineering knowledge in the planning, management, and generation of electrical power.

Resource and Energy Economics: A Journal Devoted to the Interdisciplinary Studies in the Allocation of Natural Resources. Elsevier. • Quarterly. $117 Individuals. Publishes papers that advance economic theory and empirical methods to gain novel insights into environmental problems.

World Watch: Working for a Sustainable Future. Worldwatch Institute. • Bimonthly. $25.00 per year. Emphasis is on environmental trends, including developments in population growth, climate change, human behavior, the role of government, and other factors.

PRICE SOURCES

Energy Prices and Taxes. International Energy Agency. Organisation for Economic Co-operation and Development Publications and Information Center. • Quarterly. $385 Individuals. Compiled by the International Energy Agency. Provides data on prices and taxation of petroleum products, natural gas, coal, and electricity. Diskette edition, $800.00. (Published in Paris).

RESEARCH CENTERS AND INSTITUTES

Idaho National Laboratory - Energy Policy Institute. Boise State University, 1910 University Dr., Boise, ID 83725-1014. Phone: (208)426-4845; Fax: (208)426-1830; Email: davidsolan@boisestate.edu • URL: http://epi.boisestate.edu • Energy issues important to the western U.S., including the relationships between energy and water with climate change, population and economic growth, and environmental impacts.

New York Institute of Technology - Center for Energy, Environment and Economics. Dept. of Energy Management, Harry Schure Hall, Rm. 116, Northern Blvd., Old Westbury, NY 11568-8000. Phone: (516)686-7990 or (516)686-7578; Fax: (516)686-7933; Email: ramundse@nyit.edu • URL: http://www.nyit.edu/engineering/centers/centers_energy_environment_economics • Established by the New York Institute of Technology as a major facility designed to disseminate information and conduct research into energy utilization and conservation, and to assist public, quasi-public, and private sector organizations in the practical use of present and future findings in the energy field. Conducts Master of Science in Energy Management and specialized professional certificate programs through NYIT's School of Engineering and Technology to provide interdisciplinary training in the technological, economic, sociological, and administrative skills required to implement new approaches to energy conversion and utilization.

U.S. Department of Energy - Bioenergy Feedstock Development Program - Oak Ridge National Laboratory. 1 Bethel Valley Rd., Oak Ridge, TN 37831-6006. Phone: 800-541-1625 or (865)574-4160; Fax: (865)574-0595 or (865)574-2232; Email: ighotline@hq.doe.gov • URL: http://www.ornl.gov.

University of Delaware - Center for Energy and Environmental Policy. 278 Graham Hall, Newark, DE 19716. Phone: (302)831-8405; Fax: (302)831-3098; Email: jbbyrne@udel.edu • URL: http://ceep.udel.edu • Energy, environmental, and technology policy issues focusing on social, political, and economic dimensions of technology, and natural resource use. Center research and graduate study is informed by theories and concepts drawn from the fields of political economy and environment, technology, and society. Of particular interest are analyses of climate change, sustainable development, energy and environmental policy, environmental justice, water and energy conservation, renewable energy policies, energy and environmental issues in developing nations, and environmental planning.

University of Hawaii at Manoa - Hawaii Natural Energy Institute. 1680 E West Rd., Post 109, Honolulu, HI 96822. Phone: (808)956-8890; Fax: (808)956-2336; Email: hnei@hawaii.edu • URL: http://www.hnei.hawaii.edu • Research areas include geothermal, wind, solar, hydroelectric, and other energy sources.

STATISTICS SOURCES

Annual Energy Outlook, with Projections to (year). U. S. Government Printing Office. • Annual. $39.00. Issued by the Energy Information Administration, U. S. Department of Energy (www.eia.doe.gov). Contains detailed statistics and 20-year projections for electricity, oil, natural gas, coal, and renewable energy. Text provides extensive discussion of energy issues and "Market Trends.".

Annual Energy Review. U. S. Government Printing Office. • Annual. $59.00. Issued by the Energy Information Administration, Office of Energy Markets and End Use, U. S. Department of Energy. Presents long-term historical as well as recent data on production, consumption, stocks, imports, exports, and prices of the principal energy commodities in the U. S.

Petroleum Supply Annual. U. S. Government Printing Office. • Annual. $78.00. Two volumes. Produced by the Energy Information Administration, U. S. Department of Energy. Contains worldwide data on the petroleum industry and petroleum products.

Petroleum Supply Monthly. U. S. Government Printing Office. • Monthly. Produced by the Energy Information Administration, U. S. Department of Energy. Provides worldwide statistics on a wide variety of petroleum products. Covers production, supplies, exports and imports, transportation, refinery operations, and other aspects of the petroleum industry.

Short-Term Energy Outlook: Quarterly Projections. U. S. Government Printing Office. • Semiannual. Issued by Energy Information Administration, U. S. Department of Energy. Contains forecasts of U. S. energy supply, demand, and prices.

Statistical Abstract of the United States. U. S. Government Printing Office. • Annual. $44.00. Issued by the U. S. Bureau of the Census.

Statistical Yearbook. United Nations Publications. • Annual. $125.00. Contains statistics for about 200 countries on a wide variety of economic, industrial, and demographic topics. Compiled by United Nations Statistical Office.

TRADE/PROFESSIONAL ASSOCIATIONS

Energy Storage Council. 3963 Flora Pl., 2nd Fl., Saint Louis, MO 63110. Phone: (314)495-4545; Email: info@energystoragecouncil.org • URL: http://www.energystoragecouncil.org • Promotes research, development and deployment of storage technologies within the energy storage industry. Raises awareness of the importance of storage for the future of America's electricity supply and energy security. Develops policies on key legislative and regulatory issues affecting the energy storage industry.

Industrial Energy Consumers of America. 1155 15th St. NW, Ste. 500, Washington, DC 20005. Phone: (202)223-1661 or (202)223-1420; Fax: (202)530-0659; Email: pcicio@ieca-us.org • URL: http://www.ieca-us.com • Promotes the interests of manufacturing companies and enhances their ability to compete in domestic and world markets. Supports policy development, identification and monitoring of issues and developing and implementing action plans pertaining to energy efficiency and environmental progress. Provides a forum to address state, national and international energy related issues, meet with policy makers and advocate sound policy.

National Council of Minorities in Energy. 1725 I St. NW, Ste. 300, Washington, DC 20006. Phone: 866-663-9045; Fax: (866)663-8007; Email: contact@minoritiesinenergy.org • URL: http://www.minoritiesinenergy.org • Advocates for development and utilization of minority and women-owned businesses in the energy sector and energy-related industries across the United States and in international markets. Provides information regarding opportunities in the energy industry. Advocates on regulatory and legislative issues at the federal, state and local levels. Presents methodologies to help implement access to capital and credit facilitation.

ENGINEERING

DIRECTORIES

Plunkett's Engineering and Research Industry Almanac: The Only Complete Guide to the Business of Research, Development, and Engineering. Plunkett Research Ltd. • Annual. $349.99 Individuals eBook, print and CD-ROM. Covers 500 of the largest companies involved in research, engineering and development in the biotech, electronics, aerospace and infotech industries.

PERIODICALS AND NEWSLETTERS

Tape/Disc Business. Access Intelligence L.L.C. • Monthly. $74. Magazine for dealers, manufacturers, and users of magnetic and optical media.

Tunnel Business Magazine: Covering the North American Tunneling Market. Benjamin Media Inc. • $99 Other countries. Magazine featuring tunnel construction and engineering in North America.

ENGINEERING CONSULTANTS

See also CONSULTANTS; MANAGEMENT CONSULTANTS

PERIODICALS AND NEWSLETTERS

Consulting-Specifying Engineer. Reed Elsevier Group plc Reed Business Information. • 13 times a year. $95.90 per year. Formerly *Consulting Engineer*.

The Last Word. American Consulting Engineers Council. • Description: Contains summaries of Council activities and legislative actions of interest to consulting engineers.

STATISTICS SOURCES

Salaries of Scientists, Engineers, and Technicians: A Summary of Salary Surveys. Commission on Professionals in Science and Technology. CPST

Publications. • Biennial. $100.00. A summary of salary surveys.

TRADE/PROFESSIONAL ASSOCIATIONS

American Consulting Engineers Council. 1015 15th St. NW, 8th Fl., Washington, DC 20005-2605. Phone: (202)347-7474; Fax: (202)898-0068; Email: acec@acec.org • URL: http://www.acec.org • Represents consulting engineering firms engaged in private practice. Conducts programs concerned with public relations, business practices, governmental affairs, international practice and professional liability. Compiles statistics on office practices, insurance, employment, insurance clients served and services provided. Holds professional development seminars. Conducts educational programs; maintains speakers' bureau.

APEC - Automated Procedures for Engineering Consultants, Inc. Talbott Tower, 141 N Ludlow St., Ste. 318, Dayton, OH 45402. Phone: (937)228-2602; Fax: (937)228-5652; Email: webmaster@hvacmall.com.

Association of Consulting Chemists and Chemical Engineers. PO Box 902, Murray Hill, NJ 07974-0902. Phone: (908)464-3182 or (973)729-6671; Fax: (908)464-3182 or (973)729-7088; Email: accce@chemconsult.org • URL: http://www.chemconsult.org • Serves the chemical and related industries through its expertise on a wide variety of technical and business knowledge. Provides experienced counseling for new members.

ENGINES

See also LUBRICATION AND LUBRICANTS

DIRECTORIES

Directory of African Importers of Motors and Motor Parts--Electric. EXIM Infotek Private Ltd. • $250 Individuals. Covers: 50 African importers of AC and DC motors, electric motors and spares, motor equipment, and motor parts. Entries include: Company name, postal address, telephone, fax, e-mail, website, contact person, designation, and product details.

Directory of American Manufacturers & Exporters of Engines & Engine Parts. EXIM Infotek Private Ltd. • $20 Individuals. Covers: 240 American manufacturers and exporters of auto engines, automobile engines, automotive and truck engines, automotive engines, boiler and air conditioning towers and engines, car engines, crankshafts, cylinders, cylinder sleeves, diesel engine parts, diesel engine parts and accessories, diesel engines, engines, engine aircraft modifications, engine parts, engine treatments, engines-gasoline, exhaust system parts, gasoline and diesel engines, gasoline engines, heavy duty diesel engines, industrial diesel engines, injectors, internal combustion engines, natural gas engines, piston automotive and light truck applications, piston pins, piston rings, piston-compressors, piston-engines, pistons, replacement parts for heavy duty diesel engines, steam engines, stern drive and inboard engines, timing components, truck engines, and turbine engines. Entries include: Company name, postal address, city, country, telephone, fax, e-mail and websites, contact person, designation, and product details.

Directory of American Manufacturers and Exporters of Motors and Motor Parts--Electric. EXIM Infotek Private Ltd. • Covers: 230 American manufacturers and exporters of AC and DC motors, brushless motors, air motors, electric motors, fractional horsepower motors, gear motors, hydraulic motor, integral horsepower motors, miniature motors, permanent magnet motors, servo motor, springs motors, stepping motors, stepper motors, sub-fractional horsepower motors, and submersible motors. Entries include: Company name, postal address, telephone, fax, e-mail, website, contact person, designation, and product details.

Directory of Asian Importers of Motors and Motor Parts--Electric. EXIM Infotek Private Ltd. • Covers: 150 Asian importers of DC motors, Eddy current variable speed motors, electric motor control, electric motors, geared motors, induction motors, motor equipment and parts, motor graders, motor parts and accessories, motor starters, pump and motor accessories, servo motors and controllers. Entries include: Company name, postal address, telephone, fax, e-mail, website, contact person, designation, and product details.

Directory of Chinese Manufacturers & Exporters of Engines & Engine Parts. EXIM Infotek Private Ltd. • $5 Individuals. Covers: 35 Chinese manufacturers and exporters of diesel engines, engine beds-ordinary, engine parts and accessories, engines, inlet valves, piston rings, pistons, spark plugs. Entries include: Company name, postal address, city, country, phone, fax, e-mail and websites, contact person, designation, and product details.

Directory of Chinese Manufacturers and Exporters of Motors and Motor Parts--Electric. EXIM Infotek Private Ltd. • $200 Individuals. Covers: 50 Chinese manufacturers and exporters of DC motors, electric motors, induction motors, motorcycle parts and accessories, AC motors, and sewing machine motors. Entries include: Company name, postal address, telephone, fax, e-mail, website, contact person, designation, and product details.

Directory of European Importers of Motors and Motor Parts--Electric. EXIM Infotek Private Ltd. • Covers: 160 European importers of electric motor, gas fuel equipment for motor vehicle, and motor equipment and parts. Entries include: Company name, postal address, telephone, fax, e-mail, website, contact person, designation, and product details.

Directory of Japanese Manufacturers & Exporters of Engines & Engine Parts. EXIM Infotek Private Ltd. • $15 Individuals. Covers: 130 Japanese manufacturers and exporters of diesel engines, diesel engine parts, electric equipment for diesel engines, engine parts and accessories, engine valves, engines, internal combustion engines, oil seals, parts for internal combustion engines, piston pin bushings, pistons, plugs, spark plugs, used car engines, used diesel engines, used engines and body parts, used gasoline engines, and used truck engines. Entries include: Company name, postal address, city, country, phone, fax, e-mail and websites, contact person, designation, and product details.

Directory of Japanese Manufacturers and Exporters of Motors and Motor Parts--Electric. EXIM Infotek Private Ltd. • Covers: 20 Japanese manufacturers and exporters of DC motors, electric motors, motorcycle parts and accessories, starter motors, and stepping motors. Entries include: Company name, postal address, telephone, fax, e-mail, website, contact person, designation, and product details.

Directory of Middle East Importers of Motors and Motor Parts--Electric. EXIM Infotek Private Ltd. • Covers: 170 Middle East importers of electric motors, motor equipment and parts, motor oil, and outboard motor. Entries include: Company name, postal address, telephone, fax, e-mail, website, contact person, designation, and product details.

Directory of SAARC Importers of Motors and Motor Parts--Electric. EXIM Infotek Private Ltd. • $200 Individuals. Covers: 40 companies in member countries of the South Asian Association for Regional Cooperation (SAARC) that import agitators and geared motors, Eddy current variable speed motors, electric motor control, flange mounted motors, geared and variable speed geared motors, speed controllers, induction motors, motorboard, motor graders, motor parts and accessories, motor starters, single wiper motor, swing motors, variable speed motors, and vertical deep tubewell motor. Entries include: Company name, postal address, telephone, fax, e-mail, website, contact person, designation, and product details.

Directory of South American Importers of Motors and Motor Parts--Electric. EXIM Infotek Private Ltd. • $250 Individuals. Covers: 80 South American importers of electric motors, motor equipment, and motor parts. Entries include: Company name, postal address, telephone, fax, e-mail, website, contact person, designation, and product details.

Directory of South Korean Manufacturers & Exporters of Engines & Engine Parts. EXIM Infotek Private Ltd. • $15 Individuals. Covers: 140 South Korean manufacturers and exporters of engine components/spare parts, engine parts and accessories, gaskets-various, internal combustion engines, pin-pistons, piston engines, piston brakes, used engines. Entries include: Company name, postal address, city, country, phone, fax, e-mail and websites, contact person, designation and product details.

Directory of South Korean Manufacturers and Exporters of Motors and Motor Parts--Electric. EXIM Infotek Private Ltd. • $250 Individuals. Covers: 70 South Korean manufacturers and exporters of motorcycles and mopeds. Entries include: Company name, postal address, telephone, fax, e-mail, website, contact person, designation, and product details.

Directory of Taiwanese Manufacturers & Exporters of Engines & Engine Parts. EXIM Infotek Private Ltd. • $15 Individuals. Covers: 130 Taiwanese manufacturers and exporters of engine components/spare parts, internal combustion engines, oil seals, pistons and plugs. Entries include: Company name, postal address, city, country, phone, fax, e-mail and websites, contact person, designation and product details.

Directory of Taiwanese Manufacturers and Exporters of Motors and Motor Parts--Electric. EXIM Infotek Private Ltd. • $650 Individuals. Covers: 340 Taiwanese manufacturers and exporters of electric motors below 1hp, electric motors over 1hp, explosion proof motors, motorcycle parts and accessories. Entries include: Company name, postal address, telephone, fax, e-mail, website, contact person, designation, and product details.

Fairplay World Shipping Directory. Fairplay Publications Ltd. • Daily. Covers: More than 76,000 companies worldwide engaged in some aspect of shipping, including over 10,000 ship-owners with fleets totaling over 45,000 vessels, shipbuilders and repairers, marine insurance shipping finance, protection and indemnity associations, marine equipment suppliers, and towing, salvage, and dredging; also lists marine organizations, shipbrokers, and consulting engineers and surveyors. Entries include: Company name, address, phone, fax, e-mail, URL, names of directors and executives, brief description of business; listings may also include associated and subsidiary companies and financial data.

Lloyd's Maritime Directory. Informa P.L.C. Informa Sports Group. • Annual. Covers: Over 40,000 shipowners, managers, and operators with 75,000 vessels. Also includes Marine consultants; towing, salvage, solicitors, P&I clubs; ship building and repair firms; general maritime organizations, banking and finance and more. Entries include: Firm name, address, phone, fax, e-mail, Internet; branch offices; names of principal executives; agents; parent and associated companies; and, for shipowners and lines, detailed information on ships owned, type, or capacity, etc. The former second volume of 'International Shipping and Shipbuilding Directory' is now published separately with the title 'Lloyd's List Marine Equipment Buyers' Guide' (see separate entry).

INTERNET DATABASES

Manufacturing Profiles. U. S. Bureau of the Census. Phone: (301)763-4636 or (301)763-4100; Fax: (301)763-4794; Email: webmaster@census.gov • URL: http://www.census.gov/prod/www/abs/mfg-prof.html • The Census Bureau makes available free on PDF (Portable Document Format) an annual consolidation of the entire Current Industrial Report series, presenting "all the data compiled." Contains statistics on production, shipments, inventories, consumption, exports, imports, and orders for a wide variety of manufactured products.

PERIODICALS AND NEWSLETTERS

Diesel & Gas Turbine Worldwide. Diesel and Gas Turbine Publications. • 10/year. $85. Covers engine room products and technologies in the power generation field.

Gas Turbine World. Pequot Publishing Inc. • Bimonthly. $130 Individuals.

TRADE/PROFESSIONAL ASSOCIATIONS

Association of Diesel Specialists. 400 Admiral Blvd., Kansas City, MO 64106. Phone: 888-401-1616 or (816)285-0810; Fax: (847)770-4952; Email: info@diesel.org • URL: http://diesel.org • Corporations and technically oriented professionals engaged in the sale and service of fuel injection, governor, supercharger, and turbocharger systems, and interested in improving the technology and servicing of these systems. Provides members with technical information and business management support. Sponsors a Parts Finder Program that compiles a monthly listing of obsolescent or surplus parts for sale by ADS members in the United States and Canada. Offers an ADS Nationwide Warranty Program which allows members to cooperate with each other and provide warranty service for transient customers. Conducts semiannual "TechCert" exams in cooperation with the National Institute for Automotive Service Excellence to certify diesel technicians.

ENTOMOLOGY, ECONOMIC

See ECONOMIC ENTOMOLOGY

ENTRANCE REQUIREMENTS

See COLLEGE ENTRANCE REQUIREMENTS

ENTREPRENEURIAL CAPITAL

See VENTURE CAPITAL

ENTREPRENEURIAL HISTORY

See BUSINESS HISTORY

ENTREPRENEURS AND INTRAPRENEURS

See also WOMEN EXECUTIVES

ABSTRACTS AND INDEXES

Business Periodicals Index Retrospective. EBSCO Publishing Inc. • 11/year. Quarterly and annual cumulations.

DIRECTORIES

Careers in Focus--Entrepreneurs. InfoBase Holdings Inc. • $35 Individuals hardcover. Covers: An overview of entrepreneurship, followed by a selection of jobs profiled in detail, including the nature of the job, earnings, prospects for employment, what kind of training and skills it requires, and sources for further information. Database includes: Black and white photographs.

Contemporary Entrepreneurs. Omnigraphics Inc. • Irregular. $95. Covers: Approximately 74 companies often cited as successful and the entrepreneurs who founded them. Entries include: Entrepreneur's name, year of birth, marital status, number of children, type of venture; venture's address, phone, founding, incorporation, revenues, number of employees, original investment, net worth; text describing the history, growth, and vision of the company and entrepreneurial lessons.

Directory of Registered Belgian Entrepreneurs and Companies. Cite Administrative de l'Etat. • Annual. Covers: Companies in Belgium. Entries include: Company name, address, phone, registration number, line of business, number of employees, business code.

The Entrepreneur's Sourcebook. Todd Publications. • $25. Covers: 7,000 organizations, publications, companies, and consultants that provide advice to entrepreneurs and small business owners. Database includes: List of more than 500 books, videos, CDs, and audiocassettes. Entries include: Name, address, phone, fax.

Hoover's Handbook of Emerging Companies. Dun & Bradstreet Inc. Hoover's Inc. • Annual. $213. Contains detailed profiles of 600 rapidly growing corporations. Includes indexes by industry, location, executive name, company name, and brand name.

100 Great Businesses and the Minds Behind Them. Bolinda Publishing. • NZ$39.95 Individuals. Covers: Entrepreneurs and their collection of stories from Australia and around the world.

E-BOOKS

Cases on Information Technology Entrepreneurship. Cengage Learning Inc. • 2007. eBook. Published by Information Science Reference. Offers a look into how IT can be the structural foundation of an entrepreneurship, and describes specific examples of IT as the base of a start-up company -- providing insight into the successes and failures of applying IT in innovative ways.

Entrepreneur's Showcase: Market Research for Small Businesses and the Woman Entrepreneur's Guide to Financing a Business. Cengage Learning Inc. • 2006. eBook. Published by Know!Books Press. Provides information on multiple aspects of entrepreneurship, focusing on market research for small business as well as on more gender-specific topics involved in starting a business.

ENCYCLOPEDIAS AND DICTIONARIES

Encyclopedia of Small Business. Cengage Learning Inc. • $763 Individuals. 2010. $696.00. 4th edition. Two volumes. Contains about 600 informative entries on a wide variety of topics affecting small business. Arrangement is alphabetical. eBook also available. Inquire for pricing.

Everyday Finance: Economics, Personal Money Management, and Entrepreneurship. Cengage Learning Inc. • $258 Individuals. 2008. 2 volumes. Contains 300 topical entries that are organized into 3 units: How the Economy Works: Personal Finance: Buying, Borrowing, Saving, and Insuring; and The World of Business. eBook available. Inquire for pricing.

GENERAL WORKS

Choosing the Right Business Entity. American CPE Inc. • Contains detailed training information covering methods and factors involved in selecting the most advantageous type of business entity for a new venture.

The Omaha Business Journal. Midlands Business Journal Publications. • Monthly. Business publication covering local start-ups and entrepreneurs.

Preparing an Entrepreneurial Business Plan. American CPE Inc. • Contains detailed training and instructional information on preparing and writing entrepreneurial business plans for beginning businesses. Offers insight and guidance on the process of writing the business plan, what a business plan accomplishes for start-up entrepreneurs, and how business plans can be helpful at all stages in the business life cycle. Covers topics such as the definition of a business plan, what goes into a business plan, meshing the entrepreneurial process and business planning, preparing the first draft of the plan, financing a business, redrafting and revising business plans, reaching the final draft, and more. Offers self-paced courseware and learning materials designed to enhance users' skills, interpersonal development, and professional abilities.

HANDBOOKS AND MANUALS

Standard Business Forms for the Entrepreneur. Entrepreneur Press. • Looseleaf. $59.50. A practical collection of forms useful to entrepreneurial small businesses. (Start-Up Business Guide No. E1319.).

Start-Up Business Guides. Entrepreneur Press. • Looseleaf. $59.50 each. Practical guides to starting a wide variety of small businesses.

INTERNET DATABASES

MBEMAG. Minority Business Entrepreneur Magazine. Phone: (310)540-9398; Fax: (310)792-8263; Email: webmaster@mbemag.com • URL: http://www.mbemag.com • Web site's main feature is the "MBE Business Resources Directory." This provides complete mailing addresses, phone, fax, and Web site addresses (URL) for more than 40 organizations and government agencies having information or assistance for ethnic minority and women business owners. Some other links are "Current Events," "Calendar of Events," and "Business Opportunities." Updating is bimonthly. Fees: Free.

ONLINE DATABASES

Wilson Business Abstracts Online. H.W. Wilson Co. • Indexes and abstracts 600 major business periodicals, plus the *Wall Street Journal* and the business section of the *New York Times*. Indexing is from 1982, abstracting from 1990, with the two newspapers included from 1993. Updated weekly. Inquire as to online cost and availability. (*Business Periodicals Index* without abstracts is also available online.).

PERIODICALS AND NEWSLETTERS

Business Start-Ups: Smart Ideas for Your Small Business. Entrepreneur Press. • Monthly. $14.97 per year. Provides advice for starting a small business. Includes business trends, new technology, E-commerce, and case histories ("real-life stories").

Business 2.0. Time Inc. • General business magazine emphasizing ideas, insight, and innovation.

Chief Executive Officers Newsletter: For the Entrepreneurial Manager and the Professionals Who Advise Him. Center for Entrepreneurial Management Inc. • Monthly. $96.00 per year. Looseleaf service. Formerly *Entrepreneurial Manager's Newsletter*.

Entrepreneur: The Small Business Authority. Entrepreneur Press. • Monthly. $19.97 per year. Contains advice for small business owners and prospective owners. Includes numerous franchise advertisements.

Fast Company: How Smart Business Works. Fast Company, Inc. • Monthly. $12.00 per year. Covers business management, with emphasis on creativity, leadership, innovation, career advancement, teamwork, the global economy, and the "new workplace.".

Income Opportunities.Com: The Original Small

Business - Home Office Magazine. Newline. • Monthly. $31.95 per year.

Inc.: The Magazine for Growing Companies. INC. • 10/year. $10 U.S. /year for two subscription. Edited for small office and home businesses with one to 25 employees. Covers management, office technology, and lifestyle. Incorporates *Self-Employed Professional*.

Minority Business Entrepreneur. Minority Business Entrepreneur. • Bimonthly. $25 Individuals print amd digital. Reports on issues "critical to the growth and development of minority and women-owned firms." Provides information on relevant legislation and profiles successful women and minority entrepreneurs.

RESEARCH CENTERS AND INSTITUTES

Babson College - Arthur M. Blank Center for Entrepreneurship. 231 Forest St., Wellesley Hills, MA 02481-6834. Phone: (781)233-5023; Fax: (781)239-4178; Email: jstrimaitis@babson.edu • URL: http://www.babson.edu/Academics/centers/blank-center/Pages/home.aspx • Sponsors annual Babson College Entrepreneurship Research Conference.

Baylor University - Center for Private Enterprise. PO Box 98003, Waco, TX 76798. Phone: (254)710-2263 or (254)710-6898; Fax: (254)710-1092; Email: kimberly_mencken@baylor.edu • URL: http://www.baylor.edu/business • Includes studies of entrepreneurship and women entrepreneurs.

Center for Entrepreneurial Studies & Development Inc. 1062 Maple Dr., Ste. 2, Morgantown, WV 26505. Phone: (304)293-5551; Fax: (304)293-6707; Email: info@cesd.wvu.edu • URL: http://www.cesd.wvu.edu • Inventory control systems included as a research field.

Dundalk Institute of Technology - Centre for Entrepreneurship Research. Dublin Rd., Dundalk, Louth, Ireland. Phone: 353 42 9370200; Fax: 353 42 9370201; Email: info@dkit.ie • URL: http://ww2.dkit.ie/research/research_centres/cer • Entrepreneurship, on a regional, national, and international basis.

New York University - Berkley Center for Entrepreneurial Studies. NYU Stern School of Business, Ste. 7-150, KMC, 44 W 4th St., New York, NY 10012. Phone: (212)998-0070; Fax: (212)995-4211; Email: jeffrey.carr@stern.nyu.edu • URL: http://w4.stern.nyu.edu/berkley • Factors that promote entrepreneurship and lead to the creation of new wealth and business revenues; business venturing within established firms. Topics include the major pitfalls and obstacles to start-ups, securing of venture capital, psychology and sociology of entrepreneurship, valuation and management of new ventures, technological innovation and new product development, emerging and creative industries, and cross-cultural environments that stimulate entrepreneurship.

Rensselaer Polytechnic Institute - Paul J. and Kathleen M. Severino Center for Technological Entrepreneurship. Pittsburgh Bldg., Lally School of Management, 110 8th St., Troy, NY 12180. Phone: (518)276-6842; Fax: (518)276-8661; Email: oconng@rpi.edu • URL: http://scte.rpi.edu • Technological entrepreneurship, including start-up companies to corporate venturing in Western economies and emerging markets.

Stockholm School of Economics - Center for Entrepreneurship and Business Creation. Saltmätargatan 13-17, SE-113 83 Stockholm, Sweden. Phone: 46 8 7369355; Email: info@hhs.se • URL: http://www.hhs.se/cebc/Pages/default.aspx • Entrepreneurship, business creation, and economic change.

University of California, Los Angeles - Institute for the Study of Educational Entrepreneurship. Moore Hall, Box 951521, Los Angeles, CA 90095. Phone: (310)825-2297; Email: isee@gseis.ucla.edu • URL: http://isee.gseis.ucla.edu • Relationships between private for-profit, private not-for-profit, and public organizations and their potential to advance public education reform.

University of Idaho - Center for Business Development and Entrepreneurship. College of Business & Economics, Moscow, ID 83844-3161. Phone: 800-960-3033; Fax: (208)885-8939; Email: dansmith@uidaho.edu • URL: http://www.cbehome.uidaho.edu/default.aspx?pid=32593 • Business and economics, including studies on market and labor force, regional economics.

University of Illinois at Urbana-Champaign - Bureau of Economic and Business Research. 430 Wohlers Hall, Office of Research, College of Business, 1206 S 6th St., Champaign, IL 61820. Phone: (217)333-2330; Fax: (217)333-7410; Email: lhuff@uiuc.edu • URL: http://business.illinois.edu/research • Economics and business, including studies in business expectations, health economics, forecasting and planning, innovation, entrepreneurship, consumer behavior, poverty problems, small business operations and problems, investment and growth, productivity, research methodology, organizational behavior, and international business and banking.

University of Missouri—Columbia - Business Research and Information Development Group. 410 S 6th St., 200 Engineering N, Columbia, MO 65211. Phone: (573)882-8855; Fax: (573)884-4297; Email: schmidtdc@missouri.edu • URL: http://www.bridg.org • Entrepreneurship, small business development and growth.

TRADE/PROFESSIONAL ASSOCIATIONS

American Home Business Association. 53 W 9000 S, Sandy, UT 84070. Phone: 866-396-7773 or (801)273-2350; Fax: (866)396-7773 or (801)273-2399; Email: info@homebusinessworks.com • URL: http://www.homebusinessworks.com • Offers benefits and services dedicated to supporting the needs of home business, small business and entrepreneurs. Benefits include health-auto-home insurance, legal, low long distance and 800 numbers, business line of credit, merchant accounts, tax programs, office supply and travel discounts and more. Seeks to provide members access to the best traditional benefits and timely information that is critical to conduct a successful home, small or Internet business.

Association des Femmes Chefs d'Entreprises du Cote d'Ivoire. BP 8232, Abidjan 08, Côte d'Ivoire. Phone: 225 3 327571; Email: fcem_ci@yahoo.fr • URL: http://www.fcem.org/en/pays-membres.html • Promotes women's entrepreneurial initiatives. Reinforces national associations of women business entrepreneurial potentials. Lobbies before the public and private institutions, policy makers and governments on issues that impede women's entrepreneurial potentials. Facilitates the development of business, partnership and trade. Fosters professional growth and business skills perfection. Encourages women to create enterprises.

Association des Femmes Chefs d'Entreprises du Maroc. Residence El Amri, Rue du 6 octubre, Quartie Racine, Casablanca, Morocco. Phone: 212 22 397593; Fax: 212 22 397736; Email: afem@afem.ma • URL: http://afem.ma • Promotes women's entrepreneurial initiatives. Reinforces national associations of women business entrepreneurial potentials. Lobbies before the public and private institutions, policy makers and governments on issues that impede women's entrepreneurial potentials. Facilitates the development of business, partnership and trade. Fosters professional growth and business skills perfection. Encourages women to create enterprises.

Association des Femmes d'Affaires et Chefs d'Entreprises du Gabon. B.P. 6023, Libreville, Gabon. Phone: 241 6 264216; Fax: 241 723883; Email: refegcham@yahoo.fr • URL: http://www.fcem.org/en/pays-membres.html • Promotes women's entrepreneurial initiatives. Reinforces national associations of women business entrepreneurial potentials. Lobbies before the public and private institutions, policy makers and governments on issues that impede women's entrepreneurial potentials. Facilitates the development of business, partnership and trade. Fosters professional growth and business skills perfection. Encourages women to create enterprises.

Association des Femmes Entrepreneurs Chefs d'Entreprises. Ave. Le Marinel N 9-11, Commune de la Gombe, Kinshasa, Republic of the Congo. Phone: 243 998911092; Fax: 243 3225667; Email: bismura2@yahoo.fr • URL: http://www.fcem.org/en/pays-membres.html • Promotes women's entrepreneurial initiatives. Reinforces national associations of women business entrepreneurial potentials. Lobbies before the public and private institutions, policy makers and governments on issues that impede women's entrepreneurial potentials. Facilitates the development of business, partnership and trade. Fosters professional growth and business skills perfection. Encourages women to create enterprises.

Association Mauricienne des Femmes Chefs d'Entreprise. Regency Sq., 1st Fl., 4 Conal and McIrvine St., Beau Bassin, Mauritius. Email: cheelichop@intnet.mu • URL: http://fcem.org/en/pays-membres/195-pays-membres/fiche-pays-details/afrique-membres/1517-ile-maurice-afrique-membres.html • Promotes women's entrepreneurial initiatives. Reinforces national associations of women business entrepreneurial potentials. Lobbies before the public and private institutions, policy makers and governments on issues that impede women's entrepreneurial potentials. Facilitates the development of business, partnership and trade. Fosters professional growth and business skills perfection. Encourages women to create enterprises.

Association of Business Women in Iceland. Kringlunni 7, IS-103 Reykjavik, Iceland. Email: fka@fka.is • URL: http://www.fka.is • Promotes women's entrepreneurial initiatives. Reinforces national associations of women business entrepreneurial potentials. Lobbies before the public and private institutions, policy makers and governments on issues that impede women's entrepreneurial potentials. Facilitates the development of business, partnership and trade. Fosters professional growth and business skills perfection. Encourages women to create enterprises.

Association of Slovenia Entrepreneurs. PO Box 40-95, 1000 Ljubljana, Slovenia. Phone: 386 1 5443678; Fax: 386 1 5443680; Email: marta.turk1@guest.arnes.si • URL: http://fcem.org • Promotes women's entrepreneurial initiatives. Lobbies before the public and private institutions, policy makers and governments on issues that impede women's entrepreneurial potentials. Facilitates the development of business, partnership and trade. Fosters professional growth and business skills perfection. Encourages women to create enterprises.

Association of Small and Medium Enterprises. 167 Jalan Bukit Merah, Tower 4, No.03-13, Singapore 150167, Singapore. Phone: 65 65130388; Fax: 65 65130399; Email: enquiries@edc-asme.sg • URL: http://www.asme.org.sg • Seeks to bring together entrepreneurs of various industries and service sectors for information exchange; promotes relationship between various national interest bodies; provides continuous business education and training; fosters entrepreneurship networking both locally and internationally; works toward the institutionalization of ASME as a business association network body.

Association Senegalaise des Femmes Chefs d'Entreprise. B.P. 30081, Dakar, Senegal. Phone: 221 338241010; Fax: 221 8257246; Email:

hadjadiordiop2000@yahoo.fr • URL: http://www.fcem.org/en/pays-membres.html • Promotes women's entrepreneurial initiatives. Lobbies before the public and private institutions, policy makers and governments on issues that impede women's entrepreneurial potentials. Facilitates the development of business, partnership and trade. Fosters professional growth and business skills perfection. Encourages women to create enterprises.

Beyster Institute. 9500 Gilman Dr. Otterson Hall S, Fourth Fl., La Jolla, CA 92093-0553. Phone: (858)246-0654; Email: beysterinfo@rady.ucsd.edu • URL: http://beysterinstitute.ucsd.edu • Helps business leaders build successful companies worldwide through training, education and outreach. Serves entrepreneurs by teaching them how to be effective managers and showing them how employee ownership can be adapted to fit their individual companies.

British Association of Women Entrepreneurs. 112 John Player Bldg., Stirling FK7 7RP, United Kingdom. Phone: 44 18 2725 5170; Email: deb@bawe-uk.org • URL: http://www.bawe-uk.org • Encourages the personal development of member entrepreneurs. Provides opportunities for members to expand their business through informal and formal networking. Represents and promotes British entrepreneurship worldwide.

Canadian Association of Women Executives and Entrepreneurs. 401 Bay St., Ste. 1600, Toronto, ON, Canada M5K 2Y4. Phone: (416)756-0000; Fax: (416)756-0000; Email: contact@cawee.net • URL: http://www.cawee.net • Seeks to provide opportunities for women to empower other women in the development and advancement of their business and professional lives; which fosters financial independence, professional development and personal satisfaction.

Central Association of Women Entrepreneurs. Kaisaniemenkatu 1 B a 74, FIN-00100 Helsinki, Finland. Phone: 358 40 5222252; Email: toimisto@yrittajanaiset.fi • URL: http://www.yrittajanaiset.fi • Women entrepreneurs in Finland. Promotes the participation of women in Finland's economic structure. Assists women in small business development.

Centre for Women in Business. Mt. Saint Vincent University, The Meadows, 2nd Fl., 166 Bedford Hwy., Halifax, NS, Canada B3M 2J6. Phone: 888-776-9022 or (902)457-6449; Fax: (902)443-4687; Email: cwb@msvu.ca • URL: http://www.centreforwomeninbusiness.ca/en/home/default.aspx • Represents women entrepreneurs in Canada.

Chambre Nationale des Femmes Chefs d'Entreprise. 17, Rue Abderrahamen El Jaziri, 1002 Tunis, Tunisia. Phone: 216 71 860112; Fax: 216 71 862049; Email: cnfce.tunisie@fcem.ws • URL: http://www.fcem.org/en/pays-membres.html • Represents the interests of women entrepreneurs before national and international organizations and institutions. Reinforces the presence and representation of women within employer organizations and national chambers. Promotes women entrepreneurship. Promotes exchanges, relationships, and development of regional, national and international contacts aimed at reinforcing partnerships and access to new markets.

China Entrepreneur Club. Peking University Technology Park, Innovation Ctr., Rm. 501, No. 127-1 Zhongguancun N Ave., Haidan District, Beijing 100080, Beijing, China. Phone: 86 10 62766066; Fax: 86 10 62768122; Email: international@daonong.com • URL: http://www.daonong.com/English • Promotes comprehensive social development and enhances the important role played by Chinese enterprises in the sustainable development of China and the world. Seeks to bring together visionary business leaders to advance common values, discover new drives for commercial spirit and guide businesses to the right path.

Confederation of Bolivian Private Entrepreneurs. Calle Mendez Arcos No. 117, Plz. Espana, La Paz, Bolivia. Phone: 591 2 2420999 or 591 2421254; Fax: 591 2 2421272; Email: cepb@cepb.org.bo • URL: http://www.cepb.org.bo • Represents the interests of the private entrepreneurs in Bolivia.

Economiesuisse. Verband der Schweizer Unternehmen, Hegibachstrasse 47, CH-8032 Zurich, Switzerland. Phone: 41 44 4213535; Fax: 41 44 4213434; Email: info@economiesuisse.ch • URL: http://www.economiesuisse.ch • Aims to preserve entrepreneurial freedom for all businesses, to continuously improve Switzerland's global competitiveness in manufacturing, services, and research, and to promote sustained growth as a prerequisite for a high level of employment in Switzerland. Creates an optimal economic environment for Swiss business.

Enactus Canada. 920 Yonge St., Ste. 800, Toronto, ON, Canada M4W 3C7. Phone: 800-766-8169 or (416)304-1566; Fax: (416)864-0514 • URL: http://www.enactus.ca • Young people, business owners, or engaged in entrepreneurial activities. Promotes growth and development of members' business interests. Provides support and services to businesses owned by young people; encourages communication and mutual support among collegiate entrepreneurs.

Entrepreneurs Association of Slovakia. Cukrova 14, 813 39 Bratislava, Slovakia. Phone: 421 2 59324344 or 421 2 59324343; Fax: 421 2 59324350; Email: zps@zps.sk • URL: http://www.zps.sk • Aims to contribute towards the development of modern and developed market economy; to protect entrepreneur status of business rights and free market restrictions, and to prevent political and economic measures leading to decline of equal market business background.

Entrepreneurs' Organization. 500 Montgomery St., Ste. 700, Alexandria, VA 22314. Phone: (703)519-6700; Fax: (703)519-1864; Email: info@eonetwork.org • URL: http://www.eonetwork.org • Entrepreneurs under the age of 50 who have either founded, co-founded, are a controlling shareholder of, or own a firm with annual gross revenues exceeding $1,000,000 (membership is by invitation only). Engages leading entrepreneurs to learn and grow. Serves as a focal point for networking and development of members through small group learning sessions, regular local chapter social and learning events, and global conference-based education programs.

Entrepreneurs' Organization - Pakistan Chapter. 121 Ferozepur Rd., Lahore, Pakistan. Phone: 92 42 35058218; Email: tm.admin@eolahore.org • URL: http://eoaccess.eonetwork.org/lahore/Pages/default.aspx • Represents the interests of entrepreneurs who wish to learn and grow from each other. Provides opportunities for members to connect through forums and one-on-one interactions with fellow entrepreneurs. Provides venues which will allow members to meet and learn from influential members of the community.

The Entrepreneurship Institute. 3700 Corporate Dr., Ste. 145, Columbus, OH 43231. Phone: (614)895-1153 • URL: http://www.tei.net • Provides encouragement and assistance to entrepreneurs who operate companies with revenue in excess of $1 million. Unites financial, legal, and community resources to help foster the success of companies. Promotes sharing of information and interaction between members. Operates President's forums and projects which are designed to improve communication between businesses, develop one-to-one business relationships between small and mid-size businesses and local resources, provide networking, and stimulate the growth of existing companies.

Environmental Entrepreneurs. Natural Resources Defense Council, 40 W 20th St., New York, NY 10011. Phone: (212)727-2700 or (212)727-4437; Fax: (212)727-1773; Email: yli@nrdc.org • URL: http://www.e2.org • Represents business people who believe in protecting the environment while building economic prosperity. Serves as a champion on the economic side of good environmental policy by taking an economically sound approach to environmental issues. Focuses on environmental policies that drive economic growth in a healthy direction.

European Business and Innovation Centre Network. Ave. de Tervueren 168, B-1150 Brussels, Belgium. Phone: 32 2 772 89 00; Fax: 32 2 772 9574; Email: info@ebn.eu • URL: http://www.ebn.be • Promotes business innovation and the entrepreneurial spirit in Europe.

European Confederation of Junior Enterprises. Rue Potagere 119, B-1210 Brussels, Belgium. Phone: 32 2 4201752; Email: mail@jadenet.org • URL: http://www.jadenet.org • Represents young entrepreneurs in Europe; provides training and assistance to set up new organizations, including legal and contact information.

Ewing Marion Kauffman Foundation. 4801 Rockhill Rd., Kansas City, MO 64110. Phone: (816)932-1000; Email: contact@kauffman.org • URL: http://www.kauffman.org • Works to accelerate entrepreneurship in America.

Female Europeans of Medium and Small Enterprises. Rue Jacques de Lalaing 4, B-1040 Brussels, Belgium. Phone: 32 2 2850714; Fax: 32 2 2307861 • URL: http://www.fem-online.eu • Represents female co-entrepreneurs and entrepreneurs working in small and medium-sized businesses in Europe. Seeks to improve the cultural, legal, and social position of female co-entrepreneurs and self-employed women. Acts as the European point of contact dealing with all issues related to female co-entrepreneurs or self-employed women. Aims to achieve an exchange of knowledge and experience amongst women of all EU Member states and also other European countries. Encourages an entrepreneurial spirit amongst women.

Groupement des Femmes d'Affaires de la Guinee. B.P. 3009, Conakry, Guinea. Phone: 224 453899; Fax: 224 453518; Email: cenafodgn@eti-bull.net • URL: http://www.fcem.org/en/pays-membres.html • Promotes women's entrepreneurial initiatives. Reinforces national associations of women business entrepreneurial potentials. Lobbies before the public and private institutions, policy makers and governments on issues that impede women's entrepreneurial potentials. Facilitates the development of business, partnership and trade. Fosters professional growth and business skills perfection. Encourages women to create enterprises.

Groupement des Femmes d'Affaires du Cameroun. BP 1940, Douala, Cameroon. Phone: 237 33401732; Fax: 237 33406533; Email: gfacnational@yahoo.fr • URL: http://fcem.org/en/pays-membres.html • Promotes women's entrepreneurial initiatives. Reinforces national associations of women business entrepreneurial potentials. Lobbies before the public and private institutions, policy makers and governments on issues that impede women's entrepreneurial potentials. Facilitates the development of business, partnership and trade. Fosters professional growth and business skills perfection. Encourages women to create enterprises.

Hong Kong Women Professionals and Entrepreneurs Association. Kingswell Commercial Tower, 171-173 Lockhart Rd., Rm. B, 18 Fl., Hong Kong, Hong Kong, China. Phone: 852 28822555; Fax: 852 28824673; Email: info@hkwpea.org • URL: http://www.hkwpea.org • Works to create practical and innovative learning and business opportunities for members and for others. Promotes high professional standards. Reaches out and establishes relationships with counterparts in

Mainland China and abroad.

Hrvatsko Udruženje Menadžera I Poduzetnik. Ban Josip Jelacic Square 15 / II., HR-10000 Zagreb, Croatia. Phone: 385 1 4838709; Fax: 385 1 4811787 • URL: http://www.croma.hr • Works to foster professional management practices in Croatian business and industry. Offers educational programs and business related information.

The Indus Entrepreneurs Dubai. Bldg. No. 1, DIC First Steps, Dubai Internet City, Dubai, United Arab Emirates. Phone: 971 4 3913517; Fax: 971 4 3918665; Email: tiedubai@tiedubai.org • URL: http://tiedubai.org • Works to foster and promote the spirit of entrepreneurship in Dubai. Provides a strong and innovative platform for young start-ups and aspiring entrepreneurs. Provides guidance and support through mentoring and networking.

Korean American Society of Entrepreneurs. 2882 Sand Hill Rd., Ste. 100, Menlo Park, CA 94025. Email: ben@kase.org • URL: http://www.kase.org • Brings together entrepreneurs, engineers, corporate executives, venture capitalists, and other professionals with roots or interests in Korea. Fosters and supports network of Korean Americans interested in starting or playing key roles in companies in the United States. Facilitates the professional development, networking, and mentoring of its members. Provides information on all areas related to its members' interests.

Korean Women Entrepreneurs Association. 7F, 733-24, Yeoksam-dong, Gangnam-Gu, Seoul, South Korea. Phone: 82 2 3690922; Fax: 82 2 3690950; Email: ceo@wbiz.or.kr • URL: http://www.womanbiz.or.kr • Represents Korean businesswomen and provides full-support for the growth and development of their businesses. Helps entrepreneurs gain confidence and improve their competitiveness through counseling and training. Implements government-commissioned projects.

My Own Business, Inc. 13181 Crossroads Pkwy. N, Ste. 190, City of Industry, CA 91746. Phone: (562)463-1800; Fax: (562)463-1802; Email: support@myownbusiness.org • URL: http://www.myownbusiness.org • Educates small business owners by providing free coursework. Develops, produces, implements, updates and markets educational offerings through multiple delivery channels. Seeks to expand collaborations with companies, schools, the community and other institutions. Works to support the vital social and economic contributions of small businesses by nurturing entrepreneurship and helping individuals build their own business.

National Association for Community College Entrepreneurship. Bldg. 101-R, 1 Federal St., Springfield, MA 01105. Phone: (413)306-3131; Fax: (413)755-6101; Email: wolpert@nacce.com • URL: http://www.nacce.com • Establishes entrepreneurship education as a core offering to foster economic development through community colleges. Focuses on increasing economic development through entrepreneurship education and student business incubation at the community college level.

National Association of Entrepreneurial Parents. PO Box 320722, Fairfield, CT 06825. Phone: (203)371-6212; Fax: (203)371-6212 • URL: http://www.en-parent.com • Seeks to assist "parents who are looking to balance work and family on their own terms." Facilitates networking among entrepreneurial parents; provides ad opportunities for members; organizes support groups for members; makes available discount programs and services to members.

National Association of Women Business Owners. 601 Pennsylvania Ave. NW, South Bldg., Ste. 900, Washington, DC 20004. Phone: 800-556-2926; Fax: (202)403-3788; Email: national@nawbo.org • URL: http://www.nawbo.org • Formerly Association of Women Business Owners.

National Black Chamber of Commerce. 4400 Jenifer St. NW, Ste. 331, Washington, DC 20015-2133. Phone: (202)466-6888; Fax: (202)466-4918; Email: info@nationalbcc.org • URL: http://www.nationalbcc.org • Works for the issues of economics and entrepreneurship in the African-American community.

National Coalition for Capital. 1028 33rd St. NW, Ste. 200, Washington, DC 20007. Phone: (202)337-1661 • URL: http://www.nationalcoalitionforcapital.org • Represents leaders who support economic development and job creation through long-term access to capital for entrepreneurs and emerging companies. Serves as a resource for promising small and emerging companies, entrepreneurs, investors, economic developers and other stakeholders within the nation's emerging investment infrastructure.

National Nurses in Business Association. 8941 Atlanta Ave., Ste. 202, Huntington Beach, CA 92646. Phone: 877-353-8888 • URL: http://www.nnba.net • Promotes, supports, educates, and provides a comprehensive network for nurse entrepreneurs.

Network for Teaching Entrepreneurship. 120 Wall St., 18th Fl., New York, NY 10005. • URL: http://www.nfte.com • Devoted to teaching entrepreneurship education to low-income young people, ages 11 through 18.

North America Chinese Clean-tech and Semiconductor Association. 809 Cuesta Dr., Ste. 208B, Mountain View, CA 94040-3666. • URL: http://www.nacsa.com • Represents the interests of professionals dedicated to the advancement of Chinese professionals in high-tech industries. Strengthens networking among professionals. Fosters entrepreneurship among ethnic Chinese. Promotes the exchange in the global semiconductor and information technology industries.

Organization for Entrepreneurial Development. 25 Pine St., Ste. 9, Rockaway, NJ 07866. Phone: 800-767-0999; Fax: (973)784-1099; Email: questions@oedglobal.org • URL: http://www.oedglobal.org • Offers educational and training programs that are focused on the entrepreneurial community. Collaborates with educators and educational institutions for the improvement of entrepreneurial skills and knowledge. Seeks to solicit the help and support of the business community at large in aiding the entrepreneurial community.

Rising Tide Capital. 334 Martin Luther King Dr., Jersey City, NJ 07305. Phone: (201)432-4316; Fax: (201)432-3504; Email: info@risingtidecapital.org • URL: http://risingtidecapital.org • Strives to assist entrepreneurs and communities to build tough businesses that transform lives, strengthen families and create vibrant, sustainable neighborhoods. Works to build a replicable model for high-quality entrepreneurial development services that can be locally adopted in low-wealth communities and used as a catalyst for social and economic empowerment. Connects entrepreneurs to appropriate business financing.

Russian Academy of Entrepreneurship. ul. Radio, 14, 105005 Moscow, Russia. Phone: 7 495 6322425 or 7 495 6322426; Email: priem@rusacad.ru • URL: http://www.rusacad.ru • Works to help Russian businesses compete in a market economy. Conducts economic analysis.

Seton Hill University's E-magnify. Seton Hill University, 1 Seton Hill Dr., 3rd Fl., Administration Bldg., Greensburg, PA 15601. Phone: (724)830-4625; Fax: (724)834-7131; Email: info@e-magnify.com • URL: http://www.e-magnify.com • Promotes women and business ownership. Offers a variety of entrepreneurial resources, educational programs, advocacy initiatives and networking opportunities to women entrepreneurs. Works "to strengthen the economic impact of women business owners as a collective force and to advance their growth through innovative programming in entrepreneurship and new venture creation." Provides support, education and encouragement essential for the continued growth of women-owned businesses through its services.

Turkish American Business Connection. 2784 Homestead Rd., No. 118, Santa Clara, CA 95051. Phone: (408)404-5208; Fax: (408)404-5208; Email: info@tabc-us.org • URL: http://www.tabc-us.org • Brings together Turkish-American entrepreneurs, professionals and business people. Advances the interests of Turkish-American businessmen, entrepreneurs and professionals from all industries. Promotes professional networking opportunities for and among its members.

Women Business Owners. 9594 1st Ave. NE, No. 274, Seattle, WA 98115-2012. Phone: (206)575-3232; Email: info@womenbusinessowners.org • URL: http://www.womenbusinessowners.org • Aims to empower, educate and enhance the lives of children and women business owners throughout the world. Provides programs and workshops on educating future entrepreneurs. Works to develop and encourage entrepreneurship, achievement and success in business.

Women Chiefs of Enterprises International. c/o Julie Ankers, President, Level 6 276 Pitt St., Sydney, NSW 2000, Australia. Phone: 61 2 92675220; Fax: 61 2 92674202 • URL: http://www.wcei.com.au • Represents women entrepreneurs in Australia. Encourages innovation in the development of entrepreneurial skills. Creates opportunities for business development.

Women Entrepreneurs of Canada. 720 Spadina Ave., Ste. 202, Toronto, ON, Canada M5S 2T9. Phone: 866-207-4439 or (416)921-5050; Fax: (416)929-5256; Email: wec@wec.ca • URL: http://www.wec.ca • Addresses the need of women entrepreneurs and supports their growth and development. Provides meaningful networking opportunities to connect with peers as well as the larger business community, government and the international business community. Builds entrepreneurship acumen and business leadership capacity.

ENVIRONMENT

See also AIR POLLUTION; ENVIRONMENTAL LAW; WATER POLLUTION

ABSTRACTS AND INDEXES

Environment Abstracts. University Publications of America. • Monthly. Price varies. Provides multidisciplinary coverage of the world's environmental literature. Incorporates *Acid Rain Abstracts.*

Environment Abstracts Annual: A Guide to the Key Environmental Literature of the Year. University Publications of America. • Annual. $495.00. A yearly cumulation of *Environment Abstracts.*

Excerpta Medica: Environmental Health and Pollution Control. Elsevier. • 16 times a year. Institutions, $3,246.00 per year. Section 46 of *Excerpta Medica.* Covers air, water, and land pollution and noise control.

NTIS Alerts: Environmental Pollution & Control. U.S. Department of Commerce National Technical Information Service. • Biweekly. $130 per year. Covers the following categories of environmental pollution: air, water, solid wastes, radiation, pesticides, and noise.

Social Sciences Citation Index. Thomson Reuters Corp. • Weekly. Product is accessed via *Web of Science.*

Social Sciences Index Retrospective: 1907-1983. EBSCO Publishing Inc. • Indexing for 1,000,000 articles. Coverage includes international index and social sciences and humanities index.

ALMANACS AND YEARBOOKS

Earth Almanac: An Annual Geophysical Review of the State of the Planet. Natalie Goldstein. Greenwood Publishing Group Inc. • $91.95. Provides background information, statistics, and a summary of major events relating to the atmosphere, oceans, land, and fresh water.

Land Use and Environment Law Review. Thomson West. • Annual. $1,392. Features property rights and economic allocation of natural resources.

State of the World (year). Worldwatch Institute. • Annual. $22.00. Provides yearly analysis of factors influencing the global environment.

Vital Signs: The Trends That Are Shaping Our Future (year). Worldwatch Institute. • Annual. $19. 95. Provides access to selected indicators showing social, economic, and environmental trends throughout the world. Includes data relating to food, energy, transportation, finance, population, and other topics.

CD-ROM DATABASES

Environment Abstracts on CD-ROM. University Publications of America. • Quarterly. $1,295.00 per year. Contains the following CD-ROM databases: *Environment Abstracts, Energy Abstracts,* and *Acid Rain Abstracts.* Length of coverage varies.

Social Sciences Abstracts. EBSCO Publishing Inc. • Provides indexing from 1983 and abstracting from 1994 of more than 750 periodicals covering economics, area studies, community health, public administration, public welfare, urban studies, and many other topics related to the social sciences.

Social Sciences Citation Index. Thomson Reuters Corp. • Weekly. Product is accessed via *Web of Science.*

DIRECTORIES

Directory of African Importers of Environment Protection and Pollution Control Equipment. EXIM Infotek Private Ltd. • $200 Individuals. Covers: 40 African importers of pollution control equipment, wastewater treatment, water treatment, and purifying equipment. Entries include: Company name, postal address, telephone, fax, e-mail, website, contact person, designation, and product details.

Directory of American Manufacturers and Exporters of Environment and Pollution Control Equipment. EXIM Infotek Private Ltd. • $650 Individuals. Covers: 340 American manufacturers and exporters of air filtration and cleaning equipment, environmental control and monitoring equipment, environmental products, gas absorbers, lease environmental instrument systems, oil and water separators, oil boom accessories, pollution control equipment and systems, pollution sampling equipment, portable water treatment plants, reverse osmosis, distillation water purifying equipment, waste heat recovery equipment, water pollution control equipment, water treatment equipment, water treatment for PH reduction utilizing carbon dioxide, water treatment plants and engineering services, and water treatment including ozone technology. Entries include: Company name, postal address, telephone, fax, e-mail, website, contact person, designation, and product details.

Directory of Asian Importers of Environment Protection and Pollution Control Equipment. EXIM Infotek Private Ltd. • Covers: 230 Asian importers of air cleaner, dust collectors, dust extractor systems, environment equipment, environment protection equipment, environmental monitoring equipment, environmentally conserving or improving products, noise control equipment, ozone generators, pollution control equipment, sewage treatment, water purification equipment, water treatment, water treatment equipment, water treatment plants, and purifying equipment. Entries include: Company name, postal address, telephone, fax, e-mail, website, contact person, designation, and product details.

Directory of British Importers of Environmental Protection and Pollution Control Equipment. EXIM Infotek Private Ltd. • $150 Individuals. Covers: 40 British importers of environmental protection equipment, pollution control equipment, water treatment, and purifying equipment. Entries include: Company name, postal address, telephone, fax, e-mail, website, contact person, designation, and product details.

Directory of French Importers of Environmental and Pollution Control Equipment. EXIM Infotek Private Ltd. • Covers: 30 French importers of environmental protection equipment, pollution control equipment, water treatment, and purifying equipment. Entries include: Company name, postal address, telephone, fax, e-mail, website, contact person, designation, and product details.

Directory of Japanese Importers of Environment and Pollution Control Equipment. EXIM Infotek Private Ltd. • $200 Individuals. Covers: 45 Japanese importers of dust collectors, environmental equipment, environmental protection equipment, environmentally conserving or improving products, noise control equipment, pollution control equipment, water purification equipment, water treatment, water treatment equipment, and purifying equipment. Entries include: Company name, postal address, telephone, fax, e-mail, website, contact person, designation, and product details.

Directory of Japanese Manufacturers and Exporters of Environment and Pollution Control Equipment. EXIM Infotek Private Ltd. • Covers: 20 Japanese manufacturers and exporters of air pollution systems, environmental equipment, evaporators, ion exchange equipment, and pollution control equipment. Entries include: Company name, postal address, telephone, fax, e-mail, website, contact person, designation, and product details.

Directory of Middle East Importers of Environment Protection and Pollution Control Equipment. EXIM Infotek Private Ltd. • Covers: 200 Middle East importers of environmental protection equipment, garbage disposals and compactors, pollution control equipment, water purification equipment, and water treatment equipment. Entries include: Company name, postal address, telephone, fax, e-mail, website, contact person, designation, and product details.

Directory of North American Importers of Environment Protection and Pollution Control Equipment. EXIM Infotek Private Ltd. • $200 Individuals. Covers: 50 North American importers of environmental protection equipment, pollution control equipment, water purification equipment, water treatment, and purifying equipment. Entries include: Company name, postal address, telephone, fax, e-mail, website, contact person, designation, and product details.

Directory of SAARC Importers of Environment Protection and Pollution Control Equipment. EXIM Infotek Private Ltd. • Covers: 20 companies in member countries of the South Asian Association for Regional Cooperation (SAARC) that import carbon dioxide and kitchen hood flooring systems, deionizers, environmental control equipment, environmental noise monitor, pollution control equipment, sewage cleaning equipment, sewage treatment, water purification equipment, water treatment equipment and plants. Entries include: Company name, postal address, telephone, fax, e-mail, website, contact person, designation, and product details.

Directory of South American Importers of Environment Protection and Pollution Control Equipment. EXIM Infotek Private Ltd. • $200 Individuals. Covers: 80 South American importers of environmental protection equipment, pollution control equipment, water treatment, and purifying equipment. Entries include: Company name, postal address, telephone, fax, e-mail, website, contact person, designation, and product details.

Directory of South Korean Manufacturers and Exporters of Environment and Pollution Control Equipment. EXIM Infotek Private Ltd. • $200 Individuals. Covers: 60 South Korean manufacturers and exporters of air pollution control equipment, air cleaner, noise pollution control equipment, water and sewage treatment plant. Entries include: Company name, postal address, telephone, fax, e-mail, website, contact person, designation, and product details.

Directory of Taiwanese Manufacturers and Exporters of Environment and Pollution Control Equipment. EXIM Infotek Private Ltd. • $400 Individuals. Covers: 160 Taiwanese manufacturers and exporters of air pollution control equipment, noise pollution control equipment, water and sewage treatment plant. Entries include: Company name, postal address, telephone, fax, e-mail, website, contact person, designation, and product details.

Environmental Guide to the Internet. Government Institutes. • $83 Individuals Paperback. Covers: 1,200 resources covering the environment on the Internet, including organizations, products, and resources, including discussion groups, electronic journals, newsgroups, and discussion groups. Entries include: Name, online address, description, e-mail address.

Environmental Management Information Systems Report. Donley Technology. • $389 Individuals single. Covers: 26 software systems that manage environmental data, including inventory and waste tracking, air pollution tracking, report and label generation, mapping, and help with emergency response. Entries include: Company name, address, phone, hardware and software requirements, description of system, cost.

The International Directory of Importers--Environmental Protection Equipment Importers. Interdata. • $200 Individuals print. Covers: 1,100 international firms importing environmental protection equipment. Entries include: Company name and address, contact person, email, number of employees, year established, phone and telefaxes, business activity, bank references, as well as a listing of environmental protection equipment currently being imported.

E-BOOKS

Green Technologies and Business Practices: An IT Approach. Cengage Learning Inc. • 2012. eBook. Published by IGI Global. An international platform that brings together academics, researchers, lecturers, policy makers, practitioners, and persons in decision-making positions from all backgrounds who ultimately share new theories, research findings and case studies, together enhancing understanding and collaboration of green issues in business and the role of information technologies and also analyze recent developments in theory and practice.

ENCYCLOPEDIAS AND DICTIONARIES

Encyclopedia of Environmental Science and Engineering. CRC Press. • $900.00. Two volumes. Covers 89 entries on a variety of environmental topics.

Environmental Encyclopedia. Cengage Learning Inc. • $327 Individuals. 2011. $298.00. 4th edition. Provides over 1,300 articles on all aspects of the environment. Written in non-technical style. eBook also available. Inquire for pricing.

Pollution A to Z. Cengage Learning Inc. • 2003.Two volumes. Provides encyclopedic coverage of many aspects of environmental pollution, including air, water, noise, and soil. Inquire as to price and availability.

GENERAL WORKS

The Eco-antique and Retro Guide: Supporting Local Businesses--Promoting Source Reduction and Energy Conservation--Helping Our Communities. Ariela Press. • $1 from publisher. Covers Oregon stores and other organizations that recycle, recondition, or resell, and/or promote the use of recycled materials.

INTERNET DATABASES

E: The Environmental Magazine (online). Earth Action Network. 1536 Crest Dr., Los Angeles, CA 90035. Email: eanla@aol.com • URL: http://www.emagazine.com/view/?289&printview • Bimonthly. $24.95 Individuals. Web site provides full-text articles from *E: The Environmental Magazine* for a period of about two years. Searching is provided. Alphabetical and subject links are shown for a wide variety of environmental Web sites. Fees: Free.

National Library of Medicine. National Institutes of Health. 9000 Rockville Pke., Bethesda, MD 20892. Phone: (301)496-4000; Email: nihinfo@od.nih.gov • URL: http://www.nih.gov • NLM Web site offers free access through MEDLINE ("PubMed") to about nine million references to articles appearing in some 4,000 biomedical journals, with abstracts. Search interfaces range from "simple keywords to advanced Boolean expressions." The NLM site offers many links to other sources of biomedical and technical information (the National Center for Biotechnology Information, for example). Fees: Free.

ONLINE DATABASES

Aqualine. Cambridge Scientific Abstracts L.P. • Provides online citations and abstracts to a wide variety of literature relating to the aquatic environment, including 400 journals, from 1960 to date. Updating is monthly. Inquire as to online cost and availability.

Environmental Business Journal. Environmental Business International Inc. • Contains the complete text of *Environmental Business Journal*, a monthly newsletter covering business-related information on the environmental industry.

Wilson Social Sciences Abstracts Online. H.W. Wilson Co. • Provides online abstracting and indexing of more than 500 periodicals covering area studies, community health, public administration, public welfare, urban studies, and many other social science topics. Time period is 1994 to date for abstracts and 1983 to date for indexing, with updates weekly. Inquire as to online cost and availability.

PERIODICALS AND NEWSLETTERS

Amber Waves. Economic Research Service Hazard Analysis and Critical Control Points. • Quarterly. Replaces *Agricultural Outlook; Food Review*; and *Rural America.* Provides research and analysis from the U.S. Department of Agriculture's Economic Research Service. Includes economic data on agriculture, food, trade, and environmental factors.

E Magazine: The Environmental. Earth Action Network, Inc. • Bimonthly. $20.00 per year. A popular, consumer magazine providing news, information, and commentary on a wide range of environmental issues.

Ecology. Ecological Society of America. • Monthly. $470.00 per year. All forms of life in relation to environment.

Ecology Law Quarterly. University of California Boalt Hall School of Law. • Quarterly. $35 Individuals. Journal covering ecology and law.

EM: A&WMA's Environmental Solutions That Make Good Business Sense. Air and Waste Management Association. • Monthly. Institutions, $299.00 per year; nonprofit and government agencies, $199.00 per year. Newsletter. Provides news of regulations, legislation, and technology relating to the environment, recycling, and waste control. Formerly *Environmental Manager.*

Environment: Where Science and Policy Meet. Scientists' Institute for Public Information. Taylor & Francis Group Heldref Publications. • 10 times a year. Individuals, $48.00 per year; institutions, $98.00 per year.

Environmental Business Journal: Strategic Information for a Changing Industry. Environmental Business International Inc. • Monthly. $250 Single issue. Includes both industrial and financial information relating to individual companies and to the environmental industry in general. Covers air pollution, wat es, U. S. Department of Health and Human Services. Provides conference, workshop, and symposium proceedings, as well as extensive reviews of environmental prospects.

Green Business. Annex Publishing & Printing Inc. • Bimonthly. Magazine focusing on issues related to corporate sustainable development, including energy, environmental management, and emissions trading.

International Journal of Environmental Science and Technology. Kluwer Academic Publishers. • Refereed research journal which aims to promote the theory and practice of environmental science and technology, innovation, engineering and management.

Resources. Resources for the Future. • Description: Features articles on renewable resources, energy, climate, quality of the environment, and risk assessment and management. Recurring features include organizational news and book notices.

World Watch: Working for a Sustainable Future. Worldwatch Institute. • Bimonthly. $25.00 per year. Emphasis is on environmental trends, including developments in population growth, climate change, human behavior, the role of government, and other factors.

RESEARCH CENTERS AND INSTITUTES

Center for Energy and Environmental Studies - Carnegie Mellon University Department of Engineering and Public Policy. Baker Hall 128-A, Pittsburgh, PA 15213. Phone: (412)268-5897; Fax: (412)268-1089; Email: rubin@cmu.edu.

Lawrence Berkeley National Laboratory - Environment, Health and Safety Division - Safety Advisory Committee. 1 Cyclotron Rd., MS 90R1140, Berkeley, CA 94720-8128. Phone: (510)486-7653; Fax: (510)486-7488; Email: paseidl@lbl.gov • URL: http://www.lbl.gov/ehs/sac/ • Development and implementation of environment, safety, and health policy, guidelines, codes, and regulatory interpretation of the Lawrence Berkeley National Laboratory.

New York Institute of Technology - Center for Energy, Environment and Economics. Dept. of Energy Management, Harry Schure Hall, Rm. 116, Northern Blvd., Old Westbury, NY 11568-8000. Phone: (516)686-7990 or (516)686-7578; Fax: (516)686-7933; Email: ramundse@nyit.edu • URL: http://www.nyit.edu/engineering/centers/centers_energy_environment_economics • Established by the New York Institute of Technology as a major facility designed to disseminate information and conduct research into energy utilization and conservation, and to assist public, quasi-public, and private sector organizations in the practical use of present and future findings in the energy field. Conducts Master of Science in Energy Management and specialized professional certificate programs through NYIT's School of Engineering and Technology to provide interdisciplinary training in the technological, economic, sociological, and administrative skills required to implement new approaches to energy conversion and utilization.

University of Cincinnati - Center for Health and Environmental Research. Department of Communication, 601A Teachers College, Cincinnati, OH 45221-0184. Phone: (513)556-4001; Fax: (513)556-0899; Email: depoe@uc.edu • URL: http://asweb.artsci.uc.edu/communication/checr/about/index.html • Communication processes and practices in environmental and health policy contexts, in order to enhance the understanding and quality of communication processes and practices among citizen, industry, and government participants in environmental and health policy formation and implementation. The center's research agenda includes the design, analysis, and evaluation of informational and persuasive messages and campaigns produced by and addressed to individuals and institutions which pertain to environmental and human health risk contexts and controversies; the analysis and evaluation of communication processes within environmental and health-related organizations; and the design, facilitation, and evaluation of processes of stakeholder involvement in risk-based decision-making.

University of Delaware - Center for Energy and Environmental Policy. 278 Graham Hall, Newark, DE 19716. Phone: (302)831-8405; Fax: (302)831-3098; Email: jbbyrne@udel.edu • URL: http://ceep.udel.edu • Energy, environmental, and technology policy issues focusing on social, political, and economic dimensions of technology, and natural resource use. Center research and graduate study is informed by theories and concepts drawn from the fields of political economy and environment, technology, and society. Of particular interest are analyses of climate change, sustainable development, energy and environmental policy, environmental justice, water and energy conservation, renewable energy policies, energy and environmental issues in developing nations, and environmental planning.

University of East Anglia - School of Environmental Sciences - Centre for Social and Economic Research on the Global Environment., Norwich NR4 7TJ, United Kingdom. Phone: 44 1603 593224; Fax: 44 1603 591327; Email: i.bateman@uea.ac.uk • URL: http://www.cserge.ac.uk • Environmental issues, including biodiversity, climate change, coastal zone management, environmental resource valuation, sustainable development, tropical forests, waste management and life cycle assessment, and water and wetlands.

University of Wisconsin—Madison - Molecular and Environmental Toxicology Center. 1300 University Ave., 1530 MSC, Madison, WI 53706. Phone: (608)263-4580; Fax: (608)262-5245; Email: bradfield@oncology.wisc.edu • URL: http://metc.med.wisc.edu/metc • Formerly Environmental Toxicology Center.

STATISTICS SOURCES

U.S. Industry and Trade Outlook. U.S. Department of Commerce National Technical Information Service. • Annual. Produced by the International Trade Administration, U.S. Department of Commerce, in a "public-private" partnership with DRI/McGraw-Hill and Standard & Poor's. Provides basic data, outlook for the current year, and "Long-Term Prospects" (five-year projections) for a wide variety of products and services. Includes high technology industries. Formerly *U.S. Industrial Outlook.*

TRADE/PROFESSIONAL ASSOCIATIONS

Canadian Association of Physicians for the Environment. 130 Spadina Ave., Ste. 301, Toronto, ON, Canada M5V 2L4. Phone: (416)306-2273; Fax: (416)960-9392 • URL: http://cape.ca • Physicians, allied health care practitioners, and citizens committed to a healthy and sustainable environment. Works to protect and promote human health by addressing issues of local and global environmental degradation. Provides information on children's health, greening health care, climate change, regulatory reform, and toxins.

China Environment Chamber of Commerce. 4 Districts Anhuili, 15th China Minmetals Tower. Rm.

1315, Chaoyang District, Beijing 100029, China. Phone: 86 10 84640865; Fax: 86 10 84649343; Email: cesia@cesia.org • URL: http://www.cecc-china.org • Aims to promote the sustainable development of China's environmental industry. Provides a platform for its members to share information and experience and discuss critical issues regarding environmental technology and policy.

Clean Technology and Sustainable Industries Organization. 3925 W Braker Ln., Austin, TX 78759. Email: community@ct-si.org • URL: http://www.ct-si.org • Advances the commercialization and global adoption of clean technologies and sustainable industry practices. Promotes clean technology development. Establishes programs and advocacy for clean technologies and global integration of sustainable industry practices.

Climate Group. 145 W 58th St., Ste. 2a, New York, NY 10019. Phone: (646)233-0550; Email: info@theclimategroup.org • URL: http://www.theclimategroup.org • Advances business and government leadership on climate change. Creates international effort to stop climate change. Works to accelerate international action on global warming. Promotes profitability and competitiveness among the government, business and non-profit sectors.

Environmental Industries Commission. Alliance House, 12 Caxton St., London SW1H 0QL, United Kingdom. Phone: 44 207 2224148 or 44 207 6549942; Email: info@eic-uk.co.uk • URL: http://www.eic-uk.co.uk • Provides environmental technology equipment and services suppliers with a strong and effective voice to influence the debate on the future of the industry among policy makers in Westminster, Whitehall and Brussels. Promotes constructive cooperation between the regulated, the regulators and the UK's environmental technology suppliers.

Friends of the Earth - Australia. PO Box 222, Melbourne, VIC 3065, Australia. Phone: 61 3 94198700; Fax: 61 3 94162081; Email: foe@foe.org.au • URL: http://www.foe.org.au • Serves as national organization working on environmental issues within a social framework. Works for national campaigns on climate justice, environment and population, uranium, indigenous land rights, multinationals. Local groups active on local, national, and international issues.

Friends of the Earth - Costa Rica. PO Box 12423-1000, San Jose 1000, Costa Rica. Phone: 506 2233 3925; Fax: 506 2223 3925 • URL: http://www.coecoceiba.org • Member of the organization, Friends of the Earth International. Promotes conservation of the earth's natural resources. Supports campaigns on climate change, ecological debt, forests, gender issues, genetically modified organisms, sustainable societies, and wetlands.

Friends of the Earth - England, Wales, and Northern Ireland. 26-28 Underwood St., London N1 7JQ, United Kingdom. Phone: 44 20 74901555 or 44 1714901555; Fax: 44 20 74900881 or 44 1714900881; Email: info@foe.co.uk • URL: http://www.foe.co.uk • Operates as an environmental pressure group, campaigning on a wide range of issues including climate change corporate accountability, resource use, transport, energy, waste, habitats, forests, and sustainable development. Exists to protect and improve the environment, now and for the future, through changing political policies and business practices, empowering individuals and communities to take personal and political action, and stimulating wide and intelligent public debate on sustainability issues.

Friends of the Earth - Haiti. Delmas 65, Rue Durandis, No. 2, Port-au-Prince, Haiti. Phone: 509 2137973 or 509 4019684; Fax: 509 2210172 • URL: http://www.haitisurvie.org • Member of the organization, Friends of the Earth International. Promotes conservation of the earth's natural resources, including toxic wastes, desertification, ozone, and trade. Haiti Survie has many activities: climate change campaign, the organization works on reforestation program and plant tree at the community level.

Friends of the Earth - Indonesia. Jl. Tegal Parang Utara No. 14, 12790 Jakarta, Indonesia. Phone: 62 21 79193363; Fax: 62 21 7941673; Email: informasi@walhi.or.id • URL: http://www.walhi.or.id • Members of the organization, Friends of the Earth International. Promotes conservation of the earth's natural resources, indigenous rights, marginalization of communities, pollution, climate change, and biodiversity conservation.

Friends of the Earth - Ireland. 9 Upper Mount St., Dublin 2, Dublin, Ireland. Phone: 353 1 6394652; Email: info@foe.ie • URL: http://www.foe.ie • Works to increase public awareness of environmental problems. Conducts media and educational campaigns on topics such as air pollution, toxic waste issues, alternative energy, and climate change. Maintains an information service.

Friends of the Earth - Mauritius/Maudesco. PO Box 1124, Port Louis, Mauritius. Phone: 230 4672565; Fax: 230 4248500; Email: maudesco@intnet.mu • URL: http://www.foei.org/member-groups/africa/mauritius • Member of the organization, Friends of the Earth International. Promotes conservation of the earth's natural resources. Main areas of focus are sustainable tourism, protection of the ocean/coral reefs, climate changes, solar energy, organic farming, and compost from household wastes; committed to raising awareness and capacity building.

Green Partners. • URL: http://www.greenpartnersllc.com • Represents the interests of businesses that are committed to protect the environment. Promotes environmentally an "green" concept to the business sectors. Educates businesses on ways to be environmentally friendly through classes, on-site inspections and mentorship.

Greenpeace Australia Pacific. 33 Mountain St., Level 2, Ultimo, Sydney, NSW 2007, Australia. Phone: 61 2 92816100; Fax: 61 2 92800380; Email: support.au@greenpeace.org • URL: http://www.greenpeace.org/australia • Campaigns to ensure a just, peaceful, sustainable environment for future generations. Works to end the nuclear threat by global nuclear disarmament and closure of the nuclear industry, replacing with non-radioactive alternatives; save the oceans by bringing end to overfishing, pirate fishing and commercial whaling; eliminate toxics; stop climate change by phasing out fossil fuels (oil, coal, gas) and replace with renewable energy, such as wind and solar power; save the forests.

Greenpeace Sweden. Rosenlundsgatan 29B, PO Box 151, 64104 65 Stockholm, Sweden. Phone: 46 8 7027070; Fax: 46 8 6949013; Email: info.se@greenpeace.org • URL: http://www.greenpeace.org/sweden • Regional branch of Greenpeace. Uses nonviolent, creative confrontation to expose global environmental problems and their causes. Researches solutions and alternatives to help provide a path for a green and peaceful future. Aims to ensure the ability of the earth to nurture life in all its diversity. Organizes public campaigns for the protection of oceans and ancient forest, for the phasing-out of fossil fuels and the promotion of renewable energies in order to stop climate change for the elimination of toxic chemicals against the release of genetically modified organisms into nature for nuclear disarmament and an end to nuclear contamination.

Greenpeace UK. Canonbury Villas, London N1 2PN, United Kingdom. Phone: 44 20 78658100; Fax: 44 20 78658200 • URL: http://www.greenpeace.org.uk • Individuals interested in environmental protection and peace issues. Greenpeace campaigns on global issues such as climate change, forests, oceans, toxic pollution, nuclear, genetic engineering and peace.

International Petroleum Industry Environmental Conservation Association. 209-215 Blackfriars Rd., 5th Fl., London SE1 8NL, United Kingdom. Phone: 44 20 76332388; Fax: 44 20 76332389; Email: info@ipieca.org • URL: http://www.ipieca.org • Represents 52% of worldwide oil and gas production drawn from 26 private and state-owned companies as well as 12 national, regional, international associations. Represents both upstream and downstream of the oil and gas industry on key global environmental issues, including oil spill preparedness and response, global climate change, health, fuel quality, biodiversity and social responsibility.

National Alliance of Forest Owners. 122 C St. NW, Ste. 630, Washington, DC 20001. Phone: (202)747-0759; Fax: (202)824-0770; Email: info@nafoalliance.org • URL: http://www.nafoalliance.org • Aims to protect and enhance the economic and environmental values of privately-owned forests through targeted policy advocacy at the national level. Focuses on issues for regulatory advocacy including climate change, renewable energy, environment, tax policy, land use, trade and market policy. Seeks public policies that shape environmental regulations, taxes, land use decisions, and timber and non-timber markets in ways that protect and grow forest values.

National Association of Environmental Professionals. PO Box 460, Collingswood, NJ 08108. Phone: 866-251-9902 or (856)283-7816; Fax: (856)210-1619; Email: naep@bowermanagementservices.com • URL: http://www.naep.org • Promotes ethical practice, technical competency, and professional standards in the environment field. Provides access to the latest trends in environmental research, technology, law, and policy.

Pollution Probe Foundation. 150 Ferrand Dr., Ste. 208, Toronto, ON, Canada M3C 3E5. Phone: 877-926-1907 or (416)926-1907; Fax: (416)926-1601; Email: pprobe@pollutionprobe.org • URL: http://www.pollutionprobe.org • Works to define environmental problems through research; seeks to raise public awareness of environmental issues through education; lobbies for environmental protection and remediation before government agencies and industrial associations. Focuses on smog and climate change, reduction and elimination of mercury in water, child health and the environment, indoor air quality, and water quality.

ENVIRONMENTAL LAW

ABSTRACTS AND INDEXES

Current Law Index. Cengage Learning Inc. • $1,332 Individuals. Monthly. $1269.00 per year. Produced in cooperation with the American Association of Law Libraries. Indexes more than 900 law journals, legal newspapers, and specialty publications from the U.S., Canada, U.K., Ireland, Australia, and New Zealand.

Environment Abstracts. University Publications of America. • Monthly. Price varies. Provides multidisciplinary coverage of the world's environmental literature. Incorporates *Acid Rain Abstracts*.

Environment Abstracts Annual: A Guide to the Key Environmental Literature of the Year. University Publications of America. • Annual. $495.00. A yearly cumulation of *Environment Abstracts*.

Index to Legal Periodicals and Books. H.W. Wilson Co. • Monthly. $490.00 per year. Quarterly and annual cumulations.

CD-ROM DATABASES

Environment Abstracts on CD-ROM. University Publications of America. • Quarterly. $1,295.00 per year. Contains the following CD-ROM databases: *Environment Abstracts, Energy Abstracts*, and *Acid Rain Abstracts*. Length of coverage varies.

Index to Legal Periodicals and Books. EBSCO Publishing Inc. • Contains indexing of more than 1,400 English language legal periodicals from 1981 to date and 2,500 books.

PAIS International. ProQuest L.L.C. • Monthly. $1,995.00 per year. Contains over 650,000 citations to the literature of contemporary social, political, and economic issues.

DIRECTORIES

Lawyer's Register International by Specialties and Fields of Law Including a Directory of Corporate Counsel. Lawyer's Register Publishing Co. • Annual. $359 Individuals. Referral source for law firms.

State Wildlife Laws Handbook. Government Institutes. • $127 Individuals cloth. Publication includes: Listing of state fish and wildlife agencies. Entries include: Name, address, phone. Principal content of publication is an analysis of wildlife management and protection laws for all fifty states.

INTERNET DATABASES

Lexis.com Research System. Lexis-Nexis Group. Phone: 800-227-4908 or (937)865-6800; Fax: (937)865-6909; Email: webmaster@prod.lexis-nexis.com • URL: http://www.nexis.com • Fee-based Web site offers extensive searching of a wide variety of legal sources. Additional features include Daily Opinion Service, lexis.com Bookstore, Career Center, CLE Center, Law Schools, and Practice Pages ("Pages specific to areas of specialty").

ONLINE DATABASES

Environmental Law Reporter (ELR). Environmental Law Institute. • Monthly. $1,995 Individuals /year. Provides full text online of *Environmental Law Reporter*, covering administrative materials, news, pending legislation, statutes, bibliography, etc. Time periods vary. Inquire as to online cost and availability.

LegalTrac. Cengage Learning Inc. • Online database. Provides indexing for approximately 875 titles of periodical literature relating to legal matters from 1980 to date. Corresponds to online *Legal Resource Index*. Inquire as to price and availability.

TRADE/PROFESSIONAL ASSOCIATIONS

Association of Clean Water Administrators. 1221 Connecticut Ave. NW, 2nd Fl., Washington, DC 20036. Phone: (202)756-0600; Fax: (202)756-0605.

Environmental Entrepreneurs. Natural Resources Defense Council, 40 W 20th St., New York, NY 10011. Phone: (212)727-2700 or (212)727-4437; Fax: (212)727-1773; Email: yli@nrdc.org • URL: http://www.e2.org • Represents business people who believe in protecting the environment while building economic prosperity. Serves as a champion on the economic side of good environmental policy by taking an economically sound approach to environmental issues. Focuses on environmental policies that drive economic growth in a healthy direction.

National Association of Clean Air Agencies. 444 N Capitol St. NW, Ste. 307, Washington, DC 20001. Phone: (202)624-7864; Fax: (202)624-7863; Email: 4cleanair@4cleanair.org • URL: http://www.cleanairworld.org • State, local and territorial air pollution program administrators and members of their staffs. Provides an opportunity for state and local officials who are responsible for implementing air pollution control programs established under the Clean Air Act to share air quality-related experiences and to discuss problems. Encourages communication and cooperation among federal, state, and local regulatory agencies.

EQUAL EMPLOYMENT OPPORTUNITY

See also AFFIRMATIVE ACTION PROGRAMS; EMPLOYMENT OF OLDER WORKERS; EMPLOYMENT OF WOMEN

OTHER SOURCES

BNA Fair Employment Practices. Bloomberg BNA. • Biweekly. $938.00 per year. Looseleaf service.

Human Resources Management Whole. Wolters Kluwer Law & Business CCH. • Nine looseleaf volumes. $1,572 per year. Includes monthly updates. Components are *Ideas and Trends Newsletter, Employment Relations, Compensation, Equal Employment Opportunity, Personnel Practices/ Communications* and *OSHA Compliance*. Components are available separately.

Practical Guide to Equal Employment Opportunity. ALM Media Properties LLC. • $570 two volumes. Serves as a legal manual for EEO compliance. "Volume one analyzes discrimination on the basis of race, religion, sex, age, and physical handicaps including AIDS." Provides information relating to an employer's liability in cases of sexual harassment of employees, including same-sex harassment. Covers affirmative action and reverse discrimination issues. Volume two contains model affirmative action plans, a sample EEO compliance manual, checklists, and other documents. (Law Journal Press).

PERIODICALS AND NEWSLETTERS

The Equal Employer. Y. S. Publications, Inc. • Biweekly. $245.00 per year. Newsletter on fair employment practices.

Fair Employment Compliance: A Confidential Letter to Management. Management Resources, Inc. • Semimonthly. $245.00 per year. Newsletter.

PE Update. Project Equality Inc. • Quarterly. Membership. Formerly *Project Equality Update*.

RESEARCH CENTERS AND INSTITUTES

Princeton University - Industrial Relations Section. Firestone Library, A-18-J, 1 Washington Rd., Princeton, NJ 08544. Phone: (609)258-4040; Fax: (609)258-2907; Email: c6789@princeton.edu • URL: http://www.irs.princeton.edu • Fields of research include labor supply, manpower training, unemployment, and equal employment opportunity.

EQUIPMENT LEASING

See also RENTAL SERVICES

ABSTRACTS AND INDEXES

Business Periodicals Index Retrospective. EBSCO Publishing Inc. • 11/year. Quarterly and annual cumulations.

CD-ROM DATABASES

Business Abstracts with Full Text. EBSCO Publishing Inc. • Includes full text articles from more than 460 business publications from 1982 to present. Indexing for nearly 880 publications.

DIRECTORIES

Leasing Sourcebook: The Directory of the U. S. Capital Equipment Leasing Industry. Bibliotechnology Systems and Publishing Co. • Every 12-18 months. $135.00. Lists approximately 5,200 capital equipment leasing companies.

ONLINE DATABASES

Wilson Business Abstracts Online. H.W. Wilson Co. • Indexes and abstracts 600 major business periodicals, plus the *Wall Street Journal* and the business section of the *New York Times*. Indexing is from 1982, abstracting from 1990, with the two newspapers included from 1993. Updated weekly. Inquire as to online cost and availability. (*Business Periodicals Index* without abstracts is also available online.).

PERIODICALS AND NEWSLETTERS

Equipment Leasing Newsletter. ALM Media Properties LLC. • Monthly. $549 per year. Covers a wide range of legal topics relating to the leasing of business and industrial equipment, including taxation, insurance, dealing with banks, lease securitization, and letter of credit issues. (A Law Journal Newsletter, formerly published by Leader Publications).

ERGONOMICS

See HUMAN ENGINEERING

ESTATE PLANNING

See also INHERITANCE TAX; TAX PLANNING

ABSTRACTS AND INDEXES

Insurance Periodicals Index. Specials Libraries Association, Insurance and Employees Benefits Div. NILS Publishing Co. • Annual. $250.00. Compiled by the Insurance and Employee Benefits Div., Special Libraries Association. A yearly index of over 15,000 articles from about 35 insurance periodicals. Arrangement is by subject, with an index to authors.

BIBLIOGRAPHIES

Insurance and Employee Benefits Literature. Special Libraries Association. • Bimonthly. $15.00 per year. Lists a wide variety of literature in all branches of the insurance industry. Includes annotations.

CD-ROM DATABASES

Authority Tax and Estate Planning Library. Matthew Bender and Company Inc. • Periodic revisions. Price on request. CD contains updated full text of *Bender's Payroll Tax Guide, Depreciation Handbook, Federal Income Taxation of Corporations, Tax Planning for Corporations, Modern Estate Planning, Planning for Large Estates, Murphy's Will Clauses, Tax & Estate Planning for the Elderly*, and 12 other Matthew Bender publications. The Internal Revenue Code is also included.

HANDBOOKS AND MANUALS

Modern Estate Planning. Matthew Bender and Company Inc. • $2,005 Print. Covers estate, gift, and GST taxation.

U.S. Master Estate and Gift Tax Guide. Wolters Kluwer Law & Business CCH. • Annual. $103 Quantity: 1 - 4. Covers federal estate and gift taxes, including generation-skipping transfer tax plans. Includes tax tables and sample filled-in tax return forms.

INTERNET DATABASES

CCH Essentials: An Internet Tax Research and Primary Source Library. CCH, Inc. Phone: 800-248-3248 or (773)866-6000; Fax: (773)866-3608 or (800)224-8299; Email: cust_serv@cch.com • URL: http://tax.cch.com/essentials • Fee-based Web site provides full-text coverage of federal tax law and regulations, including rulings, procedures, tax court decisions, and IRS publications, announcements, notices, and penalties. Includes explanation, analysis, tax planning guides, and a daily tax news service. Searching is offered, including citation search.

OTHER SOURCES

AACE International. Transactions of the Annual Meetings. American Assoiciation of Cost Engineers. AACE International. • Annual. Price varies. Contains texts of papers presented at AACE meetings.

Estate Planning. ALM Media Properties LLC. • $670 two volumes. Covers all legal aspects of estate planning, including wills, trusts, taxation, gifts, charitable contributions, family business considerations, and insurance. Includes forms and checklists. (Law Journal Press).

Fiduciary Tax Guide. Wolters Kluwer Law & Business CCH. • Monthly. $478.00 per year. Looseleaf service. Covers federal income taxation of estates, trusts, and beneficiaries. Provides information on gift and generation- skipping taxation.

Financial and Estate Planning: Analysis, Strategies and Checklists. Wolters Kluwer Law & Business CCH. • 4 looseleaf volumes. Price on application. services.

PERIODICALS AND NEWSLETTERS

Broker World. Insurance Publications Inc. • Bimonthly. $6.00 per year. Edited for independent insurance agents and brokers. Special feature issue topics include annuities, disability insurance, estate planning, and life insurance.

Estate Planner's Alert. Thomson RIA. • Monthly. $290 Individuals Print. Covers the tax aspects of personal finance, including home ownership, investments, insurance, retirement planning, and charitable giving. Formerly *Estate and Financial Planners Alert*.

Estate Planning Journal. Thomson RIA. • Monthly. $525 Individuals Print. Contains a variety of practical ideas and analysis of recent developments in each issue.

Financial Planning: The Magazine for Financial Service Professionals. SourceMedia Inc. • Monthly. $79.00 per year. Edited for independent financial planners and insurance agents. Covers retirement planning, estate planning, tax planning, and insurance, including long-term healthcare considerations. Special features include a Retirement Planning Issue, Mutual Fund Performance Survey, and Variable Life and Annuity Survey.

Robb Report Worth: Wealth in Perspective. CurtCo Robb Media. • Monthly. $54.95 per year. Glossy magazine featuring articles for the affluent on personal financial management, investments, estate planning, trusts, private bankers, taxes, travel, yachts, and lifestyle. Formerly *Worth: Financial Intelligence*.

TRADE/PROFESSIONAL ASSOCIATIONS

National Association of Financial and Estate Planning. 515 E 4500 S. No. G-200, Salt Lake City, UT 84107. Phone: 800-454-2649; Fax: (877)890-0929 or (801)266-9900; Email: info@accuplan.net • URL: http://www.nafep.com • Represents financial and estate planners.

ESTATE TAX

See INHERITANCE TAX

ESTIMATING

ABSTRACTS AND INDEXES

Business Periodicals Index Retrospective. EBSCO Publishing Inc. • 11/year. Quarterly and annual cumulations.

NTIS Alerts: Building Industry Technology. U.S. Department of Commerce National Technical Information Service. • Biweekly. $130 per year. Covers architecture, construction management, building materials, maintenance, furnishings, and related subjects.

CD-ROM DATABASES

ABI/INFORM. ProQuest L.L.C. • Monthly. Provides CD-ROM indexing and abstracting of worldwide business literature. Archival discs are available from 1971. Formerly *ABI/INFORM OnDisc*.

Applied Science & Business Periodicals Retrospective. EBSCO Publishing Inc. • Includes citations for more than 3 million articles detailing events, issues, and trends in business and industry.

ONLINE DATABASES

Wilson Business Abstracts Online. H.W. Wilson Co. • Indexes and abstracts 600 major business periodicals, plus the *Wall Street Journal* and the business section of the *New York Times*. Indexing is from 1982, abstracting from 1990, with the two newspapers included from 1993. Updated weekly. Inquire as to online cost and availability. (*Business Periodicals Index* without abstracts is also available online.).

PERIODICALS AND NEWSLETTERS

Design Cost Data. DC & D Technologies Inc. • Bimonthly. $149 U.S. /year plus online access to archive. Provides a preliminary cost estimating system for architects, contractors, builders, and developers, utilizing historical data. Includes case studies of actual costs. Formerly *Design Cost and Data*.

The National Estimator. Society of Cost Estimating and Analysis. • Quarterly. $30.00 per year. Covers government contract estimating.

PRICE SOURCES

Means Facilities Construction Cost Data. RSMeans. • Annual. $496.95 Individuals. Provides costs for use in building estimating.

Means Interior Cost Data. RSMeans. • Annual. $207.95 Individuals.

Means Repair and Remodeling Cost Data. RSMeans. • Annual. $163.95 Individuals.

Means Residential Cost Data. RSMeans. • Annual. $139.95 Individuals.

National Building Cost Manual. Craftsman Book Co. • Annual. $63 Individuals.

National Construction Estimator. Craftsman Book Co. • Annual. $51.63 Individuals.

TRADE/PROFESSIONAL ASSOCIATIONS

American Society of Professional Estimators. 2525 Perimeter Place Dr., Ste. 103, Nashville, TN 37214. Phone: 888-EST-MATE or (615)316-9200; Fax: (615)316-9800; Email: psmith@aspenational.org • URL: http://www.aspenational.org • Members are construction cost estimators and construction educators.

Professional Construction Estimators Association of America. PO Box 680336, Charlotte, NC 28216. Phone: 877-521-7232 or (704)489-1494; Email: pcea@pcea.org • URL: http://www.pcea.org • Members are building and construction cost estimators.

ETHICAL DRUG INDUSTRY

See PHARMACEUTICAL INDUSTRY

EUROCURRENCY

See also FOREIGN EXCHANGE

INTERNET DATABASES

Gateway to the European Union. European Union. Email: pressoffice@eurostat.cec.be • URL: http://www.europa.eu.int • Web site provides access to a wide variety of EU information, including statistics (Eurostat), news, policies, publications, key issues, and official exchange rates for the euro. Includes links to the European Central Bank, the European Investment Bank, and other institutions. Fees: Free.

ONLINE DATABASES

Banking Information Source. ProQuest L.L.C. • Provides indexing and abstracting of periodical and other literature from 1982 to date, with weekly updates. Covers the financial services industry: banks, savings institutions, investment houses, credit unions, insurance companies, and real estate organizations. Emphasis is on marketing and management. Inquire as to online cost and availability. (Formerly *FINIS: Financial Industry Information Service*.).

PERIODICALS AND NEWSLETTERS

American Banker: The Financial Services Daily. SourceMedia Inc. • Daily. $895.00 per year. Provides news of banking, investment products, mortgages, credit unions, finance, bank technology, and legal developments.

Euromoney: The Monthly Journal of International Money and Capital Markets. American Educational Systems. • Monthly. $490.00 per year. Includes print and online editions. Supplement available *Guide to World Equity Markets*.

Financial Times (London). The Financial Times, Inc. • Daily, except Sunday. $572.88 per year. An international business and financial newspaper, featuring news from London, Paris, Frankfurt, New York, and Tokyo. Includes worldwide stock and bond market data, commodity market data, and monetary/currency exchange information.

International Currency Review. World Reports Ltd. • Quarterly. $475.00 per year.

U.S. Banker. SourceMedia Inc. • Monthly. $65.00 per year. Edited for bank executives and managers. Covers a wide variety of banking and financial topics.

World Business Intelligence: Economic & Political Financial Analysts from Rundt's New York. S.J. Rundt & Associates Inc. • $885 Individuals. Magazine featuring information on international trade, country risk analyses, currencies, and political, financial, and economic intelligence. Formerly *Rundt's Weekly Intelligence*.

EURODOLLARS

See EUROCURRENCY

EUROPEAN CONSUMER MARKET

See also EUROPEAN MARKETS

ABSTRACTS AND INDEXES

Business Periodicals Index Retrospective. EBSCO Publishing Inc. • 11/year. Quarterly and annual cumulations.

CD-ROM DATABASES

ABI/INFORM. ProQuest L.L.C. • Monthly. Provides CD-ROM indexing and abstracting of worldwide business literature. Archival discs are available from 1971. Formerly *ABI/INFORM OnDisc*.

Applied Science & Business Periodicals Retrospective. EBSCO Publishing Inc. • Includes citations for more than 3 million articles detailing events, issues, and trends in business and industry.

DIRECTORIES

Market Share Reporter (MSR). Cengage Learning Inc. • $777 Individuals. 2013. $740.00. Published by Gale. Provides consumer market share data for leading companies. Also available as eBook.

World's Major Multinationals. Euromonitor International Business Reference Div. • Covers: List of major multinational companies. Entries include: Company name, address, phone; performance analysis; list of subsidiaries; market share; net profit and turnover; leading brands; and merger and acquisition information.

ONLINE DATABASES

Market Research Monitor. Euromonitor International Inc. • Contains full-text reports online from *Market Research Europe, Market Research Great Britain, Market Research International, and Retail Monitor International.* Time period is 1995 to date, with monthly updates. Inquire as to online cost and availability.

Wilson Business Abstracts Online. H.W. Wilson Co. • Indexes and abstracts 600 major business periodicals, plus the *Wall Street Journal* and the business section of the *New York Times*. Indexing is from 1982, abstracting from 1990, with the two newspapers included from 1993. Updated weekly. Inquire as to online cost and availability. (*Business Periodicals Index* without abstracts is also available online.).

PERIODICALS AND NEWSLETTERS

Advertising Age's Euromarketing. Crain Communications Inc. • Weekly. $295 Individuals. Newsletter on European advertising and marketing.

Europa 2000: The American Business Report on Europe. Wolfe Publishing, Inc. • Monthly. $119.00 per year. Newsletter on consumer and industrial marketing in a unified European Economic Community. Includes classified business opportunity advertisements and a listing by country of forthcoming major trade shows in Europe.

Pharma Business: The International Magazine of Pharmaceutical Business and Marketing. Engel Publishing Partners. • Six times a year. $235.00 per year. Circulated mainly in European countries. Coverage includes worldwide industry news, new drug products, regulations, and research developments.

STATISTICS SOURCES

European Marketing Data and Statistics. Cengage Learning Inc. • 2013. $475.00. Published by Euromonitor International. Presents essential marketing data, including demographics and consumer expenditure patterns for 44 European countries. Also available as eBook.

Eurostat Regional Yearbook. Bernan Associates. • Annual. $50.00. Published by the Commission of European Communities. Provides data on the social and economic situation in specific European areas. Includes population, employment, migration, industry, living standards, etc.

Market Share Reporter (MSR). Cengage Learning Inc. • $777 Individuals. 2013. $740.00. Published by Gale. Provides consumer market share data for leading companies. Also available as eBook.

EUROPEAN ECONOMIC COMMUNITY

See EUROPEAN MARKETS

EUROPEAN MARKETS

See also EUROPEAN CONSUMER MARKET; INTERNATIONAL BUSINESS

ABSTRACTS AND INDEXES

Business Periodicals Index Retrospective. EBSCO Publishing Inc. • 11/year. Quarterly and annual cumulations.

F & S Index: Europe. Cengage Learning Inc. • Monthly. $2,532.00 per year, including quarterly and annual cumulations. Provides annotated citations to marketing, business, financial, and industrial literature. Coverage of European business activity includes trade journals, financial magazines, business newspapers, and special reports. Formerly Predicasts F & S Index: Europe.

ALMANACS AND YEARBOOKS

Economic Survey of Europe. United Nations Economic Commission for Europe. • Semiannual. Provides yearly analysis and review of the European economy, including Eastern Europe and the USSR. Text in English.

Euroguide Yearbook of the Institutions of the European Union. Bernan Associates. • Annual. $440. Published by Editions Delta. Information on public and private institutions in the European Union contributing to European integration.

CD-ROM DATABASES

Baltia Kompass Business Disc. Kompass USA, Inc. • Provides information on more than 22,000 companies in Estonia, Latvia, and Lithuania. Classification system covers approximately 50,000 products and services.

Benelux Kompass Business Disc. Kompass USA, Inc. • Semiannual. CD-ROM provides information on more than 52,000 companies in Belgium, Netherlands, and Luxembourg. Classification system covers approximately 50,000 products and services.

East European Kompass on Disc. Kompass USA, Inc. • Provides information on more than 294,000 companies in Austria, Azerbaijan, Belarus, Croatia, Czech Republic, Estonia, Hungary, Latvia, Lithuania, Moldova, Poland, Romania, Russia, Slovakia, Slovenia, Ukraine, and Yugoslavia. Classification system covers approximately 50,000 products and services.

European Kompass on Disc. Kompass USA, Inc. • Provides information on more than 350,000 companies in Belgium, Denmark, France, Germany, Ireland, Italy, Luxembourg, Netherlands, Norway, Spain, Sweden, and UK. Classification system covers approximately 50,000 products and services.

Kompass CD-ROM Editions. Kompass USA, Inc. • Semiannual or annual. Prices vary. CD-ROM versions of Kompass international trade directories are available for each of 36 major countries and nine world regions. Searching is provided for 50,000 product/service items and for many company details.

Kompass Concord CD-ROM. Kompass USA, Inc. • Provides information on more than 105,000 companies in 17 rapidly developing East European countries: Armenia, Azerbaijan, Belarus, Bulgaria, Czech Republic, Estonia, Hungary, Kazakhstan, Kyrgyzstan, Latvia, Lithuania, Moldova, Poland, Romania, Russia, Ukraine, and Uzbekistan. Classification system covers approximately 50,000 products and services.

OECD Statistical Compendium. Organization for Economic Cooperation and Development. • Semiannual. $1,905.00 per year for 1 to 10 users. CD-ROM contains more than 730,000 monthly, quarterly, and annual time series for OECD countries, 1960 to date. Includes fully searchable data on agriculture, food, economic indicators, national accounts, employment, energy, finance, industry, technology, and foreign trade. Results can be displayed in various forms.

Scandinavian Kompass on Disc. Kompass USA, Inc. • Semiannual. CD-ROM provides information on more than 120,000 companies in Denmark, Finland, Norway, and Sweden. Classification system covers approximately 50,000 products and services.

DIRECTORIES

The Directory of EU Information Sources: The Red Book. Euroconfidentiel S. A. • Annual. $230.00. Lists publications, associations, consultants, law firms, diplomats, jounalists, and other sources of information about Europe and the European Union.

Directory of Trade and Professional Associations in the European Union - The Blue Book. Euroconfidentiel S. A. • Annual. $160.00. Includes more than 9,000 EU-related associations.

Emerging Europe Autos Directory. Business Monitor International Ltd. • $895 Individuals. Covers: 1,275 top autos executives on 443 leading automotive companies from Bosnia-Herzegovina, Bulgaria, Croatia, the Czech Republic, Estonia, Hungary, Latvia, Lithuania, Macedonia, Poland, Romania, Russia, Serbia, Slovakia, Slovenia and the Ukraine. Entries include: parent company head offices, full company name, address, phone and fax numbers, email and website address, senior contact personnel, company description and profile, nationality, and ownership status.

Emerging Europe Oil and Gas Directory. Business Monitor International Ltd. • $895 Individuals. Covers: 698 top oil and gas executives on 234 leading oil and gas companies from Emerging Europe. Entries include: Parent company head offices, full company name, address, phone and fax numbers, email and website address, senior oil and gas contact personnel, company description and profile, nationality, and ownership status.

Emerging Europe Telecommunications Directory. Business Monitor International Ltd. • $895 Individuals. Covers: 1,333 top telecommunications executives at 445 leading telecommunications companies from Emerging Europe. Entries include: parent company head offices, full company name, address, phone and fax numbers, email and website address, senior contact personnel, company description and profile, nationality, and ownership status.

The EU Institutions' Register. Routledge Reference. • £305 Individuals hardback. Covers: Over 5,900 key personnel in each of the major institutions, including: European Commission, European Parliament, Economic and Social Committee, Council of the European Union, Court of Justice, European Investment Bank, Court of Auditors, Committee of Regions and EU Agencies. Entries include: Contact information.

European International Business Academy--Membership Directory. European International Business Academy. • Covers: 300 individuals involved in international business.

European Union Encyclopedia and Directory. Routledge Reference. • Semiannual. £450 Individuals Hardback. Published by Europa. Provides directory information for major European Union organizations, with detailed descriptions of various groups or concepts in an "Encyclopedia" section. A statistics section contains a wide variety of data related to business, industry, and economics. Formerly *European Communities Encyclopedia and Directory.*

Europe's Top Quoted Companies: A Comparative Directory from Seventeen European Stock Exchanges. Kogan Page, Limited. • Annual. $325.00. Provides detailed, 5-year financial data on 850 major European companies that are publicly traded. Includes company addresses.

Guide to Business Information on Central and Eastern Europe. Taylor & Francis Ltd. • $98.95 Individuals Paperback. Covers: Twelve countries of Central and Eastern Europe. Entries include: Country overview; current developments; company name, address, phone, fax; names and titles of key personnel; industries and services; legislation; and organizations.

Guide to Business Information on Russia, the NIS, and the Baltic States. Taylor & Francis Ltd. • $104.95 Individuals Paperback. Covers: Fifteen countries of Russia, the NIS, and the Baltic States. Entries include: Current developments; company name, address, phone, fax; industries and services; legislation; and organizations.

Guide to EU Information Sources on the Internet. Euroconfidentiel S. A. • Annual. $210.00. Contains descriptions of more than 1,700 Web sites providing information relating to the European Union and European commerce and industry. Includes a quarterly e-mail newsletter with new sites and address changes.

Hoover's Handbook of World Business. Dun & Bradstreet Inc. Hoover's Inc. • Annual. $225 Individuals Hardcover. Covers: Hundreds of companies headquartered outside the U.S., including many with substantial activity in the U.S.; global enterprises, businesses that dominate their respective industries, and representative companies from all major industries. Entries include: Company name, overview, history, exchange and stock symbols, fiscal year-end date, names and titles of key personnel, name of auditors, number of employees, headquarters address, phone, fax, description of where the company does business, specific products/services/brand names produced, key competitors, 10 years of key financial data.

International Media Guide Business-Professional Publications: Europe. Kantar Media SRDS. • $553 Individuals online; 1 year. Describes 8,800 trade journals from Eastern and Western Europe, with advertising rates and circulation data.

London Business School: A SourceGuide to European Company Information. Cengage Learning Inc. • $108. Over 1,000 business information resources in 18 European countries, including trade councils, government agencies, directories, databases, newspapers, newsletters, and other media.

Major Companies of Europe. Cengage Learning Inc. • Annual. $2,980 set. Published by Graham & Whiteside. Approximately 44,640 major companies and key executives in European countries in all lines of business.

World of Information Business & Economic Europe Review. Kogan Page, Limited. • Covers: Tourist and business information, including airlines, banks, hotels, ministries and associations in Europe. Entries include: Address.

HANDBOOKS AND MANUALS

Practical Guide to Foreign Direct Investment in the European Union: The Green Book. Euroconfidentiel S. A. • Annual. $240.00. Provides coverage of national and EU business incentives. In addition to 70 charts and tables, includes EU country profiles of taxation, labor costs, and employment regulations.

INTERNET DATABASES

Financial Times: Where Information Becomes Intelligence. FT Group. Phone: (800)628-8088 • URL: http://www.ft.com • Web site provides extensive data and information relating to international business and finance, with daily updates. Includes Markets Today, Company News, Economic Indicators, Equities, Currencies, Capital Markets, Euro Prices, etc. Fees: Free (registration required).

Gateway to the European Union. European Union. Email: pressoffice@eurostat.cec.be • URL: http://www.europa.eu.int • Web site provides access to a wide variety of EU information, including statistics (Eurostat), news, policies, publications, key issues, and official exchange rates for the euro. Includes links to the European Central Bank, the European Investment Bank, and other institutions. Fees: Free.

PERIODICALS AND NEWSLETTERS

Business Week International: The World's Only International Newsweekly of Business. McGraw Hill Financial Inc. • Weekly. $95.00 per year.

Commission European Union Bulletin. Commision of the European Communities. Bernan Associates. • 11 times a year. $210.00 per year. Published by the Office of Official Publications of the European Communities. Covers all main events within the Union. Supplement available. Text in Danish, Dutch, English, French, German, Greek, Italian, Spanish, Portuguese. Formerly *Bulletin of the European Communities.*

Europa 2000: The American Business Report on Europe. Wolfe Publishing, Inc. • Monthly. $119.00 per year. Newsletter on consumer and industrial marketing in a unified European Economic Community. Includes classified business opportunity advertisements and a listing by country of forthcoming major trade shows in Europe.

European Access. European Commission-United Kingdom Offices. Chadwyck-Healey Inc. • Bimonthly. $195.00 per year. Published in England. A journal providing general coverage of developments and trends within the European Community.

European Management Journal. Elsevier. • Bimonthly. $1,162 Individuals Print. Covers a wide variety of topics, including management problems of the European Single Market.

Institutional Investor International Edition: The Magazine for International Finance and Investment. Institutional Investor Inc. Journals Group. • Monthly. $475.00 per year. Covers the international aspects of professional investing and finance. Emphasis is on Europe, the Far East, and Latin America.

International Economic Scoreboard. The Conference Board. • Description: Provides current data on the business outlook in 11 major industrial countries: Australia, Canada, France, West Germany, Italy, Japan, Korea, New Zealand, Taiwan, the United Kingdom, and the U.S. **Remarks:** A source for additional information on this indicator system and its uses is available at the Center for International Business Cycle Research, Columbia University Business School.

Market: Europe. Edimax. • Description: Profiles European consumers and provides ideas for marketing strategies. Reports on European conferences and summarizes articles from international periodicals. Recurring features include analyses of specific countries and cities.

RESEARCH CENTERS AND INSTITUTES

Free University of Berlin - Institute for East-European Studies. Garystr. 55, 14195 Berlin, Germany. Phone: 49 30 83854058; Fax: 49 30 83856419; Email: institutsrat@oei.fu-berlin.de • URL: http://www.oei.fu-berlin.de/en/index.html • Eastern, central, and southern Europe, including studies in Slavic languages and literatures, economics, law, history, geography, political sciences, sociology, education, arts, cultural studies, and Balkan studies.

Free University of Brussels - Institute for European Studies. Ave. F.D. Roosevelt 39, CP 172, B-1050 Brussels, Belgium. Phone: 32 2 6503079; Fax: 32 2 6503069; Email: iee@admin.ulb.ac.be • URL: http://www.iee-ulb.eu • European studies, including law, economics, politics.

World Health Organization - Regional Office for Europe. Marmorvej 51, DK-2100 Copenhagen, Denmark. Phone: 45 45 337000; Fax: 45 45 337001; Email: postmaster@euro.who.int • URL: http://www.euro.who.int • Works to ensure that WHO programs effectively meet the particular public health needs of Europe; serves as a liaison between national and local public health agencies and the WHO.

STATISTICS SOURCES

European Marketing Data and Statistics. Cengage Learning Inc. • 2013. $475.00. Published by Euromonitor International. Presents essential marketing data, including demographics and consumer expenditure patterns for 44 European countries. Also available as eBook.

Eurostat Regional Yearbook. Bernan Associates. • Annual. $50.00. Published by the Commission of European Communities. Provides data on the social and economic situation in specific European areas. Includes population, employment, migration, industry, living standards, etc.

TRADE/PROFESSIONAL ASSOCIATIONS

European Finance Association. Pl. de Brouckere Plein 31, B-1000 Brussels, Belgium. Phone: 32 2 2266660 or 32 2 2266665; Fax: 32 2 5121929; Email: kannel@eiasm.be • URL: http://www.efa-online.org/r/default.asp?iId=ILGLJ • Academics and practitioners interested in financial management and theory and application. Fosters dissemination and exchange of information; provides forum for presentation of research results in the areas of company finance, investment, financial markets, and banking.

European Money and Finance Forum. c/o Oesterreichische Nationalbank, Otto Wagner-Platz 3, A-1090 Vienna, Austria. Phone: 43 1 404207206; Fax: 43 1 404207298; Email: suerf@oenb.at • URL: http://www.suerf.org • Represents academics, bank economists, and interested individuals in 37 countries. Develops contacts among members in order to discuss monetary and financial questions. Sponsors research in monetary, economic, and financial areas. Aims to create an active network between professional economists, financial practitioners, central bankers and academics for the analysis and mutual understanding of monetary and financial issues. Sponsors conferences, seminars, workshops and lectures. Publishes study volumes each year.

European Round Table of Industrialists. Karabiniersplein, Pl. de Carabiniers 18a, B-1030 Brussels, Belgium. Phone: 32 2 5343100; Fax: 32 2 5347348; Email: contact@ert.eu • URL: http://www.ert.eu • Chief executive officers of large manufacturing companies headquartered in 16 European countries. Promotes an improved business climate in Europe in an attempt to expand Europe's international as well as domestic technical and industrial market. Encourages entrepreneurial initiatives.

Family Federation of Finland. PO Box 849, FIN-00101 Helsinki, Finland. Phone: 358 9 228050 or 358 9 22805101; Fax: 358 9 6121211 • URL: http://www.vaestoliitto.fi • Organizations concerned with the state of the family in Finland. Works for a social climate favorable to families, children, and demographic balance. Initiates reform legislation and strives to guide social planning, housing policy, and social services to meet the needs of families with children. Offers family and genetic counseling, infertility treatment, and child care and family planning services. Conducts occupational training courses, medical research programs and conferences. Participates in cooperative development projects and does advocacy work among decision-makers on global population issues and sexual and reproductive health and rights.

EUROPEAN UNION

See EUROPEAN MARKETS

EVALUATION OF PERFORMANCE

See RATING OF EMPLOYEES

EVENT PLANNING

See SPECIAL EVENT PLANNING

EXCHANGE, FOREIGN

See FOREIGN EXCHANGE

EXCHANGE RATES

See CURRENCY EXCHANGE RATES

EXCHANGES, COMMODITY

See COMMODITY FUTURES TRADING

EXCHANGES, STOCK

See STOCK EXCHANGES

EXCISE TAX

INTERNET DATABASES

CCH Essentials: An Internet Tax Research and Primary Source Library. CCH, Inc. Phone: 800-248-3248 or (773)866-6000; Fax: (773)866-3608 or (800)224-8299; Email: cust_serv@cch.com • URL: http://tax.cch.com/essentials • Fee-based Web site provides full-text coverage of federal tax law and regulations, including rulings, procedures, tax court decisions, and IRS publications, announcements, notices, and penalties. Includes explanation, analysis, tax planning guides, and a daily tax news service. Searching is offered, including citation search.

RESEARCH CENTERS AND INSTITUTES

University of Michigan - Stephen M. Ross School of Business - Office of Tax Policy Research. 701 Tappan St., Rm. R5380, Ann Arbor, MI 48109-1234. Phone: (734)763-3068; Fax: (734)763-4032; Email: jslemrod@umich.edu • URL: http://www.bus.umich.edu/OTPR/ • Tax policy, including compliance, capital gains, reform, international taxation, and income dynamics.

EXECUTIVE COMPENSATION

See also ADMINISTRATION; EXECUTIVES

ABSTRACTS AND INDEXES

Business Periodicals Index Retrospective. EBSCO Publishing Inc. • 11/year. Quarterly and annual cumulations.

HANDBOOKS AND MANUALS

Personnel Management: Compensation. Prentice Hall PTR. • Looseleaf. Periodic supplementation. Price on application.

INTERNET DATABASES

eComp: The Most Powerful Executive Compensation Online Research Tool. AON Consulting Inc. Phone: (212)441-2047; Fax: (212)441-1944; Email: sales@ecomp-online.com • URL: http://www.ecomponline.com • Web site provides free access to executive compensation data by company name or industry. Gives names and titles of top executives for each company, with the following information for each corporate officer: salary, bonus, long-term incentive plan data (LTIP), options granted, options expiration date, dollar value of options, and detailed options exercisable data. More extensive, customized data is available on a fee basis.

U.S. Securities and Exchange Commission. 100 F St. NE, Washington, DC 20549. Phone: 800-732-0330 or (202)942-8088; Fax: (202)942-9634; Email: webmaster@sec.gov • URL: http://www.sec.gov • SEC Web site offers free access through EDGAR to text of official corporate filings, such as annual reports (10-K), quarterly reports (10-Q), and proxies. (EDGAR is "Electronic Data Gathering, Analysis, and Retrieval System.") An example is given of how to obtain executive compensation data from proxies. Text of the daily *SEC News Digest* is offered, as are links to other government sites, non-government market regulators, and U. S. stock exchanges. Search facilities are extensive. Fees: Free.

Wageweb: Salary Survey Data On-Line. HRPDI: Human Resources Programs Development and Improvement. Phone: (804)363-1792; Fax: (804)594-3721; Email: salaries@wageweb.com • URL: http://www.wageweb.com • Web site provides salary information for more than 170 benchmark positions, including (for example) 29 information management jobs. Data shows average minimum, median, and average maximum compensation for each position, based on salary surveys. Fees: Free for national salary data; $169.00 per year for more detailed information (geographic, organization size, specific industries).

ONLINE DATABASES

EdgarPlus: SEC Basic Filings. Thomson Reuters Markets. • Online service provides full text of about 60,000 documents that have been filed with the U.S. Securities and Exchange Commission, 1987 to date, with daily updates. Filings include 6-K, 8-K, 10-K, 10-C, 10-Q, 20-F, and proxy statements. Inquire as to online cost and availability.

Wilson Business Abstracts Online. H.W. Wilson Co. • Indexes and abstracts 600 major business periodicals, plus the *Wall Street Journal* and the business section of the *New York Times*. Indexing is from 1982, abstracting from 1990, with the two newspapers included from 1993. Updated weekly. Inquire as to online cost and availability. (*Business Periodicals Index* without abstracts is also available online.).

OTHER SOURCES

Business Rankings Annual (BRA). Cengage Learning Inc. • Annual. $584 Individuals. A guide to lists and rankings appearing in major business publications. The top ten names are listed in each case.

Executive Compensation. ALM Media Properties LLC. • $570. Covers many topics relating to the legal aspects of executive compensation, including taxation, securities law, payments in stock, fringe benefits, employment agreements, and severance arrangements. (Law Journal Press).

Executive Compensation for Emerging Companies. Daniel Niehans and Shawn E. Lampron. Glasser LegalWorks. • $599 Individuals Binder/Looseleaf (Full set). Periodic Supplementation. Covers various aspects of executive compensation, with emphasis on stock option plans and stock ownership. Includes many annotated legal forms. (Emerging Growth Companies Series.).

Executive Stock Options and Stock Appreciation Rights. ALM Media Properties LLC. • $525. Coverage includes non-qualified stock options and incentive stock options. Contains sample forms and documents. (Law Journal Press).

PERIODICALS AND NEWSLETTERS

Compensation and Benefits Review: The Journal of Total Compensation Strategies. Pine Forge Press. • Bimonthly. $565 Individuals print only. Contains a summary of the latest compensation and benefits surveys, reports, and legal and regulatory developments.

Compensation and Benefits Update. Thomson RIA. • Monthly. $149.00 per year. Provides information on the latest ideas and developments in the field of employee benefits. In-depth exploration of popular benefits programs. Formerly *Benefits and Compensation Update*.

Tax Management Compensation Planning Journal. BNA Tax Management. • Monthly. $426.00 per year. Formerly *Compensation Planning Journal*.

STATISTICS SOURCES

Project Management Salary Survey. Project Management Institute. • Annual. $200.00. Gives compensation data for key project management positions in North America, according to job title, level of responsibility, number of employees supervised, and various other factors. Includes data on retirement plans and benefits.

Top Executive Compensation. The Conference Board. • Annual. $395 Nonmembers. Provides data on compensation of highest paid executives in major corporations.

TRADE/PROFESSIONAL ASSOCIATIONS

WorldatWork. 14040 N Northsight Blvd., Scottsdale, AZ 85260. Phone: 866-816-2962 or (480)922-2020 or (480)951-9191; Fax: (480)483-8352 or (866)816-2962; Email: customerrelations@worldatwork.org • URL: http://www.worldatwork.org • Dedicated to knowledge leadership in compensation, benefits and total rewards, focusing on disciplines associated with attracting, retaining and motivating employees. Offers CCP, CBP, and GRP certification and education programs, conducts surveys, research and provides networking opportunities.

EXECUTIVE EDUCATION

See EXECUTIVE TRAINING AND DEVELOPMENT

EXECUTIVE RATING

See RATING OF EMPLOYEES

EXECUTIVE RECRUITING

See RECRUITMENT OF PERSONNEL

EXECUTIVE SALARIES

See EXECUTIVE COMPENSATION

EXECUTIVE SECRETARIES

See OFFICE PRACTICE

EXECUTIVE TRAINING AND DEVELOPMENT

See also ADULT EDUCATION; BUSINESS EDUCATION; TRAINING OF EMPLOYEES

ABSTRACTS AND INDEXES

Business Periodicals Index Retrospective. EBSCO Publishing Inc. • 11/year. Quarterly and annual cumulations.

ONLINE DATABASES

Wilson Business Abstracts Online. H.W. Wilson Co. • Indexes and abstracts 600 major business periodicals, plus the *Wall Street Journal* and the business section of the *New York Times*. Indexing is from 1982, abstracting from 1990, with the two newspapers included from 1993. Updated weekly. Inquire as to online cost and availability. (*Business Periodicals Index* without abstracts is also available online.).

OTHER SOURCES

Maximizing Law Firm Profitability: Hiring, Training, and Developing Productive Lawyers. ALM Media Properties LLC. • $590 print + online + ebook. Covers subjects on how to enhance your skills as a lawyer and to develop the potential of your associates.

PERIODICALS AND NEWSLETTERS

Business Education Forum. National Business Education Association. • Four times a year. Libraries, $70.00 per year. Includes *Yearbook* and *Keying In*, a newsletter.

Executive Excellence: The Newsletter of Personal Development, Managerial Effectiveness, and Organizational Productivity. Kenneth M. Shelton, editor. Executive Excellence Publishing. • Monthly. $129.00 per year. Newsletter.

T and D Magazine. ASTD. • Monthly. Free to members; non-members, $85.00 per year.

Training: The Magazine of Covering the Human Side of Business. Nielsen Business Media Inc. • Monthly. $78.00 per year.

TRADE/PROFESSIONAL ASSOCIATIONS

ASTD. 1640 King St., Alexandria, VA 22314-2746. Phone: 800-628-2783 or (703)683-8100; Fax: (703)683-1523; Email: customercare@astd.org • URL: http://www.astd.org • Represents workplace learning and performance professionals.

Center for Management Effectiveness. PO Box 1202, Pacific Palisades, CA 90272. Phone: (310)459-6052; Email: info@cmeinc.com • URL: http://www.cmeinc.org • Participants are directors of training and management development from industry, government, and nonprofit organizations. Conducts programs for management trainers on topics such as stress management, resolution of disagreements, risk-taking, problem solving, strategic decision-making and managing change.

Ledernes Hovedeorganisation. Vermlandsgade 65, DK-2300 Copenhagen, Denmark. Phone: 45 32833283; Email: lederne@lederne.dk • URL: http://www.lederne.dk • Business managers and executives. Represents members' interests before government agencies, industry associations, and the public. Manages unemployment insurance fund for members; makes available legal services; conducts continuing professional training programs.

National Conference of Executives of the Arc. 1825 K St. NW, Ste. 1200, Washington, DC 20006. Phone: 800-433-5255 or (202)534-3700; Fax: (202)534-3731; Email: info@thearc.org • URL: http://www.thearc.org/nce • Executives of the Arc. Promotes professional development of members; seeks to enhance the lives of people with mental retardation. Provides educational opportunities and professional support to Arc executives.

EXECUTIVES

See also ADMINISTRATION; BUSINESS; CORPORATE DIRECTORS AND OFFICERS

BIBLIOGRAPHIES

Thunderbird International Business Review. Thunderbird American Graduate School of International Management. John Wiley and Sons, Inc., Journals Div. • Bimonthly. $937 Institutions print only. Journal on international business and commerce for academic scholars, business and government executives, and trade specialists. Formerly *International Executive*.

BIOGRAPHICAL SOURCES

Newsmakers. Cengage Learning Inc. • Annual. $314 Individuals. Four softbound issues and one hardbound annual. Biographical information on individuals currently in the news. Includes photographs. Formerly *Contemporary Newsmakers*. eBook also available. Contact for pricing.

Who's Who in Finance and Business. Marquis Who's Who L.L.C. • Biennial. $349 Individuals. Provides over 21,000 concise biographies of business leaders in all fields.

CD-ROM DATABASES

Business Abstracts with Full Text. EBSCO Publishing Inc. • Includes full text articles from more than 460 business publications from 1982 to present. Indexing for nearly 880 publications.

OECD Statistical Compendium. Organization for Economic Cooperation and Development. • Semiannual. $1,905.00 per year for 1 to 10 users. CD-ROM contains more than 730,000 monthly, quarterly, and annual time series for OECD countries, 1960 to date. Includes fully searchable data on agriculture, food, economic indicators, national accounts, employment, energy, finance, industry, technology, and foreign trade. Results can be displayed in various forms.

Standard & Poor's Corporations. Dialog OnDisc. • Monthly. Price on application. Produced by Standard & Poor's. Contains three CD-ROM files: Executives, Private Companies, and Public Companies, providing detailed information on more than 70,000 business executives, 55,000 private companies, and 12,000 publicly-traded corporations.

The Tax Directory. Tax Analysts. • Quarterly. $499 Individuals both volumes, web, CD or print. Updated quarterly on CD-ROM and in print; updated continually online. Covering federal, state, and international tax officials, tax practitioners, and corporate tax executives.

DIRECTORIES

Business Week--Survey of Executive Compensation Issue. The McGraw-Hill Companies Inc. • Weekly. $46.95 for 1 year. Publication includes: Executives in major industries of the United States and their compensation in salary, bonuses, stock options, stock appreciation rights. Entries include: Company name, sales, and return on equity; names and titles of chief executives, salary, and total of salary and bonus with percentage of change from prior year, long term compensation, one-year and three-year pay to performance analysis.

Directory of Top Computer Executives. Applied Computer Research Inc. • Semiannual. $345 Individuals single volume, per issue. Covers: In three volumes, over 65,000 U.S. and Canadian executives with major information technology or communications responsibilities in over 35,500 U.S. and Canadian companies. Database includes: Listings of manufacturer and model numbers of systems that are installed at each company. Entries include: Company name, address, phone, subsidiary and/or division names, major systems installed, names and titles of top information system executives, number of IT employees, number of PCs, and web address.

Directory of Washington, DC Chief Executive Officers. Labor Market Information and Research Division District of Columbia Department of Employment Services. • Annual. Covers: 200 large nongovernmental companies in the District of Columbia, selected on the basis of number of employees. Entries include: Company name, name of chief executive officer, address and the telephone numbers.

Dun's Key Decision-Makers in Hong Kong. Dun & Bradstreet Inc. • Quarterly. HK$3,850 Individuals. Covers: 10,000 directors and senior executives from leading businesses in Hong Kong. Entries include: D&B D-U-N-S number, company name, address, phone, fax, descriptive line of business, SIC codes, presence in People's Republic of China, number of employees, multiple executive names and titles, year started.

Financial Yellow Book: Who's Who at the Leading U. S. Financial Institutions. Leadership Directories Inc. • Semiannual. $465. Gives the names and titles of over 28,000 key executives in financial institutions. Includes the areas of banking, investment, money management, and insurance. Five indexes are provided: institution, executive name, geographic by state, financial service segment, and parent company.

Forbes--Chief Executive Compensation Survey Issue. Forbes Inc. • Annual. $4.95. Publication includes: List of 800 firms. Entries include: (In tabular form) Company name, name of chief executive officer, age, rank, compensation in salary and bonus, other remuneration, stock gains, total remuneration, years with company, years as chief executive, place of birth, educational and business background.

The Middle Management of German Business. Hoppenstedt Produktinformationen GmbH. • Annual. $240. Covers 60,000 middle managers at 25,000 major German companies.

Personen-Compass. Compass-Verlag. • Annual. $1,250. Covers: over 19,000 principal executives of major Austrian companies. Entries include: Name, address, affiliations.

President's Club! Presidents of Computer and Telecommunications Companies Directory. Ex-IBM Corp. • $95 per issue. Covers: over 2,200 presidents of companies, organizations, or associations involved in the computer and telecommunications industries. Entries include: Company, organization, or association name, president's name, address, and phone.

Standard & Poor's Register of Corporations, Directors and Executives. Standard & Poor's Financial Services L.L.C. • Annual. Covers: over 55,000 public and privately held corporations in the United States, including names and titles of over 400,000 officials (Volume 1); 70,000 biographies of directors and executives (Volume 2). Database includes: In Volume 3, lists of new executives, new companies, a corporate "Family Tree," Standard & Poor's 500 composite stock indices, and obituaries. Entries include: For companies--Name, address, phone, names of principal executives and accountants; primary bank, primary law firm, number of employees, estimated annual sales, outside directors, Standard Industrial Classification (SIC) code, product or service provided. For directors and executives--Name, home and principal business addresses, date and place of birth, fraternal organization memberships, business affiliations.

The Tax Directory. Tax Analysts. • Quarterly. $499 Individuals both volumes, web, CD or print. Updated quarterly on CD-ROM and in print; updated continually online. Covering federal, state, and international tax officials, tax practitioners, and corporate tax executives.

Who's Who in Canadian Business. University of Toronto Press Inc. • Annual. $192.95 Individuals plus shipping charges. Covers: About 5,400 corporate and entrepreneurial leaders, each with a detailed biography and contact information. Biographies include such information as current employment, address, education, career history, publications, favorite charities and honors. Entries include: Name, degree(s), position, and title; office address, phone, fax, e-mail, and URL; personal, education, and career data; memberships, affiliations, and other interests.

Who's Who in Chicago Business. Crain Communications Inc. • $249 Individuals Excel format. Covers 800 civic, professional, and cultural leaders in Chicago.

Who's Who in Finance and Business. Marquis Who's Who L.L.C. • Biennial. $349 Individuals. Provides over 21,000 concise biographies of business leaders in all fields.

Who's Who of Britain's Business Elite. Who's Who Publications. • $59. Includes Boards of Directors involved in the most established and successful companies in the U.K.

ENCYCLOPEDIAS AND DICTIONARIES

Business Leader Profiles for Students. Cengage Learning Inc. • $193 Individuals. Focuses on an additional 100 new business leaders to those listed in volume 1 and 25 updated profles from the first volume. Biographical profiles range from 1,250 to 2,500 words in length.

INTERNET DATABASES

Business 2.0 Web Guide to the Best Business Links. Business 2.0 Media Inc. Phone: (415)293-4800; Email: support@business2.com • URL: http://www.business2.com/webguide • Web site presents an extensive, searchable directory of links to "the best, most informative, and authoritative web pages." Twenty main categories cover business, finance, career, company information, people, and technology topics, with thousands of subtopics, all linking to Web sites recommended by experienced business researchers. Fees: Free.

EBSCO Information Services. EBSCO Publishing Inc. 10 Estes St., Ipswich, MA 01938-2106. Phone: 800-653-2726 or (978)356-6500; Fax: (978)356-6565; Email: information@ebscohost.com • URL: http://www.ebscohost.com • Fee-based Web site providing Internet access to a wide variety of databases, including business-related material. Full text is available for many periodical titles, with daily updates. Fees: Apply.

InSite 2. Intelligence Data/Thomson Financial. Phone: 800-654-0393 or (617)856-1890; Fax: (617)737-3182; Email: intelligence.data@tfn.com • URL: http://www.insite2.gale.com/ • Fee-based Web site consolidates information in a "Base Pack" consisting of Business InSite, Market InSite, and Company InSite. Optional databases are Consumer InSite, Health and Wellness InSite, Newsletter InSite, and Computer InSite. Includes fulltext content from more than 2,500 trade publications, journals, newsletters, newspapers, analyst reports, and other sources. Continuous updating. Formerly produced by The Gale Group.

ProQuest. ProQuest L.L.C. 789 E Eisenhower Pkwy., Ann Arbor, MI 48106-1346. Phone: 800-521-0600 or (734)761-4700; Fax: (734)662-4554; Email: info@proquest.com • URL: http://www.proquest.com • Fee-based Web site providing Internet access to more than 3,000 periodicals, newspapers, and other publications. Many items are available full-text, with daily updates. Includes extensive corporate and financial information. Fees: Apply.

ONLINE DATABASES

Wilson Business Abstracts Online. H.W. Wilson Co. • Indexes and abstracts 600 major business periodicals, plus the *Wall Street Journal* and the business section of the *New York Times*. Indexing is from 1982, abstracting from 1990, with the two newspapers included from 1993. Updated weekly. Inquire as to online cost and availability. (*Business Periodicals Index* without abstracts is also available online.).

PERIODICALS AND NEWSLETTERS

Academy of Management Perspectives. Academy of Management. • Quarterly. $130 /year for individuals in U.S. (print only). Contains articles relating to the practical application of management principles and theory.

Administrative Science Quarterly. Cornell University, Johnson Graduate School of Management. • Quarterly. $299 Institutions combined (print & e-access).

Boston Business Journal. American City Business Journals. • Weekly. $102 Individuals print and online. Business newspaper specializing in local and regional business for upper management and CEO's of large and mid-sized businesses.

Business Finance. Penton. • Monthly. $59.00 per year. Covers trends in finance, technology, and economics for corporate financial executives.

Business Month: The Magazine of Corporate Management. Goldhirsh Group. • Monthly. Magazine for business executives.

Business Week. The McGraw-Hill Companies Inc. • Weekly. $5 Individuals 12 issues. Magazine providing business news and intelligence for executives.

Daily Report for Executives. Bloomberg BNA. • Daily. Covers legal, regulatory, economic, and tax developments affecting corporations.

904: Northeast Florida's Business & Executive Life Authority. White Publishing Co. • Bimonthly. $9.04 Individuals. Business periodical featuring business-related articles focusing on high-profile executives and business managers.

TRADE/PROFESSIONAL ASSOCIATIONS

American Businesspersons Association. Hillsboro Executive Center North, 350 Fairway Dr., Ste. 107, Deerfield Beach, FL 33441-1834. Phone: 800-221-2168; Fax: (954)571-8582; Email: membership@assnservices.com • URL: http://www.aba-assn.com • Owners of businesses and individuals in executive, managerial, and sales capacities. Provides substantial discounts, affordable insurance, products and other special services to members.

Association of Business Executives. 5th Fl., CI Tower, St. George Sq., New Maiden, Surrey, London KT3 4TE, United Kingdom. Phone: 44 20 83292930; Fax: 44 20 83292945; Email: info@abeuk.com • URL: http://www.abeuk.com • Student membership sitting examinations.

CEO Netweavers. PO Box 700393, Dallas, TX 75370. Email: info@ceonetweavers.org • URL: http://www.ceonetweavers.org • Represents servant leader CEOs and their trusted professional service advisors. Promotes servant leadership and relationship building among members. Provides communication, brand building, education, community outreach and learning.

Chief Executives Organization. 7920 Norfolk Ave., Ste. 400, Bethesda, MD 20814-2507. Phone: (301)656-9220; Fax: (301)656-9221; Email: info@ceo.org • URL: http://www.ceo.org • Invited members of the Young Presidents' Organization who have reached the age of 49, the mandatory "retirement" age for YPO. (Young Presidents' Organization comprises presidents of corporations with gross annual revenue of at least one million dollars and a minimum of 50 employees, of nonindustrial corporations with revenue of two million dollars and 25 employees, or of banking corporations with average deposits of 15 million dollars and 25 employees. Each member must have been elected president of a corporation before reaching the age of 40.) Sponsors educational programs.

Committee of 200. 980 N Michigan Ave., Ste. 1575, Chicago, IL 60611. Phone: (312)255-0296; Fax: (312)255-0789; Email: info@c200.org • URL: http://www.c200.org • Represents women executives who are recognized as leaders in their industries (though originally intended to have a membership of 200 top-ranking businesswomen, the committee is no longer limited to 200). Encourages successful entrepreneurship by women and the active participation of women business owners and senior corporate executives in business, economic, social, and educational concerns. Seeks to strengthen the influence of women business leaders. Provides forum for exchange of ideas and enhancement of business opportunities for women.

Executive Leadership Council. 1001 N Fairfax St., Ste. 300, Alexandria, VA 22314. Phone: (703)706-5200; Email: elcinfo@elcinfo.com • URL: http://www.elcinfo.com • Provides senior African-American corporate executives with a network and leadership forum that adds perspective and direction to the achievement of excellence in business, economic and public policies for the African-American community and its corporations, and the community at large. Conducts educational and research programs.

Executive Women International. 3860 S 2300 E, Salt Lake City, UT 84109. Phone: (801)355-2800; Fax: (801)355-2852; Email: ewi@ewiconnect.com • URL: http://www.ewiconnect.com • Individuals holding key positions in business professions. Conducts networking educational and charitable programs.

Executives Association of Great Britain. The Limes, High Rd., Orsett, London RM16 3ER, United Kingdom. Phone: 44 1375 893414 • URL: http://www.eagb.co.uk • Executives of businesses in the United Kingdom. Provides a forum for the exchange of information between members.

Executives Without Borders. 281 Summer St., 5th Fl., Boston, MA 02210. Phone: 800-790-6134; Email: contactus@execwb.org • URL: http://www.executiveswithoutborders.org • Encourages businessmen and businesswomen to use their leadership positions to foster the growth of business in developing countries. Provides humanitarian aid to alleviate the effects of natural and economic disasters. Promotes cooperation and works with research institutions to find sustainable business solutions.

Financial Executives International. 1250 Headquarters Plz., West Tower, 7th Fl., Morristown, NJ 07960. Phone: 877-359-1070 or (973)765-1000; Fax: (973)765-1018; Email: membership@financialexecutives.org • URL: http://www.financialexecutives.org • Professional organization of corporate financial executives performing duties of chief financial officer, controller, treasurer, or vice-president-finance. Sponsors research activities through its affiliated Financial Executives Research Foundation. Maintains offices in Toronto, Canada, and Washington, DC.

The International Alliance for Women. 1101 Pennsylvania Ave. NW, 6th Fl., Washington, DC 20004. Phone: 888-712-5200 or (202)351-6839; Email: admin@tiaw.org • URL: http://www.tiaw.org • Local networks comprising 50,000 professional and executive women in 12 countries; individual businesswomen without a network affiliation are alliance associates. Promotes recognition of the achievements of women in business. Encourages placement of women in senior executive positions. Maintains high standards of professional competence among members. Facilitates communication on an international scale among professional women's networks and their members. Represents members' interests before policymaking business and government. Sponsors programs that support equal opportunity and enhance members' business and professional skills. Operates appointments and directors service. Maintains speakers' bureau.

International Christian Union of Business Executives. c/o Pierre Lecocq, President, 15-25 Blvd. de l'Amiral Bruix, F-75016 Paris, France. Phone: 33 1 56022121; Fax: 33 1 4526 • URL: http://www.uniapac.org • National Christian employers' associations in 29 countries. Works to promote Christian ethics and sound economic policies in both business and social sectors. Serves as liaison between members and Christian associations with common goals. Conducts biennial symposium.

International Executive Service Corps. 1900 M St. NW, Ste. 500, Washington, DC 20036. Phone: (202)589-2600; Fax: (202)326-0289; Email: iesc@iesc.org • URL: http://www.iesc.org • Provides technical and managerial assistance to enterprises, organizations and government bodies in emerging democracies and developing countries. Focuses on the knowledge, skill and experience of its 12,000 industry experts. Maintains a network of experts that includes high-level professionals drawn from nearly every area of private enterprise, government and non-governmental organizations; Geekcorps division includes experts in communications and information technology and is committed to closing the digital divide.

Japan Association of Corporate Executives. 1-4-6, Marunouchi, Chiyoda-ku, Tokyo 100-0005, Japan. Phone: 81 3 32111271 or 81 3 32840220; Fax: 81 3 32132946 or 81 3 32123774; Email: kdcontact1207@doyukai.or.jp • URL: http://www.doyukai.or.jp • Businesspersons in Japan. Formulates social, economic, policy proposals through research and discussion among members.

National Association for Female Executives. 2 Park Ave., New York, NY 10016. • URL: http://www.nafe.com • Represents and supports professional women and women business owners; provides resources and services through education, networking and public advocacy to empower members to achieve career success and financial security.

National Association of Corporate Directors. 2001 Pennsylvania Ave. NW, Ste. 500, Washington, DC 20006. Phone: (202)775-0509; Fax: (202)775-4857; Email: join@nacdonline.org • URL: http://www.nacdonline.org • Corporate directors and boards of directors; chief executive officers, presidents, accountants, lawyers, consultants, and other executives are members. Conducts research, surveys, and seminars.

National Executive Service Corps. 55 W 39th St., 12th Fl., New York, NY 10018. Phone: (212)269-1234; Fax: (212)269-0959; Email: info@nesc.org • URL: http://www.nesc.org • Provides management and business advisory services to non-profit educational, health care, social services, cultural, and religious organizations. Supplies services through experienced and senior-leveled business people who act as volunteer management consultants.

World Presidents Organization. 600 E Las Colinas Blvd., Ste. 1000, Irving, TX 75039. Phone: 800-773-7976 or (972)587-1500 or (972)587-1618; Fax: (972)587-1611; Email: membership@ypowpo.org • URL: http://www.wpo.org • Corporate executives, all of whom are former members of the Young Presidents' Organization. Functions as a graduate school for former members of YPO. Strives to provide high quality program content and to keep members well-informed on major topics through contact with the world's leading authorities. Conducts seminars.

Young Presidents' Organization. 600 E Las Colinas Blvd., Ste. 1000, Irving, TX 75039. Phone: 800-773-7976 or (972)587-1500; Fax: (972)587-1611; Email: askypo@ypo.org • URL: http://www.ypo.org • Presidents or chief executive officers of corporations with minimum of 50 employees; each member must have been elected president before his/her 40th birthday and must retire by June 30th the year after his/her 50th birthday. Assists members in becoming better presidents through education and idea exchange. Conducts courses for members and spouses, in business, arts and sciences, world affairs, and family and community life, during a given year at various locations, including graduate business schools.

EXECUTIVES, WOMEN

See WOMEN EXECUTIVES

EXERCISE EQUIPMENT INDUSTRY

See FITNESS INDUSTRY

EXPENSE CONTROL

See COST CONTROL

EXPERT SYSTEMS

See ARTIFICIAL INTELLIGENCE

EXPLOSIVES INDUSTRY

ABSTRACTS AND INDEXES

Applied Science and Technology Index. EBSCO Publishing Inc. • 11/year. Indexes a wide variety of English language technical, industrial, and engineering periodicals.

Engineering Index Monthly: Abstracting and Indexing Services Covering Sources ofthe World's Engineering Literature. Engineering Information Inc. • Monthly. Institutions, $5,279.00 per year. Provides indexing and abstracting of the world's engineering and technical literature.

F & S Index: United States. Cengage Learning Inc. • $2,659 Individuals. Monthly. $2,532.00 per year, including quarterly and annual cumulations. Provides annotated citations to marketing, business, financial, and industrial literature. Coverage of U.S. business activity includes trade journals, financial magazines, business newspapers, and special reports.

CD-ROM DATABASES

Applied Science and Technology Abstracts. EBSCO Publishing Inc. • Citations for more than 700 prominent scientific, technical, engineering, and industrial periodicals.

ONLINE DATABASES

Aerospace Database. American Institute of Aeronautics and Astronautics. • Contains abstracts of literature covering all aspects of the aerospace and aircraft industry 1983 to date. Monthly updates. Inquire as to online cost and availability.

Applied Science and Technology Index Online. H.W. Wilson Co. • Provides online indexing of 500 major scientific, technical, industrial, and engineering periodicals. Time period is 1983 to date. Monthly updates. Inquire as to online cost and availability.

RESEARCH CENTERS AND INSTITUTES

Missouri University of Science and Technology - Rock Mechanics and Explosives Research Center. 1006 Kingshighway, Rolla, MO 65409. Phone: 800-522-0938 or (573)341-4365 or (573)341-4111; Fax: (573)341-4368; Email: rockmech@mst.edu • URL: http://rockmech.mst.edu • Rock mechanics and explosives technology, including studies on applications of high-pressure water jets in cutting geologic material, ground support design, rock fracture mechanics, physical and computer modeling, static rock mechanics, dynamic rock mechanics, theory of waves in real earth materials, development of detonators, gun and rocket propellants, explosives research and development, shaped charges, and high-tech metal machining. Also studies design and behavior of excavations in salt and potash deposits, and performs field blasting experiments.

New Mexico Institute of Mining and Technology - Energetic Materials Research and Testing Center. 801 Leroy Pl., Socorro, NM 87801. Phone: (575)835-5312; Fax: (575)835-5630; Email: webmaster@emrtc.nmt.edu • URL: http://www.emrtc.nmt.edu • Research areas include the development of industrial applications for explosives as energy sources.

EXPORT-IMPORT TRADE

See also CUSTOMS HOUSE, U.S. CUSTOMS SERVICE; FOREIGN TRADE

ALMANACS AND YEARBOOKS

World Economic Outlook Reports. International Monetary Fund. • Semiannual. $110. Provides key insights into how to view unprecedented global imbalances, respond to capital account crises caused by abrupt shifts in global asset allocations, and evaluate the opportunities for all member countries, especially low-income countries, to grow.

CD-ROM DATABASES

Global Trade Atlas. Global Trade Information Services Inc. • Subscription fees are tailored. Provides government statistics on trade between the U. S. and each of more than 80 countries. Includes import-export data, trade balances, product information, market share, price data, etc.

OECD Statistical Compendium. Organization for Economic Cooperation and Development. • Semiannual. $1,905.00 per year for 1 to 10 users. CD-ROM contains more than 730,000 monthly, quarterly, and annual time series for OECD countries, 1960 to date. Includes fully searchable data on agriculture, food, economic indicators, national accounts, employment, energy, finance, industry, technology, and foreign trade. Results can be displayed in various forms.

U.S. Exports of Merchandise. U.S. Bureau of the Census, Foreign Trade Division. • Monthly and quarterly data. Provides export data in the most extensive detail available, including product, quantity, value, shipping weight, country of destination, customs district of exportation, etc.

U.S. Imports of Merchandise. U.S. Bureau of the Census, Foreign Trade Division. • Monthly. $2,400 per year. Provides import data in the most extensive detail available, including product, quantity, value, shipping weight, country of origin, customs district of entry, rate provision, etc.

USA Trade. U.S. Department of Commerce. • Monthly. $650.00 per year. Provides over 150,000 trade-related data series on CD-ROM. Includes full text of many government publications. Specific data is included on national income, labor, price indexes, foreign exchange, technical standards, and international markets. Website address is www.stat-usa.gov/.

World Trade Analyzer. Statistics Canada, International Trade Division. • $4,000. Annual. CD-ROM provides 20 years of export-import data for 800 commodities traded by the 180 member countries of the United Nations.

DIRECTORIES

AAPEX Export Interest Directory: 2008. • Lists U.S. companies that are interested in overseas markets, and exhibited at AAPEX 2008.

Afghanistan Business Law Handbook. International Business Publications, USA. • $99.95 Individuals hardcover. Covers: Information on basic business legislation, laws and climate, export-import regulations, and contacts.

Algeria Industrial and Business Directory. International Business Publications, USA. • Annual. $99.95 Individuals. Covers industrial, investment, and business contacts for conducting export-import and investment activity in the country.

Ankara Chamber of Industry Export Catalogue. Ankara Chamber of Industry. • Irregular. $5. Covers: Manufacturing and exporting companies associated with the Ankara Chamber of Industry. Entries include: Names, addresses, and products.

Arkansas Export Directory. Arkansas Economic Development Commission. • Annual. Covers: Products produced by Arkansas firms who export or are seeking to develop export sales. Entries include: Company name, address, phone.

Armenia Export-Import and Business Directory. International Business Publications, USA. • $99.95 Individuals. Covers strategic, economic, investment, export-import, and business opportunities and contact numbers.

Armenia Industrial and Business Directory.

International Business Publications, USA. • Annual. $99.95 Individuals. Covers industrial, investment and business contacts for conducting export-import and investment activity in the country.

Asia-Pacific International Business Directory of Importers. Coble International. • $455 print or CD-ROM. Covers: 32,000 importers from South Korea, Australia, Philippines, New Zealand, India, Vietnam, Sri Lanka, Japan, Kazakhstan, Malaysia, Pakistan, Singapore, Indonesia, Mauritius, South Pacific Islands, Mongolia, Hong Kong, Taiwan, Thailand, China, and Uzbekistan. Entries include: Name, address, phone, fax, primary contact person, list of products, e-mail addresses, and Web site.

Austria Export-Import Trade and Business Directory. International Business Publications, USA. • $99.95 Individuals. Contains information on strategic economic, investment, export-import, and business opportunities and contact numbers.

Azerbaijan Export-Import Trade and Business Directory. International Business Publications, USA. • $99.95 Individuals. Contains information on strategic economic, investment, export-import, and business opportunities and contact numbers.

Azerbaijan Industrial and Business Directory. International Business Publications, USA. • Annual. $99.95 Individuals. Covers industrial, investment, and business contacts for conducting export-import and investment activity in the country.

Basic Guide to Exporting. Todd Publications. • Quadrennial. $20. Covers: Sources for aid in understanding foreign business practices, government regulations, taxes, and currency. Database includes: How to evaluate a product or service's overseas potential; how to make contacts and sell overseas; how to handle financing; and how to get paid.

Belarus Export-Import Trade and Business Directory. International Business Publications, USA. • $99.95 Individuals. Contains information on strategic, economic, investment, export-import, and business opportunities and contact numbers.

Belgium Export-Import and Business Directory. International Business Publications, USA. • $99.95 Individuals. Covers information on strategic, economic, investment, export-import, and business opportunities and contact numbers.

British Export Interactive Website. Reed Business Information. • Database covers: 17,000 companies in the United Kingdom, as well as the products and services they actively export. Database includes: Full electronic commerce.

Brunei Industrial and Business Directory. International Business Publications, USA. • Annual. $99.95 Individuals. Covers industrial, investment and business contacts for conducting export-import and investment activity in the country.

Bulgarian Trade Directory. Bulgarian Chamber of Commerce and Industry. • Annual. €35 Individuals EU member. Covers: 2,000 export/import companies and 120 economic committees and ministries in Bulgaria. Entries include: Name, address, phone, description of activities.

Busconi's Worldwide Importers Directory. Small Business Publications. • Irregular. $100. Covers: Importers of Indian products, engineering goods, chemicals, pharmaceuticals, electronics, electrical goods, foodstuffs, handicrafts, jewelry, leather products, medicinal plants, spices, ready-made garments. Entries include: Contact details.

Business Directory for Foreign Visitors. TeleDiplomacy Inc. • Database covers: Businesses and immigration, import, and export issues of interest to visitors to the United States. Entries include: Contact information.

Caribbean Exporters: A Directory of Caribbean Exporters. Caribbean Export Development Agency. • $50. Covers: Approximately 1,600 exporting companies in the Caribbean community. Database includes: General information about the Caribbean community; maps. Entries include: Company name, address, phone, fax, number of employees, product/service provided.

The Caricom Exporter: A Comprehensive Buyers' Guide to Caribbean Products and Services. Caribbean Imprint Directory Service. • Annual. $50. Covers: 1,600 listings of Caribbean products and services. Database includes: A separate listing of service companies, maps, and facts-at-a-glance for each country. Entries include: Exporter name, address, telephone number, fax number, telex number, name of contact, product brand name, banker name, plant location, size of firm.

China Industrial and Business Directory. International Business Publications, USA. • Annual. $99.95 Individuals. Covers industrial, investment and business contacts for conducting export-import and investment activity in the country.

Colombia Industrial and Business Directory. International Business Publications, USA. • Annual. $99.95 Individuals. Covers industrial, investment and business contacts for conducting export-import and investment activity in the country.

Comprehensive Directory of Mexican Importers. Todd Publications. • Biennial. $75. Covers: More than 2,700 Mexican importers.

Directory of African Importers of Yarns and Threads. EXIM Infotek Private Ltd. • $300 Individuals. Covers: 90 African importers of acrylic yarn, cotton yarn and thread, embroidery threads, polyester yarn, sewing threads, synthetic yarns and thread, and wool yarn. Entries include: Company name, postal address, telephone, fax, e-mail, website, contact person, designation, and product details.

Directory of Argentine Exporters and Importers. Telmo G. Mirat. • Annual. $100 postpaid. Covers: 3,250 manufacturers, importers, and exporters in Argentina, and companies and organizations providing products and services to international traders. Entries include: Organization name, address, phone, telex, fax, description of product/service, and Brussels tariff number.

Directory of Arizona Exporters. Arizona Commerce Authority. • Annual. Covers: Arizona enterprises currently involved in international trade. Entries include: Company name, address, phone, fax, e-mail, names of principal executive, and international marketing contact, number of employees, products or services, date established, current or planned export regions.

Directory of Asian Importers of Audio Visual Training Equipment and Projectors. EXIM Infotek Private Ltd. • $300 Individuals. Covers: 60 Asian importers of audio, audio visual equipment, audio visual training equipment, LCD projector, projectors, project equipment, slides, and slide projectors. Entries include: Company name, postal address, telephone, fax, e-mail, website, contact person, designation, and product details.

Directory of Belgian Importers of American Products. American Chamber of Commerce in Belgium. • Annual. $125. Covers: 1,000 Belgian importers and distributors and 3,000 U.S. exporters of U.S. products in Belgium. Entries include: Company name, address, phone, fax, executives, products.

Directory of Caribbean Importers. Caribbean Export Development Agency. • $15. Covers: Companies importing goods in the Carribean business community. Database includes: Profiles of sixteen Caribbean countries. Entries include: Name, address, phone, products imported.

Directory of Cordoba Exporters. Imagen S.A. • Covers: Products exported from Cordoba. Entries include: Product name, company name.

Directory of Danish Importers of Office Equipment & Supplies. EXIM Infotek Private Ltd. • $10 Individuals. Covers: 50 Danish importers of accounting and bookkeeping equipment, addressing and mailing equipment, banking equipment and supplies, calculators, cash registers, copying machines and supplies, fax and duplicating papers, office equipment and supplies, office machines, time recorders and timers, and typewriters. Entries include: Company name, postal address, telephone, fax, e-mail, website, contact person, designation, and product details.

Directory of European Importers of Biological Products. EXIM Infotek Private Ltd. • $15 Individuals. Covers: 50 European importers of biological products. Entries include: Company name, postal address, telephone, fax, e-mail, website, contact person, designation, and product details.

Directory of European Importers of Hoses & Fittings. EXIM Infotek Private Ltd. • Covers: 40 European importers of hoses, hose fittings, and adaptors. Entries include: Company name, postal address, telephone, fax, e-mail, website, contact person, designation, and product details.

Directory of European Importers of Wax & Wax Products. EXIM Infotek Private Ltd. • Covers: 50 European importers of paraffin, paraffin waxes, polishes and creams. Entries include: Company name, postal address, telephone, fax, e-mail, website, contact person, designation, and product details.

Directory of Exporting Industrialists. Istanbul Chamber of Industry. • Annual. $8 Restricted circulation. Covers: Approximately 700 exporting industrialist members of the Istanbul Chamber of Industry. Entries include: Company name, address, phone, telex number; Standard Industrial Classification (SIC) code; export amounts; description of products/services offered.

Directory of Importers. IBCON S.A. • Irregular. $488 Individuals. 2,284 Mexican companies importing at least $1,000,000 a year, for their own supplies or commercial distribution with executive in charge of imports.

Directory of Indian Importers of Wax & Wax Products. EXIM Infotek Private Ltd. • Covers: 30 Indian importers of micro waxes, paraffin waxes, polishes and creams, and slack waxes. Entries include: Company name, postal address, telephone, fax, e-mail, website, contact person, designation, and product details.

Directory of International Trade & Industrial Association in the World. EXIM Infotek Private Ltd. • Covers: 2,150 international trade and industrial associations. Entries include: Company name, postal address, telephone, fax, e-mail, website, contact person, designation, and product details.

Directory of Middle East Importers of Wax & Wax Products. EXIM Infotek Private Ltd. • Covers: 40 Middle East importers of paraffin, paraffin waxes, polishes and creams. Entries include: Company name, postal address, telephone, fax, e-mail, website, contact person, designation, and product details.

Directory of St. Petersburg Free-Zone Region. Flegon Press. • $75 postpaid. Covers: import-export enterprises in St. Petersburg (formerly Leningrad) and surrounding areas in Russia. Entries include: Enterprise name, address, phone, telex, names and titles of key personnel.

Directory of Services to Exporters. IBCON S.A. • Irregular. $283 Individuals. Covers: 654 companies, associations and government agencies, located in Mexico City, that offer a variety of services needed by exporters.

Directory of South American Importers of Furnaces

and Ovens--Industrial. EXIM Infotek Private Ltd. • $150 Individuals. Covers: 20 South American importers of industrial furnaces and oven. Entries include: Company name, postal address, telephone, fax, e-mail, website, contact person, designation, and product details.

Directory of South American Importers of Wax & Wax Products. EXIM Infotek Private Ltd. • Covers: 20 South American importers of paraffin waxes, polishes and creams. Entries include: Company name, postal address, telephone, fax, e-mail, website, contact person, designation, and product details.

Directory of Taiwan's Leading Exporters. China Economic News Service. • Annual. $90. Covers: 6,000 suppliers of machinery, toys, giftware, stationery, jewelry, sporting goods, leather goods, footwear, bicycles, automobiles, hardware, building materials, electronics, computers, textiles, furniture, and lighting.

Directory of UK Exporters. Hemming Information Services. • $275 plus $9.00 shipping. Covers: 10,500 manufacturing exporters. Entries include: Named export contact, products, countries of destination, tonnage shipped and turnover.

Directory of U.S. Importers. Journal of Commerce Group. • Annual. $2,750 Master Edition CD. Covers: 32,000 importers in the United States. Database includes: Lists of world ports and international banks; trade commissions, consulates, embassies, and foreign trade zones; guide to operations of the U.S. Customs Service and company name. Entries include: Company name, address, phone, fax, names and titles of key personnel, SIC code, commodities imported, import country, U.S. port of entry, tonnage and volume indicators.

Directory of United States Importers/Directory of United States Exporters. Piers Publishing Group. • Annual. $675.00. Two volumes. $475.00 per volume. Approximately 55,000 firms with import and export interests; export and import managers, agents, and merchants in the United States; World ports; consulates and embassies. Formerly *United States Importers and Exporters Directories*.

Directory of Vendors. IBCON S.A. • Irregular. $473 Individuals. Covers: 14,640 companies that are SA corporations located in Mexico City. Entries include: Company name, address, phone, fax, industry code, Producing, Distributing, Servicing initials, name and position of the top executive.

Directory of World Trade Center & Trade Points. EXIM Infotek Private Ltd. • Covers: 280 World Trade Centers and trade points. Entries include: Company name, postal address, telephone, fax, e-mail, website, contact person, designation, and product details.

Directory of Worldwide Export-Import Promotion Center. EXIM Infotek Private Ltd. • Covers: 550 export and import promotion centers worldwide. Entries include: Company name, postal address, telephone, fax, e-mail, website, contact person, designation, and product details.

DMA's Who's Who in Hong Kong Trading Industries. Asian Market Information & Analysis Centre. • Covers: 1,500 companies in Hong Kong's trading industries. Entries include: Company name, website; contact address, phone, fax, and e-mail; contact person, job title, and e-mail address.

Export and Import Directory of Peru. Association of Peruvian Exporters. • Annual. $60. Covers: Exporters, importers, and export service firms in Peru.

Export--Buyers Guide Issue. Johnston International Publishing Corp. • Annual. $10. Publication includes: About 250 manufacturers and exporters of hardware, air conditioning and refrigeration equipment, garden supplies, sporting goods, automotive accessories, and building products. Limited to advertisers. Entries include: Company name, address, phone, telex, names of contacts.

Export Denmark. Kongeriget Danmarks Handels-Kalender. • Annual. Covers: 10,000 exporters in Denmark. Entries include: Company name, address, phone, telex number, products, trade names.

Export/Import Markets: Puerto Rico Edition. Direct Marketing & Media Group Inc. • $30. Covers: about 1,000 firms located in Puerto Rico and engaged in exporting, importing, and supplying services to international trade (including steamship lines and agents, banks, rental firms, freight forwarders, and custom house brokers). Entries include: For steamship lines and agents--Firm name, address, phone, fax, telex, name of firms represented. For others--Company name, address, phone, fax, telex, names and titles of key personnel, number of employees, product/service.

Export Mail-Order. Todd Publications. • Biennial. $20. Covers: Suppliers, overseas firms seeking exports, firms serving as export management companies, and other information to aid in choosing products to export.

Exporter Directory. People Publishing Ltd. • Annual. Covers: 2,000 export companies in New Zealand seeking overseas contacts and clients.

Finnish Export Companies. FINPRO. • Database covers: over 2,500 Finnish export companies. Database includes: Company name, address, names and titles of key personnel, products.

Global Foreign Trade Barriers to U.S. Products and Services Exports Handbook. International Business Publications, USA. • $99.95 Individuals paperback. Covers: Foreign trade barriers to the U.S. Products and services exports to various countries.

Global Trade Review Directory. Exporta Publishing & Events Ltd. • Annual. £125 Individuals non-subscribers. Covers: 450 service providers to global trade, commodity, and export finance markets. Entries include: Company contact information.

Greek Exporters. European P.L.C. • Provides specific proposals of co-operation between Greek companies and their counterparts within the Eastern European, Balkans and N.I.S. countries. Covers: Greek export companies in Eastern Europe, Balkans, and N.I.S.

Hawaii Business Abroad. Hawaii Department of Business, Economic Development, and Tourism Research and Economic Analysis Division. • Irregular. Covers: approximately 400 Hawaiian firms that export, import, maintain overseas offices, or have business activities in foreign countries. Entries include: Company name, address, phone, fax, telex, name of contact, cable address, line of business, year established, number of employees, locations of overseas offices, description of overseas activities, parent company name and address (if any), names of countries with which business is done.

Hong Kong Importer Directory. Biz Focus Company Ltd. • $240 Individuals. Covers: 4,972 importers with various product categories. Entries include: Company name, contact person, contact address, telephone number, fax number, e-mail, URL, and import products.

Hong Kong Importers List. INFOT Inc. • $80.75 CD-ROM; additional $119 for MS Access format. Covers: 15,826 selected importers and buyers from Hong Kong and P.R. China. Entries include: Company name, contact person, physical addresses, email and website addresses, telephone and fax number, and business description.

Imports and Exports of the Republic of China and Taiwan. Taiwan External Trade Development Council. • Annual. $150. Covers import commodities whose import value exceeds $200,000 (U.S. funds) annually.

The Indian Export Directory. Indian Export Trade Journal. • Annual. $120. Covers: Indian manufacturers, exporters, importers, foreign firms interested in trade with India, world chambers of commerce, trade associations, and products. Entries include: Company name, address, phone, telex, cable.

Indian Export Yearbook. M/S Sales Overseas. • Annual. $80. Covers: Importers, exporters, manufacturers, Indian agents, foreign trade statistics, Indian economy, events, government trade offices, export firms, information for tourists; exporters and importers trading with SAARC countries (Bangladesh, Bhutan, Maldives, Nepal, Pakistan, and Sri Lanka). Entries include: Contact information.

Indian Exporters Directory, Database. NIIR Project Consultancy Services. • $200 U.S. CD-ROM. Covers: 43,000+ Indian exporters. Entries include: Company name, contact person name and designation, full postal address, phone, fax, email (wherever available), website address (wherever available), activity.

Indian Importers Directory, Database. NIIR Project Consultancy Services. • $150 Individuals CD-ROM. Covers: 20,000+ Indian importers. Entries include: Company name, contact person name and designation, full postal address, phone, fax, email (wherever available), website address (wherever available), activity.

Indonesian Business Directory. PT Sumber Daya Multimedia. • $30. Database covers: 94,000 Indonesian importers, exporters, and other businesses. Entries include: Contact information, industry, and description of products and services.

Inform Katalog Export Import. Inform Katalog Spol. S.R.O. • Annual. Covers: More than 4,000 of the leading Czech exporters and importers classified by commodities.

International Directory of Importers--Africa. Croner Publications Inc. • Irregular. $225. Covers: 10,000 importers in 40 countries in Africa. Entries include: Company name, address, phone.

The International Directory of Importers - Africa. Interdata. • $250 By mail print. Covers: 9,000 firms importing in 44 African countries a broad variety of products from abrasives to zippers. Entries include: Company name and address, contact person, email, number of employees, year established, phone and telefaxes, business activity, bank references, as well as a detailed listing of products imported.

The International Directory of Importers - Asia/Pacific. Interdata. • $385 U.S. print edition. Covers: 32,000 firms importing in 22 Asian countries a broad variety of products from abrasives to zippers. Entries include: Company name and address, contact person, email, number of employees, year established, phone and telefaxes, business activity, bank references, as well as a detailed listing of products imported.

International Directory of Importers--Asia/Pacific. Croner Publications Inc. • Irregular. $350. Covers: 30,000 importers in Australia, Hong Kong, Indonesia, Japan, Malaysia, New Zealand, Pakistan, Philippines, Singapore, South Korea, Sri Lanka, Taiwan, and Thailand. Entries include: Company name, address, phone.

International Directory of Importers--Europe. Croner Publications Inc. • Irregular. $450. Covers: 54,000 importers in Austria, Belgium, Denmark, France, Holland, Italy, Norway, Spain, Sweden, Switzerland, United Kingdom, and West Germany. Entries include: Company name, address, phone.

The International Directory of Importers - Europe. Interdata. • $485 Individuals regular mail. Covers: 54,000 firms importing in 35 European countries a broad variety of products from abrasives to zippers. Entries include: Company name and address, contact person, email, number of employees, year established, phone and telefaxes, business activity, bank references, as well as a detailed listing of products imported.

International Directory of Importers--Medical, Hospital, and Surgical Equipment and Supplies. International Directory of Importers. • Annual. $295 Individuals print. Covers: 5,000 worldwide manufacturers, importers, and firms trading in medical, hospital, and surgical equipment and supplies. Entries include: Company name, address, phone, fax, email address when available, importing manager, year established.

The International Directory of Importers - Middle East. Interdata. • $250 Individuals print. Covers: 13,000 firms importing in 14 Middle East countries a broad variety of products from abrasives to zippers. Entries include: Company name and address, contact person, email, number of employees, year established, phone and telefaxes, business activity, bank references, as well as a detailed listing of products imported.

International Directory of Importers--Middle East. Croner Publications Inc. • Irregular. $225. Covers: 14,000 importers in Bahrain, Egypt, Iran, Iraq, Israel, Jordan, Kuwait, Lebanon, Oman, Qatar, Saudi Arabia, Syria, United Arab Emirates, and North/South Yemen. Entries include: Company name, address, phone.

The International Directory of Importers - North America. Interdata. • $250 Individuals print. Covers: 19,000 firms importing in North America a broad variety of products from abrasives to zippers. Entries include: Company name and address, contact person, email, number of employees, year established, phone and telefaxes, business activity, bank references, as well as a detailed listing of products imported.

International Directory of Importers--North America. Croner Publications Inc. • Irregular. $225. Covers: 20,000 importers in the United States and Canada. Entries include: Company name, address, phone.

The International Directory of Importers - Office Equipment, Stationery and Supplies Importers. Interdata. • Annual. $320 Individuals print. Covers: 7,100 international firms importing office equipment, stationery and supplies. Entries include: Company name and address, contact person, email, number of employees, year established, phone and telefaxes, business activity, bank references, as well as a listing of office equipment, stationery and supplies currently being imported.

The International Directory of Importers--Safety, Security and Fire Fighting Equipment Importers. Interdata. • $260 Individuals print edition. Covers: 3,300 international firms importing safety, security and fire fighting equipment. Entries include: Company name and address, contact person, email, number of employees, year established, phone and telefaxes, business activity, bank references, as well as a listing of safety, security and fire fighting equipment currently being imported.

The International Directory of Importers - South America. Interdata. • $250 Individuals print edition. Covers: 23,000 firms importing in 27 South American countries a broad variety of products from abrasives to zippers. Entries include: Company name and address, contact person, e-mail address, number of employees, year established, phone and telefaxes, business activity, bank references, as well as a detailed listing of products imported.

International Intertrade Index of New Imported Products. International Intertrade Index. • Monthly. $45 per year. Covers: manufacturers of new products that are announced at foreign trade fairs and available to United States importers. Entries include: Company name, address, description of new products, and prices. Subscription includes "Foreign Trade Fairs" newsletter.

International Trade Directory. Indian Export Trade Journal. • Biennial. $50. Covers: Importers, exporters, shipping, clearing agents, banks, and chambers of commerce in 150 countries. Entries include: Contact information.

International Trade Directory for Dayton, Ohio. Dayton Area Chamber of Commerce. • Biennial. $25 Members. Covers: International firms importing and exporting in Dayton. Entries include: Company name, address, phone.

Israel Agro and Biotechnology Industry Export-Import Directory. International Business Publications, USA. • Annual. $99.95 Individuals hardcover, e-book, CD-ROM. Covers: Information on strategic economic, investment, export-import, and business opportunities. Contains important export-import, government, and business contacts. Ultimate directory for conducting export-import operations in the country.

Israel IT and Telecommunication Industry Export-Import Directory. International Business Publications, USA. • Annual. $99.95 Individuals hardcover, e-book, CD-ROM. Covers: Major investment, export-import and other strategic business opportunities, contacts, and basic information for conducting business in the country.

Kansas Manufacturing Firms in Export. Kansas Department of Commerce - Office of Minority and Women Business Development. • Biennial. Covers: nearly 1,000 Kansas companies in major groups 20 through 39 of the Standard Industrial Classification (SIC). Entries include: Company name, address, phone, name of principal executive, parent or subsidiary company, number of employees, products or services.

Kazakhstan Trade Directory. Flegon Press. • $200 Complete set. Covers: Business contacts from all industrial branches and government offices, including Agriculture, Fisheries, Health Care, Science and Tourism, in Kazakhstan, the richest republic of the former Soviet Union. Database includes: Over 1,000 trade propositions and requests for partnerships. Entries include: For contacts--name, address, phone; for producers--name, address, phone, fax, telex, directors' name, output/import needs, requests for partnership.

Korean Trade Directory. Korean Foreign Trade Association. • Annual. Covers: Exporters, importers, commodities, and foreign firms established in Korea, including airline offices, marine insurance companies, shipping firms, and trade associations. Database includes: Details on trade and investment laws and regulations. Entries include: Company name, address, phone, telex, names and titles of key personnel.

Latin American Import-Export Directory. International Trade Council. • Annual. Covers: 24,500 importing and exporting companies in Argentina, Bolivia, Brazil, Chile, Panama, Paraguay, Peru, Uruguay, Venezuela, Colombia, Costa Rica, Ecuador, El Salvador, Guatemala, Honduras, Mexico, Nicaragua, and the Dominican Republic; lists top companies in Latin American markets.

Latin American Product Guide. Todd Publications. • $125. Covers: Over 10,000 exporters from 18 Latin American countries.

Made in Greece. Trade Publishing Resources. • Covers: Greek companies engaged in establishing trade and business relations in 155 countries.

Made in Malta. Malta External Trade Corp. • Annual. Covers: Over 850 manufacturing companies and service providers in Malta. Entries include: Company name, address, phone, fax, name and title of contact, number of employees, product/services, company logo.

Malaysia Exporters of Halal Products and Services Directory. Malaysia External Trade Development Corp. • Covers: 200 exporters of halal products including food and beverages, palm oil products, herbal, cosmetics, and dietary supplements.

Malaysia Exports. Malaysia External Trade Development Corp. • $60 Individuals. Includes manufacturers of a wide range of products in 31 categories that cover the agricultural & food sectors; electrical & electronics; building & construction materials; furniture; automotive components; and other sectors. Covers: 8,000 exporting companies from both manufacturing and exporting sectors.

Malta Export-Import, Economic, Financial, Trade and Industrial Development Handbook. International Business Publications, USA. • $99.95. Covers: Government programs and plans for economic, industrial, and business development in Malta.

Manufacturer Importers/Exporters. Tower Publishing Co. • $225. Covers: 5,034 manufacturing companies in Maine, Massachusetts, New Hampshire and Vermont which import or export products outside the U.S. Entries include: Company name, address, phone, fax, contact name and title, e-mail, URL, SIC code, type of office, countries to which the company exports.

The Marketing Guide to Ireland. Dun & Bradstreet International. • Annual. Covers: 4,000 Irish businesses, including 3,000 in the Republic of Ireland and 1,000 in Northern Ireland. Our new section contains exporters and importers. Entries include: Company name, address, phone, fax, name and title of up to 8 contacts, number of employees, line of business, sales turnover, parent company, importer/exporter indicator, year established.

Mexican Product Guide. Todd Publications. • Biennial. $125. Covers: Over 5,000 Mexican importers and exporters. Entries include: Company name, address, phone, fax, telex.

Michigan Exporters of Wood Products. Forest Management Division of the Michigan Dept. of Natural Resources. • Irregular. Covers: Approximately 500 sawmills and manufacturers in Michigan that want to become involved in or are currently exporting their wood products. Entries include: Company name, address, phone, fax, telex, name and title of contact, number of employees, annual amount of wood purchased, principal products manufactured, species or material used, equipment, services, and specialty.

Namibia Trade Directory. Namibia Trade Directory. • Covers: Trade and industries in Namibia. Entries include: Addresses and contact persons.

North American Directory of U.S. Importers and Canadian Importers. Coble International. • $285 print or CD-ROM. Covers: 19,000 importers in Canada and in the United States. Entries include: Name, address, phone, fax, primary contact person, list of products, e-mail addresses, and Web site.

Norway Exports--Products and Services for Development. The Export Council of Norway. • Biennial. Covers: Products and services exported in Norway in a variety of lines of business, including financial and banking services, construction, mining, electricity, manufacturing and metals, electronics, training, surveying and mapping, wood processing, water supply and electricity. Entries include: Company name, address, phone, telex number, product/service.

OFERES. Instituto Espanol de Comercio Exterior. • Weekly. Database covers: Approximately 100,000 export companies in Spain. Database includes: Company name, address, phone, fax, number of employees, export representative, languages, activity, current annual and total export volume, product sector, trademarks and brand names, trade partners.

Office Equipment, Stationery & Supplies, Packaging Importer Directory. Biz Focus Company Ltd. • $320 Individuals. Covers: 8,596 importers of accounting and invoicing machine, calculating machine, packaging and bottling machinery accessories, mailing and postal machinery and equipment, office machinery and equipment, and plastic articles for office use. Entries include: Company name, contact person, contact address, telephone number, fax number, e-mail, URL, and import products.

Official Export and Import Directory of Costa Rica. Mercadeo Profesional, S.A. • Annual. Covers: Export and import companies in Costa Rica.

Pakistan Export-Import and Business Directory. International Business Publications, USA. • $99.95 Individuals paperback. Covers: Information on strategic economic, investment, export-import, and business opportunities. Contains important export-import, government, and business contacts and more.

Perishable Products Export Control Board--Export Directory. Perishable Products Export Council Board. • Provides information and statistics of South African perishable export products.

Polish Industry Directory. Branzowy Katalog Firm-Ravi Sp. • Annual. Covers: More than 10,000 companies in Poland, including leading Polish importers/exporters. Entries include: Company name, address, phone, product/service.

Register of Arab Importers and Traders. The Amalgamated Press. • Biennial. $150. Publication includes: Arab importers, exporters, distributors, wholesalers, agents, products, services, chambers of commerce, import/export trade associations, state trading organizations, boards of trade, consulates, embassies, high commissions, banks, hotels, travel, shipping and insurance companies, newspapers. Entries include: Company or organization name, address, phone. Principal content of publication is Geography, ports, ecotomy, trade and travel in Algeria, Bahrain, Egypt, Iraq, Jordan, Kuwait, Lebanon, Libya, Mauritania, Morocco, Oman, Qatar, Saudi Arabia, Somalia, Sudan, Syria, Tunisia, United Arab Emirates, and Yemen.

Russia/CIS Exporters-Importers Directory. Business Information Agency Inc. PlanetInform. • Annual. $149 Individuals Paperback (plus shipping charge). Covers: 5,936 representatives of foreign firms and joint-venture companies in Russia. Entries include: Company name, location, detailed contact information, type of business, SIC codes, number of employees, year founded, legal status, and subsidiary indicators.

Russian Exporters and Importers--Firm Directory. International Bureau for Information and Telecommunications. • Annual. $25. Covers: 4,300 leading Russian companies trading on the international market and their exports and imports product range. Entries include: Company name, address, phone, fax, geographical area served, products or services provided.

Singapore Exporters Database. NIIR Project Consultancy Services. • $100 Individuals CD-ROM. Covers: 3,641 Singapore exporters. Entries include: Company name, full postal address, phone, fax, email (wherever available), website (wherever available), telex (wherever available).

South-Central American International Business Directory of Importers. Coble International. • $285 print or CD-ROM. Covers: 23,000 importers from the West Indies, Nicaragua, Mexico, Honduras, Guyana, El Salvador, Uruguay, Paraguay, Brazil, Guatemala, Belize, Colombia, Costa Rica, Puerto Rico, Dominican Republic, Chile, Haiti, Bahamas, Jamaica, Panama, Peru, Bolivia, Ecuador, Venezuela and Argentina. Entries include: Name, address, phone, fax, primary contact person, list of products, e-mail addresses, and Web site.

Soviet Trade Directory. Flegon Press. • $200. Covers: Over 20,000 listings of ex-Soviet plants, factories, and enterprises in all branches of industry. Entries include: Company name and address.

Taiwan Product Guide. Todd Publications. • Biennial. $125. Covers: More than 6,000 Taiwan exporters. Database includes: Taiwan government agencies and essential services available. Entries include: Company name, address, phone, fax, telex.

Telecommunications Export Guide. North American Telecommunications Association. • Irregular. $103. Publication includes: List of about 135 foreign telecommunications agencies, and federal and state government agencies concerned with exports in the United States, including Department of Commerce district offices, port authorities, and small business administration field offices. Entries include: For foreign agencies--Name of the official telecommunications agency, address, U.S. representative, customs requirements, type of electrical current, technical data and statistics. For U.S. agencies--Name, address.

Teleselekt. Austrian Federal Economic Chamber. • Semiannual. Database covers: 10,000 Austrian exporters and importers and 18,000 products. Entries include: Company name and address, management, number of employees, turnover, shares, commodities, services, and product information.

Thailand Export-Import Yellow Pages. Teleinfo Media Company Ltd. • Covers: Updated information for exporters and importers in Thailand. Entries include: Company information and contact details.

Thailand Product Guide. Todd Publications. • $95. Covers: Over 1,500 Thailand exporters. Entries include: Company name, address, phone, fax, telex.

Thailand Showcase: A Buyers' Guide. Cosmic Group of Cos. • Annual. $48 plus shipping charges. Covers: More than 3,000 companies in Thailand engaged in exporting their goods. Database includes: Overview of the Thailand economy. Entries include: Company name, address, phone.

Trade Directory for Istanbul. Istanbul Chamber of Commerce. • Annual. Covers: Exporters, importers, commission agents, and building contractors in Istanbul.

Trado Asian & African Directory. Trado Publications Private Ltd. • Annual. $115 airmail postpaid. Covers: manufacturers, exporters, and importers in Bahrain, Bangladesh, Canary Islands, Cyprus, Ethiopia, Hong Kong, India, Iran, Iraq, Japan, Jordan, Kenya, Kuwait, Liberia, Libya, Malta, Malawi, Mauritius, Nigeria, Philippines, Saudi Arabia, Sierra Leone, Singapore, Malaysia, Somalia, South Yemen, Sri Lanka, Sudan, Syria, Tanzania, Thailand, United Arab Emirates, and Zambia.

Tri-State Directory of Export Management and Trading Companies. National Association of Export Cos. • Irregular. $20 Nonmembers. Covers: 700 export management and trading companies in Connecticut, New Jersey, and New York who are National Association of Export Companies (NEXCO) members. Entries include: Company name, address, phone, fax, contact name, product specialty.

UNCTAD-Trade Analysis and Information System. United Nations Conference on Trade and Development. • Database covers: Indicators of trade control measures (tariff, para-tariff and non-tariff measures), as well as imports by suppliers at each harmonized system 6-digit level for over 160 countries. It also provides country notes of trade regimes for some 40 developing countries, describing market access conditions according to the UNCTAD coding system of Trade control measures.

U.S. Custom House Guide. UBM Global Trade. • Annual. $899 Individuals online access. Publication includes: List of ports having customs facilities, customs officials, port authorities, chambers of commerce, embassies and consulates, foreign trade zones, and other organizations; related trade services. Entries include: For each principal port--Name of organization or agency, address, phone, fax, names and titles of key personnel; description and limitations of port facilities. For service firms--Company name, address, phone, fax. Principal content is U.S. tariff schedules and customs regulations, and a "How to Import" manual.

U.S. Export Directory. Reed Business Information. • Annual. $235. Covers: Exporting companies in the U.S. Entries include: Company name, address, telecommunication information, overseas agents and subsidiaries.

U.S. Importers Product Guide. Todd Publications. • Biennial. $195. Covers: Approximately 10,000 United States import companies. Entries include: Name, address, phone, fax, name and title of contact, description of product/service.

Western States Exporters and Importers Database. Harris InfoSource. • $445. Covers: 11,500 exporting and 5,000 importing companies in Alaska, Arizona, California, Colorado, Hawaii, Idaho, Montana, New Mexico, Nevada, Oregon, Utah, Washington, and Wyoming. Entries include: Company name, address, phone, fax, toll-free, names and titles of key personnel, number of employees, geographical area served, financial data, descriptions of product/service, Standard Industrial Classification (SIC) code, year established, annual revenues, plant size, legal structure, export/import information.

Who's Who in Export. Indian Export Trade Journal. • Biennial. $25.

Wisconsin Exporters' Directory. Wisconsin Department of Commerce. • Irregular. Covers: about 1,400 Wisconsin firms that export or are interested in exporting. Entries include: Company name, address, telex, names and titles of key personnel, product and service, Standard Industrial Classification (SIC) code.

World Wide Importers Register International Buyers Directory. NIIR Project Consultancy Services. • $250 Individuals. Covers: 45,000 entries of importing firms in Europe, America, Middle East, Asia/Pacific, South/Central America and Africa. Entries include: Indian missions/embassies, e-mail, phone, fax and complete address to facilitate exporters.

Yugoslavia Export-Import Directory. Yugoslaviapublic. • Annual. Covers: Foreign trade organizations, products, services in Yugoslavia. Entries include: Name, address, phone.

GENERAL WORKS

Business Leksikon. ARCO & BK Service. • Contains a dictionary of approximately 5200 terms related to the import/export industry. Includes a directory of import and export specialists throughout Denmark.

Business Opportunities Bulletin. Mauritius Chamber of Commerce and Industry. • Monthly. Includes information on import and export products and industrial opportunities.

Proff, the Business Finder. Eniro Danmark A/S. • Contains a directory for Denmark's business-to-business trade.

HANDBOOKS AND MANUALS

United States Export Administration Regulations. U. S. Government Printing Office. • $199 U.S. Looseleaf. Includes supplements. Includes basic manual and supplementary bulletins for one year. Issued by the Bureau of Export Administration, U. S. Department of Commerce (www.doc.gov). Consists of export licensing rules and regulations.

INTERNET DATABASES

Business 2.0 Web Guide to the Best Business Links. Business 2.0 Media Inc. Phone: (415)293-4800; Email: support@business2.com • URL: http://www.business2.com/webguide • Web site presents an extensive, searchable directory of links to "the best, most informative, and authoritative web pages." Twenty main categories cover business, finance, career, company information, people, and technol-

ogy topics, with thousands of subtopics, all linking to Web sites recommended by experienced business researchers. Fees: Free.

Fedstats. Federal Interagency Council on Statistical Policy. Phone: (202)395-7254 • URL: http://www.fedstats.gov • Web site features an efficient search facility for full-text statistics produced by more than 100 federal agencies, including the Census Bureau, the Bureau of Economic Analysis, and the Bureau of Labor Statistics. Boolean searches can be made within one agency or for all agencies combined. Links are offered to international statistical bureaus, including the UN, IMF, OECD, UNESCO, Eurostat, and 20 individual countries. Fees: Free.

FreeLunch.com. Economy.com, Inc. Phone: (610)696-8700; Fax: (610)696-1678 • URL: http://www.freelunch.com • Web site provides free access to more than 200 million economic and financial data series, covering industry, demographics, labor markets, prices, retail sales, government spending, trade, interest rates, housing starts, the stock market, etc. Data is available in either chart or table form. Searching is offered. Free, but registration required. Economy.com, Inc. also offers fee-based economic analysis at *The Dismal Scientist* site (www.dismal.com).

Manufacturing Profiles. U. S. Bureau of the Census. Phone: (301)763-4636 or (301)763-4100; Fax: (301)763-4794; Email: webmaster@census.gov • URL: http://www.census.gov/prod/www/abs/mfg-prof.html • The Census Bureau makes available free on PDF (Portable Document Format) an annual consolidation of the entire Current Industrial Report series, presenting "all the data compiled." Contains statistics on production, shipments, inventories, consumption, exports, imports, and orders for a wide variety of manufactured products.

U.S. Business Advisor. Small Business Administration. Phone: (202)205-6600; Fax: (202)205-7064 • URL: http://www.sba.gov • Web site provides "a one-stop electronic link to all the information and services government provides for the business community." Covers about 60 federal agencies that exist to assist or regulate business. Detailed information is provided on financial assistance, workplace issues, taxes, regulations, international trade, and other business topics. Searching is offered. Fees: Free.

OTHER SOURCES

Investing, Licensing, and Trading. The Economist Intelligence Unit. • Semiannual. $345.00 per year for each country. Key laws, rules, and licensing provisions are explained for each of 60 countries. Information is provided on political conditions, markets, price policies, foreign exchange practices, labor, and export-import.

PERIODICALS AND NEWSLETTERS

AgExporter. U. S. Government Printing Office. • Monthly. $44 Individuals. Issued by the Foreign Agricultural Service, U. S. Department of Agriculture. Edited for U. S. exporters of farm products. Provides practical information on exporting, including overseas trade opportunities.

Amber Waves. Economic Research Service Hazard Analysis and Critical Control Points. • Quarterly. Replaces *Agricultural Outlook; Food Review*; and *Rural America.* Provides research and analysis from the U.S. Department of Agriculture's Economic Research Service. Includes economic data on agriculture, food, trade, and environmental factors.

Doing Business with Korea. Korea Chamber of Commerce and Industry. • Semiannual. Contains information on Korea's export and import status.

Export Today: The Global Business and Technology Magazine. Trade Communications Inc. • Monthly. $49.00 per year. Edited for corporate executives to provide practical information on international business and exporting.

International Trade Alert. American Association of Exporters and Importers. • Weekly. Description: Reports on trade issues as they affect importers and exporters. Contains news of actions by Customs, the Federal Drug Administration (FDA), and the Department of Commerce, CITA, CPSC, FTC, and the USDA, as well as other federal agencies and departments; and the status of regulations on imported/exported products. Also contains information on legislative activity affecting importers and exporters.

International Trade Reporter Export Reference Manual. Bloomberg BNA. • Biweekly. $874.00 per year. Looseleaf service.

Outlook for United States Agricultural Trade. U. S. Government Printing Office. • Quarterly. $15.00 per year. Issued by the Economic Research Service, U. S. Department of Agriculture. (Situation and Outlook Reports.).

RESEARCH CENTERS AND INSTITUTES

Harvard Law School International Tax Program. Harvard Law School, 1563 Massachusetts Ave., 1563 Massachusetts Ave., Cambridge, MA 02138. Phone: (617)495-3100 or (617)495-4406; Fax: (617)495-1110; Email: sfs@law.harvard.edu • URL: http://www.law.harvard.edu/programs/index.html • Studies the worldwide problems of taxation, including tax law and tax administration.

U.S. Customs and Border Protection - Office of Field Operations - Laboratories and Scientific Services Division - Research Laboratory. 7501 Boston Blvd., Ste. 113, Springfield, VA 22153. Phone: (703)921-7200; Fax: (703)921-7155; Email: cbp.labresearch@dhs.gov • URL: http://www.cbp.gov/xp/cgov/import/operations_support/labs_scientific_svcs/ • Provides technical services in support of the U.S. Customs mission in tariff and trade and in enforcement. Principal area of interest is analytical chemistry (instrumentation and methodology). Laboratory supports a field laboratory system, with affiliated laboratories in New York City, Savannah, New Orleans, Los Angeles, San Francisco, Chicago, and San Juan.

STATISTICS SOURCES

National Trade Estimate Report on Foreign Trade Barriers (year). U. S. Government Printing Office. • Annual. $47. Issued by the Office of the United States Trade Representative. "Provides quantitative estimates of the impact of foreign practices on the value of United States exports.".

Survey of Current Business. U. S. Government Printing Office. • Published by Bureau of Economic Analysis, U. S. Department of Commerce. Presents a wide variety of business and economic data.

United States Waterborne Exports and General Imports. U.S. Department of Commerce U.S. Census Bureau. • Quarterly and annual.

TRADE/PROFESSIONAL ASSOCIATIONS

Austrian Trade Commission. 120 W 45th St., 9th Fl., New York, NY 10036. Phone: (212)421-5250; Fax: (212)421-5251; Email: newyork@advantageaustria.org • Promotes U.S.-Austrian trade with particular emphasis on Austrian exports to the U.S.; identifies Austrian trade sources to meet U.S. commercial demand. Handles inquiries related to trade between the two nations and deals with issues such as customs duties, trade laws, and licensing. Compiles statistics. Sponsors trade exhibits.

Brazil-U.S. Business Council. 1615 H St. NW, Washington, DC 20062. Phone: (202)463-5729; Email: brazilcouncil@uschamber.com • URL: http://www.brazilcouncil.org • Works to provide a high-level private sector forum for the business communities of both countries to engage in substantive dialogue on trade and investment issues and communicate private sector priorities to both governments.

Brazilian Government Trade Bureau of the Consulate General of Brazil in New York. 220 E 42nd St., New York, NY 10017-5806. Phone: (917)777-7777; Fax: (212)827-0225; Email: cg.novayork@itamaraty.gov.br • URL: http://novayork.itamaraty.gov.br/en-us • Commercial Office of the Brazil Consulate in New York. Offers online match between Brazilian exporters of goods and services and U.S. importers.

British Trade Office at Consulate-General. 845 3rd Ave., New York, NY 10022. Phone: (212)745-0200; Fax: (212)745-0456 • URL: http://www.gov.uk/government/world/organisations/british-consulate-general-new-york • British government office that promotes trade with the U.S.; assists British companies selling in the U.S.; aids American companies that wish to import goods from or invest in Britain.

Cairns Chamber of Commerce. Ste. M2a, Mezzanine Level, The Pier, Pier Point Rd., Cairns, QLD 4870, Australia. Phone: 61 7 40311838; Fax: 61 7 40310883; Email: info@cairnschamber.com.au • URL: http://www.cairnschamber.com.au • Represents business in the Cairns region. Provides statistical and business advice. Works to attract investment and business relocation to the area. Provides trade and export support.

Camara de Comercio Exterior de Rosario. 1868 Cordoba St., 1st Fl., 2000 Rosario, Argentina. Phone: 54 341 4257147; Fax: 54 341 4257486; Email: ccer@commerce.com.ar • URL: http://www.commerce.com.ar • Promotes international trade for export and import businesses in the Rosario region of Argentina.

German Foods North America. 719 6th St. NW, Washington, DC 20001. Phone: 800-881-6419; Email: info@germanfoods.org • URL: http://germanfoods.org • Promotes imported German foods, beverages, and agricultural products in the U.S. and Canada through advertising, public relations programs, and promotional campaigns with supermarket chains and individual retailers. Acts as a liaison between U.S. and Canadian importers and German manufacturers and exporters. Provides assistance to German manufacturers and their importers and distributors in complying with U.S. regulations.

Innovation Norway - United States. 655 3rd Ave., Ste. 1810, New York, NY 10017-9111. Phone: (212)885-9700 or (212)421-9210; Fax: (212)885-9710 or (212)838-0374; Email: newyork@innovationnorway.no • URL: http://www.innovasjonnorge.no/Kontorer-i-utlandet/usa-newyork/ • U.S. branch of the Export Council of Norway. Assists Norwegian companies in marketing their goods and services in the U.S. Provides information to Norwegian exporters on U.S. markets, tariffs and statistics, trade constraints, and distribution channels. Establishes contacts with U.S. authorities, marketing and manufacturing firms, local lawyers, accountants, banks, patent offices, advertising and public relations agencies, consultants, and credit and debt collection agencies. Aids in establishing Norwegian subsidiaries in the U.S.

Iran National Union of Agro Products. No. 94, Keyvan Alley, Kashani St., Urmia, Iran. Phone: 98 441 3451988 or 98 441 3455780; Fax: 98 441 3455606; Email: shakor_a@iranazarfruit.com • URL: http://www.iranazarfruit.com • Represents the interests of exporters of agricultural products. Aims to create coordination in the export of fruits and vegetables and the promotion of export products. Assists members by providing facilities and marketing services for their agricultural products.

Japan Paper Exporters' Association. Kami Parupu Bldg., 3-9-11, Ginza, Chuo-ku, Tokyo, Tokyo 104-8139, Japan. Phone: 81 3 32484831; Fax: 81 3 32484834; Email: info@jpeta.or.jp • URL: http://www.jpeta.or.jp • Exporters of paper and related products. Seeks to establish and maintain a domestic and international business climate beneficial to the paper trade. Represents members' interests; gathers and disseminates information.

Japan Paper Importers' Association. Kami Papuru Bldg., 3-9-11, Ginza, Chuo-ku, Tokyo, Tokyo 104-8139, Japan. Phone: 81 3 32484831; Fax: 81 3 32484834 • URL: http://www.jpeta.or.jp • Importers of paper and related products. Seeks to establish and maintain a domestic and international business climate beneficial to the paper trade. Represents members' interests; gathers and disseminates information.

National Association of Export Companies. Grand Central Station, New York, NY 10163. Phone: 877-291-4901; Fax: (646)349-9628; Email: director@nexco.org • URL: http://www.nexco.org • Established independent international trade firms, bilateral chambers of commerce, banks, law firms, accounting firms, trade associations, insurance companies, and product/service providers; export trading companies; export management companies. Promotes expansion of U.S. trade. Promotes the participation of members in international trade. Conducts educational programs.

National Customs Brokers and Forwarders Association of America. 1200 18th St. NW, No. 901, Washington, DC 20036. Phone: (202)466-0222; Fax: (202)466-0226; Email: staff@ncbfaa.org • URL: http://www.ncbfaa.org • Formerly Customs Brokers and Forwarders Association of America.

National United States-Arab Chamber of Commerce. 1023 15th St. NW, Ste. 400, Washington, DC 20005. Phone: (202)289-5920; Fax: (202)289-5938; Email: info@nusacc.org • URL: http://www.nusacc.org • Individuals, companies, corporations, and associations interested in commercial trade relations with the Arab world. Promotes business between the United States and the Arab world; encourages policies that promote better commercial relations. Conducts research and information services on commercial opportunities, export regulations, and conditions that affect the trade and investment climate. Sponsors trade delegations; holds seminars, conferences, and training sessions; acts as a central information center. Maintains relations with U.S. and Arab governments and agencies to develop, monitor, and recommend relevant legislation.

Polish-U.S. Business Council. Chamber of Commerce of the United States, 1615 H St. NW, Washington, DC 20062-2000. Phone: 800-638-6582 or (202)659-6000; Email: press@uschamber.com • URL: http://www.uschamber.com • U.S. corporations involved in industry, agriculture, or services. Seeks to expand trade between the U.S. and Poland, and to encourage investment in Poland by U.S. firms.

Romanian-U.S. Business Council. 620 8th Ave., New York, NY 10018. Phone: (646)678-2905; Email: info@usrobc.org • URL: http://usrobc.org • Advocates American business interests with respect to U.S. Romanian trade and investments. Provides the American and Romanian business communities with a means of discussing bilateral trade and investment issues and the formulation of policy positions that will promote and expand economic relations between the two countries. Facilitates appropriate legislation and policies regarding trade between the U.S. and Romania. Has sponsored seminars on topics such as possibilities for cooperative commercial efforts in other countries and cooperation in energy development.

Southern U.S. Trade Association. 701 Poydras St., Ste. 3725, New Orleans, LA 70139. Phone: (504)568-5986; Fax: (504)568-6010; Email: susta@susta.org • URL: http://www.susta.org • The Southern U.S. Trade Association (SUSTA) promotes the export of high-value food and agricultural products internationally. SUSTA works closely on an individual basis with its export company members to develop and expand their share of agricultural export markets through partnering with the Department of Agriculture to provide southern U.S. companies discounted booth space at international trade exhibitions, and inbound and outbound trade missions. SUSTA facilitates the MAP Branded Program that reimburses up to 50% of certain international marketing and promotion expenses, including eligible tradeshows, in-store displays, and required label changes.

Swedish Trade Council. 150 N Michigan Ave., Ste. 1950, Chicago, IL 60601. Phone: (312)781-6222; Fax: (312)276-8606; Email: usa@swedishtrade.se • URL: http://www.swedishtrade.se/english • Promotes Swedish exports and assists American companies in contacting Swedish suppliers. Performs market developments studies and research, partner searches, and project management.

F

FABRICS, INDUSTRIAL

See INDUSTRIAL FABRICS INDUSTRY

FABRICS, NONWOVEN

See NONWOVEN FABRICS INDUSTRY

FACILITIES MANAGEMENT

See FACTORY MANAGEMENT

FACSIMILE SYSTEMS

ABSTRACTS AND INDEXES

Applied Science and Technology Index. EBSCO Publishing Inc. • 11/year. Indexes a wide variety of English language technical, industrial, and engineering periodicals.

Business Periodicals Index Retrospective. EBSCO Publishing Inc. • 11/year. Quarterly and annual cumulations.

DIRECTORIES

National E-mail and Fax Directory. Cengage Learning Inc. • Annual. $265 Individuals. 2009. 23rd edition. A comprehensive "one stop" source of information on contact information -- fax numbers, e-mail addresses, voice telephone numbers, and mailing addresses. Coverage spans over 151,000 major businesses, agencies and organizations in the United States.

Telecommunications Directory. Cengage Learning Inc. • Annual. $993 Individuals. Two volumes: North America and International. Cover national and international voice and data communications networks, electronic mail services, teleconferencing facilities and services, facsimile services, Internet access providers, videotex and teletext operations, transactional services, local area networks, audiotex services, microwave systems/networkers, satellite facilities, and others involved in telecommunications, including related consultants, advertisers/ marketers; associations, regulatory bodies, and publishers. Available as eBook.

ONLINE DATABASES

Applied Science and Technology Index Online. H.W. Wilson Co. • Provides online indexing of 500 major scientific, technical, industrial, and engineering periodicals. Time period is 1983 to date. Monthly updates. Inquire as to online cost and availability.

Wilson Business Abstracts Online. H.W. Wilson Co. • Indexes and abstracts 600 major business periodicals, plus the *Wall Street Journal* and the business section of the *New York Times*. Indexing is from 1982, abstracting from 1990, with the two newspapers included from 1993. Updated weekly. Inquire as to online cost and availability. (*Business Periodicals Index* without abstracts is also available online.).

PERIODICALS AND NEWSLETTERS

FAX Magazine. Technical Data Publishing Corp. • Quarterly. Price on application.

T W I C E: This Week in Consumer Electronics. Reed Elsevier Group plc Reed Business Information. • 29 times a year. $129.90 per year. Contains marketing and manufacturing news relating to a wide variety of consumer electronic products, including video, audio, telephone, and home office equipment.

FACTORY LOCATION

See LOCATION OF INDUSTRY

FACTORY MAINTENANCE

See MAINTENANCE OF BUILDINGS

FACTORY MANAGEMENT

See also TIME AND MOTION STUDY

ABSTRACTS AND INDEXES

Key Abstracts: Factory Automation. Institution of Engineering and Technology. • Monthly. $1,138. Provides international coverage of journal and proceedings literature, including publications on CAD/CAM, materials handling, robotics, and factory management.

DIRECTORIES

Directory of European Information Brokers and Consultants. Information Marketmakers Ltd. • Annual. $59. Covers: information systems brokers and consultants in Europe. Entries include: Company name, address, phone, name and title of contact, names and titles of key personnel, subject expertise, and description of products and services.

Facilities Design & Management--Directory of Consultants & Service Firms Issue. Bpi Communications Inc. • Annual. $7. Publication includes: Listing of firms offering products, services, and consulting services to facilities designers and managers.

OTHER SOURCES

First-Line Supervision. American Management Association Extension Institute. • Looseleaf. $139.00. Self-study course. Focuses on the day-to-day concerns of the first line supervisor. A self-study course.

PERIODICALS AND NEWSLETTERS

AFE Newsline elsewhere. Association for Facilities Engineering. • Bimonthly. Description: Internal newsletter of the association.

IndustryWeek: The Management Resource. Penton Media Inc. • Monthly. Edited for industrial and business managers. Covers organizational and technological developments affecting industrial management.

Production. Gardner Business Media, Inc. • Covers the latest manufacturing management issues. Discusses the strategic and financial implications of various tecnologies as they impact factory management, quality and competitiveness.

RESEARCH CENTERS AND INSTITUTES

Carnegie Mellon Research Institute-The Robotics Institute. 5000 Forbes Ave., Pittsburgh, PA 15213. Phone: (412)268-3818; Fax: (412)268-6436; Email: robotics@ri.cmu.edu • URL: http://www.ri.cmu.edu • Multidisciplinary research activities include expert systems applications, minicomputer and microcomputer systems design, genetic engineering, and transportation systems analysis.

TRADE/PROFESSIONAL ASSOCIATIONS

ASME International. 2 Park Ave., New York, NY 10016-5990. Phone: 800-843-2763 or (973)882-1170; Fax: (973)882-1717; Email: customercare@asme.org • URL: http://www.asme.org • Technical society of mechanical engineers and students. Conducts research; develops boiler, pressure vessel, and power test codes. Develops safety codes and standards for equipment. Conducts short course programs, and Identifying Research Needs Program. Maintains 19 research committees and 38 divisions.

Association for Facilities Engineering. 12801 Worldgate Dr., Ste. 500, Herndon, VA 20170. Phone: (571)203-7171; Fax: (571)766-2142; Email: info@afe.org • URL: http://www.afe.org • Professional society of plant engineers and facilities managers engaged in the management, engineering, maintenance and operation of industrial, institutional, and commercial facilities. Compiles statistics. Offers three certification programs, Certified Plant Engineer (CPE), Certified Plant Maintenance Manager (CPMM), and Certified Plant Supervisor.

European Facility Management Network. PO Box 5135, NL-1410 AC Naarden, Netherlands. Phone: 31 35 6942785; Email: eurofm@eurofm.org • URL: http://www.eurofm.org • Promotes knowledge in facility management in Europe and its application in practice, education and research.

Facility Management Association of Australia. 313 La Trobe St., Level 6, Melbourne, VIC 3000, Australia. Phone: 61 3 86416666; Fax: 61 3 86416600; Email: info@fma.com.au • URL: http://www.fma.com.au/cms • Promotes the facility management profession in Australia.

Restaurant Facility Management Association. 5600 Tennyson Pkwy., Ste. 280, Plano, TX 75024. Phone: (972)805-0905; Fax: (972)805-0906; Email: tracy@rfmaonline.com • URL: http://www.rfmaonline.com • Aims to promote the advancement of the restaurant facility management profession. Maintains professional and ethical standards among members. Provides networking to share knowledge and exchange information.

FACTORY SECURITY

See INDUSTRIAL SECURITY PROGRAMS

FAILURES, BANK

See BANK FAILURES

FAILURES, BUSINESS

See BUSINESS FAILURES

FAIR TRADE

See PRICES AND PRICING

FAIRS

See also CONCESSIONS; CONVENTIONS

DIRECTORIES

Directory of Festivals, Schools and Workshops. Chamber Music America. • Annual. Covers: over 150 chamber music workshops and schools for students, young professionals, and adult amateurs; international listings. Entries include: Name, location or address, description of program and participants sought, procedure for auditions, type of accommodations and recreational facilities, dates, age requirements, and fees as of spring 2000.

IAFE Membership Directory. International Association of Fairs and Expositions. • Annual. $125 Nonmembers. Lists member agricultural fairs in the United States and Canada. Formerly *International Association of Fairs and Expositions Directory.*

International Association of Amusement Parks and Attractions International Directory and Buyers' Guide. International Association of Amusement Parks and Attractions. • Annual. Over 1,800 member amusement parks, attractions and industry suppliers.

PERIODICALS AND NEWSLETTERS

Horseman and Fair World: Devoted to the Trotting and Pacing Horse. Horseman Publishing Co., Insite Communications. • $50.

IEG's Sponsorship Report: The International Newsletter of Event Sponsorship and Lifestyle Marketing. IEG LLC. • $499 multi-user subscription. Newsletter reporting on corporate sponsorship of special events: sports, music, festivals, and the arts. Edited for event producers, directors, and marketing personnel.

FAMILY CORPORATIONS

See CLOSELY HELD CORPORATIONS

FAMILY LAW

See also DIVORCE

ABSTRACTS AND INDEXES

Current Law Index. Cengage Learning Inc. • $1,332 Individuals. Monthly. $1269.00 per year. Produced in cooperation with the American Association of Law Libraries. Indexes more than 900 law journals, legal newspapers, and specialty publications from the U.S., Canada, U.K., Ireland, Australia, and New Zealand.

Readers' Guide to Periodical Literature. EBSCO Publishing Inc. • Provides indexing for over 400 periodicals dating back to 1983.

ALMANACS AND YEARBOOKS

American Law Yearbook. Cengage Learning Inc. • $308 Individuals. Annual. $280.00. Serves as a yearly supplement to *West's Encyclopedia of American Lawa.* Describes new legal developments in many subject areas.

CD-ROM DATABASES

Readers' Guide to Periodical Literature. EBSCO Publishing Inc. • Provides indexing for over 400 periodicals dating back to 1983.

ENCYCLOPEDIAS AND DICTIONARIES

West's Encyclopedia of American Law. Cengage Learning Inc. • 2004. eBook. Second edition. Covers a wide variety of legal topics for the general reader. Inquire for pricing.

HANDBOOKS AND MANUALS

Women and the Law. Carol H. Lefcourt, editor. Thomson West. • Annual. $691.60 Individuals book - softbound. Covers such topics as employment discrimination, pay equity (comparable worth), sexual harassment in the workplace, property rights, and child custody issues.

INTERNET DATABASES

Lexis.com Research System. Lexis-Nexis Group. Phone: 800-227-4908 or (937)865-6800; Fax: (937)865-6909; Email: webmaster@prod.lexis-nexis.com • URL: http://www.nexis.com • Fee-based Web site offers extensive searching of a wide variety of legal sources. Additional features include Daily Opinion Service, lexis.com Bookstore, Career Center, CLE Center, Law Schools, and Practice Pages ("Pages specific to areas of specialty").

ONLINE DATABASES

Contemporary Women's Issues. Cengage Learning Inc. • Provides full-text articles online from 150 periodicals and a wide variety of additional sources relating to economic, legal, social, political, education, health, and other women's issues. Time span is 1992 to date. Weekly updates. Inquire as to online cost and availability.

PERIODICALS AND NEWSLETTERS

Brandeis Law Journal. University of Louisville Louis D. Brandeis School of Law. University of Louisville. • Quarterly. $30.00 per year.

Family Advocate. American Bar Association - Family Law Section. • Quarterly. Members $39.50; non-members, $44.50 per year. Practical advice for attorneys practicing family law.

Family Court Review: An Interdisciplinary Journal. Association of Family and Conciliation Courts. Pine Forge Press. • Quarterly. Institutions, $456.00 per year.

Family Law Quarterly. American Bar Association - Family Law Section. • Quarterly. Free to members; non-members, $49.95 per year.

Family Relations: State Capitals. Wakeman/Walworth Inc. • 50 times a year. $245.00 per year; print and online editions, $350.00 per year. Newsletter. Formerly *From the State Capitals: Family Relations.*

Matrimonial Strategist. ALM Media Properties LLC. • Monthly. $429 print and online. Newsletter on legal strategy and matrimonial law.

RESEARCH CENTERS AND INSTITUTES

University of Florida - Fredric G. Levin College of Law - Center for Governmental Responsibility. 309 Vill. Dr., Gainesville, FL 32611. Phone: (352)273-0835; Fax: (352)392-1457 • URL: http://www.law.ufl.edu/academics/centers/cgr • Research fields include family law.

TRADE/PROFESSIONAL ASSOCIATIONS

American College of Counselors. 273 Glossip Ave., Highlandville, MO 65669-8133. Phone: (417)885-7632 or (417)885-7632; Fax: (417)443-3002 • URL: http://acconline.us • Formerly National Alliance for Family Life.

Association of Family and Conciliation Courts. 6525 Grand Teton Plz., Madison, WI 53719. Phone: (608)664-3750; Fax: (608)664-3751; Email: afcc@afccnet.org • URL: http://www.afccnet.org • Members are judges, attorneys, and family counselors. Promotes conciliation counseling as a complement to legal procedures.

Legal Momentum. 5 Hanover Sq., Ste. 1502, New York, NY 10004. Phone: (212)925-6635; Email: info@legalmomentum.org • URL: http://www.legalmomentum.org • Formerly NOW Legal Defense and Education Fund.

National Council of Juvenile and Family Court Judges. PO Box 8970, Reno, NV 89507-8970. Phone: (775)784-6012; Fax: (775)784-6628; Email: staff@ncjfcj.org • URL: http://www.ncjfcj.org • Judges with juvenile and family court jurisdiction and others with a professional interest in the nation's juvenile justice system. Works to further more effective administration of justice for young people through the improvement of juvenile and family court standards and practices. Sponsors continuing education programs. Compiles and disseminates research data.

FARM BUSINESS

See AGRIBUSINESS

FARM CREDIT

See AGRICULTURAL CREDIT

FARM EQUIPMENT INDUSTRY

See AGRICULTURAL MACHINERY

FARM IMPLEMENTS

See AGRICULTURAL MACHINERY

FARM INCOME

See AGRICULTURAL STATISTICS

FARM JOURNALS

See also BUSINESS JOURNALISM

ABSTRACTS AND INDEXES

Biological and Agricultural Index. H.W. Wilson Co. • 11 times a year. Annual and quarterly cumulations. Price varies.

OTHER SOURCES

Bacon's Newspaper and Magazine Directories. Cision US Inc. • Annual. $325.00 per year. Two volumes: Magazines and Newspapers. Covers print media in the United States and Canada. Formerly *Bacon's Publicity Checker.*

PERIODICALS AND NEWSLETTERS

Agronomy Journal: An International Journal. American Society of Agronomy. • Bimonthly. $216 Nonmembers.

Farm Journal: The Magazine of American Agriculture. Farm Journal Corp. • Monthly. $25 Individuals. Agricultural news magazine for people who own or operate farms or ranches.

FARM MACHINERY

See AGRICULTURAL MACHINERY

FARM MANAGEMENT

See also AGRICULTURE

OTHER SOURCES

Agricultural Law. Matthew Bender and Company Inc. • Semiannual. $2,501.00. 15 looseleaf volumes. Covers all aspects of state and federal law relating to farms, ranches and other agricultural interests. Includes five volumes dealing with agricultural estate, tax and business planning.

PERIODICALS AND NEWSLETTERS

Ag Executive. Ag Executive Inc. • Description: Focuses on financial, personnel, and risk management issues for commercial agriculture. Covers business analysis and practical management ideas for improving profitability. Includes such topics as accounting, farm business organization, financing, economic forecasting, resource/risk control, and taxes.

RESEARCH CENTERS AND INSTITUTES

Cooperative State Research, Education, and Extension Service - Small and Home-Based Business. 4435 Waterfront Ctr., 800 9th St. SW, Washington, DC 20250. Phone: (202)720-5997; Fax: (202)690-2975; Email: amclaren@csrees.usda.gov • URL: http://www.csrees.usda.gov/smallhomebasedbusiness.cfm • Women-owned and operated farms and ranches, rural entrepreneurship, small and home-based businesses.

TRADE/PROFESSIONAL ASSOCIATIONS

American Society of Farm Managers and Rural Appraisers. 950 S Cherry St., Ste. 508, Denver, CO 80246-2664. Phone: (303)758-3513; Fax: (303)758-0190; Email: info@asfmra.org • URL: http://www.asfmra.org • Professional farm managers, appraisers, lenders, consultants, educators and researchers in farm and ranch management and/or rural appraisal. Bestows registered ARA (Accredited Rural Appraiser), Accredited Agricultural Consultant (ACC), AFM (Accredited Farm Manager) and RPRA (Real Property Review Appraiser) designations. Operates management and appraisal schools, Internet course offerings. Maintains placement service.

Demeter Biodynamic Trade Association. PO Box 264, Talmage, CA 95481-0264. Email: info@demeterbta.com • URL: http://www.demeterbta.com • Represents Demeter Certified Biodynamic farms, vineyards, wineries, dairies, food processors, traders and distributors. Aims to further interest and education in Demeter Certified Biodynamic farming. Strives to promote Demeter Certified Biodynamic products in the marketplace. Supports and advocates for the protection of the Demeter certification marks.

Northwest Farm Managers Association. c/o North Dakota State University, Dept. 7000, 315 Morrill Hall, Fargo, ND 58108-6050. Phone: (701)231-8944 • URL: http://www.ag.ndsu.edu/nwfm • Represents manager-operators of commercial farms and agriculturists interested in research in farm management, marketing, and agribusiness.

FARM MARKETS

See also MARKETING

ALMANACS AND YEARBOOKS

Agricultural Policy Monitoring and Evaluation. Organization for Economic Cooperation and Development. Organisation for Economic Co-operation and Development Publications and Information Center. • Annual. Provides estimates of support to agriculture as well as chapters on agricultural policy developments.

PERIODICALS AND NEWSLETTERS

Agri Marketing: The Magazine for Professionals Selling to the Farm Market. Doane Agricultural Services Co. • Monthly. $30 Individuals.

Produce Merchandising: The Packer's Retailing and Merchandising Magazine. Vance Publishing Corp. • Monthly. $35.00 per year. Provides information and advice on the retail marketing and promotion of fresh fruits and vegetalbe.

RESEARCH CENTERS AND INSTITUTES

Texas A&M University - Agribusiness, Food, and Consumer Economics Research Center. Department of Agricultural Economics, 600 John Kimbrough Blvd., Ste. 371, 2124 TAMU, College Station, TX 77843-2124. Phone: (979)845-5911; Fax: (979)845-6378; Email: afcerc@tamu.edu • URL: http://afcerc.tamu.edu • Marketing of Texas and U.S. agricultural products. Areas include domestic and foreign market opportunities, marketing policies and strategies, international competitiveness of Texas and the U.S. in the production and marketing of traditional bulk and high value/value-added products, impact of new technologies on markets and prices, efficiency of market information systems, market structure and performance, and consumer survey research.

TRADE/PROFESSIONAL ASSOCIATIONS

North American Agricultural Marketing Officials. c/o Debra May, President, Florida Dept. of Agriculture and Consumer Services, 407 S Calhoun St., Tallahassee, FL 32399. Phone: (850)921-1727 • URL: http://www.naamo.org • Affiliated with National Association of Produce Market Managers and the National Association of State Departments of Argicutural. Formerly National Agricultural Marketing Officals.

FARM PRODUCE

See also AGRICULTURE

ABSTRACTS AND INDEXES

Field Crop Abstracts. CABI Publishing North America. • Monthly. Published in England by CABI Publishing, formerly Commonwealth Agricultural Bureaux.

CD-ROM DATABASES

AGRICOLA on SilverPlatter. Ovid Technologies Inc. • Updated monthly. Price varies. Produced by the National Agricultural Library. Provides over 4 million citations to the literature of agriculture, agricultural economics, animal sciences, entomology, fertilizer, food, forestry, nutrition, pesticides, plant science, water resources, and other topics.

Biological & Agricultural Index Plus. EBSCO Publishing Inc. • Full text of literature in biology and agriculture. Also includes podcasts, indexing and abstracts.

DIRECTORIES

American Vegetable Grower--Source Book. Meister Media Worldwide. • Annual. Publication includes: Lists of suppliers of agricultural chemicals and manufacturers and suppliers of other agricultural products, equipment, and services including packaging equipment, transportation services, direct marketing suppliers, plants and seeds, etc. Entries include: Company name, address, phone, fax, e-mail.

ENCYCLOPEDIAS AND DICTIONARIES

Encyclopedia of Food and Culture. Cengage Learning Inc. • 2003. $657.00. Three volumes. Contains 600 articles covering various aspects of food and its place in society, from agronomy to zucchini. Includes illustrations and a detailed index. eBook also available, updated in 2004.

FINANCIAL RATIOS

Annual Statement Studies. Risk Management Association. • Annual. Compiled from over 280,000 financial statements.

Annual Statement Studies: Industry Default Probabilities and Cash Flow Measures. Risk Management Association. • Annual. $405 Nonmembers. Serves as a companion volume to the original *Annual Statement Studies.* Gives probability of default estimates on a percentage scale for more than 450 industries. Includes changes in position year-by-year for eight financial statement line items and provides percentage measures of cash flow.

INTERNET DATABASES

USDA. U.S. National Institute of Standards and Technology. 100 Bureau Dr., Gaithersburg, MD 20899-1070. Phone: 800-877-8339 or (301)975-6478 or (202)720-2791; Fax: (301)975-8295; Email: inquiries@nist.gov • URL: http://www.nist.gov • The USDA home page has six sections: News and Information; What's New; About USDA; Agencies; Opportunities; Search and Help. Keyword searching is offered from the USDA home page and from various individual agency home pages. Agencies are the Economic Research Service, Agricultural Marketing Service, National Agricultural Statistics Service, National Agricultural Library, and about 12 others. Updating varies. Fees: Free.

ONLINE DATABASES

Agricola. U.S. National Agricultural Library World List of Agricultural Serials. • Covers worldwide agricultural literature. Over 3.3 million citations, 1970 to present, with monthly updates. Inquire as to online cost and availability.

CAB Abstracts. CABI. • Contains 46 specialized abstract collections covering over 10,000 journals and monographs in the areas of agriculture, horticulture, forest products, farm products, nutrition, dairy science, poultry, grains, animal health, entomology, etc. Time period is 1972 to date, with monthly updates. Inquire as to online cost and availability. *CAB Abstracts on CD-ROM* also available, with annual updating.

PERIODICALS AND NEWSLETTERS

Agricultural Research. U. S. Government Printing Office. • Monthly. $50 Individuals. Issued by the Agricultural Research Service of the U. S. Department of Agriculture. Presents results of research projects related to a wide variety of farm crops and products.

Crop Science. Crop Science Society of America. • Bimonthly. $50 Members print. Agricultural science journal.

Journal of Crop Improvement. The Haworth Press Inc. • 6/year. $396 Individuals online. Topics include plant biotechnology, plant genetics, crop productivity, quality, safety, pest control, and environmental concerns. Formerly *Journal of Crop Production.*

RESEARCH CENTERS AND INSTITUTES

New South Wales Department of Primary Industries - Orange Agricultural Institute. Forest Rd., Orange, NSW 2800, Australia. Phone: 61 2 63913800; Fax: 61 2 63913899; Email: david.michalk@dpi.nsw.gov.au • URL: http://www.dpi.nsw.gov.au/research/centres/orange • Animal health, including infectious and toxicity diseases; animal production, including sheep genetics, wool production, and vertebrate pests; plant production, including weed control and ecology, crops, pastures, and horticulture; agricultural scientific collections; plant protection, including entomology and plant pathology; biometrics; and economics.

Texas A&M AgriLife Research Center - Sonora - Texas A & M University. 7887 US Highway 87 N, San Angelo, TX 76901. Phone: (325)653-4576; Fax: (325)655-7791 • URL: http://sanangelo.tamu.edu/satellite-stations/sonora.

University of California - California Agricultural Experiment Station. 1111 Franklin St., Rm. 6402, Oakland, CA 94607-5200. Phone: (510)987-0036 or (510)987-0060; Fax: (510)465-2659 or (510)451-2317; Email: steve.nation@ucop.edu • URL: http://ucanr.org/AES.shtml • Plant and animal biology, agricultural engineering and economics, soils, and water, including basic and applied studies directed toward solving problems of agriculture involved in production, storage, and transportation of over 300 commodities produced in California. Studies problems relating to forestry, human welfare and nutrition, pest management, mosquito control, and outdoor recreation. Operates on a statewide basis, with main units on Berkeley, Davis, and Riverside campuses of the University and ten research and extension centers throughout the state.

STATISTICS SOURCES

Agricultural Statistics. U.S. Department of Agriculture National Agricultural Statistics Service. • Annual. $46 Individuals. Provides a wide variety of statistical data relating to agricultural production, supplies, consumption, prices/price-supports, foreign trade, costs, and returns, as well as farm labor, loans, income, and population. In many cases, historical data is shown annually for 10 years. In addition to farm data, includes detailed fishery statistics.

United States Census of Agriculture. U.S. Department of Agriculture National Agricultural Statistics Service. • Quinquennial. Provides uniform, comprehensive farming and ranching operations data for every U.S. state and county, including production expenses, market value of products, and operator characteristics.

Vegetables and Specialties Situation and Outlook. U. S. Government Printing Office. • Three times a year. Issued by the Economic Research Service of the U. S. Department of Agriculture. Provides current statistical information on supply, demand, and prices.

TRADE/PROFESSIONAL ASSOCIATIONS

European Lime Association. c/o IMA-Europe, Rue des Deux Eglises 26, B-1000 Brussels, Belgium. Phone: 32 2 2104410; Fax: 32 2 2104429; Email: info@eula.be • URL: http://www.eula.eu • Maintains a close relationship with the European Institutions, and the International and European Trade Associations. Represents the lime industry's views on issues, policies and strategies being developed in various areas such as industry competitiveness, environmental protection, energy consumption and climate change. Promotes lime acknowledgement in regulatory and scientific authorities.

Iran National Union of Agro Products. No. 94, Keyvan Alley, Kashani St., Urmia, Iran. Phone: 98 441 3451988 or 98 441 3455780; Fax: 98 441 3455606; Email: shakor_a@iranazarfruit.com • URL: http://www.iranazarfruit.com • Represents the interests of exporters of agricultural products. Aims to create coordination in the export of fruits and vegetables and the promotion of export products. Assists members by providing facilities and marketing services for their agricultural products.

National Alliance of Independent Crop Consultants. 349 E Nolley Dr., Collierville, TN 38017. Phone: (901)861-0511; Fax: (901)861-0512; Email: jonesnaicc@aol.com • URL: http://www.naicc.org • Independent crop consultants and contract researchers united to promote agriculture and professionalism in the field. Seeks to: assist in the formation of state and national policies relating to agricultural production and of crop management philosophies; support agricultural crop producers by the most ecologically sound, environmentally safe, and economical means. Encourages members to expand their knowledge concerning crop management practices and techniques; participates in research in this area. Provides assistance in the formation of state and regional consultant organizations; offers referral system for members. Compiles statistics; sponsors educational programs.

National Association of Produce Market Managers. PO Box 1617, Garner, NC 27529-1617. Phone: (919)779-5258 • URL: http://www.napmm.org • Produce market managers and industrial produce dealers; associate members are county agents and state employees in agriculture. Seeks to improve market conditions.

FARMERS

See also AGRICULTURE; LABOR

ABSTRACTS AND INDEXES

World Agricultural Economics and Rural Sociology Abstracts (WAERSA). CABI. • Monthly. Print and online available. Published in England by CABI Publishing. Provides worldwide coverage of the literature.

INTERNET DATABASES

USDA. U.S. National Institute of Standards and Technology. 100 Bureau Dr., Gaithersburg, MD 20899-1070. Phone: 800-877-8339 or (301)975-6478 or (202)720-2791; Fax: (301)975-8295; Email: inquiries@nist.gov • URL: http://www.nist.gov • The USDA home page has six sections: News and Information; What's New; About USDA; Agencies; Opportunities; Search and Help. Keyword searching is offered from the USDA home page and from various individual agency home pages. Agencies are the Economic Research Service, Agricultural Marketing Service, National Agricultural Statistics Service, National Agricultural Library, and about 12 others. Updating varies. Fees: Free.

PERIODICALS AND NEWSLETTERS

Amber Waves. Economic Research Service Hazard Analysis and Critical Control Points. • Quarterly. Replaces *Agricultural Outlook; Food Review*; and *Rural America*. Provides research and analysis from the U.S. Department of Agriculture's Economic Research Service. Includes economic data on agriculture, food, trade, and environmental factors.

Farm Industry News. Primedia Business Magazines and Media. • Monthly. $25.00 per year. Includes new products for farm use.

Farmer's Digest. Heartland Communications Group Inc. • 10 times a year. $17.95 per year. Current information on all phases of agriculture.

National Farmers Union News. National Farmers Union. • Description: Provides news, legislation, and tax information in relation to the farming industry.

Progressive Farmer. Progressive Farmer, Inc. • Monthly. $16 per year. Includes supplement *Rural Sportsman.*

STATISTICS SOURCES

Agricultural Statistics. U.S. Department of Agriculture National Agricultural Statistics Service. • Annual. $46 Individuals. Provides a wide variety of statistical data relating to agricultural production, supplies, consumption, prices/price-supports, foreign trade, costs, and returns, as well as farm labor, loans, income, and population. In many cases, historical data is shown annually for 10 years. In addition to farm data, includes detailed fishery statistics.

Agriculture Fact Book. U. S. Government Printing Office. • Annual. $26 Individuals. Issued by the Office of Communications, U. S. Department of Agriculture. Includes data on U. S. agriculture, farmers, food, nutrition, and rural America. Programs of the Department of Agriculture in six areas are described: rural economic development, foreign trade, nutrition, the environment, inspection, and education.

TRADE/PROFESSIONAL ASSOCIATIONS

Farm Financial Standards Council. c/o Carroll Merry, N78 W14573 Appleton Ave., No. 287, Menomonee Falls, WI 53051. Phone: (262)253-6902; Fax: (262)253-6903 • URL: http://www.ffsc.org • Aims to create and promote uniformity and integrity in financial reporting and analysis for agricultural producers. Strives to be recognized as the definitive resource of financial guidelines to benefit agricultural producers.

National Farmers Organization. 528 Billy Sunday Rd., Ste. 100, Ames, IA 50010-2508. Phone: 800-247-2110; Email: nfo@nfo.org • URL: http://www.nfo.org • Nonpartisan organization of farmers who bargain collectively to obtain contracts with buyers, processors, and exporters for the sale of farm commodities. Works to continuously improve such contracts. Conducts educational programs; maintains speakers' bureau.

National Farmers Union. 20 F St. NW, Ste. 300, Washington, DC 20001-6700. Phone: (202)554-1600; Fax: (202)554-1654 • URL: http://www.nfu.org • Farm families interested in agricultural welfare. Carries on educational, cooperative and legislative activities. Represents members' interests especially in acquiring a more equitable share of the food dollar. Assists farm families in developing self-help institutions such as cooperatives.

Turkey Farmers of Canada. Bldg. 1, Ste. 202, 7145 W Credit Ave., Mississauga, ON, Canada L5N 6J7. Phone: (905)812-3140; Fax: (905)812-9326; Email: info@tfc-edc.ca • URL: http://www.turkeyfarmersofcanada.ca • Turkey processors (3) and representatives of provincial turkey producers' organizations (8). Promotes a healthy business climate for turkey processors and growers. Sets national turkey production and supply levels. Conducts marketing programs; gathers and disseminates industry information; represents members before government agencies.

FARMS

See AGRICULTURE

FASHION INDUSTRY

See also CLOTHING INDUSTRY; WOMEN'S APPAREL

DIRECTORIES

Accessories Resources Directory. Business Journals Inc. • Annual. Covers: 1,600 manufacturers, importers, and sales representatives producing or handling belts, gloves, handbags, scarves, hosiery, jewelry, sunglasses, and umbrellas. Entries include: Company, name, address, phone, fax.

Directory of African Importers of Handkerchives, Scarves and Neckwears. EXIM Infotek Private Ltd. • $150 Individuals. Covers: 20 African importers of handkerchieves, scarves, neckwear, and neckties.

Directory of Asian Importers of Handkerchives, Scarves and Neckwears. EXIM Infotek Private Ltd. • $350 Individuals. Covers: 130 Asian importers of clothing accessories, ties, scarves, corsage, handkerchieves, neckwear, mufflers, necktie, pashmina shawls, silk neckties, silk scarves, and stoles. Entries include: Company name, postal address, telephone, fax, e-mail, website, contact person, designation, and product details.

Directory of Japanese Importers of Handkerchieves, Scarves and Neckwears. EXIM Infotek Private Ltd. • $250 Individuals. Covers: 90 Japanese importers of clothing accessories, ties, scarves, handkerchieves, neckwear, mufflers, and silk neckties. Entries include: Company name, postal address, telephone, fax, e-mail, website, contact person, designation, and product details.

Directory of Middle East Importers of Handkerchives, Scarves and Neckwears. EXIM Infotek Private Ltd. • $150 Individuals. Covers: 20 Middle East importers of handkerchieves, scarves, and neckwear.

Directory of North American Importers of Handkerchives, Scarves and Neckwears. EXIM Infotek Private Ltd. • $250 Individuals. Covers: 60 North American importers of bows, handkerchieves, scarves, neckwear, mufflers, napkins, neckties, pashmina shawls, silk scarves, and wool shawls. Entries include: Company name, postal address, telephone, fax, e-mail, website, contact person, designation, and product details.

Directory of Taiwanese Manufacturers & Exporters of Handkerchieves, Scarves & Neckwares. EXIM Infotek Private Ltd. • $5 Individuals. Covers: 20 Taiwanese manufacturers & exporters of neckties/ scarves. Entries include: Company name, postal address, city, country, phone, fax, e-mail & websites, contact person, designation, products detail.

Fashion Calendar. Ruth Finley. • Biweekly. $550 Individuals print and online. Covers: Events of interest to the fashion industry, including private and public fashion openings, and important events in other fields which are scheduled for principal fashion cities; coverage is heavily New York City, but major cities worldwide are also covered. Entries include: For openings--Event name, date, address, phone. For other events--Event name, date, time, location, phone.

The National Register of Fashion Accessories. Marche Publishing. • $200 Individuals print. Covers: Apparel accessory companies in the United States. Entries include: company name, address, phone, fax and toll free numbers, website and email addresses, officers, year established, brands, and affiliates.

The National Register of Independent Sales Reps--Apparel and Accessories. Marche Publishing. • $250 Individuals print. Covers: 1,200 representatives throughout the United States and Canada. Entries include: Company name, address, phone and fax numbers, email address, year established, lines of business, origin of companies, and quote from reps.

E-BOOKS

Fashion Supply Chain Management: Industry and Business Analysis. Cengage Learning Inc. • 2012. eBook. Published by IGI Global. Covers quantitative research on Fashion Supply Chain Management (FSCM) and exploratory studies on emerging supply chain management issues in the fashion industry.

GENERAL WORKS

Business of Fashion: Designing, Manufacturing and Marketing. Conde Nast Inc. • $100 Individuals. Business guide covering United States textile, apparel, and home fashions companies.

PERIODICALS AND NEWSLETTERS

DNR: The Men's Fashion Retail Textile Authority. Fairchild Publications. • Daily. $85.00 per year. Formerly *Daily News Record.*

GQ: Gentleman's Quarterly for Men. Conde Nast Publications. • Monthly. $15 Individuals.

Harper's Bazaar. The Hearst Corp. • Monthly. Monthly. $18.00 per year.

Tobe Report. Tobe Associates Inc. • Monthly. Edited for fashion retailers. Provides detailed information and analysis relating to current trends in the women's, children's, and men's apparel and accessories markets.

Vows: The Bridal and Wedding Business Journal. Grimes and Associates. • Bimonthly. $30 Individuals. Trade journal for bridal and wedding professionals.

Wearables Business. Penton. • Trade magazine covering the wearable segment of the promotional products industry for distributors.

TRADE/PROFESSIONAL ASSOCIATIONS

CFDA Foundation. 65 Bleecker St., 11 Fl., New York, NY 10012. Phone: (212)302-1821; Fax: (212)768-0515; Email: info@cfda.com • URL: http://www.cfda.com • Persons of "recognized ability, standing, and integrity, who are actively engaged in creative fashion design in the United States, in the fields of wearing apparel, fabrics, accessories, jewelry, or related products." (Membership is individual and does not extend to the firm or associates.) Seeks "to further the position of fashion design as a recognized branch of American art and culture, to advance its artistic and professional standards, to establish and maintain a code of ethics and practices of mutual benefit in professional, public, and trade relations, and to promote and improve public understanding and appreciation of the fashion arts through leadership in quality and taste."

FAST FOOD INDUSTRY

See also FROZEN FOOD INDUSTRY; RESTAURANTS, LUNCHROOMS, ETC.

FINANCIAL RATIOS

Annual Statement Studies. Risk Management Association. • Annual. Compiled from over 280,000 financial statements.

Annual Statement Studies: Industry Default Probabilities and Cash Flow Measures. Risk Management Association. • Annual. $405 Nonmembers. Serves as a companion volume to the original *Annual Statement Studies.* Gives probability of default estimates on a percentage scale for more than 450 industries. Includes changes in position year-by-year for eight financial statement line items and provides percentage measures of cash flow.

HANDBOOKS AND MANUALS

Pizzeria. Entrepreneur Press. • Looseleaf. $59.50. A practical guide to starting a pizza shop. Covers profit potential, start-up costs, market size evaluation, owner's time required, site selection, lease negotiation, pricing, accounting, advertising, promotion, etc. (Start-Up Business Guide No. E1006.).

Sandwich Shop/Deli. Entrepreneur Press. • Looseleaf. $59.50. A practical guide to starting a sandwich shop and delicatessen. Covers profit potential, start-up costs, market size evaluation, owner's time required, site selection, lease negotiation, pricing, accounting, advertising, promotion, etc. (Start-Up Business Guide No. E1156.).

FASTENER INDUSTRY

See also HARDWARE INDUSTRY

DIRECTORIES

Assembly Buyers Guide. Reed Elsevier Group plc Reed Business Information. • Annual. $68.00. Lists manufacturers and suppliers of equipment relating to assembly automation, fasteners, adhesives, robotics, and power tools.

Directory of American Manufacturers & Exporters of Nuts, Bolts, Screws & Fasteners. EXIM Infotek Private Ltd. • $20 Individuals. Covers: 260 American manufacturers & exporters of belt fasteners, bolts, captive screws, clevis pins, electronic & electrical enclosure closing systems, fasteners, fasteners for electronics & aerospace, fasteners-aluminum steel, fasteners-automotive, fasteners-industrial, fasteners-military specialties, fasteners-nylon, fasteners-plastic, fasteners-specialty, fasteners-spring steel, fasteners-stainless steel, fasteners-textiles, hand adjusting & fastening components, hex head bolts, marine snap fasteners, metric fasteners, military snap fasteners, nuts, nuts & bolts, pins, plastic fasteners, plastic snap fasteners, precision fasteners for military & commercial aircraft, quarter-turn fasteners, rivets, screws, self-locking nuts, special threaded & non-threaded fasteners, staples, threaded inserts & related high-tech fasteners. Entries include: Company name, postal address, city, country, telephone, fax, e-mail & websites, contact person, designation, products detail.

Directory of Chinese Manufacturers & Exporters of Nuts, Bolts, Screws & Fasteners. EXIM Infotek Private Ltd. • $5 Individuals. Covers: 40 Chinese manufacturers and exporters of bolts, chestnut kernels, fasteners, nuts and bolts, rivets, screws, slide fasteners, and washers. Entries include: Company name, postal address, city, country, phone, fax, e-mail and websites, contact person, designation, and product details.

Directory of Japanese Manufacturers & Exporters of Nuts, Bolts, Screws & Fasteners. EXIM Infotek Private Ltd. • $5 Individuals. Covers: 20 Japanese manufacturers and exporters of bifurcated rivets, bolts and nuts, bolts, fasteners, hexagon socket button head cap screws, hexagon socket cap screws, hexagon socket flat cap screws, hexagon socket set screws, industrial fasteners, rivets, screws, socket cap screws, tubular rivets, washers, and wood screws. Entries include: Company name, postal address, city, country, phone, fax, e-mail and websites, contact person, designation, and product details.

Directory of South Korean Manufacturers & Exporters of Nuts, Bolts, Screws & Fasteners. EXIM Infotek Private Ltd. • $10 Individuals. Covers: 50 South Korean manufacturers and exporters of bolts and nuts, nails, fasteners-metal, metal nuts/bolts/ washers, metal rivets, metal screws/bolts/nuts, and screws-metal. Entries include: Company name, postal address, city, country, phone, fax, e-mail and websites, contact person, designation, and product details.

Directory of Taiwanese Manufacturers & Exporters of Nuts, Bolts, Screws & Fasteners. EXIM Infotek Private Ltd. • $20 Individuals. Covers: 260 Taiwanese manufacturers and exporters of bolts and nuts, bolts, fasteners, fasteners-metal, metal nuts/ bolts/washers, metal rivets, metal screws/bolts/nuts, rivet nuts, rivets, screws, screws-metal, self-drilling screws, special screws and nuts, washers. Entries include: Company name, postal address, city, country, phone, fax, e-mail and websites, contact person, designation, and product details.

Fastener Technology International Buyers' Guide. Initial Publications Inc. • Annual. $50 Individuals print. Lists over 1,800 international manufacturers and distributors of fasteners and precision-formed parts.

The International Directory of Importers--Screws, Nuts, Bolts and Fasteners Importers. Interdata. • $200 Individuals print. Covers: 900 international firms importing screws, nuts, bolts and fasteners. Entries include: Company name and address, contact person, email, number of employees, year established, phone and telefaxes, business activity, bank references, as well as a listing of screws, nuts, bolts and fasteners currently being imported.

ONLINE DATABASES

Thomas Register Online. Thomas Publishing Company L.L.C. • Provides concise information on approximately 194,000 U. S. companies, mainly manufacturers, with over 50,000 product classifications. Indexes over 115,000 trade names. Information is updated semiannually. Inquire as to online cost and availability.

PERIODICALS AND NEWSLETTERS

Fastener Technology International. Initial Publications Inc. • Bimonthly. $40.00 per year.

Hardware Age. Reed Elsevier Group plc Reed Business Information. • Monthly. $75.00 per year.

STATISTICS SOURCES

U.S. Industry and Trade Outlook. U.S. Department of Commerce National Technical Information Service. • Annual. Produced by the International Trade Administration, U.S. Department of Commerce, in a "public-private" partnership with DRI/ McGraw-Hill and Standard & Poor's. Provides basic data, outlook for the current year, and "Long-Term Prospects" (five-year projections) for a wide variety of products and services. Includes high technology industries. Formerly *U.S. Industrial Outlook*.

TRADE/PROFESSIONAL ASSOCIATIONS

ASM International. 9639 Kinsman Rd., Materials Park, OH 44073-0002. Phone: 800-336-5152 or (440)338-5151; Email: memberservicecenter@asminternational.org • URL: http://www.asminternational.org • Metallurgists, materials engineers, executives in materials producing and consuming industries; teachers and students. Disseminates technical information about the manufacture, use, and treatment of engineered materials. Offers in-plant, home study, and intensive courses through Materials Engineering Institute.

National Fastener Distributors Association. 10842 Noel St., No. 107, Los Alamitos, CA 90720. Phone: 877-487-6332 or (714)484-7858; Fax: (562)684-0695; Email: nfda@nfda-fastener.org • URL: http://www.nfda-fastener.org • Marketers, distributors, manufacturers, and importers of the fastener industry (producers or distributors of screws, bolts, and nuts). Develops new uses for fasteners; collects and disseminates statistics and information for members; conducts membership performance surveys. Assists in the maintenance of sound and equitable relationships among members of the industry, the public, and government. Offers training and educational programs.

FATS

See OIL AND FATS INDUSTRY

FAX

See FACSIMILE SYSTEMS

FEDERAL AID

See also GRANTS-IN-AID

DIRECTORIES

Free Help from Uncle Sam to Start Your Own Business. Puma Publishing Co. • Irregular. $15.95 plus $3.00 shipping. Covers: over 100 federal programs that provide loans, services, and information to businesses. Entries include: Program name, agency name, address, phone, name of contact.

Government Assistance Almanac: The Guide to Federal, Domestic, Financial and Other Programs Covering Grants, Loans, Insurance, Personal Payments and Benefits. Omnigraphics Inc. • Annual. $275 print. Gives users updated information on all available federal domestic assistance programs. These programs represent nearly $2 trillion worth of federal assistance earmarked for distribution to consumers, children, parents, veterans, senior citizens, students, businesses, civic groups, state and local agencies, and others.

Guide to Federal Funding for Governments and Nonprofits. Thompson Publishing Group Inc. • Updated continuously; printed on request. $399. Contains detailed descriptions of federal grant programs in economic development, housing, transportation, social services, science, etc.

INTERNET DATABASES

FedWorld: A Program of the United States Department of Commerce. National Technical Information Service. Phone: 800-553-NTIS or (703)605-6000; Fax: (703)605-6900; Email: webmaster@fedworld.gov • URL: http://www.fedworld.gov • Web site offers "a comprehensive central access point for searching, locating, ordering, and acquiring government and business information." Emphasis is on searching the Web pages, databases, and government reports of a wide variety of federal agencies. Fees: Free.

FirstGov: Your First Click to the U. S. Government. General Services Administration. Phone: 800-333-4636 or (202)501-0705; Email: public.affairs@gsa.gov • URL: http://www.gsa.gov • Free Web site provides extensive links to federal agencies covering a wide variety of topics, such as agriculture, business, consumer safety, education, the environment, government jobs, grants, health, social security, statistics sources, taxes, technology, travel, and world affairs. Also provides links to federal forms, including IRS tax forms. Searching is offered, both keyword and advanced.

U.S. Business Advisor. Small Business Administration. Phone: (202)205-6600; Fax: (202)205-7064 • URL: http://www.sba.gov • Web site provides "a one-stop electronic link to all the information and services government provides for the business community." Covers about 60 federal agencies that exist to assist or regulate business. Detailed information is provided on financial assistance, workplace issues, taxes, regulations, international trade, and other business topics. Searching is offered. Fees: Free.

ONLINE DATABASES

GrantSelect. Schoolhouse Partners L.L.C. • Online service provides detailed descriptions of more than 10,000 grants offered by government and organizations in the U. S. Includes grants in a wide variety of subject fields. Contains current information with daily updates. Inquire as to online cost and availability.

OTHER SOURCES

Navy Retired Activities Branch. • A program of the U.S. Department of the Navy. Assists Navy retirees and survivors with benefits and entitlement information. Maintains speakers' bureau.

PERIODICALS AND NEWSLETTERS

Federal Assistance Monitor: Semi-Monthly Report on Federal and Private Grant Opportunities. Community Development Services. CD Publications. • Semimonthly. $339.00 per year; with online edition, $379.00 per year. Newsletter. Provides news of federal grant and loan programs for social, economic, and community purposes. Monitors grant announcements, funding, and availability. Formerly *Federal Research Report*.

Federal Grants and Contracts Weekly: Funding Opportunities in Research, Training and Services. Wolters Kluwer Law and Business. • 50 times a year. $450.00 per year. Newsletter.

Grantsmanship Center Magazine. The Grantsmanship Center. • Quarterly. Irregular. Free to qualified personnel. Contains a variety of concise articles on grant-related topics, such as program planning, proposal writing, fundraising, non-cash gifts, federal project grants, benchmarking, taxation, etc.

FEDERAL AID FOR EDUCATION

See FEDERAL AID

FEDERAL AID TO RESEARCH

See FEDERAL AID

FEDERAL BUDGET

See also NATIONAL DEBT

CD-ROM DATABASES

OECD Statistical Compendium. Organization for Economic Cooperation and Development. • Semiannual. $1,905.00 per year for 1 to 10 users. CD-ROM contains more than 730,000 monthly, quarterly, and annual time series for OECD countries, 1960 to date. Includes fully searchable data on agriculture, food, economic indicators, national accounts, employment, energy, finance, industry, technology, and foreign trade. Results can be displayed in various forms.

FINANCIAL RATIOS

Financial Report of the United States Government. U. S. Government Printing Office. • Annual. $21.00. Issued by the U. S. Treasury Department (www.treas.gov). Presents information about the financial condition and operations of the federal government. Program accounting systems of various government agencies provide data for the report.

INTERNET DATABASES

Business 2.0 Web Guide to the Best Business Links. Business 2.0 Media Inc. Phone: (415)293-4800; Email: support@business2.com • URL: http://www.business2.com/webguide • Web site presents an extensive, searchable directory of links to "the best, most informative, and authoritative web pages." Twenty main categories cover business, finance, career, company information, people, and technology topics, with thousands of subtopics, all linking to Web sites recommended by experienced business researchers. Fees: Free.

Fedstats. Federal Interagency Council on Statistical Policy. Phone: (202)395-7254 • URL: http://www.fedstats.gov • Web site features an efficient search facility for full-text statistics produced by more than 100 federal agencies, including the Census Bureau, the Bureau of Economic Analysis, and the Bureau of Labor Statistics. Boolean searches can be made within one agency or for all agencies combined. Links are offered to international statistical bureaus, including the UN, IMF, OECD, UNESCO, Eurostat, and 20 individual countries. Fees: Free.

FreeLunch.com. Economy.com, Inc. Phone: (610)696-8700; Fax: (610)696-1678 • URL: http://www.freelunch.com • Web site provides free access to more than 200 million economic and financial data series, covering industry, demographics, labor markets, prices, retail sales, government spending, trade, interest rates, housing starts, the stock market, etc. Data is available in either chart or table form. Searching is offered. Free, but registration required.

For publishers' addresses, refer to SOURCES CITED section at the back of the book.

Economy.com, Inc. also offers fee-based economic analysis at *The Dismal Scientist* site (www.dismal.com).

OTHER SOURCES

Center for Strategic and Budgetary Assessments. • Serves as nonpartisan independent research organization that analyzes military spending and national security policy issues. Provides timely, independent analyses of military budget and defense issues to the media, citizens' organizations, policy-makers, and advocacy groups. Conducts research and educational programs. Sponsors briefings and discussions on defense and military issues. Analyzes issues such as the impact of the defense budget on other national spending priorities, the American economy, and the federal deficit; the relationship between defense spending, national security, and the development of alternatives to present national security policies. Maintains internship program.

United States Government Annual Report, Fiscal Year. U. S. Government Printing Office. • Annual. Issued by the Financial Management Service, U. S. Treasury Department (www.fms.treas.gov). Contains the official report on the receipts and outlays of the federal government. Presents budgetary results at the summary level.

STATISTICS SOURCES

The AIER Chart Book. AIER Research Staff. American Institute for Economic Research. • Annual. $4 Individuals. A compact compilation of long-range charts ("Purchasing Power of the Dollar," for example, goes back to 1780) covering various aspects of the U. S. economy. Includes inflation, interest rates, debt, gold, taxation, stock prices, etc. (Economic Education Bulletin.).

Budget and Economic Outlook: Fiscal Years (10-year period). U. S. Government Printing Office. • Annual. $27. Issued by the Congressional Budget Office (CBO). Reports on fiscal policy and provides baseline projections of federal budget for 10 years. Also offers "impartial analysis with no recommendations.".

Survey of Current Business. U. S. Government Printing Office. • Published by Bureau of Economic Analysis, U. S. Department of Commerce. Presents a wide variety of business and economic data.

Treasury Bulletin. U. S. Government Printing Office. • Quarterly. $51 List Price. Issued by the Financial Management Service, U. S. Treasury Department. Provides data on the federal budget, government securities and yields, the national debt, and the financing of the federal government in general.

FEDERAL GOVERNMENT

ABSTRACTS AND INDEXES

Current Law Index. Cengage Learning Inc. • $1,332 Individuals. Monthly. $1269.00 per year. Produced in cooperation with the American Association of Law Libraries. Indexes more than 900 law journals, legal newspapers, and specialty publications from the U.S., Canada, U.K., Ireland, Australia, and New Zealand.

Social Sciences Citation Index. Thomson Reuters Corp. • Weekly. Product is accessed via *Web of Science.*

Social Sciences Index Retrospective: 1907-1983. EBSCO Publishing Inc. • Indexing for 1,000,000 articles. Coverage includes international index and social sciences and humanities index.

BIBLIOGRAPHIES

Subject Bibliography Index: A Guide to U.S. Government Information. U. S. Government Printing Office. • Annual. Free. Issued by the Superintendent of Documents. Lists currently available subject bibliographies by title and by topic. Each *Subject Bibliography* describes government books, periodicals, posters, pamphlets, and subscription services available for sale from the Government Printing Office.

CD-ROM DATABASES

OECD Statistical Compendium. Organization for Economic Cooperation and Development. • Semiannual. $1,905.00 per year for 1 to 10 users. CD-ROM contains more than 730,000 monthly, quarterly, and annual time series for OECD countries, 1960 to date. Includes fully searchable data on agriculture, food, economic indicators, national accounts, employment, energy, finance, industry, technology, and foreign trade. Results can be displayed in various forms.

Social Sciences Abstracts. EBSCO Publishing Inc. • Provides indexing from 1983 and abstracting from 1994 of more than 750 periodicals covering economics, area studies, community health, public administration, public welfare, urban studies, and many other topics related to the social sciences.

Social Sciences Citation Index. Thomson Reuters Corp. • Weekly. Product is accessed via *Web of Science.*

DIRECTORIES

Carroll's Federal & Federal Regional Directory. Caroll Publishing. • Semiannual. $500 Individuals. Lists more than 23,000 U. S. government officials throughout the country, including military installations.

Carroll's Federal Directory. Caroll Publishing. • $550 Single issue 4 issues per year. Covers approximately 37,000 executive managers in federal government offices in Washington, DC, including executive, congressional and judicial branches; members of Congress and Congressional committees and staff.

Carroll's Federal Regional Directory. Caroll Publishing. • Annual. $500 Individuals. Covers: Over 32,000 officials in federal congressional, judicial, and executive branch departments and agencies outside the District of Columbia. Database includes: Regional maps showing states covered in each federal region and Federal Information Centers. Entries include: Organization or agency name; names, addresses, and phone numbers of key personnel.

Federal Regional Yellow Book: Who's Who in the Federal Government's Departments, Agencies, Military Installations, and Service Academies Outside of Washington, DC. Leadership Directories Inc. • Semiannual. $465 Individuals annual. Lists over 35,000 federal officials and support staff at 8,000 regional offices.

Federal Staff Directory: With Biographical Information on Executive Staff Personnel. CQ Press. • Three times a year. $259.00 per year. Single copies, $149.00. Lists 35,000 staff members of federal departments and agencies, with biographies of 3,200 key executives. Includes keyword and name indexes.

Government Phone Book USA: Your Comprehensive Guide to Federal, State, County, and Local Government Offices in the United States. Omnigraphics Inc. • Annual. $265.00. Contains more than 270,000 listings of federal, state, county, and local government offices and personnel, including legislatures. Formerly *Government Directory of Addresses and Phone Numbers.*

The Internet Blue Pages: The Guide to Federal Government Web Sites. Information Today, Inc. • Annual. $34.95. Provides information on more than 1,800 Web sites used by various agencies of the federal government. Includes indexes to agencies and topics. Links to all Web sites listed are available at www.fedweb.com. (CyberAge Books.).

Judicial Staff Directory: With Biographical Information on Judges and Key Court Staff. CQ Press. • Semiannual. $450.00. $225.00 per volume. Lists 33,500 federal court personnel, including 1,900 federal judges and their staffs, including biographies of judges and key executives. Includes maps of court jurisdictions.

Judicial Yellow Book: Who's Who in Federal and State Courts. Leadership Directories Inc. • Semiannual. $465 /year. Lists more than 3,200 judges and staffs in various federal courts and 1,200 judges and staffs in state courts. Includes biographical profiles of judges.

Rhode Island Directory of Human Service Agencies & Government Agencies. Travelers Aid Society of Rhode Island. • Biennial. Covers: about 1,200 public and private nonprofit human service agencies and organizations in Rhode Island. Entries include: Agency name, address, phone, name of contact or director; description of services; hours open; eligibility requirements; ages and geographic area served; fee for service; funding.

United States Government Manual. Office of the Federal Register. • Annual. $29 Individuals. Provides information on the agencies of the executive, judicial, and legislative branches of the Federal government. Contains a section on terminated or transferred agencies. Database includes: Includes boards, commissions, committees and quasi-official agencies and organizations in which US participates.

Washington: A Comprehensive Directory of the Key Institutions and Leaders in th e National Capitol Area. Columbia Books Inc. • Annual. $149.00. Provides information on about 5,000 Washington, DC key businesses, government offices, non-profit organizations, and cultural institutions, with the names of about 25,000 principal executives. Includes Washington media, law offices, foundations, labor unions, international organizations, clubs, etc.

Washington Information Directory. CQ Press. • Annual. $175 Individuals print cloth, standing order. Covers: 10,000 governmental agencies, congressional committees, and non-governmental associations considered competent sources of specialized information. Entries include: Name of agency, committee, or association; address, phone, fax, and Internet; annotation concerning function or activities of the office; and name of contact.

INTERNET DATABASES

Business 2.0 Web Guide to the Best Business Links. Business 2.0 Media Inc. Phone: (415)293-4800; Email: support@business2.com • URL: http://www.business2.com/webguide • Web site presents an extensive, searchable directory of links to "the best, most informative, and authoritative web pages." Twenty main categories cover business, finance, career, company information, people, and technology topics, with thousands of subtopics, all linking to Web sites recommended by experienced business researchers. Fees: Free.

Fedstats. Federal Interagency Council on Statistical Policy. Phone: (202)395-7254 • URL: http://www.fedstats.gov • Web site features an efficient search facility for full-text statistics produced by more than 100 federal agencies, including the Census Bureau, the Bureau of Economic Analysis, and the Bureau of Labor Statistics. Boolean searches can be made within one agency or for all agencies combined. Links are offered to international statistical bureaus, including the UN, IMF, OECD, UNESCO, Eurostat, and 20 individual countries. Fees: Free.

FedWorld: A Program of the United States Department of Commerce. National Technical Information Service. Phone: 800-553-NTIS or (703)605-6000; Fax: (703)605-6900; Email: webmaster@fedworld.gov • URL: http://www.fedworld.gov • Web site offers "a comprehensive central access point for searching, locating, ordering, and acquiring government and business information." Emphasis is on searching the Web pages, databases, and government reports of a wide variety of federal agencies. Fees: Free.

FirstGov: Your First Click to the U. S. Government. General Services Administration. Phone: 800-333-4636 or (202)501-0705; Email: public.affairs@gsa.gov • URL: http://www.gsa.gov • Free Web site provides extensive links to federal agencies covering a wide variety of topics, such as agriculture, business, consumer safety, education, the environment, government jobs, grants, health, social security, statistics sources, taxes, technology, travel, and world affairs. Also provides links to federal forms, including IRS tax forms. Searching is offered, both keyword and advanced.

FreeLunch.com. Economy.com, Inc. Phone: (610)696-8700; Fax: (610)696-1678 • URL: http://www.freelunch.com • Web site provides free access to more than 200 million economic and financial data series, covering industry, demographics, labor markets, prices, retail sales, government spending, trade, interest rates, housing starts, the stock market, etc. Data is available in either chart or table form. Searching is offered. Free, but registration required. Economy.com, Inc. also offers fee-based economic analysis at *The Dismal Scientist* site (www.dismal.com).

Lexis.com Research System. Lexis-Nexis Group. Phone: 800-227-4908 or (937)865-6800; Fax: (937)865-6909; Email: webmaster@prod.lexis-nexis.com • URL: http://www.nexis.com • Fee-based Web site offers extensive searching of a wide variety of legal sources. Additional features include Daily Opinion Service, lexis.com Bookstore, Career Center, CLE Center, Law Schools, and Practice Pages ("Pages specific to areas of specialty").

U.S. Census Bureau: The Official Statistics. U. S. Bureau of the Census. Phone: (301)763-4636 or (301)763-4100; Fax: (301)763-4794; Email: webmaster@census.gov • URL: http://www.census.gov/prod/www/abs/mfg-prof.html • Web site is "Your Source for Social, Demographic, and Economic Information." Contains "Current U. S. Population Count," "Current Economic Indicators," and a wide variety of data under "Other Official Statistics." Keyword searching is provided. Fees: Free.

ONLINE DATABASES

Wilson Social Sciences Abstracts Online. H.W. Wilson Co. • Provides online abstracting and indexing of more than 500 periodicals covering area studies, community health, public administration, public welfare, urban studies, and many other social science topics. Time period is 1994 to date for abstracts and 1983 to date for indexing, with updates weekly. Inquire as to online cost and availability.

OTHER SOURCES

American Society of Military Comptrollers. • Civilians and military personnel who are now or who have been involved in the overall field of military comptrollership; other interested individuals. Conducts research programs. Compiles statistics; maintains speakers' bureau. Plans to establish library.

Armed Forces Sports. • Persons serving as head of the morale and welfare activities of the U.S. Army, Navy, Marines, and Air Force. Encourages physical fitness in the armed forces through a policy of "sports for all"; has established uniform rules to govern all service sports within its jurisdiction. Conducts interservice sports championship competitions. Develops and encourages spectator interest sports for the individual services. Selects and sends military athletes and teams to national and international competitions; has representative on the Executive Board and House of Delegates of the U.S. Olympic Committee, various U.S. sports governing bodies, and the International Military Sports Council. Compiles statistics.

Citizen Soldier. • Individuals concerned with military-civilian relationships within American society. Aims to help Vietnam War veterans who may have been harmed by highly toxic herbicides (including Agent Orange) that were used in Vietnam between 1962 and 1970. Works with veterans who were exposed to low-level radiation at Nevada and South Pacific A-bomb test sites and Persian Gulf War veterans suffering from unexplained chronic ailments. Represents GIs on active duty who are victims of military racism and/or sexism. Assists GIs who have been prosecuted or otherwise punished due to positive results on drug residue urine tests that CS believes to have been inaccurate because of defective laboratory work. Seeks to protect the rights of soldiers testing positive for the AIDS antibody. Advocates for veterans suffering from Persian Gulf Syndrome. Promotes a public service campaign to inform service members of their legal rights regarding the military's HIV testing program. Works with high school and college youths to address concerns on military recruiting practices. Maintains speakers' bureau. Advises GIs who wish alternatives to service in current Iraqi War.

Defense Advisory Committee on Women in the Services. • Civilians appointed by Secretary of Defense to provide recommendations to optimize utilization and quality of life for women in U.S. armed forces. Assists the Department of Defense by advising on specified matters relating to the recruitment and retention, treatment, employment, integration, and well-being of highly qualified professional women in the Services. Advises on family issues related to the recruitment and retention of a highly qualified professional military.

Inter-University Seminar on Armed Forces and Society. • Individuals from both public and private life in the academic, military, and government fields who are primarily researchers. Promotes the study of armed forces and society; provides a focal point for the exchange of information on the subject; stimulates research in the field on a cross-national basis. Compiles statistics; recommends a scholar to conduct seminars and give lectures.

National Committee for Employer Support of the Guard and Reserve. • Provides free education, consultation, and if necessary, mediation for employers of guard and reserve members. Aims to ensure the national security. Promotes cooperation and understanding between reserve component members and their civilian employers and assists in the resolution of conflicts arising from an employee's military commitment. Operates with a network of almost 4,000 volunteers throughout 56 Committees located in each state, commonwealth, territory, and the District of Columbia. Operates an ombudsman program to assist in the informal resolution of employer-employee conflicts resulting from employee participation in the National Guard and Reserve.

National Lawyers Guild - Military Law Task Force. • Counselors, attorneys, and law students concerned with military, selective service, and veterans' law. Purposes are to: assist active-duty personnel, veterans, and those affected by selective service; provide educational and political work focused on these areas of law; offer research assistance in military and veterans law; support networking among attorneys and counselors. Operates speakers' bureau; offers informal referral services and educational materials.

Naval Intelligence Professionals. • Active duty and former naval intelligence officers; enlisted personnel; civilian professionals; corporations. Objectives are to: improve naval intelligence operations; act as a clearinghouse for information on scientific and technical advances in naval intelligence; provide a forum for the exchange of ideas. Encourages readiness for those who would be involved in a national crisis mobilization.

Carroll's Federal Organization Charts. Caroll Publishing. • 8/year. $1,650 Individuals. Provides 200 large, fold-out paper charts showing personnel relationships in 2,100 federal departments and agencies. Charts are also available online and on CD-ROM.

PERIODICALS AND NEWSLETTERS

Federal Computer Week: The Newspaper for the Government Systems Community. FCW Government Technology Group. • 41 times a year. $95.00 per year.

Government Executive: Federal Government's Business Magazine. National Journal Group Inc. • Monthly. $48 Individuals. Includes management of computerized information systems in the federal government.

The Information Freeway Report: Free Business and Government Information Via Modem. Washington Researchers Ltd. • Monthly. $160.00 per year. Newsletter. Provides news of business and government databases that are available free of charge through the Internet or directly. Emphasis is on federal government databases and electronic bulletin boards (Fedworld).

Legal Times: Law and Lobbying in the Nation's Capital. ALM Media Properties LLC. • Weekly. $318.00 per year. Published in Washington, DC. Provides news relating to lawyers and the federal government. Special features cover a variety of topics relating to law firm administration.

National Journal: The Weekly on Politics and Government. National Journal Group Inc. • Weekly. $1,499 Individuals. Includes semiannual supplement *Capital Source.* A non-partisan weekly magazine on politics and government.

RESEARCH CENTERS AND INSTITUTES

United States Naval Institute. 291 Wood Rd., Annapolis, MD 21402-1213. Phone: 800-223-8764 or (410)268-6110; Fax: (410)571-1703; Email: customer@usni.org • URL: http://www.usni.org • Regular, reserve, and retired professionals in the Navy, Marine Corps, and Coast Guard; civilians interested in the advancement of the knowledge of sea power and in advancing professional, literary, and scientific knowledge in the naval and maritime services. Conducts oral history and color print program.

STATISTICS SOURCES

Statistical Abstract of the United States. U. S. Government Printing Office. • Annual. $44.00. Issued by the U. S. Bureau of the Census.

FEDERAL INSURANCE CONTRIBUTIONS ACT (FICA)

See SOCIAL SECURITY

FEDERAL REGULATION

See REGULATION OF INDUSTRY

FEDERAL RESERVE SYSTEM

See also BANKS AND BANKING

BIBLIOGRAPHIES

FED in Print: Economics and Banking Topics. Federal Reserve Bank of Philadelphia. • Semiannual. Free. Business and banking topics.

Federal Reserve Board Publications. U.S. Board of

Governors of the Federal Reserve System. • Semiannual. Free.

CD-ROM DATABASES

OECD Statistical Compendium. Organization for Economic Cooperation and Development. • Semiannual. $1,905.00 per year for 1 to 10 users. CD-ROM contains more than 730,000 monthly, quarterly, and annual time series for OECD countries, 1960 to date. Includes fully searchable data on agriculture, food, economic indicators, national accounts, employment, energy, finance, industry, technology, and foreign trade. Results can be displayed in various forms.

INTERNET DATABASES

Business 2.0 Web Guide to the Best Business Links. Business 2.0 Media Inc. Phone: (415)293-4800; Email: support@business2.com • URL: http://www.business2.com/webguide • Web site presents an extensive, searchable directory of links to "the best, most informative, and authoritative web pages." Twenty main categories cover business, finance, career, company information, people, and technology topics, with thousands of subtopics, all linking to Web sites recommended by experienced business researchers. Fees: Free.

Federal Reserve Board Publications and Education Resources. Board of Governors of the Federal Reserve System. Phone: (202)452-3000; Fax: (202)452-3819 • URL: http://www.federalreserve.gov/publications.htm • Web site provides access to statistics, surveys, and research from the Federal Reserve Board. *Federal Reserve Bulletin* articles are available as abstracts or full text (PDF) currently or from six-year archives. The link "Statistics: Releases and Historical Data" offers daily, weekly, monthly, quarterly, and annual data in great detail for interest rates, foreign exchange, consumer credit, money stock measures, industrial production indexes, bank reserves, and other items. Historical tabulations are available for various time periods. Free.

Fedstats. Federal Interagency Council on Statistical Policy. Phone: (202)395-7254 • URL: http://www.fedstats.gov • Web site features an efficient search facility for full-text statistics produced by more than 100 federal agencies, including the Census Bureau, the Bureau of Economic Analysis, and the Bureau of Labor Statistics. Boolean searches can be made within one agency or for all agencies combined. Links are offered to international statistical bureaus, including the UN, IMF, OECD, UNESCO, Eurostat, and 20 individual countries. Fees: Free.

FreeLunch.com. Economy.com, Inc. Phone: (610)696-8700; Fax: (610)696-1678 • URL: http://www.freelunch.com • Web site provides free access to more than 200 million economic and financial data series, covering industry, demographics, labor markets, prices, retail sales, government spending, trade, interest rates, housing starts, the stock market, etc. Data is available in either chart or table form. Searching is offered. Free, but registration required. Economy.com, Inc. also offers fee-based economic analysis at *The Dismal Scientist* site (www.dismal.com).

Summary of Commentary on Current Economic Conditions by Federal Reserve District. Board of Governors of the Federal Reserve System. Phone: (202)452-3000; Fax: (202)452-3819 • URL: http://www.federalreserve.gov/publications.htm • 8/year. Free Web site provides current "anecdotal information" eight times a year on economic conditions within each of the 12 Federal Reserve Districts, plus an extensive national *Summary*. Text is based on the opinions of bank officials, business executives, economists, financial market experts, and others. Typically contains views of consumer spending, manufacturing, services, credit, employment, prices, wages, and the economy in general. Usually referred to as the Beige Book.

ONLINE DATABASES

Banking Information Source. ProQuest L.L.C. • Provides indexing and abstracting of periodical and other literature from 1982 to date, with weekly updates. Covers the financial services industry: banks, savings institutions, investment houses, credit unions, insurance companies, and real estate organizations. Emphasis is on marketing and management. Inquire as to online cost and availability. (Formerly *FINIS: Financial Industry Information Service.*).

PERIODICALS AND NEWSLETTERS

American Banker: The Financial Services Daily. SourceMedia Inc. • Daily. $895.00 per year. Provides news of banking, investment products, mortgages, credit unions, finance, bank technology, and legal developments.

Central Banking: Policy, Markets, Supervision. European Business Publications Inc. • Quarterly. $260.00 per year, including annual *Central Banking Directory*. Published in England by Central Banking Publications. Reports and comments on the activities of central banks around the world. Also provides discussions of the International Monetary Fund (IMF), the Organization for Economic Cooperation and Development (OECD), the Bank for International Settlements (BIS), and the World Bank.

InvesTech Market Analyst: Technical and Monetary Investment Analysis. Investech Research. • Every three weeks. $190.00 per year. Newsletter. Provides interpretation of monetary statistics and Federal Reserve actions, especially as related to technical analysis of stock market price trends.

U.S. Banker. SourceMedia Inc. • Monthly. $65.00 per year. Edited for bank executives and managers. Covers a wide variety of banking and financial topics.

STATISTICS SOURCES

Survey of Current Business. U. S. Government Printing Office. • Published by Bureau of Economic Analysis, U. S. Department of Commerce. Presents a wide variety of business and economic data.

FEDERAL STATISTICS

See GOVERNMENT STATISTICS

FEED AND FEEDSTUFFS INDUSTRY

See also CORN INDUSTRY; FARM PRODUCE

ABSTRACTS AND INDEXES

Field Crop Abstracts. CABI Publishing North America. • Monthly. Published in England by CABI Publishing, formerly Commonwealth Agricultural Bureaux.

Nutrition Abstracts and Reviews, Series B: Livestock Feeds and Feeding. CABI Publishing North America. • Monthly. Institutions, $1,180.00 per year. Online edition available, $1,215.00 per year. Published in England by CABI Publishing. Provides worldwide coverage of the literature.

CD-ROM DATABASES

AGRICOLA on SilverPlatter. Ovid Technologies Inc. • Updated monthly. Price varies. Produced by the National Agricultural Library. Provides over 4 million citations to the literature of agriculture, agricultural economics, animal sciences, entomology, fertilizer, food, forestry, nutrition, pesticides, plant science, water resources, and other topics.

FINANCIAL RATIOS

Annual Statement Studies. Risk Management Association. • Annual. Compiled from over 280,000 financial statements.

Annual Statement Studies: Industry Default Probabilities and Cash Flow Measures. Risk Management Association. • Annual. $405 Nonmembers. Serves as a companion volume to the original *Annual Statement Studies*. Gives probability of default estimates on a percentage scale for more than 450 industries. Includes changes in position year-by-year for eight financial statement line items and provides percentage measures of cash flow.

INTERNET DATABASES

USDA. U.S. National Institute of Standards and Technology. 100 Bureau Dr., Gaithersburg, MD 20899-1070. Phone: 800-877-8339 or (301)975-6478 or (202)720-2791; Fax: (301)975-8295; Email: inquiries@nist.gov • URL: http://www.nist.gov • The USDA home page has six sections: News and Information; What's New; About USDA; Agencies; Opportunities; Search and Help. Keyword searching is offered from the USDA home page and from various individual agency home pages. Agencies are the Economic Research Service, Agricultural Marketing Service, National Agricultural Statistics Service, National Agricultural Library, and about 12 others. Updating varies. Fees: Free.

ONLINE DATABASES

CAB Abstracts. CABI. • Contains 46 specialized abstract collections covering over 10,000 journals and monographs in the areas of agriculture, horticulture, forest products, farm products, nutrition, dairy science, poultry, grains, animal health, entomology, etc. Time period is 1972 to date, with monthly updates. Inquire as to online cost and availability. *CAB Abstracts on CD-ROM* also available, with annual updating.

PERIODICALS AND NEWSLETTERS

Feed and Feeding Digest. National Grain and Feed Association. • Monthly. Membership.

Feed Bulletin. Jacobsen Publishing Co. • Daily. $750.00 per year.

Livestock and Grain Market News Branch Weekly Summary. U.S. Dept of Agriculture. Livestock and Grain Market News Branch. • Weekly. $85.00 per year. Formerly *Grain and Feed Weekly Summary and Statistics.*

PRICE SOURCES

Feedstuffs. Miller Publishing Co. • Weekly. $144 Individuals.

RESEARCH CENTERS AND INSTITUTES

University of Massachusetts at Amherst - West Experiment Station - Soil and Plant Tissue Testing Laboratory. 682 N Pleasant St., Amherst, MA 01003. Phone: (413)545-2311; Fax: (413)545-1931; Email: veneman@psis.umass.edu • URL: http://soiltest.umass.edu • Soil and plant tissue.

STATISTICS SOURCES

Agricultural Statistics. U.S. Department of Agriculture National Agricultural Statistics Service. • Annual. $46 Individuals. Provides a wide variety of statistical data relating to agricultural production, supplies, consumption, prices/price-supports, foreign trade, costs, and returns, as well as farm labor, loans, income, and population. In many cases, historical data is shown annually for 10 years. In addition to farm data, includes detailed fishery statistics.

TRADE/PROFESSIONAL ASSOCIATIONS

American Feed Industry Association. 2101 Wilson Blvd., Ste. 916, Arlington, VA 22201. Phone: (703)524-0810; Fax: (703)524-1921; Email: afia@afia.org • URL: http://www.afia.org/afia/home.aspx • Manufacturers of formula feed and pet food; suppliers to feed manufacturers; other trade related associations. Maintains Equipment Manufacturing Council.

National Grain and Feed Association. 1250 I St.

NW, Ste. 1003, Washington, DC 20005. Phone: (202)289-0873; Fax: (202)289-5388; Email: ngfa@ngfa.org • URL: http://www.ngfa.org • Formerly Grain and Feed Dealers National Association.

National Hay Association. 151 Treasure Island Causeway, No. 2, Saint Petersburg, FL 33706. Phone: 800-707-0014 or (727)367-9702; Fax: (727)367-9608; Email: haynha@aol.com • URL: http://nationalhay.org • Hay shippers, dealers, brokers, producers, and others interested in the hay industry.

FERTILIZER INDUSTRY

See also AGRICULTURAL CHEMICALS; POTASH INDUSTRY

ALMANACS AND YEARBOOKS

Association of American Plant Food Control Officials Official Publication. Services. University of Kentucky. • Annual. $60. Source of information for AAPFCO, its membership, Rules & Standards (including the model "Uniform State Fertilizer Bill" and other model bills), Uniform Policy Statements and Official Terms.

CD-ROM DATABASES

AGRICOLA on SilverPlatter. Ovid Technologies Inc. • Updated monthly. Price varies. Produced by the National Agricultural Library. Provides over 4 million citations to the literature of agriculture, agricultural economics, animal sciences, entomology, fertilizer, food, forestry, nutrition, pesticides, plant science, water resources, and other topics.

OECD Statistical Compendium. Organization for Economic Cooperation and Development. • Semiannual. $1,905.00 per year for 1 to 10 users. CD-ROM contains more than 730,000 monthly, quarterly, and annual time series for OECD countries, 1960 to date. Includes fully searchable data on agriculture, food, economic indicators, national accounts, employment, energy, finance, industry, technology, and foreign trade. Results can be displayed in various forms.

DIRECTORIES

Major Chemical and Petrochemical Companies of the World. Cengage Learning Inc. • Annual. $1,460 Individuals. 2008. 12th edition. eBook. Published by Graham & Whiteside. Contains profiles of more than 8,500 important chemical and petrochemical companies in various countries. Subject areas include general chemicals, specialty chemicals, agricultural chemicals, petrochemicals, industrial gases, and fertilizers.

FINANCIAL RATIOS

Annual Statement Studies. Risk Management Association. • Annual. Compiled from over 280,000 financial statements.

Annual Statement Studies: Industry Default Probabilities and Cash Flow Measures. Risk Management Association. • Annual. $405 Nonmembers. Serves as a companion volume to the original *Annual Statement Studies.* Gives probability of default estimates on a percentage scale for more than 450 industries. Includes changes in position year-by-year for eight financial statement line items and provides percentage measures of cash flow.

INTERNET DATABASES

Business 2.0 Web Guide to the Best Business Links. Business 2.0 Media Inc. Phone: (415)293-4800; Email: support@business2.com • URL: http://www.business2.com/webguide • Web site presents an extensive, searchable directory of links to "the best, most informative, and authoritative web pages." Twenty main categories cover business, finance, career, company information, people, and technology topics, with thousands of subtopics, all linking to Web sites recommended by experienced business researchers. Fees: Free.

Fedstats. Federal Interagency Council on Statistical Policy. Phone: (202)395-7254 • URL: http://www.fedstats.gov • Web site features an efficient search facility for full-text statistics produced by more than 100 federal agencies, including the Census Bureau, the Bureau of Economic Analysis, and the Bureau of Labor Statistics. Boolean searches can be made within one agency or for all agencies combined. Links are offered to international statistical bureaus, including the UN, IMF, OECD, UNESCO, Eurostat, and 20 individual countries. Fees: Free.

FreeLunch.com. Economy.com, Inc. Phone: (610)696-8700; Fax: (610)696-1678 • URL: http://www.freelunch.com • Web site provides free access to more than 200 million economic and financial data series, covering industry, demographics, labor markets, prices, retail sales, government spending, trade, interest rates, housing starts, the stock market, etc. Data is available in either chart or table form. Searching is offered. Free, but registration required. Economy.com, Inc. also offers fee-based economic analysis at *The Dismal Scientist* site (www.dismal.com).

Manufacturing Profiles. U. S. Bureau of the Census. Phone: (301)763-4636 or (301)763-4100; Fax: (301)763-4794; Email: webmaster@census.gov • URL: http://www.census.gov/prod/www/abs/mfg-prof.html • The Census Bureau makes available free on PDF (Portable Document Format) an annual consolidation of the entire Current Industrial Report series, presenting "all the data compiled." Contains statistics on production, shipments, inventories, consumption, exports, imports, and orders for a wide variety of manufactured products.

USDA. U.S. National Institute of Standards and Technology. 100 Bureau Dr., Gaithersburg, MD 20899-1070. Phone: 800-877-8339 or (301)975-6478 or (202)720-2791; Fax: (301)975-8295; Email: inquiries@nist.gov • URL: http://www.nist.gov • The USDA home page has six sections: News and Information; What's New; About USDA; Agencies; Opportunities; Search and Help. Keyword searching is offered from the USDA home page and from various individual agency home pages. Agencies are the Economic Research Service, Agricultural Marketing Service, National Agricultural Statistics Service, National Agricultural Library, and about 12 others. Updating varies. Fees: Free.

ONLINE DATABASES

CAB Abstracts. CABI. • Contains 46 specialized abstract collections covering over 10,000 journals and monographs in the areas of agriculture, horticulture, forest products, farm products, nutrition, dairy science, poultry, grains, animal health, entomology, etc. Time period is 1972 to date, with monthly updates. Inquire as to online cost and availability. *CAB Abstracts on CD-ROM* also available, with annual updating.

PERIODICALS AND NEWSLETTERS

Ag Professional. Doane Agricultural Services Co. • 10/year. Published to meet the business needs of the retail fertilizer and agrichemical dealer industry. Formerly *Ag Retailer Magazine.*

AgProfessional. Vance Publishing Corp. • Provides agronomic and business management solutions to retailers/distributors, professional farm managers and crop consultants, resulting in increased production and profitability in the food, fiber and energy markets.

Croplife. Meister Media. • Monthly. $36.00 per year. Formerly *Farm Chemicals.*

Dealer Progress: How Smart Agribusiness is Growing. The Fertilizer Institute. • Bimonthly. Free to qualified personnel; others, $40.00 per year. Published in association with the Fertilizer Institute. Includes information on fertilizers and agricultural chemicals, including farm pesticides. Formerly *Progress.*

PRICE SOURCES

The National Provisioner: Serving Meat, Poultry, and Seafood Processors. BNP Media. • Monthly. $85.04 Individuals. *Buyer's Guide* available. Meat, poultry and seafood newsletter.

Prices of Agricultural Products and Selected Inputs in Europe and North America. Economic Commission for Europe. United Nations Publications. • Annual. $36 Individuals.

RESEARCH CENTERS AND INSTITUTES

International Fertilizer Development Center. PO Box 2040, Muscle Shoals, AL 35662. Phone: (205)386-2874 or (256)381-6600; Fax: (256)381-7408; Email: general@ifdc.org • URL: http://www.ifdc.org • Conducts research relating to all aspects of fertilizer production, marketing, and use. Supported by the United Nations, the World Bank, and other international agencies.

Tennessee Agricultural Experiment Station - University of Tennessee, Knoxville. 103 Morgan Hall, Knoxville, TN 37996-4506. Phone: (865)974-4520; Fax: (865)974-6451; Email: AgResearch@tennessee.edu • URL: http://taes.tennessee.edu.

University of California - California Agricultural Experiment Station. 1111 Franklin St., Rm. 6402, Oakland, CA 94607-5200. Phone: (510)987-0036 or (510)987-0060; Fax: (510)465-2659 or (510)451-2317; Email: steve.nation@ucop.edu • URL: http://ucanr.org/AES.shtml • Plant and animal biology, agricultural engineering and economics, soils, and water, including basic and applied studies directed toward solving problems of agriculture involved in production, storage, and transportation of over 300 commodities produced in California. Studies problems relating to forestry, human welfare and nutrition, pest management, mosquito control, and outdoor recreation. Operates on a statewide basis, with main units on Berkeley, Davis, and Riverside campuses of the University and ten research and extension centers throughout the state.

University of Nebraska—Lincoln - Agricultural Research Division. 207 Agricultural Hall, Lincoln, NE 68583-0704. Phone: (402)472-2045; Fax: (402)472-9071; Email: aclutter2@unl.edu.

STATISTICS SOURCES

Agricultural Statistics. U.S. Department of Agriculture National Agricultural Statistics Service. • Annual. $46 Individuals. Provides a wide variety of statistical data relating to agricultural production, supplies, consumption, prices/price-supports, foreign trade, costs, and returns, as well as farm labor, loans, income, and population. In many cases, historical data is shown annually for 10 years. In addition to farm data, includes detailed fishery statistics.

Survey of Current Business. U. S. Government Printing Office. • Published by Bureau of Economic Analysis, U. S. Department of Commerce. Presents a wide variety of business and economic data.

TRADE/PROFESSIONAL ASSOCIATIONS

Association of American Plant Food Control Officials. PO Box 3160, College Station, TX 77841-3160. Phone: (573)882-0007; Fax: (979)845-1389 • URL: http://www.aapfco.org • Represents officials of state agencies concerned with enforcement of laws relating to control of sale and distribution of mixed fertilizer and fertilizer materials.

FIBER INDUSTRY

See also COTTON INDUSTRY; JUTE INDUSTRY; SYNTHETIC TEXTILE FIBER INDUSTRY; WOOL AND WORSTED INDUSTRY

ABSTRACTS AND INDEXES

NTIS Alerts: Materials Sciences. U.S. Department of Commerce National Technical Information Service. • Biweekly. $130 per year. Covers ceramics, glass, coatings, composite materials, alloys, plastics, wood, paper, adhesives, fibers, lubricants, and related subjects.

Textile Technology Index™. EBSCO Publishing Inc. • Monthly. $545 Individuals. Includes indexing and abstracts for more than 470 periodicals.

DIRECTORIES

Directory of African Importers of Fibre Products. EXIM Infotek Private Ltd. • $150 Individuals. Covers: 35 African importers of fiberglass cloth and products, fiberglass resins, fiber products, and synthetic fiber. Entries include: Company name, postal address, telephone, fax, e-mail, website, contact person, designation, and product details.

Directory of Asian Importers of Fibre Products. EXIM Infotek Private Ltd. • $500 Individuals. Covers: 190 Asian importers of acrylic fiber, carbon fiber, fiberglass materials, fiber waste, fiberglass, fiberglass cloth, fiberglass products and cloth, fiber products, fiber materials, fiberglass chopped strands, fiberglass products, high-density fiberboard, natural fiber, optic fiber, polyester fiber, polyester staple fiber, polynosic staple fiber, synthetic fiber, viscose fiber, viscose rayon staple fiber, and vulcanized fiber. Entries include: Company name, postal address, telephone, fax, e-mail, website, contact person, designation, and product details.

Directory of Australia and New Zealand Importers of Fibre and Fibre Products. EXIM Infotek Private Ltd. • $150 Individuals. Covers: 20 Australian and New Zealand importers of acrylic fibers, fiber glass grating, fiber optic cables, fiber glass, fiber glass products and cloth, fiber glass chopped strands, fiber glass products, microfibers, PU fiber glass, staple fibers, synthetic fibers, and viscose fiber. Entries include: Company name, postal address, telephone, fax, e-mail, website, contact person, designation, and product details.

Directory of Chinese Importers of Fibre Products. EXIM Infotek Private Ltd. • $150 Individuals. Covers: 20 Chinese importers of fibers, high-density fiberboard, optic fibers, polyester staple fibers, and synthetic fibers. Entries include: Company name, postal address, telephone, fax, e-mail, website, contact person, designation, and product details.

Directory of Indian Importers of Fibre Products. EXIM Infotek Private Ltd. • $200 Individuals. Covers: 45 Indian importers of acrylic fiber, fiber waste, fiberglass, fiberglass cloth, fiberglass products, staple fiber, and synthetic fiber. Entries include: Company name, postal address, telephone, fax, e-mail, website, contact person, designation, and product details.

Directory of Japanese Importers of Fibre and Fibre Products. EXIM Infotek Private Ltd. • $200 Individuals. Covers: 40 Japanese importers of fiber glass cloth, fiber products, glass fibers, natural fiber, and synthetic fiber. Entries include: Company name, postal address, telephone, fax, e-mail, website, contact person, designation, and product details.

Directory of Middle East Importers of Fibre and Fibre Products. EXIM Infotek Private Ltd. • $300 Individuals. Covers: 100 Middle East importers of acrylic fibers, fiber optic equipment, fiber glass, fiber glass cloth and products, fiber products, glass fibers, polyester fibers, polyester staple fibers, synthetic fibers, and viscose fibers. Entries include: Company name, postal address, telephone, fax, e-mail, website, contact person, designation, and product details.

Directory of SAARC Importers of Fibre and Fibre Products. EXIM Infotek Private Ltd. • $150 Individuals. Covers: 20 SAARC Countries importers of acrylic fiber, carbon fiber, fiber glass materials, fiber glass products and cloth, fiber rods and sheets, Mexican fiber, mineral fiber board, natural fiber, palmyra fiber, polyester fiber, polyester staple fiber, staple fiber, synthetic fiber, viscose fiber, and vulcanized fiber. Entries include: Company name, postal address, telephone, fax, e-mail, website, contact person, designation, and product details.

Directory of South American Importers of Fibre and Fibre Products. EXIM Infotek Private Ltd. • $200 Individuals. Covers: 30 South American importers of fiberboard products, fiber glass cloth and products, fiber products, glass fiber, and synthetic fiber. Entries include: Company name, postal address, telephone, fax, e-mail, website, contact person, designation, and product details.

Directory of South Korean Manufacturers & Exporters of Cotton, Silk, Wool Raw & Waste. EXIM Infotek Private Ltd. • $5 Individuals. Covers: 40 South Korean manufacturers and exporters of raw cotton and vegetable textile fiber, raw wool and other animal fibers, silkworms and silkworm cocoons. Entries include: Company name, postal address, city, country, phone, fax, e-mail and websites, contact person, designation, and product details.

Materials Research Centres: A World Directory of Organizations and Programmes in Materials Science. Specialist Journals. • Biennial. $445.00. Profiles of research centers in 75 countries. Materials include plastics, metals, fibers, etc.

ONLINE DATABASES

Textile Technology Index™. EBSCO Publishing Inc. • Monthly. $545 Individuals. Includes indexing and abstracts for more than 470 periodicals.

World Textiles. Elsevier. • Provides abstracting and indexing from 1970 of worldwide textile literature (periodicals, books, pamphlets, and reports). Includes U. S., European, and British patent information. Updating is monthly. Inquire as to online cost and availability.

PERIODICALS AND NEWSLETTERS

Journal of Natural Fibers. The Haworth Press Inc. • Quarterly. $400.00 per year to libraries; $45.00 per year to individuals. Covers applications, technology, research, and world markets relating to fibers from silk, wool, cotton, flax, hemp, jute, etc. Previously *Natural Fibres*, published annually.

RESEARCH CENTERS AND INSTITUTES

HERTY Advanced Materials Development Center. 110 Brampton Rd., Savannah, GA 31408. Phone: (912)963-2600; Fax: (912)963-2614; Email: info@herty.com • URL: http://www.herty.com.

Institute of Textile Technology. College of Textiles, Box 8301, N Carolina State University, 2401 Research Dr., Raleigh, NC 27695-8301. Phone: (919)513-7583; Fax: (888)348-3512; Email: wgoneal@itt.edu • URL: http://www.itt.edu • Textile materials, processes, and technology, with an emphasis on processing, instrumentation, statistical quality control, and testing of raw materials and finished products. Special attention given to yarn manufacture, carding, finishing operations, operations research applications, computer applications to manufacturing, techniques for evaluation of fiber quality, chemical treatment of raw materials, mechanical blending of fibers, environmental and energy conservation, methods of improving fabric finishes, applications of statistical methods, simulation, expert systems, processing, and interrelation of production, costs, and quality in yarn and fabric manufacture.

Texas A&M University - Agribusiness, Food, and Consumer Economics Research Center. Department of Agricultural Economics, 600 John Kimbrough Blvd., Ste. 371, 2124 TAMU, College Station, TX 77843-2124. Phone: (979)845-5911; Fax: (979)845-6378; Email: afcerc@tamu.edu • URL: http://afcerc.tamu.edu • Marketing of Texas and U.S. agricultural products. Areas include domestic and foreign market opportunities, marketing policies and strategies, international competitiveness of Texas and the U.S. in the production and marketing of traditional bulk and high value/value-added products, impact of new technologies on markets and prices, efficiency of market information systems, market structure and performance, and consumer survey research.

Textile Materials Technology. Philadelphia University, 4201 Henry Ave., Philadelphia, PA 19144. Phone: (215)951-2700; Fax: (215)951-2651; Email: admissions@philau.edu • URL: http://www.philau.edu/textilemat • Many research areas, including industrial and nonwoven textiles.

TRADE/PROFESSIONAL ASSOCIATIONS

American Fiber Manufacturers Association. 1530 Wilson Blvd., Ste. 690, Arlington, VA 22209-2418. Phone: (703)875-0432; Fax: (703)875-0907 • URL: http://www.fibersource.com/afma/afma.htm • Producers of manufactured fibers used in apparel, household goods, industrial materials, and other types of products. Represents the industry in educational, governmental, and foreign trade matters. Distributes a video depicting production and end uses of manufactured fibers.

FIBER OPTICS INDUSTRY

ABSTRACTS AND INDEXES

Applied Science and Technology Index. EBSCO Publishing Inc. • 11/year. Indexes a wide variety of English language technical, industrial, and engineering periodicals.

Key Abstracts: Optoelectronics. Institution of Engineering and Technology. • Monthly. $1,138. Provides international coverage of journal and proceedings literature relating to fiber optics, lasers, and optoelectronics in general.

Science Citation Index. Thomson Reuters Intellectual Property and Science. • Weekly. Includes *Source Index*, *Citation Index*, *Permuterm Subject Index*, and *Corporate Index*. Provides researchers, administrators, faculty, and students with quick, powerful access to the bibliographic and citation information they need to find research data, analyze trends, journals and researchers, and share their findings.

CD-ROM DATABASES

Applied Science and Technology Abstracts. EBSCO Publishing Inc. • Citations for more than 700 prominent scientific, technical, engineering, and industrial periodicals.

Science Citation Index. Thomson Reuters Intellectual Property and Science. • Weekly. Includes *Source Index*, *Citation Index*, *Permuterm Subject Index*, and *Corporate Index*. Provides researchers, administrators, faculty, and students with quick, powerful access to the bibliographic and citation information they need to find research data, analyze trends, journals and researchers, and share their findings.

DIRECTORIES

Fiber Optics Yellow Pages: The International Optical Networks/Fiberoptics Yellow Pages. Information Gatekeepers Inc. • Annual. $89.95 print. Includes manufacturers of fiber optics products. Provides a glossary and a discussion of current uses of fiber optics. Formerly *Fiber Optics Yellow Pages*.

Lightwave Buyers Guide. PennWell Corp., Advanced Technology Div. • Lists manufacturers and distributors of fiberoptic systems and components.

ONLINE DATABASES

Applied Science and Technology Index Online. H.W. Wilson Co. • Provides online indexing of 500 major scientific, technical, industrial, and engineering periodicals. Time period is 1983 to date. Monthly updates. Inquire as to online cost and availability.

PERIODICALS AND NEWSLETTERS

Fiber Optics and Communications. Information Gatekeepers Inc. • Monthly. $695.00. Emphasis on the use of fiber optics in telecommunications.

Fiber Optics News. Access Intelligence L.L.C. • Weekly. $797.00 per year. Newsletter.

Fiberoptic Product News. Reed Elsevier Group plc Reed Business Information. • Monthly. $167.75 per year. Includes annual *Directory* and five *European editions*. Provides general coverage of the fiber optics industry, for both producers and users.

Optical Fiber Technology: Materials, Devices, and Systems. Elsevier. • Bimonthly. Individuals, $210.00 per year; institutions, $777.00 per year.

Optics and Photonics News. Optical Society of America. • Monthly. $99.00 per year. Includes print and online editions.

RESEARCH CENTERS AND INSTITUTES

Fiber and Electro Optics Research Center. Virginia Polytechnic Institute and State University, Dept. of Electrical Engineering, 106 Plantation Rd., Blacksburg, VA 24061. Phone: (540)231-7203; Fax: (540)231-4561; Email: roclaus@vt.edu • URL: http://www.unirel.vt.edu/history/extension_outreach_research/technology_development_centers.html.

Massachusetts Institute of Technology - Laboratory for Information and Decision Systems. 77 Massachusetts Ave., Rm. 32-D608, Cambridge, MA 02139. Phone: (617)253-2142; Fax: (617)253-3578; Email: willsky@mit.edu • URL: http://lids.mit.edu • Research areas include data communication networks and fiber optic networks.

Stanford University - Edward L. Ginzton Laboratory. Spilker Engineering and Applied Sciences, 348 Via Pueblo Mall, Stanford, CA 94305. Phone: (650)724-2765; Fax: (650)725-2533; Email: solgaard@stanford.edu • URL: http://www.stanford.edu/group/ginzton • Research fields include low-temperature physics and superconducting electronics.

STATISTICS SOURCES

U.S. Industry and Trade Outlook. U.S. Department of Commerce National Technical Information Service. • Annual. Produced by the International Trade Administration, U.S. Department of Commerce, in a "public-private" partnership with DRI/McGraw-Hill and Standard & Poor's. Provides basic data, outlook for the current year, and "Long-Term Prospects" (five-year projections) for a wide variety of products and services. Includes high technology industries. Formerly *U.S. Industrial Outlook*.

TRADE/PROFESSIONAL ASSOCIATIONS

Optical Society of America. 2010 Massachusetts Ave. NW, Washington, DC 20036-1023. Phone: 800-766-405A or (202)223-8130; Fax: (202)223-1096; Email: info@osa.org • URL: http://www.osa.org • Persons interested in any branch of optics: research, instruction, optical applications, manufacture, distribution of optical equipment, and physiological optics. Sponsors topical meetings.

FILES AND FILING (DOCUMENTS)

See also LIBRARY MANAGEMENT; OFFICE MANAGEMENT; OFFICE PRACTICE

CD-ROM DATABASES

LISA Plus. Cambridge Scientific Abstracts L.P. • Quarterly. $2,000 per year. CD-ROM version of Library Information and Science Abstracts, providing abstracting and indexing of the world's library and information science literature, 1969 to date. Contains more than 180,000 citations.

FILMS, MOTION PICTURE

See MOTION PICTURE INDUSTRY

FILTER INDUSTRY

ABSTRACTS AND INDEXES

Applied Science and Technology Index. EBSCO Publishing Inc. • 11/year. Indexes a wide variety of English language technical, industrial, and engineering periodicals.

Current Contents: Engineering, Computing and Technology. Thomson Reuters Intellectual Property and Science. • Weekly. $730 per year. Reproductions of contents pages of technical journals. Includes *Author Index*, *Address Directory*, *Current Book Contents*, and *Title Word Index*. Formerly *Current Contents: Engineering, Technology and Applied Sciences*.

DIRECTORIES

Directory of American Manufacturers & Exporters of Filters & Strainers--Industrial. EXIM Infotek Private Ltd. • $30 Individuals. Covers: 400 American manufacturers and exporters of air filters, ceramic and iodine portable camping filters, cloth filters, compressed-air filters, cooling towers water filter systems, counter-top and under counter filters, filter media, filter pads, filter paper, filter systems and pumps, filters, fire restoration, interference filters, media filters, sand filters and replacement filter elements, screens, water filters for commercial, consumer water filters for home, business and restaurant, water filtration equipment, water filters, water filtration and purification conditioning, water filtration and purification equipment, water filtration and purification ultraviolet, water filtration equipment, water filtration treatment, water filtration and purification equipment, water purification and treatment systems, and water purifiers. Entries include: Company name, postal address, city, country, telephone, fax, e-mail and websites, contact person, designation, and product details.

Directory of South Korean Manufacturers & Exporters of Filters & Strainers--Industrial. EXIM Infotek Private Ltd. • $10 Individuals. Covers: 50 South Korean manufacturers and exporters of bolting and filter cloths/gauzes, filters, filters and strainers for processing industries, filters and strainers-metal, line filters, and water and waste water filters. Entries include: Company name, postal address, city, country, phone, fax, e-mail and websites, contact person, designation, and product details.

Directory of Taiwanese Manufacturers & Exporters of Filters & Strainers--Industrial. EXIM Infotek Private Ltd. • $10 Individuals. Covers: 80 Taiwanese manufacturers and exporters of bolting and filter cloths/gauzes, filters and strainers for processing industries, filters and strainers-metal, glue for air filters, and water and waste water filters. Entries include: Company name, postal address, city, country, phone, fax, e-mail and websites, contact person, designation, products detail.

ONLINE DATABASES

Applied Science and Technology Index Online. H.W. Wilson Co. • Provides online indexing of 500 major scientific, technical, industrial, and engineering periodicals. Time period is 1983 to date. Monthly updates. Inquire as to online cost and availability.

Thomas Register Online. Thomas Publishing Company L.L.C. • Provides concise information on approximately 194,000 U. S. companies, mainly manufacturers, with over 50,000 product classifications. Indexes over 115,000 trade names. Information is updated semiannually. Inquire as to online cost and availability.

PERIODICALS AND NEWSLETTERS

Filtration News. Eagle Publications Inc. • Bimonthly. Controlled circulation. Emphasis is on new filtration products for industrial use.

Industrial Equipment News. Thomas Publishing Company L.L.C. • Monthly. Contains new product information for manufacturing industries.

Liquid Filtration Newsletter. The McIlvaine Co. • Description: Focuses on the liquid filtration industry, providing information on technical developments and reports on individual companies in the field. Recurring features include a calendar of events and a column titled New & Different.

New Equipment Digest. Intertec Publishing. • Monthly. Magazine (tabloid) showcasing new or improved equipment, products, materials, and components. Formerly *Material Handling Engineering*.

New Equipment Reporter: New Products Industrial News. DeRoche Publications. • Monthly. Controlled circulation.

Processing. Putman Media Inc. • 14 times a year. $54.00 per year. Emphasis is on descriptions of new products for all areas of industrial processing, including valves, controls, filters, pumps, compressors, fluidics, and instrumentation.

FINANCE

See also ACCOUNTING; BUSINESS; COMPUTERS IN FINANCE; CORPORATE FINANCE; COUNTY FINANCE; FINANCIAL MANAGEMENT; INTERNATIONAL FINANCE; INVESTMENTS; MUNICIPAL FINANCE

ABSTRACTS AND INDEXES

Business Periodicals Index Retrospective. EBSCO Publishing Inc. • 11/year. Quarterly and annual cumulations.

NTIS Alerts: Business & Economics. U.S. Department of Commerce National Technical Information Service. • Biweekly. $130 per year. Covers consumer affairs, minority enterprises, marketing and economics, international commerce, banking, and finance.

Social Sciences Citation Index. Thomson Reuters Corp. • Weekly. Product is accessed via *Web of Science*.

BIOGRAPHICAL SOURCES

Who's Who in Finance and Business. Marquis Who's Who L.L.C. • Biennial. $349 Individuals. Provides over 21,000 concise biographies of business leaders in all fields.

CD-ROM DATABASES

Business Abstracts with Full Text. EBSCO Publishing Inc. • Includes full text articles from more than 460 business publications from 1982 to present. Indexing for nearly 880 publications.

OECD Statistical Compendium. Organization for Economic Cooperation and Development. • Semiannual. $1,905.00 per year for 1 to 10 users. CD-ROM contains more than 730,000 monthly, quarterly, and annual time series for OECD countries, 1960 to date. Includes fully searchable data on agriculture, food, economic indicators, national accounts, employment, energy, finance, industry, technology, and foreign trade. Results can be displayed in various forms.

Social Sciences Citation Index. Thomson Reuters Corp. • Weekly. Product is accessed via *Web of Science*.

DIRECTORIES

Accounts Receivable (Financing) Directory. Info-Group Inc. • Annual. Number of listings: 19,980.

Entries include: Name, address, phone, size of advertisement, name of owner or manager, number of employees, year first in "Yellow Pages." Compiled from telephone company "Yellow Pages," nationwide.

Airfinance Annual. Euromoney Institutional Investor P.L.C. • Annual. $450 Individuals. Covers: About 1,200 banks, finance houses, insurers, consultants, brokers, legal consultants, accountants, and leasing companies serving the aviation industry worldwide. Entries include: Company name, address, phone, e-mail, contact, key personnel, servicers provided, branch office names and locations.

American Library Association Guide to Information Access. Library and Information Technology Association. • $18.95. Publication includes: List of reference sources for areas including business and finance, consumer information, education, jobs and careers, and science and technology. Principal content of publication is a guide to general research methods.

Asia Corporate Profile and National Finance. Dataline Asia-Pacific Ltd. • Annual. $70. Covers: about 1,900 companies in Asia; includes list of the 500 largest companies. Entries include: Company name, address, phone, fax, telex, names and titles of key personnel, number of employees, financial data.

Asian Finance Directory. Mead Ventures Inc. • $195. Covers: about 400 Asian financial companies, banks, securities firms, venture capitalists, and real estate financers in the United States. Entries include: Company name, address, phone, telex, fax, names and titles of key personnel, number of employees, geographical area served, financial data, local offices, subsidiaries or parent companies, description of services provided, and description of projects.

Business and Financial News Media. Larriston Communications. • Annual. $99 book. Covers: over 300 daily newspapers with at least 50,000 in circulation and a business or finance correspondent; television stations and all-news radio stations in the largest 40 markets; periodicals of general or business and finance interest; syndicated business and financial columnists and newswriters; news and wire services; and free-lance writers whose specialties include business and financial topics. Entries include: Outlet name, address, phone, names and titles of contacts who cover business, finance, or economic news; news services used; circulation or audience figures.

Directory of Buyout Financing Sources. Buyout Publications, Inc. • Annual. $445 plus $9.00 shipping. Covers: over 1,000 sources of acquisition financing, including banks, asset-based lenders, small business investment companies, insurance companies, and venture capital firms. Entries include: Company name, address, phone, E-mail, URL, names and titles of key personnel, financial data, type of company and size requirements, underwriting criteria, equity requirements, post-closing role, information required, response time, sample transactions. Also promoted under title 'Financing Sourcebook for Buyouts & Acquisitions.'.

European Directory of Financial Information Sources. Euromonitor International Business Reference Div. • $160. Covers: Sources of financial information for companies in Europe, including official sources and publications, libraries, information services, banks and other financial institutions, accountancy firms and tax advisors, stockbrokers, stock exchanges, databases, indexes, abstracts, banking journals, and European business contacts. Entries include: Name, address, phone, fax, year founded.

Financial Review of Alien Insurers. National Association of Insurance Commissioners. • Annual. $275 per year, including updates; payment with order. Covers: alien insurance companies operating in the United States market. Entries include: Company name, address, balance sheet, operating statement, financial statement with notes, and names of auditors; description of trust account with location, valuation, and expiration date.

Fortune--Deals of the Year Issue. Time Inc. • $5. Publication includes: 50 largest United States corporate financial transactions, including mergers, acquisitions, leveraged buyouts, and debt and equity offerings. Entries include: Companies involved, value (value and percent of book value), date and type of transaction, type of industry, financial intermediary, fee charged.

The Global Directory of Financial Information Vendors. QSU Publishing. • $95. Covers: On-line financial services vendors and their operating systems. Database includes: Geographic market information and principal applications.

Guia Senior. Guia Senior. • Covers: Argentina's national government, provincial government, diplomatic corps, foreign diplomatic corps, armed forces, political groups, banks, saving banks, loan companies, stocks, investment, credit companies, financial associations, insurance companies, stock exchange, and advertising agencies.

Guide to the Canadian Financial Services Industry. Globe Interactive. • Annual. $349.99. Covers: over 800 financial service companies operating in Canada. Database includes: Executive listings with biographical information; lists of government agencies which deal with the financial services industry, industry associations, and top accounting firms in Canada. Entries include: Company name, address, phone, company officers and directors, regional offices, total assets, revenue, net income, number of branches, number of employees, Canadian Standard Industrial Classification.

Indiana Financial Institutions Directory. Indiana Bankers Association. • $35 Members. Covers: State and federal agencies associated with the financial institutions industry. Entries include: Name, address, phone, officers and directors of every Indiana bank, savings and loan and credit union, plus listings of officers, directors, total assets, deposits, correspondent banks, counties and population.

Kompass Finance. Kompass France. • Annual. $1,650. Database covers: Financial information for approximately 50,000 French industrial and commercial firms. Database includes: Company name, address, phone, products and services; financial data and alliances.

Major Financial Institutions of the World. Cengage Learning Inc. • $1,460 Individuals. 2012. 16th edition. eBook. Published by Graham & Whiteside. Contains detailed information on more than 10,000 important financial institutions in various countries. Includes banks, investment companies, and insurance companies.

The MEED Middle East Financial Directory. EMAP Business International. • Annual. $120. Covers: 4,000 banks and financial institutions in the Middle East. Entries include: Company name, address, phone, telex, financial statistics, branch offices.

Plunkett's On-Line Trading, Finance, and Investment Web Sites Almanac. Plunkett Research Ltd. • Annual. $149.99. Provides profiles and usefulness rankings of financial Web sites. Sites are rated from 1 to 5 for specific uses. Includes CD-ROM.

Project Finance Yearbook. Euromoney Institutional Investor P.L.C. • $375 Individuals. Contains innovative project finance modelling, case studies of recent ground-breaking projects, advice on managing both country and project risk, legal and contractual problems and how they were solved. Covers: Approximately 3,000 companies involved in project finance worldwide. Entries include: Name, address, phone, fax, e-mail, names and titles of key personnel.

Sunday Telegraph Business Finance Directory. Graham & Trotman Ltd. • Annual. $219. Covers: 900 institutions providing financial services for businesses and sources of financial advice. Entries include: Institution name, address, phone, telex number, contact name, requirements, conditions.

The Times 1,000: The Indispensable Annual Review of the World's Leading Industrial and Financial Companies. Times Books Ltd. • Annual. $32.50. Covers: 1,000 leading companies in the United Kingdom; 1,000 leading companies in Europe; leading firms in the United States, Canada, Australia, South Africa, Ireland, Hong Kong, and Japan. Entries include: For all companies--Company name and address. For British firms--Company name, names of chairman and managing director, sales, profits, capital, number of employees, and ranks and ratios. Listings for other firms vary in detail.

Who's Who in Asian Banking & Finance. Bibliotheque: Worldwide. • Annual. $210 plus $7.50 shipping. Covers: 1,851 prominent and influential bankers and investors and 1,552 banks and financial institutions in Asia. Entries include: For individuals--Name, address, phone, fax, current job title and function, other professional, educational, and personal background details. For companies--Name, address, phone, fax, names and titles of key personnel.

Who's Who in Finance and Business. Marquis Who's Who L.L.C. • Biennial. $349 Individuals. Provides over 21,000 concise biographies of business leaders in all fields.

World Financial System. Financial Times Healthcare. • Irregular. $165. Publication includes: Descriptions of 56 international economic organizations, including monetary, developmental, trade, and petroleum organizations. Database includes: Essays on international monetary relations from 1944 to 1992, including summaries of events, conferences, and important documents. Entries include: Name, address, name of chief executive, background, functions, member countries, structure, operations, description of activities, conferences, etc.

E-BOOKS

Business Applications and Computational Intelligence. Cengage Learning Inc. • 2005. eBook. Addresses the need for a compact overview of the diversity of applications in a number of business disciplines, and consists of chapters written by leading international researchers. Chapters cover most fields of business, including: marketing, data mining, e-commerce, production and operations, finance, decision-making, and general management.

ENCYCLOPEDIAS AND DICTIONARIES

Encyclopedia of American Business. Cengage Learning Inc. • 2013. eBook. 2 volumes. 800 essays. A guide to the nuts and bolts of business jargon. Difficult ideas are explained in straightforward language to help non-specialists, students, and general readers understand the complex and sometimes confusing concepts and terms that are used in business. Five general areas of business are covered: accounting, banking, finance, marketing, and management.

Encyclopedia of Business and Finance. Cengage Learning Inc. • 2014. $485. 3rd edition. Two volumes. Published by Macmillan Reference USA. Contains articles on accounting, business administration, banking, finance, management information systems, and marketing.

Everyday Finance: Economics, Personal Money Management, and Entrepreneurship. Cengage Learning Inc. • $258 Individuals. 2008. 2 volumes. Contains 300 topical entries that are organized into 3 units: How the Economy Works; Personal Finance: Buying, Borrowing, Saving, and Insuring; and The World of Business. eBook available. Inquire for pricing.

GENERAL WORKS

Accounting and Business Research. Routledge. • 6/year. $137 Individuals print. Publication for the banking, finance, and accounting industries.

Business I. ITHAKA JSTOR, the Journal Storage Project. • Contains more than 2 million pages from 47 titles in the fields of economics and finance, accounting, labor relations, marketing, management, operations research, and risk assessment.

Enterprise Development and Microfinance Journal. Practical Action. • Quarterly. $104 Other countries print. Journal covering small enterprise development.

Financial Concepts and Tools for Business Management. American CPE Inc. • Contains detailed training information covering basic financial concepts and their use in business management settings.

Small Business Controller. Thomson RIA. • Quarterly. $76 Individuals. Source for technical information in accounting and financial management. For financial managers in growing and emerging businesses.

INTERNET DATABASES

BanxQuote Banking, Mortgage, and Finance Center. BanxQuote, Inc. Phone: (914)722-1600; Fax: (914)722-6630; Email: info@banx.com • URL: http://www.banx.com • Daily. Web site quotes interest rates paid by banks around the country on various savings products, as well as rates paid by consumers for automobile loans, mortgages, credit cards, home equity loans, and personal loans. Also provided: stock quotes, indexes, stock options, futures trading data, economic indicators, and links to many other financial sites.

Business 2.0 Web Guide to the Best Business Links. Business 2.0 Media Inc. Phone: (415)293-4800; Email: support@business2.com • URL: http://www.business2.com/webguide • Web site presents an extensive, searchable directory of links to "the best, most informative, and authoritative web pages." Twenty main categories cover business, finance, career, company information, people, and technology topics, with thousands of subtopics, all linking to Web sites recommended by experienced business researchers. Fees: Free.

Business Week Online. McGraw-Hill. Phone: (212)512-2511; Fax: (684)842-6101 • URL: http://www.businessweek.com • Web site provides complete contents of current issue of *Business Week* plus "BW Daily" with additonal business news, financial market quotes, and corporate information from Standard & Poor's. Includes various features, such as "Banking Center" with mortgage and interest data, and "Interactive Computer Buying Guide." The "Business Week Archive" is fully searchable back to 1996.

EBSCO Information Services. EBSCO Publishing Inc. 10 Estes St., Ipswich, MA 01938-2106. Phone: 800-653-2726 or (978)356-6500; Fax: (978)356-6565; Email: information@ebscohost.com • URL: http://www.ebscohost.com • Fee-based Web site providing Internet access to a wide variety of databases, including business-related material. Full text is available for many periodical titles, with daily updates. Fees: Apply.

Factiva. Dow Jones Reuters Business Interactive, LLC. Phone: 800-369-7466 or (609)452-1511; Fax: (609)520-5770; Email: solutions@factiva.com • URL: http://www.factiva.com • Fee-based Web site provides "global news and business information through Web sites and content integration solutions." Includes Dow Jones and Reuters newswires, The Wall Street Journal, and more than 7,000 other sources of current news, historical articles, market research reports, and investment analysis. Content includes 96 major U. S. newspapers, 900 non-English sources, trade publications, media transcripts, country profiles, news photos, etc.

Fedstats. Federal Interagency Council on Statistical Policy. Phone: (202)395-7254 • URL: http://www.fedstats.gov • Web site features an efficient search facility for full-text statistics produced by more than 100 federal agencies, including the Census Bureau, the Bureau of Economic Analysis, and the Bureau of Labor Statistics. Boolean searches can be made within one agency or for all agencies combined. Links are offered to international statistical bureaus, including the UN, IMF, OECD, UNESCO, Eurostat, and 20 individual countries. Fees: Free.

The Financial Post. National Post Online. Phone: 800-805-1184 or (244)383-2300; Fax: (416)383-2443 • URL: http://www.nationalpost.com/financialpost/ • Provides a broad range of Canadian business news online, with daily updates. Includes news, opinion, and special reports, as well as "Investing," "Money Rates," "Market Watch," and "Daily Mutual Funds." Allows advanced searching (Boolean operators), with links to various other sites. Fees: Free.

FreeLunch.com. Economy.com, Inc. Phone: (610)696-8700; Fax: (610)696-1678 • URL: http://www.freelunch.com • Web site provides free access to more than 200 million economic and financial data series, covering industry, demographics, labor markets, prices, retail sales, government spending, trade, interest rates, housing starts, the stock market, etc. Data is available in either chart or table form. Searching is offered. Free, but registration required. Economy.com, Inc. also offers fee-based economic analysis at *The Dismal Scientist* site (www.dismal.com).

InSite 2. Intelligence Data/Thomson Financial. Phone: 800-654-0393 or (617)856-1890; Fax: (617)737-3182; Email: intelligence.data@tfn.com • URL: http://www.insite2.gale.com/ • Fee-based Web site consolidates information in a "Base Pack" consisting of Business InSite, Market InSite, and Company InSite. Optional databases are Consumer InSite, Health and Wellness InSite, Newsletter InSite, and Computer InSite. Includes fulltext content from more than 2,500 trade publications, journals, newsletters, newspapers, analyst reports, and other sources. Continuous updating. Formerly produced by The Gale Group.

Nexis.com. Lexis-Nexis Group. Phone: 800-227-4908 or (937)865-6800; Fax: (937)865-6909; Email: webmaster@prod.lexis-nexis.com • URL: http://www.nexis.com • Fee-based Web site offers searching of about 2.8 billion documents in some 30,000 news, business, and legal information sources. Features include a subject directory covering 1,200 topics in 34 categories and a Company Dossier containing information on more than 500,000 public and private companies. Boolean searching is offered.

ProQuest. ProQuest L.L.C. 789 E Eisenhower Pkwy., Ann Arbor, MI 48106-1346. Phone: 800-521-0600 or (734)761-4700; Fax: (734)662-4554; Email: info@proquest.com • URL: http://www.proquest.com • Fee-based Web site providing Internet access to more than 3,000 periodicals, newspapers, and other publications. Many items are available full-text, with daily updates. Includes extensive corporate and financial information. Fees: Apply.

Wall Street Journal Interactive Edition. Dow Jones & Co., Inc. 1211 Avenue of the Americas, New York, NY 10036. Phone: 800-369-5663; Email: service@dowjones.com • URL: http://new.dowjones.com • Fee-based Web site providing online searching of worldwide information from *The Wall Street Journal*. Includes "Company Snapshots," "The Journal's Greatest Hits," "Index to Market Data," "Journal Links," etc. Financial price quotes are available. Fees: $49.00 per year; $29.00 per year to print subscribers.

ONLINE DATABASES

Banking Information Source. ProQuest L.L.C. • Provides indexing and abstracting of periodical and other literature from 1982 to date, with weekly updates. Covers the financial services industry: banks, savings institutions, investment houses, credit unions, insurance companies, and real estate organizations. Emphasis is on marketing and management. Inquire as to online cost and availability. (Formerly *FINIS: Financial Industry Information Service*.).

Compustat. Standard and Poor's. • Financial data on publicly held U.S. and some foreign corporations; data held for 20 years. Inquire as to online cost and availability.

Wilson Business Abstracts Online. H.W. Wilson Co. • Indexes and abstracts 600 major business periodicals, plus the *Wall Street Journal* and the business section of the *New York Times*. Indexing is from 1982, abstracting from 1990, with the two newspapers included from 1993. Updated weekly. Inquire as to online cost and availability. (*Business Periodicals Index* without abstracts is also available online.).

OTHER SOURCES

BNA's Banking Report: Legal and Regulatory Developments in the Financial Services Industry. Bloomberg BNA. • Weekly. $1,221.00 per year. Two looseleaf volumes. Emphasis on federal regulations.

Business Rankings Annual (BRA). Cengage Learning Inc. • Annual. $584 Individuals. A guide to lists and rankings appearing in major business publications. The top ten names are listed in each case.

Finance and Accounting for Nonfinancial Managers. American Management Association Extension Institute. • $19.95. Looseleaf. Self-study course. Emphasis is on practical explanations, examples, and problem solving. Quizzes and a case study are included.

PERIODICALS AND NEWSLETTERS

Abacus: A Journal of Accounting, Finance and Business Studies. John Wiley & Sons Inc. Wiley-Blackwell. • Quarterly. $597 Institutions Australia & New Zealand, print and online. Journal covering academic and professional aspects of accounting, finance and business.

American Banker: The Financial Services Daily. SourceMedia Inc. • Daily. $895.00 per year. Provides news of banking, investment products, mortgages, credit unions, finance, bank technology, and legal developments.

Barron's: The Dow Jones Business and Financial Weekly. Dow Jones & Co., Inc. • Weekly (Mon.). $100.94 Individuals. Business and finance magazine.

Business Credit. National Association of Credit Management. • 9/year. $54 U.S.. Formerly *Credit and Financial Management*. Covers business and trade credit as well as risk management.

Business Finance. Intertec Publishing. • Quarterly. $39 Individuals. Magazine reporting on key financial issues, strategies, trends and technologies, significant to senior finance executives.

Business Money. Business Money Ltd. • Monthly. £149 Individuals single copy print, online and app. Professional magazine covering finance, business banking, and related topics.

Commercial and Financial Chronicle. William B. Dana Co. • Weekly. $140.00. per year.

Financial History: Chronicling the History of America's Capital Markets. Museum of American Finance. • Quarterly. Membership. Contains articles on early stock and bond markets and trading in the U. S., with photographs and other illustrations. Current trading in rare and unusual, obsolete stock and bond certificates is featured. Formerly *Friends of Financial History*.

Financial Markets, Institutions, and Instruments. New York University, Salomon Center. Blackwell Publishing Inc. • Five times a year. Institutions, $338.00 per year. Includes online edition. Edited to "bridge the gap between the academic and professional finance communities." Special fifth issue each year provides surveys of developments in four areas: money and banking, derivative securities, corporate finance, and fixed-income securities.

Fortune India: Indian Magazine for Business, Finance and Investment. Fortune Publications Private Ltd. • Biweekly. Rs 555 Individuals. Trade publication on premier business, finance and investment.

Fortune Magazine. Time Inc., Business Information Group. • Biweekly. $19.99 all access. Edited for top executives and upper-level managers.

Global Business and Finance Review. Global Business and Finance Review. • Semiannual. $50 Individuals. The GBFR is a referred journal specializing in global business and finance.

Investor's Business Daily. Investor's Business Daily, Inc. • Daily. $329 Individuals print. Business and financial newspaper.

Mathematical Finance: An International Journal of Mathematics, Statistics, and Financial Economics. Blackwell Publishing Inc. • Quarterly. $1,453 Institutions print only. Covers the use of sophisticated mathematical tools in financial research and practice.

Paytech. American Payroll Association. • Monthly. Membership. Covers the details and technology of payroll administration.

The Quarterly Review of Economics and Finance. JAI Press. • Quarterly. $142 Individuals. Publishes high quality manuscripts that cover topics in the areas of economics, financial economics and finance.

Schmalenbach Business Review. Verlagsgruppe Handelsblatt GmbH. • Quarterly. $135 Institutions.

U.S. Banker. SourceMedia Inc. • Monthly. $65.00 per year. Edited for bank executives and managers. Covers a wide variety of banking and financial topics.

WebFinance. SourceMedia Inc. • Semimonthly. $995.00 per year. Newsletter (also available online at www.webfinance.net). Covers the Internet-based provision of online financial services by banks, online brokers, mutual funds, and insurance companies. Provides news stories, analysis, and descriptions of useful resources.

RESEARCH CENTERS AND INSTITUTES

Agency for Healthcare Research and Quality - Center for Financing, Access, and Cost Trends. John M. Eisenberg Bldg., 540 Gaither Rd., Rockville, MD 20850. Phone: (301)427-1104; Fax: (301)427-1276; Email: joel.cohen@ahrq.hhs.gov • URL: http://www.ahrq.gov/about/cfact • Cost and financing of health care and access to health care services and related trends. Develops data sets to support policy and behavioral research and analyses.

American Institute for Economic Research. 250 Division St., Great Barrington, MA 01230-1000. Phone: 888-528-1216; Fax: (413)528-0103; Email: info@aier.org • URL: http://www.aier.org • Through research and publications, provides "information on economic and financial subjects that is useful and completely independent of special interests." Sponsors a fellowship program for graduate study of economics at the institute and in absentia.

Financial Executives Research Foundation. Financial Executives International. 1250 Headquarters Plz., West Tower, 7th Fl., Morristown, NJ 07960. Phone: (973)765-1000; Fax: (973)765-1018; Email: mhollein@financialexecutives.org • URL: http://www.financialexecutives.org • Publishes research in business management, with emphasis on corporate financial management issues. Maintains inquiry services.

London School of Economics and Political Science - Centre for Research into Economics and Finance in Southern Africa. Rm. G409, 20 Kingsway, Houghton St., London WC2A 2AE, United Kingdom. Phone: 44 20 79557505; Email: j.leape@lse.ac.uk • URL: http://www.lse.ac.uk/researchAndExpertise/units/CREFSA/home.aspx • Private capital flows in Southern Africa; financial regulation and the development of financial systems in Southern Africa; prospects for regional trade and monetary integration in the SADC.

Monash University - Centre for Research in Accounting and Finance. Wellington Rd., Bldg. 11E, Clayton, VIC 3168, Australia. Phone: 61 3 99052389; Fax: 61 3 99055475; Email: kim.langfield-smith@buseco.monash.edu.au • URL: http://www.buseco.monash.edu.au/aaf/research/ • Accounting and finance.

New York University - Salomon Center for the Study of Financial Institutions. Stern School of Business, 44 W 4th St., Ste. 9-160, New York, NY 10012. Phone: (212)998-0700; Fax: (212)995-4220; Email: mrichar0@stern.nyu.edu • URL: http://w4.stern.nyu.edu/salomon • Evaluates changing structure of financial instruments and markets and the use of these instruments and markets in financial intermediation and the management of risk by financial institutions and business corporations. Recent projects include modern portfolio management and the prudent man rule, role of financial futures and options in large financial institutions' investment portfolios, information and stock market efficiency, composition of individual investment portfolios, hedging and trading performance of new financial futures and options, new financial instruments, reforming Japan's financial markets, reconfiguration of the insurance industry, and restructuring the U.S. financial and insurance sectors.

Princeton University - Bendheim Center for Finance. Department of Economics, 26 Prospect Ave., Princeton, NJ 08540-5296. Phone: (609)258-0770; Fax: (609)258-0771; Email: jessicab@princeton.edu • URL: http://www.princeton.edu/bcf • Research areas include securities markets, portfolio analysis, credit markets, and corporate finance. Emphasis is on quantitative and mathematical perspectives.

Queen's University of Belfast - Finance and Economics Research Group. Management School, Rm. 25, G07, 25 University Sq., Belfast BT7 1NN, United Kingdom. Phone: 44 28 90975126; Email: k.close@qub.ac.uk • URL: http://www.qub-efrg.com • Economic theory; econometrics; labor economics; microstructure finance; international finance; and financial institutions, including nonprofits.

Rice University - Center for Computational Finance and Economic Systems. Department of Statistics, MS-138, Houston, TX 77251-1892. Phone: (713)348-5839; Fax: (713)348-5476; Email: ensor@rice.edu • URL: http://www.cofes.rice.edu • Computational finance and economic systems, including credit risk management, pricing financial derivatives, emerging markets, energy markets, impact of politics on world finance, and risk fundamentals and integration of risk.

Stockholm School of Economics - Department of Accounting - Center for Accounting and Managerial Finance. PO Box 6501, SE-113 83 Stockholm, Sweden. Phone: 46 8 7369000; Fax: 46 8 318186; Email: info@hhs.se • URL: http://www.economicresearch.se/amf • Accounting theory, management accounting, financial accounting, and financial markets.

Universitat Pompeu Fabra - Research Center in Financial Economics and Accounting. Ramon Trias Fargas, 25-27, E-08005 Barcelona, Spain. Phone: 34 93 5421619; Fax: 34 93 5421746; Email: xavier.freixas@upf.edu • URL: http://www.crefc.upf.edu • Financial economics, accounting, and business.

University of Amsterdam - Center for Nonlinear Dynamics in Economics and Finance. Department of Economics & Econometrics, Roetersstraat 11, 1018 Amsterdam, Netherlands. Phone: 31 20 5254217; Fax: 31 20 5254349; Email: c.h.hommes@uva.nl • URL: http://www1.fee.uva.nl/cendef • Nonlinear dynamics in economics and finance.

University of Cyprus - Center for Banking and Financial Research. School of Economics & Management, Nicosia 1678, Cyprus. Phone: 357 2 2892496; Fax: 357 2 2892421; Email: hermes@ucy.ac.cy • URL: http://www.ucy.ac.cy/hermes/en • Computational finance and economics.

STATISTICS SOURCES

Statistical Information on the Financial Services Industry. American Bankers Association. • Annual. Members, $150.00; non-members, $275.00. Presents a wide variety of data relating to banking and financial services, including consumer economics, personal finance, credit, government loans, capital markets, and international banking.

Survey of Current Business. U. S. Government Printing Office. • Published by Bureau of Economic Analysis, U. S. Department of Commerce. Presents a wide variety of business and economic data.

TRADE/PROFESSIONAL ASSOCIATIONS

Afghanistan Microfinance Association. House No 547 St. 3, Taimani Project, District 4, Kabul, Afghanistan. Phone: 93 799 308876; Email: info@ama.org.af • URL: http://www.ama.org.af • Promotes the microfinance sector of Afghanistan. Seeks to enhance the security measures between microfinance institutions (MFIs) and increase government support in terms of securing microfinance operations. Develops and delivers a number of training modules in local languages to ensure the best use of the training programs by employees of the microfinance sector.

American Accounts Payable Association. 660 N Main Ave., Ste. 200, San Antonio, TX 78205-1217. Phone: (210)630-4373; Fax: (210)630-4410; Email: membership@americanap.org • URL: http://www.americanap.org • Seeks to uphold the standards of practice in the accounts payable profession. Fosters the professional development of members. Offers comprehensive educational programs for accounts payable professionals.

American Finance Association. University of California, Haas School of Business, Berkeley, CA 94720-1900. Phone: 800-835-6770 or (781)388-8599; Fax: (781)388-8232; Email: pyle@haas.berkeley.edu • URL: http://www.afajof.org • College and university professors of economics and finance, bankers, treasurers, analysts, financiers and others interested in financial problems; libraries and other institutions. Seeks to improve public understanding of financial problems and to provide for exchange of analytical ideas. Areas of special interest include: corporate finance, investments, banking and international and public finance.

American Financial Services Association. 919 18th St. NW, Ste. 300, Washington, DC 20006. Email: info@afsamail.org • URL: http://www.afsaonline.org • Represents companies whose business is primarily direct credit lending to consumers and/or the purchase of sales finance paper on consumer goods. Has members that have insurance and retail subsidiaries; some are themselves subsidiaries of highly diversified parent corporations. Encourages the business of financing individuals and families for necessary and useful purposes at reasonable charges, including interest; promotes consumer understanding of basic money management principles as well as constructive uses of consumer credit. Includes educational services such as films, textbooks and study units for the classroom and budgeting guides for individuals and families. Compiles statistical reports; offers seminars.

American Legal Finance Association. 228 Park Ave. S, No. 23315, New York, NY 10003. Phone: (212)837-2911 • URL: http://www.americanlegalfin.com • Develops an awareness of the legal funding industry. Works to establish legal and regulatory frameworks to meet the needs and concerns of all parties interested in legal funding. Establishes and maintains ethical standards and fair business practices within the legal funding industry.

American Payroll Association. 660 N Main Ave., Ste. 100, San Antonio, TX 78205-1217. Phone: (210)226-4600 or (210)224-6406; Fax: (210)226-4027 or (210)224-6038; Email: APA@americanpayroll.org • URL: http://www.americanpayroll.org • Payroll employees. Works to increase members' skills and professionalism through education and mutual support. Represents the interest of members before legislative bodies. Conducts training courses. Operates speakers' bureau; conducts educational programs. Administers the certified payroll professional program of recognition.

Asia Pacific Loan Market Association. Jardine House, 32nd Fl., One Connaught Pl., Central, Hong Kong, Hong Kong, China. Phone: 852 28263500 • URL: http://www.aplma.com • Promotes growth and liquidity in the primary and secondary loan markets. Facilitates the standardization of primary and secondary loan documentation. Develops standard trading, settlement and valuation procedures. Organizes educational and social functions for syndicated loan professionals. Acts as a liaison between major loan market players and regional regulators.

Asset Based Finance Association. 3rd Fl., 20 Hill Rise, Surrey, Richmond TW10 6UA, United Kingdom. Phone: 44 20 8332 9955; Fax: 44 20 8332 2585 • URL: http://www.abfa.org.uk • Brokers, business agents, and factors in the United Kingdom. Promotes and protects members' interests in the fields of factoring and invoice discounting. Conducts educational and research programs. Maintains a code of conduct; fosters the advancement of knowledge and experience; awards diplomas to students. Disseminates information; compiles statistics.

Association for Financial Professionals. 4520 E West Hwy., Ste. 750, Bethesda, MD 20814. Phone: (301)907-2862; Fax: (301)907-2864 • URL: http://www.afponline.org • Seeks to establish a national forum for the exchange of concepts and techniques related to improving the management of treasury and the careers of professionals through research, education, publications and recognition of the treasury management profession through a certification program. Conducts educational programs. Operates career center.

Association of African American Financial Advisors. PO Box 4853, Capitol Heights, MD 20791. Phone: (240)396-2530; Fax: (888)392-5702; Email: info@aaafainc.cm • URL: http://aaafainc.com • Seeks to develop and foster professional relationships among African American professionals working in the financial advisory industry. Provides assistance and nurturing for those families that seek to improve their opportunities for participating and prospering financially in an economically progressive society. Strives to create support networks for minority financial professionals. Provides a forum for further education, training and visibility of its members.

Association of Corporate Treasurers of Southern Africa. PO Box 5853, Cresta 2118, South Africa. Phone: 27 11 4821512; Fax: 27 11 4821996 • URL: http://www.actsa.org.za • Provides a forum for the promotion of the common interests of corporate treasurers in Southern Africa. Provides learning and networking opportunities for its members.

Association of Corporate Treasurers Singapore. Block 51, Telok Blangah Dr., No. 06-142, Singapore 100051, Singapore. • URL: http://www.act.org.sg • Provides a platform for the exchange of ideas and information relating to treasury. Enhances treasury management skills through training and education. Facilitates a platform for dialogue between the industry and the government. Promotes the growth of the treasury profession to help Singapore develop into a financial hub in the region.

Association of Microfinance Organizations of Tajikistan. 14 Firuz St., 734003 Dushanbe, Tajikistan. Phone: 992 44 6005794; Fax: 992 44 6005793; Email: office@amfot.tj • URL: http://www.amfot.tj • Facilitates the development of the microfinance sector in Tajikistan. Serves as a forum for interrelation and network of microfinance organizations in Tajikistan. Provides professional services for training and consultations and assists in the introduction of national standards of microfinance activity.

Cayman Finance. Fidelity Financial Ctre., 2nd Fl., 1 Gecko Link, West Bay Rd., Grand Cayman, Cayman Islands. Phone: (345)623-6725; Email: enquiries@caymanfinance.ky • URL: http://caymanfinances.com • Represents Cayman's financial services industry. Promotes the integrity and quality of financial services in the Cayman Islands. Offers the media and the financial services industry with information on issues that affect Cayman's financial services.

China Association of Microfinance. RDI of CASS, Rm. 1343, 5 Jianguomennei St., Beijing 100732, Hebei, China. Phone: 86 10 8519 6476 or 86 10 8519 5660; Fax: 86 10 8519 6476; Email: cam.net@163.com • URL: http://www.chinamfi.net • Represents and supports the microfinance industry. Promotes governmental support and strengthens international cooperation on microfinance. Raises funds for microfinance development and provides financial services to populations living with poverty and low income. Enhances the management capacity of microfinance institutions.

Chinese Finance Association. Church Street Station, New York, NY 10008. • URL: http://www.tcfaglobal.org • Promotes Chinese finance, business, economy, financial institutions and financial markets.

Commercial Finance Association. 370 7th Ave., Ste. 1801, New York, NY 10001. Phone: (212)792-9390; Fax: (212)564-6053; Email: info@cfa.com • URL: http://www.cfa.com • Organizations engaged in asset-based financial services including commercial financing and factoring and lending money on a secured basis to small- and medium-sized business firms. Acts as a forum for information and consideration about ideas, opportunities and legislation concerning asset-based financial services. Seeks to improve the industry's legal and operational procedures. Offers job placement and reference services for members. Sponsors School for Field Examiners and other educational programs. Compiles statistics; conducts seminars and surveys; maintains speakers' bureau and 21 committees.

Community Financial Services Association. 515 King St., Ste. 300, Alexandria, VA 22314. Phone: 888-572-9329; Fax: (703)684-1219; Email: info@cfsaa.com • URL: http://cfsaa.com • Works to promote laws and regulations that balance the interests of the payday advance industry with consumers. Supports and encourages responsible industry practices.

Credit Builders Alliance. 1701 K St. NW, Ste. 1000, Washington, DC 20006. Phone: (202)730-9390; Fax: (202)350-9430; Email: info@creditbuildersalliance.org • URL: http://www.creditbuildersalliance.org • Represents the interests of community lenders including CDFIs, microenterprise and housing development organizations, asset building organizations and community credit unions. Provides assistance to low and moderate income individuals served by non-traditional financial and asset building institutions to build their credit and financial access. Raises awareness to open new credit building opportunities for low-income and underserved populations.

Dutch Association of Corporate Treasurers. PO Box 279, 1400 AG Bussum, Netherlands. Phone: 31 35 6954101; Fax: 31 35 6945045 • URL: http://www.dact.nl • Represents the Dutch treasury community. Promotes the development of treasury in The Netherlands.

Eastern Finance Association. PO Box 244023, Montgomery, AL 36124-4023. Phone: (850)644-4220; Fax: (850)644-4225; Email: membershipservices@blackwellpublishers.co.uk • URL: http://etnpconferences.net/efa • College and university professors and financial officers; libraries. Provides a meeting place for persons interested in any aspect of finance, including financial management, investments, and banking. Sponsors research competitions.

Finance and Leasing Association. Imperial House, 2nd Fl., 15-19 Kingsway, London WC2B 6UN, United Kingdom. Phone: 44 20 78366511; Fax: 44 20 74209600; Email: info@fla.org.uk • URL: http://www.financeleasingassociation.co.uk • Trade association representing the UK asset, consumer, and motor finance sectors. Provides high-level representation and lobbying at both national and EU levels, supported by technical information and industry statistics. Complies with the association's code of conduct, which is supported by their conciliation and arbitration schemes. Provides a focus and forum for the industry, and has a high level of member involvement in its many working groups. Organizes conferences, workshops, and training courses.

Finance Project. 1150 18th St. NW, Ste. 325, Washington, DC 20036-3856. Phone: (202)628-4200; Fax: (202)628-1293; Email: info@financeproject.org • URL: http://www.financeproject.org • Develops and disseminates information, knowledge, tools, technical assistance for improved policies, programs, financing strategies that will benefit children, families and communities.

Finance Sector Union of Australia. 341 Queen St., Melbourne, VIC 3000, Australia. Fax: 61 39 1300366378 or 61 39 1300307943; Email: fsuinfo@fsunion.org.au • URL: http://www.fsunion.org.au • Employees of private and public sector financial services companies. Works to enhance members' welfare and conditions of employment. Conducts union organization training and insurance industry research.

Financial Managers Society. 1 N La Salle St., Ste. 3100, Chicago, IL 60602-4003. Phone: 800-275-4367 or (312)578-1300; Fax: (312)578-1308; Email: info@fmsinc.org • URL: http://www.fmsinc.org • Works for the needs of finance and accounting professionals from banks, thrifts and credit unions. Offers career-enhancing education, specialized publications, national leadership opportunities and worldwide connections with other industry professionals.

Financial Markets Association. 333 2nd St. NE, No. 104, Washington, DC 20002. Phone: (202)544-6327; Email: dp-fma@starpower.net • URL: http://www.fmaweb.org • Accountants, brokers, retail and investment bankers. Dedicated to meeting the needs of the financial industry for capital markets, fiduciary services, data processing, banking, asset/

liability management, broker/dealer activities and investment advisory services. Offers educational seminars.

Financial Markets Association of Pakistan. Treasury Management Group, National Bank of Pakistan, NBP Head Office, 1st Flr.,, I.I. Chundrigar Rd., Karachi 74000, Pakistan. Phone: 92 21 143738; Fax: 92 21 1439440 • URL: http://www.fma.com.pk • Represents the interest of financial markets. Aims to promote educational, professional, ethical and social interests of the financial markets and the banking industry. Provides training and development support and conducts survey studies and research of the various fields of financial markets.

Financial Publishers Association. 15430 Endeavor Dr., Jupiter, FL 33478-6402. Phone: (561)515-8555; Fax: (561)282-4509; Email: support@financialpublishers.org • URL: http://www.financialpublishers.org • Aims to enhance the financial publishing industry's reputation for excellence. Shares knowledge of business best practices to help members. Provides financial information to guide investors.

Financial Women's Association of New York. 355 Lexington Ave., 15th Fl., New York, NY 10017. Phone: (212)297-2133; Fax: (212)370-9047 or (212)982-3008; Email: fwaoffice@fwa.org • URL: http://www.nywici.org/links/link_fwa.html • Persons of professional status in the field of finance in the New York metropolitan area. Works to promote and maintain high professional standards in the financial and business communities; provide an opportunity for members to enhance one another's professional contacts; achieve recognition of the contribution of women to the financial and business communities; encourage other women to seek professional positions within the financial and business communities. Activities include educational trips to foreign countries; college internship program including foreign student exchange; high school mentorship program; Washington and international briefings; placement service for members. Maintains speakers' bureau.

FIRST Union. 120 Church St., Onehunga, Auckland 1643, New Zealand. Phone: 64 9 6228355 or 64 9 6228351; Fax: 64 9 6228353; Email: contact@firstunion.org.nz • URL: http://www.firstunion.org.nz • Organizing union for workers in the financial services industry. Seeks to obtain optimal conditions of employment for members. Represents members in negotiations with employers.

Hospitality Financial and Technology Professionals. 11709 Boulder Ln., Ste. 110, Austin, TX 78726. Phone: 800-646-4387 or (512)249-5333; Fax: (512)249-1533; Email: membership@hftp.org • URL: http://www.hftp.org • Accountants, financial officers and MIS managers in 50 countries working in hotels, resorts, casinos, restaurants, and clubs. Develops uniform system of accounts. Conducts education, training, and certification programs; offers placement service; maintains hall of fame.

International Association of CFOs and Corporate Treasurers China. c/o Mr. Francis Ho, CLP Holdings, Group Treasury Dept., 147 Argyle St., Mongkok, Kowloon, Hong Kong, China. • URL: http://www.iacctchina.com • Promotes the development of professional corporate treasury practice in China. Fosters exchange and sharing among a network of corporate treasurers and CFOs in both mainland Chinese. Supports financial reforms in China by developing a platform for dialogue between members and financial regulators.

International Association of Financial Executives Institutes. 1003 Pasong Tamo Tower, 10th Fl., 2210 Don Chino Roces Ave., Makati City 1231, Philippines. Phone: 63 2 7280315 • URL: http://www.iafei.org • Seeks to build and improve mutual understanding internationally among financial executives through the exchange of financial information, experience, and ideas. Provides a basis for international cooperation among financial executives towards making financial systems and regulations more uniform, compatible, and harmonious worldwide. Promotes ethical considerations in the practice of financial management throughout the world.

International Factoring Association. 6627 Bay Laurel Pl., Ste. C, Avila Beach, CA 93424-0039. Phone: 800-563-1895; Fax: (805)773-0021; Email: info@factoring.org • URL: http://www.factoring.org • Represents the interests of the factoring industry. Assists the factoring community by providing information, training, purchasing power and resources. Provides opportunities for members to discuss issues and concerns in the industry.

International Network of Alternative Financial Institution. Mermoz, 11 rue MZ - 157, Dakar, Senegal. Email: claudeabsa@yahoo.fr • URL: http://www.mixmarket.org/networks/inafi • Seeks to advance microfinance programs for the poor by increasing the quality of service and performance of microfinancial institutions through counselling, research, and publications.

International Society of Financiers. 64 Brookside Dr., Hendersonville, NC 28792. Phone: (828)393-8908; Fax: (828)393-8919; Email: insofin@gmail.com • URL: http://www.insofin.com • Membership in more than 25 countries includes: real estate, minerals, commodities, and import-export brokers; corporate, industrial, and private lenders; and other financial professionals. Provides information and referrals on major domestic and international financial projects and transactions, and fosters integrity and professionalism among members.

Japan Securities Dealers' Association. 1-5-8, Kayaba-cho Nihonbashi, Chuo, Tokyo 103-0025, Japan. Phone: 81 3 3667-8537; Email: international@wan.jsda.or.jp • URL: http://www.jsda.or.jp/en • Represents securities companies and registered financial institutions. Aims to protect investors by ensuring fair and smooth trading in securities and other transactions by members of the association. Promotes the implementation of policy measures for the revitalization of the Japanese securities markets in order to contribute to the growth and development of the Japanese economy.

National Association of Commercial Finance Brokers. Hamilton House, 1 Temple Ave., London EC4Y 0HA, United Kingdom. Phone: 44 20 74892056; Email: admin@nacfb.org.uk • URL: http://www.nacfb.org • Seeks to protect consumer from fraud and malpractice in the commercial finance industry. Raises professional standards of commercial finance brokers. Provides training, education and information.

National Association of Financial Services. Tauentzienstrasse 12, D-10787 Berlin, Germany. Phone: 49 30 23003504 or 49 30 20454403; Fax: 49 30 23003562 or 49 30 20634759; Email: fifaeg@t-online.de • URL: http://www.fifa.de • Promotes the financial industry in Germany. Seeks to develop the field of financial services. Provides information on the financial industry.

National Association of Health and Educational Facilities Finance Authorities. PO Box 906, Oakhurst, NJ 07755. Phone: 888-414-5713; Fax: (888)414-5713 • URL: http://www.naheffa.com • Serves the common interests and improves effectiveness of member authorities through communication, education, and advocacy, with emphasis on issues which directly influence the availability of or access to tax-exempt financing for healthcare facilities.

National Association of Settlement Purchasers. c/o Susan Barnes, Association Administrator, 720 Collier Dr., Dixon, CA 95620. Phone: (707)888-2647; Email: susan@barnescompany.com • URL: http://www.nasp-usa.com • Finance companies that purchase structured settlements from individuals for a lump sum (structured settlements are received by individuals as redress for personal injury or other liability). Seeks to insure ethical practice in the trading of structured settlements; promotes advancement of the structured settlement purchasing industry. Serves as a clearinghouse on the purchase of structured settlements; lobbies for reform of regulations governing the trade in structured settlements.

National Business Incubation Association. 340 W State St., Unit 25, Athens, OH 45701-1565. Phone: (740)593-4331; Fax: (740)593-1996; Email: info@nbia.org • URL: http://www.nbia.org • Incubator developers and managers; corporate joint venture partners, venture capital investors; economic development professionals. (Incubators are business assistance programs providing business consulting services and financing assistance to start-up and fledgling companies.) Helps newly formed businesses to succeed. Educates businesses and investors on incubator benefits; offers specialized training in incubator formation and management. Conducts research and referral services; compiles statistics; maintains speakers' bureau; publishes information relevant to business incubation and growing companies.

NBFI and Modaraba Association of Pakistan. 602, Progressive Ctr., 30-A, Blk. 6, PEHCS, Shahrah-e-Faisal, Karachi 75400, Pakistan. Phone: 92 21 34389774; Fax: 92 21 34389775; Email: association@nbfi-modaraba.com.pk • URL: http://www.nbfi-modaraba.com.pk • Seeks to promote the Islamic way of business. Encourages public awareness of the role of modaraba in financing. Conducts surveys and analysis on the Islamic modes of business and finance. Safeguards and protects the interests of members.

PlaNet Finance US. 44 rue de Prony, 75017 Paris, France. Email: contact@planetfinance.org • URL: http://www.planetfinance.org • Works to alleviate poverty through the development of microfinance. Seeks to support and strengthen the capacity of the microfinance sector. Raises public awareness of microfinancing.

Professional Women Controllers. PO Box 23924, Washington, DC 20024. Email: info@pwcinc.org • URL: http://www.pwcinc.org • Women controllers. Promotes the advancement of women within the financial industry. Represents members' interests; facilitates networking among women controllers; and makes available educational programs.

WAM International: Women Advancing Microfinance. 402 Constitution Ave. NE, Washington, DC 20002. Phone: (202)547-4546; Email: wam.international.president@gmail.com • URL: http://waminternational.org • Promotes the advancement of women working in the microfinance industry. Seeks to extend economic opportunities to women globally and encourages active participation of women in management and governance roles.

Western Payments Alliance. 300 Montgomery St., Ste.400, San Francisco, CA 94104. Phone: (415)433-1230; Fax: (415)433-1370; Email: info@wespay.org • URL: http://www.wespay.org • Represents financial institutions and others involved in payments systems in the U.S.

Women in Housing and Finance. 400 N Washington St., Ste. 300, Alexandria, VA 22314. Phone: (703)683-4742; Fax: (703)683-0018; Email: whf@whfdc.org • URL: http://www.whfdc.org • Professionals employed in the fields of housing or finance. Provides women finance professionals with the opportunity for continued professional development through interaction with others with similar interests. Promotes educational development of women in housing and finance; provides members with services and benefits to help them attain higher levels of expertise. Sponsors social events for members; holds receptions for congressional and regulatory leaders; conducts monthly luncheon and programs featuring speakers from federal agencies, Congress and the private sector. Sponsors career development workshops. Activities are concentrated in the Washington, DC, area.

Zambia Union of Financial Institutions and Allied Workers. Luangwa House, Cairo Rd., Lusaka, Zambia. Phone: 260 211 222105; Fax: 260 211 231364; Email: zufiaw@zamnet.zm • URL: http://www.africaefuture.org/zufiaw • Exists to improve the material conditions of members and their families. Aims to strive for equality between all men and women in the sharing of all national wealth and world leisure.

FINANCE, BANK

See BANK LOANS

FINANCE COMPANIES

See also CREDIT

DIRECTORIES

Plunkett's Financial Services Industry Almanac: The Only Complete Guide to the Technologies and Companies Changing the Way the World Banks, Invest and Borrows. Plunkett Research Ltd. • Annual. $249.99 plus $9.50 shipping (includes CD-ROM). Covers: 500 of the largest investment, banking, and financial companies. Entries include: Firm name, address, phone, fax; description; and leading executives with their titles, addresses, phone numbers, E-mail addresses, Web sites, and fax numbers.

United Kingdom Business Finance Directory. Graham & Trotman Ltd. • Annual. $265. Covers: 1,500 financial institutions, banks, insurance companies, accountants, investment brokers, and job hunters in the United Kingdom. Entries include: Company name, address, phone, fax, telex number.

HANDBOOKS AND MANUALS

Moody's Bank and Finance Manual. Mergent. • Annual. $1,750 Four volumes. Includes biweekly supplements in *Moody's Bank and Finance News Report.*

INTERNET DATABASES

Federal Reserve Board Publications and Education Resources. Board of Governors of the Federal Reserve System. Phone: (202)452-3000; Fax: (202)452-3819 • URL: http://www.federalreserve.gov/publications.htm • Web site provides access to statistics, surveys, and research from the Federal Reserve Board. *Federal Reserve Bulletin* articles are available as abstracts or full text (PDF) currently or from six-year archives. The link "Statistics: Releases and Historical Data" offers daily, weekly, monthly, quarterly, and annual data in great detail for interest rates, foreign exchange, consumer credit, money stock measures, industrial production indexes, bank reserves, and other items. Historical tabulations are available for various time periods. Free.

PERIODICALS AND NEWSLETTERS

Consumer Credit and Truth-in-Lending Compliance Report. Thomson RIA. • Monthly. $183.75 per year. Newsletter. Focuses on the latest regulatory rulings and findings involving consumer lending and credit activity. Incorporates (Consumer Lending Report).

Credit Executive Letter. American Financial Services Association. • Monthly. Members, $12.00 per year; non-members, $22.00 per year.

The Secured Lender. Commercial Finance Association. • Bimonthly. $35 Members domestic. Bimonthly. Free to members.

TRADE/PROFESSIONAL ASSOCIATIONS

Accounting and Auditing Organization for Islamic Financial Institutions. Yateem Center, Blk. 304, Al Muthana Rd., Manama, Bahrain. Phone: 973 17 244 496; Fax: 973 17 250 194 • URL: http://www.aaoifi.com • Represents central banks, Islamic financial institutions, and other participants from the international Islamic banking and finance industry. Aims to uphold the accounting and auditing standards of Islamic financial institutions. Provides its members the necessary resources needed to improve and maintain the quality of service of Islamic financial institutions.

Accounting and Finance Benchmarking Consortium. 4606 FM 1960 W, Ste. 250, Houston, TX 77069-9949. Phone: (281)440-5044 • URL: http://www.afbc.org • Accounting and finance managers of corporations with an interest in benchmarking. Promotes the use of benchmarking, wherein businesses compare their processes with those of their competitors, as a means of improving corporate efficiency and profitability. Facilitates exchange of information among members; conducts target operations, procurement, development, and maintenance studies; identifies model business practices.

American Financial Services Association. 919 18th St. NW, Ste. 300, Washington, DC 20006. Email: info@afsamail.org • URL: http://www.afsaonline.org • Represents companies whose business is primarily direct credit lending to consumers and/or the purchase of sales finance paper on consumer goods. Has members that have insurance and retail subsidiaries; some are themselves subsidiaries of highly diversified parent corporations. Encourages the business of financing individuals and families for necessary and useful purposes at reasonable charges, including interest; promotes consumer understanding of basic money management principles as well as constructive uses of consumer credit. Includes educational services such as films, textbooks and study units for the classroom and budgeting guides for individuals and families. Compiles statistical reports; offers seminars.

Commercial Finance Association. 370 7th Ave., Ste. 1801, New York, NY 10001. Phone: (212)792-9390; Fax: (212)564-6053; Email: info@cfa.com • URL: http://www.cfa.com • Organizations engaged in asset-based financial services including commercial financing and factoring and lending money on a secured basis to small- and medium-sized business firms. Acts as a forum for information and consideration about ideas, opportunities and legislation concerning asset-based financial services. Seeks to improve the industry's legal and operational procedures. Offers job placement and reference services for members. Sponsors School for Field Examiners and other educational programs. Compiles statistics; conducts seminars and surveys; maintains speakers' bureau and 21 committees.

Financial Executives International. 1250 Headquarters Plz., West Tower, 7th Fl., Morristown, NJ 07960. Phone: 877-359-1070 or (973)765-1000; Fax: (973)765-1018; Email: membership@financialexecutives.org • URL: http://www.financialexecutives.org • Professional organization of corporate financial executives performing duties of chief financial officer, controller, treasurer, or vice-president-finance. Sponsors research activities through its affiliated Financial Executives Research Foundation. Maintains offices in Toronto, Canada, and Washington, DC.

National Foundation for Credit Counseling. 2000 M St. NW, Ste. 505, Washington, DC 20036. Phone: (202)677-4300 • URL: http://www.nfcc.org • Supersedes Retail Credit Institute of America.

FINANCE, COMPUTERS IN

See COMPUTERS IN FINANCE

FINANCE, CORPORATE

See CORPORATE FINANCE

FINANCE, INTERNATIONAL

See INTERNATIONAL FINANCE

FINANCE, PERSONAL

See PERSONAL FINANCE

FINANCE, PUBLIC

See PUBLIC FINANCE

FINANCIAL ANALYSIS

See also COMPUTERS IN FINANCE; FINANCIAL RATIOS

ALMANACS AND YEARBOOKS

Advances in Investment Analysis and Portfolio Management. Chung-Few Lee, editor. Elsevier. • Focus on investment analysis and portfolio theory.

CD-ROM DATABASES

InvesText. Thomson Financial. • Monthly. Contains full text on CD-ROM of investment research reports from about 630 sources, including leading brokers and investment bankers. Reports are available on both U. S. and international publicly traded corporations. Separate industry reports cover more than 50 industries. Time span is 1982 to date.

DIRECTORIES

ICC UK Company Financial Database. Dun & Bradstreet U.K. ICC Information. • Weekly. Database covers: Comprehensive analysis on 2.2 million companies with limited liability in the UK--large, medium, and small, quoted and non-quoted, public and private, from all sectors on industry and commerce. Provides data for all types of company research, providing extended profit and loss accounts and balance sheet information, new cash flow items, together with new auditors' qualification reference data, comprehensive business ratios, industrial comparisons, growth rates, and an improved credit rating system. Access to complete database of U.K. Directors with over 5 million directorships covered exact images of alt company accounts and annual returns.

Institutional Buyers of Energy Stocks. bigdough.com Inc. • Annual. $645.00. Provides detailed profiles 555 institutional buyers of petroleum-related and other energy stocks. Includes names of financial analysts and portfolio managers.

Institutional Buyers of REIT Securities. bigdough.com Inc. • Semiannual. $995.00 per year. Provides detailed profiles of about 500 institutional buyers of REIT securities. Includes names of financial analysts and portfolio managers.

Institutional Buyers of Small-Cap Stocks. bigdough.com Inc. • Annual. $295.00. Provides detailed profiles of more than 837 institutional buyers of small capitalization stocks. Includes names of financial analysts and portfolio managers.

Key British Enterprises Financial Performance. Dun & Bradstreet Inc. • Monthly. Database covers: Approximately 50,000 of the largest companies in the United Kingdom. Database includes: Company name, address, director name, parent company, product trade name, annual and export sales, number of employees, export markets, trade description, trade awards, Companies Registration Office number, pre-tax profit, net worth, total assets, current assets, current liabilities, working capital, long-term debt, return on capital, profit margin, current ratio, profit per employee, U.S. and U.K. SIC code.

Zacks Analyst Directory. Zacks Investment Research Inc. • Updated daily. Lists stockbroker investment analysts and gives the names of major U.S. corporations covered by those analysts.

Zacks Analyst Guide. Zacks Investment Research Inc. • Ranks analysts within more than 70 industry groups.

HANDBOOKS AND MANUALS

Analyst's Handbook: Composite Corporate Per Share Data by Industry. Standard & Poor's Financial Services L.L.C. • Annual. $795.00. Monthly updates.

INTERNET DATABASES

Mergent Online. Mergent Inc. 580 Kingsley Park Dr., Fort Mill, SC 29715. Phone: 800-937-1398 or (704)527-2700 or (704)559-7601; Fax: (704)559-6837 or (704)559-6960; Email: customerservice@mergent.com • URL: http://www.mergent.com • Fee-based Web site provides detailed information on 20,000 publicly-owned companies in 100 foreign countries, as well as more than 10,000 corporations listed on the New York Stock Exchange, American Stock Exchange, NASDAQ, and U.S. regional exchanges. Searching is offered on many financial variables and text fields. Weekly updating. Formerly *FIS Online*.

ONLINE DATABASES

Compustat. Standard and Poor's. • Financial data on publicly held U.S. and some foreign corporations; data held for 20 years. Inquire as to online cost and availability.

EdgarPlus: SEC Basic Filings. Thomson Reuters Markets. • Online service provides full text of about 60,000 documents that have been filed with the U.S. Securities and Exchange Commission, 1987 to date, with daily updates. Filings include 6-K, 8-K, 10-K, 10-C, 10-Q, 20-F, and proxy statements. Inquire as to online cost and availability.

InvesText. Thomson Financial. • Provides full text online of investment research reports from more than 600 sources, including leading brokers and investment bankers. Reports are available on approximately 60,000 U. S. and international corporations. Separate industry reports cover 54 industries. Time span is 1982 to date, with daily updates. Inquire as to online cost and availability.

PERIODICALS AND NEWSLETTERS

Consensus: National Futures and Financial Weekly. Consensus Inc. • Weekly. $365.00 per year. Newspaper. Contains news, statistics, and special reports relating to agricultural, industrial, and financial futures markets. Features daily basis price charts, reprints of market advice, and "The Consensus Index of Bullish Market Opinion" (charts show percent bullish of advisors for various futures).

Emerging Growth. Navellier and Associates Inc. • Monthly. $275.00 per year. Newsletter. Provides specific stock selection and model portfolio advice (conservative, moderately aggressive, and aggressive) based on quantitative analysis and modern portfolio theory.

Financial Analysts Journal. CFA Institute. • Bimonthly. $50 Members print and online. Contains important topics related to the investment industry.

Institutional Investor: The Premier of Professional Magazine Finance. Institutional Investor Inc. Journals Group. • Monthly. $445.00 per year. Includes print and online editions. Edited for portfolio managers and other investment professionals. Special feature issues include "Country Credit Ratings," "Fixed Income Trading Ranking," "All-America Research Team," and "Global Banking Ranking.".

RESEARCH CENTERS AND INSTITUTES

Columbia University - Columbia Business School - Center for Excellence in Accounting and Security Analysis. 608 Uris Hall, 3022 Broadway, New York, NY 10027. Phone: (212)854-3832; Fax: (212)316-9219; Email: ceasa@gsb.columbia.edu • URL: http://www8.gsb.columbia.edu/ceasa • Financial reporting that reflects economic reality and investment advice that communicates sound valuations.

TRADE/PROFESSIONAL ASSOCIATIONS

Association of Independent Asset Managers in Liechtenstein. PO Box 134, FL-9496 Balzers, Liechtenstein. Phone: 423 3882350; Fax: 423 3882359; Email: info@vuvl.li • URL: http://www.vuvl.li/CFDOCS/cmsout/admin/content.cfm?GroupID=141 • Aims to protect and promote the reputation of independent asset managers in Liechtenstein and abroad. Seeks to establish professional guidelines within the framework of the Asset Management Accounting. Facilitates exchange of information within the business community.

CFA Institute. 560 Ray C. Hunt Dr., Charlottesville, VA 22903-2981. Phone: 800-247-8132 or (434)951-5499; Fax: (434)951-5262; Email: info@cfainstitute.org • URL: http://www.cfainstitute.org/pages/index.aspx • Formerly Association for Investment Management and Research.

European Federation of Financial Analysts Societies. c/o Claudia Stinnes, Secretary, Mainzer Landstrasse 47a, DE-60329 Frankfurt, Germany. Phone: 49 69 264848300; Fax: 49 69 264848335; Email: info@effas.com • URL: http://effas.net • Associations and individuals active in the area of financial analysis. Objectives are to provide investors with accurate and comprehensive data on financial matters and to develop a general methodology of financial analysis based on approaches utilized in different European countries.

Farm Financial Standards Council. c/o Carroll Merry, N78 W14573 Appleton Ave., No. 287, Menomonee Falls, WI 53051. Phone: (262)253-6902; Fax: (262)253-6903 • URL: http://www.ffsc.org • Aims to create and promote uniformity and integrity in financial reporting and analysis for agricultural producers. Strives to be recognized as the definitive resource of financial guidelines to benefit agricultural producers.

Financial Managers Society. 1 N La Salle St., Ste. 3100, Chicago, IL 60602-4003. Phone: 800-275-4367 or (312)578-1300; Fax: (312)578-1308; Email: info@fmsinc.org • URL: http://www.fmsinc.org • Works for the needs of finance and accounting professionals from banks, thrifts and credit unions. Offers career-enhancing education, specialized publications, national leadership opportunities and worldwide connections with other industry professionals.

Healthcare Financial Management Association. 3 Westbrook Corporate Ctr., Ste. 600, Westchester, IL 60154. Phone: 800-252-4362 or (708)531-9600; Fax: (708)531-0032; Email: memberservices@hfma.org • URL: http://www.hfma.org • Financial management professionals employed by hospitals and long-term care facilities, public accounting and consulting firms, insurance companies, medical groups, managed care organizations, government agencies, and other organizations. Conducts conferences, including annual conference in late June and audio teleconferences. Publishes books on healthcare financial issues. A Fellowship in Healthcare Financial Management (FHFMA) as well as the Certified Healthcare Professional (CHFP) in Finance and Accounting, Financial Management of Physician Practices, Managed Care, and Patient Financial Services are offered.

Norwegian Society of Financial Analysts. PO Box 1276 VIKA, N-0111 Oslo, Norway. Phone: 47 22 129210; Fax: 47 22 129211; Email: nff@finansanalytiker.no • URL: http://www.finansanalytiker.no • Financial analysts. Acts as a forum for exchange of technical information. Conducts educational programs.

Society of Quantitative Analysts. PO Box 6, Rutledge, MO 63563. Phone: 800-918-7930; Email: sqa@sqa-us.org • URL: http://www.sqa-us.org • Works for the application of new and innovative techniques in finance, with particular emphasis on the use of quantitative techniques in investment and risk management. Sponsors a half-day program in the fall and a Fuzzy Day seminar in the spring on an exploratory topic.

FINANCIAL FUTURES TRADING

See also STOCK INDEX TRADING

ABSTRACTS AND INDEXES

Business Periodicals Index Retrospective. EBSCO Publishing Inc. • 11/year. Quarterly and annual cumulations.

DIRECTORIES

Futures Magazine SourceBook: The Most Complete List of Exchanges, Companies, Regulators, Organizations, etc., Offering Products and Services to the Futures and Options Industry. Futures Magazine Inc. • Annual. $19.50. Provides information on commodity futures brokers, trading method services, publications, and other items of interest to futures traders and money managers.

INTERNET DATABASES

BanxQuote Banking, Mortgage, and Finance Center. BanxQuote, Inc. Phone: (914)722-1600; Fax: (914)722-6630; Email: info@banx.com • URL: http://www.banx.com • Daily. Web site quotes interest rates paid by banks around the country on various savings products, as well as rates paid by consumers for automobile loans, mortgages, credit cards, home equity loans, and personal loans. Also provided: stock quotes, indexes, stock options, futures trading data, economic indicators, and links to many other financial sites.

Chicago Board of Trade: The World's Leading Futures Exchange. Chicago Board of Trade. Phone: (312)535-3500; Fax: (312)341-3392; Email: comments@cbot.com • URL: http://www.cbot.com • Web site provides a wide variety of statistics, commentary, charts, and news relating to both agricultural and financial futures trading. For example, Web page "MarketPlex: Information MarketPlace to the World" offers prices & volume, contract specifications & margins, government reports, etc. Searching is available, with daily updates for current data. Fees: Mostly free (some specialized services are fee-based).

CRB Market Overview. Commodity Research Bureau. Phone: 800-621-5271 or (312)554-8456; Fax: (312)939-4135; Email: info@crbtrader.com • URL: http://www.crbtrader.com/data/ • Web site provides free, detailed, current price quotes for about 100 futures contracts, covering Currencies, Energies, Financials, Grains, Meats, Metals, "Softs" (orange juice, coffee, etc.) and stock price indexes. Includes contract specifications and detailed prices of options on futures.

Futures Online. Futures Magazine Inc. Phone: (312)846-4600; Fax: (312)846-4638 • URL: http://www.futuresmag.com • Web site presents updates of *Futures* magazine and links to other futures-related sites.

ONLINE DATABASES

Wilson Business Abstracts Online. H.W. Wilson Co. • Indexes and abstracts 600 major business periodicals, plus the *Wall Street Journal* and the business section of the *New York Times*. Indexing is from 1982, abstracting from 1990, with the two newspapers included from 1993. Updated weekly. Inquire as to online cost and availability. (*Business Periodicals Index* without abstracts is also available online.).

OTHER SOURCES

Managing Financial Risk with Forwards, Futures, Options, and Swaps. American Management Association Extension Institute. • Looseleaf. $159.00. Self-study course. Emphasis is on practical explanations, examples, and problem solving. Quizzes and a case study are included.

PERIODICALS AND NEWSLETTERS

Futures and OTC World. Russell R. Wasendorf. • Weekly. $435.00 per year. Newsletter. Futures market information. Includes Daily Hotline Information to update advice. Formerly *Futures and Options Factors*.

Futures: News, Analysis, and Strategies for Futures, Options, and Derivatives Traders. Futures Magazine Inc. • Monthly. $39 Individuals. Edited for institutional money managers and traders, brokers, risk managers, and individual investors or speculators. Includes special feature issues on interest rates, technical indicators, currencies, charts, precious metals, hedge funds, and derivatives. Supplements available.

SFO: Stocks, Futures & Options. W and A Publishing. • Subtitle: *Official Journal for Personal Investing in Stocks, Futures, and Options*. Covers mainly speculative techniques for stocks, commodity futures, financial futures, stock index futures, foreign exchange, short selling, and various kinds of options.

Technical Analysis of Stocks & Commodities: The Traders Magazine. Technical Analysis Inc. • $89.99 Individuals Annual. 13 times a year. Covers use of personal computers for stock trading, price movement analysis by means of charts, and other technical trading methods.

PRICE SOURCES

CRB Futures Perspective: Financial Edition. Commodity Research Bureau. • Weekly. $275.00 per year. Service provides comprehensive price charts for more than 50 financial futures, from Australian Bills to Swiss Francs (includes precious metals and oil). Also provides technical analysis of price movements and market commentary. Formerly part of *CRB Futures Chart Service*.

STATISTICS SOURCES

Statistical Annual: Interest Rates, Metals, Stock Indices, Options on Financial Futures, Options on Metals Futures. Chicago Board of Trade. • Annual. Includes historical data on GNMA CDR Futures, Cash-Settled GNMA Futures, U. S. Treasury Bond Futures, U. S. Treasury Note Futures, Options on Treasury Note Futures, NASDAQ-100 Futures, Major Market Index Futures, Major Market Index MAXI Futures, Municipal Bond Index Futures, 1,000-Ounce Silver Futures, Options on Silver Futures, and Kilo Gold Futures.

TRADE/PROFESSIONAL ASSOCIATIONS

Financial Industry Regulatory Authority. 1735 K St., Washington, DC 20006. Phone: (301)590-6500; Fax: (202)293-6260; Email: francine.lee@finra.org • URL: http://www.finra.org • Formerly National Association of Securities Dealers.

National Futures Association. 300 S Riverside Plz., No. 1800, Chicago, IL 60606-6615. Phone: 800-621-3570 or (312)781-1300 or (312)781-1410; Fax: (312)781-1467; Email: information@nfa.futures.org • URL: http://www.nfa.futures.org • Futures commission merchants; commodity trading advisors; commodity pool operators; brokers and their associated persons. Works to: strengthen and expand industry self-regulation to include all segments of the futures industry; provide uniform standards to eliminate duplication of effort and conflict; remove unnecessary regulatory constraints to aid effective regulation. Conducts member qualification screening, financial surveillance, and registration. Monitors and enforces customer protection rules and uniform business standards. Maintains information center. Arbitrates customer disputes; audits non-exchange member FCM's.

FINANCIAL MANAGEMENT

See also COMPUTERS IN FINANCE; CORPORATE FINANCE

ABSTRACTS AND INDEXES

Business Periodicals Index Retrospective. EBSCO Publishing Inc. • 11/year. Quarterly and annual cumulations.

BIOGRAPHICAL SOURCES

Who's Who in Finance and Business. Marquis Who's Who L.L.C. • Biennial. $349 Individuals. Provides over 21,000 concise biographies of business leaders in all fields.

CD-ROM DATABASES

ABI/INFORM. ProQuest L.L.C. • Monthly. Provides CD-ROM indexing and abstracting of worldwide business literature. Archival discs are available from 1971. Formerly *ABI/INFORM OnDisc*.

Applied Science & Business Periodicals Retrospective. EBSCO Publishing Inc. • Includes citations for more than 3 million articles detailing events, issues, and trends in business and industry.

DIRECTORIES

America's Corporate Finance Directory. LexisNexis. • Annual. $1,399 Individuals print. Covers: Financial personnel and outside financial services relationships of 5,000 leading United States corporations and their wholly-owned United States subsidiaries. Entries include: Company name, address, phone, fax, telex, e-mail addresses, stock exchange information, earnings, total assets, size of pension/profit-sharing fund portfolio, number of employees, description of business, wholly-owned U.S. Subsidiaries of parent company; name and title of key executives; outside suppliers of financial services.

Financial Management Association: Membership/Professional Directory. Financial Management Association. • Annual. Lists 4,800 corporate financial officers and professors of financial management.

Nelson Information's Directory of Investment Managers. Nelson Information. • Annual. $595.00. Three volumes. Provides information on 2,200 investment management firms, both U.S. and foreign.

Who's Who in Finance and Business. Marquis Who's Who L.L.C. • Biennial. $349 Individuals. Provides over 21,000 concise biographies of business leaders in all fields.

GENERAL WORKS

Cost of Doing Business. Associated Equipment Distributors. • Annual. $595 Members nonparticipants. For construction equipment distributors covering business costs, sales, and financial data.

HANDBOOKS AND MANUALS

Accountant's Business Manual. American Institute of Certified Public Accountants. • $198.75. Looseleaf. Two volumes. Semiannual updates. Covers a wide variety of topics relating to financial and accounting management, including types of ownership, business planning, financing, cash management, valuation, retirement plans, estate planning, workers' compensation, unemployment insurance, social security, and employee benefits management.

Money Manager's Compliance Guide. Thompson Publishing Group Inc. • $739.00 per year. Two looseleaf volumes. Monthly updates and newletters. Edited for investment advisers and investment companies to help them be in compliance with governmental regulations, including SEC rules, restrictions based on the Employee Retirement Income Security Act (ERISA), and regulations issued by the Commodity Futures Trading Commission (CFTC).

ONLINE DATABASES

Accounting and Tax Database. ProQuest L.L.C. • Provides indexing and abstracting of the literature of accounting, taxation, and financial management, 1971 to date. Updating is weekly. Especially covers accounting, auditing, banking, bankruptcy, employee compensation and benefits, cash management, financial planning, and credit. Inquire as to online cost and availability.

American Banker Full Text. American Banker-Bond Buyer, Database Services. • Provides complete text online of the daily *American Banker*. Inquire as to cost and availability.

Banking Information Source. ProQuest L.L.C. • Provides indexing and abstracting of periodical and other literature from 1982 to date, with weekly updates. Covers the financial services industry: banks, savings institutions, investment houses, credit unions, insurance companies, and real estate organizations. Emphasis is on marketing and management. Inquire as to online cost and availability. (Formerly *FINIS: Financial Industry Information Service*.).

Financial Times Business Reports: Technology. The Economist. • A database containing the full text of articles appearing in selected Financial Times newsletters covering developments in the business aspects of new technology, especially in the computer and telecommunications industries. It is commercially available online.

Wilson Business Abstracts Online. H.W. Wilson Co. • Indexes and abstracts 600 major business periodicals, plus the *Wall Street Journal* and the business section of the *New York Times*. Indexing is from 1982, abstracting from 1990, with the two newspapers included from 1993. Updated weekly. Inquire as to online cost and availability. (*Business Periodicals Index* without abstracts is also available online.).

OTHER SOURCES

Finance and Accounting for Nonfinancial Managers. American Management Association Extension Institute. • $19.95. Looseleaf. Self-study course. Emphasis is on practical explanations, examples, and problem solving. Quizzes and a case study are included.

PERIODICALS AND NEWSLETTERS

American Banker: The Financial Services Daily. SourceMedia Inc. • Daily. $895.00 per year. Provides news of banking, investment products, mortgages, credit unions, finance, bank technology, and legal developments.

Business Finance. Penton. • Monthly. $59.00 per year. Covers trends in finance, technology, and economics for corporate financial executives.

CFO: The Magazine for Senior Financial Executives. CFO Publishing Corp. • Monthly.

Financial Executive. Financial Executives International. • Monthly. $69 Individuals. Magazine covering corporate financial management for senior executives of major corporations. Published for corporate financial officers and managers.

Financial Management (FM). Financial Management Association International. • Quarterly. $392 Institutions for Americas, online only. Covers theory and practice of financial planning, international finance, investment banking, and portfolio management. Includes *Financial Practice and Education and Contemporary Finance Digest.*

Fund Action. Institutional Investor Inc. Journals Group. • Weekly. $2,475.00 per year. Newsletter. Includes print and online editions. Edited for mutual fund executives. Covers competition among funds, aggregate statistics, new products, regulations, service providers, and other subjects of interest to fund managers.

Investment Management Mandate Pipeline. SourceMedia Inc. • Weekly. $1,295.00 per year. Newsletter. Edited for money managers and other investment professionals. Covers personnel news, investment strategies, and industry trends.

IT Cost Management Strategies: The Planning Assistant for IT Directors. Computer Economics Inc. • Monthly. $495.00 per year. Newsletter for information technology professionals. Covers data processing costs, budgeting, financial management, and related topics.

Operations Management. Institutional Investor Inc. Journals Group. • Weekly. $2,105.00 per year. Includes print and online editions. Newsletter. Edited for managers of securities clearance and settlement at financial institutions. Covers new products, technology, legalities, management practices, and other topics related to securities processing.

Robb Report Worth: Wealth in Perspective. CurtCo Robb Media. • Monthly. $54.95 per year. Glossy magazine featuring articles for the affluent on personal financial management, investments, estate planning, trusts, private bankers, taxes, travel, yachts, and lifestyle. Formerly *Worth: Financial Intelligence.*

Strategic Finance. Institute of Management Accountants. • Monthly. $220 Nonmembers. Provides articles on corporate finance, cost control, cash flow, budgeting, corporate taxes, and other financial management topics.

U.S. Banker. SourceMedia Inc. • Monthly. $65.00 per year. Edited for bank executives and managers. Covers a wide variety of banking and financial topics.

Windows in Financial Services. • Quarterly. $39.00 per year. Covers information technology applications and products for Microsoft Windows users in the financial sector.

RESEARCH CENTERS AND INSTITUTES

Financial Executives Research Foundation. Financial Executives International, 1250 Headquarters Plz., West Tower, 7th Fl., Morristown, NJ 07960. Phone: (973)765-1000; Fax: (973)765-1018; Email: mhollein@financialexecutives.org • URL: http://www.financialexecutives.org • Publishes research in business management, with emphasis on corporate financial management issues. Maintains inquiry services.

University of Pennsylvania - The Wharton School - Rodney L. White Center for Financial Research. 3254 Steinberg Hall-Dietrich Hall, Philadelphia, PA 19104-6367. Phone: (215)898-7616; Fax: (215)573-8084; Email: rlwctr@finance.wharton.upenn.edu • URL: http://rodneywhitecenter.wharton.upenn.edu • Research areas include financial management, money markets, real estate finance, and international finance.

TRADE/PROFESSIONAL ASSOCIATIONS

American Finance Association. University of California, Haas School of Business, Berkeley, CA 94720-1900. Phone: 800-835-6770 or (781)388-8599; Fax: (781)388-8232; Email: pyle@haas.berkeley.edu • URL: http://www.afajof.org • College and university professors of economics and finance, bankers, treasurers, analysts, financiers and others interested in financial problems; libraries and other institutions. Seeks to improve public understanding of financial problems and to provide for exchange of analytical ideas. Areas of special interest include: corporate finance, investments, banking and international and public finance.

Asia Catalyst. 39 W 32nd St., Ste. 1602, New York, NY 10001. Phone: (212)967-2123; Email: info@asiacatalyst.org • URL: http://www.asiacatalyst.org • Provides support services to non-governmental organizations (NGOs). Facilitates capacity-building training in personnel and financial management. Conducts fundraising, advocacy, and media outreach activities. Fosters research on human rights issues that are of direct concern to NGOs.

European Finance Association. Pl. de Brouckere Plein 31, B-1000 Brussels, Belgium. Phone: 32 2 2266660 or 32 2 2266665; Fax: 32 2 5121929; Email: kannel@eiasm.be • URL: http://www.efa-online.org/r/default.asp?iId=ILGLJ • Academics and practitioners interested in financial management and theory and application. Fosters dissemination and exchange of information; provides forum for presentation of research results in the areas of company finance, investment, financial markets, and banking.

European Financial Management and Marketing Association. 8, rue Bayen, F-75017 Paris, France. Phone: 33 1 47425272; Fax: 33 1 47425676; Email: info@efma.com • URL: http://www.efma.com • European financial organizations in 17 countries. Goals are to: establish communication among individuals working with European financial organizations and supporting the concept of marketing; encourage innovation in the field; foster initiation of financial marketing research projects; represent the interests of European financial marketing. Sponsors seminars and professional training sessions. Maintains documentation center. Compiles data on credit card systems.

Institute of Management Accountants, Cost Management Group. 10 Paragon Dr., Ste. 1, Montvale, NJ 07645-1718. Phone: 800-638-4427 or (201)573-9000; Fax: (201)474-1600; Email: ima@imanet.org • URL: http://www.imanet.org • A group within the Institute of Management Accountants. Seeks to improve the quality of corporate cost management systems. Educates business professionals about decision-making and productivity improvement. Provides a means of exchanging opinions and experiences about cost management systems. Conducts surveys; compiles statistics.

I.T. Financial Management Association. PO Box 30188, Santa Barbara, CA 93130. Phone: (805)687-7390; Fax: (805)687-7382; Email: info@itfma.com • URL: http://www.itfma.com • Individuals and corporations interested in the financial management of information technology (IT) organizations. Works for the education and improvement of members and the industry. Offers certification in IT financial management. Conducts peer studies, in-house seminars, and chargeback system reviews. Operates educational programs.

Media Financial Management Association. 550 W Frontage Rd., Ste. 3600, Northfield, IL 60093. Phone: (847)716-7000; Fax: (847)716-7004; Email: info@mediafinance.org • URL: http://www.mediafinance.org • Members are accountants and other financial personnel in the radio and television broadcasting industries. Formerly Broadcast Financial Management Association.

National Association of State and Local Equity Funds. 1970 Broadway, Ste. 250, Oakland, CA 94612. Phone: (510)444-1101; Fax: (510)444-1191; Email: info@naslef.org • URL: http://www.naslef.org • Promotes efficient management of state and local equity funds. Represents individuals, public and private corporations and professional associations with an interest in the tax credit program or an active involvement with a state or local equity fund. Fosters greater understanding of the Low Income Housing Tax Credit (LIHTC).

Native American Finance Officers Association. 1101 30th St. NW, Ste. 500, Washington, DC 20007. Phone: (202)631-2003 • URL: http://www.nafoa.org • Improves the quality of financial and business management of Native American governments and businesses. Promotes tribal sovereignty through sound financial management. Develops scholarship training and internship program for Native American students and tribal employees.

Society of Insurance Financial Management. PO Box 9001, Mount Vernon, NY 10552. Phone: (914)966-3180; Fax: (914)966-3264; Email: sifm@cinn.com • URL: http://www.sifm.org • Represents insurance company officers and employees in financial management departments. Provides a timely forum for discussing current insurance industry issues relating to financial accounting and reporting, reinsurance, taxation, regulatory developments and other relevant topics.

FINANCIAL PLANNING

See also ESTATE PLANNING; PERSONAL FINANCE; TAX PLANNING

ABSTRACTS AND INDEXES

Business Periodicals Index Retrospective. EBSCO Publishing Inc. • 11/year. Quarterly and annual cumulations.

DIRECTORIES

Professional Financial Planning Directory. Info-Group Inc. • Annual. Number of listings: 14,191. Entries include: Name, address, phone, size of advertisement, name of owner or manager, number of employees, year first in "Yellow Pages." Compiled from telephone company "Yellow Pages," nationwide.

HANDBOOKS AND MANUALS

Personal Financial Planning Handbook: With Forms and Checklists. Thomson Reuters Financial Unit. • $360 book. Looseleaf service. Biennial supplementation. Designed for professional financial planners, accountants, attorneys, insurance marketers, brokers, and bankers.

ONLINE DATABASES

Financial Times Business Reports: Technology. The Economist. • A database containing the full text of articles appearing in selected Financial Times newsletters covering developments in the business aspects of new technology, especially in the computer and telecommunications industries. It is commercially available online.

Wilson Business Abstracts Online. H.W. Wilson Co. • Indexes and abstracts 600 major business periodicals, plus the *Wall Street Journal* and the business section of the *New York Times.* Indexing is from 1982, abstracting from 1990, with the two newspapers included from 1993. Updated weekly. Inquire as to online cost and availability. (*Business Periodicals Index* without abstracts is also available online.).

OTHER SOURCES

Financial and Estate Planning: Analysis, Strategies and Checklists. Wolters Kluwer Law & Business CCH. • 4 looseleaf volumes. Price on application. services.

PERIODICALS AND NEWSLETTERS

Accounting and Financial Planning for Law Firms. ALM Media Properties LLC. • Monthly. $499 /year.

Covers budgeting, liability issues, billing systems, benefits management, and other topics relating to law firm administration. (A Law Journal Newsletter, formerly published by Leader Publications).

Bank Investment Consultant: Sales Strategies for the Financial Adviser. SourceMedia Inc. • Monthly. Controlled circulation. Covers sales and marketing techniques for bank investment and asset management divisions. Formerly *Bank Investment Marketing*.

Estate Planner's Alert. Thomson RIA. • Monthly. $290 Individuals Print. Covers the tax aspects of personal finance, including home ownership, investments, insurance, retirement planning, and charitable giving. Formerly *Estate and Financial Planners Alert*.

Financial Counseling and Planning (JFCP). Association for Financial Counseling and Planning Education. • Semiannual. Disseminates scholarly research relating to finacial planning and counseling.

Financial Management (FM). Financial Management Association International. • Quarterly. $392 Institutions for Americas, online only. Covers theory and practice of financial planning, international finance, investment banking, and portfolio management. Includes *Financial Practice* and *Education and Contemporary Finance Digest*.

Financial Planning: The Magazine for Financial Service Professionals. SourceMedia Inc. • Monthly. $79.00 per year. Edited for independent financial planners and insurance agents. Covers retirement planning, estate planning, tax planning, and insurance, including long-term healthcare considerations. Special features include a Retirement Planning Issue, Mutual Fund Performance Survey, and Variable Life and Annuity Survey.

Investment News: The Weekly Newspaper for Financial Advisers. Crain Communications Inc. • Weekly. $29.00 per year. Edited for both personal and institutional investment advisers, planners, and managers.

Money. • 13 times a year. $19.95 per year. Covers all aspects of family finance; investments, careers, shopping, taxes, insurance, consumerism, etc.

On Wall Street. SourceMedia Inc. • Monthly. $96.00 per year. Edited for securities dealers. Includes articles on financial planning, retirement planning, variable annuities, and money management, with special coverage of 401(k) plans and IRAs.

The Practical Accountant: Providing the Competitive Edge. SourceMedia Inc. • Monthly. $65.00 per year. Covers tax planning, financial planning, practice management, client relationships, and related topics.

Private Asset Management. Institutional Investor Inc. Journals Group. • Biweekly. $2,335.00 per year. Newsletter. Includes print and online editions. Edited for managers investing the private assets of wealthy ("high-net-worth") individuals. Includes marketing, taxation, regulation, and fee topics.

Treasury Manager's Report: Strategic Information for the Financial Executive. Access Intelligence L.L.C. • Biweekly. $630.00. Newsletter reporting on legal developments affecting the operations of banks, savings institutions, and other financial service organizations. Formerly *Financial Services Law Report*.

RESEARCH CENTERS AND INSTITUTES

American Institute for Economic Research. 250 Division St., Great Barrington, MA 01230-1000. Phone: 888-528-1216; Fax: (413)528-0103; Email: info@aier.org • URL: http://www.aier.org • Through research and publications, provides "information on economic and financial subjects that is useful and completely independent of special interests." Sponsors a fellowship program for graduate study of economics at the institute and in absentia.

Center for Financial Responsibility. Texas Tech University, Lubbock, TX 79409-11210. Phone: (806)742-5050; Fax: (806)742-5033 • URL: http://www.depts.ttu.edu/cfr • Research areas include financial preparation for retirement, financial education, determinants of financial satisfaction, risk tolerance, and the career preparation of retirement industry professionals.

University of Nebraska—Omaha - Nebraska Business Development Center. Mammel Hall, Ste. 200, College of Business Administration, 6708 Pine St., Omaha, NE 68182. Phone: (402)554-2521; Fax: (402)554-3473; Email: rbernier@unomaha.edu • URL: http://nbdc.unomaha.edu • Sustainable development, technology commercialization, management education, market research, marketing plans, strategic planning, financial planning, cash flow budgeting, capital budgeting, loan packaging, and rural development.

TRADE/PROFESSIONAL ASSOCIATIONS

Association for Financial Counseling and Planning Education. 1940 Duke St., Ste. 200, Alexandria, VA 22314-3452. Phone: (703)684-4484; Fax: (703)684-4485 • URL: http://www.afcpe.org • Members are researchers, academics, financial counselors and financial planners.

Association of Divorce Financial Planners. 514 Fourth St., East Northport, NY 11731-2342. Phone: 888-838-7773; Email: adfp@divorceandfinance.org • URL: http://www.divorceandfinance.org • Aims to create awareness of the benefits of divorce financial planning. Provides members with continuing education. Promotes communication, networking and peer review.

Debtors Anonymous. PO Box 920888, Needham, MA 02492-0009. Phone: 800-421-2383 or (781)453-2743; Fax: (781)453-2745; Email: office@debtorsanonymous.org • URL: http://www.debtorsanonymous.org • Fellowship of men and women who share their experience, strength, and hope with each other that they may solve their common problem of compulsive debiting. Adapts the Twelve Steps and Twelve Traditions of Alcoholics Anonymous World Services for compulsive debtors. Establishes and coordinates self help support groups for people seeking to live without incurring unsecured debt. Helps members develop workable plans for long-term financial and lifestyle goals.

Financial Planning Association. 7535 E Hampden Ave., Ste. 600, Denver, CO 80231. Phone: 800-322-4237 or (303)759-4900; Fax: (303)759-0749; Email: webfeedback@fpanet.org • URL: http://www.plannersearch.org/Pages/home.aspx • Works to support the financial planning process in order to help people achieve their goals and dreams. Believes that everyone needs objective advice to make smart financial decisions and that when seeking the advice of a financial planner, the planner should be a CFP professional.

Institute of Consumer Financial Education. PO Box 34070, San Diego, CA 92163-4070. Phone: (619)239-1401; Fax: (619)923-3284; Email: info@icfe.info • URL: http://www.financial-education-icfe.org • Aims to encourage Americans to improve spending, saving, investing, insuring, and financial planning habits to lessen their dependence on Social Security, welfare, or other individuals. Provides financial education courses to junior high and high school. Maintains a resource section of videos, books and home study courses in personal finance.

Institute of Financial Planning. 1 Redcliff St., Bristol BS1 6NP, United Kingdom. Phone: 44 117 9452470; Fax: 44 117 9292214; Email: enquiries@financialplanning.org.uk • URL: http://www.financialplanning.org.uk • Consists of IFAs, accountants, solicitors, bankers and tax-consultants. Provides holistic financial planning objectively to members of the public and to companies. Seeks to promote the profession and practice of financial planning, increase public awareness of the need for financial planning and ensure high professional and ethical standards amongst its members. Shares knowledge and skills with other professionals for the benefit of mutual clients. Confers certified financial planner license to qualified individuals. Affiliated to Certified Financial Planner Board of Standards.

International Association of Registered Financial Consultants. Financial Planning Bldg., 2507 N Verity Pkwy., Middletown, OH 45042-0506. Phone: 800-532-9060; Fax: (513)424-5752; Email: info@iarfc.org • URL: http://www.iarfc.org • Financial professionals gathered to foster public confidence in the financial planning profession. Helps financial consultants exchange planning techniques. Offers educational programs and professional certifications.

National Association of Financial and Estate Planning. 515 E 4500 S, No. G-200, Salt Lake City, UT 84107. Phone: 800-454-2649; Fax: (877)890-0929 or (801)266-9900; Email: info@accuplan.net • URL: http://www.nafep.com • Represents financial and estate planners.

National Association of Personal Financial Advisors. 3250 N Arlington Heights Rd., Ste. 109, Arlington Heights, IL 60004. Phone: 888-333-6659 or (847)483-5400; Fax: (847)483-5415; Email: info@napfa.org • URL: http://www.napfa.org • Members are full-time financial planners who are compensated on a fee-only basis.

FINANCIAL RATIOS

See also FINANCIAL ANALYSIS

CD-ROM DATABASES

CreditDisk 2.0. Fitch. • Price and frequency on application. CD-ROM provides credit research and ratings on individual banks throughout the world, with Internet updating. Includes graphic displays of rating histories and financial ratios.

FINANCIAL RATIOS

Annual Statement Studies. Risk Management Association. • Annual. Compiled from over 280,000 financial statements.

Annual Statement Studies: Industry Default Probabilities and Cash Flow Measures. Risk Management Association. • Annual. $405 Nonmembers. Serves as a companion volume to the original *Annual Statement Studies*. Gives probability of default estimates on a percentage scale for more than 450 industries. Includes changes in position year-by-year for eight financial statement line items and provides percentage measures of cash flow.

Industry Norms and Key Business Ratios. Dun & Bradstreet Inc. • Annual. Five volumes. Covers over 800 kinds of businesses, arranged by Standard Industrial Classification number. More detailed editions covering longer periods of time are also available.

Quarterly Financial Report for Manufacturing, Mining, Trade, and Selected Service Industries. U.S. Federal Trade Commission and U.S. Securities and Exchange Commission. U.S. Census Bureau Foreign Trade Division. • Quarterly. Quarterly. Report on financial results of U.S. corporations.

ONLINE DATABASES

Compustat. Standard and Poor's. • Financial data on publicly held U.S. and some foreign corporations: data held for 20 years. Inquire as to online cost and availability.

FINANCIAL SERVICES

See INVESTMENT ADVISORY SERVICES

FIRE ALARMS

See ELECTRONIC SECURITY SYSTEMS

FIRE INSURANCE

See also INSURANCE

ABSTRACTS AND INDEXES

Insurance Periodicals Index. Specials Libraries Association, Insurance and Employees Benefits Div. NILS Publishing Co. • Annual. $250.00. Compiled by the Insurance and Employee Benefits Div., Special Libraries Association. A yearly index of over 15,000 articles from about 35 insurance periodicals. Arrangement is by subject, with an index to authors.

ALMANACS AND YEARBOOKS

Insurance Almanac: Who, What, When and Where in Insurance. Criterion Publishing Co. • Annual. $195. Lists insurance agencies and brokerage firms: U.S. and Canadian insurance companies, adjusters, appraisers, auditors, investigators, insurance officials and insurance organizations.

BIBLIOGRAPHIES

Insurance and Employee Benefits Literature. Special Libraries Association. • Bimonthly. $15.00 per year. Lists a wide variety of literature in all branches of the insurance industry. Includes annotations.

ONLINE DATABASES

I.I.I. Data Base Search. Insurance Information Institute. • Provides online citations and abstracts of insurance-related literature in magazines, newspapers, trade journals, and books. Emphasis is on property and casualty insurance issues, including highway safety, product safety, and environmental liability. Inquire as to online cost and availability.

OTHER SOURCES

Best's Insurance Reports: Property-Casualty. A.M. Best Company Inc. • Annual. $750.00. Guide to over 3,200 major property/casualty companies.

BestWeek: Insurance News and Analysis. A.M. Best Company Inc. • Weekly. $495.00 per year. Newsletter. Focuses on key areas of the insurance industry.

Fire and Casualty Insurance Law Reports. Wolters Kluwer Law & Business CCH. • $870.00 per year. Looseleaf service. Semimonthly updates.

PERIODICALS AND NEWSLETTERS

Fire, Casualty and Surety Bulletin. • Monthly. $420.00 per year. Five looseleaf volumes.

NAMIC Magazine. National Association of Mutual Insurance Companies. • Quarterly. Specially packaged for property/casualty insurance executives, many of whom are members of the National Association of Mutual Insurance Companies (NAMIC). It is also designed to be of interest to underwriting, claims, and agency professionals; as well as insurance legislative contacts and management of other industry-related businesses.

STATISTICS SOURCES

Property-Casualty Insurance Facts. Insurance Information Institute. • Annual. $22.50. Formerly *Insurance Facts*.

TRADE/PROFESSIONAL ASSOCIATIONS

American Insurance Association. 2101 L St. NW, Ste. 400, Washington, DC 20037. Phone: (202)828-7100; Fax: (202)293-1219 • URL: http://www.aiadc.org/aiapub • Represents companies providing property and casualty insurance and suretyship. Monitors and reports on economic, political, and social trends; serves as a clearinghouse for ideas, advice, and technical information. Represents members' interests before state and federal legislative and regulatory bodies; coordinates members' litigation.

CPCU Society. 720 Providence Rd., Malvern, PA 19355-0709. Phone: 800-932-2728; Fax: (610)251-2780; Email: membercenter@cpcusociety.org • URL: http://www.cpcusociety.org • Serves as a professional society of individuals who have passed national examinations of the American Institute for Chartered Property Casualty Underwriters, have 3 years of work experience, have agreed to be bound by a code of ethics, and have been awarded CPCU designation. Promotes education, research, social responsibility, and professionalism in the field. Holds seminars, symposia, and workshops.

FIRE PREVENTION

See also FIRE PROTECTION

ABSTRACTS AND INDEXES

Applied Science and Technology Index. EBSCO Publishing Inc. • 11/year. Indexes a wide variety of English language technical, industrial, and engineering periodicals.

ONLINE DATABASES

Applied Science and Technology Index Online. H.W. Wilson Co. • Provides online indexing of 500 major scientific, technical, industrial, and engineering periodicals. Time period is 1983 to date. Monthly updates. Inquire as to online cost and availability.

PERIODICALS AND NEWSLETTERS

Fire and Materials: An International Journal. John Wiley and Sons, Inc., Journals Div. • 8/year. Bimonthly. Individuals, $1,215.00 per year; institutions, $1,620.00 per year. Published in England by John Wiley & Sons Ltd. Provides international coverage of subject matter.

Security Letter. Security Letter Inc. • Description: Contains "solution-oriented information on security and protection of assets from loss," particularly for executives concerned about the following: internal checks and controls, personnel practices, management of change, fraud and embezzlement, business crime trends, security, and urban terrorism. Recurring features include news of research, a calendar of events, semiannual FBI crime data, quarterly financial news of major companies in the security industry, book reviews, security and safety pointers, and a question-and-answer feature.

FIRE PROTECTION

See also FIRE PREVENTION

DIRECTORIES

Directory of African Importers of Fire Fighting Equipment & Supplies. EXIM Infotek Private Ltd. • Covers: 35 African importers of fire fighting equipment. Entries include: Company name, postal address, telephone, fax, e-mail, website, contact person, designation, and product details.

Directory of American Manufacturers & Exporters of Fire Fighting Equipment & Supplies. EXIM Infotek Private Ltd. • Covers: 250 American manufacturers and exporters of airflame, fire alarms, detectors and holder releases, fire doors, fireproof, electric valves, electronic burglary equipment, fire alarm control equipment, extinguishers and cabinets, fire apparatus, residential fire alarm, fire fighting clothing, fire fighting equipment and supplies, gloves, pumps, nozzles, reels, adapters, fire protective coatings, fire rescue blankets, fire retardant products for fabrics, paper, wood and paint, fire sprinklers, fire suppression equipment, industrial foam fire, retardant coatings and mastics, life safety systems, pumpers, rated and non-rated doors, single and double jacket, smoke detectors, smoke vents, sprinkler systems, water tankers, wireless commercial and residential burglar alarm.

Directory of Asian Importers of Fire Fighting Equipment & Supplies. EXIM Infotek Private Ltd. • $500 Individuals. Covers: 250 Asian importers of automatic fire alarm systems, CO2 gas and extinguishers, fire alarm and detection systems, fire alarm equipment, fire alarm panels, fire blankets, fire detection products, fire fighting equipment, fire fighting supplies, fire hose reel, hydrant and sprinkler systems, fire hose systems, fire hydrants, fire panels, fire protective clothing, fire resistant products, fire sensors and components, fire suppression systems, firefighting vehicles and accessories, flame detectors, optical smoke detector, security and fire fighting equipment, smoke detection systems, and smoke detectors. Entries include: Company name, postal address, telephone, fax, e-mail, website, contact person, designation, and product details.

Directory of Australia & New Zealand Importers of Fire Fighting Equipment & Supplies. EXIM Infotek Private Ltd. • $150 Individuals. Covers: 20 Australian and New Zealand importers of CO2 gas and extinguishers, electrical fire stopping and protection systems, fire alarm, fire detection for smoke, flame, heat, and gas, fire detection products, fire extinguishers, fire fighting equipment, fire fighting supplies, fire hoses, fire panels, fire proofing chemicals, fire protection equipment, fire rescue equipment, firefighting powders and foams, paramedic and trauma products, fire rescue tools, flame detection instruments, flame protection products, monitors (foam/water), and pressure protection products. Entries include: Company name, postal address, telephone, fax, e-mail, website, contact person, designation, and product details.

Directory of Chinese Manufacturers & Exporters of Fire Fighting Equipment & Supplies. EXIM Infotek Private Ltd. • Covers: 20 Chinese manufacturers and exporters of fire alarm systems, fire extinguishing systems, fire fighting equipment, fire proof materials, fire protection equipment, fireclay bricks, and flame retardant. Entries include: Company name, postal address, telephone, fax, e-mail, website, contact person, designation, and product details.

Directory of Indian Importers of Fire Fighting Equipment & Supplies. EXIM Infotek Private Ltd. • Covers: 20 Indian importers of fire alarm panels, fire alarm systems, fire detection systems, fire extinguishers, fire fighting equipment, and fire hydrants. Entries include: Company name, postal address, telephone, fax, e-mail, website, contact person, designation, and product details.

Directory of Middle East Importers of Fire Fighting Equipment & Supplies. EXIM Infotek Private Ltd. • Covers: 200 Middle East importers of fire alarm equipment and fire fighting equipment. Entries include: Company name, postal address, telephone, fax, e-mail, website, contact person, designation, and product details.

Directory of SAARC Importers of Fire Fighting Equipment & Supplies. EXIM Infotek Private Ltd. • Covers: 40 companies in member countries of the South Asian Association for Regional Cooperation (SAARC) that import fire and safety instruments, fire alarm systems, fire clothing and equipment, fire demonstration and training, fire detection and alarm systems, fire detection products, fire doors and panic hardware, fire extinguishers, fire fighting equipment, fire hose reel, hydrant and sprinkler systems, fire hose systems, fire rated shutters, fire resistant products, fire trucks and sewerage equipment, fire vehicles and accessories, firefighting uniforms, helmet, emblems, badges, tarpaulins, foam extinguishers, and smoke detection systems. Entries include: Company name, postal address, telephone, fax, e-mail, website, contact person, designation, and product details.

Directory of South American Importers of Fire Fighting Equipment. EXIM Infotek Private Ltd. • Covers: 40 South American importers of fire fighting equipment. Entries include: Company name, postal address, telephone, fax, e-mail, website, contact person, designation, and product details.

Directory of South Korean Manufacturers & Exporters of Fire Fighting Equipment & Supplies. EXIM Infotek Private Ltd. • Covers: 30 South Korean manufacturers and exporters of fire fighting equipment. Entries include: Company name, postal address, telephone, fax, e-mail, website, contact person, designation, and product details.

Directory of Taiwanese Manufacturers & Exporters of Fire Fighting Equipment & Supplies. EXIM Infotek Private Ltd. • Covers: 30 Taiwanese manufacturers and exporters of fire extinguishing systems and fire fighting equipment. Entries include: Company name, postal address, telephone, fax, e-mail, website, contact person, designation, and product details.

HANDBOOKS AND MANUALS

National Fire Codes. National Fire Protection Association. • Annual. $1,295 Individuals. Features a compilation of over 300 fire codes, standards, recommended practices, manuals, and guides on fire protection.

PERIODICALS AND NEWSLETTERS

Fire Chief: Administration, Training, Operations. Primedia Business Magazines and Media. • Monthly. $54.00 per year.

Fire Engineering: The Journal of Fire Suppression and Protection. PennWell Corp., Industrial Div. • Monthly. $19.95 per year.

Fire International: The Journal of the World's Fire Protection Services. DMG World Media Ltd. • 10 times a year. $158.00 per year. Text in English. Summaries in French, German and Spanish.

Fire Technology: An International Journal of Fire Protection Research and Engineering. National Fire Protection Association. • Quarterly. $199.00 per year.

TRADE/PROFESSIONAL ASSOCIATIONS

National Fire Protection Association. 1 Batterymarch Park, Quincy, MA 02169-7471. Phone: 800-344-3555 or (617)770-3000; Fax: (617)770-0700; Email: library@nfpa.org • URL: http://www.nfpa.org • Represents individuals from the fire service, business and industry, health care, educational and other institutions, and individuals in the fields of insurance, government, architecture, and engineering. Develops, publishes, and disseminates standards. Conducts fire safety education programs for the general public. Provides information on fire protection, prevention, and suppression; compiles annual statistics on causes and occupancies of fires, fire deaths, and fire fighter casualties. Provides field service by specialists on electricity, flammable liquids and gases, and marine fire problems. Sponsors National Fire Prevention Week each October and public education campaigns featuring Sparky the Fire Dog.

FIREARMS INDUSTRY

See also DEFENSE INDUSTRIES; MILITARY MARKET

DIRECTORIES

LAW and ORDER Magazine. Hendon Publishing Co. • Lists manufacturers, dealers, and distributors of equipment and services for police departments.

Law Enforcement Technology Directory. Cygnus Business Media Inc. • Annual. $60.00 per year. $6.00 per issue; a directory of products, equipment, services, and technology for police professionals. Includes weapons, uniforms, communications equipment, and software.

PERIODICALS AND NEWSLETTERS

American Firearms Industry. National Association of Federally Licensed Firearms Dealers. AFI Communications Group, Inc. • Monthly. $35.00 per year.

Bureau of Alcohol, Tobacco, and Firearms Quarterly Bulletin. Bureau of Alcohol, Tobacco, and Firearms, U.S. Department of the Treasury. U. S. Government Printing Office. • Quarterly. $25.00 per year. Laws and regulations.

Guns and Ammo. PRIMEDIA Inc. • Monthly. $14.97 per year.

Guns Magazine: Finest in the Firearms Field. Publishers Development Corp. • Monthly. $24.95 U.S.. Firearms information on current shooting products and trends.

Shooting Industry. Publishers Development Corp. • Monthly. $45 Other countries. Magazine serving the firearms industry.

TRADE/PROFESSIONAL ASSOCIATIONS

National Rifle Association of America. 11250 Waples Mill Rd., Fairfax, VA 22030-7400. Phone: 800-672-3888 or (703)267-1614; Fax: (703)267-3913; Email: nfmstaff@nrahq.org • URL: http://www.nrahq.org • Target shooters, hunters, gun collectors, gunsmiths, police officers, and others interested in firearms. Promotes rifle, pistol, and shotgun shooting, hunting, gun collecting, home firearm safety, and wildlife conservation. Encourages civilian marksmanship. Educates police firearms instructors. Maintains national and international records of shooting competitions; sponsors teams to compete in world championships. Also maintains comprehensive collection of antique and modern firearms. Administers the NRA Political Victory Fund. Compiles statistics; sponsors research and education programs; maintains speakers' bureau and museum. Lobbies on firearms issues.

FIRING OF EMPLOYEES

See DISMISSAL OF EMPLOYEES

FISH CULTURE

See AQUACULTURE

FISH INDUSTRY

See also SEAFOOD INDUSTRY

ABSTRACTS AND INDEXES

NTIS Alerts: Agriculture & Food. U.S. Department of Commerce National Technical Information Service. • Biweekly. $130 per year. Covers agricultural economics, horticulture, fisheries, veterinary medicine, food technology, and related subjects.

DIRECTORIES

Directory of Fisheries of the Former Soviet Union. Flegon Press. • $100. Covers: Fisheries of the former USSR, including production associations, research and design institutes, nautical and fishery schools, shipyards, fishing gear factories, netting mills, fish processing and breeding plants, fish farms, and retail fish vendors among others. Entries include: Name, address, phone, telex, managing personnel.

Fish (Tropical) Dealers Directory. InfoGroup Inc. • Annual. Number of listings: 2,236. Entries include: Name, address, phone, size of advertisement, name of owner or manager, number of employees, year first in "Yellow Pages." Compiled from telephone company "Yellow Pages," nationwide.

Major Food and Drink Companies of the World. Cengage Learning Inc. • 12th edition. eBook. Published by Graham & Whiteside. Contains profiles and trade names for more than 9,200 important food and beverage companies in various countries. In addition to foods, includes both alcoholic and nonalcoholic drink products.

INTERNET DATABASES

USDA. U.S. National Institute of Standards and Technology. 100 Bureau Dr., Gaithersburg, MD 20899-1070. Phone: 800-877-8339 or (301)975-6478 or (202)720-2791; Fax: (301)975-8295; Email: inquiries@nist.gov • URL: http://www.nist.gov • The USDA home page has six sections: News and Information; What's New; About USDA; Agencies; Opportunities; Search and Help. Keyword searching is offered from the USDA home page and from various individual agency home pages. Agencies are the Economic Research Service, Agricultural Marketing Service, National Agricultural Statistics Service, National Agricultural Library, and about 12 others. Updating varies. Fees: Free.

ONLINE DATABASES

Food Science and Technology Abstracts (online). IFIS North American Desk. • Produced by International Food Information Service. Provides about 500,000 online citations, with abstracts, to the international literature of food science, technology, commodities, engineering, and processing. Approximately 2,000 periodicals are covered. Time period is 1969 to date, with monthly updates. Inquire as to online cost and availability.

PERIODICALS AND NEWSLETTERS

Commercial Fisheries News. Compass Publications, Fisheries Division. • Monthly. $21.95 print only. Covers the commercial fishing industry in New England. Includes news of marine technology, boatbuilding, fish and lobster prices, business trends, government regulation, and other topics.

Fisheries. American Fisheries Society. • Monthly. $1,530 Institutions American Fisheries Society Pack (online only). Covers the management of fisheries and aquatic resources, including related technology.

North American Journal of Fisheries Management. American Fisheries Society. • 6/year. $55 Individuals print, North America. Covers fisheries management trends and research.

Seafood Business. Diversified Business Communications Inc. • $57 U.S.. Edited for a wide range of seafood buyers, including distributors, restaurants, supermarkets, and institutions. Special issues feature information on specific products, such as salmon or lobster.

PRICE SOURCES

Seafood Price-Current. Urner Barry Publications Inc. • Semiweekly. $756 Individuals.

RESEARCH CENTERS AND INSTITUTES

Darling Marine Center. University of Maine, 193 Clarks Cove Rd., Walpole, ME 04573. Phone: (207)563-3146; Fax: (207)563-3119; Email: darling@maine.edu • URL: http://www.dmc.maine.edu • Formerly Ira C. Darling Center for Research, Teaching, and Service.

Interactive Oceanography Division. University of California, San Diego, Scripps Institution of Oceanography, 8650 Discovery Way, La Jolla, CA 92093. Phone: (858)534-2068; Fax: (858)534-6500 • URL: http://www.iod.ucsd.edu • Formerly Marine Life Research Group.

University of California, San Diego - Scripps Institution of Oceanography. 9500 Gilman Dr., MC 0210, La Jolla, CA 92093-0210. Phone: (858)534-3624; Fax: (858)534-5306; Email: scrippsnews@

ucsd.edu • URL: http://scripps.ucsd.edu • Marine sciences, focusing on physical, chemical, biological, geological, and geophysical studies.

STATISTICS SOURCES

Agricultural Statistics. U.S. Department of Agriculture National Agricultural Statistics Service. • Annual. $46 Individuals. Provides a wide variety of statistical data relating to agricultural production, supplies, consumption, prices/price-supports, foreign trade, costs, and returns, as well as farm labor, loans, income, and population. In many cases, historical data is shown annually for 10 years. In addition to farm data, includes detailed fishery statistics.

TRADE/PROFESSIONAL ASSOCIATIONS

American Fisheries Society. 5410 Grosvenor Ln., Bethesda, MD 20814. Phone: (301)897-8616; Fax: (301)897-8096; Email: main@fisheries.org • URL: http://fisheries.org • International scientific organization of fisheries and aquatic science professionals, including fish culturists, fish biologists, water quality scientists, fish health professionals, fish technologists, educators, limnologists, and oceanographers. Promotes the development of all branches of fishery science and practice, and the conservation, development, and wise utilization of fisheries, both recreational and commercial. Strengthens professional standards by certifying fisheries scientists, stressing professional ethics, and providing forums for the exchange of scientific and management information. Represents members through written and verbal testimony before legislative and administrative bodies concerning aquatic environmental issues. Maintains over 30 committees.

Southeastern Fisheries Association. 1118-B Thomasville Rd., Tallahassee, FL 32303. Phone: (850)224-0612; Fax: (850)222-3663; Email: info@sfaonline.org • URL: http://www.sfaonline.org/ • Producers, distributors and suppliers of seafood in the South Atlantic and Gulf of Mexico areas. Disseminates information on legislation, both proposed and implemented, that affects fishermen in that area. Promotes and represents commercial fishermen's interests in legislative, industrial and environmental matters. Provides HAACP training onsite.

Sustainable Fishery Advocates. 303 Potrero St., Ste. 201, Santa Cruz, CA 95060. Phone: (831)427-1707; Fax: (309)213-4688; Email: t.ish@sustainablefishery.org • URL: http://www.sustainablefishery.org • Aims to improve the sustainability and financial performance of seafood retailers, distributors and producers. Provides innovative, market-based tools to promote the health and recovery of ocean ecosystems. Supports sustainability in the seafood industry through environmentally responsible business practices.

FITNESS INDUSTRY

ABSTRACTS AND INDEXES

Readers' Guide to Periodical Literature. EBSCO Publishing Inc. • Provides indexing for over 400 periodicals dating back to 1983.

CD-ROM DATABASES

Readers' Guide to Periodical Literature. EBSCO Publishing Inc. • Provides indexing for over 400 periodicals dating back to 1983.

DIRECTORIES

Fitness Centers Directory. InfoGroup Inc. • Annual. Number of listings: 17,012. Entries include: Name, address, phone, size of advertisement, name of owner or manager, number of employees, year first in "Yellow Pages." Compiled from telephone company "Yellow Pages," nationwide.

Fitness Management Products and Services Source Guide. Leisure Publications Inc. • Annual. $24.00. A directory of more than 1,250 fitness equipment manufacturers and suppliers of services. Includes a glossary of terms related to the fitness industry and employee wellness programs.

Looking Fit Buyers Guide. Virgo Publishing L.L.C. • Lists suppliers of products and equipment for the tanning industry.

HANDBOOKS AND MANUALS

Physical Fitness Center. Entrepreneur Press. • Looseleaf. $59.50. A practical guide to starting a physical fitness center. Covers profit potential, start-up costs, market size evaluation, owner's time required, site selection, lease negotiation, pricing, accounting, advertising, promotion, etc. (Start-Up Business Guide No. E1172.).

PERIODICALS AND NEWSLETTERS

Club Business International. Fitness Industry Association. • Monthly. Publication covering physical fitness.

Club Industry's Fitness Business Pro. Penton. • Monthly. Trade magazine covering trends and news for owners and operators of commercial health and fitness facilities.

Fitness Management. Leisure Publications Inc. • Monthly. $24.00 per year. Published for owners and managers of physical fitness centers, both commercial and corporate.

RESEARCH CENTERS AND INSTITUTES

Human Power, Biochemechanics, and Robotics Laboratory. Cornell University, Dept. of Theoretical and Applied Mechanics, 306 Kimball Hall, Ithaca, NY 14853-1503. Phone: (607)255-7108; Fax: (607)255-2011; Email: ruina@cornell.edu • URL: http://ruina.tam.cornell.edu/ • Conducts research relating to human muscle-powered machines, such as bicycles and rowers.

National Institute for Fitness and Sport. 250 University Blvd., Indianapolis, IN 46202. Phone: (317)274-3432; Fax: (317)274-7408 • URL: http://www.nifs.org • Exercise physiology, sports medicine, and health and fitness education.

University of Florida - Center for Exercise Science. PO Box 118208, Gainesville, FL 32611. Phone: (352)294-1713; Fax: (352)392-0316; Email: spowers@hhp.ufl.edu • URL: http://apk.hhp.ufl.edu/index.php/departments-centers/center-for-exercise-science-ces • Studies fitness as it relates to the general population and as it relates to athletic performance.

University of Michigan - Health Management Research Center. 1015 E Huron St., Ann Arbor, MI 48104-1688. Phone: (734)763-2462; Fax: (734)763-2206; Email: hmrc-contact@umich.edu • URL: http://www.hmrc.umich.edu • Examines the relationships between lifestyle behaviors, quality of life, organizational productivity, and health care costs.

STATISTICS SOURCES

Profiles of Success. International Health, Racquet and Sportsclub Association. • Annual. Members, $249.95; non-members, $499.95. Provides detailed financial statistics for commercial health clubs, sports clubs, and gyms.

United States Census of Service Industries. U.S. Department of Commerce U.S. Census Bureau. • Quinquennial. Various reports available.

TRADE/PROFESSIONAL ASSOCIATIONS

Association of Pool and Spa Professionals. 2111 Eisenhower Ave., Ste. 500, Alexandria, VA 22314. Phone: (703)838-0083; Fax: (703)549-0493; Email: memberservices@apsp.org • URL: http://www.apsp.org • Formerly National Spa and Pool Institute.

International Association for Worksite Health Promotion. c/o Heather Turner, Program Officer, 401 W Michigan St., Indianapolis, IN 46202. Phone: (317)637-9200; Email: iawhp@acsm.org • URL: http://www.acsm-iawhp.org • Members are physical fitness professionals hired by major corporations to conduct health and fitness programs. Formerly Association for Fitness in Business.

FIXED INCOME SECURITIES

See BONDS

FLAVORINGS

See ADDITIVES AND FLAVORINGS

FLOOR COVERINGS

DIRECTORIES

Directory of Australia and New Zealand Importers of Carpets, Durries, Floor Coverings. EXIM Infotek Private Ltd. • $150 Individuals. Covers: 30 Australian and New Zealand importers of carpets, rugs, designer rugs, floor coverings, hand knotted rugs, hand tufted rugs, handloomed wool rugs, handmade carpets, handmade woollen rugs, linoleum (vinyl), mats (grass, rattan, bamboo, cotton), and rubber floor coverings. Entries include: Company name, postal address, telephone, fax, e-mail, website, contact person, designation, and product details.

Directory of British Importers of Carpets, Durries and Floor Coverings. EXIM Infotek Private Ltd. • $200 Individuals. Covers: 25 British importers of carpets, rugs, oriental carpets, oriental rugs, and vinyl floorings. Entries include: Company name, postal address, telephone, fax, e-mail, website, contact person, designation, and product details.

Directory of Chinese Manufacturers & Exporters of Carpets, Durries, Floor Coverings. EXIM Infotek Private Ltd. • $10 Individuals. Covers: 50 Chinese manufacturers and exporters of carpets, PVC floor tiles, PVC tiles, rugs, silk carpets, and woolen carpets. Entries include: Company name, postal address, city, country, phone, fax, e-mail and websites, contact person, designation, and product details.

Directory of German Importers of Carpets, Durries and Floor Coverings. EXIM Infotek Private Ltd. • $200 Individuals. Covers: 20 German importers of carpets, rugs, coir mats, coir mattings, floor coverings, and oriental rugs. Entries include: Company name, postal address, telephone, fax, e-mail, website, contact person, designation, and product details.

Directory of Japanese Importers of Carpets, Durries, Rugs and Floor Coverings. EXIM Infotek Private Ltd. • $250 Individuals. Covers: 80 Japanese importers of carpets, rugs, floor coverings, flooring goods, and mats. Entries include: Company name, postal address, telephone, fax, e-mail, website, contact person, designation, and product details.

Directory of Taiwanese Manufacturers & Exporters of Carpets, Durries, Rugs & Floor Coverings. EXIM Infotek Private Ltd. • $5 Individuals. Covers: 20 Taiwanese manufacturers and exporters of carpets and rugs. Entries include: Company name, postal address, city, country, phone, fax, e-mail and websites, contact person, designation, and product details.

ICS Cleaning Specialists Annual Trade Directory and Buying Guide. Specialist Publications Inc. • Annual. $35. Lists about 6,000 manufacturers and distributors of floor covering installation and cleaning equipment. Formerly *Installation and Cleaning Specialists Trade Directory and Buying Guide.*

The International Directory of Importers - Floor Coverings, Carpets and Rugs Importers. Interdata. • $200 Individuals print. Covers: 1,000 international firms importing floor coverings, carpets and rugs. Entries include: Company name and address, contact person, email, number of employees, year established, phone and telefaxes, business activity, bank references, as well as a listing of floor coverings, carpets and rugs currently being imported.

NFT Directory & Buying Guide. BNP Media. • Annual. $35 Individuals. Covers: Floor covering manufacturers, distributors, retail groups and franchises, installation and technical training schools, sales agents, and products.

FINANCIAL RATIOS

Annual Statement Studies. Risk Management Association. • Annual. Compiled from over 280,000 financial statements.

Annual Statement Studies: Industry Default Probabilities and Cash Flow Measures. Risk Management Association. • Annual. $405 Nonmembers. Serves as a companion volume to the original *Annual Statement Studies*. Gives probability of default estimates on a percentage scale for more than 450 industries. Includes changes in position year-by-year for eight financial statement line items and provides percentage measures of cash flow.

INTERNET DATABASES

Manufacturing Profiles. U. S. Bureau of the Census. Phone: (301)763-4636 or (301)763-4100; Fax: (301)763-4794; Email: webmaster@census.gov • URL: http://www.census.gov/prod/www/abs/mfg-prof.html • The Census Bureau makes available free on PDF (Portable Document Format) an annual consolidation of the entire Current Industrial Report series, presenting "all the data compiled." Contains statistics on production, shipments, inventories, consumption, exports, imports, and orders for a wide variety of manufactured products.

PERIODICALS AND NEWSLETTERS

Carpet and Rug Industry. Rodman Publications. • Monthly. $42.00 per year. Edited for manufacturers and distributors of carpets and rugs.

Carpet Flooring Retail. CMP Information Ltd. • Biweekly. $92.00 per year. Formerly *Carpet and Floorcoverings Review*.

Dalton Carpet Journal. The Daily Citizen News. • Monthly. $12.00. Covers the international tufted carpet market.

Floor Covering News. RO-EL Productions Inc. • Biweekly. $25 Individuals. Magazine featuring articles of interest to floor covering retailers, distributors, and manufacturers.

Floor Covering Weekly: The Business Newspaper of the Floor Covering Industry. FCW. • 32 times a year. $61.00 per year.

ICS Cleaning Specialist. BNP Media. • Monthly. Free to qualified personnel. Written for floor covering installers and cleaners. Formerly *Installation and Cleaning Specialist*.

Oriental Rug Review. Oriental Rug Auction Review Inc. • Bimonthly. $48.00 per year.

Paint and Decorating Retailer. Paint and Decorating Retailers Association. • Monthly. $45.00 per year. Formerly *Decorating Retailer*.

STATISTICS SOURCES

United States Census of Manufactures. U.S. Department of Commerce U.S. Census Bureau. • Quinquennial. Results presented in reports, tape, CD-ROM, and Diskette files.

U.S. Industry and Trade Outlook. U.S. Department of Commerce National Technical Information Service. • Annual. Produced by the International Trade Administration, U.S. Department of Commerce, in a "public-private" partnership with DRI/McGraw-Hill and Standard & Poor's. Provides basic data, outlook for the current year, and "Long-Term Prospects" (five-year projections) for a wide variety of products and services. Includes high technology industries. Formerly *U.S. Industrial Outlook*.

TRADE/PROFESSIONAL ASSOCIATIONS

Carpet and Rug Institute. 100 S Hamilton St., Dalton, GA 30720. Phone: (706)278-3176; Fax: (706)278-8835; Email: snewberry@carpet-rug.org • URL: http://www.carpet-rug.org • Formerly Tufted Textile Manufacturers Association.

Carpet Cushion Council. 5103 Brandywine Dr., Eagleville, PA 19403. Phone: (484)687-5170; Fax: (610)885-5131; Email: info@carpetcushion.org • URL: http://www.carpetcushion.org • Works to promote the sale and use of separate carpet cushions; to act as public relations counsel for the industry; to maintain contact with various government agencies; to establish quality and performance standards. Compiles statistics; maintains speakers' bureau.

Jute Carpet Backing Council and Burlap and Jute Association. Dayton National Sales Office and Plant, 322 Davis Ave., Dayton, OH 45403. Phone: 800-543-3400 or (937)258-8000; Fax: (937)258-0029 • Affiliated with Burlap and Jute Association. Formerly Jute Carpet Backing Council.

FLORIST SHOPS

DIRECTORIES

Florist-Buyers Directory. FTD Association. • Annual. $7.00. Lists 1,200 suppliers in floral industry.

FINANCIAL RATIOS

Annual Statement Studies. Risk Management Association. • Annual. Compiled from over 280,000 financial statements.

Annual Statement Studies: Industry Default Probabilities and Cash Flow Measures. Risk Management Association. • Annual. $405 Nonmembers. Serves as a companion volume to the original *Annual Statement Studies*. Gives probability of default estimates on a percentage scale for more than 450 industries. Includes changes in position year-by-year for eight financial statement line items and provides percentage measures of cash flow.

PERIODICALS AND NEWSLETTERS

Canadian Florist Greenhouse & Nursery: The National Horticulural Business Publication. Horticulture Publications. • Monthly. $18. Magazine for commercial florists, greenhouse growers, nurseries, garden centers, interior landscapers, and craft and hobby retailers.

Florafacts. Florafax International, Inc. • Monthly. $15.00 per year.

Floral Retailing Magazine: We Build Floral Business. Vance Publishing Corp. • Monthly. $35 Individuals. Magazine for managers and buyers in the high volume retail floral industry.

Florists' Review. Florist's Review Enterprises Inc. • Monthly. $42.00 per year.

Flowers &: The Beautiful Magazine About the Business of Flowers. Teleflora. • Monthly. $38.95 per year.

STATISTICS SOURCES

United States Census of Retail Trade. U.S. Department of Commerce U.S. Census Bureau. • Quinquennial.

FLOUR INDUSTRY

See also GRAIN INDUSTRY

ABSTRACTS AND INDEXES

Flour Milling and Baking Abstracts. CCFAA Technology Ltd. • Bimonthly. Members, $275.00 per year; non-members, $325.00 per year. Includes print and online editions.

CD-ROM DATABASES

OECD Statistical Compendium. Organization for Economic Cooperation and Development. • Semiannual. $1,905.00 per year for 1 to 10 users. CD-ROM contains more than 730,000 monthly, quarterly, and annual time series for OECD countries, 1960 to date. Includes fully searchable data on agriculture, food, economic indicators, national accounts, employment, energy, finance, industry, technology, and foreign trade. Results can be displayed in various forms.

DIRECTORIES

Major Food and Drink Companies of the World. Cengage Learning Inc. • 12th edition. eBook. Published by Graham & Whiteside. Contains profiles and trade names for more than 9,200 important food and beverage companies in various countries. In addition to foods, includes both alcoholic and nonalcoholic drink products.

INTERNET DATABASES

Business 2.0 Web Guide to the Best Business Links. Business 2.0 Media Inc. Phone: (415)293-4800; Email: support@business2.com • URL: http://www.business2.com/webguide • Web site presents an extensive, searchable directory of links to "the best, most informative, and authoritative web pages." Twenty main categories cover business, finance, career, company information, people, and technology topics, with thousands of subtopics, all linking to Web sites recommended by experienced business researchers. Fees: Free.

Fedstats. Federal Interagency Council on Statistical Policy. Phone: (202)395-7254 • URL: http://www.fedstats.gov • Web site features an efficient search facility for full-text statistics produced by more than 100 federal agencies, including the Census Bureau, the Bureau of Economic Analysis, and the Bureau of Labor Statistics. Boolean searches can be made within one agency or for all agencies combined. Links are offered to international statistical bureaus, including the UN, IMF, OECD, UNESCO, Eurostat, and 20 individual countries. Fees: Free.

FreeLunch.com. Economy.com, Inc. Phone: (610)696-8700; Fax: (610)696-1678 • URL: http://www.freelunch.com • Web site provides free access to more than 200 million economic and financial data series, covering industry, demographics, labor markets, prices, retail sales, government spending, trade, interest rates, housing starts, the stock market, etc. Data is available in either chart or table form. Searching is offered. Free, but registration required. Economy.com, Inc. also offers fee-based economic analysis at *The Dismal Scientist* site (www.dismal.com).

Manufacturing Profiles. U. S. Bureau of the Census. Phone: (301)763-4636 or (301)763-4100; Fax: (301)763-4794; Email: webmaster@census.gov • URL: http://www.census.gov/prod/www/abs/mfg-prof.html • The Census Bureau makes available free on PDF (Portable Document Format) an annual consolidation of the entire Current Industrial Report series, presenting "all the data compiled." Contains statistics on production, shipments, inventories, consumption, exports, imports, and orders for a wide variety of manufactured products.

USDA. U.S. National Institute of Standards and Technology. 100 Bureau Dr., Gaithersburg, MD 20899-1070. Phone: 800-877-8339 or (301)975-6478 or (202)720-2791; Fax: (301)975-8295; Email: inquiries@nist.gov • URL: http://www.nist.gov • The USDA home page has six sections: News and Information; What's New; About USDA; Agencies; Opportunities; Search and Help. Keyword searching is offered from the USDA home page and from various individual agency home pages. Agencies are the Economic Research Service, Agricultural Marketing Service, National Agricultural Statistics Service, National Agricultural Library, and about 12 others.

Updating varies. Fees: Free.

ONLINE DATABASES

Food Science and Technology Abstracts (online). IFIS North American Desk. • Produced by International Food Information Service. Provides about 500,000 online citations, with abstracts, to the international literature of food science, technology, commodities, engineering, and processing. Approximately 2,000 periodicals are covered. Time period is 1969 to date, with monthly updates. Inquire as to online cost and availability.

PRICE SOURCES

Commercial Review. Oregon Feed and Grain Association Inc. • Weekly. $35.00 per year.

STATISTICS SOURCES

Agricultural Statistics. U.S. Department of Agriculture National Agricultural Statistics Service. • Annual. $46 Individuals. Provides a wide variety of statistical data relating to agricultural production, supplies, consumption, prices/price-supports, foreign trade, costs, and returns, as well as farm labor, loans, income, and population. In many cases, historical data is shown annually for 10 years. In addition to farm data, includes detailed fishery statistics.

Survey of Current Business. U. S. Government Printing Office. • Published by Bureau of Economic Analysis, U. S. Department of Commerce. Presents a wide variety of business and economic data.

TRADE/PROFESSIONAL ASSOCIATIONS

American Institute of Baking. 1213 Bakers Way, Manhattan, KS 66505-3999. Phone: 800-633-5137 or (785)537-4750; Fax: (785)537-1493; Email: info@aibonline.org • URL: http://www.aibonline.org • Nutrition, including effects of ingredients, processing, and baked products on physiological responses in humans; and cereal science, particularly applied technology. Contract research projects include performance characteristics of new and improved ingredients for the baking industry and product and process development utilizing laboratory and pilot bakeries.

International Association of Operative Millers. 12351 W 96th Terr., Ste. 100, Lenexa, KS 66215. Phone: (913)338-3377; Fax: (913)338-3553; Email: info@iaom.info • URL: http://www.iaom.info • Represents operation managers, plant managers, superintendents, grinders, bolters, engineers, and others engaged in the production of flour, feeds and cereal products through processing of wheat, corn, oats, rice, seeds, and spices.

National Association of Flour Distributors. 5350 Woodland Pl., Canfield, OH 44406. Phone: (330)718-6563; Fax: (877)573-1230 • URL: http://www.thenafd.com • Affiliated with National Association of Wholesaler-Distributors.

North American Millers' Association. 600 Maryland Ave. SW, Ste. 825 W, Washington, DC 20024. Phone: (202)484-2200 or (202)554-1618; Fax: (202)488-7416; Email: generalinfo@namamillers.org • URL: http://www.namamillers.org • Grain milling companies that are processors of specially blended corn, wheat, and sorghum foods that are used primarily for overseas feeding programs. Millers of wheat, corn, oats, durum, and rye flour; members' mill 95 percent of total United States capacity.

FLUIDICS INDUSTRY

See also HYDRAULIC ENGINEERING AND MACHINERY

ABSTRACTS AND INDEXES

Applied Science and Technology Index. EBSCO Publishing Inc. • 11/year. Indexes a wide variety of English language technical, industrial, and engineering periodicals.

Current Contents: Engineering, Computing and Technology. Thomson Reuters Intellectual Property and Science. • Weekly. $730 per year. Reproductions of contents pages of technical journals. Includes *Author Index, Address Directory, Current Book Contents,* and *Title Word Index.* Formerly *Current Contents: Engineering, Technology and Applied Sciences.*

Mechanical Engineering Abstracts. Cambridge Scientific Abstracts L.P. • Quarterly. $1,620 Individuals print + web edition (includes shipping). Database covering international literature on mechanical engineering, engineering management, and production engineering, including specific and theoretical applications. Formerly *ISMEC - Mechanical Engineering Abstracts.*

Science Citation Index. Thomson Reuters Intellectual Property and Science. • Weekly. Includes *Source Index, Citation Index, Permuterm Subject Index,* and *Corporate Index.* Provides researchers, administrators, faculty, and students with quick, powerful access to the bibliographic and citation information they need to find research data, analyze trends, journals and researchers, and share their findings.

CD-ROM DATABASES

Science Citation Index. Thomson Reuters Intellectual Property and Science. • Weekly. Includes *Source Index, Citation Index, Permuterm Subject Index,* and *Corporate Index.* Provides researchers, administrators, faculty, and students with quick, powerful access to the bibliographic and citation information they need to find research data, analyze trends, journals and researchers, and share their findings.

DIRECTORIES

Fluid Power Handbook and Directory. Penton Media Inc. • Biennial. Over 1,500 manufacturers and 3,000 distributors of fluid power products in the United States and Canada.

INTERNET DATABASES

Manufacturing Profiles. U. S. Bureau of the Census. Phone: (301)763-4636 or (301)763-4100; Fax: (301)763-4794; Email: webmaster@census.gov • URL: http://www.census.gov/prod/www/abs/mfg-prof.html • The Census Bureau makes available free on PDF (Portable Document Format) an annual consolidation of the entire Current Industrial Report series, presenting "all the data compiled." Contains statistics on production, shipments, inventories, consumption, exports, imports, and orders for a wide variety of manufactured products.

ONLINE DATABASES

Applied Science and Technology Index Online. H.W. Wilson Co. • Provides online indexing of 500 major scientific, technical, industrial, and engineering periodicals. Time period is 1983 to date. Monthly updates. Inquire as to online cost and availability.

FLUIDEX. Elsevier. • Produced in the Netherlands by Elsevier Science B.V. Provides indexing and abstracting of the international literature of fluid engineering and technology, 1973 to date, with monthly updates. Also known as *Fluid Engineering Abstracts.* Inquire as to online cost and availability.

Thomas Register Online. Thomas Publishing Company L.L.C. • Provides concise information on approximately 194,000 U. S. companies, mainly manufacturers, with over 50,000 product classifications. Indexes over 115,000 trade names. Information is updated semiannually. Inquire as to online cost and availability.

PERIODICALS AND NEWSLETTERS

Hydraulics and Pneumatics: The Magazine of Fluid Power and Motion Control Systems. Penton Media Inc.

Industrial Equipment News. Thomas Publishing Company L.L.C. • Monthly. Contains new product information for manufacturing industries.

National Fluid Power Association--Reporter. National Fluid Power Association. • Description: Includes articles on the fluid power market, manufacturing, people and meetings. Also includes statistics.

New Equipment Digest. Intertec Publishing. • Monthly. Magazine (tabloid) showcasing new or improved equipment, products, materials, and components. Formerly *Material Handling Engineering.*

New Equipment Reporter: New Products Industrial News. DeRoche Publications. • Monthly. Controlled circulation.

Processing. Putman Media Inc. • 14 times a year. $54.00 per year. Emphasis is on descriptions of new products for all areas of industrial processing, including valves, controls, filters, pumps, compressors, fluidics, and instrumentation.

RESEARCH CENTERS AND INSTITUTES

Fluid Power Laboratory. Ohio State University, Mechanical Engineering Department, 206 W 19th Ave., Columbus, OH 43210. Phone: (614)292-2289; Fax: (614)292-3163 • URL: http://mae.osu.edu.

Milwaukee School of Engineering - Fluid Power Institute. 1025 N Broadway St., Milwaukee, WI 53202-3109. Phone: 800-332-6763 or (414)277-7191; Fax: (414)277-7470; Email: explore@msoe.edu • URL: http://www.msoe.edu/community/academics/labs/page/1917/fluid-power-institute • Fluid power and motion control evaluation and design of components and systems, including field troubleshooting, test stand design, mathematical modeling and simulation of components and systems, including, pumps, motors, cylinders, and valves, reliability assessments of fluid power components and systems, hydraulic fluids development and contamination control programs. Conducts performance and endurance tests on components and systems including pressure drop flowrate, fatigue, and dynamic response tests. Develops national and international industrial fluid power standards.

TRADE/PROFESSIONAL ASSOCIATIONS

National Fluid Power Association. 3333 N Mayfair Rd., Ste. 211, Milwaukee, WI 53222-3219. Phone: (414)778-3344; Fax: (414)778-3361; Email: nfpa@nfpa.com • URL: http://www.nfpa.com • Manufacturers of components such as fittings used in transmitting power by hydraulic and pneumatic pumps, valves, cylinders, filters, seals; the components are used in industrial and mobile machinery in the material-handling, automotive, railway, aircraft, marine, aerospace, construction, agricultural, and other industries. Works to develop: American National Standards Institute and International Organization for Standardization; fluid power technical standards; fluid power index (industry sales); management and marketing studies. Compiles statistics. Administers and serves as secretariat to several international project groups and other fluid power organizations.

FLUORESCENT LIGHTING

See LIGHTING

FM BROADCASTING

See RADIO BROADCASTING INDUSTRY

FOOD ADDITIVES

See ADDITIVES AND FLAVORINGS

FOOD EQUIPMENT AND MACHINERY

ABSTRACTS AND INDEXES

Applied Science and Technology Index. EBSCO Publishing Inc. • 11/year. Indexes a wide variety of English language technical, industrial, and engineering periodicals.

Food Science and Technology Abstracts. Ovid Technologies Inc. • Monthly. $1,780.00 per year. Provides worldwide coverage of the literature of food technology and food production.

Foods Adlibra: Key to the World's Food Literature. General Mills, Inc. Foods Adlibra Publications. • Semimonthly. $240.00 per year. Provides journal citations and abstracts to the literature of food technology and packaging.

ALMANACS AND YEARBOOKS

Almanac of the Canning, Freezing, Preserving Industries. Food Institute. • Annual. $110 Individuals Hard Copy mail delivery or pdf email from publisher. Contains U.S. food laws and regulations and detailed production statistics.

DIRECTORIES

Directory of American Manufacturers and Exporters of Restaurant, Hotel and Catering Equipment and Supplies. EXIM Infotek Private Ltd. • Covers: 120 American manufacturers and exporters of beverage dispensers and equipment for hotels and restaurants. Entries include: Company name, postal address, telephone, fax, e-mail, website, contact person, designation, and product details.

Directory of Asian Importers of Restaurant, Hotel and Catering Equipment. EXIM Infotek Private Ltd. • $250 Individuals. Covers: 70 Asian importers of catering equipment, catering supplies, commercial kitchen equipment, cooking equipment (patio and outdoors), food service equipment, food waste disposer, hotel and restaurant equipment, hotel amenity goods, hotel equipment and supplies, microwave equipment and component, hotel and catering service requisites. Entries include: Company name, postal address, telephone, fax, e-mail, website, contact person, designation, and product details.

Directory of British Importers of Restaurant, Hotel and Catering Equipment. EXIM Infotek Private Ltd. • Covers: 25 British importers of catering equipment and supplies, cooking equipment (patio and outdoors), microwave equipment and component, restaurant and hotel equipment. Entries include: Company name, postal address, telephone, fax, e-mail, website, contact person, designation, and product details.

Directory of Middle East Importers of Restaurant, Hotel and Catering Equipment. EXIM Infotek Private Ltd. • Covers: 160 Middle East importers of catering equipment, cooking ranges and oven, restaurant and hotel equipment. Entries include: Company name, postal address, telephone, fax, e-mail, website, contact person, designation, and product details.

Directory of North American Importers of Restaurant, Hotel and Catering Equipment. EXIM Infotek Private Ltd. • $250 Individuals. Covers: 80 North American importers of bar supplies, barbecue, catering equipment and supplies, cooking equipment (patio and outdoors), cooking range and oven, food service components, painted serving trays, restaurant equipment, restaurant supplies, hotel equipment and supplies, tray and chafing dishes, wine baskets and racks. Entries include: Company name, postal address, telephone, fax, e-mail, website, contact person, designation, and product details.

Directory of South American Importers of Restaurant, Hotel and Catering Equipment. EXIM Infotek Private Ltd. • Covers: 100 South American importers of catering equipment, cooking equipment (patio and outdoors), cooking range and oven, fast food equipment, restaurant and hotel equipment. Entries include: Company name, postal address, telephone, fax, e-mail, website, contact person, designation, and product details.

Directory of Taiwanese Manufacturers and Exporters of Restaurant, Hotel and Catering Equipment. EXIM Infotek Private Ltd. • $150 Individuals. Covers: 30 Taiwanese manufacturers and exporters of catering machinery and equipment. Entries include: Company name, postal address, telephone, fax, e-mail, website, contact person, designation, and product details.

Food Processing Guide and Directory. Putman Media Inc. • Annual. $90. Lists over 5,390 food ingredient and equipment manufacturers.

Foodservice Equipment and Supplies Product Source Guide. Reed Elsevier Group plc Reed Business Information. • Annual. $35.00. Nearly 1,700 manufacturers of food service equipment and supplies. Formerly *Foodservice Equipment Buyer's Guide and Product Directory.*

Major Food and Drink Companies of the World. Cengage Learning Inc. • 12th edition. eBook. Published by Graham & Whiteside. Contains profiles and trade names for more than 9,200 important food and beverage companies in various countries. In addition to foods, includes both alcoholic and nonalcoholic drink products.

ONLINE DATABASES

Food Science and Technology Abstracts (online). IFIS North American Desk. • Produced by International Food Information Service. Provides about 500,000 online citations, with abstracts, to the international literature of food science, technology, commodities, engineering, and processing. Approximately 2,000 periodicals are covered. Time period is 1969 to date, with monthly updates. Inquire as to online cost and availability.

PERIODICALS AND NEWSLETTERS

Food Manufacturing. Advantage Business Media L.L.C. • 9/year. $54 Individuals. Edited for food processing operations managers and food engineering managers. Includes end-of-year *Food Products and Equipment Literature Review.*

Food Processing. Putman Media Inc. • Monthly. $89 others. Edited for executive and operating personnel in the food processing industry.

Food Production-Management: Monthly Publication of the Canning, Glass-Packing, As eptic, and Frozen Food Industry. CTI Publications Inc. • Monthly. $35.00 per year.

Foodservice Equipment and Supplies. Reed Elsevier Group plc Reed Business Information. • $106.90 Individuals.

RESEARCH CENTERS AND INSTITUTES

Food Industries Center. Ohio State University, 110 Parker Food Science & Technology Bldg., 2015 Fyffe Rd., Columbus, OH 43210. Phone: (614)292-6281; Fax: (614)292-0218; Email: fst@osu.edu • URL: http://www.fst.ohio-state.edu.

Institute of Food Science. Cornell University, 114 Stocking Hall, Ithaca, NY 14853-7201. Phone: (607)255-7900; Fax: (607)254-4868; Email: ddm2@cornell.edu • URL: http://www.nysaes.cornell.edu/cifs • Research areas include the chemistry and processing of food commodities, food processing engineering, food packaging, and nutrition.

National Food Processors Association Research Foundation. 1350 I (Eye) St. NW, Ste. 300, Washington, DC 20005. Phone: (202)639-5900; Fax: (202)639-5932; Email: nfpa@gmaonline.org • URL: http://www.gmaonline.org • Conducts research on food processing engineering, chemistry, microbiology, sanitation, preservation aspects, and public health factors.

STATISTICS SOURCES

U.S. Industry and Trade Outlook. U.S. Department of Commerce National Technical Information Service. • Annual. Produced by the International Trade Administration, U.S. Department of Commerce, in a "public-private" partnership with DRI/McGraw-Hill and Standard & Poor's. Provides basic data, outlook for the current year, and "Long-Term Prospects" (five-year projections) for a wide variety of products and services. Includes high technology industries. Formerly *U.S. Industrial Outlook.*

TRADE/PROFESSIONAL ASSOCIATIONS

Commercial Food Equipment Service Association. PO Box 77139, Greensboro, NC 27417. Phone: (336)346-4700; Fax: (336)346-4745 • URL: http://www.cfesa.com • Represents firms that repair food preparation equipment used by restaurants, hotels, and institutions. Provides training and education for members and their employees.

Manufacturers' Agents Association for the Foodservice Industry. 1199 Euclid Ave., Atlanta, GA 30307. Phone: (404)214-9474; Fax: (404)522-0132; Email: info@mafsi.org • URL: http://www.mafsi.org • Members are independent manufacturers' representatives who sell food service equipment and supplies. Formerly Marketing Agents for Food Service Industry.

Research and Development Associates for Military Food and Packaging Systems. 16607 Blanco Rd., Ste. 501, San Antonio, TX 78232. Phone: (210)493-8024; Fax: (210)493-8036; Email: hqs@militaryfood.org • URL: http://militaryfood.org/newsite • Industrial firms, educational institutions and related groups engged in food, food service, distribution and container research and development.

FOOD INDUSTRY

See also GROCERY BUSINESS

ABSTRACTS AND INDEXES

Applied Science and Technology Index. EBSCO Publishing Inc. • 11/year. Indexes a wide variety of English language technical, industrial, and engineering periodicals.

Food Science and Technology Abstracts. Ovid Technologies Inc. • Monthly. $1,780.00 per year. Provides worldwide coverage of the literature of food technology and food production.

Foods Adlibra: Key to the World's Food Literature. General Mills, Inc. Foods Adlibra Publications. • Semimonthly. $240.00 per year. Provides journal citations and abstracts to the literature of food technology and packaging.

NTIS Alerts: Agriculture & Food. U.S. Department of Commerce National Technical Information Service. • Biweekly. $130 per year. Covers agricultural economics, horticulture, fisheries, veterinary medicine, food technology, and related subjects.

Nutrition Abstracts and Reviews, Series A: Human and Experimental. CABI Publishing North America. • Monthly. Institutions, $1,835.00 per year. Includes single site internet access. Published in England by CABI Publishing. Provides worldwide coverage of the literature.

ALMANACS AND YEARBOOKS

The State of Food and Agriculture. Bernan Associates. • Annual. $75. Published by the Food and Agriculture Organization of the United Nations (FAO). A yearly review of world and regional agricultural and food activities. Includes tables and graphs. Text in English.

CD-ROM DATABASES

AGRICOLA on SilverPlatter. Ovid Technologies Inc. • Updated monthly. Price varies. Produced by the National Agricultural Library. Provides over 4 million citations to the literature of agriculture, agricultural economics, animal sciences, entomology, fertilizer, food, forestry, nutrition, pesticides, plant science, water resources, and other topics.

OECD Statistical Compendium. Organization for Economic Cooperation and Development. • Semiannual. $1,905.00 per year for 1 to 10 users. CD-ROM contains more than 730,000 monthly, quarterly, and annual time series for OECD countries, 1960 to date. Includes fully searchable data on agriculture, food, economic indicators, national accounts, employment, energy, finance, industry, technology, and foreign trade. Results can be displayed in various forms.

DIRECTORIES

Asia Pacific Food and Drink Directory. Business Monitor International Ltd. • $895 Individuals CD. Covers: 2,022 top food and drink executives on 688 leading food and drink companies from Asia Pacific. Entries include: Company name and address; phone, fax, email and website address; senior contact personnel; full description of company activity; local company profile; nationality; and ownership status and parentage.

Carry Out Food Service Directory. InfoGroup Inc. • Annual. Number of listings: 28,970. Entries include: Name, address, phone, size of advertisement, name of owner or manager, number of employees, year first in "Yellow Pages." Compiled from telephone company "Yellow Pages," nationwide.

Directory of American Manufacturers & Exporters of Food Additives & Aromatic Chemicals. EXIM Infotek Private Ltd. • $5 Individuals. Covers: 20 American manufacturers and exporters of aroma chemicals and chemicals for food and beverage. Entries include: Company name, postal address, city, country, phone, fax, e-mail and websites, contact person, designation, and product details.

Directory of Foreign Buyers, Importers of Food and Agro Based Products. NIIR Project Consultancy Services. • $100 Individuals CD-ROM. Covers: 1,000 buyers/importers of food and agro-based products, processed food, additives and ingredients. Entries include: Company name, full postal address, phone, fax, email (wherever available), website address (wherever available).

Directory of U.S. Meat Suppliers. United States Meat Export Federation. • Annual. Covers: U.S. packers, processors, purveyors, and exporters of red meat and red meat products. Directory is included with payment of membership dues.

Emerging Europe Food and Drink Directory. Business Monitor International Ltd. • $895 Individuals. Covers: 1,577 top food and drink executives on 559 leading food and drink companies from Emerging Europe. Entries include: parent company head offices, full company name, address, phone and fax numbers, email and website address, senior contact personnel, company description and profile, nationality, and ownership status.

European Union--Food and Drinks Directory. Trade Publishing Resources. • Covers: 100,000 brand names, 29,000 executives, and 16,000 companies engaged in importing, wholesaling, and retailing of food and drinks.

Europe's Top 1,000 Food & Drink Companies. Datamonitor. • $995. Covers: 1,000 leading food and drink companies in Europe. Entries include: Company name, address, phone, telex, names and titles of key personnel, number of employees; financial data, product/service, Standard Industrial Classification (SIC) code, production locations.

Food Business Mergers and Acquisitions. American Institute of Food Distribution, Inc. Information and Research Center. • Annual. $295 Individuals book & CD-ROM. Gives names, locations, and industry categories of all companies involved in food business mergers during the previous year.

Food Business Mergers & Acquisitions. Food Institute. • Annual. $295 Individuals print version and disk. Covers: Companies involved in food industry company mergers or take-overs, including import-export, banking, and advertising firms. Database includes: Ratings and financial information for selected firms from Moody's Investors Service. Entries include: Acquiring company name, location; acquired company name, location, products, number of units or stores.

Food Chemicals News Directory. Food Chemical News. CRC Press. • Semiannual. $497.00. Over 2,000 subsidiaries belonging to nearly 250 corporate parents plus an additional 3,000 independent processors. Formerly *Hereld's 1,500*.

Food Industry--Slovakia. I.S.M.C. Information Systems and Marketing Contacts Ltd. • $65. Covers: Companies in the food industry in Slovakia, including suppliers of technologies for food processing and packaging.

Food Processing Guide and Directory. Putman Media Inc. • Annual. $90. Lists over 5,390 food ingredient and equipment manufacturers.

Global Top 1,000 Bakery Companies. Datamonitor. • $995. Covers: 1,000 leading international bakery companies. Entries include: Company name, address, phone, telex, names and titles of key personnel, number of employees; financial data, product/service, Standard Industrial Classification (SIC) code, production locations.

Global Top 1,000 Canned Food Companies. Datamonitor. • $995. Covers: 1,000 leading international canned food companies. Entries include: Company name, address, phone, telex, names and titles of key personnel, number of employees; financial data, product/service, Standard Industrial Classification (SIC) code, production locations.

Global Top 1,000 Confectionery Companies. Datamonitor. • $995. Covers: 1,000 leading international confectionery companies. Entries include: Company name, address, phone, telex, names and titles of key personnel, number of employees; financial data, product/service, Standard Industrial Classification (SIC) code, production locations.

Global Top 1,000 Dairy Companies. Datamonitor. • $995. Covers: 1,000 leading international dairy companies. Entries include: Company name, address, phone, telex, names and titles of key personnel, number of employees; financial data, product/service, Standard Industrial Classification (SIC) code, production locations.

Global Top 1,000 Frozen Food Companies. Datamonitor. • $995. Covers: 1,000 leading international frozen food companies. Entries include: Company name, address, phone, telex, names and titles of key personnel, number of employees; financial data, product/service, Standard Industrial Classification (SIC) code, production locations.

Global Top 1,000 Ready Meals Companies. Datamonitor. • $995. Covers: 1,000 leading international companies that provide ready meals. Entries include: Company name, address, phone, telex, names and titles of key personnel, number of employees; financial data, product/service, Standard Industrial Classification (SIC) code, production locations.

The International Directory of Importers - Food & Beverage Importers. Interdata. • $320 Individuals print. Covers: 7,300 international firms importing food and beverage. Entries include: Company name and address, contact person, email, number of employees, year established, phone and telefaxes, business activity, bank references, as well as a listing of food and beverage currently being imported.

Kompass Agribusiness, Food, and Beverage. APN News & Media Group Ltd. APN Business Information Group. • Annual. $85. Covers: Agricultural food and beverage companies and their products and services.

Latin America and Caribbean Food and Drink Directory. Business Monitor International Ltd. • $975 Individuals CD. Covers: 1,642 top food and drink executives on 550 leading food and drink companies from Latin America and Caribbean. Entries include: parent company head offices, full company name, address, phone and fax numbers, email and website address, senior contact personnel, company description and profile, nationality, and ownership status.

Major Food & Drink Companies of the World. Cengage Learning Inc. • Annual. $1,460 Individuals. 2008. 12th edition. eBook. Published by Graham & Whiteside Ltd. Contains directory information on more than 9,200 of the leading food, alcoholic, and non-alcoholic drink companies worldwide.

Major Food and Drink Companies of the World. Cengage Learning Inc. • 12th edition. eBook. Published by Graham & Whiteside. Contains profiles and trade names for more than 9,200 important food and beverage companies in various countries. In addition to foods, includes both alcoholic and nonalcoholic drink products.

The Mardek Guide to the UK's Top Food & Drink Suppliers. William Reed Publishing Ltd. • Annual. $295. Covers: 260 leading companies and over 100 major subsidiaries of food and drink manufacturers in the United Kingdom. Entries include: Corporate structure, company activities, personnel, products, brands, new product launches, turnover/pre-tax profit--up to the last three year, mergers, acquisitions and disposals.

Middle East and Africa Food and Drink Directory. Business Monitor International Ltd. • $995 Individuals CD. Covers: 1,553 top food and drink executives on 459 leading food and drink companies from Middle East and Africa. Entries include: Parent company head offices, full company name, address, phone and fax numbers, email and website address, senior contact personnel, company description and profile, nationality, and ownership status.

Middle East and World Food Directory: An Essential Food Industry Resource. CPH World Media s.a.r.l. • Covers: Major organizations participating in the food, beverage, packaging and catering industries in the Middle East and worldwide. Also includes a country report describing market needs, export-import figures, and forecasts of how these industries will develop.

Plunkett's Food Industry Almanac. Plunkett Research Ltd. • $349.99 Individuals print + online. Covers: 340 leading companies in the global food industry. Entries include: Name, address, phone, fax, and key executives. Also includes analysis and information on trends, technology, and statistics in the field.

Rest of the World Food Companies. Datamonitor. • $995. Covers: Food companies in countries outside of Europe, Asia, and the U.S. Entries include: Company name, address, phone, telex, names and titles of key personnel; number of employees; financial data, product/service, Standard Industrial Classification (SIC) code, production locations.

SourceGuide to Food Industry Information. London Business School Information Service. • $50. Covers: Sources of information on the food industry available in the U.K., with some international coverage; includes statistics sources, directories, trade journals, trade associations, and online databases.

Entries include: Source name, address, phone, type of data available, price.

Top 1,000 Food & Drink Companies in Asia-Pacific. Datamonitor. • $995. Covers: 1,000 leading food and drink companies in Asia and the Pacific. Entries include: Company name, address, phone, telex, names and titles of key personnel, number of employees; financial data, product/service, Standard Industrial Classification (SIC) code, production locations.

Top 1,000 Food & Drink Companies in Latin America. Datamonitor. • $995. Covers: 1,000 leading food and drink companies in Latin America. Entries include: Company name, address, phone, telex, names and titles of key personnel, number of employees; financial data, product/service, Standard Industrial Classification (SIC) code, production locations.

Top 1,000 Food & Drink Companies in the U.S. Datamonitor. • $995. Covers: 1,000 leading food and drink companies in the U.S. Entries include: Company name, address, phone, telex, names and titles of key personnel, number of employees; financial data, product/service, Standard Industrial Classification (SIC) code, production locations.

USA Food Manufacturers Directory. Business Information Agency Inc. PlanetInform. • Annual. $149 Individuals Hard copy or PDF. Covers: 2,500 American food manufacturers of meat and meat products, bakery, beverages, and dairy products, along with 1,000 food manufacturers in Asia and Europe. Entries include: Company name, location, industry description, manufacturing indicator, contact information, SIC codes, number of employees, type of business, year founded, legal status, and subsidiary indicators.

World Food Marketing Directory. Euromonitor International Business Reference Div. • $475 Individuals. Covers: Over 2,000 retailers and wholesalers, 1,500 manufacturers, over 2,000 international and European organizations, statistical agencies, trade journals and associations, databases, and trade fairs in the grocery and food industries worldwide. Entries include: Company name, address, phone, telex, names of parent company and subsidiaries, number of employees, financial data, products and brand names handled; retailers and wholesalers include type of outlet, names and titles of key personnel.

ENCYCLOPEDIAS AND DICTIONARIES

The Business of Food: Encyclopedia of the Food and Drink Industries. Cengage Learning Inc. • 2010. eBook. Takes readers as consumers behind the scenes of the food and drink industries. Covers topics from food companies and brands to the environment, health, science and technology, culture, finance, and more. The more than 150 essay entries also cover those issues that have been and continue to be of perennial importance. Historical context is emphasized and the focus is mainly on business in the United States.

Encyclopedia of Food and Culture. Cengage Learning Inc. • 2003. $657.00. Three volumes. Contains 600 articles covering various aspects of food and its place in society, from agronomy to zucchini. Includes illustrations and a detailed index. eBook also available, updated in 2004.

FINANCIAL RATIOS

Food Retailing Industry Speaks. Food Marketing Institute. • Annual. Members, $150; non-members, $350. Provides data on overall food industry marketing performance, including retail distribution and store operations.

HANDBOOKS AND MANUALS

Progressive Grocer Guidebook. Trade Dimensions. • Annual. $375.00. Over 800 major chain and independent food retailers and wholesalers in the United States and Canada; also includes food brokers, rack jobbers, candy and tobacco distributors, and magazine distributors.

INTERNET DATABASES

Business 2.0 Web Guide to the Best Business Links. Business 2.0 Media Inc. Phone: (415)293-4800; Email: support@business2.com • URL: http://www.business2.com/webguide • Web site presents an extensive, searchable directory of links to "the best, most informative, and authoritative web pages." Twenty main categories cover business, finance, career, company information, people, and technology topics, with thousands of subtopics, all linking to Web sites recommended by experienced business researchers. Fees: Free.

Fedstats. Federal Interagency Council on Statistical Policy. Phone: (202)395-7254 • URL: http://www.fedstats.gov • Web site features an efficient search facility for full-text statistics produced by more than 100 federal agencies, including the Census Bureau, the Bureau of Economic Analysis, and the Bureau of Labor Statistics. Boolean searches can be made within one agency or for all agencies combined. Links are offered to international statistical bureaus, including the UN, IMF, OECD, UNESCO, Eurostat, and 20 individual countries. Fees: Free.

FreeLunch.com. Economy.com, Inc. Phone: (610)696-8700; Fax: (610)696-1678 • URL: http://www.freelunch.com • Web site provides free access to more than 200 million economic and financial data series, covering industry, demographics, labor markets, prices, retail sales, government spending, trade, interest rates, housing starts, the stock market, etc. Data is available in either chart or table form. Searching is offered. Free, but registration required. Economy.com, Inc. also offers fee-based economic analysis at *The Dismal Scientist* site (www.dismal.com).

ONLINE DATABASES

Applied Science and Technology Index Online. H.W. Wilson Co. • Provides online indexing of 500 major scientific, technical, industrial, and engineering periodicals. Time period is 1983 to date. Monthly updates. Inquire as to online cost and availability.

Food Science and Technology Abstracts (online). IFIS North American Desk. • Produced by International Food Information Service. Provides about 500,000 online citations, with abstracts, to the international literature of food science, technology, commodities, engineering, and processing. Approximately 2,000 periodicals are covered. Time period is 1969 to date, with monthly updates. Inquire as to online cost and availability.

OTHER SOURCES

Food Law Reports. Wolters Kluwer Law & Business CCH. • Weekly. $1,459.00 per year. Six looseleaf volumes. Covers regulation of adulteration, packaging, labeling, and additives. Formerly *Food Drug Cosmetic Law Reports.*

PERIODICALS AND NEWSLETTERS

Amber Waves. Economic Research Service Hazard Analysis and Critical Control Points. • Quarterly. Replaces *Agricultural Outlook; Food Review*; and *Rural America.* Provides research and analysis from the U.S. Department of Agriculture's Economic Research Service. Includes economic data on agriculture, food, trade, and environmental factors.

FDA Consumer. U. S. Government Printing Office. • Bimonthly. $14.00 per year. Issued by the U. S. Food and Drug Administration. Provides consumer information about FDA regulations and product safety.

Food Industry Newsletter: All the Food News That Matters. Newsletters Inc. • 26 times a year. $245.00 per year. Newsletter. A summary of key industry news for food executives.

The Food Institute Report. Food Institute. • Description: Reports on developments in the food industry, including new products, the food service industry, mergers and acquisitions, current legislation and regulations, judicial decisions, and financial and marketing information.

Food Technology. Institute of Food Technologists. • Monthly. $190 U.S. and Canada. Articles cover food product development, food ingredients, production, packaging, research, and regulation.

Journal of Agricultural and Food Information. The Haworth Press Inc. • Quarterly. Institutions, $95.00 per year. A journal for librarians and others concerned with the acquisition of information on food and agriculture.

Prepared Foods. BNP Media. • Monthly. Edited for food manufacturing management, marketing, and operations personnel.

Progressive Grocer: The Magazine of Supermarketing. Nielsen Business Media Inc.

Seafood Business. Diversified Business Communications Inc. • $57 U.S.. Edited for a wide range of seafood buyers, including distributors, restaurants, supermarkets, and institutions. Special issues feature information on specific products, such as salmon or lobster.

The Washington Agricultural Record. Washington Agricultural Record. • Description: Focuses on Washington farm issues and developments, reporting international congressional and United States Department of Agriculture (U.S.D.A.) news and international agricultural developments.

RESEARCH CENTERS AND INSTITUTES

Consumer Federation of America - Food Policy Institute. 1620 I St. NW, Ste. 200, Washington, DC 20006. Phone: (202)387-6121 or (202)737-0766; Fax: (202)265-7989; Email: cfa@consumerfed.org • URL: http://www.consumerfed.org/food-and-agriculture • National food, health, and environmental policies, including food safety, sustainable agriculture, children's nutrition, and inner-city retail food access.

Michigan State University - Institute for Food Laws and Regulations. G.M. Trout Food Science and Human Nutrition Bldg., 469 Wilson Rd., Ste. 139, East Lansing, MI 48824. Phone: (517)355-8295; Fax: (517)432-1492; Email: iflr@msu.edu • URL: http://www.iflr.msu.edu • Conducts research on the food industry, including processing, packaging, marketing, and new products.

Poland Ministry of Agriculture and Food Economy - Institute of Agricultural and Food Economics. ul. Świetokrzyska 20, 00-002 Warsaw, Poland. Phone: 48 22 5054444; Fax: 48 22 8271960; Email: andrzej.kowalski@ierigz.waw.pl • URL: http://www.ierigz.waw.pl • Agricultural and food policy, forecasting of agriculture and food economy development, farm and food industry economics, regional analyses, ownership transformations, analysis and prognosis of agricultural and food markets, and social transformation in agricultural and rural populations.

St. Joseph's University - Academy of Food Marketing. 150 Mandeville Hall, 5600 City Ave., Philadelphia, PA 19131. Phone: (610)660-1600; Fax: (610)660-1604; Email: rhiggins@sju.edu • URL: http://www.sju.edu/academics/hsb/foodmarketing/academy • Food marketing from farm gate to table, including analysis and evaluation of concepts, precepts, and practices of the food industry in America and elsewhere. Conducts special studies on problems of food marketing in urban low-income areas, in-home electronic shopping, household buying behavior, national and international food consumption, and nutrient intake. Also seeks to improve efficiency in retail and wholesale operations, evaluates procedures for development of new products, examines aspects of consumer research, analyzes the effectiveness of coupons and in-store promotions, and investigates

For publishers' addresses, refer to SOURCES CITED section at the back of the book.

bulk foods and warehouse productivity.

Secretary of Agriculture and Supply - Institute of Food Technology. Avda. Brasil 2880, Caixa Postal 139, 13070-178 Campinas, SP, Brazil. Phone: 55 19 37431700; Fax: 55 19 37431799; Email: rh@ital.sp.gov.br • URL: http://www.ital.sp.gov.br • Food science, engineering and technology, including dehydrated foods, grain storage, juices and beverages, biotechnology, meat and meat products, postharvest physiology of fruit and vegetable, food packaging, equipment design, flours and bakery products, milk and dairy products, marketing and economics, edible oils, seafood resources, and physical, chemical, biochemical, microbiological, and sensory evaluation of food products.

Texas A&M University - Agribusiness, Food, and Consumer Economics Research Center. Department of Agricultural Economics, 600 John Kimbrough Blvd., Ste. 371, 2124 TAMU, College Station, TX 77843-2124. Phone: (979)845-5911; Fax: (979)845-6378; Email: afcerc@tamu.edu • URL: http://afcerc.tamu.edu • Marketing of Texas and U.S. agricultural products. Areas include domestic and foreign market opportunities, marketing policies and strategies, international competitiveness of Texas and the U.S. in the production and marketing of traditional bulk and high value/value-added products, impact of new technologies on markets and prices, efficiency of market information systems, market structure and performance, and consumer survey research.

STATISTICS SOURCES

Agriculture Fact Book. U. S. Government Printing Office. • Annual. $26 Individuals. Issued by the Office of Communications, U. S. Department of Agriculture. Includes data on U. S. agriculture, farmers, food, nutrition, and rural America. Programs of the Department of Agriculture in six areas are described: rural economic development, foreign trade, nutrition, the environment, inspection, and education.

Standard & Poor's Industry Surveys. Standard & Poor's Financial Services L.L.C. • Semiannual. $1,800.00. Two looseleaf volumes. Includes monthly *Supplements*. Provides detailed, individual surveys of 52 major industry groups. Each survey is revised on a semiannual basis. Also includes "Monthly Investment Review" (industry group investment analysis) and monthly "Trends & Projections" (economic analysis).

Survey of Current Business. U. S. Government Printing Office. • Published by Bureau of Economic Analysis, U. S. Department of Commerce. Presents a wide variety of business and economic data.

TRADE/PROFESSIONAL ASSOCIATIONS

Food Institute. 10 Mountainview Rd., Ste. S125, Upper Saddle River, NJ 07458. Phone: (201)791-5570; Fax: (201)791-5222; Email: questions@foodinstitute.com • URL: http://www.foodinstitute.com • Growers, food processors, importers, exporters, brokers, wholesalers, supermarket chains, independent retailers, food industry suppliers, food service distributors, advertising and banking executives, and government officials. Strives to provide food industry-related information to its members.

Grocery Manufacturers Association. 1350 I St. NW, Washington, DC 20005. Phone: (202)639-5900; Fax: (202)639-5932; Email: info@gmaonline.org • URL: http://www.gmaonline.org • Absorbed Association of Sales and Marketing Companies.

Sustainable Food Trade Association. 49 Race St., New Castle, VA 24127-6397. Phone: (413)624-6678; Email: info@sustainablefoodtrade.org • URL: http://www.sustainablefoodtrade.org • Works to foster sustainable business practices in the organic food trade. Collaborates with businesses in the organic and natural foods trade to align their day-to-day business practices with sustainability principles. Provides education, research, and networking for industry leaders to create opportunities for cross-supply chain innovation and best practices.

FOOD MACHINERY

See FOOD EQUIPMENT AND MACHINERY

FOOD PACKAGING

See PACKAGING

FOOD, PROCESSED

See PROCESSED FOOD INDUSTRY

FOOD SERVICE INDUSTRY

See also RESTAURANTS, LUNCHROOMS, ETC.

DIRECTORIES

Foodservice Consultants Society International--Membership Directory. Foodservice Consultants Society International. • Annual. $450. About 950 food service consultants.

Foodservice Equipment and Supplies Product Source Guide. Reed Elsevier Group plc Reed Business Information. • Annual. $35.00. Nearly 1,700 manufacturers of food service equipment and supplies. Formerly *Foodservice Equipment Buyer's Guide and Product Directory*.

International Foodservice Manufacturers Association: Membership Directory. International Foodservice Manufacturers Association. • Annual. Manufacturers of processed foods equipment and supplies for schools, hospitals, hotels, restaurants, and institutions and related services in the foodservice industry.

INTERNET DATABASES

Advance Monthly Retail Trade Report. U. S. Census Bureau. Phone: 800-541-8345 or (301)457-4100 or (301)763-2713; Fax: (301)457-1296 or (301)457-3842; Email: naics@census.gov • URL: http://www.census.gov/epcd/www/naicstab.htm • Web pages provide monthly sales figures for a wide range of retail businesses. Advance, preliminary, and final statistics are provided for the latest month available in each case, with a previous-year comparison. Updates are monthly.

PERIODICALS AND NEWSLETTERS

Chef. Aktiebolaget Electrolux. • Monthly. $24.00 per year. Edited for executive chefs, food and beverage directors, caterers, banquet and club managers, and others responsible for food buying and food service. Special coverage of regional foods is provided.

Food Management: Ideas for Colleges, Healthcare, Schools, and Business Dining. Penton Media Inc. • Monthly. Free to qualified personel; others.

Foodservice Equipment and Supplies. Reed Elsevier Group plc Reed Business Information. • $106.90 Individuals.

Hospitality Technology: Guiding High-Growth Businesses to Best-Choice IT Solutions. Edgell Communications Inc. • 10/year. Covers information technology, computer communications, and software for foodservice and lodging enterprises.

Restaurants and Institutions. Reed Elsevier Group plc Reed Business Information. • Semimonthly. $149.00 per year. Features news, new products, recipes, menu concepts and merchandising ideas from the most successful foodservice operations around the U.S.

STATISTICS SOURCES

Annual Benchmark Report for Retail Trade and Food Services..A Detailed Summary of Retail Sales, Purchases, Accounts Receivable, Inventories, and Food Service Sales. U. S. Government Printing Office. • Annual. $13.00. Issued by the U.S. Census Bureau. Provides detailed annual and monthly retail statistics for the most recent 10 years. Includes data for various kinds of retail outlets, including automobiles, furniture, appliances, building supplies, grocery stores, drug stores, gasoline stations, clothing, sporting goods, department stores, and restaurants.

TRADE/PROFESSIONAL ASSOCIATIONS

Association for Healthcare Foodservice. 455 S Fourth St., Ste. 650, Louisville, KY 40202. Phone: 888-528-9552 or (502)574-9930 or (502)574-9934; Fax: (502)589-3602; Email: info@healthcarefoodservice.org • URL: http://www.healthcarefoodservice.org • Formerly American Society for Hospital Food Service Administrators.

Association of Correctional Food Service Affiliates. 210 N Glenoaks Blvd., Ste. C, Burbank, CA 91502. Phone: (818)843-6608; Fax: (818)843-7423 • URL: http://www.acfsa.org • Food service professionals from federal, state and county correctional institutions and vendors that serve them. Works to advance skills and professionalism through education, information and networking.

Convenience Caterers and Food Manufacturers Association. 1205 Spartan Dr., Madison Heights, MI 48071. Phone: (248)982-5379; Email: ccfma@ymail.com • URL: http://www.mobilecaterers.com • Firms and corporations engaged in the mobile catering business and in any other business catering to industrial feeding by mobile equipment; associate members are suppliers and manufacturers. Deals with common intra-industry problems through exchange of ideas, advice on legal problems, and safety standards and licensing regulations.

Dietary Managers Association. 406 Surrey Woods Dr., Saint Charles, IL 60174. Phone: 800-323-1908; Fax: (630)587-6308 • URL: http://www.anfponline.org • Dietary managers united to maintain a high level of competency and quality in dietary departments through continuing education. Provides educational programs and placement service.

Manufacturers' Agents Association for the Foodservice Industry. 1199 Euclid Ave., Atlanta, GA 30307. Phone: (404)214-9474; Fax: (404)522-0132; Email: info@mafsi.org • URL: http://www.mafsi.org • Members are independent manufacturers' representatives who sell food service equipment and supplies. Formerly Marketing Agents for Food Service Industry.

National Council of Chain Restaurants. 325 7th St. NW, Ste. 1100, Washington, DC 20004. Phone: (202)783-7971; Fax: (202)737-2849; Email: info@nrf.com • URL: http://www.nccr.net • Major multi-unit, multistate foodservice, restaurant and lodging companies in the United States.

National Restaurant Association Educational Foundation. 2055 L St. NW, Washington, DC 20036. Phone: 800-424-5156; Email: scholars@nraef.org • URL: http://www.nraef.org • Serves as an educational foundation supported by the National Restaurant Association and all segments of the foodservice industry including restaurateurs, foodservice companies, food and equipment manufacturers, distributors and trade associations. Advances the professional standards of the industry through education and research. Offers video training programs, management courses and careers information. Conducts research and maintains hall of fame.

School Nutrition Association. 120 Waterfront St., Ste. 300, National Harbor, Oxon Hill, MD 20745-1142. Phone: 800-877-8822 or (301)686-3100; Fax:

(301)686-3115; Email: servicecenter@schoolnutrition.org • URL: http://www.schoolnutrition.org • Persons engaged in school food service or related activities in public or private schools, preschools, colleges and universities. Seeks to encourage and promote the maintenance and improvement of the school food and nutrition program. Sponsors National School Lunch Week in October and National School Breakfast week in March. Distributes information on school food and nutrition programs and child nutrition legislation. Holds industry seminar, major city directors and supervisors' meeting, and annual national conference for school food service personnel. Maintains School Food Service Foundation, which conducts research and educational programs relating to child nutrition and encourages professional development of school food service personnel. Maintains hall of fame. Operates political action committee.

FOOD SERVICE, INSTITUTIONAL

See FOOD SERVICE INDUSTRY

FOOD, SNACK

See SNACK FOOD INDUSTRY

FOOD, SPECIALTY

See SPECIALTY FOOD INDUSTRY

FOOTWEAR

See SHOE INDUSTRY

FOREIGN AGRICULTURE

See also AGRICULTURE

CD-ROM DATABASES

OECD Statistical Compendium. Organization for Economic Cooperation and Development. • Semiannual. $1,905.00 per year for 1 to 10 users. CD-ROM contains more than 730,000 monthly, quarterly, and annual time series for OECD countries, 1960 to date. Includes fully searchable data on agriculture, food, economic indicators, national accounts, employment, energy, finance, industry, technology, and foreign trade. Results can be displayed in various forms.

ONLINE DATABASES

CAB Abstracts. CABI. • Contains 46 specialized abstract collections covering over 10,000 journals and monographs in the areas of agriculture, horticulture, forest products, farm products, nutrition, dairy science, poultry, grains, animal health, entomology, etc. Time period is 1972 to date, with monthly updates. Inquire as to online cost and availability. *CAB Abstracts on CD-ROM* also available, with annual updating.

PERIODICALS AND NEWSLETTERS

AgExporter. U. S. Government Printing Office. • Monthly. $44 Individuals. Issued by the Foreign Agricultural Service, U. S. Department of Agriculture. Edited for U. S. exporters of farm products. Provides practical information on exporting, including overseas trade opportunities.

IFAP Newsletter. International Federation of Agricultural Producers. • Bimonthly. Price on application.

Outlook for United States Agricultural Trade. U. S. Government Printing Office. • Quarterly. $15.00 per year. Issued by the Economic Research Service, U. S. Department of Agriculture. (Situation and Outlook Reports.).

TRADE/PROFESSIONAL ASSOCIATIONS

German Foods North America. 719 6th St. NW, Washington, DC 20001. Phone: 800-881-6419; Email: info@germanfoods.org • URL: http://germanfoods.org • Promotes imported German foods, beverages, and agricultural products in the U.S. and Canada through advertising, public relations programs, and promotional campaigns with supermarket chains and individual retailers. Acts as a liaison between U.S. and Canadian importers and German manufacturers and exporters. Provides assistance to German manufacturers and their importers and distributors in complying with U.S. regulations.

Iran National Union of Agro Products. No. 94, Keyvan Alley, Kashani St., Urmia, Iran. Phone: 98 441 3451988 or 98 441 3455780; Fax: 98 441 3455606; Email: shakor_a@iranazarfruit.com • URL: http://www.iranazarfruit.com • Represents the interests of exporters of agricultural products. Aims to create coordination in the export of fruits and vegetables and the promotion of export products. Assists members by providing facilities and marketing services for their agricultural products.

Pakistan Agriculture and Dairy Farmers Association. JK House, 32-W, Susan Rd., Madina Town, Faisalabad, Pakistan. Phone: 92 41 8721956; Fax: 92 41 8712399; Email: info@padfapak.org • URL: http://www.padfapak.org • Represents trade, commerce, industry or services in agriculture and dairy farming in Pakistan. Encourages unity, mutual understanding and high ethical standards among its members. Supports a unified approach of policies affecting the interests of agriculture and dairy farming.

FOREIGN AUTOMOBILES

See also AUTOMOBILES

ONLINE DATABASES

Ward's AutoInfoBank. Ward's Communications. • Provides weekly, monthly, quarterly, and annual statistical data from 1980 to date for U. S. and imported cars and trucks. Covers production, shipments, sales, inventories, optional equipment, etc. Updating varies by series. Inquire as to online cost and availability.

PERIODICALS AND NEWSLETTERS

Importcar: The Complete Import Service Magazine. Babcox Publications Inc. • Monthly. News on imported cars. Includes *Automotive Aftermarket Training Guide.* Formerly *Importcar and Truck.*

TRADE/PROFESSIONAL ASSOCIATIONS

American International Automobile Dealers Association. 500 Montgomery St., Ste. 800, Alexandria, VA 22314. Phone: 800-462-4232; Fax: (703)519-7810; Email: membership@aiada.org • URL: http://www.aiada.org • Trade association for America's international nameplate automobile dealerships and their employees who sell and service automobiles manufactured in the U.S. and abroad. Works to preserve a free market for international automobiles in the U.S. and is dedicated to increasing public awareness of the benefits the industry provides.

Global Automakers. 1050 K St. NW, Ste. 650, Washington, DC 20001. Phone: (202)650-5555; Email: info@globalautomakers.org • URL: http://www.globalautomakers.org • Formerly known as the Association of International Automobile Manufacturers.

FOREIGN BUSINESS

See INTERNATIONAL BUSINESS

FOREIGN COMMERCE

See FOREIGN TRADE

FOREIGN CREDIT

See also CREDIT; EXPORT-IMPORT TRADE; FOREIGN EXCHANGE

ABSTRACTS AND INDEXES

PAIS International. ProQuest L.L.C. • Monthly. $850.00 per year; cumulations three times a year. Provides topical citations to the worldwide literature of public affairs, economics, demographics, sociology, and trade. Text in English; indexed materials in English, French, German, Italian, Portuguese and Spanish.

CD-ROM DATABASES

CreditDisk 2.0. Fitch. • Price and frequency on application. CD-ROM provides credit research and ratings on individual banks throughout the world, with Internet updating. Includes graphic displays of rating histories and financial ratios.

EconLit. Ovid Technologies Inc. • Updated monthly. Lists journal articles, book reviews, disserations of economic literature. Over 1,400 journals covered.

PAIS International. ProQuest L.L.C. • Monthly. $1,995.00 per year. Contains over 650,000 citations to the literature of contemporary social, political, and economic issues.

OTHER SOURCES

Country Finance. The Economist Intelligence Unit. • Annual $425.00 per year. Discusses banking and financial conditions in each of 47 countries. Includes foreign exchange regulations, the currency outlook, sources of capital, financing techniques, and tax considerations.

PERIODICALS AND NEWSLETTERS

FCIB International Bulletin. ement. FCIB-NACM Corp. • Quarterly. Membership.

Grant's Interest Rate Observer. Grant's Financial Publishing Inc. • Biweekly. $1,025 Individuals. Newsletter containing detailed analysis of money-related topics, including interest rate trends, global credit markets, fixed-income investments, bank loan policies, and international money markets.

International Bank Credit Analyst. BCA Publications Ltd. • Monthly. $795.00 per year. "A monthly forecast and analysis of currency movements, interest rates, and stock market developments in the principal countries, based on a continuous appraisal of money and credit trends worldwide." Includes many charts and graphs providing international coverage of money, credit, and securities.

Project Finance Monthly. Infocast Inc. • Description: Provides information about the power industry. Includes industry news, financing, regulation, and contracts.

STATISTICS SOURCES

Statistical Information on the Financial Services Industry. American Bankers Association. • Annual. Members, $150.00; non-members, $275.00. Presents a wide variety of data relating to banking and financial services, including consumer economics, personal finance, credit, government loans, capital markets, and international banking.

FOREIGN EMPLOYMENT

See EMPLOYMENT IN FOREIGN COUNTRIES

FOREIGN EXCHANGE

See also CURRENCY EXCHANGE RATES; MONEY; PAPER MONEY

ALMANACS AND YEARBOOKS

World Economic Outlook Reports. International Monetary Fund. • Semiannual. $110. Provides key insights into how to view unprecedented global imbalances, respond to capital account crises caused by abrupt shifts in global asset allocations, and evaluate the opportunities for all member countries, especially low-income countries, to grow.

INTERNET DATABASES

Factiva. Dow Jones Reuters Business Interactive, LLC. Phone: 800-369-7466 or (609)452-1511; Fax: (609)520-5770; Email: solutions@factiva.com • URL: http://www.factiva.com • Fee-based Web site provides "global news and business information through Web sites and content integration solutions." Includes Dow Jones and Reuters newswires, The Wall Street Journal, and more than 7,000 other sources of current news, historical articles, market research reports, and investment analysis. Content includes 96 major U. S. newspapers, 900 non-English sources, trade publications, media transcripts, country profiles, news photos, etc.

Federal Reserve Board Publications and Education Resources. Board of Governors of the Federal Reserve System. Phone: (202)452-3000; Fax: (202)452-3819 • URL: http://www.federalreserve.gov/publications.htm • Web site provides access to statistics, surveys, and research from the Federal Reserve Board. *Federal Reserve Bulletin* articles are available as abstracts or full text (PDF) currently or from six-year archives. The link "Statistics: Releases and Historical Data" offers daily, weekly, monthly, quarterly, and annual data in great detail for interest rates, foreign exchange, consumer credit, money stock measures, industrial production indexes, bank reserves, and other items. Historical tabulations are available for various time periods. Free.

Financial Times: Where Information Becomes Intelligence. FT Group. Phone: (800)628-8088 • URL: http://www.ft.com • Web site provides extensive data and information relating to international business and finance, with daily updates. Includes Markets Today, Company News, Economic Indicators, Equities, Currencies, Capital Markets, Euro Prices, etc. Fees: Free (registration required).

Gateway to the European Union. European Union. Email: pressoffice@eurostat.cec.be • URL: http://www.europa.eu.int • Web site provides access to a wide variety of EU information, including statistics (Eurostat), news, policies, publications, key issues, and official exchange rates for the euro. Includes links to the European Central Bank, the European Investment Bank, and other institutions. Fees: Free.

Nexis.com. Lexis-Nexis Group. Phone: 800-227-4908 or (937)865-6800; Fax: (937)865-6909; Email: webmaster@prod.lexis-nexis.com • URL: http://www.nexis.com • Fee-based Web site offers searching of about 2.8 billion documents in some 30,000 news, business, and legal information sources. Features include a subject directory covering 1,200 topics in 34 categories and a Company Dossier containing information on more than 500,000 public and private companies. Boolean searching is offered.

Wall Street Journal Interactive Edition. Dow Jones & Co., Inc. 1211 Avenue of the Americas, New York, NY 10036. Phone: 800-369-5663; Email: service@dowjones.com • URL: http://new.dowjones.com • Fee-based Web site providing online searching of worldwide information from *The Wall Street Journal.* Includes "Company Snapshots," "The Journal's Greatest Hits," "Index to Market Data," "Journal Links," etc. Financial price quotes are available. Fees: $49.00 per year; $29.00 per year to print subscribers.

PERIODICALS AND NEWSLETTERS

American Banker: The Financial Services Daily. SourceMedia Inc. • Daily. $895.00 per year. Provides news of banking, investment products, mortgages, credit unions, finance, bank technology, and legal developments.

Financial Times (London). The Financial Times, Inc. • Daily, except Sunday. $572.88 per year. An international business and financial newspaper, featuring news from London, Paris, Frankfurt, New York, and Tokyo. Includes worldwide stock and bond market data, commodity market data, and monetary/currency exchange information.

Foreign Exchange Letter. Institutional Investor Inc. Journals Group. • Biweekly. $1,625.00 per year. Newsletter. Provides information on foreign exchange rates, trends, and opportunities. Edited for banks, multinational corporations, currency traders, and others concerned with money rates.

Foreign Exchange Rates. U.S. Federal Reserve System Board of Governors Publications Services. • $20 weekly.

International Market Alert. UCG Holdings L.P. • Description: Provides a fax service covering financial markets, world economy developments, foreign exchange, and U.S. interest rates.

International Monetary Fund Staff Papers. International Monetary Fund, Publication Services. • Quarterly. Individuals, $56.00 per year; students, $28.00 per year. Contains studies by IMF staff members on balance of payments, foreign exchange, fiscal policy, and related topics. Formerly *International Monetary Fund Staff Papers.*

U.S. Banker. SourceMedia Inc. • Monthly. $65.00 per year. Edited for bank executives and managers. Covers a wide variety of banking and financial topics.

World Business Intelligence: Economic & Political Financial Analysts from Rundt's New York. S.J. Rundt & Associates Inc. • $885 Individuals. Magazine featuring information on international trade, country risk analyses, currencies, and political, financial, and economic intelligence. Formerly *Rundt's Weekly Intelligence.*

TRADE/PROFESSIONAL ASSOCIATIONS

Association of Certified Treasury Managers. 52, Nagarjuna Hills, Hyderabad 500 082, Telangana, India. Phone: 91 40 23435368 or 91 40 23435374; Fax: 91 40 23352521; Email: info@actmindia.org • URL: http://www.qfinance.com/information-sources/association-of-certified-treasury-managers-india • Develops and regulates the growth of the treasury management profession. Organizes seminars, workshops, and training programs in treasury management, foreign exchange management, risk management, and allied areas. Provides placement assistance to members and students.

China-Britain Business Council. Portland House, 3rd Fl., Bressenden Pl., London SW1E 5BH, United Kingdom. Phone: 44 20 78022000; Fax: 44 20 78022029; Email: enquiries@cbbc.org • URL: http://www.cbbc.org • British companies doing business in China. Promotes British trade in China. Acts as a liaison between the British and Chinese governments and member companies.

Portuguese Chamber. 11 Belgrave Sq., 4th Fl., London SW1X 8PP, United Kingdom. Phone: 44 20 72016638; Email: info@portuguese-chamber.org.uk • URL: http://www.portuguese-chamber.org.uk • Promotes business and commerce.

FOREIGN INVESTMENTS

See also FOREIGN TRADE; INTERNATIONAL FINANCE; INVESTMENTS

BIBLIOGRAPHIES

Thunderbird International Business Review. Thunderbird American Graduate School of International Management. John Wiley and Sons, Inc., Journals Div. • Bimonthly. $937 Institutions print only. Journal on international business and commerce for academic scholars, business and government executives, and trade specialists. Formerly *International Executive.*

DIRECTORIES

Afghanistan Investment and Business Guide. International Business Publications, USA. • Annual. $99.95 Individuals hardcover. Covers: Strategic and business information, contacts, regulations and more.

Algeria Investment and Business Guide. International Business Publications, USA. • $99.95 Individuals hardcover. Covers: Basic information on economy, export-import and investment climate, opportunities, industrial development, banking, and government. Entries include: Important business contacts and business travel.

Andorra Offshore Investment and Business Guide. International Business Publications, USA. • $99.95 Individuals hardcover. Covers: Information on conducting business and investment activity in the country with offshore status.

Angola Investment and Business Guide. International Business Publications, USA. • $99.95 Individuals hardcover. Covers: Basic information on economy, export-import and investment climate, regulations, industrial development, banking, opportunities and government. Entries include: Business contacts and business travel.

Argentina Industrial and Business Directory. International Business Publications, USA. • Annual. $99.95 Individuals hardcover. Covers: Detailed information on investment, export-import business opportunities, foreign economic assistance projects, government and business contacts.

Australia Industrial and Business Directory. International Business Publications, USA. • Annual. $99.95 Individuals hardcover. Covers: Strategic industrial, investment, and business contacts for conducting export-import and investment activity in the country.

Australia Investment and Business Guide. International Business Publications, USA. • $99.95 Individuals hardcover. Covers: Basic information on economy and government, export-import activity and investment climate, regulations and industrial development, and banking. Entries include: Important business contacts and business travel.

Austria Industrial and Business Directory. International Business Publications, USA. • Annual. $99.95 Individuals hardcover. Covers: Detailed information on investment, export-import business opportunities, foreign economic assistance projects, government and business contacts.

Azerbaijan Investment and Business Guide. International Business Publications, USA. • $99.95 Individuals hardcover. Covers: Strategic and practical information on economy, export-import and investment climate, regulations and industrial development, banking, and government. Entries include: Important business contacts and business travel.

Bahrain Investment & Business Guide. International Business Publications, USA. • $99.95 Individuals hardcover. Covers: Major investment, strategic business opportunities and basic information on economy, export-import, industrial development, banking and government. Entries include: Business contacts and business travel.

Bangladesh Industrial and Business Directory. International Business Publications, USA. • Annual. $99.95 Individuals hardcover. Covers: Strategic industrial, investment and business contacts for conducting export-import and investment activity in the country.

Bangladesh Investment and Business Guide. International Business Publications, USA. • $99.95 Individuals hardcover. Covers: Practical and strategic information on economy, export-import activity, investment climate, regulations and industrial development, banking, and government. Entries include: Business contacts and business travel.

Belarus Industrial and Business Directory. International Business Publications, USA. • Annual. $99.95 Individuals hardcover. Covers: Strategic industrial, investment and business contacts for conducting export-import and investment activity in the country.

Belgium Industrial and Business Directory. International Business Publications, USA. • Annual. $99.95 Individuals hardcover. Covers: Detailed information on investment, export-import business opportunities, foreign economic assistance projects, government and business contacts.

Belize Investment & Business Guide. International Business Publications, USA. • $99.95 Individuals hardcover. Covers: Strategic business information, export-import activity in the state, regulations and industrial development, banking, government, and opportunities. Entries include: Guides for conducting investment and business contacts.

Bolivia Industrial and Business Directory. International Business Publications, USA. • Annual. $99.95 Individuals hardcover. Covers: Strategic industrial, investment and business contacts for conducting export-import and investment activity in the country.

Brazil Industrial and Business Directory. International Business Publications, USA. • Annual. $99.95 Individuals hardcopy. Covers: Strategic industrial, investment and business contacts for conducting export-import and investment activity in the country.

Cambodia Investment & Business Guide. International Business Publications, USA. • $99.95 Individuals hardcopy. Covers: Information on economy, business, export-import and investment climate, regulations and industrial development, banking, government, and opportunities. Entries include: Important business contacts and business travel.

Cameroon Industrial and Business Directory. International Business Publications, USA. • $99.95 Individuals hardcover. Covers: Strategic and practical economic and business information. Entries include: Business contacts for conducting business activity in the country.

Canada Industrial and Business Directory. International Business Publications, USA. • Annual. $99.95 Individuals hardcopy. Covers: Detailed information on investment, export-import business opportunities, foreign economic assistance projects, government and business contacts.

Chile Industrial and Business Directory. International Business Publications, USA. • Annual. $99.95 Individuals hardcopy, e-book, CD-ROM. Covers: Strategic industrial, investment and business contacts for conducting export-import and investment activity in the country.

Colombia Investment and Business Guide. International Business Publications, USA. • $99.95 Individuals hardcopy, e-book, CD-ROM. Covers: Information on economy, export-import and investment climate, regulations and industrial development, banking, and government. Entries include: Important business contacts and business travel.

Colorado Investment and Business Guide. International Business Publications, USA. • $99.95 Individuals hardcopy, e-book, CD-ROM. Covers: State economy, business, investment and export-import opportunities, government structure, mineral resources, technology, and government. Entries include: Political and business contacts.

Costa Rica Investment and Business Guide. International Business Publications, USA. • $99.95 Individuals hardcopy, e-book, CD-ROM. Covers: Strategic and business information, business contacts, and business travel. Entries include: Basic information on economy, business, export-import and investment climate, opportunities, and regulations.

Cote d'Ivoire Investment and Business Guide. International Business Publications, USA. • $99.95 Individuals hardcopy, e-book, CD-ROM. Covers: Basic information on economy, export-import and investment climate, regulations and industrial development, banking, and government. Entries include: Important business contacts and business travel.

Croatia Investment and Business Guide. International Business Publications, USA. • $99.95 Individuals hardcopy, e-book, CD-ROM. Covers: Strategic business information, export-import activity, regulations and industrial development, banking, government, and opportunities. Entries include: Important business contacts and business travel.

Cuba Investment and Business Guide. International Business Publications, USA. • $99.95 Individuals hardcopy, e-book, CD-ROM. Covers: Strategic and business information, contacts, regulations and more.

Denmark Industrial and Business Directory. International Business Publications, USA. • Annual. $99.95 Individuals hardcopy, e-book, CD-ROM. Covers: Detailed information on investment, export-import business opportunities, foreign economic assistance projects, government and business contacts.

Denmark Investment and Business Guide. International Business Publications, USA. • $99.95 Individuals hardcopy, e-book, CD-ROM. Covers: Basic information on economy, export-import and investment climate, regulations and industrial development, banking, and government. Entries include: Important business contacts and business travel.

Directory of Foreign Firms Operating in the United States. Uniworld Business Publications Inc. • Biennial. $350 Individuals hardcover plus s&h. Covers: Approximately 4,900 firms in 86 countries that own or have substantial investments in about 18,250 U.S. Companies. Entries include: Company name, address, phone, fax, name of chief executive officer, number of employees, annual sales, web address, product or service; affiliated U.S. company name, address, phone, fax, name of chief executive, number of employees, product or service, percent foreign-owned. Separate country editions are also available.

Directory of Foreign Investors That Invest in U.S.A. Property and Real Estate. Communication Network International Inc. • Biennial. $650. Covers: more than 3,500 investors. Entries include: Personal name, address; United States representative name, address, phone; approximate dollar amount of U.S. investments.

Dominica Investment and Business Guide. International Business Publications, USA. • $99.95 Individuals hardcopy, e-book, CD-ROM. Covers: Strategic information on economy, business, export-import and investment climate, regulations and industrial development, banking, government, and opportunities. Entries include: Important business contacts and business travel.

Dominican Republic Industrial and Business Directory. International Business Publications, USA. • Annual. $99.95 Individuals hardcopy, e-book, CD-ROM. Covers: Strategic industrial, investment and business contacts for conducting export-import and investment activity in the country. Contains strategic practical economic and business information.

Dubai Industrial and Business Directory. International Business Publications, USA. • $99.95 Individuals hardcopy, e-book, CD-ROM. Covers: Strategic investment and business contacts for conducting export-import activity in the country. Entries include: Strategic economic and business information.

Dubai Investment and Business Guide. International Business Publications, USA. • Annual. $99.95 Individuals hardcopy, e-book, CD-ROM. Covers: Detailed information on investment, business opportunities, foreign economic assistance projects, government and business contacts and more. An ultimate guide for starting and conducting a successful business in the country.

Ecuador Investment and Business Guide. International Business Publications, USA. • $99.95 Individuals hardcopy, e-book, CD-ROM. Covers: Strategic information on economy, business, export-import and investment climate, regulations and industrial development, banking, government, and opportunities. Entries include: Important business contacts and business travel.

Egypt Industrial and Business Directory. International Business Publications, USA. • Annual. $99.95 Individuals paperback, e-book, CD-ROM. Covers: Strategic industrial, investment and business contacts for conducting export-import and investment activity in the country.

Egypt Investment and Business Guide. International Business Publications, USA. • $99.95 Individuals hardcover, e-book, CD-ROM. Covers: Strategic and business information, contacts, regulations and more.

El Salvador Investment and Business Guide. International Business Publications, USA. • $99.95 Individuals hardcover, e-book, CD-ROM. Covers: Basic information on economy, export-import and investment climate, regulations and industrial development, banking, and government. Entries include: Important business contacts and business travel.

Eritrea Investment and Business Guide. International Business Publications, USA. • $99.95 Individuals hardcopy, e-book, CD-ROM. Covers: Strategic business information, export-import activity, regulations and industrial development, banking, government, and opportunities. Entries include: Guides for conducting investment and business contacts.

Estonia Industrial and Business Directory. International Business Publications, USA. • Annual. $99.95 Individuals paperback, e-book, CD-ROM. Covers: Strategic industrial, investment and business contacts for conducting export-import and investment activity in the country. Contains strategic practical economic and business information.

Europe's Top Quoted Companies: A Comparative Directory from Seventeen European Stock Exchanges. Kogan Page, Limited. • Annual. $325. 00. Provides detailed, 5-year financial data on 850 major European companies that are publicly traded. Includes company addresses.

Foreign Direct Investment Database. United Nations Conference on Trade and Development. • $80 Individuals. Database covers: Statistics on foreign direct investment for 196 countries. The FDI database presents aggregate inflows, outflows, inward stocks and outward stocks of foreign direct investment.

France Industrial and Business Directory. International Business Publications, USA. • Annual. $99.95 Individuals hardcopy, e-book, CD-ROM. Covers: Detailed information on investment, export-import business opportunities, foreign economic assistance projects, government and business contacts.

France Investment and Business Guide. International Business Publications, USA. • $99.95 Individuals hardcover, e-book, CD-ROM. Covers: Basic information on economy, export-import activity and investment climate, regulations and industrial development, banking, and government. Entries include: Important business contacts and business travel.

Georgia Republic Business and Industrial Directory. International Business Publications, USA. • Annual. $99.95 Individuals hardcover, e-book, CD-ROM. Covers: Strategic industrial, investment and business contacts for conducting export-import and investment activity in the country.

Germany Industrial and Business Directory. International Business Publications, USA. • Annual. $99.95 Individuals hardcover, e-book, CD-ROM. Covers: Strategic industrial, investment and business contacts for conducting export-import and investment activity in the country.

Greece Industrial and Business Directory. International Business Publications, USA. • Annual. $99.95 Individuals hardcopy, e-book, CD-ROM. Covers: Strategic industrial, investment and business contacts for conducting export-import and investment activity in the country. Contains strategic, practical economic and business information.

Hungary Investment and Business Guide. International Business Publications, USA. • $99.95 Individuals hardcopy, e-book, CD-ROM. Covers: Strategic and business information, contacts, regulations, etc. Entries include: Business contacts and business travel.

India Investment and Business Guide. International Business Publications, USA. • $99.95 Individuals hardcopy, e-book, CD-ROM. Covers: Strategic and business information, contacts, regulations and more.

Indonesia Industrial and Business Directory. International Business Publications, USA. • $99.95 Individuals hardcopy, e-book, CD-ROM. Covers: Strategic investment, industrial and business contacts for conducting investment and export-import activity in the country.

International Centre for Settlement of Investment Disputes - Annual Report. International Centre for Settlement of Investment Disputes. • Annual. Contains an overview of the activities during the past ICSID fiscal year.

Investment Opportunities in China: Chemical Industry. Pasha Publications. • $255. Covers: Approximately 530 Chinese projects in the chemical industry seeking international offshore capital investments. Entries include: Project name, address, phone, cable number; name and title of contact; financial data; description of project.

Iran Industrial and Business Directory. International Business Publications, USA. • Annual. $99.95 Individuals hardcopy, e-book, CD-ROM. Covers: Strategic industrial, investment and business contacts for conducting export-import and investment activity in the country.

Iran Investment and Business Guide. International Business Publications, USA. • $99.95 Individuals hardcopy, e-book, CD-ROM. Covers: Basic information on economy, export-import and investment climate, regulations and industrial development, banking, and government. Entries include: Business contacts and business travel.

Iraq Industrial and Business Directory. International Business Publications, USA. • Annual. $99.95 Individuals hardcopy, e-book, CD-ROM. Covers: Strategic industrial, investment and business contacts for conducting export-import and investment activity in the country. Contains strategic practical economic and business information.

Ireland Industrial and Business Directory. International Business Publications, USA. • Annual. $99.95 Individuals hardcover, e-book, CD-ROM. Covers: Strategic industrial, investment and business contacts for conducting export-import and investment activity in the country. Contains strategic practical economic and business information.

Italy Industrial and Business Directory. International Business Publications, USA. • Annual. $99.95 Individuals hardcover, e-book, CD-ROM. Covers: Strategic industrial, investment and business contacts for conducting export-import and investment activity in the country. Contains strategic, practical economic and business information.

Italy Investment and Business Guide. International Business Publications, USA. • $99.95 Individuals hardcopy, e-book, CD-ROM. Covers: Basic information on economy, export-import and investment climate, regulations and industrial development, banking, and government. Entries include: Business contacts and business travel.

Japan Industrial and Business Directory. International Business Publications, USA. • $99.95 Individuals hardcopy, e-book, CD-ROM. Covers: Customs, trade regulations and procedures.

Japan Investment and Business Guide. International Business Publications, USA. • $99.95 Individuals hardcopy, e-book, CD-ROM. Covers: Strategic information on economy, business, export-import and investment climate, regulations and industrial development, banking, government, and opportunities. Entries include: Important business contacts and business travel.

Japanese Investment in U.S. and Canadian Real Estate Directory. Mead Ventures Inc. • Annual. $295. Covers: about 550 Japanese investors, brokers, lenders, consultants, and developers in the United States and Canada; and about 275 companies in Japan. Entries include: Company name, address, phone, fax, telex, name and title of contact, geographical area served, services provided and description of projects and services.

Kenya Industrial and Business Directory. International Business Publications, USA. • Annual. $99.95 Individuals hardcopy, e-book, CD-ROM. Covers: Strategic industrial, investment and business contacts for conducting export-import and investment activity in the country. Contains strategic practical economic and business information.

Kenya Telecom Industry Investment Guide. International Business Publications, USA. • $99.95 Individuals hardcopy, e-book, CD-ROM. Covers: Kenya Telecom Industry. Entries include: Investment opportunities, regulations, and contacts.

Kyrgyzstan Industrial and Business Directory. International Business Publications, USA. • Annual. $99.95 Individuals hardcopy, e-book, CD-ROM. Covers: Strategic industrial, investment and business contacts for conducting export-import and investment activity in the country.

Labuan Offshore Investment & Business Guide. International Business Publications, USA. • $99.95 Individuals hardcopy, e-book, CD-ROM. Covers: Basic information on economy, export-import and investment climate, regulations and industrial development, banking, and government. Entries include: Important business contacts and business travel.

Latvia Industrial and Business Directory. International Business Publications, USA. • Annual. $99.95 Individuals hardcopy, e-book, CD-ROM. Covers: Strategic industrial, investment and business contacts for conducting export-import and investment activity in the country.

Latvia Investment and Business Guide. International Business Publications, USA. • $99.95 Individuals hardcopy, e-book, CD-ROM. Covers: Basic information on economy, export-import and investment climate, regulations and industrial development, banking, and government. Entries include: Business contacts and business travel.

Liechtenstein Industrial and Business Directory. International Business Publications, USA. • Annual. $99.95 Individuals hardcover, e-book, CD-ROM. Covers: Strategic industrial, investment and business contacts for conducting export-import and investment activity in the country.

Lithuania Industrial and Business Directory. International Business Publications, USA. • Annual. $99.95 Individuals hardcover, e-book, CD-ROM. Covers: Strategic industrial, investment and business contacts for conducting export-import and investment activity in the country.

Luxembourg Industrial and Business Directory. International Business Publications, USA. • Annual. $99.95 Individuals paperback, e-book, CD-ROM. Covers: Strategic industrial, investment and business contacts for conducting export-import and investment activity in the country. Contains strategic, practical economic and business information.

Malaysia Industrial and Business Directory. International Business Publications, USA. • $99.95 Individuals hardcopy, e-book, CD-ROM. Covers: Customs, trade regulations and procedures.

Mauritius Industrial and Business Directory. International Business Publications, USA. • Annual. $99.95 Individuals hardcopy, e-book, CD-ROM. Covers: Strategic industrial, investment and business contacts for conducting export-import and investment activity in the country.

Mexico Investment and Business Guide. International Business Publications, USA. • $99.95 Individuals hardcopy, e-book, CD-ROM. Covers: Strategic information on economy, business, export-import and investment climate, regulations and industrial development, banking, government, and opportunities. Entries include: Important business contacts and business travel.

Moldova Industrial and Business Directory. International Business Publications, USA. • Annual. $99.95 Individuals hardcopy, e-book, CD-ROM. Covers: Strategic industrial, investment and business contacts for conducting export-import and investment activity in the country. Contains strategic practical economic and business information.

Mongolia Industrial and Business Directory. International Business Publications, USA. • $99.95 Individuals hardcopy, e-book, CD-ROM. Covers: Strategic and practical economic and business information. Entries include: Business contacts for conducting business activity in the country.

Morocco Investment and Business Guide. International Business Publications, USA. • $99.95 Individuals hardcopy, e-book, CD-ROM. Covers: Strategic information on economy, business, export-import and investment climate, opportunities, industrial development, banking and government. Entries include: Business contacts and business travel.

Moscow City Investment and Business Guide. International Business Publications, USA. • Annual. $99.95 Individuals hardcopy, e-book, CD-ROM. Covers: Strategic and business information, contacts, regulations and more. An ultimate guide for conducting investment, export-import activity in the Moscow City.

Namibia Industrial and Business Directory. International Business Publications, USA. • Annual. $99.95 Individuals hardcopy, e-book, CD-ROM. Covers: Strategic industrial, investment and business contacts for conducting export-import and investment activity in the country. Contains strategic practical economic and business information.

Netherlands Industrial and Business Directory. International Business Publications, USA. • Annual.

$99.95 Individuals hardcover, e-book, CD-ROM. Covers: Detailed information on investment, export-import business opportunities, foreign economic assistance projects, government and business contacts.

New Caledonia Industrial and Business Directory. International Business Publications, USA. • Annual. $99.95 Individuals hardcopy, e-book, CD-ROM. Covers: Strategic industrial, investment and business contacts for conducting export-import and investment activity in the country. Contains strategic, practical economic and business information.

New Zealand Industrial and Business Directory. International Business Publications, USA. • Annual. $99.95 Individuals hardcopy, e-book, CD-ROM. Covers: Strategic industrial, investment and business contacts for conducting export-import and investment activity in the country.

Nigeria Industrial and Business Directory. International Business Publications, USA. • Annual. $99.95 Individuals hardcover. Covers: Strategic industrial, investment and business contacts for conducting export-import and investment activity in the country.

Panama Industrial and Business Directory. International Business Publications, USA. • Annual. $99.95 Individuals hardcopy, e-book, CD-ROM. Covers: Strategic industrial, investment and business contacts for conducting export-import and investment activity in the country.

Panama Investment and Business Guide. International Business Publications, USA. • $99.95 Individuals hardcopy, e-book, CD-ROM. Covers: Strategic information on economy, business, export-import and investment climate, regulations and industrial development, banking, government, and opportunities. Entries include: Important business contacts and business travel.

Peru Industrial and Business Directory. International Business Publications, USA. • Annual. $99.95 Individuals hardcopy, e-book, CD-ROM. Covers: Strategic industrial, investment and business contacts for conducting export-import and investment activity in the country. Contains strategic, practical economic and business information.

Peru Investment and Business Guide. International Business Publications, USA. • Annual. $99.95 Individuals hardcopy, e-book, CD-ROM. Covers: Strategic and business information, contacts, regulations and more. An ultimate guide for conducting investment, export-import activity in the country.

Philippines Industrial and Business Directory. International Business Publications, USA. • Annual. $99.95 Individuals hardcopy, e-book, CD-ROM. Covers: Strategic industrial, investment and business contacts for conducting export-import and investment activity in the country.

Philippines Investment and Business Guide. International Business Publications, USA. • $99.95 Individuals hardcopy, e-book, CD-ROM. Covers: Basic information on economy, export-import and investment climate, regulations and industrial development, banking, and government. Entries include: Important business contacts and business travel.

Poland Investment and Business Guide. International Business Publications, USA. • $99.95 Individuals hardcopy, e-book, CD-ROM. Covers: Strategic information on economy, business, export-import and investment climate, opportunities, industrial development, banking and government. Entries include: Business contacts and business travel.

Portugal Investment and Business Guide. International Business Publications, USA. • $99.95 Individuals hardcopy, e-book, CD-ROM. Covers: Strategic information on economy, business, export-import and investment climate, opportunities, industrial development, banking and government. Entries include: Business contacts and business travel.

Probe Directory of Foreign Direct Investment in the United States. Probe International. • Triennial. $250. Covers: over 1,500 affiliate firms in the United States which are partially or totally owned by over 800 Japanese companies. Entries include: For U.S. companies--Company name, address, phone, subsidiary names, name of executive officer, foreign investor's name, line of business/product. For foreign investors--Company name, address, names of U.S. affiliates.

Romania Investment and Business Guide. International Business Publications, USA. • $99.95 Individuals hardcopy, e-book, CD-ROM. Covers: Detailed information on investment, export-import business opportunities, foreign economic assistance projects, government and business contacts.

Russia Industrial and Business Directory. International Business Publications, USA. • Annual. $99.95 Individuals hardcopy, e-book, CD-ROM. Covers: Strategic industrial, investment and business contacts for conducting export-import and investment activity in the country.

Russia Investment and Business Guide. International Business Publications, USA. • $99.95 Individuals hardcopy, e-book, CD-ROM. Covers: Basic information on economy, export-import and investment climate, regulations and industrial development, banking, and government. Entries include: Important business contacts and business travel.

Rwanda Investment and Business Guide. International Business Publications, USA. • $99.95 Individuals hardcopy, e-book, CD-ROM. Covers: Strategic information on economy, business, export-import and investment climate, regulations and industrial development, banking, government, and opportunities. Entries include: Important business contacts and business travel.

St. Petersburg (Russia) Investment and Business Guide. International Business Publications, USA. • Annual. $99.95 Individuals hardcopy, e-book, CD-ROM. Covers: Strategic and business information, contacts, regulations and more. An ultimate guide for conducting investment, export-import activity in the country.

Sao Paulo Year Book: Amcham Yearbook Directory. American Chamber of Commerce for Brazil - Sao Paulo. • Annual. $500 Members. Covers: 5,450 member American and Brazilian firms and 20,000 individual members interested in developing trade and investment within and between the two countries; other American chambers of commerce, American organizations in Sao Paulo, government agencies, institutions, and associations. Database includes: Glossary of product terms in Portuguese; section on Brazilian business and economics; statistics. Entries include: For firms--Company name, address, phone, telex, fax, names and titles of key personnel, product/service, export and domestic sales, net worth, number of employees, registered capital, branches, affiliates abroad. For individual members--Name, title, company name, phone, home or office address, telex. For others--Name, address, phone.

Saudi Arabia Industrial and Business Directory. International Business Publications, USA. • Annual. $99.95 Individuals hardcopy, e-book, CD-ROM. Covers: Strategic industrial, investment and business contacts for conducting export-import and investment activity in the country.

Saudi Arabia Investment and Business Guide. International Business Publications, USA. • $99.95 Individuals hardcopy, e-book, CD-ROM. Covers: Strategic information on economy, business, export-import and investment climate, regulations and industrial development, banking, government, and opportunities. Entries include: Important business contacts and business travel.

Sierra Leone Investment and Business Guide. International Business Publications, USA. • $99.95 Individuals hardcopy, e-book, CD-ROM. Covers: Guide for conducting business activity in the country. Entries include: Important business information, business travel, and contacts.

Singapore Investment & Business Guide. International Business Publications, USA. • $99.95 Individuals hardcopy, e-book, CD-ROM. Covers: Basic information on economy, export-import and investment climate, regulations and industrial development, banking, and government. Entries include: Important business contacts and business travel.

Solomon Islands Investment and Business Guide. International Business Publications, USA. • $99.95 Individuals hardcopy, e-book, CD-ROM. Covers: Strategic and business information, contacts, regulations and more. An ultimate guide for conducting investment, export-import activity in the country.

South Africa Industrial and Business Directory. International Business Publications, USA. • Annual. $99.95 Individuals hardcopy, e-book, CD-ROM. Covers: Strategic industrial, investment and business contacts for conducting export-import and investment activity in the country.

South Carolina Investment and Business Guide. International Business Publications, USA. • $99.95 Individuals hardcopy, e-book, CD-ROM. Covers: Strategic and business information, contacts, regulations and more. An ultimate guide for conducting investment, export-import activity in the country.

Spain Industrial and Business Directory. International Business Publications, USA. • Annual. $99.95 Individuals hardcopy, e-book, CD-ROM. Covers: Strategic industrial, investment and business contacts for conducting export-import and investment activity in the country.

Sweden Industrial and Business Directory. International Business Publications, USA. • Annual. $99.95 Individuals hardcopy, e-book, CD-ROM. Covers: Strategic industrial, investment and business contacts for conducting export-import and investment activity in the country. Contains strategic, practical economic and business information.

Switzerland Industrial and Business Directory. International Business Publications, USA. • Annual. $99.95 Individuals hardcopy, e-book, CD-ROM. Covers: Strategic industrial, investment and business contacts for conducting export-import and investment activity in the country.

Taiwan Industrial and Business Directory. International Business Publications, USA. • Annual. $99.95 Individuals hardcopy, e-book, CD-ROM. Covers: Strategic industrial, investment and business contacts for conducting export-import and investment activity in the country.

Tajikistan Industrial and Business Directory. International Business Publications, USA. • Annual. $99.95 Individuals hardcopy, e-book, CD-ROM. Covers: Strategic industrial, investment and business contacts for conducting export-import and investment activity in the country.

Tanzania Investment and Business Guide. International Business Publications, USA. • $99.95 Individuals hardcopy, e-book, CD-ROM. Covers: Strategic information on economy, opportunities, export-import and investment climate, regulations and industrial development, banking, and government. Entries include: Business contacts and business travel.

Thailand Investment and Business Guide. International Business Publications, USA. • $99.95 Individuals hardcopy, e-book, CD-ROM. Covers:

Basic information on economy, export-import and investment climate, regulations and industrial development, banking, and government. Entries include: Important business contacts and business travel.

Trinidad and Tobago Investment and Business Guide. International Business Publications, USA. • $99.95 Individuals hardcopy, E-book and CD-ROM. Covers: Strategic and information on economy, business, export-import activity, investment climate, opportunities, industrial development, banking and government. Entries include: Business contacts, regulations, etc.

Turkey Investment and Business Guide. International Business Publications, USA. • $99.95 Individuals hardcopy, E-book and CD-ROM. Covers: Detailed information on investment, export-import business opportunities, foreign economic assistance projects, government and business contacts.

The UK/USA Investment Directory & Business Resource. BritishAmerican Business Inc. of New York and London. • Biennial. $149. Covers: Over 6,000 British and American companies and their approximately 4,000 subsidiaries in the United Kingdom and the United States. Entries include: Parent company name, address, phone, fax; name of British subsidiary in the United States, address, phone, fax; percentage of business British or American owned, number of staff, product or service provided, Standard Industrial Classification (SIC) code.

Ukraine Government and Business Contacts Handbook. International Business Publications, USA. • Annual. $99.95 Individuals hardcopy, E-book and CD-ROM. Covers: Strategic industrial, investment and business contacts for conducting export-import and investment activity in the country.

United Arab Emirates Industrial and Business Directory. International Business Publications, USA. • Annual. $99.95 Individuals hardcopy, E-book and CD-ROM. Covers: Strategic industrial, investment and business contacts for conducting export-import and investment activity in the country.

United States Industrial and Business Directory. International Business Publications, USA. • Annual. $99.95 Individuals hardcopy, E-book and CD-ROM. Covers: Detailed information on investment, export-import business opportunities, foreign economic assistance projects, government and business contacts.

Uruguay Industrial and Business Directory. International Business Publications, USA. • Annual. $99.95 Individuals hardcopy, E-book and CD-ROM. Covers: Strategic industrial, investment and business contacts for conducting export-import and investment activity in the country.

Uruguay Investment & Business Guide. International Business Publications, USA. • $99.95 Individuals hardcopy, E-book and CD-ROM. Covers: Strategic information on economy, business, export-import and investment climate, regulations and industrial development, banking, government, and opportunities. Entries include: Important business contacts and business travel.

Uzbekistan Industrial and Business Directory. International Business Publications, USA. • $99.95 Individuals hardcopy, E-book and CD-ROM. Covers: Strategic and practical economic and business information. Entries include: Business contacts for conducting business activity in the country.

Venezuela Industrial and Business Directory. International Business Publications, USA. • Annual. $99.95 Individuals hardcopy, E-book and CD-ROM. Covers: Strategic industrial, investment and business contacts for conducting export-import and investment activity in the country.

Vietnam: Business Opportunities and Risks. China Books. • A$5. Publication includes: Business contacts in Vietnam. Database includes: Maps, charts, and a bibliography. Entries include: Name, address, phone. Principal content of publication is information on the business environment, forms of foreign investment, laws, taxes, and investment regulations in Vietnam.

Vietnam Investment and Business Guide. International Business Publications, USA. • $99.95 Individuals hardcopy, E-book and CD-ROM. Covers: Strategic and business information, contacts, regulations and more. An ultimate guide for conducting investment, export-import activity in the country.

Wallis & Futuna Investment & Business Guide. International Business Publications, USA. • $99.95 Individuals hardcopy, E-book and CD-ROM. Covers: Basic information on economy, export-import and investment climate, regulations and industrial development, banking, and government. Entries include: Important business contacts and business travel.

Yugoslavia (Serbia) Industrial and Business Directory. International Business Publications, USA. • Annual. $99.95 Individuals hardcopy, E-book and CD-ROM. Covers: Strategic industrial, investment and business contacts for conducting export-import and investment activity in the country.

HANDBOOKS AND MANUALS

Practical Guide to Foreign Direct Investment in the European Union: The Green Book. Euroconfidentiel S. A. • Annual. $240.00. Provides coverage of national and EU business incentives. In addition to 70 charts and tables, includes EU country profiles of taxation, labor costs, and employment regulations.

INTERNET DATABASES

CANOE: Canadian Online Explorer. Canoe Limited Partnership. Phone: (416)947-2154; Fax: (416)947-2209 • URL: http://www.canoe.ca • Web site provides a wide variety of Canadian news and information, including business and financial data. Includes "Money," "Your Investment," "Technology," and "Stock Quotes." Allows keyword searching, with links to many other sites. Daily updating. Fees: Free.

ETF Connect. Nuveen Investments. Phone: 800-257-8787 • URL: http://www.etfconnect.com • Free Web site makes available extensive, searchable information on individual closed-end investment funds, preferred share funds, and exchange-traded index funds. Information on a particular fund is available by name or as part of a classification (high yield, investment grade, municipal, emerging markets, global equity, etc.). Fund charts are available for various time periods, as is data concerning premiums or discounts, dividends, annualized total return, credit quality, "Top 10 Holdings," and so forth.

OTHER SOURCES

Investing, Licensing, and Trading. The Economist Intelligence Unit. • Semiannual. $345.00 per year for each country. Key laws, rules, and licensing provisions are explained for each of 60 countries. Information is provided on political conditions, markets, price policies, foreign exchange practices, labor, and export-import.

World Investment Report. United Nations Publications. • Annual. Concerned with foreign direct investment, economic development, regional trends, transnational corporations, and globalization.

PERIODICALS AND NEWSLETTERS

Emerging Markets Debt Report. SourceMedia Inc. • Weekly. $895.00 per year. Newsletter. Provides information on new and prospective sovereign and corporate bond issues from developing countries. Includes an emerging market bond index and pricing data.

Emerging Markets Quarterly. Institutional Investor Inc. Journals Group. • Quarterly. Price on application. Newsletter on financial markets in developing areas, such as Africa, Latin America, Southeast Asia, and Eastern Europe. Topics include institutional investment opportunities and regulatory matters. Formerly *Emerging Markets Weekly.*

Global Money Management. Wolters Kluwer Law and Business. • Description: Reports on international fund management, including investment strategies; pension fund searches; hires for consultants, managers, and custodians; performance measurement; developing markets, and significant personnel changes.

Institutional Investor International Edition: The Magazine for International Finance and Investment. Institutional Investor Inc. Journals Group. • Monthly. $475.00 per year. Covers the international aspects of professional investing and finance. Emphasis is on Europe, the Far East, and Latin America.

Institutional Investor: The Premier of Professional Magazine Finance. Institutional Investor Inc. Journals Group. • Monthly. $445.00 per year. Includes print and online editions. Edited for portfolio managers and other investment professionals. Special feature issues include "Country Credit Ratings," "Fixed Income Trading Ranking," "All-America Research Team," and "Global Banking Ranking.".

RESEARCH CENTERS AND INSTITUTES

Bureau of International Labor Affairs - Office of International Economic Affairs - Foreign Economic Research Division. 200 Constitution Ave. NW, Rm. S-5317, Washington, DC 20210. Phone: (202)693-4887; Fax: (202)693-4851 • URL: http://www.dol.gov/ilab/programs/oiea • Effects of international economic developments, including policies that affect international trade and investment on U.S. workers. Projects have included analysis of: multilateral trade negotiations; effects on U.S. workers of foreign investment and technology transfer by multinational corporations; compensation of earnings losses for workers who are displaced by trade; changing pattern of U.S. comparative advantage in trade; and effects of trade on employment opportunities, by industry and occupational categories.

TRADE/PROFESSIONAL ASSOCIATIONS

American-Lithuanian Business Council. 701 8th St., NW Ste. 500, Washington, DC 20001. Phone: (202)973-5975; Fax: (202)659-5249; Email: info@amlithbc.org • URL: http://www.amlithbc.org • Executive firms having significant actual or potential trade involvement with Lithuania, including coverage of policy issues related to Russia, Ukraine, Belarus, Turkey, Iran, the Caucasus and Central Asia. Provides a forum for discussing trade and investment issues and formulation of policy issues to promote and expand economic relations between the U.S. and Lithuania.

Brazil-U.S. Business Council. 1615 H St. NW, Washington, DC 20062. Phone: (202)463-5729; Email: brazilcouncil@uschamber.com • URL: http://www.brazilcouncil.org • Works to provide a high-level private sector forum for the business communities of both countries to engage in substantive dialogue on trade and investment issues and communicate private sector priorities to both governments.

Camara de Comercio Argentino-Britanica en la Republica Argentina. Av. Corrientes 457, Piso 10, C1043AAE Buenos Aires, Argentina. Phone: 54 11 43942762; Fax: 54 11 43263860; Email: info@ccab.com.ar • URL: http://www.ccab.com.ar • Promotes bilateral Trade and Investment between Argentina and UK.

Iran-Netherlands Business Council. No. 254 Taleghani Ave., Tehran, Iran. Phone: 98 21 88346736; Fax: 98 21 88346736; Email: info@inbc.ir • URL:

http://www.inbc.ir/pages/default.aspx?lan=en • Promotes investment, trade, and political and cultural cooperation between Iran and Netherlands. Fosters business to business relationships between entrepreneurs of Iran and Netherlands.

Malaysian Business Council of Cambodia. No. 87, 294 St., Boeng Keng Kong 1, Phnom Penh, Cambodia. Phone: 855 23 216176; Fax: 855 23 726101; Email: mbcc.secretariat@gmail.com • URL: http://mbccambodia.org • Fosters strong business ties between Malaysia and Cambodia. Encourages the development of Malaysian investment in Cambodia. Provides a forum for meetings, discussions and interaction between the Malaysian business community and governmental personnel in Cambodia.

Middle East Investment Initiative. 500 Eighth St. NW, Washington, DC 20004. Phone: (202)799-4345; Fax: (202)799-5000 • URL: http://www.meiinitiative.org • Partners with public and private entities to offer specialized financial products in the Palestinian territories. Helps to revitalize the economy, stimulate economic activity and create jobs in the Middle East. Works to create risk insurance to address movement of products for Palestinian businesses.

Polish-U.S. Business Council. Chamber of Commerce of the United States, 1615 H St. NW, Washington, DC 20062-2000. Phone: 800-638-6582 or (202)659-6000; Email: press@uschamber.com • URL: http://www.uschamber.com • U.S. corporations involved in industry, agriculture, or services. Seeks to expand trade between the U.S. and Poland, and to encourage investment in Poland by U.S. firms.

U.S.-Pakistan Business Council. 1615 H St. NW, Washington, DC 20062. Phone: (202)463-5732; Fax: (202)822-2491; Email: uspbc@uschamber.com • URL: http://www.uspakistan.org • Fosters awareness of business opportunities in Pakistan. Increases U.S. foreign direct investment in Pakistan. Brings together Pakistani and American business leaders for discussions on business conditions and policy related issues. Provides a forum for dialogue on key economic, commercial, and other relevant issues of interest to American companies doing or planning to do business in Pakistan.

FOREIGN LANGUAGE PRESS AND NEWSPAPERS

See also BUSINESS JOURNALISM; NEWSPAPERS

ALMANACS AND YEARBOOKS

Editor & Publisher International Yearbook: Encyclopedia of the Newspaper Industry. Editor and Publisher Company Inc. • Annual. $150.00. Daily and Sunday newspapers in the United States and Canada.

DIRECTORIES

Bacon's International Directory--Western Europe. Cision US Inc. • Annual. Covers: over 16,000 consumer, business, trade, and technical publications, and about 1,000 national and regional newspapers in 12 countries of western Europe. Entries include: Publication name, address, phone, telex, translation requirements for news releases, code indicating type of publicity in which interested (new products, trade literature, etc.), frequency, circulation.

Burrelle's Media Directory: Newspapers and Related Media. BurrellesLuce. • Annual. $550.00. *Daily Newspapers* volume lists more than 2,200 daily publications in the U. S., Canada, and Mexico. *Non-Daily Newspapers* volume lists more than 10,400 items published no more than three times a week. Provides detailed descriptions, including key personnel.

Hispanic Media & Market Source. Kantar Media SRDS. • Quarterly. $445 per year. Provides detailed information on the following Hispanic advertising media in the U.S.: TV, radio, newspapers, magazines, direct mail, outdoor, and special events.

International Media Guide: Newspapers Worldwide. Kantar Media SRDS. • $553 Individuals online; 1 year. Covers over 3,400 papers in every major city in the world.

FOREIGN LAW

See INTERNATIONAL LAW AND REGULATION

FOREIGN MARKETS

See FOREIGN TRADE

FOREIGN OPERATIONS

See INTERNATIONAL BUSINESS

FOREIGN RADIO AND TELEVISION

See also FOREIGN LANGUAGE PRESS AND NEWSPAPERS; RADIO BROADCASTING INDUSTRY; TELEVISION BROADCASTING INDUSTRY

DIRECTORIES

Media Communications Association International Membership Directory. Media Communications Association - International.

PERIODICALS AND NEWSLETTERS

International Broadcast Engineer. DMG World Media Ltd. • Eight times a year. $119.00 per year.

Television International Magazine. TVI Publishing. • Bimonthly. $42.00 per year.

FOREIGN SERVICE

See DIPLOMATIC AND CONSULAR SERVICE

FOREIGN STUDY

See STUDY ABROAD

FOREIGN TRADE

See also EXPORT-IMPORT TRADE

ABSTRACTS AND INDEXES

PAIS International. ProQuest L.L.C. • Monthly. $850.00 per year; cumulations three times a year. Provides topical citations to the worldwide literature of public affairs, economics, demographics, sociology, and trade. Text in English; indexed materials in English, French, German, Italian, Portuguese and Spanish.

ALMANACS AND YEARBOOKS

Agricultural Policy Monitoring and Evaluation. Organization for Economic Cooperation and Development. Organisation for Economic Co-operation and Development Publications and Information Center. • Annual. Provides estimates of support to agriculture as well as chapters on agricultural policy developments.

Trade and Development Report (TDR). United Nations Conference on Trade and Development. • Annual. Yearly overview of trends in international trade, including an analysis of the economic and trade situation in developing countries. Published by the United Nations Conference on Trade and Development (UNCTAD).

CD-ROM DATABASES

Business Abstracts with Full Text. EBSCO Publishing Inc. • Includes full text articles from more than 460 business publications from 1982 to present. Indexing for nearly 880 publications.

Global Trade Atlas. Global Trade Information Services Inc. • Subscription fees are tailored. Provides government statistics on trade between the U. S. and each of more than 80 countries. Includes import-export data, trade balances, product information, market share, price data, etc.

OECD Statistical Compendium. Organization for Economic Cooperation and Development. • Semiannual. $1,905.00 per year for 1 to 10 users. CD-ROM contains more than 730,000 monthly, quarterly, and annual time series for OECD countries, 1960 to date. Includes fully searchable data on agriculture, food, economic indicators, national accounts, employment, energy, finance, industry, technology, and foreign trade. Results can be displayed in various forms.

PAIS International. ProQuest L.L.C. • Monthly. $1,995.00 per year. Contains over 650,000 citations to the literature of contemporary social, political, and economic issues.

USA Trade. U.S. Department of Commerce. • Monthly. $650.00 per year. Provides over 150,000 trade-related data series on CD-ROM. Includes full text of many government publications. Specific data is included on national income, labor, price indexes, foreign exchange, technical standards, and international markets. Website address is www.stat-usa.gov/.

World Trade Organization Trade Policy Review. Bernan Press. • Annual. $95. provides detailed trade information for each of 40 countries. Includes search capabilities, hypertext links, charts, tables, and graphs.

DIRECTORIES

America's International Trade: A Reference Handbook. ABC-Clio Inc. • $45 Individuals print. Covers: The importance of international trade to the American economy and the influence it has on American businesses. Publication includes: List of organizations relevant to America and international trade, such as the World Bank. Entries include: Contact data. Principal content of publication is a discussion of international trade and the American economy and businesses and international trade agreement.

Bolivia--American Chamber of Commerce--Membership Directory. U.S. Chamber of Commerce. • Annual. Covers: American and Bolivian companies and individuals interested in the development of trade within and between the two countries. Entries include: For firms--Company name, address, phone, fax, telex, cable address, names and titles of key personnel, line of business, subsidiary and branch names and locations, locations of plants or branch offices, product/service information. For individuals--Name, title, affiliation, address. Plus details on Bolivia's investment climate, economic indicators, new land reform laws, and trade agreement obligations.

Business Foundation Book: General Trade Index & Business Guide--Poland. Business Foundation Company Ltd. • Annual. $90 plus $40.00 shipping. Covers: Approximately 3,500 Polish businesses and firms seeking foreign cooperation and trade with the West. Database includes: General information on Polish industry and trade, including the Polish economy, business and labor law, finance, taxation, import/export regulations, and laws pertaining to foreign investment and business. Entries include: Abbreviated trade names; firm name, address, phone, fax, telex; year established; name and title of contact and languages spoken; line of business; proposed fields of cooperation or goods sought; number of employees; financial data.

Business: Your Partner in China Plus. Computing Center of the Ministry of Foreign Trade and Economic Cooperation. • $650. Database covers: Listings concerning China's foreign trade, including customs, commodity inspection agencies, insurance agencies, and banks. Database includes: International transport information, animal quarantine laws, and travel agencies.

California International Trade Register. Harris InfoSource. • Annual. $155. Covers: 15,656 California international trade companies. Entries include: Company name, address, county, phone, fax, web site address (on CD-ROM only), number of employees, names and titles of key executives, plant size, year established, parent company, annual sales, import/export information, Standard Industrial Classification (SIC) code, and product description.

Commercial and Industrial Directory of Switzerland. Mosse Adress AG. • Annual. $901 Individuals. Covers: 300,000 industrial, trade, and export businesses and services in Switzerland. Entries include: Company name, address, phone.

Department of Trade and Industry--The Single Market: Guide to Sources of Advice. Department of Trade and Industry. • Covers: Organizations providing information on business and trade in the European Community, including representative organizations, research and technology organizations, chambers of commerce, public sector advisers, and language advisers. Entries include: For representative organizations and research and technology organizations--Name, address, phone, name and title of contact, sectors covered, restrictions on service, type of information offered, European links. For others--Name, address, phone, type of information offered.

Directory of Arizona Exporters. Arizona Commerce Authority. • Annual. Covers: Arizona enterprises currently involved in international trade. Entries include: Company name, address, phone, fax, e-mail, names of principal executive, and international marketing contact, number of employees, products or services, date established, current or planned export regions.

Directory of Service, Industrial and Foreign Trading Companies in Egypt. International Trade Consulting Co. • $45. Covers: Companies in Egypt. Entries include: Company name, address, phone.

Finnish Trade. Federation of Finnish Trade and Commerce. • Annual. Covers: Member firms of the Federation of Finnish Commerce and Trade. Entries include: Company name, address, phone, fax, telex.

General Trade Index & Business Guide. Business Foundation Company Ltd. • Annual. $135. Publication includes: More than 3,500 public and private Polish companies seeking foreign joint ventures or foreign trade opportunities. Entries include: Company name, address, phone. Principal content of publication is information on doing business and living in Poland.

German Canadian Business and Trade Directory. German Canadian and Trade Publication. • Covers: Companies in all business sectors. Entries include: Multinational corporations, public institutions, professional associations, and importer/exporter.

Global World Trade Centers Directory. International Business Publications, USA. • $99.95 Individuals paperback. Covers: World Trade Centers located in over 100 countries.

Hoover's Handbook of World Business. Dun & Bradstreet Inc. Hoover's Inc. • Annual. $225 Individuals Hardcover. Covers: Hundreds of companies headquartered outside the U.S., including many with substantial activity in the U.S.; global enterprises, businesses that dominate their respective industries, and representative companies from all major industries. Entries include: Company name, overview, history, exchange and stock symbols, fiscal year-end date, names and titles of key personnel, name of auditors, number of employees, headquarters address, phone, fax, description of where the company does business, specific products/services/brand names produced, key competitors, 10 years of key financial data.

International Business and Trade Directories. Grey House Publishing. • $225 Individuals softcover. Covers: Approximately 8,000 directories concerned with international business and trade. Entries include: Directory title, publisher name, address, phone, fax, description of directory, ISBN, size, price, frequency, editor, U.S. Distributor.

Malaysian German Business. Malaysian-German Chamber of Commerce and Industry. • Annual. RM150 Individuals. Covers: Listings of Malaysian-German business members. Entries include: Members' contact information and activities.

Malaysian-Thai Chamber of Commerce--Handbook and Directory. Malaysian-Thai Chamber of Commerce. • Covers: Malaysian and Thai member companies and individuals.

MZM World Business Directory. MZM Publications Publishing Promotion Co. • Irregular. $154 plus airmail. Covers: companies in 33 post-socialist countries involved in international trade and business: Albania, Armenia, Azerbaijan, Bosnia & Herzegovina, Bulgaria, Belorus, China, Croatia, Cuba, Czech Republic, Slovakia, Estonia, Georgia, former East Germany, Hungary, Kazakhstan, Kirghizia, Latvia, Lithuania, North Korea, Macedonia, Moldova, Mongolia, Poland, Romania, Russia, Kaliningrad Province of Russia, Slovenia, Tadzhikistan, Turkmenistan, Ukraine, Uzbekistan, Vietnam, and Yugoslavia. Entries include: Company name, address, phone, fax, telex, number of employees, year established, subsidiary companies, description.

Sao Paulo Year Book: Amcham Yearbook Directory. American Chamber of Commerce for Brazil - Sao Paulo. • Annual. $500 Members. Covers: 5,450 member American and Brazilian firms and 20,000 individual members interested in developing trade and investment within and between the two countries; other American chambers of commerce, American organizations in Sao Paulo, government agencies, institutions, and associations. Database includes: Glossary of product terms in Portuguese; section on Brazilian business and economics; statistics. Entries include: For firms--Company name, address, phone, telex, fax, names and titles of key personnel, product/service, export and domestic sales, net worth, number of employees, registered capital, branches, affiliates abroad. For individual members--Name, title, company name, phone, home or office address, telex. For others--Name, address, phone.

Trade Directory of Nigeria. World Trade Center of Nigeria. • Triennial. Covers: Trade-related information for import/export companies, manufacturers, government representatives, lawyers, accountants, and interested individuals in Nigeria.

UNCTAD-Trade Analysis and Information System. United Nations Conference on Trade and Development. • Database covers: Indicators of trade control measures (tariff, para-tariff and non-tariff measures), as well as imports by suppliers at each harmonized system 6-digit level for over 160 countries. It also provides country notes of trade regimes for some 40 developing countries, describing market access conditions according to the UNCTAD coding system of Trade control measures.

United States Foreign Trade Sanctions Handbook. International Business Publications, USA. • $99.95 Individuals paperback. Covers: United States trade sanctions for selected countries.

Who Knows About Foreign Industries and Markets. MarketResearch.com. • Annual. $85. Covers: 2,500 U.S. experts and authorities on international trade. Entries include: Name and telephone number.

World Directory of Trade Promotion Organizations and Other Foreign Trade Bodies. International Trade Centre. • Annual. $50 Free to developing countries/economies in transition. Covers: over 1,200 international trade promotion organizations and other foreign trade bodies involved in international trade, including ministries, trade promotion organizations, import promotion offices, chambers of commerce in principal business centers and/or federations of chambers of commerce, trade associations, operational trade pointes, and selected regional and inter-regional organizations. Entries include: Organization name, address, phone, fax, telex, e-mail, URL, and codes description of services provided when available.

Yugoslavia Export-Import Directory. Yugoslaviapublic. • Annual. Covers: Foreign trade organizations, products, services in Yugoslavia. Entries include: Name, address, phone.

INTERNET DATABASES

Bureau of Economic Analysis. U. S. Department of Commerce, Bureau of Economic Analysis. Phone: (202)606-9900; Fax: (202)606-5310; Email: webmaster@bea.doc.gov • URL: http://www.bea.doc.gov • Web site includes "News Release Information" covering national, regional, and international economic estimates from the BEA. Highlights of releases appear online the same day, complete text and tables appear the next day. "Recent News Releases" section provides titles for past nine months, with links. "BEA Data and Methodology" includes "Frequently Requested NIPA Data" (national income and product accounts, such as gross domestic product and personal income). Other statistics are available. Fees: Free.

Business 2.0 Web Guide to the Best Business Links. Business 2.0 Media Inc. Phone: (415)293-4800; Email: support@business2.com • URL: http://www.business2.com/webguide • Web site presents an extensive, searchable directory of links to "the best, most informative, and authoritative web pages." Twenty main categories cover business, finance, career, company information, people, and technology topics, with thousands of subtopics, all linking to Web sites recommended by experienced business researchers. Fees: Free.

EBSCO Information Services. EBSCO Publishing Inc. 10 Estes St., Ipswich, MA 01938-2106. Phone: 800-653-2726 or (978)356-6500; Fax: (978)356-6565; Email: information@ebscohost.com • URL: http://www.ebscohost.com • Fee-based Web site providing Internet access to a wide variety of databases, including business-related material. Full text is available for many periodical titles, with daily updates. Fees: Apply.

Fedstats. Federal Interagency Council on Statistical Policy. Phone: (202)395-7254 • URL: http://www.fedstats.gov • Web site features an efficient search facility for full-text statistics produced by more than 100 federal agencies, including the Census Bureau, the Bureau of Economic Analysis, and the Bureau of Labor Statistics. Boolean searches can be made within one agency or for all agencies combined. Links are offered to international statistical bureaus, including the UN, IMF, OECD, UNESCO, Eurostat, and 20 individual countries. Fees: Free.

FedWorld: A Program of the United States Department of Commerce. National Technical Information Service. Phone: 800-553-NTIS or (703)605-6000; Fax: (703)605-6900; Email: webmaster@fedworld.gov • URL: http://www.fedworld.gov • Web site offers "a comprehensive central access point for searching, locating, ordering, and acquiring government and business information." Emphasis is on searching the Web pages, databases, and government reports of a wide variety of federal agencies. Fees: Free.

FreeLunch.com. Economy.com, Inc. Phone: (610)696-8700; Fax: (610)696-1678 • URL: http://www.freelunch.com • Web site provides free access to more than 200 million economic and financial data series, covering industry, demographics, labor markets, prices, retail sales, government spending, trade, interest rates, housing starts, the stock market, etc. Data is available in either chart or table form. Searching is offered. Free, but registration required. Economy.com, Inc. also offers fee-based economic analysis at *The Dismal Scientist* site (www.dismal.com).

InSite 2. Intelligence Data/Thomson Financial. Phone: 800-654-0393 or (617)856-1890; Fax: (617)737-3182; Email: intelligence.data@tfn.com • URL: http://www.insite2.gale.com/ • Fee-based Web site consolidates information in a "Base Pack" consisting of Business InSite, Market InSite, and Company InSite. Optional databases are Consumer InSite, Health and Wellness InSite, Newsletter InSite, and Computer InSite. Includes fulltext content from more than 2,500 trade publications, journals, newsletters, newspapers, analyst reports, and other sources. Continuous updating. Formerly produced by The Gale Group.

ProQuest. ProQuest L.L.C. 789 E Eisenhower Pkwy., Ann Arbor, MI 48106-1346. Phone: 800-521-0600 or (734)761-4700; Fax: (734)662-4554; Email: info@proquest.com • URL: http://www.proquest.com • Fee-based Web site providing Internet access to more than 3,000 periodicals, newspapers, and other publications. Many items are available full-text, with daily updates. Includes extensive corporate and financial information. Fees: Apply.

Trade Show Center. Global Sources/Trade Media Holdings Ltd. Phone: (656)574-2800; Email: service@globalsources.com • URL: http://www.globalsources.com/TRADESHW/TRDSHFRM.HTM • Free Web site provides current, detailed information on more than 1,000 major trade shows worldwide, including events in the U. S., but with an emphasis on "Asia and Greater China." Searching is offered by product, supplier, country, and month of year. Includes links to "Trade Information.".

ONLINE DATABASES

Wilson Business Abstracts Online. H.W. Wilson Co. • Indexes and abstracts 600 major business periodicals, plus the *Wall Street Journal* and the business section of the *New York Times*. Indexing is from 1982, abstracting from 1990, with the two newspapers included from 1993. Updated weekly. Inquire as to online cost and availability. (*Business Periodicals Index* without abstracts is also available online.).

OTHER SOURCES

Foreign Tax and Trade Briefs. Matthew Bender and Company Inc. • Quarterly. $1,054 book. The latest tax and trade information for over 100 foreign countries.

Trade Policy Agenda. U. S. Government Printing Office. • Annual. $45.00. Lists U. S. trade agreements "that afford increased foreign market access or reduce foreign barriers.".

Trade Policy Reviews. Bernan Press. • Annual. Each review describes "trade policies, practices, and macroeconomic situations." Prepared by the Trade Policy Review Board of the World Trade Organization.

World Trade Organization Dispute Settlement Decisions: Bernan's Annotated Reporter. Bernan Press. • 3/year. $320 2 volume set. Contains all World Trade Organization Panel Reports and Appellate Decisions since the establishment of the WTO in 1995. Includes such cases as "The Importation, Sale, and Distribution of Bananas."

PERIODICALS AND NEWSLETTERS

China Business. China Business Hong Kong. • English-language business magazine containing information involving domestic foreign trade companies, industrial-trading companies, power-enlarged enterprises, international hotels and commercial centers.

Direction of Trade Statistics (DOT). International Monetary Fund. International Monetary Fund - Data and Statistics Department. • Quarterly. Individuals, $128.00 per year; libraries, $89.00 per year. Includes *Yearbook*.

Economic Justice Report: Global Issues of Economic Justice. Ecumenical Coalition for Economic Justice. • Quarterly. Individuals, $30.00 per year; institutions, $40.00 per year. Reports on economic fairness in foreign trade. Formerly *Gatt-Fly Report*.

International Trade Reporter Export Reference Manual. Bloomberg BNA. • Biweekly. $874.00 per year. Looseleaf service.

Project Finance Monthly. Infocast Inc. • Description: Provides information about the power industry. Includes industry news, financing, regulation, and contracts.

World Trade Review: Economics, Law, International Institutions. Cambridge University Press. • Three times a year. Individuals, $48.00 pr year; institutions, $200.00 per year. Published in conjunction with the World Trade Organization (www.wto.org). Covers "issues of relevance to the multilateral trading system.".

RESEARCH CENTERS AND INSTITUTES

Bureau of International Labor Affairs - Office of International Economic Affairs - Foreign Economic Research Division. 200 Constitution Ave. NW, Rm. S-5317, Washington, DC 20210. Phone: (202)693-4887; Fax: (202)693-4851 • URL: http://www.dol.gov/ilab/programs/oiea • Effects of international economic developments, including policies that affect international trade and investment on U.S. workers. Projects have included analysis of: multilateral trade negotiations; effects on U.S. workers of foreign investment and technology transfer by multinational corporations; compensation of earnings losses for workers who are displaced by trade; changing pattern of U.S. comparative advantage in trade; and effects of trade on employment opportunities, by industry and occupational categories.

London School of Economics and Political Science - Department of International Relations - International Trade Policy Unit. Clement House, Rm. CLM 613, Houghton St., London WC2A 2AE, United Kingdom. Phone: 44 20 79557696; Fax: 44 20 79557980; Email: itpu@lse.ac.uk • URL: http://www.lse.ac.uk/internationalRelations/centresandunits/ITPU/ITPUhome.aspx • Policies and business implications of trade agreements at the multilateral, regional, and national levels.

U.S. International Trade Commission - Minerals, Metals, Machinery, and Miscellaneous Manufacturers Division. 500 E St. SW, Washington, DC 20436. Phone: (202)205-3418; Fax: (202)205-2217; Email: brookhart@usitc.gov • URL: http://www.usitc.gov • Survey data related to international trade matters, including international competitiveness of U.S. industries, especially iron and steel products, industrial minerals and nonferrous metals, machinery and general manufactured products.

University of Michigan - Erb Institute for Global Sustainable Enterprise. Dana Bldg., 440 Church St., Ann Arbor, MI 48109-1234. Phone: (734)647-9799; Fax: (734)647-8551; Email: tplyon@umich.edu • URL: http://erb.umich.edu • Understanding the complex dynamics of coupled human and natural systems in relation to economic activity. Research addresses four questions: how can dynamic interactions between nature and society, including lags and inertia, be incorporated into emerging models and conceptualizations that integrate the Earth system, human development, and sustainability; how are long-term trends in environment and development, including consumption and population, reshaping nature-society interactions in ways relevant to sustainability; what systems of incentive structures, including markets, rules, norms, and scientific information, can most effectively improve social capacity to guide interactions between nature and society toward more sustainable trajectories; and how can today's operational systems for monitoring and reporting on environmental and social conditions be integrated and extended to prove guidance for efforts to navigate a transition toward sustainability.

STATISTICS SOURCES

Agriculture Fact Book. U. S. Government Printing Office. • Annual. $26 Individuals. Issued by the Office of Communications, U. S. Department of Agriculture. Includes data on U. S. agriculture, farmers, food, nutrition, and rural America. Programs of the Department of Agriculture in six areas are described: rural economic development, foreign trade, nutrition, the environment, inspection, and education.

National Trade Estimate Report on Foreign Trade Barriers (year). U. S. Government Printing Office. • Annual. $47. Issued by the Office of the United States Trade Representative. "Provides quantitative estimates of the impact of foreign practices on the value of United States exports.".

Statistical Yearbook. United Nations Publications. • Annual. $125.00. Contains statistics for about 200 countries on a wide variety of economic, industrial, and demographic topics. Compiled by United Nations Statistical Office.

Statistics on International Trade in Services. Organization for Economic Cooperation and Development. Organisation for Economic Cooperation and Development Publications and Information Center. • Annual. $126.00. Presents a compilation and assessment of data on OECD member countries' international trade in services. Covers four major categories for 20 years: travel, transportation, government services, and other services.

Survey of Current Business. U. S. Government Printing Office. • Published by Bureau of Economic Analysis, U. S. Department of Commerce. Presents a wide variety of business and economic data.

TRADE/PROFESSIONAL ASSOCIATIONS

American-Kuwaiti Alliance. 2550 M St. NW, Washington, DC 20037. Phone: (202)429-4999; Email: info@americankuwaitialliance.org • URL: http://ww.american-kuwaitialliance.com • Aims to expand and deepen the political, commercial and cultural ties between the U.S. and Kuwait. Fosters the existing U.S.-Kuwaiti relations by facilitating expanded political relationships and policies. Promotes increased trade and commerce, and creates opportunities for American and Kuwaiti citizens to exchange cultural experiences.

American-Lithuanian Business Council. 701 8th St., NW Ste. 500, Washington, DC 20001. Phone: (202)973-5975; Fax: (202)659-5249; Email: info@amlithbc.org • URL: http://www.amlithbc.org • Executive firms having significant actual or potential trade involvement with Lithuania, including coverage of policy issues related to Russia, Ukraine, Belarus, Turkey, Iran, the Caucasus and Central Asia. Provides a forum for discussing trade and investment issues and formulation of policy issues to promote and expand economic relations between the U.S. and Lithuania.

Argentina Israel Chamber of Commerce. Phone: 54 11 43726273; Email: info@ccai.com.ar • URL: http://www.ccai.com.ar • Promotes trade between Argentina and Israel.

Argentine Chinese Chamber of Production, Industry and Commerce. Viamonte 1145 7 A, C1053ABW Buenos Aires, Argentina. Phone: 54 11 43726133; Fax: 54 11 43726133; Email: argenchina@ciudad.com.ar • URL: http://www.argenchina.org/_en_index.asp • Promotes business trade between Argentina and China.

Armenian American Chamber of Commerce. 225 E Broadway, Ste. 313C, Glendale, CA 91205. Phone: (818)247-0196; Fax: (818)247-7668; Email: aacc@armenianchamber.com • URL: http://www.armenianchamber.org • Aims to serve the needs of the business community in the United States and abroad. Assists its members, which consist of business persons, professionals and scholars in business development and networking. Advances the industrial, commercial, professional and public interests of the Armenian American community.

Association of Moroccan Professionals in America. PO Box 77254, San Francisco, CA 94107. Fax: (801)996-6334; Email: jaridati@amp-usa.org • URL: http://www.amp-usa.org • Promotes networking opportunities among Moroccan professionals. Advances the social and professional development of Moroccan professionals. Encourages bilateral commercial exchanges between the U.S. and Morocco. Provides community service and education initiatives in Morocco.

Camara de Comercio Argentino-Britanica en la Republica Argentina. Av. Corrientes 457, Piso 10, C1043AAE Buenos Aires, Argentina. Phone: 54 11 43942762; Fax: 54 11 43263860; Email: info@ccab.com.ar • URL: http://www.ccab.com.ar • Promotes bilateral Trade and Investment between Argentina and UK.

Camara de Comercio de la Republica de Cuba. Calle 21 esq. a Calle A, No. 661, Vedado, Havana, Cuba. Phone: 53 7 833-8040; Fax: 53 7 838-1324; Email: ccicuba@camara.com.cu • URL: http://www.camaracuba.cu • Represents trade, industry, finance, transport, insurance and all sectors of international businesses. Shapes policies and raises awareness of international business concerns. Fosters networking and cooperation among members.

Camara de Comercio Italiana de Rosario. Cordoba 1868, 2000 Rosario, Argentina. Phone: 54 341 4266789 or 54 341 4245691; Email: info@italrosario.com • URL: http://www.italrosario.com/ • Represent Italian business interests in Rosario, Argentina.

Camara de Industria y Comercio Argentino-Alemana. Av. Corrientes 327, C1043AAD Buenos Aires, Argentina. Phone: 54 11 52194000; Fax: 54 11 52194001; Email: ahkargentina@ahkargentina.com.ar • URL: http://www.ahkargentina.com.ar/ • Represents German business in Argentina and promotes international trade between Argentina and Germany.

Canada-Arab Business Council. 1 Rideau St., Ste. 700, Ottawa, ON, Canada K1N 8S7. Phone: (613)670-5853 • URL: http://canada-arabbusiness.org • Canadian business organizations interested in Middle East markets. Promotes business and trade between Canada and the Arab world; serves as a business advisory body to governments in Canada on matters relating to Canadian trade with the region; promotes awareness of Canada's business and commercial capabilities; seeks to advance Canada to the Region; assists members in trade and investment activities in each country in the Middle East.

Canada-China Business Council. 330 Bay St., Ste. 1501, Toronto, ON, Canada M5H 2S8. Phone: (416)954-3800; Fax: (416)954-3806; Email: ccbc@ccbc.com • URL: http://www.ccbc.com • Promotes trade and investment between Canada and the People's Republic of China; seeks to stimulate trade in goods and services, investment and technology transfer; strives to achieve stronger economic growth and a closer relationship between Canada and China; provides assistance to business; advocates for Canadian business on matters of Canada - China relations to the government and public; disseminates market information.

Canada-India Business Council. 1 St. Clair Ave. E, Ste. 302, Toronto, ON, Canada M4T 2V7. Phone: (416)214-5947; Fax: (416)214-9081; Email: info@canada-indiabusiness.ca • URL: http://canada-indiabusiness.ca • Canadian businesses trading with India. Promotes increased trade between Canada and India. Advocates for legislation conducive to trade; represents members before trade and industrial organizations and the public.

Canada - Japan Society of British Columbia. 15-555 W 12th Ave., Vancouver, BC, Canada V5Z 3X0. Phone: (604)708-3306; Fax: (604)921-8192 • URL: http://www.canadajapansociety.bc.ca • Promotes opportunities with Japan in British Columbia; seeks to provide a better understanding between the people of Canada and Japan.

China-Africa Business Council. Shimao International Ctr., Building 1, Rm. 1805, Chaoyang District, Beijing 100027, Beijing, China. Phone: 86 10 64169865 or 86 10 64166409; Fax: 86 10 64169811; Email: cabc@cabc.org.cn • URL: http://www.cabc.org.cn/enindex/index.jhtml • Promotes trade and cooperation between China and Africa. Provides business tools that are designed to strengthen business ties between the two countries. Provides members with opportunities to share experiences and strengthen their capacity to address challenges through trainings, symposiums, workshops and forums.

Federation of Euro-Asian Stock Exchanges. Borsa Istanbul Bldg., Emirgan, TR-34467 Istanbul, Turkey. Phone: 90 212 298 2160; Fax: 90 212 298 2209; Email: secretariat@feas.org • URL: http://www.feas.org • Committed to a fair, efficient and transparent market environment. Works to eliminate trade barriers, and to promote development of the Euro-Asian stock markets. Provides cross listing and trading opportunities for securities issued within member countries.

French Bruneian Business Association. Kompleks Jalan Sultan, Rm. 301-306, 3rd Fl., Jalan Sultan, Bandar Seri Begawan BS8811, Brunei. Phone: 673 2240924 or 673 2220960; Fax: 673 2243373 • URL: http://www.fbbabrunei.com • Brings together people actively involved in trade and commerce between France and Brunei Darussalam. Provides a mutual forum for French and Bruneian business partners. Disseminates economic information to members on matters of interest. Develops business opportunities between Brunei Darussalam and France.

International Economic Alliance. 1 Mifflin Pl., Ste. 400, Cambridge, MA 02138-4946. Phone: (617)418-1981; Fax: (617)812-0499 • URL: http://www.iealliance.org • Aims to further global trade, economic development and advance business relations. Brings together the world's key players and decision-makers (business and government leaders, investors and leading intellectuals) for practical, open, bi-partisan and solution-oriented exchange of ideas. Serves as a source of knowledge, facilitator of relationships, and catalyst for new business opportunities.

Iran-Netherlands Business Council. No. 254 Taleghani Ave., Tehran, Iran. Phone: 98 21 88346736; Fax: 98 21 88346736; Email: info@inbc.ir • URL: http://www.inbc.ir/pages/default.aspx?lan=en • Promotes investment, trade, and political and cultural cooperation between Iran and Netherlands. Fosters business to business relationships between entrepreneurs of Iran and Netherlands.

Ireland China Association. 28 Merrion Sq., Dublin 2, Dublin, Ireland. Phone: 353 1 6424178; Fax: 353 1 6612315; Email: info@irelandchina.org • URL: http://www.irelandchina.org • Aims to bring together Irish and Chinese businesspeople for the purpose of exploring business opportunities and making contracts. Promotes greater economic ties and increases trade and commerce between Ireland and China. Furthers the cultural links and greater knowledge of both countries.

Ireland Japan Association. 28 Merrion Sq., Dublin 2, Dublin, Ireland. Phone: 353 1 6424178; Email: info@ija.ie • URL: http://www.ija.ie • Aims to enhance and develop relations between Ireland and Japan. Promotes economic and business ties and increases trade and commerce between Ireland and Japan. Fosters mutual understanding between the peoples of both countries. Creates a forum for Irish and Japanese people to interact in both business and social environments.

Italian American Alliance for Business and Technology. 535 Griswold, Ste. 1844, Detroit, MI 48226. Phone: (248)227-6143; Email: info@iaabt.org • URL: http://iaabt.org • Serves the needs of Italian industrial companies wanting to do business in the United States and U.S. industrial companies seeking to do business in Italy. Promotes the technological, scientific, research and development, design and manufacturing capabilities of member companies. Fosters business opportunities and facilitates exchange of ideas among its members.

Latin America Trade Coalition. 1615 H St. NW, Washington, DC 20062. Phone: (202)463-5485; Fax: (202)463-3126; Email: americas@uschamber.com • URL: http://www.uschamber.com • Represents U.S. companies, farmers and business organizations. Aims to secure congressional approval of the U.S.-Colombia Trade Promotion Agreement and the U.S.-Panama Trade Promotion Agreement.

Malaysia South-South Association. Bangunan AmBank Group, 17th Fl., Jaalan Raja Chulan, 50200 Kuala Lumpur, Malaysia. Phone: 60 3 20783788; Fax: 60 3 20728411; Email: mail@massa.net.my • URL: http://www.massa.net.my • Promotes and enhances knowledge and understanding of economic, trade and investment policies and conditions of South-South countries. Acts as an informal liaison body between the private sector and the government in the promotion of trade and investment. Provides a forum for the dissemination of ideas and for the discussion of trade, economy and culture. Enhances trade and investment relations and fosters friendship and cooperation in South-South countries.

National Foreign Trade Council. 1625 K St. NW, Ste. 200, Washington, DC 20006. Phone: (202)887-0278; Fax: (202)452-8160; Email: nftcinformation@nftc.org • URL: http://www.nftc.org • Manufacturers, exporters, importers, foreign investors, banks, transportation lines, and insurance, communication, law, accounting, service, and publishing firms. Works to promote and protect American foreign trade and investment. Areas of concern include the removal of arbitrary barriers to expansion of international trade and investment; a greater awareness by the government that this expansion is essential to the economic growth of the U.S.; the formation of a cohesive, consistent international economic policy.

Pakistan Agriculture and Dairy Farmers Association. JK House, 32-W, Susan Rd., Madina Town, Faisalabad, Pakistan. Phone: 92 41 8721956; Fax: 92 41 8712399; Email: info@padfapak.org • URL: http://www.padfapak.org • Represents trade, commerce, industry or services in agriculture and dairy farming in Pakistan. Encourages unity, mutual understanding and high ethical standards among its members. Supports a unified approach of policies affecting the interests of agriculture and dairy farming.

Pakistan-Belgium Business Forum. c/o Honorary Consulate of Belgium, A-9 Mohammad Ali Bogra Rd., Bath Island, Karachi 75530, Pakistan. Phone: 92 21 35879876 or 92 21 35872941; Fax: 92 21 35861257; Email: pbbf1@cyber.net.pk • URL: http://www.pbbf.org • Promotes trade, commerce and economic cooperation between Pakistan and Belgium. Encourages mutual understanding and friendly relations of business communities. Fosters and organizes trade and investment delegations, trade fairs, exhibitions, symposia and lectures.

Swedish Business Association of Singapore. No. 05-01 Triple One Somerset, 111 Somerset Rd., Singapore 238164, Singapore. Phone: 65 67345009; Email: swedbiz@singnet.com.sg • URL: http://www.sbas.org.sg • Aims to promote the development of commerce between Singapore and Sweden.

Swiss-Argentine Chamber of Commerce. Av. Leandro N Alem 1074, Piso 10, C1001AAS Buenos Aires, Argentina. Phone: 54 11 43117187; Email: info@suiza.org.ar • URL: http://www.suiza.org.ar/select_lang.php • Promotes businesses between Argentina and Switzerland.

Taipei Business Association in Singapore. No. 06-07 SCCCI Bldg., 47 Hill St., Singapore 179365, Singapore. Phone: 65 63383916; Fax: 65 63383930; Email: tpebiz@singnet.com.sg • URL: http://www.tbas.org.sg.

U.S.-Vietnam WTO Coalition. 1101 17th St. NW, Ste. 411, Washington, DC 20036. Phone: (202)289-1912; Fax: (202)289-0519; Email: vncoalition@usasean.org • URL: http://www.usvtc.org/coalition.asp • Represents American companies, farm groups, trade associations, veterans associations and public interest organizations supportive of Vietnam's accession to the World Trade Organization and the attainment of full U.S.-Vietnam normalization.

World Trade Center Nigeria. Western House, 8th Fl., 8/10 Broad St., Lagos, Lagos, Nigeria. Phone: 234 1 8103570; Email: info@wtcnlagos.org • URL: http://www.wtcnlagos.org • Works to improve the business climate in Nigeria by pushing ideas that would make the working environment more conducive for international trade and investment. Facilitates trade and investment by disseminating information and match-making foreign business persons with their appropriate local counterparts.

FOREMEN

See FACTORY MANAGEMENT

FOREST PRODUCTS

See also HARDWOOD INDUSTRY; LUMBER INDUSTRY; PAPER INDUSTRY

ABSTRACTS AND INDEXES

Forestry Abstracts: Compiled from World Literature. CABI Publishing North America. • Monthly. Institutions, $1,435.00 per year. Print and online edition, $1,460.00 per year. Published in England by CABI Publishing. Provides worldwide coverage of the literature.

ALMANACS AND YEARBOOKS

Wood Technology-Equipment Catalog and Buyers' Guide. UBM L.L.C. • Annual. $55.00. Formerly *Forest Industries-Lumber Review and Buyers' Guide.*

CD-ROM DATABASES

AGRICOLA on SilverPlatter. Ovid Technologies Inc. • Updated monthly. Price varies. Produced by the National Agricultural Library. Provides over 4 million citations to the literature of agriculture, agricultural economics, animal sciences, entomology, fertilizer, food, forestry, nutrition, pesticides, plant science, water resources, and other topics.

DIRECTORIES

Directory of Middle East Importers of Lumber, Timber, Plywood and Hardboards. EXIM Infotek Private Ltd. • $500 Individuals. Covers: 260 Middle East importers of blockboard and hardboard, doors and windows, formica, gypsum boards, hardboard and particle board, hardwood flooring and floor tiles, laminates, hardwood lumber, softwood lumber, timber, plywood, medium-density fiberboard, millwork (wooden), veneer, poles, pilings and logs, and sawdust. Entries include: Company name, postal address, telephone, fax, e-mail, website, contact person, designation, and product details.

E-BOOKS

Encyclopedia of American Industries. Cengage Learning Inc. • 2011. $807.00. 6th edition. Three volumes. Volume one is Manufacturing Industries and volume two is Service and Non-Manufacturing Industries. Provides the history, development, and recent status of approximately 1,000 industries. Includes statistical graphs, with industry and general indexes. Also available as eBook.

INTERNET DATABASES

USDA. U.S. National Institute of Standards and Technology. 100 Bureau Dr., Gaithersburg, MD 20899-1070. Phone: 800-877-8339 or (301)975-6478 or (202)720-2791; Fax: (301)975-8295; Email: inquiries@nist.gov • URL: http://www.nist.gov • The USDA home page has six sections: News and Information; What's New; About USDA; Agencies; Opportunities; Search and Help. Keyword searching is offered from the USDA home page and from various individual agency home pages. Agencies are the Economic Research Service, Agricultural Marketing Service, National Agricultural Statistics Service, National Agricultural Library, and about 12 others. Updating varies. Fees: Free.

ONLINE DATABASES

CAB Abstracts. CABI. • Contains 46 specialized abstract collections covering over 10,000 journals and monographs in the areas of agriculture, horticulture, forest products, farm products, nutrition, dairy science, poultry, grains, animal health, entomology, etc. Time period is 1972 to date, with monthly updates. Inquire as to online cost and availability. *CAB Abstracts on CD-ROM* also available, with annual updating.

PERIODICALS AND NEWSLETTERS

Forest Products Journal (FPJ). Forest Products Society. • 8/year. $230 Members individuals:complimentary; Institutions, electronic. Peer-reviewed journal of wood science and technology.

PRICE SOURCES

Official Board Markets: "The Yellow Sheet". Mark Arzoumanian. Advanstar Communications. • Weekly. $160.00 per year. Covers the corrugated container, folding carton, rigid box and waste paper industries.

STATISTICS SOURCES

Agricultural Statistics. U.S. Department of Agriculture National Agricultural Statistics Service. • Annual. $46 Individuals. Provides a wide variety of statistical data relating to agricultural production, supplies, consumption, prices/price-supports, foreign trade, costs, and returns, as well as farm labor, loans, income, and population. In many cases, historical data is shown annually for 10 years. In addition to farm data, includes detailed fishery statistics.

Standard & Poor's Industry Surveys. Standard & Poor's Financial Services L.L.C. • Semiannual. $1,800.00. Two looseleaf volumes. Includes monthly *Supplements.* Provides detailed, individual surveys of 52 major industry groups. Each survey is revised on a semiannual basis. Also includes "Monthly Investment Review" (industry group investment analysis) and monthly "Trends & Projections" (economic analysis).

Timber Bulletin. Economic Commission for Europe. United Nations Publications. • Irregular. $30. Contains international statistics on forest products, including price, production, and foreign trade data.

U.S. Industry and Trade Outlook. U.S. Department of Commerce National Technical Information Service. • Annual. Produced by the International Trade Administration, U.S. Department of Commerce, in a "public-private" partnership with DRI/McGraw-Hill and Standard & Poor's. Provides basic data, outlook for the current year, and "Long-Term Prospects" (five-year projections) for a wide variety of products and services. Includes high technology industries. Formerly *U.S. Industrial Outlook.*

United States Timber Production, Trade, Consumption, And Price Statistics. Forest Service. U.S. Department of Agriculture. • Annual.

TRADE/PROFESSIONAL ASSOCIATIONS

American Forest and Paper Association. 1101 K St., NW, Ste. 700, Washington, DC 20005. Phone: (202)463-2700; Fax: (202)463-2785; Email: info@afandpa.org • URL: http://www.afandpa.org • National trade association of the forest, pulp, paper, paperboard and wood products industry. Represents approximately 400 member companies and related trade associations that grow, harvest, and process wood and wood fiber, manufacture pulp, paper and paperboard from both virgin and recycled fiber, and produce solid wood products.

National Alliance of Forest Owners. 122 C St. NW, Ste. 630, Washington, DC 20001. Phone: (202)747-0759; Fax: (202)824-0770; Email: info@nafoalliance.org • URL: http://www.nafoalliance.org • Aims to protect and enhance the economic and environmental values of privately-owned forests through targeted policy advocacy at the national level. Focuses on issues for regulatory advocacy including climate change, renewable energy, environment, tax policy, land use, trade and market policy. Seeks public policies that shape environmental regulations, taxes, land use decisions, and timber and non-timber markets in ways that protect and grow forest values.

National Hardwood Lumber Association. 6830 Raleigh La Grange Rd., Memphis, TN 38134-0518. Phone: 800-933-0318 or (901)377-1818; Fax: (901)382-6419 or (901)399-7581; Email: info@nhla.com • URL: http://www.nhla.com • United States, Canadian and International hardwood lumber and veneer manufacturers, distributors and consumers. Inspects hardwood lumber. Maintains inspection training school. Conducts management and marketing seminars for the hardwood industry. Promotes research in hardwood timber management and utilization. Promotes public awareness of the industry.

FORGERIES

See also COUNTERFEITING; CRIME AND CRIMINALS; FRAUD AND EMBEZZLEMENT

PERIODICALS AND NEWSLETTERS

FBI Law Enforcement Bulletin. U. S. Government Printing Office. • Monthly. $36.00 per year. Issued by Federal Bureau of Investigation, U. S. Department of Justice. Contains articles on a wide variety of law enforcement and crime topics, including computer-related crime.

FORGES

See FOUNDRIES

FORMS AND BLANKS

DIRECTORIES

Business Forms & Systems (Wholesale) Directory. InfoGroup Inc. • Annual. Number of listings: 7,565. Entries include: Company name, address, phone (including area code), size of advertisement, year first in "Yellow Pages," name of owner or manager, number of employees. Compiled from telephone company "Yellow Pages," nationwide.

Business Forms, Labels & Systems--Who's Who of Manufacturers and Suppliers. North American Publishing Co. • Annual. Covers: More than 800 manufacturers of business forms, labels, and related products, and 500 suppliers of equipment and paper used to manufacture business forms. Entries include: Company name, address, phone, fax, toll-free number, company profile.

Who's Who Among Business Printing Independents. Print Services and Distribution Association. • Annual. Covers: about 2,400 member independent manufacturers and distributors of business forms; coverage is international. Database includes: Calendar of events; description of events and seminars. Entries include: Company name, address, phone, names of executives, financial keys, branch offices or subsidiaries, member services.

ENCYCLOPEDIAS AND DICTIONARIES

Nichols Cyclopedia of Legal Forms Annotated. Thomson West. • Full set $7,451.00. Annual updates. Provides personal and business forms and alternative provisions for more than 230 law topics.

FINANCIAL RATIOS

Annual Statement Studies. Risk Management Association. • Annual. Compiled from over 280,000 financial statements.

Annual Statement Studies: Industry Default Probabilities and Cash Flow Measures. Risk Management Association. • Annual. $405 Nonmembers. Serves as a companion volume to the original *Annual Statement Studies.* Gives probability of default estimates on a percentage scale for more than 450 industries. Includes changes in position year-by-year for eight financial statement line items and provides percentage measures of cash flow.

HANDBOOKS AND MANUALS

Standard Business Forms for the Entrepreneur. Entrepreneur Press. • Looseleaf. $59.50. A practical collection of forms useful to entrepreneurial small businesses. (Start-Up Business Guide No. E1319.).

Warren's Forms of Agreements. Matthew Bender and Company Inc. • Biennial. $2,368 print. 8-volume set. A compact source of forms that business transaction lawyers are most frequently asked to document.

West's Legal Forms. Thomson West. • Annual. Selection of customizable forms suitable for drafting a wide range of legal documents. Includes detailed commentary, analysis, checklists, and library references to the Key Number System.

ONLINE DATABASES

Gale BusinessForms. Cengage Learning Inc. • Contains professionally drafted state-specific documents and forms for businesses. Covers dozens of topics, including arbitration, bills of sale, collections, confidentiality and nondisclosure, distributorships, guaranty, liens, limited liability companies, power of attorney, and technology.

OTHER SOURCES

E-Commerce and Internet Law: Treatise with Forms. Ian C. Ballon. Glasser LegalWorks. • $1,479 Individuals Binder/Looseleaf (Full Set). Periodic supplementation. Analyzes Internet legalities, including litigious matters relating to downloading, streaming, music, video, content aggregation, domain names, chatrooms, and search engines. Includes forms, contracts, checklists, sample pleadings, and an extensive glossary.

Employment Forms and Policies. Matthew Bender and Company Inc. • $150 print and e-book. Periodic supplementation available. Contains more than 300 forms, policies, and checklists for use by small or medium-sized businesses. Covers such topics as employee selection, payroll issues, benefits, performance appraisal, dress codes, and employee termination.

Fletcher Corporation Forms Annotated. Thomson West. • Annual. $5,220 hardbound (full set). Cover all aspects of corporate law.

Forms and Agreements for Architects, Engineers and Contractors. Albert Dib. Thomson West. • $2,687.25 full set. Three times a year. Five looseleaf volume. Covers evaluation of construction documents and alternative clauses. Includes pleadings for litigation and resolving of claims. (Real Property Law Series).

Forms of Business Agreements and Resolutions-Annotated, Tax Tested. Prentice Hall PTR. • Three looseleaf volumes. Periodic supplementation. Price on application.

Reproducible Copies of Federal Tax Forms and Instructions. U. S. Government Printing Office. • Annual. $64 U.S. Looseleaf. Two looseleaf volumes issued by the Internal Revenue Service (www.irs.gov). "Contains the most frequently requested tax forms and instructions," prepared especially for libraries.

PERIODICALS AND NEWSLETTERS

Business Forms, Labels and Systems. North American Publishing Co. • Semimonthly. $95.00 per year. Formerly *Business Forms and Systems.*

Print Solutions Magazine. Document Management Industries Association. • Monthly. $99 Nonmembers.

TRADE/PROFESSIONAL ASSOCIATIONS

Business Forms Management Association. 1147 Fleetwood Ave., Madison, WI 53716-1417. Phone: 888-367-3078 or (402)216-0479; Fax: (937)885-5320; Email: bfma@bfma.org • URL: http://www.bfma.org • Persons engaged in forms management work, forms procedures analysis, forms design, or in education in this field; customer service firms selling, manufacturing, or servicing forms and supplies. Provides leadership and education to businesses in areas where the forms profession has demonstrated its special competence; promotes a broader function as a component of effective management; encourages, establishes, and maintains high standards of professional education, competence, and performance; provides a means for the sharing of information through study, programs, and research.

Print Services and Distribution Association. 330 N Wabash Ave., Ste. 2000, Chicago, IL 60611. Phone: 800-230-0175; Fax: (312)673-6880 • URL: http://www.psda.org • Independent distributors, manufacturers and suppliers to the forms, business printing and document management industries. Sponsors educational and channel marketing programs. Compiles statistics.

FORWARDING COMPANIES

See FREIGHT TRANSPORT

FORWARDING FREIGHT

See FREIGHT TRANSPORT

FOUNDATIONS

See also ARTS MANAGEMENT; FUND-RAISING; GRANTS-IN-AID; NONPROFIT CORPORATIONS

ABSTRACTS AND INDEXES

Foundation Directory Online. Foundation Center. • Formerly *Foundation Grants Index.* Five plan levels with monthly, annual, and two-year subscription options.

BIBLIOGRAPHIES

Catalog of Nonprofit Literature. • Dates vary. Covers the literature of philanthropy, foundations, nonprofit organizations, fund-raising, and federal aid.

DIRECTORIES

Directory of Corporate and Foundation Givers. Taft Group. • $270. Covers: 8,000 private foundations, corporate foundations, and companies that give money to nonprofit organizations. Entries include: Foundation name, sponsoring company name, address, phone, fax, e-mail, URL, contact name; financial summary, including assets and amounts given for up to previous three years; Employer Identification Number; summary of contributions, including typical recipients, grant types, nonmonetary support types, geographic distribution; names and titles of key personnel; application procedures; grants summary including total grants, highest grant, typical grant range, and list of recent grants, giving amounts and names of recipients.

Foundation Directory. Foundation Center. • Annual. $215 Individuals main. Over 10,000 of the largest foundations in the United States, all having $1.3 million or more in assets or awarding $400,000 or more in grants in a recent year.

Foundation Reporter: Comprehensive Profiles and Giving Analyses of America's Major Private Foundations. Taft Group. • Annual. $490.00. Provides detailed information on major U. S. foundations. Eight indexes (location, grant type, recipient type, personnel, etc.).

Foundations of the 1990s: A Directory of Newly Established Foundations. • $150 plus shipping cost. Covers: Over 9,000 independent, community, and corporate foundations incorporated since 1989. Entries include: Foundation name, address, phone, name and title of contact, names of trustees and officers, application procedures, financial data, grantmaking interests and giving limitations, and grant descriptions.

Grants for Libraries & Information Services. • Available only as a downloadable file. Single use version $39.95; library use version $$99.95. Foundations and organizations which have awarded grants made the preceding year for public, academic, research, special, and school libraries; for archives and information centers; for consumer information; and for philanthropy information centers.

Guide to U.S. Foundations, Their Trustees, Officers, and Donors. Foundation Center. • Annual. $650 U.S. Directory set. Covers: over 74,000 currently active grantmaking foundations in the United States, including community and operating foundations, based on information returns to the Internal Revenue Service. Database includes: Bibliography of state and local directories of grantmaking foundations. Entries include: Foundation name, address, phone, name of principal contact, assets, amount of grants made, donor information, gifts received during most recent period reported; giving limitations, key officials, codes identifying coverage in other Foundation Center publications.

International Directory of Corporate Philanthropy. Taylor & Francis Group. • Annual. $250.00. Published by Europa Publications (www.europapublications.com). Contains profiles of about 1,000 corporate foundations and "co-ordinating organizations" in various countries of the world. Provides details of charitable activities and philanthropic expenditures.

National Directory of Corporate Giving. • Annual. $195 Individuals. Provides information on nearly

4,400 company-sponsored foundations and corporate giving programs.

Nelson Information's Directory of Plan Sponsors. Nelson Information. • Annual. Approximately 19,000 plan sponsors (corporate, union, public/government, endowment, foundation, and hospital) of investments (pensions, endowments) funds with assets over $10 million. Formerly *Nelson's Directory of Plan Sponsors and Tax-Exempt Funds.*

Washington: A Comprehensive Directory of the Key Institutions and Leaders in th e National Capitol Area. Columbia Books Inc. • Annual. $149.00. Provides information on about 5,000 Washington, DC key businesses, government offices, non-profit organizations, and cultural institutions, with the names of about 25,000 principal executives. Includes Washington media, law offices, foundations, labor unions, international organizations, clubs, etc.

Who Knows Who: Networking through Corporate Boards. Who Knows Who Publishers. • Annual. $165. Publication includes: List of over 1,000 companies noted by either Fortune magazine or Forbes magazine, or both; over 120 major foundations. Entries include: Company or foundation name, address, phone, boards of directors. Principal content of publication is lists of the companies and their boards of directors showing relationships among the companies by showing which of the board members sit on several of the companies' boards, i.e. interlocking directorates.

INTERNET DATABASES

Welcome to the Foundation Center. Foundation Center. Phone: (212)620-4230 or (212)807-3679; Fax: (212)807-3677; Email: mfn@fdncenter.org • URL: http://www.fdncenter.org • Web site provides a wide variety of information about foundations, grants, and philanthropy, with links to philanthropic organizations. "Grantmaker Information" link furnishes descriptions of available funding.

PERIODICALS AND NEWSLETTERS

Foundation News & Commentary. Council on Foundations. • Bimonthly. Bimonthly. $48.00 per year. Formerly *Foundation News.*

Nonprofit Issues. Donald W. Kramer. • Description: Presents legal information for nonprofit executives and their professional advisors.

RESEARCH CENTERS AND INSTITUTES

Connecticut Society of Certified Public Accountants Education and Research Foundation. 845 Brook St., Bldg. 2, Rocky Hill, CT 06067-3405. Phone: 800-232-2232 or (860)258-4800; Fax: (860)258-4859; Email: artr@cs-cpa.org • URL: http://www.cs-cpa.org • Accounting.

TRADE/PROFESSIONAL ASSOCIATIONS

Business and Community Foundation. 1D, 1st Fl., Shahpur Jat, New Delhi 110049, Delhi, India. Phone: 91 11 3253-6392 • URL: http://www.bcfindia.org • Promotes awareness and practice of good corporate citizenship as a business operation; promotes businesses to become an integral part of the societal process whereby people have access and control over resources to make informed choices and decisions towards a more humane, compassionate and just society in India.

Council on Foundations. 2121 Crystal Dr., Ste. 700, Arlington, VA 22202-3706. Phone: 800-673-9036 or (703)879-0600; Email: membership@cof.org • URL: http://www.cof.org • Formerly National Council on Community Foundations.

NAED National Education and Research Foundation. 1181 Corporate Lake Dr., Saint Louis, MO 63132-1716. Phone: 888-791-2512 or (314)991-9000; Fax: (314)991-3060 • URL: http://www.naed.org • Established by the National Association of Electrical Distributors to provide electrical distributor and distributor-oriented manufacturers with the opportunity to become better business people by expanding their managerial skills. Designs and conducts seminars, workshops, conferences and home study materials covering all aspects of professional management in the electrical supply industry.

FOUNDRIES

See also IRON AND STEEL INDUSTRY

DIRECTORIES

Directory of Taiwanese Manufacturers & Exporters of Castings & Forgings. EXIM Infotek Private Ltd. • $15 Individuals. Covers: 170 Taiwanese manufacturers and exporters of casting, iron castings, and steel castings. Entries include: Company name, postal address, city, country, phone, fax, e-mail and websites, contact person, designation, and product details.

Foundry Directory and Register of Forges. Metal Bulletin Inc. • Biennial. $165.00. Foundries and forges in the United Kingdom and Europe; suppliers of foundry and forging equipment, raw materials and services.

Modern Casting-Buyer's Reference. American Foundry Society. • About 1,700 manufacturers, suppliers, and distributors of foundry and metal casting equipment and products. Formerly *Modern Castings - Buyer's Guide.*

Swiss Foundry and Metalworks. Verlag fur Internationale Wirtschaftsliteratur Ltd. • Biennial. $60. Covers: Manufacturers, associations, and importers in the metal, iron, foundry and metal working industries. Entries include: Company or association name, address, phone.

FINANCIAL RATIOS

Annual Statement Studies. Risk Management Association. • Annual. Compiled from over 280,000 financial statements.

Annual Statement Studies: Industry Default Probabilities and Cash Flow Measures. Risk Management Association. • Annual. $405 Nonmembers. Serves as a companion volume to the original *Annual Statement Studies.* Gives probability of default estimates on a percentage scale for more than 450 industries. Includes changes in position year-by-year for eight financial statement line items and provides percentage measures of cash flow.

PERIODICALS AND NEWSLETTERS

Foundry Management and Technology. Penton Media Inc. • Monthly. $50 others. Coverage includes nonferrous casting technology and production.

Modern Casting. American Foundry Society. • Monthly.

RESEARCH CENTERS AND INSTITUTES

Pennsylvania State University - College of Engineering - Harold and Inge Marcus Department of Industrial and Manufacturing Engineering - Metal Casting Laboratory. 221 Leonard Bldg., University Park, PA 16802. Phone: (814)863-7290 or (814)863-5640; Fax: (814)863-4745; Email: rcv2@psu.edu • URL: http://www.ie.psu.edu • Properties and processing of cast metals and alloys, dimensional control of castings, environmental solutions for the metal casting industry.

University of Wisconsin-Madison - Cast Metals Laboratory. University of Wisconsin-Madison, Dept. of Materials Science & Engineering, 276 Materials Science & Engineering Bldg., 1509 University Ave., Madison, WI 53706-1595. Phone: (608)262-3732 or (608)262-2562; Fax: (608)262-8353; Email: msaedept@engr.wisc.edu • URL: http://www.engr.wisc.edu/mse.

STATISTICS SOURCES

Nonferrous Castings. U. S. Bureau of the Census. • Annual. (Current Industrial Reports MA-33E.).

TRADE/PROFESSIONAL ASSOCIATIONS

American Foundry Society. 1695 N Penny Ln., Schaumburg, IL 60173. Phone: 800-537-4237 or (847)824-0181; Fax: (847)824-2174 or (847)824-7848; Email: jcall@afsinc.org • URL: http://www.afsinc.org • Technical, trade and management association of foundrymen, patternmakers, technologists, and educators. Sponsors foundry training courses through the Cast Metals Institute on all subjects pertaining to the castings industry; conducts educational and instructional exhibits of foundry industry; sponsors 10 regional foundry conferences and 400 local foundry technical meetings. Maintains Technical Information Center providing literature searching and document retrieval service; and Metalcasting Abstract Service involving abstracts of the latest metal casting literature. Provides environmental services and testing; conducts research programs; compiles statistics, provides marketing information.

Casting Industry Suppliers Association. 14175 W Indian School Rd., Ste. B4-504, Goodyear, AZ 85395. Phone: (623)547-0920; Fax: (623)536-1486; Email: info@cisa.org • URL: http://www.foundry-suppliers.com/media/media?id=130743410326823318 • Manufacturers of foundry equipment and supplies such as molding machinery, dust control equipment and systems, blast cleaning machines, tumbling equipment, and related products. Fosters better trade practices; serves as industry representative before the government and the public. Encourages member research into new processes and methods of foundry operation and disseminates reports of progress in these fields. Compiles monthly statistics on booked and billed sales.

Non-Ferrous Founders' Society. 1480 Renaissance Dr., Ste. 310, Park Ridge, IL 60068. Phone: (847)299-0950; Fax: (847)299-3598; Email: nffstaff@nffs.org • URL: http://www.nffs.org • Manufacturers of brass, bronze, aluminum, and other nonferrous castings.

FOUNTAIN PENS

See WRITING INSTRUMENTS

401(k) RETIREMENT PLANS

HANDBOOKS AND MANUALS

401(k) Handbook. Thompson Publishing Group Inc. • Two looseleaf volumes. $387.00 per year, including monthly updates and newsletters. Provides detailed information on 401(k) retirement plan design, administration, employee communication, rollovers, federal regulations, plan loans, investment vehicles, and related topics. Includes a glossary.

Pension Plan Fix-It Handbook. Thompson Publishing Group Inc. • Two looseleaf volumes. $529.00 per year. Two looseleaf volumes. Monthly updates and newsletters. Serves as a comprehensive guide to pension plan administration, taxation, and federal regulation. Includes both defined benefit and defined contribution plans.

U.S. Master Pension Guide. Wolters Kluwer Law & Business CCH. • Annual. $99.95 1 - 4 (quantity). Explains IRS rules and regulations applying to 401(k) plans, 403(k) plans, ESOPs (employee stock ownership plans), IRAs, SEPs (simplified employee pension plans), Keogh plans, and nonqualified plans.

INTERNET DATABASES

Mutual Funds Interactive. Brill Editorial Services, Inc. Phone: (877)442-7455 • URL: http://www.brill.com • Web site provides specific information on individual funds in addition to general advice on mutual fund investing and 401(k) plans. Searching is provided, including links to moderated newsgroups and a chat page.

Small Business Retirement Savings Advisor. U. S. Department of Labor. Phone: (202)219-8921 • URL: http://www.dol.gov/elaws/pwbaplan.htm • Web site provides "answers to a variety of commonly asked questions about retirement saving options for small business employers." Includes a comparison chart and detailed descriptions of various plans: 401(k), SEP-IRA, SIMPLE-IRA, Payroll Deduction IRA, Keogh Profit-Sharing, Keogh Money Purchase, and Defined Benefit. Searching is offered. Fees: Free.

PERIODICALS AND NEWSLETTERS

Financial Planning: The Magazine for Financial Service Professionals. SourceMedia Inc. • Monthly. $79.00 per year. Edited for independent financial planners and insurance agents. Covers retirement planning, estate planning, tax planning, and insurance, including long-term healthcare considerations. Special features include a Retirement Planning Issue, Mutual Fund Performance Survey, and Variable Life and Annuity Survey.

IOMA's Report on Defined Contribution Plan Investing. Institute of Management and Administration. • Semimonthly. $1,189.90 per year. Newsletter. Edited for 401(k) and other defined contribution retirement plan managers, sponsors, and service providers. Reports on such items as investment manager performance, guaranteed investment contract (GIC) yields, and asset allocation trends.

IOMA's Report on Managing 401(k) Plans. Institute of Management and Administration. • Monthly. $521 print and online. Newsletter for retirement plan managers.

On Wall Street. SourceMedia Inc. • Monthly. $96.00 per year. Edited for securities dealers. Includes articles on financial planning, retirement planning, variable annuities, and money management, with special coverage of 401(k) plans and IRAs.

Plan Sponsor. Asset International, Inc. • Monthly. Edited for professional pension plan managers and executives. Defined contribution plans are emphasized.

Retirement Plans Bulletin: Practical Explanations for the IRA and Retirement Plan Professional. Universal Pensions Inc. • Monthly. $99.00 per year. Newsletter. Provides information on the rules and regulations governing qualified (tax-deferred) retirement plans.

RESEARCH CENTERS AND INSTITUTES

Center for Pension and Retirement Research. Miami University, Department of Economics, 109E Laws Hall, Oxford, OH 45056. Phone: (513)529-2850; Fax: (513)529-3308; Email: swilliamson@eh.net • Research areas include pension economics, pension plans, and retirement decisions.

Pension Research Council. The Wharton School of the University of Pennsylvania, 3620 Locust Walk, 3000 Steinberg Hall - Dietrich Hall, Philadelphia, PA 19104-6302. Phone: (215)898-7620; Fax: (215)573-3418; Email: prc@wharton.upenn.edu • URL: http://www.pensionresearchcouncil.org • Research areas include various types of private sector and public employee pension plans.

STATISTICS SOURCES

EBRI Pension Investment Report. Employee Benefit Research Institute. • Periodic Quarterly. $500 /issue for nonmembers. Irregular. Membership.

TRADE/PROFESSIONAL ASSOCIATIONS

American Benefits Council. 1501 M St. NW, Ste. 600, Washington, DC 20005-1775. Phone: (202)289-6700; Fax: (202)289-4582; Email: info@abcstaff.org • URL: http://www.americanbenefitscouncil.org • Serves as national trade association for companies concerned about federal legislation and regulations affecting all aspects of the employee benefits system. Represents the entire spectrum of the private employee benefits community and sponsors or administers retirement and health plans covering more than one hundred million Americans.

American Society of Pension Professionals and Actuaries. 4245 N Fairfax Dr., Ste. 750, Arlington, VA 22203. Phone: (703)516-9300; Fax: (703)516-9308; Email: customercare@asppa.org • URL: http://www.asppa.org • Members are involved in the pension and insurance aspects of employee benefits. Includes an Insurance and Risk Management Committee, and sponsors an annual 401(k) Workshop.

Plan Sponsor Council of America. 20 N Wacker Dr., Ste. 3700, Chicago, IL 60606. Phone: (312)419-1863; Fax: (312)419-1864; Email: psca@psca.org • URL: http://www.psca.org • Members are business firms with profit sharing and/or 401(K) plans. Affiliated with the Profit Sharing/401(K) Education Foundation. Formerly Profit Sharing Council of America.

FRAGRANCE INDUSTRY

See PERFUME INDUSTRY

FRANCHISES

See also CHAIN STORES; CONCESSIONS

DIRECTORIES

Bond's Franchise Guide. Todd Publications. • Covers: 2,000 American and 500 Canadian franchisers divided into 54 business categories. Entries include: Company name, address, phone, fax, names and titles of key personnel for 1,500 franchise operations; for all entries: Company history, size, geographic distribution, financial requirements, staff, start-up assistance and training provided, ongoing royalty fees and franchiser services, and more.

Entrepreneur's Annual Franchise 500 Issue. Entrepreneur Press. • Annual. Provides a ranking of 500 "top franchise opportunities," based on a combination of financial strength, growth rate, size, stability, number of years in business, litigation history, and other factors. Includes 17 major business categories, further divided into about 140 very specific groups (22 kinds of fast food, for example).

Franchise Opportunities Guide. International Franchise Association. • Semiannual. $12 Members per year; plus $10.00 for shipping and handling. More than 600 companies which offer franchises.

The Sourcebook of Franchise Opportunities. QSU Publishing. • Annual. $35. Covers: Over 3,000 franchising opportunities. Entries include: Franchisor name, address, phone, and profiles are included for approximately 1,000.

ENCYCLOPEDIAS AND DICTIONARIES

Encyclopedia of Small Business. Cengage Learning Inc. • $763 Individuals. 2010. $696.00. 4th edition. Two volumes. Contains about 600 informative entries on a wide variety of topics affecting small business. Arrangement is alphabetical. eBook also available. Inquire for pricing.

GENERAL WORKS

Franchising: Realities and Remedies. Harold Brown. ALM Media Properties LLC. • $399. Revised edition.

ONLINE DATABASES

Business Franchise Guide. Wolters Kluwer Law & Business CCH. • Contains extensive legal and regulatory information related to all aspects of business franchising.

OTHER SOURCES

Product Distribution Law Guide. Wolters Kluwer Law & Business CCH. • $199.00. Looseleaf service. Annual updates available. Covers the legal aspects of various methods of product distribution, including franchising.

PERIODICALS AND NEWSLETTERS

Entrepreneur: The Small Business Authority. Entrepreneur Press. • Monthly. $19.97 per year. Contains advice for small business owners and prospective owners. Includes numerous franchise advertisements.

Franchising Business and Law Alert. ALM Media Properties LLC. • Monthly. $469 per year. Provides news of legal developments affecting both franchisors and franchisees. (A Law Journal Newsletter, formerly published by Leader Publications).

Franchising World. International Franchise Association. • Monthly. $50 Individuals. Trade magazine covering topics of interest to franchise company executives and the business world. Formerly *Franchising Opportunities.*

Info Franchise Newsletter. Info Press Inc. • Description: Covers business format franchising in the U.S., Canada, and overseas; reports on trends, legislation and litigation, and on developments in the franchising business scene. Recurring features include lists of new franchisors, including descriptions, contact addresses and telephone numbers for each; and address changes of franchisor headquarters. Spotlights upcoming seminars, conferences and business opportunity shows.

ReCareering Newsletter: An Idea and Resource Guide to Second Career and Relocation Planning. Publications Plus, Inc. • Monthly. $59.00 per year. Edited for "downsized managers, early retirees, and others in career transition after leaving traditional employment." Offers advice on second careers, franchises, starting a business, finances, education, training, skills assessment, and other matters of interest to the newly unemployed.

FRAUD AND EMBEZZLEMENT

See also CRIME AND CRIMINALS; FORGERIES

ABSTRACTS AND INDEXES

Current Law Index. Cengage Learning Inc. • $1,332 Individuals. Monthly. $1269.00 per year. Produced in cooperation with the American Association of Law Libraries. Indexes more than 900 law journals, legal newspapers, and specialty publications from the U.S., Canada, U.K., Ireland, Australia, and New Zealand.

ENCYCLOPEDIAS AND DICTIONARIES

Encyclopedia of Crime and Justice. Cengage Learning Inc. • 2001. $737. 2nd edition. 4 volumes. Published by Macmillan Reference USA. Contains extensive information on a wide variety of topics pertaining to crime, criminology, social issues, and the courts. Also available as eBook.

HANDBOOKS AND MANUALS

Banking Crimes: Fraud, Money Laundering & Embezzlement. John K. Villa. Thomson West. • $369.60 Full Set. Covers fraud and embezzlement.

Private Investigator. Entrepreneur Press. • Looseleaf. $59.50. A practical guide to starting a private investigation agency. Covers profit potential, start-up costs, market size evaluation, pricing, accounting, advertising, promotion, etc. (Start-Up Business Guide No. E1320.).

Securities Crimes. Thomson West. • Annual. $798 full set. Analyzes the enfo of federal securities laws from the viewpoint of the defendant. Discusses Securities and Exchange Commission (SEC) investigations and federal sentencing guidelines. (Securities Law Series).

INTERNET DATABASES

Lexis.com Research System. Lexis-Nexis Group. Phone: 800-227-4908 or (937)865-6800; Fax: (937)865-6909; Email: webmaster@prod.lexis-nexis.com • URL: http://www.nexis.com • Fee-based Web site offers extensive searching of a wide variety of legal sources. Additional features include Daily Opinion Service, lexis.com Bookstore, Career Center, CLE Center, Law Schools, and Practice Pages ("Pages specific to areas of specialty").

OTHER SOURCES

Forensic Accounting and Financial Fraud. American Management Association Extension Institute. • Looseleaf. $159.00. Self-study course. Emphasis is on practical explanations, examples, and problem solving. Quizzes and a case study are included.

White Collar Crime: Business and Regulatory Offenses. ALM Media Properties LLC. • $740 print + online + ebook. Covers such legal matters as criminal tax cases, securities fraud, computer crime, mail fraud, bank embezzlement, criminal antitrust activities, extortion, perjury, the criminal liability of corporations, and RICO (Racketeer Influenced and Corrupt Organization Act). (Law Journal Press).

PERIODICALS AND NEWSLETTERS

Business Crimes Bulletin. ALM Media Properties LLC. • Monthly. $510 per year. Provides news of the "multifaceted world of financial and white collar crime." Covers such items as foreign corrupt practices, mail fraud, money laundering, tax fraud, securities law violations, environmental crime, and antitrust violations. Includes developments in sentencing guidelines for white collar perpetrators. (A Law Journal Newsletter, formerly published by Leader Publications).

Claims. • Monthly. $46.00 per year. Edited for insurance adjusters, risk managers, and claims professionals. Covers investigation, fraud, insurance law, and other claims-related topics.

FBI Law Enforcement Bulletin. U. S. Government Printing Office. • Monthly. $36.00 per year. Issued by Federal Bureau of Investigation, U. S. Department of Justice. Contains articles on a wide variety of law enforcement and crime topics, including computer-related crime.

Health Care Fraud and Abuse Newsletter. ALM Media Properties LLC. • Monthly. $195.00 per year. Newsletter. Provides legal news relating mainly to fraudulent or excessive medical billing practices. Covers both civil and criminal proceedings. (A Law Journal Newsletter, formerly published by Leader Publications).

STATISTICS SOURCES

Uniform Crime Reports for the United States. Federal Bureau of Investigation, U.S. Department of Justice. U. S. Government Printing Office. • Annual. $45.

TRADE/PROFESSIONAL ASSOCIATIONS

American Society of Criminology. 1314 Kinnear Rd., Ste. 212, Columbus, OH 43212-1156. Phone: (614)292-9207; Fax: (614)292-6767; Email: asc@asc41.com • URL: http://www.asc41.com • Formerly Society for the Advancement of Criminology.

North American Security Products Organization. 204 E St. NE, Washington, DC 20002. Phone: (202)608-1322; Fax: (202)547-6348; Email: smc@naspo.info • URL: http://www.naspo.info • Aims to combat fraud within the areas of brand protection, finance and identity. Fosters the development of security risk management standards to reduce financial fraud, identify document fraud and dilution of brand integrity. Enables security product firms to classify and validate their ability to deliver high, medium or basic levels of security assurance throughout their operations.

FRAUD, COMPUTER

See COMPUTER CRIME AND SECURITY

FREEDOM OF INFORMATION

ABSTRACTS AND INDEXES

Index to Legal Periodicals and Books. H.W. Wilson Co. • Monthly. $490.00 per year. Quarterly and annual cumulations.

PERIODICALS AND NEWSLETTERS

Access Reports: Freedom of Information. Access Reports Inc. • Semimonthly. $400 Individuals.

FTC Freedom of Information Log. Washington Regulatory Reporting Associates. • Weekly. $451 Individuals. Newsletter listing Freedom of Information Act requests that have been submitted to the Federal Trade Commission.

IRE Journal. Investigative Reporters and Editors. • Quarterly. $70 Nonmembers. Contains practical information relating to investigative journalism.

TRADE/PROFESSIONAL ASSOCIATIONS

American Society of Access Professionals. 1444 I St. NW, Ste. 700, Washington, DC 20005. Phone: (202)712-9054; Fax: (202)216-9646; Email: asap@bostrom.com • URL: http://www.accesspro.org • Members are individuals concerned with safeguarding freedom of information, privacy, open meetings, and fair credit reporting laws.

Electronic Frontier Foundation. 815 Eddy St., San Francisco, CA 94109. Phone: (415)436-9333; Fax: (415)436-9993; Email: info@eff.org • URL: http://www.eff.org • Promotes the creation of legal and structural approaches to help ease the assimilation of new technologies by society. Seeks to: help policymakers develop a better understanding of issues underlying telecommunications; increase public understanding of the opportunities and challenges posed by computing and telecommunications fields. Fosters awareness of civil liberties issues arising from the advancements in new computer-based communications media and supports litigation to preserve, protect, and extend First Amendment rights in computing and telecommunications technology. Maintains speakers' bureau; conducts educational programs. Encourages and supports the development of tools to endow non-technical users with access to computer-based telecommunications.

Reporters Committee for Freedom of the Press. 1101 Wilson Blvd., Ste. 1100, Arlington, VA 22209. Phone: 800-336-4243 or (703)807-2100; Fax: (703)807-2109; Email: info@rcfp.org • URL: http://www.rcfp.org • Concerned with protecting freedom of information rights for the working press.

FREIGHT, AIR

See AIR FREIGHT

FREIGHT FORWARDERS

See FREIGHT TRANSPORT

FREIGHT RATES

See also FREIGHT TRANSPORT

PERIODICALS AND NEWSLETTERS

International Freighting Weekly: Sea, Air, Rail, Road. Informa UK Ltd. • Weekly. $289.00 per year. Looseleaf service.

FREIGHT SHIPS

See SHIPS, SHIPPING AND SHIPBUILDING

FREIGHT TRANSPORT

See also AIR FREIGHT; FREIGHT RATES; TRANSPORTATION INDUSTRY

CD-ROM DATABASES

OECD Statistical Compendium. Organization for Economic Cooperation and Development. • Semiannual. $1,905.00 per year for 1 to 10 users. CD-ROM contains more than 730,000 monthly, quarterly, and annual time series for OECD countries, 1960 to date. Includes fully searchable data on agriculture, food, economic indicators, national accounts, employment, energy, finance, industry, technology, and foreign trade. Results can be displayed in various forms.

DIRECTORIES

Air Freight Directory. Air Cargo Inc. • Bimonthly. $34.50 single copy. Publication includes: Directory of more than 500 motor carriers contracting with Air Cargo, Inc. for delivery and pick up of freight. Air Cargo is a ground service specialist organization jointly owned by 18 major air carriers. Entries include: Airport city and code, firm name, address, phone, and services offered. Principal content of publication is chart of service points and rates.

American Motor Carrier Directory. UBM Global Trade. • Annual. Publication includes: Lists of all licensed Less Than Truckload (LTL) general commodity carriers in the United States; includes specialized motor carriers and related services; includes refrigerated carriers, heavy haulers, bulk haulers, riggers, and specified commodity carriers; state and federal regulatory bodies governing the trucking industry; tariff publishing bureaus; freight claim councils; industry associations, etc. Entries include: For carriers and services--Company name, address of headquarters and terminals, phones, tariffs followed, names of executives, insurance, and equipment information, services or commodities handled. Principal content of publication is listing of direct point-to-point services of LTL general commodity carriers throughout the United States and to Canada and Mexico.

National Customs Brokers and Forwarders Association of America Membership Directory. National Customs Brokers and Forwarders Association of America. • Annual. $55.00. Lists about 600 customs brokers, international air cargo agents, and freight forwarders in the U.S.

FINANCIAL RATIOS

Annual Statement Studies. Risk Management Association. • Annual. Compiled from over 280,000 financial statements.

Annual Statement Studies: Industry Default Probabilities and Cash Flow Measures. Risk Management Association. • Annual. $405 Nonmembers. Serves as a companion volume to the original *Annual Statement Studies*. Gives probability of default estimates on a percentage scale for more than 450 industries. Includes changes in position year-by-year for eight financial statement line items and provides percentage measures of cash flow.

INTERNET DATABASES

Business 2.0 Web Guide to the Best Business Links. Business 2.0 Media Inc. Phone: (415)293-4800; Email: support@business2.com • URL: http://www.business2.com/webguide • Web site presents an extensive, searchable directory of links to "the best, most informative, and authoritative web pages." Twenty main categories cover business, finance, career, company information, people, and technology topics, with thousands of subtopics, all linking to Web sites recommended by experienced business researchers. Fees: Free.

Fedstats. Federal Interagency Council on Statistical Policy. Phone: (202)395-7254 • URL: http://www.fedstats.gov • Web site features an efficient search facility for full-text statistics produced by more than 100 federal agencies, including the Census Bureau, the Bureau of Economic Analysis, and the Bureau of Labor Statistics. Boolean searches can be made within one agency or for all agencies combined. Links are offered to international statistical bureaus, including the UN, IMF, OECD, UNESCO, Eurostat, and 20 individual countries. Fees: Free.

FreeLunch.com. Economy.com, Inc. Phone: (610)696-8700; Fax: (610)696-1678 • URL: http://www.freelunch.com • Web site provides free access to more than 200 million economic and financial data series, covering industry, demographics, labor markets, prices, retail sales, government spending, trade, interest rates, housing starts, the stock market, etc. Data is available in either chart or table form. Searching is offered. Free, but registration required. Economy.com, Inc. also offers fee-based economic analysis at *The Dismal Scientist* site (www.dismal.com).

STATISTICS SOURCES

Survey of Current Business. U. S. Government Printing Office. • Published by Bureau of Economic Analysis, U. S. Department of Commerce. Presents a wide variety of business and economic data.

FRINGE BENEFITS

See also EMPLOYEE BENEFIT PLANS

ABSTRACTS AND INDEXES

Business Periodicals Index Retrospective. EBSCO Publishing Inc. • 11/year. Quarterly and annual cumulations.

ONLINE DATABASES

Wilson Business Abstracts Online. H.W. Wilson Co. • Indexes and abstracts 600 major business periodicals, plus the *Wall Street Journal* and the business section of the *New York Times*. Indexing is from 1982, abstracting from 1990, with the two newspapers included from 1993. Updated weekly. Inquire as to online cost and availability. (*Business Periodicals Index* without abstracts is also available online.).

OTHER SOURCES

Fringe Benefits Tax Guide. Wolters Kluwer Law & Business CCH. • Monthly. $539.00. Looseleaf service.

FROZEN FOOD INDUSTRY

See also CANNED FOOD INDUSTRY; FAST FOOD INDUSTRY; REFRIGERATION INDUSTRY

ABSTRACTS AND INDEXES

Food Science and Technology Abstracts. Ovid Technologies Inc. • Monthly. $1,780.00 per year. Provides worldwide coverage of the literature of food technology and food production.

Foods Adlibra: Key to the World's Food Literature. General Mills, Inc. Foods Adlibra Publications. • Semimonthly. $240.00 per year. Provides journal citations and abstracts to the literature of food technology and packaging.

ALMANACS AND YEARBOOKS

Almanac of the Canning, Freezing, Preserving Industries. Food Institute. • Annual. $110 Individuals Hard Copy mail delivery or pdf email from publisher. Contains U.S. food laws and regulations and detailed production statistics.

DIRECTORIES

Major Food and Drink Companies of the World. Cengage Learning Inc. • 12th edition. eBook. Published by Graham & Whiteside. Contains profiles and trade names for more than 9,200 important food and beverage companies in various countries. In addition to foods, includes both alcoholic and nonalcoholic drink products.

National Frozen and Refrigerated Foods Association Membership Directory. National Frozen and Refrigerated Foods Association. • Annual. $195.00. Lists products, services and personnel.

Plunkett's Food Industry Almanac. Plunkett Research Ltd. • $349.99 Individuals print + online. Covers: 340 leading companies in the global food industry. Entries include: Name, address, phone, fax, and key executives. Also includes analysis and information on trends, technology, and statistics in the field.

ONLINE DATABASES

Food Science and Technology Abstracts (online). IFIS North American Desk. • Produced by International Food Information Service. Provides about 500,000 online citations, with abstracts, to the international literature of food science, technology, commodities, engineering, and processing. Approximately 2,000 periodicals are covered. Time period is 1969 to date, with monthly updates. Inquire as to online cost and availability.

PERIODICALS AND NEWSLETTERS

Quick Frozen Foods International. E.W. Williams Publications Co. • Quarterly. $42.00 per year. Text in English, summaries in French and German.

TRADE/PROFESSIONAL ASSOCIATIONS

American Frozen Food Institute. 2000 Corporate Ridge, Ste. 1000, McLean, VA 22102. Phone: (703)821-0770; Fax: (703)821-1350; Email: info@affi.com • URL: http://www.affi.com • Frozen food processors and allied industry companies who work for the advancement of the frozen food industry. Seeks to improve consumer understanding and acceptance of frozen foods and to increase sales of frozen products through promotional and communications programs. Sponsors retail trade study, consumer and industry education on care and handling of frozen foods. Promotes a cooperative relationship between frozen food processors, suppliers and marketing associates. Represents the frozen food industry before federal, state and local governments. Conducts research to improve the quality of frozen food products.

National Frozen and Refrigerated Foods Association. 4755 Linglestown Rd., Ste. 300, Harrisburg, PA 17112. Phone: (717)657-8601; Fax: (717)657-9862; Email: info@nfraweb.org • URL: http://www.nfraweb.org • Absorbed Foodservice Organizations of Distributors. Formerly National Frozen Food Association.

FRUIT INDUSTRY

See also APPLE INDUSTRY; BANANA INDUSTRY; CITRUS FRUIT INDUSTRY

ABSTRACTS AND INDEXES

Food Science and Technology Abstracts. Ovid Technologies Inc. • Monthly. $1,780.00 per year. Provides worldwide coverage of the literature of food technology and food production.

Foods Adlibra: Key to the World's Food Literature. General Mills, Inc. Foods Adlibra Publications. • Semimonthly. $240.00 per year. Provides journal citations and abstracts to the literature of food technology and packaging.

Horticultural Science Abstracts. CABI Publishing North America. • Updated weekly online; also available in print, delivered monthly.

CD-ROM DATABASES

AGRICOLA on SilverPlatter. Ovid Technologies Inc. • Updated monthly. Price varies. Produced by the National Agricultural Library. Provides over 4 million citations to the literature of agriculture, agricultural economics, animal sciences, entomology, fertilizer, food, forestry, nutrition, pesticides, plant science, water resources, and other topics.

DIRECTORIES

Directory of Chinese Manufacturers & Exporters of Fruits & Vegetables. EXIM Infotek Private Ltd. • $15 Individuals. Covers: 150 Chinese manufacturers and exporters of apples, bamboo shoots, canned fruits, canned mushrooms, canned pineapples, carrots, cherries, dehydrated vegetables, dried carrots, dried mushrooms, dried vegetables, frozen bamboo shoots, frozen carrots, frozen fruits, frozen vegetables, fruit, garlic, garlic sprouts, ginger, grapes, green beans, vermicelli, green vegetables, lychee, mushrooms, mushrooms and fungi, onion slices, onions, onions-Chinese, oranges, pea pods, salted vegetables, strawberries, vegetable products, vegetables, and vegetables-canned. Entries include: Company name, postal address, city, country, phone, fax, e-mail and websites, contact person, designation, and product details.

Directory of Chinese Manufacturers & Exporters of Nuts & Dried Fruits. EXIM Infotek Private Ltd. • $5 Individuals. Covers: 30 Chinese manufacturers and exporters of chestnuts, dried fruits, dry fruits, nuts-dried, peanut kernels, walnuts. Entries include: Company name, postal address, city, country, phone, fax, e-mail and websites, contact person, designation, and product details.

Major Food and Drink Companies of the World. Cengage Learning Inc. • 12th edition. eBook. Published by Graham & Whiteside. Contains profiles and trade names for more than 9,200 important food and beverage companies in various countries. In addition to foods, includes both alcoholic and nonalcoholic drink products.

ENCYCLOPEDIAS AND DICTIONARIES

Encyclopedia of Food and Culture. Cengage Learning Inc. • 2003. $657.00. Three volumes. Contains 600 articles covering various aspects of food and its place in society, from agronomy to zucchini. Includes illustrations and a detailed index. eBook also available, updated in 2004.

INTERNET DATABASES

USDA. U.S. National Institute of Standards and Technology. 100 Bureau Dr., Gaithersburg, MD 20899-1070. Phone: 800-877-8339 or (301)975-6478 or (202)720-2791; Fax: (301)975-8295; Email: inquiries@nist.gov • URL: http://www.nist.gov • The USDA home page has six sections: News and Information; What's New; About USDA; Agencies; Opportunities; Search and Help. Keyword searching is offered from the USDA home page and from various individual agency home pages. Agencies are the Economic Research Service, Agricultural Marketing Service, National Agricultural Statistics Service, National Agricultural Library, and about 12 others. Updating varies. Fees: Free.

ONLINE DATABASES

Food Science and Technology Abstracts (online). IFIS North American Desk. • Produced by International Food Information Service. Provides about 500,000 online citations, with abstracts, to the international literature of food science, technology, commodities, engineering, and processing. Approximately 2,000 periodicals are covered. Time period is 1969 to date, with monthly updates. Inquire as to online cost and availability.

PERIODICALS AND NEWSLETTERS

American Fruit Grower. Meister Media. • Monthly. $27.47 per year.

American Pomological Society Journal. American Pomological Society. • Quarterly. $30 Individuals. Presents reports and general information on fruit varieties.

Fresh Produce Journal. Lockwood Press, Ltd. • Weekly (Fri.). £125 Individuals. Trade magazine for the fresh produce industry. Formerly *Fruit Trades Journal.*

The Grower: Profitable Business Strategies for Fruit and Vegetable Growers. Vance Publishing Corp. • Monthly. $45 Individuals. Magazine providing management information for the commercial fruit and vegetable producer with emphasis on management, industry trends, effective marketing, chemicals, and legislative and regulatory environments.

The Packer: Devoted to the Interest of Commericial Growers, Packers, Shippers, Receivers and Retailers of Fruits, Vegetables and Other Products. Vance Publishing Corp., Produce Div. • Weekly. $65.00 per year. Supplements available: *Brand Directory and Fresh Trends, Packer's Produce Availability and Merchandising Guide* and *Produce Services Sourcebooks.*

The Packer: The Business Newspaper of the Produce Industry. Vance Publishing Corp. • Weekly. $99 Individuals. Newspaper on produce marketing.

Produce Merchandising: The Packer's Retailing and Merchandising Magazine. Vance Publishing Corp. • Monthly. $35.00 per year. Provides information and advice on the retail marketing and promotion of fresh fruits and vegetalbe.

PRICE SOURCES

PPI Detailed Report. Periodical covering business. Bureau of Labor Statistics, U.S. Department of Labor. U. S. Government Printing Office. • Monthly. $55 Individuals.

RESEARCH CENTERS AND INSTITUTES

College of Tropical Agriculture and Human Resources. University of Hawaii at Manoa, 2515 Campus Rd., Miller Hall 110, Honolulu, HI 96822. Phone: (808)956-8234; Fax: (808)956-9105; Email: gallom@ctahr.hawaii.edu • URL: http://www.ctahr.hawaii.edu • Concerned with the production and marketing of tropical food and ornamental plant products, including pineapples, bananas, coffee, and macadamia nuts.

University of California - California Agricultural Experiment Station. 1111 Franklin St., Rm. 6402, Oakland, CA 94607-5200. Phone: (510)987-0036 or (510)987-0060; Fax: (510)465-2659 or (510)451-2317; Email: steve.nation@ucop.edu • URL: http://ucanr.org/AES.shtml • Plant and animal biology, agricultural engineering and economics, soils, and water, including basic and applied studies directed toward solving problems of agriculture involved in production, storage, and transportation of over 300 commodities produced in California. Studies problems relating to forestry, human welfare and nutrition, pest management, mosquito control, and outdoor recreation. Operates on a statewide basis, with main units on Berkeley, Davis, and Riverside campuses of the University and ten research and extension centers throughout the state.

Washington State University - Agricultural Research Center. PO Box 646240, Pullman, WA 99164-6240. Phone: (509)335-4563; Fax: (509)335-6751; Email: agresearch@wsu.edu • URL: http://arc.wsu.edu • Agriculture and food safety, including economics; biological systems engineering; agronomy and soils; animal sciences; human development; food science and human nutrition; apparel; merchandising; interior design; rural sociology; entomology; natural resource management; horticulture and landscape architecture; plant pathology; veterinary science; plant and animal biotechnology; wood materials; and low-input sustainable agriculture. Performs forage, seed, and minor pesticide testing.

STATISTICS SOURCES

Agricultural Statistics. U.S. Department of Agriculture National Agricultural Statistics Service. • Annual. $46 Individuals. Provides a wide variety of statistical data relating to agricultural production, supplies, consumption, prices/price-supports, foreign trade, costs, and returns, as well as farm labor, loans, income, and population. In many cases, historical data is shown annually for 10 years. In addition to farm data, includes detailed fishery statistics.

TRADE/PROFESSIONAL ASSOCIATIONS

National Association of Flavors and Food-Ingredient Systems. 3301 Rte. 66, Bldg. C, Ste. 205, Neptune, NJ 07753. Phone: (732)922-3218; Fax: (732)922-3590; Email: info@naffs.org • URL: http://www.naffs.org • Manufacturers of fruit and syrup toppings, flavors and stabilizers for the food industry. Formerly National Association of Fruits, Flavors and Syrups.

Tampa Bay Rare Fruit Council International. 39320 North Ave., Zephyrhills, FL 33542. Email: tampa.bay.rfci@gmail.com • URL: http://www.rarefruit.org • Individuals in 34 countries interested in propagating and raising tropical fruit plants. Formerly Rare Fruit Council.

FUEL

ABSTRACTS AND INDEXES

NTIS Alerts: Energy. U.S. Department of Commerce National Technical Information Service. • Biweekly. $130 per year. Covers electric power, batteries, fuels, geothermal energy, heating/cooling systems, nuclear technology, solar energy, energy policy, and related subjects.

CD-ROM DATABASES

Environment Abstracts on CD-ROM. University Publications of America. • Quarterly. $1,295.00 per year. Contains the following CD-ROM databases: *Environment Abstracts, Energy Abstracts,* and *Acid Rain Abstracts.* Length of coverage varies.

E-BOOKS

Macmillan Encyclopedia of Energy. Cengage Learning Inc. • 2003. eBook. Published by Macmillan Reference USA. Covers the business, technology, and history of a wide variety of energy sources. Inquire as to price and availability.

ENCYCLOPEDIAS AND DICTIONARIES

Evolution of Modern Business Series. Cengage Learning Inc. • Contains in-depth surveys on business trends and waves of industrial progress. Offers a critical look at the practices and evolution of the business world. Series includes: Curtiss-Wright, History of Black Business in America, Incorporating Women, and The Invisible Fuel: A History of Natural Gas in America. Volumes available individually.

ONLINE DATABASES

Alternative Fuel Vehicle Businesses in the World. Momentum Technologies L.L.C. • Contains detailed directory listings and contact information for dozens of businesses involved with alternative fuel vehicles in operation throughout the world. Includes business name, address, phone number, fax number, e-mail address, and web site address. Includes brief descriptions of product lines, services offered, and business type. Covers manufacturers, wholesale and retail suppliers, system design businesses, system installers, nonprofit organizations, trade organizations, and more.

OTHER SOURCES

Major Energy Companies of the World. Cengage Learning Inc. • Annual. $1,460 Individuals. 2008. 12th edition. eBook. Published by Graham & Whiteside. Contains detailed information on more than 4,850 important energy companies in various countries. Industries include electricity generation, coal, natural gas, nuclear energy, petroleum, fuel distribution, and equipment for energy production.

PERIODICALS AND NEWSLETTERS

Energy & Fuels. American Chemical Society. • Bimonthly. $1,537 Institutions. An interdisciplinary technical journal covering non-nuclear energy sources: petroleum, gas, synthetic fuels, etc.

Fuel: Science and Technology of Fuel and Energy. Elsevier. • $98 Qualified personnel.

International Journal of Energy Research. John Wiley and Sons, Inc., Journals Div. • 15 times a year. Individuals, $2,685.00 per year; institutions, $3,500.00 per year. Published in England by John Wiley & Sons Ltd.

Journal of Energy Engineering: The International Journal. Architectural Engineering Institute of ASCE. • Quarterly. $350 Individuals Online only. Contains reports on the development of scientific and engineering knowledge in the planning, management, and generation of electrical power.

STATISTICS SOURCES

Annual Energy Outlook, with Projections to (year). U. S. Government Printing Office. • Annual. $39.00. Issued by the Energy Information Administration, U. S. Department of Energy (www.eia.doe.gov). Contains detailed statistics and 20-year projections for electricity, oil, natural gas, coal, and renewable energy. Text provides extensive discussion of energy issues and "Market Trends.".

Petroleum Statement, Annual Energy Report. Energy Information Administration. U.S. Department of Energy. • Annual.

Steam Electric Market Analysis. National Mining Association. • Monthly. Free to members; non-members, $300.00 per year. Covers 400 major electric power plants, with detailed data on coal consumption and stockpiles. Shows percent of power generated by fuel type. (Publisher formerly National Coal Association.).

FUEL CELLS

See BATTERY INDUSTRY

FUEL OIL INDUSTRY

CD-ROM DATABASES

OECD Statistical Compendium. Organization for Economic Cooperation and Development. • Semiannual. $1,905.00 per year for 1 to 10 users. CD-ROM contains more than 730,000 monthly, quarterly, and annual time series for OECD countries, 1960 to date. Includes fully searchable data on agriculture, food, economic indicators, national accounts, employment, energy, finance, industry, technology, and foreign trade. Results can be displayed in various forms.

DIRECTORIES

Asia Pacific Oil and Gas Directory. Business Monitor International Ltd. • $895 Individuals. Covers: 1,329 top oil and gas executives on 445 leading oil and gas companies from Asia Pacific. Entries include: Company name and address; phone, fax, email and website address; senior contact personnel; full description of company activity; local company profile; nationality; and ownership status and parentage.

FINANCIAL RATIOS

Annual Statement Studies. Risk Management Association. • Annual. Compiled from over 280,000 financial statements.

Annual Statement Studies: Industry Default Probabilities and Cash Flow Measures. Risk Management Association. • Annual. $405 Nonmembers. Serves as a companion volume to the original *Annual Statement Studies*. Gives probability of default estimates on a percentage scale for more than 450 industries. Includes changes in position year-by-year for eight financial statement line items and provides percentage measures of cash flow.

INTERNET DATABASES

Advance Monthly Retail Trade Report. U. S. Census Bureau. Phone: 800-541-8345 or (301)457-4100 or (301)763-2713; Fax: (301)457-1296 or (301)457-3842; Email: naics@census.gov • URL: http://www.census.gov/epcd/www/naicstab.htm • Web pages provide monthly sales figures for a wide range of retail businesses. Advance, preliminary, and final statistics are provided for the latest month available in each case, with a previous-year comparison. Updates are monthly.

Business 2.0 Web Guide to the Best Business Links. Business 2.0 Media Inc. Phone: (415)293-4800; Email: support@business2.com • URL: http://www.business2.com/webguide • Web site presents an extensive, searchable directory of links to "the best, most informative, and authoritative web pages." Twenty main categories cover business, finance, career, company information, people, and technology topics, with thousands of subtopics, all linking to Web sites recommended by experienced business researchers. Fees: Free.

Fedstats. Federal Interagency Council on Statistical Policy. Phone: (202)395-7254 • URL: http://www.fedstats.gov • Web site features an efficient search facility for full-text statistics produced by more than 100 federal agencies, including the Census Bureau, the Bureau of Economic Analysis, and the Bureau of Labor Statistics. Boolean searches can be made within one agency or for all agencies combined. Links are offered to international statistical bureaus, including the UN, IMF, OECD, UNESCO, Eurostat, and 20 individual countries. Fees: Free.

FreeLunch.com. Economy.com, Inc. Phone: (610)696-8700; Fax: (610)696-1678 • URL: http://www.freelunch.com • Web site provides free access to more than 200 million economic and financial data series, covering industry, demographics, labor markets, prices, retail sales, government spending, trade, interest rates, housing starts, the stock market, etc. Data is available in either chart or table form. Searching is offered. Free, but registration required. Economy.com, Inc. also offers fee-based economic analysis at *The Dismal Scientist* site (www.dismal.com).

PERIODICALS AND NEWSLETTERS

Indoor Comfort Marketing. Industry Publications Inc. • Monthly. $30.00 per year. Formerly *Fueloil and Oil Heat with Air Conditioning*.

Oil and Gas Journal. PennWell Corp., Industrial Div. • Weekly. $84.00 per year.

STATISTICS SOURCES

Annual Benchmark Report for Retail Trade and Food Services..A Detailed Summary of Retail Sales, Purchases, Accounts Receivable, Inventories, and Food Service Sales. U. S. Government Printing Office. • Annual. $13.00. Issued by the U.S. Census Bureau. Provides detailed annual and monthly retail statistics for the most recent 10 years. Includes data for various kinds of retail outlets, including automobiles, furniture, appliances, building supplies, grocery stores, drug stores, gasoline stations, clothing, sporting goods, department stores, and restaurants.

Fuel Oil News: Source Book. • Annual. $28.00. Provides fuel (heating) oil industry data.

Petroleum Supply Annual. U. S. Government Printing Office. • Annual. $78.00. Two volumes. Produced by the Energy Information Administration, U. S. Department of Energy. Contains worldwide data on the petroleum industry and petroleum products.

Petroleum Supply Monthly. U. S. Government Printing Office. • Monthly. Produced by the Energy Information Administration, U. S. Department of Energy. Provides worldwide statistics on a wide variety of petroleum products. Covers production, supplies, exports and imports, transportation, refinery operations, and other aspects of the petroleum industry.

Survey of Current Business. U. S. Government Printing Office. • Published by Bureau of Economic Analysis, U. S. Department of Commerce. Presents a wide variety of business and economic data.

FUEL, SYNTHETIC

See SYNTHETIC FUELS

FUND-RAISING

See also FEDERAL AID; FOUNDATIONS; GRANTS-IN-AID

DIRECTORIES

Foundation Reporter: Comprehensive Profiles and Giving Analyses of America's Major Private Foundations. Taft Group. • Annual. $490.00. Provides detailed information on major U. S. foundations. Eight indexes (location, grant type, recipient type, personnel, etc.).

Guide to Federal Funding for Governments and Nonprofits. Thompson Publishing Group Inc. • Updated continuously; printed on request. $399. Contains detailed descriptions of federal grant programs in economic development, housing, transportation, social services, science, etc.

INTERNET DATABASES

Welcome to the Foundation Center. Foundation Center. Phone: (212)620-4230 or (212)807-3679; Fax: (212)807-3677; Email: mfn@fdncenter.org • URL: http://www.fdncenter.org • Web site provides a wide variety of information about foundations, grants, and philanthropy, with links to philanthropic organizations. "Grantmaker Information" link furnishes descriptions of available funding.

OTHER SOURCES

Charitable Giving and Solicitation. Thomson RIA. • $495.00 per year. Looseleaf service. Updates 13 times a year. Bulletin discusses federal tax rules pertaining to charitable contributions.

PERIODICALS AND NEWSLETTERS

Direct Marketing News. Haymarket Media Group Ltd. • Monthly. $148 U.S. /year. Includes special feature issues on catalog marketing, telephone marketing, database marketing, and fundraising. Includes monthly supplements, *DM News International*, *DRTV News*, and *TeleServices*.

FRM Weekly. Hoke Communications Inc. • Weekly. $115.00 per year.

Giving USA Update. American Association of Fund-Raising Counsel. AAFRC Trust for Philanthropy. • Quarterly. $110 Individuals. Legal, economic and social essays on philanthropy.

Grantsmanship Center Magazine. The Grantsmanship Center. • Quarterly. Irregular. Free to qualified personnel. Contains a variety of concise articles on grant-related topics, such as program planning, proposal writing, fundraising, non-cash gifts, federal project grants, benchmarking, taxation, etc.

NSFRE-News. Association of Fundraising Professionals. • Description: Covers tax-related issues affecting nonprofit organizations, conference and seminar information, educational opportunities, and chapter news.

Taft Monthly Portfolio. Taft Group. • Monthly. $75.00 per year. New ideas and proven techniques used by universitites, hospitals and other nonprofit organizations to raise philanthropic gifts. Formerly *FRI Monthly Portfolio*.

STATISTICS SOURCES

United Way Annual Report. United Way Worldwide. • Annual.

TRADE/PROFESSIONAL ASSOCIATIONS

Association of Fundraising Professionals. 4300 Wilson Blvd., Ste. 300, Arlington, VA 22203. Phone: 800-666-3863 or (703)684-0410; Fax: (703)684-0540; Email: afp@afpnet.org • URL: http://www.afpnet.org • Formerly National Society of Fundraising Executives.

DMA Nonprofit Federation. 1615 L St. NW, Ste. 1100, Washington, DC 20036. Phone: (202)861-2427; Fax: (202)628-4383; Email: aosgood@the-dma.org • URL: http://www.nonprofitfederation.org • Trade and lobbying group for non-profit organizations that use direct and online marketing to raise funds and communicate with members. Sponsors professional development conferences and seminars, lobbies on state and federal legislation, regulation, and standards related to direct marketing and related issues. Provides information about and participants in litigation affecting non-profits. Promotes the overall welfare of non-profits. Represents health care charities, social service agencies, religious groups, colleges and universities and fraternal organizations.

FUNDS, COMMUNITY

See COMMUNITY FUNDS

FUNDS, MUTUAL

See INVESTMENT COMPANIES

FUNERAL HOMES AND DIRECTORS

DIRECTORIES

NFDA Directory of Members and Transportation Guide. National Funeral Directors Association. • Annual. $35 Members print. Covers 14,000 members of state funeral director associations affiliated with the National Funeral Directors Association. Formerly *National Funeral Directors Association-Membership Listing and Resources*.

FINANCIAL RATIOS

Annual Statement Studies. Risk Management Association. • Annual. Compiled from over 280,000 financial statements.

Annual Statement Studies: Industry Default Probabilities and Cash Flow Measures. Risk Management Association. • Annual. $405 Nonmembers. Serves as a companion volume to the original *Annual Statement Studies*. Gives probability of default estimates on a percentage scale for more than 450 industries. Includes changes in position year-by-year for eight financial statement line items and provides percentage measures of cash flow.

GENERAL WORKS

Business in Calgary. Business in Calgary. • Bimonthly. $45 Individuals. Trade magazine for monument and bronze makers, and the managers of cemeteries, crematoriums, and mausoleums.

PERIODICALS AND NEWSLETTERS

American Funeral Director. Kates-Boylston Publications, Inc. • Monthly. $59.00 per year.

The Director. National Funeral Directors

Association. National Funeral Directors Association. • Monthly. Offers in-depth features on the trends, expert analysis of legislative and regulatory developments, and thought-provoking opinions by industry leaders.

TRADE/PROFESSIONAL ASSOCIATIONS

National Funeral Directors and Morticians Association. 6290 Shannon Pkwy., Union City, GA 30291. Phone: 800-434-0958 or (770)969-0064; Fax: (770)969-0505 or (404)286-6573 • URL: http://www.nfdma.com • State, district and local funeral directors and embalmers associations and their members. Promotes ethical practices; encourages just and uniform laws pertaining to funeral directing and embalming industry.

National Funeral Directors Association. 13625 Bishops Dr., Brookfield, WI 53005-6607. Phone: 800-228-6332 or (262)789-1880; Fax: (262)789-6977; Email: nfda@nfda.org • URL: http://www.nfda.org • Federation of state funeral directors' associations with individual membership of funeral directors. Seeks to enhance the funeral service profession and promote quality services to the consumers. Conducts professional education seminars and home study courses. Compiles statistics.

Selected Independent Funeral Homes. 500 Lake Cook Rd., Ste. 205, Deerfield, IL 60015. Phone: 800-323-4219; Fax: (847)236-9968 • URL: http://www.selectedfuneralhomes.org • Funeral directors. Aims to study, develop, and establish a standard of service for the benefit of its consumers. Provides a continuing forum for the exchange, development and dissemination of knowledge and information beneficial to members and the public.

FUR INDUSTRY

DIRECTORIES

Directory of Chinese Importers of Leather, Hides, Skins & Furs. EXIM Infotek Private Ltd. • Covers: 30 Chinese importers of cow leathers, hides, skins and fur, leather, mink and fox tails, pig skins, scrap sheep, and fox skin. Entries include: Company name, postal address, telephone, fax, e-mail, website, contact person, designation, and product details.

Fur Business-Retail Directory. InfoGroup Inc. • Updated continuously; printed on request. Covers fur businesses.

OTHER SOURCES

Fur World: The Newsmagazine of Fur and Better Outerware. Creative Marketing Plus, Inc. • Semimonthly. $50.00 per year. Edited for fur retailers, ranchers, pelt dealers, and manufacturers. Provides news and statistics relating to the retail and wholesale fur business.

FURNISHINGS (MEN'S CLOTHING)

See MEN'S CLOTHING INDUSTRY

FURNITURE INDUSTRY

See also OFFICE FURNITURE INDUSTRY

ABSTRACTS AND INDEXES

NTIS Alerts: Building Industry Technology. U.S. Department of Commerce National Technical Information Service. • Biweekly. $130 per year. Covers architecture, construction management, building materials, maintenance, furnishings, and related subjects.

CD-ROM DATABASES

OECD Statistical Compendium. Organization for Economic Cooperation and Development. • Semiannual. $1,905.00 per year for 1 to 10 users. CD-ROM contains more than 730,000 monthly, quarterly, and annual time series for OECD countries, 1960 to date. Includes fully searchable data on agriculture, food, economic indicators, national accounts, employment, energy, finance, industry, technology, and foreign trade. Results can be displayed in various forms.

DIRECTORIES

Casual Living--Casual Outdoor Furniture and Accessory Directory Issue. Reed Elsevier Group plc Reed Business Information. • Annual. $22.99 Individuals. Publication includes: List of manufacturers, manufacturers' representatives, and suppliers of outdoor furniture, wicker and rattan furniture, and backyard accessories, such as barbecue grills, picnic accessories, outdoor lighting, cushions and pads, patio umbrellas, vinyl refinishing and maintenance products. Entries include: Name of firm, address, phone, products.

Corridor Directory. Miller Freeman UK Ltd. • Database covers: More than 10,000 UK manufacturers, retailers, agents, wholesalers, service suppliers, and associations in the furniture and furnishings industry. Entries include: Company information.

Directory of American Manufacturers & Exporters of Furniture--All Types. EXIM Infotek Private Ltd. • $25 Individuals. Covers: 330 American manufacturers and exporters of bed frames, bed liners, bedroom furniture, bookcases, chairs, church furniture, commercial furniture, computer furniture, computer tables, custom upholstered wood furniture, decorative furniture, dining room furniture, dining tables, edge-glued furniture panels, fine home theater furniture, finished furniture, folding chairs, folding tables, furniture, furniture and supplies, furniture parts, garden furniture, hardwood furniture, hotel furniture, institution furniture, metal furniture, motel furniture, occasional furniture, occasional tables, office furniture and accessories, outdoor furniture, residential furniture, restaurant furniture, safes, school furniture, steel furniture, steel shelving, unfinished wood furniture, upholstered furniture, vault doors, wood library furniture, wrought iron furniture. Entries include: Company name, postal address, city, country, telephone, fax, e-mail and websites, contact person, designation, and product details.

Directory of American Manufacturers & Exporters of Home Furnishing Materials. EXIM Infotek Private Ltd. • $5 Individuals. Covers: 40 American manufacturers and exporters of bedspreads and sleeping bags, cleaners, cushion grips, doors, earring cushions and accessories, home furnishings, pillows, table cloths, vacuum cleaners, and wooden bedroom. Entries include: Company name, postal address, city, country, phone, fax, e-mail and websites, contact person, designation, and product details.

Directory of Chinese Manufacturers & Exporters of Furniture--All Types. EXIM Infotek Private Ltd. • $15 Individuals. Covers: 170 Chinese manufacturers and exporters of aluminum chairs, bamboo furniture, beach chairs, beds, benches, cabinets, chairs, Chinese antique furniture, coffee tables, dinner tables, foldable chairs, furniture-domestic, furniture-garden, furniture-hotel/restaurant/bar, furniture-kitchen, furniture-office, furniture, furniture-antique, furniture-outdoor, metal furniture, plastic chairs, plastic tables, racks and fittings, sofas, steel furniture, steel tube furniture, tables, wood furniture, and wooden furniture. Entries include: Company name, postal address, city, country, phone, fax, e-mail and websites, contact person, designation, and product details.

Directory of Chinese Manufacturers & Exporters of Home Furnishing Materials. EXIM Infotek Private Ltd. • $15 Individuals. Covers: 170 Chinese manufacturers and exporters of baby quilts, bath towels, beach towels, bed cloths, bed covers, bed sheets, bedding products, bedroom articles, blankets, curtains, cushion covers, cushions, doormats, down quilts, face towels, home decorations, home textiles, household textiles, kitchen towels, linen clothing, mats, mattresses, cushions and pillows, pillowcases, pillows, PVC table cloths, quilt cases, quilts, sanitary towels and baby napkins, shower curtains, silk towels, sleeping bags, table cloths, textiles-household, towels-jacquard bath, towels-plain bath, towels, and woolen blankets. Entries include: Company name, postal address, city, country, phone, fax, e-mail and websites, contact person, designation, and product details.

Directory of Japanese Manufacturers & Exporters of Furniture--All Types. EXIM Infotek Private Ltd. • $5 Individuals. Covers: 20 Japanese manufacturers and exporters of furniture, safes and strong boxes, showcases, steel furniture, upholstered furniture, and wooden furniture. Entries include: Company name, postal address, city, country, phone, fax, e-mail and websites, contact person, designation, and product details.

Directory of Japanese Manufacturers & Exporters of Home Furnishing Materials. EXIM Infotek Private Ltd. • $5 Individuals. Covers: 20 Japanese manufacturers and exporters of curtains, interior goods for housing, venetian blinds, and wallpaper. Entries include: Company name, postal address, city, country, phone, fax, e-mail and websites, contact person, designation, and product details.

Directory of South Korean Manufacturers & Exporters of Furniture--All Types. EXIM Infotek Private Ltd. • $15 Individuals. Covers: 140 South Korean manufacturers and exporters of arm-rockers, furniture and fittings for shops/stores, furniture for manufactured products, furniture/racking-industrial/lab, furniture-children, furniture-domestic, furniture-garden, furniture-hospital, furniture-hotel/restaurant/bar, furniture-kitchen, furniture-office, furniture-public places, furniture-school, furniture-ships, furniture-upholstered, knockdown furniture, metal cabinets, small furniture articles. Entries include: Company name, postal address, city, country, phone, fax, e-mail and websites, contact person, designation and product details.

Directory of Taiwanese Manufacturers & Exporters of Furniture--All Types. EXIM Infotek Private Ltd. • $40 Individuals. Covers: 690 Taiwanese manufacturers and exporters of bamboo furniture, chairs, flexible shelving systems, furniture and fittings for shops/stores, furniture fittings, furniture for manufactured products, furniture/racking-industrial/lab, furniture-cane and wicker, furniture-children, furniture-domestic, furniture-garden, furniture-hospital, furniture-hotel/restaurant/bar, furniture-institutional, furniture-kitchen, furniture-office, furniture-public places, furniture-school, furniture-upholstered, knockdown furniture, leisure folding chairs, metal cabinets, small furniture articles, store fixtures, walking cane chairs, and wooden furniture. Entries include: Company name, postal address, city, country, phone, fax, e-mail and websites, contact person, designation, and product details.

Directory of Taiwanese Manufacturers & Exporters of Home Furnishing Materials. EXIM Infotek Private Ltd. • $15 Individuals. Covers: 140 Taiwanese manufacturers and exporters of bathroom mats, crochet lace table cloths, curtains, curtain blinds, door curtains, household linens and soft furnishings, mattresses, cushions and pillows, sanitary towels and baby napkins, shower curtain cloths, table cloths, table lamps, vertical blinds, vinyl placemats, vinyl table cloths, and window curtains. Entries include: Company name, postal address, city, country, phone, fax, e-mail and websites, contact person, designation, and product details.

FDM--The Source--Woodworking Industry Directory. Reed Elsevier Group plc Reed Business

Information. • Annual. $25. Publication includes: List of over 1,800 suppliers to secondary woodworking industry; coverage includes Canada. Entries include: Company name, address, phone, fax, product lines.

Futons Directory. InfoGroup Inc. • Annual. Number of listings: 1,793. Entries include: Name, address, phone, size of advertisement, name of owner or manager, number of employees, year first in "Yellow Pages." Compiled from telephone company "Yellow Pages," nationwide.

The International Directory of Importers - Furniture and Home Furnishings Importers. Interdata. • $320 Individuals print. Covers: 5,100 international firms importing furniture and home furnishings. Entries include: Company name and address, contact person, email, number of employees, year established, phone and telefaxes, business activity, bank references, as well as a listing of furniture and home furnishings currently being imported.

Wood Digest-Showcase. Cygnus Business Media Inc. • Monthly. Publication includes: List of suppliers of materials, machinery, tools, and services for woodworking, cabinetry, casegoods, and furniture manufacturing processes (SIC 24, 25, 37, and 39). Entries include: Company name, phone number, photograph of product, services.

FINANCIAL RATIOS

Industry Norms and Key Business Ratios. Dun & Bradstreet Inc. • Annual. Five volumes. Covers over 800 kinds of businesses, arranged by Standard Industrial Classification number. More detailed editions covering longer periods of time are also available.

HANDBOOKS AND MANUALS

PVC Furniture Manufacturing. Entrepreneur Press. • Looseleaf. $59.50. A practical guide to starting a business for the manufacture of plastic furniture. Covers profit potential, start-up costs, market size evaluation, owner's time required, site selection, lease negotiation, pricing, accounting, advertising, promotion, etc. (Start-Up Business Guide No. E1262.).

INTERNET DATABASES

Advance Monthly Retail Trade Report. U. S. Census Bureau. Phone: 800-541-8345 or (301)457-4100 or (301)763-2713; Fax: (301)457-1296 or (301)457-3842; Email: naics@census.gov • URL: http://www.census.gov/epcd/www/naicstab.htm • Web pages provide monthly sales figures for a wide range of retail businesses. Advance, preliminary, and final statistics are provided for the latest month available in each case, with a previous-year comparison. Updates are monthly.

Business 2.0 Web Guide to the Best Business Links. Business 2.0 Media Inc. Phone: (415)293-4800; Email: support@business2.com • URL: http://www.business2.com/webguide • Web site presents an extensive, searchable directory of links to "the best, most informative, and authoritative web pages." Twenty main categories cover business, finance, career, company information, people, and technology topics, with thousands of subtopics, all linking to Web sites recommended by experienced business researchers. Fees: Free.

Fedstats. Federal Interagency Council on Statistical Policy. Phone: (202)395-7254 • URL: http://www.fedstats.gov • Web site features an efficient search facility for full-text statistics produced by more than 100 federal agencies, including the Census Bureau, the Bureau of Economic Analysis, and the Bureau of Labor Statistics. Boolean searches can be made within one agency or for all agencies combined. Links are offered to international statistical bureaus, including the UN, IMF, OECD, UNESCO, Eurostat, and 20 individual countries. Fees: Free.

FreeLunch.com. Economy.com, Inc. Phone: (610)696-8700; Fax: (610)696-1678 • URL: http://www.freelunch.com • Web site provides free access to more than 200 million economic and financial data series, covering industry, demographics, labor markets, prices, retail sales, government spending, trade, interest rates, housing starts, the stock market, etc. Data is available in either chart or table form. Searching is offered. Free, but registration required. Economy.com, Inc. also offers fee-based economic analysis at *The Dismal Scientist* site (www.dismal.com).

PERIODICALS AND NEWSLETTERS

FDM: For Builders of Cabinets, Fixtures, Furniture, Millwork Furniture Design a nd Manufacturing. Chartwell Communications, Inc. • Monthly. Free to qualified personnel. Edited for furniture executives, production managers, and designers. Covers the manufacturing of household, office, and institutional furniture, store fixtures, and kitchen and bathroom cabinets.

Furniture Today: The Weekly Business Newspaper of the Furniture Industry. Reed Elsevier Group plc Reed Business Information. • $119 U.S.. Furniture retailing and manufacturing magazine (tabloid).

Furniture-Today: The Weekly Business Newspaper of the Furniture Industry. Reed Elsevier Group plc Reed Business Information. • Weekly. $169.97 U.S. and Canada.

Furniture World. Towse Publishing Co. • Monthly. $19.00 per year. Formerly *Furniture World and Furniture Buyer and Decorator.*

HFN (Home Furnishing News): The Newsweekly of Home Products Retailing. Fairchild Publications. • Formerly *HFD-Home Furnishing Daily.*

Home Furnishings Business. North American Publishing Co. • Magazine publishing articles in the field of furniture retail.

Unfinished Business. Unfinished Furniture Association. • Bimonthly.

RESEARCH CENTERS AND INSTITUTES

Purdue University - Wood Research Laboratory. Department of Forestry and Natural Resources, 175 Marsteller St., West Lafayette, IN 47907-2033. Phone: (765)494-3619; Fax: (765)496-1344; Email: ehaviar@purdue.edu • URL: http://ag.purdue.edu/fnr/Pages/labwoodresearch.aspx • Use of wood and wood-base materials in engineered structures, ranging from furniture through residential and industrial/commercial building components; wood processing of wood and wood-base materials into furniture and cabinetry; structural applications of wood-base composites; and use, re-use, and care of wood in historic preservation and restoration. Research includes cross-disciplinary projects with engineering disciplines in simulation, machine vision and CAD.

STATISTICS SOURCES

Annual Benchmark Report for Retail Trade and Food Services..A Detailed Summary of Retail Sales, Purchases, Accounts Receivable, Inventories, and Food Service Sales. U. S. Government Printing Office. • Annual. $13.00. Issued by the U.S. Census Bureau. Provides detailed annual and monthly retail statistics for the most recent 10 years. Includes data for various kinds of retail outlets, including automobiles, furniture, appliances, building supplies, grocery stores, drug stores, gasoline stations, clothing, sporting goods, department stores, and restaurants.

Survey of Current Business. U. S. Government Printing Office. • Published by Bureau of Economic Analysis, U. S. Department of Commerce. Presents a wide variety of business and economic data.

TRADE/PROFESSIONAL ASSOCIATIONS

American Home Furnishings Alliance. 1912 Eastchester Dr., Ste. 100, High Point, NC 27265. Phone: (336)884-5000; Fax: (336)884-5303 • URL: http://www.ahfa.us • Furniture manufacturers seeking to provide a unified voice for the furniture industry and to aid in the development of industry personnel. Provides: market research data; industrial relations services; costs and operating statistics; transportation information; general management and information services. Compiles statistics; develops quarterly Econometric Forecast.

North American Home Furnishings Association. 500 Giuseppe Ct., Ste. 6, Roseville, CA 95678. Phone: 800-422-3778 or (916)784-7677; Fax: (916)784-7697; Email: sbradley@nahfa.org • URL: http://www.nahfa.org • Provides business services to help retailers of home furnishings grow their businesses. Provides educational programs for retail sales managers and trainers, for middle management, for owners and executives, and for family businesses.

FUTURES, FINANCIAL

See FINANCIAL FUTURES TRADING

FUTURES TRADING

See COMMODITY FUTURES TRADING

FUTURISTICS

ABSTRACTS AND INDEXES

The Futurist. World Future Society. • $89 Institutions libraries. Monthly. Individuals, $98.00 per year; libraries, $145.00 per year.

ALMANACS AND YEARBOOKS

Vital Signs: The Trends That Are Shaping Our Future (year). Worldwatch Institute. • Annual. $19.95. Provides access to selected indicators showing social, economic, and environmental trends throughout the world. Includes data relating to food, energy, transportation, finance, population, and other topics.

BIBLIOGRAPHIES

Future Survey Annual: A Guide to the Recent Literature of Trends, Forecasts, and Policy Proposals. World Future Society. • Annual. $35.00.

DIRECTORIES

World Futures Studies Federation Membership Directory. World Futures Studies Federation. • Annual. Publication includes: List of over 700 member individuals and 60 institutions with an interest in the study of the world's future. Entries include: Name, address, phone, fax, e-mail.

PERIODICALS AND NEWSLETTERS

Futures Research Quarterly. World Future Society. • Quarterly. Members, $77.00 per year; others, $99.00 per year.

The Futurist: A Journal of Forecasts, Trends, and Ideas About the Future. World Future Society. • Bimonthly. $89 Institutions.

The Trends Journal: The Authority on Trends Management. Gerald Celente, editor. Trends Research Institute. • Quarterly. $185.00 per year. Newsletter. Provides forecasts on a wide variety of economic, social, and political topics. Includes "Hot Trends to Watch.".

21.C: Scanning the Future: A Magazine of Culture, Technology, and Science. International Publishers Distributors. • Quarterly. $24.00 per year. Contains multidisciplinary articles relating to the 21st century.

World Watch: Working for a Sustainable Future. Worldwatch Institute. • Bimonthly. $25.00 per year. Emphasis is on environmental trends, including developments in population growth, climate change, human behavior, the role of government, and other factors.

RESEARCH CENTERS AND INSTITUTES

Institute for Alternative Futures. 100 N Pitt St., Ste. 307, Alexandria, VA 22314-3134. Phone: (703)684-5880; Fax: (703)684-0640; Email: futurist@altfutures.org • URL: http://www.altfutures.org • Conducts studies in the future of communications, health care, bioengineering, the legal system, etc.

Tel Aviv University - Interdisciplinary Center for Technology Analysis and Forecasting. Ramat Aviv, 69978 Tel Aviv, Israel. Phone: 972 3 6407571; Email: tsofer@eng.tau.ac.il • URL: http://ictaf.tau.ac.il/index.asp?lang=eng • Center assists decision makers through forecasting studies on issues of national interest as well as high-tech strategy, and translates findings into short-term decisions. Areas of interest include systems analysis, chemistry, economics, physics, mechanical engineering, electronics, operations research, sociology, statistics, business administration, production engineering, information science, science policy, high-tech strategy, urban planning, space and remote sensing.

G

GAMBLING INDUSTRY

DIRECTORIES

American Casino Guide. Casino Vacations. • Annual. $18.95 Individuals plus shipping charges. Covers: more than 700 casino/resorts, riverboat casinos, and Indian casinos in the U.S. Database includes: Maps, photos. Entries include: Casino name, address, phone, toll-free number, room rates, dining information, games offered, features, web site addresses.

Casino Gaming in the United States: A Research Guide. The Scarecrow Press Inc. • $95 Individuals Hardback. Covers: Bibliography of nearly 900 books, articles, periodicals, Internet sites and government publications from 1985-94 on casino gambling. Also includes state gambling agencies, associations, Indian gaming locations, consultants, and public gaming companies. Entries include: For publications--Publication title, subject, author, web site address where applicable. For organizations--Name, address, phone.

Casinos Directory. InfoGroup Inc. • Annual. Number of listings: 1,792. Entries include: Name, address, phone, size of advertisement, name of owner or manager, number of employees, year first in "Yellow Pages." Compiled from telephone company "Yellow Pages," nationwide.

Plunkett's Airline, Hotel, and Travel Industry Almanac. Plunkett Research Ltd. • Annual. $349.99. Contains profiles of 300 leading companies, including airlines, hotels, travel agencies, theme parks, cruise lines, casinos, and car rental companies.

E-BOOKS

Encyclopedia of Emerging Industries. Cengage Learning Inc. • $546 6th edition. Provides detailed information on 140 "newly flourishing" industries. Includes historical background, organizational structure, significant individuals, current conditions, major companies, work force, technology trends, research developments, and other industry facts.

PERIODICALS AND NEWSLETTERS

Bottomline. Hospitality Financial and Technology Professionals. • Bimonthly. Free to members, educational institutions and libraries; non-members, $50.00 per year. Contains articles on accounting, finance, information technology, and management for hotels, resorts, casinos, clubs, and other hospitality businesses.

Casino Chronicle: A Weekly Newsletter Focusing on the Gaming Industry. Ben Borowsky. • 48 times a year. $175.00 per year. Newsletter focusing on the Atlantic City gambling industry.

Hospitality Technology: Guiding High-Growth Businesses to Best-Choice IT Solutions. Edgell Communications Inc. • 10/year. Covers information technology, computer communications, and software for foodservice and lodging enterprises.

International Gaming and Wagering Business. Gem Communications. • Monthly. $113.00 per year.

STATISTICS SOURCES

Standard & Poor's Industry Surveys. Standard & Poor's Financial Services L.L.C. • Semiannual. $1,800.00. Two looseleaf volumes. Includes monthly *Supplements*. Provides detailed, individual surveys of 52 major industry groups. Each survey is revised on a semiannual basis. Also includes "Monthly Investment Review" (industry group investment analysis) and monthly "Trends & Projections" (economic analysis).

TRADE/PROFESSIONAL ASSOCIATIONS

National Council on Problem Gambling. 730 11th St. NW, Ste. 601, Washington, DC 20001. Phone: 800-522-4700 or (202)547-9204; Fax: (202)547-9206; Email: ncpg@ncpgambling.org • URL: http://www.ncpgambling.org • Advocates for programs and services to assist problem gamblers and their families. Formerly National Council on Compulsive Gambling.

GAMES

See TOY INDUSTRY

GAMES, MANAGEMENT

See MANAGEMENT GAMES

GARAGES

See GASOLINE SERVICE STATIONS

GARBAGE DISPOSAL

See SANITATION INDUSTRY

GARDEN SUPPLY INDUSTRY

See also LAWN CARE INDUSTRY

DIRECTORIES

Directory of Chinese Manufacturers & Exporters of Garden Tools, Equipment & Supplies. EXIM Infotek Private Ltd. • $5 Individuals. Covers: 20 Chinese manufacturers and exporters of garden decorations, garden products, garden tools, and garden tools-all kinds. Entries include: Company name, postal address, city, country, phone, fax, e-mail and websites, contact person, designation, and product details.

Directory of Taiwanese Manufacturers & Exporters of Garden Tools, Equipment & Supplies. EXIM Infotek Private Ltd. • $10 Individuals. Covers: 70 Taiwanese manufacturers and exporters of garden irrigation accessories, garden tools, and garden tools-all kinds. Entries include: Company name, postal address, city, country, phone, fax, e-mail and websites, contact person, designation, and product details.

Gardeners Directory. InfoGroup Inc. • Annual. Number of listings: 33,994. Entries include: Name, address, phone, size of advertisement, name of owner or manager, number of employees, year first in "Yellow Pages." Compiled from telephone company "Yellow Pages," nationwide.

Green Industry Pros. Cygnus Business Media Inc. • Irregular. Nine times a year. Includes retailers and distributors of lawn and garden power equipment, lawn and plant care products, patio furniture, etc. Arranged by type of product. Includes a *Product* issue.

The International Directory of Importers - Garden, Lawn and Patio Equipment and Supplies Importers. Interdata. • $295 Individuals print edition. Covers: 3,800 international firms importing garden, lawn, patio equipment and supplies. Entries include: Company name and address, contact person, email, number of employees, year established, phone and telefaxes, business activity, bank references, as well as a listing of garden, lawn, patio equipment and supplies currently being imported.

STATISTICS SOURCES

U.S. Industry and Trade Outlook. U.S. Department of Commerce National Technical Information Service. • Annual. Produced by the International Trade Administration, U.S. Department of Commerce, in a "public-private" partnership with DRI/McGraw-Hill and Standard & Poor's. Provides basic data, outlook for the current year, and "Long-Term Prospects" (five-year projections) for a wide variety of products and services. Includes high technology industries. Formerly *U.S. Industrial Outlook*.

GARMENT INDUSTRY

See CLOTHING INDUSTRY

GAS AND OIL ENGINES

See ENGINES

GAS APPLIANCES

DIRECTORIES

Kitchen and Bath Business Buyers' Guide. CMP Books. • Guide to kitchen and bath products, supplies and services. Formerly *Kitchen and Bath Business and Buyers' Guide/Almanac.*

TRADE/PROFESSIONAL ASSOCIATIONS

American Society of Gas Engineers. PO Box 66, Artesia, CA 90702. Phone: (949)733-4304; Email: asgecge@aol.com • URL: http://www.asge-national.org • Serves as professional society of engineers in the field of gas appliances and equipment.

GAS COMPANIES

See PUBLIC UTILITIES

GAS ENGINES

See ENGINES

GAS INDUSTRY

See also NATURAL GAS; PROPANE AND BUTANE GAS INDUSTRY; PUBLIC UTILITIES

CD-ROM DATABASES

OECD Statistical Compendium. Organization for Economic Cooperation and Development. • Semiannual. $1,905.00 per year for 1 to 10 users. CD-ROM contains more than 730,000 monthly, quarterly, and annual time series for OECD countries, 1960 to date. Includes fully searchable data on agriculture, food, economic indicators, national accounts, employment, energy, finance, industry, technology, and foreign trade. Results can be displayed in various forms.

DIRECTORIES

Major Chemical and Petrochemical Companies of the World. Cengage Learning Inc. • Annual. $1,460 Individuals. 2008. 12th edition. eBook. Published by Graham & Whiteside. Contains profiles of more than 8,500 important chemical and petrochemical companies in various countries. Subject areas include general chemicals, specialty chemicals, agricultural chemicals, petrochemicals, industrial gases, and fertilizers.

Oil and Gas Asia Business Directory. AP Energy Business Publications Private Ltd. • Annual. Drilling and production companies, pipeline contractors and operators, refinery, petrochemical and gas processing operators, equipment and service companies.

ENCYCLOPEDIAS AND DICTIONARIES

Manual of Oil and Gas Terms. Matthew Bender and Company Inc. • $148.00. 15th edition. Defines technical, legal, and tax terms relating to the oil and gas industry.

GENERAL WORKS

Gas Business. Society of British Gas Industries. • Quarterly. Publication covering gases.

HANDBOOKS AND MANUALS

Mergent's Public Utility Manual. Mergent Inc. • Annual. $1,995.00. Updated weekly online. Contains financial and other information concerning publicly-held utility companies (electric, gas, telephone, water).

World Gas Handbook. Energy Intelligence Group. • Annual. Contains the gas industry structure, policies, markets, and production data for each of about 50 countries. Also includes detailed profiles of 56 major gas producers.

INTERNET DATABASES

Business 2.0 Web Guide to the Best Business Links. Business 2.0 Media Inc. Phone: (415)293-4800; Email: support@business2.com • URL: http://www.business2.com/webguide • Web site presents an extensive, searchable directory of links to "the best, most informative, and authoritative web pages." Twenty main categories cover business, finance, career, company information, people, and technology topics, with thousands of subtopics, all linking to Web sites recommended by experienced business researchers. Fees: Free.

Fedstats. Federal Interagency Council on Statistical Policy. Phone: (202)395-7254 • URL: http://www.fedstats.gov • Web site features an efficient search facility for full-text statistics produced by more than 100 federal agencies, including the Census Bureau, the Bureau of Economic Analysis, and the Bureau of Labor Statistics. Boolean searches can be made within one agency or for all agencies combined. Links are offered to international statistical bureaus, including the UN, IMF, OECD, UNESCO, Eurostat, and 20 individual countries. Fees: Free.

FreeLunch.com. Economy.com, Inc. Phone: (610)696-8700; Fax: (610)696-1678 • URL: http://www.freelunch.com • Web site provides free access to more than 200 million economic and financial data series, covering industry, demographics, labor markets, prices, retail sales, government spending, trade, interest rates, housing starts, the stock market, etc. Data is available in either chart or table form. Searching is offered. Free, but registration required. Economy.com, Inc. also offers fee-based economic analysis at *The Dismal Scientist* site (www.dismal.com).

OTHER SOURCES

Federal Taxation of Oil and Gas Transactions. Matthew Bender and Company Inc. • $771 book. Covers the depletion deduction; tax treament of costs incurred in drilling; oil and gas partnerships; equipment depreciation, and more.

PERIODICALS AND NEWSLETTERS

American Gas: The Monthly Magazine of the American Gas Association. American Gas Association. • Monthly. $59 Nonmembers U.S. & Canada. Magazine for gas distribution and transmission industry senior and mid-level executives focusing on business, legislative, regulatory, and technical issues.

Biofuels Business. Sosland Publishing Co. • Magazine covering the ethanol and biodiesel industries.

Gas Utility Manager. James Informational Media Inc. • Monthly. $95 Free to qualified subscribers USA. Trade magazine covering the natural gas market for industry professionals. Formerly *Gas Utility and Pipeline Industries.*

Oil and Gas Journal. PennWell Corp., Industrial Div. • Weekly. $84.00 per year.

Oil, Gas and Energy Quarterly. Matthew Bender and Company Inc. • Quarterly. $474.00 per year. Covers latest tax ideas, techniques, and practice pointers in oil and gas taxation and accounting features.

Petroleum Management: The International Business Magazine for the Oil and Gas Industry. Management Publishing Services. • Monthly. $36. Trade magazine.

Utility Business. Penton. • Monthly. Trade magazine covering the utility industry for executives, managers and others in the electric, gas, water and telecommunications utility business.

PRICE SOURCES

AGA Rate Service. American Gas Association. • Semiannual. $175 Members. Looseleaf service.

STATISTICS SOURCES

Standard & Poor's Industry Surveys. Standard & Poor's Financial Services L.L.C. • Semiannual. $1,800.00. Two looseleaf volumes. Includes monthly *Supplements.* Provides detailed, individual surveys of 52 major industry groups. Each survey is revised on a semiannual basis. Also includes "Monthly Investment Review" (industry group investment analysis) and monthly "Trends & Projections" (economic analysis).

Survey of Current Business. U. S. Government Printing Office. • Published by Bureau of Economic Analysis, U. S. Department of Commerce. Presents a wide variety of business and economic data.

TRADE/PROFESSIONAL ASSOCIATIONS

American Gas Association. 400 N Capitol St. NW, Washington, DC 20001. Phone: (202)824-7000; Email: ggardner@aga.org • URL: http://www.aga.org • Advocates for local natural gas utility companies; provides a broad range of programs and services for member natural gas pipelines, marketers, gatherers, international gas companies and industry associates.

American Public Gas Association. 201 Massachusetts Ave. NE, Ste. C-4, Washington, DC 20002. Phone: 800-927-4204 or (202)464-2742; Fax: (202)464-0246 • URL: http://www.apga.org/ • Publicly owned gas systems; private corporations, persons or firms dealing with public gas systems are associate members. Promotes efficiency among public gas systems and protects the interests of the gas consumer. Provides information service on federal developments affecting natural gas; surveys municipal systems.

National Propane Gas Association. 1899 L St. NW, Ste. 350, Washington, DC 20036-4623. Phone: (202)466-7200; Fax: (202)466-7205; Email: info@npga.org • URL: http://www.npga.org/i4a/pages/index.cfm?pageid=1 • Represents the propane industry, including small businesses and large corporations engaged in the retail marketing of propane gas and appliances, producers and wholesalers of propane gas and equipment, manufacturers and fabricators of propane gas cylinders and tanks, propane transporters, and manufacturer's representatives. Works to promote the safe and increased use of propane; advocates in Congress and federal regulatory agencies for favorable environment for production, distributing, and marketing of propane gas. Develops safety standards and training materials for the safe use and distribution of propane gas.

GAS, LIQUEFIED PETROLEUM

See PROPANE AND BUTANE GAS INDUSTRY

GAS, NATURAL

See NATURAL GAS

GAS PIPELINES

See PIPELINE INDUSTRY

GAS RATES

See GAS INDUSTRY

GASOHOL

See FUEL

For publishers' addresses, refer to SOURCES CITED section at the back of the book.

GASOLINE ENGINES

See ENGINES

GASOLINE INDUSTRY

See also GAS INDUSTRY; PETROLEUM INDUSTRY

CD-ROM DATABASES

OECD Statistical Compendium. Organization for Economic Cooperation and Development. • Semiannual. $1,905.00 per year for 1 to 10 users. CD-ROM contains more than 730,000 monthly, quarterly, and annual time series for OECD countries, 1960 to date. Includes fully searchable data on agriculture, food, economic indicators, national accounts, employment, energy, finance, industry, technology, and foreign trade. Results can be displayed in various forms.

INTERNET DATABASES

Business 2.0 Web Guide to the Best Business Links. Business 2.0 Media Inc. Phone: (415)293-4800; Email: support@business2.com • URL: http://www.business2.com/webguide • Web site presents an extensive, searchable directory of links to "the best, most informative, and authoritative web pages." Twenty main categories cover business, finance, career, company information, people, and technology topics, with thousands of subtopics, all linking to Web sites recommended by experienced business researchers. Fees: Free.

Fedstats. Federal Interagency Council on Statistical Policy. Phone: (202)395-7254 • URL: http://www.fedstats.gov • Web site features an efficient search facility for full-text statistics produced by more than 100 federal agencies, including the Census Bureau, the Bureau of Economic Analysis, and the Bureau of Labor Statistics. Boolean searches can be made within one agency or for all agencies combined. Links are offered to international statistical bureaus, including the UN, IMF, OECD, UNESCO, Eurostat, and 20 individual countries. Fees: Free.

FreeLunch.com. Economy.com, Inc. Phone: (610)696-8700; Fax: (610)696-1678 • URL: http://www.freelunch.com • Web site provides free access to more than 200 million economic and financial data series, covering industry, demographics, labor markets, prices, retail sales, government spending, trade, interest rates, housing starts, the stock market, etc. Data is available in either chart or table form. Searching is offered. Free, but registration required. Economy.com, Inc. also offers fee-based economic analysis at *The Dismal Scientist* site (www.dismal.com).

PERIODICALS AND NEWSLETTERS

International Oil News. William F. Bland Co. • Description: Covers "timely and significant developments in the international oil business, including exploration, production, transportation, refining, and marketing.".

Lundberg Letter. Lundberg Survey Inc. • Description: Provides statistics and analysis of U.S. oil marketing primary data. Includes an in-depth single-subject profile of a development in the petroleum market in each issue. Discusses such topics as retail/wholesale pricing, market shares, and station characteristics nationwide and regionally.

Oil and Gas Journal. PennWell Corp., Industrial Div. • Weekly. $84.00 per year.

PRICE SOURCES

CPI Detailed Report: Consumer Price Index. U. S. Government Printing Office. • Monthly. $45 Individuals. Cost of living data.

STATISTICS SOURCES

Annual Energy Outlook, with Projections to (year). U. S. Government Printing Office. • Annual. $39.00. Issued by the Energy Information Administration, U. S. Department of Energy (www.eia.doe.gov). Contains detailed statistics and 20-year projections for electricity, oil, natural gas, coal, and renewable energy. Text provides extensive discussion of energy issues and "Market Trends.".

Petroleum Supply Annual. U. S. Government Printing Office. • Annual. $78.00. Two volumes. Produced by the Energy Information Administration, U. S. Department of Energy. Contains worldwide data on the petroleum industry and petroleum products.

Petroleum Supply Monthly. U. S. Government Printing Office. • Monthly. Produced by the Energy Information Administration, U. S. Department of Energy. Provides worldwide statistics on a wide variety of petroleum products. Covers production, supplies, exports and imports, transportation, refinery operations, and other aspects of the petroleum industry.

Standard & Poor's Industry Surveys. Standard & Poor's Financial Services L.L.C. • Semiannual. $1,800.00. Two looseleaf volumes. Includes monthly *Supplements*. Provides detailed, individual surveys of 52 major industry groups. Each survey is revised on a semiannual basis. Also includes "Monthly Investment Review" (industry group investment analysis) and monthly "Trends & Projections" (economic analysis).

Survey of Current Business. U. S. Government Printing Office. • Published by Bureau of Economic Analysis, U. S. Department of Commerce. Presents a wide variety of business and economic data.

Weekly Petroleum Status Report. Energy Information Administration. U. S. Government Printing Office. • Weekly. Current statistics in the context of both historical information and selected prices and forecasts.

GASOLINE SERVICE STATIONS

See also GASOLINE INDUSTRY

CD-ROM DATABASES

OECD Statistical Compendium. Organization for Economic Cooperation and Development. • Semiannual. $1,905.00 per year for 1 to 10 users. CD-ROM contains more than 730,000 monthly, quarterly, and annual time series for OECD countries, 1960 to date. Includes fully searchable data on agriculture, food, economic indicators, national accounts, employment, energy, finance, industry, technology, and foreign trade. Results can be displayed in various forms.

FINANCIAL RATIOS

Annual Statement Studies. Risk Management Association. • Annual. Compiled from over 280,000 financial statements.

Annual Statement Studies: Industry Default Probabilities and Cash Flow Measures. Risk Management Association. • Annual. $405 Nonmembers. Serves as a companion volume to the original *Annual Statement Studies*. Gives probability of default estimates on a percentage scale for more than 450 industries. Includes changes in position year-by-year for eight financial statement line items and provides percentage measures of cash flow.

INTERNET DATABASES

Advance Monthly Retail Trade Report. U. S. Census Bureau. Phone: 800-541-8345 or (301)457-4100 or (301)763-2713; Fax: (301)457-1296 or (301)457-3842; Email: naics@census.gov • URL: http://www.census.gov/epcd/www/naicstab.htm • Web pages provide monthly sales figures for a wide range of retail businesses. Advance, preliminary, and final statistics are provided for the latest month available in each case, with a previous-year comparison. Updates are monthly.

Business 2.0 Web Guide to the Best Business Links. Business 2.0 Media Inc. Phone: (415)293-4800; Email: support@business2.com • URL: http://www.business2.com/webguide • Web site presents an extensive, searchable directory of links to "the best, most informative, and authoritative web pages." Twenty main categories cover business, finance, career, company information, people, and technology topics, with thousands of subtopics, all linking to Web sites recommended by experienced business researchers. Fees: Free.

Fedstats. Federal Interagency Council on Statistical Policy. Phone: (202)395-7254 • URL: http://www.fedstats.gov • Web site features an efficient search facility for full-text statistics produced by more than 100 federal agencies, including the Census Bureau, the Bureau of Economic Analysis, and the Bureau of Labor Statistics. Boolean searches can be made within one agency or for all agencies combined. Links are offered to international statistical bureaus, including the UN, IMF, OECD, UNESCO, Eurostat, and 20 individual countries. Fees: Free.

FreeLunch.com. Economy.com, Inc. Phone: (610)696-8700; Fax: (610)696-1678 • URL: http://www.freelunch.com • Web site provides free access to more than 200 million economic and financial data series, covering industry, demographics, labor markets, prices, retail sales, government spending, trade, interest rates, housing starts, the stock market, etc. Data is available in either chart or table form. Searching is offered. Free, but registration required. Economy.com, Inc. also offers fee-based economic analysis at *The Dismal Scientist* site (www.dismal.com).

PERIODICALS AND NEWSLETTERS

Motor Age: For the Professional Automotive Import and Domestic Service Industry. Reed Elsevier Group plc Reed Business Information. • Monthly. $49.00 per year. Published for independent automotive repair shops and gasoline service stations.

Oil Express: Inside Report on Trends in Petroleum Marketing Without the Influence of Advertising. UCG Holdings L.P. • 50 times a year. $337.00 per year. Newsletter. Provides news of trends in petroleum marketing and convenience store operations. Includes *U.S. Oil Week's Price Monitor* (petroleum product prices) and *C-Store Digest* (news concerning convenience stores operated by the major oil companies) and *Fuel Oil Update*. Formerly *U.S. Oil Week*.

STATISTICS SOURCES

Annual Benchmark Report for Retail Trade and Food Services..A Detailed Summary of Retail Sales, Purchases, Accounts Receivable, Inventories, and Food Service Sales. U. S. Government Printing Office. • Annual. $13.00. Issued by the U.S. Census Bureau. Provides detailed annual and monthly retail statistics for the most recent 10 years. Includes data for various kinds of retail outlets, including automobiles, furniture, appliances, building supplies, grocery stores, drug stores, gasoline stations, clothing, sporting goods, department stores, and restaurants.

Survey of Current Business. U. S. Government Printing Office. • Published by Bureau of Economic Analysis, U. S. Department of Commerce. Presents a wide variety of business and economic data.

United States Census of Service Industries. U.S. Department of Commerce U.S. Census Bureau. • Quinquennial. Various reports available.

TRADE/PROFESSIONAL ASSOCIATIONS

Automotive Service Association. 8190 Precinct Line Rd., Ste. 100, Colleyville, TX 76034-7675. Phone: 800-272-7467 or (817)514-2900; Fax: (817)514-0770; Email: asainfo@asashop.org • URL: http://

www.asashop.org • Automotive service businesses including body, paint, and trim shops, engine rebuilders, radiator shops, brake and wheel alignment services, transmission shops, tune-up services, and air conditioning services; associate members are manufacturers and wholesalers of automotive parts, and the trade press. Represents independent business owners and managers before private agencies and national and state legislative bodies. Promotes confidence between consumer and the automotive service industry, safety inspection of motor vehicles, and better highways.

GAUGES

See TOOL INDUSTRY

GEAR INDUSTRY

See also MACHINERY

ABSTRACTS AND INDEXES

Applied Science and Technology Index. EBSCO Publishing Inc. • 11/year. Indexes a wide variety of English language technical, industrial, and engineering periodicals.

Engineering Index Monthly: Abstracting and Indexing Services Covering Sources ofthe World's Engineering Literature. Engineering Information Inc. • Monthly. Institutions, $5,279.00 per year. Provides indexing and abstracting of the world's engineering and technical literature.

F & S Index: United States. Cengage Learning Inc. • $2,659 Individuals. Monthly. $2,532.00 per year, including quarterly and annual cumulations. Provides annotated citations to marketing, business, financial, and industrial literature. Coverage of U.S. business activity includes trade journals, financial magazines, business newspapers, and special reports.

NTIS Alerts: Manufacturing Technology. U.S. Department of Commerce National Technical Information Service. • Biweekly. $130 per year. Covers computer-aided design and manufacturing (CAD/CAM), engineering materials, quality control, machine tools, robots, lasers, productivity, and related subjects.

CD-ROM DATABASES

Applied Science and Technology Abstracts. EBSCO Publishing Inc. • Citations for more than 700 prominent scientific, technical, engineering, and industrial periodicals.

DIRECTORIES

Directory of American Manufacturers & Exporters of Gears & Gears Boxes. EXIM Infotek Private Ltd. • $15 Individuals. Covers: 150 American manufacturers and exporters of custom gears, gear boxes, gears, gears-bevel, gears-helical, gears-helical and worm, gears-instruments, gears-master, gears-miter, gears-pinions, gears-plastic, gears-precision, gears-racks, gears-speed reducers, gears-spiral bevel, gears-splines, gears-sprocket, gears-spur, gears-straight and spiral bevel, gears-worms, and zerol and hypoid gears. Entries include: Company name, postal address, city, country, phone, fax, e-mail and websites, contact person, designation, and product details.

Directory of European Importers of Gears & Boxes. EXIM Infotek Private Ltd. • $10 Individuals. Covers: 90 European importers of gears and boxes. Entries include: Company name, postal address, telephone, fax, e-mail, website, contact person, designation, and product details.

Directory of South Korean Manufacturers & Exporters of Gears & Gears Boxes. EXIM Infotek Private Ltd. • $5 Individuals. Covers: 20 South Korean manufacturers and exporters of gear boxes and gears. Entries include: Company name, postal address, city, country, phone, fax, e-mail and websites, contact person, designation, and product details.

Directory of Taiwanese Manufacturers & Exporters of Gears & Gears Boxes. EXIM Infotek Private Ltd. • $10 Individuals. Covers: 70 Taiwanese manufacturers and exporters of gears, worm gear reducers.

ONLINE DATABASES

Applied Science and Technology Index Online. H.W. Wilson Co. • Provides online indexing of 500 major scientific, technical, industrial, and engineering periodicals. Time period is 1983 to date. Monthly updates. Inquire as to online cost and availability.

PERIODICALS AND NEWSLETTERS

Gear Technology: The Journal of Gear Manufacturing. Randall Publishing Inc. • Bimonthly. $45 Individuals. Edited for manufacturers, engineers, and designers of gears.

RESEARCH CENTERS AND INSTITUTES

Ohio State University - Gear and Power Transmission Research Laboratory. Department of Mechanical and Aerospace Engineering, 201 W 19th Ave., Columbus, OH 43210. Phone: (614)292-4678 or (614)688-3952; Fax: (614)292-3163; Email: kahraman.1@osu.edu • URL: http://gearlab.org • Transmission error prediction for spur and helical gears, load distribution prediction, finite element modeling, vibration signal analysis, acoustic intensity measurements, and gear testing. Supports graduate student research.

TRADE/PROFESSIONAL ASSOCIATIONS

American Gear Manufacturers Association. 1001 N Fairfax St., Ste. 500, Alexandria, VA 22314-1587. Phone: (703)684-0211; Fax: (703)684-0242; Email: foundation@agma.org • URL: http://www.agma.org • Represents manufacturers of gears, geared speed changers and related equipment; manufacturers of gear cutting and checking equipment; teachers of mechanical engineering and gearing. Conducts educational and research programs; compiles statistics and financial data. Develops technical standards for domestic and international industry.

GEMS AND GEMSTONES

See also JEWELRY BUSINESS

DIRECTORIES

Directory of Japanese Manufacturers & Exporters of Gemstones & Diamonds. EXIM Infotek Private Ltd. • $5 Individuals. Covers: 30 Japanese manufacturers and exporters of crystal, cultured pearls, diamonds, natural pearls, precious stones. Entries include: Company name, postal address, city, country, phone, fax, e-mail and websites, contact person, designation, and product details.

Directory of South Korean Manufacturers & Exporters of Gemstones & Diamonds. EXIM Infotek Private Ltd. • $5 Individuals. Covers: 20 South Korean manufacturers and exporters of colored precious stones-polished, diamond-polished, diamonds-rough, ivory/coral/pearl articles, and rough colored precious stones. Entries include: Company name, postal address, city, country, phone, fax, e-mail and websites, contact person, designation, and product details.

PERIODICALS AND NEWSLETTERS

Gems & Gemology: The Quarterly Journal of GIA. Gemological Institute of America. • Quarterly. $79.99 Individuals print only. Peer-reviewed scientific journal covering gemology and related issues: diamonds, colored stones, treatments, synthetics, identification techniques, gem instruments, innovative jewelry and lapidary arts.

Modern Jeweler. Cygnus Business Media. • Monthly. $60.00 per year. Edited for retail jewelers. Covers the merchandising of jewelry, gems, and watches. Supersedes in part *Modern Jeweler*.

Spectra. National Communication Association. • Description: Discusses forensics, interpretation, interpersonal communication, rhetoric and public address, communication theory, mass media, theater, speech and language sciences, and job advertising. Recurring features include official business of the Association, news briefs concerning members, and notices of available materials.

TRADE/PROFESSIONAL ASSOCIATIONS

American Gem Society. 8881 W Sahara Ave., Las Vegas, NV 89117. Phone: 866-805-6500 or (702)255-6500; Fax: (702)255-7420; Email: rbatson@ags.org • URL: http://www.americangemsociety.org • Represents 1,600 retail and manufacturer jewelry firms in North America dedicated to proven ethics, knowledge and consumer protection. Encourages members to pursue studies in gemology; confers titles of Registered Jeweler, Registered Supplier, Certified Gemologist, and Certified Gemologist Appraiser upon those taking recognized courses and passing extensive examinations. Sponsors national promotional programs. Conducts educational programs.

American Gem Trade Association. 3030 LBJ Fwy., Ste. 840, Dallas, TX 75234. Phone: 800-972-1162 or (214)742-4367; Fax: (214)742-7334; Email: webmaster@agta.org • URL: http://www.agta.org • Represents suppliers of natural colored gemstones; retail jewelers and jewelry manufacturers. Promotes natural colored gemstones; encourages high ethical standards among members and within the industry. Seeks to establish closer communication within the industry; works to protect consumers from fraud and to create a greater awareness of natural colored gemstones. Conducts seminars; maintains speakers' bureau.

GENERAL AGREEMENT ON TARIFFS AND TRADE (GATT)

PERIODICALS AND NEWSLETTERS

Economic Justice Report: Global Issues of Economic Justice. Ecumenical Coalition for Economic Justice. • Quarterly. Individuals, $30.00 per year; institutions, $40.00 per year. Reports on economic fairness in foreign trade. Formerly *Gatt-Fly Report*.

GENERAL AVIATION

See BUSINESS AVIATION

GENERATORS, ELECTRIC

See ELECTRICAL EQUIPMENT INDUSTRY

GENERIC DRUG INDUSTRY

See also PHARMACEUTICAL INDUSTRY

ABSTRACTS AND INDEXES

Business Periodicals Index Retrospective. EBSCO Publishing Inc. • 11/year. Quarterly and annual cumulations.

International Pharmaceutical Abstracts: Key to the World's Literature of Pharmacy. American Society of Health-System Pharmacists. • Semimonthly. $565.50 per year.

CD-ROM DATABASES

ABI/INFORM. ProQuest L.L.C. • Monthly. Provides CD-ROM indexing and abstracting of worldwide business literature. Archival discs are available from 1971. Formerly *ABI/INFORM OnDisc*.

Business Abstracts with Full Text. EBSCO Publishing Inc. • Includes full text articles from more than 460 business publications from 1982 to present. Indexing for nearly 880 publications.

International Pharmaceutical Abstracts. Ovid Technologies Inc. • Quarterly. International pharmaceutical literature from 1970 to date.

Mosby's GenRx (year). CME Inc. • Quarterly. $250. 00. CD-ROM contains detailed monographs for more than 45,000 generic and brand name prescription drugs. Includes color pill images and customizable patient education handouts.

DIRECTORIES

Red Book. American Monument Association. • Annual. $60. Covers: 7,000 retail monument dealers, suppliers of granite and marble, wholesalers, quarriers, funeral homes and cemeteries. Entries include: company; name, address, phone, fax; trade classification, names of owner or corporate officers and their titles. Available only to members of The American Monument Association.

HANDBOOKS AND MANUALS

Approved Drug Products, with Therapeutic Equivalence Evaluations. U. S. Government Printing Office. • $273 U.S.. Issued by the Food and Drug Administration, U. S. Department of Health and Human Services. Lists prescription drugs that have been approved by the FDA. Includes therapeutic equivalents to aid in containment of health costs and to serve State drug selection laws.

Physicians' Desk Reference. Medical Economics Co. • Annual. $82.95. Generally known as "PDR." Provides detailed descriptions, effects, and adverse reactions for about 4,000 prescription drugs. Includes data on more than 250 drug manufacturers, with brand name and generic name indexes and drug identification photographs. Discontinued drugs are also listed.

INTERNET DATABASES

National Library of Medicine. National Institutes of Health. 9000 Rockville Pke., Bethesda, MD 20892. Phone: (301)496-4000; Email: nihinfo@od.nih.gov • URL: http://www.nih.gov • NLM Web site offers free access through MEDLINE ("PubMed") to about nine million references to articles appearing in some 4,000 biomedical journals, with abstracts. Search interfaces range from "simple keywords to advanced Boolean expressions." The NLM site offers many links to other sources of biomedical and technical information (the National Center for Biotechnology Information, for example). Fees: Free.

Rx List: The Internet Drug Index. WebMD Health Corp. 111 8th Ave., New York, NY 10011. Phone: (212)624-3700 • URL: http://www.wbmd.com • Web site features detailed information (cost, usage, dosage, side effects, etc.) from Mosby, Inc. for about 300 major pharmaceutical products, representing two thirds of prescriptions filled in the U. S. (3,700 other products are listed). The "Top 200" drugs are ranked by number of prescriptions filled. Keyword searching is provided. Fees: Free.

ONLINE DATABASES

Derwent Drug File. Derwent Information Ltd. • Provides indexing and abstracting of the world's pharmaceutical journal literature since 1964, with weekly updates. Formerly *RINGDOC*. Inquire as to online cost and availability.

F-D-C Reports. Elsevier Business Intelligence. • An online version of "The Gray Sheet" (medical devices), "The Pink Sheet" (pharmaceuticals), "The Rose Sheet" (cosmetics), "The Blue Sheet" (biomedical), and "The Tan Sheet" (nonprescription). Contains full-text information on legal, technical, corporate, financial, and marketing developments from 1987 to date, with weekly updates. Inquire as to online cost and availability.

Wilson Business Abstracts Online. H.W. Wilson Co. • Indexes and abstracts 600 major business periodicals, plus the *Wall Street Journal* and the business section of the *New York Times*. Indexing is from 1982, abstracting from 1990, with the two newspapers included from 1993. Updated weekly. Inquire as to online cost and availability. (*Business Periodicals Index* without abstracts is also available online.).

PERIODICALS AND NEWSLETTERS

Drug Store News Continuing Education Quarterly. Lebhar-Friedman Inc. • Quarterly. $59.95 per year. Formerly *Drug Store News Chain Pharmacy*.

Generic Line. Scitec Services Inc. • Description: Focuses on the pharmaceutical industry, emphasizing generic products. Discusses regulatory, legislative, technical, and business developments of interest to generic and small pharmaceutical manufacturers. Recurring features include reports on current research and actions of pharmaceutical companies.

The Pink Sheet: Prescription Pharmaceuticals and Biotechnology. Elsevier Business Intelligence. • 51 times a year. Institutions, $1,431.00 per year. Newsletter covering business and regulatory developments affecting the pharmaceutical and biotechnology industries. Provides information on generic drug approvals and includes a drug sector stock index.

RESEARCH CENTERS AND INSTITUTES

University of Mississippi - Center for Pharmaceutical Marketing and Management. Faser Hall Rms. 128-136, School of Pharmacy, University, MS 38677. Phone: (662)915-5352 or (662)915-5948; Fax: (662)915-5262; Email: benb3@olemiss.edu • URL: http://www.pharmacy.olemiss.edu/cpmm • Proprietary and in-house marketing and management studies relating to pharmaceutical products, including formulary decision factors, generic substitution, reimbursement issues, medication compliance and consumer preferences. Conducts mail surveys, telephone interviews, focus groups, internet surveys, consumer reaction panels, and surveys of professionals at national and state meetings.

GENERIC PRODUCTS

See PRIVATE LABEL PRODUCTS

GENETIC ENGINEERING

See also BIOTECHNOLOGY

ABSTRACTS AND INDEXES

Applied Science and Technology Index. EBSCO Publishing Inc. • 11/year. Indexes a wide variety of English language technical, industrial, and engineering periodicals.

Excerpta Medica: Human Genetics. Elsevier. • Semimonthly. Section 22 of *Excerpta Medica*.

Genetics Abstracts. CSA. • Monthly. $1,595.00 per year. Includes print and online editions.

NTIS Alerts: Biomedical Technology & Human Factor Engineering. U.S. Department of Commerce National Technical Information Service. • Biweekly. $130 per year. Covers biotechnology, ergonomics, bionics, artificial intelligence, prosthetics, and related subjects.

CD-ROM DATABASES

Biotechnology Abstracts on CD-ROM. Thomson Derwent, Inc. • Quarterly. Price on application. Provides CD-ROM indexing and abstracting of the world's biotechnology journal literature since 1982, including genetic engineering topics.

DIRECTORIES

Genetic Engineering and Biotechnology Firms Worldwide Directory. Mega-Type Publishing. • Annual. $299.00. About 6,000 firms, including major firms with biotechnology divisions as well as small independent firms.

Plunkett's Biotech and Genetics Industry Almanac. Plunkett Research Ltd. • Annual. $349.99 Individuals. Provides detailed profiles of 400 leading biotech corporations. Includes information on current trends and research in the field of biotechnology/genetics.

E-BOOKS

Encyclopedia of Emerging Industries. Cengage Learning Inc. • $546 6th edition. Provides detailed information on 140 "newly flourishing" industries. Includes historical background, organizational structure, significant individuals, current conditions, major companies, work force, technology trends, research developments, and other industry facts.

ONLINE DATABASES

Applied Science and Technology Index Online. H.W. Wilson Co. • Provides online indexing of 500 major scientific, technical, industrial, and engineering periodicals. Time period is 1983 to date. Monthly updates. Inquire as to online cost and availability.

Biological Sciences Database. Cambridge Scientific Abstracts L.P. • Includes online versions of *Biotechnology Research Abstracts, Entomology Abstracts, Genetics Abstracts*, and about 20 other abstract collections. Time period is 1978 to date, with monthly updates. Inquire as to online cost and availability.

Derwent Biotechnology Abstracts. Derwent Information Ltd. • Provides indexing and abstracting of the world's biotechnology journal literature since 1982, including genetic engineering topics. Monthly updates. Inquire as to online cost and availability.

PERIODICALS AND NEWSLETTERS

Genetic Engineering News: The Information Source of the Biotechnology Industry. Mary Ann Liebert, Inc. • $666 Individuals. Newsletter. Business and financial coverage.

Genetic Technology News. John Wiley & Sons Inc. • Description: Informs corporate development and research managers of advances in genetic engineering with applications in medical, agricultural, chemical, food, and other businesses. Covers areas such as recombinant DNA, monoclonal antibodies, and interferon. Recurring features include news of research, company reports, a calendar of events, and supplements titled Market Forecasts, Patent Update, and Strategic Partners. **Remarks:** Also available as part of Biotechnology Information Package, which includes Industrial Bioprocessing (see separate listings).

Health Policy and Biomedical Research: The Blue Sheet. Elsevier Business Intelligence. • 51 times a year. $716.00 per year. Newsletter. Emphasis is on news of medical research agencies and institutions, especially the National Institutes of Health (NIH).

Washington Drug Letter. Washington Business Information Inc. • Description: Focuses on regulation and legislation affecting prescription and proprietary drugs. Monitors Food & Drug Administration (FDA) actions and new drug applications, manufacturing procedures, advertising and labeling, compliance cases, research, and testing rules.

RESEARCH CENTERS AND INSTITUTES

Baylor College of Medicine - Department of Molecular and Human Genetics. Baylor Clinic, 6620 Main St., 12th Fl., Ste. 1225, Houston, TX

77030. Phone: (713)798-7820 or (713)798-3651; Fax: (713)798-6450 or (713)798-6521; Email: abeaudet@bcm.tmc.edu • URL: http://www.bcm.edu/genetics/index.cfm?PMID=10398.

Carnegie Mellon Research Institute-The Robotics Institute. 5000 Forbes Ave., Pittsburgh, PA 15213. Phone: (412)268-3818; Fax: (412)268-6436; Email: robotics@ri.cmu.edu • URL: http://www.ri.cmu.edu • Multidisciplinary research activities include expert systems applications, minicomputer and microcomputer systems design, genetic engineering, and transportation systems analysis.

TRADE/PROFESSIONAL ASSOCIATIONS

American Genetic Association. c/o Anjanette Baker, Managing Editor, 2030 SE Marine Science Dr., Newport, OR 97365-5300. Phone: (541)867-0334; Email: agajoh@oregonstate.edu • URL: http://www.theaga.org • Represents biologists, zoologists, geneticists, botanists, and others engaged in basic and applied research in genetics. Explores transmission genetics of plants and animals.

Council for Responsible Genetics. 5 Upland Rd., Ste. 3, Cambridge, MA 02140-2717. Phone: (617)868-0870; Fax: (617)491-5344; Email: crg@gene-watch.org • URL: http://www.councilforresponsiblegenetics.org • Concerned with the social implications of genetic technologies. Formerly Committee for Responsible Genetics.

GEOTHERMAL ENERGY

ABSTRACTS AND INDEXES

Applied Science and Technology Index. EBSCO Publishing Inc. • 11/year. Indexes a wide variety of English language technical, industrial, and engineering periodicals.

Engineering Index Monthly: Abstracting and Indexing Services Covering Sources ofthe World's Engineering Literature. Engineering Information Inc. • Monthly. Institutions, $5,279.00 per year. Provides indexing and abstracting of the world's engineering and technical literature.

Environment Abstracts. University Publications of America. • Monthly. Price varies. Provides multidisciplinary coverage of the world's environmental literature. Incorporates *Acid Rain Abstracts*.

Environment Abstracts Annual: A Guide to the Key Environmental Literature of the Year. University Publications of America. • Annual. $495.00. A yearly cumulation of *Environment Abstracts*.

NTIS Alerts: Energy. U.S. Department of Commerce National Technical Information Service. • Biweekly. $130 per year. Covers electric power, batteries, fuels, geothermal energy, heating/cooling systems, nuclear technology, solar energy, energy policy, and related subjects.

ALMANACS AND YEARBOOKS

Earth Almanac: An Annual Geophysical Review of the State of the Planet. Natalie Goldstein. Greenwood Publishing Group Inc. • $91.95. Provides background information, statistics, and a summary of major events relating to the atmosphere, oceans, land, and fresh water.

CD-ROM DATABASES

Applied Science and Technology Abstracts. EBSCO Publishing Inc. • Citations for more than 700 prominent scientific, technical, engineering, and industrial periodicals.

Environment Abstracts on CD-ROM. University Publications of America. • Quarterly. $1,295.00 per year. Contains the following CD-ROM databases: *Environment Abstracts, Energy Abstracts*, and *Acid Rain Abstracts*. Length of coverage varies.

DIRECTORIES

Geothermal Energy System Businesses in the World. Momentum Technologies L.L.C. • Contains directory listings for more than 490 geothermal energy system businesses and related companies throughout the world. Includes business name, address, phone number, fax number, e-mail address, and web site address. Provides brief descriptions of product lines, services offered, and business type. Includes information on manufacturers, component makers, wholesalers, retailers, system designers, architectural services, system installers, trade associations, and more. Searchable by location, business type, company name, and keyword.

E-BOOKS

Macmillan Encyclopedia of Energy. Cengage Learning Inc. • 2003. eBook. Published by Macmillan Reference USA. Covers the business, technology, and history of a wide variety of energy sources. Inquire as to price and availability.

ONLINE DATABASES

Applied Science and Technology Index Online. H.W. Wilson Co. • Provides online indexing of 500 major scientific, technical, industrial, and engineering periodicals. Time period is 1983 to date. Monthly updates. Inquire as to online cost and availability.

Current Contents Connect. Thomson Reuters Intellectual Property and Science. • Provides online abstracts of articles listed in the tables of contents of about 7,500 journals. Coverage is very broad, including science, social science, life science, technology, engineering, industry, agriculture, the environment, economics, and arts and humanities. Time period is two years, with weekly updates. Inquire as to online cost and availability.

OTHER SOURCES

Major Energy Companies of the World. Cengage Learning Inc. • Annual. $1,460 Individuals. 2008. 12th edition. eBook. Published by Graham & Whiteside. Contains detailed information on more than 4,850 important energy companies in various countries. Industries include electricity generation, coal, natural gas, nuclear energy, petroleum, fuel distribution, and equipment for energy production.

PERIODICALS AND NEWSLETTERS

Geothermics: International Journal of Geothermal Research and Its Applications. Elsevier. • Bimonthly. $1,807 Institutions. Covers theory, exploration, development, and utilization of geothermal energy. Text and summaries in English and French.

Independent Energy: The Power Industry's Business Magazine. PennWell Corp., Industrial Div. • 10 times a year. $127.00 per year. Covers non-utility electric power plants (cogeneration) and other alternative sources of electric energy.

RESEARCH CENTERS AND INSTITUTES

Southern Methodist University - Geothermal Laboratory. Heroy Hall, Rm. 235, Department of Earth Sciences, 3225 Daniel Ave., Dallas, TX 75205. Phone: (214)768-2749; Email: blackwel@smu.edu • URL: http://smu.edu/geothermal • Temperature history of sedimentary basins, geothermal regime of North America, and geothermal systems in the Western U.S., especially, Nevada, the Cascade Range and the Snake River Plains. Oil and Gas well conversion to geothermal energy production.

University of Hawaii at Manoa - Hawaii Natural Energy Institute. 1680 E West Rd., Post 109, Honolulu, HI 96822. Phone: (808)956-8890; Fax: (808)956-2336; Email: hnei@hawaii.edu • URL: http://www.hnei.hawaii.edu • Research areas include geothermal, wind, solar, hydroelectric, and other energy sources.

STATISTICS SOURCES

Annual Energy Outlook, with Projections to (year). U. S. Government Printing Office. • Annual. $39.00. Issued by the Energy Information Administration, U. S. Department of Energy (www.eia.doe.gov). Contains detailed statistics and 20-year projections for electricity, oil, natural gas, coal, and renewable energy. Text provides extensive discussion of energy issues and "Market Trends.".

GIFT BUSINESS

DIRECTORIES

Directory of American Manufacturers & Exporters of Giftware & Novelties. EXIM Infotek Private Ltd. • $10 Individuals. Covers: 50 American manufacturers and exporters of ceramic mugs with logos, gift items, gift wrap, novelties, silverplate halloware and giftware cutlery. Entries include: Company name, postal address, city, country, phone, fax, e-mail and websites, contact person, designation, and product details.

Directory of Chinese Manufacturers & Exporters of Giftwares & Novelties. EXIM Infotek Private Ltd. • $10 Individuals. Covers: 90 Chinese manufacturers & exporters of Christmas articles, Christmas gifts, gifts, giftware, key chain, novelty, photo frames, picture frames, plastic photo frames, premiums, promotional items, souvenirs. Entries include: Company name, postal address, city, country, phone, fax, e-mail & websites, contact person, designation, products detail.

Directory of Japanese Manufacturers & Exporters of Giftware & Novelties. EXIM Infotek Private Ltd. • $5 Individuals. Covers: 30 Japanese manufacturers and exporters of gift items, gifts, giftware, souvenirs, trophies/ceremonial plates. Entries include: Company name, postal address, city, country, phone, fax, e-mail and websites, contact person, designation, and product details.

Directory of South Korean Manufacturers & Exporters of Giftware & Novelties. EXIM Infotek Private Ltd. • $5 Individuals. Covers: 40 South Korean manufacturers and exporters of albums and files, coins/medals/decorations and badges, key holders, medals, photo albums, photo frames, promotional giftware, and trophies/ceremonial plates. Entries include: Company name, postal address, city, country, phone, fax, e-mail and websites, contact person, designation, and product details.

Directory of Taiwanese Manufacturers & Exporters of Giftware & Novelties. EXIM Infotek Private Ltd. • $20 Individuals. Covers: 250 Taiwanese manufacturers and exporters of albums and files, ceramic faucet accessories, coins/medals/decorations and badges, enamel badges, gift articles, gift sets, gifts, key chains, key holders, kitchen utensils, medals, novelty glasses, photo frames, promotional giftware, religious festive seasonal gifts, solid brass quick release key chains, souvenirs, trophies/ceremonial plates. Entries include: Company name, postal address, city, country, phone, fax, e-mail and websites, contact person, designation, and product details.

Directory of Taiwanese Manufacturers & Exporters of Handicrafts & Decorative Items. EXIM Infotek Private Ltd. • $10 Individuals. Covers: 120 Taiwanese manufacturers and exporters of bronze/copper/brass and wrought iron artistic goods, candle holders, Christmas tree ornaments, Christmas tree sets, fancy metal boxes, festival articles and decorations, handicrafts, religious articles-Buddhist/Hindu, religious articles-Christian, religious articles-Jewish. Entries include: Company name, postal address, city, country, phone, fax, e-mail and websites, contact person, designation, products detail.

Gifts & Tablewares--Directory Issue. Scott's Directories. • Annual. $52.95 Individuals. Publication includes: List of approximately 1,000 manufacturers and suppliers of gift, home decor, stationery, and tableware items in Canada. Database includes: Calendar of Canadian, American,

For publishers' addresses, refer to SOURCES CITED section at the back of the book.

European, and Asian trade shows. Entries include: Company name, address, phone, fax, name, address, and phone of branches and showrooms; description of products and services; email and web sites.

Souvenirs, Gifts & Novelties Magazine--Buyer's Guide Issue. Kane Communications Inc. • Annual. Publication includes: List of 1,000 manufacturers, wholesalers, and importers of souvenirs, gifts, apparel, toys, jewelry novelty, and candle items. Entries include: Company name, address, phone, products, whether firm is manufacturer, wholesaler, or importer.

FINANCIAL RATIOS

Annual Statement Studies. Risk Management Association. • Annual. Compiled from over 280,000 financial statements.

Annual Statement Studies: Industry Default Probabilities and Cash Flow Measures. Risk Management Association. • Annual. $405 Nonmembers. Serves as a companion volume to the original *Annual Statement Studies.* Gives probability of default estimates on a percentage scale for more than 450 industries. Includes changes in position year-by-year for eight financial statement line items and provides percentage measures of cash flow.

PERIODICALS AND NEWSLETTERS

Fancy Food and Culinary Products. Talcott Communications Corp. • Monthly. $34.00 per year. Emphasizes new specialty food products and the business management aspects of the specialty food and confection industries. Includes special issues on wine, cheese, candy, "upscale" cookware, and gifts. Formerly (Fancy Foods).

Gifts and Decorative Accessories: The International Business Magazine of Gifts, Tabletop, Gourmet, Home Accessories, Greeting Card and Social Stationery. Reed Elsevier Group plc Reed Business Information. • Monthly. $53.95 per year. Includes *Annual Directory.*

Gifts and Tablewares. Scott's Directories. • Seven times a year. $47.95 per year. Includes annual *Trade Directory.*

Giftware News: The International Magazine for Gifts, China and Glass, Stationery and Home Accessories. Talcott Communications Corp. • Monthly.

Gourmet News: The Business Newspaper for the Gourmet Industry. HME News. • Monthly. $60.00 per year. Provides news of the gourmet food industry, including specialty food stores, upscale cookware shops, and gift shops.

TRADE/PROFESSIONAL ASSOCIATIONS

Gift and Home Trade Association. 2550 Sandy Plains Rd. Ste. 225, Marietta, GA 30066. Phone: 877-600-4872; Email: info@giftandhome.org • URL: http://www.giftandhome.org • Aims to ensure the viability of the gift and home industry. Promotes business practices and professional development. Establishes standards and ethical guidelines.

Gift Sales Manager Association. 14710 Quaker Bottom Rd., Sparks, MD 21152. Phone: (410)472-3593; Email: ldcolson@comcast.net • URL: http://www.giftsalesmanagers.org • Represents the interests of sales managers in the gift and home decor industry. Works to improve company operations and increase sales. Serves as a forum to exchange information and ideas among members.

GIFT TAX

HANDBOOKS AND MANUALS

U.S. Master Estate and Gift Tax Guide. Wolters Kluwer Law & Business CCH. • Annual. $103 Quantity: 1 - 4. Covers federal estate and gift taxes, including generation-skipping transfer tax plans. Includes tax tables and sample filled-in tax return forms.

INTERNET DATABASES

ACGA: Partners in Philanthropy. American Council on Gift Annuities. Phone: (317)269-6271: Fax: (317)269-6276; Email: acga@acga-web.org • URL: http://www.acga-web.org • Web site provides detailed information on gift annuities, including suggested charitable gift annuity rates for use by charities and their donors. Rates for immediate and deferred annuities are presented in the form of tables for ages 20 to 90 (and over), for both "Single Life" and "Two Lives - Joint and Survivor." Other items covered include the philosophy of gift annuities, state regulations, "What's New," and a search site. Fees: Free.

Court Filings. ProQuest LLC. 2250 Perimeter Park Dr., Ste. 300, Morrisville, NC 27560. Phone: 800-334-2564 or (919)804-6400; Fax: (919)804-6410; Email: contact@dialog.com • URL: http://www.dialog.com • The three main sections of Tax Analysts home page are "Tax News" (Today's Tax News, Feature of the Week, Tax Snapshots, Tax Calendar); "Products & Services" (Product Catalog, Press Releases); and "Public Interest" (Discussion Groups, Tax Clinic, Tax History Project). Fees: Free for coverage of current tax events; fee-based for comprehensive information. Daily updating.

Internal Revenue Service IRS.gov. Internal Revenue Service. Phone: 800-829-1040 or (202)622-5000; Fax: (202)622-5844 • URL: http://www.irs.gov • Web site provides a wide variety of tax information, including IRS forms and publications. Searching is available. Fees: Free.

OTHER SOURCES

Fiduciary Tax Guide. Wolters Kluwer Law & Business CCH. • Monthly. $478.00 per year. Looseleaf service. Covers federal income taxation of estates, trusts, and beneficiaries. Provides information on gift and generation- skipping taxation.

PERIODICALS AND NEWSLETTERS

Highlights and Documents. Tax Analysts. • Daily. $2,599.95 Individuals. Provides daily coverage of IRS, congressional, judicial, state, and international tax developments. Includes abstracts and citations for "all tax documents released within the previous 24 to 48 hours." Annual compilation available *Highlights and Documents on Microfiche.*

Tax Notes: The Weekly Tax Service. Tax Analysts. • Weekly. Weekly. $1,699.00 per year. Includes an *Annual* and compilations of previous years. Newsletter. Covers "tax news from all federal sources," including congressional committees, tax courts, and the Internal Revenue Service. Each issue contains "summaries of every document that pertains to federal tax law," with citations. Commentary is provided.

Tax Practice. Tax Analysts. • Weekly. $199.00 per year. Newsletter. Covers news affecting tax practitioners and litigators, with emphasis on federal court decisions, rules and regulations, and tax petitions. Provides a guide to Internal Revenue Service audit issues.

RESEARCH CENTERS AND INSTITUTES

University of Michigan - Stephen M. Ross School of Business - Office of Tax Policy Research. 701 Tappan St., Rm. R5380, Ann Arbor, MI 48109-1234. Phone: (734)763-3068; Fax: (734)763-4032; Email: jslemrod@umich.edu • URL: http://www.bus.umich.edu/OTPR/ • Tax policy, including compliance, capital gains, reform, international taxation, and income dynamics.

TRADE/PROFESSIONAL ASSOCIATIONS

National Tax Association-Tax Institute of America. 725 15th St. NW, Ste. 600, Washington, DC 20005-2109. Phone: (202)737-3325 or (202)261-5577; Fax: (202)737-7308; Email: natltax@aol.com • URL: http://www.ntanet.org.

GIRLS' CLOTHING

See CHILDREN'S APPAREL INDUSTRY

GLASS CONTAINER INDUSTRY

See also CONTAINER INDUSTRY; GLASS INDUSTRY; GLASSWARE INDUSTRY

CD-ROM DATABASES

OECD Statistical Compendium. Organization for Economic Cooperation and Development. • Semiannual. $1,905.00 per year for 1 to 10 users. CD-ROM contains more than 730,000 monthly, quarterly, and annual time series for OECD countries, 1960 to date. Includes fully searchable data on agriculture, food, economic indicators, national accounts, employment, energy, finance, industry, technology, and foreign trade. Results can be displayed in various forms.

INTERNET DATABASES

Business 2.0 Web Guide to the Best Business Links. Business 2.0 Media Inc. Phone: (415)293-4800; Email: support@business2.com • URL: http://www.business2.com/webguide • Web site presents an extensive, searchable directory of links to "the best, most informative, and authoritative web pages." Twenty main categories cover business, finance, career, company information, people, and technology topics, with thousands of subtopics, all linking to Web sites recommended by experienced business researchers. Fees: Free.

Fedstats. Federal Interagency Council on Statistical Policy. Phone: (202)395-7254 • URL: http://www.fedstats.gov • Web site features an efficient search facility for full-text statistics produced by more than 100 federal agencies, including the Census Bureau, the Bureau of Economic Analysis, and the Bureau of Labor Statistics. Boolean searches can be made within one agency or for all agencies combined. Links are offered to international statistical bureaus, including the UN, IMF, OECD, UNESCO, Eurostat, and 20 individual countries. Fees: Free.

FreeLunch.com. Economy.com, Inc. Phone: (610)696-8700; Fax: (610)696-1678 • URL: http://www.freelunch.com • Web site provides free access to more than 200 million economic and financial data series, covering industry, demographics, labor markets, prices, retail sales, government spending, trade, interest rates, housing starts, the stock market, etc. Data is available in either chart or table form. Searching is offered. Free, but registration required. Economy.com, Inc. also offers fee-based economic analysis at *The Dismal Scientist* site (www.dismal.com).

STATISTICS SOURCES

Survey of Current Business. U. S. Government Printing Office. • Published by Bureau of Economic Analysis, U. S. Department of Commerce. Presents a wide variety of business and economic data.

TRADE/PROFESSIONAL ASSOCIATIONS

American Scientific Glassblowers Society. PO Box 453, Machias, NY 14101. Phone: (716)353-8062; Fax: (716)353-4259; Email: natl-office@asgs-glass.org • URL: http://www.asgs-glass.org • Glassblowers with more than 5 years' experience in making scientific glass apparatus (condensers, distillation apparatus, glass-to-metal seals and vacuum devices); junior members are glassblowers with less than 5 years' professional experience; associates are persons connected with the manufacture or use of glass or glassblowing equipment in scientific work. Seeks to gather and disseminate information concerning scientific glassblowing, apparatus, equipment and materials.

National Association of Container Distributors. 800 Roosevelt Rd., Bldg. C-312, Glen Ellyn, IL 60137. Phone: (630)942-6585; Fax: (630)790-3095; Email: info@nacdmeetings.org • URL: http://www.nacd.net • Represents packaging distributors who supply bottles, lubes, pumps, sprayers, and related components. Services include warehousing and labeling.

GLASS INDUSTRY

See also GLASS CONTAINER INDUSTRY; GLASSWARE INDUSTRY; TABLEWARE

ABSTRACTS AND INDEXES

NTIS Alerts: Materials Sciences. U.S. Department of Commerce National Technical Information Service. • Biweekly. $130 per year. Covers ceramics, glass, coatings, composite materials, alloys, plastics, wood, paper, adhesives, fibers, lubricants, and related subjects.

CD-ROM DATABASES

OECD Statistical Compendium. Organization for Economic Cooperation and Development. • Semiannual. $1,905.00 per year for 1 to 10 users. CD-ROM contains more than 730,000 monthly, quarterly, and annual time series for OECD countries, 1960 to date. Includes fully searchable data on agriculture, food, economic indicators, national accounts, employment, energy, finance, industry, technology, and foreign trade. Results can be displayed in various forms.

DIRECTORIES

Directory of European Importers of Machinery for Glass and Ceramic Industry. EXIM Infotek Private Ltd. • $150 Individuals. Covers: 20 European importers of ceramic industry equipment and supplies, glass making machinery and equipment. Entries include: Company name, postal address, telephone, fax, e-mail, website, contact person, designation, and product details.

Directory of South Korean Manufacturers & Exporters of Glass, China, Ceramic & Porcelainware. EXIM Infotek Private Ltd. • $150 Individuals. Covers: 40 South Korean manufacturers and exporters of glass tableware, glassware, handmade glassware, porcelain and ceramic products, pottery, Chinaware, and shaped glass products. Entries include: Company name, postal address, telephone, fax, e-mail, website, contact person, designation, and product details.

Kompass. Kompass Deutschland Verlags- und Vertriebsgesellschaft, mbH. • Annual. $88. Covers: German products and companies specializing in coal extraction, ore mining, quarries, cement industry, glass and ceramics.

FINANCIAL RATIOS

Annual Statement Studies. Risk Management Association. • Annual. Compiled from over 280,000 financial statements.

Annual Statement Studies: Industry Default Probabilities and Cash Flow Measures. Risk Management Association. • Annual. $405 Nonmembers. Serves as a companion volume to the original *Annual Statement Studies*. Gives probability of default estimates on a percentage scale for more than 450 industries. Includes changes in position year-by-year for eight financial statement line items and provides percentage measures of cash flow.

INTERNET DATABASES

Business 2.0 Web Guide to the Best Business Links. Business 2.0 Media Inc. Phone: (415)293-4800; Email: support@business2.com • URL: http://www.business2.com/webguide • Web site presents an extensive, searchable directory of links to "the best, most informative, and authoritative web pages." Twenty main categories cover business, finance, career, company information, people, and technology topics, with thousands of subtopics, all linking to Web sites recommended by experienced business researchers. Fees: Free.

Fedstats. Federal Interagency Council on Statistical Policy. Phone: (202)395-7254 • URL: http://www.fedstats.gov • Web site features an efficient search facility for full-text statistics produced by more than 100 federal agencies, including the Census Bureau, the Bureau of Economic Analysis, and the Bureau of Labor Statistics. Boolean searches can be made within one agency or for all agencies combined. Links are offered to international statistical bureaus, including the UN, IMF, OECD, UNESCO, Eurostat, and 20 individual countries. Fees: Free.

FreeLunch.com. Economy.com, Inc. Phone: (610)696-8700; Fax: (610)696-1678 • URL: http://www.freelunch.com • Web site provides free access to more than 200 million economic and financial data series, covering industry, demographics, labor markets, prices, retail sales, government spending, trade, interest rates, housing starts, the stock market, etc. Data is available in either chart or table form. Searching is offered. Free, but registration required. Economy.com, Inc. also offers fee-based economic analysis at *The Dismal Scientist* site (www.dismal.com).

Manufacturing Profiles. U. S. Bureau of the Census. Phone: (301)763-4636 or (301)763-4100; Fax: (301)763-4794; Email: webmaster@census.gov • URL: http://www.census.gov/prod/www/abs/mfg-prof.html • The Census Bureau makes available free on PDF (Portable Document Format) an annual consolidation of the entire Current Industrial Report series, presenting "all the data compiled." Contains statistics on production, shipments, inventories, consumption, exports, imports, and orders for a wide variety of manufactured products.

PERIODICALS AND NEWSLETTERS

Glass Digest: Trade Magazine Serving the Flat Glass, Architectural Metal an d Allied Products Industry. Dialysis Inc. • Monthly. $40.00 per year.

Glass Magazine. National Glass Association. • 11/year. $34.95 Individuals.

U.S. Glass, Metal, and Glazing. AutoGlass Repair and Replacement Key Communications Inc. • Monthly. $35.00 per year. Edited for glass fabricators, glaziers, distributors, and retailers. Special feature issues are devoted to architectural glass, mirror glass, windows, storefronts, hardware, machinery, sealants, and adhesives. Regular topics include automobile glass and fenestration (window design and placement).

STATISTICS SOURCES

Survey of Current Business. U. S. Government Printing Office. • Published by Bureau of Economic Analysis, U. S. Department of Commerce. Presents a wide variety of business and economic data.

TRADE/PROFESSIONAL ASSOCIATIONS

National Glass Association. 1945 Old Gallows Rd., Ste. 750, Vienna, VA 22182. Phone: 866-342-5642 or (703)442-4890; Fax: (703)442-0630 or (703)827-0557; Email: pjames@glass.org • URL: http://www.glass.org • Manufacturers, installers, retailers, distributors and fabricators of flat, architectural, automotive and specialty glass and metal products, mirrors, shower and patio doors, windows and tabletops. Provides informational, educational and technical services.

GLASSWARE INDUSTRY

See also GLASS CONTAINER INDUSTRY; GLASS INDUSTRY; TABLEWARE

DIRECTORIES

Directory of Chinese Manufacturers & Exporters of Glassware, Chinaware, Ceramicware & Porcelainware. EXIM Infotek Private Ltd. • $10 Individuals. Covers: 100 Chinese manufacturers and exporters of artistic porcelain, ashtrays, ceramic pots, ceramic tea sets, ceramics household, Chinaware, daily use porcelain, glass art decoration, glass candle holders, glass chimneys, glass vases, glassware, porcelain and ceramic products-commercial/industrial, porcelain dolls, porcelains, porcelainware, pottery, white porcelainware. Entries include: Company name, postal address, city, country, phone, fax, e-mail and websites, contact person, designation, products detail.

The International Directory of Importers - Kitchenware, Tableware and Glassware Importers. Interdata. • $220 Individuals print. Covers: 3,000 international firms importing kitchenware, tableware and glassware. Entries include: Company name and address, contact person, email, number of employees, year established, phone and telefaxes, business activity, bank references, as well as a listing of kitchenware, tableware and glassware currently being imported.

INTERNET DATABASES

Manufacturing Profiles. U. S. Bureau of the Census. Phone: (301)763-4636 or (301)763-4100; Fax: (301)763-4794; Email: webmaster@census.gov • URL: http://www.census.gov/prod/www/abs/mfg-prof.html • The Census Bureau makes available free on PDF (Portable Document Format) an annual consolidation of the entire Current Industrial Report series, presenting "all the data compiled." Contains statistics on production, shipments, inventories, consumption, exports, imports, and orders for a wide variety of manufactured products.

TRADE/PROFESSIONAL ASSOCIATIONS

National Glass Association. 1945 Old Gallows Rd., Ste. 750, Vienna, VA 22182. Phone: 866-342-5642 or (703)442-4890; Fax: (703)442-0630 or (703)827-0557; Email: pjames@glass.org • URL: http://www.glass.org • Manufacturers, installers, retailers, distributors and fabricators of flat, architectural, automotive and specialty glass and metal products, mirrors, shower and patio doors, windows and tabletops. Provides informational, educational and technical services.

GLOVE INDUSTRY

See also CHILDREN'S APPAREL INDUSTRY; MEN'S CLOTHING INDUSTRY; WOMEN'S APPAREL

DIRECTORIES

Accessories Resources Directory. Business Journals Inc. • Annual. Covers: 1,600 manufacturers, importers, and sales representatives producing or handling belts, gloves, handbags, scarves, hosiery, jewelry, sunglasses, and umbrellas. Entries include: Company, name, address, phone, fax.

INTERNET DATABASES

Manufacturing Profiles. U. S. Bureau of the Census. Phone: (301)763-4636 or (301)763-4100; Fax: (301)763-4794; Email: webmaster@census.gov • URL: http://www.census.gov/prod/www/abs/mfg-prof.html • The Census Bureau makes available free on PDF (Portable Document Format) an annual consolidation of the entire Current Industrial Report series, presenting "all the data compiled." Contains statistics on production, shipments, inventories, consumption, exports, imports, and orders for a wide variety of manufactured products.

GLUE INDUSTRY

See ADHESIVES

GOLD

See also COINS AS AN INVESTMENT; MONEY

CD-ROM DATABASES

OECD Statistical Compendium. Organization for Economic Cooperation and Development. • Semiannual. $1,905.00 per year for 1 to 10 users. CD-ROM contains more than 730,000 monthly, quarterly, and annual time series for OECD countries, 1960 to date. Includes fully searchable data on agriculture, food, economic indicators, national accounts, employment, energy, finance, industry, technology, and foreign trade. Results can be displayed in various forms.

DIRECTORIES

Futures Magazine SourceBook: The Most Complete List of Exchanges, Companies, Regulators, Organizations, etc., Offering Products and Services to the Futures and Options Industry. Futures Magazine Inc. • Annual. $19.50. Provides information on commodity futures brokers, trading method services, publications, and other items of interest to futures traders and money managers.

INTERNET DATABASES

Business 2.0 Web Guide to the Best Business Links. Business 2.0 Media Inc. Phone: (415)293-4800; Email: support@business2.com • URL: http://www.business2.com/webguide • Web site presents an extensive, searchable directory of links to "the best, most informative, and authoritative web pages." Twenty main categories cover business, finance, career, company information, people, and technology topics, with thousands of subtopics, all linking to Web sites recommended by experienced business researchers. Fees: Free.

Fedstats. Federal Interagency Council on Statistical Policy. Phone: (202)395-7254 • URL: http://www.fedstats.gov • Web site features an efficient search facility for full-text statistics produced by more than 100 federal agencies, including the Census Bureau, the Bureau of Economic Analysis, and the Bureau of Labor Statistics. Boolean searches can be made within one agency or for all agencies combined. Links are offered to international statistical bureaus, including the UN, IMF, OECD, UNESCO, Eurostat, and 20 individual countries. Fees: Free.

FreeLunch.com. Economy.com, Inc. Phone: (610)696-8700; Fax: (610)696-1678 • URL: http://www.freelunch.com • Web site provides free access to more than 200 million economic and financial data series, covering industry, demographics, labor markets, prices, retail sales, government spending, trade, interest rates, housing starts, the stock market, etc. Data is available in either chart or table form. Searching is offered. Free, but registration required. Economy.com, Inc. also offers fee-based economic analysis at *The Dismal Scientist* site (www.dismal.com).

Futures Online. Futures Magazine Inc. Phone: (312)846-4600; Fax: (312)846-4638 • URL: http://www.futuresmag.com • Web site presents updates of *Futures* magazine and links to other futures-related sites.

PERIODICALS AND NEWSLETTERS

Bullion Advisory. Moneypower. • Monthly. $36.00 per year. Specializes in gold, silver and platinum.

Canadian Resources and PennyMines Analyst: The Canadian Newsletter for Penny-Mines Investors Who Insist on Geological Value. MPL Communications Inc. • Weekly. $145.00 per year. Newsletter. Mainly on Canadian gold mine stocks. Formerly *Canadian PennyMines Analyst*.

Futures: News, Analysis, and Strategies for Futures, Options, and Derivatives Traders. Futures Magazine Inc. • Monthly. $39 Individuals. Edited for institutional money managers and traders, brokers, risk managers, and individual investors or speculators. Includes special feature issues on interest rates, technical indicators, currencies, charts, precious metals, hedge funds, and derivatives. Supplements available.

Gold Newsletter. Jefferson Financial Inc. • Description: Reports on the relationship between gold and the economic system. Covers news of the "world gold markets, other precious metals markets, monetary reform, international economics, inflation, deflation, future of gold prices," and related economic and political matters. Remarks: Also available via e-mail.

Powell Monetary Analyst. Larson M. Powell, editor. Reserve Research Ltd. • Description: Offers investment advice concentrating on precious metals, gold coins, currencies, and mining stocks.

PRICE SOURCES

Platt's Metals Week. Platts Global Energy. • Weekly. $770 Individuals.

STATISTICS SOURCES

The AIER Chart Book. AIER Research Staff. American Institute for Economic Research. • Annual. $4 Individuals. A compact compilation of long-range charts ("Purchasing Power of the Dollar," for example, goes back to 1780) covering various aspects of the U. S. economy. Includes inflation, interest rates, debt, gold, taxation, stock prices, etc. (Economic Education Bulletin.).

Non-Ferrous Metal Data Yearbook. American Bureau of Metal Statistics. • Annual. $405.00. Provides worldwide data on approximately about 200 statistical tables covering many nonferrous metals. Includes production, consumption, inventories, exports, imports, and other data.

Standard & Poor's Industry Surveys. Standard & Poor's Financial Services L.L.C. • Semiannual. $1,800.00. Two looseleaf volumes. Includes monthly *Supplements*. Provides detailed, individual surveys of 52 major industry groups. Each survey is revised on a semiannual basis. Also includes "Monthly Investment Review" (industry group investment analysis) and monthly "Trends & Projections" (economic analysis).

Statistical Annual: Interest Rates, Metals, Stock Indices, Options on Financial Futures, Options on Metals Futures. Chicago Board of Trade. • Annual. Includes historical data on GNMA CDR Futures, Cash-Settled GNMA Futures, U. S. Treasury Bond Futures, U. S. Treasury Note Futures, Options on Treasury Note Futures, NASDAQ-100 Futures, Major Market Index Futures, Major Market Index MAXI Futures, Municipal Bond Index Futures, 1,000-Ounce Silver Futures, Options on Silver Futures, and Kilo Gold Futures.

Survey of Current Business. U. S. Government Printing Office. • Published by Bureau of Economic Analysis, U. S. Department of Commerce. Presents a wide variety of business and economic data.

United States Census of Mineral Industries. Bureau of the Census, U.S. Department of Commerce. U. S. Government Printing Office. • Quinquennial.

GOLF INDUSTRY

DIRECTORIES

Golf Course Directory. National Golf Foundation. • Annual. $199. Lists about 15,000 public and private golf facilities, with information as to size, number of holes, year opened, and practice ranges.

Golf Magazine Buyers' Guide. Times4 Media Inc. • Annual. $10 per year. Price on application. Lists golf club manufacturers, with description of products and prices.

PERIODICALS AND NEWSLETTERS

AGS Quarterly: Bulletin of the Association for Gravestone Studies. Association for Gravestone Studies. • Quarterly. Description: Concerned with the study and preservation of national and international gravestones: folk art carvings, lettering, epitaphs, shapes, materials used, and symbolism. Recurring features include articles on conservation procedures, Association news, book reviews, news of research, and regional news.

Golf Course Management. Golf Course Superintendents Association of America. • Monthly. $60 Individuals. Contains articles on golf course maintenance, equipment, landscaping, renovation, and management.

Golf Course News: The Newspaper for the Golf Course Industry. HME News. • Monthly. $60.00 per year. Edited for golf course superintendents, managers, architects, and developers.

Golf Digest: How to Play, What to Play, Where to Play. Golf Digest. • Monthly. $14.97 Individuals. A high circulation consumer magazine for golfers. Editions available in various languages. Supplement available *Golf Digest Woman*.

Golf Magazine. Time Inc. • Monthly. $19.95 Individuals. Popular consumer magazine for golfers.

Golf World Business. Golf Digest. • 9/year. $72 Individuals. Edited for retailers of golf equipment. Formerly *Golf Shop Operations*.

Golfdom. Elsevier. • Monthly. $30.00 per year. Covers marketing, financing, insurance, human resources, maintenance, environmental factors, and other aspects of golf course management. *Formerly Golf Business*.

Golfweek: America's Golf Newspaper. Golfweek. • Weekly. $34.95 Individuals U.S, print. Includes biweekly supplement, *Golfweek's Strictly Business*, covering business and marketing for the golfing industry.

STATISTICS SOURCES

U.S. Industry and Trade Outlook. U.S. Department of Commerce National Technical Information Service. • Annual. Produced by the International Trade Administration, U.S. Department of Commerce, in a "public-private" partnership with DRI/McGraw-Hill and Standard & Poor's. Provides basic data, outlook for the current year, and "Long-Term Prospects" (five-year projections) for a wide variety of products and services. Includes high technology industries. Formerly *U.S. Industrial Outlook*.

TRADE/PROFESSIONAL ASSOCIATIONS

American Society of Golf Course Architects. 125 N Executive Dr., Ste. 302, Brookfield, WI 53005-6035. Phone: (262)786-5960; Fax: (262)786-5919; Email: info@asgca.org • URL: http://www.asgca.org • Members are professional designers and architects of golf courses.

Association of Golf Merchandisers. PO Box 7247, Phoenix, AZ 85011-7247. Phone: (602)604-8250; Fax: (602)604-8251; Email: info@agmgolf.org • URL: http://www.agmgolf.org • Members are vendors of golf equipment and merchandise.

Ladies Professional Golf Association. 100 International Golf Dr., Daytona Beach, FL 32124-1092. Phone: (386)274-6200; Fax: (386)274-1099; Email: feedback@lpga.com • URL: http://www.lpga.com • Represents and promotes women golfers, teachers and competitors. Compiles statistics on tournaments, money winnings, and scoring.

National Golf Course Owners Association. 291 Seven Farms Dr., Charleston, SC 29492. Phone: 800-933-4262 or (843)881-9956; Fax: (843)881-9958; Email: info@ngcoa.org • URL: http://www.ngcoa.org • Owners and operators of privately owned golf courses. Assist members to develop more productive, efficient, and profitable golf operations. Provides information on taxation, destination golf, community relations, environmental regulations, and marketing. Offers group purchasing opportunities. Conducts educational seminars. Compiles statistics.

Professional Golfers' Association of America. 100 Ave. of the Champions, Palm Beach Gardens, FL 33418-3653. Phone: (561)624-8400 • URL: http://

www.pga.com • Recruits and trains men and women to manage a variety of golf businesses, including golf clubs, courses, and tournaments. Sponsors PGA Championship, PGA Seniors' Championship, Ryder Cup Matches, PGA Grand Slam of Golf, Club Professional Championship, PGA Foundation, and Senior Club Professional Championship; PGA Junior Championship; PGA Assistants Championship. Conducts Professional Golf Management; certifies college programs in golf management at 14 universities. Sponsors winter tournament program for club professionals including tournaments held in south Florida. Offers complementary employment services for PGA members and employers, owns and operates PGA Golf Club and PGA Learning Center.

GOURMET FOODS

See SPECIALTY FOOD INDUSTRY

GOVERNMENT ACCOUNTING

ABSTRACTS AND INDEXES

Accounting and Tax Index. ProQuest L.L.C. • Quarterly. Indexes accounting, auditing, and taxation literature appearing in journals, books, pamphlets, conference proceedings, and newsletters.

Accounting Articles. Wolters Kluwer Law & Business CCH. • Monthly. $624. Covers accounting news.

PAIS International. ProQuest L.L.C. • Monthly. $850.00 per year; cumulations three times a year. Provides topical citations to the worldwide literature of public affairs, economics, demographics, sociology, and trade. Text in English; indexed materials in English, French, German, Italian, Portuguese and Spanish.

Sage Public Administration Abstracts. EBSCO Publishing Inc. • Titles include Journal of Public Economics, Public Administration, and Public Administratioin Review.

ALMANACS AND YEARBOOKS

Research in Governmental and Nonprofit Accounting. Elsevier. • Dates vary. Price varies. 10 volumes.

CD-ROM DATABASES

PAIS International. ProQuest L.L.C. • Monthly. $1,995.00 per year. Contains over 650,000 citations to the literature of contemporary social, political, and economic issues.

INTERNET DATABASES

Rutgers Accounting Web. Rutgers University Accounting Research Center. Phone: (973)353-5172; Fax: (973)353-1283 • URL: http://www.rutgers.edu/accounting • RAW Web site provides extensive links to sources of national and international accounting information, such as the Big Six accounting firms, the Financial Accounting Standards Board (FASB), SEC filings (EDGAR), journals, publishers, software, the International Accounting Network, and "Internet's largest list of accounting firms in USA." Searching is offered. Fees: Free.

ONLINE DATABASES

Accounting and Tax Database. ProQuest L.L.C. • Provides indexing and abstracting of the literature of accounting, taxation, and financial management, 1971 to date. Updating is weekly. Especially covers accounting, auditing, banking, bankruptcy, employee compensation and benefits, cash management, financial planning, and credit. Inquire as to online cost and availability.

PERIODICALS AND NEWSLETTERS

Governing: The States and Localities. • Monthly. $39.95 per year. Edited for state and local government officials. Covers finance, office management, computers, telecommunications, environmental concerns, etc.

Journal of Government Financial Management. Association of Government Accountants. • Quarterly. $95 Individuals. *Government Accountants Journal*.

TRADE/PROFESSIONAL ASSOCIATIONS

Association of Government Accountants. 2208 Mt. Vernon Ave., Alexandria, VA 22301-1314. Phone: 800-AGA-7211 or (703)684-6931; Fax: (703)548-9367; Email: agamembers@agacgfm.org • URL: http://www.agacgfm.org • Members are employed by federal, state, county, and city government agencies. Includes accountants, auditors, budget officers, and other government finance administrators and officials.

GOVERNMENT ADMINISTRATION

See PUBLIC ADMINISTRATION

GOVERNMENT AID

See FEDERAL AID

GOVERNMENT AND BUSINESS

See REGULATION OF INDUSTRY

GOVERNMENT BONDS

See also BONDS; MUNICIPAL BONDS

CD-ROM DATABASES

OECD Statistical Compendium. Organization for Economic Cooperation and Development. • Semiannual. $1,905.00 per year for 1 to 10 users. CD-ROM contains more than 730,000 monthly, quarterly, and annual time series for OECD countries, 1960 to date. Includes fully searchable data on agriculture, food, economic indicators, national accounts, employment, energy, finance, industry, technology, and foreign trade. Results can be displayed in various forms.

DIRECTORIES

Mergent Municipal and Government Manual. Mergent Inc. • Covers all U.S. taxing jurisdictions and agencies with total long-term rated debt of $25,000,000 or over.

INTERNET DATABASES

Business 2.0 Web Guide to the Best Business Links. Business 2.0 Media Inc. Phone: (415)293-4800; Email: support@business2.com • URL: http://www.business2.com/webguide • Web site presents an extensive, searchable directory of links to "the best, most informative, and authoritative web pages." Twenty main categories cover business, finance, career, company information, people, and technology topics, with thousands of subtopics, all linking to Web sites recommended by experienced business researchers. Fees: Free.

Factiva. Dow Jones Reuters Business Interactive, LLC. Phone: 800-369-7466 or (609)452-1511; Fax: (609)520-5770; Email: solutions@factiva.com • URL: http://www.factiva.com • Fee-based Web site provides "global news and business information through Web sites and content integration solutions." Includes Dow Jones and Reuters newswires, The Wall Street Journal, and more than 7,000 other sources of current news, historical articles, market research reports, and investment analysis. Content includes 96 major U. S. newspapers, 900 non-English sources, trade publications, media transcripts, country profiles, news photos, etc.

Fedstats. Federal Interagency Council on Statistical Policy. Phone: (202)395-7254 • URL: http://www.fedstats.gov • Web site features an efficient search facility for full-text statistics produced by more than 100 federal agencies, including the Census Bureau, the Bureau of Economic Analysis, and the Bureau of Labor Statistics. Boolean searches can be made within one agency or for all agencies combined. Links are offered to international statistical bureaus, including the UN, IMF, OECD, UNESCO, Eurostat, and 20 individual countries. Fees: Free.

FreeLunch.com. Economy.com, Inc. Phone: (610)696-8700; Fax: (610)696-1678 • URL: http://www.freelunch.com • Web site provides free access to more than 200 million economic and financial data series, covering industry, demographics, labor markets, prices, retail sales, government spending, trade, interest rates, housing starts, the stock market, etc. Data is available in either chart or table form. Searching is offered. Free, but registration required. Economy.com, Inc. also offers fee-based economic analysis at *The Dismal Scientist* site (www.dismal.com).

Nexis.com. Lexis-Nexis Group. Phone: 800-227-4908 or (937)865-6800; Fax: (937)865-6909; Email: webmaster@prod.lexis-nexis.com • URL: http://www.nexis.com • Fee-based Web site offers searching of about 2.8 billion documents in some 30,000 news, business, and legal information sources. Features include a subject directory covering 1,200 topics in 34 categories and a Company Dossier containing information on more than 500,000 public and private companies. Boolean searching is offered.

Wall Street Journal Interactive Edition. Dow Jones & Co., Inc. 1211 Avenue of the Americas, New York, NY 10036. Phone: 800-369-5663; Email: service@dowjones.com • URL: http://new.dowjones.com • Fee-based Web site providing online searching of worldwide information from *The Wall Street Journal*. Includes "Company Snapshots," "The Journal's Greatest Hits," "Index to Market Data," "Journal Links," etc. Financial price quotes are available. Fees: $49.00 per year; $29.00 per year to print subscribers.

OTHER SOURCES

Fitch Insights. Fitch Investors Service, Inc. • Biweekly. $1,040.00 per year. Includes bond rating actions and explanation of actions. Provides commentary and Fitch's view of the financial markets.

Tables of Redemption Values for United States Savings Bonds, Series EE and Series E. U. S. Government Printing Office. • Semiannual. $14 U.S. single copy. Issued by the Public Debt Bureau, U. S. Treasury Department.

PERIODICALS AND NEWSLETTERS

American Banker: The Financial Services Daily. SourceMedia Inc. • Daily. $895.00 per year. Provides news of banking, investment products, mortgages, credit unions, finance, bank technology, and legal developments.

Moody's Bond Survey. Moody's Investors Service Inc. • Weekly (Mon.). Description: Presents statistical information and analysis of corporate, municipal, government, federal agency, and international bonds, preferred stock, and commercial paper. Includes ratings changes and withdrawals, calendars of recent and prospective bond offerings, and Moody's bond and preferred stock yield averages.

U.S. Banker. SourceMedia Inc. • Monthly. $65.00 per year. Edited for bank executives and managers. Covers a wide variety of banking and financial topics.

STATISTICS SOURCES

Statistical Annual: Interest Rates, Metals, Stock Indices, Options on Financial Futures, Options on Metals Futures. Chicago Board of Trade. • Annual. Includes historical data on GNMA CDR Futures, Cash-Settled GNMA Futures, U. S. Treasury Bond Futures, U. S. Treasury Note Futures, Options on Treasury Note Futures, NASDAQ-100 Futures, Major Market Index Futures, Major Market Index MAXI Futures, Municipal Bond Index Futures, 1,000-Ounce Silver Futures, Options on Silver Futures, and Kilo Gold Futures.

Stocks, Bonds, Bills, and Inflation Classic Yearbook. Ibbotson Associates. • Annual. $185. Provides detailed data from 1926 to the present on inflation and the returns from various kinds of financial investments, such as small-cap stocks and long-term government bonds.

Survey of Current Business. U. S. Government Printing Office. • Published by Bureau of Economic Analysis, U. S. Department of Commerce. Presents a wide variety of business and economic data.

Treasury Bulletin. U. S. Government Printing Office. • Quarterly. $51 List Price. Issued by the Financial Management Service, U. S. Treasury Department. Provides data on the federal budget, government securities and yields, the national debt, and the financing of the federal government in general.

GOVERNMENT BUDGET

See FEDERAL BUDGET

GOVERNMENT, COMPUTERS IN

See COMPUTERS IN GOVERNMENT

GOVERNMENT CONTRACTS

See also CONTRACTS; GOVERNMENT PURCHASING

ABSTRACTS AND INDEXES

Current Law Index. Cengage Learning Inc. • $1,332 Individuals. Monthly. $1269.00 per year. Produced in cooperation with the American Association of Law Libraries. Indexes more than 900 law journals, legal newspapers, and specialty publications from the U.S., Canada, U.K., Ireland, Australia, and New Zealand.

DIRECTORIES

Commerce Business Daily (CBD). Chicago Metropolitan Agency for Planning. • Daily. $324 per yr. for priority subscription. Covers all planned federal contracts and contract awards in excess of $25,000; coming sales of surplus government property; notices for federal prime contractors seeking subcontractors; foreign government contract announcements.

INTERNET DATABASES

Lexis.com Research System. Lexis-Nexis Group. Phone: 800-227-4908 or (937)865-6800; Fax: (937)865-6909; Email: webmaster@prod.lexis-nexis.com • URL: http://www.nexis.com • Fee-based Web site offers extensive searching of a wide variety of legal sources. Additional features include Daily Opinion Service, lexis.com Bookstore, Career Center, CLE Center, Law Schools, and Practice Pages ("Pages specific to areas of specialty").

OTHER SOURCES

Government Contracts: Law, Administration and Procedure. Matthew Bender and Company Inc. • Quarterly. $3,165. Coverage of important aspects of government contracts.

Government Contracts Reports. Wolters Kluwer Law & Business CCH. • Weekly. $2,600.00 per year. 10 looseleaf volumes. Laws and regulations affecting government contracts.

PERIODICALS AND NEWSLETTERS

Federal Grants and Contracts Weekly: Funding Opportunities in Research, Training and Services. Wolters Kluwer Law and Business. • 50 times a year. $450.00 per year. Newsletter.

Government Contractor. West DC Editorial. • Weekly. $1,700 Individuals.

Government Primecontracts Monthly. Government Data Publications Inc. • Monthly. $96.00 per year.

MBI: The National Report on Minority, Women-Owned and Disadvantaged Business. Community Development Services, Inc. CD Publications. • Semimonthly. $379.00 per year. Newsletter. Provides news of affirmative action, government contracts, minority business employment, and education/training for minorities in business. Formerly *Minorities in Business.*

The National Estimator. Society of Cost Estimating and Analysis. • Quarterly. $30.00 per year. Covers government contract estimating.

TRADE/PROFESSIONAL ASSOCIATIONS

Contract Services Association of America. 1000 Wilson Blvd., Ste. 1800, Arlington, VA 22209-3920. Phone: (703)243-2020; Fax: (703)243-3601; Email: info@csa-dc.org • URL: http://www.csa-dc.org • Formerly National Council of Technical Services Industries.

National Association of Minority Government Contractors. PO Box 44609, Washington, DC 20026. Email: info@namgc.org • URL: http://www.namgc.org • Focuses on enhancing diversification in the workplace. Provides opportunities for the federal, state and local government sector to find key resources in order to engage in contracting opportunities. Provides members with networking, information and services which will connect them with federal, state and local government contracting opportunities.

National Contract Management Association. 21740 Beaumeade Cir., Ste. 125, Ashburn, VA 20147. Phone: 800-344-8096 or (571)382-0082 or (703)448-9231; Fax: (703)448-0939; Email: wearelistening@ncmahq.org • URL: http://www.ncmahq.org • Professional individuals concerned with administration, procurement, acquisition, negotiation and management of contracts and subcontracts. Works for the education, improvement and professional development of members and nonmembers through national and chapter programs, symposia and educational materials. Offers certification in Contract Management (CPCM, CFCM, and CCCM) designations as well as a credential program. Operates speakers' bureau.

GOVERNMENT DOCUMENTS

See GOVERNMENT PUBLICATIONS

GOVERNMENT EMPLOYEES

See also BUREAUCRACY; CIVIL SERVICE; PUBLIC ADMINISTRATION

CD-ROM DATABASES

OECD Statistical Compendium. Organization for Economic Cooperation and Development. • Semiannual. $1,905.00 per year for 1 to 10 users. CD-ROM contains more than 730,000 monthly, quarterly, and annual time series for OECD countries, 1960 to date. Includes fully searchable data on agriculture, food, economic indicators, national accounts, employment, energy, finance, industry, technology, and foreign trade. Results can be displayed in various forms.

The Tax Directory. Tax Analysts. • Quarterly. $499 Individuals both volumes, web, CD or print. Updated quarterly on CD-ROM and in print; updated continually online. Covering federal, state, and international tax officials, tax practitioners, and corporate tax executives.

DIRECTORIES

Carroll's County Directory. Caroll Publishing. • Annual. $500 Individuals 2 issues per year. Covers over 51,000 officials in more than 3,000 counties; includes elected, appointed, and career office holders.

Carroll's Federal & Federal Regional Directory. Caroll Publishing. • Semiannual. $500 Individuals. Lists more than 23,000 U. S. government officials throughout the country, including military installations.

Carroll's Federal Directory. Caroll Publishing. • $550 Single issue 4 issues per year. Covers approximately 37,000 executive managers in federal government offices in Washington, DC, including executive, congressional and judicial branches; members of Congress and Congressional committees and staff.

Carroll's Federal Regional Directory. Caroll Publishing. • Annual. $500 Individuals. Covers: Over 32,000 officials in federal congressional, judicial, and executive branch departments and agencies outside the District of Columbia. Database includes: Regional maps showing states covered in each federal region and Federal Information Centers. Entries include: Organization or agency name; names, addresses, and phone numbers of key personnel.

Carroll's Municipal/County Directory. Caroll Publishing. • Semiannual. $500 Individuals. Provides listings of about 90,000 city, town, and county officials in the U. S.

Carroll's Municipal Directory. Caroll Publishing. • Annual. $500 Individuals. Covers: About 51,000 officials in more than 7,900 cities towns and villages; includes top elected council or elected board members. Entries include: Name, county name, locator phone, address, population; officials' names, titles, addresses, and phone numbers.

Carroll's State Directory. Caroll Publishing. • Annual. $500 Individuals 3 issues per year. Covers: About 70,000 state government officials in all branches of government; officers, committees and members of state legislatures; managers of boards and authorities. Entries include: Name, address, phone, fax, title.

Carroll's State Directory: CD-ROM Edition. Caroll Publishing. • Three times a year. $325.00 per year. Provides CD-ROM listings of about 43,000 state officials, plus the text of all state constitutions and biographies of all governors. Also available online.

Federal Regional Yellow Book: Who's Who in the Federal Government's Departments, Agencies, Military Installations, and Service Academies Outside of Washington, DC. Leadership Directories Inc. • Semiannual. $465 Individuals annual. Lists over 35,000 federal officials and support staff at 8,000 regional offices.

Federal Staff Directory: With Biographical Information on Executive Staff Personnel. CQ Press. • Three times a year. $259.00 per year. Single copies, $149.00. Lists 35,000 staff members of federal departments and agencies, with biographies of 3,200 key executives. Includes keyword and name indexes.

The Tax Directory. Tax Analysts. • Quarterly. $499 Individuals both volumes, web, CD or print. Updated quarterly on CD-ROM and in print;

updated continually online. Covering federal, state, and international tax officials, tax practitioners, and corporate tax executives.

United States Government Manual. Office of the Federal Register. • Annual. $29 Individuals. Provides information on the agencies of the executive, judicial, and legislative branches of the Federal government. Contains a section on terminated or transferred agencies. Database includes: Includes boards, commissions, committees and quasi-official agencies and organizations in which US participates.

INTERNET DATABASES

Business 2.0 Web Guide to the Best Business Links. Business 2.0 Media Inc. Phone: (415)293-4800; Email: support@business2.com • URL: http://www.business2.com/webguide • Web site presents an extensive, searchable directory of links to "the best, most informative, and authoritative web pages." Twenty main categories cover business, finance, career, company information, people, and technology topics, with thousands of subtopics, all linking to Web sites recommended by experienced business researchers. Fees: Free.

Fedstats. Federal Interagency Council on Statistical Policy. Phone: (202)395-7254 • URL: http://www.fedstats.gov • Web site features an efficient search facility for full-text statistics produced by more than 100 federal agencies, including the Census Bureau, the Bureau of Economic Analysis, and the Bureau of Labor Statistics. Boolean searches can be made within one agency or for all agencies combined. Links are offered to international statistical bureaus, including the UN, IMF, OECD, UNESCO, Eurostat, and 20 individual countries. Fees: Free.

FreeLunch.com. Economy.com, Inc. Phone: (610)696-8700; Fax: (610)696-1678 • URL: http://www.freelunch.com • Web site provides free access to more than 200 million economic and financial data series, covering industry, demographics, labor markets, prices, retail sales, government spending, trade, interest rates, housing starts, the stock market, etc. Data is available in either chart or table form. Searching is offered. Free, but registration required. Economy.com, Inc. also offers fee-based economic analysis at *The Dismal Scientist* site (www.dismal.com).

U.S. Census Bureau: The Official Statistics. U. S. Bureau of the Census. Phone: (301)763-4636 or (301)763-4100; Fax: (301)763-4794; Email: webmaster@census.gov • URL: http://www.census.gov/prod/www/abs/mfg-prof.html • Web site is "Your Source for Social, Demographic, and Economic Information." Contains "Current U. S. Population Count," "Current Economic Indicators," and a wide variety of data under "Other Official Statistics." Keyword searching is provided. Fees: Free.

OTHER SOURCES

Carroll's Federal Organization Charts. Caroll Publishing. • 8/year. $1,650 Individuals. Provides 200 large, fold-out paper charts showing personnel relationships in 2,100 federal departments and agencies. Charts are also available online and on CD-ROM.

Government Discrimination: Equal Protection Law and Litigation. James A. Kushner. Thomson West. • Semiannual. $708.75 full set. Covers discrimination in employment, housing, and other areas by local, state, and federal offices or agencies. (Civil Rights Series).

Government Employee Relations Report. Bloomberg BNA. • Weekly. $1,144.00 per year. Three looseleaf volumes. Concerned with labor relations in the public sector.

PERIODICALS AND NEWSLETTERS

Employee Policy for the Private and Public Sector: State Capitals. Wakeman/Walworth Inc. • Weekly. $245.00 per year; print and online editions, $350.00 per year. Newsletter. Formerly *From the State Capitals: Employee Policy for the Private and Public Sector.*

Federal Employee News Digest. Federal Employee News Digest, Inc. • Weekly. $59.00 per year. Provides essential information for federal employees.

Federal Human Resources Week: News, Strategies and Best Practices for the HR Professional. LRP Publications Library. • 48 times a year. $350.00 per year. Newsletter. Covers federal personnel issues, including legislation, benefits, budgets, and downsizing.

Government Standard. American Federation of Government Employees. • Bimonthly.

Government Union Review and Public Policy Digest. Public Service Research Foundation. • Quarterly.

Public Employee. American Federation of State, County and Municipal Employees. • 8/year. Bimonthly. Membership. Newsletter. Formerly *Public Employee Magazine.*

STATISTICS SOURCES

Public Employment. Bureau of the Census, U.S. Department of Commerce. U. S. Government Printing Office. • Annual.

Statistical Abstract of the United States. U. S. Government Printing Office. • Annual. $44.00. Issued by the U. S. Bureau of the Census.

Survey of Current Business. U. S. Government Printing Office. • Published by Bureau of Economic Analysis, U. S. Department of Commerce. Presents a wide variety of business and economic data.

TRADE/PROFESSIONAL ASSOCIATIONS

American Federation of Government Employees. 80 F St. NW, Washington, DC 20001. Phone: (202)737-8700 or (202)639-6435; Fax: (202)639-6490 or (202)639-6441; Email: comments@afge.org • URL: http://www.afge.org • Affiliated with AFL-CIO.

American Federation of State, County and Municipal Employees. 1625 L St. NW, Washington, DC 20036-5687. Phone: (202)429-1000; Fax: (202)429-1293; Email: recruiting@afscme.org • URL: http://www.afscme.org • Represents service and health care workers in the public and private sectors. Organizes for social and economic justice in the workplace and through political action and legislative advocacy.

Civil Service Employees Association. 143 Washington Ave., Albany, NY 12210. Phone: 800-342-4146 or (518)257-1000 • URL: http://cseany.org • AFL-CIO. Represents state and local government employees from all public employee classifications. Negotiates work contracts; represents members in grievances; provides legal assistance for on-the-job problems; provides advice and assistance on federal, state, and local laws affecting public employees. Conducts research, training and education programs. Compiles statistics.

Government Investment Officers Association. 10655 Park Run Dr., Ste. 120, Las Vegas, NV 89144. Phone: (702)255-3224; Fax: (702)575-6670; Email: mday@gioa.us • URL: http://www.gioa.us • Provides education and training to government investment officers to assist them in their responsibilities. Promotes educational and professional development among investment officers in state and local governments. Seeks to instill higher levels of investment management skills, ethics and efficiency. Interacts with the public investment community and other public investment officers so that members will have the opportunity to gain the skills, knowledge and contacts that will greatly aid them in discharging their duties.

National Association of Government Employees. 159 Burgin Pkwy., Quincy, MA 02169. Phone: 866-412-7762 or (617)376-0220 or (617)472-7566; Fax: (617)376-0285 or (617)472-7566; Email: membership@nage.org • URL: http://www.nage.org • Supersedes Federal Employees Veterans Association.

National Federation of Federal Employees. 805 15th St. NW, Ste. 500, Washington, DC 20005. Phone: (202)216-4420 or (202)216-4421; Fax: (202)898-1861; Email: cbythrow@nffe.org • URL: http://www.nffe.org • Independent. Opposes Social Security coverage for civil service workers. Conducts seminars on labor relations.

GOVERNMENT EXPENDITURES

See FEDERAL BUDGET

GOVERNMENT FINANCE

See PUBLIC FINANCE

GOVERNMENT HOUSING PROJECTS

See HOUSING

GOVERNMENT INVESTIGATIONS

ABSTRACTS AND INDEXES

PAIS International. ProQuest L.L.C. • Monthly. $850.00 per year; cumulations three times a year. Provides topical citations to the worldwide literature of public affairs, economics, demographics, sociology, and trade. Text in English; indexed materials in English, French, German, Italian, Portuguese and Spanish.

CD-ROM DATABASES

PAIS International. ProQuest L.L.C. • Monthly. $1,995.00 per year. Contains over 650,000 citations to the literature of contemporary social, political, and economic issues.

ENCYCLOPEDIAS AND DICTIONARIES

Encyclopedia of Crime and Justice. Cengage Learning Inc. • 2001. $737. 2nd edition. 4 volumes. Published by Macmillan Reference USA. Contains extensive information on a wide variety of topics pertaining to crime, criminology, social issues, and the courts. Also available as eBook.

Encyclopedia of Governmental Advisory Organizations. Cengage Learning Inc. • Annual. $1,178 Individuals print. Contains more than 7,300 entries describing activities and personnel. Complete contact information.

GENERAL WORKS

Congressional Investigations: Law and Practice. John C. Grabow. Wolters Kluwer Law and Business. • $95.00. Looseleaf service. Periodic supplementation.

GOVERNMENT PROCUREMENT

See GOVERNMENT PURCHASING

GOVERNMENT PUBLICATIONS

See also CENSUS REPORTS

ABSTRACTS AND INDEXES

Government Periodicals Index. ProQuest L.L.C. • An index to approximately 180 periodicals issued by various agencies of the federal government.

BIBLIOGRAPHIES

Catalog of United States Government Publications. U. S. Government Printing Office. • Updated daily.

Subject Bibliography Index: A Guide to U.S. Government Information. U. S. Government Printing Office. • Annual. Free. Issued by the Superintendent of Documents. Lists currently available subject bibliographies by title and by topic. Each *Subject Bibliography* describes government books, periodicals, posters, pamphlets, and subscription services available for sale from the Government Printing Office.

U.S. Government Books: Publications for Sale by the Government Printing Office. U. S. Government Printing Office. • Quarterly. Free. Describes best selling government documents and "new titles that reflect today's news and consumer issues.".

U.S. Government Information Catalog of New and Popular Titles. U. S. Government Printing Office. • Irregular. Free. Includes recently issued and popular publications, periodicals, and electronic products.

U.S. Government Information for Business. U. S. Government Printing Office. • Annual. Free. A selected list of currently available publications, periodicals, and electronic products on business, trade, labor, federal regulations, economics, and other topics. Also known as *Business Catalog*.

U.S. Government Subscriptions. U. S. Government Printing Office. • Quarterly. Free. Includes agency and subject indexes.

DIRECTORIES

Annuaire France Telexport. Paris Chamber of Commerce and Industry. • Annual. $179.40. Covers: Approximately 40,000 French companies involved in international trade. Entries include: Company name, address, phone, telex, names and titles of key personnel, number of employees, geographical area served, financial data, product/service, main business activity, date/type of incorporation, products imported/exported, countries of export/import.

Annual Report of the Bank Commissioner of the State of Maryland. Maryland Department of Labor, Licensing and Regulation. • Biennial. Covers: State-chartered banks and credit unions in Maryland. Entries include: Financial institution name, address, phone, fax, names and titles of key personnel, financial data.

Birmingham Chamber of Commerce--Prospect List. Birmingham Regional Chamber of Commerce. • Covers: 4,000 prospect companies for the Birmingham Chamber of Commerce. Entries include: Name, address, phone, fax.

Business Services Directory. German American Chamber of Commerce. • $10. Covers: Member firms which provide business, engineering, research, accounting, technical, marketing, and personnel management consulting services. Entries include: Company name, address, phone, fax, contact, number of employees, geographical location, foreign language capabilities, activities, history.

Caribbean Exporters: A Directory of Caribbean Exporters. Caribbean Export Development Agency. • $50. Covers: Approximately 1,600 exporting companies in the Caribbean community. Database includes: General information about the Caribbean community; maps. Entries include: Company name, address, phone, fax, number of employees, product/service provided.

Guide to State Government Services for Business in Alabama. Alabama Development Office Alabama Center for Commerce. • Quarterly. Covers: Alabama state government agencies and other public and private entities that provide economic development and other business and technical assistance in Alabama, including training, research, information, and other services.

Guide to the Port of New York-New Jersey. Port Authority of New York and New Jersey. • Annual. Covers: commercial shipping facilities at the port areas of New York and New Jersey: about 20 freight terminals; Port Authority offices and U.S. government departments; 80 international trade, maritime, and transportation associations; 385 companies providing trucking and freight hauling services; 90 warehouse facilities; 500 international freight forwarders, custom house brokers, and firms that combine the services of forwarder and broker; 55 airlines providing freight services from John F. Kennedy International Airport, LaGuardia Airport, and Newark International Airport; 75 steamship lines, steamship line agents, terminal operators and steve dores; 1,230 companies providing maritime services, e.g. international banking, marine insurance, contracting, brokering, and engineering; 180 suppliers of marine equipment; and 85 inland (i.e. interstate) freight services. Database includes: Glossary of shipping terms, customs acronyms, list of related books, reports, and periodicals; shipping information hotlines, truck routes to harbors, customs documents, hazardous materials identification symbols, and others. Entries include: For terminals--Terminal name, address, phone, owner name, terminal operator, description of facilities and services, routes of access. For Port Authority offices--Office name; names, titles, addresses, and phones of key personnel. For government departments--Department name, address, phone; name, address, phone, and name of key official for each branch office or division. For associations--Name, address, phone, brief history, description of projects and services. For trucking and freight companies--Name, address, phone, name and title of contact, geographical area served. For warehouse facilities--Company name, address, phone, telex, fax, cable address, storage capacity, description of facilities and services, including export packaging and automobile processing capabilities. For freight forwarders and custom house brokers--Company name, address, phone, telex, fax, cable address, name and title of chief officer. For air cargo services--Airline name, New York address; name, title, and phone of sales contact; address and phone of cargo operations at each airport; specialized services, cargo space available. For steamship services--Company name; name, address, phone of New York/New Jersey port area agent; types of service offered, countries served, name and location of terminal at which cargo is loaded. For others--Company name, address, phone.

International Business Quick Reference Guide. U.S. Chamber of Commerce. • $25 Members. Covers: American Chambers of Commerce abroad, foreign chambers of commerce in the U.S., embassies, overseas assistance, Commerce Departments and contacts. Chamber, department or embassy name, address, phone, contact name, title.

The Internet Blue Pages: The Guide to Federal Government Web Sites. Information Today, Inc. • Annual. $34.95. Provides information on more than 1,800 Web sites used by various agencies of the federal government. Includes indexes to agencies and topics. Links to all Web sites listed are available at www.fedweb.com. (CyberAge Books.).

Kuwait Business Guides Series III: Contacts for Kuwaiti Contracting. International Executive Reports. • $145 payment must accompany order. Covers: contact names and addresses at the Kuwaiti Task Force; U.S. Army Corps of Engineers, Kuwaiti ministries, local merchants, government offices, banks and financial institutions; local offices of foreign companies and the Kuwait Petroleum Corporation.

National Five-Digit Zip Code and Post Office Directory. United States Postal Service - National Customer Support Center. • Annual. Two volumes. Formerly National Zip Code and Post Office Directory-.

Sibbald Guide to Every Public and the Top 150 Private Companies in Oklahoma, Louisiana, and Arkansas. Acorn Press Inc. • Annual. $80 per year, plus $5.00 shipping; payment must accompany order.. Covers: 285 public and privately-held corporations and financial institutions in Oklahoma, Louisiana, and Arkansas. Entries include: Company name, address, phone, brief company history and description, names and titles of officers and directors; return on beginning equity, return on sales/revenues; condensed balance sheet, income statement for past five years, auditors, transfer agent, legal counsel, stock exchange.

Sibbald Guide to the Top 250 Public Companies and Top 250 Private Companies in Georgia, Florida, and the Carolinas. Acorn Press Inc. • Annual. $102.50 per year, plus $5.00 shipping; payment must accompany order. Covers: 500 public and privately-held corporations and financial institutions in Georgia, Florida, and North and South Carolina. Entries include: Company name, address, phone; brief company history and description, names and titles of officers and directors; return on beginning equity, return on sales/revenues; condensed balance sheet, income statement for past five years, auditors, transfer agent, legal counsel, stock exchange.

Sweden in America. Swedish-American Chamber of Commerce. • Annual. $110. Covers: companies in the U.S. with ties to Sweden. Entries include: Company name, address, phone, fax, telex, number of employees, description of product/service.

United States Government Manual. Office of the Federal Register. • Annual. $29 Individuals. Provides information on the agencies of the executive, judicial, and legislative branches of the Federal government. Contains a section on terminated or transferred agencies. Database includes: Includes boards, commissions, committees and quasi-official agencies and organizations in which US participates.

HANDBOOKS AND MANUALS

Guide to U.S. Government Publications. Cengage Learning Inc. • Annual. $662.00. Catalogs "important series, periodicals, and reference tools" published annually by the federal government. Includes references to annual reports of various agencies.

INTERNET DATABASES

FedWorld: A Program of the United States Department of Commerce. National Technical Information Service. Phone: 800-553-NTIS or (703)605-6000; Fax: (703)605-6900; Email: webmaster@fedworld.gov • URL: http://www.fedworld.gov • Web site offers "a comprehensive central access point for searching, locating, ordering, and acquiring government and business information." Emphasis is on searching the Web pages, databases, and government reports of a wide variety of federal agencies. Fees: Free.

FirstGov: Your First Click to the U. S. Government. General Services Administration. Phone: 800-333-4636 or (202)501-0705; Email: public.affairs@gsa.gov • URL: http://www.gsa.gov • Free Web site provides extensive links to federal agencies covering a wide variety of topics, such as agriculture, business, consumer safety, education, the environment, government jobs, grants, health, social security, statistics sources, taxes, technology, travel, and world affairs. Also provides links to federal forms, including IRS tax forms. Searching is offered, both keyword and advanced.

GPO Access. U. S. Government Printing Office Sales Program, Bibliographic Systems Branch. Phone: (888)293-6498 or (202)512-1530; Fax:

(202)512-1262; Email: gpoaccess@gpo.gov • URL: http://www.access.gpo.gov • Web site provides searching of the GPO's Sales Product Catalog (SPC), also known as Publications Reference File (PRF). Covers all "Government information products currently offered for sale by the Superintendent of Documents." There are also specialized search pages for individual databases, such as the *Code of Federal Regulations*, the *Federal Register*, and *Commerce Business Daily*. Updated daily. Fees: Free.

PERIODICALS AND NEWSLETTERS

Documents to the People (DttP). Government Documents Round Table. Library and Information Technology Association. • Quarterly. Official publication of the Government Documents Round Table (GODORT) of the American Library Association (ALA). DttP features articles on local, state, national, and international government information, government activities, and documents the professional activities of GODORT.

Federal Register. Office of the Federal Register. U. S. Government Printing Office. • Daily except Saturday and Sunday. $764.00 per year. Publishes regulations and legal notices issued by federal agencies, including executive orders and presidential proclamations. Issued by the National Archives and Records Administration (www.nara.gov).

Government Business. Public Sector Publishing Ltd. • Bimonthly. Magazine featuring news and case studies that explain the commercial issues affecting local and central government.

Government Publications News. Bernan Associates. • Monthly. Free. Controlled circulation newsletter providing information on recent publications from the U. S. Government Printing Office and selected international agencies.

Internet Connection: Your Guide to Government Resources. Glasser LegalWorks. • 10 times a year. $89.00 per year. Newsletter (print) devoted to finding free or low-cost U. S. Government information on the Internet. Provides detailed descriptions of government Web sites.

Small Business Preferential Subcontracts Opportunities Monthly. Government Data Publications Inc. • Monthly. $84 Individuals per year. Companies whose government contracts exceed $1,000,000 in value for construction; $500,000 for others.

GOVERNMENT PURCHASING

See also GOVERNMENT CONTRACTS; GOVERNMENT PUBLICATIONS

DIRECTORIES

United States Government Manual. Office of the Federal Register. • Annual. $29 Individuals. Provides information on the agencies of the executive, judicial, and legislative branches of the Federal government. Contains a section on terminated or transferred agencies. Database includes: Includes boards, commissions, committees and quasi-official agencies and organizations in which US participates.

OTHER SOURCES

Government Contracts Reports. Wolters Kluwer Law & Business CCH. • Weekly. $2,600.00 per year. 10 looseleaf volumes. Laws and regulations affecting government contracts.

PERIODICALS AND NEWSLETTERS

Federal Register. Office of the Federal Register. U. S. Government Printing Office. • Daily except Saturday and Sunday. $764.00 per year. Publishes regulations and legal notices issued by federal agencies, including executive orders and presidential proclamations. Issued by the National Archives and Records Administration (www.nara.gov).

Government Product News. Penton Media Inc..

Navy Supply Corps Newsletter. U. S. Government Printing Office. • Bimonthly. $31 U.S.. Newsletter issued by U. S. Navy Supply Systems Command. Provides news of Navy supplies and stores activities.

TRADE/PROFESSIONAL ASSOCIATIONS

National Association of State Procurement Officials. 201 E Main St., Ste. 1405, Lexington, KY 40507-2004. Phone: (859)514-9159; Fax: (859)514-9166; Email: headquarters@naspo.org • URL: http://www.naspo.org • Purchasing officials of the states and territories. Formerly National Association of State Purchasing Officials.

National Institute of Government Purchasing. 151 Spring St., Herndon, VA 20170-5223. Phone: 800-367-6447 or (703)736-8900; Fax: (703)736-2818; Email: info@nigp.com • URL: http://www.nigp.org.

GOVERNMENT REGULATION OF INDUSTRY

See REGULATION OF INDUSTRY

GOVERNMENT RESEARCH

See also GOVERNMENT PUBLICATIONS; GOVERNMENT STATISTICS

ABSTRACTS AND INDEXES

NTIS Alerts: Business & Economics. U.S. Department of Commerce National Technical Information Service. • Biweekly. $130 per year. Covers consumer affairs, minority enterprises, marketing and economics, international commerce, banking, and finance.

NTIS Alerts: Government Inventions for Licensing. U.S. Department of Commerce National Technical Information Service. • Biweekly. $130 per year. Covers a wide variety of industrial and technical areas.

PAIS International. ProQuest L.L.C. • Monthly. $850.00 per year; cumulations three times a year. Provides topical citations to the worldwide literature of public affairs, economics, demographics, sociology, and trade. Text in English; indexed materials in English, French, German, Italian, Portuguese and Spanish.

CD-ROM DATABASES

PAIS International. ProQuest L.L.C. • Monthly. $1,995.00 per year. Contains over 650,000 citations to the literature of contemporary social, political, and economic issues.

DIRECTORIES

Federal Research in Progress (FEDRIP). National Technical Information Service Office of Product Management. • Monthly. $450 single user subscription. Database covers: more than 150,000 federally-funded research projects currently in progress in the physical sciences, engineering, health, agriculture, and life sciences areas. Database includes: Project title, starting date, principal investigator, performing and sponsoring organization, detailed abstract, description of the research, objective, and findings (when available).

Who's Who in Governmental Research. Governmental Research Association. • Annual. $50. Lists information on governmental research organization throughout the country.

ENCYCLOPEDIAS AND DICTIONARIES

Encyclopedia of Governmental Advisory Organizations. Cengage Learning Inc. • Annual. $1,178 Individuals print. Contains more than 7,300 entries describing activities and personnel. Complete contact information.

INTERNET DATABASES

FedWorld: A Program of the United States Department of Commerce. National Technical Information Service. Phone: 800-553-NTIS or (703)605-6000; Fax: (703)605-6900; Email: webmaster@fedworld.gov • URL: http://www.fedworld.gov • Web site offers "a comprehensive central access point for searching, locating, ordering, and acquiring government and business information." Emphasis is on searching the Web pages, databases, and government reports of a wide variety of federal agencies. Fees: Free.

FirstGov: Your First Click to the U. S. Government. General Services Administration. Phone: 800-333-4636 or (202)501-0705; Email: public.affairs@gsa.gov • URL: http://www.gsa.gov • Free Web site provides extensive links to federal agencies covering a wide variety of topics, such as agriculture, business, consumer safety, education, the environment, government jobs, grants, health, social security, statistics sources, taxes, technology, travel, and world affairs. Also provides links to federal forms, including IRS tax forms. Searching is offered, both keyword and advanced.

PERIODICALS AND NEWSLETTERS

Federal Assistance Monitor: Semi-Monthly Report on Federal and Private Grant Opportunities. Community Development Services. CD Publications. • Semimonthly. $339.00 per year; with online edition, $379.00 per year. Newsletter. Provides news of federal grant and loan programs for social, economic, and community purposes. Monitors grant announcements, funding, and availability. Formerly *Federal Research Report*.

GRA Reporter. Governmental Research Association. • Quarterly. $50 /year for nonmembers. Description: Provides a research bibliography and news of members and their organizations. Recurring features include news of research, reports of meetings, and notices of publications available.

The Information Freeway Report: Free Business and Government Information Via Modem. Washington Researchers Ltd. • Monthly. $160.00 per year. Newsletter. Provides news of business and government databases that are available free of charge through the Internet or directly. Emphasis is on federal government databases and electronic bulletin boards (Fedworld).

R and D Contracts Monthly (Research and Development): A Continuously Up-dated Sales and R and D Tool For All Research Organizations and Manufacturers. Government Data Publications Inc. • Monthly. $96.00 per year. Lists recently awarded government contracts. Annual *Directory* available.

RESEARCH CENTERS AND INSTITUTES

Midwestern State University - Bureau of Business and Government Research. Dillard College of Business Administration, 3410 Taft Blvd., Wichita Falls, TX 76308. Phone: (940)397-4722; Fax: (940)397-4693; Email: john.martinez@mwsu.edu • URL: http://www.mwsu.edu/academics/business • North Texas and southwest U.S. economic and business research.

University at Albany, State University of New York - Nelson A. Rockefeller Institute of Government. 411 State St., Albany, NY 12203-1003. Phone: (518)443-5522; Fax: (518)443-5788; Email: thomas.gais@rockinst.suny.edu • URL: http://www.rockinst.org • Public policy issues, including economic development, education, public finance, environment, governance, criminal justice, health, human services, information management, faith-based social service programs, and other issues facing New York and the nation.

University of Maryland - Institute for Governmental

Service and Research, 4321 Hartwick Rd., Ste. 208, College Park, MD 20742-3225. Phone: (301)405-4905; Fax: (301)314-9258; Email: bgr@bgr.umd.edu • URL: http://www.igsr.umd.edu/about_IGSR/history.php.

GOVERNMENT RESEARCH SUPPORT

See FEDERAL AID

GOVERNMENT SERVICE

See CIVIL SERVICE

GOVERNMENT, STATE

See STATE GOVERNMENT

GOVERNMENT STATISTICS

See also BUSINESS STATISTICS; GOVERNMENT PUBLICATIONS; STATISTICS SOURCES

ABSTRACTS AND INDEXES

Current Index to Statistics: Applications, Methods, and Theory. American Statistical Association. • Annual. An index to journal articles on statistical applications and methodology.

CD-ROM DATABASES

OECD Statistical Compendium. Organization for Economic Cooperation and Development. • Semiannual. $1,905.00 per year for 1 to 10 users. CD-ROM contains more than 730,000 monthly, quarterly, and annual time series for OECD countries, 1960 to date. Includes fully searchable data on agriculture, food, economic indicators, national accounts, employment, energy, finance, industry, technology, and foreign trade. Results can be displayed in various forms.

INTERNET DATABASES

Business 2.0 Web Guide to the Best Business Links. Business 2.0 Media Inc. Phone: (415)293-4800; Email: support@business2.com • URL: http://www.business2.com/webguide • Web site presents an extensive, searchable directory of links to "the best, most informative, and authoritative web pages." Twenty main categories cover business, finance, career, company information, people, and technology topics, with thousands of subtopics, all linking to Web sites recommended by experienced business researchers. Fees: Free.

Fedstats. Federal Interagency Council on Statistical Policy. Phone: (202)395-7254 • URL: http://www.fedstats.gov • Web site features an efficient search facility for full-text statistics produced by more than 100 federal agencies, including the Census Bureau, the Bureau of Economic Analysis, and the Bureau of Labor Statistics. Boolean searches can be made within one agency or for all agencies combined. Links are offered to international statistical bureaus, including the UN, IMF, OECD, UNESCO, Eurostat, and 20 individual countries. Fees: Free.

FedWorld: A Program of the United States Department of Commerce. National Technical Information Service. Phone: 800-553-NTIS or (703)605-6000; Fax: (703)605-6900; Email: webmaster@fedworld.gov • URL: http://www.fedworld.gov • Web site offers "a comprehensive central access point for searching, locating, ordering, and acquiring government and business information." Emphasis is on searching the Web pages, databases, and government reports of a wide variety of federal agencies. Fees: Free.

FirstGov: Your First Click to the U. S. Government. General Services Administration. Phone: 800-333-4636 or (202)501-0705; Email: public.affairs@gsa.gov • URL: http://www.gsa.gov • Free Web site provides extensive links to federal agencies covering a wide variety of topics, such as agriculture, business, consumer safety, education, the environment, government jobs, grants, health, social security, statistics sources, taxes, technology, travel, and world affairs. Also provides links to federal forms, including IRS tax forms. Searching is offered, both keyword and advanced.

FreeLunch.com. Economy.com, Inc. Phone: (610)696-8700; Fax: (610)696-1678 • URL: http://www.freelunch.com • Web site provides free access to more than 200 million economic and financial data series, covering industry, demographics, labor markets, prices, retail sales, government spending, trade, interest rates, housing starts, the stock market, etc. Data is available in either chart or table form. Searching is offered. Free, but registration required. Economy.com, Inc. also offers fee-based economic analysis at *The Dismal Scientist* site (www.dismal.com).

STATISTICS SOURCES

Revenue Statistics. Organisation for Economic Co-operation and Development Publications and Information Center. • Annual. $65.00. Presents data on government revenues in OECD countries, classified by type of tax and level of government. Text in English and French.

Standard & Poor's Statistical Service. Current Statistics. Standard & Poor's Financial Services L.L.C. • Monthly. $688.00 per year. Includes 10 *Basic Statistics* sections, *Current Statistics Supplements* and *Annual Security Price Index Record.*

Statistical Abstract of the United States. U. S. Government Printing Office. • Annual. $44.00. Issued by the U. S. Bureau of the Census.

TRADE/PROFESSIONAL ASSOCIATIONS

American Statistical Association. 732 N Washington St., Alexandria, VA 22314-1943. Phone: 888-231-3473 or (703)684-1221; Fax: (703)684-2037; Email: asainfo@amstat.org • URL: http://www.amstat.org • Professional society of persons interested in the theory, methodology, and application of statistics to all fields of human endeavor.

National Association for Public Health Statistics and Information Systems. 962 Wayne Ave., Ste. 701, Silver Spring, MD 20910. Phone: (301)563-6001; Fax: (301)563-6012; Email: hq@naphsis.org • URL: http://www.naphsis.org/Pages/home.aspx • Members are officials of state and local health agencies.

GOVERNMENT SURPLUS

See SURPLUS PRODUCTS

GRADUATE WORK IN UNIVERSITIES

See also ADULT EDUCATION; BUSINESS EDUCATION; COLLEGES AND UNIVERSITIES

ABSTRACTS AND INDEXES

Current Index to Journals in Education (CIJE). Oryx Press. • Monthly. $245.00 per year. Semiannual cumulations, $475.00.

Education Index. H.W. Wilson Co. • 10 times a year. Quarterly and annual cumulations. Price varies.

Educational Administration Abstracts. Pine Forge Press. • Quarterly. $722 Institutions.

DIRECTORIES

American Universities and Colleges. American Council on Education USA. Walter de Gruyter Inc. • Quadrennial. $249.50. Two volumes. Produced in collaboration with the American Council on Education. Provides full descriptions of more than 1,900 institutions of higher learning, including details of graduate and professional programs.

Barron's Guide to Graduate Business Schools. Barron's Educational Series Inc. • Biennial. Contains profiles of more than 600 business schools offering graduate business degrees in the U. S. and Canada. Includes advice on choosing a school.

The Europa World of Learning. Routledge. • Annual. $1,500 Individuals hardback. Covers about 33,000 colleges, libraries, museums, learned societies, academies, and research institutions throughout the world. Edited by Europa Publications.

Graduate Assistantship Directory in Computing. Association for Computing Machinery. • Database covers: Fellowships and assistantships in the computer sciences offered at U.S. and Canadian educational institutions. Entries include: Institution name, address, name and title of contact, degrees offered, area of expertise, financial aid offered, stipend amount, department facilities (hardware and software), school enrollment, required exams, admission deadlines.

E-BOOKS

The College Blue Book. Cengage Learning Inc. • Annual. $572 Individuals. Published by Macmillan Reference USA. Provides detailed information on programs, degrees, and financial aid sources in the U.S. and Canada.

ONLINE DATABASES

Dissertation Abstracts Online. ProQuest L.L.C. • Citations to all dissertations accepted for doctoral degrees by accredited U.S. educational institutions, 1861 to date. Includes British theses, 1988 to date. Inquire as to online cost and availability.

Education Index Online. H.W. Wilson Co. • Indexes a wide variety of periodicals related to schools, colleges, and education, 1984 to date. Monthly updates. Inquire as to online cost and availability.

PERIODICALS AND NEWSLETTERS

AACSB Newsline. Association to Advance Collegiate Schools of Business. • Monthly. Description: Covers issues and events affecting management education, and Association projects and activities. Recurring features include notices of publications available and news of educational opportunities.

Resources in Education. Educational Resources Information Center. U. S. Government Printing Office. • Monthly. Reports on educational research.

RESEARCH CENTERS AND INSTITUTES

Pennsylvania State University - Center for the Study of Higher Education. 400 Rackley Bldg., University Park, PA 16802-3202. Phone: (814)865-9756 or (814)865-6346; Fax: (814)865-3638; Email: cshe@psu.edu • URL: http://www.ed.psu.edu/educ/cshe • Policy analysis of major trends, issues, and practices in higher education at the institutional, state, regional, and national levels. Research initiatives include postsecondary teaching, learning assessment, program review and evaluation, the impact of college on students, strategic and regional planning, organizational cultures, business-industry relationships with colleges and universities, and international higher education. Encourages interdisciplinary studies.

STATISTICS SOURCES

Global Salary Survey Report. Association to Advance Collegiate Schools of Business. • Annual. Reports aggregate salary data of business school administrators and faculty. Text in English and Spanish.

Occupational Projections and Training Data. U. S. Government Printing Office. • Biennial. $31.50. Issued by Bureau of Labor Statistics, U. S. Department of Labor. Contains projections of employment change and job openings over the next 15 years for about 500 specific occupations. Also includes the number of associate, bachelor's, master's, doctoral, and professional degrees awarded in a recent year for about 900 specific fields of study.

School Enrollment, Social and Economic Characteristics of Students. U. S. Government Printing Office. • Annual. $2.50. Issued by the U. S. Bureau of the Census. Presents detailed tabulations of data on school enrollment of the civilian noninstitutional population three years old and over. Covers nursery school, kindergarten, elementary school, high school, college, and graduate school. Information is provided on age, race, sex, family income, marital status, employment, and other characteristics.

TRADE/PROFESSIONAL ASSOCIATIONS

Association of Graduate Schools. 1200 New York Ave. NW, Ste. 550, Washington, DC 20005. Phone: (202)408-7500; Fax: (202)408-8184 • Deans of graduate studies in the 61 universities comprising the Association of American Universities. Works to consider matters of common interest relating to graduate study and research.

Consortium for Graduate Study in Management. 229 Chesterfield Business Pkwy., Chesterfield, MO 63005. Phone: (636)681-5460 or (636)681-5553; Fax: (636)681-5499 • URL: http://www.cgsm.org • Works as an alliance of American business schools and some of the country's top corporations including University of California Berkeley, University of California Los Angeles, Carnegie Mellon University, Cornell University, Dartmouth College, Indiana University-Bloomington, University of Michigan-Ann Arbor, New York University, University of North Carolina at Chapel Hill, University of Rochester, University of Southern California, Emory University, The University of Texas at Austin, University of Virginia, Washington University in St. Louis, University of Wisconsin-Madison and Yale University. Bestows award merit-based, full-tuition fellowships for up to two consecutive years of fulltime graduate business education.

Council of Graduate Schools. 1 Dupont Cir. NW, Ste. 230, Washington, DC 20036. Phone: (202)223-3791; Fax: (202)331-7157; Email: general_inquiries@cgs.nche.edu • URL: http://www.cgsnet.org • Formerly Council of Graduate Schools in the United States.

GRAFT (POLITICS)

See CRIME AND CRIMINALS

GRAIN DEALERS

See GRAIN INDUSTRY

GRAIN ELEVATORS

See GRAIN INDUSTRY

GRAIN INDUSTRY

ABSTRACTS AND INDEXES

Field Crop Abstracts. CABI Publishing North America. • Monthly. Published in England by CABI Publishing, formerly Commonwealth Agricultural Bureaux.

Food Science and Technology Abstracts. Ovid Technologies Inc. • Monthly. $1,780.00 per year. Provides worldwide coverage of the literature of food technology and food production.

Foods Adlibra: Key to the World's Food Literature. General Mills, Inc. Foods Adlibra Publications. • Semimonthly. $240.00 per year. Provides journal citations and abstracts to the literature of food technology and packaging.

CD-ROM DATABASES

AGRICOLA on SilverPlatter. Ovid Technologies Inc. • Updated monthly. Price varies. Produced by the National Agricultural Library. Provides over 4 million citations to the literature of agriculture, agricultural economics, animal sciences, entomology, fertilizer, food, forestry, nutrition, pesticides, plant science, water resources, and other topics.

OECD Statistical Compendium. Organization for Economic Cooperation and Development. • Semiannual. $1,905.00 per year for 1 to 10 users. CD-ROM contains more than 730,000 monthly, quarterly, and annual time series for OECD countries, 1960 to date. Includes fully searchable data on agriculture, food, economic indicators, national accounts, employment, energy, finance, industry, technology, and foreign trade. Results can be displayed in various forms.

DIRECTORIES

Major Food and Drink Companies of the World. Cengage Learning Inc. • 12th edition. eBook. Published by Graham & Whiteside. Contains profiles and trade names for more than 9,200 important food and beverage companies in various countries. In addition to foods, includes both alcoholic and nonalcoholic drink products.

ENCYCLOPEDIAS AND DICTIONARIES

Encyclopedia of Food and Culture. Cengage Learning Inc. • 2003. $657.00. Three volumes. Contains 600 articles covering various aspects of food and its place in society, from agronomy to zucchini. Includes illustrations and a detailed index. eBook also available, updated in 2004.

FINANCIAL RATIOS

Annual Statement Studies. Risk Management Association. • Annual. Compiled from over 280,000 financial statements.

Annual Statement Studies: Industry Default Probabilities and Cash Flow Measures. Risk Management Association. • Annual. $405 Nonmembers. Serves as a companion volume to the original *Annual Statement Studies.* Gives probability of default estimates on a percentage scale for more than 450 industries. Includes changes in position year-by-year for eight financial statement line items and provides percentage measures of cash flow.

INTERNET DATABASES

Business 2.0 Web Guide to the Best Business Links. Business 2.0 Media Inc. Phone: (415)293-4800; Email: support@business2.com • URL: http://www.business2.com/webguide • Web site presents an extensive, searchable directory of links to "the best, most informative, and authoritative web pages." Twenty main categories cover business, finance, career, company information, people, and technology topics, with thousands of subtopics, all linking to Web sites recommended by experienced business researchers. Fees: Free.

Fedstats. Federal Interagency Council on Statistical Policy. Phone: (202)395-7254 • URL: http://www.fedstats.gov • Web site features an efficient search facility for full-text statistics produced by more than 100 federal agencies, including the Census Bureau, the Bureau of Economic Analysis, and the Bureau of Labor Statistics. Boolean searches can be made within one agency or for all agencies combined. Links are offered to international statistical bureaus, including the UN, IMF, OECD, UNESCO, Eurostat, and 20 individual countries. Fees: Free.

FreeLunch.com. Economy.com, Inc. Phone: (610)696-8700; Fax: (610)696-1678 • URL: http://www.freelunch.com • Web site provides free access to more than 200 million economic and financial data series, covering industry, demographics, labor markets, prices, retail sales, government spending, trade, interest rates, housing starts, the stock market, etc. Data is available in either chart or table form. Searching is offered. Free, but registration required. Economy.com, Inc. also offers fee-based economic analysis at *The Dismal Scientist* site (www.dismal.com).

USDA. U.S. National Institute of Standards and Technology. 100 Bureau Dr., Gaithersburg, MD 20899-1070. Phone: 800-877-8339 or (301)975-6478 or (202)720-2791; Fax: (301)975-8295; Email: inquiries@nist.gov • URL: http://www.nist.gov • The USDA home page has six sections: News and Information; What's New; About USDA; Agencies; Opportunities; Search and Help. Keyword searching is offered from the USDA home page and from various individual agency home pages. Agencies are the Economic Research Service, Agricultural Marketing Service, National Agricultural Statistics Service, National Agricultural Library, and about 12 others. Updating varies. Fees: Free.

ONLINE DATABASES

Agricola. U.S. National Agricultural Library World List of Agricultural Serials. • Covers worldwide agricultural literature. Over 3.3 million citations, 1970 to present, with monthly updates. Inquire as to online cost and availability.

CAB Abstracts. CABI. • Contains 46 specialized abstract collections covering over 10,000 journals and monographs in the areas of agriculture, horticulture, forest products, farm products, nutrition, dairy science, poultry, grains, animal health, entomology, etc. Time period is 1972 to date, with monthly updates. Inquire as to online cost and availability. *CAB Abstracts on CD-ROM* also available, with annual updating.

Food Science and Technology Abstracts (online). IFIS North American Desk. • Produced by International Food Information Service. Provides about 500,000 online citations, with abstracts, to the international literature of food science, technology, commodities, engineering, and processing. Approximately 2,000 periodicals are covered. Time period is 1969 to date, with monthly updates. Inquire as to online cost and availability.

PERIODICALS AND NEWSLETTERS

Amber Waves. Economic Research Service Hazard Analysis and Critical Control Points. • Quarterly. Replaces *Agricultural Outlook; Food Review*; and *Rural America.* Provides research and analysis from the U.S. Department of Agriculture's Economic Research Service. Includes economic data on agriculture, food, trade, and environmental factors.

Livestock and Grain Market News Branch Weekly Summary. U.S. Dept of Agriculture. Livestock and Grain Market News Branch. • Weekly. $85.00 per year. Formerly *Grain and Feed Weekly Summary and Statistics.*

Milling and Baking News. Sosland Publishing Co. • Weekly. $135 print. News magazine for the breadstuffs industry.

PRICE SOURCES

Commercial Review. Oregon Feed and Grain Association Inc. • Weekly. $35.00 per year.

Nebraska Farmer. Farm Progress Companies Inc. • $26.95 Individuals.

RESEARCH CENTERS AND INSTITUTES

Cereal Disease Laboratory-U.S. Department of Agricultural Research Service. University of Minnesota, 1551 Lindig St., Saint Paul, MN 55108. Phone: (612)624-4155; Fax: (612)649-5054; Email: shahryar.kianian@ars.usda.gov • URL: http://www.cdl.umn.edu.

STATISTICS SOURCES

Agricultural Statistics. U.S. Department of Agriculture National Agricultural Statistics Service. • Annual. $46 Individuals. Provides a wide variety of statistical data relating to agricultural production, supplies, consumption, prices/price-supports, foreign trade, costs, and returns, as well as farm labor, loans, income, and population. In many cases, historical data is shown annually for 10 years. In addition to farm data, includes detailed fishery statistics.

Statistical Annual: Grains, Options on Agricultural Futures. Chicago Board of Trade. • Annual. Includes historical data on Wheat Futures, Options on Wheat Futures, Corn Futures, Options on Corn Futures, Oats Futures, Soybean Futures, Options on Soybean Futures, Soybean Oil Futures, Soybean Meal Futures.

Survey of Current Business. U. S. Government Printing Office. • Published by Bureau of Economic Analysis, U. S. Department of Commerce. Presents a wide variety of business and economic data.

United States Census of Agriculture. U.S. Department of Agriculture National Agricultural Statistics Service. • Quinquennial. Provides uniform, comprehensive farming and ranching operations data for every U.S. state and county, including production expenses, market value of products, and operator characteristics.

TRADE/PROFESSIONAL ASSOCIATIONS

Commodity Markets Council. 1300 L St. NW, Ste. 1020, Washington, DC 20005. Phone: (202)842-0400 • URL: http://www.commoditymkts.org • Represents and supports grain exchanges, boards of trade, grain companies, milling and processing companies, transportation companies, futures commission merchants, and banks.

National Grain and Feed Association. 1250 I St. NW, Ste. 1003, Washington, DC 20005. Phone: (202)289-0873; Fax: (202)289-5388; Email: ngfa@ngfa.org • URL: http://www.ngfa.org • Formerly Grain and Feed Dealers National Association.

North American Export Grain Association. 1250 I St. NW, Ste. 1003, Washington, DC 20005-3939. Phone: (202)682-4030; Fax: (202)682-4033; Email: info@naega.org • URL: http://www.naega.org • U.S. and Canadian exporters of grain and oilseeds from the United States.

GRANITE

See QUARRYING

GRANTS-IN-AID

See also ARTS MANAGEMENT; FEDERAL AID; FOUNDATIONS

ABSTRACTS AND INDEXES

Foundation Directory Online. Foundation Center. • Formerly *Foundation Grants Index*. Five plan levels with monthly, annual, and two-year subscription options.

DIRECTORIES

Annual Register of Grant Support: A Directory of Funding Sources. Information Today, Inc. • Annual. $299 Individuals Softbound. Contains information on more than 3,500 corporate, private, and public organizations that provide grants in 11 major subject areas, including 61 specific sub-categories.

Directory of Corporate and Foundation Grants. Taft Group. • $155. Covers: in two sections; Section 1 lists over 95,000 grants and their recipients. Section 2 lists over 5,500 corporate and foundation grantmakers. Entries include: Section 1--Recipient category, location, name of recipient, amount of grant, grant description, name of corporate or foundation grantmaker. Section 2--Foundation/company name, location, grants data, alpha record of grants.

Directory of Scottish Grant Making Trusts. Scottish Council for Voluntary Organisations. • Irregular. $9.50 Members. Number of listings: 524. Entries include: Company name, address, phone, grant name and subject, requirements, recipients.

Foundation Grants to Individuals. Foundation Center. • Annual. $99.95 Individuals. Nearly 10,000 foundations that make grants to individuals. Subscriptions available in one-, three-, six-month, and yearly rates.

Foundation Reporter: Comprehensive Profiles and Giving Analyses of America's Major Private Foundations. Taft Group. • Annual. $490.00. Provides detailed information on major U. S. foundations. Eight indexes (location, grant type, recipient type, personnel, etc.).

Free Money from the Federal Government for Small Businesses and Entrepreneurs. John Wiley and Sons Inc. Technical Insights. • $18.95 Individuals. Covers: Approximately 1,500 grants and funding programs from 52 government agencies. Database includes: Bibliography. Entries include: Program name, description, contact information.

FUND ME! Sources. IGW Canada Inc. • Quarterly. $495. CD-ROM, diskette. Database covers: over 2,000 programs, grants, and subsidies for research and business available in Canada from a variety of sources, including government agencies and departments, private foundations, international associations, banks, and venture capital companies. Entries include: Program title, sponsoring organization name, address, phone, areas of interest, program criteria and description, funding amount and type.

FUNDED!. IGW Canada Inc. • CD-ROM. Database covers: over 500 researchers, companies, and projects that have been awarded funds by public sector agencies and selected private sector organizations.

Government Assistance Almanac: The Guide to Federal, Domestic, Financial and Other Programs Covering Grants, Loans, Insurance, Personal Payments and Benefits. Omnigraphics Inc. • Annual. $275 print. Gives users updated information on all available federal domestic assistance programs. These programs represent nearly $2 trillion worth of federal assistance earmarked for distribution to consumers, children, parents, veterans, senior citizens, students, businesses, civic groups, state and local agencies, and others.

Grants for Libraries & Information Services. • Available only as a downloadable file. Single use version $39.95; library use version $$99.95. Foundations and organizations which have awarded grants made the preceding year for public, academic, research, special, and school libraries; for archives and information centers; for consumer information; and for philanthropy information centers.

Guide to Federal Funding for Governments and Nonprofits. Thompson Publishing Group Inc. • Updated continuously; printed on request. $399. Contains detailed descriptions of federal grant programs in economic development, housing, transportation, social services, science, etc.

Guide to Grants for Business. Associated Management Services Ltd. • Annual. $39.50. Covers: Sources of grants in the European Community and the United Kingdom, including national and local government sources, job centers, environmental organizations, energy efficiency organizations, and loan guarantee schemes. Entries include: For national and local government sources--Name, address, phone, fax, name and title of contact. For others--Name, address, phone, fax, name and title of contact, benefits, amount available, description.

Guide to U.S. Foundations, Their Trustees, Officers, and Donors. Foundation Center. • Annual. $650 U.S. Directory set. Covers: over 74,000 currently active grantmaking foundations in the United States, including community and operating foundations, based on information returns to the Internal Revenue Service. Database includes: Bibliography of state and local directories of grantmaking foundations. Entries include: Foundation name, address, phone, name of principal contact, assets, amount of grants made, donor information, gifts received during most recent period reported; giving limitations, key officials, codes identifying coverage in other Foundation Center publications.

Inside Japanese Support. Taft Group. • Annual. $199. Covers: 340 U.S. subsidiaries of Japanese firms and 40 Japan-based foundations awarding grants in the United States. Entries include: Company name, address, phone, name and title of contact, application information, program descriptions, recent grants, U.S. operating locations; Japanese parent company name, address, and financial information. Graphs and essay entitled "The Current Status of Japanese Foundations" comprise Section 1; directory information is in Section 2.

Money to Work II--Funding for Visual Artists. Art Resources International. • Irregular. $8.95 plus $3.25 shipping. Covers: about 225 organizations offering grants for painters, sculptors, photographers, printmakers, and other visual and craft artists. Entries include: Organization name, description of grant, application and selection procedures.

National Solid Waste Grants Database. RCRA Research Library. • Database covers: More than 500 grant and loan providers as well as venture capitalists interested in recycling, reuse and solid waste management. Database includes: Contact information for some Northeastern U.S. firms.

INTERNET DATABASES

FedWorld: A Program of the United States Department of Commerce. National Technical Information Service. Phone: 800-553-NTIS or (703)605-6000; Fax: (703)605-6900; Email: webmaster@fedworld.gov • URL: http://www.fedworld.gov • Web site offers "a comprehensive central access point for searching, locating, ordering, and acquiring government and business information." Emphasis is on searching the Web pages, databases, and government reports of a wide variety of federal agencies. Fees: Free.

FirstGov: Your First Click to the U. S. Government. General Services Administration. Phone: 800-333-4636 or (202)501-0705; Email: public.affairs@gsa.gov • URL: http://www.gsa.gov • Free Web site provides extensive links to federal agencies covering a wide variety of topics, such as agriculture, business, consumer safety, education, the environment, government jobs, grants, health, social security, statistics sources, taxes, technology, travel, and world affairs. Also provides links to federal forms, including IRS tax forms. Searching is offered, both keyword and advanced.

Welcome to the Foundation Center. Foundation Center. Phone: (212)620-4230 or (212)807-3679; Fax: (212)807-3677; Email: mfn@fdncenter.org • URL: http://www.fdncenter.org • Web site provides a wide variety of information about foundations, grants, and philanthropy, with links to philanthropic organizations. "Grantmaker Information" link furnishes descriptions of available funding.

ONLINE DATABASES

GrantSelect. Schoolhouse Partners L.L.C. • Online service provides detailed descriptions of more than 10,000 grants offered by government and organizations in the U. S. Includes grants in a wide variety of subject fields. Contains current information with daily updates. Inquire as to online cost and availability.

PERIODICALS AND NEWSLETTERS

Federal Assistance Monitor: Semi-Monthly Report on Federal and Private Grant Opportunities. Community Development Services. CD Publications. • Semimonthly. $339.00 per year; with online edition, $379.00 per year. Newsletter. Provides news of federal grant and loan programs for social, economic, and community purposes. Monitors grant announcements, funding, and availability. Formerly *Federal Research Report*.

Federal Grants and Contracts Weekly: Funding Opportunities in Research, Training and Services. Wolters Kluwer Law and Business. • 50 times a year. $450.00 per year. Newsletter.

Grantsmanship Center Magazine. The Grantsmanship Center. • Quarterly. Irregular. Free to qualified personnel. Contains a variety of concise articles on grant-related topics, such as program planning, proposal writing, fundraising, non-cash gifts, federal project grants, benchmarking, taxation, etc.

TRADE/PROFESSIONAL ASSOCIATIONS

Council for Aid to Education. 215 Lexington Ave., 16th Fl., New York, NY 10016-6023. Phone: (212)661-5800; Fax: (212)661-9766; Email: vse@cae.org • URL: http://www.cae.org • Works to improve quality and productivity in higher education. Supports research and promotes policy reforms in higher education. Conducts the annual Voluntary Support of Education Survey and operates the Collegiate Learning Assessment program for undergraduate education in the United States.

National Association of Student Financial Aid Administrators. 1101 Connecticut Ave. NW, Ste. 1100, Washington, DC 20036-4312. Phone: (202)785-0453; Fax: (202)785-1487; Email: web@nasfaa.org • URL: http://www.nasfaa.org • Serves as a national forum for matters related to student aid.

National Grants Management Association. 2100 M St. NW, Ste. 170, Washington, DC 20037. Phone: (202)308-9443; Email: info@ngma.org • URL: http://netforum.avectra.com/eweb/StartPage.aspx?Site=ngma&WebCode=HomePage • Strengthens the relationship between grant-making agencies and grant recipients by empowering both sides with knowledge through training, seminars, workshops, and conferences. Focuses on federal, state, and local governments and private foundations that provide grants, grants-in-aid, cooperative agreements, and subsidies.

GRAPE INDUSTRY

See FRUIT INDUSTRY

GRAPHIC ARTS INDUSTRY

See also COMMERCIAL ART; DESIGN IN INDUSTRY; LITHOGRAPHY; PRINTING AND PRINTING EQUIPMENT INDUSTRIES

ABSTRACTS AND INDEXES

Art Index. EBSCO Publishing Inc. • Quarterly. Annual cumulations. Price varies. Subject and author index to periodicals in art, architecture, industrial design, city planning, photography, and various related topics.

DIRECTORIES

Holo-Pack Holo-Print Guidebook and Business Directory: 2nd Edition. Smithers Pira. • $47.50 Individuals. Covers: Organizations around the world which supply holograms or holographic products and services.

FINANCIAL RATIOS

Annual Statement Studies. Risk Management Association. • Annual. Compiled from over 280,000 financial statements.

Annual Statement Studies: Industry Default Probabilities and Cash Flow Measures. Risk Management Association. • Annual. $405 Nonmembers. Serves as a companion volume to the original *Annual Statement Studies*. Gives probability of default estimates on a percentage scale for more than 450 industries. Includes changes in position year-by-year for eight financial statement line items and provides percentage measures of cash flow.

Printing Industries of America Ratios. Printing Industries of America - Center for Technology and Research. • Annual. $750 Members Full Set (volume 1-16). Annual financial benchmarking study.

ONLINE DATABASES

Art Index Online. H.W. Wilson Co. • Indexes a wide variety of art-related periodicals, 1984 to date. Monthly updates. Inquire as to online cost and availability.

PERIODICALS AND NEWSLETTERS

Color Publishing. PennWell Corp., Advanced Technology Div. • Bimonthly. $29.70 per year.

Graphic Arts Monthly: The Magazine of the Printing Industry. Reed Elsevier Group plc Reed Business Information. • Monthly. Free to qualified personnel; others, $142.99 per year.

In-Plant Graphics. North American Publishing Co. • Contains articles, news, and features from the print magazine, *In-Plant Graphics*. Provides information on the in-plant printing industry, covering more than 24,000 in-house reproduction departments for companies, manufacturers, government organizations, and universities in the United States. Covers topics such as publishing, pre-press, printing, binding, and mailing. Includes editorials, salary surveys, company financial information, coverage of industry happenings, and more. Includes an article archive. Provides online searchable access to the magazine's annual *Buyers' and Specifiers' Guide*, with contact information and descriptions of printers, suppliers, and manufacturers throughout the United States. Also includes searchable access to a listing of used printing equipment.

The Magazine for Electronic Publishing Professionals. Publish Media. • Monthly. $39.90 per year. Edited for professional publishers, graphic designers, and industry service providers. Covers new products and emerging technologies for the electronic publishing industry.

Step Inside Design: The World of Design from Inside Out. Dynamic Graphics Inc. • Bimonthly. $42.00 per year. Formerly *Step-by-Step Graphics*.

TAGA Newsletter. Technical Association of the Graphic Arts. • Description: Disseminates information in the graphic arts industry to members which is international in scope. Recurring features include interviews, news of research, reports of meetings, news of educational opportunities, and standards updates.

RESEARCH CENTERS AND INSTITUTES

Rochester Institute of Technology - Chester F. Carlson Center for Imaging Science. 54 Lomb Memorial Dr., Rochester, NY 14623. Phone: (585)475-5944; Fax: (585)475-5988; Email: baum@cis.rit.edu • URL: http://www.cis.rit.edu • Imaging sciences, including remote sensing, digital image processing, color science, optics, medical diagnostic imaging, visual perception, sensor development, printing technology, and astronomical imaging.

TRADE/PROFESSIONAL ASSOCIATIONS

American Institute of Graphic Arts. 164 5th Ave., New York, NY 10010-5901. Phone: (212)807-1990; Fax: (212)807-1799 • URL: http://www.aiga.org • Graphic designers, art directors, illustrators and packaging designers. Sponsors exhibits and projects in the public interest. Sponsors traveling exhibitions. Operates gallery. Maintains library of design books and periodicals; offers slide archives.

Design Management Institute. 38 Chauncy St., Ste. 800, Boston, MA 02111. Phone: (617)338-6380 • URL: http://www.dmi.org • In-house design groups and consultant design firms; individuals involved in the management of designers with in-house corporate design groups or consultant design firms. Aims to share management techniques as applied to design groups, and to facilitate better understanding by business management of the role design can play in achieving business goals. Design disciplines included are: architecture, advertising, communications, exhibit design, graphics, interior design, packaging and product design. Develops and distributes design management education materials. Sponsors seminars for design professionals. Identifies critical areas of design management study; conducts surveys and research on corporate design management. Maintains design management archive. Operates Center for Research, Center for Education, and Center for Design and Management Resources.

Print Alliance Credit Exchange. 1100 Main St., Buffalo, NY 14209. Fax: (716)878-0479 • URL: http://www.gopace.com • Manufacturers or designers of business forms or graphic media, selling to dealers, distributors, office supply, copy stores, or end users. Promotes the collection, computation, and exchange of factual ledger experience information by members. Compiles statistics.

Research and Engineering Council of NAPL. 1 Meadowlands Plz., Ste. 1511, East Rutherford, NJ 07073. Phone: 800-642-6275 or (201)634-9600; Fax: (201)634-0324; Email: webmaster@napl.org • URL: http://napl.org.

GRAPHICS, COMPUTER

See COMPUTER GRAPHICS

GRAPHITE

See MINES AND MINERAL RESOURCES

GRAPHS AND CHARTS

PERIODICALS AND NEWSLETTERS

Harvard Management Communication Letter. Harvard Business School Publishing. • Description: Provides information and techniques for managers on effective communication.

Presentations: Technology and Techniques for Effective Communication. Nielsen Business Media Inc. • Monthly. Free to qualified personnel; others, $69.00 per year. Covers the use of presentation hardware and software, including audiovisual equipment and computerized display systems. Includes an annual *Buyers Guide to Presentation Products*.

GRAVEL INDUSTRY

See QUARRYING

GREASE

See LUBRICATION AND LUBRICANTS

For publishers' addresses, refer to SOURCES CITED section at the back of the book.

GREETING CARD INDUSTRY

DIRECTORIES

Directory of Australia and New Zealand Importers of Calendars. EXIM Infotek Private Ltd. • $150 Individuals. Covers: 20 Australian and New Zealand importers of calendars, greeting cards, postcards, cards, morals, posters, prints, lithographs and etching. Entries include: Company name, postal address, telephone, fax, e-mail, website, contact person, designation, and product details.

Directory of South American Importers of Calendars, Greeting, Prints and Lithographs. EXIM Infotek Private Ltd. • $150 Individuals. Covers: 30 South American importers of calendars, greeting cards, postcards, prints, lithographs, and etchings. Entries include: Company name, postal address, telephone, fax, e-mail, website, contact person, designation, and product details.

GRINDING AND POLISHING

See ABRASIVES INDUSTRY

GROCERY BUSINESS

See also CHAIN STORES; FOOD INDUSTRY; SUPERMARKETS

CD-ROM DATABASES

OECD Statistical Compendium. Organization for Economic Cooperation and Development. • Semiannual. $1,905.00 per year for 1 to 10 users. CD-ROM contains more than 730,000 monthly, quarterly, and annual time series for OECD countries, 1960 to date. Includes fully searchable data on agriculture, food, economic indicators, national accounts, employment, energy, finance, industry, technology, and foreign trade. Results can be displayed in various forms.

DIRECTORIES

Directory of Wholesale Grocers. Chain Store Guide. • Annual. $327.00. Online edition, $747.00. Profiles over 1,100 cooperatives, voluntaries, non-sponsoring wholesalers, cash and carry warehouses, and nearly 220 service merchandisers. Covers United States and Canada.

Grocery Headquarters: The Newspaper for the Food Industry. Trend Publishing Inc. • Monthly. $80. Covers the sale and distribution of food products and other items sold in supermarkets and grocery stores. Edited mainly for retailers and wholesalers. Incorporates (Grocery Distribution).

International Private Label Directory. E.W. Williams Publications Co. • Annual. Provides information on over 2,000 suppliers of a wide variety of private label and generic products: food, over-the-counter health products, personal care items, and general merchandise.

Plunkett's Food Industry Almanac. Plunkett Research Ltd. • $349.99 Individuals print + online. Covers: 340 leading companies in the global food industry. Entries include: Name, address, phone, fax, and key executives. Also includes analysis and information on trends, technology, and statistics in the field.

Trade Dimensions' Market Scope: The Desktop Guide to Supermarket Share. Trade Dimensions. • Annual. Covers: Market share for over 1,400 supermarket chains and wholesalers. Entries include: Company name, location, number of stores in the area, market share. Syndicated market areas include 52 AC Nielsen Scantrack markets, all 64 IRI InfoScan markets, all 205 DMAs (Designated Market Areas) and 100 MSAs (government-defined), plus 48 Trade Dimensions markets.

FINANCIAL RATIOS

Food Retailing Industry Speaks. Food Marketing Institute. • Annual. Members, $150; non-members, $350. Provides data on overall food industry marketing performance, including retail distribution and store operations.

HANDBOOKS AND MANUALS

Progressive Grocer Guidebook. Trade Dimensions. • Annual. $375.00. Over 800 major chain and independent food retailers and wholesalers in the United States and Canada; also includes food brokers, rack jobbers, candy and tobacco distributors, and magazine distributors.

INTERNET DATABASES

Advance Monthly Retail Trade Report. U. S. Census Bureau. Phone: 800-541-8345 or (301)457-4100 or (301)763-2713; Fax: (301)457-1296 or (301)457-3842; Email: naics@census.gov • URL: http://www.census.gov/epcd/www/naicstab.htm • Web pages provide monthly sales figures for a wide range of retail businesses. Advance, preliminary, and final statistics are provided for the latest month available in each case, with a previous-year comparison. Updates are monthly.

Business 2.0 Web Guide to the Best Business Links. Business 2.0 Media Inc. Phone: (415)293-4800; Email: support@business2.com • URL: http://www.business2.com/webguide • Web site presents an extensive, searchable directory of links to "the best, most informative, and authoritative web pages." Twenty main categories cover business, finance, career, company information, people, and technology topics, with thousands of subtopics, all linking to Web sites recommended by experienced business researchers. Fees: Free.

Fedstats. Federal Interagency Council on Statistical Policy. Phone: (202)395-7254 • URL: http://www.fedstats.gov • Web site features an efficient search facility for full-text statistics produced by more than 100 federal agencies, including the Census Bureau, the Bureau of Economic Analysis, and the Bureau of Labor Statistics. Boolean searches can be made within one agency or for all agencies combined. Links are offered to international statistical bureaus, including the UN, IMF, OECD, UNESCO, Eurostat, and 20 individual countries. Fees: Free.

FreeLunch.com. Economy.com, Inc. Phone: (610)696-8700; Fax: (610)696-1678 • URL: http://www.freelunch.com • Web site provides free access to more than 200 million economic and financial data series, covering industry, demographics, labor markets, prices, retail sales, government spending, trade, interest rates, housing starts, the stock market, etc. Data is available in either chart or table form. Searching is offered. Free, but registration required. Economy.com, Inc. also offers fee-based economic analysis at *The Dismal Scientist* site (www.dismal.com).

PERIODICALS AND NEWSLETTERS

Food Industry Newsletter: All the Food News That Matters. Newsletters Inc. • 26 times a year. $245.00 per year. Newsletter. A summary of key industry news for food executives.

Food Trade News. Best-Met Publishing Company Inc. • Monthly. Reports on the retail food industry in Pennsylvania, Delaware, southern New Jersey and northern Maryland.

Modern Grocer. GC Publishing Co. • Monthly. $50 Individuals. Magazine for food retailers, wholesalers, distributors, brokers, manufacturers, and packers in the metro New York and New Jersey marketing area. Formerly *Modern Grocer.*

Produce Merchandising: The Packer's Retailing and Merchandising Magazine. Vance Publishing Corp. • Monthly. $35.00 per year. Provides information and advice on the retail marketing and promotion of fresh fruits and vegetalbe.

Progressive Grocer: The Magazine of Supermarketing. Nielsen Business Media Inc..

STATISTICS SOURCES

Annual Benchmark Report for Retail Trade and Food Services..A Detailed Summary of Retail Sales, Purchases, Accounts Receivable, Inventories, and Food Service Sales. U. S. Government Printing Office. • Annual. $13.00. Issued by the U.S. Census Bureau. Provides detailed annual and monthly retail statistics for the most recent 10 years. Includes data for various kinds of retail outlets, including automobiles, furniture, appliances, building supplies, grocery stores, drug stores, gasoline stations, clothing, sporting goods, department stores, and restaurants.

Survey of Current Business. U. S. Government Printing Office. • Published by Bureau of Economic Analysis, U. S. Department of Commerce. Presents a wide variety of business and economic data.

TRADE/PROFESSIONAL ASSOCIATIONS

Grocery Manufacturers Association. 1350 I St. NW, Washington, DC 20005. Phone: (202)639-5900; Fax: (202)639-5932; Email: info@gmaonline.org • URL: http://www.gmaonline.org • Absorbed Association of Sales and Marketing Companies.

National Grocers Association. 1005 N Glebe Rd., Ste. 250, Arlington, VA 22201-5758. Phone: (703)516-0700; Fax: (703)516-0115; Email: feedback@nationalgrocers.org • URL: http://www.nationalgrocers.org • Independent food retailers; wholesale food distributors servicing 29,000 food stores. Promotes industry interests and works to advance understanding, trade and cooperation among all sectors of the food industry. Represents members' interests before the government. Aids in the development of programs designed to improve the productivity and efficiency of the food distribution industry. Offers services in areas such as store planning and engineering, personnel selection and training, operations and advertising. Sponsors seminars and in-house training. Maintains liaison with Women Grocers of America, which serves as an advisory arm.

GROSS NATIONAL PRODUCT

See also NATIONAL ACCOUNTING

CD-ROM DATABASES

OECD Statistical Compendium. Organization for Economic Cooperation and Development. • Semiannual. $1,905.00 per year for 1 to 10 users. CD-ROM contains more than 730,000 monthly, quarterly, and annual time series for OECD countries, 1960 to date. Includes fully searchable data on agriculture, food, economic indicators, national accounts, employment, energy, finance, industry, technology, and foreign trade. Results can be displayed in various forms.

ENCYCLOPEDIAS AND DICTIONARIES

Worldmark Encyclopedia of National Economies. Cengage Learning Inc. • 2002. $572.00. Four volumes. Covers both the current and historical development of the economies of 200 foreign nations. Includes analysis and statistics. Also available as eBook.

INTERNET DATABASES

Bureau of Economic Analysis. U. S. Department of Commerce, Bureau of Economic Analysis. Phone: (202)606-9900; Fax: (202)606-5310; Email: webmaster@bea.doc.gov • URL: http://www.bea.doc.gov • Web site includes "News Release Information" covering national, regional, and international economic estimates from the BEA. Highlights of releases appear online the same day, complete text and tables appear the next day. "Recent News Releases" section provides titles for past nine months, with links. "BEA Data and Methodology" includes "Frequently Requested NIPA Data" (national income and product accounts, such as gross domestic product and personal income). Other statistics are available. Fees: Free.

Business 2.0 Web Guide to the Best Business Links. Business 2.0 Media Inc. Phone: (415)293-4800; Email: support@business2.com • URL: http://www.business2.com/webguide • Web site presents an extensive, searchable directory of links to "the best, most informative, and authoritative web pages." Twenty main categories cover business, finance, career, company information, people, and technology topics, with thousands of subtopics, all linking to Web sites recommended by experienced business researchers. Fees: Free.

Fedstats. Federal Interagency Council on Statistical Policy. Phone: (202)395-7254 • URL: http://www.fedstats.gov • Web site features an efficient search facility for full-text statistics produced by more than 100 federal agencies, including the Census Bureau, the Bureau of Economic Analysis, and the Bureau of Labor Statistics. Boolean searches can be made within one agency or for all agencies combined. Links are offered to international statistical bureaus, including the UN, IMF, OECD, UNESCO, Eurostat, and 20 individual countries. Fees: Free.

FreeLunch.com. Economy.com, Inc. Phone: (610)696-8700; Fax: (610)696-1678 • URL: http://www.freelunch.com • Web site provides free access to more than 200 million economic and financial data series, covering industry, demographics, labor markets, prices, retail sales, government spending, trade, interest rates, housing starts, the stock market, etc. Data is available in either chart or table form. Searching is offered. Free, but registration required. Economy.com, Inc. also offers fee-based economic analysis at *The Dismal Scientist* site (www.dismal.com).

STATISTICS SOURCES

Survey of Current Business. U. S. Government Printing Office. • Published by Bureau of Economic Analysis, U. S. Department of Commerce. Presents a wide variety of business and economic data.

GROUP INSURANCE

See HEALTH INSURANCE

GROUP MEDICAL PRACTICE

See also HEALTH CARE INDUSTRY

ABSTRACTS AND INDEXES

NTIS Alerts: Health Care. U.S. Department of Commerce National Technical Information Service. • Biweekly. $130 per year. Covers a wide variety of health care topics, including quality assurance, delivery organization, economics (costs), technology, and legislation.

CD-ROM DATABASES

Authority Health Care Law Library. Matthew Bender and Company Inc. • Periodic updates. Price on request. Full text CD-ROM provides legal information, case law, and analysis relating to health care facilities, health insurance, longterm care, Medigap, and Medicare.

DIRECTORIES

AHA Integrated Delivery Network Directory: U.S. Health Care Systems, Networks, and Alliances. American Hospital Association. • Annual. $250.00. Provides information about a wide variety of U.S. health care groups and affiliations, including hospitals, nursing homes, rehabilitation centers, psychiatric facilities, home health care agencies, clinical laboratories, outpatient facilities, and diagnostic imaging centers. Includes names of more than 8,000 key executives.

Directory of Physician Groups and Networks. Dorland Healthcare Information. • Annual. $495.00. Available only online. Approximately 8,000 independent practice associations (IPAs), physician hospital organizations (PHOs), management service organizations (MSOs), physician practice management companies (PPMCs), and group practices having 20 or more physicians.

Dorland's Directory of Health Plans. Dorland Healthcare Information. • Annual. $195.00. Published in association with the American Association of Health Plans (www.aahp.org). Lists more than 2,400 health plans, including Health Maintenance Organizations (HMOs), Preferred Provider Organizations (PPOs), and Point of Service plans (POS). Includes the names of about 9,000 health plan executives.

PERIODICALS AND NEWSLETTERS

AHA News. American Hospital Association. HealthForum. • Description: Highlights major news affecting hospitals and the health care field. Reports on legislation and regulation, court cases, surveys, and federal programs. Carries information on individual hospitals and allied hospital associations.

Group Practice Journal. American Medical Group Association. • 10/year. $75 Institutions.

Healthplan: The Magazine of Trends, Insights, and Best Practices. American Association of Health Plans. • Bimonthly. $60 Individuals. Trade magazine covering news and analysis of managed health care for HMO and PPO executives.

MGMA Connexion. Medical Group Management Association. • 10/year. $95 Individuals /year. Formerly *Medical Group Management Journal.* Provides in-depth coverage of key industry topics and advice for group practice professionals.

Modern Physician: Essential Business News for the Executive Physician. Crain Communications Inc. • Monthly. $45.00. Edited for physicians responsible for business decisions at hospitals, clinics, HMOs, and other health groups. Includes special issues on managed care, practice management, legal issues, and finance.

TRADE/PROFESSIONAL ASSOCIATIONS

American College of Medical Practice Executives. 104 Inverness Terr. E, Englewood, CO 80112-5306. Phone: 877-275-6462 or (303)799-1111; Fax: (303)643-4439; Email: acmpe@mgma.com • URL: http://www.mgma.com/about/default.aspx?id=242 • Formerly American College of Medical Group Administrators.

American Medical Group Association. 1 Prince St., Alexandria, VA 22314-3318. Phone: (703)838-0033; Fax: (703)548-1890; Email: dfisher@amga.org • URL: http://www.amga.org • Represents the interests of medical groups. Advocates for the medical groups and patients through innovation and information sharing, benchmarking, developing leadership, and improving patient care. Provides political advocacy, educational and networking programs and publications, benchmarking data services, and financial and operations assistance.

Medical Group Management Association. 104 Inverness Terr. E, Englewood, CO 80112-5306. Phone: 877-275-6462 or (303)799-1111; Fax: (303)643-4439; Email: service@mgma.com • URL: http://www.mgma.com • Represents professionals involved in the management of medical group practices and administration of other ambulatory healthcare facilities. Provides products and services that includes education, benchmarking, surveys, national advocacy and networking opportunities for members.

GROWTH STOCKS

See STOCKS

GUARANTEED WAGES

See WAGES AND SALARIES

GUIDED MISSILES

See ROCKET INDUSTRY

GUMS AND RESINS

See NAVAL STORES

GUNS

See FIREARMS INDUSTRY

For publishers' addresses, refer to SOURCES CITED section at the back of the book.

H

HABERDASHERY

See MEN'S CLOTHING INDUSTRY

HAIR CARE PRODUCTS

See COSMETICS INDUSTRY

HAIRDRESSERS

See BARBER AND BEAUTY SHOPS

HALF-TONE PROCESS

See PHOTOENGRAVING

HANDICAPPED WORKERS

See also EQUAL EMPLOYMENT OPPORTUNITY

DIRECTORIES

New Jersey Business and Agency TTY/TDD Directory. Scotch Plains Lions Club. • Annual. Covers more than 300 New Jersey businesses, government agencies, police departments, services for the handicapped (including qualified interpreters for the deaf), associations, schools, libraries, churches, and medical facilities equipped with devices which make them accessible by telephone to the hearing- and speech-impaired.

HANDBOOKS AND MANUALS

ADA Compliance Guide. Thompson Publishing Group Inc. • $499 print only. Provides detailed information for employers and others on complying with the Americans With Disabilities Act (ADA). Includes material on employment discrimination, transportation accessibility, accessibility in public accommodations, and state disability laws.

OTHER SOURCES

ADA Compliance Manual for Employers. Matthew Bender and Company Inc. • Looseleaf. $95.00. Periodic supplementation available. "Every business with more than 15 employees must comply with the Amricans with Disabilities Act." This guide provides practical advice on job requirements, accessibility, employee selection, reasonable accomodations, termination issues, and other matters.

PERIODICALS AND NEWSLETTERS

GDL Alert. Thomson RIA. • Monthly. $110.98 per year. Newsletter. Covers current legal developments of interest to employers. Formerly *Disabilities in the Workplace Alert*.

RESEARCH CENTERS AND INSTITUTES

National Institute on Disability and Rehabilitation Research - Self-Employment Technology Transfer. 52 Corbin Hall, Rural Institute on Disabilities, University of Montana, Missoula, MT 59812. Phone: 800-732-0320 or (406)268-2743; Fax: (406)243-4730; Email: nancy@ruralinstitute.umt.edu • URL: http://rtc.ruralinstitute.umt.edu/SelEm/RuSelfEm.htm • Vocational rehabilitation research, specifically, self-employment for people with disabilities.

Vecova Centre for Disability Services and Research. 3304 - 33rd St. NW, Calgary, AB, Canada T2L 2A6. Phone: (403)284-1121; Fax: (403)284-1146; Email: info@vecova.ca • URL: http://vecova.ca • Associated with University of Calgary.

TRADE/PROFESSIONAL ASSOCIATIONS

Disability Rights Center. 24 Stone St., Ste. 204, Augusta, ME 04330. Phone: 800-452-1948 or (207)626-2774; Fax: (207)621-1419; Email: advocate@drcme.org • URL: http://www.drcme.org • Represents public interest research group committed on educating society about the disability rights movement. Aims to inform the public, political activists, consumer activists, advocates, and students on the disability movement. Seeks to involve as many disabled citizens as possible in processes that directly affect their lives, to work closely with other disability-related, consumer-based advocacy groups, and to educate the public in the legitimate demands and needs of the disabled. Compiles statistics.

HANDLING OF MATERIALS

See MATERIALS HANDLING

HARASSMENT, SEXUAL

See SEXUAL HARASSMENT IN THE WORKPLACE

HARBORS

See PORTS

HARD FIBERS INDUSTRY

See FIBER INDUSTRY

HARDWARE INDUSTRY

See also FASTENER INDUSTRY; SAW INDUSTRY; TOOL INDUSTRY

DIRECTORIES

Directory of American Manufacturers & Exporters of Hardwares--All Types. EXIM Infotek Private Ltd. • $15 Individuals. Covers: 170 American manufacturers and exporters of builders' hardware, cabinet hardware, cabinet locks, door hardware, door hardware locks, door locks, electrical hardware, electronic hardware, furniture hardware, granite blocks and panels, hardware, hinges, industrial hardware, luggage hardware, metal and plastic adjustable hand levers, padlocks, panels, patch panels, structural and decorative panels, and wall panels. Entries include: Company name, postal address, city, country, phone, fax, e-mail and websites, contact person, designation, and product details.

Directory of Chinese Manufacturers & Exporters of Hardwares--All Types. EXIM Infotek Private Ltd. • $20 Individuals. Covers: 200 Chinese manufacturers and exporters of abrasive materials, abrasive paper, abrasives products, brackets, brass locks, clamps, clips, decorations-indoor, door closers, door locks, fittings, flanges, hardware, hardware fittings, hardware minerals, hardware products, hardware tools, hinges, locks, locksets, pad locks, panels, and pins. Entries include: Company name, postal address, city, country, phone, fax, e-mail and websites, contact person, designation, and product details.

Directory of Japanese Manufacturers & Exporters of Hardwares--All Types. EXIM Infotek Private Ltd. • $5 Individuals. Covers: 40 Japanese manufacturers and exporters of builders' hardware, casters, door handles, door locks, door operators, fittings, pins, and springs. Entries include: Company name, postal address, city, country, phone, fax, e-mail and websites, contact person, designation, and product details.

Directory of SAARC Importers of Hardwares--All Types. EXIM Infotek Private Ltd. • Covers: 90 companies in member countries of the South Asian Association for Regional Cooperation (SAARC) that import abrasives, anchors, blades, brass ball knob, brass collars, knobs for brass beds, brass fittings, brass hardware, builder's hardware, cabinet hardware, castor wheel, ceiling fittings, coated abrasives, curtain fittings, curtain rails, door accessories, door closers, door fittings, door handles, door locks, emery paper, furniture hardware and parts, general hardware, hardware merchants, hinges, hooded ball casters, hooks, lipped channel, cylinder lock, locks for homes and hotels, magnet catches, nails, overhead sliding door systems, pantry cupboards fittings, railings, roller doors, roller shutter spring, sand paper, spring, flat washers, taper lock bushes, tug pins, twin wheel casters, vibrator roller, water sand paper, zigzag, and engineering tools.

Directory of South American Importers of Hardwares--All Types. EXIM Infotek Private Ltd. • $35 Individuals. Covers: 500 South American importers of abrasives, builders hardware, casters, furniture hardware and parts, and locks. Entries include: Company name, postal address, telephone, fax, e-mail, website, contact person, designation, and product details.

Directory of South Korean Manufacturers & Exporters of Hardwares--All Types. EXIM Infotek Private Ltd. • $15 Individuals. Covers: 160 South Korean manufacturers and exporters of abrasive coated products, abrasive paper, brackets, clips, frame-doors (channel), haberdashery metalware, hinge-doors/trunks/hoods, ironmongery and hardware, ironmongery and hardware for furniture, locksmith articles, metal fittings, metal smallwares for various uses, nails/tacks/spikes/staples-metal, paint brushes and rollers, pins, and springs-various types. Entries include: Company name, postal address, city, country, phone, fax, e-mail and websites, contact person, designation, and product details.

Directory of Taiwanese Manufacturers & Exporters of Hardwares--All Types. EXIM Infotek Private Ltd. • $40 Individuals. Covers: 650 Taiwanese manufacturers and exporters of abrasive coated products, abrasive media, blind rivets, brass hardware, brass knobs and pulls, brass padlocks, builders' hardware, building hardware, cabinet hardware, cam locks, casters, ceramic cabinet hardware, door edge guards, door fittings, door handles, door hardware, door knob/lever handles, door locks, d-rings, furniture hardware, furniture lock sets, haberdashery metalware, home hardwares, ironmongery and hardware, ironmongery and hardware for furniture, key lock switches, locking handles, locks, locks for luggage and bags, locksmith articles, luggage hardware and accessories, metal fittings, metal smallwares for various uses, nails/tacks/spikes/staples-metal, pad locks, paint brushes and rollers, pins, plastic foot studs, plastic handles w/loops, roller strips, screen door hardware, sliders, springs, and stainless steel hardware. Entries include: Company name, postal address, city, country, telephone, fax, e-mail and websites, contact person, designation, and product details.

ProSales Buyer's Guide. DoveTale Publishers. • Annual. Price on application. A directory of equipment for professional builders.

Tools of the Trade Annual Buyers Guide. DoveTale Publishers. • Annual. Price on application. A directory of tools for the construction industry.

FINANCIAL RATIOS

Annual Statement Studies. Risk Management Association. • Annual. Compiled from over 280,000 financial statements.

Annual Statement Studies: Industry Default Probabilities and Cash Flow Measures. Risk Management Association. • Annual. $405 Nonmembers. Serves as a companion volume to the original *Annual Statement Studies.* Gives probability of default estimates on a percentage scale for more than 450 industries. Includes changes in position year-by-year for eight financial statement line items and provides percentage measures of cash flow.

National Retail Hardware Association Management Report: Cost of Doing Business Study. North American Retail Hardware Association. • Annual. Report provides information on business cost analysis.

INTERNET DATABASES

Advance Monthly Retail Trade Report. U. S. Census Bureau. Phone: 800-541-8345 or (301)457-4100 or (301)763-2713; Fax: (301)457-1296 or (301)457-3842; Email: naics@census.gov • URL: http://www.census.gov/epcd/www/naicstab.htm • Web pages provide monthly sales figures for a wide range of retail businesses. Advance, preliminary, and final statistics are provided for the latest month available in each case, with a previous-year comparison. Updates are monthly.

ONLINE DATABASES

Thomas Register Online. Thomas Publishing Company L.L.C. • Provides concise information on approximately 194,000 U. S. companies, mainly manufacturers, with over 50,000 product classifications. Indexes over 115,000 trade names. Information is updated semiannually. Inquire as to online cost and availability.

PERIODICALS AND NEWSLETTERS

Doors & Hardware. Door and Hardware Institute. • Monthly. $75 Life member. Covers the architectural openings industry.

Hardware Age. Reed Elsevier Group plc Reed Business Information. • Monthly. $75.00 per year.

Hardware Retailing: Serving Hardware, Home Center, Building Material Retailers. North American Retail Hardware Association. • Monthly. $8 Individuals. Trade magazine for hardware retailers selling do-it-yourself products. Formerly *DIY Retailing.*

STATISTICS SOURCES

Annual Benchmark Report for Retail Trade and Food Services..A Detailed Summary of Retail Sales, Purchases, Accounts Receivable, Inventories, and Food Service Sales. U. S. Government Printing Office. • Annual. $13.00. Issued by the U.S. Census Bureau. Provides detailed annual and monthly retail statistics for the most recent 10 years. Includes data for various kinds of retail outlets, including automobiles, furniture, appliances, building supplies, grocery stores, drug stores, gasoline stations, clothing, sporting goods, department stores, and restaurants.

TRADE/PROFESSIONAL ASSOCIATIONS

American Hardware Manufacturers Association. The William P. Farrell Bldg., 801 N Plaza Dr., Schaumburg, IL 60173. Phone: (847)605-1025; Fax: (847)605-1030; Email: info@ahma.org • URL: http://www.ahma.org • Represents the hardware, home improvement, lawn and garden, paint and decorating, and related industries.

Builders Hardware Manufacturers Association. 355 Lexington Ave., 15th Fl., New York, NY 10017. Phone: (212)297-2122; Fax: (212)370-9047; Email: bhma@kellencompany.com • URL: http://www.buildershardware.com • Manufacturers of builders' hardware, both contract and stock. Provides statistical services; maintains standardization program; sponsors certification programs for locks, latches, door closers and cabinet hardware. Maintains 12 product sections.

Decorative Plumbing and Hardware Association. 7508 Wisconsin Ave., 4th Fl., Bethesda, MD 20814-3561. Phone: (301)657-3642; Fax: (301)907-9326; Email: info@dpha.net • URL: http://www.dpha.net • Advances the business and professional development of independent dealers, manufacturers, representatives and others involved in the decorative plumbing and hardware industry. Offers educational programs to train staff, create career paths and provide recognition.

Door and Hardware Institute. 14150 Newbrook Dr., Ste. 200, Chantilly, VA 20151-2223. Phone: (703)222-2010; Fax: (703)222-2410; Email: membership@dhi.org • URL: http://www.dhi.org • Commercial distributors, manufacturers and specifiers involved in doors and builders' hardware (locks, door hardware, latches, hinges, and electrified products). Works with architects, contractors, and building owners. Conducts management and technical courses and membership-related surveys. Offers certification program for the Architectural Openings Industry (AHC, CDC).

North American Retail Hardware Association. 6325 Digital Way, Ste. 300, Indianapolis, IN 46278-1787. Phone: 800-772-4424 or (317)275-9400 or (317)290-0338; Fax: (317)275-9403 or (317)328-4354; Email: hwegeng@nrha.org • URL: http://www.nrha.org • Represents independent family-owned hardware/home improvement retailers. Sponsors correspondence courses in hardware and building materials retailing; conducts annual cost-of-doing-business study.

HARDWOOD INDUSTRY

See also LUMBER INDUSTRY

ABSTRACTS AND INDEXES

Forest Products Abstracts. CABI Publishing North America. • Weekly updates.

CD-ROM DATABASES

AGRICOLA on SilverPlatter. Ovid Technologies Inc. • Updated monthly. Price varies. Produced by the National Agricultural Library. Provides over 4 million citations to the literature of agriculture, agricultural economics, animal sciences, entomology, fertilizer, food, forestry, nutrition, pesticides, plant science, water resources, and other topics.

Biological & Agricultural Index Plus. EBSCO Publishing Inc. • Full text of literature in biology and agriculture. Also includes podcasts, indexing and abstracts.

OECD Statistical Compendium. Organization for Economic Cooperation and Development. • Semiannual. $1,905.00 per year for 1 to 10 users. CD-ROM contains more than 730,000 monthly, quarterly, and annual time series for OECD countries, 1960 to date. Includes fully searchable data on agriculture, food, economic indicators, national accounts, employment, energy, finance, industry, technology, and foreign trade. Results can be displayed in various forms.

DIRECTORIES

Directory of African Importers of Lumber, Timber, Plywood and Hardboards. EXIM Infotek Private Ltd. • $300 Individuals. Covers: 70 African importers of doors and windows, formica sheets, gypsum board and sheetrock, hardboard and particle board, laminates (wood), hardwood lumber, softwood lumber, timber, plywood, medium-density fiberboard, millwork (wooden), veneer, special decorative plywood, poles, pilings and logs, sawn timber, saw and saw blades, and wood. Entries include: Company name, postal address, telephone, fax, e-mail, website, contact person, designation, and product details.

Directory of South American Importers of Lumber, Timber, Plywood and Hardboards. EXIM Infotek Private Ltd. • $400 Individuals. Covers: 200 South American importers of doors and windows, gypsum boards, hardboard and particle board, hardwood flooring and floor tiles, laminates (wood), hardwood lumber, softwood lumber, timber, plywood, millwork (wooden), veneer, poles, pilings and logs. Entries include: Company name, postal address, telephone, fax, e-mail, website, contact person, designation, and product details.

Hardwood Manufacturers Association Buyers Guide. Hardwood Manufacturers Association. • provides details on members and products.

National Hardwood Lumber Association Member-

ship Directory. National Hardwood Lumber Association. • Available on website. Members are hardwood lumber and veneer manufacturers, distributors, and users.

FINANCIAL RATIOS

Annual Statement Studies. Risk Management Association. • Annual. Compiled from over 280,000 financial statements.

Annual Statement Studies: Industry Default Probabilities and Cash Flow Measures. Risk Management Association. • Annual. $405 Nonmembers. Serves as a companion volume to the original *Annual Statement Studies*. Gives probability of default estimates on a percentage scale for more than 450 industries. Includes changes in position year-by-year for eight financial statement line items and provides percentage measures of cash flow.

Industry Norms and Key Business Ratios. Dun & Bradstreet Inc. • Annual. Five volumes. Covers over 800 kinds of businesses, arranged by Standard Industrial Classification number. More detailed editions covering longer periods of time are also available.

INTERNET DATABASES

Business 2.0 Web Guide to the Best Business Links. Business 2.0 Media Inc. Phone: (415)293-4800; Email: support@business2.com • URL: http://www.business2.com/webguide • Web site presents an extensive, searchable directory of links to "the best, most informative, and authoritative web pages." Twenty main categories cover business, finance, career, company information, people, and technology topics, with thousands of subtopics, all linking to Web sites recommended by experienced business researchers. Fees: Free.

Fedstats. Federal Interagency Council on Statistical Policy. Phone: (202)395-7254 • URL: http://www.fedstats.gov • Web site features an efficient search facility for full-text statistics produced by more than 100 federal agencies, including the Census Bureau, the Bureau of Economic Analysis, and the Bureau of Labor Statistics. Boolean searches can be made within one agency or for all agencies combined. Links are offered to international statistical bureaus, including the UN, IMF, OECD, UNESCO, Eurostat, and 20 individual countries. Fees: Free.

FreeLunch.com. Economy.com, Inc. Phone: (610)696-8700; Fax: (610)696-1678 • URL: http://www.freelunch.com • Web site provides free access to more than 200 million economic and financial data series, covering industry, demographics, labor markets, prices, retail sales, government spending, trade, interest rates, housing starts, the stock market, etc. Data is available in either chart or table form. Searching is offered. Free, but registration required. Economy.com, Inc. also offers fee-based economic analysis at *The Dismal Scientist* site (www.dismal.com).

Manufacturing Profiles. U. S. Bureau of the Census. Phone: (301)763-4636 or (301)763-4100; Fax: (301)763-4794; Email: webmaster@census.gov • URL: http://www.census.gov/prod/www/abs/mfg-prof.html • The Census Bureau makes available free on PDF (Portable Document Format) an annual consolidation of the entire Current Industrial Report series, presenting "all the data compiled." Contains statistics on production, shipments, inventories, consumption, exports, imports, and orders for a wide variety of manufactured products.

USDA. U.S. National Institute of Standards and Technology. 100 Bureau Dr., Gaithersburg, MD 20899-1070. Phone: 800-877-8339 or (301)975-6478 or (202)720-2791; Fax: (301)975-8295; Email: inquiries@nist.gov • URL: http://www.nist.gov • The USDA home page has six sections: News and Information; What's New; About USDA; Agencies; Opportunities; Search and Help. Keyword searching is offered from the USDA home page and from various individual agency home pages. Agencies are the Economic Research Service, Agricultural Marketing Service, National Agricultural Statistics Service, National Agricultural Library, and about 12 others. Updating varies. Fees: Free.

ONLINE DATABASES

Agricola. U.S. National Agricultural Library World List of Agricultural Serials. • Covers worldwide agricultural literature. Over 3.3 million citations, 1970 to present, with monthly updates. Inquire as to online cost and availability.

CAB Abstracts. CABI. • Contains 46 specialized abstract collections covering over 10,000 journals and monographs in the areas of agriculture, horticulture, forest products, farm products, nutrition, dairy science, poultry, grains, animal health, entomology, etc. Time period is 1972 to date, with monthly updates. Inquire as to online cost and availability. *CAB Abstracts on CD-ROM* also available, with annual updating.

PERIODICALS AND NEWSLETTERS

Hardwood Floors. National Wood Flooring Association. Athletic Business Publications Inc. • Bimonthly. Covers the marketing and installation of hardwood flooring. Published for contractors and retailers.

National Hardwood Magazine. Miller Publishing Corp. • Monthly. $55 Individuals 1 year - US. Contains latest developments in the Hardwood Industry, both on the supplier side and in the marketplace.

NHLA Newsletter. National Hardwood Lumber Association. • Monthly. Features hardwood products, industry trends, and legislation.

RESEARCH CENTERS AND INSTITUTES

Department of Forest Biomaterials. North Carolina State University, Campus Box 8005, Raleigh, NC 27695. Phone: (919)515-5807; Fax: (919)515-6302; Email: contactfb@ncsu.edu • URL: http://cnr.ncsu.edu • Studies the mechanical and engineering properties of wood, wood finishing, wood anatomy, wood chemistry, etc.

Purdue University - Wood Research Laboratory. Department of Forestry and Natural Resources, 175 Marsteller St., West Lafayette, IN 47907-2033. Phone: (765)494-3619; Fax: (765)496-1344; Email: ehaviar@purdue.edu • URL: http://ag.purdue.edu/fnr/Pages/labwoodresearch.aspx • Use of wood and wood-base materials in engineered structures, ranging from furniture through residential and industrial/commercial building components; wood processing of wood and wood-base materials into furniture and cabinetry; structural applications of wood-base composites; and use, re-use, and care of wood in historic preservation and restoration. Research includes cross-disciplinary projects with engineering disciplines in simulation, machine vision and CAD.

STATISTICS SOURCES

AF and PA Statistical Roundup. American Forest and Paper Association. • Monthly. Members, $57.00 per year; non-members, $157.00 per year. Contains monthly statistical data for hardwood and softwood products. Formerly *NFPA Statistical Roundup*.

Agricultural Statistics. U.S. Department of Agriculture National Agricultural Statistics Service. • Annual. $46 Individuals. Provides a wide variety of statistical data relating to agricultural production, supplies, consumption, prices/price-supports, foreign trade, costs, and returns, as well as farm labor, loans, income, and population. In many cases, historical data is shown annually for 10 years. In addition to farm data, includes detailed fishery statistics.

Survey of Current Business. U. S. Government Printing Office. • Published by Bureau of Economic Analysis, U. S. Department of Commerce. Presents a wide variety of business and economic data.

TRADE/PROFESSIONAL ASSOCIATIONS

American Forest and Paper Association. 1101 K St., NW, Ste. 700, Washington, DC 20005. Phone: (202)463-2700; Fax: (202)463-2785; Email: info@afandpa.org • URL: http://www.afandpa.org • National trade association of the forest, pulp, paper, paperboard and wood products industry. Represents approximately 400 member companies and related trade associations that grow, harvest, and process wood and wood fiber, manufacture pulp, paper and paperboard from both virgin and recycled fiber, and produce solid wood products.

Appalachian Hardwood Manufacturers. 816 Eastchester Dr., High Point, NC 27262. Phone: (336)885-8315; Fax: (336)886-8865; Email: office@appalachianwood.org • URL: http://www.appalachianwood.org • Promotes Appalachian hardwoods.

Hardwood Federation. 1111 19th St. NW, Ste. 800, Washington, DC 20036. Phone: (202)463-2452; Fax: (202)463-4702 • URL: http://www.hardwoodfederation.wildapricot.org • Represents organizations engaged in the manufacturing, wholesaling or distribution of North American hardwood lumber, veneer, plywood, flooring and related products. Seeks to promote and represent the common business interests of and improve business conditions among members of the hardwood industry. Strives to maintain a healthy business environment for family businesses and small companies in the hardwood community.

National Hardwood Lumber Association. 6830 Raleigh La Grange Rd., Memphis, TN 38134-0518. Phone: 800-933-0318 or (901)377-1818; Fax: (901)382-6419 or (901)399-7581; Email: info@nhla.com • URL: http://www.nhla.com • United States, Canadian and International hardwood lumber and veneer manufacturers, distributors and consumers. Inspects hardwood lumber. Maintains inspection training school. Conducts management and marketing seminars for the hardwood industry. Promotes research in hardwood timber management and utilization. Promotes public awareness of the industry.

HARVESTING MACHINERY

See AGRICULTURAL MACHINERY

HAY INDUSTRY

See FEED AND FEEDSTUFFS INDUSTRY

HAZARDOUS MATERIALS

See also INDUSTRIAL HYGIENE; WASTE MANAGEMENT

ABSTRACTS AND INDEXES

Applied Science and Technology Index. EBSCO Publishing Inc. • 11/year. Indexes a wide variety of English language technical, industrial, and engineering periodicals.

Current Contents: Engineering, Computing and Technology. Thomson Reuters Intellectual Property and Science. • Weekly. $730 per year. Reproductions of contents pages of technical journals. Includes *Author Index, Address Directory, Current Book Contents*, and *Title Word Index*. Formerly *Current Contents: Engineering, Technology and Applied Sciences*.

Health and Safety Science Abstracts. Institute of Safety and Systems Management. Cambridge Information Group. • Monthly. Provides coverage of world literature on general safety, environmental and ecological safety, industrial hygiene and occupational safety, transportation safety, aviation and aerospace safety, and medical safety. Formerly *Safety Science Abstracts Journal.*

NTIS Alerts: Environmental Pollution & Control. U.S. Department of Commerce National Technical Information Service. • Biweekly. $130 per year. Covers the following categories of environmental pollution: air, water, solid wastes, radiation, pesticides, and noise.

CD-ROM DATABASES

Hazardous Substances Data Bank. SilverPlatter Information Inc. • Provides CD-ROM information on hazardous substances, including 140,000 chemicals in the *Registry of Toxic Effects of Chemical Substances* and 60,000 materials covered by the *Toxic Substances Control Act Initial Inventory.*

OSH-ROM: Occupational Safety and Health Information on CD-ROM. SilverPlatter Information Inc. • Price and frequency on application. Produced in Geneva by the International Occupational Safety and Health Information Centre, International Labour Organization (www.ilo.org). Provides about two million citations and abstracts to the worldwide literature of industrial safety, industrial hygiene, hazardous materials, and accident prevention. Material is included from journals, technical reports, books, government publications, and other sources. Time span varies.

DIRECTORIES

Hazardous Waste Consultant Directory of Commercial Hazardous Waste Management Facilities. Elsevier. • Annual. $115.00. List of 170 facilities that process, store, and dispose of hazardous waste materials.

Waste Age Buyers' Guide. RentPath Inc. • Annual. Manufacturers of equipment and supplies for the waste management industry.

ONLINE DATABASES

Applied Science and Technology Index Online. H.W. Wilson Co. • Provides online indexing of 500 major scientific, technical, industrial, and engineering periodicals. Time period is 1983 to date. Monthly updates. Inquire as to online cost and availability.

OTHER SOURCES

Hazardous Waste Litigation Reporter: The National Journal of Record of Hazardous Waste-Related Litigation. Andrews Publications. • Semimonthly. $875.00 per year. Newsletter. Reports on hazardous waste legal cases.

PERIODICALS AND NEWSLETTERS

Environment Advisor. J.J. Keller and Associates Inc. • Monthly. $90.00 per year. Newsletter. Formerly *Hazardous Substances Advisor.*

Golob's Environmental Business Report. World Information Systems. • Description: Provides news and analysis on environmental business, hazardous materials, waste management, and pollution prevention and control. Covers regulations, legislation and court decisions, new technology, contract opportunities and awards, and conferences.

Hazardous Materials Newsletter. John R. Cashman. • Description: Focuses on response to and control of hazardous materials emergencies, particularly appropriate tools, equipment, materials, methods, procedures, strategies, and lessons learned. Addresses leak, fire, and spill control for incident commanders and experienced responders, including incident causes, prevention, and remedial actions; decisionmaking; scene management; control and containment; response teams; and product identification and hazards. Recurring features include incident reports, a calendar of events, description of public safety agency/commercial/industrial response team operations, coverage of research sources and resources, networking ideas, and chemical and biological agents.

Hazardous Waste Consultant. Elsevier. • Seven times a year. $798.00 per year. Discusses the technical, regulatory and legal aspects of the hazardous waste industry.

Hazardous Waste/Superfund Week. Business Publishers Inc. • Description: Examines issues and developments in the hazardous waste management industry. Covers legislative and regulatory actions, technology research and development, disposal site controversies, Superfund contracting, and other news of interest. Recurring features include columns titled Slants & Trends, Business and Technology News, Grants and Contracts, calendar, Around the States, Market News, and Industrial Waste Focus.

International Journal of Environmental Science and Technology. Kluwer Academic Publishers. • Refereed research journal which aims to promote the theory and practice of environmental science and technology, innovation, engineering and management.

Nuclear Waste News: Generation-Packaging-Transportation-Processing-Disposal. Business Publishers Inc. • Weekly. $867.00. per year. Newsletter.

OSHA Required Safety Training for Supervisors. Occupational Safety and Health Administration. Business & Legal Resources, Inc. • Monthly. $99.00 per year. Newsletter. Formerly *Safetyworks for Supervisors.*

Pollution Engineering: Magazine of Environmental Control. BNP Media. • Monthly. Covers the air, water, waste and remediation environmental concerns in the Pollution Control field.

Sludge Newsletter: The Newsletter on Municipal Wastewater and Biosolids. Business Publishers Inc. • Biweekly. $409.00 per year. per year. Newsletter. Monitors sludge management developments in Washington and around the country.

RESEARCH CENTERS AND INSTITUTES

CTC Inc. 100 CTC Dr., Johnstown, PA 15904-1935. Email: info@ctc.com • URL: http://www.ctc.com • Formerly Center for Hazardous Materials Research.

Hazardous Substance Management Research Center. New Jersey Institute of Technology, University Heights, Newark, NJ 07102-1982. Phone: (973)596-3233; Fax: (973)642-7170; Email: watts@admin.njit.edu • URL: http://ycees.njit.edu/ycees/about_ycees.

University of Wisconsin—Madison - Molecular and Environmental Toxicology Center. 1300 University Ave., 1530 MSC, Madison, WI 53706. Phone: (608)263-4580; Fax: (608)262-5245; Email: bradfield@oncology.wisc.edu • URL: http://metc.med.wisc.edu/metc • Formerly Environmental Toxicology Center.

TRADE/PROFESSIONAL ASSOCIATIONS

American Conference of Governmental Industrial Hygienists. 1330 Kemper Meadow Dr., Cincinnati, OH 45240-4147. Phone: (513)742-2020 or (513)742-6163; Fax: (513)742-3355; Email: mail@acgih.org • URL: http://www.acgih.org • Members are government employees. Formerly National Conference of Governmental Industrial Hygients.

American Industrial Hygiene Association. 3141 Fairview Park Dr., Ste. 777, Falls Church, VA 22042. Phone: (703)849-8888; Fax: (703)207-3561; Email: infonet@aiha.org • URL: http://www.aiha.org • Professional society of industrial hygienists. Promotes the study and control of environmental factors affecting the health and well-being of workers. Sponsors continuing education courses in industrial hygiene, government affairs program, and public relations. Accredits laboratories. Maintains 40 technical committees and a foundation. Operates placement service. Conducts educational and research programs.

HEALTH CARE INDUSTRY

See also HEALTH INSURANCE; HEALTH MAINTENANCE ORGANIZATIONS; HOME HEALTH CARE INDUSTRY; HOSPITAL ADMINISTRATION; MEDICARE; NURSING HOMES

ABSTRACTS AND INDEXES

Business Periodicals Index Retrospective. EBSCO Publishing Inc. • 11/year. Quarterly and annual cumulations.

Cumulative Index to Nursing and Allied Health Literature. EBSCO Publishing Inc. • Includes annual *Cumulation Index.*

Index Medicus. U.S. National Library of Medicine. U. S. Government Printing Office. • Monthly. $522 Individuals. Bibliographic listing of references to current articles from approximately 3,000 of the world's biomedical journals.

NTIS Alerts: Health Care. U.S. Department of Commerce National Technical Information Service. • Biweekly. $130 per year. Covers a wide variety of health care topics, including quality assurance, delivery organization, economics (costs), technology, and legislation.

Science Citation Index. Thomson Reuters Intellectual Property and Science. • Weekly. Includes *Source Index, Citation Index, Permuterm Subject Index,* and *Corporate Index.* Provides researchers, administrators, faculty, and students with quick, powerful access to the bibliographic and citation information they need to find research data, analyze trends, journals and researchers, and share their findings.

Social Sciences Citation Index. Thomson Reuters Corp. • Weekly. Product is accessed via *Web of Science.*

Social Sciences Index Retrospective: 1907-1983. EBSCO Publishing Inc. • Indexing for 1,000,000 articles. Coverage includes international index and social sciences and humanities index.

ALMANACS AND YEARBOOKS

Annual Review of Medicine: Selected Topics in the Clinical Sciences. Annual Reviews. • Annual. $99 Individuals online only. Covers significant developments in various fields of Medicine.

Annual Review of Public Health. Annual Reviews. • Annual. $93 Individuals online only.

BIBLIOGRAPHIES

Health and Vital Statistics. U. S. Government Printing Office. • Annual. Free. Lists government publications. (GPO Subject Bibliography Number 121).

Medical & Health Care Books & Serials in Print. Grey House Publishing. • $645 Individuals Hardcover. Provides immediate access to the highly specialized publishing activity in the health sciences and allied health fields.

CD-ROM DATABASES

Authority Health Care Law Library. Matthew Bender and Company Inc. • Periodic updates. Price on request. Full text CD-ROM provides legal information, case law, and analysis relating to health care facilities, health insurance, longterm care, Medigap, and Medicare.

Healthcare QuickDisc. American Hospital Association. • Corresponds to the printed *AHA Guide,* with additional material and extensive search capabilities (400 data fields). Provides detailed information on 6,000 hospitals and hospital systems, including utilization data.

Science Citation Index. Thomson Reuters Intel-

For publishers' addresses, refer to SOURCES CITED section at the back of the book.

lectual Property and Science. • Weekly. Includes *Source Index*, *Citation Index*, *Permuterm Subject Index*, and *Corporate Index*. Provides researchers, administrators, faculty, and students with quick, powerful access to the bibliographic and citation information they need to find research data, analyze trends, journals and researchers, and share their findings.

Social Sciences Abstracts. EBSCO Publishing Inc. • Provides indexing from 1983 and abstracting from 1994 of more than 750 periodicals covering economics, area studies, community health, public administration, public welfare, urban studies, and many other topics related to the social sciences.

Social Sciences Citation Index. Thomson Reuters Corp. • Weekly. Product is accessed via *Web of Science*.

DIRECTORIES

AHA Integrated Delivery Network Directory: U.S. Health Care Systems, Networks, and Alliances. American Hospital Association. • Annual. $250.00. Provides information about a wide variety of U.S. health care groups and affiliations, including hospitals, nursing homes, rehabilitation centers, psychiatric facilities, home health care agencies, clinical laboratories, outpatient facilities, and diagnostic imaging centers. Includes names of more than 8,000 key executives.

Australian Health and Medical Industry. APN News & Media Group Ltd. APN Business Information Group. • Annual. Covers: Australian companies involved in the medical and health industry and interested in exporting their products and services.

Binley's Directory of NHS Estates & Facilities Management. Beachwood House Publishing Ltd. • Annual. £150 Individuals online version. Covers: 5,178 named personnel, located at 575 separate NHS sites. Entries include: Name, address, phone and fax numbers, email and website address.

Binley's Directory of NHS Management. Beachwood House Publishing Ltd. • Annual. £250 Individuals online version. Covers: Over 30,649 named personnel working at NHS organizations throughout the U.K. from chief executives and medical directors to estates managers, IT managers, and suppliers and purchasing managers. Database includes: Maps. Entries include: Organization name, address, NHS code, phone and fax numbers, email and website address.

Convalescent Homes Directory. InfoGroup Inc. • Annual. Number of listings: 2,178. Entries include: Name, address, phone, size of advertisement, name of owner or manager, number of employees, year first in "Yellow Pages." Compiled from telephone company "Yellow Pages," nationwide.

Dakotas-Montana Medical Directory. Jola Publications. • Biennial. $25 Individuals. Covers: Approximately 5,000 doctors, hospitals, clinics, nursing homes, and other selected health care providers in North Dakota, South Dakota, and Montana. Entries include: Doctor or facility name, address, phone.

Detwiler's Directory of Health and Medical Resources. S.M. Detwiler and Associates. • Biennial. $195.00. Lists a wide range of healthcare information resources, including more than 2,000 corporations, associations, government agencies, publishers, licensure organizations, market research firms, foundations, and institutes, as well as 6,000 publications. Indexed by type of information, publication, acronym, and 600 subject categories.

Directory of Physician Groups and Networks. Dorland Healthcare Information. • Annual. $495.00. Available only online. Approximately 8,000 independent practice associations (IPAs), physician hospital organizations (PHOs), management service organizations (MSOs), physician practice management companies (PPMCs), and group practices having 20 or more physicians.

Directory of South Korean Manufacturers & Exporters of Health Care Products & Foods. EXIM Infotek Private Ltd. • Covers: 20 South Korean manufacturers and exporters of health and diet products. Entries include: Company name, postal address, telephone, fax, e-mail, website, contact person, designation, and product details.

Dorland's Medical Directory. Access Intelligence L.L.C. • Annual. $69.95 Individuals plus $3.95 shipping. Covers: Nearly 15,000 physicians in Eastern Pennsylvania and Southern New Jersey, Northern Delaware. Also includes group practices, hospitals, healthcare facilities, and medical organizations. Entries include: For physicians--Name, office and home addresses and phone, fax numbers, email addresses, medical school attended and year graduated, medical specialties, certifications, hospital affiliations. For hospitals--Name, address, names and specialties of staff members.

Emerging Europe Pharmaceuticals and Healthcare Directory. Business Monitor International Ltd. • $895 Individuals. Covers: 2,212 top pharmaceutical executives at 794 leading pharmaceutical companies from Bosnia, Bulgaria, Croatia, the Czech Republic, Estonia, Hungary, Latvia, Lithuania, Macedonia, Poland, Romania, Russia, Serbia, Slovakia, Slovenia and the Ukraine. Entries include: Parent company head offices, full company name, address, phone and fax numbers, email and website address, senior contact personnel, company description and profile, nationality, and ownership status.

Global Health Directory. Global Health Council. • Irregular. Covers: Over 500 private voluntary organizations, universities, civic groups, professional associations, and other groups involved with global health. Entries include: Organization name, address, e-mail, website, contact name, number of employees, mission, services, regions served, publications, internships available, and volunteer information.

The HCEA Directory of Healthcare Meetings and Conventions. Healthcare Convention and Exhibitors Association. • Annual. $345 Nonmembers. Lists more than 6,000 health care meetings, most of which have an exhibit program. Formerly *Handbook-A Directory of Health Care Meetings and Conventions*.

Health Groups in Washington: A Directory. National Health Council. • Biennial. $40 Members. Covers: Over 900 professional, voluntary, consumer, insurance, union, business, and academic organizations with some impact on the development of federal health policies. Entries include: Name of organization, address, phone, e-mail address, website address, names of Washington representatives.

Hospitals Directory. InfoGroup Inc. • Annual. Number of listings: 13,914. Entries include: Name, address, phone, size of advertisement, name of owner or manager, number of employees, year first in "Yellow Pages." Compiled from telephone company "Yellow Pages," nationwide.

Journal of the American Medical Association--Physician Service Opportunities Overseas Section. American Medical Association. • Irregular. Publication includes: List of more than 60 organizations that provide assignments overseas for physicians from the United States. Entries include: Organization name, address, phone, contact person, countries served, and medical specialties sought.

Kazakhstan Health Care Directory. Flegon Press. • $100. Covers: Health care organizations, schools, provides, trade unions, and departments of health in the republic of Kazakhstan of the former Soviet Union. Entries include: Name, address, phone, fax, contact person.

Massage: A Career at Your Fingertips. Enterprise Publishing. • Triennial. $25.95 Individuals. Publication includes: Approximately 1,000 organizations involved in the massage industry, including schools, associations, massage equipment suppliers, bodywork organizations, and massage marketing companies in the United States. Entries include: For schools--Name, address, phone, hours of training required, number of in-class hours required, cost, financial aid availability, subjects covered, unique aspects of school or curriculum. For others--Name, address, phone, description of products/services offered. Principal content of publication is information on becoming a successful massage therapist.

Medical and Healthcare Marketplace Guide. IDD Inc. • Annual. $595.00. Two volumes. Provides market survey summaries for about 500 specific product and service categories (volume one: "Research Reports"). Contains profiles of nearly 5,500 pharmaceutical, medical product, and healthcare service companies (volume two: "Company Profiles").

Medical Quality Management Sourcebook. Thomson Financial Inc. • Annual. $295 Individuals. Covers: Clinical performance measurement and improvement systems, and organizations and individuals involved in patient satisfaction surveys. Database includes: Fact sheets, charts. Entries include: Company and individual name, address, phone, fax.

Medical Research Centres: A World Directory of Organizations and Programmes. Informa Group PLC. • Biennial. $470.00. Two volumes. Contains profiles of more than 7,000 medical research facilities around the world. Includes medical, dental, nursing, pharmaceutical, psychiatric, and surgical research centers.

Medicare & You Handbook. Health Care Financing Administration U.S. Department of Health & Human Service. • Irregular. Publication includes: Lists of Medicare carriers in individual states. Principal content includes discussion of what Medicare is, what its various options are, and what new benefits have been added recently.

Middle East and Africa Pharmaceuticals and Healthcare Directory. Business Monitor International Ltd. • $975 Individuals CD. Covers: 2,032 top pharmaceutical executives on 615 leading pharmaceutical companies from Algeria, Bahrain, Botswana, Egypt, Greece, Iran, Jordan, Kuwait, Lebanon, Libya, Morocco, Mozambique, Namibia, Oman, Qatar, Saudi Arabia, South Africa, Syria, Tunisia, Turkey, UAE, Yemen, Zambia and Zimbabwe. Entries include: Parent company head offices, full company name, address, phone and fax numbers, email and website address, senior contact personnel, company description and profile, nationality, and ownership status.

National Wellness Institute--Member Directory. National Wellness Institute. • Covers: more than 1,600 health and wellness promotion professionals in corporations, hospitals, colleges, government agencies, universities, community organizations, schools (K-12), and consulting firms, and managed care. Entries include: Member name, address, and phone, fax, email.

Scott's Canadian Dental Directory. Scott's Directories. • Biennial. $259 Individuals Plus Applicable Taxes + S/H. Covers: Approximately 18,000 dentists, dental suppliers, and dental laboratories and associations in Canada. Entries include: Name, address, phone, names and titles of key personnel, biographical data (for dentists), geographical area served.

Sell's Products and Services Directory. Miller Freeman UK Ltd. • Annual. $99 print. Covers: Approximately 60,000 firms in United Kingdom and Ireland, including over 8,900 suppliers of health care products, equipment, and services in the United Kingdom and industry associations. Entries include: Company name, address, phone, fax, telex, description of product/service, names and titles of key personnel.

Telehealth Buyer's Guide. Miller Freeman Inc. • Annual. $10.00. Lists sources of telecommunications and information technology products and services for the health care industry.

Wisconsin Medical Directory. Jola Publications. • Annual. $25 Individuals. Covers: Approximately 15,000 doctors, hospitals, clinics, nursing homes, and other selected health care providers in Wisconsin. Entries include: Doctor or facility name, address, phone, fax, doctors' UPINS.

Women's Health Concerns Sourcebook. Omnigraphics Inc. • Irregular. $85 Individuals Hardcover. Publication includes: Resources on women's health issues. Entries include: Publication name, address. Principal content of publication is articles on specific health issues, definitions, symptoms, risks, treatment, and answers to frequently asked questions.

E-BOOKS

Social Trends & Indicators USA. Monique D. Magee, editor. Cengage Learning Inc. • Includes data on labor, economics, the health care industry, crime, leisure, population, education, social security, and many other topics. Sources include various government agencies and major publications. Inquire for pricing.

FINANCIAL RATIOS

Industry Norms and Key Business Ratios. Dun & Bradstreet Inc. • Annual. Five volumes. Covers over 800 kinds of businesses, arranged by Standard Industrial Classification number. More detailed editions covering longer periods of time are also available.

INTERNET DATABASES

Espicom Business Intelligence Country Healthcare (MDST). ProQuest LLC. 2250 Perimeter Park Dr., Ste. 300, Morrisville, NC 27560. Phone: 800-334-2564 or (919)804-6400; Fax: (919)804-6410; Email: contact@dialog.com • URL: http://www.dialog.com • An electronic database with reports profiling health care systems in various countries. The database provides data on medical equipment, health care, and hospital services in 77 countries worldwide.

National Center for Health Statistics: Monitoring the Nation's Health. National Center for Health Statistics, Centers for Disease Control and Prevention. Phone: (301)458-4000; Email: nchsquery@cdc.gov • URL: http://www.cdc.gov/nchswww • Web site provides detailed data on diseases, vital statistics, and health care in the U. S. Includes a search facility and links to many other health-related Web sites. "Fastats A to Z" offers quick data on hundreds of topics from Accidents to Work-Loss Days, with links to Comprehensive Data and related sources. Frequent updates. Fees: Free.

National Library of Medicine. National Institutes of Health. 9000 Rockville Pke., Bethesda, MD 20892. Phone: (301)496-4000; Email: nihinfo@od.nih.gov • URL: http://www.nih.gov • NLM Web site offers free access through MEDLINE ("PubMed") to about nine million references to articles appearing in some 4,000 biomedical journals, with abstracts. Search interfaces range from "simple keywords to advanced Boolean expressions." The NLM site offers many links to other sources of biomedical and technical information (the National Center for Biotechnology Information, for example). Fees: Free.

ONLINE DATABASES

Business Media Advertising Source®. Kantar Media SRDS. • Contains in-depth information on advertising opportunities in healthcare trade media throughout the world.

Embase. Elsevier. • Worldwide medical literature, 1974 to present. Weekly updates. Inquire as to online cost and availability.

F-D-C Reports. Elsevier Business Intelligence. • An online version of "The Gray Sheet" (medical devices), "The Pink Sheet" (pharmaceuticals), "The Rose Sheet" (cosmetics), "The Blue Sheet" (biomedical), and "The Tan Sheet" (nonprescription). Contains full-text information on legal, technical, corporate, financial, and marketing developments from 1987 to date, with weekly updates. Inquire as to online cost and availability.

Gale Group PharmaBiomed Business Journals. Cengage Learning Inc. • Contains international coverage of full-text articles from trade journals on pharmaceuticals, biotechnology, and healthcare, including information on methods and techniques, business practices, new products, companies, markets, market share, research and development, regulations, and applied technologies in these fields.

Wilson Business Abstracts Online. H.W. Wilson Co. • Indexes and abstracts 600 major business periodicals, plus the *Wall Street Journal* and the business section of the *New York Times*. Indexing is from 1982, abstracting from 1990, with the two newspapers included from 1993. Updated weekly. Inquire as to online cost and availability. (*Business Periodicals Index* without abstracts is also available online.).

Wilson Social Sciences Abstracts Online. H.W. Wilson Co. • Provides online abstracting and indexing of more than 500 periodicals covering area studies, community health, public administration, public welfare, urban studies, and many other social science topics. Time period is 1994 to date for abstracts and 1983 to date for indexing, with updates weekly. Inquire as to online cost and availability.

PERIODICALS AND NEWSLETTERS

Administrative Radiology Journal: The Journal of Medical Imaging Business, Management & Administration. Glendale Publishing Corp. • Monthly. $96 Individuals. Monthly Journal of Imaging Administration for Chief Imaging M.D.'s, Imaging Department Managers, Radiation Oncology Directors, and Healthcare Administrators.

AHA News. American Hospital Association. HealthForum. • Description: Highlights major news affecting hospitals and the health care field. Reports on legislation and regulation, court cases, surveys, and federal programs. Carries information on individual hospitals and allied hospital associations.

American Dental Association Journal. American Dental Association. • Monthly. Free to members; non-members, $173.00 per year; institutions, $205.00 per year.

American Health Care Association: Provider. American Health Care Association. • Monthly. $48.00 per year. Formerly *American Health Care Association Journal*.

The Gray Sheet Reports: Medical Devices, Diagnostics and Instrumentation. Elsevier Business Intelligence. • Weekly. Institutions, $1,172.00 per year. Newsletter. Provides industry and financial news, including a medical sector stock index. Monitors regulatory developments at the Center for Devices and Radiological Health of the U. S. Food and Drug Administration.

Health Business. Public Sector Publishing Ltd. • Monthly. Magazine featuring news and case studies that explain the administrative and commercial issues affecting healthcare and hospital management.

Health Care Financing Review. U. S. Government Printing Office. • Quarterly. $48 Individuals. Issued by the Health Care Financing Administration, U. S. Department of Health and Human Services. Presents articles by professionals in the areas of health care costs and financing.

Health Care Fraud and Abuse Newsletter. ALM Media Properties LLC. • Monthly. $195.00 per year. Newsletter. Provides legal news relating mainly to fraudulent or excessive medical billing practices. Covers both civil and criminal proceedings. (A Law Journal Newsletter, formerly published by Leader Publications).

Health Care Strategic Management: The Newsletter for Hospital Strategies. The Business Word. • Monthly. $284.00 per year. Planning, marketing and resource allocation.

Health Facilities Management. American Hospital Association. Health Forum L.L.C. • Covers building maintenance and engineering for hospitals and nursing homes.

Health Forum Journal: Leadership Strategies for Healthcare Executives. Healthcare Forum. • Bimonthly. $65.00 per year.

Health Grants and Contracts Weekly: Selected Federal Project Opportunities. Wolters Kluwer Law and Business. • 50 times a year. $459.00 per year. Newsletter. Lists new health-related federal contracts and grants.

Health Industry Today: The Market Letter for Health Care Industry Vendors. The Business Word. • Monthly. $360.00 per year; online edition, $420.00 per year.

The Health Letter. Sidney M. Wolfe, editor. North America Syndicate. • Description: Addresses health topics, with discussion of cause and effect, practical counsel, and information on normal variations. Carries news of research, briefings from current medical literature, and highlights of conferences and other events.

Health Management Technology. Nelson Publishing Inc. • Monthly. $38.00 per year. Formerly *Computers in Healthcare*.

Health Marketing Quarterly. The Haworth Press Inc. • Quarterly. $580.00 per year.

Health News Daily. Elsevier Business Intelligence. • Description: Tracks developments in health care policy, legislation and regulation, insurance, pharmaceuticals, delivery, manufacturing, technology and treatment, funding, and research.

Health Policy and Biomedical Research: The Blue Sheet. Elsevier Business Intelligence. • 51 times a year. $716.00 per year. Newsletter. Emphasis is on news of medical research agencies and institutions, especially the National Institutes of Health (NIH).

Healthcare Executive. American College of Healthcare Executives. • Bimonthly. $110 Individuals in the U.S.. Focuses on critical management issues in the healthcare industry.

Healthcare Financial Management. Healthcare Financial Management Association. • Monthly. $260 Individuals.

Healthcare Marketing Report. HMR Publication Group. • $235 U.S.. Contains the latest news on winning market strategies, concepts and trends in the healthcare industry.

Healthcare Risk Management. AHC Media. • Description: Analyzes specific legal cases and trends relevant to healthcare liability. Discusses malpractice, liability for patients, staff and visitor injury, injury prevention, biomedical engineering, and medical staff credentials. Also covers high-risk areas of hospitals, hospital-owned home health and physician practices, accreditation, Medicare reimbursement, physician liability, medical records, and claims management. Recurring features include interviews, statistics, news of research, guest columns, legal briefs, and commentaries.

HealthLeaders-InterStudy. • Bimonthly. Provides broad coverage of finance, marketing, management, and technology for executives in the health care industry. Includes "Roundtable" discussions of particular health care issues. Formerly *Healthcare Business*.

HomeCare Magazine: For Business Leaders in Home Medical Equipment. Cahaba Media Group. • Monthly. $135 Canada. Magazine serving home medical equipment suppliers, including independent and chain centers specializing in home care, pharmacies or chain drug stores with home care products, and joint-ventured hospital home health care businesses. Contains industry news and new product launches and marketing strategies.

International Journal of Health Planning and Management. John Wiley and Sons, Inc., Journals Div. • Quarterly. Individuals, $960.00 per year; institutions, $1,280.00 per year. Published in England by John Wiley and Sons Ltd.

JAMA: Journal of the American Medical Association. American Medical Association. • Weekly. $111 Individuals print and online; member. Scientific general medical journal.

Medical Malpractice Law and Strategy. ALM Media Properties LLC. • Monthly. $479 per year. Covers malpractice legal issues for lawyers representing physicians and for lawyers representing patients. Includes news of judicial, legislative, and medical developments affecting malpractice strategies. (A Law Journal Newsletter, formerly published by Leader Publications).

Medical Marketing and Media. Haymarket Media, Inc. • Monthly. $148 U.S. 1-year subscription. Contains articles on marketing, direct marketing, advertising media, and sales personnel for the healthcare and pharmaceutical industries.

Medical Reference Services Quarterly. The Haworth Press Inc. • Quarterly. Institutions, $275.00 per year. An academic and practical journal for medical reference librarians.

MGMA Connexion. Medical Group Management Association. • 10/year. $95 Individuals /year. Formerly *Medical Group Management Journal*. Provides in-depth coverage of key industry topics and advice for group practice professionals.

The Milbank Quarterly: A Journal of Public Health and Health Care Policy. Milbank Memorial Fund. Blackwell Publishing Inc. • Quarterly. $268 Institutions print or online. Devoted to scholarly analysis of significant issues in health and health care policy. It presents original research, policy analysis, and commentary from academics, clinicians, and policy makers. Formerly *Health and Society*.

Modern Healthcare: The Newsmagazine for Administrators and Managers in Hospitals and Other Healthcare Institutions. Crain Communications Inc. • $159 Premium Access (Web + Data + Digital Edition).

Modern Physician: Essential Business News for the Executive Physician. Crain Communications Inc. • Monthly. $45.00. Edited for physicians responsible for business decisions at hospitals, clinics, HMOs, and other health groups. Includes special issues on managed care, practice management, legal issues, and finance.

New England Journal of Medicine. Massachusetts Medical Society. • Weekly. $179 Individuals print and online. The offical journal of the Massachusetts Medical Society.

Physicians & Computers. Moorhead Publications Inc. • Monthly. $40.00 per year. Includes material on computer diagnostics, online research, medical and non-medical software, computer equipment, and practice management.

Public Relations. Access Intelligence L.L.C. • Biweekly. $397.00 per year. Newsletter on public relations and client communications for the healthcare industry. Incorporates (Healthcare PR and Marketing News).

Strategic Health Care Marketing. Health Care Communications. • Monthly. Description: Provides news and analysis on health care services marketing, and business development. Covers strategies and techniques used by marketing innovators. Recurring features include interviews, news of research, a calendar of events, reports of meetings, and notices of publications available.

SurgiStrategies: Business Solutions for the ASC. Virgo Publishing L.L.C. • $45 Individuals. Magazine featuring Ambulatory Surgery Centers industry.

RESEARCH CENTERS AND INSTITUTES

Agency for Healthcare Research and Quality - Center for Primary Care, Prevention, and Clinical Partnerships - Partnerships for Quality Program. 540 Gaither Rd., Rockville, MD 20850. Phone: (301)427-1495; Fax: (301)427-1597; Email: charlotte.mullican@ahrq.hhs.gov • URL: http://www.ahrq.gov/about/cp3/cp3ptqual.htm • Improvement of health care services and their security, safety, outcomes, quality, effectiveness, and cost-effectiveness.

Brandeis University - Council on Health Care Economics and Policy. Schneider Institute for Health Policy, Heller School for Social Policy & Management, MS 035, 415 South St., Waltham, MA 02454-9110. Phone: (781)736-3940; Fax: (781)736-3306; Email: doonan@brandeis.edu • URL: http://council.brandeis.edu • Critical issues generated by health system change and the economic impact of such changes.

Brandeis University - Schneider Institutes for Health Policy. Heller School for Social Policy & Management, MS 035, 415 S St., Waltham, MA 02454-9110. Phone: (781)736-3901; Fax: (781)736-3905; Email: wallack@brandeis.edu • URL: http://sihp.brandeis.edu • Health care, focusing on the intersection of health behavior and systems of care, including policy studies in the areas of financing organization, value of health services, quality, high cost and high risk populations, and technology.

Canadian Institutes of Health Research - Institute of Health Services and Policy Research. 3666 McTavish, Montreal, QC, Canada H3A 1Y2. Phone: (514)398-5940; Email: info.ihspr@mcgill.ca • URL: http://www.cihr-irsc.gc.ca/e/13733.html • Supports research on problems confronting health care systems, policy-makers, and managers regarding effective health services and products.

Case Western Reserve University - Center for Health Care Research and Policy. Rammelkamp Research & Education Bldg., R221, MetroHealth Medical Ctr., 2500 Metrohealth Dr., Cleveland, OH 44109-1998. Phone: (216)778-3901; Fax: (216)778-3945; Email: rdc@case.edu • URL: http://www.chrp.org • Health care and health policy.

Columbia University - College of Physicians and Surgeons - Center for the Study of Society and Medicine. 630 W 168th St., New York, NY 10032. Phone: (212)305-4186; Fax: (212)305-6416 • URL: http://www.societyandmedicine.columbia.edu • Issues that arise in clinical and research settings, including studies in bioethics and health policy, bioethics and medical decision-making, social policy, analyses of the social history of patienthood.

Dalhousie University - Schulich School of Law - Health Law Institute. 6061 University Ave., Halifax, NS, Canada B3H 4R2. Phone: (902)494-6881; Fax: (902)494-6879; Email: hli@dal.ca • URL: http://www.dal.ca/faculty/law/hli.html • Health law and policy.

Dartmouth College - Geisel School of Medicine - Dartmouth Institute for Health Policy and Clinical Practice. 35 Centerra Pky., Lebanon, NH 03766. Phone: (603)653-0800; Fax: (603)653-0820; Email: the.dartmouth.institute@dartmouth.edu • URL: http://tdi.dartmouth.edu • Evaluative clinical science and health care delivery, including medical care epidemiology, health policy, health behavior, efficacy of medical procedures, quality of medical and surgical care, distribution of health care resources, medical interventions and consequences for patients, care at the end of life, distribution of health care resources across hospital market areas, geriatric health, and sociology of medical organizations.

Duke University - Sanford School of Public Policy - Center for Health Policy and Inequalities Research. 310 Trent Dr., Durham, NC 27705. Phone: (919)613-5430; Fax: (919)613-5466 • URL: http://chpir.org • Quantitative analysis of clinical policies, decision analysis, Bayesian statistics, health economics, disease prevention, cancer and cancer detection, stroke prevention and management, and technology assessment, including evaluation of reimbursement policies for medical procedures, hospital and health care policies, and Health Maintenance Organization (HMO) medical policies.

ECRI: Emergency Care Research Institute. 5200 Butler Pike, Plymouth Meeting, PA 19462-1298. Phone: (610)825-6000; Fax: (610)834-1275; Email: info@ecri.org • URL: http://www.ecri.org • Major research area is health care technology.

Georgia State University - Andrew Young School of Policy Studies - Georgia Health Policy Center. 14 Marietta St. NW, Ste. 221, Atlanta, GA 30303-2813. Phone: (404)413-0314; Fax: (404)413-0316; Email: ghpc@gsu.edu • URL: http://ghpc.gsu.edu • Health care policy in order to improve health care delivery systems in Georgia, focusing on children's health, end of life and long-term care improvement, and networks for rural health.

Health Policy Institute. 1200 Pressler St., Houston, TX 77025. Phone: (713)500-9494; Fax: (713)500-9493; Email: Stephen.H.Linder@uth.tmc.edu • URL: http://sph.uth.edu/research/centers/ihp.

Institute for Advanced Studies - Health Economics and Health Policy. Department of Economics & Finance, Stumpergasse 56, A-1060 Vienna, Austria. Phone: 43 1 59991127; Fax: 43 1 59991555; Email: thomas.czypionka@ihs.ac.at • URL: http://www.ihs.ac.at/vienna/ • Health economics and policy.

Institute of Medicine - Board on Global Health. Keck Ctr., 500 5th St. NW, Washington, DC 20001. Phone: (202)334-2427; Fax: (202)334-3861; Email: pkelley@nas.edu • URL: http://www.iom.edu/About-IOM/Leadership-Staff/Boards/Board-on-Global-Health.aspx • Health of populations worldwide, including developing country health issues, enhancing the U.S. role in global health, and addressing health issues that have implications for U.S. health policy.

Institute of Medicine - Board on Health Sciences Policy. Keck Ctr., 500 5th St. NW, Washington, DC 20001. Phone: (202)334-1888; Fax: (202)334-1329; Email: apope@nas.edu • URL: http://www.iom.edu/About-IOM/Leadership-Staff/Boards/Board-on-Health-Sciences-Policy.aspx • Issues affecting the science base underlying health and health care.

James Madison University - Health Communication Institute. School of Communication Studies, Harrisonburg, VA 22807. Phone: (540)568-3586; Email: gabbaras@jmu.edu • URL: http://www.jmu.edu/healthcom/index.shtml • Health communication.

Johns Hopkins University - Johns Hopkins Bloomberg School of Public Health - Department of Population, Family and Reproductive Health - Women's and Children's Health Policy Center. 615 N Wolfe St., Baltimore, MD 21205. Phone: (410)502-5450; Fax: (410)502-5831; Email: cminkovi@jhsph.edu • URL: http://www.jhsph.edu/research/centers-and-institutes/womens-and-childrens-health-policy-center • Health system reforms impacting the health of women, children, and adolescents.

Kansas State University - Community Health Institute. 1 Natatorium, Manhattan, KS 66506-0700. Phone: (785)532-7750; Email: dadx@ksu.edu • URL: http://www.k-state.edu/media/webzine/institute/communityhealth.html • Healthy and sustainable communities, healthy eating and physical activity, and quality of life.

Kenya Medical Research Institute - Center for Geographic Medicine Research-Coast. PO Box 54840-00200, Nairobi, Kenya. Phone: 254 2 2722541; Fax: 254 2 2720030; Email: director@kemri.org • URL: http://www.kemri.org/index.php/cgmr-c • Malaria and other parasitic diseases, HIV/AIDS/STI, health systems, maternal/child health, and reproductive health.

Kenya Medical Research Institute - Center for Public Health Research. PO Box 20752 – 00202, Nairobi, Kenya. Phone: 254 20 2725017; Fax: 254 20 2720030; Email: ykombe@kemri-nuitm.or.ke • URL: http://www.kemri.org/index.php/cphr • Health systems, applied human nutrition, child health, and population and behavioral studies.

Republic of Korea Ministry of Health and Welfare - Korea Institute for Health and Social Affairs. Jinhungro 235, Bulgwang-dong, Eunpyeonggu, Seoul 122-705, South Korea. Phone: 82 2 3808000; Fax: 82 2 3522181; Email: master@kihasa.re.kr • URL: http://www.kihasa.re.kr/html/jsp/english/main.jsp • National health, social welfare, and population. Also provides information and guidelines for the formulation of government policy in these fields. Health Policy, Social Insurance, Social Welfare, Population and Family, and Survey and Statistics. Also provides information and guidelines for the formulation of government policy in these fields.

Lawrence Berkeley National Laboratory - Environment, Health and Safety Division - Safety Advisory Committee. 1 Cyclotron Rd., MS 90R1140, Berkeley, CA 94720-8128. Phone: (510)486-7653; Fax: (510)486-7488; Email: paseidl@lbl.gov • URL: http://www.lbl.gov/ehs/sac/ • Development and implementation of environment, safety, and health policy, guidelines, codes, and regulatory interpretation of the Lawrence Berkeley National Laboratory.

London Metropolitan University - Faculty of Social Sciences and Humanities - Centre for Primary Health and Social Care. 166-220 Holloway Rd., London N7 8DB, United Kingdom. Phone: 44 20 71335005; Fax: 44 20 71335203; Email: r.gevorgyan@londonmet.ac.uk • URL: http://www.londonmet.ac.uk/faculties/faculty-of-social-sciences-and-humanities/research/centre-for-primary-health-and-social-care • Health in its social, political and economic context, promoting wellbeing and challenging barriers to social exclusion.

London School of Economics and Political Science - Health and Social Care Research Centre. Cowdray House, Houghton St., London WC2A 2AE, United Kingdom. Phone: 44 20 79556840; Fax: 44 20 79556803; Email: e.a.mossialos@lse.ac.uk • URL: http://www.lse.ac.uk/LSEHealthAndSocialCare/Home.aspx • Health policy, including comparative health policy; health care financing and equity; international mental health policy and practice; health policy relating to pharmaceutical industries; health economics, including economic evaluation in health care; pharmaceutical economics; healthcare technology; economics of mental health and the hospital sector; health care workforce issues; social care, focusing on long-term care finance; health and social care integration; community care for the elderly; adulthood economic outcomes of childhood problems; and healthy living centers.

Loyola University Chicago - Neiswanger Institute for Bioethics. Bldg. 120, Rm. 292, Stritch School of Medicine, 2160 S 1st Ave., Maywood, IL 60153. Phone: (708)327-9219; Fax: (708)327-9208; Email: mkuczew@lumc.edu • URL: http://hsd.luc.edu/bioethics • Bioethics and health policy.

Mahidol University - ASEAN Institute for Health Development. Salaya, Phutthamonthon, Nakhon Pathom 73170, Thailand. Phone: 66 2 4419040; Fax: 66 2 4419044; Email: directad@mahidol.ac.th • URL: http://www.aihd.mahidol.ac.th/new/en • Primary health care and quality of life networks in the ASEAN (Association of South East Asian Nations) region.

Malcolm Wiener Center for Social Policy. Harvard University, John F. Kennedy School of Government, 79 John F. Kennedy St., Cambridge, MA 02138. Phone: (617)495-1100; Fax: (617)496-9053; Email: mwcenter@harvaard.edu • URL: http://www.hks.harvard.edu • Does multidisciplinary research on health care access and financing.

Massachusetts General Hospital - Institute for Health Policy. 50 Staniford St., 9th Fl., Ste. 901, Boston, MA 02114. Phone: (617)724-4744; Fax: (617)724-4738; Email: info@instituteforhealthpolicy.org • URL: http://www.instituteforhealthpolicy.org • Health policy and health systems.

McMaster University - Centre for Health Economics and Policy Analysis. CRL Bldg., No. 282, 1280 Main St. W, Hamilton, ON, Canada L8S 4K1. Phone: (905)525-9140; Fax: (905)546-5211; Email: chepa@mcmaster.ca • URL: http://www.chepa.org • Health economics and health policy analysis, including organization, funding, and delivery of health care; the evaluation of health care programs and technologies; the measurement of health at the individual and population level; the determinants of population health; and the processes of health policy making.

Medical Research Council of South Africa - Health Systems Research Unit. PO Box 19070, Tygerberg 7505, South Africa. Phone: 27 21 9380454; Fax: 27 21 9380483; Email: cathy.mathews@mrc.ac.za • URL: http://www.mrc.ac.za/healthsystems/healthsystems.htm • Health care services, systems, interventions, and policies.

Medical University of South Carolina - Center for Health Economics and Policy Studies. CHP Research Bldg., 3rd Fl., Department of Health Sciences & Research, College of Health Professions Complex, 77 President St., Charleston, SC 29425. Phone: (843)792-3176; Fax: (843)792-1358; Email: lindrorc@musc.edu • URL: http://www.musc.edu/chp/cheps • Health economics and health policy.

National Center for Scientific Research - Research Center for Medicine, Sciences, Health and Society. CNRS UMR 8169-EHESS-Inserm U750, 7 rue Guy Môquet, F-94801 Villejuif, France. Phone: 33 1 49583636; Fax: 33 1 49583438; Email: cermes@vjf.cnrs.fr • URL: http://cermes.vjf.inserm.fr • Health and medicine, including sociology, anthropology, economics, history and history of sciences.

National Health Policy Forum. George Washington University, 2131 K St. NW, Ste. 500, Washington, DC 20037-1882. Phone: (202)872-1390; Fax: (202)862-9837; Email: nhpf@gwu.edu • URL: http://www.nhpf.org • Nonpartisan education program serving primarily senior federal legislative and executive branch health staff but also addressing the interests of state officials and their Washington representatives. Seeks to foster more informed government decision-making. Helps decision makers forge the personal acquaintances and understanding necessary for cooperation among government agencies and between government and the private sector.

National Yang-Ming University - Research Center of Health and Welfare Policy. Li-Nong St., No. 155, Section 2, Taipei 112, Taiwan. Phone: 886 2 28267000; Fax: 886 2 28205503; Email: ihw@ym.edu.tw • URL: http://www.ym.edu.tw/hwprc/engli.htm • Health and welfare policies of Taiwan.

New York University Medical Center - Institute of Community Health and Research - Center for Health and Human Rights. Bellevue C&D Bldg., Rm. 741, 462 1st Ave., New York, NY 10016. Phone: (212)562-8490; Fax: (212)562-4436 • URL: http://medicine.med.nyu.edu/dgim/sections/primary-care/health-and-human-rights-overview • Health policy related to human rights.

Ohio State University - Center for Health Outcomes, Policy and Evaluation Studies. 280G Cunz Hall, 1841 Neil Ave., Columbus, OH 43210. Phone: (614)292-2129; Fax: (614)292-3572; Email: adembe@cph.osu.edu • URL: http://cph.osu.edu/hopes • Health care policy.

Peking University - Center for Healthy Aging and Family Studies. China Ctr. for Economy Research, Beijing 100871, China. Phone: 86 10 62756914; Fax: 86 10 62756843; Email: chafs@ccer.pku.edu.cn • URL: http://www.pku.edu.cn/academic/ageing/english/indexe.htm • Healthy aging and inter-generational relationships within the family unit, as well as the economics of aging.

RAND - Center for Domestic and International Health Security. 1200 S Hayes St., Arlington, VA 22202-5050. Phone: (703)413-1100; Email: globalhealth@rand.org • URL: http://www.rand.org/health/centers/healthsecurity • Health security at the global as well as community level. Research focuses on strengthening the U.S. public health system to address emerging challenges, supporting development of health systems in the global community, and advancing health in foreign policy.

Rutgers University - Center for State Health Policy. 112 Paterson St., 5th Fl., New Brunswick, NJ 08901-1913. Phone: (732)932-3105; Fax: (732)932-0069; Email: jcantor@ifh.rutgers.edu • URL: http://www.cshp.rutgers.edu/ • State health policy issues in New Jersey, including long-term care, access to health care, racial and ethnic health disparities, health care performance measurement, and pharmaceutical policy.

Shandong University - Center for Health Management and Policy. 44 Wenhua Xi Rd., Jinan 250012, Shandong, China. Phone: 86 531 8382692; Fax: 86 531 8382693; Email: qmeng@sdu.edu.cn • URL: http://www.chmp.sdu.edu.cn/Eng • Health economics, health policy analysis, and development of health management instruments.

Stanford University - Center for Primary Care and Outcomes Research. 117 Encina Commons, Stanford, CA 94305-6019. Phone: (650)736-0815; Fax: (650)723-1919; Email: garber@stanford.edu • URL: http://healthpolicy.stanford.edu • Clinical practice and public health, including medical technology assessment, advancement of primary care policy and practice, clinical decision making and practice guideline development, patient safety and quality of care, and medical outcomes.

Texas Tech University - Center for Healthcare Innovation, Education and Research. Rawls College of Business Administration, Lubbock, TX 79409. Phone: (806)742-1236; Fax: (806)742-3434; Email: tim.huerta@ttu.edu • URL: http://chier.ba.ttu.edu/index.asp • Interdisciplinary approaches to studying healthcare safety issues and addition of electronic medical records.

University of Akron - Buchtel College of Arts and Sciences - Institute of Bioscience and Social Research. Polsky Bldg. 520, 225 S Main St., Akron, OH 44325-1915. Phone: (330)972-6765; Fax: (330)972-8675; Email: wilder@uakron.edu • URL: http://www.uakron.edu/ibsr • Healthcare policy and services.

University of Alabama at Birmingham - Lister Hill Center for Health Policy. Ryals Public Health Bldg., 1665 University Blvd., Birmingham, AL 35294-0022. Phone: (205)975-9007; Fax: (205)934-3347; Email: morrisey@uab.edu • URL: http://www.soph.uab.edu/index.php?q=listerhill • Health policy research, focusing on health care markets and managed care, maternal and child health, management in public health organizations, aging policy, and outcomes research.

University of Arkansas for Medical Sciences -

Arkansas Center for Health Improvement. Victory Bldg., Ste. 300, 1401 W Capitol, Little Rock, AR 72201. Phone: (501)526-2244; Fax: (501)526-2252 • URL: http://www.achi.net • Policies that improve the health of the citizens of Arkansas.

University of Auckland - Centre for Mental Health Research. Bldg. 505, Level 2, Faculty of Medical and Health Sciences, 85 Park Rd., Private Bag 92019, Auckland 1142, New Zealand. Phone: 64 9 3737599; Fax: 64 9 3677158; Email: b.mckenna@auckland.ac.nz • URL: http://www.fmhs.auckland.ac.nz/son/cmhr • Mental health policy, services, workforce and clinical practice.

University of Brighton - School of Applied Social Science - Social Science Policy and Research Centre. Mayfield House, Falmer, Brighton BN1 9PH, United Kingdom. Phone: 44 1273 643980; Fax: 44 1273 643496; Email: marian.barnes@brighton.ac.uk • URL: http://www.brighton.ac.uk/sass/research/ • Health and social policy issues, including neighborhood renewal, community participation, social exclusion, interagency working, health and social care, the social services workforce, third sector concerns, policing and criminal justice, transport and the environment, housing, and youth concerns.

University of British Columbia - Centre for Health Services and Policy Research. 201-2206 E Mall, Vancouver, BC, Canada V6T 1Z3. Phone: (604)822-4969; Fax: (604)822-5690; Email: mbarer@chspr.ubc.ca • URL: http://www.chspr.ubc.ca • Pharmaceuticals, primary health care, patterns of health and health care utilization, and data and infrastructure development.

University of California, Berkeley - School of Public Health - Center for Health and Public Policy Studies. 50 University Hall, No. 7360, Berkeley, CA 94720-7360. Phone: (510)643-1675; Fax: (510)643-2340; Email: chpps@berkeley.edu • URL: http://chpps.berkeley.edu • Issues in health policy and politics that affect California and the nation.

University of California, Davis - Center for Healthcare Policy and Research. 2103 Stockton Blvd., Sacramento, CA 95817. Phone: (916)734-2818; Fax: (916)734-8731 • URL: http://www.ucdmc.ucdavis.edu/chsrpc • Public health policy, including causes and prevention of adverse health outcomes, quality of care, physician-patient interaction, and cost effectiveness.

University of California, Los Angeles - Center for Health Policy Research. 10960 Wilshire Blvd., Ste. 1550, Los Angeles, CA 90024. Phone: (310)794-0909; Fax: (310)794-2686; Email: healthpolicy@ucla.edu • URL: http://healthpolicy.ucla.edu/Pages/home.aspx • Cost-effectiveness of health programs and services and their effects on health of communities and consumers; policy analysis and develops policy tools that address issues of health promotion and disease prevention.

University of California, San Francisco - Institute for Health and Aging. UCSF Box 0646, San Francisco, CA 94143-0646. Phone: (415)476-9483; Fax: (415)476-3915; Email: wendy.max@ucsf.edu • URL: http://nursing.ucsf.edu/iha • Aging health policy issues and policy alternatives; state discretionary policies in long-term care, social services, and income maintenance; private sector involvement in supporting health and social services for the elderly; effects of intergovernmental relations and state and federal fiscal conditions on services to the elderly; coordination between state and local aging programs and health planning, financing, and regulatory programs; special health and social service needs of the low-income, isolated elderly; enrollment of the elderly in health maintenance and social/health organizations; gender issues; Alzheimer's disease resources and program evaluation; AIDS; international alcohol; health promotion and injury and disease prevention; disability statistics; and health status of the elderly, with special emphasis on selected acute and chronic health conditions.

University of California, San Francisco - Institute for Health Policy Studies. 3333 California St., Ste. 265, San Francisco, CA 94118. Phone: (415)476-5255; Fax: (415)476-0705; Email: claire.brindis@ucsf.edu • URL: http://healthpolicy.ucsf.edu • Health policy and health services research.

University of California, San Francisco - Rosalind Russell Medical Research Center for Arthritis. 350 Parnassus Ave., Ste. 600, San Francisco, CA 94117. Phone: (415)476-1141; Fax: (415)476-3526; Email: rrac@medicine.ucsf.com • URL: http://www.rosalindrussellcenter.ucsf.edu • Arthritis and its probable causes, focusing on immunology, immunogenetics, and inflammation. Examines health services and policy and educational approaches and methods for arthritis patients and health professionals.

University of Chicago. 947 E 58th St., MC0926, Chicago, IL 60637-5416. Phone: (773)702-6371 or (773)702-1234; Fax: (773)702-1216 or (773)702-7222; Email: info@ssa.uchicago.edu • URL: http://pps.bsd.uchicago.edu/.

University of Cincinnati - Center for Health and Environmental Research. Department of Communication, 601A Teachers College, Cincinnati, OH 45221-0184. Phone: (513)556-4001; Fax: (513)556-0899; Email: depoe@uc.edu • URL: http://asweb.artsci.uc.edu/communication/checr/about/index.html • Communication processes and practices in environmental and health policy contexts, in order to enhance the understanding and quality of communication processes and practices among citizen, industry, and government participants in environmental and health policy formation and implementation. The center's research agenda includes the design, analysis, and evaluation of informational and persuasive messages and campaigns produced by and addressed to individuals and institutions which pertain to environmental and human health risk contexts and controversies; the analysis and evaluation of communication processes within environmental and health-related organizations; and the design, facilitation, and evaluation of processes of stakeholder involvement in risk-based decision-making.

University of Cincinnati - Institute for the Study of Health. PO Box 670840, Cincinnati, OH 45267-0840. Phone: (513)558-2756; Fax: (513)558-2744; Email: ronnie.horner@uc.edu • URL: http://www.healthinstitute.uc.edu/Templates/Home.cfm • Health policy and health services, especially cost effectiveness and health outcomes.

University of Connecticut - Center for Public Health and Health Policy - Health Policy Group. 99 Ash St., 2nd Fl., MC 7160, East Hartford, CT 06108. Phone: (860)282-8578; Fax: (860)282-8505; Email: meberle@uchc.edu • URL: http://www.publichealth.uconn.edu/policy-analysis.html • Health policy, including prevention, health promotion and primary care.

University of Connecticut - School of Medicine - Department of Community Medicine and Health Care - Center for International Community Health Studies. MC 6325, 263 Farmington Ave., Farmington, CT 06030-6325. Phone: (860)679-1570; Fax: (860)679-5464; Email: schensul@nso2.uchc.edu • URL: http://www.commed.uchc.edu/cichs • The health of underprivileged people in the U.S. and abroad, emphasizing international primary health care and community health, including international health policy, urban health in developing and developed countries, maternal and child health, health programs and problems in Peru, Sri Lanka, Kenya, Mauritius, and Connecticut, effects of economic development on health, and the role of the hospital in the developing world. Facilitates international health research for faculty and graduate students through consultation on grant proposals, networking with international contacts, advocating for researchers within international agencies, and establishing foreign research and educational placements.

University of Florida - Institute for Child Health Policy. 1329 SW 16th St., Gainesville, FL 32608. Phone: (352)265-7220; Fax: (352)265-7221 • URL: http://ichp.ufl.edu • Child health policy and family and child health care delivery issues, including development of an equitable and comprehensive child health policy model for states; development of case management programs for children with special health care needs; development of health care financing strategies, including school enrollment-based health insurance; and comprehensive program development and health services research and evaluation.

University of Houston - Health Law and Policy Institute. 100 Law Ctr., Houston, TX 77204-6060. Phone: (713)743-2101; Fax: (713)743-2117; Email: healthlaw@uh.edu • URL: http://www.law.uh.edu/healthlaw • Health issues affecting the state and nation, including health law and policy, occupational injury and illness, nonfinancial barriers to health care, and family violence and the health care system.

University of Illinois at Chicago - Institute for Health Research and Policy - Center for Health Services Research. Westside Research Office Bldg., Rm. 560 CU3, 1747 W Roosevelt Rd., MC 275, Chicago, IL 60608. Phone: (312)996-1062; Fax: (312)996-5356; Email: jzwanzig@uic.edu • URL: http://ihrp.uic.edu/center/center-health-services-research • New health care technologies, medical informatics, health manpower, observation unit medicine in the hospital emergency room, and performance of preventive through tertiary healthcare delivery at the systems, program, and specific intervention levels. Studies focus on access, appropriateness, acceptability, cost, safety, availability, effectiveness, benefits, and overall quality of healthcare. Specific topics include clinical decision-making, health information management, psychological and social sciences, and public health policy analysis.

University of Illinois at Urbana-Champaign - Bureau of Economic and Business Research. 430 Wohlers Hall, Office of Research, College of Business, 1206 S 6th St., Champaign, IL 61820. Phone: (217)333-2330; Fax: (217)333-7410; Email: lhuff@uiuc.edu • URL: http://business.illinois.edu/research • Economics and business, including studies in business expectations, health economics, forecasting and planning, innovation, entrepreneurship, consumer behavior, poverty problems, small business operations and problems, investment and growth, productivity, research methodology, organizational behavior, and international business and banking.

University of Iowa - Law, Health Policy and Disability Center. 280-1 Boyd Law Bldg., Iowa City, IA 52242-1113. Phone: (319)335-8469; Fax: (319)335-9764; Email: helen-schartz@uiowa.edu • URL: http://disability.law.uiowa.edu • Legal, health policy and employment issues facing persons with disabilities.

University of Kent at Canterbury - Centre for Health Services Studies. Cornwallis Bldg., George Allen Wing, Canterbury CT2 7NF, United Kingdom. Phone: 44 1227 824057; Fax: 44 1227 827868; Email: s.peckham@kent.ac.uk • URL: http://www.kent.ac.uk/chss • Recuperative care; aged in more care; health needs assessment for prisons; integrated health and social care for older persons, including issues, problems and solutions; stroke and rehabilitation, identification and management of risks of everyday life.

University of Leeds - Faculty of Medicine and Health - Leeds Institute of Cancer and Pathology -

Epidemiology and Biostatistics Section. Cancer Genetics Bldg., St. James's University Hospital, Leeds LS9 7TF, United Kingdom. Phone: 44 113 2064573 • URL: http://medhealth.leeds.ac.uk/info/920/epidemiology_and_biostatistics • Public health, health services and health policy.

University of Manitoba - Faculty of Medicine - Department of Community Health Sciences - Manitoba Centre for Health Policy. 408-727 McDermot Ave., Winnipeg, MB, Canada R3E 3P5. Phone: (204)789-3819; Fax: (204)789-3910; Email: info@cpe.umanitoba.ca • URL: http://umanitoba.ca/faculties/medicine/units/community_health_sciences/departmental_units/mchp • Health of Manitobans, focusing on health services, population and public health, and social determinants of health.

University of Maryland at Baltimore - Center for Vaccine Development. 685 W Baltimore St., Rm. 480, Baltimore, MD 21201-1509. Phone: (410)706-5328; Fax: (410)706-6205; Email: mlevine@medicine.umaryland.edu • URL: http://medschool.umaryland.edu/CVD • Bacterial diseases, parasitic diseases, viral diseases, novel delivery systems, combination vaccines and public health and policy.

University of Massachusetts at Worcester - Medical School - Center for Health Policy and Research. 333 South St., Shrewsbury, MA 01545. Phone: (508)856-3124; Fax: (508)856-6100; Email: chpr@umassmed.edu • URL: http://chpr.umassmed.edu • Health policy.

University of New England - Center for Health Policy, Planning and Research. Linnell Hall, 716 Stevens Ave., Portland, ME 04103. Phone: (207)221-4560; Fax: (207)523-1914; Email: rdeprez@une.edu • URL: http://www.une.edu/chppr • Healthcare improvement initiatives in communities, health systems, regions and countries, especially for patients with chronic medical conditions.

University of New Hampshire - College of Health and Human Services - New Hampshire Institute for Health Policy and Practice. Hewitt Hall, Ste. 202, 4 Library Way, Durham, NH 03824. Phone: (603)862-5031; Fax: (603)862-4457 • URL: http://chhs.unh.edu/ihpp • Health policy and practice for the citizens of New Hampshire, focusing on community health, Medicaid policy, and adolescent health.

University of New South Wales - Centre for Clinical Governance Research. AGSM Bldg., Level 1, Faculty of Medicine, Sydney, NSW 2052, Australia. Phone: 61 2 93853861; Fax: 61 2 96634926; Email: j.braithwaite@unsw.edu.au • URL: http://www.aihi.unsw.edu.au/ccgr • Role of clinicians in health care delivery and why and how this is being affected by changes in the social, legal, economic, organizational, informational and political contexts of health service organizations.

University of Pennsylvania - Leonard Davis Institute of Health Economics. Colonial Penn Ctr., 3641 Locust Walk, Philadelphia, PA 19104-6218. Phone: (215)898-5611 or (215)898-1657; Fax: (215)898-0229; Email: polsky@mail.med.upenn.edu • URL: http://ldi.upenn.edu • Research fields include health care management and cost-quality trade-offs.

University of Pennsylvania - School of Nursing - Center for Health Outcomes and Policy Research. Fagin Hall, Rm. 387, 418 Curie Blvd., Philadelphia, PA 19104-4217. Phone: (215)898-5673; Email: laiken@nursing.upenn.edu • URL: http://www.nursing.upenn.edu/chopr/Pages/default.aspx • Health care and workforce organization, financing, and outcomes; and public policies that influence nursing and health care delivery nationally and internationally.

University of Sydney - Effective Healthcare Australia. Victor Coppleson Bldg. D02, Sydney, NSW 2006, Australia. Phone: 61 2 93514378; Fax: 61 2 93515204; Email: grubin@med.usyd.edu.au • URL: http://www.eha.usyd.edu.au/ • Clinical and public health care improvement and health care policy in the Asia Pacific region.

University of Sydney - George Institute for Global Health. Missenden Rd., Sydney, NSW 2050, Australia. Phone: 61 2 96570300; Fax: 61 2 96570301; Email: info@georgeinstitute.org.au • URL: http://www.georgeinstitute.org/ • Chronic disease and injury, particularly involving the heart and vascular system; epidemiology and biostatistics; injury prevention and trauma care; mental health; and medical policy and practice.

University of Texas at Austin - Center for Health and Social Policy. Lyndon B. Johnson School of Public Affairs, Austin, TX 78713-8925. Phone: (512)232-3423; Email: cheinrich@austin.utexas.edu • URL: http://www.utexas.edu/lbj/chasp • Health and social policy.

University of Texas Medical Branch at Galveston - Institute for the Medical Humanities. 301 University Blvd., Galveston, TX 77555-1311. Phone: (409)772-2376; Fax: (409)772-5640; Email: davicker@utmb.edu • URL: http://imh.utmb.edu • History of professional medical ethics, phenomenology of aging, iconography of the life cycle, confidentiality in the doctor-patient relationship, women in medicine, ethics of research in clinical medicine, and empathy in medical practice.

University of Western Australia - Centre for Health Services Research. School of Population Health, 35 Stirling Hwy., Crawley, WA 6009, Australia. Phone: 61 8 64881307; Fax: 61 8 64881188; Email: david.preen@uwa.edu.au • URL: http://www.sph.uwa.edu.au/research/chsr • Health services policy and practice, focusing on the inequalities in health care, preventable inpatient time, best practices in surgical and procedural care, clinical safety and post-implementation surveillance.

University of Wisconsin—Madison - Center for Health System Research and Analysis. WARF Bldg., 11th Fl., 610 Walnut St., Madison, WI 53726-2397. Phone: (608)263-5722; Fax: (608)263-4523; Email: jim_robinson@chsra.wisc.edu • URL: http://www.chsra.wisc.edu • Five major research areas: quality assessment and improvement, long term care, public health policy and program evaluation, consumer decision making, and patient education and support.

Veterans Health Administration - Health Services Research and Development Service - Houston Center for Quality of Care and Utilization Studies - Health Policy and Quality Division. Veterans Affairs Medical Ctr. (152), 2002 Holcombe Blvd., Houston, TX 77030. Phone: (713)794-8623; Fax: (713)748-7359; Email: laura.petersen@va.gov • URL: http://www.hsrd.houston.med.va.gov/health-policy-quality.htm • Effects of local, state, and federal government policies on the health of populations, access to care, efficiency of care and the quality of health care.

Washington University in St. Louis - Center for Health Policy. Simon Hall, CB 1133, 1 Brookings Dr., Saint Louis, MO 63130. Phone: (314)935-8767; Fax: (314)935-9199; Email: peckw@wustl.edu • URL: http://healthpolicy.wustl.edu • Health policy, including disparities in access to care and insurance, healthcare costs, medical workforce shortages, and inefficiencies and errors in provision of medical services.

Wayne State University - College of Nursing - Office of Health Research. Cohn Bldg., Rm. 319, 5557 Cass Ave., Detroit, MI 48202. Phone: (313)577-4135; Fax: (313)577-5777; Email: n.artinian@wayne.edu • URL: http://www.nursing.wayne.edu/faculty/health-research.php • Studies innovation in health care organization and financing.

STATISTICS SOURCES

Standard & Poor's Industry Surveys. Standard & Poor's Financial Services L.L.C. • Semiannual. $1,800.00. Two looseleaf volumes. Includes monthly *Supplements*. Provides detailed, individual surveys of 52 major industry groups. Each survey is revised on a semiannual basis. Also includes "Monthly Investment Review" (industry group investment analysis) and monthly "Trends & Projections" (economic analysis).

U.S. Industry and Trade Outlook. U.S. Department of Commerce National Technical Information Service. • Annual. Produced by the International Trade Administration, U.S. Department of Commerce, in a "public-private" partnership with DRI/McGraw-Hill and Standard & Poor's. Provides basic data, outlook for the current year, and "Long-Term Prospects" (five-year projections) for a wide variety of products and services. Includes high technology industries. Formerly *U.S. Industrial Outlook*.

The Universal Healthcare Almanac: A Complete Guide for the Healthcare Professional - Facts, Figures, Analysis. Silver & Cherner, Ltd. • $195.00 per year. Looseleaf service. Quarterly updates. Includes a wide variety of health care statistics: national expenditures, hospital data, health insurance, health professionals, vital statistics, demographics, etc. Years of coverage vary, with long range forecasts provided in some cases.

TRADE/PROFESSIONAL ASSOCIATIONS

American College of Health Care Administrators. 1321 Duke St., Ste. 400, Alexandria, VA 22314. Phone: (202)536-5120; Fax: (866)874-1585; Email: mgrachek@achca.org • URL: http://www.achca.org • Formerly American College of Nursing Home Administrators.

American College of Healthcare Executives. 1 N Franklin St., Ste. 1700, Chicago, IL 60606-3529. Phone: (312)424-2800 or (312)424-9400; Fax: (312)424-0023 or (312)424-9405; Email: contact@ache.org • URL: http://www.ache.org • Formerly American College of Hospital Administrators.

American Dental Association. 211 E Chicago Ave., Chicago, IL 60611-2678. Phone: 800-947-4746 or (312)440-2500; Fax: (312)440-3542; Email: berryj@ada.org • URL: http://www.ada.org • Professional society of dentists. Encourages the improvement of the health of the public and promotes the art and science of dentistry in matters of legislation and regulations. Inspects and accredits dental schools and schools for dental hygienists, assistants, and laboratory technicians. Conducts research programs at ADA Foundation Research Institute. Produces dental health education material used in the U.S. Sponsors National Children's Dental Health Month and Give Kids a Smile Day. Compiles statistics on personnel, practice, and dental care needs and attitudes of patients with regard to dental health.

American Health Care Association. 1201 L St. NW, Washington, DC 20005. Phone: (202)842-4444; Fax: (202)842-3860 • URL: http://www.ahcancal.org/Pages/Default.aspx • Federation of state associations of long-term health care facilities. Promotes standards for professionals in long-term health care delivery and quality care for patients and residents in a safe environment. Focuses on issues of availability, quality, affordability, and fair payment. Operates as liaison with governmental agencies, Congress, and professional associations. Compiles statistics.

American Hospital Association. 155 N Wacker Dr., Chicago, IL 60606. Phone: 800-424-4301 or (312)422-3000 or (312)422-2050; Fax: (312)422-4700 • URL: http://www.aha.org • Represents health care provider organizations. Seeks to advance the health of individuals and communities. Leads, represents, and serves health care provider organizations that are accountable to the community and committed to health improvement.

American Medical Association. AMA Plaza, 330 N Wabash Ave., Chicago, IL 60611. Phone: 800-621-8335 or (312)464-4430; Fax: (312)464-5226; Email: amalibrary@ama-assn.org • URL: http://www.ama-assn.org • Represents county medical societies and physicians. Disseminates scientific information to members and the public. Informs members on significant medical and health legislation on state and national levels and represents the profession before Congress and governmental agencies. Cooperates in setting standards for medical schools, hospitals, residency programs, and continuing medical education courses. Offers physician placement service and counseling on practice management problems. Operates library that lends material and provides specific medical information to physicians. Maintains Ad-hoc committees for such topics as health care planning and principles of medical ethics.

American Nurses Credentialing Center. 8515 Georgia Ave., Ste. 400, Silver Spring, MD 20910-3492. Phone: 800-284-2378 • URL: http://www.nursecredentialing.org • Empowers nurses within their professional sphere of activity and contributes to better patient outcome. Provides Board Certification in the following nursing specialties: Acute Care Nurse Practitioner, Adult Health Clinical Nurse Specialist (formerly Med-Surg), Adult Nurse Practitioner, Adult Psychiatric and Mental Health Clinical Nurse Specialist, Adult Psychiatric and Mental Health Nurse Practitioner, Ambulatory Care Nurse, Cardiac Vascular Nurse, Nursing Case Management, Child/Adolescent Psychiatric and Mental Health Clinical Nurse Specialist, Diabetes Management, Family Nurse Practitioner, Family Psychiatric and Mental Health Nurse Practitioner, Gerontological Clinical Nurse Specialist, Gerontological Nursing, Gerontological Nurse Practitioner, Informatics Nurse, Medical-Surgical Nurse, Nurse Executive, Nursing Professional Development, Pain Management, Pediatric Clinical Nurse Specialist, Pediatric Nurse, Pediatric Nurse Practitioner, Psychiatric and Mental Health Nurse, Advanced Public/Community Health Nurse.

APhA Academy of Pharmacy Practice and Management. 2215 Constitution Ave. NW, Washington, DC 20037. Phone: 800-237-APHA or (202)628-4410 or (202)429-7557; Fax: (202)783-2351; Email: infocenter@aphanet.org • URL: http://www.pharmacist.com/apha-appm • Pharmacists concerned with rendering professional services directly to the public, without regard for status of employment or environment of practice. Formerly Academy of Pharmacy Practice and Management.

Healthcare Financial Management Association. 3 Westbrook Corporate Ctr., Ste. 600, Westchester, IL 60154. Phone: 800-252-4362 or (708)531-9600; Fax: (708)531-0032; Email: memberservices@hfma.org • URL: http://www.hfma.org • Financial management professionals employed by hospitals and long-term care facilities, public accounting and consulting firms, insurance companies, medical groups, managed care organizations, government agencies, and other organizations. Conducts conferences, including annual conference in late June and audio teleconferences. Publishes books on healthcare financial issues. A Fellowship in Healthcare Financial Management (FHFMA) as well as the Certified Healthcare Professional (CHFP) in Finance and Accounting, Financial Management of Physician Practices, Managed Care, and Patient Financial Services are offered.

Medical Group Management Association. 104 Inverness Terr. E, Englewood, CO 80112-5306. Phone: 877-275-6462 or (303)799-1111; Fax: (303)643-4439; Email: service@mgma.com • URL: http://www.mgma.com • Represents professionals involved in the management of medical group practices and administration of other ambulatory healthcare facilities. Provides products and services that includes education, benchmarking, surveys, national advocacy and networking opportunities for members.

National Association of Health and Educational Facilities Finance Authorities. PO Box 906, Oakhurst, NJ 07755. Phone: 888-414-5713; Fax: (888)414-5713 • URL: http://www.naheffa.com • Serves the common interests and improves effectiveness of member authorities through communication, education, and advocacy, with emphasis on issues which directly influence the availability of or access to tax-exempt financing for healthcare facilities.

Pharmaceutical Research and Manufacturers Association. 950 F St. NW, Ste. 300, Washington, DC 20004. Phone: (202)835-3400 • URL: http://www.phrma.org • Formerly Pharmaceutical Manufacturers Association.

HEALTH CLUB INDUSTRY

See FITNESS INDUSTRY

HEALTH FOOD INDUSTRY

See also DIET; FOOD INDUSTRY; HERBS; VITAMINS

ABSTRACTS AND INDEXES

Nutrition Abstracts and Reviews, Series A: Human and Experimental. CABI Publishing North America. • Monthly. Institutions, $1,835.00 per year. Includes single site internet access. Published in England by CABI Publishing. Provides worldwide coverage of the literature.

DIRECTORIES

Health Products Business Purchasing Guide. Cygnus Business Media. • Annual. $10.00. Listing of manufacturers, importers, exclusive distributors, brokers, and wholesalers of health food products, publishers of health food related books and magazines, and associations interested in the health foods industry. Formerly *Health Foods Business Purchasing Guide.*

FINANCIAL RATIOS

Annual Statement Studies. Risk Management Association. • Annual. Compiled from over 280,000 financial statements.

Annual Statement Studies: Industry Default Probabilities and Cash Flow Measures. Risk Management Association. • Annual. $405 Nonmembers. Serves as a companion volume to the original *Annual Statement Studies.* Gives probability of default estimates on a percentage scale for more than 450 industries. Includes changes in position year-by-year for eight financial statement line items and provides percentage measures of cash flow.

PERIODICALS AND NEWSLETTERS

Health Food Business Magazine. Target Publishing Ltd. • Monthly. £54 Individuals United Kingdom only. Trade magazine for the health food retail industry.

Health Products Business: The Business Publication of the Natural Foods In dustry. Cygnus Business Media. • Monthly. $60.00 per year.

Journal of Dietary Supplements. The Haworth Press Inc. • Quarterly. $175.00 per year to libraries; $50.00 per year to individuals. Edited with a view to both academic research and industry concerns. Sections are dedicated to health professionals, educators, and dieticians. Includes book reviews and short reviews of research appearing elsewhere. Formerly *Journal of Nutraceuticals, Functional & Medical Foods.*

HEALTH, INDUSTRIAL

See INDUSTRIAL HYGIENE

HEALTH INSURANCE

See also ACCIDENT INSURANCE; HEALTH MAINTENANCE ORGANIZATIONS; LIFE INSURANCE; LONG-TERM CARE INSURANCE; MEDICARE

ABSTRACTS AND INDEXES

Insurance Periodicals Index. Specials Libraries Association, Insurance and Employees Benefits Div. NILS Publishing Co. • Annual. $250.00. Compiled by the Insurance and Employee Benefits Div., Special Libraries Association. A yearly index of over 15,000 articles from about 35 insurance periodicals. Arrangement is by subject, with an index to authors.

ALMANACS AND YEARBOOKS

Insurance Almanac: Who, What, When and Where in Insurance. Criterion Publishing Co. • Annual. $195. Lists insurance agencies and brokerage firms; U.S. and Canadian insurance companies, adjusters, appraisers, auditors, investigators, insurance officials and insurance organizations.

BIBLIOGRAPHIES

ACLI Life Insurers Fact Book. American Council of Life Insurance. • Annual. Free. Provides statistics and information on trends in the life insurance industry.

Insurance and Employee Benefits Literature. Special Libraries Association. • Bimonthly. $15.00 per year. Lists a wide variety of literature in all branches of the insurance industry. Includes annotations.

DIRECTORIES

Business Insurance-Directory of HMOs, POSs and PPOs. Crain Communications Inc. • Annual. $149 per year. Provides detailed information on more than 600 managed care providers in the U. S., chiefly health maintenance organizations (HMOs) and preferred provider organizations (PPOs).

HANDBOOKS AND MANUALS

Medicare: Employer Health Plans. Consumer Information Center. • Free. Published by the U. S. Department of Health and Human Services. Explains the special rules that apply to Medicare beneficiaries who have employer group health plan coverage. (Publication No. 520-Y.).

Medicare Explained. Wolters Kluwer Law & Business CCH. • Annual. $67.95.

INTERNET DATABASES

Free Insurance Advice. InsWeb, Inc. 2868 Prospect Park Dr., Ste. 650, Rancho Cordova, CA 95670. Phone: (916)853-3300; Fax: (916)853-3300; Email: customercare@insweb.com • URL: http://www.insweb.com • Web site offers a wide variety of advice and information on automobile, life, health, and "other" insurance. Includes glossaries of insurance terms, Standard & Poor's ratings of individual insurance companies, and "Financial Needs Estimators." Searching is available. Fees: Free.

National Center for Health Statistics: Monitoring the Nation's Health. National Center for Health Statistics, Centers for Disease Control and Prevention. Phone: (301)458-4000; Email: nchsquery@cdc.gov • URL: http://www.cdc.gov/nchswww • Web site provides detailed data on diseases, vital statistics, and health care in the U. S. Includes a search facility and links to many other health-related Web sites. "Fastats A to Z" offers quick data on hundreds of topics from Accidents to Work-Loss Days, with links to Comprehensive Data and related sources. Frequent updates. Fees: Free.

ONLINE DATABASES

I.I.I. Data Base Search. Insurance Information Institute. • Provides online citations and abstracts of insurance-related literature in magazines, newspapers, trade journals, and books. Emphasis is on property and casualty insurance issues, including highway safety, product safety, and environmental liability. Inquire as to online cost and availability.

OTHER SOURCES

Best's Insurance Reports. A.M. Best Company Inc. • Annual. Covers life-health insurance covering about 1,750 companies, and property-casualty insurance covering over 3,200 companies. Includes subscription to both *Best's Review* and *Best's Insurance Management Reports.*

Health Care Benefits Law. ALM Media Properties LLC. • $565. Covers the legal compliance aspects of employer health care plans. Includes checklists and sample forms. (Law Journal Press).

Life, Health, and Accident Insurance Law Reports. Wolters Kluwer Law & Business CCH. • $835.00 per year. Looseleaf service. Monthly updates.

PERIODICALS AND NEWSLETTERS

Contingencies: The Magazine of the Actuarial Profession. American Academy of Actuaries. • Bimonthly. $24 Nonmembers. Provides nontechnical articles on the actuarial aspects of insurance, employee benefits, and pensions.

Drug Benefit Trends: For Pharmacy Managers and Managed HealthCare Professionals. Cliggott Publishing Co. • Monthly. Individuals, $95.00 per year; libraries, $120.00 per year; students, $40.00 per year. Covers the business of managed care drug benefits.

Guide to HMOs and Health Insurers: A Quarterly Compilation of Health Insurance Company Ratings and Analysis. Weiss Research Inc. • Quarterly. $499. Emphasis is on rating of financial safety and relative risk. Includes annual summary.

Guide to Life, Health, and Annuity Insurers: A Quarterly Compilation of Insurance Company Ratings and Analysis. Weiss Research Inc. • Quarterly. $499. Emphasis is on rating of financial safety and relative risk. Includes annual summary.

Health Care Financing Review. U. S. Government Printing Office. • Quarterly. $48 Individuals. Issued by the Health Care Financing Administration, U. S. Department of Health and Human Services. Presents articles by professionals in the areas of health care costs and financing.

Health Data Management. SourceMedia Inc. • Monthly. $98.00 per year. Covers the management and automation of clinical data and health care insurance claims. Provides news and analysis of various aspects of health care information technology for administrators of hospitals, clinics, and managed care plans.

Health Insurance Underwriter. National Association of Health Underwriters. • Monthly. Includes special feature issues on long-term care insurance, disability insurance, managed health care, and insurance office management.

Health News Daily. Elsevier Business Intelligence. • Description: Tracks developments in health care policy, legislation and regulation, insurance, pharmaceuticals, delivery, manufacturing, technology and treatment, funding, and research.

Healthcare Risk Management. AHC Media. • Description: Analyzes specific legal cases and trends relevant to healthcare liability. Discusses malpractice, liability for patients, staff and visitor injury, injury prevention, biomedical engineering, and medical staff credentials. Also covers high-risk areas of hospitals, hospital-owned home health and physician practices, accreditation, Medicare reimbursement, physician liability, medical records, and claims management. Recurring features include interviews, statistics, news of research, guest columns, legal briefs, and commentaries.

Healthplan: The Magazine of Trends, Insights, and Best Practices. American Association of Health Plans. • Bimonthly. $60 Individuals. Trade magazine covering news and analysis of managed health care for HMO and PPO executives.

Inquiry: The Journal of Health Care Organization, Provision, and Financing. Blue Cross and Blue Shield Association of the Rochester Area. • $118 Individuals print and web /year. Quarterly. Individuals, $53.00 per year; institutions, $75.00 per year.

Insurance and Technology. UBM L.L.C. • Monthly. $65.00 per year. Covers information technology and systems management as applied to the operation of life, health, casualty, and property insurance companies.

Insurance Forum: For the Unfettered Exchange of Ideas About Insurance. Joseph M. Belth, editor. Insurance Forum Inc. • Monthly. $90.00 per year. Newsletter. Provides analysis of the insurance business, including occasional special issues showing the ratings of about 1,600 life-health insurance companies, as determined by four major rating services: Duff & Phelps Credit Rating Co., Moody's Investors Service, Standard & Poor's Corp., and Weiss Research, Inc.

Risk and Insurance. LRP Publications Library. • Monthly. Price on application. Topics include risk management, workers' compensation, reinsurance, employee benefits, and managed care.

RESEARCH CENTERS AND INSTITUTES

Office of Academic Affairs, School of Public Health. University of Michigan, 1415 Washington Heights, Ann Arbor, MI 48109-2029. Phone: (734)764-5425; Fax: (734)763-5455; Email: nkjanz@umich.edu • URL: http://www.sph.umich.edu/ • Research fields include health care economics, health insurance, and long-term care.

University of Minnesota - Division of Health Policy and Management. School of Public Health, MMC 729, 420 Delaware St. SE, Minneapolis, MN 55455-0392. Phone: (612)624-6151; Fax: (612)624-2196; Email: mosco001@umn.edu • URL: http://www.sph.umn.edu/hpm • Fields of research include health insurance, consumer choice of health plans, quality of care, and long-term care.

STATISTICS SOURCES

Standard & Poor's Industry Surveys. Standard & Poor's Financial Services L.L.C. • Semiannual. $1,800.00. Two looseleaf volumes. Includes monthly *Supplements.* Provides detailed, individual surveys of 52 major industry groups. Each survey is revised on a semiannual basis. Also includes "Monthly Investment Review" (industry group investment analysis) and monthly "Trends & Projections" (economic analysis).

TRADE/PROFESSIONAL ASSOCIATIONS

Blue Cross and Blue Shield Association. 225 N Michigan Ave., Chicago, IL 60601. • URL: http://www.bcbs.com • Local Blue Cross and Blue Shield Plans in the U.S., and other licensees in Europe, Japan, and Jamaica. Aims to promote the betterment of public health and security; to secure the widest public acceptance of voluntary non-profit, prepayment of health services; to provide services to Blue Cross and Blue Shield Plans and licensees. Contracts with federal government as administrative agency for federal health programs; sponsors and conducts programs on health care and prepayment issues.

National Association of Professional Insurance Agents. 400 N Washington St., Alexandria, VA 22314. Phone: (703)836-9340; Fax: (703)836-1279; Email: web@pianet.org • URL: http://www.pianet.com • Members are independent agents in various fields of insurance. Formerly National Association of Mutual Insurance Agents.

United Agribusiness League. 54 Corporate Park, Irvine, CA 92606-5105. Phone: 800-223-4590 or (949)975-1424; Fax: (949)975-1573 or (949)975-1671; Email: marketing@aul.org • URL: http://www.ual.org • Agricultural industries and businesses. Promotes the development and common interest of the agricultural industry. Works to coordinate members' activities to advance agribusiness in general; provides services and benefits to enable members to realize greater productive efficiency. Serves as a clearinghouse on international agribusiness. Provides employee health care plans and other insurance to agribusinesses.

HEALTH MAINTENANCE ORGANIZATIONS

See also HEALTH CARE INDUSTRY; HEALTH INSURANCE

CD-ROM DATABASES

Authority Health Care Law Library. Matthew Bender and Company Inc. • Periodic updates. Price on request. Full text CD-ROM provides legal information, case law, and analysis relating to health care facilities, health insurance, longterm care, Medigap, and Medicare.

DIRECTORIES

AHA Integrated Delivery Network Directory: U.S. Health Care Systems, Networks, and Alliances. American Hospital Association. • Annual. $250.00. Provides information about a wide variety of U.S. health care groups and affiliations, including hospitals, nursing homes, rehabilitation centers, psychiatric facilities, home health care agencies, clinical laboratories, outpatient facilities, and diagnostic imaging centers. Includes names of more than 8,000 key executives.

Business Insurance-Directory of HMOs, POSs and PPOs. Crain Communications Inc. • Annual. $149 per year. Provides detailed information on more than 600 managed care providers in the U. S., chiefly health maintenance organizations (HMOs) and preferred provider organizations (PPOs).

Dorland's Directory of Health Plans. Dorland Healthcare Information. • Annual. $195.00. Published in association with the American Association of Health Plans (www.aahp.org). Lists more than 2,400 health plans, including Health Maintenance Organizations (HMOs), Preferred Provider Organizations (PPOs), and Point of Service plans (POS). Includes the names of about 9,000 health plan executives.

Health Maintenance Organization (HMO) Directory and Market Report. FIRSTMARK Inc. • Annual. $630.00. Three looseleaf volumes. Contains information relating to over 700 HMOs. Relevant market data is also provided.

National Directory of HMOs. America's Health Insurance Plans. • Annual. $125.00. Includes names of key personnel and benefit options.

HANDBOOKS AND MANUALS

Medicare and Coordinated Care Plans. Consumer Information Center. • Free. Published by the U. S. Department of Health and Human Services. Contains detailed information on services to Medicare beneficiaries from health maintenance organizations (HMOs).

INTERNET DATABASES

Free Insurance Advice. InsWeb, Inc. 2868 Prospect Park Dr., Ste. 650, Rancho Cordova, CA 95670. Phone: (916)853-3300; Fax: (916)853-3300; Email: customercare@insweb.com • URL: http://www.insweb.com • Web site offers a wide variety of advice and information on automobile, life, health, and "other" insurance. Includes glossaries of insurance terms, Standard & Poor's ratings of individual insurance companies, and "Financial Needs Estimators." Searching is available. Fees: Free.

PERIODICALS AND NEWSLETTERS

AHA News. American Hospital Association. HealthForum. • Description: Highlights major news affecting hospitals and the health care field. Reports on legislation and regulation, court cases, surveys, and federal programs. Carries information on individual hospitals and allied hospital associations.

Drug Benefit Trends: For Pharmacy Managers and Managed HealthCare Professionals. Cliggott Publishing Co. • Monthly. Individuals, $95.00 per year; libraries, $120.00 per year; students, $40.00 per year. Covers the business of managed care drug benefits.

Effective Clinical Practice. American College of Physicians. • Bimonthly. Individuals, $54.00 per year; institutions, $70.00 per year. Formerly *HMO Practice*.

Group Practice Journal. American Medical Group Association. • 10/year. $75 Institutions.

Guide to HMOs and Health Insurers: A Quarterly Compilation of Health Insurance Company Ratings and Analysis. Weiss Research Inc. • Quarterly. $499. Emphasis is on rating of financial safety and relative risk. Includes annual summary.

Health Insurance Underwriter. National Association of Health Underwriters. • Monthly. Includes special feature issues on long-term care insurance, disability insurance, managed health care, and insurance office management.

Healthcare Executive. American College of Healthcare Executives. • Bimonthly. $110 Individuals in the U.S.. Focuses on critical management issues in the healthcare industry.

Healthplan: The Magazine of Trends, Insights, and Best Practices. American Association of Health Plans. • Bimonthly. $60 Individuals. Trade magazine covering news and analysis of managed health care for HMO and PPO executives.

Medical Benefits. Wolters Kluwer Law and Business. • Description: Focuses on key developments, statistics, and studies relating to the health care system. Covers eight major topic areas: cost containment, employee benefits, employee health/ wellness, quality of care, delivery systems, government in health care, legal issues, and health care expenditure data.

Modern Physician: Essential Business News for the Executive Physician. Crain Communications Inc. • Monthly. $45.00. Edited for physicians responsible for business decisions at hospitals, clinics, HMOs, and other health groups. Includes special issues on managed care, practice management, legal issues, and finance.

RESEARCH CENTERS AND INSTITUTES

Duke University - Sanford School of Public Policy - Center for Health Policy and Inequalities Research. 310 Trent Dr., Durham, NC 27705. Phone: (919)613-5430; Fax: (919)613-5466 • URL: http://chpir.org • Quantitative analysis of clinical policies, decision analysis, Bayesian statistics, health economics, disease prevention, cancer and cancer detection, stroke prevention and management, and technology assessment, including evaluation of reimbursement policies for medical procedures, hospital and health care policies, and Health Maintenance Organization (HMO) medical policies.

Johns Hopkins University Bloomberg School of Public Health - Center for Health Services and Outcomes Research. Hampton House, 6th Fl., Department of Health Policy & Management, 624 N Broadway, Baltimore, MD 21205-1901. Phone: (410)955-6567; Fax: (410)955-0470; Email: awu@jhsph.edu • URL: http://www.jhsph.edu/research/centers-and-institutes/health-services-outcomes-research/index.html • Health services, including determinants of health outcomes; the impacts of alternative health care systems on cost and quality; effective strategies for health promotion and disease prevention; and methods of meeting the needs of high risk populations such as the poor, elderly, mentally ill, disabled, and children.

MGMA Center for Research. 104 Inverness Ter. E, Englewood, CO 80112-5306. Phone: 877-275-6462 or (303)799-1111; Fax: (303)784-6101; Email: dng@mgma.com • URL: http://www.mgma.com/cfr • Fields of research include medical group practice management. Formerly Center for Research in Ambulatory Health Care Administration.

Stratis Health. 2901 Metro Dr., Ste. 400, Bloomington, MN 55425-1525. Phone: 877-787-2847 or (952)854-3306; Fax: (952)853-8503; Email: info@stratishealth.org • URL: http://www.stratishealth.org • Physicians interested in ensuring the availability of quality health care at reasonable costs. Evaluates health care services at hospitals, retirement homes, and other facilities. Develops health care standards for hospitals and offers consultation services to operators of health care facilities to improve efficiency in services. Conducts research and development on latest treatments and medical technologies. Tests new medical technologies.

University of Chicago. 947 E 58th St., MC0926, Chicago, IL 60637-5416. Phone: (773)702-6371 or (773)702-1234; Fax: (773)702-1216 or (773)702-7222; Email: info@ssa.uchicago.edu • URL: http://pps.bsd.uchicago.edu/.

Wayne State University - College of Nursing - Office of Health Research. Cohn Bldg., Rm. 319, 5557 Cass Ave., Detroit, MI 48202. Phone: (313)577-4135; Fax: (313)577-5777; Email: n.artinian@wayne.edu • URL: http://www.nursing.wayne.edu/faculty/health-research.php • Studies innovation in health care organization and financing.

STATISTICS SOURCES

Standard & Poor's Industry Surveys. Standard & Poor's Financial Services L.L.C. • Semiannual. $1,800.00. Two looseleaf volumes. Includes monthly *Supplements*. Provides detailed, individual surveys of 52 major industry groups. Each survey is revised on a semiannual basis. Also includes "Monthly Investment Review" (industry group investment analysis) and monthly "Trends & Projections" (economic analysis).

TRADE/PROFESSIONAL ASSOCIATIONS

American Association of Preferred Provider Organizations. 222 S 1st St., Ste. 303, Louisville, KY 40202. Phone: 800-642-2515 or (502)403-1122; Fax: (502)403-1129 • URL: http://www.aappo.org • Formerly Association of Managed Healthcare Organizations.

American Medical Group Association. 1 Prince St., Alexandria, VA 22314-3318. Phone: (703)838-0033; Fax: (703)548-1890; Email: dfisher@amga.org • URL: http://www.amga.org • Represents the interests of medical groups. Advocates for the medical groups and patients through innovation and information sharing, benchmarking, developing leadership, and improving patient care. Provides political advocacy, educational and networking programs and publications, benchmarking data services, and financial and operations assistance.

HEALTH OF EMPLOYEES

See EMPLOYEE WELLNESS PROGRAMS

HEATING AND VENTILATION

See also AIR CONDITIONING INDUSTRY

ABSTRACTS AND INDEXES

NTIS Alerts: Energy. U.S. Department of Commerce National Technical Information Service. • Biweekly. $130 per year. Covers electric power, batteries, fuels, geothermal energy, heating/cooling systems, nuclear technology, solar energy, energy policy, and related subjects.

DIRECTORIES

Directory of American Manufacturers and Exporters of Boiler and Boiler Parts. EXIM Infotek Private Ltd. • Covers: 100 American manufacturers and exporters of boilers, gas boilers, oil boilers, hot water boilers, packaged steam and hot water boilers, steam and hot water boilers. Entries include: Company name, postal address, telephone, fax, e-mail, website, contact person, designation, and product details.

Directory of Asian Importers of Boiler and Boiler Parts. EXIM Infotek Private Ltd. • Covers: 120 Asian importers of boiler machinery, boilers, boilers and parts, boiler fittings, gas boiler, hot water boilers, and steam boilers. Entries include: Company name, postal address, telephone, fax, e-mail, website, contact person, designation, and product details.

Directory of Asian Importers of Heaters and Heating Equipment. EXIM Infotek Private Ltd. • Covers: 120 Asian importers of electric heaters for industry, heat detectors, heat exchangers, heaters, heating and ventilation equipment, heating elements and spare parts, heating equipment, solar energy heating products, solar water systems, thermic fluid heaters, waste heat recovery systems, and water heaters. Entries include: Company name, postal address, telephone, fax, e-mail, website, contact person, designation, and product details.

Directory of Chinese Manufacturers & Exporters of Heaters & Heating Equipment. EXIM Infotek Private Ltd. • Covers: 30 Chinese manufacturers and exporters of electric water heaters, electrical heaters, heat exchangers, heaters, plate heat exchanger, solar energy water heaters, solar water heaters, and water heaters. Entries include: Company name, postal address, telephone, fax, e-mail, website, contact person, designation, and product details.

Directory of European Importers of Heaters and Heating Equipment. EXIM Infotek Private Ltd. • Covers: 270 European importers of air heaters, copper tubes for central heating, heat exchangers, heating equipment, heating household application of iron and steel (non-electric), heating systems, and water heaters. Entries include: Company name, postal address, telephone, fax, e-mail, website, contact person, designation, and product details.

Directory of Indian Importers of Heaters and Heating Equipment. EXIM Infotek Private Ltd. • Covers: 20 Indian importers of heat exchangers, heaters, and heating equipment. Entries include: Company name, postal address, telephone, fax, e-mail, website, contact person, designation, and product details.

Directory of Japanese Importers of Heaters and Heating Equipment. EXIM Infotek Private Ltd. • Covers: 35 Japanese importers of heat exchangers, heaters, and heating equipment. Entries include: Company name, postal address, telephone, fax, e-mail, website, contact person, designation, and product details.

Directory of Middle East Importers of Boiler and Boiler Parts. EXIM Infotek Private Ltd. • $200 Individuals. Covers: 50 Middle East importers of boilers and parts, oil/gas/electric boilers, and pressure vessels. Entries include: Company name, postal address, telephone, fax, e-mail, website, contact person, designation, and product details.

Directory of Middle East Importers of Heaters and Heating Equipment. EXIM Infotek Private Ltd. • Covers: 130 Middle East importers of central heating plants and equipment, heat exchangers, and heaters. Entries include: Company name, postal address, telephone, fax, e-mail, website, contact person, designation, and product details.

Directory of North American Importers of Heaters and Heating Equipment. EXIM Infotek Private Ltd. • $300 Individuals. Covers: 120 North American importers of heat exchangers, heating and ventilation equipment, and heating elements. Entries include: Company name, postal address, telephone, fax, e-mail, website, contact person, designation, and product details.

Directory of South American Importers of Heaters and Heating Equipment. EXIM Infotek Private Ltd. • Covers: 50 South American importers of heat exchangers and heating equipment. Entries include: Company name, postal address, telephone, fax, e-mail, website, contact person, designation, and product details.

Directory of South Korean Manufacturers and Exporters of Boiler and Boiler Parts. EXIM Infotek Private Ltd. • Covers: 20 South Korean manufacturers and exporters of boilers and accessories, industrial steam boilers and accessories. Entries include: Company name, postal address, telephone, fax, e-mail, website, contact person, designation, and product details.

Directory of South Korean Manufacturers & Exporters of Heaters & Heating Equipment. EXIM Infotek Private Ltd. • $350 Individuals. Covers: 130 South Korean manufacturers and exporters of air and gas heaters, central heating equipment, central heating systems, driers, drying plants, electric heating equipment, heat exchangers, heaters, and heating machine. Entries include: Company name, postal address, telephone, fax, e-mail, website, contact person, designation, and product details.

Directory of South Korean Manufacturers & Exporters of Ventilation Equipment. EXIM Infotek Private Ltd. • $250 Individuals. Covers: 80 South Korean manufacturers and exporters of blowers and ventilators, dust and fume collectors, fans and blowers. Entries include: Company name, postal address, telephone, fax, e-mail, website, contact person, designation, and product details.

Directory of Taiwanese Manufacturers & Exporters of Heaters & Heating Equipment. EXIM Infotek Private Ltd. • $450 Individuals. Covers: 200 Taiwanese manufacturers and exporters of central heating systems, driers, drying plants, electric heating equipment, heat exchanger, heating elements and accessories, heating machine, high frequency induction heating machine, and water heaters. Entries include: Company name, postal address, telephone, fax, e-mail, website, contact person, designation, and product details.

Heating Equipment--Manufacturers Directory. InfoGroup Inc. • Annual. Number of listings: 1,419. Entries include: Name, address, phone, size of advertisement, name of owner or manager, number of employees, year first in "Yellow Pages." Compiled from telephone company "Yellow Pages," nationwide.

The International Directory of Importers - Refrigeration, Ventilation and Heating Equipment Importers. Interdata. • $260 Individuals print. Covers: 3,300 international firms importing refrigeration, ventilation and heating equipment. Entries include: Company name and address, contact person, email, number of employees, year established, phone and telefaxes, business activity, bank references, as well as a listing of refrigeration, ventilation and heating equipment currently being imported.

E-BOOKS

Macmillan Encyclopedia of Energy. Cengage Learning Inc. • 2003. eBook. Published by Macmillan Reference USA. Covers the business, technology, and history of a wide variety of energy sources. Inquire as to price and availability.

FINANCIAL RATIOS

American Supply Association Operating Performance Report. American Supply Association. • Annual. $399 Members. Report provides details on operating performance.

Annual Statement Studies. Risk Management Association. • Annual. Compiled from over 280,000 financial statements.

Annual Statement Studies: Industry Default Probabilities and Cash Flow Measures. Risk Management Association. • Annual. $405 Nonmembers. Serves as a companion volume to the original *Annual Statement Studies.* Gives probability of default estimates on a percentage scale for more than 450 industries. Includes changes in position year-by-year for eight financial statement line items and provides percentage measures of cash flow.

INTERNET DATABASES

Manufacturing Profiles. U. S. Bureau of the Census. Phone: (301)763-4636 or (301)763-4100; Fax: (301)763-4794; Email: webmaster@census.gov • URL: http://www.census.gov/prod/www/abs/mfg-prof.html • The Census Bureau makes available free on PDF (Portable Document Format) an annual consolidation of the entire Current Industrial Report series, presenting "all the data compiled." Contains statistics on production, shipments, inventories, consumption, exports, imports, and orders for a wide variety of manufactured products.

ONLINE DATABASES

Heating, Ventilation and Air Conditioning Businesses in the World. Momentum Technologies L.L.C. • Contains detailed directory listings and contact information for heating, ventilation, and air conditioning (HVAC) businesses in operation throughout the world. Includes business name, address, phone number, fax number, e-mail address, and web site address. Provides keyword search functions.

OTHER SOURCES

HPAC Techlit Selector. Penton Media Inc. • Semiannual. Free to qualified personnel. Manufacturers' catalogs and technical literature.

Major Energy Companies of the World. Cengage Learning Inc. • Annual. $1,460 Individuals. 2008. 12th edition. eBook. Published by Graham & Whiteside. Contains detailed information on more than 4,850 important energy companies in various countries. Industries include electricity generation, coal, natural gas, nuclear energy, petroleum, fuel distribution, and equipment for energy production.

PERIODICALS AND NEWSLETTERS

Air Conditioning, Heating, and Refrigeration News: The HVACR Contractor's Weekly Newsmagazine. BNP Media. • Weekly. $87.00 per year. Includes *Supplement.*

Heating/Piping/Air Conditioning Engineering: The Magazine of Mechanical Systems Engineering. Penton Media Inc. • Monthly. Covers design, specification, installation, operation, and maintenance for systems in industrial, commercial, and institutional buildings. Formerly (Heating, Piping and Air Conditioning).

RESEARCH CENTERS AND INSTITUTES

Purdue University - Ray W. Herrick Laboratories. School of Mechanical Engineering, 140 S Martin Jischke Dr., West Lafayette, IN 47907-2031. Phone: (765)494-2132; Fax: (765)494-0787; Email: rhlab@ecn.purdue.edu • URL: http://engineering.purdue.edu/Herrick/index.html • Mechanical engineering, including studies on heating, air conditioning, and refrigeration equipment and systems, engineering acoustics, noise and vibration control (including vehicle and engine noise), sound quality, positive displacement compressor technology, mechanical reliability, precision measurements, mechanics of materials, tribology, noise control materials, electro-hydraulic and engine controls, emissions, and automatic control.

STATISTICS SOURCES

Refrigeration, Air Conditioning, and Warm Air Heating Equipment. U. S. Bureau of the Census. • Annual. Provides data on quantity and value of shipments by manufacturers. Formerly *Air Conditioning and Refrigeration Equipment.* (Current Industrial Reports, MA-333M.).

TRADE/PROFESSIONAL ASSOCIATIONS

American Society of Heating, Refrigerating and Air-Conditioning Engineers. 1791 Tullie Cir. NE, Atlanta, GA 30329. Phone: 800-527-4723 or (404)636-8400; Fax: (404)321-5478; Email: ashrae@ashrae.org • URL: http://www.ashrae.org • Represents Technical society of heating, ventilating, refrigeration, and air-conditioning engineers. Sponsors numerous research programs in cooperation with universities, research laboratories, and government agencies on subjects such as human and animal environmental studies, effects of air-conditioning, quality of inside air, heat transfer, flow, and cooling processes. Conducts professional development seminars. Writes method of test standards and other standards addressing energy conservation in buildings, indoor air quality, and refrigerants. Publishes extensive literature and electronic products.

HELICOPTERS

See also AEROSPACE INDUSTRY; AVIATION INDUSTRY

HANDBOOKS AND MANUALS

Operations and Management, Guide/Safety Manual. Helicopter Association International. • Annual.

PERIODICALS AND NEWSLETTERS

AIAA Journal. American Institute of Aeronautics and Astronautics. • Monthly. $80 Members /year for members in the U.S.; print and online. Technical journal providing original archival research papers on new theoretical developments and/or experimental results in the fields of aeronautics and astronautics. For research-oriented readers.

Defence & Public Service Helicopter. Shephard Press Ltd. • Bi-monthly. $130.00 per year. Provides international coverage of both the public service (police, emergency, etc.) and military helicopter industries and markets. Includes technical, piloting, and safety topics. Formerly *Defence Helicopter.*

Helicopter News. Access Intelligence L.L.C. • Description: Reports to company executives, military leaders, and ancillary industries on the state of the helicopter industry. Tracks buying and selling information, news of contracts, and new programs. Also concerned with related issues, including EMS (Emergency Mission Support) and insurance. Recurring features include interviews and news of technology and new products. **Remarks:** Also available online and via e-mail.

Rotor & Wing. Access Intelligence L.L.C. • Monthly. *World Helicopter Resources Rotor and Wing International.*

Vertiflite. AHS International. • Bimonthly. $135 Nonmembers inside US.

RESEARCH CENTERS AND INSTITUTES

Flight Mechanics Laboratory. Texas A & M University, 701 HR Bright Bldg., College Station, TX 77843-3141. Phone: (979)862-1749; Fax: (979)845-6051; Email: saric@tamu.edu • URL: http://flight.tamu.edu.

Ohio Aerospace Institute. 22800 Cedar Point Rd., Cleveland, OH 44142. Phone: (440)962-3000; Fax: (216)962-3120 or (440)962-3120; Email: info@oai.

org • URL: http://www.oai.org • Aerospace-related research, education, and technology transfers. Formerly Ohio Aerospace Institute.

STATISTICS SOURCES

Aerospace Facts and Figures. Aerospace Industries Association of America. • Annual. $35 Individuals. Includes financial data for the aerospace industries.

TRADE/PROFESSIONAL ASSOCIATIONS

AHS International. 217 N Washington St., Alexandria, VA 22314-2538. Phone: 855-247-4685 or (703)684-6777; Fax: (703)739-9279; Email: staff@vtol.org • URL: http://www.vtol.org • Represents aircraft designers, engineers, government personnel, operators, and industry executives in over 40 countries interested in V/STOL aircraft. (V/STOL stands for Vertical/Short Takeoff and Landing.) Conducts research and educational and technical meetings concerning professional training and updated information.

HENS

See POULTRY INDUSTRY

HERBS

See also DIET; HEALTH FOOD INDUSTRY

ALMANACS AND YEARBOOKS

Herbarist. Herb Society of America. • Annual. $12.50 Members. Journal of The Herb Society of America.

CD-ROM DATABASES

Pharmacopeia of Herbs. CME Inc. • $149.00. Frequently updated CD-ROM provides searchable data on a wide variety of herbal medicines, vitamins, and amino acids. Includes information on clinical studies, contraindications, side-effects, phytoactivity, and 534 therapeutic use categories. Contains a 1,000 word glossary.

DIRECTORIES

All India Manufacturers & Exporters of Herbal Products. NIIR Project Consultancy Services. • $200 Individuals CD-ROM. Covers: 2,500+ manufacturers and exporters of herbal products in India. Entries include: Name of company, address, city, phone (wherever available), fax (wherever available), e-mail (wherever available), activities (wherever available).

Directory of Australia & New Zealand Importers of Herbs & Herbal Medicine Products. EXIM Infotek Private Ltd. • $150 Individuals. Covers: 20 Australian and New Zealand importers of Chinese herbal products, Chinese herbs, Chinese medicines, herb extracts, herb seeds, herbal cosmetics, herbal extracts, herbal medicine, herbal powders, herbal products, herbal remedies, herbal tea, herbs, legumes, medicinal herb and botanicals, natural and herbal medicines, natural cosmetic ingredients, and natural health. Entries include: Company name, postal address, telephone, fax, e-mail, website, contact person, designation, and product details.

Directory of Chinese Manufacturers & Exporters of Herbs & Herbal Medicine Products. EXIM Infotek Private Ltd. • $10 Individuals. Covers: 110 Chinese manufacturers & exporters of biological medicine, botanical extracts, burdock, Chinese herbs, Chinese medicine, Chinese medicine-traditional, ginseng, herbal extracts, herbal medicines, herbs, natural plant extracts. Entries include: Company name, postal address, city, country, phone, fax, e-mail & websites, contact person, designation, products detail.

Directory of Indian Importers of Herbs & Herbal Medicine Products. EXIM Infotek Private Ltd. • $200 Individuals. Covers: 30 Indian importers of herbs, legumes, medicinal herbs, and botanicals. Entries include: Company name, postal address, telephone, fax, e-mail, website, contact person, designation, and product details.

Directory of Japanese Manufacturers & Exporters of Herbs & Herbal Medicine Products. EXIM Infotek Private Ltd. • $5 Individuals. Covers: 20 Japanese manufacturers and exporters of agricultural medicines, and herbal medicines. Entries include: Company name, postal address, city, country, phone, fax, e-mail and websites, contact person, designation, and product details.

Directory of Middle East Importers of Herbs & Herbal Medicine Products. EXIM Infotek Private Ltd. • Covers: 20 Middle East importers of medicinal herbs and botanicals. Entries include: Company name, postal address, telephone, fax, e-mail, website, contact person, designation, and product details.

Directory of North American Importers of Herbs & Herbal Medicine Products. EXIM Infotek Private Ltd. • $300 Individuals. Covers: 60 North American importers of ayurvedic medicines, ayurvedic products, botanicals, bulk herbs, Chinese herbs, crude botanical drugs, ginseng, herb products, herb seeds, herbal cosmetics, herbal extracts, herbal products, herbal tea, herbicides, herbs, medicinal herbs, and botanical. Entries include: Company name, postal address, telephone, fax, e-mail, website, contact person, designation, and product details.

Directory of South Korean Manufacturers & Exporters of Herbs & Herbal Medicine Products. EXIM Infotek Private Ltd. • $5 Individuals. Covers: 30 South Korean manufacturers and exporters of Chinese medical preparations, herb plants, herbal medicines. Entries include: Company name, postal address, city, country, phone, fax, e-mail and websites, contact person, designation, and product details.

Directory of Taiwanese Manufacturers & Exporters of Herbs & Herbal Medicine Products. EXIM Infotek Private Ltd. • $15 Individuals. Covers: 160 Taiwanese manufacturers and exporters of Chinese medical preparations, and herbal medicines. Entries include: Company name, postal address, city, country, phone, fax, e-mail and websites, contact person, designation, and product details.

GENERAL WORKS

The Business of Herbs. Northwind Publications. • Bimonthly. $24 Individuals. Trade journal for the herb and specialty horticulture industry. Covers growing and marketing of herbs, including medicinal, culinary, fragrant, and ornamental.

PERIODICALS AND NEWSLETTERS

Herb Quarterly. EGW Publishing Co. • Quarterly. A magazine for herb enthusiasts covering all aspects of herb uses.

Journal of Dietary Supplements. The Haworth Press Inc. • Quarterly. $175.00 per year to libraries; $50.00 per year to individuals. Edited with a view to both academic research and industry concerns. Sections are dedicated to health professionals, educators, and dieticians. Includes book reviews and short reviews of research appearing elsewhere. Formerly *Journal of Nutraceuticals, Functional & Medical Foods.*

Natural Products Marketplace. Virgo Publishing L.L.C. • Monthly. $50.00 per year. Covers all aspects of the vitamin and health supplement market, including new products. Includes an annual buyer's guide, an annual compilation of industry statistics, and annual guides to vitamins and herbs.

Nutrition Industry Executive. Vitamin Retailer Magazine, Inc. • 10 times a year. $50.00 per year. Edited for manufacturers of vitamins and other dietary supplements. Covers marketing, new products, industry trends, regulations, manufacturing procedures, and related topics. Includes a directory of suppliers to the industry.

HIDE INDUSTRY

See CATTLE INDUSTRY

HIGH BLOOD PRESSURE

See HYPERTENSION

HIGH FIDELITY/STEREO

See also RADIO EQUIPMENT INDUSTRY; SOUND RECORDERS AND RECORDING

PERIODICALS AND NEWSLETTERS

The Absolute Sound: The High End Journal of Audio and Music. Absolute Multimedia Inc. • 10/year. $14.95 Individuals print. Preeminent source of expert reviews, features, and commentary on high-performance audio and music.

High Performance Review: Definitive Magazine for Audiophiles and Music Lovers. High Performance Review Publishing. • Quarterly. $15.00 per year.

Poptronics. Gernsback Publications, Inc. • Monthly. $19.99 per year. Incorporates *Electronics Now.*

Pro Audio Review: The Industry's Equipment Authority. IMAS Publishing Group. • Monthly. $24.95 /year. Provides critical product reviews of professional audio equipment and recording gear, including bench tests and user reports.

Robb Report Home Entertaining & Design. CurtCo Robb Media. • Monthly. $65. Covers "high end" home theaters, audio, video, wireless home networks, and custom installations.

The Sensible Sound. • Bimonthly. $29.00 per year. High fidelity equipment review.

Sound & Vision: Home Theater- Audio- Video- MultimediaMovies- Music. Bonnier AB. • 10/year. $12.97 10 issues. Popular magazine providing explanatory articles and critical reviews of equipment and media (CD-ROM, DVD, etc.). Supplement available *Stereo Review's Sound and Vision Buyers Guide.* Replaces *Stereo Review* and *Video Magazine.*

Stereophile: For the High Fidelity Stereo Perfectionist. PRIMEDIA Inc. • Monthly. $12.97 Individuals 12 issues. Offers authoritative reviews, informed recommendations, helpful advice, and controversial opinions, all stemming from the revolutionary idea that audio components should be judged on how they reproduce music.

T W I C E: This Week in Consumer Electronics. Reed Elsevier Group plc Reed Business Information. • 29 times a year. $129.90 per year. Contains marketing and manufacturing news relating to a wide variety of consumer electronic products, including video, audio, telephone, and home office equipment.

PRICE SOURCES

Audio. Orion Research Corp. • Annual. $179 Individuals. Quotes retail and wholesale prices of used audio equipment. Original list prices and years of manufacture are also shown.

Car Stereo. Orion Research Corp. • Annual. $144 Individuals. Quotes retail and wholesale prices of used stereo sound equipment for automobiles. Original list prices and years of manufacture are also shown.

Guitars and Musical Instruments. Orion Research Corp. • Annual. $179 Individuals. List of manufacturers of guitars and musical instruments. Original list prices and years of manufacture are also shown.

HIGH TECHNOLOGY

See TECHNOLOGY

HIGH YIELD BONDS

See JUNK BOND FINANCING

HIGHER EDUCATION

See COLLEGES AND UNIVERSITIES

HIGHWAY ACCIDENTS

See TRAFFIC ACCIDENTS AND TRAFFIC SAFETY

HIGHWAYS

See ROADS AND HIGHWAYS

HISPANIC MARKETS

See MINORITY MARKETS

HISTORY, BUSINESS

See BUSINESS HISTORY

HMOS

See HEALTH MAINTENANCE ORGANIZATIONS

HOBBY INDUSTRY

DIRECTORIES

American Craft--News Section. American Craft Council. • Bimonthly. $5 per issue. Publication includes: List of exhibitions, sales, workshops, seminars, conferences, and competitions for contemporary American craftspersons. Entries include: Event name, dates, location; name of gallery, museum, or sponsoring organization. For shows and sales--Whether juried, deadline for applications, fees, contact name and address, media accepted. For workshops, courses, conferences, etc.--Contact name and address, guest artist presiding, dates of events.

Directory of Chinese Manufacturers & Exporters of Handicrafts & Decorative Items. EXIM Infotek Private Ltd. • $25 Individuals. Covers: 310 Chinese manufacturers and exporters of antiques, arts and crafts, art decoration, artware, building decoration materials, carvings, Christmas decorations, Christmas items, Christmas tree ornaments, Christmas tree sets, crafts, craft clocks, craft products, craft works, decoration items, decorative products, figurines, folk crafts, Halloween decorations, handicrafts, hanging decorations, hanging objects, hanging pictures, metal crafts, oil paintings, sculptures, tombstones, tourist articles, vases. Entries include: Company name, postal address, city, country, phone, fax, e-mail and websites, contact person, designation, and product details.

Directory of Japanese Manufacturers & Exporters of Handicrafts & Decorative Items. EXIM Infotek Private Ltd. • $5 Individuals. Covers: 20 Japanese manufacturers and exporters of art and crafts, art handicrafts, Christmas decorations, Christmas goods, folk crafts, handicrafts, and vases. Entries include: Company name, postal address, city, country, phone, fax, e-mail and websites, contact person, designation, and product details.

Handicraft Supplies Directory. InfoGroup Inc. • Annual. Number of listings: 9,320. Entries include: Name, address, phone, size of advertisement, name of owner or manager, number of employees, year first in "Yellow Pages." Compiled from telephone company "Yellow Pages," nationwide.

iGaming Business Directory. Casino City Press. • Annual. $449.95 Book and CD Package (Standard License). Includes 2,500 iGaming sites, 679 site owners, 5,700 iGaming portal sites, site rankings, software manufacturers, and 400 affiliate programs.

Warman's Antiques & Collectibles Price Guide. Krause Publications Inc. • Annual. $20 Individuals Paperback. Covers: Over 50,000 antiques and collectibles, plus listings for collector's clubs. Database includes: 1,500 color photos. Entries include: Description, price.

FINANCIAL RATIOS

Annual Statement Studies. Risk Management Association. • Annual. Compiled from over 280,000 financial statements.

Annual Statement Studies: Industry Default Probabilities and Cash Flow Measures. Risk Management Association. • Annual. $405 Nonmembers. Serves as a companion volume to the original *Annual Statement Studies*. Gives probability of default estimates on a percentage scale for more than 450 industries. Includes changes in position year-by-year for eight financial statement line items and provides percentage measures of cash flow.

OTHER SOURCES

American Society of Military Insignia Collectors. • Represents oldest military insignia collectors group in the U.S. Promotes the collection and preservation of U.S. and foreign military insignia. Disseminates information on the symbolism and historical significance of insignia. Assists veterans and individuals in search of insignia.

PERIODICALS AND NEWSLETTERS

International Journal: The News and Views Paper for the Hobbyist. Levine Publications. • Quarterly. $52.50.

PRICE SOURCES

Kovels' on Antiques and Collectibles: The Newsletter for Dealers, Collectors, and Investors. Antiques Inc. • Monthly. $27 Individuals.

TRADE/PROFESSIONAL ASSOCIATIONS

Association of American Military Uniform Collectors. PO Box 1876, Elyria, OH 44036. Phone: (440)365-5321; Email: aamucfl@comcast.net • URL: http://naples.net/clubs/aamuc • Collectors of American military and naval uniforms (1776-present). Promotes interest in uniform preservation and heritage along with patriotic interest in the U.S. armed forces. Loans uniform displays by members to various groups, including Boy Scouts of America, Girl Scouts of the U.S.A., American Legion, and Veterans of Foreign Wars of the U.S.A. branches, public schools, libraries, and public exhibitions. Reviews the books on U.S. military uniforms.

Craft Retailers Association for Tomorrow. PO Box 293, Islamorada, FL 33036. Phone: (305)664-3650; Fax: (305)664-0199; Email: info@craftonline.org • URL: http://www.craftonline.org • Represents a network of galleries, shops and artists. Supports and encourages creativity and artistic excellence in American craftspeople. Promotes awareness of American crafts through communication programs, education, networking and marketing.

HOLIDAYS

See ANNIVERSARIES AND HOLIDAYS

HOME APPLIANCES

See ELECTRIC APPLIANCE INDUSTRY

HOME-BASED BUSINESSES

See SELF-EMPLOYMENT

HOME BUILDING INDUSTRY

See BUILDING INDUSTRY

HOME COMPUTERS

See MICROCOMPUTERS AND MINICOMPUTERS

HOME DECORATION

See INTERIOR DECORATION

HOME EDUCATION

See CORRESPONDENCE SCHOOLS AND COURSES

HOME FREEZERS

See FROZEN FOOD INDUSTRY

HOME FURNITURE INDUSTRY

See FURNITURE INDUSTRY

HOME HEALTH CARE INDUSTRY

See also HEALTH CARE INDUSTRY

CD-ROM DATABASES

Authority Health Care Law Library. Matthew Bender and Company Inc. • Periodic updates. Price on request. Full text CD-ROM provides legal information, case law, and analysis relating to health care facilities, health insurance, longterm care, Medigap, and Medicare.

DIRECTORIES

AHA Integrated Delivery Network Directory: U.S. Health Care Systems, Networks, and Alliances. American Hospital Association. • Annual. $250.00. Provides information about a wide variety of U.S. health care groups and affiliations, including hospitals, nursing homes, rehabilitation centers, psychiatric facilities, home health care agencies, clinical laboratories, outpatient facilities, and diagnostic imaging centers. Includes names of more than 8,000 key executives.

Assisted Living and Elder Care Directory. InfoGroup Inc. • Annual. Number of listings: 14,305. Entries include: Name, address, phone, size of advertisement, name of owner or manager, number of employees, year first in "Yellow Pages." Compiled from telephone company "Yellow Pages," nationwide.

Home Health Agencies Report and Directory. SMG Marketing Group Inc. • Annual. $575.00. Lists over 13,000 home healthcare agencies and corporations. Includes a market analysis and growth projections.

FINANCIAL RATIOS

Annual Statement Studies. Risk Management Association. • Annual. Compiled from over 280,000 financial statements.

Annual Statement Studies: Industry Default Probabilities and Cash Flow Measures. Risk Management Association. • Annual. $405 Nonmembers. Serves as a companion volume to the original *Annual Statement Studies*. Gives probability of default estimates on a percentage scale for more than 450 industries. Includes changes in position year-by-year for eight financial statement line items and provides percentage measures of cash flow.

PERIODICALS AND NEWSLETTERS

Continuing Care News: Supporting the Transition into Post Hospital Care. Stevenson Publishing Corp. • Monthly. $99.00 per year. Topics include insurance, legal issues, health business news, ethics, and case management. Includes annual *Buyer's Guide*.

HME News. HME News. • Monthly. Covers the home medical equipment business for dealers and manufacturers. Provides information on a wide variety of home health care supplies and equipment.

Home Health Care Dealer-Provider. CurAnt Communications Inc. • Bimonthly. Free. For home care dealer and home care pharmacies. Formerly *Home Health Care Dealer - Supplier*.

Home Health Care Services Quarterly: The Journal of Community Care. The Haworth Press Inc. • Quarterly. $535.00 per year. An academic and practical journal focusing on the marketing and administration of home care.

Home Health Line: The Home Care Industry's National Independent Newsletter. • 48 times per year. $527.00 per year. Newsletter on legislation and regulations affecting the home health care industry, with an emphasis on federal funding and Medicare programs.

Home Health Products. Stevens Publishing Corp. • 10 times a year. $99.00 per year. Covers new medical equipment products for the home care industry.

Home Healthcare Nurse: The Journal for the Home Care and Hospice Professional. The Home Healthcare Nurses Association. Lippincott Williams & Wilkins. • $49.99 Individuals. For professional nurses in the home health care field.

Homecare Magazine: The Business Magazine of the Home Health Industry. RentPath Inc. • Monthly. Edited for dealers and suppliers of home medical equipment, including pharmacies and chain stores. Includes information on new products.

Homecare News. National Association for Home Care. • Description: Reports on National Association for Home Care news plus home care industry developments for the entire industry.

Hospital Home Health: The Monthly Updates for Executives and Health Care Professionals. AHC Media. • Monthly. $399.00 per year. Newsletter for hospital-based home health agencies.

RESEARCH CENTERS AND INSTITUTES

Stratis Health. 2901 Metro Dr., Ste. 400, Bloomington, MN 55425-1525. Phone: 877-787-2847 or (952)854-3306; Fax: (952)853-8503; Email: info@stratishealth.org • URL: http://www.stratishealth.org • Physicians interested in ensuring the availability of quality health care at reasonable costs. Evaluates health care services at hospitals, retirement homes, and other facilities. Develops health care standards for hospitals and offers consultation services to operators of health care facilities to improve efficiency in services. Conducts research and development on latest treatments and medical technologies. Tests new medical technologies.

TRADE/PROFESSIONAL ASSOCIATIONS

National Association for Home Care and Hospice. 228 7th St. SE, Washington, DC 20003. Phone: (202)547-7424; Fax: (202)547-3540; Email: exec@nahc.org • URL: http://www.nahc.org • Promotes high standards of patient care in home care services. Members are durable medical providers, medical equipment and oxygen suppliers, mainly for home health care.

HOME IMPROVEMENT INDUSTRY

See also BUILDING INDUSTRY

DIRECTORIES

Directory of South Korean Manufacturers & Exporters of Home Furnishing Materials. EXIM Infotek Private Ltd. • $10 Individuals. Covers: 50 South Korean manufacturers and exporters of blankets, household linen and soft furnishings, mattresses, cushions and pillows, sanitary towels and baby napkins, and tapestries. Entries include: Company name, postal address, city, country, phone, fax, e-mail and websites, contact person, designation, and product details.

Home Design and Planning Service Directory. InfoGroup Inc. • Annual. Number of listings: 3,518. Entries include: Name, address, phone, size of advertisement, name of owner or manager, number of employees, year first in "Yellow Pages." Compiled from telephone company "Yellow Pages," nationwide.

Home Improvements Directory. InfoGroup Inc. • Annual. Number of listings: 43,179. Entries include: Name, address, phone, size of advertisement, name of owner or manager, number of employees, year first in "Yellow Pages." Compiled from telephone company "Yellow Pages," nationwide.

Remodeling--Product Guide. DoveTale Publishers. • Annual. $10. Publication includes: List of more than 2,000 manufacturers and suppliers serving the remodeling contracting industry; list of industry-related associations. Entries include: For manufacturers and suppliers--Company name, address, phone, name and title of contact, product line, geographical area served. For associations--Association name, address, phone, director.

PERIODICALS AND NEWSLETTERS

Builder: The Voice of America's Housing Industry. Finance and Housing Policy Div. DoveTale Publishers. • Monthly. $29.95 per year. Covers the home building and remodeling industry in general, including design, construction, and marketing.

Building Material Dealer. National Lumber and Building Material Dealers Association. • Monthly. $48.00 per year. Includes special feature issues on hand and power tools, lumber, roofing, kitchens, flooring, windows and doors, and insulation. Formerly *Builder Material Retailer*.

National Home Center News: News and Analysis for the Home Improvement, Building Material Industry. Lebhar-Friedman Inc. • 22 times a year. $99.00 per year. Includes special feature issues on hardware and tools, building materials, millwork, electrical supplies, lighting, and kitchens.

Remodeling: Excellence in Professional Remodeling. DoveTale Publishers. • Monthly. $44.95 per year. Covers new products, construction, management, and marketing for remodelers.

TRADE/PROFESSIONAL ASSOCIATIONS

National Association of the Remodeling Industry. PO Box 4250, Des Plaines, IL 60016. Phone: (847)298-9200; Fax: (847)298-9225; Email: info@nari.org • URL: http://www.nari.org • Represents remodeling contractors, manufacturers of remodeling/building products, lending institutions and wholesalers and distributors. Promotes the common business interests of those engaged in the home improvement and remodeling industries. Encourages ethical conduct, good business practices and professionalism in the remodeling industry. Conducts seminars, workshops and promotional programs and has developed an extensive certification program. Local chapters monitor legislations and regulations affecting the industry.

HOME OWNERSHIP

See also PERSONAL FINANCE

ABSTRACTS AND INDEXES

Readers' Guide to Periodical Literature. EBSCO Publishing Inc. • Provides indexing for over 400 periodicals dating back to 1983.

CD-ROM DATABASES

Readers' Guide to Periodical Literature. EBSCO Publishing Inc. • Provides indexing for over 400 periodicals dating back to 1983.

HANDBOOKS AND MANUALS

Complete Guide to Your Real Estate Closing: Answers to All Your Questions from Opening Escrow to Negotiating Fees to Signing Closing Papers. Sandy Gadow. McGraw Hill Financial Inc. • Date not set. $19.95. Includes sample forms and work sheets, with specific real estate closing information for all 50 states. (Teach Yourself Series).

PERIODICALS AND NEWSLETTERS

Metropolitan Home: Style for Our Generation. Hachette Filipacchi Media U.S., Inc. • Bimonthly. $17.94 per year.

Taunton's Fine Homebuilding. Taunton Press Inc. • Eight issues per year $37.95. Special interest magazine written by builders for builders - professional and homeowners. Formerly *Fine Homebuilding*.

Unique Homes: The Global Resource of Luxury Real Estate. Unique Homes, Inc. • Six times a year. $29.97 per year. Homes for sale.

STATISTICS SOURCES

American Housing Survey for the United States in (year). U. S. Government Printing Office. • Biennial. $51.00. Issued by the U. S. Census Bureau (www.census.gov). Covers both owner-occupied and renter-occupied housing. Includes data on such factors as condition of building, type of mortgage, utility costs, and housing occupied by minorities. (Current Housing Reports, H150.).

ULI Market Profiles: North America. Urban Land Institute. • Annual. Members, $249.95; nonmembers, $299.95. Provides real estate marketing data for residential, retail, office, and industrial sectors. Covers 76 U. S. metropolitan areas and 13 major foreign metropolitan areas.

TRADE/PROFESSIONAL ASSOCIATIONS

Community Associations Institute. 6402 Arlington Blvd., Ste. 500, Falls Church, VA 22042. Phone: 888-224-4321 or (703)970-9220; Fax: (703)970-9558; Email: cai-info@caionline.org • URL: http://www.caionline.org • Condominium and homeowner associations, cooperatives, and association-governed planned communities of all sizes and architectural types; community or property managers and management firms; individual homeowners; community association managers and management firms; public officials; and lawyers, accountants, engineers, reserve specialists, builder/developers and other providers of professional services and products for CAs. Seeks to educate and represent America's 250,000 residential condominium, cooperative and homeowner associations and related professionals and service providers. Aims to foster vibrant, responsive, competent community associations that promote harmony, community and responsible leadership.

National Foundation of Manufactured Home

Owners. 11 Moonrise Court, Newport Beach, CA 92663-2103. Phone: (949)791-8302; Fax: (801)365-8205; Email: jsisker@yahoo.com • URL: http://www.mfghomeowners.net • Represents 20,000,000 owners of mobile/manufactured homes. Serves as a unified national voice for mobile/manufactured homeowners and to improve communications among members, and research problems homeowners can experience. Maintains resources, include extensive collection of material, clearinghouse of information, especially on the purchase, set-up and maintenance of homes.

National Housing Conference. 1900 M St. NW, Ste. 200, Washington, DC 20036. Phone: (202)466-2121; Fax: (202)466-2122 • URL: http://www.nhc.org • Housing authority officials, community development specialists, builders, bankers, lawyers, accountants, owners, residents, insurers, architects and planners, religious organizations, labor groups, and national housing and housing-related organizations. Mobilizes support for effective programs in housing and community development as well as affordable and accessible housing for all Americans. Holds educational programs.

National Rural Housing Coalition. 1331 G St. NW, 10th Fl., Washington, DC 20005. Phone: (202)393-5229; Fax: (202)393-3034; Email: nrhc@ruralhousingcoalition.org • URL: http://ruralhousingcoalition.org • Advocates for improved government and private housing programs for people in small towns and rural areas. Develops informational and educational material; gives and coordinates testimony before congressional committees; seeks improved administrative procedures within the executive branch of the federal government. Lobbies for low-income rural housing and community facilities.

HOME TEXTILES

See LINEN INDUSTRY

HOMES FOR THE AGED

See NURSING HOMES

HONEY INDUSTRY

ABSTRACTS AND INDEXES

Apicultural Abstracts (AA). International Bee Research Association. • Quarterly. $295. Up-to-date summary of world literature on bees and beekeeping.

Bee Culture: The Magazine of American Beekeeping. The A.I. Root Co. • Monthly. $25 Individuals. Articles, reports and stories about beekeeping market. Latest industry news. Formerly *Gleanings in Bee Culture*.

DIRECTORIES

Directory of Asian Importers of Honey and Syrup. EXIM Infotek Private Ltd. • $150 Individuals. Covers: 35 Asian importers of honey, syrups, and honey products. Entries include: Company name, postal address, telephone, fax, e-mail, website, contact person, designation, and product details.

Directory of Middle East Importers of Honey and Syrup. EXIM Infotek Private Ltd. • $150 Individuals. Covers: 20 Middle East importers of honey and syrups. Entries include: Company name, postal address, telephone, fax, e-mail, website, contact person, designation, and product details.

Directory of North American Importers of Honey and Syrup. EXIM Infotek Private Ltd. • $150 Individuals. Covers: 25 North American importers of cinnamon honey, honey, and syrup. Entries include: Company name, postal address, telephone, fax, e-mail, website, contact person, designation, and product details.

INTERNET DATABASES

USDA. U.S. National Institute of Standards and Technology. 100 Bureau Dr., Gaithersburg, MD 20899-1070. Phone: 800-877-8339 or (301)975-6478 or (202)720-2791; Fax: (301)975-8295; Email: inquiries@nist.gov • URL: http://www.nist.gov • The USDA home page has six sections: News and Information; What's New; About USDA; Agencies; Opportunities; Search and Help. Keyword searching is offered from the USDA home page and from various individual agency home pages. Agencies are the Economic Research Service, Agricultural Marketing Service, National Agricultural Statistics Service, National Agricultural Library, and about 12 others. Updating varies. Fees: Free.

ONLINE DATABASES

CAB Abstracts. CABI. • Contains 46 specialized abstract collections covering over 10,000 journals and monographs in the areas of agriculture, horticulture, forest products, farm products, nutrition, dairy science, poultry, grains, animal health, entomology, etc. Time period is 1972 to date, with monthly updates. Inquire as to online cost and availability. *CAB Abstracts on CD-ROM* also available, with annual updating.

PERIODICALS AND NEWSLETTERS

American Bee Journal. Dadant and Sons Inc. • Monthly. $27.00 per year. Magazine for hobbyist and professional beekeepers.

American Beekeeping Federation Newsletter. American Beekeeping Federation. • Bimonthly. $25.00 per year. Newsletter.

Journal of Apicultural Research. International Bee Research Association. • Quarterly. £90 Individuals /year. Publishes original research articles, original theoretical papers, notes, comments and authoritative reviews on scientific aspects of the biology, ecology, natural history, conservation and culture of all types of bees.

RESEARCH CENTERS AND INSTITUTES

Agricultural Research Service, Pacific West Area - Carl Hayden Bee Research Center - Honey Bee Research Unit. 2000 E Allen Rd., Tucson, AZ 85719. Phone: (520)647-9107; Fax: (520)670-6493; Email: gloria.hoffman@ars.usda.gov • URL: http://www.ars.usda.gov/main/site_main.htm?modecode=53-42-03-00 • Biology of honey bees, including: biochemistry and physiology of bees to determine specific requirements for individual and colony growth, development, and reproduction; role of mites and microorganisms in the physiology of bees; behavior of bees, including modes of communication, structure and function of sensory receptors, and identification and roles of pheromones; pollination ecology and colony foraging dynamics of bees in crop ecosystems; development of computer simulated models; and remote sensing using radar, microwave frequencies, and other techniques to monitor the activities of bees.

Agricultural Research Service, Southern Plains Area - Kika de la Garza Subtropical Agricultural Research Center. USDA Agricultural Research Center, 2413 E Highway 83, Bldg. 200, Weslaco, TX 78596. Phone: (956)447-6301; Fax: (956)447-6345; Email: jquisenberry@welasco.ars.usda.gov • URL: http://www.ars.usda.gov.

Utah State University - Bee Biology and Systematics Laboratory. 5310 Old Main Hill, Logan, UT 84322-5310. Phone: (435)797-2524; Fax: (435)797-0461 • URL: http://www.loganbeelab.usu.edu.

STATISTICS SOURCES

Agricultural Statistics. U.S. Department of Agriculture National Agricultural Statistics Service. • Annual. $46 Individuals. Provides a wide variety of statistical data relating to agricultural production, supplies, consumption, prices/price-supports, foreign trade, costs, and returns, as well as farm labor, loans, income, and population. In many cases, historical data is shown annually for 10 years. In addition to farm data, includes detailed fishery statistics.

Sugar and Sweetener Situation and Outlook. U. S. Government Printing Office. • Three times per year. $18.00 per year. Issued by Economic Research Service, U. S. Department of Agriculture. Provides current statistical information on supply, demand, and prices.

TRADE/PROFESSIONAL ASSOCIATIONS

National Honey Packers and Dealers Association. 3301 Rte. 66, Ste. 205, Bldg. C, Neptune, NJ 07753. Phone: (732)922-3008; Fax: (732)922-3590; Email: info@nhpda.org • URL: http://www.nhpda.org • Represents cooperative and independent processors, packers, and dealers of honey at either the wholesale or retail level. Offers members information on testing facilities for honey analysis. Consults with Department of Agriculture on research programs in the field of honey marketing.

HONG KONG

See ASIAN MARKETS

HONORARY DEGREES

See ACADEMIC DEGREES

HOPS

See BREWING INDUSTRY

HOROLOGY

See CLOCK AND WATCH INDUSTRY

HOSIERY INDUSTRY

See also CHILDREN'S APPAREL INDUSTRY; CLOTHING INDUSTRY; TEXTILE INDUSTRY; WOMEN'S APPAREL

CD-ROM DATABASES

OECD Statistical Compendium. Organization for Economic Cooperation and Development. • Semiannual. $1,905.00 per year for 1 to 10 users. CD-ROM contains more than 730,000 monthly, quarterly, and annual time series for OECD countries, 1960 to date. Includes fully searchable data on agriculture, food, economic indicators, national accounts, employment, energy, finance, industry, technology, and foreign trade. Results can be displayed in various forms.

DIRECTORIES

Accessories Resources Directory. Business Journals Inc. • Annual. Covers: 1,600 manufacturers, importers, and sales representatives producing or handling belts, gloves, handbags, scarves, hosiery, jewelry, sunglasses, and umbrellas. Entries include: Company, name, address, phone, fax.

HANDBOOKS AND MANUALS

Sock Shop. Entrepreneur Press. • Looseleaf. $59.50. A practical guide to starting a store that sells stockings of various kinds. Covers profit potential, start-up costs, market size evaluation, owner's time required, site selection, lease negotiation, pricing, accounting, advertising, etc. (Start-Up Business Guide No. E1340.).

INTERNET DATABASES

Business 2.0 Web Guide to the Best Business Links. Business 2.0 Media Inc. Phone: (415)293-4800: Email: support@business2.com • URL: http://www.business2.com/webguide • Web site presents an extensive, searchable directory of links to "the best, most informative, and authoritative web pages." Twenty main categories cover business, finance, career, company information, people, and technology topics, with thousands of subtopics, all linking to Web sites recommended by experienced business researchers. Fees: Free.

Fedstats. Federal Interagency Council on Statistical Policy. Phone: (202)395-7254 • URL: http://www.fedstats.gov • Web site features an efficient search facility for full-text statistics produced by more than 100 federal agencies, including the Census Bureau, the Bureau of Economic Analysis, and the Bureau of Labor Statistics. Boolean searches can be made within one agency or for all agencies combined. Links are offered to international statistical bureaus, including the UN, IMF, OECD, UNESCO, Eurostat, and 20 individual countries. Fees: Free.

FreeLunch.com. Economy.com, Inc. Phone: (610)696-8700; Fax: (610)696-1678 • URL: http://www.freelunch.com • Web site provides free access to more than 200 million economic and financial data series, covering industry, demographics, labor markets, prices, retail sales, government spending, trade, interest rates, housing starts, the stock market, etc. Data is available in either chart or table form. Searching is offered. Free, but registration required. Economy.com, Inc. also offers fee-based economic analysis at *The Dismal Scientist* site (www.dismal.com).

PERIODICALS AND NEWSLETTERS

Hosiery News. Hosiery Association. • Monthly. Hosiery-related news including new offerings for retail, industry changes, legislative updates of hosiery-impacting laws, foreign trade and statistical information.

STATISTICS SOURCES

Survey of Current Business. U. S. Government Printing Office. • Published by Bureau of Economic Analysis, U. S. Department of Commerce. Presents a wide variety of business and economic data.

TRADE/PROFESSIONAL ASSOCIATIONS

Hosiery Association. 7421 Carmel Executive Park Dr., Ste. 200, Charlotte, NC 28226. Phone: (704)365-0913; Fax: (704)362-2056; Email: thainfo@hosieryassociation.com • URL: http://www.hosieryassociation.com • Hosiery manufacturers and suppliers. Develops standards for hosiery measurement. Sponsors annual "Celebrate Hosiery" to educate consumers on hosiery varieties. Conducts field visitations for assistance in technical areas. Compiles statistics; conducts research programs. Operates Group Purchasing Program.

HOSPITAL ADMINISTRATION

See also ADMINISTRATION; HEALTH CARE INDUSTRY; HOSPITAL EQUIPMENT

ABSTRACTS AND INDEXES

Excerpta Medica: Health Policy, Economics and Management. Elsevier. • Bimonthly. Section 36 of *Excerpta Medica.*

CD-ROM DATABASES

Authority Health Care Law Library. Matthew Bender and Company Inc. • Periodic updates. Price on request. Full text CD-ROM provides legal information, case law, and analysis relating to health care facilities, health insurance, longterm care, Medigap, and Medicare.

Healthcare QuickDisc. American Hospital Association. • Corresponds to the printed *AHA Guide*, with additional material and extensive search capabilities (400 data fields). Provides detailed information on 6,000 hospitals and hospital systems, including utilization data.

DIRECTORIES

AHA Guide to the Health Care Field. American Hospital Association. • Annual. $295.00. A directory of hospitals and health care systems.

AHA Integrated Delivery Network Directory: U.S. Health Care Systems, Networks, and Alliances. American Hospital Association. • Annual. $250.00. Provides information about a wide variety of U.S. health care groups and affiliations, including hospitals, nursing homes, rehabilitation centers, psychiatric facilities, home health care agencies, clinical laboratories, outpatient facilities, and diagnostic imaging centers. Includes names of more than 8,000 key executives.

American Hospital Directory. American Hospital Directory, Inc. • $395 Individuals single user. Database covers: Comparative data on hospitals in the U.S. Entries include: Hospital name, address, phone, fax, characteristics, financial statistics, services, accreditation status, utilization statistics, hospital web page.

Directory of Physician Groups and Networks. Dorland Healthcare Information. • Annual. $495.00. Available only online. Approximately 8,000 independent practice associations (IPAs), physician hospital organizations (PHOs), management service organizations (MSOs), physician practice management companies (PPMCs), and group practices having 20 or more physicians.

Profiles of U. S. Hospitals. Dorland Healthcare Information. • Annual. $299.00. Contains profiles of more than 6,000 community, teaching, children's, specialty, psychiatric, and rehabilitation hospitals. Emphasis is on 50 key financial and performance measures. Annual CD-ROM version with key word searching is available at $395.00.

OTHER SOURCES

Hospital Liability. ALM Media Properties LLC. • $550. Written for attorneys representing either hospitals or patients of hospitals. Covers a wide variety of legal topics relating to hospital/physician malpractice, including the expansion of HMO liability. (Law Journal Press).

PERIODICALS AND NEWSLETTERS

AHA News. American Hospital Association. HealthForum. • Description: Highlights major news affecting hospitals and the health care field. Reports on legislation and regulation, court cases, surveys, and federal programs. Carries information on individual hospitals and allied hospital associations.

Health Data Management. SourceMedia Inc. • Monthly. $98.00 per year. Covers the management and automation of clinical data and health care insurance claims. Provides news and analysis of various aspects of health care information technology for administrators of hospitals, clinics, and managed care plans.

Health Facilities Management. American Hospital Association. Health Forum L.L.C. • Covers building maintenance and engineering for hospitals and nursing homes.

Healthcare Risk Management. AHC Media. • Description: Analyzes specific legal cases and trends relevant to healthcare liability. Discusses malpractice, liability for patients, staff and visitor injury, injury prevention, biomedical engineering, and medical staff credentials. Also covers high-risk areas of hospitals, hospital-owned home health and physician practices, accreditation, Medicare reimbursement, physician liability, medical records, and claims management. Recurring features include interviews, statistics, news of research, guest columns, legal briefs, and commentaries.

Hospital Pharmacist Report. Thomson Medical Economics. • Monthly. $39.00 per year. Covers both business and clinical topics for hospital pharmacists.

Modern Physician: Essential Business News for the Executive Physician. Crain Communications Inc. • Monthly. $45.00. Edited for physicians responsible for business decisions at hospitals, clinics, HMOs, and other health groups. Includes special issues on managed care, practice management, legal issues, and finance.

Public Relations. Access Intelligence L.L.C. • Biweekly. $397.00 per year. Newsletter on public relations and client communications for the healthcare industry. Incorporates (Healthcare PR and Marketing News).

Report on Healthcare Information Management. Capital Publications, Inc. • Monthly. $358.00 per year. Newsletter. Covers management information sytems for hospitals and physicicans' groups.

Solid Waste Report: Resource Recovery-Recycling-Collection-Disposal. Business Publishers Inc. • Weekly. $627.00 per year. Newsletter. Covers regulation, business news, technology, and international events relating to solid waste management.

Trustee: The Magazine for Hospital Governing Boards. American Hospital Association. Health Forum L.L.C. • 10 times a year. $55.00 per year. Emphasis is on community health care.

RESEARCH CENTERS AND INSTITUTES

Johns Hopkins University Bloomberg School of Public Health - Center for Health Services and Outcomes Research. Hampton House, 6th Fl., Department of Health Policy & Management, 624 N Broadway, Baltimore, MD 21205-1901. Phone: (410)955-6567; Fax: (410)955-0470; Email: awu@jhsph.edu • URL: http://www.jhsph.edu/research/centers-and-institutes/health-services-outcomes-research/index.html • Health services, including determinants of health outcomes; the impacts of alternative health care systems on cost and quality; effective strategies for health promotion and disease prevention; and methods of meeting the needs of high risk populations such as the poor, elderly, mentally ill, disabled, and children.

University of Chicago. 947 E 58th St., MC0926, Chicago, IL 60637-5416. Phone: (773)702-6371 or (773)702-1234; Fax: (773)702-1216 or (773)702-7222; Email: info@ssa.uchicago.edu • URL: http://pps.bsd.uchicago.edu/.

STATISTICS SOURCES

AHA Hospital Statistics. American Hospital Association. Health Forum L.L.C. • Annual. $370 Members book/CD. Provides detailed statistical data on the nation's hospitals, including revenues, expenses, utilization, and personnel. Formerly *Hospital Statistics.*

Standard & Poor's Industry Surveys. Standard & Poor's Financial Services L.L.C. • Semiannual. $1,800.00. Two looseleaf volumes. Includes monthly *Supplements.* Provides detailed, individual surveys of 52 major industry groups. Each survey is revised on a semiannual basis. Also includes "Monthly Investment Review" (industry group investment analysis) and monthly "Trends & Projections" (economic analysis).

TRADE/PROFESSIONAL ASSOCIATIONS

American College of Healthcare Executives. 1 N Franklin St., Ste. 1700, Chicago, IL 60606-3529. Phone: (312)424-2800 or (312)424-9400; Fax: (312)424-0023 or (312)424-9405; Email: contact@ache.org • URL: http://www.ache.org • Formerly American College of Hospital Administrators.

American Hospital Association. 155 N Wacker Dr., Chicago, IL 60606. Phone: 800-424-4301 or

(312)422-3000 or (312)422-2050; Fax: (312)422-4700 • URL: http://www.aha.org • Represents health care provider organizations. Seeks to advance the health of individuals and communities. Leads, represents, and serves health care provider organizations that are accountable to the community and committed to health improvement.

American Society of Health-System Pharmacists. 7272 Wisconsin Ave., Bethesda, MD 20814. Phone: 866-279-0681 or (301)664-8700 or (301)657-3000; Fax: (301)657-1251; Email: custserv@ashp.org • URL: http://www.ashp.org • Affiliated with American Hospital Association and American Nurses Association.

HOSPITAL EQUIPMENT

See also SURGICAL INSTRUMENTS INDUSTRY; X-RAY EQUIPMENT INDUSTRY

CD-ROM DATABASES

Health Devices Journals. ECRI Institute. • Monthly. $285 each.

DIRECTORIES

The International Directory of Importers - Medical, Hospital and Surgical Equipment and Supplies Importers. Interdata. • $295 Individuals print. Covers: 4,400 international firms importing medical, hospital and surgical equipment and supplies. Entries include: Company name and address, contact person, email, number of employees, year established, phone and telefaxes, business activity, bank references, as well as a listing of medical, hospital and surgical equipment and supplies currently being imported.

Medical and Healthcare Marketplace Guide. IDD Inc. • Annual. $595.00. Two volumes. Provides market survey summaries for about 500 specific product and service categories (volume one: "Research Reports"). Contains profiles of nearly 5,500 pharmaceutical, medical product, and healthcare service companies (volume two: "Company Profiles").

INTERNET DATABASES

National Library of Medicine. National Institutes of Health. 9000 Rockville Pke., Bethesda, MD 20892. Phone: (301)496-4000; Email: nihinfo@od.nih.gov • URL: http://www.nih.gov • NLM Web site offers free access through MEDLINE ("PubMed") to about nine million references to articles appearing in some 4,000 biomedical journals, with abstracts. Search interfaces range from "simple keywords to advanced Boolean expressions." The NLM site offers many links to other sources of biomedical and technical information (the National Center for Biotechnology Information, for example). Fees: Free.

ONLINE DATABASES

F-D-C Reports. Elsevier Business Intelligence. • An online version of "The Gray Sheet" (medical devices), "The Pink Sheet" (pharmaceuticals), "The Rose Sheet" (cosmetics), "The Blue Sheet" (biomedical), and "The Tan Sheet" (nonprescription). Contains full-text information on legal, technical, corporate, financial, and marketing developments from 1987 to date, with weekly updates. Inquire as to online cost and availability.

PERIODICALS AND NEWSLETTERS

The Gray Sheet Reports: Medical Devices, Diagnostics and Instrumentation. Elsevier Business Intelligence. • Weekly. Institutions, $1,172.00 per year. Newsletter. Provides industry and financial news, including a medical sector stock index. Monitors regulatory developments at the Center for Devices and Radiological Health of the U. S. Food and Drug Administration.

Health Devices Alerts: A Summary of Reported Problems, Hazards, Recalls, and Updates. ECRI Institute. • Weekly. $3,649.40 per year. Looseleaf service. Contains reviews of health equipment problems. Includes *Health Devices Alerts Action Items, Health Devices Alerts Abstracts, Health Devices Alerts FDA Data, Health Devices Alerts Implants, Health Devices Alerts Hazards Bulletin.*

Healthcare Purchasing News: A Magazine for Hospital Materials Management Central Service, Infection Control Practitioners. Thomson Medical Economics. • Monthly. $72. Edited for personnel responsible for the purchase of medical, surgical, and hospital equipment and supplies. Features new purchasing techniques and new products. Includes news of the activities of two major purchasing associations, Health Care Material Management Society and International Association of Healthcare Central Service Materiel Management.

Medical Product Manufacturing News. Canon Communications LLC. • 5/year. Directed at manufacturers of medical devices and medical electronic equipment. Covers industry news, service news, and new products.

Surgical Products. Advantage Business Media L.L.C. • Monthly. $41.90 per year. Covers new Technology and products for surgeons and operation rooms.

STATISTICS SOURCES

Standard & Poor's Industry Surveys. Standard & Poor's Financial Services L.L.C. • Semiannual. $1,800.00. Two looseleaf volumes. Includes monthly *Supplements.* Provides detailed, individual surveys of 52 major industry groups. Each survey is revised on a semiannual basis. Also includes "Monthly Investment Review" (industry group investment analysis) and monthly "Trends & Projections" (economic analysis).

TRADE/PROFESSIONAL ASSOCIATIONS

Association for Healthcare Resource and Materials Management. 155 N Wacker Dr., Chicago, IL 60606. Phone: (312)422-3840; Fax: (312)422-4573; Email: ahrmm@aha.org • URL: http://www.ahrmm.org • Members are involved with the purchasing and distribution of supplies and equipment for hospitals and other healthcare establishments. Formerly American Society for Healthcare Materials Management.

National Association for Home Care and Hospice. 228 7th St. SE, Washington, DC 20003. Phone: (202)547-7424; Fax: (202)547-3540; Email: exec@nahc.org • URL: http://www.nahc.org • Promotes high standards of patient care in home care services. Members are durable medical providers, medical equipment and oxygen suppliers, mainly for home health care.

HOSPITALS

See HOSPITAL ADMINISTRATION

HOTEL AND MOTEL INDUSTRY

See also TRAVEL INDUSTRY

ABSTRACTS AND INDEXES

Leisure, Recreation and Tourism Abstracts. CABI Publishing North America. • Quarterly. Members, $280.00 per year; Institutions, $610.00 per year. Includes single site internet access. Provides coverage of the worldwide literature of travel, recreation, sports, and the hospitality industry.

Lodging, Restaurant and Tourism Index. Distance Learning Service. Purdue University - Consumer and Family Sciences Library. • Quarterly. $265.00 per year. Provides subject indexing to 52 periodicals related to the hospitality industry. Annual bound cumulations are available. Formerly *Lodging and Restaurant Index.*

CD-ROM DATABASES

OECD Statistical Compendium. Organization for Economic Cooperation and Development. • Semiannual. $1,905.00 per year for 1 to 10 users. CD-ROM contains more than 730,000 monthly, quarterly, and annual time series for OECD countries, 1960 to date. Includes fully searchable data on agriculture, food, economic indicators, national accounts, employment, energy, finance, industry, technology, and foreign trade. Results can be displayed in various forms.

DIRECTORIES

Business Atlanta--Hotel and Meeting Services Guide Issue. Primedia Business. • Annual. $6.50 postpaid. Covers over 150 hotels in and around the metropolitan Atlanta area, and nearly 200 Atlanta companies providing convention services.

Council on Hotel, Restaurant and Institutional Education--Member Directory and Resource Guide. International Council on Hotel, Restaurant, and Institutional Education. • Biennial. Covers: Over 2,000 educational programs and institutions in the hotel, restaurant, and tourism industries. Entries include: Name, address, phone, fax.

Goff's Business Travellers' Guide. Adprint. • Annual. $1.95. Covers: about 200 hotels in the United Kingdom. Entries include: Hotel name, address, phone, telex, fax, location, proximity of major city and airport, description of facilities, rates, whether credit cards are accepted, restaurants, symbols for amenities.

Hotel and Travel Index: The World Wide Hotel Directory. Northstar Travel Media L.L.C. • Quarterly. $185 per year. Contains concise information on more than 41,000 hotels in the U. S. and around the world. Includes 400 maps showing location of hotels and airports.

Plunkett's Airline, Hotel, and Travel Industry Almanac. Plunkett Research Ltd. • Annual. $349.99. Contains profiles of 300 leading companies, including airlines, hotels, travel agencies, theme parks, cruise lines, casinos, and car rental companies.

FINANCIAL RATIOS

Annual Statement Studies. Risk Management Association. • Annual. Compiled from over 280,000 financial statements.

Annual Statement Studies: Industry Default Probabilities and Cash Flow Measures. Risk Management Association. • Annual. $405 Nonmembers. Serves as a companion volume to the original *Annual Statement Studies.* Gives probability of default estimates on a percentage scale for more than 450 industries. Includes changes in position year-by-year for eight financial statement line items and provides percentage measures of cash flow.

INTERNET DATABASES

Business 2.0 Web Guide to the Best Business Links. Business 2.0 Media Inc. Phone: (415)293-4800; Email: support@business2.com • URL: http://www.business2.com/webguide • Web site presents an extensive, searchable directory of links to "the best, most informative, and authoritative web pages." Twenty main categories cover business, finance, career, company information, people, and technology topics, with thousands of subtopics, all linking to Web sites recommended by experienced business researchers. Fees: Free.

Fedstats. Federal Interagency Council on Statistical Policy. Phone: (202)395-7254 • URL: http://www.fedstats.gov • Web site features an efficient search facility for full-text statistics produced by more than 100 federal agencies, including the Census Bureau, the Bureau of Economic Analysis, and the Bureau of

Labor Statistics. Boolean searches can be made within one agency or for all agencies combined. Links are offered to international statistical bureaus, including the UN, IMF, OECD, UNESCO, Eurostat, and 20 individual countries. Fees: Free.

FreeLunch.com. Economy.com, Inc. Phone: (610)696-8700; Fax: (610)696-1678 • URL: http://www.freelunch.com • Web site provides free access to more than 200 million economic and financial data series, covering industry, demographics, labor markets, prices, retail sales, government spending, trade, interest rates, housing starts, the stock market, etc. Data is available in either chart or table form. Searching is offered. Free, but registration required. Economy.com, Inc. also offers fee-based economic analysis at *The Dismal Scientist* site (www.dismal.com).

PERIODICALS AND NEWSLETTERS

Bottomline. Hospitality Financial and Technology Professionals. • Bimonthly. Free to members, educational institutions and libraries; non-members, $50.00 per year. Contains articles on accounting, finance, information technology, and management for hotels, resorts, casinos, clubs, and other hospitality businesses.

The Cornell Hotel and Restaurant Administration Quarterly. Cornell University School of Hotel Administration. Pine Forge Press. • Bimonthly. Individuals, $113.00 per year; institutions, $319.00 per year.

Foodservice and Hospitality Magazine: Canada's Hospitality Business Magazine. Kostuch Publications Ltd. • Monthly. $55 Canada. Magazine for restaurant and hotel operators.

Hospitality Technology: Guiding High-Growth Businesses to Best-Choice IT Solutions. Edgell Communications Inc. • 10/year. Covers information technology, computer communications, and software for foodservice and lodging enterprises.

Hotel & Restaurant: The Accommodation, Food and Beverage Business Magazine for Southern Africa. Ramsay, Son & Parker Ltd. • Monthly. $168 Individuals. Trade magazine for the hospitality industry in South Africa.

Hotel Business. ICD Publications. • Biweekly. $260 Individuals domestic. Trade magazine covering the hotel industry.

Hotel Management. Advanstar Communications.

Resort Management and Operations: The Resort Resource. Finan Publishing. • Bimonthly. Price on application. Edited for hospitality professionals at both large and small resort facilities.

Restaurant Hospitality. Penton Media Inc. • Monthly.

STATISTICS SOURCES

Outlook for Travel and Tourism. U.S. Travel Association. • Annual. Members, $100.00; non-members, $175.00. Contains forecasts of the performance of the U. S. travel industry, including air travel, business travel, recreation (attractions), and accomodations.

Standard & Poor's Industry Surveys. Standard & Poor's Financial Services L.L.C. • Semiannual. $1,800.00. Two looseleaf volumes. Includes monthly *Supplements*. Provides detailed, individual surveys of 52 major industry groups. Each survey is revised on a semiannual basis. Also includes "Monthly Investment Review" (industry group investment analysis) and monthly "Trends & Projections" (economic analysis).

Survey of Current Business. U. S. Government Printing Office. • Published by Bureau of Economic Analysis, U. S. Department of Commerce. Presents a wide variety of business and economic data.

Trends in the Hotel Industry: U.S.A. Edition. PKF Consulting Corp. • Annual. $350 online. Provides detailed financial analysis of hotel operations in the U. S. (PKF is Pannell Kerr Forster.).

TRADE/PROFESSIONAL ASSOCIATIONS

Council for Hospitality Management Education. University of Bournemouth, Dorset House, Talbot Campus, Fern Barrow, Dorset, Poole BH12 5BB, United Kingdom. • URL: http://www.chme.co.uk • Universities and colleges which offer degree and/or HND courses in hospitality management. Represents member institutions' interests in the field of hospitality management education at HE level, EC, government, industry and professional levels. Promotes hospitality management education in general, as well as specialist levels, e.g. industrial placement, research, access to courses, etc.

Hospitality Financial and Technology Professionals. 11709 Boulder Ln., Ste. 110, Austin, TX 78726. Phone: 800-646-4387 or (512)249-5333; Fax: (512)249-1533; Email: membership@hftp.org • URL: http://www.hftp.org • Accountants, financial officers and MIS managers in 50 countries working in hotels, resorts, casinos, restaurants, and clubs. Develops uniform system of accounts. Conducts education, training, and certification programs; offers placement service; maintains hall of fame.

Hotel Technology Next Generation. 650 E Algonquin Rd., Ste. 207, Schaumburg, IL 60173. Phone: (847)303-5560; Email: info@htng.org • URL: http://www.htng.org • Promotes collaboration and partnership among hoteliers and technology providers. Serves as the voice of the global hotel community and facilitates the development of technology models for the hospitality industry. Works to increase the effectiveness and efficiency of hotels and creates a healthy ecosystem of technology suppliers.

HOUSE BUYING AND SELLING

See HOME OWNERSHIP

HOUSE DECORATION

See INTERIOR DECORATION

HOUSE OF REPRESENTATIVES

See UNITED STATES CONGRESS

HOUSE ORGANS

See also BUSINESS JOURNALISM; EDITORS AND EDITING; NEWSLETTERS

ALMANACS AND YEARBOOKS

Editor & Publisher International Yearbook: Encyclopedia of the Newspaper Industry. Editor and Publisher Company Inc. • Annual. $150.00. Daily and Sunday newspapers in the United States and Canada.

DIRECTORIES

Working Press of the Nation. R.R. Bowker L.L.C. • Annual. $530.00. $295.00 per volume. Three volumes: (1) *Newspaper Directory*; (2) *Magazine and Internal Publications Directory*; (3) *Radio and Television Directory*. Includes names of editors and other personnel.

HANDBOOKS AND MANUALS

Personnel Management: Communications. Prentice Hall PTR. • Looseleaf. Periodic supplementation. Price on application. Includes how to write effectively and how to prepare employee publications.

HOUSE-TO-HOUSE SELLING

See DIRECT MARKETING

HOUSEHOLD APPLIANCES

See ELECTRIC APPLIANCE INDUSTRY

HOUSEHOLD FURNISHINGS

See FURNITURE INDUSTRY

HOUSEHOLD PRODUCTS INDUSTRY

See CLEANING PRODUCTS INDUSTRY

HOUSES, PREFABRICATED

See PREFABRICATED HOUSE INDUSTRY

HOUSEWARES INDUSTRY

DIRECTORIES

Directory of American Manufacturers & Exporters of Houseware, Kitchenware & Tableware. EXIM Infotek Private Ltd. • $10 Individuals. Covers: 90 American manufacturers & exporters of brooms, cleaning materials, coasters, cutlery, dinnerware, flatware cutlery, gas stoves, holloware cutlery, household brooms, household cutlery, housewares, kitchen cutlery, knife sets, knives, plastic cups, plastic cutlery, plastic disposable cutlery, professional cutlery, scissors & knives, stainless steel cutlery, stainless steel flatware cutlery. Entries include: Company name, postal address, city, country, phone, fax, e-mail & websites, contact person, designation, products detail.

Directory of Chinese Manufacturers & Exporters of Houseware, Kitchenware & Tableware. EXIM Infotek Private Ltd. • $20 Individuals. Covers: 210 Chinese manufacturers and exporters of aluminum utensils, beer mugs, bottle openers, bowls, brooms and brushes for domestic use, brushes, choppers, chopsticks, coffee and tea sets, coffee mugs, coffee pots, combs, cooking utensils, cookwares, cups, cutlery, daily use goods, dinnerware, electric mosquito killer series, flasks, gas lighters, gas stoves, hangers, household goods, household plastic products, household utensils, housewares, ice cream spoons, kitchen articles-metal, kitchen products, kitchen tools, kitchen utensils, kitchenware, knives-metal, mugs, plastic household goods, plastic products for daily use, pressure cookers, scissors, stainless steel cookware sets, stainless steel kitchenware, stainless steel knives, stainless steel tableware, stainless steel utensils, tableware, trays, utensils, and vacuum flasks. Entries include: Company name, postal address, city, country, telephone, fax, e-mail and websites, contact person, designation, and product details.

Directory of Japanese Manufacturers & Exporters of Houseware, Kitchenware & Tableware. EXIM Infotek Private Ltd. • $10 Individuals. Covers: 110 Japanese manufacturers & exporters of combs, cutlery, daily use goods, gas utensils, home accessories, housing components for various system equipment, kitchen utensils, kitchenware, knives, scissors, tableware. Entries include: Company name, postal address, city, country, phone, fax, e-mail & websites, contact person, designation, products detail.

Directory of Taiwanese Manufacturers & Exporters of Houseware, Kitchenware & Tableware. EXIM Infotek Private Ltd. • $30 Individuals. Covers: 470 Taiwanese manufacturers and exporters of baskets-plastic, brooms and brushes for domestic use, cloth hangers-plastic, cutlery, decorative plastic articles, domestic articles-metal, fashion acrylic houseware, gold-plated/silverplated and pewterware, hangers, household cutlery-metal, household plastic products, kitchen articles/tableware-plastic, kitchen articles-metal, knife, knives-metal, plastic houseware, scissors, and scissors for cloth or paper cutting. Entries include: Company name, postal address, city, country, phone, fax, e-mail and websites, contact person, designation, and product details.

The International Directory of Importers - Housewares and Home Accessories Importers. Interdata. • $320 Individuals print. Covers: 6,200 international firms importing housewares and home accessories. Entries include: Company name and address, contact person, email, number of employees, year established, phone and telefaxes, business activity, bank references, as well as a listing of housewares and home accessories currently being imported.

PERIODICALS AND NEWSLETTERS

Fancy Food and Culinary Products. Talcott Communications Corp. • Monthly. $34.00 per year. Emphasizes new specialty food products and the business management aspects of the specialty food and confection industries. Includes special issues on wine, cheese, candy, "upscale" cookware, and gifts. Formerly (Fancy Foods).

Gourmet News: The Business Newspaper for the Gourmet Industry. HME News. • Monthly. $60.00 per year. Provides news of the gourmet food industry, including specialty food stores, upscale cookware shops, and gift shops.

Gourmet Retailer. Nielsen Business Media Inc. • Monthly. Free to qualified personnel; others, $75.00 per year. Covers upscale food and housewares, including confectionery items, bakery operations, and coffee.

TRADE/PROFESSIONAL ASSOCIATIONS

Cookware Manufacturers Association. PO Box 531335, Birmingham, AL 35253-1335. Phone: (205)592-0389; Fax: (205)599-5598 • URL: http://www.cookware.org • Represents manufacturers of cooking utensils and cooking accessories. Compiles statistics.

International Housewares Association. 6400 Shafer Ct., Ste. 650, Rosemont, IL 60018. Phone: (847)292-4200; Fax: (847)292-4211 • URL: http://www.housewares.org • Manufacturers and distributors of housewares and small appliances. Conducts annual market research survey of the housewares industry. Manages the international housewares show.

HOUSING

See also APARTMENT HOUSES; BUILDING INDUSTRY; CONDOMINIUMS; PREFABRICATED HOUSE INDUSTRY; REAL ESTATE BUSINESS

CD-ROM DATABASES

Newspaper Abstracts Ondisc. ProQuest L.L.C. • Monthly. $2,950.00 per year (covers 1989 to date; archival discs are available for 1985-88). Provides cover-to-cover CD-ROM indexing and abstracting of 19 major newspapers, including the *New York Times, Wall Street Journal, Washington Post, Chicago Tribune,* and *Los Angeles Times.*

OECD Statistical Compendium. Organization for Economic Cooperation and Development. • Semiannual. $1,905.00 per year for 1 to 10 users. CD-ROM contains more than 730,000 monthly, quarterly, and annual time series for OECD countries, 1960 to date. Includes fully searchable data on agriculture, food, economic indicators, national accounts, employment, energy, finance, industry, technology, and foreign trade. Results can be displayed in various forms.

Sourcebooks America CD-ROM. CACI Marketing Systems. • Annual. $1,250.00. Provides the CD-ROM version of *The Sourcebook of ZIP Code Demographics: Census Edition* and *The Sourcebook of County Demographics: Census Edition.*

DIRECTORIES

Manufactured Homes Manufacturers Directory. InfoGroup Inc. • Annual. Number of listings: 2,002. Entries include: Name, address, phone, size of advertisement, name of owner or manager, number of employees, year first in "Yellow Pages." Compiled from telephone company "Yellow Pages," nationwide.

INTERNET DATABASES

Business 2.0 Web Guide to the Best Business Links. Business 2.0 Media Inc. Phone: (415)293-4800; Email: support@business2.com • URL: http://www.business2.com/webguide • Web site presents an extensive, searchable directory of links to "the best, most informative, and authoritative web pages." Twenty main categories cover business, finance, career, company information, people, and technology topics, with thousands of subtopics, all linking to Web sites recommended by experienced business researchers. Fees: Free.

Fedstats. Federal Interagency Council on Statistical Policy. Phone: (202)395-7254 • URL: http://www.fedstats.gov • Web site features an efficient search facility for full-text statistics produced by more than 100 federal agencies, including the Census Bureau, the Bureau of Economic Analysis, and the Bureau of Labor Statistics. Boolean searches can be made within one agency or for all agencies combined. Links are offered to international statistical bureaus, including the UN, IMF, OECD, UNESCO, Eurostat, and 20 individual countries. Fees: Free.

FreeLunch.com. Economy.com, Inc. Phone: (610)696-8700; Fax: (610)696-1678 • URL: http://www.freelunch.com • Web site provides free access to more than 200 million economic and financial data series, covering industry, demographics, labor markets, prices, retail sales, government spending, trade, interest rates, housing starts, the stock market, etc. Data is available in either chart or table form. Searching is offered. Free, but registration required. Economy.com, Inc. also offers fee-based economic analysis at *The Dismal Scientist* site (www.dismal.com).

U.S. Census Bureau: The Official Statistics. U. S. Bureau of the Census. Phone: (301)763-4636 or (301)763-4100; Fax: (301)763-4794; Email: webmaster@census.gov • URL: http://www.census.gov/prod/www/abs/mfg-prof.html • Web site is "Your Source for Social, Demographic, and Economic Information." Contains "Current U. S. Population Count," "Current Economic Indicators," and a wide variety of data under "Other Official Statistics." Keyword searching is provided. Fees: Free.

OTHER SOURCES

Housing Discrimination: Law and Litigation. Robert G. Schwemm. Thomson West. • Annual. $593 full set. Covers provisions of the Fair Housing Act and related topics.

PERIODICALS AND NEWSLETTERS

Affordable Housing Finance. Alexander & Edwards Publishing. • 10/year. $119 Individuals. Provides advice and information on obtaining financing for lower-cost housing. Covers both government and private sources.

Builder: The Voice of America's Housing Industry. Finance and Housing Policy Div. DoveTale Publishers. • Monthly. $29.95 per year. Covers the home building and remodeling industry in general, including design, construction, and marketing.

Housing Affairs Letter: The Weekly Washington Report on Housing. Community Development Services, Inc. CD Publications. • Weekly. $624 print and online, 12 months. Covers mortgage activity news, including forecasts of mortgage rates.

RESEARCH CENTERS AND INSTITUTES

Insight Center for Community Economic Development. 2201 Broadway, Ste. 815, Oakland, CA 94612-3024. Phone: (510)251-2600; Fax: (510)251-0600; Email: info@insightcced.org • URL: http://insightcced.org • Aims to build economic health in vulnerable communities. Develops and promotes innovative solutions that help people and communities become, and remain, economically secure. Collaborates with foundations, nonprofits, educational institutions, government and businesses to develop, strengthen and promote programs and public policy that: lead to good jobs, strengthen early care and education systems, and enable people and communities to build financial and educational assets.

NAHB Home Innovation Research Labs. 400 Prince George's Blvd., Upper Marlboro, MD 20774. Phone: 800-638-8556 or (301)249-4000; Fax: (301)430-6180 • URL: http://www.homeinnovation.com.

University of California, Los Angeles - Richard S. Ziman Center for Real Estate. Gold Hall, Ste. B100, 110 Westwood Plz., Los Angeles, CA 90095-1481. Phone: (310)206-9424 or (213)825-3977; Fax: (310)267-5391 or (310)206-5455; Email: stuart.gabriel@anderson.ucla.edu • URL: http://www.anderson.ucla.edu/centers/ziman • Secondary mortgage markets, housing finance, growth management, infrastructure, corporate finance issues, and development industry.

STATISTICS SOURCES

American Housing Survey for the United States in (year). U. S. Government Printing Office. • Biennial. $51.00. Issued by the U. S. Census Bureau (www.census.gov). Covers both owner-occupied and renter-occupied housing. Includes data on such factors as condition of building, type of mortgage, utility costs, and housing occupied by minorities. (Current Housing Reports, H150.).

Statistical Abstract of the United States. U. S. Government Printing Office. • Annual. $44.00. Issued by the U. S. Bureau of the Census.

Statistical Yearbook. United Nations Publications. • Annual. $125.00. Contains statistics for about 200 countries on a wide variety of economic, industrial, and demographic topics. Compiled by United Nations Statistical Office.

Survey of Current Business. U. S. Government Printing Office. • Published by Bureau of Economic Analysis, U. S. Department of Commerce. Presents a wide variety of business and economic data.

U.S. Housing Markets. DoveTale Publishers. • Monthly. $345.00 per year. Includes eight interim reports. Provides data on residential building permits, apartment building completions, rental vacancy rates, sales of existing homes, average home prices, housing affordability, etc. All major U. S. cities and areas are covered.

TRADE/PROFESSIONAL ASSOCIATIONS

National Association of Home Builders - Systems Builder Council. 1201 15th St. NW, Washington, DC 20005. Phone: 800-368-5242 or (202)266-8200; Fax: (202)266-8400 • URL: http://www.nahb.org/reference_list.aspx?sectionID=815 • Formerly Home Manufacturers Councils of NAHB.

National Association of Housing and Redevelopment Officials. 630 Eye St. NW, Washington, DC 20001-3736. Phone: 877-866-2476 or (202)289-3500; Fax: (202)289-8181; Email: nahro@nahro.

org • URL: http://www.nahro.org • Formerly National Association of Housing Officials.

National Association of State and Local Equity Funds. 1970 Broadway, Ste. 250, Oakland, CA 94612. Phone: (510)444-1101; Fax: (510)444-1191; Email: info@naslef.org • URL: http://www.naslef.org • Promotes efficient management of state and local equity funds. Represents individuals, public and private corporations and professional associations with an interest in the tax credit program or an active involvement with a state or local equity fund. Fosters greater understanding of the Low Income Housing Tax Credit (LIHTC).

National Center for Housing Management. 1801 Old Reston Ave., Ste. 203, Reston, VA 20190-3356. Phone: 800-368-5625; Email: service@nchm.org • URL: http://www.nchm.org • Purposes are to upgrade and professionalize the housing management industry through training, accreditation of firms, certification of individuals, research, technical assistance, and clearinghouse activities. Funded by performance contracts with federal, state, and local agencies, grants from foundations, and contracts with public and private management and mortgage servicing organizations. Provides training for all levels of housing management and currently awards certifications for occupancy specialists and maintenance managers. Offers technical assistance in compliance with the Fair Housing Act and Section 504 of the Rehabilitation Act of 1973.

National Housing Conference. 1900 M St. NW, Ste. 200, Washington, DC 20036. Phone: (202)466-2121; Fax: (202)466-2122 • URL: http://www.nhc.org • Housing authority officials, community development specialists, builders, bankers, lawyers, accountants, owners, residents, insurers, architects and planners, religious organizations, labor groups, and national housing and housing-related organizations. Mobilizes support for effective programs in housing and community development as well as affordable and accessible housing for all Americans. Holds educational programs.

Women in Housing and Finance. 400 N Washington St., Ste. 300, Alexandria, VA 22314. Phone: (703)683-4742; Fax: (703)683-0018; Email: whf@whfdc.org • URL: http://www.whfdc.org • Professionals employed in the fields of housing or finance. Provides women finance professionals with the opportunity for continued professional development through interaction with others with similar interests. Promotes educational development of women in housing and finance; provides members with services and benefits to help them attain higher levels of expertise. Sponsors social events for members; holds receptions for congressional and regulatory leaders; conducts monthly luncheon and programs featuring speakers from federal agencies, Congress and the private sector. Sponsors career development workshops. Activities are concentrated in the Washington, DC, area.

HOUSING MANAGEMENT

See PROPERTY MANAGEMENT

HUMAN ENGINEERING

ABSTRACTS AND INDEXES

NTIS Alerts: Biomedical Technology & Human Factor Engineering. U.S. Department of Commerce National Technical Information Service. • Biweekly. $130 per year. Covers biotechnology, ergonomics, bionics, artificial intelligence, prosthetics, and related subjects.

PERIODICALS AND NEWSLETTERS

Ergonomics: An International Journal of Research and Practice in Human Factors and Ergonomics. Taylor & Francis Ltd. • Monthly. Research journal for human factors and ergonomics industry.

Human Factors and Ergonomics in Manufacturing & Service Industries. John Wiley and Sons, Inc., Journals Div. • Bimonthly. Published in England by John Wiley and Sons Ltd. Formerly *International Journal of Human Factors in Manufacturing.*

TRADE/PROFESSIONAL ASSOCIATIONS

MTM Association for Standards and Research. 1111 E Touhy Ave., Des Plaines, IL 60018. Phone: (847)299-1111; Fax: (847)299-3509; Email: webmaster@mtm.org • URL: http://www.mtm.org • Persons interested in the fields of industrial engineering, industrial psychology, and human engineering. Conducts research at accredited institutions on human motion (the physical movement of body and limb), with emphasis on examining: internal velocity, acceleration, tension, and control characteristics of a given motion under several conditions; external regularities of given groups of motion as they vary under several conditions of performance; the proper use of motion information in measuring, controlling, and improving manual activities. Also studies ergonomics and the effects of workplace environment on productivity. Provides information on fatigue, optimum methods of performance, the effect of practice on motion performance, and the use of motion information for determining allowances and predicting total performance time. Has developed computer programs for the application of Methods Time Measurement (MTM) and MTM-based work measurement systems. Conducts training courses and testing for certification of practitioners and instructors in all Association MTM Systems. Develops and makes available specialized productivity management services.

HUMAN RELATIONS

See also INDUSTRIAL PSYCHOLOGY; INDUSTRIAL RELATIONS; PERSONNEL MANAGEMENT

ABSTRACTS AND INDEXES

Current Contents: Social and Behavioral Sciences. Thomson Reuters Intellectual Property and Science. • Weekly. $730. Includes *Author Index.*

Psychological Abstracts. American Psychological Association. • Monthly. Members, $815.00 per year; individuals and institutions, $1,207.00 per year. Covers the international literature of psychology and the behavioral sciences. Includes journals, technical reports, dissertations, and other sources.

Social Sciences Citation Index. Thomson Reuters Corp. • Weekly. Product is accessed via *Web of Science.*

Social Sciences Index Retrospective: 1907-1983. EBSCO Publishing Inc. • Indexing for 1,000,000 articles. Coverage includes international index and social sciences and humanities index.

Sociological Abstracts. ProQuest L.L.C. • Monthly. A compendium of non-evaluative abstracts covering the field of sociology and related disciplines.

CD-ROM DATABASES

Social Sciences Abstracts. EBSCO Publishing Inc. • Provides indexing from 1983 and abstracting from 1994 of more than 750 periodicals covering economics, area studies, community health, public administration, public welfare, urban studies, and many other topics related to the social sciences.

Social Sciences Citation Index. Thomson Reuters Corp. • Weekly. Product is accessed via *Web of Science.*

ENCYCLOPEDIAS AND DICTIONARIES

Gale Encyclopedia of Psychology. Cengage Learning Inc. • 2000. $267.00. Second edition. Includes bibliographies arranged by topic and a glossary. More than 650 topics are covered.

GENERAL WORKS

Business Pulse. Chamber of Commerce and Industry of Western Australia. • Monthly. Journal containing information about business, employee relations, and international trade.

ONLINE DATABASES

Wilson Social Sciences Abstracts Online. H.W. Wilson Co. • Provides online abstracting and indexing of more than 500 periodicals covering area studies, community health, public administration, public welfare, urban studies, and many other social science topics. Time period is 1994 to date for abstracts and 1983 to date for indexing, with updates weekly. Inquire as to online cost and availability.

OTHER SOURCES

How to Manage Conflict in the Organization. American Management Association Extension Institute. • Looseleaf. $139.00. Self-study course. Emphasis is on practical explanations, examples, and problem solving. Quizzes and a case study are included.

PERIODICALS AND NEWSLETTERS

American Behavioral Scientist. Pine Forge Press. • Fourteen per year. Institutions, $1,425.00 per year.

Business Pulse. Chamber of Commerce and Industry of Western Australia. • Monthly. Journal containing information about business, employee relations, and international trade.

Communication Briefings: A Monthly Idea Source for Decision Makers. Briefings Publishing Group. • Monthly. $97. Presents useful ideas for communication, public relations, customer service, human resources, and employee training.

Human Communication Research. International Communication Association. Oxford University Press, Journals. • A scholarly journal of interpersonal communication.

Human Relations: Towards the Integration of Social Sciences. Tavistock Institute of Human Relations. Pine Forge Press. • Monthly. $163 Individuals print only. Contains high quality research papers of social relationships at work and organizational forms, practices and processes that affect the nature, structure and conditions of work and work organizations.

Journal of Applied Behavioral Science. Pine Forge Press. • $943 Institutions print and e-access. Quarterly. Includes print and online editions.

Organizational Dynamics: A Quarterly Review of Organizational Behavior for Management Executives. American Management Association. • Quarterly. Individuals, $77.00 per year; institutions, $171.00 per year. Covers the application of behavioral sciences to business management.

People to People. American Public Power Association. • Description: Reports on public sector labor and personnel issues, especially those concerning the electric utility industry. Summarizes case studies in public labor relations.

Teamwork: Your Personal Guide to Working Successfully with People. Dartnell Corp. • Monthly. $249 Individuals Print and Online - Annual. Offers your employees practical tips and techniques that help them work together as a cohesive unit, improve relations with other teams, and motivate themselves.

RESEARCH CENTERS AND INSTITUTES

Academia Sinica - Sun Yat-Sen Institute for Social Sciences and Philosophy. Nankang, Taipei 11529, Taiwan. Phone: 886 2 27821693; Fax: 886 2 27854160; Email: tpleung@ccvax.sinica.edu.tw • URL: http://www.sinica.edu.tw/as/intro/issp.html • Interdisciplinary studies on social sciences and humanities, including history and philosophy.

sociology, political science, economics and jurisprudence.

Australian National University - Research School of Social Sciences., Canberra, ACT 0200, Australia. Phone: 61 2 252257; Fax: 61 2 250502; Email: adam.graycar@anu.edu.au • URL: http://rsss.anu.edu.au • Demography and sociology, economics, law, history, philosophy, political science, sociology, social and political theory, research evaluation and policy, immigration and multicultural studies.

Friedrich Ebert Foundation - Latin American Social Sciences Research Institute. Av. República 500 y Diego de Almagro, Edif. Pucará, 4to. Piso, Of. 404, Casilla 17-03-367, Quito, Ecuador. Phone: 593 2 2562103; Fax: 593 2 2504337; Email: info@fes.ec • URL: http://www.fes-ecuador.org • Conducts investigations around political, social and economic problems in Latin America.

Lingnan University - Institute of Humanities and Social Sciences - Center for Public Policy Studies. Tuen Mun, Hong Kong, China. Phone: 86 852 26167182; Fax: 86 852 25910690; Email: lsho@ln.edu.hk • URL: http://www.ln.edu.hk/cpps • Labor, human capital investment, and industrial policy; urban, health and environmental policy; and socio-economic justice and collective behavior.

London School of Economics and Political Science - Centre for Philosophy of Natural and Social Science. Lakatos Bldg., Houghton St., London WC2A 2AE, United Kingdom. Phone: 44 207 9557573; Fax: 44 207 9556869; Email: philcent@lse.ac.uk • URL: http://www.lse.ac.uk/CPNSS/Home.aspx • Philosophy of natural and social science; Darwinism and the human sciences; causation; foundations of physics; economics and human values; and measuring voting power.

Mississippi State University - Social Science Research Center. 1 Research Park, Ste. 103, Starkville, MS 39759. Phone: (662)325-7127; Fax: (662)325-7966; Email: arthur.cosby@ssrc.msstate.edu • URL: http://www.ssrc.msstate.edu • Economic and social issues in Mississippi, the southeastern region and the United States, particularly social and economic development, the family and children, rural health and health policy, community development, alcohol safety, homeland security, substance abuse, traffic safety, race relations, information-age societal monitoring, natural resources, social services, and crime, delinquency and justice. Research is conducted through three divisions: Family and Children Research Unit; Mississippi Alcohol Safety Education Program; and the Mississippi Health Policy Research Center and five laboratories: Evaluation and Decision Support Laboratory, Secure Data Laboratory, Monitor Laboratory, Survey Research Laboratory, and the Unit for Community and Environmental Studies.

National Research Council - Division of Behavioral and Social Science and Education - Center for Social and Economic Studies. 500 5th St. NW, 11th Fl., Washington, DC 20001. Phone: (202)334-3730; Fax: (202)334-3829; Email: cses@nas.edu • URL: http://www7.nationalacademies.org/cses/ • Social and economic policy-related research, including racial dynamics in the U.S., urban issues, environmental decision-making, and international conflict resolution.

National Science Foundation - Directorate for Social, Behavioral, and Economic Sciences - Division of Social and Economic Sciences. 4201 Wilson Blvd., Rm. 995N, Arlington, VA 22230. Phone: (703)292-8760; Fax: (703)292-9068; Email: jmumpowe@nsf.gov • URL: http://www.nsf.gov/div/index.jsp?div=SES • Economics, law and social science, political science, sociology, measurement methods and data improvement, decision, risk, and management science. The goal of the Division is to develop basic scientific knowledge of human social behavior, interaction, and decision-making, and of social and economic systems, organizations, and institutions. The Division also supports research on the human dimensions of global environmental change and research to improve the quality and the accessibility of social and economic data resources. In addition to research proposals, programs within the Division consider proposals for doctoral dissertation support, research conferences, the acquisition of specialized research and computing equipment, group international travel, and data collection.

New York University - Center for Experimental Social Science. 19 W 4th St., 6th Fl., New York, NY 10012. Phone: (212)998-8952; Fax: (212)995-3932; Email: andrew.schotter@nyu.edu • URL: http://cess.nyu.edu • Social sciences, focusing on economic theory and/or the properties of proposed or existing economic, political, or social institutions.

Pontifical Catholic University of Peru - Center for Social, Economic, Political and Anthropological Research. Av. Universitaria Cdra. 18, San Miguel, Lima 32, Peru. Phone: 51 1 6262000; Fax: 51 1 6262815 • URL: http://cisepa.pucp.edu.pe • Social sciences, economy, sociology, anthropology and political sciences.

RAND Center for the Study of Aging. 1776 Main St., Santa Monica, CA 90407-2138. Phone: (310)393-0411; Fax: (310)451-6923; Email: diana_malouf@rand.org • URL: http://www.rand.org/labor/aging • Relationships among institutional and socioeconomic factors, health, and financial well-being among the elderly.

Society for the Study of Social Problems. University of Tennessee, 901 McClung Tower, Knoxville, TN 37996-0490. Phone: (865)689-1531; Fax: (865)689-1534 • URL: http://www.sssp1.org • An interdisciplinary community of scholars, activists, practitioners, and students endeavoring to create greater social justice through social research. Members are often social scientists working in colleges and universities, in non-profit organizations and in other applied and policy settings.

University of California, Los Angeles - Social Sciences Grant Support. 2134 Rolfe Hall, Los Angeles, CA 90095-1484. Phone: (310)825-0711; Fax: (310)206-4453; Email: aortega@ucla.edu • URL: http://www.issr.ucla.edu • Basic and policy studies on a broad spectrum of contemporary sociological, psychological, political, and economic problems and community issues. Encourages collaborative research between faculty in various social science departments of the University, as well as cooperative projects involving members of professional schools of the University and faculty of the School. Sponsors the following interdisciplinary research programs: Center for American Politics and Public Policy; Center for the Study of Urban Poverty; and Center for Social Theory and Comparative History.

University of California, Santa Barbara - Institute for Social, Behavioral, and Economic Research - Center on Police Practices and Community. 2201 N Hall, Santa Barbara, CA 93106-2150. Phone: (805)901-4439; Fax: (805)893-7995; Email: mca@coppac.ucsb.edu • URL: http://www.coppac.ucsb.edu/ • Relationships between law enforcement and society.

University of Michigan - Institute for Social Research - Inter-University Consortium for Political and Social Research. 330 Packard St., Ann Arbor, MI 48104. Phone: 888-741-7242 or (734)615-8400 or (734)615-7652; Fax: (734)647-8200; Email: netmail@icpsr.umich.edu • URL: http://www.icpsr.umich.edu/icpsrweb/landing.jsp • Cooperative partnership among institutions of higher education represented by libraries and departments of political science, history, sociology, and related disciplines concerned with the systematic study of political and social behavior. Seeks to facilitate research in the social sciences by: developing a major data repository providing access to basic research materials; conducting an advanced training program providing formal course work in methodology, research techniques, and substantive fields for advanced graduate students and faculty; stimulating new research projects; consulting in computer support needs. Makes available technical facilities to scholars from member institutions. Data repository holdings include survey, election, census, and roll call data, representing nations throughout the world.

University of North Carolina at Chapel Hill - Odum Institute for Research in Social Science. Davis Library, 2nd Fl., CB 3355, Chapel Hill, NC 27599. Phone: (919)962-3061; Fax: (919)962-2875; Email: carsey@unc.edu • URL: http://www.odum.unc.edu/odum/home2.jsp • Sociology, anthropology, psychology, political science, city and regional planning, journalism, economics, history, geography, religion, education, business administration, library science, law, public health, survey methodology, digital archives and curation, and social work.

University of Northern Iowa - College of Social and Behavioral Sciences - Center for Social and Behavioral Research. 2304 College St., Cedar Falls, IA 50614-0402. Phone: (319)273-2105; Fax: (319)273-3104; Email: gene.lutz@uni.edu • URL: http://www.uni.edu/csbr/ • Geography, history, home economics, political science, psychology, sociology, anthropology, criminology, social work, and public policy, including studies on adolescents, adult education, airline passengers, airports, educational needs assessment, elderly, environmental impact assessment, highways, human services needs assessment, outdoor recreation, radio listening habits, substance abuse, and television viewing habits. Performs feasibility studies on proposed projects such as sports complexes and auditoriums. Conducts special surveys for groups, organizations, localities, regions, and social aggregates.

University of Pennsylvania - Center for Analytical Research in Economics and the Social Sciences. 3718 Locust Walk, Philadelphia, PA 19104-6297. Phone: (215)898-5735 • URL: http://economics.sas.upenn.edu/research • Economic theory and related mathematics.

University of Tokyo - Institute of Social Science. 7-3-1 Hongo, Bunkyo-ku, Tokyo 113-0033, Japan. Phone: 81 3 58414904; Fax: 81 3 58414905; Email: webmaster@iss.u-tokyo.ac.jp • URL: http://www.iss.u-tokyo.ac.jp • Comparative contemporary law, politics, economics, and societies.

University of Wisconsin—Madison - Social Systems Research Institute. William H. Sewell Social Science Bldg., Rm. 6470, Department of Economics, 1180 Observatory Dr., Madison, WI 53706. Phone: (608)262-0446; Fax: (608)263-3876; Email: ssri@wisc.edu • URL: http://www.econ.wisc.edu/archive • Econometrics, industrial organization, international economics, labor economics, macroeconomics, public economics and economic theory.

University of York - Institute for Research in the Social Sciences. Heslington, York YO10 5DD, United Kingdom. Phone: 44 1904 321290; Fax: 44 1904 321281; Email: hdj1@york.ac.uk • URL: http://www.york.ac.uk/iriss • Health economics, social policy, housing policy, and social work.

HUMAN RESOURCES MANAGEMENT

See PERSONNEL MANAGEMENT

HUMAN RIGHTS

See CIVIL RIGHTS

HUMOR AND JOKES

See also PUBLIC SPEAKING; TOASTS

PERIODICALS AND NEWSLETTERS

Studies in American Humor. American Humor Studies Association. • Annual.

TRADE/PROFESSIONAL ASSOCIATIONS

American Humor Studies Association. Averett University, 316 Frith Hall, Danville, VA 24541. Phone: (434)791-7242 • URL: http://americanhumorstudiesassociation.wordpress.com • Academics, general readers, and professional humorists. Encourages the study and appreciation of American humor from interdisciplinary perspectives.

HYDRAULIC ENGINEERING AND MACHINERY

See also CIVIL ENGINEERING; FLUIDICS INDUSTRY

ABSTRACTS AND INDEXES

Fluid Abstracts: Civil Engineering. Elsevier. • Monthly. $3,804 Institutions print. Monthly. Institutions, $1,709.00 per year. Includes annual cumulation. Includes the literature of coastal structures. Published in England by Elsevier Science Publishing Ltd. Formerly *Civil Engineering Hydraulics Abstracts.*

ONLINE DATABASES

FLUIDEX. Elsevier. • Produced in the Netherlands by Elsevier Science B.V. Provides indexing and abstracting of the international literature of fluid engineering and technology, 1973 to date, with monthly updates. Also known as *Fluid Engineering Abstracts.* Inquire as to online cost and availability.

PERIODICALS AND NEWSLETTERS

Hydraulics and Pneumatics: The Magazine of Fluid Power and Motion Control Systems. Penton Media Inc..

TRADE/PROFESSIONAL ASSOCIATIONS

National Fluid Power Association. 3333 N Mayfair Rd., Ste. 211, Milwaukee, WI 53222-3219. Phone: (414)778-3344; Fax: (414)778-3361; Email: nfpa@nfpa.com • URL: http://www.nfpa.com • Manufacturers of components such as fittings used in transmitting power by hydraulic and pneumatic pumps, valves, cylinders, filters, seals; the components are used in industrial and mobile machinery in the material-handling, automotive, railway, aircraft, marine, aerospace, construction, agricultural, and other industries. Works to develop: American National Standards Institute and International Organization for Standardization; fluid power technical standards; fluid power index (industry sales); management and marketing studies. Compiles statistics. Administers and serves as secretariat to several international project groups and other fluid power organizations.

HYDROCARBONS

See PETROLEUM INDUSTRY

HYDROELECTRIC INDUSTRY

DIRECTORIES

Hydro Review Worldwide. PennWell Publishing Co. • Bimonthly. Provides network for sharing information regarding practical, technical and expertise on hydroelectric power.

ONLINE DATABASES

Hydro Energy Businesses in the World. Momentum Technologies L.L.C. • Contains detailed directory listings and contact information for dozens of hydro energy businesses in operation throughout the world. Includes business name, address, phone and fax numbers, and online contact addresses. Includes brief descriptions of product lines, services offered, and business type. Covers businesses providing large hydro energy systems (more than 50 KW) and smaller hydro energy systems (less than 50 KW); large and small hydro energy system components; and large and small hydroelectric turbines. Provides keyword search functions.

PERIODICALS AND NEWSLETTERS

Hydro Review: A Magazine Covering the North American Hydroelectric Industry. PennWell Hydro Group. • Covers hydroelectric power generation in North America. Supplement available *Industry Directory.*

RESEARCH CENTERS AND INSTITUTES

University of Hawaii at Manoa - Hawaii Natural Energy Institute. 1680 E West Rd., Post 109, Honolulu, HI 96822. Phone: (808)956-8890; Fax: (808)956-2336; Email: hnei@hawaii.edu • URL: http://www.hnei.hawaii.edu • Research areas include geothermal, wind, solar, hydroelectric, and other energy sources.

STATISTICS SOURCES

Annual Energy Outlook, with Projections to (year). U. S. Government Printing Office. • Annual. $39.00. Issued by the Energy Information Administration, U. S. Department of Energy (www.eia.doe.gov). Contains detailed statistics and 20-year projections for electricity, oil, natural gas, coal, and renewable energy. Text provides extensive discussion of energy issues and "Market Trends.".

TRADE/PROFESSIONAL ASSOCIATIONS

National Hydropower Association. 25 Massachusetts Ave. NW, Ste. 450, Washington, DC 20001. Phone: (202)682-1700; Fax: (202)682-9478; Email: help@hydro.org • URL: http://www.hydro.org • Represents hydrodevelopers, dam site owners, manufacturers, utilities and municipalities, individuals from the financial community (such as bankers, brokers, and investors), civil contracting firms, architects, engineering firms, and others actively involved in the promotion and development of hydropower. Promotes the development of hydroelectric energy. Participates in the regulatory process on issues such as simplified licensing procedures, purchase power rates, removal of regulatory barriers, and timely implementation of previously adopted legislation. Informs the government about the potential of hydropower and also monitors and drafts new legislation to government regulatory and legislative bodies.

HYGIENE

See INDUSTRIAL HYGIENE

HYPERTENSION

CD-ROM DATABASES

Consumer Health Complete. EBSCO Publishing Inc. • Full text of more than 250 health references, health diagrams, videos, pamphlets.

INTERNET DATABASES

National Library of Medicine. National Institutes of Health. 9000 Rockville Pke., Bethesda, MD 20892. Phone: (301)496-4000; Email: nihinfo@od.nih.gov • URL: http://www.nih.gov • NLM Web site offers free access through MEDLINE ("PubMed") to about nine million references to articles appearing in some 4,000 biomedical journals, with abstracts. Search interfaces range from "simple keywords to advanced Boolean expressions." The NLM site offers many links to other sources of biomedical and technical information (the National Center for Biotechnology Information, for example). Fees: Free.

PERIODICALS AND NEWSLETTERS

Hypertension. American Heart Association. • Individuals, $256.00 per year; institutions, $401.00 per year.

I

ICE CREAM INDUSTRY

See also DAIRY INDUSTRY

ABSTRACTS AND INDEXES

Food Science and Technology Abstracts. Ovid Technologies Inc. • Monthly. $1,780.00 per year. Provides worldwide coverage of the literature of food technology and food production.

Foods Adlibra: Key to the World's Food Literature. General Mills, Inc. Foods Adlibra Publications. • Semimonthly. $240.00 per year. Provides journal citations and abstracts to the literature of food technology and packaging.

DIRECTORIES

Major Food and Drink Companies of the World. Cengage Learning Inc. • 12th edition. eBook. Published by Graham & Whiteside. Contains profiles and trade names for more than 9,200 important food and beverage companies in various countries. In addition to foods, includes both alcoholic and nonalcoholic drink products.

ONLINE DATABASES

Food Science and Technology Abstracts (online). IFIS North American Desk. • Produced by International Food Information Service. Provides about 500,000 online citations, with abstracts, to the international literature of food science, technology, commodities, engineering, and processing. Approximately 2,000 periodicals are covered. Time period is 1969 to date, with monthly updates. Inquire as to online cost and availability.

PERIODICALS AND NEWSLETTERS

Dairy Foods. BNP Media. • Monthly. Provides broad coverage of new developments in the dairy industry, including cheese and ice cream products.

Ice Cream Reporter: The Newsletter for Ice Cream Executives. MarketResearch.com. • Monthly. $395.00 per year. Covers new products, mergers, research, packaging, etc.

The National Dipper: The Magazine for Frozen Dessert Retailers. • Bimonthly. $55.00 per year. Edited for ice cream store owners and managers. Includes industry news, new product information, statistics, and feature articles.

PRICE SOURCES

Supermarket News: The Industry's Weekly Newspaper. Fairchild Publications. • Weekly. Individuals, $196.00 per year; retailers, $45.00 per year; manufacturers, $89.00 per year.

TRADE/PROFESSIONAL ASSOCIATIONS

National Ice Cream Retailers Association. 1028 W Devon Ave., Elk Grove Village, IL 60007. Phone: 866-303-6960 or (847)301-7500; Fax: (847)301-8402 • URL: http://www.nicra.org • Represents frozen dessert retailers that operate ice cream and frozen yogurt dipping stores or parlors. Provides free and frank exchange of information among members so that all may improve their operations, increase profits and prosper.

IDENTIFICATION SYSTEMS, AUTOMATIC

See AUTOMATIC IDENTIFICATION SYSTEMS

ILLEGAL ALIENS

See IMMIGRATION AND EMIGRATION

IMAGE, CORPORATE

See CORPORATE IMAGE

IMAGING, COMPUTER

See COMPUTER IMAGING

IMMIGRATION AND EMIGRATION

See also CITIZENSHIP

ABSTRACTS AND INDEXES

Current Law Index. Cengage Learning Inc. • $1,332 Individuals. Monthly. $1269.00 per year. Produced in cooperation with the American Association of Law Libraries. Indexes more than 900 law journals, legal newspapers, and specialty publications from the U.S., Canada, U.K., Ireland, Australia, and New Zealand.

CD-ROM DATABASES

Authority Immigration Law Library. Matthew Bender and Company Inc. • Periodic revisions. Price on request. CD-ROM contains updated full text of *Immigration Case Reporter, Immigration Law and Procedure Treatise, INS Regulations,* and other immigration law publications issued by Matthew Bender.

GENERAL WORKS

U.S. Immigration and Migration Reference Library. Cengage Learning Inc. • 2004. $378.00. Five volumes. Includes *Almanac* (2 vols.), *Biographies* (2 vols.), and *Primary Sources.* Provides detailed history and information relating to U.S. immigration from "earliest times" to the present. (U-X-L imprint). eBook also available.

HANDBOOKS AND MANUALS

United States Immigration Laws, General Information. U.S. Immigration and Naturalization Service. U. S. Government Printing Office. • Irregular.

INTERNET DATABASES

Lexis.com Research System. Lexis-Nexis Group. Phone: 800-227-4908 or (937)865-6800; Fax: (937)865-6909; Email: webmaster@prod.lexis-nexis.com • URL: http://www.nexis.com • Fee-based Web site offers extensive searching of a wide variety of legal sources. Additional features include Daily Opinion Service, lexis.com Bookstore, Career Center, CLE Center, Law Schools, and Practice Pages ("Pages specific to areas of specialty").

OTHER SOURCES

Board of Immigration Appeals Interim Decisions. U.S. Immigration and Naturalization Service. U. S. Government Printing Office. • Irregular.

Business Immigration Law: Strategies for Employing Foreign Nationals. ALM Media Properties LLC. • $540 per year. Provides step-by-step employment procedures relating to the law and regulations of the State Department, the Immigration and Naturalization Service, specific visa programs, and the Labor Department. Includes guidelines and samples of forms. (Law Journal Press).

Immigration Law and Business. Sam Bernsen. Thomson West. • $552 full set. Three times a year. Three looseleaf volumes. Covers labor certification, temporary workers, applications, petitions, etc.

Immigration Law and Crimes. Dan Kesselbrenner and Lory D. Rosenberg. Thomson West. • $319.50 book. Semiannual. Looseleaf service. Covers legal representation of the foreign-born criminal defendant.

Immigration Law and Defense. National Lawyers Guild. Thomson West. • $536 book-softbound. Semiannual. Two looseleaf volumes. Covers legal defense of immigrants and aliens.

Immigration Law and Procedure. Matthew Bender and Company Inc. • $3,446. 21 looseleaf volumes. Periodic supplementation.

World Migration Report. United Nations Publications. • Annual. $39.00. Analyzes major trends in world migration, including individual country profiles.

PERIODICALS AND NEWSLETTERS

Immigration Law Report. Austin T. Fragomen and Steven C. Bell. Thomson West. • Description: Reports on U.S. immigration and nationality laws. Presents arguments that can be used in preparing Immigration and Naturalization Service (INS) cases and federal court cases. Carries analysis of material not readily available, such as internal INS policy statements and unpublished cases. Recurring features include reviews of recent decisions and regulations.

International Migration Review: A Quarterly Study-ing Sociological, Demographic, Economic, Historical, and Legislative Aspects of Human Migration Movements and Ethnic Group Relations. Center for Migration Studies. • Quarterly. Individuals, $39.00 per year; institutions, $80.00 per year.

Migration World: A Bimonthly Magazine Focusing on the Newest Immigrant and Refugee Groups; Policy and Legislation; Resources. Center for Migration Studies. • Bimonthly. $31 Individuals /year.

RESEARCH CENTERS AND INSTITUTES

Center for Migration Studies. 27 Carmine St., New York, NY 10014-4423. Phone: (212)337-3080; Fax: (646)998-4625; Email: cms@cmsny.org • URL: http://cmsny.org • A nonprofit institute whose goal is to provide a forum for debate on international migration.

TRADE/PROFESSIONAL ASSOCIATIONS

American Immigration Lawyers Association. 1331 G St. NW, Ste. 300, Washington, DC 20005-3142. Phone: (202)216-2400 or (202)507-7600; Fax: (202)783-7853; Email: executive@aila.org • URL: http://www.aila.org • Lawyers specializing in the field of immigration and nationality law. Fosters and promotes the administration of justice with particular reference to the immigration and nationality laws of the United States.

National Immigration Forum. 50 F St. NW, Ste. 300, Washington, DC 20001-1552. Phone: (202)347-0040; Fax: (202)347-0058 or (202)544-0004; Email: info@immigrationforum.org • URL: http://www.immigrationforum.org • Dedicated to extending and defending America's tradition as a nation of immigrants. Supports the reunification of families, the rescue and resettlement of refugees fleeing persecution, and the equitable treatment of immigrants under the law. Encourages immigrants to become U.S. citizens and promote cooperation and understanding between immigrants and other Americans.

IMPORT TRADE

See EXPORT-IMPORT TRADE

INCANDESCENT LAMPS

See LIGHTING

INCENTIVE MERCHANDISING

See PREMIUMS

INCOME

ALMANACS AND YEARBOOKS

National Accounts Statistics: Main Aggregates and Detailed Tables. United Nations Publications. • Annual.

CD-ROM DATABASES

OECD Statistical Compendium. Organization for Economic Cooperation and Development. • Semiannual. $1,905.00 per year for 1 to 10 users. CD-ROM contains more than 730,000 monthly, quarterly, and annual time series for OECD countries, 1960 to date. Includes fully searchable data on agriculture, food, economic indicators, national accounts, employment, energy, finance, industry, technology, and foreign trade. Results can be displayed in various forms.

Sourcebooks America CD-ROM. CACI Marketing Systems. • Annual. $1,250.00. Provides the CD-ROM version of *The Sourcebook of ZIP Code Demographics: Census Edition* and *The Sourcebook of County Demographics: Census Edition.*

INTERNET DATABASES

Bureau of Economic Analysis. U. S. Department of Commerce, Bureau of Economic Analysis. Phone: (202)606-9900; Fax: (202)606-5310; Email: webmaster@bea.doc.gov • URL: http://www.bea.doc.gov • Web site includes "News Release Information" covering national, regional, and international economic estimates from the BEA. Highlights of releases appear online the same day, complete text and tables appear the next day. "Recent News Releases" section provides titles for past nine months, with links. "BEA Data and Methodology" includes "Frequently Requested NIPA Data" (national income and product accounts, such as gross domestic product and personal income). Other statistics are available. Fees: Free.

Business 2.0 Web Guide to the Best Business Links. Business 2.0 Media Inc. Phone: (415)293-4800; Email: support@business2.com • URL: http://www.business2.com/webguide • Web site presents an extensive, searchable directory of links to "the best, most informative, and authoritative web pages." Twenty main categories cover business, finance, career, company information, people, and technology topics, with thousands of subtopics, all linking to Web sites recommended by experienced business researchers. Fees: Free.

Fedstats. Federal Interagency Council on Statistical Policy. Phone: (202)395-7254 • URL: http://www.fedstats.gov • Web site features an efficient search facility for full-text statistics produced by more than 100 federal agencies, including the Census Bureau, the Bureau of Economic Analysis, and the Bureau of Labor Statistics. Boolean searches can be made within one agency or for all agencies combined. Links are offered to international statistical bureaus, including the UN, IMF, OECD, UNESCO, Eurostat, and 20 individual countries. Fees: Free.

FreeLunch.com. Economy.com, Inc. Phone: (610)696-8700; Fax: (610)696-1678 • URL: http://www.freelunch.com • Web site provides free access to more than 200 million economic and financial data series, covering industry, demographics, labor markets, prices, retail sales, government spending, trade, interest rates, housing starts, the stock market, etc. Data is available in either chart or table form. Searching is offered. Free, but registration required. Economy.com, Inc. also offers fee-based economic analysis at *The Dismal Scientist* site (www.dismal.com).

PERIODICALS AND NEWSLETTERS

Review of Income and Wealth. John Wiley & Sons Inc. Wiley-Blackwell. • Quarterly. $326 Institutions print & online. Association journal covering research on national and economic and social accounting as related to the measurement and analysis of income and wealth.

Review of Social Economy. Association for Social Economics. Taylor & Francis Ltd. • Quarterly. $152 Individuals Print and Online. Quarterly. Subject matter is concerned with the relationships between social values and economics. Includes articles on income distribution, poverty, labor, and class.

RESEARCH CENTERS AND INSTITUTES

Boston College - Institute for Scientific Research. St. Clement's Hall, 400A, 140 Commonwealth Ave., Chestnut Hill, MA 02467. Phone: (617)552-8767; Fax: (617)552-4328; Email: patricia.doherty@bc.edu • URL: http://www.bc.edu/research/isr • Development and use of analysis tools to explain various physical phenomena in the areas of earth and space sciences, the environment, finance and economics.

Columbia University - Center for the Study of Wealth and Inequality. International Affairs Bldg., 420 W 118th St., MC 3355, New York, NY 10027. Phone: (212)854-4273; Fax: (212)854-8925; Email: ss50@columbia.edu • URL: http://iserp.columbia.edu/content/center-wealth-and-inequality • Income and wealth, along with exploring the dimensions of societal inequality in these household resources. The center's interests encompass issues of poverty, labor market behavior, public transfer programs and tax policy, in that each has a clear relevance to economic inequality, family resources, and to living standards.

STATISTICS SOURCES

Statistics of Income Bulletin. U. S. Government Printing Office. • Quarterly. $44. Current data compiled from tax returns relating to income, assets, and expenses of individuals and businesses. (U. S. Internal Revenue Service.).

Statistics of Income: Corporation Income Tax Returns. U.S. Internal Revenue Service. U. S. Government Printing Office. • Annual.

Survey of Current Business. U. S. Government Printing Office. • Published by Bureau of Economic Analysis, U. S. Department of Commerce. Presents a wide variety of business and economic data.

INCOME TAX

See also CORPORATE INCOME TAX; STATE TAXES; TAX PLANNING; TAX SHELTERS; TAXATION

ABSTRACTS AND INDEXES

Accounting and Tax Index. ProQuest L.L.C. • Quarterly. Indexes accounting, auditing, and taxation literature appearing in journals, books, pamphlets, conference proceedings, and newsletters.

ALMANACS AND YEARBOOKS

Tax Year in Review. Wolters Kluwer Law & Business CCH. • Annual. Covers the year's "major new legislative and regulatory changes.".

CD-ROM DATABASES

Authority Tax and Estate Planning Library. Matthew Bender and Company Inc. • Periodic revisions. Price on request. CD contains updated full text of *Bender's Payroll Tax Guide, Depreciation Handbook, Federal Income Taxation of Corporations, Tax Planning for Corporations, Modern Estate Planning, Planning for Large Estates, Murphy's Will Clauses, Tax & Estate Planning for the Elderly*, and 12 other Matthew Bender publications. The Internal Revenue Code is also included.

Business Abstracts with Full Text. EBSCO Publishing Inc. • Includes full text articles from more than 460 business publications from 1982 to present. Indexing for nearly 880 publications.

Federal Tax Products. U. S. Government Printing Office. • Annual. $27.00. CD-ROM issued by the Internal Revenue Service (www.irs.treas.gov/forms_pubs/). Provides current tax forms, instructions, and publications. Also includes older tax forms beginning with 1991.

OECD Statistical Compendium. Organization for Economic Cooperation and Development. • Semiannual. $1,905.00 per year for 1 to 10 users. CD-ROM contains more than 730,000 monthly, quarterly, and annual time series for OECD countries, 1960 to date. Includes fully searchable data on agriculture, food, economic indicators, national accounts, employment, energy, finance, industry, technology, and foreign trade. Results can be displayed in various forms.

The Tax Directory. Tax Analysts. • Quarterly. $499 Individuals both volumes, web, CD or print. Updated quarterly on CD-ROM and in print; updated continually online. Covering federal, state, and international tax officials, tax practitioners, and corporate tax executives.

U.S. Master Tax Guide. Wolters Kluwer Law & Business CCH. • Annual. $93.50.

DIRECTORIES

Income Tax Service Directory. InfoGroup Inc. • Annual. Number of listings: 63,898. Entries include: Name, address, phone, size of advertisement, name of owner or manager, number of employees, year first in "Yellow Pages." Compiled from telephone company "Yellow Pages," nationwide.

The Tax Directory. Tax Analysts. • Quarterly. $499 Individuals both volumes, web, CD or print. Updated quarterly on CD-ROM and in print; updated continually online. Covering federal, state, and international tax officials, tax practitioners, and corporate tax executives.

U.S. Income Tax Treaties with Foreign Countries Handbook. International Business Publications, USA. • $99.95 Individuals hardcopy, E-book and CD-ROM. Covers: US income tax treaties with Australia, Austria, Barbados, Belgium, Canada, China, Cyprus, Czech Republic, Denmark, Denmark, Egypt, Estonia, and Finland.

ENCYCLOPEDIAS AND DICTIONARIES

Dictionary of 1040 Deductions. Matthew Bender and Company Inc. • Annual. $131.00. Organized by schedule and supported by thousands of citations. Designed to quickly answer all questions about deductions.

HANDBOOKS AND MANUALS

Business Taxpayer Information Publications. U. S. Government Printing Office. • Annual. $66 U.S. Looseleaf. Two volumes, consisting of *Circular E, Employer's Tax Guide* and *Employer's Supplemental Tax Guide*. Issued by the Internal Revenue Service (http://www.irs.ustreas.gov). Includes a variety of business-related tax information, including withholding tables, tax calendars, self-employment issues, partnership matters, corporation topics, depreciation, and bankruptcy.

CCH Analysis of Top Tax Issues. Wolters Kluwer Law & Business CCH. • Annual. $49.00. Covers yearly tax changes affecting business and personal transactions, planning, and returns.

CCH Guide to Car, Travel, Entertainment, and Home Office Deductions. Wolters Kluwer Law & Business CCH. • Annual. Explains how to claim maximum tax deductions for common business expenses. Includes automobile depreciation tables, lease value tables, worksheets, and examples of filled-in tax forms.

Essentials of Federal Income Taxation for Individuals and Business. Wolters Kluwer Law & Business CCH. • Annual. $165. Covers basic tax planning and tax reduction strategies as affected by tax law changes and IRS interpretations. Includes sample filled-in forms.

Federal Withholding Tax Tables. Wolters Kluwer Law & Business CCH. • Annual. $18.00.

Tax Guide for Small Business. U.S. Department of the Treasury, Internal Revenue Service. U. S. Government Printing Office. • Annual. $11 Individuals USA List price. Contains tax information for small business owners.

Tax Preparation Service. Entrepreneur Press. • Looseleaf. $59.50. A practical guide to starting a business for the preparation of income tax returns. Covers profit potential, start-up costs, market size evaluation, owner's time required, site selection, lease negotiation, pricing, accounting, advertising, promotion, etc. (Start-Up Business Guide No. E2332.).

U.S. Master Tax Guide. Wolters Kluwer Law & Business CCH. • Annual. $93.50.

Your Federal Income Tax. U.S. Department of the Treasury, Internal Revenue Service. U. S. Government Printing Office. • Annual. $23 U.S.. Layman's guide to income tax preparation.

INTERNET DATABASES

Business 2.0 Web Guide to the Best Business Links. Business 2.0 Media Inc. Phone: (415)293-4800; Email: support@business2.com • URL: http://www.business2.com/webguide • Web site presents an extensive, searchable directory of links to "the best, most informative, and authoritative web pages." Twenty main categories cover business, finance, career, company information, people, and technology topics, with thousands of subtopics, all linking to Web sites recommended by experienced business researchers. Fees: Free.

CCH Essentials: An Internet Tax Research and Primary Source Library. CCH, Inc. Phone: 800-248-3248 or (773)866-6000; Fax: (773)866-3608 or (800)224-8299; Email: cust_serv@cch.com • URL: http://tax.cch.com/essentials • Fee-based Web site provides full-text coverage of federal tax law and regulations, including rulings, procedures, tax court decisions, and IRS publications, announcements, notices, and penalties. Includes explanation, analysis, tax planning guides, and a daily tax news service. Searching is offered, including citation search.

Court Filings. ProQuest LLC. 2250 Perimeter Park Dr., Ste. 300, Morrisville, NC 27560. Phone: 800-334-2564 or (919)804-6400; Fax: (919)804-6410; Email: contact@dialog.com • URL: http://www.dialog.com • The three main sections of Tax Analysts home page are "Tax News" (Today's Tax News, Feature of the Week, Tax Snapshots, Tax Calendar); "Products & Services" (Product Catalog, Press Releases); and "Public Interest" (Discussion Groups, Tax Clinic, Tax History Project). Fees: Free for coverage of current tax events; fee-based for comprehensive information. Daily updating.

Factiva. Dow Jones Reuters Business Interactive, LLC. Phone: 800-369-7466 or (609)452-1511; Fax: (609)520-5770; Email: solutions@factiva.com • URL: http://www.factiva.com • Fee-based Web site provides "global news and business information through Web sites and content integration solutions." Includes Dow Jones and Reuters newswires, The Wall Street Journal, and more than 7,000 other sources of current news, historical articles, market research reports, and investment analysis. Content includes 96 major U. S. newspapers, 900 non-English sources, trade publications, media transcripts, country profiles, news photos, etc.

Fedstats. Federal Interagency Council on Statistical Policy. Phone: (202)395-7254 • URL: http://www.fedstats.gov • Web site features an efficient search facility for full-text statistics produced by more than 100 federal agencies, including the Census Bureau, the Bureau of Economic Analysis, and the Bureau of Labor Statistics. Boolean searches can be made within one agency or for all agencies combined. Links are offered to international statistical bureaus, including the UN, IMF, OECD, UNESCO, Eurostat, and 20 individual countries. Fees: Free.

FedWorld: A Program of the United States Department of Commerce. National Technical Information Service. Phone: 800-553-NTIS or (703)605-6000; Fax: (703)605-6900; Email: webmaster@fedworld.gov • URL: http://www.fedworld.gov • Web site offers "a comprehensive central access point for searching, locating, ordering, and acquiring government and business information." Emphasis is on searching the Web pages, databases, and government reports of a wide variety of federal agencies. Fees: Free.

FirstGov: Your First Click to the U. S. Government. General Services Administration. Phone: 800-333-4636 or (202)501-0705; Email: public.affairs@gsa.gov • URL: http://www.gsa.gov • Free Web site provides extensive links to federal agencies covering a wide variety of topics, such as agriculture, business, consumer safety, education, the environment, government jobs, grants, health, social security, statistics sources, taxes, technology, travel, and world affairs. Also provides links to federal forms, including IRS tax forms. Searching is offered, both keyword and advanced.

FreeLunch.com. Economy.com, Inc. Phone: (610)696-8700; Fax: (610)696-1678 • URL: http://www.freelunch.com • Web site provides free access to more than 200 million economic and financial data series, covering industry, demographics, labor markets, prices, retail sales, government spending, trade, interest rates, housing starts, the stock market, etc. Data is available in either chart or table form. Searching is offered. Free, but registration required. Economy.com, Inc. also offers fee-based economic analysis at *The Dismal Scientist* site (www.dismal.com).

Internal Revenue Service IRS.gov. Internal Revenue Service. Phone: 800-829-1040 or (202)622-5000; Fax: (202)622-5844 • URL: http://www.irs.gov • Web site provides a wide variety of tax information, including IRS forms and publications. Searching is available. Fees: Free.

Nexis.com. Lexis-Nexis Group. Phone: 800-227-4908 or (937)865-6800; Fax: (937)865-6909; Email: webmaster@prod.lexis-nexis.com • URL: http://www.nexis.com • Fee-based Web site offers searching of about 2.8 billion documents in some 30,000 news, business, and legal information sources. Features include a subject directory covering 1,200 topics in 34 categories and a Company Dossier containing information on more than 500,000 public and private companies. Boolean searching is offered.

Rutgers Accounting Web. Rutgers University Accounting Research Center. Phone: (973)353-5172; Fax: (973)353-1283 • URL: http://www.rutgers.edu/accounting • RAW Web site provides extensive links to sources of national and international accounting information, such as the Big Six accounting firms, the Financial Accounting Standards Board (FASB), SEC filings (EDGAR), journals, publishers, software, the International Accounting Network, and "Internet's largest list of accounting firms in USA." Searching is offered. Fees: Free.

ONLINE DATABASES

Accounting and Tax Database. ProQuest L.L.C. • Provides indexing and abstracting of the literature of accounting, taxation, and financial management, 1971 to date. Updating is weekly. Especially covers accounting, auditing, banking, bankruptcy, employee compensation and benefits, cash management, financial planning, and credit. Inquire as to online cost and availability.

Wilson Business Abstracts Online. H.W. Wilson Co. • Indexes and abstracts 600 major business periodicals, plus the *Wall Street Journal* and the business section of the *New York Times*. Indexing is from 1982, abstracting from 1990, with the two newspapers included from 1993. Updated weekly. Inquire as to online cost and availability. (*Business Periodicals Index* without abstracts is also available online.).

OTHER SOURCES

Federal Taxes: Internal Memoranda of the IRS. Prentice Hall PTR. • Looseleaf. Periodic supplementation. Price on application.

Internal Revenue Manual: Audit and Administration. Wolters Kluwer Law & Business CCH. • Irregular. $1,254.00. Six looseleaf volumes. Reproduces IRS tax administration provisions and procedures.

IRS Publications. Wolters Kluwer Law & Business CCH. • Irregular. $352.00. Three looseleaf volumes. Periodic supplementation. Photographic reproductions of current Internal Revenue Service tax publications intended for public use.

Reproducible Copies of Federal Tax Forms and Instructions. U. S. Government Printing Office. • Annual. $64 U.S. Looseleaf. Two looseleaf volumes issued by the Internal Revenue Service (www.irs.gov). "Contains the most frequently requested tax forms and instructions," prepared especially for libraries.

PERIODICALS AND NEWSLETTERS

Highlights and Documents. Tax Analysts. • Daily. $2,599.95 Individuals. Provides daily coverage of IRS, congressional, judicial, state, and international tax developments. Includes abstracts and citations for "all tax documents released within the previous 24 to 48 hours." Annual compilation available *Highlights and Documents on Microfiche*.

Internal Revenue Bulletin. Thomson RIA. • Weekly. Description: Presents new treasury and IRS releases in full official text. Contains rulings and decisions, releases on treaties, tax legislation, administrative and procedural releases, disbarment and suspensions.

Internal Revenue Cumulative Bulletin. U. S. Government Printing Office. • Semiannual. Issued by the Internal Revenue Service. Cumulates all items of a "permanent nature" appearing in the weekly *Internal Revenue Bulletin*.

State Income Tax Alert. State Taxation Institute. • Description: Features updates on state income tax issues. Recurring features include a calendar of events, book reviews, and news of educational opportunities.

Tax Notes: The Weekly Tax Service. Tax Analysts. • Weekly. Weekly. $1,699.00 per year. Includes an *Annual* and compilations of previous years. Newsletter. Covers "tax news from all federal sources," including congressional committees, tax courts, and the Internal Revenue Service. Each issue contains "summaries of every document that pertains to federal tax law," with citations. Commentary is provided.

Tax Practice. Tax Analysts. • Weekly. $199.00 per year. Newsletter. Covers news affecting tax practitioners and litigators, with emphasis on federal court decisions, rules and regulations, and tax petitions. Provides a guide to Internal Revenue Service audit issues.

RESEARCH CENTERS AND INSTITUTES

University of Michigan - Stephen M. Ross School of Business - Office of Tax Policy Research. 701 Tappan St., Rm. R5380, Ann Arbor, MI 48109-1234. Phone: (734)763-3068; Fax: (734)763-4032; Email: jslemrod@umich.edu • URL: http://www.bus.umich.edu/OTPR/ • Tax policy, including compliance, capital gains, reform, international taxation, and income dynamics.

STATISTICS SOURCES

Statistics of Income: Corporation Income Tax Returns. U.S. Internal Revenue Service. U. S. Government Printing Office. • Annual.

Survey of Current Business. U. S. Government Printing Office. • Published by Bureau of Economic Analysis, U. S. Department of Commerce. Presents a wide variety of business and economic data.

TRADE/PROFESSIONAL ASSOCIATIONS

National Taxpayers Union. 108 N Alfred St., Alexandria, VA 22314-3053. Phone: (703)683-5700; Fax: (703)683-5722; Email: ntu@ntu.org • URL: http://www.ntu.org • Seeks to: reduce government spending; cut taxes; protect the rights of taxpayers. Claims to have helped generate federal budget cuts of over 120 billion dollars. Activities include research programs and an intense lobbying campaign in Washington, DC; has been a leader in the fights against government ventures such as: social security tax; guaranteed income; congressional and bureaucratic pay raises; federal subsidies; foreign aid; national health insurance. Works for a balanced federal budget/tax limitation constitutional amendment; federal pension reform; reduction of capital gains and personal income tax; social security reform. Has worked for airline deregulation; indexing of federal income tax, California's Proposition 13, Massachusetts Proposition 2 1/2, and other state tax cutting initiatives. Conducts annual voting study of congressmen and senators, rating their votes on spending and tax issues and presenting awards for best and worst records.

INCOME TAX, STATE

See STATE TAXES

INCORPORATION

See also CORPORATION LAW AND REGULATION

ABSTRACTS AND INDEXES

Business Periodicals Index Retrospective. EBSCO Publishing Inc. • 11/year. Quarterly and annual cumulations.

Current Law Index. Cengage Learning Inc. • $1,332 Individuals. Monthly. $1269.00 per year. Produced in cooperation with the American Association of Law Libraries. Indexes more than 900 law journals, legal newspapers, and specialty publications from the U.S., Canada, U.K., Ireland, Australia, and New Zealand.

Index to Legal Periodicals and Books. H.W. Wilson Co. • Monthly. $490.00 per year. Quarterly and annual cumulations.

ALMANACS AND YEARBOOKS

American Law Yearbook. Cengage Learning Inc. • $308 Individuals. Annual. $280.00. Serves as a yearly supplement to *West's Encyclopedia of American Lawa*. Describes new legal developments in many subject areas.

CD-ROM DATABASES

Business Abstracts with Full Text. EBSCO Publishing Inc. • Includes full text articles from more than 460 business publications from 1982 to present. Indexing for nearly 880 publications.

Index to Legal Periodicals and Books. EBSCO Publishing Inc. • Contains indexing of more than 1,400 English language legal periodicals from 1981 to date and 2,500 books.

DIRECTORIES

Directory of Incorporated (Registered) Companies in Nigeria. ICIC Ltd. • Biennial. $50. Covers: Companies from 1912 to present in Nigeria. Entries include: Company name, address.

ENCYCLOPEDIAS AND DICTIONARIES

West's Encyclopedia of American Law. Cengage Learning Inc. • 2004. eBook. Second edition. Covers a wide variety of legal topics for the general reader. Inquire for pricing.

INTERNET DATABASES

Lexis.com Research System. Lexis-Nexis Group. Phone: 800-227-4908 or (937)865-6800; Fax: (937)865-6909; Email: webmaster@prod.lexis-nexis.com • URL: http://www.nexis.com • Fee-based Web site offers extensive searching of a wide variety of legal sources. Additional features include Daily Opinion Service, lexis.com Bookstore, Career Center, CLE Center, Law Schools, and Practice Pages ("Pages specific to areas of specialty").

ONLINE DATABASES

Wilson Business Abstracts Online. H.W. Wilson Co. • Indexes and abstracts 600 major business periodicals, plus the *Wall Street Journal* and the business section of the *New York Times*. Indexing is from 1982, abstracting from 1990, with the two newspapers included from 1993. Updated weekly. Inquire as to online cost and availability. (*Business Periodicals Index* without abstracts is also available online.).

OTHER SOURCES

Formation and Financing of Emerging Companies. Daniel E. O'Connor and others. Glasser LegalWorks. • $499 Individuals Binder/Looseleaf (Full set). Periodic Supplementation. Covers incorporation, bylaws, indemnification, intellectual property, financing sources, venture capital, due diligence, bridge loans, investor rights, compliance, and other legal issues associated with company formation. (Emerging Growth Companies Series.).

Start-Up and Emerging Companies: Planning, Financing, and Operating the Successful Business, with Forms on Disk. ALM Media Properties LLC. • $925 print + online + ebook. Covers a wide variety of business and legal topics relating to new enterprises. Provides information on venture financing, formation of corporations, tax laws, limited liability companies, employee benefits, contracts, and accounting. Includes a CD-ROM containing more than 75 sample legal forms, clauses, agreements, organizational resolutions, and checklists. (Law Journal Press).

INDEPENDENT SCHOOLS

See PRIVATE SCHOOLS

INDEX TRADING

See STOCK INDEX TRADING

INDEXING

CD-ROM DATABASES

LISA Plus. Cambridge Scientific Abstracts L.P. • Quarterly. $2,000 per year. CD-ROM version of Library Information and Science Abstracts, providing abstracting and indexing of the world's library and information science literature, 1969 to date. Contains more than 180,000 citations.

DIRECTORIES

Indexer Locator. American Society for Indexing. • Annual. Lists over 200 free-lance indexers in the U. S. and their subject specialties. Formerly *Register of Indexers*.

PERIODICALS AND NEWSLETTERS

The Indexer: The International Journal of Indexing. American Society for Indexing. • Semiannual. Free to members; non-members, $65.00 per year. Devoted specifically to all aspects of indexing.

Keywords. SPSS Inc. • Monthly. $40 Individuals non-members. Description: Intended for users of SPSS, Inc. computer software. Offers advice and technical information on using SPSS products and carries data on new products. Recurring features include training schedules and publications ordering information.

TRADE/PROFESSIONAL ASSOCIATIONS

American Society for Indexing. 1628 E Southern Ave., No. 9-223, Tempe, AZ 85282. Phone:

(480)245-6750; Email: info@asindexing.org • URL: http://www.asindexing.org • Affiliated with the American Library Association, the American Society for Information Science, and other organizations.

National Federation of Advanced Information Services, c/o Jill O'Neill, Director, 1518 Walnut St., Ste. 1004, Philadelphia, PA 19102-3403. Phone: (215)893-1561; Fax: (215)893-1564 • URL: http://nfais.org • Formerly National Federation of Abstracting and Indexing Services.

INDICATORS, ECONOMIC

See ECONOMIC INDICATORS

INDIVIDUAL RETIREMENT ACCOUNTS

HANDBOOKS AND MANUALS

U.S. Master Pension Guide. Wolters Kluwer Law & Business CCH. • Annual. $99.95 1 - 4 (quantity). Explains IRS rules and regulations applying to 401(k) plans, 403(k) plans, ESOPs (employee stock ownership plans), IRAs, SEPs (simplified employee pension plans), Keogh plans, and nonqualified plans.

INTERNET DATABASES

Internal Revenue Service IRS.gov. Internal Revenue Service. Phone: 800-829-1040 or (202)622-5000; Fax: (202)622-5844 • URL: http://www.irs.gov • Web site provides a wide variety of tax information, including IRS forms and publications. Searching is available. Fees: Free.

Small Business Retirement Savings Advisor. U. S. Department of Labor. Phone: (202)219-8921 • URL: http://www.dol.gov/elaws/pwbaplan.htm • Web site provides "answers to a variety of commonly asked questions about retirement saving options for small business employers." Includes a comparison chart and detailed descriptions of various plans: 401(k), SEP-IRA, SIMPLE-IRA, Payroll Deduction IRA, Keogh Profit-Sharing, Keogh Money Purchase, and Defined Benefit. Searching is offered. Fees: Free.

PERIODICALS AND NEWSLETTERS

Financial Planning: The Magazine for Financial Service Professionals. SourceMedia Inc. • Monthly. $79.00 per year. Edited for independent financial planners and insurance agents. Covers retirement planning, estate planning, tax planning, and insurance, including long-term healthcare considerations. Special features include a Retirement Planning Issue, Mutual Fund Performance Survey, and Variable Life and Annuity Survey.

The IRA Reporter. Universal Pensions Inc. • Monthly. $115.00 per year. Newsletter. Edited for financial planners. Provides information on the rules and regulations of individual retirement accounts (IRAs).

On Wall Street. SourceMedia Inc. • Monthly. $96.00 per year. Edited for securities dealers. Includes articles on financial planning, retirement planning, variable annuities, and money management, with special coverage of 401(k) plans and IRAs.

Retirement Plans Bulletin: Practical Explanations for the IRA and Retirement Plan Professional. Universal Pensions Inc. • Monthly. $99.00 per year. Newsletter. Provides information on the rules and regulations governing qualified (tax-deferred) retirement plans.

INDUSTRIAL ADVERTISING

See also ADVERTISING; INDUSTRIAL MARKETING

CD-ROM DATABASES

Advertiser and Agency Red Books Plus. National Register Publishing Co. • Quarterly. $1,295.00 per year. The CD-ROM version of *Standard Directory of Advertisers, Standard Directory of Advertising Agencies,* and *Standard Directory of International Advertisers and Agencies.*

PERIODICALS AND NEWSLETTERS

Adweek Magazines' Technology Marketing. Nielsen Business Media Inc. • Monthly. $55.00 per year. Edited for marketing executives in high technology industries. Covers both advertising and marketing. Formerly *MC Technology Marketing Intelligence.*

B to B: The Magazine for Marketing and E-Commerce Strategists. Crain Communications Inc. • Monthly. $59.00 per year. Formerly *Advertising Age's Business Marketing.*

TRADE/PROFESSIONAL ASSOCIATIONS

Association of National Advertisers. 708 3rd Ave., 33rd Fl., New York, NY 10017. Phone: (212)697-5950; Fax: (212)687-7310 • URL: http://www.ana.net • Serves the needs of members by providing marketing and advertising industry leadership in traditional and e-marketing, legislative leadership, information resources, professional development and industry-wide networking. Maintains offices in New York City and Washington, DC.

INDUSTRIAL COATINGS

See also CORROSION CONTROL INDUSTRY; PAINT AND PAINTING

ABSTRACTS AND INDEXES

Applied Science and Technology Index. EBSCO Publishing Inc. • 11/year. Indexes a wide variety of English language technical, industrial, and engineering periodicals.

Corrosion Abstracts: Abstracts of the World's Literature on Corrosion and Corrosion Mitigation. National Association of Corrosion Engineers. CSA. • Monthly. $240 Individuals per year. Includes print and online editions. Provides abstracts of the worldwide literature of corrosion and corrosion control. Also available on CD-ROM.

CPI Digest: Key to World Literature Serving the Coatings, Plastics, Fibers, Adhesives, and Related Industries. CPI Information Services. • Monthly. $397.00 per year. Abstracts of business and technical articles for polymer-based, chemical process industries. Includes a monthly list of relevant U. S. patents. International coverage.

Current Contents: Engineering, Computing and Technology. Thomson Reuters Intellectual Property and Science. • Weekly. $730 per year. Reproductions of contents pages of technical journals. Includes *Author Index, Address Directory, Current Book Contents,* and *Title Word Index.* Formerly *Current Contents: Engineering, Technology and Applied Sciences.*

NTIS Alerts: Materials Sciences. U.S. Department of Commerce National Technical Information Service. • Biweekly. $130 per year. Covers ceramics, glass, coatings, composite materials, alloys, plastics, wood, paper, adhesives, fibers, lubricants, and related subjects.

DIRECTORIES

Industrial Paint and Powder Buyer's Guide. Business News Publishing. • Annual. Free to qualified personnel; others, $15.00. List of about 2,000 manufacturers of finishing and formulating products. Formerly *Industrial Finishing Buyer's Guide.*

McCutcheon's Functional Materials Volumes 2. Manufacturing Confectioner Publishing Corp. • Edited for product development, quality control and research and development chemists.

Paint & Coatings Buyers Guide. American Coatings Association. • $150. About 7,500 chemists, technicians, and supervisory production personnel in the decorative and protective coatings industry who are members of the 27 constituent societies of the federation.

ONLINE DATABASES

Applied Science and Technology Index Online. H.W. Wilson Co. • Provides online indexing of 500 major scientific, technical, industrial, and engineering periodicals. Time period is 1983 to date. Monthly updates. Inquire as to online cost and availability.

Thomas Register Online. Thomas Publishing Company L.L.C. • Provides concise information on approximately 194,000 U. S. companies, mainly manufacturers, with over 50,000 product classifications. Indexes over 115,000 trade names. Information is updated semiannually. Inquire as to online cost and availability.

World Surface Coatings Abstracts (Online). Paint Research Association of Great Britain. • Indexing and abstracting of the literature of paint and surface coatings, 1976 to present. Monthly updates. Inquire as to online cost and availability.

PERIODICALS AND NEWSLETTERS

Advanced Coatings and Surface Technology. Technical Insights. • Monthly. $650 Institutions. Newsletter on technical developments relating to industrial coatings.

Corrosion: Journal of Science and Engineering. National Association of Corrosion Engineers. NACE International: The Corrosion Society. • Monthly. Individuals. $160.00 per year; institutions, $290.00 per year. Covers corrosion control science, theory, engineering, and practice.

Industrial Equipment News. Thomas Publishing Company L.L.C. • Monthly. Contains new product information for manufacturing industries.

Industrial Paint and Powder: Coatings Manufacturing and Application. Reed Elsevier Group plc Reed Business Information. • Monthly. $72.90 per year. Supplement available, *Annual Buyer's Guide.* Formerly *Industrial Finishing.*

JCT: Journal of Coatings Technology. American Coatings Association. • 6/year. A forum for the exchange of research, experience, knowledge and ideas among those with a professional interest in the science, technology and manufacture of functional, protective and decorative coatings including paints, inks and related coatings and their raw materials, and similar topics.

Materials Performance: Articles on Corrosion Science and Engineering Solutions for Corrosion Problems. National Association of Corrosion Engineers. NACE International: The Corrosion Society. • Monthly. $115 Nonmembers 1-year subscription. Covers the protection and performance of materials in corrosive environments. Includes information on new materials and industrial coatings.

Modern Paint and Coatings. Chemical Week Associates. • Monthly. $52.00 per year. A comprehensive publication highlighting formulators and suppliers to the Paint, Coatings and Ink Industry.

New Equipment Digest. Intertec Publishing. • Monthly. Magazine (tabloid) showcasing new or improved equipment, products, materials, and components. Formerly *Material Handling Engineering.*

New Equipment Reporter: New Products Industrial News. DeRoche Publications. • Monthly. Controlled circulation.

Paint and Coatings Industry. BNP Media. • Monthly. Free to members, non-members, $55.00 per year. Includes annual *Raw Material and Equipment Directory and Buyers Guide.*

RESEARCH CENTERS AND INSTITUTES

Emulsion Polymers Institute. Lehigh University, Iacocca Hall, Rm. D-325, 111 Research Dr., Bethlehem, PA 18015. Phone: (610)758-3602; Fax: (610)758-5880; Email: eric.daniels@lehigh.edu • URL: http://www.lehigh.edu/inemuls/epi/ • Includes latex paint research.

International Coatings and Formulation Institute. University of Southern Mississippi, School of Polymers and High Performance Materials, Hattiesburg, MS 39406-0037. Phone: (601)266-4781; Fax: (601)266-5880; Email: shelby.f.thames@usm.edu • URL: http://www.psrc.usm.edu/icfi.

Ohio State University - Fontana Corrosion Center. 477 Watts Hall, 2041 College Rd., Columbus, OH 43210. Phone: (614)292-9857; Fax: (614)292-9857; Email: frankel.10@osu.edu • URL: http://www.matsceng.ohio-state.edu/frankel/FCC • Research areas include metal coatings and corrosion of alloys.

STATISTICS SOURCES

Paint, Varnish, and Lacquer. U. S. Bureau of the Census. • Quarterly and annual. Provides data on shipments: value, quantity, imports, and exports. Includes paint, varnish, lacquer, product finishes, and special purpose coatings. (Current Industrial Reports, MQ-28F.).

U.S. Industry and Trade Outlook. U.S. Department of Commerce National Technical Information Service. • Annual. Produced by the International Trade Administration, U.S. Department of Commerce, in a "public-private" partnership with DRI/McGraw-Hill and Standard & Poor's. Provides basic data, outlook for the current year, and "Long-Term Prospects" (five-year projections) for a wide variety of products and services. Includes high technology industries. Formerly *U.S. Industrial Outlook*.

TRADE/PROFESSIONAL ASSOCIATIONS

American Coatings Association. 1500 Rhode Island Ave. NW, Washington, DC 20005. Phone: (202)462-6272; Fax: (202)462-8549 • URL: http://www.paint.org • Formerly National Paint and Coatings Association.

Association of Industrial Metallizers, Coaters and Laminators. 201 Springs St., Fort Mill, SC 29715. Phone: (803)948-9470; Fax: (803)948-9471; Email: aimcal@aimcal.org • URL: http://www.aimcal.org • Metallizers, coaters, and laminators; producers of metallized film and/or paper on continuous rolls; manufacturers of metallizing, coating, and laminating equipment; suppliers of plastic films, papers, and adhesives. The end uses of the product are films and papers, solar control films, reflective insulation, decorative films and papers, and packaging. Monitors related legislative activities; reports on current industry developments. Conducts technical seminars.

Chemical Coaters Association International. 5040 Old Taylor Mill Rd., Taylor Mill, KY 41015. Phone: (859)356-1030; Fax: (859)356-0908 • URL: http://www.ccaiweb.com • Industrial users of organic finishing systems; suppliers of chemicals, equipment, and paints. Works toward the improvement of decorative, functional, and performance standards of chemical coatings. Encourages members to continue improvements in application technology. Provides coating industry with representation to public authorities and government agencies. Sponsors research and educational programs to control environmental pollution. Maintains placement service. Provides speaker's bureau.

NACE International: The Corrosion Society. 1440 S Creek Dr., Houston, TX 77084-4906. Phone: 800-797-6223 or (281)228-6200 or (281)228-6223; Fax: (281)228-6300; Email: firstservice@nace.org • URL: http://www.nace.org • Serves as professional technical society dedicated to reducing the economic impact of corrosion, promoting public safety, and protecting the environment by advancing the knowledge of corrosion engineering and science. Conducts programs for technical training, sponsors technical conferences, and produces standards, publications, and software. Maintains certification program for engineers, technicians, and coating inspectors.

National Association for Surface Finishing. 1155 15th St. NW, Ste. 500, Washington, DC 20005. Phone: (202)457-8404 or (703)887-7235; Fax: (202)530-0659; Email: passante@nasf.org • URL: http://www.nasf.org • Members are management personnel of metal and plastic finishing companies. Finishing includes plating, coating, polishing, rustproofing, and other processes.

Powder Coating Institute. PO Box 2112, The Woodlands, TX 77380. Phone: 800-988-COAT or (936)597-5060; Fax: (936)597-5059; Email: pci-info@powdercoating.org • URL: http://www.powdercoating.org • Individuals and businesses that manufacture, sell, or develop powder coating materials and equipment. Promotes the application and use of powder coating technology among industrial finishers; disseminates information to both consumers and the industry on the value and performance of powder coating; supports educational programs in the industrial coating/finishing field; updates members, governmental departments, and regulatory agencies on the activities and developments concerning the manufacture, application, and proper handling of powder coatings. Presents technical papers at conferences of related organizations and prepares articles for the media on the powder coating industry.

Society of Manufacturing Engineers. One SME Dr., Dearborn, MI 48121. Phone: 800-733-4763 or (313)425-3000; Fax: (313)425-3400; Email: service@sme.org • URL: http://www.sme.org • Professional society of manufacturing engineers, practitioners and management executives concerned with manufacturing technologies for improved productivity. Seeks to advance the science of manufacturing through the continuing education of manufacturing engineers, practitioners and management. Conducts expositions, international seminars and clinics.

INDUSTRIAL CONTROLS

See CONTROL EQUIPMENT INDUSTRY

INDUSTRIAL DESIGN

See DESIGN IN INDUSTRY

INDUSTRIAL DEVELOPMENT

See also DEVELOPING AREAS; ECONOMIC DEVELOPMENT; LOCATION OF INDUSTRY

DIRECTORIES

Area Development Sites & Facility Planning--Industrial Development Directory of Canada Issue. Halcyon Business Publications Inc. • Annual. $25. Publication includes: List of industrial development organizations at provincial and municipal levels. Entries include: Name, address, phone, and name and title of contact.

PERIODICALS AND NEWSLETTERS

Economic Development Monitor. Whitaker Newsletters Inc. • Biweekly. $247.00 per year. Newsletter. Covers the news of U. S. economic and industrial development, including legislation, regulation, planning, and financing.

Plants, Sites, and Parks. Reed Elsevier Group plc Reed Business Information. • Seven times a year. Free to qualified personnel; others, $43.90 per year. Covers economic development, site location, industrial parks, and industrial development programs.

Sales Prospector. Sales Prospector. • Description: Reports on planned construction of new plants, plant additions, shopping centers, commercial and institutional buildings, relocations, mergers, acquisitions, and government contracts to provide sales leads for salesmen and other businessmen. Provides name of company, location of construction, purpose, approximate dates of start and completion, name of contractor, architect, or developer, and estimate of amount of investment. Published in 28 separate editions each month for different areas of the country, plus two editions for Canada.

RESEARCH CENTERS AND INSTITUTES

Center for International Policy. 2000 M St. NW, Ste. 720, Washington, DC 20036-3327. Phone: (202)232-3317; Fax: (202)232-3440; Email: cip@ciponline.org • URL: http://www.ciponline.org • Research subjects include the International Monetary Fund, the World Bank, and other international financial institutions. Analyzes the impact of policies on social and economic conditions in developing countries.

Massachusetts Institute of Technology - Department of Urban Studies and Planning - Community Innovators Lab. Department of Urban Studies and Planning, Bldg./Rm. 9-419, 77 Massachusetts Ave., Cambridge, MA 02139. Phone: (617)253-3216; Fax: (617)258-6515; Email: colab-info@mit.edu • URL: http://web.mit.edu/colab • Provides opportunity for minority community activists and local governmental officials (10 to 12 per year) to spend a year of reflection, study, and research at the Massachusetts Institute of Technology. The Program is being redesigned to capture the potential of new information technologies for poor communities and communities of color.

TRADE/PROFESSIONAL ASSOCIATIONS

Bahamas Agricultural and Industrial Corporation. Levy Bldg., E Bay St., Nassau, Bahamas. Phone: (242)322-3740; Fax: (242)322-2123; Email: baic@bahamas.net.bs • URL: http://www.bahamas.gov.bs • Assists in the development of commerce and industry in the Bahamas and works to expand the economic opportunities available to Bahamians. Sponsors seminars; disseminates information.

International Economic Development Council. 734 15th St. NW, Ste. 900, Washington, DC 20005. Phone: (202)223-7800; Fax: (202)223-4745 • URL: http://www.iedconline.org • Works to help economic development professionals improve the quality of life in their communities. Represents all levels of government, academia, and private industry; provides a broad range of member services including research, advisory services, conferences, professional certification, professional development, publications, legislative tracking and more.

National Association of Industrial and Office Properties. 2201 Cooperative Way, Ste. 300, Herndon, VA 20171-3034. Phone: (703)904-7100; Fax: (703)904-7942 • URL: http://www.naiop.org • Members are owners and developers of business, industrial, office, and retail properties. Formerly The Association of Commercial Real Estate.

INDUSTRIAL DIAMONDS

ABSTRACTS AND INDEXES

Industrial Diamond Review. De Beers Industrial Diamond Div. • Quarterly. Free to qualified personnel. Incorporating *Industrial Diamond Abstracts*.

INDUSTRIAL DIRECTORIES

See CATALOGS AND DIRECTORIES

INDUSTRIAL DISTRIBUTION

See DISTRIBUTION

INDUSTRIAL EFFICIENCY

See TIME AND MOTION STUDY

INDUSTRIAL ENGINEERING

See also INDUSTRIAL MANAGEMENT

ABSTRACTS AND INDEXES

Applied Science and Technology Index. EBSCO Publishing Inc. • 11/year. Indexes a wide variety of English language technical, industrial, and engineering periodicals.

Business Periodicals Index Retrospective. EBSCO Publishing Inc. • 11/year. Quarterly and annual cumulations.

Engineering Index Monthly: Abstracting and Indexing Services Covering Sources ofthe World's Engineering Literature. Engineering Information Inc. • Monthly. Institutions, $5,279.00 per year. Provides indexing and abstracting of the world's engineering and technical literature.

CD-ROM DATABASES

Applied Science & Business Periodicals Retrospective. EBSCO Publishing Inc. • Includes citations for more than 3 million articles detailing events, issues, and trends in business and industry.

Applied Science and Technology Abstracts. EBSCO Publishing Inc. • Citations for more than 700 prominent scientific, technical, engineering, and industrial periodicals.

DIRECTORIES

NAEDA Buyer's Guide. North American Equipment Dealers Association. • Annual. $35 print only. List of manufacturers and suppliers of agricultural, outdoor power equipment and construction equipment.

ONLINE DATABASES

Applied Science and Technology Index Online. H.W. Wilson Co. • Provides online indexing of 500 major scientific, technical, industrial, and engineering periodicals. Time period is 1983 to date. Monthly updates. Inquire as to online cost and availability.

Wilson Business Abstracts Online. H.W. Wilson Co. • Indexes and abstracts 600 major business periodicals, plus the *Wall Street Journal* and the business section of the *New York Times*. Indexing is from 1982, abstracting from 1990, with the two newspapers included from 1993. Updated weekly. Inquire as to online cost and availability. (*Business Periodicals Index* without abstracts is also available online.).

PERIODICALS AND NEWSLETTERS

Computers and Industrial Engineering: An International Journal. Elsevier. • Monthly. Contains original contributions to the development of new computerized methodologies for solving industrial engineering problems.

NAEDA Equipment Dealer. North American Equipment Dealers Association. • Monthly. $45 Individuals ground delivery. Covers power equipment for farm, outdoor, and industrial use. Formerly *Farm and Power Equipment Dealer.*

Production. Gardner Business Media, Inc. • Covers the latest manufacturing management issues. Discusses the strategic and financial implications of various tecnologies as they impact factory management, quality and competitiveness.

RESEARCH CENTERS AND INSTITUTES

Engineering Dean's Office. University of California at Berkeley, 320 McLaughlin Hall, Berkeley, CA 94720-1700. Phone: (510)642-5771; Fax: (510)642-9178; Email: sastry@coe.berkeley.edu • URL: http://www.coe.berkeley.edu • Research fields include civil, electrical, industrial, mechanical, and other types of engineering.

Engineering Experiment Station. Purdue University, 701 W Stadium Ave., Ste. 3000, West Lafayette, IN 47907. Phone: (765)494-5345; Fax: (765)494-9321; Email: dean.of.engineering@purdue.edu • URL: http://www.ecn.purdue.edu • Research fields include chemical, civil, electrical, industrial, mechanical, and other types of engineering.

University of Florida - Engineering and Industrial Experiment Station. 300 Weil Hall, College of Engineering, Gainesville, FL 32611-6550. Phone: (352)392-6000; Fax: (352)392-9673; Email: caber@eng.ufl.edu • URL: http://www.eng.ufl.edu • Research fields include chemical, civil, electrical, industrial, mechanical, and other types of engineering.

University of Wisconsin—Madison - Center for Quality and Productivity Improvement. 3130 Engineering Centers Bldg., 1550 Engineering Dr., Madison, WI 53706. Phone: (608)263-2520; Fax: (608)263-1425; Email: carayon@ie.engr.wisc.edu • URL: http://cqpi.engr.wisc.edu • Research areas include quality management and industrial engineering.

STATISTICS SOURCES

United States Census of Service Industries. U.S. Department of Commerce U.S. Census Bureau. • Quinquennial. Various reports available.

INDUSTRIAL EQUIPMENT INDUSTRY

DIRECTORIES

Ag Equipment Power. Clintron Publishers. • Monthly. $12 Individuals. Publication includes: Featuring news agricultural equipment and technology for growers in Washington, Idaho, and Oregon. List of about 750 manufacturers, distributors, dealers, and suppliers of new and used farm machinery and chemicals; coverage limited to Washington, Oregon, and Idaho. Entries include: Company name, address, product lines.

My Little Salesman Heavy Equipment Catalog; New and Used Equipment Guide. My Little Salesman. • Monthly.

ONLINE DATABASES

Thomas Register Online. Thomas Publishing Company L.L.C. • Provides concise information on approximately 194,000 U. S. companies, mainly manufacturers, with over 50,000 product classifications. Indexes over 115,000 trade names. Information is updated semiannually. Inquire as to online cost and availability.

PERIODICALS AND NEWSLETTERS

IEEE Industry Applications Magazine. IEEE - Communications Society. • Bimonthly. Covers new industrial applications of power conversion, drives, lighting, and control. Emphasis is on the petroleum, chemical, rubber, plastics, textile, and mining industries.

Industrial Distribution: For Industrial Distributors and Their Sales Personnel. Reed Elsevier Group plc Reed Business Information. • Monthly. $109.90 per year.

Industrial Equipment News. Thomas Publishing Company L.L.C. • Monthly. Contains new product information for manufacturing industries.

New Equipment Digest. Intertec Publishing. • Monthly. Magazine (tabloid) showcasing new or improved equipment, products, materials, and components. Formerly *Material Handling Engineering.*

STATISTICS SOURCES

U.S. Industry and Trade Outlook. U.S. Department of Commerce National Technical Information Service. • Annual. Produced by the International Trade Administration, U.S. Department of Commerce, in a "public-private" partnership with DRI/McGraw-Hill and Standard & Poor's. Provides basic data, outlook for the current year, and "Long-Term Prospects" (five-year projections) for a wide variety of products and services. Includes high technology industries. Formerly *U.S. Industrial Outlook.*

TRADE/PROFESSIONAL ASSOCIATIONS

Industrial Auctioneers Association. 3213 Ayr Ln., Dresher, PA 19025. Phone: 800-805-8359 or (215)366-5450; Fax: (215)657-1964; Email: info@industrialauctioneers.org • URL: http://www.industrialauctioneers.org • Represents industrial machinery and equipment auctioneers. Promotes the use of auction sales in idle industrial equipment. Maintains ethical and professional standards among member auctioneers.

International Photovoltaic Equipment Association. PO Box 771507, Orlando, FL 32877. Phone: (407)856-9100; Email: ekus@ipvea.com • URL: http://www.ipvea.org • Represents manufacturers and suppliers of photovoltaic (PV) fabrication equipment and related raw materials used in PV ingot, wafer, cell and panel manufacturing. Fosters the development of the photovoltaic equipment manufacturing industry. Provides members with a forum for information, discussion and exchange of ideas to develop business opportunities and strategic partnerships.

INDUSTRIAL EQUIPMENT LEASING

See RENTAL SERVICES

INDUSTRIAL FABRICS INDUSTRY

See also NONWOVEN FABRICS INDUSTRY

ABSTRACTS AND INDEXES

Applied Science and Technology Index. EBSCO Publishing Inc. • 11/year. Indexes a wide variety of English language technical, industrial, and engineering periodicals.

Textile Technology Index™. EBSCO Publishing Inc. • Monthly. $545 Individuals. Includes indexing and abstracts for more than 470 periodicals.

DIRECTORIES

Industrial Fabrics Association International Membership Directory. Industrial Fabrics Association International.

Specialty Fabrics Review Buyer's Guide. Industrial Fabrics Association International. • Annual. $69 U.S. two years. Guide to services, products, and supplies for the specialty fabric industry.

FINANCIAL RATIOS

Industry Norms and Key Business Ratios. Dun & Bradstreet Inc. • Annual. Five volumes. Covers over 800 kinds of businesses, arranged by Standard Industrial Classification number. More detailed editions covering longer periods of time are also available.

ONLINE DATABASES

Applied Science and Technology Index Online. H.W. Wilson Co. • Provides online indexing of 500 major scientific, technical, industrial, and engineering periodicals. Time period is 1983 to date. Monthly updates. Inquire as to online cost and availability.

Textile Technology Index™. EBSCO Publishing Inc. • Monthly. $545 Individuals. Includes indexing and abstracts for more than 470 periodicals.

World Textiles. Elsevier. • Provides abstracting and indexing from 1970 of worldwide textile literature (periodicals, books, pamphlets, and reports). Includes U. S., European, and British patent information. Updating is monthly. Inquire as to online cost and availability.

PERIODICALS AND NEWSLETTERS

International Textile Bulletin: Nonwovens and Industrial Textiles Edition. ITS Publishing, International Textile Service. • Quarterly. $170.00 per year. Editions in Chinese, English, French, German, Italian and Spanish.

Specialty Fabrics Review. Industrial Fabrics Association International. • Monthly. $69 Two years /year in U.S.. Magazine covering the technical and industrial fabrics industries.

RESEARCH CENTERS AND INSTITUTES

Fibrous Materials Research Center. Drexel University, Dept. of Materials Engineering, 3141 Chestnut St., Philadelphia, PA 19104. Phone: (215)895-2323; Fax: (215)895-6760; Email: materials@coe.drexel.edu • URL: http://www.materials.drexel.edu • Research fields include computer-aided design of nonwoven fabrics and design curves for industrial fibers.

Institute of Textile Technology. College of Textiles, Box 8301, N Carolina State University, 2401 Research Dr., Raleigh, NC 27695-8301. Phone: (919)513-7583; Fax: (888)348-3512; Email: wgoneal@itt.edu • URL: http://www.itt.edu • Textile materials, processes, and technology, with an emphasis on processing, instrumentation, statistical quality control, and testing of raw materials and finished products. Special attention given to yarn manufacture, carding, finishing operations, operations research applications, computer applications to manufacturing, techniques for evaluation of fiber quality, chemical treatment of raw materials, mechanical blending of fibers, environmental and energy conservation, methods of improving fabric finishes, applications of statistical methods, simulation, expert systems, processing, and interrelation of production, costs, and quality in yarn and fabric manufacture.

Textile Materials Technology. Philadelphia University, 4201 Henry Ave., Philadelphia, PA 19144. Phone: (215)951-2700; Fax: (215)951-2651; Email: admissions@philau.edu • URL: http://www.philau.edu/textilemat • Many research areas, including industrial and nonwoven textiles.

INDUSTRIAL FASTENERS

See FASTENER INDUSTRY

INDUSTRIAL HYGIENE

See also INDUSTRIAL MEDICINE; INDUSTRIAL SAFETY

DIRECTORIES

Industrial Hygiene News Buyer's Guide. Rimbach Publishing Inc. • Annual. Lists about 1,000 manufacturers and suppliers of products, equipment, and services to the occupational health, industrial hygiene, and high-tech safety industry.

GENERAL WORKS

Principles of Health and Hygiene in the Workplace. Timothy J. Key and Michael A. Mueller. Lewis Publishers. • Date not set. $69.95.

INTERNET DATABASES

National Center for Health Statistics: Monitoring the Nation's Health. National Center for Health Statistics, Centers for Disease Control and Prevention. Phone: (301)458-4000; Email: nchsquery@cdc.gov • URL: http://www.cdc.gov/nchswww • Web site provides detailed data on diseases, vital statistics, and health care in the U. S. Includes a search facility and links to many other health-related Web sites. "Fastats A to Z" offers quick data on hundreds of topics from Accidents to Work-Loss Days, with links to Comprehensive Data and related sources. Frequent updates. Fees: Free.

ONLINE DATABASES

Embase. Elsevier. • Worldwide medical literature, 1974 to present. Weekly updates. Inquire as to online cost and availability.

Toxline. National Library of Medicine. • Weekly. Abstracting service covering human and animal toxicity studies, 1965 to present (older studies available in *Toxback* file). Weekly updates. Inquire as to online cost and availability.

OTHER SOURCES

Practical Guide to the Occupational Safety and Health Act. ALM Media Properties LLC. • $545 print + online + ebook. Covers the practical aspects of doing business while complying with OSHA regulations. Covers inspections, enforcement, rights of employees, the possibility of criminal prosecution, and related issues. (Law Journal Press).

PERIODICALS AND NEWSLETTERS

Environmental Toxicology: An International Journal. John Wiley and Sons, Inc., Journals Div. • Publishes in the areas of toxicity and toxicology of environmental pollutants in air, dust, sediment, soil and water, and natural toxins in the environment.

Industrial Hygiene News. Rimbach Publishing Inc. • Seven times a year. Free to qualified personnel.

Management OHS and E. Stevens Publishing Corp. • Monthly. Free to qualified personnel; others, $150.00 per year. Includes news, interviews, feature articles, legal developments, and reviews of literature. Includes *Buyer's Guide*.

Occupational Health and Safety Letter..Towards Productivity and Peace of Mind. Business Publishers Inc. • Biweekly. $317.00 per year.

TRADE/PROFESSIONAL ASSOCIATIONS

American Industrial Hygiene Association. 3141 Fairview Park Dr., Ste. 777, Falls Church, VA 22042. Phone: (703)849-8888; Fax: (703)207-3561; Email: infonet@aiha.org • URL: http://www.aiha.org • Professional society of industrial hygienists. Promotes the study and control of environmental factors affecting the health and well-being of workers. Sponsors continuing education courses in industrial hygiene, government affairs program, and public relations. Accredits laboratories. Maintains 40 technical committees and a foundation. Operates placement service. Conducts educational and research programs.

United Kingdom Forum for Organisational Health. c/o Mary Manolias, Secretary, 43 Pemberton Rd., Surrey, East Molesey KT8 9LG, United Kingdom. Phone: 44 20 89793344; Email: mary.manolias@talktalk.net • URL: http://www.ukfoh.org.uk • Professionals who share a common interest in the healthy development of organisations and includes occupational health physicians and nurses, researchers, counselors, personnel managers, general managers and occupational psychologists. Promotes the development and maintenance of the psychosocial health of organisations and of the individual within the workplace. Believes that people are the most critical resource in any organisation, supports humanisation of the workplace and recognition of ways in which individual creativity and growth contribute to organisational effectiveness.

INDUSTRIAL JOURNALISM

See BUSINESS JOURNALISM

INDUSTRIAL LOCATION

See LOCATION OF INDUSTRY

INDUSTRIAL MANAGEMENT

See also ADMINISTRATION; FACTORY MANAGEMENT; INDUSTRIAL ENGINEERING; PROJECT MANAGEMENT; RECORDS MANAGEMENT; SALES MANAGEMENT; SYSTEMS IN MANAGEMENT

ABSTRACTS AND INDEXES

Business Periodicals Index Retrospective. EBSCO Publishing Inc. • 11/year. Quarterly and annual cumulations.

CD-ROM DATABASES

Business Abstracts with Full Text. EBSCO Publishing Inc. • Includes full text articles from more than 460 business publications from 1982 to present. Indexing for nearly 880 publications.

DIRECTORIES

Reference Book of Corporate Managements. • Annual. Libraries, $650.00 per year; others, $795.00 per year. Lease basis. Management executives at over 12,000 leading United States companies.

ONLINE DATABASES

Wilson Business Abstracts Online. H.W. Wilson Co. • Indexes and abstracts 600 major business periodicals, plus the *Wall Street Journal* and the business section of the *New York Times*. Indexing is from 1982, abstracting from 1990, with the two newspapers included from 1993. Updated weekly. Inquire as to online cost and availability. (*Business Periodicals Index* without abstracts is also available online.).

OTHER SOURCES

First-Line Supervision. American Management Association Extension Institute. • Looseleaf. $139.00. Self-study course. Focuses on the day-to-day concerns of the first line supervisor. A self-study course.

PERIODICALS AND NEWSLETTERS

Executive Excellence: The Newsletter of Personal Development, Managerial Effectiveness, and Organizational Productivity. Kenneth M. Shelton, editor. Executive Excellence Publishing. • Monthly. $129.00 per year. Newsletter.

Hard at Work. Professional Training Associates Inc. • Monthly. $89.00 per year. Newsletter on common personnel problems of supervisors and office managers. Formerly *Practical Supervision*.

Harvard Management Update. Harvard Business School Publishing. • Description: Provides information on current management techniques and trends.

Human Factors and Ergonomics in Manufacturing & Service Industries. John Wiley and Sons, Inc., Journals Div. • Bimonthly. Published in England by John Wiley and Sons Ltd. Formerly *International Journal of Human Factors in Manufacturing*.

IndustryWeek: The Management Resource. Penton Media Inc. • Monthly. Edited for industrial and business managers. Covers organizational and technological developments affecting industrial management.

MIT Sloan Management Review. Sloan Management Review Association. Massachusetts Institute of Technology Department of Urban Studies and Planning Community Innovators Lab. • Quarterly. $69. A business journal that bridges the gap between management research and practice.

Production and Operations Management. Production and Operations Management Society. • Quarterly 6/year. $70 Individuals per year.

The Professional Manager. Institute of Industrial Engineers. • Bimonthly. Free to members; non-members, $24.00 per year. Features articles on the latest problem-solving techniques and trends available to industrial managers. Formerly *Industrial Management*.

RESEARCH CENTERS AND INSTITUTES

Åbo Academy University - Laboratory of Industrial Management. Biskopsgatan 8, FI-20500 Abo, Finland. Phone: 358 2 221531; Email: infowww@abo.fi • URL: http://www.abo.fi/student/en/Content/Document/document/9465 • How industrial companies operate now and in the future within different industries, especially what is offered, the organization of the companies and what capabilities are needed. There is a special focus on international industrial project-based business.

Board of Research. Babson College. 204 Babson, Babson Park, MA 02457-0310. Phone: (781)235-1200; Fax: (718)239-6416; Email: chern@babson.edu • URL: http://www.babson.edu/bor • Research areas include management, entrepreneurial characteristics, and multi-product inventory analysis.

TRADE/PROFESSIONAL ASSOCIATIONS

American Management Association. 1601 Broadway, New York, NY 10019-7420. Phone: 877-566-9441 or (212)586-8100 or (518)891-5510; Fax: (212)903-8168 or (518)891-0368; Email: customerservice@amanet.org • URL: http://www.amanet.org • Provides educational forums worldwide where members and their colleagues learn superior, practical business skills and explore best practices of world-class organizations through interaction with each other and expert faculty practitioners. Maintains a publishing program providing tools individuals use to extend learning beyond the classroom in a process of life-long professional growth and development through education.

Industrial Asset Management Council. 6625 The Corners Pkwy., Ste. 200, Peachtree Corners, GA 30092-3334. Phone: (770)325-3461; Fax: (770)263-8825; Email: info@iamc.org • URL: http://www.iamc.org • Represents the interests of industrial asset management and corporate real estate executives. Provides educational resources and networking opportunities for the leaders of the manufacturing and industrial asset management industry. Implements the best strategies for success in corporate operations.

National Management Association. 2210 Arbor Blvd., Dayton, OH 45439. Phone: (937)294-0421; Email: nma@nma1.org • URL: http://www.nma1.org • Business and industrial management personnel; membership comes from supervisory level, with the remainder from middle management and above. Seeks to develop and recognize management as a profession and to promote the free enterprise system. Prepares chapter programs on basic management, management policy and practice, communications, human behavior, industrial relations, economics, political education, and liberal education. Maintains speakers' bureau and hall of fame. Maintains educational, charitable, and research programs. Sponsors charitable programs.

Production and Operations Management Society. The University of Texas at Dallas, School of Management, 2601 N Floyd Rd., Richardson, TX 75080. Phone: (972)883-4047; Fax: (972)883-5834; Email: poms@utdallas.edu • URL: http://www.poms.org • Members are professionals and educators in fields related to operations management and production.

INDUSTRIAL MARKETING

See also INDUSTRIAL ADVERTISING; MARKETING

PERIODICALS AND NEWSLETTERS

Adweek Magazines' Technology Marketing. Nielsen Business Media Inc. • Monthly. $55.00 per year. Edited for marketing executives in high technology industries. Covers both advertising and marketing. Formerly *MC Technology Marketing Intelligence*.

Industrial Marketing Management: The International Journal of Marketing for Industrial and High-Tech Firms. Elsevier. • $1,751 Institutions. Eight times a year. Qualified personnel, $127.00 per year; institutions, $816.00 per year.

RESEARCH CENTERS AND INSTITUTES

Pennsylvania State University - Institute for the Study of Business Markets. 484 Business Bldg., Smeal College of Business, University Park, PA 16802. Phone: (814)863-2782; Fax: (814)863-0413; Email: isbm@psu.edu • URL: http://isbm.smeal.psu.edu • Research areas include international distribution channels.

INDUSTRIAL MEDICINE

See also INDUSTRIAL HYGIENE

ABSTRACTS AND INDEXES

Excerpta Medica: Occupational Health and Industrial Medicine. Elsevier. • Monthly. Section 35 of *Excerpta Medica*.

DIRECTORIES

American College of Occupational and Environmental Medicine-Membership Directory. • Annual. $195.00. Lists 6,500 medical directories and plant physicians specializing in occupational medicine and surgery; coverage includes Canada and other foreign countries. Geographically arranged.

ENCYCLOPEDIAS AND DICTIONARIES

Attorneys' Textbook of Medicine. Matthew Bender and Company Inc. • Updated quarterly. 19 volumes. $5,476.00. Detailed information on injuries and diseases. Written specifically for attorneys.

GENERAL WORKS

Principles of Health and Hygiene in the Workplace. Timothy J. Key and Michael A. Mueller. Lewis Publishers. • Date not set. $69.95.

INTERNET DATABASES

National Library of Medicine. National Institutes of Health. 9000 Rockville Pke., Bethesda, MD 20892. Phone: (301)496-4000; Email: nihinfo@od.nih.gov • URL: http://www.nih.gov • NLM Web site offers free access through MEDLINE ("PubMed") to about nine million references to articles appearing in some 4,000 biomedical journals, with abstracts. Search interfaces range from "simple keywords to advanced Boolean expressions." The NLM site offers many links to other sources of biomedical and technical information (the National Center for Biotechnology Information, for example). Fees: Free.

ONLINE DATABASES

Embase. Elsevier. • Worldwide medical literature, 1974 to present. Weekly updates. Inquire as to online cost and availability.

OTHER SOURCES

Society of Air Force Physicians. • Air Force internists, family practitioners, and specialists in emergency medicine, dermatology, allergy/immunology, and neurology. Seeks to foster advancement of the art and science of medicine in the Air Force; encourage clinical and laboratory investigation; disseminate information.

Society of Medical Consultants to the Armed Forces. • Professional society of physicians and surgeons who have been in active military service and who have acted as consultants to the Surgeons General of the Army, Navy, or Air Force. Preserves and encourages the association of civilian consultants and military medical personnel and assists in the development and maintenance of the highest standards of medical practice in the Armed Forces.

Society of Military Orthopaedic Surgeons. • Orthopedic surgeons who have served in the active or reserve military. Seeks to stimulate scholarly contribution by military medical residents; act as clearinghouse; provides opportunities for consultation with and contributions of surgeons who are retired from the military; furthers the continuing education of orthopedic surgeons and residents. Presents scientific papers at annual meeting.

Society of Military Otolaryngologists - Head and Neck Surgeons. • Otolaryngologists, head and neck surgeons and residents in training of the U.S. Army, Air Force, Navy, and former active duty members. Purposes are to further the social and professional contacts of military otolaryngologists and to advance the science and art of the field.

Uniformed Services Academy of Family Physicians. • Family physicians, teachers of family medicine, medical students, and residents in the armed services, public health service, or Indian health service. Sponsors continuing education program. Sponsors educational programs.

Attorneys' Textbook of Medicine. Matthew Bender and Company Inc. • Updated quarterly. 19 volumes. $5,476.00. Detailed information on injuries and diseases. Written specifically for attorneys.

PERIODICALS AND NEWSLETTERS

Environmental Epidemiology and Toxicology. Macmillan Publishers Ltd. Nature Publishing Group. • Quarterly. Individuals, $365.00 per year; institutions, $430.00 per year. *Formerly Environmental Epidemiology and Toxicology*.

INDUSTRIAL MORALE

See HUMAN RELATIONS

INDUSTRIAL PARKS

See INDUSTRIAL DEVELOPMENT

INDUSTRIAL PHOTOGRAPHY

See COMMERCIAL PHOTOGRAPHY

INDUSTRIAL PRODUCTIVITY

See PRODUCTIVITY

INDUSTRIAL PSYCHOLOGY

See also MENTAL HEALTH; PSYCHOLOGICAL TESTING

ABSTRACTS AND INDEXES

Business Periodicals Index Retrospective. EBSCO Publishing Inc. • 11/year. Quarterly and annual cumulations.

Psychological Abstracts. American Psychological Association. • Monthly. Members, $815.00 per year; individuals and institutions, $1,207.00 per year. Covers the international literature of psychology and the behavioral sciences. Includes journals, technical reports, dissertations, and other sources.

ALMANACS AND YEARBOOKS

International Review of Industrial and Organizational Psychology. John Wiley and Sons, Inc., Journals Div. • Annual. $154.95. Published in England by John Wiley and Sons Ltd. Contains comprehensive, state-of-the-art overview of topic areas which cover the entire spectrum of industrial and organizational psychology, including job design, work motivation, stress and new and emergent areas.

DIRECTORIES

Tests. Cengage Learning Inc. • 2008. $105.00. 6th edition. List nearly 200 publishers for over 2,000 tests. Published by Pro-Ed Inc.

ENCYCLOPEDIAS AND DICTIONARIES

Gale Encyclopedia of Psychology. Cengage Learning Inc. • 2000. $267.00. Second edition. Includes bibliographies arranged by topic and a glossary. More than 650 topics are covered.

GENERAL WORKS

Journal of Business and Psychology. Business Psychology Research Institute. Springer Science-Business Media LLC. • Quarterly. $614 Institutions print. An international outlet publishing high quality research designed to advance organizational science and practice.

PERIODICALS AND NEWSLETTERS

Journal of Business and Psychology. Business Psychology Research Institute. Springer Science-Business Media LLC. • Quarterly. $614 Institutions print. An international outlet publishing high quality research designed to advance organizational science and practice.

INDUSTRIAL PURCHASING

See PURCHASING

INDUSTRIAL REAL ESTATE

See also PROPERTY TAX; TAX SHELTERS

ABSTRACTS AND INDEXES

Business Periodicals Index Retrospective. EBSCO Publishing Inc. • 11/year. Quarterly and annual cumulations.

DIRECTORIES

Executive Guide to Specialists in Industrial and Office Real Estate. Society of Industrial and Office Realtors. • Annual. Lists approximately 5,000 corporate real estate specialists.

U.S. Real Estate Register. Barry Inc. • Annual. $95 Individuals. Covers: Real estate departments of large national companies, industrial economic/development organizations, utilities, real estate brokers, and railroads involved in commercial and industrial real estate development. Entries include: Company or organization name, address; many listings include name of contact.

ONLINE DATABASES

Wilson Business Abstracts Online. H.W. Wilson Co. • Indexes and abstracts 600 major business periodicals, plus the *Wall Street Journal* and the business section of the *New York Times.* Indexing is from 1982, abstracting from 1990, with the two newspapers included from 1993. Updated weekly. Inquire as to online cost and availability. (*Business Periodicals Index* without abstracts is also available online.).

PERIODICALS AND NEWSLETTERS

Buildings: The Source for Facilities Decision-Makers. Stamats Communications Inc. • Monthly. $70.00 per year. Serves professional building ownership/management organizations.

Business Facilities: The Location Advisor. Group C Media Inc. • Monthly. Free to qualified personnel; others, $30.00 per year. Facility planning and site selection.

Commercial Leasing Law and Strategy. ALM Media Properties LLC. • Monthly. $489 per year. Covers commercial real estate leasing developments relating to large retailers, tenant inducements, tax consequences, unbilled rent obligations, and other matters. (A Law Journal Newsletter, formerly published by Leader Publications).

Development. National Association of Industrial and Office Properties. • Quarterly. $35 /year. Focuses on issues, trends and new ideas affecting the commercial and industrial real estate development industry.

Real Estate Finance. Institutional Investor Inc. Journals Group. • Bimonthly. $350.00 per year. Covers real estate for professional investors. Provides information on complex financing, legalities, and industry trends.

Real Estate Finance and Investment. Institutional Investor Inc. Journals Group. • Weekly. $2,275.00 per year. Includes print and online editions. Newsletter for professional investors in commercial real estate. Includes information on financing, restructuring, strategy, and regulation.

Real Estate Forum: America's Premier Real Estate Business Magazine. Real Estate Media Inc. • 10/year. Emphasis on corporate and industrial real estate.

PRICE SOURCES

National Real Estate Index. CB Richard Ellis Group Inc. • Price and frequency on application. Provides reports on commercial real estate prices, rents, capitalization rates, and trends in more than 65 metropolitan areas. Time span is 12 years. Includes urban office buildings, suburban offices, warehouses, retail properties, and apartments.

RESEARCH CENTERS AND INSTITUTES

University of Illinois at Urbana-Champaign - Office of Real Estate Research. 140A Wohlers Hall, 1206 S 6th St., Champaign, IL 61820. Phone: (217)333-2278; Fax: (217)244-3102; Email: orer@illinois.edu • URL: http://business.illinois.edu/orer • Ongoing and contract studies on real estate issues, including appraisal and valuation, marketing and brokerage, environmental issues, land markets, municipal finance, property management, real estate investment, real estate financial markets, tenure choice, law, and public policy issues such as property rights, rent control, taxation, eminent domain, impact fees, etc.

STATISTICS SOURCES

ULI Market Profiles: North America. Urban Land Institute. • Annual. Members, $249.95; non-members, $299.95. Provides real estate marketing data for residential, retail, office, and industrial sectors. Covers 76 U. S. metropolitan areas and 13 major foreign metropolitan areas.

TRADE/PROFESSIONAL ASSOCIATIONS

AIR Commercial Real Estate Association. 500 N Brand Blvd., Ste. 900, Glendale, CA 91203-3315. Phone: 866-946-2472 or (213)687-8777; Fax: (213)687-8616; Email: membershipla@airea.com • URL: http://www.airea.com • Real estate men and women specializing in industrial and commercial properties; affiliate members are title companies, mortgage loan companies, public utilities, and developers. Membership concentrated in Southern California. Encourages high professional standards. Sponsors a course on industrial real estate, in cooperation with the University of California. Develops industrial multiple listing system and standard lease forms. Supports the Industrial Multiple, a clearinghouse for information on industrial listings. Maintains a computerized multiple listing system.

Industrial Asset Management Council. 6625 The Corners Pkwy., Ste. 200, Peachtree Corners, GA 30092-3334. Phone: (770)325-3461; Fax: (770)263-8825; Email: info@iamc.org • URL: http://www.iamc.org • Represents the interests of industrial asset management and corporate real estate executives. Provides educational resources and networking opportunities for the leaders of the manufacturing and industrial asset management industry. Implements the best strategies for success in corporate operations.

National Association of Industrial and Office Properties. 2201 Cooperative Way, Ste. 300, Herndon, VA 20171-3034. Phone: (703)904-7100; Fax: (703)904-7942 • URL: http://www.naiop.org • Members are owners and developers of business, industrial, office, and retail properties. Formerly The Association of Commercial Real Estate.

INDUSTRIAL RECREATION

ABSTRACTS AND INDEXES

Leisure, Recreation and Tourism Abstracts. CABI Publishing North America. • Quarterly. Members, $280.00 per year; Institutions, $610.00 per year. Includes single site internet access. Provides coverage of the worldwide literature of travel, recreation, sports, and the hospitality industry.

DIRECTORIES

Membership and Peer Network Directory. Employee Morale and Recreation Association. • Annual. Lists more than 4,500 personnel managers, recreation directors and certified administrators in employee recreation, fitness and services. Formerly *National Employee Services and Recreation Association-Membership and Peer Network Directory.*

PERIODICALS AND NEWSLETTERS

Employee Services Management: The Journal of Employee Services Recreation, Heal th and Education. Employee Services Management. • Bimonthly. Free to members; non-members, $52.00 per year.

TRADE/PROFESSIONAL ASSOCIATIONS

Employee Morale and Recreation Association. PO Box 10517, Rockville, MD 20849. • URL: http://employeemorale.org • Corporations and governmental agencies that sponsor recreation, fitness, and service programs for their employees; associate members are manufacturers and suppliers in the employee recreation market and distributors of consumer products and services. Serves as an information resource network for members nationwide. Implements and maintains a diverse range of employee services; believes that employee services, as practical solutions to work/life issues, are essential to sound business management. Conducts programs that improves relations between employees and management, increases overall productivity, boosts morale, and reduces absenteeism and turnover.

INDUSTRIAL RELATIONS

See also NEGOTIATION

ABSTRACTS AND INDEXES

Business Periodicals Index Retrospective. EBSCO Publishing Inc. • 11/year. Quarterly and annual cumulations.

Index to Legal Periodicals and Books. H.W. Wilson Co. • Monthly. $490.00 per year. Quarterly and annual cumulations.

DIRECTORIES

Directory of U. S. Labor Organizations. BNA, Inc. • $180 Individuals softcover. More than 150 national unions and professional and state employees associations engaged in labor representation.

ONLINE DATABASES

Wilson Business Abstracts Online. H.W. Wilson Co. • Indexes and abstracts 600 major business periodicals, plus the *Wall Street Journal* and the business section of the *New York Times*. Indexing is from 1982, abstracting from 1990, with the two newspapers included from 1993. Updated weekly. Inquire as to online cost and availability. (*Business Periodicals Index* without abstracts is also available online.).

OTHER SOURCES

How to Manage Conflict in the Organization. American Management Association Extension Institute. • Looseleaf. $139.00. Self-study course. Emphasis is on practical explanations, examples, and problem solving. Quizzes and a case study are included.

Labor Relations Reporter. Bloomberg BNA. • Weekly. $4,998.00 per year. Looseleaf service.

PERIODICALS AND NEWSLETTERS

HR Magazine (Human Resources): Strategies and Solutions for Human Resource Professionals. Society for Human Resource Management. • Monthly. $70. Formerly *Personnel Administrator*.

Industrial and Labor Relations Review. Cornell University ILR School. • Quarterly. Individuals, $32.00 per year; institutions, $52.00 per year; students, $16.00 per year.

Industrial Relations: A Journal of Economy and Society. University of California at Berkeley. Blackwell Publishing Inc. • 5/year. Bimonthly. Institutions, $862.00 per year. Includes online edition.

IRRA Newsletter. Labor and Employment Relations Association. • Description: Presents news of meetings, elections, and programs of this Association of business, labor, and government leaders interested in researching labor and management relationships.

RESEARCH CENTERS AND INSTITUTES

Industrial Relations Research Institute. University of Wisconsin-Madison, c, Madison, WI 53706. Phone: (608)262-1300; Fax: (608)265-4591; Email: irri@mhub.facstaff.wisc.edu • URL: http://www.wisc.edu.

Institute for Research on Labor, Employment, and the Economy. 506 E Liberty St., 3rd Fl., Ann Arbor, MI 48104-2210. Phone: (734)998-6201; Fax: (734)998-6202 • URL: http://www.irlee.umich.edu.

Princeton University - Industrial Relations Section. Firestone Library, A-18-J, 1 Washington Rd., Princeton, NJ 08544. Phone: (609)258-4040; Fax: (609)258-2907; Email: c6789@princeton.edu • URL: http://www.irs.princeton.edu • Fields of research include labor supply, manpower training, unemployment, and equal employment opportunity.

University of California, Berkeley - Institute for Research on Labor and Employment. 2521 Channing Way, No. 5555, Berkeley, CA 94720-5555. Phone: (510)643-8140 or (510)642-1705; Fax: (510)642-6432; Email: mreich@econ.berkeley.edu • URL: http://www.irle.berkeley.edu • Employment and training systems in the United States, Japan, and Europe; green economy; high performance workplaces; labor-management relations, organizational behavior, wages and related problems, economic security programs, labor market and labor mobility, social and industrial psychology, comparative developmental studies, labor history, and occupational health. Conduct interdisciplinary research program.

University of Pennsylvania - Center for Human Resources. 204 Steinberg Hall/Dietrich Hall, The Wharton School, 3620 Locust Walk, Philadelphia, PA 19104-6302. Phone: (215)898-5606; Fax: (215)898-5908; Email: cappelli@wharton.upenn.edu • URL: http://chr.wharton.upenn.edu • U.S. and international manpower issues, labor-management relations, human resources management and related areas.

TRADE/PROFESSIONAL ASSOCIATIONS

Council of Communication Management. 65 Enterprise, Aliso Viejo, CA 92656. Phone: 866-463-6226; Email: info@thecommunicationexchange.org • URL: http://www.ccmconnection.com • Formerly Industrial Communication Council.

INDUSTRIAL RESEARCH

See also RESEARCH AND DEVELOPMENT

ABSTRACTS AND INDEXES

Applied Science and Technology Index. EBSCO Publishing Inc. • 11/year. Indexes a wide variety of English language technical, industrial, and engineering periodicals.

Science Citation Index. Thomson Reuters Intellectual Property and Science. • Weekly. Includes *Source Index*, *Citation Index*, *Permuterm Subject Index*, and *Corporate Index*. Provides researchers, administrators, faculty, and students with quick, powerful access to the bibliographic and citation information they need to find research data, analyze trends, journals and researchers, and share their findings.

CD-ROM DATABASES

Science Citation Index. Thomson Reuters Intellectual Property and Science. • Weekly. Includes *Source Index*, *Citation Index*, *Permuterm Subject Index*, and *Corporate Index*. Provides researchers, administrators, faculty, and students with quick, powerful access to the bibliographic and citation information they need to find research data, analyze trends, journals and researchers, and share their findings.

DIRECTORIES

Plunkett's Engineering and Research Industry Almanac. Plunkett Research Ltd. • Annual. $349.99. Contains detailed profiles of major engineering and technology corporations. Includes CD-ROM.

ENCYCLOPEDIAS AND DICTIONARIES

Encyclopedia of Products & Industries - Manufacturing (EPIM). Cengage Learning Inc. • $978 Individuals. 2007. 2 volumes. Designed to assist college students who need to research products and the relationships between products and their industries. Includes tables, charts, and statistics. eBook available. Inquire for pricing.

ONLINE DATABASES

Applied Science and Technology Index Online. H.W. Wilson Co. • Provides online indexing of 500 major scientific, technical, industrial, and engineering periodicals. Time period is 1983 to date. Monthly updates. Inquire as to online cost and availability.

Current Contents Connect. Thomson Reuters Intellectual Property and Science. • Provides online abstracts of articles listed in the tables of contents of about 7,500 journals. Coverage is very broad, including science, social science, life science, technology, engineering, industry, agriculture, the environment, economics, and arts and humanities. Time period is two years, with weekly updates. Inquire as to online cost and availability.

PERIODICALS AND NEWSLETTERS

Industrial & Engineering Chemistry Research. American Chemical Society. • Semimonthly. $2,388 Institutions. Magazine on industrial and engineering chemistry. Formerly *Industrial and Engineering Chemistry Product Research and Development*.

Research and Development: The Voice of the Research and Development Community. Reed Elsevier Group plc Reed Business Information. • 13 times a year. $81.90 per year.

RESEARCH CENTERS AND INSTITUTES

Iowa State University of Science and Technology - Center for Industrial Research and Service. 2272 Howe Hall, Ste. 2620, Ames, IA 50011-2272. Phone: (515)294-3420; Fax: (515)294-4925; Email: rcox@iastate.edu • URL: http://www.ciras.iastate.edu • Problem areas of business, manufacturing, technology transfer, productivity, new product design, manufacturing processes, marketing, and related topics. Acts as a problem-handling facility and a clearinghouse for efforts to help Iowa's industry grow through studies highlighting not only production and management problems but also markets and profit potential of possible new developments.

INDUSTRIAL ROBOTS

See ROBOTS

INDUSTRIAL SAFETY

See also INDUSTRIAL HYGIENE; SAFETY

ABSTRACTS AND INDEXES

Health and Safety Science Abstracts. Institute of Safety and Systems Management. Cambridge Information Group. • Monthly. Provides coverage of world literature on general safety, environmental and ecological safety, industrial hygiene and occupational safety, transportation safety, aviation and aerospace safety, and medical safety. Formerly *Safety Science Abstracts Journal*.

CD-ROM DATABASES

Authority Worker's Compensation Library. Matthew Bender and Company Inc. • Periodic revisions. Price on request. CD-ROM contains updated full text of *Larson's Workmen's Compensation, Occupational Injuries and Illnesses*, and other Matthew Bender publications relating to worker's compensation laws.

OSH-ROM: Occupational Safety and Health Information on CD-ROM. SilverPlatter Information Inc. • Price and frequency on application. Produced in Geneva by the International Occupational Safety and Health Information Centre, International Labour Organization (www.ilo.org). Provides about two million citations and abstracts to the worldwide literature of industrial safety, industrial hygiene, hazardous materials, and accident prevention. Material is included from journals, technical reports, books, government publications, and other sources. Time span varies.

OTHER SOURCES

Human Resources Management Whole. Wolters Kluwer Law & Business CCH. • Nine looseleaf volumes. $1,572 per year. Includes monthly updates. Components are *Ideas and Trends Newsletter, Employment Relations, Compensation, Equal Employment Opportunity, Personnel Practices/Communications* and *OSHA Compliance*. Components are available separately.

Occupational Safety and Health Handbook: An

Employer's Guide to OSHA Laws. Matthew Bender and Company Inc. • $128. Periodic supplementation available. Covers inspections, violations, the citation process, ergonomics, hazards, equipment, and other topics relating to the law enforced by the federal Occupational Safety and Health Administration (OSHA).

Practical Guide to the Occupational Safety and Health Act. ALM Media Properties LLC. • $545 print + online + ebook. Covers the practical aspects of doing business while complying with OSHA regulations. Covers inspections, enforcement, rights of employees, the possibility of criminal prosecution, and related issues. (Law Journal Press).

PERIODICALS AND NEWSLETTERS

EHS Today. Penton Media Inc. • Monthly. $55.00 per year. Industrial safety and security management.

Industrial Safety and Hygiene News: News of Safety, Health and Hygiene, Environmental, Fire, Security and Emergency Protection Equipment. BNP Media. • Monthly. Free to qualified personnel; others, $120.00 per year.

Job Safety and Health Quarterly. U. S. Government Printing Office. • Quarterly. $17.00 per year. Issued by the Occupational Safety and Health Administration (OSHA), U. S. Department of Labor. Contains articles on employee safety and health, with information on current OSHA activities.

Professional Safety. American Society of Safety Engineers. • Monthly. $60 U.S., Canada, and Mexico. Emphasis is on research and technology in the field of accident prevention.

Safety and Health. National Safety Council. • Monthly. Qualified professionals may receive free for one year.

STATISTICS SOURCES

Report on the American Workforce. U. S. Government Printing Office. • Annual. Issued by the U. S. Department of Labor (www.dol.gov). Appendix contains tabular statistics, including employment, unemployment, price indexes, consumer expenditures, employee benefits (retirement, insurance, vacation, etc.), wages, productivity, hours of work, and occupational injuries. Annual figures are shown for up to 50 years.

TRADE/PROFESSIONAL ASSOCIATIONS

American Society of Safety Engineers. 1800 E Oakton St., Des Plaines, IL 60018. Phone: (847)699-2929; Fax: (847)768-3434; Email: customerservice@asse.org • URL: http://www.asse.org • Professional society of safety engineers, safety directors, and others concerned with accident prevention, environmental protection and safety and health programs. Sponsors National Safety Month and conducts research and educational programs. Develops/publishes ANSI safety-related standards and other technical literature. Compiles statistics; maintains job placement service.

International Association of Directional Drilling. 525 Sam Houston Pkwy. E, Ste. 525, Houston, TX 77060. Phone: (281)931-8811 or (281)288-6484; Email: dallen@iadd-intl.org • URL: http://www.iadd-intl.org • Represents the interests of the directional drilling industry. Encourages members to share ideas and develop safety and performance standards. Fosters collaboration among operators, directional drilling vendors and suppliers.

INDUSTRIAL SECURITY PROGRAMS

See also ELECTRONIC SECURITY SYSTEMS; LOCKS AND KEYS

HANDBOOKS AND MANUALS

Private Investigator. Entrepreneur Press. • Looseleaf. $59.50. A practical guide to starting a private investigation agency. Covers profit potential, start-up costs, market size evaluation, pricing, accounting, advertising, promotion, etc. (Start-Up Business Guide No. E1320.).

PERIODICALS AND NEWSLETTERS

CSO: The Resource for Security Executives. CXO Media Inc. • 10/year. $70 U.S. and Canada. Edited for corporate chief security officers (CSOs). Covers a wide variety of business security issues, including computer security, identity theft, spam, physical security, loss prevention, risk management, privacy, and investigations.

Homeland Security and Defense: Weekly Intelligence for the Global Homeland Security and Defense Community. Aviation Week Business Intelligence Services. • Weekly. $595.00 per year. Newsletter. Emphasis is on airline and airport programs (federal, state, and local). Also covers counterterrorism, protection of military units, Department of Homeland Security activities, industrial security, communications equipment, and other topics related to homeland security.

Security Letter. Security Letter Inc. • Description: Contains "solution-oriented information on security and protection of assets from loss," particularly for executives concerned about the following: internal checks and controls, personnel practices, management of change, fraud and embezzlement, business crime trends, security, and urban terrorism. Recurring features include news of research, a calendar of events, semiannual FBI crime data, quarterly financial news of major companies in the security industry, book reviews, security and safety pointers, and a question-and-answer feature.

Security Management. ASIS International. • Monthly. $60 Nonmembers print and online. Included in membership. Articles cover the protection of corporate assets, including personnel property and information security.

TRADE/PROFESSIONAL ASSOCIATIONS

ASIS International. 1625 Prince St., Alexandria, VA 22314. Phone: (703)519-6200; Fax: (703)519-6299; Email: asis@asisonline.org • URL: http://www.asisonline.org/Pages/default.aspx • ASIS is the world's largest organization dedicated to security professionals. Presents seminars and exhibits and offers a variety of educational programs on security issues in a number of fields including communications.

INDUSTRIAL TOXICOLOGY

See INDUSTRIAL HYGIENE

INDUSTRIAL WELFARE

See EMPLOYEE BENEFIT PLANS

INDUSTRY

See also BUSINESS; CORPORATIONS

ABSTRACTS AND INDEXES

Applied Science and Technology Index. EBSCO Publishing Inc. • 11/year. Indexes a wide variety of English language technical, industrial, and engineering periodicals.

BIOGRAPHICAL SOURCES

Who's Who in Finance and Business. Marquis Who's Who L.L.C. • Biennial. $349 Individuals. Provides over 21,000 concise biographies of business leaders in all fields.

CD-ROM DATABASES

D & B Business Locator. Dun & Bradstreet Inc. • Quarterly. $2,495.00 per year. CD-ROM provides concise information on more than 10 million U. S. companies or businesses. Includes data on number of employees.

OECD Statistical Compendium. Organization for Economic Cooperation and Development. • Semiannual. $1,905.00 per year for 1 to 10 users. CD-ROM contains more than 730,000 monthly, quarterly, and annual time series for OECD countries, 1960 to date. Includes fully searchable data on agriculture, food, economic indicators, national accounts, employment, energy, finance, industry, technology, and foreign trade. Results can be displayed in various forms.

USA Trade. U.S. Department of Commerce. • Monthly. $650.00 per year. Provides over 150,000 trade-related data series on CD-ROM. Includes full text of many government publications. Specific data is included on national income, labor, price indexes, foreign exchange, technical standards, and international markets. Website address is www.stat-usa.gov/.

DIRECTORIES

ABC voor Handel en Industrie. ABC voor Handel en Industries C.V. • Quarterly. Database covers: Approximately 120,000 profiles of Dutch manufacturers, importers, import agents and service providers and their products/services; also includes some 46,000 foreign houses' representatives in Holland. Entries include: Company name, address, phone, fax, telex; executive names; capital; bank affiliation; year founded; number of employees.

Advanced Manufacturing Technology. John Wiley & Sons Inc. Scientific, Technical, Medical, and Scholarly Div. (Wiley-Blackwell). • Monthly. Publication includes: List of companies involved in developing advanced manufacturing technologies such as robotics, artificial intelligence in computers, ultrasonics, lasers, and waterjet cutters; also lists sources of information and education on high-technology. Entries include: Company or organization name, address, phone, name of contact; description of process, product, or service. Principal content is articles and analysis of advanced manufacturing technology.

Alabama Industrial Directory. Alabama Development Office Alabama Center for Commerce. • Biennial. $75 Individuals print. Covers: More than 6,000 industrial companies in Alabama. Entries include: Company name, address, phone, fax number, e-mail and website addresses, NAICS code, name and title of principal executive, name and address of parent company, number of employees, product or service provided, Standard Industrial Classification (SIC) code, year established.

American Big Businesses Directory. InfoGroup Inc. • Annual. $295. Covers: 218,000 U.S. businesses with more than 100 employees, and 500,000 key executives and directors. CD-ROM version contains 160,000 top firms and 431,000 key executives. Entries include: Name, address, phone, names and titles of key personnel, number of employees, sales volume, Standard Industrial Classification (SIC) codes, subsidiaries and parent company names, stock exchanges on which traded.

American Manufacturers Directory. InfoGroup Inc. • Annual. $295. Covers: more than 150,000 manufacturing companies with 20 or more employees. CD-ROM version lists all 531,000 U.S. manufacturers, in all employee size ranges. Entries include: Company name, address, phone, contact name, Standard Industrial Classification (SIC) codes, number of employees, sales volume code, credit rating scores.

America's Corporate Families. Dun & Bradstreet Inc. • Annual. Covers approximately 12,700 U.S. corporations. Ultimate companies must meet all of the following criteria for inclusion: two or more business locations, 250 or more employees at that location or in excess of $25 million in sales volume or a tangible net worth greater than $500,000, and controlling interest in one or more subsidiary company.

The Americas Review: The Economic and Business Report. Kogan Page, Limited. • £50 Individuals. Covers: about 200 United States manufacturers and remanufacturers: includes facts on suppliers, country profiles, business guides, and directories for areas of North, Central, and South America, and all the Caribbean states and South Atlantic. Entries include: Heads of States, currencies, official languages, capital city, population, GNP, inflation, oil revenues, exports/imports, country profile, information for international visitors, name, address, phone of hotels, chambers of commerce, airlines, banks, government ministries and industrial associations.

Angola Industrial and Business Directory. International Business Publications, USA. • $99.95 Individuals hardcover. Covers: Strategic and practical economic and business information. Entries include: Business contacts for conducting business activity in the country.

Annuaire National de Fournisseurs des Administrations Francaises. Editions le Fil d'Ariane. • Annual. Covers: Over 2,00 industrial firms and merchant and service companies which are the main suppliers to the French Civil Service. Entries include: Company name, address, phone, fax, telex number, data on clients.

Antenna Industry Directory and Buyers Guide. Webcom Communications Corp. • $195 Individuals hardcopy. Covers: Over 2,000 antenna designers, manufacturers, distributors, installers, suppliers, consultants, government agencies and information sources worldwide. Entries include: Company name, address, phone, fax, email, website address, executive names and titles, year founded, sales, company description, and antenna types offered.

Argentina Industrial and Business Directory. International Business Publications, USA. • Annual. $99.95 Individuals hardcover. Covers: Detailed information on investment, export-import business opportunities, foreign economic assistance projects, government and business contacts.

Arkansas Manufacturing Directory. Arkansas Industrial Development Foundation. • Annual. $75 pre-payment required. Covers: about 2,800 firms in Arkansas. Entries include: Company name, address, phone, names of principal executives, number of employees, list of products or services, Standard Industrial Classification (SIC) codes, whether company exports, name of parent company if firm is a subsidiary.

Association of Thai Industries--Industrial Directory. Business Company Ltd. • Biennial. $350. Covers: 827 manufacturers, wholesalers, and distributors in Thailand. Entries include: Company name, address, phone, telex, and names of directors and officials.

Australia Industrial and Business Directory. International Business Publications, USA. • Annual. $99.95 Individuals hardcover. Covers: Strategic industrial, investment, and business contacts for conducting export-import and investment activity in the country.

Austria Industrial and Business Directory. International Business Publications, USA. • Annual. $99.95 Individuals hardcover. Covers: Detailed information on investment, export-import business opportunities, foreign economic assistance projects, government and business contacts.

Bangladesh Industrial and Business Directory. International Business Publications, USA. • Annual. $99.95 Individuals hardcover. Covers: Strategic industrial, investment and business contacts for conducting export-import and investment activity in the country.

Belarus Industrial and Business Directory. International Business Publications, USA. • Annual. $99.95 Individuals hardcover. Covers: Strategic industrial, investment and business contacts for conducting export-import and investment activity in the country.

Belgium Industrial and Business Directory. International Business Publications, USA. • Annual. $99.95 Individuals hardcover. Covers: Detailed information on investment, export-import business opportunities, foreign economic assistance projects, government and business contacts.

Biometric Information Directory. Grey House Publishing. • $225 Individuals softcover. Covers: 700+ manufacturers and service providers in the biometrics industry, including finger, voice, face, hand, signature, iris, vein and palm identification systems. Includes information resources such as organizations, trade & educational associations, publications, conferences, trade shows and expositions worldwide. Entries include: Name, address, phone, fax, email, website, key executives, company size and a detailed, indexed description of their product line.

Birmingham Area Industrial Directory. Birmingham Regional Chamber of Commerce. • Biennial. $55 Members. Covers: about 2,800 manufacturing establishments in 21 counties of Alabama including maps. Features pinpointer county maps. Entries include: Company name, address, phone, name of principal executive, number of employees, product/service, SIC numbers.

Bolivia Industrial and Business Directory. International Business Publications, USA. • Annual. $99.95 Individuals hardcover. Covers: Strategic industrial, investment and business contacts for conducting export-import and investment activity in the country.

Brazil Industrial and Business Directory. International Business Publications, USA. • Annual. $99.95 Individuals hardcopy. Covers: Strategic industrial, investment and business contacts for conducting export-import and investment activity in the country.

Business Forms, Labels & Systems--Who's Who of Manufacturers and Suppliers. North American Publishing Co. • Annual. Covers: More than 800 manufacturers of business forms, labels, and related products, and 500 suppliers of equipment and paper used to manufacture business forms. Entries include: Company name, address, phone, fax, toll-free number, company profile.

Businessman's Directory of the Republic of China. Taiwan Enterprise Press Ltd. • Annual. $75 airmail postpaid. Covers: Taiwan manufacturers, exporters, importers, and services.

California Manufacturers Register: 2008 Edition. San Francisco Chamber of Commerce. • Annual. $259 Nonmembers (with book and Read only CD-ROM). Covers: 34,000 manufacturing firms which are members of the California Manufacturers Association. Entries include: Contact details.

Cameroon Industrial and Business Directory. International Business Publications, USA. • $99.95 Individuals hardcover. Covers: Strategic and practical economic and business information. Entries include: Business contacts for conducting business activity in the country.

Canada Industrial and Business Directory. International Business Publications, USA. • Annual. $99.95 Individuals hardcopy. Covers: Detailed information on investment, export-import business opportunities, foreign economic assistance projects, government and business contacts.

Chile Industrial and Business Directory. International Business Publications, USA. • Annual. $99.95 Individuals hardcopy, e-book, CD-ROM. Covers: Strategic industrial, investment and business contacts for conducting export-import and investment activity in the country.

China Product Handbook. Chis Info-Consultants Company Ltd. • $300 Individuals. Covers: 20,000 famous enterprises in China, including machinery, electric, electronic, light, textile, chemical, and pharmaceutical industries. Entries include: Enterprise name, address, phone, fax, director, major products.

China's Manufacturers and Products Database. Computing Center of the Ministry of Foreign Trade and Economic Cooperation. • $3,600. Database covers: 50,000 manufacturers in China. Entries include: Contact information, office hours, executives, bankers, number of employees, contact person, registered capital, sales, list of products.

Commercial and Industrial Directory. Impresos Litograficos de Centro America. • Annual. $15. Covers: Commercial and industrial manufacturers, wholesalers, and distributors in El Salvador. Entries include: Company name, address, phone, telex, names of directors, type of company.

Commercial and Industrial Directory of Switzerland. Mosse Adress AG. • Annual. $901 Individuals. Covers: 300,000 industrial, trade, and export businesses and services in Switzerland. Entries include: Company name, address, phone.

Copying & Duplicating Machine & Supplies Directory. InfoGroup Inc. • Annual. Number of listings: 10,350. Entries include: Name, address, phone (including area code), size of advertisement, year first in "Yellow Pages." Coding indicates brands carried, specialties, or franchises held. Franchise editions also available. Compiled from telephone company "Yellow Pages," nationwide.

Copying & Duplicating Service Directory. InfoGroup Inc. • Annual. Number of listings: 20,946. Entries include: Company name, address, phone (including area code), size of advertisement, year first in "Yellow Pages," name of owner or manager, number of employees. Compiled from telephone company "Yellow Pages," nationwide.

Dalton's Baltimore/Washington Metropolitan Directory of Business/Industry. Dalton Directory. • Covers: over 8,500 companies in the Baltimore and Washington, D.C. metropolitan area, including manufacturers, law firms, hospitals, hotels, schools and colleges, accounting firms, etc. Entries include: Company name, address, phone, fax, names and titles of key personnel, number of employees, Standard Industrial Classification (SIC) code, product/service.

Denmark Industrial and Business Directory. International Business Publications, USA. • Annual. $99.95 Individuals hardcopy, e-book, CD-ROM. Covers: Detailed information on investment, export-import business opportunities, foreign economic assistance projects, government and business contacts.

Department of Trade and Industry--The Single Market: Guide to Sources of Advice. Department of Trade and Industry. • Covers: Organizations providing information on business and trade in the European Community, including representative organizations, research and technology organizations, chambers of commerce, public sector advisers, and language advisers. Entries include: For representative organizations and research and technology organizations--Name, address, phone, name and title of contact, sectors covered, restrictions on service, type of information offered, European links. For others--Name, address, phone, type of information offered.

Directory of Central Atlantic States Manufacturers. George D. Hall Company Inc. • Biennial. $83 plus $4.90 shipping (1994 edition). Covers: about 18,000 companies in Maryland, Delaware, Virginia, West Virginia, North Carolina, and South Carolina. Entries include: Company name, address, phone, name of principal executive, number of employees, products or services, Standard Industrial Classification (SIC) code.

Directory of Colorado Manufacturers. University of Colorado at Boulder Leeds School of Business Business Research Division. • $100 Individuals book; plus tax. Covers: 6,000 manufacturing firms in Colorado. Entries include: Company name, mailing address, plant address, phone, Standard Metropolitan Statistical Area (SMSA), names and titles of executives, date founded, distribution area, approximate employment, products or services.

Directory of East European Businesses. Mercury Books Gold Arrow Publications Ltd. • $74.95 plus $3.50 shipping. Covers: 2,000 leading manufacturing and engineering companies in Albania, Bulgaria, the Commonwealth of Independent States, eastern Germany, Hungary, Poland, Romania, and Czechoslovakia and Yugoslavia (prior to their separations). Entries include: Company name, address, phone, fax, telex, name and title of contact, line of business, sales, profits.

Directory of EC Industry Information Sources. Macmillan Publishers Ltd. Nature Publishing Group. • $105 plus $6.00 postage. Covers: Organizations and individuals in the European Communities responsible for specific industrial information, including finding business partners, business startups, lobbying, electronic information services, and statistics.

Directory of Florida Industries. Florida Chamber of Commerce. • Annual. Covers: About 15,300 manufacturing, mining, and processing concerns with 4 or more employees. Entries include: Company name, address, phone, names of principal executives, number of employees, products or services, Standard Industrial Classification (SIC) numbers, whether firm imports or exports.

Directory of Foreign Manufacturers in the United States. Georgia State University Business Press. • Biennial. $195 payment must accompany orders from individuals. Covers: over 7,300 United States manufacturing, mining, and petroleum companies, and the over 6,800 firms abroad that own them. Entries include: Company name, address, phone, fax, products or services, Standard Industrial Classification (SIC) codes, parent company name and address.

Directory of Industrial Suppliers. Hong Kong Productivity Council. • Annual. $280 pick up at HKPC Office. Covers: Over 3,000 industrial suppliers in Hong Kong as well as their operations in Mainland China. Entries include: Name, address, phone, fax, e-mail, URL, number of employees, turnover, and products/brand names.

Directory of Kansas Manufacturers and Products. Kansas Department of Commerce & Housing. • Biennial. $50. Covers: Approximately 2,500 manufacturers in Kansas. Entries include: Company name, address, phone, fax, name of principal executive, products or services, codes for number of employees.

Directory of Louisiana Manufacturers. Dun & Bradstreet Inc. • Annual. Covers: Over 6,500 manufacturing companies in Louisiana. Database includes: Statistical data, trade show calendar. Entries include: Company name, address, county, phone, fax, number of employees, names and titles of key executives, plant size, year established, parent company, annual sales, import and export information, Standard Industrial Classification (SIC) code, and product description.

Directory of Manufacturers of Pressure-Sensitive Tape, Label Stock, and Other Coated Products. Satas & Associates. • $99. Covers: 92 manufacturers of specialized coated tapes and labeling products. Entries include: Company name, address, phone, product/service.

Directory of North Carolina Manufacturing Firms: Federal ID 56-1611-847. Harris InfoSource. • Annual. $70 payment must accompany order. Covers: Approximately 7,200 manufacturers in North Carolina. Entries include: Company name, address, names and titles of principal executives, names and address of parent company, geographical area served, Standard Industrial Classification (SIC) code, product/service provided, number of employees, year established.

Directory of Packaging and Allied Industries. NIIR Project Consultancy Services. • $100 Individuals. Covers: 1,000 companies/industries (manufacturers and suppliers) of packaging industries, packaging raw material, packaging machineries in India. Entries include: Company name, full postal address, phone, fax, email (wherever available), website address (wherever available).

Directory of Rhode Island Manufacturers. Rhode Island Economic Development Corporation. • Annual. Covers: 2800 manufacturers in Rhode Island. Entries include: Company name, address, phone, product/service, name and title of contact, number of employees, parent company, and estimated sales.

Directory of Texas Manufacturers. University of Texas at Austin IC2 Institute Bureau of Business Research. • Annual. $139. Covers: more than 17,000 manufacturers in Texas and Texarkana, Arkansas; includes Standard Industrial Classification (SIC) manufacturing codes, products. Entries include: Company name, address, phone, toll-free number, fax number, geographical territory covered, form of company organization, number of employees, products, sales volume, SIC code. Updated monthly by "Texas Industrial Expansion" (see separate entry).

Directory of the Russian Far East. Flegon Press. • Irregular. $99. Covers: Industry in the Far East of Russia. Entries include: Company name and location, manager name, phone, telex, number of employees, products, and import/export details.

Dirigeants and Cadres. Editus S.A.R.L. • Annual. Covers: 4,500 executives in the commerce trade and industry in Luxembourg. Entries include: Names and addresses.

Dominican Republic Industrial and Business Directory. International Business Publications, USA. • Annual. $99.95 Individuals hardcopy, e-book, CD-ROM. Covers: Strategic industrial, investment and business contacts for conducting export-import and investment activity in the country. Contains strategic practical economic and business information.

Dubai Industrial and Business Directory. International Business Publications, USA. • $99.95 Individuals hardcopy, e-book, CD-ROM. Covers: Strategic investment and business contacts for conducting export-import activity in the country. Entries include: Strategic economic and business information.

Dun's Industrial Guide: The Metalworking Directory. Dun & Bradstreet Inc. • Annual. Libraries, $485; commercial institutions, $795.00. Lease basis. Three volumes. Lists about 65,000 U. S. manufacturing plants using metal and suppliers of metalworking equipment and materials. Includes names and titles of key personnel. Products, purchases, and processes are indicated.

East European Business Information. Headland Press. • Annual. $99. Covers: Organizations providing commercial and industrial information in Eastern Europe, including information on joint ventures, banking, legislation, and marketing. Entries include: Name, address, phone.

Economic Guide--Tunisia. Information Economique Africaine. • Biennial. $50. Covers: Industrial, commercial and agricultural entities in Tunisia. Entries include: Company name, address, phone.

Egypt Industrial and Business Directory. International Business Publications, USA. • Annual. $99.95 Individuals paperback, e-book, CD-ROM. Covers: Strategic industrial, investment and business contacts for conducting export-import and investment activity in the country.

ESSOR. Union Francaise d'Annuaires Professionnels. • Annual. Covers: more than 200,000 French companies involved in industry and services. Entries include: Company name, address, phone, fax, telex, names and titles of key personnel, line of business, number of employees, registered capital, sales, product descriptions, legal and administrative information.

Estonia Industrial and Business Directory. International Business Publications, USA. • Annual. $99.95 Individuals paperback, e-book, CD-ROM. Covers: Strategic industrial, investment and business contacts for conducting export-import and investment activity in the country. Contains strategic practical economic and business information.

The European Market for High Voltage Switchgear. ABS Publications. • $800. Covers: European manufacturers of high voltage switchgear (greater than 1kV). Entries include: Utility statistics, company profiles, trade production and market data for both supply and demand.

Faulkner & Gray's European Business Directory. Thomson Financial Inc. • Annual. $295. Covers: over 2,000 attorneys, accountants, consultants, search firms, translators, shippers, commercial and investment banks, and industry leaders in Europe and the U.S. interested in or presently doing business in Europe. Database includes: Profiles of 40 countries. Entries include: Company or personal name, address, phone, telex, name and title of contact, subsidiary and branch names and locations, description of service.

Florida Industries Guide. Industries Guides Inc. • Biennial. $95. Number of listings: 10,000. Entries include: Company name, address, phone, name of contact, products or services, number of employees, sic codes, fax and 800 numbers.

France Industrial and Business Directory. International Business Publications, USA. • Annual. $99.95 Individuals hardcopy, e-book, CD-ROM. Covers: Detailed information on investment, export-import business opportunities, foreign economic assistance projects, government and business contacts.

George D. Hall's Directory of New England Manufacturers. George D. Hall Company Inc. • $128 plus $4.95 shipping. Covers: about 21,000 manufacturers in Connecticut, Maine, Massachusetts, New Hampshire, Rhode Island, and Vermont. Entries include: For manufacturers--company name, address, phone, names of principal executives, Standard Industrial Classification (SIC) code, product/service, number of employees, whether firm exports or imports. For banks--Name, address, phone, names of principal executives, service, number of employees.

Georgia Industries Guide. Industries Guides Inc. • $95. Covers: Approximately 9,000 manufacturers in Georgia. Entries include: Company name, address, phone.

Georgia Manufacturing Directory. Georgia Chamber of Commerce. • Annual. $99.95 book; payment must accompany order. Covers: about 9,400 firms manufacturing products within Standard Industrial Classification (SIC) codes 20-39. Entries include: Company name, address, phone, names of principal executives, number of men and women employees, products or services, 4-digit SIC numbers, date established, market served, e-mail and web addresses.

Georgia Republic Business and Industrial Directory. International Business Publications, USA. • Annual. $99.95 Individuals hardcover, e-book, CD-ROM. Covers: Strategic industrial, investment and business contacts for conducting export-import and investment activity in the country.

Germany Industrial and Business Directory. International Business Publications, USA. • Annual. $99.95 Individuals hardcover, e-book, CD-ROM. Covers: Strategic industrial, investment and business contacts for conducting export-import and investment activity in the country.

Gibaud Directory--Industrial, Commercial and Trade Enterprises. Annuaire Gibaud. • Annual. Covers: 27,000 industrial, commercial and trade enterprises in France. Entries include: Company name, address, phone, name and title of contact, year established, number of employees, subsidiaries, manager name, product/service.

Greece Industrial and Business Directory. International Business Publications, USA. • Annual. $99.95 Individuals hardcopy, e-book, CD-ROM. Covers: Strategic industrial, investment and business contacts for conducting export-import and investment activity in the country. Contains strategic, practical economic and business information.

Gulf Coast Industrial Atlas/Directory. Industrial Info Resources Inc. • Continuous. Covers: about 2,400 heavy industrial plants (including refineries, steel mills, power plants, pulp and paper mills, terminals, docks, storage saltdomes, gas processing plants, chemical plants) and 4,800 management contacts in Florida, Alabama, Mississippi, Louisiana, and Texas. Database includes: Wall maps from Laredo, Texas to St. Marks, Florida. Entries include: For plants--Company or plant name, mailing address, street address, phone, fax, names of plant manager and purchasing agent. For engineering and service companies--Name, address, phone, fax, line of business, description of company.

Harris Manufacturers Directory 2000: National Edition. Harris InfoSource. • Annual. $565.00. Two volumes. Provides statistical and descriptive information for about 47,062 U.S. industrial firms having 100 or more employees.

Harris Minnesota Directory of Manufacturers. Dun & Bradstreet Inc. • Annual. Covers: over 11,500 manufacturers in Minnesota. Entries include: Company name, address, key executives, annual sales, phone, fax, toll-free number, number of employees, date established, Standard Industrial Classification (SIC) codes, list of products, international trade, and plant square footage.

Headquarters USA: A Directory of Contact Information for Headquarters and Other Central Offices of Major Businesses and Organizations Nationwide. Omnigraphics Inc. • $195 Individuals Hardcover - Web price. Two volumes. Volume one is alphabetical by name of business or organization. Volume two is classified by subject. Includes more than 112,000 businesses, organizations, agencies, institutions, and "high-profile" individuals. Listings include addresses, telephone numbers, fax numbers, and toll-free numbers and Web addresses where available. Formerly *Business Phone Book USA*.

Hong Kong Commercial/Industrial Guide. GTE Directories Ltd. • $30. Covers: over 200,000 suppliers of 2,000 products and services in Hong Kong; banks, importers and exporters. Entries include: Company name, address, phone, telex, fax.

Idaho Manufacturers Directory and Industrial Database. Manufacturers' News Inc. • Annual. $89 Individuals print. Covers: 2,560 manufacturers in Idaho. Entries include: Company name, address, phone, names and titles of key personnel, year established, number of employees, plant square footage, services, Standard Industry Classification (SIC) code, parent and subsidiary company information, type of in-house computer system, URL, e-mail address.

Illinois Industries Guide. Industries Guides Inc. • $95. Covers: Approximately 20,000 manufacturers in Illinois. Entries include: Company name, address, phone.

Illinois Manufacturers Directory. Manufacturers' News Inc. • Annual. $211 Individuals print; plus shipping and handling. Covers: 19,423 manufacturers and 61,317 executives in Illinois. Entries include: Company name, address, phone, titles and functions of key personnel, year established, number of employees, plant square footage, services, Standard Industrial Classification (SIC) code, parent and subsidiary company information, type of in-house computer system, fax, web address, e-mail address.

Indiana All-Business Database. Harris InfoSource. • Database covers: 21,000 manufacturing and service companies throughout Indiana.

Indonesia Industrial and Business Directory. International Business Publications, USA. • $99.95 Individuals hardcopy, e-book, CD-ROM. Covers: Strategic investment, industrial and business contacts for conducting investment and export-import activity in the country.

Industrial & Service Contacts in Ex-Soviet Union Area Republics. MZM Publications Publishing Promotion Co. • Irregular. Entries include: Company name, address, phone, telex.

Industrial/Commercial Directory of Peru. Confederacion Nacional de Comerciantes. • Annual. $50. Covers: Industrial and commercial firms in Peru. Entries include: Name, address, phone, telex, products, services.

Industrial Directory of Colombia Guide. Legis Ltda. • Annual. $18. Covers: Manufacturers, distributors, and services in Colombia. Entries include: Name, address, phone, telex.

Industrial Directory of Israel. Dun & Bradstreet Israel Ltd. • Irregular. $48. Covers: Local industries in Israel. Entries include: Address, telephone, annual sales, names and titles of key personnel, products, exports.

Industrial Market Location. Market Location Ltd. • Database covers: about 150,000 manufacturing and distribution firms and commercial businesses in the United Kingdom. Database includes: Company name, address, phone, names and titles of key personnel, number of employees, description of product/service, Standard Industrial Classification (SIC) code.

Industridata: AA Enterprises. Mercametrica Ediciones S.A. • Annual. $550 Individuals. Covers: Over 1,700 industrial, commercial, and services companies in Mexico with 251 to 500 employees. Includes banks and insurance companies. Companion volume of 'Industridata: AAA Enterprises' (see separate entry). Information from both titles is listed by postal code in 'Industridata by Zip Codes.' Entries include: Company name, location, phone, fax, telex, days and hours of operation, main products and brands, number of employees, sales, installed capacity and output for previous four years, government and foreign ownership, year established, names and titles of key personnel.

Industry--New and Expanding. Alabama Development Office Alabama Center for Commerce. • Annual. Covers: List of industrial companies announcing plans to locate or expand facilities in Alabama. Entries include: Company name, location, products or services, amount of capital investment, number of jobs created.

Iran Industrial and Business Directory. International Business Publications, USA. • Annual. $99.95 Individuals hardcopy, e-book, CD-ROM. Covers: Strategic industrial, investment and business contacts for conducting export-import and investment activity in the country.

Iraq Industrial and Business Directory. International Business Publications, USA. • Annual. $99.95 Individuals hardcopy, e-book, CD-ROM. Covers: Strategic industrial, investment and business contacts for conducting export-import and investment activity in the country. Contains strategic practical economic and business information.

Ireland Industrial and Business Directory. International Business Publications, USA. • Annual. $99.95 Individuals hardcover, e-book, CD-ROM. Covers: Strategic industrial, investment and business contacts for conducting export-import and investment activity in the country. Contains strategic practical economic and business information.

IT Legal Guide. VNU Business Publications Ltd. • Annual. $45 plus 4 postage. Covers: More than 400 manufacturers, distributors, and consultants in the United Kingdom specializing with information on 300 technology products and services for the legal profession. Database includes: List of pertinent information sources. Entries include: Name, address, phone, fax, description of products/services.

Italy Industrial and Business Directory. International Business Publications, USA. • Annual. $99.95 Individuals hardcover, e-book, CD-ROM. Covers: Strategic industrial, investment and business contacts for conducting export-import and investment activity in the country. Contains strategic, practical economic and business information.

Japan Industrial and Business Directory. International Business Publications, USA. • $99.95 Individuals hardcopy, e-book, CD-ROM. Covers: Customs, trade regulations and procedures.

Kansas Directory of Manufacturers and Products. Wichita Eagle. • Biennial. $50. Covers: Approximately 2,400 manufacturers in Kansas; includes Standard Industrial Classification (SIC) code 02, 07, 13, 14, 20, 22-39, and 49. Entries include: Company name, address, phone, telex, names and titles of key personnel, number of employees, description of products, Standard Industrial Classification (SIC) code.

Kansas Manufacturers Register. Harris InfoSource. • Annual. $145 Individuals All-Businesses Price. Covers: Over 4,900 manufacturers in Kansas. Entries include: Company name, address, phone, fax, toll-free numbers, names and titles of key personnel, number of employees, annual sales, square feet, Standard Industrial Classification (SIC) codes, products produced, year established, foreign trade, and headquarters information.

Kansas Manufacturing Firms in Export. Kansas Department of Commerce - Office of Minority and Women Business Development. • Biennial. Covers: nearly 1,000 Kansas companies in major groups 20 through 39 of the Standard Industrial Classification (SIC). Entries include: Company name, address, phone, name of principal executive, parent or subsidiary company, number of employees, products or services.

Kelly's Industrial Directory Book. Reed Business Information. • Annual. Directory of over 94,600 U.K. industrial companies.

Kentucky Directory of Manufacturers. Kentucky Cabinet for Economic Development. • Annual. $87. Covers: Approximately 5,900 manufacturing firms in Kentucky. Entries include: Company name, address, phone, names of principal executives, number of employees, products or services, date established, parent company (with name and address).

Kenya Industrial and Business Directory. International Business Publications, USA. • Annual. $99.95 Individuals hardcopy, e-book, CD-ROM. Covers: Strategic industrial, investment and business contacts for conducting export-import and investment activity in the country. Contains strategic practical economic and business information.

Kompass Deutschland: Jahrbuch der Deutschen

Wirtschaft. Kompass Deutschland Verlags- und Vertriebsgesellschaft, mbH. • Annual. Covers: Major German manufacturers, distributors, and service companies linked to 40,000 products and services. Database includes: Glossary. Entries include: Company name, address, phone, telex, names and titles of key personnel, bank, key to product and service listings, year established, symbols indicating whether company is a manufacturer, wholesaler, or agent, and whether it imports and exports, turnover, number of employees, shareholders; reference to dot-chart index.

Kompass International. Kompass France. • Annual. Covers: Over 1,500,000 commercial and industrial firms worldwide; over 500,000 prominent business and industry professionals in 64 countries.

Kraks Industrial and Commercial Directory of Denmark. Kraks Forlag A.S. • Annual. $2,765. Covers: 73,400 industrial and commercial firms in Denmark; 94,000 companies in the Register of Limited Liability Companies, the Insurance Register, and Trade Register in Denmark; public authorities, institutions, libraries, churches, hospitals, museums, schools, universities, and societies in Denmark. Entries include: Organization name, address, phone, product/service (where applicable).

Kyrgyzstan Industrial and Business Directory. International Business Publications, USA. • Annual. $99.95 Individuals hardcopy, e-book, CD-ROM. Covers: Strategic industrial, investment and business contacts for conducting export-import and investment activity in the country.

Latvia Industrial and Business Directory. International Business Publications, USA. • Annual. $99.95 Individuals hardcopy, e-book, CD-ROM. Covers: Strategic industrial, investment and business contacts for conducting export-import and investment activity in the country.

Liechtenstein Industrial and Business Directory. International Business Publications, USA. • Annual. $99.95 Individuals hardcover, e-book, CD-ROM. Covers: Strategic industrial, investment and business contacts for conducting export-import and investment activity in the country.

Lithuania Industrial and Business Directory. International Business Publications, USA. • Annual. $99.95 Individuals hardcover, e-book, CD-ROM. Covers: Strategic industrial, investment and business contacts for conducting export-import and investment activity in the country.

Luxembourg Industrial and Business Directory. International Business Publications, USA. • Annual. $99.95 Individuals paperback, e-book, CD-ROM. Covers: Strategic industrial, investment and business contacts for conducting export-import and investment activity in the country. Contains strategic, practical economic and business information.

MacRae's Blue Book. MacRae's Blue Book. • Annual. Covers: about 50,000 manufacturing firms. Entries include: Company name, address, products or services, phone, email and URL addresses.

Maine Manufacturers Register and Industrial Database. Manufacturers' News Inc. • Annual. $92 Individuals print. Covers: 2,683 manufacturers in Maine. Entries include: Company name, address, phone, names and titles of key personnel, year established, number of employees, plant square footage, services, Standard Industry Classification (SIC) code, parent and subsidiary company information, type of in-house computer system, URL, e-mail address.

Maine Manufacturing Directory. Tower Publishing Co. • Annual. $55 Individuals. Covers: Approximately 1,584 manufacturers and processors in Maine. Entries include: Company name, address, phone, fax, toll-free phone, e-mail and web addresses, names and titles of principal officers, number of employees, product or service, Standard Industrial Classification (SIC) code, parent company (if applicable), sales revenue, import/export data.

Malaysia Industrial and Business Directory. International Business Publications, USA. • $99.95 Individuals hardcopy, e-book, CD-ROM. Covers: Customs, trade regulations and procedures.

Massachusetts Manufacturers Register and Industrial Database. Manufacturers' News Inc. • Annual. $141 Individuals print. Covers: 9,577 manufacturers in Massachusetts. Entries include: Company name, address, phone, names and titles of key personnel, year established, number of employees, plant square footage, services, Standard Industry Classification (SIC) code, parent and subsidiary company information, type of in-house computer system, URL, e-mail address.

Mauritius Industrial and Business Directory. International Business Publications, USA. • Annual. $99.95 Individuals hardcopy, e-book, CD-ROM. Covers: Strategic industrial, investment and business contacts for conducting export-import and investment activity in the country.

Mergent Industrial Manual and News Reports. Mergent Inc. • Annual. $2,095 including 'News Reports.' Covers: nearly 2,000 companies listed on the New York, American, or regional stock exchanges. Entries include: Company name, headquarters address, phone, names and titles of executive officers and directors, history, Standard Industrial Classification (SIC) code, Moody's rating, and financial and statistical data.

Mergent OTC Industrial Manual. Mergent Inc. • Annual. $1,995 including 'News Reports.' Covers over 2,500 companies whose stock is traded over the counter. Includes biweekly *Moody's OTC Industrial News Report*.

Metropolitan Atlanta Manufacturing Directory. Metro Atlanta Chamber of Commerce. • Biennial. $30 Members only available in PDF document sent via email. Covers: About 4,000 firms with Standard Industrial Classification (SIC) codes 20-39 in the Atlanta metropolitan area. Entries include: Company name, address, phone, names of principal executives, number of employees, product or service provided, SIC code, date established, market served.

Michigan Industrial Directory. Dun & Bradstreet Inc. • Annual. Covers: 20,100 Michigan manufacturing companies. Database includes: Statistical data, trade show calendar. Entries include: Company name, address, county, phone, fax, number of employees, names and titles of key executives, plant size, year established, parent company, annual sales, import and export information, Standard Industrial Classification (SIC) code, and product description.

Minnesota Industries Guide. Industries Guides Inc. • $95. Covers: Approximately 10,000 manufacturers in Minnesota. Entries include: Company name, address, phone.

Moldova Industrial and Business Directory. International Business Publications, USA. • Annual. $99.95 Individuals hardcopy, e-book, CD-ROM. Covers: Strategic industrial, investment and business contacts for conducting export-import and investment activity in the country. Contains strategic practical economic and business information.

Mongolia Industrial and Business Directory. International Business Publications, USA. • $99.95 Individuals hardcopy, e-book, CD-ROM. Covers: Strategic and practical economic and business information. Entries include: Business contacts for conducting business activity in the country.

Montana Manufacturers Directory. Montana Department of Commerce Office of Trade and International Relations. • $50. Covers: Approximately 1,900 manufacturing firms in Montana. Entries include: Company name, address, phone, name of principal executive, number of employees, products or service provided.

Namibia Industrial and Business Directory. International Business Publications, USA. • Annual. $99.95 Individuals hardcopy, e-book, CD-ROM. Covers: Strategic industrial, investment and business contacts for conducting export-import and investment activity in the country. Contains strategic practical economic and business information.

Netherlands Industrial and Business Directory. International Business Publications, USA. • Annual. $99.95 Individuals hardcover, e-book, CD-ROM. Covers: Detailed information on investment, export-import business opportunities, foreign economic assistance projects, government and business contacts.

Nevada Manufacturers Directory and Industrial Database. Manufacturers' News Inc. • Annual. $86 Individuals print. Covers: 2,104 manufacturers in Nevada. Entries include: Company name, address, phone, names and titles of key personnel, year established, number of employees, plant square footage, services, Standard Industry Classification (SIC) code, parent and subsidiary company information, type of in-house computer system, URL, e-mail address.

Nevada Manufacturers Register. Harris InfoSource. • Annual. Covers: Approximately 2,800 manufacturers in Nevada plus names and titles of key executives. Entries include: Company name, address, parent name/location, telephone, fax and 800 numbers, Web site address (on CD-ROM only), number of employees, year established, annual revenue, plant size, business description, Standard Industrial Classification (SIC) codes, executive names/titles, public ownership, legal structure, import/export designators, female/minority ownership.

New Caledonia Industrial and Business Directory. International Business Publications, USA. • Annual. $99.95 Individuals hardcopy, e-book, CD-ROM. Covers: Strategic industrial, investment and business contacts for conducting export-import and investment activity in the country. Contains strategic, practical economic and business information.

New Hampshire Manufacturers Register and Industrial Database. Manufacturers' News Inc. • Annual. $93 Individuals print. Covers: 2,963 manufacturers in New Hampshire. Entries include: Company name, address, phone, names and titles of key personnel, year established, number of employees, plant square footage, services, Standard Industry Classification (SIC) code, parent and subsidiary company information, type of in-house computer system, URL, e-mail address.

New Industries and Plant Expansions Reported in Wisconsin. Wisconsin Department of Development Bureau of Information Services. • Annual. Covers: plant additions, new plants, branch plants, and relocated plants announced during the year to be built in Wisconsin; about 300 projects in recent edition. Entries include: Company name, city of new or expanded construction, type of project, square footage, type of facility (plant, office, etc.), number of workers to be added, product or service.

New Zealand Industrial and Business Directory. International Business Publications, USA. • Annual. $99.95 Individuals hardcopy, e-book, CD-ROM. Covers: Strategic industrial, investment and business contacts for conducting export-import and investment activity in the country.

Nigeria Industrial and Business Directory. International Business Publications, USA. • Annual. $99.95 Individuals hardcover. Covers: Strategic industrial, investment and business contacts for conducting export-import and investment activity in the country.

North Carolina/South Carolina Industries Guide.

Industries Guides Inc. • $95. Covers: Approximately 14,000 manufacturers in North Carolina and South Carolina. Entries include: Company name, address, phone.

Northern Ireland Trade Directory. Industrial Development Board for Northern Ireland Her Majesty's Stationary Office. • Annual. $33. Covers: Approximately 5,200 manufacturing companies in Northern Ireland. Entries include: Company name, address, phone, telex, name and title of contact, number of employees, description of product/service.

Norway Exports--Products and Services for Development. The Export Council of Norway. • Biennial. Covers: Products and services exported in Norway in a variety of lines of business, including financial and banking services, construction, mining, electricity, manufacturing and metals, electronics, training, surveying and mapping, wood processing, water supply and electricity. Entries include: Company name, address, phone, telex number, product/service.

Ohio Industrial Directory. Harris InfoSource. • Annual. $220 Individuals manufacturing price. Covers: 22,900 Ohio manufacturing companies. Database includes: Statistical data, trade show calendar. Entries include: Company name, address, county, phone, fax, number of employees, names and titles of key executives, plant size, year established, parent company, annual sales, import/export information, Standard Industrial Classification (SIC) code, and product description.

Ohio Industries Guide. Industries Guides Inc. • $95. Covers: Approximately 20,000 manufacturers in Ohio. Entries include: Company name, address, phone.

Ohio Roster. Edward Howard & Co. • $12. Covers: the 200 largest manufacturers, retailers, service companies, transportation firms, public utilities, and financial institutions headquartered in Ohio whose stock is publicly traded. Database includes: Lists of the top 20 firms by revenue, assets, net income, and biggest sales gain. Entries include: Firm name, location, total revenues, net income, total assets, earnings per share, stock exchange on which traded.

Oklahoma Directory of Manufacturers and Processors. Dun & Bradstreet Inc. • Annual. $100 Individuals. Covers: 5,000 Oklahoma manufacturers (Standard Industrial Classification (SIC) codes 20-39). Entries include: Company name, address, phone, fax, name of principal executive, employment number, date established, Standard Industrial Classification (SIC) codes, list of products or services.

Oman Chamber of Commerce and Industry--Industrial Directory. Oman Chamber of Commerce and Industry. • Provides data on companies and industrial enterprises in the Sultanate and supporting institutions to invest in the industrial sector, investment incentives and facilities as well as available investment opportunities in all areas of economic activity.

Oman Trade Directory. Oman Chamber of Commerce and Industry. • Provides information about companies and economic institutions in Oman.

Oregon Manufacturers Directory and Industrial Database. Manufacturers' News Inc. • Annual. $114 Individuals print. Covers: 6,835 manufacturers in Oregon. Entries include: Company name, address, phone, names and titles of key personnel, year established, number of employees, plant square footage, services, Standard Industry Classification (SIC) code, parent and subsidiary company information, type of in-house computer system, URL, e-mail address.

Oregon Manufacturers Register. Harris InfoSource. • Annual. Covers: Approximately 8,400 manufacturers plus key executives in Oregon. Entries include: Company, address, parent name/location, telephone, fax and 800 numbers, Web site address (on CD-ROM only), number of employees, year established, annual revenue, plant size, business description, Standard Industrial Classification (SIC) codes, executive names/titles, public ownership, legal structure, import/export designators, female/minority ownership.

Orion Blue Book--Copier. Orion Research Corp. • Annual. $130 Individuals hardbound or CD. Publication includes: List of manufacturers of copiers and other office equipment. Entries include: Company name, address, phone. Principal content of publication is a listing of 3,091 office equipment products with the original retail value, value paid to customer on trade-in when in mint condition, and average value paid to customer on trade-in.

Panama Industrial and Business Directory. International Business Publications, USA. • Annual. $99.95 Individuals hardcopy, e-book, CD-ROM. Covers: Strategic industrial, investment and business contacts for conducting export-import and investment activity in the country.

PennSuburban Chamber of Commerce--Membership Directory. PennSuburban Chamber of Commerce. • Annual. Covers: Over 900 member businesses and industries in Montgomery, Bucks, and Chester counties in Pennsylvania. Entries include: Company name, address, phone, names and titles of key personnel, number of employees, product or service provided.

Pennsylvania Industrial Directory. Dun & Bradstreet Inc. • Annual. Covers: 22,600 manufacturing establishments in Pennsylvania. Database includes: Statistical data and trade show calendar. Entries include: Company name, address, county, phone, toll-free number, number of employees, names and titles of key executives, plant size, year established, parent company, annual sales, import/export information, SIC code, and product description.

Pennsylvania Industries Guide. Industries Guides Inc. • $95. Covers: Approximately 17,000 manufacturers in Pennsylvania. Entries include: Company name, address, phone.

Peru Industrial and Business Directory. International Business Publications, USA. • Annual. $99.95 Individuals hardcopy, e-book, CD-ROM. Covers: Strategic industrial, investment and business contacts for conducting export-import and investment activity in the country. Contains strategic, practical economic and business information.

Philippines Industrial and Business Directory. International Business Publications, USA. • Annual. $99.95 Individuals hardcopy, e-book, CD-ROM. Covers: Strategic industrial, investment and business contacts for conducting export-import and investment activity in the country.

Polish Industry Directory. Branzowy Katalog Firm-Ravi Sp. • Annual. Covers: More than 10,000 companies in Poland, including leading Polish importers/exporters. Entries include: Company name, address, phone, product/service.

Process Industry Directory. Telmo G. Mirat. • Annual. $95. Covers: Argentine manufacturers, importers, and exporters of raw materials, industrial chemicals, and products for the process industry.

Qui Decide. Bottin S.A. • Annual. Covers: 200,000 commercial and industrial entities and 4,000 products and services in France. Entries include: Company name, address, phone, product/service.

R & S Annual Directory. Ricerche e Studi S.p.A. Mediobanca. • Annual. €150 Individuals European countries. Covers: Nearly 10,000 businesses forming part of 180 groups representing over a third of Italy's manufacturing industry. Database includes: Italian-English glossary. Entries include: Group name, address, phone, directors, details of shareholders, products, market shares, production facilities, sales and employees, financial data.

Racine Area Manufacturers Directory. • Annual. Covers: About 400 manufacturers in the Racine, Wisconsin, area. Entries include: Company name, address, phone, name of principal executive, number of employees, product or service provided, fax, and e-mail.

Russia Industrial and Business Directory. International Business Publications, USA. • Annual. $99.95 Individuals hardcopy, e-book, CD-ROM. Covers: Strategic industrial, investment and business contacts for conducting export-import and investment activity in the country.

SANI. CERVED S.p.A. • Daily. Database covers: about 4 million Italian industrial, commercial, agricultural, and trade companies. Database includes: Company name, address, date and type of incorporation, incorporation capital, product/service, names and titles of key personnel. CERVED stands for Centri Elettronici Reteconnessi Valutazione Elaborazione Dati.

Saudi Arabia Industrial and Business Directory. International Business Publications, USA. • Annual. $99.95 Individuals hardcopy, e-book, CD-ROM. Covers: Strategic industrial, investment and business contacts for conducting export-import and investment activity in the country.

Saudi Industrial Development Fund--National Industries Directory. Saudi Industrial Development Fund. • Covers: More than 2000 industrial plants in Saudi Arabia. Entries include: Name, address, phone, fax.

Scott's Directories: Greater Montreal and Laval Business Directory. Scott's Directories. • Annual. $229 Individuals. Covers: More than 18,000 manufacturers, distributors, wholesalers, manufacturers' representatives, contractors, transportation companies, financial institutions; legal, engineering, and architectural firms; real estate brokers, retail main offices, and special services related to industry in Montreal. Entries include: Name, postal code, phone, fax, executive names and titles, type of business or product produced, North American Standard Industrial Classification (NAICS) code, number of employees; code indicating line of business; year established.

Sectores. Databank S.p.A. • Annual. $1,300 per report. A series of reports on 100 industrial sectors in Spain. Each report includes a description of the industry, trends, size of market and market shares of individual companies, and financial data in addition to a list of names and addresses of industry suppliers.

Sell's Scottish Directory. Miller Freeman UK Ltd. • Annual. $30. Covers: 8,000 industrial and commercial firms in Scotland, including firms int he North Sea oil industry. Entries include: Company name, address, phone, telex number, type of business.

Sharjah Industrial Products Directory. Express Print Publishers. • Covers: Manufacturing firms operating in United Arab Emirates. Entries include: Company address, executives, and activities.

SIRENE. France Institut National de la Statistique et des Etudes Economiques. • Daily. Database covers: Approximately 2.5 million French industrial and commercial firms. Entries include: Firm name, address, type of incorporation, national identification code, sector of activity, number of salaried employees, quarterly business volume.

Site Selection and Industrial Development--Geo-Political Index Issue. Conway Data Inc. • Annual. $20 plus $2.00 shipping. Publication includes: List of state, county, and local governmental agencies which negotiate and administer inducements to industrial firms to locate new offices, plants, warehouses, or other facilities within their jurisdiction. Database includes: Tabulations of incentives, financing plans, etc., offered by state and local agencies. Entries include: Agency name, address, phone, name of principal executive, and indication of special services and incentives.

Site Selection--Geo-Economic Index Issue. Conway Data Inc. • $20 plus $2.00 shipping. Publication includes: List of area development bodies, including state development agencies, city and county development offices, urban renewal agencies, port and airport agencies, railroads, utilities, banks, chambers of commerce, etc.; coverage includes Canada and over 50 other countries. Entries include: Group name, phone, name of contact.

SourceGuide to Industrial Market Data. London Business School Information Service. • $100. Covers: Directories, yearbooks, journals, statistical sources, market reports, trade and research associations, libraries and information services, and databases that provide data on 14 industrial market sectors in the U.K. Entries include: Source name, address, phone, description, evaluation.

South Africa Industrial and Business Directory. International Business Publications, USA. • Annual. $99.95 Individuals hardcopy, e-book, CD-ROM. Covers: Strategic industrial, investment and business contacts for conducting export-import and investment activity in the country.

South Carolina Industrial Directory. South Carolina Department of Commerce. • Annual. Covers: nearly 4,000 industrial companies throughout South Carolina. Entries include: Company name, address, phone, parent company (if applicable), plant address, names of principal executives, whether firm exports or imports, number of employees, product or service provided, Standard Industrial Classification (SIC) code, NAICS code, email, and web addresses.

Spain Industrial and Business Directory. International Business Publications, USA. • Annual. $99.95 Individuals hardcopy, e-book, CD-ROM. Covers: Strategic industrial, investment and business contacts for conducting export-import and investment activity in the country.

Surface Coating Resin Index. European Resin Manufacturers' Association. • Triennial. $5. Covers: Manufacturers, products and trade names of surface coating resins in the United Kingdom. Entries include: Manufacturer name, address, phone, products, trade names.

Survey of Industries in Texarkana--Arkansas/Texas. Texarkana Chamber of Commerce. • Quarterly. $2. Covers: Approximately 120 Texarkana manufacturers, processors, and sales agencies. Entries include: Company name, address, phone, number of employees, name of contact person, and products/ services.

Sweden Industrial and Business Directory. International Business Publications, USA. • Annual. $99.95 Individuals hardcopy, e-book, CD-ROM. Covers: Strategic industrial, investment and business contacts for conducting export-import and investment activity in the country. Contains strategic, practical economic and business information.

Swedish Industrial Directory. Sveriges Industrieforbund. • Annual. $400. Covers: Manufacturing companies in Sweden. Entries include: Manufacturer name, address, phone.

Switzerland Industrial and Business Directory. International Business Publications, USA. • Annual. $99.95 Individuals hardcopy, e-book, CD-ROM. Covers: Strategic industrial, investment and business contacts for conducting export-import and investment activity in the country.

Taiwan Industrial and Business Directory. International Business Publications, USA. • Annual. $99.95 Individuals hardcopy, e-book, CD-ROM. Covers: Strategic industrial, investment and business contacts for conducting export-import and investment activity in the country.

Taiwan Industrial Pages. INFOT Inc. • $46.75 CD-ROM; additional $167.50 for MS Access format. Covers: 100,882 Taiwan manufacturers, factories, plants, exporters, and importers. Entries include: Email and website addresses, telephone and fax number, business titles, address, number of employees, capital, and industry.

Tajikistan Industrial and Business Directory. International Business Publications, USA. • Annual. $99.95 Individuals hardcopy, e-book, CD-ROM. Covers: Strategic industrial, investment and business contacts for conducting export-import and investment activity in the country.

Texas Industrial Expansion. University of Texas at Austin IC2 Institute Bureau of Business Research. • Monthly. $60. Covers: New and expanding manufacturing facilities in Texas in Standard Industrial Classifications (SIC) 1321, 1477, 2011-3999, 4911. Entries include: Company name, address, phone, name of principal executive square footage and cost of project when available, number of employees, products or services.

Thomas Register of American Manufacturers. Thomas Publishing Company L.L.C. • Annual. More than 168,000 manufacturing firms are listed in this 34 volume set. Volumes 1-23 list the firms under 68,000 product headings. Thomas Register is enhanced with over 8,000 manufacturers' catalogs and is available in print, CD-ROM, DVD or online. Logistics Guide, a reference manual for freight and shipping sourcing.

The Times 1,000: The Indispensable Annual Review of the World's Leading Industrial and Financial Companies. Times Books Ltd. • Annual. $32.50. Covers: 1,000 leading companies in the United Kingdom; 1,000 leading companies in Europe; leading firms in the United States, Canada, Australia, South Africa, Ireland, Hong Kong, and Japan. Entries include: For all companies--Company name and address. For British firms--Company name, names of chairman and managing director, sales, profits, capital, number of employees, and ranks and ratios. Listings for other firms vary in detail.

Trade Directory of the Former Soviet Union. Flegon Press. • Biennial. $300. Covers: over 60,000 plants, factories, and other companies in all branches of industry in the former Soviet Union. Entries include: Company name, address, phone, telex, subsidiary and branch names and locations, description of product/service, number of employees.

Turkey Industry and Trade Directory. AGT Research Development & Information Corporation Inonu Caddesi. • Annual. $112. Covers: 14,500 producers, marketers, foreign trade investment service companies, representatives, authorized sellers, and wholesalers in Turkey.

UAE Commercial Directory. Federation of UAE Chamber of Commerce & Industry. • Annual. Provides information on UAE diplomatic missions abroad, Chambers of Commerce and Industry, and lists of business establishments. Entries include: Addresses of government institutions.

UAE Industrial Directory. Federation of UAE Chamber of Commerce & Industry. • Aims to widen the industrial channels and provide all the available services in order to help industrialists, business men and investors in different fields and to consolidate trust and provide suitable ambience for cooperation between industrialists and consumers. Covers: Industrial firms and companies operating in UAE. Entries include: Company name and address.

United Arab Emirates Industrial and Business Directory. International Business Publications, USA. • Annual. $99.95 Individuals hardcopy, E-book and CD-ROM. Covers: Strategic industrial, investment and business contacts for conducting export-import and investment activity in the country.

United States Industrial and Business Directory. International Business Publications, USA. • Annual. $99.95 Individuals hardcopy, E-book and CD-ROM. Covers: Detailed information on investment, export-import business opportunities, foreign economic assistance projects, government and business contacts.

U.S. Industrial Directory. Reed. • Annual. $179 per set. Publication consists of three volumes, of which the "Telephone/Address Section" provides name, address, phone, fax, local sales offices and distributors for over 52,000 companies. Other volumes comprise the "Product Sections," with listings of suppliers categorized by product and service.

Uruguay Industrial and Business Directory. International Business Publications, USA. • Annual. $99.95 Individuals hardcopy, E-book and CD-ROM. Covers: Strategic industrial, investment and business contacts for conducting export-import and investment activity in the country.

USA Major Manufacturers Directory. Business Information Agency Inc. PlanetInform. • Annual. $199 Individuals Hard copy or PDF. Covers: 4,000 industrial and consumer product manufacturers in the U.S.A. Entries include: Company name, location, contact information, SIC codes, number of employees, type of business, year founded, legal status, and subsidiary indicators.

Utah Manufacturers Directory and Industrial Database. Manufacturers' News Inc. • Annual. $102 Individuals print. Covers: 4,504 manufacturers in Utah. Entries include: Company name, address, phone, names and titles of key personnel, year established, number of employees, plant square footage, services, Standard Industry Classification (SIC) code, parent and subsidiary company information, type of in-house computer system, URL, e-mail address.

Utah Manufacturers Register. Harris InfoSource. • Annual. Covers: Approximately 4,600 manufacturers in Utah, plus names of key executives. Entries include: Company name, address, parent name/ location, telephone, fax and 800 numbers, Web site address (on CD-ROM only), number of employees, year established, annual revenue, plant size, business description, Standard Industrial Classification (SIC) codes, executive names/titles, public ownership, legal structure, import/export designators, female/minority ownership.

Uzbekistan Industrial and Business Directory. International Business Publications, USA. • $99.95 Individuals hardcopy, E-book and CD-ROM. Covers: Strategic and practical economic and business information. Entries include: Business contacts for conducting business activity in the country.

Venezuela Industrial and Business Directory. International Business Publications, USA. • Annual. $99.95 Individuals hardcopy, E-book and CD-ROM. Covers: Strategic industrial, investment and business contacts for conducting export-import and investment activity in the country.

Vermont Manufacturers Register and Industrial Database. Manufacturers' News Inc. • Annual. $82 Individuals print. Covers: 1,698 manufacturers in Vermont. Entries include: Company name, address, phone, names and titles of key personnel, year established, number of employees, plant square footage, services, Standard Industry Classification (SIC) code, parent and subsidiary company information, type of in-house computer system, URL, e-mail address.

Virginia Industrial Directory. Florida Chamber of Commerce. • Annual. $105 Members. Covers: over 6,000 manufacturing and mining firms. Entries include: Company name, address, phone, names and titles of key personnel, number of employees, product/service provided, headquarters address (if different). Separate list of firms with foreign affiliations gives parent company, country, and product only.

Ward's Business Directory of U.S. Private and Public Companies. Cengage Learning Inc. • Annual. $3,627 Individuals five-volume set. Eight volumes. Ward's contains basic information on about 115,000 business firms, of which 90 percent are private companies. Volumes available individually.

Washington Manufacturers Directory and Industrial Database. Manufacturers' News Inc. • Annual. $118 Individuals print. Covers: 7,834 manufacturers in Washington State. Entries include: Company name, address, phone, names and titles of key personnel, year established, number of employees, plant square footage, services, Standard Industry Classification (SIC) code, parent and subsidiary company information, type of in-house computer system, URL, e-mail address.

Washington Manufacturers Register. Harris InfoSource. • Annual. Covers: 12,600 manufacturers in Washington state, plus names of key executives. Entries include: Company name, address, parent name/location, telephone, fax and 800 numbers, Web site address (on CD-ROM only), number of employees, year established, annual revenue, plant size, business description, Standard Industrial Classification (SIC) codes, executive names/titles, public ownership, legal structure, import/export designators, female/minority ownership.

Wer Liefert Was? Online. Wer liefert was GmbH. • Database covers: Products and services from over 307,356 companies in Germany, Austria, Switzerland, the Netherlands, Belgium, Luxembourg, the Czech Republic, Slovakia, Slovenia, Croatia, the UK, France, and Italy. Entries include: Company name, address, phone, product/service, managers, ISO certification, e-mail/internet address.

Western Manufacturers Database Prospect System. Harris InfoSource. • $3,125. Database covers: Manufacturers covering the western U.S. Entries include: Company number of employees, annual sales, plant size, year established, names and titles for up to 10 executives, SIC codes.

Who's Who in Finance and Business. Marquis Who's Who L.L.C. • Biennial. $349 Individuals. Provides over 21,000 concise biographies of business leaders in all fields.

Who's Who of European Business and Industry. Triumph Books Inc. • Covers: over 9,500 European business executives (volume 1) and over 1,400 companies (volume 2). Entries include: For executives--Name, biographical data. For companies--Name, address, phone, profile.

Wisconsin Industries Guide. Industries Guides Inc. • $95. Covers: Approximately 10,000 manufacturers in Wisconsin. Entries include: Company name, address, phone.

Wisconsin Manufacturers Directory. WMC Foundation. • Annual. $177 Individuals. Covers: Approximately 12,300 manufacturers in Wisconsin. Entries include: Company name, address, phone, fax, number of employees, SIC codes, names and titles of key personnel, import/export activity, product descriptions, ownership status, parent company.

World Directory of Industrial Information Sources. United Nations Publications. • $40 Individuals. Covers: Industrial information sources for the most appropriate sources of technology and equipment. It contains profiles of information providers such as information and documentation centers, banks, training institutes, development agencies and manufacturers associations that are prepared to provide entrepreneurs in developing countries with answers to their industrial needs.

Worldwide Magnetics Industry Directory. Webcom Communications Corp. • $195 Individuals hardcopy. Covers: 2,400 companies that manufacture, distribute, and assemble materials and equipment in the magnetic industry worldwide. Includes industry-wide listing of magnetic manufacturers and distributors as well as suppliers of parts, components, systems and supplies used in the manufacture and aftermarket service of the magnet and materials industry. Information on over 4,800 personnel involved in the industry.

Wyoming Directory of Manufacturing and Mining. Wyoming Business Council. • Biennial. $15. Covers: About 790 companies in mining and manufacturing; state and local organizations and government agencies that provide business assistance. Entries include: For businesses--Name of firm, address, phone, name of key executive, product or activity, parent company (if any), codes for number of employees and geographic scope, Standard Industrial Classification (SIC) code. For organizations and agencies--Name of agency or organization, address, phone, contact name or official.

Yellow Pages Industry Sourcebook. Communications Trends Inc. • Annual. $295. Publication includes: Company listings. Entries include: Company name, address, phone, description, officer names, financial data, key customers, national accounts.

Yugoslavia (Serbia) Industrial and Business Directory. International Business Publications, USA. • Annual. $99.95 Individuals hardcopy, E-book and CD-ROM. Covers: Strategic industrial, investment and business contacts for conducting export-import and investment activity in the country.

E-BOOKS

Encyclopedia of American Industries. Cengage Learning Inc. • 2011. $807.00. 6th edition. Three volumes. Volume one is Manufacturing Industries and volume two is Service and Non-Manufacturing Industries. Provides the history, development, and recent status of approximately 1,000 industries. Includes statistical graphs, with industry and general indexes. Also available as eBook.

Encyclopedia of Emerging Industries. Cengage Learning Inc. • $546 6th edition. Provides detailed information on 140 "newly flourishing" industries. Includes historical background, organizational structure, significant individuals, current conditions, major companies, work force, technology trends, research developments, and other industry facts.

ENCYCLOPEDIAS AND DICTIONARIES

Encyclopedia of Emerging Markets. Cengage Learning Inc. • Covers emerging markets and industry profiles in 33 nations worldwide. Available in print ($549) and eBook. Published June 2013.

GENERAL WORKS

How Products Are Made. Cengage Learning Inc. • $211 Individuals. 2007. Volume 7. $192. Provides easy-to-read, step-by-step descriptions of how approximately 100 different products are manufactured. eBook also available.

Industrial Revolution Reference Library. Cengage Learning Inc. • 2003. $247. Three volumes. Individual volumes are available. Includes *Industrial Revolution: Almanac; Industrial Revolution: Biographies* and *Industrial Revolution: Primary Sources.* (UXL imprint).

HANDBOOKS AND MANUALS

Mergent OTC Industrial Manual. Mergent Inc. • Annual. $1,995 including 'News Reports.' Covers over 2,500 companies whose stock is traded over the counter. Includes biweekly *Moody's OTC Industrial News Report.*

INTERNET DATABASES

Bureau of Economic Analysis. U. S. Department of Commerce, Bureau of Economic Analysis. Phone: (202)606-9900; Fax: (202)606-5310; Email: webmaster@bea.doc.gov • URL: http://www.bea.doc.gov • Web site includes "News Release Information" covering national, regional, and international economic estimates from the BEA. Highlights of releases appear online the same day, complete text and tables appear the next day. "Recent News Releases" section provides titles for past nine months, with links. "BEA Data and Methodology" includes "Frequently Requested NIPA Data" (national income and product accounts, such as gross domestic product and personal income). Other statistics are available. Fees: Free.

Business 2.0 Web Guide to the Best Business Links. Business 2.0 Media Inc. Phone: (415)293-4800; Email: support@business2.com • URL: http://www.business2.com/webguide • Web site presents an extensive, searchable directory of links to "the best, most informative, and authoritative web pages." Twenty main categories cover business, finance, career, company information, people, and technology topics, with thousands of subtopics, all linking to Web sites recommended by experienced business researchers. Fees: Free.

EBSCO Information Services. EBSCO Publishing Inc. 10 Estes St., Ipswich, MA 01938-2106. Phone: 800-653-2726 or (978)356-6500; Fax: (978)356-6565; Email: information@ebscohost.com • URL: http://www.ebscohost.com • Fee-based Web site providing Internet access to a wide variety of databases, including business-related material. Full text is available for many periodical titles, with daily updates. Fees: Apply.

Factiva. Dow Jones Reuters Business Interactive, LLC. Phone: 800-369-7466 or (609)452-1511; Fax: (609)520-5770; Email: solutions@factiva.com • URL: http://www.factiva.com • Fee-based Web site provides "global news and business information through Web sites and content integration solutions." Includes Dow Jones and Reuters newswires, The Wall Street Journal, and more than 7,000 other sources of current news, historical articles, market research reports, and investment analysis. Content includes 96 major U. S. newspapers, 900 non-English sources, trade publications, media transcripts, country profiles, news photos, etc.

Federal Reserve Board Publications and Education Resources. Board of Governors of the Federal Reserve System. Phone: (202)452-3000; Fax: (202)452-3819 • URL: http://www.federalreserve.gov/publications.htm • Web site provides access to statistics, surveys, and research from the Federal Reserve Board. *Federal Reserve Bulletin* articles are available as abstracts or full text (PDF) currently or from six-year archives. The link "Statistics: Releases and Historical Data" offers daily, weekly, monthly, quarterly, and annual data in great detail for interest rates, foreign exchange, consumer credit, money stock measures, industrial production indexes, bank reserves, and other items. Historical tabulations are available for various time periods. Free.

Fedstats. Federal Interagency Council on Statistical Policy. Phone: (202)395-7254 • URL: http://www.fedstats.gov • Web site features an efficient search facility for full-text statistics produced by more than 100 federal agencies, including the Census Bureau, the Bureau of Economic Analysis, and the Bureau of Labor Statistics. Boolean searches can be made within one agency or for all agencies combined. Links are offered to international statistical bureaus, including the UN, IMF, OECD, UNESCO, Eurostat, and 20 individual countries. Fees: Free.

FreeLunch.com. Economy.com, Inc. Phone: (610)696-8700; Fax: (610)696-1678 • URL: http://www.freelunch.com • Web site provides free access to more than 200 million economic and financial data series, covering industry, demographics, labor markets, prices, retail sales, government spending, trade, interest rates, housing starts, the stock market, etc. Data is available in either chart or table form. Searching is offered. Free, but registration required. Economy.com, Inc. also offers fee-based economic analysis at *The Dismal Scientist* site (www.dismal.com).

InSite 2. Intelligence Data/Thomson Financial. Phone: 800-654-0393 or (617)856-1890; Fax: (617)737-3182; Email: intelligence.data@tfn.com • URL: http://www.insite2.gale.com/ • Fee-based Web site consolidates information in a "Base Pack" consisting of Business InSite, Market InSite, and Company InSite. Optional databases are Consumer InSite, Health and Wellness InSite, Newsletter InSite, and Computer InSite. Includes fulltext content from more than 2,500 trade publications, journals, newsletters, newspapers, analyst reports, and other sources. Continuous updating. Formerly produced by The Gale Group.

Manufacturing Profiles. U. S. Bureau of the Census. Phone: (301)763-4636 or (301)763-4100; Fax: (301)763-4794; Email: webmaster@census.gov • URL: http://www.census.gov/prod/www/abs/mfg-prof.html • The Census Bureau makes available free on PDF (Portable Document Format) an annual consolidation of the entire Current Industrial Report series, presenting "all the data compiled." Contains statistics on production, shipments, inventories, consumption, exports, imports, and orders for a wide variety of manufactured products.

Nexis.com. Lexis-Nexis Group. Phone: 800-227-4908 or (937)865-6800; Fax: (937)865-6909; Email: webmaster@prod.lexis-nexis.com • URL: http://www.nexis.com • Fee-based Web site offers searching of about 2.8 billion documents in some 30,000 news, business, and legal information sources. Features include a subject directory covering 1,200 topics in 34 categories and a Company Dossier containing information on more than 500,000 public and private companies. Boolean searching is offered.

1997 NAICS and 1987 SIC Correspondence Tables. U. S. Census Bureau. Phone: 800-541-8345 or (301)457-4100 or (301)763-2713; Fax: (301)457-1296 or (301)457-3842; Email: naics@census.gov • URL: http://www.census.gov/epcd/www/naicstab.htm • Web site provides detailed tables for converting four-digit Standard Industrial Classification (SIC) numbers to the six-digit North American Industrial Classification System (NAICS) or vice versa: "1987 SIC Matched to 1997 NAICS" or "1997 NAICS Matched to 1987 SIC." Fees: Free.

ProQuest. ProQuest L.L.C. 789 E Eisenhower Pkwy., Ann Arbor, MI 48106-1346. Phone: 800-521-0600 or (734)761-4700; Fax: (734)662-4554; Email: info@proquest.com • URL: http://www.proquest.com • Fee-based Web site providing Internet access to more than 3,000 periodicals, newspapers, and other publications. Many items are available full-text, with daily updates. Includes extensive corporate and financial information. Fees: Apply.

Summary of Commentary on Current Economic Conditions by Federal Reserve District. Board of Governors of the Federal Reserve System. Phone: (202)452-3000; Fax: (202)452-3819 • URL: http://www.federalreserve.gov/publications.htm • 8/year. Free Web site provides current "anecdotal information" eight times a year on economic conditions within each of the 12 Federal Reserve Districts, plus an extensive national *Summary*. Text is based on the opinions of bank officials, business executives, economists, financial market experts, and others. Typically contains views of consumer spending, manufacturing, services, credit, employment, prices, wages, and the economy in general. Usually referred to as the Beige Book.

Switchboard. Switchboard, Inc. Phone: (508)898-8000; Fax: (508)898-1755; Email: webmaster@switchboard.com • URL: http://www.switchboard.com • Web site provides telephone numbers and street addresses for more than 100 million business locations and residences in the U. S. Broad industry categories are available. Fees: Free.

U.S. Census Bureau: The Official Statistics. U. S. Bureau of the Census. Phone: (301)763-4636 or (301)763-4100; Fax: (301)763-4794; Email: webmaster@census.gov • URL: http://www.census.gov/prod/www/abs/mfg-prof.html • Web site is "Your Source for Social, Demographic, and Economic Information." Contains "Current U. S. Population Count," "Current Economic Indicators," and a wide variety of data under "Other Official Statistics." Keyword searching is provided. Fees: Free.

Wall Street Journal Interactive Edition. Dow Jones & Co., Inc. 1211 Avenue of the Americas, New York, NY 10036. Phone: 800-369-5663; Email: service@dowjones.com • URL: http://new.dowjones.com • Fee-based Web site providing online searching of worldwide information from *The Wall Street Journal*. Includes "Company Snapshots," "The Journal's Greatest Hits," "Index to Market Data," "Journal Links," etc. Financial price quotes are available. Fees: $49.00 per year; $29.00 per year to print subscribers.

ONLINE DATABASES

Applied Science and Technology Index Online. H.W. Wilson Co. • Provides online indexing of 500 major scientific, technical, industrial, and engineering periodicals. Time period is 1983 to date. Monthly updates. Inquire as to online cost and availability.

Business & Industry™. Cengage Learning Inc. • A multi-industry business database with a strong global focus on company, product and industry information.

Industry Insider. Thomson Financial. • Contains full-text online industry research reports from more than 200 leading trade associations, covering 50 specific industries. Reports include extensive statistics and market research data. Inquire as to online cost and availability.

Thomas Register Online. Thomas Publishing Company L.L.C. • Provides concise information on approximately 194,000 U. S. companies, mainly manufacturers, with over 50,000 product classifications. Indexes over 115,000 trade names. Information is updated semiannually. Inquire as to online cost and availability.

OTHER SOURCES

Business Rankings Annual (BRA). Cengage Learning Inc. • Annual. $584 Individuals. A guide to lists and rankings appearing in major business publications. The top ten names are listed in each case.

PERIODICALS AND NEWSLETTERS

Fortune Magazine. Time Inc., Business Information Group. • Biweekly. $19.99 all access. Edited for top executives and upper-level managers.

IEEE Industry Applications Magazine. IEEE - Communications Society. • Bimonthly. Covers new industrial applications of power conversion, drives, lighting, and control. Emphasis is on the petroleum, chemical, rubber, plastics, textile, and mining industries.

Industries in Transition: A Newsletter Written for Growth Directed Management and Business Planners. Business Communications Co., Inc. • Monthly. $375.00 per year. Newsletter. Formerly *Growth Industry News*.

IndustryWeek: The Management Resource. Penton Media Inc. • Monthly. Edited for industrial and business managers. Covers organizational and technological developments affecting industrial management.

The Levy Institute Forecast. Forecasting Center Jerome Levy Economics Institute. • Description: Provides analyses and forecasts of U.S. business conditions. Reports on production, sales, inflation, corporate profits, and interest rates.

RESEARCH CENTERS AND INSTITUTES

National Center for Manufacturing Sciences. 3025 Boardwalk, Ann Arbor, MI 48108-3230. Phone: 800-222-6267 or (734)995-0300; Fax: (734)995-1150 or (734)995-4004; Email: info@ncms.org • Research areas include process technology and control, machine mechanics, sensors, testing methods, and quality assurance.

STATISTICS SOURCES

Manufacturing & Distribution USA. Cengage Learning Inc. • Biennial. $631 Individuals three-volume set. 2012. 7th edition. eBook. Three volumes. Presents statistics and projections relating to economic activity in more than 600 business classifications.

SRC Green Book of 5 Trend 35-Year Charts. Securities Research Co. • Annual. $150.00. Chart book presents statistical information on the stocks of 400 leading companies over a 35-year period. Each full page chart is in semi-log format to avoid visual distortion. Also includes charts of 12 leading market averages or indexes and 39 major industry groups.

Standard & Poor's Industry Surveys. Standard & Poor's Financial Services L.L.C. • Semiannual. $1,800.00. Two looseleaf volumes. Includes monthly *Supplements*. Provides detailed, individual surveys of 52 major industry groups. Each survey is revised on a semiannual basis. Also includes "Monthly Investment Review" (industry group investment analysis) and monthly "Trends & Projections" (economic analysis).

Statistical Abstract of the United States. U. S. Government Printing Office. • Annual. $44.00. Issued by the U. S. Bureau of the Census.

Statistical Yearbook. United Nations Publications. • Annual. $125.00. Contains statistics for about 200 countries on a wide variety of economic, industrial, and demographic topics. Compiled by United Nations Statistical Office.

Survey of Current Business. U. S. Government Printing Office. • Published by Bureau of Economic Analysis, U. S. Department of Commerce. Presents a wide variety of business and economic data.

United States Census of Manufactures. U.S. Department of Commerce U.S. Census Bureau. • Quinquennial. Results presented in reports, tape, CD-ROM, and Diskette files.

U.S. Industry and Trade Outlook. U.S. Department of Commerce National Technical Information Service. • Annual. Produced by the International Trade Administration, U.S. Department of Commerce, in a "public-private" partnership with DRI/McGraw-Hill and Standard & Poor's. Provides basic data, outlook for the current year, and "Long-Term Prospects" (five-year projections) for a wide variety of products and services. Includes high technology industries. Formerly *U.S. Industrial Outlook*.

TRADE/PROFESSIONAL ASSOCIATIONS

ACT and Region Chamber of Commerce and Industry. 12a Thesiger Ct., Canberra, ACT 2600, Australia. Phone: 61 2 62835200; Fax: 61 2 62822436; Email: chamber@actchamber.com.au • URL: http://www.actchamber.com.au • Represents businesses in the Australian Capital Territory of Australia.

Alliance for American Manufacturing. 711 D St. NW, 3rd Fl., Washington, DC 20004. Phone: 800-915-4609 or (202)393-3430; Email: info@aamfg.org • URL: http://www.americanmanufacturing.org • Seeks to strengthen manufacturing in the U.S. Provides research, public education, advocacy, strategic communications and coalition building around the issues that matter to America's manufacturing sector. Promotes policy solutions on priorities such as international trade, energy security, health care, retirement security, currency manipulation and other issues of mutual concern.

American Small Manufacturers Coalition. PO Box 15289, Washington, DC 20003. Phone: (202)341-7066; Fax: (202)315-3906 • URL: http://www.smallmanufacturers.org • Strives to help small manufacturers to succeed. Improves the innovativeness and productivity of America's manufacturing community. Advocates for legislative and programmatic resources to allow small manufacturers to compete in the global marketplace.

Argentine Industry Association. Av. de Mayo 1147/57, C1085ABB Buenos Aires, Argentina. Phone: 54 11 41242300; Fax: 54 11 41242301; Email: uia@uia.org.ar • URL: http://www.uia.org.ar • Represents members of industrial union in Argentina.

Australian Industry Group. Level 5, 51 Walker St., North Sydney, NSW 2060, Australia. Phone: 61 294665566; Fax: 61 294665599; Email: info@aigroup.asn.au • URL: http://www.aigroup.com.au • Promotes and develops the interests of industrial businesses.

Bunbury Chamber of Commerce and Industries. 15 Stirling St., Bunbury, WA 6230, Australia. Phone: 61 97912292; Fax: 61 97916646; Email: ceo@bcci.asn.au • URL: http://www.bunburycci.com.au • Represents business and industry in the South West region of Western Australia.

Business Industry Promotion Association of Pakistan. 455 Shadman 1, Lahore, Pakistan. Phone: 92 42 7581288; Fax: 92 42 7581288; Email: bipap@brain.net.pk • Seeks to integrate the activities of professionals in the fields of trade, industry, manufacturing, exporting, engineering, investment, finance and general services. Facilitates cooperation and networking among business professionals.

Business SA. 136 Greenhill Rd., Adelaide, SA 5061, Australia. Phone: 61 8 83000000; Fax: 61 8 83000001; Email: accoutsquery@business-sa.com • URL: http://business-sa.com • Represents businesses in South Australia; provides services to businesses and employers, including management of export transactions.

Cairns Chamber of Commerce. Ste. M2a, Mezzanine Level, The Pier, Pier Point Rd., Cairns, QLD 4870, Australia. Phone: 61 7 40311838; Fax: 61 7 40310883; Email: info@cairnschamber.com.au • URL: http://www.cairnschamber.com.au • Represents business in the Cairns region. Provides statistical and business advice. Works to attract investment and business relocation to the area. Provides trade and export support.

Camara de Comercio Argentino-Brasilena. Montevideo 770-12 Piso, 1019 Buenos Aires, Argentina. Phone: 54 11 48114503; Email: institucionales@cambras.org.ar • URL: http://www.cambras.org.ar • Represents business and commerce in Argentina.

Camara de Comercio e Industria de Trenque Lauquen. Bvard. Villegas 150, 6400 Buenos Aires, Argentina. Phone: 54 2392412000 or 54 2392431672; Fax: 54 2392430414; Email: info@lacamaradetrenque.com.ar • URL: http://www.tlauquen.com.ar • Represents business in Argentina.

Camara de Comercio, Industria Y Servicios de Carlos Casares. Avda. San Martin 318, B6530 Carlos Casares, Argentina. Fax: 54 2395451022 • URL: http://www.camaracarloscasares.com.ar • Promotes business and industry in the Carlos Casares region of Argentina.

Camara de Industria y Comercio de Matanza. Cal. Entre Rios 3026, San Justo, 1754 Buenos Aires, Argentina. Phone: 54 11 46511830; Fax: 54 11 46511830; Email: info@cicm.com.ar • URL: http://www.cicm.com.ar • Represents business in Argentina.

Camara Empresaria Parque Industrial de Pilar. Ruta 8, km. 60, Parque Industrial Pilar, Calle Del Canal Nro. 1758, 1629 Buenos Aires, Argentina. Phone: 54 230 4491994 or 54 230 4491892; Email: info@cepip.org.ar • URL: http://www.cepip.org.ar • Represents businesses in Argentina.

Camara Espanola de Comercio de la Republica Argentina. 863 Av. Belgrano, Piso 7, C1092AAI Buenos Aires, Argentina. Phone: 54 11 43355000; Fax: 54 11 43355022; Email: recepcion.cecra@cecra.com.ar • URL: http://www.cecra.com.ar • Represents Spanish-Argentine businesses in Buenos Aires.

Coffs Harbour Chamber of Commerce and Industry. The Promenade, 321 Harbour Dr., Coffs Harbour, NSW 2450, Australia. Phone: 61 2 66514101; Fax: 61 2 66514081; Email: info@coffschamber.com.au • URL: http://www.coffschamber.com.au • Represents the local interests of small, medium sized, and multinational organizations throughout the Coffs Harbour region.

Confederation of British Industry. Cannon Pl., 103 New Oxford St., London EC4N 6HN, United Kingdom. Phone: 44 20 73797400; Fax: 44 20 73797200; Email: enquiries@cbi.org.uk • URL: http://www.cbi.org.uk • Works to ensure that the government understands the intentions, needs, and problems of British business.

Confederation of Indian Industry. Secretary, 23-26 Institutional Area, Lodi Rd., New Delhi 110 003, Delhi, India. Phone: 91 011694298 or 91 11 24629997; Fax: 91 11 24626149; Email: info@cii.in • URL: http://cii.in • Industrial firms. Promotes advancement of Indian industry. Represents members' interests; gathers and disseminates information.

Confederation of Indian Industry - United Kingdom. c/o Confederation of British Industry, Centre Point, 103 New Oxford St., London WC1A 1DU, United Kingdom. Phone: 44 20 78364121 or 44 20 73797400; Fax: 44 20 78361972 • URL: http://www.cii.in • Works to create and sustain an environment conducive to growth of the Indian industry. Links the industry and the government through advisory and consultative process. Serves as a reference point for the Indian industry and the international business community.

Confederation of Swedish Enterprise. Storgatan 19, S-114 82 Stockholm, Sweden. Phone: 46 8 55343000; Fax: 46 8 55343099 • URL: http://www.svensktnaringsliv.se • Represents the interests of Swedish manufacturers. Conducts lobbying activities.

Confederation of Tanzania Industries. NIC Investment House, 9th Fl., Samora Ave., Dar es Salaam, Tanzania. Phone: 255 22 2114954 or 255 22 2123802; Fax: 255 22 2115414; Email: cti@cti.co.tz • URL: http://www.cti.co.tz • Promotes the interests of the manufacturing sector and supporting industries in Tanzania. Ensures a conducive legal, financial and economic environment in which the industry can operate effectively.

Consultants Association for the Natural Products Industry. PO Box 4014, Clovis, CA 93613-4014. Phone: (559)325-7192; Email: info@cani-consultants.org • URL: http://www.cani-consultants.org • Works to enhance the growth and integrity of the natural products industry. Offers professional services to help manufacturers, distributors, retailers, and non-profit organizations thrive in the nutraceutical marketplace. Promotes education and ethical standards for the improvement of manufacturing, distribution, marketing and advertising to help the industry develop safe and beneficial products for the public.

Coordinating Committee of Agriculture, Commercial, Industrial and Financial Associations. Route 6, 9-21, Zone 4, Level 9, 01004 Guatemala City, Guatemala. Phone: 502 2201-0000; Email: unice@cacif.org.gt • URL: http://www.cacif.org.gt.

Environmental Industries Commission. Alliance House, 12 Caxton St., London SW1H 0QL, United Kingdom. Phone: 44 207 2224148 or 44 207 6549942; Email: info@eic-uk.co.uk • URL: http://www.eic-uk.co.uk • Provides environmental technology equipment and services suppliers with a strong and effective voice to influence the debate on the future of the industry among policy makers in Westminster, Whitehall and Brussels. Promotes constructive cooperation between the regulated, the regulators and the UK's environmental technology suppliers.

Federation of Industries Products Systems and Services for Construction. Via Brenta, 13, I-00198 Rome, Italy. Phone: 39 6 8555203; Fax: 39 6 8559860; Email: finco@fincoweb.org • URL: http://www.fincoweb.org • Promotes the products systems and services used by the construction industries.

Federation of Thai Industries. Queen Sirikit National Convention Centre, 4th Fl., Zone C, 60th Rachadapisek Rd., Klongtoey, Bangkok 10110, Thailand. Phone: 66 2 3451000; Fax: 66 2 3451296; Email: information@off.fti.or.th • URL: http://www.fti.or.th • Represents the industrial enterprises in Thailand. Seeks to identify and solve problems and issues arising in the conduct of industrial enterprises.

Franco-Argentina Chamber of Commerce and Industry. Av. Libertador 498, 17e etage, C1001AAO Buenos Aires, Argentina. Phone: 54 11 43101000; Fax: 54 11 43101021; Email: ccifa@ccifa.com.ar • URL: http://www.ccifa.com.ar • Promotes business and trade between Argentine and French companies.

Geelong Chamber of Commerce. 10 Moorabool St., Geelong, VIC 3220, Australia. Phone: 61 3 52222234; Fax: 61 3 52222235 • URL: http://www.geelongchamber.com.au • Represents businesses in Geelong and the Surfcoast region of Australia.

Geosynthetics Materials Association. c/o Industrial Fabrics Association International, 1801 County Rd. B W, Roseville, MN 55113-4061. Phone: 800-225-4324 or (651)222-2508; Fax: (651)631-9334; Email: generalinfo@ifai.com • URL: http://www.ifai.com/groups/gma • Represents members of the geosynthetics industry including manufacturers, testing firms and service companies. Aims to promote the acceptance and use of geosynthetic materials in a variety of applications. Provides resources and offers networking opportunities among members.

Industrial Energy Consumers of America. 1155 15th St. NW, Ste. 500, Washington, DC 20005. Phone: (202)223-1661 or (202)223-1420; Fax: (202)530-0659; Email: pcicio@ieca-us.org • URL: http://www.ieca-us.com • Promotes the interests of manufacturing companies and enhances their ability to compete in domestic and world markets. Supports policy development, identification and monitoring of issues and developing and implementing action plans pertaining to energy efficiency and environmental progress. Provides a forum to address state, national and international energy related issues, meet with policy makers and advocate sound policy.

Industrial Society. Av. Andres Bello 2777, Piso 3, Las Condes, Santiago, Chile. Phone: 56 2 3913100; Fax: 56 2 3913200; Email: sofofa@sofofa.cl • URL: http://web.sofofa.cl • Represents the views and interests of Chilean industry and business. Promotes the advancement and expansion of the private sector.

Industrialists' Association of Panama. Apartado 0819-05411, Panama City, Panama. Phone: 507 230-0169; Email: sip@cableonda.net • URL: http://www.industriales.org.

Industry Council for Emergency Response Technologies. PO Box 42563, Washington, DC 20015-2604. Phone: (240)398-3065; Email: george.rice@theindustrycouncil.org • URL: http://www.theindustrycouncil.org • Represents the emergency communications industry in the development of emergency technology infrastructure and policy for the good of public safety and the public it serves. Conducts scientifically credible and objective research to support innovation in the 9-1-1 industry for the benefit of the public. Brings together industry leaders in order to maximize the value of research and development investment.

International Association of Directional Drilling. 525 Sam Houston Pkwy. E, Ste. 525, Houston, TX 77060. Phone: (281)931-8811 or (281)288-6484; Email: dallen@iadd-intl.org • URL: http://www.iadd-intl.org • Represents the interests of the directional drilling industry. Encourages members to share ideas and develop safety and performance standards. Fosters collaboration among operators, directional drilling vendors and suppliers.

Jamaica Manufacturers' Association. 85a Duke St., Kingston, Jamaica. Phone: (876)922-8880 or (876)922-8869; Fax: (876)922-9205; Email: jma@cwjamaica.com • URL: http://www.jma.com.jm • Promotes the development of the manufacturing sector and increase its contribution to the socio-economic welfare of the country by creating jobs and improving the standard of living for all.

MSPAlliance. 1380 E Ave., Ste. 124-376, Chico, CA 95926-7349. Phone: (530)891-1340; Fax: (530)433-5707; Email: info@mspalliance.com • URL: http://www.mspalliance.com • Aims to promote the Managed Services Industry as a true and viable profession to the IT Business Consumer. Represents providers working together in a vendor-neutral manner to define and promote the Managed Services Industry. Educates consumers on the benefits of using Managed Service Providers.

National Association of Manufacturers. 733 10th St. NW, Ste. 700, Washington, DC 20001. Phone: 800-814-8468 or (202)637-3000; Fax: (202)637-3182; Email: manufacturing@nam.org • URL: http://www.nam.org • Manufacturers and cooperating non-manufacturers having a direct interest in or relationship to manufacturing. Represents industry's views on national and international problems to government. Maintains public affairs and public relations programs. Reviews current and proposed legislation, administrative rulings and interpretations, judicial decisions and legal matters affecting industry. Maintains numerous policy groups: Human Resources Policy; Small and Medium Manufacturers; Tax Policy; Resources & Environmental Policy; Regulation and Legal Reform Policy; International Economic Affairs. Affiliated with 150 local and state trade associations of manufacturers through National Industrial Council and 250 manufacturing trade associations through the Associations Council.

National Council of Minorities in Energy. 1725 I St. NW, Ste. 300, Washington, DC 20006. Phone: 866-663-9045; Fax: (866)663-8007; Email: contact@minoritiesinenergy.org • URL: http://www.minoritiesinenergy.org • Advocates for development and utilization of minority and women-owned businesses in the energy sector and energy-related industries across the United States and in international markets. Provides information regarding opportunities in the energy industry. Advocates on regulatory and legislative issues at the federal, state and local levels. Presents methodologies to help implement access to capital and credit facilitation.

Salvadoran Association of Industrials. Calle Roma y Liverpool, Col. Roma, San Salvador, El Salvador. Phone: 503 2267-9200; Email: info@asi.com.sv • URL: http://industriaelsalvador.com • Promotes the industrial sector of El Salvador.

Self Storage Association of the United Kingdom. Priestley House, The Gullet, Nantwich CW5 5SZ, United Kingdom. Phone: 44 1270 623150; Email: admin@ssauk.com • URL: http://www.ssauk.com • Encourages members, of the Self Storage Industry, to operate their storage facilities to a recommended minimum standard. Encourages prospective self-storage operators to carry out a full research of the Industry before opening their facilities. Preserves high standards of conduct in its members and in the industry. Promotes the industry to the general public.

Spanish Confederation of Business Organisations. Calle Diego de Leon, 50, E-28006 Madrid, Spain. Phone: 34 91 5663400; Fax: 34 91 5622562; Email: ceoe@ceoe.es • URL: http://www.ceoe.es • Represents the Spanish business community in all sectors, including agriculture, industry and services.

Sudanese Chambers of Industries Association. PO Box 2565, Khartoum, Sudan. Phone: 249 1 83471717; Fax: 249 1 83471720; Email: sec.general@sudanindustry.org • URL: http://sudanindustry.org • Represents businessmen from the private industrial sector. Participates in trade agreements, workers' legislation and decision making in issues regarding the industry as well as the economy of Sudan. Encourages local and foreign investment in the industrial sector.

Tasmanian Chamber of Commerce and Industry. 309 Liverpool St., Hobart, TAS 7000, Australia. Phone: 61 3 62363600; Fax: 61 3 62311278; Email: admin@tcci.com.au • URL: http://www.tcci.com.au • Represents businesses in Tasmania, Australia.

Utility Industry Group. Southern California Edison Co., Bldg. 3-2 MD3, 4910 Rivergrade Rd., Irwindale, CA 91706. Phone: (626)543-6291; Fax: (626)302-5332 • URL: http://www.uig.org • Represents the interests of the utility industry including distribution companies, energy suppliers, service providers and their customers, supply chain participants and other interested parties. Promotes effective implementation of electronic commerce to standards committees, governmental bodies and other appropriate organizations involved in the standards setting process. Provides a forum for the exchange of ideas and solutions related to electronic commerce and its influence on the business needs of the utility industry.

Venezuelan Confederation of Industries. Ave. Araure (Principal de Chuao), Caracas 1061, Venezuela. Phone: 58 212 991-2116; Fax: 58 212 991-7737; Email: conindustria@conindustria.org • URL: http://www.conindustria.org • Represents the interests of the industrial regions and productive sectors in Venezuela.

Victorian Employers' Chamber of Commerce and Industry. 486 Albert St., Melbourne, VIC 3002, Australia. Phone: 61 3 86625333; Fax: 61 3 86625462; Email: vecci@vecci.org.au • URL: http://www.vecci.org.au • Represents businesses in Victoria, Australia.

INDUSTRY, REGULATION OF

See REGULATION OF INDUSTRY

INFANTS WEAR

See CHILDREN'S APPAREL INDUSTRY

INFLATION

See also MONEY; PRICES AND PRICING

ABSTRACTS AND INDEXES

Business Periodicals Index Retrospective. EBSCO Publishing Inc. • 11/year. Quarterly and annual cumulations.

Social Sciences Citation Index. Thomson Reuters Corp. • Weekly. Product is accessed via *Web of Science*.

Social Sciences Index Retrospective: 1907-1983. EBSCO Publishing Inc. • Indexing for 1,000,000 articles. Coverage includes international index and social sciences and humanities index.

CD-ROM DATABASES

OECD Statistical Compendium. Organization for Economic Cooperation and Development. • Semiannual. $1,905.00 per year for 1 to 10 users. CD-ROM contains more than 730,000 monthly, quarterly, and annual time series for OECD countries, 1960 to date. Includes fully searchable data on agriculture, food, economic indicators, national accounts, employment, energy, finance, industry, technology, and foreign trade. Results can be displayed in various forms.

Social Sciences Abstracts. EBSCO Publishing Inc. • Provides indexing from 1983 and abstracting from 1994 of more than 750 periodicals covering economics, area studies, community health, public administration, public welfare, urban studies, and many other topics related to the social sciences.

Social Sciences Citation Index. Thomson Reuters Corp. • Weekly. Product is accessed via *Web of Science*.

INTERNET DATABASES

Business 2.0 Web Guide to the Best Business Links. Business 2.0 Media Inc. Phone: (415)293-4800; Email: support@business2.com • URL: http://www.business2.com/webguide • Web site presents an extensive, searchable directory of links to "the best, most informative, and authoritative web pages." Twenty main categories cover business, finance, career, company information, people, and technology topics, with thousands of subtopics, all linking to Web sites recommended by experienced business researchers. Fees: Free.

Fedstats. Federal Interagency Council on Statistical Policy. Phone: (202)395-7254 • URL: http://www.fedstats.gov • Web site features an efficient search facility for full-text statistics produced by more than 100 federal agencies, including the Census Bureau, the Bureau of Economic Analysis, and the Bureau of Labor Statistics. Boolean searches can be made within one agency or for all agencies combined. Links are offered to international statistical bureaus, including the UN, IMF, OECD, UNESCO, Eurostat, and 20 individual countries. Fees: Free.

FreeLunch.com. Economy.com, Inc. Phone: (610)696-8700; Fax: (610)696-1678 • URL: http://www.freelunch.com • Web site provides free access to more than 200 million economic and financial data series, covering industry, demographics, labor markets, prices, retail sales, government spending, trade, interest rates, housing starts, the stock market, etc. Data is available in either chart or table form. Searching is offered. Free, but registration required. Economy.com, Inc. also offers fee-based economic analysis at *The Dismal Scientist* site (www.dismal.com).

ONLINE DATABASES

Wilson Business Abstracts Online. H.W. Wilson Co. • Indexes and abstracts 600 major business periodicals, plus the *Wall Street Journal* and the business section of the *New York Times*. Indexing is from 1982, abstracting from 1990, with the two newspapers included from 1993. Updated weekly. Inquire as to online cost and availability. (*Business Periodicals Index* without abstracts is also available online.).

Wilson Social Sciences Abstracts Online. H.W. Wilson Co. • Provides online abstracting and indexing of more than 500 periodicals covering area studies, community health, public administration, public welfare, urban studies, and many other social science topics. Time period is 1994 to date for abstracts and 1983 to date for indexing, with updates weekly. Inquire as to online cost and availability.

PERIODICALS AND NEWSLETTERS

Forecasts and Strategies. Access Intelligence L.L.C. • Monthly. $99.00 per year. Covers inflation, taxes and government controls.

Personal Finance. KCI Communications Inc. • Description: Contains articles on subjects of interest to those investigating personal finance strategies. Provides news, information, and suggestions on investment decisions. Covers stock and growth stock activity, individual retirement accounts, market trends and developments, and real estate. Recurring features include columns titled Capsule Advisory and Answers to Your Money Questions.

PRICE SOURCES

CPI Detailed Report: Consumer Price Index. U. S. Government Printing Office. • Monthly. $45 Individuals. Cost of living data.

STATISTICS SOURCES

ACCRA Cost of Living Index. Council for Community and Economic Research. • Quarterly. $165 Individuals. Compares price levels for 280-310 U.S. cities.

The AIER Chart Book. AIER Research Staff. American Institute for Economic Research. • Annual. $4 Individuals. A compact compilation of long-range charts ("Purchasing Power of the Dollar," for example, goes back to 1780) covering various aspects of the U. S. economy. Includes inflation, interest rates, debt, gold, taxation, stock prices, etc. (Economic Education Bulletin.).

Prices and Earnings Around the Globe. Union Bank of Switzerland. • Triennial. Free. Published in Zurich. Compares prices and purchasing power in 48 major cities of the world. Wages and hours are also compared.

Stocks, Bonds, Bills, and Inflation Classic Yearbook. Ibbotson Associates. • Annual. $185. Provides detailed data from 1926 to the present on inflation and the returns from various kinds of financial investments, such as small-cap stocks and long-term government bonds.

Survey of Current Business. U. S. Government Printing Office. • Published by Bureau of Economic Analysis, U. S. Department of Commerce. Presents a wide variety of business and economic data.

INFORMATION BROKERS

See INFORMATION INDUSTRY

INFORMATION, FREEDOM OF

See FREEDOM OF INFORMATION

INFORMATION INDUSTRY

See also ONLINE INFORMATION SYSTEMS

ABSTRACTS AND INDEXES

Applied Science and Technology Index. EBSCO Publishing Inc. • 11/year. Indexes a wide variety of English language technical, industrial, and engineering periodicals.

Business Periodicals Index Retrospective. EBSCO Publishing Inc. • 11/year. Quarterly and annual cumulations.

Computer and Information Systems Abstracts Journal: An Abstract Journal Pertaining to the Theory, Design, Fabrication and Application of Computer and Information Systems. CSA. • Monthly. $1,750 per year.

Computer Science Index. EBSCO Publishing Inc. • Quarterly. $245 per year. Contains brief abstracts of book and periodical literature covering all phases of computing, including approximately 70 specific application areas.

Information Science Abstracts. American Society for Information Science. Information Today, Inc. • Nine times a year. $725.00 per year.

Internet and Personal Computing Abstracts (print edition). EBSCO Publishing Inc. • Quarterly. $269.00 per year, including cumulative index. Provides more than 10,000 abstracts annually from both trade and academic publications. Covers computer hardware, software, product reviews, Web topics, e-commerce, networks, corporate news, security, and related topics. Formerly *Microcomputer Abstracts.*

Library Literature and Information Science Index. H.W. Wilson Co. • Quarterly. Annual cumulation. Price varies.

LISA: Library and Information Science Abstracts. R.R. Bowker L.L.C. • 13 times a year. $1,055.00 per year; includes print and online editions.

Social Sciences Citation Index. Thomson Reuters Corp. • Weekly. Product is accessed via *Web of Science.*

ALMANACS AND YEARBOOKS

Annual Society for Information Science and Technology, Information and Business Div. Martha E. Williams, editor. Information Today, Inc. • Annual. $79.95 Members. Published on behalf of the American Society for Information Science (ASIS). Covers trends in planning, basic techniques, applications, and the information profession in general.

Information Technology Outlook. Organisation for Economic Co-operation and Development Publications and Information Center. • Biennial. A review of recent developments in international markets for computer hardware, software, and services. Also examines current legal provisions for information systems security and privacy in OECD countries.

CD-ROM DATABASES

LISA Plus. Cambridge Scientific Abstracts L.P. • Quarterly. $2,000 per year. CD-ROM version of Library Information and Science Abstracts, providing abstracting and indexing of the world's library and information science literature, 1969 to date. Contains more than 180,000 citations.

Social Sciences Citation Index. Thomson Reuters Corp. • Weekly. Product is accessed via *Web of Science.*

WILSONDISC: Library Literature and Information Science Index. H.W. Wilson Co. • Quarterly. Includes unlimited access to the online version of *Library Literature.* Provides CD-ROM indexing of about 400 periodicals, covering a wide range of topics having to do with libraries, library management, and the information industry.

DIRECTORIES

The Annual Directory of the Information Industry Association. Software and Information Industry Association. • Annual. Members, $75.00; nonmembers, $125.00.

Directory of Colorado Manufacturers--Information, Science, & Technology. University of Colorado at Boulder Leeds School of Business Business Research Division. • $25 clearance price. Covers: More than 1,600 Colorado manufacturers in the information, science and technology fields. Entries include: Plant address, mailing address, telephone number, e-mail, Web address, names and titles of key personnel, NAICS code numbers, number of employees, branch and subsidiary details, area of distribution.

Information Industry Directory. Cengage Learning Inc. • Annual. $1,160 Individuals. Provides information on companies that produce and provide electronic systems, services and products.

KMWorld Buyer's Guide. Knowledge Asset Media Inc. • Semiannual. $2,395 (Basic Corporate Profile Package) One Issue — Spring 2014 Edition PLUS 6 Months Online. Controlled circulation as part of *KMWorld.* Contains corporate and product profiles related to various aspects of knowledge management and information systems. (Knowledge Asset Media is a an affiliate of Information Today, Inc.).

Major Information Technology Companies of the World. Cengage Learning Inc. • Annual. $1,460 Individuals. 2008. 11th edition. eBook. Published by Graham & Whiteside. Contains profiles of more than 8,250 leading information technology companies in various countries.

Metroplex Technology Business Council--Membership Directory. Metroplex Technology Business Council. • Provides contact information for technology provider companies.

E-BOOKS

Encyclopedia of Emerging Industries. Cengage Learning Inc. • $546 6th edition. Provides detailed information on 140 "newly flourishing" industries. Includes historical background, organizational structure, significant individuals, current conditions, major companies, work force, technology trends, research developments, and other industry facts.

Global Information Society: Operating Information Systems in a Dynamic Global Business Environment. Cengage Learning Inc. • 2006. eBook. Published by Information Science Reference. Addresses the importance of information technology management and issues in operating information systems in the global dynamic business environment. This title offers a collection of new ideas, latest technology applications and experiences in global information systems development and operations.

ENCYCLOPEDIAS AND DICTIONARIES

Encyclopedia of Communication and Information. Cengage Learning Inc. • 2003. eBook. Published by Macmillan Reference USA. Provides an overview of universal modes of communication. Inquire about price and availability.

Encyclopedia of Library and Information Science. CRC Press. • Available in print or as an online subscription.

HANDBOOKS AND MANUALS

Trade Secret Protection in an Information Age. Gale R. Peterson. Glasser LegalWorks. • Looseleaf. $149. 00, including sample forms on disk. Periodic supplementation available. Covers trade secret law relating to computer software, online databases, and multimedia products. Explanations are based on more than 1,000 legal cases. Sample forms on disk include work-for-hire examples and covenants not to compete.

INTERNET DATABASES

InfoTech Trends. Data Analysis Group. Phone: (925)462-1202; Fax: (925)462-1225; Email: support@infotechtrends.com • URL: http://www.infotechtrends.com • Web site provides both free and fee-based market research data on the information technology industry, including computers, peripherals, telecommunications, the Internet, software, CD-ROM/DVD, e-commerce, and workstations. Fees: Free for current (most recent year) data; more extensive information has various fee structures. Formerly *Computer Industry Forecasts.*

Wired News. Lycos Inc. 400-2 Totten Pond Rd., Waltham, MA 02451-2053. Phone: (781)370-2700 or (415)276-8400; Fax: (781)370-2600 or (415)276-8500; Email: press@lycos.com • URL: http://www.lycos.com • Provides summaries and full-text of "Top Stories" relating to the Internet, computers, multimedia, telecommunications, and the electronic information industry in general. These news stories are placed in the broad categories of Politics, Business, Culture, and Technology. Affiliated with *Wired* magazine. Fees: Free.

ONLINE DATABASES

Applied Science and Technology Index Online. H.W. Wilson Co. • Provides online indexing of 500 major scientific, technical, industrial, and engineering periodicals. Time period is 1983 to date. Monthly updates. Inquire as to online cost and availability.

Computer Database. Cengage Learning Inc. • Provides one year of full-text online for 150 leading computer-related publications. Also includes 70,000 product specifications and brief profiles of 13,000 computer product vendors and manufacturers. Inquire as to prices and availability.

INSPEC. Institution of Electrical Engineers. • Provides online citations, with abstracts, to the world literature of electrical engineering, electronics, optoelectronics, telecommunications, industrial controls, instrumentation, computer technology, information technology, and physics. Coverage includes more than 4,000 technical and scientific journals from 1969 to date, with weekly updating. (INSPEC is Information Services in Physics, Electronics, and Computing.) Inquire as to online cost and availability.

Wilson Business Abstracts Online. H.W. Wilson Co. • Indexes and abstracts 600 major business periodicals, plus the *Wall Street Journal* and the business section of the *New York Times*. Indexing is from 1982, abstracting from 1990, with the two newspapers included from 1993. Updated weekly. Inquire as to online cost and availability. (*Business Periodicals Index* without abstracts is also available online.).

OTHER SOURCES

E-Commerce and Internet Law: Treatise with Forms. Ian C. Ballon. Glasser LegalWorks. • $1,479 Individuals Binder/Looseleaf (Full Set). Periodic supplementation. Analyzes Internet legalities, including litigious matters relating to downloading, streaming, music, video, content aggregation, domain names, chatrooms, and search engines. Includes forms, contracts, checklists, sample pleadings, and an extensive glossary.

Information and Image Management: The State of the Industry. Association for Information and Image Management International. • Annual. $130.00. Market data with five-year forecasts. Covers electronic imaging, micrographics supplies and equipment, software, and records management services.

PERIODICALS AND NEWSLETTERS

CIO: The Magazine for Chief Information Officers. CXO Media Inc. • Monthly. $129 per year. Edited for chief information officers. Includes a monthly "Web Business" section (incorporates the former *WebMaster* periodical) and a monthly "Enterprise" section for other company executives.

EContent: Digital Content Strategies and Resources. Online Inc. • Monthly. $110.00 per year. Emphasis is on the business management and financial aspects of the digital content industry. (Formerly published by Online, Inc.).

Electronic Information Report: Empowering Industry Decision Makers Since 1979. SIMBA Information Inc. • 46 times a year. $649.00 per year. Newsletter. Provides business and financial news and trends for online services, electronic publishing, storage media, multimedia, and voice services. Includes information on relevant IPOs (initial public offerings) and mergers. Formerly *Electronic Information Week*.

Global Business and Organizational Excellence. Society of Competitive Intelligence Professionals. John Wiley and Sons, Inc., Journals Div. • Bimonthly. $931 U.S., Canada, and Mexico print only,other countries. Journal covering best practices and trends that organizations use to excel. Formerly *Competitive Intelligence Review*.

InForm. Victor O. Schinnerer and Company Inc. • Description: Reports national and state developments affecting architects and engineers.

Information Broker. Helen P. Burwell, editor. Burwell Enterprises Inc. • Description: Covers companies that offer fee-based information services and issues related to "the business" of information brokering.

Information Hotline. Science Associates/International Inc. • Monthly. $150. Description: "The oldest, most respected, continuously published newsletter." Devoted to objective coverage of trends, policy, analysis, and opinion in the information field.

Information Outlook: The Monthly Magazine of the Special Libraries Association. Special Libraries Association. • Monthly. $65.00 per year. Topics include information technology, the Internet, copyright, research techniques, library management, and professional development. Replaces *Special Libraries* and *SpeciaList*.

Information Services and Use: An International Journal. IOS Press, Inc. • Quarterly. $140 Individuals online only. An information and information technology oriented publication with a wide scope of subject matters.

The Information Society: An International Journal. Taylor & Francis Ltd. • 5/year. $209 Individuals. Five times a year. Individuals, $105.00 per year; institutions, $285.00 per year.

Information Standards Quarterly. National Information Standards Organization. • Quarterly. $130 Individuals /year. Newsletter. Reports on activities of the National Information Standards Organization.

Information Times. Software and Information Industry Association. • Monthly. Membership. Formerly *Friday Memo*.

Information Today: The Newspaper for Users and Producers of Electronic Information Services. Information Today, Inc. • 11 times a year. $68.95 per year.

Information Week: Business Innovation Powered by Technology. UBM L.L.C. • Weekly. $199.00 per year. The magazine for information systems management.

InfoWorld: Defining Technology for Business. InfoWorld Publishing. • Weekly. $195.00 per year. For personal computing professionals.

Online Newsletter. Information Intelligence Inc. • Description: Tracks developments in the fields of CD-ROM and online services. Contains news of online/CD-ROM developments and events, mergers and acquisitions, personnel movements, telecommunications and networks, new equipment and developments, microcomputer hardware and software, new and forthcoming databases, forthcoming meetings, and publications and user aids.

Report on Electronic Commerce: Online Business, Financial and Consumer Strategies and Trends. Wolters Kluwer Law and Business. • Biweekly. $1,789.00 per year. Newsletter. Includes *Daily Multimedia News Service*. Incorporates *Interactive Services Report*.

The Seybold Report. Seybold Publications. • Semimonthly. $499 /year. The definitive and independent source of information about the technologies used for publishing and printing.

Telematics and Informatics: An International Journal on Telecommunications and Internet Technology. Elsevier. • Four times a year. Institutions, $938.00 per year.

RESEARCH CENTERS AND INSTITUTES

Economic Research Service - Information Services Division. 1400 Independence Ave. SW, Washington, DC 20250. Phone: (202)694-5100; Fax: (202)245-4781; Email: rbianchi@ers.usda.gov • URL: http://www.ers.usda.gov/contact-us/management-directory.aspx#ISD • Manages and directs agency-wide information technology, communications, and administrative activities in support of the economic research and analysis mission of ERS.

STATISTICS SOURCES

U.S. Industry and Trade Outlook. U.S. Department of Commerce National Technical Information Service. • Annual. Produced by the International Trade Administration, U.S. Department of Commerce, in a "public-private" partnership with DRI/McGraw-Hill and Standard & Poor's. Provides basic data, outlook for the current year, and "Long-Term Prospects" (five-year projections) for a wide variety of products and services. Includes high technology industries. Formerly *U.S. Industrial Outlook*.

TRADE/PROFESSIONAL ASSOCIATIONS

Alpha Iota Delta. University of Detroit Mercy, 4001 W McNichols Rd., Detroit, MI 48221. Phone: (313)993-1219; Fax: (313)993-1052; Email: ulfertgw@udmercy.edu • URL: http://www.alphaiotadelta.com • Serves as honor society for men and women in decision sciences and information systems.

American Society for Information Science and Technology. 8555 16th St., Ste. 850, Silver Spring, MD 20910. Phone: (301)495-0900; Fax: (301)495-0810; Email: asis@asis.org • URL: http://www.asis.org • Members are information managers, scientists, librarians, and others who are interested in the storage, retrieval, and use of information.

Information Technology Alliance. 23940 N 73rd Pl., Scottsdale, AZ 85255. Phone: (480)515-2003; Fax: (602)294-2399 • URL: http://www.italliance.com • Represents mid-market technology professionals, consultants, and product/service providers in North America. Aims to create a community where members share information and build relationships that improve the way they do business with their clients. Protects the quality of the profession and promotes public welfare.

Library and Information Technology Association. 50 E Huron St., Chicago, IL 60611-2795. Phone: 800-545-2433; Fax: (312)280-3257; Email: lita@ala.org • URL: http://www.ala.org/lita • Affiliated with the American Library Association. Formerly Information Science and Automation Division of ALA.

MSPAlliance. 1380 E Ave., Ste. 124-376, Chico, CA 95926-7349. Phone: (530)891-1340; Fax: (530)433-5707; Email: info@mspalliance.com • URL: http://www.mspalliance.com • Aims to promote the Managed Services Industry as a true and viable profession to the IT Business Consumer. Represents providers working together in a vendor-neutral manner to define and promote the Managed Services Industry. Educates consumers on the benefits of using Managed Service Providers.

National Federation of Advanced Information Services. c/o Jill O'Neill, Director, 1518 Walnut St., Ste. 1004, Philadelphia, PA 19102-3403. Phone: (215)893-1561; Fax: (215)893-1564 • URL: http://nfais.org • Formerly National Federation of Abstracting and Indexing Services.

National Information Standards Organization. 3600 Clipper Mill Rd., Ste. 302, Baltimore, MD 21211. Phone: (301)654-2512; Fax: (410)685-5278; Email: hreid@copyright.com • URL: http://www.niso.org • Identifies, develops, maintains, and publishes technical standards to manage information in the changing environment used by libraries, publishers, and information services. Supports open access to NISO standards. Standards available at website.

INFORMATION MANAGEMENT SYSTEMS

See MANAGEMENT INFORMATION SYSTEMS

INFORMATION RETRIEVAL (DOCUMENTATION)

See ONLINE INFORMATION SYSTEMS

INFORMATION SOURCES

See also STATISTICS SOURCES

BIBLIOGRAPHIES

Booklist. Library and Information Technology Association. • Biweekly. $147.50 U.S. and Canada /year. Reviews library materials for school and public libraries. Incorporates *Reference Books Bulletin.*

Business Research Handbook: Methods and Sources for Lawyers and Business Professionals. Kathy E. Shimpock. Wolters Kluwer Law and Business. • Semiannual. $859 Individuals Looseleaf. Provides detailed advice on how to find business information. Describes a wide variety of data sources, both private and government.

Reference Books Bulletin: A Compilation of Evaluations. Mary Ellen Quinn, editor. Library and Information Technology Association. • *Booklist.*

Statistics Sources. Cengage Learning Inc. • $874 Individuals. 2012. $836.00. 37th edition. Lists sources of statistical information for more than 20,000 topics.

U.S. Government Information for Business. U. S. Government Printing Office. • Annual. Free. A selected list of currently available publications, periodicals, and electronic products on business, trade, labor, federal regulations, economics, and other topics. Also known as *Business Catalog.*

DIRECTORIES

American Companies: A Guide to Sources of Information. CBD Research Ltd. • Biennial. £78 Individuals. Covers: Business information sources from over 50 countries in North, South, and Central America and the Caribbean. Entries include: For companies--company name, address, phone, fax, telex, year established, description, countries of specialization, branch offices, and languages spoken; for publications--title, publisher, address, telephone, fax, telex, year first published, frequency; latest edition, price, page count, description, company information, types of indexes, languages, and formats available.

American Library Association Guide to Information Access. Library and Information Technology Association. • $18.95. Publication includes: List of reference sources for areas including business and finance, consumer information, education, jobs and careers, and science and technology. Principal content of publication is a guide to general research methods.

The Annual Directory of the Information Industry Association. Software and Information Industry Association. • Annual. Members, $75.00; non-members, $125.00.

Automated Sources of Information in the Department of Commerce. U.S. Department of Commerce National Technical Information Service. • $25 plus $5 handling fee (PB88-132568AHT). Diskette. Covers: Agencies of the United States Department of Commerce that produce or support online databases, electronic bulletin boards, information centers, and publications. Database includes: Agency name, address, phone, name and title of contact, information system content, titles of principal publications.

Brokers. IZUM Information Service. • Quarterly. Database covers: Approximately 22 databases currently available on information providers and/or database producers in Slovenia. Part of the INFORS database. Entries include: Database name, acronym, date status, topic, language, number of records, update frequency, source of data, host, vendor, and producer.

Business Database Finder. The Information Advisor. • Annual. $99. Covers: Business databases and online hosts. Database includes: Comparative charts/tables showing features and costs of databases. Entries include: Name of database, description of product/service.

Business Information Desk Reference: Where to Find Answers to Business Questions. Macmillan Creative Services. • $20 paper. Covers: Approximately 1,000 print materials, online databases, federal agencies, private organizations and other information sources covering 24 business areas.

Business Information Sources. Hoover's Inc. • $39. 95. Covers: Sources of business information, including books, periodicals, CD-ROMs, and online databases.

The Business of Supplier Diversity: A Handbook of Essential Contacts and Information for Navigating the Industry. Diversity Information Resources. • Annual. $129 Individuals. Covers: Business opportunity fairs, seminars, and workshops; National Supplier Development Council regional offices; Small Business Administration and Minority Business Development Administration offices; minority and women-owned business directories; and other resources for minority and women-owned businesses. Database includes: Summaries of legislation affecting minority businesses; glossary.

CINFOLINK Directory of Information Services and the Internet in China. CINFOLINK Services. • Biennial. $20 U.S. plus airmail postage within North America $2.50. Covers: nearly 400 electronic databases and information networks, approximately 225 related publication and information sources (including associations, research institutes of the Chinese Academy of Sciences, universities and colleges, and libraries), and 150 current Internet sources in China and Hong Kong. Entries include: For database services--Name, description, type of data, language, size, updating frequency, timespan; producer name and address; contact name, phone, fax; other formats, subject(s), status, price, etc. For publication sources--Name, address, phone, fax, titles produced, description.

Company Information. Bowker Ltd. • Biennial. $199 plus $15.00 shipping. Covers: Sources of company information in the United Kingdom, including print, online, and CD-ROM data sources, and organizations.

Croner's A-Z of Business Information Sources. Wolters Kluwer Ltd. • Annual. $71.50 includes first year's updates & shipping. Covers: Organizations, publications, and other sources of business information in the United Kingdom from abrasives to zinc and the aerospace industry to wire products. Entries include: Name, address, phone, telex, contact name, brief description.

Data Sources for Business and Market Analysis. Hoover's Inc. • $54.95. Covers: Sources of business information from providers including the federal government, regional and local governments, foreign sources, universities, research centers, and professional and trade associations.

Data, Where It Is and How to Get It: Directory of Business, Environment and Energy Data Sources. Coleman/Morse. • $24.95. Covers: Over 2,500 sources of information produced by the U.S. government on business, environmental and energy activities; includes experts, federal departments and agencies, data centers, and user groups. Entries include: Data sources for agriculture, banking and finance, international trade, demographics, employment, prices, income, and rural development.

Datapro Reports. Datapro Information Services Group. • Monthly. $495 minimum cost per year, depending on service. Datapro produces sixty information services covering products, vendors, markets, and technologies in large systems, microcomputers, telecommunications, data communications, word processing, software, office automation systems, copiers and duplicators, information security systems, retail automation equipment, banking automation equipment, personal computer communications, communications alternatives, and electronic publishing systems. Reports generally include descriptions and analyses of each equipment model offered by each manufacturer in the field, comparison charts, and lists of suppliers, associations, consultants, etc., with addresses and phone numbers. Individual descriptions include a summary and detailed reports on technical characteristics and operation. Reports are on looseleaf pages.

Detwiler's Directory of Health and Medical Resources. S.M. Detwiler and Associates. • Biennial. $195.00. Lists a wide range of healthcare information resources, including more than 2,000 corporations, associations, government agencies, publishers, licensure organizations, market research firms, foundations, and institutes, as well as 6,000 publications. Indexed by type of information, publication, acronym, and 600 subject categories.

Directory of Business Information. John Wiley and Sons Inc. Technical Insights. • $290 Individuals. Covers: Over 10,000 sources of business information, including publications, associations, companies, government offices, and libraries.

The Directory of Business Information Resources. Grey House Publishing. • Annual. $195 Libraries Softcover. Provides contact names as well as editorial and advertising personnel, phone and fax numbers, description, frequency, pricing information, industry's associations, newsletters, magazines, trade shows, directories, databases and industry websites of 21,000 businesses.

Directory of Canadian Information Sources. Browning Associates. • Covers: approximately 1,500 directories, market surveys, trade guides, association publications, and special periodical issues that are sources of Canadian information. Entries include: Publication title, publisher name, address, phone, frequency, price, scope of coverage, description of contents and arrangement, whether advertising is accepted, other details.

Directory of EC Industry Information Sources. Macmillan Publishers Ltd. Nature Publishing Group. • $105 plus $6.00 postage. Covers: Organizations and individuals in the European Communities responsible for specific industrial information, including finding business partners, business start-ups, lobbying, electronic information services, and statistics.

The Directory of EU Information Sources: The Red Book. Euroconfidentiel S. A. • Annual. $230.00. Lists publications, associations, consultants, law firms, diplomats, jounalists, and other sources of information about Europe and the European Union.

Directory of International Sources of Business Information. Pearson Education Ltd. • Annual. $85. Covers: Sources of business information worldwide, including business information brokers, Euro-Info centers, banks, stockbrokers, associations, embassies and councils, market research organizations, economic and statistical organizations, publishers, publications, online databases, and United Kingdom packet switching exchanges. Entries include: For business information brokers and Euro-Info centers--Name, address, phone, fax, host and databases accessed, subject areas covered, languages spoken, description of services offered. For banks, stockbrokers, associations, embassies and councils, market research organizations, economic and statistical organizations, and publications--Name, address, phone. For online databases--Name, address, phone, host. For United Kingdom packet switching exchanges--Phone. For publishers--Name, address, phone, fax, telex.

Directory of Special Libraries and Information Centers. Cengage Learning Inc. • Annual. $966 Individuals. 2010. 38th edition. eBook. Provides detailed contact and descriptive information on subject-specific resource collections maintained by government agencies, businesses, publishers, educational and nonprofit organizations, and associations worldwide.

East European Business Handbook. Euromonitor International Business Reference Div. • $190. Publication includes: List of sources of information on doing business in eastern Europe. Principal content of publication is a guide in identifying market opportunities in eastern Europe.

East European Business Information. Headland Press. • Annual. $99. Covers: Organizations providing commercial and industrial information in Eastern Europe, including information on joint ventures, banking, legislation, and marketing. Entries include: Name, address, phone.

Eastern Europe: A Directory and Sourcebook. Euromonitor International Business Reference Div. • $440. Publication includes: Lists of publishers of private research, journals and newsletters, online databases, consultants, and abstracts and indexes providing information on eastern Europe. Database includes: Economic and demographic data, analysis of business practices, markets, investment opportunities, and rankings.

Encyclopedia of Business Information Sources. Cengage Learning Inc. • Annual. $626 Individuals. Contains bibliographic information on more than 35,000 live, print, and electronic sources of information covering more than 1,100 subjects of interest to business personnel. Includes abstracts and indexes, almanacs and yearbooks, bibliographies, online databases, research centers and institutes, and more. Available as eBook.

European Business Information Sourcebook. Headland Press. • Annual. $139. Covers: Sources of European business information, including databanks, online services, market research firms, sources of official statistics, business research services, libraries, directories, magazines, and newspapers. Entries include: Name, address, phone, fax.

European Directory of Business Information Libraries. Euromonitor International Business Reference Div. • Irregular. $650. Covers: More than 2,000 European business libraries and services. Entries include: location, accessibility, fees, stock, and subject area.

European Directory of Financial Information Sources. Euromonitor International Business Reference Div. • $160. Covers: Sources of financial information for companies in Europe, including official sources and publications, libraries, information services, banks and other financial institutions, accountancy firms and tax advisors, stockbrokers, stock exchanges, databases, indexes, abstracts, banking journals, and European business contacts. Entries include: Name, address, phone, fax, year founded.

European Sources of Scientific and Technical Information. Cartermill International. • Irregular. $225. Covers: over 1,500 patents and standards offices, national offices of information, and organizations active in scientific fields in Europe, including former Soviet bloc nations. Provides English-language version of foreign terminology. Entries include: Organization name, address, phone, fax, e-mail and website addresses, year founded, name of contact, parent company, subject(s) covered, publications, library facilities, and information, consulting, and training services.

Findex: The Worldwide Directory of Market Research Reports, Studies, and Surveys. MarketResearch.com. • Annual. Provides brief annotations of market research reports and related publications from about 1,000 publishers, arranged by topic. Back of book includes Report Titles by Publisher, Publishers/Distributors Directory, Subject Index, Geography Index, and Company Index. (Formerly published by Cambridge Information Group.).

GATEWAYS. IZUM Information Service. • Monthly. Database covers: 10 databases currently available online on records on the Internet and other networks providers in Slovenia. Entries include: Database name, acronym, date status, topic, language, number of records, update frequency, source of data, host, vendor, and producer.

Great Big Book of Business Lists. Entrepreneur Press. • $34.95 Individuals paperback. Covers: Approximately 10,000 listings of business information. Entries include: Business' contact information.

The Guide: A Practical Handbook of Marketing Research Sources in the United Kingdom and Western Europe. Key Note Publications Ltd. • $165. Covers: Sources of marketing research in the United Kingdom and Western Europe, including business information sources, market research sources, advertising organizations, periodicals, newspapers, magazines, official statistical sources, online databases, and libraries. Entries include: For databases--Database name, host, producer, contents, frequency of updates. For others--Name, address, phone, fax, description.

How to Find Business Intelligence in Washington. MarketResearch.com. • $295 payment with order. Covers: over 500 government libraries, archives, offices, agencies, statistical centers, and other sources of publications, market studies, statistical summaries, and census data. Entries include: Office, agency, or organization name, address, phone, description of information, price (if any).

How to Find Information about Companies. MarketResearch.com. • Annual. $395 per volume. Covers: in Part 1, over 9,000 sources of corporate intelligence, including federal, state, and local repositories of company filings, individual industry experts, published sources, databases, CD-ROM products, and corporate research services. Entries include: Source name, address, phone, contact name, description. Parts 2 and 3 provide guidelines for company research.

How to Find Information about Private Companies. MarketResearch.com. • Irregular. $59. Covers: Organizations, publications, and individuals that collect information on private companies. Database includes: Corporate research tips. Entries include: Name, address, phone.

International Business Information on the Web: Searcher Magazine's Guide to Sites and Strategies for Global Business Research. Information Today, Inc. • $29.95. Lists directories, search engines, banks, financial institutions, news sources, government contacts, chambers of commerce, and other country-specific information. Covers: Approximately 1,000 Web sites related to international business research including general business sites in the United States and worldwide. Publication includes: URLs. Entries include: Information regarding each site.

International Directory of Business Information Sources and Services. Routledge Reference. • $240. Covers: over 4,500 chambers of commerce, government agencies, foreign trade promotion agencies, associations, research organizations, business libraries, and other sources of business information in 50 countries. Entries include: Agency name, address, phone, fax, names and titles of key personnel, name and title of contact, description.

International Directory of Marketing Information Sources. Euromonitor International Business Reference Div. • Irregular. $650. Covers: Marketing sources in major non-European industrialized countries. Entries include: Over 6,000 contacts, services, and publications.

Internet Resources and Services for International Business: A Global Guide. Greenwood Electronic Media. • $82.95 Single issue Paperback. Covers: More than 2,500 business-related Web sites, most of which are government and university sites, international. Entries include: Web site, content.

Latin American Markets: A Guide to Company and Information Sources. MarketResearch.com. • Irregular. $335. Covers: sources of information on businesses in Central America, South America, and the Caribbean. Entries include: Source name, address, phone, fax, names and titles of key personnel.

Library Journal: Reference: Print, CD-ROM, Online (year). Reed Elsevier Group plc Reed Business Information. • Annual. Issued in November as a supplement to *Library Journal.* Lists new and updated reference material, including general and trade print titles, directories, annuals, CD-ROM titles, and online sources. Includes material from more than 200 publishers, arranged by company name, with an index by subject.

Library Journal Sourcebook: The Reference For Library Products & Services. Reed Elsevier Group plc Reed Business Information. • Annual. Publication includes: List of over 600 suppliers of products and services used by libraries from abstracting to word processing equipment. Entries include: Company name, address, phone, list of products or services. Complete listings for more than 100 architectural firms; Disaster planning for librarians.

New Jersey Business Source Book. Research Communications. • Annual. $495 Individuals book with CD. Covers: Sources of New Jersey business information, including 555 of the state's top employers, 798 trade and professional associations, and 170 NJ chambers of commerce. Database includes: Information on services available to the New Jersey business community and New Jersey web sites. Entries include: For companies--Name, address, phone, e-mail, URL, description names and titles of key personnel. For associations--Name, address, phone, number of members. For chambers of commerce--Name, address, phone, fax, e-mail.

PM Directory & Reference Issue: Plumbers Buyers Guide. BNP Media. • Annual. Covers: Manufacturers, wholesalers, products, consultants, and manufacturers' representatives in the industries of plumbing, piping, and hydronic heating. Entries include: Contact name, company, address, phone, fax, and product descriptions.

Researching Markets, Industries, & Business Opportunities. MarketResearch.com. • Irregular. $245. Publication includes: Lists of sources of business and market information. Entries include: Source name, address, phone, description. Principal content of publication is discussion of methods for studying markets and industries.

SourceGuide to Food Industry Information. London Business School Information Service. • $50. Covers: Sources of information on the food industry available in the U.K., with some international coverage; includes statistics sources, directories, trade journals, trade associations, and online databases. Entries include: Source name, address, phone, type of data available, price.

For publishers' addresses, refer to SOURCES CITED section at the back of the book.

SourceGuide to Industrial Market Data. London Business School Information Service. • $100. Covers: Directories, yearbooks, journals, statistical sources, market reports, trade and research associations, libraries and information services, and databases that provide data on 14 industrial market sectors in the U.K. Entries include: Source name, address, phone, description, evaluation.

SourceGuide to Management Information. London Business School Information Service. • $50. Covers: Sources of published and unpublished information on management issues available worldwide, including journals, databases and other electronic sources, abstracting and indexing services, reference works, academic working papers, and other relevant materials. Entries include: Source name, address, phone, description.

Sources of Free Business Information. Kogan Page, Limited. • Irregular. $12.95 hardback. Covers: Free business information and how to obtain it, including taxation, business finance, grants and incentives, exporting and overseas business, general economic and business information, small business advice, legal matters, computers, and investment. Entries include: Providers of information name, address, phone.

Transnational Corporations and Labor: A Directory of Resources. WorldViews. • $12.95 plus $2.00 shipping. Covers: sources for books, periodicals, pamphlets, audiovisuals, and other educational resources on transnational corporations and labor issues; names of resources with annotations and ordering information. Entries include: Organization name, address, phone, titles of print and audio/visual material. Part of a 10 volume series (updated in "Third World Resources"), each volume covering single region or issue.

Which Business CD-ROM?. Bowker-Saur. • Annual. $259 plus $30.00 shipping. Publication includes: List of major CD-ROM publishers in the field of business; coverage includes the U.K. and Europe, with limited U.S. listings. Principal content of publication is information significant CD-ROM titles in various business fields, such as company directories, company accounts, mergers/acquisitions, business news, legislation/regulations, market research, industries, economics and finance, international trade, and business management literature. Entries include: Publisher name, address, phone.

Who Knows What: The Essential Business Resource Book. Henry Holt and Co. • $45. Covers: Approximately 5,500 businesses, special libraries, government agencies, and other organizations in the U.S. that have access to information in over 500 business-related subject areas. Entries include: Company or organization name, address, phone, fax, name and title of contact, description of services and projects.

World Database of Business Information Sources on the Internet. Euromonitor International Business Reference Div. • $690. Covers: Over 35,000 business information sources worldwide, including 12,000 organizations, 13,000 publications, 2,000 exhibitions, and 700 online databases. Entries include: Source name, contact information, description.

World Directory of Business Information Sources. Euromonitor International Business Reference Div. • $700 Individuals U.S.D. Covers: National and international Web sites of interest to business researchers, provided by trade associations, magazines, government agencies, private research firms and others.

World Directory of Industrial Information Sources. United Nations Publications. • $40 Individuals. Covers: Industrial information sources for the most appropriate sources of technology and equipment. It contains profiles of information providers such as information and documentation centers, banks, training institutes, development agencies and manufacturers associations that are prepared to provide entrepreneurs in developing countries with answers to their industrial needs.

E-BOOKS

Business Information Handbook. David Mort. Cengage Learning Inc. • 2005. Published by K.G. Saur. Serves as a general guide to the world of business information. Inquire as to price and availability.

INTERNET DATABASES

EBSCO Information Services. EBSCO Publishing Inc. 10 Estes St., Ipswich, MA 01938-2106. Phone: 800-653-2726 or (978)356-6500; Fax: (978)356-6565; Email: information@ebscohost.com • URL: http://www.ebscohost.com • Fee-based Web site providing Internet access to a wide variety of databases, including business-related material. Full text is available for many periodical titles, with daily updates. Fees: Apply.

GPO Access. U. S. Government Printing Office Sales Program, Bibliographic Systems Branch. Phone: (888)293-6498 or (202)512-1530; Fax: (202)512-1262; Email: gpoaccess@gpo.gov • URL: http://www.access.gpo.gov • Web site provides searching of the GPO's Sales Product Catalog (SPC), also known as Publications Reference File (PRF). Covers all "Government information products currently offered for sale by the Superintendent of Documents." There are also specialized search pages for individual databases, such as the *Code of Federal Regulations*, the *Federal Register*, and *Commerce Business Daily*. Updated daily. Fees: Free.

InSite 2. Intelligence Data/Thomson Financial. Phone: 800-654-0393 or (617)856-1890; Fax: (617)737-3182; Email: intelligence.data@tfn.com • URL: http://www.insite2.gale.com/ • Fee-based Web site consolidates information in a "Base Pack" consisting of Business InSite, Market InSite, and Company InSite. Optional databases are Consumer InSite, Health and Wellness InSite, Newsletter InSite, and Computer InSite. Includes fulltext content from more than 2,500 trade publications, journals, newsletters, newspapers, analyst reports, and other sources. Continuous updating. Formerly produced by The Gale Group.

Intelligence Data. Thomson Financial. Phone: 800-654-0393; Fax: (617)824-2477 • URL: http://www.intelligencedata.com • Fee-based Web site provides a wide variety of information relating to competitive intelligence, strategic planning, business development, mergers, acquisitions, sales, and marketing. "Intelliscope" feature offers searching of other Thomson units, such as Investext, MarkIntel, InSite 2, and Industry Insider. Weekly updating.

ProQuest. ProQuest L.L.C. 789 E Eisenhower Pkwy., Ann Arbor, MI 48106-1346. Phone: 800-521-0600 or (734)761-4700; Fax: (734)662-4554; Email: info@proquest.com • URL: http://www.proquest.com • Fee-based Web site providing Internet access to more than 3,000 periodicals, newspapers, and other publications. Many items are available full-text, with daily updates. Includes extensive corporate and financial information. Fees: Apply.

PubList.com: The Internet Directory of Publications. Bowes & Associates, Inc. Phone: (781)792-0999; Fax: (781)792-0988; Email: info@publist.com • URL: http://www.publist.com • "The premier online global resource for information about print and electronic publications." Provides online searching for information on more than 150,000 magazines, journals, newsletters, e-journals, and monographs. Database entries generally include title, publisher, format, address, editor, circulation, subject, and International Standard Serial Number (ISSN). Fees: Free.

Ulrichsweb.com. R.R. Bowker L.L.C. 630 Central Ave, New Providence, NJ 07974. Phone: 888-269-5372 or (908)286-1090; Email: info@bowker.com • URL: http://www.bowker.com • Web site provides fee-based access to about 250,000 serials records from the *Ulrich's International Periodicals Directory* database. Includes periodical evaluations from *Library Journal* and *Magazines for Libraries*. Monthly updates.

WilsonWeb Periodicals Databases. H.W. Wilson Co. 950 University Ave., Bronx, NY 10452-4224. Phone: 800-367-6770 or (718)588-8400 or (718)558-8400; Fax: (718)590-1617 or (800)590-1617; Email: custserv@hwwilson.com • URL: http://www.hwwilson.com • Web sites provide fee-based access to *Wilson Business Full Text, Applied Science & Technology Full Text, Biological & Agricultural Index, Library Literature & Information Science Full Text*, and *Readers' Guide Full Text, Mega Edition*. Daily updates.

OTHER SOURCES

Business Rankings Annual (BRA). Cengage Learning Inc. • Annual. $584 Individuals. A guide to lists and rankings appearing in major business publications. The top ten names are listed in each case.

PERIODICALS AND NEWSLETTERS

Business Information Alert: Sources, Strategies and Signposts for Information Professionals. Alert Publications Inc. • 10 times per year. Libraries, $162.00 per year. Newsletter for business librarians and information specialists.

The Information Advisor: Tips and Techniques for Smart Information Users. MarketResearch.com. • Monthly. $159.00 per year. Newsletter. Evaluates and discusses online, CD-ROM, and published sources of business, financial, and market research information.

The Information Report. Washington Researchers Ltd. • Description: Contains 40-140 items in each issue identifying little-known sources of information. Lists and describes directories, special libraries, booklets, seminars, studies, and other research sources available on markets, competition, federal regulation, and economic conditions. Covers government as well as corporate sources, trade, and professional organizations.

Internet Reference Services Quarterly: A Journal of Innovative Information Practice, Technologies, and Resources. The Haworth Press Inc. • Quarterly. $110.00 per year. Covers both theoretical research and practical applications.

Reference and User Services Quarterly. Reference and User Services Association of the American Library Association. • Quarterly. $65 Nonmembers /year. In addition to articles, includes reviews of databases, reference books, and library professional material. Formerly *RQ*.

TRADE/PROFESSIONAL ASSOCIATIONS

National Federation of Advanced Information Services. c/o Jill O'Neill, Director, 1518 Walnut St., Ste. 1004, Philadelphia, PA 19102-3403. Phone: (215)893-1561; Fax: (215)893-1564 • URL: http://nfais.org • Formerly National Federation of Abstracting and Indexing Services.

INFORMATION SYSTEMS, MANAGEMENT

See MANAGEMENT INFORMATION SYSTEMS

INFORMATION SYSTEMS, ONLINE

See ONLINE INFORMATION SYSTEMS

INHERITANCE TAX

See also ESTATE PLANNING

HANDBOOKS AND MANUALS

Trust Administration and Taxation. Matthew Bender and Company Inc. • Semiannual. $1,857 Individuals Book. A well-documented, practical text on the establishment, administration and taxation of trusts, covering revocable living trusts, charitable remainder trusts, and more.

U.S. Master Estate and Gift Tax Guide. Wolters Kluwer Law & Business CCH. • Annual. $103 Quantity: 1 - 4. Covers federal estate and gift taxes, including generation-skipping transfer tax plans. Includes tax tables and sample filled-in tax return forms.

INTERNET DATABASES

CCH Essentials: An Internet Tax Research and Primary Source Library. CCH, Inc. Phone: 800-248-3248 or (773)866-6000; Fax: (773)866-3608 or (800)224-8299; Email: cust_serv@cch.com • URL: http://tax.cch.com/essentials • Fee-based Web site provides full-text coverage of federal tax law and regulations, including rulings, procedures, tax court decisions, and IRS publications, announcements, notices, and penalties. Includes explanation, analysis, tax planning guides, and a daily tax news service. Searching is offered, including citation search.

Court Filings. ProQuest LLC. 2250 Perimeter Park Dr., Ste. 300, Morrisville, NC 27560. Phone: 800-334-2564 or (919)804-6400; Fax: (919)804-6410; Email: contact@dialog.com • URL: http://www.dialog.com • The three main sections of Tax Analysts home page are "Tax News" (Today's Tax News, Feature of the Week, Tax Snapshots, Tax Calendar); "Products & Services" (Product Catalog, Press Releases); and "Public Interest" (Discussion Groups, Tax Clinic, Tax History Project). Fees: Free for coverage of current tax events; fee-based for comprehensive information. Daily updating.

Internal Revenue Service IRS.gov. Internal Revenue Service. Phone: 800-829-1040 or (202)622-5000; Fax: (202)622-5844 • URL: http://www.irs.gov • Web site provides a wide variety of tax information, including IRS forms and publications. Searching is available. Fees: Free.

OTHER SOURCES

Fiduciary Tax Guide. Wolters Kluwer Law & Business CCH. • Monthly. $478.00 per year. Looseleaf service. Covers federal income taxation of estates, trusts, and beneficiaries. Provides information on gift and generation- skipping taxation.

PERIODICALS AND NEWSLETTERS

Estate Planner's Alert. Thomson RIA. • Monthly. $290 Individuals Print. Covers the tax aspects of personal finance, including home ownership, investments, insurance, retirement planning, and charitable giving. Formerly *Estate and Financial Planners Alert.*

Highlights and Documents. Tax Analysts. • Daily. $2,599.95 Individuals. Provides daily coverage of IRS, congressional, judicial, state, and international tax developments. Includes abstracts and citations for "all tax documents released within the previous 24 to 48 hours." Annual compilation available *Highlights and Documents on Microfiche.*

Tax Notes: The Weekly Tax Service. Tax Analysts. • Weekly. Weekly. $1,699.00 per year. Includes an *Annual* and compilations of previous years. Newsletter. Covers "tax news from all federal sources," including congressional committees, tax courts, and the Internal Revenue Service. Each issue contains "summaries of every document that pertains to federal tax law," with citations. Commentary is provided.

Tax Practice. Tax Analysts. • Weekly. $199.00 per year. Newsletter. Covers news affecting tax practitioners and litigators, with emphasis on federal court decisions, rules and regulations, and tax petitions. Provides a guide to Internal Revenue Service audit issues.

INJURIES

See ACCIDENTS

INK

See PRINTING INK INDUSTRY

INLAND MARINE INSURANCE

See MARINE INSURANCE

INLAND WATERWAYS

See WATERWAYS

INNOVATION, BUSINESS

See BUSINESS INNOVATION

INNOVATION IN PRODUCTS

See NEW PRODUCTS

INSECTICIDES

See PESTICIDE INDUSTRY

INSECTS

See ECONOMIC ENTOMOLOGY

INSERVICE TRAINING

See TRAINING OF EMPLOYEES

INSIDER TRADING

See also STOCKHOLDERS

ABSTRACTS AND INDEXES

Business Periodicals Index Retrospective. EBSCO Publishing Inc. • 11/year. Quarterly and annual cumulations.

Index to Legal Periodicals and Books. H.W. Wilson Co. • Monthly. $490.00 per year. Quarterly and annual cumulations.

HANDBOOKS AND MANUALS

Responsibilities of Corporate Officers and Directors Under Federal Securities Law. Wolters Kluwer Law & Business CCH. • Annual. $132 paperback. Includes discussions of indemnification, "D & O" insurance, corporate governance, and insider liability.

INTERNET DATABASES

U.S. Securities and Exchange Commission. 100 F St. NE, Washington, DC 20549. Phone: 800-732-0330 or (202)942-8088; Fax: (202)942-9634; Email: webmaster@sec.gov • URL: http://www.sec.gov • SEC Web site offers free access through EDGAR to text of official corporate filings, such as annual reports (10-K), quarterly reports (10-Q), and proxies. (EDGAR is "Electronic Data Gathering, Analysis, and Retrieval System.") An example is given of how to obtain executive compensation data from proxies. Text of the daily *SEC News Digest* is offered, as are links to other government sites, non-government market regulators, and U. S. stock exchanges. Search facilities are extensive. Fees: Free.

ONLINE DATABASES

Vickers On-Line. Vickers Stock Research Corp. • Provides detailed online information relating to insider trading and the securities holdings of institutional investors. Daily updates. Inquire as to online cost and availability.

Wilson Business Abstracts Online. H.W. Wilson Co. • Indexes and abstracts 600 major business periodicals, plus the *Wall Street Journal* and the business section of the *New York Times.* Indexing is from 1982, abstracting from 1990, with the two newspapers included from 1993. Updated weekly. Inquire as to online cost and availability. (*Business Periodicals Index* without abstracts is also available online.).

OTHER SOURCES

Ferrara on Insider Trading and The Wall. Ralph C. Ferrara. ALM Media Properties LLC. • $540. Demonstrates how firms can use "Chinese Walls" and other devices to control the dissemination of material, nonpublic information by employees. Includes "suggested guidelines for deterring insider trading by employees." (Law Journal Press).

Westlaw Journal Securities Litigation & Regulation. Thomson Reuters Westlaw. • $3,563.52 full set. Provides coverage of shareholder lawsuits against public companies.

PERIODICALS AND NEWSLETTERS

Vickers Weekly Insider Report. Vickers Stock Research Corp. • Description: Reports on stock insider transactions and maintains portfolios based on insider buy signals-96 up 68%.

RESEARCH CENTERS AND INSTITUTES

University of Chicago - Booth School of Business - Center for Research in Security Prices. 105 W Adams St., Ste. 1700, Chicago, IL 60603. Phone: (312)263-6400; Fax: (312)263-6430; Email: subscriptions@crsp.chicagobooth.edu • URL: http://www.crsp.com • Historical financial data.

University of Pennsylvania - The Wharton School - Rodney L. White Center for Financial Research. 3254 Steinberg Hall-Dietrich Hall, Philadelphia, PA 19104-6367. Phone: (215)898-7616; Fax: (215)573-8084; Email: rlwctr@finance.wharton.upenn.edu • URL: http://rodneywhitecenter.wharton.upenn.edu • Research areas include financial management, money markets, real estate finance, and international finance.

TRADE/PROFESSIONAL ASSOCIATIONS

Financial Industry Regulatory Authority. 1735 K St., Washington, DC 20006. Phone: (301)590-6500; Fax: (202)293-6260; Email: francine.lee@finra.org • URL: http://www.finra.org • Formerly National Association of Securities Dealers.

New York Stock Exchange Inc. 11 Wall St., New York, NY 10005-1905. Phone: (212)656-3000 or (212)656-2060; Fax: (212)656-2126; Email: iec@nyse.com • URL: http://www.nyse.com • Aims to add value to the capital raising and asset management process by providing a cost effective, self regulated marketplace for the trading of financial instruments. Promotes confidence in, and understanding of, industry processes and serves as a forum for discussion of relevant national and international policy issues.

North American Securities Administrators Association. 750 1st St. NE, Ste. 1140, Washington, DC 20002-8034. Phone: (202)737-0900; Fax:

(202)783-3571: Email: ri@nasaa.org • URL: http://www.nasaa.org • Represents the interests of the state, provincial and territorial securities administrators in the U.S., Canada, Mexico and Puerto Rico. Provides support to its members in government relations and with federal regulators, industry SROs and other groups.

INSOLVENCY

See BANKRUPTCY

INSTALLMENT PLAN PURCHASING

See CONSUMER CREDIT; FINANCE COMPANIES

INSTITUTIONAL FOOD SERVICE

See FOOD SERVICE INDUSTRY

INSTITUTIONAL INVESTMENTS

See also INVESTMENTS; TRUSTS AND TRUSTEES

ALMANACS AND YEARBOOKS

Advances in Investment Analysis and Portfolio Management. Chung-Few Lee, editor. Elsevier. • Focus on investment analysis and portfolio theory.

CD-ROM DATABASES

Compact D/SEC. Thomson Reuters Corp. • Monthly. Provides 200 financial data items for 12,000 U. S. publicly-held corporations filing reports with the Securities and Exchange Commission. Includes company profiles.

InvesText. Thomson Financial. • Monthly. Contains full text on CD-ROM of investment research reports from about 630 sources, including leading brokers and investment bankers. Reports are available on both U. S. and international publicly traded corporations. Separate industry reports cover more than 50 industries. Time span is 1982 to date.

DIRECTORIES

Directory of Trust Banking. Thomson Financial Publishing. • Annual. $344.00. Contains profiles of bank affiliated trust companies, independent trust companies, trust investment advisors, and trust fund managers. Provides contact information for professional personnel at more than 3,000 banking and other financial institutions.

Financial Yellow Book: Who's Who at the Leading U. S. Financial Institutions. Leadership Directories Inc. • Semiannual. $465. Gives the names and titles of over 28,000 key executives in financial institutions. Includes the areas of banking, investment, money management, and insurance. Five indexes are provided: institution, executive name, geographic by state, financial service segment, and parent company.

Futures Magazine SourceBook: The Most Complete List of Exchanges, Companies, Regulators, Organizations, etc., Offering Products and Services to the Futures and Options Industry. Futures Magazine Inc. • Annual. $19.50. Provides information on commodity futures brokers, trading method services, publications, and other items of interest to futures traders and money managers.

HedgeWorld Annual Compendium: The Hedge Fund Industry's Definitive Reference Guide. HedgeWorld. • Annual. $499.00. Contains profiles of 500 domestic and offshore hedge funds with more than $50 million in assets under management. Includes articles on "The Basics of Investing in Hedge Funds," "Beyond the Basics," and other information.

HedgeWorld Service Provider League Tables & Analyses. HedgeWorld. • Annual. $595.00. Provides quantitative and qualitative information on firms providing services to hedge funds: accountants/auditors, administrators, custodians, legal counsel, and prime brokers. Detailed categories cover banks, clearing services, consultants, derivatives business, investment companies, wealth management services, etc.

Institutional Buyers of Energy Stocks. bigdough.com Inc. • Annual. $645.00. Provides detailed profiles 555 institutional buyers of petroleum-related and other energy stocks. Includes names of financial analysts and portfolio managers.

Institutional Buyers of REIT Securities. bigdough.com Inc. • Semiannual. $995.00 per year. Provides detailed profiles of about 500 institutional buyers of REIT securities. Includes names of financial analysts and portfolio managers.

Institutional Buyers of Small-Cap Stocks. bigdough.com Inc. • Annual. $295.00. Provides detailed profiles of more than 837 institutional buyers of small capitalization stocks. Includes names of financial analysts and portfolio managers.

Major Financial Institutions of the World. Cengage Learning Inc. • $1,460 Individuals. 2012. 16th edition. eBook. Published by Graham & Whiteside. Contains detailed information on more than 10,000 important financial institutions in various countries. Includes banks, investment companies, and insurance companies.

Money Market Directory of Pension Funds and Their Investment Managers. Standard & Poors Money Market Directories. • Institutional funds and managers.

Nelson Information's Directory of Institutional Real Estate. Nelson Information. • Annual. Includes real estate investment managers, service firms, consultants, real estate investment trusts (REITs), and various institutional investors in real estate. Formerly *Nelson's Directory of Real Estate Investments*.

Nelson Information's Directory of Investment Managers. Nelson Information. • Annual. $595.00. Three volumes. Provides information on 2,200 investment management firms, both U.S. and foreign.

Nelson Information's Directory of Pension Fund Consultants. Nelson Information. • Annual. $995. Covers the pension plan sponsor industry. More than 325 worldwide consulting firms are described. Formerly *Nelson's Guide to Pension Fund Consultants*.

Nelson Information's Directory of Plan Sponsors. Nelson Information. • Annual. Approximately 19,000 plan sponsors (corporate, union, public/government, endowment, foundation, and hospital) of investments (pensions, endowments) funds with assets over $10 million. Formerly *Nelson's Directory of Plan Sponsors and Tax-Exempt Funds*.

Zacks Analyst Directory. Zacks Investment Research Inc. • Updated daily. Lists stockbroker investment analysts and gives the names of major U.S. corporations covered by those analysts.

Zacks Analyst Guide. Zacks Investment Research Inc. • Ranks analysts within more than 70 industry groups.

HANDBOOKS AND MANUALS

Money Manager's Compliance Guide. Thompson Publishing Group Inc. • $739.00 per year. Two looseleaf volumes. Monthly updates and newletters. Edited for investment advisers and investment companies to help them be in compliance with governmental regulations, including SEC rules, restrictions based on the Employee Retirement Income Security Act (ERISA), and regulations issued by the Commodity Futures Trading Commission (CFTC).

INTERNET DATABASES

Derivatives. Imagine Software Inc. 233 Broadway, 17th Fl., New York, NY 10279. Phone: (212)317-7600; Fax: (212)317-7601 • URL: http://www.derivatives.com • Web site mainly promotes proprietary software for the use of derivatives in risk management, but also provides free access to articles on a variety of derivatives-related topics.

ETF Connect. Nuveen Investments. Phone: 800-257-8787 • URL: http://www.etfconnect.com • Free Web site makes available extensive, searchable information on individual closed-end investment funds, preferred share funds, and exchange-traded index funds. Information on a particular fund is available by name or as part of a classification (high yield, investment grade, municipal, emerging markets, global equity, etc.). Fund charts are available for various time periods, as is data concerning premiums or discounts, dividends, annualized total return, credit quality, "Top 10 Holdings," and so forth.

Futures Online. Futures Magazine Inc. Phone: (312)846-4600; Fax: (312)846-4638 • URL: http://www.futuresmag.com • Web site presents updates of *Futures* magazine and links to other futures-related sites.

ONLINE DATABASES

Banking Information Source. ProQuest L.L.C. • Provides indexing and abstracting of periodical and other literature from 1982 to date, with weekly updates. Covers the financial services industry: banks, savings institutions, investment houses, credit unions, insurance companies, and real estate organizations. Emphasis is on marketing and management. Inquire as to online cost and availability. (Formerly *FINIS: Financial Industry Information Service*.).

First Call Consensus Earnings Estimates. Thomson Financial Inc. • Online service provides corporate earnings estimates for more than 2,500 U. S. companies, based on data from leading brokerage firms. Weekly updates. Inquire as to online cost and availability.

Fitch Ratings Delivery Service. Fitch. • Daily. Provides online delivery of Fitch financial ratings in three sectors: "Corporate Finance" (corporate bonds, insurance companies), "Structured Finance" (asset-backed securities), and "U.S. Public Finance" (municipal bonds).

InvesText. Thomson Financial. • Provides full text online of investment research reports from more than 600 sources, including leading brokers and investment bankers. Reports are available on approximately 60,000 U. S. and international corporations. Separate industry reports cover 54 industries. Time span is 1982 to date, with daily updates. Inquire as to online cost and availability.

Vickers On-Line. Vickers Stock Research Corp. • Provides detailed online information relating to insider trading and the securities holdings of institutional investors. Daily updates. Inquire as to online cost and availability.

Zacks Earnings Estimates. Zacks Investment Research Inc. • Provides online earnings projections for about 6,000 U. S. corporations, based on investment analysts' reports. Data is mainly from 200 major brokerage firms. Time span varies according to online provider, with daily or weekly updates. Inquire as to online cost and availability.

PERIODICALS AND NEWSLETTERS

American Banker: The Financial Services Daily. SourceMedia Inc. • Daily. $895.00 per year.

Provides news of banking, investment products, mortgages, credit unions, finance, bank technology, and legal developments.

Bank Investment Consultant: Sales Strategies for the Financial Adviser. SourceMedia Inc. • Monthly. Controlled circulation. Covers sales and marketing techniques for bank investment and asset management divisions. Formerly *Bank Investment Marketing*.

Emerging Growth. Navellier and Associates Inc. • Monthly. $275.00 per year. Newsletter. Provides specific stock selection and model portfolio advice (conservative, moderately aggressive, and aggressive) based on quantitative analysis and modern portfolio theory.

Emerging Markets Debt Report. SourceMedia Inc. • Weekly. $895.00 per year. Newsletter. Provides information on new and prospective sovereign and corporate bond issues from developing countries. Includes an emerging market bond index and pricing data.

Emerging Markets Quarterly. Institutional Investor Inc. Journals Group. • Quarterly. Price on application. Newsletter on financial markets in developing areas, such as Africa, Latin America, Southeast Asia, and Eastern Europe. Topics include institutional investment opportunities and regulatory matters. Formerly *Emerging Markets Weekly*.

Financial Management (FM). Financial Management Association International. • Quarterly. $392 Institutions for Americas, online only. Covers theory and practice of financial planning, international finance, investment banking, and portfolio management. Includes *Financial Practice* and *Education and Contemporary Finance Digest*.

Financial Markets, Institutions, and Instruments. New York University, Salomon Center. Blackwell Publishing Inc. • Five times a year. Institutions, $338.00 per year. Includes online edition. Edited to "bridge the gap between the academic and professional finance communities." Special fifth issue each year provides surveys of developments in four areas: money and banking, derivative securities, corporate finance, and fixed-income securities.

Futures: News, Analysis, and Strategies for Futures, Options, and Derivatives Traders. Futures Magazine Inc. • Monthly. $39 Individuals. Edited for institutional money managers and traders, brokers, risk managers, and individual investors or speculators. Includes special feature issues on interest rates, technical indicators, currencies, charts, precious metals, hedge funds, and derivatives. Supplements available.

Global Money Management. Wolters Kluwer Law and Business. • Description: Reports on international fund management, including investment strategies; pension fund searches; hires for consultants, managers, and custodians; performance measurement; developing markets, and significant personnel changes.

Guide to Stock Mutual Funds: A Quarterly Compilation of Mutual Fund Ratings and Analysis Covering Equity and Balanced Funds. Weiss Research Inc. • Quarterly. $438.00 per year. Emphasis is on rating of financial safety and relative risk. Includes annual summary.

High Yield Report. American Banker/Bond Buyer Inc. • Description: Examines markets for high-yield corporate bonds, work-outs, bankruptcies, and secondary markets for distressed securities. Contains pricing information for primary and secondary markets and analysis of the high-yield sector. Reports on developments affecting the senior and subordinated debt of companies in bankruptcy or working their way out of debt, detailing proposed financial restructurings. Tracks regulatory decisions affecting trade of distressed debt and funds purchased and sold. **Remarks:** Incorporates the former Distressed Debt Report.

Institutional Investor International Edition: The Magazine for International Finance and Investment. Institutional Investor Inc. Journals Group. • Monthly. $475.00 per year. Covers the international aspects of professional investing and finance. Emphasis is on Europe, the Far East, and Latin America.

Institutional Investor: The Premier of Professional Magazine Finance. Institutional Investor Inc. Journals Group. • Monthly. $445.00 per year. Includes print and online editions. Edited for portfolio managers and other investment professionals. Special feature issues include "Country Credit Ratings," "Fixed Income Trading Ranking," "All-America Research Team," and "Global Banking Ranking.".

Insurance Finance and Investment. Institutional Investor Inc. Journals Group. • Biweekly. $1,960.00 per year. Newsletter. Edited for insurance company investment managers.

Investment Dealers' Digest. SourceMedia Inc. • Weekly. $750.00 per year. Covers financial news, trends, new products, people, private placements, new issues of securities, and other aspects of the investment business. Includes feature stories.

Investment Management Mandate Pipeline. SourceMedia Inc. • Weekly. $1,295.00 per year. Newsletter. Edited for money managers and other investment professionals. Covers personnel news, investment strategies, and industry trends.

Investment News: The Weekly Newspaper for Financial Advisers. Crain Communications Inc. • Weekly. $29.00 per year. Edited for both personal and institutional investment advisers, planners, and managers.

Investor Relations Business. SourceMedia Inc. • Semimonthly. $495.00 per year. Covers the issues affecting stockholder relations, corporate public relations, and institutional investor relations.

IOMA's Report on Defined Contribution Plan Investing. Institute of Management and Administration. • Semimonthly. $1,189.90 per year. Newsletter. Edited for 401(k) and other defined contribution retirement plan managers, sponsors, and service providers. Reports on such items as investment manager performance, guaranteed investment contract (GIC) yields, and asset allocation trends.

Latin Fund Management. SourceMedia Inc. • Monthly. $495.00 per year. Newsletter (also available online at www.latinfund.net). Provides news and analysis of Latin American mutual funds, pension funds, and annuities.

Money Management Letter: Bi-Weekly Newsletter Covering the Pensions and Money Maagement Industry. Institutional Investor Inc. Journals Group. • Biweekly. $2,440.00 per year. Newsletter. Includes print and online editions. Edited for pension fund investment managers.

Mortgage-Backed Securities Letter. Securities Data Publishing. • Description: Covers developments in the structured finance markets. Analyzes transactions and their collateral; follows litigation, refinancing opportunities, and market conditions.

Outstanding Investor Digest: Perspectives and Activities of the Nation's Most Successful Money Managers. Outstanding Investor Digest, Inc. • $395.00 for 10 issues. Newsletter. Each issue features interviews with leading money managers.

Private Equity Week. Thomson Financial Inc. • Weekly. $1,495.00 per year. Provides detailed information on both prospective and completed private equity transactions. Includes news, data, commentary, trends, developments, and analysis.

Project Finance: The Magazine for Global Development. American Educational Systems. • 11 times a year. $740.00 per year. Includes print and online editions. Provides articles on the financing of the infrastructure (transportation, utilities, communications, the environment, etc). Coverage is international. Supplements available *World Export Credit Guide* and *Project Finance Book of Lists*. Formed by the merger of *Infrastructure Finance* and *Project and Trade Finance*.

Real Estate Finance and Investment. Institutional Investor Inc. Journals Group. • Weekly. $2,275.00 per year. Includes print and online editions. Newsletter for professional investors in commercial real estate. Includes information on financing, restructuring, strategy, and regulation.

Traders Magazine. SourceMedia Inc. • Monthly. $60.00 per year. Edited for institutional buy side and sell side equity traders. Covers industry news, market trends, regulatory developments, and personnel news. Serves as the official publication of the Security Traders Association.

U.S. Banker. SourceMedia Inc. • Monthly. $65.00 per year. Edited for bank executives and managers. Covers a wide variety of banking and financial topics.

RESEARCH CENTERS AND INSTITUTES

Princeton University - Bendheim Center for Finance. Department of Economics, 26 Prospect Ave., Princeton, NJ 08540-5296. Phone: (609)258-0770; Fax: (609)258-0771; Email: jessicab@princeton.edu • URL: http://www.princeton.edu/bcf • Research areas include securities markets, portfolio analysis, credit markets, and corporate finance. Emphasis is on quantitative and mathematical perspectives.

STATISTICS SOURCES

EBRI Pension Investment Report. Employee Benefit Research Institute. • Periodic Quarterly. $500 /issue for nonmembers. Irregular. Membership.

TRADE/PROFESSIONAL ASSOCIATIONS

Association of Independent Asset Managers in Liechtenstein. PO Box 134, FL-9496 Balzers, Liechtenstein. Phone: 423 3882350; Fax: 423 3882359; Email: info@vuvl.li • URL: http://www.vuvl.li/CFDOCS/cmsout/admin/content.cfm?GroupID=141 • Aims to protect and promote the reputation of independent asset managers in Liechtenstein and abroad. Seeks to establish professional guidelines within the framework of the Asset Management Accounting. Facilitates exchange of information within the business community.

CFA Institute. 560 Ray C. Hunt Dr., Charlottesville, VA 22903-2981. Phone: 800-247-8132 or (434)951-5499; Fax: (434)951-5262; Email: info@cfainstitute.org • URL: http://www.cfainstitute.org/pages/index.aspx • Formerly Association for Investment Management and Research.

Council of Institutional Investors. 888 17th St. NW, Ste. 500, Washington, DC 20006. Phone: (202)822-0800; Fax: (202)822-0801; Email: info@cii.org • URL: http://www.cii.org • Members are nonprofit organization pension plans and other nonprofit institutional investors.

INSTRUCTION OF EMPLOYEES

See TRAINING OF EMPLOYEES

INSTRUCTION, PROGRAMMED

See PROGRAMMED LEARNING

INSTRUMENTS, MUSICAL

See MUSICAL INSTRUMENTS INDUSTRY

INSTRUMENTS, SCIENTIFIC

See SCIENTIFIC APPARATUS AND INSTRUMENT INDUSTRIES

INSTRUMENTS, SURGICAL

See SURGICAL INSTRUMENTS INDUSTRY

INSULATION

See also BUILDING INDUSTRY

PERIODICALS AND NEWSLETTERS

Building Material Dealer. National Lumber and Building Material Dealers Association. • Monthly. $48.00 per year. Includes special feature issues on hand and power tools, lumber, roofing, kitchens, flooring, windows and doors, and insulation. Formerly *Builder Material Retailer*.

Roofing, Siding, Insulation. Advanstar Communications. • Monthly. $44.00 per year.

TRADE/PROFESSIONAL ASSOCIATIONS

Association for Better Insulation. 3906 Auburn Hills Dr., Greensboro, NC 27407. Phone: (603)768-3984; Fax: (270)721-0022; Email: service@betterinsulation.com • Informs homeowners about better insulation choices to help them make educated decisions. Promotes a green and more sustainable growth in the insulation industry. Acts as a proponent of green building products, environment responsibility and long term savings of energy and resources in the building industry.

National Fenestration Rating Council. 6305 Ivy Ln., Ste. 140, Greenbelt, MD 20770. Phone: (301)589-1776 or (785)862-1890; Fax: (301)589-3884; Email: info@nfrc.org • URL: http://www.nfrc.org • Individuals, organizations, and corporations interested in production, regulation, promotion, and development of technology related to fenestration products. Develops national voluntary energy performance rating system for fenestration products; coordinates certification and labeling activities to ensure uniform rating application. Promotes consumer awareness of fenestration ratings in an effort to encourage informed purchase of windows, doors, and skylights. Conducts efficiency testing. Maintains speakers' bureau; conducts educational and research programs.

National Insulation Association. 12100 Sunset Hills Rd., Ste. 330, Reston, VA 20190. Phone: (703)464-6422; Fax: (703)464-5896 • URL: http://www.insulation.org • Insulation contractors, distributors, and manufacturers.

North American Insulation Manufacturers Association. 11 Canal Center Plz., Ste. 103, Alexandria, VA 22314. Phone: (703)684-0084; Fax: (703)684-0427 • URL: http://www.naima.org • Manufacturers of fiberglass, rock wool, and slag wool insulation products. Promotes energy efficiency and environmental preservation through the use of fiberglass, rock wool, and slag wool insulation products. Encourages safe production and use of insulation materials.

INSURANCE

See also ACCIDENT INSURANCE; AUTOMOBILE INSURANCE; BUSINESS INTERRUPTION INSURANCE; CASUALTY INSURANCE; CREDIT INSURANCE; DISABILITY INSURANCE; FIRE INSURANCE; HEALTH INSURANCE; LIFE INSURANCE; LONG-TERM CARE INSURANCE; MARINE INSURANCE; PROPERTY AND LIABILITY INSURANCE; RISK MANAGEMENT; UNEMPLOYMENT INSURANCE

ABSTRACTS AND INDEXES

Business Periodicals Index Retrospective. EBSCO Publishing Inc. • 11/year. Quarterly and annual cumulations.

Insurance Periodicals Index. Specials Libraries Association, Insurance and Employees Benefits Div. NILS Publishing Co. • Annual. $250.00. Compiled by the Insurance and Employee Benefits Div., Special Libraries Association. A yearly index of over 15,000 articles from about 35 insurance periodicals. Arrangement is by subject, with an index to authors.

Social Sciences Citation Index. Thomson Reuters Corp. • Weekly. Product is accessed via *Web of Science*.

Social Sciences Index Retrospective: 1907-1983. EBSCO Publishing Inc. • Indexing for 1,000,000 articles. Coverage includes international index and social sciences and humanities index.

ALMANACS AND YEARBOOKS

Insurance Almanac: Who, What, When and Where in Insurance. Criterion Publishing Co. • Annual. $195. Lists insurance agencies and brokerage firms; U.S. and Canadian insurance companies, adjusters, appraisers, auditors, investigators, insurance officials and insurance organizations.

BIBLIOGRAPHIES

Insurance and Employee Benefits Literature. Special Libraries Association. • Bimonthly. $15.00 per year. Lists a wide variety of literature in all branches of the insurance industry. Includes annotations.

CD-ROM DATABASES

Assecuranz Compass CD-ROM. Kompass USA, Inc. • Provides detailed financial and other information on more than 21,000 insurance companies in 209 countries worldwide. Includes listings of 47,000 insurance company executives.

Business Abstracts with Full Text. EBSCO Publishing Inc. • Includes full text articles from more than 460 business publications from 1982 to present. Indexing for nearly 880 publications.

OECD Statistical Compendium. Organization for Economic Cooperation and Development. • Semiannual. $1,905.00 per year for 1 to 10 users. CD-ROM contains more than 730,000 monthly, quarterly, and annual time series for OECD countries, 1960 to date. Includes fully searchable data on agriculture, food, economic indicators, national accounts, employment, energy, finance, industry, technology, and foreign trade. Results can be displayed in various forms.

Social Sciences Abstracts. EBSCO Publishing Inc. • Provides indexing from 1983 and abstracting from 1994 of more than 750 periodicals covering economics, area studies, community health, public administration, public welfare, urban studies, and many other topics related to the social sciences.

Social Sciences Citation Index. Thomson Reuters Corp. • Weekly. Product is accessed via *Web of Science*.

DIRECTORIES

America's Corporate Finance Directory. LexisNexis. • Annual. $1,399 Individuals print. Covers: Financial personnel and outside financial services relationships of 5,000 leading United States corporations and their wholly-owned United States subsidiaries. Entries include: Company name, address, phone, fax, telex, e-mail addresses, stock exchange information, earnings, total assets, size of pension/profit-sharing fund portfolio, number of employees, description of business, wholly-owned U.S. Subsidiaries of parent company; name and title of key executives; outside suppliers of financial services.

Financial Review of Alien Insurers. National Association of Insurance Commissioners. • Annual. $275 per year, including updates; payment with order. Covers: alien insurance companies operating in the United States market. Entries include: Company name, address, balance sheet, operating statement, financial statement with notes, and names of auditors; description of trust account with location, valuation, and expiration date.

Financial Yellow Book: Who's Who at the Leading U. S. Financial Institutions. Leadership Directories Inc. • Semiannual. $465. Gives the names and titles of over 28,000 key executives in financial institutions. Includes the areas of banking, investment, money management, and insurance. Five indexes are provided: institution, executive name, geographic by state, financial service segment, and parent company.

Germany's Top 300. Frankfurter Allgemeine Zeitung GmbH. • Annual. $595. Covers: Germany's top 300 corporations, banks, and insurance companies; corporations are ranked based on their turnover; banks are ranked according to business volume; insurance companies are ranked according to premium income. Entries include: Company name, address, phone, fax ranking, products and activities, Standard Industrial Classification (SIC) codes, names of key management personnel, number of employees, turnover, pre-tax profit, net profit, cash flow, assets, investments, cash reserves, shareholders, investor relations, dividend, and high/low share price.

Insurance Marketplace: The Agents and Brokers Guide to Non-Standard and Special ty Lines, Aviation, Marine and International Insurance. The Rough Notes Company Inc. • Annual. Lists specialty, excess, and surplus insurance lines.

Major Financial Institutions of the World. Cengage Learning Inc. • $1,460 Individuals. 2012. 16th edition. eBook. Published by Graham & Whiteside. Contains detailed information on more than 10,000 important financial institutions in various countries. Includes banks, investment companies, and insurance companies.

GENERAL WORKS

Business InsuranceQuote.com. Tornado Solutions. • Offers helpful articles on topics such as adjuster claims, insurance processing, medical billing, processing software, life insurance school, and automobile fraud.

INTERNET DATABASES

Business 2.0 Web Guide to the Best Business Links. Business 2.0 Media Inc. Phone: (415)293-4800; Email: support@business2.com • URL: http://www.business2.com/webguide • Web site presents an extensive, searchable directory of links to "the best, most informative, and authoritative web pages." Twenty main categories cover business, finance, career, company information, people, and technology topics, with thousands of subtopics, all linking to Web sites recommended by experienced business researchers. Fees: Free.

Free Insurance Advice. InsWeb, Inc. 2868 Prospect Park Dr., Ste. 650, Rancho Cordova, CA 95670. Phone: (916)853-3300; Fax: (916)853-3300; Email: customercare@insweb.com • URL: http://www.insweb.com • Web site offers a wide variety of advice and information on automobile, life, health, and "other" insurance. Includes glossaries of insurance terms, Standard & Poor's ratings of individual insurance companies, and "Financial Needs Estimators." Searching is available. Fees: Free.

ONLINE DATABASES

Banking Information Source. ProQuest L.L.C. • Provides indexing and abstracting of periodical and other literature from 1982 to date, with weekly updates. Covers the financial services industry: banks, savings institutions, investment houses, credit unions, insurance companies, and real estate organizations. Emphasis is on marketing and management. Inquire as to online cost and availability. (Formerly *FINIS: Financial Industry Information Service.*).

Business Insurance. Crain Communications Inc. • Weekly. $799 Individuals data + print and digital. Contains the complete text of *Business Insurance*, a newspaper providing information on the purchase and administration of corporate insurance and self-insurance programs, including property and liability insurance, reinsurance, and employee benefit and risk management programs.

Fitch Ratings Delivery Service. Fitch. • Daily. Provides online delivery of Fitch financial ratings in three sectors: "Corporate Finance" (corporate bonds, insurance companies), "Structured Finance" (asset-backed securities), and "U.S. Public Finance" (municipal bonds).

I.I.I. Data Base Search. Insurance Information Institute. • Provides online citations and abstracts of insurance-related literature in magazines, newspapers, trade journals, and books. Emphasis is on property and casualty insurance issues, including highway safety, product safety, and environmental liability. Inquire as to online cost and availability.

Wilson Business Abstracts Online. H.W. Wilson Co. • Indexes and abstracts 600 major business periodicals, plus the *Wall Street Journal* and the business section of the *New York Times*. Indexing is from 1982, abstracting from 1990, with the two newspapers included from 1993. Updated weekly. Inquire as to online cost and availability. (*Business Periodicals Index* without abstracts is also available online.).

Wilson Social Sciences Abstracts Online. H.W. Wilson Co. • Provides online abstracting and indexing of more than 500 periodicals covering area studies, community health, public administration, public welfare, urban studies, and many other social science topics. Time period is 1994 to date for abstracts and 1983 to date for indexing, with updates weekly. Inquire as to online cost and availability.

OTHER SOURCES

Best's Insurance Reports. A.M. Best Company Inc. • Annual. Covers life-health insurance covering about 1,750 companies, and property-casualty insurance covering over 3,200 companies. Includes subscription to both *Best's Review* and *Best's Insurance Management Reports.*

Best's Insurance Reports: Property-Casualty. A.M. Best Company Inc. • Annual. $750.00. Guide to over 3,200 major property/casualty companies.

Federal Taxation of Insurance Companies. Dennis P. Van Mieghem and others. Prentice Hall PTR. • $447.00 per year. Looseleaf service. Biweekly updates.

Fire and Casualty Insurance Law Reports. Wolters Kluwer Law & Business CCH. • $870.00 per year. Looseleaf service. Semimonthly updates.

Life, Health, and Accident Insurance Law Reports. Wolters Kluwer Law & Business CCH. • $835.00 per year. Looseleaf service. Monthly updates.

PERIODICALS AND NEWSLETTERS

American Banker: The Financial Services Daily. SourceMedia Inc. • Daily. $895.00 per year. Provides news of banking, investment products, mortgages, credit unions, finance, bank technology, and legal developments.

Chartered Property and Casualty Underwriters eJournal. Society of Chartered Property and Casualty Underwriters. • Monthly. Published by the Chartered Property and Casualty Underwriters Society (CPCU). Edited for professional insurance underwriters and agents.

Claims. • Monthly. $46.00 per year. Edited for insurance adjusters, risk managers, and claims professionals. Covers investigation, fraud, insurance law, and other claims-related topics.

Contingencies: The Magazine of the Actuarial Profession. American Academy of Actuaries. • Bimonthly. $24 Nonmembers. Provides non-technical articles on the actuarial aspects of insurance, employee benefits, and pensions.

Guide to Life, Health, and Annuity Insurers: A Quarterly Compilation of Insurance Company Ratings and Analysis. Weiss Research Inc. • Quarterly. $499. Emphasis is on rating of financial safety and relative risk. Includes annual summary.

Guide to Property and Casualty Insurers: A Quarterly Compilation of Insurance Company Ratings and Analysis. Weiss Research Inc. • Quarterly. $499. Emphasis is on rating of financial safety and relative risk. Includes annual summary.

Insurance Advocate. Emanuel Levy, editor. Shea-Haarmann Cos. • Biweekly. Weekly. $59.00 per year. News and features on all aspects of insurance business for industry professionals.

Insurance and Technology. UBM L.L.C. • Monthly. $65.00 per year. Covers information technology and systems management as applied to the operation of life, health, casualty, and property insurance companies.

Insurance Finance and Investment. Institutional Investor Inc. Journals Group. • Biweekly. $1,960.00 per year. Newsletter. Edited for insurance company investment managers.

Insurance Forum: For the Unfettered Exchange of Ideas About Insurance. Joseph M. Belth, editor. Insurance Forum Inc. • Monthly. $90.00 per year. Newsletter. Provides analysis of the insurance business, including occasional special issues showing the ratings of about 1,600 life-health insurance companies, as determined by four major rating services: Duff & Phelps Credit Rating Co., Moody's Investors Service, Standard & Poor's Corp., and Weiss Research, Inc.

Insurance Networking: Strategies and Solutions for Electronic Commerce. SourceMedia Inc. • 10 times a year. Price on application. Covers information technology for the insurance industry, with emphasis on computer communications and the Internet.

InsuranceWeek. I.W. Publications, Inc. • Weekly. $30.00 per year.

Risk and Insurance. LRP Publications Library. • Monthly. Price on application. Topics include risk management, workers' compensation, reinsurance, employee benefits, and managed care.

Risk Management. Risk and Insurance Management Society. Risk and Insurance Management Society. • 10/year. $115 Individuals. Magazine featuring analysis, insight, and news for corporate risk managers.

Safe Money Report. Weiss Research Inc. • Monthly. $99.00 per year. Newsletter. Provides financial advice and current safety ratings of various banks, savings and loan companies, insurance companies, and securities dealers.

U.S. Banker. SourceMedia Inc. • Monthly. $65.00 per year. Edited for bank executives and managers. Covers a wide variety of banking and financial topics.

RESEARCH CENTERS AND INSTITUTES

Georgia State University - Center for Risk Management and Insurance Research. PO Box 4036, Atlanta, GA 30302-4036. Phone: (404)413-7515 or (404)413-7500; Fax: (404)413-7516 or (404)413-7499; Email: rwklein@gsu.edu • URL: http://rmictr.gsu.edu • Insurance, finance, and economics. Provides technical materials and policy research in the areas of health care financing, international issues, law and regulation, corporate finance, retirement financing, risk, risk management, insurance, finance, economics. Research focuses on risk management and insurance including insurance markets, catastrophe risk, financial instruments, social insurance, health care financing, retirement, law, public policy, and regulation.

University of Pennsylvania - S.S. Huebner Foundation. 3000 Steinberg Hall-Dietrich Hall, 3620 Locust Walk, Philadelphia, PA 19104-6302. Phone: (215)898-9631; Fax: (215)573-2218; Email: huebner_foundation@wharton.upenn.edu • URL: http://www.huebnergeneva.org/huebner • Awards grants for research in various areas of insurance.

STATISTICS SOURCES

Property-Casualty Insurance Facts. Insurance Information Institute. • Annual. $22.50. Formerly *Insurance Facts.*

Standard & Poor's Industry Surveys. Standard & Poor's Financial Services L.L.C. • Semiannual. $1,800.00. Two looseleaf volumes. Includes monthly *Supplements*. Provides detailed, individual surveys of 52 major industry groups. Each survey is revised on a semiannual basis. Also includes "Monthly Investment Review" (industry group investment analysis) and monthly "Trends & Projections" (economic analysis).

U.S. Industry and Trade Outlook. U.S. Department of Commerce National Technical Information Service. • Annual. Produced by the International Trade Administration, U.S. Department of Commerce, in a "public-private" partnership with DRI/McGraw-Hill and Standard & Poor's. Provides basic data, outlook for the current year, and "Long-Term Prospects" (five-year projections) for a wide variety of products and services. Includes high technology industries. Formerly *U.S. Industrial Outlook.*

TRADE/PROFESSIONAL ASSOCIATIONS

American Risk and Insurance Association. 716 Providence Rd., Malvern, PA 19355-3402. Phone: (610)640-1997; Fax: (610)725-1007; Email: aria@theinstitutes.org • URL: http://www.aria.org • Promotes education and research in the science of risk and insurance.

International Association of Insurance Professionals. 8023 E 63rd Pl., Ste. 540, Tulsa, OK 74133. Phone: 800-766-6249 or (918)294-3700; Fax: (918)294-3711 • URL: http://naiw.site-ym.com • Formerly Nationl Assoiciation of Insurance Women.

National Association of Independent Insurance Adjusters. 1880 Radcliff Ct., Tracy, CA 95376. Phone: (209)832-6962; Fax: (630)832-6964; Email: admin@naiia.com • URL: http://www.naiia.org • Claims adjusters and firms operating independently on a fee basis for all insurance companies. Originator of adjusters educational program administered by Insurance Institute of America.

National Association of Mutual Insurance Companies. 3601 Vincennes Rd., Indianapolis, IN 46268. Phone: (317)875-5250; Fax: (317)879-8408 • URL: http://www.namic.org • Affiliated with Crop Insurance Research Bureau and the Insurance Loss Control Association.

Risk and Insurance Management Society. 1065 Ave. of the Americas, 13th Fl., New York, NY 10018. Phone: 800-713-7467 or (212)286-9292; Fax: (212)986-9716; Email: lists@rims.org • URL: http://www.rims.org • Formerly American Society of Insurance Management.

Society of Insurance Financial Management. PO Box 9001, Mount Vernon, NY 10552. Phone: (914)966-3180; Fax: (914)966-3264; Email: sifm@cinn.com • URL: http://www.sifm.org • Represents insurance company officers and employees in financial management departments. Provides a timely forum for discussing current insurance industry issues relating to financial accounting and reporting, reinsurance, taxation, regulatory developments and other relevant topics.

INSURANCE, ACCIDENT

See ACCIDENT INSURANCE

INSURANCE ACTUARIES

See ACTUARIAL SCIENCE

INSURANCE AGENTS

FINANCIAL RATIOS

Annual Statement Studies. Risk Management Association. • Annual. Compiled from over 280,000 financial statements.

Annual Statement Studies: Industry Default Probabilities and Cash Flow Measures. Risk Management Association. • Annual. $405 Nonmembers. Serves as a companion volume to the original *Annual Statement Studies.* Gives probability of default estimates on a percentage scale for more than 450 industries. Includes changes in position year-by-year for eight financial statement line items and provides percentage measures of cash flow.

HANDBOOKS AND MANUALS

Responsibilities of Insurance Agents and Brokers. Matthew Bender and Company Inc. • Semiannual. $2,220 book. Covers legal responsibilities of agents and federal tax consequences of insurance arrangements.

PERIODICALS AND NEWSLETTERS

Broker World. Insurance Publications Inc. • Bimonthly. $6.00 per year. Edited for independent insurance agents and brokers. Special feature issue topics include annuities, disability insurance, estate planning, and life insurance.

Financial Planning: The Magazine for Financial Service Professionals. SourceMedia Inc. • Monthly. $79.00 per year. Edited for independent financial planners and insurance agents. Covers retirement planning, estate planning, tax planning, and insurance, including long-term healthcare considerations. Special features include a Retirement Planning Issue, Mutual Fund Performance Survey, and Variable Life and Annuity Survey.

GAMA International Journal. GAMA International. • Bimonthly. $30 for members (in addition to annual dues). Contains practical articles on the management of life insurance agencies.

Health Insurance Underwriter. National Association of Health Underwriters. • Monthly. Includes special feature issues on long-term care insurance, disability insurance, managed health care, and insurance office management.

Independent Agent. Independent Insurance Agents & Brokers of America Inc. • Monthly. $24.00 per year.

Insurance Marketing: The Ins and Outs of Recruiting and Retaining More Agents. Agent Media Corp. • Bimonthly. Controlled circulation. Provides practical advice for insurance companies on how to hire and keep sales personnel.

Resource: LOMA's Magazine for Insurance and Financial Services Management. LOMA. • Monthly. $75 Nonmembers. Contains news and information about industry operations and management.

Today's Insurance Professionals. International Association of Insurance Professionals. • Quarterly. $15 Individuals. Provides advice on professional and personal development in the insurance business. Formerly *Today's Insurance Woman.*

TRADE/PROFESSIONAL ASSOCIATIONS

National Association of Professional Insurance Agents. 400 N Washington St., Alexandria, VA 22314. Phone: (703)836-9340; Fax: (703)836-1279; Email: web@pianet.org • URL: http://www.pianet.com • Members are independent agents in various fields of insurance. Formerly National Association of Mutual Insurance Agents.

INSURANCE, AUTOMOBILE

See AUTOMOBILE INSURANCE

INSURANCE, BUSINESS INTERRUPTION

See BUSINESS INTERRUPTION INSURANCE

INSURANCE, CASUALTY

See CASUALTY INSURANCE

INSURANCE, DISABILITY

See DISABILITY INSURANCE

INSURANCE, FIRE

See FIRE INSURANCE

INSURANCE, HEALTH

See HEALTH INSURANCE

INSURANCE LAW AND REGULATION

ABSTRACTS AND INDEXES

Current Law Index. Cengage Learning Inc. • $1,332 Individuals. Monthly. $1269.00 per year. Produced in cooperation with the American Association of Law Libraries. Indexes more than 900 law journals, legal newspapers, and specialty publications from the U.S., Canada, U.K., Ireland, Australia, and New Zealand.

Index to Legal Periodicals and Books. H.W. Wilson Co. • Monthly. $490.00 per year. Quarterly and annual cumulations.

ALMANACS AND YEARBOOKS

American Law Yearbook. Cengage Learning Inc. • $308 Individuals. Annual. $280.00. Serves as a yearly supplement to *West's Encyclopedia of American Lawa.* Describes new legal developments in many subject areas.

CD-ROM DATABASES

Index to Legal Periodicals and Books. EBSCO Publishing Inc. • Contains indexing of more than 1,400 English language legal periodicals from 1981 to date and 2,500 books.

ENCYCLOPEDIAS AND DICTIONARIES

West's Encyclopedia of American Law. Cengage Learning Inc. • 2004. eBook. Second edition. Covers a wide variety of legal topics for the general reader. Inquire for pricing.

INTERNET DATABASES

Lexis.com Research System. Lexis-Nexis Group. Phone: 800-227-4908 or (937)865-6800; Fax: (937)865-6909; Email: webmaster@prod.lexis-nexis.com • URL: http://www.nexis.com • Fee-based Web site offers extensive searching of a wide variety of legal sources. Additional features include Daily Opinion Service, lexis.com Bookstore, Career Center, CLE Center, Law Schools, and Practice Pages ("Pages specific to areas of specialty").

PERIODICALS AND NEWSLETTERS

Defense Counsel Journal. International Association of Defense Counsel. • Quarterly. $87 Individuals. Scholarly and practical articles dealing with defense of civil cases, particularly those involving insurance.

Insurance Coverage Law Bulletin. ALM Media Properties LLC. • Monthly. $510. Provides news of property insurance claims management and coverage disputes. Edited for both legal and non-legal insurance professionals. (A Law Journal Newsletter, formerly published by Leader Publications).

Insurance Regulation: State Capitals. Wakeman/Walworth Inc. • 50 times a year. $245.00 per year; print and online editions, $350.00 per year. Formerly *From the State Capitals: Insurance Regulation.*

NAIC News. National Association of Insurance Commissioners. • Monthly. $200.00 per year. Newsletter covering insurance legislation and regulation.

National Insurance Law Review. NILS Publishing Co. • Quarterly. $95.00 per year. Contains insurance-related articles from major law reviews.

STATISTICS SOURCES

Property-Casualty Insurance Facts. Insurance Information Institute. • Annual. $22.50. Formerly *Insurance Facts.*

TRADE/PROFESSIONAL ASSOCIATIONS

Association of Defense Trial Attorneys. 4135 Topsail Trail, New Port Richey, FL 34652. Phone: (727)859-0350 • URL: http://www.adtalaw.com • Trial lawyers who have over five years' experience in the preparation and trial of insurance cases and the handling of insurance matters, and who possess the knowledge, skill, and facilities to provide insurance companies and self-insurers a legal service of the highest standard. Maintains current biographical data on each member.

Association of Life Insurance Counsel. 14350 Mundy Dr., Ste. 800, No. 258, Noblesville, IN 46060. Phone: (317)774-7500; Fax: (317)614-7147 • URL: http://www.alic.cc • Members are attorneys for life insurance companies.

National Association of Insurance Commissioners. 1100 Walnut St., Ste. 1500, Kansas City, MO 64106-2277. Phone: (816)842-3600; Fax: (816)783-8175 • URL: http://www.naic.org • Members are state officials involved in the regulation of insurance companies. Formerly National Convention of Insurance Commissioners.

INSURANCE, LIABILITY

See PROPERTY AND LIABILITY INSURANCE

INSURANCE, LIFE

See LIFE INSURANCE

INSURANCE, LONG-TERM CARE

See LONG-TERM CARE INSURANCE

INSURANCE, MARINE

See MARINE INSURANCE

INSURANCE, PROPERTY

See PROPERTY AND LIABILITY INSURANCE

INSURANCE, SOCIAL

See SOCIAL SECURITY

INSURANCE, TITLE

See TITLE INSURANCE

INSURANCE UNDERWRITERS

PERIODICALS AND NEWSLETTERS

National Underwriter. • Weekly. Two editions: *Life* or *Health*. $86.00 per year, each edition.

TRADE/PROFESSIONAL ASSOCIATIONS

American Institute for CPCU. 720 Providence Rd., Ste. 100, Malvern, PA 19355-3433. Phone: 800-644-2101 or (610)644-2100; Fax: (610)640-9576 • URL: http://www.aicpcu.org • Determines qualifications for professional certification of insurance personnel; conducts examinations and awards designation of Chartered Property Casualty Underwriter (CPCU).

American Insurance Association. 2101 L St. NW, Ste. 400, Washington, DC 20037. Phone: (202)828-7100; Fax: (202)293-1219 • URL: http://www.aiadc.org/aiapub • Represents companies providing property and casualty insurance and suretyship. Monitors and reports on economic, political, and social trends; serves as a clearinghouse for ideas, advice, and technical information. Represents members' interests before state and federal legislative and regulatory bodies; coordinates members' litigation.

CPCU Society. 720 Providence Rd., Malvern, PA 19355-0709. Phone: 800-932-2728; Fax: (610)251-2780; Email: membercenter@cpcusociety.org • URL: http://www.cpcusociety.org • Serves as a professional society of individuals who have passed national examinations of the American Institute for Chartered Property Casualty Underwriters, have 3 years of work experience, have agreed to be bound by a code of ethics, and have been awarded CPCU designation. Promotes education, research, social responsibility, and professionalism in the field. Holds seminars, symposia, and workshops.

Group Underwriters Association of America. c/o Roland Birkner, Co-Chairperson, 233 S Wacker Dr., Ste. 2000, Chicago, IL 60606. Phone: (312)288-7206; Email: roland.birkner@willis.com • URL: http://www.guaa.com • Promotes the study, analysis, and discussion pertaining to all matters of mutual interest in underwriting group products. Seeks to uphold the standards of practices within the group insurance industry. Provides its members the opportunities for professional development, networking and information gathering.

National Association of Insurance and Financial Advisors. 2901 Telestar Ct., Falls Church, VA 22042-1205. Phone: 877-866-2432; Email: membersupport@naifa.org • URL: http://www.naifa.org • Affiliated with Association for Advanced Life Underwriting. Formerly National Association of Life Underwriters.

Society of Financial Service Professionals. 19 Campus Blvd., Ste. 100, Newtown Square, PA 19073-3239. Phone: 800-392-6900 or (610)526-2500; Fax: (610)527-1499; Email: info@financialpro.org • URL: http://www.financialpro.org • Represents the interests of financial advisers. Fosters the development of professional responsibility. Assists clients to achieve personal and business-related financial goals. Offers educational programs, online professional resources and networking opportunities.

INSURANCE, UNEMPLOYMENT

See UNEMPLOYMENT INSURANCE

INTEGRATED CIRCUITS

See SEMICONDUCTOR INDUSTRY

INTEGRATED SYSTEMS

See SYSTEMS INTEGRATION

INTELLECTUAL PROPERTY

See also COPYRIGHT; LICENSING AGREEMENTS; TRADE SECRETS

ABSTRACTS AND INDEXES

Current Law Index. Cengage Learning Inc. • $1,332 Individuals. Monthly. $1269.00 per year. Produced in cooperation with the American Association of Law Libraries. Indexes more than 900 law journals, legal newspapers, and specialty publications from the U.S., Canada, U.K., Ireland, Australia, and New Zealand.

Index to Legal Periodicals and Books. H.W. Wilson Co. • Monthly. $490.00 per year. Quarterly and annual cumulations.

ALMANACS AND YEARBOOKS

IP Almanac. ALM Media Properties LLC. • Annual. $20.00. Provides a digest of the year's most important developments in the area of intellectual property. Also included with subscription to *IP Law and Business*.

CD-ROM DATABASES

Authority Computer and Telecommunications Law Library. Matthew Bender and Company Inc. • Quarterly. Price on request. Full text CD-ROM provides cases, analysis, sample agreements, and other information relating to computer law, telecommunications regulation (cable, broadcasting, satellite, Internet), international computer law, and computer contracts.

Authority Intellectual Property Library. Matthew Bender and Company Inc. • Quarterly. Price on request. CD-ROM contains updated full text of *Intellectual Property Counseling and Litigation, Computer Law, International Computer Law, Nimmer on Copyright, Milgrim on Trade Secrets, Patent Litigation, Patent Licensing Transactions, Trademark Protection and Practice*, and other Matthew Bender publications relating to the law of intellectual property.

DIRECTORIES

Intellectual Property World Directory. World Bureau L.L.C. • Annual. Covers: Patent, trademark, and copyright agencies and officials in over 100 countries. Entries include: Name, address, phone, fax, and e-mail address of officials responsible for intellectual property issues. Also includes statistics, reports, full cabinets, embassies, and organizational charts.

KMWorld Buyer's Guide. Knowledge Asset Media Inc. • Semiannual. $2,395 (Basic Corporate Profile Package) One Issue — Spring 2014 Edition PLUS 6 Months Online. Controlled circulation as part of *KMWorld*. Contains corporate and product profiles related to various aspects of knowledge management and information systems. (Knowledge Asset Media is a an affiliate of Information Today, Inc.).

HANDBOOKS AND MANUALS

Antitrust-Intellectual Property Handbook. Alan J. Weinschel. Glasser LegalWorks. • Looseleaf. $175.00. Periodic supplementation. Covers patent licensing, patent antitrust issues, innovation markets, intervention by government agencies, standard-setting activities, royalty arrangements, and related intellectual property/antitrust topics. Provides explanations, legal guidance, and historical background.

Intellectual Property Primary Law Sourcebook. Matthew Bender and Company Inc. • $175 print only. Provides federal copyright, patent, and trademark statutes, as well as the Leahy-Smith America Invents Act.

Protecting Trade Secrets, Patents, Copyrights, and Trademarks. Robert C. Dorr and Christopher H. Munch. Aspen Publishers, Inc. • $165.00. Looseleaf service.

INTERNET DATABASES

Lexis.com Research System. Lexis-Nexis Group. Phone: 800-227-4908 or (937)865-6800; Fax: (937)865-6909; Email: webmaster@prod.lexis-nexis.com • URL: http://www.nexis.com • Fee-based Web site offers extensive searching of a wide variety of legal sources. Additional features include Daily Opinion Service, lexis.com Bookstore, Career Center, CLE Center, Law Schools, and Practice Pages ("Pages specific to areas of specialty").

OTHER SOURCES

Cyberlaw: Intellectual Property in the Digital Millennium. ALM Media Properties LLC. • $530 per year. A basic guide to copyright as applied to the Internet and other electronic sources. (Law Journal Press).

E-Commerce and Internet Law: Treatise with Forms. Ian C. Ballon. Glasser LegalWorks. • $1,479 Individuals Binder/Looseleaf (Full Set). Periodic supplementation. Analyzes Internet legalities, including litigious matters relating to downloading, streaming, music, video, content aggregation, domain names, chatrooms, and search engines. Includes forms, contracts, checklists, sample pleadings, and an extensive glossary.

Intellectual Property and Antitrust Law. William C. Holmes. Thomson West. • Semiannual. $1,347 full set. Includes patent, trademark, and copyright practices.

Intellectual Property Law: Commercial, Creative, and Industrial Property. ALM Media Properties LLC. • $1,025 two volumes. Covers the legal aspects of patents, trade secrets, copyright, technology protection, software protection, databases, etc. Also "compares the basic principles of U.S. law with those of Asian and European law." (Law Journal Press).

Licensing of Intellectual Property. ALM Media Properties LLC. • $680. Includes such licensing topics as royalties, infringement, antitrust, trade secrets, and patent agreements. Examples of licensing agreements and sample forms (on CD-ROM) are included. (Law Journal Press).

PERIODICALS AND NEWSLETTERS

Intellectual Property Newsletter. L L Professional Publishing. • Monthly. $261.00 per year.

Intellectual Property Strategist. ALM Media Properties LLC. • Monthly. $505 print and online. Covers "business and litigation tactics" in the field of intellectual property law, including international issues. (A Law Journal Newsletter, formerly published by Leader Publications).

Intellectual Property Today. • Monthly. $96.00 per year. Covers legal developments in copyright, patents, trademarks, and licensing. Emphasizes the effect of new technology on intellectual property. Formerly *Law Works*.

IP Law and Business. ALM Media Properties LLC. • Monthly. $125.00 per year. Covers intellectual property litigation and business issues. Includes annual *IP Almanac*.

RESEARCH CENTERS AND INSTITUTES

University of Edinburgh - Arts and Humanities Research Council - Research Centre for Studies in Intellectual Property and Technology Law. School of Law, Old College, S Bridge, Edinburgh EH8 9YL, United Kingdom. Phone: 44 131 6502014; Fax: 44 131 6506317; Email: itandip@ed.ac.uk • URL: http://www.law.ed.ac.uk/ahrc/aboutus.aspx • Intellectual property, copyright, patents, technology,

For publishers' addresses, refer to SOURCES CITED section at the back of the book.

commerce, society, information technology, genetics, and medical jurisprudence and ethics.

TRADE/PROFESSIONAL ASSOCIATIONS

American Intellectual Property Law Association. 241 18th St. S, Ste. 700, Arlington, VA 22202. Phone: (703)415-0780; Fax: (703)415-0786; Email: aipla@aipla.org • URL: http://www.aipla.org/Pages/default.aspx • Voluntary bar association of lawyers practicing in the fields of patents, trademarks, copyrights, and trade secrets. Aids in the operation and improvement of U.S. patent, trademark, and copyright systems, including the laws by which they are governed and rules and regulations under which federal agencies administer those laws. Sponsors moot court and legal writing competitions.

Coalition for Intellectual Property Rights. 607 14th St. NW, Ste. 500, Washington, DC 20036. Phone: (202)466-6210; Fax: (202)466-6205; Email: amanda.lahan@cipr.org • URL: http://www.cipr.org • Aims to advance intellectual property rights in Russia, Ukraine and other states in the Commonwealth for Independent States (CIS) region. Works with government and businesses to improve IPR laws and enforcement regimes consistent with international standards. Seeks to provide support to members addressing company-specific IP issues in Russia, Ukraine, and other countries of the region.

Licensing Executives Society. 1800 Diagonal Rd., Ste. 280, Alexandria, VA 22314-2840. Email: info@les.org • URL: http://www.lesi.org • U.S. and foreign businessmen, scientists, engineers, and lawyers having direct responsibility for the transfer of technology. Maintains placement service.

INTELLIGENCE, ARTIFICIAL

See ARTIFICIAL INTELLIGENCE

INTERACTIVE MEDIA

See also MULTIMEDIA

ABSTRACTS AND INDEXES

Internet and Personal Computing Abstracts (print edition). EBSCO Publishing Inc. • Quarterly. $269.00 per year, including cumulative index. Provides more than 10,000 abstracts annually from both trade and academic publications. Covers computer hardware, software, product reviews, Web topics, e-commerce, networks, corporate news, security, and related topics. Formerly *Microcomputer Abstracts*.

DIRECTORIES

AV Market Place: The Complete Business Directory of Audio, Audio Visual, Computer Systems, Film, Video, and Programming, with Industry Yellow Pages. Information Today, Inc. • Annual. $279.50 Individuals list price. Provides information on "more than 7,500 companies that create, apply, or distribute AV equipment and services for business, education, science, and government." Multimedia, virtual reality, presentation software, and interactive video are among the categories. Formerly published by R. R. Bowker.

DV Buyer's Guide. UBM L.L.C. • Annual. $10.00. A directory of professional video products, including digital cameras, monitors, editing systems, and software.

Interactive TV Investor Buyer's Guide and Directory. Paul Kagan Associates, Inc. • Annual. Price on application. (A special issue of the periodical *Convergence*.).

E-BOOKS

Encyclopedia of Emerging Industries. Cengage Learning Inc. • $546 6th edition. Provides detailed information on 140 "newly flourishing" industries. Includes historical background, organizational structure, significant individuals, current conditions, major companies, work force, technology trends, research developments, and other industry facts.

INTERNET DATABASES

InfoTech Trends. Data Analysis Group. Phone: (925)462-1202; Fax: (925)462-1225; Email: support@infotechtrends.com • URL: http://www.infotechtrends.com • Web site provides both free and fee-based market research data on the information technology industry, including computers, peripherals, telecommunications, the Internet, software, CD-ROM/DVD, e-commerce, and workstations. Fees: Free for current (most recent year) data; more extensive information has various fee structures. Formerly *Computer Industry Forecasts*.

Wired News. Lycos Inc. 400-2 Totten Pond Rd., Waltham, MA 02451-2053. Phone: (781)370-2700 or (415)276-8400; Fax: (781)370-2600 or (415)276-8500; Email: press@lycos.com • URL: http://www.lycos.com • Provides summaries and full-text of "Top Stories" relating to the Internet, computers, multimedia, telecommunications, and the electronic information industry in general. These news stories are placed in the broad categories of Politics, Business, Culture, and Technology. Affiliated with *Wired* magazine. Fees: Free.

ONLINE DATABASES

Computer Database. Cengage Learning Inc. • Provides one year of full-text online for 150 leading computer-related publications. Also includes 70,000 product specifications and brief profiles of 13,000 computer product vendors and manufacturers. Inquire as to prices and availability.

PERIODICALS AND NEWSLETTERS

Convergence: The Journal of Research Into New Media Technologies. Reed Elsevier Group plc Reed Business Information. • Monthly. Individuals, $40.00 per year; institutions, $160.00 per year. Covers the merging of communications technologies. Includes telecommunications networks, interactive TV, multimedia, wireless phone service, and electronic information services.

DV Magazine. UBM L.L.C. • Monthly. Edited for producers and creators of digital media. Includes topics relating to video, audio, animation, multimedia, interactive design, and special effects. Covers both hardware and software, with product reviews. Formerly *Digital Video Magazine*.

InterActive Consumers. MarketResearch.com. • Monthly. $395.00 per year. Newsletter. Covers the emerging markets for digital content, products, and services. Includes market information on telecommuting, online services, the Internet, online investing, and other areas of electronic commerce.

Interactive Content: Consumer Media Strategies Monthly. Jupitermedia Corp. • Monthly. $675.00 per year; with online edition, $775.00 per year. Newsletter. Covers the broad field of providing content (information, news, entertainment) for the Internet/World Wide Web.

Interactive Update. Alexander & Associates. • Description: Provides information on the interactive entertainment industry, focusing on software.

Maximum PC. Imagine Media, Inc. • Quarterly. $29.95 per year. Provides articles and reviews relating to multimedia hardware and software. Each issue includes a CD-ROM sampler (emphasis is on games). Formed by the merger of Home PC and Boot.

Smart TV and Sound: Interactive Television and DVD-MP3-Internet Audio and Video-Satellite Television. York Publishing Inc. • Semiannual. $14.97 per year. Consumer magazine covering WebTV, PC/TV appliances, DVD players, "Smart TV," and other topics relating to interactive television, the Internet, and multimedia. Formerly *Smart TV*.

Sound & Vision: Home Theater- Audio- Video- MultimediaMovies- Music. Bonnier AB. • 10/year. $12.97 10 issues. Popular magazine providing explanatory articles and critical reviews of equipment and media (CD-ROM, DVD, etc.). Supplement available *Stereo Review's Sound and Vision Buyers Guide*. Replaces *Stereo Review* and *Video Magazine*.

RESEARCH CENTERS AND INSTITUTES

Boston University - Multimedia Communications Laboratory. Department of Electrical & Computer Engineering, 8 Saint Mary's St., Boston, MA 02215. Phone: (617)353-9877; Fax: (617)353-6440; Email: tdcl@bu.edu • URL: http://hulk.bu.edu • Research areas include interactive multimedia applications.

Carnegie Mellon University - College of Fine Arts - Studio for Creative Inquiry. 5000 Forbes Ave., Rm. 111, Pittsburgh, PA 15213-3890. Phone: (412)268-3451; Fax: (412)268-2829; Email: mmbm@andrew.cmu.edu • URL: http://studioforcreativeinquiry.org • Research areas include artificial intelligence, virtual reality, hypermedia, multimedia, and telecommunications, in relation to the arts.

International Data Corp. 5 Speen St., Ste. 1, Framingham, MA 01701-4674. Phone: 800-343-4935 or (508)872-8200; Fax: (508)935-4015 or (508)935-4271; Email: idcinfo@idc.com • URL: http://www.idc.com • Private research firm specializing in market research related to computers, multimedia, and telecommunications.

Massachusetts Institute of Technology - The Media Laboratory. Bldg. E15, 77 Massachusetts Ave., Cambridge, MA 02139-4307. Phone: (617)253-5960; Fax: (617)258-6264; Email: walter@media.mit.edu • URL: http://www.media.mit.edu • Research areas include electronic publishing, spatial imaging, human-machine interface, computer vision, and advanced television.

U.S. Department of Energy - Office of Energy Efficiency and Renewable Energy - Industrial Technologies Program - Industrial Assessment Center. School of Engineering, San Francisco State University, 1600 Holloway Ave., San Francisco, CA 94132. Phone: (415)338-6218 or (415)338-7736; Fax: (415)338-3086; Email: iac@sfsu.edu • URL: http://www.sfsu.edu/iac • Research areas include multimedia, computerized experimental arts processes, and digital sound.

University of Illinois at Chicago - Electronic Visualization Laboratory. Department of Computer Science, Rm. 1120, MC 152, 851 S Morgan St., Chicago, IL 60607-7053. Phone: (312)996-3002; Fax: (312)413-7585; Email: spiff@uic.edu • URL: http://www.evl.uic.edu • Research areas include computer graphics, virtual reality, multimedia, and interactive techniques.

University of Southern California - Integrated Media Systems Center. 306 Powell Hall of Engineering, 3737 Watt Way, Los Angeles, CA 90089-0272. Phone: (213)740-8945; Fax: (213)740-2539; Email: shahabi@usc.edu • URL: http://imsc.usc.edu • Media areas for research include education, mass communication, and entertainment.

INTEREST

See also MONEY

CD-ROM DATABASES

OECD Statistical Compendium. Organization for Economic Cooperation and Development. • Semiannual. $1,905.00 per year for 1 to 10 users. CD-ROM contains more than 730,000 monthly, quarterly, and annual time series for OECD countries, 1960 to date. Includes fully searchable data on agriculture, food, economic indicators, national accounts, employment, energy, finance, industry, technology, and foreign trade. Results can be displayed in various forms.

INTERNET DATABASES

BanxQuote Banking, Mortgage, and Finance Center. BanxQuote, Inc. Phone: (914)722-1600; Fax: (914)722-6630; Email: info@banx.com • URL: http://www.banx.com • Daily. Web site quotes interest rates paid by banks around the country on various savings products, as well as rates paid by consumers for automobile loans, mortgages, credit cards, home equity loans, and personal loans. Also provided: stock quotes, indexes, stock options, futures trading data, economic indicators, and links to many other financial sites.

Bondtalk.com: Live Talk & Analysis on the Bond Market & the Economy. Miller Tabak & Co., LLC. Phone: (212)370-0040; Email: acrescenzi@bondtalk.com • URL: http://www.bondtalk.com • Web site provides extensive, free data on the fixed income securities market, including individual bond prices, yields, interest rates, Federal Reserve information, charts, bond market news, and economic analysis. Also offered on a fee basis is "Bondtalkpro.com: The New and Enhanced Service for Market Professionals.".

Bureau of Economic Analysis. U. S. Department of Commerce, Bureau of Economic Analysis. Phone: (202)606-9900; Fax: (202)606-5310; Email: webmaster@bea.doc.gov • URL: http://www.bea.doc.gov • Web site includes "News Release Information" covering national, regional, and international economic estimates from the BEA. Highlights of releases appear online the same day, complete text and tables appear the next day. "Recent News Releases" section provides titles for past nine months, with links. "BEA Data and Methodology" includes "Frequently Requested NIPA Data" (national income and product accounts, such as gross domestic product and personal income). Other statistics are available. Fees: Free.

Business 2.0 Web Guide to the Best Business Links. Business 2.0 Media Inc. Phone: (415)293-4800; Email: support@business2.com • URL: http://www.business2.com/webguide • Web site presents an extensive, searchable directory of links to "the best, most informative, and authoritative web pages." Twenty main categories cover business, finance, career, company information, people, and technology topics, with thousands of subtopics, all linking to Web sites recommended by experienced business researchers. Fees: Free.

Business Week Online. McGraw-Hill. Phone: (212)512-2511; Fax: (684)842-6101 • URL: http://www.businessweek.com • Web site provides complete contents of current issue of *Business Week* plus "BW Daily" with additonal business news, financial market quotes, and corporate information from Standard & Poor's. Includes various features, such as "Banking Center" with mortgage and interest data, and "Interactive Computer Buying Guide." The "Business Week Archive" is fully searchable back to 1996.

Federal Reserve Board Publications and Education Resources. Board of Governors of the Federal Reserve System. Phone: (202)452-3000; Fax: (202)452-3819 • URL: http://www.federalreserve.gov/publications.htm • Web site provides access to statistics, surveys, and research from the Federal Reserve Board. *Federal Reserve Bulletin* articles are available as abstracts or full text (PDF) currently or from six-year archives. The link "Statistics: Releases and Historical Data" offers daily, weekly, monthly, quarterly, and annual data in great detail for interest rates, foreign exchange, consumer credit, money stock measures, industrial production indexes, bank reserves, and other items. Historical tabulations are available for various time periods. Free.

Fedstats. Federal Interagency Council on Statistical Policy. Phone: (202)395-7254 • URL: http://www.fedstats.gov • Web site features an efficient search facility for full-text statistics produced by more than 100 federal agencies, including the Census Bureau, the Bureau of Economic Analysis, and the Bureau of Labor Statistics. Boolean searches can be made within one agency or for all agencies combined. Links are offered to international statistical bureaus, including the UN, IMF, OECD, UNESCO, Eurostat, and 20 individual countries. Fees: Free.

FreeLunch.com. Economy.com, Inc. Phone: (610)696-8700; Fax: (610)696-1678 • URL: http://www.freelunch.com • Web site provides free access to more than 200 million economic and financial data series, covering industry, demographics, labor markets, prices, retail sales, government spending, trade, interest rates, housing starts, the stock market, etc. Data is available in either chart or table form. Searching is offered. Free, but registration required. Economy.com, Inc. also offers fee-based economic analysis at *The Dismal Scientist* site (www.dismal.com).

ONLINE DATABASES

Banking Information Source. ProQuest L.L.C. • Provides indexing and abstracting of periodical and other literature from 1982 to date, with weekly updates. Covers the financial services industry: banks, savings institutions, investment houses, credit unions, insurance companies, and real estate organizations. Emphasis is on marketing and management. Inquire as to online cost and availability. (Formerly *FINIS: Financial Industry Information Service*.).

PERIODICALS AND NEWSLETTERS

American Banker: The Financial Services Daily. SourceMedia Inc. • Daily. $895.00 per year. Provides news of banking, investment products, mortgages, credit unions, finance, bank technology, and legal developments.

Grant's Interest Rate Observer. Grant's Financial Publishing Inc. • Biweekly. $1,025 Individuals. Newsletter containing detailed analysis of money-related topics, including interest rate trends, global credit markets, fixed-income investments, bank loan policies, and international money markets.

Interest Rate Service. World Reports Ltd. • 10 times a year. $950.00 per year.

Jumbo Rate News. BauerFinancial Inc. • Description: Reports on high-yielding, insured Jumbo CD (Certificate of Deposit) rates nationwide. Analyzes each institution by current credit-worthiness, and lists current assets and capital ratios. Provides phone numbers, contacts, methods of computation, and information on how interest is paid. Also contains financial news, insights, and commentary of interest to Jumbo CD investors. Recurring features include editorials and news of interest.

Money Reporter: The Insider's Letter for Investors Whose Interest is More Interest. MPL Communications Inc. • Semimonthly. $227 /year. Supplement available, *Monthly Key Investment*. Canadian interest-bearing deposits and investments.

Moneyletter. Agora Inc. • Description: Provides assertive, do-it-yourself, individual investors with a unique market timing system, specific buy and sell recommendations, and portfolio allocation advice on no-load mutual funds. Features updates on economic and financial market, fund profiles, and articles on non-mutual fund financial planning issues.

One Hundred Highest Yields. Bankrate Inc. • Weekly. $124.00 per year. Newsletter. List CD's and money markets offered by federally insured banks. National coverage.

U.S. Banker. SourceMedia Inc. • Monthly. $65.00 per year. Edited for bank executives and managers. Covers a wide variety of banking and financial topics.

STATISTICS SOURCES

The AIER Chart Book. AIER Research Staff. American Institute for Economic Research. • Annual. $4 Individuals. A compact compilation of long-range charts ("Purchasing Power of the Dollar," for example, goes back to 1780) covering various aspects of the U. S. economy. Includes inflation, interest rates, debt, gold, taxation, stock prices, etc. (Economic Education Bulletin.).

Selected Interest Rates. U.S. Federal Reserve System Board of Governors Publications Services. • Weekly release. $20.00 per year.

Statistical Annual: Interest Rates, Metals, Stock Indices, Options on Financial Futures, Options on Metals Futures. Chicago Board of Trade. • Annual. Includes historical data on GNMA CDR Futures, Cash-Settled GNMA Futures, U. S. Treasury Bond Futures, U. S. Treasury Note Futures, Options on Treasury Note Futures, NASDAQ-100 Futures, Major Market Index Futures, Major Market Index MAXI Futures, Municipal Bond Index Futures, 1,000-Ounce Silver Futures, Options on Silver Futures, and Kilo Gold Futures.

Survey of Current Business. U. S. Government Printing Office. • Published by Bureau of Economic Analysis, U. S. Department of Commerce. Presents a wide variety of business and economic data.

Treasury Bulletin. U. S. Government Printing Office. • Quarterly. $51 List Price. Issued by the Financial Management Service, U. S. Treasury Department. Provides data on the federal budget, government securities and yields, the national debt, and the financing of the federal government in general.

INTERIOR DECORATION

See also WINDOW COVERING INDUSTRY

ABSTRACTS AND INDEXES

Art Index. EBSCO Publishing Inc. • Quarterly. Annual cumulations. Price varies. Subject and author index to periodicals in art, architecture, industrial design, city planning, photography, and various related topics.

DIRECTORIES

Decorators Directory. InfoGroup Inc. • Annual. Number of listings: 33,751. Entries include: Name, address, phone, size of advertisement, name of owner or manager, number of employees, year first in "Yellow Pages." Compiled from telephone company "Yellow Pages," nationwide.

Home Decorating Services Directory. InfoGroup Inc. • Annual. Number of listings: 33,751. Entries include: Name, address, phone, size of advertisement, name of owner or manager, number of employees, year first in "Yellow Pages." Compiled from telephone company "Yellow Pages," nationwide.

Interior Design Buyers Guide. Reed Elsevier Group plc Reed Business Information. • Annual. $16.95. Included with subscription to *Interior Design*.

The SOURCE: Commercial Buildings Products Guide. Stamats Business Media. • Annual. Lists sources of surface materials, furniture, lighting, etc., for interior designers. Formerly the annual buyers guide.

ONLINE DATABASES

Art Index Online. H.W. Wilson Co. • Indexes a wide variety of art-related periodicals, 1984 to date. Monthly updates. Inquire as to online cost and availability.

Avery Architectural Periodicals Index. Columbia University Avery Architectural and Fine Arts Library. • Indexes a wide range of periodicals related to architecture and design. Subjects include building design, building materials, interior design, housing, land use, and city planning. Time span: 1977 to date. hul URL: www-rlg.stanford.edu/cit-ave.html.

PERIODICALS AND NEWSLETTERS

Contract: The Business Magazine of Commercial and Institutional Interior Design, and Architecture, Planning and Construction. Nielsen Business Media Inc. • Monthly. $94.00 per year. Firms engaged in specifying furniture and furnishings for commercial installations. Formerly *Contract Design.*

Interior Design. Reed Elsevier Group plc Reed Business Information. • Monthly. $64.95 per year. For the professional designed, provides information on trends and new products.

Interiors and Sources. L.C. Clark Publishing Company Inc. • Bimonthly. $27.00 per year. Promotes professionalism for interior designers and design firms. Includes special features on office systems, work stations, and office furniture.

Paint and Decorating Retailer. Paint and Decorating Retailers Association. • Monthly. $45.00 per year. Formerly *Decorating Retailer.*

RESEARCH CENTERS AND INSTITUTES

Interior Design Laboratory. Lambuth University. 101 Wilder Tower, Memphis, TN 38152-3520. Phone: 800-669-2679 • URL: http://www.memphis.edu/lambuth.

TRADE/PROFESSIONAL ASSOCIATIONS

American Society of Interior Designers. 718 7th St. NW, 4th Fl., Washington, DC 20001. Phone: (202)546-3480; Fax: (202)546-3240; Email: membership@asid.org • URL: http://www.asid.org • Represents practicing professional interior designers, students and industry partners. ASID Educational Foundation sponsors scholarship competitions, finances educational research and awards special grants.

Gift and Home Trade Association. 2550 Sandy Plains Rd. Ste. 225, Marietta, GA 30066. Phone: 877-600-4872; Email: info@giftandhome.org • URL: http://www.giftandhome.org • Aims to ensure the viability of the gift and home industry. Promotes business practices and professional development. Establishes standards and ethical guidelines.

INTERNAL AUDITING

See also AUDITING

ABSTRACTS AND INDEXES

Business Periodicals Index Retrospective. EBSCO Publishing Inc. • 11/year. Quarterly and annual cumulations.

INTERNET DATABASES

Rutgers Accounting Web. Rutgers University Accounting Research Center. Phone: (973)353-5172; Fax: (973)353-1283 • URL: http://www.rutgers.edu/accounting • RAW Web site provides extensive links to sources of national and international accounting information, such as the Big Six accounting firms, the Financial Accounting Standards Board (FASB), SEC filings (EDGAR), journals, publishers, software, the International Accounting Network, and "Internet's largest list of accounting firms in USA." Searching is offered. Fees: Free.

ONLINE DATABASES

Wilson Business Abstracts Online. H.W. Wilson Co. • Indexes and abstracts 600 major business periodicals, plus the *Wall Street Journal* and the business section of the *New York Times.* Indexing is from 1982, abstracting from 1990, with the two newspapers included from 1993. Updated weekly. Inquire as to online cost and availability. (*Business Periodicals Index* without abstracts is also available online.).

PERIODICALS AND NEWSLETTERS

Internal Auditing Alert. Warren, Gorham & Lamont Inc. • Description: Presents unique coverage that includes reviews and explanations of current Institute of Internal Auditors releases, appraisals of new audit techniques, and highlights of successful audit management practices.

Internal Auditor. Institute of Internal Auditors. • Bimonthly. $75 U.S. and Canada print and online. Internal auditing.

INTERNAL PUBLICATIONS

See HOUSE ORGANS

INTERNAL REVENUE SERVICE

See INCOME TAX

INTERNATIONAL AGENCIES

See also ASSOCIATIONS; ORGANIZATION FOR ECONOMIC COOPERATION AND DEVELOPMENT; UNITED NATIONS

ABSTRACTS AND INDEXES

PAIS International. ProQuest L.L.C. • Monthly. $850.00 per year; cumulations three times a year. Provides topical citations to the worldwide literature of public affairs, economics, demographics, sociology, and trade. Text in English; indexed materials in English, French, German, Italian, Portuguese and Spanish.

United Nations Document Index. United Nations Publications. • Quarterly. Annual cumulation. Text in English.

BIBLIOGRAPHIES

Monthly Bibliography. United Nations Publications. • Monthly. $180 per year. Text in English and French.

CD-ROM DATABASES

PAIS International. ProQuest L.L.C. • Monthly. $1,995.00 per year. Contains over 650,000 citations to the literature of contemporary social, political, and economic issues.

DIRECTORIES

The Asia and Pacific Review: The Economic and Business Report. Kogan Page, Limited. • Covers: Key facts, indicators, country profile, business guide and directory for 60 countries in Asia and the Pacific. Database includes: Charts, tables and maps. Entries include: Heads of States, currencies, official languages, capital city, population, GNP, inflation, oil revenues, exports/imports, country profile, information for international visitors, name, address, phone of hotels, chambers of commerce, airlines, banks, government ministries and associations.

The EU Institutions' Register. Routledge Reference. • £305 Individuals hardback. Covers: Over 5,900 key personnel in each of the major institutions, including: European Commission, European Parliament, Economic and Social Committee, Council of the European Union, Court of Justice, European Investment Bank, Court of Auditors, Committee of Regions and EU Agencies. Entries include: Contact information.

Washington: A Comprehensive Directory of the Key Institutions and Leaders in th e National Capitol Area. Columbia Books Inc. • Annual. $149.00. Provides information on about 5,000 Washington, DC key businesses, government offices, non-profit organizations, and cultural institutions, with the names of about 25,000 principal executives. Includes Washington media, law offices, foundations, labor unions, international organizations, clubs, etc.

INTERNET DATABASES

Fedstats. Federal Interagency Council on Statistical Policy. Phone: (202)395-7254 • URL: http://www.fedstats.gov • Web site features an efficient search facility for full-text statistics produced by more than 100 federal agencies, including the Census Bureau, the Bureau of Economic Analysis, and the Bureau of Labor Statistics. Boolean searches can be made within one agency or for all agencies combined. Links are offered to international statistical bureaus, including the UN, IMF, OECD, UNESCO, Eurostat, and 20 individual countries. Fees: Free.

Publishers' Catalogues Home Page. EBSCO Publishing Inc. 10 Estes St., Ipswich, MA 01938-2106. Phone: 800-653-2726 or (978)356-6500; Fax: (978)356-6565; Email: information@ebscohost.com • URL: http://www.ebscohost.com • Provides links to the Web home pages of about 1,700 U. S. publishers (including about 80 University presses) and publishers in 48 foreign countries. "International/Multinational Publishers" are included, such as the International Monetary Fund, the World Bank, and the World Trade Organization. Publishers are arranged in convenient alphabetical lists. Searching is offered. Fees: Free.

OTHER SOURCES

World Trade Organization Dispute Settlement Decisions: Bernan's Annotated Reporter. Bernan Press. • 3/year. $320 2 volume set. Contains all World Trade Organization Panel Reports and Appellate Decisions since the establishment of the WTO in 1995. Includes such cases as "The Importation, Sale, and Distribution of Bananas."

PERIODICALS AND NEWSLETTERS

Government Publications News. Bernan Associates. • Monthly. Free. Controlled circulation newsletter providing information on recent publications from the U. S. Government Printing Office and selected international agencies.

InBusiness. American Chamber of Commerce in Romania. • Quarterly. Contains articles of interest to the U.S. and foreign business community in Romania.

World Trade Review: Economics, Law, International Institutions. Cambridge University Press. • Three times a year. Individuals, $48.00 pr year; institutions, $200.00 per year. Published in conjunction with the World Trade Organization (www.wto.org). Covers "issues of relevance to the multilateral trading system.".

RESEARCH CENTERS AND INSTITUTES

London School of Economics and Political Science - European Institute - Hellenic Observatory. Houghton St., London WC2A 2AE, United Kingdom. Phone: 44 20 79556066; Fax: 44 20 79556497; Email: k.featherstone@lse.ac.uk • URL: http://www.lse.ac.uk/europeanInstitute/research/hellenicObservatory/home.aspx • Contemporary politics, economics and society of Greece and Cyprus.

SOAS, University of London - Japan Research Centre. Russell Sq., Thornhaught St., London WC1H 0XG, United Kingdom. Phone: 44 207 8984892; Fax: 44 207 8984489; Email: centres@soas.ac.uk • URL: http://www.soas.ac.uk/jrc • Japan, including its anthropology, art and archaeology, economics, geography, gender and sexuality, history, imperialism, language and literature, law, linguistics, media, music, politics, religion and sociology.

Tohoku University - Center for Northeast Asian Studies. Kawauchi 41, Aoba-ku, Sendai 980-8576, Japan. Phone: 81 22 7956009; Fax: 81 22 7956010; Email: contasia@cneas.tohoku.ac.jp • URL: http://field.cneas.tohoku.ac.jp/index_e.html • Area studies in the Northeast Asian region, including East Asia, North Asia and Japan, particularly culture, society, economy, history, resources and the environment.

U.S. Department of the Treasury - Office of International Affairs - Office of Risk and Research Analysis. 1500 Pennsylvania Ave. NW, Washington, DC 20220. Phone: (202)622-2000; Fax: (202)622-6415 • URL: http://www.treasury.gov/about/organizational-structure/offices/International-Affairs/Pages/rra.aspx • Global economy, crisis prevention and financial vulnerabilities, and financial markets.

University of Calgary - Latin American Research Centre. Social Sciences 004, 2500 University Dr. NW, Calgary, AB, Canada T2N 1N4. Phone: (403)210-3929; Fax: (403)282-8606; Email: larc@ucalgary.ca • URL: http://larc.ucalgary.ca • Geography, archaeology, literature, business in Latin America.

University of Guelph - Ontario Public Interest Research Group-Guelph. 1 Trent Ln., Guelph, ON, Canada N1G 2W1. Phone: (519)824-2091; Fax: (519)824-8990; Email: opirg@uoguelph.ca • URL: http://www.opirgguelph.org/index.php?mode=2&linkID=1&l=0 • Social, political, economic and environmental issues of public concern.

University of New Brunswick - Canadian Research Institute for Social Policy. Keirstead Hall, Ste. 300, Fredericton, NB, Canada E3B 5A3. Phone: (506)447-3178; Fax: (506)447-3427; Email: crisp@unb.ca • URL: http://www.unb.ca/research/institutes/crisp • Social policy in Canada, especially policy affecting education, child care, and health.

University of New Hampshire - International Private Enterprise Center. Peter T. Paul College of Business & Economics, 10 Garrison Ave., Durham, NH 03824. Phone: (603)862-3354; Fax: (603)862-3383; Email: frk@christa.unh.edu • URL: http://paulcollege.unh.edu/international-private-enterprise-center • Public policy and managerial strategies to enhance private sector economic growth.

University of Oxford - St. Antony's College - Asian Studies Centre. 62 Woodstock Rd., Oxford OX2 6JF, United Kingdom. Phone: 44 1865 274559; Fax: 44 1865 274559; Email: rachel.murphy@sant.ox.ac.uk • URL: http://www.sant.ox.ac.uk/asian • Politics, economics, history, anthropology and international relations of East, Southeast, Northeast and South Asia.

University of Saskatchewan - International Centre for Northern Governance and Development. Kirk Hall, Rm. 234, 117 Science Pl., Saskatoon, SK, Canada S7N 5C8. Phone: (306)966-1665; Fax: (306)966-7780 • URL: http://artsandscience.usask.ca/icngd/ • Governance and development in three areas: capacity building for legal and judicial reform, knowledge development on market economy and social development interrelationships, and policy analysis for good governance.

TRADE/PROFESSIONAL ASSOCIATIONS

Accounting and Auditing Organization for Islamic Financial Institutions. Yateem Center, Blk. 304, Al Muthana Rd., Manama, Bahrain. Phone: 973 17 244 496; Fax: 973 17 250 194 • URL: http://www.aaoifi.com • Represents central banks, Islamic financial institutions, and other participants from the international Islamic banking and finance industry. Aims to uphold the accounting and auditing standards of Islamic financial institutions. Provides its members the necessary resources needed to improve and maintain the quality of service of Islamic financial institutions.

AIESEC Bahrain. BBIC Headquarters, Hidd Area, Manama, Bahrain. Phone: 973 17358819; Email: info.bh@aiesec.net • URL: http://www.aiesec.org/bahrain • Represents students of economics or business and related fields presently studying at affiliated universities worldwide. Aims to develop internationally educated managers. Manages the international exchange of students on internships around the world. Conducts training of members in the management of international business operations.

AIESEC Canada. 161 Eglinton Ave. E, Ste. 402, Toronto, ON, Canada M4P 1J5. Phone: (416)368-1001; Fax: (416)368-4490; Email: info2010@aiesec.ca • URL: http://aiesec.ca • Develops students through international internship exchange. Serves as a platform for young people to discover their potential so as to have a positive impact in the society.

AIESEC China. c/o Zachary Law, VP Communication, Block E, Rm. 1108, 16th St., hongguancun, Haidian mansion, Haidian District, Beijing, China. Phone: 86 10 82866532; Email: mainland.china@aiesec.net • URL: http://www.aiesec.cn • Provides leadership and work abroad opportunities. Organizes conferences and virtual tools to build networks. Contributes to the development of the communities with an overriding commitment to international co-operation and understanding. Facilitates international traineeship exchanges for its members and stakeholders.

AIESEC Kenya. PO Box 30197-00200, Nairobi, Kenya. Phone: 254 20 2608757; Email: info@aiesec.or.ke • URL: http://ke.aiesec.org • Enables students and recent graduate the opportunity to live and work in another country. Serves as a platform for young people to discover and develop their potential. Organizes conferences.

AIESEC Pakistan. 201 2nd Fl., Cotton Exchange, Bldg., II Chundrigarh Rd., Karachi, Pakistan. Phone: 92 21 35464958; Email: info@aiesec.pk • URL: http://www.aiesec.org/pakistan • Represents students of economics or business and related fields presently studying at affiliated universities worldwide. Aims to develop internationally educated managers. Manages the international exchange of students on internships around the world. Conducts training of members in the management of international business operations.

AIESEC Qatar. PO Box 24475, Doha, Qatar. Phone: (974)5542-6271; Email: qatar@aiesec.net • URL: http://www.aiesec.org/qatar • Represents students of economics or business and related fields presently studying at affiliated universities worldwide. Aims to develop internationally educated managers. Manages the international exchange of students on internships around the world. Conducts training of members in the management of international business operations.

Arab International Women's Forum. Berkeley Square House, Berkeley Sq., London W1J 6BD, United Kingdom. Phone: 44 20 78877630; Fax: 44 20 78876001 • URL: http://www.aiwfonline.com/home.aspx • Promotes the role of women in the economy and society. Serves as a link between the Arab business and professional women and their counterparts in the international community.

Argentina Israel Chamber of Commerce. Phone: 54 11 43726273; Email: info@ccai.com.ar • URL: http://www.ccai.com.ar • Promotes trade between Argentina and Israel.

Argentine Chinese Chamber of Production, Industry and Commerce. Viamonte 1145 7 A, C1053ABW Buenos Aires, Argentina. Phone: 54 11 43726133; Fax: 54 11 43726133; Email: argenchina@ciudad.com.ar • URL: http://www.argenchina.org/_en_index.asp • Promotes business trade between Argentina and China.

Asia Pacific Loan Market Association. Jardine House, 32nd Fl., One Connaught Pl., Central, Hong Kong, Hong Kong, China. Phone: 852 28263500 • URL: http://www.aplma.com • Promotes growth and liquidity in the primary and secondary loan markets. Facilitates the standardization of primary and secondary loan documentation. Develops standard trading, settlement and valuation procedures. Organizes educational and social functions for syndicated loan professionals. Acts as a liaison between major loan market players and regional regulators.

Association of Residential Cleaning Services International. c/o Ernie Hartong, 7870 Olentangy River Rd., Ste. 301, Columbus, OH 43235. Phone: (614)547-0887; Fax: (614)505-7136; Email: chris@arcsi.org • URL: http://www.arcsi.org • Represents residential cleaning service owners and professionals. Advances and improves the residential cleaning industry. Shares knowledge and information to ensure the growth and development of cleaning service businesses.

Australian Plants Society - South Australian Region. PO Box 304, Unley, SA 5061, Australia. Email: president@australianplantssa.asn.au • URL: http://www.australianplantssa.asn.au • Encourages the cultivation and study of Australian plants. Promotes the establishment of gardens in all types of soil and climates for the preservation of Australian flora. Protects Australian plants and their habitats. Represents its members in government activity.

Binational Tourism Alliance. 143 Genesee St., Buffalo, NY 14203. Phone: 877-884-2736 or (716)856-6525; Fax: (716)856-6754; Email: arlene.white@btapartners.com • URL: http://www.btapartners.com • Promotes tourism products and services and supports tourism development in Canada and the United States. Seeks to improve business opportunities and growth potential of members. Provides industry research and information, training and professional development.

Bridal Show Producers International. 2701 Del Paso Rd. 130-343, Sacramento, CA 95835. Fax: (800)573-6070 • URL: http://www.bspibridalshows.com • Represents and promotes the bridal show industry. Maintains and enhances the quality of bridal shows. Increases communications and integrity among exhibitors and producers. Fosters mutual support and camaraderie among members.

Business Network International - Suriname. Verl Hoogestraat No. 1, Paramaribo, Suriname. Phone: 597 424354 • URL: http://www.bnisuriname.com • Seeks to increase business opportunities for members. Encourages members to share ideas, contacts and business referrals. Fosters and develops personal relationships with other qualified business professionals.

Business Retention and Expansion International. PO Box 3212, Bismarck, ND 58502-3212. Email: brei@brei.org • URL: http://www.brei.org • Promotes business retention and expansion as a fundamental strategy for economic sustainability and growth. Provides leadership resources, education and networking opportunities in business retention and expansion. Fosters communication and collaboration among members.

Camara de Comercio Argentino-Brasilena. Montevideo 770-12 Piso, 1019 Buenos Aires, Argentina. Phone: 54 11 48114503; Email: institucionales@cambras.org.ar • URL: http://www.cambras.org.ar • Represents business and commerce in Argentina.

Camara de Comercio Argentino-Britanica en la Republica Argentina. Av. Corrientes 457, Piso 10, C1043AAE Buenos Aires, Argentina. Phone: 54 11 43942762; Fax: 54 11 43263860; Email: info@ccab.com.ar • URL: http://www.ccab.com.ar • Promotes bilateral Trade and Investment between Argentina and UK.

Camara de Comercio Italiana de Rosario. Cordoba 1868, 2000 Rosario, Argentina. Phone: 54 341 4266789 or 54 341 4245691; Email: info@italrosario.com • URL: http://www.italrosario.com/

• Represent Italian business interests in Rosario, Argentina.

Camara de Industria y Comercio Argentino-Alemana. Av. Corrientes 327, C1043AAD Buenos Aires, Argentina. Phone: 54 11 52194000; Fax: 54 11 52194001; Email: ahkargentina@ahkargentina.com.ar • URL: http://www.ahkargentina.com.ar/ • Represents German business in Argentina and promotes international trade between Argentina and Germany.

Camara Espanola de Comercio de la Republica Argentina. 863 Av. Belgrano, Piso 7, C1092AAI Buenos Aires, Argentina. Phone: 54 11 43355000; Fax: 54 11 43355022; Email: recepcion.cecra@cecra.com.ar • URL: http://www.cecra.com.ar • Represents Spanish-Argentine businesses in Buenos Aires.

Center for International Private Enterprise - Egypt Office. Fayoum St., No. 1, Off Cleopatra St., Heliopolis, Fl. 8, Ste. 8003, Cairo 11341, Egypt. Phone: 20 2 4143282; Fax: 20 2 4143295; Email: rzoghbi@cipe-egypt.org • URL: http://www.cipe.org • Encourages the growth of voluntary business organizations and private enterprise systems, such as chambers of commerce, trade associations, employers' organizations, and business-oriented research groups, particularly in developing countries. Creates exchanges among business leaders and institutions to strengthen the international private enterprise system. Offers leadership training for association executives.

Climate Group. 145 W 58th St., Ste. 2a, New York, NY 10019. Phone: (646)233-0550; Email: info@theclimategroup.org • URL: http://www.theclimategroup.org • Advances business and government leadership on climate change. Creates international effort to stop climate change. Works to accelerate international action on global warming. Promotes profitability and competitiveness among the government, business and non-profit sectors.

Community Managers International Association. PO Box 848, Dana Point, CA 92629-0848. Phone: (949)940-9263; Email: cmiamanager@gmail.com • URL: http://www.cmiamanager.org • Aims to promote the community management profession. Provides an environment for the exchange of ideas among members. Collaborates with other national and state organizations. Sponsors seminars and workshops.

Credit Professionals International. 10726 Manchester Rd., Ste. 210, Saint Louis, MO 63122. Phone: (314)821-9393; Fax: (314)821-7171; Email: creditpro@creditprofessionals.org • URL: http://www.creditprofessionals.org • Represents individuals employed in credit or collection departments of business firms or professional offices. Conducts educational program in credit work. Sponsors Career Club composed of members who have been involved in credit work for at least 25 years.

European Professional Women's Network. 4, rue Galvani, F-75838 Paris, France. Phone: 33 9 70446262; Email: contact@europeanpwn.net • URL: http://www.europeanpwn.net • Promotes the sustainable and innovative professional career paths of women. Raises the visibility of European women in business.

European Women's Management Development Austria. Schmiedinger strasse 67, 5020 Salzburg, Austria. Email: austria@ewmd.org • URL: http://www.ewmd.org/chapter/104 • Aims to improve the quality of management with respect to people, children, age and the cultural diversity of Europe. Provides a forum for collecting and exchanging information about trends management development in Europe and worldwide. Promotes women in management. Facilitates communication among individuals involved in the development of new role models for better work-life-balance.

European Women's Management Development Switzerland. Stockerstrasse 56, 8002 Zurich, Switzerland. Email: switzerland@ewmd.org • URL: http://www.ewmd.org • Aims to improve the quality of management with respect to people, children, age and the cultural diversity of Europe. Provides a forum for collecting and exchanging information about trends management development in Europe and worldwide. Promotes women in management. Facilitates communication among individuals involved in the development of new role models for better work-life-balance.

EWMD ITALY: European Women's Management Development. c/o EWMD Brescia, via Papa Giovanni XXIII 74, Rezzato, I-25086 Brescia, Italy. Phone: 39 30 2793124; Email: italy@ewmd.org • URL: http://www.ewmd.org/chapter/106 • Aims to improve the quality of management with respect to people, children, age and the cultural diversity of Europe. Promotes the best practices for work-life-balance management. Provides a forum for collecting and exchanging information about trends management development in Europe and worldwide. Promotes women in management. Facilitates communication among individuals involved in the development of new role models for better work-life-balance.

Franco-Argentina Chamber of Commerce and Industry. Av. Libertador 498, 17e etage, C1001AAO Buenos Aires, Argentina. Phone: 54 11 43101000; Fax: 54 11 43101021; Email: ccifa@ccifa.com.ar • URL: http://www.ccifa.com.ar • Promotes business and trade between Argentine and French companies.

HELIO International. 31-33 rue de la Colonie, 75013 Paris, France. Phone: 33 1 45802607; Email: helio@helio-international.org • URL: http://www.helio-international.org • Aims to identify, assess, measure and publicize the contribution of energy systems and policies to sustainable and equitable development. Provides independent input to the design and implementation of ecodevelopment, energy and climate projects. Designs analytical tools and promotes the creation and integration of citizen in the energy decision-making process.

International Air Filtration Certifiers Association. c/o Michael Alleman, 129 S Gallatin, Liberty, MO 64068. Phone: 888-679-1904; Fax: (816)792-8105 • URL: http://www.iafca.com • Promotes professionalism in the biological safety cabinet industry. Establishes and maintains certification program for biological safety cabinet certifiers. Provides information and guidance to legislative and regulatory agencies with regard to laws and standards affecting the industry.

International Amusement and Leisure Defense Association. PO Box 4563, Louisville, KY 40204. Phone: (502)473-0956; Fax: (502)473-7352; Email: info@ialda.org • URL: http://www.ialda.org • Promotes and protects the interests of the amusement and leisure industries. Encourages members to exchange information, share experiences and develop litigation strategies regarding the amusement and leisure industry. Serves as a clearinghouse for speakers and authors on industry-specific topics.

International Association of CFOs and Corporate Treasurers China. c/o Mr. Francis Ho, CLP Holdings, Group Treasury Dept., 147 Argyle St., Mongkok, Kowloon, Hong Kong, China. • URL: http://www.iacctchina.com • Promotes the development of professional corporate treasury practice in China. Fosters exchange and sharing among a network of corporate treasurers and CFOs in both mainland Chinese. Supports financial reforms in China by developing a platform for dialogue between members and financial regulators.

International Association of Directional Drilling. 525 Sam Houston Pkwy. E, Ste. 525, Houston, TX 77060. Phone: (281)931-8811 or (281)288-6484; Email: dallen@iadd-intl.org • URL: http://www.iadd-intl.org • Represents the interests of the directional drilling industry. Encourages members to share ideas and develop safety and performance standards. Fosters collaboration among operators, directional drilling vendors and suppliers.

International Association of Women in Family Enterprises. 1906 Vista Del Lago Dr., No. L-119, Valley Springs, CA 95252. Phone: (209)772-9200 or (209)772-2810; Fax: (209)772-2810; Email: info@iawife.com • URL: http://www.iawife.com • Aims to support women who are building and growing family businesses. Offers opportunities to help members become successful in family enterprises. Provides support, education and networking among members.

International Bridal Manufacturers Association. 118 W 20th St., 3rd Fl., New York, NY 10011-3627. Email: info@ibma.us • URL: http://ibma.us • Represents wedding apparel and accessory manufacturers. Promotes economic opportunities and fosters better relationships between manufacturers and retailers of bridal apparel. Coordinates and sets non-conflicting dates for bridal industry markets.

International Economic Alliance. 1 Mifflin Pl., Ste. 400, Cambridge, MA 02138-4946. Phone: (617)418-1981; Fax: (617)812-0499 • URL: http://www.iealliance.org • Aims to further global trade, economic development and advance business relations. Brings together the world's key players and decision-makers (business and government leaders, investors and leading intellectuals) for practical, open, bi-partisan and solution-oriented exchange of ideas. Serves as a source of knowledge, facilitator of relationships, and catalyst for new business opportunities.

International Energy Credit Association. 1500 Commerce Pkwy., Ste. C, Mount Laurel, NJ 08054. Phone: (856)380-6854; Fax: (856)439-0525 • URL: http://www.ieca.net • Credit executives of petroleum and energy related companies and vendors to the field. Conducts educational seminars.

International Factoring Association. 6627 Bay Laurel Pl., Ste. C, Avila Beach, CA 93424-0039. Phone: 800-563-1895; Fax: (805)773-0021; Email: info@factoring.org • URL: http://www.factoring.org • Represents the interests of the factoring industry. Assists the factoring community by providing information, training, purchasing power and resources. Provides opportunities for members to discuss issues and concerns in the industry.

International Janitorial Cleaning Services Association. 2011 Oak St., Wyandotte, MI 48192. Phone: (734)252-6189; Email: info@ijcsa.com • URL: http://www.ijcsanetwork.com • Represents the interests of the janitorial industry. Promotes professionalism and ethics in the janitorial and cleaning services field. Provides training and education for cleaning professionals.

International Network of Alternative Financial Institution. Mermoz, 11 rue MZ - 157, Dakar, Senegal. Email: claudeabsa@yahoo.fr • URL: http://www.mixmarket.org/networks/inafi • Seeks to advance microfinance programs for the poor by increasing the quality of service and performance of microfinancial institutions through counselling, research, and publications.

International Ombudsman Association. 111 Deer Lake Rd., Ste. 100, Deerfield, IL 60015. Phone: (847)509-7991; Fax: (847)480-9282; Email: info@ombudsassociation.org • URL: http://www.ombudsassociation.org/home.aspx • Individuals actively engaged in the practice of organizational ombudsmanry, as designated neutrals. Works to enhance the quality and value of the ombudsman function by: establishing and communicating appropriate standards of excellence for the profession; developing and disseminating ethical guidelines for organizational ombudspeople; training new and experienced ombuds practitioners in complaint handling skills and principles of effective practice; communicating the latest developments of the profession; and fostering appropriate forums to share common interests and strengthen skills.

International Society of Financiers. 64 Brookside Dr., Hendersonville, NC 28792. Phone: (828)393-8908; Fax: (828)393-8919; Email: insofin@gmail.com • URL: http://www.insofin.com • Membership in more than 25 countries includes: real estate, minerals, commodities, and import-export brokers; corporate, industrial, and private lenders; and other financial professionals. Provides information and referrals on major domestic and international financial projects and transactions, and fosters integrity and professionalism among members.

Palladium Alliance International. PO Box 81511, Billings, MT 59108. Phone: 877-473-7873; Email: info@luxurypalladium.com • URL: http://www.luxurypalladium.com • Represents experts who work with retailers, producers and manufacturers all over the world. Focuses on establishing palladium as a luxurious, precious and distinctive metal. Provides education, marketing and technical support and a vision for the advancement of palladium.

Swiss-Argentine Chamber of Commerce. Av. Leandro N Alem 1074, Piso 10, C1001AAS Buenos Aires, Argentina. Phone: 54 11 43117187; Email: info@suiza.org.ar • URL: http://www.suiza.org.ar/select_lang.php • Promotes businesses between Argentina and Switzerland.

Swiss Business Association Singapore. c/o Embassy of Switzerland, 1, Swiss Club Link, Singapore 288162, Singapore. Phone: 65 67220799 • URL: http://www.swissbusiness.org.sg • Assists Swiss companies established in Singapore in conducting, sponsoring or promoting any activity that will benefit its members. Promotes the interests of members related to trade. Encourages the growth of the Swiss trade by promoting investment, finance, commerce and industry.

Swiss Malaysian Business Association. c/o Embassy of Switzerland, 16 Persiaran Madge, 55000 Kuala Lumpur, Malaysia. Phone: 60 3 21629889; Fax: 60 3 21418410; Email: info@smba.org.my • URL: http://www.myswiss.org • Promotes and fosters bilateral trade, services and investment between Switzerland and Malaysia. Assists potential new Swiss companies in establishing their headquarters in Malaysia. Maintains and improves close trading, commercial and other links between Malaysia and Switzerland. Provides a forum for members in exchanging information and identifying and discussing issues of common interests regarding economic, industrial and commercial objectives.

SwissCham Australia. 46 Market St., Ste. 303, Sydney, NSW 2000, Australia. Phone: 61 2 92621511; Fax: 61 2 92901928 • URL: http://www.swisscham.com.au • Represents Swiss business interests in Australia.

Transmission Rebuilders Network International. 6501 E Greenway Pkwy., Ste. 103/298, Scottsdale, AZ 85254-2065. Phone: 888-582-8764; Email: info@trannybuilder.com • URL: http://www.trannybuilder.com • Advances the science of rebuilding automatic transmissions and the art of managing a transmission shop. Serves as a forum for the members to share and exchange ideas on automatic transmissions. Provides training, support and technical information based on the needs, trends and opportunities of the transmission/powertrain industry.

U.S.-Vietnam WTO Coalition. 1101 17th St. NW, Ste. 411, Washington, DC 20036. Phone: (202)289-1912; Fax: (202)289-0519; Email: vncoalition@usasean.org • URL: http://www.usvtc.org/coalition.asp • Represents American companies, farm groups, trade associations, veterans associations and public interest organizations supportive of Vietnam's accession to the World Trade Organization and the attainment of full U.S.-Vietnam normalization.

WAM International: Women Advancing Microfinance. 402 Constitution Ave. NE, Washington, DC 20002. Phone: (202)547-4546; Email: wam.international.president@gmail.com • URL: http://waminternational.org • Promotes the advancement of women working in the microfinance industry. Seeks to extend economic opportunities to women globally and encourages active participation of women in management and governance roles.

Women Chiefs of Enterprises International. c/o Julie Ankers, President, Level 6 276 Pitt St., Sydney, NSW 2000, Australia. Phone: 61 2 92675220; Fax: 61 2 92674202 • URL: http://www.wcei.com.au • Represents women entrepreneurs in Australia. Encourages innovation in the development of entrepreneurial skills. Creates opportunities for business development.

INTERNATIONAL ASSOCIATIONS

See INTERNATIONAL AGENCIES

INTERNATIONAL BUSINESS

See also EUROPEAN MARKETS; FOREIGN INVESTMENTS; FOREIGN TRADE; INTERNATIONAL MARKETING; MULTINATIONAL CORPORATIONS

ABSTRACTS AND INDEXES

F & S Index: Europe. Cengage Learning Inc. • Monthly. $2,532.00 per year, including quarterly and annual cumulations. Provides annotated citations to marketing, business, financial, and industrial literature. Coverage of European business activity includes trade journals, financial magazines, business newspapers, and special reports. Formerly Predicasts F & S Index: Europe.

F & S Index: International. Cengage Learning Inc. • $2,659 Individuals. Monthly. $2,532.00 per year, including quarterly and annual cumulations. Provides annotated citations to marketing, business, financial, and industrial literature. Coverage of international business activity includes trade journals, financial magazines, business newspapers, and special reports. Areas included are Asia, Latin America, Africa, the Middle East, Oceania, and Canada.

NTIS Alerts: Business & Economics. U.S. Department of Commerce National Technical Information Service. • Biweekly. $130 per year. Covers consumer affairs, minority enterprises, marketing and economics, international commerce, banking, and finance.

ALMANACS AND YEARBOOKS

Countries of the World and Their Leaders Yearbook. Cengage Learning Inc. • Annual. $475 Individuals. 2012. eBook. Contact publisher for pricing. Based on U.S. State Department data covering nearly 200 countries.

Political Risk Yearbook. The PRS Group Inc. • Annual. Each volume covers a separate region of the world and assesses economic and political conditions as they relate to the risk of doing business.

Research in International Business and Finance. Elsevier. • $347 Individuals Print. Publishes empirical and applied research on issues relating to International Business and International Finance.

CD-ROM DATABASES

Asia Pacific Kompass on Disc. Kompass USA, Inc. • Annual. CD-ROM provides information on more than 200,000 companies in Australia, China, Hong Kong, India, Korea, Malaysia, New Zealand, Philippines, Singapore, Thailand, and Taiwan. Classification system covers approximately 50,000 products and services.

Baltia Kompass Business Disc. Kompass USA, Inc. • Provides information on more than 22,000 companies in Estonia, Latvia, and Lithuania. Classification system covers approximately 50,000 products and services.

Benelux Kompass Business Disc. Kompass USA, Inc. • Semiannual. CD-ROM provides information on more than 52,000 companies in Belgium, Netherlands, and Luxembourg. Classification system covers approximately 50,000 products and services.

East European Kompass on Disc. Kompass USA, Inc. • Provides information on more than 294,000 companies in Austria, Azerbaijan, Belarus, Croatia, Czech Republic, Estonia, Hungary, Latvia, Lithuania, Moldova, Poland, Romania, Russia, Slovakia, Slovenia, Ukraine, and Yugoslavia. Classification system covers approximately 50,000 products and services.

European Kompass on Disc. Kompass USA, Inc. • Provides information on more than 350,000 companies in Belgium, Denmark, France, Germany, Ireland, Italy, Luxembourg, Netherlands, Norway, Spain, Sweden, and UK. Classification system covers approximately 50,000 products and services.

Kompass CD-ROM Editions. Kompass USA, Inc. • Semiannual or annual. Prices vary. CD-ROM versions of Kompass international trade directories are available for each of 36 major countries and nine world regions. Searching is provided for 50,000 product/service items and for many company details.

Kompass Concord CD-ROM. Kompass USA, Inc. • Provides information on more than 105,000 companies in 17 rapidly developing East European countries: Armenia, Azerbaijan, Belarus, Bulgaria, Czech Republic, Estonia, Hungary, Kazakhstan, Kyrgyzstan, Latvia, Lithuania, Moldova, Poland, Romania, Russia, Ukraine, and Uzbekistan. Classification system covers approximately 50,000 products and services.

Middle-East/Africa Kompass on Disc. Kompass USA, Inc. • Annual. CD-ROM provides information on more than 140,000 companies in Algeria, Bahrain, Cyprus, Egypt, Lebanon, Mauritania, Morocco, Oman, Saudi Arabia, South Africa, Tunisia, and United Arab Emirates. Classification system covers approximately 50,000 products and services.

OECD Statistical Compendium. Organization for Economic Cooperation and Development. • Semiannual. $1,905.00 per year for 1 to 10 users. CD-ROM contains more than 730,000 monthly, quarterly, and annual time series for OECD countries, 1960 to date. Includes fully searchable data on agriculture, food, economic indicators, national accounts, employment, energy, finance, industry, technology, and foreign trade. Results can be displayed in various forms.

Scandinavian Kompass on Disc. Kompass USA, Inc. • Semiannual. CD-ROM provides information on more than 120,000 companies in Denmark, Finland, Norway, and Sweden. Classification system covers approximately 50,000 products and services.

DIRECTORIES

Academy of International Business--Membership Directory. Academy of International Business. • Covers: About 3,068 members. Entries include: Name, address, phone, fax, Bitnet, discipline.

African International Business Directory of Importers. Coble International. • $285 print or CD-ROM. Covers: 9,000 importers from 42 countries in Africa. Entries include: Name, address, phone, fax, primary contact person, list of products, e-mail addresses, and Web site.

Algeria Industrial and Business Directory. International Business Publications, USA. • Annual. $99.95 Individuals. Covers industrial, investment, and business contacts for conducting export-import and investment activity in the country.

Alliance of Area Business Publications--Membership Directory. Alliance of Area Business Publications. • Annual. Covers over 70 local, state, and regional member business publications in the United States, Canada, Australia and Puerto Rico.

American Business Directory: Directory and Year Book of American Business in Ireland. American Chamber of Commerce Ireland. • Annual. Contains lists of American owned, associated, and affiliated companies in the Republic of Ireland with company listings by name and type of business.

American Business Directory for the USSR. Amtorg Trading Corp. • Publication consists of paid advertisements and business reply cards from U.S. companies wishing to do business with the U.S.S.R.

American Business in China. Caravel Inc. • Annual. $99 print edition. Publication includes: More than 1,000 U.S. firms with offices in China and Hong Kong, including Beijing, Shanghai, and Guangzhou. Database includes: Exporting to China; Marketing, Advertising and Exhibiting in China; China's major cites for foreign investments. Entries include: Company name, address, phone, fax; websites and e-mail addresses, name of contact for both U.S. Headquarters and China branch offices; and products or services provided.

American Companies in Brazil. U.S. Chamber of Commerce. • $75 plus $4.00 shipping. Covers: U.S. subsidiary and affiliate companies in Brazil. Entries include: Company name, address, phone.

American Subsidiaries and Affiliates of French Firms. French Embassy Trade Office. • $125. Covers: French firms and their American subsidiaries. Database includes: Address, telephone and fax of french parent company. Entries include: firm address, telephone and fax numbers, activity.

Armenia Export-Import and Business Directory. International Business Publications, USA. • $99.95 Individuals. Covers strategic, economic, investment, export-import, and business opportunities and contact numbers.

Armenia Industrial and Business Directory. International Business Publications, USA. • Annual. $99.95 Individuals. Covers industrial, investment and business contacts for conducting export-import and investment activity in the country.

The Asia and Pacific Review: The Economic and Business Report. Kogan Page, Limited. • Covers: Key facts, indicators, country profile, business guide and directory for 60 countries in Asia and the Pacific. Database includes: Charts, tables and maps. Entries include: Heads of States, currencies, official languages, capital city, population, GNP, inflation, oil revenues, exports/imports, country profile, information for international visitors, name, address, phone of hotels, chambers of commerce, airlines, banks, government ministries and associations.

Asia-Pacific International Business Directory of Importers. Coble International. • $455 print or CD-ROM. Covers: 32,000 importers from South Korea, Australia, Philippines, New Zealand, India, Vietnam, Sri Lanka, Japan, Kazakhstan, Malaysia, Pakistan, Singapore, Indonesia, Mauritius, South Pacific Islands, Mongolia, Hong Kong, Taiwan, Thailand, China, and Uzbekistan. Entries include: Name, address, phone, fax, primary contact person, list of products, e-mail addresses, and Web site.

Asian Business League of San Francisco--Membership Directory. Asian Business League of San Francisco. • Includes contact information of Asian-American members.

Austria in U.S.A. American Chamber of Commerce in Austria. • Periodic. €150 Members. Covers: 550 Austrian companies with U.S. Subsidiaries, branch offices, associates, joint ventures, or representations in the U.S.; American representations and Austrian-American organizations in Austria, Austrian representations in the U.S., American Chambers of Commerce in Europe, and the representation of American states in Europe. Entries include: For companies--Name, address, phone; name, address, phone of U.S. Affiliated company; name of the Austrian company's general manager; a brief description of the U.S. Company; type of business and nature of relationship.

Bahamas Chamber of Commerce--Annual Membership Directory: Business Directory. Bahamas Chamber of Commerce. • Annual. $8 plus shipping. Covers about 500 member firms in construction, manufacturing, professional and business services, sales, tourism, and transportation.

Belarus Export-Import Trade and Business Directory. International Business Publications, USA. • $99.95 Individuals. Contains information on strategic, economic, investment, export-import, and business opportunities and contact numbers.

Belgium Export-Import and Business Directory. International Business Publications, USA. • $99.95 Individuals. Covers information on strategic, economic, investment, export-import, and business opportunities and contact numbers.

Belgium-Luxembourg Chamber of Commerce in Hong Kong--Directory. Belgium-Luxembourg Chamber of Commerce in Hong Kong. • Covers: Member organizations involved in developing two-way trade between Belgium - Luxembourg and Hong Kong.

Brazilian-American Who's Who. Brazilian-American Chamber of Commerce. • Irregular. $55. Covers: more than 1,300 firms, subsidiaries, and affiliates operating and/or having interests in both the United States and Brazil. Entries include: Company name, address, names and titles of key personnel.

Bricker's International Directory: Long-Term University-Based Executive Programs. Peterson's. • Annual. Covers: Several hundred residential management development programs at academic institutions in the United States and abroad. Criteria for listing include that program must be residential, at least one week in length, in English, not introductory in content, and with emphasis on "strategic" issues and functions covering a wide range of organizations. Entries include: Name of program; sponsoring institution; location, dates, and duration of program; tuition fees; curriculum content; modes of instruction; size of classes; information on participants; living accommodations; faculty; special features; official contact.

British Firms in Germany. British Chamber of Commerce in Germany. • $200. Covers: companies in the Federal Republic of Germany which are subsidiaries of or otherwise affiliated with United Kingdom firms. Entries include: German company name and address, name and address of British affiliate or owner, code indicating products.

Brunei Industrial and Business Directory. International Business Publications, USA. • Annual. $99.95 Individuals. Covers industrial, investment and business contacts for conducting export-import and investment activity in the country.

Business Directory for Americans Abroad. TeleDiplomacy Inc. • Database covers: Businesses and immigration, import, and export issues of interest to U.S. Citizens travelling abroad. Entries include: Contact information.

Business Directory for Diplomats. TeleDiplomacy Inc. • Database covers: Businesses and immigration, import, and export issues of interest to diplomats in the Washington, DC, area. Entries include: Contact information.

Business Directory of Hong Kong. Current Publications Ltd. • Annual. $180 surface mail postpaid. Covers over 12,300 firms in Hong Kong, including manufacturers, exporters, importers, banks and financial firms, construction, transportation, service companies, professional firms and organizations, foreign government commissions and consulates in Hong Kong, and trade promotion organizations.

Business in the Arab World. National United States-Arab Chamber of Commerce. • $2 /profile. Contains series of business profiles with regulations, procedures, and contacts for each Arab country.

Business, Investor & Government Relations Directory. PIMS UK Ltd. • Quarterly. $60 per issue. Covers over 7,000 companies, organizations, and individuals involved in the financial industry in the United Kingdom, including financial press, securities analysts, stock exchanges, banks, insurance companies, related trade associations, and members of the British and European parliaments.

Business Mexico. American Chamber of Commerce of Mexico - Mexico City. • Monthly. $145 /year for nonmembers. Covers business, economic, and policy developments in Mexico. Includes statistics and research reports.

Business Who's Who of Australia (BWW). Dun and Bradstreet Marketing. • Provides information on more than 22,000 public and private companies located in Australia. It provides coverage of company activities, financial details, and key personnel, products, and services. BWW is available in print as a two-volume directory, on CD-ROM, and via the Internet.

CCBC--Membership Directory. Canada-China Business Council. • Annual. Covers: 200 Canadian companies in China. Entries include: Company profile.

Central Europe Profiled: Essential Facts on Society, Business, and Politics in Central Europe. Palgrave Macmillan. • $19.95 paperback. List of banks, stock exchanges, trade and labor associations, top industrial companies, transport and communications, social institutions, addresses, and market share.

China Business Directory. American Chamber of Commerce in Hong Kong. • Periodic. $45 for nonmembers (overseas delivery). Features China offices and contact of companies with regional headquarters in Hong Kong.

China Business Guide. American Chamber of Commerce in Hong Kong. • $40 Individuals. Covers: Companies engaged in business and trade in China. Database includes: Statistics, charts.

China Industrial and Business Directory. International Business Publications, USA. • Annual. $99.95 Individuals. Covers industrial, investment and business contacts for conducting export-import and investment activity in the country.

Colombia Industrial and Business Directory. International Business Publications, USA. • Annual. $99.95 Individuals. Covers industrial, investment and business contacts for conducting export-import and investment activity in the country.

Contact Peru. American Chamber of Commerce of Peru. • Quarterly. Covers: Member companies and American Chambers of Commerce in Latin America. Entries include: Company name, address, phone, telex.

Contacts for Kuwaiti Contracting. International Executive Reports. • $195. Covers: business contacts in Kuwait, including Kuwaiti federal and state government agencies; U.S. Defense Reconstruction Assistance Office; Kuwaiti importers, agents, banks, airlines, and hotels; and U.S., British, and German firms actively doing business in Kuwait. Entries include: Name, address.

Cotton Council International Buyers' Guide. Cotton

Council International. • Covers: Exporters of U.S. raw cotton. Entries include: Company name, addresses of exporting companies, production and ginning seasons, and official U.S. cotton standards, packaging, and transportation data.

Craighead's International Business, Travel, and Relocation Guide to 84 Countries. Cengage Learning Inc. • $775 Individuals hardcover. Publication includes: List of Web sites for children's organizations, spousal employment, telephones/ telecommunications, visa requirements, and more. Principal content of publication is detailed information on relocating or traveling to foreign countries.

Croatia Business Services Providers Leads. Business Information Agency Inc. PlanetInform. • Monthly. $50 Individuals mailing list. Covers: Croatian companies and all sub-industries that provide various services to commercial businesses, establishments, and organizations, including consulting, advertising and marketing services, and facilities maintenance.

Current Directory of International Chambers of Commerce and Industry. Current Pacific Ltd. • $150 Individuals. Covers: More than 4,000 international chambers of commerce and industry selected from major cities in more than 165 countries in territories in the world.

Czech Republic Business Services Providers Leads. Business Information Agency Inc. PlanetInform. • Monthly. $109 Individuals mailing list. Covers Czech companies and all sub-industries that provide various services to commercial businesses, establishments, and organizations, including consulting, advertising and marketing services, and facilities maintenance.

Denmark Business Services Providers Leads. Business Information Agency Inc. PlanetInform. • Monthly. $211 Individuals mailing list. Covers Danish companies and all sub-industries that provide various services to commercial businesses, establishments, and organizations, including consulting, advertising and marketing services, and facilities maintenance.

Diamond's Japan Business Directory. Diamond Lead Company Ltd. • Annual. €964.40 Single issue approximative price. Covers more than 2,000 leading Japanese firms in all lines of business; business-related government agencies and organizations.

Dictionary of International Trade. Reference Press Inc. • $16.45. Covers: More than 4,000 entries concerning international trade, including 200 trade groups, 750 acronyms and abbreviations, 180 country codes, 300 city codes, currencies for 200 countries, and a source guide for 125 publications. Database includes: Regional maps of the world. Entries include: For trade groups--name, address, phone, fax.

Directory of Affiliates & Offices of Japanese Firms in USA & Canada. Want Publishing Co. • Irregular. $190. Covers: over 6,000 Japanese-affiliated or owned firms in the U.S. and Canada.

Directory of American Business in Hong Kong. GTE Directories Ltd. • $20. Covers: American companies, their agents, and distributors in Hong Kong; US State and Port of Authority representatives in Hong Kong; products and service of the American Consulate General in Hong Kong.

Directory of American Business in South China. American Chamber of Commerce in Hong Kong. • Covers: Over 900 American companies that have regional headquarters or representative offices in Hong Kong.

Directory of American Companies Operating in Mexico. American Chamber of Commerce of Mexico - Mexico City. • Biennial. Covers: over 2,500 United States commercial and investment companies with operations in Mexico, and the 2,500 Mexican companies that represent them in Mexico. Entries include: For United States companies--Name, address, phone, fax, contact person, products, names of Mexican firm with which associated, type of affiliation. For Mexican companies--Name, address, phone, fax, contact person, products, sales, name of United States company.

Directory of Foreign Manufacturers in the United States. Georgia State University Business Press. • Biennial. $195 payment must accompany orders from individuals. Covers: over 7,300 United States manufacturing, mining, and petroleum companies, and the over 6,800 firms abroad that own them. Entries include: Company name, address, phone, fax, products or services, Standard Industrial Classification (SIC) codes, parent company name and address.

Directory of International Buyers. Auto Care Association. • Annual. $70. Covers: 650 foreign firms that attended the association's annual show. Entries include: Company name, address, name and title of contact, type of buyer.

Directory of International Corporate Giving in America and Abroad. Taft Group. • $215. Covers: 443 foreign-owned companies that support nonprofit organizations in the U.S., and 170 U.S. companies that support organizations overseas. Entries include: Corporation name, foundation name; name, title, and phone of contact; location of U.S. headquarters, number of employees, total foundation assets, name and address of overseas parent company; summary of grant support, including amounts given, geographical area and types of activities preferred, and recently funded programs.

Directory of International Sources of Business Information. Pearson Education Ltd. • Annual. $85. Covers: Sources of business information worldwide, including business information brokers, Euro-Info centers, banks, stockbrokers, associations, embassies and councils, market research organizations, economic and statistical organizations, publishers, publications, online databases, and United Kingdom packet switching exchanges. Entries include: For business information brokers and Euro-Info centers--Name, address, phone, fax, host and databases accessed, subject areas covered, languages spoken, description of services offered. For banks, stockbrokers, associations, embassies and councils, market research organizations, economic and statistical organizations, and publications--Name, address, phone. For online databases--Name, address, phone, host. For United Kingdom packet switching exchanges--Phone. For publishers--Name, address, phone, fax, telex.

Directory of U.S. Companies Doing Business in Central and Eastern Europe and the Commonwealth of Independent States. Wetherby International Co. • Quarterly. $25 postpaid. Covers: over 500 U.S. firms with operations in the Commonwealth of Independent States and Central and Eastern Europe; sources of assistance for U.S. business at the Commerce Department. Entries include: Company or agency name, address, phone, type of activity.

Directory of Websites for International Jobs. Development Concepts Inc. • $19.95 Individuals. Covers: 1,400 websites.

Doing Business in Emerging Europe. Palgrave Macmillan. • £110 Individuals Hardback. Publication includes: Additional details about conducting business in each country featured. Entries include: Name, address, phone, fax, and URL. Principal content of publication is practical information about doing business in twelve countries in eastern Europe: Belarus, Croatia, the Czech Republic, Estonia, Hungary, Latvia, Lithuania, Poland, Slovakia, Slovenia, Turkey, and Ukraine.

Doing Business in Hong Kong: Your Guide to Establishing an Office. American Chamber of Commerce in Hong Kong. • Annual. $180 Nonmembers. Provides an overview of the various factors to consider when establishing a business in Hong Kong.

Doing Business with China. Kogan Page US. • Publication includes: List of helpful business contacts in China. Entries include: Name, address, phone, fax. Principal content of publication is extensive general and business information about China.

Dominican Republic--American Chamber of Commerce--Membership Directory. U.S. Chamber of Commerce. • Covers: American and Dominican Republic companies and individuals interested in the development of trade within and between the two countries. Entries include: For firms--Company name, address, phone, fax, telex, cable address, names and titles of key personnel, line of business, subsidiary and branch names and locations, locations of plants or branch offices, product/service information. For individuals--Name, title, affiliation, address.

Dublin Business. Dublin Chamber of Commerce. • Quarterly.

Dun & Bradstreet Guide to Hong Kong Businesses. Dun & Bradstreet Inc. • Annual. $380. Covers 20,000 companies in Hong Kong, including foreign-owned companies operating in Hong Kong.

Dutch Chamber of Commerce--Business Directory. Dutch Chamber of Commerce. • Annual. Covers: 480 individual members representing 180 companies in Hong Kong and mainland China.

The East-West Business Directory. Duncan Publishing. • Irregular. $65 plus $3.50 shipping. Covers: Approximately 863 companies that have central and eastern European capital participation, located in over 20 European and North American countries, Australia, and Japan. Database includes: Lists (with addrs.) of official Eastern bloc trade missions and commercial, shipping, banking, airline, and tourist offices in the OECD countries, and an overview of investment activities of Soviet and eastern European state ent. Entries include: Company name, address, phone, telex, name and title of principal executive, number of employees, financial information, ownership structure, statistical data, products or services.

Economic World Directory of Japanese Companies in the U.S.A. Economic Salon Ltd. • Biennial. $300. Covers: about 850 companies in the United States that are subsidiaries, divisions, etc., of Japanese parent firms. Entries include: United States company name, address, phone; branch facilities, addresses, and phone numbers; financial data, type of business, names of executives, number of Japanese and United States employees, history, current company information, and similar but less extensive data on parent company.

El Salvador--American Chamber of Commerce--Membership Directory. U.S. Chamber of Commerce. • Annual. $100 Nonmembers for investment. Covers: Companies in the U.S. and El Salvador and individuals interested in the development of trade, labor law, investment regulations, economic trends, and foreign policy within and between the two countries. Entries include: For firms--Company, name, address, phone, fax, telex, cable address, names and titles of key personnel, line of business, subsidiary and branch names and locations, locations of plants or branch offices, product/ service information. For individuals--Name, title, affiliation, address.

Encyclopedia of Chinese-Foreign Joint Ventures, Contractual Joint Ventures, Foreign-Funded Enterprises. Jinghua Publishing House. • $300. Covers: Approximately 30,000 Chinese-foreign joint ventures, contractual joint ventures, and foreign-funded enterprises. Database includes: An introduction to China's laws, regulations, and rules related to Chinese-foreign joint ventures, contractual joint ventures, and foreign-funded enterprises. Entries include: Contact information.

The European Association for Business Research. European Association for Business Research, Planning, and Development in the Chemical Industry. • Annual. Includes memebers of the European Association for Business Research.

European International Business Academy--Membership Directory. European International Business Academy. • Covers: 300 individuals involved in international business.

Forbes--The Forbes International 500 Issue. Forbes Inc. • Annual. Publication includes: 500 largest foreign corporations, 50 largest corporations in the world. Entries include: For foreign companies--Company name, revenue, net income, assets, market value of common stock, location of corporate headquarters, number of employees.

Foreign Companies in Asia Yearbook. Business Monitor International Ltd. • $5,445 Individuals 40% discount. Covers: 49,270 senior executive contacts on 16,775 foreign company subsidiaries across 32 industry sectors in Asia. Entries include: full company name, address, phone and fax numbers, email and web addresses, and key contact names and titles.

Foreign Subsidiaries in Michigan. Global Business Development. • Irregular. Covers: over 930 Michigan subsidiaries of companies from outside the U.S. Entries include: Subsidiary company name, address; parent company name, address; product/service, type of establishment in Michigan.

French Companies and their Partners Abroad. DAFSA. • Annual. Covers: 80,000 French companies in France and abroad. Entries include: Company name, address, phone, ownership connections, subsidiaries, ownership percentages.

German Business CD-ROM. Datamedia GmbH. • Description: CD-ROM. Database covers: approximately 1.8 businesses in Germany. Entries include: Company name, address, phone, fax, classification information.

German Chamber of Commerce in China--Membership Directory. German Industry & Commerce Company Ltd. • 1,200 ¥ Nonmembers. Number of listings: 1,800. Entries include: Company name, address, e-mail, phone, and fax numbers.

Global Business Associations. International Business Publications, USA. • Covers: Approximately 1,000 largest business associations in over 100 countries.

Global Business Contacts Directory. International Business Publications, USA. • $99.95 Individuals. Covers: Major business and government contacts in over 100 countries.

Global Offshore Business and Investment Contacts Handbook. International Business Publications, USA. • Annual. $99.95. Covers: Business and investment contacts in 33 offshore countries and territories. Entries include: Contact details.

Global Offshore Business Laws and Regulations Handbook. International Business Publications, USA. • Annual. $99.95. Covers: Business laws and regulations for conducting business in 33 offshore countries and territories.

Global Offshore Investment and Business Guide. International Business Publications, USA. • $99.95 Individuals paperback. Comprehensive guide for conducting offshore business.

Global Offshore Tax Guide. International Business Publications, USA. • Annual. $99.95. Covers: Tax regulations guidelines for 33 offshore countries and territories.

Hawaii Business Abroad. Hawaii Department of Business, Economic Development, and Tourism Research and Economic Analysis Division. • Irregular. Covers: approximately 400 Hawaiian firms that export, import, maintain overseas offices, or have business activities in foreign countries. Entries include: Company name, address, phone, fax, telex, name of contact, cable address, line of business, year established, number of employees, locations of overseas offices, description of overseas activities, parent company name and address (if any), names of countries with which business is done.

Hoover's Handbook of World Business. Dun & Bradstreet Inc. Hoover's Inc. • Annual. $225 Individuals Hardcover. Covers: Hundreds of companies headquartered outside the U.S., including many with substantial activity in the U.S.; global enterprises, businesses that dominate their respective industries, and representative companies from all major industries. Entries include: Company name, overview, history, exchange and stock symbols, fiscal year-end date, names and titles of key personnel, name of auditors, number of employees, headquarters address, phone, fax, description of where the company does business, specific products/services/brand names produced, key competitors, 10 years of key financial data.

Houston International Business Directory. Houston Chamber of Commerce. • Annual. $20 Individuals MBS. Covers: More than 3,300 U.S. and foreign companies involved in international business activities in Houston, Texas. Entries include: Company name, address, phone, principal executives, type of business, imports/exports.

Indo-German Business Directory. Indo-German Chamber of Commerce. • Rs 1,500 for nonmembers. Includes profiles of more than 6500 members of the Indo-German Chamber of Commerce.

Indonesia Yellow Pages Business Directory. Faust Information GmbH. • Contains comprehensive business and directory information on companies in Indonesia. Includes information on more than 470,000 companies in 3000 industries and classifications. Provides data such as company name, mailing address, phone and fax numbers, e-mail address, web site address, names of contact persons, and more. Where available, includes information on product lines, services offered, and number of employees, plus financial data, brand names, company location, company background, and more. Includes keyword search functions. Allows export of data for use in spreadsheets, mailing programs, and other applications.

Initiative Europe. ICC Online Services Div. ICC Information Group Ltd. • Monthly. Covers: Small- and medium-sized businesses in Europe seeking international joint venture, partnership, and licensing agreements.

Intercompany Relations on Charts. Hoppenstedt Produktinformationen GmbH. • Shows in chart form the economic and financial relations between 700 parent companies from all over the world and their 90,000 subsidiaries.

International Business and Trade Directories. Grey House Publishing. • $225 Individuals softcover. Covers: Approximately 8,000 directories concerned with international business and trade. Entries include: Directory title, publisher name, address, phone, fax, description of directory, ISBN, size, price, frequency, editor, U.S. Distributor.

International Business in South Africa. Investor Responsibility Research Center Institute. • Annual. $500. Covers: about 600 non-U.S. companies with business links to South Africa. Database includes: Lists of companies that do business in South Africa but do not own any assets there; companies with "non equity" links to South Africa. Entries include: Name and address of parent company, line of business, names and locations of South African subsidiaries, number of employees, policies. Companies based in the United States are listed in "U.S. Business in South Africa" (see separate entry). Updated monthly for "South Africa Review Service" subscribers.

International Business Information on the Web: Searcher Magazine's Guide to Sites and Strategies for Global Business Research. Information Today, Inc. • $29.95. Lists directories, search engines, banks, financial institutions, news sources, government contacts, chambers of commerce, and other country-specific information. Covers: Approximately 1,000 Web sites related to international business research including general business sites in the United States and worldwide. Publication includes: URLs. Entries include: Information regarding each site.

International Business Opportunities Database. NIIR Project Consultancy Services. • $100 Individuals CD-ROM. Covers: 180,000+ global importers, exporters, agents, representatives, business opportunity seekers, various trade opportunities. Entries include: Company name, address, phone and fax, email, and websites.

International Business Practices Guide. University of Missouri, St. Louis.

International Dallas. Dallas Regional Chamber. • Annual. $20 Members. Covers: Listings of over 1,500 international businesses in the Dallas/Ft. Worth area, including importers, exporters, foreign-owned companies, plus trade statistics and a guide to exporting. Entries include: Company name, address, phone, fax; description; product codes; local executives; parent company.

Internet Resources and Services for International Business: A Global Guide. Greenwood Electronic Media. • $82.95 Single issue Paperback. Covers: More than 2,500 business-related Web sites, most of which are government and university sites, international. Entries include: Web site, content.

J W Business International: International Business Communications Directory. Telex-Verlag Jaeger + Waldmann GmbH. • Annual. $210. Covers: Approximately 2,000,000 companies on fax and telex worldwide in all trades and industries classified by products and services within 43 main groups. Entries include: Company name, address, fax and telex numbers; subsidiary and branch names and locations.

J W Communications CD International and J W Business CD International. Telex-Verlag Jaeger + Waldmann GmbH. • Annual. $440. Covers: Six million companies worldwide. Entries include: Company name and address, communications data, and products and services code. Country database includes dialing codes, products and services, and trade classification in four languages.

Japanese-Affiliated Companies in U.S.A. and Canada. Japan External Trade Organization. • Biennial. Covers: 9,870 Japanese firms, restaurants, and various information sources. Database includes: Area maps. Entries include: Company name, address, phone, fax, line of business, parent company, executive officers, year established.

Japanese Business in Britain. Culver Financial Surveys. • Annual. $100 2000 edition. Covers: Approximately 550 Japanese-owned, United Kingdom-registered limited companies. Entries include: Company name, address, names and titles of key personnel, number of employees, financial data, subsidiary and branch names and locations, description, ownership information, sales and profits data.

Joint Venture Directory of the New Independent States. Triumph Books Inc. • $295 payment must accompany order. Covers: about 2,650 firms in the Commonwealth of Independent States that are joint ventures between CIS companies and foreign firms. Entries include: Company name, address, phone, fax, telex, name and title of contact, product or service, names of domestic and foreign partners, capitalization, number of employees, date registered, objectives.

Joint Venture Partner Search Directory. Michigan Department of Agriculture. • Irregular. $15. Covers: more than 200 Michigan companies interested in forming international partnerships. Entries include: Company name, address, phone, Standard Industrial Classification (SIC) code, annual sales (if available), number of employees, geographical areas in which interested in conducting business.

Latvia Business Services Providers Leads. Business Information Agency Inc. PlanetInform. • Monthly. $67 Individuals mailing list. Covers Latvian companies and all sub-industries that provide various services to commercial businesses, establishments, and organizations, including consulting, advertising and marketing services, and facilities maintenance.

Lesotho Business Directory. A.C. Braby (Pty) Ltd. • Annual. Covers industrial, commercial, and service firms; trade unions; employers' organizations; societies and institutions in Lesotho.

Major Companies of Europe. Cengage Learning Inc. • Annual. $2,980 set. Published by Graham & Whiteside. Approximately 44,640 major companies and key executives in European countries in all lines of business.

Major Companies of Latin America and the Caribbean. Cengage Learning Inc. • $1,275. Includes more than 8,650 major companies in Latin America and more than 1,100 leading Caribbean firms.

Mergent International Manual and News Reports. Mergent Inc. • Financial and other information about 13,000 companies in 100 countries. Formerly *Moody's International Manual and News Reports*.

The Middle Management of German Business. Hoppenstedt Produktinformationen GmbH. • Annual. $240. Covers 60,000 middle managers at 25,000 major German companies.

MZM World Business Directory. MZM Publications Publishing Promotion Co. • Irregular. $154 plus airmail. Covers: companies in 33 post-socialist countries involved in international trade and business: Albania, Armenia, Azerbaijan, Bosnia & Herzegovina, Bulgaria, Belorus, China, Croatia, Cuba, Czech Republic, Slovakia, Estonia, Georgia, former East Germany, Hungary, Kazakhstan, Kirghizia, Latvia, Lithuania, North Korea, Macedonia, Moldova, Mongolia, Poland, Romania, Russia, Kaliningrad Province of Russia, Slovenia, Tadzhikistan, Turkmenistan, Ukraine, Uzbekistan, Vietnam, and Yugoslavia. Entries include: Company name, address, phone, fax, telex, number of employees, year established, subsidiary companies, description.

Nations of the World: A Political, Economic and Business Handbook. Grey House Publishing. • Annual. $180 Individuals softcover. Covers: Political, economic and business information for 231 nations and self-governing territories around the world. Database includes: Five regional chapters. Entries include: Key facts, political and economic issues, country profile, business information, maps, demographics, GDP figures, climate, chambers of commerce, media, travel information, and contact information for government offices.

New Zealand Trade Directory. Current Pacific Ltd. • Annual. $120 Individuals. Covers: More than 6,000 firms in New Zealand, including manufacturers, exporters, importers, distributors, food processors, banks and financial firms, tourism services, professional firms, trade promotion organizations, central and local governments, public libraries, tertiary and secondary education institutions, foreign government representations.

North American Companies Manufacturing in Scotland. Scottish Enterprise. • Covers: about 200 North American-owned companies in Scotland. Entries include: Company name, address, phone, telex, name and title of contact, number of employees, description of services.

Norway Business Services Providers Leads. Business Information Agency Inc. PlanetInform. • Monthly. $134 Individuals mailing list. Covers Norway's companies and all sub-industries that provide various services to commercial businesses, establishments, and organizations, including consulting, advertising and marketing services, and facilities maintenance.

Overseas and European Companies Manufacturing in Scotland. Scottish Enterprise. • Covers: over 130 foreign owned companies, excluding North American owned, located in Scotland. Entries include: Company name, address, phone, telex, name and title of contact, number of employees, geographical area covered, description of services.

Overseas Companies in Ireland. Industrial Development Agency of Ireland. • Updated continuously; printed on request. Computer printout. About 1,000 overseas manufacturers and international service companies with operations in Ireland. Entries include: Name and address of parent company; name, address, phone of Irish filial company, description of product or service specialty.

Probe Directory of Foreign Direct Investment in the United States. Probe International. • Triennial. $250. Covers: over 1,500 affiliate firms in the United States which are partially or totally owned by over 800 Japanese companies. Entries include: For U.S. companies--Company name, address, phone, subsidiary names, name of executive officer, foreign investor's name, line of business/product. For foreign investors--Company name, address, names of U.S. affiliates.

South-Central American International Business Directory of Importers. Coble International. • $285 print or CD-ROM. Covers: 23,000 importers from the West Indies, Nicaragua, Mexico, Honduras, Guyana, El Salvador, Uruguay, Paraguay, Brazil, Guatemala, Belize, Colombia, Costa Rica, Puerto Rico, Dominican Republic, Chile, Haiti, Bahamas, Jamaica, Panama, Peru, Bolivia, Ecuador, Venezuela and Argentina. Entries include: Name, address, phone, fax, primary contact person, list of products, e-mail addresses, and Web site.

Spanish-American Commercial Directory. IBAR. • Triennial. $60. Covers: More than 350,000 businesses in Spain, Portugal, and Latin-American countries, as well as companies in African, Asia, Australia, Canada, and Europe interested in conducting business with Latin-American countries. Entries include: Company name, address, phone.

Subsidiaries of German Firms in the U.S. German American Chamber of Commerce. • Annual. $100 Members. Covers: Over 3,500 German firms and subsidiaries in the U.S. Entries include: Name, address, phone, and telex of American firm; name and address of German parent company; percentage of German participation; number of employees; type of company (manufacturer, sales agent, etc.); and products.

Swedish Chamber of Commerce--Trade Directory. Swedish Chamber of Commerce. • Annual. Covers: 400 member companies representing Swedish, British and European companies.

Swedish Related Companies in the United States. Swedish-American Chamber of Commerce. • Annual. $24.90 Members. Covers: Swedish-related companies in the U.S. and their parent companies: lists more than 700 companies in the US; chambers of commerce, trade offices, embassies and consulates, information offices, and tourist offices. Entries include: Name of parent company, address, phone, telex, fax, name of United States subsidiary, address, phone, name and title of key executive, products.

Taiwan Business Directory. China Credit Information Service Ltd. • Annual. $160 Individuals. Covers 30,000 manufacturing, service, and trading companies in Taiwan.

Textile Month. Reed Business Information. • Biennial. $4. Covers: United Kingdom companies representing overseas manufacturers of textile machinery. Entries include: Company name, address, phone, telex, key personnel, overseas contacts, types of machinery handled.

The Thunderbird Guide to International Business Resources on the World Wide Web. Wiley Publishing Group. • $57.95 Individuals Paperback. Covers: Web sites for political and economic developments that affect trade worldwide. Derived from a study by Dean's Global Information and Technology at Thunderbird (American Graduate School of International Management). Entries include: country, category (country information, business, business topics, government resources, information providers), title, URL, and description.

Transnational Corporations and Labor: A Directory of Resources. WorldViews. • $12.95 plus $2.00 shipping. Covers: sources for books, periodicals, pamphlets, audiovisuals, and other educational resources on transnational corporations and labor issues; names of resources with annotations and ordering information. Entries include: Organization name, address, phone, titles of print and audio/visual material. Part of a 10 volume series (updated in "Third World Resources"), each volume covering single region or issue.

Trinidad & Tobago--American Chamber of Commerce--Membership Directory. U.S. Chamber of Commerce. • Annual. $80 Individuals. Covers: Companies in the U.S. and Trinidad and Tobago and individuals interested in the development of trade within and between the two countries. Entries include: For firms--Company name, address, phone, fax, telex, cable address, names and titles of key personnel, line of business, subsidiary and branch names and locations, locations of plants or branch offices, product/service information. For individuals--Name, title, affiliation, address.

Turnkey Offers from India. EEPC India. • Biennial. Covers: Companies in India involved in international projects.

U.S.-China Business Services Directory. U.S.-China Business Council. • Irregular. $35. Covers: more than 900 companies in the U. S., Hong Kong, and China providing business services to China, such as consulting firms, architectural and construction engineering firms, freight forwarding companies, and law firms. Entries include: Company name, address, phone, telex, name and title of contact, subsidiary and branch names and locations, description of products or services.

U.S. Income Tax Treaties with Foreign Countries Handbook. International Business Publications, USA. • $99.95 Individuals hardcopy, E-book and CD-ROM. Covers: US income tax treaties with Australia, Austria, Barbados, Belgium, Canada, China, Cyprus, Czech Republic, Denmark, Denmark, Egypt, Estonia, and Finland.

U.S. Investments in Germany: A Listing of American Subsidiaries in Germany. American Chamber of Commerce in Germany. • €150 Individuals print. Covers: Approximately 3,000 German subsidiaries of U.S. Firms. Entries include: Company address, management details, and SIC code.

U.S. List. American Chamber of Commerce in Austria. • Biennial. €80 Members. Covers: About 360 U.S. subsidiaries and affiliated companies located in Austria. Entries include: U.S. Parent company name and address, Austrian subsidiary or affiliated company name, address, phone, fax, managing director, line of business, e-mail, Internet-homepage address, kind of relationship.

Wansbeck Business Directory. Wansbeck Business Forum. • Covers businesses within Wansbeck Area in United Kingdom.

Who Owns Whom. Dun & Bradstreet Inc. • Annual. Covers: In four regional volumes, approximately 320,000 company affiliates and subsidiaries of more than 23,000 companies in Australia and the Far East, North America, the United Kingdom and Ireland, and Continental Europe. Entries include: Ultimate parent and country, parent name, address, phone, place of incorporation, Standard Industrial Classification (SIC) code, trade investments, direct subsidiaries.

Who's Who in International Business Education and Research. Edward Elgar Publishing Inc. • $256.50 Individuals hardbound. Covers: 150 individuals in international business education and research. Entries include: Biographical data and professional data, career summary, URL.

Who's Who of Colombian-American Business. Colombian-American Chamber of Commerce - Bogota. • Annual. $75. Covers industrial, commercial, financial, tourist, and other service companies in Bogota, Cali, Cartagena, and Medellin.

WISE International Business Directory. World Institute of Scientology Enterprises. • Covers: Business people who use L. Ron Hubbard management technology. Entries include: Contact information.

E-BOOKS

Business and Technology in China. Cengage Learning Inc. • 2011. eBook. Explores the inner workings of China's business world, highlighting the country's attempts to develop the scientific and technological base for a greener economic model.

Business Information Handbook. David Mort. Cengage Learning Inc. • 2005. Published by K.G. Saur. Serves as a general guide to the world of business information. Inquire as to price and availability.

Cases on Business and Management in the MENA Region: New Trends and Opportunities. Cengage Learning Inc. • 2012. eBook. Presents a blend of conceptual, theoretical and applied research in regard to the relationship between the Middle East and North Africa region and business and management.

Global Business: Concepts. Cengage Learning Inc. • 2013. eBook. Published by IGI Global. Examines critical issues and emerging trends in global business, with topics ranging from managing new information technology in global business operations to ethics and communication strategies.

Global Electronic Business Research: Opportunities and Directions. Cengage Learning Inc. • 2006. eBook. Published by Information Science Reference. Encourages researchers and professionals interested in SMEs (small to medium-sized enterprises) and e-commerce to address the next phase in this field. This book points to some of the impending issues concerning e-commerce in SMEs, and highlights the need to do something in order to bridge the existing divide between the two. Global Electronic Business Research raises the importance of addressing the e-commerce phenomenon in SMEs at a global level.

Global Information Society: Operating Information Systems in a Dynamic Global Business Environment. Cengage Learning Inc. • 2006. eBook. Published by Information Science Reference. Addresses the importance of information technology management and issues in operating information systems in the global dynamic business environment. This title offers a collection of new ideas, latest technology applications and experiences in global information systems development and operations.

Inside the Indian Business Mind: A Tactical Guide for Managers. Cengage Learning Inc. • Published by Praeger. This title can help Western business people enter the Indian market, make the best use of Indian labor and manufacturing facilities, and create and develop successful, long-term business relationships.

Knowledge Ecology in Global Business: Managing Intellectual Capital. Cengage Learning Inc. • Published by Information Science Reference. Provides ideas on how intellectual capital through emerging technologies can support business performance. Covers topics such as competitive strategy, human resource management, and organizational learning.

Southeast Asia's Chinese Businesses in an Era of Globalization. Cengage Learning Inc. • 2009. eBook. Published by Institute of Southeast Asian Studies. Addresses the rise of China and its impacts on Southeast Asia's economies and businesses, especially on those of ethnic Chinese.

ENCYCLOPEDIAS AND DICTIONARIES

Encyclopedia of Emerging Markets. Cengage Learning Inc. • Covers emerging markets and industry profiles in 33 nations worldwide. Available in print ($549) and eBook. Published June 2013.

Major Companies of Africa South of the Sahara. Cengage Learning Inc. • Annual. $980 Individuals. More than 2,150 major companies in South Africa are covered, plus 4,250 businesses in non-Arab countries south of the Sahara.

FINANCIAL RATIOS

Brookers Sale and Purchase of a Business Precedents. Thomson Reuters New Zealand Legal, Tax and Accounting Unit. • Contains a collection of documents and precedents needed to guide solicitors through the sale or purchase of a business in New Zealand.

GENERAL WORKS

African Business. IC Publications Ltd. • Monthly. £40 Individuals U.K.. Business publication.

African Journal of Business and Economic Research. Adonis & Abbey Publishers Ltd. • £200 Institutions print. Peer-reviewed journal covering theoretical and empirical research of business and economy of Africa.

Asian Business & Management. Palgrave Macmillan. • 5/year. $1,092 Institutions print. Peer-reviewed journal covering the field of business and management.

Asian Business Intelligence. Asian Business Intelligence Ltd. • Continuous. Covers information on market size, future growth, competitors, distribution channels, price points, and potential distributors.

Biz 2000: L&H Comprehensive Business Dictionary. Gyldendals Red Dictionaries. • Contains a detailed dictionary of business terms in Danish, English, and German. Available in four versions: Danish to English, English to Danish, Danish to German, and German to Danish.

Business Eastern Europe. The Economist Intelligence Unit. • Provides news on political, economic, and legal developments throughout the region, including business and e-business news: regulatory changes; distribution, human resources, market-entry strategies and regulatory development issues; economic and political risk analysis; company case studies; business intelligence.

Business Eastern Europe. Treasury & Risk. • Quarterly. $1,530 Individuals. Professional magazine covering business information in Eastern Europe.

Business Guide to Trinidad & Tobago. American Chamber of Commerce of Trinidad and Tobago. • Biennial. $50. Contains market entry information for foreign companies doing business in Trinidad and Tobago.

Business II. ITHAKA JSTOR, the Journal Storage Project. • Contains more than 1.3 million pages from 60 titles in the fields of international business as well as the intersections between economics and law, policy, and psychology.

Business India Intelligence. The Economist Intelligence Unit. • Provides news on political, economic, and legal developments throughout the region, including business and e-business news: regulatory changes; distribution, human resources, market-entry strategies and regulatory development issues; economic and political risk analysis; company case studies; business intelligence.

Business Lanka. Sri Lanka Export Development Board Trade Information Service. • Quarterly. $320. Provides information on Sri Lankan exports and products for business people.

Business Middle East. The Economist Intelligence Unit. • Provides news on political, economic, and legal developments throughout the region, including business and e-business news; regulatory changes; distribution, human resources, market-entry strategies and regulatory development issues; economic and political risk analysis; company case studies; business intelligence.

Business Pulse. Chamber of Commerce and Industry of Western Australia. • Monthly. Journal containing information about business, employee relations, and international trade.

Business Russia. The Economist Intelligence Unit. • Provides news on political, economic, and legal developments throughout the region, including business and e-business news: regulatory changes; distribution, human resources, market-entry strategies and regulatory development issues; political and economic risk analysis; company case studies; business intelligence.

Center for International Business and Public Policy Articles. Johns Hopkins University Center for International Business and Public Policy.

China Business Database. The Data Supplier. • Contains contact information for more than 500,000 manufacturers in China. Covers approximately 50,000 manufacturers in the automobile, motor, and machinery industry; 55,000 in the shoes, watch, bags, toys, and sports industry; 70,000 in the textiles, clothing, fabrics, garments, and fashion industry; 55,000 in the electrical, electronics, computers, and digital entertainment industry; 75,000 in the furniture, appliance, arts, jewelry, stationery, and crafts industry; and 90,000 in the chemicals, plastics, ceramics, metals, petroleum, and leather industry. Includes business name and full contact information.

European Legal Business. Legalese Ltd. • Bimonthly. $195 Individuals. Journal covering the European legal market.

France Business Database. The Data Supplier. • Contains contact information for more than 136,000 companies in France. Includes business name, full contact information, e-mail addresses, and Web site.

Germany Business Database. The Data Supplier. • Contains contact information for more than 136,000 companies in Germany. Includes business name, full contact information, e-mail addresses, Web site, and contacts.

ie: The Business of International Events. International Festivals and Events Association. • Quarterly. $50 for nonmembers. Includes industry updates, trends and issues.

India Business Database. The Data Supplier. • Contains contact information for more than 256,000 manufacturers in India. Includes business name, full contact information, e-mail addresses, and Web site.

Indonesia Business Database. The Data Supplier. • Contains contact information for more than 230,537 companies in Indonesia. Includes business name, full contact information, e-mail addresses, Web site.

International Business. Chamber of Commerce and Industry Queensland. • A$55.45. Contains guidelines to become a successful international business.

International Business Review. Elsevier. • $1,692 Institutions print. Journal describing the latest developments and advances in knowledge and practice of international business.

International Journal of Indian Culture and Business Management (IJICBM). Inderscience Publishers. • 8/year. €735 Individuals print or online only for 1 user. Journal covering field of new developments in Indian culture and their implications on business.

Introduction to the Kuwaiti Economy and Major Business Laws and Regulations. Kuwait Chamber of Commerce and Industry.

Italy Business Database. The Data Supplier. • Contains contact information for more than 80,000 companies in Italy. Includes business name, full contact information, e-mail addresses, Web site, and contacts.

Journal of International Business and Cultural Studies (JIBCS). Academic and Business Research Institute. • Journal containing manuscripts related to international business and cultural relations issues.

Journal of Translational Business Institution Management. IBIMA Publishing. • Peer-reviewed journal covering the management of transnational business institutions.

Legal Business. Legalese Ltd. • 10/year. £495 Individuals. Journal covering commercial law in Europe.

MENA Journal of Business Case Studies. IBIMA Publishing. • Peer-reviewed journal publishing information on business and corporate activities in the Middle East and North Africa region.

Mexico Business Journal. Gulf Breeze Publishing Co. • Weekly. Publication providing news and information on doing business in Mexico.

Proff, the Business Finder. Eniro Danmark A/S. • Contains a directory for Denmark's business-to-business trade.

Russia Business Services Providers Leads. Business Information Agency Inc. PlanetInform. • Monthly. $101 Individuals mailing list. Covers Russian companies and all sub-industries that provide various services to commercial businesses, establishments, and organizations, including consulting, advertising and marketing services, and facilities maintenance.

Slovenia Business Services Providers Leads. Business Information Agency Inc. PlanetInform. • Monthly. $84 Individuals mailing list. Covers Slovenian companies and all sub-industries that provide various services to commercial businesses, establishments, and organizations, including consulting, advertising and marketing services, and facilities maintenance.

South Asian Journal of Global Business Research. Emerald Group Publishing Ltd. • Peer-reviewed journal publishing articles on business and management issues facing multinational and local organizations within South Asia.

Spain Business Services Providers Leads. Business Information Agency Inc. PlanetInform. • Monthly. $230 Individuals mailing list. Covers Spanish companies and all sub-industries that provide various services to commercial businesses, establishments, and organizations, including consulting, advertising and marketing services, and facilities maintenance.

Sweden Business Services Providers Leads. Business Information Agency Inc. PlanetInform. • Monthly. $220 Individuals mailing list. Covers Swedish companies and all sub-industries that provide various services to commercial businesses, establishments, and organizations, including consulting, advertising and marketing services, and facilities maintenance.

Switzerland Business Services Providers Leads. Business Information Agency Inc. PlanetInform. • Monthly. $219 Individuals mailing list. Covers Swiss companies and all sub-industries that provide various services to commercial businesses, establishments, and organizations, including consulting, advertising and marketing services, and facilities maintenance.

U.S. Japan Business News. U.S. Japan Business News. • Weekly. $78 Individuals. Japanese language business newspaper.

Vietnam Business. Vietnam Trade Information Center Ministry of Trade. • Semimonthly. $15,000. Provides information for foreign traders and investors.

Who's Who in International Business Education and Research. Edward Elgar Publishing Inc. • $256.50 Individuals hardbound. Covers: 150 individuals in international business education and research. Entries include: Biographical data and professional data, career summary, URL.

Worldwide Business Collaborations--Consultants News and Business Opportunities. International Press Cutting Service. • Weekly. $715. Publication spotlighting international business opportunities and openings.

HANDBOOKS AND MANUALS

Guide to Doing Business in Egypt. American Chamber of Commerce in Egypt.

INTERNET DATABASES

Ebusiness Forum: Global Business Intelligence for the Digital Age. Economist Intelligence Unit (EIU), Economist Group. Phone: 800-938-4685 or (212)554-0600; Fax: (212)586-0248; Email: newyork@eiu.com • URL: http://www.ebusinessforum.com • Web site provides information relating to multinational business, with an emphasis on activities in specific countries. Includes rankings of countries for "e-business readiness," additional data on the political, economic, and business environment in 180 nations ("Doing Business in" and "Today's News Analysis.") Fees: Free, but registration is required for access to all content. Daily updates.

European Business Register (EBR). Patent- och Registreringsverket PRV InterPat. PO Box 5055, SE-102 42 Stockholm, Sweden. Phone: 46 8 782 25 00 or 46 8 782 2500; Fax: 46 8 666 02 86 or 46 8 666 0286; Email: prv.patent@prv.se • URL: http://www.prv.se • Provides online access to official company information from several European countries. The database contains company directory details, board of directors listings, company profiles, and other information.

Factiva. Dow Jones Reuters Business Interactive, LLC. Phone: 800-369-7466 or (609)452-1511; Fax: (609)520-5770; Email: solutions@factiva.com • URL: http://www.factiva.com • Fee-based Web site provides "global news and business information through Web sites and content integration solutions." Includes Dow Jones and Reuters newswires, The Wall Street Journal, and more than 7,000 other sources of current news, historical articles, market research reports, and investment analysis. Content includes 96 major U. S. newspapers, 900 non-English sources, trade publications, media transcripts, country profiles, news photos, etc.

FedWorld: A Program of the United States Department of Commerce. National Technical Information Service. Phone: 800-553-NTIS or (703)605-6000; Fax: (703)605-6900; Email: webmaster@fedworld.gov • URL: http://www.fedworld.gov • Web site offers "a comprehensive central access point for searching, locating, ordering, and acquiring government and business information." Emphasis is on searching the Web pages, databases, and government reports of a wide variety of federal agencies. Fees: Free.

Financial Times: Where Information Becomes Intelligence. FT Group. Phone: (800)628-8088 • URL: http://www.ft.com • Web site provides extensive data and information relating to international business and finance, with daily updates. Includes Markets Today, Company News, Economic Indicators, Equities, Currencies, Capital Markets, Euro Prices, etc. Fees: Free (registration required).

Nexis.com. Lexis-Nexis Group. Phone: 800-227-4908 or (937)865-6800; Fax: (937)865-6909; Email: webmaster@prod.lexis-nexis.com • URL: http://www.nexis.com • Fee-based Web site offers searching of about 2.8 billion documents in some 30,000 news, business, and legal information sources. Features include a subject directory covering 1,200 topics in 34 categories and a Company Dossier containing information on more than 500,000 public and private companies. Boolean searching is offered.

Trade Show Center. Global Sources/Trade Media Holdings Ltd. Phone: (656)574-2800; Email: service@globalsources.com • URL: http://www.globalsources.com/TRADESHW/TRDSHFRM.HTM • Free Web site provides current, detailed information on more than 1,000 major trade shows worldwide, including events in the U. S., but with an emphasis on "Asia and Greater China." Searching is offered by product, supplier, country, and month of year. Includes links to "Trade Information.".

Wall Street Journal Interactive Edition. Dow Jones & Co., Inc. 1211 Avenue of the Americas, New York, NY 10036. Phone: 800-369-5663; Email: service@dowjones.com • URL: http://new.dowjones.com • Fee-based Web site providing online searching of worldwide information from *The Wall Street Journal.* Includes "Company Snapshots," "The Journal's Greatest Hits," "Index to Market Data," "Journal Links," etc. Financial price quotes are available. Fees: $49.00 per year; $29.00 per year to print subscribers.

ONLINE DATABASES

Business Browser Asia Pacific. OneSource Information Services Inc. • Provides integrated industry information on thousands of public and private companies from countries in Asia and the Pacific Rim region.

Country Report Services. The PRS Group Inc. • Provides full text of reports describing the business risks and opportunities currently existing in more than 150 countries of the world. Contains a wide variety of statistics and forecasts relating to economics political and social conditions. Also includes demographics, tax, and currency information. Updated monthly. Inquire as to online cost and availability.

Database of the Central Archives for Finnish Business Records. Central Archives for Finnish Business Records. • Contains information about materials held at the Central Archives for Finnish Business Records, at various public institutes, and in the libraries of about 200 companies. Includes documents, drawings, photographs, and maps.

Gale Business Insights: Global. Cengage Learning Inc. • Contains broad yet detailed coverage of international business. Includes case studies, full-text articles, and data sets coupled with authoritative references and tools for analysis. Features topic overviews, interactive rankings and statistics, company histories and market share data, global industry research reports, hundreds of economic and business indicators, case studies, and full-text articles from academic journals, business periodicals, newswires, and other media outlets.

OTHER SOURCES

Country Finance. The Economist Intelligence Unit. • Annual $425.00 per year. Discusses banking and financial conditions in each of 47 countries. Includes foreign exchange regulations, the currency outlook, sources of capital, financing techniques, and tax considerations.

Doing Business in Europe. Wolters Kluwer Law & Business CCH. • Biweekly. $970 Individuals. Loose leaf series on international trade.

Foreign Labor Trends. U. S. Government Printing Office. • Irregular (50 to 60 issues per year, each on an individual country). $95.00 per year. Prepared by various American Embassies. Issued by the Bureau of International Labor Affairs, U. S. Department of Labor. Covers labor developments in important foreign countries, including trends in wages, working conditions, labor supply, employment, and unemployment.

Foreign Tax and Trade Briefs. Matthew Bender and Company Inc. • Quarterly. $1,054 book. The latest tax and trade information for over 100 foreign countries.

International Business Planning: Law and Taxation. William P. Streng and Jeswald W. Salacuse. Matthew Bender and Company Inc. • $475 book. Three looseleaf volumes. Periodic supplementation.

International Country Risk Guide. The PRS Group Inc. • Monthly. $5,701 online/print/cd-rom subscription. Provides detailed analysis of a group of countries, covering financial risks, political trends, and economic developments. More than 140 countries are covered during the course of a year, with specific business risk point ratings assigned.

International Tax Planning Manual-Corporations. Wolters Kluwer Law & Business CCH. • Two looseleaf volumes. Periodic supplementation. Price on application. Tax strategies for doing business in 42 major countries.

Investing, Licensing, and Trading. The Economist Intelligence Unit. • Semiannual. $345.00 per year for each country. Key laws, rules, and licensing provisions are explained for each of 60 countries. Information is provided on political conditions, markets, price policies, foreign exchange practices, labor, and export-import.

PERIODICALS AND NEWSLETTERS

Acquisitions Monthly. Thomson Financial Inc. • Monthly. $790.00 per year. Published in London. Provides detailed information, commentary, and statistics on merger, acquisition, and buyout activity in Europe, the U.S., and Asia.

Arabian Business. The Information & Technology Publishing Company Ltd. • Weekly. English-language business magazine for the Middle East.

Argentina Business Forecast Report. Telecommunications Insight. • Quarterly. $1,195 Individuals Single User. Business forecast report for Argentina.

BC Business Magazine. Canada Wide Magazines & Communications Ltd. • Monthly. $24.95 Individuals 12 issues. Magazine covering business for consumers in British Columbia.

Brazil Business Forecast Report. Telecommunications Insight. • Quarterly. $1,195 Individuals Single user. Business forecast report for Brazil.

Bulletin of American Mideast Business. American Mideast Business Associates. • International business magazine.

Business Beijing. Asia Systems Media Corp. • Monthly. Chinese business magazine.

Business Edge. Business Edge, Inc. • Semimonthly. $96 Individuals. Magazine covering Canada's local business scenes.

Business Ireland. Ashville Media Group. • Quarterly. Magazine featuring business in Ireland.

Business Pulse. Chamber of Commerce and Industry of Western Australia. • Monthly. Journal containing information about business, employee relations, and international trade.

Business Today Egypt. Egypt Today. • $100 Individuals Europe, US and Canada. Business magazine covering business in Egypt.

Business Week International: The World's Only International Newsweekly of Business. McGraw Hill Financial Inc. • Weekly. $95.00 per year.

Business Woman. Business Women's Committee of Armenia. • Periodic. Armenian and Russian language newspaper covering women in business.

BusinessWorld's Top 500 & the Next 500 Corporations in the Philippines. BusinessWorld Publishing Corp. • Annual. $300 postpaid. Covers 1,000 leading corporations in the Philippines selected on the basis of gross revenues.

Canadian Business. Canadian Business Media. • Biweekly. $20 per year. Edited for corporate managers and executives, this is a major periodical in Canada covering a variety of business, economic, and financial topics. Emphasis is on the top 500 Canadian corporations.

Chile Business Forecast Report. Telecommunications Insight. • Quarterly. $1,195 Individuals Single user. Business forecast report for Chile.

China-Britain Business Review. China-Britain Business Council. • Magazine featuring China-Britain trade and China economic news.

China Business. China Business Hong Kong. • English-language business magazine containing information involving domestic foreign trade companies, industrial-trading companies, power-enlarged enterprises, international hotels and commercial centers.

China Business Forecast Report. Telecommunications Insight. • Quarterly. $1,195 Individuals single user. Business forecast reports.

Colombia Business Forecast Report. Telecommunications Insight. • Quarterly. $1,195 Individuals Single user. Business forecast report for Colombia.

The Economist. The Economist Intelligence Unit. • 190 ₱ Individuals Print and Digital per week.

Egypt Business Forecast Report. Telecommunications Insight. • Quarterly. $1,195 Individuals Single user. Business forecast report for Egypt.

Energy Compass. Energy Intelligence Group. • Description: Focuses on worldwide geopolitical developments and their impact on the oil industry. Also includes marketing and trading information, political risk assessment, and current events and trends. **Remarks:** Available via fax, e-mail, or online.

Europe and Eurasia Business Committee Dispatch. Hungarian-U.S. Business Council. • Weekly. $350 /year for nonmembers. Provides information on regulations, legislation and specific industries for Central/Eastern Europe, New Independent States, Turkey and Iran.

European Business Journal. Whurr Publisher Ltd. • Quarterly. $195 Individuals. International business publication.

Export Today: The Global Business and Technology Magazine. Trade Communications Inc. • Monthly. $49.00 per year. Edited for corporate executives to provide practical information on international business and exporting.

German Business Scope. Representative of German Industry and Trade. • A biweekly online publication which describes politico-economic developments in Germany (and the European Union) from the perspective of German industry.

Global Business and Economics Review. Inderscience Enterprises Limited. • €520 Individuals print or online. Peer-reviewed journal focusing on the discussion and analysis of advanced concepts, initial treatments, and fundamental research in all fields of business and economics.

Gulf Business. Motivate Publishing. • Monthly. 15 Dh Individuals. Consumer magazine covering business in the Middle East and worldwide.

Hungary Business Forecast Report. Telecommunications Insight. • Quarterly. $1,195 Individuals Single user. Business forecast report for Hungary.

Iceland Business. Iceland Review. • Magazine covering business in Iceland.

Indonesia Business Forecast Report. Telecommunications Insight. • Quarterly. $1,195 Individuals Single user. Business forecasting reports for Indonesia.

International Market Alert. UCG Holdings L.P. • Description: Provides a fax service covering financial markets, world economy developments, foreign exchange, and U.S. interest rates.

Iran Business Forecast Report. Telecommunications Insight. • Quarterly. $1,195 Individuals Single user. Business forecast report for Iran.

Japan-U.S. Business Report. Japan Economic Institute. • Monthly. $185 /year. Provides updates on major sales and investment developments among U.S. and Japanese firms; arranged by industry groupings.

Journal of International Business Studies. Journal of International Business Studies. • Bimonthly. $498 Institutions print only, U.S.. Scholarly business journal, covering topics from e-commerce to foreign markets.

Malaysia Business Forecast Report. Telecommunications Insight. • Quarterly. $1,195 Individuals Single user. Business forecast reports for Malaysia.

Mexico Business Forecast Report. Telecommunications Insight. • Quarterly. $1,195 Individuals Single user. Business forecast report for Mexico.

Peru Business Forecast Report. Telecommunications Insight. • Quarterly. $1,195 Individuals Single user. Business forecast report for Peru.

Philippines Business Forecast Report. Telecommunications Insight. • Quarterly. $1,195 Individuals Single user. Business forecasting reports for the Phillipines.

Poland Business Forecast Report. Telecommunications Insight. • Quarterly. $1,195 Individuals Single user. Business forecast report for Poland.

Political Risk Letter. The PRS Group Inc. • Monthly. Description: Offers concise political and economic forecasts for both 18 month and 5 year time spans. Provides country risk forecasts and analysis on 100 countries around the world and provides indepth coverage on 20 countries.

Russia Business Forecast Report. Telecommunications Insight. • Quarterly. $1,195 Individuals Single user. Business forecast report for Russia.

Russian Business Magazine. Vystavochno-Ekspertno-Marketingovaya i Zakupochnaya Programma: Luchshie Tovary i Uslugina Rynkakh Rossii. • Bimonthly. $95 U.S.. Magazine covering business in Russia.

Saudi Arabia Business Forecast Report. Telecommunications Insight. • Quarterly. $1,195 Individuals Single user. Business forecast report for Saudi Arabia.

South Africa Business Forecast Report. Telecommunications Insight. • Quarterly. $1,195 Individuals Single user. Business forecast report for South Africa.

Thailand Business Forecast Report. Telecommunications Insight. • Quarterly. $1,195 Individuals Single user. Business forecasting report for Thailand.

Turkey Business Forecast Report. Telecommunications Insight. • Quarterly. $1,195 Individuals Single user. Business forecast report for Turkey.

United Arab Emirates Business Forecast Report. Telecommunications Insight. • Quarterly. $1,195 Individuals Single user. Business forecast report for the United Arab Emirates.

Vietnam Business Forecast Report. Telecommunications Insight. • Quarterly. $1,195 Individuals Single user. Business forecast report for Vietnam.

RESEARCH CENTERS AND INSTITUTES

Asian Institute of Management Policy Center. Eugenio Lopez Foundation Bldg., 3rd Fl., 123 Paseo de Roxas, Makati City 1260, Philippines. Phone: 63 2 8924011; Fax: 63 2 4039498; Email: policycenter@aim.edu • URL: http://policy.aim.edu • Business competitiveness, especially involving globalization, technological advances, and economic opportunities.

George Washington University - Center for Latin American Issues. Duques Hall, Ste. 450, 2201 G St. NW, Washington, DC 20052. Phone: (202)994-5205; Fax: (202)994-5225; Email: clai@gwu.edu • URL: http://www.gwu.edu/clai • U.S.-Latin American relations, focusing on strengthening business-government relations throughout the region, resolving differences, identifying areas for expanded relations, and managing economic and business issues.

Grand Valley State University - Michigan Small Business and Technology Development Center. 1020-L William Seidman Center, 50 Front Ave. SW, Grand Rapids, MI 49504. Phone: (616)331-7480; Fax: (616)331-7485; Email: sbtdchq@gvsu.edu • URL: http://misbtdc.org • Manufacturing, financing, and international business information (particularly the export process) for small businesses. Resources for the export process includes determining and detailing international feasibility, foreign market entry plans, and responding to international inquiries. Foreign market information includes business etiquette and negotiating, country demographics, detailed tax information, financing sources, industry specific information, intellectual property rights, market contracts, rules and regulations, specific market information, and tariff reduction schedules.

Mack Center for Technological Innovation. University of Pennsylvania, 1050 Steinberg Hall-Dietrich Hall, 3620 Locust Walk, Philadelphia, PA 19104. Phone: (215)898-2104; Fax: (215)573-2129; Email: mackcenter@wharton.upenn.edu • URL: http://www.mackcenter.wharton.upenn.edu • Conducts research related to international business. Formerly Huntsman Center for Global Competition and Innovation.

University of Illinois at Urbana-Champaign - Bureau of Economic and Business Research. 430 Wohlers Hall, Office of Research, College of Business, 1206 S 6th St., Champaign, IL 61820. Phone: (217)333-2330; Fax: (217)333-7410; Email: lhuff@uiuc.edu • URL: http://business.illinois.edu/research • Economics and business, including studies in business expectations, health economics, forecasting and planning, innovation, entrepreneurship, consumer behavior, poverty problems, small business operations and problems, investment and growth, productivity, research methodology, organizational behavior, and international business and banking.

University of Maryland at College Park - Center for Global Business Education. 2410 Van Munching Hall, Robert H. Smith School of Business, College Park, MD 20742-1815. Phone: (301)405-0200; Fax: (301)314-9526; Email: lbarnard@rhsmith.umd.edu • URL: http://www.rhsmith.umd.edu/global • Global business and management.

University of Maryland at College Park - International Communications and Negotiations Simulations. 0145 Tydings Hall, Department of Government & Politics, College Park, MD 20742. Phone: (301)405-4172; Fax: (301)314-9301; Email: dfridl@umd.edu • URL: http://www.icons.umd.edu • Focuses on the critical connections between international issues and the perspectives that different cultures bring to negotiations. Also teaches cross cultural negotiation and develops international economic, environmental, and political scenarios/curriculum materials for university and high school students.

University of Toledo - International Business Institute. 2801 W Bancroft St., 2044 Stranahan Hall, Toledo, OH 43606-3328. Phone: 800-586-5336 or (419)530-2068; Fax: (419)530-2101; Email: thomas.sharkey@utoledo.edu • URL: http://www.utoledo.edu/business/ibi/index.html • International business, exporting, foreign direct investment, international marketing, and comparative management.

University of Wisconsin—Milwaukee - International Business Center. Sheldon B. Lubar School of Business, Milwaukee, WI 53201. Phone: (414)229-6260; Fax: (414)229-5999; Email: vkp@uwm.edu • URL: http://www4.uwm.edu/business/research/ibc.cfm • International business.

STATISTICS SOURCES

International Marketing Data and Statistics. Cengage Learning Inc. • 2013. $475.00. Published by Euromonitor International. Contains statistics on population, economic factors, energy, consumer expenditures, prices, and other items affecting marketing in 160 non-European countries of the world. Also available as eBook.

TRADE/PROFESSIONAL ASSOCIATIONS

Academy of International Business. Michigan State University, The Eli Broad College of Business, 645 N Shaw Ln., Rm. 7, East Lansing, MI 48824-1121. Phone: (517)432-1452; Fax: (517)432-1009; Email: aib@aib.msu.edu • URL: http://aib.msu.edu • Consists primarily of university professors, doctoral students, researchers, writers, consultants, executives, and policy setters in the international business/trade research and education fields. Facilitates information exchange among people in academia, business, and government and encourages research activities that advance the knowledge of international business operations and increase the available body of teaching materials. Compiles an inventory of collegiate courses in international business, a survey of research projects, and statistics.

Argentine Chinese Chamber of Production, Industry and Commerce. Viamonte 1145 7 A, C1053ABW Buenos Aires, Argentina. Phone: 54 11 43726133; Fax: 54 11 43726133; Email: argenchina@ciudad.com.ar • URL: http://www.argenchina.org/_en_index.asp • Promotes business trade between Argentina and China.

Association of European Businesses. Krasnoproletarskaya ul 16, Bldg. 3, entrance 8, 4th Fl., 127473 Moscow, Russia. Phone: 7 495 2342764; Fax: 7 495 2342807; Email: info@aebrus.ru • URL: http://www.aebrus.ru • Represents and promotes the interests of European companies conducting business in the Russian Federation.

Australian Business in Europe. c/o HWL Ebsworth Lawyers, 530 Collins St., Level 26, Melbourne, VIC VIC 3000, Australia. Phone: 61 3 86443616; Fax: 3 86154300 • URL: http://www.abie.com.au • Works to provide a forum for Australians working in Europe and for European business people associated with Australian industry and commerce.

Bahrain British Business Forum. PO Box 10051, Manama, Bahrain. Phone: 973 1781-3488; Fax: 973 1781-3489; Email: bbbforum@batelco.com.bh • URL: http://bbbforum.org • Seeks to complement and improve relations between the local British and Bahraini business communities. Demonstrates to the local business community the interest and commitment of British business in Bahrain. Acts as a forum for the exchange of information related to local business opportunities.

Bermuda Business Development Agency. Maxwell Roberts Bldg., 6th Fl., 1 Church St., Hamilton HM 11, Bermuda. Phone: (441)292-0632; Fax: (441)292-1797; Email: info@bermudabda.com • URL: http://bermudabda.com • Professionals and businesses. Promotes and supports high business standards among professionals in international business.

Binational Tourism Alliance. 143 Genesee St., Buffalo, NY 14203. Phone: 877-884-2736 or (716)856-6525; Fax: (716)856-6754; Email: arlene.white@btapartners.com • URL: http://www.btapartners.com • Promotes tourism products and services and supports tourism development in Canada and the United States. Seeks to improve business opportunities and growth potential of members. Provides industry research and information, training and professional development.

Business and Community Foundation. 1D, 1st Fl., Shahpur Jat, New Delhi 110049, Delhi, India. Phone: 91 11 3253-6392 • URL: http://www.bcfindia.org • Promotes awareness and practice of good corporate citizenship as a business operation; promotes businesses to become an integral part of the societal process whereby people have access and control over resources to make informed choices and decisions towards a more humane, compassionate and just society in India.

Camara de Comercio de la Republica de Cuba. Calle 21 esq. a Calle A, No. 661, Vedado, Havana, Cuba. Phone: 53 7 833-8040; Fax: 53 7 838-1324; Email: ccicuba@camara.com.cu • URL: http://www.camaracuba.cu • Represents trade, industry, finance, transport, insurance and all sectors of international businesses. Shapes policies and raises awareness of international business concerns. Fosters networking and cooperation among members.

Camara de Industria y Comercio Argentino-Alemana. Av. Corrientes 327, C1043AAD Buenos Aires, Argentina. Phone: 54 11 52194000; Fax: 54 11 52194001; Email: ahkargentina@ahkargentina.com.ar • URL: http://www.ahkargentina.com.ar/ • Represents German business in Argentina and promotes international trade between Argentina and Germany.

Camara Espanola de Comercio de la Republica Argentina. 863 Av. Belgrano, Piso 7, C1092AAI Buenos Aires, Argentina. Phone: 54 11 43355000; Fax: 54 11 43355022; Email: recepcion.cecra@cecra.com.ar • URL: http://www.cecra.com.ar • Represents Spanish-Argentine businesses in Buenos Aires.

Canada-Arab Business Council. 1 Rideau St., Ste. 700, Ottawa, ON, Canada K1N 8S7. Phone: (613)670-5853 • URL: http://canada-arabbusiness.org • Canadian business organizations interested in Middle East markets. Promotes business and trade between Canada and the Arab world; serves as a business advisory body to governments in Canada on matters relating to Canadian trade with the region; promotes awareness of Canada's business and commercial capabilities; seeks to advance Canada to the Region; assists members in trade and investment activities in each country in the Middle East.

Canada-China Business Council. 330 Bay St., Ste. 1501, Toronto, ON, Canada M5H 2S8. Phone: (416)954-3800; Fax: (416)954-3806; Email: ccbc@ccbc.com • URL: http://www.ccbc.com • Promotes trade and investment between Canada and the People's Republic of China; seeks to stimulate trade in goods and services, investment and technology transfer; strives to achieve stronger economic growth and a closer relationship between Canada and China; provides assistance to business; advocates for Canadian business on matters of Canada - China relations to the government and public; disseminates market information.

Canada - Japan Society of British Columbia. 15-555 W 12th Ave., Vancouver, BC, Canada V5Z 3X0. Phone: (604)708-3306; Fax: (604)921-8192 • URL: http://www.canadajapansociety.bc.ca • Promotes opportunities with Japan in British Columbia; seeks to provide a better understanding between the people of Canada and Japan.

Canadian Netherlands Business and Professional Association. 600 The East Mall, Etobicoke, ON, Canada M9B 4B1. Phone: (647)478-8620; Fax: (647)478-8620; Email: info@cnbpa.ca • URL: http://www.cnbpa.ca • Business people and professionals in Canada and the Netherlands. Promotes increased trade and communication between Canada and the Netherlands. Serves as a forum for the exchange of information among members.

Center for International Private Enterprise - Egypt Office. Fayoum St., No. 1, Off Cleopatra St., Heliopolis, Fl. 8, Ste. 8003, Cairo 11341, Egypt. Phone: 20 2 4143282; Fax: 20 2 4143295; Email: rzoghbi@cipe-egypt.org • URL: http://www.cipe.org • Encourages the growth of voluntary business organizations and private enterprise systems, such as chambers of commerce, trade associations, employers' organizations, and business-oriented research groups, particularly in developing countries. Creates exchanges among business leaders and institutions to strengthen the international private enterprise system. Offers leadership training for association executives.

Center for International Private Enterprise - Russia Office. Office 318, 101 Prospekt Mira, 129085 Moscow, Russia. Phone: 7 495 3802571; Fax: 7 495 3802572; Email: eurasia@cipe.org • URL: http://www.cipe-eurasia.org • Encourages the growth of voluntary business organizations and private enterprise systems, such as chambers of commerce, trade associations, employers' organizations, and business-oriented research groups, particularly in developing countries. Creates exchanges among business leaders and institutions to strengthen the international private enterprise system. Offers leadership training for association executives.

China-Africa Business Council. Shimao International Ctr., Building 1, Rm. 1805, Chaoyang District, Beijing 100027, Beijing, China. Phone: 86 10 64169865 or 86 10 64166409; Fax: 86 10 64169811; Email: cabc@cabc.org.cn • URL: http://www.cabc.org.cn/enindex/index.jhtml • Promotes trade and cooperation between China and Africa. Provides business tools that are designed to strengthen business ties between the two countries. Provides members with opportunities to share experiences and strengthen their capacity to address challenges through trainings, symposiums, workshops and forums.

Confederation of Indian Industry - United Kingdom. c/o Confederation of British Industry, Centre Point, 103 New Oxford St., London WC1A 1DU, United Kingdom. Phone: 44 20 78364121 or 44 20 73797400; Fax: 44 20 78361972 • URL: http://www.cii.in • Works to create and sustain an environment conducive to growth of the Indian industry. Links the industry and the government through advisory and consultative process. Serves as a reference point for the Indian industry and the international business community.

Estonian Business Association. Sadama 5/7, EE-10111 Tallinn, Estonia. Email: esea@esea.ee • URL: http://www.esea.ee • Fosters active business community in the country. Develops cooperation with foreign business associations. Keeps its members updated through local and international seminars and workshops. Meets with state authorities to advance the organization's interests.

European International Business Academy. c/o EIASM, Hotel Metropole, 2nd Fl., Pl. de Brouckere Plein, 31, B-1000 Brussels, Belgium. Phone: 32 2 2266660; Fax: 32 2 5121929 • URL: http://www.eiba-online.org • Individuals and associations involved in international business. Encourages exchange of ideas; fosters communication among members; serves as an information clearinghouse for those interested in education and research of international business.

Federation of Euro-Asian Stock Exchanges. Borsa Istanbul Bldg., Emirgan, TR-34467 Istanbul, Turkey. Phone: 90 212 298 2160; Fax: 90 212 298 2209; Email: secretariat@feas.org • URL: http://www.feas.org • Committed to a fair, efficient and transparent market environment. Works to eliminate trade barriers, and to promote development of the Euro-Asian stock markets. Provides cross listing and trading opportunities for securities issued within member countries.

French Bruneian Business Association. Kompleks Jalan Sultan, Rm. 301-306, 3rd Fl., Jalan Sultan, Bandar Seri Begawan BS8811, Brunei. Phone: 673 2240924 or 673 2220960; Fax: 673 2243373 • URL: http://www.fbbabrunei.com • Brings together people actively involved in trade and commerce between France and Brunei Darussalam. Provides a mutual forum for French and Bruneian business partners. Disseminates economic information to members on matters of interest. Develops business opportunities between Brunei Darussalam and France.

German Business Council Qatar. PO Box 24481, Doha, Qatar. Phone: 974 44 311152; Fax: 974 44 311154; Email: gbcq@ahkqatar.com • URL: http://www.gbcqatar.com • Aims to promote, cultivate and assist business relations between Germany and Qatar, as well as other international business communities, by forming a platform where business representatives of both nations can meet and exchange views and ideas.

German-Chinese Business Association. Unter Sachsenhausen 10-26, D-50667 Cologne, Germany. Phone: 49 221 120370; Fax: 49 221 120417; Email: info@dcw-ev.de • URL: http://www.dcw-ev.de • Promotes mutual co-operation in the economic sphere, particularly between medium-sized Chinese and German companies. Supports intensive exchange of thoughts and experiences between all institutions and companies interested in doing business in China. Organizes information seminars on a regular basis in various cities.

German Industry UK. Ymwlch Isaf, Gwynedd, Criccieth LL52 0PW, United Kingdom. Phone: 44 1766 523113; Email: info@gi-uk.co.uk • URL: http://www.gi-uk.co.uk • Works to provide forum for the discussion and exchange of experience and views on subjects relating to industry, economy and politics. Provides sales opportunities for members.

Global Automotive Management Council. 5305 Plymouth Rd., Ann Arbor, MI 48105. Phone: (734)997-9249; Fax: (734)997-9443; Email: info@gamcinc.com • URL: http://gamcinc.com • Represents senior executives from the global automotive industry. Promotes the globalization of automotive industries through meetings, seminars and educational forums. Provides educational and networking opportunities for senior executives.

Global Sourcing Council. 750 Third Ave., 11th Fl., New York, NY 10017. Phone: (631)398-3366; Email: sanjaysrr@gmail.com • URL: http://www.gscouncil.org • Supports people and organizations with an interest in the social and economic effects of sourcing. Serves as a forum for the discussion of the social and economic impacts of global sourcing. Provides opportunities for professional networking and business development. Addresses issues relevant to any company involved in global business operations.

International Business Chamber Cambodia. Phnom Penh Tower, 12th Fl., Monivong Blvd., No. 445, Phnom Penh, Cambodia. Phone: 855 23 964455; Email: info@ibccambodia.com • URL: http://www.ibccambodia.com • Provides leadership in creating a forum for international and local businesses and business associations that have an interest in Cambodia to work together in a spirit of friendship and cooperation for mutual benefit.

International Economic Alliance. 1 Mifflin Pl., Ste. 400, Cambridge, MA 02138-4946. Phone: (617)418-1981; Fax: (617)812-0499 • URL: http://www.iealliance.org • Aims to further global trade, economic development and advance business relations. Brings together the world's key players and decision-makers (business and government leaders, investors and leading intellectuals) for practical, open, bi-partisan and solution-oriented exchange of ideas. Serves as a source of knowledge, facilitator of relationships, and catalyst for new business opportunities.

Iran-Netherlands Business Council. No. 254 Taleghani Ave., Tehran, Iran. Phone: 98 21 88346736; Fax: 98 21 88346736; Email: info@inbc.ir • URL: http://www.inbc.ir/pages/default.aspx?lan=en • Promotes investment, trade, and political and cultural cooperation between Iran and Netherlands. Fosters business to business relationships between entrepreneurs of Iran and Netherlands.

Iraqi Businessmen Union. Kahramana Sq., Baghdad, Iraq. Phone: 964 1 7193887; Email: info@ibmu-iq.org • URL: http://www.ibmu-iq.org • Aims to strengthen the relationship between businessmen in Iraq, Arab and international countries. Enhances capabilities of Iraqi businessmen through contribution and participation in conferences and symposiums. Encourages businessmen and supports them to establish development projects in Pakistan.

Ireland China Association. 28 Merrion Sq., Dublin 2, Dublin, Ireland. Phone: 353 1 6424178; Fax: 353 1 6612315; Email: info@irelandchina.org • URL: http://www.irelandchina.org • Aims to bring together Irish and Chinese businesspeople for the purpose of exploring business opportunities and making contracts. Promotes greater economic ties and increases trade and commerce between Ireland and China. Furthers the cultural links and greater knowledge of both countries.

Ireland Japan Association. 28 Merrion Sq., Dublin 2, Dublin, Ireland. Phone: 353 1 6424178; Email: info@ija.ie • URL: http://www.ija.ie • Aims to enhance and develop relations between Ireland and Japan. Promotes economic and business ties and increases trade and commerce between Ireland and Japan. Fosters mutual understanding between the peoples of both countries. Creates a forum for Irish and Japanese people to interact in both business and social environments.

Italian Business Council Qatar. PO Box 22058, Doha, Qatar. Email: ibcqatar@gmail.com • URL: http://www.itachamqatar.org • Aims to promote economical, commercial and cultural relations between Italy and Qatar. Assists Italian companies in Qatar to establish relationships with Qatari representatives in the private sector through events, meetings and seminars.

Latin America Trade Coalition. 1615 H St. NW, Washington, DC 20062. Phone: (202)463-5485; Fax: (202)463-3126; Email: americas@uschamber.com • URL: http://www.uschamber.com • Represents U.S. companies, farmers and business organizations. Aims to secure congressional approval of the U.S.-Colombia Trade Promotion Agreement and the U.S.-Panama Trade Promotion Agreement.

Malaysia South-South Association. Bangunan AmBank Group, 17th Fl., Jaalan Raja Chulan, 50200 Kuala Lumpur, Malaysia. Phone: 60 3 20783788; Fax: 60 3 20728411; Email: mail@massa.net.my • URL: http://www.massa.net.my • Promotes and enhances knowledge and understanding of economic, trade and investment policies and conditions of South-South countries. Acts as an informal liaison body between the private sector and the government in the promotion of trade and investment. Provides a forum for the dissemination of ideas and for the discussion of trade, economy and culture. Enhances trade and investment relations and fosters friendship and cooperation in South-South countries.

Malaysian Business Council of Cambodia. No. 87, 294 St., Boeng Keng Kong 1, Phnom Penh, Cambodia. Phone: 855 23 216176; Fax: 855 23 726101; Email: mbcc.secretariat@gmail.com • URL: http://mbccambodia.org • Fosters strong business ties between Malaysia and Cambodia. Encourages the development of Malaysian investment in Cambodia. Provides a forum for meetings, discussions and interaction between the Malaysian business community and governmental personnel in Cambodia.

Moscow International Business Association. Office 505, Ilyinka d.5/2, 109012 Moscow, Russia. Phone: 7 495 6200130; Fax: 7 495 6200552; Email: miba@mibas.ru • URL: http://www.mibas.ru • Strives to create an environment for Russian and foreign businessmen operating in Moscow. Boosts the Russian economy by helping businessmen engaged in productive endeavors.

National United States-Arab Chamber of Commerce. 1023 15th St. NW, Ste. 400, Washington, DC 20005. Phone: (202)289-5920; Fax: (202)289-5938; Email: info@nusacc.org • URL: http://www.nusacc.org • Individuals, companies, corporations, and associations interested in commercial trade relations with the Arab world. Promotes business between the United States and the Arab world; encourages policies that promote better commercial relations. Conducts research and information services on commercial opportunities, export regulations, and conditions that affect the trade and investment climate. Sponsors trade delegations; holds seminars, conferences, and training sessions; acts as a central information center. Maintains relations with U.S. and Arab governments and agencies to develop, monitor, and recommend relevant legislation.

Pakistan-Belgium Business Forum. c/o Honorary Consulate of Belgium, A-9 Mohammad Ali Bogra Rd., Bath Island, Karachi 75530, Pakistan. Phone: 92 21 35879876 or 92 21 35872941; Fax: 92 21 35861257; Email: pbbf1@cyber.net.pk • URL: http://www.pbbf.org • Promotes trade, commerce and economic cooperation between Pakistan and Belgium. Encourages mutual understanding and friendly relations of business communities. Fosters and organizes trade and investment delegations, trade fairs, exhibitions, symposia and lectures.

Representative of German Industry and Trade. 1776 I St. NW, Ste. 1000, Washington, DC 20006. Phone: (202)659-4777; Fax: (202)659-4779; Email: info@rgit-usa.com • URL: http://www.rgit-usa.com • Organizations representing 95% of private industry in Germany. Provides data concerning economic developments and the economic environment in Germany.

Romanian-U.S. Business Council. 620 8th Ave., New York, NY 10018. Phone: (646)678-2905; Email: info@usrobc.org • URL: http://usrobc.org • Advocates American business interests with respect to U.S. Romanian trade and investments. Provides the American and Romanian business communities with a means of discussing bilateral trade and investment issues and the formulation of policy positions that will promote and expand economic relations between the two countries. Facilitates appropriate legislation and policies regarding trade between the U.S. and Romania. Has sponsored seminars on topics such as possibilities for cooperative commercial efforts in other countries and cooperation in energy development.

South Africa China Business Association. 5 Dongzhimen Wai Dajie, Beijing 100600, China. Email: secretary@sacba-prc.org • URL: http://www.sacba-prc.org • Strives to strengthen and grow social and business ties between South Africa and China. Promotes social interaction and cultural understanding between South Africa and China through the facilitation of interactive events.

Swedish Business Association of Singapore. No. 05-01 Triple One Somerset, 111 Somerset Rd., Singapore 238164, Singapore. Phone: 65 67345009; Email: swedbiz@singnet.com.sg • URL: http://www.sbas.org.sg • Aims to promote the development of commerce between Singapore and Sweden.

SwissCham Australia. 46 Market St., Ste. 303, Sydney, NSW 2000, Australia. Phone: 61 2 92621511; Fax: 61 2 92901928 • URL: http://www.swisscham.com.au • Represents Swiss business interests in Australia.

Taipei Business Association in Singapore. No. 06-07 SCCCI Bldg., 47 Hill St., Singapore 179365, Singapore. Phone: 65 63383916; Fax: 65 63383930; Email: tpebiz@singnet.com.sg • URL: http://www.tbas.org.sg.

Transparency International Anti-corruption Center. Aygestan 9th St., House 6, 0025 Yerevan, Armenia. Phone: 374 2 10569910 or 374 2 10553069; Fax: 374 2 10571399; Email: info@transparency.am • URL: http://transparency.am • Represents corporations, organizations and individuals interested in reducing fraud and corruption in international business transactions. Raises public awareness of anticorruption measures and influences legislation regulating international business transactions. Formulates standards of integrity to govern international business dealings. Conducts anticorruption and antifraud programs.

Transparency International - Azerbaijan. Jafar Jabbarli St. 16, Apt. 7, AZ1001 Baku, Azerbaijan. Phone: 994 12 4978170; Fax: 994 12 5962038; Email: info@transparency.az • URL: http://transparency.az • Represents corporations, organizations and individuals interested in reducing fraud and corruption in international business transactions. Raises public awareness of anticorruption measures and influences legislation regulating international business transactions. Formulates standards of integrity to govern international business dealings. Conducts anticorruption and antifraud programs.

Transparency International - Bosnia and Herzegovina. Gajeva 2, 78000 Banja Luka, Bosnia and Herzegovina. Phone: 387 51 216928; Fax: 387 51 216369; Email: info@ti-bih.org • URL: http://www.ti-bih.org • Represents corporations, organizations and individuals interested in reducing fraud and corruption in international business transactions. Raises public awareness of anticorruption measures and influences legislation regulating international business transactions. Formulates standards of integrity to govern international business dealings. Conducts anticorruption and antifraud programs.

Transparency International - Brazil. Rua Francisco Leitao 339, cj 122, 05414-025 Sao Paulo, SP, Brazil. Phone: 55 11 30623436; Fax: 55 11 30623436; Email: tbrasil@transparencia.org.br • URL: http://www.transparencia.org.br • Represents corporations, organizations and individuals interested in reducing fraud and corruption in international business transactions. Raises public awareness of anticorruption measures and influences legislation regulating international business transactions. Formulates standards of integrity to govern international business dealings. Conducts anticorruption and antifraud programs.

Transparency International - Bulgaria. PO Box 72, Sofia, Bulgaria. Phone: 359 2 9867713 or 359 2 9867920; Fax: 359 2 9867834; Email: mbox@transparency.bg • URL: http://www.transparency.bg • Represents corporations, organizations and individuals interested in reducing fraud and corruption in international business transactions. Raises public awareness of anti-corruption measures and influences legislation regulating international business transactions. Formulates standards of integrity to govern international business dealings. Conducts anti-corruption and anti-fraud programs.

Transparency International - Burundi. c/o ABUCO, Ave. du 28 Novembre, No. 4611/C, Bujumbura, Burundi. Phone: 257 237686; Email: abuco@ymail.com • URL: http://www.burunditransparence.org • Aims to promote good governance and fight against corruption. Seeks to raise public awareness of anti-corruption measures and influence legislation regulating international business transactions. Formulates standards of integrity to govern international business dealings.

Transparency International - Cameroon. Nouvelle Route Bastos, rue 1.839, Yaounde, Cameroon. Phone: 237 33156378; Email: transparency@ti-cameroon.org • URL: http://www.ti-cameroon.org • Aims to promote good governance and fight against corruption. Works with coalitions of individuals and organizations to prevent corruption and reform the systems. Fosters dialogue with the government and companies.

Transparency International - Canada. Business Ethics Office - N211, Schulich School of Business, York University, 4700 Keele St., Toronto, ON, Canada M3J 1P3. Phone: (416)488-3939; Fax: (416)483-5128; Email: ti-can@transparency.ca • URL: http://www.transparency.ca • Represents corporations, organizations and individuals interested in reducing fraud and corruption in international business transactions. Raises public awareness of anticorruption measures and influences legislation regulating international business transactions. Formulates standards of integrity to govern international business dealings. Conducts anticorruption and antifraud programs.

Transparency International - Chile. Avda. Providencia 1017, Providencia, Santiago, Chile. Phone: 56 2 2364507; Fax: 56 2 2364507; Email: chiletransparente@chiletransparente.cl • URL: http://www.chiletransparente.cl • Represents corporations, organizations and individuals interested in reducing fraud and corruption in international business transactions. Raises public awareness of anticorruption measures and influences legislation regulating international business transactions. Formulates standards of integrity to govern international business dealings. Conducts anticorruption and antifraud programs.

Transparency International - Colombia. Carrera 45, No. 93-61, Barrio la Castellana, Bogota, Colombia. Phone: 57 1 6100822; Fax: 57 1 6373603; Email: transparencia@transparenciacolombia.org.co • URL: http://www.transparency.org/whoweare/contact#O_nc_colombia • Represents corporations, organizations and individuals interested in reducing fraud and corruption in international business transactions. Raises public awareness of anticorruption measures and influences legislation regulating international business transactions. Formulates standards of integrity to govern international business dealings. Conducts anticorruption and antifraud programs.

Transparency International - Costa Rica. 800 metros oeste del Restaurante Tony Romas, Urbanizacion Trejos Montealegre, San Jose, Costa Rica. Phone: 506 40340929; Email: crintegra@gmail.com • URL: http://www.transparency.org/whoweare/contact#O_nc_costarica • Represents corporations, organizations and individuals interested in reducing fraud and corruption in international business transactions. Raises public awareness of anti-corruption measures and influences legislation regulating international business transactions. Formulates standards of integrity to govern international business dealings. Conducts anti-corruption and antifraud programs.

For publishers' addresses, refer to SOURCES CITED section at the back of the book.

Transparency International - Croatia. Ilica 35, CT-10000 Zagreb, Croatia. Phone: 385 1 4830653; Fax: 385 1 4830654; Email: ti-croatia@transparency.hr • URL: http://www.transparency.hr • Represents corporations, organizations and individuals interested in reducing fraud and corruption in international business transactions. Raises public awareness of anticorruption measures and influences legislation regulating international business transactions. Formulates standards of integrity to govern international business dealings. Conducts anticorruption and antifraud programs.

Transparency International - Czech Republic. Sokolovska 260/143, CZ-180 00 Prague, Czech Republic. Phone: 420 2 24240895 or 420 2 24240897; Email: info@transparency.cz • URL: http://www.transparency.cz • Represents corporations, organizations and individuals interested in reducing fraud and corruption in international business transactions. Raises public awareness of anticorruption measures and influences legislation regulating international business transactions. Formulates standards of integrity to govern international business dealings. Conducts anticorruption and antifraud programs.

Transparency International - Denmark. c/o Mellemfolkeligt Samvirke, Faelledvej 12, DK-2200 Copenhagen, Denmark. Email: sekretariatet@transparency.dk • URL: http://transparency.dk • Represents corporations, organizations and individuals interested in reducing fraud and corruption in international business transactions. Raises public awareness of anti-corruption measures and influences legislation regulating international business transactions. Formulates standards of integrity to govern international business dealings. Conducts anti-corruption and antifraud programs.

Transparency International - Dominican Republic. Calle Wenceslao Alvarez, No. 8, Santo Domingo, Dominican Republic. Phone: (809)685-6200; Fax: (809)685-6631; Email: info@pciudadana.org • URL: http://www.pciudadana.org • Aims to promote good governance and fight against corruption. Seeks to raise public awareness of anti-corruption measures and influence legislation regulating international business transactions. Formulates standards of integrity to govern international business dealings.

Transparency International - Estonia. Telliskivi 60a, 10412 Tallinn, Estonia. Phone: 372 56678118; Email: info@transparency.ee • URL: http://www.transparency.ee • Seeks to highlight the appearance of corruption in the public and private sector. Strengthens cooperation between the institutions and private persons concerned with the fight against corruption. Analyzes the risks of corruption and proposes legislative amendments related to transparency, accountability and corruption.

Transparency International - Ethiopia. PO Box 27847, Addis Ababa, Ethiopia. Phone: 251 11 6621596 or 251 11 6555508 • URL: http://transparencyethiopia.org • Aims to promote good governance and fight against corruption. Seeks to raise public awareness of anti-corruption measures and influence legislation regulating international business transactions. Formulates standards of integrity to govern international business dealings.

Transparency International - Fiji. 72 Pratt St., Suva, Fiji. Phone: 679 3304702; Fax: 679 3303533; Email: oa@transparencyfiji.org • URL: http://www.transparencyfiji.org • Represents corporations, organizations and individuals interested in reducing fraud and corruption in international business transactions. Raises public awareness of anti-corruption measures and influences legislation regulating international business transactions. Formulates standards of integrity to govern international business dealings. Conducts anti-corruption and antifraud programs.

Transparency International - France. 14, passage Dubail, F-75010 Paris, France. Phone: 33 1 84169565; Email: contact@transparence-france.org • URL: http://www.transparence-france.org • Represents corporations, organizations and individuals interested in reducing fraud and corruption in international business transactions. Raises public awareness of anti-corruption measures and influences legislation regulating international business transactions. Formulates standards of integrity to govern international business dealings. Conducts anti-corruption and antifraud programs.

Transparency International - Georgia. 26, Rustaveli Ave., 0108 Tbilisi, Republic of Georgia. Phone: 995 32 2921403; Fax: 995 32 2920251; Email: info@transparency.ge • URL: http://www.transparency.ge • Represents corporations, organizations and individuals interested in reducing fraud and corruption in international business transactions. Raises public awareness of anti-corruption measures and influences legislation regulating international business transactions. Formulates standards of integrity to govern international business dealings. Conducts anti-corruption and antifraud programs.

Transparency International - Germany. Alte Schoenhauser Str. 44, D-10119 Berlin, Germany. Phone: 49 30 5498980; Fax: 49 30 54989822; Email: office@transparency.de • URL: http://www.transparency.de • Dedicates itself to curbing corruption in all its forms and increasing government accountability. Develops standards of integrity to govern national and international business dealings; seeks to raise public awareness of anticorruption measures and influences the government to strengthen anticorruption laws. Maintains information and documentation center; undertakes publicity campaigns; works in networks with other organizations with similar focus; most of the program work is done by volunteers.

Transparency International - Greece. Thetidos 4, GR-11528 Athens, Greece. Phone: 30 210 7224940; Fax: 30 210 7224947; Email: tihellas@otenet.gr • URL: http://www.transparency.gr • Represents corporations, organizations and individuals interested in reducing fraud and corruption in international business transactions. Raises public awareness of anticorruption measures and influences legislation regulating international business transactions. Formulates standards of integrity to govern international business dealings. Conducts anticorruption and antifraud programs.

Transparency International - Haiti. PO Box 16136, Petionville, Haiti. Phone: 509 37017089; Fax: 509 25137089; Email: heritagehaiti@yahoo.com • URL: http://www.transparency.org • Aims to promote good governance and fight against corruption. Seeks to raise public awareness of anti-corruption measures and influence legislation regulating international business transactions. Formulates standards of integrity to govern international business dealings.

Transparency International - Hungary. Falk Miksa u. 30th 4th em. 2, 1055 Budapest, Hungary. Phone: 36 1 2699534; Fax: 36 1 2699535; Email: info@transparency.hu • URL: http://www.transparency.org • Represents corporations, organizations and individuals interested in reducing fraud and corruption in international business transactions. Raises public awareness of anti-corruption measures and influences legislation regulating international business transactions. Formulates standards of integrity to govern international business dealings. Conducts anti-corruption and anti-fraud programs.

Transparency International - India. Qr.No.- 4, Lajpat Bhawan, Lajpat Nagar - IV, New Delhi 110 024, Delhi, India. Phone: 91 11 26460826; Fax: 91 11 26460824; Email: tiindia.newdelhi@gmail.com • URL: http://www.transparencyindia.org • Represents corporations, organizations and individuals interested in reducing fraud and corruption in international business transactions. Raises public awareness of anticorruption measures and influences legislation regulating international business transactions. Formulates standards of integrity to govern international business dealings. Conducts anticorruption and antifraud programs.

Transparency International - Indonesia. Jl. Senayan Bawah No. 17, 12180 Jakarta, Indonesia. Phone: 62 21 7208515; Fax: 62 21 7267815; Email: info@ti.or.id • URL: http://www.transparency.org • Represents corporations, organizations and individuals interested in reducing fraud and corruption in international business transactions. Raises public awareness of anticorruption measures and influences legislation regulating international business transactions. Formulates standards of integrity to govern international business dealings. Conducts anticorruption and antifraud programs.

Transparency International - Initiative Madagascar. Lot 11 M 98 B, Antsakaviro, Antananarivo 101, Madagascar. Phone: 261 2 2265357; Email: transparency.mg@moov.mg • URL: http://www.transparency.org/whoweare/contact/org/nc_madagascar • Represents corporations, organizations and individuals interested in reducing fraud and corruption in international business transactions. Raises public awareness of anticorruption measures and influences legislation regulating international business transactions. Formulates standards of integrity to govern international business dealings. Conducts anticorruption and antifraud programs.

Transparency International - Ireland. The Capel Bldg., Ste. 109, Dublin 7, Dublin, Ireland. Phone: 353 1 8719433; Email: info@transparency.ie • URL: http://transparency.ie • Aims to promote good governance and fight against corruption. Seeks to raise public awareness of anti-corruption measures and influence legislation regulating international business transactions. Provides anti-corruption tools, strategies and programs.

Transparency International - Israel. PO Box 39874, IL-61398 Tel Aviv, Israel. Phone: 972 3 6409176; Fax: 972 3 6409176; Email: shvil@ti-israel.org • URL: http://www.ti-israel.org • Represents corporations, organizations and individuals interested in reducing fraud and corruption in international business transactions. Raises public awareness of anti-corruption measures and influences legislation regulating international business transactions. Formulates standards of integrity to govern international business dealings. Conducts anti-corruption and antifraud programs.

Transparency International - Italy. Via Zamagna 19, I-20148 Milan, Italy. Phone: 39 2 40093560; Fax: 39 2 406829; Email: info@transparency.it • URL: http://www.transparency.org • Represents corporations, organizations and individuals interested in reducing fraud and corruption in international business transactions. Raises public awareness of anticorruption measures and influences legislation regulating international business transactions. Formulates standards of integrity to govern international business dealings. Conducts anticorruption and antifraud programs.

Transparency International - Kazakhstan. Karasai Batyr 85, 4th Fl., Office 41, 050026 Almaty, Kazakhstan. Phone: 7 327 2726981; Fax: 7 327 2726981 • URL: http://www.transparencykazakhstan.org • Represents corporations, organizations and individuals interested in reducing fraud and corruption in international business transactions. Raises public awareness of anticorruption measures and influences legislation regulating international business transactions. Formulates standards of integrity to govern international business dealings. Conducts anticorruption and antifraud programs.

Transparency International - Kenya. ACK Garden

House, 3rd Fl., Wing D, 1st Ngong Ave. off Bishops Rd., Nairobi, Kenya. Phone: 254 2 2727763 or 254 2 2730324; Fax: 254 2 2729530; Email: transparency@tikenya.org • URL: http://www.tikenya.org • Represents corporations, organizations and individuals interested in reducing fraud and corruption in international business transactions. Raises public awareness of anticorruption measures and influences legislation regulating international business transactions. Formulates standards of integrity to govern international business dealings. Conducts anticorruption and antifraud programs.

Transparency International - Korea. 1006 Pierson Bldg., 89-27 Sinmunno 2-ga, Jongno-Gu, Seoul 110-762, South Korea. Phone: 82 2 7176211; Fax: 82 2 7176210; Email: ti@ti.or.kr • URL: http://ti.or.kr/xe • Represents corporations, organizations and individuals interested in reducing fraud and corruption in international business transactions. Raises public awareness of anti-corruption measures and influences legislation regulating international business transactions. Formulates standards of integrity to govern international business dealings. Conducts anti-corruption and antifraud programs.

Transparency International - Lithuania. Didzioji St. 5, LT-01128 Vilnius, Lithuania. Phone: 370 5 2126951; Fax: 370 5 2121687; Email: info@transparency.lt • URL: http://www.transparency.org • Represents corporations, organizations and individuals interested in reducing fraud and corruption in international business transactions. Raises public awareness of anticorruption measures and influences legislation regulating international business transactions. Formulates standards of integrity to govern international business dealings. Conducts anticorruption and antifraud programs.

Transparency International - Malaysia. Wisma Pantai, Plz. Pantai, Ste. B-11-1, No. 5 Jalan 4/83A, Off Jalan Pantai Baru, 59200 Kuala Lumpur, Malaysia. Phone: 60 3 22840630; Fax: 60 3 22840690; Email: admin@transparency.org.my • URL: http://www.transparency.org • Represents corporations, organizations and individuals interested in reducing fraud and corruption in international business transactions. Raises public awareness of anticorruption measures and influences legislation regulating international business transactions. Formulates standards of integrity to govern international business dealings. Conducts anticorruption and antifraud programs.

Transparency International - Moldova. 98, 31-August 1989 St., Rm. 205, MD-2004 Chisinau, Moldova. Phone: 373 2 2203484 or 373 2 2203485; Fax: 373 2 2237876; Email: office@transparency.md • URL: http://www.transparency.md • Represents corporations, organizations and individuals interested in reducing fraud and corruption in international business transactions. Raises public awareness of anticorruption measures and influences legislation regulating international business transactions. Formulates standards of integrity to govern international business dealings. Conducts anticorruption and antifraud programs.

Transparency International - Mongolia. Bldg. of Zorig Foundation, 2nd Fl., Peace Ave. 17, Sukhbaataar District, Ulan Bator, Mongolia. Phone: 976 1 70154250; Fax: 976 1 70154250 • URL: http://www.transparency.org/country#MNG_Chapter • Represents corporations, organizations and individuals interested in reducing fraud and corruption in international business transactions. Raises public awareness of anticorruption measures and influences legislation regulating international business transactions. Formulates standards of integrity to govern international business dealings. Conducts anticorruption and antifraud programs.

Transparency International - Nepal. Newplaza, Pulalisadak, Kathmandu, Nepal. Phone: 977 1 436462 or 977 1 420412; Email: trans@tinepal.org • URL: http://www.tinepal.org • Represents corporations, organizations and individuals interested in reducing fraud and corruption in international business transactions. Raises public awareness of anti-corruption measures and influences legislation regulating international business transactions. Formulates standards of integrity to govern international business dealings. Conducts anti-corruption and antifraud programs.

Transparency International - New Zealand. Lambton Quay, Wellington, New Zealand. Email: mpetrie@ihug.co.nz • URL: http://www.transparency.org/whoweare/contact#O_nc_newzealand • Represents corporations, organizations and individuals interested in reducing fraud and corruption in international business transactions. Raises public awareness of anti-corruption measures and influences legislation regulating international business transactions. Formulates standards of integrity to govern international business dealings. Conducts anti-corruption and antifraud programs.

Transparency International - Nigeria. No. 11B Otukpo St., Gimbiya St., Area 11, Off Onitsha Crescent, Garki, Abuja, Nigeria. Email: info@ti-nigeria.org • URL: http://www.transparency.org/content/view/full/337/(filter)/n • Represents corporations, organizations and individuals interested in reducing fraud and corruption in international business transactions. Raises public awareness of anticorruption measures and influences legislation regulating international business transactions. Formulates standards of integrity to govern international business dealings. Conducts anticorruption and antifraud programs.

Transparency International - Pakistan. 5-C, 2nd Fl., Khayaban-e-Ittehad, Phase VII, D.H.A., Karachi, Pakistan. Phone: 92 21 5390408 or 92 21 5390409; Fax: 92 21 5390410; Email: ti.pakistan@gmail.com • URL: http://www.transparency.org.pk • Aims to raise public awareness of the effects of bribery and corruption. Encourages the government, government departments, municipalities, civic agencies and private-sector organizations to establish and implement laws, policies and anti-corruption programs. Enhances public transparency and accountability in administrative, financial and business transactions.

Transparency International - Papua New Guinea. PO Box 591, Port Moresby, Papua New Guinea. Phone: 675 3202188; Fax: 675 3202189 • URL: http://www.transparencypng.org.pg • Aims to combat corruption. Promotes openness, honesty and accountability in public and private dealings. Encourages research and analysis of the extent and effect of corruption in Papua New Guinea. Raises awareness of the presence and adverse effects of dishonest and corrupt practices.

Transparency International - Philippine Chapter. Philippine International Convention Center, Rm. S-370, CCP Complex, Pasay City 1000, Philippines. Phone: 63 2 5529188; Fax: 63 2 5529188; Email: transparencyinternational_ph@yahoo.com • URL: http://www.transparency.org • Represents corporations, organizations and individuals interested in reducing fraud and corruption in international business transactions. Raises public awareness of anticorruption measures and influences legislation regulating international business transactions. Formulates standards of integrity to govern international business dealings. Conducts anticorruption and antifraud programs.

Transparency International - Poland. ul. Ordynacka 9, pok. 33, 00-364 Warsaw, Poland. Phone: 48 22 8289243; Email: ti@transparency.pl • URL: http://www.transparency.pl • Represents corporations, organizations and individuals interested in reducing fraud and corruption in international business transactions. Raises public awareness of anti-corruption measures and influences legislation regulating international business transactions. Formulates standards of integrity to govern international business dealings. Conducts anti-corruption and antifraud programs.

Transparency International - Romania. 21 Nicolae Balcescu Blvd., 2nd Fl., Sector 1, 010044 Bucharest, Romania. Phone: 40 21 3177170; Fax: 40 21 3177172; Email: office@ransparency.org.ro • URL: http://www.transparency.org.ro • Represents corporations, organizations and individuals interested in reducing fraud and corruption in international business transactions. Raises public awareness of anticorruption measures and influences legislation regulating international business transactions. Formulates standards of integrity to govern international business dealings. Conducts anticorruption and antifraud programs.

Transparency International - Russia. Nikoloyamskaya ul. 6, 109240 Moscow, Russia. Phone: 7 95 9150019; Fax: 7 95 9150019; Email: info@transparency.org.ru • URL: http://www.transparency.org.ru • Represents corporations, organizations and individuals interested in reducing fraud and corruption in international business transactions. Raises public awareness of anticorruption measures and influences legislation regulating international business transactions. Formulates standards of integrity to govern international business dealings. Conducts anticorruption and antifraud programs.

Transparency International - Slovakia. Bajkalska 25, 827 18 Bratislava, Slovakia. Phone: 421 2 53417207; Fax: 421 2 53417207; Email: tis@transparency.sk • URL: http://www.transparency.sk • Represents corporations, organizations and individuals interested in reducing fraud and corruption in international business transactions. Raises public awareness of anticorruption measures and influences legislation regulating international business transactions. Formulates standards of integrity to govern international business dealings. Conducts anticorruption and antifraud programs.

Transparency International - Solomon Islands. PO Box 1665, Honiara, Solomon Islands. Email: tsi@solomon.com.sb • URL: http://www.transparency.org • Aims to promote good governance and fight against corruption. Seeks to raise public awareness of anti-corruption measures and influence legislation regulating international business transactions. Formulates standards of integrity to govern international business dealings.

Transparency International - Sri Lanka. No. 6, 37th Ln., Off Queens Rd., Colombo 3, Sri Lanka. Fax: 94 112 506419; Email: tisl@tisrilanka.org • URL: http://www.tisrilanka.org • Represents corporations, organizations and individuals interested in reducing fraud and corruption in international business transactions. Raises public awareness of anticorruption measures and influences legislation regulating international business transactions. Formulates standards of integrity to govern international business dealings. Conducts anticorruption and antifraud programs.

Transparency International - Sweden. Linnegatan 14, 6 tr, S-114 47 Stockholm, Sweden. Phone: 46 8 7914040; Email: info@transparency-se.org • URL: http://www.transparency-se.org • Represents corporations, organizations and individuals interested in reducing fraud and corruption in international business transactions. Raises public awareness of anti-corruption measures and influences legislation regulating international business transactions. Formulates standards of integrity to govern international business dealings. Conducts anti-corruption and antifraud programs.

Transparency International - Taiwan. PO Box 6-16 Mucha, Taipei 11699, Taiwan. Phone: 886 2 22362204; Fax: 886 2 22363325; Email: tict@tict.org.tw • URL: http://www.transparency.org •

Represents corporations, organizations and individuals interested in reducing fraud and corruption in international business transactions. Raises public awareness of anticorruption measures and influences legislation regulating international business transactions. Formulates standards of integrity to govern international business dealings. Conducts anticorruption and antifraud programs.

Transparency International - Uganda. Plot 3 Martyrs Ln., Ntinda, Kampala, Uganda. Phone: 256 414 255836; Fax: 256 414 341546; Email: info@tiuganda.org • URL: http://tiuganda.org • Aims to promote good governance and fight against corruption. Seeks to raise public awareness of anti-corruption measures and influence legislation regulating international business transactions. Formulates standards of integrity to govern international business dealings.

Transparency International - Ukraine. 17, Egorova St., Off. 4, 25006 Kirovograd, Ukraine. Phone: 380 522 272754; Fax: 380 522 321553; Email: info@ti-ukraine.org • URL: http://www.transparency.org • Represents corporations, organizations and individuals interested in reducing fraud and corruption in international business transactions. Raises public awareness of anti-corruption measures and influences legislation regulating international business transactions. Formulates standards of integrity to govern international business dealings. Conducts anti-corruption and antifraud programs.

Transparency International - Vanuatu. PO Box 355, Port Vila, Vanuatu. Phone: 678 25715; Fax: 678 25716; Email: transparency@vanuatu.com.vu • URL: http://www.transparencyvanuatu.org • Represents corporations, organizations and individuals interested in reducing fraud and corruption in international business transactions. Raises public awareness of anticorruption measures and influences legislation regulating international business transactions. Formulates standards of integrity to govern international business dealings. Conducts anticorruption and antifraud programs.

Transparency International - Zambia. Stand No. 3880, Kwacha Rd., Olympia Park, Lusaka, Zambia. Phone: 260 1 290080; Fax: 260 1 293649; Email: tizambia@zamnet.zm • URL: http://www.transparency.org/whoweare/contact#O_nc_zambia • Represents corporations, organizations and individuals interested in reducing fraud and corruption in international business transactions. Raises public awareness of anticorruption measures and influences legislation regulating international business transactions. Formulates standards of integrity to govern international business dealings. Conducts anti-corruption and antifraud programs.

Transparency Maldives. MF Bldg., 7th Fl., Chaandhanee Magu, Male, Maldives. Phone: 960 3304017; Fax: 960 3006062; Email: office@transparencymaldives.org • URL: http://www.transparencymaldives.org • Promotes collaboration, awareness and other initiatives to improve governance and eliminate corruption. Encourages discussion on transparency, accountability and the fight against corruption. Seeks to engage stakeholders from all sectors to raise awareness on corruption.

Transparency Mauritius. TN Tower, 6th Fl., St. Georges St., Port Louis, Mauritius. Phone: 230 2130796; Fax: 230 2130795; Email: transparency.mauritius@gmail.com • URL: http://www.transparency.org • Represents corporations, organizations and individuals interested in reducing fraud and corruption in international business transactions. Raises public awareness of anti-corruption measures and influences legislation regulating international business transactions. Formulates standards of integrity to govern international business dealings. Conducts anti-corruption and antifraud programs.

United Kingdom Science Park Association. Chesterford Research Park, Little Chesterford, Essex, Saffron Walden CB10 1XL, United Kingdom. Phone: 44 1799 532050; Fax: 44 1799 532049; Email: info@ukspa.org.uk • URL: http://www.ukspa.org.uk • Supports and encourages the startup, incubation and development of innovation led, high growth, knowledge-based businesses. Provides opportunity for larger and international businesses to develop specific and close interactions with a particular centre of knowledge creation for mutual benefit.

United States Council for International Business. 1212 Avenue of the Americas, New York, NY 10036. Phone: (212)354-4480 or (212)703-5046; Fax: (212)575-0327; Email: info@uscib.org • URL: http://www.uscib.org • Serves as the U.S. National Committee of the International Chamber of Commerce. Enables multinational enterprises to operate effectively by representing their interests to intergovernmental and governmental bodies and by keeping enterprises advised of international developments having a major impact on their operations. Serves as: U.S. representative to the International Organization of Employers; national affiliate to the U.S.A. Business and Industry Advisory Committee to the BIAC. Operates ATA Carnet export service, which enables goods to be shipped overseas duty-free for demonstration and exhibition. Sponsors seminars and luncheon briefings.

U.S.-Pakistan Business Council. 1615 H St. NW, Washington, DC 20062. Phone: (202)463-5732; Fax: (202)822-2491; Email: uspbc@uschamber.com • URL: http://www.uspakistan.org • Fosters awareness of business opportunities in Pakistan. Increases U.S. foreign direct investment in Pakistan. Brings together Pakistani and American business leaders for discussions on business conditions and policy related issues. Provides a forum for dialogue on key economic, commercial, and other relevant issues of interest to American companies doing or planning to do business in Pakistan.

INTERNATIONAL CORPORATIONS

See MULTINATIONAL CORPORATIONS

INTERNATIONAL DEVELOPMENT

See DEVELOPING AREAS

INTERNATIONAL ECONOMICS

See also ECONOMICS; INTERNATIONAL BUSINESS

ABSTRACTS AND INDEXES

PAIS International. ProQuest L.L.C. • Monthly. $850.00 per year; cumulations three times a year. Provides topical citations to the worldwide literature of public affairs, economics, demographics, sociology, and trade. Text in English; indexed materials in English, French, German, Italian, Portuguese and Spanish.

ALMANACS AND YEARBOOKS

Economic Survey of Europe. United Nations Economic Commission for Europe. • Semiannual. Provides yearly analysis and review of the European economy, including Eastern Europe and the USSR. Text in English.

State of the World (year). Worldwatch Institute. • Annual. $22.00. Provides yearly analysis of factors influencing the global environment.

BIBLIOGRAPHIES

OECD Catalogue of Publications. Organization for Economic Cooperation and Development. Organisation for Economic Co-operation and Development Publications and Information Center. • Online only. No print edition.

CD-ROM DATABASES

EconLit. Ovid Technologies Inc. • Updated monthly. Lists journal articles, book reviews, disserations of economic literature. Over 1,400 journals covered.

OECD Statistical Compendium. Organization for Economic Cooperation and Development. • Semiannual. $1,905.00 per year for 1 to 10 users. CD-ROM contains more than 730,000 monthly, quarterly, and annual time series for OECD countries, 1960 to date. Includes fully searchable data on agriculture, food, economic indicators, national accounts, employment, energy, finance, industry, technology, and foreign trade. Results can be displayed in various forms.

PAIS International. ProQuest L.L.C. • Monthly. $1,995.00 per year. Contains over 650,000 citations to the literature of contemporary social, political, and economic issues.

USA Trade. U.S. Department of Commerce. • Monthly. $650.00 per year. Provides over 150,000 trade-related data series on CD-ROM. Includes full text of many government publications. Specific data is included on national income, labor, price indexes, foreign exchange, technical standards, and international markets. Website address is www.stat-usa.gov/.

DIRECTORIES

Armenia Export-Import and Business Directory. International Business Publications, USA. • $99.95 Individuals. Covers strategic, economic, investment, export-import, and business opportunities and contact numbers.

Capital for Shipping. Informa Publishing Group. • Annual. $128.00. Published in the UK by Lloyd's List (www.lloydslist.com). Consists of a "Financial Directory" and a "Legal Directory," listing international ship finance providers and international law firms specializing in shipping. Included with subscription to *Lloyd's Shipping Economist.*

ENCYCLOPEDIAS AND DICTIONARIES

Worldmark Encyclopedia of National Economies. Cengage Learning Inc. • 2002. $572.00. Four volumes. Covers both the current and historical development of the economies of 200 foreign nations. Includes analysis and statistics. Also available as eBook.

GENERAL WORKS

Economic and Social Survey of Asia and the Pacific. United Nations Publications. • Annual. $85 print. Emphasis is on trends in economic policy and economic development strategies.

Worldwide Business Collaborations--Consultants News and Business Opportunities. International Press Cutting Service. • Weekly. $715. Publication spotlighting international business opportunities and openings.

INTERNET DATABASES

Gateway to the European Union. European Union. Email: pressoffice@eurostat.cec.be • URL: http://www.europa.eu.int • Web site provides access to a wide variety of EU information, including statistics (Eurostat), news, policies, publications, key issues, and official exchange rates for the euro. Includes links to the European Central Bank, the European Investment Bank, and other institutions. Fees: Free.

OTHER SOURCES

Consensus Forecasts: A Worldwide Survey. Consensus Economics Inc. • Monthly. Provides a survey of more than 200 "prominent"financial and economic forecasters, covering 20 major countries. Two-year forecasts for each country include future growth, inflation, interest rates, and exchange rates. Each issue contains analysis of business conditions in various countries.

World Economic and Social Survey: Trends and Policies in the World Economy. United Nations Publications. • Annual. $55.00. Includes discussion and "an extensive statistical annex of economic, trade, and financial indicators, incorporating current data and forecasts.".

World Economic Situation and Prospects. United Nations Publications. • Annual. $42 Individuals print. Serves as a supplement and update to the UN *World Economic and Social Survey*.

PERIODICALS AND NEWSLETTERS

The Economist. The Economist Intelligence Unit. • 190 ₱ Individuals Print and Digital per week.

Financial Times Currency Forecaster: Consensus Forecasts of the Worldwide Currency and Economic Outlook. Briefings Publishing Group. • Monthly. $695.00 per year. Newsletter. Provides forecasts of foreign currency exchange rates and economic conditions. Supplement available: *Mid-Month Global Financial Report*.

The George Washington International Law Review. George Washington University Law School. • Quarterly. $42 domestic. Articles dealing with a variety of topics within the area of private international comparative law and economics.

International Economic Scoreboard. The Conference Board. • Description: Provides current data on the business outlook in 11 major industrial countries: Australia, Canada, France, West Germany, Italy, Japan, Korea, New Zealand, Taiwan, the United Kingdom, and the U.S. **Remarks:** A source for additional information on this indicator system and its uses is available at the Center for International Business Cycle Research, Columbia University Business School.

International Review of Applied Economics. Routledge. • Quarterly. Individuals, $310.00 per year; institutions, $1,007.00 per year.

Review of International Political Economy. Taylor & Francis Ltd. • 6/year. $884 Institutions Online. Includes articles on international trade, finance, production, and consumption.

World Trade Review: Economics, Law, International Institutions. Cambridge University Press. • Three times a year. Individuals, $48.00 pr year; institutions, $200.00 per year. Published in conjunction with the World Trade Organization (www.wto.org). Covers "issues of relevance to the multilateral trading system.".

RESEARCH CENTERS AND INSTITUTES

Russian Academy of Sciences - Institute for International Economic and Political Studies. Novocheryemushkinskaya, 42a, 117418 Moscow, Russia. Phone: 7 499 1286780; Fax: 7 499 1208371; Email: omepi@mail.ru • URL: http://www.imepi-eurasia.ru/eng/kalendar.php • Theoretical principles and the practical problems of creating a post socialist economic order, including various aspects of foreign policy and foreign trade relations of Russia and of internal economic and political development of all post-communist countries.

University of Adelaide - Centre for International Economic Studies. School of Economics, Adelaide, SA 5005, Australia. Phone: 61 8 83134712; Fax: 61 8 82231460; Email: kym.anderson@adelaide.edu.au • URL: http://www.adelaide.edu.au/cies • International economics and closely related disciplines with relevance to the Asia-Pacific region and the global trading system, including programs on China and Indonesia; macroeconomic, monetary, and financial issues; environmental and resource economics; wine.

University of Maryland at College Park - Center for International Economics. 3105 Tydings Hall, Department of Economics, College Park, MD 20742. Phone: (301)405-3548; Fax: (301)405-3542; Email: mendozae@econ.umd.edu • URL: http://www.econ.umd.edu/about/centers/CIE • International economics.

University of St. Gallen - Swiss Institute for International Economics and Applied Economic Research. Bodanstrasse 8, CH-9000 Saint Gallen, Switzerland. Phone: 41 71 2242340; Fax: 41 71 2242298; Email: gabriela.schmid@unisg.ch • URL: http://www.siaw.unisg.ch • Applied economics, economic policy, and international economics.

University of Strathclyde - Fraser of Allander Institute. Sir William Duncan Bldg., 130 Rottenrow, Glasgow G4 0GE, United Kingdom. Phone: 44 141 5483958; Fax: 44 141 5485776; Email: fraser@strath.ac.uk • URL: http://www.strath.ac.uk/fraser • Scottish economy, including studies in regional economics, input-output analysis, econometric modeling, labor economics, and economic development. Institute's goals include: analysis and forecasting of short-term trends in the Scottish economy; long-term analysis of prospective trends in the Scottish economy (Medium Term Model); applied computable general equilibrium modeling; compilation, updating, and maintenance of the Scottish Economic Data Bank; and portfolio of applied economics research projects.

STATISTICS SOURCES

Economic Outlook Statistics. • Includes country and global forecasts of over 170 economic and business variables. Actual data is shown for two years, with forecasts up to ten years.

Economic Survey of Latin America and the Caribbean. United Nations Publications. • Annual. $25. Includes reports on economic trends in 20 Latin American countries.

OECD Economic Outlook. Organisation for Economic Co-operation and Development Publications and Information Center. • Semiannual. Price on application. $95.00 per year. Contains a wide range of economic and monetary data relating to the member countries of the Organization for Economic Cooperation and Development. Includes about 100 statistical tables and graphs, with 24-month forecasts for each of the OECD countries. Provides extensive review and analysis of recent economic trends.

OECD Economic Surveys. Organisation for Economic Co-operation and Development Publications and Information Center. • Annual. $26.00 each. These are separate, yearly reviews for each of the economies of the industrialized nations that comprise the OECD. Each edition includes forecasts, analyses, and detailed statistical tables for the country being surveyed. (The combined series, one annual volume for each nation, is available at $485.00.).

Statistics on International Trade in Services. Organization for Economic Cooperation and Development. Organisation for Economic Co-operation and Development Publications and Information Center. • Annual. $126.00. Presents a compilation and assessment of data on OECD member countries' international trade in services. Covers four major categories for 20 years: travel, transportation, government services, and other services.

World Economic Factbook. Cengage Learning Inc. • Annual. $475 Individuals E-book. Published by Euromonitor International. Presents key economic facts and figures for each of 204 countries worldwide, including details of chief industries, export-import trade, currency, political risk, household expenditures, and the economic situation in general.

World Economic Prospects. Cengage Learning Inc. • 2010. $650.00. 8th edition. Published by Euromonitor International. Ranks countries by specific economic characteristics, such as gross domestic product (GDP) per capita and short term growth prospects. Discusses the economic situation, prospects, and market potential of each of the countries.

TRADE/PROFESSIONAL ASSOCIATIONS

Global Sourcing Council. 750 Third Ave., 11th Fl., New York, NY 10017. Phone: (631)398-3366; Email: sanjaysrr@gmail.com • URL: http://www.gscouncil.org • Supports people and organizations with an interest in the social and economic effects of sourcing. Serves as a forum for the discussion of the social and economic impacts of global sourcing. Provides opportunities for professional networking and business development. Addresses issues relevant to any company involved in global business operations.

Organisation for Economic Co-Operation and Development. 2, rue Andre Pascal, F-75775 Paris, France. Phone: 33 1 45248200; Fax: 1 45248500; Email: webmaster@oecd.org • URL: http://www.oecd.org.

INTERNATIONAL FINANCE

See also FOREIGN EXCHANGE; FOREIGN INVESTMENTS; MONEY

ABSTRACTS AND INDEXES

World Banking Abstracts. Institution of European Finance. John Wiley & Sons Inc. Wiley-Blackwell. • Bimonthly. Provides worldwide coverage of articles appearing in over 400 financial publications.

ALMANACS AND YEARBOOKS

Bankers' Almanac. Reed Business Information. • Semiannual. $1,170.00. Six volumes. Lists more than 27,000 financial institutions; international coverage. Formerly *Bankers' Almanac and Yearbook*.

National Accounts Statistics: Main Aggregates and Detailed Tables. United Nations Publications. • Annual.

World Economic Outlook Reports. International Monetary Fund. • Semiannual. $110. Provides key insights into how to view unprecedented global imbalances, respond to capital account crises caused by abrupt shifts in global asset allocations, and evaluate the opportunities for all member countries, especially low-income countries, to grow.

CD-ROM DATABASES

InvesText. Thomson Financial. • Monthly. Contains full text on CD-ROM of investment research reports from about 630 sources, including leading brokers and investment bankers. Reports are available on both U. S. and international publicly traded corporations. Separate industry reports cover more than 50 industries. Time span is 1982 to date.

OECD Statistical Compendium. Organization for Economic Cooperation and Development. • Semiannual. $1,905.00 per year for 1 to 10 users. CD-ROM contains more than 730,000 monthly, quarterly, and annual time series for OECD countries, 1960 to date. Includes fully searchable data on agriculture, food, economic indicators, national accounts, employment, energy, finance, industry, technology, and foreign trade. Results can be displayed in various forms.

DIRECTORIES

The Bank Directory. Accuity Inc. • Semiannual. $1,670 Individuals. Covers: In five volumes, about 11,000 banks and 50,000 branches of United States banks, and 60,000 foreign banks and branches engaged in foreign banking; Federal Reserve system and other United States government and state government banking agencies; 500 largest North American and International commercial banks; paper and automated clearinghouses. Volumes 1 and 2 contain North American listings; volumes 3 and 4, international listings (also cited as 'Thomson International Bank Directory; volume 5, Worldwide Correspondents Guide containing key correspondent data to facilitate funds transfer. Database includes: Bank operations information, asset ranking in state and country, bank routing numbers in numeric sequence, discontinued or changed bank names in geographical sequence. Entries include: For domestic banks--Bank name, address, phone, telex, cable, date established, routing number, charter type, bank holding company affiliation, memberships in Federal Reserve System and other banking organizations, principal officers by function performed, principal correspondent banks, and key financial data (deposits, etc.). For international banks--Bank name, address, phone, fax, telex, cable, SWIFT address, transit or sort codes within home country, ownership, financial data, names and titles of key personnel, branch locations. For branches--Bank name, address, phone, charter type, ownership and other details comparable to domestic bank listings.

Europe's Top Quoted Companies: A Comparative Directory from Seventeen European Stock Exchanges. Kogan Page, Limited. • Annual. $325. 00. Provides detailed, 5-year financial data on 850 major European companies that are publicly traded. Includes company addresses.

Foreign Representatives in the U. S. Yellow Book: Who's Who in the U. S. Offices of Foreign Corporations, Foreign Nations, the Foreign Press, and Intergovernmental Organizations. Leadership Directories Inc. • Semiannual. $465 per year. Lists executives located in the U. S. for 1,200 foreign companies, 300 foreign banks and other financial institutions, 175 embassies and consulates, and 375 foreign press outlets. Includes five indexes.

Morningstar American Depositary Receipts. Morningstar Inc. • Biweekly. Looseleaf. Provides detailed profiles of 700 foreign companies having shares traded in the U. S. through American Depositary Receipts (ADRs).

Thomson World Bank Directory: International Edition. Accuity Inc. • Annual. $685 Individuals. Covers: Over 10,000 international banks and their branches in around 200 countries around the globe, including the top 1,000 U.S. Banks. Entries include: Institution name, address, phone, fax, key banking officers by functional title, directors, data established, expanded statement of condition, including a profit and loss account and historic performance ratios.

HANDBOOKS AND MANUALS

Miller European Accounting Guide. Aspen Publishers, Inc. • Annual. $159.00. Presents analysis of accounting standards in 25 European and Eastern European countries.

INTERNET DATABASES

Financial Times: Where Information Becomes Intelligence. FT Group. Phone: (800)628-8088 • URL: http://www.ft.com • Web site provides extensive data and information relating to international business and finance, with daily updates. Includes Markets Today, Company News, Economic Indicators, Equities, Currencies, Capital Markets, Euro Prices, etc. Fees: Free (registration required).

Gateway to the European Union. European Union. Email: pressoffice@eurostat.cec.be • URL: http://www.europa.eu.int • Web site provides access to a wide variety of EU information, including statistics (Eurostat), news, policies, publications, key issues, and official exchange rates for the euro. Includes links to the European Central Bank, the European Investment Bank, and other institutions. Fees: Free.

ONLINE DATABASES

Banking Information Source. ProQuest L.L.C. • Provides indexing and abstracting of periodical and other literature from 1982 to date, with weekly updates. Covers the financial services industry: banks, savings institutions, investment houses, credit unions, insurance companies, and real estate organizations. Emphasis is on marketing and management. Inquire as to online cost and availability. (Formerly *FINIS: Financial Industry Information Service.*).

InvesText. Thomson Financial. • Provides full text online of investment research reports from more than 600 sources, including leading brokers and investment bankers. Reports are available on approximately 60,000 U. S. and international corporations. Separate industry reports cover 54 industries. Time span is 1982 to date, with daily updates. Inquire as to online cost and availability.

OTHER SOURCES

Country Finance. The Economist Intelligence Unit. • Annual $425.00 per year. Discusses banking and financial conditions in each of 47 countries. Includes foreign exchange regulations, the currency outlook, sources of capital, financing techniques, and tax considerations.

International Capital Markets and Securities Regulation. Harold S. Bloomenthal. Thomson West. • $3,876 full set. Nine looseleaf volumes. Periodic supplementation. Securities regulation in industrialized nations. (Securities Law Series).

World Investment Report. United Nations Publications. • Annual. Concerned with foreign direct investment, economic development, regional trends, transnational corporations, and globalization.

PERIODICALS AND NEWSLETTERS

American Banker: The Financial Services Daily. SourceMedia Inc. • Daily. $895.00 per year. Provides news of banking, investment products, mortgages, credit unions, finance, bank technology, and legal developments.

Central Banking: Policy, Markets, Supervision. European Business Publications Inc. • Quarterly. $260.00 per year, including annual *Central Banking Directory.* Published in England by Central Banking Publications. Reports and comments on the activities of central banks around the world. Also provides discussions of the International Monetary Fund (IMF), the Organization for Economic Cooperation and Development (OECD), the Bank for International Settlements (BIS), and the World Bank.

The Economist. The Economist Intelligence Unit. • 190 ₱ Individuals Print and Digital per week.

Emerging Markets Debt Report. SourceMedia Inc. • Weekly. $895.00 per year. Newsletter. Provides information on new and prospective sovereign and corporate bond issues from developing countries. Includes an emerging market bond index and pricing data.

Emerging Markets Quarterly. Institutional Investor Inc. Journals Group. • Quarterly. Price on application. Newsletter on financial markets in developing areas, such as Africa, Latin America, Southeast Asia, and Eastern Europe. Topics include institutional investment opportunities and regulatory matters. Formerly *Emerging Markets Weekly.*

Euromoney: The Monthly Journal of International Money and Capital Markets. American Educational Systems. • Monthly. $490.00 per year. Includes print and online editions. Supplement available *Guide to World Equity Markets.*

Finance and Development. International Monetary Fund, Publication Services. • Quarterly. Free.

Financial Flows and the Developing Countries. World Bank Group. • Quarterly. $150.00 per year. Concerned mainly with debt, capital markets, and foreign direct investment. Includes statistical tables.

Financial Management (FM). Financial Management Association International. • Quarterly. $392 Institutions for Americas, online only. Covers theory and practice of financial planning, international finance, investment banking, and portfolio management. Includes *Financial Practice* and *Education and Contemporary Finance Digest.*

Financial Times (London). The Financial Times, Inc. • Daily, except Sunday. $572.88 per year. An international business and financial newspaper, featuring news from London, Paris, Frankfurt, New York, and Tokyo. Includes worldwide stock and bond market data, commodity market data, and monetary/currency exchange information.

Institutional Investor International Edition: The Magazine for International Finance and Investment. Institutional Investor Inc. Journals Group. • Monthly. $475.00 per year. Covers the international aspects of professional investing and finance. Emphasis is on Europe, the Far East, and Latin America.

Institutional Investor: The Premier of Professional Magazine Finance. Institutional Investor Inc. Journals Group. • Monthly. $445.00 per year. Includes print and online editions. Edited for portfolio managers and other investment professionals. Special feature issues include "Country Credit Ratings," "Fixed Income Trading Ranking," "All-America Research Team," and "Global Banking Ranking.".

International Bank Credit Analyst. BCA Publications Ltd. • Monthly. $795.00 per year. "A monthly forecast and analysis of currency movements, interest rates, and stock market developments in the principal countries, based on a continuous appraisal of money and credit trends worldwide." Includes many charts and graphs providing international coverage of money, credit, and securities.

International Currency Review. World Reports Ltd. • Quarterly. $475.00 per year.

International Financial Law Review. American Educational Systems. • Monthly. $750.00 per year. Includes print and online editions.

International Monetary Fund Staff Papers. International Monetary Fund, Publication Services. • Quarterly. Individuals, $56.00 per year; students, $28.00 per year. Contains studies by IMF staff members on balance of payments, foreign exchange, fiscal policy, and related topics. Formerly *International Monetary Fund Staff Papers.*

Project Finance Monthly. Infocast Inc. • Description: Provides information about the power industry. Includes industry news, financing, regulation, and contracts.

Standard and Poor's Ratings Handbook. Standard & Poor's Financial Services L.L.C. • Monthly. $275.00 per year. Newsletter. Provides news and analysis of international credit markets, including information on new bond issues. Formerly *Credit Week International Ratings.*

U.S. Banker. SourceMedia Inc. • Monthly. $65.00 per year. Edited for bank executives and managers. Covers a wide variety of banking and financial topics.

RESEARCH CENTERS AND INSTITUTES

Federal Reserve Board - Division of International Finance - Advanced Foreign Economies Section. 20th St. & Constitution Ave. NW, Washington, DC 20551. Phone: (202)452-2865; Email: paul.wood@frb.gov • URL: http://www.federalreserve.gov/econresdata/ifafe-staff.htm • Economic developments and policies in major industrial countries that affect international payments, foreign exchange markets, and U.S. economic activity and policy. Research focuses on open-economy macroeconomic issues.

University of Pennsylvania - The Wharton School - Rodney L. White Center for Financial Research. 3254 Steinberg Hall-Dietrich Hall, Philadelphia, PA 19104-6367. Phone: (215)898-7616; Fax: (215)573-8084; Email: rlwctr@finance.wharton.upenn.edu • URL: http://rodneywhitecenter.wharton.upenn.edu • Research areas include financial management, money markets, real estate finance, and international finance.

STATISTICS SOURCES

Statistical Information on the Financial Services Industry. American Bankers Association. • Annual. Members, $150.00; non-members, $275.00. Presents a wide variety of data relating to banking and financial services, including consumer economics, personal finance, credit, government loans, capital markets, and international banking.

TRADE/PROFESSIONAL ASSOCIATIONS

ACI - Financial Markets Association. 8, Rue du Mail, F-75002 Paris, France. Phone: 33 1 42975115 • URL: http://www.aciforex.org • National financial markets associations representing individuals and firms. Seeks to advance the foreign exchange and related financial businesses. Represents members at the international level; facilitates communication and cooperation among financial markets professionals and firms; sponsors educational and career development programs.

New Rules for Global Finance Coalition. 2000 M St. NW, Ste. 720, Washington, DC 20036-3327. Phone: (202)277-9390; Fax: (202)280-1141 • URL: http://www.new-rules.org • Represents the interests of development, human rights, labor, environmental, and religious organizations and scholars. Aims to reform the global financial architecture to prevent financial crises. Works to stabilize the world economy, reduce poverty and inequality, uphold fundamental rights, and protect the environment.

Union of Finance Personnel in Europe. Friedrichstrasse 169/170, D-10117 Berlin, Germany. Phone: 49 30 206256600; Fax: 49 30 206256601 • URL: http://www.finanzpersonal-europa.de/pages/default/impressum.php • Promotes the finance industry in Europe. Protects the legal, economic, and professional interests of European finance personnel.

INTERNATIONAL INSTITUTIONS

See INTERNATIONAL AGENCIES

INTERNATIONAL INVESTMENTS

See FOREIGN INVESTMENTS

INTERNATIONAL LAW AND REGULATION

ABSTRACTS AND INDEXES

Current Law Index. Cengage Learning Inc. • $1,332 Individuals. Monthly. $1269.00 per year. Produced in cooperation with the American Association of Law Libraries. Indexes more than 900 law journals, legal newspapers, and specialty publications from the U.S., Canada, U.K., Ireland, Australia, and New Zealand.

Index to Foreign Legal Periodicals. American Association of Law Libraries. University of California Press - Journals and Digital Publishing Division. • Quarterly. $725.00 per year. Annual cumulation.

Index to Legal Periodicals and Books. H.W. Wilson Co. • Monthly. $490.00 per year. Quarterly and annual cumulations.

ALMANACS AND YEARBOOKS

British Year Book of International Law. Oxford University Press. • Annual. $400. An essential work of reference for academics and practicing lawyers. It provides up-to-date information on important developments in modern international law.

Yearbook of the International Law Commission. United Nations, Department of Public Information. • Annual.

CD-ROM DATABASES

Index to Legal Periodicals and Books. EBSCO Publishing Inc. • Contains indexing of more than 1,400 English language legal periodicals from 1981 to date and 2,500 books.

INTERNET DATABASES

Lexis.com Research System. Lexis-Nexis Group. Phone: 800-227-4908 or (937)865-6800; Fax: (937)865-6909; Email: webmaster@prod.lexis-nexis.com • URL: http://www.nexis.com • Fee-based Web site offers extensive searching of a wide variety of legal sources. Additional features include Daily Opinion Service, lexis.com Bookstore, Career Center, CLE Center, Law Schools, and Practice Pages ("Pages specific to areas of specialty").

OTHER SOURCES

International Capital Markets and Securities Regulation. Harold S. Bloomenthal. Thomson West. • $3,876 full set. Nine looseleaf volumes. Periodic supplementation. Securities regulation in industrialized nations. (Securities Law Series).

World Trade Organization Dispute Settlement Decisions: Bernan's Annotated Reporter. Bernan Press. • 3/year. $320 2 volume set. Contains all World Trade Organization Panel Reports and Appellate Decisions since the establishment of the WTO in 1995. Includes such cases as "The Importation, Sale, and Distribution of Bananas."

PERIODICALS AND NEWSLETTERS

Europe and Eurasia Business Committee Dispatch. Bulgarian-U.S. Business Council. • Monthly. Provides current information on regulations, legislation and specific industries for Central/Eastern Europe, New Independent States, Turkey and Iran.

International and Comparative Law Quarterly (ICLQ). British Institute of International and Comparative Law. • Quarterly. $394 Nonmembers print & online. Journal offering coverage of comparative law as well as public and private international law.

International Financial Law Review. American Educational Systems. • Monthly. $750.00 per year. Includes print and online editions.

The International Lawyer. American Bar Association, International Law and Practice Section. • Quarterly. Free to members; non-members, $60.00 per year.

International Legal Materials. American Society of International Law. • Bimonthly. $190.00 per year.

World Trade Review: Economics, Law, International Institutions. Cambridge University Press. • Three times a year. Individuals, $48.00 pr year; institutions, $200.00 per year. Published in conjunction with the World Trade Organization (www.wto.org). Covers "issues of relevance to the multilateral trading system.".

TRADE/PROFESSIONAL ASSOCIATIONS

American Society of International Law. 2223 Massachusetts Ave. NW, Washington, DC 20008. Phone: (202)939-6000; Fax: (202)797-7133 or (202)319-1670 • URL: http://www.asil.org • Scholars, practitioners, government officials, political scientists, and specialists in subjects. Such as human rights, law of the sea, disarmament and more. Provides access to insight and information on the world of international law.

Canada-India Business Council. 1 St. Clair Ave. E, Ste. 302, Toronto, ON, Canada M4T 2V7. Phone: (416)214-5947; Fax: (416)214-9081; Email: info@canada-indiabusiness.ca • URL: http://canada-indiabusiness.ca • Canadian businesses trading with India. Promotes increased trade between Canada and India. Advocates for legislation conducive to trade; represents members before trade and industrial organizations and the public.

Canadian Netherlands Business and Professional Association. 600 The East Mall, Etobicoke, ON, Canada M9B 4B1. Phone: (647)478-8620; Fax: (647)478-8620; Email: info@cnbpa.ca • URL: http://www.cnbpa.ca • Business people and professionals in Canada and the Netherlands. Promotes increased trade and communication between Canada and the Netherlands. Serves as a forum for the exchange of information among members.

China-Britain Business Council. Portland House, 3rd Fl., Bressenden Pl., London SW1E 5BH, United Kingdom. Phone: 44 20 78022000; Fax: 44 20 78022029; Email: enquiries@cbbc.org • URL: http://www.cbbc.org • British companies doing business in China. Promotes British trade in China. Acts as a liaison between the British and Chinese governments and member companies.

Transparency, Consciousness and Citizenship. CLN 202, Bloco B, Sala 101, 70832-525 Brasilia, DF, Brazil. Phone: 55613218085; Fax: 55 55613216333; Email: mail@tcc-brasil.org.br • URL: http://www.tcc-brasil.org.br • Corporations, organizations, and individuals interested in reducing fraud and corruption in international business transactions. Seeks to: raise public awareness of anticorruption measures; influence legislation regulating international business transactions. Formulates standards of integrity to govern international business dealings; maintains network of businesses agreeing to adhere to these standards. Conducts anticorruption and antifraud programs. Sponsors research and educational activities.

Transparency International - Argentina. Piedras 547, 1070 Buenos Aires, Argentina. Phone: 54 11 43314925; Fax: 54 11 43314925; Email: comunicacion@poderciudadano.org • URL: http://www.poderciudadano.org.ar • Corporations, organizations, and individuals interested in reducing fraud and corruption in international business transactions. Seeks to raise public awareness of anticorruption measures and influence legislation regulating international business transactions. Formulates standards of integrity to govern international business dealings and maintains network of businesses agreeing to adhere to these standards. Conducts anticorruption and antifraud programs. Sponsors research and educational activities.

Transparency International - Australia. PO Box 41, Melbourne, VIC 3130, Australia. Phone: 61 3 98770369; Fax: 61 3 98771628; Email: tioz@transparency.org.au • URL: http://www.transparency.org.au • Corporations, organizations, and individuals interested in reducing fraud and corruption in international business transactions. Seeks to: raise public awareness of anticorruption measures; influence legislation regulating international business transactions. Formulates standards of integrity to govern international business dealings; maintains network of businesses agreeing to adhere to these standards. Conducts anticorruption and antifraud programs. Sponsors research and educational activities.

Transparency International - Bangladesh. House 141, Blk. E, Rd. 12, Banani, Dhaka 1213, Bangladesh. Phone: 880 2 9887884 or 880 2

8826036; Fax: 880 2 9884811; Email: info@ti-bangladesh.org • URL: http://www.ti-bangladesh.org • Corporations, organizations, and individuals interested in reducing fraud and corruption in international business transactions. Seeks to: raise public awareness of anticorruption measures; influence legislation regulating international business transactions. Formulates standards of integrity to govern international business dealings; maintains network of businesses agreeing to adhere to these standards. Conducts anticorruption and antifraud programs. Sponsors research and educational activities.

Transparency International - Brussels. E Jacqmainlaan 135, B-1000 Brussels, Belgium. Phone: 32 2 5090031; Email: info@transparencybelgium.be • URL: http://www.transparencybelgium.be • Corporations, organizations, and individuals interested in reducing fraud and corruption in international business transactions. Seeks to raise public awareness of anticorruption measures and influence legislation regulating international business transactions. Formulates standards of integrity to govern international business dealings and maintains network of businesses agreeing to adhere to these standards. Conducts anticorruption and antifraud programs. Sponsors research and educational activities.

Transparency International - South Africa. Methodist House, 114 Rissik St., Braamfontein 2017, South Africa. Phone: 27 11 4037746; Fax: 27 11 4034966 • URL: http://www.tisa.org.za • Corporations, organizations, and individuals interested in reducing fraud and corruption in international business transactions. Seeks to raise public awareness of anticorruption measures and to influence legislation regulating international business transactions. Formulates standards of integrity to govern international business dealings; maintains network of businesses agreeing to adhere to these standards. Conducts anticorruption and antifraud programs. Sponsors research and educational activities.

Transparency International - Switzerland. Schanzeneckstrasse 25, Postfach 8509, CH-3001 Bern, Switzerland. Phone: 41 31 3823550; Fax: 41 31 3825044; Email: info@transparency.ch • URL: http://www.transparency.ch/de/index.php?navid=1 • Corporations, organizations, and individuals interested in reducing fraud and corruption in international business transactions. Seeks to raise public awareness of anti-corruption measures and to influence legislation regulating international business transactions. Formulates standards of integrity to govern international business dealings; maintains network of businesses agreeing to adhere to these standards. Conducts anti-corruption and antifraud programs. Sponsors research and educational activities.

Transparency International - Thailand. Centre for Philanthropy and Civil Society, 118 Seri-Thai Rd., Bankapi, Bangkok 10240, Thailand. Phone: 66 2 3777206; Fax: 66 2 3747399 • URL: http://www.transparency-thailand.org • Represents corporations, organizations, and individuals interested in reducing fraud and corruption in international business transactions. Seeks to raise public awareness of anticorruption measures and influence legislation regulating international business transactions. Formulates standards of integrity to govern international business dealings and maintains network of businesses agreeing to adhere to these standards. Conducts anticorruption and antifraud programs. Sponsors research and educational activities.

Transparency International - Turkey. Niyazi Bey Apt., No. 30, D:5 Sisli, Istanbul, Turkey. Phone: 90 212 240 52 81; Fax: 90 212 240 52 81; Email: info@seffaflik.org • URL: http://www.seffaflik.org/index_en.asp • Corporations, individuals, organizations interested in reducing fraud and corruption in Turkish government, business and society. Seeks to raise public awareness of anticorruption measures and to influence legislation regulating transparency and good governance. Formulates standards of integrity in all sectors; maintains network of businesses agreeing to adhere to these standards. Conducts anticorruption and antifraud programs. Sponsors research and educational activities.

Transparency International - UK. 32-36 Loman St., London SE1 0EH, United Kingdom. Phone: 44 20 7922-7906; Email: info@transparency.org.uk • URL: http://www.transparency.org.uk • Corporations, organizations, and individuals interested in reducing corruption in international business transactions. Eliminates corruption, particularly its corrosive impact on development in poorer countries and corruption's role in worsening poverty, increasing political instability and undermining the rule of law and democracy. Aims to encourage business to adopt commercial practices that are ethical. Formulates standards of integrity to govern international business dealings; maintains network of businesses agreeing to adhere to these standards. Priority areas are: construction and engineering sector; corruption in the official arms trade; money laundering in the UK; transparency in the extractive industries and reform of the UK law of corruption. Conducts anticorruption programs. Undertakes research and educational activities.

Transparency International - Zimbabwe. 96 Central Ave., Causeway, Harare, Zimbabwe. Phone: 263 4 793246 or 263 4 793277; Email: tiz@transparency.org.zw • URL: http://www.transparency.org.zw • Corporations, organizations, and individuals interested in reducing fraud and corruption in international business transactions. Seeks to raise public awareness of anti-corruption measures and influence legislation regulating international business transactions. Formulates standards of integrity to govern international business dealings and maintains network of businesses agreeing to adhere to these standards. Conducts anti-corruption and antifraud programs. Sponsors research and educational activities.

INTERNATIONAL MARKETING

See also ASIAN MARKETS; CANADIAN MARKETS; EUROPEAN CONSUMER MARKET; LATIN AMERICAN MARKETS

ABSTRACTS AND INDEXES

Business Periodicals Index Retrospective. EBSCO Publishing Inc. • 11/year. Quarterly and annual cumulations.

F & S Index: Europe. Cengage Learning Inc. • Monthly. $2,532.00 per year, including quarterly and annual cumulations. Provides annotated citations to marketing, business, financial, and industrial literature. Coverage of European business activity includes trade journals, financial magazines, business newspapers, and special reports. Formerly Predicasts F & S Index: Europe.

F & S Index: International. Cengage Learning Inc. • $2,659 Individuals. Monthly. $2,532.00 per year, including quarterly and annual cumulations. Provides annotated citations to marketing, business, financial, and industrial literature. Coverage of international business activity includes trade journals, financial magazines, business newspapers, and special reports. Areas included are Asia, Latin America, Africa, the Middle East, Oceania, and Canada.

NTIS Alerts: Business & Economics. U.S. Department of Commerce National Technical Information Service. • Biweekly. $130 per year. Covers consumer affairs, minority enterprises, marketing and economics, international commerce, banking, and finance.

PAIS International. ProQuest L.L.C. • Monthly. $850.00 per year; cumulations three times a year. Provides topical citations to the worldwide literature of public affairs, economics, demographics, sociology, and trade. Text in English; indexed materials in English, French, German, Italian, Portuguese and Spanish.

ALMANACS AND YEARBOOKS

World Development Report. World Bank Group. • Annual. Covers history, conditions, and trends relating to economic globalization and localization. Includes selected data from *World Development Indicators* for 132 countries or economies. Key indicators are provided for 78 additional countries or economies.

CD-ROM DATABASES

Business Abstracts with Full Text. EBSCO Publishing Inc. • Includes full text articles from more than 460 business publications from 1982 to present. Indexing for nearly 880 publications.

PAIS International. ProQuest L.L.C. • Monthly. $1,995.00 per year. Contains over 650,000 citations to the literature of contemporary social, political, and economic issues.

World Development Report. World Bank Group. • Annual. Covers history, conditions, and trends relating to economic globalization and localization. Includes selected data from *World Development Indicators* for 132 countries or economies. Key indicators are provided for 78 additional countries or economies.

DIRECTORIES

International Media Guide: Business-Professional: Asia/Pacific, Middle East, Africa. Kantar Media SRDS. • $553 Individuals online; 1 year. Provides information on 3,800 trade publications "from Africa to the Pacific Rim," including advertising rates and circulation data.

International Media Guide Business-Professional Publications: Europe. Kantar Media SRDS. • $553 Individuals online; 1 year. Describes 8,800 trade journals from Eastern and Western Europe, with advertising rates and circulation data.

International Media Guide: Business/Professional Publications: The Americas. Kantar Media SRDS. • $553 Individuals online; 1 year. Describes over 4,400 trade publications from North, South, and Central America, with advertising rates and circulation data.

International Media Guide: Newspapers Worldwide. Kantar Media SRDS. • $553 Individuals online; 1 year. Covers over 3,400 papers in every major city in the world.

Market Share Reporter (MSR). Cengage Learning Inc. • $777 Individuals. 2013. $740.00. Published by Gale. Provides consumer market share data for leading companies. Also available as eBook.

World Market Share Reporter. Cengage Learning Inc. • $572 Individuals. Compilation of global market share data from periodical literature. Covers nearly 1,670 entries in 360 geographic worldwide locations of companies and products and services.

ONLINE DATABASES

Market Research Monitor. Euromonitor International Inc. • Contains full-text reports online from *Market Research Europe, Market Research Great Britain, Market Research International, and Retail Monitor International.* Time period is 1995 to date, with monthly updates. Inquire as to online cost and availability.

MarkIntel. Thomson Financial. • Provides the current full text online of more than 50,000 market research reports covering 54 industries, from 85 leading research firms worldwide. Reports include extensive forecasts and market analysis. Inquire as to online cost and availability.

Wilson Business Abstracts Online. H.W. Wilson Co. • Indexes and abstracts 600 major business periodicals, plus the *Wall Street Journal* and the business section of the *New York Times.* Indexing is from 1982, abstracting from 1990, with the two newspapers included from 1993. Updated weekly. Inquire as to online cost and availability. (*Business Periodicals Index* without abstracts is also available online.).

PERIODICALS AND NEWSLETTERS

Advertising Age's Euromarketing. Crain Communications Inc. • Weekly. $295 Individuals. Newsletter on European advertising and marketing.

Pharma Business: The International Magazine of Pharmaceutical Business and Marketing. Engel Publishing Partners. • Six times a year. $235.00 per year. Circulated mainly in European countries. Coverage includes worldwide industry news, new drug products, regulations, and research developments.

RESEARCH CENTERS AND INSTITUTES

Pennsylvania State University - Institute for the Study of Business Markets. 484 Business Bldg., Smeal College of Business, University Park, PA 16802. Phone: (814)863-2782; Fax: (814)863-0413; Email: isbm@psu.edu • URL: http://isbm.smeal.psu.edu • Research areas include international distribution channels.

STATISTICS SOURCES

Market Share Reporter (MSR). Cengage Learning Inc. • $777 Individuals. 2013. $740.00. Published by Gale. Provides consumer market share data for leading companies. Also available as eBook.

World Market Share Reporter. Cengage Learning Inc. • $572 Individuals. Compilation of global market share data from periodical literature. Covers nearly 1,670 entries in 360 geographic worldwide locations of companies and products and services.

TRADE/PROFESSIONAL ASSOCIATIONS

European Marketing Academy. Pl. de Brouckere Plein, 31, B-1000 Brussels, Belgium. Phone: 32 2 2266660; Fax: 32 2 5121929; Email: emac@eiasm.be • URL: http://www.emac-online.org/r/default.asp?iId=FLFDIE • Persons involved or interested in teaching or research in the field of marketing. Serves as forum for exchange of information concerning marketing; fosters improved dissemination of information; promotes international exchange in the field of marketing.

INTERNATIONAL MONETARY FUND (IMF)

ABSTRACTS AND INDEXES

PAIS International. ProQuest L.L.C. • Monthly. $850.00 per year; cumulations three times a year. Provides topical citations to the worldwide literature of public affairs, economics, demographics, sociology, and trade. Text in English; indexed materials in English, French, German, Italian, Portuguese and Spanish.

CD-ROM DATABASES

PAIS International. ProQuest L.L.C. • Monthly. $1,995.00 per year. Contains over 650,000 citations to the literature of contemporary social, political, and economic issues.

PERIODICALS AND NEWSLETTERS

Central Banking: Policy, Markets, Supervision. European Business Publications Inc. • Quarterly. $260.00 per year, including annual *Central Banking Directory.* Published in England by Central Banking Publications. Reports and comments on the activities of central banks around the world. Also provides discussions of the International Monetary Fund (IMF), the Organization for Economic Cooperation and Development (OECD), the Bank for International Settlements (BIS), and the World Bank.

IMF Survey. International Monetary Fund. • Description: Timely news on topics of general interest in the fields of international finance, country economics, trade, and commodities. Contains information on the IMF's activities, including press releases, major management speeches, and lending activity data rates.

International Monetary Fund Staff Papers. International Monetary Fund, Publication Services. • Quarterly. Individuals, $56.00 per year; students, $28.00 per year. Contains studies by IMF staff members on balance of payments, foreign exchange, fiscal policy, and related topics. Formerly *International Monetary Fund Staff Papers.*

RESEARCH CENTERS AND INSTITUTES

Center for International Policy. 2000 M St. NW, Ste. 720, Washington, DC 20036-3327. Phone: (202)232-3317; Fax: (202)232-3440; Email: cip@ciponline.org • URL: http://www.ciponline.org • Research subjects include the International Monetary Fund, the World Bank, and other international financial institutions. Analyzes the impact of policies on social and economic conditions in developing countries.

TRADE/PROFESSIONAL ASSOCIATIONS

Bretton Woods Committee. 1726 M St. NW, Ste. 200, Washington, DC 20036. Phone: (202)331-1616; Fax: (202)785-9423; Email: info@brettonwoods.org • URL: http://www.brettonwoods.org • Corporate CEOs, university administrators, former government officials, state governors, association and trade union executives, and bankers. Seeks to inform and educate the public regarding the activities of the World Bank, International Monetary Fund, and other Multinational Development Banks (MDB). Promotes U.S. participation in MDBs.

INTERNATIONAL ORGANIZATIONS

See INTERNATIONAL AGENCIES

INTERNATIONAL TAXATION

See also MULTINATIONAL CORPORATIONS; TAX SHELTERS

ABSTRACTS AND INDEXES

Accounting and Tax Index. ProQuest L.L.C. • Quarterly. Indexes accounting, auditing, and taxation literature appearing in journals, books, pamphlets, conference proceedings, and newsletters.

Business Periodicals Index Retrospective. EBSCO Publishing Inc. • 11/year. Quarterly and annual cumulations.

Index to Legal Periodicals and Books. H.W. Wilson Co. • Monthly. $490.00 per year. Quarterly and annual cumulations.

PAIS International. ProQuest L.L.C. • Monthly. $850.00 per year; cumulations three times a year. Provides topical citations to the worldwide literature of public affairs, economics, demographics, sociology, and trade. Text in English; indexed materials in English, French, German, Italian, Portuguese and Spanish.

CD-ROM DATABASES

PAIS International. ProQuest L.L.C. • Monthly. $1,995.00 per year. Contains over 650,000 citations to the literature of contemporary social, political, and economic issues.

The Tax Directory. Tax Analysts. • Quarterly. $499 Individuals both volumes, web, CD or print. Updated quarterly on CD-ROM and in print; updated continually online. Covering federal, state, and international tax officials, tax practitioners, and corporate tax executives.

DIRECTORIES

The Tax Directory. Tax Analysts. • Quarterly. $499 Individuals both volumes, web, CD or print. Updated quarterly on CD-ROM and in print; updated continually online. Covering federal, state, and international tax officials, tax practitioners, and corporate tax executives.

INTERNET DATABASES

TAXNET.PRO. Carswell. Phone: 800-387-5164 or (416)609-3800; Fax: (416)298-5082; Email: orders@carswell.com • URL: http://www.carswell.com/taxnetpro.asp • Fee-based Web site provides complete coverage of Canadian tax law and regulation, including income tax, provincial taxes, accounting, and payrolls. Daily updates. Base price varies according to product.

ONLINE DATABASES

Wilson Business Abstracts Online. H.W. Wilson Co. • Indexes and abstracts 600 major business periodicals, plus the *Wall Street Journal* and the business section of the *New York Times.* Indexing is from 1982, abstracting from 1990, with the two newspapers included from 1993. Updated weekly. Inquire as to online cost and availability. (*Business Periodicals Index* without abstracts is also available online.).

OTHER SOURCES

Foreign Tax and Trade Briefs. Matthew Bender and Company Inc. • Quarterly. $1,054 book. The latest tax and trade information for over 100 foreign countries.

International Tax Agreements. United Nations Publications. • Irregular. Price varies. Looseleaf.

Manufacturers' Tax Alert. Wolters Kluwer Law & Business CCH. • Monthly $297.00 per year. Newsletter. Covers the major tax issues affecting manufacturing companies. Includes current developments in various kind of federal, state, and international taxes: sales, use, franchise, property, and corporate income.

PERIODICALS AND NEWSLETTERS

Highlights and Documents. Tax Analysts. • Daily. $2,599.95 Individuals. Provides daily coverage of IRS, congressional, judicial, state, and international tax developments. Includes abstracts and citations for "all tax documents released within the previous 24 to 48 hours." Annual compilation available *Highlights and Documents on Microfiche.*

International Tax Journal. Wolters Kluwer Law and Business. • Quarterly. $297.00 per year. Articles, columns and tax notes pertaining to the international tax market.

International Tax Report: Maximizing Tax Opportunities Worldwide. Informa Group PLC. • Monthly. $1,100.00 per year.

Journal of Taxation of Global Transactions. Wolters Kluwer Law & Business CCH. • Quarterly. $215.00 per year. Covers tax laws affecting international business activity.

Tax Management International Forum. Bloomberg BNA. • Quarterly. $370.00 per year.

Tax Management International Journal: A Monthly Professional Review of Current International Tax Developments. BNA Tax Management. • Monthly. $426.00 per year. Semiannual *Index.*

Worldwide Tax Daily. Tax Analysts. • Weekly. $999 Individuals. Provides "news and in-depth reports on a variety of international tax topics." Summarizes tax statutes, regulations, rulings, court decisions, and treaties from various countries of the world.

RESEARCH CENTERS AND INSTITUTES

Harvard Law School International Tax Program. Harvard Law School, 1563 Massachusetts Ave., 1563 Massachusetts Ave., Cambridge, MA 02138. Phone: (617)495-3100 or (617)495-4406; Fax: (617)495-1110; Email: sfs@law.harvard.edu • URL: http://www.law.harvard.edu/programs/index.html • Studies the worldwide problems of taxation, including tax law and tax administration.

STATISTICS SOURCES

Revenue Statistics. Organisation for Economic Cooperation and Development Publications and Information Center. • Annual. $65.00. Presents data on government revenues in OECD countries, classified by type of tax and level of government. Text in English and French.

TRADE/PROFESSIONAL ASSOCIATIONS

Argentine Fiscal Associations. IFLYSIB Calle 59, 789, CC 565, B19 00BTE La Plata, Argentina. Phone: 54 221 4254904; Fax: 54 221 4257317; Email: afa@iflysib.unlp.edu.ar • URL: http://www2.ib.edu.ar/afa • Promotes the study and advancement of international and comparative law with regards to public finance, specifically international, comparative fiscal law and the financial and economic aspects of taxation.

INTERNATIONAL TRADE

See FOREIGN TRADE

INTERNET

See also COMPUTER COMMUNICATIONS; ELECTRONIC COMMERCE; ONLINE INFORMATION SYSTEMS

ABSTRACTS AND INDEXES

Business Periodicals Index Retrospective. EBSCO Publishing Inc. • 11/year. Quarterly and annual cumulations.

Computer Science Index. EBSCO Publishing Inc. • Quarterly. $245 per year. Contains brief abstracts of book and periodical literature covering all phases of computing, including approximately 70 specific application areas.

F & S Index: United States. Cengage Learning Inc. • $2,659 Individuals. Monthly. $2,532.00 per year, including quarterly and annual cumulations. Provides annotated citations to marketing, business, financial, and industrial literature. Coverage of U.S. business activity includes trade journals, financial magazines, business newspapers, and special reports.

Internet and Personal Computing Abstracts (print edition). EBSCO Publishing Inc. • Quarterly. $269.00 per year, including cumulative index. Provides more than 10,000 abstracts annually from both trade and academic publications. Covers computer hardware, software, product reviews, Web topics, e-commerce, networks, corporate news, security, and related topics. Formerly *Microcomputer Abstracts.*

Key Abstracts: Computer Communications and Storage. Institution of Engineering and Technology. • Monthly. $1,138. Provides international coverage of journal and proceedings literature, including material on optical disks and networks.

Library Literature and Information Science Index. H.W. Wilson Co. • Quarterly. Annual cumulation. Price varies.

ALMANACS AND YEARBOOKS

Annual Society for Information Science and Technology, Information and Business Div. Martha E. Williams, editor. Information Today, Inc. • Annual. $79.95 Members. Published on behalf of the American Society for Information Science (ASIS). Covers trends in planning, basic techniques, applications, and the information profession in general.

CD-ROM DATABASES

Authority Computer and Telecommunications Law Library. Matthew Bender and Company Inc. • Quarterly. Price on request. Full text CD-ROM provides cases, analysis, sample agreements, and other information relating to computer law, telecommunications regulation (cable, broadcasting, satellite, Internet), international computer law, and computer contracts.

Business Abstracts with Full Text. EBSCO Publishing Inc. • Includes full text articles from more than 460 business publications from 1982 to present. Indexing for nearly 880 publications.

OECD Statistical Compendium. Organization for Economic Cooperation and Development. • Semiannual. $1,905.00 per year for 1 to 10 users. CD-ROM contains more than 730,000 monthly, quarterly, and annual time series for OECD countries, 1960 to date. Includes fully searchable data on agriculture, food, economic indicators, national accounts, employment, energy, finance, industry, technology, and foreign trade. Results can be displayed in various forms.

WILSONDISC: Library Literature and Information Science Index. H.W. Wilson Co. • Quarterly. Includes unlimited access to the online version of *Library Literature.* Provides CD-ROM indexing of about 400 periodicals, covering a wide range of topics having to do with libraries, library management, and the information industry.

DIRECTORIES

Bibliography: A Guide to Development Research Resources. Bentz Whaley Flessner. • Annual. Covers: Online services, Internet sites, listservs, and other resources of interest to business prospectors. Entries include: Company name, address, phone, fax, e-mail, Web address, name and title of contact, biographical data, description of services/projects.

Environmental Guide to the Internet. Government Institutes. • $83 Individuals Paperback. Covers: 1,200 resources covering the environment on the Internet, including organizations, products, and resources, including discussion groups, electronic journals, newsgroups, and discussion groups. Entries include: Name, online address, description, e-mail address.

Guide to EU Information Sources on the Internet. Euroconfidentiel S. A. • Annual. $210.00. Contains descriptions of more than 1,700 Web sites providing information relating to the European Union and European commerce and industry. Includes a quarterly e-mail newsletter with new sites and address changes.

Handbook of Internet Stocks. Mergent Inc. • Annual. $19.95. Contains detailed financial information on more than 200 Internet-related corporations, including e-commerce firms and telecommunications hardware manufacturers. Lists and rankings are provided.

Harley Hahn's Internet Yellow Pages. Harley Hahn. Harley Hahn. • Annual. Lists World Wide Web sites in more than 193 categories.

International Business Information on the Web: Searcher Magazine's Guide to Sites and Strategies for Global Business Research. Information Today, Inc. • $29.95. Lists directories, search engines, banks, financial institutions, news sources, government contacts, chambers of commerce, and other country-specific information. Covers: Approximately 1,000 Web sites related to international business research including general business sites in the United States and worldwide. Publication includes: URLs. Entries include: Information regarding each site.

Internet Access Providers: An International Resource Directory. Mecklermedia Corp. • $30. Covers: 150 private companies, electronic bulletin board systems, and regional networks that offer dial-in access to the Internet. Entries include: Description.

The Internet Blue Pages: The Guide to Federal Government Web Sites. Information Today, Inc. • Annual. $34.95. Provides information on more than 1,800 Web sites used by various agencies of the federal government. Includes indexes to agencies and topics. Links to all Web sites listed are available at www.fedweb.com. (CyberAge Books.).

Internet Service Providers Directory (ISP). Info-Group Inc. • Annual. Number of listings: 27,032. Entries include: Name, address, phone, size of advertisement, name of owner or manager, number of employees, year first in "Yellow Pages." Compiled from telephone company "Yellow Pages," nationwide.

IOMA Business Directory. Institute of Management & Administration Inc. • Covers: Business Web sites. Entries include: Web links.

Library Journal: Reference: Print, CD-ROM, Online (year). Reed Elsevier Group plc Reed Business Information. • Annual. Issued in November as a supplement to *Library Journal.* Lists new and updated reference material, including general and trade print titles, directories, annuals, CD-ROM titles, and online sources. Includes material from more than 200 publishers, arranged by company name, with an index by subject.

Library Journal Sourcebook: The Reference For Library Products & Services. Reed Elsevier Group plc Reed Business Information. • Annual. Publication includes: List of over 600 suppliers of products and services used by libraries from abstracting to word processing equipment. Entries include: Company name, address, phone, list of products or services. Complete listings for more than 100 architectural firms; Disaster planning for librarians.

Major Information Technology Companies of the World. Cengage Learning Inc. • Annual. $1,460 Individuals. 2008. 11th edition. eBook. Published by Graham & Whiteside. Contains profiles of more than 8,250 leading information technology companies in various countries.

Plunkett's E-Commerce and Internet Business Almanac. Plunkett Research Ltd. • Annual. $349.99. Contains detailed profiles of 250 large companies engaged in various areas of Internet commerce, including e-business Web sites, communications equipment manufacturers, and Internet service providers. Includes CD-ROM.

Plunkett's Employers' Internet Sites with Careers Information. Plunkett Research Ltd. • Annual. $199. 99. Includes diskette.

Plunkett's On-Line Trading, Finance, and Investment Web Sites Almanac. Plunkett Research Ltd. • Annual. $149.99. Provides profiles and usefulness rankings of financial Web sites. Sites are rated from 1 to 5 for specific uses. Includes CD-ROM.

SRDS Interactive Advertising Source. Kantar Media SRDS. • Quarterly. $569.00 per year. Provides descriptive profiles, rates, audience, personnel, etc., for producers of various forms of interactive or multimedia advertising: online/Internet, CD-ROM, interactive TV, interactive cable, interactive telephone, interactive kiosk, and others.

Telehealth Buyer's Guide. Miller Freeman Inc. • Annual. $10.00. Lists sources of telecommunications and information technology products and services for the health care industry.

The Thunderbird Guide to International Business Resources on the World Wide Web. Wiley Publishing

Group. • $57.95 Individuals Paperback. Covers: Web sites for political and economic developments that affect trade worldwide. Derived from a study by Dean's Global Information and Technology at Thunderbird (American Graduate School of International Management). Entries include: country, category (country information, business, business topics, government resources, information providers), title, URL, and description.

The Wilson Guide to Internet Experts. H.W. Wilson Co. • $54.99. Covers: Noted authorities in the Internet industry. Entries include: Biographical details, office address and phone number, e-mail and Web site addresses, current projects, specialties.

World Directory of Business Information Sources. Euromonitor International Business Reference Div. • $700 Individuals U.S.D. Covers: National and international Web sites of interest to business researchers, provided by trade associations, magazines, government agencies, private research firms and others.

E-BOOKS

Semantic Web for Business: Cases and Applications. Cengage Learning Inc. • 2009. eBook. Published by Information Science Reference. Presents cases that illustrate the benefits of semantic seb technologies as applied to e-business and e-commerce scenarios. Covers topics such as business integration, organizational knowledge management, and semantic web services.

GENERAL WORKS

ISP Business | IPTB. Information Gatekeepers Inc. • Monthly. $695 U.S. and Canada print. Covers news of the business aspects of Internet service providers worldwide. Includes information on finances, marketing, mergers and acquisitions, joint ventures, technologies, customer billing and service, new products, and international developments.

INTERNET DATABASES

Business 2.0 Web Guide to the Best Business Links. Business 2.0 Media Inc. Phone: (415)293-4800; Email: support@business2.com • URL: http://www.business2.com/webguide • Web site presents an extensive, searchable directory of links to "the best, most informative, and authoritative web pages." Twenty main categories cover business, finance, career, company information, people, and technology topics, with thousands of subtopics, all linking to Web sites recommended by experienced business researchers. Fees: Free.

InfoTech Trends. Data Analysis Group. Phone: (925)462-1202; Fax: (925)462-1225; Email: support@infotechtrends.com • URL: http://www.infotechtrends.com • Web site provides both free and fee-based market research data on the information technology industry, including computers, peripherals, telecommunications, the Internet, software, CD-ROM/DVD, e-commerce, and workstations. Fees: Free for current (most recent year) data; more extensive information has various fee structures. Formerly *Computer Industry Forecasts.*

Internet.com: The E-Business and Internet Technology Network. Jupitermedia. Phone: (203)226-6967; Fax: (203)454-5840; Email: info@internet.com • URL: http://www.internet.com • Web site provides a wide variety of information relating to Internet commerce, search engines, news, Web design, servers, browsers, Java, service providers, advertising, marketing, etc. Online searching is offered. Fees: Free. (Formerly produced by Mecklermedia Corp.).

SAEGIS Internet Search. Thomson & Thomson. Phone: 800-692-8833 or (617)479-1600; Fax: (617)786-8273; Email: support@thomson-thomson.com • URL: http://www.thomson-thomson.com • Fee-based Web site provides extensive, common law screening of the World Wide Web for trademarks. Searches are performed offline, with final report delivered to user's "SAEGIS Inbox." Context of trademark within each relevant Web site is indicated, and links are provided.

Search Engine Watch. Internet.com Corp. Phone: (203)662-2800; Fax: (203)655-4686 • URL: http://www.searchenginewatch.com • Web site offers information on various aspects of search engines, including new developments, indexing systems, technology, ratings and reviews of major operators, specialty services, tutorials, news, history, "Search Engine EKGs," "Facts and Fun," etc. Online searching is provided. Formerly *A Webmaster's Guide to Search Engines.*

Wired News. Lycos Inc. 400-2 Totten Pond Rd., Waltham, MA 02451-2053. Phone: (781)370-2700 or (415)276-8400; Fax: (781)370-2600 or (415)276-8500; Email: press@lycos.com • URL: http://www.lycos.com • Provides summaries and full-text of "Top Stories" relating to the Internet, computers, multimedia, telecommunications, and the electronic information industry in general. These news stories are placed in the broad categories of Politics, Business, Culture, and Technology. Affiliated with *Wired* magazine. Fees: Free.

ONLINE DATABASES

Computer Database. Cengage Learning Inc. • Provides one year of full-text online for 150 leading computer-related publications. Also includes 70,000 product specifications and brief profiles of 13,000 computer product vendors and manufacturers. Inquire as to prices and availability.

Wilson Business Abstracts Online. H.W. Wilson Co. • Indexes and abstracts 600 major business periodicals, plus the *Wall Street Journal* and the business section of the *New York Times.* Indexing is from 1982, abstracting from 1990, with the two newspapers included from 1993. Updated weekly. Inquire as to online cost and availability. (*Business Periodicals Index* without abstracts is also available online.).

OTHER SOURCES

Cyberlaw: Intellectual Property in the Digital Millennium. ALM Media Properties LLC. • $530 per year. A basic guide to copyright as applied to the Internet and other electronic sources. (Law Journal Press).

E-Business, Internet, and Online Transactions. Michael L. Taviss and others. Glasser LegalWorks. • Looseleaf. $225.00, including CD-ROM version. Periodic Supplementation. Covers the legal aspects of online content, marketing, advertising, domain names, software licensing, and other Internet issues. Includes many sample forms. (Emerging Growth Companies Series.).

E-Commerce and Internet Law: Treatise with Forms. Ian C. Ballon. Glasser LegalWorks. • $1,479 Individuals Binder/Looseleaf (Full Set). Periodic supplementation. Analyzes Internet legalities, including litigious matters relating to downloading, streaming, music, video, content aggregation, domain names, chatrooms, and search engines. Includes forms, contracts, checklists, sample pleadings, and an extensive glossary.

Internet Payments Report. Jupitermedia Corp. • Annual. $1,095.00. Market research report. Provides data, comment, and forecasts on the collection of electronic payments ("e-money") for goods and services offered through the Internet.

Telecommunications Regulation: Cable, Broadcasting, Satellite, and the Internet. Matthew Bender and Company Inc. • Semiannual. $1,747. Four looseleaf volumes. Covers local, state, and federal regulation, with emphasis on the Telecommunications Act of 1996. Includes regulation of television, telephone, cable, satellite, computer communication, and online services. Formerly *Cable Television Law.*

World Online Markets. Jupitermedia Corp. • Annual. $1,895.00. Market research report. Provides broad coverage of worldwide Internet and online information business activities, including country-by-country data. Includes company profiles and five-year forecasts or trend projections.

PERIODICALS AND NEWSLETTERS

CIO: The Magazine for Chief Information Officers. CXO Media Inc. • Monthly. $129 per year. Edited for chief information officers. Includes a monthly "Web Business" section (incorporates the former *WebMaster* periodical) and a monthly "Enterprise" section for other company executives.

InfoAlert: Your Expert Guide to Online Business Information. Economics Press Inc. • Monthly. $129.00 per year. Newsletter. Provides information on recommended World Wide Web sites in various business, marketing, industrial, and financial areas.

The Information Advisor's Guide to Internet Research. Information Today, Inc. • 10/year. $199.95 U.S. One year subscription. Evaluates free and low-cost websites.

The Information Freeway Report: Free Business and Government Information Via Modem. Washington Researchers Ltd. • Monthly. $160.00 per year. Newsletter. Provides news of business and government databases that are available free of charge through the Internet or directly. Emphasis is on federal government databases and electronic bulletin boards (Fedworld).

Information Outlook: The Monthly Magazine of the Special Libraries Association. Special Libraries Association. • Monthly. $65.00 per year. Topics include information technology, the Internet, copyright, research techniques, library management, and professional development. Replaces *Special Libraries* and *SpeciaList.*

Information Standards Quarterly. National Information Standards Organization. • Quarterly. $130 Individuals /year. Newsletter. Reports on activities of the National Information Standards Organization.

IntdustryWeek. • Resource for manufacturing operations knowledge.

InterActive Consumers. MarketResearch.com. • Monthly. $395.00 per year. Newsletter. Covers the emerging markets for digital content, products, and services. Includes market information on telecommuting, online services, the Internet, online investing, and other areas of electronic commerce.

Interactive Content: Consumer Media Strategies Monthly. Jupitermedia Corp. • Monthly. $675.00 per year; with online edition, $775.00 per year. Newsletter. Covers the broad field of providing content (information, news, entertainment) for the Internet/World Wide Web.

Interactive Home: Consumer Technology Monthly. Jupiter Communications. • Monthly. $625.00 per year; with online edition, $725.00 per year. Newsletter on devices to bring the Internet into the average American home. Covers TV set-top boxes, game devices, telephones with display screens, handheld computer communication devices, the usual PCs, etc.

Interactive Marketing and P R News: News and Practical Advice on Using Interactive Advertising and Marketing to Sell Your Products. Access Intelligence L.L.C. • Biweekly. $495.00 per year. Newsletter. Provides information and guidance on merchandising via CD-ROM ("multimedia catalogs"), the Internet, and interactive TV. Topics include "cybermoney," addresses for e-mail marketing, "virtual malls," and other interactive subjects. Formerly *Interactive Marketing News.*

Internet and Electronic Commerce Strategies: Using Technology to Improve Your Bottom Line. Computer Economics Inc. • Monthly. Price on application. Newsletter on management strategies for making money from the Internet. Compares online marketing with traditional marketing.

Internet Business Report: Software, Tools and

Platforms. Jupitermedia Corp. • Semimonthly. $695.00 per year; with electronic software, $795.00 per year. Newsletter. Covers Internet advertising, fee collection, and attempts in general to make the Internet/World Wide Web profitable. Includes news of how businesses are using the Internet for sales promotion and public relations.

Internet Connection: Your Guide to Government Resources. Glasser LegalWorks. • 10 times a year. $89.00 per year. Newsletter (print) devoted to finding free or low-cost U. S. Government information on the Internet. Provides detailed descriptions of government Web sites.

Internet Industry Magazine. Jonas Publishing. • Semiannual. Price on application. Lists products and services for Internet service providers. Includes Internet-related articles and interviews.

Internet Law and Strategy. ALM Media Properties LLC. • Monthly. $459 per year. Primarily concerned with doing legal research online. Contains reviews of the best Web sites for lawyers. (A Law Journal Newsletter, formerly published by Leader Publications.).

Internet Marketing and Technology Report: Advising Marketing, Sales, and Corporate Executives on Online Opportunities. Computer Economics Inc. • Monthly. $387.00 per year. Newsletter. Covers strategic marketing, sales, advertising, public relations, and corporate communications, all in relation to the Internet. Includes information on "cutting-edge technology" for the Internet.

Internet Marketing Report: News and Advice to Help Companies Harness the Power of the Internet to Achieve Business Objectives. American Future Systems Inc. • Semimonthly. $299.00 per year. Newsletter. Covers Internet marketing strategy, site traffic, success stories, technology, cost control, and other Web site advertising and marketing topics.

Internet Reference Services Quarterly: A Journal of Innovative Information Practice, Technologies, and Resources. The Haworth Press Inc. • Quarterly. $110.00 per year. Covers both theoretical research and practical applications.

Internet Retailer: E-Business Strategies. Thomson Financial Inc. • 10 times a year. $98.00 per year. Trade journal on the selling of retail merchandise through the Internet. Provides information on pricing, payment systems, order management, fraud, digital imaging, advertising, Web trends, and other topics.

Journal of Website Promotion: Innovations in Internet Business Research, Theory, and Practice. The Haworth Press Inc. • Semiannual. $250.00 per year to libraries; $45.00 per year to individuals. Presents a scholarly view of such items as spam, banner ads, pop-ups, click rates, and the use of search engines for advertising.

Multimedia Schools: A Practical Journal of Technology for Education including Multimedia, CD-ROM, Online and Internet and Hardware in K-12. Information Today, Inc. • Six times a year. $39.95 per year. Edited for school librarians, media center directors, computer coordinators, and others concerned with educational multimedia. Coverage includes the use of CD-ROM sources, the Internet, online services, and library technology.

Network World: The Newsweekly of Enterprise Network Computing. Network World Inc. • Weekly. $129.00 per year. Includes special feature issues on enterprise Internets, network operating systems, network management, high-speed modems, LAN management systems, and Internet access providers.

Online Marketplace. Jupiter Communications. • Description: Keeps abreast of the fast-emerging developments in the digital marketplace and emerging interactive technologies. Reports on players and devices to provide the "inside scoop" on this marketplace. Topics include screen phones, interactive television, and smart cards, to name a few. Recurring features include interviews, and columns titled Tool Watch, Site Watch, and News Digest.

Online Searcher. Information Today, Inc. • Bimonthly. $139.00 per year. Edited for librarians, Webmasters, site designers, content managers, and others concerned with knowledge/information management. Includes critical reviews of Web sites, software, search engines, and information services. (Formerly published by Online, Inc.).

U.S. Banker. SourceMedia Inc. • Monthly. $65.00 per year. Edited for bank executives and managers. Covers a wide variety of banking and financial topics.

WebFinance. SourceMedia Inc. • Semimonthly. $995.00 per year. Newsletter (also available online at www.webfinance.net). Covers the Internet-based provision of online financial services by banks, online brokers, mutual funds, and insurance companies. Provides news stories, analysis, and descriptions of useful resources.

RESEARCH CENTERS AND INSTITUTES

Advanced Networking Research Group. Washington University, One Brookings Dr., St. Louis, MO 63130-4899. Phone: (314)935-5455; Fax: (314)935-7302; Email: jst@cs.wustl.edu • Research fields include the design of high speed internetworks and the design of host interfaces.

Columbia University - Columbia Business School - Columbia Institute for Tele-Information. Uris Hall, 3022 Broadway, New York, NY 10027. Phone: (212)854-4222; Fax: (212)854-1471; Email: noam@columbia.edu • URL: http://www8.gsb.columbia.edu/citi • Areas of research include private and public networking, the economics of networks, pricing of network access, and economics of technology adoption in the public network.

University of Southern California - Information Sciences Institute. 4676 Admiralty Way, Ste. 1001, Marina del Rey, CA 90292. Phone: (310)822-1511; Fax: (310)823-6714; Email: vcomms@usc.edu • URL: http://www.isi.edu/home • Research fields include online information and computer science, with emphasis on the World Wide Web.

STATISTICS SOURCES

Standard & Poor's Industry Surveys. Standard & Poor's Financial Services L.L.C. • Semiannual. $1,800.00. Two looseleaf volumes. Includes monthly *Supplements*. Provides detailed, individual surveys of 52 major industry groups. Each survey is revised on a semiannual basis. Also includes "Monthly Investment Review" (industry group investment analysis) and monthly "Trends & Projections" (economic analysis).

TRADE/PROFESSIONAL ASSOCIATIONS

Business Modeling and Integration Domain Task Force. Object Management Group, 109 Highland Ave., Needham, MA 02494. Phone: (781)444-0404; Fax: (781)444-0320; Email: info@omg.org • URL: http://bmi.omg.org • Aims to empower all companies, across all industries, to develop and operate business processes that span multiple applications and business partners, behind the firewall and over the Internet.

Electronic Frontier Foundation. 815 Eddy St., San Francisco, CA 94109. Phone: (415)436-9333; Fax: (415)436-9993; Email: info@eff.org • URL: http://www.eff.org • Promotes the creation of legal and structural approaches to help ease the assimilation of new technologies by society. Seeks to: help policymakers develop a better understanding of issues underlying telecommunications; increase public understanding of the opportunities and challenges posed by computing and telecommunications fields. Fosters awareness of civil liberties issues arising from the advancements in new computer-based communications media and supports litigation to preserve, protect, and extend First Amendment rights in computing and telecommunications technology. Maintains speakers' bureau; conducts educational programs. Encourages and supports the development of tools to endow non-technical users with access to computer-based telecommunications.

National Information Standards Organization. 3600 Clipper Mill Rd., Ste. 302, Baltimore, MD 21211. Phone: (301)654-2512; Fax: (410)685-5278; Email: hreid@copyright.com • URL: http://www.niso.org • Identifies, develops, maintains, and publishes technical standards to manage information in the changing environment used by libraries, publishers, and information services. Supports open access to NISO standards. Standards available at website.

INTERNET COMMERCE

See ELECTRONIC COMMERCE

INTERNSHIP PROGRAMS

TRADE/PROFESSIONAL ASSOCIATIONS

AIESEC Bahrain. BBIC Headquarters, Hidd Area, Manama, Bahrain. Phone: 973 17358819; Email: info.bh@aiesec.net • URL: http://www.aiesec.org/bahrain • Represents students of economics or business and related fields presently studying at affiliated universities worldwide. Aims to develop internationally educated managers. Manages the international exchange of students on internships around the world. Conducts training of members in the management of international business operations.

AIESEC Canada. 161 Eglinton Ave. E, Ste. 402, Toronto, ON, Canada M4P 1J5. Phone: (416)368-1001; Fax: (416)368-4490; Email: info2010@aiesec.ca • URL: http://aiesec.ca • Develops students through international internship exchange. Serves as a platform for young people to discover their potential so as to have a positive impact in the society.

AIESEC China. c/o Zachary Law, VP Communication, Block E, Rm. 1108, 16th St., hongguancun, Haidian mansion, Haidian District, Beijing, China. Phone: 86 10 82866532; Email: mainland.china@aiesec.net • URL: http://www.aiesec.cn • Provides leadership and work abroad opportunities. Organizes conferences and virtual tools to build networks. Contributes to the development of the communities with an overriding commitment to international co-operation and understanding. Facilitates international traineeship exchanges for its members and stakeholders.

AIESEC Kenya. PO Box 30197-00200, Nairobi, Kenya. Phone: 254 20 2608757; Email: info@aiesec.or.ke • URL: http://ke.aiesec.org • Enables students and recent graduate the opportunity to live and work in another country. Serves as a platform for young people to discover and develop their potential. Organizes conferences.

AIESEC Pakistan. 201 2nd Fl., Cotton Exchange, Bldg., II Chundrigarh Rd., Karachi, Pakistan. Phone: 92 21 35464958; Email: info@aiesec.pk • URL: http://www.aiesec.org/pakistan • Represents students of economics or business and related fields presently studying at affiliated universities worldwide. Aims to develop internationally educated managers. Manages the international exchange of students on internships around the world. Conducts training of members in the management of international business operations.

AIESEC Qatar. PO Box 24475, Doha, Qatar. Phone: (974)5542-6271; Email: qatar@aiesec.net • URL: http://www.aiesec.org/qatar • Represents students of economics or business and related fields presently studying at affiliated universities worldwide. Aims to develop internationally educated managers. Manages the international exchange of students on internships around the world. Conducts training of members in the management of international business operations.

AIESEC United States. 11 Hanover Sq., Ste. 1700, New York, NY 10005. Phone: (212)757-3774 • URL: http://aiesecus.org • Students of economics or business and related fields presently studying at affiliated universities worldwide. Aims to develop an internationally educated managers. Manages the international exchange of students on internships around the world. Conducts training of members in the management of international business operations.

National Society for Experiential Education. 19 Mantua Rd., Mount Royal, NJ 08061-1006. Phone: (856)423-3427; Email: nsee@talley.com • URL: http://www.nsee.org • Members include representatives of internship programs. Formerly National Society for Internships and Experential Education.

INTERPERSONAL RELATIONS

See HUMAN RELATIONS

INTERSTATE COMMERCE

See MOTOR VEHICLE LAW AND REGULATION

INTERVIEWING

See also COUNSELING

ABSTRACTS AND INDEXES

Psychological Abstracts. American Psychological Association. • Monthly. Members, $815.00 per year; individuals and institutions, $1,207.00 per year. Covers the international literature of psychology and the behavioral sciences. Includes journals, technical reports, dissertations, and other sources.

INTRANETS (COMPUTER NETWORKS)

ABSTRACTS AND INDEXES

Internet and Personal Computing Abstracts (print edition). EBSCO Publishing Inc. • Quarterly. $269.00 per year, including cumulative index. Provides more than 10,000 abstracts annually from both trade and academic publications. Covers computer hardware, software, product reviews, Web topics, e-commerce, networks, corporate news, security, and related topics. Formerly *Microcomputer Abstracts.*

INTERNET DATABASES

InfoTech Trends. Data Analysis Group. Phone: (925)462-1202; Fax: (925)462-1225; Email: support@infotechtrends.com • URL: http://www.infotechtrends.com • Web site provides both free and fee-based market research data on the information technology industry, including computers, peripherals, telecommunications, the Internet, software, CD-ROM/DVD, e-commerce, and workstations. Fees: Free for current (most recent year) data; more extensive information has various fee structures. Formerly *Computer Industry Forecasts.*

PERIODICALS AND NEWSLETTERS

Business Communications Review. Key3Media Group, Inc. • Monthly. $45.00 per year. Edited for communications managers in large end-user companies and institutions. Includes special feature issues on intranets and network management.

Communications News: Solutions for Today's Networking Decision Managers. Nelson Publishing Inc. • Monthly. Free to qualified personnel; others, $84.00 per year. Includes coverage of "Internetworking" and "Intrenetworking." Emphasis is on emerging telecommunications technologies.

Computer Economics Networking Strategies Report: Advising IT Decision Maker ractices and Current Trends. Computer Economics Inc. • Monthly. $395.00 per year. Newsletter. Edited for information technology managers. Covers news and trends relating to a variety of corporate computer network and management information systems topics. Emphasis is on costs. Formerly *Intranet and Networking Strategies Report.*

IntraNets: Enterprise Strategies and Solutions. Information Today, Inc. • $199.50 U.S.. Bimonthly. Newsletter on the use of Internet technology for local library networks.

INTRAOCULAR LENS INDUSTRY

See CONTACT LENS AND INTRAOCULAR LENS INDUSTRIES

INTRAPRENEURS

See ENTREPRENEURS AND INTRAPRENEURS

INVENTIONS

See also NEW PRODUCTS; PATENTS

ABSTRACTS AND INDEXES

NTIS Alerts: Government Inventions for Licensing. U.S. Department of Commerce National Technical Information Service. • Biweekly. $130 per year. Covers a wide variety of industrial and technical areas.

INTERNET DATABASES

United States Patent and Trademark Office. U. S. Department of Commerce. Phone: 800-786-9199 or (703)308-4357; Fax: (703)305-7786; Email: help@mbda.gov • URL: http://www.uspto.gov • Web site provides extensive information about patents and trademarks, with advanced search facilities for specific documents or names. "Special Pages" are available for "How to Search," "Trademarks-Logos-Brands," "Inventor Resources," and other topics. A complete fee schedule is available for filing applications, appeals, copies, etc.

PERIODICALS AND NEWSLETTERS

Official Gazette of the United States Patent and Trademark Office: Patents. U. S. Government Printing Office. • Weekly. Contains the Patents, Patent Office Notices, and Designs issued each week (www.uspto.gov). Annual indexes are sold separately.

TRADE/PROFESSIONAL ASSOCIATIONS

American Society of Inventors. PO Box 354, Feasterville, PA 19053. Phone: (215)546-6601; Email: info@asoi.org • URL: http://asoi.org • Engineers, scientists, businessmen, and others who are interested in a cooperative effort to serve both the short- and long-term needs of the inventor and society. Works with government and industry to improve the environment for the inventor. Aims to encourage invention and innovation; help the independent inventor become self-sufficient. Establishes a networking system for inventors and businessmen to solve problems. Sponsors educational programs.

INVENTORY CONTROL

See also PRODUCTION CONTROL

ABSTRACTS AND INDEXES

Business Periodicals Index Retrospective. EBSCO Publishing Inc. • 11/year. Quarterly and annual cumulations.

ONLINE DATABASES

Wilson Business Abstracts Online. H.W. Wilson Co. • Indexes and abstracts 600 major business periodicals, plus the *Wall Street Journal* and the business section of the *New York Times.* Indexing is from 1982, abstracting from 1990, with the two newspapers included from 1993. Updated weekly. Inquire as to online cost and availability. (*Business Periodicals Index* without abstracts is also available online.).

PERIODICALS AND NEWSLETTERS

Production and Inventory Management Journal. APICS. • Quarterly.

RESEARCH CENTERS AND INSTITUTES

Board of Research. Babson College, 204 Babson, Babson Park, MA 02457-0310. Phone: (781)235-1200; Fax: (718)239-6416; Email: chern@babson.edu • URL: http://www.babson.edu/bor • Research areas include management, entrepreneurial characteristics, and multi-product inventory analysis.

Center for Entrepreneurial Studies & Development Inc. 1062 Maple Dr., Ste. 2, Morgantown, WV 26505. Phone: (304)293-5551; Fax: (304)293-6707; Email: info@cesd.wvu.edu • URL: http://www.cesd.wvu.edu • Inventory control systems included as a research field.

University of Missouri—St. Louis - Center for Business and Industrial Studies. 220 Express Scripts Hall, 1 University Dr., Saint Louis, MO 63121-4499. Phone: (314)516-6108 or (314)516-5451; Email: ldsmith@umsl.edu • URL: http://www.umsl.edu/divisions/business/ncbis/index.html • Research fields include inventory and management control. Specific projects also include development of computer software for operations in public transit systems.

TRADE/PROFESSIONAL ASSOCIATIONS

APICS. 8430 W Bryn Mawr Ave., Ste. 1000, Chicago, IL 60631. Phone: 800-444-2742 or (773)867-1777; Fax: (773)639-3000; Email: service@apics.org • URL: http://www.apics.org • Members are professional resource managers.

North American Association of Inventory Services. PO Box 120145, Saint Paul, MN 55112. • URL: http://www.naais.com • Represents Independent inventory services; individuals interested in the inventory industry; individuals outside the industry who have performed notable service. Promotes activities aimed at enabling the inventory service to operate efficiently and maintain high standards of conduct. Provides a clearinghouse and medium for the benefit of owners of businesses and shops involving the utilization and maintenance of product inventories. Considers and deals with problems of operation and management, such as those associated with customer accounts and employment. Disseminates business information on the inventory service industry. Maintains speakers' bureau; compiles statistics.

INVESTMENT ADVISORY SERVICES

See also INVESTMENTS; STOCKS

DIRECTORIES

Money Market Directory of Pension Funds and Their Investment Managers. Standard & Poors

For publishers' addresses, refer to SOURCES CITED section at the back of the book.

Money Market Directories. • Institutional funds and managers.

HANDBOOKS AND MANUALS

Gale Business Insights Handbook Of. Cengage Learning Inc. • $627 Individuals. Examines the questions "What is social media marketing" and "How can it be used in my business?".

PERIODICALS AND NEWSLETTERS

Hulbert Financial Digest. Hulbert Financial Digest. • Monthly. Description: Provides performance ratings on more than 400 portfolios recommended by more than 145 financial newsletters, calculated on the basis of model portfolios constructed according to each newsletter's advice. Includes a timing scoreboard, analysis of newsletter performance, list of mutual funds most frequently recommended for sale or purchase, a stock market sentiment index, and a question and answer section.

Investors Intelligence. Michael Burke, editor. Chartcraft Inc. • Description: Serves as a "comprehensive and authoritative Stock Market Advisory Service dedicated to bringing the investor facts, original projections, and a cross section of the recommendations of other leading Services.".

The Moneypaper. Temper of the Times Communications, Inc. Temper of the Times Communications Inc. • Description: Contains strategies to minimize stock sales costs and articles on investing and market trends. Includes a summary of monthly financial news drawn from over 70 financial publications and advisory services. Recurring features include columns titled Summing Up, Market Outlook, and Stocktrack.

The Wall Street Digest. Donald H. Rowe The Wall Street Digest. • Description: Covers major investment areas, including stocks and bonds; foreign currencies; gold, silver, and other precious metals; real estate; tax shelters; and estate planning. Recurring features include "a digest of the month's best" investment and financial seminars, newsletter reviews, and statistics.

TRADE/PROFESSIONAL ASSOCIATIONS

Association of Independent Asset Managers in Liechtenstein. PO Box 134, FL-9496 Balzers, Liechtenstein. Phone: 423 3882350; Fax: 423 3882359; Email: info@vuvl.li • URL: http://www.vuvl.li/CFDOCS/cmsout/admin/content.cfm?GroupID=141 • Aims to protect and promote the reputation of independent asset managers in Liechtenstein and abroad. Seeks to establish professional guidelines within the framework of the Asset Management Accounting. Facilitates exchange of information within the business community.

Cayman Finance. Fidelity Financial Ctre., 2nd Fl., 1 Gecko Link, West Bay Rd., Grand Cayman, Cayman Islands. Phone: (345)623-6725; Email: enquiries@caymanfinance.ky • URL: http://caymanfinances.com • Represents Cayman's financial services industry. Promotes the integrity and quality of financial services in the Cayman Islands. Offers the media and the financial services industry with information on issues that affect Cayman's financial services.

CFA Institute. 560 Ray C. Hunt Dr., Charlottesville, VA 22903-2981. Phone: 800-247-8132 or (434)951-5499; Fax: (434)951-5262; Email: info@cfainstitute.org • URL: http://www.cfainstitute.org/pages/index.aspx • Formerly Association for Investment Management and Research.

INVESTMENT ANALYSIS

See FINANCIAL ANALYSIS

INVESTMENT BANKING

BIOGRAPHICAL SOURCES

Who's Who in Finance and Business. Marquis Who's Who L.L.C. • Biennial. $349 Individuals. Provides over 21,000 concise biographies of business leaders in all fields.

Who's Who in the Securities Industry. Economist Publishing Co. • Annual. $15.00. Lists about 1,000 investment bankers.

CD-ROM DATABASES

Buyout Financing Sources/M & A Intermediaries. SourceMedia Inc. • Annual. $895.00. Provides the CD-ROM combination of *Directory of Buyout Financing Sources* and *Directory of M & A Intermediaries*. Contains information on more than 1,000 financing sources (banks, insurance companies, venture capital firms, etc.) and 850 intermediaries (corporate acquirers, valuation firms, lawyers, accountants, etc.). Also includes back issues of *Buyouts Newsletter* and *Mergers & Acquisitions Report*. Fully searchable.

DIRECTORIES

Securities Industry Yearbook. Securities Industry and Financial Markets Association. • Annual. $110 Members. Covers: over 600 member securities firms, with about 480 of them covered in detail. Entries include: For firms covered in detail--Company name, name of parent company, address, phone, capital position and rank, number of offices and type, number of employees, area of specialization, names and titles of key personnel, number of registered representatives, departments with name of department head, dollar volume of underwriting and syndication by type, other financial data. For other firms--Company name, address, name of delegated liaison to the association.

Who's Who in Finance and Business. Marquis Who's Who L.L.C. • Biennial. $349 Individuals. Provides over 21,000 concise biographies of business leaders in all fields.

PERIODICALS AND NEWSLETTERS

Corporate Financing Week: The Newsweekly of Corporate Finance, Investment Banking and M and A. Institutional Investor Inc. Journals Group. • Weekly. $2,550.00 per year. Includes print and online editions. Newsletter for corporate finance officers. Emphasis is on debt and equity financing, mergers, leveraged buyouts, investment banking, and venture capital.

Financial Management (FM). Financial Management Association International. • Quarterly. $392 Institutions for Americas, online only. Covers theory and practice of financial planning, international finance, investment banking, and portfolio management. Includes *Financial Practice and Education and Contemporary Finance Digest*.

Investment Management Mandate Pipeline. SourceMedia Inc. • Weekly. $1,295.00 per year. Newsletter. Edited for money managers and other investment professionals. Covers personnel news, investment strategies, and industry trends.

TRADE/PROFESSIONAL ASSOCIATIONS

Association for Financial Markets in Europe. St. Michael's House, 1 George Yard, London EC3V 9DH, United Kingdom. Phone: 44 207 7439300; Fax: 44 207 7439301 • URL: http://www.afme.eu • Principal trade association in the UK for firms active in the investment banking and securities industry. Represents the interests of its members on all aspects of their business and promotes their views to the authorities in the UK, the European Union, and elsewhere.

Association of Chinese Finance Professionals. 240 Hazelwood Ave., San Francisco, CA 94127. Email: acfp_us@yahoo.com • URL: http://www.acfp.net • Promotes cooperation between U.S. and China in the fields of commercial and investment banking, asset management, insurance, corporate finance, financial planning and financial software. Provides a forum for finance professionals to exchange ideas and discuss experiences.

Financial Industry Regulatory Authority. 1735 K St., Washington, DC 20006. Phone: (301)590-6500; Fax: (202)293-6260; Email: francine.lee@finra.org • URL: http://www.finra.org • Formerly National Association of Securities Dealers.

INVESTMENT CLUBS

TRADE/PROFESSIONAL ASSOCIATIONS

Investment Education Institute. 711 W 13 Mile Rd., Ste. 900, Madison Heights, MI 48071. Phone: 877-275-6242 or (248)583-6242 or (248)654-3047; Fax: (248)583-4880; Email: service@betterinvesting.org • URL: http://www.better-investing.org • Affiliated with the National Association of Investors Corporation and conducted through various business schools. Seeks to enlarge the scope and quality of investment education, especially through investment clubs. Has held conferences for educators, financial institutions, financial writers, and corporate shareholder relations executives to gain information and to stimulate activity in these groups. Representatives from 50 investment club councils have taken a series of special courses to improve their teaching skills. Individuals and corporations have contributed funds to establish the program.

National Association of Investors Corporation. PO Box 220, Royal Oak, MI 48068-0220. Phone: 877-275-6242 or (248)583-6242; Fax: (248)583-4880; Email: service@betterinvesting.org • URL: http://www.betterinvesting.org • Affiliated with Investment Education Institute. Formerly National Association of Investment Clubs.

INVESTMENT COMPANIES

See also CLOSED-END FUNDS

ALMANACS AND YEARBOOKS

Investment Company Yearbook. Thomson Financial Inc. • Annual. $310.00. Provides an "entire history of recent events in the mutual funds industry," with emphasis on changes during the past year. About 100 pages are devoted to general information and advice for fund investors. Includes 600 full-page profiles of popular mutual funds, with brief descriptions of 10,000 others, plus 7,000 variable annuities and 500 closed-end funds. Contains a glossary of technical terms, a Web site index, and an overall book index. Also known as *Wiesenberger Investment Companies Yearbook*.

DIRECTORIES

HedgeWorld Annual Compendium: The Hedge Fund Industry's Definitive Reference Guide. HedgeWorld. • Annual. $499.00. Contains profiles of 500 domestic and offshore hedge funds with more than $50 million in assets under management. Includes articles on "The Basics of Investing in Hedge Funds," "Beyond the Basics," and other information.

HedgeWorld Service Provider League Tables & Analyses. HedgeWorld. • Annual. $595.00. Provides quantitative and qualitative information on firms providing services to hedge funds: accountants/auditors, administrators, custodians, legal counsel, and prime brokers. Detailed categories cover banks, clearing services, consultants, derivatives business, investment companies, wealth management services, etc.

Investment Counsel Association of America--Directory of Member Firms. Investment Adviser Association. • Annual. Covers: over 300 member investment counseling firms. Entries include: Name and address of firm; contact, number of clients, assets under management, staff, type of account, minimum account and fee.

Major Financial Institutions of the World. Cengage Learning Inc. • $1,460 Individuals. 2012. 16th edition. eBook. Published by Graham & Whiteside.

Contains detailed information on more than 10,000 important financial institutions in various countries. Includes banks, investment companies, and insurance companies.

Morningstar Mutual Funds. Morningstar Inc. • Twenty issues per year. $639 per year. Looseleaf service. Contains detailed information and risk-adjusted ratings on over 1,500 load and no-load, equity and fixed-income mutual funds. Annual returns are provided for up to 12 years for each fund.

Mutual Fund Profiles. Standard & Poor's Financial Services L.L.C. • Quarterly. $158.00 per year. Produced jointly with Lipper Analytical Services. Provides detailed information on approximately 800 of the largest stock funds and taxable bond funds. In addition, contains concise data on about 2,400 smaller funds and municipal bond funds.

Nelson Information's Directory of Investment Managers. Nelson Information. • Annual. $595.00. Three volumes. Provides information on 2,200 investment management firms, both U.S. and foreign.

HANDBOOKS AND MANUALS

Money Manager's Compliance Guide. Thompson Publishing Group Inc. • $739.00 per year. Two looseleaf volumes. Monthly updates and newletters. Edited for investment advisers and investment companies to help them be in compliance with governmental regulations, including SEC rules, restrictions based on the Employee Retirement Income Security Act (ERISA), and regulations issued by the Commodity Futures Trading Commission (CFTC).

Moody's Bank and Finance Manual. Mergent. • Annual. $1,750 Four volumes. Includes biweekly supplements in *Moody's Bank and Finance News Report.*

INTERNET DATABASES

The Financial Post. National Post Online. Phone: 800-805-1184 or (244)383-2300; Fax: (416)383-2443 • URL: http://www.nationalpost.com/financialpost/ • Provides a broad range of Canadian business news online, with daily updates. Includes news, opinion, and special reports, as well as "Investing," "Money Rates," "Market Watch," and "Daily Mutual Funds." Allows advanced searching (Boolean operators), with links to various other sites. Fees: Free.

FundAlarm. Roy Weitz. Phone: (818)345-7516; Fax: (818)776-1562 • URL: http://www.fundalarm.com • Web site subtitle: "Know when to hold'em, know when to fold'em, know when to walk away, know when to run." Provides lists of underperforming mutual funds ("3-ALARM Funds") and severely underperforming funds ("Most Alarming 3-ALARM Funds"). Performance is based on various benchmarks. Site also provides mutual fund news, recent manager changes, and basic data for each of about 2,100 funds. Monthly updates. Fees: Free.

Morningstar.com: Your First Second Opinion. Morningstar Inc. 22 W Washington St., Chicago, IL 60602. Phone: 800-735-0700 or (312)696-6000; Fax: (312)696-6001; Email: newsroom@morningstar.com • URL: http://www.corporate.morningstar.com • Annual. $199 Premium membership. Web site provides a broad selection of information and advice on both mutual funds and individual stocks, including financial news and articles on investment fundamentals.

Mutual Funds Interactive. Brill Editorial Services, Inc. Phone: (877)442-7455 • URL: http://www.brill.com • Web site provides specific information on individual funds in addition to general advice on mutual fund investing and 401(k) plans. Searching is provided, including links to moderated newsgroups and a chat page.

TheStreet.com: Your Insider's Look at Wall Street. TheStreet.com, Inc. Phone: 800-562-9571 or (212)321-5000; Fax: (212)321-5016 • URL: http://www.thestreet.com • Daily. Iconoclastic advice and comment on the stock market, but premium service displays a more comprehensive selection of news and analysis.

U.S. Securities and Exchange Commission. 100 F St. NE, Washington, DC 20549. Phone: 800-732-0330 or (202)942-8088; Fax: (202)942-9634; Email: webmaster@sec.gov • URL: http://www.sec.gov • SEC Web site offers free access through EDGAR to text of official corporate filings, such as annual reports (10-K), quarterly reports (10-Q), and proxies. (EDGAR is "Electronic Data Gathering, Analysis, and Retrieval System.") An example is given of how to obtain executive compensation data from proxies. Text of the daily *SEC News Digest* is offered, as are links to other government sites, non-government market regulators, and U. S. stock exchanges. Search facilities are extensive. Fees: Free.

ONLINE DATABASES

Vickers On-Line. Vickers Stock Research Corp. • Provides detailed online information relating to insider trading and the securities holdings of institutional investors. Daily updates. Inquire as to online cost and availability.

OTHER SOURCES

Fund Governance: Legal Duties of Investment Company Directors. ALM Media Properties LLC. • $580 print and online + ebook. Covers the legal obligations of directors of mutual funds and closed-end funds. (Law Journal Press).

Mergent's Annual Dividend Record. Mergent Inc. • Annual. Provides detailed dividend data, including tax information, for 12,000 stocks and 18,000 mutual funds. Covers the most recent year. Formerly *Moody's Annual Dividend Record.*

Money Fund Monitor. iMoneyNet Inc. • Provides daily and weekly performance information and rankings. Contact for pricing.

Money Fund Report. iMoneyNet Inc. • Weekly. $1,095.00 per year. Looseleaf. Contains detailed information on about 1,000 U.S. money market funds, including portfolios and yields.

PERIODICALS AND NEWSLETTERS

Financial Planning: The Magazine for Financial Service Professionals. SourceMedia Inc. • Monthly. $79.00 per year. Edited for independent financial planners and insurance agents. Covers retirement planning, estate planning, tax planning, and insurance, including long-term healthcare considerations. Special features include a Retirement Planning Issue, Mutual Fund Performance Survey, and Variable Life and Annuity Survey.

The Financial Post: Canadian's Business Voice. Financial Post Datagroup. • Daily. $200.00 per year. Provides Canadian business, economic, financial, and investment news. Features extensive price quotes from all major Canadian markets: stocks, bonds, mutual funds, commodities, and currencies. Supplement available: *Financial Post 500.* Includes annual supplement.

Fund Action. Institutional Investor Inc. Journals Group. • Weekly. $2,475.00 per year. Newsletter. Includes print and online editions. Edited for mutual fund executives. Covers competition among funds, aggregate statistics, new products, regulations, service providers, and other subjects of interest to fund managers.

Growth Fund Guide: The Investor's Guide to Dynamic Growth Funds. Growth Fund Research Inc. • Monthly. $99.00 per year. Newsletter. Covers no-load growth mutual funds.

Guide to Stock Mutual Funds: A Quarterly Compilation of Mutual Fund Ratings and Analysis Covering Equity and Balanced Funds. Weiss Research Inc. • Quarterly. $438.00 per year. Emphasis is on rating of financial safety and relative risk. Includes annual summary.

InvesTech Mutual Fund Advisor: Professional Portfolio Allocation. Investech Research. • Every three weeks. $190.00 per year. Newsletter. Contains model portfolio for mutual fund investing.

Latin Fund Management. SourceMedia Inc. • Monthly. $495.00 per year. Newsletter (also available online at www.latinfund.net). Provides news and analysis of Latin American mutual funds, pension funds, and annuities.

Moneyletter. Agora Inc. • Description: Provides assertive, do-it-yourself, individual investors with a unique market timing system, specific buy and sell recommendations, and portfolio allocation advice on no-load mutual funds. Features updates on economic and financial market, fund profiles, and articles on non-mutual fund financial planning issues.

Morningstar FundInvestor. Morningstar Inc. • Monthly. $135 Individuals 1-year subscription. Provides tables of statistical data and star ratings for leading mutual funds "The Morningstar 500" News of funds and financial planning advice for investors is also included.

Mutual Fund Advisor: The Top Performing Mutual Funds. The Mutual Fund Advisor Inc. • Monthly. Price on application. Newsletter.

Mutual Fund Letter. Investment Information Services Inc. • Monthly. $125.00 per year. Newsletter. Provides mutual fund recommendations.

Mutual Fund Market News. Dalbar Publishing Inc. • Description: Provides persons in the mutual fund industry with critical information, breaking news, industry developments, new product analyses, and changes in market share. Covers all major changes of distribution for mutual funds and related products, with emphasis on banks, broker/dealers, captive sales forces, corporate and nonprofit pensions, and direct markets. Recurring features include portfolio management strategies, letters to the editor, a calendar of events and conferences, reports of industry meetings, and columns titled Hot Off the Wire, On the Move, and Newly Registered Funds.

Mutual Fund Strategies. Progressive Investing, Inc. • Monthly. $127.00 per year. Newsletter.

Mutual Fund Trends. Growth Fund Research Inc. • Description: Provides high quality semi-log charts with multiple moving averages and relative strength line on approximately 180 top performing funds. Statistics include lows to current time and high to low. Market indicators with good records. Includes weekly telephone hot line.

Mutual Funds Update. Thomson Financial Inc. • Monthly. $325.00 per year. Provides recent performance information and statistics for approximately 10,000 mutual funds and closed-end funds as compiled from the CDA/Wiesenberger database. Includes commentary and analysis relating to the mutual fund industry. Information is provided on new funds, name changes, mergers, and liquidations.

The No-Load Fund Investor. No-Load Fund Investor Inc. • Description: Predicts which no-load and low-load funds will perform best overall in the coming year. Provides performance data for 995 no- and low-loads and recommends funds and analyzes promising new funds. Recurring features include a listing of the top 20 no-loads plus 18 model portfolios. **Remarks:** Published in conjuction with the Handbook for No-Load Investors.

STATISTICS SOURCES

Statistical Information on the Financial Services Industry. American Bankers Association. • Annual. Members, $150.00; non-members, $275.00. Presents a wide variety of data relating to banking and financial services, including consumer economics, personal finance, credit, government loans, capital markets, and international banking.

Trends in Mutual Fund Activity. Investment Company Institute. • Monthly. $400 Nonmembers per year. Contains statistical tables showing fund industry sales, redemptions, assets, cash, and other data.

U.S. Industry and Trade Outlook. U.S. Department of Commerce National Technical Information Service. • Annual. Produced by the International Trade Administration, U.S. Department of Commerce, in a "public-private" partnership with DRI/McGraw-Hill and Standard & Poor's. Provides basic data, outlook for the current year, and "Long-Term Prospects" (five-year projections) for a wide variety of products and services. Includes high technology industries. Formerly *U.S. Industrial Outlook.*

TRADE/PROFESSIONAL ASSOCIATIONS

Mutual Fund Education Alliance. 100 NW Englewood Rd., No. 130, Kansas City, MO 64118. Phone: (816)454-9422; Fax: (816)454-9322; Email: mfeamail@mfea.com • URL: http://www.mfea.com • Formerly No-Load Mutual Fund Association.

National Association of Real Estate Investment Trusts. 1875 I St. NW, Ste. 600, Washington, DC 20006-5413. Phone: 800-362-7348 or (202)739-9400; Fax: (202)739-9401; Email: baiken@nareit.com • URL: http://www.reit.com • Formerly National Association of Real Estste Investment Funds.

INVESTMENT COMPANIES, CLOSED-END

See CLOSED-END FUNDS

INVESTMENT DEALERS

See STOCK BROKERS

INVESTMENT SERVICES

See INVESTMENT ADVISORY SERVICES

INVESTMENT TRUSTS

See INVESTMENT COMPANIES

INVESTMENTS

ALMANACS AND YEARBOOKS

Advances in Investment Analysis and Portfolio Management. Chung-Few Lee, editor. Elsevier. • Focus on investment analysis and portfolio theory.

CD-ROM DATABASES

Business Abstracts with Full Text. EBSCO Publishing Inc. • Includes full text articles from more than 460 business publications from 1982 to present. Indexing for nearly 880 publications.

InvesText. Thomson Financial. • Monthly. Contains full text on CD-ROM of investment research reports from about 630 sources, including leading brokers and investment bankers. Reports are available on both U. S. and international publicly traded corporations. Separate industry reports cover more than 50 industries. Time span is 1982 to date.

DIRECTORIES

CFA Institute--Membership Directory. CFA Institute. • Annual. $150 per year. Covers: 38,000 security and financial analysts who are practicing investment analysis. Entries include: Name, firm affiliation and address, phone, fax, e-mail.

Expatriate's Guide to Savings & Investments. Public Relations Consultants Association. • Biennial. $20. Covers: Over 400 investment funds and their management companies situated outside of the United Kingdom. Entries include: Name, address, phone, fax, names and titles of key personnel, procedures, policy, financial data.

Gale Directory of Early Stage Investment. Cengage Learning Inc. • $606 print only. Covers several types of early stage investors including: venture capitalists, business incubators, angel investors and angel groups, corporate investment divisions, crowdfunding and co-operative groups.

Global Investment Funds Directory. International Business Publications, USA. • $99.95 Individuals paperback. Covers: Major investment funds interested in international ventures.

Global Pere Investors Directory. PEI London. • $1,195 Individuals. Covers: 1,200 institutions investing in unlisted real estate funds. Entries include: Contact information.

Investment Blue Book. Securities Investigations Inc. • Irregular. $145. Covers: 6,000 brokers and dealers in tax shelter plans; 2,000 sponsors of tax shelter product and suppliers of services to the industry. Entries include: Company name, address, phone, toll-free, phone, fax, name of contact.

Major Financial Institutions of the World. Cengage Learning Inc. • $1,460 Individuals. 2012. 16th edition. eBook. Published by Graham & Whiteside. Contains detailed information on more than 10,000 important financial institutions in various countries. Includes banks, investment companies, and insurance companies.

Mergent International Manual and News Reports. Mergent Inc. • Financial and other information about 13,000 companies in 100 countries. Formerly *Moody's International Manual and News Reports.*

Nelson Information's Directory of Investment Research. Nelson Information. • Annual. Covers: Over 7,000 firms; 14,000 public companies; and 9,000 analysts. Entries include: Name, address, phone, fax, names and titles of key personnel, five-year operating summary, description of business.

Plunkett's On-Line Trading, Finance, and Investment Web Sites Almanac. Plunkett Research Ltd. • Annual. $149.99. Provides profiles and usefulness rankings of financial Web sites. Sites are rated from 1 to 5 for specific uses. Includes CD-ROM.

INTERNET DATABASES

ETF Connect. Nuveen Investments. Phone: 800-257-8787 • URL: http://www.etfconnect.com • Free Web site makes available extensive, searchable information on individual closed-end investment funds, preferred share funds, and exchange-traded index funds. Information on a particular fund is available by name or as part of a classification (high yield, investment grade, municipal, emerging markets, global equity, etc.). Fund charts are available for various time periods, as is data concerning premiums or discounts, dividends, annualized total return, credit quality, "Top 10 Holdings," and so forth.

Factiva. Dow Jones Reuters Business Interactive, LLC. Phone: 800-369-7466 or (609)452-1511; Fax: (609)520-5770; Email: solutions@factiva.com • URL: http://www.factiva.com • Fee-based Web site provides "global news and business information through Web sites and content integration solutions." Includes Dow Jones and Reuters newswires, The Wall Street Journal, and more than 7,000 other sources of current news, historical articles, market research reports, and investment analysis. Content includes 96 major U. S. newspapers, 900 non-English sources, trade publications, media transcripts, country profiles, news photos, etc.

Morningstar.com: Your First Second Opinion. Morningstar Inc. 22 W Washington St., Chicago, IL 60602. Phone: 800-735-0700 or (312)696-6000; Fax: (312)696-6001; Email: newsroom@morningstar.com • URL: http://www.corporate.morningstar.com • Annual. $199 Premium membership. Web site provides a broad selection of information and advice on both mutual funds and individual stocks, including financial news and articles on investment fundamentals.

Nexis.com. Lexis-Nexis Group. Phone: 800-227-4908 or (937)865-6800; Fax: (937)865-6909; Email: webmaster@prod.lexis-nexis.com • URL: http://www.nexis.com • Fee-based Web site offers searching of about 2.8 billion documents in some 30,000 news, business, and legal information sources. Features include a subject directory covering 1,200 topics in 34 categories and a Company Dossier containing information on more than 500,000 public and private companies. Boolean searching is offered.

TheStreet.com: Your Insider's Look at Wall Street. TheStreet.com, Inc. Phone: 800-562-9571 or (212)321-5000; Fax: (212)321-5016 • URL: http://www.thestreet.com • Daily. Iconoclastic advice and comment on the stock market, but premium service displays a more comprehensive selection of news and analysis.

ONLINE DATABASES

InvesText. Thomson Financial. • Provides full text online of investment research reports from more than 600 sources, including leading brokers and investment bankers. Reports are available on approximately 60,000 U. S. and international corporations. Separate industry reports cover 54 industries. Time span is 1982 to date, with daily updates. Inquire as to online cost and availability.

Wilson Business Abstracts Online. H.W. Wilson Co. • Indexes and abstracts 600 major business periodicals, plus the *Wall Street Journal* and the business section of the *New York Times*. Indexing is from 1982, abstracting from 1990, with the two newspapers included from 1993. Updated weekly. Inquire as to online cost and availability. (*Business Periodicals Index* without abstracts is also available online.).

OTHER SOURCES

The Value Line Investment Survey. Value Line Inc. • Weekly. $598 U.S. /year. Provides detailed information and ratings for 1,700 stocks actively-traded in the U. S.

PERIODICALS AND NEWSLETTERS

AAII Journal. American Association of Individual Investors. • 10/year. $49 Individuals. Covers strategy and investment techniques.

Bank Investment Consultant: Sales Strategies for the Financial Adviser. SourceMedia Inc. • Monthly. Controlled circulation. Covers sales and marketing techniques for bank investment and asset management divisions. Formerly *Bank Investment Marketing.*

Commercial and Financial Chronicle. William B. Dana Co. • Weekly. $140.00. per year.

Financial Sentinel: Your Beacon to the World of Investing. Gulf Atlantic Publish. Inc. • Monthly. $29.95 per year. Provides "The only complete listing of all OTC Bulletin Board stocks traded, with all issues listed on the Nasdaq SmallCap Market, the Toronto, and Vancouver Stock Exchanges." Also includes investment advice and recommendations of small capitalization stocks.

Forbes. Forbes Inc. • Biweekly. $29.99 Individuals. Magazine reporting on industry, business and finance management.

Fortune India: Indian Magazine for Business, Finance and Investment. Fortune Publications Private Ltd. • Biweekly. Rs 555 Individuals. Trade publication on premier business, finance and investment.

Investment Dealers' Digest. SourceMedia Inc. • Weekly. $750.00 per year. Covers financial news.

trends, new products, people, private placements, new issues of securities, and other aspects of the investment business. Includes feature stories.

Investment Guide (IG). American Investment Services Inc. • Monthly. $59 printed version. Description: Contains analyses of stock market activity and strategies for investment. Recurring features include market statistics, Dow high-yield stock investing.

Investment News: The Weekly Newspaper for Financial Advisers. Crain Communications Inc. • Weekly. $29.00 per year. Edited for both personal and institutional investment advisers, planners, and managers.

The Investment Reporter. MPL Communications Inc. • Description: Profiles specific companies and market trends and developments, making recommendations to assist in formulating investment strategies. Includes short articles offering advice on investment decisions.

Investor's Business Daily. Investor's Business Daily, Inc. • Daily. $329 Individuals print. Business and financial newspaper.

One Hundred Highest Yields. Bankrate Inc. • Weekly. $124.00 per year. Newsletter. List CD's and money markets offered by federally insured banks. National coverage.

Outstanding Investor Digest: Perspectives and Activities of the Nation's Most Successful Money Managers. Outstanding Investor Digest, Inc. • $395.00 for 10 issues. Newsletter. Each issue features interviews with leading money managers.

Predictions: Specific Investment Forecasts and Recommendations from the World's Top Financial Experts. Lee Euler, editor. Agora Inc. • Monthly. $78.00 per year. Newsletter.

Profit Investor Portfolio: The International Magazine of Money and Style. Profit Publications, Inc. • Bimonthly. $29.95 per year. A glossy consumer magazine featuring specific investment recommendations and articles on upscale travel and shopping.

Profitable Investing. Richard E. Band, editor. Profitable Investing. • Description: Advises individuals seeking low-risk growth by providing : "a wealth of information." Discusses various stocks, mutual funds, interest income, and tax issues. Contains lists of best investments.

Richard C. Young's Intelligence Report. Access Intelligence L.L.C. • Description: Provides information for "serious, conservative investors (buy and hold as opposed to active traders)." Features investing advice and recommendations for best funds, stocks, and bonds for current or retirement income.

Robb Report Worth: Wealth in Perspective. CurtCo Robb Media. • Monthly. $54.95 per year. Glossy magazine featuring articles for the affluent on personal financial management, investments, estate planning, trusts, private bankers, taxes, travel, yachts, and lifestyle. Formerly *Worth: Financial Intelligence*.

SmartMoney: The Wall Street Journal Magazine of Personal Business. The Hearst Corp. • Monthly. $10 Individuals 12 issues. Magazine featuring practical and imaginative ideas for investing, spending and saving. Includes *Stock Trader's Almanac*.

Stanger Report: A Guide to Partnership Investing. Robert A. Stanger & Company Inc. • Quarterly. $447 Individuals Annual. Includes overall statistics on the size of the current market, quarterly fundraising, current distribution rates and coverage and latest valuation reports for closed non-traded REITs, market updates on new registrations, newly-effective issues and fund closings, secondary market transactions, and more.

PRICE SOURCES

Bank and Quotation Record. William B. Dana Co. • Monthly. $130.00 per year.

RESEARCH CENTERS AND INSTITUTES

Princeton University - Bendheim Center for Finance. Department of Economics, 26 Prospect Ave., Princeton, NJ 08540-5296. Phone: (609)258-0770; Fax: (609)258-0771; Email: jessicab@princeton.edu • URL: http://www.princeton.edu/bcf • Research areas include securities markets, portfolio analysis, credit markets, and corporate finance. Emphasis is on quantitative and mathematical perspectives.

STATISTICS SOURCES

Standard & Poor's Industry Surveys. Standard & Poor's Financial Services L.L.C. • Semiannual. $1,800.00. Two looseleaf volumes. Includes monthly *Supplements*. Provides detailed, individual surveys of 52 major industry groups. Each survey is revised on a semiannual basis. Also includes "Monthly Investment Review" (industry group investment analysis) and monthly "Trends & Projections" (economic analysis).

TRADE/PROFESSIONAL ASSOCIATIONS

American Association of Individual Investors. 625 N Michigan Ave., Chicago, IL 60611. Phone: 800-428-2244 or (312)280-0170; Fax: (312)280-9883 or (312)280-1625; Email: members@aaii.com • URL: http://www.aaii.com • Individuals who make their own investment decisions. Assists individuals in becoming effective managers of their own assets through educational programs and research. Provides programs to help individuals develop an investment philosophy and decision-making process based on their objectives, capabilities and attitudes. Offers home-study curriculum on investment topics and a videotape course on investing fundamentals and mutual funds.

Canadian Capital Markets Association. 85 Richmond St. W, Toronto, ON, Canada M5H 2C9. Phone: (416)410-1050; Email: info@ccma-acmc.ca • URL: http://www.ccma-acmc.ca • Enhances the competitiveness of the Canadian capital markets through a forum of industry experts who provide leadership and direction to the investment community. Promotes straight-through processing strategies that reduce ongoing errors and processing costs. Addresses the massive changes occurring in global securities markets such as increased on and off exchange securities trading volumes and volatility due in part to the growth of on-line trading.

CFA Institute. 560 Ray C. Hunt Dr., Charlottesville, VA 22903-2981. Phone: 800-247-8132 or (434)951-5499; Fax: (434)951-5262; Email: info@cfainstitute.org • URL: http://www.cfainstitute.org/pages/index.aspx • Formerly Association for Investment Management and Research.

Chartered Alternative Investment Analyst Association. 100 University Dr., Amherst, MA 01002-2357. Phone: (413)253-7373; Fax: (413)253-4494; Email: info@caia.org • URL: http://caia.org • Seeks to establish the Chartered Alternative Investment Analyst designation as the educational standard for the alternative investment industry. Advocates for high standards of professional conduct in the field of alternative investment analysis. Promotes professional development through continuous education. Facilitates communication among industry professionals.

European Business Angel Network. Rue de la Science 14B, B-1040 Brussels, Belgium. Phone: 32 2 626 20 60; Fax: 32 2 626 20 69; Email: info@eban.org • URL: http://www.eban.org • Encourages exchange of experience among business angels networks. Promotes recognition of business angels networks. Works to create and develop a positive environment for business angels' activities.

Financial Industry Regulatory Authority. 1735 K St., Washington, DC 20006. Phone: (301)590-6500; Fax: (202)293-6260; Email: francine.lee@finra.org • URL: http://www.finra.org • Formerly National Association of Securities Dealers.

Government Investment Officers Association. 10655 Park Run Dr., Ste. 120, Las Vegas, NV 89144. Phone: (702)255-3224; Fax: (702)575-6670; Email: mday@gioa.us • URL: http://www.gioa.us • Provides education and training to government investment officers to assist them in their responsibilities. Promotes educational and professional development among investment officers in state and local governments. Seeks to instill higher levels of investment management skills, ethics and efficiency. Interacts with the public investment community and other public investment officers so that members will have the opportunity to gain the skills, knowledge and contacts that will greatly aid them in discharging their duties.

Investment Education Institute. 711 W 13 Mile Rd., Ste. 900, Madison Heights, MI 48071. Phone: 877-275-6242 or (248)583-6242 or (248)654-3047; Fax: (248)583-4880; Email: service@betterinvesting.org • URL: http://www.better-investing.org • Affiliated with the National Association of Investors Corporation and conducted through various business schools. Seeks to enlarge the scope and quality of investment education, especially through investment clubs. Has held conferences for educators, financial institutions, financial writers, and corporate shareholder relations executives to gain information and to stimulate activity in these groups. Representatives from 50 investment club councils have taken a series of special courses to improve their teaching skills. Individuals and corporations have contributed funds to establish the program.

Japan Machinery Center for Trade and Investment. Kikai Shinkou Kaikan, 4th Fl., 3-8-5, Shiba Koen, Minato, Tokyo, Tokyo 105-0011, Japan. Phone: 81 3 34319507; Fax: 81 3 34366455 • URL: http://www.jmcti.org • Exporters of machinery. Seeks to establish and maintain a domestic and international business climate beneficial to the exportation of machinery. Represents members' interests; gathers and disseminates information.

National Coalition for Capital. 1028 33rd St. NW, Ste. 200, Washington, DC 20007. Phone: (202)337-1661 • URL: http://www.nationalcoalitionforcapital.org • Represents leaders who support economic development and job creation through long-term access to capital for entrepreneurs and emerging companies. Serves as a resource for promising small and emerging companies, entrepreneurs, investors, economic developers and other stakeholders within the nation's emerging investment infrastructure.

National Investor Relations Institute. 225 Reinekers Ln., Ste. 560, Alexandria, VA 22314. Phone: (703)562-7700 or (703)506-3570; Fax: (703)562-7701 or (703)506-3571; Email: info@niri.org • URL: http://www.niri.org • Executives engaged in investor relations. Identifies the role of the investor relations practitioner; protects a free and open market with equity and access to investors of all kinds; improves communication between corporate management and shareholders, present and future. Holds professional development seminars and conducts research programs. Maintains placement service and speakers' bureau; compiles statistics.

NBFI and Modaraba Association of Pakistan. 602, Progressive Ctr., 30-A, Blk. 6, PEHCS, Shahrah-e-Faisal, Karachi 75400, Pakistan. Phone: 92 21 34389774; Fax: 92 21 34389775; Email: association@nbfi-modaraba.com.pk • URL: http://www.nbfi-modaraba.com.pk • Seeks to promote the Islamic way of business. Encourages public awareness of the role of modaraba in financing. Conducts surveys and analysis on the Islamic modes of business and finance. Safeguards and protects the interests of members.

For publishers' addresses, refer to SOURCES CITED section at the back of the book.

Netherlands Society for Industry and Trade. Jan Van Nassaustraat 75, NL-2596 BP The Hague, Netherlands. Phone: 31 70 3141940; Fax: 31 70 3247515; Email: info@de-maatschappij.nl • URL: http://www.de-maatschappij.nl • Association of businesses and industries in the Netherlands. Promotes trade and investment. Conducts research.

INVESTMENTS, INSTITUTIONAL

See INSTITUTIONAL INVESTMENTS

INVESTMENTS, REAL ESTATE

See REAL ESTATE INVESTMENTS

IRAS

See Individual Retirement Accounts

IRON AND STEEL INDUSTRY

See also FOUNDRIES; METAL INDUSTRY

CD-ROM DATABASES

METADEX Materials Collection: Metals-Polymers-Ceramics. Cambridge Scientific Abstracts L.P. • Quarterly. Provides CD-ROM citations to the worldwide literature of materials science and metallurgy. Corresponds to *Metals Abstracts, Alloys Index, Steels Alert, Nonferrous Alert, Polymers/Ceramics/Composites Alert,* and *Engineered Materials Abstracts*. (Formerly produced by ASM International.).

OECD Statistical Compendium. Organization for Economic Cooperation and Development. • Semiannual. $1,905.00 per year for 1 to 10 users. CD-ROM contains more than 730,000 monthly, quarterly, and annual time series for OECD countries, 1960 to date. Includes fully searchable data on agriculture, food, economic indicators, national accounts, employment, energy, finance, industry, technology, and foreign trade. Results can be displayed in various forms.

DIRECTORIES

Directory of Chinese Manufacturers & Exporters of Castings and Forgings. EXIM Infotek Private Ltd. • $15 Individuals. Covers: 130 Chinese manufacturers and exporters of cast iron, cast iron fittings, cast iron pipes, cast iron products, cast steel products, casting, casting-iron, castings, die casting mould, die castings, forging, forging parts, grey cast iron, iron casting, manhole covers, nodular cast iron, precision castings, steel castings. Entries include: Company name, postal address, city, country, phone, fax, e-mail & websites, contact person, designation, products detail.

Iron and Steel International Directory. DMG World Media. • Annual. $48. Covers: Plant and equipment manufacturers in the steel industry, worldwide. Entries include: Company name, address, phone, fax, product/service provided.

FINANCIAL RATIOS

Annual Statement Studies. Risk Management Association. • Annual. Compiled from over 280,000 financial statements.

Annual Statement Studies: Industry Default Probabilities and Cash Flow Measures. Risk Management Association. • Annual. $405 Nonmembers. Serves as a companion volume to the original *Annual Statement Studies*. Gives probability of default estimates on a percentage scale for more than 450 industries. Includes changes in position year-by-year for eight financial statement line items and provides percentage measures of cash flow.

INTERNET DATABASES

Business 2.0 Web Guide to the Best Business Links. Business 2.0 Media Inc. Phone: (415)293-4800; Email: support@business2.com • URL: http://www.business2.com/webguide • Web site presents an extensive, searchable directory of links to "the best, most informative, and authoritative web pages." Twenty main categories cover business, finance, career, company information, people, and technology topics, with thousands of subtopics, all linking to Web sites recommended by experienced business researchers. Fees: Free.

Fedstats. Federal Interagency Council on Statistical Policy. Phone: (202)395-7254 • URL: http://www.fedstats.gov • Web site features an efficient search facility for full-text statistics produced by more than 100 federal agencies, including the Census Bureau, the Bureau of Economic Analysis, and the Bureau of Labor Statistics. Boolean searches can be made within one agency or for all agencies combined. Links are offered to international statistical bureaus, including the UN, IMF, OECD, UNESCO, Eurostat, and 20 individual countries. Fees: Free.

FreeLunch.com. Economy.com, Inc. Phone: (610)696-8700; Fax: (610)696-1678 • URL: http://www.freelunch.com • Web site provides free access to more than 200 million economic and financial data series, covering industry, demographics, labor markets, prices, retail sales, government spending, trade, interest rates, housing starts, the stock market, etc. Data is available in either chart or table form. Searching is offered. Free, but registration required. Economy.com, Inc. also offers fee-based economic analysis at *The Dismal Scientist* site (www.dismal.com).

Manufacturing Profiles. U. S. Bureau of the Census. Phone: (301)763-4636 or (301)763-4100; Fax: (301)763-4794; Email: webmaster@census.gov • URL: http://www.census.gov/prod/www/abs/mfg-prof.html • The Census Bureau makes available free on PDF (Portable Document Format) an annual consolidation of the entire Current Industrial Report series, presenting "all the data compiled." Contains statistics on production, shipments, inventories, consumption, exports, imports, and orders for a wide variety of manufactured products.

ONLINE DATABASES

Materials Business File™ (MBF). ProQuest LLC CSA. • Contains more than 896,000 citations, with abstracts, to worldwide literature on technical and commercial aspects of iron and steel, nonferrous metals, and relevant nonmetallic materials such as polymers, ceramics, and composites. Sources include more than 2000 technical journals, trade magazines, newspapers, news briefs, books, conference proceedings, and announcements worldwide.

PERIODICALS AND NEWSLETTERS

Advanced Materials and Processes. ASM International. • Monthly. $325 Institutions. Incorporates *Metal Progress*.Technical information and reports on new developments in the technology of engineered materials and manufacturing processes.

AISE Steel Technology. Association for Iron and Steel Technology. • Monthly. $165 U.S., Canada, and Mexico.

Metal Bulletin. Metal Bulletin Inc. • Daily. £1,395 1-year standard subscription. Provides news of international trends, prices, and market conditions for both steel and non-ferrous metal industries. (Published in England.).

Metal Bulletin Monthly. Metal Bulletin Inc. • Monthly. Edited for international metal industry business executives and senior technical personnel. Covers business, economic, and technical developments. (Published in England.).

Modern Casting. American Foundry Society. • Monthly.

Steel Times International. Quartz Business Media Ltd. • Bimonthly. £168 Individuals. Includes *Iron and Steel Directory*.

33 Metalproducing: For Primary Producers of Steel, Aluminum, and Copper-Base Alloys. Penton Media Inc. • Monthly. $65.00 per year. Covers metal production technology and methods and industry news. Includes a bimonthly *Nonferrous Supplement*.

RESEARCH CENTERS AND INSTITUTES

U.S. International Trade Commission - Minerals, Metals, Machinery, and Miscellaneous Manufacturers Division. 500 E St. SW, Washington, DC 20436. Phone: (202)205-3418; Fax: (202)205-2217; Email: brookhart@usitc.gov • URL: http://www.usitc.gov • Survey data related to international trade matters, including international competitiveness of U.S. industries, especially iron and steel products, industrial minerals and nonferrous metals, machinery and general manufactured products.

STATISTICS SOURCES

American Iron and Steel Annual Statistical Report. American Iron and Steel Institute. • Annual. $100 Individuals.

OECD Iron and Steel Industry. Organization for Economic Cooperation and Development. Organisation for Economic Co-operation and Development Publications and Information Center. • Annual. $34.00. Data for orders, production, manpower, imports, exports, consumption, prices and investment in the iron and steel industry in OECD member countries. Text in English and French.

OECD Steel Market and Outlook. Organization for Economic Cooperation and Development. Organisation for Economic Co-operation and Development Publications and Information Center. • Annual. Price varies.

Standard & Poor's Industry Surveys. Standard & Poor's Financial Services L.L.C. • Semiannual. $1,800.00. Two looseleaf volumes. Includes monthly *Supplements*. Provides detailed, individual surveys of 52 major industry groups. Each survey is revised on a semiannual basis. Also includes "Monthly Investment Review" (industry group investment analysis) and monthly "Trends & Projections" (economic analysis).

Statistics of World Trade in Steel. United Nations Economic Commission for Europe. • Annual. $90.00.

Steel Mill Products. U.S. Department of Commerce U.S. Census Bureau. • Annual. (Current Industrial Reports MA-33B).

Survey of Current Business. U. S. Government Printing Office. • Published by Bureau of Economic Analysis, U. S. Department of Commerce. Presents a wide variety of business and economic data.

TRADE/PROFESSIONAL ASSOCIATIONS

American Foundry Society. 1695 N Penny Ln., Schaumburg, IL 60173. Phone: 800-537-4237 or (847)824-0181; Fax: (847)824-2174 or (847)824-7848; Email: jcall@afsinc.org • URL: http://www.afsinc.org • Technical, trade and management association of foundrymen, patternmakers, technologists, and educators. Sponsors foundry training courses through the Cast Metals Institute on all subjects pertaining to the castings industry; conducts educational and instructional exhibits of foundry industry; sponsors 10 regional foundry conferences and 400 local foundry technical meetings. Maintains Technical Information Center providing literature searching and document retrieval service; and Metalcasting Abstract Service involving abstracts of the latest metal casting literature. Provides environmental services and testing; conducts research programs; compiles statistics, provides marketing information.

American Iron and Steel Institute. 25 Massachusetts Ave. NW, Ste. 800, Washington, DC 20001. Phone: (202)452-7100 • URL: http://www.steel.org • Represents basic manufacturers in the steel industry. Operates steel mills, blast furnaces, finishing mills, and iron ore mines. Includes products such as pig iron, steel ingots, sheets, plates, bars, shapes, strips, tin plate, nails, pipe and tubes, railroad rails, wire products, and other basic forms of ferrous metals. Conducts extensive research programs on manufacturing technology, basic materials, environmental quality control, energy, and fuels consumption. Compiles statistics.

Association of Steel Distributors. 401 N Michigan Ave., Ste. 2200, Chicago, IL 60611. Phone: (312)673-5793; Fax: (312)527-6705; Email: headquarters@steeldistributors.org • URL: http://www.steeldistributors.org • Represents wholesalers of steel and steel products. Provides the steel distribution industry a forum for ideas exchange and market information.

IRON AND STEEL SCRAP METAL INDUSTRY

CD-ROM DATABASES

OECD Statistical Compendium. Organization for Economic Cooperation and Development. • Semiannual. $1,905.00 per year for 1 to 10 users. CD-ROM contains more than 730,000 monthly, quarterly, and annual time series for OECD countries, 1960 to date. Includes fully searchable data on agriculture, food, economic indicators, national accounts, employment, energy, finance, industry, technology, and foreign trade. Results can be displayed in various forms.

DIRECTORIES

Directory of South Korean Manufacturers & Exporters of Castings & Forgings. EXIM Infotek Private Ltd. • $10 Individuals. Covers: 80 South Korean manufacturers and exporters of casting, casting-aluminum and zinc, forging, iron castings, and steel castings. Entries include: Company name, postal address, city, country, phone, fax, e-mail and websites, contact person, designation, and product details.

North American Scrap Metals Directory. Recycling Today Media Group. • Annual. $95.20 Individuals discounted price. Covers: Suppliers of scrap metal materials in North America. Entries include: Contact information.

INTERNET DATABASES

Business 2.0 Web Guide to the Best Business Links. Business 2.0 Media Inc. Phone: (415)293-4800; Email: support@business2.com • URL: http://www.business2.com/webguide • Web site presents an extensive, searchable directory of links to "the best, most informative, and authoritative web pages." Twenty main categories cover business, finance, career, company information, people, and technology topics, with thousands of subtopics, all linking to Web sites recommended by experienced business researchers. Fees: Free.

Fedstats. Federal Interagency Council on Statistical Policy. Phone: (202)395-7254 • URL: http://www.fedstats.gov • Web site features an efficient search facility for full-text statistics produced by more than 100 federal agencies, including the Census Bureau, the Bureau of Economic Analysis, and the Bureau of Labor Statistics. Boolean searches can be made within one agency or for all agencies combined. Links are offered to international statistical bureaus, including the UN, IMF, OECD, UNESCO, Eurostat, and 20 individual countries. Fees: Free.

FreeLunch.com. Economy.com, Inc. Phone: (610)696-8700; Fax: (610)696-1678 • URL: http://www.freelunch.com • Web site provides free access to more than 200 million economic and financial data series, covering industry, demographics, labor markets, prices, retail sales, government spending, trade, interest rates, housing starts, the stock market, etc. Data is available in either chart or table form. Searching is offered. Free, but registration required. Economy.com, Inc. also offers fee-based economic analysis at *The Dismal Scientist* site (www.dismal.com).

PERIODICALS AND NEWSLETTERS

Scrap. Institute of Scrap Recycling Industries. • Bimonthly. $48 Individuals companies. Magazine for the scrap processing and recycling industry. Formerly *Scrap Processing and Recycling*.

STATISTICS SOURCES

Survey of Current Business. U. S. Government Printing Office. • Published by Bureau of Economic Analysis, U. S. Department of Commerce. Presents a wide variety of business and economic data.

IRON FOUNDRIES

See FOUNDRIES

IRRIGATION

ABSTRACTS AND INDEXES

Environment Abstracts. University Publications of America. • Monthly. Price varies. Provides multidisciplinary coverage of the world's environmental literature. Incorporates *Acid Rain Abstracts*.

Environment Abstracts Annual: A Guide to the Key Environmental Literature of the Year. University Publications of America. • Annual. $495.00. A yearly cumulation of *Environment Abstracts*.

Irrigation and Drainage Abstracts. CABI Publishing North America. • Bimonthly. Published in England by CABI Publishing. Provides worldwide coverage of the literature.

CD-ROM DATABASES

Environment Abstracts on CD-ROM. University Publications of America. • Quarterly. $1,295.00 per year. Contains the following CD-ROM databases: *Environment Abstracts*, *Energy Abstracts*, and *Acid Rain Abstracts*. Length of coverage varies.

DIRECTORIES

Irrigation Association Membership Directory and Industry Buyers' Guide. Irrigation Association. • Annual. Free to members; non-members, $25.00. Includes manufacturing, distribution, contracting, consultation, research and educational information.

ONLINE DATABASES

CAB Abstracts. CABI. • Contains 46 specialized abstract collections covering over 10,000 journals and monographs in the areas of agriculture, horticulture, forest products, farm products, nutrition, dairy science, poultry, grains, animal health, entomology, etc. Time period is 1972 to date, with monthly updates. Inquire as to online cost and availability. *CAB Abstracts on CD-ROM* also available, with annual updating.

TRADE/PROFESSIONAL ASSOCIATIONS

National Water Resources Association. 3800 N Fairfax Dr., Ste. 4, Arlington, VA 22203. Phone: (703)524-1544; Fax: (703)524-1548; Email: nwra@nwra.org • URL: http://www.nwra.org • Officers of irrigation districts, canal companies, businesses, and others interested in the development, control, conservation, and utilization of water resources in the reclamation states (17 western states). Conducts legislative tracking and provides updates.

ISOTOPES

PERIODICALS AND NEWSLETTERS

Applied Radiation and Isotopes. Elsevier. • Monthly. $374 Institutions. Journal presenting isotopic and radiation techniques, especially novel ones, and those capable of a wide application in industry and medicine.

J

JANITORIAL SERVICES

See MAINTENANCE OF BUILDINGS

JAPAN

See ASIAN MARKETS

JAVA (COMPUTER PROGRAM LANGUAGE)

ABSTRACTS AND INDEXES

Internet and Personal Computing Abstracts (print edition). EBSCO Publishing Inc. • Quarterly. $269.00 per year, including cumulative index. Provides more than 10,000 abstracts annually from both trade and academic publications. Covers computer hardware, software, product reviews, Web topics, e-commerce, networks, corporate news, security, and related topics. Formerly *Microcomputer Abstracts.*

PERIODICALS AND NEWSLETTERS

Java Developer's Journal. SYS-CON Media Inc. • Monthly. $69.99 per year. Provides technical information for Java professionals.

Java Pro. Fawcette Technical Publications. • Monthly. $29.95 per year. Contains technical articles for Java developers.

JET PROPULSION

See ROCKET INDUSTRY

JEWELRY BUSINESS

See also GEMS AND GEMSTONES

DIRECTORIES

Costume Jewelry: Industry Sector Profile. Philippine-German Export Development Project Philippine Bureau of Export Trade Promotion. • Publication includes: Companies exporting costume jewelry from the Philippines. Entries include: Company name, address, phone, fax, name and title of contact, type of business, year established, subsidiary and branch names and locations, financial data, number of employees, government registrations, professional memberships, bank references, supply capability, export experience, business plan. Principal content of publication is an overview of the business environment and costume jewelry industry in the Philippines.

Directory of American Manufacturers & Exporters of Gold & Silvery Jewelry. EXIM Infotek Private Ltd. • $5 Individuals. Covers: 20 American manufacturers and exporters of gold, gold jewelry, silver, and silver jewelry. Entries include: Company name, postal address, city, country, phone, fax, e-mail and websites, contact person, designation, and product details.

Directory of American Manufacturers & Exporters of Imitation & Fashion Jewellery. EXIM Infotek Private Ltd. • $10 Individuals. Covers: 80 American manufacturers and exporters of bracelets, costume jewelry, custom jewelry, diamond cabbing and polishing equipment, earrings, fashion jewelry, hair pins, jewelry casting investments, jewelry chains, jewelry findings, jewelry tools, and necklaces. Entries include: Company name, postal address, city, country, phone, fax, e-mail and websites, contact person, designation, and product details.

Directory of Australia and New Zealand Importers of Gold and Silver Jewellery. EXIM Infotek Private Ltd. • $150 Individuals. Covers: 20 Australian and New Zealand importers of bracelet, gold, silver jewelry, gold and silver leaf mirrors, jewelry parts and components. Entries include: Company name, postal address, telephone, fax, e-mail, website, contact person, designation, and product details.

Directory of Chinese Manufacturers & Exporters of Imitation & Fashion Jewelry. EXIM Infotek Private Ltd. • $10 Individuals. Covers: 70 Chinese manufacturers and exporters of bangles, beads, bracelets, brooches, buckles, costume accessories, costume jewelry, costumes, earrings, fashion accessories, glass beads, glass ornaments, hair accessories, hair clips, hair pins, imitation jewelry, jewelry, jewelry boxes, necklaces, ornament chains, ornaments, pendants, and synthetic diamonds. Entries include: Company name, postal address, city, country, phone, fax, e-mail and websites, contact person, designation, and product details.

Directory of Japanese Manufacturers & Exporters of Imitation & Fashion Jewellery. EXIM Infotek Private Ltd. • $5 Individuals. Covers: 30 Japanese manufacturers and exporters of costume accessories, fancy goods, hair accessories, imitation jewelry, imitation pearls, personal accessories, personal ornaments. Entries include: Company name, postal address, city, country, phone, fax, e-mail and websites, contact person, designation, and product details.

Directory of South Korean Manufacturers & Exporters of Imitation & Fashion Jewellery. EXIM Infotek Private Ltd. • $15 Individuals. Covers: 150 South Korean manufacturers and exporters of bracelets, buckles, ladies belts, costume jewelry, cuff links, custom jewelry, earrings, fashion goods, fashion jewelry, hair bands, hair ornaments, hair pins, imitation jewelry, jewelry, necklaces, synthetic diamonds, synthetic jewels for watches, and tie pins. Entries include: Company name, postal address, city, country, phone, fax, e-mail and websites, contact person, designation, and product details.

Directory of Taiwanese Manufacturers & Exporters of Imitation & Fashion Jewellery. EXIM Infotek Private Ltd. • $10 Individuals. Covers: 90 Taiwanese manufacturers & exporters of bracelets, buckles, costume jewelry, cuff links, earrings, fashion goods, fashion metal accessories, hair bands, hair clips, hair ornaments, imitation jewelry, jewelry, necklaces, synthetic jewels for watches, theatrical masks for arts, craft & festivals, tie pins. Entries include: Company name, postal address, city, country, phone, fax, e-mail & websites, contact person, designation, products detail.

The International Directory of Importers - Jewelry and Costume Jewelry Importers. Interdata. • $220 Individuals print. Covers: 2,100 international firms importing jewelry and costume jewelry. Entries include: Company name and address, contact person, email, number of employees, year established, phone and telefaxes, business activity, bank references, as well as a listing of jewelry and costume jewelry currently being imported.

Jewelers' Circular/Keystone-Jewelers' Directory. Reed Elsevier Group plc Reed Business Information. • About 8,500 manufacturers, importers and wholesale jewelers providing merchandise and supplies to the jewelry retailing industry; and related trade organizations. Included with subscription to *Jewelers' Circular Keystone.*

Jewelers Directory--Supplies. InfoGroup Inc. • Annual. Number of listings: 594. Entries include: Name, address, phone, size of advertisement, name of owner or manager, number of employees, year first in "Yellow Pages." Compiled from telephone company "Yellow Pages," nationwide.

Manufacturing Jewelers Buyers' Guide. Manufacturing Jewelers and Suppliers of America. • $35 for nonmembers. Lists manufacturers and suppliers and has cross-reference by products listed.

FINANCIAL RATIOS

Annual Statement Studies. Risk Management Association. • Annual. Compiled from over 280,000 financial statements.

Annual Statement Studies: Industry Default Probabilities and Cash Flow Measures. Risk Management Association. • Annual. $405 Nonmembers. Serves as a companion volume to the original *Annual Statement Studies.* Gives probability of default estimates on a percentage scale for more than 450 industries. Includes changes in position year-by-year for eight financial statement line items and provides percentage measures of cash flow.

GENERAL WORKS

Jewelry Business Directory. Hong Kong Jewelry Manufacturers Association. • Annual. Contains more than 400 company listings, including all major Hong Kong jewelry manufacturers and related business.

INTERNET DATABASES

Advance Monthly Retail Trade Report. U. S. Census Bureau. Phone: 800-541-8345 or (301)457-4100 or (301)763-2713; Fax: (301)457-1296 or (301)457-3842; Email: naics@census.gov • URL: http://www.census.gov/epcd/www/naicstab.htm • Web pages provide monthly sales figures for a wide range of retail businesses. Advance, preliminary, and final statistics are provided for the latest month available in each case, with a previous-year comparison. Updates are monthly.

PERIODICALS AND NEWSLETTERS

Jewelers' Circular Keystone (JCK). Reed Elsevier Group plc Reed Business Information. • Monthly. $90.00 per year.

Modern Jeweler. Cygnus Business Media. • Monthly. $60.00 per year. Edited for retail jewelers. Covers the merchandising of jewelry, gems, and watches. Supersedes in part *Modern Jeweler*.

National Jeweler. Nielsen Business Media Inc. • Bimonthly. $65.00 per year. For jewelry retailers.

STATISTICS SOURCES

Annual Benchmark Report for Retail Trade and Food Services..A Detailed Summary of Retail Sales, Purchases, Accounts Receivable, Inventories, and Food Service Sales. U. S. Government Printing Office. • Annual. $13.00. Issued by the U.S. Census Bureau. Provides detailed annual and monthly retail statistics for the most recent 10 years. Includes data for various kinds of retail outlets, including automobiles, furniture, appliances, building supplies, grocery stores, drug stores, gasoline stations, clothing, sporting goods, department stores, and restaurants.

U.S. Industry and Trade Outlook. U.S. Department of Commerce National Technical Information Service. • Annual. Produced by the International Trade Administration, U.S. Department of Commerce, in a "public-private" partnership with DRI/McGraw-Hill and Standard & Poor's. Provides basic data, outlook for the current year, and "Long-Term Prospects" (five-year projections) for a wide variety of products and services. Includes high technology industries. Formerly *U.S. Industrial Outlook*.

TRADE/PROFESSIONAL ASSOCIATIONS

Jewelers' Security Alliance. 6 E 45th St., New York, NY 10017. Phone: 800-537-0067; Fax: (212)808-9168; Email: jsa2@jewelerssecurity.org • URL: http://www.jewelerssecurity.org • Formerly Jewelers Security Alliance of U.S.

Jewelers Vigilance Committee. 25 W 45th St., Ste. 1406, New York, NY 10036. Phone: (212)997-2002; Fax: (212)997-9148 • URL: http://www.jvclegal.org • Represents manufacturers, importers, wholesalers, and retailers. Combats deceptive trade practices and misleading advertising. Aims to develop and maintain high trade standards. Provides advice on markings and assists in prosecution of violations of marking, advertising, and related jewelry industry laws.

Jewelry Information Center. 120 Broadway, Ste. 2820, New York, NY 10271. Phone: 800-223-0673 or (646)658-0246; Fax: (646)658-0256; Email: info@jic.org • URL: http://www.jic.org • Represents retailers, wholesalers, and manufacturers of fine jewelry products. Conducts industry-wide promotional and educational programs; sponsors marketing seminars and consumer-oriented programs on radio, television, and print media.

Manufacturing Jewelers and Suppliers of America. 57 John L. Dietsch Sq., Attleboro Falls, MA 02763. Phone: 800-444-6572 or (401)274-3840 or (508)316-2132; Fax: (401)274-0265 or (508)316-1429; Email: info@mjsa.org • URL: http://www.mjsa.org • Formerly Manufacturing Jewelers and Silversmiths of America.

JOB ANALYSIS

ONLINE DATABASES

BusinessAnalystCrossing.com. • Offers business analyst job listings. Includes entry level business analyst, technical and business analyst jobs.

JOB DESCRIPTIONS

See also OCCUPATIONS

ENCYCLOPEDIAS AND DICTIONARIES

BLR Job Descriptions Encyclopedia. Business & Legal Resources, Inc. • $299 Individuals. $299.00. Two volumes. More than 700 prewritten job descriptions.

ONLINE DATABASES

BusinessAnalystCrossing.com. • Offers business analyst job listings. Includes entry level business analyst, technical and business analyst jobs.

JOB EVALUATION

See JOB ANALYSIS

JOB HUNTING

See also EMPLOYMENT AGENCIES AND SERVICES; JOB RESUMES

ABSTRACTS AND INDEXES

Business Periodicals Index Retrospective. EBSCO Publishing Inc. • 11/year. Quarterly and annual cumulations.

Readers' Guide to Periodical Literature. EBSCO Publishing Inc. • Provides indexing for over 400 periodicals dating back to 1983.

BIBLIOGRAPHIES

Job & Career Books. Kennedy Information Inc. • Annual. Free. Contains descriptions of selected books from various publishers on job searching and choice of career.

Job Hunter's Sourcebook. Cengage Learning Inc. • $243 Individuals. 2012. $231.00. 12th edition. Covers over 200 professions and occupations.

CD-ROM DATABASES

OECD Statistical Compendium. Organization for Economic Cooperation and Development. • Semiannual. $1,905.00 per year for 1 to 10 users. CD-ROM contains more than 730,000 monthly, quarterly, and annual time series for OECD countries, 1960 to date. Includes fully searchable data on agriculture, food, economic indicators, national accounts, employment, energy, finance, industry, technology, and foreign trade. Results can be displayed in various forms.

Readers' Guide to Periodical Literature. EBSCO Publishing Inc. • Provides indexing for over 400 periodicals dating back to 1983.

DIRECTORIES

Atlanta JobBank: The Job Hunter's Guide to Georgia. Adams Media Corp. • $17.95 Individuals Paperback. Covers: 3,900 employers in the state of Georgia, including Albany, Columbus, Macon, and Savannah. Database includes: Information on the basics of job winning and writing resumes and cover letters; electronic job search information; 330 industry associations; 90 online career resources; 235 employment services. Entries include: Firm or organization name, address, local phone, toll-free phone, fax, description of organization, subsidiaries, other locations, recorded jobline, name and title of contact, typical titles for common positions, educational backgrounds desired, number of employees, benefits offered, training programs, internships, parent company, revenues, e-mail and URL address, projected number of hires.

Boston JobBank: The Job Hunter's Guide to the Bay State. Adams Media Corp. • Annual. $17.95 Individuals Paperback. Covers: Over 7,000 employers in Massachusetts. Database includes: Information on the basics of job winning and writing resumes and cover letters; electronic job search information; 330 industry associations; 90 online career resources; 420 employment services. Entries include: Firm or organization name, address, local phone, toll-free phone, fax, e-mail, URL, recorded jobline, hours, names of management, name and title of contact, titles of common positions, entry-level positions, fringe benefits offered, stock exchange listing, description of organization, subsidiaries, location of headquarters, educational background desired, projected number of hires, training programs, internships, parent company, number of employees, revenues, other U.S. Locations, and international locations.

California Job Journal. California Job Journal. • Weekly. Covers: Employment issues and job openings in California from entry-level to executive positions. Database includes: Career guidance and job search advice. Entries include: Company name, address, phone, type of business, name and title of contact; comprehensive description of position and required skills/background, salary and/or benefits offered.

Careers in Focus--Business Managers. InfoBase Holdings Inc. • $35 Individuals hardcover. Covers: An overview of business managers, followed by a selection of jobs profiled in detail, including the nature of the job, earnings, prospects for employment, what kind of training and skills it requires, and sources for further information. Database includes: Black and white photographs.

Careers in Focus--Entrepreneurs. InfoBase Holdings Inc. • $35 Individuals hardcover. Covers: An overview of entrepreneurship, followed by a selection of jobs profiled in detail, including the nature of the job, earnings, prospects for employment, what kind of training and skills it requires, and sources for further information. Database includes: Black and white photographs.

Carolina JobBank: The Job Hunter's Guide to North and South Carolina. Adams Media Corp. • $12.21 Individuals Paperback. Covers: 4,600 employers in North Carolina and South Carolina. Database includes: Information on the basics of getting a job and writing resumes and cover letters; regional employment outlook; 330 industry associations; 90 online career resources; 280 employment services. Entries include: Firm or organization name, address, local phone, toll-free phone, fax, e-mail, URL, recorded jobline, description of organization, subsidiaries, other locations, hours, names of management, name and title of contact, location of headquarters, typical titles for common positions, educational backgrounds desired, projected number of hires, company benefits, stock exchange listing, training programs and internships, parent company, number of employees, revenues.

Chicago JobBank: The Job Hunter's Guide to Metro Chicago. Adams Media Corp. • Annual. $17.95 Individuals Paperback. Covers: About 5,500 major employers in northern and central Illinois including Aurora, Peoria, Rockford, and Springfield. Database includes: Information on the basics of job winning and writing resumes and cover letters; electronic job search information; 330 industry association; 90 online career resources, 480 employment services. Entries include: Firm or organization name, address, local phone, toll-free phone, fax, e-mail, URL, description of organization, hours, recorded jobline, subsidiaries, names of management, name and title of contact, names of management, headquarters locations, typical titles for entry-level and middle-level positions, educational backgrounds desired, company benefits, stock exchange listing, training programs, internships, parent company, number of employees, revenues, other U.S. Locations, international locations.

Complete Guide to Public Employment. Development Concepts Inc. • Triennial. $19.95 Individuals paper. Publication includes: List of federal, state, and local government agencies and departments, trade and professional associations, contracting and consulting firms, nonprofit organizations, foundations, research organizations, political support groups, and other organizations offering public service career opportunities. Entries include: Organization name, address, phone, name and title of contact. Complete title is "Complete Guide to Public Employment: Opportunities and Strategies with Federal, State, and Local Government;" Trade and Professional Associations; Contracting and Consulting Firms; Foundations; Research Organizations; and Political Support Groups.

Dallas/Ft. Worth JobBank: The Job Hunter's Guide to the Dallas-Fort Worth Metroplex. Adams Media Corp. • Annual. $9 Individuals Paperback. Covers: 4,000 employers in the Dallas/Ft. Worth, Texas, area including Abilene, Amarillo, Arlington, Garland, Irving, Lubbock, Plano. Database includes: Information on the basics of getting a job and writing resumes and cover letters; electronic job search information. Entries include: Firm or organization name, address, local phone, toll-free phone, fax, e-mail, URL, recorded jobline, hours, description of organization, subsidiaries, names of management, name and title of contact, location of headquarters, typical titles for common positions, educational backgrounds desired, company benefits, stock exchange listing, training programs, internships, parent company, number of employees, revenues, projected number of hires.

Denver JobBank: The Job Hunter's Guide to Colorado. Adams Media Corp. • $17.95 Individuals 4 used & new. Covers: 3,500 employers in Denver and the rest of Colorado including Aurora, Boulder, Colorado Springs, Lakewood. Database includes: Information on the basics of job winning and writing resumes and cover letters; searching for a job online; regional employment outlook; 330 industry associations; 90 online career resources; 150 employment services. Entries include: Firm or organization name, address, local phone, toll-free phone, fax, e-mail, URL, description of organization, subsidiaries, other locations, hours, recorded jobline, names of management, name and title of contact, headquarters location, projected number of hires; listings may also include typical titles for common positions, educational backgrounds desired, company benefits, stock exchange listing, training programs, internships, parent company, number of employees, revenues.

Directory of Websites for International Jobs. Development Concepts Inc. • $19.95 Individuals. Covers: 1,400 websites.

Federal Career Opportunities. Federal Research Service Inc. • Biweekly. $195 Individuals 26 issues, 1 year. Covers: More than 3,000 current federal job vacancies in the United States and overseas; includes permanent, part-time, and temporary positions. Entries include: Position title, location, series and grade, job requirements, special forms, announcement number, closing date, application address.

Federal Jobs Digest. Federal Jobs Digest. • $20 Individuals 3 months. Covers: Over 10,000 specific job openings in the federal government in each issue. Vacancies from over 300 Federal Agencies are covered. Entries include: Position name, title, General Schedule (GS) grade, and Wage Grade (WG), closing date for applications, announcement number, application address, phone, and name of contact.

Florida JobBank: The Job Hunter's Guide to the Sunshine State. Adams Media Corp. • $17.95 Individuals payment with order. Covers: 5,500 employers in Florida including Fort Lauderdale, Jacksonville, Miami, Orlando, Tampa. Database includes: Information on the basics of job winning and writing resumes and cover letters; electronic job search information; 330 industry associations; 90 online career resources; 285 employment services. Entries include: Firm or organization name, address, local phone, toll-free phone, fax, e-mail addresses, web addresses, description of organization, subsidiaries, hours, recorded jobline, name and title of contact, headquarters location, typical titles for common positions, educational backgrounds desired, number of projected hires, company benefits, stock exchange listing, training programs, internships, parent company, number of employees, revenues, other U.S. Locations, international locations.

HireDiversity.com. Hispanic Business Inc. • Database covers: Over 95,000 resumes of multicultural professionals and recent college graduates who are seeking employment with Fortune 500 companies; job listings with a large variety of companies. Entries include: Name, address, phone, employment history, salary requirements, level of management experience, education, geographical preference, and language.

Houston JobBank: The Job Hunter's Guide to Houston. Adams Media Corp. • Annual. $17.95 Individuals 3 used & new. Covers: Over 4,000 employers in Houston, Texas and the surrounding areas including Bayton, Beaumont, Galveston, Pasadena. Database includes: Information on the basics of job winning and writing resumes and cover letters; electronic job search information; 330 industry associations; 90 online career resources; 145 employment services. Entries include: Firm or organization name, address, local phone, toll-free phone, fax, recorded jobline, e-mail, URL, hours, name and title of contact; description of organization; headquarters location, subsidiaries, operations at the facility, names of management, typical titles for common positions, educational backgrounds desired, number of projected hires, fringe benefits offered, stock exchange listing, training programs, internships, parent company, number of employees, revenues, other U.S. locations, international locations.

The Job-Seeker's Guide to On-line Resources. Kennedy Information Inc. • $14.95 plus $4 shipping. Covers: Approximately 140 candidate databases, job-posting services, and related resources with introductory text containing tips for novices. Entries include: On-line name, address, phone, fax; e-mail address, description.

Los Angeles JobBank: The Job Hunter's Guide to Southern California. Adams Media Corp. • Annual. $16.95 Individuals Paperback. Covers: Over 7,900 southern California employers including Orange, Riverside, San Bernardino, San Diego, Santa Barbara and Ventura counties. Database includes: Information on the basics of job winning and writing resumes and cover letters; electronic job search information; 330 industry associations; 90 online career resources; 515 employment services. Entries include: Firm or organization name, address, local phone, toll-free phone, fax, e-mail, URL, recorded jobline, hours, subsidiaries, other locations, names of management, name and title of contact, description of organization, number of employees, headquarters location, typical titles for common positions, educational backgrounds desired, fringe benefits offered, stock exchange listing, training programs, internships, parent company, number of employees, revenues, corporate headquarters, and number of projected hires. Projected hires.

Metropolitan Washington DC JobBank: The Job Hunter's Guide to Washington DC. Adams Media Corp. • $17.95 Individuals Paperback. Covers: 6,900 employers in Washington, D.C., Greater Baltimore, and Northern Virginia. Database includes: Information on the basics of job winning and writing resumes and cover letters; electronic job search information; 330 industry associations; 90 online career resources; 250 employment services. Entries include: Firm or organization name, address, local phone, toll-free phone, fax, recorded jobline, name and title of contact, description of organization, subsidiaries, other locations, names of management, hours, titles for common positions, educational backgrounds desired, company benefits, stock exchange listing, location of headquarters, training programs, internships, parent company, number of employees, revenues, email and URL address, projected number of hires.

National Directory for Employment in Education. American Association for Employment in Education. • Annual. $20 Nonmembers Processing fee $2. Covers: about 600 placement offices maintained by teacher-training institutions and 300 school district personnel officers and/or superintendents responsible for hiring profesional staff. Entries include: Institution name, address, phone, contact name, email address, and website.

National JobBank. Adams Media Corp. • Annual. $475 Individuals payment with order. Covers: Over 20,000 employers nationwide. Entries include: Firm or organization name, address, local phone, toll-free phone, fax, contact name and title, description of organization, headquarters location, names of management, number of employees, other locations, subsidiaries, parent company, projected number of hires, training offered, internships, hours, recorded jobline, typical titles for common positions, educational backgrounds desired, stock exchange (if listed), fringe benefits offered. Several state and regional volumes are available and described separately.

Net Jobs. Hoover's Inc. • $12.95. Covers: Internet sites and online sources dealing with employment, including resume writing tips, interviewing advice, and classified listings. Entries include: Name, location/host.

On-Line Job Search Companion. Hoover's Inc. • $14.95. Covers: Online sources of employment opportunities. Database includes: Information on selecting a career path. Entries include: Name, location/host.

Plunkett's Employers' Internet Sites with Careers Information. Plunkett Research Ltd. • Annual. $199. 99. Includes diskette.

San Francisco Bay Area JobBank: The Job Hunter's Guide to Northern California. Adams Media Corp. • $17.95 Individuals Paperback. Covers: About 5,600 employers in the San Francisco Bay area and the Northern half of California including Oakland, Sacramento, San Jose, and Silicon Valley. Database includes: Information on the basics of job winning and writing resumes and cover letters; electronic job search information; 330 industry associations; 90 online career resources; 350 employment services. Entries include: Firm or organization name, address, local phone, toll-free phone, fax, e-mail, URL, recorded jobline, hours, description of organization, subsidiaries, other locations, number of employees, name and title of contact, headquarters location, typical titles for common positions, educational backgrounds desired, company benefits, stock exchange listing, training programs, internships, parent company, and number of employees, revenues, corporate headquarters, and number of projected hires.

Seattle JobBank: The Job Hunter's Guide to Washington. Adams Media Corp. • $17.95 Individuals Paperback. Covers: About 4,800 employers in Washington state, including Spokane, Tacoma, and Bellevue. Database includes: Information on the basics of job winning and writing resumes and cover letters; regional employment outlook; 330 industry associations; 90 online career resources; 135 employment services. Entries include: Firm or organization name, address, local phone, toll-free phone, fax, e-mail, URL, description of organization, subsidiaries, name and title of contact, headquarters location, recorded jobline, typical titles for common positions, educational backgrounds desired, projected number of hires, company benefits, stock exchange listing, training programs, internships, parent company, number of employees, revenues.

INTERNET DATABASES

Business Job Finder. Ohio State University Department of Finance. Max M. Fisher College of Business, 700 Fisher Hall, 2100 Neil Ave., Columbus, OH 43210. Phone: (614)292-5026 • URL: http://www.fisher.osu.edu • Internet site containing information on jobs in the business sector, primarily in accounting, finance, and consulting. Links to many corporations who hire extensively in this area are included for those wishing to make contacts and/or mail out resumes. Detailed information on job search aids and employer profiles are provided with job areas broken down into subject.

Business 2.0 Web Guide to the Best Business Links. Business 2.0 Media Inc. Phone: (415)293-4800; Email: support@business2.com • URL: http://www.business2.com/webguide • Web site presents an extensive, searchable directory of links to "the best, most informative, and authoritative web pages." Twenty main categories cover business, finance, career, company information, people, and technology topics, with thousands of subtopics, all linking to Web sites recommended by experienced business researchers. Fees: Free.

ONLINE DATABASES

NYU Stern School of Business. • Office of Career Development section of website provides career resources for business graduates, along with resume databases arranged by classes. Many resources restricted to Stern students and alumni.

Wilson Business Abstracts Online. H.W. Wilson Co. • Indexes and abstracts 600 major business periodicals, plus the *Wall Street Journal* and the business section of the *New York Times*. Indexing is from 1982, abstracting from 1990, with the two newspapers included from 1993. Updated weekly. Inquire as to online cost and availability. (*Business Periodicals Index* without abstracts is also available online.).

PERIODICALS AND NEWSLETTERS

ReCareering Newsletter: An Idea and Resource Guide to Second Career and Relocation Planning. Publications Plus, Inc. • Monthly. $59.00 per year. Edited for "downsized managers, early retirees, and others in career transition after leaving traditional employment." Offers advice on second careers, franchises, starting a business, finances, education, training, skills assessment, and other matters of interest to the newly unemployed.

RESEARCH CENTERS AND INSTITUTES

FHI 360 - National Institute for Work and Learning. 1825 Connecticut Ave. NW, Washington, DC 20009. Phone: (202)884-8184; Fax: (202)884-8422; Email: icharner@fhi360.org • URL: http://www.niwl.org • Research areas include adult education, training, unemployment insurance, and career development.

TRADE/PROFESSIONAL ASSOCIATIONS

Association of Executive Search Consultants. 425 5thAve., 4th Fl., New York, NY 10016. Phone: (212)398-9556; Email: info@bluesteps.com • URL: http://www.aesc.org/eweb/StartPage.aspx • Represents executive search consulting firms worldwide, establishes professional and ethical standards for its members, and serves to broaden public understanding of the executive search process. Specialized form of management consulting, conducted through an exclusive engagement with a client organization.

Minority Professional Network. PO Box 55399, Atlanta, GA 30308-5399. Phone: 888-676-6389 or (770)901-9323; Email: Support@MPNmail.com • URL: http://www.minorityprofessionalnetwork.com • Seeks to improve career counseling and placement services for minority college students.

National Association of Personnel Services. 78 Dawson Village Way, Ste. 410-201, Dawsonville, GA 30534. Phone: (706)531-0060; Fax: (866)739-4750 • URL: http://www.naps360.org • Members are private employment agencies. Formerly National Association of Personnel Consultants.

The Viscardi Center. 201 I.U. Willets Rd., Albertson, NY 11507-1599. Phone: (516)465-1400; Email: info@abilitiesonline.org • URL: http://www.viscardicenter.org • Formerly National Center for Disablity Services.

JOB INTERVIEWS

See INTERVIEWING

JOB PERFORMANCE

See RATING OF EMPLOYEES

JOB RESUMES

See also EMPLOYMENT AGENCIES AND SERVICES; JOB HUNTING

DIRECTORIES

Career Information Center. Glencoe Publishing Co. • Biennial. $778 Individuals. Organized into 13 occupational clusters (comprising 13 volumes and an index volume). Each volume includes a section listing accredited occupational educational and vocational institutions. A second section lists more than 700 occupational profiles and over 3,000 organizations with jobs in the field of work with which the volume is concerned. Database includes: Job summary chart; industry snapshots that summarize major developments; photographs; overview of the job market; job hunting information and tips. Entries include: For institutions--Name, address, programs and degrees offered. For organizations--Name, address.

HANDBOOKS AND MANUALS

Resume Writing and Career Counseling. Entrepreneur Press. • Looseleaf. $59.50. A practical guide to starting a resume writing and career counseling service. Covers profit potential, start-up costs, market size evaluation, owner's time required, site selection, pricing, accounting, advertising, promotion, etc. (Start-Up Business Guide No. E1260.).

JOB SEARCHING

See JOB HUNTING

JOB TRAINING

See TRAINING OF EMPLOYEES

JOBBERS, RACK

See RACK JOBBERS

JOBLESS COMPENSATION

See UNEMPLOYMENT INSURANCE

JOBS IN FOREIGN COUNTRIES

See EMPLOYMENT IN FOREIGN COUNTRIES

JOKES

See HUMOR AND JOKES

JOURNALISM

See also EDITORS AND EDITING; NEWSPAPERS

ALMANACS AND YEARBOOKS

Editor & Publisher International Yearbook: Encyclopedia of the Newspaper Industry. Editor and Publisher Company Inc. • Annual. $150.00. Daily and Sunday newspapers in the United States and Canada.

DIRECTORIES

Editor & Publisher Journalism Awards and Fellowship Directory. Editor and Publisher Company Inc. • Annual. Over 500 cash prizes scholarships, fellowships, and grants available to journalists and students for work on special subjects or in specific fields.

Journalism & Mass Communication Directory. Association for Education in Journalism and Mass Communication. • Annual. Lists more than 400 schools and departments of journalism and mass communication.

The Journalist's Road to Success. Dow Jones & Co. • $2 per copy. Lists more than 400 colleges and universities offering journalism/mass communications; general journalism career information; section of minority scholarships and special training programs; section on fellowships for continuing education. Formerly *Journalism Career and Scholarship Guide*.

Working Press of the Nation. R.R. Bowker L.L.C. • Annual. $530.00. $295.00 per volume. Three volumes: (1) *Newspaper Directory*; (2) *Magazine and Internal Publications Directory*; (3) *Radio and Television Directory*. Includes names of editors and other personnel.

ENCYCLOPEDIAS AND DICTIONARIES

World Press Encyclopedia. Cengage Learning Inc. • 2003. $572.00. Second edition. Two volumes. Comprehensive essays cover the background and economic framework of newspapers and other news media in about 200 countries. Covers relevant legal issues, censorship, government relations, education in journalism, status of news agencies, cable, Internet, and other media topics. eBook also available.

PERIODICALS AND NEWSLETTERS

Columbia Journalism Review. Columbia University, Graduate School of Journalism. • Bimonthly. Critical review of news media.

Editor and Publisher - The Newsmagazine of the Fourth Estate Since 1894. Editor & Publisher Magazine. • Weekly. $79 Individuals Total Access - Print and Digital. Trade journal of the newspaper industry.

IRE Journal. Investigative Reporters and Editors. • Quarterly. $70 Nonmembers. Contains practical information relating to investigative journalism.

Quill: The Magazine for Journalists. Society of Professional Journalists. • Bimonthly. $75 Individuals.

RESEARCH CENTERS AND INSTITUTES

Northwestern University - Media Management Center. 1801 Maple Ave., Ste. 5316. Evanston, IL 60208-2101. Phone: (847)491-4900; Fax: (847)491-5619; Email: mediamanagement@mmc.northwestern.edu • URL: http://www.mediamanagementcenter.org • Research areas are related to various business aspects of the newspaper industry: management, marketing, personnel, planning, accounting, and finance. A joint activity of the J. L. Kellogg Graduate School of Management and the Medill School of Journalism.

Texas Tech University - Center for Communications Research. College of Mass Communications. Lubbock, TX 79409-3082. Phone: (806)834-3117; Fax: (806)742-1085; Email: p.muhlberger@ttu.edu • URL: http://www.depts.ttu.edu/comc/ccr/index.php • Public opinion and consumer surveys, communication experiments, economic and policy studies, and television/radio production and testing, including studies on communication immunization and functions, and television personality and viewers' preference.

TRADE/PROFESSIONAL ASSOCIATIONS

Accrediting Council on Education in Journalism and Mass Communications. Stauffer-Flint Hall, 1435 Jayhawk Blvd., Lawrence, KS 66045-7575. Phone: (785)864-3973 or (785)864-3986; Fax: (785)864-5225 • URL: http://www2.ku.edu/acejmc • Consists of journalism education associations and related industry groups. Encourages cooperation between the mass media and colleges and universities in education for journalism and accredits professional programs in schools and departments of journalism. Approved list currently includes 112 colleges and universities and one university outside the country.

Association for Education in Journalism and Mass Communication. 234 Outlet Pointe Blvd., Ste. A. Columbia, SC 29210-5667. Phone: (803)798-0271; Fax: (803)772-3509; Email: aejmchq@aol.com • URL: http://www.aejmc.org • Professional organization of college and university journalism and communication teachers. Works to improve methods and standards of teaching and stimulate research. Compiles statistics on enrollments and current developments in journalism education. Maintains a listing of journalism and communication teaching positions available and teaching positions wanted, revised bimonthly.

National Press Club. National Press Bldg., 529 14th St. NW, 13th Fl., Washington, DC 20045. Phone: (202)662-7500 or (202)662-7505; Fax: (202)662-7512 • URL: http://press.org • Reporters, writers and news people employed by newspapers, wire services, magazines, radio and television stations and other forms of news media. Sponsors sports, travel and cultural events, rap sessions with news figures and authors and newsmaker breakfasts and luncheons. Offers monthly training.

JOURNALISM, BUSINESS

See BUSINESS JOURNALISM

JOURNALS, TRADE

See TRADE JOURNALS

JUDICIARY

See COURTS

JUKE BOXES

See VENDING MACHINES

JUNIOR COLLEGES

PERIODICALS AND NEWSLETTERS

Community and Junior College Libraries: The Journal for Learning Resources Centers. The Haworth Press Inc. • Quarterly. $85.00 per year.

Community College Journal. American Association of Community Colleges. • Bimonthly. $36 Members. Highlights field research, outstanding programs, college leaders, and membership activities. Formerly *Community, Technical and Junior College Journal.*

Community College Review. Dept. of Adult and Community College Education. North Carolina State University. • Quarterly. £54 Individuals print only. Contains articles on all aspects of community college administration, education, and policy.

Community College Week: The Independent Voice Serving Community, Technical and Junior Colleges. Cox, Matthews and Associates Inc. • Biweekly. $52. Covers a wide variety of current topics relating to the administration and operation of community colleges.

JUNK

See WASTE PRODUCTS

JUNK BOND FINANCING

See also BONDS; FINANCE; LEVERAGED BUYOUTS

ABSTRACTS AND INDEXES

Business Periodicals Index Retrospective. EBSCO Publishing Inc. • 11/year. Quarterly and annual cumulations.

INTERNET DATABASES

ETF Connect. Nuveen Investments. Phone: 800-257-8787 • URL: http://www.etfconnect.com • Free Web site makes available extensive, searchable information on individual closed-end investment funds, preferred share funds, and exchange-traded index funds. Information on a particular fund is available by name or as part of a classification (high yield, investment grade, municipal, emerging markets, global equity, etc.). Fund charts are available for various time periods, as is data concerning premiums or discounts, dividends, annualized total return, credit quality, "Top 10 Holdings," and so forth.

ONLINE DATABASES

Wilson Business Abstracts Online. H.W. Wilson Co. • Indexes and abstracts 600 major business periodicals, plus the *Wall Street Journal* and the business section of the *New York Times.* Indexing is from 1982, abstracting from 1990, with the two newspapers included from 1993. Updated weekly. Inquire as to online cost and availability. (*Business Periodicals Index* without abstracts is also available online.).

OTHER SOURCES

Fitch Insights. Fitch Investors Service, Inc. • Biweekly. $1,040.00 per year. Includes bond rating actions and explanation of actions. Provides commentary and Fitch's view of the financial markets.

PERIODICALS AND NEWSLETTERS

High Yield Report. American Banker/Bond Buyer Inc. • Description: Examines markets for high-yield corporate bonds, work-outs, bankruptcies, and secondary markets for distressed securities. Contains pricing information for primary and secondary markets and analysis of the high-yield sector. Reports on developments affecting the senior and subordinated debt of companies in bankruptcy or working their way out of debt, detailing proposed financial restructurings. Tracks regulatory decisions affecting trade of distressed debt and funds purchased and sold. **Remarks:** Incorporates the former Distressed Debt Report.

Moody's Bond Survey. Moody's Investors Service Inc. • Weekly (Mon.). Description: Presents statistical information and analysis of corporate, municipal, government, federal agency, and international bonds, preferred stock, and commercial paper. Includes ratings changes and withdrawals, calendars of recent and prospective bond offerings, and Moody's bond and preferred stock yield averages.

PRICE SOURCES

National Bond Summary. OTC Markets Group Inc. • Monthly, with semiannual cumulations. $504.00 per year. Includes price quotes for both active and inactive issues, with transfer agents, market makers (brokers), capital changes, name changes, and other corporate information. Formerly published by the National Quotation Bureau.

RESEARCH CENTERS AND INSTITUTES

University of Pennsylvania - The Wharton School - Rodney L. White Center for Financial Research. 3254 Steinberg Hall-Dietrich Hall, Philadelphia, PA 19104-6367. Phone: (215)898-7616; Fax: (215)573-8084; Email: rlwctr@finance.wharton.upenn.edu • URL: http://rodneywhitecenter.wharton.upenn.edu • Research areas include financial management, money markets, real estate finance, and international finance.

JURIES

See TRIALS AND JURIES

JURISTS

See LAWYERS

JURORS

See COURTS

JUTE INDUSTRY

DIRECTORIES

Directory of Taiwanese Manufacturers & Exporters of Jute, Hemp, Sisal, Burlap & Its Products. EXIM Infotek Private Ltd. • $10 Individuals. Covers: 60 Taiwanese manufacturers and exporters of canvas and duck, canvas and duck products. Entries include: Company name, postal address, city, country, phone, fax, e-mail and websites, contact person, designation, and product details.

Directory of 20 South Korean Manufacturers & Exporters of Jute, Hemp, Sisal, Burlap & Its Products. EXIM Infotek Private Ltd. • $5 Individuals. Covers: 20 South Korean manufacturers and exporters of canvas and duck, canvas and duck products. Entries include: Company name, postal address, city, country, phone, fax, e-mail and websites, contact person, designation, and product details.

PERIODICALS AND NEWSLETTERS

Journal of Natural Fibers. The Haworth Press Inc. • Quarterly. $400.00 per year to libraries; $45.00 per year to individuals. Covers applications, technology, research, and world markets relating to fibers from silk, wool, cotton, flax, hemp, jute, etc. Previously *Natural Fibres*, published annually.

JUVENILES

See YOUTH MARKET

K

KEOGH PLANS

See also SELF-EMPLOYMENT; TAX SHELTERS

ABSTRACTS AND INDEXES

Business Periodicals Index Retrospective. EBSCO Publishing Inc. • 11/year. Quarterly and annual cumulations.

HANDBOOKS AND MANUALS

Pension Plan Fix-It Handbook. Thompson Publishing Group Inc. • Two looseleaf volumes. $529.00 per year. Two looseleaf volumes. Monthly updates and newsletters. Serves as a comprehensive guide to pension plan administration, taxation, and federal regulation. Includes both defined benefit and defined contribution plans.

U.S. Master Pension Guide. Wolters Kluwer Law & Business CCH. • Annual. $99.95 1 - 4 (quantity). Explains IRS rules and regulations applying to 401(k) plans, 403(k) plans, ESOPs (employee stock ownership plans), IRAs, SEPs (simplified employee pension plans), Keogh plans, and nonqualified plans.

INTERNET DATABASES

Small Business Retirement Savings Advisor. U. S. Department of Labor. Phone: (202)219-8921 • URL: http://www.dol.gov/elaws/pwbaplan.htm • Web site provides "answers to a variety of commonly asked questions about retirement saving options for small business employers." Includes a comparison chart and detailed descriptions of various plans: 401(k), SEP-IRA, SIMPLE-IRA, Payroll Deduction IRA, Keogh Profit-Sharing, Keogh Money Purchase, and Defined Benefit. Searching is offered. Fees: Free.

ONLINE DATABASES

Wilson Business Abstracts Online. H.W. Wilson Co. • Indexes and abstracts 600 major business periodicals, plus the *Wall Street Journal* and the business section of the *New York Times*. Indexing is from 1982, abstracting from 1990, with the two newspapers included from 1993. Updated weekly. Inquire as to online cost and availability. (*Business Periodicals Index* without abstracts is also available online.).

PERIODICALS AND NEWSLETTERS

Small Business Tax News. Inside Mortgage Finance Publications. • Monthly. $139 Online. Contains latest news on tax changes, as well as detailed analysis of guidances from the IRS.

The Small Business Tax Review. A/N Group Inc. • Description: Reports tax news on such topics as new laws, court cases, IRS rulings, fringe benefits, and business and individual taxes, with emphasis on smaller businesses. Advises on financial planning and technical aspects of small business management.

KEYLESS DATA ENTRY

See AUTOMATIC IDENTIFICATION SYSTEMS

KEYS

See LOCKS AND KEYS

KITCHENS

DIRECTORIES

FDM--The Source--Woodworking Industry Directory. Reed Elsevier Group plc Reed Business Information. • Annual. $25. Publication includes: List of over 1,800 suppliers to secondary woodworking industry; coverage includes Canada. Entries include: Company name, address, phone, fax, product lines.

Kitchen Cabinets & Equipment Directory--Household. InfoGroup Inc. • Annual. Number of listings: 17,583. Entries include: Name, address, phone, size of advertisement, name of owner or manager, number of employees, year first in "Yellow Pages." Compiled from telephone company "Yellow Pages," natyonwide.

FINANCIAL RATIOS

Kitchen Cabinet Manufacturers Association Income & Expense Report. Kitchen Cabinet Manufacturers Association. • Annual. Covers 40 key operating ratios that measure company performance.

PERIODICALS AND NEWSLETTERS

Building Material Dealer. National Lumber and Building Material Dealers Association. • Monthly. $48.00 per year. Includes special feature issues on hand and power tools, lumber, roofing, kitchens, flooring, windows and doors, and insulation. Formerly *Builder Material Retailer.*

FDM: For Builders of Cabinets, Fixtures, Furniture, Millwork Furniture Design a nd Manufacturing. Chartwell Communications, Inc. • Monthly. Free to qualified personnel. Edited for furniture executives, production managers, and designers. Covers the manufacturing of household, office, and institutional furniture, store fixtures, and kitchen and bathroom cabinets.

National Home Center News: News and Analysis for the Home Improvement, Building Material Industry. Lebhar-Friedman Inc. • 22 times a year. $99.00 per year. Includes special feature issues on hardware and tools, building materials, millwork, electrical supplies, lighting, and kitchens.

TRADE/PROFESSIONAL ASSOCIATIONS

Kitchen Cabinet Manufacturers Association. 1899 Preston White Dr., Reston, VA 20191-5435. Phone: (703)264-1690; Fax: (703)620-6530 • URL: http://www.kcma.org • Serves as a national trade association representing cabinet and countertop manufacturers and suppliers to the industry. Promotes the cabinet manufacturing industry, develops standards for the industry, administers a testing and certification program, conducts education programs and meetings, provides management information and industry data, and engages in activities on behalf of members on legislative and regulatory issues.

National Kitchen and Bath Association. 687 Willow Grove St., Hackettstown, NJ 07840. Phone: 800-843-6522; Fax: (908)852-1695; Email: feedback@nkba.org • URL: http://www.nkba.org • Formerly American Institute of Kitchen Dealers.

KNIT GOODS INDUSTRY

See also TEXTILE INDUSTRY

ABSTRACTS AND INDEXES

Textile Technology Index™. EBSCO Publishing Inc. • Monthly. $545 Individuals. Includes indexing and abstracts for more than 470 periodicals.

FINANCIAL RATIOS

Annual Statement Studies. Risk Management Association. • Annual. Compiled from over 280,000 financial statements.

Annual Statement Studies: Industry Default Probabilities and Cash Flow Measures. Risk Management Association. • Annual. $405 Nonmembers. Serves as a companion volume to the original *Annual Statement Studies.* Gives probability of default estimates on a percentage scale for more than 450 industries. Includes changes in position year-by-year for eight financial statement line items and provides percentage measures of cash flow.

INTERNET DATABASES

Manufacturing Profiles. U. S. Bureau of the Census. Phone: (301)763-4636 or (301)763-4100; Fax: (301)763-4794; Email: webmaster@census.gov • URL: http://www.census.gov/prod/www/abs/mfg-prof.html • The Census Bureau makes available free on PDF (Portable Document Format) an annual consolidation of the entire Current Industrial Report series, presenting "all the data compiled." Contains statistics on production, shipments, inventories, consumption, exports, imports, and orders for a wide variety of manufactured products.

ONLINE DATABASES

Textile Technology Index™. EBSCO Publishing Inc. • Monthly. $545 Individuals. Includes indexing and abstracts for more than 470 periodicals.

World Textiles. Elsevier. • Provides abstracting and indexing from 1970 of worldwide textile literature (periodicals, books, pamphlets, and reports). Includes U. S., European, and British patent information. Updating is monthly. Inquire as to online cost and availability.

PERIODICALS AND NEWSLETTERS

DNR: The Men's Fashion Retail Textile Authority. Fairchild Publications. • Daily. $85.00 per year. Formerly *Daily News Record*.

STATISTICS SOURCES

U.S. Industry and Trade Outlook. U.S. Department of Commerce National Technical Information Service. • Annual. Produced by the International Trade Administration, U.S. Department of Commerce, in a "public-private" partnership with DRI/ McGraw-Hill and Standard & Poor's. Provides basic data, outlook for the current year, and "Long-Term Prospects" (five-year projections) for a wide variety of products and services. Includes high technology industries. Formerly *U.S. Industrial Outlook*.

TRADE/PROFESSIONAL ASSOCIATIONS

American Apparel and Footwear Association. 1601 N Kent St., Ste. 1200, Arlington, VA 22209. Phone: (703)524-1864; Fax: (703)522-6741; Email: mstorch@wewear.org • URL: http://www.wewear.org • Formerly National Knitwear Manufacturers Association.

KOSHER FOODS INDUSTRY

DIRECTORIES

Kosher Directory :Directory of Kosher Products and Services. Orthodox Union. • Over 10,000 consumer, institutional and industrial products and services produced under the rabbinical supervision of the Union.

PERIODICALS AND NEWSLETTERS

Deli News. Delicatessen Council of Southern California, Inc. Pacific Rim Publishing Co. • Monthly. $25.00 per year. Includes product news and comment related to cheeses, lunch meats, packaged fresh meats, kosher foods, gourmet-specialty items, and bakery products.

Di Yiddishe Heim/Jewish Home. Chabad Lubavitch. • Text in English and Yiddishe.

L

LABELS AND LABELING

See also PACKAGING

DIRECTORIES

Directory of Manufacturers of Pressure-Sensitive Tape, Label Stock, and Other Coated Products. Satas & Associates. • $99. Covers: 92 manufacturers of specialized coated tapes and labeling products. Entries include: Company name, address, phone, product/service.

Labels Directory. InfoGroup Inc. • Updated continuously; printed on request. Number of listings: 1,730. Entries include: Name, address, phone, size of advertisement, name of owner or manager, number of employees, year first in "Yellow Pages." Compiled from telephone company "Yellow Pages," nationwide.

Labels--Paper Directory. InfoGroup Inc. • Annual. Number of listings: 1,366. Entries include: Name, address, phone, size of advertisement, name of owner or manager, number of employees, year first in "Yellow Pages." Compiled from telephone company "Yellow Pages," nationwide.

OTHER SOURCES

Food Law Reports. Wolters Kluwer Law & Business CCH. • Weekly. $1,459.00 per year. Six looseleaf volumes. Covers regulation of adulteration, packaging, labeling, and additives. Formerly *Food Drug Cosmetic Law Reports.*

PERIODICALS AND NEWSLETTERS

PackagePrinting: For Printers and Converters of Labels, Flexible Packaging and Folding Cartons. North American Publishing Co. • Monthly. Free to qualified personnel; others, $59.00 per year. Formerly *Package Printing and Converting.*

TRADE/PROFESSIONAL ASSOCIATIONS

Printing Industries of America - Center for Technology and Research. 200 Deer Run Rd., Sewickley, PA 15143-2600. Phone: 800-910-4283 or (412)741-6860; Fax: (412)741-2311; Email: printingind@printing.org • URL: http://www.printing.org/ctr • Affiliated with Printing Industries of America.

LABOR

See also INDUSTRIAL RELATIONS; LABOR LAW AND REGULATION; LABOR UNIONS

ABSTRACTS AND INDEXES

Social Sciences Citation Index. Thomson Reuters Corp. • Weekly. Product is accessed via *Web of Science.*

Social Sciences Index Retrospective: 1907-1983. EBSCO Publishing Inc. • Indexing for 1,000,000 articles. Coverage includes international index and social sciences and humanities index.

ALMANACS AND YEARBOOKS

Advances in Industrial and Labor Relations. David Levin and Paul Gollan, editors. Elsevier. • Multiple volumes. Prices vary.

World Labour Report. International Labour Office. • Irregular. Price varies. International coverage. Reviews significant recent events and labor policy developments in the following areas: employment, human rights, labor relations, and working conditions.

CD-ROM DATABASES

Business Abstracts with Full Text. EBSCO Publishing Inc. • Includes full text articles from more than 460 business publications from 1982 to present. Indexing for nearly 880 publications.

Social Sciences Abstracts. EBSCO Publishing Inc. • Provides indexing from 1983 and abstracting from 1994 of more than 750 periodicals covering economics, area studies, community health, public administration, public welfare, urban studies, and many other topics related to the social sciences.

Social Sciences Citation Index. Thomson Reuters Corp. • Weekly. Product is accessed via *Web of Science.*

DIRECTORIES

Directory of U. S. Labor Organizations. BNA, Inc. • $180 Individuals softcover. More than 150 national unions and professional and state employees associations engaged in labor representation.

E-BOOKS

Social Trends & Indicators USA. Monique D. Magee, editor. Cengage Learning Inc. • Includes data on labor, economics, the health care industry, crime, leisure, population, education, social security, and many other topics. Sources include various government agencies and major publications. Inquire for pricing.

ENCYCLOPEDIAS AND DICTIONARIES

St. James Encyclopedia of Labor History Worldwide. Cengage Learning Inc. • $484. 2003. Two volumes. Cover 300 key events, national and international, that took place in labor history over the past 200 years. Includes illustrations, maps, a glossary, a bibliography, and indexes. St. James Press imprint. eBook also available. Inquire for pricing.

HANDBOOKS AND MANUALS

Personnel Management: Labor Relations Guide. Prentice Hall PTR. • Three looseleaf volumes. Periodic supplementation. Price on application.

ONLINE DATABASES

Wilson Business Abstracts Online. H.W. Wilson Co. • Indexes and abstracts 600 major business periodicals, plus the *Wall Street Journal* and the business section of the *New York Times.* Indexing is from 1982, abstracting from 1990, with the two newspapers included from 1993. Updated weekly. Inquire as to online cost and availability. (*Business Periodicals Index* without abstracts is also available online.).

Wilson Social Sciences Abstracts Online. H.W. Wilson Co. • Provides online abstracting and indexing of more than 500 periodicals covering area studies, community health, public administration, public welfare, urban studies, and many other social science topics. Time period is 1994 to date for abstracts and 1983 to date for indexing, with updates weekly. Inquire as to online cost and availability.

OTHER SOURCES

Labor Relations Reporter. Bloomberg BNA. • Weekly. $4,998.00 per year. Looseleaf service.

PERIODICALS AND NEWSLETTERS

International Labour Review. International Labour Office. ILO Publications Center. • $431 Institutions. Bimonthly. $80.00. Editions in English, French and Spanish.

People to People. American Public Power Association. • Description: Reports on public sector labor and personnel issues, especially those concerning the electric utility industry. Summarizes case studies in public labor relations.

Review of Social Economy. Association for Social Economics. Taylor & Francis Ltd. • Quarterly. $152 Individuals Print and Online. Quarterly. Subject matter is concerned with the relationships between social values and economics. Includes articles on income distribution, poverty, labor, and class.

RESEARCH CENTERS AND INSTITUTES

Institute for Research on Labor, Employment, and the Economy. 506 E Liberty St., 3rd Fl., Ann Arbor, MI 48104-2210. Phone: (734)998-6201; Fax: (734)998-6202 • URL: http://www.irlee.umich.edu.

RAND - Labor and Population Program. 1700 Main St., Santa Monica, CA 90407-2138. Phone: (310)393-0411 • URL: http://www.rand.org/labor • United States labor markets, demography of families and children, social welfare policy and family and child well being, social and economic functioning of the elderly, economic and social change in developing countries.

University of British Columbia - Centre for Labour and Empirical Economic Research. Department of Economics, 997-1873 E Mall, Vancouver, BC, Canada V6T 1Z1. Phone: (604)822-4870; Fax:

(604)822-5915; Email: cleer2@interchange.ubc.ca • URL: http://www.econ.ubc.ca/cleer/ • Labor markets and other sectors of the economy.

STATISTICS SOURCES

Bulletin of Labour Statistics: Supplementing the Annual Data Presented in the Year Book of Labour Statistics. International Labor Ofice. • Quarterly. $84.00 per year. Includes five Supplements. A supplement to *Yearbook of Labour Statistics.* Provides current labor and price index statistics for over 130 countries. Generally includes data for the most recent four years. Text in English, French and Spanish.

TRADE/PROFESSIONAL ASSOCIATIONS

HR Policy Association. 1100 13th St. NW, Ste. 850, Washington, DC 20005. Phone: (202)789-8670; Fax: (202)789-0064; Email: info@hrpolicy.org • URL: http://www.hrpolicy.org • Senior human resource executives of Fortune 500 companies. Conducts research and publishes findings on matters relating to federal human resources policy and its application and effects. Maintains task forces to study pending employment issues; conducts seminars, and offers a suite of labor relations and HR effectiveness training courses.

LABOR ARBITRATION

See ARBITRATION

LABOR DISCIPLINE

See EMPLOYEE DISCIPLINE

LABOR FORCE

See LABOR SUPPLY

LABOR LAW AND REGULATION

ABSTRACTS AND INDEXES

Current Law Index. Cengage Learning Inc. • $1,332 Individuals. Monthly. $1269.00 per year. Produced in cooperation with the American Association of Law Libraries. Indexes more than 900 law journals, legal newspapers, and specialty publications from the U.S., Canada, U.K., Ireland, Australia, and New Zealand.

Index to Legal Periodicals and Books. H.W. Wilson Co. • Monthly. $490.00 per year. Quarterly and annual cumulations.

ALMANACS AND YEARBOOKS

American Law Yearbook. Cengage Learning Inc. • $308 Individuals. Annual. $280.00. Serves as a yearly supplement to *West's Encyclopedia of American Lawa.* Describes new legal developments in many subject areas.

CD-ROM DATABASES

Index to Legal Periodicals and Books. EBSCO Publishing Inc. • Contains indexing of more than 1,400 English language legal periodicals from 1981 to date and 2,500 books.

ENCYCLOPEDIAS AND DICTIONARIES

West's Encyclopedia of American Law. Cengage Learning Inc. • 2004. eBook. Second edition. Covers a wide variety of legal topics for the general reader. Inquire for pricing.

INTERNET DATABASES

Lexis.com Research System. Lexis-Nexis Group. Phone: 800-227-4908 or (937)865-6800; Fax: (937)865-6909; Email: webmaster@prod.lexis-nexis.com • URL: http://www.nexis.com • Fee-based Web site offers extensive searching of a wide variety of legal sources. Additional features include Daily Opinion Service, lexis.com Bookstore, Career Center, CLE Center, Law Schools, and Practice Pages ("Pages specific to areas of specialty").

OTHER SOURCES

Contingent Workforce: Business and Legal Strategies. ALM Media Properties LLC. • $550 print and online. Covers the legal, employee benefit, and taxation aspects of alternative work arrangements (temporary employees, independent contractors, outsourcing). (Law Journal Press).

Employment Forms and Policies. Matthew Bender and Company Inc. • $150 print and e-book. Periodic supplementation available. Contains more than 300 forms, policies, and checklists for use by small or medium-sized businesses. Covers such topics as employee selection, payroll issues, benefits, performance appraisal, dress codes, and employee termination.

Labor Relations. Wolters Kluwer Law & Business CCH. • $2,589.00 per year. Seven looseleaf volumes. Weekly updates. Covers labor relations, wages and hours, state labor laws, and employment practices. Supplement available, *Labor Law Reports.* Summary Newsletter.

Labor Relations Reporter. Bloomberg BNA. • Weekly. $4,998.00 per year. Looseleaf service.

Occupational Safety and Health Handbook: An Employer's Guide to OSHA Laws. Matthew Bender and Company Inc. • $128. Periodic supplementation available. Covers inspections, violations, the citation process, ergonomics, hazards, equipment, and other topics relating to the law enforced by the federal Occupational Safety and Health Administration (OSHA).

PERIODICALS AND NEWSLETTERS

Employee Policy for the Private and Public Sector: State Capitals. Wakeman/Walworth Inc. • Weekly. $245.00 per year; print and online editions, $350.00 per year. Newsletter. Formerly *From the State Capitals: Employee Policy for the Private and Public Sector.*

Employment Law Strategist. Law Journal Newsletter. • $439 per year. Covers employment law topics, including immigration laws, repetitive stress claims, workplace violence, liability of actions of intoxicated employees, record keeping, liability for fetal injury, independent contractor, and employee issues. Monthly. 229 individuals electronic edition. Description: Reports on legal strategy and substantive developments in the area of matrimonial law, including such topics as tax considerations, custody, visitation, division of property, and valuation. Recurring features include litigation roundup and a legislative update.

Federal Register. Office of the Federal Register. U. S. Government Printing Office. • Daily except Saturday and Sunday. $764.00 per year. Publishes regulations and legal notices issued by federal agencies, including executive orders and presidential proclamations. Issued by the National Archives and Records Administration (www.nara.gov).

LABOR MARKET

See LABOR SUPPLY

LABOR ORGANIZATION

See LABOR UNIONS

LABOR PRODUCTIVITY

See PRODUCTIVITY

LABOR SUPPLY

CD-ROM DATABASES

OECD Statistical Compendium. Organization for Economic Cooperation and Development. • Semiannual. $1,905.00 per year for 1 to 10 users. CD-ROM contains more than 730,000 monthly, quarterly, and annual time series for OECD countries, 1960 to date. Includes fully searchable data on agriculture, food, economic indicators, national accounts, employment, energy, finance, industry, technology, and foreign trade. Results can be displayed in various forms.

Sourcebooks America CD-ROM. CACI Marketing Systems. • Annual. $1,250.00. Provides the CD-ROM version of *The Sourcebook of ZIP Code Demographics: Census Edition* and *The Sourcebook of County Demographics: Census Edition.*

INTERNET DATABASES

Bureau of Economic Analysis. U. S. Department of Commerce, Bureau of Economic Analysis. Phone: (202)606-9900; Fax: (202)606-5310; Email: webmaster@bea.doc.gov • URL: http://www.bea.doc.gov • Web site includes "News Release Information" covering national, regional, and international economic estimates from the BEA. Highlights of releases appear online the same day, complete text and tables appear the next day. "Recent News Releases" section provides titles for past nine months, with links. "BEA Data and Methodology" includes "Frequently Requested NIPA Data" (national income and product accounts, such as gross domestic product and personal income). Other statistics are available. Fees: Free.

Business 2.0 Web Guide to the Best Business Links. Business 2.0 Media Inc. Phone: (415)293-4800; Email: support@business2.com • URL: http://www.business2.com/webguide • Web site presents an extensive, searchable directory of links to "the best, most informative, and authoritative web pages." Twenty main categories cover business, finance, career, company information, people, and technology topics, with thousands of subtopics, all linking to Web sites recommended by experienced business researchers. Fees: Free.

Fedstats. Federal Interagency Council on Statistical Policy. Phone: (202)395-7254 • URL: http://www.fedstats.gov • Web site features an efficient search facility for full-text statistics produced by more than 100 federal agencies, including the Census Bureau, the Bureau of Economic Analysis, and the Bureau of Labor Statistics. Boolean searches can be made within one agency or for all agencies combined. Links are offered to international statistical bureaus, including the UN, IMF, OECD, UNESCO, Eurostat, and 20 individual countries. Fees: Free.

FreeLunch.com. Economy.com, Inc. Phone: (610)696-8700; Fax: (610)696-1678 • URL: http://www.freelunch.com • Web site provides free access to more than 200 million economic and financial data series, covering industry, demographics, labor markets, prices, retail sales, government spending, trade, interest rates, housing starts, the stock market, etc. Data is available in either chart or table form. Searching is offered. Free, but registration required. Economy.com, Inc. also offers fee-based economic analysis at *The Dismal Scientist* site (www.dismal.com).

OTHER SOURCES

Foreign Labor Trends. U. S. Government Printing Office. • Irregular (50 to 60 issues per year, each on an individual country). $95.00 per year. Prepared by various American Embassies. Issued by the Bureau of International Labor Affairs, U. S. Department of Labor. Covers labor developments in important foreign countries, including trends in wages, working conditions, labor supply, employment, and unemployment.

PERIODICALS AND NEWSLETTERS

Working USA: The Journal of Labor and Society. M.E. Sharpe Inc. • Quarterly. $160.00 per year to institutions; $45.00 to individuals. Provides a wide range of material on employment, labor markets, societal issues, and present-day labor unions.

RESEARCH CENTERS AND INSTITUTES

Aalborg University - Center for Labor Market Research. Fibigerstraede 1, 9220 Alborg, Denmark. Phone: 45 99409940; Fax: 45 98155346 • URL: http://www.dps.aau.dk/forskningsenheder/carma-english • Work organization, technology developments, cooperation and management styles, collective bargaining, wage and personnel policies in private enterprises and public institutions.

Princeton University - Industrial Relations Section. Firestone Library, A-18-J, 1 Washington Rd., Princeton, NJ 08544. Phone: (609)258-4040; Fax: (609)258-2907; Email: c6789@princeton.edu • URL: http://www.irs.princeton.edu • Fields of research include labor supply, manpower training, unemployment, and equal employment opportunity.

W.E. Upjohn Institute for Employment Research. 300 S Westnedge Ave., Kalamazoo, MI 49007-4686. Phone: 888-227-8569 or (269)343-5541; Fax: (269)343-7310; Email: communications@upjohn.org • URL: http://www.upjohninstitute.org • Research fields include unemployment, unemployment insurance, worker's compensation, labor productivity, profit sharing, the labor market, economic development, earnings, training, and other areas related to employment.

STATISTICS SOURCES

Quarterly Labour Force Statistics. Organization for Economic Cooperation and Development. Organisation for Economic Co-operation and Development Publications and Information Center. • Quarterly. $90.00 per year. Provides current data for OECD member countries on population, employment, unemployment, civilian labor force, armed forces, and other labor factors.

Report on the American Workforce. U. S. Government Printing Office. • Annual. Issued by the U. S. Department of Labor (www.dol.gov). Appendix contains tabular statistics, including employment, unemployment, price indexes, consumer expenditures, employee benefits (retirement, insurance, vacation, etc.), wages, productivity, hours of work, and occupational injuries. Annual figures are shown for up to 50 years.

Statistical Yearbook. United Nations Publications. • Annual. $125.00. Contains statistics for about 200 countries on a wide variety of economic, industrial, and demographic topics. Compiled by United Nations Statistical Office.

Survey of Current Business. U. S. Government Printing Office. • Published by Bureau of Economic Analysis, U. S. Department of Commerce. Presents a wide variety of business and economic data.

LABOR UNIONS

See also COLLECTIVE BARGAINING

DIRECTORIES

Directory of U. S. Labor Organizations. BNA, Inc. • $180 Individuals softcover. More than 150 national unions and professional and state employees associations engaged in labor representation.

Trade Unions of the World. Cengage Learning Inc. • $160 Individuals. Covers trade union centers, international affiliations of trade unions, and major organizations outside of the trade union centers.

Washington: A Comprehensive Directory of the Key Institutions and Leaders in th e National Capitol Area. Columbia Books Inc. • Annual. $149.00. Provides information on about 5,000 Washington, DC key businesses, government offices, non-profit organizations, and cultural institutions, with the names of about 25,000 principal executives. Includes Washington media, law offices, foundations, labor unions, international organizations, clubs, etc.

ENCYCLOPEDIAS AND DICTIONARIES

St. James Encyclopedia of Labor History Worldwide. Cengage Learning Inc. • $484. 2003. Two volumes. Cover 300 key events, national and international, that took place in labor history over the past 200 years. Includes illustrations, maps, a glossary, a bibliography, and indexes. St. James Press imprint. eBook also available. Inquire for pricing.

OTHER SOURCES

Labor Relations Reporter. Bloomberg BNA. • Weekly. $4,998.00 per year. Looseleaf service.

PERIODICALS AND NEWSLETTERS

America at Work. AFL-CIO. • 11/year. Covers information on working in America. Formerly *AFL-CIO News*.

Union Labor Report. Bloomberg BNA. • Biweekly. Description: Covers legal, legislative, and regulatory developments and trends affecting management and labor in the workplace.

Working USA: The Journal of Labor and Society. M.E. Sharpe Inc. • Quarterly. $160.00 per year to institutions; $45.00 to individuals. Provides a wide range of material on employment, labor markets, societal issues, and present-day labor unions.

TRADE/PROFESSIONAL ASSOCIATIONS

Argentine Industry Association. Av. de Mayo 1147/57, C1085ABB Buenos Aires, Argentina. Phone: 54 11 41242300; Fax: 54 11 41242301; Email: uia@uia.org.ar • URL: http://www.uia.org.ar • Represents members of industrial union in Argentina.

FIRST Union. 120 Church St., Onehunga, Auckland 1643, New Zealand. Phone: 64 9 6228355 or 64 9 6228351; Fax: 64 9 6228353; Email: contact@firstunion.org.nz • URL: http://www.firstunion.org.nz • Organizing union for workers in the financial services industry. Seeks to obtain optimal conditions of employment for members. Represents members in negotiations with employers.

Nordic Financial Unions. PO Box 720, S-101 34 Stockholm, Sweden. Phone: 46 8 6140300 or 46 8 6140302; Fax: 46 8 6113898 • URL: http://nordicfinancialunions.org • Bank and insurance employees' trade unions of Denmark, Finland, Iceland, Norway, and Sweden representing 165,000 individuals. Promotes the interests of bank and insurance employees in Scandinavia. Conducts biennial training course for shop stewards. Arranges conferences and meetings; training courses for shop stewards; carries out research, information, and lobbying activities; and has a system for economic assistance to member unions during labour conflicts.

Zambia Union of Financial Institutions and Allied Workers. Luangwa House, Cairo Rd., Lusaka, Zambia. Phone: 260 211 222105; Fax: 260 211 231364; Email: zufiaw@zamnet.zm • URL: http://www.africaefuture.org/zufiaw • Exists to improve the material conditions of members and their families. Aims to strive for equality between all men and women in the sharing of all national wealth and world leisure.

LABORATORIES

See also CLINICAL LABORATORY INDUSTRY; RESEARCH AND DEVELOPMENT

ABSTRACTS AND INDEXES

Science Citation Index. Thomson Reuters Intellectual Property and Science. • Weekly. Includes *Source Index*, *Citation Index*, *Permuterm Subject Index*, and *Corporate Index*. Provides researchers, administrators, faculty, and students with quick, powerful access to the bibliographic and citation information they need to find research data, analyze trends, journals and researchers, and share their findings.

CD-ROM DATABASES

Science Citation Index. Thomson Reuters Intellectual Property and Science. • Weekly. Includes *Source Index*, *Citation Index*, *Permuterm Subject Index*, and *Corporate Index*. Provides researchers, administrators, faculty, and students with quick, powerful access to the bibliographic and citation information they need to find research data, analyze trends, journals and researchers, and share their findings.

PERIODICALS AND NEWSLETTERS

Today's Chemist at Work. American Chemical Society. • Monthly. Institutions, $200.00 per year; others, price on application. Provide pracrtical information for chemists on day-to-day operations. Product coverage includes chemicals, equipment, apparatus, instruments, and supplies.

RESEARCH CENTERS AND INSTITUTES

Åbo Academy University - Laboratory of Industrial Management. Biskopsgatan 8, FI-20500 Abo, Finland. Phone: 358 2 221531; Email: infowww@abo.fi • URL: http://www.abo.fi/student/en/Content/Document/document/9465 • How industrial companies operate now and in the future within different industries, especially what is offered, the organization of the companies and what capabilities are needed. There is a special focus on international industrial project-based business.

U.S. Customs and Border Protection - Office of Field Operations - Laboratories and Scientific Services Division - Research Laboratory. 7501 Boston Blvd., Ste. 113, Springfield, VA 22153. Phone: (703)921-7200; Fax: (703)921-7155; Email: cbp.labresearch@dhs.gov • URL: http://www.cbp.gov/xp/cgov/import/operations_support/labs_scientific_svcs/ • Provides technical services in support of the U.S. Customs mission in tariff and trade and in enforcement. Principal area of interest is analytical chemistry (instrumentation and methodology). Laboratory supports a field laboratory system, with affiliated laboratories in New York City, Savannah, New Orleans, Los Angeles, San Francisco, Chicago, and San Juan.

LABORATORIES, CLINICAL

See CLINICAL LABORATORY INDUSTRY

LABORATORY EQUIPMENT

See SCIENTIFIC APPARATUS AND INSTRUMENT INDUSTRIES

LACE INDUSTRY

ABSTRACTS AND INDEXES

Textile Technology Index™. EBSCO Publishing Inc. • Monthly. $545 Individuals. Includes indexing and abstracts for more than 470 periodicals.

DIRECTORIES

Directory of Chinese Manufacturers & Exporters of Laces, Ribbons & Embroidery Products. EXIM Infotek Private Ltd. • $10 Individuals. Covers: 50 Chinese manufacturers & exporters of badges, embroidery-all types, embroideries, embroidery products, garlands, laces, ribbons. Entries include: Company name, postal address, city, country, phone, fax, e-mail & websites, contact person, designation, products detail.

Directory of South Korean Manufacturers & Exporters of Laces, Ribbons & Embroidery Products. EXIM Infotek Private Ltd. • $10 Individuals. Covers: 50 South Korean manufacturers and exporters of badges, embroidery-all types, embroidery/lace mending services, embroidery-hand made, lace, lace-machine made, ribbons, ribbons and tapes for industrial use, ribbons and tapes-non industrial, and trimmings/cordings/braids and fringes. Entries include: Company name, postal address, city, country, phone, fax, e-mail and websites, contact person, designation, and product details.

Directory of Taiwanese Manufacturers & Exporters of Laces, Ribbons & Embroidery Products. EXIM Infotek Private Ltd. • $15 Individuals. Covers: 180 Taiwanese manufacturers and exporters of badges, decorative trim, embroidery-all types, embroidered emblems, embroideries, embroidery, embroidery emblems, embroidery-hand made, flower tapes, lace and embroidery, lace-hand made, lace-machine made, ribbons, ribbons and tapes for industrial use, ribbons and tapes-non industrial, trimmings/cordings/braids and fringes, and woven ribbon. Entries include: Company name, postal address, city, country, phone, fax, e-mail and websites, contact person, designation, and product details.

ONLINE DATABASES

Textile Technology Index™. EBSCO Publishing Inc. • Monthly. $545 Individuals. Includes indexing and abstracts for more than 470 periodicals.

World Textiles. Elsevier. • Provides abstracting and indexing from 1970 of worldwide textile literature (periodicals, books, pamphlets, and reports). Includes U. S., European, and British patent information. Updating is monthly. Inquire as to online cost and availability.

LACQUER AND LACQUERING

See PAINT AND PAINTING

LAMB INDUSTRY

See SHEEP INDUSTRY

LAMPS

See LIGHTING

LAN

See LOCAL AREA NETWORKS

LAND COMPANIES

See REAL ESTATE BUSINESS

LAND UTILIZATION

ABSTRACTS AND INDEXES

Environment Abstracts. University Publications of America. • Monthly. Price varies. Provides multidisciplinary coverage of the world's environmental literature. Incorporates *Acid Rain Abstracts.*

Environment Abstracts Annual: A Guide to the Key Environmental Literature of the Year. University Publications of America. • Annual. $495.00. A yearly cumulation of *Environment Abstracts.*

ALMANACS AND YEARBOOKS

Earth Almanac: An Annual Geophysical Review of the State of the Planet. Natalie Goldstein. Greenwood Publishing Group Inc. • $91.95. Provides background information, statistics, and a summary of major events relating to the atmosphere, oceans, land, and fresh water.

Land Use and Environment Law Review. Thomson West. • Annual. $1,392. Features property rights and economic allocation of natural resources.

CD-ROM DATABASES

Environment Abstracts on CD-ROM. University Publications of America. • Quarterly. $1,295.00 per year. Contains the following CD-ROM databases: *Environment Abstracts, Energy Abstracts,* and *Acid Rain Abstracts.* Length of coverage varies.

OTHER SOURCES

American Land Planning Law. John Taylor and Norma Williams. Thomson West. • $1,058 Individuals full set. Examines the changing priorities in zoning and land use practices, focusing on the relationship between private activity and governmental power, and analyzing over 15,000 cases from all 50 states.

PERIODICALS AND NEWSLETTERS

Housing and Commercial Real Estate News Roundup. Urban Land Institute. • Description: Summarizes current developments in land use, real estate development, and related areas.

Land Use Law Report. Business Publishers Inc. • Monthly. $297 Individuals online. Description: Provides up-to-date information on court decisions, legislation, and regulations that impact today's most pressing land-use policy, planning, and legal issues. Readers receive in-depth coverage on zoning and planning policies, regulatory takings, undesirable land uses, environmental legislation, and much more. **Remarks:** Also available via e-mail.

LANDSCAPE ARCHITECTURE

ABSTRACTS AND INDEXES

Art Index. EBSCO Publishing Inc. • Quarterly. Annual cumulations. Price varies. Subject and author index to periodicals in art, architecture, industrial design, city planning, photography, and various related topics.

FINANCIAL RATIOS

Annual Statement Studies. Risk Management Association. • Annual. Compiled from over 280,000 financial statements.

Annual Statement Studies: Industry Default Probabilities and Cash Flow Measures. Risk Management Association. • Annual. $405 Nonmembers. Serves as a companion volume to the original *Annual Statement Studies.* Gives probability of default estimates on a percentage scale for more than 450 industries. Includes changes in position year-by-year for eight financial statement line items and provides percentage measures of cash flow.

ONLINE DATABASES

Art Index Online. H.W. Wilson Co. • Indexes a wide variety of art-related periodicals, 1984 to date. Monthly updates. Inquire as to online cost and availability.

PERIODICALS AND NEWSLETTERS

Landscape Maintenance News. Landscape Information Services. • Description: Provides landscape service companies with information to help them manage their services; covers changes and events in the industry. Covers image, customer service, advertising and marketing, estimating, mowing, poweraking, fertilization, weed control, maintenance, and miscellaneous services. Discusses trade shows, products and services, associations, and franchise opportunities. Recurring features include news of research, news of educational opportunities, book reviews, and notices of publications available.

TRADE/PROFESSIONAL ASSOCIATIONS

American Society of Landscape Architects. 636 Eye St. NW, Washington, DC 20001-3736. Phone: 888-999-2752 or (202)898-2444; Fax: (202)898-1185; Email: info@asla.org • URL: http://www.asla.org • Professional society of landscape architects. Promotes the advancement of education and skill in the art of landscape architecture as an instrument in service to the public welfare. Seeks to strengthen existing and proposed university programs in landscape architecture. Offers counsel to new and emerging programs; encourages state registration of landscape architects. Sponsors annual educational exhibit. Offers placement service; conducts specialized education and research.

LAPTOP COMPUTERS

See PORTABLE COMPUTERS

LARD INDUSTRY

See OIL AND FATS INDUSTRY

LASERDISKS

See OPTICAL DISK STORAGE DEVICES

LASERS

ABSTRACTS AND INDEXES

Journal of Current Laser Abstracts. PennWell Corp., Advanced Technology Div. • Monthly. $465 Individuals. Covers the world's literature of lasers: industrial, medical, and military. Subscription includes annual subject and author index.

Key Abstracts: Optoelectronics. Institution of Engineering and Technology. • Monthly. $1,138. Provides international coverage of journal and proceedings literature relating to fiber optics, lasers, and optoelectronics in general.

NTIS Alerts: Manufacturing Technology. U.S. Department of Commerce National Technical Information Service. • Biweekly. $130 per year. Covers computer-aided design and manufacturing (CAD/CAM), engineering materials, quality control, machine tools, robots, lasers, productivity, and related subjects.

Solid State and Superconductivity Abstracts. Cambridge Scientific Abstracts L.P. • Monthly. Covers chemistry, physics, metallurgy, resonance, materials, measurement, and superconductivity theories, applications, and problem areas. Formerly *Solid State Abstracts Journal.*

DIRECTORIES

Industrial Laser Solutions Buyer's Guide. PennWell Corp., Advanced Technology Div. • Annual. Lists industrial laser suppliers by category and geographic location. (Included with subscription to *Industrial Laser Solutions.*).

PERIODICALS AND NEWSLETTERS

Industrial Laser Solutions for Manufacturing. PennWell Corp., Advanced Technology Div. • Monthly. $300.00 per year. Covers industrial laser technology, especially machine tool applications.

Medical Laser Report. PennWell Corp. • Description: Presents news on the medical laser industry, technology, research, and markets. Recurring features include news of research, business news and product introductions.

For publishers' addresses, refer to SOURCES CITED section at the back of the book.

Optics and Laser Technology. Elsevier. • Eight times a year. Institutions, $2,115.00 per year. Published in United Kingdom.

RESEARCH CENTERS AND INSTITUTES

Massachusetts Institute of Technology - Laser Biomedical Research Center, GR Harrison Spectroscopy Laboratory, 6-205, 77 Massachusetts Ave., Cambridge, MA 02139. Phone: (617)253-8418 or (617)253-7700; Fax: (617)253-4513; Email: rrdasari@mit.edu • URL: http://web.mit.edu/spectroscopy/facilities/lbrc.html • Concerned with the medical use of lasers.

University of Central Florida - Center for Research and Education in Optics and Lasers, College of Optics & Photonics, 4000 Central Florida Blvd., Orlando, FL 32816-2700. Phone: (407)823-6800; Fax: (407)823-6880; Email: creol@creol.ucf.edu • URL: http://www.creol.ucf.edu • Photonics, nanophotonics, biophotonics, optical switching, nonlinear optics fiber optics, laser propagation, waveguides, growth of nonlinear and laser host materials, optical scattering, laser-produced plasmas, free electron lasers, opto-electronics, quantum electronics, optical sensors, correlation techniques, laser-induced damage, optical power limiting, ultra-fast phenomena (femtosecond laser interactions), nonlinear optical spectroscopy, diffractive optics, liquid crystal optics, spatial solitons, image understanding, thin film optics, X-ray lasers, diode pumped lasers, micro-lasers, and classical optics. Applications include the following: optical telecommunications, new laser sources, detection, surveillance, reconnaissance, command and control, counter and counter-counter measures, intelligence collection, and the development of improved optical components, sensor protection, optical computing, and medical lasers.

University of Tennessee at Tullahoma - Center for Laser Applications, 411 B.H. Goethert Pkwy., Tullahoma, TN 37388. Phone: (931)393-7466; Fax: (931)454-2271; Email: hof@utsi.edu • URL: http://cla.utsi.edu • In addition to research, provides technical assistance relating to the industrial use of lasers.

TRADE/PROFESSIONAL ASSOCIATIONS

Laser Institute of America, 13501 Ingenuity Dr., Ste. 128, Orlando, FL 32826. Phone: 800-345-2737 or (407)380-1553; Fax: (407)380-5588 • URL: http://www.lia.org • Formerly Laser Industry Association.

Optical Society of America, 2010 Massachusetts Ave. NW, Washington, DC 20036-1023. Phone: 800-766-405A or (202)223-8130; Fax: (202)223-1096; Email: info@osa.org • URL: http://www.osa.org • Persons interested in any branch of optics: research, instruction, optical applications, manufacture, distribution of optical equipment, and physiological optics. Sponsors topical meetings.

LATHING

See PLASTER AND PLASTERING

LATIN AMERICAN MARKETS

See also NORTH AMERICAN FREE TRADE AGREEMENT

ABSTRACTS AND INDEXES

Business Periodicals Index Retrospective. EBSCO Publishing Inc. • 11/year. Quarterly and annual cumulations.

F & S Index: International. Cengage Learning Inc. • $2,659 Individuals. Monthly. $2,532.00 per year, including quarterly and annual cumulations. Provides annotated citations to marketing, business, financial, and industrial literature. Coverage of international business activity includes trade journals, financial magazines, business newspapers, and special reports. Areas included are Asia, Latin America, Africa, the Middle East, Oceania, and Canada.

Hispanic American Periodicals Index. University of California, Los Angeles. Latin American Studies Center Publications. • Daily. $425. Annual. Indexes about 250 periodicals that regularly include material on Latin America. Supplement available.

PAIS International. ProQuest L.L.C. • Monthly. $850.00 per year; cumulations three times a year. Provides topical citations to the worldwide literature of public affairs, economics, demographics, sociology, and trade. Text in English; indexed materials in English, French, German, Italian, Portuguese and Spanish.

CD-ROM DATABASES

Business Abstracts with Full Text. EBSCO Publishing Inc. • Includes full text articles from more than 460 business publications from 1982 to present. Indexing for nearly 880 publications.

Latino-Hispanic Historical Collection. EBSCO Publishing Inc. • 60,000 historical articles, complete texts, political and religious pamphlets. Available in two series.

PAIS International. ProQuest L.L.C. • Monthly. $1,995.00 per year. Contains over 650,000 citations to the literature of contemporary social, political, and economic issues.

DIRECTORIES

Hoover's Handbook of World Business. Dun & Bradstreet Inc. Hoover's Inc. • Annual. $225 Individuals Hardcover. Covers: Hundreds of companies headquartered outside the U.S., including many with substantial activity in the U.S.; global enterprises, businesses that dominate their respective industries, and representative companies from all major industries. Entries include: Company name, overview, history, exchange and stock symbols, fiscal year-end date, names and titles of key personnel, name of auditors, number of employees, headquarters address, phone, fax, description of where the company does business, specific products/services/brand names produced, key competitors, 10 years of key financial data.

International Media Guide: Business/Professional Publications: The Americas. Kantar Media SRDS. • $553 Individuals online; 1 year. Describes over 4,400 trade publications from North, South, and Central America, with advertising rates and circulation data.

Latin America and Caribbean Autos Directory. Business Monitor International Ltd. • $975 Individuals CD. Covers: 1,145 top autos executives on 374 leading automotive companies from Argentina, Brazil, Chile, Colombia, Mexico, Peru, Venezuela, Anguilla, Antigua & Barbuda, Aruba, the Bahamas, Barbados, Bermuda, British Virgin Islands, Cayman Islands, Cuba, Dominica, Dominican Rep, French Guiana, Grenada, Guadeloupe, Guyana, Haiti, Jamaica, Martinique, Montserrat, Netherland Antilles, Puerto Rico, St Kitts, St Lucia, St Vincent, Suriname, Trinidad & Tobago, Turks & Caicos and US Virgin Islands. Entries include: parent company head offices, full company name, address, phone and fax numbers, email and website address, senior contact personnel, company description and profile, nationality, and ownership status.

Latin America and Caribbean Food and Drink Directory. Business Monitor International Ltd. • $975 Individuals CD. Covers: 1,642 top food and drink executives on 550 leading food and drink companies from Latin America and Caribbean. Entries include: parent company head offices, full company name, address, phone and fax numbers, email and website address, senior contact personnel, company description and profile, nationality, and ownership status.

Latin America & Caribbean Oil and Gas Directory. Business Monitor International Ltd. • $995 Individuals CD. Covers: 828 top oil and gas executives on 309 leading oil and gas companies from Latin America. Entries include: parent company head offices, full company name, address, phone and fax numbers, email and website address, senior contact personnel, company description and profile, nationality, and ownership status.

Latin America and Caribbean Pharmaceuticals and Healthcare Directory. Business Monitor International Ltd. • $995 Individuals CD. Covers: 1,908 top pharmaceutical executives at 598 leading pharmaceutical companies from Argentina, Brazil, Chile, Colombia, Mexico, Peru, Venezuela and the Caribbean. Entries include: parent company head offices, full company name, address, phone and fax numbers, email and website address, senior contact personnel, company description and profile, nationality, and ownership status.

Latin America and Caribbean Telecommunications Directory. Business Monitor International Ltd. • $995 Individuals CD. Covers: 2,506 top telecommunications executives at 808 leading telecommunications companies from Latin America and Caribbean. Entries include: parent company head offices, full company name, address, phone and fax numbers, email and website address, senior contact personnel, company description and profile, nationality, and ownership status.

Trade Directory of Mexico. Hoover's Inc. • Annual. $99.95. Published by IMF Editora. Contains profiles of 6,000 Mexican companies involved in foreign trade. Includes profile of Mexico and of the individual states.

GENERAL WORKS

Latin American Law and Business Report. Prentice Hall Press. • Monthly. $345 Individuals. Journal covering current business and legal developments and practices in Latin America.

ONLINE DATABASES

Chronicle of Latin American Economic Affairs (online). Latin America Data Base. • Contains the complete text online of the weekly newsletter, *Chronicle of Latin American Economic Affairs*. Provides news and analysis of trade and economic developments in Latin America, including Caribbean countries. Time period is 1986 to date, with weekly updates. Inquire as to online cost and availability.

NotiCen: Central American & Caribbean Affairs. Latin America Data Base. • An online newsletter covering economic, trade, political, and social issues in Central America. Time period is 1986 to date, with weekly updates. Inquire as to online cost and availability. Formerly EcoCentral.

Wilson Business Abstracts Online. H.W. Wilson Co. • Indexes and abstracts 600 major business periodicals, plus the *Wall Street Journal* and the business section of the *New York Times*. Indexing is from 1982, abstracting from 1990, with the two newspapers included from 1993. Updated weekly. Inquire as to online cost and availability. (*Business Periodicals Index* without abstracts is also available online.).

PERIODICALS AND NEWSLETTERS

Business Latin America: Weekly Report to Managers of Latin American Operations. The Economist Intelligence Unit. • Weekly. $1,250.00 per year. Newsletter covering Latin American business trends, politics, regulations, exchange rates, economics, and finance. Provides statistical data on foreign debt, taxes, labor costs, gross domestic product (GDP), and inflation rates.

Business Week International: The World's Only

International Newsweekly of Business. McGraw Hill Financial Inc. • Weekly. $95.00 per year.

Caribbean Business. Casiano Communications Inc. • Weekly. $35.99.

Economic and Social Progress in Latin America. Inter-American Development Bank. • Monthly. $24.95 per year. Covers developments in Latin America affecting business and trade. Text in Spanish.

Emerging Markets Quarterly. Institutional Investor Inc. Journals Group. • Quarterly. Price on application. Newsletter on financial markets in developing areas, such as Africa, Latin America, Southeast Asia, and Eastern Europe. Topics include institutional investment opportunities and regulatory matters. Formerly *Emerging Markets Weekly*.

Institutional Investor International Edition: The Magazine for International Finance and Investment. Institutional Investor Inc. Journals Group. • Monthly. $475.00 per year. Covers the international aspects of professional investing and finance. Emphasis is on Europe, the Far East, and Latin America.

International Economic Scoreboard. The Conference Board. • Description: Provides current data on the business outlook in 11 major industrial countries: Australia, Canada, France, West Germany, Italy, Japan, Korea, New Zealand, Taiwan, the United Kingdom, and the U.S. **Remarks:** A source for additional information on this indicator system and its uses is available at the Center for International Business Cycle Research, Columbia University Business School.

Latin Fund Management. SourceMedia Inc. • Monthly. $495.00 per year. Newsletter (also available online at www.latinfund.net). Provides news and analysis of Latin American mutual funds, pension funds, and annuities.

Market: Latin America. The PRS Group Inc. • Monthly. $397.00 per year ($198.00 to academic institutions). Newsletter. Provides market trend information and demographic data for Latin American countries. Includes sales trend projections for various products and services, with consumer household buying patterns and industrial expenditures. Formerly published by Market Newsletters.

Twin Plant News: The Magazine of the Maquiladora Industry. Nibbe, Hernandez and Associates Inc. • Monthly. $85.00 per year. Focuses on Mexican labor laws, taxes, economics, industrial trends, and culture. Industries featured include electronic components, plastics, automotive supplies, metals, communications, and packaging.

RESEARCH CENTERS AND INSTITUTES

Center for Latin American Studies. University of Chicago, Kelly Hall 117, 5848 S University Ave., Chicago, IL 60637. Phone: (773)702-8420; Fax: (773)702-1755; Email: clas@uchicago.edu • URL: http://clas.uchicago.edu • Includes economic inquiry on Latin America.

George Washington University - Center for Latin American Issues. Duques Hall, Ste. 450, 2201 G St. NW, Washington, DC 20052. Phone: (202)994-5205; Fax: (202)994-5225; Email: clai@gwu.edu • URL: http://www.gwu.edu/clai • U.S.-Latin American relations, focusing on strengthening business-government relations throughout the region, resolving differences, identifying areas for expanded relations, and managing economic and business issues.

Latin American and Caribbean Center-Intercultural Dance and Music Institute. Florida International University, 11200 SW 8th St., Miami, FL 33199. Phone: (305)348-2894; Fax: (305)348-3593; Email: lacc@fiu.edu • URL: http://www.lacc.fiu.edu • Research fields include economic development and trade.

University of California, Los Angeles - Latin American Center. 10349 Bunche Hall, Los Angeles, CA 90095. Phone: (310)825-4571; Fax: (310)206-6859; Email: latinamctr@international.ucla.edu • URL: http://www.international.ucla.edu/lai.

STATISTICS SOURCES

Economic Survey of Latin America and the Caribbean. United Nations Publications. • Annual. $25. Includes reports on economic trends in 20 Latin American countries.

Statistical Abstract of Latin America. University of California, Los Angeles. • Annual. $325.00. Two volumes.

Statistical Yearbook for Latin America and the Caribbean. • Annual. $79.00. Issued by the Economic Commission for Latin America and the Caribbean. Includes a wide variety of economic, industrial, and trade data for Latin American nations. Text in English and Spanish.

TRADE/PROFESSIONAL ASSOCIATIONS

Americas Society/Council of the Americas. 680 Park Ave., New York, NY 10065. Phone: (212)249-8950; Fax: (212)249-5868; Email: inforequest@as-coa.org • URL: http://www.americas-society.org • Members are U. S. corporations with business interests in Latin America. Formerly Council of the Americas.

Association of American Chambers of Commerce in Latin America. 1615 H St. NW, Washington, DC 20062-0001. Phone: (202)463-5460; Fax: (202)463-3126; Email: info@aaccla.org • URL: http://www.aaccla.org • Umbrella organization for American chambers of commerce in Latin America. Affiliated with U.S. Chamber of Commerce.

Brazilian-American Chamber of Commerce. 509 Madison Ave., Ste. 304, New York, NY 10022. Phone: (212)751-4691; Fax: (212)751-7692 or (212)751-8929 • URL: http://www.brazilcham.com • Promotes trade between Brazil and the U. S.

Brazilian Trade Bureau of the Consulate General of Brazil in New York. 220 E 42nd St., 26th Fl., New York, NY 10017-5806. Phone: (917)777-7777; Fax: (212)827-0225; Email: cg.novayork@itamaraty.gov.br • URL: http://novayork.itamaraty.gov.br/en-us • Offers assistance to American firms wishing to purchase Brazilian products, and promotes Brazilian firms and their exports. Formerly Brazilian Government Trade Bureau.

Colombian American Association. 641 Lexington Ave., Ste. 1430, New York, NY 10022. Phone: (212)233-7776; Fax: (212)233-7779; Email: info@andean-us.com • URL: http://www.colombianamerican.org • Facilitates commerce and trade between the Republic of Colombia and the U.S. Fosters and advances cultural relations and goodwill between the two nations. Encourages sound investments in Colombia by Americans and in the U.S. by Colombians. Disseminates information in the U.S. concerning Colombia.

Coltrade: Colombian Government Trade Bureau. 1901 L St. NW, Ste. 700, Washington, DC 20036. Phone: (202)887-9000; Fax: (202)223-0526; Email: coltrade@coltrade.org • URL: http://www.coltrade.org • Promotes Colombian exports to the U. S.

Latin America Trade Coalition. 1615 H St. NW, Washington, DC 20062. Phone: (202)463-5485; Fax: (202)463-3126; Email: americas@uschamber.com • URL: http://www.uschamber.com • Represents U.S. companies, farmers and business organizations. Aims to secure congressional approval of the U.S.-Colombia Trade Promotion Agreement and the U.S.-Panama Trade Promotion Agreement.

LAUNDRY INDUSTRY

See also CLEANING INDUSTRY

ABSTRACTS AND INDEXES

Textile Technology Index™. EBSCO Publishing Inc. • Monthly. $545 Individuals. Includes indexing and abstracts for more than 470 periodicals.

FINANCIAL RATIOS

Annual Statement Studies. Risk Management Association. • Annual. Compiled from over 280,000 financial statements.

Annual Statement Studies: Industry Default Probabilities and Cash Flow Measures. Risk Management Association. • Annual. $405 Nonmembers. Serves as a companion volume to the original *Annual Statement Studies*. Gives probability of default estimates on a percentage scale for more than 450 industries. Includes changes in position year-by-year for eight financial statement line items and provides percentage measures of cash flow.

ONLINE DATABASES

Textile Technology Index™. EBSCO Publishing Inc. • Monthly. $545 Individuals. Includes indexing and abstracts for more than 470 periodicals.

PERIODICALS AND NEWSLETTERS

American Coin-Op: The Magazine for Coin-Operated Laundry and Drycleaning Businessmen. Crain Communications Inc. • Monthly. Free.

TRADE/PROFESSIONAL ASSOCIATIONS

Association for Linen Management. 2161 Lexington Rd., Ste. 2, Richmond, KY 40475. Phone: 800-669-0863 or (859)624-0177; Fax: (859)624-3580 • URL: http://www.almnet.org • Formerly National Assoiciation of Institutional Laundry Managers.

Coin Laundry Association. 1 S 660 Midwest Rd., Ste. 205, Oakbrook Terrace, IL 60181. Phone: 800-570-5629 or (630)953-7920; Fax: (630)953-7925; Email: info@coinlaundry.org • URL: http://coinlaundry.org • Manufacturers of equipment or supplies used in self-service (coin-operated) laundry or dry cleaning establishments; distributors of equipment services and supplies; owners and operators of self-service laundry and/or dry cleaning stores. Compiles statistics.

Multi-Housing Laundry Association. 1500 Sunday Dr., Ste. 102, Raleigh, NC 27607. Phone: (919)861-5579; Fax: (919)787-4916; Email: nshore@mla-online.com • URL: http://www.mla-online.com • Operating and supplier companies. Strives to provide tenants with professionally operated laundry facilities. Sponsors annual convention and trade show.

LAW

ABSTRACTS AND INDEXES

Current Law Index. Cengage Learning Inc. • $1,332 Individuals. Monthly. $1269.00 per year. Produced in cooperation with the American Association of Law Libraries. Indexes more than 900 law journals, legal newspapers, and specialty publications from the U.S., Canada, U.K., Ireland, Australia, and New Zealand.

Index to Foreign Legal Periodicals. American Association of Law Libraries. University of California Press - Journals and Digital Publishing Division. • Quarterly. $725.00 per year. Annual cumulation.

Index to Legal Periodicals and Books. H.W. Wilson Co. • Monthly. $490.00 per year. Quarterly and annual cumulations.

ALMANACS AND YEARBOOKS

American Law Yearbook. Cengage Learning Inc. • $308 Individuals. Annual. $280.00. Serves as a yearly supplement to *West's Encyclopedia of American Lawa*. Describes new legal developments in many subject areas.

BIBLIOGRAPHIES

Pimsleur's Checklists of Basic American Legal Publications. American Association of Law

Libraries. Fred B. Rothman and Co. • $295 Individuals 3 volumes Looseleaf. Authoritative bibliographic source in any library having an interest in our legal process.

CD-ROM DATABASES

Index to Legal Periodicals and Books. EBSCO Publishing Inc. • Contains indexing of more than 1,400 English language legal periodicals from 1981 to date and 2,500 books.

DIRECTORIES

Commercial Bar Association Directory. Wiley Chancery. • Annual. $25. Covers: Over 700 barristers in the U.K. specializing in corporate and commercial law; includes chamber and individual members. Entries include: Chamber name, address, phone, fax, principal fields of work; associated barristers, with name, date of birth, date of call, Queen's counsel, inn, academic and professional qualifications, pubications, languages spoken.

International Business Practices Guide. University of Missouri, St. Louis.

ENCYCLOPEDIAS AND DICTIONARIES

Encyclopedia of Crime and Justice. Cengage Learning Inc. • 2001. $737. 2nd edition. 4 volumes. Published by Macmillan Reference USA. Contains extensive information on a wide variety of topics pertaining to crime, criminology, social issues, and the courts. Also available as eBook.

GENERAL WORKS

American Business Law Journal. Academy of Legal Studies in Business. • Quarterly. $852 Institutions print & online. Journal focusing on a range of topics related to business law.

Entrepreneurial Business Law Journal.

Global Business Law Review.

Legal Business. Legalese Ltd. • 10/year. £495 Individuals. Journal covering commercial law in Europe.

Legal Environments of Business. American CPE Inc. • Contains detailed training information covering legal structures and environments in which businesses operate in the United States.

HANDBOOKS AND MANUALS

The Company Secretary's Handbook. Cengage Learning Inc. • Published by Kogan Page. A practical guide that will help newly appointed company secretaries do their job efficiently and comply with company law. Covers the formation of companies, corporate governance and day-to-day administration, keeping the statutory records, annual routines and dissolution. It also includes useful addresses and examples of all the necessary official documentation.

Restatement of the Law. American Law Institute - Committee on Continuing Professional Education. • $131 hardbound. Multivolume set. Periodic supplementation. Price varies. Statements of the common law-an overview, clarification, and simplification of American law.

INTERNET DATABASES

Law.com: First in Legal News and Information. ALM Media Properties Inc. Phone: 800-888-8300 or (212)779-9200; Fax: (212)481-8110 • URL: http://www.law.com • Web site provides free, law-related, current news (National News Sites and Regional News Sites). Free searching of martindale.com lawyer locator is offered, including lawyer ratings. Fee-based premium services for the legal profession are also available.

Lexis.com Research System. Lexis-Nexis Group. Phone: 800-227-4908 or (937)865-6800; Fax: (937)865-6909; Email: webmaster@prod.lexis-nexis.com • URL: http://www.nexis.com • Fee-based Web site offers extensive searching of a wide variety of legal sources. Additional features include Daily Opinion Service, lexis.com Bookstore, Career Center, CLE Center, Law Schools, and Practice Pages ("Pages specific to areas of specialty").

ONLINE DATABASES

LegalTrac. Cengage Learning Inc. • Online database. Provides indexing for approximately 875 titles of periodical literature relating to legal matters from 1980 to date. Corresponds to online *Legal Resource Index.* Inquire as to price and availability.

RICO Business Disputes Guide. Wolters Kluwer Law & Business CCH. • Contains information on pending U.S. Supreme Court RICO cases, as well as pending federal and state legislation.

OTHER SOURCES

Quicken Business Law Partner. Broderbund and The Learning Co. • A computer software program that is capable of preparing up to 59 legal documents. The program allows the user to enter information either through the Interview method—in which documents are created based on answers to questions—or the typical Fill-in-the-Blank format. Quicken Business Law Partner prepares documents in 12 different categories, including Personal Information; Powers of Attorney; Consumer Letters; Credit Letters; Government Letters; Other Letters; Corporate Forms; Employment Forms; Small Claims Forms; Business Forms; Financial Forms; and Real Estate Forms. Business Law Partner is available on diskette or CD-ROM.

PERIODICALS AND NEWSLETTERS

Harvard Law Review. Harvard Law Review. • 8/year. $60 Individuals.

National Law Journal: The Weekly Newspaper for the Profession. ALM Media Properties LLC. • Weekly. News and analysis of the latest developments in the law and the law profession.

United States Law Week: A National Survey of Current Law. Bloomberg BNA. • Weekly. $1,152.00 per year. Covers U.S. Supreme Court proceedings and gives full text of decisions. Also provides detailed reports on important legislative and regulatory actions.

Wake Forest Journal of Business and Intellectual Property Law. Wake Forest University School of Law.

RESEARCH CENTERS AND INSTITUTES

Arizona State University - Sandra Day O'Connor College of Law - Center for Law, Science and Innovation. Armstrong Hall, 1100 S McAllister Ave., Tempe, AZ 85287. Phone: (480)965-6181 • URL: http://www.law.asu.edu/lsi • Studies the development of legal frameworks for new technologies and advancing the use of science in legal decision making.

Boston University - Center for Finance, Law and Policy. 53 Bay State Rd., 1st Fl., Boston, MA 02215. Phone: 888-285-7003 or (617)353-3023; Fax: (617)353-2444; Email: ckhurley@bu.edu • URL: http://www.bu.edu/bucflp • Research fields include banking law, regulation of depository institutions, and deposit insurance.

Radboud University Nijmegen - Faculty of Law - Business and Law Research Center. Thomas van Aquinostraat 8, NL-6500 Nijmegen, Netherlands. Phone: 31 24 3615565; Fax: 31 24 3615662; Email: oor@jur.ru.nl • URL: http://www.ru.nl/law/businessandlawresearchcentre • Business and law.

University of Edinburgh - Arts and Humanities Research Council - Research Centre for Studies in Intellectual Property and Technology Law. School of Law, Old College, S Bridge, Edinburgh EH8 9YL, United Kingdom. Phone: 44 131 6502014; Fax: 44 131 6506317; Email: itandip@ed.ac.uk • URL: http://www.law.ed.ac.uk/ahrc/aboutus.aspx • Intellectual property, copyright, patents, technology, commerce, society, information technology, genetics, and medical jurisprudence and ethics.

University of Iowa - Law, Health Policy and Disability Center. 280-1 Boyd Law Bldg., Iowa City, IA 52242-1113. Phone: (319)335-8469; Fax: (319)335-9764; Email: helen-schartz@uiowa.edu • URL: http://disability.law.uiowa.edu • Legal, health policy and employment issues facing persons with disabilities.

University of New Mexico - Institute of Public Law. 1117 Stanford NE, MSC11 6070, 1 University of New Mexico, Albuquerque, NM 87131-0001. Phone: (505)277-5006; Fax: (505)277-7064; Email: lambert@law.unm.edu • URL: http://lawschool.unm.edu/ipl/index.php • Public law and policy analysis.

University of Pennsylvania - Institute for Law and Economics. 3501 Sansom St., Philadelphia, PA 19104. Phone: (215)898-7719; Fax: (215)573-2025; Email: mwachter@law.upenn.edu • URL: http://www.law.upenn.edu/academics/institutes/ile • Applies economic analysis in law to major policy issues affecting business and government, including economic analysis of common law doctrine, taxation and tax policy, public finance, labor market regulation, antitrust, financial institutions, and commercial law and industrial organization. Jointly conducts programs with the Law and Wharton Schools and the Department of Economics.

Worcester Polytechnic Institute - Economics, Policy, and Law Research Group. Department of Social Science & Policy Studies, 100 Institute Rd., Worcester, MA 01609-2280. Phone: (508)831-5234; Fax: (508)831-5892; Email: epl@wpi.edu • URL: http://web.cs.wpi.edu/Research/trg/ • Economics, policy, and law.

TRADE/PROFESSIONAL ASSOCIATIONS

American Law Institute. 4025 Chestnut St., Philadelphia, PA 19104-3081. Phone: (215)243-1600 or (215)243-1627; Fax: (215)243-1636; Email: ali@ali.org • URL: http://www.ali.org • Judges, law teachers, and lawyers. Promotes the clarification and simplification of the law and its better adaptation to social needs by continuing work on the Restatement of the Law, model and uniform codes, and model statutes. Conducts a program of continuing legal education jointly with the American Bar Association called "ALI-ABA."

American Legal Finance Association. 228 Park Ave. S, No. 23315, New York, NY 10003. Phone: (212)837-2911 • URL: http://www.americanlegalfin.com • Develops an awareness of the legal funding industry. Works to establish legal and regulatory frameworks to meet the needs and concerns of all parties interested in legal funding. Establishes and maintains ethical standards and fair business practices within the legal funding industry.

American Society of Comparative Law. 1420 N Charles St., Baltimore, MD 21201. Phone: (410)837-4689; Fax: (410)837-4560 • URL: http://www.comparativelaw.org • Members are law schools and law-related institutes. Promotes the comparative study of law and the understanding of foreign legal systems and private international law. Supports the American Journal of Comparative Law and other publications concerning comparative, foreign, and private international law; also co-sponsors conferences in these fields.

Argentine Fiscal Associations. IFLYSIB Calle 59, 789, CC 565, B19 00BTE La Plata, Argentina. Phone: 54 221 4254904; Fax: 54 221 4257317; Email: afa@iflysib.unlp.edu.ar • URL: http://www2.ib.edu.ar/afa • Promotes the study and advancement of international and comparative law with regards to public finance, specifically international, comparative fiscal law and the financial and economic aspects of taxation.

Practising Law Institute. 1177 Avenue of the

Americas, New York, NY 10036. Phone: 800-260-4754 or (212)824-5700; Fax: (212)824-5733; Email: info@pli.edu • URL: http://www.pli.edu • Provides through publications, videotapes, forums, and live and online seminars, training for lawyers throughout the country in new developments in the law and new legal techniques. Presents over 250 seminars annually.

LAW, BUSINESS

See BUSINESS LAW

LAW, COMPUTER

See COMPUTER LAW

LAW ENFORCEMENT INDUSTRIES

See also CRIME AND CRIMINALS

DIRECTORIES

Directory of Asian Importers of Military & Police Equipment & Supplies. EXIM Infotek Private Ltd. • $250 Individuals. Covers: 70 Asian importers of ammunition, military clothing, military electronic equipment, military equipment and supplies, military surplus goods, police equipment, surplus military equipment and supplies, and traffic control systems. Entries include: Company name, postal address, telephone, fax, e-mail, website, contact person, designation, and product details.

Jane's Police and Homeland Security Equipment. IHS Global Ltd. IHS Jane's: Defense & Security Intelligence & Analysis. • Provides information on sources of more than 2,000 items of law enforcement equipment. Covers traffic control, riot control, communications, personal protection, surveillance, and other equipment categories. Includes detailed product descriptions.

LAW and ORDER Magazine. Hendon Publishing Co. • Lists manufacturers, dealers, and distributors of equipment and services for police departments.

Law Enforcement Technology Directory. Cygnus Business Media Inc. • Annual. $60.00 per year. $6.00 per issue; a directory of products, equipment, services, and technology for police professionals. Includes weapons, uniforms, communications equipment, and software.

National Directory of Law Enforcement Administrators. National Public Safety Information Bureau. • Annual. $169.00. Lists a wide variety of law enforcement administrators and institutions, including city police departments, sheriffs, prosecutors, state agencies, federal agencies, correctional institutions, college campus police departments, airport police, and harbor police.

PERIODICALS AND NEWSLETTERS

Correctional News. Emlen Publications, Inc. • Bimonthly. Free to qualified personnel. Only available online.

Corrections Today. American Correctional Association. • 6/year. $25 Individuals. Magazine covering corrections, law enforcement, and rehabilitation. Includes "Annual Architecture, Construction, and Design Issue" on prisons and other correctional facilities.

9-1-1 Magazine: Public Safety Communications and Response. Official Publications Inc. • Bimonthly. $29.95 per year. Covers technical information and applications for public safety communications personnel.

Police Chief: Professional Voice of Law Enforcement. International Association of Chiefs of Police. • Monthly. $30 per year. Subject matter includes information on law enforcement technology and new products.

Police Science and Technology Review. Jane's Information Group, Inc. • Quarterly. $57.00 per year. Includes detailed information on technology relating to surveillance, forensics, and fingerprints.

Police: The Law Enforcement Magazine. Bobit Publications. • Monthly. $25 per year. Edited for law enforcement professionals. Includes information on new technology and equipment.

RESEARCH CENTERS AND INSTITUTES

University of Tennessee at Knoxville - Municipal Technical Advisory Service Library. 600 Henley St., Ste. 120, Knoxville, TN 37996-4105. Phone: (865)974-0411; Fax: (865)974-0423; Email: steve.thompson@tennessee.edu • URL: http://www.mtas.tennessee.edu/web2012.nsf/Web/Home • Research areas include municipal finance, police administration, and public works.

STATISTICS SOURCES

Sourcebook of Criminal Justice Statistics. U. S. Government Printing Office. • Annual. $56.00. Issued by the Bureau of Justice Statistics, U. S. Department of Justice (www.usdoj.gov/bjs). Contains both crime data and corrections statistics.

TRADE/PROFESSIONAL ASSOCIATIONS

National Correctional Industries Association. 1202 N Charles St., Baltimore, MD 21201. Phone: (410)230-3972; Fax: (410)230-3981; Email: info@nationalcia.org • URL: http://www.nationalcia.org • Professional correctional industry managers, supervisors, superintendents, and others employed in the industry. Seeks to improve the effectiveness of industrial programs as they relate to the correctional process by providing a forum for the development and exchange of ideas and by providing professional reaction and guidance concerning projected ideas and programs related to correctional industry trends. Compiles statistics.

LAW, ENVIRONMENTAL

See ENVIRONMENTAL LAW

LAW, FAMILY

See FAMILY LAW

LAW FIRMS

See LAWYERS

LAW, STATE

See STATE LAW

LAWN CARE INDUSTRY

See also GARDEN SUPPLY INDUSTRY

ABSTRACTS AND INDEXES

Horticultural Science Abstracts. CABI Publishing North America. • Updated weekly online; also available in print, delivered monthly.

Readers' Guide to Periodical Literature. EBSCO Publishing Inc. • Provides indexing for over 400 periodicals dating back to 1983.

CD-ROM DATABASES

AGRICOLA on SilverPlatter. Ovid Technologies Inc. • Updated monthly. Price varies. Produced by the National Agricultural Library. Provides over 4 million citations to the literature of agriculture, agricultural economics, animal sciences, entomology, fertilizer, food, forestry, nutrition, pesticides, plant science, water resources, and other topics.

Biological & Agricultural Index Plus. EBSCO Publishing Inc. • Full text of literature in biology and agriculture. Also includes podcasts, indexing and abstracts.

Readers' Guide to Periodical Literature. EBSCO Publishing Inc. • Provides indexing for over 400 periodicals dating back to 1983.

DIRECTORIES

Green Industry Pros. Cygnus Business Media Inc. • Irregular. Nine times a year. Includes retailers and distributors of lawn and garden power equipment, lawn and plant care products, patio furniture, etc. Arranged by type of product. Includes a *Product* issue.

ONLINE DATABASES

Agricola. U.S. National Agricultural Library World List of Agricultural Serials. • Covers worldwide agricultural literature. Over 3.3 million citations, 1970 to present, with monthly updates. Inquire as to online cost and availability.

CAB Abstracts. CABI. • Contains 46 specialized abstract collections covering over 10,000 journals and monographs in the areas of agriculture, horticulture, forest products, farm products, nutrition, dairy science, poultry, grains, animal health, entomology, etc. Time period is 1972 to date, with monthly updates. Inquire as to online cost and availability. *CAB Abstracts on CD-ROM* also available, with annual updating.

PERIODICALS AND NEWSLETTERS

PRO. Braun de Mexico y Compania S.A. de C.V. • 7/year. For owners and operators of lawn maintenance service firms. Includes annual *Product* issue.

TRADE/PROFESSIONAL ASSOCIATIONS

Lawn Institute. 2 E Main St., East Dundee, IL 60118. Phone: 800-405-8873 or (847)649-5555; Fax: (847)649-5678; Email: info@thelawninstitue.org • URL: http://www.thelawninstitute.org • Producers of lawn seed and lawn products. Seeks to help bridge the gap between professional research and an increasingly sophisticated consumer. Promotes better lawns through use of quality materials, research, and education.

Outdoor Power Equipment Institute. 341 S Patrick St., Alexandria, VA 22314. Phone: (703)549-7600 • URL: http://opei.org • Manufacturers of lawn mowers, garden tractors, snow throwers, utility vehicles, chainsaws, motor tillers, shredder/grinders, edger/trimmers, leaf vacuums, log splitters, stump cutters, chippers and sprayers, and major components. Compiles statistics and forecasting information; sponsors industry trade shows; produces comprehensive consumer education materials on safety and other industry issues; hosts' annual member meeting; represents members' interests on important legislative and regulatory issues.

Professional Landcare Network. 950 Herndon Pkwy., Ste. 450, Herndon, VA 20170-5528. Phone: 800-395-2522 or (703)736-9666; Fax: (703)736-9668; Email: info@landcarenetwork.org • URL: http://www.landcarenetwork.org • Formerly Professional Lawn Care Association of America.

LAWS

See also LAW

ABSTRACTS AND INDEXES

Congressional Index. Wolters Kluwer Law & Business CCH. • Index to action on Public Bills from introduction to final disposition. Subject, author, and bill number indexes.

For publishers' addresses, refer to SOURCES CITED section at the back of the book.

Current Law Index. Cengage Learning Inc. • $1,332 Individuals. Monthly. $1269.00 per year. Produced in cooperation with the American Association of Law Libraries. Indexes more than 900 law journals, legal newspapers, and specialty publications from the U.S., Canada, U.K., Ireland, Australia, and New Zealand.

ALMANACS AND YEARBOOKS

Advertising Law Guide. Wolters Kluwer Law & Business CCH. • Monthly. $2,115. Contains full-text reporting of state and federal laws as well as federal regulations.

Securities, Commodities, and Federal Banking: 1999 in Review. Wolters Kluwer Law & Business CCH. • Irregular. $57.00. Summarizes the year's significant legal and regulatory developments.

Suggested State Legislation (SSL). Chief Officers of State Library Agencies. • Annual. A source of legislative ideas and drafting assistance for state government officials.

HANDBOOKS AND MANUALS

National Survey of State Laws. Cengage Learning Inc. • 2007. eBook. 6th edition. Provides concise state-by-state comparisons of current state laws on a wide variety of topics. Includes references to specific codes or statutes. Inquire for pricing.

United States Code. U.S. Congress. U. S. Government Printing Office. • Continual supplements. Price varies. Permanent and general public law of the United States from 1789 to the codification date.

United States Code Annotated: Crimes and Criminal Procedures. Thomson West. • $3,125.00. 15 volumes. Annual cumulation. Arranged in parallel fashion to *United States Code*. Gives abstracts of relevant federal and state court decisions pertaining to each section of the code. Supplemented by annual pocket parts.

United States Statutes at Large. U.S. Office of the Federal Register. U. S. Government Printing Office. • Annual. Congressional acts and presidential proclamations issued during the Congressional session. For all laws in force at a specific date, refer to *United States Code*.

INTERNET DATABASES

FindLaw: Internet Legal Resources. FindLaw. 610 Opperman Dr., Eagan, MN 55123. Phone: 800-455-4565 or (408)524-4799 or (650)940-4300; Fax: (800)392-6206 or (408)524-4798; Email: findlawexperience@thomsonreuters.com • URL: http://www.findlaw.com • Web site provides a wide variety of information and links relating to laws, law schools, professional development, lawyers, the U. S. Supreme Court, consultants (experts), law reviews, legal news, etc. Online searching is provided. Fees: Free.

Lexis.com Research System. Lexis-Nexis Group. Phone: 800-227-4908 or (937)865-6800; Fax: (937)865-6909; Email: webmaster@prod.lexis-nexis.com • URL: http://www.nexis.com • Fee-based Web site offers extensive searching of a wide variety of legal sources. Additional features include Daily Opinion Service, lexis.com Bookstore, Career Center, CLE Center, Law Schools, and Practice Pages ("Pages specific to areas of specialty").

PERIODICALS AND NEWSLETTERS

Congressional Record. U.S. Congress. U. S. Government Printing Office. • Daily. Daily. Indexes give names, subjects, and history of bills. Texts of bills not included.

Federal Register. Office of the Federal Register. U. S. Government Printing Office. • Daily except Saturday and Sunday. $764.00 per year. Publishes regulations and legal notices issued by federal agencies, including executive orders and presidential proclamations. Issued by the National Archives and Records Administration (www.nara.gov).

United States Law Week: A National Survey of Current Law. Bloomberg BNA. • Weekly. $1,152.00 per year. Covers U.S. Supreme Court proceedings and gives full text of decisions. Also provides detailed reports on important legislative and regulatory actions.

RESEARCH CENTERS AND INSTITUTES

Bowling Green State University - Department of Philosophy - Social Philosophy and Policy Center. 225 Troup St., Bowling Green, OH 43403. Phone: (419)372-2536; Fax: (419)372-8738; Email: fmiller@bgsu.edu • URL: http://www.bgsu.edu/offices/sppc/ • Political philosophy and public policy, drawing upon disciplines of philosophy, history, political science, law, and economics.

Brown University - A. Alfred Taubman Center for Public Policy and American Institutions. 67 George St., Box 1977, Providence, RI 02912. Phone: (401)863-2201; Fax: (401)863-2452; Email: marion_orr@brown.edu • URL: http://www.brown.edu/academics/taubman-center • Urban issues, economic and urban development, elections, mass media, social and child welfare, comparative public policy, education policy, regulation, and federalism.

Duke University - Sanford School of Public Policy - Center for Health Policy and Inequalities Research. 310 Trent Dr., Durham, NC 27705. Phone: (919)613-5430; Fax: (919)613-5466 • URL: http://chpir.org • Quantitative analysis of clinical policies, decision analysis, Bayesian statistics, health economics, disease prevention, cancer and cancer detection, stroke prevention and management, and technology assessment, including evaluation of reimbursement policies for medical procedures, hospital and health care policies, and Health Maintenance Organization (HMO) medical policies.

Federal Highway Administration - Office of Transportation Policy Studies. 1200 New Jersey Ave. SE, 8th Fl., Washington, DC 20590. Phone: (202)366-9232; Fax: (202)366-3297; Email: mary.tischer@dot.gov • URL: http://www.fhwa.dot.gov/policy/otps • Formulation of highway policy and legislative initiatives. Principal areas of research interest are highway use, performance, and requirements and the relationship of these factors to commercial highway transport; truck sizes and weights; cost allocations; transportation user charge substructures, taxing policies and subsidy issues, and the effects of these issues upon various public and private groups; and the economic characteristics of specific industries (as necessary for the formulation of highway program policy).

Massey University - Centre for Public Policy Evaluation. Private Bag, Palmerston North, New Zealand. Phone: 64 6 3505799; Fax: 64 6 3505660; Email: k.s.birks@massey.ac.nz • URL: http://turwww1.massey.ac.nz/wwcppe • Public policy and economics in the areas of education, health, law, gender issues and aspects of the policymaking process.

Robert Gordon University - Centre for Public Policy and Management. Aberdeen Business School, Garthdee Rd., Aberdeen AB10 7QE, United Kingdom. Phone: 44 1224 263111; Fax: 44 1224 263434; Email: cppm@rgu.ac.uk • URL: http://www2.rgu.ac.uk/publicpolicy/cppm • Policy analysis, social administration, management, planning, law, economics and social science.

University of Arizona - Udall Center for Studies in Public Policy. 803 E 1st St., Tucson, AZ 85719. Phone: (520)626-4393; Fax: (520)626-3664; Email: udallctr@u.arizona.edu • URL: http://udallcenter.arizona.edu • Multidisciplinary public policy research in the areas of natural resources and the environment, economic development, health care, and the effects of science and technology on public policy. Special emphasis is on U.S.-Mexico border environmental institutions and policy, American Indian policy and environmental conflict resolution in the Western U.S.

University of California, Berkeley - School of Public Health - Center for Health and Public Policy Studies. 50 University Hall, No. 7360, Berkeley, CA 94720-7360. Phone: (510)643-1675; Fax: (510)643-2340; Email: chpps@berkeley.edu • URL: http://chpps.berkeley.edu • Issues in health policy and politics that affect California and the nation.

University of Florida - Public Policy Research Center. 204 Matherly Hall, Department of Economics, Warrington College of Business Administration, Gainesville, FL 32611-7140. Phone: (352)392-3904; Fax: (352)392-7860; Email: sapping@ufl.edu • URL: http://warrington.ufl.edu/centers/pprc • Public policy on antitrust, regulation, taxation, education, and other government policy.

University of Houston - Center for Public Policy. 306 McElhinney Hall, Houston, TX 77204-5035. Phone: (713)743-3970; Fax: (713)743-3978; Email: jgranato@uh.edu • URL: http://www.uh.edu/hcpp • Economic, political, sociological, related to public policy issues, including studies in regional economics and demographics. Provides assistance to a variety of research undertaken by University faculty and initiates and sponsors surveys. Primary focus is on the eight county areas surrounding Houston.

University of Iowa - Office of the Vice President for Research and Economic Development - Public Policy Center - Health Policy Research Program. 209 S Quadrangle, 310 S Grand Ave., Iowa City, IA 52242-1192. Phone: (319)335-6867; Fax: (319)335-6801 • URL: http://ppc.uiowa.edu/health • Effects of policy initiatives and government activities on the cost, access, and quality of health care.

University of Maryland, Baltimore County - Maryland Institute for Policy Analysis and Research. 428 Public Policy Bldg., 1000 Hilltop Cir., Baltimore, MD 21250. Phone: (410)455-1080; Fax: (410)455-1084; Email: mipar_info@umbc.edu • URL: http://www.umbc.edu/mipar/ • Significant issues of public policy, including public welfare, public housing, emergency health services, health policy, computers and information management, juvenile justice, family literacy, minority contracting programs, and childcare.

University of Oxford - Centre for Socio-Legal Studies. Manor Rd., Oxford OX1 3UQ, United Kingdom. Phone: 44 1865 284220; Fax: 44 1865 284221; Email: fernanda.pirie@csls.ox.ac.uk • URL: http://www.csls.ox.ac.uk • Law and society, including studies on government, regulation, family law, business law, dispute resolution, public international law, media studies.

University of San Diego - Center for Public Interest Law. School of Law, 5998 Alcalá Park, San Diego, CA 92110. Phone: (619)260-4806; Fax: (619)260-4753 • URL: http://www.cpil.org • State regulation of business, professions, and trades, including the Public Utilities Commission, Department of Insurance, Medical Board of California, and the State Bar.

University of South Carolina at Columbia - College of Arts and Sciences - Institute for Public Service and Policy Research. 1600 Hampton St., Rm. 402, Columbia, SC 29208. Phone: (803)777-4566 or (803)777-4568; Fax: (803)777-4575; Email: roldendi@mailbox.sc.edu • URL: http://www.ipspr.sc.edu • State and local government, with special emphasis on South Carolina, urban policy, public finance and health policy.

University of Utah - Center for Public Policy and Administration. 260 S Central Campus Dr., Rm. 214, Salt Lake City, UT 84112-9154. Phone: (801)581-6781; Email: robinson@cppa.utah.edu • URL: http://cppa.utah.edu • Local and state government finance, organization, and administration; public policy research on education, health, environment, transportation, resources, energy; Western regional policy issues and regional governance.

STATISTICS SOURCES

Property-Casualty Insurance Facts. Insurance Information Institute. • Annual. $22.50. Formerly *Insurance Facts.*

TRADE/PROFESSIONAL ASSOCIATIONS

Coalition to Insure Against Terrorism. 1875 Eye St. NW, Ste. 600, Washington, DC 20006-5413. Phone: (202)739-9454; Email: info@insureagainstterrorism.org • URL: http://www.insureagainstterrorism.org • Represents organizations in the transportation, real estate, manufacturing, construction, entertainment and retail sectors. Seeks the passage of legislation that will enable the nation's insurers to provide holders with comprehensive terrorism coverage. Supports the passage of the Terrorism Risk Insurance Revision and Extension Act (TRIREA).

LAWS, ADVERTISING

See ADVERTISING LAW AND REGULATION

LAWS, BANKING

See BANKING LAW AND REGULATION

LAWYERS

See also WOMEN LAWYERS

ALMANACS AND YEARBOOKS

The Lawyer's Almanac: An Encyclopedia of Information about Law, Lawyers, and the Profession. Aspen Law. • Annual. $144.00. List of the 250 largest law firms.

BIOGRAPHICAL SOURCES

Who's Who in American Law. Marquis Who's Who L.L.C. • Biennial. $345 Individuals. Contains over 23,000 concise biographies of American lawyers, judges, and others in the legal field.

CD-ROM DATABASES

Martindale.com. LexisNexis Martindale-Hubbell. • Database of more than 1 million lawyers and law firms.

The Tax Directory. Tax Analysts. • Quarterly. $499 Individuals both volumes, web, CD or print. Updated quarterly on CD-ROM and in print; updated continually online. Covering federal, state, and international tax officials, tax practitioners, and corporate tax executives.

DIRECTORIES

American Bar Association--Directory: The Redbook. American Bar Association. • Annual. $17.95 Individuals. Covers: Approximately 7,500 lawyers active in the affairs of the Association, including officers, members of Boards of Governors and House of Delegates, section officers and council members, committee leaders, headquarters staff, state and local bars, affiliated and other legal organizations. Entries include: Section, council, or other unit name; names, addresses, and phone numbers of officers or chairpersons and members.

Capital for Shipping. Informa Publishing Group. • Annual. $128.00. Published in the UK by Lloyd's List (www.lloydslist.com). Consists of a "Financial Directory" and a "Legal Directory," listing international ship finance providers and international law firms specializing in shipping. Included with subscription to *Lloyd's Shipping Economist.*

International Business Lawyers Index/Industrial Property/Chambers of Commerce. Datapress Ltd. • Biennial. $35. Covers: 10,000 business lawyers, 10,000 chambers of commerce and industry, 2,000 official industrial property agencies, and 110 state property agencies for 140 countries. Entries include: Name, address, phone, telex numbers.

Law Firms Yellow Book: Who's Who in the Management of the Leading U. S. Law Firms. Leadership Directories Inc. • Semiannual. $465. Provides detailed information on more than 700 major U. S. law firms. Includes domestic offices, foreign offices, subsidiaries, and affiliates. There are seven indexes: geographic, subject specialty, management, administrative, law school attended, personnel, and law firm.

Lawyer's Register International by Specialties and Fields of Law Including a Directory of Corporate Counsel. Lawyer's Register Publishing Co. • Annual. $359 Individuals. Referral source for law firms.

Martindale-Hubbell Bar Register of Preeminent Lawyers. LexisNexis Martindale-Hubbell. • Annual. $195 Individuals. Lists over 9,700 &"outstanding members of the bar" in general practice and in 28 specific fields. Covers the U. S. and Canada.

The Tax Directory. Tax Analysts. • Quarterly. $499 Individuals both volumes, web, CD or print. Updated quarterly on CD-ROM and in print; updated continually online. Covering federal, state, and international tax officials, tax practitioners, and corporate tax executives.

Washington: A Comprehensive Directory of the Key Institutions and Leaders in th e National Capitol Area. Columbia Books Inc. • Annual. $149.00. Provides information on about 5,000 Washington, DC key businesses, government offices, non-profit organizations, and cultural institutions, with the names of about 25,000 principal executives. Includes Washington media, law offices, foundations, labor unions, international organizations, clubs, etc.

FINANCIAL RATIOS

Annual Statement Studies. Risk Management Association. • Annual. Compiled from over 280,000 financial statements.

Annual Statement Studies: Industry Default Probabilities and Cash Flow Measures. Risk Management Association. • Annual. $405 Nonmembers. Serves as a companion volume to the original *Annual Statement Studies.* Gives probability of default estimates on a percentage scale for more than 450 industries. Includes changes in position year-by-year for eight financial statement line items and provides percentage measures of cash flow.

HANDBOOKS AND MANUALS

ABA/BNA Lawyer's Manual on Professional Conduct. Bloomberg BNA. • Updated monthly. Available via print and web. Covers American Bar Association's model rules governing ethical practice of law.

INTERNET DATABASES

FindLaw: Internet Legal Resources. FindLaw. 610 Opperman Dr., Eagan, MN 55123. Phone: 800-455-4565 or (408)524-4799 or (650)940-4300; Fax: (800)392-6206 or (408)524-4798; Email: findlawexperience@thomsonreuters.com • URL: http://www.findlaw.com • Web site provides a wide variety of information and links relating to laws, law schools, professional development, lawyers, the U. S. Supreme Court, consultants (experts), law reviews, legal news, etc. Online searching is provided. Fees: Free.

Law.com: First in Legal News and Information. ALM Media Properties Inc. Phone: 800-888-8300 or (212)779-9200; Fax: (212)481-8110 • URL: http://www.law.com • Web site provides free, law-related, current news (National News Sites and Regional News Sites). Free searching of martindale.com lawyer locator is offered, including lawyer ratings. Fee-based premium services for the legal profession are also available.

OTHER SOURCES

Andrews' Professional Liability Litigation Reporter. Andrews Publications. • Monthly. $550.00 per year. Provides reports on lawsuits against attorneys, accountants, and investment professionals.

Marketing the Law Firm: Business Development Techniques. ALM Media Properties LLC. • Looseleaf. $510.00. Updated as needed. Covers client surveys, brochures, direct mail, Web sites, seminars, newsletters, proposals, trade shows, and other marketing avenues for both large and small law firms. (Law Journal Press).

Maximizing Law Firm Profitability: Hiring, Training, and Developing Productive Lawyers. ALM Media Properties LLC. • $590 print + online + ebook. Covers subjects on how to enhance your skills as a lawyer and to develop the potential of your associates.

PERIODICALS AND NEWSLETTERS

ABA Journal: The Lawyer's Magazine. American Bar Association. • Monthly. $75 Individuals. Includes five regular sections: news affecting lawyers, practical applications of court decisions, pratice management advice, feature articles, and lifestyle stories.

Accounting and Financial Planning for Law Firms. ALM Media Properties LLC. • Monthly. $499 /year. Covers budgeting, liability issues, billing systems, benefits management, and other topics relating to law firm administration. (A Law Journal Newsletter, formerly published by Leader Publications).

Corporate Counselor. ALM Media Properties LLC. • Monthly. $459 /year. Covers issues involved with managing the legal department of a corporation, including relations with outside counsel. (A Law Journal Newsletter, formerly published by Leader Publications).

Internet Law and Strategy. ALM Media Properties LLC. • Monthly. $459 per year. Primarily concerned with doing legal research online. Contains reviews of the best Web sites for lawyers. (A Law Journal Newsletter, formerly published by Leader Publications.).

Law Firm Inc. ALM Media Properties LLC. • Quarterly. $49.95 per year. Covers human resources, insurance, financing, marketing, compensation, recruitment, etc., as related to law firm management.

Law Firm Partnership and Benefits Report. ALM Media Properties LLC. • Monthly. $499 per year. Covers personnel issues for law firms, including compensation, partnership agreements, malpractice, employment discrimination, training, health insurance, pension plans, and other matters relating to human resources management. (A Law Journal Newsletter, formerly published by Leader Publications).

Law Technology News: Products, Systems, and Services for Legal Professionals. ALM Media Properties LLC. • Monthly. 115 Dh. Features descriptions of new technology products and services of interest to the legal profession.

Legal Times: Law and Lobbying in the Nation's Capital. ALM Media Properties LLC. • Weekly. $318.00 per year. Published in Washington, DC. Provides news relating to lawyers and the federal government. Special features cover a variety of topics relating to law firm administration.

Marketing the Law Firm. ALM Media Properties LLC. • Monthly. $475. Focuses on actions that lawyers can take to find more clients and do more business. (A Law Journal Newsletter, formerly published by Leader Publications under the title *Marketing for Lawyers*).

For publishers' addresses, refer to SOURCES CITED section at the back of the book.

National Law Journal: The Weekly Newspaper for the Profession. ALM Media Properties LLC. • Weekly. News and analysis of the latest developments in the law and the law profession.

Of Counsel: The Monthly Legal Practice Report. Wolters Kluwer Law and Business. • 12 times a year. $829.00 per year. Newsletter on the management, marketing, personnel, and compensation of law firms.

The Practical Lawyer. Committee on Continuing Professional Education. American Law Institute - Committee on Continuing Professional Education. • 6/year. $99 per year. Contains advice ondealing with the client's problem in commercial and corporate law, real estate, litigation, tax and estate planning.

The Practical Real Estate Lawyer. Committee on Continuing Professional Education. American Law Institute - Committee on Continuing Professional Education. • Bimonthly. $99 per year. Frequently includes legal forms for use in real estate practice.

Tax Practice. Tax Analysts. • Weekly. $199.00 per year. Newsletter. Covers news affecting tax practitioners and litigators, with emphasis on federal court decisions, rules and regulations, and tax petitions. Provides a guide to Internal Revenue Service audit issues.

STATISTICS SOURCES

Small Law Firm Economic Survey. Incisive Legal Intelligence. • Annual. $395.00. Provides aggregate data (benchmarks) on the economics, finances, billing, and staffing of law offices in the U. S. having "less than 12 lawyers.".

Survey of Law Firm Economics: A Management and Planning Tool. ALM Media Properties LLC. • Annual. Provides aggregate economic statistics and financial data (benchmarks) relating to the legal profession in the U. S. Includes income, expenses, hourly rates, billable hours, compensation, staffing, data by states, and trends. Most information is arranged by region, firm size, years of experience, and other factors.

U.S. Industry and Trade Outlook. U.S. Department of Commerce National Technical Information Service. • Annual. Produced by the International Trade Administration, U.S. Department of Commerce, in a "public-private" partnership with DRI/ McGraw-Hill and Standard & Poor's. Provides basic data, outlook for the current year, and "Long-Term Prospects" (five-year projections) for a wide variety of products and services. Includes high technology industries. Formerly *U.S. Industrial Outlook.*

TRADE/PROFESSIONAL ASSOCIATIONS

American College of Trial Lawyers. 19900 MacArthur Blvd., Ste. 530, Irvine, CA 92612. Phone: (949)752-1801; Fax: (949)752-1674; Email: nationaloffice@actl.com • URL: http://www.actl.com • Maintains and improves the standards of trial practice, the administration of justice and the ethics of the profession. Brings together members of the profession who are qualified and who, by reason of probity and ability, will contribute to the accomplishments and good fellowship of the College.

Defense Research Institute. 55 W Monroe St., Ste. 2000, Chicago, IL 60603-5121. Phone: (312)795-1101; Fax: (312)795-0749 • URL: http://www.dri.org • Lawyers, claims people, adjusters, insurance companies, trade associations, corporations, and "target" defendants in civil litigation, such as doctors, pharmacists, engineers, manufacturers, and other professional and skilled personnel. Seeks to increase the knowledge and improve the skills of defense lawyers and to improve the adversary system of justice. Maintains research facilities, including files of speeches, briefs, and names of expert witnesses in various fields. Maintains Expert Witness Index.

Economic Justice Institute. University of Wisconsin Law School, 975 Bascom Mall, Madison, WI 53706-1399. Phone: (608)262-2240 • URL: http://law.wisc.edu/eji • Provides advocate services for consumers and low-income families through education, research, training and representation. Aims to educate and empower consumers by providing services and information.

National Lawyers Guild. 132 Nassau St., Rm. 922, New York, NY 10038. Phone: (212)679-5100; Fax: (212)679-2811 • URL: http://www.nlg.org • Lawyers, law students, legal workers, and jailhouse lawyers dedicated to seek economic justice, social equality, and the right to political dissent. Serves as national center for progressive legal work providing training programs to both members and nonmembers. Sponsors skills seminars in different areas of law. Maintains speakers' bureau and offers legal referrals.

National Legal Aid and Defender Association. 1901 Pennsylvania Ave. NW, Ste. 500, Washington, DC 20006. Phone: (202)452-0620; Fax: (202)872-1031; Email: info@nlada.org • URL: http://www.nlada100years.org • Legal aid offices and public defender organizations representing the indigent and individual members. Provides technical and management assistance to local organizations offering legal services to poor persons in civil or criminal cases and to state and local units of government. Advocates for federally funded high quality legal services with the public, media, congress, and members of the Executive branch. Offers litigation support through amicus curiae capability to organizations providing legal services. Serves as clearinghouse for information on the provision of legal aid and defender services to persons without means to pay lawyers' fees. Sponsors training program covering substantive law, management issues and litigation skills. Matches private law firms with impact cases to facilitate increased pro bono participation.

Personal Injury Lawyers Marketing and Management Association. 607 Briarwood Dr., Ste. 4, Myrtle Beach, SC 29572. Phone: 800-497-1890 or (843)361-1700; Fax: (866)859-8126; Email: info@pilmma.org • URL: http://www.pilmma.org • Represents personal injury lawyers and disability attorneys. Provides members with the necessary tools, information and education to help grow and manage a successful contingency-based injury and disability law practice. Seeks to fulfill the marketing and management needs of members by granting access to sources of credible information and educational events.

Total Attorneys. 25 E Washington St., Ste. 510, Chicago, IL 60602. Phone: 877-349-1307; Email: solutions@totalattorneys.com • URL: http://www.totalattorneys.com • Focuses on the advancement of attorneys, paralegals and other legal support staff. Offers solo practitioners and small law firms the tools, training and network needed to collaborate with peers, connect with experts and find better work-life balance. Coordinates workshops and conferences, educational resources, legal tools, affinity partnerships and community forums.

LAYOFFS

See DISMISSAL OF EMPLOYEES

LEAD INDUSTRY

CD-ROM DATABASES

METADEX Materials Collection: Metals-Polymers-Ceramics. Cambridge Scientific Abstracts L.P. • Quarterly. Provides CD-ROM citations to the worldwide literature of materials science and metallurgy. Corresponds to *Metals Abstracts, Alloys Index, Steels Alert, Nonferrous Alert, Polymers/ Ceramics/Composites Alert,* and *Engineered Materials Abstracts.* (Formerly produced by ASM International.).

STATISTICS SOURCES

Non-Ferrous Metal Data Yearbook. American Bureau of Metal Statistics. • Annual. $405.00. Provides worldwide data on approximately about 200 statistical tables covering many nonferrous metals. Includes production, consumption, inventories, exports, imports, and other data.

U.S. Industry and Trade Outlook. U.S. Department of Commerce National Technical Information Service. • Annual. Produced by the International Trade Administration, U.S. Department of Commerce, in a "public-private" partnership with DRI/ McGraw-Hill and Standard & Poor's. Provides basic data, outlook for the current year, and "Long-Term Prospects" (five-year projections) for a wide variety of products and services. Includes high technology industries. Formerly *U.S. Industrial Outlook.*

TRADE/PROFESSIONAL ASSOCIATIONS

Non-Ferrous Metals Producers Committee. 2030 M St. NW, Ste. 800, Washington, DC 20036. Phone: (202)466-7720; Fax: (202)466-2710 • URL: http://www.arcat.com/arcatcos/cos37/arc37679.cfm • Represents domestic copper, lead, and zinc producers. Promotes the interests of copper, lead, and zinc mining and metal industries in the U.S. with emphasis on tariffs, laws, regulations, and government policies affecting international trade and foreign imports.

LEADERSHIP

DIRECTORIES

American Business Leaders from Colonial Times to the Present. ABC-Clio Inc. • $175 Individuals print. Covers: The last three centuries of visionary figures in American business.

E-BOOKS

The Accountable Leader. Cengage Learning Inc. • 2010. eBook. Published by Kogan Page. Centered around three themes -- leadership, accountability, and organizational structure -- this book highlights how most leadership related problems arise from the ineffectiveness of organizational structures that lack accountable jobs.

ENCYCLOPEDIAS AND DICTIONARIES

Encyclopedia of E-Leadership, Counseling and Training. Cengage Learning Inc. • Offers an in-depth description of key terms and concepts related to different themes, issues, and trends in educational leadership, counseling, and technology integration in modern universities and organizations worldwide.

OTHER SOURCES

First-Level Leadership: Supervising in the New Organization. American Management Association Extension Institute. • Looseleaf. $139.00. Self-study course. Emphasis is on practical explanations, examples, and problem solving. Quizzes and a case study are included.

PERIODICALS AND NEWSLETTERS

Black Business Quarterly. Cape Media. • Quarterly. Magazine featuring top black business leadership.

Executive Excellence: The Newsletter of Personal Development, Managerial Effectiveness, and Organizational Productivity. Kenneth M. Shelton, editor. Executive Excellence Publishing. • Monthly. $129.00 per year. Newsletter.

Fast Company: How Smart Business Works. Fast Company, Inc. • Monthly. $12.00 per year. Covers business management, with emphasis on creativity, leadership, innovation, career advancement, teamwork, the global economy, and the "new workplace.".

Perspective. Magna Publications Inc. • Description:

Provides administrators with guidelines for keeping their schools out of court. Examines current trends in law related to higher education, as well as past and future legal issues affecting students, faculty, administrators and the public. Recurring features include columns titled Key Case Review, Follow-Up, Resources, Legislative Note, Outside the Courts, Cross-Examination, and Cases Noted.

RESEARCH CENTERS AND INSTITUTES

Columbia University - Center on Global Brand Leadership. Uris Hall, Rm. 2M3, Columbia Business School, 3022 Broadway, New York, NY 10027. Phone: (212)854-0659; Fax: (212)854-3762; Email: bschmitt@globalbrands.org • URL: http://www8.gsb.columbia.edu/globalbrands • Challenges of branding and innovation in a global economy.

Hillsdale College - Center for Constructive Alternatives/National Leadership Institute. 33 E College St., Hillsdale, MI 49242. Phone: (517)437-7341; Fax: (517)437-3923; Email: cca@hillsdale.edu • URL: http://www.hillsdale.edu • Political theory, public policy, culture.

Middle Tennessee State University - Tennessee Center for Labor-Management Relations. 1313 Old Ft. Pky., Ste. 300, Murfreesboro, TN 37129. Phone: (615)895-4166; Fax: (615)895-9389 • URL: http://www.tnlabormgmt.org • Steward training, leadership, supervisor training, labor-management cooperation, stress management, negotiation, health and safety, worker participation, mediation, alternate dispute resolution, and diversity.

University of Illinois at Springfield - Center for State Policy and Leadership. Public Affairs Ctr., Rm. 409, 1 University Plz., MS PAC 409, Springfield, IL 62703-5407. Phone: (217)206-8417; Fax: (217)206-6542; Email: draci2@uis.edu • URL: http://cspl.uis.edu • Public problems and policies, focusing on applied research on the Illinois government, the judicial system, and state administrative agencies. Specific areas of study include social services, health policy, Illinois budgeting, public law and administrative rule making, law and public policy, patronage, capital punishment, abortion, and campaign and school financing. Also evaluates the effectiveness of government programs.

TRADE/PROFESSIONAL ASSOCIATIONS

AIESEC Canada. 161 Eglinton Ave. E, Ste. 402, Toronto, ON, Canada M4P 1J5. Phone: (416)368-1001; Fax: (416)368-4490; Email: info2010@aiesec.ca • URL: http://aiesec.ca • Develops students through international internship exchange. Serves as a platform for young people to discover their potential so as to have a positive impact in the society.

AIESEC China. c/o Zachary Law, VP Communication, Block E, Rm. 1108, 16th St., hongguancun, Haidian mansion, Haidian District, Beijing, China. Phone: 86 10 82866532; Email: mainland.china@aiesec.net • URL: http://www.aiesec.cn • Provides leadership and work abroad opportunities. Organizes conferences and virtual tools to build networks. Contributes to the development of the communities with an overriding commitment to international co-operation and understanding. Facilitates international traineeship exchanges for its members and stakeholders.

AIESEC Kenya. PO Box 30197-00200, Nairobi, Kenya. Phone: 254 20 2608757; Email: info@aiesec.or.ke • URL: http://ke.aiesec.org • Enables students and recent graduate the opportunity to live and work in another country. Serves as a platform for young people to discover and develop their potential. Organizes conferences.

Alpha Kappa Psi. 7801 E 88th St., Indianapolis, IN 46256-1233. Phone: (317)872-1553; Fax: (317)872-1567; Email: mail@akpsi.org • URL: http://www.akpsi.org • Professional fraternity - business administration. Conducts educational and charitable programs. Focuses on leadership development.

Association for Corporate Growth - Toronto Chapter. 720 Spadina Ave., Ste. 202, Toronto, ON, Canada M5S 2T9. Phone: (416)868-1881; Fax: (416)391-3633; Email: acgtoronto@acg.org • URL: http://www.acg.org/toronto • Professionals with a leadership role in strategic corporate growth. Seeks to facilitate the professional advancement of members, and the practice of corporate growth management. Fosters communication and cooperation among members; conducts continuing professional education programs.

Australian Institute of Management. 380 La Trobe St., Level 20, Melbourne, VIC 3000, Australia. Phone: 61 3 95348181; Fax: 61 3 95345050; Email: enquiry@aimvic.com.au • URL: http://www.aim.com.au • Promotes growth in management and leadership. Provides management training and consultancy services.

Center for Creative Leadership. 1 Leadership Pl., Greensboro, NC 27410-9427. Phone: (336)288-7210 or (336)545-2810; Fax: (336)282-3284; Email: info@ccl.org • URL: http://www.ccl.org • Promotes behavioral science research and leadership education.

Executive Leadership Council. 1001 N Fairfax St., Ste. 300, Alexandria, VA 22314. Phone: (703)706-5200; Email: elcinfo@elcinfo.com • URL: http://www.elcinfo.com • Provides senior African-American corporate executives with a network and leadership forum that adds perspective and direction to the achievement of excellence in business, economic and public policies for the African-American community and its corporations, and the community at large. Conducts educational and research programs.

Future Business Leaders of America - Phi Beta Lambda. 1912 Association Dr., Reston, VA 20191-1591. Phone: 800-325-2946; Fax: (866)500-5610; Email: general@fbla.org • URL: http://www.fbla-pbl.org • Maintains 4 divisions: Future Business Leaders of America for high school students preparing for business and related careers; Phi Beta Lambda for post-secondary and college men and women enrolled in business or teacher education programs; Professional Division for business persons FBLA - parents and teachers; Middle Level for students in junior high schools. Sponsors educational program and National Student Award program based on national competition for members.

Institute of Leadership and Management. Stowe House, Netherstowe, Lichfield WS13 6TJ, United Kingdom. Phone: 44 1543 266886 or 44 1543 266867; Fax: 44 1543 266811 or 44 1543 266893; Email: customer@i-l-m.com • URL: http://www.i-l-m.com • Fellows, Members and Associates - Corporate grades; Affiliates and Students Non-corporate grades. Aims to encourage and develop the science and practice of management and gain recognition of management as a profession.

International Academy of Management. 21 Pearson Ave., 08034 Barcelona, Spain. Phone: 34 93 2534200; Email: epy@iese.edu • URL: http://theiam.ws • Leaders in management from 32 countries who have been elected fellows of the IAM in recognition for their contributions to the field. Seeks to: provide a body to safeguard the objectivity and precision of management and the disciplined integration of new/progressive managerial trends; stimulate intellectual interests in management.

International PEN - Writers in Prison Committee. Brownlow House, 50/51 High Holborn, London WC1V 6ER, United Kingdom. Phone: 44 20 74050338; Fax: 44 20 74050339; Email: info@pen-international.org • URL: http://www.pen-international.org • Serves as a key resource for the writing instruments industry. Provides leadership and direction for its members by staying at the forefront of trends, education, and technology in order to promote and procure the future of writing instrument development and distribution. Offers strategic analysis of manufacturer and retail marketing efforts.

Iota Phi Lambda. 1015 15th St. NW, Ste. 1110, Washington, DC 20005. Phone: (202)462-4682; Email: iotahq@verizon.net • URL: http://iota1929.org • Business and professional civic sorority. Seeks to: develop leadership expertise among business and professional women; promote increased interest in business education among high school and college girls through planned programs and scholarships; encourage the development of personalities for all areas of leadership through provision of educational opportunities; establish and promote civic and social service activities for youth and adults. Conducts children's services and tutoring sessions. Maintains small library. Provides educational, tutorial, senior citizen, and health programs.

Junior Achievement China. Bldg. 5, Ste. 201, Unit 5, Julong Garden, 68 Xinzhongjie, Dongcheng District, Beijing 100027, Hebei, China. Phone: 86 10 65515235; Fax: 86 10 65527850; Email: beijing@jachina.org • URL: http://www.jachina.org • Educates young people to value free enterprise, business and economics. Serves as a catalyst for character, creativity and leadership development of young people. Implements principle-centered, interactive business and economic education programs.

Junior Achievement Ireland. 8 Longford Pl., Monkstown, Dublin, Dublin, Ireland. Phone: 353 1 2366644; Fax: 353 1 2803758; Email: info@jai.ie • URL: http://www.juniorachievement.ie • Aims to build a bridge between classroom and workplace. Provides young people the opportunity to participate in educational programs. Recruits persons who are qualified to teach students about business.

Junior Achievement of Canada. 1 Eva Rd., Ste. 218, Toronto, ON, Canada M9C 4Z5. Phone: 800-265-0699 or (416)622-4602; Fax: (416)622-6861 • URL: http://jacan.org • Works to help young Canadians discover leadership, entrepreneurial and workforce readiness skills to achieve highest potential as citizens for the global community.

Junior Achievement Russia. Leninsky Prospekt, 113/1 Park Pl., 3rd Fl., Ste. B-301, 117 198 Moscow, Russia. Phone: 7 95 9565810; Fax: 7 95 9565246; Email: ja-russia@inbox.ru • URL: http://www.ja-russia.ru • Promotes the growth and development of business and economic educational programs for youth. Establishes partnerships between business and educational communities.

Junior Achievement Tajikistan. 169, Lenina St., Sughd, 735700 Khujand, Tajikistan. Phone: 992 927777917; Email: ja-tajikistan@mail.ru • URL: http://www.ja-ap.org • Aims to educate and inspire young people to value free enterprise and understand the mechanisms of market economy. Facilitates innovative teaching methods of business and economics. Fosters a spirit of entrepreneurship among young people.

Social Venture Network. PO Box 29221, San Francisco, CA 94129-0221. Phone: (415)561-6501; Fax: (415)561-6435; Email: svn@svn.org • URL: http://www.svn.org • Aims to build a just and sustainable world through business. Promotes new models and leadership for socially and environmentally sustainable business through initiatives, information services and forums.

LEADING INDICATORS

See ECONOMIC INDICATORS

LEARNING, PROGRAMMED

See PROGRAMMED LEARNING

LEATHER INDUSTRY

See also LUGGAGE INDUSTRY; SHOE INDUSTRY; TANNING INDUSTRY

CD-ROM DATABASES

OECD Statistical Compendium. Organization for Economic Cooperation and Development. • Semiannual. $1,905.00 per year for 1 to 10 users. CD-ROM contains more than 730,000 monthly, quarterly, and annual time series for OECD countries, 1960 to date. Includes fully searchable data on agriculture, food, economic indicators, national accounts, employment, energy, finance, industry, technology, and foreign trade. Results can be displayed in various forms.

DIRECTORIES

American Leather Chemists Association--Membership Directory. American Leather Chemists Association. • Annual. Covers: About 500 chemists, leather technologists, and educators concerned with the tanning and leather industry. Entries include: Personal name, address; company name, address, phone, fax.

Directory of Chinese Importers of Leather, Hides, Skins & Furs. EXIM Infotek Private Ltd. • Covers: 30 Chinese importers of cow leathers, hides, skins and fur, leather, mink and fox tails, pig skins, scrap sheep, and fox skin. Entries include: Company name, postal address, telephone, fax, e-mail, website, contact person, designation, and product details.

Directory of Chinese Manufacturers & Exporters of Leather Products. EXIM Infotek Private Ltd. • $15 Individuals. Covers: 170 Chinese manufacturers and exporters of artificial leather products, bags, fashion bags, fur clothing & products, fur products, hand bags, leather articles, leather bags, leather belts, leather cases, leather clothing, leather garments, leather goods, leather jackets, leather products, leather purses, leather waist belts, purses, sheep and lamb skin leather products, and wallets. Entries include: Company name, postal address, city, country, phone, fax, e-mail and website, contact person, designation, and product details.

Directory of Japanese Manufacturers & Exporters of Leather, Hides, Skins & Furs. EXIM Infotek Private Ltd. • $5 Individuals. Covers: 20 Japanese manufacturers and exporters of artificial fur, leather, rabbit fur and skin, raw hide leather, raw hide skins (fresh, salted), raw skins, and synthetic leather. Entries include: Company name, postal address, city, country, phone, fax, e-mail and websites, contact person, designation, and product details.

Directory of Japanese Manufacturers & Exporters of Leather Products. EXIM Infotek Private Ltd. • $5 Individuals. Covers: 20 Japanese manufacturers and exporters of bags, hand bags, leather goods, and leather products. Entries include: Company name, postal address, city, country, phone, fax, e-mail and websites, contact person, designation, and product details.

Directory of South Korean Manufacturers & Exporters of Leather, Hides, Skins & Furs. EXIM Infotek Private Ltd. • $10 Individuals. Covers: 110 South Korean manufacturers & exporters of leather-reconstituted, leather-processed, PVC leathercloth, sheep & goat skins, sheep & lamb skins, skins, hides & leather, swine skins/leather. Entries include: Company name, postal address, city, country, phone, fax, e-mail & websites, contact person, designation, products detail.

Directory of South Korean Manufacturers & Exporters of Leather Products. EXIM Infotek Private Ltd. • $15 Individuals. Covers: 130 South Korean manufacturers and exporters of bags, cases and covers of leather, fancy leather goods, fur clothing and products, leather airbags/sportbags, leather clothing, leather goods for industrial use and leather waist belts. Entries include: Company name, postal address, city, country, phone, fax, e-mail and websites, contact person, designation, and product details.

Directory of South Korean Manufacturers & Exporters of Machinery for Leather & Shoe Industry. EXIM Infotek Private Ltd. • $5 Individuals. Covers: 20 South Korean manufacturers and exporters of boot and shoe making machinery/equipment, leather working and saddlery making equipment. Entries include: Company name, postal address, city, country, phone, fax, e-mail and websites, contact person, designation, and product details.

Directory of Taiwanese Manufacturers & Exporters of Leather, Hides, Skins & Furs. EXIM Infotek Private Ltd. • $20 Individuals. Covers: 190 Taiwanese manufacturers and exporters of leather-reconstituted, leather-processed, PVC leathercloth, PVC sponge leather, sheep and goat skins, sheep and lamb skins, skins, hides and leather, and swine skins/leather. Entries include: Company name, postal address, city, country, phone, fax, e-mail and websites, contact person, designation, and product details.

Directory of Taiwanese Manufacturers & Exporters of Leather Products. EXIM Infotek Private Ltd. • $20 Individuals. Covers: 280 Taiwanese manufacturers and exporters of bags, cases and covers of leather, fancy leather goods, fur clothing and products, leather airbags/sportbags, leather clothing, leather goods for industrial use, leather purses, leather waist belts. Entries include: Company name, postal address, city, country, phone, fax, e-mail and websites, contact person, designation, and product details.

Directory of Taiwanese Manufacturers & Exporters of Machinery for Leather & Shoe Industry. EXIM Infotek Private Ltd. • $10 Individuals. Covers: 100 Taiwanese manufacturers and exporters of boot and shoe making machinery/equipment, leather working and saddlery making/equipment, shoe industry equipment, tannery machinery and equipment. Entries include: Company name, postal address, city, country, phone, fax, e-mail and websites, contact person, designation, products detail.

The International Directory of Importers - Leather Goods, Footwear and Travel Accessories Importers. Interdata. • $260 Individuals print edition. Covers: 3,200 international firms importing leather goods, footwear and travel accessories. Entries include: Company name and address, contact person, email, number of employees, year established, phone and telefaxes, business activity, bank references, as well as a listing of leather goods, footwear and travel accessories currently being imported.

Leather Goods Directory--Wholesalers. InfoGroup Inc. • Annual. Number of listings: 690. Entries include: Name, address, phone, size of advertisement, name of owner or manager, number of employees, year first in "Yellow Pages." Compiled from telephone company "Yellow Pages," nationwide.

Travelware Suppliers Directory. Business Journals Inc. • Annual. $20 postpaid: payment with order. Covers: 500 manufacturers and importers that supply hardware, leather, fabrics, and other components to the luggage and leather goods industry (SIC 3161). Entries include: Company name, address, phone, fax, telex, name of principal executive, sales offices/showrooms/reps, email, URL.

World Directory of Hides, Skins & Raw Leather Importers. World-Wide Market-Link. • Irregular. $35. Covers: 400 leather importers and wholesalers in the U.S. and Canada, the United Kingdom, Australia, Austria, Belgium, Denmark, Finland, France, West Germany, Greece, Holland, Italy, Israel, Japan, Spain, Sweden, and Switzerland. Entries include: Company name, address, phone, products handled.

FINANCIAL RATIOS

Annual Statement Studies. Risk Management Association. • Annual. Compiled from over 280,000 financial statements.

Annual Statement Studies: Industry Default Probabilities and Cash Flow Measures. Risk Management Association. • Annual. $405 Nonmembers. Serves as a companion volume to the original *Annual Statement Studies.* Gives probability of default estimates on a percentage scale for more than 450 industries. Includes changes in position year-by-year for eight financial statement line items and provides percentage measures of cash flow.

INTERNET DATABASES

Business 2.0 Web Guide to the Best Business Links. Business 2.0 Media Inc. Phone: (415)293-4800; Email: support@business2.com • URL: http://www.business2.com/webguide • Web site presents an extensive, searchable directory of links to "the best, most informative, and authoritative web pages." Twenty main categories cover business, finance, career, company information, people, and technology topics, with thousands of subtopics, all linking to Web sites recommended by experienced business researchers. Fees: Free.

Fedstats. Federal Interagency Council on Statistical Policy. Phone: (202)395-7254 • URL: http://www.fedstats.gov • Web site features an efficient search facility for full-text statistics produced by more than 100 federal agencies, including the Census Bureau, the Bureau of Economic Analysis, and the Bureau of Labor Statistics. Boolean searches can be made within one agency or for all agencies combined. Links are offered to international statistical bureaus, including the UN, IMF, OECD, UNESCO, Eurostat, and 20 individual countries. Fees: Free.

FreeLunch.com. Economy.com, Inc. Phone: (610)696-8700; Fax: (610)696-1678 • URL: http://www.freelunch.com • Web site provides free access to more than 200 million economic and financial data series, covering industry, demographics, labor markets, prices, retail sales, government spending, trade, interest rates, housing starts, the stock market, etc. Data is available in either chart or table form. Searching is offered. Free, but registration required. Economy.com, Inc. also offers fee-based economic analysis at *The Dismal Scientist* site (www.dismal.com).

RESEARCH CENTERS AND INSTITUTES

Leather Research Laboratory. University of Cincinnati. 5997 Center Hill Ave., Cincinnati, OH 45224. Phone: (513)242-6300; Fax: (513)242-9797; Email: donmezk@uc.edu • URL: http://www.leatherusa.org • Automotive, upholstery, garment, apparel and chamois leather testing (physical, chemical, and toxicity).

STATISTICS SOURCES

Survey of Current Business. U. S. Government Printing Office. • Published by Bureau of Economic Analysis, U. S. Department of Commerce. Presents a wide variety of business and economic data.

TRADE/PROFESSIONAL ASSOCIATIONS

American Leather Chemists Association. 1314 50th St., Ste. 103, Lubbock, TX 79412-2940. Phone: (806)744-1798; Fax: (806)744-1785; Email: alca@leatherchemists.org • URL: http://www.leatherchemists.org • Chemists, leather technologists, and educators concerned with the tanning and leather industry. Works to devise and perfect methods for the analysis and testing of leathers and materials used in leather manufacture. Promotes advancement of chemistry and other sciences, especially their application to problems confronting the leather industry.

Leather Industries of America. 3050 K St. NW, Ste. 400, Washington, DC 20007. Phone: (202)342-8497; Fax: (202)342-8583; Email: info@leatherusa.

com • URL: http://www.leatherusa.com • Formerly Tanners' Council of America.

LEGAL FORMS

See FORMS AND BLANKS

LEGAL HOLIDAYS

See ANNIVERSARIES AND HOLIDAYS

LEGAL PROFESSION

See LAWYERS

LEGAL RIGHTS

See CIVIL RIGHTS

LEGATIONS

See DIPLOMATIC AND CONSULAR SERVICE

LEGISLATION

See LAWS

LEGISLATIVE INVESTIGATIONS

See GOVERNMENT INVESTIGATIONS

LEGISLATIVE PROCEDURE

ABSTRACTS AND INDEXES

Current Law Index. Cengage Learning Inc. • $1,332 Individuals. Monthly. $1269.00 per year. Produced in cooperation with the American Association of Law Libraries. Indexes more than 900 law journals, legal newspapers, and specialty publications from the U.S., Canada, U.K., Ireland, Australia, and New Zealand.

INTERNET DATABASES

Lexis.com Research System. Lexis-Nexis Group. Phone: 800-227-4908 or (937)865-6800; Fax: (937)865-6909; Email: webmaster@prod.lexis-nexis.com • URL: http://www.nexis.com • Fee-based Web site offers extensive searching of a wide variety of legal sources. Additional features include Daily Opinion Service, lexis.com Bookstore, Career Center, CLE Center, Law Schools, and Practice Pages ("Pages specific to areas of specialty").

RESEARCH CENTERS AND INSTITUTES

Harvard Legislative Research Bureau. Harvard University, Harvard Law School, 1541 Massachusetts Ave., Cambridge, MA 02138. Phone: (617)495-4400; Fax: (617)495-1110; Email: pgowder@law.harvard.edu • Concerned with federal and state legislation in all fields.

LEGISLATURES

ALMANACS AND YEARBOOKS

Suggested State Legislation (SSL). Chief Officers of State Library Agencies. • Annual. A source of legislative ideas and drafting assistance for state government officials.

BIOGRAPHICAL SOURCES

Who's Who in American Politics. Marquis Who's Who L.L.C. • Biennial. $349 Individuals. Contains about 27,000 biographical sketches of local, state, and national elected or appointed individuals.

DIRECTORIES

CSG State Directories I: State Elective Officials. Chief Officers of State Library Agencies. • Annual. $65 Individuals. Covers: About 8,000 state legislators, elected state executive branch officials, and state supreme court judges. Database includes: Miscellaneous state facts and term limit information. Entries include: Name, title, address, district, party affiliation, fax and facts about each state-motto, flower, bird, nickname, capitol address, bill status phone, land area, population, D. C. Liaison, term limits, election and session dates.

PERIODICALS AND NEWSLETTERS

State Legislatures. National Conference of State Legislatures. • Description: Provides a national perspective on government and policy in the each state. Features articles on public policy issues.

TRADE/PROFESSIONAL ASSOCIATIONS

Chief Officers of State Library Agencies. 201 E Main St., Ste. 1405, Lexington, KY 40507. Phone: 800-800-1910 or (859)514-9151 or (859)244-8000; Fax: (859)514-9166 or (859)244-8001; Email: lsingler@amrms.com • URL: http://www.cosla.org • Supersedes American Legislator Association.

National Conference of State Legislatures. 7700 E 1st Pl., Denver, CO 80230-7143. Phone: (303)364-7700; Fax: (303)364-7800; Email: ncslnet-admin@ncsl.org • URL: http://www.ncsl.org • Affiliated with Council of State Governments.

LEMONS

See CITRUS FRUIT INDUSTRY

LENSES, CONTACT

See CONTACT LENS AND INTRAOCULAR LENS INDUSTRIES

LENSES, INTRAOCULAR

See CONTACT LENS AND INTRAOCULAR LENS INDUSTRIES

LETTER WRITING

See BUSINESS CORRESPONDENCE

LEVERAGED BUYOUTS

See also JUNK BOND FINANCING; MERGERS AND ACQUISITIONS

ABSTRACTS AND INDEXES

Business Periodicals Index Retrospective. EBSCO Publishing Inc. • 11/year. Quarterly and annual cumulations.

CD-ROM DATABASES

Buyout Financing Sources/M & A Intermediaries. SourceMedia Inc. • Annual. $895.00. Provides the CD-ROM combination of *Directory of Buyout Financing Sources* and *Directory of M & A Intermediaries*. Contains information on more than 1,000 financing sources (banks, insurance companies, venture capital firms, etc.) and 850 intermediaries (corporate acquirers, valuation firms, lawyers, accountants, etc.). Also includes back issues of *Buyouts Newsletter* and *Mergers & Acquisitions Report*. Fully searchable.

ONLINE DATABASES

Wilson Business Abstracts Online. H.W. Wilson Co. • Indexes and abstracts 600 major business periodicals, plus the *Wall Street Journal* and the business section of the *New York Times*. Indexing is from 1982, abstracting from 1990, with the two newspapers included from 1993. Updated weekly. Inquire as to online cost and availability. (*Business Periodicals Index* without abstracts is also available online.).

OTHER SOURCES

Going Private. ALM Media Properties LLC. • $560 print + online + ebook. Discusses the legal ramifications of a publicly-owned company "going private" by way of a sale, leveraged buyout, reverse stock split, or merger. (Law Journal Press).

PERIODICALS AND NEWSLETTERS

Acquisitions Monthly. Thomson Financial Inc. • Monthly. $790.00 per year. Published in London. Provides detailed information, commentary, and statistics on merger, acquisition, and buyout activity in Europe, the U.S., and Asia.

Buyouts: The Newsletter for Management Buyouts, Leveraged Aquisitions, and Special Situations. Thomson Financial Inc. • Biweekly. $1,595.00 per year. Newsletter. Covers news and trends for the buyout industry. Provides information on deal makers and current buyout activity.

Corporate Acquisitions. ARCH Group. • Description: Summaries of trends and analysis of transactions in corporate mergers and acquisitions. Recurring features include interviews, reports of meetings, book reviews, and companies listed for sale.

Corporate Control Alert; A Report on Current Changes for Corporate Control. ALM Media Properties LLC. • Monthly. $1,595 per year. A monthly mergers and acquisitions newsletter.

Corporate Financing Week: The Newsweekly of Corporate Finance, Investment Banking and M and A. Institutional Investor Inc. Journals Group. • Weekly. $2,550.00 per year. Includes print and online editions. Newsletter for corporate finance officers. Emphasis is on debt and equity financing, mergers, leveraged buyouts, investment banking, and venture capital.

Corporate Growth. Princeton Research Institute. • Monthly. $198.00 per year.

RESEARCH CENTERS AND INSTITUTES

University of Pennsylvania - The Wharton School - Rodney L. White Center for Financial Research. 3254 Steinberg Hall-Dietrich Hall, Philadelphia, PA 19104-6367. Phone: (215)898-7616; Fax: (215)573-8084; Email: rlwctr@finance.wharton.upenn.edu • URL: http://rodneywhitecenter.wharton.upenn.edu • Research areas include financial management, money markets, real estate finance, and international finance.

University of Rochester - Bradley Policy Research Center. 305 Schlegel Hall, William E Simon Graduate School of Business, Rochester, NY 14627. Phone: (585)275-3316 or (585)275-2668; Fax: (585)275-0095; Email: sue.north@simon.rochester.edu • URL: http://www.simon.rochester.edu/faculty--research/research-center-and-conferences/bradley-policy-research-center/index.aspx • Corporate control and corporate takeovers are among the research areas covered.

LIABILITY, PRODUCT

See PRODUCT SAFETY AND LIABILITY

LIABILITY, PROFESSIONAL

See PROFESSIONAL LIABILITY

LIBRARIANS

ABSTRACTS AND INDEXES

Library Literature and Information Science Index. H.W. Wilson Co. • Quarterly. Annual cumulation. Price varies.

CD-ROM DATABASES

LISA Plus. Cambridge Scientific Abstracts L.P. • Quarterly. $2,000 per year. CD-ROM version of Library Information and Science Abstracts, providing abstracting and indexing of the world's library and information science literature, 1969 to date. Contains more than 180,000 citations.

WILSONDISC: Library Literature and Information Science Index. H.W. Wilson Co. • Quarterly. Includes unlimited access to the online version of *Library Literature.* Provides CD-ROM indexing of about 400 periodicals, covering a wide range of topics having to do with libraries, library management, and the information industry.

DIRECTORIES

Guide to Employment Sources in the Library and Information Professions. Library and Information Technology Association. • Annual. Associations and agencies offering library placement services.

PERIODICALS AND NEWSLETTERS

Information Broker. Helen P. Burwell, editor. Burwell Enterprises Inc. • Description: Covers companies that offer fee-based information services and issues related to "the business" of information brokering.

Library Administrator's Digest. The Foundation for Baltimore County Public Library Inc. • Description: Designed to keep library administrators abreast of new ideas and developments, particularly in the public library field. Recurring features include editorials and letters to the editor.

The One-Person Library: A Newsletter for Librarians and Management. Information Bridges International Inc. • Monthly. $85.00 per year. Newsletter for librarians working alone or with minimal assistance. Contains reports on library literature, management advice, case studies, book reviews, and general information.

School Library Journal. Media Source Inc. • Monthly. $130.99 1 year subscription. Provides news, information and reviews for librarians and media specialists who serve children and young adults in school and public libraries.

STATISTICS SOURCES

SLA Annual Salary Survey. Special Libraries Association. • Annual. Members, $75.00; nonmembers, $150.00. Provides data on salaries for special librarians in the U. S. and Canada, according to location, job title, industry, budget, and years of experience.

TRADE/PROFESSIONAL ASSOCIATIONS

American Library Association - Gay, Lesbian, Bisexual and Transgendered Roundtable. c/o American Library Association, 50 E Huron St., Chicago, IL 60611-2795. Phone: 800-545-2433 or (312)944-6780; Fax: (312)440-9374; Email: ala@ala.org • URL: http://www.ala.org/glbtrt/glbtrt • Promotes gay, lesbian, bisexual and transgendered professionals in the library industry.

Asian Pacific American Librarians Association. PO Box 677593, Orlando, FL 32867-7593. • URL: http://www.apalaweb.org • Librarians and information specialists of Asian Pacific descent working in the U.S.; interested persons. Provides a forum for discussing problems and concerns; supports and encourages library services to Asian Pacific communities; recruits and supports Asian Pacific Americans in the library and information science professions. Offers placement service; compiles statistics. Conducts fundraising for scholarships.

Black Caucus of the American Library Association. PO Box 1738, Hampton, VA 23669. Email: webmaster@bcala.org • URL: http://www.bcala.org • Black librarians; blacks interested in library services. Promotes librarianship; encourages active participation of blacks in library associations and boards and all levels of the profession. Monitors activities of the American Library Association with regard to its policies and programs and how they affect black librarians and library users. Reviews, analyzes, evaluates, and recommends to the ALA actions that influence the recruitment, development, advancement, and general working conditions of black librarians. Facilitates library services that meet the informational needs of black people including increased availability of materials related to social and economic concerns.

Catholic Library Association. 205 W Monroe St., Ste. 314, Chicago, IL 60606-5061. Phone: 855-739-1776 or (312)739-1776; Fax: (312)739-1778; Email: sbaron@regent.edu • URL: http://www.cathla.org • Librarians, teachers, and booksellers concerned with Catholic libraries and their specialized problems and the writing, publishing, and distribution of Catholic literature. Members represent lay and clergy in both Catholic and non-Catholic institutions.

Library and Information Technology Association. 50 E Huron St., Chicago, IL 60611-2795. Phone: 800-545-2433; Fax: (312)280-3257; Email: lita@ala.org • URL: http://www.ala.org/lita • Affiliated with the American Library Association. Formerly Information Science and Automation Division of ALA.

Middle East Librarians Association. c/o Roberta L. Dougherty, Vice President/Program Chair, Yale University Library, PO Box 208240, New Haven, CT 06520-8240. Phone: (514)398-6787 • URL: http://www.mela.us • Librarians and others interested in aspects of librarianship that support the study or dissemination of information about the Middle East since the rise of Islam. Facilitates communication among members through meetings and publications. Improves the quality of area librarianship through the development of standards for the profession and education of Middle East library specialists. Compiles and disseminates information concerning Middle East libraries and collections and represents the judgment of the members in matters affecting them. Encourages cooperation among members and Middle East libraries, especially in the acquisition of materials and the development of bibliographic controls.

LIBRARIES

See also LIBRARY MANAGEMENT

ABSTRACTS AND INDEXES

Library Literature and Information Science Index. H.W. Wilson Co. • Quarterly. Annual cumulation. Price varies.

LISA: Library and Information Science Abstracts. R.R. Bowker L.L.C. • 13 times a year. $1,055.00 per year; includes print and online editions.

ALMANACS AND YEARBOOKS

The Library and Book Trade Almanac. Information Today, Inc. • $209 Individuals Hardbound. Reviews key trends and events and provides basic statistical information. Includes financial averages: library expenditures, salaries, and book prices. Contains lists of "best books, literary prizes, winners, and bestsellers." Formerly published by R. R. Bowker.

CD-ROM DATABASES

ERIC SilverPlatter. U.S. Department of Education Institute of Education Sciences Education Resources Information Center. • Opinion papers, evaluations, speeches.

LISA Plus. Cambridge Scientific Abstracts L.P. • Quarterly. $2,000 per year. CD-ROM version of Library Information and Science Abstracts, providing abstracting and indexing of the world's library and information science literature, 1969 to date. Contains more than 180,000 citations.

WILSONDISC: Library Literature and Information Science Index. H.W. Wilson Co. • Quarterly. Includes unlimited access to the online version of *Library Literature.* Provides CD-ROM indexing of about 400 periodicals, covering a wide range of topics having to do with libraries, library management, and the information industry.

DIRECTORIES

American Library Directory (ALD). Information Today, Inc. • Annual. $369.50 Individuals hardbound; plus $25 shipping and handling. Covers: Over 36,000 U.S. and Canadian academic, public, county, provincial, and regional libraries; library systems; medical, law, and other special libraries; and libraries for the blind and physically handicapped. Separate section lists over 350 library networks and consortia and 220 accredited and unaccredited library school programs. Entries include: For libraries--Name, supporting or affiliated institution or firm name, address, phone, fax, electronic mail address, Standard Address Number (SANs), names of librarian and department heads, income, collection size, special collections, computer hardware, automated functions, and type of catalog. For library systems--Name, location. For library schools--Name, address, phone, fax, electronic mail address, director, type of training and degrees, admission requirements, tuition, faculty size. For networks and consortia--Name, address, phone, names of affiliates, name of director, function.

European Directory of Business Information Libraries. Euromonitor International Business Reference Div. • Irregular. $650. Covers: More than 2,000 European business libraries and services. Entries include: location, accessibility, fees, stock, and subject area.

Grants for Libraries & Information Services. • Available only as a downloadable file. Single use version $39.95; library use version $$99.95. Foundations and organizations which have awarded grants made the preceding year for public, academic, research, special, and school libraries; for archives and information centers; for consumer information; and for philanthropy information centers.

ENCYCLOPEDIAS AND DICTIONARIES

Encyclopedia of Library and Information Science. CRC Press. • Available in print or as an online subscription.

INTERNET DATABASES

WilsonWeb Periodicals Databases. H.W. Wilson Co. 950 University Ave., Bronx, NY 10452-4224. Phone: 800-367-6770 or (718)588-8400 or (718)558-8400; Fax: (718)590-1617 or (800)590-1617; Email: custserv@hwwilson.com • URL: http://www.hwwilson.com • Web sites provide fee-based access to *Wilson Business Full Text, Applied Science & Technology Full Text, Biological & Agricultural Index, Library Literature & Information Science Full Text,* and *Readers' Guide Full Text, Mega Edition.* Daily updates.

ONLINE DATABASES

American Library Directory Online. Information Today, Inc. • Provides information on more than 30,000 public, college, and special libraries in the U.S. and Canada, with annual updates. Includes library networks, consortia, organizations, and schools. Inquire as to online cost and availability.

ERIC. U.S. Department of Education Institute of Education Sciences Educational Resources Information Center. • Funded by the U.S. Department of Education, Institute of Education Sciences (formerly Office of Educational Research and Improvement).

Provides access to more than one million online records covering education-related journal and report literature, 1966 to date. Updating is monthly. Inquire as to online cost and availability.

OTHER SOURCES

Advances in Librarianship. Elsevier. • Irregular. Prices vary.

PERIODICALS AND NEWSLETTERS

The Journal of Academic Librarianship: Articles, Features, and Book Reviews for the Academic Library Professional. Elsevier. • $472 Institutions. Bimonthly. Qualified personnel.

Journal of Library and Information Services in Distance Learning. The Haworth Press Inc. • Quarterly. $150.00 per year to libraries; $48.00 per year to individuals.

Public Library Quarterly. The Haworth Press Inc. • Quarterly. Institutions, $141.00 per year (print and online).

TRADE/PROFESSIONAL ASSOCIATIONS

Library and Information Technology Association. 50 E Huron St., Chicago, IL 60611-2795. Phone: 800-545-2433; Fax: (312)280-3257; Email: lita@ala.org • URL: http://www.ala.org/lita • Affiliated with the American Library Association. Formerly Information Science and Automation Division of ALA.

LIBRARIES, COLLEGE AND UNIVERSITY

See COLLEGE AND UNIVERSITY LIBRARIES

LIBRARIES, PUBLIC

See LIBRARIES

LIBRARIES, SPECIAL

See SPECIAL LIBRARIES

LIBRARY AUTOMATION

See also ONLINE INFORMATION SYSTEMS

ABSTRACTS AND INDEXES

Information Science Abstracts. American Society for Information Science. Information Today, Inc. • Nine times a year. $725.00 per year.

Library Literature and Information Science Index. H.W. Wilson Co. • Quarterly. Annual cumulation. Price varies.

LISA: Library and Information Science Abstracts. R.R. Bowker L.L.C. • 13 times a year. $1,055.00 per year; includes print and online editions.

CD-ROM DATABASES

LISA Plus. Cambridge Scientific Abstracts L.P. • Quarterly. $2,000 per year. CD-ROM version of Library Information and Science Abstracts, providing abstracting and indexing of the world's library and information science literature, 1969 to date. Contains more than 180,000 citations.

WILSONDISC: Library Literature and Information Science Index. H.W. Wilson Co. • Quarterly. Includes unlimited access to the online version of *Library Literature.* Provides CD-ROM indexing of about 400 periodicals, covering a wide range of topics having to do with libraries, library management, and the information industry.

DIRECTORIES

Library Journal Sourcebook: The Reference For Library Products & Services. Reed Elsevier Group plc Reed Business Information. • Annual. Publication includes: List of over 600 suppliers of products and services used by libraries from abstracting to word processing equipment. Entries include: Company name, address, phone, list of products or services. Complete listings for more than 100 architectural firms; Disaster planning for librarians.

Library Resource Guide: A Catalog of Services and Suppliers for the Library Community. Information Today, Inc. • Annual. Free to libraries. An advertising directory listing several hundred manufacturers or distributors of library supplies, services, and equipment in such areas as audiovisual, automation, bar codes, binding, furniture, microfilm, shelving, and storage. Some book dealers, document delivery services, online services, and publishers are also included (www.libraryresource.com). Formerly published by R. R. Bowker.

OTHER SOURCES

Library Technology Reports: Expert Guides to Library Systems and Services. Library and Information Technology Association. • Bimonthly. $315.00 per year. Looseleaf service.

PERIODICALS AND NEWSLETTERS

Computers in Libraries. Information Today, Inc. • Monthly. 10 times a year. $98.95 per year.

Information Processing and Management: An International Journal. Elsevier. • $327 Individuals. Bimonthly. Qualified personnel, $301.00 per year; institutions, $1,196.00 per year. Text in English, French, German and Italian.

Information Standards Quarterly. National Information Standards Organization. • Quarterly. $130 Individuals /year. Newsletter. Reports on activities of the National Information Standards Organization.

IntraNets: Enterprise Strategies and Solutions. Information Today, Inc. • $199.50 U.S.. Bimonthly. Newsletter on the use of Internet technology for local library networks.

Multimedia Schools: A Practical Journal of Technology for Education including Multimedia, CD-ROM, Online and Internet and Hardware in K-12. Information Today, Inc. • Six times a year. $39.95 per year. Edited for school librarians, media center directors, computer coordinators, and others concerned with educational multimedia. Coverage includes the use of CD-ROM sources, the Internet, online services, and library technology.

Online Libraries and Microcomputers. Information Intelligence Inc. • Ten times a year. Individuals $43.75 per year; libraries. $62.50 per year. Newsletter. Covers library automation and electronic information (online, CD-ROM). Reviews or describes new computer hardware and software for library use.

Online Searcher. Information Today, Inc. • Bimonthly. $139.00 per year. Edited for librarians, Webmasters, site designers, content managers, and others concerned with knowledge/information management. Includes critical reviews of Web sites, software, search engines, and information services. (Formerly published by Online, Inc.).

Program: Electronic Library and Information Systems. Emerald Group Publishing Ltd. • Discusses computer applications for libraries.

Technical Services Quarterly: New Trends in Computers, Automation, and Advanced Technologies in the Technical Operation of Libraries and Information Centers. The Haworth Press Inc. • Quarterly. Institutions, $375.00 per year.

RESEARCH CENTERS AND INSTITUTES

Center for Study of Librarianship. Kent State University, Kent, OH 44242-0001. Phone: (330)672-2782; Fax: (330)672-7965; Email: dwicks@kent.edu • URL: http://www.slis.kent.edu.

TRADE/PROFESSIONAL ASSOCIATIONS

American Society for Information Science and Technology. 8555 16th St., Ste. 850, Silver Spring, MD 20910. Phone: (301)495-0900; Fax: (301)495-0810; Email: asis@asis.org • URL: http://www.asis.org • Members are information managers, scientists, librarians, and others who are interested in the storage, retrieval, and use of information.

Association for Library Collections and Technical Services. 50 E Huron St., Chicago, IL 60611. Phone: 800-545-2433 or (312)280-5037; Fax: (312)280-5033; Email: cwilt@ala.org • URL: http://www.ala.org/alcts • Offers well-integrated and forward-looking services to library and information specialists in acquisitions, cataloging, classification, preservation, and collection development and management. Offers extensive programming, regional educational events, and practical publications.

Library and Information Technology Association. 50 E Huron St., Chicago, IL 60611-2795. Phone: 800-545-2433; Fax: (312)280-3257; Email: lita@ala.org • URL: http://www.ala.org/lita • Affiliated with the American Library Association. Formerly Information Science and Automation Division of ALA.

National Information Standards Organization. 3600 Clipper Mill Rd., Ste. 302, Baltimore, MD 21211. Phone: (301)654-2512; Fax: (410)685-5278; Email: hreid@copyright.com • URL: http://www.niso.org • Identifies, develops, maintains, and publishes technical standards to manage information in the changing environment used by libraries, publishers, and information services. Supports open access to NISO standards. Standards available at website.

Public Library Association; Technology Committee. c/o American Library Association, 50 E Huron St., Chicago, IL 60611. Phone: 800-545-2433 or (312)280-5047; Fax: (312)280-5029 • URL: http://www.ala.org/pla/about/committees/pla-tech • Affiliated with the American Library Association. Formerly Public Libraries Division.

Reference and User Services Association of the American Library Association. 50 E Huron St., Chicago, IL 60611. Phone: 800-545-2433 or (312)280-4395; Fax: (312)280-5273; Email: rusa@ala.org • URL: http://www.ala.org/rusa • Affiliated with American Library Association. Formerly Reference and Adult Services Division of American Library Association.

LIBRARY MANAGEMENT

See also LIBRARIES

ABSTRACTS AND INDEXES

Library Literature and Information Science Index. H.W. Wilson Co. • Quarterly. Annual cumulation. Price varies.

ALMANACS AND YEARBOOKS

Advances in Library Administration and Organization. Delmus E. Williams and Janine Golden, editors. Emerald Group Publishing Ltd. • Annual. Price varies per volume. 31 volumes.

CD-ROM DATABASES

LISA Plus. Cambridge Scientific Abstracts L.P. • Quarterly. $2,000 per year. CD-ROM version of Library Information and Science Abstracts, providing abstracting and indexing of the world's library and information science literature, 1969 to date. Contains more than 180,000 citations.

WILSONDISC: Library Literature and Information Science Index. H.W. Wilson Co. • Quarterly. Includes unlimited access to the online version of *Library Literature.* Provides CD-ROM indexing of about 400 periodicals, covering a wide range of topics having to do with libraries, library management, and the information industry.

OTHER SOURCES

Legal Research and Law Library Management. ALM Media Properties LLC. • $565. Covers the planning and operation of libraries for law firms, including personnel selection and selection of books, periodicals, online services, microforms, and other materials. (Law Journal Press).

PERIODICALS AND NEWSLETTERS

The Bottom Line: Managing Library Finances. Emerald Group Publishing Inc., • Quarterly. $1,039.00 per year. Provides articles on the financial management of libraries: budgeting, funding, cost analysis, etc.

Collection Management: A Quarterly Journal Devoted to the Management of Library Collections. The Haworth Press Inc. • Quarterly. $235.00 per year.

Information Management Report: An International Newsletter for Information Professionals and Librarians. R.R. Bowker L.L.C. • Monthly. $505.00 per year; includes print and online editions. Incorporates *Outlook on Research Libraries.*

Information Outlook: The Monthly Magazine of the Special Libraries Association. Special Libraries Association. • Monthly. $65.00 per year. Topics include information technology, the Internet, copyright, research techniques, library management, and professional development. Replaces *Special Libraries* and *SpeciaList.*

MLS: Marketing Library Services. Information Today, Inc. • $99.95 6 issues/year. Description: Tells librarians and information professionals how to actively market their services to gain clients and to justify their existence. Discusses marketing, communication skills, fundraising, promotional events, publicity, and advocacy. Recurring features include how-to articles, case studies, news, a Customer-Based Marketing column, and book reviews.

The One-Person Library: A Newsletter for Librarians and Management. Information Bridges International Inc. • Monthly. $85.00 per year. Newsletter for librarians working alone or with minimal assistance. Contains reports on library literature, management advice, case studies, book reviews, and general information.

TRADE/PROFESSIONAL ASSOCIATIONS

Library Leadership and Management Association. 50 E Huron St., Chicago, IL 60611-2729. Phone: 800-545-2433; Fax: (312)280-2169; Email: llama@ala.org • URL: http://www.ala.org/llama/ • Affiliated with American Library Association. Formerly Library Administration Division of ALA.

LIBRARY RESEARCH

See also ONLINE INFORMATION SYSTEMS

BIBLIOGRAPHIES

American Reference Books Annual. Bohdan S. Wynar, editor. Libraries Unlimited. • Annual. $155 Individuals Hardcover. Provides librarians with insightful, critical reviews of all reference resources released in 2013 as well as some from 2012 and 2014.

Reference Books Bulletin: A Compilation of Evaluations. Mary Ellen Quinn, editor. Library and Information Technology Association. • *Booklist.*

DIRECTORIES

Directory of Special Libraries and Information Centers. Cengage Learning Inc. • Annual. $966 Individuals. 2010. 38th edition. eBook. Provides detailed contact and descriptive information on subject-specific resource collections maintained by government agencies, businesses, publishers, educational and nonprofit organizations, and associations worldwide.

Library Journal: Reference: Print, CD-ROM, Online (year). Reed Elsevier Group plc Reed Business Information. • Annual. Issued in November as a supplement to *Library Journal.* Lists new and updated reference material, including general and trade print titles, directories, annuals, CD-ROM titles, and online sources. Includes material from more than 200 publishers, arranged by company name, with an index by subject.

Library Journal Sourcebook: The Reference For Library Products & Services. Reed Elsevier Group plc Reed Business Information. • Annual. Publication includes: List of over 600 suppliers of products and services used by libraries from abstracting to word processing equipment. Entries include: Company name, address, phone, list of products or services. Complete listings for more than 100 architectural firms; Disaster planning for librarians.

PERIODICALS AND NEWSLETTERS

College and Research Libraries. Association of College and Research Libraries. • Bimonthly. $53 Nonmembers 1 year. Magazine reporting news, trends, and research of interest to academic library professionals.

Focus: On the Center for Research Libraries. Center for Research Libraries. • Bimonthly. Free. Newsletter. Provides news of Center activites.

The Information Advisor's Guide to Internet Research. Information Today, Inc. • 10/year. $199.95 U.S. One year subscription. Evaluates free and low-cost websites.

Internet Reference Services Quarterly: A Journal of Innovative Information Practice, Technologies, and Resources. The Haworth Press Inc. • Quarterly. $110.00 per year. Covers both theoretical research and practical applications.

Journal of Electronic Resources in Medical Libraries. The Haworth Press Inc. • Quarterly. $240.00 per year to libraries; $75.00 per year to individuals.

Reference and User Services Quarterly. Reference and User Services Association of the American Library Association. • Quarterly. $65 Nonmembers /year. In addition to articles, includes reviews of databases, reference books, and library professional material. Formerly *RQ.*

The Reference Librarian. The Haworth Press Inc. • Semiannual. Institutions. $325.00 per year. Two volumes.

Research Strategies: A Journal of Library Concepts and Instruction. Elsevier. • Quarterly. Individuals, $76.00 per year; institutions, $152.00 per year. Edited for librarians involved in bibliographic or library instruction.

LICENSE PLATES

See MOTOR VEHICLE LAW AND REGULATION

LICENSES

OTHER SOURCES

Broker-Dealer Regulation. David A. Lipton. Thomson West. • Semiannual. $114 per month. Focuses on the basics of stockbroker license application procedure, registration, regulation, and responsibilities. (Securities Law Series).

PERIODICALS AND NEWSLETTERS

The Licensing Letter (TLL). EPM Communications Inc. • Description: Concerned with all aspects of licensed merchandising, "the business of associating someone's name, likeness or creation with someone else&'s product or service, for a consideration." Recurring features include statistics, research, events, mechanics, available properties, and identification of licensors, licensing agents, and licensees.

TRADE/PROFESSIONAL ASSOCIATIONS

Council on Licensure, Enforcement and Regulation. 403 Marquis Ave., Ste. 200, Lexington, KY 40502. Phone: (859)269-1289; Fax: (859)231-1943; Email: clear@clearhq.org • URL: http://www.clearhq.org • Members are state government occupational and professional licensing officials. Formerly National Clearinghouse on Licensure, Enforcement and Regulation.

LICENSING AGREEMENTS

See also INTELLECTUAL PROPERTY

ABSTRACTS AND INDEXES

Current Law Index. Cengage Learning Inc. • $1,332 Individuals. Monthly. $1269.00 per year. Produced in cooperation with the American Association of Law Libraries. Indexes more than 900 law journals, legal newspapers, and specialty publications from the U.S., Canada, U.K., Ireland, Australia, and New Zealand.

Index to Legal Periodicals and Books. H.W. Wilson Co. • Monthly. $490.00 per year. Quarterly and annual cumulations.

NTIS Alerts: Government Inventions for Licensing. U.S. Department of Commerce National Technical Information Service. • Biweekly. $130 per year. Covers a wide variety of industrial and technical areas.

HANDBOOKS AND MANUALS

Antitrust-Intellectual Property Handbook. Alan J. Weinschel. Glasser LegalWorks. • Looseleaf. $175.00. Periodic supplementation. Covers patent licensing, patent antitrust issues, innovation markets, intervention by government agencies, standard-setting activities, royalty arrangements, and related intellectual property/antitrust topics. Provides explanations, legal guidance, and historical background.

INTERNET DATABASES

Lexis.com Research System. Lexis-Nexis Group. Phone: 800-227-4908 or (937)865-6800; Fax: (937)865-6909; Email: webmaster@prod.lexis-nexis.com • URL: http://www.nexis.com • Fee-based Web site offers extensive searching of a wide variety of legal sources. Additional features include Daily Opinion Service, lexis.com Bookstore, Career Center, CLE Center, Law Schools, and Practice Pages ("Pages specific to areas of specialty").

OTHER SOURCES

Investing, Licensing, and Trading. The Economist Intelligence Unit. • Semiannual. $345.00 per year for each country. Key laws, rules, and licensing provisions are explained for each of 60 countries. Information is provided on political conditions, markets, price policies, foreign exchange practices, labor, and export-import.

Licensing of Intellectual Property. ALM Media Properties LLC. • $680. Includes such licensing topics as royalties, infringement, antitrust, trade secrets, and patent agreements. Examples of licensing agreements and sample forms (on CD-ROM) are included. (Law Journal Press).

PERIODICALS AND NEWSLETTERS

Intellectual Property Today. • Monthly. $96.00 per year. Covers legal developments in copyright, patents, trademarks, and licensing. Emphasizes the effect of new technology on intellectual property. Formerly *Law Works.*

International New Product Newsletter. International New Product Newsletter. • Monthly. $25 per issue. Description: Provides "advance news of new products and processes, primarily from sources outside the U.S." Emphasizes new products which can cut costs and improve efficiency. Recurring features include the column Special Licensing Opportunities which lists new products and processes that are available for manufacture under license, or are for sale or import.

Les Nouvelles. Licensing Executives Society. • Quarterly. Description: Concerned with technological licensing and related subjects. Covers technology, patents, trademarks, and licensing "know-how" world-wide.

TRADE/PROFESSIONAL ASSOCIATIONS

Licensing Executives Society. 1800 Diagonal Rd., Ste. 280, Alexandria, VA 22314-2840. Email: info@les.org • URL: http://www.lesi.org • U.S. and foreign businessmen, scientists, engineers, and lawyers having direct responsibility for the transfer of technology. Maintains placement service.

LIFE INSURANCE

See also ACCIDENT INSURANCE; HEALTH INSURANCE

ABSTRACTS AND INDEXES

Insurance Periodicals Index. Specials Libraries Association, Insurance and Employees Benefits Div. NILS Publishing Co. • Annual. $250.00. Compiled by the Insurance and Employee Benefits Div., Special Libraries Association. A yearly index of over 15,000 articles from about 35 insurance periodicals. Arrangement is by subject, with an index to authors.

BIBLIOGRAPHIES

ACLI Life Insurers Fact Book. American Council of Life Insurance. • Annual. Free. Provides statistics and information on trends in the life insurance industry.

Insurance and Employee Benefits Literature. Special Libraries Association. • Bimonthly. $15.00 per year. Lists a wide variety of literature in all branches of the insurance industry. Includes annotations.

DIRECTORIES

Weiss Ratings Guide to Life and Annuity Insurers. Weiss Ratings, Inc. • Quarterly. Rates life insurance companies for overall safety and financial stability.

INTERNET DATABASES

Free Insurance Advice. InsWeb, Inc. 2868 Prospect Park Dr., Ste. 650, Rancho Cordova, CA 95670. Phone: (916)853-3300; Fax: (916)853-3300; Email: customercare@insweb.com • URL: http://www.insweb.com • Web site offers a wide variety of advice and information on automobile, life, health, and "other" insurance. Includes glossaries of insurance terms, Standard & Poor's ratings of individual insurance companies, and "Financial Needs Estimators." Searching is available. Fees: Free.

OTHER SOURCES

Best's Insurance Reports. A.M. Best Company Inc. • Annual. Covers life-health insurance covering about 1,750 companies, and property-casualty insurance covering over 3,200 companies. Includes subscription to both *Best's Review* and *Best's Insurance Management Reports*.

Life, Health, and Accident Insurance Law Reports. Wolters Kluwer Law & Business CCH. • $835.00 per year. Looseleaf service. Monthly updates.

PERIODICALS AND NEWSLETTERS

Broker World. Insurance Publications Inc. • Bimonthly. $6.00 per year. Edited for independent insurance agents and brokers. Special feature issue topics include annuities, disability insurance, estate planning, and life insurance.

Contingencies: The Magazine of the Actuarial Profession. American Academy of Actuaries. • Bimonthly. $24 Nonmembers. Provides non-technical articles on the actuarial aspects of insurance, employee benefits, and pensions.

GAMA International Journal. GAMA International. • Bimonthly. $30 for members (in addition to annual dues). Contains practical articles on the management of life insurance agencies.

Guide to Life, Health, and Annuity Insurers: A Quarterly Compilation of Insurance Company Ratings and Analysis. Weiss Research Inc. • Quarterly. $499. Emphasis is on rating of financial safety and relative risk. Includes annual summary.

Insurance and Technology. UBM L.L.C. • Monthly. $65.00 per year. Covers information technology and systems management as applied to the operation of life, health, casualty, and property insurance companies.

Insurance Forum: For the Unfettered Exchange of Ideas About Insurance. Joseph M. Belth, editor. Insurance Forum Inc. • Monthly. $90.00 per year. Newsletter. Provides analysis of the insurance business, including occasional special issues showing the ratings of about 1,600 life-health insurance companies, as determined by four major rating services: Duff & Phelps Credit Rating Co., Moody's Investors Service, Standard & Poor's Corp., and Weiss Research, Inc.

Insurance Marketing: The Ins and Outs of Recruiting and Retaining More Agents. Agent Media Corp. • Bimonthly. Controlled circulation. Provides practical advice for insurance companies on how to hire and keep sales personnel.

National Underwriter. • Weekly. Two editions: *Life* or *Health*. $86.00 per year, each edition.

Resource: LOMA's Magazine for Insurance and Financial Services Management. LOMA. • Monthly. $75 Nonmembers. Contains news and information about industry operations and management.

Safe Money Report. Weiss Research Inc. • Monthly. $99.00 per year. Newsletter. Provides financial advice and current safety ratings of various banks, savings and loan companies, insurance companies, and securities dealers.

RESEARCH CENTERS AND INSTITUTES

University of Pennsylvania - S.S. Huebner Foundation. 3000 Steinberg Hall-Dietrich Hall, 3620 Locust Walk, Philadelphia, PA 19104-6302. Phone: (215)898-9631; Fax: (215)573-2218; Email: huebner_foundation@wharton.upenn.edu • URL: http://www.huebnergeneva.org/huebner • Awards grants for research in various areas of insurance.

STATISTICS SOURCES

Standard & Poor's Industry Surveys. Standard & Poor's Financial Services L.L.C. • Semiannual. $1,800.00. Two looseleaf volumes. Includes monthly *Supplements*. Provides detailed, individual surveys of 52 major industry groups. Each survey is revised on a semiannual basis. Also includes "Monthly Investment Review" (industry group investment analysis) and monthly "Trends & Projections" (economic analysis).

Statistical Information on the Financial Services Industry. American Bankers Association. • Annual. Members, $150.00; non-members, $275.00. Presents a wide variety of data relating to banking and financial services, including consumer economics, personal finance, credit, government loans, capital markets, and international banking.

U.S. Industry and Trade Outlook. U.S. Department of Commerce National Technical Information Service. • Annual. Produced by the International Trade Administration, U.S. Department of Commerce, in a "public-private" partnership with DRI/McGraw-Hill and Standard & Poor's. Provides basic data, outlook for the current year, and "Long-Term Prospects" (five-year projections) for a wide variety of products and services. Includes high technology industries. Formerly *U.S. Industrial Outlook*.

TRADE/PROFESSIONAL ASSOCIATIONS

American Council of Life Insurers. 101 Constitution Ave. NW, Ste. 700, Washington, DC 20001-2133. Phone: 877-674-4659 or (202)624-2000 or (202)624-2424; Email: webadmin@acli.com • URL: http://www.acli.com • Represents the interests of legal reserve life insurance companies in legislative, regulatory and judicial matters at the federal, state and municipal levels of government and at the NAIC. Member companies hold majority of the life insurance in force in the United States.

Association of Life Insurance Counsel. 14350 Mundy Dr., Ste. 800, No. 258, Noblesville, IN 46060. Phone: (317)774-7500; Fax: (317)614-7147 • URL: http://www.alic.cc • Members are attorneys for life insurance companies.

LIMRA International. 300 Day Hill Rd., Windsor, CT 06095. Phone: 800-235-4672 or (860)285-7789; Fax: (860)285-7792; Email: customer.service@limra.com • URL: http://www.limra.com • Life insurance and financial services companies. Conducts market, consumer, economic, financial, and human resources research; monitors industry distribution systems and product and service developments. Provides executive and field management development schools and seminars. Offers human resource development consulting services, including needs analysis and program design, evaluation, and implementation.

LOMA. 2300 Windy Ridge Pkwy., Ste. 600, Atlanta, GA 30339-8443. Phone: (770)951-1770 or (770)984-3720; Fax: (770)984-6422; Email: askloma@loma.org • URL: http://www.loma.org • Life and health insurance companies and financial services in the U.S. and Canada; and overseas in 45 countries; affiliate members are firms that provide professional support to member companies. Provides research, information, training, and educational activities in areas of operations and systems, human resources, financial planning and employee development. Administers FLMI Insurance Education Program, which awards FLMI (Fellow, Life Management Institute) designation to those who complete the ten-examination program.

National Association of Insurance and Financial Advisors. 2901 Telestar Ct., Falls Church, VA 22042-1205. Phone: 877-866-2432; Email: membersupport@naifa.org • URL: http://www.naifa.org • Affiliated with Association for Advanced Life Underwriting. Formerly National Association of Life Underwriters.

National Association of Professional Insurance Agents. 400 N Washington St., Alexandria, VA 22314. Phone: (703)836-9340; Fax: (703)836-1279; Email: web@pianet.org • URL: http://www.pianet.com • Members are independent agents in various fields of insurance. Formerly National Association of Mutual Insurance Agents.

Society of Financial Service Professionals. 19 Campus Blvd., Ste. 100, Newtown Square, PA 19073-3239. Phone: 800-392-6900 or (610)526-2500; Fax: (610)527-1499; Email: info@financialpro.org • URL: http://www.financialpro.org • Represents the interests of financial advisers. Fosters the development of professional responsibility. Assists clients to achieve personal and business-related financial goals. Offers educational programs, online professional resources and networking opportunities.

LIFT TRUCKS

See MATERIALS HANDLING

LIGHTING

DIRECTORIES

Directory of American Manufacturers & Exporters of Lighting Fixtures, Lamps & Accessories. EXIM

Infotek Private Ltd. • $25 Individuals. Covers: 320 American manufacturers and exporters of architectural lighting/dimming equipment, ballasts and fixture lamps, black light lamps, emergency lighting equipment, fixtures, fixtures-lamps, flash lamps, flashlights, floor lamps, fluorescent fixtures and supplies, fluorescent lamp ballasts, fluorescent lighting fixtures, fluorescent tubes, fuel lamps, H.I.D. lamps, halogen lamps, hand lamps, high intensity lamps, incandescent lamps, indoor/outdoor lighting equipment, lamp parts, lamp shades, lamp sockets, lamps, lamps-electric, lamps-fluorescent, lamps-germicidal, light bulbs, lights for nightclubs and discotheques, lighting control equipment for theatrical, lighting equipment and supplies, lighting fixture glassware, lighting fixtures, lighting systems, low voltage lighting, portable lamps, searchlights, solar lighting, solar rail and bus waiting station lights, solar-electric lighting, store display fixtures, table lamps. Entries include: Company name, postal address, city, country, telephone, fax, e-mail and websites, contact person, designation, and product details.

Directory of Chinese Manufacturers & Exporters of Candles & Candle Products. EXIM Infotek Private Ltd. • $5 Individuals. Covers: 35 Chinese manufacturers and exporters of candle holders, candle lamps, candles, craft candles. Entries include: Company name, postal address, city, country, phone, fax, e-mail and websites, contact person, designation, and product details.

Directory of Chinese Manufacturers & Exporters of Lighting Fixtures, Lamps & Accessories. EXIM Infotek Private Ltd. • $20 Individuals. Covers: 190 Chinese manufacturers and exporters of bulbs, ceramic lamps, Christmas lights, compact fluorescent lamps, decorative lights, electric bulbs, electric lamps, electric lighting, emergency lighting, energy saving lamps, energy saving tubes, flashlights, floodlights, floor lamps, fluorescent lamps, garden lamps, glass lighting products, halogen lamps, lampholders, lamps, lanterns, lighting, lighting appliances, lighting electric appliances, lighting equipment, lighting fixtures, lighting products, metal halide lamps and ballast, neon lamps, rope lights, solar lights, solar powered lights, solar warning lights, spotlights, table lamps, and tungsten lamps. Entries include: Company name, postal address, city, country, phone, fax, e-mail and websites, contact person, designation, and product details.

Directory of Japanese Manufacturers & Exporters of Lighting Fixtures, Lamps & Accessories. EXIM Infotek Private Ltd. • $5 Individuals. Covers: 30 Japanese manufacturers and exporters of fog lamps, halogen lamps, incandescent lamps, lamps, lighting fixtures-glass, lighting fixtures, lighting fixtures and parts, mercury lamps. Entries include: Company name, postal address, city, country, phone, fax, e-mail and websites, contact person, designation, and product details.

Directory of South Korean Manufacturers & Exporters of Lighting Fixtures, Lamps & Accessories. EXIM Infotek Private Ltd. • $10 Individuals. Covers: 90 South Korean manufacturers & exporters of aluminum flashlights, bulbs-halogen, discharge & special purpose lamps, electric lamp components, filament lamps-all types, fluorescent lamps, halogen lamps, indoor electric lighting equipment, lamp accessories & parts, lamp-combination, lamps, lamp various, lighting appliances-non electric, lighting equipment-outdoor, matches, pilot lamps, portable electric lamps & accessories, sub-miniature lamps. Entries include: Company name, postal address, city, country, phone, fax, e-mail & websites, contact person, designation, products detail.

Directory of Taiwanese Manufacturers & Exporters of Lighting Fixtures, Lamps & Accessories. EXIM Infotek Private Ltd. • $30 Individuals. Covers: 450 Taiwanese manufacturers and exporters of bulbs, decoration bulbs, discharge and special purpose lamps, electric lamp components, filament lamps-all types, flash light, fluorescent lamps, fog lamps, halogen lamps, indoor electric lighting equipment, laser lights, lighting equipment-outdoor, miniature lamps, portable electric lamps and accessories, and turning lamps. Entries include: Company name, postal address, city, country, phone, fax, e-mail and websites, contact person, designation, and product details.

Home Lighting and Accessories Suppliers Directory. Doctorow Publishing. • Semiannual. $6.00 per issue. Lists almost 1,000 suppliers of residential lighting fixtures and accessories.

The International Directory of Importers - Lighting Equipment, Lamps and Accessories Importers. Interdata. • Annual. $220 Individuals print. Covers: 2,500 international firms importing lighting equipment, lamps and accessories. Entries include: Company name and address, contact person, email, number of employees, year established, phone and telefaxes, business activity, bank references, as well as a listing of lighting equipment, lamps and accessories currently being imported.

L D A: Lighting Equipment Accessories Directory. Illuminating Engineering Society of North America. • Annual. $48 U.S. /year. Lists over 800 manufacturers of lighting fixtures, controls, components, mounting devices, maintenance equipment, etc.

FINANCIAL RATIOS

Annual Statement Studies. Risk Management Association. • Annual. Compiled from over 280,000 financial statements.

Annual Statement Studies: Industry Default Probabilities and Cash Flow Measures. Risk Management Association. • Annual. $405 Nonmembers. Serves as a companion volume to the original *Annual Statement Studies.* Gives probability of default estimates on a percentage scale for more than 450 industries. Includes changes in position year-by-year for eight financial statement line items and provides percentage measures of cash flow.

INTERNET DATABASES

Manufacturing Profiles. U. S. Bureau of the Census. Phone: (301)763-4636 or (301)763-4100; Fax: (301)763-4794; Email: webmaster@census.gov • URL: http://www.census.gov/prod/www/abs/mfg-prof.html • The Census Bureau makes available free on PDF (Portable Document Format) an annual consolidation of the entire Current Industrial Report series, presenting "all the data compiled." Contains statistics on production, shipments, inventories, consumption, exports, imports, and orders for a wide variety of manufactured products.

ONLINE DATABASES

Lighting Businesses in the World. Momentum Technologies L.L.C. • Contains directory listings for hundreds of lighting businesses and related companies in operation throughout the world. Includes business name, address, phone number, fax number, e-mail address, and web site address. Provides brief descriptions of product lines, services offered, and business type. Includes information on manufacturers, component makers, wholesalers, retailers, system designers, system installers, architectural services, trade associations, and more. Covers businesses involved in fluorescent lighting, LED lighting, natural daylighting, tubular skylights, energy efficient lighting, and more. Provides keyword search functions.

PERIODICALS AND NEWSLETTERS

Home Lighting and Accessories. Doctorow Communications, Inc. • Monthly. Trade magazine of the residential lighting industry for retailers, distributors, designers, architects, specifiers, manufacturers and all lighting professionals.

IEEE Industry Applications Magazine. IEEE - Communications Society. • Bimonthly. Covers new industrial applications of power conversion, drives, lighting, and control. Emphasis is on the petroleum, chemical, rubber, plastics, textile, and mining industries.

National Home Center News: News and Analysis for the Home Improvement, Building Material Industry. Lebhar-Friedman Inc. • 22 times a year. $99.00 per year. Includes special feature issues on hardware and tools, building materials, millwork, electrical supplies, lighting, and kitchens.

STATISTICS SOURCES

U.S. Industry and Trade Outlook. U.S. Department of Commerce National Technical Information Service. • Annual. Produced by the International Trade Administration, U.S. Department of Commerce, in a "public-private" partnership with DRI/McGraw-Hill and Standard & Poor's. Provides basic data, outlook for the current year, and "Long-Term Prospects" (five-year projections) for a wide variety of products and services. Includes high technology industries. Formerly *U.S. Industrial Outlook.*

TRADE/PROFESSIONAL ASSOCIATIONS

American Lighting Association. 2050 N Stemmons Fwy., Unit 100, Dallas, TX 75207-3206. Phone: 800-605-4448 or (214)698-9898; Fax: (214)698-9899; Email: skelley@americanlightingassoc.com • URL: http://www.americanlightingassoc.com • Manufacturers, manufacturers' representatives, distributors, and retailers of residential lighting fixtures, portable lamps, component parts, accessories, and bulbs. Trains and certifies lighting consultants; conducts showroom sales seminars; disseminates marketing and merchandising information. Compiles statistics.

Professional Lighting and Sign Management Companies of America. 1100-H Brandywine Blvd., Zanesville, OH 43701-7303. Phone: (740)452-4541 • URL: http://plasmalighting.org • Represents independently owned service providers offering lighting and signage services, workmanship and expertise. Seeks to uphold the standards of practice within the lighting and sign management industry. Promotes and protects the interests of members.

LIMESTONE INDUSTRY

See also QUARRYING

FINANCIAL RATIOS

Annual Statement Studies. Risk Management Association. • Annual. Compiled from over 280,000 financial statements.

Annual Statement Studies: Industry Default Probabilities and Cash Flow Measures. Risk Management Association. • Annual. $405 Nonmembers. Serves as a companion volume to the original *Annual Statement Studies.* Gives probability of default estimates on a percentage scale for more than 450 industries. Includes changes in position year-by-year for eight financial statement line items and provides percentage measures of cash flow.

PERIODICALS AND NEWSLETTERS

Building Stone Magazine. Building Stone Institute. • Quarterly. $20 Individuals /year. Information on the natural stone industry.

TRADE/PROFESSIONAL ASSOCIATIONS

National Stone, Sand and Gravel Association. 1605 King St., Alexandria, VA 22314-2726. Phone: 800-342-1415 or (703)525-8788 or (703)526-1098; Fax: (703)525-7782; Email: info@nssga.org • URL: http://www.nssga.org • Formerly National Stone Association.

LIMITED PARTNERSHIPS

See PARTNERSHIP

LINEAR PROGRAMMING

ONLINE DATABASES

INSPEC. Institution of Electrical Engineers. • Provides online citations, with abstracts, to the world literature of electrical engineering, electronics, optoelectronics, telecommunications, industrial controls, instrumentation, computer technology, information technology, and physics. Coverage includes more than 4,000 technical and scientific journals from 1969 to date, with weekly updating. (INSPEC is Information Services in Physics, Electronics, and Computing.) Inquire as to online cost and availability.

LINEN INDUSTRY

ABSTRACTS AND INDEXES

Textile Technology Index™. EBSCO Publishing Inc. • Monthly. $545 Individuals. Includes indexing and abstracts for more than 470 periodicals.

INTERNET DATABASES

Manufacturing Profiles. U. S. Bureau of the Census. Phone: (301)763-4636 or (301)763-4100; Fax: (301)763-4794; Email: webmaster@census.gov • URL: http://www.census.gov/prod/www/abs/mfg-prof.html • The Census Bureau makes available free on PDF (Portable Document Format) an annual consolidation of the entire Current Industrial Report series, presenting "all the data compiled." Contains statistics on production, shipments, inventories, consumption, exports, imports, and orders for a wide variety of manufactured products.

ONLINE DATABASES

Textile Technology Index™. EBSCO Publishing Inc. • Monthly. $545 Individuals. Includes indexing and abstracts for more than 470 periodicals.

World Textiles. Elsevier. • Provides abstracting and indexing from 1970 of worldwide textile literature (periodicals, books, pamphlets, and reports). Includes U. S., European, and British patent information. Updating is monthly. Inquire as to online cost and availability.

LINGERIE INDUSTRY

See UNDERWEAR INDUSTRY

LIQUEFIED PETROLEUM GAS

See PROPANE AND BUTANE GAS INDUSTRY

LIQUOR INDUSTRY

See DISTILLING INDUSTRY

LIQUOR LAW AND REGULATION

ABSTRACTS AND INDEXES

Current Law Index. Cengage Learning Inc. • $1,332 Individuals. Monthly. $1269.00 per year. Produced in cooperation with the American Association of Law Libraries. Indexes more than 900 law journals, legal newspapers, and specialty publications from the U.S., Canada, U.K., Ireland, Australia, and New Zealand.

Index to Legal Periodicals and Books. H.W. Wilson Co. • Monthly. $490.00 per year. Quarterly and annual cumulations.

ALMANACS AND YEARBOOKS

American Law Yearbook. Cengage Learning Inc. • $308 Individuals. Annual. $280.00. Serves as a yearly supplement to *West's Encyclopedia of American Lawa*. Describes new legal developments in many subject areas.

CD-ROM DATABASES

Index to Legal Periodicals and Books. EBSCO Publishing Inc. • Contains indexing of more than 1,400 English language legal periodicals from 1981 to date and 2,500 books.

ENCYCLOPEDIAS AND DICTIONARIES

West's Encyclopedia of American Law. Cengage Learning Inc. • 2004. eBook. Second edition. Covers a wide variety of legal topics for the general reader. Inquire for pricing.

INTERNET DATABASES

Lexis.com Research System. Lexis-Nexis Group. Phone: 800-227-4908 or (937)865-6800; Fax: (937)865-6909; Email: webmaster@prod.lexis-nexis.com • URL: http://www.nexis.com • Fee-based Web site offers extensive searching of a wide variety of legal sources. Additional features include Daily Opinion Service, lexis.com Bookstore, Career Center, CLE Center, Law Schools, and Practice Pages ("Pages specific to areas of specialty").

OTHER SOURCES

Liquor Control Law Reporter. Wolters Kluwer Law & Business CCH. • Biweekly. Federal and state regulation and taxation of alcoholic beverages.

PERIODICALS AND NEWSLETTERS

Alcoholic Beverage Control: State Capitals. Wakeman/Walworth Inc. • 50 times a year. $245.00 per year; print and online editions, $350.00 per year. Formerly *From the State Capitals: Alcoholic Beverage Control*.

STATISTICS SOURCES

Statistical Reports. National Alcohol Beverage Control Association. • Monthly. Price on application. Includes quarterly and annual cumulations.

Uniform Crime Reports for the United States. Federal Bureau of Investigation, U.S. Department of Justice. U. S. Government Printing Office. • Annual. $45.

TRADE/PROFESSIONAL ASSOCIATIONS

National Alcohol Beverage Control Association. 4401 Ford Ave., Ste. 700, Alexandria, VA 22302-1433. Phone: (703)578-4200; Fax: (703)820-3551; Email: nabca.info@nabca.org • URL: http://www.nabca.org • Formerly Joint Committee of the States to study Alcoholic Beverage Laws.

National Conference of State Liquor Administrators. 543 Long Hill Rd., Gurnee, IL 60031. Phone: (847)721-6410 • URL: http://www.ncsla.org • State agencies administering liquor control laws and collecting beverage taxes under a license system rather than a state-controlled monopoly stores system.

LIQUOR STORES

FINANCIAL RATIOS

Annual Statement Studies. Risk Management Association. • Annual. Compiled from over 280,000 financial statements.

Annual Statement Studies: Industry Default Probabilities and Cash Flow Measures. Risk Management Association. • Annual. $405 Nonmembers. Serves as a companion volume to the original *Annual Statement Studies*. Gives probability of default estimates on a percentage scale for more than 450 industries. Includes changes in position year-by-year for eight financial statement line items and provides percentage measures of cash flow.

INTERNET DATABASES

Advance Monthly Retail Trade Report. U. S. Census Bureau. Phone: 800-541-8345 or (301)457-4100 or (301)763-2713; Fax: (301)457-1296 or (301)457-3842; Email: naics@census.gov • URL: http://www.census.gov/epcd/www/naicstab.htm • Web pages provide monthly sales figures for a wide range of retail businesses. Advance, preliminary, and final statistics are provided for the latest month available in each case, with a previous-year comparison. Updates are monthly.

PRICE SOURCES

Beverage Media. Beverage Network. Beverage Media Group. • Monthly. $78 Individuals. Wholesale prices.

STATISTICS SOURCES

Annual Benchmark Report for Retail Trade and Food Services..A Detailed Summary of Retail Sales, Purchases, Accounts Receivable, Inventories, and Food Service Sales. U. S. Government Printing Office. • Annual. $13.00. Issued by the U.S. Census Bureau. Provides detailed annual and monthly retail statistics for the most recent 10 years. Includes data for various kinds of retail outlets, including automobiles, furniture, appliances, building supplies, grocery stores, drug stores, gasoline stations, clothing, sporting goods, department stores, and restaurants.

TRADE/PROFESSIONAL ASSOCIATIONS

American Beverage Licensees. 5101 River Rd., Ste. 108, Bethesda, MD 20816-1560. Phone: (301)656-1494; Fax: (301)656-7539; Email: info@ablusa.org • URL: http://www.ablusa.org • Federation of associations of alcohol beverage retailers.

LITERARY AGENTS

See WRITERS AND WRITING

LITERARY PROPERTY

See COPYRIGHT

LITERATURE SEARCHING, ONLINE

See ONLINE INFORMATION SYSTEMS

LITHOGRAPHY

See also GRAPHIC ARTS INDUSTRY; PRINTING AND PRINTING EQUIPMENT INDUSTRIES

FINANCIAL RATIOS

Printing Industries of America Ratios. Printing Industries of America - Center for Technology and Research. • Annual. $750 Members Full Set (volume 1-16). Annual financial benchmarking study.

TRADE/PROFESSIONAL ASSOCIATIONS

National Association for Printing Leadership. 1 Meadowlands Plz., Ste. 1511, East Rutherford, NJ 07073. Phone: 800-642-6275 or (201)634-9600; Fax: (201)634-0324 or (201)986-2976; Email: jtruncale@napl.org • URL: http://www.napl.org • Text: Formerly National Association of Printers and Lithographers.

LIVESTOCK INDUSTRY

See also CATTLE INDUSTRY; MEAT INDUSTRY; SWINE INDUSTRY

ABSTRACTS AND INDEXES

Animal Breeding Abstracts: A Monthly Abstract of World Literature. CABI Publishing North America. • Monthly. $1,305.

Index Veterinarius: Comprehensive Monthly Subject and Author Index to the World's Veterinary Literature. Availabe in Print and on the Internet. CABI Publishing North America. • Monthly. Institutions, $1,660.00 per year. Annual cumulation. Includes single site internet access. Published in England by CABI Publishing. Provides worldwide coverage of the literature.

Nutrition Abstracts and Reviews, Series B: Livestock Feeds and Feeding. CABI Publishing North America. • Monthly. Institutions, $1,180.00 per year. Online edition available, $1,215.00 per year. Published in England by CABI Publishing. Provides worldwide coverage of the literature.

CD-ROM DATABASES

OECD Statistical Compendium. Organization for Economic Cooperation and Development. • Semiannual. $1,905.00 per year for 1 to 10 users. CD-ROM contains more than 730,000 monthly, quarterly, and annual time series for OECD countries, 1960 to date. Includes fully searchable data on agriculture, food, economic indicators, national accounts, employment, energy, finance, industry, technology, and foreign trade. Results can be displayed in various forms.

DIRECTORIES

Directory of African Importers of Fodder and Animal Foodstuffs. EXIM Infotek Private Ltd. • $250 Individuals. Covers: 70 African importers of animal foodstuff additives, animal foodstuff, feed additives, fodder, cereals, livestock breeding supplies, and oats. Entries include: Company name, postal address, telephone, fax, e-mail, website, contact person, designation, and product details.

Directory of Asian Importers of Fodder and Animal Foodstuffs. EXIM Infotek Private Ltd. • $450 Individuals. Covers: 210 Asian importers of alfalfa, alfalfa hay cubes, animal and foodstuff aditives, animal feeds, feed additives, animal food, cottonseed meal, feeder calves, fodder, cereals, and livestock breeding supplies, livestock products, and whey. Entries include: Company name, postal address, telephone, fax, e-mail, website, contact person, designation, and product details.

Directory of European Importers of Fodder & Animal Foodstuffs. EXIM Infotek Private Ltd. • $20 Individuals. Covers: 270 European importers of animal food meals, animal foodstuff additives, feed additives, fodder, livestock breeding supplies, and oats. Entries include: Company name, postal address, telephone, fax, e-mail, website, contact person, designation, and product details.

Directory of Japanese Importers of Fodder and Animal Foodstuffs. EXIM Infotek Private Ltd. • $200 Individuals. Covers: Japanese importers of animal foodstuff, food additives, feeder calves, fodder, cereals, and livestock products. Entries include: Company name, postal address, telephone, fax, e-mail, website, contact person, designation, and product details.

Directory of Middle East Importers of Fodder and Animal Foodstuffs. EXIM Infotek Private Ltd. • $400 Individuals. Covers: 170 Middle East importers of animal and poultry fodder, animal feeds, animal feed additives, animal feed ingredients, animal food, animal foodstuff additives, fodder, cereals, and livestock breeding supplies. Entries include: Company name, postal address, telephone, fax, e-mail, website, contact person, designation, and product details.

Directory of North American Importers of Fodder and Animal Foodstuffs. EXIM Infotek Private Ltd. • $150 Individuals. Covers: 40 North American importers of animal feed, animal food, animal foodstuff additives, animal foodstuff, feed additives, fodder, cereals, and livestock breeding supplies. Entries include: Company name, postal address, telephone, fax, e-mail, website, contact person, designation, and product details.

Directory of South American Importers of Fodder and Animal Foodstuffs. EXIM Infotek Private Ltd. • $300 Individuals. Covers: 140 South American importers of animal food, animal foodstuff additives, fodder, livestock breeding supplies, oats, and sorghum. Entries include: Company name, postal address, telephone, fax, e-mail, website, contact person, designation, and product details.

Milk Producers Directory. InfoGroup Inc. • Annual. Number of listings: 1,964. Entries include: Name, address, phone, size of advertisement, name of owner or manager, number of employees, year first in "Yellow Pages." Compiled from telephone company "Yellow Pages," nationwide.

INTERNET DATABASES

BEEF. National Cattlemen's Beef Association. Phone: (303)694-0305; Fax: (303)694-2851; Email: cows@beef.org • URL: http://www.beef.org • Web site provides detailed information from the "Cattle and Beef Handbook," including "Beef Economics" (production, sales, consumption, retail value, foreign competition, etc.). Text of monthly newsletter is also available: "The Beef Brief-Issues & Trends in the Cattle Industry." Keyword searching is offered. Fees: Free.

Business 2.0 Web Guide to the Best Business Links. Business 2.0 Media Inc. Phone: (415)293-4800; Email: support@business2.com • URL: http://www.business2.com/webguide • Web site presents an extensive, searchable directory of links to "the best, most informative, and authoritative web pages." Twenty main categories cover business, finance, career, company information, people, and technology topics, with thousands of subtopics, all linking to Web sites recommended by experienced business researchers. Fees: Free.

Fedstats. Federal Interagency Council on Statistical Policy. Phone: (202)395-7254 • URL: http://www.fedstats.gov • Web site features an efficient search facility for full-text statistics produced by more than 100 federal agencies, including the Census Bureau, the Bureau of Economic Analysis, and the Bureau of Labor Statistics. Boolean searches can be made within one agency or for all agencies combined. Links are offered to international statistical bureaus, including the UN, IMF, OECD, UNESCO, Eurostat, and 20 individual countries. Fees: Free.

FreeLunch.com. Economy.com, Inc. Phone: (610)696-8700; Fax: (610)696-1678 • URL: http://www.freelunch.com • Web site provides free access to more than 200 million economic and financial data series, covering industry, demographics, labor markets, prices, retail sales, government spending, trade, interest rates, housing starts, the stock market, etc. Data is available in either chart or table form. Searching is offered. Free, but registration required. Economy.com, Inc. also offers fee-based economic analysis at *The Dismal Scientist* site (www.dismal.com).

USDA. U.S. National Institute of Standards and Technology. 100 Bureau Dr., Gaithersburg, MD 20899-1070. Phone: 800-877-8339 or (301)975-6478 or (202)720-2791; Fax: (301)975-8295; Email: inquiries@nist.gov • URL: http://www.nist.gov • The USDA home page has six sections: News and Information; What's New; About USDA; Agencies; Opportunities; Search and Help. Keyword searching is offered from the USDA home page and from various individual agency home pages. Agencies are the Economic Research Service, Agricultural Marketing Service, National Agricultural Statistics Service, National Agricultural Library, and about 12 others. Updating varies. Fees: Free.

ONLINE DATABASES

CAB Abstracts. CABI. • Contains 46 specialized abstract collections covering over 10,000 journals and monographs in the areas of agriculture, horticulture, forest products, farm products, nutrition, dairy science, poultry, grains, animal health, entomology, etc. Time period is 1972 to date, with monthly updates. Inquire as to online cost and availability. *CAB Abstracts on CD-ROM* also available, with annual updating.

PERIODICALS AND NEWSLETTERS

Hog Farm Management: Journal of the Nation's Pork Business. Miller Publishing Co. • Monthly. Magazine serving hog producers.

Journal of Animal Science. American Society of Animal Science. • Monthly. $135 Members U.S. online. Professional journal covering animal science.

Pork: The Business Magazine for Professional Pork Producers. Vance Publishing Corp. • Monthly. $50 Individuals. Magazine on pork production and marketing.

PRICE SOURCES

The National Provisioner: Serving Meat, Poultry, and Seafood Processors. BNP Media. • Monthly. $85.04 Individuals. *Buyer's Guide* available. Meat, poultry and seafood newsletter.

STATISTICS SOURCES

Agricultural Statistics. U.S. Department of Agriculture National Agricultural Statistics Service. • Annual. $46 Individuals. Provides a wide variety of statistical data relating to agricultural production, supplies, consumption, prices/price-supports, foreign trade, costs, and returns, as well as farm labor, loans, income, and population. In many cases, historical data is shown annually for 10 years. In addition to farm data, includes detailed fishery statistics.

Survey of Current Business. U. S. Government Printing Office. • Published by Bureau of Economic Analysis, U. S. Department of Commerce. Presents a wide variety of business and economic data.

TRADE/PROFESSIONAL ASSOCIATIONS

American Society of Animal Science. PO Box 7410, Champaign, IL 61826-7410. Phone: (217)356-9050 or (212)621-4623; Email: asas@asas.org • URL: http://www.asas.org • Professional organization for animal scientist designed to help members provide effective leadership through research, extension, teaching, and service for the animal industries.

Fullblood Simmental Fleckvieh Federation. PO Box 321, Cisco, TX 76437. Phone: 855-353-2584; Fax: (855)638-2582; Email: info@fleckvieh.com • URL: http://www.fleckvieh.com • Aims to develop and promote Fullblood Simmental and Fullblood Fleckvieh cattle. Seeks to educate beef producers on the economic traits of Fullblood Simmental and Fullblood Fleckvieh cattle. Strives to promote the use of Fullblood Simmental and Fullblood Fleckvieh beef cattle genetics and to preserve and market the breeds in North America and worldwide to both purebred and commercial beef producers.

Livestock Marketing Association. 10510 NW Ambassador Dr., Kansas City, MO 64153. Phone: 800-821-2048 • URL: http://www.lmaweb.com • Livestock marketing businesses and livestock dealers. Sponsors annual World Livestock Auctioneer Championships. Offers management and promotional services.

National Cattlemen's Beef Association. 9110 E Nichols Ave., Ste. 300, Centennial, CO 80112. Phone: (303)694-0305; Fax: (303)694-2851; Email: information@beef.org • URL: http://www.beefusa.org • Represents 149 organizations of livestock marketers, growers, meat packers, food retailers, and food service firms. Conducts extensive program of promotion, education and information about beef, veal, and associated meat products. Conducts projects such as recipe testing and development, food demonstrations, food photography, educational service to colleges, experimental meat cutting methods, merchandising programs, and preparation of materials for newspapers, magazines, radio, and television.

LOANS, BANK

See BANK LOANS

LOANS, COMMERCIAL

See COMMERCIAL LENDING

LOANS, STUDENT

See SCHOLARSHIPS AND STUDENT AID

LOBBYING

See PRESSURE GROUPS

LOBSTER INDUSTRY

See also SHELLFISH INDUSTRY

ABSTRACTS AND INDEXES

Oceanic Abstracts. CSA. • Monthly. $1,645.00 per year. Includes print and online editions. Covers oceanography, marine biology, ocean shipping, and a wide range of other marine-related subject areas.

PERIODICALS AND NEWSLETTERS

Commercial Fisheries News. Compass Publications, Fisheries Division. • Monthly. $21.95 print only. Covers the commercial fishing industry in New England. Includes news of marine technology, boatbuilding, fish and lobster prices, business trends, government regulation, and other topics.

Seafood Business. Diversified Business Communications Inc. • $57 U.S.. Edited for a wide range of seafood buyers, including distributors, restaurants, supermarkets, and institutions. Special issues feature information on specific products, such as salmon or lobster.

TRADE/PROFESSIONAL ASSOCIATIONS

Maine Lobstermen's Association. 203 Lafayette Ctr., Kennebunk, ME 04043. Phone: (207)967-4555; Fax: (866)407-3770; Email: info@mainelobstermen.org • URL: http://www.mainelobstermen.org • Licensed lobstermen and supporting business. Gives Maine's lobstermen a voice and influence at the highest levels of government.

LOCAL AREA NETWORKS

See also COMPUTER COMMUNICATIONS; MICROCOMPUTERS AND MINICOMPUTERS

ABSTRACTS AND INDEXES

Business Periodicals Index Retrospective. EBSCO Publishing Inc. • 11/year. Quarterly and annual cumulations.

Computer and Information Systems Abstracts Journal: An Abstract Journal Pertaining to the Theory, Design, Fabrication and Application of Computer and Information Systems. CSA. • Monthly. $1,750 per year.

Computer Science Index. EBSCO Publishing Inc. • Quarterly. $245 per year. Contains brief abstracts of book and periodical literature covering all phases of computing, including approximately 70 specific application areas.

Inspec Direct. Institution of Engineering and Technology. • Monthly. $2,400 per year. Section C of *Science Abstracts.*

Key Abstracts: Computer Communications and Storage. Institution of Engineering and Technology. • Monthly. $1,138. Provides international coverage of journal and proceedings literature, including material on optical disks and networks.

CD-ROM DATABASES

Datapro on CD-ROM: Communications Analyst. Gartner Inc. • Monthly. Price on application. Provides detailed information on products and services for communications systems, including local area networks and voice systems.

ONLINE DATABASES

Wilson Business Abstracts Online. H.W. Wilson Co. • Indexes and abstracts 600 major business periodicals, plus the *Wall Street Journal* and the business section of the *New York Times.* Indexing is from 1982, abstracting from 1990, with the two newspapers included from 1993. Updated weekly. Inquire as to online cost and availability. (*Business Periodicals Index* without abstracts is also available online.).

PERIODICALS AND NEWSLETTERS

Computer Economics Networking Strategies Report: Advising IT Decision Maker ractices and Current Trends. Computer Economics Inc. • Monthly. $395.00 per year. Newsletter. Edited for information technology managers. Covers news and trends relating to a variety of corporate computer network and management information systems topics. Emphasis is on costs. Formerly *Intranet and Networking Strategies Report.*

CRN: The Newsweekly for Builders of Technology Solutions. CMP Worldwide Media Networks. • Monthly. Incorporates *Computer Reseller Sources and Macintosh News.* Formerly *Computer Retailer News.*

EDP Weekly: The Leading Weekly Computer News Summary. Computer Age and EDP News Services. • Weekly. $495.00 per year. Newsletter. Summarizes news from all areas of the computer and microcomputer industries.

Exploring Windows NT for Professionals. Skillsoft Ireland Ltd. • Monthly. $139.00 per year. Newsletter on the Windows operating system for networks. Formerly *Exploring Windows NT.*

Insurance Networking: Strategies and Solutions for Electronic Commerce. SourceMedia Inc. • 10 times a year. Price on application. Covers information technology for the insurance industry, with emphasis on computer communications and the Internet.

Network Computing: Computing in a Network Environment. UBM L.L.C. • Semimonthly. Free to qualified personnel.

Network: Strategies and Solutions for the Network Professional. UBM L.L.C. • 13 times a year. Free to qualified personnel. Covers network products and peripherals for computer professionals. Includes annual network managers salary survey and annual directory issue. Formerly *LAN: The Network Solutions Magazine.*

Network World: The Newsweekly of Enterprise Network Computing. Network World Inc. • Weekly. $129.00 per year. Includes special feature issues on enterprise Internets, network operating systems, network management, high-speed modems, LAN management systems, and Internet access providers.

Wireless Data News. Access Intelligence L.L.C. • Description: Provides analysis of technology, applications, marketing, and competition in the mobile communications industry. Scope is international. Recurring features include news of research.

RESEARCH CENTERS AND INSTITUTES

Columbia University - Center for Advanced Information Management. 650 W 168th St., Black Bldg. - 130, New York, NY 10032. Phone: (212)305-2944 or (212)305-5334; Fax: (212)305-0196 or (212)305-3302; Email: tomaselli@cat.columbia.edu • URL: http://www.cat.columbia.edu • Biomedical informatics, computer science, computational and systems biology, biomedical imaging.

Massachusetts Institute of Technology - Laboratory for Information and Decision Systems. 77 Massachusetts Ave., Rm. 32-D608, Cambridge, MA 02139. Phone: (617)253-2142; Fax: (617)253-3578; Email: willsky@mit.edu • URL: http://lids.mit.edu • Research areas include data communication networks and fiber optic networks.

STATISTICS SOURCES

Standard & Poor's Industry Surveys. Standard & Poor's Financial Services L.L.C. • Semiannual. $1,800.00. Two looseleaf volumes. Includes monthly *Supplements.* Provides detailed, individual surveys of 52 major industry groups. Each survey is revised on a semiannual basis. Also includes "Monthly Investment Review" (industry group investment analysis) and monthly "Trends & Projections" (economic analysis).

U.S. Industry and Trade Outlook. U.S. Department of Commerce National Technical Information Service. • Annual. Produced by the International Trade Administration, U.S. Department of Commerce, in a "public-private" partnership with DRI/McGraw-Hill and Standard & Poor's. Provides basic data, outlook for the current year, and "Long-Term Prospects" (five-year projections) for a wide variety of products and services. Includes high technology industries. Formerly *U.S. Industrial Outlook.*

TRADE/PROFESSIONAL ASSOCIATIONS

Computer and Communications Industry Association. 900 17th St. NW, Ste. 1100, Washington, DC 20006. Phone: (202)783-0070; Fax: (202)783-0534; Email: info@ccianet.org • URL: http://www.ccianet.org • Formerly Computer Industry Association.

LOCATION OF INDUSTRY

See also INDUSTRIAL DEVELOPMENT

DIRECTORIES

Craighead's International Business, Travel, and Relocation Guide to 84 Countries. Cengage Learning Inc. • $775 Individuals hardcover. Publication includes: List of Web sites for children's organizations, spousal employment, telephones/telecommunications, visa requirements, and more. Principal content of publication is detailed information on relocating or traveling to foreign countries.

Kelly's Post Office--London Business Directory. Reed Business Information. • Covers: 96,000 London businesses, 70,000 streets with postal district name, 21,000 buildings, local and regional government offices and officials, public bodies and societies, and professional firms. Entries include: Company name, address, phone, government official name, position, title.

PERIODICALS AND NEWSLETTERS

Business Facilities: The Location Advisor. Group C Media Inc. • Monthly. Free to qualified personnel; others, $30.00 per year. Facility planning and site selection.

Expansion Management: Growth Strategies for Companies on the Move. Penton Media Inc., Industry Div. • Monthly. Free to qualified personnel;

others, $40.00 per year. Subject matter is concerned with expansion and relocation of industrial facilities.

Insulation Outlook: Business Solutions for Expanding or Relocating Companies. National Insulation Association. • $98.00 per year. Covers site selection and related topics.

New Plant Report. Conway Data Inc. • Monthly. $1,800 All regions. Description: Covers new plants and plant expansions. Provides project location, company name, product to be manufactured or service performed, NAICS code, type of facility, stage of development, and (as available) number of employees, square footage, investment amount, and contact name. **Remarks:** Also available on disk and via e-mail.

Plants, Sites, and Parks. Reed Elsevier Group plc Reed Business Information. • Seven times a year. Free to qualified personnel; others, $43.90 per year. Covers economic development, site location, industrial parks, and industrial development programs.

LOCKOUTS

See STRIKES AND LOCKOUTS

LOCKS AND KEYS

See also INDUSTRIAL SECURITY PROGRAMS

PERIODICALS AND NEWSLETTERS

Keynotes. International College of Dentists. • Description: Contains news of the activities and projects of the organization, which provides networking and educational opportunities for professionals in the dental field. Recurring features include a calendar of events, reports of meetings, news of educational opportunities, and a column titled the History Corner.

National Locksmith. National Publishing Company Inc. • Monthly. $66 U.S. print and digital. Source for automotive technology, safe opening techniques, electronic security.

TRADE/PROFESSIONAL ASSOCIATIONS

Associated Locksmiths of America. 3500 Easy St., Dallas, TX 75247. Phone: 800-532-2562 or (214)819-9733; Fax: (214)819-9736; Email: mary@aloa.org • URL: http://www.aloa.org • Retail locksmiths; associate members are manufacturers and distributors of locks, keys, safes, and burglar alarms. Aims to educate and provide current information to individuals in the physical security industry. Maintains information and referral services for members; offers insurance and bonding programs. Holds annual five-day technical training classes and 3-day technical exhibit. Maintains museum.

LOCOMOTIVES

See RAILROADS

LOGGING

See LUMBER INDUSTRY

LOGISTIC RESEARCH

See OPERATIONS RESEARCH

LONG-TERM CARE INSURANCE

See also HEALTH INSURANCE; NURSING HOMES

ABSTRACTS AND INDEXES

Insurance Periodicals Index. Specials Libraries Association, Insurance and Employees Benefits Div. NILS Publishing Co. • Annual. $250.00. Compiled by the Insurance and Employee Benefits Div., Special Libraries Association. A yearly index of over 15,000 articles from about 35 insurance periodicals. Arrangement is by subject, with an index to authors.

Readers' Guide to Periodical Literature. EBSCO Publishing Inc. • Provides indexing for over 400 periodicals dating back to 1983.

BIBLIOGRAPHIES

Insurance and Employee Benefits Literature. Special Libraries Association. • Bimonthly. $15.00 per year. Lists a wide variety of literature in all branches of the insurance industry. Includes annotations.

CD-ROM DATABASES

Authority Health Care Law Library. Matthew Bender and Company Inc. • Periodic updates. Price on request. Full text CD-ROM provides legal information, case law, and analysis relating to health care facilities, health insurance, longterm care, Medigap, and Medicare.

Readers' Guide to Periodical Literature. EBSCO Publishing Inc. • Provides indexing for over 400 periodicals dating back to 1983.

INTERNET DATABASES

Free Insurance Advice. InsWeb, Inc. 2868 Prospect Park Dr., Ste. 650, Rancho Cordova, CA 95670. Phone: (916)853-3300; Fax: (916)853-3300; Email: customercare@insweb.com • URL: http://www.insweb.com • Web site offers a wide variety of advice and information on automobile, life, health, and "other" insurance. Includes glossaries of insurance terms, Standard & Poor's ratings of individual insurance companies, and "Financial Needs Estimators." Searching is available. Fees: Free.

ONLINE DATABASES

Ageline. AARP. • Provides indexing and abstracting of the literature of social gerontology, including consumer aspects, financial planning, employment, housing, health care services, mental health, social security, and retirement. Time period is 1978 to date. Inquire as to online cost and availability.

PERIODICALS AND NEWSLETTERS

Financial Planning: The Magazine for Financial Service Professionals. SourceMedia Inc. • Monthly. $79.00 per year. Edited for independent financial planners and insurance agents. Covers retirement planning, estate planning, tax planning, and insurance, including long-term healthcare considerations. Special features include a Retirement Planning Issue, Mutual Fund Performance Survey, and Variable Life and Annuity Survey.

Health Insurance Underwriter. National Association of Health Underwriters. • Monthly. Includes special feature issues on long-term care insurance, disability insurance, managed health care, and insurance office management.

RESEARCH CENTERS AND INSTITUTES

Office of Academic Affairs, School of Public Health. University of Michigan, 1415 Washington Heights, Ann Arbor, MI 48109-2029. Phone: (734)764-5425; Fax: (734)763-5455; Email: nkjanz@umich.edu • URL: http://www.sph.umich.edu/ • Research fields include health care economics, health insurance, and long-term care.

University of Minnesota - Division of Health Policy and Management. School of Public Health, MMC 729, 420 Delaware St. SE, Minneapolis, MN 55455-0392. Phone: (612)624-6151; Fax: (612)624-2196; Email: mosco001@umn.edu • URL: http://www.sph.umn.edu/hpm • Fields of research include health insurance, consumer choice of health plans, quality of care, and long-term care.

TRADE/PROFESSIONAL ASSOCIATIONS

National Association of Health Underwriters. 1212 New York Ave. NW, Ste. 1100, Washington, DC 20005. Phone: (202)552-5060; Fax: (202)747-6820; Email: info@nahu.org • URL: http://www.nahu.org • Members are engaged in the sale of health and disability insurance. Formerly International Association of Health Underwriters.

National Association of Insurance and Financial Advisors. 2901 Telestar Ct., Falls Church, VA 22042-1205. Phone: 877-866-2432; Email: membersupport@naifa.org • URL: http://www.naifa.org • Affiliated with Association for Advanced Life Underwriting. Formerly National Association of Life Underwriters.

LOW TEMPERATURE TECHNOLOGY

See CRYOGENICS

LUBRICATION AND LUBRICANTS

See also PETROLEUM INDUSTRY

ABSTRACTS AND INDEXES

NLGI Spokesman. National Lubricating Grease Institute. • Bimonthly. $65 Members. Bi-monthly. $65 per year. Information about the lubricating grease industry.

NTIS Alerts: Materials Sciences. U.S. Department of Commerce National Technical Information Service. • Biweekly. $130 per year. Covers ceramics, glass, coatings, composite materials, alloys, plastics, wood, paper, adhesives, fibers, lubricants, and related subjects.

DIRECTORIES

McCutcheon's Functional Materials Volumes 2. Manufacturing Confectioner Publishing Corp. • Edited for product development, quality control and research and development chemists.

FINANCIAL RATIOS

Annual Statement Studies. Risk Management Association. • Annual. Compiled from over 280,000 financial statements.

Annual Statement Studies: Industry Default Probabilities and Cash Flow Measures. Risk Management Association. • Annual. $405 Nonmembers. Serves as a companion volume to the original *Annual Statement Studies*. Gives probability of default estimates on a percentage scale for more than 450 industries. Includes changes in position year-by-year for eight financial statement line items and provides percentage measures of cash flow.

PERIODICALS AND NEWSLETTERS

Tribology International; The Practice and Technology of Lubrication, Wear Prevention and Friction Control. Elsevier. • Monthly. Qualified personnel, $173.00 per year; institutions, $1,528.00 per year.

TRADE/PROFESSIONAL ASSOCIATIONS

National Lubricating Grease Institute. 249 SW Noel St., Ste. 249, Lees Summit, MO 64063-2241. Phone: (816)524-2500; Fax: (816)524-2504; Email: nlgi@nlgi.org • URL: http://www.nlgi.org • Companies manufacturing or selling all types of lubricating greases; suppliers to such companies; technical and educational organizations. Promotes research and testing for the development of better lubricating greases and improved grease lubrication engineering service to industry. Collects and disseminates technical data; conducts forums and educational program. Operates the National Lubricating Grease Institute Research Fund.

LUGGAGE INDUSTRY

DIRECTORIES

Directory of Chinese Manufacturers & Exporters of Travel & Luggage Accessories. EXIM Infotek Private Ltd. • $10 Individuals. Covers: 60 Chinese manufacturers and exporters of briefcases, hardside luggage, leather briefcases, luggage carts, luggage, suitcases, suitcase accessories, travel bags, and travel goods. Entries include: Company name, postal address, city, country, phone, fax, e-mail and websites, contact person, designation, and product details.

Directory of South Korean Manufacturers & Exporters of Travel & Luggage Accessories. EXIM Infotek Private Ltd. • $10 Individuals. Covers: 70 South Korean manufacturers and exporters of leather travel goods/handbags, umbrellas and walking sticks. Entries include: Company name, postal address, city, country, phone, fax, e-mail and websites, contact person, designation, and product details.

Directory of Taiwanese Manufacturers & Exporters of Travel & Luggage Accessories. EXIM Infotek Private Ltd. • $30 Individuals. Covers: 370 Taiwanese manufacturers and exporters of all kinds of umbrellas, leather travel goods/handbags, luggage carts, travel bags, umbrellas and walking sticks. Entries include: Company name, postal address, city, country, phone, fax, e-mail and websites, contact person, designation, and product details.

FINANCIAL RATIOS

Annual Statement Studies. Risk Management Association. • Annual. Compiled from over 280,000 financial statements.

Annual Statement Studies: Industry Default Probabilities and Cash Flow Measures. Risk Management Association. • Annual. $405 Nonmembers. Serves as a companion volume to the original *Annual Statement Studies.* Gives probability of default estimates on a percentage scale for more than 450 industries. Includes changes in position year-by-year for eight financial statement line items and provides percentage measures of cash flow.

PERIODICALS AND NEWSLETTERS

Newsbreak. Leather Industries of America. • Free to members and other qualified personnel. Reports on issues and events in the luggage industry.

Travelware. Business Journals Inc. • Seven times a year. $32.00. Formerly *Luggage and Travelware.*

STATISTICS SOURCES

U.S. Industry and Trade Outlook. U.S. Department of Commerce National Technical Information Service. • Annual. Produced by the International Trade Administration, U.S. Department of Commerce, in a "public-private" partnership with DRI/McGraw-Hill and Standard & Poor's. Provides basic data, outlook for the current year, and "Long-Term Prospects" (five-year projections) for a wide variety of products and services. Includes high technology industries. Formerly *U.S. Industrial Outlook.*

TRADE/PROFESSIONAL ASSOCIATIONS

National Luggage Dealers Association. 1817 Elmdale Ave., Glenview, IL 60026. Phone: (847)998-6869; Fax: (847)998-6884; Email: inquiry@nlda.com • URL: http://www.luggagedealers.com • Represents retailers of luggage, leather goods, gifts, and handbags. Buying group producing promotional materials.

LUMBER INDUSTRY

See also FOREST PRODUCTS; HARDWOOD INDUSTRY; PLYWOOD INDUSTRY; WOODWORKING INDUSTRIES

ABSTRACTS AND INDEXES

Forest Products Abstracts. CABI Publishing North America. • Weekly updates.

Forestry Abstracts: Compiled from World Literature. CABI Publishing North America. • Monthly. Institutions, $1,435.00 per year. Print and online edition, $1,460.00 per year. Published in England by CABI Publishing. Provides worldwide coverage of the literature.

CD-ROM DATABASES

OECD Statistical Compendium. Organization for Economic Cooperation and Development. • Semiannual. $1,905.00 per year for 1 to 10 users. CD-ROM contains more than 730,000 monthly, quarterly, and annual time series for OECD countries, 1960 to date. Includes fully searchable data on agriculture, food, economic indicators, national accounts, employment, energy, finance, industry, technology, and foreign trade. Results can be displayed in various forms.

DIRECTORIES

Directory of Australia and New Zealand Importers of Lumber, Timber, Plywood and Hardwood. EXIM Infotek Private Ltd. • $150 Individuals. Covers: 40 Australian and New Zealand importers of board, construction plywood, decorative plywood, doors and windows, hardboard and particleboard, hardwood flooring, floor tiles, laminates, hardwood lumber, softwood lumber, marine plywood, medium-density fiberboards, millwork (wooden), plywood, veneer, poles, pilings and logs, sawn lumber, teak, timber, timber products, timberland products, and wood. Entries include: Company name, postal address, telephone, fax, e-mail, website, contact person, designation, and product details.

Directory of Belgium Importers of Lumber, Timber, Plywood and Hardboards. EXIM Infotek Private Ltd. • $150 Individuals. Covers: 25 Belgium importers of doors, windows, hardwood flooring, floor tiles, hardwood lumber, softwood lumber, plywood, veneer, poles, wood, pilings and logs. Entries include: Company name, postal address, telephone, fax, e-mail, website, contact person, designation, and product details.

Directory of British Importers of Lumber, Timber, Plywood and Hardboards. EXIM Infotek Private Ltd. • $250 Individuals. Covers: 80 British importers of doors, windows, hardboard, particleboard, hardwood flooring, floor tiles, wood laminates, lumber, timber, plywood, hardwood lumber, softwood lumber, plywood, veneer, poles, pilings and logs. Entries include: Company name, postal address, telephone, fax, e-mail, website, contact person, designation, and product details.

Directory of Chinese Importers of Lumber, Timber, Plywood and Hardboards. EXIM Infotek Private Ltd. • $150 Individuals. Covers: 30 Chinese importers of beechwood lumber, hardwood lumber, softwood lumber, plywood, veneer, poles, pilings and logs, sawn timber, and wood. Entries include: Company name, postal address, telephone, fax, e-mail, website, contact person, designation, and product details.

Directory of European Importers of Lumber, Timber, Plywood and Hardboards. EXIM Infotek Private Ltd. • $950 Individuals. Covers: 580 European importers of coniferous raw wood, doors and windows, glued timber, gypsum board and sheetrock, hardboard and particleboard, hardwood flooring and tiles, hardwood lumber, hardwood, laminates, wood laminates, lumber goods, timber and plywood, softwood lumber, oak flooring, oak sheets, parquet, particle boards, pinewood, planed wood, plywood and veneer, poles, pilings and logs, round logs, sawdust, softwood, solid wood, teak and mahogany wood, teak logs, veneering wood, wood particle slabs, wood sawn, and wooden moldings. Entries include: Company name, postal address, telephone, fax, e-mail, website, contact person, designation, and product details.

Directory of French Importers of Lumber, Timber, Plywood and Hardboards. EXIM Infotek Private Ltd. • $200 Individuals. Covers: 60 French importers of doors, windows, hardboard and particleboard, hardwood flooring, floor tiles, wood laminates, lumber goods, lumber, timber, plywood, hardwood lumber, softwood lumber, plywood, veneer, poles, wood, pilings and logs. Entries include: Company name, postal address, telephone, fax, e-mail, website, contact person, designation, and product details.

Directory of German Importers of Lumber, Timber, Plywood and Hardboards. EXIM Infotek Private Ltd. • $250 Individuals. Covers: 60 German importers of doors, windows, glued timber, hardboard, particleboard, hardwood flooring, floor tiles, laminates, wood laminates, lumber, timber, plywood, hardwood lumber, softwood lumber, parquet, pine wood, planed wood, veneer, poles, pilings and logs, round logs, softwood, solid wood, wood, and wooden moldings. Entries include: Company name, postal address, telephone, fax, e-mail, website, contact person, designation, and product details.

Directory of Indian Importers of Lumber, Timber, Plywood and Hardboards. EXIM Infotek Private Ltd. • $250 Individuals. Covers: 80 Indian importers of gypsum board, hard boards, wood laminates, logs, hardwood lumber, softwood lumber, particle boards, plywood, veneer, poles, pilings and logs, sheetrock, spruce logs, teak wood, timber, timber logs, veneer sheets, and wood. Entries include: Company name, postal address, telephone, fax, e-mail, website, contact person, designation, and product details.

Directory of Japanese Importers of Lumber, Timber, Plywood and Hardboards. EXIM Infotek Private Ltd. • $650 Individuals. Covers: 340 Japanese importers of bamboo shoots, bamboo and rattan (raw), doors and door frames, windows, gypsum board, hardboard, particleboard, hardwood flooring, floor tiles, hardwood products, laminated lumber, wood laminates, logs, lumber, hardwood lumber, softwood lumber, timber, plywood, medicament plywood, millwork (wooden), veneer, poles, pilings and logs, rattans, sandalwood, sawn goods, sawn timber, sheetrock, teak wood, timber, wood, wood housing products, woodchips, and wooden doors. Entries include: Company name, postal address, telephone, fax, e-mail, website, contact person, designation, and product details.

Directory of Middle East Importers of Lumber, Timber, Plywood and Hardboards. EXIM Infotek Private Ltd. • $500 Individuals. Covers: 260 Middle East importers of blockboard and hardboard, doors and windows, formica, gypsum boards, hardboard and particle board, hardwood flooring and floor tiles, laminates, hardwood lumber, softwood lumber, timber, plywood, medium-density fiberboard, millwork (wooden), veneer, poles, pilings and logs, and sawdust. Entries include: Company name, postal address, telephone, fax, e-mail, website, contact person, designation, and product details.

Directory of North American Importers of Lumber, Timber, Plywood and Hardboards. EXIM Infotek Private Ltd. • $700 Individuals. Covers: 350 North American importers of bamboo and rattan raw, doors, windows, exotic wood, forestry products, gypsum board and sheetrock, hardboard, particleboard, hardwood, hardwood flooring, hardwood floor tiles, lumber, laminates (wood), lumber (hardwood), lumber (softwood), lumber products, lumber timber and plywood, mahogany, millwork (wooden), oak vanities, plywood, veneer, poles, pilings and logs, rattan, teakwood, timber, tropical hardwood, and wicker. Entries include: Company name, postal address, telephone, fax, e-mail, website, contact person, designation, and product details.

Directory of SAARC Importers of Lumber, Timber,

Plywood and Hardboards. EXIM Infotek Private Ltd. • $200 Individuals. Covers: 60 SAARC countries importers of artificial timber, bio-fold doors, windows, board, ebonite rods and sheets, false ceiling board, formica, gypsum board, hard boards, particleboard, laminated boards, laminated wooden boards, doors, windows, laminated decorative-sheets, laminates, hardwood lumber, softwood lumber, medium-density fiberboards, particle boards, plywood, veneer, doors, plywood sheets, sawn goods, sliding doors, straw boards, swing door, teak wood, timber, timber products, white boards, window shutters, window type, and wood. Entries include: Company name, postal address, telephone, fax, e-mail, website, contact person, designation, and product details.

Lumbermens Red Book: Reference Book of the Lumbermens Credit Association. Lumbermens Credit Association Inc. • Semiannual $2,140.00 per year. Weekly supplements. Lists approximately 39,000 United States firms in the lumber and woodworking industries, with credit ratings. Available online.

Timber Harvesting--Logger's Resource Guide. Hatton-Brown Publishers Inc. • Annual. Publication includes: List manufacturers and distributors of equipment used in harvesting and handling timber, logging trade organizations and trade associations. Entries include: Firm name, division or subsidiary name, address, fax, phone, e-mail, website, year company established, names and titles of key personnel.

INTERNET DATABASES

Business 2.0 Web Guide to the Best Business Links. Business 2.0 Media Inc. Phone: (415)293-4800; Email: support@business2.com • URL: http://www.business2.com/webguide • Web site presents an extensive, searchable directory of links to "the best, most informative, and authoritative web pages." Twenty main categories cover business, finance, career, company information, people, and technology topics, with thousands of subtopics, all linking to Web sites recommended by experienced business researchers. Fees: Free.

Fedstats. Federal Interagency Council on Statistical Policy. Phone: (202)395-7254 • URL: http://www.fedstats.gov • Web site features an efficient search facility for full-text statistics produced by more than 100 federal agencies, including the Census Bureau, the Bureau of Economic Analysis, and the Bureau of Labor Statistics. Boolean searches can be made within one agency or for all agencies combined. Links are offered to international statistical bureaus, including the UN, IMF, OECD, UNESCO, Eurostat, and 20 individual countries. Fees: Free.

FreeLunch.com. Economy.com, Inc. Phone: (610)696-8700; Fax: (610)696-1678 • URL: http://www.freelunch.com • Web site provides free access to more than 200 million economic and financial data series, covering industry, demographics, labor markets, prices, retail sales, government spending, trade, interest rates, housing starts, the stock market, etc. Data is available in either chart or table form. Searching is offered. Free, but registration required. Economy.com, Inc. also offers fee-based economic analysis at *The Dismal Scientist* site (www.dismal.com).

Manufacturing Profiles. U. S. Bureau of the Census. Phone: (301)763-4636 or (301)763-4100; Fax: (301)763-4794; Email: webmaster@census.gov • URL: http://www.census.gov/prod/www/abs/mfg-prof.html • The Census Bureau makes available free on PDF (Portable Document Format) an annual consolidation of the entire Current Industrial Report series, presenting "all the data compiled." Contains statistics on production, shipments, inventories, consumption, exports, imports, and orders for a wide variety of manufactured products.

USDA. U.S. National Institute of Standards and Technology. 100 Bureau Dr., Gaithersburg, MD 20899-1070. Phone: 800-877-8339 or (301)975-6478 or (202)720-2791; Fax: (301)975-8295; Email: inquiries@nist.gov • URL: http://www.nist.gov • The USDA home page has six sections: News and Information; What's New; About USDA; Agencies; Opportunities; Search and Help. Keyword searching is offered from the USDA home page and from various individual agency home pages. Agencies are the Economic Research Service, Agricultural Marketing Service, National Agricultural Statistics Service, National Agricultural Library, and about 12 others. Updating varies. Fees: Free.

PERIODICALS AND NEWSLETTERS

Building Material Dealer. National Lumber and Building Material Dealers Association. • Monthly. $48.00 per year. Includes special feature issues on hand and power tools, lumber, roofing, kitchens, flooring, windows and doors, and insulation. Formerly *Builder Material Retailer.*

Random Lengths: The Weekly Report on North American Forest Products Markets. Random Lengths Publications, Inc. • Weekly. Information covering the wood products industry. Supplement available *Random Lengths Midweek Market Report.*

Southern Lumberman. Hatton-Brown Publishers Inc. • Monthly. $23.00 per year. Controlled circulation. A magazine for the sawmill industry.

Timber Harvesting. Hatton-Brown Publishers Inc. • 10 times a year. $40.00 per year.

STATISTICS SOURCES

Agricultural Statistics. U.S. Department of Agriculture National Agricultural Statistics Service. • Annual. $46 Individuals. Provides a wide variety of statistical data relating to agricultural production, supplies, consumption, prices/price-supports, foreign trade, costs, and returns, as well as farm labor, loans, income, and population. In many cases, historical data is shown annually for 10 years. In addition to farm data, includes detailed fishery statistics.

Survey of Current Business. U. S. Government Printing Office. • Published by Bureau of Economic Analysis, U. S. Department of Commerce. Presents a wide variety of business and economic data.

Timber Bulletin. Economic Commission for Europe. United Nations Publications. • Irregular. $30. Contains international statistics on forest products, including price, production, and foreign trade data.

TRADE/PROFESSIONAL ASSOCIATIONS

American Hardwood Export Council. 1825 Michael Faraday Dr., Reston, VA 20190. Phone: (703)435-2900; Fax: (703)435-2537; Email: msnow@ahec.org • URL: http://www.ahec.org • Represents exporting companies and hardwood trade associations that serve the hardwood lumber industry. Promotes the export of U.S. hardwood lumber worldwide.

American Lumber Standard Committee. PO Box 210, Germantown, MD 20875-0210. Phone: (301)972-1700; Fax: (301)540-8004; Email: alsc@alsc.org • URL: http://www.alsc.org • Members appointed by the Department of Commerce to represent producers, consumers, and specifiers of softwood lumber. Establishes and maintains standards for size, grade, and other matters; elects an independent board of review to approve softwood lumber grading rules and accredit agencies that audit treating plants and accredit agencies that audit pallet, box and crate manufacturers for international trade.

Hardwood Federation. 1111 19th St. NW, Ste. 800, Washington, DC 20036. Phone: (202)463-2452; Fax: (202)463-4702 • URL: http://www.hardwoodfederation.wildapricot.org • Represents organizations engaged in the manufacturing, wholesaling or distribution of North American hardwood lumber, veneer, plywood, flooring and related products. Seeks to promote and represent the common business interests of and improve business conditions among members of the hardwood industry. Strives to maintain a healthy business environment for family businesses and small companies in the hardwood community.

National Hardwood Lumber Association. 6830 Raleigh La Grange Rd., Memphis, TN 38134-0518. Phone: 800-933-0318 or (901)377-1818; Fax: (901)382-6419 or (901)399-7581; Email: info@nhla.com • URL: http://www.nhla.com • United States, Canadian and International hardwood lumber and veneer manufacturers, distributors and consumers. Inspects hardwood lumber. Maintains inspection training school. Conducts management and marketing seminars for the hardwood industry. Promotes research in hardwood timber management and utilization. Promotes public awareness of the industry.

National Lumber and Building Material Dealers Association. 2025 M St. NW, Ste. 800, Washington, DC 20036-3309. Phone: (202)367-1169; Fax: (202)367-2169; Email: info@dealer.org • URL: http://www.dealer.org • Formerly National Retail Lumber Dealers Association.

LUNCHROOMS

See RESTAURANTS, LUNCHROOMS, ETC.

LUNCHROOMS, EMPLOYEE

See EMPLOYEE LUNCHROOMS AND CAFETERIAS

A information can be obtained
v.ICGtesting.com
'n the USA
n1057310815